THE SELECTED WRITINGS OF

Lafcadio Hearn

The Selected Writings of
LAFCADIO HEARN

EDITED BY

Henry Goodman

WITH AN INTRODUCTION BY

Malcolm Cowley

A Citadel Press Book
Published by Carol Publishing Group

CONTENTS

Some Chinese Ghosts

Chita

A MEMORY OF LAST ISLAND

American Sketches

CINCINNATI

Contents vii

Lafcadio Hearn

IT WAS A SURPRISING EXPERIENCE TO REREAD HIS WORK VOLUME AFTER
volume. Some of it seemed as mannered and frilled as the fashions
of sixty years ago, and not always the best fashions; at times it might
have been copied from Paris models by an earnest but awkward provincial dressmaker. Perhaps I was expecting all of it to have this end-
of-the-century air, this charm of the faded and half-forgotten; what
surprised me was that so much of it remained new and genuine.
Unlike many authors with broader talents, he had the *métier,* the
vocation for writing, the conscience that kept him working over each
passage until it had the exact color of what he needed to say; and in
most cases the colors have proved fast. Many books written by his

famous contemporaries are becoming difficult to read. One can't help seeing that Howells followed the conventions of his day, that Frank Norris was full of romantic bad taste; but Lafcadio Hearn at his best was independent of fashion and was writing for our time as much as his own.

No American author of the nineteenth century had a stranger life. He was born in 1850 on the Ionian island of Santa Maura—the ancient Leucadia, which explains his given name—and in 1904 his ashes were buried after a Buddhist ceremony in Tokyo. His ancestry was Maltese on his mother's side and hence may be taken as a mixture of Phoenician, Arab, Norman, Spanish and Italian; on his father's side it was Anglo-Irish with—Lafcadio liked to think—a touch of Romany. He learned to say his first prayers in Italian and demotic Greek. Adopted by a wealthy great-aunt, Sarah Brenane, he was educated by private tutors in Dublin and at Catholic schools in England and France. He was a British subject until he became a naturalized Japanese at the age of forty-six; but he always thought of himself as an American writer.

"Yes;" he said in a letter to an English friend in Japan, "I have got out of touch with Europe altogether, and think of America when I make comparisons. At nineteen years of age, after my people had been reduced from riches to poverty by an adventurer,—and before I had seen anything of the world except in a year of London among the common folk,—I was dropped moneyless on the pavement of an American city to begin life. Often slept in the street, etc.," and he might have added that the "etc." included doorways, packing boxes, a stable and a rusty boiler in a vacant lot. "Worked as a servant, waiter, printer, proofreader, hack-writer, gradually pulled myself up. I never gave up my English citizenship. But I had eighteen years of American life,—and so got out of touch with Europe. For the same reason, I had to work at literature through American vehicles."

It is doubtful whether he could have survived as a writer, or survived at all, if he had started his career in another country. Besides being a very small man—five feet, three inches in height—and nearly blind, so that his life was in danger whenever he crossed a street, he was as shy as an African pygmy and as quick to take offense as the king's musketeers. He had the beginnings of a classical education and absolutely no knowledge of how to earn a living. In New York and Cincinnati he was often close to starvation, but he was always rescued in time; for that was during the Gilded Age, when American life had a sort of hurried and absent-minded ease, with few organized charities, but with more acts of casual kindness than a waif like Lafcadio would encounter in our own day. People found jobs for him, and when he lost or left the jobs they sometimes fed him like a stray kitten. The warmest shelter open to him was the Cincinnati Public Library, where the librarian asked him questions and gave him work to do. A printer named Henry Watkin promised to teach him the trade and meanwhile let him sleep behind the shop, in a box full of paper shavings.

By 1872, three years after his arrival in this country, he was working as proofreader for a small publishing house—the other men in the office called him Old Semicolon—and at night he was writing articles which he hoped to publish in the Cincinnati newspapers. He had carried the first article to Colonel John A. Cockerill, the editor of the *Enquirer.* "Do you pay for contributions?" he asked in a voice that could scarcely be heard. Cockerill said that he did and invited the big-spectacled waif into his private office. Producing a manuscript from under his very long coat, Lafcadio laid it on the table with trembling hands, "and stole away," Cockerill said, "like a distorted brownie, leaving behind him an impression that was uncanny and indescribable." The manuscript was printed, as were most of the others that Lafcadio brought into the office; sometimes his contributions filled one-fourth of the Sunday edition. Soon he was a salaried member of the *Enquirer* staff.

American daily journalism gave Hearn a chance he would have found in no other field. He had come to this country at a time when many serious writers, after fleeing to Europe, were complaining from a distance that American books had to be written and American magazines edited for a genteel audience composed chiefly of women. They forgot the newspapers, which were written for men and therefore retained more freedom of speech, besides a touch of cynicism. The newspapers of the time discussed dangerous topics like prostitution, adultery and miscegenation, which couldn't even be mentioned in the magazines. When describing crimes of violence, their reporters were advised to copy the methods of the French naturalists. Their critics were permitted to indulge in fine writing and a show of curious learning. Although newspapers overworked their staffs and paid them miserable wages—standard figures in the Middle West were $10 a week for cubs and $30 for star reporters—still they paid those wages every Saturday and thus provided the only sure livelihood for writers in revolt against the genteel tradition. Bierce, Huneker, Harold Frederic,

Stephen Crane, David Graham Phillips and Dreiser—almost all the skeptics, the bohemians and the naturalists—started their careers as newspaper men.

Hearn was a bohemian by necessity and a distant ally of the French late-romantic and decadent writers. As a newspaper man he could publish translations from Gautier and Loti that were daring for the time, besides original sketches that the magazines would have rejected as being godless or indecent (or simply overwritten). He could also publish editorials and reviews that displayed as in a showcase the fruits of his esoteric reading. On the *Enquirer* and later on the New Orleans *Times-Democrat* he became a sort of provincial Remy de Gourmont, divorced from life but pillaging the whole world of books and presenting his readers with folk tales from Arabia and India, voodoo chants and extracts from the best that was being written in Europe.

He had a purple style in his youth and the newspapers encouraged it. Describing a visit to a New Orleans hospital during a yellow-fever epidemic he would say, "The grizzled watcher of the inner gate extended his pallid palm for that eleemosynary contribution exacted from all visitors;—and it seemed to me that I beheld the gray Ferryman of Shadows himself, silently awaiting his obolus from me, also a Shadow." The *Times-Democrat* printed that without deleting an adjective or a semicolon and Hearn was inspired to use still loftier language. "The spider at last ceased to repair her web of elfin silk," he said; "years came and went with lentor inexpressible." He was proud of that last phrase, though afterwards he learned to regret it. "My first work was awfully florid," he said when he was living in Japan. "I should like now to go through many paragraphs written years ago and sober them down." But although he blamed the newspapers for encouraging the weaker side of his work, he could also thank them for printing every word of it and for teaching him habits of industry.

There was another service, too, for which he could thank the newspapers that employed him; to some extent they protected him in his conflicts with the proprieties. Hearn was so conscious of his physical handicaps that he never made love to any woman of his own race whom he regarded as his social equal; on the other hand, he felt at ease with those who were more unfortunate than himself. In Cincinnati he married a colored woman named Alethea Foley, the mother of an illegitimate child by another white man, and lived with her in a tumbledown house next door to the stables of the Adams Express Company. Soon the Hearn household was a citywide scandal, one that would have kept him from earning a living if he had been a clerk or a teacher; fortunately a reporter was not expected to observe the conventions. Although the *Enquirer* became worried and discharged him in 1875, a year after his marriage, he was soon rehired by another paper, which paid him a lower salary and thought it was getting a bargain.

Hearn separated from Alethea in 1877; no divorce was necessary because mixed marriages were not legally recognized in Ohio. That same year he went to New Orleans, where he lived for some months on the edge of starvation and nearly died of dengue, or breakbone fever. He looked like an undernourished scarecrow when he was at last hired by a struggling newspaper, the *Item,* at a cub's salary of $10 a week. That was enough to live on, in New Orleans, and four years later he became the translator and staff critic for a larger paper, the *Times-Democrat,* at a star reporter's salary of $30. There were scandals about him in New Orleans, too, probably without much basis, but kept alive by the rebellious and sensual tone of his writing. Once again his newspapers protected him and were proud to publish his work.

It was not until he went north, in 1887, and tried to live by writing for the magazines that he began to feel exposed to the full force of social condemnation. He sought refuge in Martinique, where he declared that nature itself was "nude, warm, savage and amorous," and where he felt at ease in a society of mixed races. In 1889 he spent an unhappy summer in Philadelphia and an unhappier winter in New York; then he fled across the world to Japan.

II

HEARN REACHED TOKYO IN THE YEAR 1890: THE 23D MEIJI BY THE JAPANESE system of reckoning from the return to power of the Mikado and the introduction of Western ways. The kingdom, not yet really an empire, was in a state of violent transformation, military, industrial and cultural. With schoolboys by the hundreds of thousands studying English, there was a lack of qualified instructors. Hearn had come to Japan with a vague commission from Harper and Brothers for books and magazine articles, but he always quarreled with publishers and soon he was left to live by his own resources. This time, instead of starving, he became professor of English at the government schools in Matsue, which was the capital of a backward province slowly emerging from the feudal age. His monthly salary of 100 yen, or about $45, made him one of the richer inhabitants of the little city on the Sea of Japan. All his life till then Hearn had felt himself to be marked off from the rest of mankind by his small stature, his strange appearance and especially by his uneven eyes, one blind, marbled and sunken in his skull, the other myopic and protruding, so that it looked like the single eye of an octopus. He had felt even more isolated by the scandals that had followed him since his marriage. In one of his letters he explained that, small as he was, he had powerful enemies, including Society, the Church—all the churches—and the English and American Press. "I am pretty much in the position," he continued, "of a book-keeper known to have once embezzled, or of a man who has been in prison, or of a prostitute who has been on the street. These are, none of them, you will confess, *important* persons. But what keeps them in their holes? Society, Church and public opinion—the Press." In Japan he seemed to have escaped from these real or imagined enemies. His small stature ceased to worry him there, since he was taller than most of his Japanese colleagues and since the whole country, with its small houses and dwarf trees in miniature gardens, was designed on his scale. Even his strange appearance provoked no special comments. All foreigners looked strange to the Japanese, Hearn scarcely more than the others.

His two years in Matsue were a long idyll. Hearn loved the old Japan, more of which had survived there than in the larger cities, and he found that he loved the people, too. In Matsue they returned his affection. At first they were kind to him out of curiosity and because he was the first foreigner to live among them; but there is evidence that students and professors came to have a special respect for Herun—or Hellum, or Fellun, as they called him in their different dialects. When the first winter proved unusually severe for southwestern Japan, a friend on the faculty suggested to Herun-san that marriage was the best means of keeping warm. He also produced a candidate bride, Setsu Koizumi, the only child of an impoverished family belonging to the warrior or samurai caste. After freezing for two more nights, Hearn paid a formal visit to her parents and the wedding took place with little delay. Setsu was a polite and conscientious little moon-faced woman who wasn't beautiful by Japanese or any other standards. As time went on she proved to be self-willed and given to fits of hysteria, but Hearn said to the end that he had the best wife in the world.

He supported the whole Koizumi family, including Setsu's mother, her father and her grandfather by adoption, as well as a collection of relatives who came for monthlong or yearlong visits. Although he had rescued them from poverty, his relations with the family were not one-sided; Hearn had more to give, but the Koizumis were loyal to him and gave whatever they could. Once when he had a serious attack of indigestion he learned that Setsu's father had sworn to starve himself for a year if the gods would let his son-in-law recover. It was, however, Setsu's mother who cured him by learning to cook European meals. In general the Koizumis guarded his working hours, taught him Japanese customs and kept him from being cheated; and in 1896 they formally adopted him as a son so that he could become a Japanese citizen.

By that time Hearn himself was a father. He was to have three sons and a daughter, but it was the firstborn, Kazuo, whom he idolized. On the night when the child was expected, he had knelt at his wife's bedside and prayed in broken Japanese. "Come into the world with good eyes," he had murmured again and again; but then the two mid-wives arrived and Hearn retired to a garden house. It was one o'clock in the morning when the great-grandfather, an old samurai, came dancing into the garden with his hands clasped above his head and his kimono sleeves fallen to his shoulders. "Hellum, Hellum!" he shouted. "Great treasure child is born." Later the old man used to carry Kazuo around the house while he sang at the top of his voice:

> *Urashima Taro lived a hundred and six years;*
> *Takeuchi Sukuné lived three hundred years;*
> *Tōbōsaku lived nine thousand years;*
> *Koizumi Kazuo—a million and more millions.*

Their common love for the firstborn was another bond that held the family together. Hearn, the former outcast, was now Papa-san and the center of a small community. He felt relieved from the Western burden of separateness he had carried all his life till then. "There are nearly twelve here," he said in a letter, "to whom I am Life and Food and other things. However intolerable anything else is, at home I enter into my little smiling world of old ways and thoughts and courtesies; where all is soft and gentle as something seen in sleep. It is so soft, so intangibly gentle and lovable and artless, that sometimes it seems a dream only; and then a fear comes that it might vanish away. It has become Me. When I am pleased, it laughs; when I don't feel jolly, everything is silent. Thus light and vapoury as its force seems, it is a moral force, perpetually appealing to conscience."

It was a moral force that would keep Hearn in Japan until he died. Reading his letters, honest and eloquent, and the touching book, *Father and I,* that Kazuo wrote when his own children were growing up, one can't help feeling a warm personal regard for this waif who had found a home. He was brave, honorable and loyal. When his burdens piled up imperceptibly, so that a stronger man might have been crushed by them, he carried them without complaint; he had become a good husband and father, a great teacher and a faithful subject of the Mikado. After the Matsue idyll he lost his illusions about Japan. Life was sterner in Kumamoto and Kobe and Tokyo, the cities where he lived for the next twelve years. His university career was always being threatened by intrigues in the Ministry of Education, so that sometimes he hated the Japanese government and even the people. "You can't understand my feeling of reaction in the matter of Japanese psychology," he wrote to his friend Professor Chamberlain. "It seems as if everything had suddenly become clear to me, and utterly void of emotional interest. . . . There are no depths to stir, no race-profundities to explore: all is like a Japanese river-bed, through which the stones and rocks show up all the year round,—and is never filled but in times of cataclysm and destruction."

No matter how he felt about the Japanese as a nation—and he had other moods than disillusionment—he was always faithful to his family. The children came first and especially Kazuo, who had become the center of his life. "Every year," he wrote to his future biographer, Elizabeth Bisland, "there are born some millions of boys cleverer, stronger, handsomer than mine. I may be quite a fool in my estimate of him. I do not find him very clever, quick, or anything of that sort. Perhaps there will prove to be 'nothing in him.' I cannot tell. All that I am quite sure of is that he naturally likes what is delicate, clean, refined, and kindly,—and that he naturally shrinks from whatever is coarse or selfish. . . . I must do all I can to feed the tiny light, and give it a chance to prove what it is worth. It is ME, in another birth—with renewed forces given by a strange and charming blood from the Period of the Gods." Often Hearn felt there were invisible walls that separated him from everything in Japan and even kept him from touching his first-born son. He longed to escape, if only for a few months; in the Japanese winter, shivering beside a charcoal brazier, he dreamed of being alone in Manila or some other tropical city. There was money enough for the trip, but Hearn was beginning to fear that he hadn't long to live and he wanted to provide for the family. A later plan was to take Kazuo with him for a visit to the United States, where Hearn would lecture at a university in order to pay for the boy's schooling. But Cornell, which had invited him, changed its mind about the lectures and he stayed in Tokyo to rewrite them into a book; it was *Japan: An Attempt at Interpretation,* the last and most ambitious of his works.

His attitude toward writing had changed since he became a father. In earlier years his life had formed a fairly simple pattern of frustration and aggression; he was always being hurt or offended and was always picking quarrels. He slept with a loaded revolver under his pillow and often carried it, too—although the only time he used it was on his trip from Cincinnati south, when he saw a man gouge out a kitten's eyes; he fired at the man four times and missed. Apparently he wrote to prove that, small as he was, he could outdo his enemies. He confessed something of the sort in a letter to Ellwood Hendrick, one of the few friends with whom he never fought. Hearn underlined the key statement: *"Unless somebody does or says something horribly mean to me, I can't do certain kinds of work,*—the tiresome kinds, that compel a great deal of thinking. The exact force of the hurt I can measure at the time of receiving it: 'This will be over in six months'; 'This I shall have to fight for two years'; 'This will be remembered longer.' When I begin to think about the matter afterwards, then I rush to work. I write page after page of vagaries, metaphysical, emotional, romantic,—throw them aside. Then the next day I go to work rewriting them. I rewrite and rewrite them till they begin to define and arrange themselves into a whole. . . . Pain is therefore to me of exceeding value betimes; and everybody who does me a wrong indirectly does me a right."

The letter was written from Kobe in 1895 and described an emotional pattern that was changing. Even though Hearn continued to quarrel with his associates, there had come to be something dogged and perfunctory in the process; he was merely following a ritual, like an atheist kneeling in prayer. He looked for grievances so they would make him go to work, as before; but writing had now become an end in itself and the means of providing an inheritance for Kazuo and the family. He couldn't stop working even when the doctors warned him that he was straining his heart. "Money, money, money," he often murmured; "I don't want money for myself, I only want it for my wife and children." He earned money by writing as much as he could —a book a year in addition to his teaching; but he was also trying to do his best work and the double effort killed him. His last words were in Japanese, *"Ah, byōki no tamé"*—Ah, on account of illness. After the funeral, which was conducted by a Buddhist archbishop, the family shrine was moved into Papa-san's study; and twice a day the children and later the grandchildren recited prayers before his photograph.

III

REREADING HIS WORK AFTER MANY YEARS, ONE IS IMPRESSED BY ITS LIMI-tations as well as by its workmanship and integrity. It is narrow in scope, as if his smallness and short-sightedness had been moral as well as physical qualities. Sometimes it deals with general ideas, but in an apprentice fashion and with continual nods of deference to Herbert Spencer, who was Hearn's only schoolmaster in philosophy. It is full of moods, colors and misty outlines, but lacking in pictures of daily life. Hearn complained in a letter that he knew nothing about the smallest practical matters: "Nothing, for example, about a boat, a horse, a farm, an orchard, a watch, a garden. Nothing about what a man ought to do under any possible circumstances." In short, he knew very little about the experiences of other human beings, and that is only one of his disabilities as an author. He was never able to invent a plot and often begged his friends to tell him stories so that he would have something to write about. He had little power of construction beyond the limits of a short essay or a folk tale. Of the sixteen books he published during his lifetime only one—*Japan: An Attempt at Interpretation*—is a book properly speaking. The others are either loose novelettes like *Chita* and *Youma,* in which the atmosphere is more important than the story; or else they are collections of shorter pieces that appeared or might have appeared in the magazines.

It seems to us now that Hearn started by misestimating and underestimating his own gifts. "Knowing that I have nothing resembling genius," he said in a letter to Whitman's disciple, William D. O'Connor, "and that any ordinary talent must be supplemented with some sort of curious study in order to place it above the mediocre line, I am striving to woo the Muse of the Odd, and hope to succeed in thus attracting some little attention." In another letter to O'Connor he spoke of pledging himself to the worship of the Odd, the Queer, the Strange, the Exotic, the Monstrous. "It quite suits my temperament," he added mistakenly. The great weakness of his early sketches is that they aren't sufficiently odd or monstrous or differentiated from one another. The best of them—including many reprinted in this volume—are folk tales adapted from various foreign literatures. The others keep reverting to the same situation, that of a vaguely pictured hero in love with a dead woman or with her ghost (just as Hearn was in love with the memory of his mother, who disappeared from his life when he was seven years old). They are obsessive rather than exotic; and they are written in a style that suggests the scrollwork on the ceiling of an old-fashioned theater.

After his death Hearn's reputation suffered from the collections that others made of his early newspaper work, most of which should have been allowed to sleep in the files of the Cincinnati and New Orleans press. Even the books he wrote in his later New Orleans years—*Stray Leaves from Strange Literatures, Some Chinese Ghosts* and *Chita*—though they all contained fine things and two of them are reprinted here in full, are not yet his mature writing. *Two Years in the French West Indies* (1890) is longer and richer and shows how Hearn could be carried out of himself by living among a people with whom he sympathized. Still, it was not until after his first years in Japan that he really mastered a subject and a style.

He wrote to Chamberlain in 1893, "After for years studying poetical prose, I am forced now to study simplicity. After attempting my utmost at ornamentation, I am converted by my own mistakes. The great point is to touch with simple words." That is exactly what he did in the best of his later writing. Instead of using important-sounding words to describe events that were not always important in themselves, he depended on the events to impress the reader and looked for words that would reveal them as through a clear glass. Here, for example, is a crucial paragraph from "The Story of Mimi-Nashi-Hōïchi," a Japanese legend retold in *Kwaidan*:

At that instant Hōïchi felt his ears gripped by fingers of iron, and torn off! Great as the pain was, he gave no cry. The heavy footfalls receded along the verandah,—descended into the garden,—passed out to the roadway,—ceased. From either side of his head, the blind man felt a thick warm trickling; but he dared not lift his hands.

Today we don't like the exclamation point after the first sentence, or the commas followed by dashes in the third; but Hearn was following his own theories about punctuation as a guide to the reader's voice. Primarily he was writing for the ear, not the eye; and the passage in its context sounds exactly right when read aloud. He almost always found the right words, as notably at the end of his story about a hunter who saw a pair of *oshidori,* or mandarin ducks, and killed the drake. Later the hunter felt an inner summons to revisit the same place—

. . . and there, when he came to the river-bank, he saw the female oshidori swimming alone. In the same moment the bird perceived Sonjo; but, instead of trying to escape, she swam straight towards him, looking at him the while in a strange fixed way. Then, with her own beak, she suddenly tore open her own body, and died before the hunter's eyes. . . .
Sonjo shaved his head, and became a priest.

Hearn would work for hours changing and rearranging the words in a brief and utterly simple passage like this one. "For me words have colour, form, character," he said in a letter to Chamberlain; "they have faces, ports, manners, gesticulations; they have moods, humours, eccentricities;—they have tints, tones, personalities"—and they had all these qualities in addition and largely without reference to their meanings. He thought that the letter A was blush-crimson and the letter E sky-blue; that KH wore a beard and a turban; that initial X was a mature Greek with wrinkles and that "—no—" had an innocent, lovable and childlike aspect. He was affected by "the whispering of words, the rustling of the procession of letters . . . the pouting of words, the frowning and fuming of words, the weeping, the raging and racketing and rioting of words, the noisomeness of words, the tenderness or hardness, the dryness or juiciness of words,—the interchange of values in the gold, the silver, the brass and the copper of words." Words were his David's pebbles against Goliath; they were the magic spells that protected him from a world of enemies. No labor with words was too great for him if it led to the perfect incantation.

He told a correspondent that he had worked for months on a single page before it expressed his mood and meaning. "When the best result comes, it ought to surprise you," he said in the same letter, "for our best work is out of the Unconscious." Not being one of the fortunate authors who are able to draw up and execute plans for their books as if they were building houses, Hearn had to depend on his unconscious mind for suggestions. His two problems were how to set that mind in operation and how to revise the impressions it yielded step by step. He wrote his first drafts hurriedly and set them aside; then he rewrote them time and again, finding that what he called his "latent feelings" took shape in the process of revision. "Of course," he said to Chamberlain, "it looks like big labor to rewrite every page half a dozen times. But in reality it is the least possible labor. To those with whom writing is an almost automatic exertion, the absolute fatigue is no more than that of writing a letter. The rest of the work *does itself*, without your effort. It is like spiritualism. Just move the pen, and the ghosts do the writing."

Hearn was innocently boasting when he wrote that letter; elsewhere he admitted that the process of composition was always painful for him. Perhaps it was most painful during the moments before he sat down at his desk. He used to pace up and down his study, sometimes groaning, sometimes shrieking as if he had been possessed, not by ghosts eager to do his writing, but by the spirits of women dead in childbirth. At such moments his wife and little Kazuo would rush up to him crying, "Papa, Papa!" until their voices had called him back from his nightmare. *"Gomen, gomen"*—I'm sorry, he would say, brushing his hand over his eyes. A short time later his scratchy pen would start to move rapidly over sheet after sheet of paper. Hearn wrote with his head bowed and twisted to the left and his one near-sighted eye six inches from the manuscript. He had an extraordinary faculty of absorption in his work; as long as the pen was moving he could see nothing else, hear nothing and feel nothing. He liked to write at night by an oil lamp; sometimes when the wick was turned too high, soot would cover everything in the room by midnight. Sometimes when Kazuo and his mother came into the room next morning they would find the floor under his desk covered with gorged mosquitoes, like little red beans. "It must have been very itchy," they would say; and Papa-san would answer, "I didn't feel them." His method of composition helped to confine him to small forms, essays and tales that he could finish before exhausting himself and losing contact with his subconscious; but it also gave him a sort of deep-lying honesty within his limitations. In his best work one never finds the fault of less scrupulous writers, who proclaim one emotion by the meaning of their words while suggesting another by the color and sound of their words. What they usually suggest is an absence of emotion and a disbelief in what they are saying. Hearn's writing was true not only on the surface but in depth; not only to his conscious thinking but also to the submerged feelings that gave their rhythms to his prose. It wears well because it is all of a piece.

Besides his sense of language and his patient integrity he had something else in his later years that larger talents have often lacked: a subject. Of course the subject was Japanese culture in the broad sense, and a question still being argued is whether his picture of it was true by factual standards or was dangerously romanticized. That question we can let the experts decide, but not before we have noted that each of them seems to have a different notion of the truth. To another question, whether Hearn knew Japan, there can be only one answer.

He knew Japan, not as an observer, but as a citizen, the adopted son of Japanese parents and the father of Japanese children. He knew the faults of his countrymen by adoption, although he preferred to emphasize their virtues when writing for Western magazines. He foresaw the conflict between Japan and the West. He knew what arguments would touch the Japanese mind and what explanations were necessary before English poems could be understood by Japanese students. It is not surprising to learn that the students worshiped him; when he lost his post at the Imperial University they spoke of banding together to defend him, like the forty-seven *ronin* of the Japanese legend who avenged their feudal lord and then committed suicide in front of his tomb. Some of the students took down his lectures word for word; and after his death a whole series of volumes—four in this country, five others in Japan—was compiled and published from their notes. The volumes do not prove that Hearn was a great critic or that he always preferred the best to the second-best. What they do prove is that he was a great interpreter who, belonging to English literature, could still explain it as if he formed part of a Japanese audience.

More important for us than the lectures, which have their place in the history of Japanese thought, are the eleven books in which he performed the opposite task of interpreting Japan to the West. He never claimed that the books presented a complete picture of his new country. He liked to confess that he knew very little about Japanese economics or politics and he always hated the new industrial society that was developing in the Meiji era. He liked old things, courtesy, kindness, devotion, ancestor worship; perhaps he exaggerated their importance in Japanese society. Apparently he could grope his way through the newspapers, but he couldn't read Japanese classical books or write anything more than short letters to his wife, who had no English, in the private language they called "Mr. Hearn dialect," *Herun-san kotoba*. On the other hand, he had a householder's knowledge of Japanese life, a scholar's knowledge of religious customs, and something more than that, an intimate and sympathetic grasp of Japanese legends.

He learned the legends from various sources; some of his students collected them and his wife helped more effectively, by reading old books for him and retelling the stories in their private language. Hearn put the best of them into English, with the freedom of a story-teller working from oral sources. He described his work as translation, but it was more than that, as became apparent when similar tales were merely translated by others. The result in their case was folk-lore for the laboratory, preserved in formaldehyde, whereas Hearn's version was literature. Long before coming to Japan he had shown an instinct for finding in legends the permanent archetypes of human experience—that is the secret of their power to move us—and he later proved that he knew which tales to choose and which details to emphasize, in exactly the right English. Now that so much of his work in many fields has been collected into one volume, I think it will be apparent that his folk tales are the most valuable part of it and that he is the writer in our language who can best be compared with Hans Christian Andersen and the brothers Grimm.

MALCOLM COWLEY

Sherman, Connecticut

Editor's Introduction

IN THE LOUNGE OF THE MIYAKO HOTEL, KYOTO, MORE THAN A DECADE AGO, a few young Westernized Japanese laughed when I asked about work-songs I had heard that day. On a walk across the hills to Otzu, I had stopped to listen to road-menders singing in the sun. The young men in the hotel laughed even more when I asked where I might buy recordings of the chants.

"Oh," they put me off, "those songs of the road-makers are very crude. Make fun of people they see. Road-makers express funny ideas. Not flattering."

But it had been songs of the plain people, I bethought myself, that Hearn, incredible Lafcadio Hearn, loved to use, together with many

16

other kinds, in his running accounts of the folk-ways of the Japanese, his people by adoption.

I took another tack.

What did young Japanese like themselves think of Lafcadio Hearn? Not much.

Too conservative.

In fact they didn't like him.

A reactionary—he was a reactionary. Didn't approve of the new ambitions of Japan. Didn't want to see Japan exercise her new industrial muscles. Young Japanese, proud of the growing power of their country, did not think highly of the man who disliked big-business, power-plants, and manufacturing centers. Worried them too much about Japan's making mistakes through over-self-confidence. Hearn, in short, was against making Japan up-to-date, modern.

I recalled that Yone Noguchi, the Japanese poet, praised Hearn with unbounded enthusiasm. "We Japanese," Noguchi had said, "have been regenerated by his sudden magic and baptized afresh under his transcendental rapture." And even the author of "Bushido—The Soul of Japan," Profesor Inazo Nitobe, had described Hearn as "the most eloquent and truthful interpreter of the Japanese mind. . ."

However, those admirers, I realized, had been the voices of old Japan and here, now, were the young voices of modern Japan, voices that wanted to make themselves heard in the world chorus of modernism.

For years, the folk-tales, stories, travel sketches, fantasies, and essays of Lafcadio Hearn had seemed to me like an enchanted garden in which I could always discover new pleasures. A charmed air hangs over it. Melodious sounds and sparkling colors are there in profusion; voices whisper in the scented gloom of unexpected nooks; veiled and ghostly figures arise, play their roles in some drama of ancient passion, and vanish as quietly as they had come. Enjoying the vivid shoots of observation among the flowers of Hearn's talent, I had found it pleasant to walk along the paths of firm comment laid down by Hearn as a result of his study of the societies he had known: American, Caribbean, and Japanese. My satisfaction in what I had found made it easy to overlook, in his work, the absence of "great" or "important" themes and problems.

Not that such themes are actually absent from Hearn's work. Explaining the meaning of the Japanese word, *Kokoro,* the title of one of his books, Hearn said that, written with the character indicated by him, "this word signifies also mind, in the emotional sense: spirit; courage; resolve; sentiment; affection; and inner meaning,—just as we say in English, 'the heart of things.'"

Just so. Hearn's writings entertain and excite because, without being strident or violent, they yield the inner meaning of loyalty, of the tragedy of betrayal, of fortitude in suffering, of faith in a person, an idea or an ideal. But the themes are so artfully and lightly worked into the texture of tale, or story, or travel sketch, as to seem to have no existence apart from the enchantment of the telling. Particularly fine examples of Hearn's way of dealing with such materials are to be found in his retellings from the great books of the early civilizations: the Talmud, Pantchatantra, Sacountala, the Mahabharata, Kalewala, and the like. From those books, he had come away with rare parables to which he gave new attractiveness in the forms he devised.

One of Hearn's most engaging traits, I had always felt, was his interest in the life of simple folk. A sure instinct had taken Hearn to the tales and legends loved by the people of the Orient, just as the same instinct had guided him to his enticing descriptions of the girls of Martinique. His own slum experiences in London, New York, Cincinnati, and New Orleans had deepened his sympathies for the ordinary folk, the common people. "The poor people, en masse," he told a friend, "are moral; the goodness of ten thousand years is in the marrow of their bones." Toward the end of his days, in Japan, he asserted the same sentiment: "The veritable strength of Japan still lies in the moral nature of her common people—her farmers and fishers, artisans and laborers—the patient quiet folk one sees toiling in the rice-fields, or occupied with the humblest of crafts and callings in city by-ways."

It had been Hearn's mistake, I thought as I heard the young gentlemen of Japan, to assume that Japan, imperialistic Japan, would continue to cherish its "patient quiet folk." Hearn had known that in the successful West whose excesses had driven him eastward, "refined feeling" turned a cold shoulder on commonplace facts and on the reality of simple, honest human emotions. He had seen that the cultivated classes of the West who boasted this refinement had lost, finally, the capacity to respond to the warm manifestations of feeling because they regarded feelings as "vulgar."

The young men frowning on the crude, perhaps impolite, songs of the road-menders were themselves already contaminated by the "refinement" brought them by Western influences. Gentlemen-like, they probably wanted to guard me against insult, but there was, too, the obvious distaste for anything touching "vulgar" road-makers.

As I listened to these young Japanese, I could gather that the ideas of expansionism, the hopes of great industrial successes, had turned Japanese thinking from the values so whole-heartedly appreciated by Hearn. That was it, then, Hearn, who had settled in Japan after rejecting Western commercialism and industrialism, was being rejected—had been rejected—by modern Japan. The idea struck me with its ironic impact. It might have been a story from his own pen!

But, it occurred to me, if modern Japanese turned from Hearn because they knew and disliked what he stands for, too many young Americans do not even have a talking acquaintance with his work and do not know how engaging and entertaining it is.

The dissent of the Japanese made me feel that it was time to re-read the writings of Lafcadio Hearn. I knew this would not be either a burden or a chore.

Hearn re-found, proved to be a source of renewed delight. Talk of weird stories, or stories of the strange! Without the clanking machinery of modern invention, his stories have a strangeness all their own. I was gratified to find again in his folk-tales, ghost stories, and travel sketches the qualities of imagination and novelty, of musical and incisive expression, of economical and exact phrasing. It was with new awareness that I recognized Hearn as the writer of the half-perceived, the half-felt, the tangential,—of the feeling caught on the wing. These moods of the tremulous half-light, as between dream and reality, had made their impression on the sensitive receptors of his imagination. He had caught moods and suggestions and succeeded in weaving them into the numerous types of writing welcomed by his admirers in America.

In preparing this book, the one trouble I had was in deciding what to leave out. *Chita, Boutimar, the Dove, Les Porteuses, Diplomacy, The Nun of the Temple of Amida, A Glimpse of Tendencies, The Story of Ming-Y, Esther's Choice, The Red Bridal, The Story of Mimi-Nashi-Hōïchi, The Dream of Akinosuké,* these and many, many more came thronging, veiled in mystery, fragrant and exciting as of old. How could I close my eyes and ears to stories, legends, folk-tales, and essays, all thrilling, all pleading to be included?

It was unfair, it was too much like a bureaucratic frontier guardsman, to turn back this story of doomed, unhappy lovers, or that tale of inescapable destiny. But to include them would mean to reprint almost all of Hearn's work. There was only one way to proceed: Noah's way, at the gangplank of the ark. If among the stories, essays, tales, and the others, there were some that bore too great a family resemblance, I would admit only the most vigorous, the most shapely, the most striking. Better to let new readers look for more, and let confirmed Hearn admirers refresh their memory in this sampling.

HENRY GOODMAN

Brooklyn, New York

Kwaidan

The Story of Mimi-Nashi-Hōïchi

MORE THAN SEVEN HUNDRED YEARS AGO, AT DAN-NO-URA, IN THE STRAITS
or Shimonoséki, was fought the last battle of the long contest between
the Heiké, or Taira clan, and the Genji, or Minamoto clan. There
the Heiké perished utterly, with their women and children, and their
infant emperor likewise—now remembered as Antoku Tennō. And
that sea and shore have been haunted for seven hundred years. . . .
Elsewhere I told you about the strange crabs found there, called
Heiké crabs, which have human faces on their backs, and are said
to be the spirits of Heiké warriors. But there are many strange things
to be seen and heard along that coast. On dark nights thousands of
ghostly fires hover about the beach, or flit above the waves—pale lights

which the fishermen call *Oni-bi,* or demon-fires; and, whenever the winds are up, a sound of great shouting comes from that sea, like a clamor of battle.

In former years the Heiké were much more restless than they now are. They would rise about ships passing in the night, and try to sink them; and at all times they would watch for swimmers, to pull them down. It was in order to appease those dead that the Buddhist temple, Amidaji, was built at Akamagaséki.[1] A cemetery also was made close by, near the beach; and within it were set up monuments inscribed with names of the drowned emperor and of his great vassals; and Buddhist services were regularly performed there, on behalf of the spirits of them. After the temple had been built, and the tombs erected, the Heiké gave less trouble than before; but they continued to do queer things at intervals—proving that they had not found the perfect peace.

Some centuries ago there lived at Akamagaséki a blind man named Hōïchi, who was famed for his skill in recitation and in playing upon the *biwa.*[2] From childhood he had been trained to recite and to play; and while yet a lad he had surpassed his teachers. As a professional *biwa-hōshi* he became famous chiefly by his recitations of the history of the Heiké and the Genji; and it is said that when he sang the song of the battle of Dan-no-ura "even the goblins (*kijin*) could not refrain from tears."

At the outset of his career, Hōïchi was very poor; but he found a good friend to help him. The priest of the Amidaji was fond of poetry and music; and he often invited Hōïchi to the temple, to play and recite. Afterwards, being much impresed by the wonderful skill of the lad, the priest proposed that Hōïchi should make the temple his home; and this offer was gratefully accepted. Hōïchi was given a room in the temple-building; and, in return for food and lodging, he was required only to gratify the priest with a musical performance on certain evenings, when otherwise disengaged.

---

[1] Or, Shimonoséki. The town is also known by the name of Bakkan.

[2] The *biwa,* a kind of four-stringed lute, is chiefly used in musical recitative. Formerly the professional minstrels who recited the "Heiké-Monogatari," and other tragical histories, were called *biwa-hōshi,* or "lute-priests." The origin of this appellation is not clear; but it is possible that it may have been suggested by the fact that "lute-priests," as well as blind shampooers, had their heads shaven, like Buddhist priests. The biwa is played with a kind of plectrum, called *bachi,* usually made of horn.

One summer night the priest was called away, to perform a Buddhist service at the house of a dead parishioner; and he went there with his acolyte, leaving Hōïchi alone in the temple. It was a hot night; and the blind man sought to cool himself on the verandah before his sleeping-room. The verandah overlooked a small garden in the rear of the Amidaji. There Hōïchi waited for the priest's return and tried to relieve his solitude by practicing upon his biwa. Midnight passed; and the priest did not appear. But the atmosphere was still too warm for comfort within doors; and Hōïchi remained outside. At last he heard steps approaching from the backgate. Somebody crossed the garden, advanced to the verandah, and halted directly in front of him—but it was not the priest. A deep voice called the blind man's name—abruptly and unceremoniously in the manner of a samurai summoning an inferior:

"Hōïchi!"

Hōïchi was too much startled, for the moment, to respond; and the voice called again, in a tone of harsh command:

"Hōïchi!"

"Hai!" answered the blind man, frightened by the menace in the voice—"I am blind!—I cannot know who calls!"

"There is nothing to fear," the stranger exclaimed, speaking more gently. "I am stopping near this temple, and have been sent to you with a message. My present lord, a person of exceedingly high rank, is now staying in Akamagaséki, with many noble attendants. He wished to view the scene of the battle of Dan-no-ura; and to-day he visited that place. Having heard of your skill in reciting the story of the battle, he now desires to hear your performance: so you will take your biwa and come with me at once to the house where the august assembly is waiting."

In those times, the order of a samurai was not to be lightly disobeyed. Hōïchi donned sandals, took his biwa, and went away with the stranger, who guided him deftly, but obliged him to walk very fast. The hand that guided was iron; and the clank of the warrior's stride proved him fully armed—probably some palace-guard on duty. Hōïchi's first alarm was over: he began to imagine himself in good luck;—for, remembering the retainer's assurance about a "person of exceedingly high rank," he thought that the lord who wished to hear the recitation could not be less than a *daimyō* of the first class. Presently the samurai halted; and Hōïchi became aware that they had arrived at a large gateway;—and he wondered, for he could not remember any large gate in that part of the town, except the main gate of the Amidaji. *"Kaimon!"* [3] the samurai called—and there was a sound of unbarring; and the twain passed on. They traversed a space of garden, and halted again before some entrance; and the retainer cried in a loud voice, "Within there! I have brought Hōïchi." Then came sounds of feet hurrying, and screens sliding, and rain-doors opening, and voices of women in converse. By the language of the women Hōïchi knew them to be domestics in some noble household; but he could not imagine to what place he had been conducted. Little time was allowed him for conjecture. After he had been helped to mount several stone steps, upon the last of which he was told to leave his sandals, a woman's hand guided him along interminable reaches of polished planking, and round pillared angles too many to remember, and over widths amazing of matted floor,—into the middle of some vast apartment. There he thought that many great people were assembled: the sound of the rustling of silk was like the sound of leaves in a forest. He heard also a great humming of voices—talking undertones; and the speech was the speech of courts.

Hōïchi was told to put himself at ease, and he found a kneeling-cushion ready for him. After having taken his place upon it, and tuned his instrument, the voice of a woman—whom he divined to be the *Rōjo,* or matron in charge of the female service—addressed him, saying:

"It is now required that the history of the Heiké be recited, to the accompaniment of the biwa."

Now the entire recital would have required a time of many nights: therefore Hōïchi ventured a question:

"As the whole of the story is not soon told, what portion is it augustly desired that I now recite?"

The woman's voice made answer:

"Recite the story of the battle at Dan-no-ura—for the pity of it is the most deep." [4]

Then Hōïchi lifted up his voice, and chanted the chant of the fight on the bitter sea—wonderfully making his biwa to sound like the straining of oars and the rushing of ships, the whirr and the hissing

---

[3] A respectful term, signifying the opening of a gate. It was used by samurai when calling to the guards on duty at a lord's gate for admission.

[4] Or the phrase might be rendered, "for the pity of that part is the deepest." The Japanese word for pity in the original text is *awaré.*

of arrows, the shouting and trampling of men, the crashing of steel upon helmets, the plunging of slain in the flood. And to left and right of him, in the pauses of his playing, he could hear voices murmuring praise: "How marvelous an artist!"—"Never in our own province was playing heard like this!"—"Not in all the empire is there another singer like Hōïchi!" Then fresh courage came to him, and he played and sang yet better than before; and a hush of wonder deepened about him. But when at last he came to tell the fate of the fair and helpless—the piteous perishing of the women and children—and the death-leap of Nii-no-Ama, with the imperial infant in her arms—then all the listeners uttered together one long, long shuddering cry of anguish; and thereafter they wept and wailed so loudly and so wildly that the blind man was frightened by the violence of the grief that he had made. For much time the sobbing and the wailing continued. But gradually the sounds of lamentation died away; and again, in the great stillness that followed, Hōïchi heard the voice of the woman whom he supposed to be the Rōjo.

She said:

"Although we had been assured that you were a very skillful player upon the biwa, and without an equal in recitative, we did not know that any one could be so skillful as you have proved yourself tonight. Our lord has been pleased to say that he intends to bestow upon you a fitting reward. But he desires that you shall perform before him once every night for the next six nights—after which time he will probably make his august return-journey. To-morrow night, therefore, you are to come here at the same hour. The retainer who to-night conducted you will be sent for you. . . . There is another matter about which I have been ordered to inform you. It is required that you shall speak to no one of your visits here, during the time of our lord's august sojourn at Akamagaséki. As he is traveling incognito,[5] he commands that no mention of these things be made. . . . You are now free to go back to your temple."

After Hōïchi had duly expressed his thanks, a woman's hand conducted him to the entrance of the house, where the same retainer, who had before guided him, was waiting to take him home. The retainer led him to the verandah at the rear of the temple, and there bade him farewell.

It was almost dawn when Hōïchi returned; but his absence from the

[5] "Traveling incognito" is at least the meaning of the original phrase—"making a disguised august-journey" (*shinobi no go-ryokō*).

temple had not been observed—as the priest, coming back at a very late hour, had supposed him asleep. During the day Hōïchi was able to take some rest; and he said nothing about his strange adventure. In the middle of the following night the samurai again came for him, and led him to the august assembly, where he gave another recitation with the same success that had attended his previous performance. But during this second visit his absence from the temple was accidentally discovered; and after his return in the morning he was summoned to the presence of the priest, who said to him, in a tone of kindly reproach:

"We have been very anxious about you, friend Hōïchi. To go out, blind and alone, at so late an hour, is dangerous. Why did you go without telling us? I could have ordered a servant to accompany you. And where have you been?"

Hōïchi answered, evasively:

"Pardon me, kind friend! I had to attend to some private business; and I could not arrange the matter at any other hour."

The priest was surprised, rather than pained, by Hōïchi's reticence: he felt it to be unnatural, and suspected something wrong. He feared that the blind lad had been bewitched or deluded by some evil spirits. He did not ask any more questions; but he privately instructed menservants of the temple to keep watch upon Hōïchi's movements, and to follow him in case that he should again leave the temple after dark.

On the very next night, Hōïchi was seen to leave the temple; and the servants immediately lighted their lanterns, and followed after him. But it was a rainy night, and very dark; and before the temple-folks could get to the roadway, Hōïchi had disappeared. Evidently he had walked very fast—a strange thing, considering his blindness; for the road was in a bad condition. The men hurried through the streets, making inquiries at every house which Hōïchi was accustomed to visit; but nobody could give them any news of him. At last, as they were returning to the temple by way of the shore, they were startled by the sound of a biwa, furiously played, in the cemetery of the Amidaji. Except for some ghostly fires—such as usually flitted there on dark nights—all was blackness in that direction. But the men at once hastened to the cemetery; and there, by the help of their lanterns, they discovered Hōïchi—sitting alone in the rain before the memorial tomb of Antoku Tennō, making his biwa resound, and loudly chanting the chant of the battle of Dan-no-ura. And behind him, and about him, and everywhere above the tombs, the fires of the dead were burning, like candles. Never before had so great a host of Oni-bi appeared in the sight of mortal man. . . .

"Hōïchi San!—Hōïchi San!" the servants cried— "you are bewitched! . . . Hōïchi San!"

But the blind man did not seem to hear. Strenuously he made his biwa to rattle and ring and clang;—more and more wildly he chanted the chant of the battle of Dan-no-ura. They caught hold of him;— they shouted into his ear:

"Hōïchi San!—Hōïchi San!—come home with us at once!"

Reprovingly he spoke to them:

"To interrupt me in such a manner, before this august assembly, will not be tolerated."

Whereat, in spite of the weirdness of the thing, the servants could not help laughing. Sure that he had been bewitched, they now seized him, and pulled him up on his feet, and by main force hurried him back to the temple—where he was immediately relieved of his wet clothes, by order of the priest, and reclad, and made to eat and drink. Then the priest insisted upon a full explanation of his friend's astonishing behavior.

Hōïchi long hesitated to speak. But at last, finding that his conduct had really alarmed and angered the good priest, he decided to abandon his reserve; and he related everything that had happened from the time of the first visit of the samurai.

The priest said:

"Hōïchi, my poor friend, you are now in great danger! How unfortunate that you did not tell me all this before! Your wonderful skill in music has indeed brought you into strange trouble. By this time you must be aware that you have not been visiting any house whatever, but have been passing your nights in the cemetery, among the tombs of the Heiké;—and it was before the memorial-tomb of Antoku Tennō that our people to-night found you, sitting in the rain. All that you have been imagining was illusion—except the calling of the dead. By once obeying them, you have put yourself in their power. If you obey them again, after what has already occurred, they will tear you in pieces. But they would have destroyed you, sooner or later, in any event. . . . Now I shall not be able to remain with you to-night: I am called to perform another service. But, before I go, it will be necessary to protect your body by writing holy texts upon it."

Before sundown the priest and his acolyte stripped Hōïchi: then, with their writing-brushes, they traced upon his breast and back, head and face and neck, limbs and hands and feet—even upon the soles of his feet, and upon all parts of his body—the text of the holy sutra called "Hannya-Shin-Kyō." [6] When this had been done, the priest instructed Hōïchi, saying:

"To-night, as soon as I go away, you must seat yourself on the verandah, and wait. You will be called. But, whatever may happen, do not answer, and do not move. Say nothing, and sit still—as if meditating. If you stir, or make any noise, you will be torn asunder. Do not get frightened; and do not think of calling for help—because no help could save you. If you do exactly as I tell you, the danger will pass, and you will have nothing more to fear."

After dark the priest and the acolyte went away; and Hōïchi seated himself on the verandah, according to the instructions given him. He laid his biwa on the planking beside him, and, assuming the attitude of meditation, remained quite still—taking care not to cough, or to breathe audibly. For hours he stayed thus.

Then, from the roadway, he heard the steps coming. They passed the gate, crossed the garden, approached the verandah, stopped—directly in front of him.

"Hōïchi!" the deep voice called. But the blind man held his breath, and sat motionless.

"Hōïchi!" grimly called the voice a second time. Then a third time—savagely:

"Hōïchi!"

Hōïchi remained as still as a stone—and the voice grumbled:

"No answer!—that won't do! . . . Must see where the fellow is." . . .

There was a noise of heavy feet mounting upon the verandah. The

---

[6] The smaller Pragña-Pâramitâ-Hridaya-Sutra is thus called in Japanese. Both the smaller and larger sutras called Pragña-Pâramitâ ("Transcendent Wisdom") have been translated by the late Professor Max Müller, and can be found in volume xlix of the *Sacred Books of the East* ("Buddhist Mahâyâna Sutras"). Apropos of the magical use of the text, as described in this story, it is worth remarking that the subject of the sutra is the Doctrine of the Emptiness of Forms—that is to say, of the unreal character of all phenomena or noumena. . . . "Form is emptiness; and emptiness is form. Emptiness is not different from form; form is not different from emptiness. What is form—that is emptiness. What is emptiness—that is form. . . . Perception, name, concept, and knowledge, are also emptiness. . . . There is no eye, ear, nose, tongue, body, and mind. . . . But when the envelopment of consciousness has been annihilated, then he [the seeker] becomes free from all fear, and beyond the reach of change, enjoying final Nirvâna."

feet approached deliberately—halted beside him. Then, for long minutes—during which Hōïchi felt his whole body shake to the beating of his heart—there was dead silence.

At last the gruff voice muttered close to him:

"Here is the biwa; but of the biwa-player I see—only two ears! . . . So that explains why he did not answer: he had no mouth to answer with—there is nothing left of him but his ears. . . . Now to my lord those ears I will take—in proof that the august commands have been obeyed, so far as was possible." . . .

At that instant Hōïchi felt his ears gripped by fingers of iron, and torn off. Great as the pain was, he gave no cry. The heavy footfalls receded along the verandah—descended into the garden—passed out to the roadway—ceased. From either side of his head, the blind man felt a thick warm trickling; but he dared not lift his hands. . . .

Before sunrise the priest came back. He hastened at once to the verandah in the rear, stepped and slipped upon something clammy, and uttered a cry of horror;—for he saw, by the light of his lantern, that the clamminess was blood. But he perceived Hōïchi sitting there, in the attitude of meditation—with the blood still oozing from his wounds.

"My poor Hōïchi!" cried the startled priest—"what is this? . . . You have been hurt?" . . .

At the sound of his friend's voice, the blind man felt safe. He burst out sobbing, and tearfully told his adventure of the night.

"Poor, poor Hōïchi!" the priest exclaimed—"all my fault!—my very grievous fault! . . . Everywhere upon your body the holy texts had been written—except upon your ears! I trusted my acolyte to do that part of the work; and it was very, very wrong of me not to have made sure that he had done it! . . . Well, the matter cannot now be helped; —we can only try to heal your hurts as soon as possible. . . . Cheer up, friend!—the danger is now well over. You will never again be troubled by those visitors."

With the aid of a good doctor, Hōïchi soon recovered from his injuries. The story of his strange adventure spread far and wide, and soon made him famous. Many noble persons went to Akamagaséki to hear him recite; and large presents of money were given to him—so that he became a wealthy man. . . . But from the time of his adventure, he was known only by the appellation of "Mimi-nashi-Hōïchi": Hōïchi-the-Earless.

Oshidori

THERE WAS A FALCONER AND HUNTER, NAMED SONJŌ, WHO LIVED IN THE district called Tamura-no-Gō, of the province of Mutsu. One day he went out hunting, and could not find any game. But on his way home, at a place called Akanuma, he perceived a pair of *oshidori* [1] (mandarin-ducks), swimming together in a river that he was about to cross. To kill oshidori is not good; but Sonjō happened to be very hungry, and he shot at the pair. His arrow pierced the male: the female escaped into the rushes of the farther shore, and disappeared. Sonjō took the dead bird home, and cooked it.

That night he dreamed a dreary dream. It seemed to him that a beautiful woman came into his room, and stood by his pillow, and began to weep. So bitterly did she weep that Sonjō felt as if his heart were being torn out while he listened. And the woman cried to him: "Why—oh! why did you kill him?—of what wrong was he guilty? . . . At Akanuma we were so happy together—and you killed him! . . . What harm did he ever do you? Do you even know what you have done?—oh! do you know what a cruel, what a wicked thing you have done? . . . Me too you have killed—for I will not live without my husband! . . . Only to tell you this I came." . . . Then again she wept aloud—so bitterly that the voice of her crying pierced into the marrow of the listener's bones;—and she sobbed out the words of this poem:

> *Hi kururéba*
> *Sasoëshi mono wo—*
> *Akanuma no*
> *Makomo no kuré no*
> *Hitori-né zo uki!*

[1] From ancient time, in the Far East, these birds have been regarded as emblems of conjugal affection.

At the coming of twilight I invited him to return with me—!
Now to sleep alone in the shadow of the rushes of Akanuma—
ah! what misery unspeakable! [2]

And after having uttered these verses she exclaimed: "Ah, you do not
know—you cannot know what you have done! But to-morrow, when
you go to Akanuma, you will see—you will see. . . ." So saying, and
weeping very piteously, she went away.

When Sonjō awoke in the morning, this dream remained so vivid in
his mind that he was greatly troubled. He remembered the words:
"But to-morrow, when you go to Akanuma, you will see—you will
see." And he resolved to go there at once, that he might learn whether
his dream was anything more than dream.

So he went to Akanuma; and there, when he came to the river-
bank, he saw the female oshidori swimming alone. In the same moment the bird perceived Sonjō; but, instead of trying to escape, she
swam straight toward him, looking at him the while in a strange fixed
way. Then, with her beak, she suddenly tore open her own body, and
died before the hunter's eyes. . . .

Sonjō shaved his head, and became a priest.

The Story of O-Tei

A LONG TIME AGO, IN THE TOWN OF NIIGATA, IN THE PROVINCE OF ECHIZEN,
there lived a man called Nagao Chōsei.

Nagao was the son of a physician, and was educated for his father's

[2] There is a pathetic double meaning in the third verse; for the syllables composing
the proper name Akanuma (Red Marsh) may also be read as *akanu-ma,* signifying "the
time of our inseparable (or delightful) relation." So the poem can also be thus rendered:
"When the day began to fail, I had invited him to accompany me. . . . ! Now, after the
time of that happy relation, what misery for the one who must slumber alone in the
shadow of the rushes!" The *makomo* is a sort of large rush, used for making baskets.

profession. At an early age he had been betrothed to a girl called O-Tei, the daughter of one of his father's friends; and both families had agreed that the wedding should take place as soon as Nagao had finished his studies. But the health of O-Tei proved to be weak; and in her fifteenth year she was attacked by a fatal consumption. When she became aware that she must die, she sent for Nagao to bid him farewell.

As he knelt at her bedside, she said to him:

"Nagao-Sama, my betrothed, we were promised to each other from the time of our childhood; and we were to have been married at the end of this year. But now I am going to die;—the gods know what is best for us. If I were able to live for some years longer, I could only continue to be a cause of trouble and grief to others. With this frail body, I could not be a good wife; and therefore even to wish to live, for your sake, would be a very selfish wish. I am quite resigned to die; and I want you to promise that you will not grieve. . . . Besides, I want to tell you that I think we shall meet again." . . .

"Indeed we shall meet again," Nagao answered earnestly. "And in that Pure Land there will be no pain of separation."

"Nay, nay!" she responded softly, "I meant not the Pure Land. I believe that we are destined to meet again in this world—although I shall be buried to-morrow."

Nagao looked at her wonderingly, and saw her smile at his wonder. She continued, in her gentle, dreamy voice:

"Yes, I mean in this world—in your own present life, Nagao-Sama. . . . Providing, indeed, that you wish it. Only, for this thing to happen, I must again be born a girl, and grow up to womanhood. So you would have to wait. Fifteen—sixteen years: that is a long time. . . . But, my promised husband, you are now only nineteen years old." . . .

Eager to soothe her dying moments, he answered tenderly:

"To wait for you, my betrothed, were no less a joy than a duty. We are pledged to each other for the time of seven existences."

"But you doubt?" she questioned, watching his face.

"My dear one," he answered, "I doubt whether I should be able to know you in another body, under another name—unless you can tell me of a sign or token."

"That I cannot do," she said. "Only the Gods and the Buddhas know how and where we shall meet. But I am sure—very, very sure—that, if you be not unwilling to receive me, I shall be able to come back to you. . . . Remember these words of mine." . . .

She ceased to speak; and her eyes closed. She was dead.

Nagao had been sincerely attached to O-Tei; and his grief was deep. He had a mortuary tablet made, inscribed with her *zokumyō;* [1] and he placed the tablet in his *butsudan,* [2] and every day set offerings before it. He thought a great deal about the strange things that O-Tei had said to him just before her death; and, in the hope of pleasing her spirit, he wrote a solemn promise to wed her if she could ever return to him in another body. This written promise he sealed with his seal, and placed in the butsudan beside the mortuary tablet of O-Tei.

Nevertheless, as Nagao was an only son, it was necessary that he should marry. He soon found himself obliged to yield to the wishes of his family, and to accept a wife of his father's choosing. After his marriage he continued to set offerings before the tablet of O-Tei; and he never failed to remember her with affection. But by degrees her image became dim in his memory—like a dream that is hard to recall. And the years went by.

During those years many misfortunes came upon him. He lost his parents by death—then his wife and his only child. So that he found himself alone in the world. He abandoned his desolate home, and set out upon a long journey in the hope of forgetting his sorrows.

One day, in the course of his travels, he arrived at Ikao—a mountain-village still famed for its thermal springs, and for the beautiful scenery of its neighborhood. In the village-inn at which he stopped, a young girl came to wait upon him; and, at the first sight of her face, he felt his heart leap as it had never leaped before. So strangely did she resemble O-Tei that he pinched himself to make sure that he was not dreaming. As she went and came—bringing fire and food, or arranging the chamber of the guest—her every attitude and motion revived in him some gracious memory of the girl to whom he had been pledged in his youth. He spoke to her; and she responded in a soft, clear voice of which the sweetness saddened him with a sadness of other days.

Then, in great wonder, he questioned her, saying:

"Elder Sister, so much do you look like a person whom I knew long ago, that I was startled when you first entered this room. Pardon me,

---

[1] The Buddhist term *zokumyō* (profane name) signifies the personal name, borne during life, in contradistinction to the *kaimyō* (sila-name) or *homyo* (Law-name) given after death—religious posthumous appelations inscribed upon the tomb, and upon the mortuary tablet in the parish-temple.

[2] Buddhist household shrine.

therefore, for asking what is your native place, and what is your name?"

Immediately—and in the unforgotten voice of the dead—she thus made answer:

"My name is O-Tei; and you are Nagao Chōsei of Echigo, my promised husband. Seventeen years ago, I died in Niigata: then you made in writing a promise to marry me if ever I could come back to this world in the body of a woman;—and you sealed that written promise with your seal, and put it in the butsudan, beside the tablet inscribed with my name. And therefore I came back." . . .

As she uttered these last words, she fell unconscious.

Nagao married her; and the marriage was a happy one. But at no time afterwards could she remember what she had told him in answer to his question at Ikao: neither could she remember anything of her previous existence. The recollection of the former birth—mysteriously kindled in the moment of that meeting—had again become obscured, and so thereafter remained.

Ubazakura

THREE HUNDRED YEARS AGO, IN THE VILLAGE CALLED ASAMIMURA, IN THE district called Onsengōri, in the province of Iyō, there lived a good man named Tokubei. This Tokubei was the richest person in the district, and the *muraosa,* or headman, of the village. In most matters he was fortunate; but he reached the age of forty without knowing the happiness of becoming a father. Therefore he and his wife, in the affliction of their childlessness, addressed many prayers to the divinity Fudō Myō Ō, who had a famous temple, called Saihōji, in Asamimura.

At last their prayers were heard: the wife of Tokubei gave birth to a daughter. The child was very pretty; and she received the name of

Tsuyu. As the mother's milk was deficient, a milk-nurse, called O-Sodé, was hired for the little one.

O-Tsuyu grew up to be a very beautiful girl; but at the age of fifteen she fell sick, and the doctors thought that she was going to die. In that time the nurse O-Sodé, who loved O-Tsuyu with a real mother's love, went to the temple Saihōji, and fervently prayed to Fudō-Sama on behalf of the girl. Every day, for twenty-one days, she went to the temple and prayed; and at the end of that time, O-Tsuyu suddenly and completely recovered.

Then there was great rejoicing in the house of Tokubei; and he gave a feast to all his friends in celebration of the happy event. But on the night of the feast the nurse O-Sodé was suddenly taken ill; and on the following morning, the doctor, who had been summoned to attend her, announced that she was dying.

Then the family, in great sorrow, gathered about her bed, to bid her farewell. But she said to them:

"It is time that I should tell you something which you do not know. My prayer has been heard. I besought Fudō-Sama that I might be permitted to die in the place of O-Tsuyu; and this great favor has been granted me. Therefore you must not grieve about my death. . . . But I have one request to make. I promised Fudō-Sama that I would have a cherry-tree planted in the garden of Saihōji, for a thank-offering and a commemoration. Now I shall not be able myself to plant the tree there: so I must beg that you will fulfill that vow for me. . . . Goodbye, dear friends; and remember that I was happy to die for O-Tsuyu's sake."

After the funeral of O-Sodé, a young cherry-tree—the finest that could be found—was planted in the garden of Saihōji by the parents of O-Tsuyu. The tree grew and flourished; and on the sixteenth day of the second month of the following year—the anniversary of O-Sodé's death—it blossomed in a wonderful way. So it continued to blossom for two hundred and fifty-four years—always upon the sixteenth day of the second month;—and its flowers, pink and white, were like the nipples of a woman's breasts, bedewed with milk. And the people called it *"Ubazakura,"* the Cherry-Tree of the Milk-Nurse.

Diplomacy

IT HAD BEEN ORDERED THAT THE EXECUTION SHOULD TAKE PLACE IN THE garden of the *yashiki*. So the man was taken there, and made to kneel down in a wide sanded space crossed by a line of *tobi-ishi,* or stepping-stones, such as you may still see in Japanese landscape-gardens. His arms were bound behind him. Retainers brought water in buckets, and rice-bags filled with pebbles; and they packed the rice-bags round the kneeling man—so wedging him in that he could not move. The master came, and observed the arrangements. He found them satisfactory, and made no remarks.

Suddenly the condemned man cried out to him:

"Honored sir, the fault for which I have been doomed I did not wittingly commit. It was only my very great stupidity which caused the fault. Having been born stupid, by reason of my karma, I could not always help making mistakes. But to kill a man for being stupid is wrong—and that wrong will be repaid. So surely as you kill me, so surely shall I be avenged;—out of the resentment that you provoke will come the vengeance; and evil will be rendered for evil." . . .

If any person be killed while feeling strong resentment, the ghost of that person will be able to take vengeance upon the killer. This the samurai knew. He replied very gently—almost caressingly:

"We shall allow you to frighten us as much as you please—after you are dead. But it is difficult to believe that you mean what you say. Will you try to give us some sign of your great resentment—after your head has been cut off?"

"Assuredly I will," answered the man.

"Very well," said the samurai, drawing his long sword;—"I am now going to cut off your head. Directly in front of you there is a stepping-stone. After your head has been cut off, try to bite the stepping-stone. If your angry ghost can help you to do that, some of us may be frightened. . . . Will you try to bite the stone?"

"I will bite it!" cried the man, in great anger—"I will bite it!—I will bite—"

There was a flash, a swish, a crunching thud: the bound body bowed over the rice sacks—two long blood-jets pumping from the shorn neck; —and the head rolled upon the sand. Heavily toward the stepping-stone it rolled: then, suddenly bounding, it caught the upper edge of the stone between its teeth, clung desperately for a moment, and dropped inert.

None spoke; but the retainers stared in horror at their master. He seemed to be quite unconcerned. He merely held out his sword to the nearest attendant, who, with a wooden dipper, poured water over the blade from haft to point, and then carefully wiped the steel several times with sheets of soft paper. . . . And thus ended the ceremonial part of the incident.

For months thereafter, the retainers and the domestics lived in cease-less fear of ghostly visitation. None of them doubted that the promised vengeance would come; and their constant terror caused them to hear and to see much that did not exist. They became afraid of the sound of the wind in the bamboos—afraid even of the stirring of shadows in the garden. At last, after taking counsel together, they decided to petition their master to have a Ségaki-service performed on behalf of the venge-ful spirit.

"Quite unnecessary," the samurai said, when his chief retainer had uttered the general wish. . . . "I understand that the desire of a dying man for revenge may be a cause for fear. But in this case there is nothing to fear."

The retainer looked at his master beseechingly, but hesitated to ask the reason of this alarming confidence.

"Oh, the reason is simple enough," declared the samurai, divining the unspoken doubt. "Only the very last intention of that fellow could have been dangerous; and when I challenged him to give me the sign, I diverted his mind from the desire of revenge. He died with the set purpose of biting the stepping-stone; and that purpose he was able to accomplish, but nothing else. All the rest he must have forgotten. . . . So you need not feel any further anxiety about the matter."

And indeed the dead man gave no more trouble. Nothing at all happened.

Of a Mirror and a Bell

EIGHT CENTURIES AGO, THE PRIESTS OF MUGENYAMA, IN THE PROVINCE OF Tōtōmi, wanted a big bell for their temple; and they asked the women of their parish to help them by contributing old bronze mirrors for bell-metal.

[Even to-day in the courts of certain Japanese temples, you may see heaps of old bronze mirrors contributed for such a purpose. The largest collection of this kind that I ever saw was in the court of a temple of the Jōdo sect, at Hakata, in Kyūshū: the mirrors had been given for the making of a bronze statue of Amida, thirty-three feet high.]

There was at that time a young woman, a farmer's wife, living at Mugenyama, who presented her mirror to the temple, to be used for bell-metal. But afterwards she much regretted her mirror. She remembered things that her mother had told her about it; and she remembered that it had belonged, not only to her mother but to her mother's mother and grandmother; and she remembered some happy smiles which it had reflected. Of course, if she could have offered the priests a certain sum of money in place of the mirror, she could have asked them to give back her heirloom. But she had not the money necessary. Whenever she went to the temple, she saw her mirror lying in the court-yard, behind a railing, among hundreds of other mirrors heaped there together. She knew it by the Shō-Chiku-Bai in relief on the back of it—those three fortunate emblems of Pine, Bamboo, and Plumflower, which delighted her baby-eyes when her mother first showed her the mirror. She longed for some chance to steal the mirror, and hide it— that she might thereafter treasure it always. But the chance did not come; and she became very unhappy—felt as if she had foolishly given away a part of her life. She thought about the old saying that a mirror is the Soul of a Woman (a saying mystically expressed, by the Chinese character for Soul, upon the backs of many bronze mirrors), and she feared that it was true in weirder ways than she had before imagined. But she could not dare to speak of her pain to anybody.

Now, when all the mirrors contributed for the Mugenyama bell had been sent to the foundry, the bell-founders discovered that there was one mirror among them which would not melt. Again and again they tried to melt it; but it resisted all their efforts. Evidently the woman who had given that mirror to the temple must have regretted the giving. She had not presented her offering with all her heart; and therefore her selfish soul, remaining attached to the mirror, kept it hard and cold in the midst of the furnace.

Of course everybody heard of the matter, and everybody soon knew whose mirror it was that would not melt. And because of this public exposure of her secret fault, the poor woman became very much ashamed and very angry. And as she could not bear the shame, she drowned herself, after having written a farewell letter containing these words:

When I am dead, it will not be difficult to melt the mirror and to cast the bell. But, to the person who breaks that bell by ringing it, great wealth will be given by the ghost of me.

You must know that the last wish or promise of anybody who dies in anger, or performs suicide in anger, is generally supposed to possess a supernatural force. After the dead woman's mirror had been melted, and the bell had been successfully cast, people remembered the words of that letter. They felt sure that the spirit of the writer would give wealth to the breaker of the bell; and, as soon as the bell had been suspended in the court of the temple, they went in multitude to ring it. With all their might and main they swung the ringing-beam; but the bell proved to be a good bell, and it bravely withstood their assaults. Nevertheless, the people were not easily discouraged. Day after day, at all hours, they continued to ring the bell furiously—caring nothing whatever for the protests of the priests. So the ringing became an affliction; and the priests could not endure it; and they got rid of the bell by rolling it down the hill into a swamp. The swamp was deep, and swallowed it up—and that was the end of the bell. Only its legend remains; and in that legend it is called the Mugen-Kané, or Bell of Mugen.

Now there are queer old Japanese beliefs in the magical efficacy of a certain mental operation implied, though not described, by the verb *nazoraëru*. The word itself cannot be adequately rendered by any English word; for it is used in relation to many kinds of mimetic magic, as well as in relation to the performance of many religious acts of faith. Common meanings of nazoraëru, according to dictionaries, are "to imitate," "to compare," "to liken"; but the esoteric meaning is *to substitute, in imagination, one object or action for another, so as to bring about some magical or miraculous result.*

For example: you cannot afford to build a Buddhist temple; but you can easily lay a pebble before the image of the Buddha, with the same pious feeling that would prompt you to build a temple if you were rich enough to build one. The merit of so offering the pebble becomes equal, or almost equal, to the merit of erecting a temple. . . . You cannot read the six thousand seven hundred and seventy-one volumes of the Buddhist texts; but you can make a revolving library, containing them, turn round, by pushing it like a windlass. And if you push with an earnest wish that you could read the six thousand seven hundred and seventy-one volumes, you will acquire the same merit as the reading of them would enable you to gain. . . . So much will perhaps suffice to explain the religious meanings of nazoraëru.

The magical meanings could not all be explained without a great variety of examples; but, for present purposes, the following will serve. If you should make a little man of straw, for the same reason that Sister Helen made a little man of wax—and nail it, with nails not less than five inches long, to some tree in a temple-grove at the Hour of the Ox—and if the person, imaginatively represented by that little straw man, should die thereafter in atrocious agony—that would illustrate one signification of nazoraëru. . . . Or, let us suppose that a robber has entered your house during the night, and carried away your valuables. If you can discover the footprints of that robber in your garden, and then promptly burn a very large moxa on each of them, the soles of the feet of the robber will become inflamed, and will allow him no rest until he returns, of his own accord, to put himself at your mercy. That is another kind of mimetic magic expressed by the term nazoraëru. And a third kind is illustrated by various legends of the Mugen-Kané.

After the bell had been rolled into the swamp, there was, of course, no more chance of ringing it in such wise as to break it. But persons who regretted this loss of opportunity would strike and break objects imaginatively substituted for the bell—thus hoping to please the spirit of the owner of the mirror that had made so much trouble. One of these persons was a woman called Umégaë—famed in Japanese legend because of her relation to Kajiwara Kagésué, a warrior of the Heiké clan. While the pair were traveling together, Kajiwara one day found himself in great straits for want of money; and Umégaë, remembering the tradition of the Bell of Mugen, took a basin of bronze, and, mentally representing it to be the bell, beat upon it until she broke it—crying out, at the same time, for three hundred pieces of gold. A guest of the inn where the pair were stopping made inquiry as to the cause of the banging and the crying, and, on learning the story of the trouble, actually presented Umégaë with three hundred ryō in gold. Afterwards a song was made about Umégaë's basin of bronze; and that song is sung by dancing-girls even to this day:

Umégaë no chōzubachi tataïté
O-kané ga déru naraba,
Mina San mi-uké wo
Sōré tanomimasu.

If, by striking upon the wash-basin of Umégaë, I could make honorable money come to me, then would I negotiate for the freedom of all my girl-comrades.

After this happening, the fame of the Mugen-Kané became great; and many people followed the example of Umégaë—thereby hoping to emulate her luck. Among these folk was a dissolute farmer who lived near Mugenyama, on the bank of the Ōïgawa. Having wasted his substance in riotous living, this farmer made for himself, out of the mud in his garden, a clay-model of the Mugen-Kané; and he beat the clay-bell, and broke it—crying out the while for great wealth.

Then, out of the ground before him, rose up the figure of a white-robed woman, with long loose-flowing hair, holding a covered jar. And the woman said: "I have come to answer your fervent prayer as it deserves to be answered. Take, therefore, this jar." So saying, she put the jar into his hands, and disappeared.

Into his house the happy man rushed, to tell his wife the good news. He set down in front of her the covered jar—which was heavy—

and they opened it together. And they found that it was filled, up to the very brim, with . . .

But, no!—I really cannot tell you with what it was filled.

Jikininki

ONCE, WHEN MUSŌ KOKUSHI, A PRIEST OF THE ZEN SECT, WAS JOURNEYING alone through the province of Mino, he lost his way in a mountain-district where there was nobody to direct him. For a long time he wandered about helplessly; and he was beginning to despair of finding shelter for the night, when he perceived, on the top of a hill lighted by the last rays of the sun, one of those little hermitages, called *anjitsu*, which are built for solitary priests. It seemed to be in a ruinous condition; but he hastened to it eagerly, and found that it was inhabited by an aged priest, from whom he begged the favor of a night's lodging. This the old man harshly refused; but he directed Musō to a certain hamlet, in the valley adjoining, where lodging and food could be obtained.

Musō found his way to the hamlet, which consisted of less than a dozen farm-cottages; and he was kindly received at the dwelling of the headman. Forty or fifty persons were assembled in the principal apartment, at the moment of Musō's arrival; but he was shown into a small separate room, where he was promptly supplied with food and bedding. Being very tired, he lay down to rest at an early hour; but a little before midnight he was roused from sleep by a sound of loud weeping in the next apartment. Presently the sliding-screens were gently pushed apart; and a young man, carrying a lighted lantern, entered the room, respectfully saluted him and said:

"Reverend sir, it is my painful duty to tell you that I am now the responsible head of this house. Yesterday I was only the eldest son. But when you came here, tired as you were, we did not wish that you should feel embarrassed in any way: therefore we did not tell you that father had died only a few hours before. The people whom you saw in the next room are the inhabitants of this village: they all assembled here to pay their last respects to the dead; and now they are going to another village, about three miles off—for, by our custom, no one of us may remain in this village during the night after a death has taken place. We make the proper offerings and prayers;—then we go away, leaving the corpse alone. Strange things always happen in the house where a corpse has thus been left: so we think that it will be better for you to come away with us. We can find you good lodging in the other village. But perhaps, as you are a priest, you have no fear of demons or evil spirits; and, if you are not afraid of being left alone with the body, you will be very welcome to the use of this poor house. However, I must tell you that nobody, except a priest, would dare to remain here to-night."

Musō made answer:

"For your kind intention and your generous hospitality, I am deeply grateful. But I am sorry that you did not tell me of your father's death when I came;—for, though I was a little tired, I certainly was not so tired that I should have found any difficulty in doing my duty as a priest. Had you told me, I could have performed the service before your departure. As it is, I shall perform the service after you have gone away; and I shall stay by the body until morning. I do not know what you mean by your words about the danger of staying here alone; but I am not afraid of ghosts or demons: therefore please to feel no anxiety on my account."

The young man appeared to be rejoiced by these assurances, and expressed his gratitude in fitting words. Then the other members of the family, and the folk assembled in the adjoining room, having been told of the priest's kind promises, came to thank him—after which the master of the house said:

"Now, reverend sir, much as we regret to leave you alone, we must bid you farewell. By the rule of our village, none of us can stay here after midnight. We beg, kind sir, that you will take every care of your honorable body, while we are unable to attend upon you. And if you happen to hear or see anything strange during our absence, please tell us of the matter when we return in the morning."

All then left the house, except the priest, who went to the room where the dead body was lying. The usual offerings had been set before the corpse; and a small Buddhist lamp—*tōmyō*—was burning.

The priest recited the service, and performed the funeral ceremonies—after which he entered into meditation. So meditating he remained through several silent hours; and there was no sound in the deserted village. But, when the hush of the night was at its deepest, there noiselessly entered a Shape, vague and vast; and in the same moment Musō found himself without power to move or speak. He saw that Shape lift the corpse, as with hands, and devour it, more quickly than a cat devours a rat—beginning at the head, and eating everything: the hair and the bones and even the shroud. And the monstrous Thing, having thus consumed the body, turned to the offerings, and ate them also. Then it went away, as mysteriously as it had come.

When the villagers returned next morning, they found the priest awaiting them at the door of the headman's dwelling. All in turn saluted him; and when they had entered, and looked about the room, no one expressed any surprise at the disappearance of the dead body and the offerings. But the master of the house said to Musō:

"Reverend sir, you have probably seen unpleasant things during the night: all of us were anxious about you. But now we are very happy to find you alive and unharmed. Gladly we would have stayed with you, if it had been possible. But the law of our village, as I told you last evening, obliges us to quit our houses after a death has taken place, and to leave the corpse alone. Whenever this law has been broken, heretofore, some great misfortune has followed. Whenever it is obeyed, we find that the corpse and the offerings disappear during our absence. Perhaps you have seen the cause."

Then Musō told of the dim and awful Shape that had entered the death-chamber to devour the body and the offerings. No person seemed to be surprised by his narration; and the master of the house observed:

"What you have told us, reverend sir, agrees with what has been said about this matter from ancient time."

Musō then inquired:

"Does not the priest on the hill sometimes perform the funeral-service for your dead?"

"What priest?" the young man asked.

"The priest who yesterday evening directed me to this village," answered Musō. "I called at his anjitsu on the hill yonder. He refused me lodging, but told me the way here."

The listeners looked at each other, as in astonishment; and, after a moment of silence, the master of the house said:

"Reverend sir, there is no priest and there is no anjitsu on the hill. For the time of many generations there has not been any resident-priest in this neighborhood."

Musō said nothing more on the subject; for it was evident that his kind hosts supposed him to have been deluded by some goblin. But after having bidden them farewell, and obtained all necessary information as to his road, he determined to look again for the hermitage on the hill, and so to ascertain whether he had really been deceived. He found the anjitsu without any difficulty; and, this time, its aged occupant invited him to enter. When he had done so, the hermit humbly bowed down before him, exclaiming: "Ah! I am ashamed!—I am very much ashamed!—I am exceedingly ashamed!"

"You need not be ashamed for having refused me shelter," said Musō. "You directed me to the village yonder, where I was very kindly treated; and I thank you for that favor."

"I can give no man shelter," the recluse made answer;—"and it is not for the refusal that I am ashamed. I am ashamed only that you should have seen me in my real shape—for it was I who devoured the corpse and the offerings last night before your eyes.... Know, reverend sir, that I am a *jikininki*[1]—an eater of human flesh. Have pity upon me, and suffer me to confess the secret fault by which I became reduced to this condition.

"A long, long time ago, I was a priest in this desolate region. There was no other priest for many leagues around. So, in that time, the bodies of the mountain-folk who died used to be brought here—sometimes from great distances—in order that I might repeat over them the holy service. But I repeated the service and performed the rites only as a matter of business;—I thought only of the food and the clothes that my sacred profession enabled me to gain. And because of this selfish impiety I was reborn, immediately after my death, into the state of a jikininki. Since then I have been obliged to feed upon the corpses of the people who die in this district: every one of them I must devour in the way that you saw last night. ... Now, reverend sir, let me beseech you to perform a Ségaki-service[2] for me: help me by your

[1] Literally, a man-eating goblin. The Japanese narrator gives also the Sanscrit term, *Râkshasa;* but this word is quite as vague as *jikininki,* since there are many kinds of Râkshasas. Apparently the word *jikininki* signifies here one of the Baramon-Rasetsu-Gaki—forming the twenty-sixth class of pretas enumerated in the old Buddhist books.

[2] A Ségaki-service is a special Buddhist service performed on behalf of beings supposed to have entered into the condition of *gaki* (pretas), or hungry spirits.

prayers, I entreat you, so that I may be soon able to escape from this horrible state of existence." . . .

No sooner had the hermit uttered this petition than he disappeared; and the hermitage also disappeared at the same instant. And Musō Kokushi found himself kneeling alone in the high grass, beside an ancient and moss-grown tomb, of the form called *go-rin-ishi*,[3] which seemed to be the tomb of a priest.

Mujina

ON THE AKASAKA ROAD, IN TŌKYŌ, THERE IS A SLOPE CALLED KII-NO-KUNI-zaka—which means the Slope of the Province of Kii. I do not know why it is called the Slope of the Province of Kii. On one side of this slope you see an ancient moat, deep and very wide, with high green banks rising up to some place of gardens;—and on the other side of the road extend the long and lofty walls of an imperial palace. Before the era of street-lamps and jinrikishas, this neighborhood was very lonesome after dark; and belated pedestrians would go miles out of their way rather than mount the Kii-no-kuni-zaka, alone, after sunset.

All because of a Mujina that used to walk there.

The last man who saw the Mujina was an old merchant of the Kyōbashi quarter, who died about thirty years ago. This is the story, as he told it:

One night, at a late hour, he was hurrying up the Kii-no-kuni-zaka, when he perceived a woman crouching by the moat, all alone, and weeping bitterly. Fearing that she intended to drown herself, he stopped to offer her any assistance or consolation in his power. She

---

[3] Literally, "five-circle [or 'five-zone'] stone." A funeral monument consisting of five parts superimposed—each of a different form—symbolizing the five mystic elements: Ether, Air, Fire, Water, Earth.

appeared to be a slight and graceful person, handsomely dressed; and her hair was arranged like that of a young girl of good family. "O-jochū,"[1] he exclaimed, approaching her—"O-jochū, do not cry like that! . . . Tell me what the trouble is; and if there be any way to help you, I shall be glad to help you." (He really meant what he said; for he was a very kind man.) But she continued to weep—hiding her face from him with one of her long sleeves. "O-jochū," he said again, as gently as he could—"please, please listen to me! . . . This is no place for a young lady at night! Do not cry, I implore you!—only tell me how I may be of some help to you!" Slowly she rose up, but turned her back to him, and continued to moan and sob behind her sleeve. He laid his hand lightly upon her shoulder, and pleaded: "O-jochū!—O-jochū!—O-jochū! . . . Listen to me, just for one little moment! . . . O-jochū!—O-jochū!" . . . Then that O-jochū turned round, and dropped her sleeve, and stroked her face with her hand;—and the man saw that she had no eyes or nose or mouth—and he screamed and ran away.

Up Kii-no-kuni-zaka he ran and ran; and all was black and empty before him. On and on he ran, never daring to look back; and at last he saw a lantern, so far away that it looked like the gleam of a firefly; and he made for it. It proved to be only the lantern of an itinerant soba-seller,[2] who had set down his stand by the road-side; but any light and any human companionship was good after that experience; and he flung himself down at the feet of the soba-seller, crying out, "Aa!—aa!!—aa! ! !" . . .

"Koré! koré!" roughly exclaimed the soba-man. "Here! what is the matter with you? Anybody hurt you?"

"No—nobody hurt me," panted the other—"only . . . Aa! aa!" . . .

"—Only scared you?" queried the peddler, unsympathetically. "Robbers?"

"Not robbers—not robbers," gasped the terrified man. . . . "I saw . . . I saw a woman—by the moat;—and she showed me . . . Aa! I cannot tell you what she showed me!" . . .

"Hé! Was it anything like THIS that she showed you?" cried the soba-man, stroking his own face—which therewith became like unto an Egg. . . . And, simultaneously, the light went out.

[1] O-jochū (honorable damsel)—a polite form of address used in speaking to a young lady whom one does not know.

[2] Soba is a preparation of buckwheat, somewhat resembling vermicelli.

Rokuro-Kubi

NEARLY FIVE HUNDRED YEARS AGO THERE WAS A SAMURAI, NAMED ISOGAI
Héïdazaëmon Takétsura, in the service of the Lord Kikuji, of Kyūshū.
This Isogai had inherited, from many warlike ancestors, a natural
aptitude for military exercises, and extraordinary strength. While yet
a boy he had surpassed his teachers in the art of swordsmanship, in
archery, and in the use of the spear, and had displayed all the capacities
of a daring and skillful soldier. Afterwards, in the time of the Eikyō [1]
war, he so distinguished himself that high honors were bestowed upon
him. But when the house of Kikuji came to ruin, Isogai found himself
without a master. He might then easily have obtained service under
another *daimyō;* but as he had never sought distinction for his own
sake alone, and as his heart remained true to his former lord, he
preferred to give up the world. So he cut off his hair, and became a
traveling priest—taking the Buddhist name of Kwairyō.

But always, under the *koromo* [2] of the priest, Kwairyō kept warm
within him the heart of the samurai. As in other years he had laughed
at peril, so now also he scorned danger; and in all weathers and all
seasons he journeyed to preach the good Law in places where no other
priest would have dared to go. For that age was an age of violence and
disorder; and upon the highways there was no security for the solitary
traveler, even if he happened to be a priest.

In the course of his first long journey, Kwairyō had occasion to visit
the province of Kai. One evening, as he was traveling through the
mountains of that province, darkness overtook him in a very lonesome
district, leagues away from any village. So he resigned himself to pass
the night under the stars; and having found a suitable grassy spot, by

[1] The period of Eikyō lasted from 1429 to 1441.
[2] The upper robe of a Buddhist priest is thus called.

the roadside, he lay down there, and prepared to sleep. He had always welcomed discomfort; and even a bare rock was for him a good bed, when nothing better could be found, and the root of a pine-tree an excellent pillow. His body was iron; and he never troubled himself about dews or rain or frost or snow.

Scarcely had he lain down when a man came along the road, carrying an axe and a great bundle of chopped wood. This woodcutter halted on seeing Kwairyō lying down, and, after a moment of silent observation, said to him in a tone of great surprise:

"What kind of a man can you be, good sir, that you dare to lie down alone in such a place as this? . . . There are haunters about here—many of them. Are you not afraid of Hairy Things?"

"My friend," cheerfully answered Kwairyō, "I am only a wandering priest—a 'Cloud-and-Water-Guest,' as folks call it: *Un-sui-no-ryokaku.* And I am not in the least afraid of Hairy Things—if you mean goblin-foxes, or goblin-badgers, or any creatures of that kind. As for lonesome places, I like them: they are suitable for meditation. I am accustomed to sleeping in the open air: and I have learned never to be anxious about my life."

"You must be indeed a brave man, Sir Priest," the peasant responded, "to lie down here! This place has a bad name—a very bad name. But, as the proverb has it, '*Kunshi ayayuki ni chikayorazu*' (The superior man does not needlessly expose himself to peril); and I must assure you, sir, that it is very dangerous to sleep here. Therefore, although my house is only a wretched thatched hut, let me beg of you to come home with me at once. In the way of food, I have nothing to offer you; but there is a roof at least, and you can sleep under it without risk."

He spoke earnestly; and Kwairyō, liking the kindly tone of the man, accepted this modest offer. The woodcutter guided him along a narrow path, leading up from the main road through mountain-forest. It was a rough and dangerous path—sometimes skirting precipices—sometimes offering nothing but a network of slippery roots for the foot to rest upon—sometimes winding over or between masses of jagged rock. But at last Kwairyō found himself upon a cleared space at the top of a hill, with a full moon shining overhead; and he saw before him a small thatched cottage, cheerfully lighted from within. The woodcutter led him to a shed at the back of the house, whither water had been conducted, through bamboo-pipes, from some neighboring stream; and the two men washed their feet. Beyond the shed was a vegetable garden, and a grove of cedars and bamboos; and beyond the trees appeared the glimmer of a cascade, pouring from some loftier height, and swaying in the moonshine like a long white robe.

As Kwairyō entered the cottage with his guide, he perceived four persons—men and women—warming their hands at a little fire kindled in the *ro* [3] of the principal apartment. They bowed low to the priest, and greeted him in the most respectful manner. Kwairyō wondered that persons so poor, and dwelling in such a solitude, should be aware of the polite forms of greeting. "These are good people," he thought to himself; "and they must have been taught by some one well acquainted with the rules of propriety." Then turning to his host—the *aruji* or house-master, as the others called him—Kwairyō said:

"From the kindness of your speech, and from the very polite welcome given me by your household, I imagine that you have not always been a woodcutter. Perhaps you formerly belonged to one of the upper classes?"

Smiling, the woodcutter answered:

"Sir, you are not mistaken. Though now living as you find me, I was once a person of some distinction. My story is the story of a ruined life—ruined by my own fault. I used to be in the service of a daimyō; and my rank in that service was not inconsiderable. But I loved women and wine too well; and under the influence of passion I acted wickedly. My selfishness brought about the ruin of our house, and caused the death of many persons. Retribution followed me; and I long remained a fugitive in the land. Now I often pray that I may be able to make some atonement for the evil which I did, and to re-establish the ancestral home. But I fear that I shall never find any way of so doing. Nevertheless, I try to overcome the karma of my errors by sincere repentance, and by helping, as far as I can, those who are unfortunate."

Kwairyō was pleased by this announcement of good resolve; and he said to the aruji:

"My friend, I have had occasion to observe that men, prone to folly in their youth, may in after years become very earnest in right living. In the holy sutras it is written that those strongest in wrong-doing can become, by power of good resolve, the strongest in right-doing. I do not doubt that you have a good heart; and I hope that better fortune will

---

[3] A sort of little fireplace, contrived in the floor of a room, is thus described. The *ro* is usually a square shallow cavity, lined with metal and half-filled with ashes, in which charcoal is lighted.

come to you. To-night I shall recite the sutras for your sake, and pray that you may obtain the force to overcome the karma of any past errors."

With these assurances, Kwairyō bade the aruji good-night; and his host showed him to a very small side-room, where a bed had been made ready. Then all went to sleep except the priest, who began to read the sutras by the light of a paper lantern. Until a late hour he continued to read and pray: then he opened a window in his little sleeping-room, to take a last look at the landscape before lying down. The night was beautiful: there was no cloud in the sky; there was no wind; and the strong moonlight threw down sharp black shadows of foliage, and glittered on the dews of the garden. Shrillings of crickets and bell-insects made a musical tumult; and the sound of the neighboring cascade deepened with the night. Kwairyō felt thirsty as he listened to the noise of the water; and, remembering the bamboo aqueduct at the rear of the house, he thought that he could go there and get a drink without disturbing the sleeping household. Very gently he pushed apart the sliding-screens that separated his room from the main apartment; and he saw, by the light of the lantern, five recumbent bodies—without heads!

For one instant he stood bewildered—imagining a crime. But in another moment he perceived that there was no blood, and that the headless necks did not look as if they had been cut. Then he thought to himself: "Either this is an illusion made by goblins, or I have been lured into the dwelling of a Rokuro-Kubi. . . . In the book 'Sōshinki' it is written that if one find the body of a Rokuro-Kubi without its head, and remove the body to another place, the head will never be able to join itself again to the neck. And the book further says that when the head comes back and finds that its body has been moved, it will strike itself upon the floor three times—bounding like a ball— and will pant as in great fear, and presently die. Now, if these be Rokuro-Kubi, they mean me no good;—so I shall be justified in follow-ing the instructions of the book." . . .

He seized the body of the aruji by the feet, pulled it to the window, and pushed it out. Then he went to the back door, which he found barred; and he surmised that the heads had made their exit through the smoke-hole in the roof, which had been left open. Gently unbarring the door, he made his way to the garden, and proceeded with all possible caution to the grove beyond it. He heard voices talking in the grove; and he went in the direction of the voices—stealing from shadow to shadow, until he reached a good hiding-place. Then, from behind a trunk, he caught sight of the heads—all five of them—flitting about, and chatting as they flitted. They were eating worms and insects which they found on the ground or among the trees. Presently the head of the aruji stopped eating and said:

"Ah, that traveling priest who came to-night!—how fat all his body is! When we shall have eaten him, our bellies will be well filled. . . . I was foolish to talk to him as I did;—it only set him to reciting the sutras on behalf of my soul! To go near him while he is reciting would be difficult; and we cannot touch him so long as he is praying. But as it is now nearly morning, perhaps he has gone to sleep. . . . Some one of you go to the house and see what the fellow is doing."

Another head—the head of a young woman—immediately rose up and flitted to the house, lightly as a bat. After a few minutes it came back, and cried out huskily, in a tone of great alarm:

"That traveling priest is not in the house;—he is gone! But that is not the worst of the matter. He has taken the body of our aruji; and I do not know where he has put it."

At this announcement the head of the aruji—distinctly visible in the moonlight—assumed a frightful aspect: its eyes opened monstrously; its hair stood up bristling; and its teeth gnashed. Then a cry burst from its lips; and—weeping tears of rage—it exclaimed:

"Since my body has been moved, to rejoin it is not possible! Then I must die! . . . And all through the work of that priest! Before I die I will get at that priest!—I will tear him!—I will devour him! . . . *And there he is*—behind that tree!—hiding behind that tree! See him! —the fat coward!" . . .

In the same moment the head of the aruji, followed by the other four heads, sprang at Kwairyō. But the strong priest had already armed himself by plucking up a young tree; and with that tree he struck the heads as they came—knocking them from him with tremendous blows. Four of them fled away. But the head of the aruji, though battered again and again, desperately continued to bound at the priest, and at last caught him by the left sleeve of his robe. Kwairyō, however, as quickly gripped the head by its topknot, and repeatedly struck it. It did not release its hold; but it uttered a long moan, and thereafter ceased to struggle. It was dead. But its teeth still held the sleeve; and, for all his great strength, Kwairyō could not force open the jaws.

With the head still hanging to his sleeve he went back to the house, and there caught sight of the other four Rokuro-Kubi squatting together, with their bruised and bleeding heads reunited to their bodies. But when they perceived him at the back door all screamed, "The priest! the priest!"—and fled, through the other doorway, out into the woods.

Eastward the sky was brightening; day was about to dawn; and Kwairyō knew that the power of the goblins was limited to the hours of darkness. He looked at the head clinging to his sleeve—its face all fouled with blood and foam and clay; and he laughed aloud as he thought to himself: "What a *miyagé!* [4]—the head of a goblin!" After which he gathered together his few belongings, and leisurely descended the mountain to continue his journey.

Right on he journeyed, until he came to Suwa in Shinano; and into the main street of Suwa he solemnly strode, with the head dangling at his elbow. Then women fainted, and children screamed and ran away; and there was a great crowding and clamoring until the *torité* (as the police of those days were called) seized the priest, and took him to jail. For they supposed the head to be the head of a murdered man who, in the moment of being killed, had caught the murderer's sleeve in his teeth. As for Kwairyō, he only smiled and said nothing when they questioned him. So, after having passed a night in prison, he was brought before the magistrates of the district. Then he was ordered to explain how he, a priest, had been found with the head of a man fastened to his sleeve, and why he had dared thus shamelessly to parade his crime in the sight of the people.

Kwairyō laughed long and loudly at these questions; and then he said:

"Sirs, I did not fasten the head to my sleeve: it fastened itself there— much against my will. And I have not committed any crime. For this is not the head of a man; it is the head of a goblin;—and, if I caused the death of the goblin, I did not do so by any shedding of blood, but simply by taking the precautions necessary to assure my own safety." . . . And he proceeded to relate the whole of the adventure— bursting into another hearty laugh as he told of his encounter with the five heads.

But the magistrates did not laugh. They judged him to be a hardened criminal, and his story an insult to their intelligence. Therefore, without further questioning, they decided to order his immediate execution

---

[4] A present made to friends or to the household on returning from a journey is thus called. Ordinarily, of course, the *miyagé* consists of something produced in the locality to which the journey has been made: this is the point of Kwairyō's jest.

—all of them except one, a very old man. This aged officer had made no remark during the trial; but, after having heard the opinion of his colleagues, he rose up, and said:

"Let us first examine the head carefully; for this, I think, has not yet been done. If the priest has spoken truth, the head itself should bear witness for him. . . . Bring the head here!"

So the head, still holding in its teeth the koromo that had been stripped from Kwairyō's shoulders, was put before the judges. The old man turned it round and round, carefully examined it, and discovered, on the nape of its neck, several strange red characters. He called the attention of his colleagues to these, and also bade them observe that the edges of the neck nowhere presented the appearance of having been cut by any weapon. On the contrary, the line of severance was smooth as the line at which a falling leaf detaches itself from the stem. . . . Then said the elder:

"I am quite sure that the priest told us nothing but the truth. This is the head of a Rokuro-Kubi. In the book 'Nan-hō-ï-butsu-shi' it is written that certain red characters can always be found upon the nape of the neck of a real Rokuro-Kubi. There are the characters: you can see for yourselves that they have not been painted. Moreover, it is well known that such goblins have been dwelling in the mountains of the province of Kai from very ancient time. . . . But you, sir," he exclaimed, turning to Kwairyō—"what sort of sturdy priest may you be? Certainly you have given proof of a courage that few priests possess; and you have the air of a soldier rather than of a priest. Perhaps you once belonged to the samurai-class?"

"You have guessed rightly, sir," Kwairyō responded. "Before becoming a priest, I long followed the profession of arms; and in those days I never feared man or devil. My name then was Isogai Héïdazaëmon Takétsura, of Kyūshū: there may be some among you who remember it."

At the utterance of that name, a murmur of admiration filled the court-room; for there were many present who remembered it. And Kwairyō immediately found himself among friends instead of judges— friends anxious to prove their admiration by fraternal kindness. With honor they escorted him to the residence of the daimyō, who welcomed him, and feasted him, and made him a handsome present before allowing him to depart. When Kwairyō left Suwa, he was as happy as any priest is permitted to be in this transitory world. As for the head, he took it with him—jocosely insisting that he intended it for a miyagé.

And now it only remains to tell what became of the head.

A day or two after leaving Suwa, Kwairyō met with a robber, who stopped him in a lonesome place, and bade him strip. Kwairyō at once removed his koromo, and offered it to the robber, who then first perceived what was hanging to the sleeve. Though brave, the highwayman was startled: he dropped the garment, and sprang back. Then he cried out: "You!—what kind of a priest are you? Why, you are a worse man than I am! It is true that I have killed people; but I never walked about with anybody's head fastened to my sleeve. . . . Well, Sir Priest, I suppose we are of the same calling; and I must say that I admire you! . . . Now that head would be of use to me: I could frighten people with it. Will you sell it? You can have my robe in exchange for your koromo; and I will give you five ryō for the head."

Kwairyō answered:

"I shall let you have the head and the robe if you insist; but I must tell you that this is not the head of a man. It is a goblin's head. So, if you buy it, and have any trouble in consequence, please to remember that you were not deceived by me."

"What a nice priest you are!" exclaimed the robber. "You kill men, and jest about it! . . . But I am really in earnest. Here is my robe; and here is the money;—and let me have the head. . . . What is the use of joking?"

"Take the thing," said Kwairyō. "I was not joking. The only joke—if there be any joke at all—is that you are fool enough to pay good money for a goblin's head." And Kwairyō, loudly laughing, went upon his way.

Thus the robber got the head and the koromo; and for some time he played goblin-priest upon the highways. But, reaching the neighborhood of Suwa, he there learned the real history of the head; and he then became afraid that the spirit of the Rokuro-Kubi might give him trouble. So he made up his mind to take back the head to the place from which it had come, and to bury it with its body. He found his way to the lonely cottage in the mountains of Kai; but nobody was there, and he could not discover the body. Therefore he buried the head by itself, in the grove behind the cottage; and he had a tombstone set up over the grave; and he caused a Ségaki-service to be performed on behalf of the spirit of the Rokuro-Kubi. And that tombstone—known as the Tombstone of the Rokuro-Kubi—may be seen (at least so the Japanese story-teller declares) even unto this day.

A Dead Secret

A LONG TIME AGO, IN THE PROVINCE OF TAMBA, THERE LIVED A RICH MER-
chant named Inamuraya Gensuké. He had a daughter called O-Sono.
As she was very clever and pretty, he thought it would be a pity to let
her grow up with only such teaching as the country-teachers could give
her: so he sent her, in care of some trusty attendants, to Kyōto, that she
might be trained in the polite accomplishments taught to the ladies of
the capital. After she had thus been educated, she was married to a
friend of her father's family—a merchant named Nagaraya;—and she
lived happily with him for nearly four years. They had one child—a
boy. But O-Sono fell ill and died, in the fourth year after her marriage.

On the night after the funeral of O-Sono, her little son said that his
mamma had come back, and was in the room upstairs. She had smiled
at him, but would not talk to him: so he became afraid, and ran away.
Then some of the family went upstairs to the room which had been
O-Sono's; and they were startled to see, by the light of a small lamp
which had been kindled before a shrine in that room, the figure of the
dead mother. She appeared as if standing in front of a *tansu,* or chest
of drawers, that still contained her ornaments and her wearing-apparel.
Her head and shoulders could be very distinctly seen; but from the
waist downwards the figure thinned into invisibility;—it was like an
imperfect reflection of her, and transparent as a shadow on water.

Then the folk were afraid, and left the room. Below they consulted
together; and the mother of O-Sono's husband said: "A woman is fond
of her small things; and O-Sono was much attached to her belongings.
Perhaps she has come back to look at them. Many dead persons will do
that—unless the things be given to the parish-temple. If we present
O-Sono's robes and girdles to the temple, her spirit will probably find
rest."

It was agreed that this should be done as soon as possible. So on the following morning the drawers were emptied; and all of O-Sono's ornaments and dresses were taken to the temple. But she came back the next night, and looked at the tansu as before. And she came back also on the night following, and the night after that, and every night;—and the house became a house of fear.

The mother of O-Sono's husband then went to the parish-temple, and told the chief priest all that had happened, and asked for ghostly counsel. The temple was a Zen temple; and the head-priest was a learned old man, known as Daigen Oshō.

He said: "There must be something about which she is anxious, in or near that tansu."

"But we emptied all the drawers," replied the old woman;—"there is nothing in the tansu."

"Well," said Daigen Oshō, "to-night I shall go to your house, and keep watch in that room, and see what can be done. You must give orders that no person shall enter the room while I am watching, unless I call."

After sundown, Daigen Oshō went to the house, and found the room made ready for him. He remained there alone, reading the sutras; and nothing appeared until after the Hour of the Rat.[1] Then the figure of O-Sono suddenly outlined itself in front of the tansu. Her face had a wistful look; and she kept her eyes fixed upon the tansu.

The priest uttered the holy formula prescribed in such cases, and then, addressing the figure by the *kaimyō*[2] of O-Sono, said: "I have come here in order to help you. Perhaps in that tansu there is something about which you have reason to feel anxious. Shall I try to find it for you?" The shadow appeared to give assent by a slight motion of the head; and the priest, rising, opened the top drawer. It was empty. Successively he opened the second, the third, and the fourth drawer;—he searched carefully behind them and beneath them;—he carefully examined the interior of the chest. He found nothing. But the figure remained gazing as wistfully as before. "What can she want?" thought the priest. Suddenly it occurred to him that there might be something

---

[1] The Hour of the Rat (*Né-no-Koku*), according to the old Japanese method of reckoning time, was the first hour. It corresponded to the time between our midnight and two o'clock in the morning; for the ancient Japanese hours were each equal to two modern hours.

[2] *Kaimyō*, the posthumous Buddhist name, or religious name, given to the dead.

hidden under the paper with which the drawers were lined. He re-moved the lining of the first drawer:—nothing! He removed the lining of the second and third drawers:—still nothing. But under the lining of the lowermost drawer he found—a letter. "Is this the thing about which you have been troubled?" he asked. The shadow of the woman turned toward him—her faint gaze fixed upon the letter. "Shall I burn it for you?" he asked. She bowed before him. "It shall be burned in the temple this very morning," he promised;—"and no one shall read it, except myself." The figure smiled and vanished.

Dawn was breaking as the priest descended the stairs, to find the family waiting anxiously below. "Do not be anxious," he said to them: "she will not appear again." And she never did.

The letter was burned. It was a love-letter written to O-Sono in the time of her studies at Kyōto. But the priest alone knew what was in it; and the secret died with him.

Yuki-Onna

IN A VILLAGE OF MUSASHI PROVINCE, THERE LIVED TWO WOODCUTTERS: Mosaku and Minokichi. At the time of which I am speaking, Mosaku was an old man; and Minokichi, his apprentice, was a lad of eighteen years. Every day they went together to a forest situated about five miles from their village. On the way to that forest there is a wide river to cross; and there is a ferry-boat. Several times a bridge was built where the ferry is; but the bridge was each time carried away by a flood. No common bridge can resist the current there when the river rises.

Mosaku and Minokichi were on their way home, one very cold eve-ning, when a great snowstorm overtook them. They reached the ferry; and they found that the boatman had gone away, leaving his boat on the other side of the river. It was no day for swimming; and the woodcutters took shelter in the ferryman's hut—thinking themselves lucky to find any shelter at all. There was no brazier in the hut, nor any place in which to make a fire: it was only a two-mat[1] hut, with a single door, but no window. Mosaku and Minokichi fastened the door, and lay down to rest, with their straw rain-coats over them. At first they did not feel very cold; and they thought that the storm would soon be over.

The old man almost immediately fell asleep; but the boy, Minokichi, lay awake a long time, listening to the awful wind, and the continual slashing of the snow against the door. The river was roaring; and the hut swayed and creaked like a junk at sea. It was a terrible storm; and the air was every moment becoming colder; and Minokichi shivered under his rain-coat. But at last, in spite of the cold, he too fell asleep.

He was awakened by a showering of snow in his face. The door of the hut had been forced open; and, by the snow-light (*yuki-akari*), he saw a woman in the room—a woman all in white. She was bending above Mosaku, and blowing her breath upon him;—and her breath was like a bright white smoke. Almost in the same moment she turned to Minokichi, and stooped over him. He tried to cry out, but found that he could not utter any sound. The white woman bent down over him, lower and lower, until her face almost touched him; and he saw that she was very beautiful—though her eyes made him afraid. For a little time she continued to look at him;—then she smiled, and she whispered: "I intended to treat you like the other man. But I cannot help feeling some pity for you—because you are so young. . . . You are a pretty boy, Minokichi; and I will not hurt you now. But, if you ever tell anybody—even your own mother—about what you have seen this night, I shall know it; and then I will kill you. . . . Remember what I say!"

With these words, she turned from him, and passed through the doorway. Then he found himself able to move; and he sprang up, and looked out. But the woman was nowhere to be seen; and the snow was driving furiously into the hut. Minokichi closed the door, and secured it by fixing several billets of wood against it. He wondered if the wind had blown it open;—he thought that he might have been only dreaming, and might have mistaken the gleam of the snow-light in the doorway for the figure of a white woman: but he could not be sure. He called to Mosaku, and was frightened because the old man did not answer. He put out his hand in the dark, and touched Mosaku's face, and found that it was ice! Mosaku was stark and dead. . . .

[1] That is to say, with a floor-surface of about six feet square.

By dawn the storm was over; and when the ferryman returned to his station, a little after sunrise, he found Minokichi lying senseless beside the frozen body of Mosaku. Minokichi was promptly cared for, and soon came to himself; but he remained a long time ill from the effects of the cold of that terrible night. He had been greatly frightened also by the old man's death; but he said nothing about the vision of the woman in white. As soon as he got well again, he returned to his calling—going alone every morning to the forest, and coming back at nightfall with his bundles of wood, which his mother helped him to sell.

One evening, in the winter of the following year, as he was on his way home, he overtook a girl who happened to be traveling by the same road. She was a tall, slim girl, very good-looking; and she answered Minokichi's greeting in a voice as pleasant to the ear as the voice of a song-bird. Then he walked beside her; and they began to talk. The girl said that her name was O-Yuki; [2] that she had lately lost both of her parents; and that she was going to Yedo, where she happened to have some poor relations, who might help her to find a situation as servant. Minokichi soon felt charmed by this strange girl; and the more that he looked at her, the handsomer she appeared to be. He asked her whether she was yet betrothed; and she answered, laughingly, that she was free. Then, in her turn, she asked Minokichi whether he was married, or pledged to marry; and he told her that, although he had only a widowed mother to support, the question of an "honorable daughter-in-law" had not yet been considered, as he was very young. . . . After these confidences, they walked on for a long while without speaking; but, as the proverb declares, *"Ki ga aréba, mé mo kuchi hodo ni mono wo iu"* (When the wish is there, the eyes can say as much as the mouth). By the time they reached the village, they had become very much pleased with each other; and then Minokichi asked O-Yuki to rest awhile at his house. After some shy hesitation, she went there with him; and his mother made her welcome, and prepared a warm meal for her. O-Yuki behaved so nicely that Minokichi's mother took a sudden fancy to her, and persuaded her to delay her journey to Yedo. And the natural end of the matter was that Yuki never went to Yedo at all. She remained in the house, as an "honorable daughter-in-law."

[2] This name, signifying "Snow," is not uncommon.

O-Yuki proved a very good daughter-in-law. When Minokichi's mother came to die—some five years later—her last words were words of affection and praise for the wife of her son. And O-Yuki bore Minokichi ten children, boys and girls—handsome children all of them, and very fair of skin.

The country-folk thought O-Yuki a wonderful person, by nature different from themselves. Most of the peasant-women age early; but O-Yuki, even having become the mother of ten children, looked as young and fresh as on the day when she had first come to the village.

One night, after the children had gone to sleep, O-Yuki was sewing by the light of a paper lamp; and Minokichi, watching her, said:

"To see you sewing there, with the light on your face, makes me think of a strange thing that happened when I was a lad of eighteen. I then saw somebody as beautiful and white as you are now—indeed, she was very like you." . . .

Without lifting her eyes from her work, O-Yuki responded:

"Tell me about her. . . . Where did you see her?"

Then Minokichi told her about the terrible night in the ferryman's hut—and about the White Woman that had stooped above him, smiling and whispering—and about the silent death of old Mosaku. And he said:

"Asleep or awake, that was the only time that I saw a being as beautiful as you. Of course, she was not a human being; and I was afraid of her—very much afraid—but she was so white! . . . Indeed, I have never been sure whether it was a dream that I saw, or the Woman of the Snow." . . .

O-Yuki flung down her sewing, and arose, and bowed above Minokichi where he sat, and shrieked into his face:

"It was I—I—I! Yuki it was! And I told you then that I would kill you if you ever said one word about it! . . . But for those children asleep there, I would kill you this moment! And now you had better take very, very good care of them; for if ever they have reason to complain of you, I will treat you as you deserve!" . . .

Even as she screamed, her voice became thin, like a crying of wind; —then she melted into a bright white mist that spired to the roof-beams, and shuddered away through the smoke-hole. . . . Never again was she seen.

The Story of Aoyagi

IN THE ERA OF BUMMEI [1469–86] THERE WAS A YOUNG SAMURAI CALLED Tomotada in the service of Hatakéyama Yoshimuné, the Lord of Noto. Tomotada was a native of Echizen; but at an early age he had been taken, as page, into the palace of the daimyō of Noto, and had been educated, under the supervision of that prince, for the profession of arms. As he grew up, he proved himself both a good scholar and a good soldier, and continued to enjoy the favor of his prince. Being gifted with an amiable character, a winning address, and a very handsome person, he was admired and much liked by his samurai-comrades.

When Tomotada was about twenty years old, he was sent upon a private mission to Hosokawa Masamoto, the great daimyō of Kyōto, a kinsman of Hatakéyama Yoshimuné. Having been ordered to journey through Echizen, the youth requested and obtained permission to pay a visit, on the way, to his widowed mother.

It was the coldest period of the year when he started; the country was covered with snow; and, though mounted upon a powerful horse, he found himself obliged to proceed slowly. The road which he followed passed through a mountain-district where the settlements were few and far between; and on the second day of his journey, after a weary ride of hours, he was dismayed to find that he could not reach his intended halting-place until late in the night. He had reason to be anxious;—for a heavy snowstorm came on, with an intensely cold wind; and the horse showed signs of exhaustion. But, in that trying moment, Tomotada unexpectedly perceived the thatched roof of a cottage on the summit of a near hill, where willow-trees were growing. With difficulty he urged his tired animal to the dwelling; and he loudly knocked upon the storm-doors, which had been closed against the wind. An old woman opened them, and cried out compassionately at the sight of the handsome stranger: "Ah, how pitiful!—a young gentleman traveling alone in such weather! . . . Deign, young master, to enter."

Tomotada dismounted, and after leading his horse to a shed in the rear, entered the cottage, where he saw an old man and a girl warming themselves by a fire of bamboo splints. They respectfully invited him to approach the fire; and the old folks then proceeded to warm some rice-wine, and to prepare food for the traveler, whom they ventured to question in regard to his journey. Meanwhile the young girl disappeared behind a screen. Tomotada had observed, with astonishment, that she was extremely beautiful—though her attire was of the most wretched kind, and her long, loose hair in disorder. He wondered that so handsome a girl should be living in such a miserable and lonesome place.

The old man said to him:

"Honored sir, the next village is far; and the snow is falling thickly. The wind is piercing; and the road is very bad. Therefore, to proceed further this night would probably be dangerous. Although this hovel is unworthy of your presence, and although we have not any comfort to offer, perhaps it were safer to remain to-night under this miserable roof. . . . We would take good care of your horse."

Tomotada accepted this humble proposal—secretly glad of the chance thus afforded him to see more of the young girl. Presently a coarse but ample meal was set before him; and the girl came from behind the screen, to serve the wine. She was now reclad, in a rough but cleanly robe of homespun; and her long, loose hair had been neatly combed and smoothed. As she bent forward to fill his cup, Tomotada was amazed to perceive that she was incomparably more beautiful than any woman whom he had ever before seen; and there was a grace about her every motion that astonished him. But the elders began to apologize for her, saying: "Sir, our daughter, Aoyagi,[1] has been brought up here, in the mountains, almost alone; and she knows nothing of gentle service. We pray that you will pardon her stupidity and her ignorance." Tomotada protested that he deemed himself lucky to be waited upon by so comely a maiden. He could not turn his eyes away from her—though he saw that his admiring gaze made her blush;—and he left the wine and food untasted before him. The mother said: "Kind sir, we very much hope that you will try to eat

[1] The name signifies "Green Willow";—though rarely met with, it is still in use.

and to drink a little—though our peasant-fare is of the worst—as you
must have been chilled by that piercing wind." Then, to please the
old folks, Tomotada ate and drank as he could; but the charm of the
blushing girl still grew upon him. He talked with her, and found
that her speech was sweet as her face. Brought up in the mountains
she might have been;—but, in that case, her parents must at some
time have been persons of high degree; for she spoke and moved like
a damsel of rank. Suddenly he addressed her with a poem—which was
also a question—inspired by the delight in his heart:

> *Tadzunétsuru,*
> *Hana ka toté koso,*
> *Hi wo kurasé,*
> *Akénu ni otoru*
> *Akané sasuran?*

Being on my way to pay a visit, I found that which I took
to be a flower: therefore here I spend the day. . . . Why, in
the time before dawn, the dawn-blush tint should glow—that,
indeed, I know not. [2]

Without a moment's hesitation, she answered him in these verses:

> *Izuru hi no*
> *Honoméku iro wo*
> *Waga sodé ni*
> *Tsutsumaba asu mo*
> *Kimiya tomaran.*

If with my sleeve I hide the faint fair color of the dawning
sun—then, perhaps, in the morning my lord will remain. [3]

Then Tomotada knew that she accepted his admiration; and he
was scarcely less surprised by the art with which she had uttered her

[2] The poem may be read in two ways; several of the phrases having a double meaning.
But the art of its construction would need considerable space to explain, and could
scarcely interest the Western reader. The meaning which Tomotada desired to convey
might be thus expressed: "While journeying to visit my mother, I met with a being
lovely as a flower; and for the sake of that lovely person, I am passing the day here. . . .
Fair one, wherefore that dawnlike blush before the hour of dawn?—can it mean that
you love me?"

[3] Another reading is possible; but this one gives the signification of the *answer* intended.

feelings in verse, than delighted by the assurance which the verses conveyed. He was now certain that in all this world he could not hope to meet, much less to win, a girl more beautiful and witty than this rustic maid before him; and a voice in his heart seemed to cry out urgently, "Take the luck that the gods have put in your way!" In short he was bewitched—bewitched to such a degree that, without further preliminary, he asked the old people to give him their daughter in marriage—telling them, at the same time, his name and lineage, and his rank in the train of the Lord of Noto.

They bowed down before him, with many exclamations of grateful astonishment. But, after some moments of apparent hesitation, the father replied:

"Honored master, you are a person of high position, and likely to rise to still higher things. Too great is the favor that you deign to offer us;—indeed, the depth of our gratitude therefor is not to be spoken or measured. But this girl of ours, being a stupid country-girl of vulgar birth, with no training or teaching of any sort, it would be improper to let her become the wife of a noble samurai. Even to speak of such a matter is not right. . . . But, since you find the girl to your liking, and have condescended to pardon her peasant-manners and to overlook her great rudeness, we do gladly present her to you, for an humble handmaid. Deign, therefore, to act thereafter in her regard according to your august pleasure."

Ere morning the storm had passed; and day broke through a cloudless east. Even if the sleeve of Aoyagi hid from her lover's eyes the rose-blush of that dawn, he could not longer tarry. But neither could he resign himself to part with the girl; and, when everything had been prepared for his journey, he thus addressed her parents:

"Though it may seem thankless to ask for more than I have already received, I must once again beg you to give me your daughter for wife. It would be difficult for me to separate from her now; and as she is willing to accompany me, if you permit, I can take her with me as she is. If you will give her to me, I shall ever cherish you as parents. . . . And, in the meantime, please to accept this poor acknowledgment of your kindest hospitality."

So saying, he placed before his humble host a purse of gold ryō. But the old man, after many prostrations, gently pushed back the gift, and said:

"Kind master, the gold would be of no use to us; and you will probably have need of it during your long, cold journey. Here we buy nothing; and we could not spend so much money upon ourselves, even if we wished. . . . As for the girl, we have already bestowed her as a free gift;—she belongs to you: therefore it is not necessary to ask our leave to take her away. Already she has told us that she hopes to accompany you, and to remain your servant so long as you may be willing to endure her presence. We are only too happy to know that you deign to accept her; and we pray that you will not trouble yourself on our account. In this place we could not provide her with proper clothing—much less with a dowry. Moreover, being old, we should in any event have to separate from her before long. Therefore it is very fortunate that you should be willing to take her with you now."

It was in vain that Tomotada tried to persuade the old people to accept a present: he found that they cared nothing for money. But he saw that they were really anxious to trust their daughter's fate to his hands; and he therefore decided to take her with him. So he placed her upon his horse, and bade the old folks farewell for the time being, with many sincere expressions of gratitude.

"Honored sir," the father made answer, "it is we, and not you, who have reason for gratitude. We are sure that you will be kind to our girl; and we have no fears for her sake." . . .

[Here, in the Japanese original, there is a queer break in the natural course of the narration, which therefrom remains curiously inconsistent. Nothing further is said about the mother of Tomotada, or about the parents of Aoyagi, or about the daimyō of Noto. Evidently the writer wearied of his work at this point, and hurried the story, very carelessly, to its startling end. I am not able to supply his omissions, or to repair his faults of construction; but I must venture to put in a few explanatory details, without which the rest of the tale would not hold together. . . . It appears that Tomotada rashly took Aoyagi with him to Kyōto, and so got into trouble; but we are not informed as to where the couple lived afterwards.]

. . . Now a samurai was not allowed to marry without the consent of his lord; and Tomotada could not expect to obtain this sanction before his mission had been accomplished. He had reason, under such circumstances, to fear that the beauty of Aoyagi might attract dangerous attention, and that means might be devised of taking her away from him. In Kyōto he therefore tried to keep her hidden from curious eyes. But a retainer of the Lord Hosokawa one day caught sight of Aoyagi, discovered her relation to Tomotada, and reported the matter to the daimyō. Thereupon the daimyō—a young prince, and fond of pretty faces—gave orders that the girl should be brought to the palace; and she was taken thither at once, without ceremony.

Tomotada sorrowed unspeakably; but he knew himself powerless. He was only an humble messenger in the service of a far-off daimyō; and for the time being he was at the mercy of a much more powerful daimyō, whose wishes were not to be questioned. Moreover, Tomotada knew that he had acted foolishly—that he had brought about his own misfortune, by entering into a clandestine relation which the code of the military class condemned. There was now but one hope for him—a desperate hope: that Aoyagi might be able and willing to escape and to flee with him. After long reflection, he resolved to try to send her a letter. The attempt would be dangerous, of course: any writing sent to her might find its way to the hands of the daimyō; and to send a love-letter to any inmate of the palace was an unpardonable offense. But he resolved to dare the risk; and, in the form of a Chinese poem, he composed a letter which he endeavored to have conveyed to her. The poem was written with only twenty-eight characters. But with those twenty-eight characters he was able to express all the depth of his passion, and to suggest all the pain of his loss:[4]

> *Kōshi ō-son gojin wo ou;*
> *Ryokuju namida wo tarété rakin wo hitataru;*
> *Komon hitotabi irité fukaki koto umi no gotoshi;*
> *Koré yori shorō koré rojin.*

Closely, closely the youthful prince now follows after the gem-bright maid;— The tears of the fair one, falling, have moistened all her robes. But the august lord, having once become enamoured of her—the depth of his longing is like the depth of the sea. Therefore it is only I that am left forlorn —only I that am left to wander alone.

On the evening of the day after this poem had been sent, Tomotada was summoned to appear before the Lord Hosokawa. The youth at

[4] So the Japanese story-teller would have us believe—although the verses seem commonplace in translation. I have tried to give only their general meaning: an effective literal translation would require some scholarship.

once suspected that his confidence had been betrayed; and he could not hope, if his letter had been seen by the daimyō, to escape the severest penalty. "Now he will order my death," thought Tomotada;— "but I do not care to live unless Aoyagi be restored to me. Besides, if the death sentence be passed, I can at least try to kill Hosokawa." He slipped his swords into his girdle, and hastened to the palace.

On entering the presence-room he saw the Lord Hosokawa seated upon the dais, surrounded by samurai of high rank, in caps and robes of ceremony. All were silent as statues; and while Tomotada advanced to make obeisance, the hush seemed to him sinister and heavy, like the stillness before a storm. But Hosokawa suddenly descended from the dais, and, taking the youth by the arm, began to repeat the words of the poem: "*Kōshi ō-son gojin wo ou.*" . . . And Tomotada, looking up, saw kindly tears in the prince's eyes.

Then said Hosokawa:

"Because you love each other so much, I have taken it upon myself to authorize your marriage, in lieu of my kinsman, the Lord of Noto; and your wedding shall now be celebrated before me. The guests are assembled;—the gifts are ready."

At a signal from the lord, the sliding-screens concealing a further apartment were pushed open and Tomotada saw there many dignitaries of the court, assembled for the ceremony, and Aoyagi awaiting him in bride's apparel. . . . Thus was she given back to him;—and the wedding was joyous and splendid;—and precious gifts were made to the young couple by the prince, and the members of his household.

For five happy years, after that wedding, Tomotada and Aoyagi dwelt together. But one morning Aoyagi, while talking with her husband about some household matter, suddenly uttered a great cry of pain, and then became very white and still. After a few moments she said, in a feeble voice: "Pardon me for thus rudely crying out— but the pain was so sudden! . . . My dear husband, our union must have been brought about through some karma-relation in a former state of existence; and that happy relation, I think, will bring us again together in more than one life to come. But for this present existence of ours, the relation is now ended;—we are about to be separated. Repeat for me, I beseech you, the Nembutsu-prayer—because I am dying."

"Oh! what strange wild fancies!" cried the startled husband—"you are only a little unwell, my dear one! . . . Lie down for a while, and rest; and the sickness will pass." . . .

"No, no!" she responded—"I am dying!—I do not imagine it;—I know! . . . And it were needless now, my dear husband, to hide the truth from you any longer: I am not a human being. The soul of a tree is my soul;—the heart of a tree is my heart;—the sap of the willow is my life. And some one, at this cruel moment, is cutting down my tree:—that is why I must die! . . . Even to weep were now beyond my strength!—quickly, quickly repeat the Nembutsu for me . . . quickly! . . . Ah!" . . .

With another cry of pain she turned aside her beautiful head, and tried to hide her face behind her sleeve. But almost in the same moment her whole form appeared to collapse in the strangest way, and to sink down, down, down—level with the floor. Tomotada had sprung to support her;—but there was nothing to support! There lay on the matting only the empty robes of the fair creature and the ornaments that she had worn in her hair: the body had ceased to exist. . . .

Tomotada shaved his head, took the Buddhist vows, and became an itinerant priest. He traveled through all the provinces of the empire; and, at all the holy places which he visited, he offered up prayers for the soul of Aoyagi. Reaching Echizen, in the course of his pilgrimage, he sought the home of the parents of his beloved. But when he arrived at the lonely place among the hills, where their dwelling had been, he found that the cottage had disappeared. There was nothing to mark even the spot where it had stood, except the stumps of three willows—two old trees and one young tree—that had been cut down long before his arrival.

Beside the stumps of those willow-trees he erected a memorial tomb, inscribed with divers holy texts; and he there performed many Buddhist services on behalf of the spirits of Aoyagi and of her parents.

Jiu-Roku-Zakura

Uso no yona—
Jiu-roku-zakura
Saki ni keri!

IN WAKÉGORI, A DISTRICT OF THE PROVINCE OF IYO, THERE IS A VERY
ancient and famous cherry-tree, called "Jiu-roku-zakura," "the Cherry-
tree of the Sixteenth day," because it blooms every year upon the sixteenth day of the first month (by the old lunar calendar)—and only
upon that day. Thus the time of its flowering is the Period of Great
Cold—though the natural habit of a cherry-tree is to wait for the
spring season before venturing to blossom. But the Jiu-roku-zakura
blossoms with a life that is not—or, at least, was not originally—its
own. There is the ghost of a man in that tree.

He was a samurai of Iyo; and the tree grew in his garden; and it
used to flower at the usual time—that is to say, about the end of
March or the beginning of April. He had played under that tree when
he was a child; and his parents and grandparents and ancestors had
hung to its blossoming branches, season after season for more than
a hundred years, bright strips of colored paper inscribed with poems
of praise. He himself became very old—outliving all his children; and
there was nothing in the world left for him to love except that tree.
And lo! in the summer of a certain year, the tree withered and died!

Exceedingly the old man sorrowed for his tree. Then kind neighbors
found him a young and beautiful cherry-tree, and planted it in his
garden—hoping thus to comfort him. And he thanked them, and pretended to be glad. But really his heart was full of pain; for he had
loved the old tree so well that nothing could have consoled him for the
loss of it.

At last there came to him a happy thought: he remembered a way by which the perishing tree might be saved. (It was the sixteenth day of the first month.) Alone he went into his garden, and bowed down before the withered tree, and spoke to it, saying: "Now deign, I beseech you, once more to bloom—because I am going to die in your stead." (For it is believed that one can really give away one's life to another person, or to a creature, or even to a tree, by the favor of the gods;—and thus to transfer one's life is expressed by the term *migawari ni tatsu,* "to act as a substitute.") Then under that tree he spread a white cloth, and divers coverings, and sat down upon the coverings, and performed hara-kiri after the fashion of a samurai. And the ghost of him went into the tree, and made it blossom in that same hour.

And every year it still blooms on the sixteenth day of the first month, in the season of snow.

The Dream of Akinosuké

IN THE DISTRICT CALLED TOÏCHI OF YAMATO PROVINCE, THERE USED TO live a *gōshi* named Miyata Akinosuké. . . .

[Here I must tell you that in Japanese feudal times there was a privileged class of soldier-farmers—free-holders—corresponding to the class of yeomen in England; and these were called *gōshi.*]

In Akinosuké's garden there was a great and ancient cedar-tree, under which he was wont to rest on sultry days. One very warm afternoon he was sitting under this tree with two of his friends, fellow-gōshi, chatting and drinking wine, when he felt all of a sudden very drowsy—so drowsy that he begged his friends to excuse him for taking a nap in their presence. Then he lay down at the foot of the tree, and dreamed this dream:

He thought that as he was lying there in his garden, he saw a procession, like the train of some great daimyō, descending a hill near

by, and that he got up to look at it. A very grand procession it proved
to be—more imposing than anything of the kind which he had ever seen
before; and it was advancing toward his dwelling. He observed in the
van of it a number of young men richly appareled, who were drawing a great lacquered palace-carriage, or *gosho-guruma*, hung with
bright blue silk. When the procession arrived within a short distance
of the house it halted; and a richly dressed man—evidently a person
of rank—advanced from it, approached Akinosuké, bowed to him
profoundly, and then said:

"Honored sir, you see before you a *kérai* (vassal) of the *Kokuō* of
Tokoyo.[1] My master, the King, commands me to greet you in his
august name, and to place myself wholly at your disposal. He also
bids me inform you that he augustly desires your presence at the
palace. Be therefore pleased immediately to enter this honorable
carriage, which he has sent for your conveyance."

Upon hearing these words Akinosuké wanted to make some fitting
reply; but he was too much astonished and embarrassed for speech;—
and in the same moment his will seemed to melt away from him, so
that he could only do as the kérai bade him. He entered the carriage;
the kérai took a place beside him, and made a signal; the drawers,
seizing the silken ropes, turned the great vehicle southward;—and the
journey began.

In a very short time, to Akinosuké's amazement, the carriage stopped
in front of a huge two-storied gateway (*rōmon*), of Chinese style,
which he had never before seen. Here the kérai dismounted, saying,
"I go to announce the honorable arrival"—and he disappeared. After
some little waiting, Akinosuké saw two noble-looking men, wearing
robes of purple silk and high caps of the form indicating lofty rank,
come from the gateway. These, after having respectfully saluted him,
helped him to descend from the carriage, and led him through the
great gate and across a vast garden, to the entrance of a palace
whose front appeared to extend, west and east, to a distance of miles.
Akinosuké was then shown into a reception-room of wonderful size
and splendor. His guides conducted him to the place of honor, and
respectfully seated themselves apart: while serving-maids, in costume
of ceremony, brought refreshments. When Akinosuké had partaken of

---

[1] This name "Tokoyo" is indefinite. According to circumstances it may signify any
unknown country—or that undiscovered country from whose bourn no traveler returns—
or that Fairyland of Far-Eastern fable, the Realm of Hōrai. The term *Kokuō* means the
ruler of a country—therefore a king. The original phrase, "Tokoyo no Kokuō," might
be rendered here as "the Ruler of Hōrai" or "the King of Fairyland."

the refreshments, the two purple-robed attendants bowed low before him, and addressed him in the following words—each speaking alter-nately, according to the etiquette of courts:

"It is now our honorable duty to inform you . . . as to the reason of your having been summoned hither. . . . Our master, the King, augustly desires that you become his son-in-law; . . . and it is his wish and command that you shall wed this very day . . . the August Princess, his maiden-daughter. . . . We shall soon conduct you to the presence-chamber . . . where His Augustness even now is waiting to receive you. . . . But it will be necessary that we first invest you . . . with the appropriate garments of ceremony." [2]

Having thus spoken, the attendants rose together, and proceeded to an alcove containing a great chest of gold lacquer. They opened the chest, and took from it various robes and girdles of rich material, and a *ḳamuri,* or regal headdress. With these they attired Akinosuké as befitted a princely bridegroom; and he was then conducted to the presence-room, where he saw the Kokuō of Tokoyo seated upon the *daiza,*[3] wearing the high black cap of state, and robed in robes of yellow silk. Before the daiza, to left and right, a multitude of dignitaries sat in rank, motionless and splendid as images in a temple; and Akinosuké, advancing into their midst, saluted the King with the triple prostration of usage. The King greeted him with gracious words, and then said:

"You have already been informed as to the reason of your having been summoned to Our presence. We have decided that you shall become the adopted husband of Our only daughter;—and the wedding ceremony shall now be performed."

As the King finished speaking, a sound of joyful music was heard; and a long train of beautiful court ladies advanced from behind a cur-tain, to conduct Akinosuké to the room in which his bride awaited him.

The room was immense; but it could scarcely contain the multitude of guests assembled to witness the wedding ceremony. All bowed down before Akinosuké as he took his place, facing the King's daughter, on the kneeling-cushion prepared for him. As a maiden of heaven the bride appeared to be; and her robes were beautiful as a summer sky. And the marriage was performed amid great rejoicing.

---

[2] The last phrase, according to old custom, had to be uttered by both attendants at the same time. All these ceremonial observances can still be studied on the Japanese stage.

[3] This was the name given to the estrade, or dais, upon which a feudal prince or ruler sat in state. The term literally signifies "great seat."

Afterwards the pair were conducted to a suite of apartments that had been prepared for them in another portion of the palace; and there they received the congratulations of many noble persons, and wedding gifts beyond counting.

Some days later Akinosuké was again summoned to the throne-room. On this occasion he was received even more graciously than before; and the King said to him:

"In the southwestern part of Our dominion there is an island called Raishū. We have now appointed you governor of that island. You will find the people loyal and docile; but their laws have not yet been brought into proper accord with the laws of Tokoyo; and their customs have not been properly regulated. We entrust you with the duty of improving their social condition as far as may be possible; and We desire that you shall rule them with kindness and wisdom. All preparations necessary for your journey to Raishū have already been made."

So Akinosuké and his bride departed from the palace of Tokoyo, accompanied to the shore by a great escort of nobles and officials; and they embarked upon a ship of state provided by the King. And with favoring winds they safely sailed to Raishū, and found the good people of that island assembled upon the beach to welcome them.

Akinosuké entered at once upon his new duties; and they did not prove to be hard. During the first three years of his governorship he was occupied chiefly with the framing and the enactment of laws; but he had wise counselors to help him, and he never found the work unpleasant. When it was all finished, he had no active duties to perform, beyond attending the rites and ceremonies ordained by ancient custom. The country was so healthy and so fertile that sickness and want were unknown; and the people were so good that no laws were ever broken. And Akinosuké dwelt and ruled in Raishū for twenty years more—making in all twenty-three years of sojourn, during which no shadow of sorrow traversed his life.

But in the twenty-fourth year of his governorship, a great misfortune came upon him; for his wife, who had borne him seven children —five boys and two girls—fell sick and died. She was buried, with high pomp, on the summit of a beautiful hill in the district of Hanryōkō; and a monument, exceedingly splendid, was placed above her grave. But Akinosuké felt such grief at her death that he no longer cared to live.

Now when the legal period of mourning was over, there came to Raishū, from the Tokoyo palace, a *shisha,* or royal messenger. The shisha delivered to Akinosuké a message of condolence, and then said to him:

"These are the words which our august master, the King of Tokoyo, commands that I repeat to you: 'We will now send you back to your own people and country. As for the seven children, they are the grandsons and the granddaughters of the King, and shall be fitly cared for. Do not, therefore, allow your mind to be troubled concerning them.'"

On receiving this mandate, Akinosuké submissively prepared for his departure. When all his affairs had been settled, and the ceremony of bidding farewell to his counselors and trusted officials had been concluded, he was escorted with much honor to the port. There he embarked upon the ship sent for him; and the ship sailed out into the blue sea, under the blue sky, and the shape of the island of Raishū itself turned blue, and then turned gray, and then vanished forever. . . . And Akinosuké suddenly awoke—under the cedar-tree in his own garden! . . .

For the moment he was stupefied and dazed. But he perceived his two friends still seated near him—drinking and chatting merrily. He stared at them in a bewildered way, and cried aloud:

"How strange!"

"Akinosuké must have been dreaming," one of them exclaimed, with a laugh. "What did you see, Akinosuké, that was strange?"

Then Akinosuké told his dream—that dream of three-and-twenty years' sojourn in the realm of Tokoyo in the island of Raishū;—and they were astonished, because he had really slept for no more than a few minutes.

One gōshi said:

"Indeed, you saw strange things. We also saw something strange while you were napping. A little yellow butterfly was fluttering over your face for a moment or two; and we watched it. Then it alighted on the ground beside you, close to the tree; and almost as soon as it alighted there, a big, big ant came out of a hole, and seized it and pulled it down into the hole. Just before you woke up, we saw that very butterfly come out of the hole again, and flutter over your face as before. And then it suddenly disappeared: we do not know where it went."

"Perhaps it was Akinosuké's soul," the other gōshi said;—"certainly

I thought I saw it fly into his mouth. . . . But, even if that butterfly *was* Akinosuké's soul, the fact would not explain his dream."

"The ants might explain it," returned the first speaker. "Ants are queer beings—possibly goblins. . . . Anyhow, there is a big ant's nest under that cedar-tree." . . .

"Let us look!" cried Akinosuké, greatly moved by this suggestion. And he went for a spade.

The ground about and beneath the cedar-tree proved to have been excavated, in a most surprising way, by a prodigious colony of ants. The ants had furthermore built inside their excavations; and their tiny constructions of straw, clay, and stems bore an odd resemblance to miniature towns. In the middle of a structure considerably larger than the rest there was a marvelous swarming of small ants around the body of the very big ant, which had yellowish wings and a long black head.

"Why, there is the King of my dream!" cried Akinosuké; "and there is the palace of Tokoyo! . . . How extraordinary! . . . Raishū ought to lie somewhat southwest of it—to the left of that big root. . . . Yes!—here it is! . . . How very strange! Now I am sure that I can find the mountain of Hanryōkō, and the grave of the princess." . . .

In the wreck of the nest he searched and searched, and at last dis covered a tiny mound, on the top of which was fixed a water-worn pebble, in shape resembling a Buddhist monument. Underneath it he found embedded in clay—the dead body of a female ant.

Riki-Baka

HIS NAME WAS RIKI, SIGNIFYING STRENGTH; BUT THE PEOPLE CALLED HIM Riki-the-Simple, or Riki-the-Fool—"Riki-Baka"—because he had been born into perpetual childhood. For the same reason they were kind to him—even when he set a house on fire by putting a lighted match to a mosquito-curtain, and clapped his hands for joy to see the blaze. At sixteen years he was a tall, strong lad; but in mind he remained always at the happy age of two, and therefore continued to play with very small children. The bigger children of the neighborhood, from four to seven years old, did not care to play with him, because he could not learn their songs and games. His favorite toy was a broomstick, which he used as a hobby-horse; and for hours at a time he would ride on that broomstick, up and down the slope in front of my house, with amazing peals of laughter. But at last he became troublesome by reason of his noise; and I had to tell him that he must find another playground. He bowed submissively, and then went off—sorrowfully trailing his broomstick behind him. Gentle at all times, and perfectly harmless if allowed no chance to play with fire, he seldom gave anybody cause for complaint. His relation to the life of our street was scarcely more than that of a dog or a chicken; and when he finally disappeared, I did not miss him. Months and months passed by before anything happened to remind me of Riki.

"What has become of Riki?" I then asked the old woodcutter who supplies our neighborhood with fuel. I remembered that Riki had often helped him to carry his bundles.

"Riki-Baka?" answered the old man. "Ah, Riki is dead—poor fellow! . . . Yes, he died nearly a year ago, very suddenly; the doctors said that he had some disease of the brain. And there is a strange story now about that poor Riki.

"When Riki died, his mother wrote his name, 'Riki-Baka,' in the palm of his left hand—putting 'Riki' in the Chinese character, and 'Baka' in kana. And she repeated many prayers for him—prayers that he might be reborn into some more happy condition.

"Now, about three months ago, in the honorable residence of Nanigashi-Sama, in Kōjimachi, a boy was born with characters on the palm of his left hand; and the characters were quite plain to read—'RIKI-BAKA'!

"So the people of that house knew that the birth must have happened in answer to somebody's prayer; and they caused inquiry to be made everywhere. At last a vegetable-seller brought word to them that there used to be a simple lad, called Riki-Baka, living in the Ushigomé quarter, and that he had died during the last autumn; and they sent two men-servants to look for the mother of Riki.

"Those servants found the mother of Riki, and told her what had happened; and she was glad exceedingly—for that Nanigashi house is a very rich and famous house. But the servants said that the family of Nanigashi-Sama were very angry about the word 'Baka' on the child's hand. 'And where is your Riki buried?' the servants asked. 'He is buried in the cemetery of Zendōji,' she told them. 'Please to give us some of the clay of his grave,' they requested.

"So she went with them to the temple Zendōji, and showed them Riki's grave; and they took some of the grave-clay away with them, wrapped up in a *furoshiki*.[1] . . . They gave Riki's mother some money —ten yen." . . .

"But what did they want with that clay?" I inquired.

"Well," the old man answered, "you know that it would not do to let the child grow up with that name on his hand. And there is no other means of removing characters that come in that way upon the body of a child: *you must rub the skin with clay taken from the grave of the body of the former birth.*" . . .

Hi-Mawari

ON THE WOODED HILL BEHIND THE HOUSE ROBERT AND I ARE LOOKING FOR fairy-rings. Robert is eight years old, comely, and very wise;—I am a little more than seven—and I reverence Robert. It is a glowing glorious August day; and the warm air is filled with sharp sweet scents of resin.

We do not find any fairy-rings; but we find a great many pine-cones in the high grass. . . . I tell Robert the old Welsh story of the man who went to sleep, unawares, inside of a fairy-ring, and so disappeared for seven years, and would never eat or speak after his friends had delivered him from the enchantment.

"They eat nothing but the points of needles, you know," says Robert.

[1] A square piece of cotton-goods, or other woven material, used as a wrapper in which to carry small packages.

"Who?" I ask.

"Goblins," Robert answers.

This revelation leaves me dumb with astonishment and awe. . . . But Robert suddenly cries out:

"There is a harper!—he is coming to the house!"

And down the hill we run to hear the harper. . . . But what a harper! Not like the hoary minstrels of the picture-books. A swarthy, sturdy, unkempt vagabond, with black bold eyes under scowling black brows. More like a bricklayer than a bard,—and his garments are corduroy!

"Wonder if he is going to sing in Welsh?" murmurs Robert.

I feel too much disappointed to make any remarks. The harper poses his harp—a huge instrument—upon our doorstep, sets all the strings ringing with a sweep of his grimy fingers, clears his throat with a sort of angry growl, and begins:

> *Believe me, if all those endearing young charms,*
> *Which I gaze on so fondly to-day . . .*

The accent, the attitude, the voice all fill me with repulsion unutterable—shock me with a new sensation of formidable vulgarity. I want to cry out loud, "You have no right to sing that song!" For I have heard it sung by the lips of the dearest and fairest being in my little world;—and that this rude, coarse man should dare to sing it vexes me like a mockery—angers me like an insolence. But only for a moment! . . . With the utterance of the syllables "to-day," that deep, grim voice suddenly breaks into a quivering tenderness indescribable; —then, marvelously changing, it mellows into tones sonorous and rich as the bass of a great organ—while a sensation unlike anything ever felt before takes me by the throat. . . . What witchcraft has he learned? what secret has he found—this scowling man of the road? . . . Oh! is there anybody else in the whole world who can sing like that? . . . And the form of the singer flickers and dims;—and the house, and the lawn, and all visible shapes of things tremble and swim before me. Yet instinctively I fear that man;—I almost hate him; and I feel myself flushing with anger and shame because of his power to move me thus. . . .

"He made you cry," Robert compassionately observes, to my further confusion—as the harper strides away, richer by a gift of sixpence taken without thanks. . . . "But I think he must be a gypsy. Gypsies are bad people—and they are wizards. . . . Let us go back to the wood."

We climb again to the pines, and there squat down upon the sun-flecked grass, and look over town and sea. But we do not play as before: the spell of the wizard is strong upon us both. . . .

"Perhaps he is a goblin," I venture at last, "or a fairy?"

"No," says Robert—"only a gypsy. But that is nearly as bad. They steal children, you know."

"What shall we do if he comes up here?" I gasp, in sudden terror at the lonesomeness of our situation.

"Oh, he wouldn't dare," answers Robert—"not by daylight, you know." . . .

*   *   *

Only yesterday, near the village of Takata, I noticed a flower which the Japanese call by nearly the same name as we do: *"Hi-mawari"* ('The Sunward-turning);—and over the space of forty years there thrilled back to me the voice of that wandering harper:

> *As the Sunflower turns on her god, when he sets,*
> *The same look that she turned when he rose.*

Again I saw the sun-flecked shadows on that far Welsh hill; and Robert for a moment again stood beside me, with his girl's face and his curls of gold. We were looking for fairy-rings. . . . But all that existed of the real Robert must long ago have suffered a sea-change into something rich and strange. . . . *Greater love hath no man than this, that a man lay down his life for his friend.* . . .

Hōrai

BLUE VISION OF DEPTH LOST IN HEIGHT—SEA AND SKY INTERBLENDING through luminous haze. The day is of spring, and the hour morning.

Only sky and sea—one azure enormity. . . . In the fore, ripples are catching a silvery light, and threads of foam are swirling. But a little farther off no motion is visible, nor anything save color: dim warm blue of water widening away to melt into blue of air. Horizon there is none: only distance soaring into space—infinite concavity hollowing before you, and hugely arching above you—the color deepening with the height. But far in the midway blue there hangs a faint, faint vision of palace towers, with high roofs horned and curved like moons— some shadowing of splendor strange and old, illumined by a sunshine soft as memory.

. . . What I have thus been trying to describe is a *kakēmono*—that is to say, a Japanese painting on silk, suspended to the wall of my alcove;—and the name of it is SHINKIRŌ, which signifies "Mirage." But the shapes of the mirage are unmistakable. Those are the glimmering portals of Hōrai the blest; and those are the moony roofs of the Palace of the Dragon-King;—and the fashion of them (though limned by a Japanese brush of to-day) is the fashion of things Chinese, twenty-one hundred years ago.

Thus much is told of the place in the Chinese books of that time: In Hōrai there is neither death nor pain; and there is no winter. The flowers in that place never fade, and the fruits never fail; and if a man taste of those fruits even but once, he can never again feel thirst or hunger. In Hōrai grow the enchanted plants So-rin-shi, and Riku-gō-aoi, and Ban-kon-tō, which heal all manner of sickness;—and there grows also the magical grass Yō-shin-shi, that quickens the dead: and the magical grass is watered by a fairy water of which a single drink confers perpetual youth. The people of Hōrai eat their rice out of very, very small bowls; but the rice never diminishes within those bowls—however much of it be eaten—until the eater desires no more. And the people of Hōrai drink their wine out of very, very small cups; but no man can empty one of those cups—however stoutly he may drink—until there comes upon him the pleasant drowsiness of intoxication.

All this and more is told in the legends of the time of the Shin dynasty. But that the people who wrote down those legends ever saw Hōrai, even in a mirage, is not believable. For really there are no enchanted fruits which leave the eater forever satisfied—nor any magical grass which revives the dead—nor any fountain of fairy water—nor any bowls which never lack rice—nor any cups which never lack wine. It is not true that sorrow and death never enter Hōrai;—neither is it true that there is not any winter. The winter in Hōrai is cold;—and winds then bite to the bone; and the heaping of snow is monstrous on the roofs of the Dragon-King.

Nevertheless there are wonderful things in Hōrai; and the most wonderful of all has not been mentioned by any Chinese writer. I mean the atmosphere of Hōrai. It is an atmosphere peculiar to the place; and, because of it, the sunshine in Hōrai is *whiter* than any other sunshine—a milky light that never dazzles—astonishingly clear, but very soft. This atmosphere is not of our human period: it is enormously old—so old that I feel afraid when I try to think how old it is; —and it is not a mixture of nitrogen and oxygen. It is not made of air at all, but of ghost—the substance of quintillions of quintillions of generations of souls blended into one immense translucency—souls of people who thought in ways never resembling our ways. Whatever mortal man inhales that atmosphere, he takes into his blood the thrilling of these spirits; and they change the senses within him—reshaping his notions of Space and Time—so that he can see only as they used to see, and feel only as they used to feel, and think only as they used to think. Soft as sleep are these changes of sense; and Hōrai, discerned across them, might thus be described:

Because in Hōrai there is no knowledge of great evil, the hearts of the people never grow old. And, by reason of being always young in heart, the people of Hōrai smile from birth until death—except when the Gods send sorrow among them; and faces then are veiled until the sorrow goes away. All folk in Hōrai love and trust each other, as if all were members of a single household;—and the speech of the women is like birdsong, because the hearts of them are light as the souls of birds; —and the swaying of the sleeves of the maidens at play seems a flutter of wide, soft wings. In Hōrai nothing is hidden but grief, because there is no reason for shame;—and nothing is locked away, because there could not be any theft;—and by night as well as by day all doors remain unbarred, because there is no reason for fear. And because the people are fairies—though mortal—all things in Hōrai, except the Palace of the Dragon-King, are small and quaint and queer;—and these fairy-folk do really eat their rice out of very small bowls, and drink their wine out of very, very small cups. . . .

Much of this seeming would be due to the inhalation of that ghostly atmosphere—but not all. For the spell wrought by the dead is only the charm of an Ideal, the glamour of an ancient hope;—and something of that hope has found fulfillment in many hearts—in the simple beauty of unselfish lives—in the sweetness of Woman. . . .

Evil winds from the West are blowing over Hōrai; and the magical atmosphere, alas! is shrinking away before them. It lingers now in patches only, and bands—like those long bright bands of cloud that trail across the landscapes of Japanese painters. Under these shreds of the elfish vapor you still can find Hōrai—but not elsewhere. . . . Remember that Hōrai is also called Shinkirō, which signifies Mirage— the Vision of the Intangible. And the Vision is fading—never again to appear save in pictures and poems and dreams. . . .

Some Chinese Ghosts

The Soul of the Great Bell

She hath spoken, and her words still resound in his ears.
HAO-KHIEOU-TOKOUAN: C. IX.

THE WATER-CLOCK MARKS THE HOUR IN THE TA-CHUNG SZ'—IN THE TOWER of the Great Bell: now the mallet is lifted to smite the lips of the metal monster—the vast lips inscribed with Buddhist texts from the sacred "Fa-hwa-King," from the chapters of the holy "Ling-yen-King!" Hear the great bell responding!—how mighty her voice, though tongueless!—KO-NGAI! All the little dragons on the high-tilted eaves of the green roofs shiver to the tips of their gilded tails under that deep wave of sound; all the porcelain gargoyles tremble on their carven perches; all the hundred little bells of the pagodas quiver with

89

desire to speak. KO-NGAI! All the green-and-gold tiles of the temple are
vibrating; the wooden goldfish above them are writhing against the
sky; the uplifted finger of Fo shakes high over the heads of the worshipers through the blue fog of incense! KO-NGAI!—What a thunder
tone was that! All the lacquered goblins on the palace cornices wriggle
their fire-colored tongues! And after each huge shock, how wondrous
the multiple echo and the great golden moan and, at last, the sudden
sibilant sobbing in the ears when the immense tone faints away in
broken whispers of silver—as though a woman should whisper, "Hiai!"
Even so the great bell hath sounded every day for well-nigh five hundred years—Ko-Ngai: first with stupendous clang, then with immeasurable moan of gold, then with silver murmuring of "Hiai!" And
there is not a child in all the many-colored ways of the old Chinese
city who does not know the story of the great bell—who cannot tell
you why the great bell says Ko-Ngai and Hiai!

Now, this is the story of the great bell in the Ta-chung sz', as the
same is related in the "Pe-Hiao-Tou-Choue," written by the learned
Yu-Pao-Tchen, of the City of Kwang-tchau-fu.

Nearly five hundred years ago the Celestially August, the Son of
Heaven, Yong-Lo, of the "Illustrious," or Ming, dynasty, commanded
the worthy official Kouan-Yu that he should have a bell made of such
size that the sound thereof might be heard for one hundred *li*. And he
further ordained that the voice of the bell should be strengthened with
brass, and deepened with gold, and sweetened with silver; and that
the face and the great lips of it should be graven with blessed sayings
from the sacred books, and that it should be suspended in the centre
of the imperial capital, to sound through all the many-colored ways of
the City of Pe-king.

Therefore the worthy mandarin Kouan-Yu assembled the master-
moulders and the renowned bellsmiths of the empire, and all men of
great repute and cunning in foundry work; and they measured the
materials for the alloy, and treated them skillfully, and prepared the
moulds, the fires, the instruments, and the monstrous melting-pot for
fusing the metal. And they labored exceedingly, like giants—neglecting only rest and sleep and the comforts of life; toiling both night and
day in obedience to Kouan-Yu, and striving in all things to do the
behest of the Son of Heaven.

But when the metal had been cast, and the earthen mould separated
from the glowing casting, it was discovered that, despite their great

labor and ceaseless care, the result was void of worth; for the metals had rebelled one against the other—the gold had scorned alliance with the brass, the silver would not mingle with the molten iron. Therefore the moulds had to be once more prepared, and the fires rekindled, and the metal remelted, and all the work tediously and toilsomely repeated. The Son of Heaven heard, and was angry, but spake nothing.

A second time the bell was cast, and the result was even worse. Still the metals obstinately refused to blend one with the other; and there was no uniformity in the bell, and the sides of it were cracked and fissured, and the lips of it were slagged and split asunder; so that all the labor had to be repeated even a third time, to the great dismay of Kouan-Yu. And when the Son of Heaven heard these things, he was angrier than before; and sent his messenger to Kouan-Yu with a letter upon lemon-colored silk, and sealed with the Seal of the Dragon, containing these words:

From the Mighty Yong-Lo, the Sublime Tait-Sung, the Celestial and August—whose rein is called "Ming"—to Kouan-Yu the Fuh-yin: Twice thou hast betrayed the trust we have deigned graciously to place in thee; if thou fail a third time in fulfilling our command, thy head shall be severed from thy neck. Tremble, and obey!

Now, Kouan-Yu had a daughter of dazzling loveliness, whose name —Ko-Ngai—was ever in the mouths of poets, and whose heart was even more beautiful than her face. Ko-Ngai loved her father with such love that she had refused a hundred worthy suitors rather than make his home desolate by her absence; and when she had seen the awful yellow missive, sealed with the Dragon-Seal, she fainted away with fear for her father's sake. And when her senses and her strength returned to her, she could not rest or sleep for thinking of her parent's danger, until she had secretly sold some of her jewels, and with the money so obtained had hastened to an astrologer, and paid him a great price to advise her by what means her father might be saved from the peril impending over him. So the astrologer made observations of the heavens, and marked the aspect of the Silver Stream (which we call the Milky Way), and examined the signs of the Zodiac —the Hwangtao, or Yellow Road—and consulted the table of the Five Hin, or Principles of the Universe, and the mystical books of the alchemists. And after a long silence, he made answer to her, saying: "Gold and brass will never meet in wedlock, silver and iron never will embrace, until the flesh of a maiden be melted in the crucible; until the blood of a virgin be mixed with the metals in their fusion." So Ko-Ngai returned home sorrowful at heart; but she kept secret all that she had heard, and told no one what she had done.

At last came the awful day when the third and last effort to cast the great bell was to be made; and Ko-Ngai, together with her waiting-woman, accompanied her father to the foundry, and they took their places upon a platform overlooking the toiling of the moulders and the lava of liquefied metal. All the workmen wrought their tasks in silence; there was no sound heard but the muttering of the fires. And the muttering deepened into a roar like the roar of typhoons approaching, and the blood-red lake of metal slowly brightened like the vermilion of a sunrise, and the vermilion was transmuted into a radiant glow of gold, and the gold whitened blindingly, like the silver face of a full moon. Then the workers ceased to feed the raving flame, and all fixed their eyes upon the eyes of Kouan-Yu; and Kouan-Yu prepared to give the signal to cast.

But ere ever he lifted his finger, a cry caused him to turn his head; and all heard the voice of Ko-Ngai sounding sharply sweet as a bird's song above the great thunder of the fires—"For thy sake, O my Father!" And even as she cried, she leaped into the white flood of metal; and the lava of the furnace roared to receive her, and spattered monstrous flakes of flame to the roof, and burst over the verge of the earthen crater, and cast up a whirling fountain of many-colored fires, and subsided quakingly, with lightnings and with thunders and with mutterings.

Then the father of Ko-Ngai, wild with his grief, would have leaped in after her, but that strong men held him back and kept firm grasp upon him until he had fainted away and they could bear him like one dead to his home. And the serving-woman of Ko-Ngai, dizzy and speechless for pain, stood before the furnace, still holding in her hands a shoe, a tiny, dainty shoe, with embroidery of pearls and flowers—the shoe of her beautiful mistress that was. For she had sought to grasp Ko-Ngai by the foot as she leaped, but had only been able to clutch the shoe, and the pretty shoe came off in her hand; and she continued to stare at it like one gone mad.

But in spite of all these things, the command of the Celestial and August had to be obeyed, and the work of the moulders to be finished, hopeless as the result might be. Yet the glow of the metal seemed purer and whiter than before; and there was no sign of the beautiful body that had been entombed therein. So the ponderous casting was made; and lo! when the metal had become cool, it was found that the bell was beautiful to look upon, and perfect in form, and wonderful in color above all other bells. Nor was there any trace found of the body of Ko-Ngai; for it had been totally absorbed by the precious alloy, and blended with the well-blended brass and gold, with the intermingling of the silver and the iron. And when they sounded the bell, its tones were found to be deeper and mellower and mightier than the tones of any other bell—reaching even beyond the distance of one hundred li, like a pealing of summer thunder; and yet also like some vast voice uttering a name, a woman's name—the name of Ko-Ngai!

And still, between each mighty stroke there is a long low moaning heard; and ever the moaning ends with a sound of sobbing and of complaining, as though a weeping woman should murmur, "Hiai!" And still, when the people hear that great golden moan they keep silence; but when the sharp, sweet shuddering comes in the air, and the sobbing of "Hiai!" then, indeed, do all the Chinese mothers in all the many colored ways of Pe-king whisper to their little ones: "Listen! That is Ko-Ngai crying for her shoe! That is Ko-Ngai calling for her shoe!"

The Story of Ming-Y

The ancient Words of Kouei—Master of Musicians in the Courts of the Emperor Yao: When ye make to resound the stone melodious, the Ming-Khieou— When ye touch the lyre that is called Kin, or the guitar that is called Ssé— Accompanying their sound with song— Then do the grandfather and the father return; Then do the ghosts of the ancestors come to hear.

Sang the Poet Tching-Kou: "Surely the Peach-Flowers blossom over the tomb of Sië-Thao."

DO YOU ASK ME WHO SHE WAS—THE BEAUTIFUL SIË-THAO? FOR A THOU-sand years and more the trees have been whispering above her bed of stone. And the syllables of her name come to the listener with the lisping of the leaves; with the quivering of many-fingered boughs; with the fluttering of lights and shadows; with the breath, sweet as a woman's presence, of numberless savage flowers—"Sië-Thao." But, saving the whispering of her name, what the trees say cannot be understood; and they alone remember the years of Sië-Thao. Something about her you might, nevertheless, learn from any of those *Kiang-kou-jin*—those famous Chinese story-tellers, who nightly narrate to listening crowds, in consideration of a few tsien, the legends of the past. Something concerning her you may also find in the book entitled "Kin-Kou-Ki-Koan," which signifies in our tongue: "The Marvelous Happenings of Ancient and of Recent Times." And perhaps of all things therein written, the most marvelous is this memory of Sië-Thao:

Five hundred years ago, in the reign of the Emperor Houng-Wou, whose dynasty was Ming, there lived in the City of Genii, the city of Kwang-tchau-fu, a man celebrated for his learning and for his piety, named Tien-Pelou. This Tien-Pelou had one son, a beautiful boy, who for scholarship and for bodily grace and for polite accomplishments had no superior among the youths of his age. And his name was Ming-Y.

Now when the lad was in his eighteenth summer, it came to pass that Pelou, his father, was appointed Inspector of Public Instruction at the city of Tching-tou; and Ming-Y accompanied his parents thither. Near the city of Tching-tou lived a rich man of rank, a high commissioner of the government, whose name was Tchang, and who wanted to find a worthy teacher for his children. On hearing of the arrival of the new Inspector of Public Instruction, the noble Tchang visited him to obtain advice in this matter; and happening to meet and converse with Pelou's accomplished son, immediately engaged Ming-Y as a private tutor for his family.

Now as the house of this Lord Tchang was situated several miles from town, it was deemed best that Ming-Y should abide in the house of his employer. Accordingly the youth made ready all things necessary for his new sojourn; and his parents, bidding him farewell, counseled him wisely, and cited to him the words of Lao-tseu and of the ancient sages:

By a beautiful face the world is filled with love; but Heaven may never be deceived thereby. Shouldst thou behold a woman coming from the East, look thou to the West; shouldst thou perceive a maiden approaching from the West, turn thine eyes to the East.

If Ming-Y did not heed this counsel in after days, it was only because of his youth and the thoughtlessness of a naturally joyous heart

And he departed to abide in the house of Lord Tchang, while the autumn passed, and the winter also.

When the time of the second moon of spring was drawing near, and that happy day which the Chinese call "Hoa-tchao," or "The Birthday of a Hundred Flowers," a longing came upon Ming-Y to see his parents; and he opened his heart to the good Tchang, who not only gave him the permission he desired, but also pressed into his hand a silver gift of two ounces, thinking that the lad might wish to bring some little memento to his father and mother. For it is the Chinese custom, on the feast of Hoa-tchao, to make presents to friends and relations.

That day all the air was drowsy with blossom perfume, and vibrant with the droning of bees. It seemed to Ming-Y that the path he followed had not been trodden by any other for many long years; the grass was tall upon it; vast trees on either side interlocked their mighty and moss-grown arms above him, beshadowing the way; but the leafy obscurities quivered with bird-song, and the deep vistas of the wood were glorified by vapors of gold, and odorous with flower-breathings as a temple with incense. The dreamy joy of the day entered into the heart of Ming-Y; and he sat him down among the young blossoms, under the branches swaying against the violet sky, to drink in the perfume and the light, and to enjoy the great sweet silence. Even while thus reposing, a sound caused him to turn his eyes toward a shady place where wild peach-trees were in bloom; and he beheld a young woman, beautiful as the pinkening blossoms themselves, trying to hide among them. Though he looked for a moment only, Ming-Y could not avoid discerning the loveliness of her face, the golden purity of her complexion, and the brightness of her long eyes, that sparkled under a pair of brows as daintily curved as the wings of the silkworm butterfly outspread. Ming-Y at once turned his gaze away, and, rising quickly, proceeded on his journey. But so much embarrassed did he feel at the idea of those charming eyes peeping at him through the leaves, that he suffered the money he had been carrying in his sleeve to fall, without being aware of it. A few moments later he heard the patter of light feet running behind him, and a woman's voice calling him by name. Turning his face in great surprise, he saw a comely servant-maid, who said to him, "Sir, my mistress bade me pick up and return you this silver which you dropped upon the road." Ming-Y thanked the girl gracefully, and requested her to convey his compliments to her mistress. Then he proceeded on his way through the perfumed silence, athwart the shadows that dreamed along the forgotten path, dreaming himself also, and feeling his heart beating with strange quickness at the thought of the beautiful being that he had seen.

It was just such another day when Ming-Y, returning by the same path, paused once more at the spot where the gracious figure had momentarily appeared before him. But this time he was surprised to perceive, through a long vista of immense trees, a dwelling that had previously escaped his notice—a country residence, not large, yet elegant to an unusual degree. The bright blue tiles of its curved and serrated double roof, rising above the foliage, seemed to blend their color with the luminous azure of the day; the green-and-gold designs of its carven porticos were exquisite artistic mockeries of leaves and flowers bathed in sunshine. And at the summit of terrace steps before it, guarded by great porcelain tortoises, Ming-Y saw standing the mistress of the mansion—the idol of his passionate fancy—accompanied by the same waiting-maid who had borne to her his message of gratitude. While Ming-Y looked, he perceived that their eyes were upon him; they smiled and conversed together as if speaking about him; and, shy though he was, the youth found courage to salute the fair one from a distance. To his astonishment, the young servant beckoned him to approach; and opening a rustic gate half veiled by trailing plants bearing crimson flowers, Ming-Y advanced along the verdant alley leading to the terrace, with mingled feelings of surprise and timid joy. As he drew near, the beautiful lady withdrew from sight; but the maid waited at the broad steps to receive him, and said as he ascended:

"Sir, my mistress understands you wish to thank her for the trifling service she recently bade me do you, and requests that you will enter the house, as she knows you already by repute, and desires to have the pleasure of bidding you good-day."

Ming-Y entered bashfully, his feet making no sound upon a matting elastically soft as forest moss, and found himself in a reception-chamber vast, cool, and fragrant with scent of blossoms freshly gathered. A delicious quiet pervaded the mansion; shadows of flying birds passed over the bands of light that fell through the half-blinds of bamboo; great butterflies, with pinions of fiery color, found their way in, to hover a moment about the painted vases, and pass out again into the mysterious woods. And noiselessly as they, the young mistress of the mansion entered by another door, and kindly greeted the boy, who lifted his hands to his breast and bowed low in salutation. She was taller than he had deemed her, and supplely slender as a beauteous lily; her black hair was interwoven with the creamy blossoms of the *chu-sha-kih;* her robes of pale silk took shifting tints when she moved, as vapors change hue with the changing of the light.

"If I be not mistaken," she said, when both had seated themselves after having exchanged the customary formalities of politeness, "my honored visitor is none other than Tien-chou, surnamed Ming-Y, educator of the children of my respected relative, the High Commissioner Tchang. As the family of Lord Tchang is my family also, I cannot but consider the teacher of his children as one of my own kin."

"Lady," replied Ming-Y, not a little astonished, "may I dare to inquire the name of your honored family, and to ask the relation which you hold to my noble patron?"

"The name of my poor family," responded the comely lady, "is Ping —an ancient family of the city of Tching-tou. I am the daughter of a certain Sië of Moun-hao; Sië is my name, likewise; and I was married to a young man of the Ping family, whose name was Khang. By this marriage I became related to your excellent patron; but my husband died soon after our wedding, and I have chosen this solitary place to reside in during the period of my widowhood."

There was a drowsy music in her voice, as of the melody of brooks, the murmurings of spring; and such a strange grace in the manner of her speech as Ming-Y had never heard before. Yet, on learning that she was a widow, the youth would not have presumed to remain long in her presence without a formal invitation; and after having sipped the cup of rich tea presented to him, he arose to depart. Sië would not suffer him to go so quickly.

"Nay, friend," she said; "stay yet a little while in my house, I pray

you; for, should your honored patron ever learn that you had been
here, and that I had not treated you as a respected guest, and regaled
you even as I would him, I know that he would be greatly angered.
Remain at least to supper."

So Ming-Y remained, rejoicing secretly in his heart, for Sië seemed
to him the fairest and sweetest being he had ever known, and he felt
that he loved her even more than his father and his mother. And
while they talked the long shadows of the evening slowly blended into
one violet darkness; the great citron-light of the sunset faded out; and
those starry beings that are called the "Three Councillors," who preside over life and death and the destinies of men, opened their cold
bright eyes in the northern sky. Within the mansion of Sië the
painted lanterns were lighted; the table was laid for the evening repast; and Ming-Y took his place at it, feeling little inclination to eat,
and thinking only of the charming face before him. Observing that he
scarcely tasted the dainties laid upon his plate, Sië pressed her young
guest to partake of wine; and they drank several cups together. It was
a purple wine, so cool that the cup into which it was poured became
covered with vapory dew; yet it seemed to warm the veins with
strange fire. To Ming-Y, as he drank, all things became more luminous
as by enchantment; the walls of the chamber appeared to recede, and
the roof to heighten; the lamps glowed like stars in their chains, and
the voice of Sië floated to the boy's ears like some far melody heard
through the spaces of a drowsy night. His heart swelled; his tongue
loosened; and words flitted from his lips that he had fancied he could
never dare to utter. Yet Sië sought not to restrain him; her lips gave
no smile; but her long bright eyes seemed to laugh with pleasure at
his words of praise, and to return his gaze of passionate admiration
with affectionate interest.

"I have heard," she said, "of your rare talent, and of your many
elegant accomplishments. I know how to sing a little, although I cannot claim to possess any musical learning; and now that I have the
honor of finding myself in the society of a musical professor, I will
venture to lay modesty aside, and beg you to sing a few songs with
me. I should deem it no small gratification if you would condescend
to examine my musical compositions."

"The honor and the gratification, dear lady," replied Ming-Y, "will
be mine; and I feel helpless to express the gratitude which the offer
of so rare a favor deserves."

The serving-maid, obedient to the summons of a little silver gong, brought in the music and retired. Ming-Y took the manuscripts, and began to examine them with eager delight. The paper upon which they were written had a pale yellow tint, and was light as a fabric of gossamer; but the characters were antiquely beautiful, as though they had been traced by the brush of Heï-song Ché-Tchoo himself—that divine Genius of Ink, who is no bigger than a fly; and the signatures attached to the compositions were the signatures of Youen-tchin, Kao-pien, and Thou-mou—mighty poets and musicians of the dynasty of Thang! Ming-Y could not repress a scream of delight at the sight of treasures so inestimable and so unique; scarcely could he summon resolution enough to permit them to leave his hands even for a moment.

"O Lady!" he cried, "these are veritably priceless things, surpassing in worth the treasures of all kings. This indeed is the handwriting of those great masters who sang five hundred years before our birth. How marvelously it has been preserved! Is not this the wondrous ink of which it was written: '*Po-nien-jou-chi, i-tien-jou-ki*' (After centuries I remain firm as stone, and the letters that I make like lacquer)? And how divine the charm of this composition!—the song of Kao-pien, prince of poets and Governor of Sze-tchouen five hundred years ago!"

"Kao-pien! darling Kao-pien!" murmured Sië, with a singular light in her eyes. "Kao-pien is also my favorite. Dear Ming-Y, let us chant his verses together, to the melody of old—the music of those grand years when men were nobler and wiser than to-day."

And their voices rose through the perfumed night like the voices of the wonder-birds—of the *Fung-hoang*—blending together in liquid sweetness. Yet a moment, and Ming-Y, overcome by the witchery of his companion's voice, could only listen in speechless ecstasy, while the lights of the chamber swam dim before his sight, and tears of pleasure trickled down his cheeks.

So the ninth hour passed; and they continued to converse, and to drink the cool purple wine, and to sing the songs of the years of Thang, until far into the night. More than once Ming-Y thought of departing; but each time Sië would begin, in that silver-sweet voice of hers, so wondrous a story of the great poets of the past, and of the women whom they loved, that he became as one entranced; or she would sing for him a song so strange that all his senses seemed to die except that of hearing. And at last, as she paused to pledge him in a cup of wine, Ming-Y could not restrain himself from putting his arm about her round neck and drawing her dainty head closer to him, and kissing the lips that were so much ruddier and sweeter than the wine. Then their lips separated no more;—the night grew old, and they knew it not.

The birds awakened, the flowers opened their eyes to the rising sun, and Ming-Y found himself at last compelled to bid his lovely enchantress farewell. Sië, accompanying him to the terrace, kissed him fondly and said: "Dear boy, come hither as often as you are able— as often as your heart whispers you to come. I know that you are not of those without faith and truth, who betray secrets; yet, being so young, you might also be sometimes thoughtless; and I pray you never to forget that only the stars have been the witnesses of our love. Speak of it to no living person, dearest; and take with you this little souvenir of our happy night."

And she presented him with an exquisite and curious little thing— a paper-weight in likeness of a couchant lion, wrought from a jade-stone yellow as that created by a rainbow in honor of Kong-futze. Tenderly the boy kissed the gift and the beautiful hand that gave it. "May the Spirits punish me," he vowed, "if ever I knowingly give you cause to reproach me, sweetheart!" And they separated with mutual vows.

That morning, on returning to the house of Lord Tchang, Ming-Y told the first falsehood which had ever passed his lips. He averred that his mother had requested him thenceforward to pass his nights at home, now that the weather had become so pleasant; for, though the way was somewhat long, he was strong and active, and needed both air and healthy exercise. Tchang believed all Ming-Y said, and offered no objection. Accordingly the lad found himself enabled to pass all his evenings at the house of the beautiful Sië. Each night they devoted to the same pleasures which had made their first acquaintance so charming: they sang and conversed by turns; they played at chess— the learned game invented by Wu-Wang, which is an imitation of war; they composed pieces of eighty rhymes upon the flowers, the trees, the clouds, the streams, the birds, the bees. But in all accomplishments Sië far excelled her young sweetheart. Whenever they played at chess, it was always Ming-Y's general, Ming-Y's *tsiang,* who was surrounded and vanquished; when they composed verses, Sië's poems were ever superior to his in harmony of word-coloring, in elegance of form, in classic loftiness of thought. And the themes they selected were always the most difficult—those of the poets of the Thang dynasty; the songs they sang were also the songs of five hundred years before—the songs of Youen-tchin, of Thoumou, of Kao-pien above all, high poet and ruler of the province of Sze-tchouen.

So the summer waxed and waned upon their love, and the luminous autumn came, with its vapors of phantom gold, its shadows of magical purple.

Then it unexpectedly happened that the father of Ming-Y, meeting his son's employer at Tching-tou, was asked by him: "Why must your boy continue to travel every evening to the city, now that the winter is approaching? The way is long, and when he returns in the morning he looks fordone with weariness. Why not permit him to slumber in my house during the season of snow?"

And the father of Ming-Y, greatly astonished, responded: "Sir, my son has not visited the city, nor has he been to our house all this summer. I fear that he must have acquired wicked habits, and that he passes his nights in evil company—perhaps in gaming, or in drinking with the women of the flower-boats."

But the High Commissioner returned: "Nay! that is not to be thought of. I have never found any evil in the boy, and there are no taverns nor flower-boats nor any places of dissipation in our neighborhood. No doubt Ming-Y has found some amiable youth of his own age with whom to spend his evenings, and only told me an untruth for fear that I would not otherwise permit him to leave my residence. I beg that you will say nothing to him until I shall have sought to discover this mystery; and this very evening I shall send my servant to follow after him, and to watch whither he goes."

Pelou readily assented to this proposal, and promising to visit Tchang the following morning, returned to his home. In the evening, when Ming-Y left the house of Tchang, a servant followed him unobserved at a distance. But on reaching the most obscure portion of the road, the boy disappeared from sight as suddenly as though the earth had swallowed him. After having long sought after him in vain, the domestic returned in great bewilderment to the house, and related what had taken place. Tchang immediately sent a messenger to Pelou.

In the mean time Ming-Y, entering the chamber of his beloved, was surprised and deeply pained to find her in tears. "Sweetheart," she sobbed, wreathing her arms around his neck, "we are about to be separated forever, because of reasons which I cannot tell you. From the very first I knew this must come to pass; and nevertheless it seemed to me for the moment so cruelly sudden a loss, so unexpected a misfortune, that I could not prevent myself from weeping! After this night we shall never see each other again, beloved, and I know that you will not be able to forget me while you live; but I know also that you will become a great scholar, and that honors and riches will be showered upon you, and that some beautiful and loving woman will console you for my loss. And now let us speak no more of grief; but let us pass this last evening joyously, so that your recollection of me may not be a painful one, and that you may remember my laughter rather than my tears."

She brushed the bright drops away, and brought wine and music and the melodious kin of seven silken strings, and would not suffer Ming-Y to speak for one moment of the coming separation. And she sang him an ancient song about the calmness of summer lakes reflecting the blue of heaven only, and the calmness of the heart also, before the clouds of care and of grief and of weariness darken its little world. Soon they forgot their sorrow in the joy of song and wine; and those last hours seemed to Ming-Y more celestial than even the hours of their first bliss.

But when the yellow beauty of morning came their sadness returned, and they wept. Once more Sië accompanied her lover to the terrace steps; and as she kissed him farewell, she pressed into his hand a parting gift—a little brush-case of agate, wonderfully chiseled, and worthy the table of a great poet. And they separated forever, shedding many tears.

Still Ming-Y could not believe it was an eternal parting. "No!" he thought, "I shall visit her tomorrow; for I cannot now live without her, and I feel assured that she cannot refuse to receive me." Such were the thoughts that filled his mind as he reached the house of Tchang, to find his father and his patron standing on the porch awaiting him.

Ere he could speak a word, Pelou demanded: "Son, in what place have you been passing your nights?"

Seeing that his falsehood had been discovered, Ming-Y dared not make any reply, and remained abashed and silent, with bowed head, in the presence of his father. Then Pelou, striking the boy violently with his staff, commanded him to divulge the secret; and at last, partly through fear of his parent, and partly through fear of the law which ordains that "the son refusing to obey his father shall be punished with one hundred blows of the bamboo," Ming-Y faltered out the history of his love.

Tchang changed color at the boy's tale. "Child," exclaimed the High Commissioner, "I have no relative of the name of Ping; I have never heard of the woman you describe; I have never heard even of the house which you speak of. But I know also that you cannot dare to lie to Pelou, your honored father; there is some strange delusion in all this affair."

Then Ming-Y produced the gifts that Sië had given him—the lion of yellow jade, the brush-case of carven agate, also some original compositions made by the beautiful lady herself. The astonishment of Tchang was now shared by Pelou. Both observed that the brush-case of agate and the lion of jade bore the appearance of objects that had lain buried in the earth for centuries, and were of a workmanship beyond the power of living man to imitate; while the compositions proved to be veritable master-pieces of poetry, written in the style of the poets of the dynasty of Thang.

"Friend Pelou," cried the High Commissioner, "let us immediately accompany the boy to the place where he obtained these miraculous things, and apply the testimony of our senses to this mystery. The boy is no doubt telling the truth; yet his story passes my understanding." And all three proceeded toward the place of the habitation of Sië.

But when they had arrived at the shadiest part of the road, where the perfumes were most sweet and the mosses were greenest, and the fruits of the wild peach flushed most pinkly, Ming-Y, gazing through the groves, uttered a cry of dismay. Where the azure-tiled roof had risen against the sky, there was now only the blue emptiness of air; where the green-and-gold façade had been, there was visible only the flickering of leaves under the aureate autumn light; and where the broad terrace had extended, could be discerned only a ruin—a tomb so ancient, so deeply gnawed by moss, that the name graven upon it was no longer decipherable. The home of Sië had disappeared!

All suddenly the High Commissioner smote his forehead with his hand, and turning to Pelou, recited the well-known verse of the ancient poet Tching-Kou:

"Surely the peach-flowers blossom over the tomb of Sië-Thao."

"Friend Pelou," continued Tchang, "the beauty who bewitched your son was no other than she whose tomb stands there in ruin before us! Did she not say she was wedded to Ping-Khang? There is no family of that name, but Ping-Khang is indeed the name of a broad alley in the city near. There was a dark riddle in all she said. She called herself Sië of Moun-Hiao: there is no person of that name; there is no street of that name; but the Chinese characters *Moun* and *hiao,* placed together, form the character Kiao. Listen! The alley Ping-Khang, situated in the street Kiao, was the place where dwelt the great courtesans of the dynasty of Thang! Did she not sing the songs of Kao-pien? And upon the brush-case and the paper-weight she gave your son, are there not characters which read, 'Pure object of art belonging to Kao, of the city of Pho-hai'? That city no longer exists; but the memory of Kao-pien remains, for he was governor of the province of Sze-tchouen, and a mighty poet. And when he dwelt in the land of Chou, was not his favorite the beautiful wanton Sië— Sië-Thao, unmatched for grace among all the women of her day? It was he who made her a gift of those manuscripts of song; it was he who gave her those objects of rare art. Sië-Thao died not as other women die. Her limbs may have crumbled to dust; yet something of her still lives in this deep wood—her Shadow still haunts this shadowy place."

Tchang ceased to speak. A vague fear fell upon the three. The thin mists of the morning made dim the distances of the green, and deepened the ghostly beauty of the woods. A faint breeze passed by, leaving a trail of blossom-scent—a last odor of dying flowers—thin as that which clings to the silk of a forgotten robe; and, as it passed, the trees seemed to whisper across the silence, "Sië-Thao."

Fearing greatly for his son, Pelou sent the lad away at once to the city of Kwang-tchau-fu. And there, in after years, Ming-Y obtained high dignities and honors by reason of his talents and his learning; and he married the daughter of an illustrious house, by whom he became the father of sons and daughters famous for their virtues and their accomplishments. Never could he forget Sië-Thao; and yet it is said that he never spoke of her—not even when his children begged him to tell them the story of two beautiful objects that always lay upon his writing-table: a lion of yellow jade, and a brush-case of carven agate.

The Legend of Tchi-Niu

A sound of gongs, a sound of song—the song of the builders building the dwellings of the dead:

> *Khiŭ tchi yîng-yîng.*
> *Toŭ tchi hoûng-hoûng.*
> *Tchŏ tchi tông-tông.*
> *Siŏ liŭ pîng-pîng.*

IN THE QUAINT COMMENTARY ACCOMPANYING THE TEXT OF THAT HOLY
book of Lao-tseu called "Kan-ing-p'ien" may be found a little story so
old that the name of the one who first told it has been forgotten for a
thousand years, yet so beautiful that it lives still in the memory of four
hundred millions of people, like a prayer that, once learned, is forever
remembered. The Chinese writer makes no mention of any city nor of
any province, although even in the relation of the most ancient traditions such an omission is rare; we are only told that the name of the
hero of the legend was Tong-yong, and that he lived in the years of
the great dynasty of Han, some twenty centuries ago.

Tong-yong's mother had died while he was yet an infant; and when
he became a youth of nineteen years his father also passed away, leaving
him utterly alone in the world, and without resources of any sort; for,
being a very poor man, Tong's father had put himself to great straits
to educate the lad, and had not been able to lay by even one copper coin
of his earnings. And Tong lamented greatly to find himself so destitute
that he could not honor the memory of that good father by having the
customary rites of burial performed, and a carven tomb erected upon a
propitious site. The poor only are friends of the poor; and among all
those whom Tong knew, there was no one able to assist him in defray-
ing the expenses of the funeral. In one way only could the youth obtain

money—by selling himself as a slave to some rich cultivator; and this he at last decided to do. In vain his friends did their utmost to dissuade him; and to no purpose did they attempt to delay the accomplishment of his sacrifice by beguiling promises of future aid. Tong only replied that he would sell his freedom a hundred times, if it were possible, rather than suffer his father's memory to remain unhonored even for a brief season. And furthermore, confiding in his youth and strength, he determined to put a high price upon his servitude—a price which would enable him to build a handsome tomb, but which it would be well-nigh impossible for him ever to repay.

Accordingly he repaired to the broad public place where slaves and debtors were exposed for sale, and seated himself upon a bench of stone, having affixed to his shoulders a placard inscribed with the terms of his servitude and the list of his qualifications as a laborer. Many who read the characters upon the placard smiled disdainfully at the price asked, and passed on without a word; others lingered only to question him out of simple curiosity; some commended him with hollow praise; some openly mocked his unselfishness, and laughed at his childish piety. Thus many hours wearily passed, and Tong had almost despaired of finding a master, when there rode up a high official of the province—a grave and handsome man, lord of a thousand slaves, and owner of vast estates. Reining in his Tartar horse, the official halted to read the placard and to consider the value of the slave. He did not smile, or advise, or ask any questions; but having observed the price asked, and the fine strong limbs of the youth, purchased him without further ado, merely ordering his attendant to pay the sum and to see that the necessary papers were made out.

Thus Tong found himself enabled to fulfill the wish of his heart, and to have a monument built which, although of small size, was destined to delight the eyes of all who beheld it, being designed by cunning artists and executed by skillful sculptors. And while it was yet designed only, the pious rites were performed, the silver coin was placed in the mouth of the dead, the white lanterns were hung at the door, the holy prayers were recited, and paper shapes of all things the departed might need in the land of the Genii were consumed in consecrated fire. And after the geomancers and the necromancers had chosen a burial-spot which no unlucky star could shine upon, a place of rest which no demon or dragon might ever disturb, the beautiful *chih* was built.

Then was the phantom money strewn along the way; the funeral procession departed from the dwelling of the dead, and with prayers and lamentation the mortal remains of Tong's good father were borne to the tomb.

Then Tong entered as a slave into the service of his purchaser, who allotted him a little hut to dwell in; and thither Tong carried with him those wooden tablets, bearing the ancestral names, before which filial piety must daily burn the incense of prayer, and perform the tender duties of family worship.

Thrice had spring perfumed the breast of the land with flowers, and thrice had been celebrated that festival of the dead which is called "Siu-fan-ti," and thrice had Tong swept and garnished his father's tomb and presented his fivefold offering of fruits and meats. The period of mourning had passed, yet he had not ceased to mourn for his parent. The years revolved with their moons, bringing him no hour of joy, no day of happy rest; yet he never lamented his servitude, or failed to perform the rites of ancestral worship—until at last the fever of the rice-fields laid strong hold upon him, and he could not arise from his couch; and his fellow-laborers thought him destined to die. There was no one to wait upon him, no one to care for his needs, inasmuch as slaves and servants were wholly busied with the duties of the household or the labor of the fields—all departing to toil at sunrise and returning weary only after the sundown.

Now, while the sick youth slumbered the fitful slumber of exhaustion one sultry noon, he dreamed that a strange and beautiful woman stood by him, and bent above him and touched his forehead with the long, fine fingers of her shapely hand. And at her cool touch a weird sweet shock passed through him, and all his veins tingled as if thrilled by new life. Opening his eyes in wonder, he saw verily bending over him the charming being of whom he had dreamed, and he knew that her lithe hand really caressed his throbbing forehead. But the flame of the fever was gone, a delicious coolness now penetrated every fibre of his body, and the thrill of which he had dreamed still tingled in his blood like a great joy. Even at the same moment the eyes of the gentle visitor met his own, and he saw they were singularly beautiful, and shone like splendid black jewels under brows curved like the wings of the swallow. Yet their calm gaze seemed to pass through him as light through crystal; and a vague awe came upon him, so that the question which had risen to his lips found no utterance. Then she, still caressing him, smiled and said: "I have come to restore thy strength and to be thy wife. Arise and worship with me."

Her clear voice had tones melodious as a bird's song; but in her gaze there was an imperious power which Tong felt he dare not resist. Rising from his couch, he was astounded to find his strength wholly restored; but the cool, slender hand which held his own led him away so swiftly that he had little time for amazement. He would have given years of existence for courage to speak of his misery, to declare his utter inability to maintain a wife; but something irresistible in the long dark eyes of his companion forbade him to speak; and as though his inmost thought had been discerned by that wondrous gaze, she said to him, in the same clear voice, "I will provide." Then shame made him blush at the thought of his wretched aspect and tattered apparel; but he observed that she also was poorly attired, like a woman of the people—wearing no ornament of any sort, nor even shoes upon her feet. And before he had yet spoken to her, they came before the ancestral tablets; and there she knelt with him and prayed, and pledged him in a cup of wine—brought he knew not from whence—and together they worshiped Heaven and Earth. Thus she became his wife.

A mysterious marriage it seemed, for neither on that day nor at any future time could Tong venture to ask his wife the name of her family, or of the place whence she came, and he could not answer any of the curious questions which his fellow-laborers put to him concerning her; and she, moreover, never uttered a word about herself, except to say that her name was Tchi. But although Tong had such awe of her that while her eyes were upon him he was as one having no will of his own, he loved her unspeakably; and the thought of his serfdom ceased to weigh upon him from the hour of his marriage. As through magic the little dwelling had become transformed: its misery was masked with charming paper devices—with dainty decorations created out of nothing by that pretty jugglery of which woman only knows the secret.

Each morning at dawn the young husband found a well-prepared and ample repast awaiting him, and each evening also upon his return; but the wife all day sat at her loom, weaving silk after a fashion unlike anything which had ever been seen before in that province. For as she wove, the silk flowed from the loom like a slow current of glossy gold, bearing upon its undulations strange forms of violet and crimson and jewel-green: shapes of ghostly horsemen riding upon horses, and of phantom chariots dragon-drawn, and of standards of trailing cloud. In every dragon's beard glimmered the mystic pearl; in every rider's helmet sparkled the gem of rank. And each day Tchi would weave a great piece of such figured silk; and the fame of her weaving spread abroad. From far and near people thronged to see the marvelous work; and the silk-merchants of great cities heard of it, and they sent messengers to Tchi, asking her that she should weave for them and teach them her secret. Then she wove for them, as they desired, in return for the silver cubes which they brought her; but when they prayed her to teach them, she laughed and said, "Assuredly I could never teach you, for no one among you has fingers like mine." And indeed no man could discern her fingers when she wove, any more than he might behold the wings of a bee vibrating in swift flight.

The seasons passed, and Tong never knew want, so well did his beautiful wife fulfill her promise—"I will provide"; and the cubes of bright silver brought by the silk-merchants were piled up higher and higher in the great carven chest which Tchi had bought for the storage of the household goods.

One morning, at last, when Tong, having finished his repast, was about to depart to the fields, Tchi unexpectedly bade him remain; and opening the great chest, she took out of it and gave him a document written in the official characters called *li-shu*. And Tong, looking at it, cried out and leaped in his joy, for it was the certificate of his manumission. Tchi had secretly purchased her husband's freedom with the price of her wondrous silks!

"Thou shalt labor no more for any master," she said, "but for thine own sake only. And I have also bought this dwelling, with all which is therein, and the tea-fields to the south, and the mulberry groves hard by—all of which are thine."

Then Tong, beside himself for gratefulness, would have prostrated himself in worship before her, but that she would not suffer it.

Thus he was made free; and prosperity came to him with his freedom; and whatsoever he gave to the sacred earth was returned to him centupled; and his servants loved him and blessed the beautiful Tchi, so silent and yet so kindly to all about her. But the silk-loom soon remained untouched, for Tchi gave birth to a son—a boy so beautiful that Tong wept with delight when he looked upon him. And thereafter the wife devoted herself wholly to the care of the child.

Now it soon became manifest that the boy was not less wonderful than his wonderful mother. In the third month of his age he could speak; in the seventh month he could repeat by heart the proverbs of the sages, and recite the holy prayers; before the eleventh month he could use the writing-brush with skill, and copy in shapely characters the precepts of Lao-tseu. And the priests of the temples came to behold him and to converse with him, and they marveled at the charm of the child and the wisdom of what he said; and they blessed Tong, saying: "Surely this son of thine is a gift from the Master of Heaven, a sign that the immortals love thee. May thine eyes behold a hundred happy summers!"

It was in the Period of the Eleventh Moon: the flowers had passed away, the perfume of the summer had flown, the winds were growing chill, and in Tong's home the evening fires were lighted. Long the husband and wife sat in the mellow glow—he speaking much of his hopes and joys, and of his son that was to be so grand a man, and of many paternal projects; while she, speaking little, listened to his words, and often turned her wonderful eyes upon him with an answering smile. Never had she seemed so beautiful before; and Tong, watching her face, marked not how the night waned, nor how the fire sank low, nor how the wind sang in the leafless trees without.

All suddenly Tchi arose without speaking, and took his hand in hers and led him, gently as on that strange wedding-morning, to the cradle where their boy slumbered, faintly smiling in his dreams. And in that moment there came upon Tong the same strange fear that he knew when Tchi's eyes had first met his own—the vague fear that love and trust had calmed, but never wholly cast out, like unto the fear of the gods. And all unknowingly, like one yielding to the pressure of mighty invisible hands, he bowed himself low before her, kneeling as to a divinity. Now, when he lifted his eyes again to her face, he closed them forthwith in awe; for she towered before him taller than any mortal woman, and there was a glow about her as of sunbeams, and the light of her limbs shone through her garments. But her sweet voice came to him with all the tenderness of other hours, saying:

"Lo! my beloved, the moment has come in which I must forsake thee; for I was never of mortal born, and the Invisible may incarnate themselves for a time only. Yet I leave with thee the pledge of our love —this fair son, who shall ever be to thee as faithful and as fond as thou thyself hast been. Know, my beloved, that I was sent to thee even by the Master of Heaven, in reward of thy filial piety, and that I must now return to the glory of His house: I AM THE GODDESS TCHI-NIU."

Even as she ceased to speak, the great glow faded; and Tong, re-opening his eyes, knew that she had passed away forever—mysteri-ously as pass the winds of heaven, irrevocably as the light of a flame blown out. Yet all the doors were barred, all the windows unopened. Still the child slept, smiling in his sleep. Outside, the darkness was breaking; the sky was brightening swiftly; the night was past. With splendid majesty the East threw open high gates of gold for the com-ing of the sun; and, illuminated by the glory of his coming, the vapors of morning wrought themselves into marvelous shapes of shifting color —into forms weirdly beautiful as the silken dreams woven in the loom of Tchi-Niu.

The Return of Yen-Tchin-King

Before me ran, as a herald runneth, the Leader of the Moon;
And the Spirit of the Wind followed after me—quickening his
    flight. LI-SAO

IN THE THIRTY-EIGHTH CHAPTER OF THE HOLY BOOK, "KAN-ING-P'IEN," wherein the Recompense of Immortality is considered, may be found the legend of Yen-Tchin-King. A thousand years have passed since the passing of the good Tchin-King; for it was in the period of the great-ness of Thang that he lived and died.

Now, in those days when Yen-Tchin-King was Supreme Judge of one of the Six August Tribunals one Li-hi-lié, a soldier mighty for evil, lifted the black banner of revolt, and drew after him, as a tide of de-struction, the millions of the northern provinces. And learning of these things, and knowing also that Hi-lié was the most ferocious of men, who respected nothing on earth save fearlessness, the Son of Heaven commanded Tchin-King that he should visit Hi-lié and strive to recall the rebel to duty, and read unto the people who followed after him in revolt the Emperor's letter of reproof and warning. For Tchin-King was famed throughout the provinces for his wisdom, his rectitude, and his fearlessness; and the Son of Heaven believed that if Hi-lié would listen to the words of any living man steadfast in loyalty and virtue, he would listen to the words of Tchin-King. So Tchin-King arrayed himself in his robes of office, and set his house in order; and, having embraced his wife and his children, mounted his horse and rode away alone to the roaring camp of the rebels, bearing the Emperor's letter in his bosom. "I shall return; fear not!" were his last words to the gray servant who watched him from the terrace as he rode.

And Tchin-King at last descended from his horse, and entered into the rebel camp, and, passing through that huge gathering of war, stood in the presence of Hi-lié. High sat the rebel among his chiefs encircled by the wave-lightning of swords and the thunders of ten thousand gongs: above him undulated the silken folds of the Black Dragon, while a vast fire rose bickering before him. Also Tchin-King saw that the tongues of that fire were licking human bones, and that skulls of men lay blackening among the ashes. Yet he was not afraid to look upon the fire, nor into the eyes of Hi-lié; but drawing from his bosom the roll of perfumed yellow silk upon which the words of the Emperor were written, and kissing it, he made ready to read, while the multitude became silent. Then, in a strong, clear voice he began:

The words of the Celestial and August, the Son of Heaven, the Divine Ko-Tsu-Tchin-Yao-Ti, unto the rebel Li-hi-lié and those that follow him.

And a roar went up like the roar of the sea—a roar of rage, and the hideous battle-moan, like the moan of a forest in storm—"Hoo! hoo-oo-oo-oo!"—and the sword-lightnings brake loose, and the thunder of the gongs moved the ground beneath the messenger's feet. But Hi-lié waved his gilded wand, and again there was silence. "Nay!" spake the rebel chief; "let the dog bark!" So Tchin-King spake on:

Knowest thou not, O most rash and foolish of men, that thou leadest the people only into the mouth of the Dragon of Destruction? Knowest thou not, also, that the people of my kingdom are the first-

born of the Master of Heaven? So it hath been written that he who doth needlessly subject the people to wounds and death shall not be suffered by Heaven to live! Thou who wouldst subvert those laws founded by the wise—those laws in obedience to which may happiness and prosperity alone be found—thou art committing the greatest of all crimes—the crime that is never forgiven!

O my people, think not that I your Emperor, I your Father, seek your destruction. I desire only your happiness, your prosperity, your greatness; let not your folly provoke the severity of your Celestial Parent. Follow not after madness and blind rage; hearken rather to the wise words of my messenger.

"Hoo! hoo-oo-oo-oo-oo!" roared the people, gathering fury. "Hoo! hoo-oo-oo-oo!"—till the mountains rolled back the cry like the rolling of a typhoon; and once more the pealing of the gongs paralyzed voice and hearing.

Then Tchin-King, looking at Hi-lié, saw that he laughed, and that the words of the letter would not again be listened to. Therefore he read on to the end without looking about him, resolved to perform his mission in so far as lay in his power. And having read all, he would have given the letter to Hi-lié; but Hie-lié would not extend his hand to take it. Therefore Tchin-King replaced it in his bosom, and folding his arms, looked Hi-lié calmly in the face, and waited.

Again Hi-lié waved his gilded wand; and the roaring ceased, and the booming of the gongs, until nothing save the fluttering of the Dragon banner could be heard. Then spake Hi-lié, with an evil smile:

"Tchin-King, O son of a dog! if thou dost not now take the oath of fealty, and bow thyself before me, and salute me with the salutation of Emperors—even with the *luh-kao,* the triple prostration—into that fire thou shalt be thrown."

But Tchin-King, turning his back upon the usurper, bowed himself a moment in worship to Heaven and Earth; and then rising suddenly, ere any man could lay hand upon him, he leaped into the towering flame, and stood there, with folded arms, like a God.

Then Hi-lié leaped to his feet in amazement, and shouted to his men; and they snatched Tchin-King from the fire, and wrung the flames from his robes with their naked hands, and extolled him, and praised him to his face. And even Hi-lié himself descended from his seat, and spoke fair words to him, saying: "O Tchin-King, I see thou art indeed a brave man and true, and worthy of all honor; be seated among us, I pray thee, and partake of whatever it is in our power to bestow!"

But Tchin-King, looking upon him unswervingly, replied in a voice clear as the voice of a great bell:

"Never, O Hi-lié, shall I accept aught from thy hand, save death, so long as thou shalt continue in the path of wrath and folly. And never shall it be said that Tchin-King sat him down among rebels and traitors, among murderers and robbers."

Then Hi-lié, in sudden fury, smote him with his sword; and Tchin-King fell to the earth and died, striving even in his death to bow his head toward the South—toward the place of the Emperor's palace—toward the presence of his beloved Master.

Even at the same hour the Son of Heaven, alone in the inner chamber of his palace, became aware of a Shape prostrate before his feet; and when he spake, the Shape arose and stood before him, and he saw that it was Tchin-King. And the Emperor would have questioned him; yet ere he could question, the familiar voice spake, saying:

"Son of Heaven, the mission confided to me I have performed; and thy command hath been accomplished to the extent of thy humble servant's feeble power. But even now must I depart, that I may enter the service of another Master."

And looking, the Emperor perceived that the Golden Tigers upon the wall were visible through the form of Tchin-King; and a strange coldness, like a winter wind, passed through the chamber; and the figure faded out. Then the Emperor knew that the Master of whom his faithful servant had spoken was none other than the Master of Heaven.

Also at the same hour the gray servant of Tchin-King's house beheld him passing through the apartments, smiling as he was wont to smile when he saw that all things were as he desired.

"Is it well with thee, my lord?" questioned the aged man.

And a voice answered him: "It is well"; but the presence of Tchin-King had passed away before the answer came.

So the armies of the Son of Heaven strove with the rebels. But the land was soaked with blood and blackened with fire; and the corpses of whole populations were carried by the rivers to feed the fishes of the sea; and still the war prevailed through many a long red year. Then came to aid the Son of Heaven the hordes that dwell in the desolations of the West and North—horsemen born, a nation of wild archers, each mighty to bend a two-hundred-pound bow until the ears should meet. And as a whirlwind they came against rebellion, raining raven-feathered arrows in a storm of death; and they prevailed against Hi-lié and his people. Then those that survived destruction and defeat submitted, and promised allegiance; and once more was the law of righteousness restored. But Tchin-King had been dead for many summers.

And the Son of Heaven sent word to his victorious generals that they should bring back with them the bones of his faithful servant, to be laid with honor in a mausoleum erected by imperial decree. So the generals of the Celestial and August sought after the nameless grave and found it, and had the earth taken up, and made ready to remove the coffin.

But the coffin crumbled into dust before their eyes; for the worms had gnawed it, and the hungry earth had devoured its substance, leaving only a phantom shell that vanished at touch of the light. And lo! as it vanished, all beheld lying there the perfect form and features of the good Tchin-King. Corruption had not touched him, nor had the worms disturbed his rest, nor had the bloom of life departed from his face. And he seemed to dream only—comely to see as upon the morning of his bridal, and smiling as the holy images smile, with eyelids closed, in the twilight of the great pagodas.

Then spoke a priest, standing by the grave: "O my children, this is indeed a Sign from the Master of Heaven; in such wise do the Powers Celestial preserve them that are chosen to be numbered with the Immortals. Death may not prevail over them, neither may corruption come nigh them. Verily the blessed Tchin-King hath taken his place among the divinities of Heaven!"

Then they bore Tchin-King back to his native place, and laid him with highest honors in the mausoleum which the Emperor had commanded; and there he sleeps, incorruptible forever, arrayed in his robes of state. Upon his tomb are sculptured the emblems of his greatness and his wisdom and his virtue, and the signs of his office, and the Four Precious Things and the monsters which are holy symbols mount giant guard in stone about it; and the weird Dogs of Fo keep watch before it, as before the temples of the gods.

The Tradition of the Tea-Plant

Sang a Chinese heart fourteen hundred years ago;
  There is Somebody of whom I am thinking.
  Far away there is Somebody of whom I am thinking.
  A hundred leagues of mountains lie between us:
  Yet the same Moon shines upon us, and the passing Wind
breathes upon us both.

> "Good is the continence of the eye;
> Good is the continence of the ear;
> Good is the continence of the nostrils;
> Good is the continence of the tongue;
> Good is the continence of the body;
> Good is the continence of speech;
> Good is all. . . ."

AGAIN THE VULTURE OF TEMPTATION SOARED TO THE HIGHEST HEAVEN OF
his contemplation, bringing his soul down, down, reeling and fluttering, back to the World of Illusion. Again the memory made dizzy his
thought, like the perfume of some venomous flower. Yet he had seen
the *bayadère* for an instant only, when passing through Kasí upon his
way to China—to the vast empire of souls that thirsted after the refreshment of Buddha's law, as sun-parched fields thirst for the life-giving
rain. When she called him, and dropped her little gift into his mendicant's bowl, he had indeed lifted his fan before his face, yet not quickly
enough; and the penalty of that fault had followed him a thousand
leagues—pursued after him even into the strange land to which he had
come to bear the words of the Universal Teacher. Accursed beauty!
surely framed by the Tempter of tempters, by Mara himself, for the
perdition of the just! Wisely had Bhagavat warned his disciples:

O ye Çramanas, women are not to be looked upon, And if ye chance to meet women, ye must not suffer your eyes to dwell upon them; but, maintaining holy reserve, speak not to them at all. Then fail not to whisper unto your own hearts, "Lo, we are Çramanas, whose duty it is to remain uncontaminated by the corruptions of this world, even as the Lotus, which suffereth no vileness to cling unto its leaves, though it blossom amid the refuse of the wayside ditch."

Then also came to his memory, but with a new and terrible meaning, the words of the Twentieth-and-Third of the Admonitions:

Of all attachments unto objects of desire, the strongest indeed is the attachment to form. Happily, this passion is unique; for were there any other like unto it, then to enter the Perfect Way were impossible.

How, indeed, thus haunted by the illusion of form, was he to fulfill the vow that he had made to pass a night and a day in perfect and unbroken meditation? Already the night was beginning! Assuredly, for sickness of the soul, for fever of the spirit, there was no physic save prayer. The sunset was swiftly fading out. He strove to pray:

O the Jewel in the Lotus!
Even as the tortoise withdraweth its extremities into its shell, let me, O Blessed One, withdraw my senses wholly into meditation!
O the Jewel in the Lotus!
For even as rain penetrateth the broken roof of a dwelling long uninhabited, so may passion enter the soul uninhabited by meditation.
O the Jewel in the Lotus!
Even as still water that hath deposited all its slime, so let my soul, O Tathâgata, be made pure! Give me strong power to rise above the world, O Master, even as the wild bird rises from its marsh to follow the pathway of the Sun!
O the Jewel in the Lotus!
By day shineth the sun, by night shineth the moon; shineth also the warrior in harness of war; shineth likewise in meditations the Çramana. But the Buddha at all times, by night or by day, shineth ever the same, illuminating the world.
O the Jewel in the Lotus!
Let me cease, O thou Perfectly Awakened, to remain as an Ape in

the World-Forest, forever ascending and descending in search of the fruits of folly. Swiftly as the twining of serpents, vast as the growth of lianas in a forest, are the all-encircling growths of the Plant of Desire.

O the Jewel in the Lotus!

Vain his prayer, alas! Vain also his invocation! The mystic meaning of the holy text—the sense of the Lotus, the sense of the Jewel!—had evaporated from the words, and their monotonous utterance now served only to lend more dangerous definition to the memory that tempted and tortured him. *O the jewel in her ear!* What lotus-bud more dainty than the folded flower of flesh, with its dripping of diamond-fire! Again he saw it, and the curve of the cheek beyond, luscious to look upon as beautiful brown fruit. How true the Two Hundred and Eighty-Fourth verse of the Admonitions!

So long as a man shall not have torn from his heart even the smallest rootlet of that liana of desire which draweth his thought toward women, even so long shall his soul remain fettered.

And there came to his mind also the Three Hundred and Forty-Fifth verse of the same blessed book, regarding fetters:

In bonds of rope, wise teachers have said, there is no strength; nor in fetters of wood, nor yet in fetters of iron. Much stronger than any of these is the fetter of concern for the jewelled earrings of women.

"Omniscient Gotama!" he cried—"all-seeing Tathâgata! How multiform the consolation of Thy Word! How marvelous Thy understanding of the human heart! Was this also one of Thy temptations?—one of the myriad illusions marshaled before Thee by Mara in that night when the earth rocked as a chariot, and the sacred trembling passed from sun to sun, from system to system, from universe to universe, from eternity to eternity?"

O the jewel in her ear! The vision would not go! Nay, each time it hovered before his thought it seemed to take a warmer life, a fonder look, a fairer form; to develop with his weakness; to gain force from his enervation. He saw the eyes, large, limpid, soft, and black as a deer's; the pearls in the dark hair, and the pearls in the pink mouth; the lips curling to a kiss, a flower-kiss; and a fragrance seemed to float to his senses, sweet, strange, soporific—a perfume of youth, an odor of woman. Rising to his feet, with strong resolve he pronounced again the sacred invocation; and he recited the holy words of the "Chapter of Impermanency":

Gazing upon the heavens and upon the earth, ye must say, These are not permanent. Gazing upon the mountains and the rivers, ye must say, These are not permanent. Gazing upon the forms and upon the faces of exterior beings, and beholding their growth and their development, ye must say, These are not permanent.

And, nevertheless, how sweet illusion! The illusion of the great sun; the illusion of the shadow-casting hills; the illusion of waters, formless and multiform; the illusion of—Nay, nay! what impious fancy! Accursed girl! yet, yet!—why should he curse her? Had she ever done aught to merit the malediction of an ascetic? Never, never! Only her form, the memory of her, the beautiful phantom of her, the accursed phantom of her! What was she? An illusion creating illusions, a mockery, a dream, a shadow, a vanity, a vexation of spirit! The fault, the sin, was in himself, in his rebellious thought, in his untamed memory. Though mobile as water, intangible as vapor, Thought, nevertheless, may be tamed by the Will, may be harnessed to the chariot of Wisdom—must be!—that happiness be found. And he recited the blessed verse of the "Book of the Way of the Law":

All forms are only temporary. When this great truth is fully comprehended by any one, then is he delivered from all pain. This is the Way of Purification.
All forms are subject unto pain. When this great truth is fully comprehended by any one, then is he delivered from all pain. This is the Way of Purification.
All forms are without substantial reality. When this great truth is fully comprehended by any one, then is he delivered from all pain. This is the way of . . .

Her form, too, unsubstantial, unreal, an illusion only, though comeliest of illusions? She had given him alms! Was the merit of the giver illusive also—illusive like the grace of the supple fingers that gave? Assuredly there were mysteries in the Abhi-dharma impenetrable, incomprehensible! . . . It was a golden coin, stamped with the symbol of an elephant—not more of an illusion, indeed, than the gifts of Kings to the Buddha! Gold upon her bosom also, less fine than the gold of her skin. Naked between the silken sash and the narrow breast-corselet, her young waist curved glossy and pliant as a bow. Richer the silver in her voice than in the hollow pagals that made a moonlight about her ankles! But her smile!—the little teeth like flower-stamens in the perfumed blossom of her mouth!

O weakness! O shame! How had the strong Charioteer of Resolve thus lost his control over the wild team of fancy! Was this languor of the Will a signal of coming peril, the peril of slumber? So strangely vivid those fancies were, so brightly definite, as about to take visible form, to move with factitious life, to play some unholy drama upon the stage of dreams! "O Thou Fully Awakened!" he cried aloud, "help now thy humble disciple to obtain the blessed wakefulness of perfect contemplation! let him find force to fulfill his vow! suffer not Mara to prevail against him!" And he recited the eternal verses of the "Chapter of Wakefulness":

Completely and eternally awake are the disciples of Gotama! Unceasingly, by day and night, their thoughts are fixed upon the Law.

Completely and eternally awake are the disciples of Gotama! Unceasingly, by day and night, their thoughts are fixed upon the Community.

Completely and eternally awake are the disciples of Gotama! Unceasingly, by day and night, their thoughts are fixed upon the Body.

Completely and eternally awake are the disciples of Gotama! Unceasingly, by day and night, their minds know the sweetness of perfect peace.

Completely and eternally awake are the disciples of Gotama! Unceasingly, by day and night, their minds enjoy the deep peace of meditation.

There came a murmur to his ears; a murmuring of many voices, smothering the utterances of his own, like a tumult of waters. The stars went out before his sight; the heavens darkened their infinities: all things became viewless, became blackness; and the great murmur deepened, like the murmur of a rising tide; and the earth seemed to sink from beneath him. His feet no longer touched the ground; a sense of supernatural buoyancy pervaded every fibre of his body: he felt himself floating in obscurity; then sinking softly, slowly, like a feather dropped from the pinnacle of a temple. Was this death? Nay, for all suddenly, as transported by the Sixth Supernatural Power, he stood again in light—a perfumed, sleepy light, vapory, beautiful—that bathed the marvelous streets of some Indian city. Now the nature of the murmur became manifest to him; for he moved with a mighty throng, a people of pilgrims, a nation of worshipers. But these were not of his faith; they bore upon their foreheads the smeared symbols of obscene gods! Still, he could not escape from their midst; the mile-broad human torrent bore him irresistibly with it, as a leaf is swept by the waters of the Ganges. Rajahs were there with their trains, and princes riding upon elephants, and Brahmins robed in their vestments, and swarms of voluptuous dancing-girls, moving to chant of *kabit* and *damâri*. But whither, whither? Out of the city into the sun they passed, between avenues of banyan, down colonnades of palm. But whither, whither?

Blue-distant, a mountain of carven stone appeared before them—the Temple, lifting to heaven its wilderness of chiseled pinnacles, flinging to the sky the golden spray of its decoration. Higher it grew with approach, the blue tones changed to gray, the outlines sharpened in the light. Then each detail became visible: the elephants of the pedestals standing upon tortoises of rock; the great grim faces of the capitals; the serpents and monsters writhing among the friezes; the many-headed gods of basalt in their galleries of fretted niches, tier above tier; the pictured foulnesses, the painted lusts, the divinities of abomination. And, yawning in the sloping precipice of sculpture, beneath a frenzied swarming of gods and Gopia—a beetling pyramid of limbs and bodies interlocked—the Gate, cavernous and shadowy as the mouth of Siva, devoured the living multitude.

The eddy of the throng whirled him with it to the vastness of the interior. None seemed to note his yellow robe, none even to observe his presence. Giant aisles intercrossed their heights above him; myriads of mighty pillars, fantastically carven, filed away to invisibility behind the yellow illumination of torch-fires. Strange images, weirdly sensuous, loomed up through haze of incense. Colossal figures, that at a distance assumed the form of elephants or garuda-birds, changed aspect when approached, and revealed as the secret of their design an interplaiting of the bodies of women; while one divinity rode all the monstrous allegories—one divinity or demon, eternally the same in the repetition of the sculptor, universally visible as though self-multiplied.

The huge pillars themselves were symbols, figures, carnalities; the orgiastic spirit of that worship lived and writhed in the contorted bronze of the lamps, the twisted gold of the cups, the chiseled marble of the tanks. . . .

How far had he proceeded? He knew not; the journey among those countless columns, past those armies of petrified gods, down lanes of flickering lights, seemed longer than the voyage of a caravan, longer than his pilgrimage to China! But suddenly, inexplicably, there came a silence as of cemeteries; the living ocean seemed to have ebbed away from about him, to have been engulfed within abysses of subterranean architecture! He found himself alone in some strange crypt before a basin, shell-shaped and shallow, bearing in its centre a rounded column of less than human height, whose smooth and spherical summit was wreathed with flowers. Lamps similarly formed, and fed with oil of palm, hung above it. There was no other graven image, no visible divinity. Flowers of countless varieties lay heaped upon the pavement; they covered its surface like a carpet, thick, soft; they exhaled their ghosts beneath his feet. The perfume seemed to penetrate his brain— a perfume sensuous, intoxicating, unholy; an unconquerable languor mastered his will, and he sank to rest upon the floral offerings.

The sound of a tread, light as a whisper, approached through the heavy stillness, with a drowsy tinkling of pagals, a tintinnabulation of anklets. All suddenly he felt glide about his neck the tepid smoothness of a woman's arm. *She, she!* his Illusion, his Temptation; but how transformed, transfigured!—preternatural in her loveliness, incomprehensible in her charm! Delicate as a jasmine-petal the cheek that touched his own; deep as night, sweet as summer, the eyes that watched him.

"Heart's-thief," her flower-lips whispered—"heart's-thief, how have I sought for thee! How have I found thee! Sweets I bring thee, my beloved; lips and bosom; fruit and blossom. Hast thirst? Drink from the well of mine eyes! Wouldst sacrifice? I am thine altar! Wouldst pray? I am thy God!"

Their lips touched; her kiss seemed to change the cells of his blood to flame. For a moment Illusion triumphed; Mara prevailed! . . . With a shock of resolve the dreamer awoke in the night—under the stars of the Chinese sky.

Only a mockery of sleep! But the vow had been violated, the sacred purpose unfulfilled! Humiliated, penitent, but resolved, the ascetic drew from his girdle a keen knife, and with unfaltering hands severed his eyelids from his eyes, and flung them from him.

"O Thou Perfectly Awakened!" he prayed, "thy disciple hath not been overcome save through the feebleness of the body; and his vow hath been renewed. Here shall he linger, without food or drink, until the moment of its fulfillment."

And having assumed the hieratic posture—seated himself with his lower limbs folded beneath him, and the palms of his hands upward, the right upon the left, the left resting upon the sole of his upturned foot—he resumed his meditation.

Dawn blushed; day brightened. The sun shortened all the shadows of the land, and lengthened them again, and sank at last upon his funeral pyre of crimson-burning cloud. Night came and glittered and passed. But Mara had tempted in vain. This time the vow had been fulfilled, the holy purpose accomplished.

And again the sun arose to fill the world with laughter of light; flowers opened their hearts to him; birds sang their morning hymn of fire worship; the deep forest trembled with delight; and far upon the plain, the eaves of many-storied temples and the peaked caps of the city-towers caught aureate glory. Strong in the holiness of his accomplished vow, the Indian pilgrim arose in the morning glow. He started for amazement as he lifted his hands to his eyes. What! was everything a dream? Impossible! Yet now his eyes felt no pain; neither were they lidless; not even so much as one of their lashes was lacking. What marvel had been wrought? In vain he looked for the severed lids that he had flung upon the ground; they had mysteriously vanished. But lo! there where he had cast them two wondrous shrubs were growing, with dainty leaflets eyelid-shaped, and snowy buds just opening to the East.

Then, by virtue of the supernatural power acquired in that mighty meditation, it was given the holy missionary to know the secret of that newly created plant—the subtle virtue of its leaves. And he named it, in the language of the nation to whom he brought the Lotus of the Good Law, "TE"; and he spake to it, saying:

"Blessed be thou, sweet plant, beneficent, life-giving, formed by the spirit of virtuous resolve! Lo! the fame of thee shall yet spread unto the ends of the earth; and the perfume of thy life be borne unto the uttermost parts by all the winds of heaven! Verily, for all time to come men who drink of thy sap shall find such refreshment that weariness may not overcome them nor languor seize upon them;—neither shall they know the confusion of drowsiness, nor any desire for slumber in the hour of duty or of prayer. Blessed be thou!"

And still, as a mist of incense, as a smoke of universal sacrifice, perpetually ascends to heaven from all the lands of earth the pleasant vapor of TE, created for the refreshment of mankind by the power of a holy vow, the virtue of a pious atonement.

The Tale of the Porcelain-God

It is written in the "Fong-ho-chin-tch'ouen," that whenever the artist Thsang-Kong was in doubt, he would look into the fire of the great oven in which his vases were baking, and question the Guardian-Spirit dwelling in the flame. And the Spirit of the Oven-fires so aided him with his counsels, that the porcelains made by Thsang-Kong were indeed finer and lovelier to look upon than all other porcelains. And they were baked in the years of Khang-hí— sacredly called "Jin Houang-tí."

WHO FIRST OF MEN DISCOVERED THE SECRET OF THE KAO-LING, OF THE Pe-tun-tse—the bones and the flesh, the skeleton and the skin, of the beauteous Vase? Who first discovered the virtue of the curd-white clay? Who first prepared the ice-pure bricks of tun: the gathered-hoariness of mountains that have died for age; blanched dust of the rocky bones and the stony flesh of sun-seeking Giants that have ceased to be? Unto whom was it first given to discover the divine art of porcelain?

Unto Pu, once a man, now a god, before whose snowy statues bow the myriad populations enrolled in the guilds of the potteries. But the place of his birth we know not; perhaps the tradition of it may have been effaced from remembrance by that awful war which in our own day consumed the lives of twenty millions of the Black-haired Race, and obliterated from the face of the world even the wonderful City of Porcelain itself—the City of King-te-chin, that of old shone like a jewel of fire in the blue mountain-girdle of Feou-liang.

Before his time indeed the Spirit of the Furnace had being; had issued from the Infinite Vitality; had become manifest as an emanation of the Supreme Tao. For Hoang-ti, nearly five thousand years ago, taught men to make good vessels of baked clay; and in his time all potters had learned to know the God of Oven-fires, and turned their wheels to the murmuring of prayer. But Hoang-ti had been gathered unto his fathers for thrice ten hundred years before that man was born destined by the Master of Heaven to become the Porcelain-God.

And his divine ghost, ever hovering above the smoking and the toiling of the potteries, still gives power to the thought of the shaper, grace to the genius of the designer, luminosity to the touch of the enamelist. For by his heaven-taught wisdom was the art of porcelain created; by his inspiration were accomplished all the miracles of Thao-yu, maker of the Kia-yu-ki, and all the marvels made by those who followed after him;

All the azure porcelains called *You-kouo-thien-tsing;* brilliant as a mirror, thin as paper of rice, sonorous as the melodious stone Khing, and colored, in obedience to the mandate of the Emperor Chi-tsong, "blue as the sky is after rain, when viewed through the rifts of the clouds." These were, indeed, the first of all porcelains, likewise called *Tchai-yao,* which no man, howsoever wicked, could find courage to break, for they charmed the eye like jewels of price;

And the *Jou-yao,* second in rank among all porcelains, sometimes mocking the aspect and the sonority of bronze, sometimes blue as summer waters, and deluding the sight with mucid appearance of thickly floating spawn of fish;

And the *Kouan-yao,* which are the porcelains of Magistrates, and third in rank of merit among all wondrous porcelains, colored with colors of the morning—skyey blueness, with the rose of a great dawn blushing and bursting through it, and long-limbed marsh-birds flying against the glow;

Also the *Ko-yao*—fourth in rank among perfect porcelains—of fair, faint, changing colors, like the body of a living fish, or made in the likeness of opal substance, milk mixed with fire; the work of Sing-I, elder of the immortal brothers Tchang;

Also the *Ting-yao*—fifth in rank among all perfect porcelains— white as the mourning garments of a spouse bereaved, and beautiful with a trickling as of tears—the porcelains sung of by the poet Son-tong-po;

Also the porcelains called *Pi-se-yao,* whose colors are called "hidden," being alternately invisible and visible, like the tints of ice beneath the sun—the porcelains celebrated by the far-famed singer Sin-in;

Also the wondrous *Chu-yao*—the pallid porcelains that utter a mournful cry when smitten—the porcelains chanted of by the mighty chanter, Thou-chao-ling;

Also the porcelains called *Thsin-yao,* white or blue, surface-wrinkled as the face of water by the fluttering of many fans. . . . And ye can see the fish!

Also the vases called *Tsi-hong-khi,* red as sunset after a rain; and the *T'o-t'ai-khi,* fragile as the wings of the silkworm-moth, lighter than the shell of an egg;

Also the *Kia-tsing*—fair cups pearl-white when empty, yet, by some incomprehensible witchcraft of construction, seeming to swarm with purple fish the moment they are filled with water;

Also the porcelains called *Yao-pien,* whose tints are transmuted by the alchemy of fire; for they enter blood-crimson into the heat, and change there to lizard-green, and at least come forth azure as the cheek of the sky;

Also the *Ki-tcheou-yao,* which are all violet as a summer's night; and the *Hing-yao* that sparkle with the sparklings of mingled silver and snow;

Also the *Sieouen-yao*—some ruddy as iron in the furnace, some diaphanous and ruby-red, some granulated and yellow as the rind of an orange, some softly flushed as the skin of a peach;

Also the *Tsoui-khi-yao,* crackled and green as ancient ice is; and the *Tchou-fou-yao,* which are the Porcelains of Emperors, with dragons wriggling and snarling in gold; and those yao that are pink-ribbed and have their angles serrated as the claws of crabs are;

Also the *Ou-ni-yao,* black as the pupil of the eye, and as lustrous; and the *Hou-tien-yao,* darkly yellow as the faces of men of India; and the *Ou-kong-yao,* whose color is the dead-gold of autumn-leaves;

Also the *Long-kang-yao,* green as the seedling of a pea, but bearing also paintings of sun-silvered cloud, and of the Dragons of Heaven;

Also the *Tching-hao-yao*—pictured with the amber bloom of grapes and the verdure of vine-leaves and the blossoming of poppies, or decorated in relief with figures of fighting crickets;

Also the *Khang-hi-nien-ts'ang-yao,* celestial azure sown with stardust of gold; and the *Khien-long-nien-thang-yao,* splendid in sable and silver as a fervid night that is flashed with lightnings.

Not indeed the *Long-Ouang-yao*—painted with the lascivious *Pi-hi,* with the obscene *Nan-niu-ssé-sie,* with the shameful *Tchun-hoa,* or "Pictures of Spring"; abominations created by command of the wicked Emperor Moutsong, though the Spirit of the Furnace hid his face and fled away;

But all other vases of startling form and substance, magically articulated, and ornamented with figures in relief, in cameo, in transparency —the vases with orifices belled like the cups of flowers, or cleft like the bills of birds, or fanged like the jaws of serpents, or pink-lipped as the mouth of a girl; the vases flesh-colored and purple-veined and dimpled, with ears and with earrings; the vases in likeness of mushrooms, of lotus-flowers, of lizards, of horse-footed dragons woman-faced; the vases strangely translucid, that simulate the white glimmering of grains of prepared rice, that counterfeit the vapory lacework of frost, that imitate the efflorescences of coral;

Also the statues in porcelain of divinities: the Genius of the Hearth; the Long-pinn who are the Twelve Deities of Ink; the blessed Laotseu, born with silver hair; Kong-fu-tse, grasping the scroll of written wisdom; Kouan-in, sweetest Goddess of Mercy, standing snowy-footed upon the heart of her golden lily; Chi-nong, the god who taught men how to cook; Fo, with long eyes closed in meditation, and lips smiling the mysterious smile of Supreme Beatitude; Cheou-lao, god of Longevity, bestriding his aerial steed, the white-winged stork; Pou-t'ai, Lord of Contentment and of Wealth, obese and dreamy; and that fairest Goddess of Talent, from whose beneficent hands eternally streams the iridescent rain of pearls.

And though many a secret of that matchless art that Pu bequeathed unto men may indeed have been forgotten and lost forever, the story of the Porcelain-God is remembered; and I doubt not that any of the aged *Jeou-yen-liao-kong,* any one of the old blind men of the great potteries, who sit all day grinding colors in the sun, could tell you Pu was once a humble Chinese workman, who grew to be a great artist by dint of tireless study and patience and by the inspiration of Heaven. So famed he became that some deemed him an alchemist, who possessed the secret called "White-and-Yellow," by which stones might be turned into gold; and others thought him a magician, having the ghastly power of murdering men with horror of nightmare, by hiding charmed effigies of them under the tiles of their own roofs; and others, again, averred that he was an astrologer who had discovered the mystery of those Five Hing which influence all things—those Powers that move even in the currents of the star-drift, in the milky Tien-ho, or River of the Sky. Thus, at least, the ignorant spoke of him; but even those who stood about the Son of Heaven, those whose hearts had been strengthened by the acquisition of wisdom, wildly praised the marvels of his handicraft, and asked each other if there might be an imaginable form of beauty which Pu could not evoke from that beauteous substance so docile to the touch of his cunning hand.

And one day it came to pass that Pu sent a priceless gift to the Celestial and August: a vase imitating the substance of ore-lock, all aflame with pyritic scintillation—a shape of glittering splendor with chameleons sprawling over it; chameleons of porcelain that shifted color as often as the beholder changed his position. And the Emperor, wondering exceedingly at the splendor of the work, questioned the princes and the mandarins concerning him that made it. And the princes and the mandarins answered that he was a workman named Pu, and that he was without equal among potters, knowing secrets that seemed to have been inspired either by gods or by demons. Whereupon the Son of Heaven sent his officers to Pu with a noble gift, and summoned him unto his presence.

So the humble artisan entered before the Emperor, and having performed the supreme prostration—thrice kneeling, and thrice nine times touching the ground with his forehead—awaited the command of the August.

And the Emperor spake to him, saying: "Son, thy gracious gift hath found high favor in our sight; and for the charm of that offering we have bestowed upon thee a reward of five thousand silver liang. But thrice that sum shall be awarded thee so soon as thou shalt have fulfilled our behest. Hearken, therefore, O matchless artificer! It is now our will that thou make for us a vase having the tint and the aspect of living flesh, but—mark well our desire!—*of flesh made to creep by the utterance of such words as poets utter—flesh moved by an Idea, flesh horripilated by a Thought!* Obey, and answer not! We have spoken."

Now Pu was the most cunning of all the *P'ei-se-kong,* the men who marry colors together; of all the *Hoa-yang-kong,* who draw the shapes of vase-decoration; of all the *Hoei-sse-kong,* who paint in enamel; of all the *T'ien-thsai-kong*, who brighten color; of all the *Chao-lou-kong*, who watch the furnace fires and the porcelain ovens. But he went away sorrowing from the Palace of the Son of Heaven, notwithstanding the gift of five thousand silver liang which had been given to him. For he thought to himself: "Surely the mystery of the comeliness of flesh, and the mystery of that by which it is moved, are the secrets of the Supreme Tao. How shall man lend the aspect of sentient life to dead clay? Who save the Infinite can give soul?"

Now Pu had discovered those witchcrafts of color, those surprises of grace, that make the art of the ceramist. He had found the secret of the *feng-hong*, the wizard flush of the Rose; of the *hoa-hong*, the delicious incarnadine; of the mountain-green called *chan-lou*; of the pale soft yellow termed *hiao-hoang-yeou*; and of the *hoang-kin*, which is the blazing beauty of gold. He had found those eel tints, those serpent greens, those pansy violets, those furnace crimsons, those carminates and lilacs, subtle as spirit flame, which our enamelists of the Occident long sought without success to reproduce. But he trembled at the task assigned him, as he returned to the toil of his studio, saying: "How shall any miserable man render in clay the quivering of flesh to an Idea—the inexplicable horripilation of a Thought? Shall a man venture to mock the magic of that Eternal Moulder by whose infinite power a million suns are shapen more readily than one small jar might be rounded upon my wheel?"

Yet the command of the Celestial and August might never be disobeyed; and the patient workman strove with all his power to fulfill the Son of Heaven's desire. But vainly for days, for weeks, for months, for season after season, did he strive; vainly also he prayed unto the gods to aid him; vainly he besought the Spirit of the Furnace, crying: "O thou Spirit of Fire, hear me, heed me, help me! how shall I—a miserable man, unable to breathe into clay a living soul—how shall I render in this inanimate substance the aspect of flesh made to creep by the utterance of a Word, sentient to the horripilation of a Thought?"

For the Spirit of the Furnace made strange answer to him with whispering of fire: "Vast thy faith, weird thy prayer! Has Thought feet, that man may perceive the trace of its passing? Canst thou measure me the blast of the Wind?"

Nevertheless, with purpose unmoved, nine-and-forty times did Pu seek to fulfill the Emperor's command; nine-and-forty times he strove to obey the behest of the Son of Heaven. Vainly, alas! did he consume his substance; vainly did he expend his strength; vainly did he exhaust his knowledge: success smiled not upon him; and Evil visited his home, and Poverty sat in his dwelling, and Misery shivered at his hearth.

Sometimes, when the hour of trial came, it was found that the colors had become strangely transmuted in the firing, or had faded into ashen pallor, or had darkened into the fuliginous hue of forest mould. And Pu, beholding these misfortunes, made wail to the Spirit of the Furnace, praying: "O thou Spirit of Fire, how shall I render the likeness of lustrous flesh, the warm glow of living color, unless thou aid me?"

And the Spirit of the Furnace mysteriously answered him with murmuring of fire: "Canst thou learn the art of that Infinite Enameler who hath made beautiful the Arch of Heaven—whose brush is Light; whose paints are the Colors of the Evening?"

Sometimes, again, even when the tints had not changed, after the pricked and labored surface had seemed about to quicken in the heat, to assume the vibratility of living skin—even at the last hour all the labor of the workers proved to have been wasted; for the fickle substance rebelled against their efforts, producing only crinklings grotesque as those upon the rind of a withered fruit, or granulations like those upon the skin of a dead bird from which the feathers have been rudely plucked. And Pu wept, and cried out unto the Spirit of the Furnace: "O thou Spirit of Flame, how shall I be able to imitate the thrill of flesh touched by a Thought, unless thou wilt vouchsafe to lend me thine aid?"

And the Spirit of the Furnace mysteriously answered him with muttering of fire: "Canst thou give ghost unto a stone? Canst thou thrill with a Thought the entrails of the granite hills?"

Sometimes it was found that all the work indeed had not failed; for the color seemed good, and all faultless the matter of the vase appeared to be, having neither crack nor wrinkling nor crinkling; but the pliant softness of warm skin did not meet the eye; the flesh-tinted surface offered only the harsh aspect and hard glimmer of metal. All their exquisite toil to mock the pulpiness of sentient substance had left no trace; had been brought to nought by the breath of the furnace. And Pu, in his despair, shrieked to the Spirit of the Furnace: "O thou merciless divinity! O thou most pitiless god!—thou whom I have worshiped with ten thousand sacrifices!—for what fault hast thou abandoned me?—for what error hast thou forsaken me? How may I, most wretched of men! ever render the aspect of flesh made to creep with the utterance of a Word, sentient to the titillation of a Thought, if thou wilt not aid me?"

And the Spirit of the Furnace made answer unto him with roaring of fire: "Canst thou divide a Soul? Nay! . . . Thy life for the life of thy work!—thy soul for the soul of thy Vase!"

And hearing these words Pu arose with a terrible resolve swelling at his heart, and made ready for the last and fiftieth time to fashion his work for the oven.

One hundred times did he sift the clay and the quartz, the *kao-ling* and the *tun;* one hundred times did he purify them in clearest water; one hundred times with tireless hands did he knead the creamy paste, mingling it at last with colors known only to himself. Then was the vase shapen and reshapen, and touched and retouched by the hands of Pu, until its blandness seemed to live, until it appeared to quiver and to palpitate, as with vitality from within, as with the quiver of rounded muscle undulating beneath the integument. For the hues of life were upon it and infiltrated throughout its innermost substance, imitating the carnation of blood-bright tissue, and the reticulated purple of the veins; and over all was laid the envelope of sun-colored *Pe-kia-ho,* the lucid and glossy enamel, half diaphanous, even like the substance that it counterfeited—the polished skin of a woman. Never since the making of the world had any work comparable to this been wrought by the skill of man.

Then Pu bade those who aided him that they should feed the furnace well with wood of *tcha;* but he told his resolve unto none. Yet after the oven began to glow, and he saw the work of his hands blossoming and blushing in the heat, he bowed himself before the Spirit of Flame, and murmured: "O thou Spirit and Master of Fire, I know the truth of thy words! I know that a Soul may never be divided! Therefore my life for the life of my work!—my soul for the soul of my Vase!"

And for nine days and for eight nights the furnaces were fed unceasingly with wood of *tcha;* for nine days and for eight nights men watched the wondrous vase crystallizing into being, rose-lighted by the breath of the flame. Now upon the coming of the ninth night, Pu bade all his weary comrades retire to rest, for that the work was well-nigh done, and the success assured. "If you find me not here at sunrise," he said, "fear not to take forth the vase; for I know that the task will

have been accomplished according to the command of the August."
So they departed.

But in that same ninth night Pu entered the flame, and yielded up
his ghost in the embrace of the Spirit of the Furnace, giving his life
for the life of his work—his soul for the soul of his Vase.

And when the workmen came upon the tenth morning to take forth
the porcelain marvel, even the bones of Pu had ceased to be; but
lo! the Vase lived as they looked upon it: seeming to be flesh moved by
the utterance of a Word, creeping to the titillation of a Thought. And
whenever tapped by the finger it uttered a voice and a name—the
voice of its maker, the name of its creator: PU.

And the Son of Heaven, hearing of these things, and viewing the
miracle of the vase, said unto those about him: "Verily, the Impossible
hath been wrought by the strength of faith, by the force of obedience!
Yet never was it our desire that so cruel a sacrifice should have been;
we sought only to know whether the skill of the matchless artificer
came from the Divinities or from the Demons—from heaven or from
hell. Now, indeed, we discern that Pu hath taken his place among the
gods." And the Emperor mourned exceedingly for his faithful servant.
But he ordained that godlike honors should be paid unto the spirit
of the marvelous artist, and that his memory should be revered for-
evermore, and that fair statues of him should be set up in all the
cities of the Celestial Empire, and above all the toiling of the potteries,
that the multitude of workers might unceasingly call upon his name
and invoke his benediction upon their labors.

Chita

A MEMORY OF LAST ISLAND

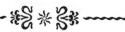

But Nature whistled with all her winds,
Did as she pleased, and went her way.

EMERSON

Je suis la vaste mêlée—
Reptile, étant l'onde; ailée,
*   Étant le vent—*
Force et fuite, haine et vie,
Houle immense, poursuivie
*   Et poursuivant.*

VICTOR HUGO

PART I

The Legend of L'Île Dernière

I

TRAVELING SOUTH FROM NEW ORLEANS TO THE ISLANDS, YOU PASS THROUGH a strange land into a strange sea, by various winding waterways. You can journey to the Gulf by lugger if you please; but the trip may be made much more rapidly and agreeably on some one of those light, narrow steamers, built especially for bayou-travel, which usually receive passengers at a point not far from the foot of old Saint Louis Street, hard by the sugar-landing, where there is ever a pushing and flocking of steam-craft—all striving for place to rest their white breasts against the levee, side by side—like great weary swans But the miniature steamboat on which you engage passage to the Gulf never lingers long in the Mississippi: she crosses the river, slips into some canal-mouth, labors along the artificial channel awhile, and then leaves it with a scream of joy, to puff her free way down many a league of heavily shadowed bayou. Perhaps thereafter she may bear you through the immense silence of drenched rice-fields, where the yellow-green level is broken at long intervals by the black silhouette of some irrigating machine;—but, whichever of the five different routes be pursued, you will find yourself more than once floating through sombre mazes of swamp-forest—past assemblages of cypresses all hoary with the parasitic tillandsia, and grotesque as gatherings of fetich-gods. Ever from river or from lakelet the steamer glides again into canal or bayou—from bayou or canal once more into lake or bay; and sometimes the swamp-forest visibly thins away from these shores into wastes of reedy morass where, even of breathless nights, the quaggy soil trembles to a sound like thunder of breakers on a coast: the storm-roar of billions of reptile voices chanting in cadence—rhythmically surging in stupendous crescendo and diminuendo—a monstrous and appalling chorus of frogs! . . .

Panting, screaming, scraping her bottom over the sand-bars—all day the little steamer strives to reach the grand blaze of blue open water below the marsh-lands; and perhaps she may be fortunate enough to enter the Gulf about the time of sunset. For the sake of passengers, she travels by day only; but there are other vessels which make the journey also by night—threading the bayou-labyrinths winter and summer: sometimes steering by the North Star—sometimes feeling the way with poles in the white season of fogs—sometimes, again, steering by that Star of Evening which in our sky glows like another moon, and drops over the silent lakes as she passes a quivering trail of silver fire.

Shadows lengthen; and at last the woods dwindle away behind you into thin bluish lines;—land and water alike take more luminous color;—bayous open into broad passes;—lakes link themselves with sea-bays;—and the ocean-wind bursts upon you—keen, cool, and full of light. For the first time the vessel begins to swing—rocking to the great living pulse of the tides. And gazing from the deck around you, with no forest walls to break the view, it will seem to you that the low land must have once been rent asunder by the sea, and strewn about the Gulf in fantastic tatters. . . .

Sometimes above a waste of wind-blown prairie-cane you see an oasis emerging—a ridge or hillock heavily umbraged with the rounded foliage of evergreen oaks:—a *chénière*. And from the shining flood also kindred green knolls arise—pretty islets, each with its beach-girdle of dazzling sand and shells, yellow-white—and all radiant with semi-tropical foliage, myrtle and palmetto, orange and magnolia. Under their emerald shadows curious little villages of palmetto huts are drowsing, where dwell a swarthy population of Orientals—Malay fishermen, who speak the Spanish-Creole of the Philippines as well as their own Tagal, and perpetuate in Louisiana the Catholic traditions of the Indies. There are girls in those unfamiliar villages worthy to inspire any statuary—beautiful with the beauty of ruddy bronze—gracile as the palmettoes that sway above them. . . . Farther seaward you may also pass a Chinese settlement: some queer camp of wooden dwellings clustering around a vast platform that stands above the water upon a thousand piles;—over the miniature wharf you can scarcely fail to observe a white sign-board painted with crimson ideographs. The great platform is used for drying fish in the sun; and the fantastic characters of the sign, literally translated, mean: "Heap—Shrimp—Plenty." . . . And finally all the land melts down into desolations of sea-marsh, whose stillness is seldom broken, except by the melancholy cry of long-legged birds, and in wild seasons by that sound which shakes all shores when the weird Musician of the Sea touches the bass keys of his mighty organ. . . .

II

BEYOND THE SEA-MARSHES A CURIOUS ARCHIPELAGO LIES. IF YOU TRAVEL by steamer to the sea-islands to-day, you are tolerably certain to enter the Gulf by Grande Pass—skirting Grande Terre, the most familiar island of all, not so much because of its proximity as because of its great crumbling fort and its graceful pharos: the stationary White-Light of Barataria. Otherwise the place is bleakly uninteresting: a wilderness of wind-swept grasses and sinewy weeds waving away from a thin beach ever speckled with drift and decaying things—worm-riddled timbers, dead porpoises. Eastward the russet level is broken by the columnar silhouette of the lighthouse, and again, beyond it, by some puny scrub timber, above which rises the angular ruddy mass of the old brick fort, whose ditches swarm with crabs, and whose sluiceways are half choked by obsolete cannon-shot, now thickly

covered with incrustation of oyster shells. . . . Around all the gray
circling of a shark-haunted sea. . . .

Sometimes of autumn evenings there, when the hollow of heaven
flames like the interior of a chalice, and waves and clouds are flying
in one wild rout of broken gold—you may see the tawny grasses all
covered with something like husks—wheat-colored husks—large, flat,
and disposed evenly along the lee-side of each swaying stalk, so as to
present only their edges to the wind. But, if you approach, those pale
husks all break open to display strange splendors of scarlet and seal-
brown, with arabesque mottlings in white and black: they change into
wondrous living blossoms, which detach themselves before your eyes
and rise in air, and flutter away by thousands to settle down farther
off, and turn into wheat-colored husks once more . . . a whirling flower-
drift of sleepy butterflies!

Southwest, across the pass, gleams beautiful Grande Isle: primitively
a wilderness of palmetto (*latanier*);—then drained, diked, and cultivated by Spanish sugar-planters; and now familiar chiefly as a bathing-
resort. Since the war the ocean reclaimed its own;—the cane-fields
have degenerated into sandy plains, over which tramways wind to
the smooth beach;—the plantation-residences have been converted into
rustic hotels, and the Negro-quarters remodeled into villages of cozy
cottages for the reception of guests. But with its imposing groves of
oak, its golden wealth of orange-trees, its odorous lanes of oleander,
its broad grazing-meadows yellow-starred with wild camomile, Grande
Isle remains the prettiest island of the Gulf; and its loveliness is exceptional. For the bleakness of Grande Terre is reiterated by most of
the other islands—Caillou, Cassetête, Calumet, Wine Island, the twin
Timbaliers, Gull Island, and the many islets haunted by the gray
pelican—all of which are little more than sand-bars covered with wiry
grasses, prairie-cane, and scrub timber. Last Island (L'Île Dernière)—
well worthy a long visit in other years, in spite of its remoteness, is
now a ghastly desolation twenty-five miles long. Lying nearly forty
miles west of Grande Isle, it was nevertheless far more populated a
generation ago: it was not only the most celebrated island of the group,
but also the most fashionable watering-place of the aristocratic South;
—to-day it is visited by fishermen only, at long intervals. Its admirable
beach in many respects resembled that of Grande Isle to-day; the
accommodations also were much similar, although finer: a charming
village of cottages facing the Gulf near the western end. The hotel

itself was a massive two-story construction of timber, containing many apartments, together with a large dining-room and dancing-hall. In rear of the hotel was a bayou, where passengers landed—"Village Bayou" it is still called by seamen;—but the deep channel which now cuts the island in two a little eastwardly did not exist while the village remained. The sea tore it out in one night—the same night when trees, fields, dwellings, all vanished into the Gulf, leaving no vestige of former human habitation except a few of those strong brick props and foundations upon which the frame houses and cisterns had been raised. One living creature was found there after the cataclysm— a cow! But how that solitary cow survived the fury of a storm-flood that actually rent the island in twain has ever remained a mystery. . . .

III

ON THE GULF SIDE OF THESE ISLANDS YOU MAY OBSERVE THAT THE TREES —when there are any trees—all bend away from the sea; and, even of bright, hot days when the wind sleeps, there is something grotesquely pathetic in their look of agonized terror. A group of oaks at Grande Isle I remember as especially suggestive: five stooping silhouettes in line against the horizon, like fleeing women with streaming garments and wind-blown hair—bowing grievously and thrusting out arms desperately northward as to save themselves from falling. And they are being pursued indeed;—for the sea is devouring the land. Many and many a mile of ground has yielded to the tireless charging of Ocean's cavalry: far out you can see, through a good glass, the porpoises at play where of old the sugar-cane shook out its million bannerets; and shark-fins now seam deep water above a site where pigeons used to coo. Men build dikes; but the besieging tides bring up their battering-rams—whole forests of drift—huge trunks of water-oak and weighty cypress. Forever the yellow Mississippi strives to build; forever the sea struggles to destroy;—and amid their eternal strife the islands and the promontories change shape, more slowly, but not less fantastically, than the clouds of heaven.

And worthy of study are those wan battle-grounds where the woods made their last brave stand against the irresistible invasion—usually at some long point of sea-marsh, widely fringed with billowing sand. Just where the waves curl beyond such a point you may discern a multitude of blackened, snaggy shapes protruding above the water—

some high enough to resemble ruined chimneys, others bearing a startling likeness to enormous skeleton-feet and skeleton-hands—with crustaceous white growths clinging to them here and there like remnants of integument. These are bodies and limbs of drowned oaks—so long drowned that the shell-scurf is inch-thick upon parts of them. Farther in upon the beach immense trunks lie overthrown. Some look like vast broken columns; some suggest colossal torsos embedded, and seem to reach out mutilated stumps in despair from their deepening graves;—and beside these are others which have kept their feet with astounding obstinacy, although the barbarian tides have been charging them for twenty years, and gradually torn away the soil above and beneath their roots. The sand around—soft beneath and thinly crusted upon the surface—is everywhere pierced with holes made by a beautifully mottled and semi-diaphanous crab, with hairy legs, big staring eyes, and milk-white claws;—while in the green sedges beyond there is a perpetual rustling, as of some strong wind beating among reeds: a marvelous creeping of "fiddlers," which the inexperienced visitor might at first mistake for so many peculiar beetles, as they run about sideways, each with his huge single claw folded upon his body like a wing-case. Year by year that rustling strip of green land grows narrower; the sand spreads and sinks, shuddering and wrinkling like a living brown skin; and the last standing corpses of the oaks, ever clinging with naked, dead feet to the sliding beach, lean more and more out of the perpendicular. As the sands subside, the stumps appear to creep; their intertwisted masses of snakish roots seem to crawl, to writhe—like the reaching arms of cephalopods. . . .

. . . Grande Terre is going: the sea mines her fort, and will before many years carry the ramparts by storm. Grande Isle is going—slowly but surely: the Gulf has eaten three miles into her meadowed land. Last Island has gone! How it went I first heard from the lips of a veteran pilot, while we sat one evening together on the trunk of a drifted cypress which some high tide had pressed deeply into the Grande Isle beach. The day had been tropically warm; we had sought the shore for a breath of living air. Sunset came, and with it the ponderous heat lifted—a sudden breeze blew—lightnings flickered in the darkening horizon—wind and water began to strive together—and soon all the low coast boomed. Then my companion began his story; perhaps the coming of the storm inspired him to speak! And as I listened to him, listening also to the clamoring of the coast, there flashed back to me recollection of a singular Breton fancy: that the

Voice of the Sea is never one voice, but a tumult of many voices—voices of drowned men—the muttering of multitudinous dead—the moaning of innumerable ghosts, all rising, to rage against the living, at the great Witch-call of storms. . . .

IV

THE CHARM OF A SINGLE SUMMER DAY ON THESE ISLAND SHORES IS SOME-thing impossible to express, never to be forgotten. Rarely, in the paler zones, do earth and heaven take such luminosity: those will best understand me who have seen the splendor of a West Indian sky. And yet there is a tenderness of tint, a caress of color, in these Gulf days which is not of the Antilles—a spirituality, as of eternal tropical spring. It must have been to even such a sky that Xenophanes lifted up his eyes of old when he vowed the Infinite Blue was God;—it was indeed under such a sky that De Soto named the vastest and grandest of Southern havens *Espiritu Santo*—the Bay of the Holy Ghost. There is a something unutterable in this bright Gulf-air that compels awe—something vital, something holy, something pantheistic: and reverentially the mind asks itself if what the eye beholds is not the Πνεύμα indeed, the Infinite Breath, the Divine Ghost, the great Blue Soul of the Unknown. All, all is blue in the calm—save the low land under your feet, which you almost forget, since it seems only as a tiny green flake afloat in the liquid eternity of day. Then slowly, caressingly, irresistibly, the witchery of the Infinite grows upon you: out of Time and Space you begin to dream with open eyes—to drift into delicious oblivion of facts—to forget the past, the present, the substantial—to comprehend nothing but the existence of that infinite Blue Ghost as something into which you would wish to melt utterly away forever. . . .

And this day-magic of azure endures sometimes for months together. Cloudlessly the dawn reddens up through a violet east: there is no speck upon the blossoming of its Mystical Rose—unless it be the silhouette of some passing gull, whirling his sickle-wings against the crimsoning. Ever, as the sun floats higher, the flood shifts its color. Sometimes smooth and gray, yet flickering with the morning gold, it is the vision of John—the apocalyptic Sea of Glass mixed with fire;—again, with the growing breeze, it takes that incredible purple tint familiar mostly to painters of West Indian scenery;—once more, under the blaze of noon, it changes to a waste of broken emerald. With evening, the horizon assumes tints of inexpressible sweetness—pearl-lights, opaline colors of milk and fire; and in the west are topaz-glowings and wondrous flushings as of nacre. Then, if the sea sleeps, it dreams of all these—faintly, weirdly—shadowing them even to the verge of heaven.

Beautiful, too, are those white phantasmagoria which, at the approach of equinoctial days, mark the coming of the winds. Over the rim of the sea a bright cloud gently pushes up its head. It rises; and others rise with it, to right and left—slowly at first; then more swiftly. All are brilliantly white and flocculent, like loose new cotton. Gradually they mount in enormous line high above the Gulf, rolling and wreathing into an arch that expands and advances—bending from horizon to horizon. A clear, cold breath accompanies its coming. Reaching the zenith, it seems there to hang poised awhile—a ghostly bridge arching the empyrean—upreaching its measureless span from either underside of the world. Then the colossal phantom begins to turn, as on a pivot of air—always preserving its curvilinear symmetry, but moving its unseen ends beyond and below the sky-circle. And at last it floats away unbroken beyond the blue sweep of the world, with a wind following after. Day after day, almost at the same hour, the white arc rises, wheels, and passes. . . .

. . . Never a glimpse of rock on these low shores;—only long sloping beaches and bars of smooth tawny sand. Sand and sea teem with vitality;—over all the dunes there is a constant susurration, a blattering and swarming of crustacea;—through all the sea there is a ceaseless play of silver lightning—flashing of myriad fish. Sometimes the shallows are thickened with minute, transparent, crab-like organisms—all colorless as gelatine. There are days also when countless medusæ drift in—beautiful veined creatures that throb like hearts, with perpetual systole and diastole of their diaphanous envelops: some, of translucent azure or rose, seem in the flood the shadows or ghosts of huge campanulate flowers;—others have the semblance of strange living vegetables—great milky tubers, just beginning to sprout. But woe to the human skin grazed by those shadowy sproutings and spectral stamens!—the touch of glowing iron is not more painful. . . . Within an hour or two after their appearance all these tremulous jellies vanish mysteriously as they came.

Perhaps, if a bold swimmer, you may venture out along a long way —once! Not twice!—even in company. As the water deepens beneath you, and you feel those ascending wave-currents of coldness arising which bespeak profundity, you will also begin to feel innumerable touches, as of groping fingers—touches of the bodies of fish, innumerable fish, fleeing toward shore. The farther you advance, the more thickly you will feel them come; and above you and around you, to right and left, others will leap and fall so swiftly as to daze the sight, like intercrossing fountain-jets of fluid silver. The gulls fly lower about you, circling with sinister squeaking cries;—perhaps for an instant your feet touch in the deep something heavy, swift, lithe, that rushes past with a swirling shock. Then the fear of the Abyss, the vast and voiceless Nightmare of the Sea, will come upon you; the silent panic of all those opaline millions that flee glimmering by will enter into you also. . . .

From what do they flee thus perpetually? Is it from the giant sawfish or the ravening shark?—from the herds of the porpoises, or from the *grande-écaille*—that splendid monster whom no net may hold—all helmed and armored in argent plate-mail?—or from the hideous devil-fish of the Gulf—gigantic, flat-bodied, black, with immense side-fins ever outspread like the pinions of a bat—the terror of luggermen, the uprooter of anchors? From all these, perhaps, and from other monsters likewise—goblin shapes evolved by Nature as destroyers, as equilibrists, as counterchecks to that prodigious fecundity, which, unhindered, would thicken the deep into one measureless and waveless ferment of being. . . . But when there are many bathers these perils are forgotten—numbers give courage—one can abandon one's self, without fear of the invisible, to the long, quivering, electrical caresses of the sea. . . .

V

THIRTY YEARS AGO, LAST ISLAND LAY STEEPED IN THE ENORMOUS LIGHT of even such magical days. July was dying;—for weeks no fleck of cloud had broken the heaven's blue dream of eternity; winds held their breath; slow wavelets caressed the bland brown beach with a sound as of kisses and whispers. To one who found himself alone, beyond the limits of the village and beyond the hearing of its voices— the vast silence, the vast light, seemed full of weirdness. And these hushes, these transparencies, do not always inspire a causeless apprehension: they are omens sometimes—omens of coming tempest. Nature—incomprehensible Sphinx!—before her mightiest bursts of rage, ever puts forth her divinest witchery, makes more manifest her awful beauty. . . .

But in that forgotten summer the witchery lasted many long days—days born in rose-light, buried in gold. It was the height of the season. The long myrtle-shadowed village was thronged with its summer population;—the big hotel could hardly accommodate all its guests;—the bathing-houses were too few for the crowds who flocked to the water morning and evening. There were diversions for all—hunting and fishing parties, yachting excursions, rides, music, games, promenades. Carriage wheels whirled flickering along the beach, seaming its smoothness noiselessly, as if muffled. Love wrote its dreams upon the sand. . . .

. . . Then one great noon, when the blue abyss of day seemed to yawn over the world more deeply than ever before, a sudden change touched the quicksilver smoothness of the waters—the swaying shadow of a vast motion. First the whole sea-circle appeared to rise up bodily at the sky; the horizon-curve lifted to a straight line; the line darkened and approached—a monstrous wrinkle, an immeasurable fold of green water, moving swift as a cloud-shadow pursued by sunlight. But it had looked formidable only by startling contrast with the previous placidity of the open: it was scarcely two feet high;—it curled slowly as it neared the beach, and combed itself out in sheets of wooly foam with a low, rich roll of whispered thunder. Swift in pursuit another followed —a third—a feebler fourth; then the sea only swayed a little, and stilled again. Minutes passed, and the immeasurable heaving recommenced—one, two, three, four . . . seven long swells this time;—and the Gulf smoothed itself once more. Irregularly the phenomenon continued to repeat itself, each time with heavier billowing and briefer intervals of quiet—until at last the whole sea grew restless and shifted color and flickered green;—the swells became shorter and changed form. Then from horizon to shore ran one uninterrupted heaving— one vast green swarming of snaky shapes, rolling in to hiss and flatten upon the sand. Yet no single cirrus-speck revealed itself through all the violet heights: there was no wind!—you might have fancied the sea had been upheaved from beneath. . . .

And indeed the fancy of a seismic origin for a windless surge would not appear in these latitudes to be utterly without foundation. On the fairest days a southeast breeze may bear you an odor singular enough to startle you from sleep—a strong, sharp smell as of fish-oil; and gazing at the sea you might be still more startled at the sudden apparition of great oleaginous patches spreading over the water, sheeting over the swells. That is, if you had never heard of the mysterious submarine oil-wells, the volcanic fountains, unexplored, that well up with the eternal pulsing of the Gulf Stream. . . .

But the pleasure-seekers of Last Island knew there must have been a "great blow" somewhere that day. Still the sea swelled; and a splendid surf made the evening bath delightful. Then, just at sundown, a beautiful cloud-bridge grew up and arched the sky with a single span of cottony pink vapor, that changed and deepened color with the dying of the iridescent day. And the cloud-bridge approached, stretched, strained, and swung round at last to make way for the coming of the gale—even as the light bridges that traverse the dreamy Têche swing open when luggermen sound through their conch-shells the long, bellowing signal of approach.

Then the wind began to blow, with the passing of July. It blew from the northeast, clear, cool. It blew in enormous sighs, dying away at regular intervals, as if pausing to draw breath. All night it blew; and in each pause could be heard the answering moan of the rising surf—as if the rhythm of the sea moulded itself after the rhythm of the air—as if the waving of the water responded precisely to the waving of the wind—a billow for every puff, a surge for every sigh.

The August morning broke in a bright sky;—the breeze still came cool and clear from the northeast. The waves were running now at a sharp angle to the shore: they began to carry fleeces, an innumerable flock of vague green shapes, wind-driven to be despoiled of their ghostly wool. Far as the eye could follow the line of the beach, all the slope was white with the great shearing of them. Clouds came, flew as in a panic against the face of the sun, and passed. All that day and through the night and into the morning again the breeze continued from the northeast, blowing like an equinoctial gale. . . .

Then day by day the vast breath freshened steadily, and the waters heightened. A week later sea-bathing had become perilous: colossal breakers were herding in, like moving leviathan-backs, twice the height of a man. Still the gale grew, and the billowing waxed mightier, and faster and faster overhead flew the tatters of torn cloud. The gray morning of the 9th wanly lighted a surf that appalled the best swimmers: the sea was one wild agony of foam, the gale was rending off the heads of the waves and veiling the horizon with a fog of salt spray. Shadowless and gray the day remained; there were mad bursts of lashing rain. Evening brought with it a sinister apparition, looming through a cloud-rent in the west—a scarlet sun in a green sky. His sanguine disk, enormously magnified, seemed barred like the body of a belted planet. A moment, and the crimson spectre vanished; and the moonless night came.

Then the Wind grew weird. It ceased being a breath; it became a Voice moaning across the world—hooting—uttering nightmare sounds —*Whoo!*—*whoo!*—*whoo!*—and with each stupendous owl-cry the mooing of the waters seeemed to deepen, more and more abysmally, through all the hours of darkness. From the northwest the breakers of the bay began to roll high over the sandy slope, into the salines;— the village bayou broadened to a bellowing flood. . . . So the tumult swelled and the turmoil heightened until morning—a morning of gray gloom and whistling rain. Rain of bursting clouds and rain of windblown brine from the great spuming agony of the sea.

The steamer *Star* was due from Saint Mary's that fearful morning. Could she come? No one really believed it—no one. And nevertheless men struggled to the roaring beach to look for her, because hope is stronger than reason. . . .

Even to-day, in these Creole islands, the advent of the steamer is the great event of the week. There are no telegraph lines, no telephones: the mail-packet is the only trustworthy medium of communication with the outer world, bringing friends, news, letters. The magic of steam has placed New Orleans nearer to New York than to the Timbaliers, nearer to Washington than to Wine Island, nearer to Chicago than to Barataria Bay. And even during the deepest sleep of waves and winds there will come betimes to sojourners in this unfamiliar archipelago a feeling of lonesomeness that is a fear, a feeling of isolation from the world of men—totally unlike that sense of solitude which haunts one in the silence of mountain-heights, or amid the eternal tumult of lofty granitic coasts: a sense of helpless insecurity. The land seems but an undulation of the sea-bed: its highest ridges do not rise more than the height of a man above the salines on either side;—the salines themselves lie almost level with the level of the flood-tides;—the tides are variable, treacherous, mysterious. But when all around and above these ever-changing shores the twin vastnesses of heaven and sea begin to utter the tremendous revelation of themselves as infinite forces in contention, then indeed this sense of separation from humanity appals. . . . Perhaps it was such a feeling which forced men, on the tenth day of August, eighteen hundred and fifty-six, to hope against hope for the coming of the *Star,* and to strain their eyes towards far-off Terrebonne. "It was a wind you could lie down on," said my friend the pilot.

. . . "Great God!" shrieked a voice above the shouting of the storm
—"*she is coming!*" . . . It was true. Down the Atchafalaya, and thence
through strange mazes of bayou, lakelet, and pass, by a rear route familiar only to the best of pilots, the frail river-craft had toiled into
Caillou Bay, running close to the main shore;—and now she was heading right for the island, with the wind aft, over the monstrous sea. On
she came, swaying, rocking, plunging—with a great whiteness wrapping her about like a cloud, and moving with her moving—a tempest-
whirl of spray;—ghost-white and like a ghost she came, for her smokestacks exhaled no visible smoke—the wind devoured it! The excitement
on shore became wild;—men shouted themselves hoarse; women
laughed and cried. Every telescope and opera-glass was directed upon
the coming apparition; all wondered how the pilot kept his feet; all
marveled at the madness of the captain.

But Captain Abraham Smith was not mad. A veteran American
sailor, he had learned to know the great Gulf as scholars know deep
books by heart: he knew the birthplace of its tempests, the mystery of
its tides, the omens of its hurricanes. While lying at Brashear City he
felt the storm had not yet reached its highest, vaguely foresaw a mighty
peril, and resolved to wait no longer for a lull. "Boys," he said, "we've
go to take her out in spite of Hell!" And they "took her out." Through
all the peril, his men stayed by him and obeyed him. By mid-morning
the wind had deepened to a roar—lowering sometimes to a rumble,
sometimes bursting upon the ears like a measureless and deafening
crash. Then the captain knew the *Star* was running a race with Death.
"She'll win it," he muttered;—"she'll stand it. . . . Perhaps they'll have
need of me to-night."

She won! With a sonorous steam-chant of triumph the brave little
vessel rode at last into the bayou, and anchored hard by her accustomed resting-place, in full view of the hotel, though not near enough
to shore to lower her gang-plank. . . . But she had sung her swan-song.
Gathering in from the northeast, the waters of the bay were already
marbling over the salines and half across the island; and still the wind
increased its paroxysmal power.

Cottages began to rock. Some slid away from the solid props upon
which they rested. A chimney tumbled. Shutters were wrenched off;
verandas demolished. Light roofs lifted, dropped again, and flapped
into ruin. Trees bent their heads to the earth. And still the storm grew
louder and blacker with every passing hour.

The *Star* rose with the rising of the waters, dragging her anchor.

Two more anchors were put out, and still she dragged—dragged in with the flood—twisting, shuddering, careening in her agony. Evening fell; the sand began to move with the wind, stinging faces like a continuous fire of fine shot; and frenzied blasts came to buffet the steamer forward, sideward. Then one of her hog-chains parted with a clang like the boom of a big bell. Then another! . . . Then the captain bade his men to cut away all her upper works, clean to the deck. Overboard into the seething went her stacks, her pilot-house, her cabins— and whirled away. And the naked hull of the *Star,* still dragging her three anchors, labored on through the darkness, nearer and nearer to the immense silhouette of the hotel, whose hundred windows were now all aflame. The vast timber building seemed to defy the storm. The wind, roaring round its broad verandas—hissing through every crevice with the sound and force of steam—appeared to waste its rage. And in the half-lull between two terrible gusts there came to the captain's ears a sound that seemed strange in that night of multitudinous terrors . . . a sound of music!

VI

. . . ALMOST EVERY EVENING THROUGHOUT THE SEASON THERE HAD BEEN dancing in the great hall;—there was dancing that night also. The population of the hotel had been augmented by the advent of families from other parts of the island, who found their summer cottages insecure places of shelter: there were nearly four hundred guests assembled. Perhaps it was for this reason that the entertainment had been prepared upon a grander plan than usual, that it assumed the form of a fashionable ball. And all those pleasure-seekers—representing the wealth and beauty of the Creole parishes—whether from Ascension or Assumption, Saint Mary's or Saint Landry's, Iberville or Terrebonne, whether inhabitants of the multi-colored and many-balconied Creole quarter of the quaint metropolis, or dwellers in the dreamy paradises of the Têche—mingled joyously, knowing each other, feeling in some sort akin—whether affiliated by blood, connaturalized by caste, or simply interassociated by traditional sympathies of class sentiment and class interest. Perhaps in the more than ordinary merriment of that evening something of nervous exaltation might have been discerned— something like a feverish resolve to oppose apprehension with gayety, to combat uneasiness by diversion. But the hours passed in mirthfulness; the first general feeling of depression began to weigh less and less upon the guests; they had found reason to confide in the solidity of the massive building; there were no positive terrors, no outspoken fears; and the new conviction of all had found expression in the words of the host himself—*"Il n'y a rien de mieux à faire que de s'amuser!"* Of what avail to lament the prospective devastation of cane-fields—to discuss the possible ruin of crops? Better to seek solace in choreographic harmonies, in the rhythm of gracious motion and of perfect melody, than hearken to the discords of the wild orchestra of storms;—wiser to admire the grace of Parisian toilettes, the eddy of trailing robes with its fairy-foam of lace, the ivorine loveliness of glossy shoulders and jewelled throats, the glimmering of satin-slippered feet—than to watch the raging of the flood without, or the flying of the wrack. . . .

So the music and the mirth went on: they made joy for themselves —those elegant guests;—they jested and sipped rich wines;—they pledged, and hoped, and loved, and promised, with never a thought of the morrow, on the night of the tenth of August, eighteen hundred and fifty-six. Observant parents were there, planning for the future bliss of their nearest and dearest;—mothers and fathers of handsome lads, lithe and elegant as young pines, and fresh from the polish of foreign university training;—mothers and fathers of splendid girls whose simplest attitudes were witcheries. Young cheeks flushed, young hearts fluttered with an emotion more puissant than the excitement of the dance;—young eyes betrayed the happy secret discreeter lips would have preserved. Slave-servants circled through the aristocratic press, bearing dainties and wines, praying permission to pass in terms at once humble and officious—always in the excellent French which well-trained house-servants were taught to use on such occasions.

. . . Night wore on: still the shining floor palpitated to the feet of the dancers; still the piano-forte pealed, and still the violins sang—and the sound of their singing shrilled through the darkness, in gaps of the gale, to the ears of Captain Smith, as he strove to keep his footing on the spray-drenched deck of the *Star*.

"Christ!" he muttered—"a dance! If that wind whips round south, there'll be another dance! . . . But I guess the *Star* will stay." . . .

Half an hour might have passed; still the lights flamed calmly, and the violins trilled, and the perfumed whirl went on. . . . And suddenly the wind veered!

Again the *Star* reeled, and shuddered, and turned, and began to drag all her anchors. But she now dragged away from the great building

and its lights—away from the voluptuous thunder of the grand piano
—even at that moment outpouring the great joy of Weber's melody
orchestrated by Berlioz: *"L'Invitation à la Valse"*—with its marvelous
musical swing!

"Waltzing!" cried the captain. "God help them!—God help us all
now! ... *The Wind waltzes tonight, with the Sea for his partner!"* ...

O the stupendous Valse-Tourbillon! O the mighty Dancer! One—
two—three! From northeast to east, from east to southeast, from southeast to south: then from the south he came, whirling the Sea in his
arms ...

... Some one shrieked in the midst of the revels;—some girl who
found her pretty slippers wet. What could it be? Thin streams of water
were spreading over the level planking—curling about the feet of the
dancers. ... What could it be? All the land had begun to quake, even
as, but a moment before, the polished floor was trembling to the pressure of circling steps;—all the building shook now; every beam uttered
its groan. What could it be? ...

There was a clamor, a panic, a rush to the windy night. Infinite
darkness above and beyond; but the lantern-beams danced far out
over an unbroken circle of heaving and swirling black water. Stealthily, swiftly, the measureless sea-flood was rising.

"Monsieurs—mesdames, ce n'est rien. Nothing serious, ladies, I assure you. ... *Mais nous en avons vu bien souvent, les inondations
comme celle-ci; ça passe vite!* The water will go down in a few hours,
ladies;—it never rises higher than this; *il n'y a pas le moindre danger,
je vous dis! Allons! il n'y a*—My God! what is that?" ...

For a moment there was a ghastly hush of voices. And through that
hush there burst upon the ears of all a fearful and unfamiliar sound,
as of a colossal cannonade—rolling up from the south, with volleying
lightnings. Vastly and swiftly, nearer and nearer it came—a ponderous
and unbroken thunder roll, terrible as the long muttering of an earthquake.

The nearest mainland—across mad Caillou Bay to the sea-marshes—
lay twelve miles north; west, by the Gulf, the nearest solid ground
was twenty miles distant. There were boats, yes!—but the stoutest
swimmer might never reach them now! ...

Then rose a frightful cry—the hoarse, hideous, indescribable cry of
hopeless fear—the despairing animal-cry man utters when suddenly
brought face to face with Nothingness, without preparation, without

consolation, without possibility of respite. . . . *Sauve qui peut!* Some wrenched down the doors; some clung to the heavy banquet-tables, to the sofas, to the billiard-tables:—during one terrible instant—against fruitless heroisms, against futile generosities—raged all the frenzy of selfishness, all the brutalities of panic. And then—then came, thundering through the blackness, the giant swells, boom on boom! . . . One crash!—the huge frame building rocks like a cradle, seesaws, crackles. What are human shrieks now?—the tornado is shrieking! Another!—chandeliers splinter; lights are dashed out; a sweeping cataract hurls in: the immense hall rises—oscillates—twirls as upon a pivot—crepitates—crumbles into ruin. Crash again!—the swirling wreck dissolves into the wallowing of another monster billow; and a hundred cottages overturn, spin in sudden eddies; quiver, disjoint and melt into the seething.

. . . So the hurricane passed—tearing off the heads of the prodigious waves, to hurl them a hundred feet in air—heaping up the ocean against the land—upturning the woods. Bays and passes were swollen to abysses; rivers regorged; the sea-marshes were changed to raging wastes of water. Before New Orleans the flood of the mile-broad Mississippi rose six feet above highest water-mark. One hundred and ten miles away, Donaldsonville trembled at the towering tide of the Lafourche. Lakes strove to burst their boundaries. Far-off river steamers tugged wildly at their cables—shivering like tethered creatures that hear by night the approaching howl of destroyers. Smokestacks were hurled overboard, pilot-houses torn away, cabins blown to fragments.

And over roaring Kaimbuck Pass—over the agony of Caillou Bay—the billowing tide rushed unresisted from the Gulf—tearing and swallowing the land in its course—ploughing out deep-sea channels where sleek herds had been grazing but a few hours before—rending islands in twain—and ever bearing with it, through the night, enormous vortex of wreck and vast wan drift of corpses. . . .

But the *Star* remained. And Captain Abraham Smith, with a long, good rope about his waist, dashed again and again into that awful surging to snatch victims from death—clutching at passing hands, heads, garments, in the cataract-sweep of the seas—saving, aiding, cheering, though blinded by spray and battered by drifting wreck, until his strength failed in the unequal struggle at last, and his men drew him aboard senseless, with some beautiful half-drowned girl safe in his arms. But well-nigh twoscore souls had been rescued by him; and the *Star* stayed on through it all.

Long years after, the weed-grown ribs of her graceful skeleton could still be seen curving up from the sand-dunes of Last Island, in valiant witness of how well she stayed.

VII

DAY BREAKS THROUGH THE FLYING WRACK, OVER THE INFINITE HEAVING OF the sea, over the low land made vast with desolation. It is a spectral dawn: a wan light, like the light of a dying sun.

The wind has waned and veered; the flood sinks slowly back to its abysses—abandoning its plunder—scattering its piteous waifs over bar and dune, over shoal and marsh, among the silences of the mango-swamps, over the long low reaches of sand-grasses and drowned weeds, for more than a hundred miles. From the shell-reefs of Pointe-au-Fer to the shallows of Pelto Bay the dead lie mingled with the high-heaped drift;—from their cypress groves the vultures rise to dispute a share of the feast with the shrieking frigate-birds and squeaking gulls. And as the tremendous tide withdraws its plunging waters, all the pirates of air follow the great white-gleaming retreat: a storm of billowing wings and screaming throats.

And swift in the wake of gull and frigate-bird the Wreckers come, the Spoilers of the dead—savage skimmers of the sea—hurricane-riders wont to spread their canvas-pinions in the face of storms; Sicilian and Corsican outlaws, Manila-men from the marshes, deserters from many navies, Lascars, marooners, refugees of a hundred nationalities—fishers and shrimpers by name, smugglers by opportunity—wild channel-finders from obscure bayous and unfamiliar chénières, all skilled in the mysteries of these mysterious waters beyond the comprehension of the oldest licensed pilot. . . .

There is plunder for all—birds and men. There are drowned sheep in multitude, heaped carcasses of kine. There are casks of claret and kegs of brandy and legions of bottles bobbing in the surf. There are billiard-tables overturned upon the sand;—there are sofas, pianos, footstools and music-stools, luxurious chairs, lounges of bamboo. There are chests of cedar, and toilet-tables of rosewood, and trunks of fine stamped leather stored with precious apparel. There are *objets de luxe* innumerable. There are children's playthings: French dolls in marvelous toilettes, and toy carts, and wooden horses, and wooden spades, and brave little wooden ships that rode out the gale in which the great Nautilus went down. There is money in notes and in coin—in purses, in pocketbooks, and in pockets: plenty of it! There are silks, satins, laces, and fine linen to be stripped from the bodies of the drowned—and necklaces, bracelets, watches, finger-rings and fine chains, brooches and trinkets. . . . *"Chi bidizza!—Oh! chi bedda mughieri! Eccu, la bidizza!"* That ball-dress was made in Paris by—But you never heard of him, Sicilian Vicenzu. . . . *"Che bella sposina!"* Her betrothal ring will not come off, Giuseppe; but the delicate bone snaps easily: your oyster-knife can sever the tendon. . . . *"Guardate! chi bedda picciota!"* Over her heart you will find it, Valentino—the locket held by that fine Swiss chain of woven hair—*"Caya manan!"* And it is not your quadroon bondsmaid, sweet lady, who now disrobes you so roughly; those Malay hands are less deft than hers—but she slumbers very far away from you, and may not be aroused from her sleep. *"Na quita mo! dalaga!—na quita maganda!"* . . . Juan, the fastenings of those diamond ear-drops are much too complicated for your peon fingers: tear them out!—*"Dispense, chulita!"* . . .

. . . Suddenly a long, mighty silver trilling fills the ears of all: there is a wild hurrying and scurrying; swiftly, one after another, the overburdened luggers spread wings and flutter away.

Thrice the great cry rings rippling through the gray air, and over the green sea, and over the far-flooded shell-reefs, where the huge white flashes are—sheet-lightning of breakers—and over the weird wash of corpses coming in.

It is the steam-call of the relief-boat, hastening to rescue the living, to gather in the dead.

The tremendous tragedy is over!

PART II

Out of the Sea's Strength

I

THERE ARE REGIONS OF LOUISIANA COAST WHOSE ASPECT SEEMS NOT OF THE present, but of the immemorial past—of that epoch when low flat reaches of primordial continent first rose into form above a Silurian Sea. To indulge this geologic dream, any fervid and breezeless day there, it is only necessary to ignore the evolutional protests of a few blue asters or a few composite flowers of the coryopsis sort, which contrive to display their rare flashes of color through the general waving of cat-heads, blood-weeds, wild cane, and marsh grasses. For, at a hasty glance, the general appearance of this marsh verdure is vague enough, as it ranges away towards the sand, to convey the idea of amphibious vegetation—a primitive flora as yet undecided whether to retain marine habits and forms, or to assume terrestrial ones;—and the occasional inspection of surprising shapes might strengthen this fancy. Queer flat-lying and many-branching things, which resemble sea-weeds in juiciness and color and consistency, crackle under your feet from time to time; the moist and weighty air seems heated rather from below than from above—less by the sun than by the radiation of a cooling world; and the mists of morning or evening appear to simulate the vapory exhalation of volcanic forces—latent, but only dozing, and uncomfortably close to the surface. And indeed geologists have actually averred that those rare elevations of the soil—which, with their heavy coronets of evergreen foliage, not only look like islands, but are so called in the French nomenclature of the coast—have been prominences created by ancient mud volcanoes.

The family of a Spanish fisherman, Feliu Viosca, once occupied and gave its name to such an islet, quite close to the Gulf-shore—the loftiest bit of land along fourteen miles of just such marshy coast as I have spoken of. Landward, it dominated a desolation that wearied the eye to look at, a wilderness of reedy sloughs, patched at intervals with ranges of bitterweed, tufts of elbow-bushes, and broad reaches of sawgrass, stretching away to a bluish-green line of woods that closed the horizon, and imperfectly drained in the driest season by a slimy little bayou that continually vomited foul water into the sea. The point had been much discussed by geologists; it proved a godsend to United States surveyors weary of attempting to take observations among quagmires, moccasins, and arborescent weeds from fifteen to twenty feet high. Savage fishermen, at some unrecorded time, had heaped upon the eminence a hill of clam-shells—refuse of a million feasts; earth again had been formed over these, perhaps by the blind agency of worms working through centuries unnumbered; and the new soil had given birth to a luxuriant vegetation. Millennial oaks interknotted their roots below its surface, and vouchsafed protection to many a frailer growth of shrub or tree—wild orange, water-willow, palmetto, locust, pomegranate, and many trailing tendrilled things, both green and gray. Then—perhaps about half a century ago—a few white fishermen cleared a place for themselves in this grove, and built a few palmetto cottages, with boat-houses and a wharf, facing the bayou. Later on this temporary fishing station became a permanent settlement: homes constructed of heavy timber and plaster mixed with the trailing moss of the oaks and cypresses took the places of the frail and fragrant huts of palmetto. Still the population itself retained a floating character: it ebbed and came, according to season and circumstances, according to luck or loss in the tilling of the sea. Viosca, the founder of the settlement, always remained; he always managed to do well. He owned several luggers and sloops, which were hired out upon excellent terms; he could make large and profitable contracts with New Orleans fish-dealers; and he was vaguely suspected of possessing more occult resources. There were some confused stories current about his having once been a daring smuggler, and having only been reformed by the pleadings of his wife Carmen—a little brown woman who had followed him from Barcelona to share his fortunes in the western world.

On hot days, when the shade was full of thin sweet scents, the place had a tropical charm, a drowsy peace. Nothing except the peculiar appearance of the line of oaks facing the Gulf could have conveyed to the visitor any suggestion of days in which the trilling of crickets and the fluting of birds had ceased, of nights when the voices of the marsh had been hushed for fear. In one enormous rank the veteran trees stood shoulder to shoulder, but in the attitude of giants overmastered —forced backward toward the marsh—made to recoil by the might of the ghostly enemy with whom they had striven a thousand years—the Shrieker, the Sky-Sweeper, the awful Sea-Wind!

Never had he given them so terrible a wrestle as on the night of the tenth of August, eighteen hundred and fifty-six. All the waves of the excited Gulf thronged in as if to see, and lifted up their voices, and pushed, and roared, until the chénière was islanded by such a billowing as no white man's eyes had ever looked upon before. Grandly the oaks bore themselves, but every fibre of their knotted thews was strained in the unequal contest and two of the giants were overthrown, upturning, as they fell, roots coiled and huge as the serpent-limbs of Titans. Moved to its entrails, all the islet trembled, while the sea magnified its menace, and reached out whitely to the prostrate trees; but the rest of the oaks stood on, and strove in line, and saved the habitations defended by them. . . .

II

BEFORE A LITTLE WAXEN IMAGE OF THE MOTHER AND CHILD—AN ODD LITTLE Virgin with an Indian face, brought home by Feliu as a gift after one of his Mexican voyages—Carmen Viosca had burned candles and prayed; sometimes telling her beads; sometimes murmuring the litanies she knew by heart; sometimes also reading from a prayer-book worn and greasy as a long-used pack of cards. It was particularly stained at one page, a page on which her tears had fallen many a lonely night—a page with a clumsy wood-cut representing a celestial lamp, a symbolic radiance, shining through darkness, and on either side a kneeling angel with folded wings. And beneath this rudely wrought symbol of the Perpetual Calm appeared in big, coarse type the title of a prayer that has been offered up through many a century, doubtless, by wives of Spanish mariners—"*Contra las Tempestades.*"

Once she became very much frightened. After a partial lull the storm had suddenly redoubled its force: the ground shook; the house quivered and creaked; the wind brayed and screamed and pushed and scuffled at the door; and the water, which had been whipping in through every crevice, all at once rose over the threshold and flooded the dwelling. Carmen dipped her finger in the watei and tasted it. It was salt!

And none of Feliu's boats had yet come in;—doubtless they had been driven into some far-away bayous by the storm. The only boat at the settlement, the *Carmencita,* had been almost wrecked by running upon a snag three days before;—there was at least a fortnight's work for the ship-carpenter of Dead Cypress Point. And Feliu was sleeping as if nothing unusual had happened—the heavy sleep of a sailor, heedless of commotions and voices. And his men, Miguel and Mateo, were at the other end of the chénière.

With a scream Carmen aroused Feliu. He raised himself upon his elbow, rubbed his eyes, and asked her, with exasperating calmness, *"Que tienes? que tienes?"* (What ails thee?)

"Oh, Feliu! the sea is coming upon us!" she answered, in the same tongue. But she screamed out a word inspired by her fear: she did not cry, *"Se nos viene el mar encima!"* but *"Se nos viene La Altura!"*—the name that conveys the terrible thought of depth swallowed up in height—the height of the *high sea.*

"No lo creo!" muttered Feliu, looking at the floor; then in a quiet, deep voice he said, pointing to an oar in the corner of the room, *"Echame ese remo."*

She gave it to him. Still reclining upon one elbow, Feliu measured the depth of the water with his thumb-nail upon the blade of the oar, and then bade Carmen light his pipe for him. His calmness reassured her. For half an hour more, undismayed by the clamoring of the wind or the calling of the sea, Feliu silently smoked his pipe and watched his oar. The water rose a little higher, and he made another mark;—then it climbed a little more, but not so rapidly; and he smiled at Carmen as he made a third mark. *"Como creia!"* he exclaimed, *"no hay porque asustarse: el agua baja!"* And as Carmen would have continued to pray, he rebuked her fears, and bade her try to obtain some rest: *"Basta ya de plegarios, querida!—vete y duerme."* His tone, though kindly, was imperative; and Carmen, accustomed to obey him, laid herself down by his side, and soon, for very weariness, slept.

It was a feverish sleep, nevertheless, shattered at brief intervals by terrible sounds—sounds magnified by her nervous condition—a sleep visited by dreams that mingled in a strange way with the impressions of the storm, and more than once made her heart stop, and start again at its own stopping. One of these fancies she never could forget—a dream about little Concha—Conchita, her first-born, who now slept far away in the old churchyard at Barcelona. She had tried to become resigned—not to think. But the child would come back night after night, though the earth lay heavy upon her—night after night, through long distances of Time and Space. Oh! the fancied clinging of infant-lips!—the thrilling touch of little ghostly hands!—those phantom-caresses that torture mothers' hearts! . . . Night after night, through many a month of pain. Then for a time the gentle presence ceased to haunt her—seemed to have lain down to sleep forever under the high bright grass and yellow flowers. Why did it return, that night of all nights, to kiss her, to cling to her, to nestle in her arms? . . .

For in her dream she thought herself still kneeling before the waxen Image, while the terrors of the tempest were ever deepening about her —raving of winds and booming of waters and a shaking of the land. And before her, even as she prayed her dream-prayer, the waxen Virgin became tall as a woman, and taller—rising to the roof and smiling as she grew. Then Carmen would have cried out for fear, but that something smothered her voice—paralyzed her tongue. And the Virgin silently stooped above her, and placed in her arms the Child—the brown Child with the Indian face. And the Child whitened in her hands and changed—seeming as it changed to send a sharp pain through her heart: an old pain linked somehow with memories of bright windy Spanish hills, and summer-scent of olive groves, and all the luminous Past;—it looked into her face with the soft dark gaze, with the unforgotten smile of . . . dead Conchita!

And Carmen wished to thank the smiling Virgin for that priceless bliss, and lifted up her eyes; but the sickness of ghostly fear returned upon her when she looked; for now the Mother seemed as a woman long dead, and the smile was the smile of fleshlessness, and the places of the eyes were voids and darknesses. . . . And the sea sent up so vast a roar that the dwelling rocked.

Carmen started from sleep to find her heart throbbing so that the couch shook with it. Night was growing gray; the door had just been opened and slammed again. Through the rain-whipped panes she discerned the passing shape of Feliu, making for the beach—a broad and bearded silhouette, bending against the wind. Still the waxen Virgin smiled her Mexican smile—but now she was only seven inches high; and her bead-glass eyes seemed to twinkle with kindliness while the flame of the last expiring taper struggled for life in the earthen socket at her feet.

III

RAIN AND A BLIND SKY AND A BURSTING SEA. FELIU AND HIS MEN, MIGUEL and Mateo, looked out upon the thundering and flashing of the monstrous tide. The wind had fallen, and the gray air was full of gulls. Behind the chénière, back to the cloudy line of low woods many miles away, stretched a wash of lead-colored water, with a green point piercing it here and there—elbow-bushes or wild cane tall enough to keep their heads above the flood. But the inundation was visibly decreasing; —with the passing of each hour more and more green patches and points had been showing themselves: by degrees the course of the bayou had become defined—two parallel winding lines of dwarf-timber and bushy shrubs traversing the water toward the distant cypress-swamps. Before the chénière all the shell-beach slope was piled with wreck—uptorn trees with the foliage still fresh upon them, splintered timbers of mysterious origin, and logs in multitude, scarred with gashes of the axe. Feliu and his comrades had saved wood enough to build a little town—working up to their waists in the surf, with ropes, poles, and boat-hooks. The whole sea was full of flotsam. *Voto á Cristo!*—what a wrecking there must have been! And to think the *Carmencita* could not be taken out!

They had seen other luggers making eastward during the morning —could recognize some by their sails, others by their gait—exaggerated in their struggle with the pitching of the sea: the *San Pablo,* the *Gasparina,* the *Enriqueta,* the *Agueda,* the *Constanza.* Ugly water, yes!—but what a chance for wreckers! . . . Some great ship must have gone to pieces;—scores of casks were rolling in the trough—casks of wine. Perhaps it was the *Manila*—perhaps the *Nautilus!*

A dead cow floated near enough for Mateo to throw his rope over one horn; and they all helped to get it out. It was a milch cow of some expensive breed; and the owner's brand had been burned upon the horns:—a monographic combination of the letters "A" and "P." Feliu said he knew that brand: Old-man Preaulx, of Belle-Isle, who kept a sort of dairy at Last Island during the summer season, used to mark all his cows that way. Strange!

But, as they worked on, they began to see stranger things—white dead faces and dead hands, which did not look like the hands or the faces of drowned sailors: the ebb was beginning to run strongly, and these were passing out with it on the other side of the mouth of the bayou;—perhaps they had been washed into the marsh during the night, when the great rush of the sea came. Then the three men left the water, and retired to higher ground to scan the furrowed Gulf;—their practiced eyes began to search the courses of the sea-currents—keen as the gaze of birds that watch the wake of the plough. And soon the casks and the drift were forgotten; for it seemed to them that the tide was heavy with human dead—passing out, processionally, to the great open. Very far, where the huge pitching of the swells was diminished by distance into a mere fluttering of ripples, the water appeared as if sprinkled with them;—they vanished and became visible again at irregular intervals, here and there—floating most thickly eastward—tossing, swaying patches of white or pink or blue or black, each with its tiny speck of flesh-color showing as the sea lifted or lowered the body. Nearer to shore there were few; but of these two were close enough to be almost recognizable: Miguel first discerned them. They were rising and falling where the water was deepest—well out in front of the mouth of the bayou, beyond the flooded sand-bars, and moving toward the shell-reef westward. They were drifting almost side by side. One was that of a Negro, apparently well attired, and wearing a white apron;—the other seemed to be a young colored girl, clad in a blue dress; she was floating upon her face; they could observe that she had nearly straight hair, braided and tied with a red ribbon. These were evidently house-servants—slaves. But from whence? Nothing could be learned until the luggers should return; and none of them was yet in sight. Still Feliu was not anxious as to the fate of his boats, manned by the best sailors of the coast. Rarely are these Louisiana fishermen lost in sudden storms; even when to other eyes the appearances are most pacific and the skies most splendidly blue, they divine some far-off danger, like the gulls; and like the gulls also, you see their light vessels fleeing landward. These men seem living barometers, exquisitely sensitive to all the invisible changes of atmospheric expansion and compression; they are not easily caught in those awful dead calms which suddenly paralyze the wings of a bark, and hold her helpless in their charmed circle, as in a nightmare, until the blackness overtakes her, and the long-sleeping sea leaps up foaming to devour her.

"*Carajo!*"

The word all at once bursts from Feliu's mouth, with that peculiar guttural snarl of the "r" betokening strong excitement—while he points to something rocking in the ebb, beyond the foaming of the shell-reef, under a circling of gulls. More dead? Yes—but something too that lives and moves, like a quivering speck of gold; and Mateo also perceives it, a gleam of bright hair—and Miguel likewise, after a moment's gazing. A living child;—a lifeless mother. *Pobrecíta!* No boat within reach, and only a mighty surf-wrestler could hope to swim thither and return!

But already, without a word, brown Feliu has stripped for the struggle;—another second, and he is shooting through the surf, head and hands tunnelling the foam-hills. . . . One—two—three lines passed!—four!—that is where they first begin to crumble white from the summit—five!—that he can ride fearlessly! . . . Then swiftly, easily, he advances, with a long, powerful breast-stroke—keeping his bearded head well up to watch for drift—seeming to slide with a swing from swell to swell—ascending, sinking—alternately presenting breast or shoulder to the wave; always diminishing more and more to the eyes of Mateo and Miguel—till he becomes a moving speck, occasionally hard to follow through the confusion of heaping waters. . . . You are not afraid of the sharks, Feliu!—no: they are afraid of you; right and left they slunk away from your coming that morning you swam for life in West-Indian waters, with your knife in your teeth, while the balls of the Cuban coast-guard were purring all around you. That day the swarming sea was warm—warm like soup—and clear, with an emerald flash in every ripple—not opaque and clamorous like the Gulf to-day. . . . Miguel and his comrade are anxious. Ropes are unrolled and interknotted into a line. Miguel remains on the beach; but Mateo, bearing the end of the line, fights his way out—swimming and wading by turns, to the farther sand-bar, where the water is shallow enough to stand in—if you know how to jump when the breaker comes.

But Feliu, nearing the flooded shell-bank, watches the white flashings—knows when the time comes to keep flat and take a long, long breath. One heavy volleying of foam—darkness and hissing as of a steam-burst; a vibrant lifting up; a rush into light—and again the volleying and the seething darkness. Once more—and the fight is won! He feels the upcoming chill of deeper water—sees before him the green quaking of unbroken swells—and far beyond him Mateo leaping on the bar—and beside him, almost within arm's-reach, a great billiard-table swaying, and a dead woman clinging there, and . . . the child.

A moment more, and Feliu has lifted himself beside the waifs. . . . How fast the dead woman clings, as if with the one power which is strong as death—the desperate force of love! Not in vain; for the frail creature bound to the mother's corpse with a silken scarf has still the strength to cry out: *"Maman! maman!"* But time is life now; and the tiny hands must be pulled away from the fair dead neck, and the scarf taken to bind the infant firmly to Feliu's broad shoulders— quickly, roughly; for the ebb will not wait. . . .

And now Feliu has a burden; but his style of swimming has totally changed;—he rises from the water like a Triton, and his powerful arms seem to spin in circles, like the spokes of a flying wheel. For now is the wrestle indeed!—after each passing swell comes a prodigious pulling from beneath—the sea clutching for its prey. But the reef is gained, is passed;—the wild horses of the deep seem to know the swimmer who has learned to ride them so well. And still the brown arms spin in an ever-nearing mist of spray; and the outer sand-bar is not far off—and there is shouting Mateo, leaping in the surf, swinging something about his head, as a vaquero swings his noose! . . . Sough! splash!—it struggles in the trough beside Feliu, and the sinewy hand descends upon it. *Tiene!—tira, Miguel!* And their feet touch land again! . . .

She is very cold, the child, and very still, with eyes closed.

"Esta muerta, Feliu?" asks Mateo.

"No!" the panting swimmer makes answer, emerging, while the waves reach whitely up the sand as in pursuit—*"no; vive!—respira todavía!"*

Behind him the deep lifts up its million hands, and thunders as in acclaim.

IV

"MADRE DE DIOS!—MI SUENO!" SCREAMED CARMEN, ABANDONING HER preparations for the morning meal, as Feliu, nude, like a marine god, rushed in and held out to her a dripping and gasping baby-girl— "Mother of God! my dream!" But there was no time then to tell of dreams; the child might die. In one instant Carmen's quick, deft hands had stripped the slender little body; and while Mateo and Feliu were finding dry clothing and stimulants, and Miguel telling how it all happened—quickly, passionately, with furious gesture—the kind and vigorous woman exerted all her skill to revive the flickering life. Soon Feliu came to aid her, while his men set to work completing the interrupted preparation of the breakfast. Flannels were heated for the friction of the frail limbs; and brandy-and-water warmed, which Carmen administered by the spoonful, skillfully as any physician—until, at last, the little creature opened her eyes and began to sob. Sobbing still, she was laid in Carmen's warm feather-bed, well swathed in woollen wrappings. The immediate danger, at least, was over; and Feliu smiled with pride and pleasure.

Then Carmen first ventured to relate her dream; and his face became grave again. Husband and wife gazed a moment into each other's eyes, feeling together the same strange thrill—that mysterious faint creeping, as of a wind passing, which is the awe of the Unknowable. Then they looked at the child, lying there, pink-cheeked with the flush of the blood returning; and such a sudden tenderness touched them as they had known long years before, while together bending above the slumbering loveliness of lost Conchita.

"Que ojos!" murmured Feliu, as he turned away—feigning hunger. . . . (He was not hungry; but his sight had grown a little dim, as with a mist.) *Que ojos!* They were singular eyes, large, dark, and wonderfully fringed. The child's hair was yellow—it was the flash of it that had saved her; yet her eyes and brows were beautifully black. She was comely, but with such a curious, delicate comeliness—totally unlike the robust beauty of Concha. . . . At intervals she would moan a little between her sobs; and at last cried out, with a thin, shrill cry: *"Maman!—oh! maman!"* Then Carmen lifted her from the bed to her lap, and caressed her, and rocked her gently to and fro, as she had done many a night for Concha—murmuring—*"Yo seré tu madre, angel mio, dulzura mia;—seré tu madrecita, palomita mia!"* (I will be thy mother, my angel, my sweet;—I will be thy little mother, my doveling.) And the long silk fringes of the child's eyes overlapped, shadowed her little cheeks; and she slept—just as Conchita had slept long ago—with her head on Carmen's bosom.

Feliu re-appeared at the inner door: at a sign, he approached cautiously, without noise, and looked.

"She can talk," whispered Carmen in Spanish: "she called her mother"—*ha llamado à su madre.*

"Y Dios tambien la ha llamado," responded Feliu, with rude pathos;—"And *God also called her.*"

"But the Virgin sent us the child, Feliu—sent us the child for Concha's sake."

He did not answer at once; he seemed to be thinking very deeply;—Carmen anxiously scanned his impassive face.

"Who knows?" he answered, at last;—"who knows? Perhaps she has ceased to belong to anyone else." . . .

One after another, Feliu's luggers fluttered in—bearing with them news of the immense calamity. And all the fishermen, in turn, looked at the child. Not one had ever seen her before.

V

TEN DAYS LATER, A LUGGER FULL OF ARMED MEN ENTERED THE BAYOU, AND moored at Viosca's wharf. The visitors were, for the most part, country gentlemen—residents of Franklin and neighboring towns, or planters from the Têche country—forming one of the numerous expeditions organized for the purpose of finding the bodies of relatives or friends lost in the great hurricane, and of punishing the robbers of the dead. They had searched numberless nooks of the coast, had given sepulture to many corpses, had recovered a large amount of jewelry, and—as Feliu afterward learned—had summarily tried and executed several of the most abandoned class of wreckers found with ill-gotten valuables in their possession, and convicted of having mutilated the drowned. But they came to Viosca's landing only to obtain information;—he was too well known and liked to be a subject for suspicion; and, moreover, he had one good friend in the crowd—Captain Harris of New Orleans, a veteran steamboat man and a market-contractor, to whom he had disposed of many a cargo of fresh pompano, sheep's-head, and Spanish-mackerel. . . . Harris was the first to step to land;—some ten of the party followed him. Nearly all had lost some relative or friend in the great catastrophe;—the gathering was serious, silent—almost grim—which formed about Feliu.

Mateo, who had come to the country while a boy, spoke English better than the rest of the chénière people;—he acted as interpreter whenever Feliu found any difficulty in comprehending or answering questions; and he told them of the child rescued that wild morning, and of Feliu's swim. His recital evoked a murmur of interest and excitement, followed by a confusion of questions. Well, they could see for themselves, Feliu said; but he hoped they would have a little patience;—the child was still weak;—it might be dangerous to startle her. "We'll arrange it just as you like," responded the captain;—"go ahead, Feliu!" . . .

All proceeded to the house, under the great trees; Feliu and Captain Harris leading the way. It was sultry and bright;—even the sea-breeze was warm; there were pleasant odors in the shade, and a soporific murmur made of leaf-speech and the hum of gnats. Only the captain entered the house with Feliu; the rest remained without— some taking seats on a rude plank bench under the oaks—others flinging themselves down upon the weeds—a few stood still, leaning upon their rifles. Then Carmen came out to them with gourds and a bucket of fresh water, which all were glad to drink.

They waited many minutes. Perhaps it was the cool peace of the place that made them all feel how hot and tired they were: conversation flagged; and the general languor finally betrayed itself in a silence so absolute that every leaf-whisper seemed to become separately audible.

It was broken at last by the guttural voice of the old captain emerging from the cottage, leading the child by the hand, and followed by Carmen and Feliu. All who had been resting rose up and looked at the child.

Standing in a lighted space, with one tiny hand enveloped by the captain's great brown fist, she looked so lovely that a general exclamation of surprise went up. Her bright hair, loose and steeped in the sun-flame, illuminated her like a halo; and her large dark eyes, gentle and melancholy as a deer's, watched the strange faces before her with shy curiosity. She wore the same dress in which Feliu had found her—a soft white fabric of muslin, with trimmings of ribbon that had once been blue; and the now discolored silken scarf, which had twice done her such brave service, was thrown over her shoulders. Carmen had washed and repaired the dress very creditably; but the tiny slim feet were bare—the brine-soaked shoes she wore that fearful night had fallen into shreds at the first attempt to remove them.

"Gentlemen," said Captain Harris—"we can find no clue to the identity of this child. There is no mark upon her clothing; and she wore nothing in the shape of jewelry—except this string of coral beads. We are nearly all Americans here; and she does not speak any English. . . . Does any one here know anything about her?"

Carmen felt a great sinking at her heart: was her new-found darling to be taken so soon from her? But no answer came to the captain's query. No one of the expedition had ever seen that child before. The coral beads were passed from hand to hand; the scarf was minutely scrutinized without avail. Somebody asked if the child could not talk German or Italian.

"*Italiano?* No!" said Feliu, shaking his head. . . . One of his lugger-men, Gioachino Sparicio, who, though a Sicilian, could speak several Italian idioms besides his own, had already essayed.

"She speaks something or other," answered the captain—"but no English. I couldn't make her understand me; and Feliu, who talks nearly all the infernal languages spoken down this way, says he can't make her understand him. Suppose some of you who know French talk to her a bit. . . . Laroussel, why don't you try?"

The young man addressed did not at first seem to notice the captain's suggestion. He was a tall, lithe fellow, with a dark, positive face: he had never removed his black gaze from the child since the moment of her appearance. Her eyes, too, seemed to be all for him—to return his scrutiny with a sort of vague pleasure, a half-savage confidence. . . . Was it the first embryonic feeling of race-affinity quickening in the little brain?—some intuitive, inexplicable sense of kindred? She shrank from Dr. Hecker, who addressed her in German, shook her head at Lawyer Solari, who tried to make her answer in Italian; and her look always went back plaintively to the dark, sinister face of Laroussel—Laroussel who had calmly taken a human life, a wicked human life, only the evening before.

"Laroussel, you're the only Creole in this crowd," said the captain: "talk to her! Talk gumbo to her! . . . I've no doubt this child knows German very well, and Italian too"—he added, maliciously—"but not in the way you gentlemen pronounce it!"

Laroussel handed his rifle to a friend, crouched down before the little girl, and looked into her face, and smiled. Her great sweet orbs shone into his one moment, seriously, as if searching; and then . . . she returned his smile. It seemed to touch something latent within the man, something rare; for his whole expression changed; and there was a caress in his look and voice none of the men could have believed possible—as he exclaimed:

"*Fais moin bo, piti.*"

She pouted up her pretty lips and kissed his black moustache.

He spoke to her again:

"*Dis moin to nom, piti;—dis moin to nom, chère.*"

Then, for the first time, she spoke, answering in her argent treble:

"*Zouzoune.*"

All held their breath. Captain Harris lifted his finger to his lips t) command silence.

"*Zouzoune? Zouzoune qui, chère?*"

"*Zouzoune, ça c'est moin, Lili!*"

"*C'est pas tout to nom, Lili;—dis moin, chère, to laut nom.*"

"*Mo pas connin laut nom.*"

"*Commente yé té pélé to maman, piti?*"

"*Maman—Maman 'Dèle.*"

"*Et comment yé té pélé to papa, chère?*"

"*Papa Zulien.*"

"*Bon! Et comment to maman té pélé to papa?—dis ça à moin, chère?*"

The child looked down, put a finger in her mouth, thought a moment, and replied:

"*Li pélé li, 'Chéri'; li pélé li, 'Papoute.'*"

"*Aïe, aïe!—c'est tout, ça?—to maman té jamain pélé li daut' chose?*"

"*Mo pas connin, moin.*"

She began to play with some trinkets attached to his watch chain;—a very small gold compass especially impressed her fancy by the trembling and flashing of its tiny needle, and she murmured, coaxingly:

"*Mo oulé ça! Donnin ça à moin.*"

He took all possible advantage of the situation, and replied at once:

"*Oui! mo va donnin toi ça si to di moin to laut nom.*"

The splendid bribe evidently impressed her greatly; for tears rose to the brown eyes as she answered:

"*Mo pas capab di' ca;—mo pas capab di' laut nom. . . . Mo oulé; mo pas capab!*"

Laroussel explained. The child's name was Lili—perhaps a contraction of Eulalie; and her pet Creole name Zouzoune. He thought she must be the daughter of wealthy people; but she could not, for some reason or other, tell her family name. Perhaps she could not pronounce it well, and was afraid of being laughed at: some of the old French names were very hard for Creole children to pronounce, so long as the little ones were indulged in the habit of talking the patois; and after a certain age their mispronunciations would be made fun of in order to accustom them to abandon the idiom of the slave-nurses, and to speak only French. Perhaps, again, she was really unable to recall the name: certain memories might have been blurred in the delicate brain by the shock of that terrible night. She said her mother's name was Adèle, and her father's Julien; but these were very common names

in Louisiana—and could afford scarcely any better clue than the innocent statement that her mother used to address her father as "dear"
(*Chéri*)—or with the Creole diminutive "little papa" (*Papoute*). Then
Laroussel tried to reach a clue in other ways, without success. He asked
her about where she lived—what the place was like; and she told him
about fig-trees in a court, and galleries, and *banquettes,* and spoke of
a *faubou'*—without being able to name any street. He asked her what
her father used to do, and was assured that he did everything—that
there was nothing he could not do. Divine absurdity of childish faith!
—infinite artlessness of childish love! . . . Probably the little girl's
parents had been residents of New Orleans—dwellers of the old
colonial quarter—the *faubourg,* the *faubou'*.

"Well, gentlemen," said Captain Harris, as Laroussel abandoned his
cross-examination in despair—"all we can do now is to make inquiries.
I suppose we'd better leave the child here. She is very weak yet, and
in no condition to be taken to the city, right in the middle of the hot
season; and nobody could care for her any better than she's being
cared for here. Then, again, seems to me that as Feliu saved her life—
and that at the risk of his own—he's got the prior claim, anyhow; and
his wife is just crazy about the child—wants to adopt her. If we can
find her relatives so much the better; but I say, gentlemen, let them
come right here to Feliu, themselves, and thank him as he ought to be
thanked, by God! That's just what I think about it."

Carmen understood the little speech;—all the Spanish charm of her
youth had faded out years before; but in the one swift look of gratitude she turned upon the captain, it seemed to blossom again;—for
that quick moment, she was beautiful.

"The captain is quite right," observed Dr. Hecker: "it would be
very dangerous to take the child away just now." There was no
dissent.

"All correct, boys?" asked the captain. . . . "Well, we've got to be
going. By-by, Zouzoune! "

But Zouzoune burst into tears. Laroussel was going too!

"Give her the thing, Laroussel! she gave you a kiss, anyhow—more
than she'd do for me," cried the captain.

Laroussel turned, detached the little compass from his watch chain,
and gave it to her. She held up her pretty face for his farewell kiss. . . .

VI

BUT IT SEEMED FATED THAT FELIU'S WAIF SHOULD NEVER BE IDENTIFIED;—diligent inquiry and printed announcements alike proved fruitless. Sea and sand had either hidden or effaced all the records of the little world they had engulfed: the annihilation of whole families, the extinction of races, had, in more than one instance, rendered vain all efforts to recognize the dead. It required the subtle perception of long intimacy to name remains tumefied and discolored by corruption and exposure, mangled and gnawed by fishes, by reptiles, and by birds;—it demanded the great courage of love to look upon the eyeless faces found sweltering in the blackness of cypress shadows, under the low palmettoes of the swamps—where gorged buzzards started from sleep, or cotton-mouths uncoiled, hissing, at the coming of the searchers. And sometimes all who had loved the lost were themselves among the missing. The full roll-call of names could never be made out;—extraordinary mistakes were committed. Men whom the world deemed dead and buried came back, like ghosts—to read their own epitaphs.

. . . Almost at the same hour that Laroussel was questioning the child in Creole patois, another expedition, searching for bodies along the coast, discovered on the beach of a low islet famed as a haunt of pelicans, the corpse of a child. Some locks of bright hair still adhering to the skull, a string of red beads, a white muslin dress, a handkerchief broidered with the initials "A. L. B."—were secured as clues; and the little body was interred where it had been found.

And, several days before, Captain Hotard, of the relief-boat *Estelle Brousseaux,* had found, drifting in the open Gulf (latitude 26° 43'; longitude 88° 17')—the corpse of a fair-haired woman, clinging to a table. The body was disfigured beyond recognition: even the slender bones of the hands had been stripped by the nibs of the sea-birds—except one finger, the third of the left, which seemed to have been protected by a ring of gold, as by a charm. Graven within the plain yellow circlet was a date—"JUILLET—1851"; and the names—"ADÈLE + JULIEN"—separated by a cross. The *Estelle* carried coffins that day; most of them were already full; but there was one for Adèle.

Who was she?—who was her Julien? . . . When the *Estelle* and many other vessels had discharged their ghastly cargoes;—when the bereaved of the land had assembled as hastily as they might for the

duty of identification;—when memories were strained almost to madness in research of names, dates, incidents—for the evocation of dead
words, resurrection of vanished days, recollection of dear promises—
then, in the confusion, it was believed and declared that the little
corpse found on the pelican island was the daughter of the wearer of
the wedding-ring: Adèle La Brierre, née Florane, wife of Dr. Julien
La Brierre, of New Orleans, who was numbered among the missing.

And they brought dead Adèle back—up shadowy river windings,
over linked brightnesses of lake and lakelet, through many a green-
glimmering bayou—to the Creole city, and laid her to rest somewhere
in the old Saint Louis Cemetery. And upon the tablet recording her
name were also graven the words:

. . . .

AUSSI À LA MÉMOIRE DE

SON MARI,

JULIEN RAYMOND LA BRIERRE,

NÉ À LA PAROISSE ST. LANDRY,

LE 29 MAI, MDCCCXXVIII;

ET DE LEUR FILLE,

EULALIE,

AGÉE DE 4 ANS ET 5 MOIS—

QUI TOUS PÉRIRENT

DANS LA GRANDE TEMPÊTE QUI

BALAYÂ L'ILE DERNIÈRE, LE

10 AOÛT, MDCCCLVI

. . . $+$ . . .

PRIEZ POUR EUX!

VII

YET SIX MONTHS AFTERWARD THE FACE OF JULIEN LA BRIERRE WAS SEEN
again upon the streets of New Orleans. Men started at the sight of
him, as at a spectre standing in the sun. And nevertheless the apparition cast a shadow. People paused, approached, half extended a hand
through old habit, suddenly checked themselves and passed on—wondering they should have forgotten, asking themselves why they had
so nearly made an absurd mistake.

It was a February day—one of those crystalline days of our snowless
Southern winter, when the air is clear and cool, and outlines sharpen

in the light as if viewed through the focus of a diamond glass;—and in that brightness Julien La Brierre perused his own brief epitaph, and gazed upon the sculptured name of drowned Adèle. Only half a year had passed since she was laid away in the high wall of tombs—in that strange colonial columbarium where the dead slept in rows, behind squared marbles lettered in black or bronze. Yet her resting-place—in the highest range—already seemed old. Under our Southern sun, the vegetation of cemeteries seems to spring into being spontaneously—to leap all suddenly into luxuriant life! Microscopic mossy growths had begun to mottle the slab that closed her in;—over its face some singular creeper was crawling, planting tiny reptile-feet into the chiseled letters of the inscription; and from the moist soil below speckled euphorbias were growing up to her—and morning-glories—and beautiful green tangled things of which he did not know the name.

And the sight of the pretty lizards, puffing their crimson pouches in the sun, or undulating athwart epitaphs, and shifting their color when approached, from emerald to ashen-gray;—the caravans of the ants, journeying to and from tiny chinks in the masonry;—the bees gathering honey from the crimson blossoms of the *crête-de-coq,* whose radicles sought sustenance, perhaps from human dust, in the decay of generations:—all that rich life of graves summoned up fancies of Resurrection, Nature's resurrection-work—wondrous transformations of flesh, marvelous transmigration of souls! . . . From some forgotten crevice of that tomb roof, which alone intervened between her and the vast light, a sturdy weed was growing. He knew that plant, as it quivered against the blue—the *chou-gras,* as Creole children call it: its dark berries form the mocking-bird's favorite food. . . . Might not its roots, exploring darkness, have found some unfamiliar nutriment within?—might it not be that something of the dead heart had risen to purple and emerald life—in the sap of translucent leaves, in the wine of the savage berries—to blend with the blood of the Wizard Singer—to lend a strange sweetness to the melody of his wooing? . . .

. . . Seldom, indeed, does it happen that a man in the prime of youth, in the possession of wealth, habituated to comforts and the elegances of life, discovers in one brief week how minute his true relation to the human aggregate—how insignificant his part as one living atom of the social organism. Seldom, at the age of twenty-eight, has one been made able to comprehend, through experience alone, that in the vast and complex Stream of Being he counts for less than a drop; and that, even as the blood loses and replaces its corpuscles, without a variance in the volume and vigor of its current, so are individual existences eliminated and replaced in the pulsing of a people's life, with never a pause in its mighty murmur. But all this, and much more, Julien had learned in seven merciless days—seven successive and terrible shocks of experience. The enormous world had not missed him; and his place therein was not void—society had simply forgotten him. So long as he had moved among them, all he knew for friends had performed their petty altruistic rôles—had discharged their small human obligations—had kept turned toward him the least selfish side of their natures—had made with him a tolerably equitable exchange of ideas and of favors; and after his disappearance from their midst, they had duly mourned for his loss—to themselves! They had played out the final act in the unimportant drama of his life: it was really asking too much to demand a repetition. . . . Impossible to deceive himself as to the feeling his unanticipated return had aroused:— feigned pity where he had looked for sympathetic welcome; dismay where he had expected surprised delight; and, oftener, airs of resignation, or disappointment ill disguised—always insincerity, politely masked or coldly bare. He had come back to find strangers in his home, relatives at law concerning his estate, and himself regarded as an intruder among the living—an unlucky guest, a revenant. . . . How hollow and selfish a world it seemed! And yet there was love in it; he had been loved in it, unselfishly, passionately, with the love of father and mother, of wife and child. . . . All buried!—all lost forever! . . . Oh! would to God the story of that stone were not a lie!—would to kind God he also were dead! . . .

Evening shadowed: the violet deepened and prickled itself with stars;—the sun passed below the west, leaving in his wake a momentary splendor of vermilion . . . our Southern day is not prolonged by gloaming. And Julien's thoughts darkened with the darkening, and as swiftly. For while there was yet light to see, he read another name that he used to know—the name of RAMIREZ. . . . *Nació en Cienfuegos, isla de Cuba.* . . . Wherefore born?—for what eternal purpose, Ramirez —in the City of a Hundred Fires? He had blown out his brains before the sepulchre of his young wife. . . . It was a detached double vault, shaped like a huge chest, and much dilapidated already:—under the continuous burrowing of the crawfish it had sunk greatly on one side, tilting as if about to fall. Out from its zigzag fissurings of brick and plaster, a sinister voice seemed to come: "*Go thou and do like-wise!* . . . *Earth groans with her burthen even now—the burthen of Man: she holds no place for thee!*"

VIII

. . . THAT VOICE PURSUED HIM INTO THE DARKNESS OF HIS CHILLY ROOM— haunted him in the silence of his lodging. And then began within the man that ghostly struggle between courage and despair, between patient reason and mad revolt, between weakness and force, between darkness and light, which all sensitive and generous natures must wage in their own souls at least once—perhaps many times—in their lives. Memory, in such moments, plays like an electric storm;—all involuntarily he found himself reviewing his life.

Incidents long forgotten came back with singular vividness: he saw the Past as he had not seen it while it was the Present;—remembrances of home, recollections of infancy, recurred to him with terrible intensity—the artless pleasures and the trifling griefs, the little hurts and the tender pettings, the hopes and the anxieties of those who loved him, the smiles and tears of slaves. . . . And his first Creole pony, a present from his father the day after he had proved himself able to recite his prayers correctly in French, without one mispronunciation— without saying *crasse* for *grâce;*—and yellow Michel, who taught him to swim and to fish and to paddle a pirogue;—and the bayou, with its wonder-world of turtles and birds and creeping things;—and his German tutor, who could not pronounce the "j";—and the songs of the cane-fields—strangely pleasing, full of quaverings and long plaintive notes, like the call of the cranes. . . . *Tou', tou' pays blanc!* . . . Afterward Camanière had leased the place;—everything must have been changed; even the songs could not be the same. *Tou', tou' pays blanc!* *—Danié qui commandé.* . . .

And then Paris; and the university, with its wild under-life—some debts, some follies; and the frequent fond letters from home to which he might have replied so much oftener;—Paris, where talent is mediocrity; Paris, with its thunders and its splendors and its seething of passion;—Paris, supreme focus of human endeavor, with its madnesses of art, its frenzied striving to express the Inexpressible, its spasmodic strainings to clutch the Unattainable, its soarings of soul-fire to the heaven of the Impossible. . . .

What a rejoicing there was at his return!—how radiant and level the long Road of the Future seemed to open before him!—everywhere friends, prospects, felicitations. Then his first serious love;—and the night of the ball at Saint Martinsville—the vision of light! Gracile as a palm, and robed at once so simply, so exquisitely in white, she had seemed to him the supreme realization of all possible dreams of beauty. . . . And his passionate jealousy; and the slap from Laroussel; and the humiliating two-minute duel with rapiers in which he learned that he had found his master. The scar was deep. Why had not Laroussel killed him then? . . . Not evil-hearted, Laroussel;—they used to salute each other afterward when they met; and Laroussel's smile was kindly. Why had he refrained from returning it? Where was Laroussel now?

For the death of his generous father, who had sacrificed so much to reform him; for the death, only a short while after, of his all-forgiving mother, he had found one sweet woman to console him with her tender words, her loving lips, her delicious caress. She had given him Zouzoune, the darling link between their lives—Zouzoune, who waited each evening with black Églantine at the gate to watch for his coming, and to cry through all the house like a bird, "*Papa, lapé vini!*—*papa Zulien apé vini!*" . . . And once that she had made him very angry by upsetting the ink over a mass of business papers, and he had slapped her (could he ever forgive himself?)—she had cried, through her sobs of astonishment and pain: "*To laimin moin?—to batté moin!*" (Thou lovest me?—thou beatest me!) Next month she would have been five years old. *To laimin moin?—to batté moin!* . . .

A furious paroxysm of grief convulsed him, suffocated him; it seemed to him that something within must burst, must break. He flung himself down upon his bed, biting the coverings in order to stifle his outcry, to smother the sounds of his despair. What crime had he ever done, O God! that he should be made to suffer thus?—was it for this he had been permitted to live? had been rescued from the sea and carried round all the world unscathed? Why should he live to remember, to suffer, to agonize? Was not Ramirez wiser?

How long the contest within him lasted, he never knew; but ere it was done, he had become, in more ways than one, a changed man. For the first—though not indeed for the last—time something of the deeper and nobler comprehension of human weakness and of human suffering had been revealed to him—something of that larger knowledge without which the sense of duty can never be fully acquired, nor the understanding of unselfish goodness, nor the spirit of tenderness. The suicide is not a coward; he is an egotist.

A ray of sunlight touched his wet pillow—awoke him. He rushed to the window, flung the latticed shutters apart, and looked out.

Something beautiful and ghostly filled all the vistas—frost-haze; and in some queer way the mist had momentarily caught and held the very color of the sky. An azure fog! Through it the quaint and checkered street—as yet but half illumined by the sun—took tones of impossible color; the view paled away through faint bluish tints into transparent purples;—all the shadows were indigo. How sweet the morning!—how well life seemed worth living! Because the sun had shown his face through a fairy-veil of frost! . . .

Who was the ancient thinker?—was it Hermes? who said:

"The Sun is Laughter; for 'tis He who maketh joyous the thoughts of men, and gladdeneth the infinite world." . . .

PART III

The Shadow of the Tide

I

CARMEN FOUND THAT HER LITTLE PET HAD BEEN TAUGHT HOW TO PRAY; for each night and morning when the devout woman began to make her orisons, the child would kneel beside her, with little hands joined, and in a voice sweet and clear murmur something she had learned by heart. Much as this pleased Carmen, it seemed to her that the child's prayers could not be wholly valid unless uttered in Spanish;—for Spanish was Heaven's own tongue—*la lengua de Dios, el idioma de Dios;* and she resolved to teach her to say the *Salve Maria* and the *Padre Nuestro* in Castilian—also her own favorite prayer to the Virgin, beginning with the words, *"Madre santísima, toda dulce y hermosa."* . . .

So Conchita—for a new name had been given to her with that terrible sea-christening—received her first lessons in Spanish; and she proved a most intelligent pupil. Before long she could prattle to Feliu; —she would watch for his return of evenings, and announce his coming with *"Aqui viene mi papacito!"*—she learned, too, from Carmen, many little caresses of speech to greet him with. Feliu's was not a joyous nature; he had his dark hours, his sombre days; yet it was rarely that he felt too sullen to yield to the little one's petting, when she would leap up to reach his neck and to coax his kiss, with—*"Dame un beso, papa!—así;—y otro! otro! otro!"* He grew to love her like his own;—was she not indeed his own, since he had won her from death? And none had yet come to dispute his claim. More and more, with the passing of weeks, months, seasons, she became a portion of his life— a part of all that he wrought for. At the first, he had had a half-formed hope that the little one might be reclaimed by relatives generous and rich enough to insist upon his acceptance of a handsome compensation; and that Carmen could find some solace in a pleasant visit to Barceloneta. But now he felt that no possible generosity could requite him for her loss; and with the unconscious selfishness of affection, he commenced to dread her identification as a great calamity.

It was evident that she had been brought up nicely. She had pretty prim ways of drinking and eating, queer little fashions of sitting in company, and of addressing people. She had peculiar notions about colors in dress, about wearing her hair; and she seemed to have already imbibed a small stock of social prejudices not altogether in harmony with the republicanism of Viosca's Point. Occasional swarthy visitors—men of the Manilla settlements—she spoke of contemptuously as *"nègues-marrons";* and once she shocked Carmen inexpressibly by stopping in the middle of her evening prayer, declaring that she wanted to say her prayers to a *white* Virgin; Carmen's Señora de Guadalupe was only a *negra!* Then, for the first time, Carmen spoke so crossly to the child as to frighten her. But the pious woman's heart smote her the next moment for that first harsh word;—and she caressed the motherless one, consoled her, cheered her, and at last explained to her—I know not how—something very wonderful about the little figurine, something that made Chita's eyes big with awe. Thereafter she always regarded the Virgin of Wax as an object mysterious and holy.

And, one by one, most of Chita's little eccentricities were gradually eliminated from her developing life and thought. More rapidly than ordinary children, because singularly intelligent, she learned to adapt herself to all the changes of her new environment—retaining only that indescribable something which to an experienced eye tells of hereditary refinement of habit and of mind:—a natural grace, a thoroughbred ease and elegance of movement, a quickness and delicacy of perception.

She became strong again and active—active enough to play a great deal on the beach, when the sun was not too fierce; and Carmen made a canvas bonnet to shield her head and face. Never had she been allowed to play so much in the sun before; and it seemed to do her good, though her little bare feet and hands became brown as copper. At first, it must be confessed, she worried her foster-mother a great deal by various queer misfortunes and extraordinary freaks;—getting bitten by crabs, falling into the bayou while in pursuit of "fiddlers," or losing herself at the conclusion of desperate efforts to run races at night with the moon, or to walk to the "end of the world." If she could only once get to the edge of the sky, she said, she "could climb up." She wanted to see the stars, which were the souls of good little children; and she knew that God would let her climb up. "Just what I am afraid of!"—thought Carmen to herself;—"He might let her climb up—a little ghost!" But one day naughty Chita received a terrible lesson—a lasting lesson—which taught her the value of obedience.

She had been particularly cautioned not to venture into a certain part of the swamp in the rear of the grove, where the weeds were very tall; for Carmen was afraid some snake might bite the child. But Chita's bird-bright eye had discerned a gleam of white in that direction; and she wanted to know what it was. The white could only be seen from one point, behind the farthest house, where the ground was high. "Never go there," said Carmen; "there is a Dead Man there—will bite you!" And yet, one day, while Carmen was unusually busy, Chita went there.

In the early days of the settlement, a Spanish fisherman had died; and his comrades had built him a little tomb with the surplus of the same bricks and other material brought down the bayou for the construction of Viosca's cottages. But no one, except perhaps some wandering duck hunter, had approached the sepulchre for years. High weeds and grasses wrestled together all about it, and rendered it totally invisible from the surrounding level of the marsh.

Fiddlers swarmed away as Chita advanced over the moist soil, each uplifting its single huge claw as it sidled off;—then frogs began to leap before her as she reached the thicker grass;—and long-legged brown insects sprang showering to right and left as she parted the tufts of the thickening verdure. As she went on, the bitter-weeds disappeared;—jointed grasses and sinewy dark plants of a taller growth rose above her head: she was almost deafened by the storm of insect shrilling, and the mosquitoes became very wicked. All at once something long and black and heavy wriggled almost from under her naked feet—squirming so horribly that for a minute or two she could not move for fright. But it slunk away somewhere, and hid itself; the weeds it had shaken ceased to tremble in its wake; and her courage returned. She felt such an exquisite and fearful pleasure in the gratification of that naughty curiosity! Then, quite unexpectedly—oh! what a start it gave her!—the solitary white object burst upon her view, leprous and ghastly as the yawn of a cottonmouth. Tombs ruin soon in Louisiana;—the one Chita looked upon seemed ready to topple down. There was a great ragged hole at one end, where wind and rain, and perhaps also the burrowing of crawfish and of worms, had loosened the bricks, and caused them to slide out of place. It seemed very black inside; but Chita wanted to know what was there. She pushed her way through a gap in the thin and rotten line of pickets, and through some tall weeds with big coarse pink flowers;—then she crouched down on hands and knees before the black hole, and peered in. It was not so black inside as she had thought; for a sunbeam slanted down through a chink in the roof; and she could see!

A brown head—without hair, without eyes, but with teeth, ever so many teeth!—seemed to laugh at her; and close to it sat a Toad, the hugest she had ever seen; and the white skin of his throat kept puffing out and going in. And Chita screamed and screamed, and fled in wild terror—screaming all the way, till Carmen ran out to meet her and carry her home. Even when safe in her adopted mother's arms, she sobbed with fright. To the vivid fancy of the child there seemed to be some hideous relation between the staring reptile and the brown death's-head, with its empty eyes, and its nightmare-smile.

The shock brought on a fever—a fever that lasted several days, and left her very weak. But the experience taught her to obey, taught her that Carmen knew best what was for her good. It also caused her to think a great deal. Carmen had told her that the dead people never frightened good little girls who stayed at home.

"*Madrecita Carmen,*" she asked, "is my mamma dead?"

"Pobrecita! ... Yes, my angel. God called her to Him—your darling mother."

"Madrecita," she asked again—her young eyes growing vast with horror—"is my own mamma now like *That?"* ... She pointed toward the place of the white gleam, behind the great trees.

"No, no, no! my darling!" cried Carmen, appalled herself by the ghastly question—"your mamma is with the dear, good, loving God, who lives in the beautiful sky—above the clouds, my darling, beyond the sun!"

But Carmen's kind eyes were full of tears; and the child read their meaning. He who teareth off the Mask of the Flesh had looked into her face one unutterable moment:—she had seen the brutal Truth, naked to the bone!

Yet there came to her a little thrill of consolation, caused by the words of the tender falsehood; for that which she had discerned by day could not explain to her that which she saw almost nightly in her slumber. The face, the voice, the form of her loving mother still lived somewhere—could not have utterly passed away; since the sweet presence came to her in dreams, bending and smiling over her, caressing her, speaking to her—sometimes gently chiding, but always chiding with a kiss. And then the child would laugh in her sleep, and prattle in Creole—talking to the luminous shadow, telling the dead mother all the little deeds and thoughts of the day. ... Why would God only let her come at night?

... Her idea of God had been first defined by the sight of a quaint French picture of the Creation—an engraving which represented a shoreless sea under a black sky, and out of the blackness a solemn and bearded gray head emerging, and a cloudy hand through which stars glimmered. God was like old Dr. de Coulanges, who used to visit the house, and talk in a voice like a low roll of thunder. ... At a later day, when Chita had been told that God was "everywhere at the same time"—without and within, beneath and above all things—this idea became somewhat changed. The awful bearded face, the huge shadowy hand, did not fade from her thought; but they became fantastically blended with the larger and vaguer notion of something that filled the world and reached to the stars—something diaphanous and incomprehensible like the invisible air, omnipresent and everlasting like the high blue of heaven. ...

II

. . . SHE BEGAN TO LEARN THE LIFE OF THE COAST.

With her acquisition of another tongue, there came to her also the understanding of many things relating to the world of the sea. She memorized with novel delight much that was told her day by day concerning the nature surrounding her—many secrets of the air, many of those signs of heaven which the dwellers in cities cannot comprehend because the atmosphere is thickened and made stagnant above them—cannot even watch because the horizon is hidden from their eyes by walls, and by weary avenues of trees with whitewashed trunks. She learned, by listening, by asking, by observing also, how to know the signs that foretell wild weather:—tremendous sunsets, scuddings and bridgings of cloud—sharpening and darkening of the sea-line—and the shriek of gulls flashing to land in level flight, out of a still transparent sky—and halos about the moon.

She learned where the sea-birds, with white bosoms and brown wings, made their hidden nests of sand—and where the cranes waded for their prey—and where the beautiful wild-ducks, plumaged in satiny lilac and silken green, found their food—and where the best reeds grew to furnish stems for Feliu's red-clay pipe—and where the ruddy sea-beams were most often tossed upon the shore—and how the gray pelicans fished all together, like men—moving in far-extending semi-circles, beating the flood with their wings to drive the fish before them.

And from Carmen she learned the fables and the sayings of the sea —the proverbs about its deafness, its avarice, its treachery, its terrific power—especially one that haunted her for all time thereafter: *Si quieres aprender á orar, entra en el mar* (If thou wouldst learn to pray, go to the sea). She learned why the sea is salt—how "the tears of women made the waves of the sea"—and how the sea has "no friends"—and how the cat's eyes change with the tides.

What had she lost of life by her swift translation from the dusty existence of cities to the open immensity of nature's freedom? What did she gain?

Doubtless she was saved from many of those little bitternesses and restraints and disappointments which all well-bred city children must suffer in the course of their training for the more or less factitious life of society:—obligations to remain very still with every nimble nerve quivering in dumb revolt;—the injustice of being found troublesome and being sent to bed early for the comfort of her elders;—the cruel necessity of straining her pretty eyes, for many long hours at a time, over grimy desks in gloomy school-rooms, though birds might twitter and bright winds flutter in the trees without;—the austere constraint and heavy drowsiness of warm churches, filled with the droning echoes of a voice preaching incomprehensible things;—the progressively augmenting weariness of lessons in deportment, in dancing, in music, in the impossible art of keeping her dresses unruffled and unsoiled. Perhaps she never had any reason to regret all these.

She went to sleep and awakened with the wild birds;—her life remained as unfettered by formalities as her fine feet by shoes. Excepting Carmen's old prayerbook—in which she learned to read a little—her childhood passed without books—also without pictures, without dainties, without music, without theatrical amusements. But she saw and heard and felt much of that which, though old as the heavens and the earth, is yet eternally new and eternally young with the holiness of beauty—eternally mystical and divine—eternally weird: the unveiled magnificence of Nature's moods—the perpetual poem hymned by wind and surge—the everlasting splendor of the sky.

She saw the quivering pinkness of waters curled by the breath of the morning—under the deepening of the dawn—like a far fluttering and scattering of rose-leaves of fire;—

Saw the shoreless, cloudless, marvelous double-circling azure of perfect summer days—twin glories of infinite deeps interreflected, while the Soul of the World lay still, suffused with a jewel-light, as of vaporized sapphire;—

Saw the Sea shift color—"change sheets"—when the viewless Wizard of the Wind breathed upon its face, and made it green;—

Saw the immeasurable panics—noiseless, scintillant—which silver, summer after summer, curved leagues of beach with bodies of little fish—the yearly massacre of migrating populations, nations of sea-trout, driven from their element by terror;—and the winnowing of shark-fins—and the rushing of porpoises—and the rising of the grande-écaille, like a pillar of flame—and the diving and pitching and fighting of the frigates and the gulls—and the armored hordes of crabs swarming out to clear the slope after the carnage and the gorging had been done;—

Saw the Dreams of the Sky—scudding mockeries of ridged foam—

and shadowy stratification of capes and coasts and promontories long-drawn-out—and imageries, multicolored, of mountain frondage, and sierras whitening above sierras—and phantom islands ringed around with lagoons of glory;—

Saw the toppling and smouldering of cloud-worlds after the enormous conflagration of sunsets—incandescence ruining into darkness; and after it a moving and climbing of stars among the blacknesses—like searching lamps;—

Saw the deep kindle countless ghostly candles as for mysterious night-festival—and a luminous billowing under a black sky, and effervescences of fire, and the twirling and crawling of phosphoric foam;—

Saw the mesmerism of the Moon;—saw the enchanted tides self-heaped in muttering obeisance before her.

Often she heard the Music of the Marsh through the night: an infinity of flutings and tinklings made by tiny amphibia—like the low blowing of numberless little tin horns, the clanking of billions of little bells;—and, at intervals, profound tones, vibrant and heavy, as of a bass-viol—the orchestra of the great frogs! And interweaving with it all, one continuous shrilling—keen as the steel speech of a saw—the stridulous telegraphy of crickets.

But always—always, dreaming or awake, she heard the huge blind Sea chanting that mystic and eternal hymn, which none may hear without awe, which no musician can learn;—

Heard the hoary Preacher—*El Pregonador*—preaching the ancient Word, the word "as a fire, and as a hammer that breaketh the rock in pieces,"—the Elohim-Word of the Sea! . . .

Unknowingly she came to know the immemorial sympathy of the mind with the Soul of the World—the melancholy wrought by its moods of gray, the reverie responsive to its vagaries of mist, the exhilaration of its vast exultings—days of windy joy, hours of transfigured light.

She felt—even without knowing it—the weight of the Silences, the solemnities of sky and sea in these low regions where all things seem to dream—waters and grasses with their momentary wavings—woods gray-webbed with mosses that drip and drool—horizons with their delusions of vapor—cranes meditating in their marshes—kites floating in the high blue. . . . Even the children were singularly quiet; and their play less noisy—though she could not have learned the difference —than the play of city children. Hour after hour, the women sewed or wove in silence. And the brown men—always barefooted, always wearing rough blue shirts—seemed, when they lounged about the wharf on idle days, as if they had told each other long ago all they knew or could ever know, and had nothing more to say. They would stare at the flickering of the current, at the drifting of clouds and buzzards—seldom looking at each other, and always turning their black eyes again, in a weary way, to sky or sea. Even thus one sees the horses and the cattle of the coast, seeking the beach to escape the whizzing flies;—all watch the long waves rolling in, and sometimes turn their heads a moment to look at one another, but always look back to the waves again, as if wondering at a mystery. . . .

How often she herself had wondered—wondered at the multiform changes of each swell as it came in—transformations of tint, of shape, of motion, that seemed to betoken a life infinitely more subtle than the strange cold life of lizards and of fishes—and sinister, and spectral. Then they all appeared to move in order—according to one law or impulse;—each had its own voice, yet all sang one and the same everlasting song. Vaguely, as she watched them and listened to them, there came to her the idea of a unity of *will* in their motion, a unity of *menace* in their utterance—the idea of one monstrous and complex life! The sea *lived*: it could crawl backward and forward; it could speak!—it only feigned deafness and sightlessness for some malevolent end. Thenceforward she feared to find herself alone with it. Was it not at her that it strove to rush, muttering, and showing its white teeth . . . just because it knew that she was all by herself? . . . *Si quieres aprender á orar, entra en el mar!* And Concha had well learned to pray. But the sea seemed to her the one Power which God could not make to obey Him as He pleased. Saying the creed one day, she repeated very slowly the opening words, *"Creo en un Dios, padre todopoderoso, Criador del cielo y de la tierra"*—and paused and thought. *Creator of Heaven and Earth?* "*Madrecita Carmen,*" she asked—"*quien entonces hizó el mar?*" (who then made the sea?)

"*Dios, mi querida,*" answered Carmen. "God, my darling. . . . All things were made by Him" (*todas las cosas fueron hechas por Él*).

Even the wicked Sea! And He had said unto it: "Thus far, and no farther." . . . Was that why it had not overtaken and devoured her when she ran back in fear from the sudden reaching out of its waves? *Thus far . . . ?* But there were times when it disobeyed—when it rushed further, shaking the world! Was it because God was then asleep—could not hear, did not see, until too late?

And the tumultuous ocean terrified her more and more: it filled her sleep with enormous nightmare;—it came upon her in dreams, mountain-shadowing—holding her with its spell, smothering her power of outcry, heaping itself to the stars.

Carmen became alarmed;—she feared that the nervous and delicate child might die in one of those moaning dreams out of which she had to arouse her, night after night. But Feliu, answering her anxiety with one of his favorite proverbs, suggested a heroic remedy:

"The world is like the sea: those who do not know how to swim in it are drowned;—and the sea is like the world," he added. . . . "Chita must learn to swim!"

And he found the time to teach her. Each morning, at sunrise, he took her into the water. She was less terrified the first time than Carmen thought she would be;—she seemed to feel confidence in Feliu; although she screamed piteously before her first ducking at his hands. His teaching was not gentle. He would carry her out, perched upon his shoulder, until the water rose to his own neck; and there he would throw her from him, and let her struggle to reach him again as best she could. The first few mornings she had to be pulled out almost at once; but after that Feliu showed her less mercy, and helped her only when he saw she was really in danger. He attempted no other instruction until she had learned that in order to save herself from being half choked by the salt water, she must not scream; and by the time she became habituated to these austere experiences, she had already learned by instinct alone how to keep herself afloat for a while, how to paddle a little with her hands. Then he commenced to train her to use them—to lift them well out and throw them forward as if reaching, to dip them as the blade of an oar is dipped at an angle, without loud splashing;—and he showed her also how to use her feet. She learned rapidly and astonishingly well. In less than two months Feliu felt really proud at the progress made by his tiny pupil: it was a delight to watch her lifting her slender arms above the water in swift, easy curves, with the same fine grace that marked all her other natural motions. Later on he taught her not to fear the sea even when it growled a little—how to ride a swell, how to face a breaker, how to dive. She only needed practice thereafter; and Carmen, who could also swim, finding the child's health improving marvelously under this new discipline, took good care that Chita should practice whenever the mornings were not too cold, or the water too rough.

With the first thrill of delight at finding herself able to glide over the water unassisted, the child's superstitious terror of the sea passed away. Even for the adult there are few physical joys keener than the exultation of the swimmer;—how much greater the same glee as newly felt by an imaginative child—a child, whose vivid fancy can lend unutterable value to the most insignificant trifles, can transform a weed-patch to an Eden! ... Of her own accord she would ask for her morning bath, as soon as she opened her eyes;—it even required some severity to prevent her from remaining in the water too long. The sea appeared to her as something that had become tame for her sake, something that loved her in a huge rough way; a tremendous playmate, whom she no longer feared to see come bounding and barking to lick her feet. And, little by little, she also learned the wonderful healing and caressing power of the monster, whose cool embrace at once dispelled all drowsiness, feverishness, weariness—even after the sultriest nights when the air had seemed to burn, and the mosquitoes had filled the chamber with a sound as of water boiling in many kettles. And on mornings when the sea was in too wicked a humor to be played with, how she felt the loss of her loved sport, and prayed for calm! Her delicate constitution changed;—the soft, pale flesh became firm and brown, the meagre limbs rounded into robust symmetry, the thin cheeks grew peachy with richer life; for the strength of the sea had entered into her; the sharp breath of the sea had renewed and brightened her young blood. . . .

. . . Thou primordial Sea, the awfulness of whose antiquity hath stricken all mythology dumb;—thou most wrinkled living Sea, the millions of whose years outnumber even the multitude of thy hoary motions;—thou omniform and most mysterious Sea, mother of the monsters and the gods—whence thine eternal youth? Still do thy waters hold the infinite thrill of that Spirit which brooded above their face in the Beginning!—still is thy quickening breath an elixir unto them that flee to thee for life—like the breath of young girls, like the breath of children, prescribed for the senescent by magicians of old— prescribed unto weazened elders in the books of the Wizards.

III

. . . EIGHTEEN HUNDRED AND SIXTY-SEVEN;—MIDSUMMER IN THE PEST-smitten city of New Orleans.

Heat motionless and ponderous. The steel-blue of the sky bleached from the furnace-circle of the horizon;—the lukewarm river ran yellow and noiseless as a torrent of fluid wax. Even sounds seemed blunted by the heaviness of the air;—the rumbling of wheels, the reverberation of footsteps, fell half-toned upon the ear, like sounds that visit a dozing brain.

Daily, almost at the same hour, the continuous sense of atmospheric oppression became thickened;—a packed herd of low-bellying clouds lumbered up from the Gulf; crowded blackly against the sun; flickered, thundered, and burst in torrential rain—tepid, perpendicular—and vanished utterly away. Then, more furiously than before, the sun flamed down;—roofs and pavements steamed; the streets seemed to smoke; the air grew suffocating with vapor; and the luminous city filled with a faint, sickly odor—a stale smell, as of dead leaves suddenly disinterred from wet mould—as of grasses decomposing after a flood. Something saffron speckled the slimy water of the gutters; sulphur some called it; others feared even to give it a name! Was it only the wind-blown pollen of some innocuous plant? I do not know; but to many it seemed as if the Invisible Destruction were scattering visible seed! . . . Such were the days; and each day the terror-stricken city offered up its hecatomb to death; and the faces of all the dead were yellow as flame!

"DÉCÉDÉ—"; "DÉCÉDÉ—"; "FALLECIO";—"DIED." . . . On the door-posts, the telegraph-poles, the pillars of verandas, the lamps—over the Government letter-boxes—everywhere glimmered the white annunciations of death. All the city was spotted with them. And lime was poured into the gutters; and huge purifying fires were kindled after sunset.

The nights began with a black heat;—there were hours when the acrid air seemed to ferment for stagnation, and to burn the bronchial tubing;—then, toward morning, it would grow chill with venomous vapors, with morbific dews—till the sun came up to lift the torpid moisture, and to fill the buildings with oven-glow. And the interminable procession of mourners and hearses and carriages again began to circulate between the centres of life and of death;—and long trains and steamships rushed from the port, with heavy burden of fugitives.

Wealth might flee; yet even in flight there was peril. Men, who might have been saved by the craft of experienced nurses at home, hurriedly departed in apparent health, unconsciously carrying in their blood the toxic principle of a malady unfamiliar to physicians of the West and North;—and they died upon their way, by the road-side, by the river-banks, in woods, in deserted stations, on the cots of quarantine hospitals. Wiser those who sought refuge in the purity of the pine forests, or in those near Gulf Islands, whence the bright sea-breath kept ever sweeping back the expanding poison into the funereal swamps, into the misty lowlands. The watering-resorts became overcrowded;—then the fishing villages were thronged—at least all which were easy to reach by steamboat or by lugger. And at last, even Viosca's Point—remote and unfamiliar as it was—had a stranger to shelter: a good old gentleman named Edwards, rather broken down in health—who came as much for quiet as for sea-air, and who had been warmly recommended to Feliu by Captain Harris. For some years he had been troubled by a disease of the heart.

Certainly the old invalid could not have found a more suitable place so far as rest and quiet were concerned. The season had early given such little promise that several men of the Point betook themselves elsewhere; and the aged visitor had two or three vacant cabins from among which to select a dwelling-place. He chose to occupy the most remote of all, which Carmen furnished for him with a cool moss bed and some necessary furniture—including a big wooden rocking-chair. It seemed to him very comfortable thus. He took his meals with the family, spent most of the day in his own quarters, spoke very little, and lived so unobtrusively and inconspicuously that his presence in the settlement was felt scarcely more than that of some dumb creature—some domestic animal—some humble pet whose relation to the family is only fully comprehended after it has failed to appear for several days in its accustomed place of patient waiting—and we know that it is dead.

IV

PERSISTENTLY AND FURIOUSLY, AT HALF-PAST TWO O'CLOCK OF AN AUGUST morning, Sparicio rang Dr. La Brierre's night-bell. He had fifty dollars in his pocket, and a letter to deliver. He was to earn another fifty dollars—deposited in Feliu's hands—by bringing the Doctor to Viosca's Point. He had risked his life for that money—and was terribly in earnest.

Julien descended in his under-clothing, and opened the letter by the light of the hall lamp. It enclosed a check for a larger fee than he had ever before received, and contained an urgent request that he would at once accompany Sparicio to Viosca's Point—as the sender was in hourly danger of death. The letter, penned in a long, quavering hand, was signed—*"Henry Edwards."*

His father's dear old friend! Julien could not refuse to go—though he feared it was a hopeless case. *Angina pectoris*—and a third attack at seventy years of age! Would it even be possible to reach the sufferer's bedside in time? *"Duè giorno—con vento"*—said Sparicio. Still, he must go; and at once. It was Friday morning;—might reach the Point Saturday night, with a good wind. . . . He roused his housekeeper, gave all needful instructions, prepared his little medicine-chest;—and long before the first rose-gold fire of day had flashed to the city spires, he was sleeping the sleep of exhaustion in the tiny cabin of a fishing-sloop.

. . . For eleven years Julien had devoted himself, heart and soul, to the exercise of that profession he had first studied rather as a polite accomplishment than as a future calling. In the unselfish pursuit of duty he had found the only possible consolation for his irreparable loss; and when the war came to sweep away his wealth, he entered the struggle valorously, not to strive against men, but to use his science against death. After the passing of that huge shock, which left all the imposing and splendid fabric of Southern feudalism wrecked forever, his profession stood him in good stead;—he found himself not only able to supply those personal wants he cared to satisfy, but also to alleviate the misery of many whom he had known in days of opulence; —the princely misery that never doffed its smiling mask, though living in secret, from week to week, on bread and orange-leaf tea;—the misery that affected condescension in accepting an invitation to dine— staring at the face of a watch (refused by the *Mont-de-Piété*) with eyes half blinded by starvation;—the misery which could afford but one robe for three marriageable daughters—one plain dress to be worn in turn by each of them, on visiting days;—the pretty misery—young, brave, sweet—asking for a "treat" of cakes too jocosely to have its asking answered—laughing and coquetting with its well-fed wooers, and crying for hunger after they were gone. Often and often, his heart had pleaded against his purse for such as these, and won its case in the silent courts of Self. But ever mysteriously the gift came—sometimes as if from the hand of a former slave; sometimes as from a remorseful creditor, ashamed to write his name. Only yellow Victorine knew; but the Doctor's housekeeper never opened those sphinx-lips of hers, until years after the Doctor's name had disappeared from the City Directory. . . .

He had grown quite thin—a little gray. The epidemic had bur-
thened him with responsibilities too multifarious and ponderous for his
slender strength to bear. The continual nervous strain of abnormally
protracted duty, the perpetual interruption of sleep, had almost prostrated even his will. Now he only hoped that, during this brief absence
from the city, he might find renewed strength to do his terrible task.

Mosquitoes bit savagely; and the heat became thicker;—and there
was yet no wind. Sparicio and his hired boy Carmelo had been walking backward and forward for hours overhead—urging the vessel yard
by yard, with long poles, through the slime of canals and bayous. With
every heavy push, the weary boy would sigh out—*"Santo Antonio!—
Santo Antonio!"*—Sullen Sparicio himself at last burst into vociferations
of ill-humor: *"Santo Antonio?—Ah! santissimu e santu diavulu! ... Sac-
ramentu pœscite vegnu un asidente!—malidittu lu Signuri!"* All through
the morning they walked and pushed, trudged and sighed and swore;
and the minutes dragged by more wearily than the shuffling of their
feet. *"Managgia Cristo co tutta a croce!"* . . . *"Santissimu e santu
diavulu!!"* . . .

But as they reached at last the first of the broad bright lakes, the
heat lifted, the breeze leaped up, the loose sail flapped and filled; and,
bending graciously as a skater, the old *San Marco* began to shoot in a
straight line over the blue flood. Then, while the boy sat at the tiller,
Sparicio lighted his tiny charcoal furnace below, and prepared a simple
meal—delicious yellow macaroni, flavored with goats' cheese; some
fried fish, that smelled appetizingly; and rich black coffee, of Oriental
fragrance and thickness. Julien ate a little, and lay down to sleep again.
This time his rest was undisturbed by the mosquitoes; and when he
woke, in the cooling evening, he felt almost refreshed. The *San Marco*
was flying into Barataria Bay. Already the lantern in the lighthouse
tower had begun to glow like a little moon; and right on the rim of
the sea, a vast and vermilion sun seemed to rest his chin. Gray pelicans
came flapping around the mast;—sea-birds sped hurtling by, their
white bosoms rose-flushed by the western glow. . . . Again Sparicio's
little furnace was at work—more fish, more macaroni, more black coffee; also a square-shouldered bottle of gin made its appearance. Julien
ate less sparingly at this second meal; and smoked a long time on deck
with Sparicio, who suddenly became very good-humored, and chatted
volubly in bad Spanish, and in much worse English. Then while the
boy took a few hours' sleep, the Doctor helped delightedly in ma-
neuvering the little vessel. He had been a good yachtsman in other

years; and Sparicio declared he would make a good fisherman. By midnight the *San Marco* began to run with a long, swinging gait;—she had reached deep water. Julien slept soundly; the steady rocking of the sloop seemed to soothe his nerves.

"After all," he thought to himself, as he rose from his little bunk next morning—"something like this is just what I needed." . . . The pleasant scent of hot coffee greeted him;—Carmelo was handing him the tin cup containing it, down through the hatchway. After drinking it he felt really hungry;—he ate more macaroni than he had ever eaten before. Then, while Sparicio slept, he aided Carmelo; and during the middle of the day he rested again. He had not had so much uninterrupted repose for many a week. He fancied he could feel himself getting strong. At supper-time it seemed to him he could not get enough to eat—although there was plenty for everybody.

All day long there had been exactly the same wave-crease distorting the white shadow of the *San Marco's* sail upon the blue water;—all day long they had been skimming over the liquid level of a world so jewel-blue that the low green ribbon-strips of marsh land, the far-off fleeing lines of pine-yellow sand beach, seemed flaws or breaks in the perfected color of the universe;—all day long had the cloudless sky revealed through all its exquisite transparency that inexpressible tenderness which no painter and no poet can ever re-image—that unutterable sweetness which no art of man may ever shadow forth, and which none may ever comprehend—though we feel it to be in some strange way akin to the luminous and unspeakable charm that makes us wonder at the eyes of a woman when she loves.

Evening came; and the great dominant celestial tone deepened;—the circling horizon filled with ghostly tints—spectral greens and grays, and pearl-lights and fish-colors. . . . Carmelo, as he crouched at the tiller, was singing, in a low, clear alto, some tristful little melody. Over the sea, behind them, lay, black-stretching, a long low arm of island-shore;—before them flamed the splendor of sun-death; they were sailing into a mighty glory—into a vast and awful light of gold.

Shading his vision with his fingers, Sparicio pointed to the long lean limb of land from which they were fleeing, and said to La Brierre:

"Look-a, Doct-a! Last-a Islan'!"

Julien knew it;—he only nodded his head in reply, and looked the other way—into the glory of God. Then, wishing to divert the fisherman's attention to another theme, he asked what was Carmelo singing. Sparicio at once shouted to the lad:

"Ha! . . . ho! Carmelo!—*Santu diavulu*! . . . Sing-a loud-a! Doct-a lik-a! sing-a! sing!!" . . . "He sing-a nicee"—added the boatman, with his peculiar dark smile. And then Carmelo sang, loud and clearly, the song he had been singing before—one of those artless Mediterranean ballads, full of caressing vowel-sounds, and young passion, and melancholy beauty:

> *M' ama ancor, beltà fulgente,*
> *Come tu m' amasti allor;—*
> *Ascoltar non dei gente,*
> *Solo interroga il tuo cor. . . .*

"He sing-a nicee—mucha bueno!" murmured the fisherman. And then, suddenly—with a rich and splendid basso that seemed to thrill every fibre of the planking—Sparicio joined in the song:

> *M' ama pur d' amore eterno,*
> *Nè delitto sembri a te;*
> *T' assicuro che l' inferno*
> *Una favola sol è. . . .*

All the roughness of the man was gone! To Julien's startled fancy, the fishers had ceased to be;—lo! Carmelo was a princely page; Sparicio, a king! How perfectly their voices married together!—they sang with passion, with power, with truth, with that wondrous natural art which is the birthright of the rudest Italian soul. And the stars throbbed out in the heaven; and the glory died in the west; and the night opened its heart; and the splendor of the eternities fell all about them. Still they sang; and the *San Marco* sped on through the soft gloom, ever slightly swerved by the steady blowing of the southeast wind in her sail;—always wearing the same crimpling-frill of wave-spray about her prow—always accompanied by the same smooth-backed swells—always spinning out behind her the same long trail of interwoven foam. And Julien looked up. Ever the night thrilled more and more with silent twinklings;—more and more multitudinously lights pointed in the eternities;—the Evening Star quivered like a great drop of liquid white fire ready to fall;—Vega flamed as a pharos lighting the courses ethereal—to guide the sailing of the suns, and the swarming of fleets of worlds. Then the vast sweetness of that violet night entered into his blood—filled him with that awful joy, so near akin to sadness, which the sense of the Infinite brings—when one feels the poetry of the Most Ancient and Most Excellent of Poets, and then is smitten at once with the contrast-thought of the sickliness and selfishness of Man —of the blindness and brutality of cities, whereinto the divine blue light never purely comes, and the sanctification of the Silences never descends . . . furious cities, walled away from heaven. . . . Oh! if one could only sail on thus always, always through such a night—through such a star-sprinkled violet night, and hear Sparicio and Carmelo sing, even though it were the same melody always, always the same song!

. . . "Scuza, Doct-a!—look-a out!" Julien bent down, as the big boom, loosened, swung over his head. The San Marco was rounding into shore—heading for her home. Sparicio lifted a huge conch-shell from the deck, put it to his lips, filled his deep lungs, and flung out into the night—thrice—a profound, mellifluent, booming horn-tone. A minute passed. Then, ghostly faint, as an echo from very far away, a triple blowing responded. . . .

And a long purple mass loomed and swelled into sight, heightened, approached—land and trees black-shadowing, and lights that swung. . . . The *San Marco* glided into a bayou—under a high wharfing of timbers, where a bearded fisherman waited, and a woman. Sparicio flung up a rope.

The bearded man caught it by the lantern-light, and tethered the *San Marco* to her place. Then he asked, in a deep voice:

"*Has traido al Doctor?*"

"*Si, si!*" answered Sparicio. . . . "*Y el viejo?*"

"*Aye! pobre!*" responded Feliu—"*hace tres dias que esta muerto.*"

Henry Edwards was dead!

He had died very suddenly, without a cry or a word, while resting in his rocking-chair—the very day after Sparicio had sailed. They had made him a grave in the marsh—among the high weeds, not far from the ruined tomb of the Spanish fisherman. But Sparicio had fairly earned his hundred dollars.

V

SO THERE WAS NOTHING TO DO AT VIOSCA'S POINT EXCEPT TO REST. FELIU and all his men were going to Barataria in the morning on business;— the Doctor could accompany them there, and take the Grand Island steamer Monday for New Orleans. With this intention Julien retired—

not sorry for being able to stretch himself at full length on the good bed prepared for him, in one of the unoccupied cabins. But he woke before day with a feeling of intense prostration, a violent headache, and such an aversion for the mere idea of food that Feliu's invitation to breakfast at five o'clock gave him an internal qualm. Perhaps a touch of malaria. In any case he felt it would be both dangerous and useless to return to town unwell; and Feliu, observing his condition, himself advised against the journey. Wednesday he would have another opportunity to leave; and in the meanwhile Carmen would take good care of him. . . . The boats departed, and Julien slept again.

The sun was high when he rose up and dressed himself, feeling no better. He would have liked to walk about the place, but felt nervously afraid of the sun. He did not remember having ever felt so broken down before. He pulled a rocking-chair to the window, tried to smoke a cigar. It commenced to make him feel still sicker, and he flung it away. It seemed to him the cabin was swaying, as the *San Marco* swayed when she first reached the deep water.

A light rustling sound approached—a sound of quick feet treading the grass: then a shadow slanted over the threshold. In the glow of the open doorway stood a young girl—gracile, tall—with singularly splendid eyes—brown eyes peeping at him from beneath a golden riot of loose hair.

"*M'sieu-le-Docteur, maman d'mande si vous n'avez bisoin d'que'que chose?*" . . . She spoke the rude French of the fishing villages, where the language lives chiefly as a *baragouin*, mingled often with words and forms belonging to many other tongues. She wore a loose-falling dress of some light stuff, steel-gray in color;—boys' shoes were on her feet.

He did not reply;—and her large eyes grew larger for wonder at the strange fixed gaze of the physician, whose face had visibly bleached—blanched to corpse-pallor. Silent seconds passed; and still the eyes stared—flamed as if the life of the man had centralized and focussed within them.

His voice had risen to a cry in his throat, quivered and swelled one passionate instant, and failed—as in a dream when one strives to call, and yet can only moan. . . . *She!* Her unforgotten eyes, her brows, her lips!—the oval of her face!—the dawn-light of her hair! . . . Adèle's own poise—her own grace!—even the very turn of her neck—even the bird-tone of her speech! . . . Had the grave sent forth a Shadow to haunt him?—could the perfidious Sea have yielded up its dead? For one terrible fraction of a minute, memories, doubts, fears, mad fancies, went pulsing through his brain with a rush like the rhythmic throbbing of an electric stream;—then the shock passed, the Reason spoke: "Fool!—count the long years since you first saw her thus!—count the years that have gone since you looked upon her last! And Time has never halted, silly heart!—neither has Death stood still!"

... *"Plait-il?"*—the clear voice of the young girl asked. She thought he had made some response she could not distinctly hear.

Mastering himself an instant, as the heart faltered back to its duty, and the color remounted to his lips, he answered her in French:

"Pardon me!—I did not hear ... you gave me such a start!" ... But even then another extraordinary fancy flashed through his thought;—and with the *tutoiement* of a parent to a child, with an irresistible outburst of such tenderness as almost frightened her, he cried: "Oh! merciful God!—how like her! ... Tell me, darling, your name;—tell me who you are?" (*Dis-moi qui tu es, mignonne;—dis-moi ton nom.*)

... Who was it had asked her the same question, in another idiom—ever so long ago? The man with the black eyes and nose like an eagle's beak—the one who gave her the compass. Not *this* man—no!

She answered, with the timid gravity of surprise:

"Chita Viosca."

He still watched her face, and repeated the name slowly—reiterated it in a tone of wonderment: "Chita Viosca?—Chita Viosca!"

"C'est à dire ..." she said, looking down at her feet—"Concha—Conchita." His strange solemnity made her smile—the smile of shyness that knows not what else to do. But it was the smile of dead Adèle.

"Thanks, my child," he exclaimed of a sudden—in a quick, hoarse, changed tone. (He felt that his emotion would break loose in some wild way, if he looked upon her longer.) "I would like to see your mother this evening; but I now feel too ill to go out. I am going to try to rest a little."

"Nothing I can bring you?" She asked;—"some fresh milk?"

"Nothing now, dear: if I need anything later, I will tell your mother when she comes."

"Mamma does not understand French very well."

"No importa, Conchita;—le hablaré en Español."

"Bien, entonces!" she responded, with the same exquisite smile. *"Adios, señor!"* ...

But as she turned in going, his piercing eye discerned a little brown speck below the pretty lobe of her right ear—just in the peachy curve between neck and cheek. . . . His own little Zouzoune had a birthmark like that!—he remembered the faint pink trace left by his fingers above and below it the day he had slapped her for overturning his ink-bottle. . . . *"To laimin moin?—to batté moin!"*

"Chita!—Chita!"

She did not hear. . . . After all, what a mistake he might have made! Were not Nature's coincidences more wonderful than fiction? Better to wait—to question the mother first, and thus make sure.

Still—there were so many coincidences! The face, the smile, the eyes, the voice, the whole charm;—then that mark—and the fair hair. Zouzoune had always resembled Adèle so strangely! That golden hair was a Scandinavian bequest to the Florane family;—the tall daughter of a Norwegian sea-captain had once become the wife of a Florane. Viosca?—who ever knew a Viosca with such hair? Yet again, these Spanish emigrants sometimes married blonde German girls. . . . Might be a case of atavism, too. Who was this Viosca? If that was his wife—the little brown Carmen—whence Chita's sunny hair? . . .

And this was part of that same desolate shore whither the Last Island dead had been drifted by that tremendous surge! On a clear day, with a good glass, one might discern from here the long blue streak of that ghastly coast. . . . Somewhere—between here and there. . . . Merciful God! . . .

. . . But again! That bivouac-night before the fight at Chancellorsville, Laroussel had begun to tell him such a singular story. . . . Chance had brought them—the old enemies—together; made them dear friends in the face of Death. How little he had comprehended the man!—what a brave, true, simple soul went up that day to the Lord of Battles! . . . What was it—that story about the little Creole girl saved from Last Island—that story which was never finished? . . . Eh! what a pain!

Evidently he had worked too much, slept too little. A decided case of nervous prostration. He must lie down, and try to sleep. These pains in the head and back were becoming unbearable. Nothing but rest could avail him now.

He stretched himself under the mosquito curtain. It was very still, breathless, hot! The venomous insects were thick;—they filled the room with a continuous ebullient sound, as if invisible kettles were boiling overhead. A sign of storm. . . . Still, it was strange!—he could not perspire. . . .

Then it seemed to him that Laroussel was bending over him—Laroussel in his cavalry uniform. *"Bonjour, camarade!—nous allons avoir un bien mauvais temps, mon pauvre Julien."* How! bad weather?—*"Comment un mauvais temps?"* . . . He looked in Laroussel's face. There was something so singular in his smile. Ah! yes—he remembered now: it was the wound! . . . *"Un vilain temps!"* whispered Laroussel. Then he was gone. . . . Whither?

"Chéri!" . . .

The whisper roused him with a fearful start. . . . Adèle's whisper! So she was wont to rouse him sometimes in the old sweet nights—to crave some little attention for ailing Eulalie—to make some little confidence she had forgotten to utter during the happy evening. . . . No, no! It was only the trees. The sky was clouding over. The wind was rising. . . . How his heart beat! how his temples pulsed! Why, this was fever! Such pains in the back and head!

Still his skin was dry—dry as parchment—burning. He rose up; and a bursting weight of pain at the base of the skull made him reel like a drunken man. He staggered to the little mirror nailed upon the wall, and looked. How his eyes glowed;—and there was blood in his mouth! He felt his pulse—spasmodic, terribly rapid. Could it possibly—? . . . No: this must be some pernicious malarial fever! The Creole does not easily fall a prey to the great tropical malady—unless after a long absence in other climates. True! he had been four years in the army! But this was 1867. . . . He hesitated a moment; then—opening his medicine-chest, he measured out and swallowed thirty grains of quinine.

Then he lay down again. His head pained more and more;—it seemed as if the cervical vertebræ were filled with fluid iron. And still his skin remained dry as if tanned. Then the anguish grew so intense as to force a groan with almost every aspiration. . . . Nausea—and the stinging bitterness of quinine rising in his throat;—dizziness, and a brutal wrenching within his stomach. Everything began to look pink; —the light was rose-colored. It darkened more—kindled with deepening tint. Something kept sparkling and spinning before his sight, like a firework. . . . Then a burst of blood mixed with a chemical bitterness filled his mouth; the light became scarlet as claret. . . . This—this was . . . not malaria. . . .

VI

... CARMEN KNEW WHAT IT WAS; BUT THE BRAVE LITTLE WOMAN WAS NOT afraid of it. Many a time before she had met it face to face, in Havanese summers; she knew how to wrestle with it;—she had torn Feliu's life away from its yellow clutch, after one of those long struggles that strain even the strength of love. Now she feared mostly for Chita. She had ordered the girl under no circumstances to approach the cabin.

Julien felt that blankets had been heaped upon him—that some gentle hand was bathing his scorching face with vinegar and water. Vaguely also there came to him the idea that it was night. He saw the shadow-shape of a woman moving against the red light upon the wall; —he saw there was a lamp burning.

Then the delirium seized him: he moaned, sobbed, cried like a child —talked wildly at intervals in French, in English, in Spanish.

"*Mentira!*—you could not be her mother.... Still, if you were—And she must not come in here—*jamas!* ... Carmen, did you know Adèle —Adèle Florane? So like her—so like—God only knows how like! ... Perhaps I think I know;—but I do not—do not know justly, fully— how like! ... *Si! si!—es el vómito!—yo lo conozco, Carmen!* ... She must not die twice.... I died twice.... I am going to die again. She only once. Till the heavens be no more she will not rise.... *Moi, au contraire, il faut que je me lève toujours!* They need me so much;— the slate is always full; the bell will never stop. They will ring that bell for men when I am dead.... So will I rise again!—*resurgam!* ... How could I save him?—could not save myself. It was a bad case—at seventy years! ... There! *Qui ça?*" ...

He saw Laroussel again—reaching out a hand to him through a whirl of red smoke. He tried to grasp it, and could not.... "*N'importe, mon ami*," said Laroussel—"*tu vas la voir bientôt.*" Who was he to see soon?—"*qui donc*, Laroussel?" But Laroussel did not answer. Through the red mist he seemed to smile;—then passed.

For some hours Carmen had trusted she could save her patient— desperate as the case appeared to be. His was one of those rapid and violent attacks, such as often despatch their victims in a single day. In the Cuban hospitals she had seen many and many terrible examples: strong young men—soldiers fresh from Spain—carried panting to the fever wards at sunrise; carried to the cemeteries at sunset. Even troopers riddled with revolutionary bullets had lingered longer. . . . Still, she had believed she might save Julien's life: the burning forehead once began to bead, the burning hands grew moist.

But now the wind was moaning;—the air had become lighter, thinner, cooler. A storm was gathering in the east; and to the fever-stricken man the change meant death. . . . Impossible to bring the priest of the Caminada now; and there was no other within a day's sail. She could only pray; she had lost all hope in her own power to save.

Still the sick man raved; but he talked to himself at longer intervals, and with longer pauses between his words;—his voice was growing more feeble, his speech more incoherent. His thought vacillated and distorted, like flame in a wind.

Weirdly the past became confounded with the present; impressions of sight and of sound interlinked in fantastic affinity—the face of Chita Viosca, the murmur of the rising storm. Then flickers of spectral lightning passed through his eyes, through his brain, with every throb of the burning arteries; then utter darkness came—a darkness that surged and moaned, as the circumfluence of a shadowed sea. And through and over the moaning pealed one multitudinous human cry, one hideous interblending of shoutings and shriekings. . . . A woman's hand was locked in his own. . . . "Tighter," he muttered, "tighter still, darling! hold as long as you can!" It was the tenth night of August, eighteen hundred and fifty-six. . . .

"*Chéri!*"

Again the mysterious whisper startled him to consciousness—the dim knowledge of a room filled with ruby-colored light—and the sharp odor of vinegar. The house swung round slowly;—the crimson flame of the lamp lengthened and broadened by turns;—then everything turned dizzily fast—whirled as if spinning in a vortex. . . . Nausea unutterable; and a frightful anguish as of teeth devouring him within—tearing more and more furiously at his breast. Then one atrocious wrenching, rending, burning—and the gush of blood burst from lips and nostrils in a smothering deluge. Again the vision of lightnings, the swaying, and the darkness of long ago. "Quick!— quick!—hold fast to the table, Adèle!—never let go!" . . .

. . . Up—up—up!—what! higher yet? Up to the red sky! Red— black-red . . . heated iron when its vermilion dies. So, too, the frightful flood! And noiseless. Noiseless because heavy, clammy—thick, warm, sickening . . . blood? Well might the land quake for the weight of

such a tide! . . . Why did Adèle speak Spanish? Who prayed for
him? . . .

"Alma de Cristo santísima santifícame!
"Sangre de Cristo, embriágame!
"O buen Jesus, oye me!" . . .

Out of the darkness into—such a light! An azure haze! Ah!—the
delicious frost! . . . All the streets were filled with the sweet blue
mist. . . . Voiceless the City and white;—crooked and weed-grown its
narrow ways! . . . Old streets of tombs, these. . . . Eh! how odd a custom!—a night-bell at every door. Yes, of course!—a *night*-bell!—the
Dead are Physicians of Souls: they may be summoned only by night
—called up from the darkness and silence. . . . Yet *she?*—might he not
dare to ring for her even by day? . . . Strange he had deemed it day!—
why, it was black, starless. . . . And it was growing queerly cold. . . .
How should he ever find her now? It was so black . . . so cold! . . .

"Chéri!"
All the dwelling quivered with the mighty whisper.
Outside, the great oaks were trembling to their roots;—all the shore
shook and blanched before the calling of the sea.
And Carmen, kneeling at the feet of the dead, cried out, alone in the
night:
"O Jesus misericordioso!—tened compasion de él!"

American Sketches

CINCINNATI

────────── ❧ ✳ ❧ ──────────

Gibbeted

THE EXECUTION OF JAMES MURPHY, YESTERDAY AFTERNOON, AT DAYTON, FOR the murder of Colonel William Dawson, in that city, on the night of August 31, 1875, was an event, it must be said, which the people of Montgomery County had long looked forward to with no small degree of satisfaction. The murder was of itself peculiarly atrocious, from the fact that it was actually committed without a shadow of provocation. The victim was a worthy and popular citizen, and the feeling of the public in regard to the crime was sufficiently evinced in the fact that the city authorities, subsequent to the arrest of Murphy, were obliged to call out the militia that the claim of legal justice to deal with the criminal might be protected. Colonel Dawson, it may be remembered, was murdered apparently for no other reason than that he refused a drunken party permission to intrude upon the quiet enjoyments of a private wedding party. The Colonel was Superintendent of the Champion Plow Works, at Dayton, and the bridegroom being an employee of the company, the Colonel had, by request, assumed the management of the wedding ball. When Murphy was refused admittance, he induced one of his companions, Lewis Meyers, to entice the Colonel out of doors on the pretext of getting a drink; and soon after the invitation had been accepted, Murphy struck Dawson, and during the subsequent scuffle, suddenly plunged a long knife up to the hilt in the Colonel's left side. The victim of this cowardly assault lived but a few moments afterward, and died without being able to positively identify his assassin.

Circumstantial evidence, notwithstanding, clearly pointed to Murphy as the criminal, and to Meyers as his accomplice; the former being sentenced to death, and the latter, being convicted of manslaughter, to a term of two years in the State Penitentiary. Sentence was passed on the 28th of April, the jury having disagreed upon the first trial, in February, which necessitated a second.

The youth of the prisoner—he was only nineteen years of age—did not, strange as it may seem, excite any marked degree of sympathy for his miserable fate. He was a fair skinned, brown haired, beardless lad, with rather large features, a firm, vicious mouth; sullen, steady gray eyes, shadowed by a habitual frown; a rather bold forehead, half concealed by a mass of curly locks, brushed down,—a face, in short, that, notwithstanding its viciousness, was not devoid of a certain coarse regularity. His parents were hard-working Irish people, but his own features showed little evidence of Celtic blood.

Perhaps the dogged obstinacy of the prisoner in denying, almost to the last, his evident crime, had no little to do with the state of public feeling in regard to him. Moreover, he had long been notorious in the city as a worthless loafer and precocious ruffian, perpetually figuring in some street fight, drunken brawl or brutal act of violence. For a considerable period of time, previous to the murder of Colonel Dawson, he had been the boasted leader of a band of young roughs, from nineteen to twenty years of age, who were known in Dayton as the "chain-gang."

The boy's mother had died while he was yet young; but he did not lack a home, and the affection of an old father, and of brothers and sisters—the latter of whom he is said to have cruelly abused in fits of drunken passion. In this connection it would of course be in order, religiously, to discourse upon the results of neglecting early admonitions; and philosophically, upon the evidence that the unfortunate lad had inherited an evil disposition, whereof the tendencies were not to be counteracted by any number of admonitions. But the facts in the case, as they appeared to the writer, were simply that a poor, ignorant, passionate boy, with a fair, coarse face, had in the heat of drunken anger taken away the life of a fellow-being, and paid the penalty of his brief crime, by a hundred days of mental torture, and a hideous death.

Perhaps there are many readers of this article, who may have perused and shuddered at the famous tale of the "Iron Shroud." You may remember that the victim, immured in the walls of a dungeon, lighted by seven windows, finds that each successive day of his imprisonment, one of the windows disappears forever. There are first seven, then six, then five, then four, then three, then two, then but one—dim and shadowy;—and then the night-black darkness that prefigures the formless gloom of the Shadow of Death. And through the thick darkness boom, hour after hour, the abysmal tones of a giant bell, announcing to the victim the incessant approach of the fearful midnight when the walls shall crush his bones to shapelessness. No one ever read that tale of the Castle of Tolfi without experiencing such horrors as make the flesh creep. Yet the agony therein depicted by a cunning writer is, after all, but a very slight exaggeration of the torture to which condemned criminals are periodically subjected in our prisons— not for seven days, forsooth, but for one hundred. This is the mercy of the law!—to compel the wretched victim to await the slow but inevitable approach of the grimmest and most ignominious of deaths for one hundred days. Fancy the ghastly mental computation of time which he must make to his own heart—"ninety-nine—ninety-eight— ninety-seven—ninety-six—ninety-five," until at last the allotment of life is reduced to a miserable seven days, as frightfully speedy as those of the Man in the Iron Shroud. And then the black scaffold with the blacker mystery below the drop, the sea of curious and unsympathetic faces, the moment of supreme suspense after his eyes are veiled from the light of the world by the sable hood. But this pyramid of agony is not absolutely complete until apexed by the vision of a fragile rope, the sudden hush of horror, and the bitterest period of agony twice endured. It is cruel folly to assert that because the criminal be ignorant, uneducated, phlegmatic, unimaginative, he is incapable of acutely feeling the torture of hideous suspense. That was asserted, nevertheless, and frequently asserted yesterday, by spectators of the execution. We did not think so. The victim was young and strong, a warm-blooded, passionate boy, with just that coarse animal vitality which makes men cling most strongly to life, as a thing to be enjoyed in the mere fact of possession—the mere ability to hear, see, feel.

The incidents of the prisoner's jail life during the last week—how he ate, drank, smoked, talked—might be very fully dwelt on as matters of strictly local interest, but may be briefly dismissed in these columns. There is, however, one story connected with that jail-life too strange and peculiar to be omitted. It seems that young Murphy learned to entertain a special affection for Tom Hellriggle, a Deputy Sheriff of Montgomery County, who had attended him kindly since his removal from the jail-room to a cell on the third floor, which opened in the rear of the scaffold. One night recently, Murphy said to Hellriggle, confidentially: "I knew I was going to be hanged, long ago. Do you know that I knew it before I was sentenced?"

"Why, how did you know that?" curiously asked the deputy.

Then the lad told him that during the intervals of the trials, one night between 12 and 1 o'clock, he heard the voice of a woman crying weirdly and wildly in the darkness, and so loudly that the sound filled all the jail-room, and that many of the men awoke and shuddered.

"You remember that, don't you?" asked the lad.

"I do," said the deputy; "and I also remember that there was no living woman in the jail-room that night."

"So," continued the boy, "they asked me if I heard it, and I said yes; but I pretended I did not know what it was. I believe I said no human being could cry so fearfully as that. But I did know what it was, Tom —*I saw the woman.*"

"Who was it?" asked Tom, earnestly.

"It was my mother. And I knew why she cried so strangely. She was crying for me."

There are few men who enter the condemned cell and leave it for the gallows without having entertained during the interval a strong desire to take their own lives, and are for the most part deterred from so doing rather by the religious dread of a dim and vague Something after death, than by any physical fear. So it appears to have been with Murphy. When all hope, except the hope of pardon from the All-forgiving Father, was dead within him, and the Governor of Ohio had refused to grant a reprieve or commutation of sentence, then the prisoner listened much more calmly to the admonitions of Father

Murphy, a fat, kindly, red-cheeked Irish priest, who took a heartfelt interest in the "spiritual welfare" of his namesake. He soon expressed repentance for his crime, and even agreed to confess all publicly—an act, all the circumstances properly considered, which really evinced more manhood than the act of "dying game" with the secret.

Shortly afterward he handed to Deputy Sheriff Hellriggle a small, keen knife, which he had managed to conceal, despite all the vigilance of his guards. "I would not take my own life, now," he said, "though I were to be hung twice over." Yet at the time the poor fellow probably had little idea that he would actually suffer the penalty of the law twice. It was evident, however, that he had frequently premeditated suicide, as in a further conversation with his guard he pointed out certain ingenious and novel modes of self-destruction which he had planned. That the criminal possessed no ordinary amount of nerve and self-control under the most trying circumstances, can not for a moment be questioned; nor can it be truthfully averred that his courage was merely the result of stolid phlegm and natural insensibility. None of the family, indeed, appear to inherit oversensitive organizations, as a glance at the faces of visitors to the condemned cell sufficiently satisfied us. When James' eldest brother, a ruddily-featured young man of twenty, visited the prisoner day before yesterday, he mounted the black scaffold erected outside the cell-door, and after a few humorous remarks, actually executed a double-shuffle dance upon the trap-door, until Sheriff Patton, hearing the noise, at once turned him out of the corridor. But James' actions in jail, his last farewell to his relations, his sensitiveness in regard to certain reports afloat concerning his past career and lastly, the very fact that his nerve did finally yield under a fearful and wholly unexpected pressure, all tend to show that his nature was by no means so brutally unfeeling as had been alleged.

The scaffold had been erected at the rear end of the central corridor of the jail hospital ward in the third story of the building, immediately without the cell-room in which the prisoner had been confined subsequent to his removal from the gloomier jail-room below, where he had heard the loud knocking of the carpenters' hammers, and the hum of saws—sounds of which the grim significance was fully recognized by him without verbal interpretation. "Ah, they are putting up the gallows!" he said. "The noise don't frighten me much, though." To the reporter who visited the long, white corridor by lamp-light, with the tall, black-draped and ebon-armed apparition at its further end, these preparations for an execution under roof, instead of beneath the clear sky, and in the pure air, seemed somewhat strange and mysteriously horrible. It is scarcely necessary to describe the mechanism of the scaffold, further than to observe—that the trap-door was closed by curved bolts, the outer ends of which were inserted into or withdrawn from shallow sockets in the framework at either side of the door, by foot-pressure upon a lever, which connected with the inner ends of the bolts, and worked them like the handles of huge pincers. The rope did, however, attract considerable attention from all who examined it previous to the execution. It seemed no thicker than a strong clothes-line, though actually three eighths of an inch, and appeared wholly unequal to the task for which it had been expressly manufactured from unbleached hemp. Yet Sheriff Gerard, of Putnam County, who had officiated at five executions, and was considered an authority upon such matters, had had it well tested with a keg of nails and other heavy weights, and believed it sufficiently strong. A bucket of water was suspended to it for some twenty-four hours, in order to remove its slight elasticity. But the bucket turned slowly around at intervals, and, under the constant pressure and motion, it seems that the rope became worn and weakened at the point of its insertion into the cross-beam. The drop-length was regulated to three feet and a half.

The unfortunate boy's mental impressions, yesterday morning, must assuredly have consisted of a strange and confused vision of solemn images and mysterious events. From the opening door of his cell he could plainly perceive every mechanical detail of the black gibbet, with its dismal hangings of sable muslin. Sisters of Charity, in dark robes; solemn-faced priests, with snowy Roman collars; Sheriffs and Deputy Sheriffs of austere countenance, which appeared momentarily to become yet more severe; policemen in full dress whispering in knots along the white corridor, a score of newspaper correspondents and reporters scattered through the crowd, writing and questioning and occasionally stealing peeps at the prisoner through the open door; calm-visaged physicians consulting together over open watches, as though eager to feel the last pulsations of the dying heart; undertakers, professional, cool and sad, adorned with silver crosses, which stood in the corner of one hospital room—these and other figures thronged the scene of death and disgrace while without a bright sun and a clear sky appeared for the last time to the wandering eyes of the condemned. He had early in the morning gone through the necessary formal preparations of being shaved, bathing, and putting on the neat suit of black cloth for which he had been measured a few days before. He had slept soundly all night; after having listened to the merry music of the city band, playing before the snowy-columned Court-house, but his sleep was probably consequent upon physical and mental exhaustion from haunting fear, rather than a natural and healthy slumber. He had risen at 7 o'clock, made a full confession in the presence of the Sheriff, heard mass, listened to Father Murphy's admonitions, ate a light breakfast, and smoked several cigars. Father Murphy's admonitions, delivered in simple language, and a strong old-country brogue, seemed to us passive listeners somewhat peculiar, especially when he stated that the "flesh and blood of Jesus Christ, which not even the angels were worthy to eat," would give strength to the poor lad "to meet his God at half-past 1 o'clock." But if ever religious faith comforted the last moments of a young criminal, it did in this instance; and it was owing to the kindly but powerful efforts of the little priest that the youth made a full confession of his crime. This is the confession:

Montgomery County Jail,
Dayton, O., August 24, 1876.
To Warren Munger and Elihu Thompson, my Attorneys:
  I will now say to you, and the public in general, that ever since you became my attorneys, at all times until today, I have denied that I struck and killed William Dawson, for which crime I am now under sentence of death. This statement I have made you in the mistaken hope and belief that it might do me some good, and I therefore put the blame on another person—Charles Tredtin. Now that all hope is gone, I have to say that you have done all you could for me as my attorneys, and that I feel satisfied with your efforts in my behalf. I am willing now to make public all I know about the murder of Colonel William Dawson, and I desire to make the statement, for I am now about to die, and do not want to die with a lie upon my lips. I do not wish Tredtin to be pointed out as long as he lives as the person who stabbed Colonel Dawson; and I desire also that justice may be done Meyers, who is entirely innocent, and was not connected in any way with the killing of Dawson. The following are the facts:
  On the evening of the murder, Jim Allen, John Petty, George Petty, Charles Hooven and myself were at a dance on McClure street. From there I and Hooven and George Petty went down the street to Bar-

low's Hall, where there was a dance going on, but of which we did not know until we arrived there. We went in and went up to the bar, and had a drink of beer. About fifteen minutes after this, Gerdes and I started up to get into the ball-room, but before we started Kline, Petty and Tredtin had gone up. When we got within two or three steps of the top of the first stairway I met Brunner there on duty as door-keeper, and he asked me if I had a pass. I told him no, and then he said, "You'll have to go down stairs." I said, "All right." Then Dawson grabbed hold of me and said, "Get down, or I'll throw you down." I jerked away from him, laughed at him, and went down stairs. Then Gerdes and I went and saw the man who got married, and asked him if he couldn't let me up stairs. He said, "Yes, of course I can;" and I then went up with Gerdes and the man who got married, and he told Brunner to let me in. We went into the ball-room, where Kline, Tredtin and Petty were standing. Then Kline said, "Where's that big son of a bitch that was going to throw you down stairs?" and I said, "What do you want to know for?" He then said, "I want to know." Then I said, "There he is; whatever you want to say to him, say it." Then Kline said, "Oh, you big son of a bitch!" After about half an hour Petty and I went down stairs to the bar-room. Gerdes, Tredtin and Kline came down there, where I saw them, but whether they came together or not I don't know. Kline, Petty and I drank beer together. We all five then went back up stairs. Dawson and Meyers went down stairs, into the bar-room; then we five followed on down, and went out at the side door on the street. We then began talking about the occurrence on the stairway between Dawson and myself, and some one said, but I don't recollect who it was, "Damn him, we'll get him before morning." I don't recollect that there was anything more said. Meyers was not with us then on the street, or at all in any way connected with us or our party that evening. All five of us then went back together up stairs, where we saw Meyers and Dawson. We staid there some five or ten minutes, when we saw Meyers and Dawson go down stairs and then we five followed after them, and saw them go out of the side door on the street, and we followed them out. Kline said to me and Petty near the corner of the side street and Fifth street, "You go down this side of the street and we'll go down the other." Petty and I followed after Meyers and Dawson, some distance behind them, while Kline, Gerdes and Tredtin went across to the north side of the street, and went down west on that side of Fifth street. We saw Meyers and Dawson try to get in at the big gate at Weidner's, and then they turned and came east toward Petty and myself. We met them between Weidner's and Pearl street. When we came together Dawson sort of turned around, and I struck him with both fists in the breast; Petty struck Meyers, and Meyers caught hold of a post and prevented himself from falling into the gutter, and then straightened himself up and ran away eastward, and Petty started across the street as soon as Meyers ran. My strokes in Dawson's breast staggered him, and he didn't recover himself until after Meyers and Petty had left. About the time Dawson recovered himself, Kline and Tredtin ran in and struck Dawson too. My passions were now aroused. I drew my knife out of my inside breast coat pocket and stabbed Colonel Dawson. I did it on the instant, and took no second thought about it. I do not remember of hearing Dawson say anything before or after I cut him. He may have said something, but I did not hear him. The purpose of our party of five in following Meyers and Dawson out was to lick them both. I saw Gerdes about the middle of the street coming towards us, but he didn't get up to us. Which way Kline and Tredtin went I do not know. Dawson started east on Fifth street on a run. I was facing the east when I cut Dawson. After Dawson ran I was alone on the sidewalk, when Funk came up and struck at me with his club. I dodged him and struck at him with my knife, but don't know whether I cut his clothes or not. I then wheeled and started to run west. As I run he threw his club at me, and as I started to run across the street, I fell over the hitching-post in front of Weidner's, and there I dropped my cap and knife. Funk fired at me with a pistol, and shot at me just as I fell. I got up and started to run across the street, and Funk fired a second time at me as I was about to enter the alley on the north side of Fifth street. I stood in the alley awhile, and then I went home to my father's house, where I was afterward arrested by the police. Whiskey and bad company have been the ruination of me, and the cause of all my bad luck. I had drank a good deal that night of beer and whiskey.

This is a true and correct statement about the murder, and is all I wish to say about the matter.

JAMES MURPHY

He also dictated a letter of thanks to Sheriff Patton, his deputies, and all who had been kind to him during his confinement. Sheriff Patton himself paid for the prisoner's coffin, a very neat one.

At half-past 1 o'clock, Deputy Sheriff Freeman appeared at the door of the cell-room, which opened directly upon the ladder leading to the scaffold, and observed in a low, steady voice: "Time's up, Jim; the Sheriff wants you." The prisoner immediately responded, "All right; I am ready;" and walked steadily up the steps of the ladder, accompanied by Fathers Murphy and Carey. His arms had been pinioned at the elbows by a strong bandage of black calico. Probably he looked at that moment younger and handsomer than he had ever appeared before; and a hum of audible surprise at his appearance passed through the spectators. Accompanied by his confessor and Father Carey he walked steadily to the front of the platform; and after looking quietly and calmly upon the faces below, spoke in a deep, clear, bold voice, pausing between each sentence to receive some suggestion from the priest at his left side.

"Gentlemen, I told a lie in the Court-house by saying Tredtin was guilty.

"I think I am guilty"—with a determined nod of the head.

"I return thanks to Sheriff Patton, his deputies and all my friends.

"I forgive all my enemies and ask their forgiveness.

"If there is anyone here who has any hard feelings toward me, I ask their forgiveness.

"This is my last request.

"Gentlemen, I want all young men to take warning by me. Drink and bad company brought me here to-day.

"And I ask the forgiveness of Mrs. Dawson and her children, whom I injured in passion, when I did not know what I was doing.

"I believe Jesus Christ will save me."

Sheriff Patton then read in a quiet, steady voice, the death-warrant. It was heavily bordered in black, and bore a great sable seal. "It is my solemn duty," said the Sheriff, "to execute the sentence passed upon you by the Court:

"State of Ohio, Montgomery County—to Wilham Patton, Sheriff: Whereas, at the January Term, 1876, of the Court of Common Pleas, within and for the County of Montgomery and State of Ohio, to-wit, on the 28th day of April, 1876, upon a full and impartial trial, one James Murphy, now in your custody, was found guilty of deliberate and premeditated murder of one William Dawson, in manner and form as found in a true bill of indictment by the grand jury on the 30th day of October, 1875; and whereas the Court aforesaid, at the term aforesaid, to-wit, on the 12th day of May, 1876, upon conviction aforesaid, ordered, adjudged and sentenced the said James Murphy to

be imprisoned in the County jail until the 25th of August, 1876, and that on that day, between the hours of 10 A.M. and 4 P.M., he be taken from said jail, and hanged by the neck until he be dead, this is therefore to command that you keep the said James Murphy in safe and secure custody until said day, August 25, 1876; and that on said day, between said hours, you take said James Murphy, and in the place and manner provided by law, hang him by the neck until he be dead. Of this warrant, and all your proceedings thereon, you shall make due return forthwith thereafter.

"Witness: JOHN S. ROBERTSON, *Clerk of said Court.*

"And the seal thereof of the city of Dayton, in said County, this 20th day of June, 1876.

"(Seal Court of Common Pleas.)

"JOHN S. ROBERTSON, Clerk."

In the meantime Deputy Sheriff Freeman adjusted the thin noose about the prisoner's neck, and pinioned his lower limbs. "James Murphy, good-bye, and may God bless you!" observed Patton in a whisper, handing the black cap to a deputy. At this moment the representative of the *Commercial* succeeded in obtaining admittance to the little audience of physicians in rear of the scaffold; and took up his position immediately to the left of the trap-door. The next instant the Sheriff pressed the lever with his foot, the drop opened as though in electric response, the thin rope gave way at the crossbeam above, and the body of the prisoner fell downward and backward on the floor of the corridor, behind the scaffold screen. "My God, my God!" cried Freeman, with a subdued scream; "give me that other rope, quick." It had been laid away for use "in case the first rope should break," we were told.

The poor young criminal had fallen on his back, apparently unconscious, with the broken rope about his neck, and the black cap veiling his eyes. The reporter knelt beside him and felt his pulse. It was beating slowly and regularly. Probably the miserable boy thought then, if he could think at all, he was really dead—dead in darkness, for his eyes were veiled—dead and blind to this world, but about to open his eyes upon another. The awful hush immediately following his fall might have strengthened this dim idea. But then came gasps, and choked sobs from the spectators; the hurrying of feet, and the horrified voice of Deputy Freeman calling, "For God's sake, get me that other rope, quick!" Then a pitiful groan came from beneath the black cap.

"My God! Oh, my God!"

"Why, I ain't dead—I ain't dead!"

"Are you hurt, my child?" inquired Father Murphy.

"No, father, I'm not dead; I'm not hurt. What are they going to do with me?"

No one had the heart to tell him, lying there blind and helpless and ignorant even of what had occurred. The reporter, who still kept his hand on the boy's wrist, suddenly felt the pulsation quicken horribly, the rapid beating of intense fear; the youth's whole body trembled violently. "His pulse is one hundred and twenty," whispered the physician.

"What's the good of leaving me here in this misery?" cried the lad. "Take me out of this, I tell you."

In the meantime they had procured the other rope—a double thin rope with two nooses—and fastened it strongly over the crossbeam. The prisoner had fallen through the drop precisely at 1.44½ P.M.; the second noose was ready within four minutes later. Then the deputies descended from the platform and lifted the prostrate body up.

"Don't carry me," groaned the poor fellow, "I can walk—let me walk."

But they carried him up again, Father Murphy supporting his head. The unfortunate wanted to see the light once more, to get one little glimpse of the sun, the narrow world within the corridor, and the faces before the scaffold. They took off his ghastly mask while the noose was being readjusted. His face was livid, his limbs shook with terror, and he suddenly seized Deputy Freeman desperately by the coat, saying in a husky whisper, "What are you going to do with me?" They tried to unfasten his hand, but it was the clutch of death-fear. Then the little Irish priest whispered firmly in his ear, "Let go, my son; let go, like a man—be a man; die like a man." And he let go. But they had to support him at arm's length while the Sheriff pressed the trap-lever—six and one-half minutes after the first fall. It was humanely rapid work then.

The body fell heavily, with a jerk, turned about once, rocked backward and forward, and became almost still. From the corridor only the head was visible—turned from the audience. Father Murphy sprinkled holy water upon the victim. The jugular veins became enlarged, and the neck visibly swelled below the black cap. At this time the pulse was beating steadily at 100; the wrist felt hot and moist, and we noticed the hand below it tightly clutched a little brass crucifix, placed there by the priest at the last moment. Gradually the pulse became fainter. Five minutes later, Dr. Crum, the jail physician, holding the right wrist, announced it at eighty-four. In ten minutes from the moment of the drop it sunk to sixty. In sixteen minutes the heart only fluttered, and the pulse became imperceptible. In seventeen minutes Dr. Crum, after a stethoscopic examination, made the official announcement of death.

The body was at once cut down by Sheriff Patton, and deposited in the handsome coffin designed for it. Half an hour later we returned to the jail, and examined the dead face. It was perfectly still, as the face of a sleeper, calm and undisfigured. It was perhaps slightly swollen, but quite natural, and betrayed no evidence of pain. The rope had cut deeply into the flesh of the neck, and the very texture of the hemp was redly imprinted on the skin. A medical examination showed the neck to have been broken.

Levee Life

ALONG THE RIVER-BANKS ON EITHER SIDE OF THE LEVEE SLOPE, WHERE THE brown water year after year climbs up to the ruined sidewalks, and pours into the warehouse cellars, and paints their grimy walls with streaks of water-weed green, may be studied a most curious and interesting phase of life—the life of a community within a community, —a society of wanderers who have haunts but not homes, and who are only connected with the static society surrounding them by the common bond of State and municipal law. It is a very primitive kind of life; its lights and shadows are alike characterized by a half savage simplicity; its happiness or misery is almost purely animal; its pleasures are wholly of the hour, neither enhanced nor lessened by anticipations of the morrow. It is always pitiful rather than shocking; and

it is not without some little charm of its own—the charm of a thoughtless existence, whose virtues are all original, and whose vices are for
the most part foreign to it. A great portion of this levee-life haunts
also the subterranean hovels and ancient frame buildings of the district lying east of Broadway to Culvert street, between Sixth and
Seventh streets. But, on a cool spring evening, when the levee is bathed
in moonlight, and the torch-basket lights dance redly upon the water,
and the clear air vibrates to the sonorous music of the deep-toned
steam-whistle, and the sound of wild banjo-thrumming floats out
through the open doors of the levee dance-houses, then it is perhaps
that one can best observe the peculiarities of this grotesquely-pictur-
esque roustabout life.

Probably less than one-third of the stevedores and 'longshoremen
employed in our river traffic are white; but the calling now really belongs by right to the Negroes, who are by far the best roustabouts and
are unrivaled as firemen. The white stevedores are generally tramps,
willing to work only through fear of the workhouse; or, sometimes
laborers unable to obtain other employment, and glad to earn money
for the time being at any employment. On board the boats, the whites
and blacks mess separately and work under different mates, there
being on an average about twenty-five roustabouts to every boat which
unloads at the Cincinnati levee. Cotton boats running on the Lower
Mississippi will often carry sixty or seventy deck-hands, who can some
seasons earn from forty-five dollars to sixty dollars per month. On the
Ohio boats the average wages paid to roustabouts will not exceed $30
per month. 'Longshoremen earn fifteen and twenty cents per hour,
according to the season. These are frequently hired by Irish contractors,
who undertake to unload a boat at so much per package; but the first-
class boats generally contract with the 'longshoremen directly through
the mate, and sometimes pay twenty-five cents per hour for such labor.
"Before Freedom," as the colored folks say, white laborers performed
most of the roustabout labor on the steamboats; the Negroes are now
gradually monopolizing the calling, chiefly by reason of their peculiar
fitness for it. Generally speaking, they are the best porters in the world;
and in the cotton States, it is not uncommon, we are told, to see Negro
levee hands for a wager, carry five-hundred-pound cotton-bales on
their backs to the wharf-boat. River men, to-day, are recognizing the
superior value of Negro labor in steamboat traffic, and the colored
roustabouts are now better treated, probably, than they have been since
the war. Under the present laws, too, they are better protected. It used

at one time to be a common thing for some ruffianly mate to ship sixty or seventy stevedores, and, after the boat had taken in all her freight, to hand the poor fellows their money and land them at some small town, or even in the woods, hundreds of miles from their home. This can be done no longer with legal impunity.

Roustabout life in the truest sense is, then, the life of the colored population of the Rows, and, partly, of Bucktown—blacks and mulattoes from all parts of the States, but chiefly from Kentucky and Eastern Virginia, where most of them appear to have toiled on the plantations before Freedom; and echoes of the old plantation life still live in their songs and their pastimes. You may hear old Kentucky slave songs chanted nightly on the steamboats, in that wild, half-melancholy key peculiar to the natural music of the African race; and you may see the old slave dances nightly performed to the air of some ancient Virginia-reel in the dance-houses of Sausage Row, or the "ball-rooms" of Bucktown. There is an intense uniqueness about all this pariah existence; its boundaries are most definitely fixed; its enjoyments are wholly sensual, and many of them are marked by peculiarities of a strictly local character. Many of their songs, which have never appeared in print, treat of levee life in Cincinnati, of all the popular steamboats running on the "Muddy Water," and of the favorite roustabout haunts on the river bank and in Bucktown. To collect these curious songs, or even all the most popular of them, would be a labor of months, and even then a difficult one, for the colored roustabouts are in the highest degree suspicious of a man who approaches them with a note-book and pencil. Occasionally, however, one can induce an intelligent steamboatman to sing a few river songs by an innocent bribe in the shape of a cigar or a drink. and this we attempted to do with considerable success during a few spare evenings last week, first, in a popular roustabout haunt on Broadway, near Sixth, and afterward in a dingy frame cottage near the corner of Sixth and Culvert streets. Unfortunately some of the most curious of these songs are not of a character to admit of publication in the columns of a daily newspaper; but others which we can present to our readers may prove interesting. Of these the following song, *Number Ninety-Nine,* was at one time immensely popular with the steamboatmen. The original resort referred to was situated on Sixth and Culvert street, where Kirk's building now stands. We present the song with some necessary emendations:

You may talk about yer railroads,
Yer steamboats and can-el
If 't hadn't been for Liza Jane
There wouldn't bin no hell.
  Chorus—Oh, ain't I gone, gone, gone,
      Oh, ain't I gone, gone, gone,
      Oh, ain't I gone, gone, gone,
          Way down de ribber road.

Whar do you get yer whisky?
Whar do you get yer rum?
I got it down in Bucktown,
  At Number Ninety-nine.
  Chorus—Oh, ain't I gone, gone, gone, etc.

I went down to Bucktown,
  Nebber was dar before,
Great big niggah knocked me down,
  But Katy barred the door.
  Chorus—Oh, ain't I gone, gone, gone, etc.

She hugged me, she kissed me,
  She told me not to cry;
She said I wus de sweetest thing
  Dat ebber libbed or died.
  Chorus—Oh, ain't I gone, gone, gone, etc.

· · ·

Yonder goes the Wildwood,
  She's loaded to the guards,
But yonder comes the Fleetwood,
  An' she's the boat for me.
  Chorus—Oh, ain't I gone, gone, gone, etc.

The words, "'Way down to Rockingham," are sometimes substituted in the chorus, for "'way down de ribber road."

One of the most popular roustabout songs now sung on the Ohio is the following. The air is low, and melancholy, and when sung in unison by the colored crew of a vessel leaving or approaching port, has a strange, sad sweetness about it which is very pleasing. The two-fold character of poor Molly, at once good and bad, is somewhat typical of the stevedore's sweetheart:

> *Molly was a good gal and a bad gal, too.*
> > *Oh Molly, row, gal.*
> *Molly was a good gal and a bad gal, too,*
> > *Oh Molly, row, gal.*

> *I'll row dis boat and I'll row no more,*
> > *Row, Molly, row, gal.*
> *I'll row dis boat, and I'll go on shore,*
> > *Row, Molly, row, gal.*

> *Captain on the biler deck a-heaving of the lead,*
> > *Oh Molly, row, gal.*
> *Calling to the pilot to give her, "Turn ahead,"*
> > *Row, Molly, row, gal.*

Here is another to a slow and sweet air. The chorus, when well sung, is extremely pretty:

> *Shawneetown is burnin' down,*
> > *Who tole you so?*
> *Shawneetown is burnin' down,*
> > *Who tole you so?*

> *Cythie, my darlin' gal,*
> > *Who tole you so?*
> *Cythie, my darlin' gal,*
> > *How do you know?*

Chorus—*Shawneetown is burnin', etc.*

> *How the h—l d'ye 'spect me to hold her,*
> > *Way down below?*
> *I've got no skin on either shoulder,*
> > *Who tole you so?*

Chorus—*Shawneetown is burnin', etc.*

De houses dey is all on fire,
   Way down below.
De houses dey is all on fire,
   Who tole you so?

Chorus—Shawneetown is burnin', etc.

My old missus tole me so,
   Way down below.
An' I b'lieve what ole missus says,
   Way down below.

Chorus—Shawneetown is burnin', etc.

The most melancholy of all these plaintive airs is that to which the song "Let her go by" is commonly sung. It is generally sung on leaving port, and sometimes with an affecting pathos inspired of the hour, while the sweethearts of the singers watch the vessel gliding down stream.

I'm going away to New Orleans!
Good-by, my lover, good-by!
I'm going away to New Orleans!
Good-by, my lover, good-by!
   Oh, let her go by!

She's on her way to New Orleans!
Good-by, my lover, good-by!
She bound to pass the Robert E. Lee,
Good-by, my lover, good-by!
   Oh, let her go by!

I'll make dis trip and I'll make no more!
Good-by, my lover, good-by!
I'll roll dese barrels, I'll roll no more!
Good-by, my lover, good-by!
   Oh, let her go by!

An' if you are not true to me,
Farewell, my lover, farewell!

An' if you are not true to me,
Farewell, my lover, farewell!
Oh, let her go by!

The next we give is of a somewhat livelier description. It has, we
believe, been printed in a somewhat different form in certain song
books. We give it as it was sung to us in a Broadway saloon:

I come down the mountain,
An' she come down the lane,
An' all that I could say to her
Was, "Good-by, 'Liza Jane."

Chorus—Farewell, 'Liza Jane!
Farewell, 'Liza Jane!
Don't throw yourself away, for I
Am coming back again.

I got up on a house-top,
An' give my horn a blow;
Thought I heerd Miss Dinah say,
"Yonder comes your beau."
[Chorus.]

Ef I'd a few more boards,
To build my chimney higher,
I'd keep aroun' the country gals,
Chunkin' up the fire.
[Chorus.]

The following are fragments of rather lengthy chants, the words
being almost similar in both, but the choruses and airs being very
different. The air of the first is sonorous and regularly slow, like a
sailor's chant when heaving anchor, the air of the next is quick and
lively.

Belle-a-Lee's got no time,
Oh, Belle! oh, Belle!
Robert E. Lee's got railroad time,
Oh, Belle! oh, Belle!

Wish I was in Mobile Bay,
  Oh, Belle! oh, Belle!
Rollin' cotton by de day,
  Oh, Belle! oh, Belle!

        .   .   .

I wish I was in Mobile Bay,
Rollin' cotton by de day,
    Stow'n' sugar in de hull below,
      Below, belo-ow,
    Stow'n' sugar in de hull below!

De Natchez is a new boat; she's just in her prime,
Beats any oder boat on de New Orleans line.
    Stow'n' sugar in de hull below, &c.

Engineer, t'rough de trumpet, gives de firemen news,
Couldn' make steam for de fire in de flues.
    Stow'n' sugar in de hull below, &c.

Cap'n on de biler deck, a scratchin' of his head,
Hollers to de deck hand to heave de larbo'rd lead.
    Stow'n' sugar in de hull below, &c.

        .   .   .

Perhaps the prettiest of all these songs is *The Wandering Steam-boatman.* Which, like many other roustabout songs, rather frankly illustrates the somewhat loose morality of the calling:

      I am a wandering steamboatman,
        And far away from home;
      I fell in love with a pretty gal,
        And she in love with me.

      She took me to her parlor
        And cooled me with her fan;
      She whispered in her mother's ear:
        "I love the steamboatman."

John Morgan come to Danville and cut a mighty dash,
Las' time I saw him, he was under whip an' lash,
'Long come a rebel at a sweepin' pace,
Whar 're ye goin', Mr. Rebel? "I'm goin' to Camp Chase."
                    Limber Jim, etc.

Way beyond de sun and de moon,
White gal tole me I were too soon.
White gal tole me I come to soon,
An' nigger gal called me an ole d—d fool.
                    Limber Jim, etc.

Eighteen pennies hidden in a fence,
Cynthiana gals ain't got no sense;
Every time they go from home
Comb thar heads wid an ole jaw bone.
                    Limber Jim, etc.

Had a little wife an' didn' inten' to keep her;
Showed her a flatboat an' sent her down de ribber;
Head like a fodder-shock, mouf like a shovel,
Put yerself wid yaller gal, put yerself in troubble.
                    Limber Jim, etc.

I went down to Dinah's house, Dinah was in bed,
Hoisted de window an' poked out her head;
T'rowed, an' I hit in her de eyeball,—bim;
"Walk back, Mr. Nigger; don't do dat again."
                    Limber Jim, etc.

Gambling man in de railroad line,
Saved my ace an' played my nine;
If you want to know my name,
My name's High-low-jack-in-the-game.
                    Limber Jim,
                        Shiloh!
                    Talk it again,
                        Shiloh!
                    You dancing girl,
                        Shiloh!

Sure's you're born,
   Shiloh!

Grease my heel with butter in the fat,
I can talk to Limber Jim better'n dat.
   Limber Jim,
      Shiloh!
   Limber Jim,
      Shiloh!
   Walk back in love,
      Shiloh!
   My turtle dove,
      Shiloh!

[Patting Juba]—And you can't go yonder,
      Limber Jim!
   And you can't go yonder,
      Limber Jim!
   And you can't go-oo-o!

One fact worth mentioning about these Negro singers is, that they can mimic the Irish accent to a degree of perfection which an American, Englishman or German could not hope to acquire. At the request of Patrolman Tighe and his partner, the same evening that we interviewed Limber Jim, a very dark mulatto, named Jim Delaney, sang for us in capital style that famous Irish ditty known as "The hat me fahther wor-re." Yet Jim, notwithstanding his name, has little or no Irish blood in his veins; nor has his companion, Jim Harris, who joined in the rollicking chorus:

'Tis the raylics of ould dacency,
The hat me fahther wor-r-re.

Jim Delaney would certainly make a reputation for Irish specialties in a minstrel troupe; his mimicry of Irish character is absolutely perfect, and he possesses a voice of great flexibility, depth and volume. He "runs" on the river.

On the southeast corner of Culvert and Sixth streets, opposite to the house in which we were thus entertained by Limber Jim and his friends, stands Kirk's building, now occupied jointly by Kirk and

Ryan. Two stories beneath this building is now the most popular dance-house of the colored steamboatmen and their "girls." The building and lot belong to Kirk; but Ryan holds a lease on the basement and half of the upper building. Recently the landlord and the lease-holder had a falling out, and are at bitter enmity; but Ryan seems to have the upper hand in the matter, and is making considerable money from the roustabouts. He has closed up the old side entrance, admission to the ballroom being now obtainable only through the bar-room, and the payment of ten cents. A special policeman has been wisely hired by the proprietor to preserve order below, and the establishment is, generally speaking, well conducted for an establishment of the kind. The amount of patronage it receives depends almost wholly upon the condition of the river traffic; during the greater part of the week the attendance is somewhat slim, but when the New Orleans boats come in the place is crowded to overflowing. Beside the admittance fee of ten cents, an additional dime is charged to all the men for every set danced—the said dime to be expended in "treating partners." When the times are hard and money scarce, the girls often pay the fees for their men in order to make up sets.

With its unplastered and windowless limestone walls; sanded floor; ruined ceiling, half plank, half cracked plaster; a dingy black counter in one corner, and rude benches ranged along the walls, this dancing-room presented rather an outlandish aspect when we visited it. At the corner of the room opposite "the bar," a long bench was placed, with its face to the wall; and upon the back of this bench, with their feet inwardly reclining upon the seat, sat the musicians. A well-dressed, neatly-built mulatto picked the banjo, and a somewhat lighter colored musician led the music with a fiddle, which he played remarkably well and with great spirit. A short, stout Negress, illy dressed, with a rather good-natured face and a bed shawl tied about her head, played the bass viol, and that with no inexperienced hand. This woman is known to the police as Anna Nun.

The dancers were in sooth a motley crew: the neat dresses of the girls strongly contrasting with the rags of the poorer roustabouts, some of whom were clad only in shirt, pants and shocking hats. Several wickedly handsome women were smoking stogies. Bill Williams, a good-natured black giant, who keeps a Bucktown saloon, acted for a while as Master of Ceremonies. George Moore, the colored Democrat who killed, last election day, the leader of a party who attacked his house, figured to advantage in the dance, possessing wonderful activity in spite of his heavy bulk. The best performer on the floor was a stumpy little roustabout named Jem Scott, who is a marvelous jig-dancer, and can waltz with a tumbler full of water on his head without spilling a drop. One-fourth of the women present were white, including two girls only about seventeen years old, but bearing physiognomical evidence of precocious vice. The best-looking girl in the room was a tall, lithe quadroon named Mary Brown, with auburn hair, gray eyes, a very fair skin, and an air of quiet innocence wholly at variance with her reputation. A short, supple mulatto girl, with a blue ribbon in her hair, who attracted considerable admiration, and was famous for dancing "breakdowns," had but recently served a term in the penitentiary for grand larceny. Another woman present, a gigantic Negress, wearing a red plaid shawl, and remarkable for an immense head of frizzly hair, was, we were informed, one of the most adroit thieves known to the police. It was a favorite trick of hers to pick a pocket while dancing, and hide the stolen money in her hair.

"How many of those present do you suppose carry knives?" we asked Patrolman Tighe.

"All of them," was the reply. "All the men, and women, too, carry knives or razors; and many of them pistols as well. But they seldom quarrel, except about a girl. Their great vice is thieving; and the fights down here are generally brought about by white roughs who have no business in this part of town except crime."

The musicians struck up that weird, wild, lively air, known perhaps to many of our readers as the "Devil's Dream," and in which "the musical ghost of a cat chasing the spectral ghost of a rat" is represented by a succession of "miauls" and "squeaks" on the fiddle. The dancers danced a double quadrille, at first, silently and rapidly; but warming with the wild spirit of the music, leaped and shouted, swinging each other off the floor, and keeping time with a precision which shook the building in time to the music. The women, we noticed, almost invariably embraced the men about the neck in swinging, the men clasping them about the waist. Sometimes the men advancing leaped and crossed legs with a double shuffle, and with almost sightless rapidity. Then the music changed to an old Virginia reel, and the dancing changing likewise, presented the most grotesque spectacle imaginable. The dancing became wild; men patted juba and shouted, the Negro women danced with the most fantastic grace, their bodies describing almost incredible curves forward and backward; limbs intertwined rapidly in a wrestle with each other and with the music; the room presented a tide of swaying bodies and tossing arms, and flying hair. The white female dancers seemed heavy, cumbersome, ungainly by contrast with their dark companions; the spirit of the music was not upon them; they were abnormal to the life about them. Once more the music changed—to some popular Negro air, with the chorus—

> *Don't get weary,*
> *I'm goin' home.*

The musicians began to sing; the dancers joined in; and the dance terminated with a roar of song, stamping of feet, "patting juba," shouting, laughing, reeling. Even the curious spectators involuntarily kept time with their feet; it was the very drunkenness of music, the intoxication of the dance. Amid such scenes does the roustabout find his heaven; and this heaven is certainly not to be despised.

The great dancing resort for steamboatmen used to be Pickett's, on Sausage Row; but year after year the river came up and flooded all the grimy saloons on the Rows, and, departing, left behind it alluvial deposits of yellow mud, and the Spirit of Rheumatic Dampness. So, about two months ago, Pickett rented out his old quarters, partly as a barber-shop, partly as a shooting-gallery, and moved into the building, No. 91 Front street, between Ludlow and Lawrence. He has had the whole building renovated throughout, and painted the front very handsomely. The basement on the river side is now used for a dancing-room; but the room is very small, and will not accommodate half of the dancers who used to congregate in the old building. The upper part of the building the old man rents out to river men and their wives or mistresses, using the second floor for a restaurant and dining rooms, which are very neatly fitted up. Whatever may have been the old man's sins, Pickett has a heart full of unselfish charity sufficient to cover them all. Year after year, through good or ill-fortune, he has daily fed and maintained fifty or sixty homeless and needy steamboatmen. Sometimes when the river trade "looks up," and all the boats are running on full time, some grateful levee hand repays his benefactor, but it is very seldom. And the old man never asks for it or expects it; he only says: "Boys, when you want to spend your money, spend it here." Although now very old, and almost helpless from a rupture, Pickett has yet but to rap on the counter of his saloon to enforce instantaneous quiet. The roustabouts will miss the old man when he is gone—the warm corner to sleep in, the simple but plentiful meal when out of a berth, and the rough kindness of his customary answer to a worthless, hungry, and shivering applicant for food and lodging. "G—d d—n you, you don't deserve it; but come in and behave yourself." The day is not far off when there will be great mourning along the levee.

With the exception of Ryan's dance-house, and one or two Bucktown lodging-houses, the roustabouts generally haunt the Rows, principally Sausage Row, from Broadway to Ludlow street. Rat Row, from Walnut to Main, is more especially the home of the white tramps and roustabouts. Here is situated the celebrated "Blazing Stump," otherwise called St. James Restaurant, which is kept by a Hollander, named Venneman. Venneman accommodates only white men, and endeavors to keep an orderly house; but the "Blazing Stump" must always remain a resort for thieves, burglars, and criminals of every description. The "Stump" is No. 13 Rat Row. No. 16 is a lodging house for colored roustabouts, kept by James Madison. No. 12 is a policy shop; although it pretends to be a saloon; and the business is so cunningly conducted that the police cannot, without special privilege, succeed in closing up the business. No. 10, which used to be known as Buckner's, is another haunt for colored roustabouts. They have a pet crow attached to the establishment, which is very plucky, and can whip all the cats and dogs in the neighborhood. It waddles about on the sidewalk of sunny days, pecking fiercely at any stranger who meddles with it, but the moment it sees the patrolmen coming along the levee it runs into the house.

No. 7—Goodman's clothing store—is said to be a "fence." At the west end of the row is Captain Dilg's celebrated hostelry, a popular and hospitable house, frequented by pilots and the most respectable class of river men. At the eastern terminus of the row is the well known Alhambra saloon, a great resort for colored steamboatmen, where large profits are realized on cigars and whisky of the cheapest kind. The contractors who hire roustabouts frequently have a private understanding with the proprietor of some levee coffee-house or saloon, and always go there to pay off their hands. Then the first one treats, then another, and so on until all the money just made by a day's heavy labor is lying in the counter drawer, and the roustabouts are helplessly boozy.

Of the two rows Sausage Row is perhaps the most famous. No. 1 is kept by old Barney Hodke, who has made quite a reputation by keeping a perfectly orderly house in a very disorderly neighborhood. No. 2

is Cottonbrook's clothing store, *alias* the "American Clothing Store," whereof the proprietor is said to have made a fortune by selling cheap clothing to the Negro stevedores. No. 3 is Mrs. Sweeney's saloon and boarding house, an orderly establishment for the entertainment of river men. No. 4 is an eating- and lodging-house for roustabouts, kept by Frank Fortner, a white man. No. 6 is a barber-shop for colored folks, with a clothing-store next to it. No. 7 is a house of ill-fame, kept by a white woman, Mary Pearl, who boards several unfortunate white girls. This is a great resort for colored men.

No. 8 is Maggie Sperlock's. Maggie has another saloon in Bucktown. She is a very fat and kind-hearted old mulatto woman, who is bringing up half a dozen illegitimate children, abandoned by their parents. One of these, a very pretty boy, is said to be the son of a white lady, who moves in good society, by a colored man.

No. 9 is now Chris. Meyer's; it was known as "Schwabe Kate's" when Meyer's wife lived. This is the great resort for German tramps.

Next in order come a barber-shop and shooting-gallery—"Long Branch" and "Saratoga." These used to be occupied by Pickett.

A few doors east of this is Chas. Redman's saloon, kept by a crippled soldier. This is another great roustabout haunt, where robberies are occasionally committed. And a little further east is Pickett's new hotel. On these two Rows Officers Brazil and Knox have made no less than two hundred and fifty-six arrests during the past two years. The most troublesome element is, of course, among the white tramps.

A number of the colored men are adroit thieves; these will work two or three months and then "lay off" until all their money has found its way to whisky-shops and brothels. The little clothing and shoe stores along the levee are almost daily robbed of some articles by such fellows, who excel in ingenious confidence dodges. A levee hand with extinct cigar will, for example, walk into a shoe shop with a "Say, bohss, giv a fellah a light." While the "bohss" is giving a light to the visitor, who always takes care to stand between the proprietor and the doorway, a confederate sneaks off with a pair of shoes. A fellow called "China Robinson," who hangs about Madison's, is said to be famous at such tricks. The police officers, however, will not allow any known sluggard or thief to loaf about the levee for more than thirty days without employment. There is always something to do for those who wish to do it, and roustabouts who persist in idleness and dirt, after one or two friendly warnings, get sent to the Workhouse.

Half of the colored 'longshoremen used at one time to wear only a coat and pants, winter and summer; but now they are a little more careful of themselves, and fearful of being sent to the Workhouse to be cleaned up. Consequently, when Officer Brazil finds a very ragged and dirty specimen of levee life on the Row, he has seldom occasion to warn him more than once to buy himself a shirt and a change of garments.

Generally speaking, the women give very little trouble. Some of the white girls now living in Pickett's barracks or in Bucktown brothels are of respectable parentage. Two of the most notorious are sisters, who have a sad history. They are yet rather handsome. All these women are morphine eaters, and their greatest dread is to be sent to the Workhouse, and being thus deprived of this stimulant. Some who were sent to the Workhouse, we were told, had died there from want of it. The white girls of the Row soon die, however, under any circumstances; their lives are often fairly burnt out with poisonous whisky and reckless dissipation before they have haunted the levee more than two or three years. After a fashion, the roustabouts treat their women kindly, with a rough good nature that is peculiar to them; many of the women are really married. But faithfulness to a roustabout husband is considered quite an impossible virtue on the levee. The stevedores are mostly too improvident and too lazy to support their "gals." While the men are off on a trip, a girl will always talk about what she will be able to buy "when my man comes back—if he has any money." When the lover does come back, sometimes after a month's absence, he will perhaps present his "gal" with fifty cents, or at most a dollar, and thinks he has done generously by her. We are speaking in general terms, of course, and alluding to the mass of the colored roustabouts who "run on the river" all their lives, and have no other calling. It is needless to say that there are thrifty and industrious stevedores who support their families well, and will finally leave the river for some more lucrative employment.

Such is a glimpse of roustabout life. They know of no other life; they can understand no other pleasures. Their whole existence is one vision of anticipated animal pleasure or of animal misery; of giant toil under the fervid summer sun; of toil under the icy glare of the winter moon; of fiery drinks and drunken dreams; of the madness of music and the intoxication of fantastic dances; of white and dark mistresses awaiting their coming at the levees, with waving of brightly colored garments; of the deep music of the great steam whistles; of the torch-basket fires redly dancing upon the purple water, the white stars sailing overhead, the passing lights of well known cabins along the dark river banks, and the mighty panting of the iron heart of the great vessel, bearing them day after day and night after night to fresh scenes of human frailty, and nearer to that Dim Levee slope, where weird boats ever discharge ghostly freight, and depart empty.

Violent Cremation

"ONE WOE DOTH TREAD UPON ANOTHER'S HEEL," SO FAST THEY FOLLOW. Scarcely have we done recording the particulars of one of the greatest conflagrations that has occurred in our city for years than we are called upon to describe the foulest murder that has ever darkened the escutcheon of our State. A murder so atrocious and so horrible that the soul sickens at its revolting details—a murder that was probably hastened by the fire; for, though vengeance could be the only prompter of two of the accused murderers, fear of a dreadful secret coming to light may have been partly the impelling motive that urged on the third to the bloody deed, as will be found further along in our story. The scene of the awful deed was H. Freiberg's tannery on Livingston street and Gamble alley, just west of Central avenue, and immediately opposite the ruins of M. Werk & Co.'s candle factory. The dramatis personæ: Herman Schilling, the murdered man, and Andreas Egner, George Rufer, and Frederick Egner, his suspected murderers.

The story, as near as we can obtain it, and divested of unnecessary verbiage, is as follows: Herman Schilling, the deceased, has been employed by Mr. Freiberg for some time, and formerly boarded with the elder Egner, who keeps a saloon and boarding-house at No. 153 Findlay street, on the lot immediately west of the tannery, and connected with it by means of a gate. Egner possessed a daughter Julia, about fifteen years of age, whose morals, from common report, were none of the best, and she and the deceased became very intimate. In fact, so intimate did they become that Schilling was found by the father, late one night, in her bedroom, under circumstances that proved that they were criminally so, and Schilling only escaped the father's vengeance at the time by jumping through the window to the ground and temporary safety. Egner claimed that Schilling had seduced his daughter, which charge was denied by the accused, who, while admitting his criminal connection with the girl, alleged that he was not the first or only one so favored. At all events, the girl became pregnant and died at the Hospital on the 6th of August last from cancer of the vulva, being seven months advanced in pregnancy at the time. The same day Egner and his son Frederick attacked Schilling in the tanyard with oak barrel staves, and in all probability would have killed him then and there but for the interposition of bystanders. Schilling had the Egners arrested for this assault and battery and they were tried and convicted before Squire True, each being fined $50 and costs for the offense, and being held in $200 bonds to keep the peace toward him for one year. After the trial the elder Egner swore, in his own barroom, that he would have Schilling's life for the wrong he had done him, and he has repeated these threats on several occasions since. After the discovery of his criminal intimacy with the girl, Schilling left Egner's house and took his meals thereafter at the house of C. Westenbrock, 126 Findlay street, and sleeping in a room in a shed of the tannery. Last Saturday night Schilling left Westenbrock's house about 10 o'clock for his sleeping apartment, and as far as is now known this was the last time he was seen alive by any one who knew him except his murderers. About half past ten o'clock a stout youth of 16, named John Hollerbach, residing on Central avenue, just above Livingston street, came home and entered his residence by the rear of its yard, opening on Gamble alley. He proceeded to his room in the back of the second floor of the dwelling, and disrobed for bed. He had scarcely done so when he heard the noise of a violent scuffle, apparently proceeding from the alley back of his house, and hastily donning his garments again he dashed down stairs, to find that the noise came from the stable of the tannery, and knowing Schilling well he called to him in German: "Herman, is that you?" The reply came, "Yes, John. John, John, come and help me, some one is killing me," uttered as if the speaker was being choked or stifled. "Who is it," was the next query. The answer was so indistinct that nothing could be made of it and Hollerbach shouted "Murder, murder, let that man alone or I will come in and shoot you." No response was made to this threat save the gurgling noise of the strangling man, and Hollerbach frightened almost to death, started out the alley and down Livingston street in quest of a policeman. He saw the light of the lantern of the private watchman of Werk's place, but not knowing that he had the power of arrest, so runs the boy's strange story, he did not call his attention to the matter, and after vainly seeking for a policeman on several streets without calling or making any outcry for them, he returned to his room, passing by the stable where the foul deed had been committed, hearing, he thought, a dragging noise as he went by. Upon regaining his room he was afraid to go to sleep, and sat up all night in fear and trembling.

About seven o'clock yesterday morning, Schilling's boarding boss, Westenbrock, who is also an employee of Mr. Freiberg, came to the grated Gamble alley gateway of the tannery to groom the horse in the stable. He found the gate locked, and called for Schilling. Of course he received no response, until his repeated calls attracted the attention of Hollerbach, who looked out of his window and said, "I shouldn't wonder if Herman was killed last night." "Come here and climb the gate," said Westenbrock. Hollerbach did as desired, and opening the gate admitted his partner. The pair at once found that a dreadful deed of blood had been committed. The stable showed signs of a desperate conflict, being splashed with gore, while a six-pronged pitchfork standing against its side was smeared with blood and hair, as was a broom and a large stick near by. Traces of blood were found leading from the stable to the door of the boiler-room, a distance of over one hundred feet, and upon examination these traces were found to lead directly to the door of the gas chamber of the furnace. The horror-struck men stood appalled for a moment as the realization of their worst fears burst upon them, and then spread the news with all the speed possible. Messengers were dispatched to the Oliver street Station-house, and Lieutenant Bierbaum arrived on the scene about half-past eight o'clock, accompanied by Officer Knoeppe. It did not take them long to determine that the body of the murdered man had been thrown into the furnace, and, aided by the spectators who had gathered to the scene by hundreds, they dampened the fire with water and then fished for the remains. These were found to consist of the head and a portion of the trunk and intestines, burned to a crisp and beyond recognition. Suspicion at once fell upon the Egners, from the fact that the gate in the fence between the tannery and their yard *was wide open* when Westenbrock and Hollerbach entered the premises. They were at once arrested and taken to the Oliver street Station-house, where a charge of suspicion of murder was placed against their names. Coroner Maley was notified and responded promptly to the call. No Constable being on the ground, he appointed Samuel Bloom special, and impaneled the following jury: John Cutter, Henry Britt, George Gould, Dennis O'Keefe, John Wessel and B. F. Schott. They adjourned until this morning at nine o'clock, the remains meanwhile being transferred to Habig's undertaking establishment, on West Sixth street. An *Enquirer* reporter visited the establishment some hours later, accompanied by Dr. Maley, and examined all so far discovered of Herman Schilling's charred corpse. The hideous mass of reeking cinders, despite all the efforts of the brutal murderers to hide their ghastly crime, remain sufficiently intact to bear frightful witness against them.

On lifting the coffin-lid a powerful and penetrating odor, strongly resembling the smell of burnt beef, yet heavier and fouler, filled the room and almost sickened the spectators. But the sight of the black remains was far more sickening. Laid upon the clean white lining of the coffin they rather resembled great shapeless lumps of half-burnt bituminous coal than aught else at the first hurried glance; and only a closer investigation could enable a strong-stomached observer to detect their ghastly character—masses of crumbling human bones, strung together by half-burnt sinews, or glued one upon another by a hideous adhesion of half-molten flesh, boiled brains and jellied blood mingled with coal. The skull had burst like a shell in the fierce furnace-heat; and the whole upper portion seemed as though it had been *blown out* by the steam from the boiling and bubbling brains. Only the posterior portion of the occipital and parietal bones, the inferior and superior maxillary, and some of the face-bones remained—the upper portions of the skull bones being jagged, burnt brown in some spots, and in others charred to black ashes. The brain had all boiled away, save a small wasted lump at the base of the skull about the size of a lemon. It was crisped and still warm to the touch. On pushing the finger through the crisp, the interior felt about the consistency of banana fruit, and the yellow fibers seemed to writhe like worms in the Coroner's hands. The eyes were cooked to bubbled crisps in the blackened sockets, and the bones of the nose were gone, leaving a hideous hole.

So covered were the jaws and lower facial bones with coal, crusted blood and gummy flesh, that the Coroner at first supposed the lower maxillary to have been burned away. On tearing away the frightful skull-mask of mingled flesh and coal and charred gristle, however, the grinning teeth shone ghastly white, and both jaws were found intact.

They were set together so firmly that it was found impossible to separate them, without reducing the whole mass to ashes. For so great
had been the heat, that the Coroner was able to crumble one of the
upper teeth in his fingers.

Besides the fragments of the skull have been found six ribs of the
right side and four of the left; the middle portion of the spinal
column; the liver, spleen and kidneys; the pelvic bones; the right and
left humerus; the femoral bones, and the tibia and fibula of both legs.
The body had burst open at the chest, and the heart and lungs had
been entirely consumed. The liver was simply roasted and the kidneys
fairly fried. There is a horrible probability that the wretched victim
was forced into the furnace alive, and suffered all the agonies of the
bitterest death which man can die, while wedged in the flaming flue.
His teeth were so terribly clenched that more than one spectator of
the hideous skull declared that only the most frightful agony could
have set those jaws together. Perhaps, stunned and disabled by the
murderous blows of his assailants, the unconscious body of the poor
German was forced into the furnace. Perhaps the thrusts of the assassin's pitchfork, wedging him still further into the fiery hell, or perhaps the first agony of burning when his bloody garments took fire,
revived him to meet the death of flame. Fancy the shrieks for mercy,
the mad expostulation, the frightful fight for life, the superhuman
struggles for existence—a century of agony crowded into a moment—
the shrieks growing feebler—the desperate struggles dying into feeble
writhings. And through all the grim murderers, demoniacally pitiless,
devilishly desperate, gasping with their exertions to destroy a poor
human life, looking on in silent triumph! Peering into the furnace
until the skull exploded and the steaming body burst, and the fiery
flue hissed like a hundred snakes! It may not be true—we hope for
poor humanity's sake it cannot be true; but the frightful secrets of
that fearful night are known only to the criminals and their God. They
may be brought to acknowledge much; but surely never so much as
that we have dared to hint at.

Immediately after the arrest of the Egners the police got news that
a man named George Rufer, who had been employed in the tannery,
had been discharged Saturday evening, and that he had blamed Schilling for his dismissal. Search was made for him at his residence, No.
90 Logan street, but that he had gone out, and his wife, in response
to questions, at first stated that he had not left the house after supper.
Afterward she convicted herself, saying that he had gone to Spring

street, to a friend's house, in company with her, and that he had re-tired at 10 o'clock.

The news of the terrible affair spread with great celerity, and though its horrible features seemed too awful for belief, for once a story passed through a dozen lips without gathering anything by the transi-tion, reality for once distancing the most fervid imagination. By noon the streets in the vicinity of the scene were thronged with people who eagerly caught at the slightest word dropped by any one conversant with the story of the murder, and repeated it with bated breath to fresh groups of earnest listeners. The day was fine, and in the afternoon hundreds who visited the locality merely to view the ruins of the fire learned of the still more terrible affair, and aided in swelling the crowd that swayed to and fro around the tannery like waves of the sea. About half past four o'clock the rain, which had been threatening for some time, began to descend in a lively manner, and this dispersed the throng, much to the relief of the police on guard around the premises.

About five o'clock Lieutenant Bierbaum started out on a fresh search for Rufer. Before he reached his residence, however, he found him on his way to the Station-house, he having been arrested by officers Paulus and Knoeppe at the corner of Logan and Findlay streets. When taken to the Station-house he was confronted by Colonel Kiersted, who or-dered him to be stripped and examined. His face was scratched and contused in a terrible manner, and presented every appearance of his having been engaged in a fearful and prolonged struggle. He appeared cool and collected, considering the fearful nature of the suspicion against him. His clothing did not present any traces of blood until he had removed his pantaloons; then the knees of his drawers were found stiffened with gore. He quickly exclaimed: "That is blood from the hides I handled." A gout of blood was also found on the breast of his undershirt.

His story was told partly in broken English and partly in German, and was substantially as follows: "Last Saturday night Mr. Freiberg told me that work was slack, and that he would have to let me go for a few days. Well, after supper I took my little child and I went down to Mr. Egner's and I had a glass of beer, and then I paid Mr. Egner my beer-bill. After I had had a couple of more beers, about nine o'clock, I took my child and started home. I stopped at a frame grocery at the corner of Logan and Findlay and took a couple of glasses more of beer and one of wine, and then I went to bed. Sunday morning I got up about 7 o'clock and after breakfast I started to walk to Columbia to see the superintendent of a furniture factory there about getting a job of work. I could not find the superintendent, as two men told me he lived over the river. I met no one in Columbia that I knew, and I started to walk home after getting some beer. I got tired, and got into the street cars and rode to the Elm street depot and then started home, when I was arrested. I did not have any trouble with Schilling. I last saw him dressing hides when I left the tannery Saturday evening. He had been in the habit of working at night. I did not know where he slept. I once heard Egner talking about Schilling and his daughter Julia's seduction, and he said that Schilling ought to be run through with a pitchfork. Another time I heard the son Fred talking about the same thing, and he said that Schilling ought to have a rope tied around his neck and be held over the hot furnace."

When asked how he accounted for the scratches on his face, he became contradictory, first saying that he got them by jumping from a shed the night of the fire at Werk's factory, then that he refused to give his wife any money Saturday night, and that she and him had a fight, and that she had torn his face with her nails, and again that he had fallen down on the street. He is a man about five feet seven inches high, with a sinewy and strong frame, and is about thirty seven years old. Our portrait is a fair reproduction of his appearance last night in his cell at the Station-house.

The most damning report against him is that the deceased, Herman Schilling, was cognizant of the fact that "Rufer had set fire" to M. Werk & Co.'s candle factory Friday night last, and that he intended to apprise the police of his information. How true this report is we cannot now state, but if true it would afford conclusive evidence of the reason that inclined him to share in the deep damnation of the murder.

The elder Egner is a German, about forty-three years old, slight and spare in figure, and with a forbidding but determined look. His son is a beardless boy, without any distinguishing characteristics save a sullen look of stolid indifference to his fate. His tale is that he played "tag," "catcher," etc., up till nine o'clock Saturday night, slept soundly during the night, hearing no noise, and awakening at seven o'clock in the morning and only hearing of the murder about eight o'clock.

Egner keeps a coffee-house and a cooper-shop, just west of the tannery, his saloon being at No. 153 Findlay street.

The deceased, Herman Schilling, was a native of Westphalia, twenty-five years old, about five feet eight inches high, finely proportioned, ruddy-faced, with dark mustache and cross-eyes. He was generally spoken of yesterday evening as a very good, companionable kind of a man. He was unmarried, and has no relations that we could learn of in this city.

The premises on which the bloody deed was enacted comprise a stable, harness, carriage, and sleeping-room of the deceased, together with two large tan-bark sheds and a boiler shed, in which is situated the furnace wherein Schilling was cremated. The stable adjoins Gamble alley, and is about eight by ten feet square, with a loft not much higher than a man's head. It is occupied by but one horse, and presents every indication of a terrible and bloody struggle. Adjoining it is a room used for storing harness, and it is probable that in this room the murderers laid in wait for their prey. Next, west, is the carriage room; and, by means of a door in its west partition, access is had to the room used by the deceased as his sleeping apartment. These rooms form an offset to the tan-bark sheds, and west of these is the boiler, furnace and engine rooms. Between these buildings and the others of the tannery is a large yard running east and west. To guard the premises are three immense and savage mastiffs.

Judging by all the evidence the murderers were familiar with the premises and its canine guardians; for, were they not, they could not have gained access to them without encountering the dogs, and being probably torn into fragments by them. They in all probability entered through the gate leading from Egner's to the tanyard, and ensconced themselves in the harness-room, which they knew their victim must pass on his way to his lodging. When he entered, as was his wont, by the small gate opening on Gamble alley, they were peering through the open door of the harness-room awaiting their opportunity. A few more steps in the darkness and silence, and the watchman's throat is suddenly seized with a grasp of iron. Then commences the terrible struggle for life.

The night is pitch dark, fit gloom for the dark deed it veils. The victim is a young and powerful man, muscled like Hercules; but he has been wholly taken by surprise, he is unarmed, and he finds by the strength of the grasp on his throat that his antagonist is more than a match for him in mere brute force. A stunning blow from behind suddenly shows him that he has two enemies to deal with; and then for the first time, perhaps, the terrible knowledge of the fact that his life is sought, first dawns upon him. Then indeed it became a fierce fight for dear life. The stable shows that the victim, despairing of his ability to cope with his savage assailants, sought refuge behind the horse's hoofs: hoping at least to thus gain a moment's time to shriek for help. But here the indications are that the contest was hottest. The side of the stable is in places deeply indented by the prongs of the pitchfork—indented by such thrusts as only immense force could give —thrusts which were designed to let out the life of the victim. It was the noise of this struggle that attracted the attention of young Hollerbach, and—who knows?—but that his version of what he saw and heard of it has yet to be told in full. Certainly it seems singular that he should behave himself in the remarkable manner he states. At the hour he names as the time of the murder a dozen saloons in the immediate vicinity were in full blast and filled with patrons. Aye, even the house in which he slept—no, did not sleep, but watched—has a bar-room in it, which kept open until after midnight, and volunteers to rescue the victim could have been obtained by scores. Mr. John Hollerbach evidently knows much more than he has told of this fearful crime. It is preposterous to think that any man in his sane mind would act as he says he did. When the life of the dying man had so far ebbed that he could no longer resist his fate his murderers thought of the best place to dispose of the body, the furnace.

Within a hundred feet of the stable is the boiler-room, and this boiler is heated by a furnace of peculiar construction, being built on the principle of an air furnace for melting iron. Its fuel is tanbark, emptied in a grate through two circular openings in its top, and provided with a brick flue through which its gases pass into a chamber underneath the boiler where they are ignited. Into this chamber is a square damper opening of about twelve inches across, and to this narrow door the victim was carried by his slayers. The fire in the furnace had been dampened down, but the villains know well its mechanism, and, forcing the body through the narrow door, they endeavor to push it through into the flue. In this, however, they were balked by its size, and their next work was to arrange the furnace so that its fire would burn the remains to ashes. How well they succeeded our story has told.

The circumstantial evidence is all as yet there is to found a suspicion on, but we must say that it appears to be of the most conclusive kind. Especially is this the fact in the case of Andreas Egner.

The grimy boards forming the floor of the loft of the stable are covered with festoons of heavy cobwebs; and through the chinks hayseed has been constantly drifting down and lodging in the glutinous film spun by the gray spiders below. Moreover, the floor of the stable is thickly covered with poplar shavings. Suspicion being once fastened upon Andreas Egner, search was made in his house for articles of clothing or other things which might serve as a clue for tracing up the crime. A bundle of clothes was one of the first things pounced upon, including an old hat, a pair of low shoes, and a well-worn pair of coarse cassimere pants. The pants bore great stains of candle-grease, but there were no stains of blood, although some strange dark spots warranted a keen investigation. Yet the other garments afforded terrible witness against him. His hat was found to be covered with just such cobwebs and hay-seed as hung from the roof of the stable; and his shoes were found full of the very poplar shavings which covered the stable-floor.

Rufer's clothes, which are also in the hands of the police, afford only the evidence of blood, but there is plenty of it. It has stained the bosom of his coarse checked shirt a muddy red. It has trickled in thick streams upon the legs of his jeans, and stained them dark below the knees. He accounts for the blood on his shirt by the fact that it has been a part of his duties in the tannery to handle fresh hides. The gore on his pants he declares to have come from the veins of a chicken which he had killed the night before. There does not seem to be anything more than a general suspicion against the boy Fred Egner.

There are several instances connected with the scene of the horrible tragedy which must come under the head of circumstantial evidence. We have already referred to the great size and ferocity of the dogs guarding the premises, and their peculiar quietness during the performance of the hideous crime as conclusive proof that the murderers must have both been very familiar with the premises and the mastiffs. When we visited the tannery late last evening in company with Messrs. Farny and Duveneck to take sketches of the buildings, we found it impossible to gain entrance by reason of the dogs' ferocity. Another curious fact is the condition in which the horse, the dumb witness of that frightful crime, was found this morning—shuddering and trembling from head to hoofs, his eyes wild with terror. Petting and caressing availed nothing; and the whole forenoon the animal was in a perfect tremor of fear.

The five-pronged fork, used by the murderers either to kill their victim, or to stuff his body into the furnace, was found in the stable, with blood and hair still adhering to it, and a suspender-buckle on the fourth prong. It is curious that a similar suspender-buckle was found among the ashes of the furnace.

Besides the fork, a long stake, sharpened to a spear-like point and dyed at the smaller end with blood, appears to have served in the deed of murder. A small broom had evidently been used to brush up the blood, as it was completely coated with thickly crusted gore. How it happened that the murderers could have been careless enough to leave such damning evidence against them, we can scarcely imagine.

John Hollerbach, by order of Chief Kiersted was arrested in his bed at two o'clock this morning by Lieutenant Benninger, and locked up in the Oliver street Station-house as a witness. He stuck to his apocryphal story. In conversation with a reporter this morning Rufer said if he had killed Schilling, he would have put him in a better place—a tank of salt-water under the tannery, where he never would have smelt. Would that tank not be a good place to drag for bloody clothes?

The following witnesses will be examined at the Coroner's inquest this morning: Wm. Hollerbach, Jr., C. Westenbrock, N. Westenbrock, Ban Fruink, Jos. Schlingrop, R. Mellenbrook, Henry Korte, E. Kerr, Wm. Osterhage, Henry Kote, Jr., Isadore Freiberg, Henry Freiberg.

George Rufer stated that his wife was at the house of her sister, Mrs. Peter Eckert, the officers who were sent in search of her having failed to find her at her home on Dunlap street.

Rufer couldn't tell where Mrs. Eckert lived. Lieutenant Wersel, without any guide except that the husband of Mrs. Eckert was a potter, set out in search of her, and after a tramp of three or four miles, calling at a dozen houses, found her on Western avenue.

She stated that Mrs. Rufer was not with her, had not been with her, that they were not on good terms, and did not visit each other. This leaves the whereabouts of Mrs. Rufer still a mystery.

A little after midnight an officer of the Oliver street Station came running into the Station-house with a statement that rumors were afloat that a band had organized to take the prisoners out of their cells and lynch them. A good reserve of police was afterward kept at the station.

Dolly: An Idyl of the Levee

"THE LORD ONLY," ONCE OBSERVED OFFICER PATSY BRAZIL, "KNOWS WHAT Dolly's real name is."

Dolly was a brown, broad-shouldered girl of the levee, with the lithe strength of a pantheress in her compactly-knit figure, and owning one of those peculiar faces which at once attract and puzzle by their very uniqueness—a face that possessed a strange comeliness when viewed at certain angles, especially half-profile, and that would have seemed very soft and youthful but for the shadow of its heavy black brows, perpetually knitted Medusa-wise, as though by everlasting pain, above a pair of great, dark, keen, steady eyes. It was a face, perhaps, rather Egyptian than aught else; fresh with a youthful roundness, and sweetened by a sensitive, passionate, pouting mouth.

Moreover, Dolly's odd deportment and peculiar attire were fancifully suggestive of those wanton Egyptian women whose portraits were limned on mighty palace walls by certain ancient and forgotten artists—some long-limbed, gauze-clad girls who seem yet to move with a snakish and fantastic grace; others, strong-limbed and deep-bosomed, raimented in a single, close-fitting robe, and wearing their ebon hair loosely flowing in a long thick mass. Dolly appeared to own the elfish grace of the former, together with the more mortal form of the latter. She must have made her own dresses, for no such dresses could have been purchased with love or with money, they were very antique and very graceful. Her favorite dress, a white robe, with a zig-zag border of purple running around the bottom, fitted her almost closely from shoulder to knee, following the sinuous outline of her firm figure, and strongly recalling certain pictures in the Egyptian Department of a famous German work upon the Costumes of Antiquity. Of course Dolly knew nothing of Antiquity or of Egypt—in fact she could neither read nor write; but she had an instinctive æsthetic taste which surmounted those obstacles to good taste in dress which ignorance and fashion jointly create. Her prehistoric aspect was further heightened by her hair,—long, black, thick as a mane, and betraying by its tendency to frizzle the strong tinge of African blood in Dolly's veins. This she generally wore loose to the waist,—a mass so heavy and dense that a breeze could not wave it, and so deeply dark as to recall those irregular daubs of solid black paint whereby the painters of the pyramid-chambers represented the locks of weird court dames. Dolly was very careful of this strange hair; but she indulged, from time to time, in the savage luxury of greasing it with butter. Occasionally, too, she arranged it in a goblin sort of way, by combing it up perpendicularly, so that it flared above her head as though imbued with an electric life of its own. Perhaps she inherited the tendency to these practices from her African blood.

In fact, Dolly was very much of a little savage, despite the evidence of her natural æsthetic taste in dress. The very voluptuousness and freedom of her movements had something savage about it, and she had a wild love for violent physical exercises. She could manage a pair of oars splendidly, and was so perfect a shot that knowing steamboatmen were continually fleecing newcomers by inducing them to bet heavily against Dolly's abilities in the Sausage Row shooting-gallery. Turning her back to the mark, with a looking-glass hung before her, Dolly could fire away all day, and never miss making the drum rattle. Then she could swim like a Tahitian, and before daybreak on sultry summer mornings often stole down to the river to strike out in the moon-silvered current. "Ain't you ashamed to be seen that way?" reproachfully inquired an astonished police officer, one morning, upon encountering Dolly coming up the levee, with a single wet garment clinging about her, and wringing out the water from her frizzly hair.

"Only the pretty moon saw me," replied Dolly, turning her dark eyes gratefully to the rich light.

Dolly was a much better character, on the whole, than her sisters of the levee, chiefly because she seldom quarreled, never committed theft, and seldom got tipsy. Smoke she did, incessantly; for tobacco is a necessity of life on the Row. It was an odd fact that she had no confidants, and never talked about herself. Her reticence, comparative sobriety, and immunity from arrest, together with the fact that she never lacked money enough for the necessities of life, occasioned a peculiar, unpleasant feeling toward her among the other women, which expressed itself in the common saying that Dolly was "putting on airs."

Once it became suddenly fashionable on the Row to adorn windows with pots containing some sort of blossoming weed, which these dusky folks euphemistically termed "flowers." Dolly at once "put on airs" by refusing to conform to the growing custom.

"Why don't you have any flower-pots in your window?" curiously queried Patsy Brazil.

"Because," said Dolly, "I ain't a-going to be so d—d mean to the flowers. The Row ain't no place for flowers."

One of her greatest pleasures was to pet a little bandy-legged Negro child, whose parents nobody knew, and whom old fat Maggie Sperlock had adopted. She would spend whole hours amusing the little fellow, romping and laughing with him, and twisting her extraordinary hair into all sorts of fantastic horns and goblin devices in order to amuse him. Then she taught him the names of all the great white boats, and the names of the far cities they sailed from, and the odd symbolism of the Negro steamboat slang. When a long vessel swept by, plowing up the yellow current in curving furrows about her prow, and leaving in her rear a long line of low-hanging nimbus-clouds, Dolly would cry: "See, Tommy, how proud the old gal is to-day; she's got a fine *ruffle* on. Look at her *switch,* Tommy; see how the old gal's curling her hair out behind her." Dolly could not read the names of the boats, but she knew by heart their gleaming shapes, and the varying tones of their wild, deep voices. So she taught the child to know them, too, until to his infantile fancy they became, as it were, great aquatic things, which slept only at the levee, and moved upon the river through the white moonlight with an awfully pulsating life of their own. She likewise made out of a pine plank for Tommy, a funny little vessel, with a cunning stern-wheel to it, which flung up the water bravely as the child drew it along the shore with a cotton string. And Dolly had no end of terrible stories to tell Tommy, about Voudoos—she called them "hoodoos"—people who gathered heads of snakes, and spiders, and hideous creeping things to make venomous charms with, by steeping them in whisky until the foul liquor became "green as grass." Tommy would have become frightened out of his little life at these tales, but that Dolly gave him a dried rabbit's foot in a bag to hang round his neck; for Dolly, like all the colored folks of the levee, believed a rabbit's foot to be a sure charm against all evil.

Of course Dolly had "her man"—a rather good-looking yellow roustabout known along the levee as Aleck. In the summer time, when the river was "lively," as the steamboatmen say, she was rather faithful to Aleck; but when the watery highway was all bound in ice, and there was no money on the Row, and Aleck was away on the Lower Mississippi or perhaps out of work, Dolly was decidedly immoral in her mode of life. But Aleck could scarcely expect her to be otherwise, for his money went almost as fast as it came. It was generally a feast or a famine with him. He did come home one spring with forty-odd dollars in his pocket—quite a fortune, he thought it, and a new silver watch for Dolly; but that was, perhaps, the great pecuniary event of his career. Somehow or other the watch did not keep perfect time, and poor Dolly, who knew far more about steamboats than she did about watches, opened the chronometer "to see what was the matter with it."

"Why, it's got a little hair wound around its guts," said Dolly; "of course it won't go right." Then she pulled out the mainspring. "Such a doggoned funny looking hair," further observed Dolly.

Unlike the other women of the levee, however, Dolly had a little respect for her own person, and did not sell her favors indiscriminately. On the contrary, she managed for a long time to maintain a certain comparative reputation for respectability. And when she did, at last, become utterly abandoned, perhaps the Great Father of each one of us, black and white, fully pardoned all her poor errors.

For it came to pass in this wise: Aleck one summer evening, became viciously drunk at a Bucktown ball, and got into a free fight, wherein one roustabout, to use Dolly's somewhat hyperbolic expression, "was shot and cut all to pieces." Aleck was only charged at the Hammond Street Police Station with being drunk and disorderly, but inasmuch as it was not his first offense of the kind, he was sentenced to pay a fine of fifty dollars, and to be imprisoned in the Workhouse for a period of thirty days. When the Black Maria had rolled away, and the gaping crowd of loafers had dispersed, after satisfying their unsympathetic curiosity, Dolly wandered into the City Park, and sitting down upon one of the little stone lions at the fountain, cried silently over the broken watch which Aleck had given her. She arose with the resolve to pay Aleck's fine as soon as the thirty days of his Workhouse sentence had expired, and went slowly back to the Row.

Now when Dolly had fairly resolved upon doing a thing, it was generally done. We dare not say too much about how Dolly had resolved to earn that fifty dollars in thirty days—about the only way, indeed, that it was remotely possible for her to earn it on the Row. Those who know the social life of the Row will, however, understand the difficulties in Dolly's way. The sudden change in her habits, the recklessness of her life—compared with what it had been; the apparently absolute loss of all the little self-respect she once had, at once excited the surprise of her companions and of the police officers, who watch closely every habitant of the levee. She bought food only when she could not beg it, seldom paid for a cigar, and seemed to become a ubiquitous character in all the worst haunts of the Row, by night and day.

"If you keep on this way, Dolly," finally exclaimed Patsy Brazil, "I'll 'vag' you." It was then nearly thirty days since Aleck had been sentenced. Patsy, kindly but always firm, never threatened in vain, and Dolly knew it.

It is hardly necessary to say, however, that Dolly had not been able to earn the amount of Aleck's fine, nor is it necessary to state how much she had earned, when Patrolman Brazil was obliged to threaten her with the Workhouse. She had one recourse left, however,—to sell her dresses and her furniture, consisting of a stove, a bed, and an ancient clock—for much less than their pitiful value. She did sell them, and returned from the second-hand store to her bare room, to fall into an exhausted sleep on the floor, hungry and supperless, but happy in the possession of enough money to pay "her man's fine." And Aleck again found himself a free man.

He felt grateful enough to Dolly not to get drunk for a week, which be naturally considered no small piece of self-abnegation in return for his freedom. A keener-eyed man in a blue uniform with brass buttons, who looked into Dolly's great hollow eyes and sunken face with a muttered "God help her!" better understood how dearly that freedom had been purchased. Hunger and sleeplessness had sapped the vitality of Dolly's nervous though vigorous organization. At last Aleck got work on a Maysville packet boat, and sailed away from the levee, and from the ghost of what was once Dolly, waving a red, ragged handkerchief from her window in defiance of Pickett's orders. Just before the regular starting time some one had "tolled" the boat's bell.

"Who's fooling with that bell," exclaimed Dolly, suddenly dropping her cigar. "It's bad luck to do that." She often thought of the bell again, when week after week the vessel regularly steamed up to the long wharfboat—without Aleck. Aleck had told her that he intended to "see God's people"—the roustabout term for visiting one's home; but she never thought he would have remained away from her so long.

At last one evening while sitting at Pickett's door, filing some little shirt-studs for Aleck out of a well-bleached beef bone, some one told her how Aleck had got married up at Maysville, and what "a tip-top weddin'" it was. Dolly said nothing, but picked up her beef bones and her little file and went up stairs.

"They never die round here," said Patsy Brazil, "until their will's gone. The will dies first." And Dolly's will was dead.

Some women of the levee picked her thin body up from the floor of the empty room and carried her to a bed. Then they sent for old Judge Fox, the gray-haired Negro preacher, who keeps a barber-shop on Sausage Row. The old Negro's notions of theology were probably peculiar to himself, yet he had comforted more than one dying woman. He closed his shop at once, and came to pray and sing for Dolly, but she heeded neither the prayers nor the strange slave-hymns that he sang. The evening gray deepened to night purple; the moon looked in through the open window at Dolly's thin face; the river reflected its shining ripple on the whitewashed walls within, and through all the sound of the praying and singing there boomed up from below the furious thrumming of banjos and bass viols, and the wild thunder of the dancers' feet. Down stairs the musicians were playing the tune, *Big Ball Up Town;* upstairs the women were chanting to a weirdly sweet air, *My Jesus Arose.*

> *Oh, ain't I mighty glad my Jesus arose,*
> *Oh, ain't I mighty glad my Jesus arose,*
> *Oh, ain't I mighty glad my Jesus arose*
>   *To send me up on high.*

> *Here comes my pilgrim Jesus,*
> *A-riding a milk-white horse;*
> *He's rode him to the east and he's rode him*
>   *to the west,*
> *And to every other quarter of the world.*
>   *Oh, ain't I mighty glad, etc.*

> *Here comes my master Jesus,*
> *With heaven in his view,*
> *He's goin' home to glory,*
> *And bids this world adieu.*
>   *Oh, ain't I mighty glad, etc.*

He'll blow out the sun and burn up the world,
  And turn that moon to blood,
  And sinners in ——

"Hush," said Dolly, rising with a desperate effort. "Ain't that the old gal talking?"

A sound deeper and sweeter and wilder than the hymned melody or the half-savage music below, filled all the moonlit levee—the steam-song of the Maysville packet coming in.

"Help me up!" gasped Dolly—"it's the old gal blowing off steam; it's Aleck; it's my man—my man!"

Then she sunk back suddenly, and lay very still—in the stillness of the Dreamless Sleep.

When they went to lay her out, they found something tightly clutched in one little bony hand—so tightly that it required no inconsiderable exertion to force the fingers open.

It was an old silver watch, with the main-spring pulled out.

Some Pictures of Poverty

That shattered roof, and this naked floor;
  A table, a broken chair;
And a wall so blank, my shadow I thank
  For sometimes falling there.

WEST SEVENTH, NOS. 206, 208 AND 210, AND THE MYSTERIOUS BUILDINGS IN the rear, running back to the alley, is a locality of such picturesque wretchedness as, perhaps, may not be found elsewhere within the city limits,—not even in the labyrinthine hollows of the famous Negro quarter in the East End. Narrow hallways, from whose irregular sides the plaster has fallen away in shapeless patches, lead through the frame cottages, fronting on Seventh street, into a species of double court-yard in the rear, whose northern end is bounded by a block of three-story frames, usually termed the Barracks, and inhabited by the poorest of the poor. Within the court itself is situated one of the strangest, most irregular, and most outlandish wooden edifices possible to imagine. It might have been a country farmhouse in days before the city had crept up north and west from the river; but now inclosed in the heart of a block, its dingy colorlessness and warped deformity suggest a mediæval rather than a modern haunt of poverty—one of those tottering hovels which crowd humbly and beseechingly about the elder Cathedrals of the old world, like so many Miseries seeking refuge under the shadow of a great Faith. The good planks have warped and bent with age, the building has shrunken and shriveled up paralytically. All its joints are rheumatic, all its features haggard and wretched. It seems to have once undulated throughout its whole gaunt length, as though the solid soil had surged under it in the groundswell of some forgotten earthquake. There is probably no true right angle in its whole composition. The angles of its windows and doors all present extraordinary obliqueness or acuteness, as in the outlines of a child's first attempt to draw a house; and no child ever drew plans more seemingly impossible and out of plumb than the withered front of this building. Molded by the irresistible pressure of the contracting walls, the narrow stairways have been squeezed up at one side, and down on the other, while the feet of dead generations of poor and children of the poor have worn deep hollows in every step. The floors slope like the cabins of vessels riding over a long swell; and one marvels how objects of furniture maintain an upright attitude in the tottering house. Part of the crooked basement appears to have sunk into the ground, as the newer pavement of the courtyard rises nearly two feet above the level of the lower floors. The northern end of this floor has ceased to be inhabitable; the southern end has its dwellers, ancient poor, who dwell with memories and their dead.

Here the Overseer is a frequent and welcome visitor, and here commenced a round of observation at once painful and picturesque. The little rickety door opened into a room small and dark; the plasterless ceiling might easily be touched with the hand, and, excepting the deep gray square of light afforded by one tiny window, the gloom was illumined only by one spot of crimson light which issued from the jaws of a shattered stove, throwing out a broad ray of red across the heavy smoke which floated through the dark.

There was the voice of a child crying in the darkness; and the voices of an aged Negro couple, seated on either side of that wavering line of ruddy light across the smoke, came huskily in greeting to the visitor's ears. The husband had beheld his eightieth year and the smiles of his children's children; the wife's years were scarcely fewer. Age had brought with it the helplessness of weakness, and the silent resignation which best befits both. They spoke a little to us of a Virginian plantation, where each had first known the other sixty years ago; of the old master who had given them manumission, and of little memories kindled into life by some kindly questions. We could not see their faces in the night on either side of the thin stream of red light, but their voices, speaking to us through the dimness and the smoke, bore something of a sad poetry with them—the poetry of two lives meeting in the summer and sunlight of strong youth, and knowing little knowledge save that of the tie which bound each to the other faster and firmer, as the summer and sunshine faded out, and the great Shadow, which is the End, approached to draw them nearer to each other in the darkness.

. . . There was light up stairs in a tiny crooked room, which the Overseer entered after cautious gropings along a creaking corridor whose floor had been eaten through in unexpected places by hungry pauper rats. The room—lighted partly by a flaring candle, with "winding-sheet" drippings, and partly by some thin, yellow flames, which wrestled weakly together within a ruined monkey-stove for the possession of a fresh lump of fuel—had an eastward slope; the old whitewash upon the walls had turned to the hue of strong tallow; a quantity of coal had been piled up into one corner within a foot of the greasy ceiling, and long articles of worn-out raiment, hung about the chamber, seemed to maintain in their tattered outlines a certain goblin mockery of withered bodies they might have clothed. Beside the fire sat two women. In the rounded outline of one figure, draped thinly in neat garments, spoke the presence of youth and comeliness; but the face was hooded in shadow and veiled with a veil. The other face stood out in strong relief under the mingled light from the coal fire and candle flame. It was the face of an aged woman, with ashen hair,—a face sharply profiled, with a wreck of great beauty in its outlines, that strong beauty of wild races which leaves the faces of the aged keenly aquiline when the forms of youth have withered away.

"This old lady," observed the Overseer, smiling, "is upwards of seventy-two years of age. She has the blood of the Indian races in her veins, and is quite proud of it, too."

The outlines of the thin, fine face, with its penetrating eyes, bore a shadowy testimony to the speaker's words, against the fact that such a story has not unfrequently been offered to conceal the source of a yet darker tinge in the veins. All her kin were dead and lost to her; but there were poor friends to aid her, and the city, also, bestowed its charity. Many held her wise in weird ways, and sought her counsel against unforeseen straits; and many also, like the silent visitor at her side, loved the pleasure of converse with her, and talks of the old days. Speaking pleasantly of her earlier years, with that picturesque minuteness of detail natural to minds which live most strongly in memories, the aged woman said that as she grew older, the remembrances of childhood seemed to grow clearer to her. "For within the last few years," said the good lady, "I can remember the face of my mother, who died when I was a child."

And there was something so sadly pathetic in this memory of seventy years—this sudden rekindling of a forgotten recollection in the mind of that gray woman, sitting alone, with shadows and shadowy thoughts—that the writer could not but ask:

"Can you describe that recollection to me?"

"I remember her face," slowly came the answer, "only as the face of a beautiful dead woman, with closed eyelids, and long hair, all dark, and flowing back darkly against a white pillow. And I remember this only because of a stronger memory. I remember a hired girl, seated on a little plank bridge lying across a shallow branch of water. She was washing a white cap and a long white dress. Some one asked her who was dead, pointing to the white things; and when she answered, I knew it was my mother."

. . . Passing from corridor to corridor, and room to room, throughout the buildings on the Groesbeck property, the actual novelty of the experience soon gave place to consciousness of the fact that poverty in Cincinnati is not only marked by precisely the same features characteristic of pauperism in the metropolitan cities, but that its habits and haunts, its garments and furniture, its want and suffering, even the localities wherein it settles, are stamped by a certain recognizable uniformity even here. So strikingly similar were the conditions of tenants in the Groesbeck property, that a description of one apartment would suffice for a dozen; and having passed through many rooms, the recollections of each were so blended together in the mind, by reason of their general resemblance, that only by the aid of some peculiarly painful or eccentric incident could the memory of any one be perfectly disentangled from the mass of impressions. The same rickety room, the same cracked stove, the same dingy walls bearing fantastic tapestry of faded rags and grotesque shadow-silhouettes of sharp profiles; the same pile of city coal in one corner, the same ghastly candle stuck in the same mineral water bottle, and decorated with a winding sheet; the same small, unmade bed and battered cupboard at its foot; the same heavily warm atmosphere and oppressive smell, seemed to greet the visitor everywhere. Even the faces of the aged women gradually impressed one as having nearly all been molded according to one pattern. As the circle of observation widened, however, these resemblances commenced to diverge in various directions; forcing the observer to recognize strongly marked lines between certain classes of city poor. Aged Irish people who need city charity, form, for example, a class by themselves, and rather a large one. They are usually far better housed and more comfortably situated in regard to furniture and household necessaries than are the poorest colored people.

These characteristics and classes began to make themselves manifest ere the Overseer had made his last call in the Seventh street barracks, among some good old women telling their beads, who called down benedictions upon him in their native Erse. Afterward the definition of these features of poverty became clearer and clearer, especially during the last round of visits in the East End.

. . . The Overseer said that there used to be a very wonderful Negro woman in the Groesbeck buildings, who was said to be a hundred and seventeen years old, and had been brought to the States from Africa by a slave-trader while a vigorous young woman, so that she remembered many interesting things—the tropical trees and strange animals, the hive-shaped huts of her people, the roar of lions in the night, the customs of the tribe, and some fragments of their wild tongue. But we could not find her; and subsequently learned with dismay that she was accustomed to speak of Washington. Then after a brief round of calls in the frames east of Vicker's Church, which left with us visions of other ancient women with sharp faces and of a young mother with two infants lying upon the framework of a broken bedstead, without mattresses or blankets, we visited a tottering framework on East Eighth street, not far from Crippen alley. Its interior presented no novel aspect of decaying wood and fallen plaster and crooked stairs; but one peaked and withered face which peered out upon us from behind a candle, tremblingly held at a creaking door, wore a look so woe-begone that for days afterward it haunted the memory like a ghost.

Within the piteous room, by the yellow light of a dip candle, the

face seemed to force its misery upon observation involuntarily yet irresistibly. There were shadows about the eyes and long lines about the
mouth which betrayed a torpor of hope, a life frozen into apathy by
the chill of long-protracted disappointment. She looked at the visitor
with a sort of ghastly tremor, like one so accustomed to an atmosphere
of wretchedness that the pressure of a cheerful being becomes an actual
infliction by contrast.

"How's the old man?" quoth the Overseer, pleasantly.

She shrugged her bony shoulders wearily, and replied in a husky
voice, bitter as a winter wind, that he had gone to the Poorhouse. The
husband of eighty years had left her in a fit of weak anger; they could
not "get along together;" "*he* was too fretful and childish."

"H'm," sympathetically ejaculated the Overseer. "No other relatives
living, eh?"

The old woman smiled a weird smile, and taking the candle, approached an old chest of drawers, so rickety that it had been propped
against the miserable bed to prevent its falling upon the floor. After a
hurried search in the bottom drawers she brought out a letter in a faded
envelope, and handed it to the visitors. It had been dated from a mining
village in the far West, in years gone by. The papers had a greasy look
and a dull hue of age; the writing had turned pale. It told of a happy
marriage and prospects of wealth, fair success in the race for fortune
and promises of assistance from a strong son.

"That was the last," she muttered, "——, 1849."

How many times that letter had been fondly read and re-read until
its paper had become too old to crepitate when the withered hand
crushed it in miserable despair, only perhaps to remorsefully stroke it
smooth again and press out the obscuring creases. Years came and went
wearily; want came and passed not away; winter after winter, each
seemingly sharper than the last, whitened the street without, and
shrieked in ghostly fashion at the keyhole; the little mining village in
the far West had grown to a great city; but the Silence remained forever unbroken, and trust in the hand that had written the faded yellow
words, "Dear mother," slowly died out, as the red life of an ember dies
out in the gray ash. And when the door closed with a dry groan behind
the departing feet of the Overseer, we felt strangely certain that the old
letter would be once more read that night by a throbbing candle flame,
ere returned to its dusty resting-place in the dusty room.

. . . These wanderings in the haunts of the poor, among shadowy
tenement houses and dilapidated cottages, and blind, foul alleys with

quaint names suggesting deformity and darkness, somehow compelled a phantasmal retrospect of the experience, which clings to the mind with nightmare tenacity. It came in the form of a grisly and spectral vision— a dream of reeling buildings of black plank, with devious corridors and deformed stairways; with interminable suites of crooked rooms, having sloping floors and curving walls; with crazy stoves and heavy smells; with long rags and ragged gowns haunting the pale walls like phantom visitors or elfish mockeries of the dead; and all the chambers haunted by sharp shadows and sharp faces that made them piteous with the bitterness of withered hopes, or weird by fearful waiting for the coming of the dreamless slumber, as a great Shadow, which, silently falling over lesser darknesses, absorbs them into Itself. The fearsome fancy of thus waiting for the end in loneliness—with only the company of memories, and the wild phantasmagory wrought upon the walls by firelight; wondering, possibly, at the grimness of one's shadow; peering, perhaps, into some clouded fragment of quicksilvered glass to watch the skull-outline slowly wearing its way through the flesh-mask of the face—brought with it a sense of strange chill, such as might follow the voiceless passing of a spirit.

. . . "Sixteen years in bed," said the Overseer with one of those looks which appear to demand a sympathetic expression of commiseration from the person addressed under penalty of feeling that you have committed a breach of etiquette. The scene lay in the second story of a sooty frame, perched on the ragged edge of Eggleston Avenue Hill. The sufferer was an aged man, whose limbs and body were swollen by disease to a monstrous size, and for whom the mercy of death could not have been far distant. The room was similar to other rooms already described, excepting that in the center of the weak floor a yawning, ragged hole had been partly covered by a broken-bottomed washtub; and the conventional figure of the Aged Woman, with weirdly-sharp features, was not absent. The slowly dying man moaned feebly at intervals, and muttered patient prayers in the Irish tongue.

"Betther, is it?" said the Aged Woman, in a husky whisper, casting, with her hands uplifted, a crooked shadow, as of Walpurgis Night, upon the wall: "Shure, honey, the Lord knows there's no more betther fur the likes iv him."

"Trying to get him to sleep, I suppose," nodded the Overseer, lowering his voice to a sympathetic whisper.

"No whisht, honey; it's afeared we are of Her," pointing to the hole in the floor, "the Divil down below."

There came up through the broken planking, even as she spoke, a voice of cursing, the voice of a furious woman, and a sound of heavy blows, mingled with the cry of a beaten child. Some little one was being terribly whipped, and its treble was strained to that hoarse scream which betrays an agony of helpless pain and fear, and pleading to merciless ears. To the listener it seemed that the whipping would never end. The sharp blows descended without regularity in a rapid shower which seemed to promise that the punishment could only be terminated by fatigue on the part of the punisher; the screams gradually grew hoarser and hoarser, with longer intervals between each until they ceased altogether, and only a choking gurgle was audible. Then the sound of whipping ceased; there was a sudden noise as of something flung heavily down, and then another hoarse curse.

"Why, she must be killing her children," muttered the Overseer.

"To be sure she is," whispered the Aged Woman, looking awfully at the hole in the floor as though fearing lest the "Divil" might suddenly rise up through it.

"But how often does this thing go on?"

"How often, is it? Shure there's no ind to it at all, at all. Ah, she bates the childher whinever she takes a dhrap too much, bad cess to her!—an' may God forgive me fur spakin' that word—an' she's dhrunk all the time, so she is, night and day. Thin, if I wor to spake a word to the Divil, she breaks up the flure undher us wid a pole; an' many's the night I've stud over the hole, thryin' to kape the flure down, an' she a-breaking it up betune me feet."

The very grotesqueness of this misery only rendered it all the more hideous, and one felt it impossible to smile at the trembling terror of the poor old creature. After all, it seemed to us there might be a greater horror in store for the helpless poor, than that of awaiting death among the shadows alone. This haggard woman, working and watching by her dying husband, in shivering fear of the horror below; the moans of the poor sufferer, the agonized scream of the tortured child, the savage whipping and violent cursing, the broken floor pried up in drunken fury,—all seemed the sights and sounds of a hideous dream, rather than the closing scene of a poor life's melodrama.

We visited Her—a strong, broad, flamboyant-haired woman, with hard, bloated features, and words haunted by the odor of spirits. Ignorant of what we had already heard, she brought the children forward for the visitor's admiration. They were not hungry-looking or thin, but there were written in their faces little tragedies of another character than hunger or cold can write. They watched with frightened eyes their mother's slightest action. Their little features were molded in the strictest obedience to the varying expression of her own. She smiled in the effort to seem agreeable, and they smiled also, poor little souls; but such smiles! God help them!

... Why should gray-haired folk, half palsied by the tightening grasp of the Skeleton's hand, mutually related in the strong kinship of misfortune, themselves the subject of sustaining charity, strive to do each other evil? We received ample evidence that they do. The Overseer daily hears jealous complaints from withered lips about alleged immoral conduct or imposition upon the part of other city poor. Wretched creatures supported by the city's alms in wretched hovels, seem so anxious to deprive other wretched creatures even of the comforts possible to be enjoyed in wretched hovels. It occurred to one, on hearing these whispered stories, that there must be something more than is ordinarily supposed in those quaint proverbs regarding the gossipy and mischief-making tendencies of venerable people. But happily for the unfortunate, the keen Overseer absorbs little of such gossip, though seeming patiently attentive to all who receive charity from his hand. Understanding the poor failings of human nature, he humors them when he can, rather than inflict pain by rebuke.

... There was a pretty pathos in the little evidences of æsthetic taste peculiar to the Negro people which no degree of misery seems capable of crushing out, and which encounters one in the most unlikely places and in the midst of the uttermost wretchedness. It was nothing short of startling to find that a certain iron railing which guards the opening of a cellar stairway in Bucktown, bore on its lower part that unmistakable Greek border-design which is formed by a single line worked into a beautiful labyrinth of right angles, and which Athenian women embroidered upon their robes three thousand years ago. But it was even more startling to find one's self, in an underground den, face to face with a very faded engraving of the famous face known to art by the name of "Beatrice Cenci," or a pale print after Raphael Morghen. One little picture we noticed on the wall of a miserable frame shanty near Culvert street, which had become little better than an outline under the dimming veil of dinginess and dust, had been carefully fixed into a frame evidently cut out of kindling wood with a penknife. It was an engraving of the head of one of Raphael's Madonnas. In extraordinary contrast hung, nailed to the plank wall beneath it, a ferrotype portrait of some rude-featured white lad; and a frightful chromo, representing

acter; and shuns as much as possible the transaction of business with it
—which contents the Creoles perfectly well. They seem to tolerate those
who understand them, and to abominate those who do not, and propose
to live in the good old way as long as possible—marrying and giving
in marriage, aiding one another in a good brotherly way, and keeping
themselves to themselves. If there is one virtue they possess remarkably,
it is the virtue of minding their own affairs—which, alas! cannot always
be said of all other people who dwell in New Orleans.

Nothing, perhaps, can be funnier than the contrast of character
brought out by the attempt of a stiff-mannered stranger to do business
with a typical Creole, especially if the latter be of the fair sex. Let us
imagine, for example, the episode of renting a house to a foreigner—
somebody whom chance or curiosity has prompted to seek quarters in
the old-fashioned part of the city. The stranger is a little phlegmatic;
the woman is as much the opposite as any human being could well be
—a little dark, tropically dark, but quite attractive, with magnetic eyes,
an electric tongue, and an utter indifference to those ordinary feelings
which prompt landladies to play the agreeable;—proud as a queen, and
quite as determined to show her own individuality as the stranger is
to conceal his own. She has a nice little house; and the stranger would
like to rent it. She would also like to rent it; but only according to her
own original idea of conditions, and she would never think of concealing her inmost feelings on the subject. She is determined that nobody shall impose upon her, and that fact she proposes to explain very
forcibly forthwith; the stranger appears to be a good sort of man, but
appearances are so deceitful in this wicked world!

SHE—"Ah, yes, monsieur, I have a nice little house. Let me beg of
you to wait a moment until I open the other door, so that you can enter
my parlor."

HE—"But what is the rent of the house?"

SHE (in a voice sweeter than the sweetest honey)—"One minute!—
this way, monsieur—come in; be seated, if you please."

HE—"But what is the rent of—"

SHE (shutting the door, and placing herself before it like a statue of
animated bronze, and suddenly changing the sweet voice for a deep
and extraordinarily vibrant alto)—"Ah, now, monsieur, let us at once
understand one another. I have a nice little house. Good! You want
a nice little house. Good! Let us understand one another. In the first
place, I do not rent my house to everybody, monsieur. Oh, no, no,
No!!" (*crescendo*).

HE—"But what is the rent of—"

SHE (imperiously, terrifying him into silence with a flash of her black eyes)—"Do not interrupt me, monsieur. Three things I require from a tenant. Do you know what the first is? No?—then I will tell you. Cash, Cash, CASH! (*crescendo*)—right here in my hand—in advance—ah, yes, all the time in advance."

HE (very timidly)—"Yes, certainly—I know—of course!—I expected; —but what is—"

SHE (in a voice like the deepest tone of a passionately agitated harp) —"*Attends, donc, monsieur.* The second thing which I require from a tenant is a guarantee that he will stay. Ah, yes! I am not one of those who rent houses for a week, or a month, or six months. *Mon Dieu, non!* I must have people who STAY, STAY, STAY (*pianissimo*); and they must stay a long, long time. You must not come to me if you want a house only for—"

HE (with a last and desperate effort, which happens to be partially successful)—"O madam, I want to stay for a number of years in the house, if I take it; but I cannot take it until I have seen it."

SHE—"You shall see it, monsieur, you shall see it (parenthetically). Now the third thing which I require from a tenant is absolute cleanliness, absolute, absolute! No spitting on the walls, no dirt upon the doors, no grease upon the planking, no *cochonnerie* in the yard. You understand me, monsieur? Yes!—you shall see the house: these are the keys."

HE—"But what is the rent of—"

SHE (frightening him into motionlessness by a sudden gypsy-like gesture)—"Ah, monsieur, but I cannot trust you with these keys. No; my servant shall go with you. I cannot have all the doors of my house left open. No; I have had too much experience. My servant shall go with you. She shall bring me back my keys. Marie! come here! Go, monsieur, see the house!"

HE (resignedly)—"Thanks, but may I ask what is—"

SHE (with a superb gesture of withering disgust and another of terrible determination)—"Do you not know, sir, that I would rather shut the house up until the last day of the world than rent it to the *canaille!* Ah! the *canaille! Monsieur!* Ah! the *canaille,* the *canaille!*"

(These last words, with an inexpressible look of horror upon her face, which would make the stranger laugh if he were not afraid to laugh.)

HE—"And the rent is—"

SHE (sweetly as a rose-fed nightingale)—"Twenty-five dollars to a responsible party, monsieur."

The stranger is by this time fairly mesmerized. He has listened to a sermon, heard an oration, received a reproof, watched a most marvelous piece of natural acting by a beautiful woman, and felt his own will and purpose completely crushed out of him by the superior vitality and will-power of this wonderful creature, whose gestures, graceful as a *bayadère's,* seemed to weave a spell of magnetism about him. He sees the house; pays faithfully in advance; gives proper recommendations; and never forgets the three requisites which his landlady taught him as forcibly as though she had burned the words into his brain with a red-hot iron.

The Dawn of the Carnival

THE NIGHT COMETH IN WHICH WE TAKE NO NOTE OF TIME, AND FORGET that we are living in a practical age which mostly relegates romance to printed pages and merriment to the stage. Yet what is more romantic than the Night of the Masked Ball—the too brief hours of light, music, and fantastic merriment which seem to belong to no century and yet to all? Somehow or other, in spite of all the noisy frolic of such nights, the spectacle of a Mardi Gras Ball impresses one at moments as a ghastly and unreal scene. The apparitions of figures which belong to other ages; the Venetian mysteries of the domino; the witchery of beauty half-veiled; the tantalizing salutes from enigmatic figures you cannot recognize; the pretty mockeries whispered into your ear by some ruddy lips whose syllabling seems so strangely familiar and yet defies recognition; the King himself seated above the shifting rout impenetrable as a Sphinx; and the kaleidoscopic changing and flashing of colors as the merry crowd whirls and sways under the musical breath of the orchestra—seem hardly real, hardly possible to belong in any manner to the prosaic life of the century. Even the few unimpassional spectators who remain maskless and motionless form so strange a contrast that they seem like watchers in a haunted palace silently gazing upon a shadowy festival which occurs only once a year in the great hall exactly between the hours of twelve and three. While the most beautiful class of costumes seem ghostly only in that they really do belong to past ages, the more grotesque and outlandish sort seem strangely suggestive of a goblin festival. And above all the charms of the domino! Does it not seem magical that a woman can, by a little bright velvet and shimmering silk, thus make herself a fairy? And the glorious Night is approaching—this quaint old-time night, star-jeweled, fantastically robed; and the blue river is bearing us fleets of white boats thronged with strangers who doubtless are dreaming of lights and music, the tepid, perfumed air of Rex's Palace, and the motley rout of merry ghosts, droll goblins, and sweet fairies, who will dance the dance of the Carnival until blue day puts out at once the trembling tapers of the stars and the lights of the great ball.

Creole Servant Girls

CREOLE COLORED SERVANTS ARE VERY PECULIAR. THEY ARE USUALLY INTELLI-gent, active, shrewd, capable. They generally perform well whatever they undertake. They are too intelligent to be dishonest, knowing the probable consequences. They comprehend a look, an expression, as well as an order; they will fulfill a wish before it is expressed. They see everything, and hear everything, and say nothing. They are consummate actresses, and can deceive even the elect. They can ape humility, simulate affection, pretend ignorance, and feign sorrow so that the imitation is really better than the reality would be, and serves the same purpose. They can tell a lie with the prettiest grace imaginable, or tell a truth in such a manner that it appears to be a lie. They read character with astonishing quickness, and once acquainted with the disposition of their employer will always anticipate his humors and make themselves pliable to his least wish. They are the most admirable waiting-machines which ever existed;—absolutely heartless, without a particle of affection or real respect for an employer or his children, yet simulating love and respect so well that no possible fault can be found with them. Once initiated into the ways of a household, it is seldom necessary to give them an order. They know everything that is required, and everything is done. If regularly paid and well treated, they will remain in a family for a generation. They demand a great deal of liberty when not actually employed, and will not remain in a house when they are not wholly free after working hours to go out or in as they please. They know everything that is going on, and a great deal more than they have any business to know. If they consider their employer discreet, they will furnish him unasked with the strangest secret news. They possess family histories capable of doing infinite mischief, but seldom make use of them, except among each other. To strangers they are absolutely deaf and blind—neither bribes nor promises will extort information from them when asked by persons they do not know. They can keep people at a distance without offending; and become familiar to any extent without making themselves disagreeable. They can be superlatively vicious, and yet appear to be supremely virtuous. They can also be dangerous enemies—and there is no denying the fact that their enmity is to be dreaded. They speak several languages, and sing weird songs. They will do anything that any imagination can conceive for money; and are very friendly, indeed, as long as the money holds out. They are actually very cleanly, oddly superstitious, and very diligent. They have a way of working very hard without appearing to work, and of doing little or no work while appearing to be working themselves to death. Their virtues are simply the result of a great natural shrewdness, which appears to have been handed down from old times, with the Latin blood that beats in the veins of French-speaking quadroons and mulattresses. They will not steal; but they have no moral scruples when the infringement of morality does not involve public disgrace and legal punishment. They do not like American or English-speaking people; and it is probable that none but Creoles know how to manage them. The type is fast disappearing; but it certainly affords one of the most extraordinary studies of human nature possible to conceive.

Why Crabs Are Boiled Alive

AND FOR WHY YOU NOT HAVE OF CRAB? BECAUSE ONE MUST DEM BOIL 'LIVE?
It is all vat is of most beast to tell so. How you make for dem kill so
you not dem boil? You not can cut dem de head off, for dat dey have
not of head. You not can break to dem de back, for dat dey not be
only all back. You not can dem bleed until dey die, for dat dey not
have blood. You not can stick to dem troo de brain, for dat dey be
same like you—dey not have of brain.

Voices of Dawn

A dreadful sound is in his ears.—Job xv, 21.

THERE HAVE NEVER BEEN SO MANY FRUIT-PEDDLERS AND VIAND-PEDDLERS OF
all sorts as at the present time—an encouraging sign of prosperity and
the active circulation of money.

With the first glow of sunlight the street resounds with their cries;
and, really, the famous "Book of London Cries" contains nothing
more curious than some of these vocal advertisements—these musical
announcements, sung by Italians, Negroes, Frenchmen, and Spaniards.
The vendor of fowls pokes in his head at every open window with
cries of "Chick-EN, Madamma, Chick-EN!" and the seller of "Lem-

ONS—fine Lem-ONS!" follows in his footsteps. The peddlers of "Ap-PULLS!" of "Straw-BARE-eries!" and "Black-Brees!"—all own sonorous voices. There is a handsome Italian with a somewhat ferocious pair of black eyes, who sells various oddities, and has adopted the word *lagniappe* for his war-cry—pronouncing it Italianwise.

He advances noiselessly to open windows and doors, plunges his blazing black glance into the interior, and suddenly queries in a deep bass, like a clap of thunder, "LAGNIAPPA, Madama-a!—la-gniap-PA!" Then there is the Cantelope Man, whose cry is being imitated by all the children:

> *Cantel-lope-ah!*
> *Fresh and fine,*
> *Jus from the vine,*
> *Only a dime!*

There are also two peddlers, the precise meaning of whose cries we have never been able to determine. One shouts, or seems to shout, "A-a-a-a-ah! she got." Just what "she got" we have not yet been able to determine; but we fancy it must be disagreeable, as the crier's rival always shouts—"I-I-I!—I want nothing!" with a tremendous emphasis on the I. There is another fellow who seems to shout something which is not exactly proper for modest ears to hear; but he is really only announcing that he has fine potatoes for sale. Then there is the Clothes-pole Man, whose musical, quavering cry is heard at the distance of miles on a clear day, "Clo-ho-ho-ho-ho-ho-ho-ho-se-poles!" As a trilling tenor he is simply marvelous. The "Coaly-coaly" Man, a merry little Gascon, is too well known as a singer to need any criticism; but he is almost ubiquitous. There is also the fig-seller, who crieth in such a manner that his "Fresh figs!" seems to be "Ice crags!" And the fan-sellers, who intend to call, "Cheap fans!" but who really seem to yell "Jap-ans!" and "Chapped hands!" Then there is the seller of "Tow-wells" and the sellers of "Ochre-A" who appear to deal in but one first-class quality of paint, if we dare believe the mendacious sounds which reach our ears; neither must we forget the vendors of "Tom-ate-toes!" Whose toes? we should like to know.

These are new cries, with perhaps three exceptions;—with the old cries added to the list—the *"calas"* and the *"plaisir"* and other Creole calls, we might "spread out" over another column. If any one has a little leisure and a little turn for amusement, he can certainly have plenty of fun while listening to the voices of the peddlers entering his room together with the first liquid gold of sunrise.

The Last of the Voudoos

IN THE DEATH OF JEAN MONTANET, AT THE AGE OF NEARLY A HUNDRED years, New Orleans lost, at the end of August, the most extraordinary African character that ever gained celebrity within her limits. Jean Montanet, or Jean La Ficelle, or Jean Latanié, or Jean Racine, or Jean Grisgris, or Jean Macaque, or Jean Bayou, or "Voudoo John," or "Bayou John," or "Doctor John" might well have been termed "The Last of the Voudoos"; not that the strange association with which he was affiliated has ceased to exist with his death, but that he was the last really important figure of a long line of wizards or witches whose African titles were recognized, and who exercised an influence over the colored population. Swarthy occultists will doubtless continue to elect their "queens" and high-priests through years to come, but the influence of the public school is gradually dissipating all faith in witchcraft, and no black hierophant now remains capable of manifesting such mystic knowledge or of inspiring such respect as Voudoo John exhibited and compelled. There will never be another "Rose," another "Marie," much less another Jean Bayou.

It may reasonably be doubted whether any other Negro of African birth who lived in the South had a more extraordinary career than that of Jean Montanet. He was a native of Senegal, and claimed to have been a prince's son, in proof of which he was wont to call attention to a number of parallel scars on his cheek, extending in curves from the edge of either temple to the corner of the lips. This fact seems to me partly confirmatory of his statement, as Berenger-Feraud dwells at some length on the fact that the Bambaras, who are probably the finest Negro race in Senegal, all wear such disfigurations. The scars are made by gashing the cheeks during infancy, and are considered a sign of race. Three parallel scars mark the freemen of the tribe; four distinguish their captives or slaves. Now Jean's face had, I am told, three scars, which would prove him a free-born Bambara, or at least a member of some free tribe allied to the Bambaras, and living upon their territory. At all events, Jean possessed physical characteristics answering to those by which the French ethnologists in Senegal distinguish the Bambaras. He was of middle height, very strongly built, with broad shoulders, well-developed muscles, an inky black skin, retreating forehead, small bright eyes, a very flat nose, and a woolly beard, gray only during the last few years of his long life. He had a resonant voice and a very authoritative manner.

At an early age he was kidnapped by Spanish slavers, who sold him at some Spanish port, whence he was ultimately shipped to Cuba. His West-Indian master taught him to be an excellent cook, ultimately became attached to him, and made him a present of his freedom. Jean soon afterward engaged on some Spanish vessel as ship's cook, and in the exercise of this calling voyaged considerably in both hemispheres. Finally tiring of the sea, he left his ship at New Orleans, and began life on shore as a cotton-roller. His physical strength gave him considerable advantage above his fellow-blacks; and his employers also discovered that he wielded some peculiar occult influence over the Negroes, which made him valuable as an overseer or gang leader. Jean, in short, possessed the mysterious obi power, the existence of which has been recognized in most slave-holding communities, and with which many a West-Indian planter has been compelled by force of circumstances to effect a compromise. Accordingly Jean was permitted many liberties which other blacks, although free, would never have presumed to take. Soon it became rumored that he was a seer of no small powers, and that he could tell the future by the marks upon bales of cotton. I have never been able to learn the details of this queer method of telling fortunes; but Jean became so successful in the exercise of it that thousands of colored people flocked to him for predictions and counsel, and even white people, moved by curiosity or by doubt, paid him to prophesy for them. Finally he became wealthy enough to abandon the levee and purchase a large tract of property on the Bayou Road, where he built a house. His land extended from Prieur Street on the Bayou Road as far as Roman, covering the greater portion of an extensive square, now well built up. In those days it was a marshy green plain, with a few scattered habitations.

At his new home Jean continued the practice of fortune-telling, but combined it with the profession of Creole medicine, and of arts still more mysterious. By-and-by his reputation became so great that he was able to demand and obtain immense fees. People of both races and both sexes thronged to see him—many coming even from far-away Creole towns in the parishes, and well-dressed women, closely veiled, often knocked at his door. Parties paid from ten to twenty dollars for advice, for herb medicines, for recipes to make the hair grow, for cataplasms supposed to possess mysterious virtues, but really made with scraps of shoe-leather triturated into paste, for advice what ticket to buy in the Havana Lottery, for aid to recover stolen goods, for love powers, for counsel in family troubles, for charms by which to obtain revenge upon an enemy. Once Jean received a fee of fifty dollars for a potion. "It was water," he said to a Creole confidant, "with some common herbs boiled in it. I hurt nobody; but if folks want to give me fifty dollars, I take the fifty dollars every time!" His office furniture consisted of a table, a chair, a picture of the Virgin Mary, an elephant's tusk, some shells which he said were African shells and enabled him to read the future, and a pack of cards in each of which a small hole had been burned. About his person he always carried two small bones wrapped around with a black string, which bones he really appeared to revere as fetiches. Wax candles were burned during his performances; and as he bought a whole box of them every few days during "flush times," one can imagine how large the number of his clients must have been. They poured money into his hands so generously that he became worth at least $50,000!

Then, indeed, did this possible son of a Bambara prince begin to live more grandly than any black potentate of Senegal. He had his carriage and pair, worthy of a planter, and his blooded saddle-horse, which he rode well, attired in a gaudy Spanish costume, and seated upon an elaborately decorated Mexican saddle. At home, where he ate and drank only the best—scorning claret worth less than a dollar the *litre*—he continued to find his simple furniture good enough for him; but he had at least fifteen wives—a harem worthy of Boubakar-Segou. White folks might have called them by a less honorific name, but Jean declared them his legitimate spouses according to African ritual. One of the curious features in modern slavery was the ownership of blacks by freedmen of their own color, and these Negro slave-holders were usually savage and merciless masters. Jean was not; but it was by right of slave purchase that he obtained most of his wives, who bore him children in great multitude. Finally he managed to woo and win a white woman of the lowest class, who might have been, after a fashion, the Sultana-Validé of this Seraglio. On grand occasions Jean used to distribute largess among the colored population of his neighborhood in the shape of food—bowls of *gombo* or dishes of *jimbalaya*. He did it for popularity's sake in those days, perhaps; but in after-years, during the great epidemics, he did it for charity, even when so much reduced in circumstances that he was himself obliged to cook the food to be given away.

But Jean's greatness did not fail to entail certain cares. He did not know what to do with his money. He had no faith in banks, and had seen too much of the darker side of life to have much faith in human nature. For many years he kept his money under-ground, burying or taking it up at night only, occasionally concealing large sums so well that he could never find them again himself; and now, after many years, people still believe there are treasures entombed somewhere in the neighborhood of Prieur Street and Bayou Road. All business negotiations of a serious character caused him much worry, and as he found many willing to take advantage of his ignorance, he probably felt small remorse for certain questionable actions of his own. He was notoriously bad pay, and part of his property was seized at last to cover a debt. Then, in an evil hour, he asked a man without scruples to teach him how to write, believing that financial misfortunes were mostly due to ignorance of the alphabet. After he had learned to write his name, he was innocent enough one day to place his signature by request at the bottom of a blank sheet of paper, and, lo! his real estate passed from his possession in some horribly mysterious way. Still he had some money left, and made heroic efforts to retrieve his fortunes. He bought other property, and he invested desperately in lottery tickets. The lottery craze finally came upon him, and had far more to do with his ultimate ruin than his losses in the grocery, the shoe-maker's shop, and other establishments into which he had put several thousand dollars as the silent partner of people who cheated him. He might certainly have continued to make a good living, since people still sent for him to cure them with his herbs, or went to see him to have their fortunes told; but all his earnings were wasted in tempting fortune. After a score of seizures and a long succession of evictions, he was at last obliged to seek hospitality from some of his numerous children; and of all he had once owned nothing remained to him but his African shells, his elephant's tusk, and the sewing-machine table that had served him to tell fortunes and to burn wax candles upon. Even these, I think, were attached a day or two before his death, which occurred at the house of his daughter by the white wife, an intelligent mulatto with many children of her own.

Jean's ideas of religion were primitive in the extreme. The conversion of the chief tribes of Senegal to Islam occurred in recent years, and it is probable that at the time he was captured by slavers his people were still in a condition little above gross fetichism. If during his years of servitude in a Catholic colony he had imbibed some notions of Romish Christianity, it is certain at least that the Christian ideas were always subordinated to the African—just as the image of the Virgin Mary was used by him merely as an auxiliary fetich in his witchcraft, and was considered as possessing much less power than the "elephant's toof." He was in many respects a humbug; but he may have sincerely believed in the efficacy of certain superstitious rites of his own. He stated that he had a Master whom he was bound to obey; that he could read the will of this Master in the twinkling of the stars; and often of clear nights the neighbors used to watch him standing alone at some street corner staring at the welkin, pulling his woolly beard, and talking in an unknown language to some imaginary being. Whenever Jean indulged in this freak, people knew that he needed money badly, and would probably try to borrow a dollar or two from some one in the vicinity next day.

Testimony to his remarkable skill in the use of herbs could be gathered from nearly every one now living who became well acquainted with him. During the epidemic of 1878, which uprooted the old belief in the total immunity of Negroes and colored people from yellow fever, two of Jean's children were "taken down." "I have no money," he said, "but I can cure my children," which he proceeded to do with the aid of some weeds plucked from the edge of the Prieur Street gutters. One of the herbs, I am told, was what our Creoles call the "parasol." "The children were playing on the *banquette* next day," said my informant.

Montanet, even in the most unlucky part of his career, retained the superstitious reverence of colored people in all parts of the city. When he made his appearance even on the American side of Canal Street to doctor some sick person, there was always much subdued excitement among the colored folks, who whispered and stared a great deal, but were careful not to raise their voices when they said, "Dar's Hoodoo John!" That an unlettered African slave should have been able to achieve what Jean Bayou achieved in a civilized city, and to earn the wealth and the reputation that he enjoyed during many years of his life, might be cited as a singular evidence of modern popular credulity, but it is also proof that Jean was not an ordinary man in point of natural intelligence.

New Orleans Superstitions

I

THE QUESTION "WHAT IS VOUDOOISM?" COULD SCARCELY BE ANSWERED to-day by any resident of New Orleans unfamiliar with the life of the African west coast, or the superstitions of Hayti, either through study or personal observation. The old generation of planters in whose day Voudooism had a recognized existence—so dangerous as a motive power for black insurrection that severe measures were adopted against it—has passed away; and the only person I ever met who had, as a child in his colored nurse's care, the rare experience of witnessing a Voudoo ceremonial, died some three years ago, at the advanced age of seventy-six. As a religion—an imported faith—Voudooism in Louisiana is really dead; the rites of its serpent worship are forgotten; the meaning of its strange and frenzied chants, whereof some fragments linger as refrains in Negro song, is not now known even to those who remember the words; and the story of its former existence is only revealed to the folklorists by the multitudinous débris of African superstition which it has left behind it. These only I propose to consider now; for what is to-day called Voudooism in New Orleans means, not an African cultus, but a curious class of Negro practices, some possibly derived from it, and others which bear resemblance to the magic of the Middle Ages. What could be more mediæval, for instance, than molding a waxen heart, and sticking pins in it, or melting it slowly before a fire, while charms are being repeated with the hope that as the waxen heart melts or breaks, the life of some enemy will depart? What, again, could remind us more of thirteenth-century superstition than the burning of a certain number of tapers to compel some absent person's return, with the idea that before the last taper is consumed a mysterious mesmerism will force the wanderer to cross rivers and mountains if necessary on his or her way back?

The fear of what are styled "Voudoo charms" is much more widely spread in Louisiana than any one who had conversed only with educated residents might suppose; and the most familiar superstition of this class is the belief in what I might call *pillow magic,* which is the supposed art of causing wasting sicknesses or even death by putting certain objects into the pillow of the bed in which the hated person sleeps. Feather pillows are supposed to be particularly well adapted to this kind of witchcraft. It is believed that by secret spells a "Voudoo" can cause some monstrous kind of bird or nondescript animal to shape itself into being out of the pillow feathers—like the *tupilek* of the Esquimau *iliseenek* (witchcraft). It grows very slowly, and by night only; but when completely formed, the person who has been using the pillow dies. Another practice of pillow witchcraft consists in tearing a living bird asunder—usually a cock—and putting portions of the wings into the pillow. A third form of the black-art is confined to putting certain charms or fetiches—consisting of bones, hair, feathers, rags, strings, or some fantastic combination of these and other trifling objects—into any sort of a pillow used by the party whom it is desired to injure. The pure Africanism of this practice needs no comment. Any exact idea concerning the use of each particular kind of charm I have not been able to discover; and I doubt whether those who practise such fetichism know the original African beliefs connected with it. Some say that putting grains of corn into a child's pillow "prevents it from growing any more"; others declare that a bit of cloth in a grown person's pillow will cause wasting sickness; but different parties questioned by me gave each a different signification to the use of similar charms. Putting an open pair of scissors under the pillow before going to bed is supposed to insure a pleasant sleep in spite of fetiches; but the surest way to provide against being "hoodooed," as American residents call it, is to open one's pillow from time to time. If any charms are found, they must be first sprinkled with salt, then burned. A Spanish resident told me that their eldest daughter had been unable to sleep for weeks, owing to a fetich that had been put into her pillow by a spiteful colored domestic. After the object had been duly exorcised and burned, all the young lady's restlessness departed. A friend of mine living in one of the country parishes once found a tow string in his pillow, into the fibers of which a great number of feather stems had either been introduced or had introduced themselves. He wished to retain it as a curiosity, but no sooner did he exhibit it to some acquaintance than it was denounced as a Voudoo "trick," and my friend was actually compelled to burn it in the presence of witnesses. Everybody knows or ought to know that feathers in pillows have a natural tendency to cling and form clots or lumps of more or less curious form, but the discovery of these in some New Orleans households is enough to create a panic. They are viewed as incipient Voudoo tupileks. The sign of the cross is made over them by Catholics, and they are promptly committed to the flames.

Pillow magic alone, however, is far from being the only recognized form of maleficent Negro witchcraft. Placing charms before the entrance of a house or room, or throwing them over a wall into a yard, is believed to be a deadly practice. When a charm is laid before a room door or hall door, oil is often poured on the floor or pavement in front of the threshold. It is supposed that whoever *crosses an oil line* falls into the power of the Voudoos. To break the oil charm, sand or salt should be strewn upon it. Only a few days before writing this article a very intelligent Spaniard told me that shortly after having discharged a dishonest colored servant he found before his bedroom door one evening a pool of oil with a charm lying in the middle of it, and a candle burning near it. The charm contained some bones, feathers, hairs, and rags—all wrapped together with a string—and a dime. No superstitious person would have dared to use that dime; but my friend, not being superstitious, forthwith put it into his pocket.

The presence of that coin I can only attempt to explain by calling attention to another very interesting superstition connected with New Orleans fetichism. The Negroes believe that in order to make an evil charm operate it is necessary *to sacrifice something*. Wine and cake are left occasionally in dark rooms, or candies are scattered over the sidewalk, by those who want to make their fetich hurt somebody. If food or sweetmeats are thus thrown away, they must be abandoned without a parting glance; the witch or wizard must not look back while engaged in the sacrifice.

Scattering dirt before a door, or making certain figures on the wall of a house with chalk, or crumbling dry leaves with the fingers and

scattering the fragments before a residence, are also forms of a maleficent conjuring which sometimes cause serious annoyance. Happily the
conjurers are almost as afraid of the counter-charms as the most superstitious persons are of the conjuring. An incident which occurred recently in one of the streets of the old quarter known as "Spanish Town"
afforded me ocular proof of the fact. Through malice or thoughtlessness, or possibly in obedience to secret orders, a young Negro girl had
been tearing up some leaves and scattering them on the sidewalk in
front of a cottage occupied by a French family. Just as she had dropped
the last leaf the irate French woman rushed out with a broom and a
handful of salt, and began to sweep away the leaves, after having flung
salt both upon them and upon the little Negress. The latter actually
screamed with fright, and cried out, *"Oh, pas jeté plis disel après moin,
madame! pas bisoin jeté disel après moin; mo pas pé vini icite encore."*
(Oh, madam, don't throw any more salt after me; you needn't throw
any more salt after me; I won't come here any more.)

Another strange belief connected with these practices was well illustrated by a gift made to my friend Professor William Henry by a Negro
servant for whom he had done some trifling favor. The gift consisted
of a "frizzly hen"—one of those funny little fowls whose feathers all
seem to curl. "Mars'r Henry, you keep dat frizzly hen, an' ef eny niggers
frow eny *conjure* in your yard, *dat frizzly hen will eat de conjure."*
Some say, however, that one is not safe unless he keeps two frizzly hens.

The naughty little Negress at whom the salt was thrown seemed to
fear the salt more than the broom pointed at her. But she was not yet
fully educated, I suspect, in regard to superstitions. The Negro's terror
of a broom is of very ancient date—it may have an African origin. It
was commented upon by Moreau de Saint-Méry in his work on San
Domingo, published in 1796. "What especially irritates the Negro," he
wrote, "is to have a broom passed over any part of his body. He asks at
once whether the person imagined that he was dead, and remains convinced that the act shortens his life." Very similar ideas concerning the
broom linger in New Orleans. To point either end of a broom at a person is deemed bad luck; and many an ignorant man would instantly
knock down or violently abuse the party who should point a broom at
him. Moreover, the broom is supposed to have mysterious power as a
means of getting rid of people. "If you are pestered by visitors whom
you would wish never to see again, sprinkle salt on the floor after they
go, and sweep it out by the same door through which they have gone,
and they will never come back." To use a broom in the evening is bad

luck: *balayer le soir, on balaye sa fortune* (to sweep in the evening is to sweep your good luck away), remains a well-quoted proverb.

I do not know of a more mysterious disease than muscular atrophy in certain forms, yet it is by no means uncommon either in New Orleans or in the other leading cities of the United States. But in New Orleans, among the colored people, and among many of the uneducated of other races, the victim of muscular atrophy is believed to be the victim of Voudooism. A notion is prevalent that Negro witches possess knowledge of a secret poison which may terminate life instantly or cause a slow "withering away," according as the dose is administered. A Frenchman under treatment for paralysis informed me that his misfortune was certainly the work of Voudoos, and that his wife and child had died through the secret agency of Negro wizards. Mental aberration is also said to be caused by the administration of poisons whereof some few Negroes are alleged to possess the secret. In short, some very superstitious persons of both races live in perpetual dread of imaginary Voudoos, and fancy that the least ailment from which they suffer is the work of sorcery. It is very doubtful whether any knowledge of those animal or vegetable poisons which leave no trace of their presence in the blood, and which may have been known to some slaves of African birth, still lingers in Louisiana, wide-spread as is the belief to the contrary. During the last decade there have been a few convictions of blacks for the crime of poisoning, but there was nothing at all mysterious or peculiar about these cases, and the toxic agent was invariably the most vulgar of all—arsenic, or some arsenious preparation in the shape of rat poison.

II

THE STORY OF THE FRIZZLY HEN BRINGS ME TO THE SUBJECT OF SUPERSTItions regarding animals. Something of the African, or at least of the San Domingan, worship of the cock seems to have been transplanted hither by the blacks, and to linger in New Orleans under various metamorphoses. A Negro charm to retain the affections of a lover consists in tying up the legs of the bird to the head, and plunging the creature alive into a vessel of gin or other spirits. Tearing the live bird asunder is another cruel charm, by which some Negroes believe that a sweetheart may become magically fettered to the man who performs the quartering. Here, as in other parts of the world, the crowing hen is killed, the hooting of the owl presages death or bad luck, and the crowing of the cock by day presages the arrival of company. The wren (*roitelet*) must not be killed: *c'est zozeau bon Dié* (it is the good God's bird)—a belief, I think, of European origin.

It is dangerous to throw hair-combings away instead of burning them, because birds may weave them into their nests, and while the nest remains the person to whom the hair belonged will have a continual headache. It is bad luck to move a cat from one house to another; seven years' bad luck to kill a cat; and the girl who steps, accidentally or otherwise, on a cat's tail need not expect to be married the same year. The apparition of a white butterfly means good news. The neighing of a horse before one's door is bad luck. When a fly bothers one very persistently, one may expect to meet an acquaintance who has been absent many years.

There are many superstitions about marriage, which seem to have a European origin, but are not less interesting on that account. "Twice a bridesmaid, never a bride," is a proverb which needs no comment. The bride must not keep the pins which fastened her wedding dress. The husband must never take off his wedding ring: to take it off will insure him bad luck of some kind. If a girl who is engaged accidentally lets a knife fall, it is a sign that her lover is coming. Fair or foul weather upon her marriage day augurs a happy or unhappy married life.

The superstitions connected with death may be all imported, but I have never been able to find a foreign origin for some of them. It is bad luck to whistle or hum the air that a band plays at a funeral. If a funeral stops before your house, it means that the dead wants company. It is bad luck to cross a funeral procession, or to count the number of carriages in it; if you do count them, you may expect to die after the expiration of as many weeks as there were carriages at the funeral. If at the cemetery there be any unusual delay in burying the dead, caused by any unlooked-for circumstances, such as the tomb proving too small to admit the coffin, it is a sign that the deceased is selecting a companion from among those present, and one of the mourners must soon die. It is bad luck to carry a spade through a house. A bed should never be placed with its foot pointing toward the street door, for corpses leave the house feet foremost. It is bad luck to travel with a priest; this idea seems to me of Spanish importation; and I am inclined to attribute a similar origin to the strange tropical superstition about the banana, which I obtained, nevertheless, from an Italian. You must not *cut* a banana, but simply break it with the fingers, because in cutting it you *cut the cross*. It does not require a very powerful imagination to discern in a severed section of the fruit the ghostly suggestion of a crucifixion.

Some other Creole superstitions are equally characterized by naïve beauty. Never put out with your finger the little red spark that tries to linger on the wick of a blown-out candle: just so long as it burns, some soul in purgatory enjoys rest from torment. Shooting-stars are souls escaping from purgatory: if you can make a good wish three times before the star disappears, the wish will be granted. When there is sunshine and rain together, a colored nurse will tell the children, *"Gadé! djabe apé batte so femme."* (Look! the devil's beating his wife!)

I will conclude this little paper with selections from a list of superstitions which I find widely spread, not citing them as of indubitable Creole origin, but simply calling attention to their prevalence in New Orleans, and leaving the comparative study of them to folklorists.

Turning the foot suddenly in walking means bad or good luck. If the right foot turns, it is bad luck; if the left, good. This superstition seems African, according to a statement made by Moreau de Saint-Méry. Some reverse the conditions, making the turning of the left foot bad luck. It is also bad luck to walk about the house with one shoe on and one shoe off, or, as a Creole acquaintance explained it to me, *"c'est appeler sa mère ou son père dans le tombeau"* (It is calling one's mother or one's father into the grave). An itching in the right palm means coming gain; in the left, coming loss.

Never leave a house by a different door from that by which you entered it; it is "carrying away the good luck of the place." Never live in a house you build before it has been rented for at least a year. When an aged person repairs his or her house, he or she is soon to die. Never pass a child through a window; it stops his growth. Stepping over a child does the same; therefore, whoever takes such a step inadvertently must step back again to break the evil spell. Never tilt a rocking-chair when it is empty. Never tell a bad dream before breakfast, unless you want it "to come true"; and never pare the nails on Monday morning before taking a cup of coffee. A funny superstition about windows is given me in this note by a friend: *"Il ne faut pas faire passer un enfant par la fenêtre, car avant un an il y en aura un autre"* (A child must not be passed through a window, for if so passed you will have another child before the lapse of a year.) This proverb, of course, interests only those who desire small families, and as a general rule Creoles are proud of large families, and show extraordinary affection toward their children.

If two marriages are celebrated simultaneously, one of the husbands will die. Marry at the time of the moon's waning and your good luck will wane also. If two persons think and express the same thought at the same time, one of them will die before the year passes. To chop up food in a pot with a knife means a dispute in the house. If you have a ringing in your ears, some person is speaking badly of you; call out the names of all whom you suspect, and when the ringing stops at the utterance of a certain name, you know who the party is. If two young girls are combing the hair of a third at the same time, it may be taken for granted that the youngest of the three will soon die. If you want to make it stop raining, plant a cross in the middle of the yard and sprinkle it with salt. The red-fish has the print of St. Peter's fingers on its tail. If water won't boil in the kettle, there may be a toad or a toad's egg in it. Never kill a spider in the afternoon or evening, but always kill the spider unlucky enough to show himself early in the morning, for the old French proverb says:

Araignée du matin—chagrin;
Araignée du midi—plaisir;
Araignée du soir—espoir

(A spider seen in the morning is a sign of grief; a spider seen at noon, of joy; a spider seen in the evening, of hope).

Even from this very brief sketch of New Orleans superstitions the reader may perceive that the subject is peculiar enough to merit th attention of experienced folklorists. It might be divided by a comp tent classifier under three heads: I. Negro superstitions confined to th black and colored population; II. Negro superstitions which have proved contagious, and have spread among the uneducated classes of whites; III. Superstitions of Latin origin imported from France, Spain, and Italy. I have not touched much upon superstitions inherited from English, Irish, or Scotch sources, inasmuch as they have nothing especially local in their character here. It must be remembered that the refined classes have no share in these beliefs, and that, with a few really rational exceptions, the practices of Creole medicine are ignored by educated persons. The study of Creole superstitions has only an ethnological value, and that of Creole medicine only a botanical one, in so far as it is related to empiricism.

All this represents an under side of New Orleans life; and if anything of it manages to push up to the surface, the curious growth makes itself visible only by some really pretty blossoms of feminine superstition in regard to weddings or betrothal rings, or by some dainty sprigs of child-lore, cultivated by those colored nurses who tell us that the little chickens throw up their heads while they drink to thank the good God for giving them water.

Caribbean Sketches

'Ti Canotié

I

ONE MIGHT ALMOST SAY THAT COMMERCIAL TIME IN SAINT PIERRE IS measured by cannon-shots—by the signal-guns of steamers. Every such report announces an event of extreme importance to the whole population. To the merchant it is a notification that mails, money, and goods have arrived;—to consuls and Government officials it gives notice of fees and dues to be collected;—for the host of lightermen, longshoremen, port laborers of all classes, it promises work and pay;—for all it signifies the arrival of food. The island does not feed itself: cattle, salt meats, hams, lard, flour, cheese, dried fish, all come from abroad—particularly from America. And in the minds of the colored population the American steamer is so intimately associated with the idea of those great tin cans in which food stuffs are brought from the United States, that the onomatope applied to the can, because of the sound outgiven by it when tapped—*bom!*—is also applied to the ship itself. The English or French or Belgian steamer, however large, is only known as *packett-à, bâtiment-là;* but the American steamer is always the "bom-ship"—*bâtiment-bom-à;* or, the "food-ship"—*bâtiment-mangé-à.* . . . You hear women and men asking each other, as the shock of the gun flaps through all the town, *"Mi! gadé ça qui là, chè?"*—and if the answer be, *"Mais c'est bom-là, chè,—bom-mangé-à ka rivé"* (Why, it is the bom, dear—the food-bom that has come), great is the exultation.

Again, because of the sound of her whistle, we find a steamer called in this same picturesque idiom, *bâtiment-cône*—"the horn-ship." There is even a song, of which the refrain is:

> *Bom-là rivé, chè—*
> *Bâtiment-cône-là rivé.*

. . . But of all the various classes of citizens, those most joyously excited by the coming of a great steamer—whether she be a "bom" or not—are the *'ti canotié,* who swarm out immediately in little canoes of their own manufacture to dive for coins which passengers gladly throw into the water for the pleasure of witnessing the graceful spectacle. No sooner does a steamer drop anchor—unless the water be very rough indeed—than she is surrounded by a fleet of the funniest little boats imaginable, full of naked urchins screaming Creole.

These *'ti canotié*—these little canoe-boys and professional divers—are, for the most part, sons of boatmen of color, the real *canotiers.* I cannot find who first invented the *'ti canot:* the shape and dimensions of the little canoe are fixed according to a tradition several generations old; and no improvements upon the original model seem to have ever been attempted, with the sole exception of a tiny water-tight box contrived sometimes at one end, in which the *palettes,* or miniature paddles, and various other trifles may be stowed away. The actual cost of material for a canoe of this kind seldom exceeds twenty-five or thirty cents; and, nevertheless, the number of canoes is not very large —I doubt if there be more than fifteen in the harbor;—as the families of Martinique boatmen are all so poor that twenty-five sous are difficult to spare, in spite of the certainty that the little son can earn fifty times the amount within a month after owning a canoe.

For the manufacture of a canoe an American lard-box or kerosene-oil box is preferred by reason of its shape; but any well-constructed shipping-case of small size would serve the purpose. The top is removed; the sides and the corners of the bottom are sawn out at certain angles; and the pieces removed are utilized for the sides of the bow and stern—sometimes also in making the little box for the paddles, or palettes, which are simply thin pieces of tough wood about the form and size of a cigar-box lid. Then the little boat is tarred and varnished: it cannot sink—though it is quite easily upset. There are no seats. The boys (there are usually two to each canot) simply squat down in the bottom—facing each other. They can paddle with surprising swiftness over a smooth sea; and it is a very pretty sight to witness one of their prize contests in racing—which take place every 14th of July. . . .

II

. . . IT WAS FIVE O'CLOCK IN THE AFTERNOON: THE HORIZON BEYOND THE harbor was turning lemon-color;—and a thin warm wind began to come in weak puffs from the southwest—the first breaths to break the immobility of the tropical air. Sails of vessels becalmed at the entrance of the bay commenced to flap lazily: they might belly after sundown.

The *La Guayra* was in port, lying well out: her mountainous iron mass rising high above the modest sailing craft moored in her vicinity —barks and brigantines and brigs and schooners and barkentines. She had lain before the town the whole afternoon, surrounded by the entire squadron of 'ti canots; and the boys were still circling about her flanks, although she had got up steam and was lifting her anchor. They had been very lucky, indeed, that afternoon—all the little canotiers;—even many yellow lads, not fortunate enough to own canoes, had swum out to her in hope of sharing the silver shower falling from her saloon-deck. Some of these, tired out, were resting themselves by sitting on the slanting cables of neighboring ships. Perched naked thus —balancing in the sun, against the blue of sky or water, their slender bodies took such orange from the mellowing light as to seem made of some self-luminous substance—flesh of sea-fairies. . . .

Suddenly the *La Guayra* opened her steam-throat and uttered such a "moo" that all the mornes cried out for at least a minute after;—and the little fellows perched on the cables of the sailing craft tumbled into the sea at the sound and struck out for shore. Then the water all at once burst backward in immense frothing swirls from beneath the stern of the steamer; and there arose such a heaving as made all the little canoes dance. The *La Guayra* was moving. She moved slowly at first, making a great fuss as she turned round: then she began to settle down to her journey very majestically—just making the water pitch a little behind her, as the hem of a woman's robe tosses lightly at her heels while she walks.

And, contrary to custom, some of the canoes followed after her. A dark handsome man, wearing an immense Panama hat, and jeweled rings upon his hands, was still throwing money; and still the boys dived for it. But only one of each crew now plunged; for, though the *La Guayra* was yet moving slowly, it was a severe strain to follow her, and there was no time to be lost.

The captain of the little band—black Maximilien, ten years old, and his comrade Stéphane—nicknamed "*Ti Chabin*," because of his bright hair—a slim little yellow boy of eleven—led the pursuit, crying always, "*Encò, Missié—encò!*" ...

The *La Guayra* had gained fully two hundred yards when the handsome passenger made his final largess—proving himself quite an expert in flinging coin. The piece fell far short of the boys, but near enough to distinctly betray a yellow shimmer as it twirled to the water. That was gold!

In another minute the leading canoe had reached the spot, the other canotiers voluntarily abandoning the quest—for it was little use to contend against Maximilien and Stéphane, who had won all the canoe contests last 14th of July. Stéphane, who was the better diver, plunged.

He was much longer below than usual, came up at quite a distance, panted as he regained the canoe, and rested his arms upon it. The water was so deep there, he could not reach the coin the first time, though he could see it: he was going to try again—it was gold, sure enough.

"*Fouinq! ça fond içitt!*" he gasped.

Maximilien felt all at once uneasy. Very deep water, and perhaps sharks. And sunset not far off! The *La Guayra* was diminishing in the offing.

"*Boug-là 'lé fai nou néyé!—laissé y, Stéphane!*" he cried. (The fellow wants to drown us. *Laissé*—leave it alone.)

But Stéphane had recovered breath, and was evidently resolved to try again. It was gold!

"Mais ça c'est lò!"

"Assez, non!" screamed Maximilien. *"Pa plongé 'ncò, moin ka di ou! Ah! foute!"* ...

Stéphane had dived again!

... And where were the others? *"Bon-Dié, gadé oti yo yé!"* They were almost out of sight—tiny specks moving shoreward. ... The *La Guayra* now seemed no bigger than the little packet running between Saint Pierre and Fort-de-France.

Up came Stéphane again, at a still greater distance than before—holding high the yellow coin in one hand. He made for the canoe, and Maximilien paddled toward him and helped him in. Blood was streaming from the little diver's nostrils, and blood colored the water he spat from his mouth.

"Áh! moin té ka di ou laissé y!" cried Maximilien, in anger and alarm. ... *"Gàdé, gàdé sang-à ka coulé nans nez ou—nans bouche ou! ... Mi oti lézautt!"*

Lézautt, the rest, were no longer visible.

"Et mi oti nou yé!" cried Maximilien again. They had never ventured so far from shore.

But Stéphane answered only, *"C'est lò!"* For the first time in his life he held a piece of gold in his fingers. He tied it up in a little rag attached to the string fastened about his waist—a purse of his own invention—and took up his paddles, coughing the while and spitting crimson.

"Mi! mi!—mi oti nou yé!" reiterated Maximilien. "Bon-Dié! look where we are!"

The Place had become indistinct;—the lighthouse, directly behind half an hour earlier, now lay well south: the red light had just been kindled. Seaward, in advance of the sinking orange disk of the sun, was the *La Guayra,* passing to the horizon. There was no sound from the shore: about them a great silence had gathered—the Silence of seas, which is a fear. Panic seized them: they began to paddle furiously.

But Saint Pierre did not appear to draw any nearer. Was it only an effect of the dying light, or were they actually moving toward the semicircular cliffs of Fond-Corré? ... Maxmilien began to cry. The little chabin paddled on—though the blood was still trickling over his breast.

Maximilien screamed out to him:

"*Ou pa ka pagayé—anh?—ou ni bousoin dòmi?*" (Thou dost not paddle, eh?—thou wouldst go to sleep?)

"*Si! moin ka pagayé—epi fò!*" (I am paddling, and hard, too!) responded Stéphane. . . .

"*Ou ka pagayé!—ou ka menti!*" (Thou art paddling!—thou liest!) vociferated Maximilien. . . . "And the fault is all thine. I cannot, all by myself, make the canoe to go in water like this! The fault is all thine: I told thee not to dive, thou stupid!"

"*Ou fou!*" cried Stéphane, becoming angry. "*Moin ka pagayé!*" (I am paddling.)

"Beast! never may we get home so! Paddle, thou lazy;—paddle, thou nasty!"

"*Macaque* thou!—monkey!"

"*Chabin!*—must be *chabin,* for to be stupid so!"

"Thou black monkey!—thou species of *ouistiti!*"

"Thou tortoise-of-the-land!—thou slothful more than *molocoye!*"

"Why, thou cursed monkey, if thou sayest I do not paddle, thou dost not know how to paddle!" . . .

. . . But Maximilien's whole expression changed: he suddenly stopped paddling, and stared before him and behind him at a great violet band broadening across the sea northward out of sight; and his eyes were big with terror as he cried out:

"*Mais ni qui chose qui douôle, içitt!*" . . . (There is something queer, Stéphane; there is something queer.) . . .

"Ah! you begin to see now, Maximilien!—it is the current!"

"A devil-current, Stéphane. . . . We are drifting: we will go to the horizon!" . . .

To the horizon—"*nou kallé l'horizon!*"—a phrase of terrible picturesqueness. . . . In the Creole tongue, "to the horizon" signifies to the Great Open—into the measureless sea.

"*C'est pa lapeine pagayé atouèlement,*" (It is no use to paddle now) sobbed Maximilien, laying down his palettes.

"*Si! si!*" said Stéphane, reversing the motion; "paddle with the current."

"With the current! It runs to La Dominique!"

"*Pouloss,*" phlegmatically returned Stéphane—"*ennou!*" (Let us make for La Dominique!)

"Thou fool!—it is more than past forty kilometres. . . . *Stéphane, mi! gadé!—mi qui gouôs requ'em!*"

A long black fin cut the water almost beside them, passed, and vanished—a *requin* indeed! But, in his patois, the boy almost reëchoed the name as uttered by quaint Père Dutertre, who, writing of strange fishes more than two hundred years ago, says it is called REQUIEM, because for the man who findeth himself alone with it in the midst of the sea, surely a requiem must be sung.

"Do not paddle, Stéphane!—do not put thy hand in the water again!"

III

... THE LA GUAYRA WAS A POINT ON THE SKY-VERGE;—THE SUN'S FACE had vanished. The silence and the darkness were deepening together.

"*Si lanmè ka vini plis fò, ça nou ké fai?*" (If the sea roughens, what are we to do?) asked Maximilien.

"Maybe we will meet a steamer," answered Stéphane: "the *Orinoco* was due to-day."

"And if she pass in the night?"

"They can see us." ...

"No, they will not be able to see us at all. There is no moon."

"They have lights ahead."

"I tell thee, they will not see us at all—*pièss! pièss! pièss!*"

"Then they will hear us cry out."

"No—we cannot cry so loud. One can hear nothing but a steam-whistle or a cannon, with the noise of the wind and the water and the machine. ... Even on the Fort-de-France packet one cannot hear for the machine. And the machine of the *Orinoco* is more big than the church of the 'Centre.'"

"Then we must try to get to La Dominique."

... They could now feel the sweep of the mighty current;—it even seemed to them that they could hear it—a deep low whispering. At long intervals they saw lights—the lights of houses in Pointe-Prince, in Fond-Canonville—in Au Prêcheur. Under them the depth was un-fathomed:—hydrographic charts mark it *sans-fond*. And they passed the great cliffs of Aux Abymes, under which lies the Village of the Abysms.

The red glare in the west disappeared suddenly as if blown out;—the rim of the sea vanished into the void of the gloom;—the night narrowed about them, thickening like a black fog. And the invisible, irresistible power of the sea was now bearing them away from the tall coast—over profundities unknown—over the sans-fond—out "to the horizon."

IV

. . . BEHIND THE CANOE A LONG THREAD OF PALE LIGHT QUIVERED AND twisted: bright points from time to time mounted up, glowered like eyes, and vanished again;—glimmerings of faint flame wormed away on either side as they floated on. And the little craft no longer rocked as before;—they felt another and a larger motion—long slow ascents and descents enduring for minutes at a time;—they were riding the great swells—*riding the horizon.*

Twice they were capsized. But happily the heaving was a smooth one, and their little canoe could not sink: they groped for it, found it, righted it, and climbed in, and baled out the water with their hands.

From time to time they both cried out together, as loud as they could—*"Sucou!—sucou!—sucou!"*—hoping that some one might be looking for them. . . . The alarm had indeed been given; and one of the little steam-packets had been sent out to look for them—with torch-fires blazing at her bows; but she had taken the wrong direction.

"Maximilien," said Stéphane, while the great heaving seemed to grow vaster—*"fau nou ka prié Bon-Dié!"* . . .

Maximilien answered nothing.

"Fau prié Bon-Dié!" (We must pray to the Bon-Dié!) repeated Stéphane.

"Pa lapeine, li pas pè ouè nou atò!" (It is not worth while: He cannot see us now!) answered the little black. . . . In the immense darkness even the loom of the island was no longer visible.

"O Maximilien!—Bon-Dié ka ouè toutt, ka connaitt toutt!" (He sees all; He knows all!) cried Stéphane.

"Y pa pè ouè non pièss atouèelement, moin ben sur!" (He cannot see us at all now—I am quite sure!) irreverently responded Maximilien. . . .

"Thou thinkest the Bon-Dié like thyself!—He has not eyes like thou," protested Stéphane. *"Li pas ka tini coulè; li pas ka tini ziél!"* (He has not color; He has not eyes!) continued the boy, repeating the text of his Catechism—the curious Creole Catechism of old Père Goux of Carbet. (Quaint priest and quaint catechism have both passed away.)

"Moin pa save si li ka tini coulè!" (I know not if He has not color!)

answered Maximilien. "But what I well know is that if He has not eyes, He cannot see. . . . *Fouinq!*—how idiot!"

"Why, it is in the Catechism!" cried Stéphane. . . . " '*Bon-Dié, li conm vent: vent tout-patout, et nou pa save ouè li;—li ka touché nou —li ka boulvésé lanmè.*' " (The Good-God is like the Wind: the Wind is everywhere, and we cannot see It;—It touches us—It tosses the sea.)

"If the Bon-Dié is the Wind," responded Maximilien, "then pray thou the Wind to stay quiet."

"The Bon-Dié is not the Wind," cried Stéphane: "He is *like* the Wind, but He is not the Wind." . . .

"Ah! *soc-soc!—fouinq!* . . . More better past praying to care we be not upset again and eaten by sharks."

.   .   .

. . . Whether the little chabin prayed either to the Wind or to the Bon-Dié, I do not know. But the Wind remained very quiet all that night—seemed to hold its breath for fear of ruffling the sea. And in the Mouillage of Saint Pierre furious American captains swore at the Wind because it would not fill their sails.

V

PERHAPS, IF THERE HAD BEEN A BREEZE, NEITHER STÉPHANE NOR MAXImilien would have seen the sun again. But they saw him rise.

Light pearled in the east, over the edge of the ocean, ran around the rim of the sky and yellowed: then the sun's brow appeared;—a current of gold gushed rippling across the sea before him;—and all the heaven at once caught blue fire from horizon to zenith. Violet from flood to cloud the vast recumbent form of Pelée loomed far behind— with long reaches of mountaining: pale grays o'ertopping misty blues. And in the north another lofty shape was towering—strangely jagged and peaked and beautiful—the silhouette of Dominica: a sapphire saw! . . . No wandering clouds:—over far Pelée only a shadowy piling of nimbi. . . . Under them the sea swayed dark as purple ink—a token of tremendous depth. . . . Still a dead calm, and no sail in sight.

"*Ça c'est la Dominique,*" said Maximilien.—"*Ennou pou ouivage-à!*" They had lost their little palettes during the night;—they used their naked hands, and moved swiftly. But Dominica was many and many a mile away. Which was the nearer island, it was yet difficult to say;—

in the morning sea-haze, both were vapory—difference of color was largely due to position. . . .

Sough!—sough!—sough!—A bird with a white breast passed overhead; and they stopped paddling to look at it—a gull. Sign of fair weather!—it was making for Dominica.

"Moin ni ben faim," murmured Maximilien. Neither had eaten since the morning of the previous day—most of which they had passed sitting in their canoe.

"Moin ni anni soif," said Stéphane. And besides his thirst he complained of a burning pain in his head, always growing worse. He still coughed, and spat out pink threads after each burst of coughing.

The heightening sun flamed whiter and whiter: the flashing of waters before his face began to dazzle like a play of lightning. . . . Now the islands began to show sharper lines, stronger colors; and Dominica was evidently the nearer;—for bright streaks of green were breaking at various angles through its vapor-colored silhouette, and Martinique still remained all blue.

. . . Hotter and hotter the sun burned; more and more blinding became his reverberation. Maximilien's black skin suffered least; but both lads, accustomed as they were to remaining naked in the sun, found the heat difficult to bear. They would gladly have plunged into the deep water to cool themselves but for fear of sharks;—all they could do was to moisten their heads, and rinse their mouths with sea-water.

Each from his end of the canoe continually watched the horizon. Neither hoped for a sail, there was no wind; but they looked for the coming of steamers—the *Orinoco* might pass, or the English packet, or some one of the small Martinique steamboats might be sent out to find them.

Yet hours went by; and there still appeared no smoke in the ring of the sky—never a sign in all the round of the sea, broken only by the two huge silhouettes. . . . But Dominica was certainly nearing;—the green lights were spreading through the luminous blue of her hills. . . . Their long immobility in the squatting posture began to tell upon the endurance of both boys—producing dull throbbing aches in thighs, hips, and loins. . . . Then, about midday, Stéphane declared he could not paddle any more;—it seemed to him as if his head must soon burst open with the pain which filled it: even the sound of his own voice hurt him—he did not want to talk.

VI

. . . AND ANOTHER OPPRESSION CAME UPON THEM—IN SPITE OF ALL THE pains, and the blinding dazzle of waters, and the biting of the sun: the oppression of drowsiness. They began to doze at intervals—keeping their canoe balanced in some automatic way—as cavalry soldiers, overweary, ride asleep in the saddle.

But at last, Stéphane, awaking suddenly with a paroxysm of coughing, so swayed himself to one side as to overturn the canoe; and both found themselves in the sea.

Maximilien righted the craft, and got in again; but the little chabin twice fell back in trying to raise himself upon his arms. He had become almost helplessly feeble. Maximilien, attempting to aid him, again overturned the unsteady little boat; and this time it required all his skill and his utmost strength to get Stéphane out of the water. Evidently Stéphane could be of no more assistance;—the boy was so weak he could not even sit up straight.

"*Aïe! ou ké jété nou encò,*" panted Maximilien—"*metté ou toutt longue.*"

Stéphane slowly let himself down, so as to lie nearly all his length in the canoe—one foot on either side of Maximilien's hips. Then he lay very still for a long time—so still that Maximilien became uneasy.

"*Ou ben malade?*" he asked. . . . Stéphane did not seem to hear: his eyes remained closed.

"*Stéphane!*" cried Maximilien, in alarm—"*Stéphane!*"

"*C'est lò, papoute,*" murmured Stéphane, without lifting his eyelids—"*ça c'est lò!—ou pa janmain ouè yon bel pièce conm ça?*" (It is gold, little father. . . . Didst thou ever see a pretty piece like that? . . . No, thou wilt not beat me, little father?—no, papoute!)

"*Ou ka dòmi, Stéphane?*"—queried Maximilien, wondering—"art asleep?"

But Stéphane opened his eyes and looked at him so strangely! Never had he seen Stéphane look that way before.

"*Ça ou ni, Stéphane?*—what ails thee?—*aïe! Bon-Dié, Bon-Dié!*"

"Bon-Dié!"—muttered Stéphane, closing his eyes again at the sound of the great Name—"He has no color;—He is like the Wind." . . .

"*Stéphane!*" . . .

"He feels in the dark;—He has not eyes." . . .

"Stéphane, pa pàlé çà!!"

"He tosses the sea. . . . He has no face;—He lifts up the dead . . . and the leaves." . . .

"Ou fou!" cried Maximilien, bursting into a wild fit of sobbing— "Stéphane, thou art mad!"

And all at once he became afraid of Stéphane—afraid of all he said —afraid of his touch—afraid of his eyes, . . . he was growing like a zombi!

But Stéphane's eyes remained closed;—he ceased to speak.

. . . About them deepened the enormous silence of the sea;—low swung the sun again. The horizon was yellowing: day had begun to fade. Tall Dominica was now half green; but there yet appeared no smoke, no sail, no sign of life.

And the tints of the two vast Shapes that shattered the rim of the light shifted as if evanescing—shifted like tones of West Indian fishes —of *pisquette* and *congre*—of *caringue* and *gouôs-zié* and *balaou*. Lower sank the sun;—cloud-fleeces of orange pushed up over the edge of the west;—a thin warm breath caressed the sea—sent long lilac shudderings over the flanks of the swells. Then colors changed again: violet richened to purple;—greens blackened softly;—grays smouldered into smoky gold. And the sun went down.

VII

AND THEY FLOATED INTO THE FEAR OF THE NIGHT TOGETHER. AGAIN THE ghostly fires began to wimple about them: naught else was visible but the high stars.

Black hours passed. From minute to minute Maximilien cried out: *"Sucou! sucou!"* Stéphane lay motionless and dumb: his feet, touching Maximilien's naked hips, felt singularly cold.

. . . Something knocked suddenly against the bottom of the canoe— knocked heavily—making a hollow loud sound. It was not Stéphane; —Stéphane lay still as a stone: it was from the depth below. Perhaps a great fish passing.

It came again—twice—shaking the canoe like a great blow. Then Stéphane suddenly moved—drew up his feet a little—made as if to speak: *"Ou . . ."*; but the speech failed at his lips—ending in a sound like the moan of one trying to call out in sleep;—and Maximilien's heart almost stopped beating. . . . Then Stéphane's limbs straightened again; he made no more movement;—Maximilien could not even hear him breathe. . . . All the sea had begun to whisper.

A breeze was rising;—Maximilien felt it blowing upon him. All at once it seemed to him that he had ceased to be afraid—that he did not care what might happen. He thought about a cricket he had one day watched in the harbor—drifting out with the tide, on an atom of dead bark—and he wondered what had become of it. Then he understood that he himself was the cricket—still alive. But some boy had found him and pulled off his legs. There they were—his own legs, pressing against him: he could still feel the aching where they had been pulled off; and they had been dead so long they were now quite cold. . . . It was certainly Stéphane who had pulled them off. . . .

The water was talking to him. It was saying the same thing over and over again—louder each time, as if it thought he could not hear. But he heard it very well: *"Bon-Dié, li conm vent . . . li ka touché nou . . . nou pa save ouè li."* (But why had the Bon-Dié shaken the wind?) *"Li pa ka tini zié,"* answered the water. . . . *Ouille!*—He might all the same care not to upset folks in the sea! . . . *Mi!* . . .

But even as he thought these things, Maximilien became aware that a white, strange, bearded face was looking at him: the Bon-Dié was there—bending over him with a lantern—talking to him in a language he did not understand. And the Bon-Dié certainly had eyes—great gray eyes that did not look wicked at all. He tried to tell the Bon-Dié how sorry he was for what he had been saying about him;—but found he could not utter a word. He felt great hands lift him up to the stars, and lay him down very near them—just under them. They burned blue-white, and hurt his eyes like lightning:—he felt afraid of them. . . . About him he heard voices—always speaking the same language, which he could not understand. . . . "Poor little devils!—poor little devils!" Then he heard a bell ring; and the Bon-Dié made him swallow something nice and warm;—and everything became black again. The stars went out! . . .

. . . Maximilien was lying under an electric-light on board the great steamer *Rio de Janeiro,* and dead Stéphane beside him. . . . It was four o'clock in the morning.

La Grande Anse

I

WHILE AT THE VILLAGE OF MORNE ROUGE, I WAS FREQUENTLY IMPRESSED by the singular beauty of young girls from the northeast coast—all *porteuses,* who passed almost daily, on their way from Grande Anse to Saint Pierre and back again—a total trip of thirty-five miles. . . . I knew they were from Grande Anse, because the village baker, at whose shop they were wont to make brief halts, told me a good deal about them: he knew each one by name. Whenever a remarkably attractive girl appeared, and I would inquire whence she came, the invariable reply (generally preceded by that peculiarly intoned French "Ah!" signifying, "Why, you certainly ought to know!") was "Grande Anse." . . . *Ah! c'est de Grande Anse, ça!* And if any commonplace, uninteresting type showed itself, it would be signaled as from somewhere else—Gros-Morne, Capote, Marigot, perhaps—but never from Grande Anse. The Grande Anse girls were distinguishable by their clear yellow or brown skins, lithe light figures, and a particular grace in their way of dressing. Their short robes were always of bright and pleasing colors, perfectly contrasting with the ripe fruit-tint of nude limbs and faces: I could discern a partiality for white stuffs with apricot-yellow stripes, for plaidings of blue and violet, and various patterns of pink and mauve. They had a graceful way of walking under their trays, with hands clasped behind their heads, and arms uplifted in the manner of caryatides. An artist would have been wild with delight for the chance to sketch some of them. . . . On the whole, they conveyed the impression that they belonged to a particular race, very different from that of the chief city or its environs.

"Are they all banana-colored at Grande Anse?" I asked—"and all as pretty as these?"

"I was never at Grande Anse," the little baker answered, "although I have been forty years in Martinique; but I know there is a fine class of young girls there: *il y a une belle jeunesse là, mon cher!*"

Then I wondered why the youth of Grande Anse should be any finer than the youth of other places; and it seemed to me that the baker's own statement of his never having been there might possibly furnish a clue. . . . Out of the thirty-five thousand inhabitants of Saint Pierre and its suburbs, there are at least twenty thousand who never have been there, and most probably never will be. Few dwellers of the west coast visit the east coast: in fact, except among the white Creoles, who represent but a small percentage of the total population, there are few persons to be met with who are familiar with all parts of their native island. It is so mountainous, and traveling is so wearisome, that populations may live and die in adjacent valleys without climbing the intervening ranges to look at one another. Grande Anse is only about twenty miles from the principal city; but it requires some considerable inducement to make the journey on horseback; and only the professional carrier-girls, plantation messengers, and colored people of peculiarly tough constitution attempt it on foot. Except for the transportation of sugar and rum, there is practically no communication by sea between the west and the northeast coast—the sea is too dangerous—and thus the populations on either side of the island are more or less isolated from each other, besides being further subdivided and segregated by the lesser mountain chains crossing their respective territories. . . . In view of all these things I wondered whether a community so secluded might not assume special characteristics within two hundred years—might not develop into a population of some yellow, red, or brown type, according to the predominant element of the original race-crossing.

II

I HAD LONG BEEN ANXIOUS TO SEE THE CITY OF THE PORTEUSES, WHEN THE opportunity afforded itself to make the trip with a friend obliged to go thither on some important business;—I do not think I should have ever felt resigned to undertake it alone. With a level road the distance might be covered very quickly, but over mountains the journey is slow and wearisome in the perpetual tropic heat. Whether made on horseback or in a carriage, it takes between four and five hours to go from Saint Pierre to Grande Anse, and it requires a longer time to return, as the road is then nearly all uphill. The young porteuse travels almost as rapidly; and the barefooted black postman, who carries the mails in a square box at the end of a pole, is timed on leaving Morne Rouge at 4 A.M. to reach Ajoupa-Bouillon a little after six, and leaving Ajoupa-Bouillon at half-past six to reach Grande Anse at half-past eight, including many stoppages and delays on the way.

Going to Grande Anse from the chief city, one can either hire a horse or carriage at Saint Pierre, or ascend to Morne Rouge by the public conveyance, and there procure a vehicle or animal, which latter is the cheaper and easier plan. About a mile beyond Morne Rouge, where the old Calebasse road enters the public highway, you reach the highest point of the journey—the top of the enormous ridge dividing the northeast from the western coast, and cutting off the trade-winds from sultry Saint Pierre. By climbing the little hill, with a tall stone cross on its summit, overlooking the Champ-Flore just here, you can perceive the sea on both sides of the island at once—lapis lazuli blue. From this elevation the road descends by a hundred windings and lessening undulations to the eastern shore. It sinks between mornes wooded to their summits—bridges a host of torrents and ravines—passes gorges from whence colossal trees tower far overhead, through heavy streaming of lianas, to mingle their green crowns in magnificent gloom. Now and then you hear a low long sweet sound like the deepest tone of a silver flute—a bird-call, the cry of the *siffleur-de-montagne;* then all is stillness. You are not likely to see a white face again for hours, but at intervals a porteuse passes, walking very swiftly, or a field-hand heavily laden; and these salute you either by speech or a lifting of the hand to the head. . . . And it is very pleasant to hear the greetings and to see the smiles of those who thus pass,— the fine brown girls bearing trays, the dark laborers bowed under great burdens of bamboo-grass—*Bonjou', Missié!* Then you should reply, if the speaker be a woman and pretty, "Good-day, dear" (*bon-jou', chè*), or, "Good-day, my daughter" (*mafi*), even if she be old; while if the passer-by be a man, your proper reply is, "Good-day, my son" (*monfi*). . . . They are less often uttered now than in other years, these kindly greetings, but they still form part of the good and true Creole manners.

The feathery beauty of the tree-ferns shadowing each brook, the grace of bamboo and arborescent grasses, seem to decrease as the road descends—but the palms grow taller. Often the way skirts a precipice dominating some marvelous valley prospect; again it is walled in by high green banks or shrubby slopes which cut off the view; and always it serpentines so that you cannot see more than a few hundred feet of the white track before you. About the fifteenth kilometre a glorious landscape opens to the right, reaching to the Atlantic;—the road still winds very high; forests are billowing hundreds of yards below it, and rising miles away up the slopes of mornes, beyond which, here and there, loom strange shapes of mountain—shading off from misty green to violet and faintest gray. And through one grand opening in this multicolored surging of hills and peaks you perceive the gold-yellow of canefields touching the sky-colored sea. Grande Anse lies somewhere in that direction. . . . At the eighteenth kilometre you pass a cluster of little country cottages, a church, and one or two large buildings framed in shade-trees—the hamlet of Ajoupa-Bouillon. Yet a little farther, and you find you have left all the woods behind you. But the road continues its bewildering curves around and between low mornes covered with cane or cocoa plants: it dips down very low, rises again, dips once more;—and you perceive the soil is changing color; it is taking a red tint like that of the land of the American cotton-belt. Then you pass the Rivière Falaise (marked "Filasse" upon old maps)—with its shallow crystal torrent flowing through a very deep and rocky channel—and the Capote and other streams; and over the yellow rim of cane-hills the long blue bar of the sea appears, edged landward with a dazzling fringe of foam. The heights you have passed are no longer verdant, but purplish or gray —with Pelée's cloud-wrapped enormity overtopping all. A very strong warm wind is blowing upon you—the trade-wind, always driving the clouds west: this is the sunny side of Martinique, where gray days and heavy rains are less frequent. Once or twice more the sea disappears and reappears, always over canes; and then, after passing a bridge and turning a last curve, the road suddenly drops down to the shore and into the burgh of Grande Anse.

III

LEAVING MORNE ROUGE AT ABOUT EIGHT IN THE MORNING, MY FRIEND AND I reached Grande Anse at half-past eleven. Everything had been arranged to make us comfortable. I was delighted with the airy corner room, commanding at once a view of the main street and of the sea—

a very high room, all open to the trade-winds—which had been prepared to receive me. But after a long carriage ride in the heat of a
tropical June day, one always feels the necessity of a little physical
exercise. I lingered only a minute or two in the house, and went out
to look at the little town and its surroundings.

As seen from the highroad, the burgh of Grande Anse makes a
long patch of darkness between the green of the coast and the azure
of the water: it is almost wholly black and gray—suited to inspire an
etching. High slopes of cane and meadow rise behind it and on either
side, undulating up and away to purple and gray tips of mountain
ranges. North and south, to left and right, the land reaches out in two
high promontories, mostly green, and about a mile apart—the Pointe
du Rochet and the Pointe de Séguinau, or Croche-Mort, which latter
name preserves the legend of an insurgent slave, a man of color, shot
dead upon the cliff. These promontories form the semicircular bay of
Grande Anse. All this Grande Anse, or "Great Creek," valley is an
immense basin of basalt; and narrow as it is, no less than five streams
water it, including the Rivière de la Grande Anse.

There are only three short streets in the town. The principal, or
Grande Rue, is simply a continuation of the national road; there is a
narrower one below, which used to be called the Rue de la Paille,
because the cottages lining it were formerly all thatched with cane
straw; and there is one above it, edging the cane-fields that billow
away to the meeting of morne and sky. There is nothing of architectural interest, and all is sombre—walls and roofs and pavements. But
after you pass through the city and follow the southern route that
ascends the Séguinau promontory, you can obtain some lovely landscape views—a grand surging of rounded mornes, with farther violet
peaks, truncated or horned, pushing up their heads in the horizon
above the highest flutterings of cane; and looking back above the
town, you may see Pelée all unclouded—not as you see it from the
other coast, but an enormous ghostly silhouette, with steep sides and
almost square summit, so pale as to seem transparent. Then if you
cross the promontory southward, the same road will lead you into
another beautiful valley, watered by a broad rocky torrent—the Valley of the Rivière du Lorrain. This clear stream rushes to the sea
through a lofty opening in the hills; and looking westward between
them, you will be charmed by the exquisite vista of green shapes piling and pushing up one behind another to reach a high blue ridge
which forms the background—a vision of tooth-shaped and fantastical

mountains—part of the great central chain running south and north through nearly the whole island. It is over those blue summits that the wonderful road called "La Trace" winds between primeval forest walls.

But the more you become familiar with the face of the little town itself, the more you are impressed by the strange swarthy tone it preserves in all this splendid expanse of radiant tinting. There are only two points of visible color in it—the church and hospital, built of stone, which have been painted yellow: as a mass in the landscape, lying between the dead-gold of the cane-clad hills and the delicious azure of the sea, it remains almost black under the prodigious blaze of light. The foundations of volcanic rock, three or four feet high, on which the frames of the wooden dwellings rest, are black; and the sea-wind appears to have the power of blackening all timber-work here through any coat of paint. Roofs and façades look as if they had been long exposed to coal-smoke, although probably no one in Grande Anse ever saw coal; and the pavements of pebbles and cement are of a deep ash-color, full of micaceous scintillation, and so hard as to feel disagreeable even to feet protected by good thick shoes. By and by you notice walls of black stone, bridges of black stone, and perceive that black forms an element of all the landscape about you. On the roads leading from the town you note from time to time masses of jagged rock or great boulders protruding through the green of the slopes, and dark as ink. These black surfaces also sparkle. The beds of all the neighboring rivers are filled with dark gray stones; and many of these, broken by those violent floods which dash rocks together—deluging the valleys, and strewing the soil of the bottom-lands (*fonds*) with dead serpents—display black cores. Bare crags projecting from the green cliffs here and there are soot-colored, and the outlying rocks of the coast offer a similar aspect. And the sand of the beach is funereally black—looks almost like powdered charcoal; and as you walk over it, sinking three or four inches every step, you are amazed by the multitude and brilliancy of minute flashes in it, like a subtle silver effervescence.

This extraordinary sand contains ninety per cent of natural steel, and efforts have been made to utilize it industrially. Some years ago a company was formed, and a machine invented to separate the metal from the pure sand—an immense revolving magnet, which, being set in motion under a sand shower, caught the ore upon it. When the covering thus formed by the adhesion of the steel became of a certain thickness, the simple interruption of an electric current precipitated the metal into appropriate receptacles. Fine bars were made from this volcanic steel, and excellent cutting tools manufactured from it: French metallurgists pronounced the product of peculiar excellence, and nevertheless the project of the company was abandoned. Political disorganization consequent upon the establishment of universal suffrage frightened capitalists who might have aided the undertaking under a better condition of affairs; and the lack of large means, coupled with the cost of freight to remote markets, ultimately baffled this creditable attempt to found a native industry.

Sometimes after great storms bright brown sand is flung up from the sea-depths; but the heavy black sand always reappears again to make the universal color of the beach.

IV

BEHIND THE ROOMY WOODEN HOUSE IN WHICH I OCCUPIED AN APARTMENT there was a small garden-plot surrounded with a hedge strengthened by bamboo fencing, and radiant with flowers of the *loseille-bois*—the Creole name for a sort of begonia, whose closed bud exactly resembles a pink and white dainty bivalve shell, and whose open blossom imitates the form of a butterfly. Here and there, on the grass, were nets drying, and nasses—curious fish-traps made of split bamboos interwoven and held in place with *mibi* stalks (the *mibi* is a liana heavy and tough as copper wire); and immediately behind the garden hedge appeared the white flashing of the surf. The most vivid recollection connected with my trip to Grande Anse is that of the first time that I went to the end of that garden, opened the little bamboo gate, and found myself overlooking the beach—an immense breadth of soot-black sand, with pale green patches and stripings here and there upon it—refuse of cane thatch, decomposing rubbish spread out by old tides. The one solitary boat owned in the community lay there before me, high and dry. It was the hot period of the afternoon; the town slept; there was no living creature in sight; and the booming of the surf drowned all other sounds; the scent of the warm strong sea-wind annihilated all other odors. Then, very suddenly, there came to me a sensation absolutely weird, while watching the strange wild sea roaring over its beach of black sand—the sensation of seeing something unreal, looking at something that had no more tangible existence than a memory! Whether suggested by the first white vision of the surf over the bamboo hedge—or by those old green tide-lines on the desolation of the black beach—or by some tone of the speaking of the sea —or something indefinable in the living touch of the wind—or by all of these, I cannot say;—but slowly there became defined within me the thought of having beheld just such a coast very long ago, I could not tell where—in those child-years of which the recollections gradually become indistiguishable from dreams.

Soon as darkness comes upon Grande Anse the face of the clock in the church-tower is always lighted: you see it suddenly burst into yellow glow above the roofs and the cocoa-palms—just like a pharos. In my room I could not keep the candle lighted because of the sea-wind; but it never occurred to me to close the shutters of the great broad windows—sashless, of course, like all the glassless windows of Martinique;—the breeze was too delicious. It seemed full of something vitalizing that made one's blood warmer, and rendered one full of contentment—full of eagerness to believe life all sweetness. Likewise, I found it soporific—this pure, dry, warm wind. And I thought there could be no greater delight in existence than to lie down at night, with all the windows open—and the Cross of the South visible from my pillow—and the seawind pouring over the bed—and the tumultuous whispering and muttering of the surf in one's ears—to dream of that strange sapphire sea white-bursting over its beach of black sand.

V

CONSIDERING THAT GRANDE ANSE LIES ALMOST OPPOSITE TO SAINT PIERRE, at a distance of less than twenty miles even by the complicated windings of the national road, the differences existing in the natural conditions of both places are remarkable enough. Nobody in Saint Pierre sees the sun rise, because the mountains immediately behind the city continue to shadow its roofs long after the eastern coast is deluged with light and heat. At Grande Anse, on the other hand, those tremendous sunsets which delight west coast dwellers are not visible at all; and during the briefer West Indian days Grande Anse is all wrapped in darkness as early as half-past four—or nearly an hour before the orange light has ceased to flare up the streets of Saint Pierre from the sea;—since the great mountain range topped by Pelée cuts off all the slanting light from the east valleys. And early as folks rise in Saint Pierre, they rise still earlier at Grande Anse—before the sun emerges from the rim of the Atlantic: about half-past four, doors are being opened and coffee is ready. At Saint Pierre one can enjoy a sea bath till seven or half-past seven o'clock, even during the time of the sun's earliest rising, because the shadow of the mornes still reaches out upon the bay;—but bathers leave the black beach of Grande Anse by six o'clock; for once the sun's face is up, the light, leveled straight at the eyes, becomes blinding. Again, at Saint Pierre it rains almost every twenty-four hours for a brief while, during at least the greater part of the year; at Grande Anse it rains more moderately and less often. The atmosphere at Saint Pierre is always more or less impregnated with vapor, and usually an enervating heat prevails, which makes exertion unpleasant; at Grande Anse the warm wind keeps the skin comparatively dry, in spite of considerable exercise. It is quite rare to see a heavy surf at Saint Pierre, but it is much rarer not to see it at Grande Anse. . . . A curious fact concerning custom is that few white Creoles care to bathe in front of the town, notwithstanding the superb beach and magnificent surf, both so inviting to one accustomed to the deep still water and rough pebbly shore of Saint Pierre. The Creoles really prefer their rivers as bathing-places; and when willing to take a sea bath, they will walk up and down hill for kilometres in order to reach some river mouth, so as to wash off in the fresh-water afterwards. They say that the effect of sea-salt upon the skin gives *boutons chards* (what we call "prickly heat"). Friends took me all the way to the mouth of the Lorrain one morning that I might have the experience of such a double bath; but after leaving the tepid sea, I must confess the plunge into the river was something terrible—an icy shock which cured me of all further desire for river baths. My willingness to let the sea-water dry upon me was regarded as an eccentricity.

VI

IT MAY BE SAID THAT ON ALL THIS COAST THE OCEAN, PERPETUALLY MOVED by the blowing of the trade-winds, never rests—never hushes its roar. Even in the streets of Grande Anse, one must in breezy weather lift one's voice above the natural pitch to be heard; and then the breakers come in lines more than a mile long, between the Pointe du Rochet and the Pointe de Séguinau—every unfurling a thunder-clap. There is no traveling by sea. All large vessels keep well away from the dangerous coast. There is scarcely any fishing; and although the sea is thick with fish, fresh fish at Grande Anse is a rare luxury. Communication with Saint Pierre is chiefly by way of the national road, winding over mountain ridges two thousand feet high; and the larger portion of merchandise is transported from the chief city on the heads of young women. The steepness of the route soon kills draught-horses and ruins the toughest mules. At one time the managers of a large estate at Grande Anse attempted the experiment of sending their sugar to Saint Pierre in iron carts drawn by five mules; but the animals could not endure the work. Cocoa can be carried to Saint Pierre by the porteuses, but sugar and rum must go by sea, or not at all; and the risks and difficulties of shipping these seriously affect the prosperity of all the north and northeast coast. Planters have actually been ruined by inability to send their products to market during a protracted spell of rough weather. A railroad has been proposed and planned: in a more prosperous era it might be constructed, with the result of greatly developing all the Atlantic side of the island, and converting obscure villages into thriving towns.

Sugar is very difficult to ship; rum and tafia can be handled with less risk. It is nothing less than exciting to watch a shipment of tafia from Grande Anse to Saint Pierre.

A little vessel approaches the coast with extreme caution, and anchors in the bay some hundred yards beyond the breakers. She is what they call a *pirogue* here, but not at all what is called a pirogue in the United States: she has a long narrow hull, two masts, no deck; she has usually a crew of five, and can carry thirty barrels of tafia. One of the pirogue men puts a great shell to his lips and sounds a call, very mellow and deep, that can be heard over the roar of the waves far up among the hills. The shell is one of those great spiral shells, weighing seven or eight pounds—rolled like a scroll, fluted and scalloped about the edges, and pink-pearled inside—such as are sold in America for mantel-piece ornaments—the shell of a lambi. Here you can often see the lambi crawling about with its nacreous house upon its back: an enormous sea-snail with a yellowish back and rose-colored belly, with big horns and eyes in the tip of each horn—very pretty eyes, having a golden iris. This creature is a common article of food; but its thick white flesh is almost compact as cartilage, and must be pounded before being cooked.[1]

---

[1] Y *batt li conm lambi*—"he beat him like a lambi"—is an expression that may often be heard in a Creole court from witnesses testifying in a case of assault and battery. One must have seen a lambi pounded to appreciate the terrible picturesqueness of the phrase.

At the sound of the blowing of the lambi-shell, wagons descend to the beach, accompanied by young colored men running beside the mules. Each wagon discharges a certain number of barrels of tafia, and simultaneously the young men strip. They are slight, well built, and generally well muscled. Each man takes a barrel of tafia, pushes it before him into the surf, and then begins to swim to the pirogue— impelling the barrel before him. I have never seen a swimmer attempt to convey more than one barrel at a time; but I am told there are experts who manage as many as three barrels together—pushing them forward in line, with the head of one against the bottom of the next. It really requires much dexterity and practice to handle even one barrel or cask. As the swimmer advances he keeps close as possible to his charge—so as to be able to push it forward with all his force against each breaker in succession—making it dive through. If it once glide well out of his reach while he is in the breakers, it becomes an enemy, and he must take care to keep out of its way—for if a wave throws it at him, or rolls it over him, he may be seriously injured; but the expert seldom abandons a barrel. Under the most favorable conditions, man and barrel will both disappear a score of times before the clear swells are reached, after which the rest of the journey is not difficult. Men lower ropes from the pirogue, the swimmer passes them under his barrel, and it is hoisted aboard.

. . . Wonderful surf-swimmers these men are;—they will go far out for mere sport in the roughest kind of a sea, when the waves, abnormally swollen by the peculiar conformation of the bay, come rolling in thirty and forty feet high. Sometimes, with the swift impulse of ascending a swell, the swimmer seems suspended in air as it passes beneath him, before he plunges into the trough beyond. The best swimmer is a young capre who cannot weigh more than a hundred and twenty pounds. Few of the Grande Anse men are heavily built; they do not compare for stature and thew with those longshoremen at Saint Pierre who can be seen any busy afternoon on the landing, lifting heavy barrels at almost the full reach of their swarthy arms.

. . . There is but one boat owned in the whole parish of Grande Anse—a fact due to the continual roughness of the sea. It has a little mast and sail, and can hold only three men. When the water is somewhat less angry than usual, a colored crew take it out for a fishing expedition. There is always much interest in this event; a crowd gathers on the beach; and the professional swimmers help to bring the little craft beyond the breakers. When the boat returns after a disappearance of several hours, everybody runs down from the village to meet it. Young colored women twist their robes up about their hips, and wade out to welcome it: there is a display of limbs of all colors on such occasions, which is not without grace, that untaught grace which tempts an artistic pencil. Every *bonne* and every house-keeper struggles for the first chance to buy the fish;—young girls and children dance in the water for delight, all screaming, *"Rhalé bois-canot!"* . . . Then as the boat is pulled through the surf and hauled up on the sand, the pushing and screaming and crying become irritating and deafening; the fishermen lose patience and say terrible things. But nobody heeds them in the general clamoring and haggling and furious bidding for the *pouèssonouge,* the *dorades,* the *volants* (beautiful purple-backed flying-fish with silver bellies, and fins all transparent, like the wings of dragon-flies). There is great bargaining even for a young shark—which makes very nice eating cooked after the Creole fashion. So seldom can the fishermen venture out that each trip makes a memorable event for the village.

The Saint Pierre fishermen very seldom approach the bay, but they do much fishing a few miles beyond it, almost in front of the Pointe du Rochet and the Roche à Bourgaut. There the best flying-fish are caught—and besides edible creatures, many queer things are often brought up by the nets: monstrosities such as the coffre-fish, shaped almost like a box, of which the lid is represented by an extraordinary conformation of the jaws;—and the *barrique-de-vin* (wine-cask), with round boneless body, secreting in a curious vesicle a liquor precisely resembling wine lees;—and the "needle-fish" (*aiguille de mer*), less thick than a Faber lead-pencil, but more than twice as long;—and huge cuttle-fish and prodigious eels. One conger secured off this coast measured over twenty feet in length, and weighed two hundred and fifty pounds—a veritable sea-serpent. . . . But even the fresh-water inhabitants of Grande Anse are amazing. I have seen crawfish by actual measurement fifty centimetres long, but these were not considered remarkable. Many are said to much exceed two feet from the tail to the tip of the claws and horns. They are of an iron-black color, and have formidable pincers with serrated edges and tip-points inwardly converging, which cannot crush like the weapons of a lobster, but which will cut the flesh and make a small ugly wound. At first sight one not familiar with the crawfish of these regions can hardly believe he is not viewing some variety of gigantic lobster instead of the common fresh-water crawfish of the east coast. When the head, tail, legs, and cuirass have all been removed, after boiling, the curved trunk has still the size and weight of a large pork sausage.

These creatures are trapped by lantern-light. Pieces of manioc root tied fast to large bowlders sunk in the river are the only bait;—the crawfish will flock to eat it upon any dark night, and then they are caught with scoop-nets and dropped into covered baskets.

VII

ONE WHOSE IDEAS OF THE PEOPLE OF GRANDE ANSE HAD BEEN FORMED ONLY by observing the young porteuses of the region on their way to the other side of the island, might expect on reaching this little town to find its population yellow as that of a Chinese city. But the dominant hue is much darker, although the mixed element is everywhere visible; and I was at first surprised by the scarcity of those clear bright skins I supposed to be so numerous. Some pretty children—notably a pair of twin-sisters, and perhaps a dozen school-girls from eight to ten years of age—displayed the same characteristics I have noted in the adult porteuses of Grande Anse; but within the town itself this brighter element is in the minority. The predominating race element of the whole commune is certainly colored (Grande Anse is even memorable because of the revolt of its *hommes de couleur* some fifty years ago);—but the colored population is not concentrated in the town; it belongs rather to the valleys and the heights surrounding the *chef-lieu*. Most of the porteuses are country girls, and I found that even those living in the village are seldom visible on the streets except when departing upon a trip or returning from one. An artist wishing to study the type might, however, pass a day at the bridge of the Rivière Falaise to advantage, as all the carrier-girls pass it at certain hours of the morning and evening.

But the best possible occasion on which to observe what my friend the baker called *la belle jeunesse,* is a confirmation day—when the bishop drives to Grande Anse over the mountains, and all the population turns out in holiday garb, and the bells are tapped like tam-tams, and triumphal arches—most awry to behold!—span the roadway, bearing in clumsiest lettering the welcome, *"Vive Monseigneur."* On that event, the long procession of young girls to be confirmed—all in white robes, white veils, and white satin slippers—is a numerical surprise. It is a moral surprise also—to the stranger at least; for it reveals the struggle of a poverty extraordinary with the self-imposed obligations of a costly ceremonialism.

No white children ever appear in these processions: there are not half a dozen white families in the whole urban population of about seven thousand souls; and those send their sons and daughters to Saint Pierre or Morne Rouge for their religious training and education. But many of the colored children look very charming in their costume of confirmation;—you could not easily recognize one of them as the same little bonne who brings your morning cup of coffee, or another as the daughter of a plantation *commandeur* (overseer's assistant)—a brown slip of a girl who will probably never wear shoes again. And many of those white shoes and white veils have been obtained only by the hardest physical labor and self-denial of poor parents and relatives: fathers, brothers, and mothers working with cutlass and hoe in the snake-swarming cane-fields;—sisters walking barefooted every day to Saint Pierre and back to earn a few francs a month.

. . . While watching such a procession it seemed to me that I could discern in the features and figures of the young confirmants something of a prevailing type and tint, and I asked an old planter beside me if he thought my impression correct.

"Partly," he answered; "there is certainly a tendency toward an attractive physical type here, but the tendency itself is less stable than you imagine; it has been changed during the last twenty years within my own recollection. In different parts of the island particular types appear and disappear with a generation. There is a sort of race-fermentation going on, which gives no fixed result of a positive sort for any great length of time. It is true that certain elements continue to dominate in certain communes, but the particular characteristics come and vanish in the most mysterious way. As to color, I doubt if any correct classification can be made, especially by a stranger. Your eyes give you general ideas about a red type, a yellow type, a brown type; but to the more experienced eyes of a Creole, accustomed to live in the country districts, every individual of mixed race appears to have a particular color of his own. Take, for instance, the so-called *capre* type, which furnishes the finest physical examples of all—you, a stranger, are at once impressed by the general red tint of the variety; but you do not notice the differences of that tint in different persons, which are more difficult to observe than shade-differences of yellow or brown. Now, to me, every capre or capresse has an individual color; and I do not believe that in all Martinique there are two half-breeds

—not having had the same father and mother—in whom the tint is precisely the same."

VIII

I THOUGHT GRANDE ANSE THE MOST SLEEPY PLACE I HAD EVER VISITED. I suspect it is one of the sleepiest in the whole world. The wind, which tans even a Creole of Saint Pierre to an unnatural brown within forty-eight hours of his sojourn in the village, has also a peculiarly somno-lent effect. The moment one has nothing particular to do, and ventures to sit down idly with the breeze in one's face, slumber comes; and everybody who can spare the time takes a long nap in the afternoon, and little naps from hour to hour. For all that, the heat of the east coast is not enervating, like that of Saint Pierre; one can take a great deal of exercise in the sun without feeling much the worse. Hunting excursions, river fishing parties, surf-bathing, and visits to neighbor-ing plantations are the only amusements; but these are enough to make existence very pleasant at Grande Anse. The most interesting of my own experiences were those of a day passed by invitation at one of the old colonial estates on the hills near the village.

It is not easy to describe the charm of a Creole interior, whether in the city or the country. The cool shadowy court, with its wonderful plants and fountain of sparkling mountain water, or the lawn, with its ancestral trees—the delicious welcome of the host, whose fraternal easy manner immediately makes you feel at home—the coming of the children to greet you, each holding up a velvety brown cheek to be kissed, after the old-time custom—the romance of the unconventional chat, over a cool drink, under the palms and the ceibas—the visible earnestness of all to please the guest, to inwrap him in a very atmos-phere of quiet happiness—combine to make a memory which you will never forget. And maybe you enjoy all this upon some exquisite site, some volcanic summit, overlooking slopes of a hundred greens—mountains far winding in blue and pearly shadowing—rivers singing seaward behind curtains of arborescent reeds and bamboos—and, per-haps, Pelée, in the horizon, dreaming violet dreams under her foulard of vapors—and, encircling all, the still sweep of the ocean's azure bending to the verge of day.

. . . My host showed or explained to me all that he thought might interest a stranger. He had brought to me a nest of the *carouge,* a bird which suspends its home, hammock-fashion, under the leaves of the banana-tree;—showed me a little *fer-de-lance,* freshly killed by one of his field hands; and a field lizard (*zanoli té* in Creole), not green like the lizards which haunt the roofs of Saint Pierre, but of a beautiful brown bronze, with shifting tints; and eggs of the zanoli, little soft oval things from which the young lizards will perhaps run out alive as fast as you open the shells; and the *matoutou-falaise,* or spider of the cliffs, of two varieties, red or almost black when adult, and bluish silvery tint when young—less in size than the tarantula, but equally hairy and venomous; and the *crabe-c'est-ma-faute* (the "Through-my-fault Crab"), having one very small and one very large claw, which latter it carries folded up against its body, so as to have suggested the idea of a penitent striking his bosom, and uttering the sacramental words of the Catholic confession, "Through my fault, through my fault, through my most grievous fault." ... Indeed I cannot recollect one-half of the queer birds, queer insects, queer reptiles, and queer plants to which my attention was called. But speaking of plants, I was impressed by the profusion of the *zhèbe-moin-misé*—a little sensitive-plant I had rarely observed on the west coast. On the hillsides of Grande Anse it prevails to such an extent as to give certain slopes its own peculiar greenish-brown color. It has many-branching leaves, only one inch and a half to two inches long, but which recall the form of certain common ferns; these lie almost flat upon the ground. They fold together upward from the central stem at the least touch, and the plant thus makes itself almost imperceptible;—it seems to live so, that you feel guilty of murder if you break off a leaf. It is called *Zhèbe-moin-misé,* or "Plant-did-I-amuse-myself," because it is supposed to tell naughty little children who play truant, or who delay much longer than is necessary in delivering a message, whether they deserve a whipping or not. The guilty child touches the plant, and asks, *"Ess moin amisé moin?"* (Did I amuse myself?); and if the plant instantly shuts its leaves up, that means, "Yes, you did!" Of course the leaves invariably close; but I suspect they invariably tell the truth, for all colored children, in Grande Anse at least, are much more inclined to play than work.

The kind old planter likewise conducted me over the estate. He took me through the sugar-mill, and showed me, among other more recent inventions, some machinery devised nearly two centuries ago by the ingenious and terrible Père Labat, and still quite serviceable, in spite of all modern improvements in sugar-making;—took me through the *rhummerie,* or distillery, and made me taste some colorless rum which had the aroma and something of the taste of the most delicate gin;—and finally took me into the *cases-à-vent,* or "wind-houses"—built as places of refuge during hurricanes. Hurricanes are rare, and more rare in this century by far than during the previous one; but this part of the island is particularly exposed to such visitations, and almost every old plantation used to have one or two cases-à-vent. They were always built in a hollow, either natural or artificial, below the land-level—with walls of rock several feet thick, and very strong doors, but no windows. My host told me about the experiences of his family in some case-à-vent during a hurricane which he recollected. It was found necessary to secure the door within by means of strong ropes; and the mere task of holding it taxed the strength of a dozen power-ful men: it would bulge in under the pressure of the awful wind—swelling like the side of a barrel; and had not its planks been made of a wood tough as hickory, they would have been blown into splinters.

I had long desired to examine a plantation drum, and see it played upon under conditions more favorable than the excitement of a holi-day *caleinda* in the villages, where the amusement is too often termi-nated by a *voum* (general row) or a *goumage* (a serious fight);—and when I mentioned this wish to the planter he at once sent word to his commandeur, the best drummer in the settlement, to come up to the house and bring his instrument with him. I was thus enabled to make the observations necessary, and also to take an instantaneous photograph of the drummer in the very act of playing.

The old African dances, the caleinda and the *bélé* (which latter is accompanied by chanted improvisation) are danced on Sundays to the sound of the drum on almost every plantation in the island. The drum, indeed, is an instrument to which the country-folk are so much attached that they swear by it—*Tambou!* being the oath uttered upon all ordinary occasions of surprise or vexation. But the instrument is quite as often called *ka,* because made out of a quarter-barrel, or quart—in the patois *ka.* Both ends of the barrel having been removed, a wet hide, well wrapped about a couple of hoops, is driven on, and in drying the stretched skin obtains still further tension. The other end of the ka is always left open. Across the face of the skin a string is tightly stretched, to which are attached, at intervals of about an inch apart, very short thin fragments of bamboo or cut feather stems. These lend a certain vibration to the tones.

In the time of Père Labat the Negro drums had a somewhat differ-ent form. There were then two kinds of drums—a big tamtam and a little one, which used to be played together. Both consisted of skins tightly stretched over one end of a wooden cylinder, or a section of hollow tree trunk. The larger was from three to four feet long with a diameter of fifteen to sixteen inches; the smaller, called *baboula*,[2] was of the same length, but only eight or nine inches in diameter. Père Labat also speaks, in his West Indian travels, of another musical instrument, very popular among the Martinique slaves of his time— "a sort of guitar" made out of a half-calabash or *couï,* covered with some kind of skin. It had four strings of silk or catgut, and a very long neck. The tradition of this African instrument is said to survive in the modern *banza* (*banza nèg Guinée*).

The skillful player (*bel tambouyé*) straddles his ka stripped to the waist, and plays upon it with the finger-tips of both hands simultaneously—taking care that the vibrating string occupies a horizontal position. Occasionally the heel of the naked foot is pressed lightly or vigorously against the skin, so as to produce changes of tone. This is called "giving heel" to the drum—*baill y talon.* Meanwhile a boy keeps striking the drum at the uncovered end with a stick, so as to produce a dry clattering accompaniment. The sound of the drum itself, well played, has a wild power that makes and masters all the excitement of the dance—a complicated double roll, with a peculiar billowy rising and falling. The Creole onomatopes, "b'lip-b'lib-b'lib-b'lip," do not fully render the roll;—for each "b'lip" or "b'lib" stands really for a series of sounds too rapidly filliped out to be imitated by articulate speech. The tapping of a ka can be heard at surprising distances; and experienced players often play for hours at a time without exhibiting wearisomeness, or in the least diminishing the volume of sound produced.

It seems there are many ways of playing—different measures familiar to all these colored people, but not easily distinguished by anybody else; and there are great matches sometimes between celebrated tambouyé. The same commandè whose portrait I took while playing told me that he once figured in a contest of this kind, his rival being a drummer from the neighboring burgh of Marigot. . . . "*Aie, aïe, yaïe! mon chè!—y fai tambou-à pàlé!*" said the commandè, describing the execution of his antagonist;—"my dear, he just made that drum

---

[2] Moreau de Saint-Méry writes, describing the drums of the Negroes of Saint Domingue: "*Le plus court de ces tambours est nommé Bamboula, attendu qu'il est formé quelquefois d'un très-gros bambou.*" (*Description de la partie française de Saint Domingue,* vol. I, p. 44.)

talk! I thought I was going to be beaten for sure; I was trembling all the time—*aïe, yaïe-yaïe!* Then he got off that ka. I mounted it; I thought a moment; then I struck up the 'River-of-the-Lizard'—*mais, mon chè, yon larivie-Léza toutt pi!*—such a River-of-the-Lizard, ah! just perfectly pure! I gave heel to that ka; I worried that ka;—I made it mad;—I made it crazy;—I made it talk;—I won!"

During some dances a sort of chant accompanies the music—a long sonorous cry, uttered at intervals of seven or eight seconds, which perfectly times a particular measure in the drum roll. It may be the burden of a song, or a mere improvisation:

> *Oh! yoïe-yoïe!*
>
> (*Drum roll.*)
>
> *Oh! missié-à!*
>
> (*Drum roll.*)
>
> *Y bel tambouyé!*
>
> (*Drum roll.*)
>
> *Aie, ya, yaie!*
>
> (*Drum roll.*)
>
> *Joli tambouyé!*
>
> (*Drum roll.*)
>
> *Chauffé tambou-à!*
>
> (*Drum roll.*)
>
> *Géné tambou-à!*
>
> (*Drum roll.*)
>
> *Crazé tambou-à!* etc., etc.

. . . The *crieur*, or chanter, is also the leader of the dance. The caleinda is danced by men only, all stripped to the waist, and twirling heavy sticks in a mock fight. Sometimes, however—especially at the great village gatherings, when the blood becomes overheated by tafia—the mock fight may become a real one; and then even cutlasses are brought into play.

But in the old days, those improvisations which gave one form of dance its name, *bélé* (from the French *bel air*), were often remarkable rhymeless poems, uttered with natural simple emotion, and full of picturesque imagery. I cite part of one, taken down from the dictation of a common field-hand near Fort-de-France. I offer a few lines of the Creole first, to indicate the form of the improvisation. There is a dancing pause at the end of each line during the performance:

Toutt fois lanmou vini lacase moin
Pou pàlé moin, moin ka reponne:
"Khé moin deja placé."
Moin ka crié, "Sécou! les voisinages!"
Moin ka crié, "Sécou! la gàde royale!"
Moin ka crié, "Sécou! la gendàmerie!
Lanmou pouend yon poignâ pou poignadé moin!"

The best part of the composition, which is quite long, might be rendered as follows:

Each time that Love comes to my cabin
To speak to me of love, I make answer.
"My heart is already placed."
I cry out, "Help, neighbors! help!"
I cry out, "Help, *la Garde Royale!"*
I cry out, "Help, help, gendarmes!
Love takes a poniard to stab me;
How can Love have a heart so hard
To thus rob me of my health!"
When the officer of police comes to me
To hear me tell him the truth,
To have him arrest my Love;—
When I see the Garde Royale
Coming to arrest my sweet heart,
I fall down at the feet of the Garde Royale,—
I pray for mercy and forgiveness.
"Arrest me instead, but let my dear Love go!"
How, alas! with this tender heart of mine,
Can I bear to see such an arrest made!
No, no! I would rather die!
Dost not remember, when our pillows lay close
    together,
How we told each to the other all that our hearts
    thought?
    ... etc.

The stars were all out when I bid my host good-bye;—he sent his black servant along with me to carry a lantern and keep a sharp watch for snakes along the mountain road.

IX

... ASSUREDLY THE CITY OF SAINT PIERRE NEVER COULD HAVE SEEMED MORE quaintly beautiful than as I saw it on the evening of my return, while the shadows were reaching their longest, and sea and sky were turning lilac. Palm-heads were trembling and masts swaying slowly against an enormous orange sunset—yet the beauty of the sight did not touch me! The deep level and luminous flood of the bay seemed to me for the first time a dead water;—I found myself wondering whether it could form a part of that living tide by which I had been dwelling, full of foam-lightnings and perpetual thunder. I wondered whether the air about me—heavy and hot and full of faint leafy smells—could ever have been touched by the vast pure sweet breath of the wind from the sunrising. And I became conscious of a profound, unreasoning, absurd regret for the somnolent little black village of that bare east coast— where there are no woods, no ships, no sunsets, . . . only the ocean roaring forever over its beach of black sand.

Les Porteuses

I

WHEN YOU FIND YOURSELF FOR THE FIRST TIME, UPON SOME UNSHADOWED day, in the delightful West Indian city of Saint Pierre—supposing that you own the sense of poetry, the recollections of a student—there is apt to steal upon your fancy an impression of having seen it all before, ever so long ago—you cannot tell where. The sensation of some happy dream you cannot wholly recall might be compared to this feeling. In the simplicity and solidity of the quaint architecture—in the eccentricity of bright narrow streets, all aglow with warm coloring—in the tints of roof and wall, antiquated by streakings and patchings of

is. . . . Let me tell you something about that highest type of professional female carrier, which is to the *charbonnière,* or coaling-girl, what the thorough-bred racer is to the draught-horse—the type of porteuse selected for swiftness and endurance to distribute goods in the interior parishes, or to sell on commission at long distances. To the same class naturally belong those country carriers able to act as porteuses of plantation produce, fruits, or vegetables—between the nearer ports and their own interior parishes. . . . Those who believe that great physical endurance and physical energy cannot exist in the tropics do not know the Creole carrier-girl.

IV

AT A VERY EARLY AGE—PERHAPS AT FIVE YEARS—SHE LEARNS TO CARRY small articles upon her head—a bowl of rice—a *dobanne,* or red earthen decanter, full of water—even an orange on a plate; and before long she is able to balance these perfectly without using her hands to steady them. (I have often seen children actually run with cans of water upon their heads, and never spill a drop.) At nine or ten she is able to carry thus a tolerably heavy basket, or a *trait* (a wooden tray with deep outward sloping sides) containing a weight of from twenty to thirty pounds; and is able to accompany her mother, sister, or cousin on long peddling journeys—walking barefoot twelve and fifteen miles a day. At sixteen or seventeen she is a tall robust girl—lithe, vigorous, tough—all tendon and hard flesh;—she carries a tray or a basket of the largest size, and a burden of one hundred and twenty to one hundred and fifty pounds weight;—she can now earn about thirty francs (about six dollars) a month, *by walking fifty miles a day,* as an itinerant seller.

Among her class there are figures to make you dream of Atalanta;—and all, whether ugly or attractive as to feature, are finely shapen as to body and limb. Brought into existence by extraordinary necessities of environment, the type is a peculiarly local one—a type of human thoroughbred representing the true secret of grace: economy of force. There are no corpulent porteuses for the long interior routes; all are built lightly and firmly as racers. There are no old porteuses;—to do the work even at forty signifies a constitution of astounding solidity. After the full force of youth and health is spent, the poor carrier must seek lighter labor;—she can no longer compete with the girls. For in this calling the young body is taxed to its utmost capacity of strength, endurance, and rapid motion.

As a general rule, the weight is such that no well-freighted porteuse can, unassisted, either "load" or "unload" (*châgé* or *déchâgé,* in Creole phrase); the effort to do so would burst a blood vessel, wrench a nerve, rupture a muscle. She cannot even sit down under her burden without risk of breaking her neck: absolute perfection of the balance is necessary for self-preservation. A case came under my own observation of a woman rupturing a muscle in her arm through careless haste in the mere act of aiding another to unload.

And no one not a brute will ever refuse to aid a woman to lift or to relieve herself of her burden;—you may see the wealthiest merchant, the proudest planter, gladly do it;—the meanness of refusing, or of making any conditions for the performance of his little kindness has only been imagined in those strange Stories of Devils wherewith the oral and uncollected literature of the Creole abounds.[1]

V

PREPARING FOR HER JOURNEY, THE YOUNG MÀCHANNE (MARCHANDE) PUTS on the poorest and briefest chemise in her possession, and the most worn of her light calico robes. These are all she wears. The robe is

---

[1] Extract from the "Story of Marie," as written from dictation:

. . . *Manman-à té ni yon gouôs jà à caïe-li. Jà-la té touôp lou'de pou Marie. Cé té li menm manman là qui té kallé pouend dileau. Yon jou y pouend jà-la pou y té allé pouend dileau. Lhè manman-à rivé bò la fontaine, y pa trouvé pésonne pou châgé y. Y rété; y ka crié, "Toutt bon Chritien, vini châgé moin!"*

. . . *Lhè manman rété y ouè pa té ni piess bon Chritien pou châgé y. Y rété; y crié: "Pouloss, si pa ni bon Chritien, ni mauvais Chritien! toutt mauvais Chritien vini châgé moin!"*

Lhè y fini di ça, y ouè yon diabe qui ka vini, ka di conm ça, "Pou mon châgé ou, ça ou ké baill moin?" Manman-là di,—y ré ponne, "Moin pa ni arien!" Diabe-la réponne y, "Y fau ba moin Marie pou moin pé châge ou."

. . . This mamma had a great jar in her house. The jar was too heavy for Marie. It was this mamma herself who used to go for water. One day she took that jar to go for water. When this mamma had got to the fountain, she could not find any one to load her. She stood there, crying out, "Any good Christian, come load me!"

. . . As the mamma stood there she saw there was not a single good Christian to help her load. She stood there, and cried out: "Well, then, if there are no good Christians, there are bad Christians. Any bad Christian, come and load me!"

The moment she said that, she saw a devil coming, who said to her, "If I load you, what will you give me?" This mamma answered, and said, "I have nothing!" The devil answered her, "Must give me Marie if you want me to load you."

drawn upward and forward, so as to reach a little below the knee, and is confined thus by a waist-string, or a long kerchief bound tightly round the loins. Instead of a Madras or painted turban-kerchief, she binds a plain *mouchoir* neatly and closely about her head; and if her hair be long, it is combed back and gathered into a loop behind. Then, with a second mouchoir of coarser quality she makes a pad, or, as she calls it, *tòche*, by winding the kerchief round her fingers as you would coil up a piece of string;—and the soft mass, flattened with a patting of the hand, is placed upon her head, over the coiffure. On this the great loaded trait is poised.

She wears no shoes! To wear shoes and do her work swiftly and well in such a land of mountains would be impossible. She must climb thousands and descend thousands of feet every day—march up and down slopes so steep that the horses of the country all break down after a few years of similar journeying. The girl invariably outlasts the horse—though carrying an equal weight. Shoes, unless extraordinarily well made, would shift place a little with every change from ascent to descent, or the reverse, during the march—would yield and loosen with the ever-varying strain—would compress the toes—produce corns, bunions, raw places by rubbing, and soon cripple the porteuse. Remember, she has to walk perhaps fifty miles between dawn and dark, under a sun to which a single hour's exposure, without the protection of an umbrella, is perilous to any European or American—the terrible sun of the tropics! Sandals are the only conceivable footgear suited to such a calling as hers; but she needs no sandals: the soles of her feet are toughened so as to feel no asperities, and present to sharp pebbles a surface at once yielding and resisting, like a cushion of solid *caoutchouc*.

Besides her load, she carries only a canvas purse tied to her girdle on the right side, and on the left a very small bottle of rum, or white *tafia*—usually the latter, because it is so cheap. . . . For she may not always find the Gouyave Water to drink—the cold clear pure stream conveyed to the fountains of Saint Pierre from the highest mountains by a beautiful and marvelous plan of hydraulic engineering: she will have to drink betimes the common spring-water of the bamboo-fountains on the remoter high-roads; and this may cause dysentery if swallowed without a spoonful of spirits. Therefore she never travels without a little liquor.

VI

. . . SO!—SHE IS READY: "CHÂGÉ MOIN, SOUPLÈ, CHÈ!" SHE BENDS TO LIFT the end of the heavy trait: some one takes the other—*yon!—dè!—toua!* —it is on her head. Perhaps she winces an instant;—the weight is not perfectly balanced; she settles it with her hands—gets it in the exact place. Then, all steady—lithe, light, half naked—away she moves with a long springy step. So even her walk that the burden never sways; yet so rapid her motion that however good a walker you may fancy yourself to be you will tire out after a sustained effort of fifteen minutes to follow her uphill. Fifteen minutes!—and she can keep up that pace without slackening—save for a minute to eat and drink at midday— for at least twelve hours and fifty-six minutes, the extreme length of a West Indian day. She starts before dawn; tries to reach her resting-place by sunset: after dark, like all her people, she is afraid of meeting zombis.

Let me give you some idea of her average speed under an average weight of one hundred and twenty-five pounds—estimates based partly upon my own observations, partly upon the declarations of the trust-worthy merchants who employ her, and partly on the assertion of habitants of the burghs or cities named—all of which statements perfectly agree. From Saint Pierre to Basse-Pointe, by the national road, the distance is a trifle less than twenty-seven kilometres and three quarters. She makes the transit easily in three hours and a half; and returns in the afternoon, after an absence of scarcely more than eight hours. From Saint Pierre to Morne Rouge—two thousand feet up in the mountains (an ascent so abrupt that no one able to pay carriage-fare dreams of attempting to walk it)—the distance is seven kilo-metres and three quarters. She makes it in little more than an hour. But this represents only the beginning of her journey. She passes on to Grande Anse, twenty-one and three-quarter kilometres away. But she does not rest there: she returns at the same pace, and reaches Saint Pierre before dark. From Saint Pierre to Gros-Morne the distance to be twice traversed by her is more than thirty-two kilometres. A jour-ney of sixty-four kilometres—daily, perhaps—forty miles! And there are many màchannes who make yet longer trips—trips of three or four days' duration;—these rest at villages upon their route.

VII

SUCH TRAVEL IN SUCH A COUNTRY WOULD BE IMPOSSIBLE BUT FOR THE excellent national roads—limestone highways, solid, broad, faultlessly graded—that wind from town to town, from hamlet to hamlet, over mountains, over ravines; ascending by zigzags to heights of twenty-five hundred feet; traversing the primeval forests of the interior; now skirting the dizziest precipices, now descending into the loveliest valleys. There are thirty-one of these magnificent routes, with a total length of 488,052 metres (more than 303 miles), whereof the construction required engineering talent of the highest order—the building of bridges beyond counting, and devices the most ingenious to provide against dangers of storms, floods, and land-slips. Most have drinking-fountains along their course at almost regular intervals—generally made by the Negroes, who have a simple but excellent plan for turning the water of a spring through bamboo pipes to the roadway. Each road is also furnished with milestones, or rather kilometre-stones; and the drainage is perfect enough to assure of the highway becoming dry within fifteen minutes after the heaviest rain, so long as the surface is maintained in tolerably good condition. Well-kept embankments of earth (usually covered with a rich growth of mosses, vines, and ferns), or even solid walls of masonry, line the side that overhangs a dangerous depth. And all these highways pass through landscapes of amazing beauty—visions of mountains so many-tinted and so singular of outline that they would almost seem to have been created for the express purpose of compelling astonishment. This tropic Nature appears to call into being nothing ordinary: the shapes which she evokes are always either gracious or odd—and her eccentricities, her extravagances, have a fantastic charm, a grotesqueness as of artistic whim. Even where the landscape-view is cut off by high woods the forms of ancient trees—the infinite interwreathing of vine growths all on fire with violence of blossom-color—the enormous green outbursts of *balisiers,* with leaves ten to thirteen feet long—the columnar solemnity of great *palmistes*—the pliant quivering exquisiteness of bamboo—the furious splendor of roses run mad—more than atone for the loss of the horizon. Sometimes you approach a steep covered with a growth of what, at first glance, looks precisely like fine green fur: it is a first-growth of young bamboo. Or you see a hillside covered with huge green feathers, all shelving down and overlapping as in the tail of some unutterable bird: these are baby ferns. And where the road leaps some deep ravine with a double or triple bridge of white stone, note well what delicious shapes spring up into sunshine from the black profundity on either hand! Palmiform you might hastily term them— but no palm was ever so gracile; no palm ever bore so dainty a head of green plumes light as lace! These likewise are ferns (rare survivors, maybe, of that period of monstrous vegetation which preceded the apparition of man), beautiful tree-ferns, whose every young plume, unrolling in a spiral from the bud, at first assumes the shape of a crozier —a crozier of emerald! Therefore are some of this species called "archbishop-trees," no doubt. . . . But one might write for a hundred years of the sights to be seen upon such a mountain road.

VIII

IN EVERY SEASON, IN ALMOST EVERY WEATHER, THE PORTEUSE MAKES HER journey—never heeding rain;—her goods being protected by double and triple waterproof coverings well bound down over her trait. Yet these tropical rains, coming suddenly with a cold wind upon her heated and almost naked body, are to be feared. To any European or unacclimated white such a wetting, while the pores are all open during a profuse perspiration, would probably prove fatal: even for white natives the result is always a serious and protracted illness. But the porteuse seldom suffers in consequence: she seems proof against fevers, rheumatisms, and ordinary colds. When she does break down, however, the malady is a frightful one—a pneumonia that carries off the victim within forty-eight hours. Happily, among her class, these fatalities are very rare.

And scarcely less rare than such sudden deaths are instances of failure to appear on time. In one case, the employer, a Saint Pierre shopkeeper, on finding his marchande more than an hour late, felt so certain something very extraordinary must have happened that he sent out messengers in all directions to make inquiries. It was found that the woman had become a mother when only halfway upon her journey home. . . . The child lived and thrived;—she is now a pretty chocolate-colored girl of eight, who follows her mother every day from their mountain *ajoupa* down to the city, and back again—bearing a little trait upon her head.

Murder for purposes of robbery is not an unknown crime in Martinique; but I am told the porteuses are never molested. And yet some of these girls carry merchandise to the value of hundreds of francs; and all carry money—the money received for goods sold, often a considerable sum. This immunity may be partly owing to the fact that they travel during the greater part of the year only by day—and usually in company. A very pretty girl is seldom suffered to journey unprotected: she has either a male escort or several experienced and powerful women with her. In the cacao season—when carriers start from Grande Anse as early as two o'clock in the morning, so as to reach Saint Pierre by dawn—they travel in strong companies of twenty or twenty-five, singing on the way. As a general rule the younger girls at all times go two together—keeping step perfectly as a pair of blooded fillies; only the veterans, or women selected for special work by reason of extraordinary physical capabilities, go alone. To the latter class belong certain girls employed by the great bakeries of Fort-de-France and Saint Pierre: these are veritable caryatides. They are probably the heaviest-laden of all, carrying baskets of astounding size far up into the mountains before daylight, so as to furnish country families with fresh bread at an early hour; and for this labor they receive about four dollars (twenty francs) a month and one loaf of bread per diem. . . . While stopping at a friend's house among the hills, some two miles from Fort-de-France, I saw the local bread-carrier halt before our porch one morning, and a finer type of the race it would be difficult for a sculptor to imagine. Six feet tall—strength and grace united throughout her whole figure from neck to heel; with that clear black skin which is beautiful to any but ignorant or prejudiced eyes; and the smooth, pleasing, solemn features of a sphinx—she looked to me, as she towered there in the gold light, a symbolic statue of Africa. Seeing me smoking one of those long thin Martinique cigars called *bouts,* she begged one; and, not happening to have another, I gave her the price of a bunch of twenty—ten sous. She took it without a smile, and went her way. About an hour and a half later she came back and asked for me—to present me with the finest and largest mango I had ever seen, a monster mango. She said she wanted to see me eat it, and sat down on the ground to look on. While eating it, I learned that she had walked a whole mile out of her way under that sky of fire, just to bring her little gift of gratitude.

IX

FORTY TO FIFTY MILES A DAY, ALWAYS UNDER A WEIGHT OF MORE THAN A hundred pounds—for when the trait has been emptied she puts in stones for ballast;—carrying her employer's merchandise and money over the mountain ranges, beyond the peaks, across the ravines, through the tropical forest, sometimes through by-ways haunted by the *fer-de-lance*—and this in summer or winter, the season of rains or the season of heat, the time of fevers or the time of hurricanes, at a franc a day! . . . How does she live upon it?

There are twenty sous to the franc. The girl leaves Saint Pierre with her load at early morning. At the second village, Morne Rouge, she halts to buy one, two, or three biscuits at a sou apiece; and reaching Ajoupa-Bouillon later in the forenoon, she may buy another biscuit or two. Altogether she may be expected to eat five sous of biscuit or bread before reaching Grande Anse, where she probably has a meal waiting for her. This ought to cost her ten sous—especially if there be meat in her *ragoût:* which represents a total expense of fifteen sous for eatables. Then there is the additional cost of the cheap liquor, which she must mix with her drinking-water, as it would be more than dangerous to swallow pure cold water in her heated condition; two or three sous more. This almost makes the franc. But such a hasty and really erroneous estimate does not include expenses of lodging and clothing;—she may sleep on the bare floor sometimes, and twenty francs a year may keep her in clothes; but she must rent the floor and pay for the clothes out of that franc. As a matter of fact she not only does all this upon her twenty sous a day, but can even economize something which will enable her, when her youth and force decline, to start in business for herself. And her economy will not seem so wonderful when I assure you that thousands of men here—huge men muscled like bulls and lions—live upon an average expenditure of five sous a day. One sou of bread, two sous of manioc flour, one sou of dried codfish, one sou of tafia: such is their meal.

There are women carriers who earn more than a franc a day—women with a particular talent for selling, who are paid on commission—from ten to fifteen per cent. These eventually make themselves independent in many instances;—they continue to sell and bargain in person, but hire a young girl to carry the goods.

X

... "OU 'LÈ MÀCHANNE!" RINGS OUT A RICH ALTO, RESONANT AS THE TONE of a gong, from behind the balisiers that shut in our garden. There are two of them—no, three—Maiyotte, Chéchelle, and Rina. Maiyotte and Chéchelle have just arrived from Saint Pierre;—Rina comes from Gros-Morne with fruits and vegetables. Suppose we call them all in, and see what they have got. Maiyotte and Chéchelle sell on commission; Rina sells for her mother, who has a little garden at Gros-Morne. ... "Bonjou', Maiyotte;—bonjou', Chéchelle! coument ou kallé, Rina, chè!" ... Throw open the folding-doors to let the great trays pass. ... Now all three are unloaded by old Théréza and by young Adou;—all the packs are on the floor, and the waterproof wrappings are being uncorded, while Ah-Manmzell, the adopted child, brings the rum and water for the tall walkers.

... "Oh, what a medley, Maiyotte!" ... Inkstands and wooden cows; purses and paper dogs and cats; dolls and cosmetics; pins and needles and soap and toothbrushes; candied fruits and smoking-caps; pelotes of thread, and tapes, and ribbons, and laces and Madeira wine; cuffs, and collars, and dancing-shoes, and tobacco sachets. ... But what is in that little flat bundle? Presents for your guêpe, if you have one. ... Jesis-Maïa!—the pretty foulards! Azure and yellow in checkerings; orange and crimson in stripes; rose and scarlet in plaidings; and bronze tints, and beetle-tints of black and green.

"Chéchelle, what a bloucoutoum if you should ever let that tray fall —aïe yaïe yaïe!" Here is a whole shop of crockeries and porcelains;— plates, dishes, cups—earthenware canaris and dobannes; and gift-mugs and cups bearing Creole girls' names—all names that end in ine: "Micheline," "Honorine," "Prospérine" [you will never sell that, Chéchelle: there is not a Prospérine this side of Saint Pierre], "Azaline," "Leontine," "Zéphyrine," "Albertine," "Chrysaline," "Florine," "Coralline," "Alexandrine." ... And knives and forks, and cheap spoons, and tin coffee-pots, and tin rattles for babies, and tin flutes for horrid little boys—and pencils and note-paper and envelopes! ...

... "Oh, Rina, what superb oranges!—fully twelve inches round! ... and these, which look something like our mandarins, what do you call them?" "Zorange-macaque!" (monkey-oranges). And here are avocados—beauties!—guavas of three different kinds—tropical cherries (which have four seeds instead of one)—tropical raspberries, whereof the entire eatable portion comes off in one elastic piece, lined with something like white silk. . . . Here are fresh nutmegs: the thick green case splits in equal halves at a touch; and see the beautiful heart within—deep dark glossy red, all wrapped in a bright net-work of flat blood-colored fibre, spun over it like branching veins. . . . This big heavy red-and-yellow thing is a *pomme-cythère:* the smooth cuticle, bitter as gall, covers a sweet juicy pulp, interwoven with something that seems like cotton thread. . . . Here is a *pomme-cannelle:* inside its scaly covering is the most delicious yellow custard conceivable, with little black seeds floating in it. This larger *corossol* has almost as delicate an interior, only the custard is white instead of yellow. . . . Here are *christophines*—great pear-shaped things, white and green, according to kind, with a peel prickly and knobby as the skin of a horned toad; but they stew exquisitely. And *mélongènes,* or egg-plants; and *palmistepith,* and *chadèques,* and *pommes-d'Haïti*—and roots that at first sight look all alike, but they are not: there are *camanioc,* and *couscous,* and *choux-caraïbes,* and *zignames,* and various kinds of *patates* among them. Old Théréza's magic will transform these shapeless muddy things, before evening, into pyramids of smoking gold— into odorous porridges that will look like messes of molten amber and liquid pearl;—for Rina makes a good sale.

Then Chéchelle manages to dispose of a tin coffee-pot and a big canari. . . . And Maiyotte makes the best sale of all; for the sight of a funny *biscuit* doll has made Ah-Manmzell cry and smile so at the same time that I should feel unhappy for the rest of my life if I did not buy it for her. I know I ought to get some change out of that six francs;—and Maiyotte, who is black but comely as the tents of Kedar, and the curtains of Solomon, seems to be aware of the fact.

Oh, Maiyotte, how plaintive that pretty sphinx face of yours, now turned in profile;—as if you knew you looked beautiful thus—with the great gold circlets of your ears glittering and swaying as you bend! And why are you so long, so long untying that poor little canvas purse? —fumbling and fingering it?—is it because you want me to think of the weight of that trait and the sixty kilometres you must walk, and the heat, and the dust, and all the disappointments? Ah, you are cunning, Maiyotte! No, I do not want the change!

XI

. . . TRAVELING TOGETHER, THE PORTEUSES OFTEN WALK IN SILENCE FOR hours at a time;—this is when they feel weary. Sometimes they sing—most often when approaching their destination;—and when they chat, it is in a key so high-pitched that their voices can be heard to a great distance in this land of echoes and elevations.

But she who travels alone is rarely silent: she talks to herself or to inanimate things;—you may hear her talking to the trees, to the flowers—talking to the high clouds and the far peaks of changing color—talking to the setting sun!

Over the miles of the morning she sees, perchance, the mighty Piton Gélé, a cone of amethyst in the light; and she talks to it: *"Ou jojoll, oui!—moin ni envie monté assou ou, pou moin ouè bien, bien!"* (Thou art pretty, pretty, aye!—I would I might climb thee, to see far, far off!)

By a great grove of palms she passes;—so thickly mustered they are that against the sun their intermingled heads form one unbroken awning of green. Many rise straight as masts; some bend at beautiful angles, seeming to intercross their long pale single limbs in a fantastic dance; others curve like bows: there is one that undulates from foot to crest, like a monster serpent poised upon its tail. She loves to look at that one—*joli-pié-bois-là!*—talks to it as she goes by—bids it good-day.

Or, looking back as she ascends, she sees the huge blue dream of the sea—the eternal haunter, that ever becomes larger as she mounts the road; and she talks to it: *"Mi lanmé ka gadé moin!"* (There is the great sea looking at me!) *"Màché toujou deïë moin, lanmè!"* (Walk after me, O Sea!)

Or she views the clouds of Pelée, spreading gray from the invisible summit, to shadow against the sun; and she fears the rain, and she talks to it: *"Pas mouillé moin, laplie-à! Quitté moin rivé avant mouillé moin!"* (Do not wet me, O Rain! Let me get there before thou wettest me!)

Sometimes a dog barks at her, menaces her bare limbs; and she talks to the dog: *"Chien-a, pas mòdé moin, chien—anh! Moin pa fé ou arien, chien, pou ou mòdé moin!"* (Do not bite, O Dog! Never did I anything to thee that thou shouldst bite me, O Dog! Do not bite me, dear! Do not bite me, doudoux!)

Sometimes she meets a laden sister traveling the opposite way. . . . "*Coument ou yé, chè?*" she cries. (How art thou, dear?) And the other makes answer, "*Toutt douce chè—et ou?*" (All sweetly, dear—and thou?) And each passes on without pausing: they have no time!

. . . It is perhaps the last human voice she will hear for many a mile. After that only the whisper of the grasses—*graïe-gras, graïe-gras!*—and the gossip of the canes—*chououa, chououa!*—and the husky speech of the *pois-Angole, ka babillé conm yon vié fenme*—that babbles like an old woman;—and the murmur of the filao-trees, like the murmur of the River of the Washerwomen.

XII

. . . SUNDOWN APPROACHES: THE LIGHT HAS TURNED A RICH YELLOW;—long black shapes lie across the curving road, shadows of balisier and palm, shadows of tamarind and Indian-reed, shadows of *ceiba* and giant-fern. And the porteuses are coming down through the lights and darknesses of the way from far Grande Anse, to halt a moment in this little village. They are going to sit down on the roadside here, before the house of the baker; and there is his great black workman, Jean-Marie, looking for them from the doorway, waiting to relieve them of their loads. . . . Jean-Marie is the strongest man in all the Champ-Flore: see what a torso—as he stands there naked to the waist! . . . His day's work is done; but he likes to wait for the girls, though he is old now, and has sons as tall as himself. It is a habit: some say that he had a daughter once—a porteuse like those coming, and used to wait for her thus at that very doorway until one evening that she failed to appear, and never returned till he carried her home in his arms dead—stricken by a serpent in some mountain path where there was none to aid. . . . The roads were not as good then as now.

. . . Here they come, the girls—yellow, red, black. See the flash of the yellow feet where they touch the light! And what impossible tint the red limbs take in the changing glow! . . . Finotte, Pauline, Médelle—all together, as usual—with Ti-Clé trotting behind, very tired. . . . Never mind, Ti-Clé!—you will outwalk your cousins when you are a few years older—pretty Ti-Clé. . . . Here come Cyrillia and Zabette, and Féfé and Dodotte and Fevriette. And behind them are coming the two *chabines*—golden girls: the twin-sisters who sell silks and threads and foulards; always together, always wearing robes and kerchiefs of similar color—so that you can never tell which is Lor-rainie and which Édoualise.

And all smile to see Jean-Marie waiting for them, and to hear his deep kind voice calling, *"Coument ou yé, chè? coument ou kallé?"* . . . (How art thou, dear?—how goes it with thee?)

And they mostly make answer, *"Toutt douce, chè—et ou?"* (All sweetly, dear—and thou?) But some, over-weary, cry to him, *"Ah, déchâgé moin vite, chè! moin lasse, lasse!"* (Unload me quickly, dear; for I am very, very weary.) Then he takes off their burdens, and fetches bread for them, and says foolish little things to make them laugh. And they are pleased, and laugh, just like children, as they sit right down on the road there to munch their dry bread.

. . . So often have I watched that scene! . . . Let me but close my eyes one moment, and it will come back to me—through all the thousand miles—over the graves of the days. . . .

Again I see the mountain road in the yellow glow, banded with umbrages of palm. Again I watch the light feet coming—now in shadow, now in sun—soundlessly as falling leaves. Still I can hear the voices crying, *"Ah! déchâgé moin vite, chè!—moin lasse!"*—and see the mighty arms outreach to take the burdens away.

. . . Only, there is a change—I know not what! . . . All vapory the road is, and the fronds, and the comely coming feet of the bearers, and even this light of sunset—sunset that is ever larger and nearer to us than dawn, even as death than birth. And the weird way appeareth a way whose dust is the dust of generations;—and the Shape that waits is never Jean-Marie, but one darker and stronger;—and these are surely voices of tired souls who cry to Thee, thou dear black Giver of the perpetual rest, *"Ah! déchâgé moin vite, chè!—moin lasse!"*

Les Blanchisseuses

I

WHOEVER STOPS FOR A FEW MONTHS IN SAINT PIERRE IS CERTAIN, SOONER or later, to pass an idle half-hour in that charming place of Martinique idlers—the beautiful Savane du Fort—and, once there, is equally certain to lean a little while over the mossy parapet of the river-wall to watch the *blanchisseuses* at work. It has a curious interest, this spectacle of primitive toil: the deep channel of the Roxelane winding under the palm-crowned heights of the Fort; the blinding whiteness of linen laid out to bleach for miles upon the huge boulders of porphyry and prismatic basalt; and the dark bronze-limbed women, with faces hidden under immense straw hats, and knees in the rushing torrent—all form a scene that makes one think of the earliest civilizations. Even here, in this modern colony, it is nearly three centuries old; and it will probably continue thus at the Rivière des Blanchisseuses for fully another three hundred years. Quaint as certain weird Breton legends whereof it reminds you—especially if you watch it before daybreak while the city still sleeps—this fashion of washing is not likely to change. There is a local prejudice against new methods, new inventions, new ideas;—several efforts at introducing a less savage style of washing proved unsuccessful; and an attempt to establish a steam-laundry resulted in failure. The public were quite contented with the old ways of laundrying, and saw no benefits to be gained by forsaking them;—while the washers and ironers engaged by the laundry proprietor at higher rates than they had ever obtained before soon wearied of indoor work, abandoned their situations, and returned with a sense of relief to their ancient way of working out in the blue air and the wind of the hills, with their feet in the mountain-water and their heads in the awful sun.

... It is one of the sights of Saint Pierre—this daily scene at the River of the Washerwomen: everybody likes to watch it;—the men, because among the blanchisseuses there are not a few decidedly handsome girls; the women probably because a woman feels always interested in woman's work. All the white bridges of the Roxelane are dotted with lookers-on during fine days, and particularly in the morning, when every *bonne* on her way to and from the market stops a moment to observe or to greet those blanchisseuses whom she knows. Then one hears such a calling and clamoring—such an inter-crossing of cries from the bridge to the river, and the river to the bridge. "... *Ouill! Noémi!*" ... "*Coument ou yé, chè?*" ... "*Eh! Pascaline!*" ... "*Bonjou', Youtte!—Dédé!—Fifi!—Henrillia!*" ... "*Coument ou kallé, Cyrillia?*" ... "*Toutt douce, chè!—et Ti Mémé?*" ... "*Y bien; —oti Ninotte?*" ... "*Bo ti manmaille pou moin, chè—ou tanne?*" ... But the bridge leading to the market of the Fort is the poorest point of view; for the better classes of blanchisseuses are not there: only the lazy, the weak, or non-professionals—house-servants, who do washing at the river two or three times a month as part of their family-service—are apt to get so far down. The experienced professionals and early risers secure the best places and choice of rocks; and among the hundreds at work you can discern something like a physical gradation. At the next bridge the women look better, stronger; more young faces appear; and the further you follow the river-course towards the Jardin des Plantes, the more the appearance of the blanchisseuses improves—so that within the space of a mile you can see well exemplified one natural law of life's struggle—the best chances to the best constitutions.

You might also observe, if you watch long enough, that among the blanchisseuses there are few sufficiently light of color to be classed as bright mulatresses,—the majority are black or of that dark copper-red race which is perhaps superior to the black Creole in strength and bulk; for it requires a skin insensible to sun as well as the toughest of constitutions to be a blanchisseuse. A *porteuse* can begin to make long trips at nine or ten years, but no girl is strong enough to learn the washing-trade until she is past twelve. The blanchisseuse is the hardest worker among the whole population;—her daily labor is rarely less than thirteen hours, and during the greater part of that time she is working in the sun, and standing up to her knees in water that descends quite cold from the mountain peaks. Her labor makes her perspire profusely; and she can never venture to cool herself by fur-

ther immersion without serious danger of pleurisy. The trade is said
to kill all who continue at it beyond a certain number of years: *"Nou
ka mò toutt dleau"* (we all die of the water), one told me, replying to
a question. No feeble or light-skinned person can attempt to do a
single day's work of this kind without danger; and a weak girl,
driven by necessity to do her own washing, seldom ventures to go to
the river. Yet I saw an instance of such rashness one day. A pretty
sangmêlée, perhaps about eighteen or nineteen years old—whom I
afterwards learned had just lost her mother and found herself thus
absolutely destitute—began to descend one of the flights of stone steps
leading to the river, with a small bundle upon her head; and two or
three of the blanchisseuses stopped their work to look at her. A tall
capresse inquired mischievously:

"Ou vini pou pouend yon bain?" (Coming to take a bath?) For
the river is a great bathing-place.

"Non; moin vini lavé." (No; I am coming to wash.)

"Aïe! aïe! aïe!—y vini lavé!" . . . And all within hearing laughed
together. "Are you crazy, girl?—*ess ou fou?*" The tall capresse
snatched the bundle from her, opened it, threw a garment to her
nearest neighbor, another to the next one, dividing the work among a
little circle of friends, and said to the stranger, *"Non ké lavé toutt ça
ba ou bien vite, chè—va, amisé ou!"* (We'll wash this for you very
quickly, dear—go and amuse yourself!) These kind women even did
more for the poor girl;—they subscribed to buy her a good breakfast,
when the food-seller—the *màchanne-mangé*—made her regular round
among them, with fried fish and eggs and manioc flour and bananas.

II

ALL OF THE MULTITUDE WHO WASH CLOTHING AT THE RIVER ARE NOT
professional blanchisseuses. Hundreds of women, too poor to pay for
laundrying, do their own work at the Roxelane;—and numerous
bonnes there wash the linen of their mistresses as a regular part of
their domestic duty. But even if the professionals did not always occupy a certain well-known portion of the channel, they could easily
be distinguished from others by their rapid and methodical manner
of work, by the ease with which immense masses of linen are handled by them, and, above all, by their way of whipping it against
the rocks. Furthermore, the greater number of professionals are like-

wise teachers, mistresses *(bou'geoises)* and have their apprentices beside them—young girls from twelve to sixteen years of age. Among these *apprenti,* as they are called in the patois, there are many attractive types, such as idlers upon the bridges like to look at.

If, after one year of instruction, the apprentice fails to prove a good washer, it is not likely she will ever become one; and there are some branches of the trade requiring a longer period of teaching and of practice. The young girl first learns simply to soap and wash the linen in the river, which operation is called "rubbing" *(frotté* in Creole); —after she can do this pretty well, she is taught the curious art of whipping it *(fessé).* You can hear the sound of the fessé a great way off, echoing and reëchoing among the mornes: it is not a sharp, smacking noise, as the name might seem to imply, but a heavy hollow sound exactly like that of an axe splitting dry timber. In fact, it so closely resembles the latter sound that you are apt on first hearing it to look up at the mornes with the expectation of seeing woodmen there at work. And it is not made by striking the linen with anything, but only by lashing it against the sides of the rocks. . . . After a piece has been well rubbed and rinsed, it is folded up into a peculiar sheaf-shape, and seized by the closely gathered end for the fessé. Then the folding process is repeated on the reverse, and the other end whipped. This process expels suds that rinsing cannot remove: it must be done very dexterously to avoid tearing or damaging the material. By an experienced hand the linen is never torn; and even pearl and bone buttons are much less often broken than might be supposed. The singular echo is altogether due to the manner of folding the article for the fessé.

After this, all the pieces are spread out upon the rocks, in the sun, for the "first bleaching" *(pouèmiè lablanie).* In the evening they are gathered into large wooden trays or baskets, and carried to what is called the "lye-house" *(lacaïe lessive)*—overlooking the river from a point on the Fort bank opposite to the higher end of the Savane. Here each blanchisseuse hires a small or a large vat, or even several— according to the quantity of work done—at two, three, or ten sous, and leaves her washing to steep in lye *(coulé* is the Creole word used) during the night. There are watchmen to guard it. Before daybreak it is rinsed in warm water; then it is taken back to the river—is rinsed again, bleached again, blued and starched. Then it is ready for ironing. To press and iron well is the most difficult part of the trade. When an apprentice is able to iron a gentleman's shirt nicely, and a pair of white pantaloons, she is considered to have finished her time; —she becomes a journey-woman *(ouvouïyé).*

Even in a country where wages are almost incredibly low, the blanchisseuse earns considerable money. There is no fixed scale of prices: it is even customary to bargain with these women beforehand. Shirts and white pantaloons figure at six and eight cents in laundry bills; but other washing is much cheaper. I saw a lot of thirty-three pieces—including such large ones as sheets, bed-covers, and several *douillettes* (the long Martinique trailing robes of one piece from neck to feet)—for which only three francs was charged. Articles are frequently stolen or lost by house-servants sent to do washing at the river; but very seldom indeed by the regular blanchisseuses. Few of them can read or write or understand owners' marks on wearing apparel; and when you see at the river the wilderness of scattered linen, the seemingly enormous confusion, you cannot understand how these women manage to separate and classify it all. Yet they do this admirably—and for that reason perhaps more than any other, are able to charge fair rates;—it is false economy to have your washing done by the house-servant;—with the professionals your property is safe. And cheap as her rates are, a good professional can make from twenty-five to thirty francs a week; averaging fully a hundred francs a month —as much as many a white clerk can earn in the stores of Saint Pierre, and quite as much (considering local differences in the purchasing power of money) as sixty dollars per month would represent in the United States.

Probably the ability to earn large wages often tempts the blanchisseuse to continue at her trade until it kills her. The "water-disease," as she calls it *(maladie-dleau),* makes its appearance after middle-life: the feet, lower limbs, and abdomen swell enormously, while the face becomes almost fleshless;—then, gradually, tissues give way, muscles yield, and the whole physical structure crumbles.

Nevertheless, the blanchisseuse is essentially a sober liver—never a drunkard. In fact, she is sober from rigid necessity: she would not dare to swallow one mouthful of spirits while at work with her feet in the cold water;—everybody else in Martinique, even the little children, can drink rum; the blanchisseuse cannot, unless she wishes to die of a congestion. Her strongest refreshment is *mabi*—a mild, effervescent, and, I think, rather disagreeable, beer made from molasses.

III

ALWAYS BEFORE DAYBREAK THEY RISE TO WORK, WHILE THE VAPORS OF the mornes fill the air with scent of mouldering vegetation—clayey odors—grassy smells: there is only a faint gray light, and the water of the river is very chill. One by one they arrive, barefooted, under their burdens built up tower-shape on their trays;—silently as ghosts they descend the steps to the river-bed, and begin to unfold and immerse their washing. They greet each other as they come, then become silent again; there is scarcely any talking: the hearts of all are heavy with the heaviness of the hour. But the gray light turns yellow; the sun climbs over the peaks: light changes the dark water to living crystal; and all begin to chatter a little. Then the city awakens; the currents of its daily life circulate again—thinly and slowly at first, then swiftly and strongly—up and down every yellow street, and through the Savane, and over the bridges of the river. Passers-by pause to look down, and cry *"bonjou', chè!"* Idle men stare at some pretty washer, till she points at them and cries: *"Gadé Missié-à ka guetté nou!—anh!—anh!—anh!"* And all the others look up and repeat the groan—*"anh!—anh!—anh!"* till the starers beat a retreat. The air grows warmer; the sky-blue takes fire: the great light makes joy for the washers; they shout to each other from distance to distance, jest, laugh, sing. Gusty of speech these women are: long habit of calling to one another through the roar of the torrent has given their voices a singular sonority and force: it is well worth while to hear them sing. One starts the song—the next joins her; then another and another, till all the channel rings with the melody from the bridge of the Jardin des Plantes to the Pont-bois:

> *C'est moin qui té ka lavé*
> *Passé, raccommodé:*
> *Y té néf hè disouè*
> *Ou metté moin derhò,—*
> *Yche moin assous bouas moin;—*
> *Laplie té ka tombé—*
> *Léfan moin assous tête moin!*
> *Doudoux, ou m'abandonne!*
> *Moin pa ni pèsonne pou soigné moin.·*

... A melancholy chant [1]—originally a Carnival improvisation made to bring public shame upon the perpetrator of a cruel act;—but it contains the story of many of these lives—the story of industrious affectionate women temporarily united to brutal and worthless men in a country where legal marriages are rare. Half of the Creole songs which I was able to collect during a residence of nearly two years in the island touch upon the same sad theme. Of these, *"Chè Manman Moin,"* a great favorite still with the older blanchisseuses, has a simple pathos unrivaled, I believe, in the oral literature of this people. Here is an attempt to translate its three rhymeless stanzas into prose; but the childish sweetness of the patois original is lost:

CHÈ MANMAN MOIN

I

... Dear mamma, once you were young like I;—dear papa, you also have been young;—dear great elder brother, you too have been young. Ah! let me cherish this sweet friendship!—so sick my heart is—yes, 't is very, very ill, this heart of mine: love, only love can make it well again. ...

II

O cursed eyes he praised that led me to him! O cursed lips of mine which ever repeated his name! O cursed moment in which I gave up my heart to the ingrate who no longer knows how to love. ...

III

Doudoux, you swore to me by Heaven!—doudoux, you swore to me by your faith! ... And now you cannot come to me? ... Oh! my heart is withering with pain! ... I was passing by the cemetery;—I saw my name upon a stone—all by itself. I saw two white roses; and in a moment one faded and fell before me. ... So my forgotten heart will be! ...

---

[1] It was I who washed and ironed and mended;—at nine o'clock at night thou didst put me out-of-doors, with my child in my arms—the rain was falling—with my poor straw mattress upon my head! ... Doudoux! thou dost abandon me! ... I have none to care for me.

The air is not so charming, however, as that of a little song which every Creole knows, and which may be often heard still at the river: I think it is the prettiest of all Creole melodies. *"To-to-to"* (patois for the French *toc*) is an onomatope for the sound of knocking at a door.

> To, to, to!—*"Ça qui là?"*
> *"C'est moin-mênme, lanmou;—*
> *Ouvé lapott ba moin!"*
>
> To, to, to!—*"Ça qui là?"*
> *"C'est moin-mênme, lanmou,*
> *Qui ka ba ou khè moin!"*
>
> To, to, to!—*"Ça qui là?"*
> *"C'est moin-mênme, lanmou,*
> *Laplie ka mouillé moin!"*

To-to-to! "Who taps there?"—" 'T is mine own self Love: open the door for me."

To-to-to! "Who taps there?"—" 'T is mine own self Love, who give my heart to thee."

To-to-to! "Who taps there?"—" 'T is mine own self Love: open thy door to me;—the rain is wetting me!" . . .

. . . But it is more common to hear the blanchisseuses singing merry, jaunty, sarcastic ditties—Carnival compositions—in which the African sense of rhythmic melody is more marked: *"Marie-Clémence maudi," "Loéma tombé," "Quand ou ni ti mari jojoll."*

At midday the màchanne-mangé comes, with her girls—carrying trays of fried fish, and *akras,* and cooked beans, and bottles of mabi. The blanchisseuses buy, and eat with their feet in the water, using rocks for tables. Each has her little tin cup to drink her mabi in. . . . Then the washing and the chanting and the booming of the fessé begin again. Afternoon wanes;—school-hours close; and children of many beautiful colors come to the river, and leap down the steps crying, *"Eti! manman!"—"Sésé!"—"Nenneine!"* calling their elder sisters, mothers, and godmothers: the little boys strip naked to play in the water awhile. . . . Toward sunset the more rapid and active workers begin to gather in their linen, and pile it on trays. Large patches of bald rock appear again. . . . By six o'clock almost the whole bed of the river is bare;—the women are nearly all gone. A few linger awhile on the Savane, to watch the last-comer. There is always a great laugh at the last to leave the channel: they ask her if she has not forgotten "to lock up the river."

"*Ou fèmé lapòte lariviè, chè—anh?*"

"*Ah! oui, chè!—moin fèmé y, ou tanne?—moin ni laclé-à!*" (Oh, yes, dear. I locked it up—you hear?—I've got the key!)

But there are days and weeks when they do not sing—times of want or of plague, when the silence of the valley is broken only by the sound of linen beaten upon the rocks, and the great voice of the Roxelane, which will sing on when the city itself shall have ceased to be, just as it sang one hundred thousand years ago. . . . "Why do they not sing to-day?" I once asked during the summer of 1887—a year of pestilence. "*Yo ka pensé toutt lanmizè yo—toutt lapeine yo,*" I was answered. (They are thinking of all their trouble, all their misery.) Yet in all seasons, while youth and strength stay with them, they work on in wind and sun, mist and rain, washing the linen of the living and the dead—white wraps for the newly born, white robes for the bride, white shrouds for them that pass into the Great Silence. And the torrent that wears away the ribs of the perpetual hills wears away their lives—sometimes slowly, slowly as black basalt is worn—sometimes suddenly—in the twinkling of an eye.

For a strange danger ever menaces the blanchisseuse—the treachery of the stream! . . . Watch them working, and observe how often they turn their eyes to the high northeast, to look at Pelée. Pelée gives them warning betimes. When all is sunny in Saint Pierre, and the harbor lies blue as lapis-lazuli, there may be mighty rains in the region of the great woods and the valleys of the higher peaks; and thin streams swell to raging floods which burst suddenly from the altitudes, rolling down rocks and trees and wreck of forests, uplifting crags, devastating slopes. And sometimes, down the ravine of the Roxelane, there comes a roar as of eruption, with a rush of foaming water like a moving mountain-wall; and bridges and buildings vanish with its passing. In 1865 the Savane, high as it lies above the river-bed, was flooded;—and all the bridges were swept into the sea.

So the older and wiser blanchisseuses keep watch upon Pelée; and if a blackness gather over it, with lightnings breaking through, then—however fair the sun shine on Saint Pierre—the alarm is given, the miles of bleaching linen vanish from the rocks in a few minutes, and every one leaves the channel. But it has occasionally happened that Pelée gave no such friendly signal before the river rose: thus lives have been lost. Most of the blanchisseuses are swimmers, and good ones— I have seen one of the girls swim almost out of sight in the harbor, during an idle hour;—but no swimmer has any chances in a rising of the Roxelane: all overtaken by it are stricken by rocks and drift;— *yo crazé,* as a Creole term expresses it—a term signifying to crush, to bray, to dash to pieces.

. . . Sometimes it happens that one who has been absent at home for a brief while returns to the river only to meet her comrades fleeing from it—many leaving their linen behind them. But she will not abandon the linen entrusted to her: she makes a run for it—in spite of warning screams—in spite of the vain clutching of kind rough fingers. She gains the river-bed;—the flood has already reached her waist, but she is strong; she reaches her linen—snatches it up, piece by piece, scattered as it is—"one!—two!—five!—seven!";—there is a roaring in her ears—"eleven!—thirteen!" she has it all . . . but now the rocks are moving! For one instant she strives to reach the steps, only a few yards off;—another, and the thunder of the deluge is upon her—and the crushing crags—and the spinning trees. . . .

Perhaps before sundown some *canotier* may find her floating far in the bay—drifting upon her face in a thousand feet of water—with faithful dead hands still holding fast the property of her employer.

Japan

STORIES OF JAPANESE LIFE

At a Railway Station

Seventh day of the sixth Month;—
twenty-sixth of Meiji

YESTERDAY A TELEGRAM FROM FUKUOKA ANNOUNCED THAT A DESPERATE criminal captured there would be brought for trial to Kumamoto to-day, on the train due at noon. A Kumamoto policeman had gone to Fukuoka to take the prisoner in charge.

Four years ago a strong thief entered some house by night in the Street of the Wrestlers, terrified and bound the inmates, and carried away a number of valuable things. Tracked skillfully by the police, he was captured within twenty-four hours—even before he could dispose of his plunder. But as he was being taken to the police station he burst his bonds, snatched the sword of his captor, killed him, and escaped. Nothing more was heard of him until last week.

Then a Kumamoto detective, happening to visit the Fukuoka prison, saw among the toilers a face that had been four years photographed upon his brain.

"Who is that man?" he asked the guard.

"A thief," was the reply—"registered here as Kusabé."

The detective walked up to the prisoner and said:

"Kusabé is not your name. Nomura Teïchi, you are needed in Kumamoto for murder."

The felon confessed all.

I went with a great throng of people to witness the arrival at the station. I expected to hear and see anger; I even feared possibilities of violence. The murdered officer had been much liked; his relatives would certainly be among the spectators; and a Kumamoto crowd is not very gentle. I also thought to find many police on duty. My anticipations were wrong.

The train halted in the usual scene of hurry and noise—scurry and clatter of passengers wearing *geta*—screaming of boys wanting to sell Japanese newspapers and Kumamoto lemonade. Outside the barrier we waited for nearly five minutes. Then, pushed through the wicket by a police-sergeant, the prisoner appeared—a large, wild-looking man, with head bowed down, and arms fastened behind his back. Prisoner and guard both halted in front of the wicket; and the people pressed forward to see—but in silence. Then the officer called out:

"Sugihara San! Sugihara O-Kibi! Is she present?"

A slight, small woman standing near me, with a child on her back, answered, *"Hai!"* and advanced through the press. This was the widow of the murdered man; the child she carried was his son. At a wave of the officer's hand the crowd fell back, so as to leave a clear space about the prisoner and his escort. In that space the woman with the child stood facing the murderer. The hush was of death.

Not to the woman at all, but to the child only, did the officer then speak. He spoke low, but so clearly that I could catch every syllable:

"Little one, this is the man who killed your father four years ago. You had not yet been born; you were in your mother's womb. That you have no father to love you now is the doing of this man. Look at him—[here the officer, putting a hand to the prisoner's chin, sternly forced him to lift his eyes]—look well at him, little boy! Do not be afraid. It is painful; but it is your duty. Look at him!"

Over the mother's shoulder the boy gazed with eyes widely open, as in fear; then he began to sob; then tears came; but steadily and obediently he still looked—looked—looked—straight into the cringing face.

The crowd seemed to have stopped breathing.

I saw the prisoner's features distort; I saw him suddenly dash himself down upon his knees despite his fetters, and beat his face into the dust, crying out the while in a passion of hoarse remorse that made one's heart shake:

"Pardon! Pardon! Pardon me, little one! That I did—not for hate was it done, but in mad fear only, in my desire to escape. Very, very wicked I have been; great unspeakable wrong have I done you! But now for my sin I go to die. I wish to die; I am glad to die! Therefore, O little one, be pitiful!—forgive me!"

The child still cried silently. The officer raised the shaking criminal; the dumb crowd parted left and right to let them by. Then, quite suddenly, the whole multitude began to sob. And as the bronzed guardian passed, I saw what I had never seen before—what few men ever see—what I shall probably never see again—the tears of a Japanese policeman.

The crowd ebbed, and left me musing on the strange morality of the spectacle. Here was justice unswerving yet compassionate—forcing knowledge of a crime by the pathetic witness of its simplest result. Here was desperate remorse, praying only for pardon before death. And here was a populace—perhaps the most dangerous in the Empire when angered—comprehending all, touched by all, satisfied with the contrition and the shame, and filled, not with wrath, but only with the great sorrow of the sin—through simple deep experience of the difficulties of life and the weaknesses of human nature.

But the most significant, because the most Oriental, fact of the episode was that the appeal to remorse had been made through the criminal's sense of fatherhood—that potential love of children which is so large a part of the soul of every Japanese.

There is a story that the most famous of all Japanese robbers, Ishikawa Goëmon, once by night entering a house to kill and steal, was charmed by the smile of a baby which reached out hands to him, and that he remained playing with the little creature until all chance of carrying out his purpose was lost.

It is not hard to believe this story. Every year the police records tell of compassion shown to children by professional criminals. Some months ago a terrible murder case was reported in the local papers—the slaughter of a household by robbers. Seven persons had been literally hewn to pieces while asleep; but the police discovered a little boy quite unharmed, crying alone in a pool of blood; and they found evidence unmistakable that the men who slew must have taken great care not to hurt the child.

The Nun of the Temple of Amida

WHEN O-TOYO'S HUSBAND—A DISTANT COUSIN, ADOPTED INTO HER FAMILY for love's sake—had been summoned by his lord to the capital, she did not feel anxious about the future. She felt sad only. It was the first time since their bridal that they had ever been separated. But she had her father and mother to keep her company, and, dearer than either—though she would never have confessed it even to herself—her little son. Besides, she always had plenty to do. There were many household duties to perform, and there was much clothing to be woven—both silk and cotton.

Once daily at a fixed hour, she would set for the absent husband, in his favorite room, little repasts faultlessly served on dainty lacquered trays—miniature meals such as are offered to the ghosts of the ancestors, and to the gods.[1] These repasts were served at the east side of the room, and his kneeling-cushion placed before them. The reason

---

[1] Such a repast, offered to the spirit of the absent one loved, is called a *Kagé-zen;* lit., "Shadow-tray." The word *zen* is also used to signify the meal served on the lacquered tray—which has feet, like a miniature table. So that the term "Shadow-feast" would be a better translation of *Kagé-zen.*

they were served at the east side was because he had gone east. Before removing the food, she always lifted the cover of the little soup-bowl to see if there was vapor upon its lacquered inside surface. For it is said that if there be vapor on the inside of the lid covering food so offered, the absent beloved is well. But if there be none, he is dead—because that is a sign that his soul has returned by itself to seek nourishment. O-Toyo found the lacquer thickly beaded with vapor day by day.

The child was her constant delight. He was three years old, and fond of asking questions to which none but the gods know the real answers. When he wanted to play, she laid aside her work to play with him. When he wanted to rest, she told him wonderful stories, or gave pretty pious answers to his questions about those things which no man can ever understand. At evening, when the little lamps had been lighted before the holy tablets and the images, she taught his lips to shape the words of filial prayer. When he had been laid to sleep, she brought her work near him, and watched the still sweetness of his face. Sometimes he would smile in his dreams; and she knew that Kwannon the divine was playing shadowy play with him, and she would murmur the Buddhist invocation to that Maid "who look-eth forever down above the sound of prayer."

Sometimes, in the season of very clear days, she would climb the mountain of Dakeyama, carrying her little boy on her back. Such a trip delighted him much, not only because of what his mother taught him to see, but also of what she taught him to hear. The sloping way was through groves and woods, and over grassed slopes, and around queer rocks; and there were flowers with stories in their hearts, and trees holding tree-spirits. Pigeons cried "korup-korup"; and doves sobbed "owaō, owaō"; and cicadae wheezed and fluted and tinkled.

All those who wait for absent dear ones make, if they can, a pilgrimage to the peak called Dakeyama. It is visible from any part of the city; and from its summit several provinces can be seen. At the very top is a stone of almost human height and shape, perpendicularly set up; and little pebbles are heaped before it and upon it. And near by there is a small Shintō shrine erected to the spirit of a princess of other days. For she mourned the absence of one she loved, and used to watch from this mountain for his coming until she pined away and was changed into a stone. The people therefore built the shrine; and lovers of the absent still pray there for the return of those dear to them; and each, after so praying, takes home one of the little peb-

bles heaped there. And when the beloved one returns, the pebble must
be taken back to the pebble-pile upon the mountain-top, and other
pebbles with it, for a thank-offering and commemoration.

Always ere O-Toyo and her son could reach their home after such
a day, the dusk would fall softly about them; for the way was long,
and they had to both go and return by boat through the wilderness of
rice-fields round the town—which is a slow manner of journeying.
Sometimes stars and fireflies lighted them; sometimes also the moon
—and O-Toyo would softly sing to her boy the Izumo child-song to
the moon:

> *Nono-San,*
> *Little Lady Moon,*
> *How old are you?*
> *"Thirteen days—*
> *Thirteen and nine."*
> *That is still young,*
> *And the reason must be*
> *For that bright red obi,*
> *So nicely tied,*[2]
> *And that nice white girdle*
> *About your hips.*
> *Will you give it to the horse?*
> *"Oh, no, no!"*
> *Will you give it to the cow?*
> *"Oh, no, no!"* [3]

And up to the blue night would rise from all those wet leagues of
labored field that great soft bubbling chorus which seems the very
voice of the soil itself—the chant of the frogs. And O-Toyo would

---

[2] Because an obi or girdle of very bright color can be worn only by children.

[3] Nono-San,
    or
O-Tsuki-San
Ikutsu?
"Jiu-san—
Kokonotsu."
Sore wa mada
Wakai yo,
Wakai ye mo
Dori

Akai iro no
Obi to,
Shiro iro no
Obi to
Koshi ni shanto
Musun de.
Uma ni yaru?
  "Iyaiya!"
Ushi ni yaru?
  "Iyaiya!"

interpret its syllables to the child: *Mé kayui! mé kayui!* ("Mine eyes tickle; I want to sleep.")

All those were happy hours.

II

THEN TWICE, WITHIN THE TIME OF THREE DAYS, THOSE MASTERS OF LIFE and death whose ways belong to the eternal mysteries struck at her heart. First she was taught that the gentle husband for whom she had so often prayed never could return to her—having been returned unto that dust out of which all forms are borrowed. And in another little while she knew her boy slept so deep a sleep that the Chinese physician could not waken him. These things she learned only as shapes are learned in lightning flashes. Between and beyond the flashes was that absolute darkness which is the pity of the gods.

It passed; and she rose to meet a foe whose name is Memory. Before all others she could keep her face, as in other days, sweet and smiling. But when alone with this visitant, she found herself less strong. She would arrange little toys and spread out little dresses on the matting, and look at them, and talk to them in whispers, and smile silently. But the smile would ever end in a burst of wild, loud weeping; and she would beat her head upon the floor, and ask foolish questions of the gods.

One day she thought of a weird consolation—that rite the people name *Toritsu-banashi*—the evocation of the dead. Could she not call back her boy for one brief minute only? It would trouble the little soul; but would he not gladly bear a moment's pain for her dear sake? Surely!

[To have the dead called back one must go to some priest—Buddhist or Shintō—who knows the rite of incantation. And the mortuary tablet, or *ihai*, of the dead must be brought to that priest.

Then ceremonies of purification are performed; candles are lighted and incense is kindled before the ihai; and prayers or parts of sutras are recited; and offerings of flowers and of rice are made. But, in this case, the rice must not be cooked.

And when everything has been made ready, the priest, taking in his left hand an instrument shaped like a bow, and striking it rapidly with his right, calls upon the name of the dead, and cries out the words, *Kitazo yo! kitazo yo! kitazo yo!* meaning, "I have come."[4] And, as he cries, the tone of his voice gradually changes until it becomes the very voice of the dead person—for the ghost enters into him.

Then the dead will answer questions quickly asked, but will cry continually: "Hasten, hasten! for this my coming back is painful, and I have but a little time to stay!" And having answered, the ghost passes; and the priest falls senseless upon his face.

Now to call back the dead is not good. For by calling them back their condition is made worse. Returning to the underworld, they must take a place lower than that which they held before.

To-day these rites are not allowed by law. They once consoled; but the law is a good law, and just—since there exist men willing to mock the divine which is in human hearts.]

So it came to pass that O-Toyo found herself one night in a lonely little temple at the verge of the city—kneeling before the ihai of her boy, and hearing the rite of incantation. And presently, out of the lips of the officiant there came a voice she thought she knew—a voice loved above all others—but faint and very thin, like a sobbing of wind.

And the thin voice cried to her:

"Ask quickly, quickly, mother! Dark is the way and long; and I may not linger."

Then tremblingly she questioned:

"Why must I sorrow for my child? What is the justice of the gods?"

And there was answer given:

"O mother, do not mourn me thus! That I died was only that you might not die. For the year was a year of sickness and of sorrow—and it was given me to know that you were to die; and I obtained by prayer that I should take your place.[5]

"O mother, never weep for me! It is not kindness to mourn for the dead. Over the River of Tears *(Namida-no-Kawa)* their silent road is; and when mothers weep, the flood of that river rises, and the soul cannot pass, but must wander to and fro.

"Therefore, I pray you, do not grieve, O mother mine! Only give me a little water sometimes."

[4] Whence the Izumo saying about one who too often announces his coming: "Thy talk is like the talk of necromancy!"—*Toritsu-banashi no yona.*

[5] *Migawari*, "substitute," is the religious term.

III

<small>FROM THAT HOUR SHE WAS NOT SEEN TO WEEP. SHE PERFORMED, LIGHTLY</small>
and silently, as in former days, the gentle duties of a daughter.

Seasons passed; and her father thought to find another husband for her. To the mother, he said:

"If our daughter again have a son, it will be great joy for her, and for all of us."

But the wiser mother made answer:

"Unhappy she is not. It is impossible that she marry again. She has become as a little child, knowing nothing of trouble or sin."

It was true that she had ceased to know real pain. She had begun to show a strange fondness for very small things. At first she had found her bed too large—perhaps through the sense of emptiness left by the loss of her child; then, day by day, other things seemed to grow too large—the dwelling itself, the familiar rooms, the alcove and its great flower-vases—even the household utensils. She wished to eat her rice with miniature chopsticks out of a very small bowl such as children use.

In these things she was lovingly humored; and in other matters she was not fantastic. The old people consulted together about her constantly. At last the father said:

"For our daughter to live with strangers might be painful. But as we are aged, we may soon have to leave her. Perhaps we could provide for her by making her a nun. We might build a little temple for her."

Next day the mother asked O-Toyo:

"Would you not like to become a holy nun, and to live in a very, very small temple, with a very small altar, and little images of the Buddhas? We should be always near you. If you wish this, we shall get a priest to teach you the sutras."

O-Toyo wished it, and asked that an extremely small nun's dress be got for her. But the mother said:

"Everything except the dress a good nun may have made small. But she must wear a large dress—that is the law of Buddha."

So she was persuaded to wear the same dress as other nuns.

IV

THEY BUILT FOR HER A SMALL AN-DERA, OR NUN'S-TEMPLE, IN AN EMPTY
court where another and larger temple, called *Amida-ji,* had once
stood. The An-dera was also called Amida-ji, and was dedicated to
Amida-Nyōrai and to other Buddhas. It was fitted up with a very
small altar and with miniature altar furniture. There was a tiny copy
of the sutras on a tiny reading-desk, and tiny screens and bells and
kakemono. And she dwelt there long after her parents had passed
away. People called her the *Amida-ji no Bikuni*—which means "The
Nun of the Temple of Amida."

A little outside the gate there was a statue of Jizō. This Jizō was
a special Jizō—the friend of sick children. There were nearly always
offerings of small rice-cakes to be seen before him. These signified
that some sick child was being prayed for; and the number of the
rice-cakes signified the number of the years of the child. Most often
there were but two or three cakes; rarely there were seven or ten.
The Amida-ji no Bikuni took care of the statue, and supplied it with
incense-offerings, and flowers from the temple garden; for there was
a small garden behind the An-dera.

After making her morning round with her alms-bowl, she would
usually seat herself before a very small loom, to weave cloth much too
narrow for serious use. But her webs were bought always by certain
shopkeepers who knew her story; and they made her presents of very
small cups, tiny flower-vases, and queer dwarf-trees for her garden.

Her greatest pleasure was the companionship of children; and this
she never lacked. Japanese child-life is mostly passed in temple courts;
and many happy childhoods were spent in the court of the Amida-ji.
All the mothers in that street liked to have their little ones play there,
but cautioned them never to laugh at the *Bikuni-San.* "Sometimes her
ways are strange," they would say; "but that is because she once had a
little son, who died, and the pain became too great for her mother's
heart. So you must be very good and respectful to her."

Good they were, but not quite respectful in the reverential sense.
They knew better than to be that. They called her "Bikuni-San" always,
and saluted her nicely; but otherwise they treated her like one of themselves. They played games with her; and she gave them tea in extremely
small cups, and made for them heaps of rice-cakes not much bigger

than peas, and wove upon her loom cloth of cotton and cloth of silk for the robes of their dolls. So she became to them as a blood-sister.

They played with her daily till they grew too big to play, and left the court of the temple of Amida to begin the bitter work of life, and to become the fathers and mothers of children whom they sent to play in their stead. These learned to love the Bikuni-San like their parents had done. And the Bikuni-San lived to play with the children of the children of the children of those who remembered when her temple was built.

The people took good heed that she should not know want. There was always given to her more than she needed for herself. So she was able to be nearly as kind to the children as she wished, and to feed extravagantly certain small animals. Birds nested in her temple, and ate from her hand, and learned not to perch upon the heads of the Buddhas.

Some days after her funeral, a crowd of children visited my house. A little girl of nine years spoke for them all:

"Sir, we are asking for the sake of the Bikuni-San who is dead. A very large *haka* (tombstone) has been set up for her. It is a nice haka. But we want to give her also a very, very small haka, because in the time she was with us she often said that she would like a very little haka. And the stone-cutter has promised to cut it for us, and to make it very pretty, if we can bring the money. Therefore perhaps you will honorably give something."

"Assuredly," I said. "But now you will have nowhere to play."

She answered, smiling:

"We shall still play in the court of the temple of Amida. She is buried there. She will hear our playing, and be glad."

Haru

HARU WAS BROUGHT UP, CHIEFLY AT HOME, IN THAT OLD-FASHIONED WAY which produced one of the sweetest types of woman the world has ever seen. This domestic education cultivated simplicity of heart, natural grace of manner, obedience, and love of duty as they were never cultivated but in Japan. Its moral product was something too gentle and beautiful for any other than the old Japanese society: it was not the most judicious preparation for the much harsher life of the new—in which it still survives. The refined girl was trained for the condition of being theoretically at the mercy of her husband. She was taught never to show jealousy, or grief, or anger—even under circumstances compelling all three; she was expected to conquer the faults of her lord by pure sweetness. In short, she was required to be almost superhuman—to realize, at least in outward seeming, the ideal of perfect unselfishness. And this she could do with a husband of her own rank, delicate in discernment —able to divine her feelings, and never to wound them.

Haru came of a much better family than her husband; and she was a little too good for him, because he could not really understand her. They had been married very young, had been poor at first, and then had gradually become well-off, because Haru's husband was a clever man of business. Sometimes she thought he had loved her most when they were less well-off; and a woman is seldom mistaken about such matters.

She still made all his clothes; and he commended her needle-work. She waited upon his wants; aided him to dress and undress; made everything comfortable for him in their pretty home; bade him a charming farewell as he went to business in the morning, and welcomed him upon his return; received his friends exquisitely; managed his household matters with wonderful economy; and seldom asked any favors that cost money. Indeed she scarcely needed such favors; for he was never ungenerous, and liked to see her daintily dressed—looking like some beautiful silver moth robed in the folding of its own wings—and to take her to theatres and other places of amusement. She accompanied him to pleasure-resorts famed for the blossoming of cherry-trees in spring, or the shimmering of fireflies on summer nights, or the crimsoning of maples in autumn. And sometimes they would pass a day together at Maiko, by the sea, where the pines seem to sway like dancing girls; or an afternoon at Kiyomidzu, in the old, old summer-house, where everything is like a dream of five hundred years ago—and where there is a great shadowing of high woods, and a song of water leaping cold and clear from caverns, and always the plaint of flutes unseen, blown softly in the antique way—a tone-caress of peace and sadness blending, just as the gold light glooms into blue over a dying sun.

Except for such small pleasures and excursions, Haru went out seldom. Her only living relatives, and also those of her husband, were far away in other provinces; and she had few visits to make. She liked to be at home, arranging flowers for the alcoves or for the gods, decorating the rooms, and feeding the tame gold-fish of the garden-pond, which would lift up their heads when they saw her coming.

No child had yet brought new joy or sorrow into her life. She looked, in spite of her wife's coiffure, like a very young girl; and she was still simple as a child—notwithstanding that business capacity in small things which her husband so admired that he often condescended to ask her counsel in big things. Perhaps the heart then judged for him better than the pretty head; but, whether intuitive or not, her advice never proved wrong. She was happy enough with him for five years—during which time he showed himself as considerate as any young Japanese merchant could well be towards a wife of finer character than his own.

Then his manner suddenly became cold—so suddenly that she felt assured the reason was not that which a childless wife might have reason to fear. Unable to discover the real cause, she tried to persuade herself that she had been remiss in her duties; examined her innocent conscience to no purpose; and tried very, very hard to please. But he remained unmoved. He spoke no unkind words—though she felt behind his silence the repressed tendency to utter them. A Japanese of the better class is not very apt to be unkind to his wife in words. It is thought to be vulgar and brutal. The educated man of normal disposition will even answer a wife's reproaches with gentle phrases. Common politeness, by the Japanese code, exacts this attitude from every manly man; moreover, it is the only safe one. A refined and sensitive woman will not long

submit to coarse treatment; a spirited one may even kill herself because
of something said in a moment of passion, and such a suicide disgraces
the husband for the rest of his life. But there are slow cruelties worse
than words, and safer—neglect or indifference, for example, of a sort
to arouse jealousy. A Japanese wife has indeed been trained never to
show jealousy; but the feeling is older than all training—old as love, and
likely to live as long. Beneath her passionless mask the Japanese wife
feels like her Western sister—just like that sister who prays and prays,
even while delighting some evening assembly of beauty and fashion, for
the coming of the hour which will set her free to relieve her pain alone.

Haru had cause for jealousy; but she was too much of a child to
guess the cause at once; and her servants too fond of her to suggest it.
Her husband had been accustomed to pass his evenings in her company,
either at home or elsewhere. But now, evening after evening, he went
out by himself. The first time he had given her some business pretexts;
afterwards he gave none, and did not even tell her when he expected
to return. Latterly, also, he had been treating her with silent rudeness.
He had become changed—"as if there was a goblin in his heart"—the
servants said. As a matter of fact he had been deftly caught in a snare
set for him. One whisper from a geisha had numbed his will; one smile
blinded his eyes. She was far less pretty than his wife; but she was very
skillful in the craft of spinning webs—webs of sensual delusion which
entangle weak men, and always tighten more and more about them
until the final hour of mockery and ruin. Haru did not know. She suspected no wrong till after her husband's strange conduct had become
habitual—and even then only because she found that his money was
passing into unknown hands. He had never told her where he passed
his evenings. And she was afraid to ask, lest he should think her jealous.
Instead of exposing her feelings in words, she treated him with such
sweetness that a more intelligent husband would have divined all. But,
except in business, he was dull. He continued to pass his evenings away;
and as his conscience grew feebler, his absences lengthened. Haru had
been taught that a good wife should always sit up and wait for her
lord's return at night; and by so doing she suffered from nervousness,
and from the feverish conditions that follow sleeplessness, and from the
lonesomeness of her waiting after the servants, kindly dismissed at the
usual hour, had left her with her thoughts. Once only, returning very
late, her husband said to her: "I am sorry you should have sat up so
late for me; do not wait like that again!" Then, fearing he might really
have been pained on her account, she laughed pleasantly, and said: "I

was not sleepy, and I am not tired; honorably please not to think about me." So he ceased to think about her—glad to take her at her word; and not long after that he stayed away for one whole night. The next night he did likewise, and a third night. After that third night's absence he failed even to return for the morning meal; and Haru knew the time had come when her duty as a wife obliged her to speak.

She waited through all the morning hours, fearing for him, fearing for herself also; conscious at last of the wrong by which a woman's heart can be most deeply wounded. Her faithful servants had told her something; the rest she could guess. She was very ill, and did not know it. She knew only that she was angry—selfishly angry, because of the pain given her—cruel, probing, sickening pain. Midday came as she sat thinking how she could say least selfishly what it was now her duty to say—the first words of reproach that would ever have passed her lips. Then her heart leaped with a shock that made everything blur and swim before her sight in a whirl of dizziness—because there was a sound of kuruma-wheels and the voice of a servant calling: "Honorable-return-is!"

She struggled to the entrance to meet him, all her slender body a-tremble with fever and pain, and terror of betraying that pain. And the man was startled, because instead of greeting him with the accustomed smile, she caught the bosom of his silk robe in one quivering little hand—and looked into his face with eyes that seemed to search for some shred of a soul—and tried to speak, but could utter only the single word, *"Anata?"* ("Thou?"). Almost in the same moment her weak grasp loosened, her eyes closed with a strange smile; and even before he could put out his arms to support her, she fell. He sought to lift her. But something in the delicate life had snapped. She was dead.

There were astonishments, of course, and tears, and useless callings of her name, and much running for doctors. But she lay white and still and beautiful, all the pain and anger gone out of her face, and smiling as on her bridal day.

Two physicians came from the public hospital—Japanese military surgeons. They asked straight hard questions—questions that cut open the self of the man down to the core. Then they told him truth cold and sharp as edged steel—and left him with his dead.

The people wondered he did not become a priest—fair evidence that his conscience had been awakened. By day he sits among his bales of Kyōto silks and Ōsaka figured goods—earnest and silent. His clerks think him a good master; he never speaks harshly. Often he works far into the night; and he has changed his dwelling-place. There are strangers in the pretty house where Haru lived; and the owner never visits it. Perhaps because he might see there one slender shadow, still arranging flowers, or bending with iris-grace above the goldfish in his pond. But wherever he rest, sometime in the silent hours he must see the same soundless presence near his pillow—sewing, smoothing, softly seeming to make beautiful the robes he once put on only to betray. And at other times—in the busiest moments of his busy life—the clamor of the great shop dies; the ideographs of his ledger dim and vanish; and a plaintive little voice, which the gods refuse to silence, utters into the solitude of his heart, like a question, the single word—"*Anata?*"

Kimiko

Wasuraruru
Mi naran to omō
Kokoro koso
Wasuré nu yori mo
Omoi nari-keré.[1]

I

THE NAME IS ON A PAPER-LANTERN AT THE ENTRANCE OF A HOUSE IN THE Street of the Geisha.

Seen at night the street is one of the queerest in the world. It is narrow as a gangway; and the dark shining woodwork of the house-fronts, all tightly closed—each having a tiny sliding door with paper-panes that look just like frosted glass—makes you think of first-class passenger-

[1] "To wish to be forgotten by the beloved is a soul-task harder far than trying not to forget." (Poem by Kimiko.)

cabins. Really the buildings are several stories high; but you do not observe this at once—especially if there be no moon—because only the lower stories are illuminated up to their awnings, above which all is darkness. The illumination is made by lamps behind the narrow paper-paned doors, and by the paper-lanterns hanging outside—one at every door. You look down the street between two lines of these lanterns—lines converging far-off into one motionless bar of yellow light. Some of the lanterns are egg-shaped, some cylindrical; others four-sided or six-sided; and Japanese characters are beautifully written upon them. The street is very quiet—silent as a display of cabinet-work in some great exhibition after closing-time. This is because the inmates are mostly away—attending banquets and other festivities. Their life is of the night.

The legend upon the first lantern to the left as you go south is *Kinoya: uchi O-Kata*; and that means "The House of Gold wherein O-Kata dwells." The lantern to the right tells of the House of Nishimura, and of a girl Miyotsuru—which name signifies "The Stork Magnificently Existing." Next upon the left comes the House of Kajita; and in that house are Kohana, the Flower-Bud, and Hinako, whose face is pretty as the face of a doll. Opposite is the House Nagaye, wherein live Kimika and Kimiko. . . . And this luminous double litany of names is half-a-mile long.

The inscription on the lantern of the last-named house reveals the relationship between Kimika and Kimiko—and yet something more; for Kimiko is styled *Ni-dai-me*, an honorary untranslatable title which signifies that she is only Kimiko No. 2. Kimika is the teacher and mistress: she has educated two geisha, both named, or rather renamed by her, Kimiko; and this use of the same name twice is proof positive that the first Kimiko—*Ichi-dai-me*—must have been celebrated. The professional appellation borne by an unlucky or unsuccessful geisha is never given to her successor.

If you should ever have good and sufficient reason to enter the house—pushing open that lantern-slide of a door which sets a gong-bell ringing to announce visits—you might be able to see Kimika, provided her little troupe be not engaged for the evening. You would find her a very intelligent person, and well worth talking to. She can tell, when she pleases, the most remarkable stories—real flesh-and-blood stories—true stories of human nature. For the Street of the Geisha is full of traditions—tragic, comic, melodramatic; every house has its memories; and Kimika knows them all. Some are very, very terrible; and some would make you laugh;

and some would make you think. The story of the first Kimiko belongs to the last class. It is not one of the most extraordinary; but it is one of the least difficult for Western people to understand.

II

THERE IS NO MORE ICHI-DAI-ME KIMOKO: SHE IS ONLY A REMEMBRANCE. Kimika was quite young when she called that Kimiko her professional sister.

"An exceedingly wonderful girl," is what Kimika says of Kimiko. To win any renown in her profession, a geisha must be pretty or very clever; and the famous ones are usually both—having been selected at a very early age by their trainers according to the promise of such qualities. Even the commoner class of singing-girls must have some charm in their best years—if only that *beauté du diable* which inspired the Japanese proverb that even a devil is pretty at eighteen.[2] But Kimiko was much more than pretty. She was according to the Japanese ideal of beauty; and that standard is not reached by one woman in a hundred thousand. Also she was more than clever: she was accomplished. She composed very dainty poems—could arrange flowers exquisitely, perform tea-ceremonies faultlessly, embroider, make silk mosaic: in short, she was genteel. And her first public appearance made a flutter in the fast world of Kyōto. It was evident that she could make almost any conquest she pleased, and that fortune was before her.

But it soon became evident, also, that she had been perfectly trained for her profession. She had been taught how to conduct herself under almost any possible circumstances; for what she could not have known Kimika knew everything about: the power of beauty, and the weakness of passion; the craft of promises and the worth of indifference; and all the folly and evil in the hearts of men. So Kimiko made few mistakes and shed few tears. By and by she proved to be, as Kimika wished— slightly dangerous. So a lamp is to night-fliers: otherwise some of them would put it out. The duty of the lamp is to make pleasant things visible: it has no malice. Kimiko had no malice, and was not too dangerous. Anxious parents discovered that she did not want to enter into respectable families, nor even to lend herself to any serious romances. But she was not particularly merciful to that class of youths who sign documents

---

[2] *Oni mo jiuhachi, azami no hana.* There is a similar saying of a dragon: *ja mo hatachi* (even a dragon at twenty).

with their own blood, and ask a dancing-girl to cut off the extreme end of the little finger of her left hand as a pledge of eternal affection. She was mischievous enough with them to cure them of their folly. Some rich folks who offered her lands and houses on condition of owning her, body and soul, found her less merciful. One proved generous enough to purchase her freedom unconditionally, at a price which made Kimika a rich woman; and Kimiko was grateful—but she remained a geisha. She managed her rebuffs with too much tact to excite hate, and knew how to heal despairs in most cases. There were exceptions, of course. One old man, who thought life not worth living unless he could get Kimiko all to himself, invited her to a banquet one evening, and asked her to drink wine with him. But Kimika, accustomed to read faces, deftly substituted tea (which has precisely the same color) for Kimiko's wine, and so instinctively saved the girl's precious life—for only ten minutes later the soul of the silly host was on its way to the Meido alone, and doubtlessly greatly disappointed. . . . After that night Kimika watched over Kimiko as a wildcat guards her kitten.

The kitten became a fashionable mania, a craze—a delirium—one of the great sights and sensations of the period. There is a foreign prince who remembers her name: he sent her a gift of diamonds which she never wore. Other presents in multitude she received from all who could afford the luxury of pleasing her; and to be in her good graces, even for a day, was the ambition of the "gilded youth." Nevertheless she allowed no one to imagine himself a special favorite, and refused to make any contracts for perpetual affection. To any protests on the subject she answered that she knew her place. Even respectable women spoke not unkindly of her—because her name never figured in any story of family unhappiness. She really kept her place. Time seemed to make her more charming. Other geisha grew into fame, but no one was even classed with her. Some manufacturers secured the sole right to use her photograph for a label; and that label made a fortune for the firm.

But one day the startling news was abroad that Kimiko had at last shown a very soft heart. She had actually said good-bye to Kimika, and had gone away with somebody able to give her all the pretty dresses she could wish for—somebody eager to give her social position also, and to silence gossip about her naughty past—somebody willing to die for her ten times over, and already half-dead for love of her. Kimika said that a fool had tried to kill himself because of Kimiko, and that Kimiko had taken pity on him, and nursed him back to foolishness. Taiko Hideyoshi had said that there were only two things in this world which he feared—a fool and a dark night. Kimika had always been afraid of a fool; and a fool had taken Kimiko away. And she added, with not unselfish tears, that Kimiko would never come back to her: it was a case of love on both sides for the time of several existences.

Nevertheless, Kimika was only half right. She was very shrewd indeed; but she had never been able to see into certain private chambers in the soul of Kimiko. If she could have seen, she would have screamed for astonishment.

III

BETWEEN KIMIKO AND OTHER GEISHA THERE WAS A DIFFERENCE OF GENTLE blood. Before she took a professional name, her name was Ai, which, written with the proper character, means love. Written with another character the same word-sound signifies grief. The story of Ai was a story of both grief and love.

She had been nicely brought up. As a child she had been sent to a private school kept by an old samurai—where the little girls squatted on cushions before little writing-tables twelve inches high, and where the teachers taught without salary. In these days when teachers get better salaries than civil-service officials, the teaching is not nearly so honest or so pleasant as it used to be. A servant always accompanied the child to and from the schoolhouse, carrying her books, her writing-box, her kneeling cushion, and her little table.

Afterwards she attended an elementary public school. The first "modern" textbooks had just been issued—containing Japanese translations of English, German, and French stories about honor and duty and heroism, excellently chosen, and illustrated with tiny innocent pictures of Western people in costumes never of this world. Those dear pathetic little textbooks are now curiosities: they have long been superseded by pretentious compilations much less lovingly and sensibly edited. Ai learned well. Once a year, at examination time, a great official would visit the school, and talk to the children as if they were all his own, and stroke each silky head as he distributed the prizes. He is now a retired statesman, and has doubtless forgotten Ai; and in the schools of to-day nobody caresses little girls, or gives them prizes.

Then came those reconstructive changes by which families of rank were reduced to obscurity and poverty; and Ai had to leave school. Many great sorrows followed, till there remained to her only her mother and an infant sister. The mother and Ai could do little but weave; and by weaving alone they could not earn enough to live. House and lands first—then, article by article, all things not necessary to existence—heirlooms, trinkets, costly robes, crested lacquer-ware—passed cheaply to those whom misery makes rich, and whose wealth is called by the people *Namida no kane*—"the Money of Tears." Help from the living was scanty—for most of the samurai-families of kin were in like distress. But when there was nothing left to sell—not even Ai's little school-books—help was sought from the dead.

For it was remembered that the father of Ai's father had been buried with his sword, the gift of a *daimyō*; and that the mountings of the weapon were of gold. So the grave was opened, and the grand hilt of curious workmanship exchanged for a common one, and the ornaments of the lacquered sheath removed. But the good blade was not taken, because the warrior might need it. Ai saw his face as he sat erect in the great red-clay urn which served in lieu of coffin to the samurai of high rank when buried by the ancient rite. His features were still recognizable after all those years of sepulture; and he seemed to nod a grim assent to what had been done as his sword was given back to him.

At last the mother of Ai became too weak and ill to work at the loom; and the gold of the dead had been spent. Ai said: "Mother, I know there is but one thing now to do. Let me be sold to the dancing-girls." The mother wept, and made no reply. Ai did not weep, but went out alone.

She remembered that in other days, when banquets were given in her father's house, and dancers served the wine, a free geisha named Kimika had often caressed her. She went straight to the house of Kimika. "I want you to buy me," said Ai; "and I want a great deal of money." Kimika laughed, and petted her, and made her eat, and heard her story —which was bravely told, without one tear. "My child," said Kimika, "I cannot give you a great deal of money; for I have very little. But this I can do: I can promise to support your mother. That will be better than to give her much money for you—because your mother, my child, has been a great lady, and therefore cannot know how to use money cunningly. Ask your honored mother to sign the bond—promising that you will stay with me till you are twenty-four years old, or until such time as you can pay me back. And what money I can now spare, take home with you as a free gift."

Thus Ai became a geisha; and Kimika renamed her Kimiko, and kept the pledge to maintain the mother and child-sister. The mother died before Kimiko became famous; the little sister was put to school. Afterwards those things already told came to pass.

The young man who had wanted to die for love of a dancing-girl was worthy of better things. He was an only son; and his parents, wealthy and titled people, were willing to make any sacrifice for him— even that of accepting a geisha for daughter-in-law. Moreover they were not altogether displeased with Kimiko, because of her sympathy for their boy.

Before going away, Kimiko attended the wedding of her young sister, Umé, who had just finished school. She was good and pretty. Kimiko had made the match, and used her wicked knowledge of men in making it. She chose a very plain, honest, old-fashioned merchant— a man who could not have been bad, even if he tried. Umé did not question the wisdom of her sister's choice, which time proved fortunate.

IV

IT WAS IN THE PERIOD OF THE FOURTH MOON THAT KIMIKO WAS CARRIED away to the home prepared for her—a place in which to forget all the unpleasant realities of life—a sort of fairy-palace lost in the charmed repose of great shadowy silent high-walled gardens. Therein she might have felt as one reborn, by reason of good deeds, into the realm of Hōrai. But the spring passed, and the summer came—and Kimiko remained simply Kimiko. Three times she had contrived, for reasons unspoken, to put off the wedding-day.

In the period of the eighth moon, Kimiko ceased to be playful, and told her reasons very gently but very firmly: "It is time that I should say what I have long delayed saying. For the sake of the mother who gave me life, and for the sake of my little sister, I have lived in hell. All that is past; but the scorch of the fire is upon me, and there is no power that can take it away. It is not for such as I to enter into an honored family—nor to bear you a son—nor to build up your house. . . . Suffer me to speak; for in the knowing of wrong I am very, very much wiser than you. . . . Never shall I be your wife to become your shame. I am your companion only, your play-fellow, your guest of an hour—and this not for any gifts. When I shall be no longer with you—nay! certainly that day must come!—you will have clearer sight. I shall still be dear to you, but not in the same way as now—which is foolishness. You will remember these words out of my heart. Some true sweet lady will be chosen for you, to become the mother of your children. I shall see them; but the place of a wife I shall never take, and the joy of a mother I must never know. I am only your folly, my beloved—an illusion, a dream, a shadow flitting across your life. Somewhat more in later time I may become, but a wife to you never—neither in this existence nor in the next. Ask me again—and I go."

In the period of the tenth moon, and without any reason imaginable, Kimiko disappeared—vanished—utterly ceased to exist.

V

NOBODY KNEW WHEN OR HOW OR WHITHER SHE HAD GONE. EVEN IN THE neighborhood of the home she had left, none had seen her pass. At first it seemed that she must soon return. Of all her beautiful and precious things—her robes, her ornaments, her presents: a fortune in themselves —she had taken nothing. But weeks passed without word or sign; and it was feared that something terrible had befallen her. Rivers were dragged, and wells were searched. Inquiries were made by telegraph and by letter. Trusted servants were sent to look for her. Rewards were offered for any news—especially a reward to Kimika, who was really attached to the girl, and would have been only too happy to find her without any reward at all. But the mystery remained a mystery. Application to the authorities would have been useless: the fugitive had done no wrong, broken no law; and the vast machinery of the imperial police-system was not to be set in motion by the passionate whim of a boy. Months grew into years; but neither Kimika, nor the little sister in Kyōto, nor any one of the thousands who had known and admired the beautiful dancer, ever saw Kimiko again.

But what she had foretold came true; for time dries all tears and quiets all longing; and even in Japan one does not really try to die twice for the same despair. The lover of Kimiko became wiser; and there was found for him a very sweet person for wife, who gave him a son. And other years passed; and there was happiness in the fairy-home where Kimiko had once been.

There came to that home one morning, as if seeking alms, a traveling nun; and the child, hearing her Buddhist cry of "Ha—i! ha—i!" ran to the gate. And presently a house-servant, bringing out the customary gift of rice, wondered to see the nun caressing the child, and whispering to him. Then the little one cried to the servant, "Let me give!" and the nun pleaded from under the veiling shadow of her great straw hat: "Honorably allow the child to give me." So the boy put the rice into the mendicant's bowl. Then she thanked him, and asked: "Now will you say again for me the little word which I prayed you to tell your honored father?" And the child lisped: "Father, one whom you will never see again in this world, says that her heart is glad because she has seen your son."

The nun laughed softly, and caressed him again, and passed away swiftly; and the servant wondered more than ever, while the child ran to tell his father the words of the mendicant.

But the father's eyes dimmed as he heard the words, and he wept over his boy. For he, and only he, knew who had been at the gate—and the sacrificial meaning of all that had been hidden.

Now he thinks much, but tells his thought to no one.

He knows that the space between sun and sun is less than the space between himself and the woman who loved him.

He knows it were vain to ask in what remote city, in what fantastic riddle of narrow nameless streets, in what obscure little temple known only to the poorest poor, she waits for the darkness before the Dawn of the Immeasurable Light—when the Face of the Teacher will smile upon her—when the Voice of the Teacher will say to her, in tones of sweetness deeper than ever came from human lover's lips: "O my daughter in the Law, thou hast practiced the perfect way; thou hast believed and understood the highest truth; therefore come I now to meet and to welcome thee!"

The Red Bridal

FALLING IN LOVE AT FIRST SIGHT IS LESS COMMON IN JAPAN THAN IN THE
West; partly because of the peculiar constitution of Eastern society, and
partly because much sorrow is prevented by early marriages which parents arrange. Love suicides, on the other hand, are not infrequent; but
they have the particularity of being nearly always double. Moreover,
they must be considered, in the majority of instances, the results of improper relationships. Still, there are honest and brave exceptions; and
these occur usually in country districts. The love in such a tragedy may
have evolved suddenly out of the most innocent and natural boy-and-
girl friendship, and may have a history dating back to the childhood of
the victims. But even then there remains a very curious difference between a Western double suicide for love and a Japanese *jōshi*. The Oriental suicide is not the result of a blind, quick frenzy of pain. It is not
only cool and methodical: it is sacramental. It involves a marriage of
which the certificate is death. The twain pledge themselves to each other
in the presence of the gods, write their farewell letters, and die. No
pledge can be more profoundly sacred than this. And therefore, if it
should happen that, by sudden outside interference and by medical skill,
one of the pair is snatched from death, that one is bound by the most
solemn obligation of love and honor to cast away life at the first possible opportunity. Of course, if both are saved, all may go well. But it
were better to commit any crime of violence punishable with half a
hundred years of state prison than to become known as a man who,
after pledging his faith to die with a girl, had left her to travel to the
Meido alone. The woman who should fail in her vow might be partially forgiven; but the man who survived a jōshi through interference,
and allowed himself to live on because his purpose was once frustrated,
would be regarded all his mortal days as a perjurer, a murderer, a bestial coward, a disgrace to human nature. I knew of one such case—but

I would now rather try to tell the story of an humble love affair which happened at a village in one of the eastern provinces.

I

THE VILLAGE STANDS ON THE BANK OF A BROAD BUT VERY SHALLOW RIVER, the stony bed of which is completely covered with water only during the rainy season. The river traverses an immense level of rice-fields, open to the horizon north and south, but on the west walled in by a range of blue peaks, and on the east by a chain of low wooded hills. The village itself is separated from these hills only by half a mile of rice-fields; and its principal cemetery, the adjunct of a Buddhist temple dedicated to Kwannon-of-the-Eleven-Faces, is situated upon a neighboring summit. As a distributing centre, the village is not unimportant. Besides several hundred thatched dwellings of the ordinary rustic style, it contains one whole street of thriving two-story shops and inns with handsome tiled roofs. It possesses also a very picturesque *ujigami,* or Shintō parish temple, dedicated to the Sun-Goddess, and a pretty shrine, in a grove of mulberry-trees, dedicated to the Deity of Silkworms.

There was born in this village, in the seventh year of Meiji, in the house of one Uchida, a dyer, a boy called Tarō. His birthday happened to be an *aku-nichi,* or unlucky day—the seventh of the eighth month, by the ancient Calendar of Moons. Therefore his parents, being old-fashioned folk, feared and sorrowed. But sympathizing neighbors tried to persuade them that everything was as it should be, because the calendar had been changed by the Emperor's order, and according to the new calendar the day was a *kitsu-nichi,* or lucky day. These representations somewhat lessened the anxiety of the parents; but when they took the child to the ujigami, they made the gods a gift of a very large paper lantern, and besought earnestly that all harm should be kept away from their boy. The *kannushi,* or priest, repeated the archaic formulas required, and waved the sacred *gohei* above the little shaven head, and prepared a small amulet to be suspended about the infant's neck; after which the parents visited the temple of Kwannon on the hill, and there also made offerings, and prayed to all the Buddhas to protect their first-born.

II

WHEN TARŌ WAS SIX YEARS OLD, HIS PARENTS DECIDED TO SEND HIM TO THE new elementary school which had been built at a short distance from the village. Tarō's grandfather bought him some writing-brushes, paper, a book, and a slate, and early one morning led him by the hand to the school. Tarō felt very happy, because the slate and the other things delighted him like so many new toys, and because everybody had told him that the school was a pleasant place, where he would have plenty of time to play. Moreover, his mother had promised to give him many cakes when he should come home.

As soon as they reached the school—a big two-story building with glass windows—a servant showed them into a large bare apartment, where a serious-looking man was seated at a desk. Tarō's grandfather bowed low to the serious-looking man, and addressed him as *Sensei*, and humbly requested him to teach the little fellow kindly. The Sensei rose up, and bowed in return, and spoke courteously to the old man. He also put his hand on Tarō's head, and said nice things. But Tarō became all at once afraid. When his grandfather had bid him good-bye, he grew still more afraid, and would have liked to run away home; but the master took him into a large, high, white room, full of girls and boys sitting on benches, and showed him a bench, and told him to sit down. All the boys and girls turned their heads to look at Tarō, and whispered to each other, and laughed. Tarō thought they were laughing at him, and began to feel very miserable. A big bell rang; and the master, who had taken his place on a high platform at the other end of the room, ordered silence in a tremendous way that terrified Tarō. All became quiet, and the master began to speak. Tarō thought he spoke most dreadfully. He did not say that school was a pleasant place: he told the pupils very plainly that it was not a place for play, but for hard work. He told them that study was painful, but that they must study in spite of the pain and the difficulty. He told them about the rules which they must obey, and about the punishments for disobedience or carelessness. When they all became frightened and still, he changed his voice altogether, and began to talk to them like a kind father—promising to love them just like his own little ones. Then he told them how the school had been built by the august command of His Imperial Majesty, that the boys and girls of the country might become wise men and good women, and how dearly they should love their noble Emperor, and be happy even to give their lives for his sake. Also he told them how they should love their parents, and how hard their parents had to work for the means of sending them to school, and how wicked and ungrateful it would be to idle during study-hours. Then he began to call them each by name, asking questions about what he had said.

Tarō had heard only a part of the master's discourse. His small mind was almost entirely occupied by the fact that all the boys and girls had looked at him and laughed when he had first entered the room. And the mystery of it all was so painful to him that he could think of little else, and was therefore quite unprepared when the master called his name.

"Uchida Tarō, what do you like best in the world?"

Tarō started, stood up, and answered frankly, "Cake."

All the boys and girls again looked at him and laughed; and the master asked reproachfully: "Uchida Tarō, do you like cake more than you like your parents? Uchida Tarō, do you like cake better than your duty to His Majesty our Emperor?"

Then Tarō knew that he had made some great mistake; and his face became very hot, and all the children laughed, and he began to cry. This only made them laugh still more; and they kept on laughing until the master again enforced silence, and put a similar question to the next pupil. Tarō kept his sleeve to his eyes, and sobbed.

The bell rang. The master told the children they would receive their first writing-lesson during the next class-hour from another teacher, but that they could first go out and play for a while. He then left the room; and the boys and girls all ran out into the school-yard to play, taking no notice whatever of Tarō. The child felt more astonished at being thus ignored than he had felt before on finding himself an object of general attention. Nobody except the master had yet spoken one word to him; and now even the master seemed to have forgotten his existence. He sat down again on his little bench, and cried and cried; trying all the while not to make a noise, for fear the children would come back to laugh at him.

Suddenly a hand was laid upon his shoulder; a sweet voice was speaking to him; and turning his head, he found himself looking into the most caressing pair of eyes he had ever seen—the eyes of a little girl about a year older than he.

"What is it?" she asked him tenderly.

Tarō sobbed and snuffled helplessly for a moment, before he could answer: "I am very unhappy here. I want to go home."

"Why?" questioned the girl, slipping an arm about his neck.

"They all hate me; they will not speak to me or play with me."

"Oh, no!" said the girl. "Nobody dislikes you at all. It is only because you are a stranger. When I first went to school, last year, it was just the same with me. You must not fret."

"But all the others are playing; and I must sit in here," protested Tarō.

"Oh, no, you must not. You must come and play with me. I will be your playfellow. Come!"

Tarō at once began to cry out loud. Self-pity and gratitude and the delight of new-found sympathy filled his little heart so full that he really could not help it. It was so nice to be petted for crying.

But the girl only laughed, and led him out of the room quickly, because the little mother soul in her divined the whole situation. "Of course you may cry, if you wish," she said; "but you must play, too!" And oh, what a delightful play they played together!

But when school was over, and Tarō's grandfather came to take him home, Tarō began to cry again, because it was necessary that he should bid his little playmate good-bye.

The grandfather laughed, and exclaimed, "Why, it is little Yoshi— Miyahara O-Yoshi! Yoshi can come along with us, and stop at the house a while. It is on her way home."

At Tarō's house the playmates ate the promised cake together; and O-Yoshi mischievously asked, mimicking the master's severity, "Uchida Tarō, do you like cake better than *me?*"

III

O-YOSHI'S FATHER OWNED SOME NEIGHBORING RICE-LANDS, AND ALSO KEPT a shop in the village. Her mother, a samurai, adopted into the Miyahara family at the time of the breaking up of the military caste, had borne several children, of whom O-Yoshi, the last, was the only survivor. While still a baby, O-Yoshi lost her mother. Miyahara was past middle age; but he took another wife, the daughter of one of his own farmers—a young girl named Ito O-Tama. Though swarthy as new copper, O-Tama was a remarkably handsome peasant girl, tall, strong, and active; but the choice caused surprise, because O-Tama could neither read nor write.

The surprise changed to amusement when it was discovered that almost from the time of entering the house she had assumed and maintained absolute control. But the neighbors stopped laughing at Miyahara's docility when they learned more about O-Tama. She knew her husband's interests better than he, took charge of everything, and managed his affairs with such tact that in less than two years she had doubled his income. Evidently, Miyahara had got a wife who was going to make him rich. As a step-mother she bore herself rather kindly, even after the birth of her first boy. O-Yoshi was well cared for, and regularly sent to school.

While the children were still going to school, a long-expected and wonderful event took place. Strange tall men with red hair and beards —foreigners from the West—came down into the valley with a great multitude of Japanese laborers, and constructed a railroad. It was carried along the base of the low hill range, beyond the rice-fields and mulberry groves in the rear of the village; and almost at the angle where it crossed the old road leading to the temple of Kwannon, a small station-house was built; and the name of the village was painted in Chinese characters upon a white signboard erected on a platform. Later, a line of telegraph-poles was planted, parallel with the railroad. And still later, trains came, and shrieked, and stopped, and passed—nearly shaking the Buddhas in the old cemetery off their lotus-flowers of stone.

The children wondered at the strange, level, ash-strewn way, with its double lines of iron shining away north and south into mystery; and they were awe-struck by the trains that came roaring and screaming and smoking, like storm-breathing dragons, making the ground quake as they passed by. But this awe was succeeded by curious interest—an interest intensified by the explanations of one of their school-teachers, who showed them, by drawings on the blackboard, how a locomotive engine was made; and who taught them, also, the still more marvelous operation of the telegraph, and told them how the new western capital and the sacred city of Kyōto were to be united by rail and wire, so that the journey between them might be accomplished in less than two days, and messages sent from the one to the other in a few seconds.

Tarō and O-Yoshi became very dear friends. They studied together, played together, and visited each other's homes. But at the age of eleven O-Yoshi was taken from school to assist her step-mother in the household; and thereafter Tarō saw her but seldom. He finished his own studies at fourteen, and began to learn his father's trade. Sorrows came.

After having given him a little brother, his mother died; and in the same year, the kind old grandfather who had first taken him to school followed her; and after these things the world seemed to him much less bright than before. Nothing further changed his life till he reached his seventeenth year. Occasionally he would visit the home of the Miyahara, to talk with O-Yoshi. She had grown up into a slender, pretty woman; but for him she was still only the merry playfellow of happier days.

IV

ONE SOFT SPRING DAY, TARŌ FOUND HIMSELF FEELING VERY LONESOME, AND the thought came to him that it would be pleasant to see O-Yoshi. Probably there existed in his memory some constant relation between the sense of lonesomeness in general and the experience of his first school-day in particular. At all events, something within him—perhaps that a dead mother's love had made, or perhaps something belonging to other dead people—wanted a little tenderness, and he felt sure of receiving the tenderness from O-Yoshi. So he took his way to the little shop. As he approached it, he heard her laugh, and it sounded wonderfully sweet. Then he saw her serving an old peasant, who seemed to be quite pleased, and was chatting garrulously. Tarō had to wait, and felt vexed that he could not at once get O-Yoshi's talk all for himself; but it made him a little happier even to be near her. He looked and looked at her, and suddenly began to wonder why he had never before thought how pretty she was. Yes, she was really pretty—more pretty than any other girl in the village. He kept on looking and wondering, and always she seemed to be growing prettier. It was very strange; he could not understand it. But O-Yoshi, for the first time, seemed to feel shy under that earnest gaze, and blushed to her little ears. Then Tarō felt quite sure that she was more beautiful than anybody else in the whole world, and sweeter, and better, and that he wanted to tell her so; and all at once he found himself angry with the old peasant for talking so much to O-Yoshi, just as if she were a common person. In a few minutes the universe had been quite changed for Tarō, and he did not know it. He only knew that since he last saw her O-Yoshi had become divine; and as soon as the chance came, he told her all his foolish heart, and she told him hers. And they wondered because their thoughts were so much the same; and that was the beginning of great trouble.

V

THE OLD PEASANT WHOM TARŌ HAD ONCE SEEN TALKING TO O-YOSHI HAD
not visited the shop merely as a customer. In addition to his real calling he was a professional *nakōdo*, or match-maker, and was at that very
time acting in the service of a wealthy rice dealer named Okazaki Yaïchirō. Okazaki had seen O-Yoshi, had taken a fancy to her, and had
commissioned the nakōdo to find out everything possible about her, and
about the circumstances of her family.

Very much detested by the peasants, and even by his more immediate
neighbors in the village, was Okazaki Yaïchirō. He was an elderly man,
gross, hard-featured, with a loud, insolent manner. He was said to be
malignant. He was known to have speculated successfully in rice during a period of famine, which the peasant considers a crime, and never
forgives. He was not a native of the *ken*, nor in any way related to its
people, but had come to the village eighteen years before, with his wife
and one child, from some western district. His wife had been dead two
years, and his only son, whom he was said to have treated cruelly, had
suddenly left him, and gone away, nobody knew whither. Other unpleasant stories were told about him. One was that, in his native western province, a furious mob had sacked his house and his godowns, and
obliged him to fly for his life. Another was that, on his wedding night,
he had been compelled to give a banquet to the god Jizō.

It is still customary in some provinces, on the occasion of the marriage of a very unpopular farmer, to make the bridegroom feast Jizō.
A band of sturdy young men force their way into the house, carrying
with them a stone image of the divinity, borrowed from the highway
or from some neighboring cemetery. A large crowd follows them. They
deposit the image in the guest-room, and they demand that ample offerings of food and of saké be made to it at once. This means, of course,
a big feast for themselves, and it is more than dangerous to refuse. All
the uninvited guests must be served till they can neither eat nor drink
any more. The obligation to give such a feast is not only a public rebuke: it is also a lasting public disgrace.

In his old age, Okazaki wished to treat himself to the luxury of a
young and pretty wife; but in spite of his wealth he found this wish
less easy to gratify than he had expected. Various families had check-
mated his proposals at once by stipulating impossible conditions. The

Headman of the village had answered, less politely, that he would sooner give his daughter to an *oni* (demon). And the rice dealer would probably have found himself obliged to seek for a wife in some other district, if he had not happened, after these failures, to notice O-Yoshi. The girl much more than pleased him; and he thought he might be able to obtain her by making certain offers to her people, whom he supposed to be poor. Accordingly, he tried, through the nakōdo, to open negotiations with the Miyahara family.

O-Yoshi's peasant stepmother, though entirely uneducated, was very much the reverse of a simple woman. She had never loved her stepdaughter, but was much too intelligent to be cruel to her without reason. Moreover, O-Yoshi was far from being in her way. O-Yoshi was a faithful worker, obedient, sweet-tempered, and very useful in the house. But the same cool shrewdness that discerned O-Yoshi's merits also estimated the girl's value in the marriage market. Okazaki never suspected that he was going to deal with his natural superior in cunning. O-Tama knew a great deal of his history. She knew the extent of his wealth. She was aware of his unsuccessful attempts to obtain a wife from various families, both within and without the village. She suspected that O-Yoshi's beauty might have aroused a real passion, and she knew that an old man's passion might be taken advantage of in a large number of cases. O-Yoshi was not wonderfully beautiful, but she was a really pretty and graceful girl, with very winning ways; and to get another like her, Okazaki would have to travel far. Should he refuse to pay well for the privilege of obtaining such a wife, O-Tama knew of younger men who would not hesitate to be generous. He might have O-Yoshi, but never upon easy terms. After the repulse of his first advances, his conduct would betray him. Should he prove to be really enamoured, he could be forced to do more than any other resident of the district could possibly afford. It was therefore highly important to discover the real strength of his inclination, and to keep the whole matter, in the mean time, from the knowledge of O-Yoshi. As the reputation of the nakōdo depended on professional silence, there was no likelihood of his betraying the secret.

The policy of the Miyahara family was settled in a consultation between O-Yoshi's father and her stepmother. Old Miyahara would have scarcely presumed, in any event, to oppose his wife's plans; but she took the precaution of persuading him, first of all, that such a marriage ought to be in many ways to his daughter's interest. She discussed with him the possible financial advantages of the union. She represented that there were, indeed, unpleasant risks, but that these could be provided against by making Okazaki agree to certain preliminary settlements. Then she taught her husband his rôle. Pending negotiations, the visits of Tarō were to be encouraged. The liking of the pair for each other was a mere cobweb of sentiment that could be brushed out of existence at the required moment; and meantime it was to be made use of. That Okazaki should hear of a likely young rival might hasten desirable conclusions.

It was for these reasons that, when Tarō's father first proposed for O-Yoshi in his son's name, the suit was neither accepted nor discouraged. The only immediate objection offered was that O-Yoshi was one year older than Tarō, and that such a marriage would be contrary to custom—which was quite true. Still, the objection was a weak one, and had been selected because of its apparent unimportance.

Okazaki's first overtures were at the same time received in such a manner as to convey the impression that their sincerity was suspected. The Miyahara refused to understand the nakōdo at all. They remained astonishingly obtuse even to the plainest assurances, until Okazaki found it politic to shape what he thought a tempting offer. Old Miyahara then declared that he would leave the matter in his wife's hands, and abide by her decision.

O-Tama decided by instantly rejecting the proposal, with every appearance of scornful astonishment. She said unpleasant things. There was once a man who wanted to get a beautiful wife very cheap. At last he found a beautiful woman who said she ate only two grains of rice every day. So he married her; and every day she put into her mouth only two grains of rice; and he was happy. But one night, on returning from a journey, he watched her secretly through a hole in the roof, and saw her eating monstrously—devouring mountains of rice and fish, and putting all the food into a hole in the top of her head under her hair. Then he knew that he had married the Yama-Omba.

O-Tama waited a month for the results of her rebuff—waited very confidently, knowing how the imagined value of something wished for can be increased by the increase of the difficulty of getting it. And, as she expected, the nakōdo at last reappeared. This time Okazaki approached the matter less condescendingly than before; adding to his first offer, and even volunteering seductive promises. Then she knew she was going to have him in her power. Her plan of campaign was not complicated, but it was founded upon a deep instinctive knowledge of the uglier side of human nature; and she felt sure of success. Promises were for fools; legal contracts involving conditions were traps for the simple. Okazaki should yield up no small portion of his property before obtaining O-Yoshi.

VI

TARŌ'S FATHER EARNESTLY DESIRED HIS SON'S MARRIAGE WITH O-YOSHI, AND he had tried to bring it about in the usual way. He was surprised at not being able to get any definite answer from the Miyahara. He was a plain, simple man; but he had the intuition of sympathetic natures, and the unusually gracious manner of O-Tama, whom he had always disliked, made him suspect that he had nothing to hope. He thought it best to tell his suspicions to Tarō, with the result that the lad fretted himself into a fever. But O-Yoshi's stepmother had no intention of reducing Tarō to despair at so early a stage of her plot. She sent kindly worded messages to the house during his illness, and a letter from O-Yoshi, which had the desired effect of reviving all his hopes. After his sickness, he was graciously received by the Miyahara, and allowed to talk to O-Yoshi in the shop. Nothing, however, was said about his father's visit.

The lovers had also frequent chances to meet at the ujigami court, whither O-Yoshi often went with her stepmother's last baby. Even among the crowd of nurse-girls, children, and young mothers, they could exchange a few words without fear of gossip. Their hopes received no further serious check for a month, when O-Tama pleasantly proposed to Tarō's father an impossible pecuniary arrangement. She had lifted a corner of her mask, because Okazaki was struggling wildly in the net she had spread for him, and by the violence of the struggles she knew the end was not far off. O-Yoshi was still ignorant of what was going on; but she had reason to fear that she would never be given to Tarō. She was becoming thinner and paler.

Tarō one morning took his child-brother with him to the temple court, in the hope of an opportunity to chat with O-Yoshi. They met; and he told her that he was feeling afraid. He had found that the little wooden amulet which his mother had put about his neck when he was a child had been broken within the silken cover.

"That is not bad luck," said O-Yoshi. "It is only a sign that the august gods have been guarding you. There has been sickness in the village; and you caught the fever, but you got well. The holy charm shielded you: that is why it was broken. Tell the kannushi to-day: he will give you another."

Because they were very unhappy, and had never done harm to anybody, they began to reason about the justice of the universe.

Tarō said: "Perhaps in the former life we hated each other. Perhaps I was unkind to you, or you to me. And this is our punishment. The priests say so."

O-Yoshi made answer with something of her old playfulness: "I was a man then, and you were a woman. I loved you very, very much; but you were very unkind to me. I remember it all quite well."

"You are not a Bosatsu," returned Tarō, smiling despite his sorrow; "so you cannot remember anything. It is only in the first of the ten states of Bosatsu that we begin to remember."

"How do you know I am not a Bosatsu?"

"You are a woman. A woman cannot be a Bosatsu."

"But is not Kwan-ze-on Bosatsu a woman?"

"Well, that is true. But a Bosatsu cannot love anything except the *kyō*."

"Did not Shaka have a wife and a son? Did he not love them?"

"Yes; but you know he had to leave them."

"That was very bad, even if Shaka did it. But I don't believe all those stories. And would you leave me, if you could get me?"

So they theorized and argued, and even laughed betimes: it was so pleasant to be together. But suddenly the girl became serious again, and said:

"Listen! Last night I saw a dream. I saw a strange river, and the sea. I was standing, I thought, beside the river, very near to where it flowed into the sea. And I was afraid, very much afraid, and did not know why. Then I looked, and saw there was no water in the river, no water in the sea, but only the bones of the Buddhas. But they were all moving, just like water.

"Then again I thought I was at home, and that you had given me a beautiful gift-silk for a kimono, and that the kimono had been made. And I put it on. And then I wondered, because at first it had seemed of many colors, but now it was all white; and I had foolishly folded it upon me as the robes of the dead are folded, to the left. Then I went to the homes of all my kinsfolk to say good-bye; and I told them I was going to the Meido. And they all asked me why; and I could not answer."

"That is good," responded Tarō; "it is very lucky to dream of the dead. Perhaps it is a sign we shall soon be husband and wife."

This time the girl did not reply; neither did she smile.

Tarō was silent a minute; then he added: "If you think it was not a good dream, Yoshi, whisper it all to the nanten plant in the garden: then it will not come true."

But on the evening of the same day Tarō's father was notified that Miyahara O-Yoshi was to become the wife of Okazaki Yaïchirō.

VII

O-TAMA WAS REALLY A VERY CLEVER WOMAN. SHE HAD NEVER MADE ANY serious mistakes. She was one of those excellently organized beings who succeed in life by the perfect ease with which they exploit inferior natures. The full experience of her peasant ancestry in patience, in cunning, in crafty perception, in rapid foresight, in hard economy, was concentrated into a perfect machinery within her unlettered brain. That machinery worked faultlessly in the environment which had called it into existence, and upon the particular human material with which it was adapted to deal—the nature of the peasant. But there was another nature which O-Tama understood less well, because there was nothing in her ancestral experience to elucidate it. She was a strong disbeliever in all the old ideas about character distinctions between samurai and *heimin*. She considered there had never been any differences between the military and the agricultural classes, except such differences of rank as laws and customs had established; and these had been bad. Laws and customs, she thought, had resulted in making all the former samurai class more or less helpless and foolish; and secretly she despised all *shizoku*. By their incapacity for hard work and their absolute ignorance of business methods, she had seen them reduced from wealth to misery. She had seen the pension bonds given them by the new government pass from their hands into the clutches of cunning speculators of the most vulgar class. She despised weakness; she despised incapacity; and she deemed the commonest vegetable seller a much superior being to the ex-Karō obliged in his old age to beg assistance from those who had formerly cast off their footgear and bowed their heads to the mud whenever he passed by. She did not consider it an advantage for O-Yoshi to have had a samurai mother: she attributed the girl's delicacy to that cause, and thought her descent a misfortune. She had clearly read in O-Yoshi's character all that could be read by one not of a superior caste; among other facts, that nothing would be gained by needless harshness to the child, and the implied quality was not one that she disliked. But there were other qualities in O-Yoshi that she had never clearly perceived—a profound though well-controlled sensitiveness to moral wrong, an unconquerable self-respect, and a latent reserve of will power that could triumph over any physical pain. And thus it happened that the behavior of O-Yoshi, when told she would have to become the wife of Okazaki, duped her stepmother, who was prepared to encounter a revolt. She was mistaken.

At first the girl turned white as death. But in another moment she blushed, smiled, bowed down, and agreeably astonished the Miyahara by announcing, in the formal language of filial piety, her readiness to obey the will of her parents in all things. There was no further appearance even of secret dissatisfaction in her manner; and O-Tama was so pleased that she took her into confidence, and told her something of the comedy of the negotiations, and the full extent of the sacrifices which Okazaki had been compelled to make. Furthermore, in addition to such trite consolations as are always offered to a young girl betrothed without her own consent to an old man, O-Tama gave her some really priceless advice how to manage Okazaki. Tarō's name was not even once mentioned. For the advice O-Yoshi dutifully thanked her stepmother, with graceful prostrations. It was certainly admirable advice. Almost any intelligent peasant girl, fully instructed by such a teacher as O-Tama, might have been able to support existence with Okazaki. But O-Yoshi was only half a peasant girl. Her first sudden pallor and her subsequent crimson flush, after the announcement of the fate reserved for her, were caused by two emotional sensations of which O-Tama was far from suspecting the nature. Both represented much more complex and rapid thinking than O-Tama had ever done in all her calculating experience.

The first was a shock of horror accompanying the full recognition of the absolute moral insensibility of her stepmother, the utter hopelessness of any protest, the virtual sale of her person to that hideous old man for the sole motive of unnecessary gain, the cruelty and the shame of the transaction. But almost as quickly there rushed to her consciousness an equally complete sense of the need of courage and strength to the face the worst, and of subtlety to cope with strong cunning. It was then she smiled. And as she smiled, her young will became steel, of the sort that severs iron without turning edge. She knew at once exactly what to do—her samurai blood told her that; and she plotted only to gain the time and the chance. And she felt already so sure of triumph that she had to make a strong effort not to laugh aloud. The light in her eyes completely deceived O-Tama, who detected only a manifestation of satisfied feeling, and imagined the feeling due to a sudden perception of advantages to be gained by a rich marriage.

It was the fifteenth day of the ninth month; and the wedding was to be celebrated upon the sixth of the tenth month. But three days later, O-Tama, rising at dawn, found that her stepdaughter had disappeared during the night. Tarō Uchida had not been seen by his father since the afternoon of the previous day. But letters from both were received a few hours afterwards.

VIII

THE EARLY MORNING TRAIN FROM KYŌTO WAS IN; THE LITTLE STATION WAS full of hurry and noise—clattering of *geta*, humming of converse, and fragmentary cries of village boys selling cakes and luncheons: "*Kwashi yoros—!*" "*Sushi yoros—!*" "*Bentō yoros—!*" Five minutes, and the geta clatter, and the banging of carriage doors, and the shrilling of the boys stopped, as a whistle blew and the train jolted and moved. It rumbled out, puffed away slowly northward, and the little station emptied itself. The policeman on duty at the wicket banged it to, and began to walk up and down the sanded platform, surveying the silent rice-fields.

Autumn had come—the Period of Great Light. The sun glow had suddenly become whiter, and shadows sharper, and all outlines clear as edges of splintered glass. The mosses, long parched out of visibility by the summer heat, had revived in wonderful patches and bands of bright soft green over all shaded bare spaces of the black volcanic soil; from every group of pine-trees vibrated the shrill wheeze of the *tsuku-tsuku-bōshi;* and above all the little ditches and canals was a silent flickering of tiny lightnings—zigzag soundless flashings of emerald and rose and azure-of-steel—the shooting of dragon-flies.

Now, it may have been due to the extraordinary clearness of the morning air that the policeman was able to perceive, far up the track, looking north, something which caused him to start, to shade his eyes with his hand, and then to look at the clock. But, as a rule, the black eye of a Japanese policeman, like the eye of a poised kite, seldom fails to perceive the least unusual happening within the whole limit of its vision. I remember that once, in far-away Oki, wishing, without being myself observed, to watch a mask-dance in the street before my inn, I poked a small hole through a paper window of the second story, and peered at the performance. Down the street stalked a policeman, in snowy uniform and havelock; for it was midsummer. He did not appear even to see the dancers or the crowd through which he walked without so much as turning his head to either side. Then he suddenly halted, and fixed his gaze exactly on the hole in my *shōji;* for at that hole he had seen an eye which he had instantly decided, by reason of its shape, to be a foreign eye. Then he entered the inn, and asked questions about my passport, which had already been examined.

What the policeman at the village station observed, and afterwards reported, was that, more than half a mile north of the station, two persons had reached the railroad track by crossing the ricefields, apparently after leaving a farmhouse considerably to the northwest of the village. One of them, a woman, he judged by the color of her robe and girdle to be very young. The early express train from Tōkyō was then due in a few minutes, and its advancing smoke could be perceived from the station platform. The two persons began to run quickly along the track upon which the train was coming. They ran on out of sight round a curve.

Those two persons were Tarō and O-Yoshi. They ran quickly, partly to escape the observation of that very policeman, and partly so as to meet the Tōkyō express as far from the station as possible. After passing the curve, however, they stopped running, and walked, for they could see the smoke coming. As soon as they could see the train itself, they stepped off the track, so as not to alarm the engineer, and waited, hand in hand. Another minute, and the low roar rushed to their ears, and they knew it was time. They stepped back to the track again, turned, wound their arms about each other, and lay down cheek to cheek, very softly and quickly, straight across the inside rail, already ringing like an anvil to the vibration of the hurrying pressure.

The boy smiled. The girl, tightening her arms about his neck, spoke in his ear:

"For the time of two lives, and of three, I am your wife; you are my husband, Tarō Sama."

Tarō said nothing, because almost at the same instant, notwithstanding frantic attempts to halt a fast train without airbrakes in a distance of little more than a hundred yards, the wheels passed through both—cutting evenly, like enormous shears.

IX

THE VILLAGE PEOPLE NOW PUT BAMBOO CUPS FULL OF FLOWERS UPON THE single gravestone of the united pair, and burn incense-sticks, and repeat prayers. This is not orthodox at all, because Buddhism forbids jōshi, and the cemetery is a Buddhist one; but there is religion in it—a religion worthy of profound respect.

You ask why and how the people pray to those dead. Well, all do not pray *to* them, but lovers do, especially unhappy ones. Other folk only decorate the tomb and repeat pious texts. But lovers pray there for supernatural sympathy and help. I was myself obliged to ask why, and I was answered simply, *"Because those dead suffered so much."*

So that the idea which prompts such prayers would seem to be at once more ancient and more modern than Buddhism—the Idea of the eternal Religion of Suffering.

The Case of O-Dai

Honor thy father and thy mother. (DEUT. v, 16.)
Hear the instruction of thy father, and forsake not the law of thy mother. (PROVERBS 1, 8.)

I

O-DAI PUSHED ASIDE THE LAMPLET AND THE INCENSE-CUP AND THE WATER vessel on the Buddha-shelf, and opened the little shrine before which they had been placed. Within were the *ihai,* the mortuary tablets of her people—five in all; and a gilded figure of the Bodhisattva Kwannon stood smiling behind them. The ihai of the grandparents occupied the left side; those of the parents the right; and between them was a smaller tablet, bearing the *kaimyo* of a child-brother with whom she used to play and quarrel, to laugh and cry, in other and happier years. Also the shrine contained a *makēmono,* or scroll, inscribed with the spirit-names of many ancestors. Before that shrine, from her infancy, O-Dai had been wont to pray.

The tablets and the scroll signified more to her faith in former time—very much more—than remembrance of a father's affection and a mother's caress;—more than any remembrance of the ever-loving, ever-patient, ever-smiling elders who had fostered her babyhood, carried her pickaback to every temple-festival, invented her pleasures, consoled her small sorrows, and soothed her fretfulness with song;—more than the memory of the laughter and the tears, the cooing and the calling and the running of the dear and mischievous little brother;—more than all the traditions of the ancestors.

For those objects signified the actual viewless presence of the lost—the haunting of invisible sympathy and tenderness—the gladness and the grief of the dead in the joy and the sorrow of the living. When, in other time, at evening dusk, she was wont to kindle the lamplet before them, how often had she seen the tiny flame astir with a motion not its own!

Yet the ihai is even more than a token to pious fancy. Strange possibilities of transmutation, transubstantiation, belong to it. It serves as temporary body for the spirit between death and birth: each fibre of its incense-penetrated wood lives with a viewless life-potential. The will of the ghost may quicken it. Sometimes, through power of love, it changes to flesh and blood. By help of the ihai the buried mother returns to suckle her babe in the dark. By help of the ihai, the maid consumed upon the funeral pyre may return to wed her betrothed—even to bless him with a son. By power of the ihai, the dead servant may come back from the dust of his rest to save his lord from ruin. Then, after love or loyalty has wrought its will, the personality vanishes;—the body again becomes, to outward seeming, only a tablet.

All this O-Dai ought to have known and remembered. Maybe she did; for she wept as she took the tablets and the scroll out of the shrine, and dropped them from a window into the river below. She did not dare to look after them as the current whirled them away.

II

O-DAI HAD DONE THIS BY ORDER OF TWO ENGLISH MISSIONARY-WOMEN WHO, by various acts of seeming kindness, had persuaded her to become a Christian. (Converts are always commanded to bury or to cast away their ancestral tablets.) These missionary-women—the first ever seen in the province—had promised O-Dai, their only convert, an allowance of three yen a month, as assistant—because she could read and write. By the toil of her hands she had never been able to earn more than two yen a month; and out of that sum she had to pay a rent of twenty-five sen for the use of the upper floor of a little house, belonging to a dealer in second-hand goods. Thither, after the death of her parents, she had taken her loom, and the ancestral tablets. She had been obliged to work very hard indeed in order to live. But with three yen a month she could live very well; and the missionary-women had a room for her. She did not think that the people would mind her change of religion.

As a matter of fact they did not much care. They did not know anything about Christianity, and did not want to know: they only laughed at the girl for being so foolish as to follow the ways of the foreign women. They regarded her as a dupe, and mocked her without malice. And they continued to laugh at her good-humoredly enough, until the day when she was seen to throw the tablets into the river. Then they stopped laughing. They judged the act in itself, without discussing its motives. Their judgment was instantaneous, unanimous, and voiceless. They said no word of reproach to O-Dai. They merely ignored her existence.

The moral resentment of a Japanese community is not always a hot resentment—not the kind that quickly burns itself out. It may be cold. In the case of O-Dai it was cold and silent and heavy like a thickening of ice. No one uttered it. It was altogether spontaneous, instinctive. But the universal feeling might have been thus translated into speech:

Human society, in this most eastern East, has been held together from immemorial time by virtue of that cult which exacts the gratitude of the present to the past, the reverence of the living for the dead, the affection of the descendant for the ancestor. Far beyond the visible world extends the duty of the child to the parent, of the servant to the master, of the subject to the sovereign. Therefore do the dead preside in the family council, in the communal assembly, in the high seats of judgment, in the governing of cities, in the ruling of the land.

Against the Virtue Supreme of Filial Piety—against the religion of the Ancestors—against all faith and gratitude and reverence and duty —against the total moral experience of her race—O-Dai has sinned the sin that cannot be forgiven. Therefore shall the people account her a creature impure—less deserving of fellowship than the Éta—less worthy of kindness than the dog in the street or the cat upon the roof; since even these, according to their feebler light, observe the common law of duty and affection.

O-Dai has refused to her dead the word of thankfulness, the whisper of love, the reverence of a daughter. Therefore, now and forever, the living shall refuse to her the word of greeting, the common salutation, the kindly answer.

O-Dai has mocked the memory of the father who begot her, the memory of the mother whose breasts she sucked, the memory of the elders who cherished her childhood, the memory of the little one who called her Sister. She has mocked at love: therefore all love shall be denied her, all offices of affection.

To the spirit of the father who begot her, to the spirit of the mother who bore her, O-Dai has refused the shadow of a roof, and the vapor of food, and the offering of water. Even so to her shall be denied the shelter of a roof, and the gift of food, and the cup of refreshment.

And even as she cast out the dead, the living shall cast her out. As a carcass shall she be in the way—as the small carrion that none will turn to look upon, that none will bury, that none will pity, that none will speak for in prayer to the Gods and the Buddhas. As a Gaki she shall be—as a Shōjiki-Gaki—seeking sustenance in refuse-heaps. Alive into hell shall she enter;—yet shall her hell remain the single hell, the solitary hell, the hell Kodoku, that spheres the spirit accurst in solitude of fire. . . .

III

UNEXPECTEDLY THE MISSIONARY-WOMEN INFORMED O-DAI THAT SHE WOULD have to take care of herself. Perhaps she had done her best; but she certainly had not been to them of any use whatever, and they required a capable assistant. Moreover, they were going away for some time, and could not take her with them. Surely she could not have been so foolish as to think that they were going to give her three yen per month merely for being a Christian! . . .

O-Dai cried; and they advised her to be brave, and to walk in the paths of virtue. She said that she could not find employment: they told her that no industrious and honest person need ever want for work in this busy world. Then, in desperate terror, she told them truths which they could not understand, and energetically refused to believe. She spoke of a danger imminent; and they answered her with all the harshness of which they were capable—believing that she had confessed herself utterly depraved. In this they were wrong. There was no atom of vice in the girl: an amiable weakness and a childish trustfulness were the worst of her faults. Really she needed help—needed it quickly—needed it terribly. But they could understand only that she wanted money; and that she had threatened to commit sin if she did not get it. They owed her nothing, as she had always been paid in advance; and they imagined excellent reasons for denying her further aid of any sort.

So they put her into the street. Already she had sold her loom. She had nothing more to sell except the single robe upon her back, and a few pair of useless *tabi,* or cleft stockings, which the missionary-women had obliged her to buy, because they thought that it was immodest for a young girl to be seen with naked feet. (They had also obliged her to twist her hair into a hideous back-knot, because the Japanese style of wearing the hair seemed to them ungodly.)

What becomes of the Japanese girl publicly convicted of offending against filial piety? What becomes of the English girl publicly convicted of unchastity? . . .

Of course, had she been strong, O-Dai might have filled her sleeves with stones, and thrown herself into the river—which would have been an excellent thing to do under the circumstances. Or she might have cut her throat—which is more respectable, as the act requires both nerve and skill. But, like most converts of her class, O-Dai was weak: the courage of the race had failed in her. She wanted still to see the sun; and she was not of the sturdy type able to wrestle with the earth for that privilege. Even after fully abjuring her errors, there was left but one road for her to travel.

Said the person who bought the body of O-Dai at a third of the price prayed for:

"My business is an exceedingly shameful business. But even into this business no woman can be received who is known to have done the thing that you have done. If I were to take you into my house, no visitors would come; and the people would probably make trouble. Therefore to Osaka, where you are not known, you shall be sent; and the house in Osaka will pay the money. . . ."

So vanished forever O-Dai—flung into the furnace of a city's lust . . . Perhaps she existed only to furnish one example of facts that every foreign missionary ought to try to understand.

The Story of O-Kamé

O-KAMÉ, DAUGHTER OF THE RICH GONYÉMON OF NAGOSHI, IN THE PROVINCE of Tosa, was very fond of her husband, Hachiyémon. She was twenty-two, and Hachiyémon twenty-five. She was so fond of him that people imagined her to be jealous. But he never gave her the least cause for jealousy; and it is certain that no single unkind word was ever spoken between them.

Unfortunately the health of O-Kamé was feeble. Within less than two years after her marriage, she was attacked by a disease, then prevalent in Tosa, and the best doctors were not able to cure her. Persons seized by this malady could not eat or drink; they remained constantly drowsy and languid, and troubled by strange fancies. And, in spite of constant care, O-Kamé grew weaker and weaker, day by day, until it became evident, even to herself, that she was going to die.

Then she called her husband, and said to him:

"I cannot tell you how good you have been to me during this miserable sickness of mine. Surely no one could have been more kind. But that only makes it all the harder for me to leave you now. . . . Think! I am not yet even twenty-five—and I have the best husband in all this world—and yet I must die! . . . Oh, no, no! it is useless to talk to me about hope; the best Chinese doctors could do nothing for me. I did think to live a few months longer; but when I saw my face this morning in the mirror, I knew that I must die to-day—yes, this very day. And there is something that I want to beg you to do for me—if you wish me to die quite happy."

"Only tell me what it is," Hachiyémon answered; "and if it be in my power to do, I shall be more than glad to do it."

"No, no—you will not be glad to do it," she returned; "you are still so young! It is difficult—very, very difficult—even to ask you to do such a thing; yet the wish for it is like a fire burning in my breast. I must speak it before I die. . . . My dear, you know that sooner or later, after I am dead, they will want you to take another wife. Will you promise me—can you promise me—not to marry again? . . ."

"Only that!" Hachiyémon exclaimed. "Why, if that be all that you wanted to ask for, your wish is very easily granted. With all my heart I promise you that no one shall ever take your place."

"*Aa! Uréshiya!*" cried O-Kamé, half-rising from her couch;—"oh, how happy you have made me!"

And she fell back dead.

Now the health of Hachiyémon appeared to fail after the death of O-Kamé. At first the change in his aspect was attributed to natural grief, and the villagers only said, "How fond of her he must have been!" But, as the months went by, he grew paler and weaker, until at last he became so thin and wan that he looked more like a ghost than a man. Then people began to suspect that sorrow alone could not explain this sudden decline of a man so young. The doctors said that Hachiyémon was not suffering from any known form of disease: they could not account for his condition; but they suggested that it might have been caused by some very unusual trouble of mind. Hachiyémon's parents questioned him in vain;—he had no cause for sorrow, he said, other than what they already knew. They counseled him to remarry; but he protested that nothing could ever induce him to break his promise to the dead.

Thereafter Hachiyémon continued to grow visibly weaker, day by day; and his family despaired of his life. But one day his mother, who

felt sure that he had been concealing something from her, adjured him
so earnestly to tell her the real cause of his decline, and wept so bitterly
before him, that he was not able to resist her entreaties.

"Mother," he said, "it is very difficult to speak about this matter, either
to you or to any one; and, perhaps, when I have told you everything,
you will not be able to believe me. But the truth is that O-Kamé can
find no rest in the other world, and that the Buddhist services repeated
for her have been said in vain. Perhaps she will never be able to rest
unless I go with her on the long black journey. For every night she returns, and lies down by my side. Every night, since the day of her funeral, she has come back. And sometimes I doubt if she be really dead;
for she looks and acts just as when she lived—except that she talks to
me only in whispers. And she always bids me tell no one that she
comes. It may be that she wants me to die; and I should not care to
live for my own sake only. But it is true, as you have said, that my
body really belongs to my parents, and that I owe to them the first
duty. So now, mother, I tell you the whole truth. . . . Yes: every night
she comes, just as I am about to sleep; and she remains until dawn.
As soon as she hears the temple-bell, she goes away."

When the mother of Hachiyémon had heard these things, she was
greatly alarmed; and, hastening at once to the parish-temple, she told
the priest all that her son had confessed, and begged for ghostly help.
The priest, who was a man of great age and experience, listened without surprise to the recital, and then said to her:

"It is not the first time that I have known such a thing to happen;
and I think that I shall be able to save your son. But he is really in
great danger. I have seen the shadow of death upon his face; and, if
O-Kamé return but once again, he will never behold another sunrise.
Whatever can be done for him must be done quickly. Say nothing of
the matter to your son; but assemble the members of both families as
soon as possible, and tell them to come to the temple without delay.
For your son's sake it will be necessary to open the grave of O-Kamé."

So the relatives assembled at the temple; and when the priest had
obtained their consent to the opening of the sepulchre, he led the way
to the cemetery. Then, under his direction, the tombstone of O-Kamé
was shifted, the grave opened, and the coffin raised. And when the
coffin-lid had been removed, all present were startled; for O-Kamé sat
before them with a smile upon her face, seeming as comely as before
the time of her sickness; and there was not any sign of death upon
her. But when the priest told his assistants to lift the dead woman out

of the coffin, the astonishment changed to fear; for the corpse was blood-warm to the touch, and still flexible as in life, notwithstanding the squatting posture in which it had remained so long.[1]

It was borne to the mortuary chapel; and there the priest, with a writing-brush, traced upon the brow and breast and limbs of the body the Sanscrit characters (*Bonji*) of certain holy talismanic words. And he performed a Ségaki service for the spirit of O-Kamé, before suffering her corpse to be restored to the ground.

She never again visited her husband; and Hachiyémon gradually recovered his health and strength. But whether he always kept his promise, the Japanese story-teller does not say.

Common Sense

ONCE THERE LIVED UPON THE MOUNTAIN CALLED ATAGOYAMA, NEAR KYŌTO, a certain learned priest who devoted all his time to meditation and the study of the sacred books. The little temple in which he dwelt was far from any village; and he could not, in such a solitude, have obtained without help the common necessaries of life. But several devout country people regularly contributed to his maintenance, bringing him each month supplies of vegetables and of rice.

Among these good folk there was a certain hunter, who sometimes visited the mountain in search of game. One day, when this hunter had brought a bag of rice to the temple, the priest said to him:

"Friend, I must tell you that wonderful things have happened here since the last time I saw you. I do not certainly know why such things should have happened in my unworthy presence. But you are aware that I have been meditating, and reciting the sutras daily, for many years; and it is possible that what has been vouchsafed me is due to the merit obtained through these religious exercises. I am not sure of

---

[1] The Japanese dead are placed in a sitting posture in the coffin, which is almost square in form.

this. But I am sure that Fugen Bosatsu (Samantabhadra Bodhisattva) comes nightly to this temple, riding upon his elephant. . . . Stay here with me this night, friend; then you will be able to see and to worship the Buddha."

"To witness so holy a vision," the hunter replied, "were a privilege indeed! Most gladly I shall stay, and worship with you."

So the hunter remained at the temple. But while the priest was engaged in his religious exercises, the hunter began to think about the promised miracle, and to doubt whether such a thing could be. And the more he thought, the more he doubted. There was a little boy in the temple—an acolyte—and the hunter found an opportunity to question the boy.

"The priest told me," said the hunter, "that Fugen Bosatsu comes to this temple every night. Have you also seen Fugen Bosatsu?"

"Six times, already," the acolyte replied, "I have seen and reverently worshiped Fugen Bosatsu."

This declaration only served to increase the hunter's suspicions, though he did not in the least doubt the truthfulness of the boy. He reflected, however, that he would probably be able to see whatever the boy had seen; and he waited with eagerness for the hour of the promised vision.

Shortly before midnight the priest announced that it was time to prepare for the coming of Fugen Bosatsu. The doors of the little temple were thrown open; and the priest knelt down at the threshold, with his face to the east. The acolyte knelt at his left hand, and the hunter respectfully placed himself behind the priest.

It was the night of the twentieth of the ninth month—a dreary, dark, and very windy night; and the three waited a long time for the coming of Fugen Bosatsu. But at last a point of white light appeared, like a star, in the direction of the east; and this light approached quickly—growing larger and larger as it came, and illuminating all the slope of the mountain. Presently the light took shape—the shape of a being divine, riding upon a snow-white elephant with six tusks. And, in another moment, the elephant with its shining rider arrived before the temple, and there stood towering, like a mountain of moonlight—wonderful and weird.

Then the priest and the boy, prostrating themselves, began with exceeding fervor to repeat the holy invocation to Fugen Bosatsu. But suddenly the hunter rose up behind them, bow in hand; and, bending his bow to the full, he sent a long arrow whizzing straight at the luminous Buddha, into whose breast it sank up to the very feathers.

Immediately, with a sound like a thunder-clap, the white light vanished, and the vision disappeared. Before the temple there was nothing but windy darkness.

"O miserable man!" cried out the priest, with tears of shame and despair. "O most wretched and wicked man!—what have you done? —what have you done?"

But the hunter received the reproaches of the priest without any sign of compunction or of anger. Then he said, very gently:

"Reverend sir, please try to calm yourself, and listen to me. You thought that you were able to see Fugen Bosatsu because of some merit obtained through your constant meditations and your recitation of the sutras. But if that had been the case, the Buddha would have appeared to you only—not to me, nor even to the boy. I am an ignorant hunter, and my occupation is to kill;—and the taking of life is hateful to the Buddhas. How, then, should I be able to see Fugen Bosatsu? I have been taught that the Buddhas are everywhere about us, and that we remain unable to see them because of our ignorance and our imperfections. You—being a learned priest of pure life— might indeed acquire such enlightenment as would enable you to see the Buddhas; but how should a man who kills animals for his livelihood find the power to see the divine? Both I and this little boy could see all that you saw. And let me now assure you, reverend sir, that what you saw was not Fugen Bosatsu, but a goblinry intended to deceive you—perhaps even to destroy you. I beg that you will try to control your feelings until daybreak. Then I will prove to you the truth of what I have said."

At sunrise the hunter and the priest examined the spot where the vision had been standing, and they discovered a thin trail of blood. And after having followed this trail to a hollow some hundred paces away, they came upon the body of a great badger, transfixed by the hunter's arrow.

The priest, although a learned and pious person, had easily been deceived by a badger. But the hunter, an ignorant and irreligious man, was gifted with strong common sense; and by mother-wit alone he was able at once to detect and to destroy a dangerous illusion.

TRAVEL

———————— ✻ ————————

My First Day in the Orient

"DO NOT FAIL TO WRITE DOWN YOUR FIRST IMPRESSIONS AS SOON AS POSsible," said a kind English professor whom I had the pleasure of meeting soon after my arrival in Japan: "they are evanescent, you know; they will never come to you again, once they have faded out; and yet of all the strange sensations you may receive in this country you will feel none so charming as these." I am trying now to reproduce them from the hasty notes of the time, and find that they were even more fugitive than charming; something has evaporated from all my recollections of them—something impossible to recall. I neglected the friendly advice, in spite of all resolves to obey it: I could not, in those first weeks, resign myself to remain indoors and write, while there was yet so much to see and hear and feel in the sun-steeped ways of the wonderful Japanese city. Still, even could I revive all the lost sensations of those first experiences, I doubt if I could express and fix them in words. The first charm of Japan is intangible and volatile as a perfume.

It began for me with my first *kuruma*-ride out of the European quarter of Yokohama into the Japanese town; and so much as I can recall of it is hereafter set down.

I

IT IS WITH THE DELICIOUS SURPRISE OF THE FIRST JOURNEY THROUGH Japanese streets—unable to make one's kuruma-runner understand anything but gestures, frantic gestures to roll on anywhere, everywhere, since all is unspeakably pleasurable and new—that one first receives the real sensation of being in the Orient, in this Far East so much read of, so long dreamed of, yet, as the eyes bear witness, heretofore all unknown. There is a romance even in the first full consciousness of this rather commonplace fact; but for me this consciousness is transfigured inexpressibly by the divine beauty of the day. There is some charm unutterable in the morning air, cool with the coolness of Japanese spring and wind-waves from the snowy cone of Fuji; a charm perhaps due rather to softest lucidity than to any positive tone—an atmospheric limpidity extraordinary, with only a suggestion of blue in it, through which the most distant objects appear focused with amazing sharpness. The sun is only pleasantly warm; the *jinrikisha,* or *kuruma,* is the most cosy little vehicle imaginable; and the street-vistas, as seen above the dancing white mushroom-shaped hat of my sandaled runner, have an allurement of which I fancy that I could never weary.

Elfish everything seems; for everything as well as everybody is small, and queer, and mysterious: the little houses under their blue roofs, the little shop-fronts hung with blue, and the smiling little people in their blue costumes. The illusion is only broken by the occasional passing of a tall foreigner, and by divers shop-signs bearing announcements in absurd attempts at English. Nevertheless such discords only serve to emphasize reality; they never materially lessen the fascination of the funny little streets.

'Tis at first a delightfully odd confusion only, as you look down one of them, through an interminable flutter of flags and swaying of dark blue drapery, all made beautiful and mysterious with Japanese or Chinese lettering. For there are no immediately discernible laws of construction or decoration: each building seems to have a fantastic prettiness of its own; nothing is exactly like anything else, and all is bewilderingly novel. But gradually, after an hour passed in the quarter, the eye begins to recognize in a vague way some general plan in the construction of these low, light, queerly gabled wooden houses, mostly unpainted, with their first stories all open to the street, and thin strips of roofing sloping above each shop-front, like awnings, back to the miniature balconies of paper-screened second stories. You begin to understand the common plan of the tiny shops, with their matted floors well raised above the street level, and the general perpendicular arrangement of sign-lettering, whether undulating on drapery or glimmering on gilded and lacquered sign-boards. You observe that the same rich dark blue which dominates in popular costume rules also in shop draperies, though there is a sprinkling of other tints— bright blue and white and red (no greens or yellows). And then you note also that the dresses of the laborers are lettered with the same wonderful lettering as the shop draperies. No arabesques could produce such an effect. As modified for decorative purposes, these ideographs have a speaking symmetry which no design without a meaning could possess. As they appear on the back of a workman's frock— pure white on dark blue—and large enough to be easily read at a great distance (indicating some guild or company of which the wearer is a member or employee), they give to the poor cheap garment a factitious appearance of splendor.

And finally, while you are still puzzling over the mystery of things, there will come to you like a revelation the knowledge that most of the amazing picturesqueness of these streets is simply due to the profusion of Chinese and Japanese characters in white, black, blue, or gold, decorating everything—even surfaces of doorposts and paper screens. Perhaps, then, for one moment, you will imagine the effect of English lettering substituted for those magical characters; and the mere idea will give to whatever æsthetic sentiment you may possess a brutal shock, and you will become, as I have become, an enemy of the Romaji-Kwai—that society founded for the ugly utilitarian purpose of introducing the use of English letters in writing Japanese.

II

AN IDEOGRAPH DOES NOT MAKE UPON THE JAPANESE BRAIN ANY IMPRESSION similar to that created in the Occidental brain by a letter or combination of letters—dull, inanimate symbols of vocal sounds. To the Japanese brain an ideograph is a vivid picture: it lives; it speaks; it gesticulates. And the whole space of a Japanese street is full of such living characters—figures that cry out to the eyes, words that smile or grimace like faces.

What such lettering is, compared with our own lifeless types, can be understood only by those who have lived in the farther East. For even the printed characters of Japanese or Chinese imported texts give no suggestion of the possible beauty of the same characters as modified for decorative inscriptions, for sculptural use, or for the commonest advertising purposes. No rigid convention fetters the fancy of the calligrapher or designer: each strives to make his characters more beautiful than any others; and generations upon generations of artists have been toiling from time immemorial with like emulation, so that through centuries and centuries of tireless effort and study, the primitive hieroglyph or ideograph has been evolved into a thing of beauty indescribable. It consists only of a certain number of brush-strokes; but in each stroke there is an undiscoverable secret art of grace, proportion, imperceptible curve, which actually makes it seem alive, and bears witness that even during the lightning-moment of its creation the artist felt with his brush for the ideal shape of the stroke *equally along its entire length,* from head to tail. But the art of the strokes is not all; the art of their combination is that which produces the enchantment, often so as to astonish the Japanese themselves. It is not surprising, indeed, considering the strangely personal, animate, esoteric aspect of Japanese lettering, that there should be wonderful legends of calligraphy, relating how words written by holy experts became incarnate, and descended from their tablets to hold converse with mankind.

III

MY KURUMAYA CALLS HIMSELF "CHA." HE HAS A WHITE HAT WHICH LOOKS like the top of an enormous mushroom; a short blue wide-sleeved

jacket; blue drawers, close-fitting as "tights," and reaching to his
ankles; and light straw sandals bound upon his bare feet with cords
of palmetto-fibre. Doubtless he typifies all the patience, endurance, and
insidious coaxing powers of his class. He has already manifested his
power to make me give him more than the law allows; and I have
been warned against him in vain. For the first sensation of having a
human being for a horse, trotting between shafts, unwearyingly bobbing up and down before you for hours, is alone enough to evoke a
feeling of compassion. And when this human being, thus trotting between shafts, with all his hopes, memories, sentiments, and compre-
hensions, happens to have the gentlest smile, and the power to return
the least favor by an apparent display of infinite gratitude, this compassion becomes sympathy, and provokes unreasoning impulses to
self-sacrifice. I think the sight of the profuse perspiration has also
something to do with the feeling, for it makes one think of the cost of
heartbeats and muscle-contractions, likewise of chills, congestions, and
pleurisy. Cha's clothing is drenched; and he mops his face with a small
sky-blue towel, with figures of bamboo-sprays and sparrows in white
upon it, which towel he carries wrapped about his wrist as he runs.

That, however, which attracts me in Cha—Cha considered not as a
motive power at all, but as a personality—I am rapidly learning to discern in the multitudes of faces turned toward us as we roll through
these miniature streets. And perhaps the supremely pleasurable impression of this morning is that produced by the singular gentleness
of popular scrutiny. Everybody looks at you curiously; but there is
never anything disagreeable, much less hostile in the gaze: most commonly it is accompanied by a smile or half smile. And the ultimate
consequence of all these kindly curious looks and smiles is that the
stranger finds himself thinking of fairy-land. Hackneyed to the degree
of provocation this statement no doubt is: everybody describing the
sensations of his first Japanese day talks of the land as fairy-land, and
of its people as fairy-folk. Yet there is a natural reason for this unanimity in choice of terms to describe what is almost impossible to describe more accurately at the first essay. To find one's self suddenly in
a world where everything is upon a smaller and daintier scale than
with us—a world of lesser and seemingly kindlier beings, all smiling
at you as if to wish you well—a world where all movement is slow
and soft, and voices are hushed—a world where land, life, and sky are
unlike all that one has known elsewhere—this is surely the realization,

for imaginations nourished with English folklore, of the old dream of a World of Elves.

IV

THE TRAVELER WHO ENTERS SUDDENLY INTO A PERIOD OF SOCIAL CHANGE—especially change from a feudal past to a democratic present—is likely to regret the decay of things beautiful and the ugliness of things new. What of both I may yet discover in Japan I know not; but to-day, in these exotic streets, the old and the new mingle so well that one seems to set off the other. The line of tiny white telegraph poles carrying the world's news to papers printed in a mixture of Chinese and Japanese characters; an electric bell in some tea-house with an Oriental riddle of text pasted beside the ivory button; a shop of American sewing-machines next to the shop of a maker of Buddhist images; the establishment of a photographer beside the establishment of a manufacturer of straw sandals: all these present no striking incongruities, for each sample of Occidental innovation is set into an Oriental frame that seems adaptable to any picture. But on the first day, at least, the Old alone is new for the stranger, and suffices to absorb his attention. It then appears to him that everything Japanese is delicate, exquisite, admirable—even a pair of common wooden chopsticks in a paper bag with a little drawing upon it; even a package of toothpicks of cherry-wood, bound with a paper wrapper wonderfully lettered in three different colors; even the little sky-blue towel, with designs of flying sparrows upon it, which the jinrikisha man uses to wipe his face. The bank bills, the commonest copper coins, are things of beauty. Even the piece of plaited colored string used by the shopkeeper in tying up your last purchase is a pretty curiosity. Curiosities and dainty objects bewilder you by their very multitude: on either side of you, wherever you turn your eyes, are countless wonderful things as yet incomprehensible.

But it is perilous to look at them. Every time you dare to look, something obliges you to buy it—unless, as may often happen, the smiling vender invites your inspection of so many varieties of one article, each specially and all unspeakably desirable, that you flee away out of mere terror at your own impulses. The shopkeeper never asks you to buy; but his wares are enchanted, and if you once begin buying you are lost. Cheapness means only a temptation to commit bankruptcy; for the resources of irresistible artistic cheapness are inexhaustible. The largest steamer that crosses the Pacific could not maintain what you wish to purchase. For, although you may not, perhaps, confess the fact to yourself, what you really want to buy is not the contents of a shop; you want the shop and the shopkeeper, and streets of shops with their draperies and their habitants, the whole city and the bay and the mountains begirdling it, and Fujiyama's white witchery overhanging it in the speckless sky, all Japan, in very truth, with its magical trees and luminous atmosphere, with all its cities and towns and temples, and forty millions of the most lovable people in the universe.

Now there comes to my mind something I once heard said by a practical American on hearing of a great fire in Japan: "Oh! those people can afford fires; their houses are so cheaply built." It is true that the frail wooden houses of the common people can be cheaply and quickly replaced; but that which was within them to make them beautiful cannot—and every fire is an art tragedy. For this is the land of infinite hand-made variety; machinery has not yet been able to introduce sameness and utilitarian ugliness in cheap production (except in response to foreign demand for bad taste to suit vulgar markets) and each object made by the artist or artisan differs still from all others, even of his own making. And each time something beautiful perishes by fire, it is a something representing an individual idea.

Happily the art impulse itself, in this country of conflagrations, has a vitality which survives each generation of artists, and defies the flame that changes their labor to ashes or melts it to shapelessness. The idea whose symbol has perished will reappear again in other creations —perhaps after the passing of a century—modified, indeed, yet recognizably of kin to the thought of the past. And every artist is a ghostly worker. Not by years of groping and sacrifice does he find his highest expression; the sacrificial past is within him; his art is an inheritance; his fingers are guided by the dead in the delineation of a flying bird, of the vapors of mountains, of the colors of the morning and the evening, of the shape of branches and the spring burst of flowers: generations of skilled workmen have given him their cunning, and revive in the wonder of his drawing. What was conscious effort in the beginning became unconscious in later centuries—becomes almost automatic in the living man—becomes the art instinctive. Wherefore, one colored print by a Hokusai or Hiroshige, originally sold for less than a cent, may have more real art in it than many a Western painting valued at more than the worth of a whole Japanese street.

V

HERE ARE HOKUSAI'S OWN FIGURES WALKING ABOUT IN STRAW RAIN-COATS, and immense mushroom-shaped hats of straw, and straw sandals— bare-limbed peasants, deeply tanned by wind and sun; and patient-faced mothers with smiling bald babies on their backs, toddling by upon their *geta* (high, noisy, wooden clogs), and robed merchants squatting and smoking their little brass pipes among the countless riddles of their shops.

Then I notice how small and shapely the feet of the people are— whether bare brown feet of peasants, or beautiful feet of children wearing tiny, tiny geta, or feet of young girls in snowy tabi. The *tabi*, the white digitated stocking, gives to a small light foot a mythological aspect—the white cleft grace of the foot of a fauness. Clad or bare, the Japanese foot has the antique symmetry: it has not yet been distorted by the infamous footgear which has deformed the feet of Occidentals.

. . . Of every pair of Japanese wooden clogs, one makes in walking a slightly different sound from the other, as *kring* to *krang;* so that the echo of the walker's steps has an alternate rhythm of tones. On a pavement, such as that of a railway station, the sound obtains immense sonority; and a crowd will some times intentionally fall into step, with the drollest conceivable result of drawling wooden noise.

VI

"TERA E YUKE!"

I have been obliged to return to the European hotel—not because of the noon-meal, as I really begrudge myself the time necessary to eat it, but because I cannot make Cha understand that I want to visit a Buddhist temple. Now Cha understands; my landlord has uttered the mystical words:

"Tera e yuke!"

A few minutes of running along broad thoroughfares lined with gardens and costly ugly European buildings; then passing the bridge of a canal stocked with unpainted sharp-prowed craft of extraordinary construction, we again plunge into narrow low bright pretty streets— into another part of the Japanese city. And Cha runs at the top of his speed between more rows of little ark-shaped houses, narrower above than below; between other unfamiliar lines of little open shops. And always over the shops little strips of blue-tiled roof slope back to the paper-screened chamber of upper floors; and from all the façades hang draperies dark blue, or white, or crimson—foot-breadths of texture covered with beautiful Japanese lettering, white on blue, red on black, black on white. But all this flies by swiftly as a dream. Once more we cross a canal; we rush up a narrow street rising to meet a hill, and Cha, halting suddenly before an immense flight of broad stone steps, sets the shafts of his vehicle on the ground that I may dismount, and, pointing to the steps, exclaims:

"Tera!"

I dismount, and ascend them, and, reaching a broad terrace, find myself face to face with a wonderful gate, topped by a tilted, peaked, many-cornered Chinese roof. It is all strangely carven, this gate. Dragons are intertwined in a frieze above its open doors; and the panels of the doors themselves are similarly sculptured; and there are gargoyles—grotesque lion heads—protruding from the eaves. And the whole is gray, stone-colored; to me, nevertheless, the carvings do not seem to have the fixity of sculpture; all the snakeries and dragonries appear to undulate with a swarming motion, elusively, in eddyings as of water.

I turn a moment to look back through the glorious light. Sea and sky mingle in the same beautiful pale clear blue. Below me the billowing of bluish roofs reaches to the verge of the unruffled bay on the right, and to the feet of the green wooded hills flanking the city on two sides. Beyond that semicircle of green hills rises a lofty range of serrated mountains, indigo silhouettes. And enormously high above the line of them towers an apparition indescribably lovely—one solitary snowy cone, so filmily exquisite, so spiritually white, that but for its immemorially familiar outline, one would surely deem it a shape of cloud. Invisible its base remains, being the same delicious tint as the sky: only above the eternal snow-line its dreamy cone appears, seeming to hang, the ghost of a peak, between the luminous land and the luminous heaven—the sacred and matchless mountain, Fujiyama.

And suddenly, a singular sensation comes upon me as I stand before this weirdly sculptured portal—a sensation of dream and doubt. It seems to me that the steps, and the dragon-swarming gate, and the blue sky arching over the roofs of the town, and the ghostly beauty of

Fuji, and the shadow of myself there stretching upon the gray masonry, must all vanish presently. Why such a feeling? Doubtless because the forms before me—the curved roofs, the coiling dragons, the Chinese grotesqueries of carving—do not really appear to me as things new, but as things dreamed: the sight of them must have stirred to life forgotten memories of picture-books. A moment, and the delusion vanishes; the romance of reality returns, with freshened consciousness of all that which is truly and deliciously new; the magical transparencies of distance, the wondrous delicacy of the tones of the living picture, the enormous height of the summer blue, and the white soft witchery of the Japanese sun.

VII

I PASS ON AND CLIMB MORE STEPS TO A SECOND GATE WITH SIMILAR gargoyles and swarming of dragons, and enter a court where graceful votive lanterns of stone stand like monuments. On my right and left two great grotesque stone lions are sitting—the lions of Buddha, male and female. Beyond is a long low light building, with curved and gabled roof of blue tiles, and three wooden steps before its entrance. Its sides are simple wooden screens covered with thin white paper. This is the temple.

On the steps I take off my shoes; a young man slides aside the screens closing the entrance, and bows me a gracious welcome. And I go in, feeling under my feet a softness of matting thick as bedding. An immense square apartment is before me, full of an unfamiliar sweet smell—the scent of Japanese incense; but after the full blaze of the sun, the paper-filtered light here is dim as moonshine; for a minute or two I can see nothing but gleams of gilding in a soft gloom. Then, my eyes becoming accustomed to the obscurity, I perceive against the paper-paned screens surrounding the sanctuary on three sides shapes of enormous flowers cutting like silhouettes against the vague white light. I approach and find them to be paper flowers— symbolic lotus-blossoms beautifully colored, with curling leaves gilded on the upper surface and bright green beneath. At the dark end of the apartment, facing the entrance, is the altar of Buddha, a rich and lofty altar, covered with bronzes and gilded utensils clustered to right and left of a shrine like a tiny gold temple. But I see no statue; only a mystery of unfamiliar shapes of burnished metal, relieved against darkness, a darkness behind the shrine and altar—whether recess or inner sanctuary I cannot distinguish.

The young attendant who ushered me into the temple now approaches, and, to my great surprise, exclaims in excellent English, pointing to a richly decorated gilded object between groups of candelabra on the altar:

"That is the shrine of Buddha."

"And I would like to make an offering to Buddha," I respond.

"It is not necessary," he says, with a polite smile.

But I insist; and he places the little offering for me upon the altar. Then he invites me to his own room, in a wing of the building—a large luminous room, without furniture, beautifully matted. And we sit down upon the floor and chat. He tells me he is a student in the temple. He learned English in Tōkyō, and speaks it with a curious accent, but with fine choice of words. Finally he asks me:

"Are you a Christian?"

And I answer truthfully:

"No."

"Are you a Buddhist?"

"Not exactly."

"Why do you make offerings if you do not believe in Buddha?"

"I revere the beauty of his teaching, and the faith of those who follow it."

"Are there Buddhists in England and America?"

"There are, at least, a great many interested in Buddhist philosophy."

And he takes from an alcove a little book, and gives it to me to examine. It is an English copy of Olcott's "Buddhist Catechism."

"Why is there no image of Buddha in your temple?" I ask.

"There is a small one in the shrine upon the altar," the student answers; "but the shrine is closed. And we have several large ones. But the image of Buddha is not exposed here every day—only upon festal days. And some images are exposed only once or twice a year."

From my place, I can see, between the open paper screens, men and women ascending the steps, to kneel and pray before the entrance of the temple. They kneel with such naïve reverence, so gracefully and so naturally, that the kneeling of our Occidental devotees seems a clumsy stumbling by comparison. Some only join their hands; others clap them three times loudly and slowly; then they bow their heads, pray silently for a moment, and rise and depart. The shortness of the prayers impresses me as something novel and interesting. From time to time I hear the clink and rattle of brazen coin cast into the great wooden money-box at the entrance.

I turn to the young student, and ask him:
"Why do they clap their hands three times before they pray?"
He answers:
"Three times for the Sansai, the Three Powers: Heaven, Earth, Man."
"But do they clap their hands to call the Gods, as Japanese clap their hands to summon their attendants?"
"Oh, no!" he replies. "The clapping of hands represents only the awakening from the Dream of the Long Night." [1]
"What night? what dream?"
He hesitates some moments before making answer:
"The Buddha said: All beings are only dreaming in this fleeting world of unhappiness."
"Then the clapping of hands signifies that in prayer the soul awakens from such dreaming?"
"Yes."
"You understand what I mean by the word 'soul'?"
"Oh, yes! Buddhists believe the soul always was—always will be."
"Even in Nirvana?"
"Yes."
While we are thus chatting the Chief Priest of the temple enters—a very aged man—accompanied by two young priests, and I am presented to them; and the three bow very low, showing me the glossy crowns of their smoothly shaven heads, before seating themselves in the fashion of gods upon the floor. I observe they do not smile; these are the first Japanese I have seen who do not smile: their faces are impassive as the faces of images. But their long eyes observe me very closely, while the student interprets their questions, and while I attempt to tell them something about the translations of the Sutras in our "Sacred Books of the East," and about the labors of Beal and Burnouf and Feer and Davids and Kern, and others. They listen without

[1] I do not think this explanation is correct; but it is interesting, as the first which I obtained upon the subject. Properly speaking, Buddhist worshipers should not clap the hands, but only rub them softly together. Shintō worshipers always clap their hands four times.

change of countenance, and utter no word in response to the young student's translation of my remarks. Tea, however, is brought in and set before me in a tiny cup, placed in a little brazen saucer, shaped like a lotus-leaf; and I am invited to partake of some little sugar-cakes (*kwashi*), stamped with a figure which I recognize as the Swastika, the ancient Indian symbol of the Wheel of the Law.

As I rise to go, all rise with me; and at the steps the student asks for my name and address.

"For," he adds, "you will not see me here again, as I am going to leave the temple. But I will visit you."

"And your name?" I ask.

"Call me Akira," he answers.

At the threshold I bow my good-bye; and they all bow very, very low—one blue-black head, three glossy heads like balls of ivory. And as I go, only Akira smiles.

VIII

"TERA?" QUERIES CHA, WITH HIS IMMENSE WHITE HAT IN HIS HAND, AS I resume my seat in the jinrikisha at the foot of the steps. Which no doubt means, do I want to see any more temples? Most certainly I do: I have not yet seen Buddha.

"Yes, tera, Cha."

And again begins the long panorama of mysterious shops and tilted eaves, and fantastic riddles written over everything. I have no idea in what direction Cha is running. I only know that the streets seem to become always narrower as we go, and that some of the houses look like great wicker work pigeon-cages only, and that we pass over several bridges before we halt again at the foot of another hill. There is a lofty flight of steps here also, and before them a structure which I know is both a gate and a symbol, imposing, yet in no manner resembling the great Buddhist gateway seen before. Astonishingly simple all the lines of it are: it has no carving, no coloring, no lettering upon it; yet it has a weird solemnity, an enigmatic beauty. It is a *torii*.

"*Miya*," observes Cha. Not a tera this time, but a shrine of the gods of the more ancient faith of the land—a *miya*.

I am standing before a Shintō symbol; I see for the first time, out of a picture at least, a torii. How describe a torii to those who have never looked at one even in a photograph or engraving? Two lofty columns, like gate-pillars, supporting horizontally two cross-beams, the lower and lighter beam having its ends fitted into the columns a little distance below their summits; the uppermost and larger beam supported upon the tops of the columns, and projecting well beyond them to right and left. That is a torii: the construction varying little in design, whether made of stone, wood, or metal. But this description can give no correct idea of the appearance of a torii, of its majestic aspect, of its mystical suggestiveness as a gateway. The first time you see a noble one, you will imagine, perhaps, that you see the colossal model of some beautiful Chinese letter towering against the sky; for all the lines of the thing have the grace of an animated ideograph—have the bold angles and curves of characters made with four sweeps of a master-brush.[2]

Passing the torii I ascend a flight of perhaps one hundred stone steps, and find at their summit a second torii, from whose lower cross-beam hangs festooned the mystic *shimenawa*. It is in this case a hempen rope of perhaps two inches in diameter through its greater length, but tapering off at either end like a snake. Sometimes the shimenawa is made of bronze, when the torii itself is of bronze; but according to tradition it should be made of straw, and most commonly is. For it represents the straw rope which the deity Futo-tama-no-mikoto stretched behind the Sun-Goddess, Ama-terasu-oho-mi-Kami, after Ame-no-ta-jikara-wo-no-Kami, the Heavenly-Hand-Strength-God, had pulled her out, as is told in that ancient myth of Shintō which Professor Chamberlain has translated.[3] And the shimenawa, in its commoner and simpler form, has pendent tufts of straw along its entire length, at regular intervals, because originally made, tradition declares, of grass pulled up by the roots which protruded from the twist of it.

Advancing beyond this torii, I find myself in a sort of park or pleasure-ground on the summit of the hill. There is a small temple on the right; it is all closed up; and I have read so much about the disappointing vacuity of Shintō temples that I do not regret the ab-

---

[2] Various writers, following the opinion of the Japanologue Satow, have stated that the *torii* was originally a bird-perch for fowls offered up to the gods at Shintō shrines— "not as food, but to give warning of daybreak." The etymology of the word is said to be "bird-rest" by some authorities; but Aston, not less of an authority, derives it from words which would give simply the meaning of a gateway. See Chamberlain's *Things Japanese*, pp. 429, 430.

[3] Professor Basil Hall Chamberlain has held the extraordinary position of Professor of *Japanese* in the Imperial University of Japan—no small honor to English philology!

sence of its guardian. And I see before me what is infinitely more interesting—a grove of cherry-trees covered with something unutterably beautiful—a dazzling mist of snowy blossoms clinging like summer cloud-fleece about every branch and twig; and the ground beneath them, and the path before me, is white with the soft, thick, odorous snow of fallen petals.

Beyond this loveliness are flower-plots surrounding tiny shrines; and marvelous grotto-work, full of monsters—dragons and mythologic beings chiseled in the rock; and miniature landscape work with tiny groves of dwarf trees, and lilliputian lakes, and microscopic brooks and bridges and cascades. Here, also, are swings for children. And here are belvederes, perched on the verge of the hill, wherefrom the whole fair city, and the whole smooth bay speckled with fishing-sails no bigger than pin-heads, and the far, faint, high promontories reaching into the sea, are all visible in one delicious view—blue-penciled in a beauty of ghostly haze indescribable.

Why should the trees be so lovely in Japan? With us, a plum- or cherry-tree in flower is not an astonishing sight; but here it is a miracle of beauty so bewildering that, however much you may have previously read about it, the real spectacle strikes you dumb. You see no leaves—only one great filmy mist of petals. Is it that the trees have been so long domesticated and caressed by man in this land of the Gods, that they have acquired souls, and strive to show their gratitude, like women loved, by making themselves more beautiful for man's sake? Assuredly they have mastered men's hearts by their loveliness, like beautiful slaves. That is to say, Japanese hearts. Apparently there have been some foreign tourists of the brutal class in this place, since it has been deemed necessary to set up inscriptions in English announcing that "It is forbidden to injure the trees."

IX

"Tera?"

"Yes, Cha, tera."

But only for a brief while do I traverse Japanese streets. The houses separate, become scattered along the feet of the hills: the city thins away through little valleys, and vanishes at last behind. And we follow a curving road overlooking the sea. Green hills slope steeply down to the edge of the way on the right; on the left, far below, spreads a vast stretch of dun sand and salty pools to a line of surf so distant that it is discernible only as a moving white thread. The tide is out; and thousands of cockle-gatherers are scattered over the sands, at such distances that their stooping figures, dotting the glimmering sea-bed, appear no larger than gnats. And some are coming along the road before us, returning from their search with well-filled baskets—girls with faces almost as rosy as the faces of English girls.

As the jinrikisha rattles on, the hills dominating the road grow higher. All at once Cha halts again before the steepest and loftiest flight of temple steps I have yet seen.

I climb and climb and climb, halting perforce betimes, to ease the violent aching of my quadriceps muscles; reach the top completely out of breath; and find myself between two lions of stone; one showing his fangs, the other with jaws closed. Before me stands the temple, at the farther end of a small bare plateau surrounded on three sides by low cliffs—a small temple, looking very old and gray. From a rocky height to the left of the building, a little cataract rumbles down into a pool, ringed in by a palisade. The voice of the water drowns all other sounds. A sharp wind is blowing from the ocean: the place is chill even in the sun, and bleak, and desolate, as if no prayer had been uttered in it for a hundred years.

Cha taps and calls, while I take off my shoes upon the worn wooden steps of the temple; and after a minute of waiting, we hear a muffled step approaching and a hollow cough behind the paper screens. They slide open; and an old white-robed priest appears, and motions me, with a low bow, to enter. He has a kindly face; and his smile of welcome seems to me one of the most exquisite I have ever been greeted with. Then he coughs again, so badly that I think if I ever come here another time, I shall ask for him in vain.

I go in, feeling that soft, spotless, cushioned matting beneath my feet with which the floors of all Japanese buildings are covered. I pass the indispensable bell and lacquered reading-desk; and before me I see other screens only, stretching from floor to ceiling. The old man, still coughing, slides back one of these upon the right, and waves me into the dimness of an inner sanctuary, haunted by faint odors of incense. A colossal bronze lamp, with snarling gilded dragons coiled about its columnar stem, is the first object I discern; and, in passing it, my shoulder sets ringing a festoon of little bells suspended from the lotus-shaped summit of it. Then I reach the altar, gropingly, unable yet to distinguish forms clearly. But the priest, sliding back screen after screen, pours in light upon the gilded brasses and the inscriptions; and I look for the image of the Deity or presiding Spirit between the altar-groups of convoluted candelabra. And I see—only a mirror, a round, pale disk of polished metal, and my own face therein, and behind this mockery of me a phantom of the far sea.

Only a mirror! Symbolizing what? Illusion? or that the Universe exists for us solely as the reflection of our own souls? or the old Chinese teaching that we must seek the Buddha only in our own hearts? Perhaps some day I shall be able to find out all these things.

As I sit on the temple steps, putting on my shoes preparatory to going, the kind old priest approaches me again, and, bowing, presents a bowl. I hastily drop some coins in it, imagining it to be a Buddhist almsbowl, before discovering it to be full of hot water. But the old man's beautiful courtesy saves me from feeling all the grossness of my mistake. Without a word, and still preserving his kindly smile, he takes the bowl away, and, returning presently with another bowl, empty, fills it with hot water from a little kettle, and makes a sign to me to drink.

Tea is most usually offered to visitors at temples; but this little shrine is very, very poor; and I have a suspicion that the old priest suffers betimes for want of what no fellow-creature should be permitted to need. As I descend the windy steps to the roadway I see him still looking after me, and I hear once more his hollow cough.

Then the mockery of the mirror recurs to me. I am beginning to wonder whether I shall ever be able to discover that which I seek—outside of myself! That is, outside of my own imagination.

X

"TERA?" ONCE MORE QUERIES CHA.

"Tera, no—it is getting late. Hotel, Cha."

But Cha, turning the corner of a narrow street, on our homeward route, halts the jinrikisha before a shrine or tiny temple scarcely larger than the smallest of Japanese shops, yet more of a surprise to me than any of the larger sacred edifices already visited. For, on either side of the entrance, stand two monster-figures, nude, blood-red, demoniac, fearfully muscled, with feet like lions, and hands brandishing gilded thunderbolts, and eyes of delirious fury; the guardians of holy things, the Ni-Ō, or "Two Kings."[4] And right between these crimson monsters a young girl stands looking at us; her slight figure, in robe of silver gray and girdle of iris-violet, relieved deliciously against the twilight darkness of the interior. Her face, impassive and curiously delicate, would charm wherever seen; but here, by strange contrast with the frightful grotesqueries on either side of her, it produces an effect unimaginable. Then I find myself wondering whether my feeling of repulsion toward those twin monstrosities be altogether just, seeing that so charming a maiden deems them worthy of veneration. And they even cease to seem ugly as I watch her standing there between them, dainty and slender as some splendid moth, and always naïvely gazing at the foreigner, utterly unconscious that they might have seemed to him both unholy and uncomely.

What are they? Artistically they are Buddhist transformations of Brahma and of Indra. Enveloped by the absorbing, all-transforming magical atmosphere of Buddhism, Indra can now wield his thunderbolts only in defense of the faith which has dethroned him: he has become a keeper of the temple gates; nay, has even become a servant of Bosatsu (Bodhisattvas), for this is only a shrine of Kwannon, Goddess of Mercy, not yet a Buddha.

"Hotel, Cha, hotel!" I cry out again, for the way is long, and the sun sinking—sinking in the softest imaginable glow of topazine light. I have not seen Shaka (so the Japanese have transformed the name Sakya-Muni); I have not looked upon the face of the Buddha. Perhaps I may be able to find his image to-morrow, somewhere in this wilderness of wooden streets, or upon the summit of some yet unvisited hill.

The sun is gone; the topaz-light is gone; and Cha stops to light his lantern of paper; and we hurry on again, between two long lines of painted paper lanterns suspended before the shops: so closely set, so

---

[4] These Ni-Ō. however, the first I saw in Japan, were very clumsy figures. There are magnificent Ni-Ō to be seen in some of the great temple gateways in Tōkyō, Kyōto, and elsewhere. The grandest of all are those in the Ni-Ō Mon, or "Two Kings' Gate," of the huge Todaiji temple at Nara. They are eight hundred years old. It is impossible not to admire the conception of stormy dignity and hurricane-force embodied in those colossal figures.

Prayers are addressed to the Ni-Ō, especially by pilgrims. Most of their statues are disfigured by little pellets of white paper, which people chew into a pulp and then spit at them. There is a curious superstition that if the pellet sticks to the statue the prayer is heard: if, on the other hand, it falls to the ground, the prayer will not be answered.

level those lines are, that they seem two interminable strings of pearls of fire. And suddenly a sound—solemn, profound, mighty—peals to my ears over the roofs of the town, the voice of the *tsurigane,* the great temple-bell of Nogiyama.

All too short the day seemed. Yet my eyes have been so long dazzled by the great white light, and so confused by the sorcery of that interminable maze of mysterious signs which made each street-vista seem a glimpse into some enormous *grimoire,* that they are now weary even of the soft glowing of all these paper lanterns, likewise covered with characters that look like texts from a Book of Magic. And I feel at last the coming of that drowsiness which always follows enchantment.

XI

"AMMA-KAMISHIMO-GO-HYAKMON!"

A woman's voice ringing through the night, chanting in a tone of singular sweetness words of which each syllable comes through my open window like a wavelet of flute-sound. My Japanese servant, who speaks a little English, has told me what they mean, those words:

"Amma-kamishimo-go-hyakmon!"

And always between these long, sweet calls I hear a plaintive whistle, one long note first, then two short ones in another key. It is the whistle of the *amma,* the poor blind woman who earns her living by shampooing the sick or the weary, and whose whistle warns pedestrians and drivers of vehicles to take heed for her sake, as she cannot see. And she sings also that the weary and the sick may call her in.

"Amma-kamishimo-go-hyakmon!"

The saddest melody, but the sweetest voice. Her cry signifies that for the sum of "five hundred mon" she will come and rub your weary body "above and below," and make the weariness or the pain go away. Five hundred mon are the equivalent of five sen (Japanese cents); there are ten rin to a sen, and ten mon to one rin. The strange sweetness of the voice is haunting—makes me even wish to have some pains, that I might pay five hundred mon to have them driven away.

I lie down to sleep, and I dream. I see Chinese texts—multitudinous, weird, mysterious—fleeing by me, all in one direction; ideographs white and dark, upon sign-boards, upon paper screens, upon backs of sandaled men. They seem to live, these ideographs, with conscious life; they are moving their parts, moving with a movement as of insects, monstrously, like *phasmidæ*. I am rolling always through low, narrow, luminous streets, in a phantom jinrikisha, whose wheels make no sound. And always, always, I see the huge white mushroom-shaped hat of Cha dancing up and down before me as he runs.

The Dream of a Summer Day

I

THE HOTEL SEEMED TO ME A PARADISE, AND THE MAIDS THEREOF CELESTIAL beings. This was because I had just fled away from one of the Open Ports, where I had ventured to seek comfort in a European hotel, supplied with all "modern improvements." To find myself at ease once more in a *yukata*, seated upon cool, soft matting, waited upon by sweet-voiced girls, and surrounded by things of beauty, was therefore like a redemption from all the sorrows of the nineteenth century. Bamboo-shoots and lotus-bulbs were given me for breakfast, and a fan from heaven for a keepsake. The design upon that fan represented only the white rushing burst of one great wave on a beach, and sea-birds shooting in exultation through the blue overhead. But to behold it was worth all the trouble of the journey. It was a glory of light, a thunder of motion, a triumph of sea-wind—all in one. It made me want to shout when I looked at it.

Between the cedarn balcony pillars I could see the course of the pretty gray town following the shore-sweep—and yellow lazy junks asleep at anchor—and the opening of the bay between enormous green cliffs—and beyond it the blaze of summer to the horizon. In that horizon there were mountain shapes faint as old memories. And all things but the gray town, and the yellow junks, and the green cliffs, were blue.

Then a voice softly toned as a wind-bell began to tinkle words of courtesy into my reverie, and broke it; and I perceived that the mistress of the palace had come to thank me for the *chadai*,[1] and I prostrated myself before her. She was very young, and more than pleasant to look upon—like the moth-maidens, like the butterfly-women, of Kunisada. And I thought at once of death; for the beautiful is sometimes a sorrow of anticipation.

She asked whither I honorably intended to go, that she might order a *kuruma* for me. And I made answer:

"To Kumamoto. But the name of your house I much wish to know, that I may always remember it."

"My guest-rooms," she said, "are augustly insignificant, and my maidens honorably rude. But the house is called the House of Urashima. And now I go to order a kuruma."

The music of her voice passed; and I felt enchantment falling all about me—like the thrilling of a ghostly web. For the name was the name of the story of a song that bewitches men.

II

ONCE YOU HEAR THE STORY, YOU WILL NEVER BE ABLE TO FORGET IT. Every summer when I find myself on the coast—especially of very soft, still days—it haunts me most persistently. There are many native versions of it which have been the inspiration for countless works of art. But the most impressive and the most ancient is found in the "Manyefushifu," a collection of poems dating from the fifth to the ninth century. From this ancient version the great scholar Aston translated it into prose, and the great scholar Chamberlain into both prose and verse. But for English readers I think the most charming form of it is Chamberlain's version written for children, in the "Japanese Fairy-Tale Series"—because of the delicious colored pictures by native artists. With that little book before me, I shall try to tell the legend over again in my own words.

Fourteen hundred and sixteen years ago, the fisher-boy Urashima Tarō left the shore of Suminoyé in his boat.

Summer days were then as now—all drowsy and tender blue, with

[1] A little gift of money, always made to a hotel by the guest shortly after his arrival.

only some light, pure white clouds hanging over the mirror of the sea. Then, too, were the hills the same—far blue soft shapes melting into the blue sky. And the winds were lazy.

And presently the boy, also lazy, let his boat drift as he fished. It was a queer boat, unpainted and rudderless, of a shape you probably never saw. But still, after fourteen hundred years, there are such boats to be seen in front of the ancient fishing-hamlets of the coast of the Sea of Japan.

After long waiting, Urashima caught something, and drew it up to him. But he found it was only a tortoise.

Now a tortoise is sacred to the Dragon God of the Sea, and the period of its natural life is a thousand—some say ten thousand—years. So that to kill it is very wrong. The boy gently unfastened the creature from his line, and set it free, with a prayer to the gods.

But he caught nothing more. And the day was very warm; and sea and air and all things were very, very silent. And a great drowsiness grew upon him—and he slept in his drifting boat.

Then out of the dreaming of the sea rose up a beautiful girl—just as you can see her in the picture to Professor Chamberlain's "Urashima"—robed in crimson and blue, with long black hair flowing down her back even to her feet, after the fashion of a prince's daughter fourteen hundred years ago.

Gliding over the waters she came, softly as air, and she stood above the sleeping boy in the boat, and woke him with a light touch, and said:

"Do not be surprised. My father, the Dragon King of the Sea, sent me to you, because of your kind heart. For to-day you set free a tortoise. And now we will go to my father's palace in the island where summer never dies; and I will be your flower-wife if you wish; and we shall live there happily forever."

And Urashima wondered more and more as he looked upon her; for she was more beautiful than any human being, and he could not but love her. Then she took one oar, and he took another, and they rowed away together—just as you may still see, off the far western coast, wife and husband rowing together, when the fishing-boats flit into the evening gold.

They rowed away softly and swiftly over the silent blue water down into the south—till they came to the island where summer never dies —and to the palace of the Dragon King of the Sea.

[Here the text of the little book suddenly shrinks away as you read,

and faint blue ripplings flood the page; and beyond them in a fairy
horizon you can see the long low soft shore of the island, and peaked
roofs rising through evergreen foliage—the roofs of the Sea God's
palace—like the palace of the Mikado Yuriaku, fourteen hundred and
sixteen years ago.]

There strange servitors came to receive them in robes of ceremony
—creatures of the Sea, who paid greeting to Urashima as the son-
in-law of the Dragon King.

So the Sea God's daughter became the bride of Urashima; and it
was a bridal of wondrous splendor; and in the Dragon Palace there
was great rejoicing.

And each day for Urashima there were new wonders and new
pleasures: wonders of the deepest deep brought up by the servants of
the Ocean God; pleasures of that enchanted land where summer never
dies. And so three years passed.

But in spite of all these things, the fisher-boy felt always a heaviness
at his heart when he thought of his parents waiting alone. So that at
last he prayed his bride to let him go home for a little while only, just
to say one word to his father and mother—after which he would
hasten back to her.

At these words she began to weep; and for a long time she continued to weep silently. Then she said to him: "Since you wish to go,
of course you must go. I fear your going very much; I fear we shall
never see each other again. But I will give you a little box to take with
you. It will help you to come back to me if you will do what I tell
you. Do not open it. Above all things, do not open it—no matter what
may happen! Because, if you open it, you will never be able to come
back, and you will never see me again."

Then she gave him a little lacquered box tied about with a silken
cord. [And that box can be seen unto this day in the temple of Kana-
gawa, by the seashore; and the priests there also keep Urashima Tarō's
fishing-line, and some strange jewels which he brought back with him
from the realm of the Dragon King.]

But Urashima comforted his bride, and promised her never, never
to open the box—never even to loosen the silken string. Then he
passed away through the summer light over the ever-sleeping sea; and
the shape of the island where summer never dies faded behind him
like a dream; and he saw again before him the blue mountains of
Japan, sharpening in the white glow of the northern horizon.

Again at last he glided into his native bay; again he stood upon its

beach. But as he looked, there came upon him a great bewilderment—
a weird doubt.

For the place was at once the same, and yet not the same. The cottage of his fathers had disappeared. There was a village; but the shapes of the houses were all strange, and the trees were strange, and the fields, and even the faces of the people. Nearly all remembered landmarks were gone; the Shintō temple appeared to have been rebuilt in a new place; the woods had vanished from the neighboring slopes. Only the voice of the little stream flowing through the settlement, and the forms of the mountains, were still the same. All else was unfamiliar and new. In vain he tried to find the dwelling of his parents; and the fisherfolk stared wonderingly at him; and he could not remember having ever seen any of those faces before.

There came along a very old man, leaning on a stick, and Urashima asked him the way to the house of the Urashima family. But the old man looked quite astonished, and made him repeat the question many times, and then cried out:

"Urashima Tarō! Where do you come from that you do not know the story? Urashima Tarō! Why, it is more than four hundred years since he was drowned, and a monument is erected to his memory in the graveyard. The graves of all his people are in that graveyard—the old graveyard which is not now used any more. Urashimo Tarō! How can you be so foolish as to ask where his house is?" And the old man hobbled on, laughing at the simplicity of his questioner.

But Urashima went to the village graveyard—the old graveyard that was not used any more—and there he found his own tombstone, and the tombstones of his father and his mother and his kindred, and the tombstones of many others he had known. So old they were, so moss-eaten, that it was very hard to read the names upon them.

Then he knew himself the victim of some strange illusion, and he took his way back to the beach—always carrying in his hand the box, the gift of the Sea God's daughter. But what was this illusion? And what could be in that box? Or might not that which was in the box be the cause of the illusion? Doubt mastered faith. Recklessly he broke the promise made to his beloved; he loosened the silken cord; he opened the box!

Instantly, without any sound, there burst from it a white cold spectral vapor that rose in the air like a summer cloud, and began to drift away swiftly into the south, over the silent sea. There was nothing else in the box.

And Urashima then knew that he had destroyed his own happiness
—that he could never again return to his beloved, the daughter of the
Ocean King. So that he wept and cried out bitterly in his despair.

Yet for a moment only. In another, he himself was changed. An icy
chill shot through all his blood; his teeth fell out; his face shriveled;
his hair turned white as snow; his limbs withered; his strength ebbed;
he sank down lifeless on the sand, crushed by the weight of four hundred winters.

Now in the official annals of the Emperors it is written that "in
the twenty-first year of the Mikado Yuriaku, the boy Urashima of
Midzunoyé, in the district of Yosa, in the province of Tango, a descendant of the divinity Shimanemi, went to Elysium [Hōrai] in a
fishing-boat." After this there is no more news of Urashima during
the reigns of thirty-one emperors and empresses—that is, from the
fifth until the ninth century. And then the annals announce that "in
the second year of Tenchiyō, in the reign of the Mikado Go-Junwa,
the boy Urashima returned, and presently departed again, none knew
whither." [2]

III

THE FAIRY MISTRESS CAME BACK TO TELL ME THAT EVERYTHING WAS READY,
and tried to lift my valise in her slender hands—which I prevented
her from doing, because it was heavy. Then she laughed, but would
not suffer that I should carry it myself, and summoned a sea-creature
with Chinese characters upon his back. I made obeisance to her; and
she prayed me to remember the unworthy house despite the rudeness
of the maidens. "And you will pay the kurumaya," she said, "only
seventy-five sen."

Then I slipped into the vehicle; and in a few minutes the little gray
town had vanished behind a curve. I was rolling along a white road
overlooking the shore. To the right were pale brown cliffs; to the left
only space and sea.

Mile after mile I rolled along that shore, looking into the infinite
light. All was steeped in blue—a marvelous blue, like that which
comes and goes in the heart of a great shell. Glowing blue sea met

<hr>

[2] See *The Classical Poetry of the Japanese*, by Professor Chamberlain, in Trübner's
Oriental Series. According to Western chronology, Urashima went fishing in 477 A.D.,
and returned in 825.

hollow blue sky in a brightness of electric fusion; and vast blue apparitions—the mountains of Higo—angled up through the blaze, like masses of amethyst. What a blue transparency! The universal color was broken only by the dazzling white of a few high summer clouds, motionlessly curled above one phantom peak in the offing. They threw down upon the water snowy tremulous lights. Midges of ships creeping far away seemed to pull long threads after them—the only sharp lines in all that hazy glory. But what divine clouds! White purified spirits of clouds, resting on their way to the beatitude of Nirvana? Or perhaps the mists escaped from Urashima's box a thousand years ago?

The gnat of the soul of me flitted out into that dream of blue, 'twixt sea and sun—hummed back to the shore of Suminoyé through the luminous ghosts of fourteen hundred summers. Vaguely I felt beneath me the drifting of a keel. It was the time of the Mikado Yuriaku. And the Daughter of the Dragon King said tinklingly, "Now we will go to my father's palace where it is always blue." "Why always blue?" I asked. "Because," she said, "I put all the clouds into the Box." "But I must go home," I answered resolutely. "Then," she said, "you will pay the kurumaya only seventy-five sen."

Wherewith I woke into Doyō, or the Period of Greatest Heat, in the twenty-sixth year of Meiji—and saw proof of the era in a line of telegraph poles reaching out of sight on the land side of the way. The kuruma was still fleeing by the shore, before the same blue vision of sky, peak, and sea; but the white clouds were gone!—and there were no more cliffs close to the road, but fields of rice and of barley stretching to far-off hills. The telegraph lines absorbed my attention for a moment, because on the top wire, and only on the top wire, hosts of little birds were perched, all with their heads to the road, and nowise disturbed by our coming. They remained quite still, looking down upon us as mere passing phenomena. There were hundreds and hundreds in rank, for miles and miles. And I could not see one having its tail turned to the road. Why they sat thus, and what they were watching or waiting for, I could not guess. At intervals I waved my hat and shouted, to startle the ranks. Whereupon a few would rise up fluttering and chippering, and drop back again upon the wire in the same position as before. The vast majority refused to take me seriously.

The sharp rattle of the wheels was drowned by a deep booming; and as we whirled past a village I caught sight of an immense drum under an open shed, beaten by naked men.

"O kurumaya!" I shouted—"that—what is it?"

He, without stopping, shouted back:

"Everywhere now the same thing is. Much time-in rain has not been: so the gods-to prayers are made, and drums are beaten."

We flashed through other villages; and I saw and heard more drums of various sizes, and from hamlets invisible, over miles of parching rice-fields, yet other drums, like echoings, responded.

IV

THEN I BEGAN TO THINK ABOUT URASHIMA AGAIN. I THOUGHT OF THE pictures and poems and proverbs recording the influence of the legend upon the imagination of a race. I thought of an Izumo dancing-girl I saw at a banquet acting the part of Urashima, with a little lacquered box whence there issued at the tragical minute a mist of Kyōto incense. I thought about the antiquity of the beautiful dance—and therefore about vanished generations of dancing-girls—and therefore about dust in the abstract; which, again, led me to think of dust in the concrete, as bestirred by the sandals of the kurumaya to whom I was to pay only seventy-five sen. And I wondered how much of it might be old human dust, and whether in the eternal order of things the motion of hearts might be of more consequence than the motion of dust. Then my ancestral morality took alarm; and I tried to persuade myself that a story which had lived for a thousand years, gaining fresher charm with the passing of every century, could only have survived by virtue of some truth in it. But what truth? For the time being I could find no answer to this question.

The heat had become very great; and I cried:

"O kurumaya! the throat of Selfishness is dry; water desirable is."

He, still running, answered:

"The Village of the Long Beach inside of—not far—a great gush-water is. There pure august water will be given."

I cried again:

"O kurumaya!—those little birds as-for, why this way always facing?"

He, running still more swiftly, responded:
"All birds wind-to facing sit."
I laughed first at my own simplicity; then at my forgetfulness—remembering I had been told the same thing, somewhere or other, when a boy. Perhaps the mystery of Urashima might also have been created by forgetfulness.

I thought again about Urashima. I saw the Daughter of the Dragon King waiting vainly in the palace made beautiful for his welcome—and the pitiless return of the Cloud, announcing what had happened—and the loving uncouth sea-creatures, in their garments of great ceremony, trying to comfort her. But in the real story there was nothing of all this; and the pity of the people seemed to be all for Urashima. And I began to discourse with myself thus:
Is it right to pity Urashima at all? Of course he was bewildered by the gods. But who is not bewildered by the gods? What is Life itself but a bewilderment? And Urashima in his bewilderment doubted the purpose of the gods, and opened the box. Then he died without any trouble, and the people built a shrine to him as Urashima Miō-jin. Why, then, so much pity?
Things are quite differently managed in the West. After disobeying Western gods, we have still to remain alive and to learn the height and the breadth and the depth of superlative sorrow. We are not allowed to die quite comfortably just at the best possible time: much less are we suffered to become after death small gods in our own right. How can we pity the folly of Urashima after he had lived so long alone with visible gods?
Perhaps the fact that we do may answer the riddle. This pity must be self-pity; wherefore the legend may be the legend of a myriad souls. The thought of it comes just at a particular time of blue light and soft wind—and always like an old reproach. It has too intimate relation to a season and the feeling of a season not to be also related to something real in one's life, or in the lives of one's ancestors. But what was the real something? Who was the Daughter of the Dragon King? Where was the island of unending summer? And what was the cloud in the box?
I cannot answer all those questions. I know this only—which is not at all new:

I have memory of a place and a magical time in which the Sun and the Moon were larger and brighter than now. Whether it was of this life or of some life before I cannot tell. But I know the sky was very much more blue, and nearer to the world—almost as it seems to become above the masts of a steamer steaming into equatorial summer. The sea was alive, and used to talk—and the Wind made me cry out for joy when it touched me. Once or twice during the other years, in divine days lived among the peaks, I have dreamed just for a moment that the same wind was blowing—but it was only a remembrance.

Also in that place the clouds were wonderful, and of colors for which there are no names at all—colors that used to make me hungry and thirsty. I remember, too, that the days were ever so much longer than these days—and that every day there were new wonders and new pleasures for me. And all that country and time were softly ruled by One who thought only of ways to make me happy. Sometimes I would refuse to be made happy, and that always caused her pain, although she was divine; and I remember that I tried very hard to be sorry. When day was done, and there fell the great hush of the night before moonrise, she would tell me stories that made me tingle from head to foot with pleasure. I have never heard any other stories half so beautiful. And when the pleasure became too great, she would sing a weird little song which always brought sleep. At last there came a parting day; and she wept, and told me of a charm she had given that I must never, never lose, because it would keep me young, and give me power to return. But I never returned. And the years went; and one day I knew that I had lost the charm, and had become ridiculously old.

V

THE VILLAGE OF THE LONG BEACH IS AT THE FOOT OF A GREEN CLIFF NEAR THE road, and consists of a dozen thatched cottages clustered about a rocky pool, shaded by pines. The basin overflows with cold water, supplied by a stream that leaps straight from the heart of the cliff—just as folks imagine that a poem ought to spring straight from the heart of a poet. It was evidently a favorite halting-place, judging by the number of kuruma and of people resting. There were benches under the trees; and, after having allayed thirst, I sat down to smoke and to look at the women washing clothes and the travelers refreshing themselves at the pool—while my kurumaya stripped, and proceeded to dash buckets of cold water over his body. Then tea was brought me by a young man with a baby on his back; and I tried to play with the baby, which said "Ah, bah!"

Such are the first sounds uttered by a Japanese babe. But they are purely Oriental; and in Romaji should be written *Aba*. And, as an utterance untaught, *Aba* is interesting. It is in Japanese child-speech the word for "good-bye"—precisely the last we would expect an infant to pronounce on entering into this world of illusion. To whom or to what is the little soul saying good-bye?—to friends in a previous state of existence still freshly remembered?—to comrades of its shadowy journey from nobody-knows-where? Such theorizing is tolerably safe, from a pious point of view, since the child can never decide for us. What its thoughts were at that mysterious moment of first speech, it will have forgotten long before it has become able to answer questions.

Unexpectedly, a queer recollection came to me—resurrected, perhaps, by the sight of the young man with the baby, perhaps by the song of the water in the cliff: the recollection of a story:

Long, long ago there lived somewhere among the mountains a poor wood-cutter and his wife. They were very old, and had no children. Every day the husband went alone to the forest to cut wood, while the wife sat weaving at home.

One day the old man went farther into the forest than was his custom, to seek a certain kind of wood; and he suddenly found himself at the edge of a little spring he had never seen before. The water was strangely clear and cold, and he was thirsty; for the day was hot, and he had been working hard. So he doffed his great straw hat, knelt down, and took a long drink. That water seemed to refresh him in a most extraordinary way. Then he caught sight of his own face in the spring, and started back. It was certainly his own face, but not at all as he was accustomed to see it in the old mirror at home. It was the face of a very young man! He could not believe his eyes. He put up both hands to his head, which had been quite bald only a moment before. It was covered with thick black hair. And his face had become smooth as a boy's; every wrinkle was gone. At the same moment he discovered himself full of new strength. He stared in astonishment at the limbs that had been so long withered by age; they were now shapely and hard with dense young muscle. Unknowingly he had drunk at the Fountain of Youth; and that draught had transformed him.

First, he leaped high and shouted for joy; then he ran home faster than he had ever run before in his life. When he entered his house his wife was frightened—because she took him for a stranger; and when he told her the wonder, she could not at once believe him. But after a long time he was able to convince her that the young man she now saw before her was really her husband; and he told her where the spring was, and asked her to go there with him.

Then she said: "You have become so handsome and so young that you cannot continue to love an old woman; so I must drink some of that water immediately. But it will never do for both of us to be away from the house at the same time. Do you wait here while I go." And she ran to the woods all by herself.

She found the spring and knelt down, and began to drink. Oh! how cool and sweet that water was! She drank and drank and drank, and stopped for breath only to begin again.

Her husband waited for her impatiently; he expected to see her come back changed into a pretty slender girl. But she did not come back at all. He got anxious, shut up the house, and went to look for her.

When he reached the spring, he could not see her. He was just on the point of returning when he heard a little wail in the high grass near the spring. He searched there and discovered his wife's clothes and a baby—a very small baby, perhaps six months old!

For the old woman had drunk too deeply of the magical water; she had drunk herself far back beyond the time of youth into the period of speechless infancy.

He took up the child in his arms. It looked at him in a sad, wondering way. He carried it home—murmuring to it—thinking strange, melancholy thoughts.

In that hour, after my reverie about Urashima, the moral of this story seemed less satisfactory than in former time. Because by drinking too deeply of life we do not become young.

Naked and cool my kurumaya returned, and said that because of the heat he could not finish the promised run of twenty-five miles, but that he had found another runner to take me the rest of the way. For so much as he himself had done, he wanted fifty-five sen.

It was really very hot—more than 100° I afterwards learned; and far away there throbbed continually, like a pulsation of the heat itself, the sound of great drums beating for rain. And I thought of the Daughter of the Dragon King.

"Seventy-five sen, she told me," I observed; "and that promised to be done has not been done. Nevertheless, seventy-five sen to you shall be given—because I am afraid of the gods."

And behind a yet unwearied runner I fled away into the enormous blaze—in the direction of the great drums.

Fuji-No-Yama

Kité miréba,
Sahodo madé nashi,
Fuji no Yama!
Seen on close approach, the mountain of Fuji
does not come up to expectation.
JAPANESE PROVERBIAL PHILOSOPHY

THE MOST BEAUTIFUL SIGHT IN JAPAN, AND CERTAINLY ONE OF THE MOST beautiful in the world, is the distant apparition of Fuji on cloudless days —more especially days of spring and autumn, when the greater part of the peak is covered with late or with early snows. You can seldom distinguish the snowless base, which remains the same color as the sky: you perceive only the white cone seeming to hang in heaven; and the Japanese comparison of its shape to an inverted half-open fan is made wonderfully exact by the fine streaks that spread downward from the notched top, like shadows of fan-ribs. Even lighter than a fan the vision appears—rather the ghost or dream of a fan;—yet the material reality a hundred miles away is grandiose among the mountains of the globe. Rising to a height of nearly 12,500 feet, Fuji is visible from thirteen provinces of the Empire. Nevertheless it is one of the easiest of lofty mountains to climb; and for a thousand years it has been scaled every summer by multitudes of pilgrims. For it is not only a sacred mountain, but the most sacred mountain of Japan—the holiest eminence of the land that is called Divine—the Supreme Altar of the Sun;—and to ascend it at least once in a lifetime is the duty of all who reverence the

ancient gods. So from every district of the Empire pilgrims annually
wend their way to Fuji; and in nearly all the provinces there are
pilgrim-societies—Fuji-Kō—organized for the purpose of aiding those
desiring to visit the sacred peak. If this act of faith cannot be performed
by everybody in person, it can at least be performed by proxy. Any
hamlet, however remote, can occasionally send one representative to
pray before the shrine of the divinity of Fuji, and to salute the rising
sun from that sublime eminence. Thus a single company of Fuji-pilgrims
may be composed of men from a hundred different settlements.

By both of the national religions Fuji is held in reverence. The Shintō
deity of Fuji is the beautiful goddess Ko-no-hana-saku-ya-himé—she
who brought forth her children in fire without pain, and whose name
signifies "Radiant-blooming-as-the-flowers-of-the-trees," or, according to
some commentators, "Causing-the-flowers-to-blossom-brightly." On the
summit is her temple; and in ancient books it is recorded that mortal
eyes have beheld her hovering, like a luminous cloud, above the verge
of the crater. Her viewless servants watch and wait by the precipices to
hurl down whosoever presumes to approach her shrine with unpurified
heart. . . . Buddhism loves the grand peak because its form is like the
white bud of the Sacred Flower—and because the eight cusps of its top,
like the eight petals of the Lotus, symbolize the Eight Intelligences of
Perception, Purpose, Speech, Conduct, Living, Effort, Mindfulness, and
Contemplation.

But the legends and traditions about Fuji, the stories of its rising out
of the earth in a single night—of the shower of pierced jewels once
flung down from it—of the first temple built upon its summit eleven
hundred years ago—of the Luminous Maiden that lured to the crater
an Emperor who was never seen afterward, but is still worshiped at a
little shrine erected on the place of his vanishing—of the sand that daily
rolled down by pilgrim feet nightly reascends to its former position—
have not all these things been written in books? There is really very
little left for me to tell about Fuji except my own experience of climbing it.

I made the ascent by way of Gotemba—the least picturesque, but perhaps also the least difficult of the six or seven routes open to choice.
Gotemba is a little village chiefly consisting of pilgrim-inns. You reach
it from Tōkyō in about three hours by the Tōkaidō railway, which
rises for miles as it approaches the neighborhood of the mighty volcano.
Gotemba is considerably more than two thousand feet above the sea,
and therefore comparatively cool in the hottest season. The open coun-

try about it slopes to Fuji; but the slope is so gradual that the table-land seems almost level to the eye. From Gotemba in perfectly clear weather the mountain looks uncomfortably near—formidable by proximity— though actually miles away. During the rainy season it may appear and disappear alternately many times in one day—like an enormous spectre. But on the gray August morning when I entered Gotemba as a pilgrim, the landscape was muffled in vapors; and Fuji was totally invisible. I arrived too late to attempt the ascent on the same day; but I made my preparations at once for the day following, and engaged a couple of gōriki (strong-pull men), or experienced guides. I felt quite secure on seeing their broad honest faces and sturdy bearing. They supplied me with a pilgrim-staff, heavy blue tabi (that is to say, cleft-stockings, to be used with sandals), a straw hat shaped like Fuji, and the rest of a pilgrim's outfit;—telling me to be ready to start with them at four o'clock in the morning.

What is hereafter set down consists of notes taken on the journey, but afterwards amended and expanded—for notes made while climbing are necessarily hurried and imperfect.

I

August 24th, 1897

FROM STRINGS STRETCHED ABOVE THE BALCONY UPON WHICH MY INN-ROOM opens, hundreds of towels are hung like flags—blue towels and white, having printed upon them in Chinese characters the names of pilgrim-companies and of the divinity of Fuji. These are gifts to the house, and serve as advertisements. . . . Raining from a uniformly gray sky. Fuji always invisible.

August 25th

3.30 A.M.—No sleep;—tumult all night of parties returning late from the mountain, or arriving for the pilgrimage;—constant clapping of hands to summon servants;—banqueting and singing in the adjoining chambers, with alarming bursts of laughter every few minutes. . . . Breakfast of soup, fish, and rice. Gōriki arrive in professional costume, and find me ready. Nevertheless they insist that I shall undress again and put on heavy underclothing;—warning me that even when it is Doyō (the period of greatest summer heat) at the foot of the mountain, it is Daikan (the period of greatest winter cold) at the top. Then they

start in advance, carrying provisions and bundles of heavy clothing. . . .
A kuruma waits for me, with three runners—two to pull, and one to
push, as the work will be hard uphill. By kuruma I can go to the height
of five thousand feet.

Morning black and slightly chill, with fine rain; but I shall soon be
above the rain-clouds. . . . The lights of the town vanish behind us;—
the kuruma is rolling along a country-road. Outside of the swinging
penumbra made by the paper-lantern of the foremost runner, nothing
is clearly visible; but I can vaguely distinguish silhouettes of trees and,
from time to time, of houses—peasants' houses with steep roofs.

Gray wan light slowly suffuses the moist air;—day is dawning through
drizzle. . . . Gradually the landscape defines with its colors. The way
lies through thin woods. Occasionally we pass houses with high thatched
roofs that look like farmhouses; but cultivated land is nowhere visible. . . .

Open country with scattered clumps of trees—larch and pine. Nothing
in the horizon but scraggy tree-tops above what seems to be the rim of
a vast down. No sign whatever of Fuji. . . . For the first time I notice
that the road is black—black sand and cinders apparently, volcanic cinders: the wheels of the kuruma and the feet of the runners sink into
it with a crunching sound.

The rain has stopped, and the sky becomes a clearer gray. . . . The
trees decrease in size and number as we advance.

What I have been taking for the horizon, in front of us, suddenly
breaks open, and begins to roll smokily away to left and right. In the
great rift part of a dark-blue mass appears—a portion of Fuji. Almost
at the same moment the sun pierces the clouds behind us; but the road
now enters a copse covering the base of a low ridge, and the view is
cut off. . . . Halt at a little house among the trees—a pilgrims' resting-
place—and there find the gōriki, who have advanced much more rapidly than my runners, waiting for us. Buy eggs, which a gōriki rolls up
in a narrow strip of straw matting;—tying the matting tightly with
straw cord between the eggs—so that the string of eggs has somewhat
the appearance of a string of sausages. . . . Hire a horse.

Sky clears as we proceed;—white sunlight floods everything. Road reascends; and we emerge again on the moorland. And, right in front, Fuji appears—naked to the summit—stupendous—startling as if newly risen from the earth. Nothing could be more beautiful. A vast blue cone —warm-blue, almost violet through the vapors not yet lifted by the sun —with two white streaklets near the top which are great gullies full of snow, though they look from here scarcely an inch long. But the charm of the apparition is much less the charm of color than of symmetry—a symmetry of beautiful bending lines with a curve like the curve of a cable stretched over a space too wide to allow of pulling taut. (This comparison did not at once suggest itself: the first impression given me by the grace of those lines was an impression of femininity;—I found myself thinking of some exquisite sloping of shoulders toward the neck.) I can imagine nothing more difficult to draw at sight. But the Japanese artist, through his marvelous skill with the writing-brush—the skill inherited from generations of calligraphists—easily faces the riddle: he outlines the silhouette with two flowing strokes made in the fraction of a second, and manages to hit the exact truth of the curves—much as a professional archer might hit a mark, without consciously taking aim, through long exact habit of hand and eye.

II

I SEE THE GŌRIKI HURRYING FORWARD FAR AWAY—ONE OF THEM CARRYING the eggs round his neck! . . . Now there are no more trees worthy of the name—only scattered stunted growths resembling shrubs. The black road curves across a vast grassy down; and here and there I see large black patches in the green surface—bare spaces of ashes and scoriæ; showing that this thin green skin covers some enormous volcanic deposit of recent date. . . . As a matter of history, all this district was buried two yards deep in 1707 by an eruption from the side of Fuji. Even in the far-off Tōkyō the rain of ashes covered roofs to a depth of sixteen centimetres. There are no farms in this region, because there is little true soil; and there is no water. But volcanic destruction is not eternal destruction; eruptions at last prove fertilizing; and the divine "Princess-who-causes-the-flowers-to-blossom-brightly" will make this waste to smile again in future hundreds of years.

. . . The black openings in the green surface become more numerous and larger. A few dwarf-shrubs still mingle with the coarse grass. . . .

The vapors are lifting; and Fuji is changing color. It is no longer a glowing blue, but a dead sombre blue. Irregularities previously hidden by rising ground appear in the lower part of the grand curves. One of these to the left—shaped like a camel's hump—represents the focus of the last great eruption.

The land is not now green with black patches, but black with green patches; and the green patches dwindle visibly in the direction of the peak. The shrubby growths have disappeared. The wheels of the ku-ruma, and the feet of the runners sink deeper into the volcanic sand. . . . The horse is now attached to the kuruma with ropes, and I am able to advance more rapidly. Still the mountain seems far away; but we are really running up its flank at a height of more than five thousand feet.

Fuji has ceased to be blue of any shade. It is black—charcoal-black—a frightful extinct heap of visible ashes and cinders and slaggy lava. . . . Most of the green has disappeared. Likewise all of the illusion. The tremendous naked black reality—always becoming more sharply, more grimly, more atrociously defined—is a stupefaction, a nightmare. . . . Above—miles above—the snow patches glare and gleam against that blackness—hideously. I think of a gleam of white teeth I once saw in a skull—a woman's skull—otherwise burnt to a sooty crisp.

So one of the fairest, if not the fairest of earthly visions, resolves itself into a spectacle of horror and death. . . . But have not all human ideals of beauty, like the beauty of Fuji seen from afar, been created by forces of death and pain?—are not all, in their kind, but composites of death, beheld in retrospective through the magical haze of inherited memory?

III

THE GREEN HAS UTTERLY VANISHED;—ALL IS BLACK. THERE IS NO ROAD—only the broad waste of black sand sloping and narrowing up to those dazzling, grinning patches of snow. But there is a track—a yellowish track made by thousands and thousands of cast-off sandals of straw (*waraji*), flung aside by pilgrims. Straw sandals quickly wear out upon this black grit; and every pilgrim carries several pairs for the journey. Had I to make the ascent alone, I could find the path by following that wake of broken sandals—a yellow streak zigzagging up out of sight across the blackness.

6.40 A.M.—We reach Tarōbō, first of the ten stations on the ascent: height, six thousand feet. The station is a large wooden house, of which two rooms have been fitted up as a shop for the sale of staves, hats, raincoats, sandals—everything pilgrims need. I find there a peripatetic photographer offering for sale photographs of the mountain which are really very good as well as very cheap. . . . Here the gōriki take their first meal; and I rest. The kuruma can go no farther; and I dismiss my three runners, but keep the horse—a docile and surefooted creature; for I can venture to ride him up to Ni-gō-goséki, or Station No. 2½.

Start for No. 2½ up the slant of black sand, keeping the horse at a walk. No. 2½ is shut up for the season. . . . Slope now becomes steep as a stairway, and further riding would be dangerous. Alight and make ready for the climb. Cold wind blowing so strongly that I have to tie on my hat tightly. One of the gōriki unwinds from about his waist a long stout cotton girdle, and giving me one end to hold, passes the other over his shoulder for the pull. Then he proceeds over the sand at an angle, with a steady short step, and I follow; the other guide keeping closely behind me to provide against any slip.

There is nothing very difficult about this climbing, except the weariness of walking through sand and cinders: it is like walking over dunes. . . . We mount by zigzags. The sand moves with the wind; and I have a slightly nervous sense—the feeling only, not the perception; for I keep my eyes on the sand—of height growing above depth. . . . Have to watch my steps carefully, and to use my staff constantly, as the slant is now very steep. . . . We are in a white fog—passing through clouds! Even if I wished to look back, I could see nothing through this vapor; but I have not the least wish to look back. The wind has suddenly ceased— cut off, perhaps, by a ridge; and there is a silence that I remember from West Indian days: the Peace of High Places. It is broken only by the crunching of the ashes beneath our feet. I can distinctly hear my heart beat. . . . The guide tells me that I stoop too much—orders me to walk upright, and always in stepping to put down the heel first. I do this, and find it relieving. But climbing through this tiresome mixture of ashes and sand begins to be trying. I am perspiring and panting. The guide bids me keep my honorable mouth closed, and breathe only through my honorable nose.

We are out of the fog again. . . . All at once I perceive above us, at
a little distance, something like a square hole in the face of the mountain
—a door! It is the door of the third station—a wooden hut half-buried
in black drift. . . . How delightful to squat again—even in a blue cloud
of wood-smoke and under smoke-blackened rafters! Time, 8.30 A.M.
Height, 7085 feet.

In spite of the wood-smoke the station is comfortable enough inside;
there are clean mattings and even kneeling-cushions. No windows, of
course, nor any other opening than the door; for the building is half-
buried in the flank of the mountain. We lunch. . . . The station-keeper
tells us that recently a student walked from Gotemba to the top of the
mountain and back again—in *geta!* Geta are heavy wooden sandals, or
clogs, held to the foot only by a thong passing between the great and
the second toe. The feet of that student must have been made of steel!
Having rested, I go out to look around. Far below white clouds are
rolling over the landscape in huge fluffy wreaths. Above the hut, and
actually trickling down over it, the stable cone soars to the sky. But the
amazing sight is the line of the monstrous slope to the left—a line that
now shows no curve whatever, but shoots down below the clouds, and
up to the gods only know where (for I cannot see the end of it), straight
as a tightened bowstring. The right flank is rocky and broken. But as
for the left—I never dreamed it possible that a line so absolutely straight
and smooth, and extending for so enormous a distance at such an amazing angle, could exist even in a volcano. That stupendous pitch gives
me a sense of dizziness, and a totally unfamiliar feeling of wonder. Such
regularity appears unnatural, frightful; seems even artificial—but artificial upon a superhuman and demoniac scale. I imagine that to fall
thence from above would be to fall for leagues. Absolutely nothing to
take hold of. But the gōriki assure me that there is no danger on that
slope: it is all soft sand.

IV

THOUGH DRENCHED WITH PERSPIRATION BY THE EXERTION OF THE FIRST
climb, I am already dry, and cold. . . . Up again. . . . The ascent is at
first through ashes and sand as before; but presently large stones begin
to mingle with the sand; and the way is always growing steeper. . . . I
constantly slip. There is nothing firm, nothing resisting to stand upon:

loose stones and cinders roll down at every step. . . . If a big lava-block were to detach itself from above! . . . In spite of my helpers and of the staff, I continually slip, and am all in perspiration again. Almost every stone that I tread upon turns under me. How is it that no stone ever turns under the feet of the gōriki? *They* never slip—never make a false step—never seem less at ease than they would be in walking over a matted floor. Their small brown broad feet always poise upon the shingle at exactly the right angle. They are heavier men than I; but they move lightly as birds. . . . Now I have to stop for rest every half-a-dozen steps. . . . The line of broken straw sandals follows the zigzags we take. . . . At last—at last another door in the face of the mountain. Enter the fourth station, and fling myself down upon the mats. Time, 10.30 A.M. Height, only 7937 feet;—yet it seemed such a distance!

Off again. . . . Way worse and worse. . . . Feel a new distress due to the rarefaction of the air. Heart beating as in a high fever. . . . Slope has become very rough. It is no longer soft ashes and sand mixed with stones, but stones only—fragments of lava, lumps of pumice, scoriæ of every sort, all angled as if freshly broken with a hammer. All would likewise seem to have been expressly shaped so as to turn upside-down when trodden upon. Yet I must confess that they never turn under the feet of the gōriki. . . . The cast-off sandals strew the slope in ever-increasing numbers. . . . But for the gōriki I should have had ever so many bad tumbles: they cannot prevent me from slipping; but they never allow me to fall. Evidently I am not fitted to climb mountains. . . . Height, 8659 feet—but the fifth station is shut up! Must keep zigzagging on to the next. Wonder how I shall ever be able to reach it! . . . And there are people still alive who have climbed Fuji three and four times, *for pleasure!* . . . Dare not look back. See nothing but the black stone always turning under me, and the bronzed feet of those marvelous gōriki who never slip, never pant, and never perspire. . . . Staff begins to hurt my hand. . . . Gōriki push and pull: it is shameful of me, I know, to give them so much trouble. . . . Ah! sixth station!—may all the myriads of the gods bless my gōriki! Time, 2.07 P.M. Height, 9317 feet.

Resting, I gaze through the doorway at the abyss below. The land is now dimly visible only through rents in a prodigious wilderness of white clouds; and within these rents everything looks almost black. . . . The horizon has risen frightfully—has expanded monstrously. . . . My gōriki warn me that the summit is still miles away. I have been too slow. We must hasten upward.

Certainly the zigzag is steeper than before. . . . With the stones now mingle angular rocks; and we sometimes have to flank queer black bulks that look like basalt. . . . On the right rises, out of sight, a jagged black hideous ridge—an ancient lava-stream. The line of the left slope still shoots up, straight as a bow-string. . . . Wonder if the way will become any steeper;—doubt whether it can possibly become any rougher. Rocks dislodged by my feet roll down soundlessly;—I am afraid to look after them. Their noiseless vanishing gives me a sensation like the sensation of falling in dreams. . . .

There is a white gleam overhead—the lowermost verge of an immense stretch of snow. . . . Now we are skirting a snow-filled gully—the lowermost of those white patches which, at first sight of the summit this morning, seemed scarcely an inch long. It will take an hour to pass it. . . . A guide runs forward, while I rest upon my staff, and returns with a large ball of snow. What curious snow! Not flaky, soft, white snow, but a mass of transparent globules—exactly like glass beads. I eat some, and find it deliciously refreshing. . . . The seventh station is closed. How shall I get to the eighth? . . . Happily, breathing has become less difficult. . . . The wind is upon us again, and black dust with it. The gōriki keep close to me, and advance with caution. . . . I have to stop for rest at every turn on the path;—cannot talk for weariness. . . . I do not feel;—I am much too tired to feel. . . . How I managed it, I do not know;—but I have actually got to the eighth station! Not for a thousand millions of dollars will I go one step farther to-day. Time, 4.40 P.M. Height, 10,693 feet.

V

IT IS MUCH TOO COLD HERE FOR REST WITHOUT WINTER CLOTHING; AND now I learn the worth of the heavy robes provided by the guides. The robes are blue, with big white Chinese characters on the back, and are padded thickly as bed-quilts; but they feel light; for the air is really like the frosty breath of February. . . . A meal is preparing;—I notice that charcoal at this elevation acts in a refractory manner, and that a fire can be maintained only by constant attention. . . . Cold and fatigue sharpen appetite: we consume a surprising quantity of Zō-sui—rice boiled with eggs and a little meat. By reason of my fatigue and of the hour, it has been decided to remain here for the night.

Tired as I am, I cannot but limp to the doorway to contemplate the amazing prospect. From within a few feet of the threshold, the ghastly slope of rocks and cinders drops down into a prodigious disk of clouds miles beneath us—clouds of countless forms, but mostly wreathings and fluffy pilings;—and the whole huddling mass, reaching almost to the horizon, is blinding white under the sun. (By the Japanese, this tremendous cloud-expanse is well named Wata-no-Umi, "the Sea of Cotton.") The horizon itself—enormously risen, phantasmally expanded—seems halfway up above the world: a wide luminous belt ringing the hollow vision. Hollow, I call it, because extreme distances below the sky-line are sky-colored and vague—so that the impression you receive is not of being on a point under a vault, but of being upon a point rising into a stupendous blue sphere, of which this huge horizon would represent the equatorial zone. To turn away from such a spectacle is not possible. I watch and watch until the dropping sun changes the colors —turning the Sea of Cotton into a Fleece of Gold. Half-round the horizon a yellow glory grows and burns. Here and there beneath it, through cloud-rifts, colored vaguenesses define: I now see golden water, with long purple headlands reaching into it, with ranges of violet peaks thronging behind it;—these glimpses curiously resembling portions of a tinted topographical map. Yet most of the landscape is pure delusion. Even my guides, with their long experience and their eagle-sight, can scarcely distinguish the real from the unreal;—for the blue and purple and violet clouds moving under the Golden Fleece, exactly mock the outlines and the tones of distant peaks and capes: you can detect what is vapor only by its slowly shifting shape. . . . Brighter and brighter glows the gold. Shadows come from the west—shadows flung by cloud-pile over cloud-pile; and these, like evening shadows upon snow, are violaceous blue. . . . Then orange-tones appear in the horizon; then smouldering crimson. And now the greater part of the Fleece of Gold has changed to cotton again—white cotton mixed with pink. . . . Stars thrill out. The cloud-waste uniformly whitens;—thickening and packing to the horizon. The west glooms. Night rises; and all things darken except that wondrous unbroken world-round of white—the Sea of Cotton.

The station-keeper lights his lamps, kindles a fire of twigs, prepares our beds. Outside it is bitterly cold, and, with the fall of night, becoming colder. Still I cannot turn away from that astounding vision. . . . Countless stars now flicker and shiver in the blue-black sky. Nothing whatever of the material world remains visible, except the black slope of the peak before my feet. The enormous cloud-disk below continues white; but to all appearance it has become a liquidly level white, without forms—a white flood. It is no longer the Sea of Cotton. It is a Sea of Milk, the Cosmic Sea of ancient Indian legend—and always self-luminous, as with ghostly quickenings.

VI

SQUATTING BY THE WOOD FIRE, I LISTEN TO THE GŌRIKI AND THE STATION-keeper telling of strange happenings on the mountain. One incident discussed I remember reading something about in a Tōkyō paper: I now hear it retold by the lips of a man who figured in it as a hero.

A Japanese meteorologist named Nonaka attempted last year the rash undertaking of passing the winter on the summit of Fuji for purposes of scientific study. It might not be difficult to winter upon the peak in a solid observatory furnished with a good stove, and all necessary comforts; but Nonaka could afford only a small wooden hut, in which he would be obliged to spend the cold season *without fire!* His young wife insisted on sharing his labors and dangers. The couple began their sojourn on the summit toward the close of September. In mid-winter news was brought to Gotemba that both were dying.

Relatives and friends tried to organize a rescue-party. But the weather was frightful; the peak was covered with snow and ice; the chances of death were innumerable; and the gōriki would not risk their lives. Hundreds of dollars could not tempt them. At last a desperate appeal was made to them as representatives of Japanese courage and hardihood: they were assured that to suffer a man of science to perish, without making even one plucky effort to save him, would disgrace the country; —they were told that the national honor was in their hands. This appeal brought forward two volunteers. One was a man of great strength and daring, nicknamed by his fellow-guides *Oni-guma,* "the Demon-Bear," the other was the elder of my gōriki. Both believed that they were going to certain destruction. They took leave of their friends and kindred, and drank with their families the farewell cup of water—*midzu-no-sakazuki*—in which those about to be separated by death pledge each other. Then, after having thickly wrapped themselves in cotton-wool, and made all possible preparation for ice-climbing, they started—taking with them a brave army-surgeon who had offered his services, without fee, for the rescue. After surmounting extraordinary difficulties, the party reached the hut; but the inmates refused to open! Nonaka protested that he would rather die than face the shame of failure in his undertaking; and his wife said that she had resolved to die with her husband. Partly by forcible, and partly by gentle means, the pair were restored to a better state of mind. The surgeon administered medicines and cordials; the patients, carefully wrapped up, were strapped to the backs of the guides; and the descent was begun. My gōriki, who carried the lady, believes that the gods helped him on the ice-slopes. More than once, all thought themselves lost; but they reached the foot of the mountain without one serious mishap. After weeks of careful nursing, the rash young couple were pronounced out of danger. The wife suffered less, and recovered more quickly, than the husband.

The gōriki have cautioned me not to venture outside during the night without calling them. They will not tell me why; and their warning is peculiarly uncanny. From previous experiences during Japanese travel, I surmise that the danger implied is supernatural; but I feel that it would be useless to ask questions.

The door is closed and barred. I lie down between the guides, who are asleep in a moment, as I can tell by their heavy breathing. I cannot sleep immediately;—perhaps the fatigues and the surprises of the day have made me somewhat nervous. I look up at the rafters of the black roof—at packages of sandals, bundles of wood, bundles of many indistinguishable kinds there stowed away or suspended, and making queer shadows in the lamplight. . . . It is terribly cold, even under my three quilts; and the sound of the wind outside is wonderfully like the sound of great surf—a constant succession of bursting roars, each followed by a prolonged hiss. The hut, half buried under tons of rock and drift, does not move; but the sand does, and trickles down between the rafters; and small stones also move after each fierce gust, with a rattling just like the clatter of shingle in the pull of a retreating wave.

4 A.M.—Go out alone, despite last evening's warning, but keep close to the door. There is a great and icy blowing. The Sea of Milk is unchanged: it lies far below this wind. Over it the moon is dying. . . . The guides, perceiving my absence, spring up and join me. I am reproved for not having awakened them. They will not let me stay outside alone: so I turn in with them.

Dawn: a zone of pearl grows round the world. The stars vanish; the sky brightens. A wild sky, with dark wrack drifting at an enormous height. The Sea of Milk has turned again into Cotton—and there are wide rents in it. The desolation of the black slope—all the ugliness of slaggy rock and angled stone—again defines. . . . Now the cotton becomes disturbed;—it is breaking up. A yellow glow runs along the east like the glare of a wind-blown fire. . . . Alas! I shall not be among the fortunate mortals able to boast of viewing from Fuji the first lifting of the sun! Heavy clouds have drifted across the horizon at the point where he should rise. . . . Now I know that he has risen; because the upper edges of those purple rags of cloud are burning like charcoal. But I have been so disappointed!

More and more luminous the hollow world. League-wide heapings of cottony cloud roll apart. Fearfully far away there is a light of gold upon water: the sun here remains viewless, but the ocean sees him. It is not a flicker, but a burnished glow;—at such a distance ripplings are invisible. . . . Farther and farther scattering, the clouds unveil a vast gray and blue landscape;—hundreds and hundreds of miles throng into vision at once. On the right I distinguish Tōkyō Bay, and Kamakura, and the holy island of Enoshima (no bigger than the dot over this letter "i");—on the left the wilder Suruga coast, and the blue-toothed promontory of Idzu, and the place of the fishing-village where I have been summering—the merest pin-point in that tinted dream of hill and shore. Rivers appear but as sun-gleams on spider-threads;—fishing-sails are white dust clinging to the gray-blue glass of the sea. And the picture alternately appears and vanishes while the clouds drift and shift across it, and shape themselves into spectral islands and mountains and valleys of all Elysian colors. . . .

VII

6.40 A.M.—START FOR THE TOP. . . . HARDEST AND ROUGHEST STAGE OF THE journey, through a wilderness of lava-blocks. The path zigzags between ugly masses that project from the slope like black teeth. The trail of castaway sandals is wider than ever. . . . Have to rest every few minutes. . . . Reach another long patch of the snow that looks like glass-beads, and eat some. The next station—a half-station—is closed; and the ninth has ceased to exist. . . . A sudden fear comes to me, not of the ascent, but of the prospective descent by a route which is too steep even to permit of comfortably sitting down. But the guides assure me that there will be no difficulty, and that most of the return journey will be by another way—over the interminable level which I wondered at yesterday—nearly all soft sand, with very few stones. It is called the *hashiri* (glissade) and we are to descend at a run! . . .

All at once a family of field-mice scatter out from under my feet in panic; and the gōriki behind me catches one, and gives it to me. I hold the tiny shivering life for a moment to examine it, and set it free again. These little creatures have very long pale noses. How do they live in this waterless desolation—and at such an altitude—especially in the season of snow? For we are now at a height of more than eleven thousand feet! The gōriki say that the mice find roots growing under the stones. . . .

Wilder and steeper;—for me, at least, the climbing is sometimes on all fours. There are barriers which we surmount with the help of ladders. There are fearful places with Buddhist names, such as the Sai-no-Kawara, or Dry Bed of the River of Souls—a black waste strewn with heaps of rock, like those stone-piles which, in Buddhist pictures of the under-world, the ghosts of children build. . . .

Twelve thousand feet, and something—the top! Time, 8.20 A.M. . . . Stone huts! Shintō shrine with torii; icy well, called the Spring of Gold; stone tablet bearing a Chinese poem and the design of a tiger; rough walls of lava-blocks round these things—possibly for protection against the wind. Then the huge dead crater—probably between a quarter of a mile and half-a-mile wide, but shallowed up to within three or four hundred feet of the verge by volcanic detritus—a cavity horrible even in the tones of its yellow crumbling walls, streaked and stained with every hue of scorching. I perceive that the trail of straw sandals ends *in* the crater. Some hideous overhanging cusps of black lava—like the broken edges of monstrous cicatrix—project on two sides several hundred feet above the opening; but I certainly shall not take the trouble to climb them. Yet these—seen through the haze of a hundred miles—through the soft illusion of blue spring weather—appear as the opening snowy petals of the bud of the Sacred Lotus! . . . No spot in this world can be more horrible, more atrociously dismal, than the cindered tip of the Lotus as you stand upon it.

But the view—the view for a hundred leagues—and the light of the far faint dreamy world—and the fairy vapors of morning—and the marvelous wreathings of cloud: all this, and only this, consoles me for the

labor and the pain. . . . Other pilgrims, earlier climbers—poised upon
the highest crag, with faces turned to the tremendous East—are clapping their hands in Shintō prayer, saluting the mighty Day. . . . The
immense poetry of the moment enters into me with a thrill. I know that
the colossal vision before me has already become a memory ineffaceable
—a memory of which no luminous detail can fade till the hour when
thought itself must fade, and the dust of these eyes be mingled with the
dust of the myriad million eyes that also have looked in ages forgotten
before my birth, from the summit supreme of Fuji to the Rising of
the Sun.

FOLK CULTURE

—————————— ❧ ❋ ❧ ——————————

A Woman's Diary

RECENTLY THERE WAS PUT INTO MY HANDS A SOMEWHAT REMARKABLE manuscript—seventeen long narrow sheets of soft paper, pierced with a silken string, and covered with fine Japanese characters. It was a kind of diary, containing the history of a woman's married life, recorded by herself. The writer was dead; and the diary had been found in a small work-box (*haribako*) which had belonged to her.

The friend who lent me the manuscript gave me leave to translate as much of it as I might think worth publishing. I have gladly availed myself of this unique opportunity to present in English the thoughts and feelings, joys and sorrows, of a simple woman of the people—just

445

as she herself recorded them in the frankest possible way, never dreaming that any foreign eye would read her humble and touching memoir.

But out of respect to her gentle ghost, I have tried to use the manuscript in such a way only as could not cause her the least pain if she were yet in the body, and able to read me. Some parts I have omitted, because I thought them sacred. Also I have left out a few details relating to customs or to local beliefs that the Western reader could scarcely understand, even with the aid of notes. And the names, of course, have been changed. Otherwise I have followed the text as closely as I could—making no changes of phrase except when the Japanese original could not be adequately interpreted by a literal rendering.

In addition to the facts stated or suggested in the diary itself, I could learn but very little of the writer's personal history. She was a woman of the poorest class; and from her own narrative it appears that she remained unmarried until she was nearly thirty. A younger sister had been married several years previously; and the diary does not explain this departure from custom. A small photograph found with the manuscript shows that its author never could have been called good-looking; but the face has a certain pleasing expression of shy gentleness. Her husband was a *kozukai*,[1] employed in one of the great public offices, chiefly for night duty, at a salary of ten yen per month. In order to help him to meet the expenses of housekeeping, she made cigarettes for a tobacco dealer.

The manuscript shows that she must have been at school for some years: she could write the *kana* very nicely, but she had not learned many Chinese characters—so that her work resembles the work of a schoolgirl. But it is written without mistakes, and skillfully. The dialect is of Tōkyō—the common speech of the city people—full of idiomatic expressions, but entirely free from coarseness.

Some one might naturally ask why this poor woman, so much occupied with the constant struggle for mere existence, should have taken the pains to write down what she probably never intended to be read. I would remind such a questioner of the old Japanese teaching that literary composition is the best medicine for sorrow; and I would remind him also of the fact that, even among the poorest classes, poems are still composed upon all the occasions of joy or pain. The

---

[1] A *kozukai* is a manservant chiefly employed as doorkeeper and messenger. The term is rendered better by the French word *concierge* than by our English word "porter"; but neither expression exactly meets the Japanese meaning.

latter part of the diary was written in lonely hours of illness; and I suppose that she then wrote chiefly in order to keep her thoughts composed at a time when solitude had become dangerous for her. A little before her death, her mind gave way; and these final pages probably represent the last brave struggle of the spirit against the hopeless weakness of the flesh.

I found that the manuscript was inscribed, on the outside sheet, with the title, *"Mukashi-banashi"* (A Story of Old Times). According to circumstances, the word *mukashi* may signify either "long ago," in reference to past centuries, or "old times," in reference to one's own past life. The latter is the obvious meaning in the present case.

MUKASHI-BANASHI

On the evening of the twenty-fifth day of the ninth month of the twenty-eighth year of Meiji [1895], the man of the opposite house came and asked:

"As for the eldest daughter of this family, is it agreeable that she be disposed of in marriage?"

Then the answer was given:

"Even though the matter were agreeable [to our wishes], no preparation for such an event has yet been made." [2]

The man of the opposite house said:

"But as no preparation is needed in this case, will you not honorably give her to the person for whom I speak? He is said to be a very steady man; and he is thirty-eight years of age. As I thought your eldest girl to be about twenty-six, I proposed her to him. . . ."

"No—she is twenty-nine years old," was answered.

"Ah! . . . That being the case, I must again speak to the other party; and I shall honorably consult with you after I have seen him."

So saying, the man went away.

---

[2] The reader must understand that "the man of the opposite house" is acting as *nakōdo*, or match-maker, in the interest of a widower who wishes to remarry. By the statement, "No preparation has been made," the father means that he is unable to provide for his daughter's marriage, and cannot furnish her with a bridal outfit—clothing, household furniture, etc.—as required by custom. The reply that "no preparation is needed" signifies that the proposed husband is willing to take the girl without any marriage gifts.

Next evening the man came again—this time with the wife of
Okada-Shi [3] [a friend of the family]—and said:
"The other party is satisfied;—so, if you are willing, the match can
be made."
Father replied:
"As the two are, both of them, *shichi-séki-kin* [seven-red-metal],[4]
they should have the same nature;—so I think that no harm can come
of it."
The match-maker asked:
"Then how would it be to arrange for the *miai* [5] to-morrow?"
Father said:
"I suppose that everything really depends upon the *En* (karma-
relation formed in previous states of existence). . . . Well, then, I beg that
you will honorably meet us to-morrow evening at the house of Okada."
Thus the betrothal promise was given on both sides.

The person of the opposite house wanted me to go with him next
evening to Okada's; but I said that I wished to go with my mother
only, as from the time of taking such a first step one could not either
retreat or advance.
When I went with mother to the house, we were welcomed in with
the words, *"Kochira ël"* Then [my future husband and I] greeted
each other for the first time. But somehow I felt so much ashamed
that I could not look at him.
Then Okada-Shi said to Namiki-Shi [the proposed husband]: "Now
that you have nobody to consult with at home, would it not be well
for you to snatch your luck where you find it, as the proverb says—
'Zen wa isogé'?"
The answer was made:
"As for me, I am well satisfied; but I do not know what the feeling
may be on the other side."

[3] Throughout this manuscript, except in one instance, the more respectful form
Sama never occurs after a masculine name, the popular form *Shi* being used even
after the names of kindred.
[4] The father has evidently been consulting a fortune-telling book, such as the *San-
zé-so*, or a professional diviner. The allusion to the astrologically determined natures, or
temperaments, of the pair could scarcely be otherwise explained.
[5] *Miai* is a term used to signify a meeting arranged in order to enable the parties
affianced to see each other before the wedding-day.

"If it be honorably deigned to take me as it is honorably known that I am . . ." [6] I said.

The match-maker said:

"The matter being so, what would be a good day for the wedding?"

[Namiki-Shi answered:]

"Though I can be at home to-morrow, perhaps the first day of the tenth month would be a better day."

But Okada-Shi at once said:

"As there is cause for anxiety about the house being unoccupied while Namiki-Shi is absent [on night-duty], to-morrow would perhaps be the better day—would it not?"

Though at first that seemed to me much too soon, I presently remembered that the next day was a *Taian-nichi* [7] [perfectly fortunate day]: so I gave my consent; and we went home.

When I told father, he was not pleased. He said that it was too soon, and that a delay of at least three or four days ought to have been allowed. Also he said that the direction [8] was not lucky, and that other conditions were not favorable.

I said:

"But I have already promised; and I cannot now ask to have the day changed. Indeed it would be a great pity if a thief were to enter

---

[6] Meaning: "I am ready to become your wife, if you are willing to take me as you have been informed that I am—a poor girl without money or clothes."

[7] Lucky and unlucky days were named and symbolized as follows according to the old Japanese astrological system:

SENKATSU: forenoon good; afternoon bad.

TOMOBIKI: forenoon good; afternoon good at the beginning and at the end, but bad in the middle.

SENPU: forenoon bad; afternoon good.

BUTSUMETSU: wholly unlucky.

TAIAN: altogether good.

SHAKŌ: all unlucky, except at noon.

[8] This statement also implies that a professional diviner has been consulted. The reference to the direction, or *hogaku,* can be fully understood only by those conversant with the old Chinese nature-philosophy.

the house in [his] absence. As for the matter of the direction being unlucky, even though I should have to die on that account, I would not complain; for I should die in my own husband's house. . . . And to-morrow," I added, "I shall be too busy to call on Goto [her brother-in-law]: so I must go there now."

I went to Goto's; but, when I saw him, I felt afraid to say exactly what I had come to say. I suggested it only by telling him:

"To-morrow I have to go to a strange house."

Goto immediately asked:

"As an honorable daughter-in-law [bride]?"

After hesitating, I answered at last:

"Yes."

"What kind of a person?" Goto asked.

I answered:

"If I had felt myself able to look at him long enough to form any opinion, I would not have put mother to the trouble of going with me."

"*Ané-San* [Elder Sister]!" he exclaimed; "then what was the use of going to see him at all? . . . But," he added, in a more pleasant tone, "let me wish you luck."

"Anyhow," I said, "to-morrow it will be."

And I returned home.

Now the appointed day having come—the twenty-eighth day of the ninth month—I had so much to do that I did not know how I should ever be able to get ready. And as it had been raining for several days, the roadway was very bad, which made matters worse for me—though, luckily, no rain fell on that day. I had to buy some little things; and I could not well ask mother to do anything for me—much as I wished for her help—because her feet had become very weak by reason of her great age. So I got up very early and went out alone, and did the best I could: nevertheless, it was two o'clock in the afternoon before I got everything ready.

Then I had to go to the hair-dresser's to have my hair dressed, and to go to the bath-house—all of which took time. And when I came back to dress, I found that no message had yet been received from Namiki-Shi; and I began to feel a little anxious. Just after we had finished supper, the message came. I had scarcely time to say good-bye to all: then I went out—leaving my home behind forever—and walked with mother to the house of Okada-Shi.

There I had to part even from mother; and the wife of Okada-Shi taking charge of me, I accompanied her to the house of Namiki-Shi in Funamachi.

The wedding ceremony of the *sansan-kudo-no-saka-zuki* [9] having been performed without any difficulty, and the time of the *o-hiraki* [honorable-blossoming] [10] having come more quickly than I had expected, the guests all returned home.

So we two were left, for the first time, each alone with the other—sitting face to face: my heart beat wildly; [11] and I felt abashed in such a way as could not be expressed by means of ink and paper.

Indeed, what I felt can be imagined only by one who remembers leaving her parents' home for the first time, to become a bride—a daughter-in-law in a strange house.

Afterward, at the hour of meals, I felt very much distressed [embarrassed]. . . .

Two or three days later, the father of my husband's former wife [who was dead] visited me, and said:

"Namiki-Shi is really a good man—a moral, steady man; but as he is also very particular about small matters and inclined to find fault, you had better always be careful to try to please him."

Now as I had been carefully watching my husband's ways from the beginning, I knew that he was really a very strict man, and I resolved so to conduct myself in all matters as never to cross his will.

The fifth day of the tenth month was the day for our *satogaëri*, [12] and for the first time we went out together, calling at Goto's on the

---

[9] Literally: a "thrice-three-nine-times-wine-cup."

[10] At a Japanese wedding it is customary to avoid the use of any word to which an unlucky signification attaches, or of any words suggesting misfortune in even an indirect way. The word *sumu* ("to finish," or "to end"); the word *kaëru*, "to return" (suggesting divorce), as well as many others, are forbidden at weddings. Accordingly, the term *o-hiraki* has long been euphemistically substituted for the term *oitoma* ("honorable leave-taking," i.e., "farewell"), in the popular etiquette of wedding assemblies.

[11] "I felt a tumultuous beating within my breast," would perhaps be a closer rendering of the real sense; but it would sound oddly artificial by comparison with the simple Japanese utterance: *"Ato ni wa futari sashi-mukai to nari, muné uchi-sawagi; sono bazukashisa hisshi ni tsukushi-gatashi."*

[12] From *sato*, "the parental home," and *kaeri*, "to return." The first visit of a bride to her parents, after marriage, is thus called.

way. After we left Goto's, the weather suddenly became bad, and it began to rain. Then we borrowed a paper umbrella, which we used as an *aigasa;* [13] and though I was very uneasy lest any of my former neighbors should see us walking thus together, we luckily reached my parents' house, and made our visit of duty, without any trouble at all. While we were in the house, the rain fortunately stopped.

On the ninth day of the same month I went with him to the theatre for the first time. We visited the Engiza at Akasaka, and saw a performance by the Yamaguchi company.

On the eighth day of the eleventh month, we made a visit to Asakusa-temple,[14] and also went to the [Shintō temple of the] O-Tori-Sama.
During this last month of the year I made new spring robes for my husband and myself: then I learned for the first time how pleasant such work was, and I felt very happy.

On the twenty-fifth day we visited the temple of Tenjin-Sama,[15] and walked about the grounds there.

On the eleventh day of the first month of the twenty-ninth year [1896], called at Okada's.
On the twelfth day we paid a visit to Goto's, and had a pleasant time there.
On the ninth day of the second month we went to the Mizaki theatre to see the play "Imosé-Yama." On our way to the theatre we met Goto-Shi unexpectedly; and he went with us. But unluckily it began to rain as we were returning home, and we found the roads very muddy.

[13] *Aigasa,* a fantastic term compounded from the verb *au,* "to accord," "to harmonize," and the noun *ḳasa,* "an umbrella." It signifies one umbrella used by two persons—especially lovers: an umbrella-of-loving-accord. To understand the wife's anxiety about being seen walking with her husband under the borrowed umbrella, the reader must know that it is not yet considered decorous for wife and husband even to walk side by side in public. A newly wedded pair, using a single umbrella in this way, would be particularly liable to have jests made at their expense—jests that might prove trying to the nerves of a timid bride.
[14] She means the great Buddhist temple of Kwannon—the most popular, and perhaps the most famous, Buddhist temple in Tōkyō.
[15] In the Ōkubo quarter. The shrine is shadowed by a fine grove of trees.

On the twenty-second day of the same month [we had our] photograph taken at Amano's.

On the twenty-fifth day of the third month we went to the Haruki theatre, and saw the play "Uguisuzuka."

During the month it was agreed that all of us [kindred, friends, and parents] should make up a party, and enjoy our *hanami* [16] together; but this could not be managed.

On the tenth day of the fourth month, at nine o'clock in the morning, we two went out for a walk. We first visited the Shōkonsha [Shintō shrine] at Kudan: thence we walked to Uyéno [park]; and from there we went to Asakusa, and visited the Kwannon temple; and we also prayed at the Monzéki [Higashi Hongwanji]. Thence we had intended to go round to Asakusa-Okuyama; but we thought that it would be better to have dinner first—so we went to an eating-house. While we were dining, we heard such a noise of shouting and screaming that we thought there was a great quarrel outside. But the trouble was really caused by a fire in one of the *misémono* [shows]. The fire spread quickly, even while we were looking at it; and nearly all the show-buildings in that street were burnt up. . . . We left the eating-house soon after, and walked about the Asakusa grounds, looking at things.

[Here follows, in the original manuscript, the text of a little poem, composed by the writer herself:]

Imado no watashi nité
Aimita koto mo naki hito ni,
Fushigi ni Miméguri-Inari,
Kaku mo fūtu ni naru nomika.
Hajimé no omoi ni hikikaëté,
Itsushika-kokoro mo Sumidagawa.
Tsugai hanarénu miyakodori,
Hito mo urayaméba wagami mo mata,
Sakimidarétaru doté no hana yori mo,
Hana ni mo mashita sono hito to

---

[16] That is to say, "It was agreed that we should all go together to see the flowers." The word *hanami* (flower-seeing) might be given to any of the numerous flower-festivals of the year, according to circumstances; but it here refers to the season of cherry blossoms. Throughout this diary the dates are those of the old lunar calendar.

Shirahigé-Yashiro ni naru madé mo.
Soïtogétashi to inorinenji!

[*Freely translated*] [17]
Having been taken across the Imado-Ferry, I strangely met
at [the temple of] Miméguri-Inari with a person whom I had
never seen before. Because of this meeting our relation is now
even more than the relation of husband and wife. And my first
anxious doubt, "For how long—?" having passed away, my
mind has become [clear] as the Sumida River. Indeed we are
now like a pair of Miyako-birds [always together]; and I even
think that I deserve to be envied. [To see the flowers we went
out; but] more than the pleasure of viewing a whole shore in
blossom is the pleasure that I now desire—always to dwell with
this person, dearer to me than any flower, until we enter the
Shirahigé-Yashiro. That we may so remain together, I suppli-
cate the Gods!

. . . Then we crossed the Azuma bridge on our homeward way; and
we went by steamer to the *kaichō* [festival] of the temple of the Soga-
Kyōdi,[18] and prayed that love and concord should continue always
between ourselves and our brothers and sisters. It was after seven
o'clock that evening when we got home.
On the twenty-fifth day of the same month we went to the Roku-
mono-no-Yosé.[19]

[17] A literal rendering is almost impossible. There is a ferry, called the Ferry of Imado,
over the Sumidagawa; but the reference here is really neither to the ferry nor to the
ferryman, but to the *nakōdo,* or match-maker, who arranged for the marriage. Miméguri-
Inari is the popular name of a famous temple of the God of Rice, in Mukojima; but
there is an untranslatable play here upon the name, suggesting a lovers' meeting. The
reference to the Sumidagawa also contains a play upon the syllables *sumi*—the verb
sumi signifying "to be clear." Shirahigé-Yashiro (White-Haired Temple) is the name
of a real and very celebrated Shintō shrine in the city; but the name is here used chiefly
to express the hope that the union may last into the period of hoary age. Besides these
suggestions, we may suppose that the poem contains allusions to the actual journey
made—over the Sumidagawa by ferry, and thence to the various temples named. From
old time, poems of like meaning have been made about these places; but the lines above
given are certainly original, with the obvious exception of a few phrases which have
become current coin in popular poetry.
[18] The Soga Brothers were famous heroes of the twelfth century. The word *kaichō*
signifies the religious festival during which the principal image of a temple is exposed
to view.
[19] Name of a public hall at which various kinds of entertainments are given, more
especially recitations by professional story-tellers.

· · ·

On the second day of the fifth month we visited [the gardens at] Ōkubo to see the azaleas in blossom.

On the sixth day of the same month we went to see a display of fireworks at the Shōkonsha.

So far we had never had any words between us nor any disagreement; [20] and I had ceased to feel bashful when we went out visiting or sight-seeing. Now each of us seemed to think only of how to please the other; and I felt sure that nothing would ever separate us. . . . May our relation always be thus happy!

The eighteenth day of the sixth month, being the festival of the Suga-jinja,[21] we were invited to my father's house. But as the hairdresser did not come to dress my hair at the proper time, I was much annoyed. However, I went with O-Tori-San [a younger sister] to father's. Presently O-Kō-San [a married sister] also came;—and we had a pleasant time. In the evening Goto-Shi [husband of O-Kō] joined us; and, last of all, came my husband, for whom I had been waiting with anxious impatience. And there was one thing that made me very glad. Often when he and I were to go out together, I had proposed that we should put on the new spring robes which I had made; but he had as often refused—preferring to wear his old kimono. Now, however, he wore the new one—having felt obliged to put it on because of father's invitation. . . . All of us being thus happily assembled, the party became more and more enjoyable; and when we had at last to say good-bye, we only regretted the shortness of the summer night.

These are the poems which we composed that evening:

Futa-fūfu
Sorōté iwō
Ujigami no
Matsuri mo kyō wa
Nigiwai ni kéri.

BY NAMIKI [THE HUSBAND]

Two wedded couples having gone together to worship at

---

[20] Literally: "there never yet having been any waves nor even wind between us."

[21] The Shintō parish-temple, or more correctly, district-temple of the Yotsuya quarter. Each quarter, or district, of the city has its tutelar divinity, or Ujigami. Suga-jinja is the Ujigami-temple of Yotsuya.

the temple, the parish-festival to-day has been merrier than ever before.

> *Ujigami no*
> *Matsuri médétashi*
> *Futa-fūfu.*

[ALSO BY THE HUSBAND]

Fortunate indeed for two married couples has been the parish-temple festival!

> *Ikutosé mo,*
> *Nigiyaka narishi,*
> *Ujigami no,*
> *Matsuri ni sorō,*
> *Kyō no uréshisa.*

[BY THE WIFE]

Though for ever so many years it has always been a joyous occasion, the festival of our parish-temple to-day is more pleasant than ever before, because of our being thus happily assembled together.

> *Matsuri toté,*
> *Ikka atsumaru,*
> *Tanoshimi wa!*
> *Géni Ujigami no*
> *Mégumi narikéri.*

[BY THE WIFE]

To-day being a day of festival, and all of us meeting together—what a delight! Surely by the favor of the tutelar God [Ujigami] this has come to pass.

> *Futa-fūfu*
> *Sorōté kyō no*
> *Shitashimi mo,*
> *Kami no mégumi zo*
> *Médéta kari-kéri.*

[BY THE WIFE]

Two wedded pairs being to-day united in such friendship as this—certainly it has happened only through the favor of the Gods!

Ujigami no
Mégumi mo fukaki
Fūfu-zuré.

[BY THE WIFE]

Deep indeed is the favor of the tutelar God to the two
married couples.

Matsuri toté,
Tsui ni shitatéshi
Iyō-gasuri,
Kyō tanoshimi ni
Kiru to omoëba.

[BY THE WIFE]

This day being a day of festival, we decided to put on, for
the joyful meeting, the robes of Iyogasuri,[22] that had been
made alike.

Omoïkya!
Hakarazu sōro
Futa-fūfu;
Nani ni tatōën
Kyō no kichi-jitsu.

BY GOTO [THE BROTHER-IN-LAW]

How could we have thought it! Here unexpectedly the
two married couples meet together. What can compare with
the good fortune of this day?

Matsuri toté
Hajimété sorō
Futa-fūfu,
Nochi no kaëri zo
Ima wa kanashıki.

BY O-KŌ [THE MARRIED SISTER]

This day being a day of festival, here for the first time two
wedded pairs have met. Already I find myself sorrowing at
the thought that we must separate again.

[22] Iyogasuri is the name given to a kind of dark-blue cotton-cloth, with a sprinkling
of white in small patterns, manufactured at Iyo, in Shikoku.

Furu-sato no
Matsuri ni sorō
Futa-fūfu:
Katarō ma saë
Natsu mo mijika yo!

BY O-KŌ

At the old parental home, two married couples have met together in holiday celebration. Alas! that the time of our happy converse should be only one short summer night!

On the fifth day of the seventh month, went to the Kanazawa-tei,[23] where Harimadayū was then reciting; and we heard him recite the *jōruri* called "Sanjūsangendō."

On the first day of the eighth month we went to the [Buddhist] temple of Asakusa [Kwannon] to pray—that day being the first anniversary [*isshūki*] of the death of my husband's former wife. Afterward we went to an eel-house, near the Azuma bridge, for dinner; and while we were there—just about the hour of noon—an earthquake took place. Being close to the river, the house rocked very much; and I was greatly frightened.

Remembering that when we went to Asakusa before, in the time of cherry blossoms, we had seen a big fire, this earthquake made me feel anxious;—I wondered whether lightning would come next.[24]

About two o'clock we left the eating-house, and went to the Asakusa park. From there we went by street-car to Kanda; and we stopped awhile at a cool place in Kanda, to rest ourselves. On our way home we called at father's, and it was after nine o'clock when we got back.

The fifteenth day of the same month was the festival of the Hachiman-jinja;[25] and Goto, my sister, and the younger sister of Goto came

---

[23] The Kanazawa-tei is a public hall in the Yotsuya quarter. Harimadayū is the professional name of a celebrated chanter of the dramatic recitations called *jōruri* and *gidayū*—in which the reciter, or chanter, mimes the voices and action of many different characters.

[24] She alludes to a popular saying of Buddhist origin: *Jishin, kwaji, kaminari, misoka, kikin, yamai no naki kuni é yuku* (Let us go to the Land where there is neither earthquake, nor fire, nor lightning, nor any last day of the month, nor famine, nor sickness).

[25] Ujigami of the Ushigomé district.

to the house. I had hoped that we could all go to the temple together; but that morning my husband had taken a little too much wine—so we had to go without him. After worshiping at the temple, we went to Goto's house; and I stopped there awhile before returning home.

In the ninth month, on the occasion of the Higan [26] festival, I went alone to the [Buddhist] temple to pray.

On the twenty-first day of the tenth month, O-Taka-San [probably a relative] came from Shidzuoka. I wanted to take her to the theatre the next day; but she was obliged to leave Tōkyō early in the morning. However, my husband and I went to the Ryūsei theatre on the following evening; and we saw the play called Matsumaë Bidan Teichū-Kagami." [27]

* * *

On the twenty-second day of the sixth month I began to sew a kimono which father had asked me to make for him; but I felt ill, and could not do much. However, I was able to finish the work on the first day of the new year [1897].

. . . Now we were very happy because of the child that was to be born. And I thought how proud and glad my parents would be at having a grandchild for the first time.

* * *

On the tenth day of the fifth month I went out with mother to worship Shiogama-Sama,[28] and also to visit Sengakuji. There we saw the tombs of the Shijin-shichi Shi [Forty-seven Rōnin], and many relics of their history. We returned by railroad, taking the train from Shinagawa to Shinjiku. At Shiochō-Sanchōmé I parted from mother, and I got home by six o'clock.

* * *

[26] Festival of the "Farther Shore" (that is to say, Paradise). There are two great Buddhist festivals thus called—the first representing a period of seven days during the spring equinox; the second, a period of seven days during the autumnal equinox.

[27] This drama is founded upon the history of a famous rice merchant named Matsumaëya Gorōbei.

[28] Shiogama-Daimyōjin, a Shintō deity, to whom women pray for easy delivery in child-birth. Shrines of this divinity may be found in almost every province of Japan.

On the eighth day of the sixth month, at four o'clock in the afternoon, a boy was born. Both mother and child appeared to be as well as
could be wished; and the child much resembled my husband; and its
eyes were large and black. . . . But I must say that it was a very small
child; for, though it ought to have been born in the eighth month, it
was born indeed in the sixth. . . . At seven o'clock in the evening of
the same day, when the time came to give the child some medicine,
we saw, by the light of the lamp, that he was looking all about, with
his big eyes wide open. During that night the child slept in my
mother's bosom. As we had been told that he must be kept very warm,
because he was only a seven-months' child, it was decided that he
should be kept in the bosom by day as well as by night.

Next day—the ninth day of the sixth month—at half-past six o'clock
in the afternoon, he suddenly died. . . .

"Brief is the time of pleasure, and quickly turns to pain; and whatsoever is born must necessarily die"; [29]—that, indeed, is a true saying
about this world.

Only for one day to be called a mother!—to have a child born only
to see it die! . . . Surely, I thought, if a child must die within two days
after birth, it were better that it should never be born.

From the twelfth to the sixth month I had been so ill!—then at last
I had obtained some ease, and joy at the birth of a son; and I had received so many congratulations about my good fortune;—and, nevertheless, he was dead! . . . Indeed, I suffered great grief.

On the tenth day of the sixth month the funeral took place, at the
temple called Senpukuji, in Ōkubo, and a small tomb was erected.

The poems composed at that time [30] were the following:

Omoïkya!
Mi ni saë kaënu
Nadéshiko ni,
Wakaréshi sodé no
Tsuyu no tamoto wo!

If I could only have known! Ah, this parting with the

[29] *"Uréshiki ma wa wazuka nité, mata kanashimi to henzuru; umaréru mono wa
kanarazu shizu"*: A Buddhist text that has become a Japanese proverb.
[30] Composed by the bereaved mother herself, as a discipline against grief.

flower,[31] for which I would so gladly have given my own life, has left my sleeves with the dew!

> *Samidaré ya!*
> *Shimérigachi naru*
> *Sodé no tamoto wo.*

Oh! the month of rain! [32] All things become damp;—the ends of my sleeves are wet.

Some little time afterward, people told me that if I planted the *sotoba* [33] upside down, another misfortune of this kind would not come to pass. I had a great many sorrowful doubts about doing such a thing; but at last, on the ninth day of the eighth month, I had the sotoba reversed. . . .

On the eighth day of the ninth month we went to the Akasaka theatre.

On the eighteenth day of the tenth month I went by myself to the Haruki theatre in Hongō, to see the play of "Ōkubo Hikozaëmon." [34] There, having carelessly lost my sandal-ticket [*gésoku-fuda*], I had to remain until after everybody else had left. Then I was at last able to get my sandals, and to go home; but the night was so black that I felt very lonesome on the way.

On the day of the Sekku,[35] in the first month [1898], I was talking

[31] *Nadéshiko* literally means a pink; but in poetry the word is commonly used in the meaning of "baby."

[32] Samidaré is the name given to the old fifth month, or, more strictly speaking, to a rainy period occurring in that month. The verses are, of course, allusive, and their real meaning might be rendered thus: "Oh! the season of grief! All things now seem sad: the sleeves of my robe are moist with my tears!"

[33] The *sotoba* is a tall wooden lath, inscribed with Buddhist texts, and planted above a grave.

[34] It would be unfair to suppose that this visit to the theatre was made only for pleasure; it was made rather in the hope of forgetting pain, and probably by order of the husband.
Ōkubo Hikozaëmon was the favorite minister and adviser of the Shōgun Iyemitsu. Numberless stories of his sagacity and kindness are recorded in popular literature; and in many dramas the notable incidents of his official career are still represented.

[35] There are five holidays thus named in every year. These *go-sekku* are usually called: Jinjitsu (the seventh of the first month), Joki (the third of the third month), Tango

with Hori's aunt and the wife of our friend Uchimi, when I suddenly felt a violent pain in my breast, and, being frightened, I tried
to reach a talisman [o-ma-mori] of Suitengū,[36] which was lying upon
the wardrobe. But in the same moment I fell senseless. Under kind
treatment I soon came to myself again; but I was ill for a long time
after.

· · ·

The tenth day of the fourth month being the holiday Sanjiu-nen-
Sai,[37] we arranged to meet at father's. I was to go there first with
Jiunosuké [perhaps a relative], and there wait for my husband, who
had to go to the office that morning for a little while. He met us at
father's house about half-past eight: then the three of us went out
together to look at the streets. We passed through Kōjimachi to Naka-
tamachi, and went by way of the Sakurada-Mon to the Hibiya-
Metsuké, and thence from Ginzadōri by way of the Mégané-Bashi to
Uyéno. After looking at things there, we again went to the Mégané-
Bashi; but then I felt so tired that I proposed to return, and my husband agreed, as he also was very tired. But Jiunosuké said: "As I do
not want to miss this chance to see the Daimyō-procession,[38] I must
go on to Ginza." So there we said good-bye to him, and we went to a
little eating-house [tempura-ya], where we were served with fried fish;
and, as luck would have it, we got a good chance to see the Daimyō-
procession from that very house. We did not get back home that
evening until half-past six o'clock.

From the middle of the fourth month I had much sorrow on account of a matter relating to my sister Tori [the matter is not men-
tioned].

· · ·

(the fifth of the fifth month), Tanabata (the seventh of the seventh month), and
Choyo (the ninth of the ninth month).

[36] A divinity half-Buddhist, half-Shintō, in origin, but now popularly considered
Shintō. This god is especially worshiped as a healer, and a protector against sickness.
His principal temple in Tōkyō is in the Nihonbashi district.

[37] A festival in commemoration of the thirtieth anniversary of the establishment of
Tōkyō as the Imperial capital, instead of Kyōto.

[38] Daimyō-no-g yoretsu. On the festival mentioned there was a pageant representing
feudal princes traveling in state, accompanied by their retainers and servants. The real
armor, costumes, and weapons of the period before Meiji were effectively displayed on
this occasion.

On the nineteenth day of the eighth month of the thirty-first year of Meiji [1898] my second child was born, almost painlessly—a girl; and we named her Hatsu.

We invited to the *shichiya* [39] all those who had helped us at the time of the child's birth. Mother afterwards remained with me for a couple of days; but she was then obliged to leave me, because my sister Kō was suffering from severe pains in the chest. Fortunately my husband had his regular vacation about the same time; and he helped me all he could—even in regard to washing and other matters; but I was often greatly troubled because I had no woman with me. . . . When my husband's vacation was over, mother came often, but only while my husband was away. The twenty-one days [the period of danger] thus passed; but mother and child continued well.

Up to the time of one hundred days after my daughter's birth, I was constantly anxious about her, because she often seemed to have a difficulty in breathing. But that passed off at last, and she appeared to be getting strong.

Still, we were unhappy about one matter—a deformity: Hatsu had been born with a double thumb on one hand. For a long time we could not make up our minds to take her to a hospital, in order to have an operation performed. But at last a woman living near our house told us of a very skillful surgeon in [the quarter of] Shinjiku; and we decided to go to him. My husband held the child on his lap during the operation. I could not bear to see the operation; and I waited in the next room, my heart full of pain and fear, wondering how the matter would end. But [when all was over] the little one did not appear to suffer any pain; and she took the breast as usual a few minutes after. So the matter ended more fortunately than I had thought possible.

At home she continued to take her milk as before, and seemed as if nothing had been done to her little body. But as she was so very young we were afraid that the operation might in some way cause her to be sick. By way of precaution, I went with her to the hospital every day for about three weeks; but she showed no sign of sickness.

---

[39] A congratulatory feast, held on the evening of the seventh day after the birth of a child. Relatives and friends invited usually make small presents to the baby.

On the third day of the third month of the thirty-second year [1899], on the occasion of the *hatsu-sekku*,[40] we received presents of *Dairi* and of *hina,* both from father's house and from Goto's—also the customary gifts of congratulations: a *tansu* [chest of drawers], a *kyōdai* [mirror-stand], and a *haribako* [work-box: literally: "needle-box"].[41] We ourselves on the same occasion bought for her a *chadai* [teacup stand], a *zen* [lacquered tray], and some other little things. Both Goto and Jiunosuké came to see us on that day; and we had a very happy gathering.

On the third day of the fourth month we visited the temple Ana-Hachiman [Shintō shrine in the district of Waséda] to pray for the child's health. . . .

On the twenty-ninth day of the fourth month Hatsu appeared to be unwell: so I wanted to have her examined by a doctor.

A doctor promised to come the same morning, but he did not come, and I waited for him in vain all that day. Next day again I waited, but he did not come. Toward evening Hatsu became worse, and seemed to be suffering great pain in her breast, and I resolved to take her to a doctor early next morning. All through that night I was very uneasy about her, but at daybreak she seemed to be better. So I went out alone, taking her on my back, and walked to the office of a doctor in Akasaka. But when I asked to have the child examined, I was told that I must wait, as it was not yet the regular time for seeing patients.

While I was waiting, the child began to cry worse than ever before; she would not take the breast, and I could do nothing to soothe her, either by walking or resting, so that I was greatly troubled. At last the doctor came, and began to examine her; and in the same moment I noticed that her crying grew feebler, and that her lips were becoming paler and paler. Then, as I could not remain silent, seeing her thus, I had to ask, "How is her condition?" "She cannot live until evening," he answered. "But could you not give her medicine?" I asked. "If she could drink it," he replied.

I wanted to go back home at once, and send word to my husband

---

[40] The first annual Festival of Girls is thus called.

[41] All the objects here mentioned are toys—toys appropriate to the occasion. The *Dairi* are old-fashioned toy-figures, representing an emperor and empress in ancient costume. *Hina* are dolls.

and to my father's house; but the shock had been too much for me—all my strength suddenly left me. Fortunately a kind old woman came to my aid, and carried my umbrella and other things, and helped me to get into a jinrikisha, so that I was able to return home by jinrikisha. Then I sent a man to tell my husband and my father. Mita's wife came to help me; and with her assistance everything possible was done to help the child. . . . Still my husband did not come back. But all our pain and trouble was in vain.

So, on the second day of the fifth month of the thirty-second year, my child set out on her journey to the Jūmanokudō [42]—never to return to this world.

And we, her father and mother, were yet living—though we had caused her death by neglecting to have her treated by a skilled doctor! This thought made us both sorrow greatly; and we often reproached ourselves in vain.

But the day after her death the doctor said to us: "Even if that disease had been treated from the beginning by the best possible means, your child could not have lived more than about a week. If she had been ten or eleven years old, she might possibly have been saved by an operation; but in this case no operation could have been attempted—the child was too young." Then he explained to us that the child had died from a *jinzōen*.[43] . . .

Thus all the hopes that we had, and all the pains that we took in caring for her, and all the pleasure of watching her grow during those nine months—all were in vain!

But we two were at last able to find some ease from our sorrow by reflecting that our relation to this child, from the time of some former life, must have been very slight and weak.[44]

In the loneliness of that weary time, I tried to express my heart by writing some verses after the manner of the story of Miyagino and Shinobu in the *gidayū-bon:* [45]

[42] Another name for the Buddhist Paradise of the West—the heaven of Amida (Amiytâbha).

[43] Nephritis.

[44] Or, "very thin and loose"—the Karma-relation being emblematically spoken of as a bond or tie. She means, of course, that the loss of the child was the inevitable consequence of some fault committed in a previous state of existence.

[45] *Gidayū-bon*, "the book of the *gidayū*." There are many gidayū books. Gidayū is

Koré, kono uchi é enzukishi wa,
Omoi kaëséba itsutosé maë;
Kondo mōkéshi wa onago no ko,
Kawaii mono toté sodatsuru ka to;—
Waga mi no nari wa uchi-wasuré,
Sodatéshi koto mo, nasaké nai.
Kōshita koto to wa tsuyushirazu,
Kono Hatsu wa buji ni sodatsuru ka.
Shubi yō seijin shita naraba,
Yagaté muko wo tori
Tanoshimashō dōshité to.
Monomi yusan wo tashinandé,
Wagako daiji to,
Otto no koto mo, Hatsu no koto mo,
Koïshi natsukashi omō no wo;—
Tanoshimi-kurashita kai mo nō.
Oyako ni narishi wa uréshii ga,
Sakidatsu koto wo miru haha no
Kokoro mo suishité tamoi no to!

—Té wo tori-kawasu fūfuga nagéki,
Nagéki wo tachi-giku mo,
Morai nakishité omotéguchi
Shōji mo nururu bakari nari.

Here in this house it was that I married him;—well I remember the day—five years ago. Here was born the girl-baby —the loved one whom we hoped to rear. Caring then no longer for my person [heedless of how I dressed when I went out]—thinking only of how to bring her up—I lived. How pitiless [this doom of mine]! Never had I even dreamed that such a thing could befall me: my only thoughts were as to how my Hatsu could best be reared. When she grows up, I thought, soon we shall find her a good husband, to make her life happy. So, never going out for pleasure-seeking, I studied only how to care for my little one—how to love and to cherish my husband and my Hatsu. Vain now, alas! this hoped-

the name given to a kind of musical drama. In the dramatic composition here referred to, the characters Miyagino and Shinobu are sisters, who relate their sorrows to each other.

for joy of living only for her sake. . . . Once having known the delight of the relation of mother and child, deign to think of the heart of the mother who sees her child die before her![46]

[All of the foregoing is addressed to the spirit of the dead child.— Translator.]

Now, while husband and wife, each clasping the hands of the other, make lament together, if any one pausing at the entrance should listen to their sorrow, surely the paper window would be moistened by tears from without.

About the time of Hatsu's death, the law concerning funerals was changed for the better; and permission was given for the burning of corpses in Ōkubo. So I asked Namiki to have the body sent to the temple of which his family had always been parishioners—providing that there should be no [legal] difficulty about the matter. Accordingly the funeral took place at Monjōji—a temple belonging to the Asakusa branch of the Hongwanji Shinshū; and the ashes were there interred.

My sister Kō was sick in bed with a rather bad cold at the time of Hatsu's death; but she visited us very soon after the news had reached her. And she called again a few days later to tell us that she had become almost well, and that we had no more cause to feel anxious about her.

As for myself, I felt a dread of going out anywhere; and I did not leave the house for a whole month. But as custom does not allow one to remain always indoors, I had to go out at last; and I made the required visit to father's and to my sister's.

·   ·   ·

Having become quite ill, I hoped that mother would be able to help me. But Kō was again sick, and Yoshi [a younger sister here mentioned for the first time] and mother had both to attend her constantly: so I could get no aid from father's house. There was no one to help me except some of my female neighbors, who attended me out of pure kindness, when they could spare the time. At last I got Hori-

[46] That is, before she herself (the mother) dies;—there is a colloquial phrase in the Japanese text. *"Ko ga oya ni sakidatsu"* is the common expression: "the child goes before the parents"; that is to say, dies before the parents.

Shi to engage a good old woman to assist me; and under her kind care I began to get well. About the beginning of the eighth month I felt much stronger. . . .

On the fourth day of the ninth month my sister Kō died of consumption.

It had been agreed beforehand that if an unexpected matter [47] came to pass, my younger sister Yoshi should be received in the place of Kō. As Goto-Shi found it inconvenient to live altogether alone, the marriage took place on the eleventh day of the same month; and the usual congratulations were offered.

On the last day of the same month Okada-Shi suddenly died.

We found ourselves greatly troubled [pecuniarily embarrassed] by the expenses that all these events caused us.

When I first heard that Yoshi had been received so soon after the death of Kō, I was greatly displeased. But I kept my feelings hidden, and I spoke to the man as before.

In the eleventh month Goto went alone to Sapporo.

On the second day of the second month, thirty-third year of Meiji [1900], Goto-Shi returned to Tōkyō; and on the fourteenth day of the same month he went away again to the Hokkaidō [Yezo], taking Yoshi with him.

. . .

On the twentieth day of the second month, at six o'clock in the morning, my third child—a boy—was born. Both mother and child were well.

We had expected a girl, but it was a boy that was born; so, when my husband came back from his work, he was greatly surprised and pleased to find that he had a boy.

But the child was not well able to take the breast: so we had to nourish him by means of a feeding-bottle.

On the seventh day after the boy's birth, we partly shaved his head. And in the evening we had the *shichiya* [seventh-day festival]—but, this time, all by ourselves.

[47] A euphemistic expression for death.

My husband had caught a bad cold some time before; and he could not go to work next morning, as he was coughing badly. So he remained in the house.

Early in the morning the child had taken his milk as usual. But, about ten o'clock in the forenoon, he seemed to be suffering great pain in his breast; and he began to moan so strangely that we sent a man for a doctor. Unfortunately the doctor that we asked to come was out of town; and we were told that he would not come back before night. Therefore, we thought that it would be better to send at once for another doctor; and we sent for one. He said that he would come in the evening. But, about two o'clock in the afternoon, the child's sickness suddenly became worse; and a little before three o'clock—the twenty-seventh day of the second month—*aënaku!* [48]—my child was dead, having lived for only eight days. . . .

I thought to myself that, even if this new misfortune did not cause my husband to feel an aversion for me, thus having to part with all my children, one after another, must be the punishment of some wrong done in the time of a former life. And, so thinking, I knew that my sleeves would never again become dry—that the rain [of tears] would never cease—that never again in this world would the sky grow clear for me.

And more and more I wondered whether my husband's feelings would not change for the worse, by reason of his having to meet such trouble, over and over again, on my account. I felt anxious about his heart, because of what already was in my own.

Nevertheless, he only repeated the words, *"Temméï itashikata koré naku"*: "From the decrees of Heaven there is no escape."

I thought that I should be better able to visit the tomb of my child if he were buried in some temple near us. So the funeral took place at the temple called Sempukuji in Ōkubo; and the ashes were buried there. . . .

Tanoshimi mo
Samété hakanashi
Haru no yumé! [49]

---

[48] *Aënaku* is an adjective signifying, according to circumstances, "feeble," or "transitory," or "sad." Its use here might best be rendered by some such phrase as "Piteous to say!"

[49] Her poem bears no date.

All the delight having perished, hopeless I remain: it was only a dream of Spring![50]

[No date.]

... I wonder whether it was because of the sorrow that I suffered —my face and limbs became slightly swollen during the fortnight [51] after my boy's death. It was nothing very serious, after all, and it soon went away. . . . Now the period of twenty-one days [the period of danger] is past. . . .

Here the poor mother's diary ends. The closing statement regarding the time of twenty-one days from the birth of her child leaves it probable that these last lines were written on the thirteenth or fourteenth day of the third month. She died on the twenty-eighth of the same month.

I doubt if any one not really familiar with the life of Japan can fully understand this simple history. But to imagine the merely material conditions of the existence here recorded should not be difficult: —the couple occupying a tiny house of two rooms—one room of six mats and one of three;—the husband earning barely one pound per month;—the wife sewing, washing, cooking (outside the house, of course);—no comfort of fire, even during the period of greatest cold. I estimate that the pair must have lived at an average cost of about seven pence a day, not including house-rent. Their pleasures were indeed very cheap: a payment of two-pence admitted them to theatres or to gidayū-recitations; and their sight-seeing was done on foot. Yet even these diversions were luxuries for them. Expenses represented by the necessary purchase of clothing, or by the obligation of making presents to kindred upon the occasion of a marriage or a birth or a death, could only have been met by heroic economy. Now it is true that thousands of poor folk in Tōkyō live still more cheaply than this —live upon a much smaller income than one pound per month—and nevertheless remain always clean, neat, and cheerful. But only a very

[50] A necessarily free translation;—the lines might also be read thus: "Having awakened, all the joy fleets and fades;—it was only a dream of Spring." The verb saméru, very effectively used here, allows of this double rendering; for it means either "to awake" or "to fade." The adjective hakanashi also has a double meaning: according to circumstances it may signify either "fleeting" (evanescent) or "hopeless" (wretched).

[51] Literally: "the first two nanuka": one nanuka representing a period of seven successive days from the date of death.

strong woman can easily bear and bring up children under such conditions—conditions much more hazardous than those of the harder but healthier peasant-life of the interior. And, as might be supposed, the weakly fail and perish in multitude.

Readers of the diary may have wondered at the eagerness shown by so shy and gentle a woman to become thus suddenly the wife of a total stranger, about whose character she knew absolutely nothing. A majority of Japanese marriages, indeed, are arranged for in the matter-of-fact way here described, and with the aid of a nakōdo; but the circumstances, in this particular case, were exceptionally discomforting. The explanation is pathetically simple. All good girls are expected to marry; and to remain unmarried after a certain age is a shame and a reproach. The dread of such reproach, doubtless, impelled the writer of the diary to snatch at the first chance of fulfilling her natural destiny. She was already twenty-nine years old;—another such chance might never have offered itself.

To me the chief significance of this humble confession of struggle and failure is not in the utterance of anything exceptional, but in the expression of something as common to Japanese life as blue air and sunshine. The brave resolve of the woman to win affection by docility and by faultless performance of duty, her gratitude for every small kindness, her childlike piety, her supreme unselfishness, her Buddhist interpretation of suffering as the penalty for some fault committed in a previous life, her attempts to write poetry when her heart was breaking—all this, indeed, I find touching, and more than touching. But I do not find it exceptional. The traits revealed are typical—typical of the moral nature of the woman of the people. Perhaps there are not many Japanese women of the same humble class who could express their personal joy and pain in a record at once so artless and pathetic; but there are millions of such women inheriting—from ages and ages of unquestioning faith—a like conception of life as duty, and an equal capacity of unselfish attachment.

Out of the Street

I

"THESE," SAID MANYEMON, PUTTING ON THE TABLE A ROLL OF WONDER-
fully written Japanese manuscript, "are Vulgar Songs. If they are to
be spoken of in some honorable book, perhaps it will be good to say
that they are Vulgar, so that Western people may not be deceived."

Next to my house there is a vacant lot, where washermen (*senta-
kuya*) work in the ancient manner,—singing as they work, and whipping the wet garments upon big flat stones. Every morning at daybreak
their singing wakens me; and I like to listen to it, though I cannot
often catch the words. It is full of long, queer, plaintive modulations.
Yesterday, the apprentice—a lad of fifteen—and the master of the
washermen were singing alternately, as if answering each other; the
contrast between the tones of the man, sonorous as if boomed through
a conch, and the clarion alto of the boy, being very pleasant to hear.
Whereupon I called Manyemon and asked him what the singing was
about.
"The song of the boy," he said, "is an old song:

> *Things never changed since the Time of the Gods:*
> *The flowing of water, the Way of Love.*

I heard it often when I was myself a boy."
"And the other song?"
"The other song is probably new:

> *Three years thought of her,*
> *Five years sought for her;*
> *Only for one night held her in my arms.*

A very foolish song!"

"I don't know," I said. "There are famous Western romances containing nothing wiser. And what is the rest of the song?"

"There is no more: that is the whole of the song. If it be honorably desired, I can write down the songs of the washermen, and the songs which are sung in this street by the smiths and the carpenters and the bamboo-weavers and the rice-cleaners. But they are all nearly the same."

Thus came it to pass that Manyemon made for me a collection of Vulgar Songs.

By "vulgar" Manyemon meant written in the speech of the common people. He is himself an adept at classical verse, and despises the *hayari-uta,* or ditties of the day; it requires something very delicate to please him. And what pleases him I am not qualified to write about; for one must be a very good Japanese scholar to meddle with the superior varieties of Japanese poetry. If you care to know how difficult the subject is, just study the chapter on prosody in Aston's "Grammar of the Japanese Written Language," or the introduction to Professor Chamberlain's "Classical Poetry of the Japanese." Her poetry is the one original art which Japan has certainly not borrowed either from China or from any other country; and its most refined charm is the essence, irreproducible, of the very flower of the language itself: hence the difficulty of representing, even partially, in any Western tongue, its subtler delicacies of sentiment, allusion, and color. But to understand the compositions of the people, no scholarship is needed: they are characterized by the greatest possible simplicity, directness, and sincerity. The real art of them, in short, is their absolute artlessness. That was why I wanted them. Springing straight from the heart of the eternal youth of the race, these little gushes of song, like the untaught poetry of every people, utter what belongs to all human experience rather than to the limited life of a class or a time; and even in their melodies still resound the fresh and powerful pulsings of their primal source.

Manyemon had written down forty-seven songs; and with his help I made free renderings of the best. They were very brief, varying from seventeen to thirty-one syllables in length. Nearly all Japanese poetical metre consists of simple alternations of lines of five and seven syllables; the frequent exceptions which popular songs offer to this rule

being merely irregularities such as the singer can smooth over either
by slurring or by prolonging certain vowel sounds. Most of the songs
which Manyemon had collected were of twenty-six syllables only;
being composed of three successive lines of seven syllables each, followed by one of five, thus:

> *Ka-mi-yo ko-no-ka-ta*
> *Ka-wa-ra-nu mo-no wa:*
> *Mi-dzu no na-ga-ré to*
> *Ko-i no mi-chi.*[1]

Among various deviations from this construction I found 7-7-7-7-5,
5-7-7-7-5, and 7-5-7-5, and 5-7-5; but the classical five-line form
(*tanka*), represented by 5-7-5-7-7, was entirely absent.

Terms indicating gender were likewise absent; even the expressions
corresponding to "I" and "you" being seldom used, and the words
signifying "beloved" applying equally to either sex. Only by the conventional value of some comparison, the use of a particular emotional
tone, or the mention of some detail of costume, was the sex of the
speaker suggested, as in this verse:

> *I am the water-weed drifting,—finding no place of attachment:*
> *Where, I wonder, and when, shall my flower begin to bloom?*

Evidently the speaker is a girl who wishes for a lover: the same
simile uttered by masculine lips would sound in Japanese ears much
as would sound in English ears a man's comparison of himself to a
violet or to a rose. For the like reason, one knows that in the following song the speaker is not a woman:

> *Flowers in both my hands,—flowers of plum and cherry:*
> *Which will be, I wonder, the flower to give me fruit?*

Womanly charm is compared to the cherry flower and also to the
plum flower; but the quality symbolized by the plum flower is moral
always rather than physical. The verse represents a man strongly
attracted by two girls: one, perhaps a dancer, very fair to look upon;

[1] Literally, "God-Age-since not-changed-things as-for: water-of flowing and love-of
way."

the other beautiful in character. Which shall he choose to be his companion for life?

One more example:

> *Too long, with pen in hand, idling, fearing, and doubting,*
> *I cast my silver pin for the test of the tatamizan.*

Here we know from the mention of the hairpin that the speaker is a woman, and we can also suppose that she is a geisha; the sort of divination called *tatamizan* being especially popular with dancing-girls. The rush covering of floor-mats (*tatami*), woven over a frame of thin strings, shows on its upper surface a regular series of lines about three fourths of an inch apart. The girl throws her pin upon a mat, and then counts the lines it touches. According to their number she deems herself lucky or unlucky. Sometimes a little pipe—geishas' pipes are usually of silver—is used instead of the hairpin.

The theme of all the songs was love, as indeed it is of the vast majority of the Japanese *chansons des rues et des bois;* even songs about celebrated places usually contain some amatory suggestion. I noticed that almost every simple phase of the emotion, from its earliest budding to its uttermost ripening, was represented in the collection; and I therefore tried to arrange the pieces according to the natural passional sequence. The result had some dramatic suggestiveness.

II

THE SONGS REALLY FORM THREE DISTINCT GROUPS, EACH CORRESPONDING TO a particular period of that emotional experience which is the subject of all. In the first group of seven the surprise and pain and weakness of passion find utterance; beginning with a plaintive cry of reproach and closing with a whisper of trust.

1

You, by all others disliked!—oh, why must my heart thus like you?

2

This pain which I cannot speak of to any one in the world:
Tell me who has made it—whose do you think the fault?

3

Will it be night forever?—I lose my way in this darkness:
Who goes by the path of Love must always go astray!

4

Even the brightest lamp, even the light electric,
Cannot lighten at all the dusk of the Way of Love.

5

Always the more I love, the more it is hard to say so:
Oh! how happy I were should the loved one say it first!

6

Such a little word!—only to say, "I love you"!
Why, oh, why do I find it hard to say like this? [2]

7

Clicked-to [3] *the locks of our hearts; let the keys remain in our bosoms.*

After which mutual confidence the illusion naturally deepens; suffering yields to a joy that cannot disguise itself, and the keys of the heart are thrown away: this is the second stage.

I

The person who said before, "I hate my life since I saw you,"
Now after union prays to live for a thousand years.

2

You and I together—lilies that grow in a valley;

[2] Inimitably simple in the original:
> *Horeta wai na to*
> *Sukoshi no koto ga:*
> *Nazé ni kono yō ni*
> *Iinikui?*

[3] In the original this is expressed by an onomatope, *pinto,* imitating the sound of the fastening of the lock of a *tansu,* or chest of drawers:
> *Pinto kokoro ni*
> *Jōmai oroshi:*
> *Kagi wa tagai no*
> *Muné ni aru.*

This is our blossoming time—but nobody knows the fact.

3

Receiving from his hand the cup of the wine of greeting,
Even before I drink, I feel that my face grows red.

4

I cannot hide in my heart the happy knowledge that fills it;
Asking each not to tell, I spread the news all round.[4]

5

All crows alike are black, everywhere under heaven.
The person that others like, why should not I like too?

6

Going to see the beloved, a thousand ri are as one ri;[5]
Returning without having seen, one ri is a thousand ri.

7

Going to see the beloved, even the water of rice-fields[6]
Ever becomes, as I drink, nectar of gods[7] *to the taste.*

8

You, till a hundred years; I, until nine and ninety;
Together we still shall be in the time when the hair turns white.

9

Seeing the face, at once the folly I wanted to utter

---

[4] Much simpler in the original:

> *Muné ni tsutsumenu*
> *Uréshii koto wa;—*
> *Kuchidomé shinagara*
> *Furéaruku.*

[5] One *ri* is equal to about two and a half English miles.

[6] In the original *dorota;* literally "mud rice-fields"—meaning rice-fields during the time of flushing, before the grain has fairly grown up. The whole verse reads:

> *Horeté kayoyeba*
> *Dorota no midzu mo*
> *Noméba kanro no*
> *Aji ga suru.*

[7] *Kanro,* a Buddhist word, properly written with two Chinese characters signifying "sweet dew." The real meaning is *amrita,* the drink of the gods.

All melts out of my thought, and somehow the tears come first.[8]

10

Crying for joy made wet my sleeve that dries too quickly:
'T is not the same with the heart—that cannot dry so soon!

11

To Heaven, with all my soul I prayed to prevent your going;
Already, to keep you with me, answers the blessed rain.

So passes the period of illusion. The rest is doubt and pain; only the love remains to challenge even death:

1

Parted from you, my beloved, I go alone to the pine-field;
There is dew of night on the leaves; there is also dew of tears.

2

Even to see the birds flying freely above me
Only deepens my sorrow—makes me thoughtful the more.

3

Coming? or coming not? Far down the river gazing—
Only yomogi *shadows*[9] *astir in the bed of the stream.*

4

Letters come by the post; photographs give me the shadow!
Only one thing remains which I cannot hope to gain.

5

If I may not see the face, but only look at the letter,
Then it were better far only in dreams to see.

[8] *Iitai guchi sayé*
    Kao miriya kiyété
     Tokaku namida ga
        Saki ni deru.

The use of *tokaku* ("somehow," for "some reason or other") gives a peculiar pathos to the utterance.

[9] The plant *yomogi* (*Artemisia vulgaris*) grows wild in many of the half-dry beds of the Japanese rivers.

6

Though his body were broken to pieces, though his bones on the shore were bleaching,
I would find my way to rejoin him, after gathering up the bones.[10]

III

THUS WAS IT THAT THESE LITTLE SONGS, COMPOSED IN DIFFERENT GENERAtions and in different parts of Japan by various persons, seemed to shape themselves for me into the ghost of a romance—into the shadow of a story needing no name of time or place or person, because eternally the same, in all times and places.

Manyemon asks which of the songs I like best; and I turn over his manuscript again to see if I can make a choice. Without, in the bright spring air, the washers are working; and I hear the heavy *pon-pon* of the beating of wet robes, regular as the beating of a heart. Suddenly, as I muse, the voice of the boy soars up in one long, clear, shrill, splendid rocket-tone—and breaks—and softly trembles down in coruscations of fractional notes; singing the song that Manyemon remembers hearing when he himself was a boy:

> *Things never changed since the Time of the Gods:*
> *The flowing of water, the Way of Love.*

"I think that is the best," I said. "It is the soul of all the rest."
"*Hin no nusubito, koi no uta,*" interpretatively murmurs Manyemon. "Even as out of poverty comes the thief, so out of love the song!"

[10] *Mi wa kuda kuda ni*
Honé wo isobé ni
Sarasoto mama yo
Hiroi atsumété
Sōté misho.

The only song of this form in the collection. The use of the verb *soi* implies union as husband and wife.

The Romance of the Milky Way

AMONG THE MANY CHARMING FESTIVALS CELEBRATED BY OLD JAPAN, THE most romantic was the festival of Tanabata-Sama, the Weaving-Lady of the Milky Way. In the chief cities her holiday is now little observed; and in Tōkyō it is almost forgotten. But in many country districts, and even in villages near the capital, it is still celebrated in a small way. If you happen to visit an old-fashioned country town or village, on the seventh day of the seventh month (by the ancient calendar), you will probably notice many freshly-cut bamboos fixed upon the roofs of the houses, or planted in the ground beside them, every bamboo having attached to it a number of strips of colored paper. In some very poor villages you might find that these papers are white, or of one color only; but the general rule is that the papers should be of five or seven different colors. Blue, green, red, yellow, and white are the tints commonly displayed. All these papers are inscribed with short poems written in praise of Tanabata and her husband Hiko-boshi. After the festival the bamboos are taken down and thrown into the nearest stream, together with the poems attached to them.

To understand the romance of this old festival, you must know the legend of those astral divinities to whom offerings used to be made, even by the Imperial Household, on the seventh day of the seventh month. The legend is Chinese. This is the Japanese popular version of it:

The great god of the firmament had a lovely daughter, Tanabata-tsumé, who passed her days in weaving garments for her august parent. She rejoiced in her work, and thought that there was no greater pleasure than the pleasure of weaving. But one day, as she sat before her loom at the door of her heavenly dwelling, she saw a handsome peasant lad pass by, leading an ox, and she fell in love with him. Her august father, divining her secret wish, gave her the youth for a husband. But the wedded lovers became too fond of each other, and neglected their duty to the god of the firmament, the sound of the shuttle was no longer heard, and the ox wandered, unheeded, over the plains of heaven. Therefore the great god was displeased, and he separated the pair. They were sentenced to live thereafter apart, with the Celestial River between them; but it was permitted them to see each other once a year, on the seventh night of the seventh moon. On that night—providing the skies be clear—the birds of heaven make, with their bodies and wings, a bridge over the stream; and by means of that bridge the lovers can meet. But if there be rain, the River of Heaven rises, and becomes so wide that the bridge cannot be formed. So the husband and wife cannot always meet, even on the seventh night of the seventh month; it may happen, by reason of bad weather, that they cannot meet for three or four years at a time. But their love remains immortally young and eternally patient; and they continue to fulfill their respective duties each day without fault—happy in their hope of being able to meet on the seventh night of the next seventh month.

To ancient Chinese fancy, the Milky Way was a luminous river—the River of Heaven—the Silver Stream. It has been stated by Western writers that Tanabata, the Weaving-Lady, is a star in Lyra; and the Herdsman, her beloved, a star in Aquila, on the opposite side of the galaxy. But it were more correct to say that both are represented, to Far-Eastern imagination, by groups of stars. An old Japanese book puts the matter thus plainly:

Kengyū [the Ox-Leader] *is on the west side of the Heavenly River, and is represented by three stars in a row, and looks like a man leading an ox. Shokujo* [the Weaving-Lady] *is on the east side of the Heavenly River: three stars so placed as to appear like the figure of a woman seated at her loom. . . . The former presides over all things relating to agriculture; the latter, over all that relates to women's work.*

In an old book called Zatsuwa-Shin, it is said that these deities were of earthly origin. Once in this world they were man and wife, and lived in China; and the husband was called Isshi, and the wife Hakuyō. They especially and most devoutly reverenced the Moon. Every clear evening, after sundown, they waited with eagerness to see her rise. And when she began to sink towards the horizon, they would climb to the top of a hill near their house, so that they might be able to gaze upon her face as long as possible. Then, when she at last disappeared from view, they would mourn together. At the age of ninety and nine, the wife died; and her spirit rode up to heaven on a magpie, and there became a star. The husband, who was then one hundred and three years old, sought consolation for his bereavement in looking at the Moon; and when he welcomed her rising and mourned her setting, it seemed to him as if his wife were still beside him.

One summer night, Hakuyō—now immortally beautiful and young —descended from heaven upon her magpie, to visit her husband; and he was made very happy by that visit. But from that time he could think of nothing but the bliss of becoming a star, and joining Hakuyō beyond the River of Heaven. At last he also ascended to the sky, riding upon a crow; and there he became a star-god. But he could not join Hakuyō at once, as he had hoped;—for between his allotted place and hers flowed the River of Heaven; and it was not permitted for either star to cross the stream, because the Master of Heaven (Ten-Tei) daily bathed in its waters. Moreover, there was no bridge. But on one day every year—the seventh day of the seventh month—they were allowed to see each other. The Master of Heaven goes always on that day to the Zenhōdo, to hear the preaching of the law of Buddha; and then the magpies and the crows make, with their hovering bodies and outspread wings, a bridge over the Celestial Stream; and Hakuyō crosses that bridge to meet her husband.

There can be little doubt that the Japanese festival called Tanabata was originally identical with the festival of the Chinese Weaving-Goddess, Tchi-Niu; the Japanese holiday seems to have been especially a woman's holiday, from the earliest times; and the characters with which the word Tanabata is written signify a weaving-girl. But as both of the star deities were worshiped on the seventh day of the seventh month, some Japanese scholars have not been satisfied with the common explanation of the name, and have stated that it was originally composed with the word *tané* (seed, or grain), and the word *hata,* (loom). Those who accept this etymology make the appellation, Tanabata-Sama, plural instead of singular, and render it as "the deities of grain and of the loom"; that is to say, those presiding over agriculture and weaving. In old Japanese pictures the star-gods are represented according to this conception of their respective attributes;— Hikoboshi being figured as a peasant lad leading an ox to drink of the Heavenly River, on the farther side of which Orihimé (Tanabata) appears, weaving at her loom. The garb of both is Chinese; and the first Japanese pictures of these divinities were probably copied from some Chinese original.

In the oldest collection of Japanese poetry extant—the Manyōshū, dating from 760 A.D.—the male divinity is usually called Hikoboshi, and the female Tanabata-tsumé; but in later times both have been called Tanabata. In Izumo the male deity is popularly termed O-Tanabata Sama, and the female Mé-Tanabata Sama. Both are still known by many names. The male is called Kaiboshi as well as Hikoboshi and Kengyū; while the female is called Asagao-himé (Morning Glory Princess),[1] Ito-ori-himé (Thread-Weaving Princess), Momoko-himé (Peach-Child Princess), Takimono-himé (Incense Princess), and Sasagani-himé (Spider Princess). Some of these names are difficult to explain—especially the last, which reminds us of the Greek legend of Arachne. Probably the Greek myth and the Chinese story have nothing whatever in common; but in old Chinese books there is recorded a curious fact which might well suggest a relationship. In the time of the Chinese Emperor Ming Hwang (whom the Japanese call Gensō), it was customary for the ladies of the court, on the seventh day of the seventh month, to catch spiders and put them into an incense-box for purposes of divination. On the morning of the eighth day the box was opened and if the spiders had spun thick webs during the night the omen was good. But if they had remained idle the omen was bad.

There is a story that, many ages ago, a beautiful woman visited the dwelling of a farmer in the mountains of Izumo, and taught to the only daughter of the household an art of weaving never before known. One evening the beautiful stranger vanished away; and the people knew that they had seen the Weaving-Lady of Heaven. The daughter of the farmer became renowned for her skill in weaving. But she would never marry—because she had been the companion of Tanabata-Sama.

Then there is a Chinese story—delightfully vague—about a man who once made a visit, unawares, to the Heavenly Land. He had observed that every year, during the eighth month, a raft of precious wood came floating to the shore on which he lived, and he wanted to

[1] *Asagao* (literally, "morning-face") is the Japanese name for the beautiful climbing plant which we call "morning glory."

know where that wood grew. So he loaded a boat with provisions for a two years' voyage, and sailed away in the direction from which the rafts used to drift. For months and months he sailed on, over an always placid sea; and at last he arrived at a pleasant shore, where wonderful trees were growing. He moored his boat, and proceeded alone into the unknown land, until he came to the bank of a river whose waters were bright as silver. On the opposite shore he saw a pavilion; and in the pavilion a beautiful woman sat weaving; she was white like moonshine, and made a radiance all about her. Presently he saw a handsome young peasant approaching, leading an ox to the water; and he asked the young peasant to tell him the name of the place and the country. But the youth seemed to be displeased by the question, and answered in a severe tone: "If you want to know the name of this place, go back to where you came from, and ask Gen-Kum-Pei." [2] So the voyager, feeling afraid, hastened to his boat, and returned to China. There he sought out the sage Gen-Kum-Pei, to whom he related the adventure. Gen-Kum-Pei clapped his hands for wonder, and exclaimed, "So it was you! . . . On the seventh day of the seventh month I was gazing at the heavens, and I saw that the Herdsman and the Weaver were about to meet;—but between them was a new Star, which I took to be a Guest-Star. Fortunate man! you have been to the River of Heaven, and have looked upon the face of the Weaving-Lady! . . ."

It is said that the meeting of the Herdsman and the Weaver can be observed by any one with good eyes; for whenever it occurs those stars burn with five different colors. That is why offerings of five colors are made to the Tanabata divinities, and why the poems composed in their praise are written upon paper of five different tints.

But, as I have said before, the pair can meet only in fair weather. If there be the least rain upon the seventh night, the River of Heaven will rise, and the lovers must wait another whole year. Therefore the rain that happens to fall on Tanabata night is called Namida no Amé, "The Rain of Tears."

When the sky is clear on the seventh night, the lovers are fortunate; and their stars can be seen to sparkle with delight. If the star Kengyū then shines very brightly, there will be great rice crops in the autumn. If the star Shokujo looks brighter than usual, there will be a prosperous time for weavers, and for every kind of female industry.

[2] This is the Japanese reading of the Chinese name.

In Old Japan it was generally supposed that the meeting of the pair signified good fortune to mortals. Even to-day, in many parts of the country, children sing a little song on the evening of the Tanabata festival—*Tenki ni nari!* (O weather, be clear!) In the province of Iga the young folks also sing a jesting song at the supposed hour of the lovers' meeting:

> *Tanabata ya!*
> *Amari isogaba,*
> *Korobubéshi!* [3]

But in the province of Izumo, which is a very rainy district, the contrary belief prevails; and it is thought that if the sky be clear on the seventh day of the seventh month, misfortune will follow. The local explanation of this belief is that if the stars can meet, there will be born from their union many evil deities who will afflict the country with drought and other calamities.

The festival of Tanabata was first celebrated in Japan on the seventh day of the seventh month of Tembyō Shōhō (A.D. 755). Perhaps the Chinese origin of the Tanabata divinities accounts for the fact that their public worship was at no time represented by many temples.

I have been able to find record of only one temple to them, called Tanabata-jinja, which was situated at a village called Hoshiai-mura, in the province of Owari, and surrounded by a grove called Tanabata-mori.[4]

Even before Tembyō Shōhō, however, the legend of the Weaving-Maiden seems to have been well known in Japan; for it is recorded that on the seventh night of the seventh year of Yōrō (A.D. 723) the poet Yamagami no Okura composed the song:

> *Amanogawa,*
> *Ai-muki tachité,*
> *Waga koïshi*
> *Kimi kimasu nari—*
> *Himo-toli makina!* [5]

[3] "Ho! Tanabata! if you hurry too much, you will tumble down!"
[4] There is no mention, however, of any such village in any modern directory.
[5] For a translation and explanation of this song, see *infra*, page 491.

It would seem that the Tanabata festival was first established in Japan eleven hundred and fifty years ago, as an Imperial Court festival only, in accordance with Chinese precedent. Subsequently the nobility and the military classes everywhere followed imperial example; and the custom of celebrating the *Hoshi-matsuri,* or Star Festival —as it was popularly called—spread gradually downwards, until at last the seventh day of the seventh month became, in the full sense of the term, a national holiday. But the fashion of its observance varied considerably at different eras and in different provinces.

The ceremonies at the Imperial Court were of the most elaborate character: a full account of them is given in the Kōji Kongen—with explanatory illustrations. On the evening of the seventh day of the seventh month, mattings were laid down on the east side of that portion of the Imperial Palace called the *Seir-yōden;* and upon these mattings were placed four tables of offerings to the Star-deities. Besides the customary food-offerings, there were placed upon these tables ricewine, incense, vases of red lacquer containing flowers, a harp and flute, and a needle with five eyes, threaded with threads of five different colors. Black-lacquered oil-lamps were placed beside the tables, to illuminate the feast. In another part of the grounds a tub of water was so placed as to reflect the light of the Tanabata-stars; and the ladies of the Imperial Household attempted to thread a needle by the reflection. She who succeeded was to be fortunate during the following year.

The court-nobility (*Kugé*) were obliged to make certain offerings to the Imperial House on the day of the festival. The character of these offerings, and the manner of their presentation, were fixed by decree. They were conveyed to the palace upon a tray, by a veiled lady of rank, in ceremonial dress. Above her, as she walked, a great red umbrella was borne by an attendant. On the tray were placed seven *tanzaku* (longilateral slips of fine tinted paper for the writing of poems); seven *kudzu*-leaves;[6] seven inkstones; seven strings of *sōmen* (a kind of vermicelli); fourteen writing-brushes; and a bunch of yam-leaves gathered at night, and thickly sprinkled with dew. In the palace grounds the ceremony began at the Hour of the Tiger—4 A.M. Then the inkstones were carefully washed—prior to preparing the ink for the writing of poems in praise of the Star-deities—and each one set upon a kudzu-leaf. One bunch of bedewed yam-leaves was then laid upon every inkstone; and

[6] *Pueraria Thunbergiana.*

with this dew, instead of water, the writing ink was prepared. All the ceremonies appear to have been copied from those in vogue at the Chinese court in the time of the Emperor Ming-Hwang.

It was not until the time of the Tokugawa Shōgunate that the Tanabata festival became really a national holiday; and the popular custom of attaching tanzaku of different colors to freshly cut bamboos, in celebration of the occasion, dates only from the era of Bunsei (1818). Previously the tanzaku had been made of a very costly quality of paper and the old aristocratic ceremonies had been not less expensive than elaborate. But in the time of the Tokugawa Shōgunate a very cheap paper of various colors was manufactured; and the holiday ceremonies were suffered to assume an inexpensive form, in which even the poorest classes could indulge.

The popular customs relating to the festival differed according to locality. Those of Izumo—where all classes of society, samurai or common folk, celebrated the holiday in much the same way—used to be particularly interesting; and a brief account of them will suggest something of the happy aspects of life in feudal times. At the Hour of the Tiger, on the seventh night of the seventh month, everybody was up; and the work of washing the inkstones and writing-brushes was performed. Then, in the household garden, dew was collected upon yam-leaves. This dew was called *Amanogawa no suzuki* (drops from the River of Heaven); and it was used to make fresh ink for writing the poems which were to be suspended to bamboos planted in the garden. It was usual for friends to present each other with new inkstones at the time of the Tanabata festival; and if there were any new inkstones in the house, the fresh ink was prepared in these. Each member of the family then wrote poems. The adults composed verses, according to their ability, in praise of the Star-deities; and the children either wrote dictation or tried to improvise. Little folk too young to use the writing-brush without help had their small hands guided, by parent or elder sister or elder brother, so as to shape on a tanzaku the character of some single word or phrase relating to the festival—such as *Amanogawa,* or *Tanabata,* or *Kasasagi no Hashi* (the Bridge of Magpies). In the garden were planted two freshly cut bamboos, with branches and leaves entire —a male bamboo (*otoko-daké*) and a female bamboo (*onna-daké*). They were set up about six feet apart, and to a cord extended between them were suspended paper-cuttings of five colors, and skeins of dyed thread of five colors. The paper-cuttings represented upper-robes—kimono. To the leaves and branches of the bamboos were tied the tanzaku on which poems had been written by the members of the family. And upon a table, set between the bamboos, or immediately before them, were placed vessels containing various offerings to the Star-deities—fruits, sōmen, rice-wine, and vegetables of different kinds, such as cucumbers and watermelons.

But the most curious Izumo custom relating to the festival was the *Nému-nagashi*, or "Sleep-wash-away" ceremony. Before daybreak the young folks used to go to some stream, carrying with them bunches composed of *némuri*-leaves and bean-leaves mixed together. On reaching the stream, they would fling their bunches of leaves into the current, and sing a little song:

> *Nému wa, nagaré yo!*
> *Mamé no ha wa, tomaré!*

These verses might be rendered in two ways; because the word *nému* can be taken in the meaning either of *némuri* (sleep), or of *némuri-gi* or *némunoki,* the "sleep-plant" (mimosa),—while the syllables *mamé,* as written in kana, can signify either "bean," or "activity," or "strength," "vigor," "health," etc. But the ceremony was symbolical, and the intended meaning of the song was: "Drowsiness, drift away! Leaves of vigor, remain!" After this, all the young folk would jump into the water, to bathe or swim, in token of their resolve to shed all laziness for the coming year, and to maintain a vigorous spirit of endeavor.

Yet it was probably in Yédo (now Tōkyō) that the Tanabata festival assumed its most picturesque aspects. During the two days that the celebration lasted—the sixth and seventh of the seventh month—the city used to present the appearance of one vast bamboo grove; fresh bamboos, with poems attached to them, being erected upon the roofs of the houses. Peasants were in those days able to do a great business in bamboos, which were brought into town by hundreds of wagonloads for holiday use. Another feature of the Yédo festival was the children's procession, in which bamboos, with poems attached to them, were carried about the city. To each such bamboo there was also fastened a red plaque on which were painted, in Chinese characters, the names of the Tanabata stars.

But almost everywhere, under the Tokugawa régime, the Tanabata festival used to be a merry holiday for the young people of all classes—

a holiday beginning with lantern displays before sunrise, and lasting well into the following night. Boys and girls on that day were dressed in their best, and paid visits of ceremony to friends and neighbors.

The moon of the seventh month used to be called *Tanabata-tsuki,* or "The Moon of Tanabata." And it was also called *Fumi-tsuki,* or "The Literary Moon," because during the seventh month poems were everywhere composed in praise of the Celestial Lovers.

I think that my readers ought to be interested in the following selection of ancient Japanese poems, treating of the Tanabata legend. All are from the "Manyōshū." The "Manyōshū" or "Gathering of a Myriad Leaves," is a vast collection of poems composed before the middle of the eighth century. It was compiled by Imperial order, and completed early in the ninth century. The number of the poems which it contains is upwards of four thousand; some being "long poems" (*naga-uta*), but the great majority *tanka,* or compositions limited to thirty-one syllables; and the authors were courtiers or high officials. The first eleven tanka hereafter translated were composed by Yamagami no Okura, Governor of the province of Chikuzen more than eleven hundred years ago. His fame as a poet is well deserved, for not a little of his work will bear comparison with some of the finer epigrams of the Greek Anthology. The following verses, upon the death of his little son Furubi, will serve as an example:

> *Wakakeréba*
> *Nichi-yuki shiraji:*
> *Mahi wa sému,*
> *Shitabé no tsukahi*
> *Ohité-tohorasé.*

As he is so young, he cannot know the way. . . . To the messenger of the Underworld I will give a bribe, and entreat him, saying: "Do thou kindly take the little one upon thy back along the road."

Eight hundred years earlier, the Greek poet Diodorus Zonas of Sardis had written:

Do thou, who rowest the boat of the dead in the water of this reedy lake, for Hades, stretch out thy hand, dark Charon, to the son of Kiny-

*ras, as he mounts the ladder by the gangway, and receive him. For his
sandals will cause the lad to slip, and he fears to set his feet naked on
the sand of the shore.*

But the charming epigram of Diodorus was inspired only by a myth—
for the "son of Kinyras" was no other than Adonis—whereas the verses
of Okura express for us the yearning of a father's heart.

Though the legend of Tanabata was indeed borrowed from China,
the reader will find nothing Chinese in the following compositions. They
represent the old classic poetry at its purest, free from alien influence;
and they offer us many suggestions as to the condition of Japanese life
and thought twelve hundred years ago. Remembering that they were
written before any modern European literature had yet taken form, one
is startled to find how little the Japanese written language has changed
in the course of so many centuries. Allowing for a few obsolete words,
and sundry slight changes of pronunciation, the ordinary Japanese
reader to-day can enjoy these early productions of his native muse with
about as little difficulty as the English reader finds in studying the poets
of the Elizabethan era. Moreover, the refinement and the simple charm
of the "Manyōshū" compositions have never been surpassed, and seldom
equaled, by later Japanese poets.

As for the forty-odd tanka which I have translated, their chief attraction lies, I think, in what they reveal to us of the human nature of their
authors. Tanabata-tsumé still represents for us the Japanese wife, wor-
shipfully loved;—Hikoboshi appears to us with none of the luminosity
of the god, but as the young Japanese husband of the sixth or seventh
century, before Chinese ethical convention had begun to exercise its restraints upon life and literature. Also these poems interest us by their
expression of the early feeling for natural beauty. In them we find the
scenery and the seasons of Japan transported to the Blue Plain of High
Heaven;—the Celestial Stream with its rapids and shallows, its sudden
risings and clamorings within its stony bed, and its water-grasses bending in the autumn wind, might well be the Kamogawa;—and the mists
that haunt its shores are the very mists of Arashiyama. The boat of
Hikoboshi, impelled by a single oar working upon a wooden peg, is
not yet obsolete; and at many a country ferry you may still see the *hiki-
funé* in which Tanabata-tsumé prayed her husband to cross in a night
of storm—a flat broad barge pulled over the river by cables. And maids
and wives still sit at their doors in country villages, on pleasant autumn

days, to weave as Tanabata-tsumé wove for the sake of her lord and lover.

It will be observed that, in most of these verses, it is not the wife who dutifully crosses the Celestial River to meet her husband, but the husband who rows over the stream to meet the wife; and there is no reference to the Bridge of Birds. . . . As for my renderings, those readers who know by experience the difficulty of translating Japanese verse will be the most indulgent, I fancy. The Romaji system of spelling has been followed (except in one or two cases where I thought it better to indicate the ancient syllabication after the method adopted by Aston); and words or phrases necessarily supplied have been enclosed in parentheses.

> *Amanogawa*
> *Ai-muki tachité,*
> *Waga koïshi*
> *Kimi kimasu nari*
> *Himo-toki makéna!*

He is coming, my long-desired lord, whom I have been waiting to meet here, on the banks of the River of Heaven. . . . The moment of loosening my girdle is nigh! [7]

> *Hisakata no* [8]
> *Ama no kawasé ni,*
> *Funé ukété,*
> *Koyoï ka kimi ga*
> *Agari kimasan?*

Over the Rapids of the Everlasting Heaven, floating in his boat, my lord will doubtless deign to come to me this very night.

[7] The last line alludes to a charming custom of which mention is made in the most ancient Japanese literature. Lovers, ere parting, were wont to tie each other's inner girdle (*himo*) and pledge themselves to leave the knot untouched until the time of their next meeting. This poem is said to have been composed in the seventh year of Yōrō—A.D. 723 —eleven hundred and eighty-two years ago.

[8] *Hisakata-no* is a "pillow-word" used by the old poets in relation to celestial objects; and it is often difficult to translate. Mr. Aston thinks that the literal meaning of *hisakata* is simply "long-hard," in the sense of long-enduring—*hisa* (long), *katai* (hard, or firm); so that hisakata-no would have the meaning of "firmamental." Japanese commentators, however, say that the term is composed with the three words, *hi* (sun), *sasu* (shine), and *kata* (side);—and this etymology would justify the rendering of hisakata-no by some such expression as "light-shedding," "radiance-giving." On the subject of pillow-words, see Aston's *Grammar of the Japanese Written Language.*

Kazé kumo wa
Futatsu no kishi ni
Kayoëdomo,
Waga toho-tsuma no
Koto zo kayowanu!

Though winds and clouds to either bank may freely come or go, between myself and my far-away spouse no message whatever may pass.

Tsubuté [9] *ni mo*
Nagé koshitsu-béki,
Amanogawa
Hédatéréba ka mo,
Amata subé-naki!

To the opposite bank one might easily fling a pebble; yet, being separated from him by the River of Heaven, alas! to hope for a meeting (except in autumn) is utterly useless.

Aki-kazé no
Fukinishi hi yori
"Itsushika" to—;
Waga machi koïshi
Kimi zo kimaséru.

From the day that the autumn wind began to blow (I kept saying to myself), "Ah! when shall we meet?"—but now my beloved, for whom I waited and longed, has come indeed!

Amanogawa
Ito kawa-nami wa
Tatanédomo,
Samorai gatashi—
Chikaki kono sé wo.

Though the waters of the River of Heaven have not greatly risen, (yet to cross) this near stream and to wait upon (my lord and lover) remains impossible.

Sodé furaba
Mi mo kawashitsu-béku

9 The old text has *tabuté.*

Chika-kerédo,
Wataru subé nashi,
Aki nishi aranéba.

Though she is so near that the waving of her (long) sleeves can be distinctly seen, yet there is no way to cross the stream before the season of autumn.

Kagéroï no
Honoka ni miété
Wakarénaba;—
Motonaya koïn
Aü-toki madé wa!

When we were separated, I had seen her for a moment only —and dimly as one sees a flying midge; [10] now I must vainly long for her as before, until time of our next meeting!

Hikoboshi no
Tsuma mukaë-buné
Kogizurashi—
Ama-no-Kawara ni
Kiri no tatéru wa.

Methinks that Hikoboshi must be rowing his boat to meet his wife—for a mist (as of oar-spray) is rising over the course of the Heavenly Stream.

Kasumi tatsu
Ama-no-Kawara ni,
Kimi matsu to—
Ikayō hodo ni
Mono-suso nurenu.

While awaiting my lord on the misty shore of the River of Heaven, the skirts of my robe have somehow become wet.

Amanogawa,
Mi-tsu no nami oto
Sawagu-nari:
Waga matsu-kimi no
Funadé-surashi mo.

On the River of Heaven, at the place of the august ferry,

---

[10] *Kagéroï* is an obsolete form of *kagéro,* meaning an ephemera.

the sound of the water has become loud: perhaps my long-awaited lord will soon be coming in his boat.

> *Tanabata no*
> *Sodé maku yoï no*
> *Akatoki wa,*
> *Kawasé no tazu wa*
> *Nakazu to mo yoshi.*

As Tanabata (slumbers) with her long sleeves rolled up, until the reddening of the dawn, do not, O storks of the river-shallows, awaken her by your cries.[11]

> *Amanogawa*
> *Kiri-tachi-wataru:*
> *Kyō, kyō, to—*
> *Waga matsu-koïshi*
> *Funadé-surashi!*

(She sees that) a mist is spreading across the River of Heaven. . . . "To-day, to-day," she thinks, "my long-awaited lord will probably come over in his boat."

> *Amanogawa,*
> *Yasu no watari ni,*
> *Funé ukété;—*
> *Waga tachi-matsu to*
> *Imo ni tsugé koso.*

By the ferry of Yasu, on the River of Heaven, the boat is floating: I pray you tell my younger sister [12] that I stand here and wait.

> *O-sora yo*
> *Kayō waré sura,*
> *Na ga yué ni,*
> *Amanokawa-ji no*
> *Nazumité zo koshi.*

Though I (being a Star-god) can pass freely to and fro,

[11] Literally, "not to cry out (will be) good"—but a literal translation of the poem is scarcely possible.

[12] That is to say, "wife." In archaic Japanese the word *imo* signified both "wife" and "younger sister." The term might also be rendered "darling" or "beloved."

through the great sky—yet to cross over the River of Heaven, for your sake, was weary work indeed!

> *Yachihoko no*
> *Kami no mi-yo yori*
> *Tomoshi-zuma;—*
> *Hito-shiri ni keri*
> *Tsugitéshi omoëba.*

From the august Age of the God-of-Eight-Thousand-Spears,[13] she had been my spouse in secret [14] only; yet now, because of my constant longing for her, our relation has become known to men.

> *Amé tsuchi to*
> *Wakaréshi toki yo*
> *Onoga tsuma;*
> *Shika zo té ni aru*
> *Aki matsu aré wa.*

From the time when heaven and earth were parted, she has been my own wife;—yet, to be with her, I must always wait till autumn.[15]

> *Waga kōru*
> *Niho no omo wa*
> *Koyoï mo ka*
> *Ama-no-kawara ni*
> *Ishi-makura makan.*

With my beloved, of the ruddy-tinted cheeks,[16] this night indeed will I descend into the bed of the River of Heaven, to sleep on a pillow of stone.

---

[13] Yachihoko-no-Kami, who has many other names, is the Great God of Izumo, and is commonly known by his appellation Oho-kuni-nushi-no-Kami, or the "Deity-Master-of-the-Great-Land." He is locally worshiped also as the god of marriage—for which reason, perhaps, the poet thus refers to him.

[14] Or, "my seldom-visited spouse." The word *tsuma* (*zuma*), in ancient Japanese, signified either wife or husband; and this poem might be rendered so as to express either the wife's or the husband's thoughts.

[15] By the ancient calendar, the seventh day of the seventh month would fall in the autumn season.

[16] The literal meaning is *"béni-tinted face"*—that is to say, a face of which the cheeks and lips have been tinted with *béni,* a kind of rouge.

Amanogawa.
Mikomori-gusa no
Aki-kazé ni
Nabikafu miréba,
Toki kitarurashi.

When I see the water-grasses of the River of Heaven bend in the autumn wind (I think to myself): "The time (for our meeting) seems to have come."

Waga séko ni
Ura-koi oréba,
Amanogawa
Yo-funé kogi-toyomu
Kaji no 'to kikoyu.

When I feel in my heart a sudden longing for my husband,[17] then on the River of Heaven the sound of the rowing of the night-boat is heard, and the plash of the oar resounds.

Tō-zuma to
Tamakura kawashi
Nétaru yo wa,
Tori-gané na naki
Akéba aku to mo!

In the night when I am reposing with my (now) far-away spouse, having exchanged jewel-pillows[18] with her, let not the cock crow, even though the day should dawn.

Yorozu-yo ni
Tazusawari ité
Ai mi-domo,
Omoi-sugu-béki
Koi naranaku ni.

Though for a myriad ages we should remain hand-in-hand and face to face, our exceeding love could never come to an

[17] In ancient Japanese the word *séko* signified either husband or elder brother. The beginning of the poem might also be rendered thus: "When I feel a secret longing for my husband," etc.

[18] "To exchange jewel-pillows" signifies to use each other's arms for pillows. This poetical phrase is often used in the earliest Japanese literature. The word for jewel, *tama*, often appears in compounds as an equivalent of "precious," "dear," etc.

end. (Why then should Heaven deem it necessary to part us?)

Waga tamé to,
Tanabata-tsumé no,
Sono yado ni,
Oréru shirotai
Nuït ken kamo?

The white cloth which Tanabata hath woven for my sake, in that dwelling of hers, is now, I think, being made into a robe for me.

Shirakumo no
I-ho é kakurité
Tō-kédomo,
Yoï-sarazu min
Imo ga atari wa.

Though she be far-away, and hidden from me by five hundred layers of white cloud, still shall I turn my gaze each night toward the dwelling-place of my younger sister (wife).

Aki saréba
Kawagiri tatéru
Amanogawa,
Kawa ni muki-ité
Kru [19] *yo zo ōki!*

When autumn comes, and the river-mists spread over the Heavenly Stream, I turn toward the river, (and long); and the nights of my longing are many!

Hito-tosé ni
Nanuka no yo nomi
Aü-hito no—
Koï mo tsuki-néba
Sayo zo aké ni keru!

But once in the whole year, and only upon the seventh night (of the seventh month), to meet the beloved person— and lo! The day has dawned before our mutual love could express itself! [20]

---

[19] For *kofuru.*
[20] Or "satisfy itself." A literal rendering is difficult.

Toshi no koï
Koyoï tsukushíté,
Asu yori wa,
Tsuné no gotoku ya
Waga koï oran.

The love-longing of one whole year having ended to-night,
every day from to-morrow I must again pine for him as before!

Hikoboshi to
Tanabata-tsumé to
Koyoï aü;—
Ama-no-Kawa to ni
Nami tatsu-na yumé!

Hikoboshi and Tanabata-tsumé are to meet each other to-
night;—ye waves of the River of Heaven, take heed that ye
do not rise!

Aki-kazé no
Fuki tadayowasu
Shirakumo wa,
Tanabata-tsumé no
Amatsu hiré kamo?

Oh! that white cloud driven by the autumn-wind—can it
be the heavenly hiré [21] of Tanabata-tsumé?

Shiba-shiba mo
Ai minu kimi wo,
Amanogawa
Funa-dé haya séyo
Yo no fukénu ma ni.

Because he is my not-often-to-be-met beloved, hasten to row
the boat across the River of Heaven ere the night be advanced.

---

[21] At different times, in the history of Japanese female costume, different articles of
dress were called by this name. In the present instance, the *hiré* referred to was probably
a white scarf, worn about the neck and carried over the shoulders to the breast, where
its ends were either allowed to hang loose, or were tied into an ornamental knot. The
hiré was often used to make signals with, much as handkerchiefs are waved today for
the same purpose;—and the question uttered in the poem seems to signify: "Can that
be Tanabata waving her scarf—to call me?" In very early times, the ordinary costumes
worn were white.

Amanogawa
Kiri tachi-watari
Hikoboshi no
Kaji no 'to kikoyu
Yo no fuké-yukéba.

Late in the night, a mist spreads over the River of Heaven;
and the sound of the oar [22] of Hikoboshi is heard.

Amanogawa
Kawa 'to sayakéshi:
Hikoboshi no
Haya kogu funé no
Nami no sawagi ka?

On the River of Heaven a sound of plashing can be distinctly heard: is it the sound of the rippling made by Hikoboshi quickly rowing his boat?

Kono yūbé,
Furikuru amé wa,
Hikoboshi no
Haya kogu funé no
Kaï no chiri ka mo.

Perhaps this evening shower is but the spray (flung down)
from the oar of Hikoboshi, rowing his boat in haste.

Asu yori wa
Waga tama-doko wo
Uchi haraï,
Kimi to inézuté
Hitori ka mo nen!

From to-morrow, alas! after having put my jewel-bed in
order, no longer reposing with my lord, I must sleep alone!

Kazé fukité,
Kawa-nami tachinu;—

---

[22] Or, "the creaking of the oar." (The word *kaji* to-day means "helm";—the single
oar, or scull, working upon a pivot, and serving at once for rudder and oar, being now
called *ro*.) The mist passing across the Amanogawa is, according to commentators, the
spray from the Star-god's oar.

Hiki-funé ni
Watari mo kimasé
Yo no fukénu ma ni.

The wind having risen, the waves of the river have become
high;—this night cross over in a towboat,[23] I pray thee, before
the hour be late!

Amanogawa
Nami wa tatsutomo,
Waga funé wa
Iza kogi iden
Yo no fukénu ma ni.

Even though the waves of the River of Heaven run high, I
must row over quickly, before it becomes late in the night.

Inishié ni
Oritéshi hata wo;
Kono yūbé
Koromo ni nuïté—
Kimi matsu aré wo!

Long ago I finished weaving the material; and, this evening, having finished sewing the garment for him—(why
must) I still wait for my lord?

Amanogawa
Sé wo hayami ka mo?
Nubatama no [24]
Yo wa fuké ni tsutsu,
Awanu Hikoboshi!

Is it that the current of the River of Heaven (has become
too) rapid? The jet-black night advances—and Hikoboshi has
not come!

---

[23] Literally, "pull-boat" (*hiki-funé*)—a barge or boat pulled by a rope.

[24] *Nubatama no yo* might better be rendered by some such phrase as "the berry-black
night"—but the intended effect would be thus lost in translation. *Nubatama-no* (a
"pillow-word") is written with characters signifying "like the black fruits of Karasu-
Ōgi"; and the ancient phrase "nubatama no yo" therefore may be said to have the same
meaning as our expressions "jet-black night," or "pitch-dark night."

Watashi-mori,
Funé haya watasé;—
Hito-tosé ni
Futatabi kayō
Kimi naranaku ni!

Oh, ferryman, make speed across the stream!—my lord is not one who can come and go twice in a year!

Aki kazé no
Fukinishi hi yori,
Amanogawa
Kawasé ni dédachi;—
Matsu to tsugé koso!

On the very day that the autumn-wind began to blow, I set out for the shallows of the River of Heaven;—I pray you, tell my lord that I am waiting here still!

Tanabata no
Funanori surashi,—
Maso-kagami,
Kiyoki tsuki-yo ni
Kumo tachi-wataru.

Methinks Tanabata must be coming in her boat; for a cloud is even now passing across the clear face of the moon.[25]

And yet it has been gravely asserted that the old Japanese poets could find no beauty in starry skies! . . .

Perhaps the legend of Tanabata, as it was understood by those old poets, can make but a faint appeal to Western minds. Nevertheless, in the silence of transparent nights, before the rising of the moon, the charm of the ancient tale sometimes descends upon me, out of the scintillant sky—to make me forget the monstrous facts of science, and the stupendous horror of Space. Then I no longer behold the Milky Way as that awful Ring of the Cosmos, whose hundred million suns are powerless to lighten the Abyss, but as the very Amanogawa itself—the River

[25] Composed by the famous poet Ōtomo no Sukuné Yakamochi, while gazing at the Milky Way, on the seventh night of the seventh month of the tenth year of Tampyo (A.D. 738). The pillow-word in the third line (*maso-kagami*) is untranslatable.

Celestial. I see the thrill of its shining stream, and the mists that hover along its verge, and the water-grasses that bend in the winds of autumn. White Orihimé I see at her starry loom, and the Ox that grazes on the farther shore;—and I know that the falling dew is the spray from the Herdsman's oar. And the heaven seems very near and warm and human; and the silence about me is filled with the dream of a love unchanging, immortal—forever yearning and forever young, and forever left unsatisfied by the paternal wisdom of the gods.

ESSAYS

─────────────── ❧ ✳ ❧ ───────────────

Of the Eternal Feminine

For metaphors of man we search the skies,
And find our allegory in all the air;—
We gaze on Nature with Narcissus-eyes,
Enamoured of our shadow everywhere.

WATSON

I

WHAT EVERY INTELLIGENT FOREIGNER DWELLING IN JAPAN MUST SOONER OR
later perceive is, that the more the Japanese learn of our æsthetics and
of our emotional character generally, the less favorably do they seem

to be impressed thereby. The European or American who tries to talk to them about Western art, or literature, or metaphysics will feel for their sympathy in vain. He will be listened to politely; but his utmost eloquence will scarcely elicit more than a few surprising comments, totally unlike what he hoped and expected to evoke. Many successive disappointments of this sort impel him to judge his Oriental auditors very much as he would judge Western auditors behaving in a similar way. Obvious indifference to what we imagine the highest expression possible of art and thought, we are led by our own Occidental experiences to take for proof of mental incapacity. So we find one class of foreign observers calling the Japanese a race of children; while another, including a majority of those who have passed many years in the country, judge the nation essentially materialistic, despite the evidence of its religions, its literature, and its matchless art. I cannot persuade myself that either of these judgments is less fatuous than Goldsmith's observation to Johnson about the Literary Club: "There can now be nothing new among us; we have traveled over one another's minds." A cultured Japanese might well answer with Johnson's famous retort: "Sir, you have not yet traveled over *my* mind, I promise you!" And all such sweeping criticisms seem to me due to a very imperfect recognition of the fact that Japanese thought and sentiment have been evolved out of ancestral habits, customs, ethics, beliefs, directly the opposite of our own in some cases, and in all cases strangely different. Acting on such psychological material, modern scientific education cannot but accentuate and develop race differences. Only half-education can tempt the Japanese to servile imitation of Western ways. The real mental and moral power of the race, its highest intellect, strongly resists Western influence; and those more competent than I to pronounce upon such matters assure me that this is especially observable in the case of superior men who have traveled or been educated in Europe. Indeed, the results of the new culture have served more than aught else to show the immense force of healthy conservatism in that race superficially characterized by Rein as a race of children. Even very imperfectly understood, the causes of this Japanese attitude to a certain class of Western ideas might well incite us to reconsider our own estimate of those ideas, rather than to tax the Oriental mind with incapacity. Now, of the causes in question, which are multitudinous, some can only be vaguely guessed at. But there is at least one—a very important one—which we may safely study, because a recognition of it is forced upon any one who passes a few years in the Far East.

II

"TEACHER, PLEASE TELL US WHY THERE IS SO MUCH ABOUT LOVE AND marrying in English novels; it seems to us very, very strange."

This question was put to me while I was trying to explain to my literature class—young men from nineteen to twenty-three years of age —why they had failed to understand certain chapters of a standard novel, though quite well able to understand the logic of Jevons and the psychology of James. Under the circumstances, it was not an easy question to answer; in fact, I could not have replied to it in any satisfactory way had I not already lived for several years in Japan. As it was, though I endeavored to be concise as well as lucid, my explanation occupied something more than two hours.

There are few of our society novels that a Japanese student can really comprehend; and the reason is, simply, that English society is something of which he is quite unable to form a correct idea. Indeed, not only English society, in a special sense, but even Western life, in a general sense, is a mystery to him. Any social system of which filial piety is not the moral cement; any social system in which children leave their parents in order to establish families of their own; any social system in which it is considered not only natural but right to love wife and child more than the authors of one's being; any social system in which marriage can be decided independently of the will of parents, by the mutual inclination of the young people themselves; any social system in which the mother-in-law is not entitled to the obedient service of the daughter-in-law, appears to him of necessity a state of life scarcely better than that of the birds of the air and the beasts of the field, or at best a sort of moral chaos. And all this existence, as reflected in our popular fiction, presents him with provoking enigmas. Our ideas about love and our solicitude about marriage furnish some of these enigmas. To the young Japanese, marriage appears a simple, natural duty, for the due performance of which his parents will make all necessary arrangements at the proper time. That foreigners should have so much trouble about getting married is puzzling enough to him; but that distinguished authors should write novels and poems about such matters, and that those novels and poems should be vastly admired, puzzles him infinitely more—seems to him "very, *very* strange."

My young questioner said "strange" for politeness' sake. His real thought would have been more accurately rendered by the word "indecent." But when I say that to the Japanese mind our typical novel appears indecent, highly indecent, the idea thereby suggested to my English readers will probably be misleading. The Japanese are not morbidly prudish. Our society novels do not strike them as indecent because the theme is love. The Japanese have a great deal of literature about love. No; our novels seem to them indecent for somewhat the same reason that the Scripture text, "For this cause shall a man leave his father and mother, and shall cleave unto his wife," appears to them one of the most immoral sentences ever written. In other words, their criticism requires a sociological explanation. To explain fully why our novels are, to their thinking, indecent, I should have to describe the whole structure, customs, and ethics of the Japanese family, totally different from anything in Western life; and to do this even in a superficial way would require a volume. I cannot attempt a complete explanation; I can only cite some facts of a suggestive character.

To begin with, then, I may broadly state that a great deal of our literature, besides its fiction, is revolting to the Japanese moral sense, not because it treats of the passion of love *per se,* but because it treats of that passion in relation to virtuous maidens, and therefore in relation to the family circle. Now, as a general rule, where passionate love is the theme in Japanese literature of the best class, it is not that sort of love which leads to the establishment of family relations. It is quite another sort of love—a sort of love about which the Oriental is not prudish at all—the *mayoi,* or infatuation of passion, inspired by merely physical attraction; and its heroines are not the daughters of refined families, but mostly hetæræ, or professional dancing-girls. Neither does this Oriental variety of literature deal with its subject after the fashion of sensuous literature in the West—French literature, for example: it considers it from a different artistic standpoint, and describes rather a different order of emotional sensations.

A national literature is of necessity reflective; and we may presume that what it fails to portray can have little or no outward manifestation in the national life. Now, the reserve of Japanese literature regarding that love which is the great theme of our greatest novelists and poets is exactly paralleled by the reserve of Japanese society in regard to the same topic. The typical woman often figures in Japanese romance as a heroine; as a perfect mother; as a pious daughter, willing to sacrifice all for duty; as a loyal wife, who follows her husband into battle, fights by his side, saves his life at the cost of her own; never as a sentimental maiden, dying, or making others die, for love. Neither do we find her on literary exhibition as a dangerous beauty, a charmer of men; and in the real life of Japan she has never appeared in any such rôle. Society, as a mingling of the sexes, as an existence of which the supremely refined charm is the charm of woman, has never existed in the East. Even in Japan, society, in the special sense of the word, remains masculine. Nor is it easy to believe that the adoption of European fashions and customs within some restricted circles of the capital indicates the beginning of such a social change as might eventually remodel the national life according to Western ideas of society. For such a remodeling would involve the dissolution of the family, the disintegration of the whole social fabric, the destruction of the whole ethical system—the breaking-up, in short, of the national life.

Taking the word "woman" in its most refined meaning, and postulating a society in which woman seldom appears, a society in which she is never placed "on display," a society in which wooing is utterly out of the question, and the faintest compliment to wife or daughter is an outrageous impertinence, the reader can at once reach some startling conclusions as to the impression made by our popular fiction upon members of that society. But, although partly correct, his conclusions must fall short of the truth in certain directions, unless he also possess some knowledge of the restraints of that society and of the ethical notions behind the restraints. For example, a refined Japanese never speaks to you about his wife (I am stating the general rule), and very seldom indeed about his children, however proud of them he may be. Rarely will he be heard to speak about any of the members of his family, about his domestic life, about any of his private affairs. But if he should happen to talk about members of his family, the persons mentioned will almost certainly be his parents. Of them he will speak with a reverence approaching religious feeling, yet in a manner quite different from that which would be natural to an Occidental, and never so as to imply any mental comparison between the merits of his own parents and those of other men's parents. But he will not talk about his wife even to the friends who were invited as guests to his wedding. And I think I may safely say that the poorest and most ignorant Japanese, however dire his need, would never dream of trying to obtain aid or to invoke pity by the mention of his wife—perhaps not even of his wife and children. But he would not hesitate to ask help for the sake of his parents or his grandparents. Love of wife and child, the strongest of all sentiments with the Occidental, is judged by the Oriental to be a selfish affection. He professes to be ruled by a higher sentiment—duty: duty, first, to his Emperor; next, to his parents. And since love can be classed only as an ego-altruistic feeling, the Japanese thinker is not wrong in his refusal to consider it the loftiest of motives, however refined or spiritualized it may be.

In the existence of the poorer classes of Japan there are no secrets; but among the upper classes family life is much less open to observation than in any country of the West, not excepting Spain. It is a life of which foreigners see little, and know almost nothing, all the essays which have been written about Japanese women to the contrary notwithstanding.[1] Invited to the home of a Japanese friend, you may or may not see the family. It will depend upon circumstances. If you see any of them, it will probably be for a moment only, and in that event you will most likely see the wife. At the entrance you give your card to the servant, who retires to present it, and presently returns to usher you into the *zashiki,* or guest-room, always the largest and finest apartment in a Japanese dwelling, where your kneeling-cushion is ready for you, with a smoking-box before it. The servant brings you tea and cakes. In a little time the host himself enters, and after the indispensable salutations conversation begins. Should you be pressed to stay for dinner, and accept the invitation, it is probable that the wife will do you the honor, as her husband's friend, to wait upon you during an instant. You may or may not be formally introduced to her; but a glance at her dress and coiffure should be sufficient to inform you at once who she is, and you must greet her with the most profound respect. She will probably impress you (especially if your visit be to a samurai home) as a delicately refined and very serious person, by no means a woman of the much-smiling and much-bowing kind. She will say extremely little, but will salute you, and will serve you for a moment with a natural grace of which the mere spectacle is a revelation, and glide away again, to remain invisible until the instant of your departure, when she will reappear at the entrance to wish you good-bye. During other successive visits you may have similar charming glimpses of her; perhaps, also some rarer glimpses of the aged father and mother; and if a much favored visitor, the children may at last come to greet you, with wonderful politeness and sweetness. But the innermost intimate life of that family will never be revealed to you. All that

[1] I do not, however, refer to those extraordinary persons who make their short residence in teahouses and establishments of a much worse kind, and then go home to write books about the women of Japan.

you see to suggest it will be refined, courteous, exquisite, but of the relation of those souls to each other you will know nothing. Behind the beautiful screens which mask the further interior, all is silent, gentle mystery. There is no reason, to the Japanese mind, why it should be otherwise. Such family life is sacred; the home is a sanctuary, of which it were impious to draw aside the veil. Nor can I think this idea of the sacredness of home and of the family relation in any wise inferior to our highest conception of the home and the family in the West.

Should there be grown-up daughters in the family, however, the visitor is less likely to see the wife. More timid, but equally silent and reserved, the young girls will make the guest welcome. In obedience to orders, they may even gratify him by a performance upon some musical instrument, by exhibiting some of their own needlework or painting, or by showing to him some precious or curious objects among the family heirlooms. But all submissive sweetness and courtesy are inseparable from the high-bred reserve belonging to the finest native culture. And the guest must not allow himself to be less reserved. Unless possessing the privilege of great age, which would entitle him to paternal freedom of speech, he must never venture upon personal compliment, or indulge in anything resembling light flattery. What would be deemed gallantry in the West may be gross rudeness in the East. On no account can the visitor compliment a young girl about her looks, her grace, her toilette, much less dare address such a compliment to the wife. But, the reader may object, there are certainly occasions upon which a compliment of some character cannot be avoided. This is true, and on such an occasion politeness requires, as a preliminary, the humblest apology for making the compliment, which will then be accepted with a phrase more graceful than our "Pray do not mention it"; that is, the rudeness of making a compliment at all.

But here we touch the vast subject of Japanese etiquette, about which I must confess myself still profoundly ignorant. I have ventured thus much only in order to suggest how lacking in refinement much of our Western society fiction must appear to the Oriental mind.

To speak of one's affection for wife or children, to bring into conversation anything closely related to domestic life, is totally incompatible with Japanese ideas of good breeding. Our open acknowledgment, or rather exhibition, of the domestic relation consequently appears to cultivated Japanese, if not absolutely barbarous, at least uxorious. And this sentiment may be found to explain not a little in

Japanese life which has given foreigners a totally incorrect idea about the position of Japanese women. It is not the custom in Japan for the husband even to walk side by side with his wife in the street, much less to give her his arm, or to assist her in ascending or descending a flight of stairs. But this is not any proof upon his part of want of affection. It is only the result of a social sentiment totally different from our own; it is simply obedience to an etiquette founded upon the idea that public displays of the marital relation are improper. Why improper? Because they seem to Oriental judgment to indicate a confession of personal, and therefore selfish sentiment. For the Oriental the law of life is duty. Affection must, in every time and place, be subordinated to duty. Any public exhibition of personal affection of a certain class is equivalent to a public confession of moral weakness. Does this mean that to love one's wife is a moral weakness? No; it is the duty of a man to love his wife; but it is moral weakness to love her more than his parents, or to show her, in public, more attention than he shows to his parents. Nay, it would be a proof of moral weakness to show her even the *same* degree of attention. During the lifetime of the parents her position in the household is simply that of an adopted daughter, and the most affectionate of husbands must not even for a moment allow himself to forget the etiquette of the family.

Here I must touch upon one feature of Western literature never to be reconciled with Japanese ideas and customs. Let the reader reflect for a moment how large a place the subject of kisses and caresses and embraces occupies in our poetry and in our prose fiction; and then let him consider the fact that in Japanese literature these have *no existence whatever*. For kisses and embraces are simply unknown in Japan as tokens of affection, if we except the solitary fact that Japanese mothers, like mothers all over the world, lip and hug their little ones betimes. After babyhood there is no more hugging or kissing. Such actions, except in the case of infants, are held to be highly immodest. Never do girls kiss one another; never do parents kiss or embrace their children who have become able to walk. And this rule holds good of all classes of society, from the highest nobility to the humblest peasantry. Neither have we the least indication throughout Japanese literature of any time in the history of the race when affection was more demonstrative than it is to-day. Perhaps the Western reader will find it hard even to imagine a literature in the whole course of which no mention is made of kissing, of embracing, even of pressing a loved hand; for hand-clasping is an action as totally foreign to Japanese im-

pulse as kissing. Yet on these topics even the naïve songs of the coun·
try folk, even the old ballads of the people about unhappy lovers, are
quite as silent as the exquisite verses of the court poets. Suppose we
take for an example the ancient popular ballad of Shuntokumaru,
which has given origin to various proverbs and household words familiar throughout western Japan. Here we have the story of two betrothed lovers, long separated by a cruel misfortune, wandering in
search of each other all over the Empire, and at last suddenly meeting
before Kiomidzu Temple by the favor of the gods. Would not any
Aryan poet describe such a meeting as a rushing of the two into each
other's arms, with kisses and cries of love? But how does the old Japanese ballad describe it? In brief, the twain only sit down together *and
stroke each other a little.* Now, even this reserved form of caress is an
extremely rare indulgence of emotion. You may see again and again
fathers and sons, husbands and wives, mothers and daughters, meeting
after years of absence, yet you will probably never see the least approach to a caress between them. They will kneel down and salute
each other, and smile, and perhaps cry a little for joy; but they will
neither rush into each other's arms, nor utter extraordinary phrases of
affection. Indeed, such terms of affection as "my dear," "my darling,"
"my sweet," "my love," "my life," do not exist in Japanese, nor any
terms at all equivalent to our emotional idioms. Japanese affection is
not uttered in words; it scarcely appears even in the tone of voice: it is
chiefly shown in acts of exquisite courtesy and kindness. I might add
that the opposite emotion is under equally perfect control; but to illustrate this remarkable fact would require a separate essay.

III

HE WHO WOULD STUDY IMPARTIALLY THE LIFE AND THOUGHT OF THE
Orient must also study those of the Occident from the Oriental point of
view. And the results of such a comparative study he will find to be in
no small degree retroactive. According to his character and his faculty
of perception, he will be more or less affected by those Oriental influences to which he submits himself. The conditions of Western life will
gradually begin to assume for him new, undreamed-of meanings, and
to lose not a few of their old familiar aspects. Much that he once
deemed right and true he may begin to find abnormal and false. He
may begin to doubt whether the moral ideals of the West are really the

highest. He may feel more than inclined to dispute the estimate placed by Western custom upon Western civilization. Whether his doubts be final is another matter: they will be at least rational enough and powerful enough to modify permanently some of his prior convictions—among others his conviction of the moral value of the Western worship of Woman as the Unattainable, the Incomprehensible, the Divine, the ideal of *"la femme que tu ne connaîtras pas,"* [2]—the ideal of the Eternal Feminine. For in this ancient East the Eternal Feminine does not exist at all. And after having become quite accustomed to live without it, one may naturally conclude that it is not absolutely essential to intellectual health, and may even dare to question the necessity for its perpetual existence upon the other side of the world.

IV

TO SAY THAT THE ETERNAL FEMININE DOES NOT EXIST IN THE FAR EAST IS to state but a part of the truth. That it could be introduced thereinto, in the remotest future, is not possible to imagine. Few, if any, of our ideas regarding it can even be rendered into the language of the country: a language in which nouns have no gender, adjectives no degrees of comparison, and verbs no persons; a language in which, says Professor Chamberlain, the absence of personification is "a characteristic so deep-seated and so all-pervading as to interfere even with the use of neuter nouns in combination with transitive verbs." "In fact," he adds "most metaphors and allegories are incapable of so much as explanation to Far-Eastern minds"; and he makes a striking citation from Wordsworth in illustration of his statement. Yet even poets much more lucid than Wordsworth are to the Japanese equally obscure. I remember the difficulty I once had in explaining to an advanced class this simple line from the well-known ballad of Tennyson—

She is more beautiful than day.

My students could understand the use of the adjective "beautiful" to qualify "day," and the use of the same adjective, separately, to qualify the word "maid." But that there could exist in any mortal mind the least idea of analogy between the beauty of day and the beauty of a

[2] A phrase from Baudelaire.

young woman was quite beyond their understanding. In order to convey to them the poet's thought, it was necessary to analyze it psychologically—to prove a possible nervous analogy between two modes of pleasurable feeling excited by two different impressions.

Thus, the very nature of the language tells us how ancient and how deeply rooted in racial character are those tendencies by which we must endeavor to account—if there be any need of accounting at all—for the absence in this Far East of a dominant ideal corresponding to our own. They are causes incomparably older than the existing social structure, older than the idea of the family, older than ancestor worship, enormously older than that Confucian code which is the reflection rather than the explanation of many singular facts in Oriental life. But since beliefs and practices react upon character, and character again must react upon practices and beliefs, it has not been altogether irrational to seek in Confucianism for causes as well as for explanations. Far more irrational have been the charges of hasty critics against Shintō and against Buddhism as religious influences opposed to the natural rights of woman. The ancient faith of Shintō has been at least as gentle to woman as the ancient faith of the Hebrews. Its female divinities are not less numerous than its masculine divinities, nor are they presented to the imagination of worshipers in a form much less attractive than the dreams of Greek mythology. Of some, like Sotohori-no-Iratsumé, it is said that the light of their beautiful bodies passes through their garments; and the source of all life and light, the eternal Sun, is a goddess, fair Ama-terasu-oho-mi-kami. Virgins serve the ancient gods, and figure in all the pageants of the faith; and in a thousand shrines throughout the land the memory of woman as wife and mother is worshiped equally with the memory of man as hero and father. Neither can the later and alien faith of Buddhism be justly accused of relegating woman to a lower place in the spiritual world than monkish Christianity accorded her in the West. The Buddha, like the Christ, was born of a virgin; the most lovable divinities of Buddhism, Jizō excepted, are feminine, both in Japanese art and in Japanese popular fancy; and in the Buddhist as in the Roman Catholic hagiography, the lives of holy women hold honored place. It is true that Buddhism, like early Christianity, used its utmost eloquence in preaching against the temptation of female loveliness; and it is true that in the teaching of its founder, as in the teaching of Paul, social and spiritual supremacy is accorded to the man. Yet, in our search for texts on this topic, we must not overlook the host of instances of favor shown by the Buddha to women of all classes, nor that remarkable legend of a later text, in which a dogma denying to woman the highest spiritual opportunities is sublimely rebuked.

In the eleventh chapter of the Sutra of the Lotus of the Good Law, it is written that mention was made before the Lord Buddha of a young girl who had in one instant arrived at supreme knowledge; who had in one moment acquired the merits of a thousand meditations, and the proofs of the essence of all laws. And the girl came and stood in the presence of the Lord.

But the Bodhissattva Pragnakuta doubted, saying, "I have seen the Lord Sakyamuni in the time when he was striving for supreme enlightenment, and I know that he performed good works innumerable through countless æons. In all the world there is not one spot so large as a grain of mustard-seed where he had not surrendered his body for the sake of living creatures. Only after all this did he arrive at enlightenment. Who then may believe this girl could in one moment have arrived at supreme knowledge?"

And the venerable priest Sariputra likewise doubted, saying, "It may indeed happen, O Sister, that a woman fulfill the six perfect virtues; but as yet there is no example of her having attained to Buddhaship, because a woman cannot attain to the rank of Bodhissattva."

But the maiden called upon the Lord Buddha to be her witness. And instantly in the sight of the assembly her sex disappeared; and she manifested herself as a Bodhissattva, filling all directions of space with the radiance of the thirty-two signs. And the world shook in six different ways. And the priest Sariputra was silent.

V

BUT TO FEEL THE REAL NATURE OF WHAT IS SURELY ONE OF THE GREATEST obstacles to intellectual sympathy between the West and the Far East, we must fully appreciate the immense effect upon Occidental life of this ideal which has no existence in the Orient. We must remember what that ideal has been to Western civilization—to all its pleasures and refinements and luxuries; to its sculpture, painting, decoration, architecture, literature, drama, music; to the development of countless industries. We must think of its effect upon manners, customs, and the language of taste, upon conduct and ethics, upon endeavor, upon philosophy and religion, upon almost every phase of public and private life—in short, upon national character. Nor should we forget that the many influences interfused in the shaping of it—Teutonic, Celtic, Scandinavian, classic, or mediæval, the Greek apotheosis of human beauty, the Christian worship of the mother of God, the exaltations of chivalry, the spirit of the Renascence steeping and coloring all the pre-existing idealism in a new sensuousness—must have had their nourishment, if not their birth, in a race feeling ancient as Aryan speech, and as alien to the most eastern East.

Of all these various influences combined to form our ideal, the classic element remains perceptibly dominant. It is true that the Hellenic conception of human beauty, so surviving, has been wondrously informed with a conception of soul beauty never of the antique world nor of the Renascence. Also it is true that the new philosophy of evolution, forcing recognition of the incalculable and awful cost of the Present to the Past, creating a totally new comprehension of duty to the Future, enormously enhancing our conception of character values, has aided more than all preceding influences together toward the highest possible spiritualization of the ideal of woman. Yet, however further spiritualized it may become through future intellectual expansion, this ideal must in its very nature remain fundamentally artistic and sensuous.

We do not see Nature as the Oriental sees it, and as his art proves that he sees it. We see it less realistically, we know it less intimately, because, save through the lenses of the specialist, we contemplate it anthropomorphically. In one direction, indeed, our æsthetic sense has been cultivated to a degree incomparably finer than that of the Oriental; but that direction has been passional. We have learned something of the beauty of Nature through our ancient worship of the beauty of woman. Even from the beginning it is probable that the perception of human beauty has been the main source of all our æsthetic sensibility. Possibly we owe to it likewise our idea of proportion; [3] our exaggerated appreciation of regularity; our fondness for parallels, curves, and all geometrical symmetries. And in the long process of our æsthetic evolution, the ideal of woman has at last become for us an æsthetic abstraction. Through the illusion of that abstraction only do we perceive the charms of our world, even as forms might be perceived through some tropic atmosphere whose vapors are iridescent.

Nor is this all. Whatsoever has once been likened to woman by art

[3] On the origin of the idea of bilateral symmetry, see Herbert Spencer's essay, "The Sources of Architectural Types."

or thought has been strangely informed and transformed by that momentary symbolism: wherefore, through all the centuries Western fancy has been making Nature more and more feminine. Whatsoever delights us imagination has feminized—the infinite tenderness of the sky, the mobility of waters, the rose of dawn, the vast caress of Day, Night, and the lights of heaven—even the undulations of the eternal hills. And flowers, and the flush of fruit, and all things fragrant, fair, and gracious; the genial seasons with their voices; the laughter of streams, and whisper of leaves, and ripplings of song within the shadows; all sights, or sounds, or sensations that can touch our love of loveliness, of delicacy, of sweetness, of gentleness, make for us vague dreams of woman. Where our fancy lends masculinity to Nature, it is only in grimness and in force—as if to enhance by rugged and mighty contrasts the witchcraft of the Eternal Feminine. Nay, even the terrible itself if fraught with terrible beauty—even Destruction if only shaped with the grace of destroyers—becomes for us feminine. And not beauty alone, of sight or sound, but well-nigh all that is mystic, sublime, or holy, now makes appeal to us through some marvelously woven intricate plexus of passional sensibility. Even the subtlest forces of our universe speak to us of woman; new sciences have taught us new names for the thrill her presence wakens in the blood, for that ghostly shock which is first love, for the eternal riddle of her fascination.

Thus, out of simple human passion, through influences and transformations innumerable, we have evolved a cosmic emotion, a feminine pantheism.

VI

AND NOW MAY NOT ONE VENTURE TO ASK WHETHER ALL THE CONSEquences of this passional influence in the æsthetic evolution of our Occident have been in the main beneficial? Underlying all those visible results of which we boast as art triumphs, may there not be lurking invisible results, some future revelation of which will cause more than a little shock to our self-esteem? Is it not quite possible that our æsthetic faculties have been developed even abnormally in one direction by the power of a single emotional idea which has left us nearly, if not totally blind to many wonderful aspects of Nature? Or rather, must not this be the inevitable effect of the extreme predominance of one particular emotion in the evolution of our æsthetic sensibility? And finally, one may surely be permitted to ask if the predominating influence itself has been the highest possible, and whether there is not a higher, known perhaps to the Oriental soul.

I may only suggest these questions, without hoping to answer them satisfactorily. But the longer I dwell in the East, the more I feel growing upon me the belief that there are exquisite artistic faculties and perceptions, developed in the Oriental, of which we can know scarcely more than we know of those unimaginable colors, invisible to the human eye, yet proven to exist by the spectroscope. I think that such a possibility is indicated by certain phases of Japanese art.

Here it becomes as difficult as dangerous to particularize. I dare hazard only some general observations. I think this marvelous art asserts that, out of the infinitely varied aspects of Nature, those which for us hold no suggestion whatever of sex character, those which cannot be looked at anthropomorphically, those which are neither masculine nor feminine, but neuter or nameless, are those most profoundly loved and comprehended by the Japanese. Nay, he sees in Nature much that for thousands of years has remained invisible to us; and we are now learning from him aspects of life and beauties of form to which we were utterly blind before. We have finally made the startling discovery that his art—notwithstanding all the dogmatic assertions of Western prejudice to the contrary, and notwithstanding the strangely weird impression of unreality which at first it produced—is never a mere creation of fantasy, but a veritable reflection of what has been and of what is: wherefore we have recognized that it is nothing less than a higher education in art simply to look at his studies of bird life, insect life, plant life, tree life. Compare, for example, our very finest drawings of insects with Japanese drawings of similar subjects. Compare Giacomelli's illustrations to Michelet's "L'Insecte" with the commonest Japanese figures of the same creatures decorating the stamped leather of a cheap tobacco pouch or the metal work of a cheap pipe. The whole minute exquisiteness of the European engraving has accomplished only an indifferent realism, while the Japanese artist, with a few dashes of his brush, has seized and reproduced, with an incomprehensible power of interpretation, not only every peculiarity of the creature's shape, but every special characteristic of its motion. Each figure flung from the Oriental painter's brush is a lesson, a revelation, to perceptions unbeclouded by prejudice, an opening of the eyes of those who can see, though it be only a spider in a wind-shaken web, a dragon-fly riding a sunbeam, a pair of crabs running through sedge, the trembling of a fish's fins in a clear current, the lilt of a flying wasp, the pitch of a flying duck, a mantis in fighting position, or a semi toddling up a cedar branch to sing. All this art is alive, intensely alive, and our corresponding art looks absolutely dead beside it.

Take, again, the subject of flowers. An English or German flower painting, the result of months of trained labor, and valued at several hundred pounds, would certainly not compare as a nature study, in the higher sense, with a Japanese flower painting executed in twenty brush strokes, and worth perhaps five sen. The former would represent at best but an ineffectual and painful effort to imitate a massing of colors. The latter would prove a perfect memory of certain flower shapes instantaneously flung upon paper, without any model to aid, and showing, not the recollection of any individual blossom, but the perfect realization of a general law of form expression, perfectly mastered, with all its moods, tenses, and inflections. The French alone, among Western art critics, seem fully to understand these features of Japanese art; and among all Western artists it is the Parisian alone who approaches the Oriental in his methods. Without lifting his brush from the paper, the French artist may sometimes, with a single wavy line, create the almost speaking figure of a particular type of man or woman. But this high development of faculty is confined chiefly to humorous sketching; it is still either masculine or feminine. To understand what I mean by the ability of the Japanese artist, my reader must imagine just such a power of almost instantaneous creation as that which characterizes certain French work, applied to almost every subject except individuality, to nearly all recognized general types, to all aspects of Japanese nature, to all forms of native landscape, to clouds and flowing water and mists, to all the life of woods and fields, to all the moods of seasons and the tones of horizons and the colors of the morning and the evening. Certainly, the deeper spirit of this magical art seldom reveals itself at first sight to unaccustomed eyes, since it appeals to so little in Western æsthetic experience. But by gentle degrees it will so enter into an appreciative and unprejudiced mind as to modify profoundly therein almost every preëxisting sentiment in relation to the beautiful. All of its meaning will indeed require many years to master, but something of its reshaping power will be felt in a much shorter time when the sight of an American illustrated magazine or of any illustrated European periodical has become almost unbearable.

Psychological differences of far deeper import are suggested by other facts, capable of exposition in words, but not capable of interpretation through Western standards of æsthetics or Western feeling of any sort. For instance, I have been watching two old men planting young trees in the garden of a neighboring temple. They sometimes spend nearly an hour in planting a single sapling. Having fixed it in the ground, they retire to a distance to study the position of all its lines, and consult together about it. As a consequence, the sapling is taken up and replanted in a slightly different position. This is done no less than eight times before the little tree can be perfectly adjusted into the plan of the garden. Those two old men are composing a mysterious thought with their little trees, changing them, transferring them, removing or replacing them, even as a poet changes and shifts his words, to give to his verse the most delicate or the most forcible expression possible.

In every large Japanese cottage there are several alcoves, or *tokonoma*, one in each of the principal rooms. In these alcoves the art treasures of the family are exhibited.[4] Within each toko a kakemono is hung; and upon its slightly elevated floor (usually of polished wood) are placed flower vases and one or two artistic objects. Flowers are arranged in the toko vases according to ancient rules which Mr. Condɔr's beautiful book will tell you a great deal about; and the kakemono and the art objects there displayed are changed at regular intervals, according to occasion and season. Now, in a certain alcove, I have at various times seen many different things of beauty: a Chinese statuette of ivory, an incense vase of bronze—representing a cloud-riding pair of dragons—the wood carving of a Buddhist pilgrim resting by the wayside and mopping his bald pate, masterpieces of lacquer ware and lovely Kyōto porcelains, and a large stone placed on a pedestal of heavy, costly wood, expressly made for it. I do not know whether you could see any beauty in that stone; it is neither hewn nor polished, nor does it possess the least imaginable intrinsic value. It is simply a gray water-worn stone from the bed of a stream. Yet it cost more than

4 The *tokonoma*, or *toko*, is said to have been first introduced into Japanese architecture about four hundred and fifty years ago, by the Buddhist priest Eisai, who had studied in China. Perhaps the alcove was originally devised and used for the exhibition of sacred objects; but to-day, among the cultivated, it would be deemed in very bad taste to display either images of the gods or sacred paintings in the toko of a guest-room. The toko is still, however, a sacred place in a certain sense. No one should ever step upon it, or squat within it, or even place in it anything not pure, or anything offensive to taste. There is an elaborate code of etiquette in relation to it. The most honored among guests is always placed nearest to it; and guests take their places, according to rank, nearer to or further from it.

one of those Kyōto vases which sometimes replace it, and which you would be glad to pay a very high price for.

In the garden of the little house I now occupy in Kumamoto, there are about fifteen rocks, or large stones, of as many shapes and sizes. They also have no real intrinsic value, not even as possible building material. And yet the proprietor of the garden paid for them something more than seven hundred and fifty Japanese dollars, or considerably more than the pretty house itself could possibly have cost. And it would be quite wrong to suppose the cost of the stones due to the expense of their transportation from the bed of the Shirakawa. No; they are worth seven hundred and fifty dollars only because they are considered beautiful to a certain degree, and because there is a large local demand for beautiful stones. They are not even of the best class, or they would have cost a great deal more. Now, until you can perceive that a big rough stone may have more æsthetic suggestiveness than a costly steel engraving, that it is a thing of beauty and a joy forever, you cannot begin to understand how a Japanese sees Nature. "But what," you may ask, "can be beautiful in a common stone?" Many things; but I will mention only one—irregularity.

In my little Japanese house, the *fusuma,* or sliding screens of opaque paper between room and room, have designs at which I am never tired of looking. The designs vary in different parts of the dwelling; I will speak only of the fusuma dividing my study from a smaller apartment. The ground color is a delicate cream-yellow; and the golden pattern is very simple—the mystic-jewel symbols of Buddhism scattered over the surface by pairs. But no two sets of pairs are placed at exactly the same distance from each other; and the symbols themselves are curiously diversified, never appearing twice in exactly the same position or relation. Sometimes one jewel is transparent, and its fellow opaque; sometimes both are opaque or both diaphanous; sometimes the transparent one is the larger of the two; sometimes the opaque is the larger; sometimes both are precisely the same size; sometimes they overlap, and sometimes do not touch; sometimes the opaque is on the left, sometimes on the right; sometimes the transparent jewel is above, sometimes below. Vainly does the eye roam over the whole surface in search of a repetition, or of anything resembling regularity, either in distribution, juxtaposition, grouping, dimensions, or contrasts. And throughout the whole dwelling nothing resembling regularity in the various decorative designs can be found. The ingenuity by which it is avoided is amazing—rises to the dignity of genius. Now, all this is a common characteristic of Japanese decorative art; and after having lived a few years under its influences, the sight of a regular pattern upon a wall, a carpet, a curtain, a ceiling, upon any decorated surface, pains like a horrible vulgarism. Surely, it is because we have so long been accustomed to look at Nature anthropomorphically that we can still endure mechanical ugliness in our own decorative art, and that we remain insensible to charms of Nature which are clearly perceived even by the eyes of the Japanese child, wondering over its mother's shoulder at the green and blue wonder of the world.

"He," saith a Buddhist text, "who discerns that nothingness is law—such a one hath wisdom."

A Glimpse of Tendencies

I

THE FOREIGN CONCESSION OF AN OPEN PORT OFFERS A STRIKING CONTRAST to its Far-Eastern environment. In the well-ordered ugliness of its streets one finds suggestions of places not on this side of the world— just as though fragments of the Occident had been magically brought oversea: bits of Liverpool, of Marseilles, of New York, of New Orleans, and bits also of tropical towns in colonies twelve or fifteen thousand miles away. The mercantile buildings—immense by comparison with the low light Japanese shops—seem to utter the menace of financial power. The dwellings, of every conceivable design—from that of an Indian bungalow to that of an English or French country-manor, with turrets and bow-windows—are surrounded by commonplace gardens of clipped shrubbery; the white roadways are solid and level as tables, and bordered with boxed-up trees. Nearly all things conventional in England or America have been domiciled in these districts. You see church-steeples and factory-chimneys and telegraph-poles and street-lamps. You see warehouses of imported brick with iron shutters, and shop fronts with plate-glass windows, and sidewalks, and cast-iron railings. There are morning and evening and weekly newspapers; clubs and reading-rooms and bowling-alleys; billiard halls and barrooms; schools and bethels. There are electric-light and telephone companies; hospitals, courts, jails, and a foreign police. There are foreign lawyers, doctors, and druggists, foreign grocers, confectioners, bakers, dairymen; foreign dressmakers and tailors; foreign school-teachers and music-teachers. There is a town-hall, for municipal business and public meetings of all kinds—likewise for amateur theatricals or lectures and concerts; and very rarely some dramatic company, on a tour of the world, halts there awhile to make men laugh and women cry like they used to do at home. There are cricket-grounds, racecourses, public parks—or, as we should call them in England, "squares"—yachting associations, athletic societies, and swimming-baths. Among the familiar noises are the endless tinkling of piano-practice, the crashing of a town-band, and an occasional wheezing of accordions: in fact, one misses only the organ-grinder. The population is English, French, German, American, Danish, Swedish, Swiss, Russian, with a thin sprinkling of Italians and Levantines. I had almost forgotten the Chinese. They are present in multitude, and have a little corner of the district to themselves. But the dominant element is English and American—the English being in the majority. All the faults and some of the finer qualities of the masterful races can be studied here to better advantage than beyond seas—because everybody knows all about everybody else in communities so small—mere oases of Occidental life in the vast unknown of the Far East. Ugly stories may be heard which are not worth writing about; also stories of nobility and generosity—about good brave things done by men who pretend to be selfish, and wear conventional masks to hide what is best in them from public knowledge.

But the domains of the foreigner do not stretch beyond the distance of an easy walk, and may shrink back again into nothing before many years—for reasons I shall presently dwell upon. His settlements developed precociously—almost like "mushroom cities" in the great American West—and reached the apparent limit of their development soon after solidifying.

About and beyond the concession, the "native town"—the real Japanese city—stretches away into regions imperfectly known. To the average settler this native town remains a world of mysteries; he may not think it worth his while to enter it for ten years at a time. It has no interest for him, as he is not a student of native customs, but simply a man of business; and he has no time to think how queer it all is. Merely to cross the concession line is almost the same thing as to cross the Pacific Ocean—which is much less wide than the difference between the races. Enter alone into the interminable narrow maze of Japanese streets, and the dogs will bark at you, and the children stare at you as if you were the only foreigner they ever saw. Perhaps they will even call after you "Ijin," "Tōjin," or "Ke-tōjin,"—the last of which signifies "hairy foreigner," and is not intended as a compliment.

II

FOR A LONG TIME THE MERCHANTS OF THE CONCESSIONS HAD THEIR OWN way in everything, and forced upon the native firms methods of business to which no Occidental merchant would think of submitting— methods which plainly expressed the foreign conviction that all Japanese were tricksters. No foreigner would then purchase anything until it had been long enough in his hands to be examined and reëxamined and "exhaustively" examined—or accept any order for imports unless the order were accompanied by "a substantial payment of bargain money." [1] Japanese buyers and sellers protested in vain; they found themselves obliged to submit. But they bided their time—yielding only with the determination to conquer. The rapid growth of the foreign town, and the immense capital successfully invested therein, proved to them how much they would have to learn before being able to help themselves. They wondered without admiring, and traded with the foreigners or worked for them, while secretly detesting them. In Old Japan the merchant ranked below the common peasant; but these foreign invaders assumed the tone of princes and the insolence of conquerors. As employers they were usually harsh, and sometimes brutal. Nevertheless they were wonderfully wise in the matter of making money; they lived like kings and paid high salaries. It was desirable that young men should suffer in their service for the sake of learning things which would have to be learned to save the country from passing under foreign rule. Some day Japan would have a mercantile marine of her own, and foreign banking agencies, and foreign credit, and be well able to rid herself of these haughty strangers: in the meanwhile they should be endured as teachers.

[1] See *Japan Mail*, July 21, 1895.

So the import and export trade remained entirely in foreign hands, and it grew from nothing to a value of hundreds of millions; and Japan was well exploited. But she knew that she was only paying to learn; and her patience was of that kind which endures so long as to be mistaken for oblivion of injuries. Her opportunities came in the natural order of things. The growing influx of aliens seeking fortune gave her the first advantage. The inter-competition for Japanese trade broke down old methods; and new firms being glad to take orders and risks without "bargain-money," large advance-payments could no longer be exacted. The relations between foreigners and Japanese simultaneously improved—as the latter showed a dangerous capacity for sudden combination against ill-treatment, could not be cowed by revolvers, would not suffer abuse of any sort, and knew how to dispose of the most dangerous rowdy in the space of a few minutes. Already the rougher Japanese of the ports, the dregs of the populace, were ready to assume the aggressive on the least provocation.

Within two decades from the founding of the settlements, those foreigners who once imagined it a mere question of time when the whole country would belong to them, began to understand how greatly they had underestimated the race. The Japanese had been learning wonderfully well—"nearly as well as the Chinese." They were supplanting the small foreign shopkeepers; and various establishments had been compelled to close because of Japanese competition. Even for large firms the era of easy fortune-making was over; the period of hard work was commencing. In early days all the personal wants of foreigners had necessarily been supplied by foreigners—so that a large retail trade had grown up under the patronage of the wholesale trade. The retail trade of the settlements was evidently doomed. Some of its branches had disappeared; the rest were visibly diminishing.

To-day the economic foreign clerk or assistant in a business house cannot well afford to live at the local hotels. He can hire a Japanese cook at a very small sum per month, or can have his meals sent him from a Japanese restaurant at five to seven sen per plate. He lives in a house constructed in "semi-foreign style," and owned by a Japanese. The carpets or mattings on his floor are of Japanese manufacture. His furniture is supplied by a Japanese cabinet-maker. His suits, shirts, shoes, walking-cane, umbrella, are "Japanese make": even the soap on his washstand is stamped with Japanese ideographs. If a smoker, he buys his Manilla cigars from a Japanese tobacconist half a dollar cheaper per box than any foreign house would charge him for the same quality. If he wants books he can buy them at much lower prices from a Japanese than from a foreign book-dealer—and select his purchases from a much larger and better-selected stock. If he wants a photograph taken he goes to a Japanese gallery: no foreign photographer could make a living in Japan. If he wants curios he visits a Japanese house;—the foreign dealer would charge him a hundred per cent dearer.

On the other hand, if he be a man of family, his daily marketing is supplied by Japanese butchers, fishmongers, dairymen, fruit-sellers, vegetable dealers. He may continue for a time to buy English or American hams, bacon, canned goods, etc., from some foreign provision dealer; but he has discovered that Japanese stores now offer the same class of goods at lower prices. If he drinks good beer, it probably comes from a Japanese brewery; and if he wants a good quality of ordinary wine or liquor, Japanese storekeepers can supply it at rates below those of the foreign importer. Indeed, the only things he cannot buy from the Japanese houses are just those things which he cannot afford—high-priced goods such as only rich men are likely to purchase. And finally, if any of his family become sick, he can consult a Japanese physician who will charge him a fee perhaps one tenth less than he would have had to pay a foreign physician in former times. Foreign doctors now find it very hard to live—unless they have something more than their practice to rely upon. Even when the foreign doctor brings down his fee to a dollar a visit, the high-class Japanese doctor can charge two, and still crush competition; for he furnishes the medicine himself at prices which would ruin a foreign apothecary. There are doctors and doctors, of course, as in all countries; but the German-speaking Japanese physician capable of directing a public or military hospital is not easily surpassed in his profession; and the average foreign physician cannot possibly compete with him. He furnishes no prescriptions to be taken to a drugstore: his drugstore is either at home or in a room of the hospital he directs.

These facts, taken at random out of a multitude, imply that foreign shops, or as we call them in America, "stores," will soon cease to be. The existence of some has been prolonged only by needless and foolish trickery on the part of some petty Japanese dealers—attempts to sell abominable decoctions in foreign bottles under foreign labels, to adulterate imported goods, or to imitate trademarks. But the common sense of the Japanese dealers, as a mass, is strongly opposed to such immorality, and the evil will soon correct itself. The native store-keepers can honestly undersell the foreign ones, because able not only to underlive them, but to make fortunes during the competition. This has been for some time well recognized in the concessions. But the delusion prevailed that the great exporting and importing firms were impregnable; that they could still control the whole volume of commerce with the West; and that no Japanese companies could find means to oppose the weight of foreign capital, or to acquire the business methods according to which it was employed. Certainly the retail trade would go. But that signified little. The great firms would remain and multiply, and would increase their capacities.

III

DURING ALL THIS TIME OF OUTWARD CHANGES THE REAL FEELING BETWEEN the races—the mutual dislike of Oriental and Occidental—had continued to grow. Of the nine or ten English papers published in the open ports, the majority expressed, day after day, one side of this dislike, in the language of ridicule or contempt; and a powerful native press retorted in kind, with dangerous effectiveness. If the "anti-Japanese" newspapers did not actually represent—as I believe they did—an absolute majority in sentiment, they represented at least the weight of foreign capital, and the preponderant influences of the settlements. The English "pro-Japanese" newspapers, though conducted by shrewd men, and distinguished by journalistic abilities of no common order, could not appease the powerful resentment provoked by the language of their contemporaries. The charges of barbarism or immorality printed in English were promptly answered by the publication in Japanese dailies of the scandals of the open ports—for all the millions of the empire to know. The race question was carried into Japanese politics by a strong anti-foreign league; the foreign concessions were openly denounced as hotbeds of vice; and the national anger became so formidable that only the most determined action on the part of the government could have prevented disastrous happenings. Nevertheless oil was still poured on the smothered fire by foreign editors, who at the outbreak of the war with China openly took the part of China. This policy was pursued throughout the campaign. Reports of imaginary reverses were printed recklessly; undeniable victories were unjustly belittled; and after the war had been decided, the cry was raised that the Japanese "had been allowed to become dangerous." Later on, the interference of Russia was applauded, and the sympathy of England condemned by men of English blood. The effect of such utterances at such a time was that of insult never to be forgiven upon a people who never forgive. Utterances of hate they were, but also utterances of alarm—alarm excited by the signing of those new treaties, bringing all aliens under Japanese jurisdiction—and fear, not ill-founded, of another anti-foreign agitation with the formidable new sense of national power behind it. Premonitory symptoms of such agitation were really apparent in a general tendency to insult or jeer at foreigners, and in some rare but exemplary acts of violence. The government again found it necessary to issue proclamations and warnings against such demonstrations of national anger; and they ceased almost as quickly as they began. But there is no doubt that their cessation was due largely to recognition of the friendly attitude of England as a naval power, and the worth of her policy to Japan in a moment of danger to the world's peace. England, too, had first rendered treaty-revision possible—in spite of the passionate outcries of her own subjects in the Far East; and the leaders of the people were grateful. Otherwise the hatred between settlers and Japanese might have resulted quite as badly as had been feared.

In the beginning, of course, this mutual antagonism was racial, and therefore natural; and the irrational violence of prejudice and malignity developed at a later day was inevitable with the ever-increasing conflict of interests. No foreigner really capable of estimating the conditions could have seriously entertained any hope of a rapprochement. The barriers of racial feeling, of emotional differentiation, of language, of manners and beliefs, are likely to remain insurmountable for centuries. Though instances of warm friendship, due to the mutual attraction of exceptional natures able to divine each other intuitively, might be cited, the foreigner, as a general rule, understands the Japanese quite as little as the Japanese understands him. What is worse for the alien than miscomprehension is the simple fact that he is in the position of an invader. Under no ordinary circumstances need he expect to be treated like a Japanese; and this not merely because he has more money at his command, but because of his race. One price for the foreigner, another for the Japanese, is the common regulation—except in those Japanese stores which depend almost exclusively upon foreign trade. If you wish to enter a Japanese theatre, a figure-show, any place of amusement, or even an inn, you must pay a virtual tax upon your nationality. Japanese artisans, laborers, clerks, will not work for you at Japanese rates—unless they have some other object in view than wages Japanese hotel-keepers—except in those hotels built and furnished especially for European or American travelers—will not make out your bill at regular prices. Large hotel-companies have been formed which maintain this rule—companies controlling scores of establishments throughout the country, and able to dictate terms to local storekeepers and to the smaller hostelries. It has been generously confessed that foreigners ought to pay higher than Japanese for accommodation, since they give more trouble; and this is true. But under even these facts race-feeling is manifest. Those innkeepers who build for Japanese custom only, in the great centres, care nothing for foreign custom, and often lose by it—partly because well-paying native guests do not like hotels patronized by foreigners, and partly because the Western guest wants all to himself the room which can be rented more profitably to a Japanese party of five or eight. Another fact not generally understood in connection with this is that in Old Japan the question of recompense for service was left to honor. The Japanese innkeeper always supplied (and in the country often still supplies) food at scarcely more than cost; and his real profit depended upon the conscience of the customer. Hence the importance of the *chadai*, or present of tea-money, to the hotel. From the poor a very small sum, from the rich a larger sum, was expected—according to services rendered. In like manner the hired servant expected to be remunerated according to his master's ability to pay, even more than according to the value of the work done; the artist preferred, when working for a good patron, never to name a price: only the merchant tried to get the better of his customers by bargaining—the immoral privilege of his class. It may be readily imagined that the habit of trusting to honor for payment produced no good results in dealing with Occidentals. All matters of buying and selling we think of as "business"; and business in the West is not conducted under purely abstract ideas of morality, but at best under relative and partial ideas of morality. A generous man extremely dislikes to have the price of an article which he wants to buy left to his conscience; for, unless he knows exactly the value of the material and the worth of the labor, he feels obliged to make such overpayment as will assure him that he has done more than right; while the selfish man takes advantage of the situation to give as nearly next to nothing as he can. Special rates have to be made, therefore, by the Japanese in all dealings with foreigners. But the dealing itself is made more or less aggressive, according to circumstance, because of race antagonism. The foreigner has not only to pay higher rates for every kind of skilled labor; but he must sign costlier leases, and submit to higher rents. Only the lowest class of Japanese servants can be hired even at high wages by a foreign household; and their stay is usually brief, as they dislike the service required of them. Even the apparent eagerness of educated Japanese to enter foreign employ is generally misunderstood; their veritable purpose being simply, in most cases, to fit themselves for the same sort of work in Japanese business houses, stores, and hotels. The average Japanese would prefer to work fifteen hours a day for one of his own countrymen than eight hours a day for a foreigner paying higher wages. I have seen graduates of the university working as servants; but they were working only to learn special things.

IV

REALLY THE DULLEST FOREIGNER COULD NOT HAVE BELIEVED THAT A PEOPLE of forty millions, uniting all their energies to achieve absolute national independence, would remain content to leave the management of their country's import and export trade to aliens—especially in view of the feeling in the open ports. The existence of foreign settlements in Japan, under consular jurisdiction, was in itself a constant exasperation to national pride—an indication of national weakness. It had so been proclaimed in print—in speeches by members of the anti-foreign league —in speeches made in parliament. But knowledge of the national desire to control the whole of Japanese commerce, and the periodical manifestations of hostility to foreigners as settlers, excited only temporary uneasiness. It was confidently asserted that the Japanese could only injure themselves by any attempt to get rid of foreign negotiators. Though alarmed at the prospect of being brought under Japanese law, the merchants of the concessions never imagined a successful attack upon large interests possible, except by violation of that law itself. It signified little that the Nippon Yusen Kwaisha had become, during the war, one of the largest steamship companies in the world; that Japan was trading directly with India and China; that Japanese banking agencies were being established in the great manufacturing centres abroad; that Japanese merchants were sending their sons to Europe and America for a sound commercial education. Because Japanese lawyers were gaining a large foreign clientèle; because Japanese shipbuilders, architects, engineers had replaced foreigners in government service, it did not at all follow that the foreign agents controlling the import and export trade with Europe and America could be dispensed with. The machinery of commerce would be useless in Japanese hands; and capacity for other professions by no means augured latent capacity for business. The foreign capital invested in Japan could not be successfully threatened by any combinations formed against it. Some Japanese houses might carry on a small import business; but the export trade required a thorough knowledge of business conditions on the other side of the world, and such connections and credits as the Japanese could not obtain. Nevertheless the self-confidence of the foreign importers and exporters was rudely broken in July, 1895, when a British house having brought suit against a Japanese company in a Japanese court, for refusal to accept delivery of goods ordered, and having won a judgment for nearly thirty thousand dollars, suddenly found itself confronted and menaced by a guild whose power had never been suspected. The Japanese firm did not appeal against the decision of the court: it expressed itself ready to pay the whole sum at once—if required. But the guild to which it belonged informed the triumphant plaintiffs that a compromise would be to their advantage. Then the English house discovered itself threatened with a boycott which could utterly ruin it—a boycott operating in all the industrial centres of the Empire. The compromise was promptly effected at considerable loss to the foreign firm; and the settlements were dismayed. There was much denunciation of the immorality of the proceeding.[2] But it was a proceeding against which the law could do nothing; for boycotting cannot be satisfactorily dealt with under the law; and it afforded proof positive that the Japanese were able to force foreign forms to submit to their dictation—by foul means if not by fair. Enormous guilds had been organized by the great industries—combinations whose moves, perfectly regulated by telegraph, could ruin opposition, and could set at defiance even the judgment of tribunals. The

[2] A Kobé merchant of great experience, writing to the *Kobé Chronicle* of August 7, 1895, observed: "I am not attempting to defend boycotts; but I firmly believe from what has come to my knowledge that in each and every case there has been provocation irritating the Japanese, rousing their feelings and their sense of justice, and driving them to combination as a defense."

Japanese had attempted boycotting in previous years with so little success that they were deemed incapable of combination. But the new situation showed how well they had learned through defeat, and that with further improvement of organization they could reasonably expect to get the foreign trade under control—if not into their own hands. It would be the next great step toward the realization of the national desire—*Japan only for the Japanese*. Even though the country should be opened to foreign settlement, foreign investments would always be at the mercy of Japanese combinations.

V

THE FOREGOING BRIEF ACCOUNT OF EXISTING CONDITIONS MAY SUFFICE TO prove the evolution in Japan of a social phenomenon of great significance. Of course the prospective opening of the country under new treaties, the rapid development of its industries, and the vast annual increase in the volume of trade with America and Europe, will probably bring about some increase of foreign settlers; and this temporary result might deceive many as to the inevitable drift of things. But old merchants of experience even now declare that the probable further expansion of the ports will really mean the growth of a native competitive commerce that must eventually dislodge foreign merchants. ' The foreign settlements, as communities, will disappear: there will remain only some few great agencies, such as exist in all the chief ports of the civilized world; and the abandoned streets of the concessions, and the costly foreign houses on the heights, will be peopled and tenanted by Japanese. Large foreign investments will not be made in the interior. And even Christian mission-work must be left to native missionaries; for just as Buddhism never took definite form in Japan until the teaching of its doctrines was left entirely to Japanese priests—so Christianity will never take any fixed shape till it has been so remodeled as to harmonize with the emotional and social life of the race. Even thus remodeled it can scarcely hope to exist except in the form of a few small sects.

The social phenomenon exhibited can be best explained by a simile. In many ways a human society may be compared biologically with an individual organism. Foreign elements introduced forcibly into the system of either, and impossible to assimilate, set up irritations and partial disintegration, until eliminated naturally or removed artificially.

Japan is strengthening herself through elimination of disturbing elements; and this natural process is symbolized in the resolve to regain possession of all the concessions, to bring about the abolishment of consular jurisdiction, to leave nothing under foreign control within the Empire. It is also manifested in the dismissal of foreign employés, in the resistance offered by Japanese congregations to the authority of foreign missionaries, and in the resolute boycotting of foreign merchants. And behind all this race-movement there is more than race-feeling: there is also the definite conviction that foreign help is proof of national feebleness, and that the Empire remains disgraced before the eyes of the commercial world, so long as its import and export trade are managed by aliens. Several large Japanese firms have quite emancipated themselves from the domination of foreign middlemen; large trade with India and China is being carried on by Japanese steamship companies; and communication with the Southern States of America is soon to be established by the Nippon Yusen Kwaisha, for the direct importation of cotton. But the foreign settlements remain constant sources of irritation; and their commercial conquest by untiring national effort will alone satisfy the country, and will prove, even better than the war with China, Japan's real place among nations. That conquest, I think, will certainly be achieved.

VI

WHAT OF THE FUTURE OF JAPAN? NO ONE CAN VENTURE ANY POSITIVE prediction on the assumption that existing tendencies will continue far into that future. Not to dwell upon the grim probabilities of war, or the possibility of such internal disorder as might compel indefinite suspension of the constitution, and lead to a military dictatorship—a resurrected Shogunate in modern uniform—great changes there will assuredly be, both for better and for worse. Supposing these changes normal, however, one may venture some qualified predictions, based upon the reasonable supposition that the race will continue, through rapidly alternating periods of action and reaction, to assimilate its new-found knowledge with the best relative consequences.

Physically, I think, the Japanese will become before the close of the next century much superior to what they now are. For such belief there are three good reasons. The first is that the systematic military and gymnastic training of the able-bodied youth of the Empire ought in a few generations to produce results as marked as those of the military system in Germany—increase in stature, in average girth of chest, in muscular development. Another reason is that the Japanese of the cities are taking to a richer diet—a flesh diet; and that a more nutritive food must have physiological results favoring growth. Immense numbers of little restaurants are everywhere springing up, in which "Western Cooking" is furnished almost as cheaply as Japanese food. Thirdly, the delay of marriage necessitated by education and by military service must result in the production of finer and finer generations of children. As immature marriages become the exception rather than the rule, children of feeble constitution will correspondingly diminish in number. At present the extraordinary differences of stature noticeable in any Japanese crowd seem to prove that the race is capable of great physical development under a severer social discipline.

Moral improvement is hardly to be expected—rather the reverse. The old moral ideals of Japan were at least quite as noble as our own; and men could really live up to them in the quiet benevolent times of patriarchal government. Untruthfulness, dishonesty, and brutal crime were rarer than now, as official statistics show; the percentage of crime having been for some years steadily on the increase—which proves of course, among other things, that the struggle for existence has been intensified. The old standard of chastity, as represented in public opinion, was that of a less developed society than our own; yet I do not believe it can be truthfully asserted that the moral conditions were worse than with us. In one respect they were certainly better; for the virtue of Japanese wives was generally in all ages above suspicion.[3]

[3] The statement has been made that there is no word for chastity in the Japanese language. This is true in the same sense only that we might say there is no word for chastity in the English language—because such words as honor, virtue, purity, chastity have been adopted into English from other languages. Open any good Japanese-English dictionary and you will find many words for chastity. Just as it would be ridiculous to deny that the word "chastity" is modern English, because it came to us through the French from the Latin, so it is ridiculous to deny that Chinese moral terms, adopted into the Japanese tongue more than a thousand years ago, are Japanese to-day. The statement, like a majority of missionary statements on these subjects, is otherwise misleading; for the reader is left to infer the absence of an adjective as well as a noun—and the purely Japanese adjectives signifying chaste are numerous. The word most commonly used applies to both sexes—and has the old Japanese sense of firm, strict, resisting, honorable. The deficiency of abstract terms in a language by no means implies the deficiency of concrete moral ideas—a fact which has been vainly pointed out to missionaries more than once.

If the morals of men were much more open to reproach, it is not necessary to cite Lecky for evidence as to whether a much better state of things prevails in the Occident. Early marriages were encouraged to guard young men from temptations to irregular life; and it is only fair to suppose that in a majority of cases this result was obtained. Concubinage, the privilege of the rich, had its evil side; but it had also the effect of relieving the wife from the physical strain of rearing many children in rapid succession. The social conditions were so different from those which Western religion assumes to be the best possible, that an impartial judgment of them cannot be ecclesiastical. One fact is indisputable—that they were unfavorable to professional vice; and in many of the larger fortified towns—the seats of princes—no houses of prostitution were suffered to exist. When all things are fairly considered, it will be found that Old Japan might claim, in spite of her patriarchal system, to have been less open to reproach even in the matter of sexual morality than many a Western country. The people were better than their laws asked them to be. And now that the relations of the sexes are to be regulated by new codes—at a time when new codes are really needed—the changes which it is desirable to bring about cannot result in immediate good. Sudden reforms are not made by legislation. Laws cannot directly create sentiment; and real social progress can be made only through change of ethical feeling developed by long discipline and training. Meanwhile increasing pressure of population and increasing competition must tend, while quickening intelligence, to harden character and develop selfishness.

Intellectually there will doubtless be great progress, but not a progress so rapid as those who think that Japan has really transformed herself in thirty years would have us believe. However widely diffused among the people, scientific education cannot immediately raise the average of practical intelligence to the Western level. The common capacity must remain lower for generations. There will be plenty of remarkable exceptions, indeed; and a new aristocracy of intellect is coming into existence. But the real future of the nation depends rather upon the general capacity of the many than upon the exceptional capacity of the few. Perhaps it depends especially upon the development of the mathematical faculty, which is being everywhere assiduously cultivated. At present this is the weak point; hosts of students being yearly debarred from the more important classes of higher study through inability to pass in mathematics. At the Imperial naval and military colleges, however, such results have been obtained as suffice to show that this weakness will eventually be remedied. The most difficult branches of scientific study will become less formidable to the children of those who have been able to distinguish themselves in such branches.

In other respects, some temporary retrogression is to be looked for. Just so certainly as Japan has attempted that which is above the normal limit of her powers, so certainly must she fall back to that limit—or, rather, below it. Such retrogression will be natural as well as necessary: it will mean nothing more than a recuperative preparation for stronger and loftier efforts. Signs of it are even now visible in the working of certain state departments—notably in that of education. The idea of forcing upon Oriental students a course of study above the average capacity of Western students; the idea of making English the language, or at least one of the languages of the country; and the idea of changing ancestral modes of feeling and thinking for the better by such training, were wild extravagances. Japan must develop her own soul: she cannot borrow another. A dear friend whose life has been devoted to philology once said to me while commenting upon the deterioration of manners among the students of Japan: "Why, the English language itself has been a demoralizing influence!" There was much depth in that observation. Setting the whole Japanese nation to study English (the language of a people who are being forever preached to about their "rights," and never about their "duties") was almost an imprudence. The policy was too wholesale as well as too sudden. It involved great waste of money and time, and it helped to sap ethical sentiment. In the future Japan will learn English, just as England learns German. But if this study has been wasted in some directions, it has not been wasted in others. The influence of English has effected modifications in the native tongue, making it richer, more flexible, and more capable of expressing the new forms of thought created by the discoveries of modern science. This influence must long continue. There will be a considerable absorption of English—perhaps also of French and German words—into Japanese: indeed this absorption is already marked in the changing speech of the educated classes, not less than in the colloquial of the ports which is mixed with curious modifications of foreign commercial words. Furthermore, the grammatical structure of Japanese is being influenced; and though I cannot agree with a clergyman who lately declared that the use of the passive voice by Tōkyō street-urchins announcing the fall of Port Arthur—("*Ryojunko ga senryo serareta!*")—represented the working of "divine providence," I do think it afforded some proof that the Japanese language, assimilative like the genius of the race, is showing capacity to meet all demands made upon it by the new conditions.

Perhaps Japan will remember her foreign teachers more kindly in the twentieth century. But she will never feel toward the Occident, as she felt toward China before the Meiji era, the reverential respect due by ancient custom to a beloved instructor; for the wisdom of China was voluntarily sought, while that of the West was thrust upon her by violence. She will have some Christian sects of her own; but she will not remember our American and English missionaries as she remembers even now those great Chinese priests who once educated her youth. And she will not preserve relics of our sojourn, carefully wrapped in septuple coverings of silk, and packed away in dainty whitewood boxes, because we had no new lesson of beauty to teach her—nothing by which to appeal to her emotions.

Industrial Danger

EVERYWHERE THE COURSE OF HUMAN CIVILIZATION HAS BEEN SHAPED BY the same evolutional law; and as the earlier history of the ancient European communities can help us to understand the social conditions of Old Japan, so a later period of the same history can help us to divine something of the probable future of the New Japan. It has been shown by the author of "La Cité Antique" that the history of all the ancient Greek and Latin communities included four revolutionary periods.[1] The first revolution had everywhere for its issue the with-

[1] Not excepting Sparta. The Spartan society was evolutionally much in advance of the Ionian societies; the Dorian patriarchal clan having been dissolved at some very early

drawal of political power from the priest-king, who was nevertheless allowed to retain the religious authority. The second revolutionary period witnessed the breaking up of the gens or γένος, the enfranchisement of the client from the authority of the patron, and several important changes in the legal constitution of the family. The third revolutionary period saw the weakening of the religious and military aristocracy, the entrance of the common people into the rights of citizenship, and the rise of a democracy of wealth—presently to be opposed by a democracy of poverty. The fourth revolutionary period witnessed the first bitter struggles between rich and poor, the final triumph of anarchy, and the consequent establishment of a new and horrible form of despotism—the despotism of the popular Tyrant.

To these four revolutionary periods, the social history of Old Japan presents but two correspondences. The first Japanese revolutionary period was represented by the Fujiwara usurpation of the Imperial civil and military authority—after which event the aristocracy, religious and military, really governed Japan down to our own time. All the events of the rise of the military power and the concentration of authority under the Tokugawa Shōgunate properly belong to the first revolutionary period. At the time of the opening of Japan, society had not evolutionally advanced beyond a stage corresponding to that of the antique Western societies in the seventh or eighth century before Christ. The second revolutionary period really began only with the reconstruction of society in 1871. But within the space of a single generation thereafter, Japan entered upon her third revolutionary period. Already the influence of the elder aristocracy is threatened by the sudden rise of a new oligarchy of wealth—a new industrial power probably destined to become omnipotent in politics. The disintegration (now proceeding) of the clan, the changes in the legal constitution of the family, the entrance of the people into the enjoyment of political rights, must all tend to hasten the coming transfer of power. There is every indication that, in the present order of things, the third revolutionary period will run its course rapidly; and then a fourth revolutionary period, fraught with serious danger, would be in immediate prospect.

---

period. Sparta kept its Kings; but affairs of civil justice were regulated by the Senate, and affairs of criminal justice by the ephors, who also had the power to declare war and to make treaties of peace. After the first great revolution of Spartan history the King was deprived of power in civil matters, in criminal matters, and in military matters: he retained his sacerdotal office. (See for details, *La Cité Antique*, pp. 285–87.)

Consider the bewildering rapidity of recent changes—from the reconstruction of society in 1871 to the opening of the first national parliament in 1891. Down to the middle of the nineteenth century the nation had remained in the condition common to European patriarchal communities twenty-six hundred years ago: society had indeed entered upon a second period of integration, but had traversed only one great revolution. And then the country was suddenly hurried through two more social revolutions of the most extraordinary kind—signalized by the abolition of the daimiates, the suppression of the military class, the substitution of a plebeian for an aristocratic army, popular enfranchisement, the rapid formalism of a new commonalty, industrial expansion, the rise of a new aristocracy of wealth and popular representation in government! Old Japan had never developed a wealthy and powerful middle class: she had not even approached that stage of industrial development which, in the ancient European societies, naturally brought about the first political struggles between rich and poor. Her social organization made industrial oppression impossible: the commercial classes were kept at the bottom of society—under the feet even of those who, in more highly evolved communities, are most at the mercy of money-power. But now those commercial classes, set free and highly privileged, are silently and swiftly ousting the aristocratic ruling-class from power—are becoming supremely important. And under the new order of things, forms of social misery, never before known in the history of the race, are being developed. Some idea of this misery may be obtained from the fact that the number of poor people in Tōkyō unable to pay their annual resident-tax is upwards of fifty thousand; yet the amount of the tax is only about twenty sen, or five pence English money. Prior to the accumulation of wealth in the hands of the minority there was never any such want in any part of Japan—except, of course, as a temporary consequence of war.

The early history of European civilization supplies analogies. In the Greek and Latin communities, up to the time of the dissolution of the gens, there was no poverty in the modern meaning of that word. Slavery, with some few exceptions, existed only in the mild domestic form; there were yet no commercial oligarchies, and no industrial oppressions; and the various cities and states were ruled, after political power had been taken from the early kings, by military aristocracies which also exercised religious functions. There was yet little trade in the modern signification of the term; and money, as current coinage, came into circulation only in the seventh century before Christ. Misery did not exist. Under any patriarchal system, based upon ancestor-worship, there is no misery, as a consequence of poverty, except such as may be temporarily created by devastation or famine. If want thus comes, it comes to all alike. In such a state of society everybody is in the service of somebody, and receives in exchange for service all the necessaries of life: there is no need for any one to trouble himself about the question of living. Also, in such a patriarchal community, which is self-sufficing, there is little need of money: barter takes the place of trade. . . . In all these respects, the condition of Old Japan offered a close parallel to the conditions of patriarchal society in ancient Europe. While the *uji* or clan existed, there was no misery except as a result of war, famine, or pestilence. Throughout society—excepting the small commercial class—the need of money was rare; and such coinage as existed was little suited to general circulation. Taxes were paid in rice and other produce. As the lord nourished his retainers, so the samurai cared for his dependants, the farmer for his laborers, the artisan for his apprentices and journeymen, the merchant for his clerks. Everybody was fed; and there was no need, in ordinary times at least, for any one to go hungry. It was only with the breaking-up of the clan-system in Japan that the possibilities of starvation for the worker first came into existence. And as, in antique Europe, the en-franchised client-class and plebeian-class developed, under like condi-tions, into a democracy clamoring for suffrage and all political rights, so in Japan have the common people developed the political instinct, in self-protection.

It will be remembered how, in Greek and Roman society, the aris-tocracy founded upon religious tradition and military power had to give way to an oligarchy of wealth, and how there subsequently came into existence a democratic form of government—democratic, not in the modern, but in the old Greek meaning. At a yet later day the results of popular suffrage were the breaking-up of this democratic government, and the initiation of an atrocious struggle between rich and poor. After that strife had begun there was no more security for life or property until the Roman conquest enforced order. . . . Now it seems not unlikely that there will be witnessed in Japan, at no very distant day, a strong tendency to repeat the history of the old Greek anarchies. With the constant increase of poverty and pressure of popu-lation, and the concomitant accumulation of wealth in the hands of a new industrial class, the peril is obvious. Thus far the nation has patiently borne all changes, relying upon the experience of its past, and trusting implicitly to its rulers. But should wretchedness be so permitted to augment that the question of how to keep from starving becomes imperative for the millions, the long patience and the long trust may fail. And then, to repeat a figure effectively used by Professor Huxley, the Primitive Man, finding that the Moral Man has landed him in the valley of the shadow of death, may rise up to take the management of affairs into his own hands, and fight savagely for the right of existence. As popular instinct is not too dull to divine the first cause of this misery in the introduction of Western industrial methods, it is unpleasant to reflect what such an upheaval might signify. But nothing of moment has yet been done to ameliorate the condition of the wretched class of operatives, now estimated to exceed half a million.

M. de Coulanges has pointed out [2] that the absence of individual liberty was the real cause of the disorders and the final ruin of the Greek societies. Rome suffered less, and survived, and dominated—because within her boundaries the rights of the individual had been more respected. . . . Now the absence of individual freedom in modern Japan would certainly appear to be nothing less than a national danger. For those very habits of unquestioning obedience, and loyalty, and respect for authority, which made feudal society possible, are likely to render a true democratic régime impossible, and would tend to bring about a state of anarchy. Only races long accustomed to personal liberty—liberty to think about matters of ethics apart from matters of government—liberty to consider questions of right and wrong, justice and injustice, independently of political authority—are able to face without risk the peril now menacing Japan. For should social disintegration take in Japan the same course which it followed in the old European societies—unchecked by any precautionary legislation—and so bring about another social revolution, the consequence could scarcely be less than utter ruin. In the antique world of Europe, the total disintegration of the patriarchal system occupied centuries: it was slow, and it was normal—not having been brought about by external forces. In Japan, on the contrary, this disintegration is taking place under enormous outside pressure, operating with the rapidity of electricity and steam. In Greek societies the changes were effected in about three hundred years; in Japan it is hardly more than thirty years since the

[2] *La Cité Antique,* pp. 400–01.

patriarchal system was legally dissolved and the industrial system re-shaped; yet already the danger of anarchy is in sight, and the popula-tion—astonishingly augmented by more than ten millions—already begins to experience all the forms of misery developed by want under industrial conditions.

It was perhaps inevitable that the greatest freedom accorded under the new order of things should have been given in the direction of greatest danger. Though the Government cannot be said to have done much for any form of competition within the sphere of its own direct control, it has done even more than could have been reasonably ex-pected on behalf of national industrial competition. Loans have been lavishly advanced, subsidies generously allowed; and, in spite of vari-ous panics and failures, the results have been prodigious. Within thirty years the value of articles manufactured for export has risen from half a million to five hundred million yen. But this immense development has been effected at serious cost in other directions. The old methods of family production—and therefore most of the beautiful industries and arts, for which Japan has been so long famed—now seem doomed beyond hope; and instead of the ancient kindly relations between master and workers, there have been brought into existence—with no legislation to restrain inhumanity—all the horrors of factory-life at its worst. The new combinations of capital have actually reëstablished servitude, under harsher forms than ever were imagined under the feudal era; the misery of the women and children subjected to that servitude is a public scandal, and proves strange possibilities of cruelty on the part of a people once renowned for kindness—kindness even to animals.

There is now a humane outcry for reform; and earnest efforts have been made, and will be made, to secure legislation for the protection of operatives. But, as might be expected, these efforts have been hitherto strongly opposed by manufacturing companies and syndicates with the declaration that any Government interference with factory management will greatly hamper, if not cripple, enterprise, and hinder competition with foreign industry. Less than twenty years ago the very same arguments were used in England to oppose the efforts then being made to improve the condition of the industrial classes; and that op-position was challenged by Professor Huxley in a noble address, which every Japanese legislator would do well to read to-day. Speaking of the reforms in progress in 1888, the professor said:

If it is said that the carrying out of such arrangements as those indicated must enhance the cost of production, and thus handicap the producer in the race of competition, I venture, in the first place, to doubt the fact; but, if it be so, it results that industrial society has to face a dilemma, either alternative of which threatens destruction.

On the one hand, a population, the labor of which is sufficiently remunerated, may be physically and morally healthy, and socially stable, but may fail in industrial competition by reason of the dearness of its produce. On the other hand, a population, the labor of which is insufficiently remunerated, must become physically and morally unhealthy, and socially unstable; and though it may succeed for a while in competition, by reason of the cheapness of its produce, it must in the end fall, through hideous misery and degradation, to utter ruin.

Well, if these be the only alternatives, let us for ourselves and our children choose the former, and, if need be, starve like men. But I do not believe that a stable society, made up of healthy, vigorous, instructed, and self-ruling people would ever incur serious risk of that fate. They are not likely to be troubled with many competitors of the same character just yet; and they may be safely trusted to find ways of holding their own.[3]

If the future of Japan could depend upon her army and her navy, upon the high courage of her people and their readiness to die by the hundred thousand for ideals of honor and of duty, there would be small cause for alarm in the present state of affairs. Unfortunately her future must depend upon other qualities than courage, other abilities than those of sacrifice; and her struggle hereafter must be one in which her social traditions will place her at an immense disadvantage. The capacity for industrial competition cannot be made to depend upon the misery of women and children; it must depend upon the intelligent freedom of the individual; and the society which suppresses this freedom, or suffers it to be suppressed, must remain too rigid for competition with societies in which the liberties of the individual are strictly maintained. While Japan continues to think and to act by groups, even by groups of industrial companies, so long she must always continue incapable of her best. Her ancient social experience is not sufficient to avail her for the future international struggle—rather it must sometimes impede her as so much dead weight: dead, in the ghostliest sense of the word—the viewless pressure upon her

[3] "The Struggle for Existence in Human Society," *Collected Essays*, vol. IX, pp. 218-19.

life of numberless vanished generations. She will have not only to strive against colossal odds in her rivalry with more plastic and more forceful societies; she will have to strive much more against the power of her phantom past.

Yet it were a grievous error to imagine that she has nothing further to gain from her ancestral faith. All her modern successes have been aided by it, and all her modern failures have been marked by needless breaking with its ethical custom. She could compel her people, by a simple fiat, to adopt the civilization of the West, with all its pain and struggle, only because that people had been trained for ages in submission and loyalty and sacrifice; and the time has not yet come in which she can afford to cast away the whole of her moral past. More freedom indeed she requires—but freedom restrained by wisdom; freedom to think and act and strive for self as well as for others—not freedom to oppress the weak, or to exploit the simple. And the new cruelties of her industrial life can find no justification in the traditions of her ancient faith, which exacted absolute obedience from the dependant, but equally required the duty of kindness from the master. In so far as she has permitted her people to depart from the way of kindness, she herself has surely departed from the Way of the Gods. . . .

And the domestic future appears dark. Born of that darkness, an evil dream comes oftentimes to those who love Japan: the fear that all her efforts are being directed, with desperate heroism, only to prepare the land for the sojourn of peoples older by centuries in commercial experience; that her thousands of miles of railroads and telegraphs, her mines and forges, her arsenals and factories, her docks and fleets, are being put in order for the use of foreign capital; that her admirable army and her heroic navy may be doomed to make their last sacrifices in hopeless contest against some combination of greedy states, provoked or encouraged to aggression by circumstances beyond the power of Government to control. . . . But the statesmanship that has already guided Japan through so many storms should prove able to cope with this gathering peril.

WEIRD TALES

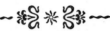

The Mirror Maiden

IN THE PERIOD OF THE ASHIKAGA SHŌGUNATE THE SHRINE OF OGAWACHI-
Myōjin, at Minami-Isé, fell into decay; and the daimyō of the district,
the Lord Kitahataké, found himself unable, by reason of war and other
circumstances, to provide for the reparation of the building. Then the
Shintō priest in charge, Matsumura Hyōgo, sought help at Kyōto from
the great daimyō Hosokawa, who was known to have influence with
the Shōgun. The Lord Hosokawa received the priest kindly, and promised to speak to the Shōgun about the condition of Ogawachi-Myōjin.
But he said that, in any event, a grant for the restoration of the temple
could not be made without due investigation and considerable delay;
and he advised Matsumura to remain in the capital while the matter

544

was being arranged. Matsumura therefore brought his family to Kyōto, and rented a house in the old Kyōgoku quarter.

This house, although handsome and spacious, had been long unoccupied. It was said to be an unlucky house. On the northeast side of it there was a well; and several former tenants had drowned themselves in that well, without any known cause. But Matsumura, being a Shintō priest, had no fear of evil spirits; and he soon made himself very comfortable in his new home.

In the summer of that year there was a great drought. For months no rain had fallen in the Five Home-Provinces; the river-beds dried up, the wells failed; and even in the capital there was a dearth of water. But the well in Matsumura's garden remained nearly full; and the water —which was very cold and clear, with a faint bluish tinge—seemed to be supplied by a spring. During the hot season many people came from all parts of the city to beg for water; and Matsumura allowed them to draw as much as they pleased. Nevertheless the supply did not appear to be diminished.

But one morning the dead body of a young servant, who had been sent from a neighboring residence to fetch water, was found floating in the well. No cause for a suicide could be imagined; and Matsumura, remembering many unpleasant stories about the well, began to suspect some invisible malevolence. He went to examine the well, with the intention of having a fence built around it; and while standing there alone he was startled by a sudden motion in the water, as of something alive. The motion soon ceased; and then he perceived, clearly reflected in the still surface, the figure of a young woman, apparently about nineteen or twenty years of age. She seemed to be occupied with her toilette: he distinctly saw her touching her lips with *béni*.[1] At first her face was visible in profile only; but presently she turned towards him and smiled. Immediately he felt a strange shock at his heart, and a dizziness came upon him like the dizziness of wine, and everything became dark, except that smiling face—white and beautiful as moonlight, and always seeming to grow more beautiful, and to be drawing him down—down —down into the darkness. But with a desperate effort he recovered his will and closed his eyes. When he opened them again, the face was gone, and the light had returned; and he found himself leaning down over the curb of the well. A moment more of that dizziness—a moment more of that dazzling lure—and he would never again have looked upon the sun. . . .

[1] A kind of rouge, now used only to color the lips.

Returning to the house, he gave orders to his people not to approach the well under any circumstances, or allow any person to draw water from it. And the next day he had a strong fence built round the well.

About a week after the fence had been built, the long drought was broken by a great rain-storm, accompanied by wind and lightning and thunder—thunder so tremendous that the whole city shook to the rolling of it, as if shaken by an earthquake. For three days and three nights the downpour and the lightnings and the thunder continued; and the Kamogawa rose as it had never risen before, carrying away many bridges. During the third night of the storm, at the Hour of the Ox, there was heard knocking at the door of the priest's dwelling, and the voice of a woman pleading for admittance. But Matsumura, warned by his experience at the well, forbade his servants to answer the appeal. He went himself to the entrance, and asked:

"Who calls?"

A feminine voice responded:

"Pardon! it is I,—Yayoi! [2] . . . I have something to say to Matsumura Sama—something of great moment. Please open!" . . .

Matsumura half opened the door, very cautiously; and he saw the same beautiful face that had smiled upon him from the well. But it was not smiling now: it had a very sad look.

"Into my house you shall not come," the priest exclaimed: "You are not a human being, but a Well-Person. . . . Why do you thus wickedly try to delude and destroy people?"

The Well-Person made answer in a voice musical as a tinkling of jewels (*tama-wokorogasu-koë*):

"It is of that very matter that I want to speak. . . . I have never wished to injure human beings. But from ancient time a Poison-Dragon dwelt in that well. He was the Master of the Well; and because of him the well was always full. Long ago I fell into the water there, and so became subject to him; and he had power to make me lure people to death, in order that he might drink their blood. But now the Heavenly Ruler has commanded the Dragon to dwell hereafter in the lake called Torii-no-Iké, in the Province of Shinshū; and the gods have decided that he shall never be allowed to return to this city. So to-night, after he had gone away, I was able to come out, to beg for your kindly help. There is now very little water in the well, because of the Dragon's departure; and if you will order search to be made, my body will be found there.

[2] This name, though uncommon, is still in use.

I pray you to save my body from the well without delay; and I shall certainly return your benevolence." . . .
So saying, she vanished into the night.

Before dawn the tempest had passed; and when the sun arose there was no trace of cloud in the pure blue sky. Matsumura sent at an early hour for well-cleaners to search the well. Then, to everybody's surprise, the well proved to be almost dry. It was easily cleaned; and at the bottom of it were found some hair-ornaments of a very ancient fashion, and a metal mirror of curious form—but no trace of any body, animal or human.

Matsumura imagined, however, that the mirror might yield some explanation of the mystery; for every such mirror is a weird thing, having a soul of its own—and the soul of a mirror is feminine. This mirror, which seemed to be very old, was deeply crusted with scurf. But when it had been carefully cleaned, by the priest's order, it proved to be of rare and costly workmanship; and there were wonderful designs upon the back of it—also several characters. Some of the characters had become indistinguishable; but there could still be discerned part of a date, and ideographs signifying, "third month, the third day." Now the third month used to be termed Yayoi (meaning, the Month of Increase); and the third day of the third month, which is a festival day, is still called Yayoi-no-sekku. Remembering that the Well-Person called herself "Yayoi," Matsumura felt almost sure that his ghostly visitant had been none other than the Soul of the Mirror.

He therefore resolved to treat the mirror with all the consideration due to a Spirit. After having caused it to be carefully repolished and re-silvered, he had a case of precious wood made for it, and a particular room in the house prepared to receive it. On the evening of the same day that it had been respectfully deposited in that room, Yayoi herself unexpectedly appeared before the priest as he sat alone in his study. She looked even more lovely than before; but the light of her beauty was now soft as the light of a summer moon shining through pure white clouds. After having humbly saluted Matsumura, she said in her sweetly tinkling voice:

"Now that you have saved me from solitude and sorrow, I have come to thank you. . . . I am indeed, as you supposed, the Spirit of the Mirror. It was in the time of the Emperor Saimei that I was first brought here from Kudara; and I dwelt in the august residence until the time of the Emperor Saga, when I was augustly bestowed upon the Lady Kamo,

Naishinnō of the Imperial Court.[3] Thereafter I became an heirloom ir the House of Fujiwara, and so remained until the period of Hōgen when I was dropped into the well. There I was left and forgotten during the years of the great war.[4] The Master of the Well [5] was a venomous Dragon, who used to live in a lake that once covered a great part of this district. After the lake had been filled in, by government order in order that houses might be built upon the place of it, the Dragon took possession of the well; and when I fell into the well I became subject to him; and he compelled me to lure many people to their deaths. But the gods have banished him forever. . . . Now I have one more favor to beseech: I entreat that you will cause me to be offered up to the Shōgun, the Lord Yoshimasa, who by descent is related to my former possessors. Do me but this last great kindness, and it will bring you good-fortune. . . . But I have also to warn you of a danger. In this house, after to-morrow, you must not stay, because it will be destroyed." . . . And with these words of warning Yayoi disappeared.

Matsumura was able to profit by this premonition. He removed his people and his belongings to another district the next day; and almost immediately afterwards another storm arose, even more violent than the first, causing a flood which swept away the house in which he had been residing.

Some time later, by favor of the Lord Hosokawa, Matsumura was enabled to obtain an audience of the Shōgun Yoshimasa, to whom he presented the mirror, together with a written account of its wonderful history. Then the prediction of the Spirit of the Mirror was fulfilled; for the Shōgun, greatly pleased with this strange gift, not only bestowed costly presents upon Matsumura, but also made an ample grant of money for the rebuilding of the Temple of Ogawachi-Myōjin.

[3] The Emperor Saimei reigned from 655 to 662 (A.D.); the Emperor Saga from 810 to 842. Kudara was an ancient kingdom in southwestern Korea, frequently mentioned in early Japanese history. A Naishinnō was of Imperial blood. In the ancient court-hierarchy there were twenty-five ranks or grades of noble ladies;—that of Naishinnō was seventh in order of precedence.

[4] For centuries the wives of the emperors and the ladies of the Imperial Court were chosen from the Fujiwara clan. The period called Hōgen lasted from 1156 to 1159: the war referred to is the famous war between the Taira and Minamoto clans.

[5] In old-time belief every lake or spring had its invisible guardian, supposed to sometimes take the form of a serpent or dragon. The spirit of a lake or pond was commonly spoken of as Iké-no-Mushi, the Master of the Lake. Here we find the title "Master" given to a dragon living in a well; but the guardian of wells is really the god Suÿin.

The Reconciliation

THERE WAS A YOUNG SAMURAI OF KYŌTO [1] WHO HAD BEEN REDUCED TO poverty by the ruin of his lord, and found himself obliged to leave his home, and to take service with the Governor of a distant province. Before quitting the capital, this samurai divorced his wife—a good and beautiful woman—under the belief that he could better obtain promotion by another alliance. He then married the daughter of a family of some distinction, and took her with him to the district whither he had been called.

But it was in the time of the thoughtlessness of youth, and the sharp experience of want, that the samurai could not understand the worth of the affection so lightly cast away. His second marriage did not prove a happy one; the character of his new wife was hard and selfish; and he soon found every cause to think with regret of Kyōto days. Then he discovered that he still loved his first wife—loved her more than he could ever love the second; and he began to feel how unjust and how thankless he had been. Gradually his repentance deepened into a remorse that left him no peace of mind. Memories of the woman he had wronged—her gentle speech, her smiles, her dainty, pretty ways, her faultless patience—continually haunted him. Sometimes in dreams he saw her at her loom, weaving as when she toiled night and day to help him during the years of their distress: more often he saw her kneeling alone in the desolate little room where he had left her, veiling her tears with her poor worn sleeve. Even in the hours of official duty, his thoughts would wander back to her: then he would ask himself how she was living, what she was doing. Something in his heart assured him that she could not accept another hus-

[1] The original story is to be found in the curious volume entitled *Konséki-Monogatari.*

band, and that she never would refuse to pardon him. And he secretly resolved to seek her out as soon as he could return to Kyōto—then to beg her forgiveness, to take her back, to do everything that a man could do to make atonement. But the years went by.

At last the Governor's official term expired, and the samurai was free. "Now I will go back to my dear one," he vowed to himself. "Ah, what a cruelty—what a folly to have divorced her!" He sent his second wife to her own people (she had given him no children); and hurrying to Kyōto, he went at once to seek his former companion—not allowing himself even the time to change his traveling-garb.

When he reached the street where she used to live, it was late in the night—the night of the tenth day of the ninth month;—and the city was silent as a cemetery. But a bright moon made everything visible; and he found the house without difficulty. It had a deserted look: tall weeds were growing on the roof. He knocked at the sliding-doors, and no one answered. Then, finding that the doors had not been fastened from within, he pushed them open, and entered. The front room was matless and empty: a chilly wind was blowing through crevices in the planking; and the moon shone through a ragged break in the wall of the alcove. Other rooms presented a like forlorn condition. The house, to all seeming, was unoccupied. Nevertheless, the samurai determined to visit one other apartment at the farther end of the dwelling—a very small room that had been his wife's favorite resting-place. Approaching the sliding-screen that closed it, he was startled to perceive a glow within. He pushed the screen aside, and uttered a cry of joy; for he saw her there—sewing by the light of a paper-lamp. Her eyes at the same instant met his own; and with a happy smile she greeted him—asking only: "When did you come back to Kyōto? How did you find your way here to me, through all those black rooms?" The years had not changed her. Still she seemed as fair and young as in his fondest memory of her;—but sweeter than any memory there came to him the music of her voice, with its trembling of pleased wonder.

Then joyfully he took his place beside her, and told her all:—how deeply he repented his selfishness—how wretched he had been without her—how constantly he had regretted her—how long he had hoped and planned to make amends;—caressing her the while, and asking her forgiveness over and over again. She answered him, with loving gentleness, according to his heart's desire—entreating him to cease all self-reproach. It was wrong, she said, that he should have allowed himself to suffer on her account: she had always felt that she was not worthy to be his wife. She knew that he had separated from her, notwithstanding, only because of poverty; and while he lived with her, he had always been kind; and she had never ceased to pray for his happiness. But even if there had been a reason for speaking of amends, this honorable visit would be ample amends;—what greater happiness than thus to see him again, though it were only for a moment?

"Only for a moment!" he answered, with a glad laugh—"say, rather, for the time of seven existences! My loved one, unless you forbid, I am coming back to live with you always—always—always! Nothing shall ever separate us again. Now I have means and friends: we need not fear poverty. To-morrow my goods will be brought here; and my servants will come to wait upon you; and we shall make this house beautiful. . . . To-night," he added, apologetically, "I came thus late—without even changing my dress—only because of the longing I had to see you, and to tell you this." She seemed greatly pleased by these words; and in her turn she told him about all that had happened in Kyōto since the time of his departure—excepting her own sorrows, of which she sweetly refused to speak. They chatted far into the night: then she conducted him to a warmer room, facing south—a room that had been their bridal chamber in former time. "Have you no one in the house to help you?" he asked, as she began to prepare the couch for him. "No," she answered, laughing cheerfully: "I could not afford a servant;—so I have been living all alone." "You will have plenty of servants to-morrow," he said—"good servants—and everything else that you need." They lay down to rest—not to sleep: they had too much to tell each other;—and they talked of the past and the present and the future, until the dawn was gray. Then, involuntarily, the samurai closed his eyes, and slept.

When he awoke, the daylight was streaming through the chinks of the sliding-shutters; and he found himself, to his utter amazement, lying upon the naked boards of a mouldering floor. . . . Had he only dreamed a dream? No: she was there;—she slept. . . . He bent above her—and looked—and shrieked—for the sleeper had no face! . . . Before him, wrapped in its grave-sheet only, lay the corpse of a woman—a corpse so wasted that little remained save the bones, and the long black tangled hair.

• •

Slowly—as he stood shuddering and sickening in the sun—the icy horror yielded to despair so intolerable, a pain so atrocious, that he clutched at the mocking shadow of a doubt. Feigning ignorance of the neighborhood, he ventured to ask his way to the house in which his wife had lived.

"There is no one in that house," said the person questioned. "It used to belong to the wife of a samurai who left the city several years ago. He divorced her in order to marry another woman before he went away; and she fretted a great deal, and so became sick. She had no relatives in Kyōto, and nobody to care for her; and she died in the autumn of the same year—on the tenth day of the ninth month. . . ."

Story of a Tengu

IN THE DAYS OF THE EMPEROR GO-REIZEI,[1] THERE WAS A HOLY PRIEST LIVING in the temple of Saito, on the mountain called Hiyei-Zan, near Kyōto. One summer day this good priest, after a visit to the city, was returning to his temple by way of Kita-no-Ōji, when he saw some boys ill-treating a kite. They had caught the bird in a snare, and were beating it with sticks. "Oh, the poor creature!" compassionately exclaimed the priest;—why do you torment it so, children?" One of the boys made answer: "We want to kill it to get the feathers." Moved by pity, the priest persuaded the boys to let him have the kite in exchange for a fan that he was carrying; and he set the bird free. It had not been seriously hurt, and was able to fly away.

[1] This story may be found in the curious old Japanese book called "Jikkun-Shō." The same legend has furnished the subject of an interesting No-play, called "Dai-É" (The Great Assembly).

In Japanese popular art, the Tengu are commonly represented either as winged men with beak-shaped noses, or as birds of prey. There are different kinds of Tengu; but all are supposed to be mountain-haunting spirits, capable of assuming many forms, and occasionally appearing as crows, vultures, or eagles. Buddhism appears to class the Tengu among the Mârakâyikas.

Happy at having performed this Buddhist act of merit, the priest then resumed his walk. He had not proceeded very far when he saw a strange monk come out of a bamboo-grove by the roadside, and hasten toward him. The monk respectfully saluted him, and said: "Sir, through your compassionate kindness my life has been saved; and I now desire to express my gratitude in a fitting manner." Astonished at hearing himself thus addressed, the priest replied: "Really, I cannot remember to have ever seen you before: please tell me who you are." "It is not wonderful that you cannot recognize me in this form," returned the monk: "I am the kite that those cruel boys were tormenting at Kita-no-Ōji. You saved my life; and there is nothing in this world more precious than life. So I now wish to return your kindness in some way or other. If there be anything that you would like to have, or to know, or to see—anything that I can do for you, in short—please to tell me; for as I happen to possess, in a small degree, the Six Supernatural Powers, I am able to gratify almost any wish that you can express." On hearing these words, the priest knew that he was speaking with a Tengu; and he frankly made answer: "My friend, I have long ceased to care for the things of this world: I am now seventy years of age;—neither fame nor pleasure has any attraction for me. I feel anxious only about my future birth; but as that is a matter in which no one can help me, it were useless to ask about it. Really, I can think of but one thing worth wishing for. It has been my lifelong regret that I was not in India in the time of the Lord Buddha, and could not attend the great assembly on the holy mountain Gridhrakûta. Never a day passes in which this regret does not come to me, in the hour of morning or of evening prayer. Ah, my friend! if it were possible to conquer Time and Space, like the Bodhissattvas, so that I could look upon that marvelous assembly, how happy I should be!" "Why," the Tengu exclaimed, "that pious wish of yours can easily be satisfied. I perfectly well remember the assembly on the Vulture Peak; and I can cause everything that happened there to reappear before you, exactly as it occurred. It is our greatest delight to represent such holy matters. . . . Come this way with me!"

And the priest suffered himself to be led to a place among pines, on the slope of a hill. "Now," said the Tengu, "you have only to wait here for awhile, with your eyes shut. Do not open them until you hear the voice of the Buddha preaching the Law. Then you can look. But when you see the appearance of the Buddha, you must not allow

your devout feelings to influence you in any way;—you must not bow
down, nor pray, nor utter any such exclamation as, 'Even so, Lord!'
or, 'O thou Blessed One!' You must not speak at all. Should you make
even the least sign of reverence, something very unfortunate might
happen to me." The priest gladly promised to follow these injunc-
tions; and the Tengu hurried away as if to prepare the spectacle.

The day waned and passed, and the darkness came; but the old
priest waited patiently beneath a tree, keeping his eyes closed. At last
a voice suddenly resounded above him—a wonderful voice, deep and
clear like the pealing of a mighty bell—the voice of the Buddha Sâkya-
muni proclaiming the Perfect Way. Then the priest, opening his eyes
in a great radiance, perceived that all things had been changed: the
place was indeed the Vulture Peak—the holy Indian mountain Gridhrakûta; and the time was the time of the Sutra of the Lotus of the
Good Law. Now there were no pines about him, but strange shining
trees made of the Seven Precious Substances, with foliage and fruit of
gems;—and the ground was covered with Mandârava and Manjûshaka
flowers showered from heaven;—and the night was filled with fragrance and splendor and the sweetness of the great Voice. And in
mid-air, shining as a moon above the world, the priest beheld the
Blessed One seated upon the Lion-throne, with Samantabhadra at his
right hand, and Mañjusrî at his left—and before them assembled—
immeasurably spreading into Space, like a flood of stars—the hosts of
the Mahâsattvas and the Bodhissattvas with their countless following:
"gods, demons, Nâgas, goblins, men, and beings not human." Sâriputra
he saw, and Kâsyapa, and Ânanda, with all the disciples of the Tathâgata—and the Kings of the Devas—and the Kings of the Four Directions, like pillars of fire—and the great Dragon-Kings—and the
Gandharvas and Garudas—and the Gods of the Sun and the Moon
and the Wind—and the shining myriads of Brahma's heaven. And incomparably further than even the measureless circling of the glory of
these, he saw—made visible by a single ray of light that shot from
the forehead of the Blessed One to pierce beyond uttermost Time—
the eighteen hundred thousand Buddha-fields of the Eastern Quarter
with all their habitants—and the beings in each of the Six States of
Existence—and even the shapes of the Buddhas extinct, that had
entered into Nirvâna. These, and all the gods, and all the demons, he
saw bow down before the Lion-throne; and he heard that multitude
incalculable of beings praising the Sutra of the Lotus of the Good

Law—like the roar of a sea before the Lord. Then forgetting utterly his pledge—foolishly dreaming that he stood in the very presence of the very Buddha—he cast himself down in worship with tears of love and thanksgiving; crying out with a loud voice, "O thou Blessed One!" . . .

Instantly with a shock as of earthquake the stupendous spectacle disappeared; and the priest found himself alone in the dark, kneeling upon the grass of the mountain-side. Then a sadness unspeakable fell upon him, because of the loss of the vision, and because of the thoughtlessness that had caused him to break his word. As he sorrowfully turned his steps homeward, the goblin-monk once more appeared before him, and said to him in tones of reproach and pain: "Because you did not keep the promise which you made to me, and heedlessly allowed your feelings to overcome you, the Gohō-tendo, who is the Guardian of the Doctrine, swooped down suddenly from heaven upon us, and smote us in great anger, crying out, 'How do ye dare thus to deceive a pious person?' Then the other monks, whom I had assembled, all fled in fear. As for myself, one of my wings has been broken—so that now I cannot fly." And with these words the Tengu vanished forever.

Of a Promise Kept

"I SHALL RETURN IN THE EARLY AUTUMN," SAID AKANA SOYĒMON [1] SEVERAL hundred years ago—when bidding good-bye to his brother by adoption, young Hasébé Samon. The time was spring; and the place was the village of Kato in the province of Harima. Akana was an Izumo samurai; and he wanted to visit his birthplace.

Hasébé said:

"Your Izumo—the Country of the Eight-Cloud Rising [2]—is very

[1] Related in the *Ugétsu Monogatari.*
[2] One of the old poetical names for the province of Izumo, or Unshu.

distant. Perhaps it will therefore be difficult for you to promise to return here upon any particular day. But, if we were to know the exact day, we should feel happier. We could then prepare a feast of welcome and we could watch at the gateway for your coming."

"Why, as for that," responded Akana, "I have been so much accustomed to travel that I can usually tell beforehand how long it will take me to reach a place; and I can safely promise you to be here upon a particular day. Suppose we say the day of the festival Chōyō?"

"That is the ninth day of the ninth month," said Hasébé;—"then the chrysanthemums will be in bloom, and we can go together to look at them. How pleasant! . . . So you promise to come back on the ninth day of the ninth month?"

"On the ninth day of the ninth month," repeated Akana, smiling farewell. Then he strode away from the village of Kato in the province of Harima;—and Hasébé Samon and the mother of Hasébé looked after him with tears in their eyes.

"Neither the Sun nor the Moon," says an old Japanese proverb, "ever halt upon their journey." Swiftly the months went by; and the autumn came—the season of chrysanthemums. And early upon the morning of the ninth day of the ninth month Hasébé prepared to welcome his adopted brother. He made ready a feast of good things, bought wine, decorated the guest-room, and filled the vases of the alcove with chrysanthemums of two colors. Then his mother, watching him, said: "The province of Izumo, my son, is more than one hundred *ri*[3] from this place; and the journey thence over the mountains is difficult and weary; and you cannot be sure that Akana will be able to come to-day. Would it not be better, before you take all this trouble, to wait for his coming?" "Nay, mother!" Hasébé made answer —"Akana promised to be here to-day: he could not break a promise! And if he were to see us beginning to make preparation after his arrival, he would know that we had doubted his word; and we should be put to shame."

The day was beautiful, the sky without a cloud, and the air so pure that the world seemed to be a thousand miles wider than usual. In the morning many travelers passed through the village—some of them samurai; and Hasébé, watching each as he came, more than once imagined that he saw Akana approaching. But the temple-bells

[3] A *ri* is about equal to two and a half English miles.

sounded the hour of midday; and Akana did not appear. Through the afternoon also Hasébé watched and waited in vain. The sun set; and still there was no sign of Akana. Nevertheless Hasébé remained at the gate, gazing down the road. Later his mother went to him, and said: "The mind of a man, my son—as our proverb declares—may change as quickly as the sky of autumn. But your chrysanthemum-flowers will still be fresh to-morrow. Better now to sleep; and in the morning you can watch again for Akana, if you wish." "Rest well, mother," returned Hasébé;—"but I still believe that he will come." Then the mother went to her own room; and Hasébé lingered at the gate.

The night was pure as the day had been: all the sky throbbed with stars; and the white River of Heaven shimmered with unusual splendor. The village slept;—the silence was broken only by the noise of a little brook, and by the far-away barking of peasants' dogs. Hasébé still waited—waited until he saw the thin moon sink behind the neighboring hills. Then at last he began to doubt and to fear. Just as he was about to reënter the house, he perceived in the distance a tall man approaching—very lightly and quickly; and in the next moment he recognized Akana.

"Oh!" cried Hasébé, springing to meet him—"I have been waiting for you from the morning until now! . . . So you really did keep your promise after all. . . . But you must be tired, poor brother!—come in;—everything is ready for you." He guided Akana to the place of honor in the guest-room, and hastened to trim the lights, which were burning low. "Mother," continued Hasébé, "felt a little tired this evening, and she has already gone to bed; but I shall awaken her presently." Akana shook his head, and made a little gesture of disapproval. "As you will, brother," said Hasébé; and he set warm food and wine before the traveler. Akana did not touch the food or the wine, but remained motionless and silent for a short time. Then, speaking in a whisper—as if fearful of awakening the mother, he said:

"Now I must tell you how it happened that I came thus late. When I returned to Izumo I found that the people had almost forgotten the kindness of our former ruler, the good Lord Enya, and were seeking the favor of the usurper Tsunéhisa, who had possessed himself of the Tonda Castle. But I had to visit my cousin, Akana Tanji, though he had accepted service under Tsunéhisa, and was living, as a retainer, within the castle grounds. He persuaded me to present myself before Tsunéhisa: I yielded chiefly in order to observe the character of the new ruler, whose face I had never seen. He is a skilled soldier, and of great courage; but he is cunning and cruel. I found it necessary to let him know that I could never enter into his service. After I left his presence he ordered my cousin to detain me—to keep me confined within the house. I protested that I had promised to return to Harima upon the ninth day of the ninth month; but I was refused permission to go. I then hoped to escape from the castle at night; but I was constantly watched; and until to-day I could find no way to fulfill my promise...."

"Until to-day!" exclaimed Hasébé in bewilderment;—"the castle is more than a hundred ri from here!"

"Yes," returned Akana; "and no living man can travel on foot a hundred ri in one day. But I felt that, if I did not keep my promise, you could not think well of me; and I remembered the ancient proverb, *Tama yoku ichi nichi ni sen ri wo yuku*' (The soul of a man can journey a thousand ri in a day). Fortunately I had been allowed to keep my sword;—thus only was I able to come to you.... Be good to our mother."

With these words he stood up, and in the same instant disappeared.

Then Hasébé knew that Akana had killed himself in order to fulfill the promise.

At earliest dawn Hasébé Samon set out for the Castle Tonda, in the province of Izumo. Reaching Matsué, he there learned that, on the night of the ninth day of the ninth month, Akana Soyëmon had performed harakiri in the house of Akana Tanji, in the grounds of the castle. Then Hasébé went to the house of Akana Tanji, and reproached Akana Tanji for the treachery done, and slew him in the midst of his family, and escaped without hurt. And when the Lord Tsunéhisa had heard the story, he gave commands that Hasébé should not be pursued. For, although an unscrupulous and cruel man himself, the Lord Tsunéhisa could respect the love of truth in others, and could admire the friendship and the courage of Hasébé Samon.

Sources and Bibliography

SOURCES

Kwaidan

This collection of stories was published in book form in 1904 by Houghton Mifflin Company. Two of the selections had previously been printed in magazines: "The Story of Mimi-Nashi-Hōïchi" in *Atlantic Monthly*, August 1903, and "The Dream of Akinosuké" in *Atlantic Monthly*, March 1904.

Some Chinese Ghosts

Published as a book in 1887 by Roberts Bros. "The Legend of Tchi-Niu" had first appeared in *Harper's Bazaar*, October 31, 1885.

Chita

First appeared in *Harper's New Monthly Magazine*, April 1888.

American Sketches

"Gibbeted" from *Cincinnati Commercial*, August 26, 1876.

"Levee Life" from *Cincinnati Commercial*, March 17, 1876.

"Violent Cremation" from *Cincinnati Enquirer*, November 9, 1874.

"Dolly: An Idyl of the Levee" from *Cincinnati Commercial*, August 27, 1876.

"Some Pictures of Poverty" from *Cincinnati Commercial*, January 7, 1877.

"A Creole Type" from *New Orleans Item*, May 6, 1879.

"The Dawn of the Carnival" from *New Orleans Item*, February 2, 1880.

"Creole Servant Girls" from *New Orleans Item*, December 20, 1880.

"Why Crabs Are Boiled Alive" from *New Orleans Item*, October 5, 1879.

"Voices of Dawn" from *New Orleans Item*, July 22, 1881.

"The Last of the Voudoos" from *Harpers Weekly*, November 7, 1885.

"New Orleans Superstitions" from *Harpers Weekly*, December 25, 1886.

Caribbean Sketches

Published in *Martinique Sketches* by Harper & Bros. in 1890. "La Grande Anse" had originally appeared in *Harpers Weekly*, November 1889, and "Les Porteuses" in *Harpers Weekly*, July 1889.

Japan

"At a Railway Station" from *Kokoro*, published 1896 by Houghton Mifflin Company.

"The Nun of the Temple of Amida" from *Kokoro*.

"Haru" from *Kokoro*.

"Kimiko" from *Kokoro*.

"The Red Bridal" from *Atlantic*, July 1894.

"The Case of O-Dai" from *A Japanese Miscellany*, published 1901 by Little, Brown & Company.

"The Story of O-Kamé" from *Kotto*, published 1902 by Macmillan Co.

"Common Sense" from *Kotto*.

"My First Day in the Orient" from *Times-Democrat*, February 7 and 14, 1892.

"The Dream of a Summer Day" from *Japan Weekly Mail*, July 28, 1894.

"Fuji-No-Yama" from *Exotics and Retrospectives*, published 1898 by Little, Brown & Company.

"A Woman's Diary" from *Kotto*, published 1902 by Macmillan Co.

"Out of the Street" from *Gleanings in Buddha-Fields*, published 1897 by Houghton Mifflin Company.

"The Romance of the Milky Way" from *Atlantic Monthly*, August 1905.

"Of the Eternal Feminine" from *Atlantic*, December 1893.

"A Glimpse of Tendencies" from *Kokoro*.

"Industrial Danger" from *Japan: an Attempt at Interpretation*, published 1904 by Macmillan Co.

"The Mirror Maiden" from *The Romance of the Milky Way and Other Studies and Stories*, published 1905 by Houghton Mifflin Company.

The Reconciliation" from *Shadowings*, published 1900 by Little, Brown & Company.

"Story of a Tengu" from *In Ghostly Japan*, published 1899 by Little, Brown & Company.

"Of a Promise Kept" from *A Japanese Miscellany*, published 1901 by Little, Brown & Company.

BIBLIOGRAPHY

─────────── ❧ ✳ ❧ ───────────

Books

BAREL, LEONA (QUEYROUZE): *The Idyl—My personal reminiscences of Lafcadio Hearn.* The Hokuseido Press, Tokyo, 1933.

BISLAND, ELIZABETH: *The Life and Letters of Lafcadio Hearn.* 2 vols, Houghton Mifflin, Boston, 1906.

BISLAND, ELIZABETH: *The Japanese Letters of Lafcadio Hearn.* Houghton Mifflin, Boston, 1910.

GOULD, GEORGE M.: *Concerning Lafcadio Hearn.* Jacobs & Company, Philadelphia, 1908.

HENDRICK, ELLWOOD: *Lafcadio Hearn.* The N. Y. Public Library, 1929.

KENNARD, NINA H.: *Lafcadio Hearn;* containing some letters from Lafcadio Hearn to his half-sister, Mrs. Atkinson. Appleton & Company, New York, 1918.

KIRKWOOD, KENNETH PORTER: *Unfamiliar Lafcadio Hearn.* The Hokuseido Press, Tokyo, 1936.

564

KOIZUMI, KAZUO: *Father and I; Memories of Lafcadio Hearn.* Houghton Mifflin, Boston, 1935.

LEWIS, OSCAR: *Hearn and His Biographers;* the record of a literary controversy; together with a group of letters from Lafcadio Hearn to Joseph Tunison. Westgate Press, San Francisco, 1930.

MCWILLIAMS, VERA SEELEY: *Lafcadio Hearn.* Houghton Mifflin, Boston, 1946.

TEMPLE, JEAN: *Blue Ghost, a Study of Lafcadio Hearn.* Jonathan Cape and Harrison Smith, New York, 1931.

TINKER, EDW. LAROCQUE: *Lafcadio Hearn's American Days.* Dodd, Mead & Co., New York, 1924.

Articles

AMENOMORI, NOBUSHIGE: "Lafcadio Hearn, the Man." *Atlantic Monthly,* 96:510-25, 1905.

BALL, CHARLES E.: "Lafcadio Hearn, an appreciation," being a lecture delivered before *La Société Internationale de Philologie, Sciences, et Beaux Arts,* on 11 May, 1926. Caxton Book Shop, London, 1926.

BLANCK, JACOB: "Avatar—Hearn or Saltus?" *Publishers Weekly,* 131: 2498-99, 1937.

BOYNTON, PERCY H.: "Lafcadio Hearn." *Virginia Quarterly Review,* 3:418-34, 1927.

BOYNTON, PERCY H.: "Lafcadio Hearn." Chapter III, 51-73, in *More Contemporary Americans,* University of Chicago Press, 1927.

GORMAN, HERBERT S.: "Lafcadio Hearn." Chapter VII, 125-35, in *The Procession of Masks,* B. J. Brimmer Co., Boston, 1923.

GOULD, GEORGE M., M.D.: "Lafcadio Hearn." Chapter VI, 209-37, in *Biographic Clinics,* Vol. IV, P. Blakiston's Son & Co., Philadelphia, 1906.

GOULD, GEORGE M., M.D.: "Lafcadio Hearn. A study of his Personality and Art." *Putnam's Monthly* (new series), 1:97-107; 156-66, 1906.

HANEY, JOHN LOUIS: "Lafcadio Hearn." Pages 279-80 in *The Story of Our Literature,* Scribners, New York, 1923.

HARTING, HUGH: "American Days of Lafcadio Hearn." *Landmark,* 9:113-16, London, 1927.

HEARNE, WILLIAM T.: Eight-page biography of Lafcadio Hearn, in *Brief History and Genealogy of the Hearne Family,* Independence, Missouri, 1907.

HUNEKER, JAMES: "The Cult of the Nuance: Lafcadio Hearn." Chapter

XIII, 240-48, in *Ivory, Apes and Peacocks,* Chas. Scribners Sons, New York, 1915.

JOSEPHSON, MATTHEW: "An Enemy of the West: Lafcadio Hearn." Chapter VI, 199-231, in *Portrait of the Artist as American,* Harcourt Brace, New York, 1930.

KOIZUMI, SETSUKO (MRS. HEARN): "The Last Days of Lafcadio Hearn." *Atlantic Monthly,* 119:349-51, 1917.

KOIZUMI, SETSUKO: "Reminiscences of Lafcadio Hearn." *Atlantic Monthly,* 122:342-51, 1918.

KIRKWOOD, KENNETH PORTER: "Lafcadio Hearn's Ancestry." *Cultural Nippon,* Vol. VI, No. 4, Tokyo, 1938.

KOWAKAMI, K. K.: "Lafcadio Hearn—lover or hater of Japan." *Japan,* 15:13-14; 44, San Francisco, January 1926.

KENT, CHARLES W.: "Biography of Lafcadio Hearn." Pages 2341-6 in *Library of Southern Literature,* Vol. VI, Martin & Hoyt Co., New Orleans, 1909.

MONAHAN, MICHAEL: "The Humor of Hearn in 'Letters from the Raven.'" Section III, 195-198, in *Adventures in Life and Letters,* George H. Doran Co., New York, 1912.

MONAHAN, MICHAEL: "A Note on Lafcadio Hearn." Pages 193-98 in *New Adventures,* Doran Co., New York, 1917.

MORDELL, ALBERT: "The Ideas of Lafcadio Hearn." Chapter XVII, 237-43, in *The Erotic Motive in Literature,* Boni & Liveright, 1919.

MORE, PAUL ELMER: Pages 46-72 in *Shelburn Essays—Second Series,* G. P. Putnam Sons, New York, 1905.

NICOLL, W. ROBERTSON: "Lafcadio Hearn: An Unconventional Life." Chapter XXXVII, 331-37, in *A Bookman's Letters,* Hodder & Stoughton, London and New York, 1913.

OGILVIE, J. S.: A story about Lafcadio Hearn, No. 45 in *The Man in the Street (Stories from the New York Times),* J. S. Ogilvie Publishing Co., New York, 1902.

PATTEE, FRED LEWIS: "Lafcadio Hearn." Chapter XIV, 217-28, in *The New American Literature,* Century Company, New York, 1930.

PATTEE, FRED LEWIS: "The Essayists." Chapter XVIII, 420-28; 434-35; 437, in *A History of American Literature,* Century Company, New York, 1915.

TINKER, EDW. LAROCQUE: "Lafcadio Hearn." Pages 484-87, in *Dictionary of American Biography,* Vol. VIII, Scribners, 1932.

OF LITERATURE

ROBERT SCHOLES
Brown University

CARL H. KLAUS
The University of Iowa

MICHAEL SILVERMAN
Brown University

UNIVERSITY PRESS ♔ 1978

Library of Congress Cataloging in Publication Data

Main entry under title:
Elements of literature.

Includes index.
1. Literature—Collections. I. Scholes, Robert
II. Klaus, Carl H. III. Silverman, Michael, 1938-
PN6014.E4   808.8   77-2743
ISBN 0-19-502265-3 pbk.

Printed in the United States of America

Acknowledgments

E. M. Forster. "Our Graves at Gallipoli" from *Abinger Harvest*. Copyright 1936, 1964 by E. M. Forster. Reprinted by permission of Harcourt Brace Jovanovich, Inc.

Robert Frost. From *The Poetry of Robert Frost*, edited by Edward Connery Lathem. Copyright 1923, 1930, 1939, © 1969 by Holt, Rinehart and Winston. Copyright 1936, 1951, © 1958 by Robert Frost. Copyright © 1964, 1967 by Lesley Frost Ballantine. Reprinted by permission of Holt, Rinehart and Winston, Publishers.

Dick Gregory. "If You Had to Kill Your Own Hog" from *The Shadow That Scares Me*. Copyright © 1968 by Dick Gregory. Reprinted by permission of Doubleday & Company, Inc.

Michael S. Harper. "History as Apple Tree" from *Song: I Want a Witness*. © 1972 by Michael S. Harper. Reprinted by permission of the University of Pittsburgh Press. "This is my Son's Song" and "Blue Ruth: America" from *History Is Your Own Heartbeat:* "mahalia: MAHALIA" and "Roland" from *Nightmare Becomes Responsibility*. Reprinted by permission of The University of Illinois Press and the author.

Ernest Hemingway. "Hills like White Elephants" from *Men Without Women*. Copyright 1927 by Charles Scribner's Sons. Reprinted by permission of Charles Scribner's Sons.

Herodotus. From *The Histories*, trans. Aubrey de Sélincourt. Copyright © 1954 by the Estate of Aubrey de Sélincourt, copyright © 1972 by A. R. Burn. Reprinted by permission of Penguin Books Ltd.

Gerald Manley Hopkins. From *The Poems of Gerald Manley Hopkins*, fourth ed., edited by W. H. Gardner and N. H. Mackenzie. Reprinted by permission of Oxford University Press, Inc.

A. E. Housman. From "A Shropshire Lad" (Authorized Edition) in *The Collected Poems of A. E. Housman*. Copyright 1939, 1940, © 1965 by Holt, Rinehart and Winston, copyright © 1967, 1968 by Robert E. Symons. Reprinted by permission of Holt, Rinehart and Winston, Publishers.

Langston Hughes. From *Selected Poems*: "Spirituals," copyright 1947 by Langston Hughes. "I, Too," copyright 1926 by Alfred A. Knopf, Inc., renewed 1954 by Langston Hughes. "Early Evening Quarrel," copyright 1942 by Alfred A. Knopf, Inc. "Aunt Sue's Stories," copyright 1926 by Alfred A. Knopf, Inc., renewed 1954 by Langston Hughes. "Trumpet Player," copyright 1947 by Langston Hughes. "Young Sailor", copyright 1926 by Alfred A. Knopf, Inc., renewed 1954 by Langston Hughes. All reprinted by permission of Alfred A. Knopf, Inc.

Henrik Ibsen. "A Doll's House" from *Ghosts and Three Other Plays*, trans. Michael Meyer. Copyright © 1966 by Michael Meyer. Reprinted by permission of Doubleday & Company, Inc.

Shirley Jackson. "The Lottery" from *The Lottery*; appeared originally in *The New Yorker*. Copyright 1948, 1949 by Shirley Jackson, renewed © 1976 by Laurence Hyman, Barry Hyman, Mrs. Sarah Webster, and Mrs. Joanne Schnurer. Reprinted by permission of Farrar, Straus & Giroux, Inc.

James Joyce. "The Boarding House" and "Clay" from *Dubliners*; published originally by B. W. Huesch, Inc. in 1916. Copyright © 1967 by the Estate of James Joyce. All rights reserved. Reprinted by permission of The Viking Press.

Franz Kafka. "On Parables" and "An Imperial Message" from *Parables and Paradoxes*, trans. Willa and Edwin Muir. Copyright © 1946, 1947, 1948, 1953, 1954, 1958 by Schocken Books Inc. Reprinted by permission of Schocken Books Inc.

William Knott. "Survival of the Fittest Groceries." Copyright © 1977 by the Heirs of William Knott's Estate. Reprinted by permission of Bill Knott.

D. H. Lawrence. "The Rocking-Horse Winner" from *The Complete Short Stories of D. H. Lawrence*, Volume III. Copyright 1933 by the Estate of D. H. Lawrence, © 1961 by Angelo Ravagli and C. M. Weekley, Executors of the Estate of Frieda Lawrence Ravagli. "The Christening" from *The Complete Short Stories of D. H. Lawrence*, Volume I. All Rights Reserved. "Piano" (2 versions) from *The Complete Poems of D. H. Lawrence*, edited by Vivian de Sola Pinto and F. Warren Roberts. Copyright © 1964, 1971 by Angelo Ravagli and C. M. Weekley, Executors of The Estate of Frieda Lawrence Ravagli. "Cocksure Women and Hensure Men" from *Phoenix II* by D. H. Lawrence. Copyright 1928 by Forum Publishing Co., copyright © 1956 by Frieda Lawrence Ravagli. All reprinted by permission of The Viking Press.

Ursula D. Le Guin. "The Ones Who Walk Away from Omelas" from *The Wind's Twelve Quarters*. Copyright © 1973, 1975 by Ursula K. Le Guin. Reprinted by permission of the author and the author's agent, Virginia Kidd.

Doris Lessing. "A Sunrise on the Veld" from *African Stories*. Copyright © 1951, 1953, 1954, 1957, 1958, 1962, 1963, 1964, 1965 by Doris Lessing. Reprinted by permission of Simon & Schuster, Division of Gulf & Western Corporation.

Philip Levine. "Ricky" from *The Iowa Review*. "For Fran" from *On the Edge* (The Stonewall Press). Copyright 1963 by Philip Levine. Reprinted by permission of the author. "Losing You" and "Hold Me" from *1933*; "Losing You" appeared originally in *Poetry*, "Hold Me" in *American Poetry Review*. Copyright © 1974 by Philip Levine. Reprinted by permission of Atheneum Publishers. "No One Remembers" from *The Names of the Lost*; appeared originally in *The New Yorker*. Copyright © 1976 by Philip Levine. Reprinted by permission of Atheneum Publishers.

Livy. From *The Early History of Rome*, trans. Aubrey de Sélincourt. Copyright © 1960 by the Estate of Aubrey de Sélincourt. Reprinted by permission of Penguin Books Ltd.

Norman Mailer. "A Statement for *Architectural Forum*" from *Cannibals and Christians*. Copyright © 1964 by Urban America, Inc. Reprinted by permission of the author and the author's agent, Scott Meredith Literary Agency, Inc., 745 Third Avenue, New York, N.Y. 10022.

Bernard Malamud. "The Magic Barrel" from *The Magic Barrel*. Copyright © 1954, 1958 by Bernard Malamud. Reprinted by permission of Farrar, Straus & Giroux, Inc.

Katherine Mansfield. "Six Years After" from *The Short Stories of Katherine Mansfield*. Copyright 1923 by Alfred A. Knopf, Inc., renewed 1951 by John Middleton Murry. Reprinted by permission of Alfred A. Knopf, Inc.

W. S. Merwin. "Envoy from d'Aubigné," "Tale," and "Elegy" from *The Carrier of Ladders*; "Envoy from d'Aubigné" appeared originally in *The New Yorker*. Copyright © 1969, 1970 by W. S. Merwin. "Separation" and "Departure's Girl Friend" from *The Moving Target*; "Separation" appeared originally in *The New Yorker*. Copyright © 1961, 1962, 1963 by W. S. Merwin. "When You Go Away" and "For a Coming Extinction" from *The Lice*. Copyright © 1966, 1967 by W. S. Merwin. All poems reprinted by permission of Atheneum Publishers.

Molière. *The Misanthrope*, trans. Richard Wilbur. Copyright © 1954, 1955 by Richard Wilbur. Reprinted by permission of Harcourt Brace Jovanovich, Inc.
  Caution: Professionals and amateurs are hereby warned that this translation, being fully protected under the copyright laws of the United States of America, the British Empire, including the Dominion of Canada, and all other countries which are signatories to the Universal Copyright Convention and the International Copyright Union, is subject to royalty. All rights, including professional, amateur, motion picture, recitation, lecturing, public reading, radio broadcasting, and television are strictly reserved. Particular emphasis is laid on the question of readings, permission for which must be secured from the author's agent in writing. Inquiries on professional rights should be addressed to Mr. Gilbert Parker, Curtis Brown, Ltd., 575 Madison Avenue, New York, N.Y. 10022. The amateur acting rights are controlled exclusively by the Dramatists Play Service, Inc., 440 Park Avenue, New York, N.Y. 10016. No amateur performance may be given without obtaining in advance the written permission of the Dramatists Play Service, Inc., and paying the requisite fee.

Marianne Moore. "A Jellyfish" from *The Complete Poems of Marianne Moore*. Copyright © 1959 by Marianne Moore. Reprinted by permission of The Viking Press. From *Collected Poems*: "Poetry," "A Grave," "The Fish," copyright 1935 by Marianne Moore, renewed 1963 by Marianne Moore and T. S. Eliot; "Nevertheless", copyright 1944 by Marianne Moore, renewed 1972 by Marianne Moore. Reprinted by permission of Macmillan Publishing Co., Inc.

Flannery O'Connor. "Everything That Rises Must Converge" from *Everything That Rises Must Converge*. Copyright © 1961, 1965 by the Estate of Mary Flannery O'Connor. Reprinted by permission of Farrar Straus & Giroux, Inc.

Frank O'Connor. "Guests of the Nation" from *More Stories by Frank O'Connor*. Published in 1954 by Alfred A. Knopf, Inc., and reprinted by permission of the publisher.

Tillie Olsen. "Tell Me a Riddle" from *Tell Me a Riddle*. Copyright © 1960, 1961 by Tillie Olsen. Reprinted by permission of Delacorte Press/Seymour Lawrence.

George Orwell. "Shooting an Elephant" from *Shooting an Elephant and Other Essays*. Copyright 1945, 1946, 1949, 1950 by Sonia Brownell Orwell, copyright 1973, 1974 by Sonia Orwell. Reprinted by permission of Harcourt Brace Jovanovich, Inc.

Ovid. From *Metamorphoses*, Book X, trans. Mary M. Innes. Copyright © 1955 by Mary M. Innes. Reprinted by permission of Penguin Books Ltd.

Dorothy Parker. "You Were Perfectly Fine" from *The Portable Dorothy Parker*. Copyright 1929, © 1957 by Dorothy Parker. Reprinted by permission of The Viking Press.

Petronius. From *Satyricon*, trans. William Arrowsmith. Copyright © 1959 by William Arrowsmith. Reprinted by permission of The University of Michigan Press.

Harold Pinter. "A Slight Ache" from *Three Plays*. Copyright © 1961 by Harold Pinter. Reprinted by permission of Grove Press, Inc.

Sylvia Plath. From *Ariel*: "Daddy," "Kindness," and "Edge," copyright © 1963 by Ted Hughes; "Sheep in Fog," "Words," copyright © 1965 by Ted Hughes. Reprinted by permission of Harper & Row, Publishers, Inc.

Katherine Anne Porter. "Rope" from *Flowering Judas and Other Stories*. Copyright 1930, 1958 by Katherine Anne Porter. Reprinted by permission of Harcourt Brace Jovanovich, Inc.

Adrienne Rich. From *Poems, Selected and New, 1950–1974*. Copyright © 1975, 1973, 1971, 1969, 1966 by W. W. Norton & Company, Inc., copyright © 1967, 1963, 1962, 1961, 1960, 1959, 1958, 1957, 1956, 1955, 1954, 1953, 1952, 1951 by Adrienne Rich. Reprinted by permission of W. W. Norton & Company, Inc.

Edward Arlington Robinson. "Reuben Bright" from *The Children of the Night*. Reprinted by permission of Charles Scribner's Sons.

Theodore Roethke. From *The Collected Poems of Theodore Roethke*: "The Premonition," copyright 1941 by Theodore Roethke; "Dolor," copyright 1943 by Modern Poetry Association, Inc.; "Elegy for Jane," copyright 1950 by Theodore Roethke; "The Walking," copyright 1953 by Theodore Roethke; "I Knew a Woman," copyright 1954 by Theodore Roethke; "The Manifestation," copyright © 1959 by Beatrice Roethke, Administratrix for the Estate of Theodore Roethke. Reprinted by permission of Doubleday & Company, Inc.

George Bernard Shaw. "Arms and the Man". Copyright 1898, 1913, 1926, 1931, 1933, 1941 by George Bernard Shaw, copyright 1905 by Brentano's, copyright 1958 by the Public Trustee as Executor of the Estate of George Bernard Shaw. Reprinted by permission of Dodd, Mead & Company, Inc. and the Society of Authors for the Estate of George Bernard Shaw.

Gary Snyder. "Looking at Pictures to Be Put Away" from *The Back Country*. Copyright © 1968 by Gary Snyder. "It Was When" from *Regarding Wave*. Copyright © 1970 by Gary Snyder. Reprinted by permission of New Directions Publishing Corporation. "Mid-August at Sourdough Mountain Lookout," "An Autumn Morning in Shokoku-ji," and "Riprap" are reprinted by permission of Gary Snyder.

Sophocles. *Oedipux Rex*, trans. Dudley Fitts and Robert Fitzgerald. Copyright 1949 by Harcourt Brace Jovanovich, Inc. Reprinted by permission of the publisher.

Caution: All rights, including professional, amateur, motion picture, recitation, lecturing, public reading, radio broadcasting, and television are strictly reserved. Inquiries on all rights should be addressed to Harcourt Brace Jovanovich, Inc., 757 Third Avenue, New York, N.Y. 10017.

Wallace Stevens. From *The Collected Poems of Wallace Stevens:* "Of Modern Poetry," copyright 1942 by Wallace Stevens, renewed 1970 by Holly Stevens; "Sunday Morning," "The Snow Man," and "A High-Toned Old Christian Woman," copyright 1923, renewed 1951 by Wallace Stevens. "Of Mere Being" from *Opus Posthumous.* Copyright © 1957 by Elsie Stevens and Holly Stevens. All reprinted by permission of Alfred A. Knopf, Inc.

August Strindberg. "The Stronger" from *Six Plays by Strindberg, trans. Elizabeth Sprigge. Copyright* © 1955 by Elizabeth Sprigg. Reprinted by permission of Curtis Brown, Ltd.

Tacitus. From *The Annals of Imperial Rome,* trans. Michael Grant. Copyright © 1956, 1959, 1971 by Michael Grant Publications Ltd. Reprinted by permission of Penguin Books Ltd.

Dylan Thomas. From *The Poems of Dylan Thomas.* Copyright 1939, 1946 by New Directions Publishing Corporation, copyright 1952 by Dylan Thomas. Reprinted by permission of New Directions Publishing Corporation.

Lewis Thomas. "The Iks" from *The Lives of a Cell.* Copyright © 1973 by The Massachusetts Medical Society. Reprinted by permission of The Viking Press.

James Thurber. "The Moth and the Star" from *Fables for Our Time;* originally printed in *The New Yorker.* Copyright © 1940 by James Thurber, copyright © 1968 by Helen Thurber. Reprinted by permission of Mrs. James Thurber.

Mark Twain. "In the Animals' Court" from *The Works of Mark Twain: What Is Man?,* published for the Iowa Center for Textual Studies by the University of California Press. Reprinted by permission of the University of Iowa Press.

John Updike. "Tomorrow and Tomorrow and So Forth" from *The Same Door;* originally published in *The New Yorker.* Copyright © 1955 by John Updike. Reprinted by permission of Alfred A. Knopf, Inc.

Kurt Vonnegut, Jr. "Harrison Bergeron" from *Welcome to the Monkey House;* originally published in *Fantasy and Science Fiction.* Copyright © 1961 by Kurt Vonnegut, Jr. Reprinted by permission of Delacorte Press/Seymour Lawrence.

Eudora Welty. "Why I Live at the P.O." from *A Curtain of Green and Other Stories.* Copyright 1941, 1969 by Eudora Welty. Reprinted by permission of Harcourt Brace Jovanovich, Inc.

E. B. White. "Spring" from *One Man's Meat.* Copyright 1941 by E. B. White. Reprinted by permission of Harper & Row, Publishers, Inc.

Tennessee Williams. *Cat on a Hot Tin Roof.* Copyright © 1954, 1955, 1971, 1975 by Tennessee Williams. Reprinted by permission of New Directions Publishing Corporation.

William Carlos Williams. From *Collected Earlier Poems:* "The Widow's Lament in Springtime," "To Elsie," "Nantucket," "This Is Just to Say," "The Last Words of My English Grandmother," and "The Red Wheelbarrow," copyright 1938 by New Directions Publishing Corporation. "Landscape with the Fall of Icarus" from *Pictures from Brueghel and Other Poems.* Copyright 1960 by William Carlos Williams. All reprinted by permission of New Directions Publishing Corporation.

Virginia Woolf. "The Death of the Moth" from *The Death of the Moth and Other Essays.* Copyright 1942 by Harcourt Brace Jovanovich, Inc., copyright 1970 by Marjorie T. Parsons, Executrix. Reprinted by permission of the publisher.

William Butler Yeats. From *Collected Poems:* "The Song of Wandering Aengus," copyright 1906 by Macmillan Publishing Co., Inc., renewed 1934 by William Butler Yeats; "A Coat," "The Dolls," copyright 1916 by Macmillan Publishing Co., Inc., renewed 1944 by Bertha Georgie Yeats; "The Wild Swans at Coole," "The Fisherman," copyright 1919 by Macmillan Publishing Co., Inc., renewed 1947 by Bertha Georgie Yeats; "Sailing to Byzantium," copyright 1928 by Macmillan Publishing Co., Inc., renewed 1956 by Georgie Yeats; "For Anne Gregory," "After Long Silence," copyright 1933 by Macmillan Publishing Co., renewed 1961 by Bertha Georgie Yeats; "The Circus Animals' Desertion," copyright 1940 by Georgie Yeats, renewed 1968 by Bertha Georgie Yeats, Michael Butler Yeats and Anne Yeats. All reprinted by permission of Macmillan Publishing Co., Inc.

Preface

In the reading of literature there are two indispensable conditions. The literature has to be interesting, and the reader has to be understanding. Thus in making this anthology we have tried to do these two things: get as many outstanding works of literature as we can between the covers of a single book; and give as much help as we can to people who want to learn how to understand and enjoy works of literature. To these ends we have gathered together here a collection of nineteen essays, fifty-seven stories, one hundred eighty poems, and eleven plays by major writers from the classical period to the contemporary period. And for each of these forms of literature we have prepared separate explanatory discussions, each approximately thirty pages in length. Our commitment to the understanding of literature has also moved us to include a special section on the contemporary art form—film—that is most closely related to the literary forms included in this book. Beyond these guides to understanding we have provided a glossary of critical terms after the text of the book, and an introduction that explains the unified view of literary forms on which our anthology is based. Thus we have no further explanations to offer in this Preface. But we do have a number of people to thank for helping us to put this book together.

For their good advice about the table of contents and the critical apparatus, we are grateful to Professors Charles L. Byrd (University of Texas), Betsy Colquitt (Texas Christian University), Nancy Comley (Brown University), Paul Diehl (University of Iowa), Wayne Franklin (University of Iowa), Raymond Fredman (Cuyahoga Community College), Lynn Garrett (Louisiana State University), Quentin Gehle (Virginia Polytechnic Institute), Miriam Gilbert (University of Iowa), Ray Heffner (University of Iowa), Donald Lawler (East Carolina University), Richard Lloyd-Jones (University of Iowa), Neill Megaw (University of Texas), Charles Molesworth (Queens College), James Nardin (Louisiana State University), Robert Root (Central

Michigan University), Audrey Roth (Miami Dade Community College), Nicholas A. Sharp (Virginia Commonwealth University), Michael Squires (Virginia Polytechnic Institute), and Gary Tate (Texas Christian University). For her generous aid in preparing the manuscript, we are grateful to Dorothy Corder (University of Iowa). For his fine theatrical drawings, we are grateful to A. G. Smith of Detroit, Michigan. And for their expert work in bringing this book into print, we are indebted to all the good people at Oxford University Press, especially Jean Shapiro, Permissions Editor, Mary Ellen Evans, Coordinating Editor, Evan Konecky, Production Editor, Frederick Schneider, Art Director, and John Wright, our Sponsoring Editor.

R.S.
C.H.K.
M.S.

Contents

2. FICTION

3. POETRY

5. FILM

Introduction
The Forms of Literature

Literature begins in the creative possibilities of human language and in the desire of human beings to use their language creatively. Though its origin lies in the joy of creation, literature can be intensely serious. It can use its formal beauty as a way of enabling us to contemplate the most painful and terrible aspects of existence, or as a way of celebrating those things we value most highly in life. In the end, literature enriches our lives because it increases our capacities for understanding and communication. It helps us to find meaning in our world and to express it and share it with others. And this is the most humane activity of our existence.

But we cannot exercise our humanity automatically. Just as no person is born knowing his or her language, so no one who learns a language is immediately capable of responding to the complexities of literature in that language. Response to the fully developed forms of literature must be learned, and it demands more skill from us than ordinary reading and writing. But the more we develop that skill, the more enlightening, enriching, and enjoyable our experience of literature becomes.

To help you understand and enjoy your reading, we have prepared critical introductions to the four forms of literature—essay, fiction, poetry, and drama—that have dominated our culture for hundreds of years. Following each of those introductions you will find representative selections of literary works in each of the four forms. But before turning to the individual forms, let us first consider how the four forms are related to one another. Once you have in mind a comprehensive view of the forms, you will then be in a better position to understand each one of them.

In each of these forms authors use words to convey their views of experience. In that basic sense all of the forms arise out of a common human impulse—to find meaning in experience and to share it with others.

But each of the forms achieves that basic purpose in a distinctly different way. In understanding how each of the forms uses words, we can begin by making two essential kinds of distinctions about the language of literature. First, we can distinguish between the ways in which the words in literary works relate to the world of experience. Second, we can distinguish between the ways in which those words are communicated to a reader.

In defining how words relate to the world of experience, we can observe that they are used either to create imaginary people and events, or to give immediate expression to ideas and feelings about experience. Consider, for instance, the opening words of "The Boarding House," by James Joyce:

> Mrs Mooney was a butcher's daughter. She was a woman who was quite able to keep things to herself: a determined woman. She had married her father's foreman and opened a butcher's shop near Spring Gardens. But as soon as his father-in-law was dead Mr Mooney began to go to the devil.

In these sentences, Joyce first sketches the character of Mrs. Mooney and then begins to tell the events of her married life. In this way his words create an imaginary world for us—a world with specific people, places, and events. Similarly, in a play a dramatist uses words to create an imaginary world through the lines he writes for the characters to speak, as in this bit of dialogue from Strindberg's *The Stronger*:

> MRS. X   Do you know, Amelia, I really believe now you would have done better to stick to him. Don't forget I was the first who told you to forgive him. Do you remember? Then you would be married now and have a home. Think how happy you were that Christmas when you stayed with your fiancé's people in the country. How warmly you spoke of domestic happiness! . . .

In just these few lines the words of Mrs. X imply a complex human relationship between herself, Amelia, and a man to whom Amelia had been engaged but had not married. As we read those lines we wonder exactly why Amelia broke off her engagement, and we also wonder why Mrs. X harasses her about it. Thus the words of Mrs. X not only create an imaginary world, but they also arouse our curiosity about it. This process of engaging our interest in an imaginary world is one of the major uses of language in literature.

But words can also be used to express ideas and feelings in a more simple and immediate way. When William Wordsworth titled a sonnet "Composed upon Westminster Bridge, September 3, 1802," he wanted to convey the impression that he was transcribing his ideas and feelings about the city of London without any intervening imaginary world, so he describes:

This City now doth, like a garment, wear
The beauty of the morning; silent, bare,

Ships, towers, domes, theatres, and temples lie
Open unto the fields, and to the sky;
All bright and glittering in the smokeless air.

And then he expresses his own feelings on that occasion:

Ne'er saw I, never felt, a Calm so deep!

Similarly, in his essay "Shooting an Elephant," George Orwell describes the corpse of an Indian coolie who had been killed by an elephant, and then he tells us his feelings about the experinece:

> His face was coated with mud, the eyes wide open, the teeth bared and grinning with an expression of unendurable agony. (Never tell me, by the way, that the dead look peaceful. Most of the corpses I have seen looked devilish.)

This process of arousing our sympathy for ideas and feelings about experience is another one of the major uses of language in literature.

In addition to distinguishing between the ways in which words are used in literature, we can also distinguish between the ways in which they are communicated to a reader. Either they are addressed directly to the reader or they are overheard by the reader. This distinction is comparable to the difference between the ways in which we ordinarily hear words in our own common experience. Sometimes people speak directly to us, and sometimes we overhear them speaking to others, or possibly even to themselves. So in some cases the words of a literary work are addressed directly to us, as in that last parenthetical statement by Orwell, or they seem to be addressed to us, as in the passage by Joyce. But in other cases it is clear that we readers are overhearing words meant for someone else, as when we listen to Mrs. X speaking to Amelia, or when we overhear Wordsworth in his "Intimations" Ode become so carried away by the singing of the birds and by his own feelings that he speaks to the birds themselves:

Then sing, ye Birds, sing, sing a joyous song!

These basic possibilities of literary expression can be clarified by a simple diagram:

words used to create imaginary persons and events

words addressed directly to the reader	words overheard by the reader

words used to express ideas and feelings

The vertical axis refers to the way words are used in literature, and the horizontal axis to the ways in which words are communicated to the reader. Within those coordinates, we can locate each literary form according to the unique way it uses words and communicates them to the reader.

The essay in its purest form uses words to establish ideas addressed directly by the essayist to the reader. On this basis we can see that its essential quality is persuasion and that it belongs in the lower left-hand area of the diagram. The poem in its purest form uses words to express feelings addressed by a speaker talking or thinking to himself or herself rather than to the reader. Its essential quality, then, is meditation, and it belongs in the lower right-hand area of the diagram. A story uses words to create a view of imaginary persons and events through the report of a storyteller to the reader. Its essential quality is narration, and it belongs in the upper left-hand area. And a play uses words to create action through the dialogue of imaginary persons talking to one another rather than to the reader. Thus the essential quality of drama is interaction, and it belongs in the upper right-hand area of the diagram. Once the forms and their qualities have been defined and located, the diagram looks like this:

```
              words used to create imaginary persons and events
                    STORY          |     PLAY
                  (narration)      |   (interaction)

        words                      |                        words
 addressed directly  ——————————————+——————————————          overheard
    to the reader                  |                      by the reader

                    ESSAY          |     POEM
                  (persuasion)     |   (meditation)
              words used to express ideas and feelings
```

With this diagram and the accompanying definitions, we can visualize immediately the unique literary quality of each form as distinguished from the others. But the diagram can take us farther in our study if we realize that it also represents the proximity of the four forms to one another. Within each of the literary forms all four possibilities exist again as emphases or strategies, as you will see when we examine each form in more detail later in the text.

Once you have mastered the four literary forms, you will also be in a position to appreciate an art form which incorporates elements of those forms, but which is peculiar to contemporary culture because it is the result of a technological breakthrough of the past one hundred years: the motion picture film. Because film is related to literature, we have devoted a special section to it in this book. Film, of course, is essentially visual, and therefore there can be no film in this printed text. But you will find discussion of one of the most important films of our time—*Citizen Kane*—and the ways it should be viewed, along with still-shot illustrations that such a discussion requires. As a preparation for that study, let us return to our diagram of the literary forms to see what it can tell us about the relationship of literature and film.

Just as the diagram enabled us to recognize that each of the literary forms can take on aspects or qualities of any of the other literary forms, so it can help us to see that film can also assume the qualities of any of the literary forms. Like essays, films can be persuasive—indeed, they are perhaps the strongest propaganda device ever invented; and, like poems, they can be lyrical and meditative; but most "movies"—the films we encounter when we "go to the movies"—have more in common with stories and plays than with essays and poems. That is, they tend to emphasize persons and events, offering us something which is partly *narration*—"told" by the camera which shapes everything we see—but also presented as an *interaction* among characters who behave as though the camera were not present at all. The camera and all the visual quality of film prevent it from even fitting into the above diagram, which is a representation of the verbal forms only. But we should note also that the spectacular and audio-visual part of drama, as we encounter it on the stage, is already beyond the purely verbal universe in which essays, poems, and stories find their being.

Literature, after all, is not really a closed field, though we may sometimes pretend that it is for our own critical convenience. Nor is this book, though it has, like all books, its beginning, middle, and end, intended to circumscribe the world of literature and close it off. For literature always says to us what the poet John Donne said about the forgiveness of his sins in "A Hymn to God the Father":

When Thou hast done, Thou hast not done,
  For I have more.

1
ESSAY

Elements of the Essay

THE ESSAY AS A FORM OF LITERATURE

Yes, we intend to discuss the essay as a form of literature. That may surprise you, since you have probably read numerous essays that you would not consider literary at all. Well, to tell the truth, many essays are not literary in any respect. Many are completely practical pieces of writing, designed to report something, or explain something, or make a case for something. Those essays usually go about their business in a no-nonsense, matter-of-fact way, because they are meant to get something done in the world—and get it done quickly. So, they are likely to be systematically organized, factually detailed, closely reasoned, and plainly written. Their form is as downright efficient as a chair, a bowl, or a candlestick. But usefulness can also become a pretext for beauty. The carpenter, the potter, and the candlestick maker can look beyond the immediate utility of their products and transform them into works of art.

Essayists, too, can look beyond their immediate purpose. George Orwell, for example, wanted "to make political writing into an art." His commitment to that goal was, in fact, so strong that he "could not do the work of writing . . . even a long magazine article, if it were not also an esthetic experience." Thus he was not content simply "to push the world in a certain direction." He also wanted to create "pleasure in the impact of one sound on another, in the firmness of good prose or the rhythm of a good story." And that is exactly what he achieved, as you can see if you turn to "Shooting an Elephant" (in our collection of essays)—an essay that has not only a political point to make but also a "good story" to tell. Many essayists are out to change the world, but some like Orwell seek to do so by using literary rather than purely utilitarian forms of composition.

And some essayists are not out to change the world at all: some are completely indifferent to immediate circumstances or practical ends. They have a point to make—every essayist does—but they are not bent on persuading us to believe something or to do something about the world. Instead of rousing us to action, such writers may lead us to contemplation or even to idle imagination. Virginia Woolf, for example, had this to say about the purpose of the essay:

> The principle which controls it is simply that it should give us pleasure; the desire which impels us when we take it from the shelf is simply to receive pleasure. Everything in an essay must be subdued to that end.

Pleasure is probably the last thing you expect of an essay, but it was certainly the first thing on her mind. And the kind of pleasure she had in mind was what we commonly expect of literature—that it temporarily remove us from the world of everyday affairs by immersing us in the world of the imagination:

> It should lay us under a spell with its first word, and we should only wake, refreshed, with its last. In the interval we may pass through the most various experiences of amusement, surprise, interest, indignation; we may soar to the heights of fantasy with Lamb or plunge to the depths of wisdom with Bacon, but we must never be roused. The essay must lap us about and draw its curtain across the world.

And that is exactly what she achieved, as you can see if you turn to "The Death of the Moth" (in our essay collection)—an essay that will lay you under its spell and lead you to contemplation, though it is only about the demise of a common insect. Essayists like Woolf seek to create an experience that is valuable for its own sake, and they do so by using language imaginatively, as in other forms of literature.

The essay is at last a very flexible form and has been so ever since it originated with the sixteenth-century French writer Montaigne. He used it as a means of exploring himself and his ideas about human experience, and his essays were, in a sense, a means of thinking on paper, of trying things out in writing. And he deliberately emphasized their tentative and informal quality by calling them *essais*, a term he derived from the French verb *essayer*—to try. The term "essay" has since come to be used as a catch-all for non-fictional prose works of limited length; but that description of the form turns out to be misleading. Some essays *are* fictional, as you can see by looking at the outlandish story told by Lamb in "The Dissertation upon Roast Pig" (in our essay anthology), and some essays are much longer than any of those we have collected for this anthology. Essays may be long or short, factual or fictional, practical or playful. They may serve any purpose and take any form that an essayist wants to try out. In this text we shall be concerned with essays that use *literary* forms of composition, whatever their purpose may be. Thus we will begin our study of the essay by considering its form in relation to the other forms of literature.

THE ESSAY AND OTHER FORMS OF LITERATURE

In relating the essay to the other literary forms, we can begin by looking again at the diagram we used in the general introduction to this book. That diagram, you will recall, locates and defines each form according to the unique way it uses words and communicates them to the reader. The essay in its pure form uses words to establish ideas that are addressed directly by the essayist to the reader. Thus, its essential quality is persuasion. But the diagram, as we said earlier, also represents the proximity of the four forms to one another. Each of the forms is capable of using the elements, techniques, or even strategies of the other forms. The essay, then, is not confined to the form of straightforward persuasion; it may also be narrative, or dramatic, or poetic in form. Or an essay may involve a combination of the forms; and the longer it is, the more likely it will be to combine the various possibilities of form in rich and complex ways. But before trying to work with those long and formally complicated essays, make sure you have mastered the simpler forms we shall be discussing here and elsewhere in this book.

In its pure form the essay explicitly attempts to *persuade* us of something by means of an appeal and argument that the author addresses directly to us, much as any public speaker would address an audience. In a *narrative* essay the author becomes a narrator, a storyteller, who reports directly to us on persons and events. A narrative essay sees its subject in time and presents it in the form of history. A *dramatic* essay may take one of two possible forms. It may take the form of a dialogue between two or more characters, in which case the author is present, if at all, only to perform the duties of a director: to set the scene and identify the characters whose words and actions are to be witnessed by the reader. Or it may take the form of a monologue rather than of a dialogue. We use the term "monologue" here because the speaker in this kind of essay is a dramatic character rather than the author—or, we might say, the speaker is a character whom the author is impersonating. An essay is *poetic* to the extent that its author or speaker appears to be talking to himself rather than to others. A poetic essay takes the form of a meditation "overheard" by the reader.

These definitions might seem to imply that only the pure form of the essay has a persuasive purpose, but this is not the case. In one sense or another all essays have a persuasive purpose, for they are, after all, views—ways of looking at a thing rather than the thing itself. When essayists describe something, they record what *they* see from *their* angle of vision, from their point of view in space and time, because they cannot do otherwise. They can describe something only as they see it, not as anyone else sees it, nor as it is. Yet, in choosing to describe something, they implicitly ask us to take their word for what it looks like. The same is true of essayists who narrate events or report information. They ask us to take their words for things. *Persuasion,* then, is at the heart of all essays, but some essayists acknowledge this and proceed directly about their persuasive business, while others play down their persuasive intention, or use indirect means to attain their ends. Some essays are argumentative, while others are narrative, dramatic, or poetic.

These distinctions may be used to identify the form of any literary essay; and once the form is identified it will suggest the appropriate critical approach. In the pages that follow, we shall discuss the elements of each form and show how to analyze each form by looking at representative essays. Before doing so, however, it is necessary that we get another perspective on the literary essay by considering the relation between the essayist and the reader, for that relation, as we have just seen, is central to the nature of the essay.

THE ESSAYIST AND THE READER

When reading an essay we often feel as though the author is speaking directly to us. Thus, in the previous section, we compared the essayist to a speaker addressing an audience. Sometimes, of course, the essayist does not address us directly, and yet we still have the sense that we hear someone speaking as we read the words to ourselves. And we usually take it for granted that the speaker we hear is the same person as the essayist. That equation, as you can see, is implicit in the opening sentences of this section. When you first read those sentences, you probably did not stop to question the assumption, since it appears to be a perfectly reasonable one to make. After all, the essayist wrote the piece, and so the essayist must be the same person that we hear speaking. But if you think about the matter a bit, you will see that essayists are not exactly the same in their essays as they are in real life. They cannot be, since in essays they are made of words, rather than of flesh and blood. Thus the particular personality conveyed in an essay is always in some sense a *fiction,* and we call it a "fiction" because we want to emphasize its imaginative nature. It is something created out of words alone.

Essayists can create any impression of themselves that they wish. They can appear stuffy or relaxed, serious or flippant, confident or nervous, wise or foolish. The possibilities are limitless and they are a product not only of *what* essayists have to say but also of *how* they say it. Thus it is important to listen carefully to the style of their prose—to hear the particular words they choose and the particular way they choose to put them together in sentences and sequences of sentences. Listen, for example, to these two passages and try to imagine what kind of person you hear speaking in each:

> I once heard a swell story about Gary Cooper. The person I heard the story from did this terrific Gary Cooper imitation, and it may be that when I tell you the story (which I am about to), it will lose something in print. It may lose everything, in fact.

> We have lived through the era when happiness was a warm puppy, and the era when happiness was a dry martini, and now we have come to the era when happiness is "knowing what your uterus looks like." For this slogan, and for what is perhaps the apotheosis of the do-it-yourself movement in America, we have the Los Angeles Self-Help Clinic to thank: this group of women has been sending its emissaries around the country with a large supply of plastic specula for sale and detailed instructions on how women can perform their own gynecological examinations and abortions.

You probably had no trouble hearing the difference between those two persons, for they speak in two very different styles. And you can detect those differences just by looking at their opening sentences. One uses the first-person singular ("I"), the other the first-person plural ("We"). One speaks in a casual idiom ("heard a swell story"), the other in lofty language ("have lived through the era"). One favors a simple sentence ("I heard a story"), the other a series of parallel clauses and phrases ("We have lived through the era when happiness was, and we have come to the era when happiness is . . ."). One expresses its opinion in a jaunty adjective ("swell"), the other through a jarring comparison ("warm puppy"—"dry martini"—" 'knowing what your uterus looks like' "). Thus, one essay sounds conversational and straightforward, the other oratorical and complex. Or, you might say, one sounds casual and spontaneous, the other formal and ingenious. No matter how you characterize the two pieces, they sound like the voices of entirely different essayists. But in fact they are two voices of a single essayist—Nora Ephron. And she created them for two different essays appearing only five months apart in the same magazine, *Esquire.*

Why, you might ask, would Nora Ephron choose to create two such different impressions of herself, especially when she is writing for the same group of readers? You might also want to know which of those personalities is closer to the real Nora Ephron. But we cannot answer either question with any degree of certainty. Only Nora Ephron could answer, and she is not likely to let us in on the secret of her art or of herself. It is clear, however, that those two different selves—or two different aspects of her self—control the way we perceive and respond to the subject of each essay. In each case the subject is not presented directly to us but is filtered through the style, the point of view, of a particular personality. Thus, in the first passage, she makes us eager to hear that story about Gary Cooper by telling us that it is "swell," but she does not lead us to expect that the story will be filled with great significance, because she does not seem to take the story that seriously. It is simply a "swell" story.

Now imagine how you would respond if she had begun her essay this way:

> We have lived through the era when Gary Cooper was a movie star, and the era when other stars imitated Gary Cooper, and now we have come to the era when people are telling legendary stories about Gary Cooper.

Then you might well expect to hear a story filled with serious cultural significance. Actually, the story does turn out to be culturally significant, as you will see when you read the whole essay and our discussion of it. Apparently, however, Ephron does not want us to anticipate its significance, and so she creates a personality that puts us at ease rather than putting us on notice. The role she plays determines the kind of response we make. In this way the particular personality created by the essayist in turn creates in us a reciprocal personality, or role, that we enact in the process of our reading. And as we read we must continually adjust ourselves to the emerging aspects of the essayist's *fictional self*. In this respect the act of reading an essay is much like carrying on any human relationship: it depends on give and take, on action and reaction. But we cannot react appropriately unless we are attentive to the other person.

Once we are attentive to an essayist's fictional self, we can also respond appropriately to that essayist's literary form. The form of a literary essay, no less than its subject, is shaped by the particular personality through which it is conveyed. And when we have responded appropriately to the form of an essay, we can authentically experience its meaning. Remembering this, we will now present five essays and commentaries to illustrate and to explain the basic forms of the literary essay and to show the kinds of interpretation we recommend for studying and appreciating them.

Five Essays and Commentaries

THE ESSAY AS ARGUMENT: PERSUASION

At the heart of all essays is the idea of persuasion. But many an essay wears its heart on its sleeve and boldly declares its persuasive purpose. These argumentative essays are admittedly out to make a case for something. Their basic form, therefore, is direct and simple: a point to be established, together with some support for the point. The point may precede the evidence; it may follow; or it may be closely interwoven with supportive materials. It may be stated boldly or subtly. Thus your first analytic task should be to isolate the point and restate it as clearly as possible. This task may also involve discovering and restating separate sub-points.

Once the main points have been identified, it is necessary to examine the supporting material. In a literary essay the principal form of support is *analogy*. Other kinds of essays may resort to statistical evidence, expert testimony, and other such non-literary appeals. But literary persuasion depends upon appeals to common experience in the form of analogies that relate the topic to comparable situations. Thus your second analytic task should be to identify the analogies and examine how they have been elaborated and applied to support the point of the essay. At this stage of the analysis, you should be concerned particularly with the appropriateness of the analogies and the tact with which they have been applied. Do they fit, or are they forced? The question of tact will then lead you naturally to consider the implied personality of the essayist and its appropriateness to the persuasive situation. Your final analytic tasks should be to examine the style and tone of voice you hear speaking in the essay, and to consider the reciprocal role you are invited to take.

Once you have examined these elements of the argumentative essay, you will be in a fair position to decide whether you feel persuaded by a genuine insight, or manipulated by an offensive procedure. It is possible, of course, that you may encounter a foolish or fraudulent presentation of a view you had previously held. That creates no real problem. But when you are confronted by an essay that seems to lead you to a view you do not wish to adopt, you have some real thinking to do. In this situation you are engaged in a fruitful conflict with another mind, and you should begin formulating your own response. Here, for example, is an argumentative essay which presents a view of the nature of women that many readers may not accept. It was written in the 1920s in response to the women's rights movement—specifically, the movement for their right to vote, which was then a critical issue in English political life. Though it was occasioned by a specific political question, it actually addresses itself to even more fundamental issues about women—and men—issues still being debated today. When you have finished reading it, take some time to consider its elements and formulate your own response before you look at our analysis.

D. H. LAWRENCE
1885–1930
Cocksure Women and Hensure Men

It seems to me there are two aspects to women. There is the demure and the dauntless. Men have loved to dwell, in fiction at least, on the demure maiden whose inevitable reply is: Oh, yes, if you please, kind sir! The demure maiden, the demure spouse, the demure mother—this is still the ideal. A few maidens, mistresses and mothers *are* demure. A few pretend to be. But the vast majority are not. And they don't pretend to be. We don't expect a girl skilfully driving her car to be demure, we expect her to be dauntless. What good would demure and maidenly Members of Parliament be, inevitably responding: Oh, yes, if you please, kind sir!—Though of course there are masculine members of that kidney.—And a demure telephone girl? Or even a demure stenographer? Demureness, to be sure, is outwardly becoming, it is an outward mark of femininity, like bobbed hair. But it goes with inward dauntlessness. The girl who has got to make her way in life has got to be dauntless, and if she has a pretty, demure manner with it, then lucky girl. She kills two birds with two stones.

With the two kinds of femininity go two kinds of confidence: There are the women who are cocksure, and the women who are hensure. A really up-to-date woman is a cocksure woman. She doesn't have a doubt nor a qualm. She is the modern type. Whereas the old-fashioned demure woman was sure as a hen is sure, that is, without knowing anything about it. She went quietly and busily clucking around, laying the eggs and mothering the chickens in a kind of anxious dream that still was full of sureness. But not mental sureness. Her sureness was a physical condition, very soothing, but a condition out of which she could easily be startled or frightened.

It is quite amusing to see the two kinds of sureness in chickens. The cockerel is, naturally, cocksure. He crows because he is *certain* it is day. Then the hen peeps out from under her wing. He marches to the door of the hen-house and pokes out his head assertively: *Ah ha! daylight, of course, just as I said!*—and he majestically steps down the chicken ladder towards *terra firma*, knowing that the hens will step cautiously after him, drawn by his confidence. So after him, cautiously, step the hens. He crows again: *Ha-ha! here we are!*—It is indisputable, and the hens accept it entirely. He marches towards the house. From the house a person ought to appear, scattering corn. Why does the person not appear? The cock will see to it. He is cocksure. He gives a loud crow in the doorway, and the person appears. The hens are suitably impressed but immediately devote all their henny consciousness to the scattered corn, pecking absorbedly, while the cock runs and fusses, cocksure that he is responsible for it all.

So the day goes on. The cock finds a tit-bit, and loudly calls the hens. They scuffle up in henny surety, and gobble the tit-bit. But when they find a juicy morsel for themselves, they devour it in silence, hensure. Unless, of course, there are little chicks, when they most anxiously call the brood. But in her own dim surety, the hen is really much surer than the cock, in a different way. She marches off to lay her egg, she secures obstinately the nest she wants, she lays her egg at last, then steps forth again with prancing confidence, and gives that most assured of all sounds, the hensure cackle of a bird who has laid her egg. The cock, who is never so sure about anything as the hen is about the egg she has laid, immediately starts to cackle like the female of his species. He is pining to be hensure, for hensure is so much surer than cocksure.

Nevertheless, cocksure is boss. When the chicken-hawk appears in the sky, loud are the cockerel's calls of alarm. Then the hens scuffle under the verandah, the cock ruffles his feathers on guard. The hens are numb with fear, they say: Alas, there is no health in us! How wonderful to be a cock so bold!—And they huddle, numbed. But their very numbness is hensurety.

Just as the cock can cackle, however, as if he had laid the egg, so can the hen bird crow. She can more or less assume his cocksureness. And yet she is never so easy, cocksure, as she used to be when she was hensure. Cocksure, she is cocksure, but uneasy. Hensure, she trembles, but is easy.

It seems to me just the same in the vast human farmyard. Only nowadays all the cocks are cackling and pretending to lay eggs, and all the hens are crowing and pretending to call the sun out of bed. If women today are cocksure, men are hensure. Men are timid, tremulous, rather soft and submissive, easy in their very henlike tremulousness. They only want to be spoken to gently. So the women step forth with a good loud *cock-a-doodle-do!*

The tragedy about cocksure women is that they are more cocky, in their assurance, than the cock himself. They never realize that when the cock gives his loud crow in the morning, he listens acutely afterwards, to hear if some other wretch of a cock dare crow defiance, challenge. To the cock, there is always defiance, challenge, danger and death on the clear air; or the possibility thereof.

But alas, when the hen crows, she listens for no defiance or challenge. When she says *cock-a-doodle-do!* then it is unanswerable. The cock listens for an answer, alert. But the hen knows she is unanswerable. *Cock-a-doodle-do!* and there it is, take it or leave it!

And it is this that makes the cocksureness of women so dangerous, so devastating. It is really out of scheme, it is not in relation to the rest of things. So we have the tragedy of cocksure women. They find, so often, that instead of having laid an egg, they have laid a vote, or an empty ink-bottle, or some other absolutely unhatchable object, which means nothing to them.

It is the tragedy of the modern woman. She becomes cocksure, she puts all her passion and energy and years of her life into some effort or assertion, without ever listening for the denial which she ought to take into count. She is cocksure, but she is a hen all the time. Frightened of her own henny self, she rushes to mad lengths about votes, or welfare, or sports, or business: she is marvellous, out-manning the man. But alas, it is all fundamentally disconnected. It is all an attitude, and one day the attitude will become a weird cramp, a pain, and then it will collapse. And when it has collapsed, and she looks at the eggs she has laid, votes, or miles of typewriting, years of business efficiency—suddenly, because she is a hen and not a cock, all she has done will turn into pure nothingness to her. Suddenly it all falls out of relation to her basic henny self, and she realizes she has lost her life. The lovely henny surety, the hensureness which is the real bliss of every female, has been denied her: she had never had it. Having lived her life with such utmost strenuousness and cocksure-ness, she has missed her life altogether. Nothingness!

A Commentary

In this essay Lawrence has taken a very strong position on a crucial aspect of modern life. His is not a popular position; but rather than judging the essay in the light of current public opinion, we should try to take the piece on its own terms. In thinking about the essay itself we must first make sure that we understand the main point, and then consider how Lawrence attempts to support it. The point is actually complicated enough that we need to break it down into its separate but related parts. Lawrence asserts that

A. Modern women are in general unhappy;
B. They have in general attempted to play a masculine role in society;
C. B is the cause of A.

Lawrence himself never formulates his points in this naked and direct way. Very few essayists do. Instead, they dress up their attitudes so as to make them attractive and to give them as much protection as possible. This is true especially of literary essayists, since they hope to engage our permanent interest in their art as well as to persuade us for the moment. Thus, the process of analysis is particularly important for understanding literary essays. In our analysis we will first examine the structure of Lawrence's essay, and then consider the way he uses analogy within that structure to make a case for his point about modern women.

In the opening paragraph Lawrence distinguishes between two kinds of women: the "demure" and the "dauntless." He further suggests that most women, modern women in particular, are dauntless rather than demure. This paragraph is not overtly evaluative; it merely seeks to persuade us that the distinction is valid without insisting that either type of womanhood is superior to the other. If anything, it suggests that women *must* be dauntless if they want to get on in modern society. In view of what we have already established as to the real point of the essay, is it possible that Lawrence is trying to mislead us here? Is he trying to soften our resistance by asserting a proposition that most of us would willingly accept?

The second paragraph moves from kinds of women to kinds of "confidence" or sureness. Here Lawrence employs an old expression—"cocksure"—and he coins a new one to balance it—"hensure." With these terms he introduces the main argument of his essay—an analogy. It is an analogy, we note, that relates human life to the life of chickens. Then Lawrence devotes paragraphs 3, 4, 5, and 6 to a description of the farmyard side of the analogy. His description is shrewd, lively, knowing. Its charm derives partly from the way he has allowed the human to interpenetrate with the non-human. These chickens have all sorts of feelings and attitudes that we think of as the exclusive property of higher orders of creation. This animates farmyard life for us and makes the analogy interesting in itself. But it is also subtly preparing the way for the persuasive purpose of the analogy.

In the first sentence of paragraph 7, Lawrence closes the analogical circuit by turning his attention from the animal farmyard to the "vast human farmyard"—and then the flow of value judgments begins. Thoughts and images oscillate back and forth, generating ludicrous images like that of women who "find that instead of having laid an egg, they have laid a vote, or an empty ink bottle, or some other absolutely unhatchable object, which means nothing to them." In the final paragraph Lawrence has completed the transfer of fowl characteristics to human beings, so that he can speak of woman's "basic henny self," and he has expanded the "nothing" in the sentence just quoted above to the "Nothingness!" with which the essay concludes.

If women *are* basically henny, and if they *are* actually behaving in a cocksure manner, then of course it is only *natural* that they must be unhappy—since they are behaving unnaturally. Lawrence's "human farmyard" is a device to turn the abstraction "unnatural" into something concrete and vivid. And it does achieve concreteness and vividness. But does it persuade? And to what extent does its value to us depend on its persuasiveness?

The persuasiveness of this essay depends chiefly on the power of the analogy used by Lawrence. How appropriate is it? How tactfully does he use it? The question of appropriateness takes us away from the essay to the world of our own experience, and leads us to consider human nature as we understand it. The question of tact relates more directly to the internal workings of the essay itself. Given a certain amount of truth or appropriateness in the analogy, we must ask whether the essayist has kept tactfully within those limits or not. In the case of Lawrence's essay, each different reader is likely to have a markedly different reaction. Men and women, in fact, may react quite differently. (Would this support Lawrence's view?) Without hoping to settle the matter here, we might say that there is enough truth in Lawrence's analogy to make it interesting—and persuasive to some extent. Further, it seems to us that Lawrence's humor operates in a tactful way to prevent the analogy from being pressed too hard. Humor lightens the persuasive touch, here. Finally, the vigor with which Lawrence develops the analogy, and the animation of his farmyard, work to engage us—to stimulate us to respond. His view may be too neat or too ingenious to accept, yet it is presented too vigorously to dismiss.

Before reaching a final assessment of the essay, we should conclude our study of its elements by examining the particular personality that Lawrence creates for himself and the role that it compels us to take as readers. The opening sentence is a good place to begin. What is the effect of his beginning with "It seems to me" and not with the assertion, "There are two aspects to women"? That opening expression is disarming, is it not? It makes us feel that we are dealing with an individual person, a real person like ourselves, one who has opinions about things but realizes that they are opinions and not eternal truths. And Lawrence uses this same disarming phrase in the opening sentence of that crucial seventh paragraph. But compare the tone of these two sentences with the tone of the concluding sentences in the essay: powerful assertions with no hesitations or doubts, there. On closer inspection we can see that even in the first sentence itself we have both diffidence and confidence. While Lawrence disarms us with "It seems to me," he quickly goes on to generalize about a difficult and dangerous subject: the nature of woman. And from that point on he develops the theme rapidly, enlivening his views with a variety of tones of voice. Consider, for instance, the special tone required for "Oh, yes, if you please, kind sir."

For the most part Lawrence talks straight at us in a very conversational manner. He implies that our role, as readers, is to meet him on his own level. We are not asked to have a lot of book-learning, but we are supposed to have eyes in our head. That farmyard analogy will work best for folks who know enough about life to know that eggs don't grow in little gray boxes. In fact, if we come to share that downright, almost folksy attitude of the farmyard section, the essay may seem to us very convincing indeed. But notice, too, that after he has lulled us into that agreeable role, he shifts his tone of voice in the last four paragraphs and becomes much more serious about the whole matter. Consider, for example, how different the tone of voice is in these two passages:

> So the day goes on. The cock finds a tit-bit, and loudly calls the hens. They scuffle up in henny surety, and gobble the tit-bit.

> It is the tragedy of the modern woman. She becomes cocksure, she puts all her passion and energy and years of life into some effort or assertion, without ever listening for the denial which she ought to take into count.

When he shifts to that serious tone, we have to call on a more serious part of ourselves and bring a more complex view of human nature to bear on the subject in order to resist its persuasiveness. When we do this, and assert our own view on the matter, we make a response that is both active and critical.

THE ESSAY AS STORY: HISTORY

Even though there is a persuasive dimension to the narrative essay, it is best approached first of all through its narrative elements. The basic elements of narration are a story and a storyteller. In a story we have characters and events, arranged in time so as to move toward some climax and resolution. The essayist presents this movement and tells the story by means of description, dialogue, and commentary. By observing the stages in the movement of the plot, and by noting the implications of description, dialogue, and commentary, we can begin to understand a narrative essay.

But the narrative essay differs from the story itself in that it is built around a specific event or situation that has existed in time and space, and it is presented as a kind of record of that event or situation. The story told in an essay may be highly personal, moving toward autobiography, or as impersonal as a journalistic "story" of current events. It may focus on a particular event or sequence of events; or it may concentrate on a place or person, becoming a travelogue or character sketch. But its essence lies ultimately in its telling us the "truth" about something that is itself actual or historical. The "truth" of this kind of essay includes not only accuracy with respect to factual data but also depth of insight into the causes and meanings of events, the motives and values of the personages represented. In the essay as story, the journalist's "where" and "when" become the historian's "how" and "why." And the historian's interpretation is the persuasive point of a narrative essay. Thus, in reading a narrative essay you should make a special point of looking for the essayist's interpretation, and you should be attentive to the essayist's personality in the process of both telling the story and interpreting it.

Here follows a narrative essay whose author you have already glimpsed briefly during our discussion of the essayist and the reader. When you have finished reading it, take some time to consider its elements and gather your own thoughts about it before you look at our commentary. You might also want to consider the "truth" it offers in relation to the point of Lawrence's essay.

NORA EPHRON
1941–
The Hurled Ashtray

I once heard a swell story about Gary Cooper. The person I heard the story from did this terrific Gary Cooper imitation, and it may be that when I tell you the story (which I am about to), it will lose something in print. It may lose everything, in fact. But enough. The story was that Gary Cooper was in a London restaurant at a large table of friends. He was sitting in a low chair, with his back to the rest of the room, so no one in the restaurant even knew that he was tall, much less that he was Gary Cooper. Across the way was a group of Teddy boys (this episode took place long long ago, you see), and they were all misbehaving and making nasty remarks about a woman at Cooper's table. Cooper turned around to give them his best mean-and-threatening stare, but they went right on. Finally he got up, very very slowly, so slowly that it took almost a minute for him to go from this short person in a low chair to a ten-foot-tall man with Gary Cooper's head on top of his shoulders. He loped over to the table of Teddy boys, looked down at them, and said, "Wouldja mind sayin' that agin?" The men were utterly cowed and left the restaurant shortly thereafter.

Well, you had to be there.

I thought of Gary Cooper and his way with words the other day. Longingly. Because in the mail, from an editor of *New York* magazine, came an excerpt from a book by Michael Korda called *Male Chauvinism: How It Works* (Random House). I have no idea whether Korda's book is any good at all, but the excerpt was fascinating, a sort of reverse-twist update on Francis Macomber, as well as a pathetic contrast to the Gary Cooper story. It seems that Korda, his wife, and another woman were having dinner in a London restaurant recently. Across the way was a table of drunks doing sensitive things like sniggering and leering and throwing bread balls at Mrs. Korda, who is a looker. Her back was to them, and she refused to acknowledge their presence, instead apparently choosing to let the flying bread balls bounce off her back onto the floor. Then, one of the men sent over a waiter with a silver tray. On it was a printed card, the kind you can buy in novelty shops, which read: "I want to sleep with you! Tick off your favorite love position from the list below, and return this card with your telephone number. . . ." Korda tore up the card before his wife could even see it, and then, consumed with rage, he picked up an ashtray and threw it at the man who had sent the card. A fracas ensued, and before long, Korda, his wife, and their woman friend were out on the street. Mrs. Korda was furious.

"If you ever do that again," she screamed, "I'll leave you! Do you think I couldn't have handled that, or ignored it? Did I ask you to come to my defense against some poor stupid drunk? You didn't even think, you just reacted like a male chauvinist. You leapt up to defend *your* woman, *your* honor, you made me seem cheap and foolish and powerless. . . . God Almighty, can't you see it was none of your business! Can't you understand how it makes me feel? I don't mind being hassled by some drunk, I can take that, but to be treated like a chattel, to be robbed of any right to decide for myself whether I'd been insulted, or how badly, to have you react for me because I'm *your* woman . . . that's really sickening, it's like being a slave." Korda repeats the story (his wife's diatribe is even longer in the original version) and then, in a *mea culpa* that is only too reminiscent of the sort that used to appear in 1960s books by white liberals about blacks, he concludes that his wife is doubtless right, that men do tend to treat women merely as appendages of themselves.

Before printing the article, *New York* asked several couples—including my husband and me—what our reaction was to what happened, and what we would have done under the circumstances. My initial reaction to the entire business was that no one ever sends me notes like that in restaurants. I sent that off to the editor, but a few days later I got to thinking about the story, and it began to seem to me that the episode just might be a distillation of everything that has happened to men and women as a result of the women's movement, and if not that, at least a way to write about etiquette after the revolution, and if not that, nothing at all. Pulled as I was by these three possibilities, I told the story over dinner to four friends and asked for their reaction. The first, a man, said that he thought Mrs. Korda was completely right. The second, a woman, said she thought Korda's behavior was totally understandable. The third, a man, said that both parties had behaved badly. The fourth, my friend Martha, said it was the second most boring thing she had ever heard, the most boring being a story I had just told her about a fight my college roommate had with a cabdriver at Kennedy Airport.

In any case, before any serious discussion of the incident of the hurled ashtray, I would like to raise some questions for which I have no answers. I raise them simply because if that story were fed into a computer, the only possible response it could make is We Do Not Have Sufficient Information to Make an Evaluation. For example:

Do the Kordas have a good marriage?

Was the heat working in their London hotel room the night of the fracas?

Was it raining out?

What did the second woman at the table look like? Was she as pretty as Mrs. Korda? Was she ugly? Was part of Michael Korda's reaction—and his desire to assert possession of his wife—the result of the possibility that he suspected the drunks thought he was with someone funny-looking?

What kind of a tacky restaurant is it where a waiter delivers a dirty message on a silver tray?

What about a woman who ignores flying bread balls? Wasn't her husband justified in thinking she would be no more interested in novelty cards?

Did Michael Korda pay the check before or after throwing the ashtray? Did he tip the standard 15 percent?

Since the incident occurs in London, a city notorious for its rampant homoerotic behavior, and since the table of drunks was all male, isn't it possible that the printed card was in fact intended not for Mrs. Korda but for Michael? In which case how should we now view his response, if at all?

There might be those who would raise questions about the ashtray itself: was it a big, heavy ashtray, these people might ask, or a dinky little round one? Was it glass or was it plastic? These questions are irrelevant.

In the absence of answers to any of the above, I would nonetheless like to offer some random musings. First, I think it is absurd for Mrs. Korda to think that she and she alone was involved in the incident.

Yes, it might have been nice had her husband consulted her; and yes, it would have been even nicer had he turned out to be Gary Cooper, or failing that, Dave DeBusschere, or even Howard Cosell—anyone but this suave flinger of ashtrays he turned out to be. But the fact remains that the men at the table *were* insulting Korda, and disturbing his dinner, as well as hers. Their insult was childish and Korda's reaction was ludicrous, but Mrs. Korda matched them all by reducing a complicated and rather interesting emotional situation to a tedious set of movement platitudes.

Beyond that—and the Kordas quite aside, because God Almighty (as Mrs. Korda might put it) knows what it is they are into—I wonder whether there is any response a man could make in that situation which would not disappoint a feminist. Yes, I want to be treated as an equal and not as an appendage or possession or spare rib, but I also want to be taken care of. Isn't any man sitting at a table with someone like me damned whatever he does? If the drunks in question are simply fools, conventioneers with funny paper hats, I suppose that a possible reaction would be utter cool. But if they were truly insulting and disturbing, some response does seem called for. Some wild and permanent gesture of size. But on whose part? And what should it consist of? And how tall do you have to be to bring it off? And where is the point that a mild show of strength becomes crude macho vulgarity; where does reserve veer off into passivity?

Like almost every other question in this column, I have no positive answer. But I think that if I ever found myself in a similar situation, and if it was truly demeaning, I would prefer that my husband handle it. My husband informs me, after some consideration, that the Gary Cooper approach would not work. But he could, for example, call over the captain and complain discreetly, perhaps even ask that our table be moved. He could hire a band of aging Teddy boys to find out where the drunks were staying and short-sheet all their beds. Or—and I think I prefer this—he could produce, from his jacket pocket, a printed card from a novelty shop reading: "I'm terribly sorry, but as you can see by looking at our dinner companion, my wife and I have other plans."

I'm going out to have those cards made up right now.

A Commentary

In this essay Ephron is concerned, as her title suggests, with an event: she has a story to tell. And like any essayist, she also has a persuasive purpose, a point to make. Her purpose, like that of any narrative essayist, is to offer an interpretation of the story—an interpretation that uses the story as a means of commenting on some aspect of experience. Before we can understand her point, however, we must examine the story itself—its plot, its characters, its dialogue—as well as her method of narrating it.

The story of "the hurled ashtray" is relatively brief: it takes up only about 20 percent of her essay. In other narrative essays the story may consume a much greater share of the piece—in some, almost the entire piece. Brief as it is, her story is lively—violent, even—and it turns out to have a surprising twist. Our first task is to identify the principal parts of her narrative, to see how they are proportioned to one another and how they are put together. Looked at in this way, her narrative seems to fall into two roughly equal sections: the scene inside the restaurant, and the scene outside the restaurant. Within these manageable sections we can consider the basic elements of narration—*description, dialogue*, and *commentary*—and examine the effects they create.

Description predominates in the first section, and it moves quickly from the quiet scene of "Korda, his wife, and another woman . . . having dinner" to the noisy climax that winds up with "Korda, his wife, and their woman friend . . . out on the street." But Ephron takes us through that rapid sequence of events by way of a carefully structured process. She moves back and forth from one table to the other, repeatedly shifting the focus of our attention, as though we were spectators at a tennis match. And each glimpse of the contestants gives us heavily loaded details that move us to sympathy for the Kordas and disgust with those "drunks" at the other table. Thus, when the first section ends with the statement that "Mrs. Korda was furious," we probably assume that she is outraged with the injustice of the whole situation.

The second section completely reverses our assumption. Mrs. Korda, we discover to our surprise, is not angry at the drunks who abused her, nor is she angry at the restaurant for letting them abuse her. Mrs. Korda is angry with Mr. Korda—for coming to her defense! On top of that, we get another shock when we discover that Mrs. Korda is not the stoically restrained person we thought her to be. The silent lady of the first section becomes a screaming fury in the second. Her true nature—her character—is revealed entirely in dialogue, or, more accurately, in monologue, since she runs on uninterruptedly until Ephron cuts off the diatribe, telling us parenthetically that it was "even longer in the original version." And if we examine Mrs. Korda's monologue in detail, we discover that from beginning to end—from calling her husband a "male chauvinist" to calling herself a "slave"—it is filled with the language and attitudes of the woman's movement. Given the content, intensity, and length of that outburst, she seems to be portrayed as a raving feminist. And that appears to be the point of the story. But then Ephron gives us yet another surprise, when she tells us that Mr. Korda, after thinking about his wife's behavior, considered it to be "doubtless right."

By this point we might very well be confused. No one in the story seems to act sensibly. Everyone, in fact, behaves excessively, as if they were completely out of control. Thus, the story seems to make no sense at all, until in the next paragraph Ephron gives us the first hint of her interpretation:

> . . . I got to thinking about the story, and it began to seem to me that the episode just might be a distillation of everything that has happened to men and women as a result of the women's movement, and if not that, at least a way to write about etiquette after the revolution.

Once she provides that brief commentary, we can begin to see the point of the story. Then we can see that our confusion is appropriate, since everyone in the story is mixed up about etiquette, not knowing how to behave in a difficult social situation. And their problem seems to arise from the clash of masculine and feminist standards of behavior.

After giving us that insight into the Korda episode, Ephron gives us another perspective on it by telling us another story about another dinner table episode, in this case a dinner at which she asked four of her friends to give *their* reactions to the Korda story. Her story of that dinner table conversation is quite brief, but the details are significant, for they reveal not only that each of her friends had a completely different judgment of the Korda episode, but also that their judgments had nothing to do with their sex. One man, for example, "thought Mrs. Korda was completely right," while the other man "said that both parties had behaved badly." Thus her report of the conversation reinforces the point of her story about the Kordas. Not only are the Kordas mixed up about etiquette, but so is everyone else, including Ephron and her friends.

Once we grasp the meaning of the Korda story and its sequel, we can see why Ephron begins her essay with that story about Gary Cooper. The Cooper story, we might say, is an example—"a distillation"—of how men and women got on before the feminist revolution. In that little restaurant episode, no one is confused as to how to handle a difficult social situation. Everyone, in fact, is sure of the way to behave. Gary Cooper reacts like a "cocksure" male, and his woman like a "hensure" female. Cooper is able to handle those Teddy boys calmly and swiftly simply by ruffling his feathers a bit, and the woman at his table does not make any fuss about the matter. She is satisfied with her "henny" role. Thus, the Cooper story seems to represent a past era when men and women got on easily with one another because they were comfortable with their traditional roles. Perhaps that is why Ephron calls the Cooper episode a "swell story." Perhaps that is why she thinks "longingly" of Cooper "and his way with words." Surely that must be why she thinks of the Korda story "as a pathetic contrast to the Gary Cooper story." She seems to long for that simpler time before the "revolution," before women became "cocksure" and men turned "hensure."

At this stage in our analysis, we might be tempted to say that the Ephron essay makes the same point as the Lawrence. Certainly they are concerned with the same basic issue—with the psychological and social consequences of changes that have taken place in the traditional roles of men and women. But they do not invite us to take the same attitude toward those changes. Lawrence is opposed to them, and he reveals that opposition both in the clear-cut logic of his analogy and in the clear-cut language of his judgments. Ephron, however, is not clear-cut in her response to the problem. She appears to take a definite stand only because we have restricted our analysis to the narrative elements of her essay. We have done so because a narrative essay should be approached through the story it tells. As we have seen, Ephron tells us three stories rather than one, and that has complicated our analytical procedure. But we must still examine both her commentary on the Korda story and the personality she projects in the essay before we can be certain of exactly what she wants us to think about "etiquette after the revolution."

When we look for the commentary in a narrative essay, we may expect to find it at almost any point. It may precede the story, or be interwoven with the story, or follow the story. And it may be conveyed explicitly or implicitly. As we have seen, Ephron implicitly comments on the Korda story through the stories she tells before and after it. She also gives us a significant bit of implicit commentary when she introduces the Korda story by describing it as "a sort of reverse-twist update on Francis Macomber." In that comment she alludes to Hemingway's fictional story, "The Short Happy Life of Francis Macomber," which tells of a married couple whose problems are caused not by the man's being too protective a husband to suit his wife's image of herself, but by the husband's being too weak a man to satisfy his wife's image of him. Thus the old masculine code of behavior seems to have been as troublesome as the new feminist one for men and women. Gary Cooper, after all, may have been a rare bird rather than a typical rooster. And that is the first hint that Ephron is not taking the same position as Lawrence.

If we turn now to her explicit, extended commentary, most of which follows the third story, we can see just how reluctant she is to take a definite stand. She begins by raising a lengthy series of questions to which she says "I have no answers." All those questions seek information about the Kordas and the immediate circumstances of their story—information that might help her to make a clear-cut evaluation of it. Lacking answers, she then professes only "to offer some random musings." But among those musings she makes a very telling statement of her personal feelings when she says, "Yes, I want to be treated as an equal and not as an appendage or possession or spare rib, but I also want to be taken care of." The very form of her statement—"I want this, but I also want that"—reveals that she finds herself in a dilemma. She is torn between feminist beliefs and a feminine desire for masculine protection. She wants to have it both ways. But when she tries to imagine how both those aspirations might be fulfilled in an actual situation, she once again acknowledges that "I have no positive answers." Thus she does not take a clear-cut stand on how men and women should behave in the wake of "the revolution." Rather, she raises a vexing problem in social behavior for which she can offer no solution other than the facetious one she proposes at the end, and so her essay concludes with a comic response to the hopelessness of the situation.

Once we confront that comic response, we might wonder just how seriously she takes the problem and how seriously she wants us to take it. But those matters can be determined only by examining the personality Ephron projects in the essay. Since she is a woman writing "about etiquette after the revolution," she is likely to be very self-conscious about the role she plays, about the etiquette she follows, about the kind of woman she appears to be in the essay; and we might assess her personality with an eye to those concerns. She opens her essay, as we noted earlier, by appearing to be a casual and spontaneous person: she does not stand on formalities. But in the second and third sentences she appears also to be a bit unsure of herself, worried about her ability to tell the Cooper story, afraid that "it will lose something in print." And when she has finished telling it, she says, "Well, you had to be there," as though to imply that she thinks she has flubbed the story.

In fact, however, Ephron handles the story quite well, carefully building up the situation to prepare for its climax. For this reason her apologetic manner seems hard to explain, until we discover in the opening of the third paragraph that she "longingly" thinks about Gary Cooper's "way with words." Then it becomes clear that Cooper is one of her heroes, and that all along she has been acting the role of a diffident feminine admirer. Indeed, once she has disposed of the Cooper story she appears to become quite self-confident. She does not, for example, show any qualms about telling the Korda story, or that of the dinner conversation with her friends. And while she may not have the answers to all the questions she raises about the Kordas, she does not hesitate to register some firm judgments about them: "Korda's reaction was ludicrous, but Mrs. Korda matched them all by reducing a complicated and rather interesting emotional situation to a tedious set of movement platitudes." Nothing diffident, there. That sounds like a tough-minded social critic doing her thing, and she retains that tone until the end, when she considers how she would like her husband to handle a difficult situation. Then she becomes somewhat tentative, when she says, for example, "I think . . . I would prefer that my husband handle it," or "he could . . . call over the captain and complain discreetly, perhaps even ask that our table be moved." Finally she turns playful, resolving the question by "going out to have those cards made up right now."

To summarize our impression of her personality: we notice that she begins diffidently when speaking about Gary Cooper, becomes confident when speaking about the Kordas, and then turns diffident again when speaking about herself and her husband. In effect she displays both sides of the personality she revealed when she spoke of wanting "to be treated as an equal," but also wanting "to be taken care of." Thus, in the alternation of her personality, in its play back and forth between those two aspects, we can see just how torn she is in her feelings toward the matter of social behavior, and therefore how difficult things have become for *her* "as a result of the women's movement." Her facetiousness at the end seems to be simply a way of keeping her sense of humor about it. Men and women, she seems to be telling us, have perenially had difficulty getting on with one another, and their difficulties have been compounded by the women's movement, so that the only thing we can do to keep our sanity is to imagine playful solutions to the eternal problem.

THE ESSAY AS POEM: MEDITATION

When we are meditating, we are in a sense engaged in a conversation with ourselves. We are talking to ourselves, seeking to discover the truth about something. Whatever our concern may be—whether we are contemplating ourselves, or someone else, or some aspect of our world—we usually try out various ways of thinking about it. We do so because we are in search of truth rather than in possession of it. The same is true of a meditative writer. The author of a meditative essay is in a sense thinking on paper, trying things out. In that sense a meditative essay comes closest to the kind of writing that Montaigne had in mind when he coined the word "essay" to describe his personal explorations. Because it is a means of exploration, the meditative essay is less concerned with persuading us about something than with revealing the author's process of thinking about something. In this respect the meditative essay has a distinctly different purpose from the other kinds we have discussed, and particularly from the argumentative essay. Yet the meditative essay, like the argumentative, is concerned with attitudes and ideas, and thus it is important to distinguish its form from that of the argumentative essay.

The major differences can be seen in the way the two forms relate the essayist to the reader. In the argumentative essay the author has mastered a subject and now expects to give us the benefit of that mastery, actively seeking to move us around to his point of view. That sureness of purpose also makes for a clear and straightforward development within the argumentative essay. In a meditative essay, on the other hand, the author pays less attention to us as readers, for he is not concerned primarily to move us in a specific direction. In fact, the meditative author may not always be sure of exactly where his thoughts will take him; they may even lead him into digressions away from what appears to be his main subject. The meditative essayist often connects ideas by an associative process, with no worry about an outline organized to lead clearly from assumptions to conclusions.

The meditative essay differs from the argumentative also in its use of images and details. In the argumentative essay, as we have seen, the important images are used as analogies to structure and support an argument. In the meditative essay, however, the images and details become *symbols,* and their meanings are primarily suggestive rather than persuasive. The meditative essayist, in fact, repeatedly observes, and describes, and then thinks about things, allowing one image or thought to produce another through the mysterious generative powers of the mind. For this reason as we read a meditative essay we are likely to find it more rewarding to concentrate on the texture of its prose than on the structure of the essay as a whole. Indeed, the structure will most likely be determined by the images themselves: it will be organized associatively rather than persuasively. Even so, we will leave a good meditative essay enriched, though not in possession of anything so neat as a coin with a motto stamped upon it. Here, for example, is a meditative essay that will enrich your thoughts about things. When you have finished reading it, take some time to consider the process of its thought before you look at our commentary.

E. B. WHITE
1899–
Spring [April 1941]

Notes on springtime and on anything else that comes to mind of an intoxicating nature.

There is considerable doubt at this writing that my hog has been bred, although she has been keeping company. Her condition is watched with interest by pigmen hereabouts, who are awaiting (as I am) the beginning of the month to see who is right. I will announce the results of this contest later if I think of it. Last year she had seven, on a Sunday. They were blithe and bonny and good and gay, except the runt—who was merely blithe and good and gay.

Anne Carroll Moore, of the New York Public Library, writes me that a representative of Superman, Inc., paid a call on the children's room the other day. He was an average-sized man (nothing super) and was armed with a large poster depicting Superman (full strength) with a list of recommended books. The list included *Robin Hood* and *King Arthur.* He told Miss Moore that the boys and girls would read those books if they knew that Superman approved of them. He said his hero carried great weight now, and that teachers in public schools frequently commanded instant obedience from their pupils by invoking Superman. As far as I could gather from Miss Moore's letter, he didn't say anything about Louisa May Alcott, author of *Little Supermen* and *Little Superwomen*.

This family, incidentally, has just finished reading *Little Women* aloud. It was our after-dinner mint of the winter of 1940–41; reading time, three months and ten days. One of the wrenching experiences that a person can wish on himself nowadays is to read about Europe in terms of Amy and Laurie.

The intoxication of spring is a figure of speech to most creatures, but to a lamb it means a real drunk. The very young lambs who stick to a straight milk diet keep their feet pretty well, but the older ones (the ones of high school age) stagger back from the pasture and after weaving about the barnyard for a few minutes, collapse. They froth at the mouth, and you can hear them grind their teeth forty feet away. It is a glorious jag, this spring drunk. I keep my syringe loaded with tea, and administer it—between paragraphs—to the worst cases. This year is not as bad as last year, for I have fewer lambs and more tea.

Haven't seen a snake yet, but I haven't been across to the rock pile and lifted a rock.

A pair of starlings are renovating the knothole in the Balm o' Gilead on the front lawn, redecorating and trying to get everything done (eggs laid, birds hatched and launched) before the arrival of the flickers, who walk right in regardless.

There is a stanza in Robert Frost's poem "Two Tramps in Mud Time" which describes an April moment when air and sky have a vernal feeling, but suddenly a cloud crosses the path of the sun and a bitter little wind finds you out, and you're back in the middle of March. Everyone who has lived in the country knows that sort of moment— the promise of warmth, the raised hope, the ruthless rebuff.

There is another sort of day which needs celebrating in song—the day of days when spring at last holds up her face to be kissed, deliberate and unabashed. On that day no wind blows either in the hills or in the mind; no chill finds the bone. It is a day which can come only in a northern climate, where there has been a long background of frigidity, a long deficiency of sun.

We've just been through this magical moment—which was more

than a moment and was a whole morning—and it lodges in memory like some old romance, with the same subtlety of tone, the same enrichment of the blood, and the enchantment and the mirth and the indescribable warmth. Even before breakfast I felt that the moment was at hand, for when I went out to the barn to investigate twins I let the kitchen door stay open, lazily, instead of closing it behind me. This was a sign. The lambs had nursed and the ewe was lying quiet. One lamb had settled itself on the mother's back and was a perfect miniature of the old one—they reminded me of a teapot we have, whose knob is a tiny replica of the pot itself. The barn seemed warmer and sweeter than usual, but it was early in the day, and the hint of springburst was still only a hint, a suggestion, a nudge. The full impact wasn't felt until the sun had climbed higher. Then came, one after another, the many small caresses which added up to the total embrace of warmth and life—a laziness and contentment in the behavior of animals and people, a tendency of man and dog to sit down somewhere in the sun. In the driveway, a deep rut which for the past week had held three or four inches of water and which had alternately frozen and thawed, showed clear indications of drying up. On the window ledge in the living room, the bare brown forsythia cuttings suddenly discovered the secret of yellow. The goose, instead of coming off her nest and joining her loud companions, settled down on her eleven eggs, pulled some feathers from her breast, and resigned herself to the twenty-eight-day grind. When I went back through the kitchen I noticed that the air that had come in was not like an invader but like a friend who had stopped by for a visit.

Sugaring operations, conducted by the minor, have been under way for some time. Sap has been running strong. Last Sunday morning we had homemade syrup on pancakes, and the consensus of opinion was that the trees were maples but maybe not sugar maples. Anyway they were not hemlocks, everybody agreed on that, hopefully. Today I received some syrup from a lady who lives in New Hampshire. It had the genuine flavor. There is something rather wonderful about our own though—a strange woody taste (and the recollection of an early morning figure starting out into the snowy woods with his buckets and his dog).

Whenever I tell about spring, or any delights which I experience, or the pleasant country, I think of a conversation I had with a friend in the city shortly before I left. "I trust," he said with an ugly leer, "that you will spare the reading public your little adventures in contentment."

Of all the common farm operations none is more ticklish and confining than tending a brooder stove. All brooder stoves are whimsical, and some of them are holy terrors. Mine burns coal, and has only a fair record. With its check draft that opens and closes, this stove occupies my dreams from midnight, when I go to bed, until five o'clock, when I get up, pull a shirt and a pair of pants on over my pajamas, and stagger out into the dawn to read the thermometer under the hover and see that my 254 little innocents are properly disposed in a neat circle round their big iron mama. If I am lucky the thermometer registers 88° and the chicks are happily eating their favorite breakfast cereal, which costs $2.65 a bag; but there is an even chance that during the night a wandering wind has come along, whipped up the stove to 110°, burned up all the coal and left a pot full of half dead ashes. In this event the thermometer now registers 68° and the chicks are standing round with their collars turned up, blowing on their hands and looking like a snow-removal gang under the El on a bitter winter's midnight.

For mothering chicks, a stove has one real advantage over a hen: it stays in one place and you always know where it is. Right there its advantage ceases. In all other respects a hen is ahead of any stove that was ever built. A hen's thermostat is always in perfect order, and her warmth has that curious indefinable quality of sociability which I believe means a lot to a chick and keeps its bowels in nice condition. A hen, moreover, is draft proof. When she gathers her little charges under her feathers, floor drafts are eliminated. A hen has a larger vocabulary than a stove and can communicate ideas more readily— which is desirable even though some of a hen's ideas are flighty and many of her suspicions unfounded. And of course a hen is a good provider and does a lot of spade work which the ordinary stove of today is incapable of. She doesn't have to be shaken down, and red-hot coals never roll out of her on to the dry floor.

Anyone with a fire on his mind is in a sort of trance. I have seen suburbanites on commuting trains who bore the unmistakable mark of the firemaker. Cooks have it—those who still cook over real fires. But the operator of a brooder stove has it to a pitiful degree. On his fire depends not simply the safety of the plumbing or the comfort of the tenants; his fire is a matter of life and death to hundreds of babies. If it lags even fifteen degrees they will crowd together in a corner and die from suffocation. If ever you are in the country in the spring of the year and see a face that is not as other faces, you can bet you are looking at a man who has a brooder stove on his mind.

In this spring of 1941 a man tends his fire in a trance that is all the deeper because of its dreamlike unreality, things being as they are in the world. I sometimes think I am crazy—everybody else fighting and dying or working for a cause or writing to his senator, and me looking after some Barred Rock chickens. But the land, and the creatures that go with it, are what is left that is good, and they are the authors of the book that I find worth reading; and anyway a man has to live according to his lights even if his lights are the red coals in the base of a firepot. On Sunday the sixth of April, the day the German spring drive started in the Balkans, a clinker started forming on one side of my grate, and for the next three days (or until I found out what was the trouble) I had a sick fire on my hands. I was trying to finish up something I had been writing, working against time, and so I had to stay up late in the evening to do my work and then get up early in the morning to make sure I still had a warm brooder; so for three days I hardly slept at all and began to feel the uneasy symptoms and the lightheadedness of brain fag. On the afternoon of the third day I was crouched carefully in front of the stove, trying for the hundredth time to figure out why a well-shaken and freshly fueled fire wouldn't take hold as it should. The thermometer had dropped to 68° and the infants, ready for bed, were chilly and were not forming the charmed circle that is indispensable to their night health but were huddled in a big black mass against one wall.

For a moment I felt as though I might be about to have what folks hereabouts call a "foolish spell," and just at that juncture somebody knocked. I unbuttoned the door and it was my boy to say that supper was ready and that "the war news was very bad." For just a second I felt licked and bewildered and afraid. But it didn't last. I soon knew that the remaining warmth in this stubborn stove was all I had to pit against the Nazi idea of *Frühling*. I boosted the fire a little, loaded about a hundred chicks into a basket in the half darkness and distributed them round the edge of the hover in a more strategic position for sleeping. Then I ate and went to bed. At eleven I got up, took a flashlight, and went out to renew my vigil in this strange cooling world. From eleven to twelve I just sat, listening to the faint stirrings of the tiny forms and occasionally reading the meter. It had sagged off four degrees.

At twelve I began experiments with a new form of poker. At twelve-thirty I located the clinker. By one o'clock I had broken it up and fished out a bucketful of dead ashes. Then I loaded another batch of chicks into the basket to lighten the congested area (like any good traffic cop) and heard that most wonderful sound—the healthy breathing of a fire that had been given up for dead.

Countries are ransacked, valleys drenched with blood. Though it seems untimely I still publish my belief in the egg, the contents of the egg, the warm coal, and the necessity for pursuing whatever fire delights and sustains you.

A Commentary

This meditative essay does have its narrative and persuasive dimensions. The story of the clinker in the brooder provides some narrative tension in the last half of the essay. And the whole piece tends toward the establishment of a case for certain domestic values in the midst of an international crisis—a world war in fact. But it lacks the tone of persuasion, and if we trace the movement of the essay from beginning to end, we can readily discover its dominant meditative quality. It does not have the pace of a story or the structure of an argument. It moves abruptly from one item to the next—from the condition of a hog to a letter about Superman, from *Little Women* to lambs, from snakes to starlings.

Actually, White prepares us for this process in his opening sentence, which is so casual, so unpremeditated, that it is not even a complete sentence—merely a fragment. What could be more appropriate, though, for someone who is making "Notes on Springtime"? The phrase following these words is the clearest announcement of White's meditative intention: "and on anything else that comes to mind." Yet he restricts himself somewhat by adding the final phrase: "of an intoxicating nature." We may expect, then, that he will confine his meditation within the limits defined by "springtime" and "intoxication." Still, both these themes leave him plenty of room to move around in. Since much of the reader's pleasure in a meditative essay comes from watching the author move around, we will begin our analysis by looking briefly at the opening sections, to see how White is moved by the suggestions—the associative power—of words, images, and ideas. Then we can go to the later sections for a more detailed sense of meditative movement.

The first two entries following White's announcement of his subject seem at first sight to be entirely unrelated. And in a sense they are. Yet, when we look at them in the light of the entire essay, we see that they establish a rhythm that later becomes more insistent: the movement from natural details to reminders of an unnatural world, from the "blithe and bonny and good and gay" to "a representative of Superman, Inc." But what, we might ask, does "Superman" have to do with "Spring"? Nothing and everything, for White is continually contrasting his idea of spring with the "Nazi idea of *Frühling*" (German for "spring"). When we make this connection, we can reclaim the word that lies behind "Superman"—the German equivalent "Übermensch," a favorite expression of the Nazis in describing themselves. Thus the Nazi idea of spring would be a new world ruled by Supermen. Now we can see why White chooses to note that the "representative" was, after all, only "an average-sized man (nothing super)."

With these few cues, we can readily see how White gets to his third entry and the movement that takes place within it, from the coziness of the family reading a peaceable novel about more innocent times to the "wrenching experiences." And then back again to "the intoxication of spring" and its effect on the lambs. From then on, the going is easy, since the next several entries stay exclusively with the joys of nature in spring.

Now we turn to the long section that begins with the difficulties of "tending a brooder stove," since this will provide us with a basis for more sharply distinguishing the meditative essay through a contrast with Lawrence's directly persuasive piece. Notice that White uses farmyard images similar to those used by Lawrence in "Cocksure Women and Hensure Men." But Lawrence uses his farmyard as an analogy to support an argument: it is a generalized farmyard, though concrete in detail. White's chickens are specific, and exist in a direct relation with the meditator himself. They have a kind of historical reality, like the characters in a narrative essay. Yet this episode of the chickens is important simply because it happened to the meditative author of the essay. It is presented with almost no dialogue and little action. Both story and ideas are subordinated to White's ruminations.

Consider, for example, White's comments on the relative merits of hens and stoves. Here he lets his mind play whimsically with the comparison. He is not out to prove anything. What, then, *is* the effect of this paragraph, and how has White achieved it? We can begin to answer those questions by looking at some of his statements on the merits of a hen:

1. "A hen's thermostat is always in perfect order."
2. "A hen . . . is draft proof."
3. "She doesn't have to be shaken down."
4. "and red-hot coals never roll out of her on to the dry floor."

This list of the hen's advantages is amusing rather than persuasive, for White has been considering the hen as a *kind* of stove, with all the equipment that a stove might have. The ideas of shaking down a hen, and having a hen start a fire by laying hot coals, are in themselves ludicrous; they carry none of the persuasive bite of Lawrence's idea of a woman laying an empty ink-bottle. Lawrence's image is sarcastic, satirical, and therefore an attempt to persuade. White's images satirize neither hen nor stove; they are amusing feats of the imagination in a playful mood.

Now consider these two statements:

1. "A hen has a larger vocabulary than a stove."
2. "A hen is a good provider and does a lot of spade work which the ordinary stove of today is incapable of."

In the first of these, White has placed both hen and stove on an equal footing as communicating creatures (after all, a stove makes noises, too). He has reduced the difference in *kind* to a difference in degree. In his benevolent perspective, both stove and chicken are assumed to have something to say to those who will listen, and with mock-judiciousness he awards the hen credit for using more words than the stove. In the second statement he follows a similar procedure but adds more humorous implications: first, that even though the *ordinary* stove may not be able to scratch up food for chicks ("spade work"), some *extraordinary* stove might well be able to; and second, that this extraordinary stove may be a real possibility in the future, since only the ordinary stove of *today* is incapable of such feats. Here, of course, he is also taking pleasure in using that salesman's cliché, "the ordinary stove of today" in such an absurd context. White also gains an effect by understating a dimension that another writer might sentimentalize as mother love. In assessing the advantages of hen-heat as compared with stove-heat, he reminds us that the hen's "warmth has that curious indefinable quality of sociability which I believe means a lot to a chick and keeps its bowels in nice condition." The term "sociability" as a quality of heat is unexpected but richly appropriate, and the picture of a contented chick as one whose bowels are "in nice condition" is unsentimental but not without charm.

As the essay moves along, the general reflections on fires and chickens become mixed with more intrusions from the outside world. The meditator is clearly supposed to be White himself, and his job of writing conflicts with his job of chick-tending. Also the news of World War II impinges more insistently than earlier upon his personal pursuits. The death and destruction of war now become explicitly poised against the warmth and life of the brooder: "I soon knew that the remaining warmth in this stubborn stove was all I had to pit against the Nazi idea of *Frühling.*"

The last paragraph of the essay summarizes these ideas and glances back at an earlier paragraph, in which White's "friend" asked that he "spare the reading public your little adventures in contentment." When we focus on this statement we can see this essay as a kind of dialogue, since the whole meditation is a response to the friend's request—especially that final paragraph, in which White asserts that he will continue to publish his little adventures, and that even in a time of international cataclysm it is necessary to pursue "whatever fire delights and sustains you." In this paragraph the egg and the coal finally become symbols of all the things that make life worth living, the things that White feels we must be concerned with in order to remain human. To this point his meditation has led him, and he closes not with an appeal to us but with an assertion in behalf of himself: "I still publish." In this meditation, then, he persuades not us but himself, and we overhear the associative pattern of his meditative process. We see the subject *through* him, and what we perceive of *it* is always in relation to *him.*

THE ESSAY AS PLAY: DIALOGUE

The dialogue is an ancient literary form that has perennially been used as a means of presenting ideas. Most of Plato's philosophy, for example, has come down to us in the form of dialogues involving Socrates and other

Athenians or visitors to Athens. During the seventeenth century, Izaak Walton used the form in *The Complete Angler* to present his ideas on the contemplative value of fishing, and John Dryden used the form in "An Essay of Dramatic Poesy" to present his ideas on the purpose and structure of drama.

The dialogue is also a popular contemporary form. We frequently encounter it in the newspaper columns of syndicated journalists who use it as a means of commenting on current events. Art Buchwald, for example, repeatedly constructs imaginary dialogues as a means of expressing his opinions on political affairs in Washington. We also encounter the dialogue in published transcripts of interviews, hearings, and other oral events. And as we know from the Watergate transcripts, the actual dialogue can be edited so as to influence public opinion. In all these instances, in fact, the dialogue is used primarily as a persuasive means of presenting ideas, and can thus be considered a form of the essay.

The dialogue, of course, is related to the play in that it presents us with characters speaking to one another; and like a play it also has a plot as well as a setting. For this reason we call it a *dramatic* essay. In the dramatic essay, however, character, plot, and setting are used not so much to create an imitation of experience as to make a persuasive statement about some aspect of experience. Thus, when reading a dramatic essay you should examine its elements to discover what they can tell you about the author's ideas. Since the author does not speak directly (except to set the scene), you will have to pay particular attention to the characters themselves. In some essays the author's view will be spoken by one character, who dominates the others in the dialogue. In other essays, the author's view will be conveyed by all the characters in the dialogue.

The dramatic essay presented here was written for British readers in 1922, when England was contemplating a small war with Turkey—and many British servicemen had died there less than a decade earlier in the Battle of Gallipoli. Although the war contemplated in 1922 did not materialize, the essay seems to have relevance beyond its immediate occasion. When you have finished reading it, take some time to consider its elements and gather your own thoughts about it before you look at our commentary. You might also want to consider the truth it offers in relation to the final meditations on war in White's essay.

E. M. FORSTER
1879–1970
Our Graves in Gallipoli

Scene: the summit of Achi Baba, an exposed spot, looking out across the Dardanelles towards Asia and the East. In a crevice between the rocks lie two graves covered by a single heap of stones. No monument marks them, for they

*escaped notice during the official survey, and the heap of stones has blended into
the desolate and austere outline of the hill. The peninsula is turning towards the
sun, and as the rays strike Achi Baba the graves begin to speak.*

FIRST GRAVE   We are important again upon earth. Each morning men
mention us.

SECOND GRAVE   Yes, after seven years' silence.

FIRST GRAVE   Every day some eminent public man now refers to the
"sanctity of our graves in Gallipoli."

SECOND GRAVE   Why do the eminent men speak of "our" graves, as if they
were themselves dead? It is we, not they, who lie on Achi Baba.

FIRST GRAVE   They say "our" out of geniality and in order to touch the great
heart of the nation more quickly. *Punch,* the great-hearted jester,
showed a picture lately in which the Prime Minister of England, Lloyd
George, fertile in counsels, is urged to go to war to protect "the sanctity
of our graves in Gallipoli." The elderly artist who designed that picture
is not dead and does not mean to die. He hopes to illustrate this war as
he did the last, for a sufficient salary. Nevertheless he writes "our"
graves, as if he was inside one, and all persons of position now say the
same.

SECOND GRAVE   If they go to war, there will be more graves.

FIRST GRAVE   That is what they desire. That is what Lloyd George, prudent
in counsels, and lion-hearted Churchill, intend.

SECOND GRAVE   But where will they dig them?

FIRST GRAVE   There is still room over in Chanak. Also, it is well for a nation
that would be great to scatter its graves all over the world. Graves in
Ireland, graves in Irak, Russia, Persia, India, each with its inscription
from the Bible or Rupert Brooke. When England thinks fit, she can
launch an expedition to protect the sanctity of her graves, and can follow
that by another expedition to protect the sanctity of the additional
graves. That is what Lloyd George, prudent in counsels, and lion-
hearted Churchill, have planned. Churchill planned this expedition to
Gallipoli, where I was killed. He planned the expedition to Antwerp,
where my brother was killed. Then he said that Labour is not fit to
govern. Rolling his eyes for fresh worlds, he saw Egypt, and fearing that
peace might be established there, he intervened and prevented it.
Whatever he undertakes is a success. He is Churchill the Fortunate, ever
in office, and clouds of dead heroes attend him. Nothing for schools,
nothing for houses, nothing for the life of the body, nothing for the
spirit. England cannot spare a penny for anything except for her heroes'
graves.

SECOND GRAVE   Is she really putting herself to so much expense on our
account?

FIRST GRAVE   For us, and for the Freedom of the Straits. That water flowing below us now—it must be thoroughly free. What freedom is, great men are uncertain, but all agree that the water must be free for all nations; if in peace, then for all nations in peace; if in war, then for all nations in war.

SECOND GRAVE   So all nations now support England.

FIRST GRAVE   It is almost inexplicable. England stands alone. Of the dozens of nations into which the globe is divided, not a single one follows her banner, and even her own colonies hang back.

SECOND GRAVE   Yes . . . inexplicable. Perhaps she fights for some other reason.

FIRST GRAVE   Ah, the true reason of a war is never known until all who have fought in it are dead. In a hundred years' time we shall be told. Meanwhile seek not to inquire. There are rumours that rich men desire to be richer, but we cannot know.

SECOND GRAVE   If rich men desire more riches, let them fight. It is reasonable to fight for our desires.

FIRST GRAVE   But they cannot fight. They must not fight. There are too few of them. They would be killed. If a rich man went into the interior of Asia and tried to take more gold or more oil, he might be seriously injured at once. He must persuade poor men, who are numerous, to go there for him. And perhaps this is what Lloyd George, fertile in counsels, has decreed. He has tried to enter Asia by means of the Greeks. It was the Greeks who, seven years ago, failed to join England after they had promised to do so, and our graves in Gallipoli are the result of this. But Churchill the Fortunate, ever in office, ever magnanimous, bore the Greeks no grudge, and he and Lloyd George persuaded their young men to enter Asia. They have mostly been killed there, so English young men must be persuaded instead. A phrase must be thought of, and "the Gallipoli graves" is the handiest. The clergy must wave their Bibles, the old men their newspapers, the old women their knitting, the unmarried girls must wave white feathers, and all must shout, "Gallipoli graves, Gallipoli graves, Gallipoli, Gally Polly, Gally Polly," until the young men are ashamed and think, What sound can that be but my country's call? and Chanak receives them.

SECOND GRAVE   Chanak is to sanctify Gallipoli.

FIRST GRAVE   It will make our heap of stones for ever England, apparently.

SECOND GRAVE   It can scarcely do that to my portion of it. I was a Turk.

FIRST GRAVE   What! a Turk! You a Turk? And I have lain beside you for seven years and never known!

SECOND GRAVE   How should you have known? What is there to know except that I am your brother?

FIRST GRAVE   I am yours . . .

SECOND GRAVE   All is dead except that. All graves are one. It is their unity
    that sanctifies them, and some day even the living will learn this.
FIRST GRAVE   Ah, but why can they not learn it while they are still alive?

*His comrade cannot answer this question. Achi Baba passes beneath the sun, and
so long as there is light warlike preparations can be seen on the opposite coast.
Presently all objects enter into their own shadows, and through the general veil
thus formed the stars become apparent.*

A Commentary

The intention of Forster's essay is clearly persuasive, just as its form is clearly
dramatic. According to the analytic procedures we have been recommend-
ing and using in this book, the form of any given essay dictates the critical
approach to be used in understanding it. This means that we should
examine Forster's essay in terms of its dramatic elements. The basic
elements of drama are character, plot, and setting. Our analysis, then, will
focus on the nature of the characters, their situation, and the movement—
the plot—of their dialogue.

   In the dramatic essay it is often the case that one or more of the
characters embodies the opinions of the essayist. Thus, an analysis
of the two Graves should help us to understand Forster's persuasive
method. We might first ask ourselves whether we discern any significant
differences between the two Graves, whether we can distinguish them as
"characters." They are certainly not distinguished by having special names
or physical qualities; in fact, all such individualizing characteristics are
deliberately suppressed. Nevertheless, the two are different. First Grave
does most of the talking. Second Grave confines himself to brief remarks
and questions. First Grave is the most indignant, and his indignation shows
in the heavy sarcasm of his dialogue. Second Grave is calmer, more
resigned. First Grave is unusually well informed and up-to-date on English
politics—particularly for a grave. Second Grave, at least on the basis of his
questions, seems to be out of touch. Now that we have made these
distinctions, we can see part of Forster's persuasive strategy. Second Grave
is, in a sense, the straight man, who makes it possible for First Grave to
voice Forster's opinions.

   We have put off remarking on an obvious point of distinction between
the two characters—that one is English, the other a Turk—for this
difference is related to plot. And plot, like character, is also related to
Forster's persuasive technique. Throughout most of the dialogue First Grave
is clearly in control of things. But when Second Grave reveals his nationality,
First Grave is taken completely by surprise—and we are, too. This is the
climax in the plot of the dialogue, for it produces a sudden reversal in which

First Grave learns that Second Grave is not a "friend" but an "enemy". This surprise is related to the type of dramatic revelation that we often encounter in the concluding scenes of a play. In this dialogue it serves to work a turn from the political to the personal, and from the specific discussion of one possible war to a more general appeal for understanding and brotherhood among all men. In this respect it bears an interesting relation to White's meditations on war and his attempts to oppose its destructiveness by seeking to understand and sustain life among all natural creatures.

The two graves in Forster's essay never comment on their own natural surroundings, but the particular setting in which they are located contributes to the significance of their dialogue. The scene, we must remember, is overlooking the Dardanelles, a strait often referred to as the dividing line between East and West, Asia and Europe. These speakers represent the opposite sides of that great cultural chasm, and their conversation recalls the history of wars fought in that part of the world. In particular, First Grave's use of heroic epithets reminds us of Homer's epic poem about a great East/West struggle that took place on that very ground, not far away: the Trojan War.

In Homer's *Iliad* the names of the leaders and heroes are always linked with their special qualities, as in "Odysseus never-at-a-loss," or "Hector tamer of horses." In Forster's dialogue First Grave seems to know his Homer, for he adopts the Homeric technique to name the contemporary war lords of his country, England. He calls Lloyd George "prudent in counsels" and Churchill "lion-hearted." But Churchill is not only called "lion-hearted" and "Fortunate"; he is also referred to as "ever in office"—a phrase that moves from heroic to satiric, as in fact do all these epithets when applied not to the fighting heroes of an epic poem but to sedentary politicians who send other men off to their death in combat.

There is, finally, a third voice in this dialogue: that of the scene-setter, who has the first and the last word. This is Forster's chance to have his say, but he does not comment specifically on the meaning of the dialogue—he lets the dialogue speak for itself. He does, however, describe the setting sun—that symbol of the waning British Empire—and contrasts it with the stars, which are always present but only "become apparent" when the sun's glare gives way to shadows. In particular the closing "stage direction," with its symbolism of sun and stars, brings a poetic and meditative dimension to the essay. The sun moves, the stars abide. In the light of the sun, "warlike preparations" are made; the stars remain, becoming visible only when the "objects enter into their own shadows." In the light of the stars, "all graves are one." In this brief essay we thus have dramatic form used to make a persuasive argument against a specific war, and growing out of the argument is a more enduring meditation on the brevity of all life and the futility of life based on hostility rather than on brotherhood.

THE DRAMATIC ESSAY AS MONOLOGUE: IMPERSONATION

The dramatic essay, as we said earlier, may take the form of a dialogue between two or more characters, or the form of a monologue involving only one character. We refer to the single speaker as a character because we want to make clear that the speaker is not to be identified with the author. Nor are the opinions of the speaker to be confused with those of the author. The speaker is a character whom the author is impersonating.

Impersonation is a specialized form of the role playing that takes place in any essay. As we said in our discussion of the essayist and the reader, every essayist projects a particular personality that calls upon us to respond in a particular way; and in our discussion of the sample essays we have seen that essayists usually project personalities that will directly serve their persuasive purposes. They may present themselves as experts, or concerned citizens, or sensitive human beings, or perplexed and puzzled spectators of the world. But whatever role they play, they usually try to put their best foot forward. They usually project an admirable personality that we are expected to regard as an aspect of their true self.

Sometimes, however, essayists choose to project a disagreeable or despicable personality, one that appears to be stupid or downright evil. In such cases they are engaged in the act of impersonation, and they expect us to view the speaker as a character different from themselves. They expect us also to regard the speaker's opinions as different from their own. Thus the speaker and the essayist exist not in a direct but in an ironic relation to each other. And that ironic situation creates special problems for us as readers. It may be easy for us to recognize an abominable character and an abominable view of things. But how are we to proceed from that recognition to an awareness of the author's view, the right view? The good is hardly ever the simple opposite of the bad. Ordinarily the author's opinion is expressed at some point in an ironic essay, and we must be on the alert for it, since it may be interwoven with the views of the dramatic character. But it may not be expressed at all, and in that case we must bring an active intelligence and imagination to our reading, so as to formulate the right view on our own.

The ironic essay can be a most powerful persuasive form, but it is also a dangerous one. It is powerful and dangerous for the same reason; it depends on our active response as readers. If we see through the irony to the real view being advocated, our response will be the more intense because of our necessary engagement in the interpretive process. On the other hand, if we fail to detect the irony we will not only miss the point but we will also be baffled or outraged, or both. Daniel Defoe was once imprisoned because influential men misinterpreted an ironic essay he wrote on sensitive political and religious issues.

No writer has ever mastered the technique of the ironic essay more thoroughly than Defoe's contemporary, Jonathan Swift. We think it appropriate, then, to conclude our selection of illustrative essays with Swift's masterpiece of impersonative persuasion, "A Modest Proposal." We offer no commentary because we do not want you to miss the challenging experience of interpreting this essay on your own. But if you find yourself baffled or outraged, you may find it helpful to think about the questions that follow the essay.

JONATHAN SWIFT
1667–1745
A Modest Proposal

for Preventing the Children of Poor People in Ireland
from Being a Burden to Their Parents or Country,
and for Making Them Beneficial to the Public

It is a melancholy object to those who walk through this great town, or travel in the country, when they see the streets, the roads and cabin-doors crowded with beggars of the female sex, followed by three, four, or six children, all in rags, and importuning every passenger for an alms. These mothers, instead of being able to work for their honest livelihood, are forced to employ all their time in strolling, to beg sustenance for their helpless infants, who, as they grow up, either turn thieves for want of work, or leave their dear native country to fight for the Pretender in Spain, or sell themselves to the Barbadoes.

I think it is agreed by all parties that this prodigious number of children, in the arms, or on the backs, or at the heels of their mothers, and frequently of their fathers, is in the present deplorable state of the kingdom a very great additional grievance; and therefore whoever could find out a fair, cheap, and easy method of making these children sound and useful members of the commonwealth would deserve so well of the public as to have his statue set up for a preserver of the nation.

But my intention is very far from being confined to provide only for the children of professed beggars; it is of a much greater extent, and shall take in the whole number of infants at a certain age who are born of parents in effect as little able to support them as those who demand our charity in the streets.

As to my own part, having turned my thoughts for many years upon this important subject, and maturely weighed the several schemes of other projectors, I have always found them grossly mistaken in their computation. It is true a child just dropped from its dam may be supported by her milk for a solar year with little other nourishment, at most not above the value of two shillings, which the mother may certainly get, or the value in scraps, by her lawful occupation of begging, and it is exactly at one year old that I propose to provide for them, in such a manner as, instead of being a charge upon their parents, or the parish, or wanting food and raiment for the rest of their lives, they shall, on the contrary, contribute to the feeding and partly to the clothing of many thousands.

There is likewise another great advantage in my scheme, that it will prevent those voluntary abortions, and that horrid practice of women murdering their bastard children, alas, too frequent among us, sacrificing the poor innocent babes, I doubt, more to avoid the expense than the shame, which would move tears and pity in the most savage and inhuman breast.

The number of souls in Ireland being usually reckoned one million and a half, of these I calculate there may be about two hundred thousand couples whose wives are breeders, from which number I subtract thirty thousand couples who are able to maintain their own children, although I apprehend there cannot be so many under the present distresses of the kingdom, but this being granted, there will remain an hundred and seventy thousand breeders. I again subtract fifty thousand for those women who miscarry, or whose children die by accident or disease within the year. There only remain an hundred and twenty thousand children of poor parents annually born: the question therefore is, how this number shall be reared, and provided for, which as I have already said, under the present situation of affairs is utterly impossible by all the methods hitherto proposed, for we can neither employ them in handicraft or agriculture; we neither build houses (I mean in the country), nor cultivate land: they can very seldom pick up a livelihood by stealing until they arrive at six years old, except where they are of towardly parts, although I confess they learn the rudiments much earlier, during which time they can however be properly looked upon only as probationers, as I have been informed by a principal gentleman in the County of Cavan, who protested to me that he never knew above one or two instances under the age of six, even in a part of the kingdom so renowned for the quickest proficiency in that art.

I am assured by our merchants that a boy or a girl before twelve years old, is no saleable commodity, and even when they come to this age, they will not yield above three pounds, or three pounds and half-a-crown at most on the Exchange, which cannot turn to account either to the parents or the kingdom, the charge of nutriment and rags having been at least four times that value.

I shall now therefore humbly propose my own thoughts, which I hope will not be liable to the least objection.

I have been assured by a very knowing American of my acquaintance in London, that a young healthy child well nursed is at a year old a most delicious, nourishing and wholesome food, whether stewed, roasted, baked, or boiled, and I make no doubt that it will equally serve in a fricassee, or a ragout.

I do therefore humbly offer it to public consideration, that of the hundred and twenty thousand children already computed, twenty thousand may be reserved for breed, whereof only one fourth part to be males, which is more than we allow to sheep, black-cattle, or swine, and my reason is that these children are seldom the fruits of marriage, a circumstance not much regarded by our savages, therefore one male will be sufficient to serve four females. That the remaining hundred thousand may at a year old be offered in sale to the persons of quality, and fortune, through the kingdom, always advising the mother to let them suck plentifully in the last month, so as to render them plump, and fat for a good table. A child will make two dishes at an entertainment for friends, and when the family dines alone, the fore or hind quarter will make a reasonable dish, and seasoned with a little pepper or salt will be very good boiled on the fourth day, especially in winter.

I have reckoned upon a medium, that a child just born will weigh twelve pounds, and in a solar year if tolerably nursed increaseth to twenty-eight pounds.

I grant this food will be somewhat dear, and therefore very proper for landlords, who, as they have already devoured most of the parents, seem to have the best title to the children.

Infant's flesh will be in season throughout the year, but more plentiful in March, and a little before and after, for we are told by a grave[1] author, an eminent French physician, that fish being a prolific diet, there are more children born in Roman Catholic countries about nine months after Lent than at any other season; therefore reckoning a year after Lent, the markets will be more glutted than usual, because the number of Popish infants is at least three to one in this kingdom, and therefore it will have one other collateral advantage by lessening the number of Papists among us.

I have already computed the charge of nursing a beggar's child (in which list I reckon all cottagers, labourers, and four-fifths of the farmers) to be about two shillings *per annum*, rags included, and I believe no gentleman would repine to give ten shillings for the carcass of a good fat child, which, as I have said, will make four

---

1. Rabelais.

dishes of excellent nutritive meat, when he hath only some particular friend of his own family to dine with him. Thus the Squire will learn to be a good landlord and grow popular among his tenants, the mother will have eight shillings net profit, and be fit for work until she produces another child.

Those who are more thrifty (as I must confess the times require) may flay the carcass; the skin of which artifically dressed, will make admirable gloves for ladies, and summer boots for fine gentlemen.

As to our city of Dublin, shambles may be appointed for this purpose, in the most convenient parts of it, and butchers we may be assured will not be wanting, although I rather recommend buying the children alive, and dressing them hot from the knife, as we do roasting pigs.

A very worthy person, a true lover of his country, and whose virtues I highly esteem was lately pleased, in discoursing on this matter to offer a refinement upon my scheme. He said that many gentlemen of this kingdom, having of late destroyed their deer, he conceived that the want of venison might be well supplied by the bodies of young lads and maidens, not exceeding fourteen years of age, nor under twelve, so great a number of both sexes in every county being now ready to starve, for want of work and service: and these to be disposed of by their parents if alive, or otherwise by their nearest relations. But with due deference to so excellent a friend, and so deserving a patriot, I cannot be altogether in his sentiments. For as to the males, my American acquaintance assured me from frequent experience that their flesh was generally tough and lean, like that of our schoolboys, by continual exercise, and their taste disagreeable, and to fatten them would not answer the charge. Then as to the females, it would, I think with humble submission, be a loss to the public, because they soon would become breeders themselves: and besides, it is not improbable that some scrupulous people might be apt to censure such a practice (although indeed very unjustly) as a little bordering upon cruelty, which I confess, hath always been with me the strongest objection against any project, howsoever well intended.

But in order to justify my friend, he confessed that this expedient was put into his head by the famous Psalmanazar, a native of the island Formosa, who came from thence to London, above twenty years ago, and in conversation told my friend that in his country when any young person happened to be put to death, the executioner sold the carcass to persons of quality, as a prime dainty, and that, in his time, the body of a plump girl of fifteen, who was crucified for an attempt to poison the emperor, was sold to his

Imperial Majesty's Prime Minister of State, and other great Mandarins of the Court, in joints from the gibbet, at four hundred crowns.
Neither indeed can I deny that if the same use were made of several
plump young girls in this town who, without one single groat to
their fortunes, cannot stir abroad without a chair, and appear at the
playhouse and assemblies in foreign fineries, which they never will
pay for, the kingdom would not be the worse.

Some persons of a desponding spirit are in great concern about
that vast number of poor people, who are aged, diseased, or maimed,
and I have been desired to employ my thoughts what course may be
taken to ease the nation of so grievous an encumbrance. But I am not
in the least pain upon that matter, because it is very well known that
they are every day dying, and rotting, by cold, and famine, and filth,
and vermin, as fast as can be reasonably expected. And as to the
younger labourers they are now in almost as hopeful a condition.
They cannot get work, and consequently pine away from want of
nourishment, to a degree that if at any time they are accidentally
hired to common labour, they have not strength to perform it; and
thus the country and themselves are in a fair way of being soon
delivered from the evils to come.

I have too long digressed, and therefore shall return to my subject.
I think the advantages by the proposal which I have made are
obvious and many, as well as of the highest importance.

For first, as I have already observed, it would greatly lessen the
number of Papists, with whom we are yearly over-run, being the
principal breeders of the nation, as well as our most dangerous
enemies, and who stay at home on purpose with a design to deliver
the kingdom to the Pretender, hoping to take their advantage by the
absence of so many good Protestants, who have chosen rather to
leave their country than stay at home and pay tithes against their
conscience to an idolatrous Episcopal curate.

Secondly, the poorer tenants will have something valuable of their
own, which by law may be made liable to distress, and help to pay
their landlord's rent, their corn and cattle being already seized, and
money a thing unknown.

Thirdly, whereas the maintenance of an hundred thousand children, from two years old, and upwards, cannot be computed at less
than ten shillings a piece *per annum*, the nation's stock will be
thereby increased fifty thousand pounds *per annum*, besides the
profit of a new dish, introduced to the tables of all gentlemen of
fortune in the kingdom, who have any refinement in taste, and the
money will circulate among ourselves, the goods being entirely of
our own growth and manufacture.

Fourthly, the constant breeders, besides the gain of eight shillings sterling *per annum*, by the sale of their children, will be rid of the charge of maintaining them after the first year.

Fifthly, this food would likewise bring great custom to taverns, where the vintners will certainly be so prudent as to procure the best receipts for dressing it to perfection, and consequently have their houses frequented by all the fine gentlemen, who justly value themselves upon their knowledge in good eating; and a skilful cook, who understands how to oblige his guests, will contrive to make it as expensive as they please.

Sixthly, this would be a great inducement to marriage, which all wise nations have either encouraged by rewards, or enforced by laws and penalties. It would increase the care and tenderness of mothers towards their children, when they were sure of a settlement for life, to the poor babes, provided in some sort by the public to their annual profit instead of expense. We should soon see an honest emulation among the married women, which of them could bring the fattest child to the market. Men would become as fond of their wives, during the time of their pregnancy, as they are now of their mares in foal, their cows in calf, or sows when they are ready to farrow, nor offer to beat or kick them (as it is too frequent a practice) for fear of a miscarriage.

Many other advantages might be enumerated. For instance, the addition of some thousand carcasses in our exportation of barrelled beef; the propagation of swine's flesh, and improvement in the art of making good bacon, so much wanted among us by the great destruction of pigs, too frequent at our tables, are no way comparable in taste or magnificence to a well-grown, fat yearling child, which roasted whole will make a considerable figure at a Lord Mayor's feast, or any other public entertainment. But this and many others I omit, being studious of brevity.

Supposing that one thousand families in this city would be constant customers for infants' flesh, besides others who might have it at merry meetings, particularly weddings and christenings; I compute that Dublin would take off annually about twenty thousand carcasses, and the rest of the kingdom (where probably they will be sold somewhat cheaper) the remaining eighty thousand.

I can think of no one objection that will possibly be raised against this proposal, unless it should be urged that the number of people will be thereby much lessened in the kingdom. This I freely own, and it was indeed one principal design in offering it to the world. I desire the reader will observe, that I calculate my remedy *for this one individual Kingdom of* Ireland, *and for no other that ever was, is, or, I think, ever can be upon earth.* Therefore let no man talk to me of other expedients: *Of taxing our absentees at five shillings a pound: Of using neither clothes, nor household furniture, except what is of our own growth and manufacture: Of utterly rejecting the materials and instruments that promote foreign luxury: Of curing the expensiveness of pride, vanity, idleness, and gaming in our women: Of introducing a vein of parsimony, prudence, and temperance: Of learning to love our country,* wherein we differ even from Laplanders, and the inhabitants of Topinamboo: *Of quitting our animosities and factions, nor act any longer like the* Jews, who were murdering one another at the very moment their city was taken: *Of being a little cautious not to sell our country and consciences for nothing: Of teaching landlords to have at least one degree of mercy towards their tenants.* Lastly, *of putting a spirit of honesty, industry, and skill into our shopkeepers, who, if a resolution could now be taken to buy only our native goods, would immediately unite to cheat and exact upon us in the price, the measure and the goodness, nor could ever yet be brought to make one fair proposal of just dealing, though often and earnestly invited to it.*

Therefore I repeat, let no man talk to me of these and the like expedients, till he hath at least a glimpse of hope that there will ever be some hearty and sincere attempt to put them in practice.

But as to myself, having been wearied out for many years with offering vain, idle, visionary thoughts, and at length utterly despairing of success, I fortunately fell upon this proposal, which as it is wholly new, so it hath something solid and real, of no expense and little trouble, full in our own power, and whereby we can incur no danger in disobliging England. For this kind of commodity will not bear exportation, the flesh being of too tender a consistence to admit a long continuance in salt, *although perhaps I could name a country which would be glad to eat up our whole nation without it.*

After all I am not so violently bent upon my own opinion as to reject any offer, proposed by wise men, which shall be found equally innocent, cheap, easy and effectual. But before some thing of that kind shall be advanced in contradiction to my scheme, and offering a better, I desire the author, or authors, will be pleased maturely to consider two points. First, as things now stand, how they will be able to find food and raiment for a hundred thousand useless mouths and backs? And secondly, there being a round million of creatures in human figure, throughout this kingdom, whose whole subsistence put into a common stock would leave them in debt two millions of pounds sterling; adding those who are beggars by profession, to the bulk of farmers, cottagers, and labourers with their wives and children, who are beggars in effect; I desire those politicians who dislike my overture, and may perhaps be so bold to attempt an answer, that they will first ask the parents of these mortals whether they would not at this day think it a great happiness to have been sold for food at a year old, in the manner I prescribe, and thereby have avoided such a perpetual scene of misfortunes as they have since gone through, by the oppression of landlords, the impossibility of paying rent without money or trade, the want of common sustenance, with neither house nor clothes to cover them from the inclemencies of weather, and the most inevitable prospect of entailing the like, or greater miseries upon their breed for ever.

I profess in the sincerity of my heart that I have not the least personal interest in endeavouring to promote this necessary work, having no other motive than the *public good of my country, by advancing our trade, providing for infants, relieving the poor, and giving some pleasure to the rich.* I have no children by which I can propose to get a single penny; the youngest being nine years old, and my wife past child-bearing.

Questions on the Swift Essay

1. A "proposal" always involves a proposer. What is the character of the proposer? Do we perceive his character to be the same throughout the essay?

2. How is our impression of the proposer affected by the content of his statements? by the style of his statements?

3. When does the proposer actually offer his proposal? What does he do before making his proposal? What does he do after making his proposal? How does the order in which he does things affect our impression of him and his proposal?

4. What are the main parts of the essay? How is the structure of the essay related to the persuasive strategy of the proposer?

5. What kinds of arguments does the proposer use in behalf of his proposal? How does he answer the possible objections that might be raised against his proposal? How does he refute alternative proposals to his?

Up to this point our questions have taken the essay as a literal piece of persuasion rather than an impersonation. The following questions take the piece as a dramatic monologue, an ironic essay.

6. How are we able to distinguish between the proposer and Swift? How can we tell that the speaker is a character rather than Swift himself?

7. What details of style will help us to make this distinction?

8. How has Swift attempted to ensure our rejection of the proposer's views?

9. What can we take to be Swift's own view of the matter?

10. How has Swift attempted to indicate his real views?

11. To what extent does an ironic essay like this depend upon the author and reader sharing certain values without question or reservation? Can we discover any such values explicitly or implicitly present in Swift's essay?

Understanding can lead to admiration, and admiration can lead to imitation.

12. Could you use Swift's technique to write a "modest proposal" of your own about some contemporary situation?

13. If you write a "modest proposal," consider how the act of assuming an alien and hostile personality has shaped your compositional task and helped or hindered your expression. Does your essay have any dimension other than the persuasive? Does Swift's?

Approaching an Essay

We hope that the ways that we have been suggesting here for dealing with essays will help in your reading and study of the essays in the collection to follow. Just to make sure that our procedures are clear, we will summarize them briefly, so that you can use them as a guide when you turn to our collection of essays.

1. In approaching an essay you should first read it through for your own pleasure. Following this first reading, review it quickly and assign it tentatively to one of five types.

2. If the essay is directly *persuasive—argumentative*—read it a second time, more analytically than the first time. Then examine its arrangement to see how the author has structured his persuasion.

   Examine its arguments, particularly any analogies used or assertions made, for (a) their accuracy in themselves, and (b) the extent of their relevance to the point being made.

   Consider any assumptions required by these assertions or analogies. Are you willing to grant these assumptions?

   Then consider the personality of the essayist and the kind of role it invites you to play. How does your perception of the essayist's personality affect your response to the essayist's ideas?

   Finally, formulate your response to the view presented and evaluate the presentation.

3. If the essay is *narrative,* pay attention to its narrative elements in your second reading. Try to divide the story into its meaningful parts and consider the way description, dialogue, and commentary work in each part—how they contribute to the events being narrated.

   After you have focused on these elements, look for passages of special thematic import in which the author steps back from the story to comment on its significance, to offer an interpretation of the story.

   Consider the persuasive force of the story in supporting the ideas the author is proposing.

   Then consider the implied personality of the essayist both during the narrative sections and the interpretive parts, and how that affects your response to the essay.

   Finally, you might ask yourself if you find the essay convincing—both as narrative and persuasion.

4. If the essay is *meditative,* your re-readings should be especially close and careful in their attention to the associative play of mind with words, images, and ideas.

Consider how one detail generates, or suggests, another, and explain, if you can, the process that leads the author from one detail or idea to the next.

The sort of examination that we think of as appropriate for poetry is appropriate for the meditative essay as well. Pay special attention, then, to tone and imagery.

Only after you have made an investigation of this kind should you begin to ask questions about the *persuasive* dimension of the essay.

5. If the essay is in *dialogue* form, your second reading should concentrate on its dramatic elements—character, setting, and plot.

You should consider whether any one character seems to speak with the author's authority behind him; and if you feel this to be the case, investigate the details that have led you to that view, in order to determine whether the evidence is really sufficient for this to be an appropriate response.

Be alert for any words of scene-setting, as this may be a way of inserting some narrative commentary into a dialogue. The scene-setter may speak with the author's voice.

Finally, look for some dramatic movement toward a climax, in order to determine the relation between the dramatic form and the persuasive purpose of the essay.

6. If the essay is an *impersonation*, if it is *ironic,* pay close attention to the character of the speaker. Try to determine how your impression of the speaker's character is influenced by his style. Consider how the speaker's ideas shape your impression of his character.

Once you have established the speaker's character and ideas, figure out what you believe to be the author's opinion on the matter. (The author's ideas may be embedded in the essay itself, but you may also have to formulate them on your own.)

7. Any essay may in fact be a combination of the basic forms, and the longer it is, the more likely is it to combine the various possibilities in rich and complex ways. Try to be tactful and vary your approach to suit the variations in the work you are reading. Remember that reading an essay or any other work of literature, like carrying on a human relationship, requires attentiveness, flexibility, and responsiveness.

8. When you read poetry, drama, and fiction, be alert for the essay-like dimensions of these literary forms. The ability to analyze the essay with sense and sensibility will stand you in good stead in dealing with every form of literature.

A Collection of Essays

JOSEPH ADDISON

1672–1719

Marraton and Yaratilda

Felices errore suo.[1]

LUCANUS

The Americans believe that all creatures have souls, not only men and women, but brutes, vegetables, nay, even the most inanimate things, as stocks[2] and stones. They believe the same of all the works of art, as of knives, boats, looking glasses: and that as any of these things perish, their souls go into another world, which is habited by the ghosts of men and women. For this reason they always place by the corpse of their dead friend a bow and arrows, that he may make use of the souls of them in the other world, as he did of their wooden bodies in this. How absurd soever such an opinion as this may appear, our European philosophers have maintained several notions altogether as improbable. Some of Plato's followers in particular, when they talk of the world of ideas, entertain us with substances and beings no less extravagant and chimerical. Many Aristotelians have likewise spoken as unintelligibly of their substantial forms. I shall only instance Albertus

1. Happy in their error.
2. Logs, or blocks of wood.

The Spectator, No. 56.

51

Magnus, who in his dissertation upon the loadstone, observing that fire will destroy its magnetic virtues, tells us that he took particular notice of one as it lay glowing amidst an heap of burning coals, and that he perceived a certain blue vapor to arise from it, which he believed might be the substantial form, that is, in our West Indian phrase, the soul of the loadstone.

There is a tradition among the Americans, that one of their countrymen descended in a vision to the great repository of souls, or, as we call it here, to the other world; and that upon his return he gave his friends a distinct account of everything he saw among those regions of the dead. A friend of mine, whom I have formerly mentioned, prevailed upon one of the interpreters of the Indian kings, to inquire of them if possible, what tradition they have among them of this matter; which, as well as he could learn by those many questions which he asked them at several times, was in substance as follows.

The visionary, whose name was Marraton, after having travelled for a long space under an hollow mountain, arrived at length on the confines of this world of spirits; but could not enter it by reason of a thick forest made up of bushes, brambles, and pointed thorns, so perplexed and interwoven with one another, that it was impossible to find a passage through it. Whilst he was looking about for some track or pathway that might be worn in any part of it, he saw an huge lion couched under the side of it, who kept his eye upon him in the same posture as he watches for his prey. The Indian immediately started back, whilst the lion rose with a spring, and leaped towards him. Being wholly destitute of all other weapons, he stooped down to take up an huge stone in his hand: but to his infinite surprise grasped nothing, and found the supposed stone to be only the apparition of one. If he was disappointed on this side, he was as much pleased on the other, when he found the lion, which had seized on his left shoulder, had no power to hurt him, and was only the ghost of that ravenous creature which it appeared to be. He no sooner got rid of his impotent enemy, but he marched up to the wood, and after having surveyed it for some time, endeavored to press into one part of it that was a little thinner than the rest; when again, to his great surprise, he found the bushes made no resistance, but that he walked through briers and brambles with the same ease as through the open air; and, in short, that the whole wood was nothing else but a wood of shades. He immediately concluded, that this huge thicket of thorns and brakes was designed as a kind of fence or quick-set hedge to the ghosts it enclosed; and that probably their soft substances might be torn by these subtle points and prickles, which were too weak to make any impressions in flesh and blood. With this thought he resolved to travel through this intricate wood; when by degrees he felt a gale of perfumes breathing upon him, that grew stronger and sweeter in proportion as he advanced. He had not proceeded much farther when he observed the thorns and briers to end, and give place to a thousand beautiful green trees covered with blossoms of the finest scents and colors, that formed a wilderness of sweets, and were a kind of lining to those ragged scenes which he had before passed through.   As he was coming out of this delightful part of the wood, and entering upon the plains it enclosed, he saw several horsemen rushing by him, and a little while after heard the cry of a pack of dogs. He had not listened long before he saw the apparition of a milk-white steed, with a young man on the back of it, advancing upon full stretch after the souls of about an hundred beagles that were hunting down the ghost of an hare, which ran away before them with an unspeakable swiftness. As the man on the milk-white steed came by him, he looked upon him very attentively, and found him to be the young prince Nicaragua, who died about half a year before, and by reason of his great virtues was at that time lamented over all the western parts of America.

He had no sooner got out of the wood, but he was entertained with such a landscape of flowery plains, green meadows, running streams, sunny hills, and shady vales, as were not to be represented by his own expressions, nor, as he said, by the conceptions of others. This happy region was peopled with innumerable swarms of spirits, who applied themselves to exercises and diversions according as their fancies led them. Some of them were tossing the figure of a quoit; others were pitching the shadow of a bar; others were breaking the apparition of a horse; and multitudes employing themselves upon ingenious handicrafts with the souls of departed utensils; for that is the name which in the Indian language they give their tools when they are burnt or broken. As he travelled through this delightful scene, he was very often tempted to pluck the flowers that rose everywhere about him in the greatest variety and profusion, having never seen several of them in his own country; but he quickly found, that though they were objects of his sight, they were not liable to his touch. He at length came to the side of a great river, and being a good fisherman himself, stood upon the banks of it some time to look upon an angler that had taken a great many shapes of fishes, which lay flouncing up and down by him.

I should have told my reader, that this Indian had been formerly married to one of the greatest beauties of his country, by whom he had several children. This couple were so famous for their love and constancy to one another, that the Indians to this day, when they give a married man joy of his wife, wish that they may live together like Marraton and Yaratilda. Marraton had not stood long by the fisherman when he saw the shadow of his beloved Yaratilda, who had for some time fixed her eye upon him, before he discovered her. Her arms were stretched out towards him, floods of tears ran down her eyes; her looks, her hands, her voice called him over to her; and at the same time seemed to tell him that the river was unpassable. Who can describe the passion made up of joy, sorrow, love, desire, astonishment, that rose in the Indian upon the sight of his dear Yaratilda? He could express it by nothing but his tears, which ran like a river down his cheeks as he looked upon her. He had not stood in this posture long, before he plunged into the stream that lay before him; and finding it to be nothing but the phantom of a river, stalked on the bottom of it till he arose on the other side. At his approach Yaratilda flew into his arms, whilst Marraton wished himself disencumbered of that body which kept her from his embraces. After many questions and endearments on both sides, she conducted him to a bower which she had dressed with her own hands with all the ornaments that could be met with in those blooming regions. She had made it gay beyond imagination, and was every day adding something new to it. As Marraton stood astonished at the unspeakable beauty of her habitation, and ravished with the fragrancy that came from every part of it, Yaratilda told him that she was preparing this bower for his reception, as well knowing that his piety to his God, and his faithful dealing towards men, would certainly bring him to that happy place, whenever his life should be at an end. She then brought two of her children to him, who died some years before, and resided with her in the same delightful bower; advising him to breed up those others which were still with him in such a manner, that they might hereafter all of them meet together in this happy place.

The tradition tells us further, that he had afterwards a sight of those dismal habitations which are the portion of ill men after death; and mentions several molten seas of gold, in which were plunged the souls of barbarous Europeans, who put to the sword so many thousands of poor Indians for the sake of that precious metal: but having already touched upon the chief points of this tradition, and exceeded the measure of my paper, I shall not give any further account of it.

CHARLES LAMB
1775–1834
A Dissertation upon Roast Pig

Mankind, says a Chinese manuscript, which my friend M. was obliging enough to read and explain to me, for the first seventy thousand ages ate their meat raw, clawing or biting it from the living animal, just as they do in Abyssinia to this day. This period is not obscurely hinted at by their great Confucius in the second chapter of his Mundane Mutations, where he designates a kind of golden age by the term Cho-fang, literally the Cooks' holiday. The manuscript goes on to say, that the art of roasting, or rather broiling (which I take to be the elder brother), was accidentally discovered in the manner following. The swineherd, Ho-ti, having gone out into the woods one morning, as his manner was, to collect mast for his hogs, left his cottage in the care of his eldest son Bo-bo, a great lubberly boy, who being fond of playing with fire, as younkers of his age commonly are, let some sparks escape into a bundle of straw, which kindling quickly, spread the conflagration over every part of their poor mansion, till it was reduced to ashes. Together with the cottage (a sorry antediluvian make-shift of a building, you may think it), which was of much more importance, a fine litter of new-farrowed pigs, no less than nine in number, perished. China pigs have been esteemed a luxury all over the East from the remotest periods that we read of. Bo-bo was in the utmost consternation, as you may think, not so much for the sake of the tenement, which his father and he could easily build up again with a few dry branches, and the labour of an hour or two, at any time, as for the loss of the pigs. While he was thinking what he should say to his father, and wringing his hands over the smoking remnants of one of those untimely sufferers, an odour assailed his nostrils, unlike any scent which he had before experienced. What could it proceed from? not from the burnt cottage—he had smelt that smell before—indeed this was by no means the first accident of the kind which had occurred through the negligence of this unlucky young fire-brand. Much less did it resemble that of any known herb, weed, or flower. A premonitory moistening at the same time overflowed his nether lip. He knew not what to think. He next stooped down to feel the pig, if there were any signs of life in it. He burnt his fingers, and to cool them he applied them in his booby fashion to his mouth. Some of the crums of the scorched skin had come away with his fingers, and for the first time in his life (in the world's life indeed, for before him no man had known it) he tasted—*crackling!* Again he felt and fumbled at the pig. It did not burn him so much now, still he licked his fingers from a sort of habit. The truth at length broke into his slow understanding, that it was the pig that smelt so, and the pig that tasted so delicious; and, surrendering himself up to the newborn pleasure, he fell to tearing up whole handfuls of the scorched skin with the flesh next to it, and was cramming it down his throat in his beastly fashion, when his sire entered amid the smoking rafters, armed with retributory cudgel, and finding how affairs stood, began to rain blows upon the young rogue's shoulders, as thick as hail-stones, which Bo-bo heeded not any more than if they had been flies. The tickling pleasure, which he experienced in his lower regions, had rendered him quite callous to any inconveniences he might feel in those remote quarters. His father might lay on, but he could not beat him from his pig, till he had fairly made an end of it, when, becoming a little more sensible of his situation, something like the following dialogue ensued.

"You graceless whelp, what have you got there devouring? Is it not enough that you have burnt me down three houses with your dog's tricks, and be hanged to you, but you must be eating fire, and I know not what—what have you got there, I say?"

"O father, the pig, the pig, do come and taste how nice the burnt pig eats."

The ears of Ho-ti tingled with horror. He cursed his son, and he cursed himself that ever he should beget a son that should eat burnt pig.

Bo-bo, whose scent was wonderfully sharpened since morning, soon raked out another pig, and fairly rendering it asunder, thrust the lesser half by main force into the fists of Ho-ti, still shouting out "Eat, eat, eat the burnt pig, father, only taste—O Lord," with such-like barbarous ejaculations, cramming all the while as if he would choke.

Ho-ti trembled in every joint while he grasped the abominable thing, wavering whether he should not put his son to death for an unnatural young monster, when the crackling scorching his fingers, as it had done his son's, and applying the same remedy to them, he in his turn tasted some of its flavour, which, make what sour mouths he would for a pretense, proved not altogether displeasing to him. In conclusion (for the manuscript here is a little tedious) both father and son fairly sat down to the mess, and never left off till they had despatched all that remained of the litter.

Bo-bo was strictly enjoined not to let the secret escape, for the neighbours would certainly have stoned them for a couple of abominable wretches, who could think of improving upon the good meat which God had sent them. Nevertheless, strange stories got about. It was observed that Ho-ti's cottage was burnt down now more frequently than ever. Nothing but fires from this time forward. Some would break out in broad day, others in the night-time. As often as the sow farrowed, so sure was the house of Ho-ti to be in a blaze; and Ho-ti himself, which was the more remarkable, instead of chastising his son, seemed to grow more indulgent to him than ever. At length they were watched, the terrible mystery discovered, and father and son summoned to take their trial at Pekin, then an inconsiderable assize town. Evidence was given, the obnoxious food itself produced in court, and verdict about to be pronounced, when the foreman of the jury begged that some of the burnt pig, of which the culprits stood accused, might be handed into the box. He handled it, and they all handled it, and burning their fingers, as Bo-bo and his father had done before them, and nature prompting to each of them the same remedy, against the face of all the facts, and the clearest charge which judge had ever given, to the surprise of the whole court, townsfolk, strangers, reporters, and all present—without leaving the box, or any manner of consultation whatever, they brought in a simultaneous verdict of Not Guilty.

The judge, who was a shrewd fellow, winked at the manifest iniquity of the decision: and, when the court was dismissed, went privily, and bought up all the pigs that could be had for love or money. In a few days his Lordship's town house was observed to be on fire. The thing took wing, and now there was nothing to be seen but fires in every direction. Fuel and pigs grew enormously dear all over the district. The insurance offices one and all shut up shop. People built slighter and slighter every day, until it was feared that the very science of architecture would in no long time be lost to the world. Thus this custom of firing houses continued, till in process of time, says my manuscript, a sage arose, like our Locke, who made a discovery, that the flesh of swine, or indeed of any animal, might be cooked (*burnt*, as they called it) without the necessity of consuming a whole house to dress it. Then first began the rude form of a gridiron. Roasting by the string, or spit, came in a century or two later, I forget in whose dynasty. By such slow degrees, concludes the manuscript, do the most useful, and seemingly the most obvious arts, make their way among mankind.

Without placing too implicit faith in the account above given, it must be agreed, that if a worthy pretext for so dangerous an experiment as setting houses on fire (especially in these days) could be assigned in favour of any culinary object, that pretext and excuse might be found in ROAST PIG.

Of all the delicacies in the whole *mundus edibilis*,[1] I will maintain it to be the most delicate—*princeps obsoniorum*.[2]

I speak not of your grown porkers—things between pig and pork—those hobbydehoys—but a young and tender suckling—under a moon old—guiltless as yet of the sty—with no original speck of the *amor immunditiæ*,[3] the hereditary failing of the first parent, yet manifest—his voice as yet not broken, but something between a childish treble, and a grumble—the mild forerunner, or *præludium*, of a grunt.

He must be roasted. I am not ignorant that our ancestors ate them seethed, or boiled—but what a sacrifice of the exterior tegument!

1. The world of food.
2. The most noble food.
3. The love of filth.

There is no flavour comparable, I will contend, to that of the crisp, tawny, well-watched, not over-roasted, *crackling*, as it is well called—the very teeth are invited to their share of the pleasure at this banquet in overcoming the coy, brittle resistance—with the adhesive oleaginous—O call it not fat—but an indefinable sweetness growing up to it—the tender blossoming of fat—fat cropped in the bud—taken in the shoot—in the first innocence—the cream and quintessence of the child-pig's yet pure food—the lean, no lean, but a kind of animal manna—or, rather, fat and lean (if it must be so) so blended and running into each other, that both together make but one ambrosian result, or common substance.

Behold him, while he is doing—it seemeth rather a refreshing warmth, than a scorching heat, that he is so passive to. How equably he twirleth round the string! Now he is just done. To see the extreme sensibility of that tender age, he hath wept out his pretty eyes—radiant jellies—shooting stars—

See him in the dish, his second cradle, how meek he lieth! wouldst thou have had this innocent grow up to the grossness and indocility which too often accompany maturer swinehood? Ten to one he would have proved a glutton, a sloven, an obstinate, disagreeable animal—wallowing in all manner of filthy conversation—from these sins he is happily snatched away—

> Ere sin could blight, or sorrow fade,
> Death came with timely care—

his memory is odoriferous—no clown curseth, while his stomach half rejecteth, the rank bacon—no coalheaver bolteth him in reeking sausages—he hath a fair sepulchre in the grateful stomach of the judicious epicure—and for such a tomb might be content to die.

He is the best of Sapors. Pine-apple is great. She is indeed almost too transcendent—a delight, if not sinful, yet so like to sinning, that really a tender-conscienced person would do well to pause—too ravishing for mortal taste, she woundeth and excoriateth the lips that approach her—like lovers' kisses, she biteth—she is a pleasure bordering on pain from the fierceness and insanity of her relish—but she stoppeth at the palate—she meddleth not with the appetite—and the coarsest hunger might barter her consistently for a mutton chop.

Pig—let me speak his praise—is no less provocative of the appetite, than he is satisfactory to the criticalness of the censorious palate. The strong man may batten on him, and the weakling refuseth not his mild juices.

Unlike to mankind's mixed characters, a bundle of virtues and vices, inexplicably intertwisted, and not to be unravelled without hazard, he is—good throughout. No part of him is better or worse than another. He helpeth, as far as his little means extend, all around. He is the least envious of banquets. He is all neighbours' fare.

I am one of those, who freely and ungrudgingly impart a share of the good things of this life which fall to their lot (few as mine are in this kind) to a friend. I protest I take as great an interest in my friend's pleasures, his relishes, and proper satisfactions, as in mine own. "Presents," I often say, "endear Absents." Hares, pheasants, partridges, snipes, barn-door chicken (those "tame villatic fowl"), capons, plovers, brawn, barrels of oysters, I dispense as freely as I receive them. I love to taste them, as it were, upon the tongue of my friend. But a stop must be put somewhere. One would not, like Lear, "give every thing." I make my stand upon pig. Methinks it is an ingratitude to the Giver of all good flavours, to extra-domiciliate, or send out of the house, slightingly, (under pretext of friendship, or I know not what) a blessing so particularly adapted, predestined, I may say, to my individual palate—It argues an insensibility.

I remember a touch of conscience in this kind at school. My good old aunt, who never parted from me at the end of a holiday without stuffing a sweet-meat, or some nice thing, into my pocket, had dismissed me one evening with a smoking plum-cake, fresh from the oven. In my way to school (it was over London bridge) a grey-headed old begger saluted me (I have no doubt at this time of day he was a counterfeit). I had no pence to console him with, and in the vanity of self-denial, and the very coxcombry of charity, school-boy-like, I made him a present of—the whole cake! I walked on a little, buoyed up, as one is on such occasions, with a sweet soothing of self-satisfaction; but before I had got to the end of the bridge, my better feelings returned, and I burst into tears, thinking how ungrateful I had been to my good aunt, to go and give her good gift away to a stranger that I had never seen before, and who might be a bad man for aught I knew; and then I thought of the pleasure my aunt would be taking in thinking that I—I myself, and not another—would eat her nice cake—and what should I say to her the next time I saw her—how naughty I was to part with her pretty present—and the odour of that spicy cake came back upon my recollection, and the pleasure and the curiosity I had taken in seeing her make it, and her joy when she sent it to the oven, and how disappointed she would feel that I had never had a bit of it in my mouth at last—and I blamed my impertinent spirit of alms-giving, and out-of-place hypocrisy of goodness, and above all I wished never to see the face again of that insidious, good-for-nothing, old grey imposter.

Our ancestors were nice in their method of sacrificing these tender victims. We read of pigs whipt to death with something of a shock, as we hear of any other obsolete custom. The age of discipline is gone by, or it would be curious to inquire (in a philosophical light merely) what effect this process might have towards intenerating and dulcifying a substance, naturally so mild and dulcet as the flesh of young pigs. It looks like refining a violet. Yet we should be cautious, while we condemn the inhumanity, how we censure the wisdom of the practice. It might impart a gusto—

I remember an hypothesis, argued upon by the young students, when I was at St. Omer's, and maintained with much learning and pleasantry on both sides, "Whether, supposing that the flavour of a pig who obtained his death by whipping (*per flagellationem extremam*[4]) superadded a pleasure upon the palate of a man more intense than any possible suffering we can conceive in the animal, is man justified in using that method of putting the animal to death?" I forget the decision.

His sauce should be considered. Decidedly, a few bread crums, done up with his liver and brains, and a dash of mild sage. But, banish, dear Mrs. Cook, I beseech you, the whole onion tribe. Barbecue your whole hogs to your palate, steep them in shalots, stuff them out with plantations of the rank and guilty garlic; you cannot poison them, or make them stronger than they are—but consider, he is a weakling—a flower.

4. By the greatest beating.

HENRY DAVID THOREAU
1817–1862
The War of the Ants

One day when I went out to my wood-pile, or rather my pile of stumps, I observed two large ants, the one red, the other much larger, nearly half an inch long, and black, fiercely contending with one another. Having once got hold they never let go, but struggled and wrestled and rolled on the chips incessantly. Looking farther, I was surprised to find that the chips were covered with such combatants, that it was not a *duellum*, but a *bellum*, a war between two races of ants, the red always pitted against the black, and frequently two red ones to one black. The legions of these Myrmidons covered all the hills and vales in my wood-yard, and the ground was already strewn with the dead and dying, both red and black. It was the only battle which I have ever witnessed, the only battle-field I ever trod while the battle was raging; internecine war; the red republicans on the one hand, and the

From *Walden, or Life in the Woods.*

black imperialists on the other. On every side they were engaged in deadly combat, yet without any noise that I could hear, and human soldiers never fought so resolutely. I watched a couple that were fast locked in each other's embraces, in a little sunny valley amid the chips, now at noonday prepared to fight till the sun went down, or life went out. The smaller red champion had fastened himself like a vise to his adversary's front, and through all the tumblings on that field never for an instant ceased to gnaw at one of his feelers near the root, having already caused the other to go by the board; while the stronger black one dashed him from side to side, and, as I saw on looking nearer, had already divested him of several of his members. They fought with more pertinacity than bulldogs. Neither manifested the least disposition to retreat. It was evident that their battle-cry was "Conquer or die." In the meanwhile there came along a single red ant on the hillside of this valley, evidently full of excitement, who either had despatched his foe, or had not yet taken part in the battle; probably the latter, for he had lost none of his limbs; whose mother had charged him to return with his shield or upon it. Or perchance he was some Achilles, who had nourished his wrath apart, and had now come to avenge or rescue his Patroclus. He saw this unequal combat from afar,—for the blacks were nearly twice the size of the red,—he drew near with rapid pace till he stood on his guard within half an inch of the combatants; then, watching his opportunity, he sprang upon the black warrior, and commenced his operations near the root of his right fore leg, leaving the foe to select among his own members; so there were three united for life, as if a new kind of attraction had been invented which put all other locks and cements to shame. I should not have wondered by this time to find that they had their respective musical bands stationed on some eminent chip, and playing their national airs the while, to excite the slow and cheer the dying combatants. I was myself excited somewhat even as if they had been men. The more you think of it, the less the difference. And certainly there is not the fight recorded in Concord history, at least, if in the history of America, that will bear a moment's comparison with this, whether for the numbers engaged in it, or for the patriotism and heroism displayed. For numbers and for carnage it was an Austerlitz or Dresden. Concord fight! Two killed on the patriots' side, and Luther Blanchard wounded! Why here every ant was a Buttrick,—"Fire! for God's sake fire!"—and thousands shared the fate of Davis and Hosmer. There was not one hireling there. I have no doubt that it was a principle they fought for, as much as our ancestors, and not to avoid a three-penny tax on their tea; and the results of this battle will be as important and memorable to those whom it concerns as those of the battle of Bunker Hill, at least.

I took up the chip on which the three I have particularly described were struggling, carried it into my house, and placed it under a tumbler on my window-sill, in order to see the issue. Holding a microscope to the first-mentioned red ant, I saw that, though he was assiduously gnawing at the near fore leg of his enemy, having severed his remaining feeler, his own breast was all torn away, exposing what vitals he had there to the jaws of the black warrior, whose breastplate was apparently too thick for his to pierce; and the dark carbuncles of the sufferer's eyes shone with ferocity such as war only could excite. They struggled half an hour longer under the tumbler, and when I looked again the black soldier had severed the heads of his foes from their bodies, and the still living heads were hanging on either side of him like ghastly trophies at his saddle-bow, still apparently as firmly fastened as ever, and he was endeavoring with feeble struggles, being without feelers and with only the remnant of a leg, and I know not how many other wounds, to divest himself of them; which at length, after half an hour or more, he accomplished. I raised the glass, and he went off over the window-sill in that crippled state. Whether he finally survived that combat, and spent the remainder of his days in some Hôtel des Invalides, I do not know; but I thought that his industry would not be worth much thereafter. I never learned which party was victorious, nor the cause of the war; but I felt for the rest of that day as if I had had my feelings excited and harrowed by witnessing the struggle, the ferocity and carnage, of a human battle before my door.

Kirby and Spence tell us that the battles of ants have long been celebrated and the date of them recorded, though they say that Huber is the only modern author who appears to have witnessed them. "Æneas Sylvius," say they, "after giving a very circumstantial account of one contested with great obstinacy by a great and small species on the trunk of a pear tree," adds that " 'this action was fought in the pontificate of Eugenius the Fourth, in the presence of Nicholas Pistoriensis, an eminent lawyer, who related the whole history of the battle with the greatest fidelity.' A similar engagement between great and small ants is recorded by Olaus Magnus, in which the small ones, being victorious, are said to have buried the bodies of their own soldiers, but left those of their giant enemies a prey to the birds. This event happened previous to the expulsion of the tyrant Christiern the Second from Sweden." The battle which I witnessed took place in the Presidency of Polk, five years before the passage of Webster's Fugitive-Slave Bill.

MARK TWAIN

1835–1910

In the Animals' Court

THE RABBIT. The testimony showed, (1), that the Rabbit, having declined to volunteer, was enlisted by compulsion, and (2) deserted in the face of the enemy on the eve of battle. Being asked if he had anything to say for himself before sentence of death should be passed upon him for violating the military law forbidding cowardice and desertion, he said he had not desired to violate that law, but had been obliged to obey a higher law which took precedence of it and set it aside. Being asked what law that was, he answered, "the law of God, which denies courage to the rabbit."

Verdict of the Court. To be disgraced in the presence of the army; stripped of his uniform; marched to the scaffold, bearing a placard marked "Coward," and hanged.

II

THE LION. The testimony showed that the Lion, by his splendid courage and matchless strength and endurance, saved the battle.

Verdict of the Court. To be given a dukedom, his statue to be set up, his name to be writ in letters of gold at the top of the roll in the Temple of Fame.

III

THE FOX. The testimony showed that he had broken the divine law, "Thou shalt not steal." Being asked for his defence, he pleaded that he had been obliged to obey the divine law, "The Fox shall steal."

Verdict of the Court. Imprisonment for life.

IV

THE HORSE. The evidence showed that he had spent many days and nights, unwatched, in the paddock with the poultry, yet had triumphed over temptation.

Verdict of the Court. Let his name be honored; let his deed be praised throughout the land by public proclamation.

V

THE WOLF. The evidence showed that he had transgressed the law "Thou shalt not kill." In arrest of judgment, he pleaded the law of his nature.

Verdict of the Court. Death.

VI

THE SHEEP. The evidence showed that he had had manifold temptations to commit murder and massacre, yet had not yielded.

Verdict of the Court. Let his virtue be remembered forever.

VII

THE MACHINE. *The Court:* Prisoner, it is charged and proven that you are poorly contrived and badly constructed. What have you to say to this?

Answer. I did not contrive myself, I did not construct myself.

The Court. It is charged and proven that you have moved when you should not have moved; that you have turned out of your course when you should have gone straight; that you have moved swiftly through crowds when the law and the public weal forbade a speed like that; that you leave a stench behind you wherever you go, and you persist in this, although you know it is improper and that other machines refrain from doing it. What have you to say to these things?

Answer. I am a machine. I am slave to the law of my make, I have to obey it, under all conditions. I do nothing, of myself. My forces are set in motion by outside influences, I never set them in motion myself.

The Court. You are discharged. Your plea is sufficient. You are a pretty poor thing, with some good qualities and some bad ones; but to attach personal merit to conduct emanating from the one set, and personal demerit to conduct emanating from the other set would be unfair and unjust. To a machine, that is—to a machine.

GEORGE ORWELL
1903–1950
Shooting an Elephant

In Moulmein, in lower Burma, I was hated by large numbers of people—the only time in my life that I have been important enough for this to happen to me. I was sub-divisional police officer of the town, and in an aimless, petty kind of way anti-European feeling was very bitter. No one had the guts to raise a riot, but if a European woman went through the bazaars alone somebody would probably spit betel juice over her dress. As a police officer I was an obvious target and was baited whenever it seemed safe to do so. When a nimble Burman tripped me up on the football field and the referee (another Burman) looked the other way, the crowd yelled with hideous laughter. This happened more than once. In the end the sneering yellow faces of young men that met me everywhere, the insults hooted after me when I was at a safe distance, got badly on my nerves. The young Buddhist priests were the worst of all. There were several thousands of them in the town and none of them seemed to have anything to do except stand on street corners and jeer at Europeans.

All this was perplexing and upsetting. For at that time I had already made up my mind that imperialism was an evil thing and the sooner I chucked up my job and got out of it the better. Theoretically—and secretly, of course—I was all for the Burmese and all against their oppressors, the British. As for the job I was doing, I hated it more bitterly than I can perhaps make clear. In a job like that you see the dirty work of Empire at close quarters. The wretched prisoners huddling in the stinking cages of the lock-ups, the gray, cowed faces of the long-term convicts, the scarred buttocks of the men who had been flogged with bamboos—all these oppressed me with an intolerable sense of guilt. But I could get nothing into perspective. I was young and ill educated and I had had to think out my problems in the utter silence that is imposed on every Englishman in the East. I did not even know that the British Empire is dying, still less did I know that it is a great deal better than the younger empires that are going to supplant it. All I knew was that I was stuck between my hatred of the empire I served and my rage against the evil-spirited little beasts who tried to make my job impossible. With one part of my mind I thought of the British Raj as an unbreakable tyranny, as something clamped down, in *saecula saeculorum,* upon the will of prostrate peoples; with another part I thought that the greatest joy in the world would be to drive a bayonet into a Buddhist priest's guts. Feelings like these are the normal by-products of imperialsim; ask any Anglo-Indian official, if you can catch him off duty.

One day something happened which in a roundabout way was enlightening. It was a tiny incident in itself, but it gave me a better glimpse than I had had before of the real nature of imperialism—the real motives for which despotic governments act. Early one morning the sub-inspector at a police station the other end of the town rang me up on the 'phone and said that an elephant was ravaging the bazaar. Would I please come and do something about it? I did not know what I could do, but I wanted to see what was happening and I got on to a pony and started out. I took my rifle, an old .44 Winchester and much too small to kill an elephant, but I thought the noise might be useful *in terrorem.*[1] Various Burmans stopped me on the way and told me about the elephant's doings. It was not, of course, a wild elephant, but a tame one which had gone "must."[2] It had been chained up, as tame elephants always are when their attack of "must" is due, but on the

---

1. To provoke fear.
2. Condition of frenzy to which male elephants are subject at irregular intervals.

previous night it had broken its chain and escaped. Its mahout,[3] the only person who could manage it when it was in that state, had set out in pursuit, but had taken the wrong direction and was now twelve hours' journey away, and in the morning the elephant had suddenly reappeared in the town. The Burmese population had no weapons and were quite helpless against it. It had already destroyed somebody's bamboo hut, killed a cow and raided some fruit-stalls and devoured the stock; also it had met the municipal rubbish van and, when the driver jumped out and took to his heels, had turned the van over and inflicted violences upon it.

The Burmese sub-inspector and some Indian constables were waiting for me in the quarter where the elephant had been seen. It was a very poor quarter, a labyrinth of squalid bamboo huts, thatched with palm-leaf, winding all over a steep hillside. I remember that it was a cloudy, stuffy morning at the beginning of the rains. We began questioning the people as to where the elephant had gone and, as usual, failed to get any definite information. That is invariably the case in the East; a story always sounds clear enough at a distance, but the nearer you get to the scene of events the vaguer it becomes. Some of the people said the elephant had gone in one direction, some said that he had gone in another, some professed not even to have heard of any elephant. I had almost made up my mind that the whole story was a pack of lies, when we heard yells a little distance away. There was a loud, scandalized cry of "Go away, child! Go away this instant!" and an old woman with a switch in her hand came around the corner of a hut, violently shooing away a crowd of naked children. Some more women followed, clicking their tongues and exclaiming; evidently there was something that the children ought not to have seen. I rounded the hut and saw a man's dead body sprawling in the mud. He was an Indian, a black Dravidian coolie, almost naked, and he could not have been dead many minutes. The people said that the elephant had come suddenly upon him round the corner of the hut, caught him with its trunk, put its foot on his back and ground him into the earth. This was the rainy season and the ground was soft, and his face had scored a trench a foot deep and a couple of yards long. He was lying on his belly with arms crucified and head sharply twisted to one side. His face was coated with mud, the eyes wide open, the teeth bared and grinning with an expression of unendurable agony. (Never tell me, by the way, that the dead look peaceful. Most of the corpses I have seen looked devilish.) The friction of the great beast's foot had stripped the skin from the back as neatly as one skins a rabbit. As soon as I saw the dead man I sent an orderly to a friend's house nearby to borrow an

3. Elephant keeper.

elephant rifle. I had already sent back the pony, not wanting it to go mad with fright and throw me if it smelt the elephant.

The orderly came back in a few minutes with a rifle and five cartridges, and meanwhile some Burmans had arrived and told us that the elephant was in the paddy fields below, only a few hundred yards away. As I started forward practically the whole population of the quarter flocked out of the houses and followed me. They had seen the rifle and were all shouting excitedly that I was going to shoot the elephant. They had not shown much interest in the elephant when he was merely ravaging their homes, but it was different now that he was going to be shot. It was a bit of fun to them, as it would be to an English crowd; besides they wanted the meat. It made me vaguely uneasy. I had no intention of shooting the elephant—I had merely sent for the rifle to defend myself if necessary—and it is always unnerving to have a crowd following you. I marched down the hill, looking and feeling a fool, with the rifle over my shoulder and an ever-growing army of people jostling at my heels. At the bottom, when you got away from the huts, there was a metalled road and beyond that a miry waste of paddy fields a thousand yards across, not yet ploughed but soggy from the first rains and dotted with coarse grass. The elephant was standing eight yards from the road, his left side toward us. He took not the slightest notice of the crowd's approach. He was tearing up bunches of grass, beating them against his knees to clean them, and stuffing them into his mouth.

I had halted on the road, As soon as I saw the elephant I knew with perfect certainty that I ought not to shoot him. It is a serious matter to shoot a working elephant—it is comparable to destroying a huge and costly piece of machinery—and obviously one ought not to do it if it can possibly be avoided. And at that distance, peacefully eating, the elephant looked no more dangerous than a cow. I thought then and I think now that his attack of "must" was already passing off; in which case he would merely wander harmlessly about until the mahout came back and caught him. Moreover, I did not in the least want to shoot him. I decided that I would watch him for a little while to make sure that he did not turn savage again, and then go home.

But at that moment I glanced round at the crowd that had followed me. It was an immense crowd, two thousand at the least and growing every minute. It blocked the road for a long distance on either side. I looked at the sea of yellow faces above the garish clothes—faces all happy and excited over this bit of fun, all certain that the elephant was going to be shot. They were watching me as they would watch a conjurer about to perform a trick. They did not like me, but with the magical rifle in my hands I was momentarily worth watching. And suddenly I realized that I should have to shoot the elephant after all.

The people expected it of me and I had got to do it; I could feel their two thousand wills pressing me forward, irresistibly. And it was at this moment, as I stood there with my rifle in my hands, that I first grasped the hollowness, the futility of the white man's dominion in the East. Here was I, the white man with his gun, standing in front of the unarmed native crowd—seemingly the leading actor of the piece; but in reality I was only an absurd puppet pushed to and fro by the will of those yellow faces behind. I perceived in this moment that when the white man turns tyrant it is his own freedom that he destroys. He becomes a sort of hollow, posing dummy, the conventionalized figure of a sahib. For it is the condition of his rule that he shall spend his life in trying to impress the "natives," and so in every crisis he has got to do what the "natives" expect of him. He wears a mask, and his face grows to fit it. I had got to shoot the elephant. I had committed myself to doing it when I sent for the rifle. A sahib has got to act like a sahib; he has got to appear resolute, to know his own mind and do definite things. To come all that way, rifle in hand, with two thousand people marching at my heels, and then to trail feebly away, having done nothing—no, that was impossible. The crowd would laugh at me. And my whole life, every white man's life in the East, was one long struggle not to be laughed at.

But I did not want to shoot the elephant. I watched him beating his bunch of grass against his knees with that preoccupied grandmotherly air that elephants have. It seemed to me that it would be murder to shoot him. At that age I was not squeamish about killing animals, but I had never shot an elephant and never wanted to. (Somehow it always seems worse to kill a *large* animal.) Besides, there was the beast's owner to be considered. Alive, the elephant was worth at least a hundred pounds; dead, he would only be worth the value of his tusks, five pounds, possibly. But I had got to act quickly. I turned to some experienced-looking Burmans who had been there when we arrived, and asked them how the elephant had been behaving. They all said the same thing: he took no notice of you if you left him alone, but he might charge if you went too close to him.

It was perfectly clear to me what I ought to do. I ought to walk up to within, say, twenty-five yards of the elephant and test his behavior. If he charged, I could shoot; if he took no notice of me, it would be safe to leave him until the mahout came back. But also I knew that I was going to do no such thing. I was a poor shot with a rifle and the ground was soft mud into which one would sink at every step. If the elephant charged and I missed him, I should have about as much chance as a toad under a steam-roller. But even then I was not thinking particularly of my own skin, only of the watchful yellow faces behind. For at that moment, with the crowd watching me, I was not afraid in the ordinary sense, as I would have been if I had been alone. A white man mustn't be frightened in front of "natives"; and so, in general, he isn't frightened. The sole thought in my mind was that if anything went wrong those two thousand Burmans would see me pursued, caught, trampled on, and reduced to a grinning corpse like that Indian up the hill. And if that happened it was quite probable that some of them would laugh. That would never do. There was only one alternative. I shoved the cartridges into the magazine and lay down on the road to get a better aim.

The crowd grew very still, and a deep, low, happy sigh, as of people who see the theater curtain go up at last, breathed from innumerable throats. They were going to have their bit of fun after all. The rifle was a beautiful German thing with cross-hair sights. I did not then know that in shooting an elephant one would shoot to cut an imaginary bar running from ear-hole to ear-hole. I ought, therefore, as the elephant was sideways on, to have aimed straight at his ear-hole; actually I aimed several inches in front of this, thinking the brain would be further forward.

When I pulled the trigger I did not hear the bang or feel the kick—one never does when a shot goes home—but I heard the devilish roar of glee that went up from the crowd. In that instant, in too short a time, one would have thought, even for the bullet to get there, a mysterious, terrible change had come over the elephant. He neither stirred nor fell, but every line of his body had altered. He looked suddenly stricken, shrunken, immensely old, as though the frightful impact of the bullet had paralyzed him without knocking him down. At last, after what seemed a long time—it might have been seconds, I dare say—he sagged flabbily to his knees. His mouth slobbered. An enormous senility seemed to have settled upon him. One could have imagined him thousands of years old. I fired again into the same spot. At the second shot he did not collapse but climbed with desperate slowness to his feet and stood weakly upright, with legs sagging and head drooping. I fired a third time. That was the shot that did for him. You could see the agony of it jolt his whole body and knock the last remnant of strength from his legs. But in falling he seemed for a moment to rise, for as his hind legs collapsed beneath him he seemed to tower upward like a huge rock toppling, his trunk reaching skyward like a tree. He trumpeted, for the first and only time. And then down he came, his belly toward me, with a crash that seemed to shake the ground even where I lay.

I got up. The Burmans were already racing past me across the mud. It was obvious that the elephant would never rise again, but he was not dead. He was breathing very rhythmically with long rattling gasps, his great mound of a side painfully rising and falling. His mouth was wide open—I could see far down into caverns of pale pink throat. I waited a long time for him to die, but his breathing did not weaken. Finally I fired my two remaining shots into the spot where I thought his heart must be. The thick blood welled out of him like red velvet, but still he did not die. His body did not even jerk when the shots hit him, the tortured breathing continued without a pause. He was dying, very slowly and in great agony, but in some world remote from me where not even a bullet could damage him further. I felt that I had got to put an end to that dreadful noise. It seemed dreadful to see the great beast lying there, powerless to move and yet powerless to die, and not even to be able to finish him. I sent back for my small rifle and poured shot after shot into his heart and down his throat. They seemed to make no impression. The tortured gasps continued as steadily as the ticking of a clock.

In the end I could not stand it any longer and went away. I heard later that it took him half an hour to die. Burmans were bringing dahs and baskets even before I left, and I was told they had stripped his body almost to the bones by the afternoon.

Afterward, of course, there were endless discussions about the shooting of the elephant. The owner was furious, but he was only an Indian and could do nothing. Besides, legally I had done the right thing, for a mad elephant has to be killed, like a mad dog, if its owner fails to control it. Among the Europeans opinion was divided. The older men said I was right, the younger men said it was a damn shame to shoot an elephant for killing a coolie, because an elephant was worth more than any damn Coringhee coolie. And afterward I was very glad that the coolie had been killed; it put me legally in the right and it gave me a sufficient pretext for shooting the elephant. I often wondered whether any of the others grasped that I had done it solely to avoid looking a fool.

VIRGINIA WOOLF
1882–1941
The Death of the Moth

Moths that fly by day are not properly to be called moths; they do not excite that pleasant sense of dark autumn nights and ivy-blossom which the commonest yellow-underwing asleep in the shadow of the curtain never fails to rouse in us. They are hybrid creatures, neither gay like butterflies nor sombre like their own species. Nevertheless the present specimen, with his narrow hay-coloured wings, fringed with a tassel of the same colour, seemed to be content with life. It was a pleasant morning, mid-September, mild, benignant, yet with a keener breath than that of the summer months. The plough was already scoring the field opposite the window, and where the share had been, the earth was pressed flat and gleamed with moisture. Such vigour came rolling in from the fields and the down beyond that it was difficult to keep the eyes strictly turned upon the book. The rooks too were keeping one of their annual festivities; soaring round the tree tops until it looked as if a vast net with thousands of black knots in it had been cast up into the air; which, after a few moments sank slowly down upon the trees until every twig seemed to have a knot at the end of it. Then, suddenly, the net would be thrown into the air again in a wider circle this time, with the utmost clamour and vociferation, as though to be thrown into the air and settle slowly down upon the tree tops were a tremendously exciting experience.

The same energy which inspired the rooks, the ploughmen, the horses, and even, it seemed, the lean bare-backed downs, sent the moth fluttering from side to side of his square of the window-pane. One could not help watching him. One was, indeed, conscious of a queer feeling of pity for him. The possibilities of pleasure seemed that morning so enormous and so various that to have only a moth's part in life, and a day moth's at that, appeared a hard fate, and his zest in enjoying his meagre opportunities to the full, pathetic. He flew vigorously to one corner of his compartment, and, after waiting there a second, flew across to the other. What remained for him but to fly to a third corner and then to a fourth? That was all he could do, in spite of the size of the downs, the width of the sky, the far-off smoke of houses, and the romantic voice, now and then, of a steamer out at sea. What he could do he did. Watching him, it seemed as if a fibre, very thin but pure, of the enormous energy of the world had been thrust into his frail and diminutive body. As often as he crossed the pane, I could fancy that a thread of vital light became visible. He was little or nothing but life.

Yet, because he was so small, and so simple a form of the energy that was rolling in at the open window and driving its way through so many narrow and intricate corridors in my own brain and in those of other human beings, there was something marvellous as well as pathetic about him. It was as if someone had taken a tiny bead of pure life and decking it as lightly as possible with down and feathers, had set it dancing and zigzagging to show us the true nature of life. Thus displayed one could not get over the strangeness of it. One is apt to forget all about life, seeing it humped and bossed and garnished and cumbered so that it has to move with the greatest circumspection and dignity. Again, the thought of all that life might have been had he been born in any other shape caused one to view his simple activities with a kind of pity.

After a time, tired by his dancing apparently, he settled on the window ledge in the sun, and, the queer spectacle being at an end, I forgot about him. Then, looking up, my eye was caught by him. He was trying to resume his dancing, but seemed either so stiff or so awkward that he could only flutter to the bottom of the window-pane; and when he tried to fly across it he failed. Being intent on other matters I watched these futile attempts for a time without thinking, unconsciously waiting for him to resume his flight, as one waits for a machine, that has stopped momentarily, to start again without considering the reason of its failure. After perhaps a seventh attempt he slipped from the wooden ledge and fell, fluttering his wings, on to his back on the window sill. The helplessness of his attitude roused me. It flashed upon me that he was in difficulties; he could no longer raise himself; his legs struggled vainly. But, as I stretched out a pencil, meaning to help him to right himself, it came over me that the failure and awkwardness were the approach of death. I laid the pencil down again.

The legs agitated themselves once more. I looked as if for the enemy against which he struggled. I looked out of doors. What had happened there? Presumably it was mid-day, and work in the fields had stopped. Stillness and quiet had replaced the previous animation. The birds had taken themselves off to feed in the brooks. The horses stood still. Yet the power was there all the same, massed outside indifferent, impersonal, not attending to anything in particular. Somehow it was opposed to the little hay-coloured moth. It was useless to try to do anything. One could only watch the extraordinary efforts made by those tiny legs against an oncoming doom which could, had it chosen, have submerged an entire city, not merely a city, but masses of human beings; nothing, I knew, had any chance against death. Nevertheless after a pause of exhaustion the legs fluttered again. It was superb this last protest, and so frantic that he succeeded at last in righting himself. One's sympathies, of course, were all on the side of life. Also, when there was nobody to care or to know, this gigantic effort on the part of an insignificant little moth, against a power of such magnitude, to retain what no one else valued or desired to keep, moved one strangely. Again, somehow, one saw life, a pure bead. I lifted the pencil again, useless though I knew it to be. But even as I did so, the unmistakable tokens of death showed themselves. The body relaxed, and instantly grew stiff. The struggle was over. The insignificant little creature now knew death. As I looked at the dead moth, this minute wayside triumph of so great a force over so mean an antagonist filled me with wonder. Just as life had been strange a few minutes before, so death was now as strange. The moth having righted himself now lay most decently and uncomplainingly composed. O yes, he seemed to say, death is stronger than I am.

JAMES THURBER
1894–1961
The Moth and the Star

A young and impressionable moth once set his heart on a certain star. He told his mother about this and she counseled him to set his heart on a bridge lamp instead. "Stars aren't the thing to hang around," she said; "lamps are the thing to hang around." "You get somewhere that way," said the moth's father. "You don't get anywhere chasing stars." But the moth would not heed the words of either parent. Every evening at dusk when the star came out he would start flying toward it and every morning at dawn he would crawl back home worn out with his vain endeavor. One day his father said to him, "You haven't burned a wing in months, boy, and it looks to me as if you were never going to. All your brothers have been badly burned flying around street lamps and all your sisters have been terribly singed flying around house lamps. Come on, now, get out of here and get yourself scorched! A big strapping moth like you without a mark on him!"

The moth left his father's house, but he would not fly around street lamps and he would not fly around house lamps. He went right on trying to reach the star, which was four and one-third light years, or twenty-five trillion miles, away. The moth thought it was just caught in the top branches of an elm. He never did reach the star, but he went right on trying, night after night, and when he was a very, very old moth he began to think that he really had reached the star and he went around saying so. This gave him a deep and lasting pleasure, and he lived to a great old age. His parents and his brothers and his sisters had all been burned to death when they were quite young.

Moral: Who flies afar from the sphere of our sorrow is here today and here tomorrow.

JAMES BALDWIN
1924–
Stranger in the Village

From all available evidence no black man had ever set foot in this tiny Swiss village before I came. I was told before arriving that I would probably be a "sight" for the village; I took this to mean that people of my complexion were rarely seen in Switzerland, and also that city people are always something of a "sight" outside of the city. It did not occur to me—possibly because I am an American—that there could be people anywhere who had never seen a Negro.

It is a fact that cannot be explained on the basis of the inaccessibility of the village. The village is very high, but it is only four hours from

Milan and three hours from Lausanne. It is true that it is virtually unknown. Few people making plans for a holiday would elect to come here. On the other hand, the villagers are able, presumably, to come and go as they please—which they do: to another town at the foot of the mountain, with a population of approximately five thousand, the nearest place to see a movie or go to the bank. In the village there is no movie house, no bank, no library, no theater; very few radios, one jeep, one station wagon; and, at the moment, one typewriter, mine, an invention which the woman next door to me here had never seen. There are about six hundred people living here, all Catholic—I conclude this from the fact that the Catholic church is open all year round, whereas the Protestant chapel, set off on a hill a little removed from the village, is open only in the summertime when the tourists arrive. There are four or five hotels, all closed now, and four or five *bistros,* of which, however, only two do any business during the winter. These two do not do a great deal, for life in the village seems to end around nine or ten o'clock. There are a few stores, butcher, baker, *épicerie,* a hardware store, and a money-changer—who cannot change travelers' checks, but must send them down to the bank, an operation which takes two or three days. There is something called the *Ballet Haus,* closed in the winter and used for God knows what, certainly not ballet, during the summer. There seems to be only one schoolhouse in the village, and this for the quite young children; I suppose this to mean that their older brothers and sisters at some point descend from these mountains in order to complete their education—possibly, again, to the town just below. The landscape is absolutely forbidding, mountains towering on all four sides, ice and snow as far as the eye can reach. In this white wilderness, men and women and children move all day, carrying washing, wood, buckets of milk or water, sometimes skiing on Sunday afternoons. All week long boys and young men are to be seen shoveling snow off the rooftops, or dragging wood down from the forest in sleds.

The village's only real attraction, which explains the tourist season, is the hot spring water. A disquietingly high proportion of these tourists are cripples, or semi-cripples, who come year after year—from other parts of Switzerland, usually—to take the waters. This lends the village, at the height of the season, a rather terrifying air of sanctity, as though it were a lesser Lourdes. There is often something beautiful, there is always something awful, in the spectacle of a person who has lost one of his faculties, a faculty he never questioned until it was gone, and who struggles to recover it. Yet people remain people, on crutches or indeed on deathbeds; and wherever I passed, the first summer I was here, among the native villagers or among the lame, a wind passed with me—of astonishment, curiosity, amusement, and outrage. That first summer I stayed two weeks and never intended to return. But I did return in the winter, to work; the village offers, obviously, no distractions whatever and has the further advantage of being extremely cheap. Now it is winter again, a year later, and I am here again. Everyone in the village knows my name, though they scarcely ever use it, knows that I come from America—though, this, apparently, they will never really believe: black men come from Africa—and everyone knows that I am the friend of the son of a woman who was born here, and that I am staying in their chalet. But I remain as much a stranger today as I was the first day I arrived, and the children shout *Neger! Neger!* as I walk along the streets.

It must be admitted that in the beginning I was far too shocked to have any real reaction. In so far as I reacted at all, I reacted by trying to be pleasant—it being a great part of the American Negro's education (long before he goes to school) that he must make people "like" him. This smile-and-the-world-smiles-with-you routine worked about as well in this situation as it had in the situation for which it was designed, which is to say that it did not work at all. No one, after all, can be liked whose human weight and complexity cannot be, or has not been, admitted. My smile was simply another unheard-of phenomenon which allowed them to see my teeth—they did not, really, see my smile and I began to think that, should I take to snarling, no one would notice any difference. All of the physical characteristics of the Negro which had caused me, in America, a very different and almost forgotten pain were nothing less than miraculous—or infernal—in the eyes of the village people. Some thought my hair was the color of tar, that it had the texture of wire, or the texture of cotton. It was jocularly suggested that I might let it all grow long and make myself a winter coat. If I sat in the sun for more than five minutes some daring creature was certain to come along and gingerly put his fingers on my hair, as though he were afraid of an electric shock, or put his hand on my hand, astonished that the color did not rub off. In all of this, in which it must be conceded there was the charm of genuine wonder and in which there was certainly no element of intentional unkindness, there was yet no suggestion that I was human: I was simply a living wonder.

I knew that they did not mean to be unkind, and I know it now; it is necessary, nevertheless, for me to repeat this to myself each time that I walk out of the chalet. The children who shout *Neger!* have no way of knowing the echoes this sound raises in me. They are brimming with good humor and the more daring swell with pride when I stop to speak with them. Just the same, there are days when I cannot pause and smile, when I have no heart to play with them; when, indeed, I mutter sourly to myself, exactly as I muttered on the street of a city these children have never seen, when I was no bigger than these children are now: *Your* mother *was a nigger*. Joyce is right about history being a nightmare—but it may be the nightmare from which no one *can* awaken. People are trapped in history and history is trapped in them.

There is a custom in the village—I am told it is repeated in many villages—of "buying" African natives for the purpose of converting them to Christianity. There stands in the church all year round a small box with a slot for money, decorated with a black figurine, and into this box the villagers drop their francs. During the *carnaval* which precedes Lent, two village children have their faces blackened—out of which bloodless darkness their blue eyes shine like ice—and fantastic horsehair wigs are placed on their blond heads; thus disguised, they solicit among the villagers for money for the missionaries in Africa. Between the box in the church and the blackened children, the village "bought" last year six or eight African natives. This was reported to me with pride by the wife of one of the *bistro* owners and I was careful to express astonishment and pleasure at the solicitude shown by the village for the souls of black folk. The *bistro* owner's wife beamed with a pleasure far more genuine than my own and seemed to feel that I might now breathe more easily concerning the souls of at least six of my kinsmen.

I tried not to think of these so lately baptized kinsmen, of the price paid for them, or the peculiar price they themselves would pay, and said nothing about my father, who having taken his own conversion too literally never, at bottom, forgave the white world (which he described as heathen) for having saddled him with a Christ in whom, to judge at least from their treatment of him, they themselves no longer believed. I thought of white men arriving for the first time in an African village, strangers there, as I am a stranger here, and tried to imagine the astounded populace touching their hair and marveling at the color of their skin. But there is a great difference between being the first white man to be seen by Africans and being the first black man to be seen by whites. The white man takes the astonishment as tribute, for he arrives to conquer and to convert the natives, whose inferiority in relation to himself is not even to be questioned; whereas I, without a thought of conquest, find myself among a people whose culture controls me, has even, in a sense, created me, people who have cost me more in anguish and rage than they will ever know, who yet do not even know of my existence. The astonishment with which I might have greeted them, should they have stumbled into my African village a few hundred years ago, might have rejoiced their hearts. But the astonishment with which they greet me today can only poison mine.

And this is so despite everything I may do to feel differently, despite my friendly conversations with the *bistro* owner's wife, despite their three-year-old son who has at last become my friend, despite the *saluts* and *bonsoirs* which I exchange with people as I walk, despite the fact that I know that no individual can be taken to task for what history is doing, or has done. I say that the culture of these people controls me—but they can scarcely be held responsible for European culture. America comes out of Europe, but these people have never seen America, nor have most of them seen more of Europe than the hamlet at the foot of their mountain. Yet they move with an authority which I shall never have; and they regard me, quite rightly, not only as a stranger in their village but as a suspect latecomer, bearing no credentials, to everything they have—however unconsciously— inherited.

For this village, even were it incomparably more remote and incredibly more primitive, is the West, the West onto which I have been so strangely grafted. These people cannot be, from the point of view of power, strangers anywhere in the world; they have made the modern world, in effect, even if they do not know it. The most illiterate among them is related, in a way that I am not, to Dante, Shakespeare, Michelangelo, Aeschylus, Da Vinci, Rembrandt, and Racine; the cathedral at Chartres says something to them which it cannot say to me, as indeed would New York's Empire State Building, should anyone here ever see it. Out of their hymns and dances come Beethoven and Bach. Go back a few centuries and they are in their full glory—but I am in Africa, watching the conquerors arrive.

The rage of the disesteemed is personally fruitless, but it is also absolutely inevitable; this rage, so generally discounted, so little understood even among the people whose daily bread it is, is one of the things that makes history. Rage can only with difficulty, and never entirely, be brought under the domination of the intelligence and is therefore not susceptible to any arguments whatever. This is a fact which ordinary representatives of the *Herrenvolk*, having never felt this rage and being unable to imagine it, quite fail to understand. Also, rage cannot be hidden, it can only be dissembled. This dissembling deludes the thoughtless, and strengthens rage and adds, to rage, contempt. There are, no doubt, as many ways of coping with the resulting complex of tensions as there are black men in the world, but no black man can hope ever to be entirely liberated from this internal warfare—rage, dissembling, and contempt having inevitably accompanied his first realization of the power of white men. What is crucial here is that, since white men represent in the black man's world so heavy a weight, white men have for black men a reality which is far from being reciprocal; and hence all black men have toward all white men an attitude which is designed, really, either to rob the white man of the jewel of his naïveté, or else to make it cost him dear.

The black man insists, by whatever means he finds at his disposal, that the white man cease to regard him as an exotic rarity and recognize him as a human being. This is a very charged and difficult moment, for there is a great deal of will power involved in the white man's naïveté. Most people are not naturally reflective any more than they are naturally malicious, and the white man prefers to keep the black man at a certain human remove because it is easier for him thus to preserve his simplicity and avoid being called to account for crimes committed by his forefathers, or his neighbors. He is inescapably aware, nevertheless, that he is in a better position in the world than black men are, nor can he quite put to death the suspicion that he is hated by black men therefor. He does not wish to be hated, neither does he wish to change places, and at this point in his uneasiness he can scarcely avoid having recourse to those legends which white men have created about black men, the most usual effect of which is that the white man finds himself enmeshed, so to speak, in his own language which describes hell, as well as the attributes which lead one to hell, as being as black as night.

Every legend, moreover, contains its residuum of truth, and the root function of language is to control the universe by describing it. It is of quite considerable significance that black men remain, in the imagination, and in overwhelming numbers in fact, beyond the disciplines of salvation; and this despite the fact that the West has been "buying" African natives for centuries. There is, I should hazard, an instantaneous necessity to be divorced from this so visibly unsaved stranger, in whose heart, moreover, one cannot guess what dreams of vengeance are being nourished; and, at the same time, there are few things on earth more attractive than the idea of the unspeakable liberty which is allowed the unredeemed. When, beneath the black mask, a human being begins to make himself felt one cannot escape a certain awful wonder as to what kind of human being it is. What one's imagination makes of other people is dictated, of course, by the laws of one's own personality and it is one of the ironies of black-white relations that, by means of what the white man imagines the black man to be, the black man is enabled to know who the white man is.

I have said, for example, that I am as much a stranger in this village today as I was the first summer I arrived, but this is not quite true. The villagers wonder less about the texture of my hair than they did then, and wonder rather more about me. And the fact that their wonder now exists on another level is reflected in their attitudes and in their eyes. There are the children who make those delightful, hilarious, sometimes astonishing grave overtures of friendship in the unpredictable fashion of children; other children, having been taught that the devil is a black man, scream in genuine anguish as I approach. Some of the older women never pass without a friendly greeting, never pass, indeed, if it seems that they will be able to engage me in conversation; other women look down or look away or rather contemptuously smirk. Some of the men drink with me and suggest that I learn how to ski—partly, I gather, because they cannot imagine what I would look like on skis—and want to know if I am married, and ask questions about my *métier*. But some of the men have accused *le sale nègre*— behind my back—of stealing wood and there is already in the eyes of some of them that peculiar, intent, paranoiac malevolence which one sometimes surprises in the eyes of American white men when, out walking with their Sunday girl, they see a Negro male approach.

There is a dreadful abyss between the streets of this village and the streets of the city in which I was born, between the children who shout *Neger!* today and those who shouted *Nigger!* yesterday—the abyss is experience, the American experience. The syllable hurled behind me today expresses, above all, wonder: I am a stranger here. But I am not a stranger in America and the same syllable riding on the American air expresses the war my presence has occasioned in the American soul.

For this village brings home to me this fact: that there was a day, and not really a very distant day, when Americans were scarcely Americans at all but discontented Europeans, facing a great unconquered continent and strolling, say, into a marketplace and seeing black men for the first time. The shock this spectacle afforded is suggested, surely, by the promptness with which they decided that these black men were not really men but cattle. It is true that the necessity on the part of the settlers of the New World of reconciling their moral assumptions with the fact—and the necessity—of slavery enhanced immensely the charm of this idea, and it is also true that this idea expresses, with a truly American bluntness, the attitude which to varying extents all masters have had toward all slaves.

But between all former slaves and slave-owners and the drama which begins for Americans over three hundred years ago at James-town, there are at least two differences to be observed. The American Negro slave could not suppose, for one thing, as slaves in past epochs had supposed and often done, that he would ever be able to wrest the power from his master's hands. This was a supposition which the modern era, which was to bring about such vast changes in the aims and dimensions of power, put to death; it only begins, in unprece-dented fashion, and with dreadful implications, to be resurrected today. But even had this supposition persisted with undiminished force, the American Negro slave could not have used it to lend his condition dignity, for the reason that this supposition rests on another: that the slave in exile yet remains related to his past, has some means—if only in memory—of revering and sustaining the forms of his former life, is able, in short, to maintain his identity.

This was not the case with the American Negro slave. He is unique among the black men of the world in that his past was taken from him, almost literally, at one blow. One wonders what on earth the first slave found to say to the first dark child he bore. I am told that there are Haitians able to trace their ancestry back to African kings, but any American Negro wishing to go back so far will find his journey through time abruptly arrested by the signature on the bill of sale which served as the entrance paper for his ancestor. At the time—to say nothing of the circumstances—of the enslavement of the captive black man who was to become the American Negro, there was not the remotest possibility that he would ever take power from his master's hands. There was no reason to suppose that his situation would ever change, nor was there, shortly, anything to indicate that his situation had ever been different. It was his necessity, in the words of E. Franklin Frazier, to find a "motive for living under American culture or die." The identity of the American Negro comes out of this extreme situation, and the evolution of this identity was a source of the most intolerable anxiety in the minds and the lives of his masters.

For the history of the American Negro is unique also in this: that the question of his humanity, and of his rights therefore as a human being, became a burning one for several generations of Americans, so burning a question that it ultimately became one of those used to divide the nation. It is out of this argument that the venom of the epithet *Nigger!* is derived. It is an argument which Europe has never had, and hence Europe quite sincerely fails to understand how or why the argument arose in the first place, why its effects are so frequently disastrous and always so unpredictable, why it refuses until today to be entirely settled. Europe's black possessions remained—and do remain—in Europe's colonies, at which remove they represented no threat whatever to European identity. If they posed any problem at all for the European conscience, it was a problem which remained comfortingly abstract: in effect, the black man, *as a man*, did not exist for Europe. But in America, even as a slave, he was an inescapable part of the general social fabric and no American could escape having an attitude toward him. Americans attempt until today to make an abstraction of the Negro, but the very nature of these abstractions reveals the tremendous effects the presence of the Negro has had on the American character.

When one considers the history of the Negro in America it is of the greatest importance to recognize that the moral beliefs of a person, or a people, are never really as tenuous as life—which is not moral—very often causes them to appear; these create for them a frame of reference and a necessary hope, the hope being that when life has done its worst they will be enabled to rise above themselves and to triumph over life. Life would scarcely be bearable if this hope did not exist. Again, even when the worst has been said, to betray a belief is not by any means to have put oneself beyond its power; the betrayal of a belief is not the same thing as ceasing to believe. If this were not so there would be no moral standards in the world at all. Yet one must also recognize that morality is based on ideas and that all ideas are dangerous—dangerous because ideas can only lead to action and where the action leads no man can say. And dangerous in this respect: that confronted with the impossibility of remaining faithful to one's beliefs, and the equal impossibility of becoming free of them, one can be driven to the most inhuman excesses. The ideas on which American beliefs are based are not, though Americans often seem to think so, ideas which originated in America. They came out of Europe. And the establishment of democracy on the American continent was scarcely as radical a break with the past as was the necessity, which Americans faced, of broadening this concept to include black men.

This was, literally, a hard necessity. It was impossible, for one thing, for Americans to abandon their beliefs, not only because these beliefs alone seemed able to justify the sacrifices they had endured and the blood that they had spilled, but also because these beliefs afforded them their only bulwark against a moral chaos as absolute as the physical chaos of the continent it was their destiny to conquer. But in the situation in which Americans found themselves, these beliefs threatened an idea which, whether or not one likes to think so, is the very warp and woof of the heritage of the West, the idea of white supremacy.

Americans have made themselves notorious by the shrillness and the brutality with which they have insisted on this idea, but they did not invent it; and it has escaped the world's notice that those very excesses of which Americans have been guilty imply a certain, unprecedented uneasiness over the idea's life and power, if not, indeed, the idea's validity. The idea of white supremacy rests simply on the fact that white men are the creators of civilization (the present civilization, which is the only one that matters; all previous civilizations are simply "contributions" to our own) and are therefore civilization's guardians and defenders. Thus it was impossible for Americans to accept the black man as one of themselves, for to do so was to jeopardize their status as white men. But not so to accept him was to deny his human reality, his human weight and complexity, and the strain of denying the overwhelmingly undeniable forced Americans into rationalizations so fantastic that they approached the pathological.

At the root of the American Negro problem is the necessity of the American white man to find a way of living with the Negro in order to be able to live with himself. And the history of this problem can be reduced to the means used by Americans—lynch law and law, segregation and legal acceptance, terrorization and concession—either to come to terms with this necessity, or to find a way around it, or (most usually) to find a way of doing both these things at once. The resulting spectacle, at once foolish and dreadful, led someone to make the quite accurate observation that "the Negro-in-America is a form of insanity which overtakes white men."

In this long battle, a battle by no means finished, the unforeseeable effects of which will be felt by many future generations, the white man's motive was the protection of his identity; the black man was motivated by the need to establish an identity. And despite the terrorization which the Negro in America endured and endures sporadically until today, despite the cruel and totally inescapable ambivalence of his status in his country, the battle for his identity has long ago been won. He is not a visitor to the West, but a citizen there, an American; as American as the Americans who despise him, the Americans who fear him, the Americans who love him—the Americans who became less than themselves, or rose to be greater than themselves by virtue of the fact that the challenge he represented was inescapable. He is perhaps the only black man in the world whose relationship to white men is more terrible, more subtle, and more meaningful than the relationship of bitter possessed to uncertain possessor. His survival depended, and his development depends, on his ability to turn his peculiar status in the Western world to his own advantage and, it may be, to the very great advantage of that world. It remains for him to fashion out of his experience that which will give him sustenance, and a voice.

The cathedral of Chartres, I have said, says something to the people of this village which it cannot say to me; but it is important to understand that this cathedral says something to me which it cannot say to them. Perhaps they are struck by the power of the spires, the glory of the windows; but they have known God, after all, longer than I have known him, and in a different way, and I am terrified by the slippery bottomless well to be found in the crypt, down which heretics were hurled to death, and by the obscene, inescapable gargoyles jutting out of the stone and seeming to say that God and the devil can never be divorced. I doubt that the villagers think of the devil when they face a cathedral because they have never been identified with the devil. But I must accept the status which myth, if nothing else, gives me in the West before I can hope to change the myth.

Yet, if the American Negro has arrived at his identity by virtue of the absoluteness of his estrangement from his past, American white men still nourish the illusion that there is some means of recovering the European innocence, of returning to a state in which black men do not exist. This is one of the greatest errors Americans can make. The identity they fought so hard to protect has, by virtue of that battle, undergone a change: Americans are as unlike any other white people in the world as it is possible to be. I do not think, for example, that it is too much to suggest that the American vision of the world—which allows so little reality, generally speaking, for any of the darker forces in human life, which tends until today to paint moral issues in glaring black and white—owes a great deal to the battle waged by Americans to maintain between themselves and black men a human separation which could not be bridged. It is only now beginning to be borne in on us—very faintly, it must be admitted, very slowly, and very much against our will—that this vision of the world is dangerously inaccurate, and perfectly useless. For it protects our moral high-mindedness at the terrible expense of weakening our grasp of reality. People who shut their eyes to reality simply invite their own destruction, and anyone who insists on remaining in a state of innocence long after that innocence is dead turns himself into a monster.

The time has come to realize that the interracial drama acted out on the American continent has not only created a new black man, it has created a new white man, too. No road whatever will lead Americans back to the simplicity of this European village where white men still have the luxury of looking on me as a stranger. I am not, really, a stranger any longer for any American alive. One of the things that distinguishes Americans from other people is that no other people has ever been so deeply involved in the lives of black men, and vice versa. This fact faced, with all its implications, it can be seen that the history of the American Negro problem is not merely shameful, it is also something of an achievement. For even when the worst has been said, it must also be added that the perpetual challenge posed by this problem was always, somehow, perpetually met. It is precisely this black-white experience which may prove of indispensable value to us in the world we face today. This world is white no longer, and it will never be white again.

DICK GREGORY

1932–

If You Had to Kill Your Own Hog

My momma could never understand how white folks could twist the words of the Bible around to justify racial segregation. Yet she could read the Ten Commandments, which clearly say, "Thou shalt not kill," and still justify eating meat. Momma couldn't read the newspaper very well, but she sure could interpret the Word of God. "God meant you shouldn't kill people," she used to say. But I insisted, "Momma, He didn't say that. He said, 'Thou shalt not kill.' If you leave that statement alone, a whole lot of things would be safe from killing. But if you are going to twist the words about killing to mean what you want them to mean, then let white folks do the same thing with justifying racial segregation."

"You can't live without eating meat," Momma would persist. "You'd starve." I couldn't buy that either. You get milk from a cow without killing it. You do not have to kill an animal to get what you need from it. You get wool from the sheep without killing it. Two of the strongest animals in the jungle are vegetarians—the elephant and the gorilla. The first two years are the most important years of a man's life, and during that period he is not involved with eating meat. If you suddenly become very ill, there is a good chance you will be taken off a meat diet. So it is a myth that killing is necessary for survival. The day I decide that I must have a piece of steak to nourish my body, I will also give the cow the same right to nourish herself on human beings.

There is so little basic difference between animals and humans. The process of reproduction is the same for chickens, cattle, and humans. If suddenly the air stopped circulating on the earth, or the sun collided with the earth, animals and humans would die alike. A nuclear holocaust will wipe out all life. Life in the created order is basically the same and should be respected as such. It seems to me the Bible says it is wrong to kill—period.

If we can justify *any* kind of killing in the name of religion, the door is opened for all kinds of other justifications. The fact of killing animals is not as frightening as our human tendency to justify it—to kill and not even be aware that we are taking life. It is sobering to realize that when you misuse one of the least of Nature's creatures, like the chicken, you are sowing the seed for misusing the highest of Nature's creatures, man.

Animals and humans suffer and die alike. If you had to kill your own hog before you ate it, most likely you would not be able to do it. To hear the hog scream, to see the blood spill, to see the baby being taken away from its momma, and to see the look of death in the animal's eye would turn your stomach. So you get the man at the packing house to do the killing for you. In like manner, if the wealthy aristocrats who are perpetrating conditions in the ghetto actually heard the screms of ghetto suffering, or saw the slow death of hungry little kids, or witnessed the strangulation of manhood and dignity, they could not continue the killing. But the wealthy are protected from such horror. They have people to do the killing for them. The wealthy profit from the daily murders of ghetto life but they do not see them. Those who immerse themselves in the daily life of the ghetto see the suffering— the social workers, the police, the local merchants, and the bill collectors. But the people on top never really see.

By the time you see a piece of meat in the butcher shop window, all the blood and suffering have been washed away. When you order a steak in the restaurant, the misery has been forgotten and you see the finished product. You see a steak with butter and parsley on it. It looks appetizing and appealing and you are pleased enough to eat it. You never even consider the suffering which produced your meal or the other animals killed that day in the slaughterhouse. In the same way, all the wealthy aristocrats ever see of the black community is the finished product, the window dressing, the steak on the platter— Ralph Bunche and Thurgood Marshall. The United Nations or the Supreme Court bench is the restaurant and the ghetto street corner is the slaughterhouse.

Life under ghetto conditions cuts short life expectancy. The Negro's life expectancy is shorter than the white man's. The oppressor benefits from continued oppression financially; he makes more money so that he can eat a little better. I see no difference between a man killing a chicken and a man killing a human being, by overwork and forcing ghetto conditions upon him, both so that he can eat a little better. If you can justify killing to eat meat, you can justify the conditions of the ghetto. I cannot justify either one.

Every time the white folks made my momma mad, she would grab the Bible and find something bitter in it. She would come home from the rich white folks' house, after they had just called her "nigger," or patted her on the rump or caught her stealing some steaks, open her Bible and read aloud, "It is easier for a camel to pass through the eye of a needle than for a rich man to get into Heaven." When you get involved with distorting the words of the Bible, you don't have to be bitter. The same tongue can be used to bless and curse men.

MICHAEL J. ARLEN
1930–
Life and Death in
the Global Village

He was shot in secrecy, away from cameras. No strange slow-motion scenes, as when the young Japanese student, sword in hand, rushed across the stage to lunge at a Socialist politician, or when Verwoerd, the South African, was shot at and for whole crazy moments (it seems so long ago; so many people shot at since then) the cameras swirled and danced around the tumbling, stampeding bodies of the crowd— and then John Kennedy was killed, his life made to disappear right there before us, frame by frame, the projector slowing down, s-l-o-w-i-n-g d-o-w-n, s—l—o—w—i—n—g d—o—w—n as we watched (three consecutive days we watched), gathered in little tight-gutted bands around the television set, meals being cooked somehow, children put to bed, sent out to play, our thought of abandonment and despair and God knows what else focusing on the images of the television set, television itself taking on (we were told later) the aspect of a national icon, a shrine, an exorciser of grief; we were never so close (we were told later) as in those days just after Dallas. It could not have been quite close enough, it seems, or lasted long enough. The man who was shot in Memphis on Thursday of last week was standing on a second-floor balcony of a motel, the Lorraine, leaning over the railing of the balcony in front of his room, which was No. 306. (We have been told it was No. 306.) He was shot once and killed by a man who fired his rifle (a Remington 30.06), apparently, from inside a bathroom window of a rooming house some two hundred feet away. The address of the rooming house is 420 South Main Street. There was no film record of the act, no attendant Zapruder to witness for us the body falling and other memorabilia, but most of us found out about it by television, and it is by television that most of us have been connected with whatever it is that really happened, or is happening now. Television connects—the global village. We sit at home— We had been out, actually, a party full of lawyers, and had come back early and turned on the eleven-o'clock news. "I have a dream . . ." young Dr. King was chanting, "that one day on the red hills of Georgia . . . ." CBS's Joseph Benti said that Dr. King had been shot and killed, was dead. The President was speaking. "I ask every citizen to reject the blind violence that has struck Dr. King, who lived by non-violence," he said. They showed us pictures of Dr. King in Montgomery. They showed us pictures of the outside of the Lorraine Motel.

The telephone rang. A friend of my wife's. "Have you heard?" she said. I said we'd heard. "It's so horrible," she said. And then, "I can't believe it." And then, "I feel we're all mad." I held the phone against my ear, mumbling the usual things, feeling, in part, her grief, her guilt, her sense of lunacy—whatever it was—and, in part, that adrenalin desire we strangers have who have been separate in our cabins all the long sea voyage to somehow touch each other at the moment that the ship goes down. She talked some more. "I'm keeping you from watching," she said at last. I mumbled protests, and we said good-by and disconnected. We will all meet for dinner three weekends hence and discuss summer rentals on the Vineyard.

All over the country now the members of the global village sit before their sets, and the voices and faces out of the sets speak softly, earnestly, reasonably, sincerely to us, in order once again (have four and a half years really gone by since Dallas?) to bind us together, to heal, to mend, to take us forward. The President appears. His face looks firmer, squarer, straighter now than it has looked in months. "We can achieve nothing by lawlessness and divisiveness among the American people," he says. "It's only by joining together and only by working together we can continue to move toward equality and fulfillment for all of our people." The Vice-President speaks. "The cause for which he marched and worked, I am sure, will find a new strength. The plight of discrimination, poverty, and neglect must be erased from America," he says. Former Vice-President Richard Nixon is expected to release a statement soon. There are brief pictures of a coffin being slid onto a plane. The Field Foundation, one hears, has just undertaken to donate a million dollars to the civil-rights movement. Dr. Ralph Bunche asks for "an effort of unparalleled determination, massiveness, and urgency to convert the American ideal of equality into reality."

The television sets hum in our midst. Gray smoke, black smoke begins to rise from blocks of buildings in Washington and Chicago. Sirens whine outside our windows in the night. The voices out of Memphis seem to be fainter now; the pictures of that little nondescript motel, the railing, the bathroom window are already being shown to us less frequently today. Down below us on the sidewalk, six blue-helmeted policemen are gathered in a group. Three police cars are parked farther down the street. The television beams out at us a Joel McCrea movie. Detroit and Newark have been remembered. Responsible decisions have been made in responsible places. The President is working now "to avoid catastrophe." The cartoons are on this morning. The air is very bright outside. The day is sunny. All day long the sirens sound. The television hums through its schedule. There is a circus on Channel 4. Back from the dime store, my daughter asks one of the helmeted policemen if anything has happened. He seems surprised. No, nothing, he says. A squad car drives slowly, slowly by. A bowling exhibition is taking place on Channel 7. Another movie—and then the news. Great waves of smoke, clouds, billowing waves are suddenly pouring out of buildings. The sounds of bells and sirens. Mayor Daley speaks. Mayor Daley declares a curfew. Six Negro boys are running down a street, carrying armfuls of clothes. Police cars streak by. More smoke. The news is over. We are reenveloped in a movie. We sit there on the floor and absorb the hum of television. Last summer it inflamed our passions, did it not? This time the scenes of black men running past the smoking buildings of Chicago are handled briefly, almost dreamily—a light caress by cameras and announcers. The coffin—one wonders where the coffin is at present, who is with it. Boston University announces that ten new scholarships for "underprivileged students" have just been created. The Indian Parliament pays tribute. The voices of reason and reordering rise out of the civic temples of the land and float through the air and the airwaves into our homes. Twenty-one House Republicans have issued an "urgent appeal" for passage of the new civil-rights bill. "With whom will we stand? The man who fired the gun? Or the man who fell before it?" Senator Edward Brooke, of Massachusetts, asks. The City Council of Chicago meets and passes a resolution to build a "permanent memorial." Senator Robert Kennedy deplores the rise in violence.

There was a moment the other evening when (just for a few seconds) everybody stopped talking, when (just for a few seconds) the television stopped its humming and soothing and filling of silences and its preachments of lessons-we-have-just-learned and how-we-must-all-march-together—and (just for a few seconds) Mrs. King appeared; she was speaking about her husband, her dead husband. She spoke; she seemed so alive with him—it's marvelous how that sometimes happens between people; he really had been alive, and one knew it then—and for a few scant moments, just at that time, and afterward, sitting there looking at the set, that very imperfect icon, that very imperfect connector of people (will somebody really have the nerve to say this week that we are a nation "united in grief"?), one could almost hear the weeping out there, of real people in real villages, and the anger, this time, of abandonment.

And then the sounds came back—the sounds of one's own life. The weather man came on. A Negro minister on Channel 13 was talking about the need to implement the recommendations of the President's new Commission on Civil Disorders. He *had* been alive . . . hadn't he? Later that night, one could hear the sirens—very cool and clear—and, somewhere nearby (around the corner? blocks away?), the sounds of footsteps running.

JOAN DIDION
1935–
On Going Home

I am home for my daughter's first birthday. By "home" I do not mean the house in Los Angeles where my husband and I and the baby live, but the place where my family is, in the Central Valley of California. It is a vital although troublesome distinction. My husband likes my family but is uneasy in their house, because once there I fall into their ways, which are difficult, oblique, deliberately inarticulate, not my husband's ways. We live in dusty houses ("D-U-S-T," he once wrote with his finger on surfaces all over the house, but no one noticed it) filled with mementos quite without value to him (what could the Canton dessert plates mean to him? how could he have known about the assay scales, why should he care if he did know?), and we appear to talk exclusively about people we know who have been committed to mental hospitals, about people we know who have been booked on drunk-driving charges, and about property, particularly about property, land, price per acre and C-2 zoning and assessments and freeway access. My brother does not understand my husband's inability to perceive the advantage in the rather common real-estate transaction known as "sale-leaseback," and my husband in turn does not understand why so many of the people he hears about in my father's house have recently been committed to mental hospitals or booked on drunk-driving charges. Nor does he understand that when we talk about sale-leasebacks and right-of-way condemnations we are talking in code about the things we like best, the yellow fields and the cottonwoods and the rivers rising and falling and the mountain roads closing when the heavy snow comes in. We miss each other's points, have another drink and regard the fire. My brother refers to my husband, in his presence, as "Joan's husband." Marriage is the classic betrayal.

Or perhaps it is not any more. Sometimes I think that those of us who are now in our thirties were born into the last generation to carry the burden of "home," to find in family life the source of all tension and drama. I had by all objective accounts a "normal" and a "happy" family situation, and yet I was almost thirty years old before I could talk to my family on the telephone without crying after I had hung up. We did not fight. Nothing was wrong. And yet some nameless anxiety colored the emotional charges between me and the place that I came from. The question of whether or not you could go home again was a very real part of the sentimental and largely literary baggage with which we left home in the fifties; I suspect that it is irrelevant to the children born of the fragmentation after World War II. A few weeks ago in a San Francisco bar I saw a pretty young girl on crystal take off her clothes and dance for the cash prize in an "amateur-topless" contest. There was no particular sense of moment about this, none of the effect of romantic degradation, of "dark journey," for which my generation strived so assiduously. What sense could that girl possibly make of, say, *Long Day's Journey into Night?* Who is beside the point?

That I am trapped in this particular irrelevancy is never more apparent to me than when I am home. Paralyzed by the neurotic lassitude engendered by meeting one's past at every turn, around every corner, inside every cupboard, I go aimlessly from room to room. I decide to meet it head-on and clean out a drawer, and I spread the contents on the bed. A bathing suit I wore the summer I was seventeen. A letter of rejection from *The Nation,* an aerial photograph of the site for a shopping center my father did not build in 1954. Three teacups hand-painted with cabbage roses and signed "E.M.," my grandmother's initials. There is no final solution for letters of rejection from *The Nation* and teacups hand-painted in 1900. Nor is there any answer to snapshots of one's grandfather as a young man on skis, surveying around Donner Pass in the year 1910. I smooth out the snapshot and look into his face, and do and do not see my own. I close the drawer, and have another cup of coffee with my mother. We get along very well, veterans of a guerrilla war we never understood.

Days pass. I see no one. I come to dread my husband's evening call, not only because he is full of news of what by now seems to me our remote life in Los Angeles, people he has seen, letters which require attention, but because he asks what I have been doing, suggests uneasily that I get out, drive to San Francisco or Berkeley. Instead I drive across the river to a family graveyard. It has been vandalized since my last visit and the monuments are broken, overturned in the dry grass. Because I once saw a rattlesnake in the grass I stay in the car and listen to a country-and-Western station. Later I drive with my father to a ranch he has in the foothills. The man who runs his cattle on it asks us to the roundup, a week from Sunday, and although I know that I will be in Los Angeles I say, in the oblique way my family talks, that I will come. Once home I mention the broken monuments in the graveyard. My mother shrugs.

I go to visit my great-aunts. A few of them think now that I am my cousin, or their daughter who died young. We recall an anecdote about a relative last seen in 1948, and they ask if I still like living in New York City. I have lived in Los Angeles for three years, but I say that I do. The baby is offered a horehound drop, and I am slipped a dollar bill "to buy a treat." Questions trail off, answers are abandoned, the baby plays with the dust motes in a shaft of afternoon sun.

It is time for the baby's birthday party: a white cake, strawberry-marshmallow ice cream, a bottle of champagne saved from another party. In the evening, after she has gone to sleep, I kneel beside the crib and touch her face, where it is pressed against the slats, with mine. She is an open and trusting child, unprepared for and unaccustomed to the ambushes of family life, and perhaps it is just as well that I can offer her little of that life. I would like to give her more. I would like to promise her that she will grow up with a sense of her cousins and of rivers and of her great-grandmother's teacups, would like to pledge her a picnic on a river with fried chicken and her hair uncombed, would like to give her *home* for her birthday, but we live differently now and I can promise her nothing like that. I give her a xylophone and a sundress from Madeira, and promise to tell her a funny story.

NORMAN MAILER
1923–
A Statement for *Architectural Forum*

The essence of totalitarianism is that it beheads. It beheads individuality, variety, dissent, extreme possibility, romantic faith; it blinds vision, deadens instinct; it obliterates the past. It makes factories look like college campuses or mental hospitals, where once factories had the specific beauty of revealing their huge and sometimes brutal function. It makes the new buildings on college campuses look like factories. It depresses the average American with the unconscious recognition that he is installed in a gelatin of totalitarian environment which is bound to deaden his most individual efforts. This new architecture, this totalitarian architecture, destroys the past. There is no trace of the forms which lived in the centuries before us, none of their arrogance, their privilege, their aspiration, their canniness, their creations, their vulgarities. We are left with less and less sense of the lives of men and women who came before us. So we are less able to judge the psychotic values of the present: overkill, fallout shelters, and adjurations . . . to drink a glass of milk each day. . . .

People who admire the new architecture find it of value because it obliterates the past. They are sufficiently totalitarian to wish to avoid the consequences of the past. Which of course is not to say that they see themselves as totalitarian. The totalitarian passion is an unconscious one. Which liberal, fighting for bigger housing and additional cubic feet of air space in elementary schools, does not see himself as a benefactor? Can he comprehend that the somewhat clammy pleasure he obtains from looking at the completion of the new school—that architectural horror!—is a reflection of a buried and ugly pleasure, a totalitarian glee that the Gothic knots and Romanesque oppressions which entered his psyche through the schoolhouses of his youth have now been excised? But those architectural wounds, those forms from his childhood, not only shamed him and scored him, but marked upon him as well a wound from culture itself—its buried message of the cruelty and horror which were rooted in the majesties of the past. Now the flat surfaces, blank ornamentation, and pastel colors of the new schoolhouses will maroon his children in an endless hallway of the present. A school is an *arena* to a child. Let it look like what it should be, mysterious, even gladiatorial, rather than look like a reception center for war brides. The totalitarian impulse not only washes away distinctions but looks for a style in buildings, in clothing, and in the ornamentations of tools, appliances, and daily objects which will diminish one's sense of function and reduce one's sense of reality by reducing such emotions as awe, dread, beauty, pity, terror, calm, horror, and harmony. By dislocating us from the most powerful emotions of reality, totalitarianism leaves us further isolated in the empty landscapes of psychosis, precisely that inner landscape of void and dread which we flee by turning to totalitarian styles of life. The totalitarian liberal looks for new schools and more desks; the real liberal looks for more difficult books to force upon the curriculum. A good school can survive in a converted cow barn.

Yes, the people who admire the new architecture are looking to eject into their environment and landscape the same deadness and monotony life has put into them. A vast deadness and a huge monotony, a nausea without spasm, has been part of the profit of American life in the last fifteen years—we will pay in the next fifteen as this living death is disgorged into the buildings our totalitarian managers will manage to erect for us.

Our commodities are swollen in price by false, needless and useless labor. Modern architecture is the child of this fact. It works with a currency which (measured in terms of the skilled and/or useful labor going into a building) is worth half the real value of nineteenth-century money. The mechanical advances in construction hardly begin to make up for the wastes of advertising, public relations, building union covenants, city grafts, land costs, and the anemia of a dollar dimished by armaments and taxes. In this context the formulas of modern architecture have triumphed, and her bastards—those new office skyscrapers—proliferate everywhere: one suspects the best reason is that modern architecture offers a pretext to a large real-estate operator to stick up a skyscraper at a fraction of the money it should cost, so helps him to conceal the criminal fact that we are being given a stricken building, a denuded, aseptic, unfinished work, stripped of ornament, origins, prejudices, not even a peaked roof or spire to engage the heavens.

It is too cheap to separate Mafia architects with their Mussolini Modern (concrete dormitories on junior-college campuses) from serious modern architects. No, I think Le Corbusier and Wright and all the particular giants of the Bauhaus are the true villains; the Mafia architects are their proper sons; modern architecture at its best is even more anomalous than at its worst, for it tends to excite the Faustian and empty appetites of the architect's ego rather than reveal an artist's vision of our collective desire for shelter which is pleasurable, substantial, intricate, intimate, delicate, detailed, foibled, rich in gargoyle, guignol, false closet, secret stair, witch's hearth, attic, grandeur, kitsch, a world of buildings as diverse as the need within the eye. Beware: the ultimate promise of modern architecture is collective sightlessness for the species.

LEWIS THOMAS
1913–
The Iks

The small tribe of Iks, formerly nomadic hunters and gatherers in the mountain valleys of northern Uganda, have become celebrities, literary symbols for the ultimate fate of disheartened, heartless mankind at large. Two disastrously conclusive things happened to them: the government decided to have a national park, so they were compelled by law to give up hunting in the valleys and become famers on poor hillside soil, and then they were visited for two years by an anthropologist who detested them and wrote a book about them.

The message of the book is that the Iks have transformed themselves into an irreversibly disagreeable collection of unattached, brutish creatures, totally selfish and loveless, in response to the dismantling of their traditional culture. Moreover, this is what the rest of us are like in our inner selves, and we will all turn into Iks when the structure of our society comes all unhinged.

The argument rests, of course, on certain assumptions about the core of human beings, and is necessarily speculative. You have to agree in advance that man is fundamentally a bad lot, out for himself alone, displaying such graces as affection and compassion only as learned habits. If you take this view, the story of the Iks can be used to confirm it. These people seem to be living together, clustered in small, dense villages, but they are really solitary, unrelated individuals with no evident use for each other. They talk, but only to make ill-tempered demands and cold refusals. They share nothing. They never sing. They turn the children out to forage as soon as they can walk, and desert the elders to starve whenever they can, and the foraging children snatch food from the mouths of the helpless elders. It is a mean society.

They breed without love or even casual regard. They defecate on each other's doorsteps. They watch their neighbors for signs of misfortune, and only then do they laugh. In the book they do a lot of laughing, having so much bad luck. Several times they even laughed at the anthropologist, who found this especially repellent (one senses, between the lines, that the scholar is not himself the world's luckiest man). Worse, they took him into the family, snatched his food, defecated on his doorstep, and hooted dislike at him. They gave him two bad years.

It is a depressing book. If as he suggests, there is only Ikness at the center of each of us, our sole hope for hanging on to the name of humanity will be in endlessly mending the structure of our society, and it is changing so quickly and completely that we may never find the thread in time. Meanwhile, left to ourselves alone, solitary, we will become the same joyless, zestless, untouching lone animals.

But this may be too narrow a view. For one thing, the Iks are extraordinary. They are absolutely astonishing, in fact. The anthropologist has never seen people like them anywhere, nor have I. You'd think, if they were simply examples of the common essence of mankind, they'd seem more recognizable. Instead, they are bizarre, anomalous. I have known my share of peculiar, difficult, nervous, grabby people, but I've never encountered any genuinely, consistently detestable human beings in all my life. The Iks sound more like abnormalities, maladies.

I cannot accept it. I do not believe that the Iks are representative of isolated, revealed man, unobscured by social habits. I believe their behavior is something extra, something laid on. This unremitting, compulsive repellence is a kind of complicated ritual. They must have learned to act this way; they copied it, somehow.

I have a theory, then. The Iks have gone crazy.

The solitary Ik, isolated in the ruins of an exploded culture, has built a new defense for himself. If you live in an unworkable society you can make up one of your own, and this is what the Iks have done. Each Ik has become a group, a one-man tribe on its own, a constituency.

Now everything falls into place. This is why they do seem, after all, vaguely familiar to all of us. We've seen them before. This is precisely the way groups of one size or another, ranging from committees to nations, behave. It is, of course, this aspect of humanity that has lagged behind the rest of evolution, and this is why the Ik seems so primitive. In his absolute selfishness, his incapacity to give anything away, no matter what, he is a successful committee. When he stands at the door of his hut, shouting insults at his neighbors in a loud harangue, he is city addressing another city.

Cities have all the Ik characteristics. They defecate on doorsteps, in rivers and lakes, their own or anyone else's. They leave rubbish. They detest all neighboring cities, give nothing away. They even build institutions for deserting elders out of sight.

Nations are the most Iklike of all. No wonder the Iks seem familiar. For total greed, rapacity, heartlessness, and irresponsibility there is nothing to match a nation. Nations, by law, are solitary, self-centered, withdrawn into themselves. There is no such thing as affection between nations, and certainly no nation ever loved another. They bawl insults from their doorsteps, defecate into whole oceans, snatch all the food, survive by detestation, take joy in the bad luck of others, celebrate the death of others, live for the death of others.

That's it, and I shall stop worrying about the book. It does not signify that man is a sparse, inhuman thing at his center. He's all right. It only says what we've always known and never had enough time to worry about, that we haven't yet learned how to stay human when assembled in masses. The Ik, in his despair, is acting out this failure, and perhaps we should pay closer attention. Nations have themselves become too frightening to think about, but we might learn some things by watching these people.

ANNIE DILLARD
1945–
The Death of a Moth

Transfiguration in a Candle Flame

I live alone with two cats, who sleep on my legs. There is a yellow one, and a black one whose name is Small. In the morning I joke to the black one, Do you remember last night? Do you remember? I throw them both out before breakfast, so I can eat.

There is a spider, too, in the bathroom, of uncertain lineage, bulbous at the abdomen and drab, whose six-inch mess of web works, works somehow, works miraculously, to keep her alive and me amazed. The web is in a corner behind the toilet, connecting tile wall to tile wall. The house is new, the bathroom immaculate, save for the spider, her web, and the sixteen or so corpses she's tossed to the floor.

The corpses appear to be mostly sow bugs, those little armadillo creatures who live to travel flat out in houses, and die round. In addition to sow-bug husks, hollow and sipped empty of color, there are what seem to be two or three wingless moth bodies, one new flake of earwig, and three spider carcasses crinkled and clenched.

I wonder on what fool's errand an earwig, or a moth, or a sow bug, would visit that clean corner of the house behind the toilet; I have not noticed any blind parades of sow bugs blundering into corners. Yet they do hazard there, at a rate of more than one a week, and the spider thrives. Yesterday she was working on the earwig, mouth on gut; today he's on the floor. It must take a certain genius to throw things away from there, to find a straight line through that sticky tangle to the floor.

Today the earwig shines darkly, and gleams, what there is of him: a dorsal curve of thorax and abdomen, and a smooth pair of pincers by which I knew his name. Next week, if the other bodies are any indication, he'll be shrunk and gray, webbed to the floor with dust. The sow bugs beside him are curled and empty, fragile, a breath away from brittle fluff. The spiders lie on their sides, translucent and ragged, their legs drying in knots. The moths stagger against each other, headless, in a confusion of arcing strips of chitin like peeling varnish, like a jumble of buttresses for cathedral vaults, like nothing resembling moths, so that I would hesitate to call them moths, except that I have had some experience with the figure Moth reduced to a nub.

Two summers ago I was camped alone in the Blue Ridge Mountains of Virginia. I had hauled myself and gear up there to read, among other things, *The Day on Fire*, by James Ullman, a novel about Rimbaud that had made me want to be a writer when I was sixteen; I was hoping it would do it again. So I read every day sitting under a tree by my tent, while warblers sang in the leaves overhead and bristle worms trailed their inches over the twiggy dirt at my feet; and I read every night by candlelight, while barred owls called in the forest and pale moths seeking mates massed round my head in the clearing, where my light made a ring.

Moths kept flying into the candle. They would hiss and recoil, reeling upside down in the shadows among my cooking pans. Or they would singe their wings and fall, and their hot wings, as if melted, would stick to the first thing they touched—a pan, a lid, a spoon—so that the snagged moths could struggle only in tiny arcs, unable to flutter free. These I could release by a quick flip with a stick; in the morning I would find my cooking stuff decorated with torn flecks of moth wings, ghostly triangles of shiny dust here and there on the aluminum. So I read, and boiled water, and replenished candles, and read on.

One night a moth flew into the candle, was caught, burnt dry, and held. I must have been staring at the candle, or maybe I looked up where a shadow crossed my page; at any rate, I saw it all. A golden female moth, a biggish one with a two-inch wingspread, flapped into the fire, dropped abdomen into the wet wax, stuck, flamed, and frazzled in a second. Her moving wings ignited like tissue paper, like angels' wings, enlarging the circle of light in the clearing and creating out of the darkness the sudden blue sleeves of my sweater, the green leaves of jewelweed by my side, the ragged red trunk of a pine; at once the light contracted again and the moth's wings vanished in a fine, foul smoke. At the same time, her six legs clawed, curled, blackened, and ceased, disappearing utterly. And her head jerked in spasms, making a spattering noise; her antennae crisped and burnt away and her heaving mouthparts cracked like pistol fire. When it was all over, her head was, so far as I could determine, gone, gone the long way of her wings and legs. Her head was a hole lost to time. All that was left was the glowing horn shell of her abdomen and thorax—a fraying, partially collapsed gold tube jammed upright in the candle's round pool.

And then this moth-essence, this spectacular skeleton, began to act as a wick. She kept burning. The wax rose in the moth's body from her soaking abdomen to her thorax to the shattered hole where her head should have been, and widened into flame, a saffron-yellow flame that robed her to the ground like an immolating monk. That candle had two wicks, two winding flames of identical light, side by side. The moth's head was fire. She burned for two hours, until I blew her out.

She burned for two hours without changing, without swaying or kneeling—only glowing within, like a building fire glimpsed through silhouetted walls, like a hollow saint, like a flame-faced virgin gone to God, while I read by her light, kindled, while Rimbaud in Paris burnt out his brain in a thousand poems, while night pooled wetly at my feet.

So. That is why I think those hollow shreds on the bathroom floor are moths. I believe I know what moths look like, in any state.

I have three candles here on the table which I disentangle from the plants and light when visitors come. The cats avoid them, although Small's tail caught fire once; I rubbed it out before she noticed. I don't mind living alone. I like eating alone and reading. I don't mind sleeping alone. The only time I mind being alone is when something is funny; then, when I am laughing at something funny, I wish someone were around. Sometimes I think it is pretty funny that I sleep alone.

2
FICTION

The Elements of Fiction

FICTION, FACT, AND TRUTH

A fiction is a made-up story. This definition covers a lot of territory. It includes the homemade lies we tell to protect ourselves from annoying scrutiny, and the casual jokes we hear and re-tell as polite (or impolite) conversation, as well as great visionary works of literature like Milton's *Paradise Lost* or the Bible itself. Yes, we are saying that the Bible is fiction; but before you either bristle with smug piety or nod with complacent skepticism, read a few words more. The Bible is fiction because it is a made-up story. This does not mean that it necessarily lacks truth. Nor does it mean that the Bible may not contain fact. The relation between fact and fiction is by no means as simple as one might think; and, since it is very important to an understanding of fiction, it must be considered with some care.

Fact and fiction are old acquaintances. They are both derivatives of Latin words. Fact comes from *facere*—to make or do. Fiction comes from *fingere*—to make or shape. Plain enough words, one would think—not necessarily loaded with overtones of approval or disapproval. But their fortunes in the world of words have not been equal. Fact has prospered. In our ordinary conversation, "fact" is associated with those pillars of verbal society, "reality" and "truth." "Fiction," on the other hand, is known to consort with such suspicious characters as "unreality" and "falsehood." Still, if we look into the matter, we can see that the relation of "fact" and "fiction" with "the real" and "the true" is not exactly what appears on the surface. Fact still means for us quite literally "a thing done." And fiction has never lost its meaning of "a thing made." But in what sense do things done or things made partake of truth or reality? A thing done has no real existence once it has been done. It may have consequences, and there may be many records that point to its former existence (think of the Civil War, for example); but once it is done its existence is finished. A thing made, on the other hand, exists until it decays or is destroyed. Once it is finished, its existence begins (think of a Civil War story like Stephen Crane's *Red Badge of Courage*, for example). Fact, finally, has no real existence, while fiction may last for centuries.

We can see this rather strange relation between fact and fiction more clearly if we consider one place where the two come together: the place we call history. The word "history" itself hides a double meaning. It comes from a Greek word that originally meant inquiry or investigation. But it soon acquired the two meanings that interest us here: on the one hand, history can mean "things that have happened"; on the other, it can refer to "a recorded version of things that are supposed to have happened." That is, history can mean both the events of the past and the story of these events: fact—or fiction. The very word "story" lurks in the word "history," and is derived from it. What begins as investigation must end as story. Fact, in order to survive, must become fiction. Seen in this way, fiction is not the opposite of fact, but its complement. It gives a more lasting shape to the vanishing deeds of men.

But this is, in fact, only one aspect of fiction. We *do* think of it also as something quite different from historical records or mere data. We think of it not just as made but as made-up, a non-natural, unreal product of the human imagination. It is helpful to see fiction in both the ways outlined here. It can be very factual, maintaining the closest possible correspondence between its story and things that have actually happened in the world. Or it can be very fanciful, defying our sense of life's ordinary possibilities.

Taking these two extremes as the opposite ends of a whole spectrum of fictional possibilities, between the infra-red of pure history and the ultra-violet of pure imagination, we can distinguish many shades of coloration. But all are fragments of the white radiance of truth, which is present in both history books and fairy tales, but only partly present in each—fragmented by the prism of fiction, without which we should not be able to see it at all. For truth is like ordinary light, present everywhere but invisible, and we must break it to behold it. To fracture truth in a purposeful and pleasing way—that is the job of the writer of fiction, with whatever shades from the spectrum he or she chooses to work.

FICTION: EXPERIENCE AND ANALYSIS

Though fiction itself has a real existence—a book has weight and occupies space—our experience of fiction is unreal. When we are reading a story we are not "doing" anything. We have stopped the ordinary course of our existence, severed our connections with friends and family, in order to withdraw temporarily into a private and unreal world. Our experience of fiction is more like dreaming than like our normal waking activity. It makes us physically inert yet exercises our imagination. In terms of our performing any action in it, this special world is absolutely unreal, whether we are reading a history book or a science fiction story. We can do nothing to affect either the Battle of Waterloo or the War of the Worlds. And yet, in a way, we participate. We are engaged and involved in the events we are reading about, even though powerless to alter them. We *experience* the events of a story, but without the consequences—emerging from John Hersey's *Hiroshima*, for example, without a scratch on our bodies. Emotionally, however, and intellectually, we are different. We have experienced something.

All discussion of literature, all classes and instruction in literary matters, can have only one valid end: to prepare us for our part in the literary experience. Just as the dull routine exercises and repetitive practice for an athletic event or a dramatic performance are devoted to the end of physical and mental readiness for the actual game or play, exercises in literature are preparations for the act of reading. The successful athlete must do much "instinctively," moving faster than thought to make the most of his time. The painstaking analysis of "game movies" by football coach and players, the searching criticism of each player's reactions to every situation, the drill to counteract past errors—all these wait upon the test of the game itself. Then ability, experience, and training will reveal their quality. It is similar with reading. Classroom, teacher, the artificially assembled anthology—all these must give place to that final confrontation between individual reader and story. Except that this is not a struggle like an athletic contest, but something more intimate and more rewarding. Ideally, it is a kind of consummation—an embrace.

Everything that follows in this section is intended to help readers toward an enriched experience of fiction. Such special terminology as is presented is presented not because critical terminology is an important object of study. Its acquisition is not an end in itself. We learn terminology in order to analyze more accurately. We learn the process of analysis in order to read better.

THE SPECTRUM OF FICTION

The fictional spectrum mentioned earlier can be of use in the analysis of fiction, so long as we remember that it is just a metaphor, a handy linguistic tool to be discarded when it becomes more of a hindrance to understanding than a help. In terms of this metaphor, you will remember, it was possible to think of fiction as resembling the spectrum of color to be found in ordinary light, but in the fictional spectrum the ends were not infra-red and ultra-violet but history and fantasy.

Now only a recording angel, taking note of all the deeds of men without distorting or omitting anything, could be called a "pure" historian. And only a kind of deity, creating a world out of his own imagination, could be called a "pure" fantasist. Both ends of the spectrum are invisible to mortal eyes. All history recorded by men becomes fictional. All human fantasy involves some resemblance—however far-fetched—to life. For the student of fiction, then, the *combination* of historical and imaginative materials becomes crucial. This is so because our understanding of fiction depends on our grasping the way in which any particular work is related to life.

Life itself is neither tragic nor comic, neither sentimental nor ironic. It is a sequence of sensations, action, thoughts, and events that we try to tame with language. Every time we say a word about our existence we are engaged in this taming process. An art like fiction is a highly developed method of domestication, in which life is not merely subdued but is asked to perform tricks as well. The tricks, if well done, please us in a very complicated way. In the first place they *please* because their order and intelligibility are a welcome relief from the confusions and pressures of daily existence. In the second place this artificial order may be mastered by us and used to help *make sense of our own experience.* Having read Hemingway or Lawrence, we will begin to recognize certain situations in our existence as having a family resemblance to situations we have encountered in the pages of Lawrence or Hemingway.

Literature offers us an "escape" from life, but also provides us with new equipment for our inevitable return. It offers us an "imitation" of life. It helps us understand life, and life helps us understand fiction. We recognize aspects of ourselves and our situations in the more ordered perspectives of fiction, and we also see ideal and debased extremes of existence—both possible and impossible—that are interesting in themselves and interestingly different from our own experience. Fiction interests us because of the complicated ways in which it is at once like and unlike life—which is what we mean when we call it an "imitation." Our experience of fiction, then, involves both pleasure and understanding. We may think of understanding either as a result of the pleasurable experience of fiction or as a necessary preliminary to that pleasure. But no matter how we view the complicated relation between pleasure and understanding, we must recognize that the two are inseparable in the reading of fiction.

Now it happens that education has more to do with understanding than with pleasure. This is regrettable, perhaps, but unavoidable. In our study of fiction, then, we must concentrate on understanding, and hope that pleasure will follow because of the connection between the two. Understanding a work of fiction begins with recognizing what kind of fiction it is. This is where the notion of a spectrum becomes useful. We can adjust to the special qualities of any given work more readily if we begin it with a clear and flexible view of fictional possibilities.

Any attempt to give every shade of fiction a place would be cumbersome and misleading. What we want is a rough scale only, with the primary possibilities noted and located in relation to one another. Between the extremes of history and fantasy on such a scale we might locate two major points of reference something like this:

history   realism   romance   fantasy

"Realism" and "romance" are names of the two principal ways that fiction can be related to life. Realism is a matter of perception. The realist presents his impressions of the world of experience. A part of his vocabulary and other technical instruments he shares with the social scientists—especially the psychologists and sociologists. The realistic writer seeks always to give the reader a sense of the way things are, but he feels that a made-up structure of character and event can do better justice to the way things are than any attempt to copy reality directly. The realist's truth is a bit more general and typical than the reporter's fact. It may also be more vivid and memorable.

Romance is a matter of vision. The romancer presents not so much his impressions of the world as his ideas about it. The ordinary world is seen at a greater distance, and its shape and color are deliberately altered by the lenses and filters of philosophy and fantasy. In the world of romance, ideas are allowed to play less encumbered by data. Yet, though "what is" often gives way in romance to "what ought to be" or "might be," *ought* and *might* always imply what *is* by their distortion of it.

Realism and romance are not absolutely different: they share some qualities between them. Realism itself is more romantic than history or journalism. (It is not reality, after all, but real*ism*.) And romance is more realistic than fantasy. Many important works of fiction are rich and complicated blends of romance and realism. In fact, it is possible to say that the greatest works are those that successfully blend the realist's perception and the romancer's vision, giving us fictional worlds remarkably close to our sense of the actual, but skillfully shaped so as to make us intensely aware of the meaningful potential of existence.

FICTIONAL MODES AND PATTERNS

The usefulness of the concept of a fictional spectrum will depend upon our ability to adapt it to various works of fiction. Such adaptation will inevitably require a certain amount of complication. The additional concepts of fictional modes and patterns will be a step in that direction. The spectrum assumed that romance diverges from realism in one way only, along that line which leads from history to fantasy. But it is possible to see this divergence in a more complete way by observing that there are actually two quite different modes of what we have been calling romance.

We may begin by noting that there are two obvious ways that reality can be distorted by fiction, that it can be made to appear better or worse than we actually believe it to be. These distortions are ways of seeing certain aspects of reality more clearly at the expense of others. They can present a "true" picture of either the heroic or the debased side of human existence. A fictional work that presents a world better than the real world is in the mode of romance. A work that presents a fictional world worse than the real world is in the mode of anti-romance, or satire. Because they represent certain potentialities that we recognize as present in our world, both these distorted views depend on our sense of the actual to achieve their effects.

The world of romance emphasizes beauty and order. The world of satire emphasizes ugliness and disorder. The relations between individual characters and these distorted worlds constitute a crucial element of fiction, for these relations determine certain patterns or master plots that affect the shaping of the particular plot of every story. One of these master patterns deals with the kind of character who begins out of harmony with his world and is gradually educated or initiated into a harmonious situation in it. This pattern may operate in either the ordered world of romance or the chaotic world of satire, but the same pattern will have a quite different effect on us when we observe it working out in such different situations. Education that adapts the inept or foolish character for a role in the orderly world presents a comic rise that we observe with approval and pleasure. An initiation into a world of ugliness and disorder, however, amounts to corruption, an ironic rise to what Milton called a "bad eminence"; and we react with disapproval and disgust. (For some reason we find both reactions pleasurable.)

Another master pattern reverses this process of accommodation and presents us with change of another sort: the character who begins in harmony with his world but is finally rejected or destroyed by it. Again, depending on our view of the world presented, we react differently. The heroic figure who falls from his position in the orderly world through some flaw in his character is *tragic*. The lowly creature whose doom is the result of his unfortunate virtue or delicacy is *pathetic*. His fall is, ironically, a kind of rise. (It is traditionally assumed, for complicated reasons, that tragedy is superior to pathos. That assumption is not made here. These patterns are presented as descriptions only, not evaluations.)

The *comic* rise and the *tragic* fall are straightforward because the values of the orderly world represent human virtue raised to a heroic power. The *satiric* rise and *pathetic* fall are ironic because of the inverted values of the debased world. Satire and pathos debase the world in order to criticize it. Tragedy and comedy elevate it to make it acceptable. The two romantic patterns promote resignation. The two satiric patterns promote opposition.

One other pair of fictional patterns may be added to the two already considered. When characters begin and end in a harmonious relation to their respective worlds, the fictional pattern is one not of change but of movement. The characters will have adventures or encounters but will not make any fundamental change in themselves or their relation to the world around them. In this kind of story the hero himself will not be as important as the things he meets. In the romantic world the adventures of the hero will take the form of a quest or voyage that ends with his triumphant return and/or his marriage to the heroine. This pattern moves us to admiration of the wonderful, offering us more of an escape from the actual than a criticism of it. In the satiric world the adventures of a born anti-hero or rogue will parody the quest pattern, often reflecting the chaos of the debased world by becoming endless themselves. Stories of this kind are likely to end when the rogue heads for new territory or another tour of the familiar chaos. This picaresque pattern moves us to recognition and acceptance of the chaotic.

Thus, we have distinguished three pairs of fictional patterns, or six kinds in all: the comic and the satiric rise; the tragic and the pathetic fall; the heroic (romantic) and the anti-heroic (picaresque) quest. But we have done this only with regard to the fantasy worlds of romance and satire, leaving open the question of what happens as these patterns are introduced into a more realistic fictional universe. What happens is, naturally, very complicated indeed. These neat, schematic distinctions fade; the various patterns combine and interact; and values themselves are called into question: rise and fall, success and failure—all become problematic. And this problematic quality is one of the great sources of interest in realistic fiction. Realism uses the familiar patterns of education, expulsion, and quest, but often in such a way as to call into question the great issues of whether the education is beneficial, the expulsion or death justified, the quest worthwhile. Our recognition of the traces of traditional patterns in realistic fiction will be of use, then, mainly in helping us to see what questions are being raised.

Viewed historically, realism developed later than romance and satire; thus it will be useful for us to see realistic fiction as combining the elements of its predecessors in various ways. It would be a mistake, however, to think of realism as superseding the earlier forms just because it uses some of their elements in a new way. In fact, the development of realism has led to a kind of counterflow of realistic elements into the older forms of fiction, re-invigorating them with its problematical qualities. The reader of contemporary fiction in particular will require the flexibility of response that can be attained by careful attention to the workings of traditional patterns in modern fiction. But our discernment of these patterns in any work of fiction will depend on our grasp of the specific elements of that work. We must be alert to the way that *its* characters, *its* plot, and *its* point of view adapt the traditional elements we have been considering.

PLOT

Fiction is movement. A story is a story because it tells about a process of change. A person's situation changes. Or the person is changed in some way. Or our understanding of the person changes. These are the essential movements of fiction. Learning to read stories involves learning to "see" these movements, to follow them, and to interpret them. In the classroom we often—perhaps too often—put our emphasis on interpretation. But you cannot interpret what you cannot see. Thus, before getting into more complicated questions of interpretation, we want to give the plainest and most direct advice possible about how to perceive and follow fictional plotting. This advice includes things to be done while reading and things to be done after a first reading. A good story may be experienced pleasurably many times, and often a second or third reading will be more satisfying in every respect than the first time through.

1. *Look at beginnings and endings.* Movement in fiction is always movement *from* and *to*. A grasp of the start and the finish should lead to a sense of the direction taken to get *from* start *to* finish.

2. *Isolate the central characters.* The things that happen in fiction happen *to* somebody. A few major characters or even a single central character may be the real focus of our concern. Explore the situation of the major characters (or central character) at the beginning and at the end of the story. The nature of the changes revealed by this exploration should begin to suggest what the story is all about.

3. *Note the stages in all important changes.* If a character has moved from one situation to another, or one state of mind to another, the steps leading to the completed change should be illuminating. Through them the reader can get to "how" and "why." But, as always, "what" comes first.

4. *Note the things working against the movement of the story.* Usually, the interest of a story may be seen as the product of two forces: the things that work to move it toward its end, and those that work against that movement, delaying its completion. If the story moves toward a marriage, for example, consider what things delay the happy occasion. When we see the obstacles clearly, we should have a better sense of the direction of the plot itself.

5. *In a long story or novel, consider the various lines of action.* A complex fiction is likely to involve a number of actions, each with its own central character. The actions may or may not interact. The central character in one line of action may be insignificant in another. By isolating the various lines of action and separating them from one another in our

thoughts, we should gain a better sense of those things that connect them. Often these connections will lead us to thematic relations that cast a direct light on the meaning of the whole fiction.

6. *Note carefully characters or events that seem to make no contribution to plot or movement.* This negative advice is a way of moving from the plot to the meaning of a story. Often elements that are not important in the plot have a special thematic importance.

CHARACTER

The greatest mistake we can make in dealing with characters in fiction is to insist on their "reality." No character in a book is a real person. Not even if he is in a history book and is called Ulysses S. Grant. Characters in fiction are *like* real people. They are also unlike them. In realistic fiction, which includes most novels and short stories, writers have tried to emphasize the lifelikeness of their characters. This means that such writers have tried to surround these characters with details drawn from contemporary life. And they have tried to restrict the events of their narrative to things likely to happen in ordinary life. As a result, the writers of realistic fiction have had to abandon certain kinds of plots that are too fanciful for characters supposed to typify ordinary life. Such writers have tried to draw the reader away from his interest in the movement of fiction and to lead him toward an interest in character for its own sake.

Using the newly developed ideas we have learned to call psychology and sociology, the realistic writers have offered us instruction in human nature. The motivation of characters, the workings of conscience and consciousness, have been made the focal point of most novels and short stories. Perhaps the most extreme movement in this direction has been the development of the stream of consciousness technique, through which fiction writers offer us a version of mental process at the level where impressions of things seen and heard converge with confused thoughts and longings arising from the subconscious mind. In reading this kind of fiction we must check the validity of its characterization against our own sense of the way people behave. The best realists always offer us a shock of recognition through which we share their perception of human behavior.

It may be useful for us to think of character as a function of two impulses: the impulse to individualize and the impulse to typify. Great and memorable characters are the result of a powerful combination of these two impulses. We remember the special, individualizing quirks—habitual patterns of speech, action, or appearance—and we remember the way the character represents something larger than himself. These individualizing touches are part of the storyteller's art. They amuse us or engage our sympathy for the character. The typifying touches are part of a story's meaning. In realistic fiction a character is likely to be representative of a social class, a race, a profession; or he may be a recognizable psychological type, analyzable in terms of this or that "complex" or "syndrome." Or he may be a mixture of social and psychological qualities. In allegorical fiction the characters are more likely to represent philosophical positions. In a story of adventure we will encounter types belonging to the traditional pattern of romantic quest: hero, heroine, villain, monster.

The important thing for a reader to remember about characterization is that there are many varieties—and many combinations of the varieties. An adventure story may have an important realistic or allegorical dimension that will be observable in its characterizations. Characters in realistic novels may also be meaningful as illustrations of philosophical ideas or attitudes. As readers we must be alert and ready to respond to different kinds of characterization on their own terms. A story by Jorge Luis Borges and a story by James Joyce are not likely to yield equally to the same kind of reading. It is the reader's business to adapt himself to whatever fictional world he enters. It is the writer's business to make such adaptation worthwhile.

MEANING

More often than not, when we talk about a story after our experience of it, we talk about its meaning. In the classroom, "What is the theme of this work?" is a favorite question. This interpretive aspect of literary analysis is the most difficult, we should say, for the reason that in order to attempt it we must not only look carefully at the work itself but also look away from the work toward the world of ideas and experiences. Discovering themes or meanings in a work involves us in making connections between the work and the world outside it. These connections *are* the meaning. The great problem for the interpreter, then, becomes that of the validity of the thematic materials he discovers. Are these ideas *really* there? we want to know. Are they being "read out" of the story or "read into" it? Is any given set of connections between story and world necessarily implied by the story itself or are they arbitrarily imposed by an overly clever interpreter?

A story is always particular, always an instance. How do we properly move from any given instance to a general notion? When is it legitimate to conclude from the presence of a husband and wife in a story (for example) that the story is "about" marriage—that it makes a statement or raises a question about this aspect of human relations? It is impossible to provide a single method that will always work. In fact, as T. S. Eliot once observed, "There is no method except to be very intelligent." But there are certain procedures that will frequently prove helpful, even for the very intelligent.

If we isolate everything that is not just narration, description, or dialogue, some clues are likely to appear in a story. The title of a work is often a striking instance of this kind of material. Sometimes it will point our thinking about the work in a particular direction, or it will emphasize for us the importance of a particular element in the work. Like the title, passages in the writing that are themselves commentary or interpretation are of especial importance for thematic discussion.

Often, however, interpretive passages will not be presented directly by a narrator, with all his authority behind them. They will be spoken instead by a character, and this means that we must assess the reliability of the character before we decide to accept his interpretation as valid. Sometimes the narrator will be characterized to the extent that we must question even *his* reliability. In similar ways narration and description may also be colored by thematic materials. A character or a scene may be presented by the author so as to lead us toward a certain way of thinking about the materials presented. A school called "Dotheboys Hall" or a teacher named "Gradgrind" is presented to us with a name that carries some not too subtle advice as to how we are to understand the presentation.

In less obvious cases, where the author refrains from direct commentary, we must look for subtler clues. Patterns of repetition, ironic juxtaposition, the tone of the narration—devices like these must lead us to the connections between the particular world of the book and the generalized world of ideas. And the more delicate and subtle the story is, the more delicate our interpretation must be. Thus, taking care that our interpretation is rooted in the work itself is only one aspect of the problem.

The other aspect involves the outside knowledge that the interpreter brings to the work. If the story is realistic it will be understood best by those readers whose experience has equipped them with information about the aspect of reality toward which the story points. This does not mean that one must have lived the life of a black American to understand "Battle Royal" or "Sonny's Blues." But these stories do depend on the reader's having some understanding of injustice and prejudice, and some sense of the way impersonal social forces can act destructively upon individuals and even whole groups of human beings.

Often a realistic story may point to an aspect of life we have encountered but never understood, and the fiction may help us clarify and order that experience. D. H. Lawrence's story "The Christening" can teach us something about personal relations, especially the way that a strong father can dominate and inhibit the lives of his children, causing them to hate him. But Lawrence requires us to bring some experience of family life to that story, for without that it must remain virtually meaningless for the reader. Fantasy and adventure are the principal ingredients of the child's literary diet, for the reason that the child lacks the experience that would make realism meaningful to him, and he lacks the learning necessary for the interpretation of complex allegorical fiction.

Often, however, allegorical fiction takes the form of fantasy or adventure, so that it can be read by the child "at one level" and by the adult on two.

Jonathan Swift's *Gulliver's Travels* has been read in that way for over two centuries. D. H. Lawrence's "The Rocking-Horse Winner" is an exciting story about a boy with a kind of magical power, but it is also a criticism of an excessively materialistic society. Kurt Vonnegut's "Harrison Bergeron" may seem to be just a strangely imagined vision of the future, and yet it asks to be read as an allegory that raises questions about the ability of a country like the United States to deliver on its promises to equalize human life while promoting human freedom. We call such modern allegories "fabulation," and we recognize their ancient ancestors in the simple fable and the homely parable. These two early forms of fiction will be discussed in the next part of this section, and a number of examples of modern fabulation will be found in the anthology of short stories that concludes our study of fiction.

Fiction generates its meanings in innumerable ways, but always in terms of some movement from the particular characters and events of the story to general ideas or human situations suggested by them. The reader comes to an understanding of a fictional work by locating the relevant generalities outside the work and fitting them to the specific instances within the work. The process of understanding can be crudely represented as a sequence something like this:

1. The reader determines whether the work points mainly toward experience itself (i.e., is "realistic"), or toward ideas about experience (i.e., is "allegorical"), or is self-contained.

2. Using the clues in the work, the reader sifts his or her store of general notions drawn from experience or systematic thought to find those appropriate to the specific materials of the story.

3. He or she checks back against the story to test the relevance of the general notions summoned up.

4. He or she seeks for the way the story refines, qualifies, questions, or reinforces those notions.

Something like the process described—performed not a single time but in rapid oscillation into the work and back out—should leave the reader with an understanding of the story and with an enriched store of general notions that he has been led to develop in order to understand. In addition to acquiring new notions, the reader may have refined his attitudes toward his old notions and toward experience itself. Fiction is justified not as a means of conveying ideas but as a means of generating attitudes toward ideas. The meaning of fiction must finally be seen in terms of emotions directed toward impressions of experience or toward ideas about life.

POINT OF VIEW: PERSPECTIVE AND LANGUAGE

Point of view is a technical term for the way a story is told. A stage play normally has no particular point of view: no one stands between the audience and the action. But if we *read* a play, the stage directions—the words of someone who is not a character—provide the beginnings of a special point of view. A story told all in dialogue would be similarly without a point of view. But as soon as a descriptive phrase is added—such as "he said *cruelly*" or "she *whined viciously*"—we begin to have a special viewpoint. A voice outside the action is reaching us, shaping our attitude toward the events being presented. In our experience of fiction, the attitude we develop toward the events presented, and our understanding of those events, will usually be controlled by the author through his or her technical management of point of view.

For convenience we may divide the subject of fictional viewpoint into two related parts—one dealing with the nature of the storyteller in any given fiction, the other dealing with his language. Obviously the two are not really separate. Certain kinds of narration require certain kinds of language—Huck Finn must talk like Huck Finn—but we may consider them apart for analytical purposes.

The nature of the storyteller is itself far from a simple matter. It involves such things as the extent to which he is himself a character whose personality affects our understanding of his statements, and the extent to which his view of events is limited in time and space or in his ability to see into the minds of various characters. The complications and refinements in fictional point of view can be classified at considerable length. But for the reader the classifications themselves are less important than his awareness of many possibilities. The reader's problem comes down to knowing how to take the things presented to him. This means paying special attention to any limitations in the narrator's viewpoint. If the viewpoint in the story is "partial"—in the sense of incomplete or in the sense of biased—the reader must be ready to compensate in appropriate ways.

The language of narration presents a similar problem for the reader—that is, a problem of adjustment and compensation. Of all the dimensions of language that can be considered, two are especially important for the reader of fiction. Both these dimensions may be seen as ways in which wit—or artistic intelligence—operates through language. One has to do with *tone*, or the way unstated attitudes are conveyed through language. The other has to do with *metaphor*, or the way language can convey the richest and most delicate kinds of understanding by bringing together different images and ideas. Consider first this small passage from Virginia Woolf's novel *Mrs. Dalloway:*

> But Sir William Bradshaw stopped at the door to look at a picture. He looked
> in the corner for the engraver's name. His wife looked too. Sir William
> Bradshaw was so interested in art.

What is the tone of this? Sarcastic, we should say. The paragraph asks us to be critical of the Bradshaws, but it does not do so directly. It uses the indirection of verbal irony in which the real meaning is different from the apparent sense of the words. The last sentence might be read aloud with a drawn-out emphasis on the word "soooo." How do we know this? How do we supply the appropriate tone of voice for words that we see on the page but do not hear prounounced? We pay attention to the clues given. In *Mrs. Dalloway* the Bradshaws appear in a similar light several times; so that by this, their last appearance, we have been prepared to regard them unsympathetically. But just on the strength of these four sentences we should be able to catch the tone.

The banal "Dick and Jane" sentence patterns reinforce the banality of an approach to art by way of the artist's name. Sir William looks not at the picture itself but at the signature. The implication of this action is that (a) he cannot tell who the artist is by considering the work alone, and (b) he attaches too much importance to the name. His interest in art is fraudulent. Thus, the statement that he is "so" interested in art conflicts with both the actions narrated and the tone of the narration. We resolve the conflict by reading the sentence as *ironic,* meaning the opposite of what it seems to say, and acquiring thereby a sarcastic tone. The way his wife's behavior mechanically mimics his own adds another satiric dimension to the little scene.

As an earlier passage in the novel has revealed, she has no life of her own but has been reduced by him to the status of an object:

> Fifteen years ago she had gone under. It was nothing you could put your
> finger on; there had been no scene, no snap; only the slow sinking,
> water-logged, of her will into his.

Thus, the short sentence—"His wife looked too"—picks up the earlier statement about the "submersion" of her will in his, and reminds us of it with satiric brevity. Catching the tone of a passage in a matter of paying attention to clues in sentence pattern and choice of words, and also of keeping in mind the whole context of the story we are reading. The more we read a particular author, the better we become at catching her tone—at perceiving the emotional shades that color the sense of her words.

The second passage quoted from *Mrs. Dalloway* (which comes first in the book) is also a good introductory example of a writer's use of metaphor. The expression "gone under" has been used often enough to refer to defeat or failure—so often, in fact, that it is quite possible to use it without any sense that it is metaphorical. But actually the notion of drowning—going under water to the point of death—is present in the expression. A writer who, like

Virginia Woolf, is sensitive to metaphor, can pick up the submerged (!) implications of such an expression and use them to strengthen her meaning: "the slow sinking, water-logged, of her will into his." The metaphor—which implicitly compares her to a floating object and him to the engulfing waters—conveys a sense of how slowly and inexorably this process has taken place, and it generates in us an appropriate feeling of horror at a human being's lingering destruction.

Similar metaphors can be used in different ways. In another part of the same novel, Virginia Woolf employs the metaphor of drowning in a related but distinct context. When Peter Walsh, who wanted to marry Clarissa Dalloway in his youth, returns from India to tell her that he is in love with a young woman whom he intends to marry, Mrs. Dalloway reacts in this way:

> "In love!" she said. That he at his age should be sucked under in his little bow-tie by that monster! And there's no flesh on his neck; his hands are red; and he's six months older than I am! her eye flashed back to her; but in her heart she felt, all the same, he is in love. He has that, she felt; he is in love.

Love is seen here as a monstrous whirlpool that sucks people under. It is dangerous and destructive: one loses one's identity when sucked in by that monster. But it is also heroic to be involved in such dangerous matters. While her "eye" tells Mrs. Dalloway that Peter is unheroic and even ridiculous, with his little bow tie and skinny neck, her "heart" accepts the heroism of this venture. It is absurd to "be sucked under" in a "little bow-tie," but it is also intensely real: "He has that, she felt; he is in love." By comparing these two metaphors of drowning we can see more accurately certain dimensions of Virginia Woolf's view of marriage: it involves a submergence or submission, but a violent conquest by an emotional whirlpool is superior to a "slow sinking, water-logged," of one will into another. We need not go outside the novel to understand this discrimination, but when we learn or remember that in a state of depression Ms. Woolf took her own life by drowning, we get a hint of why this metaphor has such intensity in her hands.

These uses of the metaphor of drowning are actually just brief examples of the way metaphorical possibilities can be exploited in the language of fiction. We present now a fuller example of metaphorical development, for the student to explore. Marcel Proust's multi-volume novel, *The Remembrance of Things Past*, is constructed upon the recovery of the past in the memory of the central character and narrator, Marcel. The process of recollection is described in a famous passage in which, on being given a piece of cake (a *madeleine*) dipped in tea, Marcel suddenly finds that the taste of this morsel has brought to mind much that he had forgotten. In the part of this passage quoted here, Marcel first discusses the persistence of sensations of taste and smell, and then considers the manner in which recollection can emerge from these sensations. The passage should be read with an eye to the metaphors (including similes) operative in it:

> But when from a long-distant past nothing subsists, after the people are dead, after the things are broken and scattered, still, alone, more fragile, but with more vitality, more unsubstantial, more persistent, more faithful, the smell and taste of things remain poised a long time, like souls, ready to remind us, waiting and hoping for their moment, amid the ruins of all the rest; and bear unfaltering, in the tiny and almost impalpable drop of their essence, the vast structure of recollection.
>
> And once I had recognised the taste of the crumb of madeleine soaked in her decoction of lime-flowers which my aunt used to give me (although I did not yet know and must long postpone the discovery of why this memory made me so happy) immediately the old grey house upon the street, where her room was, rose up like the scenery of a theatre, to attach itself to the little pavilion, opening on to the garden, which had been built out behind it for my parents (the isolated panel which until that moment had been all that I could see); and with the house the town, from morning to night and in all weathers, the Square where I was sent before luncheon, the streets along which I used to run errands, the country roads we took when it was fine. And just as the Japanese amuse themselves by filling a porcelain bowl with water and steeping in it little crumbs of paper which until then are without character or form, but, the moment they become wet, stretch themselves and bend, take on colour and distinctive shape, become flowers or houses or people, permanent and recognisable, so in that moment all the flowers in our garden and in M. Swann's park, and the water-lilies on the Vivonne and the good folk of the village and their little dwellings and the parish church and the whole of Combray and of its surroundings, taking their proper shapes and growing solid, sprang into being, town and gardens alike, from my cup of tea.

While it is not our intention to encroach too much on what should be matter for the student's consideration and discussion, we should point out two of the principal metaphors in the passage and offer a suggestion or two about them. The first is the comparison of the smell and taste of things to "souls" in whose "essence" a shape or structure is housed. Proust is here using an ancient Greek notion of the soul as an essence that gives its shape to the body it inhabits. The second, the final metaphor of the passage, takes the form of an extended analogy: "*just as* the Japanese . . . *so* in that moment. . . ." In examining Proust's use of this particular metaphor, the student might begin by considering the ways in which the metaphor is appropriate to the situation—that is, to both the eating of a cake dipped in tea and the ensuing recovery of the past. Beyond that, he might consider how the Japanese paper metaphor is related to the soul metaphor, and how both of these are related to the theatrical simile ("like the scenery") that links them.

Finally, this consideration of metaphor should lead back to an awareness of tone. Though this passage is a translation from the original French, it captures the tone of the original with high fidelity. How would you describe this tone? How should the passage sound if read aloud? What is the function of the repeated use of "and" in the last sentence (which is the last sentence in a whole section of the book)? How is the tone related to the metaphoric structure and the meaning of the passage? In sum, how do these two most important dimensions of the art of language—tone and metaphor—operate in this passage to control the response of a sensitive and careful reader?

In getting at this question the student might try to paraphrase the passage without its metaphors and tonal qualities. Considering such a paraphrase, he might then ask to what extent the meaning *is* paraphrasable, and to what extent the meaning requires the images and rhythms of the passage itself.

DESIGN: JUXTAPOSITION AND REPETITION IN THE STRUCTURE OF FICTION

When we look at a painting up close, we can see its details clearly and the texture of its brush strokes, but we cannot really see it as a whole. When we back away, we lose our perception of these minute qualities but gain, with this new perspective, a sense of its design. Similarly, as we read a story, we are involved in its details. And in a story we are involved especially because we experience it as a flow of words in time, bringing us impressions and ideas, moving us emotionally and stirring us intellectually. It is natural to back away from a painting and see it as a whole. But it is less natural and more difficult to get a similar perspective on a book. We can never "see" it all at once. Yet design is an important part of the writer's art, and a sense of design is essential to a full reading experience.

Design in fiction takes many forms, but these may be seen as mainly of two kinds. One has to do with juxtaposition: with what is put next to what in the arrangement of the story. The other has to do with repetition: with images, ideas, or situations that are repeated—often with interesting variations—in the course of the narrative. Juxtaposition is more important in some kinds of fiction than it is in others. If a single action is presented in a simple, chronological arrangement, the order of events is not likely to assume any special significance. But if the action is rearranged in time so that we encounter events out of their chronological sequence—through flashbacks or some other device—the order should be given some attention. We must look for reasons behind this manipulation of chronology by the author. Why has he chosen to place this particular scene from the "past" next to this particular scene in the "present"? Similarly, if we are following two actions in one story, now one and now the other, we should look for reasons why an incident from one sequence should be placed next to a particular incident in the other.

Often we will find interesting parallels: similar situations that amount to a kind of repetition with variation. If character A gets into a situation and takes one kind of action, while character B, in a similar situation, takes a different action, we should be able to compare the two and contrast their distincitve behavior, thus learning more about both. This kind of comparison can also lead us quite properly to generalizations about the meaning of a work.

Significant kinds of repetition occur also in sections of a story that are not placed next to one another. This kind of repetition is an important element of design, and serves to tie separate parts of a story together, enriching and strengthening the whole structure. Structure in fiction is a very complicated notion, because it involves so many factors. We can think of structure in one sense as the elements that shape our experience as we move through the story. In this sense structure is close to plot. We can also think of structure as the elements that enable us to see a meaningful pattern in the whole work. In this sense structure is close to design. For if plot has to do with the dynamics or movement of fiction, design has to do with the statics of fiction—the way we see a whole story after we have stopped moving through it. When we become aware of design in reading, so that one part of a story reminds us of parts we have read earlier, we are actually involved in a movement counter to our progress through from beginning to end. Plot wants to move us along; design wants to delay our movement, to make us pause and "see." The counteraction of these two forces is one of the things which enriches our experience of fiction.

Design is often a matter of the repetition of images or metaphors. In considering the metaphors of drowning in *Mrs. Dalloway*, we have already begun an examination of the way metaphoric design can tie together quite different characters and situations. Now we present a striking example of a rather different use of repetition in the design of a story. This is a case in which two episodes in the life of the same character—separated both by pages of our reading and by weeks in the life of the character—are brought together into powerful contrast by means of repetition with variation.

At the end of the second chapter of James Joyce's novel *A Portrait of the Artist as a Young Man*, the young man of the title, Stephen Dedalus, has been led by the urgings of physical desire into the arms of a prostitute. This is the last paragraph of that chapter:

> With a sudden movement she bowed his head and joined her lips to his and he read the meaning of her movements in her frank uplifted eyes. It was too much for him. He closed his eyes, surrendering himself to her, body and mind, conscious of nothing in the world but the dark pressure of her softly parting lips. They pressed upon his brain as upon his lips as though they were the vehicle of vague speech; and between them he felt an unknown and timid pressure, darker than the swoon of sin, softer than sound or odour.

By the end of the third chapter, Joyce has taken Stephen Dedalus through a period of disgust, remorse, and repentance. In the last paragraphs of the chapter we find Stephen receiving Holy Communion:

He knelt before the altar with his classmates, holding the altar cloth with them over a living rail of hands. His hands were trembling, and his soul trembled as he heard the priest pass with the ciborium from communicant to communicant.
—*Corpus Domini nostri.*
Could it be? He knelt there sinless and timid: and he would hold upon his tongue the host and God would enter his purified body.
—*In vitam eternam. Amen.*
Another life! A life of grace and virtue and happiness! It was true.
—*Corpus Domini nostri.*
The ciborium had come to him.

In the last sentence of the second chapter, Stephen felt the woman's tongue, pressing through her kiss—"an unknown and timid pressure." In the last lines of the third chapter, his tongue receives the body of Our Lord. Could the contrast be made more striking, or more rich in emotional and intellectual implications? Design here is powerfully carrying out Joyce's intention, which is to make us see Stephen poised between sinful and holy extremes, both of which attract him powerfully but neither of which can hold him finally—as the later chapters demonstrate. The focus on tongues in these two episodes is the crucial repeated element that makes the contrast Joyce wishes. And in the context of the whole story, it reminds us that tongues are not only for kissing or receiving the sacrament. They are also instruments of expression. Stephen ultimately must strive to express himself as an artist of languages, using his gift of tongues. In these two episodes, Stephen has been passive, the receiver. Later he will learn to speak out.

What we have been considering is the way that an object—in this case the tongue—can by its use in a fictional design acquire a metaphorical value that points in the direction of meaning. When this happens, the object becomes a symbol. The process of symbolism will be examined further in the commentary on "Clay" below.

Early Forms of Fiction

KINDS OF STORY

Long before the modern novel and short story developed, human beings were telling one another stories, acting them and singing them, too. When systems of writing were developed, stories began to be recorded for future times. In this brief section we present some illustrative examples of the ancestors of modern fiction, since modern works of fiction usually offer us a combination of elements that were more distinctly separated in these earlier forms. In order to isolate these elements for inspection, we include, first, three different kinds of story: the myth, the fable (or parable), and the tale; followed by examples of three different types of characterization.

In the study of fiction it is never really possible to separate plot from character. After all, a character *is* what he or she does; and a story must be about *someone*. In the most primitive forms of fiction—myth and legend—it is impossible to say whether the character or the plot is the center of interest, since the character is known specifically for the action that defines his or her mythic or legendary status. In more sophisticated forms, as we shall see later on, character can be presented in terms of description, analysis, and a few illustrative actions, without anything like a complete story being required.

Myth

Myths are expressions in narrative form of the deepest human concerns. The myths of primitive peoples are closely associated with their religious beliefs and tribal values. The Orpheus myth presented here is based on ancient celebrations of the fertility/sterility cycle that follows the annual march of the seasons. But the myth has already been given a personal touch; it is also the story of any husband mourning the loss of a beloved wife, a story of death and bereavement.

The following two versions of the Orpheus myth are, first, the plainest possible telling (by C. S. Lewis) of the events that compose the myth; and, second, a modern translation of the sophisticated Roman poet Ovid's elaboration of the mythic story. Taken together, the two versions allow us to see how different the "same story" may appear when it is told differently. Some people prefer the plain version; others, the fancy one. Ask yourself which one you prefer. Can you locate any specific parts of Ovid's version that seem to you especially effective or, on the other hand, too elaborate for your taste? Do you find anything lacking in the plain version?

C. S. LEWIS
1898–1963
Orpheus

There was a man who sang and played the harp so well that even beasts and trees crowded to hear him. And when his wife died he went down alive into the land of the dead and made music before the King of the Dead till even he had compassion and gave him back his wife, on condition that he led her up out of that land without once looking back to see her until they came out into the light. But when they were nearly out, one moment too soon, the man looked back, and she vanished from him forever.

OVID
43 B.C.–?A.D. 17
Orpheus

From there Hymen, clad in his saffron robes, was summoned by Orpheus, and made his way across the vast reaches of the sky to the shores of the Cicones. But Orpheus' invitation to the god to attend his marriage was of no avail, for though he was certainly present, he did not bring good luck. His expression was gloomy, and he did not sing his accustomed refrain. Even the torch he carried sputtered and smoked, bringing tears to the eyes, and no amount of tossing could make it burn. The outcome was even worse than the omens foretold: for while the new bride was wandering in the meadows, with her band of naiads, a serpent bit her ankle, and she sank lifeless to the ground. The Thracian poet mourned her loss; when he had wept for her to the full in the upper world, he made so bold as to descend through the gate of Taenarus to the Styx, to try to rouse the sympathy of the shades as well. There he passed among the thin ghosts, the wraiths of the dead, till he reached Persephone and her lord, who holds sway over these dismal regions, the king of the shades. Then, accompanying his words with the music of his lyre, he said:

"Deities of this lower world, to which all we of mortal birth descend, if I have your permission to dispense with rambling insincerities and speak the simple truth, I did not come here to see the dim haunts of Tartarus, nor yet to chain Medusa's monstrous dog, with its three heads and snaky ruff. I came because of my wife, cut off before she reached her prime when she trod on a serpent and it poured its poison into her veins. I wished to be strong enough to endure my grief, and I will not deny that I tried to do so; but Love was too much for me. He is a god well-known in the world above; whether he may be so here too, I do not know, but I imagine that he is familiar to you also and, if there is any truth in the story of that rape of long ago, then you yourselves were brought together by Love. I beg you, by these awful regions, by this boundless chaos, and by the silence of your vast realms, weave again Eurydice's destiny, brought too swiftly to a close. We mortals and all that is ours are fated to fall to you, and after a little time, sooner or later, we hasten to this one abode. We are all on our way here, this is our final home, and yours the most lasting sway over the human race. My wife, like the rest, when she has completed her proper span of years will, in the fullness of time, come within your power. I ask as a gift from you only the enjoyment of her: but if the fates refuse her a reprieve, I have made up my mind that I do not wish to return either. You may exult in my death as well as hers!"

As he sang these words to the music of his lyre, the bloodless ghosts were in tears: Tantalus made no effort to reach the waters that ever shrank away, Ixion's wheel stood still in wonder, the vultures ceased to gnaw Tityus' liver, the daughters of Danaus rested from their pitchers, and Sisyphus sat idle on his rock. Then for the first time, they say, the cheeks of the Furies were wet with tears, for they were overcome by his singing. The king and queen of the underworld could not bear to refuse his pleas. They called Eurydice. She was among the ghosts who had but newly come, and walked slowly because of her injury. Thracian Orpheus received her, but on condition that he must not look back until he had emerged from the valleys of Avernus, or else the gift he had been given would be taken from him.

Up the sloping path, through the mute silence they made their way, up the steep dark track, wrapped in impenetrable gloom, till they had almost reached the surface of the earth. Here, anxious in case his wife's strength be failing and eager to see her, the lover looked behind him, and straightway Eurydice slipped back into the depths. Orpheus stretched out his arms, straining to clasp her and be clasped; but the hapless man touched nothing but yielding air. Eurydice, dying now a second time, uttered no complaint against her husband. What was there to complain of, but that she had been loved? With a last farewell which scarcely reached his ears, she fell back again into the same place from which she had come.

At his wife's second death, Orpheus was completely stunned. He was like that timid fellow who, when he saw three-headed Cerberus led along, chained by the middle one of his three necks, was turned to stone in every limb, and lost his fear only when he lost his original nature too: or like Olenus and hapless Lethaea, once fond lovers, now stones set on well-watered Ida, all because Lethaea was too confident in her beauty, while Olenus sought to take her guilt upon his own shoulders, and wished to be considered the culprit. In vain did the poet long to cross the Styx a second time, and prayed that he might do so. The ferryman thrust him aside. For seven days, unkempt and neglected, he sat on the river bank, without tasting food: grief, anxiety and tears were his nourishment. Then he retired to lofty Rhodope and windswept Haemus, complaining of the cruelty of the gods of Erebus.

Fable and Parable

The fable and parable are ancient forms of fiction that share two important elements. They are very short, and they are allegorical in nature. That is, they tell, very briefly, a story about one thing while really directing attention to something else. Thus, there are always "two levels" to the fable and parable—a *literal* level and a *figurative* level.

In the fables of Aesop (a Greek of very ancient times) the literal level always involves animals, and the figurative level always points toward some aspect of human social behavior. Aesop invariably concludes his fable with a moral generalization that brings home the figurative point made by the fable. Jesus, on the other hand, usually bases his parables on some ordinary human action. He tells an anecdote about human behavior which is intended to illustrate a moral or spiritual truth at the figurative level. As Jesus explains in the Parable of the Sower, a parable has a hidden meaning that can function as a kind of test. Those who are enlightened will understand. Those who are not, will fail to comprehend. If and when they finally see the light, they will join the enlightened.

These little allegorical fictions are related to such truly primitive forms as the riddle. In ancient rituals, initiation often involved the answering of riddles as a qualification test for admission to the inner circle. The parable works in somewhat the same way. The fable, on the other hand, is a more socialized form: it is related to the primitive proverb—and, indeed, many a "moral" attached to the end of a fable also circulates on its own as a maxim or proverb.

You could, for instance, invent a story to go before such familiar sayings as "Look before you leap" or "He who hesitates is lost." You could also retell the stories of Aesop and Jesus so as to make different points from those made in the originals. You might even suggest alternatives to the morals or spiritual values regularly attached to the fables and parables presented here. Kurt Vonnegut (whose modern fable "Harrison Bergeron" you may read later in this volume) has rather impudently suggested, for instance, that the whole life story of Jesus may be read as a fable leading to a moral like this one: You shouldn't hassle a kid whose family has connections. Could you rewrite or reinterpret the fables or parables presented here, or invent others of your own?

FABLES OF AESOP
c. 620–c. 560 B.C.
The Wolf and the Mastiff

A Wolf, who was almost skin and bone—so well did the dogs of the neighborhood keep guard—met, one moonshiny night, a sleek Mastiff, who was, moreover, as strong as he was fat. Bidding the Dog good-night very humbly, he praised his good looks. "It would be easy for you," replied the Mastiff, "to get as fat as I am if you liked." "What shall I have to do?" asked the Wolf. "Almost nothing," answered the Dog. They trotted off together, but, as they went along, the Wolf noticed a bare spot on the Dog's neck. "What is that mark?" said he. "Oh, the merest trifle," answered the Dog; "the collar which I wear when I am tied up is the cause of it." "Tied up!" exclaimed the Wolf, with a sudden stop; "tied up? Can you not always then run where you please?" "Well, not quite always," said the Mastiff; "but what can that matter?" "It matters much to me, " rejoined the Wolf, and, leaping away, he ran once more to his native forest.

Moral: Better starve free, than be a fat slave.

The Dog in the Manger

A Dog was lying in a Manger full of hay. An Ox, being hungry, came near and was going to eat of the hay. The Dog, getting up and snarling at him, would not let him touch it. "Surly creature," said the Ox, "you cannot eat the hay yourself, and yet you will let no one else have any."

Moral: People often grudge others what they cannot enjoy themselves.

The Fox and the Grapes

A famished Fox saw some clusters of ripe black grapes hanging from a trellised vine. She resorted to all her tricks to get at them, but wearied herself in vain, for she could not reach them. At last she turned away, beguiling herself of her disappointment and saying: "The Grapes are sour, and not ripe as I thought."

Moral: It is easy to despise what we cannot have.

PARABLES OF JESUS
The Sower and the Seed

And when much people were gathered together, and were come to him out of every city, he spake by a parable: A sower went out to sow his seed: and as he sowed, some fell by the way side; and it was trodden down, and the fowls of the air devoured it. And some fell upon a rock; and as soon as it was sprung up, it withered away, because it lacked moisture. And some fell among thorns; and the thorns sprang up with it, and choked it. And other fell on good ground, and sprang up, and bare fruit an hundredfold. And when he had said these things, he cried, He that hath ears to hear, let him hear. And his disciples asked him, saying, What might this parable be? And he said, Unto you it is given to know the mysteries of the kingdom of God: but to others in parables; that seeing they might not see, and hearing they might not understand. Now the parable is this: The seed is the word of God. Those by the way side are they that hear; then cometh the devil, and taketh away the word out of their hearts, lest they should believe and be saved. They on the rock are they, which, when they hear, receive the word with joy; and these have no root, which for a while believe, and in time of temptation fall away. And that which fell among thorns are they, which, when they have heard, go forth, and are choked with cares and riches and pleasures of this life, and bring no fruit to perfection. But that on the good ground are they, which in an honest and good heart, having heard the word, keep it, and bring forth fruit with patience.

These excerpts are from the King James version of the Gospel according to Luke, chapters 8, 10, and 15.

The Good Samaritan

And, behold, a certain lawyer stood up, and tempted him, saying, Master, what shall I do to inherit eternal life? He said unto him, What is written in the law? how readest thou? And he answering said, Thou shalt love the Lord thy God with all thy heart, and with all thy soul, and with all thy strength, and with all thy mind; and thy neighbour as thyself. And he said unto him, Thou hast answered right: this do, and thou shalt live. But he, willing to justify himself, said unto Jesus, And who is my neighbour? And Jesus answering said, A certain man went down from Jerusalem to Jericho, and fell among thieves, which stripped him of his raiment, and wounded him, and departed, leaving him half dead. And by chance there came down a certain priest that way: and when he saw him, he passed by on the other side. And likewise a Levite, when he was at the place, came and looked on him, and passed by on the other side. But a certain Samaritan, as he journeyed, came where he was: and when he saw him, he had compassion on him, and went to him, and bound up his wounds, pouring in oil and wine, and set him on his own beast, and brought him to an inn, and took care of him. And on the morrow when he departed, he took out two pence, and gave them to the host, and said unto him, Take care of him; and whatsoever thou spendest more, when I come again, I will repay thee. Which now of these three, thinkest thou, was neighbour unto him that fell among the thieves? And he said, He that shewed mercy on him. Then said Jesus unto him, Go, and do thou likewise.

Three Parables on Lost and Found

Then drew near unto him all the publicans and sinners for to hear him. And the Pharisees and scribes murmured, saying, This man receiveth sinners, and eateth with them.

And he spake this parable unto them, saying, What man of you, having an hundred sheep, if he lose one of them, doth not leave the ninety and nine in the wilderness, and go after that which is lost, until he find it? And when he hath found it, he layeth it on his shoulders, rejoicing. And when he cometh home, he calleth together his friends and neighbours, saying unto them, Rejoice with me; for I have found my sheep which was lost. I say unto you, that likewise joy shall be in heaven over one sinner that repenteth, more than over ninety and nine just persons, which need no repentance.

Either what woman having ten pieces of silver, if she lose one piece, doth not light a candle, and sweep the house, and seek diligently till she find it? And when she hath found it, she calleth her friends and her neighbours together, saying, Rejoice with me; for I have found the piece which I had lost. Likewise, I say unto you, there is joy in the presence of the angels of God over one sinner that repenteth.

And he said, A certain man had two sons: and the younger of them said to his father, Father, give me the portion of goods that falleth to me. And he divided unto them his living. And not many days after the younger son gathered all together, and took his journey into a far country, and there wasted his substance with riotous living. And when he had spent all, there arose a mighty famine in that land; and he began to be in want. And he went and joined himself to a citizen of that country; and he sent him into his fields to feed swine. And he would fain have filled his belly with the husks that the swine did eat: and no man gave unto him. And when he came to himself, he said, How many hired servants of my father's have bread enough and to spare, and I perish with hunger! I will arise and go to my father, and will say unto him, Father, I have sinned against heaven, and before thee, and am no more worthy to be called thy son: make me as one of thy hired servants. And he arose, and came to his father. But when he was yet a great way off, his father saw him, and had compassion, and ran, and fell on his neck, and kissed him. And the son said unto him, Father, I have sinned against heaven, and in thy sight, and am no more worthy to be called thy son. But the father said to his servants, Bring forth the best robe, and put it on him; and put a ring on his hand, and shoes on his feet: and bring hither the fatted calf, and kill it; and let us eat, and be merry: for this my son was dead, and is alive again; he was lost, and is found. And they began to be merry. Now his elder son was in the field: and as he came and drew nigh to the house, he heard musick and dancing. And he called one of the servants, and asked what these things meant. And he said unto him, Thy brother is come; and thy father hath killed the fatted calf, because he hath received him safe and sound. And he was angry, and would not go in: therefore came his father out, and intreated him. And he answering said to his father, Lo, these many years do I serve thee, neither transgressed I at any time thy commandment: and yet thou never gavest me a kid, that I might make merry with my friends: but as soon as this thy son was come, which hath devoured thy living with harlots, thou hast killed for him the fatted calf. And he said unto him, Son, thou art ever with me, and all that I have is thine. It was meet that we should make merry, and be glad: for this thy brother was dead, and is alive again; and was lost, and is found.

The Tale

The tale is a complete story that exists for its own sake, because it is "a good story." Even though it may make a point or illustrate an argument, and thus be reduced to a kind of fable or parable, there is always something about its own form that justifies it for us whether it has a moral or not. The tale, of all the ancient forms of story, is also the most deeply rooted in everyday life. The tale turns on points of human behavior, and thus tends to focus on the things that move people most immediately: love, money, and social position.

Of all the early forms of short fiction, the tale is the one most concerned to produce an emotional reaction in an audience. The simplest tales call for either laughter or tears from their audience. More complicated fictions call for both—or something in between that partakes of both. The greatest tales seem always to have an ironic dimension. They exploit the difference between what humans hope for and what they get, or between what they say and what they do, producing either the pathetic irony of frustrated dreams or the ironic comedy of satire and ridicule.

More modern fictions have been frequently based upon the difference between what a character thinks to be true about the world and what is actually the case. Such an ironic gap between appearance and reality may lead to the realistic story of education. The ancient tales seldom if ever took this form. Most of them were in fact simple stories of hopes and wishes fulfilled, like many fairy tales. But the two tales included for examination here are not so simple. Although both have "happy endings," neither is a simple story of wish fulfillment.

The tale began as an oral form, and both examples here preserve some oral quality. The first, taken from the *Satyricon* of the first-century (A.D.) Roman courtier Petronius, is presented as a story that proves a point, but it is also considered a real anecdote, of "something that happened in our own time." In the hands of Petronius the tale reveals its connection to the ancient form of the joke, as well as to the fable and parable. The second, taken from the *Decameron* of Giovanni Boccaccio (a Florentine of the fourteenth century), is also presented as a story told aloud to an audience. And it, too, is said to be a real story about real people. In Boccaccio's case, this "reality" is insisted upon even more, through the device of naming a real person, known to the audience, who is alleged to be the authority for the tale's authenticity.

The hundred stories of the *Decameron* are presented as being told to one another by a group of ladies and gentlemen, to while away the time they must spend in the country avoiding a siege of plague in the city of Florence. The stories were called *novelli*, or novels, by Boccaccio, since they were supposed to be "new" or "novel" stories set in contemporary places, rather than traditional tales retold. Many of them, however, were far from new, but Boccaccio modernized them as best he could, and the very best, like the tale included here, he must have shaped himself.

The word "novel" became the word for short story in all the Romance languages, as opposed to the word "romance," which meant long story. When the English took over these words, they made a different distinction, designating both "novel" and "romance" as terms for long fictions in prose, but thinking of the novel as being closer to ordinary life—more realistic— and romance as extraordinary or fantastic. But the *novello* of Boccaccio is the ancestor not of the modern novel but of the modern short story. It is just a step from "Federigo and Giovanna" to certain stories of Maupassant —but it took humanity almost five centuries to manage that little step.

PETRONIUS
First century A.D.
The Widow of Ephesus

Meanwhile Eumolpus, our spokesman in the hour of danger and the author of our present reconciliation, anxious that our gaiety should not be broken, began, in a sudden movement of silence, to gibe at the fickleness of women, the wonderful ease with which they became infatuated, their readiness to abandon their children for their lovers, and so forth. In fact, he declared, no woman was so chaste or faithful that she couldn't be seduced; sooner or later she would fall head over heels in love with some passing stranger. Nor, he added, was he thinking so much of the old tragedies and the classics of love betrayed as of something that had happened in our own time; in fact, if we were willing to hear, he would be delighted to tell the story. All eyes and ears were promptly turned to our narrator, and he began:

Once upon a time there was a certain married woman in the city of Ephesus whose fidelity to her husband was so famous that the women from all the neighboring towns and villages used to troop into Ephesus merely to stare at this prodigy. It happened, however, that her husband one day died. Finding the normal custom of following the cortege with hair unbound and beating her breast in public quite inadequate to express her grief, the lady insisted on following the corpse right into the tomb, an underground vault of the Greek type, and there set herself to guard the body, weeping and wailing night and day. Although in her extremes of grief she was clearly courting death from starvation, her parents were utterly unable to persuade her to leave, and even the magistrates, after one last supreme attempt, were rebuffed and driven away. In short, all Ephesus had gone into mourning for this extraordinary woman, all the more since the lady was now passing her fifth consecutive day without once tasting food. Beside the failing woman sat her devoted maid, sharing her mistress' grief and relighting the lamp whenever it flickered out. The whole city could speak, in fact, of nothing else: here at last, all classes alike agreed, was the one true example of conjugal fidelity and love.

In the meantime, however, the governor of the province gave orders that several thieves should be crucified in a spot close by the vault where the lady was mourning her dead husband's corpse. So, on the following night, the soldier who had been assigned to keep watch on the crosses so that nobody could remove the thieves' bodies for burial suddenly noticed a light blazing among the tombs and heard the sounds of groaning. And prompted by a natural human curiosity to know who or what was making those sounds, he descended into the vault.

But at the sight of a strikingly beautiful woman, he stopped short in terror, thinking he must be seeing some ghostly apparition out of hell. Then, observing the corpse and seeing the tears on the lady's face and the scratches her fingernails had gashed in her cheeks, he realized what it was: a widow, in inconsolable grief. Promptly fetching his little supper back down to the tomb, he implored the lady not to persist in her sorrow or break her heart with useless mourning. All men alike, he reminded her, have the same end; the same resting place awaits us all. He used, in short, all those platitudes we use to comfort the suffering and bring them back to life. His consolations, being unwelcome, only exasperated the widow more; more violently than ever she beat her breast, and tearing out her hair by the roots, scattered it over the dead man's body. Undismayed, the soldier repeated his arguments and pressed her to take some food, until the little maid, quite overcome by the smell of the wine, succumbed and stretched out her hand to her tempter. Then, restored by the food and wine, she began herself to assail her mistress' obstinate refusal.

"How will it help you," she asked the lady, "if you faint from hunger? Why should you bury yourself alive, and go down to death before the Fates have called you? What does Vergil say?—

> Do you suppose the shades and ashes of the dead are by such sorrow touched?

No, begin your life afresh. Shake off these woman's scruples; enjoy the light while you can. Look at that corpse of your poor husband:

doesn't it tell you more eloquently than any words that you should live?"

None of us, of course, really dislikes being told that we must eat, that life is to be lived. And the lady was no exception. Weakened by her long days of fasting, her resistance crumbled at last, and she ate the food the soldier offered her as hungrily as the little maid had eaten earlier.

Well, you know what temptations are normally aroused in a man on a full stomach. So the soldier, mustering all those blandishments by means of which he had persuaded the lady to live, now laid determined siege to her virtue. And chaste though she was, the lady found him singularly attractive and his arguments persuasive. As for the maid, she did all she could to help the soldier's cause, repeating like a refrain the appropriate line of Vergil:

If love is pleasing, lady, yield yourself to love.

To make the matter short, the lady's body soon gave up the struggle; she yielded and our happy warrior enjoyed a total triumph on both counts. That very night their marriage was consummated, and they slept together the second and the third night too, carefully shutting the door of the tomb so that any passing friend or stranger would have thought the lady of famous chastity had at last expired over her dead husband's body.

As you can perhaps imagine, our soldier was a very happy man, utterly delighted with his lady's ample beauty and that special charm that a secret love confers. Every night, as soon as the sun had set, he bought what few provisions his slender pay permitted and smuggled them down to the tomb. One night, however, the parents of one of the crucified thieves, noticing that the watch was being badly kept, took advantage of our hero's absence to remove their son's body and bury it. The next morning, of course, the soldier was horror-struck to discover one of the bodies missing from its cross, and ran to tell his mistress of the horrible punishment which awaited him for neglecting his duty. In the circumstances, he told her, he would not wait to be tried and sentenced, but would punish himself then and there with his own sword. All he asked of her was that she make room for another corpse and allow the same gloomy tomb to enclose husband and lover together.

Our lady's heart, however, was no less tender than pure. "God forbid," she cried, "that I should have to see at one and the same time the dead bodies of the only two men I have ever loved. No, better far, I say, to hang the dead than kill the living." With these words, she gave orders that her husband's body should be taken from its bier and strung up on the empty cross. The soldier followed this good advice, and the next morning the whole city wondered by what miracle the dead man had climbed up on the cross.

GIOVANNI BOCCACCIO
1313–1375
Federigo and Giovanna

It is now my turn to speak, dearest ladies, and I shall gladly do so with a tale similar in part to the one before, not only that you may know the power of your beauty over the gentle heart, but because you may learn yourselves to be givers of rewards when fitting, without allowing Fortune always to dispense them, since Fortune most often bestows them, not discreetly but lavishly.

You must know then that Coppo di Borghese Domenichi, who was and perhaps still is one of our fellow citizens, a man of great and revered authority in our days both from his manners and his virtues (far more than from nobility of blood), a most excellent person worthy of eternal fame, and in the fullness of his years delighted often to speak of past matters with his neighbors and other men. And this he could do better and more orderly and with a better memory and more ornate speech than anyone else.

Among other excellent things, he was wont to say that in the past there was in Florence a young man named Federigo, the son of Messer Filippo Alberighi, renowned above all other young gentlemen of Tuscany for his prowess in arms and his courtesy. Now, as most often happens to gentlemen, he fell in love with a lady named Monna Giovanna, in her time held to be one of the gayest and most beautiful women ever known in Florence. To win her love, he went to jousts and tourneys, made and gave feasts, and spent his money without stint. But she, no less chaste than beautiful, cared nothing for the things he did for her nor for him who did them.

Now as Federigo was spending far beyond his means and getting nothing in, as easily happens, his wealth failed and he remained poor with nothing but a little farm, on whose produce he lived very penuriously, and one falcon which was among the best in the world. More in love than ever, but thinking he would never be able to live in the town any more as he desired, he went to Campi where his farm was. There he spent his time hawking, asked nothing of anybody, and patiently endured his poverty.

Now while Federigo was in this extremity it happened one day that Monna Giovanna's husband fell ill, and seeing death come upon him, made his will. He was a very rich man and left his estate to a son who was already growing up. And then, since he had greatly loved Monna Giovanna, he made her his heir in case his son should die without legitimate children; and so died.

Monna Giovanna was now a widow, and as is customary with our women, she went with her son to spend the year in a country house she had near Federigo's farm. Now the boy happened to strike up a friendship with Federigo, and delighted in dogs and hawks. He often saw Federigo's falcon fly, and took such great delight in it that he very much wanted to have it, but did not dare ask for it, since he saw how much Federigo prized it.

While matters were in this state, the boy fell ill. His mother was very much grieved, as he was her only child and she loved him extremely. She spent the day beside him, trying to help him, and often asked him if there was anything he wanted, begging him to say so, for if it were possible to have it, she would try to get it for him. After she had many times made this offer, the boy said:

"Mother, if you can get me Federigo's falcon, I think I should soon be better."

The lady paused a little at this, and began to think what she should do. She knew that Federigo had loved her for a long time, and yet had never had one glance from her, and she said to herself:

"How can I send or go and ask for this falcon, which is, from what I hear, the best that ever flew, and moreover his support in life? How can I be so thoughtless as to take this away from a gentleman who has no other pleasure left in life?"

Although she knew she was certain to have the bird for the asking, she remained in embarrassed thought, not knowing what to say, and did not answer her son. But at length love for her child got the upper hand and she determined that to please him in whatever way it might be, she would not send, but go herself for it and bring it back to him. So she replied:

"Be comforted, my child, and try to get better somehow. I promise you that tomorrow morning I will go for it, and bring it to you."

The child was so delighted that he became a little better that same day. And on the morrow the lady took another woman to accompany her, and as if walking for exercise went to Federigo's cottage, and asked for him. Since it was not the weather for it, he had not been hawking for some days, and was in his garden employed in certain work there. When he heard that Monna Giovanna was asking for him at the door, he was greatly astonished, and ran there happily. When she saw him coming, she got up to greet him with womanly charm, and when Federigo had courteously saluted her, she said:

"How do you do, Federigo? I have come here to make amends for the damage you have suffered through me by loving me more than was needed. And in token of this, I intend to dine today familiarly with you and my companion here."

"Madonna," replied Federigo humbly, "I do not remember ever to have suffered any damage through you, but received so much good that if I was ever worth anything it was owing to your worth and the love I bore it. Your generous visit to me is so precious to me that I could spend again all that I have spent; but you have come to a poor host."

So saying, he modestly took her into his house, and from there to his garden. Since there was nobody else to remain in her company, he said:

"Madonna, since there is nobody else, this good woman, the wife of this workman, will keep you company, while I go to set the table."

Now, although his poverty was extreme, he had never before realised what necessity he had fallen into by his foolish extravagance in spending his wealth. But he repented of it that morning when he could find nothing with which to do honour to the lady, for love of whom he had entertained vast numbers of men in the past. In his anguish he cursed himself and his fortune and ran up and down like a man out of his senses, unable to find money or anything to pawn. The hour was late and his desire to honour the lady extreme, yet he would not apply to anyone else, even to his own workman; when suddenly his eye fell upon his falcon, perched on a bar in the sitting room. Having no one to whom he could appeal, he took the bird, and finding it plump, decided it would be food worthy such a lady. So, without further thought, he wrung its neck, made his little maid servant quickly pluck and prepare it, and put it on a spit to roast. He spread the table with the whitest napery, of which he had some left, and returned to the lady in the garden with a cheerful face, saying that the meal he had been able to prepare for her was ready.

The lady and her companion arose and went to table, and there together with Federigo, who served it with the greatest devotion, they ate the good falcon, not knowing what it was. They left the table and spent some time in cheerful conversation, and the lady, thinking the time had now come to say what she had come for, spoke fairly to Federigo as follows:

"Federigo, when you remember your former life and my chastity, which no doubt you considered harshness and cruelty, I have no doubt that you will be surprised at my presumption when you hear what I have come here for chiefly. But if you had children, through whom you could know the power of parental love, I am certain that you would to some extent excuse me.

"But, as you have no child, I have one, and I cannot escape the common laws of mothers. Compelled by their power, I have come to ask you—against my will, and against all good manners and duty—for a gift, which I know is something especially dear to you, and reasonably so, because I know your straitened fortune has left you no other pleasure, no other recreation, no other consolation. This gift is your falcon, which has so fascinated my child that if I do not take it to him, I am afraid his present illness will grow so much worse that I may lose him. Therefore I beg you, not by the love you bear me (which holds you to nothing), but by your own nobleness, which has shown itself so much greater in all courteous usage than is wont in other men, that you will be pleased to give it me, so that through this gift I may be able to say that I have saved my child's life, and thus be ever under an obligation to you."

When Federigo heard the lady's request and knew that he could not serve her, because he had given her the bird to eat, he began to weep in her presence, for he could not speak a word. The lady at first thought that his grief came from having to part with his good falcon, rather than from anything else, and she was almost on the point of retraction. But she remained firm and waited for Federigo's reply after his lamentation. And he said:

"Madonna, ever since it has pleased God that I should set my love upon you, I have felt that Fortune has been contrary to me in many things, and have grieved for it. But they are all light in comparison with what she has done to me now, and I shall never be at peace with her again when I reflect that you came to my poor house, which you never deigned to visit when it was rich, and asked me for a little gift, and Fortune has so acted that I cannot give it to you. Why this cannot be, I will briefly tell you.

"When I heard that you in your graciousness desired to dine with me and I thought of your excellence and your worthiness, I thought it right and fitting to honor you with the best food I could obtain; so, remembering the falcon you asked me for and its value, I thought it a meal worthy of you, and today you had it roasted on the dish and set forth as best I could. But now I see that you wanted the bird in another form, it is such a grief to me that I cannot serve you that I think I shall never be at peace again."

And after saying this, he showed her the feathers and the feet and the beak of the bird in proof. When the lady heard and saw all this, she first blamed him for having killed such a falcon to make a meal for a woman; and then she inwardly commended his greatness of soul which no poverty could or would be able to abate. But, having lost all hope of obtaining the falcon, and thus perhaps the health of her son, she departed sadly and returned to the child. Now, either from disappointment at not having the falcon or because his sickness must inevitably have led to it, the child died not many days later, to the mother's extreme grief.

Although she spent some time in tears and bitterness, yet, since she had been left very rich and was still young, her brothers often urged her to marry again. She did not want to do so, but as they kept on pressing her, she remembered the worthiness of Federigo and his last act of generosity, in killing such a falcon to do her honor.

"I will gladly submit to marriage when you please," she said to her brothers, "but if you want me to take a husband, I will take no man but Federigo degli Alberighi."

At this her brothers laughed at her, saying:

"Why, what are you talking about, you fool? Why do you want a man who hasn't a penny in the world?"

But she replied:

"Brothers, I know it is as you say, but I would rather have a man who needs money than money which needs a man."

Seeing her determination, the brother, who knew Federigo's good qualities, did as she wanted, and gave her with all her wealth to him, in spite of his poverty. Federigo, finding that he had such a woman, whom he loved so much, with all her wealth to boot, as his wife, was more prudent with his money in the future, and ended his days happily with her.

TYPES OF CHARACTER

One of the major lines of development in the history of fiction may be traced in the examples presented here. As humans have developed their knowledge of the social and psychological forces conditioning human behavior, they have learned to write about people with greater insight into the motives behind their actions. Of course, the more we have discovered about the extent to which human actions are indeed conditioned by forces beyond our control, the less heroic our fictional characters have become.

If we think of Orpheus, that mythic hero whose story was presented earlier, as the most ancient kind of characterization, we can trace a steady movement in types of character from ancient times to the modern era. First, the mythic figures, who can deal even with the gods face to face; then heroes, whose brave deeds affect the fate of kingdoms; then social types, such as one might encounter on the street or at home; and, finally, individuals who are unique. This is not a simple progression through time: the Germanic and Scandinavian peoples (including the Anglo-Saxons) were still writing a heroic kind of fiction a thousand years after sophisticated Greeks had developed characterizations of different social types. But the general tendency is clear: a movement from heroic figures, defined by their valorous deeds, toward social and psychological portraiture.

When English and French writers of the seventeenth century rediscovered ways of writing about social types and historic individuals, the features of characterization that we recognize in the realistic modern novel and short story were finally achieved, and a recognizably modern fiction could begin its development. As we shall see later on, this development culminated in the fictional achievements of the nineteenth and twentieth centuries.

Legendary Hero

The Legendary Hero is to be found in the writings of certain historians who emphasize battlefield heroics in their histories. These writers are poised between the world of myth and the world of science, between fantastic invention and sober recording. Their heroes in a sense are actual historical personages, in that people bearing those names may well have lived and even been present at the events described. But the deeds recounted are so colored by myth and epic poetry that no modern historian dares to accept them uncritically.

The first historian represented here is the Greek Herodotus (fifth century B.C.), called the "father of history" because he was the first to call his writing *Histories* (or, more literally, *Inquiries*) and to attempt a kind of historical research—not easy in a world with few written records of the past. He has also been called, by later historians, the "father of lies." Our second historian is the Roman, Livy (first century B.C.) who, like Herodotus, loved a good story whether it was entirely accurate or not.

The tendency to make legendary heroes out of more ordinary or more complicated human beings did not die with the fall of Rome. It was one of the most powerful forces operating in European literature during the Middle Ages, and it is still powerful wherever folk literature flourishes. Historians and folklore scholars have shown how strongly the popular image of General Custer was colored by the same heroic pattern you will find in the stories of Leonidas and Horatius. The more recent bumper sticker, "Custer Died for Your Sins" suggests—with tongue in cheek—that we should see Custer in a rather different mythic pattern. But whenever a modern folk singer tries to cash in on an actual event, the result is likely to be a song about a figure cast in the old heroic mold, made into a "legend in his own time."

HERODOTUS
Fifth Century B.C.
Leonidas

The Greeks at Thermopylae had their first warning of the death that was coming with the dawn from the seer Megistias, who read their doom in the victims of sacrifice; deserters, too, came in during the night with news of the Persian flank movement, and lastly, just as day was breaking, the look-out men came running from the hills. In council of war their opinions were divided, some urging that they must not abandon their post, others the opposite. The result was that the army split: some dispersed, contingents returning to their various cities, while others made ready to stand by Leonidas. It is said that Leonidas himself dismissed them, to spare their lives, but thought it unbecoming for the Spartans under his command to desert the post which they had originally come to guard. I myself am inclined to think that he dismissed them when he realized that they had no heart for the fight and were unwilling to take their share of the danger; at the same time honor forbade that he himself should go. And indeed by remaining at his post he left a great name behind him, and Sparta did not lose her prosperity, as might otherwise have happened; for right at the outset of the war the Spartans had been told by the Delphic oracle that either their city must be laid waste by the foreigner or a Spartan king be killed. The prophecy was in hexameter verse and ran as follows:

Hear your fate, O dwellers in Sparta of the wide spaces;
Either your famed, great town must be sacked by Perseus' sons,
Or, if that be not, the whole land of Lacedaemon
Shall mourn the death of a king of the house of Heracles,
For not the strength of lions or of bulls shall hold him,
Strength against strength; for he has the power of Zeus,
And will not be checked till one of these two he has consumed.

I believe it was the thought of this oracle, combined with his wish to lay up for the Spartans a treasure of fame in which no other city should share, that made Leonidas dismiss those troops; I do not think that they deserted, or went off without orders, because of a difference of opinion. Moreover, I am strongly supported in this view by the case of the seer Megistias, who was with the army—an Acarnanian, said to be of the clan of Melampus—who foretold the coming doom from his inspection of the sacrificial victims. He quite plainly received orders from Leonidas to quit Thermopylae, to save him from sharing the army's fate. He refused to go, but he sent his only son, who was serving with the forces.

Thus it was that the confederate troops, by Leonidas' orders, abandoned their posts and left the pass, all except the Thespians and the Thebans who remained with the Spartans. The Thebans were detained by Leonidas as hostages very much against their will; but the Thespians of their own accord refused to desert Leonidas and his

men, and stayed, and died with them. They were under the command of Demophilus the son of Diadromes.

In the morning Xerxes poured a libation to the rising sun, and then
waited till it was well up before he began to move forward. This was
according to Ephilates' instructions, for the way down from the ridge
is much shorter and more direct than the long and circuitous ascent.
As the Persian army advanced to the assault, the Greeks under
Leonidas, knowing that they were going to their deaths, went out
into the wider part of the pass much further than they had done
before; in the previous days' fighting they had been holding the wall
and making sorties from behind it into the narrow neck, but now
they fought outside the narrows. Many of the invaders fell; behind
them the company commanders plied their whips indiscriminately,
driving the men on. Many fell into the sea and were drowned, and
still more were trampled to death by their friends. No one could
count the number of the dead. The Greeks, who knew that the enemy
were on their way round by the mountain track and that death was
inevitable, put forth all their strength and fought with fury and
desperation. By this time most of their spears were broken, and they
were killing Persians with their swords.

In the course of that fight Leonidas fell, having fought most
gallantly, and many distinguished Spartans with him—their names I
have learned, as those of men who deserve to be remembered;
indeed, I have learned the names of all the three hundred. Amongst
the Persian dead, too, were many men of high distinction, including
two brothers of Xerxes, Habrocomes and Hyperanthes, sons of
Darius by Artanes' daughter Phratagune. Artanes, the son of Hys-
taspes and grandson of Arsames, was Darius' brother; as Phratagune
was his only child, his giving her to Darius was equivalent to giving
him his entire estate.

There was a bitter struggle over the body of Leonidas; four times
the Greeks drove the enemy off, and at last by their valour rescued it.
So it went on, until the troops with Ephialtes were close at hand; and
then, when the Greeks knew that they had come, the character of the
fighting changed. They withdrew again into the narrow neck of the
pass, behind the wall, and took up a position in a single compact
body—all except the Thebans—on the little hill at the entrance to the
pass, where the stone lion in memory of Leonidas stands today. Here
they resisted to the last, with their swords, if they had them, and, if
not, with their hands and teeth, until the Persians, coming on from
the front over the ruins of the wall and closing in from behind, finally
overwhelmed them with missile weapons.

Of all the Spartans and Thespians who fought so valiantly the most signal proof of courage was given by the Spartan Dieneces. It is said that before the battle he was told by a native of Trachis that, when the Persians shot their arrows, there were so many of them that they hid the sun. Dieneces, however, quite unmoved by the thought of the strength of the Persian army, merely remarked: "This is pleasant news that the stranger from Trachis brings us: if the Persians hide the sun, we shall have our battle in the shade." He is said to have left on record other sayings, too, of a similar kind, by which he will be remembered. After Dieneces the greatest distinction was won by two Spartan brothers, Alpheus and Maron, the sons of Orsiphantus; and of the Thespians the man to gain the highest glory was a certain Dithyrambus, the son of Harmatides.

The dead were buried where they fell, and with them the men who had been killed before those dismissed by Leonidas left the pass. Over them is this inscription, in honor of the whole force:

Four thousand here from Pelops' land
Against three million once did stand.

The Spartans have a special epitaph; it runs:

Go tell the Spartans, you who read:
We took their orders, and are dead.

For the seer Megistias there is the following:

Here lies Megistias, who died
When the Mede passed Spercheius' tide.
A prophet; yet he scorned to save
Himself, but shared the Spartans' grave.

The columns with the epitaphs inscribed on them were erected in honor of the dead by the Amphictyons—though the epitaph upon the seer Megistias was the work of Simonides, the son of Leoprepes, who put it there for friendship's sake.

LIVY
59 B.C.–A.D. 17

Horatius

On the approach of the Etruscan army, the Romans abandoned their farmsteads and moved into the city. Garrisons were posted. In some sections the city walls seemed sufficient protection, in others the barrier of the Tiber. The most vulnerable point was the wooden bridge, and the Etruscans would have crossed it and forced an entrance into the city, had it not been for the courage of one man, Horatius Cocles—that great soldier whom the fortune of Rome gave to be her shield on that day of peril. Horatius was on guard at the bridge when the Janiculum was captured by a sudden attack. The enemy forces came pouring down the hill, while the Roman troops, throwing away their weapons, were behaving more like an undisciplined rabble than a fighting force. Horatius acted promptly: as his routed comrades approached the bridge, he stopped as many as he could catch and compelled them to listen to him. "By God," he cried, "can't you see that if you desert your post escape is hopeless? If you leave the bridge open in your rear, there will soon be more of them in the Palatine and the Capitol than on the Janiculum." Urging them with all the power at his command to destroy the bridge by fire or steel or any means they could muster, he offered to hold up the Etruscan advance, so far as was possible, alone. Proudly he took his stand at the outer end of the bridge; conspicuous amongst the rout of fugitives, sword and shield ready for action, he prepared himself for close combat, one man against an army. The advancing enemy paused in sheer astonishment at such reckless courage. Two other men, Spurius Lartius and Titus Herminius, both aristocrats with a fine military record, were ashamed to leave Horatius alone, and with their support he won through the first few minutes of desperate danger. Soon, however, he forced them to save themselves and leave him; for little was now left of the bridge, and the demolition squads were calling them back before it was too late. Once more Horatius stood alone; with defiance in his eyes he confronted the Etruscan chivalry, challenging one after another to single combat, and mocking them all as tyrants' slaves who, careless of their own liberty, were coming to destroy the liberty of others. For a while they hung back, each waiting for his neighbor to make the first move, until shame at the unequal battle drove them to action, and with a fierce cry they hurled their spears at the solitary figure which barred their way. Horatius caught the missiles on his shield and, resolute as ever, straddled the bridge and held his ground. The Etruscans moved forward, and would have thrust him aside by the sheer weight of numbers, but their advance was suddenly checked by the crash of the falling bridge and the simultaneous shout of triumph from the Roman soldiers who had done their work in time. The Etruscans could only stare in bewilderment as Horatius, with a prayer to Father Tiber to bless him and his sword, plunged fully armed into the water and swam, through the missiles which fell thick about him, safely to the other side where his friends were waiting to receive him. It was a noble piece of work—legendary, maybe, but destined to be celebrated in story through the years to come.

For such courage the country showed its gratitude. A statue of Horatius was placed in the Comitium, and he was granted as much land as he could drive a plough round in a day. In addition to public honours many individuals marked their admiration of his exploit in the very hard times which were to follow, by going short themselves in order to contribute something, whatever they could afford, to his support.

The Social Type

The word "characters" was used by the Greek writer Theophrastus (fourth century B.C.) to describe his collection of sketches of typical Athenian social types. The sketches that have come down to us are comic and satirical, apparently designed for recitation at parties and other social functions. They are fictional in two senses. First, they are slightly exaggerated portraits, and, second, they represent a "type" of behavior rather than the actions of any individual person. The exaggeration, in fact, comes from the putting together of so many similar traits as the sketch of a single character. Yet each trait represents a kind of actual behavior. The types represented by Theophrastus are not social types in the sense of being defined by class or trade; they are behavioral types who violate the standards of good manners in some particular way.

In seventeenth-century England there was a great revival of "Character"-making. The inspiration for this came from the rediscovery of the work of Theophrastus himself, but the nature of the English Characters changed the form somewhat. In the two samples presented here (modernized a bit but quite faithful to the originals), you will find the work of Thomas Overbury and some friends of his, which sees each Character as linked to a particular profession or trade. One question to ask in considering these is how the Overburian Character differs from the Theophrastian. Another is how authentically historical these Characters may be. Are these types confined to ancient Athens and the England of three centuries ago? Or do they represent human functions sufficiently universal to be recognized today? Would it be possible to produce contemporary imitations of Theophrastus or Overbury? Overbury's own definition of a Character offers some clues as to how to proceed:

> . . . it is a picture (real or personal) quaintly drawn in various colors, all of them heightened by one shadowing.
>   It is a quick and soft touch of many strings, all shutting up in one musical close. It is wit's descant [variation] on any plain song.

THEOPHRASTUS

Fourth century B.C.

The Rough

Roughness is coarse conduct, whether in word or act. The rough takes an oath lightly and is insensible to insult and ready to give it. In character he is a sort of town bully, obscene in manner, ready for anything and everything. He is willing, sober and without a mask, to dance the vulgar cordax[1] in comic chorus. At a show he goes around from man to man and collects the pennies, quarrelling with the spectators who present a pass and therefore insist on seeing the performance free.

He is the sort of man to keep a hostelry,[2] or brothel, or to farm the taxes. There is no business he considers beneath him, but he is ready to follow the trade of crier, cook, or gambler. He does not support his mother, is caught at theft and spends more time in jail than in his home. He is the type of man who collects a crowd of bystanders and harangues them in a loud brawling voice; while he is talking, some are going and others coming, without listening to him; to one part of the moving crowd he tells the beginning of his story, to another part a sketch of it, and to another part a mere fragment. He regards a holiday as the fittest time for the full exhibition of his roughness.

He is a great figure in the courts as plaintiff or defendant. Sometimes he excuses himself on oath from trial but later he appears with a bundle of papers in the breast of his cloak, and a file of documents in his hands. He enjoys the role of generalissimo in a band of rowdy loafers; he lends his followers money and on every quarter collects a penny interest per day. He visits the bakeshops, the markets for fresh and pickled fish, collects his tribute from them, and stuffs it in his cheek.

1. Lewd dance
2. Innkeepers were in ill-repute in antiquity.

The Gross Man

Grossness is such neglect of one's person as gives offense to others. The gross man is one who goes about with an eczema, or white eruption, or diseased nails, and says that these are congenital ailments; for his father had them, and his grandfather, too, and it would be hard to foist an outsider upon their family. He's very apt to have sores on his shins and bruises on his toes, and to neglect these things so that they grow worse.

His armpits are hairy like an animal's for a long distance down his sides; his teeth are black and decayed. As he eats, he blows his nose with his fingers. As he talks, he drools, and has no sooner drunk wine than up it comes. After bathing he uses rancid oil to anoint himself; and when he goes to the marketplace, he wears a thick tunic and a thin outer garment disfigured with spots of dirt.

When his mother goes to consult the soothsayer, he utters words of evil omen; and when people pray and offer sacrifices to the gods he lets the goblet fall, laughing as though he had done something amusing. When there's playing on the flute, he alone of the company claps his hands, singing an accompaniment and upbraiding the musician for stopping so soon.

Often he tries to spit across the table,—only to miss the mark and hit the butler.

THOMAS OVERBURY
1581–1613
A Mere Scholar

A mere scholar is an intelligible ass, or a silly fellow in black that speaks sentences more familiarly than sense. The antiquity of his University is his creed, and the excellency of his College (though but for a match of football) is an article of his faith. He speaks Latin better than his mother tongue, and is a stranger in no part of the world but in his own country. He does usually tell great stories of himself to small purpose, for they are commonly ridiculous, be they true or false. His ambition is that he either is, or shall be, a graduate, but if he ever gets a fellowship, he has then no fellow. In spite of all logic he dare swear and maintain it, that a cuckold and a townsman are *termini convertibles*,[1] though his mother's husband be an Alderman. He was never begotten (as it seems) without much wrangling, for his whole life is spent in *Pro & Contra*.[2] His tongue goes always before his wit, like a gentleman-usher, but somewhat faster. That he is a complete gallant in all points, from head to toe, witness his horsemanship and the wearing of his weapons. He is commonly long-winded, able to speak more with ease than any man can hear with patience.

University jests are his universal discourse, and his news the demeanor of the Proctors. His phrase, the apparel of his mind, is made up of diverse shreds like a cushion, and when it goes plainest

1. I.e., that a deceived husband and a man who lives in town are identical concepts.
2. Disputation

has a rash outside and rough linings. The current of his speech is closed with an "*ergo*," and whatever be the question, the truth is on his side. 'Tis a wrong to his reputation to be ignorant of anything, and yet he knows not that he knows nothing. He gives directions for husbandry from Virgil's *Georgics*; for cattle, from his *Bucolics*; for warlike strategems, from his *Aeneid* or Caesar's *Commentaries*. He orders all things by the book, is skillful in all trades, and thrives in none. He is led more by his ears than his understanding, taking the sound of words for their true sense. His ill luck is not so much in being a fool, as in being put to such pains to express it to the world; for what in others is natural, in him (with much ado) is artificial. His poverty is his happiness, for it makes some men believe that he is none of fortune's favorites. That learning which he has, was in his youth put in backwards like an enema, and 'tis now like ware mislaid in a peddler's pack: he has it, but knows not where it is. In a word, he is the index of a man, and the title page of a scholar, or a Puritan in morality; much in profession, nothing in practice.

A Jailer

Is a creature mistaken in the making, for he should be a tiger. But the shape being thought too terrible, it is covered, and he wears the mask of a man, yet retains the qualities of his former fierceness, currishness, and ravenousness. Of that red earth of which he was fashioned, this piece was the basest. Of the rubbish which was left and thrown aside came a jailer. Or if God had something else to do than to regard such trash, his descent, then, is more ancient but more ignoble, for he comes of the race of those angels that fell with Lucifer from heaven, whither he never (or hardly ever) returns. Of all his bunches of keys not one has the power to open that door. For a jailer's soul stands not upon those two pillars that support heaven (justice and mercy), it rather sits upon those two footstools of hell, wrong and cruelty. He is a judge's slave, a prisoner is his. In this they differ: he is a voluntary one, the other compelled. He is the hangman of the law with a lame hand, and if the law gave him all his limbs perfect, he would strike those on whom he is glad to fawn. In fighting against a debtor he is a creditor's second, but observes not the laws of the dueller's code, for his play is foul and he takes base advantages. His conscience and his shackles hang up together and are made very nearly of the same metal, saving that the one is harder than the other and has one property greater than iron, for it never melts. He distills money out of the poor's tears, and grows fat by their curses. No man coming to the practical part of hell can discharge it better, because here he does nothing but study the theory of it. His house is a picture of hell, and the original of the Letters Patent of his office stand exemplified there. A chamber of lousy beds is better worth to him than the best acre of corn-land in England. Two things are hard to him (nay, almost impossible), *viz:* to save all his prisoners that none ever escape, and to be saved himself. His ears are stopped to the cries of others, and God's to his. And good reason, for lay the life of a man in one scale, and his fees in another—he will lose the first to find the second. He must look for no mercy (if he desires justice to be done to him) for he shows none; and I think he cares less, because he knows heaven has no need of jailers. The doors there want no porters, for they stand ever open. If it were possible for all creatures in the world to sleep every night, he only and a Tyrant cannot. That blessing is taken from them, and this curse comes instead: to be ever in fear, and ever hated. What estate can be worse?

The Historical Personage

As we have seen, the earliest historians were interested especially in presenting heroic figures taken from a legendary past. Even in ancient times, however, certain writers made a serious effort to describe the events of their own times and to record the lives of important people for posterity. Little more than a century after Livy wrote, Tacitus, his fellow Roman, produced a brilliant study of Imperial Rome, which, though it is heightened with the colors of rhetoric, is also valuable as documentation of Rome in the time of Nero. We have excerpted from the *Annals* of Tacitus two passages dealing with the life and death of Seneca, a famous playwright and philosopher, who had been Nero's tutor and became his victim. Even in a modern translation we can appreciate how Tacitus used language to create dramatic scenes and to color events and situations with his own harshly ironical view of life.

The other two portraits of individuals presented here are modern English translations from the eighteenth-century French *Memoirs* of Louis de Rouvroy, Duc de Saint-Simon. Less formal than Tacitus, and less dramatic, Saint-Simon offers posterity intimate sketches of life at the court of Louis XIV. The portraits or sketches of Saint-Simon were written roughly a century after the Characters of the Englishman Thomas Overbury. It will be in instructive to compare the work of Overbury and Saint-Simon, to see what distinguishes the memoir-sketch of an actual historical personage from the invented character-type produced by Overbury and his friends. Certainly, in both cases, we find a fierce delight in capturing the unpleasant detail, but the methods are interestingly different. And, taken together, they show very clearly where the realistic characterizations of modern fiction have their roots.

TACITUS
55(?)–117(?) A.D.

Seneca

Burrus' death undermined Seneca's influence. Decent standards carried less weight when one of their two advocates was gone. Now Nero listened to more disreputable advisers. These attacked Seneca, first for his wealth, which was enormous and excessive for any subject, they said, and was still increasing; secondly, for the grandeur of his mansions and beauty of his gardens, which outdid even the emperor's; and thirdly, for his alleged bids for popularity. They also charged Seneca with allowing no one to be called eloquent but himself. "He is always writing poetry," they suggested, "now that Nero has become fond of it. He openly disparages the emperor's amusements, underestimates him as a charioteer, and makes fun of his singing. How long must merit at Rome be conferred by Seneca's certificate alone? Surely Nero is a boy no longer! He is a grown man and ought to discharge his tutor. His ancestors will teach him all he needs." Seneca knew of these attacks. People who still had some decency told him of them. Nero increasingly avoided his company.

Seneca, however, requested an audience, and when it was granted, this is what he said. "It is nearly fourteen years, Caesar, since I became associated with your rising fortunes, eight since you became emperor. During that time you have showered on me such distinctions and riches that, if only I could retire to enjoy them unpretentiously, my prosperity would be complete.

"May I quote illustrious precedents drawn from your rank, not mine? Your great-great-grandfather Augustus allowed Marcus Agrippa to withdraw to Mytilene, and allowed Gaius Maecenas the equivalent of retirement at Rome itself. The one his partner in wars, the other the bearer of many anxious burdens at Rome, they were greatly rewarded, for great services. I have had no claim on your generosity, except my learning. Though acquired outside the glare of public life, it has brought me the wonderful recompense and distinction of having assisted in your early education.

"But you have also bestowed on me measureless favours, and boundless wealth. Accordingly, I often ask myself: 'Is it I, son of a provincial non-senator, who am accounted a national leader? Is it my unknown name which has come to glitter among ancient and glorious pedigrees? Where is my old self, that was content with so little? Laying out these fine gardens? Grandly inspecting these estates? Wallowing in my vast revenues?' I can only find one excuse. It was not for me to obstruct your munificence.

"But we have both filled the measure—you, of what an emperor can give his friend, and I, of what a friend may receive from his emperor. Anything more will breed envy. Your greatness is far above all such mortal things. But I am not; so I crave your help. If, in the field or on a journey, I were tired, I should want a stick. In life's journey, I need just such a support.

"For I am old and cannot do the lightest work. I am no longer equal to the burden of my wealth. Order your agents to take over my property and incorporate it in yours. I do not suggest plunging myself into poverty, but giving up the things that are too brilliant and dazzle me. The time now spent on gardens and mansions shall be devoted to the mind. You have abundant strength. For years the supreme power has been familiar to you. We older friends may ask for our rest. This, too, will add to your glory—that you have raised to the heights men content with lower positions."

The substance of Nero's reply was this. "My first debt to you is that I can reply impromptu to your premeditated speech. For you taught me to improvise as well as to make prepared orations. True, my great-great-grandfather Augustus permitted Agrippa and Maecenas to rest after their labors. But he did so when he was old enough to assure them, by his prestige, of everything—of whatever kind—that he had given them. Besides, he certainly deprived neither of the rewards which they had earned from him in the wars and crises of Augustus' youthful years. If my life had been warlike, you too would have fought for me. But you gave what our situation demanded: wisdom, advice, philosophy, to support me as boy and youth. Your gifts to me will endure as long as life itself! My gifts to you, gardens and mansions and revenues, are liable to circumstances.

"They may seem extensive. But many people far less deserving than you have had more. I omit, from shame, to mention ex-slaves who flaunt greater wealth. I am even ashamed that you, my dearest friend, are not the richest of all men. You are still vigorous and fit for State affairs and their rewards. My reign is only beginning. Or do you think you have reached your limit? If so you must rank yourself below Lucius Vitellius, thrice consul, and my generosity below that of Claudius, and my gifts as inferior to the lifelong savings of Lucius Volusius Saturninus (II).

"If youth's slippery paths lead me astray, be at hand to call me back! You equipped my manhood; devote even greater care to guiding it! If you return my gifts and desert your emperor, it is not your unpretentiousness, your retirement, that will be on everyone's lips, but *my* meanness, your dread of *my* brutality. However much your self-denial were praised, no philosopher could becomingly gain credit from an action damaging to his friend's reputation."

Then he clasped and kissed Seneca. Nature and experience had fitted Nero to conceal hatred behind treacherous embraces. Seneca expressed his gratitude (all conversations with autocrats end like that). But he abandoned the customs of his former ascendancy. Terminating his large receptions, he dismissed his entourage, and rarely visited Rome. Ill-health or philosophical studies kept him at home, he said. . . .

Seneca's death followed. It delighted the emperor. Nero had no proof of Seneca's complicity but was glad to use steel against him when poison had failed. The only evidence was a statement of Antonius Natalis that he had been sent to visit the ailing Seneca and complain because Seneca had refused to receive Piso. Natalis had conveyed the message that friends ought to have friendly meetings; and Seneca had answered that frequent meetings and conversations would benefit neither, but that his own welfare depended on Piso's.

A colonel of the Guard, Gavius Silvanus, was ordered to convey this report to Seneca and ask whether he admitted that those were the words of Natalis and himself. Fortuitously or intentionally, Seneca had returned that day from Campania and halted at a villa four miles from Rome. Towards evening the officer arrived. Surrounding the villa with pickets, he delivered the emperor's message to Seneca as he dined with his wife Pompeia Paulina and two friends. Seneca replied as follows: "Natalis was sent to me to protest, on Piso's behalf, because I would not let him visit me. I answered excusing myself on grounds of health and love of quiet. I could have had no reason to value any private person's welfare above my own. Nor am I a flatterer. Nero knows this exceptionally well. He has had more frankness than servility from Seneca!"

The officer reported this to Nero in the presence of Poppaea and Tigellinus, intimate counsellors of the emperor's brutalities. Nero asked if Seneca was preparing for suicide. Gavius Silvanus replied that he had noticed no signs of fear or sadness in his words or features. So Silvanus was ordered to go back and notify him of the death-sentence. According to one source,[1] he did not return by the way he had come but made a detour to visit the commander of the Guard, Faenius Rufus; he showed Faenius the emperor's orders asking if he should obey them; and Faenius, with that ineluctable weakness which they all revealed, told him to obey. For Silvanus was himself one of the conspirators—and now he was adding to the crimes which he had conspired to avenge. But he shirked communicating or witnessing the atrocity. Instead he sent in one of his staff-officers to tell Seneca he must die.

Unperturbed, Seneca asked for his will. But the officer refused.

1. Fabius Rusticus

Then Seneca turned to his friends. "Being forbidden," he said, "to show gratitude for your services, I leave you my one remaining possession, and my best: the pattern of my life. If you remember it, your devoted friendship will be rewarded by a name for virtuous accomplishments." As he talked—and sometimes in sterner and more imperative terms—he checked their tears and sought to revive their courage. Where had their philosophy gone, he asked, and that resolution against impending misfortunes which they had devised over so many years? "Surely nobody was unaware that Nero was cruel!" he added. "After murdering his mother and brother, it only remained for him to kill his teacher and tutor."

These words were evidently intended for public hearing. Then Seneca embraced his wife and, with a tenderness very different from his philosophical imperturbability, entreated her to moderate and set a term to her grief, and take just consolation, in her bereavement, from contemplating his well-spent life. Nevertheless, she insisted on dying with him, and demanded the executioner's stroke. Seneca did not oppose her brave decision. Indeed, loving her wholeheartedly, he was reluctant to leave her for ill-treatment. "Solace in life was what I commended to you," he said. "But you prefer death and glory. I will not grudge your setting so fine an example. We can die with equal fortitude. But yours will be the nobler end."

Then, each with one incision of the blade, he and his wife cut their arms. But Seneca's aged body, lean from austere living, released the blood too slowly. So he also severed the veins in his ankles and behind his knees. Exhausted by severe pain, he was afraid of weakening his wife's endurance by betraying his agony—or of losing his own self-possession at the sight of her sufferings. So he asked her to go into another bedroom. But even in his last moments his eloquence remained. Summoning secretaries, he dictated a dissertation. (It has been published in his own words, so I shall refrain from paraphrasing it.)

Nero did not dislike Paulina personally. In order, therefore, to avoid increasing his ill-repute for cruelty, he ordered her suicide to be averted. So, on instructions from the soldiers, slaves and ex-slaves bandaged her arms and stopped the bleeding. She may have been unconscious. But discreditable versions are always popular, and some took a different view—that as long as she feared there was no appeasing Nero, she coveted the distinction of dying with her husband, but when better prospects appeared life's attractions got the better of her. She lived on for a few years, honorably loyal to her husband's memory, with pallid features and limbs which showed how much vital blood she had lost.

Meanwhile Seneca's death was slow and lingering. Poison, such as was formerly used to execute State criminals at Athens, had long been prepared; and Seneca now entreated his well-tried doctor, who was also an old friend,[1] to supply it. But when it came, Seneca drank it without effect. For his limbs were already cold and numbed against the poison's action. Finally he was placed in a bath of warm water. He sprinkled a little of it on the attendant slaves, commenting that this was his libation to Jupiter. Then he was carried into a vapor-bath, where he suffocated. His cremation was without ceremony, in accordance with his own instructions about his death—written at the height of his wealth and power.

1. Annaeus Statius

DUC DE SAINT-SIMON
1675–1755

Two Portraits

Princesse d'Harcourt

The Princesse d'Harcourt was a sort of personage whom it is good to make known, in order better to lay bare a Court which did not scruple to receive such as she. She had once been beautiful and gay; but though not old, all her grace and beauty had vanished. The rose had become an ugly thorn. At the time I speak of she was a tall, fat creature, mightily brisk in her movements, with a complexion like milk-porridge; great, ugly, thick lips, and hair like tow, always sticking out and hanging down in disorder, like all the rest of her fittings out. Dirty, slatternly, always intriguing, pretending, enterprising, quarrelling—always low as the grass or high as the rainbow, according to the person with whom she had to deal: she was a blonde Fury, nay more, a harpy: she had all the effrontery of one, and the deceit and violence; all the avarice and the audacity; moreover, all the gluttony, and all the promptitude to relieve herself from the effects thereof; so that she drove out of their wits those at whose house she dined; was often a victim of her confidence; and was many a time sent to the devil by the servants of M. du Maine and M. le Grand. She, however, was never in the least embarrassed, tucked up her petticoats and went her way; then returned, saying she had been unwell. People were accustomed to it.

Whenever money was to be made by scheming and bribery, she was there to make it. At play she always cheated, and if found out stormed and raged; but pocketed what she had won. People looked upon her as they would have looked upon a fishfag, and did not like to commit themselves by quarrelling with her.

Sometimes the Duchesse de Bourgogne used to send about twenty Swiss guards, with drums, into her chamber, who roused her from her first sleep by their horrid din. Another time—and these scenes were always at Marly—they waited until very late for her to go to bed and sleep. She lodged not far from the post of the Captain of the Guards, who was at that time the Maréchal de Lorges. It had snowed very hard, and had frozen. Madame la Duchesse de Bourgogne and her suite gathered snow from the terrace which is on a level with their lodgings; and, in order to be better supplied, waked up to assist them, the Maréchal's people, who did not let them want for ammunition. Then, with a false key, and lights, they gently slipped into the chamber of the Princesse d'Harcourt; and, suddenly drawing the curtains of her bed, pelted her amain with snowballs. The filthy creature, waking up with a start, bruised and stifled in snow, with which even her ears were filled, with disheveled hair, yelling at the top of her voice, and wriggling like an eel, without knowing where to hide, formed a spectacle that diverted people more than half an hour: so that at last the nymph swam in her bed, from which the water flowed everywhere, slushing all the chamber. It was enough to make one die of laughter.

She was very violent with her servants, beat them, and changed them every day. Upon one occasion, she took into her service a strong and robust chambermaid, to whom, from the first day of her arrival, she gave many slaps and boxes on the ear. The chambermaid said nothing, but after submitting to this treatment for five or six days, conferred with the other servants; and one morning, while in her mistress's room, locked the door without being perceived, said something to bring down punishment upon her, and at the first box on the ear she received, flew upon the Princesse d'Harcourt, gave her no end of thumps and slaps, knocked her down, kicked her, mauled her from her head to her feet, and when she was tired of this exercise, left her on the ground, all torn and disheveled, howling like a devil.

Madame de Montespan

On Wednesday, the 27th of May, 1707, at three o'clock in the morning, Madame de Montespan, aged sixty, died very suddenly at the waters of Bourbon. Her death made much stir, although she had long retired from the Court and from the world, and preserved no trace of the commanding influence she had so long possessed. I need not go back beyond my own experience, and to the time of her reign as mistress of the King. I will simply say, because the anecdote is little known, that her conduct was more the fault of her husband than her own. She warned him as soon as she suspected the King to be in love with her; and told him when there was no longer any doubt upon her mind. She assured him that a great entertainment that the King gave was in her honor. She pressed him, she entreated him in the most eloquent manner, to take her away to his estates of Guyenne, and leave her there until the King had forgotten her or chosen another mistress. It was all to no purpose; and Montespan was not long before repentance seized him; for his torment was that he loved her all his life, and died still in love with her—although he would never consent to see her again after the first scandal.

At last God touched her. Her sin had never been accompanied by forgetfulness; she used often to leave the King to go and pray in her cabinet; nothing could ever make her evade any fast-day or meagre day; her austerity in fasting continued amidst all her dissipation. She gave alms, was esteemed by good people, never gave way to doubt or impiety; but she was imperious, haughty and overbearing, full of mockery, and of all the qualities by which beauty with the power it bestows is naturally accompanied. Being resolved at last to take advantage of an opportunity which had been given her against her will, she put herself in the hands of Père de la Tour, that famous General of the Oratory. From that moment to the time of her death her conversion continued steadily, and her penitence augmented.

Little by little she gave almost all she had to the poor. She worked for them several hours a day, making stout shirts and such things for them. Her table, that she had loved to excess, became the most frugal; her fasts multiplied; she would interrupt her meals in order to go and pray. Her mortifications were continued; her chemises and her sheets were of rough linen, of the hardest and thickest kind, but hidden under others of ordinary kind. She unceasingly wore bracelets, garters, and a girdle, all armed with iron points, which oftentimes inflicted wounds upon her; and her tongue, formerly so dangerous, had also its peculiar penance imposed on it.

She received the last sacrament with an ardent piety. The fear of death which all her life had so continually troubled her, disappeared suddenly, and disturbed her no more. She died, without regret, occupied only with thoughts of eternity, and with a sweetness and tranquility that accompanied all her actions.

Madame de Montespan was bitterly regretted by all the poor of the province, amongst whom she spread an infinity of alms, as well as amongst others of different degree.

Three Stories and Commentaries

INTRODUCTION

These three stories are intended to illustrate something of the range and variety of modern short fiction. The commentaries illustrate ways in which the procedures outlined at the beginning of this section may be employed in the reading of specific texts. They may also be thought of as developments or refinements of those procedures. In preparing them we have sought not to put the stories mechanically through every analytical process mentioned earlier, but rather to fit the relevant and useful procedures to the appropriate aspects of each story.

In the anthology section ahead, students and teachers will find an even greater range of fiction for discussion and study. The examples of analysis offered here should suggest approaches that may apply to other stories but should not be allowed to limit the analytical procedures applied to the stories to come. Every discussion of a story must be adapted to that particular story. There is no single analytical method that works for everything. In considering these examples of critical analysis, it might be especially appropriate to ask why each discussion takes the form it does, emphasizing the aspects of the story it does, and whether it leaves out anything important about the story it treats.

GUY DE MAUPASSANT
1850–1893
Moonlight

His warlike name well suited the Abbé Marignan.[1] He was a tall thin priest, full of zeal, his soul always exalted but just. All his beliefs were fixed; they never wavered. He sincerely believed that he understood his God, entered into His plans, His wishes, His intentions.

As he strode down the aisle of his little country church, sometimes a question would take shape in his mind: "Now why has God done that?" He would seek the answer stubbornly, putting himself in

1. The Battle of Marignan (1515) was a great and bloody victory for Francis I and France.

Translated by R.S., with valuable advice and criticism from Peter Clothier and the students in his University of Iowa Translation Workshop.

God's place, and he nearly always found it. He was not one of those who murmur with an air of pious humility, "O Lord, your designs are impenetrable!" He would say to himself: "I am the servant of God, I should know His purposes, and if I don't know them I should divine them."

Everything in nature seemed to him created with an absolute and admirable logic. The "why" and the "because" always balanced out. Dawns existed to make waking up a pleasure, days to ripen the crops, rain to water them, evening to prepare for slumber, and the night was dark for sleeping.

The four seasons were perfectly fitted to all the needs of agriculture; and it would never have occurred to the priest to suspect that nature has no intentions at all, and that, on the contrary, every living thing has bowed to the hard necessities of times, climates, and matter itself.

But he hated women, he hated them unconsciously and despised them by instinct. He often repeated the words of Christ: "Woman, what have I to do with thee?" and he added, "You'd think that not even God himself was happy with that particular piece of work." Woman for him was precisely that child twelve times unclean of whom the poet speaks. She was the temptress who had ensnared the first man and who still continued her damnable work—a weak creature, dangerous, curiously disturbing. And even more than her devilish body he hated her loving soul.

He had often felt the yearning affection of women, and, even though he knew himself invulnerable, he was exasperated by this need to love which always trembled in them.

God, in his opinion, had made woman only to tempt man and test him. Thus man should approach her with great care, ever fearful of traps. She was, in fact, even shaped like a trap, with her arms extended and her lips parted for a man.

He was indulgent only of nuns, made inoffensive by their vows; and he treated even them severely, because he felt stirring in the depths of their fettered hearts—those hearts so humbled—that eternal yearning which still sought him out, even though he was a priest.

He felt it in their gaze—more steeped in piety than that of monks—in their religious ecstasy tainted with sex, in their transports of love for Christ, which infuriated him because it was woman's love, fleshly love. He felt it—this wicked yearning—even in their docility, in the sweetness of their voices in talking to him, in their lowered eyes, and in their submissive tears when he rebuffed them rudely.

And he shook out his soutane on leaving the gates of a convent and strode quickly away as though fleeing from danger.

He had a niece who lived with her mother in a little house nearby. He was determined to make her a Sister of Charity.

She was pretty, light-headed, and impish. When the Abbé preached, she laughed; and when he got angry at her she kissed him eagerly, clasping him to her heart while he tried instinctively to escape this embrace which nevertheless gave him a taste of sweet happiness, waking deep within him those paternal impulses which slumber in every man.

Often he spoke to her of God—of his God—while walking beside her along country lanes. She scarcely listened but looked at the sky, the grass, the flowers, with a lively joy which showed in her eyes. Sometimes she leaped to catch some flying thing and brought it back to him, crying: "Look, uncle, how pretty it is. I want to pet it." And this impulse to "pet bugs" or nuzzle lilac blossoms disturbed, annoyed, sickened the priest, who discerned in it that ineradicable yearning which always springs up in the female heart.

Then, it happened that one day the sacristan's wife, who kept house for the Abbé Marignan, cautiously told him that his niece had a lover. The news shocked him terribly and he stopped, choking, with his face full of soap, for he was busy shaving.

When he recovered so that he could think and speak, he shouted: "It is not true, you are lying, Mélanie!"

But the good woman put her hand on her heart: "May the Good Lord strike me dead if I'm lying, M. le Curé. She goes out there every night, I tell you, as soon as your sister's in bed. They meet down by the river. You've only to go and watch there between ten and midnight."

He stopped scraping his chin and started walking up and down violently, as he always did in his hours of solemn meditation. When he tried to finish shaving he cut himself three times between the nose and the ear.

All day he was silenced, swollen with indignation and rage. To his fury as a priest, confronted by love, the invincible, was added the exasperation of a strict father, of a guardian, of a confessor fooled, cheated, tricked by a child. He shared that self-centered feeling of suffocation experienced by parents whose daughter tells them she has—without them and despite them—chosen a husband.

After dinner he tried to read a bit, but he could not get into it. He got more and more exasperated. When ten o'clock struck he took down his walking stick, a formidable oaken cudgel he always used when making his evening rounds to visit the sick. And he smiled as he looked at this big club, whirling it about fiercely in his great countryman's fist. Then, suddenly, he raised it and, gritting his teeth, brought it down on a chair, knocking its splintered back to the floor.

He opened the door to go out, but stopped on the sill, surprised by a splendor of moonlight such as he had rarely seen.

And, endowed as he was with an exalted spirit—such as those poetical dreamers the Fathers of the Church might have had—he was immediately distracted, moved by the glorious and serene beauty of the pale night.

In his little garden, all bathed in soft light, the ordered ranks of his fruit trees traced on the path the shadows of their slender limbs, lightly veiled with foliage, while the giant honeysuckle, clinging to the wall of the house, exhaled a delicious, sugary breath that floated through the calm clear air like a ghostly perfume.

He began to breathe deeply, drinking the air as a drunkard drinks wine, and he took a few slow, dreaming, wondering steps, almost forgetting his niece.

When he reached the open country, he stopped to contemplate the fields all flooded with tender light, bathed in the delicate and languid charm that calm nights have. Incessantly the frogs gave out their short metallic note, and distant nightingales, inspiring dream not thought, blended their unstrung tune—a rapid throbbing music made for kisses—with the enchantment of the moonlight.

The Abbé pressed on, losing heart, though he could not tell why. He felt feeble, suddenly drained; he wanted to sit down, to stay there, to contemplate, to admire God in His handiwork.

Below, following the undulations of the little river, a tall line of poplars wound like a snake. A fine mist, a white vapor which the moonbeams pierced and turned to glowing silver, hung around and above the banks wrapping the whole tortuous watercourse in a sort of delicate and transparent gauze.

The priest halted again, struck to the depths of his soul by an irresistible wave of yearning.

And a doubt, a vague disturbance, came over him. He sensed within himself another of those questions he sometimes posed.

Why had God done this? Since the night is intended for sleep, for unconsciousness, for repose, for oblivion, why make it more charming than the day, sweeter than dawn or evening? And why this slow and seductive moon, which is more poetic than the sun and seems intended by its very delicacy to illumine things too fragile and mysterious for daylight, why should it come to make the shadows so transparent?

Why should the loveliest of songbirds not go to sleep with the others but linger on to sing in the disturbing shade?

Why this half-veil thrown over the world? Why this thrill in the heart, this stirring of the soul, this languor of the flesh?

Why this display of delights that men never see, since they are asleep in their beds? For whom was it intended, this sublime spectacle, this flood of poetry poured from the sky over the earth?

And the Abbé found no answer.

But then, down below, on the edge of the fields, under the vault of trees drenched with glowing mist, two shadows appeared, walking side by side.

The man was taller and held the neck of his lover and sometimes kissed her forehead. Their sudden appearance brought the still countryside to life, and it enfolded the young lovers like a setting divinely made for them. They seemed, the pair, a single being, the being for whom this calm and silent night was intended, and they moved toward the priest like a living answer, the answer to his question, flung back by his Master.

He stood still, his heart pounding in confusion, and he felt as if he were looking at a biblical scene, like the love of Ruth and Boaz, like the accomplishment of the will of God as presented in one of the great scenes of holy scripture. In his head echoed verses of the Song of Songs: the passionate cries, the calls of the flesh, all the ardent poetry of this poem that seethes with passionate yearning.

And he said to himself: "Perhaps God has made such nights to veil the loves of men with ideal beauty."

He recoiled before the couple who kept walking arm in arm. It was certainly his niece. But he asked himself now if he was not on the verge of disobeying God. Must not God permit love since He lavished upon it such visible splendor?

And he fled, distraught, almost ashamed, as if he had entered a temple where he had no right to be.

A Commentary

This tale is essentially realistic. The events are ordinary, the geography recognizable; the characters can be assigned to a particular time, place, religion, and class. But the imposition of a pattern on this realistic material moves it in the direction of comic romance. It contains no detail presented for its own sake or as documentation of a way of life. Every piece of information given to us contributes to the comic pattern of the plot. We can see this if we consider the central character and what we know about him.

In this uncomplicated tale the Abbé Marignan is not only the central character, he is almost the only character. His niece and the housekeeper, Mélanie, exist only to the extent that they contribute to the Abbé's story.

And the Abbé's story, if we consider its beginning and end, is a story of education, of a change in attitude. The change involves a dramatic shift in the priest's view of women and love.

The story falls naturally into three sections of nearly equal length, of which the first is entirely devoted to the presentation of the Abbé's character. Even here a striking selectivity prevails. We learn about two facets of this character only: one is the nature of the priest's religious belief, presented in the first paragraph and elaborated in the next three; the other is the priest's attitude toward women and love, presented in the fourth paragraph and elaborated in the next five. These two attributes are absolutely vital to the story because his attitude toward love must be changed— this is what the story is "about"—and his religious belief is the lever by means of which the change is accomplished. All the information in the first four paragraphs prepares us for the priest's mental process as we follow it in the closing paragraphs of the story.

If we accept the justice of the priest's comic education, we accept with it a particular view of life. There is a touch of satire as well as comedy in this tale. The priest's view of the workings of the universe is being subjected to an ironic scrutiny that is implicit in the way the story is worked out, and is almost explicit in the point of view from which the story is told. Even the priest's name, Marignan, is touched with irony for those who recognize what it alludes to, since the victor of the Battle of Marignan, Francis I, was defeated and captured in his next campaign, as the Abbé is in *his* little struggle.

Exactly what is our perspective on the events of this little tale? We look into the mind of the Abbé but we do not see things from his point of view. The narrator has his own perspective which is revealed to us by the allusion to the Battle of Marignan and by other means. Consider the fourth paragraph:

> The four seasons were perfectly fitted to all the needs of agriculture; and it would never have occurred to the priest to suspect that nature has no intentions at all, and that, on the contrary, every living thing has bowed to the hard necessities of times, climates, and matter itself.

Up to the semicolon, we are receiving a report on the priest's view—actually a continuation of the preceding paragraph. But after the semicolon, we are being given another view of the world, one which "would never have occurred" to the Abbé himself. This other viewpoint—the narrator's—is in direct opposition to the priest's. Where the Abbé sees God's intentions everywhere, the narrator sees a nature without plan or purpose but still determining the quality of existence. There is a touch of naturalism in this view (a satiric hint of a chaotic, destructive world), which is counteracted by the purposeful pattern of the story itself.

The narrator's views are closest to the surface in this paragraph, but once we are alert to them we can see them operating more subtly elsewhere. In the very first paragraph, for instance, the last two sentences are so emphatic in their repetition that they acquire a somewhat mocking tone. In them we learn not only that the priest's views are "fixed," but also that they "never wavered." We learn that the Abbé entered not only into God's "plans," but also into "His wishes, His intentions." This underlining of the rigidity and presumption of the priest's beliefs prepares us for his comeuppance and at the same time makes us unconsciously begin to wish for it.

Some of the metaphors used by the narrator also enrich the meaning of the work. The last sentence employs a simile which is appropriate and ironic. The priest flees from this love scene "as if he had entered into a temple where he had no right to be." The word "entered" (pénétré), of course, echoes ironically the penetration of the priest into God's designs, and is an interesting example of such designed repetition, but this penetration in the last sentence of the story is part of a metaphoric structure—an analogy introduced by the expression "as if." The key word in the simile is "temple." The priest does not flee from a scene that outrages religion in order to take sanctuary in his church. In a comic reversal he flees from a scene which is itself religious, as he now understands it, and where he is the infidel profaning holy ground. This image of the temple, we should also note, has been prepared for by our first sight of the two lovers, under the "vault" of the trees.

Other metaphors operate with comparable subtlety. Consider the priest's first vision of this scene, as he pauses above it and looks at the winding river and the poplars lining its banks. The narrator, in describing the trees, says they "wound like a snake" (serpentait). He must have chosen this expression specifically to remind us of a similar idyllic love scene—the Garden of Eden—which also had its serpent. The suggestion is delicate and rich. The priest usually thinks of woman as "the temptress who had ensnared the first man," but in this scene nature itself and finally God seem to have conspired to surround this "sin" with beauty. And the Abbé enters a world in which he is as much an alien as the devil in paradise, though his intention is not to tempt but to prevent a fall.

Although this story is essentially a plot, it is not without design. The early sample of the Abbé's reasoning process is repeated at the end with its startling new conclusion that God "must permit love." And the temple simile in the last sentence reminds us of two related scenes: the Abbé striding so confidently down the aisle of his own church, and the Abbé leaving a convent of nuns with that same stride, after having shaken its contaminating dust of femininity off his soutane. He, who had been too pure to accept these nuns as his spiritual equals, is finally seen as profaning a temple of love. The design and the tone reinforce in various subtle ways the irony of the plot. The strength of this little story lies in the way all these elements cooperate to achieve its comic effect.

JAMES JOYCE

1882–1941

Clay

The matron had given her leave to go out as soon as the women's tea was over and Maria looked forward to her evening out. The kitchen was spick and span: the cook said you could see yourself in the big copper boilers. The fire was nice and bright and on one of the side-tables were four very big barmbracks. These barmbracks seemed uncut; but if you went closer you would see that they had been cut into long thick even slices and were ready to be handed round at tea. Maria had cut them herself.

Maria was a very, very small person indeed but she had a very long nose and a very long chin. She talked a little through her nose, always soothingly: *Yes, my dear,* and *No, my dear.* She was always sent for when the women quarrelled over their tubs and always succeeded in making peace. One day the matron had said to her:

—Maria, you are a veritable peace-maker!

And the sub-matron and two of the Board ladies had heard the compliment. And Ginger Mooney was always saying what she wouldn't do to the dummy who had charge of the irons if it wasn't for Maria. Everyone was so fond of Maria.

The women would have their tea at six o'clock and she would be able to get away before seven. From Ballsbridge to the Pillar, twenty minutes; from the Pillar to Drumcondra, twenty minutes; and twenty minutes to buy the things. She would be there before eight. She took out her purse with the silver clasps and read again the words *A Present from Belfast.* She was very fond of that purse because Joe had brought it to her five years before when he and Alphy had gone to Belfast on a Whit-Monday trip. In the purse were two half-crowns and some coppers. She would have five shillings clear after paying tram fare. What a nice evening they would have, all the children singing! Only she hoped that Joe wouldn't come in drunk. He was so different when he took any drink.

Often he had wanted her to go and live with them; but she would have felt herself in the way (though Joe's wife was ever so nice with her) and she had become accustomed to the life of the laundry. Joe was a good fellow. She had nursed him and Alphy too; and Joe used often say:

—Mamma is mamma but Maria is my proper mother.

After the break-up at home the boys had got her that position in the *Dublin by Lamplight* laundry, and she liked it. She used to have such a bad opinion of Protestants but now she thought they were very nice people, a little quiet and serious, but still very nice people to live with. Then she had her plants in the conservatory and she liked looking after them. She had lovely ferns and wax-plants and, whenever anyone came to visit her, she always gave the visitor one or two slips from her conservatory. There was one thing she didn't like and that was the tracts on the walls; but the matron was such a nice person to deal with, so genteel.

When the cook told her everything was ready she went into the women's room and began to pull the big bell. In a few minutes the women began to come in by twos and threes, wiping their steaming hands in their petticoats and pulling down the sleeves of their blouses over their red steaming arms. They settled down before their huge mugs which the cook and the dummy filled up with hot tea, already mixed with milk and sugar in huge tin cans. Maria superintended the distribution of the barmbrack and saw that every woman got her four slices. There was a great deal of laughing and joking during the meal. Lizzie Fleming said Maria was sure to get the ring and, though Fleming had said that for so many Hallow Eves, Maria had to laugh and say she didn't want any ring or man either; and when she laughed her grey-green eyes sparkled with disappointed shyness and the tip of her nose nearly met the tip of her chin. Then Ginger Mooney lifted up her mug of tea and proposed Maria's health while all the other women clattered with their mugs on the table, and said she was sorry she hadn't a sup of porter to drink it in. And Maria laughed again till the tip of her nose nearly met the tip of her chin and till her minute body nearly shook itself asunder because she knew that Mooney meant well though, of course, she had the notions of a common woman.

But wasn't Maria glad when the women had finished their tea and the cook and the dummy had begun to clear away the tea-things! She went into her little bedroom and, remembering that the next morning was a mass morning, changed the hand of the alarm from seven to six. Then she took off her working skirt and her house-boots and laid her best skirt out on the bed and her tiny dress-boots beside the foot of the bed. She changed her blouse too and, as she stood before the mirror, she thought of how she used to dress for mass on Sunday morning when she was a young girl; and she looked with quaint affection at the diminutive body which she had so often adorned. In spite of its years she found it a nice tidy little body.

When she got outside the streets were shining with rain and she was glad of her old brown raincloak. The tram was full and she had to sit on the little stool at the end of the car, facing all the people, with her toes barely touching the floor. She arranged in her mind all she was going to do and thought how much better it was to be independent and to have your own money in your pocket. She hoped they would have a nice evening. She was sure they would but she could not help thinking what a pity it was Alphy and Joe were not speaking. They were always falling out now but when they were boys together they used to be the best of friends: but such was life.

She got out of her tram at the Pillar and ferreted her way quickly among the crowds. She went into Downes's cake-shop but the shop was so full of people that it was a long time before she could get herself attended to. She bought a dozen of mixed penny cakes, and at last came out of the shop laden with a big bag. Then she thought what else would she buy: she wanted to buy something really nice. They would be sure to have plenty of apples and nuts. It was hard to know what to buy and all she could think of was cake. She decided to buy some plumcake but Downes's plumcake had not enough almond icing on top of it so she went over to a shop in Henry Street. Here she was a long time in suiting herself and the stylish young lady behind the counter, who was evidently a little annoyed by her, asked her was it wedding-cake she wanted to buy. That made Maria blush and smile at the young lady; but the young lady took it all very seriously and finally cut a thick slice of plumcake, parcelled it up and said:

—Two-and-four, please.

She thought she would have to stand in the Drumcondra tram because none of the young men seemed to notice her but an elderly gentleman made room for her. He was a stout gentleman and he wore a brown hard hat; he had a square red face and a greying moustache. Maria thought he was a colonel-looking gentleman and she reflected how much more polite he was than the young men who simply stared straight before them. The gentleman began to chat with her about Hallow Eve and the rainy weather. He supposed the bag was full of good things for the little ones and said it was only right that the youngsters should enjoy themselves while they were young. Maria agreed with him and favoured him with demure nods and hems. He was very nice with her, and when she was getting out at the Canal Bridge she thanked him and bowed, and he bowed to her and raised his hat and smiled agreeably; and while she was going up along the terrace, bending her tiny head under the rain, she thought how easy it was to know a gentleman even when he has a drop taken.

Everybody said: O, here's Maria! when she came to Joe's house. Joe was there, having come home from business, and all the children had their Sunday dresses on. There were two big girls in from next door and games were going on. Maria gave the bag of cakes to the eldest boy, Alphy, to divide and Mrs Donnelly said it was too good of her to bring such a big bag of cakes and made all the children say:

—Thanks, Maria.

But Maria said she had brought something special for papa and mamma, something they would be sure to like, and she began to look for her plumcake. She tried in Downes's bag and then in the pockets of her raincloak and then on the hallstand but nowhere could she find it. Then she asked all the children had any of them eaten it—by mistake, of course—but the children all said no and looked as if they did not like to eat cakes if they were to be accused of stealing. Everybody had a solution for the mystery and Mrs Donnelly said it was plain that Maria had left it behind her in the tram. Maria, remembering how confused the gentleman with the greyish moustache had made her, coloured with shame and vexation and disappointment. At the thought of the failure of her little surprise and of the two and fourpence she had thrown away for nothing she nearly cried outright.

But Joe said it didn't matter and made her sit down by the fire. He was very nice with her. He told her all that went on in his office, repeating for her a smart answer which he had made to the manager. Maria did not understand why Joe laughed so much over the answer he had made but she said that the manager must have been a very overbearing person to deal with. Joe said he wasn't so bad when you knew how to take him, that he was a decent sort so long as you didn't rub him the wrong way. Mrs Donnelly played the piano for the children and they danced and sang. Then the two next-door girls handed round the nuts. Nobody could find the nutcrackers and Joe was nearly getting cross over it and asked how did they expect Maria to crack nuts without a nutcracker. But Maria said she didn't like nuts and that they weren't to bother about her. Then Joe asked would she take a bottle of stout and Mrs Donnelly said there was port wine too in the house if she would prefer that. Maria said she would rather they didn't ask her to take anything: but Joe insisted.

So Maria let him have his way and they sat by the fire talking over old times and Maria thought she would put in a good word for Alphy. But Joe cried that God might strike him stone dead if ever he spoke a word to his brother again and Maria said she was sorry she had mentioned the matter. Mrs Donnelly told her husband it was a great shame for him to speak that way of his own flesh and blood but Joe said that Alphy was no brother of his and there was nearly being a row on the head of it. But Joe said he would not lose his temper on account of the night it was and asked his wife to open some more stout. The two next-door girls had arranged some Hallow Eve games and soon everything was merry again. Maria was delighted to see the children so merry and Joe and his wife in such good spirits. The next-door girls put some saucers on the table and then led the children up to the table, blindfold. One got the prayer-book and the other three got the water; and when one of the next-door girls got the ring Mrs Donnelly shook her finger at the blushing girl as much as to say: *O, I know all about it!* They insisted then on blindfolding Maria and leading her up to the table to see what she would get; and, while they were putting on the bandage, Maria laughed and laughed again till the top of her nose nearly met the tip of her chin.

They led her up to the table amid laughing and joking and she put her hand out in the air as she was told to do. She moved her hand about here and there in the air and descended on one of the saucers. She a felt a soft wet substance with her fingers and was surprised that nobody spoke or took off her bandage. There was a pause for a few seconds; and then a great deal of scuffling and whispering. Somebody said something about the garden, and at last Mrs Donnelly said something very cross to one of the next-door girls and told her to throw it out at once: that was no play. Maria understood that it was wrong that time and so she had to do it over again: and this time she got the prayer-book .

After that Mrs Donnely played Miss McCloud's Reel for the children and Joe made Maria take a glass of wine. Soon they were all quite merry again and Mrs Donnelly said Maria would enter a convent before the year was out because she had got the prayer-book. Maria had never seen Joe so nice to her as he was that night, so full of pleasant talk and reminiscences. She said they were all very good to her.

At last the children grew tired and sleepy and Joe asked Maria would she not sing some little song before she went, one of the old songs. Mrs Donnelly said *Do, please, Maria!* and so Maria had to get up and stand beside the piano. Mrs Donnelly bade the children be quiet and listen to Maria's song. Then she played the prelude and said *Now, Maria!* and Maria, blushing very much, began to sing in a tiny quavering voice. She sang *I Dreamt that I Dwelt*, and when she came to the second verse she sang again:

I dreamt that I dwelt in marble halls
  With vassals and serfs at my side
And of all who assembled within those walls
  That I was the hope and the pride.
I had riches too great to count, could boast
  Of a high ancestral name,
But I also dreamt, which pleased me most,
  That you loved me still the same.

But no one tried to show her her mistake; and when she had ended her song Joe was very much moved. He said that there was no time like the long ago and no music for him like poor old Balfe, whatever other people might say; and his eyes filled up so much with tears that he could not find what he was looking for and in the end he had to ask his wife to tell him where the corkscrew was.

A Commentary *by R. S.*

I can remember vividly my first encounter with "Clay," and this is partly why I have included it here. I was a freshman in college, and my roommate handed me the anthology they were using in his English class and asked me what I made of one story that baffled him. The story was "Clay," and I remember that it baffled me as well. It was not like the stories I knew and admired—by Poe, O. Henry, Maupassant. It seemed to me to have no plot and to be about nothing in particular. By one of those ironies that operate in life as well as in art, I have since devoted a good deal of my time to studying Joyce. So "Clay" is here both because I know it well and respect it and because I can remember so well what it was like not to understand it.

Like "Moonlight" it is realistic, dealing with ordinary people and situations. It is, in fact, much more concerned to document a kind of reality than to tell a crisp and comic tale. It is more realistic than "Moonlight" and more pathetic than comic in its effect. As the Abbé Marignan's story is amusing, Maria's is sad. And as his story is one of education, hers is one of revelation. He *learns* from his experience; she *is revealed* to us through her experience, but without any increase in awareness on her part. The Abbé's day, after all, is an extraordinary one in his life. Maria's is merely typical. Nothing of great importance happens in it. This is one reason why "Clay" can be so baffling. It is hard to "see" a story in it, since nothing of any consequence happens. Nevertheless, it is a story, and it will respond to a careful consideration of its elements.

To begin with the matter of plot, it is not easy to find one in "Clay," but one is there all the same. Part of it has to do with the Halloween game that Maria and the others play. The game is not explained but there are enough clues in the story for us to reconstruct its method. We first hear of the game while Maria is still at the laundry:

> There was a great deal of laughing and joking during the meal. Lizzie Fleming said Maria was sure to get the ring and, though Fleming had said that for so many Hallow Eves, Maria had to laugh and say she didn't want any ring or any man either; and when she laughed her grey-green eyes sparkled with disappointed shyness and the tip of her nose nearly met the tip of her chin.

Later, Maria plays the game at her brother's house, so that, taken together, the two scenes make the beginning and end of a line of action in the story. And, since the title points directly toward the second of these scenes, we are surely right to consider it important. In this scene we first learn more about the operation of the game, as the children and the next-door girls play it:

> The next-door girls put some saucers on the table and then led the children up to the table, blindfold. One got the prayer-book and the other three got the water; and when one of the next-door girls got the ring Mrs Donnelly shook her finger at the blushing girl as much as to say: *O, I know all about it!*

And later, after the game has gone "wrong" once and been played over, Maria is gently teased by Mrs Donnelly also:

> ... Mrs Donnelly said Maria would enter a convent before the year was out because she had got the prayer-book.

The game, as we can reconstruct it from the clues in these three passages, is a simple, fortunetelling affair. A blindfolded person chooses among three saucers and the choice indicates the future event. The ring indicates marriage, the prayerbook foretells entering the Church, and the water—we are not told, but I should guess a sea voyage. In reading this story we must continue to perform exactly this kind of reconstruction. Where Maupassant told us everything he wanted us to know in the most direct way possible, Joyce is *in*direct, making us do a good deal of interpretive labor ourselves. But having figured out the game, we must now arrive at an understanding of its significance in Maria's story.

At the beginning of this line of action, Maria was teased by Lizzie Fleming about being "sure to get the ring"—which would mean marriage. At the end she is teased about having got the prayerbook, which means a life of chaste seclusion from the world. But between these moments, Maria has actually made her real selection:

> They led her up to the table amid laughing and joking and she put out her hand out in the air as she was told to do. She moved her hand about here and there in the air and descended on one of the saucers. She felt a soft wet substance with her fingers and was surprised that nobody spoke or took off her bandage. There was a pause for a few seconds; and then a great deal of scuffling and whispering. Somebody said something about the garden, and at last Mrs Donnelly said something very cross to one of the next-door girls and told her to throw it out at once: that was no play. Maria understood that it was wrong that time and so she had to do it over again: and this time she got the prayer-book.

By calling his story "Clay," Joyce made sure that we would be able to understand this episode and its significance, even though Maria herself, from whose point of view we are perceiving things, never realizes what substance she has encountered. The next-door girls have played a trick on her by putting clay into one of the saucers. We know what the ring, prayerbook, and water signify in this game. But clay is not regularly a part of it. Its significance is a matter for our interpretation. Clearly, we will not be far wrong if we associate it with death, realizing that Maria is not likely to marry or enter a convent, but certainly is destined to die and become clay—as are we all. Clay is the substance out of which the first man was made. It conveys the essence of human frailty. Indeed, "that was no play." The clay intrudes on this Halloween scene like a ghostly presence, reminding us of the reality of death and decomposition. Thus, with some scrutiny, this strand of the action becomes both clear and meaningful. But at least one other must be accounted for. If we are to grasp the entire story we must understand such episodes as Maria admiring her body in the mirror, Maria responding to the "colonel-looking gentlemen," Maria losing her plum-cake, and Maria mistaking the verses of her song.

Since the mistake in singing is the very last thing in "Clay," we might well consider it for possible revelations. What mistake does Maria make? "When she came to the second verse she sang again: . . . . But no one tried to show her her mistake." She repeats the first verse, which is to say, she leaves out the second. What does she leave out? The omitted second verse goes this way:

> I dreamt that suitors sought my hand,
>   That knights on bended knee,
> And with vows no maiden heart could withstand,
>   They pledged their faith to me.
> And I dreamt that one of that noble band,
>   Came forth my heart to claim,
> But I also dreamt, which charmed me most,
>   That you loved me all the same.

Joyce could have told us what was in this verse that Maria omitted, but he chose simply to leave out what she left out and include the verse she repeated. He made sure we knew she had left something out, but he did not tell us its nature. As with the game, he insists that we do the work of interpretation, which in this case includes research into "I Dreamt that I Dwelt," so that we can supply the missing verse. He continually requires us to share the work of constructing this story in order to understand it. But what does the missing verse tell us? It tells us that Maria unconsciously rebelled at singing "suitors sought my hand"; that a subject such as "vows that no maiden heart could withstand" bothered her enough that she repressed it and "forgot" the second verse. Can we relate this to the other episodes in the story?

When Lizzie Fleming teased her and predicted she would "get the ring,"

Maria "had to laugh and say she didn't want any ring or man either." But she adorns her "nice tidy little body," and she gets so flustered by an inebriated "colonel-looking gentleman" that she misplaces her plumcake while talking to him. In its very different way from Maupassant's, Joyce's story is also about feminine *tendresse*, or "yearning." The missing verse fits into this pattern perfectly. Maria is a reluctant spinster, homely as a Halloween witch, with the tip of her nose nearly meeting the tip of her chin. She feels superior to the "common" women who work in the *Dublin by Lamplight* laundry (a title intended to suggest that the laundresses have been reclaimed from a distinctly "fallen" status), but she takes several drinks when Joe "makes" her. Her appetites are more like those of the "common" women than she would admit. All in all, she is a pathetic figure—a "peacemaker" whose "children" have quarreled so bitterly that she is powerless to reconcile them, and whose suspicions that the children ate her missing plumcake turn them temporarily against her and perhaps lead to the trick by the next-door girls. Clay certainly, common clay.

The title of this story points much more insistently toward its meaning than does the title of "Moonlight" (though the French title, "Clair de lune," is stronger than its English equivalent in suggesting a metaphoric "light" in the sense of mental illumination). Like the title of "Moonlight," the title of "Clay" points toward something that is present in the story, but this clay of Joyce's story is more richly and subtly meaningful than Maupassant's moonlight. The substance, clay, acquires metaphorical suggestions of mortality and common human weakness. The object in the story—that dish of clay in the Halloween game—becomes a symbol for these complicated qualities. And symbolism is the richest and most complicated of metaphorical processes.

Metaphorical possibilities range from the simple and straightforward simile to the symbol. The simile indicates precisely the nature of the comparison it makes with words like "as" and "so." But the symbol opens out from an object or image in the direction of an unspecified meaning. We should add that though the meaning of a symbol is extensive and not precisely limited, this meaning is always directed and controlled in some way. A symbol in a work of fiction, like the clay in this story, cannot be made to "mean" anything we happen to associate with the word "clay." Only those associations both suggested by the substance clay and actually related to Maria's fictional situation belong in our interpretation of the story. Meanings like "mortality" and "common weakness" are traditionally associated with clay in Western tradition, from the Bible on, and clay is used to symbolize similar things in other cultures as well. But we must demonstrate a connection between these traditional meanings and the story in order to establish their appropriateness. Plot, character, and symbol work together to shape our final understanding of the story.

We should note in passing that "Clay" is a special kind of short story in that it is actually part of a sequence of stories put together by its author for a purpose beyond that realizable in any single short piece. In this case, Joyce called his sequence *Dubliners* and meant it as a representation of life in his native city of Dublin. In its proper setting, the meaning of "Clay" chimes with the meaning of the other stories, as Maria's spinsterhood and common humanity are echoed by and contrasted with the situations and qualities of other Dubliners. But even though it gains in resonance when placed in *Dubliners*, "Clay" is sufficient to be of interest by itself.

Aside from its central symbol, Joyce is sparing of metaphor in "Clay." But he is very careful about his control of tone. The tone he establishes at the beginning never falters. How should it be described? "The kitchen was spick and span. . . . The fire was nice and bright." What kind of prose is this? Or consider the short fourth paragraph:

> And the sub-matron and two of the Board ladies had heard the compliment. And Ginger Mooney was always saying what she wouldn't do to the dummy who had charge of the irons if it wasn't for Maria. Everyone was so fond of Maria.

The syntactical pattern of "And . . . and . . . . And" is just one facet of the excessive simplicity of this prose. It is echoed by the quality of cliché that we find in phrases like "spick and span" or "nice and bright." Though Maria herself is not telling this story to us, the narrator is using language closely approaching her own. That is one reason why any striking use of metaphor has been ruled out. Complicated sentences, complex words, and brilliant turns of phrase are all inappropriate here. Joyce said once that he had written *Dubliners* in a style of "scrupulous meanness." That expression is exactly appropriate to the style of "Clay."

In the paragraph we are considering, this linguistic situation is actually somewhat like the one in the first paragraph quoted from *Mrs. Dalloway* in the section on point of view (see p. 114 above): simple, even banal language; and a "so" in the last sentence. Is the tone of the two paragraphs—or of the two "so's"—exactly the same? I think not. The excessive simplicity of Virginia Woolf's prose at this point is entirely devoted to mockery of Sir William Bradshaw. But Joyce's simplicity is in considerable part devoted to giving us Maria's own view of her situation. Her view is undoubtedly limited. Everyone is not *so* fond of her as she would like to think. But we are not really standing off from her and subjecting her to an ironic scrutiny. We are *with* her to some extent here, as well as detached from her. The paragraph in *Mrs. Dalloway* is almost pure satire. The paragraph in "Clay" is pathos mainly, with perhaps a slight admixture of satire.

All the way through the story, Joyce keeps very close not only to a style of language appropriate to Maria, but also to Maria's perspective. Only rarely, as when Maria responds to Lizzie's teasing, does he tell us directly something she could not perceive herself. And there, when he tells us her "eyes sparkled with disappointed shyness," he is giving us an important clue to the "disappointed" quality of her spinsterhood. Usually he avoids such direct transcendence of Maria's perspective and makes us do the work of inference ourselves. Even at the end, when he tells us something that Maria does not know—that she has left out a verse of the song—he does not tell us what is in the verse, for to do so would take us too far from her perspective. By holding us so close to the viewpoint of his central character, Joyce makes it necessary for us to infer a good deal in order to achieve a distance from her sufficient to focus on her with the clarity of detachment. In effect, he makes us see Maria with a double vision, engaged and detached, sympathetic and ironic. And not only Maria but the other characters as well must be seen in this way. Joe, at the close of the story, weeping so much he cannot find the corkscrew to open another bottle, could be seen as a caricature only—another drunken, sentimental, stage Irishman. But Joe's booze-induced sentimentality is also genuine warmth—a mixture of the genuine and the spurious which is, for better or worse, very common in life. Joyce leaves the evaluation to us.

The comic clarity of Maupassant does make, in a sense, a better story. The delicacy and complexity of Joyce make a more realistic one. Fortunately, we do not have to choose between one and the other. We can have both ways, and many more, whenever we want.

Design in "Clay" is mainly a matter of the organization of parts to bear on the revelation of Maria's common disappointments. The central symbol of the clay itself, which is established in the story's climactic episode, is the pivot around which everything else turns. The story appears to us to be almost a plotless, designless "slice of life," and we have to look carefully to note the care of its construction. Actually, design operates much more powerfully in Dubliners as a whole than in any single story. The arrangement of stories was very carefully worked out by Joyce to achieve certain juxtapositions, and the stories are designed so that each contains elements that repeat and echo their counterparts in the others. The larger any work is, the more important plot and design become as elements of coherence. A collection of stories, which has no plot, must depend extensively on design for its structural interconnections. But Joyce preferred design to plot, and his longest narratives, Ulysses and Finnegans Wake, are scantily plotted and elaborately designed.

You will encounter another story from Dubliners in the anthology section that follows. At that point, it should be interesting to see how the two stories work together, treating similar thematic materials with a similar technique—yet managing to be entirely unique.

JORGE LUIS BORGES

1899–

Theme of the Traitor and the Hero

> So the Platonic year
> Whirls out new right and wrong,
> Whirls in the old instead;
> All men are dancers and their tread
> Goes to the barbarous clangour of a gong.
> W. B. Yeats: *The Tower*

Under the notable influence of Chesterton (contriver and embellisher of elegant mysteries) and the palace counselor Leibniz (inventor of the pre-established harmony), in my idle afternoons I have imagined this story plot which I shall perhaps write some-day and which already justifies me somehow. Details, rectifications, adjustments are lacking; there are zones of the story not yet revealed to me; today, January 3rd, 1944, I seem to see it as follows:

The action takes place in an oppressed and tenacious country: Poland, Ireland, the Venetian Republic, some South American or Balkan state . . . Or rather it has taken place, since, though the narrator is contemporary, his story occurred towards the middle or the beginning of the nineteenth century. Let us say (for narrative convenience) Ireland; let us say in 1824. The narrator's name is Ryan; he is the great-grandson of the young, the heroic, the beautiful, the assassinated Fergus Kilpatrick, whose grave was mysteriously violated, whose name illustrated the verses of Browning and Hugo, whose statue presides over a gray hill amid red marshes.

Kilpatrick was a conspirator, a secret and glorious captain of conspirators: like Moses, who from the land of Moab glimpsed but could not reach the promised land, Kilpatrick perished on the eve of the victorious revolt which he had premeditated and dreamt of. The first centenary of his death draws near; the circumstances of the crime are enigmatic; Ryan, engaged in writing a biography of the hero, discovers that the enigma exceeds the confines of a simple police investigation. Kilpatrick was murdered in a theater; the British police never found the killer; the historians maintain that this scarcely soils their good reputation, since it was probably the police themselves who had him killed. Other facets of the enigma disturb Ryan. They are of a cyclic nature: they seem to repeat or combine events of remote regions, or remote ages. For example, no one is unaware that the officers who examined the hero's body found a sealed letter in which he was warned of the risk of attending the theater that evening; likewise Julius Caesar, on his way to the place where his friends' daggers awaited him, received a note he never read, in which the treachery was declared along with the traitors' names. Caesar's wife, Calpurnia, saw in a dream the destruction of a tower decreed him by the Senate; false and anonymous rumors on the eve of Kilpatrick's death publicized throughout the country that the circular tower of Kilgarvan had burned, which could be taken as a presage, for he had been born in Kilgarvan. These parallelisms (and others) between the story of Caesar and the story of an Irish conspirator lead Ryan to suppose the existence of a secret form of time, a pattern of repeated lines. He thinks of the decimal history conceived by Condorcet, of the morphologies proposed by Hegel, Spengler and Vico, of Hesiod's men, who degenerate from gold to iron. He thinks of the transmigration of souls, a doctrine that lends horror to Celtic literature and that Caesar himself attributed to the British druids: he thinks that, before having been Fergus Kilpatrick, Fergus Kilpatrick was Julius Caesar. He is rescued from these circular labyrinths by a curious finding, a finding which then sinks him into other, more inextricable and heterogeneous labyrinths: certain words uttered by a beggar who spoke with Fergus Kilpatrick the day of his death were prefigured by Shakespeare in the tragedy *Macbeth*. That history should have copied history was already sufficiently astonishing; that history should copy literature was inconceivable. . . . Ryan finds that, in 1814, James Alexander Nolan, the oldest of the hero's companions, had translated the principal dramas of Shakespeare into Gaelic; among these was *Julius Caesar*. He also discovers in the archives the manuscript of an article by Nolan on the Swiss *Festspiele:* vast and errant theatrical representations which require thousands of actors and repeat historical episodes in the very cities and mountains where they took place. Another unpublished document reveals to him that, a few days before the end, Kilpatrick, presiding over the last meeting, had signed the order for the execution of a traitor whose name had been deleted from the records. This order does not accord with Kilpatrick's merciful nature. Ryan investigates the matter (this investigation is one of the gaps in my plot) and manages to decipher the enigma.

Kilpatrick was killed in a theater, but the entire city was a theater as well, and the actors were legion, and the drama crowned by his death extended over many days and many nights. This is what happened:

On the 2nd of August, 1824, the conspirators gathered. The country was ripe for revolt; something, however, always failed: there was a traitor in the group. Fergus Kilpatrick had charged James Nolan with the responsibility of discovering the traitor. Nolan carried out his assignment: he announced in the very midst of the meeting that the traitor was Kilpatrick himself. He demonstrated the truth of his accusations with irrefutable proof; the conspirators condemned their president to die. He signed his own sentence, but begged that his punishment not harm his country.

It was then that Nolan conceived his strange scheme. Ireland idolized Kilpatrick; the most tenuous suspicion of his infamy would have jeopardized the revolt; Nolan proposed a plan which made of the traitor's execution an instrument for the country's emancipation. He suggested that the condemned man die at the hands of an unknown assassin in deliberately dramatic circumstances which would remain engraved in the imagination of the people and would hasten the revolt. Kilpatrick swore he would take part in the scheme, which gave him the occasion to redeem himself and for which his death would provide the final flourish.

Nolan, urged on by time, was not able to invent all the circumstances of the multiple execution; he had to plagiarize another dramatist, the English enemy William Shakespeare. He repeated scenes from *Macbeth,* from *Julius Caesar.* The public and secret enactment comprised various days. The condemned man entered Dublin, discussed, acted, prayed, reproved, uttered words of pathos, and each of these gestures, to be reflected in his glory, had been pre-established by Nolan. Hundreds of actors collaborated with the protagonist; the role of some was complex; that of others momentary. The things they did and said endure in the history books, in the impassioned memory of Ireland. Kilpatrick, swept along by this minutely detailed destiny which both redeemed him and destroyed him, more than once enriched the text of his judge with improvised acts and words. Thus the populous drama unfolded in time, until on the 6th of August, 1824, in a theater box with funereal curtains prefiguring Lincoln's, a long-desired bullet entered the breast of the traitor and hero, who, amid two effusions of sudden blood, was scarcely able to articulate a few foreseen words.

In Nolan's work, the passages imitated from Shakespeare are the *least* dramatic; Ryan suspects that the author interpolated them so that in the future someone might hit upon the truth. He understands that he too forms part of Nolan's plot. . . . After a series of tenacious hesitations, he resolves to keep his discovery silent. He publishes a book dedicated to the hero's glory; this too, perhaps, was foreseen.

A Commentary

The first paragraph of Borges's story indicates unmistakably how far removed it is from the realism of Maupassant and Joyce. Instead of presenting us with a character situated in a world, it presents us with an idea for a "story plot which I shall perhaps write someday." This story does not pretend to be a slice of life. It does not even pretend to be a finished story: "Details, rectifications, adjustments are lacking; there are zones of the story not yet revealed to me." It is hard to see how fiction could insist more resolutely on its fictional character. Moreover, despite its shortness, the story consists of a number of separate plots or lines of action. The narrator himself, whom we might call *Borges* (italicized to distinguish him from the author, Borges), is telling us about Ryan, a man who is trying to write a biography. Ryan, himself a narrator, is trying to write the life of his ancestor Fergus Kilpatrick. In particular, Ryan is trying to account for the mysterious manner of Kilpatrick's death in a theater.

In the first sentence *Borges* tells us he has "imagined" this story under the influence of two other writers: Chesterton, author of the still popular "Father Brown" detective-mysteries, and Leibniz (or Leibnitz), a politician-mathematician-historian-philosopher who developed a theory in which the world is seen as an arrangement of harmoniously related substances. By notifying us that a mystery writer and a philosopher have inspired this tale, *Borges* suggests that we should be alert for clues and ideas. The story offers us a mystery about the death of Fergus Kilpatrick, complete with clues and solution; and the solution suggests a certain view of the world, a philosophical position.

Along with Ryan, the detective-biographer, we follow the clues about the murder of Fergus Kilpatrick. We discover not only that James Nolan was responsible for his death but that Nolan also stage-managed all the events surrounding that death: "Kilpatrick was killed in a theater, but the entire city was a theater as well." Nolan, who was an expert on the Swiss *Festspiele*, had arranged a gigantic play. But this one, with its cast of thousands, was not a reenactment of history in the form of fiction. It was fiction becoming history: "The things they did and said endure in the history books." The whole episode, which also prefigured the actual death of Lincoln, is referred to as Nolan's "work"—which it is, since he created it. *Borges*'s story closes with this paragraph:

> In Nolan's work, the passages imitated from Shakespeare are the *least* dramatic; Ryan suspects that the author interpolated them so that in the future someone might hit upon the truth. He understands that he too forms part of Nolan's plot . . . After a series of tenacious hesitations, he resolves to keep his discovery silent. He publishes a book dedicated to the hero's glory; this too, perhaps, was foreseen.

Ryan, the historian, has set out to discover historical truth about certain characters who lived in the past. He will then put them in a history book. What he discovers, however, is that he himself is perhaps a character in a fictional work designed by James Nolan; and his part is not that of truthful historian but of deceitful falsifier of history. He accepts the role as Kilpatrick accepted his, and plays the assigned part. But of course this part was really assigned by *Borges*, who tells us that he has made the whole thing up "in my idle afternoons." And behind this fictional *Borges* there stands another Borges who has made up this one, idle afternoons and all. And perhaps behind that one. . . .

We end, finally, as characters in someone's great design ourselves, as we sit reading Borges's pages, wondering whether the world is really organized according to a "pre-established harmony". The quotation from Yeats, which is set before the story as its epigraph, proposes a cyclical theory of history. It is taken from a poem, "Nineteen Hundred and Nineteen," written by the poet during the Irish "Troubles," which began with an uprising, like many others plotted in Ireland, but ended in success—only to be followed by civil war.

The poem, which Yeats included in his volume *The Tower*, is appropriate to the story in a very immediate way. But its main purpose is to add its voice to the cyclical theory of history that Borges is proposing in his story. The story is not a logical argument for this view. It merely asks "What if . . . ?" If history moves in cycles according to a pre-established harmony, then the sort of thing presented here might well occur. Questions like, "Does this sort of thing actually occur?" are left open to our thought. But Borges directs our thought along these lines. Instead of simply moving continually from old to new, history may—as Yeats suggests—whirl out the new and whirl in the old. It may move not in a line but in a circle or spiral. Borges's story can be seen as a variation on this theme in the philosophy of history.

Thus, in his tale Borges displays no special interest in the psychology of his characters or in the specific sociology of their environment. His Ireland is not Joyce's. Nor is it Yeats's. It is not even necessarily Ireland. It could be Poland or "some South American or Balkan state," as long as it is "oppressed and tenacious." The crowded plot and elaborate design of this little story overwhelm the characters. Idea and pattern, and the idea *of* pattern, dominate our vision. Borges has moved far from realism in telling us the stories of Ryan, Kilpatrick, and Nolan. Their tragi-comic histories exist for us mainly as a way of encouraging a pleasurable speculation—what Poe called "ratiocination." Philosophy can be seen as a serious playing with ideas. Borges embraces this playfulness and makes philosophy into fiction.

The title of this fable also encourages us to take a detached and speculative view of its "theme." What are traitors and heroes, it asks? One answer proposed is that traitors and heroes are people whom the history books present as traitors and heroes. Kilpatrick, of course, could be seen as either or both: his death being the execution of a traitor and the martyrdom of a hero who redeems himself by playing a role. Which is the "real" Kilpatrick? And is James Alexander Nolan, the stage-manager and executioner, a hero or traitor? And Ryan, who falsifies history for the sake of an ideal?

Whereas Joyce took a day in the life of an insignificant person and presented it with great care and seriousness, Borges takes the ideas of philosophers of history (like those he mentions: Condorcet, Hegel, Spengler, and Vico) and plays a fictional game with them. The possibilities of fiction are as various as man himself, and are continually renewed and refreshed by writers who offer us new perspectives on the universe. What every writer of fiction proposes to us is his own view of the world. He may look at it with a microscope or an inverted telescope. His lenses may be clear or colored. He may seek a photographic verisimilitude or offer us idealization or caricature. But every genuine writer of fiction offers us refined perception or expanded vision. It is because fiction enlarges and enhances our dealings with reality that we cherish it so highly.

In the stories in the anthology that follows, you will find two groups of tales that may be related to this one. This story is a modern kind of fable, similar to others collected under the heading "Fabulation." But it is also a "Metafiction," a story about the processes involved in creating fiction and in writing history. Thus, if this fable has a moral, it is a metafictional one, one that asks us to wonder whether there is really any difference between acting on the stage of history and performing in a theater. Borges suggests that in believing that we have separated the factual from the fictional in writing, we may have made a great mistake—or created yet another fiction.

A Collection of Modern Fiction

Fabulation, Realism, The Realistic Novella, Metafiction

FABULATION: *INTRODUCTION*

Modern fabulation looks back to the ancient forms of fable and parable, but instead of leading us toward a clear moral or spiritual conclusion, modern fabling may simply raise a question or play with an idea. Thus, Kafka's parables bear upon the impossibility of reaching final interpretations: they grow out of the gap between literal and figurative levels of meaning, a gap crossed so easily in the fables of Aesop or the parables of Jesus. What all the works of fabulation here collected have in common is a concern for ideas and values rather than for the social surface of existence or the psychological depths of character—or even our notion of what is possible or impossible in this world. Some of these modern tales and fables approach realism in one way or another. There is a good deal of social detail in "The Rocking-Horse Winner," for instance, or in "The Magic Barrel." In fact, each one of them has its realistic dimensions. But in every case there is at least one break with what we recognize as normal or probable; there is some moving away from realism for the sake of ideas that may ordinarily be concealed by the surface of reality.

The justification for this kind of fabling lies precisely in the way that it can open up questions of value for us, and prompt us to consider the assumptions upon which we act. Where ancient fables tried to settle questions of behavior, modern fables try to unsettle, to disturb, patterns of thought and action that have become so habitual that they conceal important dimensions of existence. In studying or discussing such tales it is most important to ask what ideas and values are called into question by the tale in question. Often, the best way to do that is to locate the most *fabulous* elements in each work and ask why the author chose to break with ordinary probabilities or possibilities at this particular point. To take the simplest and most graphic illustration, why should Merwin decide to describe in painstaking detail the *un*-chopping of a tree? With this question in mind, it should be possible to examine the way any given feature of a fable relates to the larger concerns of the whole story.

FRANZ KAFKA
1883–1924
On Parables

Many complain that the words of the wise are always merely parables and of no use in daily life, which is the only life we have. When the sage says: "Go over," he does not mean that we should cross to some actual place, which we could do anyhow if the labor were worth it; he means some fabulous yonder, something unknown to us, something that he cannot designate more precisely either, and therefore cannot help us here in the very least. All these parables really set out to say merely that the incomprehensible is incomprehensible, and we know that already. But the cares we have to struggle with every day: that is a different matter.

Concerning this a man once said: Why such reluctance? If you only followed the parables you yourselves would become parables and with that rid of all your daily cares.

Another said: I bet that is also a parable.

The first said: You have won.

The second said: But unfortunately only in parable.

The first said: No, in reality: in parable you have lost.

Translated by Willa and Edwin Muir

An Imperial Message

The emperor, so a parable runs, has sent a message to you, the humble subject, the insignificant shadow cowering in the remotest distance before the imperial sun; the Emperor from his deathbed has sent a message to you alone. He has commanded the messenger to kneel down by the bed, and has whispered the message to him; so much store did he lay on it that he ordered the messenger to whisper it back into his ear again. Then by a nod of the head he has confirmed that it is right. Yes, before the assembled spectators of his death—all the obstructing walls have been broken down, and on the spacious and loftily mounting open staircases stand in a ring the great princes of the Empire—before all these he has delivered his message. The messenger immediately sets out on his journey; a powerful, an indefatigable man; now pushing with his right arm, now with his left, he cleaves a way for himself through the throng; if he encounters resistance he points to his breast, where the symbol of the sun glitters; the way is made easier for him than it would be for any other man. But the multitudes are so vast; their numbers have no end. If he could reach the open fields how fast he would fly, and soon doubtless you would hear the welcome hammering of his fists on your door. But instead how vainly does he wear out his strength; still he is only making his way through the chambers of the innermost palace; never will he get to the end of them; and if he succeeded in that nothing would be gained; he must next fight his way down the stair; and if he succeeded in that nothing would be gained; the courts would still have to be crossed; and after the courts the second outer palace; and once more stairs and courts; and once more another palace; and so on for thousands of years; and if at last he should burst through the outermost gate—but never, never can that happen—the imperial capital would lie before him, the center of the world, crammed to bursting with its own sediment. Nobody could fight his way through here even with a message from a dead man. But you sit at your window when evening falls and dream it to yourself.

Translated by Willa and Edwin Muir

D. H. LAWRENCE
1885–1930
The Rocking-Horse Winner

There was a woman who was beautiful, who started with all the advantages, yet she had no luck. She married for love, and the love turned to dust. She had bonny children, yet she felt they had been thrust upon her, and she could not love them. They looked at her coldly, as if they were finding fault with her. And hurriedly she felt she must cover up some fault in herself. Yet what it was that she must cover up she never knew. Nevertheless, when her children were present, she always felt the centre of her heart go hard. This troubled her, and in her manner she was all the more gentle and anxious for her children, as if she loved them very much. Only she herself knew that at the centre of her heart was a hard little place that could not feel love, no, not for anybody. Everybody else said of her: "She is such a good mother. She adores her children." Only she herself, and her children themselves, knew it was not so. They read it in each other's eyes.

There were a boy and two little girls. They lived in a pleasant house, with a garden, and they had discreet servants, and felt themselves superior to anyone in the neighbourhood.

Although they lived in style, they felt always an anxiety in the house. There was never enough money. The mother had a small income, and the father had a small income, but not nearly enough for the social position which they had to keep up. The father went into town to some office. But though he had good prospects, these prospects never materialised. There was always the grinding sense of the shortage of money, though the style was always kept up.

At last the mother said: "I will see if I can't make something." But she did not know where to begin. She racked her brains, and tried this thing and the other, but could not find anything successful. The failure made deep lines come into her face. Her children were growing up, they would have to go to school. There must be more money, there must be more money. The father, who was always very handsome and expensive in his tastes, seemed as if he never *would* be able to do anything worth doing. And the mother, who had a great belief in herself, did not succeed any better, and her tastes were just as expensive.

And so the house came to be haunted by the unspoken phrase: *There must be more money! There must be more money!* The children could hear it all the time, though nobody said it aloud. They heard it at Christmas, when the expensive and splendid toys filled the nursery. Behind the shining modern rocking-horse, behind the smart doll's house, a voice would start whispering: "There *must* be more money! There *must* be more money!" And the children would stop playing, to listen for a moment. They would look into each other's eyes, to see if they had all heard. And each one saw in the eyes of the other two that they too had heard. "There *must* be more money! There *must* be more money!"

It came whispering from the springs of the still-swaying rocking-horse, and even the horse, bending his wooden, champing head, heard it. The big doll, sitting so pink and smirking in her new pram, could hear it quite plainly, and seemed to be smirking all the more self-consciously because of it. The foolish puppy, too, that took the place of the teddy-bear, he was looking so extraordinarily foolish for no other reason but that he heard the secret whisper all over the house: "There *must* be more money!"

Yet nobody ever said it aloud. The whisper was everywhere, and therefore no one spoke it. Just as no one ever says: "We are breathing!" in spite of the fact that breath is coming and going all the time.

"Mother," said the boy Paul one day, "why don't we keep a car of our own? Why do we always use uncle's, or else a taxi?"

"Because we're the poor members of the family," said the mother.

"But why *are* we, mother?"

"Well—I suppose," she said slowly and bitterly, "it's because your father has no luck."

The boy was silent for some time.

"Is luck money, mother?" he asked, rather timidly.

"No, Paul. Not quite. It's what causes you to have money."

"Oh!" said Paul vaguely. "I thought when Uncle Oscar said *filthy lucker*, it meant money."

"*Filthy lucre* does mean money," said the mother. "But it's lucre, not luck."

"Oh!" said the boy. "Then what *is* luck, mother?"

"It's what causes you to have money. If you're lucky you have money. That's why it's better to be born lucky than rich. If you're rich, you may lose your money. But if you're lucky, you will always get more money."

"Oh! Will you? And is father not lucky?"

"Very unlucky, I should say," she said bitterly.

The boy watched her with unsure eyes.

"Why?" he asked.

"I don't know. Nobody ever knows why one person is lucky and another unlucky."

"Don't they? Nobody at all? Does *nobody* know?"

"Perhaps God. But He never tells."

"He ought to, then. And aren't you lucky either, mother?"

"I can't be, if I married an unlucky husband."

"But by yourself, aren't you?"

"I used to think I was, before I married. Now I think I am very unlucky indeed."

"Why?"

"Well—never mind! Perhaps I'm not really," she said.

The child looked at her to see if she meant it. But he saw, by the lines of her mouth, that she was only trying to hide something from him.

"Well, anyhow," he said stoutly, "I'm a lucky person."

"Why?" said his mother, with a sudden laugh.

He stared at her. He didn't even know why he had said it.

"God told me," he asserted, brazening it out.

"I hope He did, dear!" she said, again with a laugh, but rather bitter.

"He did, mother!"

"Excellent!" said the mother, using one of her husband's exclamations.

The boy saw she did not believe him; or rather, that she paid no attention to his assertion. This angered him somewhere, and made him want to compel her attention.

He went off by himself, vaguely, in a childish way, seeking for the clue to "luck." Absorbed, taking no heed of other people, he went about with a sort of stealth, seeking inwardly for luck. He wanted luck, he wanted it, he wanted it. When the two girls were playing dolls in the nursery, he would sit on his big rocking-horse, charging madly into space, with a frenzy that made the little girls peer at him uneasily. Wildly the horse careered, the waving dark hair of the boy tossed, his eyes had a strange glare in them. The little girls dared not speak to him.

When he had ridden to the end of his mad little journey, he climbed down and stood in front of his rocking-horse, staring fixedly into its lowered face. Its red mouth was slightly open, its big eye was wide and glassy-bright.

"Now!" he would silently command the snorting steed. "Now, take me to where there is luck! Now take me!"

And he would slash the horse on the neck with the little whip he had asked Uncle Oscar for. He *knew* the horse could take him to where there was luck, if only he forced it. So he would mount again and start on his furious ride, hoping at last to get there. He knew he could get there.

"You'll break your horse, Paul!" said the nurse.

"He's always riding like that! I wish he'd leave off!" said his elder sister Joan.

But he only glared down on them in silence. Nurse gave him up. She could make nothing of him. Anyhow, he was growing beyond her.

One day his mother and his Uncle Oscar came in when he was on one of his furious rides. He did not speak to them.

"Hallo, you young jockey! Riding a winner?" said his uncle.

"Aren't you growing too big for a rocking-horse? You're not a very little boy any longer, you know," said his mother.

But Paul only gave a blue glare from his big, rather close-set eyes. He would speak to nobody when he was in full tilt. His mother watched him with an anxious expression on her face.

At last he suddenly stopped forcing his horse into the mechanical gallop and slid down.

"Well, I got there!" he announced fiercely, his blue eyes still flaring, and his sturdy long legs straddling apart.

"Where did you get to?" asked his mother.

"Where I wanted to go," he flared back at her.

"That's right, son!" said Uncle Oscar. "Don't you stop till you get there. What's the horse's name?"

"He doesn't have a name," said the boy.

"Gets on without all right?" asked the uncle.

"Well, he has different names. He was called Sansovino last week."

"Sansovino, eh? Won the Ascot. How did you know this name?"

"He always talks about horse-races with Bassett," said Joan.

The uncle was delighted to find that his small nephew was posted with all the racing news. Bassett, the young gardener, who had been wounded in the left foot in the war and had got his present job through Oscar Cresswell, whose batman he had been, was a perfect blade of the "turf." He lived in the racing events, and the small boy lived with him.

Oscar Cresswell got it all from Bassett.

"Master Paul comes and asks me, so I can't do more than tell him, sir," said Bassett, his face terribly serious, as if he were speaking of religious matters.

"And does he ever put anything on a horse he fancies?"

"Well—I don't want to give him away—he's a young sport, a fine sport, sir. Would you mind asking him himself? He sort of takes a pleasure in it, and perhaps he'd feel I was giving him away, sir, if you don't mind."

Bassett was serious as a church.

The uncle went back to his nephew and took him off for a ride in the car.

"Say, Paul, old man, do you ever put anything on a horse?" the uncle asked.

The boy watched the handsome man closely.

"Why, do you think I oughtn't to?" he parried.

"Not a bit of it! I thought perhaps you might give me a tip for the Lincoln."

The car sped on into the country, going down to Uncle Oscar's place in Hampshire.

"Honour bright?" said the nephew.

"Honour bright, son!" said the uncle.

"Well, then, Daffodil."

"Daffodil! I doubt it, sonny. What about Mirza?"

"I only know the winner," said the boy. "That's Daffodil."

"Daffodil, eh?"

There was a pause. Daffodil was an obscure horse comparatively.

"Uncle!"

"Yes, son?"

"You won't let it go any further, will you? I promised Bassett."

"Bassett be damned, old man! What's he got to do with it?"

"We're partners. We've been partners from the first. Uncle, he lent me my first five shillings, which I lost. I promised him, honour bright, it was only between me and him; only you gave me that ten-shilling note I started winning with, so I thought you were lucky. You won't let it go any further, will you?"

The boy gazed at his uncle from those big, hot, blue eyes, set rather close together. The uncle stirred and laughed uneasily.

"Right you are, son! I'll keep your tip private. Daffodil, eh? How much are you putting on him?"

"All except twenty pounds," said the boy. "I keep that in reserve."

The uncle thought it a good joke.

"You keep twenty pounds in reserve, do you, you young romancer? What are you betting, then?"

"I'm betting three hundred," said the boy gravely. "But it's between you and me, Uncle Oscar! Honour bright?"

The uncle burst into a roar of laughter.

"It's between you and me all right, you young Nat Gould," he said, laughing. "But where's your three hundred?"

"Bassett keeps it for me. We're partners."

"You are, are you! And what is Bassett putting on Daffodil?"

"He won't go quite as high as I do, I expect. Perhaps he'll go a hundred and fifty."

"What, pennies?" laughed the uncle.

"Pounds," said the child, with a surprised look at his uncle. "Bassett keeps a bigger reserve than I do."

Between wonder and amusement Uncle Oscar was silent. He pursued the matter no further, but he determined to take his nephew with him to the Lincoln races.

"Now, son," he said, "I'm putting twenty on Mirza, and I'll put five on for you on any horse you fancy. What's your pick?"

"Daffodil, uncle."

"No, not the fiver on Daffodil!"

"I should if it was my own fiver," said the child.

"Good! Good! Right you are! A fiver for me and a fiver for you on Daffodil."

The child had never been to a race-meeting before, and his eyes were blue fire. He pursed his mouth tight and watched. A Frenchman just in front had put his money on Lancelot. Wild with excitement, he flayed his arms up and down, yelling "Lancelot! Lancelot!" in his French accent.

Daffodil came in first, Lancelot second, Mirza third. The child, flushed and with eyes blazing, was curiously serene. His uncle brought him four five-pound notes, four to one.

"What am I do with these?" he cried, waving them before the boy's eyes.

"I suppose we'll talk to Bassett," said the boy. "I expect I have fifteen hundred now; and twenty in reserve; and this twenty."

His uncle studied him for some moments.

"Look here, son!" he said. "You're not serious about Bassett and that fifteen hundred, are you?"

"Yes, I am. But it's between you and me, uncle. Honour bright?"

"Honour bright all right, son! But I must talk to Bassett."

"If you'd like to be a partner, uncle, with Bassett and me, we could all be partners. Only, you'd have to promise, honour bright, uncle, not to let it go beyond us three. Bassett and I are lucky, and you must be lucky, because it was your ten shillings I started winning with. . . ."

Uncle Oscar took both Bassett and Paul into Richmond Park for an afternoon, and there they talked.

"It's like this, you see, sir," Bassett said. "Master Paul would get me talking about racing events, spinning yarns, you know, sir. And he was always keen on knowing if I'd made or if I'd lost. It's about a year since, now, that I put five shillings on Blush of Dawn for him: and we lost. Then the luck turned, with that ten shillings he had from you: that we put on Singhalese. And since that time, it's been pretty steady, all things considering. What do you say, Master Paul?"

"We're all right when we're sure," said Paul. "It's when we're not quite sure that we go down."

"Oh, but we're careful then," said Bassett.

"But when are you *sure*?" smiled Uncle Oscar.

"It's Master Paul, sir," said Bassett in a secret, religious voice. "It's as if he had it from heaven. Like Daffodil, now, for the Lincoln. That was as sure as eggs."

"Did you put anything on Daffodil?" asked Oscar Cresswell.

"Yes, sir. I made my bit."

"And my nephew?"

Bassett was obstinately silent, looking at Paul.

"I made twelve hundred, didn't I, Bassett? I told uncle I was putting three hundred on Daffodil."

"That's right," said Bassett, nodding.

"But where's the money?" asked the uncle.

"I keep it safe locked up, sir. Master Paul he can have it any minute he likes to ask for it."

"What, fifteen hundred pounds?"

"And twenty! And *forty*, that is, with the twenty he made on the course."

"It's amazing!" said the uncle.

"If Master Paul offers you to be partners, sir, I would, if I were you: if you'll excuse me," said Bassett.

Oscar Cresswell thought about it.

"I'll see the money," he said.

They drove home again, and, sure enough, Bassett came round to the garden-house with fifteen hundred pounds in notes. The twenty pounds reserve was left with Joe Glee, in the Turf Commission deposit.

"You see, it's all right, uncle, when I'm *sure!* Then we go strong, for all we're worth. Don't we, Bassett?"

"We do that, Master Paul."

"And when are you sure?" said the uncle, laughing.

"Oh, well, sometimes I'm *absolutely* sure, like about Daffodil," said the boy; "and sometimes I have an idea; and sometimes I haven't even an idea, have I, Bassett? Then we're careful, because we mostly go down."

"You do, do you! And when you're sure, like about Daffodil, what makes you sure, sonny?"

"Oh, well, I don't know," said the boy uneasily. "I'm sure, you know, uncle; that's all."

"It's as if he had it from heaven, sir," Bassett reiterated.

"I should say so!" said the uncle.

But he became a partner. And when the Leger was coming on Paul was "sure" about Lively Spark, which was a quite inconsiderable horse. The boy insisted on putting a thousand on the horse, Bassett was for five hundred, and Oscar Cresswell two hundred. Lively Spark came in first, and the betting had been ten to one against him. Paul had made ten thousand.

"You see," he said, "I was absolutely sure of him."

Even Oscar Cresswell had cleared two thousand.

"Look here, son," he said, "this sort of thing makes me nervous."

"It needn't, uncle! Perhaps I shan't be sure again for a long time."

"But what are you going to do with your money?" asked the uncle.

"Of course," said the boy, "I started it for mother. She said she had no luck, because father is unlucky, so I thought if *I* was lucky, it might stop whispering."

"What might stop whispering?"

"Our house. I *hate* our house for whispering."

"What does it whisper?"

"Why—why"—the boy fidgeted—"why, I don't know. But it's always short of money, you know, uncle."

"I know it, son, I know it."

"You know people send mother writs, don't you, uncle?"

"I'm afraid I do," said the uncle.

"And then the house whispers, like people laughing at you behind your back. It's awful, that is! I thought if I was lucky——"

"You might stop it," added the uncle.

The boy watched him with big blue eyes, that had an uncanny cold fire in them, and he said never a word.

"Well, then!" said the uncle. "What are we doing?"

"I shouldn't like mother to know I was lucky," said the boy.

"Why not, son?"

"She'd stop me."

"I don't think she would."

"Oh!"—and the boy writhed in an odd way—"I *don't* want her to know, uncle."

"All right, son! We'll manage it without her knowing."

They managed it very easily. Paul, at the other's suggestion, handed over five thousand pounds to his uncle, who deposited it with the family lawyer, who was then to inform Paul's mother that a relative had put five thousand pounds into his hands, which sum was to be paid out a thousand pounds at a time, on the mother's birthday, for the next five years.

"So she'll have a birthday present of a thousand pounds for five successive years," said Uncle Oscar. "I hope it won't make it all the harder for her later."

Paul's mother had her birthday in November. The house had been "whispering" worse than ever lately, and, even in spite of his luck, Paul could not bear up against it. He was very anxious to see the effect of the birthday letter, telling his mother about the thousand pounds.

When there were no visitors, Paul now took his meals with his parents, as he was beyond the nursery control. His mother went into town nearly every day. She had discovered that she had an odd knack of sketching furs and dress materials, so she worked secretly in the studio of a friend who was the chief "artist" for the leading drapers. She drew the figures of ladies in furs and ladies in silk and sequins for the newspaper advertisements. This young woman artist earned several thousand pounds a year, but Paul's mother only made several hundreds, and she was again dissatisfied. She so wanted to be first in something, and she did not succeed, even in making sketches for drapery advertisements.

She was down to breakfast on the morning of her birthday. Paul watched her face as she read her letters. He knew the lawyer's letter. As his mother read it, her face hardened and became more expressionless. Then a cold, determined look came on her mouth. She hid the letter under the pile of others, and said not a word about it.

"Didn't you have anything nice in the post for your birthday, mother?" said Paul.

"Quite moderately nice," she said, her voice cold and absent.

She went away to town without saying more.

But in the afternoon Uncle Oscar appeared. He said Paul's mother had had a long interview with the lawyer, asking if the whole five thousand could not be advanced at once, as she was in debt.

"What do you think, uncle?" said the boy.

"I leave it to you, son."

"Oh, let her have it, then! We can get some more with the other," said the boy.

"A bird in the hand is worth two in the bush, laddie!" said Uncle Oscar.

"But I'm sure to *know* for the Grand National; or the Lincolnshire; or else the Derby. I'm sure to know for *one* of them," said Paul.

So Uncle Oscar signed the agreement, and Paul's mother touched the whole five thousand. Then something very curious happened. The voices in the house suddenly went mad, like a chorus of frogs on a spring evening. There were certain new furnishings, and Paul had a tutor. He was *really* going to Eton, his father's school, in the following autumn. There were flowers in the winter, and a blossoming of the luxury Paul's mother had been used to. And yet the voices in the house, behind the sprays of mimosa and almondblossom, and from under the piles of iridescent cushions, simply trilled and screamed in a sort of ecstasy: "There *must* be more money! Oh-h-h; there *must* be more money. Oh, now, now-w! Now-w-w—there *must* be more money!—more than ever! More than ever!"

It frightened Paul terribly. He studied away at his Latin and Greek with his tutor. But his intense hours were spent with Bassett. The Grand National had gone by: he had not "known," and had lost a hundred pounds. Summer was at hand. He was in agony for the Lincoln. But even for the Lincoln he didn't "know," and he lost fifty pounds. He became wild-eyed and strange, as if something were going to explode in him.

"Let it alone, son! Don't you bother about it!" urged Uncle Oscar. But it was as if the boy couldn't really hear what his uncle was saying.

"I've got to know for the Derby! I've got to know for the Derby!" the child reiterated, his big blue eyes blazing with a sort of madness.

His mother noticed how overwrought he was.

"You'd better go to the seaside. Wouldn't you like to go now to the seaside, instead of waiting? I think you'd better," she said, looking down at him anxiously, her heart curiously heavy because of him.

But the child lifted his uncanny blue eyes.

"I couldn't possibly go before the Derby, mother!" he said. "I couldn't possibly!"

"Why not?" she said, her voice becoming heavy when she was opposed. "Why not? You can still go from the seaside to see the Derby with your Uncle Oscar, if that's what you wish. No need for you to wait here. Besides, I think you care too much about these races. It's a bad sign. My family has been a gambling family, and you won't know till you grow up how much damage it has done. But it has done damage. I shall have to send Bassett away, and ask Uncle Oscar not to talk racing to you, unless you promise to be reasonable about it: go away to the seaside and forget it. You're all nerves!"

"I'll do what you like, mother, so long as you don't send me away till after the Derby," the boy said.

"Send you away from where? Just from this house?"

"Yes," he said, gazing at her.

"Why, you curious child, what makes you care about this house so much, suddenly? I never knew you loved it."

He gazed at her without speaking. He had a secret within a secret, something he had not divulged, even to Bassett or to his Uncle Oscar.

But his mother, after standing undecided and a little bit sullen for some moments, said:

"Very well, then! Don't go to the seaside till after the Derby, if you don't wish it. But promise me you won't let your nerves go to pieces. Promise you won't think so much about horse-racing and *events*, as you call them!"

"Oh no," said the boy casually. "I won't think much about them, mother. You needn't worry. I wouldn't worry, mother, if I were you."

"If you were me and I were you," said his mother, "I wonder what we *should* do!"

"But you know you needn't worry, mother, don't you?" the boy repeated.

"I should be awfully glad to know it," she said wearily.

"Oh, well, you *can*, you know. I mean, you *ought* to know you needn't worry," he insisted.

"Ought I? Then I'll see about it," she said.

Paul's secret of secrets was his wooden horse, that which had no name. Since he was emancipated from a nurse and a nursery-governess, he had had his rocking-horse removed to his own bedroom at the top of the house.

"Surely you're too big for a rocking-horse!" his mother had remonstrated.

"Well, you see, mother, till I can have a *real* horse, I like to have *some* sort of animal about," had been his quaint answer.

"Do you feel he keeps you company?" she laughed.

"Oh yes! He's very good, he always keeps me company, when I'm there," said Paul.

So the horse, rather shabby, stood in an arrested prance in the boy's bedroom.

The Derby was drawing near, and the boy grew more and more

tense. He hardly heard what was spoken to him, he was very frail, and his eyes were really uncanny. His mother had sudden strange seizures of uneasiness about him. Sometimes, for half an hour, she would feel a sudden anxiety about him that was almost anguish. She wanted to rush to him at once, and know he was safe.

Two nights before the Derby, she was at a big party in town, when one of her rushes of anxiety about her boy, her first-born, gripped her heart till she could hardly speak. She fought with the feeling, might and main, for she believed in common sense. But it was too strong. She had to leave the dance and go downstairs to telephone to the country. The children's nursery-governess was terribly surprised and startled at being rung up in the night.

"Are the children all right, Miss Wilmot?"

"Oh yes, they are quite all right."

"Master Paul? Is he all right?"

"He went to bed as right as a trivet. Shall I run up and look at him?"

"No," said Paul's mother reluctantly. "No! Don't trouble. It's all right. Don't sit up. We shall be home fairly soon." She did not want her son's privacy intruded upon.

"Very good," said the governess.

It was about one o'clock when Paul's mother and father drove up to their house. All was still. Paul's mother went to her room and slipped off her white fur cloak. She had told her maid not to wait up for her. She heard her husband downstairs, mixing a whisky and soda.

And then, because of the strange anxiety at her heart, she stole upstairs to her son's room. Noiselessly she went along the upper corridor. Was there a faint noise? What was it?

She stood, with arrested muscles, outside his door, listening. There was a strange, heavy, and yet not loud noise. Her heart stood still. It was a soundless noise, yet rushing and powerful. Something huge, in violent, hushed motion. What was it? What in God's name was it? She ought to know. She felt that she knew the noise. She knew what it was.

Yet she could not place it. She couldn't say what it was. And on and on it went, like a madness.

Softly, frozen with anxiety and fear, she turned the doorhandle.

The room was dark. Yet in the space near the window, she heard and saw something plunging to and fro. She gazed in fear and amazement.

Then suddenly she switched on the light, and saw her son, in his green pyjamas, madly surging on the rocking-horse. The blaze of light suddenly lit him up, as he urged the wooden horse, and lit her up, as she stood, blonde, in her dress of pale green and crystal, in the doorway.

"Paul!" she cried. "Whatever are you doing?"

"It's Malabar!" he screamed in a powerful, strange voice. "It's Malabar!"

His eyes blazed at her for one strange and senseless second, as he ceased urging his wooden horse. Then he fell with a crash to the ground, and she, all her tormented motherhood flooding upon her, rushed to gather him up.

But he was unconscious, and unconscious he remained, with some brain-fever. He talked and tossed, and his mother sat stonily by his side.

"Malabar! It's Malabar! Bassett, Bassett, I *know*! It's Malabar!"

So the child cried, trying to get up and urge the rocking-horse that gave him his inspiration.

"What does he mean by Malabar?" asked the heart-frozen mother.

"I don't know," said the father stonily.

"What does he mean by Malabar?" she asked her brother Oscar.

"It's one of the horses running for the Derby," was the answer.

And, in spite of himself, Oscar Cresswell spoke to Bassett, and himself put a thousand on Malabar: at fourteen to one.

The third day of the illness was critical: they were waiting for a change. The boy, with his rather long, curly hair, was tossing ceaselessly on the pillow. He neither slept nor regained consciousness, and his eyes were like blue stones. His mother sat, feeling her heart had gone, turned actually into a stone.

In the evening, Oscar Cresswell did not come, but Bassett sent a message, saying could he come up for one moment, just one moment? Paul's mother was very angry at the intrusion, but on second thoughts she agreed. The boy was the same. Perhaps Bassett might bring him to consciousness.

The gardener, a shortish fellow with a little brown moustache and sharp little brown eyes, tiptoed into the room, touched his imaginary cap to Paul's mother, and stole to the bedside, staring with glittering, smallish eyes at the tossing, dying child.

"Master Paul!" he whispered. "Master Paul! Malabar came in first all right, a clean win. I did as you told me. You've made over seventy thousand pounds, you have; you've got over eighty thousand. Malabar came in all right, Master Paul."

"Malabar! Malabar! Did I say Malabar, mother? Did I say Malabar? Do you think I'm lucky, mother? I knew Malabar, didn't I? Over eighty thousand pounds! I call that lucky, don't you, mother? Over eighty thousand pounds! I knew, didn't I know I knew? Malabar came in all right. If I ride my horse till I'm sure, then I tell you, Bassett, you can go as high as you like. Did you go for all you were worth, Bassett?"

"I went a thousand on it, Master Paul."

"I never told you, mother, that if I can ride my horse, and *get there*, then I'm absolutely sure—oh, absolutely! Mother, did I ever tell you? I *am* lucky!"

"No, you never did," said his mother.

But the boy died in the night.

And even as he lay dead, his mother heard her brother's voice saying to her: "My God, Hester, you're eighty-odd thousand to the good, and a poor devil of a son to the bad. But, poor devil, poor devil, he's best gone out of a life where he rides his rocking-horse to find a winner."

ELIZABETH BOWEN
1899–1973
The Demon Lover

Towards the end of her day in London Mrs. Drover went round to her shut-up house to look for several things she wanted to take away. Some belonged to herself, some to her family, who were by now used to their country life. It was late August; it had been a steamy, showery day: at the moment the trees down the pavement glittered in an escape of humid yellow afternoon sun. Against the next batch of clouds, already piling up ink-dark, broken chimneys and parapets stood out. In her once familiar street, as in any unused channel, an unfamiliar queerness had silted up; a cat wove itself in and out of railings, but no human eye watched Mrs. Drover's return. Shifting some parcels under her arm, she slowly forced round her latchkey in an unwilling lock, then gave the door, which had warped, a push with her knee. Dead air came out to meet her as she went in.

The staircase window having been boarded up, no light came down into the hall. But one door, she could just see, stood ajar, so she went quickly through into the room and unshuttered the big window in there. Now the prosaic woman, looking about her, was more perplexed than she knew by everything that she saw, by traces of her long former habit of life—the yellow smoke-stain up the white marble mantelpiece, the ring left by a vase on the top of the escritoire; the bruise in the wallpaper where, on the door being thrown open widely, the china handle had always hit the wall. The piano, having gone away to be stored, had left what looked like claw-marks on its part of the parquet. Though not much dust had seeped in, each object wore a film of another kind; and, the only ventilation being the chimney, the whole drawing-room smelled of the cold hearth. Mrs. Drover put down her parcels on the escritoire and left the room to proceed upstairs; the things she wanted were in a bedroom chest.

She had been anxious to see how the house was—the part-time caretaker she shared with some neighbours was away this week on his holiday, known to be not yet back. At the best of times he did not look in often, and she was never sure that she trusted him. There were some cracks in the structure, left by the last bombing, on which she was anxious to keep an eye. Not that one could do anything—

A shaft of refracted daylight now lay across the hall. She stopped dead and stared at the hall table—on this lay a letter addressed to her.

She thought first—then the caretaker *must* be back. All the same, who, seeing the house shuttered, would have dropped a letter in at the box? It was not a circular, it was not a bill. And the post office redirected, to the address in the country, everything for her that came through the post. The caretaker (even if he *were* back) did not know she was due in London to-day—her call here had been planned to be a surprise—so his negligence in the manner of this letter, leaving it to wait in the dusk and the dust, annoyed her. Annoyed, she picked up the letter, which bore no stamp. But it cannot be important, or they would know . . . She took the letter rapidly upstairs with her, without a stop to look at the writing till she reached what had been her bedroom, where she let in light. The room looked over the garden and other gardens: the sun had gone in; as the clouds sharpened and lowered, the trees and rank lawns seemed already to smoke with dark. Her reluctance to look again at the letter came from the fact that she felt intruded upon—and by someone contemptuous of her ways. However, in the tenseness preceding the fall of rain she read it: it was a few lines.

> DEAR KATHLEEN,
> You will not have forgotten that to-day is our anniversary, and the day we said. The years have gone by at once slowly and fast. In view of the fact that nothing has changed, I shall rely upon you to keep your promise. I was sorry to see you leave London, but was satisfied that you would be back in time. You may expect me, therefore, at the hour arranged.
>
> Until then . . .
>
> K.

Mrs. Drover looked for the date: it was to-day's. She dropped the letter on to the bed-springs, then picked it up to see the writing again—her lips, beneath the remains of lipstick, beginning to go white. She felt so much the change in her own face that she went to the mirror, polished a clear patch in it and looked at once urgently and stealthily in. She was confronted by a woman of forty-four, with eyes starting out under a hat-brim that had been rather carelessly pulled down. She had not put on any more powder since she left the shop where she ate her solitary tea. The pearls her husband had given her on their marriage hung loose round her now rather thinner throat, slipping into the V of the pink wool jumper her sister knitted last autumn as they sat round the fire. Mrs. Drover's most normal expression was one of controlled worry, but of assent. Since the birth of the third of her little boys, attended by a quite serious illness, she had had an intermittent muscular flicker to the left of her mouth, but in spite of this she could always sustain a manner that was at once energetic and calm.

Turning from her own face as precipitately as she had gone to meet it, she went to the chest where the things were, unlocked it, threw up the lid and knelt to search. But as rain began to come crashing down she could not keep from looking over her shoulder at the stripped bed on which the letter lay. Behind the blanket of rain the clock of the church that still stood struck six—with rapidly heightening apprehension, she counted each of the slow strokes. "The hour arranged . . . My God," she said, "*what* hour? How should I . . . ? After twenty-five years. . . ."

The young girl talking to the soldier in the garden had not ever completely seen his face. It was dark; they were saying good-bye under a tree. Now and then—for it felt, from not seeing him at this intense moment, as though she had never seen him at all—she verified his presence for these few moments longer by putting out a hand, which he each time pressed, without very much kindness, and painfully, on to one of the breast buttons of his uniform. That cut of the button on the palm of her hand was, principally, what she was to carry away. This was so near the end of a leave from France that she could only wish him already gone. It was August 1916. Being not kissed, being drawn away from and looked at intimidated Kathleen till she imagined spectral glitters in the place of his eyes. Turning away and looking back up the lawn she saw, through branches of trees, the drawing-room window alight: she caught a breath for the moment when she could go running back there into the safe arms of her mother and sister, and cry: "What shall I do, what shall I do? He has gone."

Hearing her catch her breath, her fiancé said, without feeling: "Cold?"

"You're going away such a long way."

"Not so far as you think."

"I don't understand?"

"You don't have to," he said. "You will. You know what we said."

"But that was—suppose you—I mean, suppose."

"I shall be with you," he said, "sooner or later. You won't forget that. You need do nothing but wait."

Only a little more than a minute later she was free to run up the silent lawn. Looking in through the window at her mother and sister, who did not for the moment perceive her, she already felt that unnatural promise drive down between her and the rest of all human kind. No other way of having given herself could have made her feel so apart, lost and foresworn. She could not have plighted a more sinister troth.

Kathleen behaved well when, some months later, her fiancé was reported missing, presumed killed. Her family not only supported her but were able to praise her courage without stint because they could not regret, as a husband for her, the man they knew almost nothing about. They hoped she would, in a year or two, console herself—and had it been only a question of consolation things might have gone much straighter ahead. But her trouble, behind just a little grief, was a complete dislocation from everything. She did not reject other lovers, for these failed to appear: for years she failed to attract men—and with the approach of her thirties she became natural enough to share her family's anxiousness on this score. She began to put herself out, to wonder; and at thirty-two she was very greatly relieved to find herself being courted by William Drover. She married him, and the two of them settled down in this quiet, arboreal part of Kensington: in this house the years piled up, her children were born and they all lived till they were driven out by the bombs of the next war. Her movements as Mrs. Drover were circumscribed, and she dismissed any idea that they were still watched.

As things were—dead or living the letter-writer sent her only a threat. Unable, for some minutes, to go on kneeling with her back exposed to the empty room, Mrs. Drover rose from the chest to sit on an upright chair whose back was firmly against the wall. The desuetude of her former bedroom, her married London home's whole air of being a cracked cup from which memory, with its reassuring power, had either evaporated or leaked away, made a crisis—and at just this crisis the letter-writer had, knowledgeably, struck. The hollowness of the house this evening cancelled years on years of voices, habits and steps. Through the shut windows she only heard rain fall on the roofs around. To rally herself, she said she was in a mood—and, for two or three seconds shutting her eyes, told herself that she had imagined the letter. But she opened them—there it lay on the bed.

On the supernatural side of the letter's entrance she was not permitting her mind to dwell. Who, in London, knew she meant to call at the house to-day? Evidently, however, this had been known. The caretaker, *had* he come back, had had no cause to expect her: he would have taken the letter in his pocket, to forward it, at his own time, through the post. There was no other sign that the caretaker had been in—but, if not? Letters dropped in at doors of deserted houses do not fly or walk to tables in halls. They do not sit on the dust of empty tables with the air of certainty that they will be found. There is needed some human hand—but nobody but the caretaker had a key. Under circumstances she did not care to consider, a house can be entered without a key. It was possible that she was not alone now. She might be being waited for, downstairs. Waited for—until when? Until "the hour arranged." At least that was not six o'clock: six has struck.

She rose from the chair and went over and locked the door.

The thing was, to get out. To fly? No, not that: she had to catch her train. As a woman whose utter dependability was the keystone of her family life she was not willing to return to the country, to her husband, her little boys and her sister, without the objects she had come up to fetch. Resuming work at the chest she set about making up a number of parcels in a rapid, fumbling-decisive way. These, with her shopping parcels, would be too much to carry; these meant a taxi—at the thought of the taxi her heart went up and her normal breathing resumed. I will ring up the taxi now; the taxi cannot come too soon: I shall hear the taxi out there running its engine, till I walk calmly down to it through the hall. I'll ring up—But no: the telephone is cut off . . . She tugged at a knot she had tied wrong.

The idea of flight . . . He was never kind to me, not really. I don't remember him kind at all. Mother said he never considered me. He was set on me, that was what it was—not love. Not love, not meaning a person well. What did he do, to make me promise like that? I can't remember— But she found that she could.

She remembered with such dreadful acuteness that the twenty-five years since then dissolved like smoke and she instinctively looked for the weal left by the button on the palm of her hand. She remembered not only all that he said and did but the complete suspension of *her* existence during that August week. I was not myself—they all told me so at the time. She remembered—but with one white burning blank as where acid has dropped on a photograph: *under no conditions* could she remember his face.

So, wherever he may be waiting, I shall not know him. You have no time to run from a face you do not expect.

The thing was to get to the taxi before any clock struck what could be the hour. She would slip down the street and round the side of the square to where the square gave on the main road. She would return in the taxi, safe, to her own door, and bring the solid driver into the house with her to pick up the parcels from room to room. The idea of the taxi driver made her decisive, bold: she unlocked her door, went to the top of the staircase and listened down.

She heard nothing—but while she was hearing nothing the *passé* air of the staircase was disturbed by a draught that travelled up to her face. It emanated from the basement: down there a door or window was being opened by someone who chose this moment to leave the house.

The rain had stopped; the pavements steamily shone as Mrs. Drover let herself out by inches from her own front door into the empty street. The unoccupied houses opposite continued to meet her look with their damaged stare. Making towards the thoroughfare and the taxi, she tried not to keep looking behind. Indeed, the silence was so intense—one of those creeks of London silence exaggerated this summer by the damage of war—that no tread could have gained on hers unheard. Where her street debouched on the square where people went on living she grew conscious of and checked her unnatural pace. Across the open end of the square two buses impassively passed each other; women, a perambulator, cyclists, a man wheeling a barrow signalized, once again, the ordinary flow of life. At the square's most populous corner should be—and was—the short taxi rank. This evening, only one taxi—but this, although it presented its blank rump, appeared already to be alertly waiting for her. Indeed, without looking round the driver started his engine as she panted up from behind and put her hand on the door. As she did so, the clock struck seven. The taxi faced the main road: to make the trip back to her house it would have to turn—she had settled back on the seat and the taxi *had* turned before she, surprised by its knowing movement, recollected that she had not "said where." She leaned forward to scratch at the glass panel that divided the driver's head from her own.

The driver braked to what was almost a stop, turned round and slid the glass panel back: the jolt of this flung Mrs. Drover forward till her face was almost into the glass. Through the aperture driver and passenger, not six inches between them, remained for an eternity eye to eye. Mrs. Drover's mouth hung open for some seconds before she could issue her first scream. After that she continued to scream freely and to beat with her gloved hands on the glass all round at the taxi, accelerating without mercy, made off with her into the hinterland of deserted streets.

JORGE LUIS BORGES
1899–

The Lottery in Babylon

Like all men in Babylon, I have been proconsul; like all, a slave. I have also known omnipotence, opprobrium, imprisonment. Look: the index finger on my right hand is missing. Look: through the rip in my cape you can see a vermilion tatoo on my stomach. It is the second symbol, Beth. This letter, on nights when the moon is full, gives me power over men whose mark is Gimmel, but it subordinates me to the men of Aleph, who on moonless nights owe obedience to those marked with Gimmel. In the half light of dawn, in a cellar, I have cut the jugular vein of sacred bulls before a black stone. During a lunar year I have been declared invisible. I shouted and they did not answer me; I stole bread and they did not behead me. I have known what the Greeks do not know, incertitude. In a bronze chamber, before the silent handkerchief of the strangler, hope has been faithful to me, as has panic in the river of pleasure. Heraclides Ponticus tells with amazement that Pythagoras remembered having been Pyrrhus and before that Euphorbus and before that some other mortal. In order to remember similar vicissitudes I do not need to have recourse to death or even to deception.

I owe this almost atrocious variety to an institution which other republics do not know or which operates in them in an imperfect and secret manner: the lottery. I have not looked into its history; I know that the wise men cannot agree. I know of its powerful purposes what a man who is not versed in astrology can know about the moon. I come from a dizzy land where the lottery is the basis of reality. Until today I have thought as little about it as I have about the conduct of indecipherable divinities or about my heart. Now, far from Babylon and its beloved customs, I think with a certain amount of amazement about the lottery and about the blasphemous conjectures which veiled men murmur in the twilight.

My father used to say that formerly—a matter of centuries, of years?—the lottery in Babylon was a game of plebeian character. He recounted (I don't know whether rightly) that barbers sold, in exchange for copper coins, squares of bone or of parchment adorned with symbols. In broad daylight a drawing took place. Those who won received silver coins without any other test of luck. The system was elementary, as you can see.

Naturally these "lotteries" failed. Their moral virtue was nil. They were not directed at all of man's faculties, but only at hope. In the face

Translated by John M. Fein.

of public indifference, the merchants who founded these venal lotteries began to lose money. Someone tried a reform: The interpolation of a few unfavorable tickets in the list of favorable numbers. By means of this reform, the buyers of numbered squares ran the double risk of winning a sum and of paying a fine that could be considerable. This slight danger (for every thirty favorable numbers there was one unlucky one) awoke, as is natural, the interest of the public. The Babylonians threw themselves into the game. Those who did not acquire chances were considered pusillanimous, cowardly. In time, that justified disdain was doubled. Those who did not play were scorned, but also the losers who paid the fine were scorned. The Company (as it came to be known then) had to take care of the winners, who could not cash in their prizes if almost the total amount of the fines was unpaid. It started a lawsuit against the losers. The judge condemned them to pay the original fine and costs or spend several days in jail. All chose jail in order to defraud the Company. The bravado of a few is the source of the omnipotence of the Company and of its metaphysical and ecclesiastical power.

A little while afterward the lottery lists omitted the amounts of fines and limited themselves to publishing the days of imprisonment that each unfavorable number indicated. That laconic spirit, almost unnoticed at the time, was of capital importance. *It was the first appearance in the lottery of nonmonetary elements.* The success was tremendous. Urged by the clientele, the Company was obliged to increase the unfavorable numbers.

Everyone knows that the people of Babylon are fond of logic and even of symmetry. It was illogical for the lucky numbers to be computed in round coins and the unlucky ones in days and nights of imprisonment. Some moralists reasoned that the possession of money does not always determine happiness and that other forms of happiness are perhaps more direct.

Another concern swept the quarters of the poorer classes. The members of the college of priests multiplied their stakes and enjoyed all the vicissitudes of terror and hope; the poor (with reasonable or unavoidable envy) knew that they were excluded from that notoriously delicious rhythm. The just desire that all, rich and poor, should participate equally in the lottery, inspired an indignant agitation, the memory of which the years have not erased. Some obstinate people did not understand (or pretended not to understand) that it was a question of a new order, of a necessary historical stage. A slave stole a crimson ticket, which in the drawing credited him with the burning of his tongue. The legal code fixed that same penalty for the one who stole a ticket. Some Babylonians argued that he deserved the burning irons in his status of a thief; others, generously, that the executioner should apply it to him because chance had determined it that way. There were disturbances, there were lamentable drawings of blood, but the masses of Babylon finally imposed their will against the opposition of the rich. The people achieved amply its generous purposes. In the first place, it caused the Company to accept total power. (That unification was necessary, given the vastness and complexity of the new operations.) In the second place, it made the lottery secret, free and general. The mercenary sale of chances was abolished. Once initiated in the mysteries of Baal, every free man automatically participated in the sacred drawings, which took place in the labyrinths of the god every sixty nights and which determined his destiny until the next drawing. The consequences were incalculable. A fortunate play could bring about his promotion to the council of wise men or the imprisonment of an enemy (public or private) or finding, in the peaceful darkness of his room, the woman who begins to excite him and whom he never expected to see again. A bad play: mutilation, different kinds of infamy, death. At times one single fact—the vulgar murder of C, the mysterious apotheosis of B—was the happy solution of thirty or forty drawings. To combine the plays was difficult, but one must remember that the individuals of the Company were (and are) omnipotent and astute. In many cases the knowledge that certain happinesses were the simple product of chance would have diminished their virtue. To avoid that obstacle, the agents of the Company made use of the power of suggestion and magic. Their steps, their maneuverings, were secret. To find out about the intimate hopes and terrors of each individual, they had astrologists and spies. There were certain stone lions, there was a sacred latrine called Qaphqa, there were fissures in a dusty aqueduct which, according to general opinion, *led to the Company*; malignant or benevolent persons deposited information in these places. An alphabetical file collected these items of varying truthfulness.

Incredibly, there were complaints. The Company, with its usual discretion, did not answer directly. It preferred to scrawl in the rubbish of a mask factory a brief statement which now figures in the sacred scriptures. This doctrinal item observed that the lottery is an interpolation of chance in the order of the world and that to accept errors is not to contradict chance: it is to corroborate it. It likewise observed that those lions and that sacred receptacle, although not disavowed by the Company (which did not abandon the right to consult them), functioned without official guarantee.

This declaration pacified the public's restlessness. It also produced other effects, perhaps unforeseen by its writer. It deeply modified the spirit and the operations of the Company. I don't have much time left; they tell us that the ship is about to weigh anchor. But I shall try to explain it.

However unlikely it might seem, no one had tried out before then a general theory of chance. Babylonians are not very speculative. They revere the judgments of fate, they deliver to them their lives, their hopes, their panic, but it does not occur to them to investigate fate's labyrinthine laws nor the gyratory spheres which reveal it. Nevertheless, the *unofficial* declaration that I have mentioned inspired many discussions of judicial-mathematical character. From some one of them the following conjecture was born: if the lottery is an intensification of chance, a periodical infusion of chaos in the cosmos, would it not be right for chance to intervene in all stages of the drawing and not in one alone? Is it not ridiculous for chance to dictate someone's death and have the circumstances of that death—secrecy, publicity, the fixed time of an hour or a century—not subject to chance? These just scruples finally caused a considerable reform, whose complexities (aggravated by centuries' practice) only a few specialists understand, but which I shall try to summarize, at least in a symbolic way.

Let us imagine a first drawing, which decrees the death of a man. For its fulfillment one proceeds to another drawing, which proposes (let us say) nine possible executors. Of these executors, four can initiate a third drawing which will tell the name of the executioner, two can replace the adverse order with a fortunate one (finding a treasure, let us say), another will intensify the death penalty (that is, will make it infamous or enrich it with tortures), others can refuse to fulfill it. This is the symbolic scheme. In reality *the number of drawings is infinite*. No decision is final, all branch into others. Ignorant people suppose that infinite drawings require an infinite time; actually it is sufficient for time to be infinitely subdivisible, as the famous parable of the contest with the tortoise teaches. This infinity harmonizes admirably with the sinuous numbers of Chance and with the Celestial Archetype of the Lottery, which the Platonists adore. Some warped echo of our rites seems to have resounded on the Tiber: Ellus Lampridius, in the *Life of Antoninus Heliogabalus*, tells that this emperor wrote on shells the lots that were destined for his guests, so that one received ten pounds of gold and another ten flies, ten dormice, ten bears. It is permissible to recall that Heliogabalus was brought up in Asia Minor, among the priests of the eponymous god.

There are also impersonal drawings, with an indefinite purpose. One decrees that a sapphire of Taprobana be thrown into the waters of the Euphrates; another, that a bird be released from the roof of a tower; another, that each century there be withdrawn (or added) a grain of sand from the innumerable ones on the beach. The consequences are, at times, terrible.

Under the beneficent influence of the Company, our customs are saturated with chance. The buyer of a dozen amphoras of Damascene wine will not be surprised if one of them contains a talisman or a snake. The scribe who writes a contract almost never fails to introduce some erroneous information. I myself, in this hasty declaration, have falsified some splendor, some atrocity. Perhaps, also, some mysterious monotony . . . Our historians, who are the most penetrating on the globe, have invented a method to correct chance. It is well known that the operations of this method are (in general) reliable, although, naturally, they are not divulged without some portion of deceit. Furthermore, there is nothing so contaminated with fiction as the history of the Company. A paleographic document, exhumed in a temple, can be the result of yesterday's lottery or of an age-old lottery. No book is published without some discrepany in each one of the copies. Scribes take a secret oath to omit, to interpolate, to change. The indirect lie is also cultivated.

The Company, with divine modesty, avoids all publicity. Its agents, as is natural, are secret. The orders which it issues continually (perhaps incessantly) do not differ from those lavished by imposters. Moreover, who can brag about being a mere imposter? The drunkard who improvises an absurd order, the dreamer who awakens suddenly and strangles the woman who sleeps at his side, do they not execute, perhaps, a secret decision of the Company? That silent functioning, comparable to God's, gives rise to all sorts of conjectures. One abominably insinuates that the Company has not existed for centuries and that the sacred disorder of our lives is purely hereditary, traditional. Another judges it eternal and teaches that it will last until the last night, when the last god annihilates the world. Another declares that the Company is omnipotent, but that it only has influence in tiny things: in a bird's call, in the shadings of rust and of dust, in the half dreams of dawn. Another, in the words of masked heresiarchs, *that it has never existed and will not exist.* Another, no less vile, reasons that it is indifferent to affirm or deny the reality of the shadowy corporation, because Babylon is nothing else than an infinite game of chance.

BERNARD MALAMUD
1914–
The Magic Barrel

Not long ago there lived in uptown New York, in a small, almost meager room, though crowded with books, Leo Finkle, a rabbinical student in the Yeshivah University. Finkle, after six years of study, was to be ordained in June and had been advised by an acquaintance that he might find it easier to win himself a congregation if he were married. Since he had no present prospects of marriage, after two tormented days of turning it over in his mind, he called in Pinye Salzman, a marriage broker whose two-line advertisement he had read in the *Forward*.

The matchmaker appeared one night out of the dark fourth-floor hallway of the graystone rooming house where Finkle lived, grasping a black, strapped portfolio that had been worn thin with use. Salzman, who had been long in the business, was of slight but dignified build, wearing an old hat, and an overcoat too short and tight for him. He smelled frankly of fish, which he loved to eat, and although he was missing a few teeth, his presence was not displeasing, because of an amiable manner curiously contrasted with mournful eyes. His voice, his lips, his wisp of beard, his bony fingers were animated, but give him a moment of repose and his mild blue eyes revealed a depth of sadness, a characteristic that put Leo a little at ease although the situation, for him, was inherently tense.

He at once informed Salzman why he had asked him to come, explaining that his home was in Cleveland, and that but for his parents, who had married comparatively late in life, he was alone in the world. He had for six years devoted himself almost entirely to his studies, as a result of which, understandably, he had found himself without time for a social life and the company of young women. Therefore he thought it the better part of trial and error—of embarrassing fumbling—to call in an experienced person to advise him on these matters. He remarked in passing that the function of the marriage broker was ancient and honorable, highly approved in the Jewish community, because it made practical the necessary without hindering joy. Moreover, his own parents had been brought together by a matchmaker. They had made, if not a financially profitable marriage—since neither had possessed any worldly goods to speak of—at least a successful one in the sense of their everlasting devotion to each other. Salzman listened in embarrassed surprise, sensing a sort of apology. Later, however, he experienced a glow of pride in his work, an emotion that had left him years ago, and he heartily approved of Finkle.

The two went to their business. Leo had led Salzman to the only clear place in the room, a table near a window that overlooked the lamp-lit city. He seated himself at the matchmaker's side but facing him, attempting by an act of will to suppress the unpleasant tickle in his throat. Salzman eagerly unstrapped his portfolio and removed a loose rubber band from a thin packet of much-handled cards. As he flipped through them, a gesture and sound that physically hurt Leo, the student pretended not to see and gazed steadfastly out the window. Although it was still February, winter was on its last legs, signs of which he had for the first time in years begun to notice. He now observed the round white moon, moving high in the sky through a cloud menagerie, and watched with half-open mouth as it penetrated a huge hen, and dropped out of her like an egg laying itself. Salzman, though pretending through eyeglasses he had just slipped on, to be engaged in scanning the writing on the cards, stole occasional glances at the young man's distinguished face, noting with pleasure the long, severe scholar's nose, brown eyes heavy with learning, sensitive yet ascetic lips, and a certain, almost hollow quality of the dark cheeks. He gazed around at shelves upon shelves of books and let out a soft, contented sigh.

When Leo's eyes fell upon the cards, he counted six spread out in Salzman's hand.

"So few?" he asked in disappointment.

"You wouldn't believe me how much cards I got in my office," Salzman replied. "The drawers are already filled to the top, so I keep them now in a barrel, but is every girl good for a new rabbi?"

Leo blushed at this, regretting all he had revealed of himself in a curriculum vitae he had sent to Salzman. He had thought it best to acquaint him with his strict standards and specifications, but in having done so, felt he had told the marriage broker more than was absolutely necessary.

He hesitantly inquired, "Do you keep photographs of your clients on file?"

"First comes family, amount of dowry, also what kind promises," Salzman replied, unbuttoning his tight coat and settling himself in the chair. "After comes pictures, rabbi."

"Call me Mr. Finkle. I'm not yet a rabbi."

Salzman said he would, but instead called him doctor, which he changed to rabbi when Leo was not listening too attentively.

Salzman adjusted his horn-rimmed spectacles, gently cleared his throat and read in an eager voice the contents of the top card:

"Sophie P. Twenty four years. Widow one year. No children. Educated high school and two years college. Father promises eight thousand dollars. Has wonderful wholesale business. Also real estate. On the mother's side comes teachers, also one actor. Well known on Second Avenue."

Leo gazed up in surprise. "Did you say a widow?"

"A widow don't mean spoiled, rabbi. She lived with her husband maybe four months. He was a sick boy she made a mistake to marry him."

"Marrying a widow has never entered my mind."

"This is because you have no experience. A widow, especially if she is young and healthy like this girl, is a wonderful person to marry. She will be thankful to you the rest of her life. Believe me, if I was looking now for a bride, I would marry a widow."

Leo reflected, then shook his head.

Salzman hunched his shoulders in an almost imperceptible gesture of disappointment. He placed the card down on the wooden table and began to read another:

"Lily H. High school teacher. Regular. Not a substitute. Has savings and new Dodge car. Lived in Paris one year. Father is successful dentist thirty-five years. Interested in professional man. Well Americanized family. Wonderful opportunity."

"I knew her personally," said Salzman. "I wish you could see this girl. She is a doll. Also very intelligent. All day you could talk to her about books and theyater and what not. She also knows current events."

"I don't believe you mentioned her age?"

"Her age?" Salzman said, raising his brows. "Her age is thirty-two years."

Leo said after a while, "I'm afraid that seems a little too old."

Salzman let out a laugh. "So how old are you, rabbi?"

"Twenty-seven."

"So what is the difference, tell me, between twenty-seven and thirty-two? My own wife is seven years older than me. So what did I suffer?—Nothing. If Rothschild's a daughter wants to marry you, would you say on account her age, no?"

"Yes," Leo said dryly.

Salzman shook off the no in the yes. "Five years don't mean a thing. I give you my word that when you will live with her for one week you will forget her age. What does it mean five years—that she lived more and knows more than somebody who is younger? On this girl, God bless her, years are not wasted. Each one that it comes makes better the bargain."

"What subject does she teach in high school?"

"Languages. If you heard the way she speaks French, you will think it is music. I am in the business twenty-five years, and I recommend her with my whole heart. Believe me, I know what I'm talking, rabbi."

"What's on the next card?" Leo said abruptly.

Salzman reluctantly turned up the third card:

"Ruth K. Nineteen years. Honor student. Father offers thirteen thousand cash to the right bridegroom. He is a medical doctor. Stomach specialist with marvelous practice. Brother in law owns own garment business. Particular people."

Salzman looked as if he had read his trump card.

"Did you say nineteen?" Leo asked with interest.

"On the dot."

"Is she attractive?" He blushed. "Pretty?"

Salzman kissed his finger tips. "A little doll. On this I give you my word. Let me call the father tonight and you will see what means pretty."

But Leo was troubled. "You're sure she's that young?"

"This I am positive. The father will show you the birth certificate."

"Are you positive there isn't something wrong with her?" Leo insisted.

"Who says there is wrong?"

"I don't understand why an American girl her age should go to a marriage broker."

A smiled spread over Salzman's face.

"So for the same reason you went, she comes."

Leo flushed. "I am pressed for time."

Salzman, realizing he had been tactless, quickly explained. "The father came, not her. He wants she should have the best, so he looks around himself. When we will locate the right boy he will introduce him and encourage. This makes a better marriage than if a young girl without experience takes for herself. I don't have to tell you this."

"But don't you think this young girl believes in love?" Leo spoke uneasily.

Salzman was about to guffaw but caught himself and said soberly, "Love comes with the right person, not before."

Leo parted dry lips but did not speak. Noticing that Salzman had snatched a glance at the next card, he cleverly asked, "How is her health?"

"Perfect," Salzman said, breathing with difficulty. "Of course, she is a little lame on her right foot from an auto accident that it happened to her when she was twelve years, but nobody notices on account she is so brilliant and also beautiful."

Leo got up heavily and went to the window. He felt curiously bitter and upbraided himself for having called in the marriage broker. Finally, he shook his head.

"Why not?" Salzman persisted, the pitch of his voice rising.

"Because I detest stomach specialists."

"So what do you care what is his business? After you marry her do you need him? Who says he must come every Friday night in your house?"

Ashamed of the way the talk was going, Leo dismissed Salzman, who went home with heavy, melancholy eyes.

Though he had felt only relief at the marriage broker's departure, Leo was in low spirits the next day. He explained it as arising from

Salzman's failure to produce a suitable bride for him. He did not care for his type of clientele. But when Leo found himself hesitating whether to seek out another matchmaker, one more polished than Pinye, he wondered if it could be—his protestations to the contrary, and although he honored his father and mother—that he did not, in essence, care for the matchmaking institution? This thought he quickly put out of mind yet found himself still upset. All day he ran around in the woods—missed an important appointment, forgot to give out his laundry, walked out of a Broadway cafeteria without paying and had to run back with the ticket in his hand; had even not recognized his landlady in the street when she passed with a friend and courteously called out, "A good evening to you, Doctor Finkle." By nightfall, however, he had regained sufficient calm to sink his nose into a book and there found peace from his thoughts.

Almost at once there came a knock on the door. Before Leo could say enter, Salzman, commercial cupid, was standing in the room. His face was gray and meager, his expression hungry, and he looked as if he would expire on his feet. Yet the marriage broker managed, by some trick of the muscles, to display a broad smile.

"So good evening. I am invited?"

Leo nodded, disturbed to see him again, yet unwilling to ask the man to leave.

Beaming still, Salzman laid his portfolio on the table. "Rabbi, I got for you tonight good news."

"I've asked you not to call me rabbi. I'm still a student."

"Your worries are finished. I have for you a first-class bride."

"Leave me in peace concerning this subject." Leo pretended lack of interest.

"The world will dance at your wedding."

"Please, Mr. Salzman, no more."

"But first must come back my strength," Salzman said weakly. He fumbled with the portfolio straps and took out of the leather case an oily paper bag, from which he extracted a hard, seeded roll and a small, smoked whitefish. With a quick motion of his hand he stripped the fish out of its skin and began ravenously to chew. "All day in a rush," he muttered.

Leo watched him eat.

"A sliced tomato you have maybe?" Salzman hesitantly inquired.

"No."

The marriage broker shut his eyes and ate. When he had finished he carefully cleaned up the crumbs and rolled up the remains of the fish, in the paper bag. His spectacled eyes roamed the room until he discovered, amid some piles of books, a one-burner gas stove. Lifting his hat he humbly asked, "A glass tea you got, rabbi?"

Conscience-stricken, Leo rose and brewed the tea. He served it with a chunk of lemon and two cubes of lump sugar, delighting Salzman.

After he had drunk his tea, Salzman's strength and good spirits were restored.

"So tell me, rabbi," he said amiably, "you considered some more the three clients I mentioned yesterday?"

"There was no need to consider."

"Why not?"

"None of them suits me."

"What then suits you?"

Leo let it pass because he could give only a confused answer.

Without waiting for a reply, Salzman asked, "You remember this girl I talked to you—the high school teacher?"

"Age thirty-two?"

But, surprisingly, Salzman's face lit in a smile. "Age twenty-nine."

Leo shot him a look. "Reduced from thirty-two?"

"A mistake," Salzman avowed. "I talked today with the dentist. He took me to his safety deposit box and showed me the birth certificate. She was twenty-nine years last August. They made her a party in the mountains where she went for her vacation. When her father spoke to me the first time I forgot to write the age and I told you thirty-two, but now I remember this was a different client, a widow."

"The same one you told me about? I thought she was twenty-four?"

"A different. Am I responsible that the world is filled with widows?"

"No, but I'm not interested in them, nor for that matter, in school teachers."

Salzman pulled his clasped hands to his breast. Looking at the ceiling he devoutly exclaimed, "Yiddishe kinder, what can I say to somebody that he is not interested in high school teachers? So what then you are interested?"

Leo flushed but controlled himself.

"In what else will you be interested," Salzman went on, "if you not interested in this fine girl that she speaks four languages and has personally in the bank ten thousand dollars? Also her father guarantees further twelve thousand. Also she has a new car, wonderful clothes, talks on all subjects, and she will give you a first-class home and children. How near do we come in our life to paradise?"

"If she's so wonderful, why wasn't she married ten years ago?"

"Why?" said Salzman with a heavy laugh. "—Why? Because she is *partikiler*. This is why. She wants the *best*."

Leo was silent, amused at how he had entangled himself. But Salzman had aroused his interest in Lily H., and he began seriously to consider calling on her. When the marriage broker observed how intently Leo's mind was at work on the facts he had supplied, he felt certain they would soon come to an agreement.

Late Saturday afternoon, conscious of Salzman, Leo Finkle walked with Lily Hirschorn along Riverside Drive. He walked briskly and erectly, wearing with distinction the black fedora he had that morning taken with trepidation out of the dusty hat box on his closet shelf, and the heavy black Saturday coat he had thoroughly whisked clean. Leo also owned a walking stick, a present from a distant relative, but quickly put temptation aside and did not use it. Lily, petite and not unpretty, had on something signifying the approach of spring. She was au courant, animatedly, with all sorts of subjects, and he weighed her words and found her surprisingly sound—score another for Salzman, whom he uneasily sensed to be somewhere around, hiding perhaps high in a tree along the street, flashing the lady signals with a pocket mirror; or perhaps a cloven-hoofed Pan, piping nuptial ditties as he danced his invisible way before them, strewing wild buds on the walk and purple grapes in their path, symbolizing fruit of a union, though there was of course still none.

Lily startled Leo by remarking, "I was thinking of Mr. Salzman, a curious figure, wouldn't you say?"

Not certain what to answer, he nodded.

She bravely went on, blushing, "I for one am grateful for his introducing us. Aren't you?"

He courteously replied, "I am."

"I mean," she said with a little laugh—and it was all in good taste, or at least gave the effect of being not in bad—"do you mind that we came together so?"

He was not displeased with her honesty, recognizing that she meant to set the relationship aright, and understanding that it took a certain amount of experience in life, and courage, to want to do it quite that way. One had to have some sort of past to make that kind of beginning.

He said that he did not mind. Salzman's function was traditional and honorable—valuable for what it might achieve, which, he pointed out, was frequently nothing.

Lily agreed with a sigh. They walked on for a while and she said after a long silence, again with a nervous laugh, "Would you mind if I asked you something a little bit personal? Frankly, I find the subject fascinating." Although Leo shrugged, she went on half embarrassedly, "How was it that you came to your calling? I mean was it a sudden passionate inspiration?"

Leo after a time, slowly replied, "I was always interested in the Law."

"You saw revealed in it the presence of the Highest?"

He nodded and changed the subject. "I understand that you spent a little time in Paris, Miss Hirschorn?"

"Oh, did Mr. Salzman tell you, Rabbi Finkle?" Leo winced but she went on, "It was ages ago and almost forgotten. I remember I had to return for my sister's wedding."

And Lily would not be put off. "When," she asked in a trembly voice, "did you become enamored of God?"

He stared at her. Then it came to him that she was talking not about Leo Finkle, but of a total stranger, some mystical figure, perhaps even passionate prophet that Salzman had dreamed up for her—no relation to the living or dead. Leo trembled with rage and weakness. The trickster had obviously sold her a bill of goods, just as he had him, who'd expected to become acquainted with a young lady of twenty-nine, only to behold, the moment he laid eyes upon her strained and anxious face, a woman past thirty-five and aging rapidly. Only his self-control had kept him this long in her presence.

"I am not," he said gravely, "a talented religious person," and in seeking words to go on, found himself possessed by shame and fear. "I think," he said in a strained manner, "that I came to God not because I loved Him, but because I did not."

This confession he spoke harshly because its unexpectedness shook him.

Lily wilted. Leo saw a profusion of loaves of bread go flying like ducks high over his head, not unlike the winged loaves by which he had counted himself to sleep last night. Mercifully, then, it snowed, which he would not put past Salzman's machinations.

He was infuriated with the marriage broker and swore he would throw him out of the room the minute he reappeared. But Salzman did not come that night, and when Leo's anger had subsided, an unaccountable despair grew in its place. At first he thought this was caused by his disappointment in Lily, but before long it became evident that he had involved himself with Salzman without a true knowledge of his own intent. He gradually realized—with an emptiness that seized him with six hands—that he had called in the broker to find him a bride because he was incapable of doing it himself. This terrifying insight he had derived as a result of his meeting and conversation with Lily Hirschorn. Her probing questions had somehow irritated him into revealing—to himself more than her—the true nature of his relationship to God, and from that it had come upon him, with shocking force, that apart from his parents, he had never loved anyone. Or perhaps it went the other way, that he did not love God so well as he might, because he had not loved man. It seemed to Leo that his whole life stood starkly revealed and he saw himself for the first time as he truly was—unloved and loveless. This bitter but somehow not fully unexpected revelation brought him to a point of panic, controlled only by extraordinary effort. He covered his face with his hands and cried.

The week that followed was the worst of his life. He did not eat and lost weight. His beard darkened and grew ragged. He stopped attending seminars and almost never opened a book. He seriously considered leaving the Yeshivah, although he was deeply troubled at the thought of the loss of all his years of study—saw them like pages torn from a book, strewn over the city—and at the devastating effect of this decision upon his parents. But he had lived without knowledge of himself, and never in the Five Books and all the Commentaries—mea culpa—had the truth been revealed to him. He did not know where to turn, and in all this desolating loneliness there was no *to whom*, although he often thought of Lily but not once could bring himself to go downstairs and make the call. He became touchy and irritable, especially with his landlady, who asked him all manner of personal questions; on the other hand, sensing his own disagreeableness, he waylaid her on the stairs and apologized abjectly, until mortified, she ran from him. Out of this, however, he drew the consolation that he was a Jew and that a Jew suffered. But gradually, as the long and terrible week drew to a close, he regained his composure and some idea of purpose in life: to go on as planned. Although he was imperfect, the ideal was not. As for his quest of a bride, the thought of continuing afflicted him with anxiety and heartburn, yet perhaps with this new knowledge of himself he would be more successful than in the past. Perhaps love would now come to him and a bride to that love. And for this sanctified seeking who needed a Salzman?

The marriage broker, a skeleton with haunted eyes, returned that very night. He looked, withal, the picture of frustrated expectancy—as if he had steadfastly waited the week at Miss Lily Hirschorn's side for a telephone call that never came.

Casually coughing, Salzman came immediately to the point: "So how did you like her?"

Leo's anger rose and he could not refrain from chiding the matchmaker: "Why did you lie to me, Salzman?"

Salzman's pale face went dead white, the world had snowed on him.

"Did you not state that she was twenty-nine?" Leo insisted.

"I give you my word—"

"She was thirty-five, if a day. *At least* thirty-five."

"Of this don't be too sure. Her father told me—"

"Never mind. The worst of it was that you lied to her."

"How did I lie to her, tell me?"

"You told her things about me that weren't true. You made me out to be more, consequently less than I am. She had in mind a totally different person, a sort of semi-mystical Wonder Rabbi."

"All I said, you was a religious man."

"I can imagine."

Salzman sighed. "This is my weakness that I have," he confessed. "My wife says to me I shouldn't be a salesman, but when I have two fine people that they would be wonderful to be married, I am so happy that I talk too much." He smiled wanly. "This is why Salzman is a poor man."

Leo's anger left him. "Well, Salzman, I'm afraid that's all."

The marriage broker fastened hungry eyes on him.

"You don't want any more a bride?"

"I do," said Leo, "but I have decided to seek her in a different way. I am no longer interested in an arranged marriage. To be frank, I now admit the necessity of premarital love. That is, I want to be in love with the one I marry."

"Love?" said Salzman, astounded. After a moment he remarked, "For us, our love is our life, not for the ladies. In the ghetto they—"

"I know, I know," said Leo. "I've thought of it often. Love, I have said to myself, should be a by-product of living and worship rather than its own end. Yet for myself I find it necessary to establish the level of my need and fulfill it."

Salzman shrugged but answered, "Listen, rabbi, if you want love, this I can find for you also. I have such beautiful clients that you will love them the minute your eyes will see them."

Leo smiled unhappily. "I'm afraid you don't understand."

But Salzman hastily unstrapped his portfolio and withdrew a manila packet from it.

"Pictures," he said, quickly laying the envelope on the table.

Leo called after him to take the pictures away, but as if on the wings of the wind, Salzman had disappeared.

March came. Leo had returned to his regular routine. Although he felt not quite himself yet—lacked energy—he was making plans for a more active social life. Of course it would cost something, but he was an expert in cutting corners; and when there was no corners left he would make circles rounder. All the while Salzman's pictures had lain on the table, gathering dust. Occasionally as Leo sat studying, or enjoying a cup of tea, his eyes fell on the manila envelope, but he never opened it.

The days went by and no social life to speak of developed with a member of the opposite sex—it was difficult, given the circumstances of his situation. One morning Leo toiled up the stairs to his room and stared out the window at the city. Although the day was bright his view of it was dark. For some time he watched the people in the street below hurrying along and then turned with a heavy heart to his little room. On the table was the packet. With a sudden relentless gesture he tore it open. For a half-hour he stood by the table in a state of excitement, examining the photographs of the ladies Salzman had included. Finally, with a deep sigh he put them down. There were six, of varying degrees of attractiveness, but look at them long enough and they all became Lily Hirschorn: all past their prime, all starved behind bright smiles, not a true personality in the lot. Life, despite their frantic yoohooings, had passed them by; they were pictures in a brief case that stank of fish. After a while, however, as Leo attempted to return the photographs into the envelope, he found in it another, a snapshot of the type taken by a machine for a quarter. He gazed at it a moment and let out a cry.

Her face deeply moved him. Why, he could at first not say. It gave him the impression of youth—spring flowers, yet age—a sense of having been used to the bone, wasted; this came from the eyes, which were hauntingly familiar, yet absolutely strange. He had a vivid impression that he had met her before, but try as he might he could not place her although he could almost recall her name, as if he had read it in her own handwriting. No, this couldn't be; he would have remembered her. It was not, he affirmed, that she had an extraordinary beauty—no, though her face was attractive enough; it was that *something* about her moved him. Feature for feature, even some of the ladies of the photographs could do better; but she leaped forth to his heart—had *lived*, or wanted to—more than just wanted, perhaps regretted how she had lived—had somehow deeply suffered: it could be seen in the depths of those reluctant eyes, and from the way the light enclosed and shone from her, and within her, opening realms of possibility: this was her own. Her he desired. His head ached and eyes narrowed with the intensity of his gazing, then as if an obscure fog had blown up in the mind, he experienced fear of her and was aware that he had received an impression, somehow, of evil. He shuddered, saying softly, it is thus with us all. Leo brewed some tea in a small pot and sat sipping it without sugar, to calm himself. But before he had finished drinking, again with excitement he examined the face and found it good: good for Leo Finkle. Only such a one could understand him and help him seek whatever he was seeking. She might, perhaps, love him. How she had happened to be among the discards in Salzman's barrel he could never guess, but he knew he must urgently go find her.

Leo rushed downstairs, grabbed up the Bronx telephone book, and searched for Salzman's home address. He was not listed, nor was his office. Neither was he in the Manhattan book. But Leo remembered having written down the address on a slip of paper after he had read Salzman's advertisement in the "personals" column of the *Forward*. He ran up to his room and tore through his papers, without luck. It was exasperating. Just when he needed the matchmaker he was nowhere to be found. Fortunately Leo remembered to look in his wallet. There on a card he found his name written and a Bronx address. No phone number was listed, the reason—Leo now recalled—he had originally communicated with Salzman by letter. He got on his coat, put a hat on over his skull cap and hurried to the subway station. All the way to the far end of the Bronx he sat on the edge of his seat. He was more than once tempted to take out the picture and see if the girl's face was as he remembered it, but he refrained, allowing the snapshot to remain in his inside coat pocket, content to have her so close. When the train pulled into the station he was waiting at the door and bolted out. He quickly located the street Salzman had advertised.

The building he sought was less than a block from the subway, but it was not an office building, nor even a loft, nor a store in which one could rent office space. It was a very old tenement house. Leo found Salzman's name in pencil on a soiled tag under the bell and climbed three dark flights to his apartment. When he knocked, the door was opened by a thin, asthmatic, gray-haired woman, in felt slippers.

"Yes?" she said, expecting nothing. She listened without listening. He could have sworn he had seen her, too, before but knew it was an illusion.

"Salzman—does he live here? Pinye Salzman," he said, "the matchmaker?"

She stared at him a long minute. "Of course."

He felt embarrassed. "Is he in?"

"No." Her mouth, though left open, offered nothing more.

"The matter is urgent. Can you tell me where his office is?"

"In the air." She pointed upward.

"You mean he has no office?" Leo asked.

"In his socks."

He peered into the apartment. It was sunless and dingy, one large room divided by a half-open curtain, beyond which he could see a sagging metal bed. The near side of a room was crowded with rickety chairs, old bureaus, a three-legged table, racks of cooking utensils, and all the apparatus of a kitchen. But there was no sign of Salzman or his magic barrel, probably also a figment of the imagination. An odor of frying fish made Leo weak to the knees.

"Where is he?" he insisted. "I've got to see your husband."

At length she answered, "So who knows where he is? Every time he thinks a new thought he runs to a different place. Go home, he will find you."

"Tell him Leo Finkle."

She gave no sign she had heard.

He walked downstairs, depressed.

But Salzman, breathless, stood waiting at his door.

Leo was astounded and overjoyed. "How did you get here before me?"

"I rushed."

"Come inside."

They entered. Leo fixed tea, and a sardine sandwich for Salzman. As they were drinking he reached behind him for the packet of pictures and handed them to the marriage broker.

Salzman put down his glass and said expectantly, "You found somebody you like?"

"Not among these."

The marriage broker turned away.

"Here is the one I want." Leo held forth the snapshot.

Salzman slipped on his glasses and took the picture into his trembling hand. He turned ghastly and let out a groan.

"What's the matter?" cried Leo.

"Excuse me. Was an accident this picture. She isn't for you."

Salzman frantically shoved the manila packet into his portfolio. He thrust the snapshot into his pocket and fled down the stairs.

Leo, after momentary paralysis, gave chase and cornered the marriage broker in the vestibule. The landlady made hysterical outcries but neither of them listened.

"Give me back the picture, Salzman."

"No." The pain in his eyes was terrible.

"Tell me who she is then."

"This I can't tell you. Excuse me."

He made to depart, but Leo, forgetting himself, seized the matchmaker by his tight coat and shook him frenziedly.

"Please," sighed Salzman. *"Please."*

Leo ashamedly let him go. "Tell me who she is," he begged. "It's very important for me to know."

"She is not for you. She is a wild one—wild, without shame. This is not a bride for a rabbi."

"What do you mean wild?"

"Like an animal. Like a dog. For her to be poor was a sin. This is why to me she is dead now."

"In God's name, what do you mean?"

"Her I can't introduce to you," Salzman cried.

"Why are you so excited?"

"Why, he asks," Salzman said, bursting into tears. "This is my baby, my Stella, she should burn in hell."

Leo hurried up to bed and hid under the covers. Under the covers he thought his life through. Although he soon fell asleep he could not sleep her out of his mind. He woke, beating his breast. Though he prayed to be rid of her, his prayers went unanswered. Through days of torment he endlessly struggled not to love her; fearing success, he escaped it. He then concluded to convert her to goodness, himself to God. The idea alternately nauseated and exalted him.

He perhaps did not know that he had come to a final decision until he encountered Salzman in a Broadway cafeteria. He was sitting alone at a rear table, sucking the bony remains of a fish. The marriage broker appeared haggard, and transparent to the point of vanishing.

Salzman looked up at first without recognizing him. Leo had grown a pointed beard and his eyes were weighted with wisdom.

"Salzman," he said, "love has at last come to my heart."

"Who can love from a picture?" mocked the marriage broker.

"It is not impossible."

"If you can love her, then you can love anybody. Let me show you some new clients that they just sent me their photographs. One is a little doll."

"Just her I want," Leo murmured.

"Don't be a fool, doctor. Don't bother with her."

"Put me in touch with her, Salzman," Leo said humbly. "Perhaps I can be of service."

Salzman had stopped eating and Leo understood with emotion that it was now arranged.

Leaving the cafeteria, he was, however, afflicted by a tormenting suspicion that Salzman had planned it all to happen this way.

Leo was informed by letter that she would meet him on a certain corner, and she was there one spring night, waiting under a street lamp. He appeared, carrying a small bouquet of violets and rosebuds. Stella stood by the lamp post, smoking. She wore white with red shoes, which fitted his expectations, although in a troubled moment he had imagined the dress red, and only the shoes white. She waited uneasily and shyly. From afar he saw that her eyes—clearly her father's—were filled with desperate innocence. He pictured, in her, his own redemption. Violins and lit candles revolved in the sky. Leo ran forward with flowers outthrust.

Around the corner, Salzman, leaning against a wall, chanted prayers for the dead.

SHIRLEY JACKSON
1919–1965
The Lottery

The morning of June 27th was clear and sunny, with the fresh warmth of a full-summer day; the flowers were blossoming profusely and the grass was richly green. The people of the village began to gather in the square, between the post office and the bank, around ten o'clock; in some towns there were so many people that the lottery took two days and had to be started on June 26th, but in this village, where there were only about three hundred people, the whole lottery took only about two hours, so it could begin at ten o'clock in the morning and still be through in time to allow the villagers to get home for noon dinner.

The children assembled first, of course. School was recently over for the summer, and the feeling of liberty sat uneasily on most of them; they tended to gather together quietly for a while before they broke into boisterous play, and their talk was still of the classroom and the teacher, of books and reprimands. Bobby Martin had already stuffed his pockets full of stones, and the other boys soon followed his example, selecting the smoothest and roundest stones; Bobby and Harry Jones and Dickie Delacroix—the villagers pronounced this name "dellacroy"—eventually made a great pile of stones in one corner of the square and guarded it against the raids of the other boys. The girls stood aside, talking among themselves, looking over their shoulders at the boys, and the very small children rolled in the dust or clung to the hands of their older brothers or sisters.

Soon the men began to gather surveying their own children, speaking of planting and rain, tractors and taxes. They stood together, away from the pile of stones in the corner, and their jokes were quiet and they smiled rather than laughed. The women, wearing faded house dresses and sweaters, came shortly after their menfolk. They greeted one another and exchanged bits of gossip as they went to join their husbands. Soon the women, standing by their husbands, began to call to their children, and the children came reluctantly, having to be called four or five times. Bobby Martin ducked under his mother's grasping hand and ran, laughing, back to the pile of stones. His father spoke up sharply, and Bobby came quickly and took his place between his father and his oldest brother.

The lottery was conducted—as were the square dances, the teen-age club, the Halloween program—by Mr. Summers, who had time and energy to devote to civic activities. He was a round-faced, jovial man and he ran the coal business, and people were sorry for him, because he had no children and his wife was a scold. When he arrived in the square, carrying the black wooden box, there was a murmur of conversation among the villagers, and he waved and called, "Little late today, folks." The postmaster, Mr. Graves, followed him, carrying a three-legged stool, and the stool was put in the center of the square and Mr. Summers set the black box down on it. The villagers kept their distance, leaving a space between themselves and the stool, and when Mr. Summers said, "Some of you fellows want to give me a hand?" there was a hesitation before two men, Mr. Martin and his oldest son, Baxter, came forward to hold the box steady on the stool while Mr. Summers stirred up the papers inside it.

The original paraphernalia for the lottery had been lost long ago, and the black box now resting on the stool had been put into use even before Old Man Warner, the oldest man in town, was born. Mr. Summers spoke frequently to the villagers about making a new box, but no one liked to upset even as much tradition as was represented by the black box. There was a story that the present box had been made with some pieces of the box that had preceded it, the one that had been constructed when the first people settled down to make a village here. Every year, after the lottery, Mr. Summers began talking again about a new box, but every year the subject was allowed to fade off without anything's being done. The black box grew shabbier each year; by now it was no longer completely black but splintered badly along one side to show the original wood color, and in some places faded or stained.

Mr. Martin and his oldest son, Baxter, held the black box securely on the stool until Mr. Summers had stirred the papers thoroughly with his hand. Because so much of the ritual had been forgotten or discarded, Mr. Summers had been successful in having slips of paper substituted for the chips of wood that had been used for generations. Chips of wood, Mr. Summers had argued, had been all very well when the village was tiny, but now that the population was more than three hundred and likely to keep on growing, it was necessary to use something that would fit more easily into the black box. The night before the lottery, Mr. Summers and Mr. Graves made up the slips of paper and put them into the box, and it was then taken to the safe of Mr. Summers' coal company and locked up until Mr. Summers was ready to take it to the square next morning. The rest of the year, the box was put away, sometimes one place, sometimes another; it had spent one year in Mr. Graves' barn and another year underfoot in the post office, and sometimes it was set on a shelf in the Martin grocery and left there.

There was a great deal of fussing to be done before Mr. Summers declared the lottery open. There were the lists to make up—of heads of families, heads of households in each family, members of each household in each family. There was the proper swearing-in of Mr. Summers by the postmaster, as the official of the lottery; at one time, some people remembered, there had been a recital of some sort, performed by the official of the lottery, a perfunctory, tuneless chant that had been rattled off duly each year; some people believed that the official of the lottery used to stand just so when he said or sang it, others believed that he was supposed to walk among the people, but years and years ago this part of the ritual had been allowed to lapse. There had been, also, a ritual salute, which the official of the lottery had had to use in addressing each person who came up to draw from the box, but this also had changed with time, until now it was felt necessary only for the official to speak to each person approaching. Mr. Summers was very good at all this; in his clean white shirt and blue jeans, with one hand resting carelessly on the black box, he seemed very proper and important as he talked interminably to Mr. Graves and the Martins.

Just as Mr. Summers finally left off talking and turned to the assembled villagers, Mrs. Hutchinson came hurriedly along the path to the square, her sweater thrown over her shoulders, and slid into place in the back of the crowd. "Clean forgot what day it was," she said to Mrs. Delacroix, who stood next to her, and they both laughed softly. "Thought my old man was out back stacking wood," Mrs. Hutchinson went on, "and then I looked out the window and the kids were gone, and then I remembered it was the twenty-seventh and came a-running." She dried her hands on her apron, and Mrs. Delacroix said, "You're in time, though. They're still talking away up there."

Mrs. Hutchinson craned her neck to see through the crowd and found her husband and children standing near the front. She tapped Mrs. Delacroix on the arm as a farewell and began to make her way through the crowd. The people separated good-humoredly to let her through; two or three people said, in voices just loud enough to be heard across the crowd, "Here comes your Mrs., Hutchinson," and "Bill, she made it after all." Mrs. Hutchinson reached her husband, and Mr. Summers, who had been waiting, said cheerfully. "Thought we were going to have to get on without you, Tessie." Mrs. Hutchinson said, grinning, "Wouldn't have me leave m'dishes in the sink, now, would you, Joe?" and soft laughter ran through the crowd as the people stirred back into position after Mrs. Hutchinson's arrival.

"Well, now," Mr. Summers said soberly, "guess we better get started, get this over with, so's we can go back to work. Anybody ain't here?"

"Dunbar," several people said. "Dunbar, Dunbar."

Mr. Summers consulted his list. "Clyde Dunbar," he said. "That's right. He's broke his leg, hasn't he? Who's drawing for him?"

"Me, I guess," a woman said, and Mr. Summers turned to look at her. "Wife draws for her husband," Mrs. Summers said. "Don't you have a grown boy to do it for you, Janey?" Although Mr. Summers and everyone else in the village knew the answer perfectly well, it was the business of the official of the lottery to ask such questions formally. Mr. Summers waited with an expression of polite interest while Mrs. Dunbar answered.

"Horace's not but sixteen yet," Mrs. Dunbar said regretfully. "Guess I gotta fill in for the old man this year."

"Right," Mr. Summers said. He made a note on the list he was holding. Then he asked, "Watson boy drawing this year?"

A tall boy in the crowd raised his hand. "Here," he said. "I'm drawing for m'mother and me." He blinked his eyes nervously and ducked his head as several voices in the crowd said things like "Good fellow, Jack," and "Glad to see your mother's got a man to do it."

"Well," Mr. Summers said, "guess that's everyone. Old Man Warner make it?"

"Here," a voice said, and Mr. Summers nodded.

A sudden hush fell on the crowd as Mr. Summers cleared his throat and looked at the list. "All ready?" he called. "Now, I'll read the names—heads of families first—and the men come up and take a paper out of the box. Keep the paper folded in your hand without looking at it until everyone has had a turn. Everything clear?"

The people had done it so many times that they only half listened to the directions; most of them were quiet, wetting their lips, not looking around. Then Mr. Summers raised one hand high and said, "Adams." A man disengaged himself from the crowd and came forward. "Hi, Steve," Mr. Summers said, and Mr. Adams said, "Hi, Joe." They grinned at one another humorlessly and nervously. Then Mr. Adams reached into the black box and took out a folded paper. He held it firmly by one corner as he turned and went hastily back to his place in the crowd, where he stood a little apart from his family, not looking down at his hand.

"Allen," Mr. Summers said. "Anderson. . . . Bentham."

"Seems like there's no time at all between lotteries any more," Mrs. Delacroix said to Mrs. Graves in the back row. "Seems like we got through with the last one only last week."

"Time sure goes fast," Mrs. Graves said.

"Clark. . . . Delacroix."

"There goes my old man," Mrs. Delacroix said. She held her breath while her husband went forward.

"Dunbar," Mr. Summers said, and Mrs. Dunbar went steadily to the box while one of the women said, "Go on, Janey," and another said, "There she goes."

"We're next," Mrs. Graves said. She watched while Mr. Graves came around from the side of the box, greeted Mr. Summers gravely, and selected a slip of paper from the box. By now, all through the crowd there were men holding the small folded papers in their large hands, turning them over and over nervously. Mrs. Dunbar and her two sons stood together, Mrs. Dunbar holding the slip of paper.

"Harburt. . . . Hutchinson."

"Get up there, Bill," Mrs. Hutchinson said, and the people near her laughed.

"Jones."

"They do say," Mr. Adams said to Old Man Warner, who stood next to him, "that over in the north village they're talking of giving up the lottery."

Old Man Warner snorted. "Pack of crazy fools," he said. "Listening to the young folks, nothing's good enough for *them*. Next thing you know, they'll be wanting to go back to living in caves, nobody work any more, live *that* way for a while. Used to be a saying about 'Lottery in June, corn be heavy soon.' First thing you know, we'd all be eating stewed chickweed and acorns. There's *always* been a lottery," he added petulantly. "Bad enough to see young Joe Summers up there joking with everybody."

"Some places have already quit lotteries," Mrs. Adams said.

"Nothing but trouble in *that*," Old Man Warner said stoutly. "Pack of young fools."

"Martin." And Bobby Martin watched his father go forward. "Overdyke. . . . Percy."

"I wish they'd hurry," Mrs. Dunbar said to her older son. "I wish they'd hurry."

"They're almost through," her son said.

"You get ready to run tell Dad," Mrs. Dunbar said.

Mr. Summers called his own name and then stepped forward precisely and selected a slip from the box. Then he called, "Warner."

"Seventy-seventh year I been in the lottery," Old Man Warner said as he went through the crowd. "Seventy-seventh time."

"Watson." The tall boy came awkwardly through the crowd. Someone said, "Don't be nervous, Jack," and Mr. Summers said, "Take your time, son."

"Zanini."

After that, there was a long pause, a breathless pause, until Mr. Summers, holding his slip of paper in the air, said, "All right, fellows." For a minute, no one moved, and then all the slips of paper were opened. Suddenly, all the women began to speak at once, saying,

"Who is it?" "Who's got it?" "Is it the Dunbars?" "Is it the Watsons?" Then the voices began to say, "It's Hutchinson. It's Bill," "Bill Hutchinson's got it."

"Go tell your father," Mrs. Dunbar said to her older son.

People began to look around to see the Hutchinsons. Bill Hutchinson was standing quiet, staring down at the paper in his hand. Suddenly, Tessie Hutchinson shouted to Mr. Summers, "You didn't give him time enough to take any paper he wanted. I saw you. It wasn't fair!"

"Be a good sport, Tessie," Mrs. Delacroix called, and Mrs. Graves said, "All of us took the same chance."

"Shut up, Tessie," Bill Hutchinson said.

"Well, everyone," Mr. Summers said, "That was done pretty fast, and now we've got to be hurrying a little more to get done in time." He consulted his next list. "Bill," he said, "you draw for the Hutchinson family. You got any other households in the Hutchinsons?"

"There's Don and Eva," Mrs. Hutchinson yelled. "Make *them* take their chance!"

"Daughters draw with their husbands' families, Tessie," Mr. Summers said gently. "You know that as well as anyone else."

"It wasn't *fair*," Tessie said.

"I guess not, Joe," Bill Hutchinson said regretfully. "My daughter draws with her husband's family, that's only fair. And I've got no other family except the kids."

"Then, as far as drawing for families is concerned, it's you," Mr. Summers said in explanation, "and as far as drawing for households is concerned, that's you, too. Right?"

"Right," Bill Hutchinson said.

"How many kids, Bill?" Mr. Summers asked formally.

"Three," Bill Hutchinson said. "There's Bill, Jr., and Nancy, and little Dave. And Tessie and me."

"All right, then," Mr. Summers said. "Harry, you got their tickets back?"

Mr. Graves nodded and held up the slips of paper. "Put them in the box, then," Mr. Summers directed. "Take Bill's and put it in."

"I think we ought to start over," Mrs. Hutchinson said, as quietly as she could. "I tell you it wasn't *fair*. You didn't give him time enough to choose. *Every*body saw that."

Mr. Graves had selected the five slips and put them in the box, and he dropped all the papers but those onto the ground, where the breeze caught them and lifted them off.

"Listen, everybody," Mrs. Hutchinson was saying to the people around her.

"Ready, Bill?" Mr. Summers asked, and Bill Hutchinson, with one quick glance around at his wife and children, nodded.

"Remember," Mr. Summers said, "Take the slips and keep them folded until each person has taken one. Harry, you help little Dave." Mr. Graves took the hand of the little boy, who came willingly with him up to the box. "Take a paper out of the box, Davy," Mr. Summers said. Davy put his hand into the box and laughed. "Take just *one* paper," Mr. Summers said. "Harry, you hold it for him." Mr. Graves took the child's hand and removed the folded paper from the tight fist and held it while little Dave stood next to him and looked up at him wonderingly.

"Nancy next," Mr. Summers said. Nancy was twelve, and her school friends breathed heavily as she went forward, switching her skirt, and took a slip daintily from the box. "Bill, Jr.," Mr. Summers said, and Billy, his face red and his feet overlarge, nearly knocked the box over as he got a paper out. "Tessie," Mr. Summers said. She hesitated for a minute, looking around defiantly, and then set her lips and went up to the box. She snatched a paper out and held it behind her.

"Bill," Mr. Summers said, and Bill Hutchinson reached into the box and felt around, bringing his hand out at last with the slip of paper in it.

The crowd was quiet. A girl whispered, "I hope it's not Nancy," and the sound of the whisper reached the edges of the crowd.

"It's not the way it used to be," Old Man Warner said clearly. "People ain't the way they used to be."

"All right," Mr. Summers said. "Open the papers. Harry, you open little Dave's."

Mr. Graves opened the slip of paper and there was a general sigh through the crowd as he held it up and everyone could see that it was blank. Nancy and Bill, Jr., opened theirs at the same time, and both beamed and laughed, turning around to the crowd and holding their slips of paper above their heads.

"Tessie," Mr. Summers said. There was a pause, and then Mr. Summers looked at Bill Hutchinson, and Bill unfolded his paper and showed it. It was blank.

"It's Tessie," Mr. Summers said, and his voice was hushed. "Show us her paper, Bill."

Bill Hutchinson went over to his wife and forced the slip of paper out of her hand. It had a black spot on it, the black spot Mr. Summers had made the night before with the heavy pencil in the coal-company office. Bill Hutchinson held it up, and there was a stir in the crowd.

"All right, folks," Mr. Summers said. "Let's finish quickly."

Although the villagers had forgotten the ritual and lost the original black box, they still remembered to use stones. The pile of stones the boys had made earlier was ready; there were stones on the ground with the blowing scraps of paper that had come out of the box. Mrs. Delacroix selected a stone so large she had to pick it up with both hands and turned to Mrs. Dunbar. "Come on," she said. "Hurry up."

Mrs. Dunbar had small stones in both hands, and she said, gasping for breath, "I can't run at all. You'll have to go ahead and I'll catch up with you."

The children had stones already, and someone gave little Davy Hutchinson a few pebbles.

Tessie Hutchinson was in the center of a cleared space by now, and she held her hands out desperately as the villagers moved in on her. "It isn't fair," she said. A stone hit her on the side of the head.

Old Man Warner was saying, "Come on, come on, everyone." Steve Adams was in the front of the crowd of villagers, with Mrs. Graves beside him.

"It isn't fair, it isn't right," Mrs. Hutchinson screamed, and then they were upon her.

KURT VONNEGUT, JR.
1922–
Harrison Bergeron

The year was 2081, and everybody was finally equal. They weren't only equal before God and the law. They were equal every which way. Nobody was smarter than anybody else. Nobody was better looking than anybody else. Nobody was stronger or quicker than anybody else. All this equality was due to the 211th, 212, and 213th Amendments to the Constitution, and to the unceasing vigilance of agents of the United States Handicapper General.

Some things about living still weren't quite right, though. April, for instance, still drove people crazy by not being springtime. And it was in that clammy month that the H-G men took George and Hazel Bergeron's fourteen-year-old son, Harrison, away.

It was tragic, all right, but George and Hazel couldn't think about it very hard. Hazel had a perfectly average intelligence, which meant she couldn't think about anything except in short bursts. And George, while his intelligence was way above normal, had a little mental handicap radio in his ear. He was required by law to wear it at all times. It was tuned to a government transmitter. Every twenty seconds or so, the transmitter would send out some sharp noise to keep people like George from taking unfair advantage of their brains.

George and Hazel were watching television. There were tears on Hazel's cheeks, but she's forgotten for the moment what they were about.

On the television screen were ballerinas.

A buzzer sounded in George's head. His thoughts fled in panic, like bandits from a burglar alarm.

"That was a real pretty dance, that dance they just did," said Hazel.

"Huh?" said George.

"That dance—it was nice," said Hazel.

"Yup," said George. He tried to think a little about the ballerinas. They weren't really very good—no better than anybody else would have been, anyway. They were burdened with sashweights and bags of birdshot, and their faces were masked, so that no one, seeing a free and graceful gesture or a pretty face, would feel like something the cat drug in. George was toying with the vague notion that maybe dancers shouldn't be handicapped. But he didn't get very far with it before another noise in his ear radio scattered his thoughts.

George winced. So did two out of the eight ballerinas.

Hazel saw him wince. Having no mental handicap herself, she had to ask George what the latest sound had been.

"Sounded like somebody hitting a milk bottle with a ball peen hammer," said George.

"I'd think it would be real interesting, hearing all the different sounds," said Hazel, a little envious. "All the things they think up."

"Um," said George.

"Only, if I was Handicapper General, you know what I would do?" said Hazel. Hazel, as a matter of fact, bore a strong resemblance to the Handicapper General, a woman named Diana Moon Glampers. "If I was Diana Moon Glampers," said Hazel, "I'd have chimes on Sunday—just chimes. Kind of in honor of religion."

"I could think, if it was just chimes," said George.

"Well—maybe make 'em real loud," said Hazel. "I think I'd make a good Handicapper General."

"Good as anybody else," said George.

"Who knows better'n I do what normal is?" said Hazel.

"Right," said George. He began to think glimmeringly about his abnormal son who was now in jail, about Harrison, but a twenty-one-gun salute in his head stopped that.

"Boy!" said Hazel, "That was a doozy, wasn't it?"

It was such a doozy that George was white and trembling, and tears stood on the rims of his red eyes. Two of the eight ballerinas had collapsed to the studio floor, were holding their temples.

"All of a sudden you look so tired," said Hazel. "Why don't you stretch out on the sofa, so's you can rest your handicap bag on the pillows, honeybunch." She was referring to the forty-seven pounds of birdshot in a canvas bag, which was padlocked around George's neck. "Go on and rest the bag for a little while," she said. "I don't care if you're not equal to me for a while."

George weighed the bag with his hands. "I don't mind it," he said. "I don't notice it any more. It's just a part of me."

"You been so tired lately—kind of wore out," said Hazel. "If there was just some way we could make a little hole in the bottom of the bag, and just take out a few of them lead balls. Just a few."

"Two years in prison and two thousand dollars fine for every ball I took out," said George. "I don't call that a bargain."

"If you could just take a few out when you came home from work," said Hazel. "I mean—you don't compete with anybody around here. You just set around."

"If I tried to get away with it," said George, "then other people'd get away with it—and pretty soon we'd be right back to the dark ages again, with everybody competing against everybody else. You wouldn't like that, would you?"

"I'd hate it," said Hazel.

"There you are," said George. "The minute people start cheating on laws, what do you think happens to society?"

If Hazel hadn't been able to come up with an answer to this question, George couldn't have supplied one. A siren was going off in his head.

"Reckon it'd fall all apart," said Hazel.

"What would?" said George blankly.

"Society," said Hazel uncertainly. "Wasn't that what you just said?"

"Who knows?" said George.

The television program was suddenly interrupted for a news bulletin. It wasn't clear at first as to what the bulletin was about, since the announcer, like all announcers, had a serious speech impediment. For about half a minute, and in a state of high excitement, the announcer tried to say, "Ladies and gentlemen—"

He finally gave up, handed the bulletin to a ballerina to read.

"That's all right—" Hazel said of the announcer, "he tried. That's the big thing. He tried to do the best he could with what God gave him. He should get a nice raise for trying so hard."

"Ladies and gentlemen—" said the ballerina, reading the bulletin. She must have been extraordinarily beautiful, because the mask she wore was hideous. And it was easy to see that she was the strongest and most graceful of all the dancers, for her handicap bags were as big as those worn by two-hundred-pound men.

And she had to apologize at once for her voice, which was a very unfair voice for a woman to use. Her voice was a warm, luminous, timeless melody. "Excuse me—" she said, and she began again, making her voice absolutely uncompetitive.

"Harrison Bergeron, age fourteen," she said in a grackle squawk, "has just escaped from jail, where he was held on suspicion of plotting to overthrow the government. He is a genius and an athlete, is under-handicapped, and should be regarded as extremely danger-ous."

A police photograph of Harrison Bergeron was flashed on the screen-upside down, then sideways, upside down again, then right side up. The picture showed the full length of Harrison against a background calibrated in feet and inches. He was exactly seven feet tall.

The rest of Harrison's appearance was Halloween and hardware. Nobody had ever borne heavier handicaps. He had outgrown hin-drances faster than the H-G men could think them up. Instead of a lit-tle ear radio for a mental handicap, he wore a tremendous pair of earphones, and spectacles with thick wavy lenses. The spectacles were intended to make him not only half blind, but to give him whanging headaches besides.

Scrap metal was hung all over him. Ordinarily, there was a certain symmetry, a military neatness to the handicaps issued to strong people, but Harrison looked like a walking junkyard. In the race of life, Harrison carried three hundred pounds.

And to offset his good looks, the H-G men required that he wear at all times a red rubber ball for a nose, keep his eyebrows shaved off, and cover his even white teeth with black caps at snaggle-tooth random.

"If you see this boy," said the ballerina, "do not—I repeat, do not—try to reason with him."

There was the shriek of a door being torn from its hinges.

Screams and barking cries of consternation came from the television set. The photograph of Harrison Bergeron on the screen jumped again and again, as though dancing to the tune of an earthquake.

George Bergeron correctly identified the earthquake, and well he might have—for many was the time his own home had danced to the same crashing tune. "My God—" said George, "that must be Harrison!"

The realization was blasted from his mind instantly by the sound of an atuomobile collision in his head.

When George could open his eyes again, the photograph of Harrison was gone. A living, breathing Harrison filled the screen.

Clanking, clownish, and huge, Harrison stood in the center of the studio. The knob of the uprooted studio door was still in his hand. Ballerinas, technicians, musicians, and announcers cowered on their knees before him, expecting to die.

"I am the Emperor!" cried Harrison. "Do you hear? I am the Emperor! Everybody must do what I say at once!" He stamped his foot and the studio shook.

"Even as I stand here—" he bellowed, "crippled, hobbled, sickened—I am a greater ruler than any man who ever lived! Now watch me become what I *can* become!"

Harrison tore the straps of his handicap harness like wet tissue paper, tore straps guaranteed to support five thousand pounds.

Harrison's scrap-iron handicaps crashed to the floor.

Harrison thrust his thumbs under the bar of the padlock that secured his head harness. The bar snapped like celery. Harrison smashed his headphones and spectacles against the wall.

He flung away his rubber-ball nose, revealed a man that would have awed Thor, the god of thunder.

"I shall now select my Empress!" he said, looking down on the cowering people. "Let the first woman who dares rise to her feet claim her mate and her throne!"

A moment passed, and then a ballerina arose, swaying like a willow.

Harrison plucked the mental handicap from her ear, snapped off her physical handicaps with marvelous delicacy. Last of all, he removed her mask.

She was blindingly beautiful.

"Now—" said Harrison, taking her hand "shall we show the people the meaning of the word dance? Music!" he commanded.

The musicians scrambled back into their chairs, and Harrison stripped them of their handicaps, too. "Play your best," he told them, "and I'll make you barons and dukes and earls."

The music began. It was normal at first—cheap, silly, false. But Harrison snatched two musicians from their chairs, waved them like batons as he sang the music as he wanted it played. He slammed them back into their chairs.

The music began again and was much improved.

Harrison and his Empress merely listened to the music for a while—listened gravely, as though synchronizing their heartbeats with it.

They shifted their weights to their toes.

Harrison placed his big hands on the girl's tiny waist, letting her sense the weightlessness that would soon be hers.

And then, in an explosion of joy and grace, into the air they sprang!

Not only were the laws of the land abandoned, but the law of gravity and the laws of motion as well.

They reeled, whirled, swiveled, flounced, capered, gamboled, and spun.

They leaped like deer on the moon.

The studio ceiling was thirty feet high, but each leap brought the dancers nearer to it.

It became their obvious intention to kiss the ceiling.

They kissed it.

And then, neutralizing gravity with love and pure will, they remained suspended in air inches below the ceiling, and they kissed each other for a long, long time.

It was then that Diana Moon Glampers, the Handicapper General, came into the studio with a double-barreled ten-gauge shotgun. She fired twice, and the Emperor and the Empress were dead before they hit the floor.

Diana Moon Glampers loaded the gun again. She aimed it at the musicians and told them they had ten seconds to get their handicaps back on.

It was then that the Bergerons' television tube burned out.

Hazel turned to comment about the blackout to George. But George had gone out into the kitchen for a can of beer.

George came back in with the beer, paused while a handicap signal shook him up. And then he sat down again. "You been crying?" he said to Hazel.

"Yup," she said.

"What about?" he said.

"I forget," she said. "Something real sad on television."

"What was it?" he said.

"It's all kind of mixed up in my mind," said Hazel.

"Forget sad things," said George.

"I always do," said Hazel.

"That's my girl," said George. He winced. There was the sound of a rivetting gun in his head.

"Gee—I could tell that one was a doozy," said Hazel.

"You can say that again," said George.

"Gee—" said Hazel. "I could tell that one was a doozy."

W. S. MERWIN
1927–
Unchopping a Tree

Start with the leaves, the small twigs, and the nests that have been shaken, ripped, or broken off by the fall; these must be gathered and attached once again to their respective places. It is not arduous work, unless major limbs have been smashed or mutilated. If the fall was carefully and correctly planned, the chances of anything of the kind happening will have been reduced. Again, much depends upon the size, age, shape, and species of the tree. Still, you will be lucky if you can get through this stage without having to use machinery. Even in the best of circumstances it is a labor that will make you wish often that you had won the favor of the universe of ants, the empire of mice, or at least a local tribe of squirrels, and could enlist their labors and their talents. But no, they leave you to it. They have learned, with time. This is men's work. It goes without saying that if the tree was hollow in whole or in part, and contained old nests of bird or mammal or insect, or hoards of nuts or such structures as wasps or bees build for their survival, the contents will have to be repaired where necessary, and reassembled, insofar as possible, in their original order, including the shells of nuts already opened. With spiders' webs you must simply do the best you can. We do not have the spider's weaving equipment, nor any substitute for the leaf's living bond with its point of attachment and nourishment. It is even harder to simulate the latter when the leaves have once become dry—as they are bound to do, for this is not the labor of a moment. Also it hardly needs saying that this is the time for repairing any neighboring trees or bushes or other growth that may have been damaged by the fall. The same rules apply. Where neighboring trees were of the same species it is difficult not to waste time conveying a detached leaf back to the wrong tree. Practice, practice. Put your hope in that.

Now the tackle must be put into place, or the scaffolding, depending on the surroundings and the dimensions of the tree. It is ticklish work. Almost always it involves, in itself, further damage to the area, which will have to be corrected later. But as you've heard, it can't be helped. And care now is likely to save you considerable trouble later. Be careful to grind nothing into the ground.

At last the time comes for the erecting of the trunk. By now it will scarcely be necessary to remind you of the delicacy of this huge skeleton. Every motion of the tackle, every slight upward heave of the trunk, the branches, their elaborately re-assembled panoply of leaves (now dead) will draw from you an involuntary gasp. You will watch for a leaf or a twig to be snapped off yet again. You will listen for the nuts to shift in the hollow limb and you will hear whether they are indeed falling into place or are spilling in disorder—in which case, or in the event of anything else of the kind—operations will have to cease, of course, while you correct the matter. The raising itself is no small enterprise, from the moment when the chains tighten around the old bandages until the bole hangs vertical above the stump, splinter above splinter. Now the final straightening of the splinters themselves can take place (the preliminary work is best done while the wood is still green and soft, but at times when the splinters are not badly twisted most of the straightening is left until now, when the torn ends are face to face with each other). When the splinters are perfectly complementary the appropriate fixative is applied. Again we have no duplicate of the original substance. Ours is extremely strong, but it is rigid. It is limited to surfaces, and there is no play in it. However the core is not the part of the trunk that conducted life from the roots up into the branches and back again. It was relatively inert. The fixative for this part is not the same as the one for the outer layers and the bark, and if either of these is involved in the splintered section they must receive applications of the appropriate adhesives. Apart from being incorrect and probably ineffective, the core fixative would leave a scar on the bark.

When all is ready the splintered trunk is lowered onto the splinters of the stump. This, one might say, is only the skeleton of the resurrection. Now the chips must be gathered, and the sawdust, and returned to their former positions. The fixative for the wood layers will be applied to chips and sawdust consisting only of wood. Chips and sawdust consisting of several substances will receive applications of the correct adhesives. It is as well, where possible, to shelter the materials from the elements while working. Weathering makes it harder to identify the smaller fragments. Bark sawdust in particular the earth lays claim to very quickly. You must find your own ways of coping with this problem. There is a certain beauty, you will notice at moments, in the pattern of the chips as they are fitted back into place. You will wonder to what extent it should be described as natural, to what extent man-made. It will lead you on to speculations about the parentage of beauty itself, to which you will return.

The adhesive for the chips is translucent, and not so rigid as that for the splinters. That for the bark and its subcutaneous layers is transparent and runs into the fibers on either side, partially dissolving them into each other. It does not set the sap flowing again but it does pay a kind of tribute to the preoccupations of the ancient thoroughfares. You could not roll an egg over the joints but some of the mine-shafts would still be passable, no doubt. For the first exploring insect who raises its head in the tight echoless passages. The day comes when it is all restored, even to the moss (now dead) over the wound. You will sleep badly, thinking of the removal of the scaffolding that must begin the next morning. How you will hope for sun and a still day!

The removal of the scaffolding or tackle is not so dangerous, perhaps, to the surroundings, as its installation, but it presents problems. It should be taken from the spot piece by piece as it is detached, and stored at a distance. You have come to accept it there, around the tree. The sky begins to look naked as the chains and struts one by one vacate their positions. Finally the moment arrives when the last sustaining piece is removed and the tree stands again on its own. It is as though its weight for a moment stood on your heart. You listen for a thud of settlement, a warning creak deep in the intricate joinery. You cannot believe it will hold. How like something dreamed it is, standing there all by itself. How long will it stand there now? The first breeze that touches its dead leaves all seems to flow into your mouth. You are afraid the motion of the clouds will be enough to push it over. What more can you do? What more can you do?

But there is nothing more you can do.

Others are waiting.

Everything is going to have to be put back.

URSULA K. LE GUIN
1929–

The Ones Who Walk Away from Omelas

(Variations on a theme by William James)

With a clamor of bells that set the swallows soaring, the Festival of Summer came to the city Omelas, bright-towered by the sea. The rigging of the boats in harbor sparkled with flags. In the streets between houses with red roofs and painted walls, between old moss-grown gardens and under avenues of trees, past great parks and public buildings, processions moved. Some were decorous: old people in long stiff robes of mauve and grey, grave master workmen, quiet, merry women carrying their babies, and chatting as they walked. In other streets the music beat faster, a shimmering of gong and tambourine, and the people went dancing, the procession was a dance. Children dodged in and out, their high calls rising like the swallows' crossing flights over the music and the singing. All the processions wound towards the north side of the city, where on the great water-meadow called the Green Fields boys and girls, naked in the bright air, with mud-stained feet and ankles and long, lithe arms, exercised their restive horses before the race. The horses wore no gear at all but a halter without bit. Their manes were braided with streamers of silver, gold, and green. They flared their nostrils and pranced and boasted to one another; they were vastly excited, the horse being the only animal who has adopted our ceremonies as his own. Far off to the north and west the mountains stood up half encircling Omelas on her bay. The air of morning was so clear that the snow still crowning the Eighteen Peaks burned with white-gold fire across the miles of sunlit air, under the dark blue of the sky. There was just enough wind to make the banners that marked the racecourse snap and flutter now and then. In the silence of the broad green meadows one could hear the music winding through the city streets, farther and nearer and ever approaching, a cheerful faint sweetness of the air that from time to time trembled and gathered together and broke out into the great joyous clanging of the bells.

Joyous! How is one to tell about joy? How describe the citizens of Omelas?

They were not simple folk, you see, though they were happy. But we do not say the words of cheer much any more. All smiles have become archaic. Given a description such as this one tends to make certain assumptions. Given a description such as this one tends to look next for the King, mounted on a splendid stallion and surrounded by his noble knights, or perhaps in a golden litter borne by great-muscled slaves. But there was no king. They did not use swords, or keep slaves. They were not barbarians. I do not know the rules and laws of their society, but I suspect that they were singularly few. As they did without monarchy and slavery, so they also got on without the stock exchange, the advertisement, the secret police, and the bomb. Yet I repeat that these were not simple folk, not dulcet shepherds, noble savages, bland utopians. They were not less complex than us. The trouble is that we have a bad habit, encouraged by pedants and sophisticates, of considering happiness as something rather stupid. Only pain is intellectual, only evil interesting. This is the treason of the artist: a refusal to admit the banality of evil and the terrible boredom of pain. If you can't lick 'em, join 'em. If it hurts, repeat it. But to praise despair is to condemn delight, to embrace violence is to lose hold of everything else. We have almost lost hold; we can no longer describe a happy man, nor make any celebration of joy. How can I tell you about the people of Omelas? They were not naïve and happy children—though their children were, in fact, happy. They were mature, intelligent, passionate adults whose lives were not wretched. O miracle! but I wish I could describe it better. I wish I could convince you. Omelas sounds in my words like a city in a fairy tale, long ago and far away, once upon a time. Perhaps it would be best if you imagined it as your own fancy bids, assuming it will rise to the occasion, for certainly I cannot suit you all. For instance, how about technology? I think that there would be no cars or helicopters in and above the streets; this follows from the fact that the people of Omelas are happy people. Happiness is based on a just discrimination of what is necessary, what is neither necessary nor destructive, and what is destructive. In the middle category, however—that of the unnecessary but undestructive, that of comfort, luxury, exuberance, etc.—they could perfectly well have central heating, subway trains, washing machines, and all kinds of marvelous devices not yet invented here, floating light-sources, fuelless power, a cure for the common cold. Or they could have none of that: it doesn't matter. As you like it. I incline to think that people from towns up and down the coast have been coming in to Omelas during the last days before the Festival on very fast little trains and double-decked trams, and that the train station of Omelas is actually the handsomest building in town, though plainer than the magnificent Farmers' Market. But even granted trains, I fear that Omelas so far strikes some of you as goody-goody. Smiles, bells, parades, horses, bleh. If so, please add an orgy. If an orgy would help, don't hesitate. Let us not, however, have temples from which issue beautiful nude priests and priestesses already half in ecstasy and ready to copulate with any man or woman, lover or stranger, who desires union with the deep godhead of the blood, although that was my first idea. But really it would be better not to have any temples in Omelas—at least, not manned temples. Religion yes, clergy no. Surely the beautiful nudes can just wander about, offering themselves like divine soufflés to the hunger of the needy and the rapture of the flesh. Let them join the processions. Let tambourines be struck above the copulations, and the glory of desire be proclaimed upon the gongs, and (a not unimportant point) let the offspring of these delightful rituals be beloved and looked after by all. One thing I know there is none of in Omelas is guilt. But what else should there be? I thought at first there were no drugs, but that is puritanical. For those who like it, the faint insistent sweetness of *drooz* may perfume the ways of the city, *drooz* which first brings a great lightness and brilliance to the mind and limbs, and then after some hours a dreamy languor, and wonderful visions at last of the very arcana and inmost secrets of the Universe, as well as exciting the pleasure of sex beyond all belief; and it is not habit-forming. For more modest tastes I think there ought to be beer. What else, what else belongs in the joyous city? The sense of victory, surely, the celebration of courage. But as we did without clergy, let us do without soldiers. The joy built upon successful slaughter is not the right kind of joy; it will not do; it is fearful and it is trivial. A boundless and generous contentment, a magnanimous triumph felt not against some outer enemy but in communion with the finest and fairest in the souls of all men everywhere and the splendor of the world's summer: this is what swells the hearts of the people of Omelas, and the victory they celebrate is that of life. I really don't think many of them need to take *drooz*.

Most of the processions have reached the Green Fields by now. A marvelous smell of cooking goes forth from the red and blue tents of the provisioners. The faces of small children are amiably sticky; in the benign grey beard of a man a couple of crumbs of rich pastry are entangled. The youths and girls have mounted their horses and are beginning to group around the starting line of the course. An old woman, small, fat, and laughing, is passing out flowers from a basket, and tall young men wear her flowers in their shining hair. A child of nine or ten sits at the edge of the crowd, alone, playing on a wooden flute. People pause to listen, and they smile, but they do not speak to him, for he never ceases playing and never sees them, his dark eyes wholly rapt in the sweet, thin magic of the tune.

He finishes, and slowly lowers his hands holding the wooden flute.

As if that little private silence were the signal, all at once a trumpet sounds from the pavilion near the starting line: imperious, melancholy, piercing. The horses rear on their slender legs, and some of them neigh in answer. Sober-faced, the young riders stroke the horses' necks and soothe them, whispering, "Quiet, quiet, there my beauty, my hope. . . ." They begin to form in rank along the starting line. The crowds along the racecourse are like a field of grass and flowers in the wind. The Festival of Summer has begun.

Do you believe? Do you accept the festival, the city, the joy? No? Then let me describe one more thing.

In a basement under one of the beautiful public buildings of Omelas, or perhaps in the cellar of one of its spacious private homes, there is a room. It has one locked door, and no window. A little light seeps in dustily between cracks in the boards, secondhand from a cobwebbed window somewhere across the cellar. In one corner of the little room a couple of mops, with stiff, clotted, foul-smelling heads, stand near a rusty bucket. The floor is dirt, a little damp to the touch, as cellar dirt usually is. The room is about three paces long and two wide: a mere broom closet or disused tool room. In the room a child is sitting. It could be a boy or a girl. It looks about six, but actually is nearly ten. It is feeble-minded. Perhaps it was born defective, or perhaps it has become imbecile through fear, malnutrition, and neglect. It picks its nose and occasionally fumbles vaguely with its toes or genitals, as it sits hunched in the corner farthest from the bucket and the two mops. It is afraid of the mops. It finds them horrible. It shuts its eyes, but it knows the mops are still standing there; and the door is locked; and nobody will come. The door is always locked; and nobody ever comes, except that sometimes—the child has no understanding of time or interval—sometimes the door rattles terribly and opens, and a person, or several people, are there. One of them may come in and kick the child to make it stand up. The others never come close, but peer in at it with frightened, disgusted eyes. The food bowl and the water jug are hastily filled, the door is locked, the eyes disappear. The people at the door never say anything, but the child, who has not always lived in the tool room, and can remember sunlight and its mother's voice, sometimes speaks. "I will be good," it says. "Please let me out. I will be good!" They never answer. The child used to scream for help at night, and cry a good deal, but now it only makes a kind of whining, "eh-haa, eh-haa," and it speaks less and less often. It is so thin there are no calves to its legs; its belly protrudes; it lives on a half-bowl of corn meal and grease a day. It is naked. Its buttocks and thighs are a mass of festered sores, as it sits in its own excrement continually.

They all know it is there, all the people of Omelas. Some of them have come to see it, others are content merely to know it is there. They all know that it has to be there. Some of them understand why, and some do not, but they all understand that their happiness, the beauty of their city, the tenderness of their friendships, the health of their children, the wisdom of their scholars, the skill of their makers, even the abundance of their harvest and the kindly weathers of their skies, depends wholly on this child's abominable misery.

This is usually explained to children when they are between eight and twelve, whenever they seem capable of understanding; and most of those who come to see the child are young people, though often enough an adult comes, or comes back, to see the child. No matter how well the matter has been explained to them, these young spectators are always shocked and sickened at the sight. They feel disgust, which they had thought themselves superior to. They feel anger, outrage, impotence, despite all the explanations. They would like to do something for the child. But there is nothing they can do. If the child were brought up into the sunlight out of that vile place, if it were cleaned and fed and comforted, that would be a good thing, indeed; but if it were done, in that day and hour all the prosperity and beauty and delight of Omelas would wither and be destroyed. Those are the terms. To exchange all the goodness and grace of every life in Omelas for that single, small improvement: to throw away the happiness of thousands for the chance of the happiness of one: that would be to let guilt within the walls indeed.

The terms are strict and absolute; there may not even be a kind word spoken to the child.

Often the young people go home in tears, or in a tearless rage, when they have seen the child and faced this terrible paradox. They may brood over it for weeks or years. But as time goes on they begin to realize that even if the child could be released, it would not get much good of its freedom: a little vague pleasure of warmth and food, no doubt, but little more. It is too degraded and imbecile to know any real joy. It has been afraid too long even to be free of fear. Its habits are too uncouth for it to respond to humane treatment. Indeed, after so long it would probably be wretched without walls about it to protect it, and darkness for its eyes, and its own excrement to sit in. Their tears at the bitter injustice dry when they begin to perceive the terrible justice of reality, and to accept it. Yet it is their tears and anger, the trying of their generosity and the acceptance of their helplessness, which are perhaps the true source of the splendor of their lives. Theirs is no vapid, irresponsible happiness. They know that they, like the child, are not free. They know compassion. It is the existence of the child, and their knowledge of its existence, that makes possible the nobility of their architecture, and poignancy of their music, the profundity of their science. It is because of the child that they are so gentle with children. They know that if the wretched one were not there snivelling in the dark, the other one, the flute-player, could make no joyful music as the young riders line up in their beauty for the race in the sunlight of the first morning of summer.

Now do you believe in them? Are they not more credible? But there is one more thing to tell, and this is quite incredible.

At times one of the adolescent girls or boys who go to see the child does not go home to weep or rage, does not, in fact, go home at all. Sometimes also a man or woman much older falls silent for a day or two, and then leaves home. These people go out into the street, and walk down the street alone. They keep walking, and walk straight out of the city of Omelas, through the beautiful gates. They keep walking across the farmlands of Omelas. Each one goes alone, youth or girl, man or woman. Night falls; the traveler must pass down village streets, between the houses with yellow-lit windows, and on out into the darkness of the fields. Each alone, they go west or north, towards the mountains. They go on. They leave Omelas, they walk ahead into the darkness, and they do not come back. The place they go towards is a place even less imaginable to most of us than the city of happiness. I cannot describe it at all. It is possible that it does not exist. But they seem to know where they are going, the ones who walk away from Omelas.

DONALD BARTHELME
1932–
The Indian Uprising

We defended the city as best we could. The arrows of the Comanches came in clouds. The war clubs of the Comanches clattered on the soft, yellow pavements. There were earthworks along the Boulevard Mark Clark and the hedges had been laced with sparkling wire. People were trying to understand. I spoke to Sylvia. "Do you think this is a good life?" The table held apples, books, long-playing records. She looked up. "No."

Patrols of paras and volunteers with armbands guarded the tall, flat buildings. We interrogated the captured Comanche. Two of us forced his head back while another poured water into his nostrils. His body jerked, he choked and wept. Not believing a hurried, careless, and exaggerated report of the number of casualties in the outer districts where trees, lamps, swans had been reduced to clear fields of fire we issued entrenching tools to those who seemed trustworthy and turned the heavy-weapons companies so that we could not be surprised from that direction. And I sat there getting drunker and drunker and more in love and more in love. We talked.

"Do you know Fauré's 'Dolly'?"

"Would that be Gabriel Fauré?"

"It would."

"Then I know it," she said. "May I say that I play it at certain times, when I am sad, or happy, although it requires four hands."

"How is that managed?"

"I accelerate," she said, "ignoring the time signature."

And when they shot the scene in the bed I wondered how you felt under the eyes of the cameramen, grips, juicers, men in the mixing booth: excited? stimulated? And when they shot the scene in the shower I sanded a hollow-core door working carefully against the illustrations in texts and whispered instructions from one who had already solved the problem. I had made after all other tables, one while living with Nancy, one while living with Alice, one while living with Eunice, one while living with Marianne.

Red men in waves like people scattering in a square startled by something tragic or a sudden, loud noise accumulated against the barricades we had made of window dummies, silk, thoughtfully planned job descriptions (including scales for the orderly progress of other colors), wine in demijohns, and robes. I analyzed the composition of the barricade nearest me and found two ashtrays, ceramic, one dark brown and one dark brown with an orange blur at the lip; a tin frying pan; two-litre bottles of red wine; three-quarter-litre bottles of Black & White, aquavit, cognac, vodka, gin, Fad #6 sherry; a hollow-core door in birch veneer on black wrought-iron legs; a blanket, red-orange with faint blue stripes; a red pillow and a blue pillow; a woven straw wastebasket; two glass jars for flowers; corkscrews and can openers; two plates and two cups, ceramic, dark brown; a yellow-and-purple poster; a Yugoslavian carved flute, wood, dark brown; and other items. I decided I knew nothing.

The hospitals dusted wounds with powders the worth of which was not quite established, other supplies having been exhausted early in the first day. I decided I knew nothing. Friends put me in touch with a Miss R., a teacher, unorthodox they said, excellent they said, successful with difficult cases, steel shutters on the windows made the house safe. I had just learned via an International Distress Coupon that Jane had been beaten up by a dwarf in a bar on Tenerife but Miss R. did not allow me to speak of it. "You know nothing," she said, "you feel nothing, you are locked in a most savage and terrible ignorance, I despise you, my boy, *mon cher*, my heart. You may attend but you must not attend now, you must attend later, a day or a week or an hour, you are making me ill. . . ." I nonevaluated these remarks as Korzybski instructed. But it was difficult. Then they pulled back in a feint near the river and we rushed into that sector with a reinforced battalion hastily formed among the Zouaves and cabdrivers. This unit was crushed in the afternoon of a day that began with spoons and letters in hallways and under windows where men tasted the history of the heart, cone-shaped muscular organ that maintains *circulation of the blood.*

But it is you I want now, here in the middle of this Uprising, with the streets yellow and threatening, short, ugly lances with fur at the throat and inexplicable shell money lying in the grass. It is when I am with you that I am happiest, and it is for you that I am making this hollow-core door table with black wrought-iron legs. I held Sylvia by her bear-claw necklace. "Call off your braves," I said. "We have many years left to live." There was a sort of muck running in the gutters, yellowish, filthy stream suggesting excrement, or nervousness, a city that does not know what it has done to deserve baldness, errors, infidelity. "With luck you will survive until matins," Sylvia said. She ran off down the Rue Chester Nimitz, uttering shrill cries.

Then it was learned that they had infiltrated our ghetto and that the people of the ghetto instead of resisting had joined the smooth, well-coördinated attack with zipguns, telegrams, lockets, causing that portion of the line held by the I.R.A. to swell and collapse. We sent more heroin into the ghetto, and hyacinths, ordering another hundred thousand of the pale, delicate flowers. On the map we considered the situation with its strung-out inhabitants and merely personal emotions. Our parts were blue and their parts were green. I showed the blue-and-green map to Sylvia. "Your parts are green," I said. "You gave me heroin first a year ago," Sylvia said. She ran off down George C. Marshall Allée, uttering shrill cries. Miss R. pushed me into a large room painted white (jolting and dancing in the soft light, and I was excited! and there were people watching!) in which there were two chairs. I sat in one chair and Miss R. sat in the other. She wore a blue dress containing a red figure. There was nothing exceptional about her. I was disappointed by her plainness, by the bareness of the room, by the absence of books.

The girls of my quarter wore long blue mufflers that reached to their knees. Sometimes the girls hid Comanches in their rooms, the blue mufflers together in a room creating a great blue fog. Block opened the door. He was carrying weapons, flowers, loaves of bread. And he was friendly, kind, enthusiastic, so I related a little of the history of torture, reviewing the technical literature quoting the best modern sources, French, German, and American, and pointing out the flies which had gathered in anticipation of some new, cool color.

"What is the situation?" I asked.

"The situation is liquid," he said. "We hold the south quarter and they hold the north quarter. The rest is silence."

"And Kenneth?"

"That girl is not in love with Kenneth," Block said frankly. "She is in love with his coat. When she is not wearing it she is huddling under it. Once I caught it going down the stairs by itself. I looked inside. Sylvia."

Once I caught Kenneth's coat going down the stairs by itself but the coat was a trap and inside a Comanche who made a thrust with his short, ugly knife at my leg which buckled and tossed me over the balustrade through a window and into another situation. Not believing that your body brilliant as it was and your fat, liquid spirit distinguished and angry as it was were stable quantities to which one could return on wires more than once, twice, or another number of times I said: "See the table?"

In Skinny Wainwright Square the forces of green and blue swayed and struggled. The referees ran out on the field trailing chains. And then the blue part would be enlarged, the green diminished. Miss R. began to speak. "A former king of Spain, a Bonaparte, lived for a time in Bordentown, New Jersey. But that's no good." She paused. "The ardor aroused in men by the beauty of women can only be satisfied by God. That is *very* good (it is Valéry) but it is not what I have to teach you, goat, muck, filth, heart of my heart." I showed the table to Nancy. "See the table?" She stuck out her tongue red as a cardinal's hat. "I made such a table once," Block said frankly. "People all over America have made such tables. I doubt very much whether one can enter an American home without finding at least one such table, or traces of its having been there, such as faded places in the carpet." And afterward in the garden the men of the 7th Cavalry played Gabrieli, Albinoni, Marcello, Vivaldi, Boccherini. I saw Sylvia. She wore a yellow ribbon, under a long blue muffler. "Which side are you on," I cried, "after all?"

"The only form of discourse of which I approve," Miss R. said in her dry, tense voice, "is the litany. I believe our masters and teachers as well as plain citizens should confine themselves to what can safely be said. Thus when I hear the words *pewter, snake, tea, Fad #6 sherry, serviette, fenestration, crown, blue* coming from the mouth of some public official, or some raw youth, I am not disappointed. Vertical organization is also possible," Miss R. said, "as in

pewter
snake
tea
Fad #6 sherry
serviette
fenestration
crown
blue.

I run to liquids and colors," she said, "but you, you may run to something else, my virgin, my darling, my thistle, my poppet, my own. Young people," Miss R. said, "run to more and more unpleasant combinations as they sense the nature of our society. Some people," Miss R. said, "run to conceits or wisdom but I hold to the hard, brown, nutlike word. I might point out that there is enough aesthetic excitement here to satisfy anyone but a damned fool." I sat in solemn silence.

Fire arrows lit my way to the post office in Patton Place where members of the Abraham Lincoln Brigade offered their last, exhausted letters, postcards, calendars. I opened a letter but inside was a Comanche flint arrowhead play by Frank Wedekind in an elegant gold chain and congratulations. Your earring rattled against my spectacles when I leaned forward to touch the soft, ruined place where the hearing aid had been. "Pack it in! Pack it in!" I urged, but the men in charge of the Uprising refused to listen to reason or to understand that it was real and that our water supply had evaporated and that our credit was no longer what it had been, once.

We attached wires to the testicles of the captured Comanche. And I sat there getting drunker and drunker and more in love and more in love. When we threw the switch he spoke. His name, he said, was Gustave Aschenbach. He was born at L—, a country town in the province of Silesia. He was the son of an upper official in the judicature, and his forebears had all been officers, judges, departmental functionaries. . . . And you can never touch a girl in the same way more than once, twice, or another number of times however much you may wish to hold, wrap, or otherwise fix her hand, or look, or some other quality, or incident, known to you previously. In Sweden the little Swedish children cheered when we managed nothing more remarkable than getting off a bus burdened with packages, bread and liver-paste and beer. We went to an old church and sat in the royal box. The organist was practicing. And then into the graveyard next to the church. *Here lies Anna Pedersen, a good woman.* I threw a mushroom on the grave. The officer commanding the garbage dump reported by radio that the garbage had begun to move.

Jane! I heard via an International Distress Coupon that you were beaten up by a dwarf in a bar on Tenerife. That doesn't sound like you, Jane. Mostly you kick the dwarf in his little dwarf groin before he can get his teeth into your tasty and nice-looking leg, don't you, Jane? Your affair with Harold is reprehensible, you know that, don't you, Jane? Harold is married to Nancy. And there is Paula to think about (Harold's kid), and Billy (Harold's other kid). I think your values are peculiar, Jane! Strings of language extend in every direction to bind the world into a rushing, ribald whole.

And you can never return to felicities in the same way, the brilliant body, the distinguished spirit recapitulating moments that occur once, twice, or another number of times in rebellions, or water. The rolling consensus of the Comanche nation smashed our inner defenses on three sides. Block was firing a greasegun from the upper floor of a building designed by Emery Roth & Sons. "See the table?" "Oh, pack it in with your bloody table!" The city officials were tied to trees. Dusky warriors padded with their forest tread into the mouth of the mayor. "Who do you want to be?" I asked Kenneth and he said he wanted to be Jean-Luc Godard but later when time permitted conversations in large lighted rooms, whispering galleries with black-and-white Spanish rugs and problematic sculpture on calm, red catafalques. The sickness of the quarrel lay thick in the bed. I touched your back, the white, raised scars.

We killed a great many in the south suddenly with helicopters and rockets but we found that those we had killed were children and more came from the north and from the east and from other places where there are children preparing to live. "Skin," Miss R. said softly in the white, yellow room. "This is the Clemency Committee. And would you remove your belt and shoelaces." I removed my belt and shoelaces and looked (rain shattering from a great height the prospects of silence and clear, neat rows of houses in the subdivisions) into their savage black eyes, paint, feathers, beads.

REALISM: *INTRODUCTION*

Even the wildest fantasy has something real about it. But works of fiction that we call "realistic" are real in a particular way. They present a world defined by certain ideas about the way social forces work upon individual human beings, and they show us characters whose inner lives conform to certain notions about human psychology. It would be impossible to define exactly what these "certain" ideas and notions are, but it is necessary to say something about them—at least in a rough and tentative way.

In earlier literature, individual characters are often shown struggling against fate or chance to achieve fame or happiness. Realism begins when writers can identify "society" as the thing against which individuals must struggle. When the romantic ideal of a unique and free personality confronts a deterministic view of social forces, realism is born. In realistic fictions we see individuals in conflict with social groups, with the class structure, the family structure, the political system. The short story—as opposed to the larger novel—specializes in loneliness, in the need for love and companionship that is seldom adequately achieved; and in the desire to retain an individual free will in the face of the enormous pressures of an indifferent or actively hostile world.

In a very definite way, realistic writers are the historians of their times—not chroniclers of the deeds of the great and powerful but witnesses to the quality of ordinary life. Two European writers showed the rest of the Western world how realism in short fiction could be achieved: Guy de Maupassant in France and Anton Chekhov in Russia. English, Irish, and American short story writers learned from them. And the Americans, in particular, learned well.

In the short story, skill with language itself counts for more than it needs to in longer fiction. The shorter a story is, the more closely it can draw upon the resources of poetry in its language. But a story, especially a realistic one, is not a poem. It must have a strong narrative structure or design, and it must get to the roots of human feeling and behavior in a way that convinces us of its human truth: truth to the way things are, to the surface of life, as well as truth to the inner lives of individuals, and the social structures in which individual lives grow or are stifled.

The range of tones and techniques employed by the writers represented here is in fact extraordinary. The interaction of individuals which is at the heart of realism can be presented in the detached, behavioral report of a Hemingway—with no interpretive commentary—or in the rich, engaged recital of a Lawrence, in which the commentary explores emotions that the characters feel but could never articulate for themselves. There are light stories with comic touches here, and heavy stories that bring us close to tears. But all these works of realistic fiction are designed to enlarge our sympathies by broadening our understanding. The end of realism is compassion.

GUY de MAUPASSANT

1850–1893

The Diamond Necklace

She was one of those pretty, charming young ladies, born, as if through an error of destiny, into a family of clerks. She had no dowry, no hopes, no means of becoming known, appreciated, loved, and married by a man either rich or distinguished; and she allowed herself to marry a petty clerk in the office of the Board of Education.

She was simple, not being able to adorn herself; but she was unhappy, as one out of her class; for women belong to no caste, no race; their grace, their beauty, and their charm serving them in the place of birth and family. Their inborn finesse, their instinctive elegance, their suppleness of wit are their only aristocracy, making some daughters of the people the equal of great ladies.

She suffered incessantly, feeling herself born for all delicacies and luxuries. She suffered from the poverty of her apartment, the shabby walls, the worn chairs, and the faded stuffs. All these things, which another woman of her station would not have noticed, tortured and angered her. The sight of the little Breton, who made this humble home, awoke in her sad regrets and desperate dreams. She thought of quiet antechambers, with their Oriental hangings, lighted by high, bronze torches, and of the two great footmen in short trousers who sleep in the large armchairs, made sleepy by the heavy air from the heating apparatus. She thought of large drawing-rooms, hung in old silks, of graceful pieces of furniture carrying bric-à-brac of inestimable value, and of the little perfumed coquettish apartments, made for five o'clock chats with most intimate friends, men known and sought after, whose attention all women envied and desired.

When she seated herself for dinner, before the round table where the tablecloth had been used three days, opposite her husband who uncovered the tureen with a delighted air, saying: "Oh! the good potpie! I know nothing better than that—" she would think of the elegant dinners, of the shining silver, of the tapestries peopling the walls with ancient personages and rare birds in the midst of fairy forests; she thought of the exquisite food served on marvelous dishes, of the whispered gallantries, listened to with the smile of the sphinx, while eating the rose-colored flesh of the trout or a chicken's wing.

She had neither frocks nor jewels, nothing. And she loved only those things. She felt that she was made for them. She had such a desire to please, to be sought after, to be clever, and courted.

She had a rich friend, a schoolmate at the convent, whom she did not like to visit, she suffered so much when she returned. And she wept for whole days from chagrin, from regret, from despair, and disappointment.

One evening her husband returned elated bearing in his hand a large envelope.

"Here," he said, "here is something for you."

She quickly tore open the wrapper and drew out a printed card on which were inscribed these words:

> The Minister of Public Instruction and Madame George Ramponneau ask the honor of Mr. and Mrs. Loisel's company Monday evening, January 18, at the Minister's residence.

Instead of being delighted, as her husband had hoped, she threw the invitation spitefully upon the table murmuring:

"What do you suppose I want with that?"

"But, my dearie, I thought it would make you happy. You never go out, and this is an occasion, and a fine one! I had a great deal of trouble to get it. Everybody wishes one, and it is very select; not many are given to employees. You will see the whole official world there."

She looked at him with an irritated eye and declared impatiently:

"What do you suppose I have to wear to such a thing as that?"

He had not thought of that; he stammered:

"Why, the dress you wear when we go to the theater. It seems very pretty to me—"

He was silent, stupefied, in dismay, at the sight of his wife weeping. Two great tears fell slowly from the corners of his eyes toward the corners of his mouth; he stammered:

"What is the matter? What is the matter?"

By a violent effort, she had controlled her vexation and responded in a calm voice, wiping her moist cheeks:

"Nothing. Only I have no dress and consequently I cannot go to this affair. Give your card to some colleague whose wife is better fitted out than I."

He was grieved, but answered:

"Let us see, Matilda. How much would a suitable costume cost, something that would serve for other occasions, something very simple?"

She reflected for some seconds, making estimates and thinking of a sum that she could ask for without bringing with it an immediate refusal and a frightened exclamation from the economical clerk.

Finally she said, in a hesitating voice:

"I cannot tell exactly, but it seems to me that four hundred francs ought to cover it."

He turned a little pale, for he had saved just this sum to buy a gun that he might be able to join some hunting parties the next summer, on the plains at Nanterre, with some friends who went to shoot larks up there on Sunday. Nevertheless, he answered:

"Very well. I will give you four hundred francs. But try to have a pretty dress."

The day of the ball approached and Mme. Loisel seemed sad, disturbed, anxious. Nevertheless, her dress was nearly ready. Her husband said to her one evening:

"What is the matter with you? You have acted strangely for two or three days."

And she responded: "I am vexed not to have a jewel, not one stone, nothing to adorn myself with. I shall have such a poverty-laden look. I would prefer not to go to this party."

He replied: "You can wear some natural flowers. At this season they look very *chic*. For ten francs you can have two or three magnificent roses."

She was not convinced. "No," she replied, "there is nothing more humiliating than to have a shabby air in the midst of rich women."

Then her husband cried out: "How stupid we are! Go and find your friend Mrs. Forestier and ask her to lend you her jewels. You are well enough acquainted with her to do this."

She uttered a cry of joy: "It is true!" she said. "I had not thought of that."

The next day she took herself to her friend's house and related her story of distress. Mrs. Forestier went to her closet with the glass doors, took out a large jewel-case, brought it, opened it, and said: "Choose, my dear."

She saw at first some bracelets, then a collar of pearls, then a Venetian cross of gold and jewels and of admirable workmanship. She tried the jewels before the glass, hesitated, but could neither decide to take them nor leave them. Then she asked:

"Have you nothing more?"

"Why, yes. Look for yourself. I do not know what will please you."

Suddenly she discovered, in a black satin box, a superb necklace of diamonds, and her heart beat fast with an immoderate desire. Her hands trembled as she took them up. She placed them about her throat against her dress, and remained in ecstasy before them. Then she asked, in a hesitating voice, full of anxiety:

"Could you lend me this? Only this?"

"Why, yes, certainly."

She fell upon the neck of her friend, embraced her with passion, then went away with her treasure.

The day of the ball arrived. Mme. Loisel was a great success. She was the prettiest of all, elegant, gracious, smiling, and full of joy. All the men noticed her, asked her name, and wanted to be presented. All the members of the Cabinet wished to waltz with her. The Minister of Education paid her some attention.

She danced with enthusiasm, with passion, intoxicated with pleasure, thinking of nothing, in the triumph of her beauty, in the glory of her success, in a kind of cloud of happiness that came of all this homage, and all this admiration, of all these awakened desires, and this victory so complete and sweet to the heart of woman.

She went home toward four o'clock in the morning. Her husband had been half asleep in one of the little salons since midnight, with three other gentlemen whose wives were enjoying themselves very much.

He threw around her shoulders the wraps they had carried for the coming home, modest garments of everyday wear, whose poverty clashed with the elegance of the ball costume. She felt this and wished to hurry away in order not to be noticed by the other women who were wrapping themselves in rich furs.

Loisel retained her: "Wait," said he. "You will catch cold out there. I am going to call a cab."

But she would not listen and descended the steps rapidly. When they were in the street, they found no carriage; and they began to seek for one, hailing the coachmen whom they saw at a distance.

They walked along toward the Seine, hopeless and shivering. Finally they found on the dock one of those old, noctural *coupés* that one sees in Paris after nightfall, as if they were ashamed of their misery by day.

It took them as far as their door in Martyr street, and they went wearily up to their apartment. It was all over for her. And on his part, he remembered that he would have to be at the office by ten o'clock.

She removed the wraps from her shoulders before the glass, for a final view of herself in her glory. Suddenly she uttered a cry. Her necklace was not around her neck.

Her husband, already half undressed, asked: "What is the matter?"

She turned toward him excitedly:

"I have—I have—I no longer have Mrs. Forestier's necklace."

He arose in dismay: "What! How is that? It is not possible."

And they looked in the folds of the dress, in the folds of the mantle, in the pockets, everywhere. They could not find it.

He asked: "You are sure you still had it when we left the house?"

"Yes, I felt it in the vestibule as we came out."

"But if you had lost it in the street, we should have heard it fall. It must be in the cab."

"Yes. It is probable. Did you take the number?"

"No. And you, did you notice what it was?"

"No."

They looked at each other utterly cast down. Finally, Loisel dressed himself again.

"I am going," said he, "over the track where we went on foot, to see if I can find it."

And he went. She remained in her evening gown, not having the force to go to bed, stretched upon a chair, without ambition or thoughts.

Toward seven o'clock her husband returned. He had found nothing.

He went to the police and to the cab offices, and put an advertisement in the newspapers, offering a reward; he did everything that afforded them a suspicion of hope.

She waited all day in a state of bewilderment before this frightful disaster. Loisel returned at evening with his face harrowed and pale; and had discovered nothing.

"It will be necessary," said he, "to write to your friend that you have broken the clasp of the necklace and that you will have it repaired. That will give us time to turn around."

She wrote as he dictated.

At the end of a week, they had lost all hope. And Loisel, older by five years, declared:

"We must take measures to replace this jewel."

The next day they took the box which had inclosed it, to the jeweler whose name was on the inside. He consulted his books:

"It is not I, Madame," said he, "who sold this necklace; I only furnished the casket."

Then they went from jeweler to jeweler seeking a necklace like the other one, consulting their memories, and ill, both of them, with chagrin and anxiety.

In a shop of the Palais-Royal, they found a chaplet of diamonds which seemed to them exactly like the one they had lost. It was valued at forty thousand francs. They could get it for thirty-six thousand.

They begged the jeweler not to sell it for three days. And they made an arrangement by which they might return it for thirty-four thousand francs if they found the other one before the end of February.

Loisel possessed eighteen thousand francs which his father had left him. He borrowed the rest.

He borrowed it, asking for a thousand francs of one, five hundred of another, five louis of this one, and three louis of that one. He gave notes, made ruinous promises, took money of usurers and the whole race of lenders. He compromised his whole existence, in fact, risked his signature, without even knowing whether he could make it good or not, and, harassed by anxiety for the future, by the black misery which surrounded him, and by the prospect of all physical privations and moral torture, he went to get the new necklace, depositing on the merchant's counter thirty-six thousand francs.

When Mrs. Loisel took back the jewels to Mrs. Forestier, the latter said to her in a frigid tone:

"You should have returned them to me sooner, for I might have needed them."

She did open the jewel-box as her friend feared she would. If she should perceive the substitution, what would she think? What should she say? Would she take her for a robber?

Mrs. Loisel now knew the horrible life of necessity. She did her part, however, completely heroically. It was necessary to pay this frightful debt. She would pay it. They sent away the maid; they changed their lodgings; they rented some rooms under a mansard roof.

She learned the heavy cares of a household, the odious work of a kitchen. She washed the dishes, using her rosy nails upon the greasy pots and the bottoms of the stewpans. She washed the soiled linen, the chemises and dishcloths, which she hung on the line to dry; she took down the refuse to the street each morning and brought up the water, stopping at each landing to breathe. And, clothed like a woman of the people she went to the grocer's, the butcher's, and the fruiterer's, with her basket on her arm, shopping, haggling to the last sou her miserable money.

Every month it was necessary to renew some notes, thus obtaining time, and to pay others.

The husband worked evenings, putting the books of some merchants in order, and nights he often did copying at five sous a page.

And this life lasted for ten years.

At the end of ten years, they had restored all, all, with interest of the usurer, and accumulated interest besides.

Mrs. Loisel seemed old now. She had become a strong, hard woman, the crude woman of the poor household. Her hair badly dressed, her skirts awry, her hands red, she spoke in a loud tone, and washed the floors with large pails of water. But sometimes, when her husband was at the office, she would seat herself before the window and think of that evening party of former times, of that ball where she was so beautiful and so flattered.

How would it have been if she had not lost that necklace? Who knows? Who knows? How singular is life, and how full of changes! How small a thing will ruin or save one!

One Sunday, as she was taking a walk in the Champs-Elysées to rid herself of the cares of the week, she suddenly perceived a woman walking with a child. It was Mrs. Forestier, still young, still pretty, still attractive. Mrs. Loisel was affected. Should she speak to her? Yes, certainly. And now that she had paid, she would tell her all. Why not?

She approached her. "Good morning, Jeanne."

Her friend did not recognize her and was astonished to be so familiarly addressed by this common personage. She stammered:

"But, Madame—I do not know— You must be mistaken—"

"No, I am Matilda Loisel."

Her friend uttered a cry of astonishment: "Oh! my poor Matilda! How you have changed—"

"Yes, I have had some hard days since I saw you; and some miserable ones—and all because of you—"

"Because of me? How is that?"

"You recall the diamond necklace that you loaned me to wear to the Commissioner's ball?"

"Yes, very well."

"Well, I lost it."

"How is that, since you returned it to me?"

"I returned another to you exactly like it. And it has taken us ten years to pay for it. You can understand that it was not easy for us who have nothing. But it is finished and I am decently content."

Madame Forestier stopped short. She said:

"You say that you bought a diamond necklace to replace mine?"

"Yes. You did not perceive it then? They were just alike."

And she smiled with a proud and simple joy. Madame Forestier was touched and took both her hands as she replied:

"Oh! my poor Matilda! Mine were false. They were not worth over five hundred francs!"

ANTON CHEKHOV

1860–1904

Heartache

"To whom shall I tell my sorrow?"[1]

Evening twilight. Large flakes of wet snow are circling lazily about the street lamps which have just been lighted, settling in a thin soft layer on roofs, horses' backs, peoples' shoulders, caps. Iona Potapov, the cabby, is all white like a ghost. As hunched as a living body can be, he sits on the box without stirring. If a whole snowdrift were to fall on him, even then, perhaps he would not find it necessary to shake it off. His nag, too, is white and motionless. Her immobility, the angularity of her shape, and the sticklike straightness of her legs make her look like a penny gingerbread horse. She is probably lost in thought. Anyone who has been torn away from the plow, from the familiar gray scenes, and cast into this whirlpool full of monstrous lights, of ceaseless uproar and hurrying people, cannot help thinking.

Iona and his nag have not budged for a long time. They had driven out of the yard before dinnertime and haven't had a single fare yet. But now evening dusk is descending upon the city. The pale light of the street lamps changes to a vivid color and the bustle of the street grows louder.

"Sleigh to the Vyborg District!" Iona hears. "Sleigh!"

Iona starts, and through his snow-plastered eyelashes sees an officer in a military overcoat with a hood.

"To the Vyborg District!" repeats the officer. "Are you asleep, eh? To the Vyborg District!"

As a sign of assent Iona gives a tug at the reins, which sends layers of snow flying from the horse's back and from his own shoulders. The officer gets into the sleigh. The driver clucks to the horse, cranes his neck like a swan, rises in his seat and, more from habit than necessity, flourishes his whip. The nag, too, stretches her neck, crooks her sticklike legs and irresolutely sets off.

"Where are you barging in, damn you?" Iona is promptly assailed by shouts from the massive dark wavering to and fro before him. "Where the devil are you going? Keep to the right!"

"Don't you know how to drive? Keep to the right," says the officer with vexation.

A coachman driving a private carriage swears at him; a pedestrian who was crossing the street and brushed against the nag's nose with his shoulder, looks at him angrily and shakes the snow off his sleeve. Iona fidgets on the box as if sitting on needles and pins, thrusts out his

1. From an old Russian song comparable to a Negro Spiritual.

elbows and rolls his eyes like a madman, as though he did not know where he was or why he was there.

"What rascals they all are," the officer jokes. "They are doing their best to knock into you or be trampled by the horse. It's a conspiracy."

Iona looks at his fare and moves his lips. He wants to say something, but the only sound that comes out is a wheeze.

"What is it?" asks the officer.

Iona twists his mouth into a smile, strains his throat and croaks hoarsely: "My son, sir . . . er, my son died this week."

"H'm, what did he die of?"

Iona turns his whole body around to his fare and says, "Who can tell? It must have been a fever. He lay in the hospital only three days and then he died. . . . It is God's will."

"Get over, you devil!" comes out of the dark. "Have you gone blind, you old dog? Keep your eyes peeled!"

"Go on, go on," says the officer. "We shan't get there until tomorrow at this rate. Give her the whip!"

The driver cranes his neck again, rises in his seat, and with heavy grace swings his whip. Then he looks around at the officer several times, but the latter keeps his eyes closed and is apparently indisposed to listen. Letting his fare off in the Vyborg District, Iona stops by a teahouse and again sits motionless and hunched on the box. Again the wet snow paints him and his nag white. One hour passes, another . . .

Three young men, two tall and lanky, one short and hunchbacked, come along swearing at each other and loudly pound the pavement with their galoshes.

"Cabby, to the Police Bridge!" the hunchback shouts in a cracked voice. "The three of us . . . twenty kopecks!"

Iona tugs at the reins and clucks to his horse. Twenty kopecks is not fair, but his mind is not on that. Whether it is a ruble or five kopecks, it is all one to him now, so long as he has a fare. . . . The three young men, jostling each other and using foul language, go up to the sleigh and all three try to sit down at once. They start arguing about which two are to sit and who shall be the one to stand. After a long ill-tempered and abusive altercation, they decide that the hunchback must stand up because he is the shortest.

"Well, get going," says the hunchback in his cracked voice, taking up his station and breathing down Iona's neck. "On your way! What a cap you've got, brother! You won't find a worse one in all Petersburg—"

"Hee, hee . . . hee, hee . . ." Iona giggles, "as you say—"

"Well, then, 'as you say,' drive on. Are you going to crawl like this all the way, eh? D'you want to get it in the neck?"

"My head is splitting," says one of the tall ones. "At the Duk-masovs' yesterday, Vaska and I killed four bottles of cognac between us."

"I don't get it, why lie?" says the other tall one angrily. "He is lying like a trouper."

"Strike me dead, it's the truth!"

"It is about as true as that a louse sneezes."

"Hee, hee," giggles Iona. "The gentlemen are feeling good!"

"Faugh, the devil take you!" cries the hunchback indignantly. "Will you get a move on, you old pest, or won't you? Is that the way to drive? Give her a crack of the whip! Giddap, devil! Giddap! Let her feel it!"

Iona feels the hunchback's wriggling body and quivering voice behind his back. He hears abuse addressed to him, sees people, and the feeling of loneliness begins little by little to lift from his heart. The hunchback swears till he chokes on an elaborate three-decker oath and is overcome by cough. The tall youths begin discussing a certain Nadezhda Petrovna. Iona looks round at them. When at last there is a lull in the conversation for which he has been waiting, he turns around and says: "This week . . . er . . . my son died."

"We shall all die," says the hunchback, with a sigh wiping his lips after his coughing fit. "Come, drive on, drive on. Gentlemen, I simply cannot stand this pace! When will he get us there?"

"Well, you give him a little encouragement. Biff him in the neck!"

"Do you hear, you old pest? I'll give it to you in the neck. If one stands on ceremony with fellows like you, one may as well walk. Do you hear, you old serpent? Or don't you give a damn what we say?"

And Iona hears rather than feels the thud of a blow on his neck.

"Hee, hee," he laughs. "The gentlemen are feeling good. God give you health!"

"Cabby, are you married?" asks one of the tall ones.

"Me? Hee, hee! The gentlemen are feeling good. The only wife for me now is the damp earth . . . Hee, haw, haw! The grave, that is! . . . Here my son is dead and me alive . . . It is a queer thing, death comes in at the wrong door . . . It don't come for me, it comes for my son. . . ."

And Iona turns round to tell them how his son died, but at that point the hunchback gives a sigh of relief and announces that, thank God, they have arrived at last. Having received his twenty kopecks, for a long while Iona stares after the revelers, who disappear into a dark entrance. Again he is alone and once more silence envelops him. The grief which has been allayed for a brief space comes back again and wrenches his heart more cruelly than ever. There is a look of anxiety and torment in Iona's eyes as they wander restlessly over the crowds moving to and fro on both sides of the street. Isn't there someone among those thousands who will listen to him? But the crowds hurry past, heedless of him and his grief. His grief is immense, boundless. If his heart were to burst and his grief to pour out, it seems that it would flood the whole world, and yet no one sees it. It has found a place for itself in such an insignificant shell that no one can see it in broad daylight.

Iona notices a doorkeeper with a bag and makes up his mind to speak to him.

"What time will it be, friend?" he asks.

"Past nine. What have you stopped here for? On your way!"

Iona drives a few steps away, hunches up and surrenders himself to his grief. He feels it is useless to turn to people. But before five minutes are over, he draws himself up, shakes his head as though stabbed by a sharp pain and tugs at the reins . . . He can bear it no longer.

"Back to the yard!" he thinks. "To the yard!"

And his nag, as though she knew his thoughts, starts out at a trot. An hour and a half later, Iona is sitting beside a large dirty stove. On the stove, on the floor, on benches are men snoring. The air is stuffy and foul. Iona looks at the sleeping figures, scratches himself and regrets that he has come home so early.

"I haven't earned enough to pay for the oats," he reflects. "That's what's wrong with me. A man that knows his job . . . who has enough to eat and has enough for his horse don't need to fret."

In one of the corners a young driver gets up, hawks sleepily and reaches for the water bucket.

"Thirsty?" Iona asks him.

"Guess so."

"H'm, may it do you good, but my son is dead, brother . . . did you hear? This week in the hospital. . . . What a business!"

Iona looks to see the effect of his words, but he notices none. The young man has drawn his cover over his head and is already asleep. The old man sighs and scratches himself. Just as the young man was thirsty for water so he thirsts for talk. It will soon be a week since his son died and he hasn't talked to anybody about him properly. He ought to be able to talk about it, taking his time, sensibly. He ought to tell how his son was taken ill, how he suffered, what he said before he died, how he died. . . . He ought to describe the funeral, and how he went to the hospital to fetch his son's clothes. His daughter Anisya is still in the country. . . . And he would like to talk about her, too. Yes, he has plenty to talk about now. And his listener should gasp and moan and keen. . . . It would be even better to talk to women. Though they are foolish, two words will make them blubber.

"I must go out and have a look at the horse," Iona thinks. "There will be time enough for sleep. You will have enough sleep, no fear. . . ."

He gets dressed and goes into the stable where his horse is standing. He thinks about oats, hay, the weather. When he is alone, he dares not think his son. It is possible to talk about him with someone, but to think of him when one is alone, to evoke his image is unbearably painful.

"You chewing?" Iona asks his mare seeing her shining eyes. "There, chew away, chew away. . . . If we haven't earned enough for oats, we'll eat hay. . . . Yes. . . . I've grown too old to drive. My son had ought to be driving, not me. . . . He was a real cabby. . . . He had ought to have lived. . . ."

Iona is silent for a space and then goes on: "That's how it is, old girl. . . . Kuzma Ionych is gone. . . . Departed this life. . . . He went and died to no purpose. . . . Now let's say you had a little colt, and you were that little colt's own mother. And suddenly, let's say, that same little colt departed this life. . . . You'd be sorry, wouldn't you?"

The nag chews, listens and breathes on her master's hands. Iona is carried away and tells her eveything.

O. HENRY

1862–1910

The Gift of the Magi

One dollar and eighty-seven cents. That was all. And sixty cents of it was in pennies. Pennies saved one and two at a time by bulldozing the grocer and the vegetable man and the butcher until one's cheeks burned with the silent imputation of parsimony that such close dealing implied. Three times Della counted it. One dollar and eighty-seven cents. And the next day would be Christmas.

There was clearly nothing to do but flop down on the shabby little couch and howl. So Della did it. Which instigates the moral reflection that life is made up of sobs, sniffles, and smiles, with sniffles predominating.

While the mistress of the home is gradually subsiding from the first stage to the second, take a look at the home. A furnished flat at $8 per week. It did not exactly beggar description, but it certainly had that word on the lookout for the mendicancy squad.

In the vestibule below was a letter-box into which no letter would go, and an electric button from which no mortal finger could coax a ring. Also appertaining thereunto was a card bearing the name "Mr. James Dillingham Young."

The "Dillingham" had been flung to the breeze during a former period of prosperity when its possessor was being paid $30 per week. Now, when the income was shrunk to $20, the letters of "Dillingham" looked blurred, as though they were thinking seriously of contracting to a modest and unassuming D. But whenever Mr. James Dillingham Young came home and reached his flat above he was called "Jim" and greatly hugged by Mrs. James Dillingham Young, already introduced to you as Della. Which is all very good.

Della finished her cry and attended to her cheeks with the powder rag. She stood by the window and looked out dully at a gray cat walking a gray fence in a gray backyard. Tomorrow would be Christmas Day, and she had only $1.87 with which to buy Jim a present. She had been saving every penny she could for months, with this result. Twenty dollars a week doesn't go far. Expenses had been greater than she had calculated. They always are. Only $1.87 to buy a present for Jim. Her Jim. Many a happy hour she had spent planning for something nice for him. Something fine and rare and sterling, something just a little bit near to being worthy of the honor of being owned by Jim.

There was a pier-glass between the windows of the room. Perhaps you have seen a pier-glass in an $8 flat. A very thin and very agile person may, by observing his reflection in a rapid sequence of longitudinal strips, obtain a fairly accurate conception of his looks. Della, being slender, had mastered the art.

Suddenly she whirled from the window and stood before the glass. Her eyes were shining brilliantly, but her face had lost its color within twenty seconds. Rapidly she pulled down her hair and let it fall to its full length.

Now, there were two possessions of the James Dillingham Youngs in which they both took a mighty pride. One was Jim's gold watch that had been his father's and his grandfather's. The other was Della's hair. Had the Queen of Sheba lived in the flat across the airshaft, Della would have let her hair hang out the window some day to dry just to depreciate Her Majesty's jewels and gifts. Had King Solomon been the janitor, with all his treasures piled up in the basement, Jim would have pulled out his watch every time he passed, just to see him pluck at his beard from envy.

So now Della's beautiful hair fell about her rippling and shining like a cascade of brown waters. It reached below her knee and made itself almost a garment for her. And then she did it up again nervously and quickly. Once she faltered for a minute and stood still while a tear or two splashed on the worn red carpet.

On went her old brown jacket; on went her old brown hat. With a whirl of skirts and with the brilliant sparkle still in her eyes, she fluttered out the door and down the stairs to the street.

Where she stopped the sign read: "Mme. Sofronie. Hair Goods of All Kinds." One flight up Della ran, and collected herself, panting. Madame, large, too white, chilly, hardly looked the "Sofronie."

"Will you buy my hair?" asked Della.

"I buy hair," said Madame. "Take yer hat off and let's have a sight at the looks of it."

Down rippled the brown cascade.

"Twenty dollars," said Madame, lifting the mass with a practised hand.

"Give it to me quick," said Della.

Oh, and the next two hours tripped by on rosy wings. Forget the hashed metaphor. She was ransacking the stores for Jim's present.

She found it at last. It surely had been made for Jim and no one else. There was no other like it in any of the stores, and she had turned all of them inside out. It was a plantinum fob chain simple and chaste in design, properly proclaiming its value by substance alone and not by meretricious ornamentation—as all good things should do. It was even worthy of The Watch. As soon as she saw it she knew that it must be Jim's. It was like him. Quietness and value—the description applied to both. Twenty-one dollars they took from her for it, and she hurried home with the 87 cents. With that chain on his watch Jim might be properly anxious about the time in any company. Grand as the watch was, he sometimes looked at it on the sly on account of the old leather strap that he used in place of a chain.

When Della reached home her intoxication gave way a little to prudence and reason. She got out her curling irons and lighted the gas and went to work repairing the ravages made by generosity added to love. Which is always a tremendous task, dear friends—a mammoth task.

Within forty minutes her head was covered with tiny, close-lying curls that made her look wonderfully like a truant schoolboy. She looked at her reflection in the mirror long, carefully, and critically.

"If Jim doesn't kill me," she said to herself, "before he takes a second look at me, he'll say I look like a Coney Island chorus girl. But what could I do—oh! what could I do with a dollar and eighty-seven cents?"

At 7 o'clock the coffee was made and the frying-pan was on the back of the stove hot and ready to cook the chops.

Jim was never late. Della doubled the fob chain in her hand and sat on the corner of the table near the door that he always entered. Then she heard his step on the stair away down on the first flight, and she turned white for just a moment. She had a habit of saying little silent prayers about the simplest everyday things, and now she whispered: "Please God, make him think I am still pretty."

The door opened and Jim stepped in and closed it. He looked thin and very serious. Poor fellow, he was only twenty-two—and to be burdened with a family! He needed a new overcoat and he was without gloves.

Jim stopped inside the door, as immovable as a setter at the scent of quail. His eyes were fixed upon Della, and there was an expression in them that she could not read, and it terrified her. It was not anger, nor surprise, nor disapproval, nor horror, nor any of the sentiments that she had been prepared for. He simply stared at her fixedly with that peculiar expression on his face.

Della wriggled off the table and went for him.

"Jim, darling," she cried, "don't look at me that way. I had my hair cut off and sold it because I couldn't have lived through Christmas without giving you a present. It'll grow out again—you won't mind, will you? I just had to do it. My hair grows awfully fast. Say 'Merry Christmas!' Jim, and let's be happy. You don't know what a nice—what a beautiful, nice gift I've got for you."

"You've cut off your hair?" asked Jim, laboriously, as if he had not arrived at that patent fact yet even after the hardest mental labor.

"Cut if off and sold it," said Della. "Don't you like me just as well, anyhow? I'm me without my hair, ain't I?"

Jim looked about the room curiously.

"You say your hair is gone?" he said, with an air almost of idiocy.

"You needn't look for it," said Della. "It's sold, I tell you—sold and gone, too. It's Christmas Eve, boy. Be good to me, for it went for you. Maybe the hairs of my head were numbered," she went on with a sudden serious sweetness, "but nobody could ever count my love for you. Shall I put the chops on, Jim?"

Out of his trance Jim seemed quickly to wake. He enfolded his Della. For ten seconds let us regard with discreet scrutiny some inconsequential object in the other direction. Eight dollars a week or a million a year—what is the difference? A mathematician or a wit would give you the wrong answer. The magi brought valuable gifts, but that was not among them. This dark assertion will be illuminated later on.

Jim drew a package from his overcoat pocket and threw it upon the table.

"Don't make any mistake, Dell," he said, "about me. I don't think there's anything in the way of a haircut or a shave or a shampoo that could make me like my girl any less. But if you'll unwrap that package you may see why you had me going a while at first."

White fingers and nimble tore at the string and paper. And then an ecstatic scream of joy; and then, alas! a quick feminine change to hysterical tears and wails, necessitating the immediate employment of all the comforting powers of the lord of the flat.

For there lay The Combs—the set of combs, side and back, that Della had worshipped for long in a Broadway window. Beautiful combs, pure tortoise shell, with jewelled rims—just the shade to wear in the beautiful vanished hair. They were expensive combs, she knew, and her heart had simply craved and yearned over them without the least hope of possession. And now, they were hers, but the tresses that should have adorned the coveted adornments were gone.

But she hugged them to her bosom, and at length she was able to look up with dim eyes and a smile and say: "My hair grows so fast, Jim!"

And then Della leaped up like a little singed cat and cried, "Oh, oh!"

Jim had not yet seen his beautiful present. She held it out to him eagerly upon her open palm. The dull precious metal seemed to flash with a reflection of her bright and ardent spirit.

"Isn't it dandy, Jim? I hunted all over town to find it. You'll have to look at the time a hundred times a day now. Give me your watch. I want to see how it looks on it."

Instead of obeying, Jim tumbled down on the couch and put his hands under the back of his head and smiled.

"Dell," said he, "let's put our Christmas presents away and keep 'em a while. They're too nice to use just at present. I sold the watch to get the money to buy your combs. And now suppose you put the chops on."

The magi, as you know, were wise men—wonderfully wise men— who brought gifts to the Babe in the manger. They invented the art of giving Christmas presents. Being wise, their gifts were no doubt wise ones, possibly bearing the privilege of exchange in case of duplication. And here I have lamely related to you the uneventful chronicle of two foolish children in a flat who most unwisely sacrificed for each other the greatest treasures of their house. But in a last word to the wise of these days let it be said that of all who give gifts these two were the wisest. Of all who give and receive gifts, such as they are wisest. Everywhere they are wisest. They are the magi.

JAMES JOYCE
1882–1941
The Boarding House

Mrs Mooney was a butcher's daughter. She was a woman who was quite able to keep things to herself: a determined woman. She had married her father's foreman and opened a butcher's shop near Spring Gardens. But as soon as his father-in-law was dead Mr Mooney began to go to the devil. He drank, plundered the till, ran headlong into debt. It was no use making him take the pledge: he was sure to break out again a few days after. By fighting his wife in the presence of customers and by buying bad meat he ruined his business. One night he went for his wife with the cleaver and she had to sleep in a neighbour's house.

After that they lived apart. She went to the priest and got a separation from him with care of the children. She would give him neither money nor food nor house-room; and so he was obliged to enlist himself as a sheriff's man. He was a shabby stooped little drunkard with a white face and a white moustache and white eyebrows, pencilled above his little eyes, which were pink-veined and raw; and all day long he sat in the bailiff's room, waiting to be put on a job. Mrs Mooney, who had taken what remained of her money out of the butcher business and set up a boarding house in Hardwicke Street, was a big imposing woman. Her house had a floating population made up of tourists from Liverpool and the Isle of Man and, occasionally, *artistes* from the music halls. Its resident population was made up of clerks from the city. She governed the house cunningly and firmly, knew when to give credit, when to be stern and when to let things pass. All the resident young men spoke of her as *The Madam*.

Mrs Mooney's young men paid fifteen shillings a week for board and lodgings (beer or stout at dinner excluded). They shared in common tastes and occupations and for this reason they were very chummy with one another. They discussed with one another the chances of favourites and outsiders. Jack Mooney, the Madam's son, who was clerk to a commission agent in Fleet Street, had the reputation of being a hard case. He was fond of using soldiers' obscenities: usually he came home in the small hours. When he met his friends he had always a good one to tell them and he was always sure to be on to a good thing—that is to say, a likely horse or a likely *artiste*. He was also handy with the mits and sang comic songs. On Sunday nights there would often be a reunion in Mrs Mooney's front drawing-room. The music-hall *artistes* would oblige; and Sheridan played waltzes and polkas and vamped accompaniments. Polly Mooney, the Madam's daughter, would also sing. She sang:

> *I'm a . . . naughty girl.*
> *You needn't sham:*
> *You know I am.*

Polly was a slim girl of nineteen; she had light soft hair and a small full mouth. Her eyes, which were grey with a shade of green through them, had a habit of glancing upwards when she spoke with anyone, which made her look like a little perverse madonna. Mrs Mooney had first sent her daughter to be a typist in a corn-factor's office but, as a disreputable sheriff's man used to come every other day to the office, asking to be allowed to say a word to his daughter, she had taken her daughter home again and set her to do housework. As Polly was very lively the intention was to give her the run of the young men. Besides, young men like to feel that there is a young woman not very far away. Polly, of course, flirted with the young men but Mrs Mooney, who was a shrewd judge, knew that the young men were only passing the time away: none of them meant business. Things went on so for a long time and Mrs Mooney began to think of sending Polly back to typewriting when she noticed that something was going on between Polly and one of the young men. She watched the pair and kept her own counsel.

Polly knew that she was being watched, but still her mother's persistent silence could not be misunderstood. There had been no open complicity between mother and daughter, no open understanding but, though people in the house began to talk of the affair, still Mrs Mooney did not intervene. Polly began to grow a little strange in her manner and the young man was evidently perturbed. At last, when she judged it to be the right moment, Mrs Mooney intervened. She dealt with moral problems as a cleaver deals with meat: and in this case she had made up her mind.

It was a bright Sunday morning of early summer, promising heat, but with a fresh breeze blowing. All the windows of the boarding house were open and the lace curtains ballooned gently towards the street beneath the raised sashes. The belfry of George's Church sent out constant peals and worshippers, singly or in groups, traversed the little circus before the church, revealing their purpose by their self-contained demeanour no less than by the little volumes in their gloved hands. Breakfast was over in the boarding house and the table of the breakfast-room was covered with plates on which lay yellow streaks of eggs with morsels of bacon-fat and bacon-rind. Mrs Mooney sat in the straw arm-chair and watched the servant Mary remove the breakfast things. She made Mary collect the crusts and pieces of broken bread to help to make Tuesday's bread-pudding. When the table was cleared, the broken bread collected, the sugar and butter safe under lock and key, she began to reconstruct the interview which she had had the night before with Polly. Things were as she had suspected: she had been frank in her questions and Polly had been frank in her answers. Both had been somewhat awkward, of course. She had been made awkward by her not wishing to receive the news in too cavalier a fashion or to seem to have connived and Polly had been made awkward not merely because allusions of that kind always made her awkward but also because she did not wish it to be thought that in her wise innocence she had divined the intention behind her mother's tolerance.

Mrs Mooney glanced instinctively at the little gilt clock on the mantelpiece as soon as she had become aware through her revery that the bells of George's Church had stopped ringing. It was seventeen minutes past eleven: she would have lots of time to have the matter out with Mr Doran and then catch short twelve at Marlborough Street. She was sure she would win. To begin with she had all the weight of social opinion on her side: she was an outraged mother. She had allowed him to live beneath her roof, assuming that he was a man of honour, and he had simply abused her hospitality. He was thirty-four or thirty-five years of age, so that youth could not be pleaded as his excuse; nor could ignorance be his excuse since he was a man who had seen something of the world. He had simply taken advantage of Polly's youth and inexperience: that was evident. The question was: What reparation would he make?

There must be reparation made in such cases. It is all very well for the man: he can go his ways as if nothing had happened, having had his moment of pleasure, but the girl has to bear the brunt. Some mothers would be content to patch up such an affair for a sum of money; she had known cases of it. But she would not do so. For her only one reparation could make up for the loss of her daughter's honour: marriage.

She counted all her cards again before sending Mary up to Mr Doran's room to say that she wished to speak with him. She felt sure she would win. He was a serious young man, not rakish or loud-voiced like the others. If it had been Mr Sheridan or Mr Meade or Bantam Lyons her task would have been much harder. She did not think he would face publicity. All the lodgers in the house knew something of the affair; details had been invented by some. Besides, he had been employed for thirteen years in a great Catholic wine-merchant's office and publicity would mean for him, perhaps, the loss of his sit. Whereas if he agreed all might be well. She knew he had a good screw for one thing and she suspected he had a bit of stuff put by.

Nearly the half-hour! She stood up and surveyed herself in the pier-glass. The decisive expression of her great florid face satisfied her and she thought of some mothers she knew who could not get their daughters off their hands.

Mr Doran was very anxious indeed this Sunday morning. He had made two attempts to shave but his hand had been so unsteady that he had been obliged to desist. Three days' reddish beard fringed his jaws and every two or three minutes a mist gathered on his glasses so that he had to take them off and polish them with his pocket-handkerchief. The recollection of his confession of the night before was a cause of acute pain to him; the priest had drawn out every ridiculous detail of the affair and in the end had so magnified his sin that he was almost thankful at being afforded a loophole of reparation. The harm was done. What could he do now but marry her or run away? He could not brazen it out. The affair would be sure to be talked of and his employer would be certain to hear of it. Dublin is such a small city: everyone knows everyone else's business. He felt his heart leap warmly in his throat as he heard in his excited imagination old Mr Leonard calling out in his rasping voice: *Send Mr Doran here, please.*

All his long years of service gone for nothing! All his industry and diligence thrown away! As a young man he had sown his wild oats, of course; he had boasted of his free-thinking and denied the existence of God to his companions in public-houses. But that was all passed and done with . . . nearly. He still bought a copy of *Reynolds's Newspaper* every week but he attended to his religious duties and for nine-tenths of the year lived a regular life. He had money enough to settle down on; it was not that. But the family would look down on her. First of all there was her disreputable father and then her mother's boarding house was beginning to get a certain fame. He had a notion that he was being had. He could imagine his friends talking of the affair and laughing. She *was* a little vulgar; some times she said *I seen* and *If I had've known*. But what would grammar matter if he really loved her? He could not make up his mind whether to like her or despise her for what she had done. Of course he had done it too. His instinct urged him to remain free, not to marry. Once you are married you are done for, it said.

While he was sitting helplessly on the side of the bed in shirt and trousers she tapped lightly at his door and entered. She told him all, that she had made a clean breast of it to her mother and that her mother would speak with him that morning. She cried and threw her arms round his neck, saying:

—O Bob! Bob! What am I to do? What am I to do at all?

She would put an end to herself, she said.

He comforted her feebly, telling her not to cry, that it would be all right, never fear. He felt against his shirt the agitation of her bosom.

It was not altogether his fault that it had happened. He remembered well, with the curious patient memory of the celibate, the first casual caresses her dress, her breath, her fingers had given him. Then late one night as he was undressing for bed she had tapped at his door, timidly. She wanted to relight her candle at his for hers had been blown out by a gust. It was her bath night. She wore a loose open combing-jacket of printed flannel. Her white instep shone in the opening of her furry slippers and the blood glowed warmly behind her perfumed skin. From her hands and wrists too as she lit and steadied her candle a faint perfume arose.

On nights when he came in very late it was she who warmed up his dinner. He scarcely knew what he was eating, feeling her beside him alone, at night, in the sleeping house. And her thoughtfulness! If the night was anyway cold or wet or windy there was sure to be a little tumbler of punch ready for him. Perhaps they could be happy together. . . .

They used to go upstairs together on tiptoe, each with a candle, and on the third landing exchange reluctant goodnights. They used to kiss. He remembered well her eyes, the touch of her hand and his delirium. . . .

But delirium passes. He echoed her phrase, applying it to himself: *What am I to do?* The instinct of the celibate warned him to hold back. But the sin was there; even his sense of honour told him that reparation must be made for such a sin.

While he was sitting with her on the side of the bed Mary came to the door and said that the missus wanted to see him in the parlour. He stood up to put on his coat and waistcoat, more helpless than ever. When he was dressed he went over to her to comfort her. It would be all right, never fear. He left her crying on the bed and moaning softly: *O my God!*

Going down the stairs his glasses became so dimmed with moisture that he had to take them off and polish them. He longed to ascend through the roof and fly away to another country where he would never hear again of his trouble, and yet a force pushed him downstairs step by step. The implacable faces of his employer and of the Madam stared upon his discomfiture. On the last flight of stairs he passed Jack Mooney who was coming up from the pantry nursing two bottles of *Bass.* They saluted coldly; and the lover's eyes rested for a second or two on a thick bulldog face and a pair of thick short arms. When he reached the foot of the staircase he glanced up and saw Jack regarding him from the door of the return-room.

Suddenly he remembered the night when one of the music-hall *artistes,* a little blond Londoner, had made a rather free allusion to Polly. The reunion had been almost broken up on account of Jack's violence. Everyone tried to quiet him. The music-hall *artiste,* a little paler than usual, kept smiling and saying that there was no harm meant: but Jack kept shouting at him that if any fellow tried that sort of a game on with *his* sister he'd bloody well put his teeth down his throat, so he would.

.   .   .   .

Polly sat for a little time on the side of the bed, crying. Then she dried her eyes and went over to the looking-glass. She dipped the end of the towel in the water-jug and refreshed her eyes with the cool water. She looked at herself in profile and readjusted a hairpin above her ear. Then she went back to the bed again and sat at the foot. She regarded the pillows for a long time and the sight of them awakened in her mind secret, amiable memories. She rested the nape of her neck against the cool iron bed-rail and fell into a revery. There was no longer any perturbation visible on her face.

She waited on patiently, almost cheerfully, without alarm, her memories gradually giving place to hopes and visions of the future. Her hopes and visions were so intricate that she no longer saw the white pillows on which her gaze was fixed or remembered that she was waiting for anything.

At last she heard her mother calling. She started to her feet and ran to the banisters.

—Polly! Polly!

—Yes, mamma?

—Come down, dear. Mr Doran wants to speak to you.

Then she remembered what she had been waiting for.

D. H. LAWRENCE
1885–1930
The Christening

The mistress of the British School stepped down from her school gate, and instead of turning to the left as usual, she turned to the right. Two women who were hastening home to scramble their husbands' dinners together—it was five minutes to four—stopped to look at her. They stood gazing after her for a moment; then they glanced at each other with a woman's little grimace.

To be sure, the retreating figure was ridiculous: small and thin, with a black straw hat, and a rusty cashmere dress hanging full all round the skirt. For so small and frail and rusty a creature to sail with slow, deliberate stride was also absurd. Hilda Rowbotham was less than thirty, so it was not years that set the measure of her pace; she had heart disease. Keeping her face, that was small with sickness, but not uncomely, firmly lifted and fronting ahead, the young woman sailed on past the market-place, like a black swan of mournful disreputable plumage.

She turned into Berryman's, the bakers. The shop displayed bread and cakes, sacks of flour and oatmeal, flitches of bacon, hams, lard and sausages. The combination of scents was not unpleasing. Hilda Rowbotham stood for some minutes nervously tapping and pushing a large knife that lay on the counter, and looking at the tall, glittering brass scales. At last a morose man with sandy whiskers came down the step from the house-place.

"What is it?" he asked, not apologising for his delay.

"Will you give me sixpennyworth of assorted cakes and pastries— and put in some macaroons, please?" she asked, in remarkably rapid and nervous speech. Her lips fluttered like two leaves in a wind, and her words crowded and rushed like a flock of sheep at a gate.

"We've got no macaroons," said the man churlishly.

He had evidently caught that word. He stood waiting.

"Then I can't have any, Mr. Berryman. Now I do feel disappointed. I like those macaroons, you know, and it's not often I treat myself. One gets so tired of trying to spoil oneself, don't you think? It's less profitable even than trying to spoil somebody else." She laughed a quick little nervous laugh, putting her hand to her face.

"Then what'll you have?" asked the man, without the ghost of an answering smile. He evidently had not followed, so he looked more glum than ever.

"Oh, anything you've got," replied the schoolmistress, flushing slightly. The man moved slowly about, dropping the cakes from various dishes one by one into a paper bag.

"How's that sister o' yours getting on?" he asked, as if he were talking to the flour-scoop.

"Whom do you mean?" snapped the schoolmistress.

"The youngest," answered the stooping, pale-faced man, with a note of sarcasm.

"Emma! Oh, she's very well, thank you!" The schoolmistress was very red, but she spoke with sharp, ironical defiance. The man grunted. Then he handed her the bag, and watched her out of the shop without bidding her "Good afternoon."

She had the whole length of the main street to traverse, a half-mile of slow-stepping torture, with shame flushing over her neck. But she carried her white bag with an appearance of steadfast unconcern. When she turned into the field she seemed to droop a little. The wide valley opened out from her, with the far woods withdrawing into twilight, and away in the centre the great pit steaming its white smoke and chuffing as the men were being turned up. A full rose-coloured moon, like a flamingo flying low under the far, dusky east, drew out of the mist. It was beautiful, and it made her irritable sadness soften, diffuse.

Across the field, and she was at home. It was a new, substantial cottage, built with unstinted hand, such a house as an old miner could build himself out of his savings. In the rather small kitchen a woman of dark, saturnine complexion sat nursing a baby in a long white gown; a young woman of heavy, brutal cast stood at the table, cutting bread and butter. She had a downcast, humble mien that sat unnaturally on her, and was strangely irritating. She did not look round when her sister entered. Hilda put down the bag of cakes and left the room, not having spoken to Emma, nor to the baby, nor to Mrs. Carlin, who had come in to help for the afternoon.

Almost immediately the father entered from the yard with a dust-pan full of coals. He was a large man, but he was going to pieces. As he passed through, he gripped the door with his free hand to steady himself, but turning, he lurched and swayed. He began putting the coals on the fire, piece by piece. One lump fell from his hands and smashed on the white hearth. Emma Rowbotham looked round, and began in a rough, loud voice of anger: "Look at you!" Then she consciously moderated her tones. "I'll sweep it up in a minute—don't you bother; you'll only be going head-first into the fire."

Her father bent down nevertheless to clear up the mess he had made, saying, articulating his words loosely and slavering in his speech:

"The lousy bit of a thing, it slipped between my fingers like a fish."

As he spoke he went tilting towards the fire. The dark-browed woman cried out; he put his hand on the hot stove to save himself; Emma swung round and dragged him off.

"Didn't I tell you!" she cried roughly. "Now, have you burnt yourself?"

She held tight hold of the big man, and pushed him into his chair.

"What's the matter?" cried a sharp voice from the other room. The speaker appeared, a hard well-favoured woman of twenty-eight. "Emma, don't speak like that to father." Then, in a tone not so cold, but just as sharp: "Now, father, what have you been doing?"

Emma withdrew to her table sullenly.

"It's nöwt," said the old man, vainly protesting. "It's nöwt at a'. Get on wi' what you're doin'."

"I'm afraid 'e's burnt 'is 'and," said the black-browed woman, speaking of him with a kind of hard pity, as if he were a cumbersome child. Bertha took the old man's hand and looked at it, making a quick tut-tutting noise of impatience.

"Emma, get that zinc ointment—and some white rag," she commanded sharply. The younger sister put down her loaf with the knife in it, and went. To a sensitive observer, this obedience was more intolerable than the most hateful discord. The dark woman bent over the baby and made silent, gentle movements of motherliness to it. The little one smiled and moved on her lap. It continued to move and twist.

"I believe this child's hungry," she said. "How long is it since he had anything?"

"Just afore dinner," said Emma dully.

"Good gracious!" exclaimed Bertha. "You needn't starve the child now you've got it. Once every two hours it ought to be fed, as I've told you; and now it's three. Take him, poor little mite—I'll cut the bread." She bent and looked at the bonny baby. She could not help herself: she smiled, and pressed its cheek with her finger, and nodded to it, making little noises. Then she turned and took the loaf from her sister. The woman rose and gave the child to its mother. Emma bent over the little sucking mite. She hated it when she looked at it, and saw it as a symbol, but when she felt it, her love was like fire in her blood.

"I should think 'e canna be comin'," said the father uneasily, looking up at the clock.

"Nonsense, father—the clock's fast! It's but half-past four! Don't fidget!" Bertha continued to cut the bread and butter.

"Open a tin of pears," she said to the woman, in a much milder tone. Then she went into the next room. As soon as she was gone, the old man said again: "I should ha'e thought he'd 'a' been 'ere by now, if he means comin'."

Emma, engrossed, did not answer. The father had ceased to consider her, since she had become humbled.

"'E'll come—'e'll come!" assured the stranger.

A few minutes later Bertha hurried into the kitchen, taking off her apron. The dog barked furiously. She opened the door, commanded the dog to silence, and said: "He will be quiet now, Mr. Kendal."

"Thank you," said a sonorous voice, and there was the sound of a bicycle being propped against a wall. A clergyman entered, a big-boned, thin, ugly man of nervous manner. He went straight to the father.

"Ah—how are you—" he asked musically, peering down on the great frame of the miner, ruined by locomotor ataxy.

His voice was full of gentleness, but he seemed as if he could not see distinctly, could not get things clear.

"Have you hurt your hand?" he said comfortingly, seeing the white rag.

"It wor nöwt but a pestered bit o' coal as dropped, an' I put my hand on th' hub. I thought tha worna commin'."

The familiar "tha", and the reproach, were unconscious retaliation on the old man's part. The minister smiled, half wistfully, half indulgently. He was full of vague tenderness. Then he turned to the young mother, who flushed sullenly because her dishonoured breast was uncovered.

"How are you?" he asked, very softly and gently, as if she were ill and he were mindful of her.

"I'm all right," she replied, awkwardly taking his hand without rising, hiding her face and the anger that rose in her.

"Yes—yes"—he peered down at the baby, which sucked with distended mouth upon the firm breast. "Yes, yes." He seemed lost in a dim musing.

Coming to, he shook hands unseeingly with the woman.

Presently they all went into the next room, the minister hesitating to help his crippled old deacon.

"I can go by myself, thank yer," testily replied the father.

Soon all were seated. Everybody was separated in feeling and isolated at table. High tea was spread in the middle kitchen, a large, ugly room kept for special occasions.

Hilda appeared last, and the clumsy, raw-boned clergyman rose to meet her. He was afraid of this family, the well-to-do old collier, and the brutal, self-willed children. But Hilda was queen among them. She was the clever one, and had been to college. She felt responsible for the keeping up of a high standard of conduct in all the members of the family. There was a difference between the Rowbothams and the common collier folk. Woodbine Cottage was a superior house to most—and was built in pride by the old man. She, Hilda, was a college-trained schoolmistress; she meant to keep up the prestige of her house in spite of blows.

She had put on a dress of green voile for this special occasion. But she was very thin; her neck protruded painfully. The clergyman, however, greeted her almost with reverence, and, with some assumption of dignity, she sat down before the tray. At the far end of the table sat the broken, massive frame of her father. Next to him was the youngest daughter, nursing the restless boy. The minister sat between Hilda and Bertha, hulking his bony frame uncomfortably.

There was a great spread on the table of tinned fruits and tinned salmon, ham and cakes. Miss Rowbotham kept a keen eye on everything: she felt the importance of the occasion. The young mother who had given rise to all this solemnity ate in sulky discomfort, snatching sullen little smiles at her child, smiles which came, in spite of her, when she felt its little limbs stirring vigorously on her lap. Bertha, sharp and abrupt, was chiefly concerned with the baby. She scorned her sister, and treated her like dirt. But the infant was a streak of light to her. Miss Rowbotham concerned herself with the function and the conversation. Her hands fluttered; she talked in little volleys, exceedingly nervous. Towards the end of the meal, there came a pause. The old man wiped his mouth with his red handkerchief, then, his blue eyes going fixed and staring, he began to speak, in a loose, slobbering fashion, charging his words at the clergyman.

"Well, mester—we'n axed you to come here ter christen this childt, an' you'n come, an' I'm sure we're very thankful. I can't see lettin' the poor blessed childt miss baptizing, an' they aren't for goin' to church wi't——" He seemed to lapse into a muse. "So," he resumed, "we'n axed you to come here to do the job. I'm not sayin' as it's not 'ard on us, it is. I'm breakin' up, an' mother's gone. I don't like leavin' a girl o' mine in a situation like 'ers is, but what the Lord's done, He's done an' it's no matter murmuring. . . . There's one thing to be thankful for an' we *are* thankful for it: they never need know the want of bread.'

Miss Rowbotham, the lady of the family, sat very stiff and pained during this discourse. She was sensitive to so many things that she was bewildered. She felt her young sister's shame, then a kind of swift protecting love for the baby, a feeling that included the mother; she was at a loss before her father's religious sentiment, and she felt and resented bitterly the mark upon the family, against which the common folk could lift their fingers. Still she winced from the sound of her father's words. It was a painful ordeal.

"It is hard for you," began the clergyman in his soft, lingering, unworldly voice. "It is hard for you to-day, but the Lord gives comfort in His time. A man child is born unto us, therefore let us rejoice and be glad. If sin has entered in among us, let us purify our hearts before the Lord. . . ."

He went on with his discourse. The young mother lifted the whimpering infant, till its face was hid in her loose hair. She was hurt, and a little glowering anger shone in her face. But nevertheless her fingers clasped the body of the child beautifully. She was stupefied with anger against this emotion let loose on her account.

Miss Bertha rose and went to the little kitchen, returning with water in a china bowl. She placed it there among the tea-things.

"Well, we're all ready," said the old man, and the clergyman began to read the service. Miss Bertha was godmother, the two men godfathers. The old man sat with bent head. The scene became impressive. At last Miss Bertha took the child and put it in the arms of the clergyman. He, big and ugly, shone with a kind of unreal love. He had never mixed with life, and women were all unliving, Biblical things to him. When he asked for the name, the old man lifted his head fiercely. "Joseph William, after me," he said, almost out of breath.

"Joseph William, I baptise thee . . ." resounded the strange, full, chanting voice of the clergyman. The baby was quite still.

"Let us pray!" It came with relief to them all. They knelt before their chairs, all but the young mother, who bent and hid herself over her baby. The clergyman began his hesitating, struggling prayer.

Just then heavy footsteps were heard coming up the path, ceasing at the window. The young mother, glancing up, saw her brother, black in his pit dirt, grinning in through the panes. His red mouth curved in a sneer; his fair hair shone above his blackened skin. He caught the eye of his sister and grinned. Then his black face disappeared. He had gone on into the kitchen. The girl with the child sat still and anger filled her heart. She herself hated now the praying clergyman and the whole emotional business; she hated her brother bitterly. In anger and bondage she sat and listened.

Suddenly her father began to pray. His familiar, loud, rambling voice made her shut herself up and become even insentient. Folks said his mind was weakening. She believed it to be true, and kept herself always disconnected from him.

"We ask Thee, Lord," the old man cried, "to look after this childt. Fatherless he is. But what does the earthly father matter before Thee? The childt is Thine, he is Thy childt. Lord, what father has a man but Thee? Lord, when a man says he is a father, he is wrong from the first word. For Thou art the Father, Lord. Lord, take away from us the conceit that our children are ours. Lord, Thou art Father of this childt as is fatherless here. O God, Thou bring him up. For I have stood between Thee and my children; I've had *my* way with them, Lord; I've stood between Thee and my children; I've cut 'em off from Thee because they were mine. And they've grown twisted, because of me. Who is their father, Lord, but Thee? But I put myself in the way, they've been plants under a stone, because of me. Lord, if it hadn't been for me, they might ha' been trees in the sunshine. Let me own it, Lord. I've done 'em mischief. It would ha' been better if they'd never known no father. No man is a father, Lord: only Thou art. They can never grow beyond Thee, but I hampered them. Lift 'em up again, and undo what I've done to my children. And let this young childt be like a willow tree beside the waters, with no father but Thee, O God. Aye, an' I wish it had been so with my children, that they'd had no father but Thee. For I've been like a stone upon them, and they rise up and curse me in their wickedness. But let me go, an' lift Thou them up, Lord . . ."

The minister, unaware of the feelings of a father, knelt in trouble, hearing without understanding the special language of fatherhood. Miss Rowbotham alone felt and understood a little. Her heart began to flutter; she was in pain. The two younger daughters kneeled unhearing, stiffened and impervious. Bertha was thinking of the baby; and the young mother thought of the father of her child, whom she hated. There was a clatter outside in the scullery. There the youngest son made as much noise as he could, pouring out the water for his wash, muttering in deep anger:

"Blortin', slaverin' old fool!"

And while the praying of his father continued, his heart was burning with rage. On the table was a paper bag. He picked it up and read: "John Berryman—Bread, Pastries, etc." Then he grinned with a grimace. The father of the baby was baker's man at Berryman's. The prayer went on in the middle kitchen. Laurie Rowbotham gathered together the mouth of the bag, inflated it, and burst it with his fist. There was a loud report. He grinned to himself. But he writhed at the same time with shame and fear of his father.

The father broke off from his prayer; the party shuffled to their feet. The young mother went into the scullery.

"What art doin', fool?" she said.

The collier youth tipped the baby under the chin, singing:

> "Pat-a-cake, pat-a-cake, baker's man,
> Bake me a cake as fast as you can. . . ."

The mother snatched the child away. "Shut thy mouth," she said, the colour coming into her cheek.

> "Prick it and stick it and mark it with P,
> And put it i' th' oven for baby an' me. . . ."

He grinned, showing a grimy, and jeering and unpleasant red mouth, and white teeth.

"I s'll gi'e thee a dab ower th' mouth," said the mother of the baby grimly. He began to sing again, and she struck out at him.

"Now what's to do?" said the father, staggering in.

The youth began to sing again. His sister stood sullen and furious.

"Why does *that* upset you?" asked the eldest Miss Rowbotham, sharply, of Emma the mother. "Good gracious, it hasn't improved your temper."

Miss Bertha came in, and took the bonny baby.

The father sat big and unheeding in his chair, his eyes vacant, his physique wrecked. He let them do as they would, he fell to pieces. And yet some power, involuntary, like a curse, remained in him. The very ruin of him was like a lodestone that held them in its control. The wreck of him still dominated the house, in his dissolution even he compelled their being. They had never lived; his life, his will had always been upon them and contained them. They were only half-individuals.

The day after the christening he staggered in at the doorway declaring, in a loud voice, with joy in life still: "The daisies light up the earth, they clap their hands in multitudes, in praise of the morning." And his daughters shrank, sullen.

KATHERINE MANSFIELD

1888–1918

Six Years After

It was not the afternoon to be on deck—on the contrary. It was exactly the afternoon when there is no snugger place than a warm cabin, a warm bunk. Tucked up with a rug, a hot-water bottle and a piping hot cup of tea she would not have minded the weather in the least. But he—hated cabins, hated to be inside anywhere more than was absolutely necessary. He had a passion for keeping, as he called it, above board, especially when he was travelling. And it wasn't surprising, considering the enormous amount of time he spent cooped up in the office. So, when he rushed away from her as soon as they got on board and came back five minutes later to say he had secured two deck chairs on the lee side and the steward was undoing the rugs, her voice through the high sealskin collar murmured "Good"; and because he was looking at her, she smiled with bright eyes and blinked quickly, as if to say, "Yes, perfectly all right— absolutely," and she meant it.

"Then we'd better—" said he, and he tucked her hand inside his arm and began to rush her off to where the two chairs stood. But she just had time to breathe. "Not so fast, Daddy, please," when he remembered too and slowed down.

Strange! They had been married twenty-eight years, and it was still an effort to him, each time, to adapt his pace to hers.

"Not cold, are you?" he asked, glancing sideways at her. Her little nose, geranium pink above the dark fur, was answer enough. But she thrust her free hand into the velvet pocket of her jacket and murmured gaily, "I shall be glad of my rug."

He pressed her tighter to his side—a quick, nervous pressure. He knew, of course, that she ought to be down in the cabin; he knew that it was no afternoon for her to be sitting on deck, in this cold and raw mist, lee side or no lee side, rugs or no rugs, and he realized how she must be hating it. But he had come to believe that it really was easier for her to make these sacrifices than it was for him. Take their present case, for instance. If he had gone down to the cabin with her, he would have been miserable the whole time, and he couldn't have helped showing it. At any rate, she would have found him out. Whereas, having made up her mind to fall in with his ideas, he would have betted anybody she would even go so far as to enjoy the experience. Not because she was without personality of her own. Good Lord! She was absolutely brimming with it. But because . . . but here his thoughts always stopped. Here they always felt the need of a cigar, as it were. And, looking at the cigar-tip, his fine blue eyes narrowed. It was a law of marriage, he supposed. . . . All the same, he always felt guilty when he asked these sacrifices of her. That was what the quick pressure meant. His being said to her being: "You do understand, don't you?" and there was an answering tremor of her fingers, "I *understand*."

Certainly, the steward—good little chap—had done all in his power to make them comfortable. He had put up their chairs in whatever warmth there was and out of the smell. She did hope he would be tipped adequately. It was on occasions like these (and her life seemed to be full of such occasions) that she wished it was the woman who controlled the purse.

"Thank you, steward. That will do beautifully."

"Why are stewards so often delicate-looking?" she wondered, as her feet were tucked under. "This poor little chap looks as though he'd got a chest, and yet one would have thought . . . the sea air. . . ."

The button of the pigskin purse was undone. The tray was tilted. She saw sixpences, shillings, half-crowns.

"I should give him five shillings," she decided, "and tell him to buy himself a good nourishing—"

He was given a shilling, and he touched his cap and seemed genuinely grateful.

Well, it might have been worse. It might have been sixpence. It might, indeed. For at that moment Father turned towards her and said, half-apologetically, stuffing the purse back, "I gave him a shilling. I think it was worth it, don't you?"

"Oh, quite! Every bit!" said she.

It is extraordinary how peaceful it feels on a little steamer once the bustle of leaving port is over. In a quarter of an hour one might have been at sea for days. There is something almost touching, childish, in the way people submit themselves to the new conditions. They go to bed in the early afternoon, they shut their eyes and "it's night" like little children who turn the table upside down and cover themselves with the table-cloth. And those who remain on deck—they seem to be always the same, those few hardened men travellers—pause, light their pipes, stamp softly, gaze out to sea, and their voices are subdued as they walk up and down. The long-legged little girl chases after the red-cheeked boy, but soon both are captured; and the old sailor, swinging an unlighted lantern, passes and disappears. . . .

He lay back, the rug up to his chin and she saw he was breathing deeply. Sea air! If anyone believed in sea air, it was he. He had the strongest faith in its tonic qualities. But the great thing was, according to him, to fill the lungs with it the moment you came on board. Otherwise, the sheer strength of it was enough to give you a chill. . . .

She gave a small chuckle, and he turned to her quickly. "What is it?"

"It's your cap," she said. "I never can get used to you in a cap. You look such a thorough burglar."

"Well, what the deuce am I to wear?" He shot up one grey eyebrow and wrinkled his nose. "It's a very good cap, too. Very fine specimen of its kind. It's got a very rich white satin lining." He paused. He declaimed, as he had hundreds of times before at this stage, "Rich and rare were the gems she wore."

But she was thinking he really was childishly proud of the white satin lining. He would like to have taken off his cap and made her feel it. "Feel the quality!" How often had she rubbed between finger and thumb his coat, his shirt cuff, tie, sock, linen handkerchief, while he said that.

She slipped down more deeply into her chair.

And the little steamer pressed on, pitching gently, over the grey, unbroken, gently-moving water, that was veiled with slanting rain.

Far out, as though idly, listlessly, gulls were flying. Now they settled on the waves, now they beat up into the rainy air, and shone against the pale sky like the lights within a pearl. They looked cold and lonely. How lonely it will be when we have passed by, she thought. There will be nothing but the waves and those birds and rain falling.

She gazed through the rust-spotted railing along which big drops trembled, until suddenly she shut her lips. It was as if a warning voice inside her had said, "Don't look!"

"No, I won't," she decided. "It's too depressing, much too depressing."

But immediately, she opened her eyes and looked again. Lonely birds, water lifting, white pale sky—how were they changed?

And it seemed to her there was a presence far out there, between the sky and the water; someone very desolate and longing watched them pass and cried as if to stop them—but cried to her alone.

"Mother!"

"Don't leave me," sounded the cry. "Don't forget me! You are forgetting me, you know you are!" And it was as though from her own breast there came the sound of childish weeping.

"My son—my precious child—it isn't true!"

Sh! How was it possible that she was sitting there on that quiet steamer beside Father and at the same time she was hushing and holding a little slender boy—so pale—who had just waked out of a dreadful dream?

"I dreamed I was in a wood—somewhere far away from everybody,—and I was lying down and a great blackberry vine grew over me. And I called and called to you—and you wouldn't come—you wouldn't come—so I had to lie there for ever."

What a terrible dream! He had always had terrible dreams. How often, years ago, when he was small, she had made some excuse and escaped from their friends in the dining-room or the drawing-room to come to the foot of the stairs and listen. "Mother!" And when he was asleep, his dream had journeyed with her back into the circle of lamplight; it had taken its place there like a ghost. And now—

Far more often—at all times—in all places—like now, for instance—she never settled down, she was never off her guard for a moment but she heard him. He wanted her. "I am coming as fast as I can! As fast as I can!" But the dark stairs have no ending, and the worst dream of all—the one that is always the same—goes for ever and ever uncomforted.

This is anguish! How is it to be borne? Still, it is not the idea of her suffering which is unbearable—it is his. Can one do nothing for the dead? And for a long time the answer had been— Nothing!

. . . But softly without a sound the dark curtain has rolled down. There is no more to come. That is the end of the play. But it can't end like that—so suddenly. There must be more. No, it's cold, it's still. There is nothing to be gained by waiting.

But—did he go back again? Or, when the war was over, did he come home for good? Surely, he will marry—later on—not for several years. Surely, one day I shall remember his wedding and my first grandchild—a beautiful dark-haired boy born in the early morning— a lovely morning—spring!

"Oh, Mother, it's not fair to me to put these ideas into my head! Stop, Mother, stop! When I think of all I have missed, I can't bear it."

"I can't bear it!" She sits up breathing the words and tosses the dark rug away. It is colder than ever, and now the dusk is falling, falling like ash upon the pallid water.

And the little steamer, growing determined, throbbed on, pressed on, as if at the end of the journey there waited. . . .

DOROTHY PARKER

1893–1967

You Were Perfectly Fine

The pale young man eased himself carefully into the low chair, and rolled his head to the side, so that the cool chintz comforted his cheek and temple.

"Oh, dear," he said. "Oh, dear, oh, dear, oh, dear. Oh."

The clear-eyed girl, sitting light and erect on the couch, smiled brightly at him.

"Not feeling so well today?" she said.

"Oh, I'm great," he said. "Corking, I am. Know what time I got up? Four o'clock this afternoon, sharp. I kept trying to make it, and every time I took my head off the pillow, it would roll under the bed. This isn't my head I've got on now. I think this is something that used to belong to Walt Whitman. Oh, dear, oh, dear, oh, dear."

"Do you think maybe a drink would make you feel better?" she said.

"The hair of the mastiff that bit me?" he said. "Oh, no, thank you. Please never speak of anything like that again. I'm through. I'm all, all through. Look at that hand; steady as a humming-bird. Tell me, was I very terrible last night?"

"Oh, goodness," she said, "everybody was feeling pretty high. You were all right."

"Yeah," he said. "I must have been dandy. Is everybody sore at me?"

"Good heavens, no," she said. "Everyone thought you were terribly funny. Of course, Jim Pierson was a little stuffy, there for a minute at dinner. But people sort of held him back in his chair, and got him calmed down. I don't think anybody at the other tables noticed it at all. Hardly anybody."

"He was going to sock me?" he said. "Oh, Lord. What did I do to him?"

"Why, you didn't do a thing," she said. "You were perfectly fine. But you know how silly Jim gets, when he thinks anybody is making too much fuss over Elinor."

"Was I making a pass at Elinor?" he said. "Did I do that?"

"Of course you didn't," she said. "You were only fooling, that's all. She thought you were awfully amusing. She was having a marvelous time. She only got a little tiny bit annoyed just once, when you poured the clam-juice down her back."

"My God," he said. "Clam-juice down that back. And every vertebra a little Cabot. Dear God. What'll I ever do?"

"Oh, she'll be all right," she said. "Just send her some flowers, or something. Don't worry about it. It isn't anything."

"No, I won't worry," he said. "I haven't got a care in the world. I'm sitting pretty. Oh, dear, oh, dear. Did I do any other fascinating tricks at dinner?"

"You were fine," she said. "Don't be so foolish about it. Everybody was crazy about you. The maître d'hôtel was a little worried because you wouldn't stop singing, but he really didn't mind. All he said was, he was afraid they'd close the place again, if there was so much noise.

But he didn't care a bit, himself. I think he loved seeing you have such a good time. Oh, you were just singing away, there, for about an hour. It wasn't so terribly loud, at all."

"So I sang," he said. "That must have been a treat. I sang."

"Don't you remember?" she said. "You just sang one song after another. Everybody in the place was listening. They loved it. Only you kept insisting that you wanted to sing some song about some kind of fusiliers or other, and everybody kept shushing you, and you'd keep trying to start it again. You were wonderful. We were all trying to make you stop singing for a minute, and eat something, but you wouldn't hear of it. My, you were funny."

"Didn't I eat any dinner?" he said.

"Oh, not a thing," she said. "Every time the waiter would offer you something, you'd give it right back to him, because you said that he was your long-lost brother, changed in the cradle by a gypsy band, and that anything you had was his. You had him simply roaring at you."

"I bet I did," he said. "I bet I was comical. Society's Pet, I must have been. And what happened then, after my overwhelming success with the waiter?"

"Why, nothing much," she said. "You took a sort of dislike to some old man with white hair, sitting across the room, because you didn't like his necktie and you wanted to tell him about it. But we got you out, before he got really mad."

"Oh, we got out," he said. "Did I walk?"

"Walk? Of course you did," she said. "You were absolutely all right. There was that nasty stretch of ice on the sidewalk, and you did sit down awfully hard, you poor dear. But good heavens, that might have happened to anybody."

"Oh, surely," he said. "Mrs. Hoover or anybody. So I fell down on the sidewalk. That would explain what's the matter with my— Yes. I see. And then what, if you don't mind?"

"Ah, now, Peter!" she said. "You can't sit there and say you don't remember what happened after that! I did think that maybe you were just a little tight at dinner—oh, you were perfectly all right, and all that, but I did know you were feeling pretty gay. But you were so serious, from the time you fell down—I never knew you to be that way. Don't you know, how you told me I had never seen your real self before? Oh, Peter, I just couldn't bear it, if you didn't remember that lovely long ride we took together in the taxi! Please, you do remember that, don't you? I think it would simply kill me, if you didn't."

"Oh, yes," he said. "Riding in the taxi. Oh, yes, sure. Pretty long ride, hmm?"

"Round and round and round the park," she said. "Oh, and the trees were shining so in the moonlight. And you said you never knew before that you really had a soul."

"Yes," he said. "I said that. That was me."

"You said such lovely, lovely things," she said. "And I'd never known, all this time, how you had been feeling about me, and I'd never dared to let you see how I felt about you. And then last night—oh, Peter dear, I think that taxi ride was the most important thing that ever happened to us in our lives."

"Yes," he said. "I guess it must have been."

"And we're going to be so happy," she said. "Oh, I just want to tell everybody! But I don't know—I think maybe it would be sweeter to keep it all to ourselves."

"I think it would be," he said.

"Isn't it lovely?" she said.

"Yes," he said. "Great."

"Lovely!" she said.

"Look here," he said, "do you mind if I have a drink? I mean, just medicinally, you know. I'm off the stuff for life, so help me. But I think I feel a collapse coming on."

"Oh, I think it would do you good," she said. "You poor boy, it's a shame you feel so awful. I'll go make you a highball."

"Honestly," he said, "I don't see how you could ever want to speak to me again, after I made such a fool of myself, last night. I think I'd better go join a monastery in Tibet."

"You crazy idiot!" she said. "As if I could ever let you go away now! Stop talking like that. You were perfectly fine."

She jumped up from the couch, kissed him quickly on the forehead, and ran out of the room.

The pale young man looked after her and shook his head long and slowly, then dropped it in his damp and trembling hands.

"Oh, dear," he said. "Oh, dear, oh, dear, oh dear."

KATHERINE ANNE PORTER

1894–

Rope

On the third day after they moved to the country he came walking back from the village carrying a basket of groceries and a twenty-four-yard coil of rope. She came out to meet him, wiping her hands on her green smock. Her hair was tumbled, her nose was scarlet with sunburn; he told her that already she looked like a born country woman. His gray flannel shirt stuck to him, his heavy shoes were dusty. She assured him he looked like a rural character in a play.

Had he brought the coffee? She had been waiting all day long for coffee. They had forgot it when they ordered at the store the first day.

Gosh, no, he hadn't. Lord, now he'd have to go back. Yes, he would if it killed him. He thought, though, he had everything else. She reminded him it was only because he didn't drink coffee himself. If he did he would remember it quick enough. Suppose they ran out of cigarettes? Then she saw the rope. What was that for? Well, he thought it might do to hang clothes on, or something. Naturally she asked him if he thought they were going to run a laundry? They already had a fifty-foot line hanging right before his eyes? Why, hadn't he noticed it, really? It was a blot on the landscape to her.

He thought there were a lot of things a rope might come in handy for. She wanted to know what, for instance. He thought a few seconds, but nothing occurred. They could wait and see, couldn't they? You need all sorts of strange odds and ends around a place in the country. She said, yes, that was so; but she thought just at that time when every penny counted, it seemed funny to buy more rope. That was all. She hadn't meant anything else. She hadn't just seen, not at first, why he felt it was necessary.

Well, thunder, he had bought it because he wanted to, and that was all there was to it. She thought that was reason enough, and couldn't understand why he hadn't said so, at first. Undoubtedly it would be useful, twenty-four yards of rope, there were hundreds of things, she couldn't think of any at the moment, but it would come in. Of course. As he had said, things always did in the country.

But she was a little disappointed about the coffee, and oh, look, look, look at the eggs! Oh, my, they're all running! What had he put on top of them? Hadn't he known eggs mustn't be squeezed? Squeezed, who had squeezed them, he wanted to know. What a silly thing to say. He had simply brought them along in the basket with the other things. If they got broke it was the grocer's fault. He should know better than to put heavy things on top of eggs.

She believed it was the rope. That was the heaviest thing in the pack, she saw him plainly when he came in from the road, the rope was a big package on top of everything. He desired the whole wide world to witness that this was not a fact. He had carried the rope in one hand and the basket in the other, and what was the use of her having eyes if that was the best they could do for her?

Well, anyhow, she could see one thing plain: no eggs for breakfast. They'd have to scramble them now, for supper. It was too damned bad. She had planned to have steak for supper. No ice, meat wouldn't keep. He wanted to know why she couldn't finish breaking the eggs in a bowl and set them in a cool place.

Cool place! if he could find one for her, she'd be glad to set them there. Well, then, it seemed to him they might very well cook the meat at the same time they cooked the eggs and then warm up the meat for tomorrow. The idea simply choked her. Warmed-over meat, when they might as well have had it fresh. Second best and scraps and makeshifts, even to the meat! He rubbed her shoulder a little. It doesn't really matter so much, does it, darling? Sometimes when they were playful, he would rub her shoulder and she would arch and purr. This time she hissed and almost clawed. He was getting ready to say that they could surely manage somehow when she turned on him and said, if he told her they could manage somehow she would certainly slap his face.

He swallowed the words red hot, his face burned. He picked up the rope and started to put it on the top shelf. She would not have it on the top shelf, the jars and tins belonged there; positively she would not have the top shelf cluttered up with a lot of rope. She had borne all the clutter she meant to bear in the flat in town, there was space here at least and she meant to keep things in order.

Well, in that case, he wanted to know what the hammer and nails were doing up there? And why had she put them there when she knew very well he needed that hammer and those nails upstairs to fix the window sashes? She simply slowed down everything and made double work on the place with her insane habit of changing things around and hiding them.

She was sure she begged his pardon, and if she had had any reason to believe he was going to fix the sashes this summer she would have left the hammer and nails right where he put them; in the middle of the bedroom floor where they could step on them in the dark. And now if he didn't clear the whole mess out of there she would throw them down the well.

Oh, all right, all right—could he put them in the closet? Naturally not, there were brooms and mops and dustpans in the closet, and why couldn't he find a place for his rope outside her kitchen? Had he stopped to consider there were seven God-forsaken rooms in the house, and only one kitchen?

He wanted to know what of it? And did she realize she was making a complete fool of herself? And what did she take him for, a three-year-old idiot? The whole trouble with her was she needed something weaker than she was to heckle and tyrannize over. He wished to God now they had a couple of children she could take it out on. Maybe he'd get some rest.

Her face changed at this, she reminded him he had forgot the coffee and had bought a worthless piece of rope. And when she thought of all the things they actually needed to make the place even decently fit to live in, well, she could cry, that was all. She looked so forlorn, so lost and despairing he couldn't believe it was only a piece of rope that was causing all the racket. What *was* the matter, for God's sake?

Oh, would he please hush and go away, and *stay* away, if he could, for five minutes? By all means, yes, he would. He'd stay away indefinitely if she wished. Lord, yes, there was nothing he'd like better than to clear out and never come back. She couldn't for the life of her see what was holding him, then. It was a swell time. Here she was, stuck, miles from a railroad, with a half-empty house on her hands, and not a penny in her pocket, and everything on earth to do; it seemed the God-sent moment for him to get out from under. She was surprised he hadn't stayed in town as it was until she had come out and done the work and got things straightened out. It was his usual trick.

It appeared to him that this was going a little far. Just a touch out of bounds, if she didn't mind his saying so. Why the hell had he stayed in town the summer before? To do a half-dozen extra jobs to get the money he had sent her. That was it. She knew perfectly well they couldn't have done it otherwise. She had agreed with him at the time. And that was the only time so help him he had ever left her to do anything by herself.

Oh, he could tell that to his great-grandmother. She had her notion of what had kept him in town. Considerably more than a notion, if he wanted to know. So, she was going to bring all that up again, was she? Well, she could just think what she pleased. He was tired of explaining. It may have looked funny but he had simply got hooked in, and what could he do? It was impossible to believe that she was going to take it seriously. Yes, yes, she knew how it was with a man: if he was left by himself a minute, some woman was certain to kidnap him. And naturally he couldn't hurt her feelings by refusing!

Well, what was she raving about? Did she forget she had told him those two weeks alone in the country were the happiest she had known for four years? And how long had they been married when she said that? All right, shut up! If she thought that hadn't stuck in his craw.

She hadn't meant she was happy because she was away from him. She meant she was happy getting the devilish house nice and ready for him. That was what she had meant, and now look! Bringing up something she had said a year ago simply to justify himself for forgetting her coffee and breaking the eggs and buying a wretched piece of rope they couldn't afford. She really thought it was time to drop the subject, and now she wanted only two things in the world. She wanted him to get that rope from underfoot, and go back to the village and get her coffee, and if he could remember it, he might bring a metal mitt for the skillets, and two more curtain rods, and if there were any rubber gloves in the village, her hands were simply raw, and a bottle of milk of magnesia from the drugstore.

He looked out at the dark blue afternoon sweltering on the slopes, and mopped his forehead and sighed heavily and said, if only she could wait a minute for *anything*, he was going back. He had said so, hadn't he, the very instant they found he had overlooked it?

Oh, yes, well . . . run along. She was going to wash windows. The country was so beautiful! She doubted they'd have a moment to enjoy it. He meant to go, but he could not until he had said that if she wasn't such a hopeless melancholiac she might see that this was only for a few days. Couldn't she remember anything pleasant about the other summers? Hadn't they ever had any fun? She hadn't time to talk about it, and now would he please not leave that rope lying around for her to trip on? He picked it up, somehow it had toppled off the table, and walked out with it under his arm.

Was he going this minute? He certainly was. She thought so. Sometimes it seemed to her he had second sight about the precisely perfect moment to leave her ditched. She had meant to put the mattresses out to sun, if they put them out this minute they would get at least three hours, he must have heard her say that morning she meant to put them out. So of course he would walk off and leave her to it. She supposed he thought the exercise would do her good.

Well, he was merely going to get her coffee. A four-mile walk for two pounds of coffee was ridiculous, but he was perfectly willing to do it. The habit was making a wreck of her, but if she wanted to wreck herself there was nothing he could do about it. If he thought it was coffee that was making a wreck of her, she congratulated him: he must have a damned easy conscience.

Conscience or no conscience, he didn't see why the mattresses couldn't very well wait until tomorrow. And anyhow, for God's sake, were they living *in* the house, or were they going to let the house ride them to death? She paled at this, her face grew livid about the mouth, she looked quite dangerous, and reminded him that housekeeping was no more her work than it was his: she had other work to do as well, and when did he think she was going to find time to do it at this rate?

Was she going to start on that again? She knew as well as he did that his work brought in the regular money, hers was only occasional, if they depended on what *she* made—and she might as well get straight on this question once for all!

That was positively not the point. The question was, when both of them were working on their own time, was there going to be a division of the housework, or wasn't there? She merely wanted to know, she had to make her plans. Why, he thought that was all arranged. It was understood that he was to help. Hadn't he always, in summers?

Hadn't he, though? Oh, just hadn't he? And when, and where, and doing what? Lord, what an uproarious joke!

It was such a very uproarious joke that her face turned slightly purple, and she screamed with laughter. She laughed so hard she had to sit down, and finally a rush of tears spurted from her eyes and poured down into the lifted corners of her mouth. He dashed towards her and dragged her up to her feet and tried to pour water on her head. The dipper hung by a string on a nail and he broke it loose. Then he tried to pump water with one hand while she struggled in the other. So he gave it up and shook her instead.

She wrenched away, crying out for him to take his rope and go to hell, she had simply given him up: and ran. He heard her high-heeled bedroom slippers clattering and stumbling on the stairs.

He went out around the house and into the lane; he suddenly realized he had a blister on his heel and his shirt felt as if it were on fire. Things broke so suddenly you didn't know where you were. She could work herself into a fury about simply nothing. She was terrible, damn it: not an ounce of reason. You might as well talk to a sieve as that woman when she got going. Damned if he'd spend his life humoring her! Well, what to do now? He would take back the rope and exchange it for something else. Things accumulated, things were mountainous, you couldn't move them or sort them out or get rid of them. They just lay and rotted around. He'd take it back. Hell, why should he? He wanted it. What was it anyhow? A piece of rope. Imagine anybody caring more about a piece of rope than about a man's feelings. What earthly right had she to say a word about it? He remembered all the useless, meaningless things she bought for herself: Why? because I wanted it, that's why! He stopped and selected a large stone by the road. He would put the rope behind it. He would put it in the tool-box when he got back. He'd heard enough about it to last him a life-time.

When he came back she was leaning against the post box beside the road waiting. It was pretty late, the smell of broiled steak floated nose high in the cooling air. Her face was young and smooth and fresh-looking. Her unmanageable funny black hair was all on end. She waved to him from a distance, and he speeded up. She called out that supper was ready and waiting, was he starved?

You bet he was starved. Here was the coffee. He waved it at her. She looked at his other hand. What was that he had there?

Well, it was the rope again. He stopped short. He had meant to exchange it but forgot. She wanted to know why he should exchange it, if it was something he really wanted. Wasn't the air sweet now, and wasn't it fine to be here?

She walked beside him with one hand hooked into his leather belt. She pulled and jostled him a little as he walked, and leaned against him. He put his arm clear around her and patted her stomach. They exchanged wary smiles. Coffee, coffee for the Ootsum-Wootsums! He felt as if he were bringing her a beautiful present.

He was a love, she firmly believed, and if she had had her coffee in the morning, she wouldn't have behaved so funny . . . There was a whippoorwill still coming back, imagine, clear out of season, sitting in the crab-apple tree calling all by himself. Maybe his girl stood him up. Maybe she did. She hoped to hear him once more, she loved whippoorwills . . . He knew how she was, didn't he?

Sure, he knew how she was.

F. SCOTT FITZGERALD
1896–1941
Babylon Revisited

"And where's Mr. Campbell?" Charlie asked.

"Gone to Switzerland. Mr. Campbell's a pretty sick man, Mr. Wales."

"I'm sorry to hear that. And George Hardt?" Charlie inquired.

"Back in America, gone to work."

"And where is the Snow Bird?"

"He was in here last week. Anyway, his friend, Mr. Schaeffer, is in Paris."

Two familiar names from the long list of a year and a half ago. Charlie scribbled an address in his notebook and tore out the page.

"If you see Mr. Schaeffer, give him this," he said. "It's my brother-in-law's address. I haven't settled on a hotel yet."

He was not really disappointed to find Paris was so empty. But the stillness in the Ritz bar was strange and portentous. It was not an American bar any more—he felt polite in it, and not as if he owned it. It had gone back into France. He felt the stillness from the moment he got out of the taxi and saw the doorman, usually in a frenzy of activity at this hour, gossiping with a *chasseur* by the servants' entrance.

Passing through the corridor, he heard only a single, bored voice in the once-clamorous women's room. When he turned into the bar he traveled the twenty feet of green carpet with his eyes fixed straight ahead by old habit; and then, with his foot firmly on the rail, he turned and surveyed the room, encountering only a single pair of eyes that fluttered up from a newspaper in the corner. Charlie asked for the head barman, Paul, who in the latter days of the bull market had come to work in his own custom-built car—disembarking, however, with due nicety at the nearest corner. But Paul was at his country house today and Alix giving him information.

"No, no more," Charlie said, "I'm going slow these days."

Alix congratulated him: "You were going pretty strong a couple of years ago."

"I'll stick to it all right," Charlie assured him. "I've stuck to it for over a year and a half now."

"How do you find conditions in America?"

"I haven't been to America for months. I'm in business in Prague, representing a couple of concerns there. They don't know about me down there."

Alix smiled.

"Remember the night of George Hardt's bachelor dinner here?" said Charlie. "By the way, what's become of Claude Fessenden?"

Alix lowered his voice confidentially: "He's in Paris, but he doesn't come here any more. Paul doesn't allow it. He ran up a bill of thirty thousand francs, charging all his drinks and his lunches, and usually his dinner, for more than a year. And when Paul finally told him he had to pay, he gave him a bad check."

Alix shook his head sadly.

"I don't understand it, such a dandy fellow. Now he's all bloated up—" He made a plump apple of his hands.

Charlie watched a group of strident queens installing themselves in a corner.

"Nothing affects them," he thought. "Stocks rise and fall, people loaf or work, but they go on forever." The place oppressed him. He called for the dice and shook with Alix for the drink.

"Here for long, Mr. Wales?"

"I'm here for four or five days to see my little girl."

"Oh-h! You have a little girl?"

Outside, the fire-red, gas-blue, ghost-green signs shone smokily through the tranquil rain. It was late afternoon and the streets were in movement; the *bistros* gleamed. At the corner of the Boulevard des Capucines he took a taxi. The Place de la Concorde moved by in pink majesty; they crossed the logical Seine, and Charlie felt the sudden provincial quality of the Left Bank.

Charlie directed his taxi to the Avenue de l'Opéra, which was out of his way. But he wanted to see the blue hour spread over the magnificent façade, and imagine that the cab horns, playing endlessly the first few bars of *Le Plus que Lent*, were the trumpets of the Second

Empire. They were closing the iron grill in front of Brentano's Book-store, and people were already at dinner behind the trim little bourgeois hedge of Duval's. He had never eaten at a really cheap restaurant in Paris. Five-course dinner, four francs fifty, eighteen cents, wine included. For some odd reason he wished that he had.

As they rolled on to the Left Bank and he felt its sudden provincialism, he thought, "I spoiled this city for myself. I didn't realize it, but the days came along one after another, and then two years were gone, and everything was gone, and I was gone."

He was thirty-five, and good to look at. The Irish mobility of his face was sobered by a deep wrinkle between his eyes. As he rang his brother-in-law's bell in the Rue Palatine, the wrinkle deepened till it pulled down his brows; he felt a cramping sensation in his belly. From behind the maid who opened the door darted a lovely little girl of nine who shrieked "Daddy!" and flew up, struggling like a fish, into his arms. She pulled his head around by one ear and set her cheek against his.

"My old pie," he said.

"Oh, daddy, daddy, daddy, daddy, dads, dads, dads!"

She drew him into the salon, where the family waited, a boy and a girl his daughter's age, his sister-in-law and her husband. He greeted Marion with his voice pitched carefully to avoid either feigned enthusiasm or dislike, but her response was more frankly tepid, though she minimized her expression of unalterable distrust by directing her regard toward his child. The two men clasped hands in a friendly way and Lincoln Peters rested his for a moment on Charlie's shoulder.

The room was warm and comfortably American. The three children moved intimately about, playing through the yellow oblongs that led to other rooms; the cheer of six o'clock spoke in the eager smacks of the fire and the sounds of French activity in the kitchen. But Charlie did not relax; his heart sat up rigidly in his body and he drew confidence from his daughter, who from time to time came close to him, holding in her arms the doll he had brought.

"Really extremely well," he declared in answer to Lincoln's question. "There's a lot of business there that isn't moving at all, but we're doing even better than ever. In fact, damn well. I'm bringing my sister over from America next month to keep house for me. My income last year was bigger than it was when I had money. You see, the Czechs—"

His boasting was for a specific purpose; but after a moment, seeing a faint restiveness in Lincoln's eye, he changed the subject:

"Those are fine children of yours, well brought up, good manners."

"We think Honoria's a great little girl too."

Marion Peters came back from the kitchen. She was a tall woman with worried eyes, who had once possessed a fresh American loveliness. Charlie had never been sensitive to it and was always surprised when people spoke of how pretty she had been. From the first there had been an instinctive antipathy between them.

"Well, how do you find Honoria?" she asked.

"Wonderful. I was astonished how much she's grown in ten months. All the children are looking well."

"We haven't had a doctor for a year. How do you like being back in Paris?"

"It seems very funny to see so few Americans around."

"I'm delighted," Marion said vehemently. "Now at least you can go into a store without their assuming you're a millionaire. We've suffered like everybody, but on the whole it's a good deal pleasanter."

"But it was nice while it lasted," Charlie said. "We were a sort of royalty, almost infallible, with a sort of magic around us. In the bar this afternoon"—he stumbled, seeing his mistake—"there wasn't a man I knew."

She looked at him keenly. "I should think you'd have had enough of bars."

"I only stayed a minute. I take one drink every afternoon, and no more."

"Don't you want a cocktail before dinner?" Lincoln asked.

"I take only one drink every afternoon, and I've had that."

"I hope you keep to it," said Marion.

Her dislike was evident in the coldness with which she spoke, but Charlie only smiled; he had larger plans. Her very aggressiveness gave him an advantage, and he knew enough to wait. He wanted them to initiate the discussion of what they knew had brought him to Paris.

At dinner he couldn't decide whether Honoria was most like him or her mother. Fortunate if she didn't combine the traits of both that had brought them to disaster. A great wave of protectiveness went over him. He thought he knew what to do for her. He believed in character; he wanted to jump back a whole generation and trust in character again as the eternally valuable element. Everything else wore out.

He left soon after dinner, but not to go home. He was curious to see Paris by night with clearer and more judicious eyes than those of other days. He bought a *strapontin* for the Casino and watched Josephine Baker go through her chocolate arabesques.

After an hour he left and strolled toward Montmartre, up the Rue Pigalle into the Place Blanche. The rain had stopped and there were a few people in evening clothes disembarking from taxis in front of cabarets, and *cocottes* prowling singly or in pairs, and many Negroes. He passed a lighted door from which issued music, and stopped with the sense of familiarity; it was Bricktop's, where he had parted with so many hours and so much money. A few doors farther on he found another ancient rendezvous and incautiously put his head inside. Immediately an eager orchestra burst into sound, a pair of professional dancers leaped to their feet and a maître d'hôtel swooped toward him, crying, "Crowd just arriving, sir!" But he withdrew quickly.

"You have to be damn drunk," he thought.

Zelli's was closed, the bleak and sinister cheap hotels surrounding it were dark; up in the Rue Blanche there was more light and a local, colloquial French crowd. The Poet's Cave had disappeared, but the two great mouths of the Café of Heaven and the Café of Hell still yawned—even devoured, as he watched, the meager contents of a tourist bus—a German, a Japanese, and an American couple who glanced at him with frightened eyes.

So much for the effort and ingenuity of Montmartre. All the catering to vice and waste was on an utterly childish scale, and he suddenly realized the meaning of the word "dissipate"—to dissipate into thin air; to make nothing out of something. In the little hours of the night every move from place to place was an enormous human jump, an increase of paying for the privilege of slower and slower motion.

He remembered thousand-franc notes given to an orchestra for playing a single number, hundred-franc notes tossed to a doorman for calling a cab.

But it hadn't been given for nothing.

It had been given, even the most wildly squandered sum, as an offering to destiny that he might not remember the things most worth remembering, the things that now he would always remember—his child taken from his control, his wife escaped to a grave in Vermont.

In the glare of a *brasserie* a woman spoke to him. He bought her some eggs and coffee, and then, eluding her encouraging stare, gave her a twenty-franc note and took a taxi to his hotel.

II

He woke upon a fine fall day—football weather. The depression of yesterday was gone and he liked the people on the streets. At noon he sat opposite Honoria at Le Grand Vatel, the only restaurant he could think of not reminiscent of champagne dinners and long luncheons that began at two and ended in a blurred and vague twilight.

"Now, how about vegetables? Oughtn't you to have some vegetables?"

"Well, yes."

"Here's *épinards* and *chou-fleur* and carrots and *haricots.*"

"I'd like *chou-fleur.*"

"Wouldn't you like to have two vegetables?"

"I usually only have one at lunch."

The waiter was pretending to be inordinately fond of children. *"Qu'elle est mignonne la petite! Elle parle exactement comme une Française."*

"How about dessert? Shall we wait and see?"

The waiter disappeared. Honoria looked at her father expectantly.

"What are we going to do?"

"First, we're going to that toy store in the Rue Saint-Honoré and buy you anything you like. And then we're going to the vaudeville at the Empire."

She hesitated. "I like it about the vaudeville, but not the toy store."

"Why not?"

"Well, you brought me this doll." She had it with her. "And I've got lots of things. And we're not rich any more, are we?"

"We never were. But today you are to have anything you want."

"All right," she agreed resignedly.

When there had been her mother and a French nurse he had been inclined to be strict; now he extended himself, reached out for a new tolerance; he must be both parents to her and not shut any of her out of communication.

"I want to get to know you," he said gravely. "First let me introduce myself. My name is Charles J. Wales, of Prague."

"Oh, daddy!" her voice cracked with laughter.

"And who are you, please?" he persisted, and she accepted a rôle immediately: "Honoria Wales, Rue Palatine, Paris."

"Married or single?"

"No, not married. Single."

He indicated the doll. "But I see you have a child, madame."

Unwilling to disinherit it, she took it to her heart and thought quickly: "Yes, I've been married, but I'm not married now. My husband is dead."

He went on quickly, "And the child's name?"

"Simone. That's after my best friend at school."

"I'm very pleased that you're doing so well at school."

"I'm third this month," she boasted. "Elsie"—that was her cousin—"is only about eighteenth, and Richard is about at the bottom."

"You like Richard and Elsie, don't you?"

"Oh, yes. I like Richard quite well and I like her all right."

Cautiously and casually he asked: "And Aunt Marion and Uncle Lincoln—which do you like best?"

"Oh, Uncle Lincoln, I guess."

He was increasingly aware of her presence. As they came in, a murmur of ". . . adorable" followed them, and now the people at the next table bent all their silences upon her, staring as if she were something no more conscious than a flower.

"Why don't I live with you?" she asked suddenly. "Because mamma's dead?"

"You must stay here and learn more French. It would have been hard for daddy to take care of you so well."

"I don't really need much taking care of any more. I do everything for myself."

Going out of the restaurant, a man and a woman unexpectedly hailed him.

"Well, the old Wales!"

"Hello there, Lorraine. . . . Dunc."

Sudden ghosts out of the past: Duncan Schaeffer, a friend from college. Lorraine Quarrles, a lovely, pale blonde of thirty; one of a crowd who had helped them make months into days in the lavish times of three years ago.

"My husband couldn't come this year," she said, in answer to his question. "We're poor as hell. So he gave me two hundred a month and told me I could do my worst on that. . . . This your little girl?"

"What about coming back and sitting down?" Duncan asked.

"Can't do it." He was glad for an excuse. As always, he felt Lorraine's passionate, provocative attraction, but his own rhythm was different now.

"Well, how about dinner?" she asked.

"I'm not free. Give me your address and let me call you."

"Charlie, I believe you're sober," she said judicially. "I honestly believe he's sober, Dunc. Pinch him and see if he's sober."

Charlie indicated Honoria with his head. They both laughed.

"What's your address?" said Duncan skeptically.

He hesitated, unwilling to give the name of his hotel.

"I'm not settled yet. I'd better call you. We're going to see the vaudeville at the Empire."

"There! That's what I want to do," Lorraine said. "I want to see some clowns and acrobats and jugglers. That's just what we'll do, Dunc."

"We've got to do an errand first," said Charlie. "Perhaps we'll see you there."

"All right, you snob. . . . Good-by, beautiful little girl."

"Good-by."

Honoria bobbed politely.

Somehow, an unwelcome encounter. They liked him because he

was functioning, because he was serious; they wanted to see him, because he was stronger than they were now, because they wanted to draw a certain sustenance from his strength.

At the Empire, Honoria proudly refused to sit upon her father's folded coat. She was already an individual with a code of her own, and Charlie was more and more absorbed by the desire of putting a little of himself into her before she crystallized utterly. It was hopeless to try to know her in so short a time.

Between the acts they came upon Duncan and Lorraine in the lobby where the band was playing.

"Have a drink?"

"All right, but not up at the bar. We'll take a table."

"The perfect father."

Listening abstractedly to Lorraine, Charlie watched Honoria's eyes leave their table, and he followed them wistfully about the room, wondering what they saw. He met her glance and she smiled.

"I liked that lemonade," she said.

What had she said? What had he expected? Going home in a taxi afterward, he pulled her over until her head rested against his chest.

"Darling, do you ever think about your mother?"

"Yes, sometimes," she answered vaguely.

"I don't want you to forget her. Have you got a picture of her?"

"Yes, I think so. Anyhow, Aunt Marion has. Why don't you want me to forget her?"

"She loved you very much."

"I loved her too."

They were silent for a moment.

"Daddy, I want to come and live with you," she said suddenly.

His heart leaped; he had wanted it to come like this.

"Aren't you perfectly happy?"

"Yes, but I love you better than anybody. And you love me better than anybody, don't you, now that mummy's dead?"

"Of course I do. But you won't always like me best, honey. You'll grow up and meet somebody your own age and go marry him and forget you ever had a daddy."

"Yes, that's true," she agreed tranquilly.

He didn't go in. He was coming back at nine o'clock and he wanted to keep himself fresh and new for the thing he must say then.

"When you're safe inside, just show yourself in that window."

"All right. Good-by, dads, dads, dads, dads."

He waited in the dark street until she appeared, all warm and glowing, in the window above and kissed her fingers out into the night.

III

They were waiting. Marion sat behind the coffee service in a dignified black dinner dress that just faintly suggested mourning. Lincoln was walking up and down with the animation of one who had already been talking. They were as anxious as he was to get into the question. He opened it almost immediately:

"I suppose you know what I want to see you about—why I really came to Paris."

Marion played with the black stars on her necklace and frowned.

"I'm awfully anxious to have a home," he continued. "And I'm awfully anxious to have Honoria in it. I appreciate your taking in Honoria for her mother's sake, but things have changed now"—he hesitated and then continued more forcibly—"changed radically with me, and I want to ask you to reconsider the matter. It would be silly for me to deny that about three years ago I was acting badly—"

Marion looked up at him with hard eyes.

"—but all that's over. As I told you, I haven't had more than a drink a day for over a year, and I take that drink deliberately, so that the idea of alcohol won't get too big in my imagination. You see the idea?"

"No," said Marion succinctly.

"It's a sort of stunt I set myself. It keeps the matter in proportion."

"I get you," said Lincoln. "You don't want to admit it's got any attraction for you."

"Something like that. Sometimes I forget and don't take it. But I try to take it. Anyway, I couldn't afford to drink in my position. The people I represent are more than satisfied with what I've done, and I'm bringing my sister over from Burlington to keep house for me, and I want awfully to have Honoria too. You know that even when her mother and I weren't getting along well we never let anything that happened touch Honoria. I know she's fond of me and I know I'm able to take care of her and—well, there you are. How do you feel about it?"

He knew that now he would have to take a beating. It would last an hour or two hours, and it would be difficult, but if he modulated his inevitable resentment to the chastened attitude of the reformed sinner, he might win his point in the end.

Keep your temper, he told himself. You don't want to be justified. You want Honoria.

Lincoln spoke first: "We've been talking it over ever since we got your letter last month. We're happy to have Honoria here. She's a dear little thing, and we're glad to be able to help her, but of course that isn't the question—"

Marion interrupted suddenly. "How long are you going to stay sober, Charlie?" she asked.

"Permanently, I hope."

"How can anybody count on that?"

"You know I never did drink heavily until I gave up business and came over here with nothing to do. Then Helen and I began to run around with—"

"Please leave Helen out of it. I can't bear to hear you talk about her like that."

He stared at her grimly; he had never been certain how fond of each other the sisters were in life.

"My drinking only lasted about a year and a half—from the time we came over until I—collapsed."

"It was time enough."

"It was time enough," he agreed.

"My duty is entirely to Helen," she said. "I try to think what she would have wanted me to do. Frankly, from the night you did that terrible thing you haven't really existed for me. I can't help that. She was my sister."

"Yes."

"When she was dying she asked me to look out for Honoria. If you hadn't been in a sanitarium then, it might have helped matters."

He had no answer.

"I'll never in my life be able to forget that morning when Helen knocked at my door, soaked to the skin and shivering and said you'd locked her out."

Charlie gripped the sides of the chair. This was more difficult than he expected; he wanted to launch out into a long expostulation and explanation, but he only said: "The night I locked her out—" and she interrupted, "I don't feel up to going over that again."

After a moment's silence Lincoln said: "We're getting off the subject. You want Marion to set aside her legal guardianship and give you Honoria. I think the main point for her is whether she has confidence in you or not."

"I don't blame Marion," Charlie said slowly, "but I think she can have entire confidence in me. I had a good record up to three years ago. Of course, it's within human possibilities I might go wrong any time. But if we wait much longer I'll lose Honoria's childhood and my chance for a home." He shook his head, "I'll simply lose her, don't you see?"

"Yes, I see," said Lincoln.

"Why didn't you think of all this before?" Marion asked.

"I suppose I did, from time to time, but Helen and I were getting along badly. When I consented to the guardianship, I was flat on my back in a sanitarium and the market had cleaned me out. I knew I'd acted badly, and I thought if it would bring any peace to Helen, I'd agree to anything. But now it's different. I'm functioning, I'm behaving damn well, so far as—".

"Please don't swear at me," Marion said.

He looked at her, startled. With each remark the force of her dislike became more and more apparent. She had built up all her fear of life into one wall and faced it toward him. This trivial reproof was possibly the result of some trouble with the cook several hours before. Charlie became increasingly alarmed at leaving Honoria in this atmosphere of hostility against himself; sooner or later it would come out, in a word here, a shake of the head there, and some of that distrust would be irrevocably implanted in Honoria. But he pulled his temper down out of his face and shut it up inside him; he had won a point, for Lincoln realized the absurdity of Marion's remark and asked her lightly since when she had objected to the word "damn."

"Another thing," Charlie said: "I'm able to give her certain advantages now. I'm going to take a French governess to Prague with me. I've got a lease on a new apartment—"

He stopped, realizing that he was blundering. They couldn't be expected to accept with equanimity the fact that his income was again twice as large as their own.

"I suppose you can give her more luxuries than we can," said Marion. "When you were throwing away money we were living along watching every ten francs. . . . I suppose you'll start doing it again."

"Oh, no," he said. "I've learned. I worked hard for ten years, you know—until I got lucky in the market, like so many people. Terribly lucky. It won't happen again."

There was a long silence. All of them felt their nerves straining, and for the first time in a year Charlie wanted a drink. He was sure now that Lincoln Peters wanted him to have his child.

Marion shuddered suddenly; part of her saw that Charlie's feet were planted on the earth now, and her own maternal feeling recognized the naturalness of his desire; but she had lived for a long time with a prejudice—a prejudice founded on a curious disbelief in her sister's happiness, and which, in the shock of one terrible night, had turned to hatred for him. It had all happened at a point in her life where the discouragement of ill health and adverse circumstances made it necessary for her to believe in tangible villainy and a tangible villain.

"I can't help what I think!" she cried out suddenly. "How much you were responsible for Helen's death, I don't know. It's something you'll have to square with your own conscience."

An electric current of agony surged through him; for a moment he was almost on his feet, an unuttered sound echoing in his throat. He hung on to himself for a moment, another moment.

"Hold on there," said Lincoln uncomfortably. "I never thought you were responsible for that."

"Helen died of heart trouble," Charlie said dully.

"Yes, heart trouble." Marion spoke as if the phrase had another meaning for her.

Then, in the flatness that followed her outburst, she saw him plainly and she knew he had somehow arrived at control over the situation. Glancing at her husband, she found no help from him, and as abruptly as if it were a matter of no importance, she threw up the sponge.

"Do what you like!" she cried, springing up from her chair. "She's your child. I'm not the person to stand in your way. I think if it were my child I'd rather see her—" She managed to check herself. "You two decide it. I can't stand this. I'm sick. I'm going to bed."

She hurried from the room; after a moment Lincoln said:

"This has been a hard day for her. You know how strongly she feels—" His voice was almost apologetic: "When a woman gets an idea in her head."

"Of course."

"It's going to be all right. I think she sees now that you—can provide for the child, and so we can't very well stand in your way or Honoria's way."

"Thank you, Lincoln."

"I'd better go along and see how she is."

"I'm going."

He was still trembling when he reached the street, but a walk down the Rue Bonaparte to the *quais* set him up, and as he crossed the Seine, fresh and new by the *quai* lamps, he felt exultant. But back in his room he couldn't sleep. The image of Helen haunted him. Helen whom he had loved so until they had senselessly begun to abuse each other's love, tear it into shreds. On that terrible February night that Marion remembered so vividly, a slow quarrel had gone on for hours. There was a scene at the Florida, and then he attempted to take her home, and then she kissed young Webb at a table; after that there was what she had hysterically said. When he arrived home alone he turned the key in the lock in wild anger. How could he know she would arrive an hour later alone, that there would be a snowstorm in which she wandered about in slippers, too confused to find a taxi? Then the aftermath, her escaping pneumonia by a miracle, and all the attendant horror. They were "reconciled," but that was the beginning of the end, and Marion, who had seen with her own eyes and who imagined it to be one of many scenes from her sister's martyrdom, never forgot.

Going over it again brought Helen nearer, and in the white, soft light that steals upon half sleep near morning he found himself talking to her again. She said that he was perfectly right about Honoria and that she wanted Honoria to be with him. She said she was glad he was being good and doing better. She said a lot of other things—very friendly things—but she was in a swing in a white dress, and swinging faster and faster all the time, so that at the end he could not hear clearly all that she said.

IV

He woke up feeling happy. The door of the world was open again. He made plans, vistas, futures for Honoria and himself, but suddenly he grew sad, remembering all the plans he and Helen had made. She had not planned to die. The present was the thing—work to do and someone to love. But not to love too much, for he knew the injury that a father can do to a daughter or a mother to a son by attaching them too closely: afterward, out in the world, the child would seek in the marriage partner the same blind tenderness and, failing probably to find it, turn against love and life.

It was another bright, crisp day. He called Lincoln Peters at the bank where he worked and asked if he could count on taking Honoria when he left for Prague. Lincoln agreed that there was no reason for delay. One thing—the legal guardianship. Marion wanted to retain that a while longer. She was upset by the whole matter, and it would oil things if she felt that the situation was still in her control for another year. Charlie agreed, wanting only the tangible, visible child.

Then the question of a governess. Charles sat in a gloomy agency and talked to a cross Béarnaise and to a buxom Breton peasant, neither of whom he could have endured. There were others whom he would see tomorrow.

He lunched with Lincoln Peters at Griffons, trying to keep down his exultation.

"There's nothing quite like your own child," Lincoln said. "But you understand how Marion feels too."

"She's forgotten how hard I worked for seven years there," Charlie said. "She just remembers one night."

"There's another thing." Lincoln hesitated. "While you and Helen were tearing around Europe throwing money away, we were just getting along. I didn't touch any of the prosperity because I never got ahead enough to carry anything but my insurance. I think Marion felt there was some kind of injustice in it—you not even working toward the end, and getting richer and richer."

"It went just as quick as it came," said Charlie.

"Yes, a lot of it stayed in the hands of *chasseurs* and saxophone players and maîtres d'hôtel—well, the big party's over now. I just said that to explain Marion's feeling about those crazy years. If you drop in about six o'clock tonight before Marion's too tired, we'll settle the details on the spot."

Back at his hotel, Charlie found a *pneumatique* that had been redirected from the Ritz bar where Charlie had left his address for the purpose of finding a certain man.

> DEAR CHARLIE: You were so strange when we saw you the other day that I wondered if I did something to offend you. If so, I'm not conscious of it. In fact, I have thought about you too much for the last year, and it's always been in the back of my mind that I might see you if I came over here. We *did* have such good times that crazy spring, like the night you and I stole the butcher's tricycle, and the time we tried to call on the president and you had the old derby rim and the wire cane. Everybody seems so old lately, but I don't feel old a bit. Couldn't we get together some time today for old time's sake? I've got a vile hang-over for the moment, but will be feeling better this afternoon and will look for you about five in the sweatshop at the Ritz.
>
> Always devotedly,
>
> LORRAINE.

His first feeling was one of awe that he had actually, in his mature years, stolen a tricycle and pedaled Lorraine all over the Étoile between the small hours and dawn. In retrospect it was a nightmare. Locking out Helen didn't fit in with any other act of his life, but the tricycle incident did—it was one of many. How many weeks or months of dissipation to arrive at that condition of utter irresponsibility?

He tried to picture how Lorraine had appeared to him then—very attractive; Helen was unhappy about it, though she said nothing. Yesterday, in the restaurant, Lorraine had seemed trite, blurred, worn away. He emphatically did not want to see her, and he was glad Alix had not given away his hotel address. It was a relief to think, instead, of Honoria, to think of Sundays spent with her and of saying good morning to her and of knowing she was there in his house at night, drawing her breath in the darkness.

At five he took a taxi and bought presents for all the Peters—a piquant cloth doll, a box of Roman soldiers, flowers for Marion, big linen handkerchiefs for Lincoln.

He saw, when he arrived in the apartment, that Marion had accepted the inevitable. She greeted him now as though he were a recalcitrant member of the family, rather than a menacing outsider. Honoria had been told she was going; Charlie was glad to see that her tact made her conceal her excessive happiness. Only on his lap did she whisper her delight and the question "When?" before she slipped away with the other children.

He and Marion were alone for a minute in the room, and on an impulse he spoke out boldly:

"Family quarrels are bitter things. They don't go according to any rules. They're not aches or wounds; they're more like splits in the skin that won't heal because there's not enough material. I wish you and I could be on better terms."

"Some things are hard to forget," she answered. "It's a question of confidence." There was no answer to this and presently she asked, "When do you propose to take her?"

"As soon as I can get a governess. I hoped the day after tomorrow."

"That's impossible. I've got to get her things in shape. Not before Saturday."

He yielded. Coming back into the room, Lincoln offered him a drink.

"I'll take my daily whisky," he said.

It was warm here, it was a home, people together by a fire. The children felt very safe and important; the mother and father were serious, watchful. They had things to do for the children more important than his visit here. A spoonful of medicine was, after all, more important than the strained relations between Marion and himself. They were not dull people, but they were very much in the grip of life and circumstances. He wondered if he couldn't do something to get Lincoln out of his rut at the bank.

A long peal at the door-bell; the *bonne à tout faire* passed through and went down the corridor. The door opened upon another long ring, and then voices, and the three in the salon looked up expectantly; Richard moved to bring the corridor within his range of vision, and Marion rose. Then the maid came back along the corridor, closely followed by the voices, which developed under the light into Duncan Schaeffer and Lorraine Quarrles.

They were gay, they were hilarious, they were roaring with laughter. For a moment Charlie was astounded; unable to understand how they ferreted out the Peters' address.

"Ah-h-h-!" Duncan wagged his finger roguishly at Charlie. "Ah-h-h!"

They both slid down another cascade of laughter. Anxious and at a loss, Charlie shook hands with them quickly and presented them to Lincoln and Marion. Marion nodded, scarcely speaking. She had drawn back a step toward the fire; her little girl stood beside her, and Marion put an arm about her shoulder.

With growing annoyance at the intrusion, Charlie waited for them to explain themselves. After some concentration Duncan said:

"We came to invite you out to dinner. Lorraine and I insist that all this shishi, cagy business 'bout your address got to stop."

Charlie came closer to them, as if to force them backward down the corridor.

"Sorry, but I can't. Tell me where you'll be and I'll phone you in half an hour."

This made no impression. Lorraine sat down suddenly on the side of a chair, and focusing her eyes on Richard, cried, "Oh, what a nice little boy! Come here, little boy." Richard glanced at his mother, but did not move. With a perceptible shrug of her shoulders, Lorraine turned back to Charlie:

"Come and dine. Sure your cousins won' mine. See you so sel'om. Or solemn."

"I can't," said Charlie sharply. "You two have dinner and I'll phone you."

Her voice became suddenly unpleasant. "All right, we'll go. But I remember once when you hammered on my door at four A.M. I was enough of a good sport to give you a drink. Come on, Dunc."

Still in slow motion, with blurred, angry faces, with uncertain feet, they retired along the corridor.

"Good night," Charlie said.

"Good night!" responded Lorraine emphatically.

When he went back into the salon Marion had not moved, only now her son was standing in the circle of her other arm. Lincoln was still swinging Honoria back and forth like a pendulum from side to side.

"What an outrage!" Charlie broke out. "What an absolute outrage!"

Neither of them answered. Charlie dropped into an armchair, picked up his drink, set it down again and said:

"People I haven't seen for two years having the colossal nerve—"

He broke off. Marion had made the sound "Oh!" in one swift, furious breath, turned her body from him with a jerk and left the room.

Lincoln set down Honoria carefully.

"You children go in and start your soup," he said, and when they obeyed, he said to Charlie:

"Marion's not well and she can't stand shocks. That kind of people make her really physically sick."

"I didn't tell them to come here. They wormed your name out of somebody. They deliberately—"

"Well, it's too bad. It doesn't help matters. Excuse me a minute."

Left alone, Charlie sat tense in his chair. In the next room he could hear the children eating, talking in monosyllables, already oblivious to the scene between their elders. He heard a murmur of conversation from a farther room and then the ticking bell of a telephone receiver picked up, and in a panic he moved to the other side of the room and out of earshot.

In a minute Lincoln came back. "Look here, Charlie. I think we'd better call off dinner for tonight. Marion's in bad shape."

"Is she angry with me?"

"Sort of," he said, almost roughly. "She's not strong and—"

"You mean she's changed her mind about Honoria?"

"She's pretty bitter right now. I don't know. You phone me at the bank tomorrow."

"I wish you'd explain to her I never dreamed these people would come here. I'm just as sore as you are."

"I couldn't explain anything to her now."

Charlie got up. He took his coat and hat and started down the corridor. Then he opened the door of the dining room and said in a strange voice, "Good night, children."

Honoria rose and ran around the table to hug him.

"Good night, sweetheart," he said vaguely, and then trying to make his voice more tender, trying to conciliate something, "Good night, dear children."

v

Charlie went directly to the Ritz bar with the furious idea of finding Lorraine and Duncan, but they were not there, and he realized that in any case there was nothing he could do. He had not touched his drink at the Peters, and now he ordered a whisky-and-soda. Paul came over to say hello.

"It's a great change," he said sadly. "We do about half the business we did. So many fellows I hear about back in the States lost everything, maybe not in the first crash, but then in the second. Your friend George Hardt lost every cent, I hear. Are you back in the States?"

"No, I'm in business in Prague."

"I heard that you lost a lot in the crash."

"I did," and he added grimly, "but I lost everything I wanted in the boom."

"Selling short."

"Something like that."

Again the memory of those days swept over him like a nightmare— the people they had met travelling; then people who couldn't add a row of figures or speak a coherent sentence. The little man Helen had consented to dance with at the ship's party, who had insulted her ten feet from the table; the women and girls carried screaming with drink or drugs out of public places—

—The men who locked their wives out in the snow, because the snow of twenty-nine wasn't real snow. If you didn't want it to be snow, you just paid some money.

He went to the phone and called the Peters' apartment; Lincoln answered.

"I called up because this thing is on my mind. Has Marion said anything definite?"

"Marion's sick," Lincoln answered shortly. "I know this thing isn't altogether your fault, but I can't have her go to pieces about it. I'm afraid we'll have to let it slide for six months; I can't take the chance of working her up to this state again."

"I see."

"I'm sorry, Charlie."

He went back to his table. His whisky glass was empty, but he shook his head when Alix looked at it questioningly. There wasn't much he could do now except send Honoria some things; he would send her a lot of things tomorrow. He thought rather angrily that this was just money—he had given so many people money. . . .

"No, no more," he said to another waiter. "What do I owe you?"

He would come back some day; they couldn't make him pay forever. But he wanted his child, and nothing was much good now, beside that fact. He wasn't young any more, with a lot of nice thoughts and dreams to have by himself. He was absolutely sure Helen wouldn't have wanted him to be so alone.

WILLIAM FAULKNER
1897–1963
A Rose for Emily

I

When Miss Emily Grierson died, our whole town went to her funeral: the men through a sort of respectful affection for a fallen monument, the women mostly out of curiosity to see the inside of her house, which no one save an old manservant—a combined gardener and cook—had seen in at least ten years.

It was a big, squarish frame house that had once been white, decorated with cupolas and spires and scrolled balconies in the heavily lightsome style of the seventies, set on what had once been our most select street. But garages and cotton gins had encroached and obliterated even the august names of that neighborhood; only Miss Emily's house was left, lifting its stubborn and coquettish decay above the cotton wagons and the gasoline pumps—an eyesore among eyesores. And now Miss Emily had gone to join the representatives of those august names where they lay in the cedar-bemused cemetery among the ranked and anonymous graves of Union and Confederate soldiers who fell at the battle of Jefferson.

Alive, Miss Emily had been a tradition, a duty, and a care; a sort of hereditary obligation upon the town, dating from that day in 1894 when Colonel Sartoris, the mayor—he who fathered the edict that no Negro woman should appear on the streets without an apron— remitted her taxes, the dispensation dating from the death of her father on into perpetuity. Not that Miss Emily would have accepted charity. Colonel Sartoris invented an involved tale to the effect that Miss Emily's father had loaned money to the town, which the town, as a matter of business, preferred this way of repaying. Only a man of Colonel Sartoris' generation and thought could have invented it, and only a woman could have believed it.

When the next generation, with its more modern ideas, became mayors and aldermen, this arrangement created some little dissatisfaction. On the first of the year they mailed her a tax notice. February came, and there was no reply. They wrote her a formal letter, asking her to call at the sheriff's office at her convenience. A week later the mayor wrote her himself, offering to call or to send his car for her, and received in reply a note on paper of an archaic shape, in a thin, flowing calligraphy in faded ink, to the effect that she no longer went out at all. The tax notice was also enclosed, without comment.

They called a special meeting of the Board of Aldermen. A deputation waited upon her, knocked at the door through which no visitor had passed since she ceased giving china-painting lessons eight or ten years earlier. They were admitted by the old Negro into a dim hall from which a stairway mounted into still more shadow. It smelled of dust and disuse—a close, dank smell. The Negro led them into the parlor. It was furnished in heavy, leather-covered furniture. When the Negro opened the blinds of one window, they could see that the leather was cracked; and when they sat down, a faint dust rose sluggishly about their thighs, spinning with slow motions in the single sun-ray. On a tarnished gilt easel before the fireplace stood a crayon portrait of Miss Emily's father.

They rose when she entered—a small, fat woman in black, with a thin gold chain descending to her waist and vanishing into her belt, leaning on an ebony cane with a tarnished gold head. Her skeleton was small and spare; perhaps that was why what would have been merely plumpness in another was obesity in her. She looked bloated, like a body long submerged in motionless water, and of that pallid hue. Her eyes, lost in the fatty ridges of her face, looked like two small pieces of coal pressed into a lump of dough as they moved from one face to another while the visitors stated their errand.

She did not ask them to sit. She just stood in the door and listened quietly until the spokesman came to a stumbling halt. Then they could hear the invisible watch ticking at the end of the gold chain.

Her voice was dry and cold. "I have no taxes in Jefferson. Colonel Sartoris explained it to me. Perhaps one of you can gain access to the city records and satisfy yourselves."

"But we have. We are the city authorities, Miss Emily. Didn't you get a notice from the sheriff, signed by him?"

"I received a paper, yes," Miss Emily said. "Perhaps he considers himself the sheriff . . . I have no taxes in Jefferson."

"But there is nothing on the books to show that, you see. We must go by the—"

"See Colonel Sartoris." (Colonel Sartoris had been dead almost ten years.) "I have no taxes in Jefferson. Tobe!" The Negro appeared. "Show these gentlemen out."

II

So she vanquished them, horse and foot, just as she had vanquished their fathers thirty years before about the smell. That was two years after her father's death and a short time after her sweetheart—the one we believed would marry her—had deserted her. After her father's death she went out very little; after her sweetheart went away, people hardly saw her at all. A few of the ladies had the temerity to call, but were not received, and the only sign of life about the place was the Negro man—a young man then—going in and out with a market basket.

"Just as if a man—any man—could keep a kitchen properly," the ladies said; so they were not surprised when the smell developed. It was another link between the gross, teeming world and the high and mighty Griersons.

A neighbor, a woman, complained to the mayor, Judge Stevens, eighty years old.

"But what will you have me do about it, madam?" he said.

"Why, send her word to stop it," the woman said. "Isn't there a law?"

"I'm sure that won't be necessary," Judge Stevens said. "It's probably just a snake or a rat that nigger of hers killed in the yard. I'll speak to him about it."

The next day he received two more complaints, one from a man who came in diffident deprecation. "We really must do something about it, Judge. I'd be the last one in the world to bother Miss Emily, but we've got to do something." That night the Board of Aldermen met—three graybeards and one younger man, a member of the rising generation.

"It's simple enough," he said. "Send her word to have her place cleaned up. Give her a certain time to do it in, and if she don't . . ."

"Dammit, sir," Judge Stevens said, "will you accuse a lady to her face of smelling bad?"

So the next night, after midnight, four men crossed Miss Emily's lawn and slunk about the house like burglars, sniffing along the base of the brickwork and at the cellar openings while one of them performed a regular sowing motion with his hand out of a sack slung from his shoulder. They broke open the cellar door and sprinkled lime there, and in all the outbuildings. As they recrossed the lawn, a window that had been dark was lighted and Miss Emily sat in it, the light behind her, and her upright torso motionless as that of an idol. They crept quietly across the lawn and into the shadow of the locusts that lined the street. After a week or two the smell went away.

That was when people had begun to feel really sorry for her. People in our town, remembering how old lady Wyatt, her great-aunt, had gone completely crazy at last, believed that the Griersons held themselves a little too high for what they really were. None of the young men were quite good enough for Miss Emily and such. We had long thought of them as a tableau, Miss Emily a slender figure in white in the background, her father a spraddled silhouette in the fore-ground, his back to her and clutching a horsewhip, the two of them framed by the back-flung front door. So when she got to be thirty and was still single, we were not pleased exactly, but vindicated; even with insanity in the family she wouldn't have turned down all of her chances if they had really materialized.

When her father died, it got about that the house was all that was left to her; and in a way, people were glad. At last they could pity Miss Emily. Being left alone, and a pauper, she had become humanized. Now she too would know the old thrill and the old despair of a penny more or less.

The day after his death all the ladies prepared to call at the house and offer condolence and aid, as is our custom. Miss Emily met them at the door, dressed as usual and with no trace of grief on her face. She told them that her father was not dead. She did that for three days, with the ministers calling on her, and the doctors, trying to persuade her to let them dispose of the body. Just as they were about to resort to law and force, she broke down, and they buried her father quickly.

We did not say she was crazy then. We believed she had to do that. We remembered all the young men her father had driven away, and we knew that with nothing left, she would have to cling to that which had robbed her, as people will.

III

She was sick for a long time. When we saw her again, her hair was cut short, making her look like a girl, with a vague resemblance to those angels in colored church windows—sort of tragic and serene.

The town had just let the contracts for paving the sidewalks, and in the summer after her father's death they began the work. The construction company came with niggers and mules and machinery, and a foreman named Homer Barron, a Yankee—a big, dark, ready man, with a big voice and eyes lighter than his face. The little boys would follow in groups to hear him cuss the niggers, and the niggers singing in time to the rise and fall of picks. Pretty soon he knew everybody in town. Whenever you heard a lot of laughing anywhere about the square, Homer Barron would be in the center of the group. Presently we began to see him and Miss Emily on Sunday afternoons driving in the yellow-wheeled buggy and the matched team of bays from the livery stable.

At first we were glad that Miss Emily would have an interest, because the ladies all said, "Of course a Grierson would not think seriously of a Northerner, a day laborer." But there were still others, older people, who said that even grief could not cause a real lady to forget noblesse oblige—without calling it noblesse oblige. They just said, "Poor Emily. Her kinsfolk should come to her." She had some kin in Alabama; but years ago her father had fallen out with them over the estate of old lady Wyatt, the crazy woman, and there was no communication between the two families. They had not even been represented at the funeral.

And as soon as the old people said, "Poor Emily," the whispering began. "Do you suppose it's really so?" they said to one another. "Of course it is. What else could . . ." This behind their hands; rustling of craned silk and satin behind jalousies closed upon the sun of Sunday afternoon as the thin, swift clop-clop-clop of the matched team passed: "Poor Emily."

She carried her head high enough—even when we believed that she was fallen. It was as if she demanded more than ever the recognition of her dignity as the last Grierson; as if it had wanted that touch of earthiness to reaffirm her imperviousness. Like when she bought the rat poison, the arsenic. That was over a year after they had begun to say "Poor Emily," and while the two female cousins were visiting her.

"I want some poison," she said to the druggist. She was over thirty then, still a slight woman, though thinner than usual, with cold, haughty black eyes in a face the flesh of which was strained across the temples and about the eye-sockets as you imagine a lighthouse-keeper's face ought to look. "I want some poison," she said.

"Yes, Miss Emily. What kind? For rats and such? I'd recom—"

"I want the best you have. I don't care what kind."

The druggist named several. "They'll kill anything up to an elephant. But what you want is—"

"Arsenic," Miss Emily said. "Is that a good one?"

"Is . . . arsenic? Yes, ma'am. But what you want—"

"I want arsenic."

The druggist looked down at her. She looked back at him, erect, her face like a strained flag. "Why, of course," the druggist said. "If that's what you want. But the law requires you to tell what you are going to use it for."

Miss Emily just stared at him, her head tilted back in order to look him eye for eye, until he looked away and went and got the arsenic and wrapped it up. The Negro delivery boy brought her the package; the druggist didn't come back. When she opened the package at home there was written on the box, under the skull and bones: "For rats."

IV

So the next day we all said, "She will kill herself"; and we said it would be the best thing. When she had first begun to be seen with Homer Barron, we had said, "She will marry him." Then we said, "She will persuade him yet," because Homer himself had remarked—he liked men, and it was known that he drank with the younger men in the Elks' Club—that he was not a marrying man. Later we said, "Poor

Emily" behind the jalousies as they passed on Sunday afternoon in the glittering buggy, Miss Emily with her head high and Homer Barron with his hat cocked and a cigar in his teeth, reins and whip in a yellow glove.

Then some of the ladies began to say that it was a disgrace to the town and a bad example to the young people. The men did not want to interfere, but at last the ladies forced the Baptist minister—Miss Emily's people were Episcopal—to call upon her. He would never divulge what happened during that interview, but he refused to go back again. The next Sunday they again drove about the streets, and the following day the minister's wife wrote to Miss Emily's relations in Alabama.

So she had blood-kin under her roof again and we sat back to watch developments. At first nothing happened. Then we were sure that they were to be married. We learned that Miss Emily had been to the jeweler's and ordered a man's toilet set in silver, with the letters H.B. on each piece. Two days later we learned that she had bought a complete outfit of men's clothing, including a nightshirt, and we said, "They are married." We were really glad. We were glad because the two female cousins were even more Grierson than Miss Emily had ever been.

So we were not surprised when Homer Barron—the streets had been finished some time since—was gone. We were a little disappointed that there was not a public blowing-off, but we believed that he had gone on to prepare for Miss Emily's coming, or to give her a chance to get rid of the cousins. (By that time it was a cabal, and we were all Miss Emily's allies to help circumvent the cousins.) Sure enough, after another week they departed. And, as we had expected all along, within three days Homer Barron was back in town. A neighbor saw the Negro man admit him at the kitchen door at dusk one evening.

And that was the last we saw of Homer Barron. And of Miss Emily for some time. The Negro man went in and out with the market basket, but the front door remained closed. Now and then we would see her at a window for a moment, as the men did that night when they sprinkled the lime, but for almost six months she did not appear on the streets. Then we knew that this was to be expected too; as if that quality of her father which had thwarted her woman's life so many times had been too virulent and too furious to die.

When we next saw Miss Emily, she had grown fat and her hair was turning gray. During the next few years it grew grayer and grayer until it attained an even pepper-and-salt iron-gray, when it ceased turning. Up to the day of her death at seventy-four it was still that vigorous iron-gray, like the hair of an active man.

From that time on her front door remained closed, save for a period of six or seven years, when she was about forty, during which she gave lessons in china-painting. She fitted up a studio in one of the downstairs rooms, where the daughters and granddaughters of Colonel Sartoris' contemporaries were sent to her with the same regularity and in the same spirit that they were sent to church on Sundays with a twenty-five-cent piece for the collection plate. Meanwhile her taxes had been remitted.

Then the newer generation became the backbone and the spirit of the town, and the painting pupils grew up and fell away and did not send their children to her with boxes of color and tedious brushes and pictures cut from the ladies' magazines. The front door closed upon the last one and remained closed for good. When the town got free postal delivery, Miss Emily alone refused to let them fasten the metal numbers above her door and attach a mailbox to it. She would not listen to them.

Daily, monthly, yearly we watched the Negro grow grayer and more stooped, going in and out with the market basket. Each December we sent her a tax notice, which would be returned by the post office a week later, unclaimed. Now and then we would see her in one of the downstairs windows—she had evidently shut up the top floor of the house—like the carven torso of an idol in a niche, looking or not looking at us, we could never tell which. Thus she passed from generation to generation—dear, inescapable, impervious, tranquil, and perverse.

And so she died. Fell ill in the house filled with dust and shadows, with only a doddering Negro man to wait on her. We did not even know she was sick; we had long since given up trying to get any information from the Negro. He talked to no one, probably not even to her, for his voice had grown harsh and rusty, as if from disuse.

She died in one of the downstairs rooms, in a heavy walnut bed with a curtain, her gray head propped on a pillow yellow and moldy with age and lack of sunlight.

V

The Negro met the first of the ladies at the front door and let them in, with their hushed, sibilant voices and their quick, curious glances, and then he disappeared. He walked right through the house and out the back and was not seen again.

The two female cousins came at once. They held the funeral on the second day, with the town coming to look at Miss Emily beneath a mass of bought flowers, with the crayon face of her father musing profoundly above the bier and the ladies sibilant and macabre; and the very old men—some in their brushed Confederate uniforms—on the porch and the lawn, talking of Miss Emily as if she had been a contemporary of theirs, believing that they had danced with her and courted her perhaps, confusing time with its mathematical progression, as the old do, to whom all the past is not a diminishing road but, instead, a huge meadow which no winter ever quite touches, divided from them now by the narrow bottle-neck of the most recent decade of years.

Already we knew that there was one room in that region above stairs which no one had seen in forty years, and which would have to be forced. They waited until Miss Emily was decently in the ground before they opened it.

The violence of breaking down the door seemed to fill this room with pervading dust. A thin, acrid pall as of the tomb seemed to lie everywhere upon this room decked and furnished as for a bridal: upon the valance curtains of faded rose color, upon the rose-shaded lights, upon the dressing table, upon the delicate array of crystal and the man's toilet things backed with tarnished silver, silver so tarnished that the monogram was obscured. Among them lay a collar and tie, as if they had just been removed, which, lifted, left upon the surface a pale crescent in the dust. Upon a chair hung the suit, carefully folded; beneath it the two mute shoes and the discarded socks.

The man himself lay in the bed.

For a long while we just stood there, looking down at the profound and fleshless grin. The body had apparently once lain in the attitude of an embrace, but now the long sleep that outlasts love, that conquers even the grimace of love, had cuckolded him. What was left of him, rotted beneath what was left of the nightshirt, had become inextricable from the bed in which he lay; and upon him and upon the pillow beside him lay that even coating of the patient and biding dust.

Then we noticed that in the second pillow was the indentation of a head. One of us lifted something from it, and leaning forward, that faint and invisible dust dry and acrid in the nostrils, we saw a long strand of iron-gray hair.

ERNEST HEMINGWAY

1899–1961

Hills like White Elephants

The hills across the valley of the Ebro were long and white. On this side there was no shade and no trees and the station was between two lines of rails in the sun. Close against the side of the station there was the warm shadow of the building and a curtain, made of strings of bamboo beads, hung across the open door into the bar, to keep out flies. The American and the girl with him sat at a table in the shade, outside the building. It was very hot and the express from Barcelona would come in forty minutes. It stopped at this junction for two minutes and went on to Madrid.

"What should we drink?" the girl asked. She had taken off her hat and put it on the table.

"It's pretty hot," the man said.

"Let's drink beer."

"Dos cervezas," the man said into the curtain.

"Big ones?" a woman asked from the doorway.

"Yes. Two big ones."

The woman brought two glasses of beer and two felt pads. She put the felt pads and the beer glasses on the table and looked at the man and the girl. The girl was looking off at the line of hills. They were white in the sun and the country was brown and dry.

"They look like white elephants," she said.

"I've never seen one," the man drank his beer.

"No, you wouldn't have."

"I might have," the man said. "Just because you say I wouldn't have doesn't prove anything."

The girl looked at the bead curtain. "They've painted something on it," she said. "What does it say?"

"Anis del Toro. It's a drink."

"Could we try it?"

The man called "Listen" through the curtain. The woman came out from the bar.

"Four reales."

"We want two Anis del Toro."

"With water?"

"Do you want it with water?"

"I don't know," the girl said. "Is it good with water?"

"It's all right."

"You want them with water?" asked the woman.

"Yes, with water."

"It tastes like licorice," the girl said and put the glass down.

"That's the way with everything."

"Yes," said the girl. "Everything tastes of licorice. Especially all the things you've waited so long for, like absinthe."

"Oh, cut it out."

"You started it," the girl said. "I was being amused. I was having a fine time."

"Well, let's try and have a fine time."

"All right. I was trying. I said the mountains looked like white elephants. Wasn't that bright?"

"That was bright."

"I wanted to try this new drink. That's all we do, isn't it—look at things and try new drinks?"

"I guess so."

The girl looked across at the hills.

"They're lovely hills," she said. "They don't really look like white elephants. I just meant the coloring of their skin through the trees."

"Should we have another drink?"

"All right."

The warm wind blew the bead curtain against the table.

"The beer's nice and cool," the man said.

"It's lovely," the girl said.

"It's really an awfully simple operation, Jig," the man said. "It's not really an operation at all."

The girl looked at the ground the table legs rested on.

"I know you wouldn't mind it, Jig. It's really not anything. It's just to let the air in."

The girl did not say anything.

"I'll go with you and I'll stay with you all the time. They just let the air in and then it's all perfectly natural."

"Then what will we do afterward?"

"We'll be fine afterward. Just like we were before."

"What makes you think so?"

"That's the only thing that bothers us. It's the only thing that's made us unhappy."

The girl looked at the bead curtain, put her hand out and took hold of two of the strings of beads.

"And you think then we'll be all right and be happy."

"I know we will. You don't have to be afraid. I've known lots of people that have done it."

"So have I," said the girl. "And afterward they were all so happy."

"Well," the man said, "if you don't want to you don't have to. I wouldn't have you do it if you didn't want to. But I know it's perfectly simple."

"And you really want to?"

"I think it's the best thing to do. But I don't want you to do it if you don't really want to."

"And if I do it you'll be happy and things will be like they were and you'll love me?"

"I love you now. You know I love you."

"I know. But if I do it, then it will be nice again if I say things are like white elephants, and you'll like it?"

"I'll love it. I love it now but I just can't think about it. You know how I get when I worry."

"If I do it you won't ever worry?"

"I won't worry about that because it's perfectly simple."

"Then I'll do it. Because I don't care about me."

"What do you mean?"

"I don't care about me."

"Well, I care about you."

"Oh, yes. But I don't care about me. And I'll do it and then everything will be fine."

"I don't want you to do it if you feel that way."

The girl stood up and walked to the end of the station. Across, on the other side, were fields of grain and trees along the banks of the Ebro. Far away, beyond the river, were mountains. The shadow of a cloud moved across the field of grain and she saw the river through the trees.

"And we could have all this," she said. "And we could have everything and every day we make it more impossible."

"What did you say?"

"I said we could have everything."

"We can have everything."

"No, we can't."

"We can have the whole world."

"No, we can't."

"We can go everywhere."

"No, we can't. It isn't ours any more."

"It's ours."

"No, it isn't. And once they take it away, you never get it back."

"But they haven't taken it away."

"We'll wait and see."

"Come on back in the shade," he said. "You mustn't feel that way."

"I don't feel any way," the girl said. "I just know things."

"I don't want you to do anything that you don't want to do—"

"Nor that isn't good for me," she said. "I know. Could we have another beer?"

"All right. But you've got to realize—"

"I realize," the girl said. "Can't we maybe stop talking?"

They sat down at the table and the girl looked across at the hills on the dry side of the valley and the man looked at her and at the table.

"You've got to realize," he said, "that I don't want you to do it if you don't want to. I'm perfectly willing to go through with it if it means anything to you."

"Doesn't it mean anything to you? We could get along."

"Of course it does. But I don't want anybody but you. I don't want any one else. And I know it's perfectly simple."

"Yes, you know it's perfectly simple."

"It's all right for you to say that, but I do know it."

"Would you do something for me now?"

"I'd do anything for you."

"Would you please please please please please please please stop talking?"

He did not say anything but looked at the bags against the wall of the station. There were labels on them from all the hotels where they had spent nights.

"But I don't want you to," he said, "I don't care anything about it."

"I'll scream," the girl said.

The woman came out through the curtains with two glasses of beer and put them down on the damp felt pads. "The train comes in five minutes," she said.

"What did she say?" asked the girl.

"That the train is coming in five minutes."

The girl smiled brightly at the woman, to thank her.

"I'd better take the bags over to the other side of the station," the man said. She smiled at him.

"All right. Then come back and we'll finish the beer."

He picked up the two heavy bags and carried them around the station to the other tracks. He looked up the tracks but could not see the train. Coming back, he walked through the barroom, where people waiting for the train were drinking. He drank an Anis at the bar and looked at the people. They were all waiting reasonably for the train. He went out through the bead curtain. She was sitting at the table and smiled at him.

"Do you feel better?" he asked.

"I feel fine," she said. "There's nothing wrong with me. I feel fine."

FRANK O'CONNOR
1903–1966
Guests of the Nation

I

At dusk the big Englishman, Belcher, would shift his long legs out of the ashes and say "Well, chums, what about it?" and Noble or me would say "All right, chum" (for we had picked up some of their curious expressions), and the little Englishman, Hawkins, would light the lamp and bring out the cards. Sometimes Jeremiah Donovan would come up and supervise the game and get excited over Hawkins's cards, which he always played badly, and shout at him as if he was one of our own, "Ah, you divil, you, why didn't you play the tray?"

But ordinarily Jeremiah was a sober and contented poor devil like the big Englishman, Belcher, and was looked up to only because he was a fair hand at documents, though he was slow enough even with them. He wore a small cloth hat and big gaiters over his long pants, and you seldom saw him with his hands out of his pockets. He reddened when you talked to him, tilting from toe to heel and back, and looking down all the time at his big farmer's feet. Noble and me used to make fun of his broad accent, because we were from the town.

I couldn't at the time see the point of me and Noble guarding Belcher and Hawkins at all, for it was my belief that you could have planted that pair down anywhere from this to Claregalway and they'd have taken root there like a native weed. I never in my short experience seen two men to take to the country as they did.

They were handed on to us by the Second Battalion when the search for them became too hot, and Noble and myself, being young, took over with a natural feeling of responsibility, but Hawkins made us look like fools when he showed that he knew the country better than we did.

"You're the bloke they calls Bonaparte," he says to me. "Mary Brigid O'Connell told me to ask you what you done with the pair of her brother's socks you borrowed."

For it seemed, as they explained it, that the Second used to have little evenings, and some of the girls of the neighborhood turned in, and, seeing they were such decent chaps, our fellows couldn't leave the two Englishmen out of them. Hawkins learned to dance "The Walls of Limerick," "The Siege of Ennis," and "The Waves of Tory" as well as any of them, though, naturally, we couldn't return the compliment, because our lads at that time did not dance foreign dances on principle.

So whatever privileges Belcher and Hawkins had with the Second they just naturally took with us, and after the first day or two we gave up all pretense of keeping a close eye on them. Not that they could have got far, for they had accents you could cut with a knife and wore khaki tunics and overcoats with civilian pants and boots. But it's my belief that they never had any idea of escaping and were quite content to be where they were.

It was a treat to see how Belcher got off with the old woman of the house where we were staying. She was a great warrant to scold, and cranky even with us, but before ever she had a chance of giving our guests, as I may call them, a lick of her tongue, Belcher had made her his friend for life. She was breaking sticks, and Belcher, who hadn't been more than ten minutes in the house, jumped up from his seat and went over to her.

"Allow me, madam," he says, smiling his queer little smile, "please allow me"; and he takes the bloody hatchet. She was struck too paralytic to speak, and after that, Belcher would be at her heels, carrying a bucket, a basket, or a load of turf, as the case might be. As Noble said, he got into looking before she leapt, and hot water, or any little thing she wanted, Belcher would have it ready for her. For such a huge man (and though I am five foot ten myself I had to look up at him) he had an uncommon shortness—or should I say lack?—of speech. It took us some time to get used to him, walking in and out, like a ghost, without a word. Especially because Hawkins talked enough for a platoon, it was strange to hear big Belcher with his toes in the ashes come out with a solitary "Excuse me, chum," or "That's right, chum." His one and only passion was cards, and I will say for him that he was a good cardplayer. He could have fleeced myself and Noble, but whatever we lost to him Hawkins lost to us, and Hawkins played with the money Belcher gave him.

Hawkins lost to us because he had too much old gab, and we probably lost to Belcher for the same reason. Hawkins and Noble would spit at one another about religion into the early hours of the morning, and Hawkins worried the soul out of Noble, whose brother was a priest, with a string of questions that would puzzle a cardinal. To make it worse, even in treating of holy subjects, Hawkins had a deplorable tongue. I never in all my career met a man who could mix such a variety of cursing and bad language into an argument. He was a terrible man, and a fright to argue. He never did a stroke of work, and when he had no one else to talk to, he got stuck in the old woman.

He met his match in her, for one day when he tried to get her to complain profanely of the drought, she gave him a great come-down by blaming it entirely on Jupiter Pluvius (a deity neither Hawkins nor I had ever heard of, though Noble said that among the pagans it was believed that he had something to do with the rain). Another day he was swearing at the capitalists for starting the German war when the old lady laid down her iron, puckered up her little crab's mouth, and said: "Mr. Hawkins, you can say what you like about the war, and think you'll deceive me because I'm only a simple poor country-woman, but I know what started the war. It was the Italian Count that stole the heathen divinity out of the temple in Japan. Believe me, Mr. Hawkins, nothing but sorrow and want can follow the people that disturb the hidden powers."

A queer old girl, all right.

II

We had our tea one evening, and Hawkins lit the lamp and we all sat into cards. Jeremiah Donovan came in too, and sat down and watched us for a while, and it suddenly struck me that he had no great love for the two Englishmen. It came as a great surprise to me, because I hadn't noticed anything about him before.

Late in the evening a really terrible argument blew up between Hawkins and Noble, about capitalists and priests and love of your country.

"The capitalists," says Hawkins with an angry gulp, "pays the priests to tell you about the next world so as you won't notice what the bastards are up to in this."

"Nonsense, man!" says Noble, losing his temper. "Before ever a capitalist was thought of, people believed in the next world."

Hawkins stood up as though he was preaching a sermon.

"Oh, they did, did they?" he says with a sneer. "They believed all the things you believe, isn't that what you mean? And you believe that God created Adam, and Adam created Shem, and Shem created Jehoshaphat. You believe all that silly old fairytale about Eve and Eden and the apple. Well, listen to me, chum. If you're entitled to hold a silly belief like that, I'm entitled to hold my silly belief—which is that the first thing your God created was a bleeding capitalist, with morality and Rolls-Royce complete. Am I right, chum?" he says to Belcher.

"You're right, chum," says Belcher with his amused smile, and got up from the table to stretch his long legs into the fire and stroke his moustache. So, seeing that Jeremiah Donovan was going, and that there was no knowing when the argument about religion would be over, I went out with him. We strolled down to the village together, and then he stopped and started blushing and mumbling and saying I ought to be behind, keeping guard on the prisoners. I didn't like the tone he took with me, and anyway I was bored with life in the cottage, so I replied by asking him what the hell we wanted guarding them at all for. I told him I'd talked it over with Noble, and that we'd both rather be out with a fighting column.

"What use are those fellows to us?" says I.

He looked at me in surprise and said: "I thought you knew we were keeping them as hostages."

"Hostages?" I said.

"The enemy have prisoners belonging to us," he says, "and now they're talking of shooting them. If they shoot our prisoners, we'll shoot theirs."

"Shoot them?" I said.

"What else did you think we were keeping them for?" he says.

"Wasn't it very unforeseen of you not to warn Noble and myself of that in the beginning?" I said.

"How was it?" says he. "You might have known it."

"We couldn't know it, Jeremiah Donovan," says I. "How could we when they were on our hands so long?"

"The enemy have our prisoners as long and longer," says he.

"That's not the same thing at all," says I.

"What difference is there?" says he.

I couldn't tell him, because I knew he wouldn't understand. If it was only an old dog that was going to the vet's, you'd try and not get too fond of him, but Jeremiah Donovan wasn't a man that would ever be in danger of that.

"And when is this thing going to be decided?" says I.

"We might hear tonight," he says. "Or tomorrow or the next day at latest. So if it's only hanging round here that's a trouble to you, you'll be free soon enough."

It wasn't the hanging round that was a trouble to me at all by this time. I had worse things to worry about. When I got back to the cottage the argument was still on. Hawkins was holding forth in his best style, maintaining that there was no next world, and Noble was maintaining that there was; but I could see that Hawkins had had the best of it.

"Do you know what, chum?" he was saying with a saucy smile. "I think you're just as big a bleeding unbeliever as I am. You say you believe in the next world, and you know just as much about the next world as I do, which is sweet damn-all. What's heaven? You don't know. Where's heaven? You don't know. You know sweet damn-all! I ask you again, do they wear wings?"

"Very well, then," says Noble, "they do. Is that enough for you? They do wear wings."

"Where do they get them, then? Who makes them? Have they a factory for wings? Have they a sort of store where you hands in your chit and takes your bleeding wings?"

"You're an impossible man to argue with," says Noble. "Now, listen to me—" And they were off again.

It was long after midnight when we locked up and went to bed. As I blew out the candle I told Noble what Jeremiah Donovan was after telling me. Noble took it very quietly. When we'd been in bed about an hour he asked me did I think we ought to tell the Englishmen. I didn't think we should, because it was more than likely that the English wouldn't shoot our men, and even if they did, the brigade officers, who were always up and down with the Second Battalion and knew the Englishmen well, wouldn't be likely to want them plugged. "I think so too," says Noble. "It would be great cruelty to put the wind up them now."

"It was very unforeseen of Jeremiah Donovan anyhow," says I.

It was next morning that we found it so hard to face Belcher and Hawkins. We went about the house all day scarcely saying a word.

Belcher didn't seem to notice; he was stretched into the ashes as usual, with his usual look of waiting in quietness for something unforeseen to happen, but Hawkins noticed and put it down to Noble's being beaten in the argument of the night before.

"Why can't you take a discussion in the proper spirit?" he says severely. "You and your Adam and Eve! I'm a Communist, that's what I am. Communist or anarchist, it all comes to much the same thing." And for hours he went round the house, muttering when the fit took him. "Adam and Eve! Adam and Eve! Nothing better to do with their time than picking bleeding apples!"

III

I don't know how we got through that day, but I was very glad when it was over, the tea things were cleared away, and Belcher said in his peaceable way: "Well, chums, what about it?" We sat round the table and Hawkins took out the cards, and just then I heard Jeremiah Donovan's footstep on the path and a dark presentiment crossed my mind. I rose from the table and caught him before he reached the door.

"What do you want?" I asked.

"I want those two soldier friends of yours," he says, getting red.

"Is that the way, Jeremiah Donovan?" I asked.

"That's the way. There were four of our lads shot this morning, one of them a boy of sixteen."

"That's bad," I said.

At that moment Noble followed me out, and the three of us walked down the path together, talking in whispers. Feeney, the local intelligence officer, was standing by the gate.

"What are you going to do about it?" I asked Jeremiah Donovan.

"I want you and Noble to get them out; tell them they're being shifted again; that'll be the quietest way."

"Leave me out of that," says Noble under his breath.

Jeremiah Donovan looks at him hard.

"All right," he says. "You and Feeney get a few tools from the shed and dig a hole by the far end of the bog. Bonaparte and myself will be after you. Don't let anyone see you with the tools. I wouldn't like it to go beyond ourselves."

We saw Feeney and Noble go round to the shed and went in ourselves. I left Jeremiah Donovan to do the explanations. He told them that he had orders to send them back to the Second Battalion. Hawkins let out a mouthful of curses, and you could see that though Belcher didn't say anything, he was a bit upset too. The old woman was for having them stay in spite of us, and she didn't stop advising them until Jeremiah Donovan lost his temper and turned on her. He had a nasty temper, I noticed. It was pitch-dark in the cottage by this time, but no one thought of lighting the lamp, and in the darkness the two Englishmen fetched their topcoats and said good-bye to the old woman.

"Just as a man makes a home of a bleeding place, some bastard at headquarters thinks you're too cushy and shunts you off," says Hawkins, shaking her hand.

"A thousand thanks, madam," says Belcher. "A thousand thanks for everything"—as though he'd made it up.

We went round to the back of the house and down towards the bog. It was only then that Jeremiah Donovan told them. He was shaking with excitement.

"There were four of our fellows shot in Cork this morning and now you're to be shot as a reprisal."

"What are you talking about?" snaps Hawkins. "It's bad enough being mucked about as we are without having to put up with your funny jokes."

"It isn't a joke," says Donovan. "I'm sorry, Hawkins, but it's true," and begins on the usual rigmarole about duty and how unpleasant it is.

I never noticed that people who talk a lot about duty find it much of a trouble to them.

"Oh, cut it out!" says Hawkins.

"Ask Bonaparte," says Donovan, seeing that Hawkins isn't taking him seriously. "Isn't it true, Bonaparte?"

"It is," I say, and Hawkins stops.

"Ah, for Christ's sake, chum."

"I mean it, chum," I say.

"You don't sound as if you meant it."

"If he doesn't mean it, I do," says Donovan, working himself up.

"What have you against me, Jeremiah Donovan?"

"I never said I had anything against you. But why did your people take out four of our prisoners and shoot them in cold blood?"

He took Hawkins by the arm and dragged him on, but it was impossible to make him understand that we were in earnest. I had the Smith and Wesson in my pocket and I kept fingering it and wondering what I'd do if they put up a fight for it or ran, and wishing to God they'd do one or the other. I knew if they did run for it, that I'd never fire on them. Hawkins wanted to know was Noble in it, and when we said yes, he asked us why Noble wanted to plug him. Why did any of us want to plug him? What had he done to us? Weren't we all chums? Didn't we understand him and didn't he understand us? Did we imagine for an instant that he'd shoot us for all the so-and-so officers in the so-and-so British Army?

By this time we'd reached the bog, and I was so sick I couldn't even answer him. We walked along the edge of it in the darkness, and every now and then Hawkins would call a halt and begin all over again, as if he was wound up, about our being chums, and I knew that nothing but the sight of the grave would convince him that we had to do it. And all the time I was hoping that something would happen; that they'd run for it or that Noble would take over the responsibility from me. I had the feeling that it was worse on Noble than on me.

IV

At last we saw the lantern in the distance and made towards it. Noble was carrying it, and Feeney was standing somewhere in the darkness behind him, and the picture of them so still and silent in the bogland brought it home to me that we were in earnest, and banished the last bit of hope I had.

Belcher, on recognizing Noble, said: "Hallo, chum," in his quiet way, but Hawkins flew at him at once, and the argument began all over again, only this time Noble had nothing to say for himself and stood with his head down, holding the lantern between his legs.

It was Jeremiah Donovan who did the answering. For the twentieth time, as though it was haunting his mind, Hawkins asked if anybody thought he'd shoot Noble.

"Yes, you would," says Jeremiah Donovan.

"No, I wouldn't, damn you!"

"You would, because you'd know you'd be shot for not doing it."

"I wouldn't, not if I was to be shot twenty times over. I wouldn't shoot a pal. And Belcher wouldn't—isn't that right, Belcher?"

"That's right, chum," Belcher said, but more by way of answering the question than of joining in the argument. Belcher sounded as though whatever unforeseen thing he'd always been waiting for had come at last.

"Anyway, who says Noble would be shot if I wasn't? What do you think I'd do if I was in his place, out in the middle of a blasted bog?"

"What would you do?" asks Donovan.

"I'd go with him wherever he was going, of course. Share my last bob with him and stick by him through thick and thin. No one can ever say of me that I let down a pal."

"We had enough of this," says Jeremiah Donovan, cocking his revolver. "Is there any message you want to send?"

"No, there isn't."

"Do you want to say your prayers?"

Hawkins came out with a cold-blooded remark that even shocked me and turned on Noble again.

"Listen to me, Noble," he says. "You and me are chums. You can't come over to my side, so I'll come over to your side. That show you I mean what I say? Give me a rifle and I'll go along with you and the other lads."

Nobody answered him. We knew that was no way out.

"Hear what I'm saying?" he says. "I'm through with it. I'm a deserter or anything else you like. I don't believe in your stuff, but it's no worse then mine. That satisfy you?"

Noble raised his head, but Donovan began to speak and he lowered it again without replying.

"For the last time, have you any messages to send?" says Donovan in a cold, excited sort of voice.

"Shut up, Donovan! You don't understand me, but these lads do. They're not the sort to make a pal and kill a pal. They're not the tools of any capitalist."

I alone of the crowd saw Donovan raise his Webley to the back of Hawkins's neck, and as he did so I shut my eyes and tried to pray. Hawkins had begun to say something else when Donovan fired, and as I opened my eyes at the bang, I saw Hawkins stagger at the knees and lie out flat at Noble's feet, slowly and as quiet as a kid falling asleep, with the lantern-light on his lean legs and bright farmer's boots. We all stood very still, watching him settle out in the last agony.

Then Belcher took out a handkerchief and began to tie it about his own eyes (in our excitement we'd forgotten to do the same for Hawkins), and, seeing it wasn't big enough, turned and asked for the loan of mine. I gave it to him and he knotted the two together and pointed with his foot at Hawkins.

"He's not quite dead," he says. "Better give him another."

Sure enough, Hawkins's left knee is beginning to rise. I bend down and put my gun to his head; then, recollecting myself, I get up again. Belcher understands what's in my mind.

"Give him his first," he says. "I don't mind. Poor bastard, we don't know what's happening to him now."

I knelt and fired. By this time I didn't seem to know what I was doing. Belcher, who was fumbling a bit awkwardly with the handker-chiefs, came out with a laugh as he heard the shot. It was the first time I heard him laugh and it sent a shudder down my back; it sounded so unnatural.

"Poor bugger!" he said quietly. "And last night he was so curious about it all. It's very queer, chums, I always think. Now he knows as much about it as they'll ever let him know, and last night he was all in the dark."

Donovan helped him to tie the handkerchiefs about his eyes.

"Thanks, chum," he said. Donovan asked if there were any messages he wanted sent.

"No, chum," he says. "Not for me. If any of you would like to write to Hawkins's mother, you'll find a letter from her in his pocket. He and his mother were great chums. But my missus left me eight years ago. Went away with another fellow and took the kid with her. I like the feeling of a home, as you may have noticed, but I couldn't start again after that."

It was an extraordinary thing, but in those few minutes Belcher said more than in all the weeks before. It was just as if the sound of the shot had started a flood of talk in him and he could go on the whole night like that, quite happily, talking about himself. We stood round like fools now that he couldn't see us any longer. Donovan looked at Noble, and Noble shook his head. Then Donovan raised his Webley, and at that moment Belcher gives his queer laugh again. He may have thought we were talking about him, or perhaps he noticed the same thing I'd noticed and couldn't understand it.

"Excuse me, chums," he says. "I feel I'm talking the hell of a lot, and so silly, about my being so handy about a house and things like that. But this thing came me suddenly. You'll forgive me, I'm sure."

"You don't want to say a prayer?" asked Donovan.

"No, chum," he says. "I don't think it would help. I'm ready, and you boys want to get it over."

"You understand that we're only doing our duty?" says Donovan.

Belcher's head was raised like a blind man's, so that you could only see his chin and the tip of his nose in the lantern-light.

"I never could make out what duty was myself," he said. "I think you're all good lads, if that's what you mean. I'm not complaining."

Noble, just as if he couldn't bear any more of it, raised his fist at Donovan, and in a flash Donovan raised his gun and fired. The big man went over like a sack of meal, and this time there was no need of a second shot.

I don't remember much about the burying, but that it was worse than all the rest because we had to carry them to the grave. It was all mad lonely with nothing but a patch of lantern-light between ourselves and the dark, and birds hooting and screeching all round, disturbed by the guns. Noble went through Hawkins's belongings to find the letter from his mother, and then joined his hands together. He did the same with Belcher. Then, when we'd filled in the grave, we separated from Jeremiah Donovan and Feeney and took our tools back to the shed. All the way we didn't speak a word. The kitchen was dark and cold as we'd left it, and the old woman was sitting over the hearth, saying her beads. We walked past her into the room, and Noble struck a match to light the lamp. She rose quietly and came to the doorway with all her cantankerousness gone.

"What did ye do with them?" she asked in a whisper, and Noble started so that the match went out in his hand.

"What's that?" he asked without turning round.

"I heard ye," she said.

"What did you hear?" asked Noble.

"I heard ye. Do ye think I didn't hear ye, putting the spade back in the houseen?"

Noble struck another match and this time the lamp lit for him.

"Was that what ye did to them?" she asked.

Then, by God, in the very doorway, she fell on her knees and began praying, and after looking at her for a minute or two Noble did the same by the fireplace. I pushed my way out past her and left them at it. I stood at the door, watching the stars and listening to the shrieking of the birds dying out over the bogs. It is so strange what you feel at times like that you can't describe it. Noble says he saw everything ten times the size, as though there were nothing in the whole world but that little patch of bog with the two Englishmen stiffening into it, but with me it was as if the patch of bog where the Englishmen were was a million miles away, and even Noble and the old woman, mumbling behind me, and the birds and the bloody stars were all far away, and I was somehow very small and very lost and lonely like a child astray in the snow. And anything that happened me afterwards, I never felt the same about again.

EUDORA WELTY

1909–

Why I Live at the P.O.

I was getting along fine with Mama, Papa-Daddy and Uncle Rondo until my sister Stella-Rondo just separated from her husband and came back home again. Mr. Whitaker! Of course I went with Mr. Whitaker first, when he first appeared here in China Grove, taking "Pose Yourself" photos, and Stella-Rondo broke us up. Told him I was one-sided. Bigger on one side than the other, which is a deliberate, calculated falsehood: I'm the same. Stella-Rondo is exactly twelve months to the day younger than I am and for that reason she's spoiled.

She's always had anything in the world she wanted and then she'd throw it away. Papa-Daddy gave her this gorgeous Add-a-Pearl necklace when she was eight years old and she threw it away playing baseball when she was nine, with only two pearls.

So as soon as she got married and moved away from home the first thing she did was separate! From Mr. Whitaker! This photographer with the popeyes she said she trusted. Came home from one of those towns up in Illinois and to our complete surprise brought this child of two.

Mama said she like to make her drop dead for a second. "Here you had this marvelous blond child and never so much as wrote your mother a word about it," says Mamma. "I'm thoroughly ashamed of you." But of course she wasn't.

Stella-Rondo just calmly takes off this *hat*, I wish you could see it. She says, "Why, Mama, Shirley-T.'s adopted, I can prove it."

"How?" says Mama, but all I says was, "H'm!" There I was over the hot stove, trying to stretch two chickens over five people and a completely unexpected child into the bargain, without one moment's notice.

"What do you mean—'H'm!'?" says Stella-Rondo, and Mama says, "I heard that, Sister."

I said that oh, I didn't mean a thing, only that whoever Shirley-T. was, she was the spit-image of Papa-Daddy if he'd cut off his beard, which of course he'd never do in the world. Papa-Daddy's Mama's papa and sulks.

Stella-Rondo got furious! She said, "Sister, I don't need to tell you you got a lot of nerve and always did have and I'll thank you to make no future reference to my adopted child whatsoever."

"Very well," I said. "Very well, very well. Of course I noticed at once she looks like Mr. Whitaker's side too. That frown. She looks like a cross between Mr. Whitaker and Papa-Daddy."

"Well, all I can say is she isn't."

"She looks exactly like Shirley Temple to me," says Mama, but Shirley-T. just ran away from her.

So the first thing Stella-Rondo did at the table was turn Papa-Daddy against me.

"Papa-Daddy," she says. He was trying to cut up his meat. "Papa-Daddy!" I was taken completely by surprise. Papa-Daddy is about a million years old and's got this long-long beard. "Papa-Daddy, Sister says she fails to understand why you don't cut off your beard."

So Papa-Daddy l-a-y-s down his knife and fork! He's real rich. Mama says he is, he says he isn't. So he says, "Have I heard correctly? You don't understand why I don't cut off my beard?"

"Why," I says, "Papa-Daddy, of course I understand, I did not say any such of a thing, the idea!"

He says, "Hussy!"

I says, "Papa-Daddy, you know I wouldn't any more want you to cut off your beard than the man in the moon. It was the farthest thing from my mind! Stella-Rondo sat there and made that up while she was eating breast of chicken."

But he says, "So the postmistress fails to understand why I don't cut off my beard. Which job I got you through my influence with the government. 'Bird's nest'—is that what you call it?"

Not that it isn't the next to smallest P.O. in the entire state of Mississippi.

I says, "Oh, Papa-Daddy," I says, "I didn't say any such of a thing, I never dreamed it was a bird's nest, I have always been grateful though this is the next to smallest P.O. in the state of Mississippi, and I do not enjoy being referred to as a hussy by my own grandfather."

But Stella-Rondo says, "Yes, you did say it too. Anybody in the world could of heard you, that had ears."

"Stop right there," says Mama, looking at *me*.

So I pulled my napkin straight back through the napkin ring and left the table.

As soon as I was out of the room Mama says, "Call her back, or she'll starve to death," but Papa-Daddy says, "This is the beard I started growing on the Coast when I was fifteen years old." He would of gone on till nightfall if Shirley-T. hadn't lost the Milky Way she ate in Cairo.

So Papa-Daddy says, "I am going out and lie in the hammock, and you can all sit here and remember my words: I'll never cut off my beard as long as I live, even one inch, and I don't appreciate it in you at all." Passed right by me in the hall and went straight out and got in the hammock.

It would be a holiday. It wasn't five minutes before Uncle Rondo suddenly appeared in the hall in one of Stella-Rondo's flesh-colored kimonos, all cut on the bias, like something Mr. Whitaker probably thought was gorgeous.

"Uncle Rondo!" I says. "I didn't know who that was! Where are you going?"

"Sister," he says, "get out of my way, I'm poisoned."

"If you're poisoned stay away from Papa-Daddy," I says. "Keep out of the hammock, Papa-Daddy will certainly beat you on the head if you come within forty miles of him. He thinks I deliberately said he ought to cut off his beard after he got me the P.O., and I've told him and told him and told him, and he acts like he just don't hear me. Papa-Daddy must of gone stone deaf."

"He picked a fine day to do it then," says Uncle Rondo, and before you could say "Jack Robinson" flew out in the yard.

What he'd really done, he'd drunk another bottle of that prescription. He does it every single Fourth of July as sure as shooting, and it's horribly expensive. Then he falls over in the hammock and snores. So he insisted on zigzagging right on out to the hammock, looking like a half-wit.

Papa-Daddy woke up with this horrible yell and right there without moving an inch he tried to turn Uncle Rondo against me. I heard every word he said. Oh, he told Uncle Rondo I didn't learn to read till I was eight years old and he didn't see how in the world I ever got the mail put up at the P.O., much less read it all, and he said if Uncle Rondo could only fathom the lengths he had gone to to get me that job! And he said on the other hand he thought Stella-Rondo had a brilliant mind and deserved credit for getting out of town. All the time he was just lying there swinging as pretty as you please and looping out his beard, and poor Uncle Rondo was *pleading* with him to slow down the hammock, it was making him as dizzy as a witch to watch it. But that's what Papa-Daddy likes about a hammock. So Uncle Rondo was too dizzy to get turned against me for the time being. He's Mama's only brother and is a good case of a one-track mind. Ask anybody. A certified pharmacist.

Just then I heard Stella-Rondo raising the upstairs window. While she was married she got this peculiar idea that it's cooler with the windows shut and locked. So she has to raise the window before she can make a soul hear her outdoors.

So she raises the window and says, "*Oh!*" You would have thought she was mortally wounded.

Uncle Rondo and Papa-Daddy didn't even look up, but kept right on with what they were doing. I had to laugh.

I flew up the stairs and threw the door open! I says, "What in the wide world's the matter, Stella-Rondo? You mortally wounded?"

"No," she says, "I'm not mortally wounded but I wish you would do me the favor of looking out that window there and telling me what you see."

So I shade my eyes and look out the window.

"I see the front yard," I says.

"Don't you see any human beings?" she says.

"I see Uncle Rondo trying to run Papa-Daddy out of the hammock," I says. "Nothing more. Naturally, it's so suffocating-hot in the house, with all the windows shut and locked, everybody who cares to stay in their right mind will have to go out and get in the hammock before the Fourth of July is over."

"Don't you notice anything different about Uncle Rondo?" asks Stella-Rondo.

"Why, no, except he's got on some terrible-looking flesh-colored contraption I wouldn't be found dead in, is all I can see," I says.

"Never mind, you won't be found dead in it, because it happens to be part of my trousseau, and Mr. Whitaker took several dozen photographs of me in it," says Stella-Rondo. "What on earth could Uncle Rondo *mean* by wearing part of my trousseau out in the broad open daylight without saying so much as 'Kiss my foot,' *knowing* I only got home this morning after my separation and hung my negligee up on the bathroom door, just as nervous as I could be?"

"I'm sure I don't know, and what do you expect me to do about it?" I says. "Jump out the window?"

"No, I expect nothing of the kind. I simply declare that Uncle Rondo looks like a fool in it, that's all," she says. "It makes me sick to my stomach."

"Well, he looks as good as he can," I says. "As good as anybody in reason could." I stood up for Uncle Rondo, please remember. And I said to Stella-Rondo, "I think I would do well not to criticize so freely if I were you and came home with a two-year-old child I had never said a word about, and no explanation whatever about my separation."

"I asked you the instant I entered this house not to refer one more time to my adopted child, and you gave me your word of honor you would not," was all Stella-Rondo would say, and started pulling out every one of her eyebrows with some cheap Kress tweezers.

So I merely slammed the door behind me and went down and made some green-tomato pickle. Somebody had to do it. Of course Mama had turned both the niggers loose; she always said no earthly power could hold one anyway on the Fourth of July, so she wouldn't even try. It turned out that Jaypan fell in the lake and came within a very narrow limit of drowning.

So Mama trots in. Lifts up the lid and says, "H'm! Not very good for your Uncle Rondo in his precarious condition, I must say. Or poor little adopted Shirley-T. Shame on you!"

That made me tired. I says, "Well, Stella-Rondo had better thank her lucky stars it was her instead of me came trotting in with that very peculiar-looking child. Now if it had been me that trotted in from Illinois and brought a peculiar-looking child of two, I shudder to think of the reception I'd of got, much less controlled the diet of an entire family."

"But you must remember, Sister, that you were never married to Mr. Whitaker in the first place and didn't go up to Illinois to live," says Mama, shaking a spoon in my face. "If you had I would of been just as overjoyed to see you and your little adopted girl as I was to see Stella-Rondo, when you wound up with your separation and came on back home."

"You would not," I says.

"Don't contradict me, I would," says Mama.

But I said she couldn't convince me though she talked till she was blue in the face. Then I said, "Besides, you know as well as I do that that child is not adopted."

"She most certainly is adopted," says Mama, stiff as a poker.

I says, "Why, Mama, Stella-Rondo had her just as sure as anything in this world, and just too stuck up to admit it."

"Why, Sister," said Mama. "Here I thought we were going to have a pleasant Fourth of July, and you start right out not believing a word your own baby sister tells you!"

"Just like Cousin Annie Flo. Went to her grave denying the facts of life," I remind Mama.

"I told you if you ever mentioned Annie Flo's name I'd slap your face," says Mama, and slaps my face.

"All right, you wait and see," I says.

"I," says Mama, "I prefer to take my children's word for anything when it's humanly possible." You ought to see Mama, she weighs two hundred pounds and has real tiny feet.

Just then something perfectly horrible occurred to me.

"Mama," I says, "can that child talk?" I simply had to whisper! "Mama, I wonder if that child can be—you know—in any way? Do you realize," I says, "that she hasn't spoken one single, solitary word to a human being up to this minute? This is the way she looks," I says, and I looked like this.

Well, Mama and I just stood there and stared at each other. It was horrible!

"I remember well that Joe Whitaker frequently drank like a fish," says Mama. "I believed to my soul he drank *chemicals*." And without another word she marches to the foot of the stairs and calls Stella-Rondo.

"Stella-Rondo? O-o-o-o-o! Stella-Rondo!"

"What?" says Stella-Rondo from upstairs. Not even the grace to get up off the bed.

"Can that child of yours talk?" asks Mama.

Stella-Rondo says, "Can she what?"

"Talk! Talk!" says Mama. "Burdyburdyburdyburdy!"

So Stella-Rondo yells back, "Who says she can't talk?"

"Sister says so," says Mama

"You didn't have to tell me, I know whose word of honor don't mean a thing in this house," says Stella-Rondo.

And in a minute the loudest Yankee voice I ever heard in my life yells out, "OE'm Pop-OE the Sailor-r-r-r Ma-a-an!" and then somebody jumps up and down in the upstairs hall. In another second the house would of fallen down.

"Not only talks, she can tap-dance!" calls Stella-Rondo. "Which is more than some people I won't name can do."

"Why, the little precious darling thing!" Mama says, so surprised. "Just as smart as she can be!" Starts talking baby talk right there. Then she turns on me. "Sister, you ought to be thoroughly ashamed! Run upstairs this instant and apologize to Stella-Rondo and Shirley-T."

"Apologize for what?" I says. "I merely wondered if the child was normal, that's all. Now that she's proved she is, why, I have nothing further to say."

But Mama just turned on her heel and flew out, furious. She ran right upstairs and hugged the baby. She believed it was adopted. Stella-Rondo hadn't done a thing but turn her against me from upstairs while I stood there helpless over the hot stove. So that made Mama, Papa-Daddy and the baby all on Stella-Rondo's side.

Next, Uncle Rondo.

I must say that Uncle Rondo has been marvelous to me at various times in the past and I was completely unprepared to be made to jump out of my skin, the way it turned out. Once Stella-Rondo did something perfectly horrible to him—broke a chain letter from Flanders Field—and he took the radio back he had given her and gave it to me. Stella-Rondo was furious! For six months we all had to call her Stella instead of Stella-Rondo, or she wouldn't answer. I always thought Uncle Rondo had all the brains of the entire family. Another time he sent me to Mammoth Cave, with all expenses paid.

But this would be the day he was drinking that prescription, the Fourth of July.

So at supper Stella-Rondo speaks up and says she thinks Uncle Rondo ought to try to eat a little something. So finally Uncle Rondo said he would try a little cold biscuits and ketchup, but that was all. So *she* brought it to him.

"Do you think it wise to disport with ketchup in Stella-Rondo's flesh-colored kimono?" I says. Trying to be considerate! If Stella-Rondo couldn't watch out for her trousseau, somebody had to.

"Any objections?" asks Uncle Rondo, just about to pour out all the ketchup.

"Don't mind what she says, Uncle Rondo," says Stella-Rondo. "Sister has been devoting this solid afternoon to sneering out my bedroom window at the way you look."

"What's that?" says Uncle Rondo. Uncle Rondo has got the most terrible temper in the world. Anything is liable to make him tear the house down if it comes at the wrong time.

So Stella-Rondo says, "Sister says, 'Uncle Rondo certainly does look like a fool in that pink kimono!' "

Do you remember who it was really said that?

Uncle Rondo spills out all the ketchup and jumps out of his chair and tears off the kimono and throws it down on the dirty floor and puts his foot on it. It had to be sent all the way to Jackson to the cleaners and re-pleated.

"So that's your opinion of your Uncle Rondo, is it?" he says. "I look like a fool, do I? Well, that's the last straw. A whole day in this house with nothing to do, and then to hear you come out with a remark like that behind my back!"

"I didn't say any such of a thing, Uncle Rondo," I says, "and I'm not saying who did, either. Why, I think you look all right. Just try to take care of yourself and not talk and eat at the same time," I says. "I think you better go lie down."

"Lie down my foot," says Uncle Rondo. I ought to of known by that he was fixing to do something perfectly horrible.

So he didn't do anything that night in the precarious state he was in—just played Casino with Mama and Stella-Rondo and Shirley-T. and gave Shirley-T. a nickel with a head on both sides. It tickled her nearly to death, and she called him "Papa." But at 6:30 A.M. the next morning, he threw a whole five-cent package of some unsold one-inch firecrackers from the store as hard as he could into my bedroom and they every one went off. Not one bad one in the string. Anybody else, there'd be one that wouldn't go off.

Well, I'm just terribly susceptible to noise of any kind, the doctor has always told me I was the most sensitive person he had ever seen in his whole life, and I was simply prostrated. I couldn't eat! People tell me they heard it as far as the cemetery, and old Aunt Jep Patterson, that had been holding her own so good, thought it was Judgment Day and she was going to meet her whole family. It's usually so quiet here.

And I'll tell you it didn't take me any longer than a minute to make up my mind what to do. There I was with the whole entire house on Stella-Rondo's side and turned against me. If I have anything at all I have pride.

So I just decided I'd go straight down to the P.O. There's plenty of room there in the back, I says to myself.

Well! I made no bones about letting the family catch on to what I was up to. I didn't try to conceal it.

The first thing they knew, I marched in where they were all playing Old Maid and pulled the electric oscillating fan out by the plug, and everything got real hot. Next I snatched the pillow I'd done the needlepoint on right off the davenport from behind Papa-Daddy. He went "Ugh!" I beat Stella-Rondo up the stairs and finally found my charm bracelet in her bureau drawer under a picture of Nelson Eddy.

"So that's the way the land lies," says Uncle Rondo. There he was, piecing on the ham. "Well, Sister, I'll be glad to donate my army cot if you got any place to set it up, providing you'll leave right this minute and let me get some peace." Uncle Rondo was in France.

"Thank you kindly for the cot and 'peace' is hardly the word I would select if I had to resort to firecrackers at 6:30 A.M. in a young girl's bedroom," I says back to him. "And as to where I intend to go, you seem to forget my position as postmistress of China Grove, Mississippi," I says. "I've always got the P.O."

Well, that made them all sit up and take notice.

I went out front and started digging up some four-o'clocks to plant around the P.O.

"Ah-ah-ah!" says Mama, raising the window. "Those happen to be my four-o'clocks. Everything planted in that star is mine. I've never known you to make anything grow in your life."

"Very well," I says. "But I take the fern. Even you, Mama, can't stand there and deny that I'm the one watered that fern. And I happen to know where I can send in a box top and get a packet of one thousand mixed seeds, no two the same kind, free."

"Oh, where?" Mama wants to know.

But I says, "Too late. You 'tend to your house, and I'll 'tend to mine. You hear things like that all the time if you know how to listen to the radio. Perfectly marvelous offers. Get anything you want free."

So I hope to tell you I marched in and got that radio, and they could of all bit a nail in two, especially Stella-Rondo, that it used to belong to, and she well knew she couldn't get it back, I'd sue for it like a shot. And I very politely took the sewing-machine motor I helped pay the most on to give Mama for Christmas back in 1929, and a good big calendar, with the first-aid remedies on it. The thermometer and the Hawaiian ukulele certainly were rightfully mine, and I stood on the step-ladder and got all my watermelon-rind preserves and every fruit and vegetable I'd put up, every jar. Then I began to pull the tacks out of the bluebird wall vases on the archway to the dining room.

"Who told you you could have those, Miss Priss?" says Mama, fanning as hard as she could.

"I bought 'em and I'll keep track of 'em," I says. "I'll tack 'em up one on each side the post-office window, and you can see 'em when you come to ask me for your mail, if you're so dead to see 'em."

"Not I! I'll never darken the door to that post office again if I live to be a hundred," Mama says. "Ungrateful child! After all the money we spent on you at the Normal."

"Me either," says Stella-Rondo. "You can just let my mail lie there and *rot*, for all I care. I'll never come and relieve you of a single, solitary piece."

"I should worry," I says. "And who you think's going to sit down and write you all those big fat letters and postcards, by the way? Mr. Whitaker? Just because he was the only man ever dropped down in China Grove and you got him—unfairly—is he going to sit down and write you a lengthy correspondence after you come home giving no rhyme nor reason whatsoever for your separation and no explanation for the presence of that child? I may not have your brilliant mind, but I fail to see it."

So Mama says, "Sister, I've told you a thousand times that Stella-Rondo simply got homesick, and this child is far too big to be hers," and she says, "Now, why don't you all just sit down and play Casino?"

Then Shirley-T. sticks out her tongue at me in this perfectly horrible way. She has no more manners than the man in the moon. I told her she was going to cross her eyes like that some day and they'd stick.

"It's too late to stop me now," I says. "You should have tried that yesterday. I'm going to the P.O. and the only way you can possibly see me is to visit me there."

So Papa-Daddy says, "You'll never catch me setting foot in that post office, even if I should take a notion into my head to write a letter some place." He says, "I won't have you reachin' out of that little old window with a pair of shears and cuttin' off any beard of mine. I'm too smart for you!"

"We all are," says Stella-Rondo.

But I said, "If you're so smart, where's Mr. Whitaker?"

So then Uncle Rondo says, "I'll thank you from now on to stop reading all the orders I get on postcards and telling everybody in China Grove what you think is the matter with them," but I says, "I draw my own conclusions and will continue in the future to draw them." I says, "If people want to write their inmost secrets on penny postcards, there's nothing in the wide world you can do about it, Uncle Rondo."

"And if you think we'll ever *write* another postcard you're sadly mistaken," says Mama.

"Cutting off your nose to spite your face then," I says. "But if you're all determined to have no more to do with the U.S. mail, think of this: What will Stella-Rondo do now, if she wants to tell Mr. Whitaker to come after her?"

"Wah!" says Stella-Rondo. I knew she'd cry. She had a conniption fit right there in the kitchen.

"It will be interesting to see how long she holds out," I says. "And now—I am leaving."

"Good-bye," says Uncle Rondo.

"Oh, I declare," says Mama, "to think that a family of mine should quarrel on the Fourth of July, or the day after, over Stella-Rondo leaving old Mr. Whitaker and having the sweetest little adopted child! It looks like we'd all be glad!"

"Wah!" says Stella-Rondo, and has a fresh conniption fit.

"*He* left *her*—you mark my words," I says. "That's Mr. Whitaker. I know Mr. Whitaker. After all, I knew him first. I said from the beginning he'd up and leave her. I foretold every single thing that's happened."

"Where did he go?" asks Mama.

"Probably to the North Pole, if he knows what's good for him," I says.

But Stella-Rondo just bawled and wouldn't say another word. She flew to her room and slammed the door.

"Now look what you've gone and done, Sister," says Mama. "You go apologize."

"I haven't got time, I'm leaving," I says.

"Well, what are you waiting around for?" asks Uncle Rondo.

So I just picked up the kitchen clock and marched off, without saying "Kiss my foot" or anything, and never did tell Stella-Rondo good-bye.

There was a nigger girl going along on a little wagon right in front.

"Nigger girl," I says, "come help me haul these things down the hill, I'm going to live in the post office."

Took her nine trips in her express wagon. Uncle Rondo came out on the porch and threw her a nickel.

And that's the last I've laid eyes on any of my family or my family laid eyes on me for five solid days and nights. Stella-Rondo may be telling the most horrible tales in the world about Mr. Whitaker, but I haven't heard them. As I tell everybody, I draw my own conclusions.

But oh, I like it here. It's ideal, as I've been saying. You see, I've got everything cater-cornered, the way I like it. Hear the radio? All the war news. Radio, sewing machine, book ends, ironing board and that great big piano lamp—peace, that's what I like. Butter-bean vines planted all along the front where the strings are.

Of course, there's not much mail. My family are naturally the main people in China Grove, and if they prefer to vanish from the face of the earth, for all the mail they get or the mail they write, why, I'm not going to open my mouth. Some of the folks here in town are taking up for me and some turned against me. I know which is which. There are always people who will quit buying stamps just to get on the right side of Papa-Daddy.

But here I am, and here I'll stay. I want the world to know I'm happy.

And if Stella-Rondo should come to me this minute, on bended knees, and *attempt* to explain the incidents of her life with Mr. Whitaker, I'd simply put my fingers in both my ears and refuse to listen.

RALPH ELLISON
1914–
Battle Royal

It goes a long way back, some twenty years. All my life I had been looking for something, and everywhere I turned someone tried to tell me what it was. I accepted their answers too, though they were often in contradiction and even self-contradictory. I was naïve. I was looking for myself and asking everyone except myself questions which I, and only I, could answer. It took me a long time and much painful boomeranging of my expectations to achieve a realization everyone else appears to have been born with: That I am nobody but myself. But first I had to discover that I am an invisible man!

And yet I am no freak of nature, nor of history. I was in the cards, other things having been equal (or unequal) eighty-five years ago. I am not ashamed of my grandparents for having been slaves. I am only ashamed of myself for having at one time been ashamed. About eighty-five years ago they were told that they were free, united with others of our country in everything pertaining to the common good, and, in everything social, separate like the fingers of the hand. And they believed it. They exulted in it. They stayed in their place, worked hard, and brought up my father to do the same. But my grandfather is the one. He was an odd old guy, my grandfather, and I am told I take after him. It was he who caused the trouble. On his deathbed he called my father to him and said, "Son, after I'm gone I want you to keep up the good fight. I never told you, but our life is a war and I have been a traitor all my born days, a spy in the enemy's country ever since I give up my gun back in the Reconstruction. Live with your head in the lion's mouth. I want you to overcome 'em with yeses, undermine 'em with grins, agree 'em to death and destruction, let 'em swoller you till they vomit or bust wide open." They thought the old man had gone out of his mind. He had been the meekest of men. The younger children were rushed from the room, the shades drawn and the flame of the lamp turned so low that it sputtered on the wick like the old man's breathing. "Learn it to the younguns," he whispered fiercely; then he died.

But my folks were more alarmed over his last words than over his dying. It was as though he had not died at all, his words caused so much anxiety. I was warned emphatically to forget what he had said and, indeed, this is the first time it has been mentioned outside the family circle. It had a tremendous effect upon me, however. I could never be sure of what he meant. Grandfather had been a quiet old man who never made any trouble, yet on his deathbed he had called himself a traitor and a spy, and he had spoken of his meekness as a dangerous activity. It became a constant puzzle which lay unanswered in the back of my mind. And whenever things went well for me I remembered my grandfather and felt guilty and uncomfortable. It was as though I was carrying out his advice in spite of myself. And to make it worse, everyone loved me for it. I was praised by the most lily-white men of the town. I was considered an example of desirable conduct— just as my grandfather had been. And what puzzled me was that the old man had defined it as *treachery*. When I was praised for my conduct I felt a guilt that in some way I was doing something that was really against the wishes of the white folks, that if they had understood they would have desired me to act just the opposite, that I should have been sulky and mean, and that that really would have been what they wanted, even though they were fooled and thought they wanted me to act as I did. It made me afraid that some day they would look upon me as a traitor and I would be lost. Still I was more afraid to act any other way because they didn't like that at all. The old man's words were like a curse. On my graduation day I delivered an oration in which I showed that humility was the secret, indeed, the very essence of progress. (Not that I believed this—how could I, remembering my grandfather?—I only believed that it worked.) It was a great success. Everyone praised me and I was invited to give the speech at a gathering of the town's leading white citizens. It was a triumph for our whole community.

It was in the main ballroom of the leading hotel. When I got there I discovered that it was on the occasion of a smoker, and I was told that since I was to be there anyway I might as well take part in the battle royal to be fought by some of my schoolmates as part of the entertainment. The battle royal came first.

All of the town's big shots were there in their tuxedoes, wolfing down the buffet foods, drinking beer and whiskey and smoking black cigars. It was a large room with a high ceiling. Chairs were arranged in neat rows around three sides of a portable boxing ring. The fourth side was clear, revealing a gleaming space of polished floor. I had some misgivings over the battle royal, by the way. Not from a distaste for fighting, but because I didn't care too much for the other fellows who were to take part. They were tough guys who seemed to have no grandfather's curse worrying their minds. No one could mistake their toughness. And besides, I suspected that fighting a battle royal might detract from the dignity of my speech. In those pre-invisible days I visualized myself as a potential Booker T. Washington. But the other fellows didn't care too much for me either, and there were nine of them. I felt superior to them in my way, and I didn't like the manner in which we were all crowded together into the servants' elevator. Nor did they like my being there. In fact, as the warmly lighted floors flashed past the elevator we had words over the fact that I, by taking part in the fight, had knocked one of their friends out of a night's work.

We were led out of the elevator through a rococo hall into an anteroom and told to get into our fighting togs. Each of us was issued a pair of boxing gloves and ushered out into the big mirrored hall, which we entered looking cautiously about us and whispering, lest we might accidentally be heard above the noise of the room. It was foggy with cigar smoke. And already the whiskey was taking effect. I was shocked to see some of the most important men of the town quite tipsy. They were all there—bankers, lawyers, judges, doctors, fire chiefs, teachers, merchants. Even one of the more fashionable pastors. Something we could not see was going on up front. A clarinet was vibrating sensuously and the men were standing up and moving eagerly forward. We were a small tight group, clustered together, our bare upper bodies touching and shining with anticipatory sweat; while up front the big shots were becoming increasingly excited over something we still could not see. Suddenly I heard the school superintendent, who had told me to come, yell, "Bring up the shines gentlemen! Bring up the little shines!"

We were rushed up to the front of the ballroom, where it smelled even more strongly of tobacco and whiskey. Then we were pushed into place. I almost wet my pants. A sea of faces, some hostile, some amused, ringed around us, and in the center, facing us, stood a magnificent blonde—stark naked. There was dead silence. I felt a blast of cold air chill me. I tried to back away, but they were behind me and around me. Some of the boys stood with lowered heads, trembling. I felt a wave of irrational guilt and fear. My teeth chattered, my skin turned to goose flesh, my knees knocked. Yet I was strongly attracted and looked in spite of myself. Had the price of looking been blindness, I would have looked. The hair was yellow like that of a circus kewpie doll, the face heavily powdered and rouged, as though to form an abstract mask, the eyes hollow and smeared a cool blue, the color of a baboon's butt. I felt a desire to spit upon her as my eyes brushed slowly over her body. Her breasts were firm and round as the domes of East Indian temples, and I stood so close as to see the fine skin texture and beads of pearly perspiration glistening like dew around the pink and erected buds of her nipples. I wanted at one and the same time to run from the room, to sink through the floor, or go to her and cover her from my eyes and the eyes of the others with my body; to feel the soft thighs, to caress her and destroy her, to love her and murder her, to hide from her, and yet to stroke where below the small American flag tatooed upon her belly her thighs formed a capital V. I had a notion that of all in the room she saw only me with her impersonal eyes.

And then she began to dance, a slow sensuous movement; the

smoke of a hundred cigars clinging to her like the thinnest of veils. She seemed like a fair bird-girl girdled in veils calling to me from the angry surface of some gray and threatening sea. I was transported. Then I became aware of the clarinet playing and the big shots yelling at us. Some threatened us if we looked and others if we did not. On my right I saw one boy faint. And now a man grabbed a silver pitcher from a table and stepped close as he dashed ice water upon him and stood him up and forced two of us to support him as his head hung and moans issued from his thick bluish lips. Another boy began to plead to go home. He was the largest of the group, wearing dark red fighting trunks much too small to conceal the erection which projected from him as though in answer to the insinuating low-registered moaning of the clarinet. He tried to hide himself with his boxing gloves.

And all the while the blonde continued dancing, smiling faintly at the big shots who watched her with fascination, and faintly smiling at our fear. I noticed a certain merchant who followed her hungrily, his lips loose and drooling. He was a large man who wore diamond studs in a shirtfront which swelled with the ample paunch underneath, and each time the blonde swayed her undulating hips he ran his hand through the thin hair of his bald head and, with his arms upheld, his posture clumsy like that of an intoxicated panda, wound his belly in a slow and obscene grind. This creature was completely hypnotized. The music had quickened. As the dancer flung herself about with a detached expression on her face, the men began reaching out to touch her. I could see their beefy fingers sink into the soft flesh. Some of the others tried to stop them and she began to move around the floor in graceful circles, as they gave chase, slipping and sliding over the polished floor. It was mad. Chairs went crashing, drinks were spilt, as they ran laughing and howling after her. They caught her just as she reached a door, raised her from the floor, and tossed her as college boys are tossed at a hazing, and above her red, fixed-smiling lips I saw the terror and disgust in her eyes, almost like my own terror and that which I saw in some of the other boys. As I watched, they tossed her twice and her soft breasts seemed to flatten against the air and her legs flung wildly as she spun. Some of the more sober ones helped her to escape. And I started off the floor, heading for the anteroom with the rest of the boys.

Some were still crying and in hysteria. But as we tried to leave we were stopped and ordered to get into the ring. There was nothing to do but what we were told. All ten of us climbed under the ropes and allowed ourselves to be blindfolded with broad bands of white cloth. One of the men seemed to feel a bit sympathetic and tried to cheer us up as we stood with our backs against the ropes. Some of us tried to grin. "See that boy over there?" one of the men said. "I want you to run across at the bell and give it to him right in the belly. If you don't get him, I'm going to get you. I don't like his looks." Each of us was told the same. The blindfolds were put on. Yet even then I had been going over my speech. In my mind each word was as bright as flame. I felt the cloth pressed into place, and frowned so that it would be loosened when I relaxed.

But now I felt a sudden fit of blind terror. I was unused to darkness. It was as though I had suddenly found myself in a dark room filled with poisonous cottonmouths. I could hear the bleary voices yelling insistently for the battle royal to begin.

"Get going in there!"

"Let me at that big nigger!"

I strained to pick up the school superintendent's voice, as though to squeeze some security out of that slightly more familiar sound.

"Let me at those black sonsabitches!" someone yelled.

"No, Jackson, no!" another voice yelled. "Here, somebody, help me hold Jack."

"I want to get at that ginger-colored nigger. Tear him limb from limb," the first voice yelled.

I stood against the ropes trembling. For in those days I was what they called ginger-colored, and he sounded as though he might crunch me between his teeth like a crisp ginger cookie.

Quite a struggle was going on. Chairs were being kicked about and I could hear voices grunting as with a terrific effort. I wanted to see, to see more desperately than ever before. But the blindfold was as tight as a thick skin-puckering scab and when I raised my gloved hands to push the layers of white aside a voice yelled, "Oh, no you don't, black bastard! Leave that alone!"

"Ring the bell before Jackson kills him a coon!" someone boomed in the sudden silence. And I heard the bell clang and the sound of the feet scuffling forward.

A glove smacked against my head. I pivoted, striking out stiffly as someone went past, and felt the jar ripple along the length of my arm to my shoulder. Then it seemed as though all nine of the boys had turned upon me at once. Blows pounded me from all sides while I struck out as best I could. So many blows landed upon me that I wondered if I were not the only blindfolded fighter in the ring, or if the man called Jackson hadn't succeeded in getting me after all.

Blindfolded, I could no longer control my motions. I had no dignity. I stumbled about like a baby or a drunken man. The smoke had become thicker and with each new blow it seemed to sear and further restrict my lungs. My saliva became like hot bitter glue. A glove connected with my head, filling my mouth with warm blood. It was everywhere. I could not tell if the moisture I felt upon my body was sweat or blood. A blow landed hard against the nape of my neck. I felt myself going over, my head hitting the floor. Streaks of blue light filled the black world behind the blindfold. I lay prone, pretending that I was knocked out, but felt myself seized by hands and yanked to my feet. "Get going, black boy! Mix it up!" My arms were like lead, my head smarting from blows. I managed to feel my way to the ropes and held on, trying to catch my breath. A glove landed in my mid-section and I went over again, feeling as though the smoke had become a knife jabbed into my guts. Pushed this way and that by the legs milling around me, I finally pulled erect and discovered that I could see the black, sweat-washed forms weaving in the smoky-blue atmosphere like drunken dancers weaving to the rapid drum-like thuds of blows.

Everyone fought hysterically. It was complete anarchy. Everybody fought everybody else. No group fought together for long. Two, three, four, fought one, then turned to fight each other, were themselves attacked. Blows landed below the belt and in the kidney, with the gloves open as well as closed, and with my eye partly opened now there was not so much terror. I moved carefully, avoiding blows, although not too many to attract attention, fighting from group to group. The boys groped about like blind, cautious crabs crouching to protect their mid-sections, their heads pulled in short against their shoulders, their arms stretched nervously before them, with their fists testing the smoke-filled air like the knobbed feelers of hypersensitive snails. In one corner I glimpsed a boy violently punching the air and heard him scream in pain as he smashed his hand against a ring post. For a second I saw him bent over holding his hand, then going down as a blow caught his unprotected head. I played one group against the other, slipping in and throwing a punch then stepping out of range while pushing the others into the melee to take the blows blindly aimed at me. The smoke was agonizing and there were no rounds, no bells at three minute intervals to relieve our exhaustion. The room spun round me, a swirl of lights, smoke, sweating bodies surrounded by tense white faces. I bled from both nose and mouth, the blood spattering upon my chest.

The men kept yelling, "Slug him, black boy! Knock his guts out!"

"Uppercut him! Kill him! Kill that big boy!"

Taking a fake fall, I saw a boy going down heavily beside me as though we were felled by a single blow, saw a sneaker-clad foot shoot into his groin as the two who had knocked him down stumbled upon him. I rolled out of range, feeling a twinge of nausea.

The harder we fought the more threatening the men became. And yet, I had begun to worry about my speech again. How would it go? Would they recognize my ability? What would they give me?

I was fighting automatically when suddenly I noticed that one after another of the boys was leaving the ring. I was surprised, filled with panic, as though I had been left alone with an unknown danger. Then I understood. The boys had arranged it among themselves. It was the custom for the two men left in the ring to slug it out for the winner's prize. I discovered this too late. When the bell sounded two men in tuxedoes leaped into the ring and removed the blindfold. I found myself facing Tatlock, the biggest of the gang. I felt sick at my stomach. Hardly had the bell stopped ringing in my ears than it clanged again and I saw him moving swiftly toward me. Thinking of nothing else to do I hit him smash on the nose. He kept coming, bringing the rank sharp violence of stale sweat. His face was a black blank of a face, only his eyes alive—with hate of me and aglow with a feverish terror from what had happened to us all. I became anxious. I wanted to deliver my speech and he came at me as though he meant to beat it out of me. I smashed him again and again, taking his blows as they came. Then on a sudden impulse I struck him lightly and as we clinched, I whispered, "Fake like I knocked you out, you can have the prize."

"I'll break your behind," he whispered hoarsely.

"For *them?*"

"For *me*, sonofabitch!"

They were yelling for us to break it up and Tatlock spun me half around with a blow, and as a joggled camera sweeps in a reeling scene, I saw the howling red faces crouching tense beneath the cloud of blue-gray smoke. For a moment the world wavered, unraveled, flowed, then my head cleared and Tatlock bounced before me. That fluttering shadow before my eyes was his jabbing left hand. Then falling forward, my head against his damp shoulder, I whispered,

"I'll make it five dollars more."

"Go to hell!"

But his muscles relaxed a trifle beneath my pressure and I breathed, "Seven?"

"Give it to your ma," he said, ripping me beneath the heart.

And while I still held him I butted him and moved away. I felt myself bombarded with punches. I fought back with hopeless desperation. I wanted to deliver my speech more than anything else in the world, because I felt that only these men could judge truly my ability, and now this stupid clown was ruining my chances. I began fighting carefully now, moving in to punch him and out again with my greater speed. A lucky blow to his chin and I had him going too—until I heard a loud voice yell, "I got my money on the big boy."

Hearing this, I almost dropped my guard. I was confused: Should I try to win against the voice out there? Would not this go against my speech, and was not this a moment for humility, for nonresistance? A blow to my head as I danced about sent my right eye popping like a jack-in-the-box and settled my dilemma. The room went red as I fell. It was a dream fall, my body languid and fastidious as to where to land, until the floor became impatient and smashed up to meet me. A moment later I came to. An hypnotic voice said FIVE emphatically. And I lay there, hazily watching a dark red spot of my own blood shaping itself into a butterfly, glistening and soaking into the soiled gray world of the canvas.

When the voice drawled TEN I was lifted up and dragged to a chair. I sat dazed. My eye pained and swelled with each throb of my pounding heart and I wondered if now I would be allowed to speak. I was wringing wet, my mouth still bleeding. We were grouped along the wall now. The other boys ignored me as they congratulated Tatlock and speculated as to how much they would be paid. One boy whimpered over his smashed hand. Looking up front, I saw attendants in white jackets rolling the portable ring away and placing a small square rug in the vacant space surrounded by chairs. Perhaps, I thought, I will stand on the rug to deliver my speech.

Then the M.C. called to us, "Come on up here boys and get your money."

We ran forward to where the men laughed and talked in their chairs, waiting. Everyone seemed friendly now.

"There it is on the rug," the man said. I saw the rug covered with coins of all dimensions and a few crumpled bills. But what excited me, scattered here and there, were the gold pieces.

"Boys, it's all yours," the man said. "You get all you grab."

"That's right, Sambo," a blond man said, winking at me confidentially.

I trembled with excitement, forgetting my pain. I would get the gold and the bills, I thought. I would use both hands. I would throw my body against the boys nearest me to block them from the gold.

"Get down around the rug now," the man commanded, "and don't anyone touch it until I give the signal."

"This ought to be good," I heard.

As told, we got around the square rug on our knees. Slowly the man raised his freckled hand as we followed it upward with our eyes.

I heard, "These niggers look like they're about to pray!"

Then, "Ready," the man said. "Go!"

I lunged for a yellow coin lying on the blue design of the carpet, touching it and sending a surprised shriek to join those rising around me. I tried frantically to remove my hand but could not let go. A hot, violent force tore through my body, shaking me like a wet rat. The rug was electrified. The hair bristled up on my head as I shook myself free. My muscles jumped, my nerves jangled, writhed. But I saw that this was not stopping the other boys. Laughing in fear and embarrassment, some were holding back and scooping up the coins knocked off by the painful contortions of the others. The men roared above us as we struggled.

"Pick it up, goddamnit, pick it up!" someone called like a bass-voiced parrot. "Go on, get it!"

I crawled rapidly around the floor, picking up the coins, trying to avoid the coppers and to get greenbacks and the gold. Ignoring the shock by laughing, as I brushed the coins off quickly, I discovered that I could contain the electricity—a contradiction, but it works. Then the men began to push us onto the rug. Laughing embarrassedly, we struggled out of their hands and kept after the coins. We were all wet and slippery and hard to hold. Suddenly I saw a boy lifted into the air, glistening with sweat like a circus seal, and dropped, his wet back landing flush upon the charged rug, heard him yell and saw him literally dance upon his back, his elbows beating a frenzied tatoo upon the floor, his muscles twitching like the flesh of a horse stung by many flies. When he finally rolled off, his face was gray and no one stopped him when he ran from the floor amid booming laughter.

"Get the money," the M.C. called. "That's good hard American cash!"

And we snatched and grabbed, snatched and grabbed. I was careful not to come too close to the rug now, and when I felt the hot whiskey breath descend upon me like a cloud of foul air I reached out and grabbed the leg of a chair. It was occupied and I held on desperately.

"Leggo, nigger! Leggo!"

The huge face wavered down to mine as he tried to push me free. But my body was slippery and he was too drunk. It was Mr. Colcord, who owned a chain of movie houses and "entertainment palaces." Each time he grabbed me I slipped out of his hands. It became a real struggle. I feared the rug more than I did the drunk, so I held on, surprising myself for a moment by trying to topple *him* upon the rug. It was such an enormous idea that I found myself actually carrying it out. I tried not to be obvious, yet when I grabbed his leg, trying to tumble him out of the chair, he raised up roaring with laughter, and, looking at me with soberness dead in the eye, kicked me viciously in the chest. The chair leg flew out of my hand I felt myself going and rolled. It was as though I had rolled through a bed of hot coals. It seemed a whole century would pass before I would roll free, a century in which I was seared through the deepest levels of my body to the fearful breath within me and the breath seared and heated to the point of explosion. It'll all be over in a flash, I thought as I rolled clear It'll all be over in a flash.

But not yet, the men on the other side were waiting, red faces swollen as though from apoplexy as they bent forward in their chairs.

Seeing their fingers coming toward me I rolled away as a fumbled football rolls off the receiver's fingertips, back into the coals. That time I luckily sent the rug sliding out of place and heard the coins ringing against the floor and the boys scuffling to pick them up and the M.C. calling, "All right, boys, that's all. Go get dressed and get your money."

I was limp as a dish rag. My back felt as though it had been beaten with wires.

When we had dressed the M.C. came in and gave us each five dollars, except Tatlock, who got ten for being last in the ring. Then he told us to leave. I was not to get a chance to deliver my speech, I thought. I was going out into the dim alley in despair when I was stopped and told to go back. I returned to the ballroom, where the men were pushing back their chairs and gathering in groups to talk.

The M.C. knocked on a table for quiet. "Gentlemen," he said, "we almost forgot an important part of the program. A most serious part, gentlemen. This boy was brought here to deliver a speech which he made at his graduation yesterday . . ."

"Bravo!"

"I'm told that he is the smartest boy we've got out there in Greenwood. I'm told that he knows more big words than a pocket-sized dictionary."

Much applause and laughter.

"So now, gentlemen, I want you to give him your attention."

There was still laughter as I faced them, my mouth dry, my eye throbbing. I began slowly, but evidently my throat was tense, because they began shouting, "Louder! Louder!"

"We of the younger generation extol the wisdom of that great leader and educator," I shouted, "who first spoke these flaming words of wisdom: 'A ship lost at sea for many days suddenly sighted a friendly vessel. From the mast of the unfortunate vessel was seen a signal: "Water, water; we die of thirst!" The answer from the friendly vessel came back: "Cast down your bucket where you are." The captain of the distressed vessel, at last heeding the injunction, cast down his bucket, and it came up full of fresh sparkling water from the mouth of the Amazon River.' And like him I say, and in his words, 'To those of my race who depend upon bettering their condition in a foreign land, or who underestimate the importance of cultivating friendly relations with the Southern white man, who is his next-door neighbor, I would say: "Cast down your bucket where you are"—cast it down in making friends in every manly way of the people of all races by whom we are surrounded . . .' "

I spoke automatically and with such fervor that I did not realize that the men were still talking and laughing until my dry mouth, filling up with blood from the cut, almost strangled me. I coughed, wanting to stop and go to one of the tall brass, sand-filled spittoons to relieve myself, but a few of the men, especially the superintendent, were listening and I was afraid. So I gulped it down, blood, saliva and all, and continued. (What powers of endurance I had during those days! What enthusiasm! What a belief in the rightness of things!) I spoke even louder in spite of the pain. But still they talked and still they laughed, as though deaf with cotton in dirty ears. So I spoke with greater emotional emphasis. I closed my ears and swallowed blood until I was nauseated. The speech seemed a hundred times as long as before, but I could not leave out a single word. All had to be said, each memorized nuance considered, rendered. Nor was that all. Whenever I uttered a word of three or more syllables a group of voices would yell for me to repeat it. I used the phrase "social responsibility" and they yelled:

"What's the word you say, boy?"

"Social responsibility," I said.

"What?"

"Social . . ."

"Louder."

". . . responsibility."

"More!"

"Respon—"

"Repeat!"

"—sibility."

The room filled with the uproar of laughter until, no doubt, distracted by having to gulp down my blood, I made a mistake and yelled a phrase I had often seen denounced in newspaper editorials, heard debated in private.

"Social . . ."

"What?" they yelled.

". . .equality—"

The laughter hung smokelike in the sudden stillness. I opened my eyes, puzzled. Sounds of displeasure filled the room. The M.C. rushed forward. They shouted hostile phrases at me. But I did not understand.

A small dry mustached man in the front row blared out, "Say that slowly, son!"

"What sir?"

"What you just said!"

"Social responsibility, sir," I said.

"You weren't being smart, were you, boy?" he said, not unkindly.

"No, sir!"

"You sure that about 'equality' was a mistake?"

"Oh, yes, sir," I said. "I was swallowing blood."

"Well, you had better speak more slowly so we can understand. We mean to do right by you, but you've got to know your place at all times. All right, now, go on with your speech."

I was afraid. I wanted to leave but I wanted also to speak and I was afraid they'd snatch me down.

"Thank you sir," I said, beginning where I had left off, and having them ignore me as before.

Yet when I finished there was a thunderous applause. I was surprised to see the superintendent come forth with a package wrapped in white tissue paper, and, gesturing for quiet, address the men.

"Gentlemen, you see that I did not overpraise this boy. He makes a good speech and some day he'll lead his people in the proper paths. And I don't have to tell you that that is important in these days and times. This is a good, smart boy, and so to encourage him in the right direction, in the name of the Board of Education I wish to present him a prize in the form of this . . ."

He paused, removing the tissue paper and revealing a gleaming calfskin brief case.

". . . in the form of this first-class article from Shad Whitmore's shop."

"Boy," he said, addressing me, "take this prize and keep it well. Consider it a badge of office. Prize it. Keep developing as you are and some day it will be filled with important papers that will help shape the destiny of your people."

I was so moved that I could hardly express my thanks. A rope of bloody saliva forming a shape like an undiscovered continent drooled upon the leather and I wiped it quickly away. I felt an importance that I had never dreamed.

"Open it and see what's inside," I was told.

My fingers a-tremble, I complied, smelling the fresh leather and finding an official-looking document inside. It was a scholarship to the state college for Negroes. My eyes filled with tears and I ran awkwardly off the floor.

I was overjoyed; I did not even mind when I discovered that the gold pieces I had scrambled for were brass pocket tokens advertising a certain make of automobile.

When I reached home everyone was excited. Next day the neighbors came to congratulate me. I even felt safe from grandfather, whose deathbed curse usually spoiled my triumphs. I stood beneath his photograph with my brief case in hand and smiled triumphantly into his stolid black peasant's face. It was a face that fascinated me. The eyes seemed to follow everywhere I went.

That night I dreamed I was at a circus with him and that he refused to laugh at the clowns no matter what they did. Then later he told me to open my brief case and read what was inside and I did, finding an official envelope stamped with the state seal; and inside the envelope I found another and another, endlessly, and I thought I would fall of weariness. "Them's years," he said. "Now open that one." And I did and in it I found an engraved document containing a short message in letters of gold. "Read it," my grandfather said. "Out loud."

"To Whom It May Concern," I intoned. "Keep This Nigger-Boy Running."

I awoke with the old man's laughter ringing in my ears.

(It was a dream I was to remember and dream again for many years after. But at that time I had no insight into its meaning. First I had to attend college.)

DORIS LESSING

1919–

A Sunrise on the Veld

Every night that winter he said aloud into the dark of the pillow: Half-past four! Half-past four! till he felt his brain had gripped the words and held them fast. Then he fell asleep at once, as if a shutter had fallen; and lay with his face turned to the clock so that he could see it first thing when he woke.

It was half-past four to the minute, every morning. Triumphantly pressing down the alarm-knob of the clock, which the dark half of his mind had outwitted, remaining vigilant all night and counting the hours as he lay relaxed in sleep, he huddled down for a last warm moment under the clothes, playing with the idea of lying abed for this once only. But he played with it for the fun of knowing that it was a weakness he could defeat without effort; just as he set the alarm each night for the delight of the moment when he woke and stretched his limbs, feeling the muscles tighten, and thought: Even my brain— even that! I can control every part of myself.

Luxury of warm rested body, with the arms and legs and fingers waiting like soldiers for a word of command! Joy of knowing that the precious hours were given to sleep voluntarily!—for he had once stayed awake three nights running, to prove that he could, and then worked all day, refusing even to admit that he was tired; and now sleep seemed to him a servant to be commanded and refused.

The boy stretched his frame full-length, touching the wall at his head with his hands, and the bedfoot with his toes; then he sprang out, like a fish leaping from water. And it was cold, cold.

He always dressed rapidly, so as to try and conserve his night-warmth till the sun rose two hours later; but by the time he had on his clothes his hands were numbed and he could scarcely hold his shoes. These he could not put on for fear of waking his parents, who never came to know how early he rose.

As soon as he stepped over the lintel, the flesh of his soles contracted on the chilled earth, and his legs began to ache with cold. It was night: the stars were glittering, the trees standing black and still. He looked for signs of day, for the greying of the edge of a stone, or a lightening in the sky where the sun would rise, but there was nothing yet. Alert as an animal he crept past the dangerous window, standing poised with his hand on the sill for one proudly fastidious moment, looking in at the stuffy blackness of the room where his parents lay.

Feeling for the grass-edge of the path with his toes, he reached inside another window further along the wall, where his gun had been set in readiness the night before. The steel was icy, and numbed fingers slipped along it, so that he had to hold it in the crook of his arm for safety. Then he tiptoed to the room where the dogs slept, and was fearful that they might have been tempted to go before him; but they were waiting, their haunches crouched in reluctance at the cold, but ears and swinging tails greeting the gun ecstatically. His warning undertone kept them secret and silent till the house was a hundred yards back: then they bolted off into the bush, yelping excitedly. The boy imagined his parents turning in their beds and muttering: Those dogs again! before they were dragged back in sleep; and he smiled scornfully. He always looked back over his shoulder at the house before he passed a wall of trees that shut it from sight. It looked so low and small, crouching there under a tall and brilliant sky. Then he turned his back on it, and on the frowsting sleepers, and forgot them.

He would have to hurry. Before the light grew strong he must be four miles away; and already a tint of green stood in the hollow of a leaf, and the air smelled of morning and the stars were dimming.

He slung the shoes over his shoulder, veld *skoen* that were crinkled and hard with the dews of a hundred mornings. They would be necessary when the ground became too hot to bear. Now he felt the chilled dust push up between his toes, and he let the muscles of his feet spread and settle into the shapes of the earth; and he thought: I could walk a hundred miles on feet like these! I could walk all day, and never tire!

He was walking swiftly through the dark tunnel of foliage that in day-time was a road. The dogs were invisibly ranging the lower travelways of the bush, and he heard them panting. Sometimes he felt a cold muzzle on his leg before they were off again, scouting for a trail to follow. They were not trained, but free-running companions of the hunt, who often tired of the long stalk before the final shots, and went off on their own pleasure. Soon he could see them, small and wild-looking in a wild strange light, now that the bush stood trembling on the verge of colour, waiting for the sun to paint earth and grass afresh.

The grass stood to his shoulders; and the trees were showering a faint silvery rain. He was soaked; his whole body was clenched in a steady shiver.

Once he bent to the road that was newly scored with animal trails, and regretfully straightened, reminding himself that the pleasure of tracking must wait till another day.

He began to run along the edge of a field, noting jerkily how it was filmed over with fresh spiderweb, so that the long reaches of great black clods seemed netted in glistening grey. He was using the steady lope he had learned by watching the natives, the run that is a dropping of the weight of the body from one foot to the next in a slow balancing movement that never tires, nor shortens the breath; and he felt the blood pulsing down his legs and along his arms, and the exultation and pride of body mounted in him till he was shutting his teeth hard against a violent desire to shout his triumph.

Soon he had left the cultivated part of the farm. Behind him the bush was low and black. In front was a long vlei, acres of long pale grass that sent back a hollowing gleam of light to a satiny sky. Near him thick swathes of grass were bent with the weight of water, and diamond drops sparkled on each frond.

The first bird woke at his feet and at once a flock of them sprang into the air calling shrilly that day had come; and suddenly, behind him, the bush woke into song, and he could hear the guinea fowl calling far ahead of him. That meant they would now be sailing down from their trees into thick grass, and it was for them he had come: he was too late. But he did not mind. He forgot he had come to shoot. He set his legs wide, and balanced from foot to foot, and swung his gun up and down in both hands horizontally, in a kind of improvised exercise, and let his head sink back till it was pillowed in his neck muscles, and watched how above him small rosy clouds floated in a lake of gold.

Suddenly it all rose in him: it was unbearable. He leapt up into the air, shouting and yelling wild, unrecognisable noises. Then he began to run, not carefully, as he had before, but madly, like a wild thing. He was clean crazy, yelling mad with the joy of living and a superfluity of youth. He rushed down the vlei under a tumult of crimson and gold, while all the birds of the world sang about him. He ran in great leaping strides, and shouted as he ran, feeling his body rise into the crisp rushing air and fall back surely on to sure feet; and thought briefly, not believing that such a thing could happen to him, that he could break his ankle any moment, in this thick tangled grass. He cleared bushes like a duiker, leapt over rocks; and finally came to a dead stop at a place where the ground fell abruptly away below him to the river. It had been a two-mile-long dash through waist-high growth, and he was breathing hoarsely and could no longer sing. But he poised on a rock and looked down at stretches of water that gleamed through stooping trees, and thought suddenly, I am fifteen! Fifteen! The words came new to him; so that he kept repeating them wonderingly, with swelling excitement; and he felt the years of his life with his hands, as if he were counting marbles, each one hard and separate and compact, each one a wonderful shining thing. That was what he was: fifteen years of this rich soil, and this slow-moving water, and air that smelt like a challenge whether it was warm and sultry at noon, or as brisk as cold water, like it was now.

There was nothing he couldn't do, nothing! A vision came to him, as he stood there, like when a child hears the word "eternity" and tries to understand it, and time takes possession of the mind. He felt his life ahead of him as a great and wonderful thing, something that was his; and he said aloud, with the blood rising to his head: all the great men of the world have been as I am now, and there is nothing I can't become, nothing I can't do; there is no country in the world I cannot make part of myself, if I choose. I contain the world. I can make of it what I want. If I choose, I can change everything that is going to happen: it depends on me, and what I decide now.

The urgency, and the truth and the courage of what his voice was saying exulted him so that he began to sing again, at the top of his voice, and the sound went echoing down the river gorge. He stopped for the echo, and sang again: stopped and shouted. That was what he was!—he sang, if he chose; and the world had to answer him.

And for minutes he stood there, shouting and singing and waiting for the lovely eddying sound of the echo; so that his own new strong thoughts came back and washed round his head, as if someone were answering him and encouraging him; till the gorge was full of soft voices clashing back and forth from rock to rock over the river. And then it seemed as if there was a new voice. He listened, puzzled, for it was not his own. Soon he was leaning forward, all his nerves alert, quite still: somewhere close to him there was a noise that was no joyful bird, nor tinkle of falling water, nor ponderous movement of cattle.

There it was again. In the deep morning hush that held his future and his past, was a sound of pain, and repeated over and over: it was a kind of shortened scream, as if someone, something, had no breath to scream. He came to himself, looked about him, and called for the dogs. They did not appear: they had gone off on their own business, and he was alone. Now he was clean sober, all the madness gone. His heart beating fast, because of that frightened screaming, he stepped carefully off the rock and went towards a belt of trees. He was moving cautiously, for not so long ago he had seen a leopard in just this spot.

At the edge of the trees he stopped and peered, holding his gun ready; he advanced, looking steadily about him, his eyes narrowed. Then, all at once, in the middle of a step, he faltered, and his face was puzzled. He shook his head impatiently, as if he doubted his own sight.

There, between two trees, against a background of gaunt black rocks, was a figure from a dream, a strange beast that was horned and drunken-legged, but like something he had never even imagined. It seemed to be ragged. It looked like a small buck that had black ragged tufts of fur standing up irregularly all over it, with patches of raw flesh beneath . . . but the patches of rawness were disappearing under moving black and came again elsewhere; and all the time the creature screamed, in small gasping screams, and leaped drunkenly from side to side, as if it were blind.

Then the boy understood: it *was* a buck. He ran closer, and again stood still, stopped by a new fear. Around him the grass was whispering and alive. He looked wildly about, and then down. The ground was black with ants, great energetic ants that took no notice of him, but hurried and scurried towards the fighting shape, like glistening black water flowing through the grass.

And, as he drew in his breath and pity and terror seized him, the beast fell and the screaming stopped. Now he could hear nothing but one bird singing, and the sound of the rustling, whispering ants.

He peered over at the writhing blackness that jerked convulsively with the jerking nerves. It grew quieter. There were small twitches from the mass that still looked vaguely like the shape of a small animal.

It came into his mind that he should shoot it and end its pain; and he raised the gun. Then he lowered it again. The buck could no longer feel; its fighting was a mechanical protest of the nerves. But it was not that which made him put down the gun. It was a swelling feeling of rage and misery and protest that expressed itself in the thought: if I had not come it would have died like this: so why should I interfere? All over the bush things like this happen; they happen all the time; this is how life goes on, by living things dying in anguish. He gripped the gun between his knees and felt in his own limbs the myriad swarming pain of the twitching animal that could no longer feel, and set his teeth, and said over and over again under his breath: I can't stop it. I can't stop it. There is nothing I can do.

He was glad that the buck was unconscious and had gone past suffering so that he did not have to make a decision to kill it even when he was feeling with his whole body: this is what happens, this is how things work.

It was right—that was what he was feeling. *It was right and nothing could alter it.*

The knowledge of fatality, of what has to be, had gripped him and for the first time in his life; and he was left unable to make any movement of brain or body, except to say: "Yes, yes. That is what living is." It had entered his flesh and his bones and grown in to the furthest corners of his brain and would never leave him. And at that moment he could not have performed the smallest action of mercy, knowing as he did, having lived on it all his life, the vast unalterable, cruel veld, where at any moment one might stumble over a skull or crush the skeleton of some small creature.

Suffering, sick, and angry, but also grimly satisfied with his new stoicism, he stood there leaning on his rifle, and watched the seething black mound grow smaller. At his feet, now, were ants trickling back with pink fragments in their mouths, and there was a fresh acid smell in his nostrils. He sternly controlled the uselessly convulsing muscles of his empty stomach, and reminded himself: the ants must eat too! At the same time he found that the tears were streaming down his face, and his clothes were soaked with the sweat of that other creature's pain.

The shape had grown small. Now it looked like nothing recognisable. He did not know how long it was before he saw the blackness thin, and bits of white showed through, shining in the sun—yes, there was the sun, just up, glowing over the rocks. Why, the whole thing could not have taken longer than a few minutes.

He began to swear, as if the shortness of the time was in itself unbearable, using the words he had heard his father say. He strode forward, crushing ants with each step, and brushing them off his clothes, till he stood above the skeleton, which lay sprawled under a small bush. It was clean-picked. It might have been lying there years, save that on the white bone were pink fragments of gristle. About the bones ants were ebbing away, their pincers full of meat.

The boy looked at them, big black ugly insects. A few were standing and gazing up at him with small glittering eyes.

"Go away!" he said to the ants, very coldly. "I am not for you—not just yet, at any rate. Go away." And he fancied that the ants turned and went away.

He bent over the bones and touched the sockets in the skull; that was where the eyes were, he thought incredulously, remembering the liquid dark eyes of a buck. And then he bent the slim foreleg bone, swinging it horizontally in his palm.

That morning, perhaps an hour ago, this small creature had been stepping proud and free through the bush, feeling the chill on its hide even as he himself had done, exhilarated by it. Proudly stepping the earth, tossing its horns, frisking a pretty white tail, it had sniffed the cold morning air. Walking like kings and conquerors it had moved throug this free-held bush, where each blade of grass grew for it alone, and where the river ran pure sparkling water for its slaking.

And then—what had happened? Such a swift surefooted thing could surely not be trapped by a swarm of ants?

The boy bent curiously to the skeleton. Then he saw that the back leg that lay uppermost and strained out in the tension of death, was snapped midway in the thigh, so that broken bones jutted over each other uselessly. So that was it! Limping into the ant-masses it could not escape, once it had sensed the danger. Yes, but how had the leg been broken? Had it fallen, perhaps? Impossible, a buck was too light and graceful. Had some jealous rival horned it?

What could possibly have happened? Perhaps some Africans had thrown stones at it, as they do, trying to kill it for meat, and had broken its leg. Yes, that must be it.

Even as he imagined the crowd of running, shouting natives, and the flying stones, and the leaping buck, another picture came into his mind. He saw himself, on any one of these bright ringing mornings, drunk with excitement, taking a snap shot at some half-seen buck. He saw himself with the gun lowered, wondering whether he had missed or not; and thinking at last that it was late, and he wanted his breakfast, and it was not worth while to track miles after an animal that would very likely get away from him in any case.

For a moment he would not face it. He was a small boy again, kicking sulkily at the skeleton, hanging his head, refusing to accept the responsibility.

Then he straightened up, and looked down at the bones with an odd expression of dismay, all the anger gone out of him. His mind went quite empty: all around him he could see trickles of ants disappearing into the grass. The whispering noise was faint and dry, like the rustling of a cast snakeskin.

At last he picked up his gun and walked homewards. He was telling himself half defiantly that he wanted his breakfast. He was telling himself that it was getting very hot, much too hot to be out roaming the bush.

Really, he was tired. He walked heavily, not looking where he put his feet. When he came within sight of his home he stopped, knitting his brows. There was something he had to think out. The death of that small animal was a thing that concerned him, and he was by no means finished with it. It lay at the back of his mind uncomfortably.

Soon, the very next morning, he would get clear of everybody and go to the bush and think about it.

JAMES BALDWIN
1924–
Sonny's Blues

I read about it in the paper, in the subway, on my way to work. I read it, and I couldn't believe it, and I read it again. Then perhaps I just stared at it, at the newsprint spelling out his name, spelling out the story. I stared at it in the swinging lights of the subway car, and in the faces and bodies of the people, and in my own face, trapped in the darkness which roared outside.

It was not to be believed, and I kept telling myself that as I walked from the subway station to the high school. And at the same time I couldn't doubt it. I was scared, scared for Sonny. He became real to me again. A great block of ice got settled in my belly and kept melting there slowly all day long, while I taught my classes algebra. It was a special kind of ice. It kept melting, sending trickles of ice water all up and down my veins, but it never got less. Sometimes it hardened and seemed to expand until I felt my guts were going to come spilling out or that I was going to choke or scream. This would always be at a moment when I was remembering some specific thing Sonny had once said or done.

When he was about as old as the boys in my classes, his face had been bright and open, there was a lot of copper in it; and he'd had wonderfully direct brown eyes, and great gentleness and privacy. I wondered what he looked like now. He had been picked up, the evening before, in a raid on an apartment downtown, for peddling and using heroin.

I couldn't believe it: but what I mean by that is that I couldn't find any room for it anywhere inside me. I had kept it outside me for a long time. I hadn't wanted to know. I had had suspicions, but I didn't name them, I kept putting them away. I told myself that Sonny was wild, but he wasn't crazy. And he'd always been a good boy, he hadn't ever turned hard or evil or disrespectful, the way kids can, so quick, so quick, especially in Harlem. I didn't want to believe that I'd ever see my brother going down, coming to nothing, all that light in his face gone out, in the condition I'd already seen so many others. Yet it had happened and here I was, talking about algebra to a lot of boys who might, every one of them for all I knew, be popping off needles every time they went to the head. Maybe it did more for them than algebra could.

I was sure that the first time Sonny had ever had horse, he couldn't have been much older than these boys were now. These boys, now, were living as we'd been living then, they were growing up with a rush and their heads bumped abruptly against the low ceiling of their actual possibilities. They were filled with rage. All they really knew were two darknesses, the darkness of their lives, which was now closing in on them, and the darkness of the movies, which had blinded them to that other darkness, and in which they now, vindictively, dreamed, at once more together than they were at any other time, and more alone.

When the last bell rang, the last class ended, I let out my breath. It seemed I'd been holding it for all that time. My clothes were set—I may have looked as though I'd been sitting in a steam bath, all dressed up, all afternoon. I sat alone in the classroom a long time. I listened to the boys outside, downstairs, shouting and cursing and laughing. Their laughter struck me for perhaps the first time. It was not the joyous laughter which—God knows why—one associates with children. It was mocking and insular, its intent was to denigrate. It was disenchanted, and in this, also, lay the authority of their curses. Perhaps I was listening to them because I was thinking about my brother and in them I heard my brother. And myself.

One boy was whistling a tune, at once very complicated and very simple, it seemed to be pouring out of him as though he were a bird, and it sounded very cool and moving through all that harsh, bright air, only just holding its own through all those other sounds.

I stood and walked over to the window and looked down into the courtyard. It was the beginning of the spring, and the sap was rising in the boys. A teacher passed through them every now and again, quickly, as though he or she couldn't wait to get out of that courtyard, to get those boys out of their sight and off their minds. I started collecting my stuff. I thought I'd better get home and talk to Isabel.

The courtyard was almost deserted by the time I got downstairs. I saw this boy standing in the shadow of a doorway, looking just like Sonny. I almost called his name. Then I saw that it wasn't Sonny, but somebody we used to know, a boy from around our block. He'd been Sonny's friend. He'd never been mine, having been too young for me, and, anyway, I'd never liked him. And now, even though he was a grown-up man, he still hung around that block, still spent hours on the street corner, was always high and raggy. I used to run into him from time to time, and he'd often work around to asking me for a quarter or fifty cents. He always had some real good excuse, too, and I always gave it to him, I don't know why.

But now, abruptly, I hated him. I couldn't stand the way he looked at me, partly like a dog, partly like a cunning child. I wanted to ask him what the hell he was doing in the school courtyard.

He sort of shuffled over to me, and he said, "I see you got the papers. So you already know about it."

"You mean about Sonny? Yes, I already know about it. How come they didn't get you?"

He grinned. It made him repulsive and it also brought to mind what he'd looked like as a kid. "I wasn't there. I stay away from them people."

"Good for you." I offered him a cigarette and I watched him through the smoke. "You come all the way down here just to tell me about Sonny?"

"That's right." He was sort of shaking his head and his eyes looked strange, as though they were about to cross. The bright sun deadened his damp dark brown skin and it made his eyes look yellow and showed up the dirt in his conked hair. He smelled funky. I moved a little away from him and I said, "Well, thanks. But I already know about it and I got to get home."

"I'll walk you a little ways," he said. We started walking. There were a couple of kids still loitering in the courtyard and one of them said good night to me and looked strangely at the boy beside me.

"What're you going to do?" he asked me. "I mean, about Sonny?"

"Look. I haven't seen Sonny for over a year, I'm not sure I'm going to do anything. Anyway, what the hell *can* I do?"

"That's right," he said quickly, "ain't nothing you can do. Can't much help old Sonny no more, I guess."

It was what I was thinking and so it seemed to me he had no right to say it.

"I'm surprised at Sonny, though," he went on—he had a funny way of talking, he looked straight ahead as though he were talking to himself—"I thought Sonny was a smart boy, I thought he was too smart to get hung."

"I guess he thought so, too," I said sharply, "and that's how he got hung. And how about you? You're pretty goddamn smart, I bet."

Then he looked directly at me, just for a minute. "I ain't smart," he said. "If I was smart, I'd have reached for a pistol a long time ago."

"Look. Don't tell *me* your sad story, if it was up to me, I'd give you one." Then I felt guilty—guilty probably, for never having supposed that the poor bastard *had* a story of his own, much less a sad one, and I asked, quickly, "What's going to happen to him now?"

He didn't answer this. He was off by himself someplace. "Funny thing," he said, and from his tone we might have been discussing the quickest way to get to Brooklyn, "when I saw the papers this morning, the first thing I asked myself was if I had anything to do with it. I felt sort of responsible."

I began to listen more carefully. The subway station was on the corner, just before us, and I stopped. He stopped, too. We were in front of a bar and he ducked slightly, peering in, but whoever he was looking for didn't seem to be there. The juke box was blasting away with something black and bouncy, and I half watched the barmaid as she danced her way from the juke box to her place behind the bar. And I watched her face as she laughingly responded to something someone said to her, still keeping time to the music. When she smiled one saw the little girl, one sensed the doomed, still-struggling woman beneath the battered face of the semi-whore.

"I never *give* Sonny nothing," the boy said finally, "but a long time ago I come to school high and Sonny asked me how it felt." He paused, I couldn't bear to watch him, I watched the barmaid, and I listened to the music which seemed to be causing the pavement to shake. "I told him it felt great." The music stopped, the barmaid paused and watched the juke box until the music began again. "It did."

All this was carrying me someplace I didn't want to go. I certainly didn't want to know how it felt. It filled everything, the people, the houses, the music, the dark, quick-silver barmaid, with menace; and this menace was their reality.

"What's going to happen to him now?" I asked again.

"They'll send him away someplace and they'll try to cure him." He shook his head. "Maybe he'll even think he's kicked the habit. Then they'll let him loose"—He gestured, throwing his cigarette into the gutter. "That's all."

"What do you mean, that's *all?*"

But I knew what he meant.

"I *mean,* that's *all.*" He turned his head and looked at me, pulling down the corners of his mouth. "Don't you know what I mean?" he asked, softly.

"How the hell *would* I know what you mean?" I almost whispered it, I don't know why.

"That's right," he said to the air, "how would *he* know what I mean?" He turned toward me again, patient and calm, and yet I somehow felt him shaking, shaking as though he were going to fall apart. I felt that ice in my guts again, the dread I'd felt all afternoon; and again I watched the barmaid, moving about the bar, washing glasses, and singing. "Listen. They'll let him out and then it'll just start over again. That's what I mean."

"You mean—they'll let him out. And then he'll just start working his way back in again. You mean he'll never kick the habit. Is that what you mean?"

"That's right," he said, cheerfully. "*You* see what I mean."

"Tell me," I said at last, "why does he want to die? He must want to die, he's killing himself, why does he want to die?"

He looked at me in surprise. He licked his lips. "He don't want to die. He wants to live. Don't nobody want to die, ever."

Then I wanted to ask him—too many things. He could not have answered, or if he had, I could not have borne the answers. I started walking. "Well, I guess it's none of my business."

"It's going to be rough on old Sonny," he said. We reached the subway station. "This is your station?" he asked. I nodded. I took one step down. "Damn!" he said, suddenly. I looked up at him. He grinned again. "Damn if I didn't leave all my money home. You ain't got a dollar on you, have you? Just for a couple of days, is all."

All at once something inside gave and threatened to come pouring out of me. I didn't hate him any more. I felt that in another moment I'd start crying like a child.

"Sure," I said. "Don't sweat." I looked in my wallet and didn't have a dollar, I only had a five. "Here," I said. "That hold you?"

He didn't look at it—he didn't want to look at it. A terrible, closed look came over his face, as though he were keeping the number on the bill a secret from him and me. "Thanks," he said, and now he was dying to see me go. "Don't worry about Sonny. Maybe I'll write him or something."

"Sure," I said. "You do that. So long."

"Be seeing you," he said. I went on down the steps.

And I didn't write Sonny or send him anything for a long time. When I finally did, it was just after my little girl died, he wrote me back a letter which made me feel like a bastard.

Here's what he said:

> Dear brother,
>   You don't know how much I needed to hear from you. I wanted to write you many a time but I dug how much I must have hurt you and so I didn't write. But now I feel like a man who's been trying to climb

up out of some deep, real deep and funky hole and just saw the sun up there, outside. I got to get outside.

I can't tell you much about how I got here. I mean I don't know how to tell you. I guess I was afraid of something or I was trying to escape from something and you know I have never been very strong in the head (smile). I'm glad Mama and Daddy are dead and can't see what's happened to their son and I swear if I'd known what I was doing I would never have hurt you so, you and a lot of other fine people who were nice to me and who believed in me.

I don't want you to think it had anything to do with me being a musician. It's more than that. Or maybe less than that. I can't get anything straight in my head down here and I try not to think about what's going to happen to me when I get outside again. Sometimes I think I'm going to flip and *never* get outside and sometime I think I'll come straight back. I tell you one thing, though, I'd rather blow my brains out than go through this again. But that's what they all say, so they tell me. If I tell you when I'm coming to New York and if you could meet me, I sure would appreciate it. Give my love to Isabel and the kids and I was sure sorry to hear about little Gracie. I wish I could be like Mama and say the Lord's will be done, but I don't know it seems to me that trouble is the one thing that never does get stopped and I don't know what good it does to blame it on the Lord. But maybe it does some good if you believe it.

Your brother,
SONNY

Then I kept in constant touch with him and I sent him whatever I could and I went to meet him when he came back to New York. When I saw him, many things I thought I had forgotten came flooding back to me. This was because I had begun, finally, to wonder about Sonny, about the life that Sonny lived inside. This life, whatever it was, had made him older and thinner and it had deepened the distant stillness in which he had always moved. He looked very unlike my baby brother. Yet, when he smiled, when we shook hands, the baby brother I'd never known looked out from the depths of his private life, like an animal waiting to be coaxed into the light.

"How you been keeping?" he asked me.

"All right. And you?"

"Just fine." He was smiling all over his face. "It's good to see you again."

"It's good to see you."

The seven years' difference in our ages lay between us like a chasm: I wondered if these years would ever operate between us as a bridge. I was remembering, and it made it hard to catch my breath, that I had been there when he was born; and I had heard the first words he had ever spoken. When he started to walk, he walked from our mother straight to me. I caught him just before he fell when he took the first steps he ever took in this world.

"How's Isabel?"

"Just fine. She's dying to see you."

"And the boys?"

"They're fine, too. They're anxious to see their uncle."

"Oh, come on. You know they don't remember me."

"Are you kidding? Of course they remember you."

He grinned again. We got into a taxi. We had a lot to say to each other, far too much to know how to begin.

As the taxi began to move, I asked, "You still want to go to India?"

He laughed. "You still remember that. Hell, no. This place is Indian enough for me."

"It used to belong to them," I said.

And he laughed again. "They damn sure knew what they were doing when they got rid of it."

Years ago, when he was around fourteen, he'd been all hipped on the idea of going to India. He read books about people sitting on rocks, naked, in all kinds of weather, but mostly bad, naturally, and walking barefoot through hot coals and arriving at wisdom. I used to say that it sounded to me as though they were getting away from wisdom as fast as they could. I think he sort of looked down on me for that.

"Do you mind," he asked, "if we have the driver drive alongside the park? On the west side—I haven't seen the city in so long."

"Of course not," I said. I was afraid that I might sound as though I were humoring him, but I hoped he wouldn't take it that way.

So we drove along, between the green of the park and the stony, lifeless elegance of hotels and apartment buildings, toward the vivid, killing streets of our childhood. These streets hadn't changed, though housing projects jutted up out of them now like rocks in the middle of a boiling sea. Most of the houses in which we had grown up had vanished, as had the stores from which we had stolen, the basements in which we had first tried sex, the rooftops from which we had hurled tin cans and bricks. But houses exactly like the houses of our past yet dominated the landscape, boys exactly like the boys we once had been found themselves smothering in these houses, came down into the streets for light and air and found themselves encircled by disaster. Some escaped the trap, most didn't. Those who got out always left something of themselves behind, as some animals amputate a leg and leave it in the trap. It might be said, perhaps, that I had escaped, after all, I was a schoolteacher; or that Sonny had, he hadn't lived in Harlem for years. Yet, as the cab moved uptown through streets which seemed, with a rush, to darken with dark people, and as I covertly studied Sonny's face, it came to me that what we both were seeking through our separate cab windows was that part of ourselves which had been left behind. It's always at the hour of trouble and confrontation that the missing member aches.

We hit 110th Street and started rolling up Lenox Avenue. And I'd known this avenue all my life, but it seemed to me again, as it had seemed on the day I'd first heard about Sonny's trouble, filled with a hidden menace which was its very breath of life.

"We almost there," said Sonny.

"Almost." We were both too nervous to say anything more.

We live in a housing project. It hasn't been up long. A few days after it was up it seemed uninhabitably new, now, of course, it's already rundown. It looked like a parody of the good, clean, faceless life—God knows the people who live in it do their best to make it a parody. The beat-looking grass lying around isn't enough to make their lives green, the hedges will never hold out the streets, and they know it. The big windows fool no one, they aren't big enough to make space out of no space. They don't bother with the windows, they watch the TV screen instead. The playground is most popular with the children who don't play at jacks, or skip rope, or roller skate, or swing, and they can be found in it after dark. We moved in partly because it's not too far from where I teach, and partly for the kids; but it's really just like the houses in which Sonny and I grew up. The same things happen, they'll have the same things to remember. The moment Sonny and I started into the house I had the feeling that I was simply bringing him back into the danger he had almost died trying to escape.

Sonny has never been talkative. So I don't know why I was sure he'd be dying to talk to me when supper was over the first night. Everything went fine, the oldest boy remembered him, and the youngest boy liked him, and Sonny had remembered to bring something for each of them; and Isabel, who is really much nicer than I am, more open and giving, had gone to a lot of trouble about dinner and was genuinely glad to see him. And she'd always been able to tease Sonny in a way that I haven't. It was nice to see her face so vivid again and to hear her laugh and watch her make Sonny laugh. She wasn't, or, anyway, she didn't seem to be, at all uneasy or embarrassed. She chatted as though there were no subject which had to be avoided and she got Sonny past his first, faint stiffness. And thank God she was there, for I was filled with that icy dread again. Everything I did seemed awkward to me, and everything I said sounded freighted with hidden meaning. I was trying to remember everything I'd heard about dope addiction and I couldn't help watching Sonny for signs. I wasn't doing it out of malice. I was trying to find out something about my brother. I was dying to hear him tell me he was safe.

"Safe!" my father grunted, whenever Mama suggested trying to move to a neighborhood which might be safer for children. "Safe, hell! Ain't no place safe for kids, nor nobody."

He always went on like this, but he wasn't, ever, really as bad as he sounded, not even on weekends, when he got drunk. As a matter of fact, he was always on the lookout for "something a little better," but he died before he found it. He died suddenly, during a drunken weekend in the middle of the war, when Sonny was fifteen. He and Sonny hadn't ever got on too well. And this was partly because Sonny was the apple of his father's eye. It was because he loved Sonny so much and was frightened for him, that he was always fighting with him. It doesn't do any good to fight with Sonny. Sonny just moves back, inside himself, where he can't be reached. But the principal reason that they never hit it off is that they were so much alike. Daddy was big and rough and loud-talking, just the opposite of Sonny, but they both had—that same privacy.

Mama tried to tell me something about this, just after Daddy died. I was home on leave from the army.

This was the last time I ever saw my mother alive. Just the same, this picture gets all mixed up in my mind with pictures I had of her when she was younger. The way I always see her is the way she used to be on a Sunday afternoon, say, when the old folks were talking after the big Sunday dinner. I always see her wearing pale blue. She'd be sitting on the sofa. And my father would be sitting in the easy chair, not far from her. And the living room would be full of church folks and relatives. There they sit, in chairs all around the living room, and the night is creeping up outside, but nobody knows it yet. You can see the darkness growing against the windowpanes and you hear the street noises every now and again, or maybe the jangling beat of a tambourine from one of the churches close by, but it's real quiet in the room. For a moment nobody's talking, but every face looks darkening, like the sky outside. And my mother rocks a little from the waist, and my father's eyes are closed. Everyone is looking at something a child can't see. For a minute they've forgotten the children. Maybe a kid is lying on the rug, half asleep. Maybe somebody's got a kid in his lap and is absent-mindedly stroking the kid's head. Maybe there's a kid, quiet and big-eyed, curled up in a big chair in the corner. The silence, the darkness coming, and the darkness in the faces frighten the child obscurely. He hopes that the hand which strokes his forehead will never stop—will never die. He hopes that there will never come a time when the old folks won't be sitting around the living room, talking about where they've come from, and what they've seen, and what's happened to them and their kinfolk.

But something deep and watchful in the child knows that this is bound to end, is already ending. In a moment someone will get up and turn on the light. Then the old folks will remember the children and they won't talk any more that day. And when light fills the room, the child is filled with darkness. He knows that every time this happens he's moved just a little closer to that darkness outside. The darkness outside is what the old folks have been talking about. It's what they've come from. It's what they endure. The child knows that they won't talk any more because if he knows too much about what's happened to *them*, he'll know too much too soon, about what's going to happen to *him*.

The last time I talked to my mother, I remember I was restless. I wanted to get out and see Isabel. We weren't married then and we had a lot to straighten out between us.

There Mama sat, in black, by the window. She was humming an old church song, *Lord, you brought me from a long ways off*. Sonny was out somewhere. Mama kept watching the streets.

"I don't know," she said, "If I'll ever see you again, after you go off from here. But I hope you'll remember the things I tried to teach you."

"Don't talk like that," I said, and smiled. "You'll be here a long time yet."

She smiled, too, but she said nothing. She was quiet for a long time. And I said, "Mama, don't you worry about nothing. I'll be writing all the time, and you be getting the checks. . . ."

"I want to talk to you about your brother," she said, suddenly. "If anything happens to me, he ain't going to have nobody to look out for him."

"Mama," I said, "ain't nothing going to happen to you *or* Sonny. Sonny's all right. He's a good boy and he's got good sense."

"It ain't a question of his being a good boy," Mama said, "nor of his having good sense. It ain't only the bad ones, nor yet the dumb ones that gets sucked under." She stopped, looking at me. "Your Daddy once had a brother," she said, and she smiled in a way that made me feel she was in pain. "You didn't never know that, did you?"

"No," I said. "I never knew that," and I watched her face.

"Oh, yes," she said, "your Daddy had a brother." She looked out of the window again. "I know you never saw your Daddy cry. But *I* did—many a time, through all these years."

I asked her, "What happened to his brother? How come nobody's ever talked about him?"

This was the first time I ever saw my mother look old.

"His brother got killed," she said, "when he was just a little younger than you are now. I knew him. He was a fine boy. He was maybe a little full of the devil, but he didn't mean nobody no harm."

Then she stopped, and the room was silent, exactly as it had sometimes been on those Sunday afternoons. Mama kept looking out into the streets.

"He used to have a job in the mill," she said, "and, like all young folks, he just liked to perform on Saturday nights. Saturday nights, him and your father would drift around to different places, go to dances and things like that, or just sit around with people they knew, and your father's brother would sing, he had a fine voice, and play along with himself on his guitar. Well, this particular Saturday night, him and your father was coming home from some place, and they were both a little drunk and there was a moon that night, it was bright like day. Your father's brother was feeling kind of good, and he was whistling to himself, and he had his guitar slung over his shoulder. They was coming down a hill, and beneath them was a road that turned off from the highway. Well, your father's brother, being always kind of frisky, decided to run down this hill, and he did, with that guitar banging and clanging behind him, and he ran across the road, and he was making water behind a tree. And your father was sort of amused at him and he was still coming down the hill, kind of slow. Then he heard a car motor and that same minute his brother stepped from behind the tree, into the road, in the moonlight. And he started to cross the road. And your father started to run down the hill, he says he don't know why. This car was full of white men. They was all drunk, and when they seen your father's brother they let out a great whoop and holler and they aimed the car straight at him. They was having fun, they just wanted to scare him, the way they do sometimes, you know. But they was drunk. And I guess the boy, being drunk, too, and scared, kind of lost his head. By the time he jumped it was too late. Your father says he heard his brother scream when the car rolled over him, and he heard the wood of that guitar when it give, and he heard them strings go flying, and he heard them white men shouting, and the car kept on a-going and it ain't stopped till this day. And, time your father got down the hill, his brother weren't nothing but blood and pulp."

Tears were gleaming on my mother's face. There wasn't anything I could say.

"He never mentioned it," she said, "because I never let him mention it before you children. Your Daddy was like a crazy man that night and for many a night thereafter. He says he never in his life seen anything as dark as that road after the lights of that car had gone away. Weren't nothing, weren't nobody on that road, just your Daddy and his brother and that busted guitar. Oh, yes. Your Daddy never did really get right again. Till the day he died he weren't sure but that every white man he saw was the man that killed his brother."

She stopped and took out her handkerchief and dried her eyes and looked at me.

"I ain't telling you all this," she said, "to make you scared or bitter or to make you hate nobody. I'm telling you this because you got a brother. And the world ain't changed."

I guess I didn't want to believe this. I guess she saw this in my face. She turned away from me, toward the window again, searching those streets.

"But I praise my Redeemer," she said at last, "that he called your Daddy home before me. I ain't saying it to throw no flowers at myself, but, I declare, it keeps me from feeling too cast down to know I helped your father get safely through this world. Your father always acted like he was the roughest, strongest man on earth. And everybody took him to be like that. But if he hadn't had *me* there—to see his tears!"

She was crying again. Still, I couldn't move. I said, "Lord, Lord, Mama, I didn't know it was like that."

"Oh, honey," she said, "there's a lot that you don't know. But you are going to find it out." She stood up from the window and came over to me. "You got to hold on to your brother," she said, "and don't let him fall, no matter what it looks like is happening to him and no matter how evil you gets with him. You going to be evil with him many a time. But don't you forget what I told you, you hear?"

"I won't forget," I said. "Don't you worry, I won't forget. I won't let nothing happen to Sonny."

My mother smiled as though she were amused at something she saw in my face. Then, "You may not be able to stop nothing from happening. But you got to let him know you's *there*."

Two days later I was married, and then I was gone. And I had a lot of things on my mind and I pretty well forgot my promise to Mama until I got shipped home on a special furlough for her funeral.

And, after the funeral, with just Sonny and me alone in the empty kitchen, I tried to find out something about him.

"What do you want to do?" I asked him.

"I'm going to be a musician," he said.

For he had graduated, in the time I had been away, from dancing to the juke box to finding out who was playing what, and what they were doing with it, and he had bought himself a set of drums.

"You mean, you want to be a drummer?" I somehow had the feeling that being a drummer might be all right for other people but not for my brother Sonny.

"I don't think," he said, looking at me very gravely, "that I'll ever be a good drummer. But I think I can play a piano."

I frowned. I'd never played the role of the older brother quite so seriously before, had scarcely ever, in fact, *asked* Sonny a damn thing. I sensed myself in the presence of something I didn't really know how to handle, didn't understand. So I made my frown a little deeper as I asked: "What kind of musician do you want to be?"

He grinned. "How many kinds do you think there are?"

"Be *serious*," I said.

He laughed, throwing his head back, and then looked at me. "I *am* serious."

"Well, then, for Christ's sake, stop kidding around and answer a serious question. I mean, do you want to be a concert pianist, you want to play classical music and all that, or—or, what?" Long before I finished he was laughing again. "For Christ's *sake*, Sonny!"

He sobered, but with difficulty. "I'm sorry. But you sound so—scared!" And he was off again.

"Well, you may think it's funny now, baby, but it's not going to be so funny when you have to make your living at it, let me tell you *that*." I was furious because I knew he was laughing at me and I didn't know why.

"No," he said, very sober now, and afraid, perhaps, that he'd hurt me, "I don't want to be a classical pianist. That isn't what interests me. I mean"—he paused, looking hard at me, as though his eyes would help me to understand, and then gestured helplessly, as though perhaps his hand would help—"I mean, I'll have a lot of studying to do, and I'll have to study *everything*, but I mean, I want to play *with*—jazz musicians." He stopped. "I want to play jazz," he said.

Well, the word had never before sounded as heavy, as real, as it sounded that afternoon in Sonny's mouth. I just looked at him and I was probably frowning a real frown by this time. I simply couldn't see why on earth he'd want to spend his time hanging around night clubs, clowning around on bandstands, while people pushed each other around a dance floor. It seemed—beneath him, somehow. I had never thought about it before, had never been forced to, but I suppose I had always put jazz musicians in a class with what Daddy called "good-time people."

"Are you *serious*?"

"Hell, *yes*, I'm serious."

He looked more helpless than ever, and annoyed, and deeply hurt.

I suggested, helpfully: "You mean—like Louis Armstrong?"

His face closed as though I'd struck him. "No. I'm not talking about none of that old-time, down home crap."

"Well, look, Sonny, I'm sorry, don't get mad. I just don't altogether get it, that's all. Name somebody—you know, a jazz musician you admire."

"Bird."

"Who?"

"Bird! Charlie Parker! Don't they teach you nothing in the goddamn army?"

I lit a cigarette. I was surprised and then a little amused to discover that I was trembling. "I've been out of touch," I said. "You'll have to be patient with me. Now. Who's this Parker character?"

"He's just one of the greatest jazz musicians alive," said Sonny, sullenly, his hands in his pockets, his back to me. "Maybe *the* greatest," he added, bitterly, "that's probably why *you* never heard of him."

"All right," I said, "I'm ignorant. I'm sorry. I'll go out and buy all the cat's records right away, all right?"

"It don't," said Sonny, with dignity, "make any difference to me. I don't care what you listen to. Don't do me no favors."

I was beginning to realize that I'd never seen him so upset before. With another part of my mind I was thinking that this would probably turn out to be one of those things kids go through and that I shouldn't make it seem important by pushing it too hard. Still, I didn't think it would do any harm to ask: "Doesn't all this take a lot of time? Can you make a living at it?"

He turned back to me and half leaned, half sat, on the kitchen table. "Everything takes time," he said, "and—well, yes, sure, I can make a living at it. But what I don't seem to be able to make you understand is that it's the only thing I want to do."

"Well, Sonny," I said gently, "you know people can't always do exactly what they want to do—"

"*No*, I don't know that," said Sonny, surprising me. "I think people *ought* to do what they want to do, what else are they alive for?"

"You getting to be a big boy," I said desperately, "it's time you started thinking about your future."

"I'm thinking about my future," said Sonny, grimly. "I think about it all the time."

I gave up. I decided, if he didn't change his mind, that we could always talk about it later. "In the meantime," I said, "you got to finish school." We had already decided that he'd have to move in with Isabel and her folks. I knew this wasn't the ideal arrangement because Isabel's folks are inclined to be dicty and they hadn't especially wanted Isabel to marry me. But I didn't know what else to do. "And we have to get you fixed up at Isabel's."

There was a long silence. He moved from the kitchen table to the window. "That's a terrible idea. You know it yourself."

"Do you have a *better* idea?"

He just walked up and down the kitchen for a minute. He was as tall as I was. He had started to shave. I suddenly had the feeling that I didn't know him at all.

He stopped at the kitchen table and picked up my cigarettes. Looking at me with a kind of mocking, amused defiance, he put one between his lips. "You mind?"

"You smoking already?"

He lit the cigarette and nodded, watching me through the smoke. "I just wanted to see if I'd have the courage to smoke in front of you." He grinned and blew a great cloud of smoke to the ceiling. "It was easy." He looked at my face. "Come on, now. I bet you was smoking at my age, tell the truth."

I didn't say anything but the truth was on my face, and he laughed. But now there was something very strained in his laugh. "Sure. And I bet that ain't all you was doing."

He was frightening me a little. "Cut the crap," I said. "We already decided that you was going to go and live at Isabel's. Now what's got into you all of a sudden?"

"*You* decided it," he pointed out. "*I* didn't decide nothing." he stopped in front of me, leaning against the stove, arms loosely folded. "Look, brother. I don't want to stay in Harlem no more, I really don't." He was very earnest. He looked at me, then over toward the kitchen window. There was something in his eyes I'd never seen before, some thoughtfulness, some worry all his own. He rubbed the muscle of one arm. "It's time I was getting out of here."

"Where do you want to *go*, Sonny?"

"I want to join the army. Or the navy, I don't care. If I say I'm old enough, they'll believe me."

Then I got mad. It was because I was so scared. "You must be crazy. You goddamn fool, what the hell do you want to go and join the *army* for?"

"I just told you. To get out of Harlem."

"Sonny, you haven't even finished *school*. And if you really want to be a musician, how do you expect to study if you're in the *army*?"

He looked at me, trapped, and in anguish. "There's ways. I might be able to work out some kind of deal. Anyway, I'll have the G.I. Bill when I come out."

"*If* you come out." We stared at each other. "Sonny, please. Be reasonable. I know the setup is far from perfect. But we got to do the best we can."

"I ain't learning nothing in school," he said. "Even when I go." He turned away from me and opened the window and threw his cigarette out into the narrow alley. I watched his back. "At least, I ain't learning nothing you'd want me to learn." He slammed the window so hard I thought the glass would fly out, and turned back to me. "And I'm sick of the stink of these garbage cans!"

"Sonny, I said, "I know how you feel. But if you don't finish school now, you're going to be sorry later that you didn't." I grabbed him by the shoulders. "And you only got another year. It ain't so bad. And I'll come back and I swear I'll help you do *whatever* you want to do. Just try to put up with it till I come back. Will you please do that? For me?"

He didn't answer and he wouldn't look at me.

"Sonny. You hear me?"

He pulled away. "I hear you. But you never hear anything *I* say."

I didn't know what to say to that. He looked out of the window and then back at me. "OK," he said, and sighed. "I'll try."

Then I said, trying to cheer him up a little, "They got a piano at Isabel's. You can practice on it."

And as a matter of fact, it did cheer him up for a minute. "That's right," he said to himself. "I forgot that." His face relaxed a little. But the worry, the thoughtfulness, played on it still, the way shadows play on a face which is staring into the fire.

But I thought I'd never hear the end of that piano. At first, Isabel would write me, saying how nice it was that Sonny was so serious about his music and how, as soon as he came in from school, or wherever he had been when he was supposed to be at school, he went straight to that piano and stayed there until suppertime. And, after supper, he went back to that piano and stayed there until everybody went to bed. He was at that piano all day Saturday and all day Sunday. Then he bought a record player and started playing records. He'd play one record over and over again, all day long sometimes, and he'd improvise along with it on the piano. Or he'd play one section of the record, one chord, one change, one progression, then he'd do it on the piano. Then back to the record. Then back to the piano.

Well, I really don't know how they stood it. Isabel finally confessed that it wasn't like living with a person at all, it was like living with sound. And the sound didn't make any sense to her, didn't make any sense to any of them—naturally. They began, in a way, to be afflicted by this presence that was living in their home. It was as though Sonny were some sort of god, or monster. He moved in an atmosphere which wasn't like theirs at all. They fed him and he ate, he washed himself, he walked in and out of their door; he certainly wasn't nasty or unpleasant or rude, Sonny isn't any of those things; but it was as though he were all wrapped up in some cloud, some fire, some vision all his own; and there wasn't any way to reach him.

At the same time, he wasn't really a man yet, he was still a child, and they had to watch out for him in all kinds of ways. They certainly couldn't throw him out. Neither did they dare to make a great scene about that piano because even they dimly sensed, as I sensed, from so many thousands of miles away, that Sonny was at that piano playing for his life.

But he hadn't been going to school. One day a letter came from the school board, and Isabel's mother got it—there had, apparently, been other letters but Sonny had torn them up. This day, when Sonny came in, Isabel's mother showed him the letter and asked where he'd been spending his time. And she finally got it out of him that he'd been down in Greenwich Village, with musicians and other characters, in a white girl's apartment. And this scared her and she started to scream at him, and what came up, once she began—though she denies it to this day—was what sacrifices they were making to give Sonny a decent home and how little he appreciated it.

Sonny didn't play the piano that day. By evening, Isabel's mother had calmed down but then there was the old man to deal with, and Isabel herself. Isabel says she did her best to be calm but she broke down and started crying. She says she just watched Sonny's face. She could tell, by watching him, what was happening with him. And what was happening was that they penetrated his cloud, they had reached him. Even if their fingers had been a thousand times more gentle than human fingers ever are, he could hardly help feeling that they had stripped him naked and were spitting on that nakedness. For he also had to see that his presence, that music, which was life or death to him, had been torture for them and that they had endured it, not at all for his sake, but only for mine. And Sonny couldn't take that. He can take it a little better today than he could then but he's still not very good at it and, frankly, I don't know anybody who is.

The silence of the next few days must have been louder than the sound of all the music ever played since time began. One morning, before she went to work, Isabel was in his room for something and she suddenly realized that all of his records were gone. And she knew for certain that he was gone. And he was. He went as far as the navy would carry him. He finally sent me a postcard from someplace in Greece, and that was the first I knew that Sonny was still alive. I didn't see him any more until we were both back in New York and the war had long been over.

He was a man by then, of course, but I wasn't willing to see it. He came by the house from time to time, but we fought almost every time we met. I didn't like the way he carried himself, loose and dreamlike all the time, and I didn't like his friends, and his music seemed to be merely an excuse for the life he led. It sounded just that weird and disordered.

Then we had a fight, a pretty awful fight, and I didn't see him for months. By and by I looked him up, where he was living, in a furnished room in the Village, and I tried to make it up. But there were lots of other people in the room, and Sonny just lay on his bed, and he wouldn't come downstairs with me, and he treated these other people as though they were his family and I weren't. So I got mad and then he got mad, and then I told him that he might just as well be dead as live the way he was living. Then he stood up and he told me not to worry about him any more in life, that he *was* dead as far as I was concerned. Then he pushed me to the door, and the other people looked on as though nothing were happening, and he slammed the door behind me. I stood in the hallway, staring at the door. I heard somebody laugh in the room and then the tears came to my eyes. I started down the steps, whistling to keep from crying, I kept whistling to myself, *You going to need me, baby, one of these cold, rainy days.*

I read about Sonny's trouble in the spring. Little Grace died in the fall. She was a beautiful little girl. But she only lived a little over two years. She died of polio and she suffered. She had a slight fever for a couple of days, but it didn't seem like anything and we just kept her in bed. And we would certainly have called the doctor, but the fever dropped, she seemed to be all right. So we thought it had just been a cold. Then, one day, she was up, playing, Isabel was in the kitchen fixing lunch for the two boys when they'd come in from school, and she heard Grace fall down in the living room. When you have a lot of children you don't always start running when one of them falls, unless they start screaming or something. And, this time, Grace was quiet. Yet, Isabel says that when she heard that *thump* and then that silence, something happened in her to make her afraid. And she ran to the living room and there was little Grace on the floor, all twisted up, and the reason she hadn't screamed was that she couldn't get her breath. And when she did scream, it was the worst sound, Isabel says, that she's ever heard in all her life, and she still hears it sometimes in her dreams. Isabel will sometimes wake me up with a low, moaning, strangled sound, and I have to be quick to awaken her and hold her to me and where Isabel is weeping against me seems a mortal wound.

I think I may have written Sonny the very day that little Grace was buried. I was sitting in the living room in the dark, by myself, and I suddenly thought of Sonny. My trouble made his real.

One Saturday afternoon, when Sonny had been living with us, or, anyway, been in our house, for nearly two weeks, I found myself wandering aimlessly about the living room, drinking from a can of beer, and trying to work up the courage to search Sonny's room. He was out, he was usually out whenever I was home, and Isabel had taken the children to see their grandparents. Suddenly I was standing still in front of the living-room window, watching Seventh Avenue. The idea of searching Sonny's room made me still. I scarcely dared to admit to myself what I'd be searching for. I didn't know what I'd do if I found it. Or if I didn't.

On the sidewalk across from me, near the entrance to a barbecue joint, some people were holding an old-fashioned revival meeting. The barbecue cook, wearing a dirty white apron, his conked hair reddish and metallic in the pale sun, and a cigarette between his lips, stood in the doorway, watching them. Kids and older people paused in their errands and stood there, along with some older men and a couple of very tough-looking women who watched everything that happened on the avenue, as though they owned it, or were maybe owned by it. Well, they were watching this, too. The revival was being carried on by three sisters in black, and a brother. All they had were their voices and their Bibles and a tambourine. The brother was testifying and while he testified two of the sisters stood together, seeming to say, Amen, and the third sister walked around with the tambourine outstretched and a couple of people dropped coins into it. Then the brother's testimony ended, and the sister who had been taking up the collection dumped the coins into her palm and transferred them to the pocket of her long black robe. Then she raised both hands, striking the tambourine against the air, and then against one hand, and she started to sing. And the two other sisters and the brother joined in.

It was strange, suddenly, to watch, though I had been seeing these street meetings all my life. So, of course, had everybody else down there. Yet, they paused and watched and listened and I stood still at the window. " 'Tis the old ship of Zion," they sang, and the sister with the tambourine kept a steady, jangling beat, "it has rescued many a thousand!" Not a soul under the sound of their voices was hearing this song for the first time, not one of them had been rescued. Nor had they seen much in the way of rescue work being done around them. Neither did they especially believe in the holiness of the three sisters and the brother, they knew too much about them, knew where they lived, and how. The woman with the tambourine, whose voice dominated the air, whose face was bright with joy, was divided by very little from the woman who stood watching her, a cigarette between her heavy, chapped lips, her hair a cuckoo's nest, her face scarred and swollen from many beatings, and her black eyes glittering like coal. Perhaps they both knew this, which was why, when, as rarely, they addressed each other, they addressed each other as Sister. As the singing filled the air, the watching, listening faces underwent a change, the eyes focusing on something within; the music seemed to soothe a poison out of them; and time seemed, nearly, to fall away from the sullen, belligerent, battered faces, as though they were fleeing back to their first condition, while dreaming of their last. The barbecue cook half shook his head and smiled, and dropped his cigarette and disappeared into his joint. A man fumbled in his pockets for change and stood holding it in his hand impatiently, as though he had just remembered a pressing appointment further up the avenue. He looked furious. Then I saw Sonny, standing on the edge of the crowd. He was carrying a wide, flat notebook with a green cover, and it made him look, from where I was standing, almost like a schoolboy. The coppery sun brought out the copper in his skin, he was very faintly smiling, standing very still. Then the singing stopped, the tambourine turned into a collection plate again. The furious man dropped in his coins and vanished, so did a couple of the women, and Sonny dropped some change in the plate, looking directly at the woman with a little smile. He started across the avenue, toward the house. He has a slow, loping walk, something like the way Harlem hipsters walk, only he's imposed on this his own half-beat. I had never really noticed it before.

I stayed at the window, both relieved and apprehensive. As Sonny disappeared from my sight, they began singing again. And they were still singing when his key turned in the lock.

"Hey," he said.

"Hey, yourself. You want some beer?"

"No. Well, maybe." But he came up to the window and stood beside me, looking out. "What a warm voice," he said.

They were singing *If I could only hear my mother pray again!*

"Yes," I said, "and she can sure beat that tambourine."

"But what a terrible song," he said, and laughed. He dropped his notebook on the sofa and disappeared into the kitchen. "Where's Isabel and the kids?"

"I think they went to see their grandparents. You hungry?"

"No." He came back into the living room with his can of beer. "You want to come someplace with me tonight?"

I sensed, I don't know how, that I couldn't possibly say no. "Sure. Where?"

He sat down on the sofa and picked up his notebook and started leafing through it. "I'm going to sit in with some fellows in a joint in the Village."

"You mean, you're going to play, tonight?"

"That's right." He took a swallow of his beer and moved back to the window. He gave me a sidelong look. "If you can stand it."

"I'll try," I said.

He smiled to himself, and we both watched as the meeting across the way broke up. The three sisters and the brother, heads bowed, were singing *God be with you till we meet again.* The faces around them were very quiet. Then the song ended. The small crowd dispersed. We watched the three women and the one man walk slowly up the avenue.

"When she was singing before," said Sonny, abruptly, "her voice reminded me for a minute of what heroin feels like sometimes—when it's in your veins. It makes you feel sort of warm and cool at the same time. And distant. And—and sure." He sipped his beer, very deliberately not looking at me. I watched his face. "It makes you feel—in control. Sometimes you've got to have that feeling."

"Do you?" I sat down slowly in the easy chair.

"Sometimes." He went to the sofa and picked up his notebook again. "Some people do."

"In order," I asked, "to play?" And my voice was very ugly, full of contempt and anger.

"Well"—he looked at me with great, troubled eyes, as though, in fact, he hoped his eyes would tell me things he could never otherwise say—"they *think* so. And *if* they think so—!"

"And what do *you* think?" I asked.

He sat on the sofa and put his can of beer on the floor. "I don't know," he said, and I couldn't be sure if he were answering my question or pursuing his thoughts. His face didn't tell me. "It's not so much to *play.* It's to *stand* it, to be able to make it at all. On any level." He frowned and smiled: "In order to keep from shaking to pieces."

"But these friends of yours," I said, "they seem to shake themselves to pieces pretty goddamn fast."

"Maybe." He played with the notebook. And something told me that I should curb my tongue, that Sonny was doing his best to talk, and I should listen. "But of course you only know the ones that've gone to pieces. Some don't—or at least they haven't *yet* and that's just about all *any* of us can say." He paused. "And then there are some who just live, really, in hell, and they know it and they see what's happening and they go right on. I don't know." He sighed, dropped the notebook, folded his arms. "Some guys, you can tell from the way they play, they on something *all* the time. And you can see that, well, it makes something real for them. But of course," he picked up his beer from the floor and sipped it and put the can down again, "they *want* to, too, you've got to see that. Even some of them that say they don't—*some,* not all."

"And what about you?" I asked—I couldn't help it. "What about you? Do *you* want to?"

He stood up and walked to the window and remained silent for a long time. Then he sighed. "Me," he said. Then: "While I was downstairs before, on my way here, listening to that woman sing, it struck me all of a sudden how much suffering she must have had to go through—to sing like that. It's *repulsive* to think you have to suffer that much."

I said: "But there's no way not to suffer—is there, Sonny?"

"I believe not," he said, and smiled, "but that's never stopped anyone from trying." He looked at me. "Has it?" I realized, with this mocking look, that there stood between us, forever, beyond the power of time or forgiveness, the fact that I had held silence—so long!—when he had needed human speech to help him. He turned back to the window. "No, there's no way not to suffer. But you try all kinds of ways to keep from drowning in it, to keep on top of it, and to make it seem—well, like *you*. Like you did something, all right, and now you're suffering for it. You know?" I said nothing. "Well you know," he said, impatiently, "why *do* people suffer? Maybe it's better to do something to give it a reason, *any* reason."

"But we just agreed," I said, "that there's no way not to suffer. Isn't it better, then, just to—take it?"

"But nobody just takes it," Sonny cried, "that's what I'm telling you! *Everybody* tries not to. You're just hung up on the *way* some people try—it's not *your* way!"

The hair on my face began to itch, my face felt wet. "That's not true," I said, "that's not true. I don't give a damn what other people do, I don't even care how they suffer. I just care how *you* suffer." And he looked at me. "Please believe me," I said, "I don't want to see you—die—trying not to suffer."

"I won't," he said, flatly, "die trying not to suffer. At least, not any faster than anybody else."

"But there's no need," I said, trying to laugh, "is there, in killing yourself?"

I wanted to say more, but I couldn't. I wanted to talk about will power and how life could be—well, beautiful. I wanted to say that it was all within; but was it? Or, rather, wasn't that exactly the trouble? And I wanted to promise that I would never fail him again. But it would all have sounded—empty words and lies.

So I made the promise to myself and prayed that I would keep it.

"It's terrible sometimes, inside," he said, "that's what's the trouble. You walk these streets, black and funky and cold, and there's not really a living ass to talk to, and there's nothing shaking, and there's no way of getting it out—that storm inside. You can't talk it and you can't make love with it, and when you finally try to get with it and play it, you realize *nobody's* listening. So *you've* got to listen. You got to find a way to listen."

And then he walked away from the window and sat on the sofa again, as though all the wind had suddenly been knocked out of him. "Sometimes you'll do *anything* to play, even cut your mother's throat."

He laughed and looked at me. "Or your brother's." Then he sobered "Or your own." Then: "Don't worry. I'm all right now and I think I'll *be* all right. But I can't forget—where I've been. I don't mean just the physical place I've been, I mean where I've *been*. And *what* I've been."

"What have you been, Sonny?" I asked.

He smiled—but sat sideways on the sofa, his elbow resting on the back, his fingers playing with his mouth and chin, not looking at me. "I've been something I didn't recognize, didn't know I could be. Didn't know anybody could be." He stopped, looking inward, looking helplessly young, looking old. "I'm not talking about it now because I feel *guilty* or anything like that—maybe it would be better if I did. I don't know. Anyway, I can't really talk about it. Not to you, not to anybody." And now he turned and faced me. "Sometimes, you know, and it was actually when I was most out of the world, I felt that I was in it, that I was *with* it, really, and I could play or I didn't really have to *play*, it just came out of me, it was there. And I don't know how I played, thinking about it now, but I know I did awful things, those times, sometimes, to people. Or it wasn't that I *did* anything to them—it was that they weren't real." He picked up the beer can; it was empty; he rolled it between his palms: "And other times—well, I needed a fix, I needed to find a place to lean, I needed to clear a space to *listen*—and I couldn't find it, and I—went crazy, I did terrible things to *me*, I was terrible *for* me." He began pressing the beer can between his hands, I watched the metal begin to give. It glittered, as he played with it, like a knife, and I was afraid he would cut himself, but I said nothing. "Oh well. I can never tell you. I was all by myself at the bottom of something, stinking and sweating and crying and shaking, and I smelled it, you know? *My* stink, and I thought I'd die if I couldn't get away from it and yet, all the same, I knew that everything I was doing was just locking me in with it. And I didn't know," he paused, still flattening the beer can, "I didn't know, I still *don't* know, something kept telling me that maybe it was good to smell your own stink, but I didn't think that *that* was what I'd been trying to do—and—who can stand it?" And he abruptly dropped the ruined beer can, looking at me with a small, still smile, and then rose, walking to the window as though it were the lodestone rock. I watched his face, he watched the avenue. "I couldn't tell you when Mama died—but the reason I wanted to leave Harlem so bad was to get away from drugs. And then, when I ran away, that's what I was running from—really. When I came back, nothing had changed, *I* hadn't changed, I was just—older." And he stopped, drumming with his fingers on the windowpane. The sun had vanished, soon darkness would fall. I watched his face. "It can come again," he said, almost as though speaking to himself. Then he turned to me. "It can come again," he repeated. "I just want you to know that."

"All right," I said at last. "So it can come again. All right."

He smiled, but the smile was sorrowful. "I had to try to tell you," he said.

"Yes," I said. "I understand that."

"You're my brother," he said, looking straight at me, and not smiling at all.

"Yes," I repeated, "yes. I understand that."

He turned back to the window, looking out. "All that hatred down there," he said, "all that hatred and misery and love. It's a wonder it doesn't blow the avenue apart."

We went to the only night club on a short, dark street, downtown. We squeezed through the narrow, chattering, jam-packed bar to the entrance of the big room, where the bandstand was. And we stood there for a moment, for the lights were very dim in this room and we couldn't see. Then, "Hello, boy," said a voice, and an enormous black man, much older than Sonny or myself, erupted out of all that atmospheric lighting and put an arm around Sonny's shoulder. "I been sitting right here," he said, "waiting for you."

He had a big voice, too, and heads in the darkness turned toward us.

Sonny grinned and pulled a little away, and said, "Creole, this is my brother. I told you about him."

Creole shook my hand. "I'm glad to meet you, son," he said, and it was clear that he was glad to meet me *there*, for Sonny's sake. And he smiled. "You got a real musician in *your* family," and he took his arm from Sonny's shoulder and slapped him, lightly, affectionately, with the back of his hand.

"Well. Now I've heard it all," said a voice behind us. This was another musician, and a friend of Sonny's, a coal-black, cheerful-looking man, built close to the ground. He immediately began confiding to me, at the top of his lungs, the most terrible things about Sonny, his teeth gleaming like a lighthouse and his laugh coming up out of him like the beginning of an earthquake. And it turned out that everyone at the bar knew Sonny, or almost everyone; some were musicians, working there, or nearby, or not working, some were simply hangers-on, and some were there to hear Sonny play. I was introduced to all of them and they were all very polite to me. Yet, it was clear that, for them, I was only Sonny's brother. Here, I was in Sonny's world. Or, rather: his kingdom. Here, it was not even a question that his veins bore royal blood.

They were going to play soon, and Creole installed me, by myself, at a table in a dark corner. Then I watched them, Creole, and the little black man, and Sonny, and the others, while they horsed around, standing just below the bandstand. The light from the bandstand spilled just a little short of them and, watching them laughing and gesturing and moving about, I had the feeling that they, nevertheless, were being most careful not to step into that circle of light too suddenly: that if they moved into the light too suddenly, without thinking, they would perish in flame. Then, while I watched, one of them, the small, black man, moved into the light and crossed the bandstand and started fooling around with his drums. Then—being funny and being, also, extremely ceremonious—Creole took Sonny by the arm and led him to the piano. A woman's voice called Sonny's name, and a few hands started clapping. And Sonny, also being funny and being ceremonious, and so touched, I think, that he could have cried, but neither hiding it nor showing it, riding it like a man, grinned, and put both hands to his heart and bowed from the waist.

Creole then went to the bass fiddle and a lean, very bright-skinned brown man jumped up on the bandstand and picked up his horn. So there they were, and the atmosphere on the bandstand and in the room began to change and tighten. Someone stepped up to the microphone and announced them. Then there were all kinds of murmurs. Some people at the bar shushed others. The waitress ran around, frantically getting in the last orders, guys and chicks got closer to each other, and the lights on the bandstand, on the quartet, turned to a kind of indigo. Then they all looked different there. Creole looked about him for the last time, as though he were making certain that all his chickens were in the coop, and then he—jumped and struck the fiddle. And there they were.

All I know about music is that not many people ever really hear it. And even then, on the rare occasions when something opens within, and the music enters, what we mainly hear, or hear corroborated, are personal, private, vanishing evocations. But the man who creates the music is hearing something else, is dealing with the roar rising from the void and imposing order on it as it hits the air. What is evoked in him, then, is of another order, more terrible because it has no words, and triumphant, too, for that same reason. And his triumph, when he triumphs, is ours. I just watched Sonny's face. His face was troubled, he was working hard, but he wasn't with it. And I had the feeling that, in a way, everyone on the bandstand was waiting for him, both waiting for him and pushing him along. But as I began to watch Creole, I realized that it was Creole who held them all back. He had them on a short rein. Up there, keeping the beat with his whole body, wailing on the fiddle, with his eyes half closed, he was listening to everything, but he was listening to Sonny. He was having a dialogue with Sonny. He wanted Sonny to leave the shore line and strike out for the deep water. He was Sonny's witness that deep water and drowning were not the same thing—he had been there, and he knew. And he wanted Sonny to know. He was waiting for Sonny to do the things on the keys which would let Creole know that Sonny was in the water.

And, while Creole listened, Sonny moved, deep within, exactly like someone in torment. I had never before thought of how awful the relationship must be between the musician and his instrument. He has to fill it, this instrument, with the breath of life, his own. He has to make it do what he wants it to do. And a piano is just a piano. It's made out of so much wood and wires and little hammers and big ones, and ivory. While there's only so much you can do with it, the only way to find this out is to try to try and make it do everything.

And Sonny hadn't been near a piano for over a year. And he wasn't on much better terms with his life, not the life that stretched before him now. He and the piano stammered, started one way, got scared, stopped; started another way, panicked, marked time, started again; then seemed to have found a direction, panicked again, got stuck. And the face I saw on Sonny I'd never seen before. Everything had been burned out of it, and, at the same time, things usually hidden were being burned in, by the fire and fury of the battle which was occurring in him up there.

Yet, watching Creole's face as they neared the end of the first set, I had the feeling that something had happened, something I hadn't heard. Then they finished, there was scattered applause, and then, without an instant's warning, Creole started into something else, it was almost sardonic, it was Am I Blue. And, as though he commanded, Sonny began to play. Something began to happen. And Creole let out the reins. The dry, low, black man said something awful on the drums, Creole answered, and the drums talked back. Then the horn insisted, sweet and high, slightly detached perhaps, and Creole listened, commenting now and then, dry, and driving, beautiful and calm and old. Then they all came together again, and Sonny was part of the family again. I could tell this from his face. He seemed to have found, right there beneath his fingers, a damn brand-new piano. It seemed that he couldn't get over it. Then, for a while, just being happy with Sonny, they seemed to be agreeing with him that brand-new pianos certainly were a gas.

Then Creole stepped forward to remind them that what they were playing was the blues. He hit something in all of them, he hit something in me, myself, and the music tightened and deepened, apprehension began to beat the air. Creole began to tell us what the blues were all about. They were not about anything very new. He and his boys up there were keeping it new, at the risk of ruin, destruction, madness, and death, in order to find new ways to make us listen. For, while the tale of how we suffer, and how we are delighted, and how we may triumph is never new, it always must be heard. There isn't any other tale to tell, it's the only light we've got in all this darkness.

And this tale, according to that face, that body, those strong hands on those strings, has another aspect in every country, and a new depth in every generation. Listen, Creole seemed to be saying, listen. Now these are Sonny's blues. He made the little black man on the drums know it, and the bright, brown man on the horn. Creole wasn't trying any longer to get Sonny in the water. He was wishing him Godspeed. Then he stepped back, very slowly, filling the air with the immense suggestion that Sonny speak for himself.

Then they all gathered around Sonny, and Sonny played. Every now and again one of them seemed to say, Amen. Sonny's fingers filled the air with life, his life. But that life contained so many others. And Sonny went all the way back, he really began with the spare, flat statement of the opening phrase of the song. Then he began to make it his. It was very beautiful because it wasn't hurried and it was no longer a lament. I seemed to hear with what burning he had made it his, with what burning we had yet to make it ours, how we could cease lamenting. Freedom lurked around us and I understood, at last, that he could help us to be free if we would listen, that he would never be free until we did. Yet, there was no battle in his face now. I heard what he had gone through, and would continue to go through until he came to rest in earth. He had made it his: that long line, of which we knew only Mama and Daddy. And he was giving it back, as everything must be given back, so that, passing through death, it can live forever. I saw my mother's face again, and felt, for the first time, how the stones of the road she had walked on must have bruised her feet. I saw the moonlit road where my father's brother died. And it brought something else back to me, and carried me past it. It saw my little girl again and felt Isabel's tears again, and I felt my own tears begin to rise. And I was yet aware that this was only a moment, that the world waited outside, as hungry as a tiger, and that trouble stretched above us, longer than the sky.

Then it was over. Creole and Sonny let out their breath, both soaking wet, and grinning. There was a lot of applause and some of it was real. In the dark, the girl came by and I asked her to take drinks to the bandstand. There was a long pause, while they talked up there in the indigo light and after a while I saw the girl put a Scotch and milk on top of the piano for Sonny. He didn't seem to notice it, but just before they started playing again, he sipped from it and looked toward me, and nodded. Then he put it back on top of the piano. For me, then, as they began to play again, it glowed and shook above my brother's head like the very cup of trembling.

FLANNERY O'CONNOR

1925–1964

Everything That Rises Must Converge

Her doctor had told Julian's mother that she must lose twenty pounds on account of her blood pressure, so on Wednesday nights Julian had to take her downtown on the bus for a reducing class at the Y. The reducing class was designed for working girls over fifty, who weighed from 165 to 200 pounds. His mother was one of the slimmer ones, but she said ladies did not tell their age or weight. She would not ride the buses by herself at night since they had been integrated, and because the reducing class was one of her few pleasures, necessary for her health, and *free*, she said Julian could at least put himself out to take her, considering all she did for him. Julian did not like to consider all she did for him, but every Wednesday night he braced himself and took her.

She was almost ready to go, standing before the hall mirror, putting on her hat, while he, his hands behind him, appeared pinned to the door frame, waiting like Saint Sebastian for the arrows to begin piercing him. The hat was new and had cost her seven dollars and a half. She kept saying, "Maybe I shouldn't have paid that for it. No, I shouldn't have. I'll take it off and return it tomorrow. I shouldn't have bought it."

Julian raised his eyes to heaven. "Yes, you should have bought it," he said. "Put it on and let's go." It was a hideous hat. A purple velvet flap came down on one side of it and stood up on the other; the rest of it was green and looked like a cushion with the stuffing out. He decided it was less comical than jaunty and pathetic. Everything that gave her pleasure was small and depressed him.

She lifted the hat one more time and set it down slowly on top of her head. Two wings of gray hair protruded on either side of her florid face, but her eyes, sky-blue, were as innocent and untouched by experience as they must have been when she was ten. Were it not that she was a widow who had struggled fiercely to feed and clothe and put him through school and who was supporting him still, "until he got on his feet," she might have been a little girl that he had to take to town.

"It's all right, it's all right," he said. "Let's go." He opened the door himself and started down the walk to get her going. The sky was a dying violet and the houses stood out darkly against it, bulbous liver-colored monstrosities of a uniform ugliness though no two were alike. Since this had been a fashionable neighborhood forty years ago, his mother persisted in thinking they did well to have an apartment in it. Each house had a narrow collar of dirt around it in which sat, usually, a grubby child. Julian walked with his hands in his pockets, his head down and thrust forward and his eyes glazed with the determination to make himself completely numb during the time he would be sacrificed to her pleasure.

The door closed and he turned to find the dumpy figure, surmounted by the atrocious hat, coming toward him. "Well," she said, "you only live once and paying a little more for it, I at least won't meet myself coming and going."

"Some day I'll start making money," Julian said gloomily—he knew he never would—"and you can have one of those jokes whenever you take the fit." But first they would move. He visualized a place where the nearest neighbors would be three miles away on either side.

"I think you're doing fine," she said, drawing on her gloves. "You've only been out of school a year. Rome wasn't built in a day."

She was one of the few members of the Y reducing class who arrived in hat and gloves and who had a son who had been to college. "It takes time," she said, "and the world is in such a mess. This hat looked better on me than any of the others, though when she brought it out I said, 'Take that thing back. I wouldn't have it on my head,' and she said, 'Now wait till you see it on,' and when she put it on me, I said, 'We-ull,' and she said, 'If you ask me, that hat does something for you and you do something for the hat, and besides,' she said, 'with that hat, you won't meet yourself coming and going.' "

Julian thought he could have stood his lot better if she had been selfish, if she had been an old hag who drank and screamed at him. He walked along, saturated in depression, as if in the midst of his martyrdom he had lost his faith. Catching sight of his long, hopeless, irritated face, she stopped suddenly with a grief-stricken look, and pulled back on his arm. "Wait on me," she said. "I'm going back to the house and take this thing off and tomorrow I'm going to return it. I was out of my head. I can pay the gas bill with the seven-fifty."

He caught her arm in a vicious grip. "You are not going to take it back," he said. "I like it."

"Well," she said, "I don't think I ought . . ."

"Shut up and enjoy it," he muttered, more depressed than ever.

"With the world in the mess it's in," she said, "it's a wonder we can enjoy anything. I tell you, the bottom rail is on the top."

Julian sighed.

"Of course," she said, "if you know who you are, you can go

anywhere." She said this every time he took her to the reducing class. "Most of them in it are not our kind of people," she said, "but I can be gracious to anybody. I know who I am."

"They don't give a damn for your graciousness," Julian said savagely. "Knowing who you are is good for one generation only. You haven't the foggiest idea where you stand now or who you are."

She stopped and allowed her eyes to flash at him. "I most certainly do know who I am," she said, "and if you don't know who you are, I'm ashamed of you."

"Oh hell," Julian said.

"Your great-grandfather was a former governor of this state," she said. "Your grandfather was a prosperous landowner. Your grandmother was a Godhigh."

"Will you look around you," he said tensely, "and see where you are now?" and he swept his arm jerkily out to indicate the neighborhood, which the growing darkness at least made less dingy.

"You remain what you are," she said. "Your great-grandfather had a plantation and two hundred slaves."

"There are no more slaves," he said irritably.

"They were better off when they were," she said. He groaned to see that she was off on that topic. She rolled onto it every few days like a train on an open track. He knew every stop, every junction, every swamp along the way, and knew the exact point at which her conclusion would roll majestically into the station: "It's ridiculous. It's simply not realistic. They should rise, yes, but on their own side of the fence."

"Let's skip it," Julian said.

"The ones I feel sorry for," she said, "are the ones that are half white. They're tragic."

"Will you skip it?"

"Suppose we were half white. We would certainly have mixed feelings."

"I have mixed feelings now," he groaned.

"Well let's talk about something pleasant," she said. "I remember going to Grandpa's when I was a little girl. Then the house had double stairways that went up to what was really the second floor—all the cooking was done on the first. I used to like to stay down in the kitchen on account of the way the walls smelled. I would sit with my nose pressed against the plaster and take deep breaths. Actually the place belonged to the Godhighs but your grandfather Chestny paid the mortgage and saved it for them. They were in reduced circumstances," she said, "but reduced or not, they never forgot who they were."

"Doubtless that decayed mansion reminded them," Julian muttered. He never spoke of it without contempt or thought of it without longing. He had seen it once when he was a child before it had been sold. The double stairways had rotted and been torn down. Negroes were living in it. But it remained in his mind as his mother had known it. It appeared in his dreams regularly. He would stand on the wide porch, listening to the rustle of oak leaves, then wander through the high-ceilinged hall into the parlor that opened onto it and gaze at the worn rugs and faded draperies. It occurred to him that it was he, not she, who could have appreciated it. He preferred its threadbare elegance to anything he could name and it was because of it that all the neighborhoods they had lived in had been a torment to him—whereas she had hardly known the difference. She called her insensitivity "being adjustable."

"And I remember the old darky who was my nurse, Caroline. There was no better person in the world. I've always had a great respect for my colored friends," she said. "I'd do anything in the world for them and they'd . . ."

"Will you for God's sake get off that subject?" Julian said. When he got on a bus by himself, he made it a point to sit down beside a Negro, in reparation as it were for his mother's sins.

"You're mighty touchy tonight," she said. "Do you feel all right?"

"Yes I feel all right," he said. "Now lay off."

She pursed her lips. "Well, you certainly are in a vile humor," she observed. "I just won't speak to you at all."

They had reached the bus stop. There was no bus in sight and Julian, his hands still jammed in his pockets and his head thrust forward, scowled down the empty street. The frustration of having to wait on the bus as well as ride on it began to creep up his neck like a hot hand. The presence of his mother was borne in upon him as she gave a pained sigh. He looked at her bleakly. She was holding herself very erect under the preposterous hat, wearing it like a banner of her imaginary dignity. There was in him an evil urge to break her spirit. He suddenly unloosened his tie and pulled it off and put it in his pocket.

She stiffened. "Why must you look like *that* when you take me to town?" she said. "Why must you deliberately embarrass me?"

"If you'll never learn where you are," he said, "you can at least learn where I am."

"You look like a—thug," she said.

"Then I must be one," he murmured.

"I'll just go home," she said. "I will not bother you. If you can't do a little thing like that for me . . ."

Rolling his eyes upward, he put his tie back on. "Restored to my class," he muttered. He thrust his face toward her and hissed, "True culture is in the mind, the *mind*," he said, and tapped his head, "the mind."

"It's in the heart," she said, "and in how you do things and how you do things is because of who you *are*."

"Nobody in the damn bus cares who you are."

"I care who I am," she said icily.

The lighted bus appeared on top of the next hill and as it approached, they moved out into the street to meet it. He put his hand under her elbow and hoisted her up on the creaking step. She entered with a little smile, as if she were going into a drawing room where everyone had been waiting for her. While he put in the tokens, she sat down on one of the broad front seats for three which faced the aisle. A thin woman with protruding teeth and long yellow hair was sitting on the end of it. His mother moved up beside her and left room for Julian besides herself. He sat down and looked at the floor across the aisle where a pair of thin feet in red and white canvas sandals were planted.

His mother immediately began a general conversation meant to attract anyone who felt like talking. "Can it get any hotter?" she said and removed from her purse a folding fan, black with a Japanese scene on it, which she began to flutter before her.

"I reckon it might could," the woman with the protruding teeth said, "but I know for a fact my apartment couldn't get no hotter."

"It must get the afternoon sun," his mother said. She sat forward and looked up and down the bus. It was half filled. Everybody was white. "I see we have the bus to ourselves," she said. Julian cringed.

"For a change," said the woman across the aisle, the owner of the red and white canvas sandals. "I come on one the other day and they were thick as fleas—up front and all through."

"The world is in a mess everywhere," his mother said. "I don't know how we've let it get in this fix."

"What gets my goat is all those boys from good families stealing automobile tires," the woman with the protruding teeth said. "I told my boy, I said you may not be rich but you been raised right and if I ever catch you in any such mess, they can send you on to the reformatory. Be exactly where you belong."

"Training tells," his mother said. "Is your boy in high school?"

"Ninth grade," the woman said.

"My son just finished college last year. He wants to write but he's selling typewriters until he gets started," his mother said.

The woman leaned forward and peered at Julian. He threw her such a malevolent look that she subsided against the seat. On the floor across the aisle there was an abandoned newspaper. He got up and got it and opened it out in front of him. His mother discreetly continued the conversation in a lower tone but the woman across the aisle said in a loud voice, "Well that's nice. Selling typewriters is close to writing. He can go right from one to the other."

"I tell him," his mother said, "that Rome wasn't built in a day."

Behind the newspaper Julian was withdrawing into the inner compartment of his mind where he spent most of his time. This was a kind of mental bubble in which he established himself when he could not bear to be a part of what was going on around him. From it he could see out and judge but in it he was safe from any kind of penetration from without. It was the only place where he felt free of the general idiocy of his fellows. His mother had never entered it but from it he could see her with absolute clarity.

The old lady was clever enough and he thought that if she had started from any of the right premises, more might have been expected of her. She lived according to the laws of her own fantasy world, outside of which he had never seen her set foot. The law of it was to sacrifice herself for him after she had first created the necessity to do so by making a mess of things. If he had permitted her sacrifices, it was only because her lack of foresight had made them necessary. All of her life had been a struggle to act like a Chestny without the Chestny goods, and to give him everything she thought a Chestny ought to have; but since, said she, it was fun to struggle, why complain? And when you had won, as she had won, what fun to look back on the hard times! He could not forgive her that she had enjoyed the struggle and that she thought *she* had won.

What she meant when she said she had won was that she had brought him up successfully and had sent him to college and that he had turned out so well—good looking (her teeth had gone unfilled so that his could be straightened), intelligent (he realized he was too intelligent to be a success), and with a future ahead of him (there was of course no future ahead of him). She excused his gloominess on the grounds that he was still growing up and his radical ideas on his lack of practical experience. She said he didn't yet know a thing about "life," that he hadn't even entered the real world—when already he was as disenchanted with it as a man of fifty.

The further irony of all this was that in spite of her, he had turned out so well. In spite of going to only a third-rate college, he had, on his own initiative, come out with a first-rate education; in spite of growing up dominated by a small mind, he had ended up with a large one; in spite of all her foolish views, he was free of prejudice and unafraid to face facts. Most miraculous of all, instead of being blinded by love for her as she was for him, he had cut himself emotionally free of her and could see her with complete objectivity. He was not dominated by his mother.

The bus stopped with a sudden jerk and shook him from his

meditation. A woman from the back lurched forward with little steps and barely escaped falling in his newspaper as she righted herself. She got off and a large Negro got on. Julian kept his paper lowered to watch. It gave him a certain satisfaction to see injustice in daily operation. It confirmed his view that with a few exceptions there was no one worth knowing within a radius of three hundred miles. The Negro was well dressed and carried a briefcase. He looked around and then sat down on the other end of the seat where the woman with the red and white canvas sandals was sitting. He immediately unfolded a newspaper and obscured himself behind it. Julian's mother's elbow at once prodded insistently into his ribs. "Now you see why I won't ride on these buses by myself," she whispered.

The woman with the red and white canvas sandals had risen at the same time the Negro sat down and had gone further back in the bus and taken the seat of the woman who had got off. His mother leaned forward and cast her an approving look.

Julian rose, crossed the aisle, and sat down in the place of the woman with the canvas sandals. From this position, he looked serenely across at his mother. Her face had turned an angry red. He stared at her, making his eyes the eyes of a stranger. He felt his tension suddenly lift as if he had openly declared war on her.

He would have liked to get in conversation with the Negro and to talk with him about art or politics or any subject that would be above the comprehension of those around them, but the man remained entrenched behind his paper. He was either ignoring the change of seating or had never noticed it. There was no way for Julian to convey his sympathy.

His mother kept her eyes fixed reproachfully on his face. The woman with the protruding teeth was looking at him avidly as if he were a type of monster new to her.

"Do you have a light?" he asked the Negro.

Without looking away from his paper, the man reached in his pocket and handed him a packet of matches.

"Thanks," Julian said. For a moment he held the matches foolishly. A NO SMOKING sign looked down upon him from over the door. This alone would not have deterred him; he had no cigarettes. He had quit smoking some months before because he could not afford it. "Sorry," he muttered and handed back the matches. The Negro lowered the paper and gave him an annoyed look. He took the matches and raised the paper again.

His mother continued to gaze at him but she did not take advantage of his momentary discomfort. Her eyes retained their battered look. Her face seemed to be unnaturally red, as if her blood pressure had risen. Julian allowed no glimmer of sympathy to show on his face.

Having got the advantage, he wanted desperately to keep it and carry it through. He would have liked to teach her a lesson that would last her a while, but there seemed no way to continue the point. The Negro refused to come out from behind his paper.

Julian folded his arms and looked stolidly before him, facing her but as if he did not see her, as if he had ceased to recognize her existence. He visualized a scene in which the bus having reached their stop, he would remain in his seat and when she said, "Aren't you going to get off?" he would look at her as at a stranger who had rashly addressed him. The corner they got off on was usually deserted, but it was well lighted and it would not hurt her to walk by herself the four blocks to the Y. He decided to wait until the time came and then decide whether or not he would let her get off by herself. He would have to be at the Y at ten to bring her back, but he could leave her wondering if he was going to show up. There was no reason for her to think she could always depend on him.

He retired again into the high-ceilinged room sparsely settled with large pieces of antique furniture. His soul expanded momentarily but then he became aware of his mother across from him and the vision shriveled. He studied her coldly. Her feet in little pumps dangled like a child's and did not quite reach the floor. She was training on him an exaggerated look of reproach. He felt completely detached from her. At that moment he could with pleasure have slapped her as he would have slapped a particularly obnoxious child in his charge.

He began to imagine various unlikely ways by which he could teach her a lesson. He might make friends with some distinguished Negro professor or lawyer and bring him home to spend the evening. He would be entirely justified but her blood pressure would rise to 300. He could not push her to the extent of making her have a stroke, and moreover, he had never been successful at making any Negro friends. He had tried to strike up an acquaintance on the bus with some of the better types, with ones that looked like professors or ministers or lawyers. One morning he had sat down next to a distinguished-looking dark brown man who had answered his questions with a sonorous solemnity but who had turned out to be an undertaker. Another day he had sat down beside a cigar-smoking Negro with a diamond ring on his finger, but after a few stilted pleasantries, the Negro had rung the buzzer and risen, slipping two lottery tickets into Julian's hand as he climbed over him to leave.

He imagined his mother lying desperately ill and his being able to secure only a Negro doctor for her. He toyed with that idea for a few minutes and then dropped it for a momentary vision of himself participating as a sympathizer in a sit-in demonstration. This was possible but he did not linger with it. Instead, he approached the ultimate horror. He brought home a beautiful suspiciously Negroid woman. Prepare yourself, he said. There is nothing you can do about it. This is the woman I've chosen. She's intelligent, dignified, even good, and she's suffered and she hasn't thought it *fun*. Now persecute us, go ahead and persecute us. Drive her out of here, but remember, you're driving me too. His eyes were narrowed and through the indignation he had generated, he saw his mother across the aisle, purple-faced, shrunken to the dwarf-like proportions of her moral nature, sitting like a mummy beneath the ridiculous banner of her hat.

He was tilted out of his fantasy again as the bus stopped. The door opened with a sucking hiss and out of the dark a large, gaily dressed, sullen-looking colored woman got on with a little boy. The child, who might have been four, had on a short plaid suit and a Tyrolean hat with a blue feather in it. Julian hoped that he would sit down beside him and that the woman would push in beside his mother. He could think of no better arrangement.

As she waited for her tokens, the woman was surveying the seating possibilities—he hoped with the idea of sitting where she was least wanted. There was something familiar-looking about her but Julian could not place what it was. She was a giant of a woman. Her face was set not only to meet opposition but to seek it out. The downward tilt of her large lower lip was like a warning sign: DON'T TAMPER WITH ME. Her bulging figure was encased in a green crepe dress and her feet overflowed in red shoes. She had on a hideous hat. A purple velvet flap came down on one side of it and stood up on the other; the rest of it was green and looked like a cushion with the stuffing out. She carried a mammoth red pocketbook that bulged throughout as if it were stuffed with rocks.

To Julian's disappointment, the little boy climbed up on the empty seat beside his mother. His mother lumped all children, black and white, into the common category, "cute," and she thought little Negroes were on the whole cuter than little white children. She smiled at the little boy as he climbed on the seat.

Meanwhile the woman was bearing down upon the empty seat beside Julian. To his annoyance, she squeezed herself into it. He saw his mother's face change as the woman settled herself next to him and he realized with satisfaction that this was more objectionable to her than it was to him. Her face seemed almost gray and there was a look of dull recognition in her eyes, as if suddenly she had sickened at some awful confrontation. Julian saw that it was because she and the woman had, in a sense, swapped sons. Though his mother would not realize the symbolic significance of this, she would feel it. His amusement showed plainly on his face.

The woman next to him muttered something unintelligible to

herself. He was conscious of a kind of bristling next to him, muted growling like that of an angry cat. He could not see anything but the red pocketbook upright on the bulging green thighs. He visualized the woman as she had stood waiting for her tokens—the ponderous figure, rising from the red shoes upward over the solid hips, the mammoth bosom, the haughty face, to the green and purple hat.

His eyes widened.

The vision of the two hats, identical, broke upon him with the radiance of a brilliant sunrise. His face was suddenly lit with joy. He could not believe that Fate had thrust upon his mother such a lesson. He gave a loud chuckle so that she would look at him and see that he saw. She turned her eyes on him slowly. The blue in them seemed to have turned a bruised purple. For a moment he had an uncomfortable sense of her innocence, but it lasted only a second before principle rescued him. Justice entitled him to laugh. His grin hardened until it said to her as plainly as if he were saying aloud: Your punishment exactly fits your pettiness. This should teach you a permanent lesson.

Her eyes shifted to the woman. She seemed unable to bear looking at him and to find the woman preferable. He became conscious again of the bristling presence at his side. The woman was rumbling like a volcano about to become active. His mother's mouth began to twitch slightly at one corner. With a sinking heart, he saw incipient signs of recovery on her face and realized that this was going to strike her suddenly as funny and was going to be no lesson at all. She kept her eyes on the woman and an amused smile came over her face as if the woman were a monkey that had stolen her hat. The little Negro was looking up at her with large fascinated eyes. He had been trying to attract her attention for some time.

"Carver!" the woman said suddenly. "Come heah!"

When he saw that the spotlight was on him at last, Carver drew his feet up and turned himself toward Julian's mother and giggled.

"Carver!" the woman said. "You heah me? Come heah!"

Carver slid down from the seat but remained squatting with his back against the base of it, his head turned slyly around toward Julian's mother, who was smiling at him. The woman reached a hand across the aisle and snatched him to her. He righted himself and hung backwards on her knees, grinning at Julian's mother. "Isn't he cute?" Julian's mother said to the woman with the protruding teeth.

"I reckon he is," the woman said without conviction.

The Negress yanked him upright but he eased out of her grip and shot across the aisle and scrambled, giggling wildly, onto the seat beside his love.

"I think he likes me," Julian's mother said, and smiled at the woman. It was the smile she used when she was being particularly gracious to an inferior. Julian saw everything lost. The lesson had rolled off her like rain on a roof.

The woman stood up and yanked the little boy off the seat as if she were snatching him from contagion. Julian could feel the rage in her at having no weapon like his mother's smile. She gave the child a sharp slap across his leg. He howled once and then thrust his head into her stomach and kicked his feet against her shins. "Behave," she said vehemently.

The bus stopped and the Negro who had been reading the newspaper got off. The woman moved over and set the little boy down with a thump between herself and Julian. She held him firmly by the knee. In a moment he put his hands in front of his face and peeped at Julian's mother through his fingers.

"I see yoooooooo!" she said and put her hand in front of her face and peeped at him.

The woman slapped his hand down. "Quit yo' foolishness," she said, "before I knock the living Jesus out of you!"

Julian was thankful that the next stop was theirs. He reached up and pulled the cord. The woman reached up and pulled it at the same time. Oh my God, he thought. He had the terrible intuition that when they got off the bus together, his mother would open her purse and give the little boy a nickel. The gesture would be as natural to her as breathing. The bus stopped and the woman got up and lunged to the front, dragging the child, who wished to stay on, after her. Julian and his mother got up and followed. As they neared the door, Julian tried to relieve her of her pocketbook.

"No," she murmured, "I want to give the little boy a nickel."

"No!" Julian hissed. "No!"

She smiled down at the child and opened her bag. The bus door opened and the woman picked him up by the arm and descended with him, hanging at her hip. Once in the street she set him down and shook him.

Julian's mother had to close her purse while she got down the bus step but as soon as her feet were on the ground, she opened it again and began to rummage inside. "I can't find but a penny," she whispered, "but it looks like a new one."

"Don't do it!" Julian said fiercely between his teeth. There was a streetlight on the corner and she hurried to get under it so that she could better see into her pocketbook. The woman was heading off rapidly down the street with the child still hanging backward on her hand.

"Oh little boy!" Julian's mother called and took a few quick steps and caught up with them just beyond the lamppost. "Here's a bright new penny for you," and she held out the coin, which shone bronze in the dim light.

The huge woman turned and for a moment stood, her shoulders lifted and her face frozen with frustrated rage, and stared at Julian's mother. Then all at once she seemed to explode like a piece of machinery that had been given one ounce of pressure too much. Julian saw the black fist swing out with the red pocketbook. He shut his eyes and cringed as he heard the woman shout, "He don't take nobody's pennies!" When he opened his eyes, the woman was disappearing down the street with the little boy staring wide-eyed over her shoulder. Julian's mother was sitting on the sidewalk.

"I told you not to do that," Julian said angrily. "I told you not to do that!"

He stood over her for a minute, gritting his teeth. Her legs were stretched out in front of her and her hat was on her lap. He squatted down and looked her in the face. It was totally expressionless. "You got exactly what you deserved," he said. "Now get up."

He picked up her pocketbook and put what had fallen out back in it. He picked the hat up off her lap. The penny caught his eye on the sidewalk and he picked that up and let it drop before her eyes into the purse. Then he stood up and leaned over and held his hands out to pull her up. She remained immobile. He sighed. Rising about them on either side were black apartment buildings, marked with irregular rectangles of light. At the end of the block a man came out of a door and walked off in the opposite direction. "All right," he said, "suppose somebody happens by and wants to know why you're sitting on the sidewalk?"

She took the hand and, breathing hard, pulled heavily up on it and then stood for a moment, swaying slightly as if the spots of light in the darkness were circling around her. Her eyes, shadowed and confused, finally settled on his face. He did not try to conceal his irritation. "I hope this teaches you a lesson," he said. She leaned forward and her eyes raked his face. She seemed trying to determine his identity. Then, as if she found nothing familiar about him, she started off with a headlong movement in the wrong direction.

"Aren't you going on to the Y?" he asked.

"Home," she muttered.

"Well, are we walking?"

For answer she kept going. Julian followed along, his hands behind him. He saw no reason to let the lesson she had had go without backing it up with an explanation of its meaning. She might as well be made to understand what had happened to her. "Don't think that was just an uppity Negro woman," he said. "That was the whole colored race which will no longer take your condescending pennies. That was your black double. She can wear the same hat as you, and to be sure," he added gratuitously (because he thought it was funny), "it looked better on her than it did on you. What all this means," he said, "is that the old world is gone. The old manners are obsolete and your graciousness is not worth a damn." He thought bitterly of the house that had been lost for him. "You aren't who you think you are," he said.

She continued to plow ahead, paying no attention to him. Her hair had come undone on one side. She dropped her pocketbook and took no notice. He stooped and picked it up and handed it to her but she did not take it.

"You needn't act as if the world had come to an end," he said, "because it hasn't. From now on you've got to live in a new world and face a few realities for a change. Buck up," he said, "it won't kill you."

She was breathing fast.

"Let's wait on the bus," he said.

"Home," she said thickly.

"I hate to see you behave like this," he said. "Just like a child. I should be able to expect more of you." He decided to stop where he was and make her stop and wait for a bus. "I'm not going any farther," he said, stopping. "We're going on the bus."

She continued to go on as if she had not heard him. He took a few steps and caught her arm and stopped her. He looked into her face and caught his breath. He was looking into a face he had never seen before. "Tell Grandpa to come get me," she said.

He stared, stricken.

"Tell Caroline to come get me," she said.

Stunned, he let her go and she lurched forward again, walking as if one leg were shorter than the other. A tide of darkness seemed to be sweeping her from him. "Mother!" he cried. "Darling, sweetheart, wait!" Crumpling, she fell to the pavement. He dashed forward and fell at her side, crying, "Mamma, Mamma!" He turned her over. Her face was fiercely distorted. One eye, large and staring, moved slightly on the left as if it had become unmoored. The other remained fixed on him, raked his face again, found nothing and closed.

"Wait here, wait here!" he cried and jumped up and began to run for help toward a cluster of lights he saw in the distance ahead of him. "Help, help!" he shouted, but his voice was thin, scarcely a thread of sound. The lights drifted farther away the faster he ran and his feet moved numbly as if they carried him nowhere. The tide of darkness seemed to sweep him back to her, postponing from moment to moment his entry into the world of guilt and sorrow.

JOHN UPDIKE
1932–
Tomorrow and Tomorrow and So Forth

Whirling, talking, 11D began to enter Room 109. From the quality of the class's excitement Mark Prosser guessed it would rain. He had been teaching high school for three years, yet his students still impressed him; they were such sensitive animals. They reacted so infallibly to merely barometric pressure.

In the doorway, Brute Young paused while little Barry Snyder giggled at his elbow. Barry's stagy laugh rose and fell, dipping down toward some vile secret that had to be tasted and retasted, then soaring like a rocket to proclaim that he, little Barry, shared such a secret with the school's fullback. Being Brute's stooge was precious to Barry. The fullback paid no attention to him; he twisted his neck to stare at something not yet coming through the door. He yielded heavily to the procession pressing him forward.

Right under Prosser's eyes, like a murder suddenly appearing in an annalistic frieze of kings and queens, someone stabbed a girl in the back with a pencil. She ignored the assault saucily. Another hand yanked out Geoffrey Langer's shirt-tail. Geoffrey, a bright student, was uncertain whether to laugh it off or defend himself with anger, and made a weak, half-turning gesture of compromise, wearing an expression of distant arrogance that Prosser instantly coördinated with baffled feelings he used to have. All along the line, in the glitter of key chains and the acute angles of turned-back shirt cuffs, an electricity was expressed which simple weather couldn't generate.

Mark wondered if today Gloria Armstrong wore that sweater, an ember-pink angora, with very brief sleeves. The virtual sleevelessness was the disturbing factor: the exposure of those two serene arms to the air, white as thighs against the delicate wool.

His guess was correct. A vivid pink patch flashed through the jiggle of arms and shoulders as the final knot of youngsters entered the room.

"Take your seats," Mr. Prosser said. "Come on. Let's go."

Most obeyed, but Peter Forrester, who had been at the center of the group around Gloria, still lingered in the doorway with her, finishing some story, apparently determined to make her laugh or gasp. When she did gasp, he tossed his head with satisfaction. His orange hair, preened into a kind of floating bang, bobbed. Mark had always disliked redheaded males, with their white eyelashes and puffy faces and thyroid eyes, and absurdly self-confident mouths. A race of bluffers. His own hair was brown.

When Gloria, moving in a considered, stately way, had taken her seat, and Peter had swerved into his, Mr. Prosser said, "Peter Forrester."

"Yes?" Peter rose, scrabbling through his book for the right place.

"Kindly tell the class the exact meaning of the words 'Tomorrow, and tomorrow, and tomorrow / Creeps in this petty pace from day to day.' "

Peter glanced down at the high-school edition of *Macbeth* lying open on his desk. One of the duller girls tittered expectantly from the back of the room. Peter was popular with the girls; girls that age had minds like moths.

"Peter. With your book shut. We have all memorized this passage for today. Remember?" The girl in the back of the room squealed in delight. Gloria laid her own book face-open on her desk, where Peter could see it.

Peter shut his book with a bang and stared into Gloria's. "Why," he said at last, "I think it means pretty much what it says."

"Which is?"

"Why, that tomorrow is something we often think about. It creeps into our conversation all the time. We couldn't make any plans without thinking about tomorrow."

"I see. Then you would say that Macbeth is here referring to the, the date-book aspect of life?"

Geoffrey Langer laughed, no doubt to please Mr. Prosser. For a moment, he *was* pleased. Then he realized he had been playing for laughs at a student's expense.

His paraphrase had made Peter's reading of the lines seem more ridiculous than it was. He began to retract. "I admit—"

But Peter was going on; redheads never know when to quit. "Macbeth means that if we quit worrying about tomorrow, and just live for today, we could appreciate all the wonderful things that are going on under our noses."

Mark considered this a moment before he spoke. He would not be sarcastic. "Uh, without denying that there is truth in what you say, Peter, do you think it likely that Macbeth, in his situation, would be expressing such"—he couldn't help himself—"such sunny sentiments?"

Geoffrey laughed again. Peter's neck reddened; he studied the floor. Gloria glared at Mr. Prosser, the indignation in her face clearly meant for him to see.

Mark hurried to undo his mistake. "Don't misunderstand me, please," he told Peter. "I don't have all the answers myself. But it seems to me the whole speech, down to 'Signifying nothing,' is saying that life is—well, a *fraud*. Nothing wonderful about it."

"Did Shakespeare really think that?" Geoffrey Langer asked, a nervous quickness pitching his voice high.

Mark read into Geoffrey's question his own adolescent premonitions of the terrible truth. The attempt he must make was plain. He told Peter he could sit down and looked through the window toward the steadying sky. The clouds were gaining intensity. "There is," Mr. Prosser slowly began, "much darkness in Shakespeare's work, and no play is darker than 'Macbeth.' The atmosphere is poisonous, oppressive. One critic has said that in this play, humanity suffocates." He felt himself in danger of suffocating, and cleared his throat.

"In the middle of his career, Shakespeare wrote plays about men like Hamlet and Othello and Macbeth—men who aren't allowed by their society, or bad luck, or some minor flaw in themselves, to become the great men they might have been. Even Shakespeare's comedies of this period deal with a world gone sour. It is as if he had seen through the bright, bold surface of his earlier comedies and histories and had looked upon something terrible. It frightened him, just as some day it may frighten some of you." In his determination to find the right words, he had been staring at Gloria, without meaning to. Embarrassed, she nodded, and, realizing what had happened, he smiled at her.

He tried to make his remarks gentler, even diffident. "But then I think Shakespeare sensed a redeeming truth. His last plays are serene and symbolical, as if he had pierced through the ugly facts and reached a realm where the facts are again beautiful. In this way, Shakespeare's total work is a more complete image of life than that of any other writer, except perhaps for Dante, an Italian poet who wrote several centuries earlier." He had been taken far from the Macbeth soliloquy. Other teachers had been happy to tell him how the kids made a game of getting him talking. He looked toward Geoffrey. The boy was doodling on his tablet, indifferent. Mr. Prosser concluded, "The last play Shakespeare wrote is an extraordinary poem called 'The Tempest.' Some of you may want to read it for your next book reports—the ones due May 10th. It's a short play."

The class had been taking a holiday. Barry Snyder was snicking BBs off the blackboard and glancing over at Brute Young to see if he noticed. "Once more, Barry," Mr. Prosser said, "and out you go." Barry blushed, and grinned to cover the blush, his eyeballs sliding toward Brute. The dull girl in the rear of the room was putting on lipstick. "Put that away, Alice," Prosser said. "This isn't a beauty parlor." Sejak, the Polish boy who worked nights, was asleep at his desk, his cheek white with pressure against the varnished wood, his mouth sagging sidewise. Mr. Prosser had an impulse to let him sleep. But the impulse might not be true kindness, but just the self-congratulatory, kindly pose in which he sometimes discovered himself. Besides, one breach of discipline encouraged others. He strode down the aisle and squeezed Sejak's shoulder; the boy awoke. A mumble was growing at the front of the room.

Peter Forrester was whispering to Gloria, trying to make her laugh. The girl's face, though, was cool and solemn, as if a thought had been provoked in her head—as if there lingered there something of what Mr. Prosser had been saying. With a bracing sense of chivalrous intercession, Mark said, "Peter. I gather from this noise that you have something to add to your theories."

Peter responded courteously. "No, sir. I honestly don't understand the speech. Please, sir, what *does* it mean?"

This candid admission and odd request stunned the class. Every white, round face, eager, for once, to learn, turned toward Mark. He said, "I don't know. I was hoping *you* would tell *me*."

In college, when a professor made such a remark, it was with grand effect. The professor's humility, the necessity for creative interplay between teacher and student were dramatically impressed upon the group. But to 11D, ignorance in an instructor was as wrong as a hole in a roof. It was as if Mark had held forty strings pulling forty faces taut toward him and then had slashed the strings. Heads waggled, eyes dropped, voices buzzed. Some of the discipline problems, like Peter Forrester, smirked signals to one another.

"Quiet!" Mr. Prosser shouted. "All of you. Poetry isn't arithmetic. There's no single right answer. I don't want to force my own impression on you; that's not why I'm here." The silent question, *Why are you here?*, seemed to steady the air with suspense. "I'm here," he said, "to let you teach yourselves."

Whether or not they believed him, they subsided, somewhat. Mark judged he could safely reassume his human-among-humans pose. He perched on the edge of the desk, informal, friendly, and frankly beseeching. "Now, honestly. Don't any of you have some personal feeling about the lines that you would like to share with the class and me?"

One hand, with a flowered handkerchief balled in it, unsteadily rose. "Go ahead, Teresa," Mr. Prosser said. She was a timid, sniffly girl whose mother was a Jehovah's Witness.

"It makes me think of cloud shadows," Teresa said.

Geoffrey Langer laughed. "Don't be rude, Geoff," Mr. Prosser said sideways, softly, before throwing his voice forward: "Thank you, Teresa. I think that's an interesting and valid impression. Cloud movement has something in it of the slow, monotonous rhythm one feels in the line 'Tomorrow, and tomorrow, and tomorrow.' It's a very gray line, isn't it, class?" No one agreed or disagreed.

Beyond the windows actual clouds were bunching rapidly, and erratic sections of sunlight slid around the room. Gloria's arm, crooked gracefully above her head, turned gold. "Gloria?" Mr. Prosser asked.

She looked up from something on her desk with a face of sullen radiance. "I think what Teresa said was very good," she said, glaring in the direction of Geoffrey Langer. Geoffrey snickered defiantly. "And I have a question. What does 'petty pace' mean?"

"It means the trivial day-to-day sort of life that, say, a bookkeeper or a bank clerk leads. Or a schoolteacher," he added, smiling.

She did not smile back. Thought wrinkles irritated her perfect brow. "But Macbeth has been fighting wars, and killing kings, and being a king himself, and all," she pointed out.

"Yes, but it's just these acts Macbeth is condemning as 'nothing.' Can you see that?"

Gloria shook her head. "Another thing I worry about—isn't it silly for Macbeth to be talking to himself right in the middle of this war, with his wife just dead, and all?"

"I don't think so, Gloria. No matter how fast events happen, thought is faster."

His answer was weak; everyone knew it, even if Gloria hadn't mused, supposedly to herself, but in a voice the entire class could hear, "It seems so *stupid*."

Mark winced, pierced by the awful clarity with which his students saw him. Through their eyes, how queer he looked, with his chalky hands, and his horn-rimmed glasses, and his hair never slicked down, all wrapped up in "literature," where, when things get rough, the king mumbles a poem nobody understands. He was suddenly conscious of a terrible tenderness in the young, a frightening patience and faith. It was so good of them not to laugh him out of the room. He looked down and rubbed his fingertips together, trying to erase the chalk dust. The class noise sifted into unnatural quiet. "It's getting late," he said finally. "Let's start the recitations of the memorized passage. Bernard Amilson, you begin."

Bernard had trouble enunciating, and his rendition began " 'T'mau 'n' t'mau 'n' t'mau.' " It was reassuring, the extent to which the class tried to repress its laughter. Mr. Prosser wrote "A" in his marking book opposite Bernard's name. He always gave Bernard A on recitations, despite the school nurse, who claimed there was nothing organically wrong with the boy's mouth.

It was the custom, cruel but traditional, to deliver recitations from the front of the room. Alice, when her turn came, was reduced to a helpless state by the first funny face Peter Forrester made at her. Mark let her hang up there a good minute while her face ripened to cherry redness, and at last relented. "Alice, you may try it later." Many of the class knew the passage gratifyingly well, though there was a tendency to leave out the line "To the last syllable of recorded time" and to turn "struts and frets" into "frets and struts" or simply "struts and struts." Even Sejak, who couldn't have looked at the passage before he came to class, got through it as far as "And then is heard no more."

Geoffrey Langer showed off, as he always did, by interrupting his own recitation with bright questions. " 'Tomorrow, and tomorrow, and tomorrow,' " he said, " 'creeps in'—shouldn't that be *'creep* in,' Mr. Prosser?"

"It is 'creeps.' The trio is in effect singular. Go on. Without the footnotes." Mr. Prosser was tired of coddling Langer. The boy's black hair, short and stiff, seemed deliberately ratlike.

" 'Creepsss in this petty pace from day to day, to the last syllable of recorded time, and all our yesterdays have lighted fools the way to dusty death. Out, out—' "

"No, no!" Mr. Prosser jumped out of his chair. "This is poetry. Don't mushmouth it! Pause a little after 'fools.' " Geoffrey looked genuinely startled this time, and Mark himself did not quite understand his annoyance and, mentally turning to see what was behind him, seemed to glimpse in the humid undergrowth the two stern eyes of the indignant look Gloria had thrown Geoffrey. He glimpsed himself in the absurd position of acting as Gloria's champion in her private war with this intelligent boy. He sighed apologetically. "Poetry is made up of lines," he began, turning to the class. Gloria was passing a note to Peter Forrester.

The rudeness of it! To pass notes during a scolding that she herself had caused! Mark caged in his hand the girl's frail wrist and ripped the note from her fingers. He read it to himself, letting the class see he was reading it, though he despised such methods of discipline. The note went:

> Pete—I think you're *wrong* about Mr. Prosser. I think he's wonderful and I get a lot out of his class. He's heavenly with poetry. I think I love him. I really do *love* him. So there.

Mr. Prosser folded the note once and slipped it into his side coat pocket. "See me after class, Gloria," he said. Then, to Geoffrey, "Let's try it again. Begin at the beginning."

While the boy was reciting the passage, the buzzer sounded the end of the period. It was the last class of the day. The room quickly emptied, except for Gloria. The noise of lockers slamming open and books being thrown against metal and shouts drifted in.

"Who has a car?"

"Lend me a cig, pig."

"We can't have practice in this slop."

Mark hadn't noticed exactly when the rain started, but it was coming down hard now. He moved around the room with the window pole, closing windows and pulling down shades. Spray bounced in on his hands. He began to talk to Gloria in a crisp voice that, like his device of shutting the windows, was intended to protect them both from embarrassment.

"About note passing." She sat motionless at her desk in the front of the room, her short, brushed-up hair like a cool torch. From the way she sat, her naked arms folded at her breasts and her shoulders hunched, he felt she was chilly. "It is not only rude to scribble when a teacher is talking, it is stupid to put one's words down on paper, where they look much more foolish than they might have sounded if spoken." He leaned the window pole in its corner and walked toward his desk.

"And about love. 'Love' is one of those words that illustrate what happens to an old, overworked language. These days, with movie stars and crooners and preachers and psychiatrists all pronouncing the word, it's come to mean nothing, you see, whereas once the word signified a quite explicit thing—a desire to share all you own and are with someone else. It is time we coined a new word to mean that, and when you think up the word *you* want to use, I suggest that you be economical with it. Treat it as something you can spend only once—if not for your own sake, for the good of the language." He walked over to his own desk and dropped two pencils on it, as if to say, "That's all."

"I'm sorry," Gloria said.

Rather surprised, Mr. Prosser said, "Don't be."

"But you don't understand."

"Of course I don't. I probably never did. At your age, I was like Geoffrey Langer."

"I bet you weren't." The girl was almost crying; he was sure of that.

"Come on, Gloria. Run along. Forget it." She slowly cradled her books between her bare arm and her sweater, and left the room with that melancholy shuffling teen-age gait, so that her body above her thighs seemed to float over the desktops.

What was it, Mark asked himself, these kids were after? What did they want? Glide, he decided, the quality of glide. To slip along, always in rhythm, always cool, the little wheels humming under you, going nowhere special. If Heaven existed, that's the way it would be there.

He's heavenly with poetry. They loved the word. Heaven was in half their songs.

"Christ, he's humming." Strunk, the physical ed teacher, had come into the room without Mark's noticing. Gloria had left the door ajar.

"Ah," Mark said, "a fallen angel, full of grit."

"What the hell makes you so happy?"

"I'm not happy, I'm just heavenly. I don't know why you don't appreciate me."

"Say." Strunk came up an aisle with a disagreeably effeminate waddle, pregnant with gossip. "Did you hear about Murchison?"

"No." Mark mimicked Strunk's whisper.

"He got the pants kidded off him today."

"Oh dear."

Strunk started to laugh, as he always did before beginning a story. "You know what a goddam lady's man he thinks he is?"

"You bet," Mark said, although Strunk said that about every male member of the faculty.

"You have Gloria Angstrom, don't you?"

"You bet."

"Well, this morning Murky intercepts a note she was writing, and the note says what a damn neat guy she thinks Murchison is and how she *loves* him!" Strunk waited for Mark to say something, and then, when he didn't, continued, "You could see he was tickled pink. But—get this—it turns out at lunch that the same damn thing happened to Fryeburg in history yesterday!" Strunk laughed and cracked his knuckles viciously. "The girl's too dumb to have thought it up herself. We all think it was Peter Forrester's idea."

"Probably was," Mark agreed. Strunk followed him out to his locker, describing Murchison's expression when Fryeburg (in all innocence, mind you) told what had happened to him.

Mark turned the combination of his locker, 18–24–3. "Would you excuse me, Dave?" he said. "My wife's in town waiting."

Strunk was too thick to catch Mark's anger. "I got to get over to the gym. Can't take the little darlings outside in the rain; their mommies'll write notes to teacher." He waddled down the hall and wheeled at the far end, shouting, "Now don't tell You-know-who!"

Mr. Prosser took his coat from the locker and shrugged it on. He placed his hat upon his head. He fitted his rubbers over his shoes, pinching his fingers painfully, and lifted his umbrella off the hook. He thought of opening it right there in the vacant hall, as a kind of joke, and decided not to. The girl had been almost crying; he was sure of that.

THE REALISTIC NOVELLA: *INTRODUCTION*

The modern "novella" lies between the short story and the novel in length, though actually most novellas are closer to being long stories than short novels. The novella as a fictional form has something of the short story's tightness of structure as well as something of the novel's richness and depth of characterization. Tillie Olsen's "Tell Me a Riddle" ranges widely in time and space, like a novel, while focusing on a dramatic family situation, like many short stories. But it does not concentrate on a single incident; rather, it captures the rhythm of two lives, and sees those lives as a part of history. Some novellas, like Franz Kafka's well-known "Metamorphosis," take the form of expanded fabulations. Tillie Olsen's "Tell Me a Riddle" falls within the realistic tradition: it is a miniature novel.

TILLIE OLSEN
1913–
Tell Me a Riddle
"These Things Shall Be"

1

For forty-seven years they had been married. How deep back the stubborn, gnarled roots of the quarrel reached, no one could say—but only now, when tending to the needs of others no longer shackled them together, the roots swelled up visible, split the earth between them, and the tearing shook even to the children, long since grown.

Why now, why now? wailed Hannah.

As if when we grew up weren't enough, said Paul.

Poor Ma. Poor Dad. It hurts so for both of them, said Vivi. They never had very much; at least in old age they should be happy.

Knock their heads together, insisted Sammy; tell 'em: you're too old for this kind of thing; no reason not to get along now.

Lennie wrote to Clara: They've lived over so much together; what could possibly tear them apart?

Something tangible enough.

Arthritic hands, and such work as he got, occasional. Poverty all his life, and there was little breath left for running. He could not, could not turn away from this desire: to have the troubling of responsibility, the fretting with money, over and done with; to be free, to be *care*free where success was not measured by accumulation, and there was use for the vitality still in him.

There was a way. They could sell the house, and with the money join his lodge's Haven, cooperative for the aged. Happy communal life, and was he not already an official; had he not helped organize it, raise funds, served as a trustee?

But she—would not consider it.

"What do we need all this for?" he would ask loudly, for her hearing aid was turned down and the vacuum was shrilling. "Five rooms" (pushing the sofa so she could get into the corner) "furniture" (smoothing down the rug) "floors and surfaces to make work. Tell me, why do we need it?" And he was glad he could ask in a scream.

"Because I'm use't."

"Because you're use't. This is a reason, Mrs. Word Miser? Used to can get unused!"

"Enough unused I have to get used to already. . . . Not enough words?" turning off the vacuum a moment to hear herself answer. "Because soon enough we'll need only a little closet, no windows, no furniture, nothing to make work, but for worms. Because now I want room. . . . Screech and blow like you're doing, you'll need that closet even sooner. . . . Ha, again!" for the vacuum bag wailed, puffed half up, hung stubbornly limp. "This time fix it so it stays; quick before the phone rings and you get too important-busy."

But while he struggled with the motor, it seethed in him. Why fix it? Why have to bother? And if it can't be fixed, have to wring the mind with how to pay the repair? At the Haven they come in with their own machines to clean your room or your cottage; you fish, or play cards, or make jokes in the sun, not with knotty fingers fight to mend vacuums.

Over the dishes, coaxingly: "For once in your life, to be free, to have everything done for you, like a queen."

"I never liked queens."

"No dishes, no garbage, no towel to sop, no worry what to buy, what to eat."

"And what else would I do with my empty hands? Better to eat at my own table when I want, and to cook and eat how I want."

"In the cottages they buy what you ask, and cook it how you like. *You* are the one who always used to say: better mankind born without mouths and stomachs than always to worry for money to buy, to shop, to fix, to cook, to wash, to clean."

"How cleverly you hid that you heard. I said it then because eighteen hours a day I ran. And you never scraped a carrot or knew a dish towel sops. Now—for you and me—who cares? A herring out of a jar is enough. But when *I* want, and nobody to bother." And she turned off her ear button, so she would not have to hear.

But as *he* had no peace, juggling and rejuggling the money to figure:

how will I pay for this now?; prying out the storm windows (there they take care of this); jolting in the streetcar on errands (there I would not have to ride to take care of this or that); fending the patronizing relatives just back from Florida (at the Haven it matters what one is, not what one can afford), he gave *her* no peace.

"Look! In their bulletin. A reading circle. Twice a week it meets."

"Haumm," her answer of not listening.

"A reading circle. Chekhov they read that you like, and Peretz. Cultured people at the Haven that you would enjoy."

"Enjoy!" She tasted the word. "Now, when it pleases you, you find a reading circle for me. And forty years ago when the children were morsels and there was a Circle, did you stay home with them once so I could go? Even once? You trained me well. I do not need others to enjoy. Others!" Her voice trembled. "Because *you* want to be there with others. Already it makes me sick to think of you always around others. Clown, grimacer, floormat, yesman, entertainer, whatever they want of you."

And now it was he who turned on the television loud so he need not hear.

Old scar tissue ruptured and the wounds festered anew. Chekhov indeed. She thought without softness of that young wife, who in the deep night hours while she nursed the current baby, and perhaps held another in her lap, would try to stay awake for the only time there was to read. She would feel again the weather of the outside on his cheek when, coming late from a meeting, he would find her so, and stimulated and ardent, sniffing her skin, coax: "I'll put the baby to bed, and you—put the book away, don't read, don't read."

That had been the most beguiling of all the "don't read, put your book away" her life had been. Chekhov indeed!

"Money?" She shrugged him off. "Could we get poorer than once we were? And in America, who starves?"

But as still he pressed:

"Let me alone about money. Was there ever enough? Seven little ones—for every penny I had to ask—and sometimes, remember, there was nothing. But always *I* had to manage. Now *you* manage. Rub your nose in it good."

But from those years she had had to manage, old humiliations and terrors rose up, lived again, and forced her to relive them. The children's needings; that grocer's face or this merchant's wife she had had to beg credit from when credit was a disgrace; the scenery of the long blocks walked around when she could not pay; school coming, and the desperate going over the old to see what could yet be remade; the soups of meat bones begged "for-the-dog" one winter. . . .

Enough. Now they had no children. Let him wrack his head for how they would live. She would not exchange her solitude for anything. Never again to be forced to move to the rhythms of others.

For in this solitude she had won to a reconciled peace.

Tranquillity from having the empty house no longer an enemy, for it stayed clean—not as in the days when it was her family, the life in it, that had seemed the enemy: tracking, smudging, littering, dirtying, engaging her in endless defeating battle—and on whom her endless defeat had been spewed.

The few old books, memorized from rereading; the pictures to ponder (the magnifying glass superimposed on her heavy eyeglasses). Or if she wishes, when he is gone, the phonograph, that if she turns up very loud and strains, she can hear: the ordered sounds and the struggling.

Out in the garden, growing things to nurture. Birds to be kept out of the pear tree, and when the pears are heavy and ripe, the old fury of work, for all must be canned, nothing wasted.

And her one social duty (for she will not go to luncheons or meetings) the boxes of old clothes left with her, as with a life-practised eye for finding what is still wearable within the worn (again the magnifying glass superimposed on the heavy glasses) she scans and sorts—this for rag or rummage, that for mending and cleaning, and this for sending away.

Being able at last to live within, and not move to the rhythms of others, as life had helped her to: denying; removing; isolating; taking the children one by one; then deafening, half-blinding—and at last, presenting her solitude.

And in it she had won to a reconciled peace.

Now he was violating it with his constant campaigning: *Sell the house and move to the Haven.* (You sit, you sit—there too you could sit like a stone.) He was making of her a battleground where old grievances tore. (Turn on your ear button—I am talking.) And stubbornly she resisted—so that from wheedling, reasoning manipulation, it was bitterness he now started with.

And it came to where every happening lashed up a quarrel.

"I will sell the house anyway," he flung at her one night. "I am putting it up for sale. There will be a way to make you sign."

The television blared, as always it did on the evenings he stayed home, and as always it reached her only as noise. She did not know if the tumult was in her or outside. Snap! she turned the sound off. "Shadows," she whispered to him, pointing to the screen, "look, it is only shadows." And in a scream: "Did you say that you will sell the house? Look at me, not at that. I am no shadow. You cannot sell without me."

"Leave on the television. I am watching."

"Like Paulie, like Jenny, a four-year-old. Staring at shadows. You cannot sell the house."

"I will. We are going to the Haven. There you would not hear the television when you do not want it. I could sit in the social room and watch. You could lock yourself up to smell your unpleasantness in a room by yourself—for who would want to come near you?"

"No, no selling." A whisper now.

"The television is shadows. Mrs. Enlightened! Mrs. Cultured! A world comes into your house—and it is shadows. People you would never meet in a thousand lifetimes. Wonders. When you were four years old, yes, like Paulie, like Jenny, did you know of Indian dances, alligators, how they use bamboo in Malaya? No, you scratched in your dirt with the chickens and thought Olshana was the world. Yes, Mrs. Unpleasant, I will sell the house, for there better can we be rid of each other than here."

She did not know if the tumult was outside, or in her. Always a ravening inside, a pull to the bed, to lie down, to succumb.

"Have you thought maybe Ma should let a doctor have a look at her?" asked their son Paul after Sunday dinner, regarding his mother crumpled on the couch, instead of, as was her custom, busying herself in Nancy's kitchen.

"Why not the President too?"

"Seriously, Dad. This is the third Sunday she's lain down like that after dinner. Is she that way at home?"

"A regular love affair with the bed. Every time I start to talk to her."

Good protective reaction, observed Nancy to herself. The workings of hos-til-ity.

"Nancy could take her. I just don't like how she looks. Let's have Nancy arrange an appointment."

"You think she'll go?" regarding his wife gloomily. "All right, we have to have doctor bills, we have to have doctor bills." Loudly: "Something hurts you?"

She startled, looked to his lips. He repeated: "Mrs. Take It Easy, something hurts?"

"Nothing. . . . Only you."

"A woman of honey. That's why you're lying down?"

"Soon I'll get up to do the dishes, Nancy."

"Leave them, Mother, I like it better this way."

"Mrs. Take It Easy, Paul says you should start ballet. You should go to see a doctor and ask: how soon can you start ballet?"

"A doctor?" she begged. "Ballet?"

"We're talking, Ma," explained Paul, "you don't seem any too well. It would be a good idea for you to see a doctor for a checkup."

"I get up now to do the kitchen. Doctors are bills and foolishness, my son. I need no doctors."

"At the Haven," he could not resist pointing out, "a doctor is *not* bills. He lives beside you. You start to sneeze, he is there before you open up a Kleenex. You can be sick there for free, all you want."

"Diarrhea of the mouth, is there a doctor to make you dumb?"

"Ma. Promise me you'll go. Nancy will arrange it."

"It's all of a piece when you think of it," said Nancy, "the way she attacks my kitchen, scrubbing under every cup hook, doing the inside of the oven so I can't enjoy Sunday dinner, knowing that half-blind or not, she's going to find every speck of dirt. . . ."

"Don't, Nancy, I've told you—it's the only way she knows to be useful. What did the *doctor* say?"

"A real fatherly lecture. Sixty-nine is young these days. Go out, enjoy life, find interests. Get a new hearing aid, this one is antiquated. Old age is sickness only if one makes it so. Geriatrics, Inc."

"So there was nothing physical."

"Of course there was. How can you live to yourself like she does without there being? Evidence of a kidney disorder, and her blood count is low. He gave her a diet, and she's to come back for follow-up and lab work. . . . But he was clear enough: Number One prescription—start living like a human being. . . . When I think of your dad, who could really play the invalid with that arthritis of his, as active as a teenager, and twice as much fun. . . ."

"You didn't tell me the doctor says your sickness is in you, how you live." He pushed his advantage. "Life and enjoyments you need better than medicine. And this diet, how can you keep it? To weigh each morsel and scrape away each bit of fat, to make this soup, that pudding. There, at the Haven, they have a dietician, they would do it for you."

She is silent.

"You would feel better there, I know it," he says gently. "There there is life and enjoyments all around."

"What is the matter, Mr. Importantbusy, you have no card game or meeting you can go to?"—turning her face to the pillow.

For a while he cut his meetings and going out, fussed over her diet, tried to wheedle her into leaving the house, brought in visitors:

"I should come to a fashion tea. I should sit and look at pretty babies in clothes I cannot buy. This is pleasure?"

"Always you are better than everyone else. The doctor said you should go out. Mrs. Brem comes to you with goodness and you turn her away."

"Because *you* asked her to, she asked me."

"They won't come back. People you need, the doctor said. Your own cousins I asked; they were willing to come and make peace as if nothing had happened. . . ."

"No more crushers of people, pushers, hypocrites, around me. No more in *my* house. You go to them if you like."

"Kind he is to visit. And you, like ice."

"A babbler. All my life around babblers. Enough!"

"She's even worse, Dad? Then let her stew a while," advised Nancy. "You can't let it destroy you; it's a psychological thing, maybe too far gone for any of us to help."

So he let her stew. More and more she lay silent in bed, and sometimes did not even get up to make the meals. No longer was the tongue-lashing inevitable if he left the coffee cup where it did not belong, or forgot to take out the garbage or mislaid the broom. The birds grew bold that summer and for once pocked the pears, undisturbed.

A bellyful of bitterness and every day the same quarrel in a new way and a different old grievance the quarrel forced her to enter and relive. And the new torment: I am not really sick, the doctor said it, then why do I feel so sick?

One night she asked him: "You have a meeting tonight? Do not go. Stay . . . with me."

He had planned to watch "This Is Your Life," but half sick himself from the heavy heat, and sickening therefore the more after the brooks and woods of the Haven, with satisfaction he grated:

"Hah, Mrs. Live Alone And Like It wants company all of a sudden. It doesn't seem so good the time of solitary when she was a girl exile in Siberia. 'Do not go. Stay with me.' A new song for Mrs. Free As A Bird. Yes, I am going out, and while I am gone chew this aloneness good, and think how you keep us both from where if you want people, you do not need to be alone."

"Go, go. All your life you have gone without me."

After him she sobbed curses he had not heard in years, old-country curses from their childhood: Grow, oh shall you grow like an onion, with your head in the ground. Like the hide of a drum shall you be, beaten in life, beaten in death. Oh shall you be like a chandelier, to hang, and to burn. . . .

She was not in their bed when he came back. She lay on the cot on the sun porch. All week she did not speak or come near him; nor did he try to make peace or care for her.

He slept badly, so used to her next to him. After all the years, old harmonies and dependencies deep in their bodies; she curled to him, or he coiled to her, each warmed, warming, turning as the other turned. The nights a long embrace.

It was not the empty bed or the storm that woke him, but a faint singing. She was singing. Shaking off the drops of rain, the lightning riving her lifted face, he saw her so; the cot covers on the floor.

"This is a private concert?" he asked. "Come in, you are wet."

"I can breathe now," she answered; "my lungs are rich." Though indeed the sound was hardly a breath.

"Come in, come in." Loosing the bamboo shades. "Look how wet you are." Half helping, half carrying her, still faint-breathing her song.

A Russian love song of fifty years ago.

He had found a buyer, but before he told her, he called together those children who were close enough to come. Paul, of course, Sammy from New Jersey, Hannah from Connecticut, Vivi from Ohio.

With a kindling of energy for her beloved visitors, she arrayed the house, cooked and baked. She was not prepared for the solemn after-dinner conclave, they too probing in and tearing. Her frightened eyes watched from mouth to mouth as each spoke.

His stories were eloquent and funny of her refusal to go back to the doctor; of the scorned invitations; of her stubborn silence or the bile "like a Niagara"; of her contrariness: "If I clean it's no good how I cleaned; if I don't clean, I'm still a master who thinks he has a slave."

(Vinegar he poured on me all his life; I am well marinated; how can I be honey now?)

Deftly he marched in the rightness for moving to the Haven; their money from social security free for visiting the children, not sucked into daily needs and into the house; the activities in the Haven for him; but mostly the Haven for *her:* her health, her need of care, distraction, amusement, friends who shared her interests.

"This does offer an outlet for Dad," said Paul; "he's always been an active person. And economic peace of mind isn't to be sneezed at, either. I could use a little of that myself."

But when they asked: "And you, Ma, how do you feel about it?" could only whisper:

"For him it is good. It is not for me. I can no longer live between people."

"You lived all your life *for* people," Vivi cried.

"Not with." Suffering doubly for the unhappiness on her children's faces.

"You have to find some compromise," Sammy insisted. "Maybe sell the house and buy a trailer. After forty-seven years there's surely some way you can find to live in peace."

"There is no help, my children. Different things we need."

"Then live alone!" He could control himself no longer. "I have a buyer for the house. Half the money for you, half for me. Either alone or with me to the Haven. You think I can live any longer as we are doing now?"

"Ma doesn't have to make a decision this minute, however you feel Dad," Paul said quickly, "and you wouldn't want her to. Let's let it lay a few months, and then talk some more."

"I think I can work it out to take Mother home with me for a while," Hannah said. "You both look terrible, but especially you, Mother. I'm going to ask Phil to have a look at you."

"Sure," cracked Sammy. "What's the use of a doctor husband if you can't get free service out of him once in a while for the family? And absence might make the heart . . . you know."

"There was something after all," Paul told Nancy in a colorless voice. "That was Hannah's Phil calling. Her gall bladder. . . . Surgery."

"Her *gall* bladder. If that isn't classic. 'Bitter as gall'—talk of psychosom——"

He stepped closer, put his hand over her mouth, and said in the same colorless, plodding voice. "We have to get Dad. They operated at once. The cancer was everywhere, surrounding the liver, everywhere. They did what they could . . . at best she has a year. Dad . . . we have to tell him."

2

Honest in his weakness when they told him, and that she was not to know. "I'm not an actor. She'll know right away by how I am. Oh that poor woman. I am old too, it will break me into pieces. Oh that poor woman. She will spit on me: 'So my sickness was how I live.' Oh Paulie, how she will be, that poor woman. Only she should not suffer. . . . I can't stand sickness, Paulie, I can't go with you."

But went. And play-acted.

"A grand opening and you did not even wait for me. . . . A good thing Hannah took you with her."

"Fashion teas I needed. They cut out what tore in me; just in my throat something hurts yet. . . . Look! so many flowers, like a funeral.

Vivi called, did Hannah tell you? And Lennie from San Francisco, and Clara; and Sammy is coming." Her gnome's face pressed happily into the flowers.

> It is impossible to predict in these cases, but once over the immediate effects of the operation, she should have several months of comparative well-being.
> *The money, where will come the money?*
> Travel with her, Dad. Don't take her home to the old associations. The other children will want to see her.
> *The money, where will I wring the money?*
> Whatever happens, she is not to know. No, you can't ask her to sign papers to sell the house; nothing to upset her. Borrow instead, then after. . . .
> *I had wanted to leave you each a few dollars to make life easier, as other fathers do. There will be nothing left now. (Failure! you and your "business is exploitation." Why didn't you make it when it could be made?—Is that what you're thinking, Sammy?)*
> Sure she's unreasonable, Dad—but you have to stay with her; if there's to be any happiness in what's left of her life, it depends on you.
> *Prop me up, children, think of me, too. Shuffled, chained with her, bitter woman. No Haven, and the little money going. . . . How happy she looks, poor creature.*

The look of excitement. The straining to hear everything (the new hearing aid turned full). Why are you so happy, dying woman?

How the petals are, fold on fold, and the gladioli color. The autumn air.

Stranger grandsons, tall above the little gnome grandmother, the little spry grandfather. Paul in a frenzy of picture-taking before going.

She, wandering the great house. Feeling the books; laughing at the maple shoemaker's bench of a hundred years ago used as a table. The ear turned to music.

"Let us go home. See how good I walk now." "One step from the hospital," he answers, "and she wants to fly. Wait till Doctor Phil says."

"Look—the birds too are flying home. Very good Phil is and will not show it, but he is sick of sickness by the time he comes home."

"Mrs. Telepathy, to read minds," he answers; "read mine what it says: when the trunks of medicines become a suitcase, then we will go."

The grandboys, they do not know what to say to us. . . . Hannah, she runs around here, there, when is there time for herself?

Let us go home. Let us go home.

Musing; gentleness—*but for the incidents of the rabbi in the hospital, and of the candles of benediction.*

Of the rabbi in the hospital:

Now tell me what happened, Mother.

From the sleep I awoke, Hannah's Phil, and he stands there like a devil in a dream and calls me by name. I cannot hear. I think he prays. Go away, please, I tell him, I am not a believer. Still he stands, while my heart knocks with fright.

You scared *him*, Mother. He thought you were delirious.

Who sent him? Why did he come to me?

It is a custom. The men of God come to visit those of their religion they might help. The hospital makes up the list for them—race, religion—and you are on the Jewish list.

Not for rabbis. At once go and make them change. Tell them to write: Race, human; Religion, none.

And of the candles of benediction:

Look how you have upset yourself, Mrs. Excited Over Nothing. Pleasant memories you should leave.

Go in, go back to Hannah and the lights. Two weeks I saw candles and said nothing. But she asked me.

So what was so terrible? She forgets you never did, she asks you to light the Friday candles and say the benediction like Phil's mother when she visits. If the candles give her pleasure, why shouldn't she have the pleasure?

Not for pleasure she does it. For emptiness. Because his family does. Because all around her do.

That is not a good reason too? But you did not hear her. For heritage, she told you. For the boys, from the past they should have tradition.

Superstition! From our ancestors, savages, afraid of the dark, of themselves: mumbo words and magic lights to scare away ghosts.

She told you: how it started does not take away the goodness. For centuries, peace in the house it means.

Swindler! does she look back on the dark centuries? Candles bought instead of bread and stuck into a potato for a candlestick? Religion that stifled and said: in Paradise, woman, you will be the footstool of your husband, and in life—poor chosen Jew—ground under, despised, trembling in cellars. And cremated. And cremated.

This is religion's fault? You think you are still an orator of the 1905 revolution? Where are the pills for quieting? Which are they?

Heritage. How have we come from our savage past, how no longer to be savages—this to teach. To look back and learn what humanizes man—this to teach. To smash all ghettos that divide us—not to go back, not to go back—this to teach. Learned books in the house, will humankind live or die, and she gives to her boys—superstition.

Hannah that is so good to you. Take your pill, Mrs. Excited For Nothing, swallow.

Heritage! But when did I have time to teach? Of Hannah I asked only hands to help.

Swallow.

Otherwise—musing; gentleness.

Not to travel. To go home.

The children want to see you. We have to show them you are as thorny a flower as ever.

Not to travel.

Vivi wants you should see her new baby. She sent the tickets—airplane tickets—a Mrs. Roosevelt she wants to make of you. To Vivi's we have to go.

A new baby. How many warm, seductive babies. She holds him stiffly, *away* from her, so that he wails. And a long shudder begins, and the sweat beads on her forehead.

"Hush, shush," croons the grandfather, lifting him back. "You should forgive your grandmamma, little prince, she has never held a baby before, only seen them in glass cases. Hush, shush."

"You're tired, Ma," says Vivi. "The travel and the noisy dinner. I'll take you to lie down."

(*A long travel from, to, what the feel of a baby evokes.*)

In the airplane, cunningly designed to encase from motion (no wind, no feel of flight), she had sat severely and still, her face turned to the sky through which they cleaved and left no scar.

So this was how it looked, the determining, the crucial sky, and this was how man moved through it, remote above the dwindled earth, the concealed human life. Vulnerable life, that could scar.

There was a steerage ship of memory that shook across a great, circular sea: clustered, ill human beings; and through the thick-stained air, tiny fretting waters in a window round like the airplane's—sun round, moon round. (The round thatched roofs of Olshana.) Eye round—like the smaller window that framed distance the solitary year of exile when only her eyes could travel, and no voice spoke. And the polar winds hurled themselves across snows trackless and endless and white—like the clouds which had closed together below and hidden the earth.

Now they put a baby in her lap. Do not ask me, she would have liked to beg. Enough the worn face of Vivi, the remembered grandchildren. I cannot, cannot. . . .

Cannot what? Unnatural grandmother, not able to make herself embrace a baby.

She lay there in the bed of the two little girls, her new hearing aid turned full, listening to the sound of the children going to sleep, the baby's fretful crying and hushing, the clatter of dishes being washed and put away. They thought she slept. Still she rode on.

It was not that she had not loved her babies, her children. The love—the passion of tending—had risen with the need like a torrent; and like a torrent drowned and immolated all else. But when the need was done—oh the power that was lost in the painful damming back and drying up of what still surged, but had nowhere to go. Only the thin pulsing left that could not quiet, suffering over lives one felt, but could no longer hold nor help.

On that torrent she had borne them to their own lives, and the riverbed was desert long years now. Not there would she dwell, a memoried wraith. Surely that was not all, surely there was more. Still the springs, the springs were in her seeking. Somewhere an older power that beat for life. Somewhere coherence, transport, meaning. If they would but leave her in the air now stilled of clamor, in the reconciled solitude, to journey on.

And they put a baby in her lap. Immediacy to embrace, and the breath of *that* past: warm flesh like this that had claims and nuzzled away all else and with lovely mouths devoured; hot-living like an animal—intensely and now; the turning maze; the long drunkenness; the drowning into needing and being needed. Severely she looked back—and the shudder seized her again, and the sweat. Not that way. Not there, not now could she, not yet. . . .

And all that visit, she could not touch the baby.

"Daddy, is it the . . . sickness she's like that?" asked Vivi. "I was so glad to be having the baby—for her. I told Tim, it'll give her more happiness than anything, being around a baby again. And she hasn't played with him once."

He was not listening, "Aahh little seed of life, little charmer," he crooned, "Hollywood should see you. A heart of ice you would melt. Kick, kick. The future you'll have for a ball. In 2050 still kick. Kick for your grandaddy then."

Attentive with the older children; sat through their performances (command performance; we command you to be the audience); helped Ann sort autumn leaves to find the best for a school program; listened gravely to Richard tell about his rock collection, while her lips mutely formed the words to remember: *igneous, sedimentary, metamorphic;* looked for missing socks, books, and bus tickets; watched the children whoop after their grandfather who knew how to tickle, chuck, lift, toss, do tricks, tell secrets, make jokes, match riddle for riddle. (Tell me a riddle, Grammy. I know no riddles, child.)

Scrubbed sills and woodwork and furniture in every room; folded the laundry; straightened drawers; emptied the heaped baskets waiting for ironing (while he or Vivi or Tim nagged: You're supposed to rest here, you've been sick) but to none tended or gave food—and could not touch the baby.

After a week she said: "Let us go home. Today call about the tickets."

"You have important business, Mrs. Inahurry? The President waits to consult with you?" He shouted, for the fear of the future raced in him. "The clothes are still warm from the suitcase, your children cannot show enough how glad they are to see you, and you want home. There is plenty of time for home. We cannot be with the children at home."

"Blind to around you as always: the little ones sleep four in a room because we take their bed. We are two more people in a house with a new baby, and no help."

"Vivi is happy so. The children should have their grandparents a while, she told to me. I should have my mommy and daddy. . . ."

"Babbler and blind. Do you look at her so tired? How she starts to talk and she cries? I am not strong enough yet to help. Let us go home."

(To reconciled solitude.)

For it seemed to her the crowded noisy house was listening to her, listening for her. She could feel it like a great ear pressed under her heart. And everything knocked: quick constant raps: let me in, let me in.

How was it that soft reaching tendrils also became blows that knocked?

C'mon, Grandma, I want to show you. . . .

Tell me a riddle, Grandma. (*I know no riddles.*)

Look, Grammy, he's so dumb he can't even find his hands. (Dody and the baby on a blanket over the fermenting autumn mould.)

I made them—for you. (Ann) (Flat paper dolls with aprons that lifted on scalloped skirts that lifted on flowered pants; hair of yarn and great ringed questioning eyes.)

Watch me, Grandma. (Richard snaking up the tree, hanging exultant, free, with one hand at the top. Below Dody hunching over in pretend-cooking.) (*Climb too, Dody, climb and look.*)

Be my nap bed, Grammy. (The "No!" too late.) Morty's abandoned heaviness, while his fingers ladder up and down her hearing-aid cord to his drowsy chant: eentsiebeentsiespider. (*Children trust.*)

It's to start off your own rock collection, Grandma. That's a trilobite fossil, 200 million years old (millions of years on a boy's mouth) and that one's obsidian, black glass.

Knocked and knocked.

> Mother, I *told* you the teacher said we had to bring it back all filled out this morning. Didn't you even ask Daddy? Then tell *me* which plan and I'll check it: evacuate or stay in the city or wait for you to come and take me away. (Seeing the look of straining to hear.) It's for Disaster, Grandma. (*Children trust.*)
>
> Vivi in the maze of the long, the lovely drunkenness. The old old noises: baby sounds; screaming of a mother flayed to exasperation; children quarreling; children playing; singing; laughter.

And Vivi's tears and memories, spilling so fast, half the words not understood.

She had started remembering out loud deliberately, so her mother would know the past was cherished, still lived in her.

Nursing the baby: My friends marvel, and I tell them, oh it's easy to be such a cow. I remember how beautiful my mother seemed nursing my brother, and the milk just flows. . . . Was that Davy? It must have been Davy. . . .

Lowering a hem: How did you ever . . . when I think how you made everything we wore . . . Tim, just think, seven kids and Mommy sewed everything . . . do I remember you sang while you sewed? That white dress with the red apples on the skirt you fixed over for me, was it Hannah's or Clara's before it was mine?

Washing sweaters: Ma, I'll never forget, one of those days so nice you washed clothes outside; one of the first spring days it must have been. The bubbles just danced while you scrubbed, and we chased after, and you stopped to show us how to blow our own bubbles with green onion stalks . . . you always. . . .

"Strong onion, to still make you cry after so many years," her father said, to turn the tears into laughter.

While Richard bent over his homework: Where is it now, do we still have it, the Book of the Martyrs? It always seemed so, well—exalted, when you'd put it on the round table and we'd all look at it together; there was even a halo from the lamp. The lamp with the beaded fringe you could move up and down; they're in style again, pulley lamps like that, but without the fringe. You know the book I'm talking about, Daddy, the Book of the Martyrs, the first picture was a bust of Socrates? I wish there was something like that for the children, Mommy, to give them what you. . . . (And the tears splashed again.)

(What I intended and did not? Stop it, daughter, stop it, leave that time. And he, the hypocrite, sitting there with tears in his eyes—it was nothing to you then, nothing.)

. . . The time you came to school and I almost died of shame because of your accent and because I knew you knew I was ashamed; how could I? . . . Sammy's harmonica and you danced to it once, yes you did, you and Davy squealing in your arms. . . . That time you bundled us up and walked us down to the railway station to stay the night 'cause it was heated and we didn't have any coal, that winter of the strike, you didn't think I remembered that, did you, Mommy? . . . How you'd call us out to see the sunsets. . . .

Day after day, the spilling memories. Worse now, questions, too. Even the grandchildren: Grandma, in the olden days, when you were little. . . .

It was the afternoons that saved.

While they thought she napped, she would leave the mosaic on the wall (of children's drawings, maps, calendars, pictures, Ann's cardboard dolls with their great ringed questioning eyes) and hunch in the girls' cupboard, on the low shelf where the shoes stood, and the girls' dresses covered.

For that while she would painfully sheathe against the listening house, the tendrils and noises that knocked, and Vivi's spilling memories. Sometimes it helped to braid and unbraid the sashes that dangled, or to trace the pattern on the hoop slips.

Today she had jacks and children under jet trails to forget. Last night, Ann and Dody silhouetted in the window against a sunset of flaming man-made clouds of jet trail, their jacks ball accenting the peaceful noise of dinner being made. Had she told them, yes she had told them of how they played jacks in her village though there was no ball, no jacks. Six stones, round and flat, toss them out, the seventh on the back of the hand, toss, catch and swoop up as many as possible, toss again. . . .

Of stones (repeating Richard) there are three kinds: earth's fire jetting; rock of layered centuries; crucibled new out of the old (*igneous, sedimentary, metamorphic*). But there was that other—frozen to black glass, never to transform or hold the fossil memory . . . (let not my seed fall on stone). There was an ancient man who fought to heights a great rock that crashed back down eternally—eternal labor, freedom, labor . . . (stone will perish, but the word remain). And you, David, who with a stone slew, screaming: Lord, take my heart of stone and give me flesh

Who was screaming? Why was she back in the common room of the prison, the sun motes dancing in the shafts of light, and the informer being brought in, a prisoner now, like themselves. And Lisa leaping, yes, Lisa, the gentle and tender, biting at the betrayer's jugular. Screaming and screaming.

No, it is the children screaming. Another of Paul and Sammy's terrible fights?

In Vivi's house. Severely: you are in Vivi's house.

Blows, screams, a call: "Grandma!" For her? Oh please not for her. Hide, hunch behind the dresses deeper. But a trembling little body hurls itself beside her—surprised, smothered laughter, arms surround her neck, tears rub dry on her cheek, and words too soft to understand whisper into her ear (Is this where you hide too, Grammy? It's my secret place, we have a secret now).

And the sweat beads, and the long shudder seizes.

It seemed the great ear pressed inside now, and the knocking. "We have to go home," she told him, "I grow ill here."

"It's your own fault, Mrs. Bodybusy, you do not rest, you do too much." He raged, but the fear was in his eyes. "It was a serious operation, they told you to take care. . . . All right, we will go to where you can rest."

But where? Not home to death, not yet. He had thought to Lennie's, to Clara's; beautiful visits with each of the children. She would have to rest first, be stronger. If they could but go to Florida—it glittered before him, the never-realized promise of Florida. California: of course. (The money, the money, dwindling!) Los Angeles first for sun and rest, then to Lennie's in San Francisco.

He told her the next day. "You saw what Nancy wrote: snow and wind back home, a terrible winter. And look at you—all bones and a swollen belly. I called Phil: he said: 'A prescription, Los Angeles sun and rest.' "

She watched the words on his lips. "You have sold the house," she cried, "that is why we do not go home. That is why you talk no more of the Haven, why there is money for travel. After the children you will drag me to the Haven."

"The Haven! Who thinks of the Haven any more? Tell her, Vivi, tell Mrs. Suspicious: a prescription, sun and rest, to make you healthy. . . . And how could I sell the house without *you?*"

At the place of farewells and greetings, of winds of coming and winds of going, they say their good-byes.

They look back at her with the eyes of others before them: Richard with her own blue blaze; Ann with the nordic eyes of Tim; Morty's dreaming brown of a great-grandmother he will never know; Dody with the laughing eyes of him who had been her springtide love (who stands beside her now); Vivi's, all tears.

The baby's eyes are closed in sleep.

Good-bye, my children.

3

It is to the back of the great city he brought her, to the dwelling places of the cast-off old. Bounded by two lines of amusement piers to the north and to the south, and between a long straight paving rimmed with black benches facing the sand—sands so wide the ocean is only a far fluting.

In the brief vacation season, some of the boarded stores fronting the sands open, and families, young people and children, may be seen. A little tasselled tram shuttles between the piers, and the lights of roller coasters prink and tweak over those who come to have sensation made in them.

The rest of the year it is abandoned to the old, all else boarded up and still; seemingly empty, except the occasional days and hours when the sun, like a tide, sucks them out of the low rooming houses, casts them onto the benches and sandy rim of the walk—and sweeps them into decaying enclosures once again.

A few newer apartments glint among the low bleached squares. It is in one of these Lennie's Jeannie has arranged their rooms. "Only a few miles north and south people pay hundreds of dollars a month for just this gorgeous air, Grandaddy, just this ocean closeness."

She had been ill on the plane, lay ill for days in the unfamiliar room. Several times the doctor came by—left medicine she would not take. Several times Jeannie drove in the twenty miles from work, still in her Visiting Nurse uniform, the lightness and brightness of her like a healing.

"Who can believe it is winter?" he asked one morning. "Beautiful it is outside like an ad. Come, Mrs. Invalid, come to taste it. You are well enough to sit in here, you are well enough to sit outside. The doctor said it too."

But the benches were encrusted with people, and the sands at the sidewalk's edge. Besides, she had seen the far ruffle of the sea: "there take me," and though she leaned against him, it was she who led.

Plodding and plodding, sitting often to rest, he grumbling. Patting the sand so warm. Once she scooped up a handful, cradling it close to her better eye; peered, and flung it back. And as they came almost to the brink and she could see the glistening wet, she sat down, pulled off her shoes and stockings, left him and began to run. "You'll catch cold," he screamed, but the sand in his shoes weighed him down—he who had always been the agile one—and already the white spray creamed her feet.

He pulled her back, took a handkerchief to wipe off the wet and the sand. "Oh no," she said, "the sun will dry," seized the square and smoothed it flat, dropped on it a mound of sand, knotted the kerchief corners and tied it to a bag—"to look at with the strong glass" (for the first time in years explaining an action of hers)—and lay down with the little bag against her cheek, looking toward the shore that nurtured life as it first crawled toward consciousness the millions of years ago.

He took her one Sunday in the evil-smelling bus, past flat miles of blister houses, to the home of relatives. Oh what is this? she cried as the light began to smoke and the houses to dim and recede. Smog, he said, everyone knows but you. . . . Outside he kept his arms about her, but she walked with hands pushing the heavy air as if to open it, whispered: who has done this? sat down suddenly to vomit at the curb and for a long while refused to rise.

One's age as seen on the altered face of those known in youth. Is this they he has come to visit? This Max and Rose, smooth and pleasant, introducing them to polite children, disinterested grandchildren, "the whole family, once a month on Sundays. And why not? We have the room, the help, the food."

Talk of cars, of houses, of success: this son that, that daughter this. And *your* children? Hastily skimped over, the intermarriages, the obscure work—"my doctor son-in-law, Phil"—all he has to offer. She silent in a corner. (Car-sick like a baby, he explains.) Years since he has taken her to visit anyone but the children, and old apprehensions prickle: "no incidents," he silently begs, "no incidents." He itched to tell them. "A very sick woman," significantly, indicating her with his eyes, "a very sick woman." Their restricted faces did not react. "Have you thought maybe she'd do better at Palm Springs?" Rose asked. "Or at least a nicer section of the beach, nicer people, a pool." Not to have to say "money" he said instead: "would she have sand to look at through a magnifying glass?" and went on, detail after detail, the old habit betraying of parading the queerness of her for laughter.

After dinner—the others into the living room in men- or women-clusters or into the den to watch TV—the four of them alone. She sat close to him, and did not speak. Jokes, stories, people they had known, beginning of reminiscence, Russia fifty-sixty years ago. Strange words across the Duncan Phyfe table: *hunger; secret meetings; human rights; spies; betrayals; prison; escape*—interrupted by one of the grandchildren: "Commercial's on; any Coke left? Gee, you're missing a real hair-raiser." And then a granddaughter (Max proudly: "look at her, an American queen") drove them home on her way back to U.C.L.A. No incident—except that there had been no incidents.

The first few mornings she had taken with her the magnifying glass, but he would sit only on the benches, so she rested at the foot, where slatted bench shadows fell, and unless she turned her hearing aid down, other voices invaded.

Now on the days when the sun shone and she felt well enough, he took her on the tram to where the benches ranged in oblongs, some with tables for checkers or cards. Again the blanket on the sand in the striped shadows, but she no longer brought the magnifying glass. He played cards, and she lay in the sun and looked towards the waters; or they walked—two blocks down to the scaling hotel, two blocks back—past chili-hamburger stands, open-doored bars, Next-to-New and perpetual rummage sale stores.

Once, out of the aimless walkers, slow and shuffling like themselves, someone ran unevenly towards them, embraced, kissed, wept: "dear friends, old friends." A friend of *hers,* not his: Mrs. Mays who had lived next door to them in Denver when the children were small.

Thirty years are compressed into a dozen sentences; and the present, not even in three. All is told: the children scattered; the husband dead; she lives in a room two blocks up from the sing hall—and points to the domed auditorium jutting before the pier. The leg? phlebitis; the heavy breathing? that, one does not ask. She, too, comes to the benches each day to sit. And tomorrow, tomorrow, are they going to the community sing? Of course he would have heard of it, everybody goes—the big doings they wait for all week. They have never been? She will come to them for dinner tomorrow and they will all go together.

So it is that she sits in the wind of the singing, among the thousand-various faces of age.

She had turned off her hearing aid at once they came into the auditorium—as she would have wished to turn off sight.

One by one they streamed by and imprinted on her—and though the savage zest of their singing came voicelessly soft and distant, the faces still roared—the faces densened the air—chorded into

children-chants, mother-croons, singing of the chained
love serenades, Beethoven storms, mad Lucia's scream
drunken joy-songs, keens for the dead, work-singing

> *while from floor to balcony to dome a bare-footed sore-covered little girl threaded the sound-thronged tumult, danced her ecstasy of grimace to flutes that scratched at a cross-roads village wedding*

Yes, faces became sound, and the sound became faces; and faces and sound became weight—pushed, pressed

"Air"—her hands claw his.

"Whenever I enjoy myself. . . ." Then he saw the gray sweat on her face. "Here. Up. Help me, Mrs. Mays," and they support her out to where she can gulp the air in sob after sob.

"A doctor, we should get for her a doctor."

"Tch, it's nothing," says Ellen Mays, "I get it all the time. You've missed the tram; come to my place. Fix your hearing aid, honey . . . close . . . tea. My view. See, she *wants* to come. Steady now, that's how." Adding mysteriously: "Remember your advice, easy to keep your head above water, empty things float. Float."

The singing a fading march for them, tall woman with a swollen leg, weaving little man, and the swollen thinness they help between.

The stench in the hall: mildew? decay? "We sit and rest then climb. My gorgeous view. We help each other and here we are."

The stench along into the slab of room. A washstand for a sink, a box with oilcloth tacked around for a cupboard, a three-burner gas plate. Aritificial flowers, colorless with dust. Everywhere pictures foaming: wedding, baby, party, vacation, graduation, family pictures. From the narrow couch under a slit of window, sure enough the view: lurching rooftops and a scallop of ocean heaving, preening, twitching under the moon.

"While the water heats. Excuse me . . . down the hall." Ellen Mays has gone.

"You'll live?" he asks mechanically, sat down to feel his fright; tried to pull her alongside.

She pushed him away. "For air," she said; stood clinging to the dresser. Then, in a terrible voice:

After a lifetime of room. Of many rooms.

Shhh.

You remember how she lived. Eight children. And now one room   like a coffin.

She pays rent!

Shrinking the life of her   into one room   like a coffin   Rooms and rooms like this   I lie on the quilt and hear them talk

Please, Mrs. Orator-without-Breath.

Once you went for coffee   I walked   I saw   A Balzac   a Chekhov to write it   Rummage   Alone   On scraps

Better old here than in the old country!

On scraps   Yet they sang like   like   Wondrous!

Humankind   one has to believe So strong   for what? To rot   not grow?

Your poor lungs beg you. They sob between each word.

Singing.   Unused   the life in them.   She   in this poor room—with her   pictures Max You The children Everywhere unused the life And who has meaning? Century after century still all in us   not to grow?

Coffins, rummage, plants: sick woman. Oh lay down. We will get for you a doctor.

"And when will it end. Oh, *the end."* *That* nightmare thought, and this time she writhed, crumpled against him, seized his hand (for a moment again the weight, the soft distant roaring of humanity) and on the strangled-for breath, begged: "Man . . . we'll   destroy ourselves?"

And looking for answer—in the helpless pity and fear for her (for *her*) that distorted his face—she understood the last months, and knew that she was dying.

4

"Let us go home," she said after several days.

"You are in training for a cross-country run? That is why you do not even walk across the room? Here, like a prescription Phil said, till you are stronger from the operation. You want to break doctor's orders?"

She saw the fiction was necessary to him, was silent; then: "At home I will get better. If the doctor here says?"

"And winter? And the visits to Lennie and to Clara? All right," for he saw the tears in her eyes, "I will write Phil, and talk to the doctor."

Days passed. He reported nothing. Jeannie came and took her out for air, past the boarded concessions, the hooded and tented amusement rides, to the end of the pier. They watched the spent waves feeding the new, the gulls in the clouded sky; even up where they sat, the wind-blown sand stung.

She did not ask to go down the crooked steps to the sea.

Back in her bed, while he was gone to the store, she said: "Jeannie, this doctor, he is not one I can ask questions. Ask him for me, can I go home?"

Jeannie looked at her, said quickly: "Of course, poor Granny. You want your own things around you, don't you? I'll call him tonight. . . . Look, I've something to show you," and from her purse unwrapped a large cookie, intricately shaped like a little girl. "Look at the curls—can you hear me well, Granny?—and the darling eyelashes. I just came from a house where they were baking them."

"The dimples, there in the knees," she marveled, holding it to the better light, turning, studying, "like art. Each singly they cut, or a mold?"

"Singly," said Jeannie, "and if it is a child only the mother can make them. Oh Granny, it's the likeness of a real little girl who died yesterday—Rosita. She was three years old. *Pan del Muerto*, the Bread of the Dead. It was the custom in the part of Mexico they came from."

Still she turned and inspected. "Look, the hollow in the throat, the little cross necklace. . . . I think for the mother it is a good thing to be busy with such bread. You know the family?"

Jeannie nodded. "On my rounds. I nursed. . . . Oh Granny, it is like a party; they play songs she liked to dance to. The coffin is lined with pink velvet and she wears a white dress. There are candles. . . ."

"In the house?" Surprised, "They keep her in the house?"

"Yes," said Jeannie, "and it is against the health law. I think she is . . . prepared there. The father said it will be sad to bury her in this country; in Oaxaca they have a feast night with candles each year; everyone picnics on the graves of those they loved until dawn."

"Yes, Jeannie, the living must comfort themselves." And closed her eyes.

"You want to sleep, Granny?"

"Yes, tired from the pleasure of you. I may keep the Rosita? There stand it, on the dresser, where I can see; something of my own around me."

In the kitchenette, helping her grandfather unpack the groceries, Jeannie said in her light voice:

"I'm resigning my job, Grandaddy."

"Ah, the lucky young man. Which one is he?"

"Too late. You're spoken for." She made a pyramid of cans, unstacked, and built again.

"Something is wrong with the job?"

"With me. I can't be"—she searched for the word—"What they call professional enough. I let myself feel things. And tomorrow I have to report a family. . . ." The cans clicked again. "It's not that, either. I just don't know what I want to do, maybe go back to school, maybe go to art school. I thought if you went to San Francisco I'd come along and talk it over with Momma and Daddy. But I don't see how you can go. She wants to go home. She asked me to ask the doctor."

The doctor told her himself. "Next week you may travel, when you are a little stronger." But next week there was the fever of an infection, and by the time that was over, she could not leave the bed—a rented hospital bed that stood beside the double bed he slept in alone now.

Outwardly the days repeated themselves. Every other afternoon and evening he went out to his newfound cronies, to talk and play cards. Twice a week, Mrs. Mays came. And the rest of the time, Jeannie was there.

By the sickbed stood Jeannie's FM radio. Often into the room the shapes of music came. She would lie curled on her side, her knees drawn up, intense in listening (Jeannie sketched her so, coiled, convoluted like an ear), then thresh her hand out and abruptly snap the radio mute—still to lie in her attitude of listening, concealing tears.

Once Jeannie brought in a young Marine to visit, a friend from high-school days she had found wandering near the empty pier. Because Jeannie asked him to, gravely, without self-consciousness, he sat himself cross-legged on the floor and performed for them a dance of his native Samoa.

Long after they left, a tiny thrumming sound could be heard where, in her bed, she strove to repeat the beckon, flight, surrender of his hands, the fluttering footbeats, and his low plaintive calls.

Hannah and Phil sent flowers. To deepen her pleasure, he placed one in her hair. "Like a girl," he said, and brought the hand mirror so she could see. She looked at the pulsing red flower, the yellow skull face; a desolate, excited laugh shuddered from her, and she pushed the mirror away—but let the flower burn.

The week Lennie and Helen came, the fever returned. With it the excited laugh, and incessant words. She, who in her life had spoken but seldom and then only when necessary (never having learned the easy, social uses of words), now in dying, spoke incessantly.

In a half-whisper: "Like Lisa she is, your Jeannie. Have I told you of Lisa who taught me to read? Of the highborn she was, but noble in herself. I was sixteen; they beat me; my father beat me so I would not go to her. It was forbidden, she was a Tolstoyan. At night, past dogs that howled, terrible dogs, my son, in the snows of winter to the road, I to ride in her carriage like a lady, to books. To her, life was holy, knowledge was holy, and she taught me to read. They hung her. Everything that happens one must try to understand why. She killed one who betrayed many. Because of betrayal, betrayed all she lived and believed. In one minute she killed, before my eyes (there is so much blood in a human being, my son), in prison with me. All that happens, one must try to understand.

"The name?" Her lips would work. "The name that was their pole star; the doors of the death houses fixed to open on it; I read of it my year of penal servitude. Thuban!" very excited, "Thuban, in ancient Egypt the pole star. Can you see, look out to see it, Jeannie, if it swings around *our* pole star that seems to *us* not to move.

"Yes, Jeannie, at your age my mother and grandmother had already buried children . . . yes, Jeannie, it is more than oceans between Olshana and you . . . yes, Jeannie, they danced, and for all the bodies they had they might as well be chickens, and indeed, they scratched and flapped their arms and hopped.

"And Andrei Yefimitch, who for twenty years had never known of it and never wanted to know, said as if he wanted to cry: but why my dear friend this malicious laughter?" Telling to herself half-memorized phrases from her few books. "Pain I answer with tears and cries, baseness with indignation, meanness with repulsion . . . for life may be hated or wearied of, but never despised."

Delirious: "Tell me, my neighbor, Mrs. Mays, the pictures never lived, but what of the flowers? Tell them who ask: no rabbis, no ministers, no priests, no speeches, no ceremonies: ah, false—let the living comfort themselves. Tell Sammy's boy, he who flies, tell him to go to Stuttgart and see where Davy has no grave. And what?" A conspirator's laugh. "And what? where millions have no graves—save air."

In delirium or not, wanting the radio on; not seeming to listen, the words still jetting, wanting the music on. Once, silencing it abruptly as of old, she began to cry, unconcealed tears this time. "You have pain, Granny?" Jeannie asked.

"The music," she said, "still it is there and we do not hear; knocks, and our poor human ears too weak. What else, what else we do not hear?"

Once she knocked his hand aside as he gave her a pill, swept the bottles from her bedside table: "no pills, let me feel what I feel," and laughed as on his hands and knees he groped to pick them up.

Nighttimes her hand reached across the bed to hold his.

A constant retching began. Her breath was too faint for sustained speech now, but still the lips moved:

> When no longer necessary   to injure others
> Pick   pick pick   Blind chicken
> As a human being   responsibility

"David!" imperious, "Basin!" and she would vomit, rinse her mouth, the wasted throat working to swallow, and begin the chant again.

She will be better off in the hospital now, the doctor said.

He sent the telegrams to the children, was packing her suitcase, when her hoarse voice startled. She had roused, was pulling herself to sitting.

"Where now?" she asked. "Where now do you drag me?"

"You do not even have to have a baby to go this time," he soothed, looking for the brush to pack. "Remember, after Davy you told me—worthy to have a baby for the pleasure of the rest in the hospital?"

"Where now? Not home yet?" Her voice mourned. "Where *is* my home?"

He rose to ease her back. "The doctor, the hospital," he started to explain, but deftly, like a snake, she had slithered out of bed and stood swaying, propped behind the night table.

"Coward," she hissed, "runner."

"You stand," he said senselessly.

"To take me there and run. Afraid of a little vomit."

He reached her as she fell. She struggled against him, half slipped from his arms, pulled herself up again.

"Weakling," she taunted, "to leave me there and run. Betrayer. All your life you have run."

He sobbed, telling Jeannie. "A Marilyn Monroe to run for her virtue. Fifty-nine pounds she weighs, the doctor said, and she beats at me like a Dempsey. Betrayer, she cries, and I running like a dog when she calls; day and night, running to her, her vomit, the bedpan. . . ."

"She needs you, Grandaddy," said Jeannie. "Isn't that what they call love? I'll see if she sleeps, and if she does, poor worn-out darling, we'll have a party, you and I: I brought us rum babas."

They did not move her. By her bed now stood the tall hooked pillar that held the solutions—blood and dextrose—to feed her veins. Jeannie moved down the hall to take over the sickroom, her face so radiant, her grandfather asked her once: "you are in love?" (Shameful the joy, the pure overwhelming joy from being with her grandmother; the peace, the serenity that breathed.) "My darling escape," she answered incoherently, "my darling Granny"—as if that explained.

Now one by one the children came, those that were able. Hannah, Paul, Sammy. Too late to ask: and what did you learn with your living, Mother, and what do we need to know?

Clara, the eldest, clenched:

> Pay me back, Mother, pay me back for all you took from me. Those others you crowded into your heart. The hands I needed to be for you, the heaviness, the responsibility.
>
> Is this she? Noises the dying make, the crablike hands crawling over the covers. The ethereal singing.
>
> She hears that music, that singing from childhood; forgotten sound—not heard since, since. . . . And the hardness breaks like a cry: Where did we lose each other, first mother, singing mother?

Annulled: the quarrels, the gibing, the harshness between; the fall into silence and the withdrawal.
I do not know you, Mother. Mother, I never knew you.

Lennie, suffering not alone for her who was dying, but for that in her which never lived (for that which in him might never live). From him too, unspoken words: *good-bye Mother who taught me to mother myself.*

Not Vivi, who must stay with her children; not Davy, but he is already here, having to die again with *her* this time, for the living take their dead with them when they die.

Light she grew, like a bird, and, like a bird, sound bubbled in her throat while the body fluttered in agony. Night and day, asleep or awake (though indeed there was no difference now) the songs and the phrases leaping.

And he, who had once dreaded a long dying (from fear of himself, from horror of the dwindling money) now desired her quick death profoundly, for *her* sake. He no longer went out, except when Jeannie forced him; no longer laughed, except when, in the bright kitchenette, Jeannie coaxed his laughter (and she, who seemed to hear nothing else, would laugh too, conspiratorial wisps of laughter).

Light, like a bird, the fluttering body, the little claw hands, the beaked shadow on her face; and the throat, bubbling, straining.

He tried not to listen, as he tried not to look on the face in which only the forehead remained familiar, but trapped with her the long nights in that little room, the sounds worked themselves into his consciousness, with their punctuation of death swallows, whimpers, gurglings.

Even in reality (swallow) *life's lack of it*
Slaveships   deathtrains   clubs   eeenough
The bell   summon what ennobles
78,000 in one minute (whisper of a scream) *78,000 human beings   we'll destroy ourselves?*

"Aah, Mrs. Miserable," he said, as if she could hear, "all your life working, and now in bed you lie, servants to tend, you do not even need to call to be tended, and still you work. Such hard work it is to die? Such hard work?"

The body threshed, her hand clung in his. A melody, ghost-thin, hovered on her lips, and like a guilty ghost, the vision of her bent in listening to it, silencing the record instantly he was near. Now, heedless of his presence, she floated the melody on and on.

"Hid it from me," he complained, "how many times you listened to remember it so?" And tried to think when she had first played it, or first begun to silence her few records when he came near—but could reconstruct nothing. There was only this room with its tall hooked pillar and its swarm of sounds.

No man one   except through others
Strong   with the not yet   in the now
Dogma dead   war dead   one country

"It helps, Mrs. Philosopher, words from books? It helps?" And it seemed to him that for seventy years she had hidden a tape recorder, infinitely microscopic, within her, that it had coiled infinite mile on mile, trapping every song, every melody, every word read, heard, and spoken—and that maliciously she was playing back only what said nothing of him, of the children, of their intimate life together.

"Left us indeed, Mrs. Babbler," he reproached, "you who called others babbler and cunningly saved your words. A lifetime you tended and loved, and now not a word of us, for us. Left us indeed? Left me."

And he took out his solitaire deck, shuffled the cards loudly, slapped them down.

Lift high   banner of reason (tatter of an orator's voice)   *justice freedom   light*
Humankind   life worthy   capacities
Seeks (blur of shudder) *belong   human being*

"Words, words," he accused, "and what human beings did *you* seek around you, Mrs. Live Alone, and what humankind think worthy?"

Though even as he spoke, he remembered she had not always been isolated, had not always wanted to be alone (as he knew there had been a voice before this gossamer one; before the hoarse voice that broke from silence to lash, make incidents, shame him—a girl's voice of eloquence that spoke their holiest dreams). But again he could reconstruct, image, nothing of what had been before, or when, or how, it had changed.

Ace, queen, jack. The pillar shadow fell, so, in two tracks; in the mirror depths glistened a moonlike blob, the empty solution bottle. And it worked in him: *of reason and justice and freedom . . . Dogma dead:* he remembered the full quotation, laughed bitterly. "Hah, good you do not know what you say; good Victor Hugo died and did not see it, his twentieth century."

Deuce, ten, five. Dauntlessly she began a song of their youth of belief:

These things shall be, a loftier race
than e'er the world hath known shall rise
with flame of freedom in their souls
and light of knowledge in their eyes

King, four jack. "In the twentieth century, huh!"

> They shall be gentle, brave and strong
> to spill no drop of blood, but dare
>
> all   on earth and fire and sea and air

"To spill no drop of blood, hah! So, cadaver, and you too, cadaver Hugo, 'in the twentieth century ignorance will be dead, dogma will be dead, war will be dead, and for all mankind one country—of fulfilment?' Hah!"

> And every life (long strangling cough) shall
> be a song

The cards fell from his fingers. Without warning, the bereavement and betrayal he had sheltered—compounded through the years—hidden even from himself—revealed itself,
>   uncoiled,
>   released,
>   *sprung*

and with it the monstrous shapes of what had actually happened in the century.

A ravening hunger or thirst seized him. He groped into the kitchenette, switched on all three lights, piled a tray—"you have finished your night snack, Mrs. Cadaver, now I will have mine." And he was shocked at the tears that splashed on the tray.

"Salt tears. For free. I forgot to shake on salt?"

Whispered: "Lost, how much I lost."

Escaped to the grandchildren whose childhoods were childish, who had never hungered, who lived unravaged by disease in warm houses of many rooms, had all the school for which they cared, could walk on any street, stood a head taller than their grandparents, towered above—beautiful skins, straight backs, clear straightforward eyes. "Yes, you in Olshana," he said to the town of sixty years ago, "they would be nobility to you."

And was this not the dream then, come true in ways undreamed? he asked.

And are there no other children in the world? he answered, as if in her harsh voice.

And the flame of freedom, the light of knowledge?

And the drop, to spill no drop of blood?

And he thought that at six Jeannie would get up and it would be his turn to go to her room and sleep, that he could press the buzzer and she would come now; that in the afternoon Ellen Mays was coming, and this time they would play cards and he could marvel at how rouge can stand half an inch on the cheek; that in the evening the doctor would come, and he could beg him to be merciful, to stop the feeding solutions, to let her die.

To let her die, and with her their youth of belief out of which her bright, betrayed words foamed; stained words, that on her working lips came stainless.

Hours yet before Jeannie's turn. He could press the buzzer and wake her to come now; he could take a pill, and with it sleep; he could pour more brandy into his milk glass, though what he had poured was not yet touched.

Instead he went back, checked her pulse, gently tended with his knotty fingers as Jeannie had taught.

She was whimpering; her hand crawled across the covers for his. Compassionately he enfolded it, and with his free hand gathered up the cards again. Still was there thirst or hunger ravening in him.

That world of their youth—dark, ignorant, terrible with hate and disease—how was it that living in it, in the midst of corruption, filth, treachery, degradation, they had not mistrusted man nor themselves; had believed so beautifully, so . . . falsely?

"Aaah, children," he said out loud, "how we believed, how we belonged." And he yearned to package for each of the children, the grandchildren, for everyone, *that joyous certainty, that sense of mattering, of moving and being moved, of being one and indivisible with the great of the past, with all that freed, ennobled.* Package it, stand on corners, in front of stadiums and on crowded beaches, knock on doors, give it as a fabled gift.

"And why not in cereal boxes, in soap packages?" he mocked himself. "Aah. You have taken my senses, cadaver."

Words foamed, died unsounded. Her body writhed; she made kissing motions with her mouth. (Her lips moving as she read, poring over the Book of the Martyrs, the magnifying glass superimposed over the heavy eyeglasses.) *Still she believed?* "Eva!" he whispered. "Still you believed? You lived by it? These Things Shall Be?"

"One pound soup meat," she answered distinctly, "one soup bone."

"My ears heard you. Ellen Mays was witness: 'Humankind . . . one has to believe.'" Imploringly: "Eva!"

"Bread, day-old." She was mumbling. "Please, in a wooden box . . . for kindling. The thread, hah, the thread breaks. Cheap thread"—and a gurgling, enormously loud, began in her throat.

"I ask for stone; she gives me bread—day-old." He pulled his hand away, shouted: "Who wanted questions? Everything you have to wake?" Then dully, "Ah, let me help you turn, poor creature."

Words jumbled, cleared. In a voice of crowded terror:

"Paul, Sammy, don't fight.

"Hannah, have I ten hands?

"How can I give it, Clara, how can I give it if I don't have?"

"You lie," he said sturdily, "there was joy too." Bitterly: "Ah how cheap you speak of us at the last."

As if to rebuke him, as if her voice had no relationship with her flailing body, she sang clearly, beautifully, a school song the children had taught her when they were little; begged:

"Not look   my hair   where they cut. . . ."

(The crown of braids shorn.) And instantly he left the mute old woman poring over the Book of the Martyrs; went past the mother treading at the sewing machine, singing with the children; past the girl in her wrinkled prison dress, hiding her hair with scarred hands, lifting to him her awkward, shamed, imploring eyes of love; and took her in his arms, dear, personal, fleshed, in all the heavy passion he had loved to rouse from her.

"Eva!"

Her little claw hand beat the covers. How much, how much can a man stand? He took up the cards, put them down, circled the beds, walked to the dresser, opened, shut drawers, brushed his hair, moved his hand bit by bit over the mirror to see what of the reflection he could blot out with each move, and felt that at any moment he would die of what was unendurable. Went to press the buzzer to wake Jeannie, looked down, saw on Jeannie's sketch pad the hospital bed, with *her;* the double bed alongside, with him; the tall pillar feeding into her veins, and their hands, his and hers, clasped, feeding each other. And as if he had been instructed he went to his bed, lay down, holding the sketch (as if it could shield against the monstrous shapes of loss, of betrayal, of death) and with his free hand took hers back into his.

So Jeannie found them in the morning.

That last day the agony was perpetual. Time after time it lifted her almost off the bed, so they had to fight to hold her down. He could not endure and left the room; wept as if there never would be tears enough.

Jeannie came to comfort him. In her light voice she said: Grand-addy, Grandaddy don't cry. She is not there, she promised me. On the last day, she said she would go back to when she first heard music, a little girl on the road of the village where she was born. She promised me. It is a wedding and they dance, while the flutes so joyous and vibrant tremble in the air. Leave her there, Grandaddy, it is all right. She promised me. Come back, come back and help her poor body to die.

For two of that generation
Seevya and Genya
Infinite, dauntless,
*   incorruptible*

Death deepens the wonder

METAFICTION: *INTRODUCTION*

Metafiction is really a special case of fabulation. A metafiction is a fictional experiment that either explores or questions the nature of fiction itself. Jorge Luis Borges's "Theme of the Traitor and the Hero," in our earlier discussion of "Three Stories and Commentaries," is a good example of one type of metafiction. In the present section you will find five more examples—each one different, and each raising some question about the nature of fiction or the relation between fiction and experience.

First, Henry James raises the question of how the appearance of reality is achieved in fiction. Then Isak Dinesen considers both the relation of the writer to the audience and that of fictional role-playing to real existence. James asks how we capture the real in fiction. Dinesen wonders what would happen if someone played a fictional role in reality (a theme similar to that of the Borges story). Julio Cortázar returns to the question of fiction and reality, but asks whether reality can ever be more than a fiction that we create for ourselves. Barth uses the metaphor of a funhouse to talk about the problems of writing, and in a critical commentary on his own story he ridicules the rules usually provided for the guidance of aspiring young writers. Finally, Coover, by describing very "realistically" an "impossible" event, raises all these questions in yet another way.

These experiments in metafiction should make an appropriate place to conclude—at least temporarily—our brief investigation of the art of fiction. For all the stories collected here can be referred to in seeking answers to the questions raised in these five works.

HENRY JAMES
1843–1916
The Real Thing

When the porter's wife who used to answer the house-bell, announced "A gentleman and a lady, sir," I had, as I often had in those days—the wish being father to the thought—an immediate vision of sitters. Sitters my visitors in this case proved to be; but not in the sense I should have preferred. There was nothing at first however to indicate that they mightn't have come for a portrait. The gentleman, a man of fifty, very high and very straight, with a moustache slightly grizzled and a dark grey walking-coat admirably fitted, both of which I noted professionally—I don't mean as a barber or yet as a tailor—would have struck me as a celebrity if celebrities often were striking. It was a truth of which I had for some time been conscious that a figure with a good deal of frontage was, as one might say, almost never a public institution. A glance at the lady helped to remind me of this paradoxi-

cal law: she also looked too distinguished to be a "personality." Moreover one would scarcely come across two variations together.

Neither of the pair immediately spoke—they only prolonged the
preliminary gaze suggesting that each wished to give the other a
chance. They were visibly shy; they stood there letting me take them
in—which, as I afterwards perceived, was the most practical thing
they could have done. In this way their embarrassment served their
cause. I had seen people painfully reluctant to mention that they
desired anything so gross as to be represented on canvas; but the
scruples of my new friends appeared almost insurmountable. Yet the
gentleman might have said "I should like a portrait of my wife," and
the lady might have said "I should like a portrait of my husband."
Perhaps they weren't husband and wife—this naturally would make
the matter more delicate. Perhaps they wished to be done together—in
which case they ought to have brought a third person to break the
news.

"We come from Mr. Rivet," the lady finally said with a dim smile
that had the effect of a moist sponge passed over a "sunk" piece of
painting, as well as of a vague allusion to vanished beauty. She was as
tall and straight, in her degree, as her companion, and with ten years
less to carry. She looked as sad as a woman could look whose face was
not charged with expression; that is her tinted oval mask showed
waste as an exposed surface shows friction. The hand of time had
played over her freely, but to an effect of elimination. She was slim and
stiff, and so well-dressed, in dark blue cloth, with lappets and pockets
and buttons, that it was clear she employed the same tailor as her
husband. The couple had an indefinable air of prosperous thrift—they
evidently got a good deal of luxury for their money. If I was to be one of
their luxuries, it would behoove me to consider my terms.

"Ah, Claude Rivet recommended me?" I echoed; and I added that it
was very kind of him, though I could reflect that, as he only painted
landscape, this wasn't a sacrifice.

The lady looked very hard at the gentleman, and the gentleman
looked round the room. Then, staring at the door a moment and
stroking his moustache, he rested his pleasant eyes on me with the
remark: "He said you were the right one."

"I try to be, when people want to sit."

"Yes, we should like to," said the lady anxiously.

"Do you mean together?"

My visitors exchanged a glance. "If you could do anything with *me* I
suppose it would be double," the gentleman stammered.

"Oh, yes, there's naturally a higher charge for two figures than for
one."

"We should like to make it pay," the husband confessed.

"That's very good of you," I returned, appreciating so unwonted a sympathy—for I supposed he meant pay the artist.

A sense of strangeness seemed to dawn on the lady. "We mean for the illustrations—Mr. Rivet said you might put one in."

"Put in—an illustration?" I was equally confused.

"Sketch her off, you know," said the gentleman, colouring.

It was only then that I understood the service Claude Rivet had rendered me; he had told them how I worked in black and white, for magazines, for storybooks, for sketches of contemporary life, and consequently had copious employment for models. These things were true, but it was not less true—I may confess it now; whether because the aspiration was to lead to everything or to nothing I leave the reader to guess—that I couldn't get the honours, to say nothing of the emoluments, of a great painter of portraits out of my head. My "illustrations" were my pot-boilers; I looked to a different branch of art—far and away the most interesting it had always seemed to me—to perpetuate my fame. There was no shame in looking to it also to make my fortune; but that fortune was by so much further from being made from the moment my visitors wished to be "done" for something. I was disappointed; for in the pictorial sense I had immediately seen them. I had seized their type—I had already settled what I would do with it. Something that wouldn't absolutely have pleased them, I afterwards reflected.

"Ah, you're—you're—a—?" I began as soon as I had mastered my surprise. I couldn't bring out the dingy word "models": it seemed so little to fit the case.

"We haven't had much practice," said the lady.

"We've got to *do* something, and we've thought that an artist in your line might perhaps make something of us," her husband threw off. He further mentioned that they didn't know many artists and that they had gone first, on the off chance—he painted views of course, but sometimes put in figures; perhaps I remembered—to Mr. Rivet, whom they had met a few years before at a place in Norfolk where he was sketching.

"We used to sketch a little ourselves," the lady hinted.

"It's very awkward, but we absolutely *must* do something," her husband went on.

"Of course we're not so *very* young," she admitted with a wan smile.

With the remark that I might as well know something more about them the husband had handed me a card extracted from a neat new pocket-book—their appurtenances were all of the freshest—and inscribed with the words "Major Monarch." Impressive as these words were they didn't carry my knowledge much further; but my visitor presently added: "I've left the army and we've had the misfortune to lose our money. In fact our means are dreadfully small."

"It's awfully trying—a regular strain," said Mrs. Monarch.

They evidently wished to be discreet—to take care not to swagger because they were gentlefolk. I felt them willing to recognise this as something of a drawback, at the same time that I guessed at an underlying sense—their consolation in adversity—that they *had* their points. They certainly had; but these advantages struck me as preponderantly social; such, for instance, as would help to make a drawing-room look well. However, a drawing-room was always, or ought to be, a picture.

In consequence of his wife's allusion to their age Major Monarch observed: "Naturally it's more for the figure that we thought of going in. We can still hold ourselves up." On the instant I saw that the figure was indeed their strong point. His "naturally" didn't sound vain, but it lighted up the question. "*She* has the best one," he continued, nodding at his wife with a pleasant after-dinner absence of circumlocution. I could only reply, as if we were in fact sitting over our wine, that this didn't prevent his own from being very good; which led him in turn to make answer: "We thought that if you ever have to do people like us we might be something like it. *She* particularly—for a lady in a book, you know."

I was so amused by them that, to get more of it, I did my best to take their point of view; and though it was an embarrassment to find myself appraising physically, as if they were animals on hire or useful blacks, a pair whom I should have expected to meet only in one of the relations in which criticism is tacit, I looked at Mrs. Monarch judicially enough to be able to exclaim after a moment with conviction: "Oh, yes, a lady in a book!" She was singularly like a bad illustration.

"We'll stand up, if you like," said the Major; and he raised himself before me with a really grand air.

I could take his measure at a glance—he was six feet two and a perfect gentleman. It would have paid any club in process of formation and in want of a stamp to engage him at a salary to stand in the principal window. What struck me at once was that in coming to me they had rather missed their vocation; they could surely have been turned to better account for advertising purposes. I couldn't of course see the thing in detail, but I could see them make somebody's fortune—I don't mean their own. There was something in them for a waistcoat-maker, an hotel-keeper or a soap-vendor. I could imagine "We always use it" pinned on their bosoms with the greatest effect; I had a vision of the brilliancy with which they would launch a table d'hôte.

Mrs. Monarch sat still, not from pride but from shyness, and presently her husband said to her: "Get up, my dear, and show how smart you are." She obeyed, but she had no need to get up to show it. She walked to the end of the studio and then came back blushing, her fluttered eyes on the partner of her appeal. I was reminded of an incident I had accidentally had a glimpse of in Paris—being with a friend there, a dramatist about to produce a play, when an actress came to him to ask to be entrusted with a part. She went through her paces before him, walked up and down as Mrs. Monarch was doing. Mrs. Monarch did it quite as well, but I abstained from applauding. It was very odd to see such people apply for such poor pay. She looked as if she had ten thousand a year. Her husband had used the word that described her: she was in the London current jargon essentially and typically "smart." Her figure was, in the same order of ideas, conspicuously and irreproachably "good." For a woman of her age her waist was surprisingly small; her elbow moreover had the orthodox crook. She held her head at the conventional angle, but why did she come to *me*? She ought to have tried on jackets at a big shop. I feared my visitors were not only destitute but "artistic"—which would be a great complication. When she sat down again I thanked her, observing that what a draughtsman most valued in his model was the faculty of keeping quiet.

"Oh, *she* can keep quiet," said Major Monarch. Then he added jocosely: "I've always kept her quiet."

"I'm not a nasty fidget, am I?" It was going to wring tears from me, I felt, the way she hid her head, ostrich-like, in the other broad bosom.

The owner of this expanse addressed his answer to me. "Perhaps it isn't out of place to mention—because we ought to be quite businesslike, oughtn't we?—that when I married her she was known as the Beautiful Statue."

"Oh dear!" said Mrs. Monarch ruefully.

"Of course I should want a certain amount of expression," I rejoined.

"Of *course!*"—and I had never heard such unanimity.

"And then I suppose you know that you'll get awfully tired."

"Oh, we *never* get tired!" they eagerly cried.

"Have you had any kind of practice?"

They hesitated—they looked at each other. "We've been photographed—*immensely*," said Mrs. Monarch.

"She means the fellows have asked us themselves," added the Major.

"I see—because you're so good-looking."

"I don't know what they thought, but they were always after us."

"We always got our photographs for nothing," smiled Mrs. Monarch.

"We might have brought some, my dear," her husband remarked.

"I'm not sure we have any left. We've given quantities away," she explained to me.

"With our autographs and that sort of thing," said the Major.

"Are they to be got in the shops?" I inquired as a harmless pleasantry.

"Oh, yes, *hers*—they used to be."

"Not now," said Mrs. Monarch with her eyes on the floor.

II

I could fancy the "sort of thing" they put on the presentation copies of their photographs, and I was sure they wrote a beautiful hand. It was odd how quickly I was sure of everything that concerned them. If they were now so poor as to have to earn shillings and pence they could never have had much of a margin. Their good looks had been their capital, and they had good-naturedly made the most of the career that this resource marked out for them. It was in their faces, the blankness, the deep intellectual repose of the twenty years of country-house visiting that had given them pleasant intonations. I could see the sunny drawing-rooms, sprinkled with periodicals she didn't read, in which Mrs. Monarch had continuously sat; I could see the wet shrubberies in which she had walked, equipped to admiration for either exercise. I could see the rich covers the Major had helped to shoot and the wonderful garments in which, late at night, he repaired to the smoking-room to talk about them. I could imagine their leggings and waterproofs, their knowing tweeds and rugs, their rolls of sticks and cases of tackle and neat umbrellas; and I could evoke the exact appearance of their servants and the compact variety of their luggage on platforms of country stations.

They gave small tips, but they were liked; they didn't do anything themselves, but they were welcome. They looked so well everywhere; they gratified the general relish for stature, complexion and "form." They knew it without fatuity or vulgarity, and they respected themselves in consequence. They weren't superficial; they were thorough and kept themselves up—it had been their line. People with such a taste for activity had to have some line. I could feel how even in a dull house they could have been counted on for the joy of life. At present something had happened—it didn't matter what, their little income had grown less, it had grown least—and they had to do something for pocket-money. Their friends could like them, I made out, without liking to support them. There was something about them that represented credit—their clothes, their manners, their type; but if credit is a large empty pocket in which an occasional chink reverberates, the chink at least must be audible. What they wanted of me was help to make it so. Fortunately they had no children—I soon divined that. They would also perhaps wish our relations to be kept secret: this was why it was "for the figure"—the reproduction of the face would betray them.

I liked them—I felt, quite as their friends must have done—they were so simple; and I had no objection to them if they would suit. But somehow with all their perfections I didn't easily believe in them. After all they were amateurs, and the ruling passion of my life was the detestation of the amateur. Combined with this was another perversity—an innate preference for the represented subject over the real one: the defect of the real one was so apt to be a lack of representation. I liked things that appeared; then one was sure. Whether they *were* or not was a subordinate and almost always a profitless question. There were other considerations, the first of which was that I already had two or three recruits in use, notably a young person with big feet, in alpaca, from Kilburn, who for a couple of years had come to me regularly for my illustrations and with whom I was still—perhaps ignobly—satisfied. I frankly explained to my visitors how the case stood, but they had taken more precautions than I supposed. They had reasoned out their opportunity, for Claude Rivet had told them of the projected *édition de luxe* of one of the writers of our day—the rarest of the novelists—who, long neglected by the mul-titudinous vulgar and dearly prized by the attentive (need I mention Philip Vincent?), had had the happy fortune of seeing, late in life, the dawn and then the full light of a higher criticism; an estimate in which on the part of the public there was something really of expiation. The edition preparing, planned by a publisher of taste, was practically an act of high reparation; the woodcuts with which it was to be enriched were the homage of English art to one of the most independent representatives of English letters. Major and Mrs. Monarch confessed to me they had hoped I might be able to work *them* into my branch of the enterprise. They knew I was to do the first of the books, *Rutland Ramsay*, but I had to make clear to them that my participation in the rest of the affair—this first book was to be a test—must depend on the satisfaction I should give. If this should be limited my employers would drop me with scarce common forms. It was therefore a crisis for me, and naturally I was making special preparations, looking about for new people, should they be necessary, and securing the best types. I admitted however that I should like to settle down to two or three good models who would do for everything.

"Should we have often to—a—put on special clothes?" Mrs. Monarch timidly demanded.

"Dear, yes—that's half the business."

"And should we be expected to supply our own costumes?"

"Oh, no; I've got a lot of things. A painter's models put on—or put off—anything he likes."

"And you mean—a—the same?"

"The same?"

Mrs. Monarch looked at her husband again.

"Oh, she was just wondering," he explained, "if the costumes are in *general* use." I had to confess that they were, and I mentioned further that some of them—I had a lot of genuine greasy last-century things—had served their time, a hundred years ago, on living world-stained men and women; on figures not perhaps so far removed, in that vanished world, from *their* type, the Monarchs,' *quoi!* of a breeched and bewigged age. "We'll put on anything that *fits*," said the Major.

"Oh, I arrange that—they fit in the pictures."

"I'm afraid I should do better for the modern books. I'd come as you like," said Mrs. Monarch.

"She has got a lot of clothes at home: they might do for contemporary life," her husband continued.

"Oh, I can fancy scenes in which you'd be quite natural." And indeed I could see the slipshod rearrangements of stale properties—the stories I tried to produce pictures for without the exasperation of reading them—whose sandy tracts the good lady might help to people. But I had to return to the fact that for this sort of work—the daily mechanical grind—I was already equipped: the people I was working with were fully adequate.

"We only thought we might be more like *some* characters," said Mrs. Monarch mildly, getting up.

Her husband also rose; he stood looking at me with a dim wistfulness that was touching in so fine a man. "Wouldn't it be rather a pull sometimes to have—a—to have—?" He hung fire; he wanted me to help him by phrasing what he meant. But I couldn't—I didn't know. So he brought it out awkwardly: "The *real* thing; a gentleman, you know, or a lady." I was quite ready to give a general assent—I admitted that there was a great deal in that. This encouraged Major Monarch to say, following up his appeal with an unacted gulp: "It's awfully hard—we've tried everything." The gulp was communicative; it proved too much for his wife. Before I knew it Mrs. Monarch had dropped again upon a divan and burst into tears. Her husband sat down beside her, holding one of her hands; whereupon she quickly dried her eyes with the other, while I felt embarrassed as she looked up at me. "There isn't a confounded job I haven't applied for—waited for—prayed for. You can fancy we'd be pretty bad first. Secretaryships and that sort of thing? You might as well ask for a peerage. I'd be *anything*—I'm strong; a messenger or a coal-heaver. I'd put on a gold-laced cap and open carriage-doors in front of the haberdasher's; I'd hang about a station to carry portmanteaus; I'd be a postman. But they won't *look* at you; there are thousands as good as yourself already on the ground. *Gentlemen,* poor beggars, who've drunk their wine, who've kept their hunters!"

I was as reassuring as I knew how to be, and my visitors were presently on their feet again while, for the experiment, we agreed on an hour. We were discussing it when the door opened and Miss Churm came in with a wet umbrella. Miss Churm had to take the omnibus to Maida Vale and then walk half a mile. She looked a trifle blowsy and slightly splashed. I scarcely ever saw her come in without thinking afresh how odd it was that, being so little in herself, she should yet be so much in others. She was a meagre little Miss Churm, but was such an ample heroine of romance. She was only a freckled cockney, but she could represent everything, from a fine lady to a shepherdess; she had the faculty as she might have had a fine voice or long hair. She couldn't spell and she loved beer, but she had two or three "points," and practice, and a knack, and mother-wit, and a whimsical sensibility, and a love of the theatre, and seven sisters, and not an ounce of respect, especially for the *h*. The first thing my visitors saw was that her umbrella was wet, and in their spotless perfection they visibly winced at it. The rain had come on since their arrival.

"I'm all in a soak; there *was* a mess of people in the 'bus. I wish you lived near a stytion," said Miss Churm. I requested her to get ready as quickly as possible, and she passed into the room in which she always changed her dress. But before going out she asked me what she was to get into this time.

"It's the Russian princess, don't you know?" I answered; "the one with the 'golden eyes,' in black velvet, for the long thing in the *Cheapside.*"

"Golden eyes? I *say!*" cried Miss Churm, while my companions watched her with intensity as she withdrew. She always arranged herself, when she was late, before I could turn round; and I kept my visitors a little on purpose, so that they might get an idea, from seeing her, what would be expected of themselves. I mentioned that she was quite my notion of an excellent model—she was really very clever.

"Do you think she looks like a Russian princess?" Major Monarch asked with lurking alarm.

"When I make her, yes."

"Oh, if you have to *make* her—!" he reasoned, not without point.

"That's the most you can ask. There are so many who are not makeable."

"Well, now, *here's* a lady"—and with a persuasive smile he passed his arm into his wife's—"who's already made!"

"Oh, I'm not a Russian princess," Mrs. Monarch protested a little coldly. I could see she had known some and didn't like them. There at once was a complication of a kind I never had to fear with Miss Churm.

This young lady came back in black velvet—the gown was rather rusty and very low on her lean shoulders—and with a Japanese fan in her red hands. I reminded her that in the scene I was doing she had to look over someone's head. "I forget whose it is; but it doesn't matter. Just look over a head."

"I'd rather look over a stove," said Miss Churm; and she took her station near the fire. She fell into position, settled herself into a tall attitude, gave a certain backward inclination to her head and certain forward droop to her fan, and looked, at least to my prejudiced sense, distinguished and charming, foreign and dangerous. We left her looking so while I went downstairs with Major and Mrs. Monarch.

"I believe I could come about as near it as that," said Mrs. Monarch.

"Oh, you think she's shabby, but you must allow for the alchemy of art."

However, they went off with an evident increase of comfort founded on their demonstrable advantage in being the real thing. I could fancy them shuddering over Miss Churm. She was very droll about them when I went back, for I told her what they wanted.

"Well, if *she* can sit I'll tyke to bookkeeping," said my model.

"She's very ladylike," I replied as an innocent form of aggravation.

"So much the worse for *you*. That means she can't turn round."

"She'll do for the fashionable novels."

"Oh, yes, she'll *do* for them!" my model humorously declared. "Ain't they bad enough without her?" I had often sociably denounced them to Miss Churm.

III

It was for the elucidation of a mystery in one of these works that I first tried Mrs. Monarch. Her husband came with her, to be useful if necessary—it was sufficiently clear that as a general thing he would prefer to come with her. At first I wondered if this were for "propriety's" sake—if he were going to be jealous and meddling. The idea was too tiresome, and if it had been confirmed it would speedily have brought our acquaintance to a close. But I soon saw there was nothing in it and that if he accompanied Mrs. Monarch it was—in addition to the chance of being wanted—simply because he had nothing else to do. When they were separate his occupation was gone, and they never *had* been separate. I judged rightly that in their awkward situation their close union was their main comfort and that this union had no weak spot. It was a real marriage, an encouragement to the hesitating, a nut for pessimists to crack. Their address was humble—I remember afterwards thinking it had been the only thing about them that was really professional—and I could fancy the lamentable lodgings in which the Major would have been left alone. He could sit there more or less grimly with his wife—he couldn't sit there anyhow without her.

He had too much tact to try and make himself agreeable when he couldn't be useful; so when I was too absorbed in my work to talk he simply sat and waited. But I liked to hear him talk—it made my work, when not interrupting it, less mechanical, less special. To listen to him was to combine the excitement of going out with the economy of staying at home. There was only one hindrance—that I seemed not to know any of the people this brilliant couple had known. I think he wondered extremely, during the term of our intercourse, whom the deuce I *did* know. He hadn't a stray sixpence of an idea to fumble for, so we didn't spin it very fine; we confined ourselves to questions of leather and even of liquor—saddlers and breeches-makers and how to get excellent claret cheap—and matters like "good trains" and the habits of small game. His lore on these last subjects was astonishing—he managed to interweave the station-master with the ornithologist. When he couldn't talk about greater things he could talk cheerfully about small, and since I couldn't accompany him into reminiscences of the fashionable world he could lower the conversation without a visible effort to my level.

So earnest a desire to please was touching in a man who could so easily have knocked one down. He looked after the fire and had an opinion on the draught of the stove without my asking him, and I could see that he thought many of my arrangements not half knowing. I remember telling him that if I were only rich I'd offer him a salary to come and teach me how to live. Sometimes he gave a random sigh of which the essence might have been: "Give me even such a bare old barrack as *this*, and I'd do something with it!" When I wanted to use him he came alone; which was an illustration of the superior courage of women. His wife could bear her solitary second floor, and she was in general more discreet; showing by various small reserves that she was alive to the propriety of keeping our relations markedly professional—not letting them slide into sociability. She wished it to remain clear that she and the Major were employed, not cultivated, and if she approved of me as a superior, who could be kept in his place, she never thought me quite good enough for an equal.

She sat with great intensity, giving the whole of her mind to it, and was capable of remaining for an hour almost as motionless as before a photographer's lens. I could see she had been photographed often, but somehow the very habit that made her good for that purpose unfitted her for mine. At first I was extremely pleased with her ladylike air, and it was a satisfaction, on coming to follow her lines, to see how good they were and how far they could lead the pencil. But after a little skirmishing I began to find her too insurmountably stiff; do what I would with it my drawing looked like a photograph or a copy of a photograph. Her figure had no variety of expression—she herself had no sense of variety. You may say that this was my business and was only a question of placing her. Yet I placed her in every conceivable position and she managed to obliterate their differences. She was always a lady certainly, and into the bargain was always the same lady. She was the real thing, but always the same thing. There were moments when I rather writhed under the serenity of her confidence that she *was* the real thing. All her dealings with me and all her husband's were an implication that this was lucky for *me*. Meanwhile I found myself trying to invent types that approached her own, instead of making her own transform itself—in the clever way that was not impossible for instance to poor Miss Churm. Arrange as I would and take the precautions I would, she always came out, in my pictures, too tall—landing me in the dilemma of having represented a fascinating woman as seven feet high, which (out of respect perhaps to my own very much scantier inches) was far from my idea of such a personage.

The case was worse with the Major—nothing I could do would keep *him* down, so that he became useful only for representation of brawny giants. I adored variety and range, I cherished human accidents, the illustrative note; I wanted to characterise closely, and the thing in the world I most hated was the danger of being ridden by a type. I had quarrelled with some of my friends about it; I had parted company with them for maintaining that one *had* to be, and that if the type was beautiful—witness Raphael and Leonardo—the servitude was only a gain. I was neither Leonardo nor Raphael—I might only be a presumptuous young modern searcher; but I held that everything was to be sacrificed sooner than character. When they claimed that the obsessional form could easily *be* character I retorted, perhaps superficially, "Whose?" It couldn't be everybody's—it might end in being nobody's.

After I had drawn Mrs. Monarch a dozen times I felt surer even than before that the value of such a model as Miss Churm resided precisely in the fact that she had no positive stamp, combined of course with the other fact that what she did have was a curious and inexplicable talent for imitation. Her usual appearance was like a curtain which she could draw up at request for a capital performance. This performance was simply suggestive; but it was a word to the wise—it was vivid and pretty. Sometimes even I thought it, though she was plain herself, too insipidly pretty; I made it a reproach to her that the figures drawn from her were monotonously (*bêtement*, as we used to say) graceful. Nothing made her more angry: it was so much her pride to feel she could sit for characters that had nothing in common with each other. She would accuse me at such moments of taking away her "reputy-tion."

It suffered a certain shrinkage, this queer quantity, from the repeated visits of my new friends. Miss Churm was greatly in demand, never in want of employment, so I had no scruple in putting her off occasionally, to try them more at my ease. It was certainly amusing at first to do the real thing—it was amusing to do Major Monarch's trousers. They *were* the real thing, even if he did come out colossal. It was amusing to do his wife's back hair—it was so mathematically neat—and the particular "smart" tension of her tight stays. She lent herself especially to positions in which the face was somewhat averted or blurred; she abounded in ladylike back views and *profils perdus*. When she stood erect she took naturally one of the attitudes in which court painters represent queens and princesses; so that I found myself wondering whether, to draw out this accomplish-ment, I couldn't get the editor of the *Cheapside* to publish a really royal romance, "A Tale of Buckingham Palace." Sometimes, however, the real thing and the make-believe came into contact; by which I mean that Miss Churm, keeping an appointment or coming to make one on days when I had much work in hand, encountered her invidious rivals. The encounter was not on their part, for they noticed her no more than if she had been the housemaid; not from intentional loftiness, but simply because as yet, professionally, they didn't know how to fraternise, as I could imagine they would have liked—or at least that the Major would. They couldn't talk about the omnibus—they always walked; and they didn't know what else to try—she wasn't interested in good trains or cheap claret. Besides, they must have felt—in the air—that she was amused at them, secretly derisive of their ever knowing how. She wasn't a person to conceal the limits of her faith if she had had a chance to show them. On the other hand Mrs. Monarch didn't think her tidy; for why else did she take pains to say to me—it was going out of the way, for Mrs. Monarch—that she didn't like dirty women?

One day when my young lady happened to be present with my other sitters—she even dropped in, when it was convenient, for a chat—I asked her to be so good as to lend a hand in getting tea, a service with which she was familiar and which was one of a class that, living as I did in a small way, with slender domestic resources, I often appealed to my models to render. They liked to lay hands on my property, to break the sitting, and sometimes the china—it made them feel Bohemian. The next time I saw Miss Churm after this incident she surprised me greatly by making a scene about it—she accused me of having wished to humiliate her. She hadn't resented the outrage at the time, but had seemed obliging and amused, enjoying the comedy of asking Mrs. Monarch, who sat vague and silent, whether she would have cream and sugar, and putting an exaggerated simper into the question. She had tried intonations—as if she too wished to pass for the real thing—till I was afraid my other visitors would take offence.

Oh, they were determined not to do this, and their touching patience was the measure of their great need. They would sit by the hour, uncomplaining, till I was ready to use them; they would come back on the chance of being wanted and would walk away cheerfully if it failed. I used to go to the door with them to see in what magnificent order they retreated. I tried to find other employment for them—I introduced them to several artists. But they didn't "take," for reasons I could appreciate, and I became rather anxiously aware that after such disappointments they fell back upon me with a heavier weight. They did me the honour to think me most *their* form. They weren't romantic enough for the painters, and in those days there were few serious workers in black-and-white. Besides, they had an eye to the great job I had mentioned to them—they had secretly set their hearts on supplying the right essence for my pictorial vindication of our fine novelist. They knew that for this undertaking I should want no costume effects, none of the frippery of past ages—that it was a case in which everything would be contemporary and satirical and presumably genteel. If I could work them into it their future would be assured, for the labour would of course be long and the occupation steady.

One day Mrs. Monarch came without her husband—she explained his absence by his having had to go to the City. While she sat there in her usual relaxed majesty there came at the door a knock which I immediately recognised as the subdued appeal of a model out of work. It was followed by the entrance of a young man whom I at once saw to be a foreigner and who proved in fact an Italian acquainted with no English word but my name, which he uttered in a way that made it seem to include all others. I hadn't then visited his country, nor was I proficient in his tongue; but as he was not so meanly constituted—what Italian is?—as to depend only on that member for expression he conveyed to me, in familiar but graceful mimicry, that he was in search of exactly the employment in which the lady before me was engaged. I was not struck with him at first, and while I continued to draw I dropped few signs of interest or encouragement. He stood his ground, however—not importunately, but with a dumb dog-like fidelity in his eyes that amounted to innocent impudence, the manner of a devoted servant—he might have been in the house for years—unjustly suspected. Suddenly it struck me that this very attitude and expression made a picture; whereupon I told him to sit down and wait till I should be free. There was another picture in the way he obeyed me, and I observed as I worked that there were others still in the way he looked wonderingly, with his head thrown back, about the high studio. He might have been crossing himself in Saint Peter's. Before I finished I said to myself, "The fellow's a bankrupt orange-monger, but a treasure."

When Mrs. Monarch withdrew he passed across the room like a flash to open the door for her, standing there with the rapt, pure gaze of the young Dante spellbound by the young Beatrice. As I never insisted, in such situations, on the blankness of the British domestic, I reflected that he had the making of a servant—and I needed one, but couldn't pay him to be only that—as well as of a model; in short I resolved to adopt my bright adventurer if he would agree to officiate in the double capacity. He jumped at my offer, and in the event my rashness—for I had really known nothing about him—wasn't brought home to me. He proved a sympathetic though a desultory ministrant, and had in a wonderful degree the *sentiment de la pose*. It was uncultivated, instinctive, a part of the happy instinct that had guided him to my door and helped him to spell out my name on the card nailed to it. He had had no other introduction to me than a guess, from the shape of my high north window, seen outside, that my place was a studio and that as a studio it would contain an artist. He had wandered to England in search of fortune, like other itinerants, and had embarked, with a partner and a small green handcart, on the sale of penny ices. The ices had melted away and the partner had dissolved in their train. My young man wore tight yellow trousers with reddish stripes and his name was Oronte. He was sallow but fair, and when I put him into some old clothes of my own he looked like an Englishman. He was as good as Miss Churm, who could look, when requested, like an Italian.

IV

I thought Mrs. Monarch's face slightly convulsed when, on her coming back with her husband, she found Oronte installed. It was strange to have to recognise in a scrap of a lazzarone a competitor to her magnificent Major. It was she who scented danger first, for the Major was anecdotically unconscious. But Oronte gave us tea, with a hundred eager confusions—he had never been concerned in so queer a process—and I think she thought better of me for having at last an "establishment." They saw a couple of drawings that I had made of the establishment, and Mrs. Monarch hinted that it never would have struck her he had sat for them. "Now the drawings you make from *us*, they look exactly like us," she reminded me, smiling in triumph; and I recognised that this was indeed just their defect. When I drew the Monarchs I couldn't anyhow get away from them—get into the character I wanted to represent; and I hadn't the least desire my model should be discoverable in my picture. Miss Churm never was, and Mrs. Monarch thought I hid her, very properly, because she was vulgar; whereas if she was lost it was only as the dead who go to heaven are lost—in the gain of an angel the more.

By this time I had got a certain start with "Rutland Ramsay," the first novel in the great projected series; that is, I had produced a dozen drawings, several with the help of the Major and his wife, and I had sent them in for approval. My understanding with the publishers, as I have already hinted, had been that I was to be left to do my work, in this particular case, as I liked, with the whole book committed to me; but my connexion with the rest of the series was only contingent. There were moments when, frankly, it *was* a comfort to have the real thing under one's hand; for there were characters in "Rutland Ramsay" that were very much like it. There were people presumably as erect as the Major and women of as good a fashion as Mrs. Monarch. There was a great deal of country-house life—treated, it is true, in a fine fanciful ironical generalised way—and there was a considerable implication of knickerbockers and kilts. There were certain things I had to settle at the outset; such things for instance as the exact appearance of the hero and the particular bloom and figure of the heroine. The author of course gave me a lead, but there was a margain for interpretation. I took the Monarchs into my confidence, I told them frankly what I was about, I mentioned my embarrassments and alternatives. "Oh, take *him*!" Mrs. Monarch murmured sweetly, looking at her husband; and "What could you want better than my wife?" the Major inquired with the comfortable candour that now prevailed between us.

I wasn't obliged to answer these remarks—I was only obliged to place my sitters. I wasn't easy in mind, and I postponed a little timidly perhaps the solving of my question. The book was a large canvas, the other figures were numerous, and I worked off at first some of the episodes in which the hero and the heroine were not concerned. When once I had set *them* up I should have to stick to them—I couldn't make my young man seven feet high in one place and five feet nine in another. I inclined on the whole to the latter measurement, though the Major more than once reminded me that *he* looked about as young as any one. It was indeed quite possible to arrange him, for the figure, so that it would have been difficult to detect his age. After the spontaneous Oronte had been with me a month, and after I had given him to understand several times over that his native exuberance would presently constitute an insurmountable barrier to our further intercourse, I waked to a sense of his heroic capacity. He was only five feet seven, but the remaining inches were latent. I tried him almost secretly at first, for I was really rather afraid of the judgement my other models would pass on such a choice. If they regarded Miss Churm as little better than a snare what would they think of the representation of a person so little the real thing as an Italian street-vendor of a protagonist formed by a public school?

If I went a little in fear of them it wasn't because they bullied me, because they had got an oppressive foothold, but because in their really pathetic decorum and mysteriously permanent newness they counted on me so intensely. I was therefore very glad when Jack Hawley came home: he was always of such good counsel. He painted badly himself, but there was no one like him for putting his finger on the place. He had been absent from England for a year; he had been somewhere—I don't remember where—to get a fresh eye. I was in a good deal of dread of any such organ, but we were old friends; he had been away for months and a sense of emptiness was creeping into my life. I hadn't dodged a missile for a year.

He came back with a fresh eye, but with the same old black velvet blouse, and the first evening he spent in my studio we smoked cigarettes till the small hours. He had done no work himself, he had only got the eye; so the field was clear for the production of my little things. He wanted to see what I had produced for the *Cheapside*, but he was disappointed in the exhibition. That at least seemed the meaning of two or three comprehensive groans which, as he lounged on my big divan, his leg folded under him, looking at my latest drawings, issued from his lips with the smoke of the cigarette.

"What's the matter with you?" I asked.

"What's the matter with *you*?"

"Nothing save that I'm mystified."

"You are indeed. You're quite off the hinge. What's the meaning of this new fad?" And he tossed me, with visible irreverence, a drawing in which I happened to have depicted both my elegant models. I asked if he didn't think it good, and he replied that it struck him as execrable, given the sort of thing I had always represented myself to him as wishing to arrive at; but I let that pass—I was so anxious to see exactly what he meant. The two figures in the picture looked colossal, but I supposed this was *not* what he meant, inasmuch as, for aught he knew to the contrary, I might have been trying for some such effect. I maintained that I was working exactly in the same way as when he last had done me the honour to tell me I might do something some day. "Well, there's a screw loose somewhere," he answered; "wait a bit and I'll discover it." I depended upon him to do so: where else was the fresh eye? But he produced at last nothing more luminous than "I don't know—I don't like your types." This was lame for a critic who had never consented to discuss with me anything but the question of execution, the direction of strokes and the mystery of values.

"In the drawings you've been looking at I think my types are very handsome."

"Oh, they won't do!"   "I've been working with new models."

"I see you have. *They* won't do."

"Are you very sure of that?"

"Absolutely—they're stupid."

"You mean *I* am—for I ought to get round that."

"You *can't*—with such people. Who are they?"

"I told him, so far as was necessary, and he concluded heartlessly: "*Ce sont des gens qu'il faut mettre à la porte.*"

"You've never seen them; they're awfully good"—I flew to their defence.

"Not seen them? Why all this recent work of yours drops to pieces with them. It's all I want to see of them."

"No one else has said anything against it—the *Cheapside* people are pleased."

"Every one else is an ass, and the *Cheapside* people the biggest asses of all. Come, don't pretend at this time of day to have pretty illusions about the public, especially about publishers and editors. It's not for *such* animals you work—it's for those who know, *coloro che sanno;* so keep straight for *me* if you can't keep straight for yourself. There was a certain sort of thing you used to try for—and a very good thing it was. But this twaddle isn't *in* it." When I talked with Hawley later about "Rutland Ramsay" and its possible successors he declared that I must get back into my boat again or I should go to the bottom. His voice in short was the voice of warning.

I noted the warning, but I didn't turn my friends out of doors. They bored me a good deal; but the very fact that they bored me admonished me not to sacrifice them—if there was anything to be done with them—simply to irritation. As I look back at this phase they seem to me to have pervaded my life not a little. I have a vision of them as most of the time in my studio, seated against the wall on an old velvet bench to be out of the way, and resembling the while a pair of patient courtiers in a royal ante-chamber. I'm convinced that during the coldest weeks of the winter they held their ground because it saved them fire. Their newness was losing its gloss, and it was impossible not to feel them objects of charity. Whenever Miss Churm arrived they went away, and after I was fairly launched in "Rutland Ramsay" Miss Churm arrived pretty often. They managed to express to me tacitly that they supposed I wanted her for the low life of the book, and I let them suppose it, since they had attempted to study the work—it was lying about the studio—without discovering that it dealt only with the highest circles. They had dipped into the most brilliant of our novelists without deciphering many passages. I still took an hour from them, now and again, in spite of Jack Hawley's warning: it would be time enough to dismiss them, if dismissal should be necessary, when the rigour of the season was over. Hawley had made their acquaintance—he had met them at my fireside—and thought them a ridiculous pair. Learning that he was a painter they tried to approach him, to show him too that they were the real thing; but he looked at them, across the big room, as if they were miles away: they were a compendium of everything he most objected to in the social system of his country. Such people as that, all convention and patent-leather, with ejaculations that stopped conversation, had no business in a studio. A studio was a place to learn to see, and how could you see through a pair of feather-beds?

The main inconvenience I suffered at their hands was that at first I was shy of letting it break upon them that my artful little servant had begun to sit to me for "Rutland Ramsay." They knew I had been odd enough—they were prepared by this time to allow oddity to artists—to pick a foreign vagabond out of the streets when I might have had a person with whiskers and credentials; but it was some time before they learned how high I rated his accomplishments. They found him in an attitude more than once, but they never doubted I was doing him as an organ-grinder. There were several things they never guessed, and one of them was that for a striking scene in the novel, in which a footman briefly figured, it occurred to me to make use of Major Monarch as the menial. I kept putting this off, I didn't like to ask him to don the livery—besides the difficulty of finding a livery to fit him. At last, one day late in the winter, when I was at work on the despised Oronte, who caught one's idea on the wing, and was in the glow of feeling myself go very straight, they came in, the Major and his wife, with their society laugh about nothing (there was less and less to laugh at); came in like country-callers—they always reminded me of that—who have walked across the park after church and are presently persuaded to stay to luncheon. Luncheon was over, but they could stay to tea—I knew they wanted it. The fit was on me, however, and I couldn't let my ardour cool and my work wait, with the fading daylight, while my model prepared it. So I asked Mrs. Monarch if she would mind laying it out—a request which for an instant brought all the blood to her face. Her eyes were on her husband's for a second, and some mute telegraphy passed between them. Their folly was over the next instant; his cheerful shrewdness put an end to it. So far from pitying their wounded pride, I must add, I was moved to give it as complete a lesson as I could. They bustled about together and got out the cups and saucers and made the kettle boil. I know they felt as if they were waiting on my servant, and when the tea was prepared I said: "He'll have a cup, please—he's tired." Mrs. Monarch brought him one where he stood, and he took it from her as if he had been a gentleman at a party squeezing a crush-hat with an elbow.

Then it came over me that she had made a great effort for me—made it with a kind of nobleness—and that I owed her a compensation. Each time I saw her after this I wondered what the compensation could be. I couldn't go on doing the wrong thing to oblige them. Oh, it *was* the wrong thing, the stamp of the work for which they sat—Hawley was not the only person to say it now. I sent in a large number of the drawings I had made for "Rutland Ramsay," and I received a warning that was more to the point than Hawley's. The artistic adviser of the house for which I was working was of opinion that many of my illustrations were not what had been looked for. Most of these illustrations were the subjects in which the Monarchs had figured. Without going into the question of what *had* been looked for, I had to face the fact that at this rate I shouldn't get the other books to do. I hurled myself in despair on Miss Churm—I put her through all her paces. I not only adopted Oronte publicly as my hero, but one morning when the Major looked in to see if I didn't require him to finish a *Cheapside* figure for which he had begun to sit the week before, I told him I had changed my mind—I'd do the drawing from my man. At this my visitor turned pale and stood looking at me. "Is *he* your idea of an English gentleman?" he asked.

I was disappointed, I was nervous, I wanted to get on with my work; so I replied with irritation: "Oh my dear Major—I can't be ruined for *you!*"

It was a horrid speech, but he stood another moment—after which, without a word, he quitted the studio. I drew a long breath, for I said to myself that I shouldn't see him again. I hadn't told him definitely that I was in danger of having my work rejected, but I was vexed at his not having felt the catastrophe in the air, read with me the moral of our fruitless collaboration, the lesson that in the deceptive atmosphere of art even the highest respectability may fail of being plastic.

I didn't owe my friends money, but I did see them again. They reappeared together three days later, and, given all the other facts, there was something tragic in that one. It was a clear proof they could find nothing else in life to do. They had threshed the matter out in a dismal conference—they had digested the bad news that they were not in for the series. If they weren't useful to me even for the *Cheapside*, their function seemed difficult to determine, and I could only judge at first that they had come, forgivingly, decorously, to take a last leave. This made me rejoice in secret that I had little leisure for a scene; for I had placed both my other models in position together and I was pegging away at a drawing from which I hoped to derive glory. It had been suggested by the passage in which Rutland Ramsay, drawing up a chair to Artemisia's piano-stool, says extraordinary things to her while she ostensibly fingers out a difficult piece of music. I had done Miss Churm at the piano before—it was an attitude in which she knew how to take on an absolutely poetic grace. I wished the two figures to "compose" together with intensity, and my little Italian had entered perfectly into my conception. The pair were vividly before me, the piano had been pulled out; it was a charming show of blended youth and murmured love, which I had only to catch and keep. My visitors stood and looked at it, and I was friendly to them over my shoulder.

They made no response, but I was used to silent company and went on with my work, only a little disconcerted—even though exhilarated by the sense that *this* was at least the ideal thing—at not having got rid of them after all. Presently I heard Mrs. Monarch's sweet voice beside or rather above me: "I wish her hair were a little better done." I looked up and she was staring with a strange fixedness at Miss Churm, whose back was turned to her. "Do you mind my just touching it?" she went on—a question which made me spring up for an instant as with the instinctive fear that she might do the young lady a harm. But she quieted me with a glance I shall never forget—I confess I should like to have been able to paint *that*—and went for a moment to my model. She spoke to her softly; laying a hand on her shoulder and bending over her; and as the girl, understanding, gratefully assented, she disposed her rough curls, with a few quick passes, in such a way as to make Miss Churm's head twice as charming. It was one of the most heroic personal services I've ever seen rendered. Then Mrs. Monarch turned away with a low sigh and, looking about her as if for something to do, stooped to the floor with a noble humility and picked up a dirty rag that had dropped out of my paint-box.

The Major meanwhile had also been looking for something to do, and, wandering to the other end of the studio, saw before him my breakfast-things neglected, unremoved. "I say, can't I be useful *here?*" he called out to me with an irrepressible quaver. I assented with a laugh that I fear was awkward, and for the next ten minutes, while I worked, I heard the light clatter of china and the tinkle of spoons and glass. Mrs. Monarch assisted her husband—they washed up my crockery, they put it away. They wandered off into my little scullery, and I afterwards found that they had cleaned my knives and that my slender stock of plate had an unprecedented surface. When it came over me, the latent eloquence of what they were doing, I confess that my drawing was blurred for a moment—the picture swam. They had accepted their failure, but they couldn't accept their fate. They had bowed their heads in bewilderment to the perverse and cruel law in virtue of which the real thing could be so much less precious than the unreal; but they didn't want to starve. If my servants were my models, then my models might be my servants. They would reverse the parts—the others would sit for the ladies and gentlemen and *they* would do the work. They would still be in the studio—it was an intense dumb appeal to me not to turn them out. "Take us on," they wanted to say—"we'll do *anything*."

My pencil dropped from my hand; my sitting was spoiled and I got rid of my sitters, who were also evidently rather mystified and awestruck. Then, alone with the Major and his wife I had a most uncomfortable moment. He put their prayer into a single sentence: "I say, you know—just let *us* do for you, can't you?" I couldn't—it was dreadful to see them emptying my slops; but I pretended I could, to oblige them, for about a week. Then I gave them a sum of money to go away, and I never saw them again. I obtained the remaining books, but my friend Hawley repeats that Major and Mrs. Monarch did me a permanent harm, got me into false ways. If it be true I'm content to have paid the price—for the memory.

ISAK DINESEN
1885–1962
A Consolatory Tale

Charles Despard, the scribe, walked into a small café in Paris, and there found a friend and compatriot dining sedately at a table by the window. He sat down face to face with him, drew a deep sigh of relief and ordered an absinthe. Till he had got it and tasted it he did not speak, but listened attentively to a few commonplace remarks from his companion.

It snowed outside. The wayfarers' footsteps were inaudible upon the thin layer of snow on the pavement; the earth was dumb and dead. But the air was intensely alive. In the dark intervals between the street lamps the falling snow made itself known to the wanderers in a multitudinous, crystalline, icy touch on eyelashes and mouth. But around the gas-lit lantern-panes it sprang into sight, a whirl of little, transilluminated wings, which seemed to dance both up and down, a small white world-system, like a hectic, silent, elfish bee-hive. The

Cathedral of Notre Dame loomed tall and grim, a rock, slanting upward infinitely into the blind night.

Charlie had just had a great success with a new book, and was making money. He was not good at spending it, for he had been poor all his life, and had no expensive tastes, and when he looked at other people to learn from them, the ways in which they were getting rid of their earnings most often seemed to him silly and insipid. So he left his wealth in the hands of the bankers, as with people mysteriously keen on and experienced in this side of existence, and was himself generally short of cash. By this time his wife had gone back to her own people, and he had no regular establishment, but travelled about. He felt at home in most places, but still had in his heart a constant, slight nostalgia for London, and his old life there.

He was silent now, and shy of human society, subject to that particular sadness which is expressed in the old saying: *omne animal post coitum triste*. For to Charlie the pursuit of writing, and that of love-making, were closely related. It would happen to him to hear a tune, or smell a scent, and to say to himself: "I have heard this tune, or smelled that scent before, at a time when I was either deeply in love, or at work on a book; I cannot call to mind which. But I remember that I was then, at the height of my vitality, pouring forth my being in harmony and ecstasy, and that everything seemed to be, unwontedly and blissfully, in its right place." So he sat by the table like a man with whom a love-affair has just come to its end, chilled and exhausted, with a strong sense of the emptiness and vanity of all human ambitions. All the same, he was pleased to have met his friend, with whom he was always in good understanding.

Charlie was a small, slight man, and looked very young for his years, but his convive was smaller than he, and of indefinable age, although the poet knew him to be ten or fifteen years older than he. He was so neatly made, with delicate hands, feet and ears, finely chiselled features, a noble little mouth, a fresh complexion and a melodious voice, that he might have passed as a miniature model of the human figure made for a museum. His clothes were well cut and decorous; his high hat lay on a shelf behind him, above his coat and umbrella.

His name was Æneas Snell, or so he called himself, but in spite of his easy and debonair manner his origin and past life were obscure even to his friends. He was said by some to have been a cleric, and unfrocked at an early stage of that career. Later in life he had become a doctor of skin diseases, and had done well in the profession. He had travelled much in Europe, Africa and Asia, and knew many cities and men. No great events, either fortunate or sad, seemed ever to have come to him personally but it had been his fate to have strange happenings, dramas and catastrophes take place where he was. He had been through the plague in Egypt and in the service of an Indian Prince during the mutiny, and he was secretary to the Duke of Choiseul de Praslin at the time when this nobleman murdered his wife. At the present moment he acted as bailiff to a great parvenu of Paris. His friends sometimes wondered that a man of so much talent and experience should all his life have felt content in the service of other people, but Æneas explained the case by pointing to the phlegm or passivity of his nature. He could not, he said, on his own find sufficient reason for doing a thing ever to do it, but the fact that he was being asked or told to do so by somebody else was to him quite a plausible reason for taking it on. He did well as a bailiff and had his employer's confidence in everything. Something in his carriage and manner suggested that by taking on this work he was conferring an honour both on himself and on his master, and this trait strongly appealed to the rich French gentleman. He was a pleasant companion, an attentive, patient listener and a skilful reconteur; he would not let his own person play any big role in his tales, but he would tell even his strangest story as if it had taken place before his own eyes, which indeed it might often have done.

When Charlie had drunk his absinthe, he became more communicative; he leaned his arm on the table and his chin in his hand, and slowly and gravely said: "Thou shalt love thy art with all thy heart, and with all thy soul, and with all thy mind. And thou shalt love thy public as thyself." And after a while he added: "All human relationships have in them something monstrous and cruel. But the relation of the artist to the public is amongst the most monstrous. Yes, it is as terrible as marriage." At that he gave Æneas a deep, bitter and harassed glance, as if he did see, in him, his public incarnated.

"For," he went on, "we are, the artist and the public, much against our own will, dependent upon one another for our very existence." Here again Charlie's eyes, dark with pain, fired a deadly accusation at his friend. Æneas felt the poet to be in such a dangerous state of mind that anything but a trivial remark might throw him off his balance. "If it be so," he said, "has not your public made you a pleasant existence?" But even these words so bewildered Charlie that he sat in silence for a long time. "My God," he said at last, "do you think that I am talking of my daily bread—of this glass, or of my coat and cravat? For the love of Christ, try to understand what I say. Nay, we are, each of us, awaiting the consent, or the co-operation of the other to be brought into existence at all. Where there is no work of art to look at, or to listen to, there can be no public either; that is clear, I suppose, even to you? And as to the work of art, now—does a painting exist at which no one looks?—does a book exist which is never read? No, Æneas, they have got to be looked at; they have got to be read. And again by the very act of being looked at, or of being read, they bring into existence that formidable being, the spectator, that which, sufficiently multiplied—and we want it multiplied, miserable creatures that we are—will become the public. And so there we are, as you see, at the mercy of it." "In that case," said Æneas, "do show a little mercy to one another." "Mercy? What are you talking about?" said Charlie, and fell into deep thought. After a long pause he said, very slowly: "We cannot show mercy to one another. The public cannot be merciful to an artist; if it were merciful it would not be the public. Thank God for that, in any case. Neither can an artist be merciful to his public, or it has, at least, never been tried.

"No," he said, "I shall explain to you how it does stand with us. All works of art are beautiful and perfect. And all of them are, at the same time, hideous, ludicrous, complete failures. At the moment when I begin a book it is always lovely. I look at it, and I see that it is good. While I am at the first chapter of it it is so well balanced, there is such sweet agreement between the various parts, as to make its entirety a marvellous harmony and generally, at that time, the last chapter of the book is the finest of all. But it is also, from the very moment it is begun, followed by a horrible shadow, a loathsome, sickening deformity, which all the same is like it, and does at times—yes, does often— change places with it, so that I myself will not recognize my work, but will shrink from it, like the farm wife from the changeling in her cradle, and cross myself at the idea that I have ever held it to be my own flesh and bone. Yes, in short and in truth, every work of art is both the idealization and the perversion, the caricature of itself. And the public has power to make it, for good or evil, the one or the other. When the heart of the public is moved and shaken by it, so that with tears of contrition and pride they acclaim it as a masterpiece, it becomes that masterpiece which I did myself at first see. And when they denounce it as insipid and worthless, it becomes worthless. But when they will not look at it at all—*voilà*, as they say in this town, it does not exist. In vain shall I cry to them: 'Do you see nothing there?' They will answer me, quite correctly: 'Nothing at all, yet all that is I see.' Æneas, if the case of the artist be so with his public, it is not good to paint or to write books.

"But do not imagine," he said after a time, "that I have no compassion with the public, or am not aware of my guilt towards them. I do have compassion with them, and it weighs on my mind. I have had to read the Book of Job, to get strength to bear my responsibility at all." "Do you see yourself in the place of Job, Charlie?" asked Æneas. "No," said Charlie solemnly and proudly, "in the place of the Lord.

"I have behaved to my reader," he went on slowly, "as the Lord behaves to Job. I know, none so well, none so well as I, how the Lord needs Job as a public, and cannot do without him. Yes, it is even doubtful whether the Lord be not more dependent upon Job than Job upon the Lord. I have laid a wager with Satan about the soul of my reader. I have marred his path and turned terrors upon him, caused him to ride on the wind and dissolved his substance, and when he waited for light there was darkness. And Job does not want to be the Lord's public any more than my public wishes to be so to me." Charlie sighed and looked down into his glass, then lifted it to his lips and emptied it.

"Still," he said, "in the end the two are reconciled; it is good to read about. For the Lord in the whirlwind pleads the defense of the artist, and of the artist only. He blows up the moral scruples and the moral sufferings of his public; he does not attempt to justify his show by any argument on right and wrong. 'Wilt thou disannul my judgment?' asks the Lord. 'Knowest thou the ordinances of heaven? Hast thou walked in the search of the depth? Canst thou lift up thy voice to the clouds? Canst thou bind the sweet influence of the Pleiades?' Yes, he speaks about the horrors and abominations of existence, and airily asks his public if they, too, will play with them as with a bird, and let their young persons do the same. And Job indeed is the ideal public. Who amongst us will ever again find a public like that? Before such arguments he bows his head and foregoes his grievance; he sees that he is better off, and safer, in the hands of the artist than with any other power of the world, and he admits that he has uttered what he understood not." Charlie made a pause. "The Lord did the same thing to me, once," he said gravely, sighed and went on: "I have read the Book of Job many times," Charlie concluded, "at night, when I could not sleep. And I have slept badly these last months." He sat silent, lost in remembrance.

"But all the same I wonder," he said after a long pause, "what is the meaning of the whole thing. Why may we not give up painting and writing, and give the public peace? What good do we do them, in the end? What good, in the end, is art to man? Vanity, vanity, all is vanity."

Æneas by this time had finished his dinner, and was quietly sipping his coffee. "Monsieur Kohl, my principal," he said, "is himself a dilettante of pictures, and keen to make a gallery in his hotel. But as he has no real knowledge of painting, and no leisure to learn about it, the selection of his pictures used to vex and trouble him. Now, however, I have on his behalf gone round to the painters, one by one, and have asked each of them to sell me the one picture which, out of all he has ever painted, he personally holds to be the best. Our gallery is growing, and it is going to be very fine."

"He is wrong," said Charlie gloomily. "The artist himself cannot say which is his finest work. Even if your artists be honest people, and you have not foisted upon you the picture which they cannot sell to anybody else—such as you deserve to have—they cannot tell." "No, they cannot tell," said Æneas. "But a collection of pictures, each of which has been picked by the painter as the finest he has ever painted, may well, in the end, tickle the curiosity of the public, and fetch its price at a sale."

"And you yourself," said Charlie bitterly, "you go on the errand of a rich dilettante from one artist to another. But you have never, upon your own, painted a picture, or bought one. When, in time, you quit this world of ours, you might as well not have lived." Æneas nodded his head. "What do you nod your head at?" asked Charlie. "At what you are saying," said Æneas. "I might as well not have lived."

Charlie had now rid himself of the restlessness and chagrin that had beset him as he first came into the café, and he felt that it would be pleasanter to listen than to go on speaking. He also found that he was hungry, and ordered dinner. By the time when he had finished his soup he leaned back in his chair, glanced round the room as if he saw it for the first time, and in a low and languid voice, like that of a convalescent, said to Æneas: "Can you not even tell me a story?"

Æneas stirred his coffee with his spoon, and picked up the sugar left on the bottom of the cup. He put the napkin to his small mouth, folded it and laid it on the table. "Yes, I can tell you a story," he said. He sat for a minute or two, ransacking his memory. During that time, although he kept so quiet, he was changed; the prim bailiff faded away, and in his seat sat a deep and dangerous little figure, consolidated, alert and ruthless—the story-teller of all the ages. "Yes," he said at last, and smiled, "I can tell you a consolatory story," and in a sweet and modulated voice he began.

When I was a young man, I was in the employ of an esteemed firm of carpet dealers in London, and was by them designated to travel to Persia, there to buy up a consignment of ancient carpets. But by the dispensations of destiny I became, for two years, during a period of political unrest and intrigue, when the English and the Russians vied for the greater influence with the Persian Court, physician in ordinary to the ruler of Persia, Mahommed Shah, a highly deserving Prince. He suffered great distress from erysipelas, a disease against which I had been happy enough to find a cure. The present Shah, Nasrud-Din Mirza, was then heir-apparent to the throne.

Nasrud-Din was a lively young Prince, keen on progress and reform, and of a willful and fantastic mind. He was ambitious to know the conditions and circumstances of his subjects, from the highest to the poorest, and gave himself or his surroundings no rest in this pursuit. He had studied the tales of the Arabian Nights, and from this reading he fancied for himself the role of the Caliph Haroun of Bagdad. So he would often, in imitation of this classical histrionic, all by himself, and in the disguise of a beggar, a peddler or a juggler, wander through his town of Teheran, and visit the market-place or the taverns of it. He listened to the talk of the labourers, water-carriers and prostitutes there, in order to get from them their true opinion on the office-holders and placement, and upon the custody of justice in the kingdom.

This caprice of the Prince caused much alarm and distress to his old Councillors. For they thought it an untenable and paradoxical state of things that a Prince should be so *au fait* with the doings and sentiments of his people, and one quite likely to upset the whole ancient system of the country. They represented to him the dangers to which he exposed himself, and the injustice that, in his intrepidity, he was doing to the realm of Persia, which might thus wantonly suffer the saddest bereavement. But the more they talked the keener Prince Nasrud-Din became upon his fancy. The ministers then had recourse to other measures. They took care that he should be, wherever he went, secretly followed by armed guards; they also bribed his valets and pages to discover in what disguise he would go, and to what part of the city he would betake himself, and often the beggar or the prostitute with whom the Prince entered into talk had been pre-instructed by the judicious old men. Of this Nasrud-Din knew nothing, and the Councillors dreaded his wrath, should he find out, so that even amongst themselves they kept silent upon their wiles.

Now it came to pass, by the time when I was at Court, that the old High Minister Mirza Aghai one day sought audience with the Prince, and solemnly imparted to him news of a strange and sinister nature.

There was, he said, in the town of Teheran a man, in face, stature and voice so like the Prince Nasrud-Din that the Queen, his mother, would hardly know the one from the other. Moreover, the stranger in all his ways minutely imitated and copied the manner and habits of the Prince. This man had for some months been walking through the poorest quarters of the city, in the disguise of a beggar, similar to that which the Prince was wont to wear, had seated himself by the gates or the walls, and there questioned and held forth to the people. Did not the fact, the old Minister asked, prove the danger of the Prince's sport? For what would lie behind it? The mystificator was either a tool in the hands of the Shah's enemies, set by them to sow discontent and rebellion amongst the populace, or he was an imposter of unheard temerity, working upon some dark scheme of his own, and possibly nurturing the horrible plan of doing away with the heir to the throne, and of passing himself off to the people as the Prince. The old man had let all the foes of the Royal House pass muster in his mind. Before him had then risen the shadow of a great lord, cousin to the Shah and decapitated in a rebellion twenty years ago, and he remembered to have heard that a posthumous son had been born to the outlaw's name. This youth, Mirza Aghai reflected, might well endeavour to revenge his father, and to get his own back. He begged his young lord to renounce his excursions until such time as the intriguer should have been seized and punished.

Nasrud-Din listened to the Chamberlain's proposal and played with the silken tassels of his sword-knot. What, he asked, did this strange plotter, the double of himself, tell the people, and what impression had he made upon them? "My lord," said Mirza Aghai, "What exactly he has told the people I cannot report, partly because his sayings seem to be deep and twofold, so that those who have heard them do not remember them, and partly because he really does not say much. But the impression which he has made is sure to be very profound. For he is not content to investigate their lot, but has set himself upon sharing it with them. He is known to have slept by the walls on winter nights, to have lived upon the leavings which the portionless paupers have spared to him, and, when they had nothing to give, to have kept fast for a whole day. He frequents the cheapest prostitutes of the city in order to convince the poor of his compassion and fellow-feeling. Yes, to insinuate himself with the lowest of your townfolk, under your favour, he keeps company with a girl who, in the tavern of a market-place, gives performances with a donkey. And all this, my Prince, within your effigy."

The Prince was a gay and gallant young man; it amused him to vex the old, cautious men of his father's Court, and Mirza Aghai's tale to him contained the promise of a rare adventure. When he had thought the matter over, he told the Minister that he would not forego the chance of meeting his *Doppelgänger*. He would go himself to speak with him, and detect the truth about him. He forbade the old men to interfere with his plan, and this time took such precautions that it became impossible to them to impede or control him. In vain did Mirza Aghai beseech him to give up so perilous a project. The only concession which in the end they wrested from him was the promise that he would go about well armed, and that he would take with him one attendant in whom he could trust.

I was, just then, seeing much of the young Prince. For Prince Nasrud-Din had on his left cheekbone a mole, the size of a cherry. It was slightly disfiguring in itself, and it was naturally in his way when he wished to go about incognito. So after he had watched my cure of his father, the Shah, he called upon me to rid him of the nevus. The treatment was slow; I had time to entertain the Prince with the narratives that he loved, and I held, by the nature of things, a big bag of tales which belongs to our classic Western civilization, and were new to him.

The Prince was also afraid of growing fat, so that at times he would eat very little. The Queen, his mother, who thought that he had never been more lovable than when, as a baby, he had been fat, took much trouble with the purveyors and the chefs of the royal household, to make them bring and prepare such rare dishes as might tempt her son's appetite. Now she saw that when I was relating my stories to him the Prince would sit long over his food, and she graciously entreated me to keep him company at table. I told the Prince as much as I could remember of the *Divina Commedia,* and of a few of Shakespeare's tragedies, together with the whole of the *Mysteries of Paris,* by Eugene Sue, that I had read just before I left Europe. During our talks on such works of art I gained his confidence, and when by this time he was to choose a companion in his secret expeditions he asked me to go with him.

He took pleasure in having me dressed up as a Persian beggar, in a big cloak and slippers, and with a flap over one eye. Each of us kept a poniard in his belt and a pistol in his breast; the Prince made me a present of my poniard, which had a silver hilt, set with turquoises. The old Minister Mirza Aghai then approached me, and promised me his gratitude and a permanent and lucrative office at Court should I, in the end, succeed in turning the mind of Nasrud-Din from his caprice. But I had no faith in my power to turn the mind of a Prince, nor had I any wish to do so.

We thus wandered through the streets and the slums of Teheran, during some evenings of early spring. On the terraces of the Royal Gardens the peach trees were already in blossom, and in the grass there were crocus and jonquils. But the air was sharp and the night frost not far away.

Within the city of Teheran the evenings of this season are wonderfully blue. The ancient grey walls, the planes and olive trees in the gardens, the people in their drab garments and the long, slow files of heavy-laden camels coming home through the gates—all seem to float in a delicate mist of azure.

The Prince and I visited strange places, and made the acquaintance of dancers, thieves, bawds and soothsayers. We had various long discussions on religion and love, and many times we also laughed together, for we were both young. But for a while we did not find the man on whose track we walked; neither did we, anywhere, hear much of him. Still we knew the name by which he called himself, which was the same as the Prince had used as a beggar. And in the end, one evening, we were guided by a small boy to a market-place, close to the oldest gate of the town, where, we were told, the plotter by this hour was wont to seat himself. By the well of the place the bare-legged child stopped, and pointed to a small figure sitting on the ground at some distance. He gave us a clear, steady glance, said: "I will go no farther," and ran off.

We paused for a moment, and felt our knives and pistols. It was a poor and vile square; narrow streets led to it; the houses were pitiable and decayed; the air filled with nauseous smells; the ground broken and dusty. The ragged inhabitants of the streets had come from their work, and in the last hour of daylight were lounging and chatting in the open, or drawing water from the well. A few of them were buying wine by the counter of an open tavern, and we did so too, asking for the cheapest that the innkeeper had to sell, since we were ourselves beggars tonight. As we drank, we kept an eye on the man upon the ground.

There was an old crooked fig tree growing out from a creek in the wall, and he sat beneath it. No crowd surrounded him, as we had been led to expect. But while I watched him I saw the wayfarers slacken their pace as they passed him. One and another amongst them stood still and exchanged a few words with him before they walked on, and each of them seemed to turn his face half away from the beggar, and to hold himself, in his nearness, with reverence and awe. As slowly I took in the whole scene before me, I thought it to be in some way unusual and striking. The place was as low and miserable as any I had walked through in the town, yet there was dignity in the atmosphere of it, and a stillness as of anticipation and confidence. The children played together without fighting or crying, the women prattled and laughed lowly and gaily, and the water-drawers waited patiently for one another.

The innkeeper was talking with a donkey driver, who had brought him two big baskets of fresh beans, cabbage and lettuce. The donkey driver said: "And what do you imagine that they will be dining on at the palace tonight?" "On what will they be dining?" said the innkeeper. "That is not easy to tell. They may be having a peacock, stuffed with olives. They may eat carps' tongues, cooked in red wine. Or they will be partaking of a fat-rumped, cinnamon-stewed sheep." "Yes, by God," said the ass driver. We smiled at the description of these extraordinary dishes, which were obviously dainties to the poor. Prince Nasrud-Din paid for his wine, draped his mendicant's cloak over his head, and without a word went forth and seated himself a little way from the stranger. I took the place next to him, by the wall.

The man for whom we had so long searched, and of whom we had talked so much between us, was a still person; he did not lift his eyes to look at the newcomers. He sat on the earth with his legs crossed, his head bent, and his folded hands resting on the ground in front of him. His beggar's bowl stood beside him, and it was empty.

He had on a large cloak, like that which the Prince wore, only more tattered and patched. It had a hood to it, which partly covered his head, but while he sat so quiet, his eyes downcast, I had time to study his face. It was true that he bore a likeness to the Prince. He was a dark, slight young man, a few years older than Nasrud-Din, of such age as the Prince would assume in his role of beggar. He had long, black eyelashes, and a small thin black beard, similar to the beard which the Prince used to put on with his beggar's disguise, only it was really growing on his face. Upon his left cheekbone he had a brown mole, the size of a cherry, and I saw, because I had experience in that matter, that it was put on artifically, with skill. As to his countenance and manner, he was in no way like the daring and dangerous conspirator whom I had expected to meet. His face was peaceful, so that indeed I do not remember to have set eyes on a more serene human physiognomy. It was also singularly vacant of shrewdness, or even of much intelligence. That dignity and collectedness which, a moment ago, I had been surprised to find in the market-place around him, were repeated within the figure of the man himself, as if these qualities were concentrated in, or issuing from, the ragged and lean beggar's form. Perhaps, I reflected, there are few things which will impart as great dignity to a man's appearance as the air of complete content and self-sufficiency.

When we had thus sat together in silence for a while, it happened that a poor funeral procession came along, on its way to the burial ground outside the walls, the corpse on a litter and covered with a cloth, a few mourners following it, and some idlers of the street strolling behind. As they caught sight of the beggar under the fig tree, they again seemed to be seized with some kind of fear or veneration; they swerved a little in their course as they passed, but they did not speak to him.

When they had gone by, the beggar lifted his head, gazed at the air before him, and in a low and gentle voice said: "Life and Death are two locked caskets, each of which contains the key to the other."

The Prince started as he heard his voice, so like was his mode of speaking, even to a slight snuffle within it, to his own. After a moment, he himself spoke to the stranger. "I am a beggar like you," he said, "and have come here to collect such alms as merciful people will give me. Let us not waste our time while we wait for them, but talk about our lives. Is your life as a beggar of so little value to you that you would be content to exchange it for death?" The beggar seemed unprepared for so energetic an address. He did not answer for a minute or two, then gently wagged his head and said: "Not at all."

Here an old poor woman came staggering across the square towards us, approaching the beggar in the shy and submissive manner of the others, turning her face away as she spoke to him. She was pressing a loaf of bread to her bosom, and as she stopped she held it out to him in both her hands. "For the mercy of God," she said, "take this bread and eat it. We have seen that you have sat here by the wall for two days, and have had nothing to eat. Now I am an old woman, the poorest of the poor here, and I think that you will not refuse alms from me." The beggar softly lifted his hand to reject the gift. "Nay," he said "take back your bread. I will not eat tonight. For I know of a beggar, my brother in mendicancy, who sat by the town wall for three full days, and was given nothing. I will experience myself what he did then feel and think." "Oh, God," sighed the old woman, "if you will not eat the bread I shall not eat it myself either, but I shall give it to the cart-bullocks which come in by the gate, and are tired and hungry." And with that she staggered away again.

When she had gone, the Prince once more turned to the beggar. "You are wrong," he said. "No beggar of the town has sat by the wall for three days and has been given nothing. I have asked for alms myself, you know, and have never been without food even for the length of a day. The people of Teheran are not so hard-hearted nor so indigent as to let the meanest of beggars starve for three days." To this the beggar answered not a word.

It was now growing colder. The great space above our heads was still glass-clear and filled with sweet light; innumerable bats had come out from holes in the wall and were noiselessly cruising within it, high and low. But the earth and everything belonging to it lay in a blue shadow, as if it had been finely enamelled with lazulite. The beggar drew his old cloak round him and shivered. "It would be better for us," I said, "to seek a little shelter in the gate itself." "Nay, I shall not go there," said the beggar. "The gatekeepers chase away beggars from the gate with a bastinado." "You are wrong once more," said the Prince. "I, who am a beggar myself, have sought shelter in the gates, and no gate-keeper has ever told me to go away. For it is the law that poor and homeless people may sit within the gates of my city, when the traffic of the day is done."

The beggar for a minute thought his words over; then he turned his head and looked at him. "Are you the Prince Nasrud-Din?" he asked him.

Prince Nasrud-Din was startled and confused by the beggar's straight question; his hand went to his knife, as my hand to my own.

But after a second he haughtily looked him in the face. "Yes, I am Nasrud-Din," he said. "You must know my face, since you have counterfeited it. You must have followed me for a long time, and closely, in order to assume my part in the eyes of my people with so much skill. I have known about your game, too, for some time. Your motive for playing it, only, I do not know. I have come here tonight to learn it from your own lips."

The beggar did not answer at once; then again he shook his head. "Heigh-ho, my gentle lord," he said. "May you rightly say so, when I have donned that very attire and semblance, which you yourself think most dissimilar to your own, and most likely to conceal you, and to beguile the people of your town? Might not I as justly charge you yourself with having, in your greatness, mimicked my humble countenance, and embezzled my beggar's appearance? Aye, it is true that I have once seen you, at a distance, in your mendicant's clothes, but I have learned more from those who followed and watched you. It is true, too, that I have made use of the likeness that God deigned to create between you and me. I have profited by it to be proud, and grateful to God, where before I was cast down. Will a Prince blame his servant for that?"

"And who," asked the Prince with a penetrating glance at the beggar, "do the people of the market-place and the streets believe you to be?" The beggar threw a quick, furtive glance round him to all sides. "Hush, my lord, speak low," he said. "The people of the market-place and the streets dare not for their lives let me know who they believe me to be. Did you not see them turning away their heads and cast down their eyes as they passed by or spoke to me? They know that I will not be known; they are afraid that, if ever I find out who they believe me to be, my wrath against them shall be so terrible that I shall go away, never to come back to them."

At these words the Prince coloured and became silent. At last he said gravely: "They all believe you to be Prince Nasrud-Din?" The beggar for a moment showed his white teeth in a smile. "Yes, they believe me to be Prince Nasrud-Din," he said. "They think that I have got a palace to live in, and may go back there whenever I wish. They believe that I have got a cellar filled with wine, my table laid with rich food, my chests filled with garments of silk and fur."

"Who then," the Prince asked, "are you, who have been made proud and thankful to God in playing to be me?" "I am what I look," said the beggar. "I am a beggar of Teheran. As such I was born. My mother was a beggarwoman, and she thrashed the profession into me before I weighed as much as a cat. I have asked for alms in the streets, and by the walls of the city all my life." "What is your name, beggar?" the Prince asked. "I am named Fath," said the beggar.

"And have you not," the Prince asked after a silence, "planned to get into that palace of which you speak, upon the strength of the likeness between you and me?" "No," said Fath. "Have you not endeavoured," the Prince asked again, "to gain influence and power with the people and to serve your ambition by means of that likeness?" "No," said Fath. He sat for a while in thought; then he said: "No. I am a beggar, and may be clever in the trade of a beggar. But about the other things I know not, and I care for none of them. I should be sadly troubled if I were to deal with them. I have gained power over the people, that is true, and it is likely that they would do what I wish, but what would I wish them to do?"

"What have you been doing, then," asked the Prince, "after you had so cleverly studied my looks and ways and had made the people of Teheran believe that you are Prince Nasrud-Din?" "I have," said Fath, "been asking for alms in the streets, and by the walls of the city." He looked at the Prince, and exclaimed: "What have you done to the mole on your cheek?" The Prince held his hand to his cheek. "I have had it removed," he said. Fath lifted his own hand to his cheek. "The people will not like that," he said gravely.

"But wherefore do you slander my people," asked the Prince, "and make out the lot of the beggars of my town harder than it is? Why did you tell that a beggar had sat for three days by the wall, and had received nothing, and that you yourself wished to know what he felt thereby?" "As God lives," said Fath, "it is no slander, but the truth." "Who," the Prince asked him severely, "was the beggar who was so cruelly treated?" "My lord, it was I, myself," said Fath, "in the days before I had seen you."

"But now tell me, for that I do not understand," said the Prince, "why you will accept nothing from the townsfolk by this time, when you have brought them to offer you the best they have got? Why did you refuse the loaf of bread which the old woman took to you and send her away so sad?" Fath thought his words over. "Good, my lord," he said. "With your permission, I perceive that you know but little about beggary. You, I suppose, all your life have had as much as you wanted to eat. If I take what they offer me, how long will they go on offering it? And how long will they believe, then, that I have got, in my palace, the richest food, and all the delicacies of the world, from the east to the west?"

The Prince was silent for a while; then he began to laugh. "By the tombs of my fathers, Fath," he said, "I took you for a fool, but now I think that you are the shrewdest man in my kindgom. For see, my courtiers and my friends demand from me offices, distinctions and gold, and when they have got them they leave me in peace. But a beggar of Teheran has harnessed me to his waggon, and from now on, awake or asleep, I shall be labouring for Fath. If I conquer a province, if I shoot a lion, if I write a poem, or if I marry the daughter of the Sultan of Zanzibar—it will all be one: it will all serve to the greater glory of Fath."

Fath looked at the Prince beneath his long eyelashes. "It may be said," he said, "and now you have said it. But I may hold, as against that, that you yourself have made Fath, and all there is of him. You did not, when you walked the streets as a beggar, endeavour to be any wiser or greater, any nobler or more magnanimous than the other beggars of the town. You made yourself just one of them, and took good care not to differ from them in any way, in order to hoax your people, and to listen, unobserved, to their talk. Therefore, now, I am no more than a common beggar either. Awake or asleep I am but the beggar's mask of Prince Nasrud-Din." "That, too, may be said," said the Prince.

"I beseech you, Prince," Fath went on solemnly, "to conquer provinces, to kill lions, to write poems. I have seen to it that the name of Prince Nasrud-Din, and that the renown of his loving-kindness, have been great with the paupers of Teheran. See to it now that the name of Fath, and his reputation for gallantry and wit, be great amongst the Kings and the Princes. As you kill a lion, remember that the heart of Fath rejoices at your bravery. And when you have married the Sultan's daughter, how highly will not the people think of you, as they still watch you sitting by the wall, all through the cold night, in order to share their hard lot. How highly will they not think of you when, to partake of the sorry fate of the poorest, you still sit down and talk with the prostitutes of these streets." "Do the prostitutes of these streets," the Prince asked, "embrace you with ardour, now, and shiver with ecstasy in your arms? Come, you ought to tell me, since I myself know nothing about it, and since their shiverings are in some way my own due." "Nay, I cannot tell you," said Fath. "I know no more about it than you do. I dare not embrace them; they are wise, and may know the embrace of a great lord." "So you stand in awe of my women, Fath?" said the Prince. "You, who showed no fear when I denounced myself to you." "My lord," said Fath, "man and woman are two locked caskets, of which each contains the key to the other."

"Hold out your hands, Fath," said the Prince, and as the beggar did so he lifted his mendicant's wallet from his belt and emptied it into the outstretched hands. Fath kept the coins in his palms, and looked at them. "Is that gold?" he asked. "Yes," said the Prince. "I have heard of it," said Fath. "I know it to be very powerful."

He hung his head, and sat for a long time, mournfully, in deep silence. "I see now," he said at last, "why you have come here tonight. You mean to put an end to my grandeur. You will have me sell my honour, and my great name with the people, for this mighty and dangerous metal." "No, by my sword," said the Prince, "I had no such thing in my mind." "What am I to do with the gold, then?" Fath asked. "Indeed, Fath," said the Prince, somewhat embarrassed, "that is a question which I have not been asked before. If you have no use for it yourself, you may give it to the poor of the market-place." Fath sat still, gazing at the gold. "I might," he said, "like the man in the tale of the forty thieves, ask for a loan of a beggar's bowl, and when I give it back by mistake leave a piece of gold at the bottom of it, so as to convince the people of my opulence. But my lord, it would do myself, or them, no good. They would want more, and more than you have given me, and more than you could ever give me. They would no longer love me, as they do now, and no more believe in my compassion, or in my wisdom. Take it back, the beggar begs you. The gold is better with you than with me."

"What can I do for you, then?" the Prince asked. Fath thought his words over, and his face lightened up, like the face of a child.

"Listen, my great lord," he said. "There is one scene which I have often pictured to myself; you can make it come true if you want to. Some day let the finest regiment of your horsemen ride through the market-place, your captain at the head of it. Then I shall seat myself in the place, and when they come I shall not move, or get out of their way. So command your captain, as he sees me, to pull up his horse in great surprise and dread, and to stop the whole regiment, in order that they shall not touch me; yes, to stop it so suddenly that the fiery horses all rear at it. But command him further, when I make a sign with my hand, to ride on, and over me, all the same—only tell him to use a little caution, so that the horses shall not hurt me. This is what you can do for me, my lord."

"What wild fancy of yours is that, Fath?" the Prince asked and smiled. "It has never happened that my horsemen have ridden over one of the people in the streets, or in the market-place." "Yes, it has happened, my lord," said Fath; "in that way my mother was killed."

The Prince sat for some time in thought. "Vanity, vanity, all is vanity," he said in the end. "I have before now, at Court, learned much about the vanity of men. But I have learned more from you, a beggar, tonight. It seems to me, now, that vanity may feed the starving, and keep warm the beggar in his ragged cloak. Is it so, Fath?" "You see, my lord," said Fath, "it will be written in the books, in a hundred years, that Nasrud-Din was such a Prince, and ruled his kingdom of Persia in such a way, that his poorest subjects did hold their vanity fully gratified as they starved, in their beggars' cloaks, by the walls of Teheran."

The Prince once more draped his cloak about him and drew it over his head.

"I shall go back now," he said. "Good night, Fath. I should have liked to come here again, on an evening, to talk with you. But in the end my visits would ruin your prestige. I will see to it that you shall sit in peace, from now, by your wall. And God be with you."

As he was about to go, he stopped. "One more word, before I go," he said with some hauteur. "It has come to my ear that you visit the woman who, in the tavern of the market-place, gives performances with a donkey. It is well that the people should learn of my wish to know their conditions, and even to share them with them. But you are taking a great liberty with our person when you make us tread, so to say, in the footsteps of an ass. From tonight you must see the woman no more." I had not guessed this particular instance in the beggar's scheme to have impressed itself so deeply on the Prince's mind; now I saw that it had shocked and offended him, and that he felt Fath to have made light of things really great and elevated. But then he was not only a Prince, but a young man.

At his word Fath looked highly bewildered and dismayed; he gazed down and wrung his hands. "Oh, my lord," he cried, "this command of yours comes hard on me. The woman is my wife. It is by the gains of her craft that I live."

The Prince stood for a long time looking at him. "Fath," he said at last, in a very gentle and royal manner, "when, in the matter between you and me, I give in to you in everything, I cannot myself say whether it be from weakness, or from some kind of strength. Tell me, my beggar of Teheran, what in your heart you hold it to be." "My master," said Fath, "you and I, the rich and the poor of this world, are two locked caskets, of which each contains the key to the other."

As we walked back in the late evening I felt that the Prince was thoughtful and disturbed in his soul. I said to him: "You will, Your Highness, tonight have learned something new as to the greatness and the power of Princes." Prince Nasrud-Din did not answer me for a while. But when we had come out of the narrow, evil-smelling streets and were entering the richer and statelier quarters of the city, he said: "I shall no more walk in my town in disguise."

In this way we came back to the Royal Palace about midnight, and had supper there together.

Here Æneas finished his story. He leaned back in his chair, took out cigarette-paper and tobacco, and rolled himself a cigarette.

Charlie had listened to the tale observantly, without a word, his eyes on the table. At the silence of his friend he looked up, like a child waking from its sleep. He remembered that there was tobacco in the world, and after Æneas' example he slowly rolled and lighted a cigarette. The two small gentlemen, each at his side of the table, smoked on in peace, and gazed at the faint blue tobacco smoke.

"Yes, a good tale," said Charlie, and after a little while added: "I shall go home now. I believe that I shall sleep tonight." But when he had come to the end of his cigarette he, too, leaned back in his chair thoughtfully. "No," he said. "Not a very good tale, really, you know. But it has moments in it that might be worked up, and from which one might construct a fine tale."

JULIO CORTÁZAR
1914–
Blow-up

It'll never be known how this has to be told, in the first person or in the second, using the third person plural or continually inventing modes that will serve for nothing. If one might say: I will see the moon rose, or: we hurt me at the back of my eyes, and especially: you the blond woman was the clouds that race before my your his our yours their faces. What the hell.

Seated ready to tell it, if one might go to drink a bock over there, and the typewriter continue by itself (because I use the machine), that would be perfection. And that's not just a manner of speaking. Perfection, yes, because here is the aperture which must be counted also as a machine (of another sort, a Contax 1.1.2) and it is possible that one machine may know more about another machine than I, you, she—the blond—and the clouds. But I have the dumb luck to know that if I go this Remington will sit turned to stone on top of the table with the air of being twice as quiet that mobile things have when they are not moving. So, I have to write. One of us all has to write, if this is going to get told. Better that it be me who am dead, for I'm less compromised than the rest; I who see only the clouds and can think without being distracted, write without being distracted (there goes another, with a grey edge) and remember without being distracted, I who am dead (and I'm alive, I'm not trying to fool anybody, you'll see when we get to the moment, because I have to begin some way and I've begun with this period, the last one back the one at the beginning, which in the end is the best of the periods when you want to tell something).

All of a sudden I wonder why I have to tell this, but if one begins to

Translated by Paul Blackburn.

wonder why he does all he does do, if one wonders why he accepts an invitation to lunch (now a pigeon's flying by and it seems to me a sparrow), or why when someone has told us a good joke immediately there starts up something like a tickling in the stomach and we are not at peace until we've gone into the office across the hall and told the joke over again; then it feels good immediately, one is fine, happy, and can get back to work. For I imagine that no one has explained this, that really the best thing is to put aside all decorum and tell it, because, after all's done, nobody is ashamed of breathing or of putting on his shoes; they're things that you do, and when something weird happens, when you find a spider in your shoe or if you take a breath and feel like a broken window, then you have to tell what's happening, tell it to the guys at the office or to the doctor. Oh, doctor, every time I take a breath . . . Always tell it, always get rid of that tickle in the stomach that bothers you.

And now that we're finally going to tell it, let's put things a little bit in order, we'd be walking down the staircase in this house as far as Sunday, November 7, just a month back. One goes down five floors and stands then in the Sunday in the sun one would not have suspected of Paris in November, with a large appetite to walk around, to see things, to take photos (because we were photographers, I'm a photographer). I know that the most difficult thing is going to be finding a way to tell it, and I'm not afraid of repeating myself. It's going to be difficult because nobody really knows who it is telling it, if I am I or what actually occurred or what I'm seeing (clouds, and once in a while a pigeon) or if, simply, I'm telling a truth which is only my truth, and then is the truth only for my stomach, for this impulse to go running out and to finish up in some manner with this, whatever it is.

We're going to tell it slowly, what happens in the middle of what I'm writing is coming already. If they replace me, if, so soon, I don't know what to say, if the clouds stop coming and something else starts (because it's impossible that this keep coming, clouds passing continually and occasionally a pigeon), if something out of all this . . . And after the "if" what am I going to put if I'm going to close the sentence structure correctly? But if I begin to ask questions, I'll never tell anything, maybe to tell would be like an answer, at least for someone who's reading it.

Roberto Michel, French-Chilean, translator and in his spare time an amateur photographer, left number 11, rue Monsieur-le-Prince Sunday November 7 of the current year (now there're two small ones passing, with silver linings). He had spent three weeks working on the French version of a treatise on challenges and appeals by José Norberto Allende, professor at the University of Santiago. It's rare that there's wind in Paris, and even less seldom a wind like this that swirled around corners and rose up to whip at old wooden venetian blinds behind what astonished ladies commented variously on how unreliable the weather had been these last few years. But the sun was out also, riding the wind and friend of the cats, so there was nothing that would keep me from taking a walk along the docks of the Seine and taking photos of the Conservatoire and Sainte-Chapelle. It was hardly ten o'clock, and I figured that by eleven the light would be good, the best you can get in the fall; to kill some time I detoured around by the Isle Saint-Louis and started to walk along the quai d'Anjou. I stared for a bit at the hôtel de Lauzun, I recited bits from Apollinaire which always get into my head whenever I pass in front of the hôtel de Lauzun (and at that I ought to be remembering the other poet, but Michel is an obstinate beggar), and when the wind stopped all at once and the sun came out at least twice as hard (I mean warmer, but really it's the same thing), I sat down on the parapet and felt terribly happy in the Sunday morning.

One of the many ways of contesting level-zero, and one of the best, is to take photographs, an activity in which one should start becoming an adept very early in life, teach it to children since it requires discipline, aesthetic education, a good eye and steady fingers. I'm not talking about waylaying the lie like any old reporter, snapping the stupid silhouette of the VIP leaving number 10 Downing Street, but in all ways when one is walking about with a camera, one has almost a duty to be attentive, to not lose that abrupt and happy rebound of sun's rays off an old stone, or the pigtails-flying run of a small girl going home with a loaf of bread or a bottle of milk. Michel knew that the photographer always worked as a permutation of his personal way of seeing the world as other than the camera insidiously imposed upon it (now a large cloud is by, almost black), but he lacked no confidence in himself, knowing that he had only to go out without the Contax to recover the keynote of distraction, the sight without a frame around it, light without the diaphragm aperture or 1/250 sec. Right now (what a word, *now*, what a dumb lie) I was able to sit quietly on the railing overlooking the river watching the red and black motor-boats passing below without it occurring to me to think photo-graphically of the scenes, nothing more than letting myself go in the letting go of objects, running immobile in the stream of time. And then the wind was not blowing.

After, I wandered down the quai de Bourbon until getting to the end of the isle where the intimate square was (intimate because it was small, not that it was hidden, it offered its whole breast to the river and the sky), I enjoyed it, a lot. Nothing there but a couple and, of course, pigeons; maybe even some of those which are flying past now so that I'm seeing them. A leap up and I settled on the wall, and let myself turn about and be caught and fixed by the sun, giving it my face and ears and hands (I kept my gloves in my pocket). I had no desire to shoot pictures, and lit a cigarette to be doing something; I think it was that moment when the match was about to touch the tobacco that I saw the young boy for the first time.

What I'd thought was a couple seemed much more now a boy with his mother, although at the same time I realized that it was not a kid and his mother, and that it was a couple in the sense that we always allegate to couples when we see them leaning up against the parapets or embracing on the benches in the squares. As I had nothing else to do, I had more than enough time to wonder why the boy was so nervous, like a young colt or a hare, sticking his hands into his pockets, taking them out immediately, one after the other, running his fingers through his hair, changing his stance, and especially why was he afraid, well, you could guess that from every gesture, a fear suffocated by his shyness, an impulse to step backwards which he telegraphed, his body standing as if it were on the edge of flight, holding itself back in a final, pitiful decorum.

All this was so clear, ten feet away—and we were alone against the parapet at the tip of the island—that at the beginning the boy's fright didn't let me see the blond very well. Now, thinking back on it, I see her much better at that first second when I read her face (she'd turned around suddenly, swinging like a metal weathercock, and the eyes, the eyes were there), when I vaguely understood what might have been occurring to the boy and figured it would be worth the trouble to stay and watch (the wind was blowing their words away and they were speaking in a low murmur). I think that I know how to look, if it's something I know, and also that every looking oozes with mendacity, because it's that which expels us furthest outside ourselves, without the least guarantee, whereas to smell, or (but Michel rambles on to himself easily enough, there's no need to let him harangue on this way). In any case, if the likely inaccuracy can be seen beforehand, it becomes possible again to look; perhaps it suffices to choose between looking and the reality looked at, to strip things of all their unnecessary clothing. And surely all this is difficult besides.

As for the boy I remember the image before his actual body (that will clear itself up later), while now I am sure that I remember the woman's body much better than the image. She was thin and willowy, two unfair words to describe what she was, and was wearing an almost-black fur coat, almost long, almost handsome. All the morning's wind (now it was hardly a breeze and it wasn't cold) had blown through her blond hair which pared away her white, bleak face—two unfair words—and put the world at her feet and horribly alone in front of her dark eyes, her eyes fell on things like two eagles, two leaps into nothingness, two puffs of greem slime. I'm not describing anything, it's more a matter of trying to understand it. And I said two puffs of green slime.

Let's be fair, the boy was well enough dressed and was sporting yellow gloves which I would have sworn belonged to his older brother, a student of law or sociology; it was pleasant to see the fingers of the gloves sticking out of his jacket pocket. For a long time I didn't see his face, barely a profile, not stupid—a terrified bird, a Fra Filippo angel, rice pudding with milk—and the back of an adolescent who wants to take up judo and has had a scuffle or two in defense of an idea or his sister. Turning fourteen, perhaps fifteen, one would guess that he was dressed and fed by his parents but without a nickel in his pocket, having to debate with his buddies before making up his mind to buy a coffee, a cognac, a pack of cigarettes. He'd walk through the streets thinking of the girls in his class, about how good it would be to go to the movies and see the latest film, or to buy novels or neckties or bottles of liquor with green and white labels on them. At home (it would be a respectable home, lunch at noon and romantic landscapes on the walls, with a dark entryway and a mahogany umbrella stand inside the door) there'd be the slow rain of time, for studying, for being mama's hope, for looking like dad, for writing to his aunt in Avignon. So that there was a lot of walking the streets, the whole of the river for him (but without a nickel) and the mysterious city of fifteen-year-olds with its signs in doorways, its terrifying cats, a paper of fried potatoes for thirty francs, the pornographic magazine folded four ways, a solitude like the emptiness of his pockets, the eagerness for so much that was incomprehensible but illumined by a total love, by the availability analogous to the wind and the streets.

This biography was of the boy and of any boy whatsoever, but this particular one now, you could see he was insular, surrounded solely by the blond's presence as she continued talking with him. (I'm tired of insisting, but two long ragged ones just went by. That morning I don't think I looked at the sky once, because what was happening with the boy and the woman appeared so soon I could do nothing but look at them and wait, look at them and . . .) To cut it short, the boy was agitated and one could guess without too much trouble what had just occurred a few minutes before, at most half-an-hour. The boy had come onto the tip of the island, seen the woman and thought her marvelous. The woman was waiting for that because she was there waiting for that, or maybe the boy arrived before her and she saw him from one of the balconies or from a car and got out to meet him, starting the conversation with whatever, from the beginning she was sure that he was going to be afraid and want to run off, and that, naturally, he'd stay, stiff and sullen, pretending experience and the pleasure of the adventure. The rest was easy because it was happening ten feet away from me, and anyone could have gauged the stages of the game, the derisive, competitive fencing; its major attraction was not that it was happening but in foreseeing its denouement. The boy would try to end it by pretending a date, an obligation, whatever, and would go stumbling off disconcerted, wishing he were walking with some assurance, but naked under the mocking glance which would follow him until he was out of sight. Or rather, he would stay there, fascinated or simply incapable of taking the initiative, and the woman would begin to touch his face gently, muss his hair, still talking to him voicelessly, and soon would take him by the arm to lead him off, unless he, with an uneasiness beginning to tinge the edge of desire, even his stake in the adventure, would rouse himself to put his arm around her waist and to kiss her. Any of this could have happened, though it did not, and perversely Michel waited, sitting on the railing, making the settings almost without looking at the camera, ready to take a picturesque shot of a corner of the island with an uncommon couple talking and looking at one another.

Strange how the scene (almost nothing: two figures there mismatched in their youth) was taking on a disquieting aura. I thought it was I imposing it, and that my photo, if I shot it, would reconstitute things in their true stupidity. I would have liked to know what he was thinking, a man in a grey hat sitting at the wheel of a car parked on the dock which led up to the footbridge, and whether he was reading the paper or asleep. I had just discovered him because people inside a parked car have a tendency to disappear, they get lost in that wretched, private cage stripped of the beauty that motion and danger give it. And nevertheless, the car had been there the whole time, forming part (or deforming that part) of the isle. A car: like saying a lighted streetlamp, a park bench. Never like saying wind, sunlight, those elements always new to the skin and the eyes, and also the boy and the woman, unique, put there to change the island, to show it to me in another way. Finally, it may have been that the man with the newspaper also became aware of what was happening and would, like me, feel that malicious sensation of waiting for everything to happen. Now the woman had swung around smoothly, putting the young boy between herself and the wall, I saw them almost in profile, and he was taller, though not much taller, and yet she dominated him, it seemed like she was hovering over him (her laugh, all at once, a whip of feathers), crushing him just by being there, smiling, one hand taking a stroll though the air. Why wait any longer? Aperture at sixteen, a sighting which would not include the horrible black car, but yes, that tree, necessary to break up too much grey space . . .

I raised the camera, pretended to study a focus which did not include them, and waited and watched closely, sure that I would finally catch the revealing expression, one that would sum it all up, life that is rhythmed by movement but which a stiff image destroys, taking time in cross section, if we do not choose the essential imperceptible fraction of it. I did not have to wait long. The woman was getting on with the job of handcuffing the boy smoothly, stripping from him what was left of his freedom a hair at a time, in an incredibly slow and delicious torture. I imagined the possible endings (now a small fluffy cloud appears, almost alone in the sky), I saw their arrival at the house (a basement apartment probably, which she would have filled with large cushions and cats) and conjectured the boy's terror and his desperate decision to play it cool and to be led off pretending there was nothing new in it for him. Closing my eyes, if I did in fact close my eyes, I set the scene: the teasing kisses, the woman mildly repelling the hands which were trying to undress her, like in novels, on a bed that would have a lilac-colored comforter, on the other hand she taking off his clothes, plainly mother and son under a milky yellow light, and everything would end up as usual, perhaps, but maybe everything would go otherwise, and the initiation of the adolescent would not happen, she would not let it happen, after a long prologue wherein the awkwardnesses, the exasperating caresses, the running of hands over bodies would be resolved in who knows what, in a separate and solitary pleasure, in a petulant denial mixed with the art of tiring and disconcerting so much poor innocence. It might go like that, it might very well go like that; that woman was not looking for the boy as a lover, and at the same time she was dominating him toward some end impossible to understand if you do not imagine it as a cruel game, the desire to desire without satisfaction, to excite herself for someone else, someone who in no way could be that kid.

Michel is guilty of making literature, of indulging in fabricated unrealities. Nothing pleases him more than to imagine exceptions to the rule, individuals outside the species, not-always-repugnant monsters. But that woman invited speculation, perhaps giving clues enough for the fantasy to hit the bullseye. Before she left, and now that she would fill my imaginings for several days, for I'm given to ruminating, I decided not to lose a moment more. I got it all into the view-finder (with the tree, the railing, the eleven-o'clock sun) and took the shot. In time to realize that they both had noticed and stood there looking at me, the boy surprised and as though questioning, but she was irritated, her face and body flat-footedly hostile, feeling robbed, ignominiously recorded on a small chemical image.

I might be able to tell it in much greater detail but it's not worth the trouble. The woman said that no one had the right to take a picture without permission, and demanded that I hand her over the film. All this in a dry, clear voice with a good Parisian accent, which rose in color and tone with every phrase. For my part, it hardly mattered whether she got the roll of film or not, but anyone who knows me will tell you, if you want anything from me, ask nicely. With the result that I restricted myself to formulating the opinion that not only was photography in public places not prohibited, but it was looked upon with decided favor, both private and official. And while that was getting said, I noticed on the sly how the boy was falling back, sort of actively backing up though without moving, and all at once (it seemed almost incredible) he turned and broke into a run, the poor kid, thinking that he was walking off and in fact in full flight, running past the side of the car, disappearing like a gossamer filament of angel-spit in the morning air.

But filaments of angel-spittle are also called devil-spit, and Michel had to endure rather particular curses, to hear himself called meddler and imbecile, taking great pains meanwhile to smile and to abate with simple movements of his head such a hard sell. As I was beginning to get tired, I heard the car door slam. The man in the grey hat was there, looking at us. It was only at that point that I realized he was playing a part in the comedy.

He began to walk toward us, carrying in his hand the paper he had been pretending to read. What I remember best is the grimace that twisted his mouth askew, it covered his face with wrinkles, changed somewhat both in location and shape because his lips trembled and the grimace went from one side of his mouth to the other as though it were on wheels, independent and involuntary. But the rest stayed fixed, a flour-powdered clown or bloodless man, dull dry skin, eyes deepset, the nostrils black and prominently visible, blacker than the eyebrows or hair or the black necktie. Walking cautiously as though the pavement hurt his feet; I saw patent-leather shoes with such thin soles that he must have felt every roughness in the pavement. I don't know why I got down off the railing, nor very well why I decided to not give them the photo, to refuse that demand in which I guessed at their fear and cowardice. The clown and the woman consulted one another in silence: we made a perfect and unbearable triangle, something I felt compelled to break with a crack of a whip. I laughed in their faces and began to walk off, a little more slowly, I imagine, than the boy. At the level of the first houses, beside the iron footbridge, I turned around to look at them. They were not moving, but the man had dropped his newspaper; it seemed to me that the woman, her back to the parapet, ran her hands over the stone with the classical and absurd gesture of someone pursued looking for a way out.

What happened after that happened here, almost just now, in a room on the fifth floor. Several days went by before Michel developed the photos he'd taken on Sunday; his shots of the Conservatoire and of Sainte-Chapelle were all they should be. Then he found two or three proof-shots he'd forgotten, a poor attempt to catch a cat perched astonishingly on the roof of a rambling public urinal, and also the shot of the blond and the kid. The negative was so good that he made an enlargement; the enlargement was so good that he made one very much larger, almost the size of a poster. It did not occur to him (now one wonders and wonders) that only the shots of the Conservatoire were worth so much work. Of the whole series, the snapshot of the tip of the island was the only one which interested him; he tacked up the enlargement on one wall of the room, and the first day he spent some time looking at it and remembering, that gloomy operation of comparing the memory with the gone reality; a frozen memory, like any photo, where nothing is missing, not even, and especially, nothingness, the true solidifier of the scene. There was the woman, there was the boy, the tree rigid above their heads, the sky as sharp as the stone of the parapet, clouds and stones melded into a single substance and inseparable (now one with sharp edges is going by, like a thunderhead). The first two days I accepted what I had done, from the photo itself to the enlargement on the wall, and didn't even question that every once in a while I would interrupt my translation of José Norberto Allende's treatise to encounter once more the woman's face, the dark splotches on the railing. I'm such a jerk; it had never occurred to me that when we look at a photo from the front, the eyes reproduce exactly the position and the vision of the lens; it's these things that are taken for granted and it never occurs to anyone to think about them. From my chair, with the typewriter directly in front of me, I looked at the photo ten feet away, and then it occurred to me that I had hung it exactly at the point of view of the lens. It looked very good that way; no doubt, it was the best way to appreciate a photo, though the angle from the diagonal doubtless has its pleasures and might even divulge different aspects. Every few minutes, for example when I was unable to find the way to say in good French what José Norberto Allende was saying in very good Spanish, I raised my eyes and looked at the photo; sometimes the woman would catch my eye, sometimes the boy, sometimes the pavement where a dry leaf had fallen admirably situated to heighten a lateral section. Then I rested a bit from my labors, and I enclosed myself again happily in that morning in which the photo was drenched, I recalled ironically the angry picture of the woman demanding I give her the photograph, the boy's pathetic and ridiculous flight, the entrance on the scene of the man with the white face. Basically, I was satisfied with myself; my part had not been too brilliant, and since the French have been given the gift of the sharp response, I did not see very well why I'd chosen to leave without a complete demonstration of the rights, privileges and prerogatives of citizens. The important thing, the really important thing was having helped the kid to escape in time (this in case my theorizing was correct, which was not sufficiently proven, but the running away itself seemed to show it so). Out of plain meddling, I had given him the opportunity finally to take advantage of his fright to do something useful; now he would be regretting it, feeling his honor impaired, his manhood diminished. That was better than the attentions of a woman capable of looking as she had looked at him on that island. Michel is something of a puritan at times, he believes that one should not seduce someone from a position of strength. In the last analysis, taking that photo had been a good act.

Well, it wasn't because of the good act that I looked at it between paragraphs while I was working. At that moment I didn't know the reason, the reason I had tacked the enlargement onto the wall; maybe all fatal acts happen that way, and that is the condition of their fulfillment. I don't think the almost-furtive trembling of the leaves on the tree alarmed me. I was working on a sentence and rounded it out successfully. Habits are like immense herbariums, in the end an enlargement of 32 x 28 looks like a movie screen, where, on the tip of the island, a woman is speaking with a boy and a tree is shaking its dry leaves over their heads.

But her hands were just too much. I had just translated: "In that case, the second key resides in the intrinsic nature of difficulties which societies . . ." —when I saw the woman's hand beginning to stir slowly, finger by finger. There was nothing left of me, a phrase in French which I would never have to finish, a typewriter on the floor, a chair that squeaked and shook, fog. The kid had ducked his head like boxers do when they've done all they can and are waiting for the final blow to fall; he had turned up the collar of his overcoat and seemed more a prisoner than ever, the perfect victim helping promote the catastrophe. Now the woman was talking into his ear, and her hand opened again to lay itself against his cheekbone, to caress and caress it, burning it, taking her time. The kid was less startled than he was suspicious, once or twice he poked his head over the woman's shoulder and she continued talking, saying something that made him look back every few minutes toward that area where Michel knew the car was parked and the man in the grey hat, carefully eliminated from the photo but present in the boy's eyes (how doubt that now) in the words of the woman, in the woman's hands, in the vicarious presence of the woman. When I saw the man come up, stop near them and look at them, his hands in his pockets and a stance somewhere between disgusted and demanding, the master who is about to whistle in his dog after a frolic in the square, I understood, if that was to understand, what had to happen now, what had to have happened then, what would have to happen at that moment, among these people, just where I had poked my nose in to upset an established order, interfering innocently in that which had not happened, but which was now going to happen, now was going to be fulfilled. And what I had imagined earlier was much less horrible than the reality, that woman, who was not there by herself, she was not caressing or propositioning or encouraging for her own pleasure, to lead the angel away with his tousled hair and play the tease with his terror and his eager grace. The real boss was waiting there, smiling petulantly, already certain of the business; he was not the first to send a woman in the vanguard, to bring him the prisoners manacled with flowers. The rest of it would be so simple, the car, some house or another, drinks, stimulating engravings, tardy tears, the awakening in hell. And there was nothing I could do, this time I could do absolutely nothing. My strength had been a photograph, that, there, where they were taking their revenge on me, demonstrating clearly what was going to happen. The photo had been taken, the time had run out, gone; we were so far from one another, the abusive act had certainly already taken place, the tears already shed, and the rest conjecture and sorrow. All at once the order was inverted, they were alive, moving, they were deciding and had decided, they were going to their future; and I on this side, prisoner of another time, in a room on the fifth floor, to not know who they were, that woman, that man, and that boy, to be only the lens of my camera, something fixed, rigid, incapable of intervention. It was horrible, their mocking me, deciding it before my impotent eye, mocking me, for the boy again was looking at the flour-faced clown and I had to accept the fact that he was going to say yes, that the proposition carried money with it or a gimmick, and I couldn't yell for him to run, or even open the road to him again with a new photo, a small and almost meek intervention which would ruin the framework of drool and perfume. Everything was going to resolve itself right there, at that moment; there was like an immense silence which had nothing to do with physical silence. It was stretching it out, setting itself up. I think I screamed, I screamed terribly, and that at that exact second I realized that I was beginning to move toward them, four inches, a step, another step, the tree swung its branches rhythmically in the foreground, a place where the railing was tarnished emerged from the frame, the woman's face turned toward me as though surprised, was enlarging, and then I turned a bit, I mean that the camera turned a little, and without losing sight of the woman, I began to close in on the man who was looking at me with the black holes he had in places of eyes, surprised and angered both, he looked, wanting to nail me onto the air, and at that instant I happened to see something like a large bird outside the focus that was flying in a single swoop in front of the picture, and I leaned up against the wall of my room and was happy because the boy had just managed to escape, I saw him running off, in focus again, sprinting with his hair flying in the wind, learning finally to fly across the island, to arrive at the footbridge, return to the city. For the second time he'd escaped them, for the second time I was helping him to escape, returning him to his precarious paradise. Out of breath, I stood in front of them; no need to step closer, the game was played out. Of the woman you could see just maybe a shoulder and a bit of the hair, brutally cut off by the frame of the picture; but the man was directly center, his mouth half open, you could see a shaking black tongue, and he lifted his hands slowly, bringing them into the foreground, an instant still in perfect focus, and then all of him a lump that blotted out the island, the tree, and I shut my eyes, I didn't want to see any more, and I covered my face and broke into tears like an idiot.

Now there's a big white cloud, as on all these days, all this untellable time. What remains to be said is always a cloud, two clouds, or long hours of a sky perfectly clear, a very clean, clear rectangle tacked up with pins on the wall of my room. That was what I saw when I opened my eyes and dried them with my fingers: the clear sky, and then a cloud that drifted in from the left, passed gracefully and slowly across and disappeared on the right. And then another, and for a change sometimes, everything gets grey, all one enormous cloud, and suddenly the splotches of rain cracking down, for a long spell you can see it raining over the picture, like a spell of weeping reversed, and little by little, the frame becomes clear, perhaps the sun comes out, and again the clouds begin to come, two at a time, three at a time. And the pigeons once in a while, and a sparrow or two.

JOHN BARTH
1930–
Lost in the Funhouse

For whom is the funhouse fun? Perhaps for lovers. For Ambrose it is *a place of fear and confusion.* He has come to the seashore with his family for the holiday, *the occasion of their visit is Independence Day, the most important secular holiday of the United States of America.* A single straight underline is the manuscript mark for italic type, *which in turn* is the printed equivalent to oral emphasis of words and phrases as well as the customary type for titles of complete works, not to mention. Italics are also employed, in fiction stories especially, for "outside," intrusive, or artificial voices, such as radio announcements, the texts of telegrams and newspaper articles, et cetera. They should be used *sparingly*. If passages originally in roman type are italicized by someone repeating them, it's customary to acknowledge the fact. *Italics mine*.

Ambrose was "at that awkward age." His voice came out high-pitched as a child's if he let himself get carried away; to be on the safe side, therefore, he moved and spoke with *deliberate calm* and *adult gravity*. Talking soberly of unimportant or irrelevant matters and listening consciously to the sound of your own voice are useful habits for maintaining control in this difficult interval. *Enroute* to Ocean City he sat in the back seat of the family car with his brother Peter, age fifteen, and Magda G——, age fourteen, a pretty girl and exquisite young lady, who lived not far from them on B—— Street in the town of D——, Maryland. Initials, blanks, or both were often substituted for proper names in nineteenth-century fiction to enhance the illusion of reality. It is as if the author felt it necessary to delete the names for reasons of tact or legal liability. Interestingly, as with other aspects of realism, it is an *illusion* that is being enhanced, by purely artificial means. Is it likely, does it violate the principle of verisimilitude, that a thirteen-year-old boy could make such a sophisticated observation? A girl of fourteen is *the psychological coeval* of a boy of fifteen or sixteen; a thirteen-year-old boy, therefore, even one precocious in some other respects, might be three years *her emotional junior*.

Thrice a year—on Memorial, Independence, and Labor Days—the family visits Ocean City for the afternoon and evening. When Ambrose and Peter's father was their age, the excursion was made by train, as mentioned in the novel *The 42nd Parallel* by John Dos Passos. Many families from the same neighborhood used to travel together, with dependent relatives and often with Negro servants; schoolfuls of children swarmed through the railway cars; everyone shared everyone else's Maryland fried chicken, Virginia ham, deviled eggs, potato salad, beaten biscuits, iced tea. Nowadays (that is, in 19—, the year of our story) the journey is made by automobile—more comfortably and quickly though without the extra fun though without the *camaraderie* of a general excursion. It's all part of the deterioration of American life, their father declares; Uncle Karl supposes that when the boys take *their* families to Ocean City for the holidays they'll fly in Autogiros. Their mother, sitting in the middle of the front seat like Magda in the second, only with her arms on the seat-back behind the men's shoulders, wouldn't want the good old days back again, the steaming trains and stuffy long dresses; on the other hand she can do without Autogiros, too, if she has to become a grandmother to fly in them.

Description of physical appearance and mannerisms is one of several standard methods of characterization used by writers of fiction. It is also important to "keep the senses operating"; when a detail from one of the five senses, say visual, is "crossed" with a detail from another, say auditory, the reader's imagination is oriented to the scene, perhaps unconsciously. This procedure may be compared to the way surveyors and navigators determine their positions by two or more compass bearings, a process known as triangulation. The brown hair on Ambrose's mother's forearms gleamed in the sun like. Though right-handed, she took her left arm from the seat-back to press the dashboard cigar lighter for Uncle Karl. When the glass bead in its handle glowed red, the lighter was ready for use. The smell of Uncle Karl's cigar smoke reminded one of. The fragrance of the ocean came strong to the picnic ground where they always stopped for lunch, two miles inland from Ocean City. Having to pause for a full hour almost within sound of the breakers was difficult for Peter and Ambrose when they were younger; even at their present age it was not easy to keep their anticipation, *stimulated by the briny spume,* from turning into short temper. The Irish author James Joyce, in his unusual novel entitled *Ulysses,* now available in this country, uses the adjectives *snot-green* and *scrotum-tightening* to describe the sea. Visual; auditory; tactile; olfactory; gustatory. Peter and Ambrose's father, while steering their black 1936 LaSalle sedan with one hand, could with the other remove the first cigarette from a white pack of Lucky Strikes and, more remarkably, light it with a match forefingered from its book and thumbed against the flint paper without being detached. The matchbook cover merely advertised U. S. War Bonds and Stamps. A fine metaphor, simile, or other figure of speech, in addition to its obvious "first-order" relevance to the thing it describes, will be seen upon reflection to have a second order of significance: it may be drawn from the *milieu* of the action, for example, or be particularly appropriate to the sensibility of the narrator, even hinting to the reader things of which the narrator is unaware; or it may cast further and subtler lights upon the things it describes, sometimes ironically qualifying the more evident sense of the comparison.

To say that Ambrose's and Peter's mother was *pretty* is to accomplish nothing; the reader may acknowledge the proposition, but his imagination is not engaged. Besides, Magda was also pretty, yet in an altogether different way. Although she lived on B—— Street she had very good manners and did better than average in school. Her figure was very well developed for her age. Her right hand lay casually on the plush upholstery of the seat, very near Ambrose's left leg, on which his own hand rested. The space between their legs, between her right and his left leg, was out of the line of sight of anyone sitting on the other side of Magda, as well as anyone glancing into the rear-view mirror. Uncle Karl's face resembled Peter's—rather, vice versa. Both had dark hair and eyes, short husky statures, deep voices. Magda's left hand was probably in a similar position on her left side. The boys' father is difficult to describe; no particular feature of his appearance or manner stood out. He wore glasses and was principal of a T—— County grade school. Uncle Karl was a masonry contractor.

Although Peter must have known as well as Ambrose that the latter, because of his position in the car, would be the first to see the electrical towers of the power plant at V——, the halfway point of their trip, he leaned forward and slightly toward the center of the car and pretended to be looking for them through the flat pinewoods and tuckahoe creeks along the highway. For as long as the boys could remember, "looking for the Towers" had been a feature of the first half of their excursions to Ocean City, "looking for the standpipe" of the second. Though the game was childish, their mother preserved the tradition of rewarding the first to see the Towers with a candy-bar or piece of fruit. She insisted now that Magda play the game; the prize, she said, was "something hard to get nowadays." Ambrose decided not to join in; he sat far back in his seat. Magda, like Peter, leaned forward. Two sets of straps were discernible through the shoulders of her sun dress; the inside right one, a brassiere-strap, was fastened or shortened with a small safety pin. The right armpit of her dress, presumably the left as well, was damp with perspiration. The simple strategy for being first to espy the Towers, which Ambrose had understood by the age of four, was to sit on the right-hand side of the car. Whoever sat there, however, had also to put up with the worst of the sun, and so Ambrose, without mentioning the matter, chose sometimes the one and sometimes the other. Not impossibly Peter had never caught on to the trick, or thought that his brother hadn't simply because Ambrose on occasion preferred shade to a Baby Ruth or tangerine.

The shade-sun situation didn't apply to the front seat, owing to the windshield; if anything the driver got more sun, since the person on the passenger side not only was shaded below by the door and dashboard but might swing down his sunvisor all the way too.

"Is that them?" Magda asked. Ambrose's mother teased the boys for letting Magda win, insinuating that "somebody [had] a girlfriend." Peter and Ambrose's father reached a long thin arm across their mother to butt his cigarette in the dashboard ashtray, under the lighter. The prize this time for seeing the Towers first was a banana. Their mother bestowed it after chiding their father for wasting a half-smoked cigarette when everything was so scarce. Magda, to take the prize, moved her hand from so near Ambrose's that he could have touched it as though accidentally. She offered to share the prize, things like that were so hard to find; but everyone insisted it was hers alone.

Ambrose's mother sang an iambic trimeter couplet from a popular song, femininely rhymed:

> "What's good is in the Army;
> What's left will never harm me."

Uncle Karl tapped his cigar ash out the ventilator window; some particles were sucked by the slipstream back into the car through the rear window on the passenger side. Magda demonstrated her ability to hold a banana in one hand and peel it with her teeth. She still sat forward; Ambrose pushed his glasses back onto the bridge of his nose with his left hand, which he then negligently let fall to the seat cushion immediately behind her. He even permitted the single hair, gold, on the second joint of his thumb to brush the fabric of her skirt. Should she have sat back at that instant, his hand would have been caught under her.

Plush upholstery prickles uncomfortably through gabardine slacks in the July sun. The function of the *beginning* of a story is to introduce the principal characters, establish their initial relationships, set the scene for the main action, expose the background of the situation if necessary, plant motifs and foreshadowings where appropriate, and initiate the first complication or whatever of the "rising action." Actually, if one imagines a story called "The Funhouse," or "Lost in the Funhouse," the details of the drive to Ocean City don't seem especially relevant. The *beginning* should recount the events between Ambrose's first sight of the funhouse early in the afternoon and his entering it with Magda and Peter in the evening. The *middle* would narrate all relevant events from the time he goes in to the time he loses his way; middles have the double and contradictory function of delaying the climax while at the same time preparing the reader for it and fetching him to it. Then the *ending* would tell what Ambrose does while he's lost, how he finally finds his way out, and what everybody makes of the experience. So far there's been no real dialogue, very little sensory detail, and nothing in the way of a *theme*. And a long time has gone by already without anything happening; it makes a person wonder. We haven't even reached Ocean City yet: we will never get out of the funhouse.

The more closely an author identifies with the narrator, literally or metaphorically, the less advisable it is, as a rule, to use the first-person narrative viewpoint. Once three years previously the young people *aforementioned* played Niggers and Masters in the backyard; when it was Ambrose's turn to be Master and theirs to be Niggers Peter had to go serve his evening papers; Ambrose was afraid to punish Magda alone, but she led him to the whitewashed Torture Chamber between the woodshed and the privy in the Slaves Quarters; there she knelt sweating among bamboo rakes and dusty Mason jars, pleadingly embraced his knees, and while bees droned in the lattice as if on an ordinary summer afternoon, purchased clemency at a surprising price set by herself. Doubtless she remembered nothing of this event; Ambrose on the other hand seemed unable to forget the least detail of his life. He even recalled how, standing beside himself with awed impersonality in the reeky heat, he'd stared the while at an empty cigar box in which Uncle Karl kept stone-cutting chisels: beneath the words *El Producto;* a laureled, loose-toga'd lady regarded the sea from a marble bench; beside her, forgotten or not yet turned to, was a five-stringed lyre. Her chin reposed on the back of her right hand; her left depended negligently from the bench-arm. The lower half of the scene and lady was peeled away; the words EXAMINED BY ____ were inked there into the wood. Nowadays cigar boxes are made of pasteboard. Ambrose wondered what Magda would have done, Ambrose wondered what Magda would do when she sat back on his hand as he resolved she should. Be angry. Make a teasing joke of it. Give no sign at all. For a long time she leaned forward, playing cow-poker with Peter against Uncle Karl and Mother and watching for the first sign of Ocean City. At nearly the same instant, picnic ground and Ocean City standpipe hove into view; an Amoco filling station on their side of the road cost Mother and Uncle Karl fifty cows and the game; Magda bounced back, clapping her right hand on Mother's right arm; Ambrose moved clear "in the nick of time."

At this rate our hero, at this rate our protagonist will remain in the funhouse forever. Narrative ordinarily consists of alternating dramatization and summarization. One symptom of nervous tension, paradoxically, is repeated and violent yawning; neither Peter nor Magda nor Uncle Karl nor Mother reacted in this manner. Although they were no longer small children, Peter and Ambrose were each given a dollar to spend on boardwalk amusements in addition to what money of their own they'd brought along. Magda too, though she protested she had ample spending money. The boys' mother made a little scene out of distributing the bills; she pretended that her sons and Magda were small children and cautioned them not to spend the sum too quickly or in one place. Magda promised with a merry laugh and, having both hands free, took the bill with her left. Peter laughed also and pledged in a falsetto to be a good boy. His imitation of a child was not clever. The boys' father was tall and thin, balding, fair-complexioned. Assertions of that sort are not effective; the reader may acknowledge the proposition, but. We should be much farther along than we are; something has gone wrong; not much of this preliminary rambling seems relevant. Yet everyone begins in the same place; how is it that most go along without difficulty but a few lose their way?

"Stay out from under the boardwalk," Uncle Karl growled from the side of his mouth. The boys' mother pushed his shoulder *in mock annoyance.* They were all standing before Fat May the Laughing Lady who advertised the funhouse. Larger than life, Fat May mechanically shook, rocked on her heels, slapped her thighs, while recorded laughter—uproarious, female—came amplified from a hidden loudspeaker. It chuckled, wheezed, wept; tried in vain to catch its breath; tittered, groaned, exploded raucous and anew. You couldn't hear it without laughing yourself, no matter how you felt. Father came back from talking to a Coast-Guardsman on duty and reported that the surf was spoiled with crude oil from tankers recently torpedoed offshore. Lumps of it, difficult to remove, made tarry tidelines on the beach and stuck on swimmers. Many bathed in the surf nevertheless and came out speckled; others paid to use a municipal pool and only sunbathed on the beach. We would do the latter. We would do the latter. We would do the latter.

Under the boardwalk, matchbook covers, grainy other things. What is the story's theme? Ambrose is ill. He perspires in the dark passages; candied apples-on-a-stick, delicious-looking, disappointing to eat. Funhouses need men's and ladies' rooms at intervals. Others perhaps have also vomited in corners and corridors; may even have had bowel movements liable to be stepped in in the dark. The word *fuck* suggests suction and/or and/or flatulence. Mother and Father; grandmothers and grandfathers on both sides; great-grandmothers and great-grandfathers on four sides, et cetera. Count a generation as thirty years: in approximately the year when Lord Baltimore was granted charter to the province of Maryland by Charles I, five hundred twelve women—English, Welsh, Bavarian, Swiss—of every class and character, received into themselves the penises the intromittent organs of five hundred twelve men, ditto, in every circumstance and posture, to conceive the five hundred twelve ancestors of the two hundred fifty-six ancestors of the et cetera et cetera et cetera et cetera et cetera et cetera et cetera et cetera of the author, of the narrator, of this story, *Lost in the Funhouse.* In alleyways, ditches, canopy beds, pinewoods, bridal suites, ship's cabins, coach-and-fours, coaches-and-four, sultry toolsheds; on the cold sand under boardwalks, littered with *El Producto* cigar butts, treasured with Lucky Strike cigarette stubs, Coca-Cola caps, gritty turds, cardboard lollipop sticks, matchbook covers warning that A Slip of the Lip Can Sink a Ship. The shluppish whisper, continuous as seawash round the globe, tidelike falls and rises with the circuit of dawn and dusk.

Magda's teeth. She *was* left-handed. Perspiration. They've gone all the way, through, Magda and Peter, they've been waiting for hours with Mother and Uncle Karl while Father searches for his lost son; they draw french-fried potatoes from a paper cup and shake their heads. They've named the children they'll one day have and bring to Ocean City on holidays. Can spermatozoa properly be thought of as male animalcules when there are no female spermatozoa? They grope through hot, dark windings, past Love's Tunnel's fearsome obstacles. Some perhaps lose their way.

Peter suggested then and there that they do the funhouse; he had been through it before, so had Magda, Ambrose hadn't and suggested, his voice cracking on account of Fat May's laughter, that they swim first. All were chuckling, couldn't help it; Ambrose's father, Ambrose's and Peter's father came up grinning like a lunatic with two boxes of syrup-coated popcorn, one for Mother, one for Magda; the men were to help themselves. Ambrose walked on Magda's right; being by nature left-handed, she carried the box in her left hand. Up front the situation was reversed.

"What are you limping for?" Magda inquired of Ambrose. He supposed in a husky tone that his foot had gone to sleep in the car. Her teeth flashed. "Pins and needles?" It was the honeysuckle on the lattice of the former privy that drew the bees. Imagine being stung there. How long is this going to take?

The adults decided to forego the pool; but Uncle Karl insisted they change into swimsuits and do the beach. "He wants to watch the pretty girls," Peter teased, and ducked behind Magda from Uncle Karl's pretended wrath. "You've got all the pretty girls you need right here," Magda declared, and Mother said: "Now that's the gospel truth." Magda scolded Peter, who reached over her shoulder to sneak some popcorn. "Your brother and father aren't getting any." Uncle Karl wondered if they were going to have fireworks that night, what with the shortages. It wasn't the shortages, Mr. M____ replied; Ocean City had fireworks from pre-war. But it was too risky on account of the enemy submarines, some people thought.

"Don't seem like Fourth of July without fireworks," said Uncle Karl. The inverted tag in dialogue writing is still considered permissible with proper names or epithets, but sounds old-fashioned with personal pronouns. "We'll have 'em again soon enough," predicted the boys' father. Their mother declared she could do without fireworks: they reminded her too much of the real thing. Their father said all the more reason to shoot off a few now and again. Uncle Karl asked *rhetorically* who needed reminding, just look at people's hair and skin.

"The oil, yes," said Mrs. M____.

Ambrose had a pain in his stomach and so didn't swim but enjoyed watching the others. He and his father burned red easily. Magda's figure was exceedingly well developed for her age. She too declined to swim, and got mad, and became angry when Peter attempted to drag her into the pool. She always swam, he insisted; what did she mean not swim? Why did a person come to Ocean City?

"Maybe I want to lay here with Ambrose," Magda teased.

Nobody likes a pedant.

"Aha," said Mother. Peter grabbed Magda by one ankle and ordered Ambrose to grab the other. She squealed and rolled over on the beach blanket. Ambrose pretended to help hold her back. Her tan was darker than even Mother's and Peter's. "Help out, Uncle Karl!" Peter cried. Uncle Karl went to seize the other ankle. Inside the top of her swimsuit, however, you could see the line where the sunburn ended and, when she hunched her shoulders and squealed again, one nipple's auburn edge. Mother made them behave themselves. "You should certainly know," she said to Uncle Karl. Archly. "That when a lady says she doesn't feel like swimming, a gentleman doesn't ask questions." Uncle Karl said excuse *him*; Mother winked at Magda; Ambrose blushed; stupid Peter kept saying "Phooey on *feel like!*" and tugging at Magda's ankle; then even he got the point, and cannonballed with a holler into the pool.

"I swear," Magda said, in mock *in feigned* exasperation.

The diving would make a suitable literary symbol. To go off the high board you had to wait in a line along the poolside and up the ladder. Fellows tickled girls and goosed one another and shouted to the ones at the top to hurry up, or razzed them for bellyfloppers. Once on the springboard some took a great while posing or clowning or deciding on a dive or getting up their nerve; others ran right off. Especially among the younger fellows the idea was to strike the funniest pose or do the craziest stunt as you fell; a thing that got harder to do as you kept on and kept on. But whether you hollered *Geronimo!* or *Sieg heil!*, held your nose or "rode a bicycle," pretended to be shot or did a perfect jacknife or changed your mind halfway down and ended up with nothing, it was over in two seconds, after all that wait. Spring, pose, splash. Spring, neat-o, splash. Spring, aw fooey, splash.

The grown-ups had gone on; Ambrose wanted to converse with Magda; she was remarkably well developed for her age; it was said that that came from rubbing with a turkish towel, and there were other theories. Ambrose could think of nothing to say except how good a diver Peter was, who was showing off for her benefit. You could pretty well tell by looking at their bathing suits and arm muscles how far along the different fellows were. Ambrose was glad he hadn't gone in swimming, the cold water shrank you up so. Magda pretended to be uninterested in the diving; she probably weighed as much as he did. If you knew your way around in the funhouse like your own bedroom, you could wait until a girl came along and then slip away without ever getting caught, even if her boyfriend was right with her. She'd think *he* did it! It would be better to be the boyfriend, and act outraged, and tear the funhouse apart.

Not act; *be*.

"He's a master diver," Ambrose said. In feigned admiration. "You really have to slave away at it to get that good." What would it matter anyhow if he asked her right out whether she remembered, even teased her with it as Peter would have?

There's no point in going farther; this isn't getting anybody anywhere; they haven't even come to the funhouse yet. Ambrose is off the track, in some new or old part of the place that's not supposed to be used; he strayed into it by some one-in-a-million chance, like the time the roller coaster car left the tracks in the nineteen-teens against all the laws of physics and sailed over the boardwalk in the dark. And they can't locate him because they don't know where to look. Even the designer and operator have forgotten this other part, that winds around on itself like a whelk shell. That winds around the right part like the snakes on Mercury's caduceus. Some people, perhaps, don't "hit their stride" until their twenties, when the growing-up business is over and women appreciate other things besides wisecracks and teasing and strutting. Peter didn't have one-tenth the imagination *he* had, not one-tenth. Peter did this naming-their-children thing as a joke, making up names like Aloysius and Murgatroyd, but Ambrose knew *exactly* how it would feel to be married and have children of your own, and be a loving husband and father, and go comfortably to work in the mornings and to bed with your wife at night, and wake up with her there. With a breeze coming through the sash and birds and mockingbirds singing in the Chinese-cigar trees. His eyes watered, there aren't enough ways to say that. He would be quite famous in his line of work. Whether Magda was his wife or not, one evening when he was wise-lined and gray at the temples he'd smile gravely, at a fashionable dinner party, and remind her of his youthful passion. The time they went with his family to Ocean City; the *erotic fantasies* he used to have about her. How long ago it seemed, and childish! Yet tender, too, *n'est-ce pas?* Would she have imagined that the world-famous whatever remembered how many strings were on the lyre on the bench beside the girl on the label of the cigar box he'd stared at in the toolshed at age ten while she, age eleven. Even then he had felt *wise beyond his years*; he'd stroked her hair and said in his deepest voice and correctest English, as to a dear child: "I shall never forget this moment."

But though he had breathed heavily, groaned as if ecstatic, what he'd really felt throughout was an odd detachment, as though some one else were Master. Strive as he might to be transported, he heard his mind take notes upon the scene: *This is what they call* passion. *I am experiencing it.* Many of the digger machines were out of order in the penny arcades and could not be repaired or replaced for the duration. Moreover the prizes, made now in USA, were less interesting than formerly, pasteboard items for the most part, and some of the machines wouldn't work on white pennies. The gypsy fortune-teller machine might have provided a foreshadowing of the climax of this story if Ambrose had operated it. It was even dilapidateder than most: the silver coating was worn off the brown metal handles, the glass windows around the dummy were cracked and taped, her kerchiefs and silks long-faded. If a man lived by himself, he could take a department-store mannequin with flexible joints and modify her in certain ways. *However:* by the time he was that old he'd have a real woman. There was a machine that stamped your name around a white-metal coin with a star in the middle: *A___*. His son would be the second, and when the lad reached thirteen or so he would put a strong arm around his shoulder and tell him calmly: "It is perfectly normal. We have all been through it. It will not last forever." Nobody knew how to be what they were right. He'd smoke a pipe, teach his son how to fish and softcrab, assure him he needn't worry about himself. Magda would certainly give, Magda would certainly yield a great deal of milk, although guilty of occasional solecisms. It don't taste so bad. Suppose the lights came on now!

The day wore on. You think you're yourself, but there are other persons in you. Ambrose gets hard when Ambrose doesn't want to, *and obversely*. Ambrose watches them disagree; Ambrose watches him watch. In the funhouse mirror-room you can't see yourself go on forever, because no matter how you stand, your head gets in the way. Even if you had a glass periscope, the image of your eye would cover up the thing you really wanted to see. The police will come; there'll be a story in the papers. That must be where it happened. Unless he can find a surprise exit, an unofficial backdoor or escape hatch opening on an alley, say, and then stroll up to the family in front of the funhouse and ask where everybody's been; *he's* been out of the place for ages. That's just where it happened, in that last lighted room: Peter and Magda found the right exit; he found one that you weren't supposed to find and strayed off into the works somewhere. In a perfect funhouse you'd be able to go only one way, like the divers off the highboard; getting lost would be impossible; the doors and halls would work like minnow traps or the valves in veins.

On account of German U-boats, Ocean City was "browned out": streetlights were shaded on the seaward side; shop-windows and boardwalk amusement places were kept dim, not to silhouette tankers and Liberty-ships for torpedoing. In a short story about Ocean City, Maryland, during World War II, the author could make use of the image of sailors on leave in the penny arcades and shooting galleries, sighting through the crosshairs of toy machine guns at swastika'd subs, while out in the black Atlantic a U-boat skipper squints through his periscope at real ships outlined by the glow of penny arcades. After dinner the family strolled back to the amusement end of the boardwalk. The boys' father had burnt red as always and was masked with Noxema, a minstrel in reverse. The grown-ups stood at the end of the boardwalk where the Hurricane of '33 had cut an inlet from the ocean to Assawoman Bay.

"Pronounced with a long *o*," Uncle Karl reminded Magda with a wink. His shirt sleeves were rolled up; Mother punched his brown biceps with the arrowed heart on it and said his mind was naughty. Fat May's laugh came suddenly from the funhouse, as if she'd just got the joke; the family laughed too at the coincidence. Ambrose went under the boardwalk to search for out-of-town matchbook covers with the aid of his pocket flashlight; he looked out from the edge of the North American continent and wondered how far their laughter carried over the water. Spies in rubber rafts; survivors in lifeboats. If the joke had been beyond his understanding, he could have said: "*The laughter was over his head.*" And let the reader see the serious wordplay on second reading.

He turned the flashlight on and then off at once even before the woman whooped. He sprang away, heart athud, dropping the light. What had the man grunted? Perspiration drenched and chilled him by the time he scrambled up to the family. "See anything?" his father asked. His voice wouldn't come; he shrugged and violently brushed sand from his pants legs.

"Let's ride the old flying horses!" Magda cried. I'll never be an author. It's been forever already, everybody's gone home, Ocean City's deserted, the ghost-crabs are tickling across the beach and down the littered cold streets. And the empty halls of clapboard hotels and abandoned funhouses. A tidal wave; an enemy air raid; a monster-crab swelling like an island from the sea. *The inhabitants fled in terror.* Magda clung to his trouser leg; he alone knew the maze's secret. "He gave his life that we might live," said Uncle Karl with a scowl of pain, as he. The fellow's hands had been tattooed; the woman's legs, the woman's fat white legs had. *An astonishing coincidence.* He yearned to tell Peter. He wanted to throw up for excitement. They hadn't even chased him. He wished he were dead.

One possible ending would be to have Ambrose come across another lost person in the dark. They'd match their wits together against the funhouse, struggle like Ulysses past obstacle after obstacle, help and encourage each other. Or a girl. By the time they found the exit they'd be closest friends, sweethearts if it were a girl; they'd know each other's inmost souls, be bound together *by the cement of shared adventure;* then they'd emerge into the light and it would turn out that his friend was a Negro. A blind girl. President Roosevelt's son. Ambrose's former archenemy.

Shortly after the mirror room he'd groped along a musty corridor, his heart already misgiving him at the absence of phosphorescent arrows and other signs. He's found a crack of light—not a door, it turned out, but a seam between the plyboard wall panels—and squinting up to it, espied a small old man, *in appearance not unlike* the photographs at home of Ambrose's late grandfather, nodding upon a stool beneath a bare, speckled bulb. A crude panel of toggle- and knife-switches hung beside the open fuse box near his head; elsewhere in the little room were wooden levers and ropes belayed to boat cleats. At the time, Ambrose wasn't lost enough to rap or call; later he couldn't find that crack. Now it seemed to him that he'd possibly dozed off for a few minutes somewhere along the way; certainly he was exhausted from the afternoon's sunshine and the evening's problems; he couldn't be sure he hadn't dreamed part or all of the sight. Had an old black wall fan droned like bees and shimmied two flypaper streamers? Had the funhouse operator—gentle, somewhat sad and tired-appearing, in expression not unlike the photographs at home of Ambrose's late Uncle Konrad—murmured in his sleep? Is there really such a person as Ambrose, or is he a figment of the author's imagination? Was it Assawoman Bay or Sinepuxent? Are there other errors of fact in this fiction? Was there another sound besides the little slap slap of thigh on ham, like water sucking at the chine-boards of a skiff?

When you're lost, the smartest thing to do is stay put till you're found, hollering if necessary. But to holler guarantees humiliation as well as rescue; keeping silent permits some saving of face—you can act surprised at the fuss when your rescuers find you and swear you weren't lost, if they do. What's more you might find your own way yet, *however belatedly.*

"Don't tell me your foot's still asleep!" Magda exclaimed as the three young people walked from the inlet to the area set aside for ferris wheels, carrousels, and other carnival rides, they having decided in favor of the vast and ancient merry-go-round instead of the funhouse. What a sentence, everything was wrong from the outset. People don't know what to make of him, he doesn't know what to make of himself, he's only thirteen, *athletically and socially inept,* not astonishingly bright, but there are antennae; he has . . . some sort of receivers in his head; things speak to him, he understands more than he should, the world winks at him through its objects, grabs grinning at his coat. Everybody else is in on some secret he doesn't know; they've forgotten to tell him. Through simple *procrastination* his mother put off his baptism until this year. Everyone else had it done as a baby; he'd assumed the same of himself, as had his mother, so she claimed, until it was time for him to join Grace Methodist-Protestant and the oversight came out. He was mortified, but pitched sleepless through his private catechizing, intimidated by the ancient mysteries, a thirteen year old would never say that, resolved to experience conversion like St. Augustine. When the water touched his brow and Adam's sin left him, he contrived by a strain like defecation to bring tears into his eyes—but felt nothing. There was some simple, radical difference about him; he hoped it was genius, feared it was madness, devoted himself to amiability and inconspicuousness. Alone on the seawall near his house he was seized by the terrifying transports he'd thought to find in toolshed, in Communion-cup. The grass was alive! The town, the river, himself, were not imaginary; time roared in his ears like wind; the world was *going on!* This part ought to be dramatized. The Irish author James Joyce once wrote. Ambrose M____ is going to scream.

There is no *texture of rendered sensory detail*, for one thing. The faded distorting mirrors beside Fat May; the impossibility of choosing a mount when one had but a single ride on the great carrousel; the *vertigo attendant on his recognition* that Ocean City was worn out, the place of fathers and grandfathers, straw-boatered men and parasoled ladies survived by their amusements. Money spent, the three paused at Peter's insistence beside Fat May to watch the girls get their skirts blown up. The object was to tease Magda, who said: "I swear, Peter M____, you've got a one-track mind! Amby and me aren't *interested* in such things." In the tumbling-barrel, too, just inside the Devil's-mouth entrance to the funhouse, the girls were upended and their boyfriends and others could see up their dresses if they cared to. Which was the whole point, Ambrose realized. Of the entire funhouse! If you looked around, you noticed that almost all the people on the boardwalk were paired off into couples except the small children; in a way, that was the whole point of Ocean City! If you had X-ray eyes and could see everything going on at that instant under the boardwalk and in all the hotel rooms and cars and alleyways, you'd realize that all that normally *showed*, like restaurants and dance halls and clothing and test-your-strength machines, was merely preparation and intermission. Fat May screamed.

Because he watched the goings-on from the corner of his eye, it was Ambrose who spied the half-dollar on the boardwalk near the tumbling-barrel. Losers weepers. The first time he'd heard some people moving through a corridor not far away, just after he'd lost sight of the crack of light, he'd decided not to call to them, for fear they'd guess he was scared and poke fun; it sounded like roughnecks; he'd hoped they'd come by and he could follow in the dark without their knowing. Another time he'd heard just one person, unless he imagined it, bumping along as if on the other side of the plywood; perhaps Peter coming back for him, or Father, or Magda lost too. Or the owner and operator of the funhouse. He'd called out once, as though merrily: "Anybody know where the heck we are?" But the query was too stiff, his voice cracked, when the sounds stopped he was terrified: maybe it was a queer who waited for fellows to get lost, or a longhaired filthy monster that lived in some cranny of the funhouse. He stood rigid for hours it seemed like, scarcely respiring. His future was shockingly clear, in outline. He tried holding his breath to the point of unconsciousness. There ought to be a button you could push to end your life absolutely without pain; disappear in a flick, like turning out a light. He would push it instantly! He despised Uncle Karl. But he despised his father too, for not being what he was supposed to be. Perhaps his father hated *his* father, and so on, and his son would hate him, and so on. Instantly!

Naturally he didn't have nerve enough to ask Magda to go through the funhouse with him. With incredible nerve and to everyone's surprise he invited Magda, quietly and politely, to go through the funhouse with him. "I warn you, I've never been through it before," he added, *laughing easily;* "but I reckon we can manage somehow. The important thing to remember, after all, is that it's meant to be a *fun*house; that is, a place of amusement. If people really got lost or injured or too badly frightened in it, the owner'd go out of business. There'd even be lawsuits. No character in a work of fiction can make a speech this long without interruption or acknowledgment from the other characters."

Mother teased Uncle Karl: "Three's a crowd, I always heard." But actually Ambrose was relieved that Peter now had a quarter too. Nothing was what it looked like. Every instant, under the surface of the Atlantic Ocean, millions of living animals devoured one another. Pilots were falling in flames over Europe; women were being forcibly raped in the South Pacific. His father should have taken him aside and said: "There is a simple secret to getting through the funhouse, as simple as being first to see the Towers. Here it is. Peter does not know it; neither does your Uncle Karl. You and I are different. Not surprisingly, you've often wished you weren't. Don't think I haven't noticed how unhappy your childhood has been! But you'll understand, when I tell you, why it had to be kept secret until now. And you won't regret not being like your brother and your uncle. *On the contrary!*" If you knew all the stories behind all the people on the boardwalk, you'd see that *nothing* was what it looked like. Husbands and wives often hated each other; parents didn't necessarily love their children; et cetera. A child took things for granted because he had nothing to compare his life to and everybody acted as if things were as they should be. Therefore each saw himself as the hero of the story, when the truth might turn out to be that he's the villain, or the coward. And there wasn't one thing you could do about it!

Hunchbacks, fat ladies, fools—that no one chose what he was was unbearable. In the movies he'd meet a beautiful young girl in the funhouse; they'd have hairs-breadth escapes from real dangers; he'd do and say the right things; she also; in the end they'd be lovers; their dialogue lines would match up; he'd be perfectly at ease; she'd not only like him well enough, she'd think he was *marvelous*; she'd lie awake thinking about *him*, instead of vice versa—the way *his* face looked in different lights and how he stood and exactly what he'd said—and yet that would be only one small episode in his wonderful life, among many many others. Not a *turning point* at all. What had happened in the toolshed was nothing. He hated, he loathed his parents! One reason for not writing a lost-in-the-funhouse story is that either everybody's felt what Ambrose feels, in which case it goes without saying, or else no normal person feels such things, in which case Ambrose is a freak. "Is anything more tiresome, in fiction, than the problems of sensitive adolescents?" And it's all too long and rambling, as if the author. For all a person knows the first time through, the end could be just around any corner; perhaps, *not impossibly* it's been within reach any number of times. On the other hand he may be scarcely past the start, with everything yet to get through, an intolerable idea.

Fill in: His father's raised eyebrows when he announced his decision to do the funhouse with Magda. Ambrose understands now, but didn't then, that his father was wondering whether he knew what the funhouse was *for*—especially since he didn't object, as he should have, when Peter decided to come along too. The ticket-woman, witchlike, mortifying him when inadvertently he gave her his name-coin instead of the half-dollar, then unkindly calling Magda's attention to the birthmark on his temple: "Watch out for him, girlie, he's a marked man!" She wasn't even cruel, he understood, only vulgar and insensitive. Somewhere in the world there was a young woman with such splendid understanding that she'd see him entire, like a poem or story, and find his words so valuable after all that when he confessed his apprehensions she would explain why they were in fact the very things that made him precious to her . . . and to Western

Civilization! There was no such girl, the simple truth being. Violent yawns as they approached the mouth. Whispered advice from an old-timer on a bench near the barrel: "Go crabwise and ye'll get an eyeful without upsetting!" Composure vanished at the first pitch: Peter hollered joyously, Magda tumbled, shrieked, clutched her skirt; Ambrose scrambled crabwise, tight-lipped with terror, was soon out, watched his dropped name-coin slide among the couples. Shamefaced he saw that to get through expeditiously was not the point; Peter feigned assistance in order to trip Magda up, shouted "I see Christmas!" when her legs went flying. The old man, his latest betrayer, cackled approval. A dim hall then of black-thread cobwebs and recorded gibber: he took Magda's elbow to steady her against revolving discs set in the slanted floor to throw your feet out from under, and explained to her in a calm, deep voice his theory that each phase of the funhouse was triggered either automatically, by a series of photoelectric devices, or else manually by operators stationed at peepholes. But he lost his voice thrice as the discs unbalanced him; Magda was anyhow squealing; but at one point she clutched him about the waist to keep from falling, and her right cheek pressed for a moment against his belt-buckle. Heroically he drew her up, it was his chance to clutch her close as if for support and say: "I love you." He even put an arm lightly about the small of her back before a sailor-and-girl pitched into them from behind, sorely treading his left big toe and knocking Magda asprawl with them. The sailor's girl was a string-haired hussy with a loud laugh and light blue drawers; Ambrose realized that he wouldn't have said "I love you" anyhow, and was smitten with self-contempt. How much better it would be to be that common sailor! A wiry little Seaman 3rd, the fellow squeezed a girl to each side and stumbled hilarious into the mirror room, closer to Magda in thirty seconds than Ambrose had got in thirteen years. She giggled at something the fellow said to Peter; she drew her hair from her eyes with a movement so womanly it struck Ambrose's heart; Peter's smacking her backside then seemed particularly coarse. But Magda made a pleased indignant face and cried, "All right for *you,* mister!" and pursued Peter into the maze without a backward glance. The sailor followed after, leisurely, drawing his girl against his hip; Ambrose understood not only that they were all so relieved to be rid of his burdensome company that they didn't even notice his absence, but that he himself shared their relief. Stepping from the treacherous passage at last into the mirror-maze, he saw once again, more clearly than ever, how readily he deceived himself into supposing he was a person. He even foresaw, wincing at his dreadful self-knowledge, that he would repeat the deception, at ever-rarer intervals, all his wretched life, so fearful were the alternatives. Fame, madness, suicide; perhaps all three. It's not believable that so young a boy could articulate that reflection, and in fiction the merely true must always yield to the plausible. Moreover, the symbolism is in places heavy-footed. Yet Ambrose M__ understood, as few adults do, that the famous loneliness of the great was no popular myth but a general truth—furthermore, that it was as much cause as effect.

All the preceding except the last few sentences is exposition that should've been done earlier or interspersed with the present action instead of lumped together. No reader would put up with so much with such *prolixity*. It's interesting that Ambrose's father, though presumably an intelligent man (as indicated by his role as grade-school principal), neither encouraged nor discouraged his sons at all in any way—as if he either didn't care about them or cared all right but didn't know how to act. If this fact should contribute to one of them's becoming a celebrated but wretchedly unhappy scientist, was it a good thing or not? He too might someday face the question; it would be useful to know whether it had tortured his father for years, for example, or never once crossed his mind.

In the maze two important things happened. First, our hero found a name-coin someone else had lost or discarded: *AMBROSE,* suggestive of the famous lightship and of his late grandfather's favorite dessert, which his mother used to prepare on special occasions out of coconut, oranges, grapes, and what else. Second, as he wondered at the endless replication of his image in the mirrors, second, as he *lost himself in the reflection* that the necessity for an observer makes perfect observation impossible, better make him eighteen at least, yet that would render other things unlikely, he heard Peter and Magda chuckling somewhere together in the maze. "Here!" "No, here!" they shouted to each other; Peter said, "Where's Amby?" Magda murmured. "Amb?" Peter called. In a pleased, friendly voice. He didn't reply. The truth was, his brother was a *happy-go-lucky youngster* who'd've been better off with a regular brother of his own, but who seldom complained of his lot and was generally cordial. Ambrose's throat ached; there aren't enough different ways to say that. He stood quietly while the two young people giggled and thumped through the glittering maze, hurrah'd their discovery of its exit, cried out in joyful alarm at what next beset them. Then he set his mouth and followed after, as he supposed, took a wrong turn, strayed into the pass *wherein he lingers yet.*

The action of conventional dramatic narrative may be represented by a diagram called Freitag's Triangle:

or more accurately by a variant of that diagram:

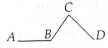

in which *AB* represents the exposition, *B* the introduction of conflict, *BC* the "rising action," complication, or development of the conflict, *C* the climax, or turn of the action, *CD* the dénouement, or resolution of the conflict. While there is no reason to regard this pattern as an absolute necessity, like many other conventions it became conventional because great numbers of people over many years learned by trial and error that it was effective; one ought not to forsake it, therefore, unless one wishes to forsake as well the effect of drama or has clear cause to feel that deliberate violation of the "normal" pattern can better can better effect that effect. This can't go on much longer; it can go on forever. He died telling stories to himself in the dark; years later, when that vast unsuspected area of the funhouse came to light, the first expedition found his skeleton in one of its labyrinthine corridors and mistook it for part of the entertainment. He died of starvation telling himself stories in the dark; but unbeknownst unbeknownst to him, an assistant operator of the funhouse, happening to overhear him, crouched just behind the plyboard partition and wrote down his every word. The operator's daughter, an exquisite young woman with a figure unusually well developed for her age, crouched just behind the partition and transcribed his every word. Though she had never laid eyes on him, she recognized that here was one of Western Culture's truly great imaginations, the eloquence of whose suffering would be an inspiration to unnumbered. And her heart was torn between her love for the misfortunate young man (yes, she loved him, though she had never laid though she knew him only—but how well!—through his words, and the deep, calm voice in which he spoke them) between her love et cetera and her womanly intuition that only in suffering and isolation could he give voice et cetera. Lone dark dying. Quietly she kissed the rough plyboard, and a tear fell upon the page. Where she had written in shorthand *Where she had written in shorthand* Where she had written in shorthand *Where she* et cetera. A long time ago we should have passed the apex of Freitag's Triangle and made brief work of the *dénouement*; the plot doesn't rise by meaningful steps but winds upon itself, digresses, retreats, hesitates, sighs, collapses, expires. The climax of the story must be it's protagonist's discovery of a way to get through the funhouse. But he has found none, may have ceased to search.

What relevance does the war have to the story? Should there be fireworks outside or not?

Ambrose wandered, languished, dozed. Now and then he fell into his habit of rehearsing to himself the unadventurous story of his life, narrated from the third-person point of view, from his earliest memory parenthesis of maple leaves stirring in the summer breath of tidewater Maryland end of parenthesis to the present moment. Its principle events, on this telling, would appear to have been *A, B, C,* and *D.*

He imagined himself years hence, successful, married, at ease in the world, the trials of his adolescence far behind him. He has come to the seashore with his family for the holiday: how Ocean City has changed! But at one seldom at one ill-frequented end of the boardwalk a few derelict amusements survive from times gone by: the great carrousel from the turn of the century, with its monstrous griffins and mechanical concert band; the roller coaster rumored since 1916 to have been condemned; the mechanical shooting gallery in which only the image of our enemies changed. His own son laughs with Fat May and wants to know what a funhouse is; Ambrose hugs the sturdy lad close and smiles around his pipestem at his wife.

The family's going home. Mother sits between Father and Uncle Karl, who teases him good-naturedly who chuckles over the fact that the comrade with whom he'd fought his way shoulder to shoulder through the funhouse had turned out to be a blind Negro girl—to their mutual discomfort, as they'd opened their souls. But such are the walls of custom, which even. Whose arm is where? How must it feel. He dreams of a funhouse vaster by far than any yet constructed; but by then they may be out of fashion, like steamboats and excursion trains. Already quaint and seedy: the draperied ladies on the frieze of the carrousel are his father's father's mooncheeked dreams; if he thinks of it more he will vomit his apple-on-a-stick.

He wonders: will he become a regular person? Something has gone wrong; his vaccination didn't take; at the Boy-Scout initiation campfire he only pretended to be deeply moved, as he pretends to this hour that it is not so bad after all in the funhouse, and that he has a little limp. How long will it last? He envisions a truly astonishing funhouse, incredibly complex yet utterly controlled from a great central switchboard like the console of a pipe organ. Nobody had enough imagination. He could design such a place himself, wiring and all, and he's only thirteen years old. He would be its operator: panel lights would show what was up in every cranny of its cunning of its multifarious vastness; a switch-flick would ease this fellow's way, complicate that's, to balance things out; if anyone seemed lost or frightened, all the operator had to do was.

He wishes he had never entered the funhouse. But he has. Then he wishes he were dead. But he's not. Therefore he will construct funhouses for others and be their secret operator—though he would rather be among the lovers for whom funhouses are designed.

ROBERT COOVER
1932–
The Hat Act

In the middle of the stage: a plain table.

A man enters, dressed as a magician with black cape and black silk hat. Doffs hat in wide sweep to audience, bows elegantly.

Applause.

He displays inside of hat. It is empty. He thumps it. It is clearly empty. Places hat on table, brim up. Extends both hands over hat, tugs back sleeves exposing wrists, snaps fingers. Reaches in, extracts a rabbit.

Applause.

Pitches rabbit into wings. Snaps fingers over hat again, reaches in, extracts a dove.

Applause.

Pitches dove into wings. Snaps fingers over hat, reaches in, extracts another rabbit. No applause. Stuffs rabbit hurriedly back in hat, snaps fingers, reaches in, extracts another hat, precisely like the one from which it came.

Applause.

Places second hat alongside first one. Snaps fingers over new hat, withdraws a third hat, exactly like the first two.

Light applause.

Snaps fingers over third hat, withdraws a fourth hat, again identical.

No applause. Does not snap fingers. Peers into fourth hat, extracts a fifth one. In fifth, he finds a sixth. Rabbit appears in third hat. Magician extracts seventh hat from sixth. Third hat rabbit withdraws a second rabbit from first hat. Magician withdraws eighth hat from seventh, ninth from eighth, as rabbits extract other rabbits from other hats. Rabbits and hats are everywhere. Stage is one mad turmoil of hats and rabbits.

Laughter and applause.

Frantically, magician gathers up hats and stuffs them into each other, bowing, smiling at audience, pitching rabbits three and four at a time into wings, smiling, bowing. It is a desperate struggle. At first, it is difficult to be sure he is stuffing hats and pitching rabbits faster than they are reappearing. Bows, stuffs, pitches, smiles, perspires.

Laughter mounts.

Slowly the confusion diminishes. Now there is one small pile of hats and rabbits. Now there are no rabbits. At last there are only two hats. Magician, perspiring from overexertion, gasping for breath, staggers to table with two hats.

Light applause, laughter.

Magician, mopping brow with silk handkerchief, stares in perplexity at two remaining hats. Pockets handkerchief. Peers into one hat, then into other. Attempts tentatively to stuff first into second, but in vain. Attempts to fit second into first, but also without success. Smiles weakly at audience. No applause. Drops first hat to floor, leaps on it until crushed. Wads crushed hat in fist, attempts once more to stuff it into second hat. Still, it will not fit.

Light booing, impatient applause.

Trembling with anxiety, magician pressed out first hat, places it brim up on table, crushes second hat on floor. Wads second hat, tries desperately to jam it into first hat. No, it will not fit. Turns irritably to pitch second hat into wings.

Loud booing.

Freezes. Pales. Returns to table with both hats, first in fair condition brim up, second still in a crumpled wad. Faces hats in defeat. Bows head as though to weep silently.

Hissing and booing.

Smile suddenly lights magician's face. He smoothes out second hat and places it firmly on his head, leaving first hat bottomside-up on table. Crawls up on table and disappears feet first into hat.

Surprised applause.

Moments later, magician's feet poke up out of hat on table, then legs, then torso. Last part to emerge is magician's head, which, when lifted from table, brings first hat with it. Magician doffs first hat to audience, shows it is empty. Second hat has disappeared. Bows deeply.

Enthusiastic and prolonged applause, cheers.

Magician returns hat to head, thumps it, steps behind table. Without removing hat, reaches up, snaps fingers, extracts rabbit from top of hat.

Applause.

Pitches rabbit into wings. Snaps fingers, withdraws dove from top of hat.

Sprinkling of applause.

Pitches dove into wings. Snaps fingers, extracts lovely assistant from top of hat.

Astonished but enthusiastic applause and whistles.

Lovely assistant wears high feathery green hat, tight green halter, little green shorts, black net stockings, high green heels. Smiles coyly at whistles and applause, scampers bouncily offstage.

Whistling and shouting, applause.

Magician attempts to remove hat, but it appears to be stuck. Twists and writhes in struggle with stuck hat.

Mild laughter.

Struggle continues. Contortions. Grimaces.

Laughter.

Finally, magician requests two volunteers from audience. Two large brawny men enter stage from audience, smiling awkwardly.

Light applause and laughter.

One large man grasps hat, other clutches magician's legs. They pull cautiously. The hat does not come off. They pull harder. Still, it is stuck. They tug now with great effort, their heavy faces reddening, their thick neck muscles taut and throbbing. Magician's neck stretches, snaps in two: POP! Large men tumble apart, rolling to opposite sides of stage, one with body, other with hat containing magician's severed head.

Screams of terror.

Two large men stand, stare aghast at handiwork, clutch mouths.

Shrieks and screams.

Decapitated body stands.

Shrieks and screams.

Zipper in front of decapitated body opens, magician emerges. He is as before, wearing same black cape and same black silk hat. Pitches deflated decapitated body into wings. Pitches hat and head into wings. Two large men sigh with immense relief, shake heads as though completely baffled, smile faintly, return to audience. Magician doffs hat and bows.

Wild applause, shouts, cheers.

Lovely assistant, still in green costume, enters, carrying glass of water.

Applause and whistling.

Lovely assistant acknowledges whistling with coy smile, sets glass of water on table, stands dutifully by. Magician hands her his hat, orders her by gesture to eat it.

Whistling continues.

Lovely assistant smiles, bites into hat, chews slowly.

Laughter and much whistling.

She washes down each bit of hat with water from glass she has brought in. Hat at last is entirely consumed, except for narrow silk band left on table. Sighs, pats slender exposed tummy.

Laughter and applause, excited whistling.

Magician invites young country boy in audience to come to stage. Young country boy steps forward shyly, stumbling clumsily over own big feet. Appears confused and utterly abashed.

Loud laughter and catcalls.

Young country boy stands with one foot on top of other, staring down redfaced at his hands, twisting nervously in front of him.

Laughter and catcalls increase.

Lovely assistant sidles up to boy, embraces him in motherly fashion. Boy ducks head away, steps first on foot, then on other, wrings hands.

More laughter and catcalls, whistles.

Lovely assistant winks broadly at audience, kisses young country boy on cheek. Boy jumps as though scalded, trips over own feet, and falls to floor.

Thundering laughter.

Lovely assistant helps boy to his feet, lifting him under armpits. Boy, ticklish, struggles and giggles helplessly.

Laughter (as before).

Magician raps table with knuckles. Lovely assistant releases hysterical country boy, returns smiling to table. Boy resumes awkward stance, wipes his runny nose with back of his hand, sniffles.

Mild laughter and applause.

Magician hands lovely assistant narrow silk band of hat she has eaten. She stuffs band into her mouth, chews thoughtfully, swallows with some difficulty, shudders. She drinks from glass. Laughter and shouting have fallen away to expectant hush. Magician grasps nape of lovely assistant's neck, forces her head with its feathered hat down between her stockinged knees. He releases grip and her head springs back to upright position. Magician repeats action slowly. Then repeats action rapidly four or five times. Looks inquiringly at lovely assistant. Her face is flushed from exertion. She meditates, then shakes head: no. Magician again forces her head to her knees, releases grip, allowing head to snap back to upright position. Repeats this two or three times. Looks inquiringly at lovely assistant. She smiles and nods. Magician drags abashed young country boy over behind lovely assistant and invites him to reach into lovely assistant's tight green shorts. Young country boy is flustered beyound belief.

Loud laughter and whistling resumes.

Young country boy, in desperation, tries to escape. Magician captures him and drags him once more behind lovely assistant.

Laughter etc. (as before).

Magician grasps country boy's arm and thrusts it forcibly into assistant's shorts. Young country boy wets pants.

Hysterical laughter and catcalls.

Lovely assistant grimaces once. Magician, smiling, releases grip on agonizingly embarrassed country boy. Boy withdraws hand. In it, he finds he is holding magician's original black silk hat, entirely whole, narrow silk band and all.

Wild applause and footstamping, laughter and cheers.

Magician winks broadly at audience, silencing them momentarily, invites young country boy to don hat. Boy ducks head shyly. Magician insists. Timidly, grinning foolishly, country boy lifts hat to head. Water spills out, runs down over his head, and soaks young country boy.

Laughter, applause, wild catcalls.

Young country boy, utterly humiliated, drops hat and turns to run offstage, but lovely assistant is standing on his foot. He trips and falls to his face.

Laughter, etc. (as before).

Country boy crawls abjectly offstage on his stomach. Magician, laughing heartily with audience, pitches lovely assistant into wings, picks up hat from floor. Brushes hat on sleeve, thumps it two or three times, returns it with elegant flourish to his head.

Appreciative applause.

Magician steps behind table. Carefully brushes off one space on table. Blows away dust. Reaches for hat. But again, it seems to be stuck. Struggles feverishly with hat.

Mild laughter.

Requests volunteers. Same two large men as before enter. One quickly grasps hat, other grasps magician's legs. They tug furiously, but in vain.

Laughter and applause.

First large man grabs magician's head under jaw. Magician appears to be protesting. Second large man wraps magician's legs around his waist. Both pull apart with terrific strain, their faces reddening, the veins in their temples throbbing. Magician's tongue protrudes, hands flutter hopelessly.

Laughter and applause.

Magician's neck stretches. But it does not snap. It is now several feet long. Two large men strain mightily.

Laughter and applause.

Magician's eyes pop like bubbles from their sockets.

Laughter and applause.

Neck snaps at last. Large men tumble head over heels with respective bloody burdens to opposite sides of stage. Expectant amused hush falls over audience. First large man scrambles to his feet, pitches head and hat into wings, rushes to assist second large man. Together they unzip decapitated body. Lovely assistant emerges.

Surprised laughter and enthusiastic applause, whistling.

Lovely assistant pitches deflated decapitated body into wings. Large men ogle her and make mildly obscene gestures for audience.

Mounting laughter and friendly catcalls.

Lovely assistant invites one of two large men to reach inside her tight green shorts.

Wild whistling.

Both large men jump forward eagerly, tripping over each other and tumbling to floor in angry heap. Lovely assistant winks broadly at audience.

Derisive catcalls.

Both men stand, face each other, furious. First large man spits at second. Second pushes first. First returns push, toppling second to floor. Second leaps to feet, smashes first in nose. First reels, wipes blood from nose, drives fist into second's abdomen.

Loud cheers.

Second weaves confusedly, crumples miserably to floor clutching abdomen. First kicks second brutally in face.

Cheers and mild laughter.

Second staggers blindly to feet, face a mutilated mess. First smashes second back against wall, knees him in groin. Second doubles over, blinded with pain. First clips second with heel of hand behind ear. Second crumples to floor, dead.

Prolonged cheering and applause.

First large man acknowledges applause with self-conscious bow. Flexes knuckles. Lovely assistant approaches first large man, embraces him in motherly fashion, winks broadly at audience.

Prolonged applause and whistling.

Large man grins and embraces lovely assistant in unmotherly fashion, as she makes faces of mock astonishment for audience.

Shouting and laughter, wild whistling.

Lovely assistant frees self from large man, turns plump hindquarters to him, and bends over, her hands on her knees, her shapely legs straight. Large man grins at audience, pats lovely assistant's green clad rear.

Wild shouting, etc. (as before).

Large man reaches inside lovely assistant's tight green shorts, rolls his eyes, and grins obscenely. She grimaces and wiggles rear briefly.

Wild shouting, etc. (as before).

Large man withdraws hand from inside lovely assistant's shorts, extracting magician in black cape and black silk hat.

Thunder of astonished applause.

Magician bows deeply, doffing hat to audience.

Prolonged enthusiastic applause, cheering.

Magician pitches lovely assistant and first large man into wings. Inspects second large man, lying dead on stage. Unzips him and young country boy emerges, flushed and embarrassed. Young country boy creeps abjectly offstage on stomach.

Laughter and catcalls, more applause.

Magician pitches deflated corpse of second large man into wings. Lovely assistant reenters, smiling, dressed as before in high feathery hat, tight green halter, green shorts, net stockings, high heels.

Applause and whistling.

Magician displays inside of hat to audience as lovely assistant points to magician. He thumps hat two or three times. It is empty. Places hat on table, and invites lovely assistant to enter it. She does so.

Vigorous applause.

Once she has entirely disappeared, magician extends both hands over hat, tugs back sleeves exposing wrists, snaps fingers. Reaches in, extracts one green high-heeled shoe.

Applause.

Pitches shoe into wings. Snaps fingers over hat again. Reaches in, withdraws a second shoe.

Applause.

Pitches shoe into wings. Snaps finger over hat. Reaches in, withdraws one long net stocking.

Applause and scattered whistling.

Pitches stocking into wings. Snaps fingers over hat. Reaches in, extracts a second black net stocking.

Applause and scattered whistling.

Pitches stocking into wings. Snaps fingers over hat. Reaches in, pulls out high feathery hat.

Increased applause and whistling, rhythmic stamping of feet.

Pitches hat into wings. Snaps fingers over hat. Reaches in, fumbles briefly.

Light laughter.

Withdraws green halter, displays it with grand flourish.

Enthusiastic applause, shouting, whistling, stamping of feet.

Pitches halter into wings. Snaps fingers over hat. Reaches in, fumbles. Distant absorbed gaze.

Burst of laughter.

Withdraws green shorts, displays them with elegant flourish.

Tremendous crash of applause and cheering, whistling.

Pitches green shorts into wings. Snaps fingers over hat. Reaches in. Prolonged fumbling. Sound of a slap. Withdraws hand hastily, a look of astonished pain on his face. Peers inside.

Laughter.

Head of lovely assistant pops out of hat, pouting indignantly.

Laughter and applause.

With difficulty, she extracts one arm from hat, then other arm. Pressing hands down against hat brim, she wriggles and twists until one naked breast pops out of hat.

Applause and wild whistling.

The other breast: POP!

More applause and whistling.

She wriggles free to the waist. She grunts and struggles, but is unable to free her hips. She looks pathetically, but uncertainly at magician. He tugs and pulls but she seems firmly stuck.

Laughter.

He grasps lovely assistant under armpits and plants feet against hat brim. Strains. In vain.

Laughter.

Thrusts lovely assistant forcibly back into hat. Fumbles again. Loud slap.

Laughter increases.

Magician returns slap soundly.

Laughter ceases abruptly, some scattered booing.

Magician reaches into hat, withdraws one unstockinged leg. He reaches in again, pulls out one arm. He tugs on arm and leg, but for all his effort cannot extract the remainder.

Scattered booing, Some whistling.

Magician glances uneasily at audience, stuffs arm and leg back into hat. He is perspiring. Fumbles inside hat. Withdraws nude hindquarters of lovely assistant.

Burst of cheers and wild whistling.

Smiles uncomfortably at audience. Tugs desperately on plump hindquarters, but rest will not follow.

Whistling diminishes, increased booing.

Jams hindquarters back into hat, mops brow with silk handkerchief.

Loud unfriendly booing.

Pockets handkerchief. Is becoming rather frantic. Grasps hat and thumps it vigorously, shakes it. Places it once more on table, brim up. Closes eyes as though in incantations, hands extended over hat. Snaps fingers several times, reaches in tenuously. Fumbles. Loud slap. Withdraws hand hastily in angry astonishment. Grasps hat. Gritting teeth, enfuriated, hurls hat to floor, leaps on it with both feet. Something crunches. Hideous piercing shriek.

Screams and shouts.

Magician, aghast, picks up hat, stares into it. Pales.

Violent screaming and shouting.

Magician gingerly sets hat on floor, and kneels, utterly appalled and grief-stricken, in front of it. Weeps silently.

Weeping, moaning, shouting.

Magician huddles miserably over crushed hat, weeping convulsively. First large man and young country boy enter timidly, soberly, from wings. They are pale and frightened. They peer uneasily into hat. They start back in horror. They clutch their mouths, turn away, and vomit.

Weeping, shouting, vomiting, accusations of murder.

Large man and country boy tie up magician, drag him away.

Weeping, retching.

Large man and country boy return, lift crushed hat gingerly, and trembling uncontrollably, carry it at arms's length into wings.

Momentary increase of weeping, retching, moaning, then dying away of sound of silence.

Country boy creeps onto stage, alone, sets up placard against table and facing audience, then creeps abjectly away.

THIS ACT IS CONCLUDED
THE MANAGEMENT REGRETS THERE
WILL BE NO REFUND

3
POETRY

The Elements of Poetry

INTRODUCTION

The Poetry Game

If you ask a poet, "What good is it? I mean, what earthly good is it?" you may get an answer like Marianne Moore's "I, too, dislike it," or W. H. Auden's "Poetry makes nothing happen." The modern poet is not likely to make grandiose claims for his craft. And we shall try not to betray that honest and tough-minded attitude. Poetry is essentially a game, with artificial rules, and it takes two—a writer and a reader—to play it. If the reader is reluctant, the game will not work.

Physical games have their practical aspects. They help make sound bodies to go with the sound minds so much admired by philosophers of education. A language game like poetry also has uses, but they are by-products rather than its proper ends. Poetry exercises a valuable though perhaps "unsound" side of the mind: imagination. (It takes an exercise of the imagination, for example, to get at what Bob Dylan means by a "hard rain.") Poetry can also be used to develop the student's ability to control and respond to language. But it is a game first of all, where—as Robert Frost said—"the work is play for mortal stakes."

A game can require great exertion, but it must reward that exertion with pleasure or there is no playing it. Anyone who has ever responded to a nursery rhyme, or to a Beatles record, or to Pete Seeger singing a ballad, has experienced the fundamental pleasure of poetry. More complicated and sophisticated poems offer essentially the same kind of pleasure. We labor to understand the rules of the game so that we need not think about them when we are playing. We master technique to make our execution easier. When we are really proficient the work becomes play.

521

The Qualities of Poetry

Part of the pleasure of poetry lies in its relation to music. It awakens in us a fundamental response to rhythmic repetitions of various kinds. Learning to read poetry is partly a matter of learning to respond to subtle and delicate rhythmic patterns as well as to the most obvious and persistant ones. But poetry is not just a kind of music. It is a special combination of musical and linguistic qualities—of sounds regarded both as pure sound and as meaningful speech. In particular, poetry is expressive language. It does for us what Samuel Beckett's character Watt wanted done for him:

> Not that Watt desired information, for he did not. But he desired words to be applied to his situation, to Mr Knott, to the house, to the grounds, to his duties, to the stairs, to his bedroom, to the kitchen, and in a general way to the conditions of being in which he found himself.

Poetry applies words to our situations, to the conditions of being in which we find ourselves. By doing so, it gives us pleasure because it helps us articulate our states of mind. The poets we value are important because they speak for us and help us learn to speak for ourselves. A revealing instance of a poet's learning to apply words to his own situation, and finding in their order and symmetry a soothing pleasure, has been recorded by James Joyce. Here we see a child of nine years making an important discovery about the nature and uses of poetry:

> [Bray: in the parlour of the house in Martello Terrace]
> MR VANCE   (comes in with a stick) . . . O, you know, he'll have to apologise, Mrs Joyce.
> MRS JOYCE   O yes . . . Do you hear that, Jim?
> MR VANCE   Or else—if he doesn't—the eagles'll come and pull out his eyes.
> MRS JOYCE   O, but I'm sure he will apologise.
> JOYCE   (under the table, to himself)
> —Pull out his eyes,
> Apologise,
> Apologise,
> Pull out his eyes.
>
> Apologise,
> Pull out his eyes,
> Pull out his eyes,
> Apologise.

The coincidence of sound that links the four-word phrase "pull-out-his-eyes" with the four-syllable word "apologise" offers the child a refuge from Mr Vance far more secure than the table under which he is hiding. In his novel *A Portrait of the Artist as a Young Man*, Joyce used this moment from his own life to illustrate Stephen's vocation for verbal art.

As a poem the child's effort is of course a simple one, but it achieves a real

effect because of the contrast between the meanings of its two basic lines
that sound so much alike. Gentle "apologise" and fierce "pull out his eyes"
ought not to fit together so neatly, the poem implies; and in doing so it
makes an ethical criticism of Mr Vance, who, after all, coupled them in the
first place. Young Joyce's deliberate wit has made a poem from the old
man's witless tirade.

Marianne Moore qualifies her dislike of poetry this way:

I, too, dislike it: there are things that are important beyond
          all this fiddle.
   Reading it, however, with a perfect contempt of it, one
          discovers in
   it after all, a place for the genuine.
      Hands that can grasp, eyes
      that can dilate, hair that can rise
          if it must, these things are important not because a

high-sounding interpretation can be put upon them but
          because they are
   useful. . . .

   And Auden adds,

. . . poetry makes nothing happen: it survives
In the valley of its making where executives
Would never want to tamper: flows on south
From ranches of isolation and the busy griefs,
Raw towns that we believe and die in; it survives,
A way of happening, a mouth.

He concludes the poem "In Memory of W. B. Yeats," from which these lines
are taken, with some advice to poets that suggests the kinds of thing poetry
can do:

Follow, poet, follow right
To the bottom of the night,
With your unconstraining voice
Still persuade us to rejoice;

With the farming of a verse
Make a vineyard of the curse,
Sing of human unsuccess
In a rapture of distress;

In the deserts of the heart
Let the healing fountain start,
In the prison of his days
Teach the free man how to praise.

Poetry, then, is a kind of musical word game that we value because of its expressive qualities. Not all poems are equally musical, or equally playful, or equally expressive. Nor are they necessarily musical, playful, or expressive in the same way. But we may consider these three qualities as the basic constituents of poetry so that we may examine some of the various ways in which poets combine and modify them in making different kinds of poems. Recognizing various poetic possibilities is important to the student of poetry because the greatest single problem for the reader of a poem is the problem of tact.

Tact

Tact acknowledges the diversity of poetry. A tactful approach to a poem must be appropriate to the special nature of the poem under consideration. Reading a poem for the first time ought to be a little like meeting a person for the first time. An initial exploratory conversation may lead to friendship, dislike, indifference, or any of dozens of other shades of attitude from love to hate. If the relation progresses, it will gain in intimacy as surface politeness is replaced by exchange of ideas and feelings at a deeper level.

We need, of course, to speak the same language if we are to communicate in any serious way. For most of us, this means we make friends with people who speak English and we read poems written in English. But speaking the same language means more than just inheriting or acquiring the same linguistic patterns. Some poems, like some people, seem to talk to us not merely in our native language but in our own idiom as well. We understand them easily and naturally. Others speak in ways that seem strange and puzzling. With poems, as with people, our first response to the puzzling should be a polite effort to eliminate misunderstanding. We need not adopt any false reverence before the poems of earlier ages. An old poem may be as much of a bore as an old person. But we should treat the aged with genuine politeness, paying attention to their words, trying to adjust to their idiom. This may turn out to be very rewarding, or it may not. But only after we have understood are we entitled to reject—or accept—any utterance.

Since the English language itself has changed considerably over the centuries and continues to change, we must often make a greater effort to understand an older poem than a modern one. Also, notions of what poetry is and should be have changed in the past and continue to change. The poetry game has not always been played with the same linguistic equipment or under the same rules. The difference between a love lyric by an Elizabethan sonneteer and a contemporary poem of love may be as great as the difference between Elizabethan tennis and modern tennis. The Elizabethans played tennis indoors, in an intricately walled court which required great finesse to master all its angles. The modern game is flat and open, all power serves and rushes to the net. Which ought to remind us that Robert Frost likened free verse (verse with unrhymed, irregular lines) to playing tennis with the net down. Such a game would make points easy to score but would not be much fun to play. Poetry, like tennis, depends on artificial rules and hindrances. These arbitrary restrictions are what give it its game-like quality.

Unlike the rules of tennis, however, the rules of poetry have never really been written down. Although critics have frequently tried to produce a "poetics" that would operate like a code of rules, they have always failed because poetry is always changing. In fact poetic "rules" are not really rules but conventions that change perpetually and must change perpetually to prevent poems from being turned out on a mass scale according to formulas. Every poet learns from his predecessors, but any poet who merely imitates them produces flat, stale poems. A poet is above all a man who finds a unique idiom, a special voice for his own poetry. The tactful reader quickly picks up the conventions operating in any particular poem and pays careful attention to the idiom of every poet, so that he can understand and appreciate or criticize each separate poetic performance.

The following parts of this discussion are designed to help the student of poetry to acquire tact. They are arranged to present certain basic elements drawn from the whole system of poetic conventions. Tact itself cannot be taught because it is of the spirit. But if the instinct for it is there, tact can be developed and refined through conscious effort. In the pages that follow, the student may consider consciously and deliberately the kinds of intellectual and emotional adjustments that the expert reader of poetry makes effortlessly and instantaneously.

EXPRESSION

Drama and Narration

Drama usually implies actors on a stage impersonating characters who speak to one another in a sequence of situations or scenes. A short poem with a single speaker, thus, is dramatic only in a limited sense. Nevertheless, *some* poems are very dramatic; the element of drama in them must be grasped if we are to understand them at all. And *all* poems are dramatic to some extent, however slight.

We approach the dramatic element in poetry by assuming that every poem shares some qualities with a speech in a play: that it is spoken aloud by a "speaker" who is a character in a situation which implies a certain relationship with other characters; and we assume that this speech is "overheard" by an audience. We may have to modify these assumptions. The poem may finally be more like a soliloquy or unspoken thought than like a part of a dialogue. Or it may seem more like a letter or a song than a speech. Still, in approaching our poem we must make a tentative decision about who the speaker is, what his situation is, and whom he seems to be addressing. In poems that are especially dramatic, the interest of the poem will depend on the interest of the character and situation presented. But because dramatic poems are very short and compressed in comparison with plays, the reader must usually do a good deal of guessing or inferring in order to grasp the elements of character and situation. The good reader will make plausible inferences; the inadequate reader will guess wildly, breaking the rules of plausibility and spoiling the inferential game.

Consider the following lines from the beginning of a dramatic poem. This imaginary speech is assigned by the title of the poem to a painter who lived in Renaissance Italy. Brother Filippo Lippi was a Carmelite friar and an important painter, whose work was sponsored by the rich and powerful Florentine banker Cosimo di Medici.

Fra Lippo Lippi

I am poor brother Lippo, by your leave!
You need not clap your torches to my face.
Zooks, what's to blame? you think you see a monk!
What, 't is past midnight, and you go the rounds,
And here you catch me at an alley's end
Where sportive ladies leave their doors ajar?
The Carmine's my cloister: hunt it up,
Do,—harry out, if you must show your zeal,
Whatever rat, there, haps on his wrong hole,
10   And nip each softling of a wee white mouse,
Weke, weke, that's crept to keep him company!
Aha, you know your betters! Then, you'll take
Your hand away that 's fiddling on my throat,
And please to know me likewise. Who am I?
Why, one, sir, who is lodging with a friend
Three streets off—he 's a certain . . . how d' ye call?
Master—a . . . Cosimo of the Medici,
I' the house that caps the corner. Boh! you were best!
Remember and tell me, the day you 're hanged,
20   How you affected such a gullet's-gripe!
But you, sir, it concerns you that your knaves
Pick up a manner nor discredit you:
Zooks, are we pilchards, that they sweep the streets
And count fair prize what comes into their net?
He 's Judas to a tittle, that man is!
Just such a face! Why, sir, you make amends.
Lord, I 'm not angry! Bid your hangdogs go
Drink out this quarter-florin to the health
Of the munificent House that harbours me
30   (And many more beside, lads! more beside!)
And all 's come square again. I 'd like his face—
His, elbowing on his comrade in the door
With the pike and lantern,—for the slave that holds

John Baptist's head a-dangle by the hair
With one hand ("Look, you, now," as who should say)
And his weapon in the other, yet unwiped!
It 's not your chance to have a bit of chalk,
A wood-coal or the like? or you should see!
Yes, I'm the painter, since you style me so.

Now consider, in order, each of these questions:

1. From these lines, what can we infer about the situation and its development?

2. Who is Lippo speaking to in the opening lines?

3. At what time of day and in what sort of neighborhood does this scene take place?

4. Would we be justified in making an inference about what Lippo has been up to? What inference might we make?

5. What is Lippo talking about when he says in line 18, "Boh! you were best!"? And whom does he say it to? What produced the action which Lippo refers to here?

6. In line 21 he addresses a different person in "you, sir." Who is he addressing?

7. What kind of man do the details in these lines suggest is speaking in this poem?

8. How would you describe the whole progress of the situation? How might the events presented in these 39 lines be re-told in the form of a story narrated by an observer of the action?

This series of questions—and their answers—should suggest the kind of inferential activity that many dramatic poems require of their readers. The words of such a poem are points of departure, and the actual poem is the one we create with our imaginative but logical response to the poet's words. The poet—Robert Browning—offers us the pleasure of helping to create his poem, and also the pleasure of entering a world remote from our own in time and space. Dramatic poems like Browning's do not so much apply words to our situations as take us out of ourselves into situations beyond our experience. When we speak Lippo's words aloud, or read them imaginatively, we are refreshed by this assumption of a strange role and this expression of a personality other than our own. In a sense, our minds are expanded, and we return to ourselves enriched by the experience. Yet even the strangest characters will often express ideas and attitudes that we recognize as related to our own, related to certain moods or conditions of being in which we have found ourselves. Every citizen who has had to explain an awkward situation to a policeman has something in common with Lippo Lippi as he begins to speak.

The line between the dramatic and narrative elements in a poem is not always clear. But a narrative poem gives us a story as told by a narrator from a perspective outside the action, while a dramatic poem presents a fragment of an action (or story) through the voice (or point of view) of a character involved in that action. The principal speaker in a narrative poem addresses us—the audience—directly, telling us about the situation and perhaps offering us introductions to characters who function as dramatic elements in the poem. In the days when long stories were recited aloud by bardic poets, verse was the natural form for narration, because it provided easily memorizable units of composition and a regular, flowing rhythm into which these units might be fitted. But now that printing has converted most of the audience for fiction from listeners to readers, most stories are told in prose. The only narrative verse form that is really alive today is the ballad, which justifies its use of rhyme and rhythm by being set to music and sung. Verse meant to be sung has its own rules or conventions, which will be discussed later on. But here we can talk about the narrative element in ballads and other forms of fiction in verse, and how versified fiction differs from the kind of story we expect to find in prose.

If we think of a dramatic poem as something like a self-sufficient fragment torn from a play, which through its compression encourages us to fill out its dramatic frame by acts of inference and imagination—then we may think of a narrative poem as related to prose fiction in a similar way. In comparison to stories, narrative poems are compressed and elliptical, shifting their focus, concentrating on striking details, and leaving us to make appropriate connections and draw appropriate conclusions. In fact, there is a strong tendency toward the dramatic in short verse narratives—a tendency to present more dialogue or action in relation to description than we would expect to find in prose fiction dealing with the same subject matter.

Actually, we find poetic elements in much prose fiction and fictional elements in many poems. Here we are concerned mainly with the special problems posed by the compressed and elliptical form taken by fiction in short poems such as this one, by E. A. Robinson:

Reuben Bright

Because he was a butcher and thereby
Did earn an honest living (and did right)
I would not have you think that Reuben Bright
Was any more a brute than you or I;
For when they told him that his wife must die,

He stared at them, and shook with grief and fright,
And cried like a great baby half that night,
And made the women cry to see him cry.

And after she was dead, and he had paid
10   The singers and the sexton and the rest,
He packed a lot of things that she had made
Most mournfully away in an old chest
Of hers, and put some chopped-up cedar boughs
In with them, and tore down the slaughter-house.

The poem is narrative for the reason that the speaker addresses us from a perspective outside the action and undertakes to comment for our benefit on the character and situation presented: Reuben earns an "honest" living; he did "right." Yet the narrator presents just two incidents from the whole of Bright's life, and he makes no final interpretation or commentary on Bright's climactic act. It is left for us to conclude that only by destroying the place of butchery could this butcher express his anguish at the death of his beloved wife. And it is left for us to note the irony involved in this presentation of an act of destructive violence as evidence that the butcher is not "any more a brute than you or I." It is also left for us to note the pathos of this gesture by which the butcher tries to dissociate himself from that death which has claimed his wife. The compactness and brevity characteristic of poetry often move narration in the direction of drama.

Consider the combination of drama and narration in the following poem by D. H. Lawrence:

Piano

Softly, in the dusk, a woman is singing to me;
Taking me back down the vista of years, till I see
A child sitting under the piano, in the boom of the tingling strings
And pressing the small, poised feet of a mother who smiles as she sings.

In spite of myself, the insidious mastery of song
Betrays me back, till the heart of me weeps to belong
To the old Sunday evenings at home, with winter outside
And hymns in the cosy parlour, the tinkling piano our guide.
So now it is vain for the singer to burst into clamour
10   With the great black piano appassionato. The glamour
Of childish days is upon me, my manhood is cast
Down in the flood of remembrance, I weep like a child for the past.

Here the speaker seems to be addressing us directly as a narrator. But he is describing a scene in which he is the central character, and describing it in the present tense as something in progress. Drama is always *now*. Narrative is always *then*. But this scene mingles now *and* then, bringing together two pianos, and two pianists; linking the speaker's childish self with his present manhood. In a sense, the poem depends on its combination of now and then, drama and narration, for its effect—uniting now and then, man and child, in its last clause: "I weep like a child for the past."

Because this is a poem, tightly compressed, it is possible for us to miss an essential aspect of the dramatic situation it presents. Why is it "vain" for the singer to play the piano "appassionato"? Why does he say that his "manhood" is cast down? What does this phrase mean? These elliptical references seem intended to suggest that the woman at the piano is in some sense wooing the man who listens, attempting to arouse his passion through her performance. But ironically, she only reminds him of his mother, casting down his manhood, reducing him from a lover to a son, from a man to a child.

It is interesting to compare this poem by D. H. Lawrence to an early version. Looking at the early draft, we might consider Lawrence's revisions as an attempt to achieve a more satisfactory combination of narrative and drama, and a more intense poem. The early version tells quite a different story from the later one—almost the opposite story. And it contains much that Lawrence eliminated. Examine the revisions in detail. What does each change accomplish? Which changes are most important, most effective?

The Piano
(*Early version*)

Somewhere beneath that piano's superb sleek black
Must hide my mother's piano, little and brown, with the back
That stood close to the wall, and the front's faded silk both torn,
And the keys with little hollows, that my mother's fingers had worn.

Softly, in the shadows, a woman is singing to me
Quietly, through the years I have crept back to see
A child sitting under the piano, in the boom of the shaking strings
Pressing the little poised feet of the mother who smiles as she sings.

The full throated woman has chosen a winning, living song
10   And surely the heart that is in me must belong
To the old Sunday evenings, when darkness wandered outside
And hymns gleamed on our warm lips, as we watched mother's fingers glide.

Or this is my sister at home in the old front room
Singing love's first surprised gladness, alone in the gloom.
She will start when she sees me, and blushing, spread out her hands
To cover my mouth's raillery, till I'm bound in her shame's heartspun bands.

A woman is singing me a wild Hungarian air
And her arms, and her bosom, and the whole of her soul is bare,
And the great black piano is clamouring as my mother's never could clamour
20   And my mother's tunes are devoured of this music's ravaging glamour.

Description and Meditation

Description is the element in poetry closest to painting and sculpture. Poets like Edmund Spenser, Keats, and Tennyson have been very sensitive to this relationship: Spenser maintained that the Poet's wit "passeth Painter farre," while Keats admitted that a painted piece of Greek pottery could "express a flowery tale more sweetly than our rhyme." In fact, describing with words has both advantages and disadvantages in comparison to plastic representation. Words are rich in meaning and suggestion but weak for rendering precise spatial relations and shades of color. Therefore, what descriptive words do best is convey an attitude or feeling through the objects that they describe.

Take a very simple description from a short poem by William Carlos Williams:

a red wheel
barrow

glazed with rain
water

beside the white
chickens.

We sense a word game here in the arbitrary arrangement of the words in lines, as they lead us to consider a visual image dominated by contrasting colors and textures—feathery white and glazed red, animate and inanimate things. But it is hard to sense distinctly any attitude conveyed by the description, which seems like a poor substitute for a painting.

Here is the entire poem:

so much depends
upon

a red wheel
barrow

glazed with rain
water

beside the white
chickens.

Now we can see how the description itself depends upon the assertion "so much depends" for its animation. The assertion directs our search for meaning, and conveys the speaker's attitude toward the objects described. We may wonder how anything at all can "depend" on such insignificant objects, and yet this very response is a response not just to a description but to a poem as well. The poem is created by the distance between this sweeping statement and the apparent insignificance of the objects it refers to. We understand, finally, that the poet is using this distance to make us feel his concern for trivial things, his sense that there is beauty in humble objects; and beyond that, he is encouraging us to share his alertness to the beautiful in things that are neither artful nor conventionally pretty. He is advising us to keep our eyes open, and he does it not with a direct admonition but with a description charged with the vigor of his own response to the visible world.

It is of the essence of poetic description that it come to us charged with the poet's feelings and attitudes. Sometimes these will be made explicit by statement or commentary in the poem. Sometimes they will remain implicit, matters of tone, rhythm, and metaphor. Consider these four opening lines from a poem by Tennyson. What attitudes or emotions are conveyed by them, and how are they conveyed?

The woods decay, the woods decay and fall,
The vapours weep their burthen to the ground,
Man comes and tills the field and lies beneath,
And after many a summer dies the swan.

The topic is decay and death, presented in terms of generalized natural description. In line 1 the continuing process of decay is emphasized by the exact repetition of a whole clause. In line 2 the vapors are presented as sentient creatures who weep. In line 3 the whole adult life of man is compressed into just nine words, few seconds, a patch of earth. In the climactic position, reserved by an inversion of normal syntax for the very last place in the sentence, comes the death of the swan. The life and death of man is thus surrounded by decay and death in other natural things, and in this way is reduced, distanced. It is not horrible but natural, and characterized by a melancholy beauty.

These lines of description serve in the poem as the beginning of a dramatic monologue. The nature of the speaker and his situation (as we come to understand them) help us to refine our grasp of the tone and the attitude these lines convey toward the objects they describe. Here is the opening verse-paragraph of the poem:

Tithonus

The woods decay, the woods decay and fall,
The vapours weep their burthen to the ground,
Man comes and tills the field and lies beneath,
And after many a summer dies the swan.
Me only cruel immortality
Consumes: I wither slowly in thine arms,
Here at the quiet limit of the world,

A white-haired shadow roaming like a dream
The ever-silent spaces of the East,
10   Far-folded mists, and gleaming halls of morn.

The speaker is Tithonus, a mythological prince who became the lover of the dawn goddess; she made him immortal but could not prevent him from growing older throughout eternity. In the light of lines 5 and 6, the first four lines are enriched with the wistful envy of one who is unable to die. At the close of the poem (some seventy lines later) the speaker returns to the images of line 3 in speaking of "happy men that have the power to die" and of "the grassy barrows of the happier dead." He asks for release so that he can become "earth in earth" and forget his unhappy existence.

The melancholy beauty of the opening lines becomes more lovely and less sad as we move toward the conclusion of the poem with its powerful projection of man's return to earth as the most desirable of consummations. Behind the dramatic speaker in the poem—the mythological Tithonus— stands the poet, reminding us that death is natural and the appropriate end of life. In this poem, description and drama collaborate to suggest rather than state a meaning.

Serious English poetry has often embodied in particular poems a movement from description to overt meditation. This movement is frequently found in religious poetry, as poets move from contemplation of created things to an awareness of the Creator. William Wordsworth was a master— prehaps *the* master—of this kind of poetic movement in English. Thus, a selection from Wordsworth makes a fitting conclusion to this discussion of description and meditation. The poem is a sonnet (see the note on this form in the introduction to Shakespeare in our Selection of Poets), in which the first eight lines (the *octet*) are devoted to description of nature and the last six (the *sestet*) take the form of a meditation on Wordsworth's daughter Caroline. The expression "Abraham's bosom" in the poem refers of course to heaven. In the New Testament (Luke 16:22) we are told that the righteous will join the patriarch Abraham in heaven after death.

It is a beauteous evening, calm and free,
The holy time is quiet as a Nun
Breathless with adoration; the broad sun
Is sinking down in its tranquillity;
The gentleness of heaven broods o'er the Sea:
Listen! the mighty Being is awake,
And doth with his eternal motion make
A sound like thunder—everlastingly.
Dear Child! dear Girl! that walkest with me here,
10   If thou appear untouched by solemn thought,
Thy nature is not therefore less divine:
Thou liest in Abraham's bosom all the year;
And worshipp'st at the Temple's inner shrine,
God being with thee when we know it not.

WORD GAMES

Language can be used to help us perceive relations that connect disparate things, or to help us make discriminations that separate similar things. In poetry these two aspects of language take the form of metaphorical comparison and ironic contrast. Metaphor and irony are the twin bases of poetical language. This means that a good reader of poetry must be especially alert and tactful in his responses to metaphorical and ironic language.

It is because poetry places such stress on these crucial dimensions of language that it is of such great use in developing linguistic skills in its readers. It makes unusual demands and offers unusual rewards. The kind of skill it takes to be a first-rate reader of poetry cannot be acquired by reading a textbook like this one, any more than the ability to play the piano can be acquired in a few lessons. Continuing practice is the most important factor in a performing art like piano playing—and reading poetry (even silently, to oneself) has many of the qualities and satisfactions of a performing art.

In the sections that follow on metaphoric and ironic language we have not tried to present an exhaustive list of poetical devices to be carefully noted and memorized. We have tried to examine some of the main varieties of metaphoric and ironic language, with a view toward establishing an awareness of these two crucial varieties of poetical word-play. To move from awareness to expertise, the student must read many poems and consider them carefully.

Some Varieties of Metaphorical Language

SIMILE

This is the easiest form of metaphor to perceive because in it both of the images or ideas being joined are stated and explicity linked by the word as or like or a similar linking-word. Similes are often quite simple:

O my Love's like a red, red rose

But even a statement of resemblance as simple and direct as this one of Robert Burns's asks us to consider the ways in which his beloved is like a rose—and not a white or yellow rose, but a red rose. And not just a red rose but a "red, red" rose. What the redness of the rose has to do with the qualities of the speaker's beloved is the first question this simile poses for us. In the poem, the simile is further complicated by a second line:

O my Love's like a red, red rose,
    That's newly sprung in June;

Here we are asked to associate the freshness of the flower and its early blooming with the qualities of the speaker's beloved. In the poem, the next two lines add a second image, compounding the simile:

O my Love's like the melodie
   That's sweetly played in tune.

The first image emphasizes the spontaneous naturalness of the beloved, the second her harmonious composure. Both roses and sweet melodies are pleasing; so that, in a sense, the poet is using his similies to make the simple statement that his beloved is pleasing to behold. But the simile is also saying that she has a complicated kind of appeal: like the rose, to sight and smell; like the melody, to the sense of sound; like the rose, a natural fresh quality; like the melody, a deliberate artfulness which intends to please. The simile also conveys to us the strength of the poet's feeling; his choice of images tells us something about the qualities of his feeling for her, because it is *he* who has found these words—which themselves have some of the qualities of spontaneous freshness and tuneful order.

A single simile can also be elaborated: as in the traditional epic simile, in which the illustrative image is often extensive enough to require the construction *as . . . so*, or *like . . . thus*. An extended simile, by multiplying possible points of contact between the thing presented and the illustrative image, can often become very complicated indeed, with the illustrative image itself becoming a thing to be illustrated or developed with other images still. Consider, for example, this epic simile from Book IV of Spenser's *Faerie Queene:*

27

Like as the tide that comes from th' Ocean main,
Flows up the Shanon with contrary force,
And overruling him in his own reign,
Drives back the current of his kindly course,
And makes it seem to have some other source:
But when the flood is spent, then back again
His borrowed waters forced to redisbourse
He sends the sea his own with double gain
And tribute eke withall, as to his Soveraine.

28

Thus did the battle vary to and fro . . .

METAPHOR
The word "metaphor" is used both as a general term for all kinds of poetic linking of images and ideas, and as a specific term for such linking when the thing and image are not presented as a direct analogy (A is *like* B) but by

discussing one in terms of the other (A *is* B-ish, or A B's; Albert *is* a dog or Albert *barked* at me). For example, within the epic simile from Spenser, we can find metaphor at work. The simile involves describing a hand-to-hand combat in terms of the ebb and flow of tides where the River Shannon meets the Atlantic Ocean. The ebb and flow of the waters illustrates the shifting tide of battle (as this metaphor become a cliché usually puts it). But this basic simile in Spenser is enriched by the idea of Shannon and Ocean as hostile potentates engaged in a struggle, with the Ocean tide invading the river and "overruling him in his own reign."

The struggle of potentates is itself further complicated by a financial metaphor. The phrase "when the flood is spent" means literally when the incoming tide has expended its force and lost its momentum. But Spenser chooses to use the financial overtones in the word "spent" to further adorn his metaphor. From "spent" he moves to "borrowed" and "redisburse," and the concept of repayment with 100 percent interest in the expression "double gain." This transaction between Ocean and Shannon can be seen as a combat or a loan. Finally, Spenser merges these two metaphors in the last line of the stanza, by calling this double payment the "tribute" of a lesser feudal power to a higher. And here Spenser actually turns his metaphor into a simile within the basic simile, with the expression "*as to his Soveraine.*"

This kind of interweaving of similes and metaphors is playful and decorative in its intent. The metaphors seem to emerge naturally and blend easily with one another. But these graceful arabesques tell us nothing much about the course of the combat of the two warriors, beyond the suggestion that the fight ebbs and flows. Their struggle is not so much described as dignified by this heroic comparison to two sovereign forces of nature.

In poems that depend heavily on metaphoric processes for their interest, the subtle interaction of images and ideas almost defies analysis; yet such poems may depend upon our attempts to follow their metaphoric threads. For us to understand such a poem, to feel it, we must start our thoughts along the lines indicated by the metaphors. Consider Shakespeare's sonnet 73 as an example of this kind of poem:

That time of year thou may'st in me behold
When yellow leaves, or none, or few, do hang
Upon those boughs which shake against the cold—
Bare ruin'd choirs where late the sweet birds sang.
In me thou see'st the twilight of such day
As after Sunset fadeth in the West,
Which by and by black night doth take away,
Death's second self, that seals up all in rest.
In me thou see'st the glowing of such fire
10   That on the ashes of his youth doth lie,
As the death-bed whereon it must expire,

Consumed with that which it was nourish'd by.
This thou perceiv'st, which makes thy love more strong
To love that well which thou must leave ere long.

The images of the first twelve lines are all elaborations of the simple
notion that the speaker is getting old. The last two lines are a dramatic
assertion, also rather simple. The speaker tells his listener that the listener
will love him all the more, precisely because old age and death threaten their
relationship. We can infer that the speaker is older than the listener, and in
terms of the dramatic situation we are entitled to wonder whether these
self-assured words are merely wishful thinking, or an appraisal of the
listener's attitude. How does the imagery of the first twelve lines contribute
to the situation and to our understanding of it? We have in these lines three
separate but related metaphors, each developed for four lines. The speaker
says, in effect, "You see in me—autumn; you see in me—twilight; you see
in me—embers."

These three metaphors for aging have in common certain qualities: a
growing coldness and darkness; suggestions of finality and impending
extinction. But each image generates its own attitude and emphasizes a
different aspect of the aging process. The first four lines suggest an analogy
between an aging person and trees whose leaves have fallen, leaving them
exposed to cold winds. And the bare trees suggest, by a further reach of
metaphor, a ruined and desolate church. Above all, this complex metaphor
generates sympathy for the speaker, a sympathy based on our concern for
lost beauty, for destruction of spiritual things, and for victims of the forces
of nature.

The next four lines, focusing on the twilight after sunset, emphasize the
threat of coming darkness. By another extension of metaphor, "black night"
is called "Death's second self." The brevity of the time between sunset and
night increases our sense of sympathetic urgency, and the introduction of
"Death" takes us full circle through the metaphors back to their object, an
aging man. The next four lines also introduce a complex metaphor. The
speaker compares himself to the glowing embers of a dying fire which lies
upon "the ashes of his youth." The fire becomes human, here, and returns
us again to the life of the speaker.

This image is the most intense of the three, because it likens the arrival of
age not merely to a seasonal change, worked by the passage of time, but to
the consumption or destruction of matter which can never be restored to its
original state. The ashes of the fire lying upon its deathbed are forcible
reminders that the speaker's body will soon lie upon a deathbed, and will
become ashes, to be returned to the ashes and dust of the grave. It is the
emotional force of all "This" which the speaker maintains in the next-to-last
line that the listener must perceive. And the confidence of the assertion is

partly the confidence of a poet who still has his poetical power. He can still sing like a sweet bird and move his hearer with his poetry. The imagery justifies the dramatic situation, and the situation intensifies the significance of the imagery.

THE CONCEIT

It is useful to think of the conceit as an extension of the simile in which aspects of the basic analogy are developed with a kind of relentless ingenuity. The "metaphysical" poets of the late sixteenth and the seventeenth century specialized in witty conceits. Here, for example, John Donne combines a dramatic situation with development of a conceit so that the images become an argument persuading his lady listener to give in.

The Flea

Mark but this flea, and mark in this,
How little that which thou deny'st me is;
Me it sucked first, and now sucks thee,
And in this flea, our two bloods mingled be;
Confess it, this cannot be said
A sin, or shame, or loss of maidenhead,
　Yet this enjoys before it woo,
　And pampered swells with one blood made of two,
　And this, alas, is more than we would do.

10　Oh stay, three lives in one flea spare,
Where we almost, nay more than married are.
This flea is you and I, and this
Our marriage bed, and marriage temple is;
Though parents grudge, and you, we are met,
And cloistered in these living walls of jet.
　Though use make you apt to kill me,
　Let not to this, self murder added be,
　And sacrilege, three sins in killing three.

Cruel and sudden, hast thou since
20　Purpled thy nail, in blood of innocence?
In what could this flea guilty be,
Except in that drop which it sucked from thee?
Yet thou triumph'st, and say'st that thou
Find'st not thyself, nor me the weaker now;
　'Tis true, then learn how false, fears be;
　Just so much honour, when thou yield'st to me,
　Will waste, as this flea's death took life from thee.

In the first two lines the speaker makes the basic analogy between the flea's having bitten both himself and the lady, and the act of love-making to which he would like to persuade her. In the rest of the poem he develops the analogy as an argument in a changing dramatic context. At the start of stanza two, the lady has threatened to kill the flea. By stanza three she has done so. And meanwhile the speaker has imaginatively transformed the flea into a marriage bed, a temple, a cloister, and a figure of the Holy Trinity (three in one); so that the flea's destruction can be hyperbolically described as murder, suicide, and sacrilege. All in preparation for the turn of the argument in the last three lines of the poem. Donne's conceit is both ingenious and playful in this poem. It is witty in more than one sense.

THE SYMBOL

The symbol can be seen as an extension of the metaphor. In it, instead of saying that A is B-ish, or calling an A a B, the poet presents us with one half of the analogy only, and requires us to supply the missing part. This invites the reader to be creative and imaginative in a situation controlled by the poet. Bob Dylan's "Hard Rain" is a symbolic poem. And here is a symbolic poem by W. B. Yeats:

The Dolls

A doll in the doll-maker's house
Looks at the cradle and bawls:
'That is an insult to us.'
But the oldest of all the dolls,
Who had seen, being kept for show,
Generations of his sort,
Out-screams the whole shelf: 'Although
There's not a man can report
Evil of this place,
10   The man and the woman bring
Hither, to our disgrace,
A noisy and filthy thing.'
Hearing him groan and stretch
The doll-maker's wife is aware
Her husband has heard the wretch,
And crouched by the arm of his chair,
She murmurs into his ear,
Head upon shoulder leant:
'My dear, my dear, O dear,
20   It was an accident.'

This whole incident stands in a metaphoric relation to something else. In other words, the poem is only apparently about dolls and doll-makers. It is really about something symbolized by the incident narrated. What? And how do we go about determining what? We must work very carefully from the situation toward possible analogies in the world of ideas and experience, first exploring the situation and images in the poem. The situation derives from the doll-maker's unique role as creator of two kinds of small, man-shaped objects: dolls and children. The dolls in their lifeless perfection resent the noise and filth produced by an actual human child. The human baby is, in fact, as the doll-maker's wife apologetically points out, not "made" in the same sense as dolls are made. Birth is an "accident"; dolls are deliberately constructed. The situation leads us outward until we see it as an illustration of the opposition between art and life, between the ideal and the real. The doll-maker himself thus symbolizes any artist who is obliged to live in the real world but create idealized objects, or any person who faces the impossible problem of realizing his ideas—or idealizing reality.

Having got this far from the concrete situation of the poem, the reader is in a position to return and consider the ways in which Yeats has used language to control his tone and charge the scene with emotion. How should we react to the various characters in this little drama? What, finally, should our attitude be toward the real/ideal conflict that the drama illustrates?

THE PUN

Often subjected to abuse as a "low" form of wit, the pun is essentially a kind of metaphor that can be used lightly and facetiously or for more serious purposes. Consider some verses by Thomas Hood (selected by William Empson to exemplify punning techniques):

How frail is our uncertain breath!
The laundress seems full hale, but death
Shall her 'last linen' bring;
The groom will die, like all his kind;
And even the stable boy will find
This life no stable thing. . . .

Cook, butler, Susan, Jonathan,
The girl that scours the pot and pan
And those that tend the steeds,
10   All, all shall have another sort
Of service after this—in short
The one the parson reads.

These puns on "stable" and "service" are playful but not funny. They use the basic device of the pun—dissimilar meanings for the same "word" or rather the same sound—to convey an attitude toward an idea. That both the life of a servant and his funeral are somehow included in that one piece of language—"service"—brings home to us the interconnection of life and death—which is the point of the poem.

Shakespeare was a master of the pun as of other metaphorical devices. Hamlet's bitter, punning responses to his uncle's smooth speeches are deadly serious and powerfully dramatic in their witty compression of his resentment.

KING   . . . But now, my cousin Hamlet, and my son—
HAMLET [Aside]   A little more than kin and less than kind!
KING   How is it that the clouds still hang on you?
HAMLET   Not so, my lord. I am too much i' the sun.

Hamlet and the King are more than *kin* (twice related: uncle/nephew and stepfather/son) but Hamlet feels they are not kindred spirits, not the same *kind*. And being called *son* by his father's murderer rouses all Hamlet's bitterness, causing him to return the King's metaphorical question about Hamlet's emotional weather with a pun that brings the metaphor back to the literal with a sarcastic bite: I am too much in the *son*.

The Language of Animation and Personification

In addition to their playful or ingenious aspects, the various metaphorical devices help to generate the qualities of compression and intensity that we value in much poetry. Similar qualities are often achieved by other means, such as animation and personification.

ANIMATION

Animation confers on objects or creatures a greater degree of awareness or purposefulness than we normally credit them with. When Tennyson writes, "The vapours weep their burthen to the ground," he gives life to the vapours, animating them with an emotion, sadness, that only living creatures experience. Less lovely scenes can also be intensified by animation. Consider these lines from Samuel Johnson's "Vanity of Human Wishes," which describe the treatment accorded the portraits of a statesman whose power has waned. Those who were honored to gaze at his features, now that no more is to be gained from the man, suddenly find the likeness ugly:

From every room descends the painted face,
That hung the bright palladium of the place;
And, smoked in kitchens, or in auctions sold,
To better features yields the frame of gold;
For now no more we trace in every line
Heroic worth, benevolence divine;
The form distorted justifies the fall,
And detestation rids th' indignant wall.

In that last line Johnson intensifies his satire by animating the very wall on which the picture hangs—it, even, is indignant and wishes to be rid of these odious features. The removal itself is effected by a person who has dwindled into an attitude—"detestation."

PERSONIFICATION

In this example from Dr. Johnson, we have a kind of reverse personification—as a human being becomes an abstract idea. Personification usually works the other way, clothing abstractions with the attributes of personality. Of all the ideas presented as sentient beings, Love has been most frequently selected. In mythology, Love figures as the boy-god Cupid or Eros, offering poets a ready-made personification which they have often used. The mechanical use of traditional personification can be a dull and dreary thing. But observe Sir Philip Sidney as he personifies Love in this sonnet, and finds ways to make concrete a whole range of other abstractions such as reverence, fear, hope, will, memory, and desire. If Love is personified here, these other notions are objectified—turned into material objects.

I on my horse, and Love on me doth try
    Our horsemanships, while by strange work I prove
    A horseman to my horse, a horse to Love;
    And now man's wrongs in me, poor beast, descry.

The reins wherewith my rider doth me tie,
    Are humbled thoughts, which bit of reverence move,
    Curb'd in with fear, but with gilt boss above
    Of hope, which makes it seem fair to the eye.

The wand is will; thou, fancy, saddle art,
10   Girt fast by memory, and while I spur
    My horse, he spurs with sharp desire my heart:

He sits me fast, however I do stir:
    And now hath made me to his hand so right,
    That in the manage my self takes delight.

The dominant image of Love as horseman provides the subordinate imagery for making concrete the other abstractions which serve to amplify this picture of a love-ridden man. The effectiveness of the poem depends on the ingenuity with which the poet has matched the objects and ideas to one another, relating all to the dominant personification of Love. Like Spenser's epic simile, Sidney's personification seems to breed subordinate metaphors easily, gracefully, and naturally.

The Anti-Metaphorical Language of Irony

Verbal irony may be said to start with simple negation of resemblance in situations where resemblance is customarily insisted upon: as in Shakespeare's sonnet 130, which begins,

My mistress' eyes are nothing like the sun;
Coral is far more red than her lips red:
If snow be white, why then her breasts are dun;
If hairs be wires, black wires grow on her head.

The anti-similes of the first three lines serve the same function as the ugly metaphor in line 4. All four lines present attacks on what the speaker will name in the last line as "false compare"—the misuse by poets of the metaphorical dimension of poetical language.

Usually, however, irony is not so straightforward. In fact, we normally think of it as involving some indirection or misleading of the reader—some gap between what the words *seem* to be saying and what they *are* saying. Thus, in this Shakespearean sonnet, after eight more lines of plain speaking about an ordinary human female, the speaker concludes,

And yet, by heaven, I think my love as rare
As any she belied by false compare.

What we might have taken as disparagement of the lady turns out to be praise after all. She is not uglier than the others; she just has a lover who won't exaggerate her beauty with the usual clichés. Thus, there is an irony in the disparity between the apparent disparagement of the lady in the first part of the poem and the praise of her at the end. We can see, then, in those opening lines, a kind of understatement, which works finally to convince us of the lady's beauty more effectively than a conventionally exaggerated simile of "false compare" would have done. (The entire sonnet may be found in our Selection of Poets.)

Understatement and overstatement are two of the most frequently used kinds of verbal irony. When Swift causes a character to observe (in prose), "Last Week I saw a Woman *flay'd*, and you will hardly believe, how much it altered her Person for the worse"—the main thing that strikes us is the awful inadequacy of the sentiment for the event. Disparity, contrast, incongruity—these things are at the heart of verbal irony. And, perhaps at the heart of that heart lies the notion that all words are inadequate for the representation of things. The poet as maker of metaphors may be seen as a genuine magician, bringing new things into the world, or as a charlatan pretending with feeble words to unite things that are essentially separate. Metaphor emphasizes the creative dimension of language, irony its tricky dimension.

For example, in Marvell's "To His Coy Mistress" the exaggerated protestations of the extent that the speaker's love would require "Had we but world enough and time" are all based on the view that of course we do *not* have world enough and time. Even before we get there, we sense the presence of the "But" on which the poem will make its turn:

But at my back I always hear
Time's winged chariot hurrying near;

The contrast between what the speaker *would* do:

Two hundred years should go to praise
Thine eyes, and on thy forehead gaze:
Two hundred to adore each breast:
And thirty thousand to the rest;

and what he *does* urge:

Now let us sport us while we may,

is an ironic one, enhanced by the extreme distance in time between hundreds or thousands of years and "Now." (Marvell's poem may be found in our Selection of Poets.)

Irony can also take the form of metaphorical overstatement, as it does in Alexander Pope's description of coffee being poured into a China cup:

From silver spouts the grateful liquors glide,
While China's earth receives the smoking tide.

These lines are metaphorical in that they present one thing (pouring a cup of coffee) in terms of another image (a kind of burning flood pouring over the mainland of China); but they are ironic in that the equation is made mainly so that we will perceive the disparity between the two images and enjoy their incongruity. Something of this reverse anti-metaphorical wit is present in many metaphors. John Donne's "The Flea" has a witty, ironic dimension derived from the inappropriateness of his basic image. To call a flea a temple is to establish a very far-fetched metaphor. The conceits used by Donne and other "metaphysical" poets of his time often have an ironic dimension.

Samuel Johnson characterized the metaphysical poets precisely in terms of this dimension—a special and extreme form of "wit" based on the "discovery of occult resemblances in things apparently unlike," and resulting in poems in which "the most heterogeneous ideas are yoked by violence together." Johnson's description emphasizes ("yoked by violence") the tension between metaphoric comparison and ironic contrast in many metaphysical conceits. Conceits tend to be witty, cerebral, unnatural; while metaphors are serious, imaginative, and natural. The metaphors of Romantic poetry are perceptions of relationships felt actually to exist. Metaphysical conceits often establish powerful but artificial relationships where one would least expect to find them.

Linking incongruous things is a feature of most kinds of witty poetry. A simple list with one incongruous element can serve to indict a whole way of life, as when Alexander Pope surveys the debris on a lady's dressing table:

Puffs, Powders, Patches, Bibles, Billet-doux

The inclusion of Bibles among love letters and cosmetics suggests a confusion between worldly and spiritual values—a failure to distinguish between true and false worth. The list is funny, but in an ironic and satiric way—as is this list of possible calamities from the same poem:

Whether the nymph shall break Diana's law,
Or some frail China jar receive a flaw;
Or stain her honour or her new brocade;
Forget her prayers or miss a masquerade;
Or lose her heart or necklace at a ball; . . .

Here Pope mixes several serious matters of the spirit with trivial and worldly items. The breaking of Diana's law of chastity is equated with damage to a jar. A single verb, "stain," governs two objects—"honour" and "brocade"—of different qualities and intensities. By this manipulation of grammar Pope makes us forcibly aware of the frivolousness of an attitude toward life which equates things that properly should have different values. He brings those two objects under that one verb so that we will feel a powerful urge to part them in our minds, resolving the incongruity by separating the elements he has brought together.

Another kind of incongruity is that achieved by Byron in such passages as this one, which presents a romantic lover trying to keep his mind on his beloved while his stomach is attacked by seasickness;

"Sooner shall heaven kiss earth—(here he fell sicker)
    Oh, Julia! what is every other woe?—
(For God's sake let me have a glass of liquor;
    Pedro, Battista, help me down below.)
Julia my love—(you rascal, Pedro, quicker)—
    Oh, Julia—(this curst vessel pitches so)—
Beloved Julia, hear me still beseeching!"
(Here he grew inarticulate with retching.)

The irony here is more a matter of drama than of language; but the difference between the language of the speaker's romantic assertions and his cries to his servants, supports the dramatic irony. The narrator points up the contrast by mis-rhyming "retching" with "beseeching" in the last two lines.

Beyond Metaphor and Irony

Much of the best contemporary poetry presents combinations of images and ideas so stretched and disconnected that they go beyond metaphor and yet so serious and appropriate they transcend irony also. The difficulty in understanding many modern poems stems from a profusion of images that seem ironically disconnected, but nevertheless suggest genuine metaphorical connection. We can find a relatively simple illustration in a few lines from a ballad by W. H. Auden entitled "As I Walked Out One Evening":

The glacier knocks in the cupboard,
  The desert sighs in the bed
And the crack in the tea-cup opens
  A lane to the land of the dead.

Here Auden seems to be operating with ironic incongruities—the glacier in the cupboard and so on—but this collection of incongruities adds up to a quite coherent statement about the absurd and empty horror that threatens much of modern life. Such a collection of images seems to combine qualities of conceit and symbol with ironic incongruity, leaving us to resolve the problem of whether these assertions are ironic overstatements or powerful metaphors for our condition.

A poem composed of a number of these high-tension ironic metaphors can be immediately intelligible in a general way and still difficult to reduce to prose sense at every point. But we should make the effort to establish prose sense—or possible prose senses—for each image and situation in such a poem, because even if we do not succeed entirely, we will be testing the ultimate intelligibility of the poem, the durability of its interest. As with certain kinds of modern art, it is sometimes hard to separate the fraudulent from the real in contemporary poetry. If we cannot discover intelligibility and coherence in a poem, if its images and situations do not enhance one another, we are confronted by either a fraudulent poem or a poem that is beyond us—one that we have not as yet learned how to read. Differences in poetic quality cannot be demonstrated conclusively, yet they exist. The following poem by a young American poet, William Knott, is offered as a problem in intelligibility and evaluation. Does it make sense? Does it work? Is it good?

Survival of the Fittest Groceries

The violence in the newspapers is pure genius
A daily gift to the reader
From some poet who wants to keep in good with us
Brown-noser wastepaperbasket-emptier

I shot 437 people that day
2 were still alive when I killed them
Why do people want to be exhumed movie-stars
I mean rats still biting them, the flesh of comets, why do they walk around like that?

I'm going to throw all of you into the refrigerator
10   And leave you to claw it out with the vegetables and meats

MUSIC

The musical element in poetry is the hardest to talk about because it is non-verbal. Our responses to rhythm and to pleasing combinations of sounds are in a sense too immediate, too fundamental to be comprehended in words. Yet music is important in all poetry, and for most poetry written before the last half-century it is crucial. Therefore, we must try to get some sort of verbal grasp of this poetical element, simply in order to do justice to most poetic achievement. Students generally prefer discussing one aspect of poetry to another in an order something like this:

1. ideas
2. situations
3. language
4. metrics

But if we are concerned about what makes poetry poetry rather than another kind of composition, we should probably reverse this order. If a piece of writing is neither especially rhythmical nor especially ironic or metaphorical in its language, it is not poetry, regardless of its dramatic situations or the ideas it presents.

In our experience, students are not only least interested in metrics of all the elements of poetry; they are also least competent in it. To demonstrate this, one need only ask them to translate a few sentences of prose into a simple, versified equivalent. Most will find this very difficult to do. No wonder they don't like poetry. They can't hear it properly. Fortunately, the fundamentals of versification are teachable to some extent, and should be part of any poetical curriculum. In the pages that follow, these fundamentals are presented in a fairly simple way, with a minimum of special terminology.

Metrics

Metrics has to do with all rhythmical effects in poetry. In English versification this means that it is largely a matter of accents and pauses. The pauses are determined by the usual grammatical principles that govern our speech and writing, and are indicated by the usual grammatical symbols: periods, commas, and so on. But one new factor is added. The end of a line of verse is itself a mark of punctuation. If a line ends with a regular mark of punctuation we call it *end-stopped*. If the last word of a line is followed by no punctuation and is part of a continuing grammatical unit like a prepositional phrase, we call the line *run-on*, or *enjambed*. In end-stopped lines, the line-end works *with* the punctuation and reinforces it, making each line a tight unit of thought. In enjambed lines the line-end works *against* the punctuation, throwing certain words into a prominence that they would not ordinarily have. The enjambed line really adds a special kind of poetical punctuation to the language: something at once more and less than a comma. Poets who use free verse forms with no regular rhythm are very dependent on enjambment to give their words a special poetical quality.

Reconsider the little poem by Williams:

so much depends
upon

a red wheel
barrow

glazed with rain
water

beside the white
chickens.

If we write this out as prose we get

So much depends upon a red wheelbarrow, glazed
with rainwater, beside the white chickens.

This is a simple, declarative prose sentence, with a couple of adjectival phrases tacked on, set off with commas. Has anything been lost by this rearrangement of the poem on the page? Decidedly so. The assertion being made is much less convincing in plain prose. The free-verse form of the sentence uses its line-endings to work against the prose movement, slowing it up, and providing a metrical equivalent for the visual highlighting of the images. Just where we would bring the words closest together in prose— making single words out of "wheel" and "barrow," "rain" and "water"— Williams has pulled them apart by breaking the line in mid-word.

The poem may or may not carry us to final agreement with its assertion, but in the free-verse form it certainly convinces us of the speaker's earnestness. We get a sense of how much he cares about what he is saying from the care with which he has spaced out his words. And when we read the poem aloud, with little pauses at line-ends, it carries us further toward conviction than the same sentence in its prosaic form.

That is a simple illustration of how poetry's special line-end punctuation can group words in a rhythm different from the rhythm of normal speech or prose. Here is a further illustration of how a poet can use the line-end to achieve an ironic effect virtually unduplicatable in prose. E. E. Cummings begins a poem this way:

pity this busy monster, manunkind,
not.

The first word of the second line absolutely reverses the meaning of the first line. We pause, with a comma, at the end of line 1. We stop entirely, with a period, after the first word of line 2. We hover, thus, with the wrong meaning until we are given the word that changes it, whereupon we stop to contemplate the admonition offered us in the whole opening sentence. Consider it rearranged as plain prose:

Pity this busy monster, manunkind, not.

or more prosaically,

Do not pity this busy monster, manunkind.

or still more prosaically,

Do not pity this busy, unkind monster, man.

By unraveling the poetical arrangement and combination of the words, we have destroyed the force of the admonition, taking away its suspense and eliminating the recoil in the original last word.

In verse that is not markedly rhythmical, unusual pauses and arrangements of words are the principal metrical device. In verse that is regularly rhythmical, however, the rhythm or meter itself is the crucial metrical element. Poetical arrangement does something to prosaic language, but not so much as does rhythm, which lifts an utterance and moves it in the direction of music. Just as the line-end pauses in a poem can work with or against the normal grammatical pauses of speech and prose, poetic rhythm can work both with and against our normal patterns of pronunciation.

In speech we begin with standard grammatical pronunciations for words. Take the word "defense." Normally we pronounce this word by accenting the first syllable lightly and the second syllable heavily. Indicating light accent by $\cup$ and heavy accent by $—$, we pronounce the word this way:

$\overset{\cup}{de}\overset{—}{fense}$. That is grammatical accent or grammatical stress. But in certain situations we might change this pronunciation for purposes of emphasis, as in, "It's not offense that's important, it's defense." Here we pronounce the word defense. This is not grammatical stress but rhetorical stress. We have altered the usual pattern of light and heavy accent in order to make a point. (Grammar, or course, keeps changing, and the repeated use of one particular rhetorical pattern can eventually alter standard pronunciation. Broadcasts of football and basketball games, for instance, are helping to make defense the standard way to accent the word.)

Both grammatical and rhetorical stress operate in poetry, where they are complicated by a third kind of accent, which we may call poetical stress. Poetical stress is a regular system of accents which establishes the basic rhythm of a poem. There are only two fundamental systems of poetic stress in English verse, though they have many variations. Most frequently, English verse simply alternates light and heavy accents, giving every other syllable the same stress. Like this:

The woods decay, the woods decay and fall

Less frequently, English verse uses two light syllables between each heavy stress. Like this:

The Assyrian came down like the wolf on the fold

And his cohorts were gleaming in purple and gold

The rhythm of this second metrical pattern is more insistent than that of the first. The simple da-dum, da-dum of "The woods decay" is more like the spoken language than the da-da-dum, da-da-dum of "like the wolf on the fold."

When discussing metrics it is useful to have a term for the units that are repeated to make the pattern. It is customary to call these units *feet*. In the first example above, we have five repeated units in the line, five feet divided this way:

The woods | decay, | the woods | decay | and fall

In the second example each line has four feet, divided like this:

And his co | horts were gleam | ing in pur | ple and gold

In describing metrical patterns we usually state the number of feet in the basic line and name the standard foot in each line. The traditional name for the foot used in the first example (da-dum) is the *iamb*. The traditional name for the foot used in the second example (da-da-dum) is the *anapest*. In referring to the number of feet in the basic line of a poem, it is customary to use numerical prefixes derived from the Greek. Thus,

```
one-foot line  =  mono  + meter  = monometer
two-foot line  =    di  + meter  = dimeter
three-foot line =   tri  + meter  = trimeter
four-foot line  = tetra  + meter  = tetrameter
five-foot line  = penta  + meter  = pentameter
six-foot line  =  hexa  + meter  = hexameter
```

We could skip the Greek and talk about such things as "lines with ten syllables that go da-dum" and so on, but it is finally easier to learn the accepted terms and say simply "iambic pentameter."

The iamb and the anapest each have a variant foot which is made by placing the accented syllable at the beginning of each foot rather than at the end. These are called the *trochee* (dum-da) and the *dactyl* (dum-da-da). They are not used very consistenly for one good reason. Rhyme in poetry is pleasing only if it includes the last accented syllable in a line *and all the unaccented syllables that follow it.* Thus, if you write,

Upon a mid | night drear | y once

You need find only a one-syllable rhyme for your rhyming line, such as:

Upon a midnight dreary once
I tried my hand at kicking punts

But if you use the trochee, and write

Once u | pon a | midnight | dreary

then you must rhyme

Once upon a midnight dreary
Of kicking punts my foot was weary.

The trochaic foot can, in fact, grow quite wearisome if carried through to the rhyme word consistently; so we often get a variation that looks like this:

Tiger, Tiger burning bright

In the forests of the night

These lines first appear trochaic (dum-da) and end by looking iambic (da-dum). (Though, actually the second line is more complicated in a way we will consider later on.) The two lines could be made fully iambic by a very slight change in each:

O, Tiger, Tiger burning bright

Within the forest of the night

or we could make them fully trochaic by this kind of alteration:

Tiger, Tiger burning brightly,

Roaming through the forest nightly

In order to name the metrical pattern of "Tiger, Tiger" we must supply an imaginary unaccented syllable at one end of the line or the other, like this:

x Ti | ger, Ti | ger, burn | ing bright

or this:

Tiger, | Tiger, | burning | bright x |

These maneuverings strongly suggest that the special terminology of metrical analysis is not important in itself, and that beyond the major distinction between the two-syllable foot and the three-syllable foot, we need not be terribly fussy in classifying. What, then, is the use of all these special terms?

The art of metrics involves a poet's ability to generate and maintain a consistent meter without destroying normal patterns of grammar and syntax. To succeed metrically a poet must make language dance without making it unnatural. And a really crucial aspect of this art is perceptible only when we have the terminology to recognize it. Any absolutely regular meter quickly becomes boring through repetition. But a totally irregular poem is totally without the kind of interest and pleasure that rhythm provides.

All good poets who work in regular meters introduce metrical variations into their poems. The simplest way to understand this is to see the variations as substitutions of a different sort of foot for the one called for by the established meter of the poem. (The second line of Blake's "Tiger, Tiger" is not quite the same as the first. Can you devise alternative ways to describe its rhythm? The whole poem may be found in our Selection of Poets.) As an example of metrical variation, consider this stanza from a poem by A. E. Housman:

With rue my heart is laden

For golden friends I had

For many a rose-lipt maiden

And many a lightfoot lad.

The meter is basically iambic, complicated a little by the extra syllable of a feminine rhyme in alternate lines (laden, maiden—two-syllable rhymes are called *feminine*). But the basic meter is varied by the addition of one anapestic foot in lines three and four.

The second (and last) stanza of that poem goes like this:

By brooks too broad for leaping
    The lightfoot boys are laid;
The rose-lipt girls are sleeping
    In fields where roses fade.

This looks almost absolutely regular—iambic trimeter with alternate feminine rhyme—but it is not quite. Both grammar and rhetoric urge us to accent and elongate the sound of the word "too" in the first line. Thus the line must be scanned (analyzed metrically) this way:

by brooks | too broad | for leaping

The second foot of this line has two accented syllables and no unaccented one. This is a kind of foot that is often used as a substitute but never as the metrical basis for a whole poem. Its technical name is *spondee*. Housman has used the spondee here for a slight variation of his rhythm—one that is almost unnoticeable to the analytic eye but works subtly on the ear to prevent the rhythm from becoming monotonous.

Having noticed that substitution, we might notice also that in both stanzas the words "lightfoot" and "rose-lipt" work gently in a spondaic direction. In both stanzas these words appear so that the heavy accent of the iamb falls on their first syllable. But that second syllable is a word in its own right, and one that might well take a heavy accent in another metrical situation, such as this:

⌣ — ⌣ — ⌣
My foot is weary,

⌣ — ⌣ — ⌣
My eye is teary,

⌣ — ⌣ — ⌣
My lip is beery.

"Foot" and "lip" (or "lipt") can both take heavy accents. In Housman's stanzas the syllables "foot" and "lipt," falling where we would expect light accents, actually result in something between heavy and light.

The basic terminology of metrical analysis establishes only the simple distinction between heavy and light, thus it cannot take us too far into any metrical subtleties. In scansion, however, we need to consider subtleties, and should probably be ready to use at least one more symbol to indicate a stress between heavy and light. Using a combination of the two stress marks we already have in operation to indicate an intermediate stress, we might re-scan the first stanza this way:

⌣̄ — ⌣ — ⌣̄ — ⌣
With rue my heart is laden

⌣ — ⌣ — ⌣̄ —
for golden friends I had,

⌣ — ⌣⌣ — ⌣̄ — ⌣
For many a rose-lipt maiden

⌣ — ⌣⌣ — ⌣̄ —
And many a lightfoot lad.

Then we could point out that the intermediate accents on lipt and foot make the last feet of lines 3 and 4 partially spondaic.

Thus far we have considered the metrics of this little poem only in terms of its pleasing variation within a firmly established pattern. We can see how the pattern is established in the first two lines of the first stanza, and then varies subtly in most of the succeeding lines, until the pattern reasserts itself in the perfectly regular last line. Now, we are in a position to deal with the question of the relation of the metrics to the meaning of the poem. The poem makes a simple statement about sadness felt for the death of those who were once agile and pretty. But death is never mentioned. It is evoked metaphorically through words like "laid" and "sleeping." These metaphors are very gentle, suggesting more the peace of the grave than any decay or destruction. In the second stanza the speaker also suggests delicately the frustration and sadness felt by those in the world of the living. The unleapable brooks symbolize things unachievable in life; the fading roses symbolize the impermanence of living things. The peace of the dead is ironically contrasted with the sadness of the living. The speaker is finally rueful not just because his golden friends are dead but because *he* is alive.

How does the meter relate to all this? Iambic trimeter calls for a good deal of rhyme—a rhyming sound every third foot. The addition of feminine rhymes in alternate lines makes for even more rhyming syllables. If we compare this metrical situation with that in another poem (by Ben Jonson) about death and decay, we should notice something about the effect of meter.

Slow, slow, fresh fount, keep time with my salt tears;
   Yet slower, yet; O faintly gentle springs;
List to the heavy part the music bears,
   Woe weeps out her division when she sings:
     Droop herbs and flowers;
     Fall grief in showers;
     Our beauties are not ours.
      O, I could still,
Like melting snow upon some craggy hill,
    Drop, drop, drop, drop,
Since nature's pride is now a withered daffodil.

How should this first line be scanned? Something like this:

$$\bar{}\ \bar{}\ \mid\ \bar{}\ \bar{}\ \mid\ \breve{}\ \bar{}\ \mid\ \cup\ \cup\ \mid\ \bar{}\ \bar{}$$
Slow, slow, | fresh fount, | keep time | with my | salt tears;

Here we have that rarity, a line almost completely spondaic—with only a suggestion of iambs in the third and fourth feet. An iambic pattern establishes itself gradually in the poem, but the verse is dominated by spondees, even in the short lines:

$$\bar{}\quad\bar{}\quad\cup\ \bar{}\ (\cup)$$
Droop herbs and flowers;

$$\bar{}\ \bar{}\ \cup\ \bar{}\ (\cup)$$
Fall grief in showers;

$$\bar{}\ \bar{}\ \cup\ \bar{}\ \bar{}\ \text{-}\ (\cup)$$
Our beauties are not ours.[1]

In addition to this spondaic domination, the lines are frequently broken by pauses—those indicated by the punctuation, as well as those which naturally follow imperatives like "droop" and "fall." These pauses and the spondees work together to give the poem a slow, hesitant, funereal movement like the sound of muffled drums. This meter works in a metaphoric or harmonious relation to the sense of the poem, which is a direct utterance of grief over seasonal decay and the death it symbolizes.

    Now, how does this compare to the movement of the Housman poem? Housman's iambic trimeter, virtually pauseless except for line-ends, is a much lighter, almost gay meter. The stresses bounce regularly, the lines

1. These rhyme words can all be scanned as either one or two syllables.

flow smoothly, the rhymes chime insistently. This pattern establishes an ironic or contrasting relation to the mournful sense of the words, but is perfectly appropriate because the words themselves are finally ironic. Housman deals with death lightly, easily, if wryly. Jonson works hard to make us respond seriously and sadly. The frequent pauses, the heavy spondees, the varying length of the lines—all these work to reinforce the sadness and seriousness of Jonson's words. Both poems have a pronounced musical dimension, but Housman's is like a spritely ballad meter and Jonson's is like a funeral dirge.

Before considering rhyme and other sound effects further, we need to look at one last important dimension of metrics. The standard line of English verse which is meant to be spoken rather than sung is a line of five iambic feet—iambic pentameter. This is the basic line of Chaucer's *Canterbury Tales*, of Spenser's *Faerie Queene*, of Shakespeare's plays, of Milton's *Paradise Lost*, of the satires of Dryden and Pope, of Byron's *Don Juan*, of Wordsworth's *Prelude*, of Browning's *The Ring and the Book*. This line often appears unrhymed, as in Shakespeare's plays (for the most part), *Paradise Lost*, and *The Prelude;* or in pairs of rhymed lines. Technically, the unrhymed iambic pentameter line is called blank verse; the paired rhymes are called couplets. In both these iambic pentameter lines, an important element is the mid-line pause or *caesura*. Varying the location of the *caesura* is an important way of preventing monotony in blank verse and pentameter couplets. Consider, for example, these opening lines of Book II of *Paradise Lost:*

> High on a Throne of Royal State, which far
> Outshone the wealth of *Ormus* and of *Ind,*
> Or where the gorgeous East with richest hand
> Show'rs on her Kings *Barbaric* Pearl and Gold,
> Satan exalted sat, by merit rais'd
> To that bad eminence; and from despair
> Thus high uplifted beyond hope, aspires
> Beyond thus high, insatiate to pursue
> Vain war with Heav'n, and by success untaught
> 10 His proud imaginations thus display'd.

If we locate the obvious *caesurae*—those indicated by internal punctuation marks—we find this situation:

> line 1 . . . end of 4th foot
> line 2 . . . none
> line 3 . . . none
> line 4 . . . none
> line 5 . . . end of 3rd foot
> line 6 . . . end of 3rd foot

line 7 . . . end of 4th foot
line 8 . . . end of 2nd foot
line 9 . . . end of 2nd foot
line 10 . . . none

In reading the poem aloud, we will find ourselves pausing slightly, at some point in nearly every line, whether a pause is indicated by punctuation or not. Thus, we can mark the whole passage this way, using a single slash for a slight pause and two for a noticeable one, three for a full stop.

High on a throne of Royal State,// which far
Outshone/ the wealth of *Ormus*/ and of *Ind*,
Or where the gorgeous East/ with richest hand
Show'rs on her kings/ *Barbaric* Pearl and Gold,
Satan exalted sat,// by merit rais'd
To that bad eminence;/// and from despair
Thus high uplifted beyond hope,// aspires
Beyond thus high,// insatiate to pursue
Vain war with Heav'n,// and by success untaught
10 His proud imaginations/ thus display'd.

By varying end-stopped lines with enjambed, and deploying caesurae of varying strengths at different points in his line, Milton continually shifts his pauses to prevent the march of his lines from growing wearisome. He also uses substitute feet frequently—especially a trochee or spondee in the first foot of a line. We count three trochees and one spondee in the first feet of these ten lines. Check this count yourself.

Now consider Alexander Pope's use of enjambment, caesura, and substitution of feet in the following lines. Pope uses a tight form, with punctuation coming nearly always at the end of each couplet. These closed couplets (as opposed to enjambed or open couplets) in iambic pentameter are called "heroic" couplets because they were the standard verse form of Restoration heroic drama (but they might better be called satiric, because they have been most successful in the satiric poems of Dryden, Pope, and Samuel Johnson).

In such a tight form as the heroic couplet, great skill is needed to avoid monotony. When we read only the real masters of such a form, we tend to take such skill for granted, but it is far from easy. Here we find Pope talking about poetic blunders and poetic skill, modulating his own verse deftly to illustrate the points he is making. (The *Alexandrine* referred to is an iambic hexameter line, occasionally used for variety in English iambic pentameter forms.) These two passages from Pope's "Essay on Criticism" are printed here widely spaced, to allow the student to write in his or her own scansion.

These equal syllables alone require,
Though oft the ear the open vowels tire;
While expletives their feeble aid do join;
And ten low words oft creep in one dull line:
While they ring round the same unvaried chimes,
With sure returns of still expected rhymes;
Where'er you find "the cooling western breeze,"
In the next line, it "whispers through the trees:"
If crystal streams "with pleasing murmurs creep,"
10 The reader's threatened (not in vain) with "sleep:"
Then, at the last and only couplet fraught
With some unmeaning thing they call a thought,
A needless Alexandrine ends the song
That, like a wounded snake, drags its slow length along.

True ease in writing comes from art, not chance,
As those move easiest who have learned to dance.
'Tis not enough no harshness gives offence,
The sound must seem an Echo to the sense:
Soft is the strain when Zephyr gently blows,
And the smooth stream in smoother numbers flows;
But when loud surges lash the sounding shore,
The hoarse, rough verse should like the torrent roar:
When Ajax strives some rock's vast weight to throw,
10 The line too labours, and the words move slow;
Not so, when swift Camilla scours the plain,
Flies o'er th' unbending corn, and skims along the main.

Rhyme is an important element in musical poetry, but much less so in dramatic poetry—where it can be too artificial—or in meditative poetry. Associated with rhyme as elements designed to generate a pleasure in sound which is almost purely aesthetic are such devices as alliteration and assonance. Alliteration is the repetition of the same sound at the beginning of words in the same line or adjacent lines. Assonance is the repetition of vowel sounds in the same or adjacent lines. For full rhyme we require the same vowel sounds which end in the same consonantal sounds. "Fight" and "foot" are alliterative. "Fight" and "bike" are assonant. "Fight" and "fire" are both assonant and alliterative but do not make a rhyme. "Fight" and "bite" make a rhyme. Consider the metrical and sonic effects in this stanza of a poem by Swinburne:

Till the slow sea rise and the sheer cliff crumble,
   Till terrace and meadow the deep gulfs drink,
Till the strength of the waves of the high tides humble
   The fields that lessen, the rocks that shrink,
Here now in his triumph where all things falter,
   Stretched out on the spoils that his own hand spread,
As a god self-slain on his own strange altar,
      Death lies dead.

The meter is mainly a mixture of anapests and spondees—an exotic combination of rapid and slow feet. Can you discern any particular pattern in the way the feet are combined? Is there variation in the pattern? What do rhyme, assonance, and alliteration contribute to the pattern?

In addition to its purely aesthetic or decorative effect, designed to charm the reader out of a critical posture and into a receptive one, rhyme can be used for just the opposite effect. In satiric or comic verse, strained rhymes are often used to awaken the reader's wits and give him a comic kind of pleasure. Ogden Nash often combines strained rhymes with lines of awkwardly unequal length for especially absurd effects. But something similar can be achieved within fairly strict formal limits. In the following stanza from Byron's *Don Juan*, we find the poet using feminine and even triple rhyme with deliberate clumsiness:

'Tis pity learned virgins ever wed
   With persons of no sort of education,
Or gentlemen, who, though well born and bred,
   Grow tired of scientific conversation:
I don't choose to say much upon this head,
   I'm a plain man, and in a single station,
But—Oh! ye lords of ladies intellectual,
Inform us truly, have they not hen-peck'd you all?

The last rhyme in particular is surprising, audacious, and deliberately strained—echoing in this way the sense of the stanza. Like imagery and metrics, rhyme can be used harmoniously or ironically, to establish or to break a mood.

Before closing, we should note that it is customary to indicate the rhyme scheme of any given poetic selection by assigning letters of the alphabet to each rhyming sound, repeating each letter as the sound is repeated. The rhyme scheme of the Byron stanza we just considered would be designated this way: *ababababcc*, with *a* standing for the sounds in *wed*, *bred*, and *head*; *b*, for . . . *ation*; and *c*, for . . . *ectual* and . . . *eck'd you all*. And in the Swinburne quoted just above, the rhyme scheme is simply *ababcdcd*.

Approaching a Poem

We do not, if we are honest, keep in readiness a number of different approaches to poems or to people. We try to keep our integrity. But at the same time we must recognize and accept the otherness that we face. In getting to know a person or a poem we make the kind of accommodation that we have called tact. But we do not pretend, we do not emote falsely, and we try not to make stock responses to surface qualities. We do not judge a man by his clothes or even by his skin. We do not judge a poem by words or ideas taken out of their full poetic context. We do not consider a statement in a poem without attention to its dramatic context, the overtones generated by its metaphors and ironies, the mood established by its metrics. And we try to give each element of every poem its proper weight.

Obviously, there can be no single method for treating every poem with tact. What is required is a flexible procedure through which we can begin to understand the nature of any poem. The suggestions below are intended to facilitate such a procedure. Like everything else in this book they should serve as a scaffolding only—a temporary structure inside of which the real building takes shape. Like any scaffolding, this one must be discarded as soon as it becomes constricting or loses its usefulness. Like good manners learned by rote, this procedure will never amount to anything until it is replaced by naturally tactful behavior. Then it will have served its purpose.

1. Try to grasp the expressive dimension of the poem first. This means especially getting a clear sense of the nature and situation of the speaker. What are the circumstances under which he or she says, writes, or thinks these words? Who hears them? Are they part of an ongoing action which is implied by them?

2. Consider the relative importance of the narrative-dramatic dimension and the descriptive-meditative dimension in the poem. Is the main interest psychological or philosophical—in character or in idea? Or is the poem's verbal playfulness or music its main reason for being? How do the nature of the speaker and the situation in which he speaks color the ideas and attitudes presented?

3. After you have a sense of the poem's larger, expressive dimension, re-read it with particular attention to the play of language. Consider the way that metaphor and irony color the ideas and situations. How does the language work to characterize the speaker or to color the ideas presented with shadings of attitude? How important is sheer word-play

or verbal wit in the poem? How well do the images and ideas fit together and reinforce one another in a metaphoric or ironic way?

4. Re-read the poem yet again with special attention to its musical dimension. To the extent that it seems important, analyze the relation of rhythm and rhyme to the expressive dimension of the poem.

5. Throughout this process, reading the poem aloud can be helpful in establishing emphases and locating problems. Parts of a poem that are not fully understood will prove troublesome in the reading. Questions of tone and attitude will become more insistent in oral performance. Thus, it is advisable to work toward a reading performance as a final check on the degree to which we have mastered situation, ideas, images, attitudes, and music. An expert may be able to read through a piece of piano music and hear in his mind a perfect performance of it. Most of us need to tap out the notes before we can grasp melodies, harmonies, and rhythms with any sureness. Reading poetry aloud helps us to establish our grasp of it—especially if a patient and knowledgeable teacher is there to correct our performance and encourage us to try again.

One last piece of advice, in the form of some lines by the Spanish poet Antonio Machado, translated by Robert Bly:

People possess four things
that are no good at sea
anchor, rudder, oars
and the fear of going down.

A Selection of Poets

INTRODUCTION

The poems collected here are intended as an introduction to the work of twenty-nine poets. For each we have provided at least five poems: enough for a student to get some sense of how that poet uses the English language to create poetry. We have not attempted to provide translations from other languages, since a translation into English must either become a new poem or fail utterly. Poetry, as Robert Frost remarked, is what gets lost in translation.

The poets are presented in the chronological order of their birth dates. They range in time and place from William Shakespeare, who wrote his sonnets in England before the year 1590, to Michael Harper, a black American whose first volume of poetry was published in 1970. Still, this is not a "history of poetry in English." What this collection is and what it is not should be clarified here.

These selections do not constitute anyone's choice of the greatest English and American poets. Some of the greatest, indeed, have been excluded here. Spenser, Milton, and Pope—to name but three—were omitted for the reason that most of their best work is found in long poems, and even their shorter works are inaccessible to the beginning student of poetry without a deadening amount of annotation. (Along with others not anthologized here, these three poets are, however, represented in the discussion of poetic elements just completed; and all poets represented are listed in the Index.)

In other cases we have excluded certain poets in order to be able to include more work by the poets who are represented here. That is to say, we have reduced the number of poets who might have been "covered" in order to give adequate representation to each poet whose work is included. Every good poet has a style of his or her own, an idiom that we come to recognize as we read more than a poem or two by that poet. This process is important, for as we master a poet's language and become at ease with it, our understanding and pleasure deepen—and our own linguistic skill grows with such mastery.

This selection deliberately emphasizes modern poetry—and particularly the poetry of twentieth-century America. Modern American poetry has been emphasized partly because it is so rich and varied and vigorous, partly because it requires less annotation for modern American students than the poetry of other times and places. If it is sometimes "difficult," the difficulties are chiefly such as will respond better to careful reading than to research. The world out of which it comes and to which it refers is, after all, our own.

Still, we have sought to represent adequately the important pre-modern schools of lyric poetry: the Petrarchan sonnet sequence in Shakespeare, metaphysical poetry in Donne and Marvell, Cavalier verse in Herrick, Romantic and Victorian English poetry in Blake, Wordsworth, Keats, Tennyson, and Browning. All these poets have much that is important to say to us, and they have said it in words that can outlive, as Shakespeare said, "the gilded monuments of princes."

"Modern" poetry, as we understand it, begins in the nineteenth century—even while Queen Victoria was still on her throne—with Whitman and Dickinson in the United States, Hopkins, Housman, and Yeats in England and Ireland. But there is always a continuity. Poets have always learned their craft from the work of their admired predecessors. For the student of poetry the trail leads ever backward until it crosses over to the continent of Europe; for the earliest English poets learned much from the poets of Italy, Rome, and Greece, and the Biblical Psalmists, whose rhythms still echo in contemporary American writing. There are worlds here, to be entered and enjoyed, since each poet offers us, in Donne's words, "a little world made cunning / Of elements." Enter and enjoy!

WILLIAM SHAKESPEARE
1564–1616

With a Note on the Sonnet

The sonnet was invented by Italians to plague Englishmen—or so some poets have maintained. It is a special form of verse that requires a good deal of intricate rhyming—which is easier to do in Italian than in English. Nevertheless, once domesticated in the sixteenth century, the sonnet form has persisted in English poetry with surprising vigor and is still alive today, though at its lowest ebb in four hundred years. Its rules are relatively few. A fourteen-line sequence of iambic pentameter verse has become the norm, even though the early sonneteers did not always adhere to this measure. The tightest rhyme schemes require just four or five sounds, in one combination or another, at the end of all fourteen lines.

In structure, most sonnets may be seen as variations on two basic patterns—and these are patterns of thought as well as of grammar and rhyme. One pattern is called *Italian* (or *Petrarchan* after its first important practitioner), the other *English* (or *Shakespearean*). In the Petrarchan structure the poem is divided into two major units of thought, syntax, and rhyme: the first eight lines, called the *octave*, and the last six, called the *sestet*. Here is an example of a Petrarchan sonnet by an American poet of the nineteenth century: Henry Wadsworth Longfellow's "Milton."

I pace the sounding sea-beach and behold
How the voluminous billows roll and run,
Upheaving and subsiding, while the sun
Shines through their sheeted emerald far unrolled
And the ninth wave, slow gathering fold by fold
All its loose-flowing garments into one,
Plunges upon the shore, and floods the dun
Pale reach of sands, and changes them to gold.
So in majestic cadence rise and fall
The mighty undulations of thy song,
O sightless Bard, England's Mæonides!
And ever and anon, high over all
Uplifted, a ninth wave superb and strong,
Floods all the soul with its melodious seas.

Longfellow uses the octet for a single sentence that flows on—barely slowed by punctuation (a few commas)—until the mighty wave it describes breaks in the seventh and eighth lines. The sestet then turns the wave into an epic simile describing the epic poet Milton's verse. Actually, the sestet is composed of two sentences, each of three lines. The rhyme scheme is very strict: *a bb a bb a* for the octet, and *c e d c e d* for the sestet. Thus, the rhymes, the sentence-structure, and the thought patterns all reinforce one another.

John Milton (1608–1674) himself tended to work in a quite different way. Although he composed sonnets in both Italian and English, following a variety of rhyme schemes, he did not work often or comfortably in this form. His most regular sonnets are on subjects of trivial consequence, and when he wrote on a subject of great importance to him he was apt to set his syntax working against the sonnet form, just as he breaks the iambic line with heavy pauses when writing long narrative poems (as our discussion of a passage from *Paradise Lost* on pp. 556–57 indicates). Here is a sonnet that Milton wrote on his own blindness. While it is less regular than Longfellow's, it concludes with one of those "ninth wave" lines of which Longfellow wrote—a line so memorable that it has become a permanent part of the language.

When I consider how my light is spent
Ere half my days, in this dark world and wide,
And that one talent which is death to hide,
Lodged with me useless, though my soul more bent
To serve therewith my Maker, and present
My true account, lest he returning chide,
"Doth God exact day-labour, light denied?"
I fondly ask; but Patience, to prevent
That murmur, soon replies, "God doth not need
Either man's work or his own gifts; who best
Bear his mild yoke, they serve him best. His state
Is kingly. Thousands at his bidding speed
And post o'er land and ocean without rest:
They also serve who only stand and wait."

In the Shakespearean sonnet the poem's fourteen lines are divided into twelve and two, and end with a rhymed couplet. In the hands of Shakespeare himself the couplet is a potent force: the whole meaning of a poem may turn on it. The first twelve lines, as we saw in sonnet 73 (discussed on pp. 536–37 above) may be subdivided in various ways, often into three quatrains, so that the whole poem will rhyme *abab cdcd efef gg*, and each of the four rhyming units will be a separate grammatical and conceptual unit as well—either a whole sentence or a major independent clause.

When the English borrowed (or stole) the sonnet from Italy they acquired a special "Petrarchan" subject matter along with the form. A true Petrarchan sonneteer might produce a whole sequence of sonnets—a hundred or more—devoted to a single subject matter: the poet's love for a lady who refuses to accept him as her lover. (See, for example, Sidney's sonnet 49 from *Astrophil and Stella*, quoted above, p. 542.) The poet describes his sufferings at great length—his fever, chills, pallor—and the lady's beauties at similar length. Often this description takes the form of a "blazon," which is a formal recounting of said beauties, one by one: eyes, nose, lips, teeth, bosom, and so on. Relics of the blazon are found in many love poems written after the English poets had escaped the domination of Italy. Shakespeare himself toyed with the Petrarchan conventions, writing to a man about his "beauties" and refusing to depict his "mistress" in the conventional way.

The Shakespearean form has been the most popular among English poets, and they have turned it to a variety of uses, serious and frivolous. We shall give one of these poets the last word on the sonnet at this point, after a reminder to watch for the progress of the sonnet throughout this anthology, noting its transformations in the modern poets. Gerard Manley Hopkins wrote sonnets in a slightly disguised form, as the attentive reader will discover. Here is William Wordsworth's view of the sonnet, expressed in Shakespearean form. The names mentioned by Wordsworth include some Italian poets of the Middle Ages and Renaissance, and the Portugese poet Camöens, as well as England's Shakespeare, Spenser, and Milton.

Scorn not the Sonnet; Critic, you have frowned,
Mindless of its just honours; with this key
Shakespeare unlocked his heart; the melody
Of this small lute gave ease to Petrarch's wound;
A thousand times this pipe did Tasso sound;
With it Camöens soothed an exile's grief;
The Sonnet glittered a gay myrtle leaf
Amid the cypress with which Dante crowned
His visionary brow: a glow-worm lamp,
It cheered mild Spenser, called from Faery-land
To struggle through dark ways; and when a damp
Fell round the path of Milton, in his hand
The Thing became a trumpet; whence he blew
Soul-animating strains—alas, too few!

Shakespeare's Sonnets

18

Shall I compare thee to a summer's day?
Thou art more lovely and more temperate.
Rough winds do shake the darling buds of May,
And summer's lease hath all too short a date.
Sometime too hot the eye of heaven shines,

And often is his gold complexion dimmed;
And every fair from fair sometimes declines,
By chance, or nature's changing course, untrimmed:
But thy eternal summer shall not fade
10   Nor lose possession of that fair thou ow'st,
Nor shall Death brag thou wand'rest in his shade
When in eternal lines to time thou grow'st.
    So long as men can breathe or eyes can see,
    So long lives this, and this gives life to thee.

29

When, in disgrace with Fortune and men's eyes,
I all alone beweep my outcast state,
And trouble deaf heaven with my bootless cries
And look upon myself and curse my fate,
Wishing me like to one more rich in hope,
Featured like him, like him with friends possessed,
Desiring this man's art, and that man's scope,
With what I most enjoy contented least;
Yet in these thoughts myself almost despising,
10   Haply I think on thee, and then my state,
Like to the lark at break of day arising
From sullen earth, sings hymns at heaven's gate;
    For thy sweet love remembered such wealth brings
    That then I scorn to change my state with kings.

55

Not marble nor the gilded monuments
Of princes shall outlive this powerful rime,
But you shall shine more bright in these contents
Than unswept stone, besmeared with sluttish time.
When wasteful war shall statues overturn,
And broils root out the work of masonry,
Nor Mars his sword nor war's quick fire shall burn
The living record of your memory.
'Gainst death and all oblivious enmity
10   Shall you pace forth; your praise shall still find room
Even in the eyes of all posterity
That wear this world out to the ending doom.
    So, till the judgment that yourself arise,
    You live in this, and dwell in lovers' eyes.

65

Since brass, nor stone, nor earth, nor boundless sea,
But sad mortality o'ersways their power,
How with this rage shall beauty hold a plea,
Whose action is no stronger than a flower?
O, how shall summer's honey breath hold out
Against the wrackful siege of batt'ring days,
When rocks impregnable are not so stout,
Nor gates of steel so strong but Time decays?
O fearful meditation: where, alack,
10   Shall Time's best jewel from Time's chest lie hid?
Or what strong hand can hold his swift foot back,
Or who his spoil of beauty can forbid?
    O, none, unless this miracle have might,
    That in black ink my love may still shine bright.

94

They that have power to hurt and will do none,
That do not do the thing they most do show,
Who, moving others, are themselves as stone,
Unmovèd, cold, and to temptation slow;
They rightly do inherit heaven's graces
And husband nature's riches from expense;
They are the lords and owners of their faces,
Others but stewards of their excellence.
The summer's flower is to the summer sweet,
10   Though to itself it only live and die;
But if that flower with base infection meet,
The basest weed outbraves his dignity:
    For sweetest things turn sourest by their deeds;
    Lilies that fester smell far worse than weeds.

130

My mistress' eyes are nothing like the sun;
Coral is far more red than her lips' red;
If snow be white, why then her breasts are dun;
If hairs be wires, black wires grow on her head.
I have seen roses damasked, red and white,
But no such roses see I in her cheeks;
And in some perfumes is there more delight

Than in the breath that from my mistress reeks.
I love to hear her speak; yet well I know
10   That music hath a far more pleasing sound:
I grant I never saw a goddess go;
My mistress, when she walks, treads on the ground.
   And yet, by heaven, I think my love as rare
   As any she belied with false compare.

JOHN DONNE
1573–1631

With a Note on Metaphysical Poetry

We have learned to call a certain group of seventeenth-century English poets "metaphysical" because of Dr. Samuel Johnson, the eighteenth-century critic, poet, and lexicographer, who complained that these poets used strained and unnatural language in which heterogeneous ideas were "yoked by violence together." Johnson's adjective has stuck to these poets, even though his criticism of them is not always accepted. Donne, in particular, has been a favorite of modern readers, perhaps because in his work the metaphysical impulse is always colored by strong erotic or religious feeling. His love poetry is no Petrarchan ritual, nor is his religious poetry in any way perfunctory. In Donne's view, God himself, as Creator of this world and Author of the Bible, was a kind of "metaphysical" poet, too, as we can see in this quotation from one of Donne's *Devotions*, a sequence of prose meditations he wrote during a serious illness. Donne's words describe the metaphysical impulse perfectly. They are worth the close attention they require.

From **Devotion 19**

My God, my God, thou art a direct God, may I not say a literal God, a God that wouldst be understood literally and according to the plain sense of all that thou sayest? but thou art also (Lord, I intend it to thy glory, and let no profane misinterpreter abuse it to thy diminution), thou art a figurative, a metaphorical God too; a God in whose words there is such a height of figures, such voyages, such peregrinations to fetch remote and precious metaphors, such extensions, such spreadings, such curtains of allegories, such third heavens of hyperboles, so harmonious elocutions, so retired and so reserved expressions, so commanding persuasions, so persuading commandments, such sinews even in thy milk, and such things in thy words, as all profane authors seem of the seed of the serpent that creeps, thou art the Dove that flies. O, what words but thine can express the inexpressible texture and composition of thy word, in which to one man that argument that binds his faith to believe that to be the word of God, is the reverent simplicity of the word, and to another the majesty of the word; and in which two men equally pious may meet, and one wonder that all should not understand it, and the other as much that any man should. So, Lord, thou givest us the same earth to labour on and to lie in, a house and a grave of the same earth; so, Lord, thou givest us the same word for our satisfaction and for our inquisition, for our instruction and for our admiration too; for there are places that thy servants Hierom[1] and Augustine would scarce believe (when they grew warm by mutual letters) of one another, that they understood them, and yet both Hierom and Augustine call upon persons whom they knew to be far weaker than they thought one another (old women and young maids) to read the Scriptures, without confining them to these or those places. Neither art thou thus a figurative, a metaphorical God in thy word only, but in thy works too. The style of thy works, the phrase of thine actions, is metaphorical. The institution of thy whole worship in the old law was a continual allegory; types and figures overspread all, and figures flowed into figures, and poured themselves out into farther figures; circumcision carried a figure of baptism, and baptism carries a figure of that purity which we shall have in perfection in the new Jerusalem. Neither didst thou speak and work in this language only in the time of thy prophets; but since thou spokest in thy Son it is so too. How often, how much more often, doth thy Son call himself a way, and a light, and a gate, and a vine, and bread, than the Son of God, or of man? How much oftener doth he exhibit a metaphorical Christ, than a real, a literal? This hath occasioned thine ancient servants, whose delight it was to write after thy copy, to proceed the same way in their expositions of the Scriptures, and in their composing both of public liturgies and of private prayers to thee, to make their accesses to thee in such a kind of language as thou wast pleased to speak to them, in a figurative, in a metaphorical language, in which manner I am bold to call the comfort which I receive now in this sickness in the indication of the concoction and maturity thereof, in certain clouds and recidences, which the physicians observe, a discovering of land from sea after a long and tempestuous voyage.

1. St. Jerome, like St. Augustine, one of the early Fathers of the Church

Love Poems

The Good Morrow

I wonder, by my troth, what thou and I
Did, till we loved? Were we not weaned till then,
But sucked on country pleasures, childishly?
Or snorted we in the seven sleepers' den?
'Twas so; but this, all pleasures fancies be.
If ever any beauty I did see,
Which I desired, and got, 'twas but a dream of thee.

And now good morrow to our waking souls,
Which watch not one another out of fear;
10   For love all love of other sights controls,
And makes one little room an everywhere.
Let sea-discoverers to new worlds have gone,
Let maps to other, worlds on worlds have shown,
Let us possess one world; each hath one, and is one.

My face in thine eye, thine in mine appears,
And true plain hearts do in the faces rest;
Where can we find two better hemispheres
Without sharp North, without declining West?
Whatever dies was not mixed equally;
20   If our two loves be one, or thou and I
Love so alike that none do slacken, none can die.

The Sun Rising

Busy old fool, unruly sun,
Why doest thou thus
Through windows and through curtains call on us?
Must to thy motions lovers' seasons run?
Saucy pedantic wretch, go chide
Late schoolboys and sour prentices,
Go tell court-huntsmen that the king will ride,
Call country ants to harvest offices;
Love, all alike, no season knows, nor clime,
10   Nor hours, days, months, which are the rags of time.

Thy beams, so reverend, and strong
Why shouldst thou think?
I could eclipse and cloud them with a wink,

But that I would not lose her sight so long;
    If her eyes have not blinded thine,
    Look, and tomorrow late tell me
      Whether both the Indias of spice and mine
      Be where thou left'st them, or lie here with me.
Ask for those kings whom thou saw'st yesterday,
20   And thou shalt hear, all here in one bed lay.

      She is all states, and all princes I;
        Nothing else is.
Princes do but play us; compared to this,
All honor's mimic, all wealth alchemy.
      Thou, sun, art half as happy as we,
      In that the world's contracted thus;
        Thine age asks ease, and since thy duties be
        To warm the world, that's done in warming us.
Shine here to us, and thou art everywhere;
30   This bed thy center is, these walls thy sphere.

The Canonization

For God's sake hold your tongue and let me love;
    Or chide my palsy or my gout,
My five gray hairs or ruined fortune flout,
    With wealth your state, your mind with arts improve,
      Take you a course, get you a place,
      Observe His Honour, or His Grace,
Or the King's real, or his stamped face
    Contemplate; what you will, approve,
    So you will let me love.

10   Alas, alas, who's injured by my love?
    What merchant's ships have my sighs drown'd?
Who says my tears have overflow'd his ground?
    When did my colds a forward spring remove?
      When did the heats which my veins fill
      Add one more to the plaguey Bill?[1]
Soldiers find wars, and Lawyers find out still
    Litigious men, which quarrels move,
    Though she and I do love.

1. List of those dead of the plague

Call us what you will, we are made such by love;
20   Call her one, me another fly,
We are tapers too, and at our own cost die,
    And we in us find th' Eagle and the Dove.
        The Phoenix[2] riddle hath more wit
        By us: we two being one, are it.
So to one neutral thing both sexes fit;
    We die and rise the same, and prove
    Mysterious by this love.

We can die by it, if not live by love,
    And if unfit for tombs and hearse
30   Our legend be, it will be fit for verse;
    And if no piece of Chronicle we prove,
        We'll build in sonnets pretty rooms;
        As well a well-wrought urn becomes
The greatest ashes, as half-acre tombs,
    And by these hymns, all shall approve
    Us *Canonized* for Love;

And thus invoke us: You whom reverend love
    Made one another's hermitage;
You, to whom love was peace, that now is rage;
40   Who did the whole world's soul contract, and drove
        Into the glasses of your eyes
        (So made such mirrors and such spies
That they did all to you epitomize);
    Countries, Towns, Courts: Beg from above
    A pattern of your love!

2. Mythical bird of no sex that lived a thousand years,
then burned itself and was reborn from the ashes

The Relic

When my grave is broke up again
Some second guest to entertain
(For graves have learned that womanhead
To be to more than one a bed)
    And he that digs it spies
A bracelet of bright hair about the bone,
    Will he not let us alone,
And think that there a loving couple lies,
Who thought that this device might be some way

10   To make their souls at the last busy day
    Meet at this grave, and make a little stay?

        If this fall in a time or land
        Where mis-devotion doth command,
        Then he that digs us up will bring
        Us to the bishop and the king
            To make us relics; then
    Thou shalt be a Mary Magdalen,[1] and I
          A something else thereby.
    All women shall adore us, and some men;
20   And since at such time miracles are sought,
    I would have that age by this paper taught
    What miracles we harmless lovers wrought.

        First, we loved well and faithfully,
        Yet knew not what we loved, nor why;
        Difference of sex no more we knew
        Than our guardian angels do;
          Coming and going, we
    Perchance might kiss, but not between those meals;
        Our hands ne'er touched the seals
30   Which nature, injured by late law, sets free.
    These miracles we did; but now, alas,
    All measure and all language I should pass,
    Should I tell what a miracle she was.

1. In Christian tradition Mary Magdalene was a prostitute
who reformed to follow Jesus—which suggests that
the "something else" in the next line refers to Christ.

Holy Sonnets

5

I am a little world made cunningly
Of elements, and an angelic sprite;
But black sin hath betrayed to endless night
My world's both parts, and O, both parts must die.
You which beyond that heaven which was most high
Have found new spheres, and of new lands can write,
Pour new seas in mine eyes, that so I might
Drown my world with my weeping earnestly,
Or wash it if it must be drowned no more.

10   But O, it must be burnt! Alas, the fire
Of lust and envy have burnt it heretofore,
And made it fouler; let their flames retire,
And burn me, O Lord, with a fiery zeal
Of Thee and Thy house, which doth in eating heal.

7

At the round earth's imagin'd corners, blow
Your trumpets, angels, and arise, arise
From death, you numberless infinities
Of souls, and to your scatter'd bodies go,
All whom the flood did, and fire shall o'erthrow,
All whom war, dearth, age, agues, tyrannies,
Despair, law, chance hath slain, and you whose eyes
Shall behold God and never taste death's woe.
But let them sleep, Lord, and me mourn a space,
10   For if above all these my sins abound,
'Tis late to ask abundance of thy grace
When we are there. Here on this lowly ground
Teach me how to repent, for that's as good
As if thou'dst seal'd my pardon with thy blood.

ROBERT HERRICK
1591–1674

With a Note on Cavalier Poetry

England in the seventeenth century was deeply divided both politically and religiously. The same impulse that brought Puritans to the American Colonies seeking religious freedom led to a Puritan rebellion against the King and the Church of England. Commanded by Oliver Cromwell, the Puritans deposed the King of England, Charles I, and later executed him. But after a few decades his son, who had been in exile in France, returned to be crowned as Charles II in 1660.

The wars of this era were aspects of a class struggle as well as of a religious one, and they anticipated the revolutions that came a century later in America and France. The King's strongest defenders were members of the hereditary aristocracy, of conservative and Catholic tendencies. His opponents were drawn mainly from the rising middle class, and were more radically Protestant, often Puritan. The greatest poet of the era was the Puritan John Milton, but the other side was neither mute nor inglorious when it came to verse. Those who sympathized with the King, whether they went into exile or stayed home in England, were called "Cavaliers." Some of them wrote elegant verse, more light than serious, so that the term "Cavalier Poetry" came to refer to a kind of light lyric, often advocating a *carpe diem* attitude.

Carpe diem, a Latin phrase meaning literally "seize the day," is a familiar theme in poetry from ancient times to the present. To "seize the day" means to disregard the future, including any "hereafter," so that one might expect the poets of this theme to ignore religion. But life is not so simple. Some Cavalier poets were also men of strong religious faith, though they wrote neither religious epics nor holy sonnets.

Robert Herrick was such a poet. And the last seventeenth-century poet included in this anthology, Andrew Marvell, managed a blend of Metaphysical and Cavalier attitudes and techniques so neat and elegant that he has been classified under both headings. There is a lesson in this about classification of poetic schools in general. Such conceptual guides must never be applied too rigidly. No good poet will stay put calmly in a box. But let Herrick sum up for us his own approach to poetry, in a little poem he used as preface to a volume of his verse.

I sing of Brooks, of Blossoms, Birds, and Bowers:
Of April, May, of June, and July-Flowers.
I sing of May-poles, Hock-carts, Wassails, Wakes,
Of Bride-grooms, Brides, and of their Bridal-cakes.
I write of Youth, of Love, and have access
By these, to sing of cleanly-wantonness.
I sing of Dews, of Rains, and piece by piece
Of Balm, of Oil, of Spice, and Amber-Greece.
I sing of Times trans-shifting; and I write
10   How Roses first came red, and Lilies white.
I write of Groves, of Twilights, and I sing
The Court of Mab, and of the Fairy-King.
I write of Hell; I sing (and ever shall)
Of Heaven, and hope to have it after all.

Delight in Disorder

A sweet disorder in the dress
Kindles in clothes a wantonness.
A lawn[1] about the shoulders thrown
Into a fine distraction;
An erring lace, which here and there

---

1. Fine linen (as a scarf)

Enthralls the crimson stomacher[2];
A cuff neglectful, and thereby
Ribbons to flow confusedly;
A winning wave, deserving note,
10 In the tempestuous petticoat;
A careless shoestring, in whose tie
I see a wild civility
Do more bewitch me than when art
Is too precise in every part.

2. Separate piece for the center front of a bodice

Upon Julia's Clothes

Whenas in silks my Julia goes
Then, then (methinks) how sweetly flows
That liquefaction of her clothes.

Next, when I cast mine eyes and see
That brave vibration each way free;
O how that glittering taketh me!

To the Virgins, to Make Much of Time

Gather ye rosebuds while ye may,
    Old time is still a-flying,
And this same flower that smiles to-day,
    To-morrow will be dying.

The glorious lamp of heaven, the sun,
    The higher he's a-getting,
The sooner will his race be run,
    And nearer he's to setting.

That age is best which is the first,
10   When youth and blood are warmer;
But being spent, the worse, and worst
    Times still succeed the former.

Then be not coy, but use your time,
    And while ye may, go marry;
For having lost but once your prime,
    You may for every tarry.

Corinna's Going A-Maying[1]

Get up, get up for shame, the blooming morn
Upon her wings presents the god unshorn.[2]
    See how Aurora[3] throws her fair
    Fresh-quilted colors through the air:
    Get up, sweet-slug-a-bed, and see
    The dew bespangling herb and tree.
Each flower has wept, and bowed toward the east,
Above an hour since; yet you not drest,
    Nay! not so much as out of bed?
    When all the birds have matins said,
    And sung their thankful hymns: 'tis sin,
    May, profanation to keep in,
When as a thousand virgins on this day
Spring, sooner than the lark, to fetch in May.

Rise; and put on your foliage, and be seen
To come forth, like the springtime, fresh and green;
    And sweet as Flora.[4] Take no care
    For jewels for your gown, or hair:
    Fear not; the leaves will strew
    Gems in abundance upon you:
Besides, the childhood of the day has kept,
Against[5] you come, some orient pearls[6] unwept:
    Come, and receive them while the light
    Hangs on the dew-locks of the night:
    And Titan[7] on the eastern hill
    Retires himself, or else stands still
Till you come forth. Wash, dress, be brief in praying:
Few beads[8] are best, when once we go a-Maying.

Come, my Corinna, come; and coming, mark
How each field turns a street; each street a park
    Made green, and trimmed with trees: see how

1. May Day observances go back to pagan times, when they
related to fertility rites. In Herrick's time they continued to
have a religious or ritual overtone.
2. Apollo's locks were never cut.
3. The dawn
4. Goddess of flowers
5. Until
6. Dew
7. Sun
8. Rosary beads, prayers

Devotion gives each house a bough,
Or branch: each porch, each door, ere this,
An ark,[9] a tabernacle is
Made up of white-thorn neatly interwove;
As if here were those cooler shades of love.
Can such delights be in the street,
And open fields, and we not see 't?
Come, we'll abroad; and let's obey
40   The proclamation made for May:
And sin no more, as we have done, by staying;
But my Corinna, come, let's go a-Maying.

There's not a budding boy, or girl, this day,
But is got up, and gone to bring in May.
A deal of youth, ere this, is come
Back, and with white-thorn laden home.
Some have dispatched their cakes and cream,
Before that we have left to dream:[10]
And some have wept, and wooed, and plighted troth,
50   And chose their priest, ere we can cast off sloth:
Many a green[11] gown has been given;
Many a kiss, both odd and even:
Many a glance too has been sent
From out the eye, Love's firmament:
Many a jest told of the keys betraying
This night, and locks picked, yet we're not a-Maying.

Come, let us go, while we are in our prime;
And take the harmless folly of the time.
We shall grow old apace, and die
60   Before we know our liberty.
Our life is short; and our days run
As fast away as does the sun:
And as a vapor, or a drop of rain
Once lost, can ne'er be found again:
So when or you or I are made
A fable, song, or fleeting shade;
All love, all liking, all delight
Lies drowned with us in endless night.
Then while time serves, and we are but decaying;
70   Come, my Corinna, come, let's go a-Maying.

9. Hebrew Ark of the Covenant (see Ex. 25: 10–21)
10. Left off dreaming
11. From lying in the grass

The Bad Season Makes the Poet Sad

Dull to myself, and almost dead to these
My many fresh and fragrant mistresses:
Lost to all music now, since everything
Puts on the semblance here of sorrowing.
Sick is the land to th' heart, and doth endure
More dangerous faintings by her desp'rate cure.
But if that golden age would come again,
And Charles[1] here rule, as he before did reign;
If smooth and unperplexed the seasons were,
10   As when the sweet Maria livèd here;
I should delight to have my curls half drowned
In Tyrian dews, and head with roses crowned;
And once more yet, ere I am laid out dead,
Knock at a star with my exalted head.

1. Charles I, the Stuart king deprived of power
by the Puritan faction (and beheaded in 1649, after this poem
was written). His queen, Henrietta Maria, is mentioned
in line 10.

ANDREW MARVELL

1621–1678

To His Coy Mistress

Had we but world enough, and time,
This coyness, lady, were no crime.
We would sit down, and think which way
To walk, and pass our long love's day.
Thou by the Indian Ganges' side
Should'st rubies find: I by the tide
Of Humber would complain. I would
Love you ten years before the Flood,
And you should, if you please, refuse
10   Till the conversion of the Jews.
My vegetable love should grow
Vaster than empires, and more slow.
An hundred years should go to praise
Thine eyes, and on thy forehead gaze;
Two hundred to adore each breast,
But thirty thousand to the rest;
An age at least to every part,
And the last age should show your heart.
For, lady, you deserve this state,

20 Nor would I love at lower rate.
     But at my back I always hear
   Time's wingèd chariot hurrying near:
   And yonder all before us lie
   Deserts of vast eternity.
   Thy beauty shall no more be found;
   Nor, in thy marble vault, shall sound
   My echoing song: then worms shall try
   That long-preserved virginity.
   And your quaint honor turn to dust,
30 And into ashes all my lust.
   The grave's a fine and private place,
   But none, I think, do there embrace.
     Now, therefore, while the youthful hue
   Sits on thy skin like morning dew,
   And while thy willing soul transpires
   At every pore with instant fires,
   Now let us sport us while we may;
   And now, like amorous birds of prey,
   Rather at once our Time devour,
40 Than languish in his slow-chapt power.
   Let us roll all our strength and all
   Our sweetness up into one ball,
   And tear our pleasures with rough strife
   Thorough the iron gates of life.
   Thus, though we cannot make our sun
   Stand still, yet we will make him run.

The Garden

   How vainly men themselves amaze
   To win the palm, the oak, or bays;
   And their incessant labors see
   Crowned from some single herb, or tree,
   Whose short and narrow-vergèd shade
   Does prudently their toils upbraid;
   While all flowers and all trees do close
   To weave the garlands of repose!

   Fair Quiet, have I found thee here,
10 And Innocence, thy sister dear!
   Mistaken long, I sought you then
   In busy companies of men.
   Your sacred plants, if here below,

Only among the plants will grow;
Society is all but rude
To this delicious solitude.

No white nor red was ever seen
So amorous as this lovely green.
Fond lovers, cruel as their flame,
20   Cut in these trees their mistress' name:
Little, alas! they know or heed
How far these beauties hers exceed!
Fair trees! wheres'e'er your barks I wound
No name shall but your own be found.

When we have run our passion's heat,
Love hither makes his best retreat.
The gods, that mortal beauty chase,
Still in a tree did end their race;
Apollo hunted Daphne so,
30   Only that she might laurel grow;
And Pan did after Syrinx speed,
Not as a nymph, but for a reed.

What wondrous life is this I lead!
Ripe apples drop about my head;
The luscious clusters of the vine
Upon my mouth do crush their wine;
The nectarine, and curious peach,
Into my hands themselves do reach;
Stumbling on melons, as I pass,
40   Ensnar'd with flowers, I fall on grass.

Meanwhile, the mind, from pleasure less,
Withdraws into its happiness:
The mind, that ocean where each kind
Does straight its own resemblance find;
Yet it creates, transcending these,
Far other worlds, and other seas;
Annihilating all that's made
To a green thought in a green shade.

Here at the fountain's sliding foot,
50   Or at some fruit-tree's mossy root,
Casting the body's vest aside,
My soul into the boughs does glide:

There like a bird it sits, and sings,
Then whets and combs its silver wings;
And, till prepared for longer flight,
Waves in its plumes the various light.

Such was that happy garden-state,
While man there walked without a mate:
After a place so pure and sweet,
60   What other help could yet be meet?
But 'twas beyond a mortal's share
To wander solitary there:
Two paradises 'twere in one,
To live in paradise alone.

How well the skillful gardener drew
Of flowers, and herbs, this dial new;
Where, from above, the milder sun
Does through a fragrant zodiac run;
And, as it works, the industrious bee
70   Computes its time as well as we.
How could such sweet and wholesome hours
Be reckoned but with herbs and flowers!

The Gallery

Clora, come view my soul, and tell
Whether I have contrived it well.
Now all its several lodgings lie
Composed into one gallery;
And the great arras-hangings, made
Of various faces, by are laid;
That, for all furniture; you'll find
Only your picture in my mind.

Here thou art painted in the dress
10   Of an inhuman Murderess;
Examining upon our hearts
Thy fertile shop of cruel arts:
Engines more keen than ever yet
Adornéd tyrant's cabinet;
Of which the most tormenting are
Black eyes, red lips, and curléd hair.

But, on the other side, th'art drawn
Like to Aurora in the dawn;
When in the east she slumb'ring lies,
20   And stretches out her milky thighs;
While all the morning choir does sing,
And manna falls, and roses spring;
And, at thy feet, the wooing doves
Sit pérfecting their harmless loves.

Like an enchantress here thou show'st,
Vexing thy restless lover's ghost;
And, by a light obscure, dost rave
Over his entrails, in the cave;
Divining thence, with horrid care,
30   How long thou shalt continue fair;
And (when informed) them throw'st away,
To be the greedy vulture's prey.

But, against that, thou sit'st a float
Like Venus in her pearly boat.
The halcyons,[1] calming all that's nigh,
Betwixt the air and water fly.
Or, if some rolling Wave appears,
A mass of ambergris it bears.
Nor blows more wind than what may well
40   Convoy the perfume to the smell.

These pictures and a thousand more,
Of thee, my gallery does store;
In all the forms thou can'st invent,
Either to please me, or torment:
For thou alone to people me,
Art grown a num'rous colony;
And a collection choicer far
Than or White-hall's, or Mantua's were.

But, of these pictures and the rest,
50   That at the entrance likes me best:
Where the same posture, and the look
Remains, with which I first was took.
A tender shepherdess, whose hair

---

1. Birds fabled to calm breezes

Hangs loosely playing in the air,
Transplanting flow'rs from the green hill,
To crown her head, and bosom fill.

The Fair Singer

To make a final conquest of all me,
Love did compose so sweet an enemy,
In whom both beauties to my death agree,
Joyning themselves in fatal harmony;
That while she with her eyes my heart does bind,
She with her voice might captivate my mind.

I could have fled from one but singly fair:
My dis-intangled soul itself might save,
Breaking the curléd trammels of her hair.
10   But how should I avoid to be her slave,
Whose subtle art invisibly can wreath
My fetters of the very air I breath?

It had been easie fighting in some plain,
Where victory might hang in equal choice.
But all resistance against her is vain,
Who has th' advantage both of eyes and voice.
And all my forces needs must be undone,
She having gainéd both the wind and sun.

The Coronet

When for the thorns with which I long, too long,
    With many a piercing wound,
    My Saviour's head have crown'd
I seek with garlands to redress that wrong:
    Through every garden, every mead,
I gather flow'rs (my fruits are only flow'rs)
    Dismantling all the fragrant tow'rs
That once adorn'd my shepherdess's head.
And now when I have summed up all my store,
10   Thinking (so I my self deceive)
    So rich a chaplet thence to weave
As never yet the King of glory wore:
    Alas I find the serpent old
    That, twining in his speckled breast,

About the flow'rs disguised does fold,
With wreaths of fame and interest.
Ah, foolish man, that would'st debase with them,
And mortal glory, heaven's diadem!
But Thou who only could'st the serpent tame
20   Either his slippery knots at once untie,
And disintangle all his winding snare:
Or shatter too with him my curious frame:
And let these wither, so that he may die,
Though set with skill and chosen out with care.
That they, while Thou on both their spoils dost tread,
May crown Thy feet, that could not crown Thy head.

WILLIAM BLAKE
1757–1827

With a Note on Romantic Poetry

England's Romantic poets (of whom the greatest are Blake, Wordsworth, Coleridge, Byron, Keats, and Shelley) constitute the most important single influence on later poetry in English. Though the poetic style and the values of each poet may show striking differences, the Romantic poets as a group tended to be radical in their politics (in sympathy with the American and French revolutions, against royalty and slavery) and transcendental in their philosophy, seeing nature as symbolic of the Creator's presence, and natural creation as analogous to the lesser creations of imaginative human beings.

These poets were part of a larger Romantic or transcendental movement, with philosophical roots in Germany and political roots in France. In America, poets and men of letters like Emerson, Bryant, and Thoreau were a part of this same movement of mind, which strongly influenced Whitman and through him most later American poetry. We are all children of the Romantic movement, no matter how rebellious we may be.

The Clod and the Pebble

"Love seeketh not itself to please,
   Nor for itself hath any care,
   But for another gives its ease,
   And builds a heaven in hell's despair."

So sung a little clod of clay,
Trodden with the cattle's feet,
But a pebble of the brook
Warbled out these metres meet:

"Love seeketh only self to please,
10   To bind another to its delight,
Joys in another's loss of ease,
And builds a hell in heaven's despite."

The Chimney-Sweeper

A little black thing among the snow,
Crying "weep, weep" in notes of woe!
"Where are thy father and mother, say?"—
"They are both gone up to church to pray.

"Because I was happy upon the heath,
And smiled among the winter's snow,
They clothed me in the clothes of death,
And taught me to sing the notes of woe.

"And because I am happy, and dance and sing,
10   They think they have done me no injury,
And are gone to praise God and his Priest and King,
Who make up a heaven of our misery."

The Sick Rose

O Rose, thou art sick:
The invisible worm,
That flies in the night,
In the howling storm,

Has found out thy bed
Of crimson joy;
And his dark secret love
Does thy life destroy.

The Tyger

Tyger! Tyger! burning bright
In the forests of the night,
What immortal hand or eye
Could frame thy fearful symmetry?

In what distant deeps or skies
Burnt the fire of thine eyes?
On what wings dare he aspire?
What the hand dare seize the fire?

And what shoulder, and what art,
10   Could twist the sinews of thy heart?
And when thy heart began to beat,
What dread hand? and what dread feet?

What the hammer? what the chain?
In what furnace was thy brain?
What the anvil? what dread grasp
Dare its deadly terrors clasp?

When the stars threw down their spears,
And water'd heaven with their tears,
Did he smile his work to see?
20   Did he who made the Lamb make thee?

Tyger! Tyger! burning bright
In the forests of the night,
What immortal hand or eye,
Dare frame thy fearful symmetry?

London

I wander through each charter'd[1] street,
Near where the charter'd Thames does flow,
And mark in every face I meet
Marks of weakness, marks of woe.

1. Pre-empted or rented

In every cry of every man,
In every infant's cry of fear,
In every voice in every ban,
The mind-forg'd manacles I hear.

How the chimney-sweeper's cry
10 Every blackening church appalls;
And the hapless soldier's sigh
Runs in blood down palace walls.

But most through midnight streets I hear
How the youthful harlot's curse
Blasts the new born infant's tear,
And blights with plagues the marriage hearse.

Auguries of Innocence

To see a world in a grain of sand
And a heaven in a wild flower,
Hold infinity in the palm of your hand,
And eternity in an hour.

A robin redbreast in a cage
Puts all heaven in a rage.
A dove-house filled with doves and pigeons
Shudders hell through all its regions.
A dog starved at his master's gate
10 Predicts the ruin of the state.
A horse misused upon the road
Calls to heaven for human blood.
Each outcry of the hunted hare
A fiber from the brain does tear.
A skylark wounded in the wing,
A cherubim does cease to sing;
The game cock clipped and armed for fight
Does the rising sun affright.
Every wolf's and lion's howl
20 Raises from hell a human soul.
The wild deer wandering here and there,
Keeps the human soul from care.
The lamb misused breeds public strife
And yet forgives the butcher's knife.
The bat that flits at close of eve

Has left the brain that won't believe.
The owl that calls upon the night
Speaks the unbeliever's fright.
He who shall hurt the little wren
30 Shall never be beloved by men.
He who the ox to wrath has moved
Shall never be by woman loved.
The wanton boy that kills the fly
Shall feel the spider's enmity.
He who torments the chafer's sprite
Weaves a bower in endless night.
The caterpillar on the leaf
Repeats to thee thy mother's grief.
Kill not the moth nor butterfly,
40 For the last judgment draweth nigh.
He who shall train the horse to war
Shall never pass the polar bar.
The beggar's dog and widow's cat,
Feed them and thou wilt grow fat.
The gnat that sings his summer's song
Poison gets from slander's tongue.
The poison of the snake and newt
Is the sweat of envy's foot.
The poison of the honey bee
50 Is the artist's jealousy.
The prince's robes and beggar's rags
Are toadstools on the miser's bags.
A truth that's told with bad intent
Beats all the lies you can invent.
It is right it should be so;
Man was made for joy and woe;
And when this we rightly know,
Through the world we safely go.
Joy and woe are woven fine,
60 A clothing for the soul divine;
Under every grief and pine
Runs a joy with silken twine.
The babe is more than swadling bands,
Throughout all these human lands;
Tools were made, and born were hands,
Every farmer understands.
Every tear from every eye
Becomes a babe in eternity;
This is caught by females bright,

70 And returned to its own delight.
The bleat, the bark, bellow, and roar
Are waves that beat on heaven's shore.
The babe that weeps the rod beneath
Writes revenge in realms of death.
The beggar's rags, fluttering in air,
Does to rags the heavens tear.
The soldier, armed with sword and gun,
Palsied strikes the summer's sun.
The poor man's farthing is worth more
80 Than all the gold on Afric's shore.
One mite wrung from the lab'rer's hands
Shall buy and sell the miser's lands;
Or, if protected from on high,
Does that whole nation sell and buy.
He who mocks the infant's faith
Shall be mocked in age and death.
He who shall teach the child to doubt
The rotting grave shall never get out.
He who respects the infant's faith
90 Triumphs over hell and death.
The child's toys and the old man's reasons
Are the fruits of the two seasons.
The questioner, who sits so sly
Shall never know how to reply.
He who replies to words of doubt
Doth put the light of knowledge out.
The strongest poison ever known
Came from Caesar's laurel crown.
Naught can deform the human race
100 Like to the armour's iron brace.
When gold and gems adorn the plow
To peaceful arts shall envy bow.
A riddle, or the cricket's cry,
Is to doubt a fit reply.
The emmet's inch and eagle's mile
Make lame philosophy to smile.
He who doubts from what he sees
Will ne'er believe, do what you please.
If the sun and moon should doubt,
110 They'd immediately go out.
To be in a passion you good may do,
But no good if a passion is in you.
The whore and gambler, by the state

Licensed, build that nation's fate.
The harlot's cry from street to street
Shall weave Old England's winding sheet.
The winner's shout, the loser's curse,
Dance before dead England's hearse.
Every night and every morn
120   Some to misery are born.
Every morn and every night
Some are born to sweet delight.
Some are born to sweet delight,
Some are born to endless night.
We are led to believe a lie
When we see not through the eye,
Which was born in a night to perish in a night,
When the soul slept in beams of light.
God appears, and God is light,
130   To those poor souls who dwell in night,
But does a human form display
To those who dwell in realms of day.

WILLIAM WORDSWORTH
1770–1850
To My Sister

It is the first mild day of March;
Each minute sweeter than before,
The redbreast sings from the tall larch
That stands beside our door.

There is a blessing in the air,
Which seems a sense of joy to yield
To the bare trees, and mountains bare,
And grass in the green field.

My sister! ('tis a wish of mine)
10   Now that our morning meal is done,
Make haste, your morning task resign;
Come forth and feel the sun.

Edward will come with you; —and, pray,
Put on with speed your woodland dress;
And bring no book: for this one day
We'll give to idleness.

No joyless forms shall regulate
Our living calendar:
We from to-day, my Friend, will date
20   The opening of the year.

Love, now a universal birth,
From heart to heart is stealing.
From earth to man, from man to earth:
—It is the hour of feeling.

One moment now may give us more
Than years of toiling reason:
Our minds shall drink at every pore
The spirit of the season.

Some silent laws our hearts will make,
30   Which they shall long obey:
We for the year to come may take
Our temper from to-day.

And from the blessèd power that rolls
About, below, above,
We'll frame the measure of our souls:
They shall be tuned to love.

Then come, my Sister! come, I pray,
With speed put on your woodland dress;
And bring no book: for this one day
40   We'll give to idleness.

I Wandered Lonely as a Cloud

I wandered lonely as a cloud
That floats on high o'er vales and hills,
When all at once I saw a crowd,
A host, of golden daffodils;
Beside the lake, beneath the trees,
Fluttering and dancing in the breeze.

Continuous as the stars that shine
And twinkle on the milky way,
They stretched in never-ending line
10   Along the margin of a bay:

Ten thousand saw I at a glance,
Tossing their heads in sprightly dance.

The waves beside them danced; but they
Out-did the sparkling waves in glee:
A poet could not but be gay,
In such a jocund company:
I gazed—and gazed—but little thought
What wealth the show to me had brought:

For oft, when on my couch I lie
20   In vacant or in pensive mood,
They flash upon that inward eye
Which is the bliss of solitude;
And then my heart with pleasure fills,
And dances with the daffodils.

Ode

Intimations of Immortality from Recollections
of Early Childhood

> The Child is father of the Man;
> And I could wish my days to be
> Bound each to each by natural piety.

I

There was a time when meadow, grove, and stream,
The earth, and every common sight,
            To me did seem
        Apparelled in celestial light,
The glory and the freshness of a dream.
It is not now as it hath been of yore;—
        Turn whereso'er I may,
            By night or day,
The things which I have seen I now can see no more.

II

10   The Rainbow comes and goes,
            And lovely is the Rose,
            The Moon doth with delight
Look round her when the heavens are bare,

Waters on a starry night
Are beautiful and fair;
The sunshine is a glorious birth;
But yet I know, where'er I go,
That there hath past away a glory from the earth.

III

Now, while the birds thus sing a joyous song,
20   And while the young lambs bound
As to the tabor's sound,
To me alone there came a thought of grief:
A timely utterance gave that thought relief,
And I again am strong:
The cataracts blow their trumpets from the steep;
No more shall grief of mine the season wrong;
I hear the Echoes through the mountains throng,
The Winds come to me from the fields of sleep,
And all the earth is gay;
30   Land and sea
Give themselves up to jollity.
And with the heart of May
Doth every Beast keep holiday;—
Thou Child of Joy,
Shout round me, let me hear thy shouts, thou happy Shepherd-boy!

IV

Ye blessèd Creatures, I have heard the call
Ye to each other make; I see
The heavens laugh with you in your jubilee;
My heart is at your festival,
40   My head hath its coronal,
The fulness of your bliss, I feel—I feel it all.
Oh evil day! if I were sullen
While Earth herself is adorning,
This sweet May-morning,
And the Children are culling
On every side,
In a thousand valleys far and wide,
Fresh flowers; while the sun shines warm,
And the Babe leaps up on his Mother's arm:—
50   I hear, I hear, with joy I hear!
—But there's a Tree, of many, one,
A single Field which I have looked upon,

Both of them speak of something that is gone:
  The Pansy at my feet
  Doth the same tale repeat:
Whither is fled the visionary gleam?
Where is it now, the glory and the dream?

V

Our birth is but a sleep and a forgetting:
The Soul that rises with us, our life's Star,
60 Hath had elsewhere its setting,
   And cometh from afar:
  Not in entire forgetfulness,
  And not in utter nakedness,
But trailing clouds of glory do we come
  From God, who is our home:
Heaven lies about us in our infancy!
Shades of the prison-house begin to close
  Upon the growing Boy,
But He beholds the light, and whence it flows,
70 He sees it in his joy;
The Youth, who daily farther from the east
  Must travel, still is Nature's Priest,
  And by the vision splendid
  Is on his way attended;
At length the Man perceives it die away,
And fade into the light of common day.

VI

Earth fills her lap with pleasures of her own;
Yearnings she hath in her own natural kind,
And, even with something of a Mother's mind,
80 And no unworthy aim,
  The homely Nurse doth all she can
To make her Foster-child, her Inmate Man,
  Forget the glories he hath known,
And that imperial palace whence he came.

VII

Behold the Child among his new-born blisses,
A six years' Darling of a pigmy size!
See, where 'mid work of his own hand he lies,
Fretted by sallies of his mother's kisses,

With light upon him from his father's eyes!
90   See, at his feet, some little plan or chart,
Some fragment from his dream of human life,
Shaped by himself with newly-learned art;
        A wedding or a festival,
        A mourning or a funeral;
            And this hath now his heart,
        And unto this he frames his song.
            Then will he fit his tongue
To dialogues of business, love, or strife;
        But it will not be long
100   Ere this be thrown aside,
        And with new joy and pride
The little Actor cons another part;
Filling from time to time his "humorous stage"
With all the Persons, down to palsied Age,
That Life brings with her in her equipage;
        As if his whole vocation
        Were endless imitation.

            VIII

Thou, whose exterior semblance doth belie
        Thy Soul's immensity;
110   Thou best Philosopher, who yet dost keep
Thy heritage, thou Eye among the blind,
That, deaf and silent, read'st the eternal deep,
Haunted for ever by the eternal mind, —
        Mighty Prophet! Seer blest!
        On whom those truths do rest,
Which we are toiling all our lives to find,
In darkness lost, the darkness of the grave,
Thou, over whom thy Immortality
Broods like the Day, a Master o'er a Slave,
120   A Presence which is not to be put by;
Thou little Child, yet glorious in the might
Of heaven-born freedom on thy being's height,
Why with such earnest pains dost thou provoke
The years to bring the inevitable yoke,
Thus blindly with thy blessedness at strife?
Full soon thy Soul shall have her earthly freight,
And custom lie upon thee with a weight,
Heavy as frost, and deep almost as life!

IX

O joy! that in our embers
Is something that doth live,
That nature yet remembers
What was so fugitive!
The thought of our past years in me doth breed
Perpetual benediction: not indeed
For that which is most worthy to be blest;
Delight and liberty, the simple creed
Of Childhood, whether busy or at rest,
With new-fledged hope still fluttering in his breast:—
Not for these I raise
The song of thanks and praise:
But for those obstinate questionings
Of sense and outward things,
Fallings from us, vanishings;
Blank misgivings of a Creature
Moving about in worlds not realised,
High instincts before which our mortal Nature
Did tremble like a guilty Thing surprised:
But for those first affections,
Those shadowy recollections,
Which, be they what they may,
Are yet the fountain-light of all our day,
Are yet a master-light of all our seeing;
Uphold us, cherish, and have power to make
Our noisy years seem moments in the being
Of the eternal Silence: truths that wake,
To perish never:
Which neither listlessness, nor mad endeavour,
Nor Man nor Boy,
Nor all that is at enmity with joy,
Can utterly abolish or destroy!
Hence in a season of calm weather
Though inland far we be,
Our Souls have sight of that immortal sea
Which brought us hither,
Can in a moment travel thither,
And see the Children sport upon the shore,
And hear the mighty waters rolling evermore.

X

Then sing, ye Birds, sing, sing a joyous song!
    And let the young Lambs bound
170   As to the tabor's sound!
We in thought will join your throng,
    Ye that pipe and ye that play,
    Ye that through your hearts today
    Feel the gladness of the May!
What though the radiance which was once so bright
Be now for ever taken from my sight,
    Though nothing can bring back the hour
Of splendour in the grass, of glory in the flower;
    We will grieve not, rather find
180   Strength in what remains behind;
    In the primal sympathy
    Which having been must ever be;
    In the soothing thoughts that spring
    Out of human suffering;
    In the faith that looks through death,
In years that bring the philosophic mind.

XI

And O, ye Fountains, Meadows, Hills, and Groves,
Forebode not any severing of our loves!
Yet in my heart of hearts I feel your might;
190 I only have relinquished one delight
To live beneath your more habitual sway.
I love the Brooks which down their channels fret,
Even more than when I tripped lightly as they;
The innocent brightness of a new-born Day
    Is lovely yet;
The Clouds that gather round the setting sun
Do take a sober colouring from an eye
That hath kept watch o'er man's mortality;
Another race hath been, and other palms are won.
200 Thanks to the human heart by which we live,
Thanks to its tenderness, its joys, and fears,
To me the meanest flower that blows can give
Thoughts that do often lie too deep for tears.

Two Sonnets

4

Composed upon Westminster Bridge,
September 3, 1802

Earth has not anything to show more fair:
Dull would he be of soul who could pass by
A sight so touching in its majesty:
This City now doth, like a garment, wear
The beauty of the morning; silent, bare,
Ships, towers, domes, theatres, and temples lie
Open unto the fields, and to the sky;
All bright and glittering in the smokeless air.
Never did sun more beautifully steep
10   In his first splendour, valley, rock, or hill;
Ne'er saw I, never felt, a calm so deep!
The river glideth at his own sweet will:
Dear God! the very houses seem asleep;
And all that mighty heart is lying still!

14

The world is too much with us; late and soon,
Getting and spending, we lay waste our powers:
Little we see in Nature that is ours;
We have given our hearts away, a sordid boon!
This Sea that bares her bosom to the moon;
The winds that will be howling at all hours,
And are up-gathered now like sleeping flowers;
For this, for everything, we are out of tune;
It moves us not.—Great God! I'd rather be
10   A Pagan suckled in a creed outworn;
So might I, standing on this pleasant lea,
Have glimpses that would make me less forlorn;
Have sight of Proteus rising from the sea;
Or hear old Triton blow his wreathèd horn.

JOHN KEATS
1795–1821

Bright Star

Bright star! would I were steadfast as thou art—
  Not in lone splendor hung aloft the night
And watching, with eternal lids apart
  Like Nature's patient sleepless Eremite,[1]
The moving waters at their priestlike task
  Of pure ablution round earth's human shores,
Or gazing on the new soft fallen mask
  Of snow upon the mountains and the moors—
No—yet still steadfast, still unchangeable,
  Pillowed upon my fair love's ripening breast,
To feel forever its soft fall and swell,
  Awake forever in a sweet unrest,
Still, still to hear her tender-taken breath,
And so live ever—or else swoon to death.

1. Religious hermit

On the Sonnet

If by dull rhymes our English must be chained,
  And, like Andromeda,[1] the Sonnet sweet
Fettered, in spite of painèd loveliness;
Let us find out, if we must be constrained,
  Sandals more interwoven and complete
To fit the naked foot of poesy;
Let us inspect the lyre, and weigh the stress
Of every chord, and see what may be gained
  By ear industrious, and attention meet;
Misers of sound and syllable, no less
Than Midas of his coinage, let us be
  Jealous of dead leaves in the bay-wreath crown;
So, if we may not let the Muse be free,
  She will be bound with garlands of her own.

1. Ethiopian princess chained as prey for a monster
   and rescued by Perseus, who then married her

Ode to a Nightingale

1

My heart aches, and a drowsy numbness pains
  My sense, as though of hemlock I had drunk,
Or emptied some dull opiate to the drains
  One minute past, and Lethe-wards[1] had sunk:
'Tis not through envy of thy happy lot,
  But being too happy in thine happiness,—
    That thou, light-wingèd Dryad[2] of the trees,
      In some melodious plot
Of beechen green, and shadows numberless,
Singest of summer in full-throated ease.

2

O, for a draught of vintage! that hath been
  Cool'd a long age in the deep-delved earth,
Tasting of Flora[3] and the country green,
  Dance, and Provençal song, and sunburnt mirth!
O for a beaker full of the warm South,
  Full of the true, the blushful Hippocrene,[4]
    With beaded bubbles winking at the brim,
      And purple-stained mouth;
That I might drink, and leave the world unseen,
And with thee fade away into the forest dim:

3

Fade far away, dissolve, and quite forget
  What thou among the leaves hast never known,
The weariness, the fever, and the fret
  Here, where men sit and hear each other groan;
Where palsy shakes a few, sad, last gray hairs,
  Where youth grows pale, and spectre-thin, and dies;
    Where but to think is to be full of sorrow
      And leaden-eyed despairs,
Where Beauty cannot keep her lustrous eyes,
Or new Love pine at them beyond tomorrow.

1. Toward Lethe, the river of Hades whose waters cause forgetfulness
2. Wood nymph
3. Goddess of flowers: personification for flowers
4. Fountain of the Muses on Mt. Helicon

4

Away! away! for I will fly to thee,
  Not charioted by Bacchus[5] and his pards,
But on the viewless wings of Poesy,
  Though the dull brain perplexes and retards:
Already with thee! tender is the night,
  And haply the Queen-Moon is on her throne,
    Cluster'd around by all her starry fays;
      But here there is no light,
Save what from heaven is with the breezes blown
40   Through verdurous glooms and winding mossy ways.

5

I cannot see what flowers are at my feet,
  Nor what soft incense hangs upon the boughs,
But, in embalmèd darkness, guess each sweet
  Wherewith the seasonable month endows
The grass, the thicket, and the fruit-tree wild;
  White hawthorn, and the pastoral eglantine;
    Fast fading violets cover'd up in leaves;
      And mid-May's eldest child,
The coming musk-rose, full of dewy wine,
50   The murmurous haunt of flies on summer eves.

6

Darkling I listen; and, for many a time
  I have been half in love with easeful Death,
Call'd him soft names in many a musèd rhyme,
  To take into the air my quiet breath;
Now more than ever seems it rich to die,
  To cease upon the midnight with no pain,
    While thou art pouring forth thy soul abroad
      In such an ecstasy!
Still wouldst thou sing, and I have ears in vain—
60   To thy high requiem become a sod.

7

Thou wast not born for death, immortal Bird!
  No hungry generations tread thee down;
The voice I hear this passing night was heard

5. God of wine, whose chariot is drawn by leopards

In ancient days by emperor and clown:
Perhaps the self-same song that found a path
   Through the sad heart of Ruth,[6] when, sick for home,
     She stood in tears amid the alien corn;
      The same that oft-times hath
Charm'd magic casements, opening on the foam
70   Of perilous seas, in faery lands forlorn.

8

Forlorn! the very word is like a bell
   To toll me back from thee to my sole self!
Adieu! the fancy cannot cheat so well
   As she is fam'd to do, deceiving elf.
Adieu! adieu! thy plaintive anthem fades
Past the near meadows, over the still stream,
   Up the hill-side; and now 'tis buried deep
     In the next valley-glades:
Was it a vision, or a waking dream?
80   Fled is that music:—Do I wake or sleep?

6. In the Bible, Ruth forsook her native land to live in Israel
with Naomi, her mother-in-law.

Ode on a Grecian Urn

1

Thou still unravish'd bride of quietness,
   Thou foster-child of silence and slow time,
Sylvan historian, who canst thus express
   A flowery tale more sweetly than our rhyme:
What leaf-fring'd legend haunts about thy shape
  Of deities or mortals, or of both,
    In Tempe[1] or the dales of Arcady?[1]
What men or gods are these? What maidens loth?
   What mad pursuit? What struggle to escape?
10   What pipes and timbrels?[2] What wild ecstasy?

1. In Greek poetry, symbols of pastoral beauty
2. Tambourines

2

Heard melodies are sweet, but those unheard
    Are sweeter; therefore, ye soft pipes, play on;
Not to the sensual ear, but, more endear'd,
    Pipe to the spirit ditties of no tone;
Fair youth, beneath the trees, thou canst not leave
    Thy song, nor ever can those trees be bare;
        Bold Lover, never, never canst thou kiss,
Though winning near the goal—yet, do not grieve;
    She cannot fade, though thou hast not thy bliss,
20   For ever wilt thou love, and she be fair!

3

Ah, happy, happy boughs! that cannot shed
    Your leaves, nor ever bid the Spring adieu;
And, happy melodist, unwearièd,
    For ever piping songs for ever new;
More happy love! more happy, happy love!
    For ever warm and still to be enjoy'd,
        For ever panting, and for ever young;
All breathing human passion far above,
    That leaves a heart high-sorrowful and cloy'd,
30   A burning forehead, and a parching tongue.

4

Who are these coming to the sacrifice?
    To what green altar, O mysterious priest,
Lead'st thou that heifer lowing at the skies,
    And all her silken flanks with garlands drest?
What little town by river or sea shore,
    Or mountain-built with peaceful citadel,
        Is emptied of this folk, this pious morn?
And, little town, thy streets for evermore
    Will silent be; and not a soul to tell
40   Why thou art desolate, can e'er return.

5

O Attic shape! Fair attitude! with brede
    Of marble men and maidens overwrought,
With forest branches and the trodden weed;
    Thou, silent form, dost tease us out of thought
As doth eternity: Cold Pastoral!
    When old age shall this generation waste,

Thou shalt remain, in midst of other woe
Than ours, a friend to man, to whom thou say'st,
    "Beauty is truth, truth beauty,"—that is all
50   Ye know on earth, and all ye need to know.

Ode to Autumn

1

Season of mists and mellow fruitfulness!
    Close bosom-friend of the maturing sun;
Conspiring with him how to load and bless
    With fruit the vines that round the thatch-eaves run;
To bend with apples the moss'd cottage-trees,
    And fill all fruit with ripeness to the core;
      To swell the gourd, and plump the hazel shells
With a sweet kernel; to set budding more
And still more, later flowers for the bees,
10 Until they think warm days will never cease;
    For summer has o'er-brimm'd their clammy cells.

2

Who hath not seen thee oft amid thy store?
    Sometimes whoever seeks abroad may find
Thee sitting careless on a granary floor,
    Thy hair soft-lifted by the winnowing wind;
Or on a half-reap'd furrow sound asleep,
    Drowsed with the fume of poppies, while thy hook
      Spares the next swath and all its twinèd flowers;
    And sometimes like a gleaner thou dost keep
20 Steady thy laden head across a brook;
Or by a cider-press, with patient look,
    Thou watchest the last oozings, hours by hours.

3

Where are the songs of Spring? Aye, where are they?
    Think not of them,—thou hast thy music too,
While barred clouds bloom the soft-dying day
    And touch the stubble-plains with rosy hue;
Then in a wailful choir the small gnats mourn
    Among the river-sallows, borne aloft
      Or sinking as the light wind lives or dies;

30   And full-grown lambs loud bleat from hilly bourn;
Hedge-crickets sing, and now with treble soft
The redbreast whistles from a garden-croft:
    And gathering swallows twitter in the skies.

ALFRED, LORD TENNYSON
1809–1892
Ulysses

It little profits that an idle king,
By this still hearth, among these barren crags,
Match'd with an aged wife, I mete and dole
Unequal laws unto a savage race,
That hoard, and sleep, and feed, and know not me.
I cannot rest from travel: I will drink
Life to the lees: all times I have enjoy'd
Greatly, have suffer'd greatly, both with those
That loved me, and alone; on shore, and when
10   Thro' scudding drifts the rainy Hyades
Vext the dim sea: I am become a name;
For always roaming with a hungry heart
Much have I seen and known: cities of men,
And manners, climates, councils, governments,
Myself not least, but honour'd of them all;
And drunk delight of battle with my peers,
Far on the ringing plains of windy Troy.
I am a part of all that I have met;
Yet all experience is an arch wherethro'
20   Gleams that untravell'd world, whose margin fades
For ever and for ever when I move.
How dull it is to pause, to make an end,
To rust unburnish'd, not to shine in use!
As tho' to breathe were life. Life piled on life
Were all too little, and of one to me
Little remains: but every hour is saved
From that eternal silence, something more,
A bringer of new things; and vile it were
For some three suns to store and hoard myself,
30   And this gray spirit yearning in desire
To follow knowledge like a sinking star,
Beyond the utmost bound of human thought.
    This is my son, mine own Telemachus,
To whom I leave the sceptre and the isle—

Well-lov'd of me, discerning to fulfil
This labour, by slow prudence to make mild
A rugged people, and thro' soft degrees
Subdue them to the useful and the good.
Most blameless is he, centred in the sphere
40 Of common duties, decent not to fail
In offices of tenderness, and pay
Meet adoration to my household gods,
When I am gone. He works his work, I mine.
   There lies the port; the vessel puffs her sail:
There gloom the dark broad seas. My mariners,
Souls that have toil'd, and wrought, and thought with me—
That ever with a frolic welcome took
The thunder and the sunshine, and opposed
Free hearts, free foreheads—you and I are old;
50 Old age hath yet his honour and his toil;
Death closes all: but something ere the end,
Some work of noble note, may yet be done,
Not unbecoming men that strove with Gods.
The lights begin to twinkle from the rocks:
The long day wanes: the slow moon climbs: the deep
Moans round with many voices. Come, my friends,
'Tis not too late to seek a newer world.
Push off, and sitting well in order smite
The sounding furrows; for my purpose holds
60 To sail beyond the sunset, and the baths
Of all the western stars, until I die.
It may be that the gulfs will wash us down:
It may be we shall touch the Happy Isles,
And see the great Achilles, whom we knew.
Tho' much is taken, much abides; and tho'
We are not now that strength which in old days
Moved earth and heaven; that which we are, we are;
One equal temper of heroic hearts,
Made weak by time and fate, but strong in will
70 To strive, to seek, to find, and not to yield.

The Eagle

Fragment

He clasps the crag with crooked hands;
Close to the sun in lonely lands,
Ring'd with the azure world, he stands.

The wrinkled sea beneath him crawls;
He watches from his mountain walls,
And like a thunderbolt he falls.

Tears, Idle Tears

Tears, idle tears, I know not what they mean,
Tears from the depth of some divine despair
Rise in the heart, and gather to the eyes,
In looking on the happy Autumn-fields,
And thinking of the days that are no more.

Fresh as the first beam glittering on a sail,
That brings our friends up from the underworld,
Sad as the last which reddens over one
That sinks with all we love below the verge;
10   So sad, so fresh, the days that are no more.

Ah, sad and strange as in dark summer dawns
The earliest pipe of half-awaken'd birds
To dying ears, when unto dying eyes
The casement slowly grows a glimmering square;
So sad, so strange, the days that are no more.

Dear as remember'd kisses after death,
And sweet as those by hopeless fancy feign'd
On lips that are for others; deep as love,
Deep as first love, and wild with all regret;
20   O Death in Life, the days that are no more.

From **In Memoriam**

7

Dark house, by which once more I stand
    Here in the long unlovely street,
    Doors, where my heart was used to beat
So quickly, waiting for a hand,

A hand that can be clasp'd no more—
    Behold me, for I cannot sleep,

And like a guilty thing I creep
At earliest morning to the door.

He[1] is not here; but far away
10   The noise of life begins again,
     And ghastly thro' the drizzling rain
On the bald street breaks the blank day.

8

A happy lover who has come
     To look on her that loves him well,
     Who 'lights and rings the gateway bell,
And learns her gone and far from home;

He saddens, all the magic light
     Dies off at once from bower and hall,
     And all the place is dark, and all
The chambers emptied of delight:

So find I every pleasant spot
10   In which we two were wont to meet,
     The field, the chamber and the street,
For all is dark where thou are not.

115

Now fades the last long streak of snow,
     Now burgeons every maze of quick
     About the flowering squares, and thick
By ashen roots the violets blow.

Now rings the woodland loud and long,
     The distance takes a lovelier hue,
     And drown'd in yonder living blue
The lark becomes a sightless song.

Now dance the lights on lawn and lea,
10   The flocks are whiter down the vale,
     And milkier every milky sail
On winding stream or distant sea;

1. Arthur Henry Hallam, Tennyson's friend,
   whose death inspired a sequence of poems
   entitled *In Memoriam A. H. H.*

Where now the seamew pipes, or dives
    In yonder greening gleam, and fly
    The happy birds, that change their sky
To build and brood; that live their lives

From land to land; and in my breast
    Spring wakens too; and my regret
    Becomes an April violet,
20   And buds and blossoms like the rest.

To Virgil

*Written at the Request of the Mantuans[1] for
the Nineteenth Centenary of Virgil's Death*

I

Roman Virgil, thou that singest
    Ilion's lofty temples robed in fire,
Ilion falling, Rome arising,
    wars, and filial faith, and Dido's pyre;

II

Landscape-lover, lord of language
    more than he that sang the Works and Days,
All the chosen coin of fancy
    flashing out from many a golden phrase;

III

Thou that singest wheat and woodland,
    tilth and vineyard, hive and horse and herd;
All the charm of all the Muses
    often flowering in a lonely word;

IV

Poet of the happy Tityrus
    piping underneath his beechen bowers;
Poet of the poet-satyr
    whom the laughing shepherd bound with flowers;

1. Citizens of Virgil's birthplace in Italy

V

Chanter of the Pollio, glorying
    in the blissful years again to be,
Summers of the snakeless meadow,
    unlaborious earth and oarless sea;

VI

Thou that seëst Universal
    Nature moved by Universal Mind;
Thou majestic in thy sadness
    at the doubtful doom of human kind;

VII

Light among the vanish'd ages;
    star that gildest yet this phantom shore;
Golden branch amid the shadows,
    kings and realms that pass to rise no more;

VIII

Now thy Forum roars no longer,
    fallen every purple Cæsar's dome—
Tho' thine ocean-roll of rhythm
    sound for ever of Imperial Rome—

IX

Now the Rome of slaves hath perish'd,
    and the Rome of freemen holds her place,
I, from out the Northern Island
    sunder'd once from all the human race,

X

I salute thee, Mantovano,[2]
    I that loved thee since my day began,
Wielder of the stateliest measure[3]
    ever moulded by the lips of man.

2. Citizen of Mantua
3. Dactylic hexameter, used by Virgil, in the *Aeneid*,
   in imitation of Homer, as imitated by Tennyson in this poem.

ROBERT BROWNING

1812–1889

Soliloquy of the Spanish Cloister

Gr-r-r—there go, my heart's abhorrence!
  Water your damned flower-pots, do!
If hate killed men, Brother Lawrence,
  God's blood, would not mine kill you!
What? your myrtle-bush wants trimming?
  Oh, that rose has prior claims—
Needs its leaden vase filled brimming?
  Hell dry you up with its flames!

At the meal we sit together;
10   *Salve tibi!*[1] I must hear
Wise talk of the kind of weather,
  Sort of season, time of year:
Not a plenteous cork-crop: scarcely
  Dare we hope oak-galls, I doubt;
What's the Latin name for "parsley"?
  What's the Greek name for Swine's Snout?

Whew! We'll have our platter burnished,
  Laid with care on our own shelf!
With a fire-new spoon we're furnished,
20   And a goblet for ourself,
Rinsed like something sacrificial
  Ere 'tis fit to touch our chaps—
Marked with L. for our initial!
  (He-he! There his lily snaps!)

Saint, forsooth! While brown Dolores
  Squats outside the Convent bank
With Sanchicha, telling stories,
  Steeping tresses in the tank,
Blue-black, lustrous, thick like horsehairs,
30   —Can't I see his dead eye glow,
Bright as 'twere a Barbary corsair's?
  (That is, if he'd let it show!)

When he finishes refection,
  Knife and fork he never lays

1. Greetings to you!

614

Cross-wise, to my recollection,
  As do I, in Jesu's praise.
I, the Trinity illustrate,
  Drinking watered orange-pulp—
In three sips the Arian[2] frustrate;
40   While he drains his at one gulp!

Oh, those melons! if he's able
  We're to have a feast; so nice!
One goes to the Abbot's table,
  All of us get each a slice.
How go on your flowers? None double?
  Not one fruit-sort can you spy?
Strange!—And I, too, at such trouble,
  Keep them close-nipped on the sly!

There's a great text in Galatians,[3]
50   Once you trip on it, entails
Twenty-nine distinct damnations,
  One sure, if another fails;
If I trip him just a-dying,
  Sure of heaven as sure can be,
Spin him round and send him flying
  Off to hell, a Manichee?[4]

Or, my scrofulous French novel
  On grey paper with blunt type!
Simply glance at it, you grovel
60   Hand and foot in Belial's[5] gripe;
If I double down its pages
  At the woeful sixteenth print,
When he gathers his greengages,
  Ope a sieve and slip it in't?

Or, there's Satan!—one might venture
  Pledge one's soul to him, yet leave
Such a flaw in the indenture
  As he'd miss till, past retrieve,

2. Follower of the heretic Arius, who denied the Trinity
3. One of St. Paul's Epistles
4. Follower of the heretic Mani
5. A devil

Blasted lay that rose-acacia
70   We're so proud of! *Hy, Zy, Hine....*
'St, there's Vespers!⁶ *Plena gratia*
    Ave, Virgo! Gr-r-r—you swine!

6. Evening prayers. The speaker intones "Hail Virgin, full of grace."

My Last Duchess

Ferrara

That's my last Duchess painted on the wall,
Looking as if she were alive. I call
That piece a wonder, now: Frà Pandolf's hands
Worked busily a day, and there she stands.
Will't please you sit and look at her? I said
"Frà Pandolf" by design, for never read
Strangers like you that pictured countenance,
The depth and passion of its earnest glance,
But to myself they turned (since none puts by
10   The curtain I have drawn for you, but I)
And seemed as they would ask me, if they durst,
How such a glance came there; so, not the first
Are you to turn and ask thus. Sir, 'twas not
Her husband's presence only, called that spot
Of joy into the Duchess' cheek; perhaps
Frà Pandolf chanced to say, "Her mantle laps
Over my lady's wrist too much," or "Paint
Must never hope to reproduce the faint
Half-flush that dies along her throat": such stuff
20   Was courtesy, she thought, and cause enough
For calling up that spot of joy. She had
A heart—how shall I say?—too soon made glad,
Too easily impressed: she liked whate'er
She looked on, and her looks went everywhere.
Sir, 'twas all one! My favour at her breast,
The dropping of the daylight in the West,
The bough of cherries some officious fool
Broke in the orchard for her, the white mule
She rode with round the terrace—all and each
30   Would draw from her alike the approving speech.
Or blush, at least. She thanked men,—good! but thanked
Somehow—I know not how—as if she ranked
My gift of a nine-hundred-years-old name
With anybody's gift. Who'd stoop to blame

This sort of trifling? Even had you skill
In speech—(which I have not)—to make your will
Quite clear to such an one, and say, "Just this
Or that in you disgusts me; here you miss,
Or there exceed the mark"—and if she let
40   Herself be lessoned so, nor plainly set
Her wits to yours, forsooth, and made excuse,
—E'en then would be some stooping; and I choose
Never to stoop. Oh sir, she smiled, no doubt,
Whene'er I passed her; but who passed without
Much the same smile? This grew; I gave commands;
Then all smiles stopped together. There she stands
As if alive. Will't please you rise? We'll meet
The company below, then. I repeat,
The Count your master's known munificence
50   Is ample warrant that no just pretence
Of mine for dowry will be disallowed;
Though his fair daughter's self, as I avowed
At starting, is my object. Nay, we'll go
Together down, sir. Notice Neptune, though,
Taming a sea-horse, thought a rarity,
Which Claus of Innsbruck cast in bronze for me!

The Bishop Orders His Tomb at Saint Praxed's Church

Rome, 15—

Vanity, saith the preacher, vanity!
Draw round my bed: is Anselm keeping back?
Nephews—sons mine . . . ah God, I know not! Well—
She, men would have to be your mother once,
Old Gandolf envied me, so fair she was!
What's done is done, and she is dead beside,
Dead long ago, and I am Bishop since,
And as she died so must we die ourselves,
And thence ye may perceive the world's a dream.
10   Life, how and what is it? As here I lie
In this state-chamber, dying by degrees,
Hours and long hours in the dead night, I ask,
"Do I live, am I dead?" Peace, peace seems all.
Saint Praxed's ever was the church for peace;
And so, about this tomb of mine. I fought
With tooth and nail to save my niche, ye know:
—Old Gandolf cozened me, despite my care;

Shrewd was that snatch from out the corner South
He graced his carrion with, God curse the same!
20   Yet still my niche is not so cramped but thence
One sees the pulpit o' the epistle-side,
And somewhat of the choir, those silent seats,
And up into the aery dome where live
The angels, and a sunbeam's sure to lurk:
And I shall fill my slab of basalt there,
And 'neath my tabernacle take my rest,
With those nine columns round me, two and two,
The odd one at my feet where Anselm stands:
Peach-blossom marble all, the rare, the ripe
30   As fresh-poured red wine of a mighty pulse.
—Old Gandolf with his paltry onion-stone,
Put me where I may look at him! True peach,
Rosy and flawless: how I earned the prize!
Draw close: that conflagration of my church
—What then? So much was saved if aught were missed!
My sons, ye would not be my death? Go dig
The white-grape vineyard where the oil-press stood,
Drop water gently till the surface sink,
And if ye find . . . Ah God, I know not, I! . . .
40   Bedded in store of rotten fig-leaves soft,
And corded up in a tight olive-frail,
Some lump, ah God, of *lapis lazuli*,
Big as a Jew's head cut off at the nape,
Blue as a vein o'er the Madonna's breast . . .
Sons, all have I bequeathed you, villas, all,
That brave Frascati villa with its bath,
So, let the blue lump poise between my knees,
Like God the Father's globe on both his hands
Ye worship in the Jesu Chruch so gay,
50   For Gandolf shall not choose but see and burst!
Swift as a weaver's shuttle fleet our years:
Man goeth to the grave, and where is he?
Did I say basalt for my slab, sons? Black—
'Twas ever antique-black I meant! How else
Shall ye contrast my frieze to come beneath?
The bas-relief in bronze ye promised me,
Those Pans and Nymphs ye wot of, and perchance
Some tripod, thyrsus, with a vase or so,
The Savior at his sermon on the mount,
60   Saint Praxed in a glory, and one Pan
Ready to twitch the Nymph's last garment off,

And Moses with the tables . . . but I know
Ye mark me not! What do they whisper thee,
Child of my bowels, Anselm? Ah, ye hope
To revel down my villas while I gasp
Bricked o'er with beggar's moldy travertine
Which Gandolf from his tomb-top chuckles at!
Nay, boys, ye love me—all of jasper, then!
'Tis jasper ye stand pledged to, lest I grieve.
70 My bath must needs be left behind, alas!
One block, pure green as a pistachio-nut,
There's plenty jasper somewhere in the world—
And have I not Saint Praxed's ear to pray
Horses for ye, and brown Greek manuscripts,
And mistresses with great smooth marbly limbs?
—That's if ye carve my epitaph aright,
Choice Latin, picked phrase, Tully's every word,
No gaudy ware like Gandolf's second line—
Tully, my masters? Ulpian serves his need!
80 And then how I shall lie through centuries,
And hear the blessed mutter of the mass,
And see God made and eaten all day long,
And feel the steady candle-flame, and taste
Good, strong, thick, stupefying incense-smoke!
For as I lie here, hours of the dead night,
Dying in state and by such slow degrees,
I fold my arms as if they clasped a crook,
And stretch my feet forth straight as stone can point,
And let the bedclothes, for a mortcloth, drop
90 Into great laps and folds of sculptor's-work:
And as yon tapers dwindle, and strange thoughts
Grow, with a certain humming in my ears,
About the life before I lived this life,
And this life too, popes, cardinals and priests,
Saint Praxed at his sermon on the mount,
Your tall pale mother with her talking eyes,
And new-found agate urns as fresh as day,
And marble's language, Latin pure, discreet,
—Aha, ELUCESCEBAT[1] quoth our friend?
100 No Tully, said I, Ulpian at the best!
Evil and brief hath been my pilgrimage.
All *lapis*, all, sons! Else I give the Pope

1. He was famous: not in the pure Latin of Cicero (Tully)
   but in the debased style of Ulpian.

My villas! Will ye ever eat my heart?
Ever your eyes were as a lizard's quick,
They glitter like your mother's for my soul,
Or ye would heighten my impoverished frieze,
Piece out its starved design, and fill my vase
With grapes, and add a visor and a Term,
And to the tripod ye would tie a lynx
110 That in his struggle throws the thyrsus down,
To comfort me on my entablature
Whereon I am to lie till I must ask,
"Do I live, am I dead?" There, leave me, there!
For ye have stabbed me with ingratitude
To death—ye wish it—God, ye wish it! Stone—
Gritstone, a-crumble! Clammy squares which sweat
As if the corpse they keep were oozing through—
And no more *lapis* to delight the world!
Well, go! I bless ye. Fewer tapers there,
120 But in a row: and, going, turn your backs
—Aye, like departing altar-ministrants,
And leave me in my church, the church for peace,
That I may watch at leisure if he leers—
Old Gandolf—at me, from his onion-stone,
As still he envied me, so fair she was!

The Lost Mistress

I

All's over, then: does truth sound bitter
  As one at first believes?
Hark, 'tis the sparrows' good-night twitter
  About your cottage eaves!

II

And the leaf-buds on the vine are wooly,
  I noticed that, to-day;
One day more bursts them open fully
  —You know the red turns grey.

III

To-morrow we meet the same then, dearest?
10   May I take your hand in mine?

Mere friends are we,—well, friends the merest
  Keep much that I resign:

     IV

For each glance of the eye so bright and black,
  Though I keep with heart's endeavour,—
Your voice, when you wish the snowdrops back,
  Though it stay in my soul for ever!—

     V

Yet I will but say what mere friends say,
  Or only a thought stronger;
I will hold your hand but as long as all may,
20   Or so very little longer!

Humility

What girl but, having gathered flowers,
Stript the beds and spoilt the bowers,
From the lapful light she carries
Drops a careless bud?—nor tarries
To regain the waif and stray:
"Store enough for home"—she'll say.

So say I too: give your lover
Heaps of loving—under, over,
Whelm him—make the one the wealthy!
10 Am I all so poor who—stealthy
Work it was!—picked up what fell:
Not the worst bud—who can tell?

Poetics

"So say the foolish!" Say the foolish so, Love?
  "Flower she is, my rose"—or else "My very swan is she"—
Or perhaps "Yon maid-moon, blessing earth below, Love,
  That art thou!"—to them, belike: no such vain words from me.

"Hush, rose, blush! no balm like breath," I chide it:
  "Bend thy neck its best, swan,—hers the whiter curve!"
Be the moon the moon: my Love I place beside it:
  What is she? Her human self,—no lower word will serve.

Summmum Bonum[1]

All the breath and the bloom of the year in the bag of one bee:
  All the wonder and wealth of the mine in the heart of one gem:
In the core of one pearl all the shade and the shine of the sea:
  Breath and bloom, shade and shine,—wonder, wealth, and—how far
      above them—
          Truth, that's brighter than gem,
          Trust, that's purer than pearl,—
Brightest truth, purest trust in the universe—all were for me
          In the kiss of one girl.

1. "The Greatest Good"

WALT WHITMAN
1818–1892

With a Note on American Poetry

Whitman is the first American poet in this anthology, and in many ways he is truly the first poet of America, though many men and women wrote poetry on this continent before him. Whitman had the courage to break with English meters and rhymes, and go back to the Biblical Psalmists for inspiration. He broke with the English language, too, writing in what is clearly American. And he chose his subject matter more as a journalist would than as traditional poets have chosen it. He wrote easily—too easily, some would say; and he wrote a lot—too much, some would say. Yet much of what he wrote remains memorable today, and the poets of the future whom he called upon in this little poem heard him and answered.

Poets to Come

Poets to come! orators, singers, musicians to come!
Not to-day is to justify me and answer what I am for,
But you, a new brood, native, athletic, continental, greater than before known,
Arouse! for you must justify me.

I myself but write one or two indicative words for the future,
I but advance a moment only to wheel and hurry back in the darkness.

I am a man who, sauntering along without fully stopping, turns a casual look upon
      you and then averts his face,
Leaving it to you to prove and define it,
Expecting the main things from you.

I Hear America Singing

I hear America singing, the varied carols I hear,
Those of mechanics, each one singing his as it should be blithe and strong,
The carpenter singing his as he measures his plank or beam,
The mason singing his as he makes ready for work, or leaves off work.
The boatman singing what belongs to him in his boat, the deckhand singing on
    the steamboat deck,
The shoemaker singing as he sits on his bench, the hatter singing as he stands,
The wood-cutter's song, the ploughboy's on his way in the morning, or at noon
    intermission or at sundown,
The delicious singing of the mother, or of the young wife at work, or of the girl
    sewing or washing,
Each singing what belongs to him or her and to none else,
10 The day what belongs to the day—at night the party of young fellows, robust,
    friendly,
Singing with open mouths their strong melodious songs.

Crossing Brooklyn Ferry

1

Flood-tide below me! I see you face to face!
Clouds of the west—sun there half an hour high—I see you also face to face.

Crowds of men and women attired in the usual costumes, how curious you are to
    me!
On the ferry-boats the hundreds and hundreds that cross, returning home, are
    more curious to me than you suppose,
And you that shall cross from shore to shore years hence are more to me, and more
    in my meditations, than you might suppose.

2

The impalpable sustenance of me from all things at all hours of the day,
The simple, compact, well-join'd scheme, myself disintegrated, every one
    disintegrated yet part of the scheme,
The similitudes of the past and those of the future,
The glories strung like beads on my smallest sights and hearings, on the walk in
    the street and the passage over the river,
10 The current rushing so swiftly and swimming with me far away,
The others that are to follow me, the ties between me and them,
The certainty of others, the life, love, sight, hearing of others.

Others will enter the gates of the ferry and cross from shore to shore,
Others will watch the run of the flood-tide,
Others will see the shipping of Manhattan north and west, and the heights of
  Brooklyn to the south and east,
Others will see the islands large and small;
Fifty years hence, others will see them as they cross, the sun half an hour high,
A hundred years hence, or ever so many hundred years hence, others will see
  them,
Will enjoy the sunset, the pouring-in of the flood-tide, the falling-back to the sea of
  the ebb-tide.

3

20 It avails not, time nor place—distance avails not,
I am with you, you men and women of a generation, or ever so many generations
  hence,
Just as you feel when you look on the river and sky, so I felt,
Just as any of you is one of a living crowd, I was one of a crowd,
Just as you are refresh'd by the gladness of the river and the bright flow, I was
  refresh'd,
Just as you stand and lean on the rail, yet hurry with the swift current, I stood yet
  was hurried,
Just as you look on the numberless masts of ships and the thick-stemm'd pipes of
  steamboats, I look'd.

I too many and many a time cross'd the river of old,
Watched the Twelfth-month sea-gulls, saw them high in the air floating with
  motionless wings, oscillating their bodies,
Saw how the glistening yellow lit up parts of their bodies and left the rest in strong
  shadow,
30 Saw the slow-wheeling circles and the gradual edging toward the south,
Saw the reflection of the summer sky in the water,
Had my eyes dazzled by the shimmering track of beams,
Look'd at the fine centrifugal spokes of light round the shape of my head in the
  sunlit water,
Look'd on the haze on the hills southward and south-westward,
Look'd on the vapor as it flew in fleeces tinged with violet,
Look'd toward the lower bay to notice the vessels arriving,
Saw their approach, saw aboard those that were near me,
Saw the white sails of schooners and sloops, saw the ships at anchor,
The sailors at work in the rigging or out astride the spars,
40 The round masts, the swinging motion of the hulls, the slender serpentine
  pennants,
The large and small steamers in motion, the pilots in their pilot-houses,

The white wake left by the passage, the quick tremulous whirl of the wheels,
The flags of all nations, the falling of them at sunset,
The scallop-edged waves in the twilight, the ladled cups, the frolicsome crests and
    glistening,
The stretch afar growing dimmer and dimmer, the gray walls of the granite
    storehouses by the docks,
On the river the shadowy group, the big steam-tug closely flank'd on each side by
    the barges, the hay-boat, the belated lighter,
On the neighboring shore the fires from the foundry chimneys burning high and
    glaringly into the night,
Casting their flicker of black contrasted with wild red and yellow light over the
    tops of houses and down into the clefts of streets.

4

These and all else were to me the same as they are to you,
50 I loved well those cities, loved well the stately and rapid river,
The men and women I saw were all near to me,
Others the same—others who look back on me because I look'd forward to them,
(The time will come, though I stop here to-day and to-night.)

5

What is it then between us?
What is the count of the scores or hundreds of years between us?

Whatever it is, it avails not—distance avails not, and place avails not,
I too lived, Brooklyn of ample hills was mine,
I too walk'd the streets of Manhattan island, and bathed in the waters around it,
I too felt the curious abrupt questionings stir within me,
60 In the day among crowds of people sometimes they came upon me,
In my walks home late at night or as I lay in my bed they came upon me,
I too had been struck from the float forever held in solution,
I too had receiv'd identity by my body,
That I was I knew was of my body, and what I should be I knew I should be of my
    body.

6

It is not upon you alone the dark patches fall,
The dark threw its patches down upon me also,
The best I had done seem'd to me blank and suspicious,
My great thoughts as I supposed them, were they not in reality meagre?
Nor is it you alone who know what it is to be evil,
70 I am he who knew what it was to be evil,

I too knitted the old knot of contrariety,
Blabb'd, blush'd, resented, lied, stole, grudg'd,
Had guile, anger, lust, hot wishes I dared not speak,
Was wayward, vain, greedy, shallow, sly, cowardly, malignant,
The wolf, the snake, the hog, not wanting in me,
The cheating look, the frivolous word, the adulterous wish, not wanting,
Refusals, hates, postponements, meanness, laziness, none of these wanting,
Was one with the rest, the days and haps of the rest,
Was call'd by my nighest name by clear loud voices of young men as they saw me
approaching or passing,
80   Felt their arms on my neck as I stood, or the negligent leaning of their flesh against
me as I sat,
Saw many I loved in the street or ferry-boat or public assembly, yet never told
them a word,
Lived the same life with the rest, the same old laughing, gnawing, sleeping,
Play'd the part that still looks back on the actor or actress,
The same old role, the role that is what we make it, as great as we like,
Or as small as we like, or both great and small.

7

Closer yet I approach you,
What thought you have of me now, I had as much of you—I laid in my stores in
advance,
I consider'd long and seriously of you before you were born.

Who was to know what should come home to me?
90   Who knows but I am enjoying this?
Who knows, for all the distance, but I am as good as looking at you now, for all you
cannot see me?

8

Ah, what can ever be more stately and admirable to me than mast-hemm'd
Manhattan?
River and sunset and scallop-edg'd waves of flood-tide?
The sea-gulls oscillating their bodies, the hay-boat in the twilight, and the belated
lighter?
What gods can exceed these that clasp me by the hand, and with voices I love call
me promptly and loudly by my nighest name as I approach?
What is more subtle than this which ties me to the woman or man that looks in my
face?
Which fuses me into you now, and pours my meaning into you?

We understand then do we not?
What I promis'd without mentioning it, have you not accepted?
100   What the study could not teach—what the preaching could not accomplish is
        accomplish'd, is it not?

        9

Flow on, river! flow with the flood-tide, and ebb with the ebb-tide!
Frolic on, crested and scallop-edg'd waves!
Gorgeous clouds of the sunset! drench with your splendor me, or the men and
        women generations after me!
Cross from shore to shore, countless crowds of passengers!
Stand up, tall masts of Mannahatta! stand up, beautiful hills of Brooklyn!
Throb, baffled and curious brain! throw out questions and answers!
Suspend here and everywhere, eternal float of solution!
Gaze, loving and thirsty eyes, in the house or street or public assembly!
Sound out, voices of young men! loudly and musically call me by my nighest
        name!
110   Live, old life! play the part that looks back on the actor or actress!
Play the old role, the role that is great or small according as one makes it!
Consider, you who peruse me, whether I may not in unknown ways be looking
        upon you;
Be firm, rail over the river, to support those who lean idly, yet haste with the
        hasting current;
Fly on, sea-birds! fly sideways, or wheel in large circles high in the air;
Receive the summer sky, you water, and faithfully hold it till all downcast eyes
        have time to take it from you!
Diverge, fine spokes of light, from the shape of my head, or any one's head, in the
        sunlit water!
Come on, ships from the lower bay! pass up or down, white-sail'd schooners,
        sloops, lighters!
Flaunt away, flags of all nations! be duly lower'd at sunset!
Burn high your fires, foundry chimneys! cast black shadows at nightfall! cast red
        and yellow light over the tops of the houses!
120   Appearances, now or henceforth, indicate what you are,
You necessary film, continue to envelop the soul,
About my body for me, and your body for you, be hung out divinest aromas,
Thrive, cities—bring your freight, bring your shows, ample and sufficient rivers,
Expand, being than which none else is perhaps more spiritual,
Keep your places, objects than which none else is more lasting.

You have waited, you always wait, you dumb, beautiful ministers,
We receive you with free sense at last, and are insatiate henceforward,
Not you any more shall be able to foil us, or withhold yourselves from us,

We use you, and do not cast you aside—we plant you permanently within us,
130   We fathom you not—we love you—there is perfection in you also,
You furnish your parts toward eternity,
Great or small, you furnish your parts toward the soul.

The World below the Brine

The world below the brine,
Forests at the bottom of the sea, the branches and leaves,
Sea-lettuce, vast lichens, strange flowers and seeds, the thick tangle, openings,
    and pink turf,
Different colors, pale gray and green, purple, white, and gold, the play of light
    through the water,
Dumb swimmers there among the rocks, coral, gluten, grass, rushes, and the
    aliment of the swimmers,
Sluggish existences grazing there suspended, or slowly crawling close to the
    bottom,
The sperm-whale at the surface blowing air and spray, or disporting with his
    flukes,
The leaden-eyed shark, the walrus, the turtle, the hairy sea-leopard, and the
    sting-ray,
Passions there, wars, pursuits, tribes, sight in those ocean-depths, breathing that
    thick-breathing air, as so many do,
10   The change thence to the sight here, and to the subtle air breathed by beings like
    us who walk this sphere,
The change onward from ours to that of beings who walk other spheres.

The Dalliance of the Eagles

Skirting the river road, (my forenoon walk, my rest,)
Skyward in air a sudden muffled sound, the dalliance of the eagles,
The rushing amorous contact high in space together,
The clinching interlocking claws, a living, fierce, gyrating wheel,
Four beating wings, two beaks, a swirling mass tight grappling,
In tumbling turning clustering loops, straight downward falling,
Till o'er the river pois'd, the twain yet one, a moment's lull,
A motionless still balance in the air, then parting, talons loosing,
Upward again on slow-firm pinions slanting, their separate diverse flight,
10   She hers, he his, pursuing.

A Sight in Camp in the Daybreak Gray and Dim

A sight in camp in the daybreak gray and dim,
As from my tent I emerge so early sleepless,
As slow I walk in the cool fresh air the path near by the hospital tent,
Three forms I see on stretchers lying, brought out there untended lying,
Over each the blanket spread, ample brownish woolen blanket,
Gray and heavy blanket, folding, covering all.

Curious I halt and silent stand,
Then with light fingers I from the face of the nearest the first just lift the blanket;
Who are you elderly man so gaunt and grim, with well-gray'd hair, and flesh all
    sunken about the eyes?
10   Who are you my dear comrade?

Then to the second I step—and who are you my child and darling?
Who are you sweet boy with cheeks yet blooming?

Then to the third—a face nor child nor old, very calm, as of beautiful yellow-white
    ivory;
Young man I think I know you—I think this face is the face of the Christ himself,
Dead and divine and brother of all, and here again he lies.

Who Learns My Lesson Complete?

Who learns my lesson complete?
Boss, journeyman, apprentice, churchman and atheist,
The stupid and the wise thinker, parents and offspring, merchant, clerk, porter
    and customer,
Editor, author, artist, and schoolboy—draw nigh and commence;
It is no lesson—it lets down the bars to a good lesson,
And that to another, and every one to another still.

The great laws take and effuse without argument,
I am of the same style, for I am their friend,
I love them quits and quits, I do not halt and make salaams.

10   I lie abstracted and hear beautiful tales of things and the reasons of things.
They are so beautiful I nudge myself to listen.

I cannot say to any person what I hear—I cannot say it to myself—it is very
    wonderful.

It is no small matter, this round and delicious globe moving so exactly in its orbit
    for ever and ever, without one jolt or the untruth of a single second,
I do not think it was made in six days, nor in ten thousand years, nor ten billions
    of years,
Nor plann'd and built one thing after another as an architect plans and builds a
    house.

I do not think seventy years is the time of a man or woman,
Nor that seventy millions of years is the time of a man or woman,
Nor that years will ever stop the existence of me, or any one else.

Is it wonderful that I should be immortal? as every one is immortal;
20 I know it is wonderful, but my eyesight is equally wonderful, and how I was
    conceived in my mother's womb is equally wonderful,
And pass'd from a babe in the creeping trance of a couple of summers and winters
    to articulate and walk—all this is equally wonderful.

And that my soul embraces you this hour, and we affect each other without ever
    seeing each other, and never perhaps to see each other, is every bit as
    wonderful.

And that I can think such thoughts as these is just as wonderful,
And that I can remind you, and you think them and know them to be true, is just
    as wonderful.

And that the moon spins round the earth and on with the earth, is equally
    wonderful,
And that they balance themselves with the sun and stars is equally wonderful.

The Ox-Tamer

In a far-away northern county in the placid pastoral region,
Lives my farmer friend, the theme of my recitative, a famous tamer of oxen,
There they bring him the three-year-olds and the four-year-olds to break them,
He will take the wildest steer in the world and break him and tame him,
He will go fearless without any whip where the young bullock chafes up and down
    the yard,
The bullock's head tosses restless high in the air with raging eyes,
Yet see you! how soon his rage subsides—how soon this tamer tames him;
See you! on the farms hereabout a hundred oxen young and old, and he is the man
    who has tamed them,
They all know him, all are affectionate to him;
10 See you! some are such beautiful animals, so lofty looking;

Some are buff-color'd, some mottled, one has a white line running along his back,
    some are brindled,
Some have wide flaring horns (a good sign)—see you! the bright hides,
See, the two with stars on their foreheads—see, the round bodies and broad backs,
How straight and square they stand on their legs—what fine sagacious eyes!
How they watch their tamer—they wish him near them—how they turn to look
    after him!
What yearning expression! how uneasy they are when he moves away from them;
Now I marvel what it can be he appears to them, (books, politics, poems,
    depart—all else departs,)
I confess I envy only his fascination—my silent, illiterate friend,
Whom a hundred oxen love there in his life on farms,
20   In the northern county far, in the placid pastoral region.

As I Sit Writing Here

As I sit writing here, sick and grown old,
Not my least burden is that dulness of the years, querilities,
Ungracious glooms, aches, lethargy, constipation, whimpering *ennui*,
May filter in my daily songs.

EMILY DICKINSON
1830–1886
[Success Is Counted Sweetest]

Success is counted sweetest
By those who ne'er succeed.
To comprehend a nectar
Requires sorest need.

Not one of all the purple Host
Who took the Flag today
Can tell the definition
So clear of Victory

As he defeated—dying—
10   On whose forbidden ear
The distant strains of triumph
Burst agonized and clear!

[I Never Hear the Word]

I never hear the word "escape"
Without a quicker blood,
A sudden expectation,
A flying attitude!

I never hear of prisons broad
By soldiers battered down,
But I tug childish at my bars
Only to fail again!

[I'm "Wife"—I've Finished That]

I'm "wife"—I've finished that—
That other state—
I'm Czar—I'm "Woman" now—
It's safer so—

How odd the Girl's life looks
Behind this soft Eclipse—
I think that Earth feels so
To folks in Heaven—now—

This being comfort—then
10   That other kind—was pain—
But why compare?
I'm "Wife"! Stop there!

[What Is—"Paradise"]

What is—"Paradise"—
Who live there—
Are they "Farmers"—
Do they "hoe"—
Do they know that this is "Amherst"—
And that I—am coming—too—

Do they wear "new shoes"—in "Eden"—
Is it always pleasant—there—
Won't they scold us—when we're hungry—
10   Or tell God—how cross we are—

You are sure there's such a person
As "a Father"—in the sky—
So if I get lost—there—ever—
Or do what the nurse calls "die"—
I shan't walk the "Jasper"—barefoot—
Ransomed folks—won't laugh at me—
Maybe—"Eden" a'nt so lonesome
As New England used to be!

[I Heard a Fly Buzz]

I heard a Fly buzz—when I died—
The Stillness in the Room
Was like the Stillness in the Air—
Between the Heaves of Storm—

The Eyes around—had wrung them dry—
And Breaths were gathering firm
For that last Onset—when the King
Be witnessed—in the Room—

I willed my Keepsakes—Signed away
10   What portion of me be
Assignable—and then it was
There interposed a Fly—

With Blue—uncertain stumbling Buzz—
Between the light—and me—
And then the Windows failed—and then
I could not see to see—

[The Heart Asks Pleasure—First]

The Heart asks Pleasure—first—
And then—Excuse from Pain—
And then—those little Anodynes
That deaden suffering—

And then—to go to sleep—
And then—if it should be
The will of its Inquisitor
The privilege to die—

[Because I Could Not Stop for Death]

Because I could not stop for Death—
He kindly stopped for me—
The Carriage held but just Ourselves—
And Immortality.

We slowly drove—He knew no haste
And I had put away
My labor and my leisure too,
For His Civility—

We passed the School, where Children strove
10   At Recess—in the Ring—
We passed the Fields of Gazing Grain—
We passed the Setting Sun—

Or rather—He passed Us—
The Dews drew quivering and chill—
For only Gossamer, my Gown—
My Tippet—only Tulle—

We paused before a House that seemed
A Swelling of the Ground—
The Roof was scarcely visible—
20   The Cornice—in the Ground—

Since then—'tis Centuries—and yet
Feels shorter than the Day
I first surmised the Horses' Heads
Were toward Eternity—

[A Narrow Fellow in the Grass]

A narrow Fellow in the Grass
Occasionally rides—
You may have met Him—did you not
His notice sudden is—

The Grass divides as with a Comb—
A spotted shaft is seen—
And then it closes at your feet
And opens further on—

He likes a Boggy Acre
10   A Floor too cool for Corn—
Yet when a Boy, and Barefoot—
I more than once at Noon

Have passed, I thought, a Whip lash
Unbraiding in the Sun
When stooping to secure it
It wrinkled, and was gone—

Several of Nature's People
I know, and they know me—
I feel for them a transport
20   Of cordiality—

But never met this Fellow
Attended, or alone
Without a tighter breathing
And Zero at the Bone—

GERARD MANLEY HOPKINS
1844–1889
God's Grandeur

The world is charged with the grandeur of God.
   It will flame out, like shining from shook foil;
   It gathers to a greatness, like the ooze of oil
Crushed. Why do men then now not reck his rod?
Generations have trod, have trod, have trod;
   And all is seared with trade; bleared, smeared with toil;
   And wears man's smudge and shares man's smell: the soil
Is bare now, nor can foot feel, being shod.

And for all this, nature is never spent;
10   There lives the dearest freshness deep down things;
And though the last lights off the black West went
   Oh, morning, at the brown brink eastward, springs—
Because the Holy Ghost over the bent
   World broods with warm breast and with ah! bright wings.

The Windhover

To Christ Our Lord

I caught this morning morning's minion, king-
   dom of daylight's dauphin, dapple-dawn-drawn Falcon, in his riding
   Of the rolling level underneath him steady air, and striding
High there, how he rung upon the rein of a wimpling wing
In his ecstasy! then off, off forth on swing,
   As a skate's heel sweeps smooth on a bow-bend: the hurl and gliding
   Rebuffed the big wind. My heart in hiding   .
Stirred for a bird,—the achieve of, the mastery of the thing!

   Brute beauty and valour and act, oh, air, pride, plume, here
10   Buckle! AND the fire that breaks from thee then, a billion
Times told lovelier, more dangerous, O my chevalier!

   No wonder of it: shéer plód makes plough down sillion
Shine, and blue-bleak embers, ah my dear,
   Fall, gall themselves, and gash gold-vermilion.

Pied Beauty

Glory be to God for dappled things—
   For skies of couple-colour as a brinded cow;
     For rose-moles all in stipple upon trout that swim;
Fresh-firecoal chestnut-falls; finches' wings;
   Landscape plotted and pieced—fold, fallow, and plough;
     And áll trádes, their gear and tackle and trim.
All things counter, original, spare, strange;
   Whatever is fickle, freckled (who knows how?)
     With swift, slow; sweet, sour; adazzle, dim;
10   He fathers-forth whose beauty is past change:
                    Praise him.

Spring and Fall: To a Young Child

Márgarét, are you gríeving
Over Goldengrove unleaving?
Leáves, líke the things of man, you
With your fresh thoughts care for, can you?
Ah! ás the heart grows older
It will come to such sights colder
By and by, nor spare a sigh

Though worlds of wanwood leafmeal lie;
And yet you will weep and know why.
10   Now no matter, child, the name:
Sórrow's spríngs áre the same.
Nor mouth had, no nor mind, expressed
What heart heard of, ghost guessed:
It ís the blight man was born for,
It is Margaret you mourn for.

[Thou Art Indeed Just, Lord]

> Justus quidem tu es, Domine, si disputem tecum: verumtamen
> justa loquar ad te: Quare via impiorum prosperatur? &c.[1]

Thou are indeed just, Lord, if I contend
With thee; but, sir, so what I plead is just.
Why do sinners' ways prosper? and why must
Disappointment all I endeavor end?

Wert thou my enemy, O thou my friend,
How wouldst thou worse, I wonder, than thou dost
Defeat, thwart me? Oh, the sots and thralls of lust
Do in spare hours more thrive than I that spend,

Sir, life upon thy cause. See, banks and brakes
10   Now, leavèd how thick! lacèd thay are again
With fretty chervil, look, and fresh wind shakes

Them; birds build—but not I build; no, but strain,
Time's eunuch, and not breed one work that wakes.
Mine, O thou lord of life, send my roots rain.

1. Quoted from the Biblical prophet Jeremiah, and translated
   in the first three lines of the poem.

A. E. HOUSMAN
1859–1936
From A Shropshire Lad

2

Loveliest of trees, the cherry now
Is hung with bloom along the bough,
And stands about the woodland ride
Wearing white for Eastertide.

Now, of my threescore years and ten,
Twenty will not come again,
And take from seventy springs a score,
It only leaves me fifty more.

And since to look at things in bloom
10   Fifty springs are little room,
About the woodlands I will go
To see the cherry hung with snow.

13

When I was one-and-twenty
    I heard a wise man say,
"Give crowns and pounds and guineas
    But not your heart away;
Give pearls away and rubies
    But keep your fancy free."
But I was one-and-twenty,
    No use to talk to me.

When I was one-and-twenty
10   I heard him say again,
"The heart out of the bosom
    Was never given in vain;
'Tis paid with sighs a plenty
    And sold for endless rue."
And I am two-and-twenty,
    And oh, 'tis true, 'tis true.

18

Oh, when I was in love with you,
    Then I was clean and brave,
And miles around the wonder grew
    How well did I behave.

And now the fancy passes by,
    And nothing will remain,
And miles around they'll say that I
    Am quite myself again.

19

To an Athlete Dying Young

The time you won your town the race
We chaired you through the market-place;
Man and boy stood cheering by,
And home we brought you shoulder-high.

To-day, the road all runners come,
Shoulder-high we bring you home,
And set you at your threshold down,
Townsman of a stiller town.

Smart lad, to slip betimes away
10   From fields where glory does not stay
And early though the laurel grows
It withers quicker than the rose.

Eyes the shady night has shut
Cannot see the record cut,
And silence sounds no worse than cheers
After earth has stopped the ears:

Now you will not swell the rout
Of lads that wore their honours out,
Runners whom renown outran
20   And the name died before the man.

So set, before its echoes fade,
The fleet foot on the sill of shade,
And hold to the low lintel up
The still-defended challenge-cup.

And round that early-laurelled head
Will flock to gaze the strengthless dead,
And find unwithered on its curls
The garland briefer than a girl's.

27

"Is my team ploughing,
    That I was used to drive
And hear the harness jingle
    When I was man alive?"

Ay, the horses trample,
  The harness jingles now;
No change though you lie under
  The land you used to plough.

"Is football playing
10   Along the river shore,
With lads to chase the leather,
  Now I stand up no more?"

Ay, the ball is flying,
  The lads play heart and soul;
The goal stands up, the keeper
  Stands up to keep the goal.

"Is my girl happy,
  That I thought hard to leave,
And has she tired of weeping
20   As she lies down at eve?"

Ay, she lies down lightly,
  She lies not down to weep:
Your girl is well contented.
  Be still, my lad, and sleep.

"Is my friend hearty,
  Now I am thin and pine,
And has he found to sleep in
  A better bed than mine?"

Yes, lad, I lie easy,
30   I lie as lads would choose;
I cheer a dead man's sweetheart,
  Never ask me whose.

62

"Terence, this is stupid stuff:
You eat your victuals fast enough;
There can't be much amiss, 'tis clear,
To see the rate you drink your beer.
But oh, good Lord, the verse you make,
It gives a chap the belly-ache.
The cow, the old cow, she is dead;

It sleeps well, the horned head:
We poor lads, 'tis our turn now
To hear such tunes as killed the cow.
Pretty friendship 'tis to rhyme
Your friends to death before their time
Moping melancholy mad:
Come, pipe a tune to dance to, lad."

   Why, if 'tis dancing you would be,
There's brisker pipes than poetry.
Say, for what were hop-yards meant,
Or why was Burton built on Trent?
Oh many a peer of England brews
Livelier liquor than the Muse,
And malt does more than Milton can
To justify God's ways to man.
Ale, man, ale's the stuff to drink
For fellows whom it hurts to think:
Look into the pewter pot
To see the world as the world's not.
And faith, 'tis pleasant till 'tis past:
The mischief is that 'twill not last.
Oh I have been to Ludlow fair
And left my necktie God knows where,
And carried half-way home, or near,
Pints and quarts of Ludlow beer:
Then the world seemed none so bad,
And I myself a sterling lad;
And down in lovely muck I've lain,
Happy till I woke again.
Then I saw the morning sky:
Heigho, the tale was all a lie;
The world, it was the old world yet,
I was I, my things were wet,
And nothing now remained to do
But begin the game anew.

   Therefore, since the world has still
Much good, but much less good than ill,
And while the sun and moon endure
Luck's a chance, but trouble's sure,
I'd face it as a wise man would,
And train for ill and not for good.

'Tis true the stuff I bring for sale
50   Is not so brisk a brew as ale:
Out of a stem that scored the hand
I wrung it in a weary land.
But take it: if the smack is sour,
The better for the embittered hour;
It should do good to heart and head
When your soul is in my soul's stead;
And I will friend you, if I may,
In the dark and cloudy day.

There was a king reigned in the East:
60   There, when kings will sit to feast,
They get their fill before they think
With poisoned meat and poisoned drink.
He gathered all that springs to birth
From the many-venomed earth;
First a little, thence to more,
He sampled all her killing store;
And easy, smiling, seasoned sound,
Sate the king when healths went round.
They put arsenic in his meat
70   And stared aghast to watch him eat;
They poured strychnine in his cup
And shook to see him drink it up:
They shook, they stared as white's their shirt:
Them it was their poison hurt.
—I tell the tale that I heard told.
Mithridates, he died old.

WILLIAM BUTLER YEATS
1865–1939
The Song of Wandering Aengus

I went out to the hazel wood,
Because a fire was in my head,
And cut and peeled a hazel wand,
And hooked a berry to a thread;
And when white moths were on the wing,
And moth-like stars were flickering out,
I dropped the berry in a stream
And caught a little silver trout.

When I had laid it on the floor
10   I went to blow the fire aflame,
But something rustled on the floor,
And some one called me by my name:
It had become a glimmering girl
With apple blossom in her hair
Who called me by my name and ran
And faded through the brightening air.

Though I am old with wandering
Through hollow lands and hilly lands,
I will find out where she has gone,
20   And kiss her lips and take her hands;
And walk among long dappled grass,
And pluck till time and times are done
The silver apples of the moon,
The golden apples of the sun.

A Coat

I made my song a coat
Covered with embroideries
Out of old mythologies
From heel to throat;
But the fools caught it,
Wore it in the world's eyes
As though they'd wrought it.
Song, let them take it,
For there's more enterprise
10   In walking naked.

The Wild Swans at Coole

The trees are in their autumn beauty,
The woodland paths are dry,
Under the October twilight the water
Mirrors a still sky;
Upon the brimming water among the stones
Are nine-and-fifty swans.

The nineteenth autumn has come upon me
Since I first made my count;
I saw, before I had well finished,

10 All suddenly mount
And scatter wheeling in great broken rings
Upon their clamorous wings.

I have looked upon those brilliant creatures,
And now my heart is sore.
All's changed since I, hearing at twilight,
The first time on this shore,
The bell-beat of their wings above my head,
Trod with a lighter tread.

Unwearied still, lover by lover,
20 They paddle in the cold
Companionable streams or climb the air;
Their hearts have not grown old;
Passion or conquest, wander where they will,
Attend upon them still.

But now they drift on the still water,
Mysterious, beautiful;
Among what rushes will they build,
By what lake's edge or pool
Delight men's eyes when I awake some day
30 To find they have flown away?

The Fisherman

Although I can see him still,
The freckled man who goes
To a grey place on a hill
In grey Connemara clothes
At dawn to cast his flies,
It's long since I began
To call up to the eyes
This wise and simple man.

All day I'd looked in the face
10 What I had hoped 'twould be
To write for my own race
And the reality;
The living men that I hate,
The dead man that I loved,
The craven man in his seat,

The insolent unreproved,
And no knave brought to book
Who has won a drunken cheer,
The witty man and his joke
20   Aimed at the commonest ear,
The clever man who cries
The catch-cries of the clown,
The beating down of the wise
And great Art beaten down.

Maybe a twelvemonth since
Suddenly I began,
In scorn of this audience,
Imagining a man,
And his sun-freckled face,
30   And grey Connemara cloth,
Climbing up to a place
Where stone is dark under froth,
And the down-turn of his wrist
When the flies drop in the stream;
A man who does not exist,
A man who is but a dream;
And cried, "Before I am old
I shall have written him one
Poem maybe as cold
40   And passionate as the dawn."

Sailing to Byzantium[1]

That is no country for old men. The young
In one another's arms, birds in the trees
—Those dying generations—at their song,
The salmon-falls, the mackerel-crowded seas,
Fish, flesh, or fowl, commend all summer long
Whatever is begotten, born, and dies.
Caught in that sensual music all neglect
Monuments of unaging intellect.

An aged man is but a paltry thing,
10   A tattered coat upon a stick, unless
Soul clap its hands and sing, and louder sing
For every tatter in its mortal dress,

1. Now Istanbul

Nor is there singing school but studying
Monuments of its own magnificence;
And therefore I have sailed the seas and come
To the holy city of Byzantium.

O sages standing in God's holy fire
As in the gold mosaic of a wall,
Come from the holy fire, perne in a gyre,[2]
20   And be the singing-masters of my soul.
Consume my heart away; sick with desire
And fastened to a dying animal
It knows not what it is; and gather me
Into the artifice of eternity.

Once out of nature I shall never take
My bodily form from any natural thing,
But such a form as Grecian goldsmiths make
Of hammered gold and gold enamelling
To keep a drowsy emperor awake;
30   Or set upon a golden bough to sing
To lords and ladies of Byzantium
Of what is past, or passing, or to come.

2. Revolve in a spiral

For Anne Gregory

"Never shall a young man,
Thrown into despair
By those great honey-coloured
Ramparts at your ear,
Love you for yourself alone
And not your yellow hair."

"But I can get a hair-dye
And set such colour there,
Brown, or black, or carrot,
10   That young men in despair
May love me for myself alone
And not my yellow hair."

"I heard an old religious man
But yesternight declare
That he had found a text to prove

That only God, my dear,
Could love you for yourself alone
And not your yellow hair."

After Long Silence

Speech after long silence; it is right,
All other lovers being estranged or dead,
Unfriendly lamplight hid under its shade,
The curtains drawn upon unfriendly night,
That we descant and yet again descant
Upon the supreme theme of Art and Song:
Bodily decrepitude is wisdom; young
We loved each other and were ignorant.

The Circus Animals' Desertion

I

I sought a theme and sought for it in vain,
I sought it daily for six weeks or so.
Maybe at last, being but a broken man,
I must be satisfied with my heart, although
Winter and summer till old age began
My circus animals[1] were all on show,
Those stilted boys, that burnished chariot,
Lion and woman and the Lord knows what.

II

What can I but enumerate old themes?
First that sea-rider Oisin led by the nose
Through three enchanted islands, allegorical dreams,
Vain gaiety, vain battle, vain repose,
Themes of the embittered heart, or so it seems,
That might adorn old songs or courtly shows;
But what cared I that set him on to ride,
I, starved for the bosom of his faery bride?

And then a counter-truth filled out its play,
The Countess Cathleen was the name I gave it;
She, pity-crazed, had given her soul away,

1. In the course of the poem, Yeats alludes to much of
   his previous work, especially his mythological
   and symbolic figures.

20   But masterful Heaven had intervened to save it.
     I thought my dear must her own soul destroy,
     So did fanaticism and hate enslave it,
     And this brought forth a dream and soon enough
     This dream itself had all my thought and love.

     And when the Fool and Blind Man stole the bread
     Cuchulain fought the ungovernable sea;
     Heart-mysteries there, and yet when all is said
     It was the dream itself enchanted me:
     Character isolated by a deed
30   To engross the present and dominate memory.
     Players and painted stage took all my love,
     And not those things that they were emblems of.

              III

     Those masterful images because complete
     Grew in pure mind, but out of what began?
     A mound of refuse or the sweeping of a street,
     Old kettles, old bottles, and a broken can,
     Old iron, old bones, old rags, that raving slut
     Who keeps the till. Now that my ladder's gone,
     I must lie down where all the ladders start,
40   In the foul rag-and-bone shop of the heart.

ROBERT FROST

1875–1963

After Apple-picking

My long two-pointed ladder's sticking through a tree
Toward heaven still,
And there's a barrel that I didn't fill
Beside it, and there may be two or three
Apples I didn't pick upon some bough.
But I am done with apple-picking now.
Essence of winter sleep is on the night,
The scent of apples: I am drowsing off.
I cannot rub the strangness from my sight
10   I got from looking through a pane of glass
I skimmed this morning from the drinking trough
And held against the world of hoary grass.

It melted, and I let it fall and break.
But I was well
Upon my way to sleep before it fell,
And I could tell
What form my dreaming was about to take.
Magnified apples appear and disappear,
Stem end and blossom end,
20   And every fleck of russet showing clear.
My instep arch not only keeps the ache,
It keeps the pressure of a ladder-round.
I feel the ladder sway as the boughs bend.
And I keep hearing from the cellar bin
The rumbling sound
Of load on load of apples coming in.
For I have had too much
Of apple-picking: I am overtired
Of the great harvest I myself desired.
30   There were ten thousand thousand fruit to touch,
Cherish in hand, lift down, and not let fall.
For all
That struck the earth,
No matter if not bruised or spiked with stubble,
Went surely to the cider-apple heap
As of no worth.
One can see what will trouble
This sleep of mine, whatever sleep it is.
Were he not gone,
40   The woodchuck could say whether it's like his
Long sleep, as I describe its coming on,
Or just some human sleep.

Stopping by Woods on a Snowy Evening

Whose woods these are I think I know.
His house is in the village, though;
He will not see me stopping here
To watch his woods fill up with snow.

My little horse must think it queer
To stop without a farmhouse near
Between the woods and frozen lake
The darkest evening of the year.

He gives his harness bells a shake
10   To ask if there is some mistake.
The only other sound's the sweep
Of easy wind and downy flake.

The woods are lovely, dark, and deep,
But I have promises to keep,
And miles to go before I sleep,
And miles to go before I sleep.

Two Tramps in Mud Time

Out of the mud two strangers came
And caught me splitting wood in the yard.
And one of them put me off my aim
By hailing cheerily "Hit them hard!"
I knew pretty well why he dropped behind
And let the other go on a way.
I knew pretty well what he had in mind:
He wanted to take my job for pay.

Good blocks of oak it was I split,
10   As large around as the chopping block;
And every piece I squarely hit
Fell splinterless as a cloven rock.
The blows that a life of self-control
Spares to strike for the common good,
That day, giving a loose to my soul,
I spent on the unimportant wood.

The sun was warm but the wind was chill.
You know how it is with an April day
When the sun is out and the wind is still,
20   You're one month on in the middle of May.
But if you so much as dare to speak,
A cloud comes over the sunlit arch,
A wind comes off a frozen peak,
And you're two months back in the middle of March.

A bluebird comes tenderly up to alight
And turns to the wind to unruffle a plume,
His song so pitched as not to excite
A single flower as yet to bloom.
It is snowing a flake: and he half knew

30 Winter was only playing possum.
    Except in color he isn't blue,
    But he wouldn't advise a thing to blossom.

    The water for which we may have to look
    In summertime with a witching wand,
    In every wheelrut's now a brook,
    In every print of a hoof a pond.
    Be glad of water, but don't forget
    The lurking frost in the earth beneath
    That will steal forth after the sun is set
40 And show on the water its crystal teeth.

    The time when most I loved my task
    These two must make me love it more
    By coming with what they came to ask.
    You'd think I never had felt before
    The weight of an ax-head poised aloft,
    The grip on earth of outspread feet,
    The life of muscles rocking soft
    And smooth and moist in vernal heat.

    Out of the woods two hulking tramps
50 (From sleeping God knows where last night,
    But not long since in the lumber camps).
    They thought all chopping was theirs of right.
    Men of the woods and lumberjacks,
    They judged me by their appropriate tool.
    Except as a fellow handled an ax,
    They had no way of knowing a fool.

    Nothing on either side was said.
    They knew they had but to stay their stay
    And all their logic would fill my head:
60 As that I had no right to play
    With what was another man's work for gain.
    My right might be love but theirs was need.
    And where the two exist in twain
    Theirs was the better right—agreed.

    But yield who will to their separation,
    My object in living is to unite
    My avocation and my vocation
    As my two eyes make one in sight.

Only where love and need are one,
70 And the work is play for mortal stakes,
Is the deed ever really done
For Heaven and the future's sakes.

Design

I found a dimpled spider, fat and white,
On a white heal-all, holding up a moth
Like a white piece of rigid satin cloth—
Assorted characters of death and blight
Mixed ready to begin the morning right,
Like the ingredients of a witches' broth—
A snow-drop spider, a flower like a froth,
And dead wings carried like a paper kite.

What had that flower to do with being white,
10 The wayside blue and innocent heal-all?
What brought the kindred spider to that height,
Then steered the white moth thither in the night?
What but design of darkness to appall?—
If design govern in a thing so small.

Provide, Provide

The witch that came (the withered hag)
To wash the steps with pail and rag,
Was once the beauty Abishag,[1]

The picture pride of Hollywood.
Too many fall from great and good
For you to doubt the likelihood.

Die early and avoid the fate.
Or if predestined to die late,
Make up your mind to die in state.

10 Make the whole stock exchange your own!
If need be occupy a throne,
Where nobody can call *you* crone.

1. Biblical beauty brought in to warm dying King David

Some have relied on what they knew;
Others on simply being true.
What worked for them might work for you.

No memory of having starred
Atones for later disregard,
Or keeps the end from being hard.

Better to go down dignified
20   With boughten friendship at your side
Than none at all. Provide, provide!

WALLACE STEVENS
1879–1955
Sunday Morning

I

Complacencies of the peignoir, and late
Coffee and oranges in a sunny chair,
And the green freedom of a cockatoo
Upon a rug mingle to dissipate
The holy hush of ancient sacrifice.
She dreams a little, and she feels the dark
Encroachment of that old catastrophe,
As a calm darkens among water-lights.
The pungent oranges and bright, green wings
10   Seem things in some procession of the dead,
Winding across wide water, without sound.
The day is like wide water, without sound,
Stilled for the passing of her dreaming feet
Over the seas, to silent Palestine,
Dominion of the blood and sepulchre.

II

Why should she give her bounty to the dead?
What is divinity if it can come
Only in silent shadows and in dreams?
Shall she not find in comforts of the sun,
20   In pungent fruit and bright, green wings, or else
In any balm or beauty of the earth,
Things to be cherished like the thought of heaven?
Divinity must live within herself:
Passions of rain, or moods in falling snow;

Grievings in loneliness, or unsubdued
Elations when the forest blooms; gusty
Emotions on wet roads on autumn nights;
All pleasures and all pains, remembering
The bough of summer and the winter branch.
30   These are the measures destined for her soul.

III

Jove in the clouds had his inhuman birth.
No mother suckled him, no sweet land gave
Large-mannered motions to his mythy mind.
He moved among us, as a muttering king,
Magnificent, would move among his hinds,
Until our blood, commingling, virginal,
With heaven, brought such requital to desire
The very hinds discerned it, in a star.
Shall our blood fail? Or shall it come to be
40   The blood of paradise? And shall the earth
Seem all of paradise that we shall know?
The sky will be much friendlier then than now,
A part of labor and a part of pain,
And next in glory to enduring love,
Not this dividing and indifferent blue.

IV

She says, "I am content when wakened birds,
Before they fly, test the reality
Of misty fields, by their sweet questionings;
But when the birds are gone, and their warm fields
50   Return no more, where, then, is paradise?"
There is not any haunt of prophecy,
Nor any old chimera of the grave,
Neither the golden underground, nor isle
Melodious, where spirits gat them home,
Nor visionary south, nor cloudy palm
Remote on heaven's hill, that has endured
As April's green endures; or will endure
Like her remembrance of awakened birds,
Or her desire for June and evening, tipped
60   By the consummation of the swallow's wings.

V

She says, "But in contentment I still feel
The need of some imperishable bliss."
Death is the mother of beauty; hence from her,
Alone, shall come fulfilment to our dreams
And our desires. Although she strews the leaves
Of sure obliteration on our paths,
The path sick sorrow took, the many paths
Where triumph rang its brassy phrase, or love
Whispered a little out of tenderness,
70   She makes the willow shiver in the sun
For maidens who were wont to sit and gaze
Upon the grass, relinquished to their feet.
She causes boys to pile new plums and pears
On disregarded plate. The maidens taste
And stray impassioned in the littering leaves.

VI

Is there no change of death in paradise?
Does ripe fruit never fall? Or do the boughs
Hang always heavy in that perfect sky,
Unchanging, yet so like our perishing earth,
80   With rivers like our own that seek for seas
They never find, the same receding shores
That never touch with inarticulate pang?
Why set the pear upon those river-banks
Or spice the shores with odors of the plum?
Alas, that they should wear out colors there,
The silken weavings of our afternoons,
And pick the strings of our insipid lutes!
Death is the mother of beauty, mystical,
Within whose burning bosom we devise
90   Our earthly mothers waiting, sleeplessly.

VII

Supple and turbulent, a ring of men
Shall chant in orgy on a summer morn
Their boisterous devotion to the sun,
Not as a god, but as a god might be,
Naked among them, like a savage source.

Their chant shall be a chant of paradise,
Out of their blood, returning to the sky;
And in their chant shall enter, voice by voice,
The windy lake wherein their lord delights,
100 The trees, like serafin, and echoing hills,
That choir among themselves long afterward.
They shall know well the heavenly fellowship
Of men that perish and of summer morn.
And whence they came and whither they shall go
The dew upon their feet shall manifest.

VIII

She hears, upon that water without sound,
A voice that cries, "The tomb in Palestine
Is not the porch of spirits lingering.
It is the grave of Jesus, where he lay."
110 We live in an old chaos of the sun,
Or old dependency of day and night,
Or island solitude, unsponsored, free,
Of that wide water, inescapable.
Deer walk upon our mountains, and the quail
Whistle about us their spontaneous cries;
Sweet berries ripen in the wilderness;
And, in the isolation of the sky,
At evening, casual flocks of pigeons make
Ambiguous undulations as they sink,
120 Downward to darkness, on extended wings.

The Snow Man

One must have a mind of winter
To regard the frost and the boughs
Of the pine-trees crusted with snow;

And have been cold a long time
To behold the junipers shagged with ice,
The spruces rough in the distant glitter

Of the January sun; and not to think
Of any misery in the sound of the wind,
In the sound of a few leaves,

10 Which is the sound of the land
    Full of the same wind
    That is blowing in the same bare place

    For the listener, who listens in the snow,
    And, nothing himself, beholds
    Nothing that is not there and the nothing that is.

A High-Toned Old Christian Woman

    Poetry is the supreme fiction, madame.
    Take the moral law and make a nave of it
    And from the nave build haunted heaven. Thus,
    The conscience is converted into palms,
    Like windy citherns hankering for hymns.
    We agree in principle. That's clear. But take
    The opposing law and make a peristyle,
    And from the peristyle project a masque
    Beyond the planets. Thus, our bawdiness,
10 Unpurged by epitaph, indulged at last,
    Is equally converted into palms,
    Squiggling like saxophones. And palm for palm,
    Madame, we are where we began. Allow,
    Therefore, that in the planetary scene
    Your disaffected flagellants, well-stuffed,
    Smacking their muzzy bellies in parade,
    Proud of such novelties of the sublime,
    Such tink and tank and tunk-a-tunk-tunk,
    May, merely may, madame, whip from themselves
20 A jovial hullabaloo among the spheres.
    This will make widows wince. But fictive things
    Wink as they will. Wink most when widows wince.

Of Modern Poetry

    The poem of the mind in the act of finding
    What will suffice. It has not always had
    To find: the scene was set; it repeated what
    Was in the script.
                        Then the theatre was changed
    To something else. Its past was a souvenir.

It has to be living, to learn the speech of the place.
It has to face the men of the time and to meet
The women of the time. It has to think about war
And it has to find what will suffice. It has
10 To construct a new stage. It has to be on that stage
And, like an insatiable actor, slowly and
With meditation, speak words that in the ear,
In the delicatest ear of the mind, repeat,
Exactly, that which it wants to hear, at the sound
Of which, an invisible audience listens,
Not to the play, but to itself, expressed
In an emotion as of two people, as of two
Emotions becoming one. The actor is
A metaphysician in the dark, twanging
20 An instrument, twanging a wiry string that gives
Sounds passing through sudden rightness, wholly
Containing the mind, below which it cannot descend,
Beyond which it has no will to rise.
                              It must
Be the finding of a satisfaction, and may
Be of a man skating, a woman dancing, a woman
Combing. The poem of the act of the mind.

Of Mere Being

The palm at the end of the mind,
Beyond the last thought, rises
In the bronze decor,

A gold-feathered bird
Sings in the palm, without human meaning,
Without human feeling, a foreign song.

You know then that it is not the reason
That makes us happy or unhappy.
The bird sings. Its feathers shine.

10 The palm stands on the edge of space.
The wind moves slowly in the branches.
The bird's fire-fangled feathers dangle down.

WILLIAM CARLOS WILLIAMS
1883–1963

The Widow's Lament in Springtime

Sorrow is my own yard
where the new grass
flames as it has flamed
often before but not
with the cold fire
that closes round me this year.
Thirtyfive years
I lived with my husband.
The plumtree is white today
10 with masses of flowers.
Masses of flowers
load the cherry branches
and color some bushes
yellow and some red
but the grief in my heart
is stronger than they
for though they were my joy
formerly, today I notice them
and turned away forgetting.
20 Today my son told me
that in the meadows,
at the edge of the heavy woods
in the distance, he saw
trees of white flowers.
I feel that I would like
to go there
and fall into those flowers
and sink into the marsh near them.

To Elsie

The pure products of America
go crazy—
mountain folk from Kentucky

or the ribbed north end of
Jersey
with its isolate lakes and

659

valleys, its deaf-mutes, thieves
old names
and promiscuity between

10 devil-may-care men who have taken
to railroading
out of sheer lust of adventure—

and young slatterns, bathed
in filth
from Monday to Saturday

to be tricked out that night
with gauds
from imaginations which have no

peasant traditions to give them
20 character
but flutter and flaunt

sheer rags—succumbing without
emotion
save numbed terror

under some hedge of choke-cherry
or viburnum—
which they cannot express—

Unless it be that marriage
perhaps
30 with a dash of Indian blood

will throw up a girl so desolate
so hemmed round
with disease or murder

that she'll be rescued by an
agent—
reared by the state and

sent out at fifteen to work in
some hard-pressed
house in the suburbs—

40 some doctor's family, some Elsie—
    voluptuous water
    expressing with broken

    brain the truth about us—
    her great
    ungainly hips and flopping breasts

    addressed to cheap
    jewelry
    and rich young men with fine eyes

    as if the earth under our feet
50 were
    an excrement of some sky

    and we degraded prisoners
    destined
    to hunger until we eat filth

    while the imagination strains
    after deer
    going by fields of goldenrod in

    the stifling heat of September
    Somehow
60 it seems to destroy us

    It is only in isolate flecks that
    something
    is given off

    No one
    to witness
    and adjust, no one to drive the car

Nantucket

Flowers through the window
lavender and yellow

changed by white curtains—
Smell of cleanliness—

Sunshine of late afternoon—
On the glass tray

a glass pitcher, the tumbler
turned down, by which

a key is lying—And the
10   immaculate white bed

This Is Just to Say

I have eaten
the plums
that were in
the icebox

and which
you were probably
saving
for breakfast

Forgive me
10   they were delicious
so sweet
and so cold

The Last Words of My English Grandmother

There were some dirty plates
and a glass of milk
beside her on a small table
near the rank, disheveled bed—

Wrinkled and nearly blind
she lay and snored
rousing with anger in her tones
to cry for food,

Gimme something to eat—
10   They're starving me—
I'm all right I won't go
to the hospital. No, no, no

Give me something to eat
Let me take you
to the hospital, I said
and after you are well

you can do as you please.
She smiled, Yes
you do what you please first
20   then I can do what I please—

Oh, oh, oh! she cried
as the ambulance men lifted
her to the stretcher—
Is this what you call

making me comfortable?
By now her mind was clear—
Oh you think you're smart
you young people,

she said, but I'll tell you
you don't know anything.
Then we started.
On the way

we passed a long row
of elms. She looked at them
awhile out of
the ambulance window and said,

What are all those
fuzzy-looking things out there?
Trees? Well, I'm tired
40   of them and rolled her head away.

Landscape with the Fall of Icarus[1]

According to Brueghel
when Icarus fell
it was spring

---

1. Second poem from a series based on the paintings
   of the Flemish artist Pieter Brueghel. This painting
   shows the mythical youth Icarus, son of Daedalus,
   falling into the sea after the wings made for him by
   his father had melted. W. H. Auden has also based a
   poem on this painting.

a farmer was ploughing
his field
the whole pageantry

of the year was
awake tingling
near

10   the edge of the sea
concerned
with itself

sweating in the sun
that melted
the wings' wax

unsignificantly
off the coast
there was

a splash quite unnoticed
20   this was
Icarus drowning

MARIANNE MOORE
1887–1972
Poetry

I, too, dislike it: there are things that are important beyond
        all this fiddle.
    Reading it, however, with a perfect contempt for it, one
        discovers in
    it after all, a place for the genuine.
        Hands that can grasp, eyes
        that can dilate, hair that can rise
            if it must, these things are important not because a

high-sounding interpretation can be put upon them but
        because they are
    useful. When they become so derivative as to become
        unintelligible,
    the same thing may be said for all of us, that we

10   do not admire what
          we cannot understand: the bat
              holding on upside down or in quest of something to

eat, elephants pushing, a wild horse taking a roll, a tireless
              wolf under
      a tree, the immovable critic twitching his skin like a
              horse that feels a flea, the base-
      ball fan, the statistician—
          nor is it valid
              to discriminate against 'business documents and

school-books';[1] all these phenomena are important. One
              must make a distinction
      however: when dragged into prominence by half poets,
              the result is not poetry,
20   nor till the poets among us can be
          'literalists of
          the imagination'[2]—above
              insolence and triviality and can present

for inspection, imaginary gardens with real toads in them,
          shall we have
      it. In the meantime, if you demand on the one hand,
      the raw material of poetry in
              all its rawness and
              that which is on the other hand
                  genuine, then you are interested in poetry.

1. Tolstoy in his *Diary* writes: "Where the boundary between prose and
   poetry lies, I shall never be able to understand. . . . Poetry is verse:
   prose is not verse. Or else poetry is everything with the exception
   of business documents and school books."—*From Miss Moore's notes*
2. W. B. Yeats in his essay "William Blake and the Imagination"
   speaks of Blake as a "too literal realist of the imagination, as
   others are of nature."—*From Miss Moore's notes*

A Grave

Man looking into the sea,
taking the view from those who have as much right to it as
      you have to it yourself,
it is human nature to stand in the middle of a thing,
but you cannot stand in the middle of this;
the sea has nothing to give but a well excavated grave.

The firs stand in a procession, each with an emerald turkey
    foot at the top,
reserved as their contours, saying nothing;
repression, however, is not the most obvious characteristic of
    the sea;
the sea is a collector, quick to return a rapacious look.
10 There are others besides you who have worn that look—
whose expression is no longer a protest; the fish no longer
    investigate them
for their bones have not lasted:
men lower nets, unconscious of the fact that they are desecrating
    a grave,
and row quickly away—the blades of the oars
moving together like the feet of water-spiders as if there were
    no such thing as death.
The wrinkles progress among themselves in a phalanx—beautiful
    under networks of foam,
and fade breathlessly while the sea rustles in and out of the
    seaweed;
the birds swim through the air at top speed, emitting catcalls
    as heretofore—
the tortoise-shell scourges about the feet of the cliffs, in motion
    beneath them;
20 and the ocean, under the pulsation of lighthouses and noise
    of bell-buoys,
advances as usual, looking as if it were not that ocean in
    which dropped things are bound to sink—
in which if they turn and twist, it is neither with volition nor
    consciousness.

The Fish

wade
through black jade.
   Of the crow-blue mussel-shells, one keeps
   adjusting the ash-heaps;
      opening and shutting itself like

an
injured fan.
   The barnacles which encrust the side
   of the wave, cannot hide
10   there for the submerged shafts of the

sun,
split like spun
   glass, move themselves with spotlight swiftness
   into the crevices—
      in and out, illuminating

the
turquoise sea
   of bodies. The water drives a wedge
   of iron through the iron edge
20   of the cliff; whereupon the stars,

pink
rice-grains, ink-
   bespattered jelly-fish, crabs like green
   lilies, and submarine
      toadstools, slide each on the other.

All
external
   marks of abuse are present on this
   defiant edifice—
30   all the physical features of

ac-
cident—lack
   of cornice, dynamite grooves, burns, and
   hatchet strokes, these things stand
      out on it; the chasm-side is

dead.
Repeated
   evidence has proved that it can live
   on what can not revive
40   its youth. The sea grows old in it.

A Jellyfish

Visible, invisible,
   a fluctuating charm
an amber-tinctured amethyst
   inhabits it, your arm

approaches and it opens
   and it closes; you had meant
to catch it and it quivers;
   you abandon your intent.

Nevertheless

you've seen a strawberry
   that's had a struggle; yet
   was, where the fragments met,

a hedgehog or a star-
   fish for the multitude
   of seeds. What better food

than apple-seeds—the fruit
   within the fruit—locked in
   like counter-curved twin

10 hazel-nuts? Frost that kills
   the little rubber-plant-
   leaves of *kok-saghyz* stalks, can't

harm the roots; they still grow
   in frozen ground. Once where
   there was a prickly-pear-

leaf clinging to barbed wire,
   a root shot down to grow
   in earth two feet below;

as carrots form mandrakes
20   or a ram's-horn root sometimes. Victory won't come

to me unless I go
   to it; a grape-tendril
   ties a knot in knots till

knotted thirty times,—so
   the bound twig that's undergone and over-gone, can't stir.

The weak overcomes its
   menace, the strong over-
30   comes itself. What is there

like fortitude! What sap
   went through that little thread
    to make the cherry red!

T. S. ELIOT
1888–1965
The Love Song of J. Alfred Prufrock

> S'io credessi che mia risposta fosse
> A persona che mai tornasse al mondo,
> Questa fiamma staria senza più scosse.
> Ma per ciò che giammai de questo fondo
> Non tornò vivo alcun, s'i'odo il vero
> Senza tema d'infamia ti rispondo.[1]

Let us go then, you and I,
When the evening is spread out against the sky
Like a patient etherized upon a table;
Let us go, through certain half-deserted streets,
The muttering retreats
Of restless nights in one-night cheap hotels
And sawdust restaurants with oyster-shells:
Streets that follow like a tedious argument
Of insidious intent
10 To lead you to an overwhelming question....
Oh, do not ask, 'What is it?'
Let us go and make our visit.
In the room the women come and go
Talking of Michelangelo.

The yellow fog that rubs its back upon the window-panes,
The yellow smoke that rubs its muzzle on the window-panes,
Licked its tongue into the corners of the evening,
Lingered upon the pools that stand in drains,
Let fall upon its back the soot that falls from chimneys,

---

1. "If I believed that my answer were to a person who should ever return
   to the world, this flame would stand without further movement;
   but since never one returns alive from this deep, if I hear true,
   I answer you without fear of infamy." *Inferno*, xxvii, 61–66. These words
   are the response a damned soul in Hell makes when a question is put to him.

20   Slipped by the terrace, made a sudden leap,
      And seeing that it was a soft October night,
      Curled once about the house, and fell asleep.

      And indeed there will be time
      For the yellow smoke that slides along the street
      Rubbing its back upon the window-panes;
      There will be time, there will be time
      To prepare a face to meet the faces that you meet;
      There will be time to murder and create,
      And time for all the works and days of hands
30   That lift and drop a question on your plate;
      Time for you and time for me,
      And time yet for a hundred indecisions,
      And for a hundred visions and revisions,
      Before the taking of a toast and tea.

      In the room the women come and go
      Talking of Michelangelo.

      And indeed there will be time
      To wonder, 'Do I dare?' and, 'Do I dare?'
      Time to turn back and descend the stair,
40   With a bald spot in the middle of my hair—
      (They will say: 'How his hair is growing thin!')
      My morning coat, my collar mounting firmly to the chin,
      My necktie rich and modest, but asserted by a simple pin—
      (They will say: 'But how his arms and legs are thin!')
      Do I dare
      Disturb the universe?
      In a minute there is time
      For decisions and revisions which a minute will reverse.

      For I have known them all already, known them all—
50   Have known the evenings, mornings, afternoons,
      I have measured out my life with coffee spoons;
      I know the voices dying with a dying fall
      Beneath the music from a farther room.
            So how should I presume?

      And I have known the eyes already, known them all—
      The eyes that fix you in a formulated phrase,
      And when I am formulated, sprawling on a pin,
      When I am pinned and wriggling on the wall,

Then how should I begin
60   To spit out all the butt-ends of my days and ways?
        And how should I presume?

And I have known the arms already, known them all—
Arms that are braceleted and white and bare
(But in the lamplight, downed with light brown hair!)
Is it perfume from a dress
That makes me so digress?
Arms that lie along a table, or wrap about a shawl.
        And should I then presume?
        And how should I begin?

        .   .   .

70   Shall I say, I have gone at dusk through narrow streets
And watched the smoke that rises from the pipes
Of lonely men in shirt-sleeves, leaning out of the windows? . . .

I should have been a pair of ragged claws
Scuttling across the floors of silent seas.

        .   .   .

And the afternoon, the evening, sleeps so peacefully!
Smoothed by long fingers,
Asleep . . . tired . . . or it malingers,
Stretched on the floor, here beside you and me.
Should I, after tea and cakes and ices,
80   Have the strength to force the moment to its crisis?
But though I have wept and fasted, wept and prayed,
Though I have seen my head (grown slightly bald) brought
            in upon a platter,[2]
I am no prophet—and here's no great matter;
I have seen the moment of my greatness flicker,
And I have seen the eternal Footman hold my coat, and
        snicker,
And in short, I was afraid.
And would it have been worth it, after all,
After the cups, the marmalade, the tea,
Among the porcelain, among some talk of you and me,

2. The head of John the Baptist was "brought in upon a platter" at
   the request of Salome as a reward for her dancing before Herod.

90   Would it have been worth while,
To have bitten off the matter with a smile,
To have squeezed the universe into a ball
To roll it toward some overwhelming question,
To say: 'I am Lazarus, come from the dead,
Come back to tell you all, I shall tell you all'—
If one, settling a pillow by her head,
     Should say: 'That is not what I meant at all.
     That is not it, at all.'

And would it have been worth it, after all,
100   Would it have been worth while,
After the sunsets and the dooryards and the sprinkled streets,
After the novels, after the teacups, after the skirts that trail
     along the floor—
And this, and so much more?—
It is impossible to say just what I mean!
But as if a magic lantern threw the nerves in patterns on a
     screen:
Would it have been worth while
If one, settling a pillow or throwing off a shawl,
And turning toward the window, should say:
     'That is not it at all,
110   That is not what I meant, at all.'

     . . .

No! I am not Prince Hamlet, nor was meant to be;
Am an attendant lord, one that will do
To swell a progress,[3] start a scene or two,
Advise the prince; no doubt, an easy tool,
Deferential, glad to be of use,
Politic, cautious, and meticulous;
Full of high sentence, but a bit obtuse;
At times, indeed, almost ridiculous—
Almost, at times, the Fool.
120 I grow old. . . . I grow old. . . .
I shall wear the bottoms of my trousers rolled.

Shall I part my hair behind? Do I dare to eat a peach?
I shall wear white flannel trousers, and walk upon the beach.
I have heard the mermaids singing, each to each.

3. Ceremonial procession at a royal court

I do not think that they will sing to me.

I have seen them riding seaward on the waves
Combing the white hair of the waves blown back
When the wind blows the water white and black.

We have lingered in the chambers of the sea
130   By sea-girls wreathed with seaweed red and brown
Till human voices wake us, and we drown.

Morning at the Window

They are rattling breakfast plates in basement kitchens,
And along the trampled edges of the street
I am aware of the damp souls of housemaids
Sprouting despondently at area gates.

   The brown waves of fog toss up to me
Twisted faces from the bottom of the street,
And tear from a passer-by with muddy skirts
An aimless smile that hovers in the air
And vanishes along the level of the roofs.

The Hollow Men

      A penny for the Old Guy

    I

We are the hollow men
We are the stuffed men
Leaning together
Headpiece filled with straw. Alas!
Our dried voices, when
We whisper together
Are quiet and meaningless
As wind in dry grass
Or rats' feet over broken glass
10   In our dry cellar

   Shape without form, shade without colour,
Paralysed force, gesture without motion;

   Those who have crossed

With direct eyes, to death's other Kingdom
Remember us—if at all—not as lost
Violent souls, but only
As the hollow men
The stuffed men.

II

Eyes I dare not meet in dreams
20 In death's dream kingdom
These do not appear:
There, the eyes are
Sunlight on a broken column
There, is a tree swinging
And voices are
In the wind's singing
More distant and more solemn
Than a fading star.

    Let me be no nearer
30 In death's dream kingdom
Let me also wear
Such deliberate disguises
Rat's coat, crowskin, crossed staves
In a field
Behaving as the wind behaves
No nearer—

    Not that final meeting
In the twilight kingdom

III

This is the dead land
40 This is cactus land
Here the stone images
Are raised, here they receive
The supplication of a dead man's hand
Under the twinkle of a fading star.

    Is it like this
In death's other kingdom
Waking alone
At the hour when we are

Trembling with tenderness
50 Lips that would kiss
Form prayers to broken stone.

IV

The eyes are not here
There are no eyes here
In this valley of dying stars
In this hollow valley
This broken jaw of our lost kingdoms

   In this last of meeting places
We grope together
And avoid speech
60 Gathered on this beach of the tumid river

   Sightless, unless
The eyes reappear
As the perpetual star
Multifoliate rose
Of death's twilight kingdom
The hope only
Of empty men.

V

Here we go round the prickly pear
Prickly pear prickly pear
70 *Here we go round the prickly pear*
At five o'clock in the morning.

   Between the idea
And the reality
Between the motion
And the act
Falls the Shadow
                For Thine is the Kingdom

   Between the conception
And the creation
80 Between the emotion
And the response
Falls the Shadow
                Life is very long

Between the desire
And the spasm
Between the potency
And the existence
Between the essence
And the descent
90   Falls the Shadow
        For Thine is the Kingdom

  For Thine is
Life is
For Thine is the

  This is the way the world ends
This is the way the world ends
This is the way the world ends
Not with a bang but a whimper.

Journey of the Magi

"A cold coming we had of it,
Just the worst time of the year
For a journey, and such a long journey:
The ways deep and the weather sharp,
The very dead of winter."
And the camels galled, sore-footed, refractory,
Lying down in the melting snow.
There were times we regretted
The summer palaces on slopes, the terraces,
10   And the silken girls bringing sherbet.
Then the camel men cursing and grumbling
And running away, and wanting their liquor and women,
And the night-fires going out, and the lack of shelters,
And the cities hostile and the towns unfriendly
And the villages dirty and charging high prices:
A hard time we had of it.
At the end we preferred to travel all night,
Sleeping in snatches,
With the voices singing in our ears, saying
20   That this was all folly.

  Then at dawn we came down to a temperate valley,
Wet, below the snow line, smelling of vegetation;
With a running stream and a water-mill beating the darkness,

And three trees on the low sky,
And an old white horse galloped away in the meadow.
Then we came to a tavern with vine-leaves over the lintel,
Six hands at an open door dicing for pieces of silver,
And feet kicking the empty wine-skins.
But there was no information, and so we continued
30   And arrived at evening, not a moment too soon
Finding the place; it was (you may say) satisfactory.

   All this was a long time ago, I remember,
And I would do it again, but set down
This set down
This: were we led all that way for
Birth or Death? There was a Birth, certainly,
We had evidence and no doubt. I had seen birth and death,
But had thought they were different; this Birth was
Hard and bitter agony for us, like Death, our death.
40   We returned to our places, these Kingdoms,
But no longer at ease here, in the old dispensation,
With an alien people clutching their gods.
I should be glad of another death.

Macavity: The Mystery Cat

Macavity's a Mystery Cat: he's called the Hidden Paw—
For he's the master criminal who can defy the Law.
He's the bafflement of Scotland Yard, the Flying Squad's despair:
For when they reach the scene of the crime—*Macavity's not there!*

   Macavity, Macavity, there's no one like Macavity,
He's broken every human law, he breaks the law of gravity.
His powers of levitation would make a fakir stare,
And when you reach the scene of crime—*Macavity's not there!*
You may seek him in the basement, you may look up in the air—
10   But I tell you once and once again, *Macavity's not there!*

   Macavity's a ginger cat, he's very tall and thin;
You would know him if you saw him, for his eyes are sunken in.
His brow is deeply lined with thought, his head is highly domed;
His coat is dusty from neglect, his whiskers are uncombed.
He sways his head from side to side, with movements like a snake;
And when you think he's half asleep, he's always wide awake.

   Macavity, Macavity, there's no one like Macavity,

For he's a fiend in feline shape, a monster of depravity.
You may meet him in a by-street, you may see him in the square—
20   But when a crime's discovered, then *Macavity's not there!*

He's outwardly respectable. (They say he cheats at cards.)
And his footprints are not found in any file of Scotland Yard's.
And when the larder's looted, or the jewel-case is rifled,
Or when the milk is missing, or another Peke's been stifled,
Or the greenhouse glass is broken, and the trellis past repair—
Ay, there's the wonder of the thing! *Macavity's not there!*

And when the Foreign Office find a Treaty's gone astray,
Or the Admiralty lose some plans and drawings by the way,
There may be a scrap of paper in the hall or on the stair—
30   But it's useless to investigate—*Macavity's not there!*
And when the loss has been disclosed, the Secret Service say:
"It *must* have been Macavity!"—but he's a mile away.
You'll be sure to find him resting, or a-licking of his thumbs,
Or engaged in doing complicated long division sums.

Macavity, Macavity, there's no one like Macavity,
There never was a Cat of such deceitfulness and suavity.
He always has an alibi, and one or two to spare:
At whatever time the deed took place—MACAVITY WASN'T THERE!
And they say that all the Cats whose wicked deeds are widely known
40   (I might mention Mungojerrie, I might mention Griddlebone)
Are nothing more than agents for the Cat who all the time
Just controls their operations: the Napoleon of Crime!

LANGSTON HUGHES
1902–1967

Aunt Sue's Stories

Aunt Sue has a head full of stories.
Aunt Sue has a whole heart full of stories.
Summer nights on the front porch
Aunt Sue cuddles a brown-faced child to her bosom
And tells him stories.

Black slaves
Working in the hot sun,
And black slaves

Walking in the dewy night,
10 And black slaves
Singing sorrow songs on the banks of a mighty river
Mingle themselves softly
In the flow of old Aunt Sue's voice,
Mingle themselves softly
In the dark shadows that cross and recross
Aunt Sue's stories.

And the dark-faced child, listening,
Knows that Aunt Sue's stories are real stories.
He knows that Aunt Sue never got her stories
20 Out of any book at all,
But that they came
Right out of her own life.

The dark-faced child is quiet
Of a summer night
Listening to Aunt Sue's stories.

Spirituals

Rocks and the firm roots of trees.
The rising shafts of mountains.
Something strong to put my hands on.

    Sing, O Lord Jesus!
    Song is a strong thing.
    I heard my mother singing
    When life hurt her:

Gonna ride in my chariot some day!

    The branches rise
10   From the firm roots of trees.
    The mountains rise
    From the solid lap of earth.
    The waves rise
    From the dead weight of sea.

Sing, O black mother!
Song is a strong thing.

Early Evening Quarrel

Where is that sugar, Hammond,
I sent you this morning to buy?
I say, where is that sugar
I sent you this morning to buy?
Coffee without sugar
Makes a good woman cry.

I ain't got no sugar, Hattie,
I gambled your dime away.
Ain't got no sugar, I
10   *Done gambled that dime away.*
If you's a wise woman, Hattie,
You ain't gonna have nothin to say.

I ain't no wise woman, Hammond.
I am evil and mad.
Ain't no sense in a good woman
Bein treated so bad.

I don't treat you bad, Hattie,
Neither does I treat you good.
But I reckon I could treat you
20   *Worser if I would.*

Lawd, these things we women
Have to stand!
I wonder is there nowhere a
Do-right man?

Young Sailor

He carries
His own strength
And his own laughter,
His own today
And his own hereafter—
This strong young sailor
Of the wide seas.

What is money for?
To spend, he says.
10   And wine?

To drink.
And women?
To love.
And today?
For joy.
And the green sea
For strength,
And the brown land
For laughter.

20   And nothing hereafter.

Trumpet Player

The Negro
With the trumpet at his lips
His dark moons of weariness
Beneath his eyes
Where the smoldering memory
Of slave ships
Blazed to the crack of whips
About his thighs.

The Negro
10   With the trumpet at his lips
Has a head of vibrant hair
Tamed down,
Patent-leathered now
Until it gleams
Like jet—
Were jet a crown.

The music
From the trumpet at his lips
Is honey
20   Mixed with liquid fire.
The rhythm
From the trumpet at his lips
Is ecstasy
Distilled from old desire—

Desire
That is longing for the moon
Where the moonlight's but a spotlight

In his eyes,
Desire
30 That is longing for the sea
Where the sea's a bar-glass
Sucker size.

The Negro
With the trumpet at his lips
Whose jacket
Has a *fine* one-button roll,
Does not know
Upon what riff the music slips
Its hypodermic needle
40 To his soul—

But softly
As the tune comes from his throat
Trouble
Mellows to a golden note.

I, Too

I, too, sing America.

I am the darker brother.
They send me to eat in the kitchen
When company comes,
But I laugh,
And eat well,
And grow strong.

Tomorrow,
I'll be at the table
10 When company comes.
Nobody'll dare
Say to me,
"Eat in the kitchen,"
Then.

Besides,
They'll see how beautiful I am
And be ashamed—

I, too, am America.

W. H. AUDEN
1907–1973
Who's Who

A shilling life will give you all the facts:
How Father beat him, how he ran away,
What were the struggles of his youth, what acts
Made him the greatest figure of his day:
Of how he fought, fished, hunted, worked all night,
Though giddy, climbed new mountains; named a sea:
Some of the last researchers even write
Love made him weep his pints like you and me.

With all his honours on, he sighed for one
10   Who, say astonished critics, lived at home;
Did little jobs about the house with skill
And nothing else; could whistle; would sit still
Or potter round the garden; answered some
Of his long marvellous letters but kept none.

On This Island

Look, stranger, on this island now
The leaping light for your delight discovers,
Stand stable here
And silent be,
That through the channels of the ear
May wander like a river
The swaying sound of the sea.

Here at the small field's ending pause
When the chalk wall falls to the foam and its tall ledges
10   Oppose the pluck
And knock of the tide,
And the shingle scrambles after the suck-
-ing surf,
And the gull lodges
A moment on its sheer side.

Far off like floating seeds the ships
Diverge on urgent voluntary errands,
And the full view

Indeed may enter
20 And move in memory as now these clouds do,
That pass the harbour mirror
And all the summer through the water saunter.

As I Walked Out One Evening

As I walked out one evening,
   Walking down Bristol Street,
The crowds upon the pavement
   Were fields of harvest wheat.

And down by the brimming river
   I heard a lover sing
Under an arch of the railway:
   'Love has no ending.

'I'll love you, dear, I'll love you
10   Till China and Africa meet,
And the river jumps over the mountain
   And the salmon sing in the street,

'I'll love you till the ocean
   Is folded and hung up to dry
And the seven stars go squawking
   Like geese about the sky.

'The years shall run like rabbits,
   For in my arms I hold
The Flower of the Ages,
20   And the first love of the world.'

But all the clocks in the city
   Began to whirr and chime:
'O let not Time deceive you,
   You cannot conquer Time.

'In the burrows of the Nightmare
   Where Justice naked is,
Time watches from the shadow
   And coughs when you would kiss.

'In headaches and in worry
30 Vaguely life leaks away,

And Time will have his fancy
    To-morrow or to-day.

'Into many a green valley
    Drifts the appalling snow;
Time breaks the threaded dances
    And the diver's brilliant bow.

'O plunge your hands in water,
    Plunge them in up to the wrist;
Stare, stare in the basin
40   And wonder what you've missed.

'The glacier knocks in the cupboard,
    The desert sighs in the bed,
And the crack in the tea-cup opens
    A lane to the land of the dead.

'Where the beggars raffle the banknotes
    And the Giant is enchanting to Jack,
And the Lily-white Boy is a Roarer,
    And Jill goes down on her back.

'O look, look in the mirror,
50   O look in your distress;
Life remains a blessing
    Although you cannot bless.

'O stand, stand at the window
    As the tears scald and start;
You shall love your crooked neighbour
    With your crooked heart.'

It was late, late in the evening,
    The lovers they were gone;
The clocks had ceased their chiming,
60   And the deep river ran on.

Musée des Beaux Arts[1]

About suffering they were never wrong,
The Old Masters: how well they understood
Its human position; how it takes place
While someone else is eating or opening a window or just walking dully along;
How, when the aged are reverently, passionately waiting
For the miraculous birth, there always must be
Children who did not specially want it to happen, skating
On a pond at the edge of the wood:
They never forgot
10   That even the dreadful martyrdom must run its course
Anyhow in a corner, some untidy spot
Where the dogs go on with their doggy life and the torturer's horse
Scratches its innocent behind on a tree.

In Brueghel's *Icarus,* for instance: how everything turns away
Quite leisurely from the disaster; the ploughman may
Have heard the splash, the forsaken cry,
But for him it was not an important failure; the sun shone
As it had to on the white legs disappearing into the green
Water; and the expensive delicate ship that must have seen
20   Something amazing, a boy falling out of the sky,
Had somewhere to get to and sailed calmly on.

1. Museum of Fine Arts. See also note to William Carlos Williams's poem
on Brueghel's "Icarus," above.

In Memory of W. B. Yeats

(d. Jan. 1939)

I

He disappeared in the dead of winter:
The brooks were frozen, the airports almost deserted,
And snow disfigured the public statues;
The mercury sank in the mouth of the dying day.
What instruments we have agree
The day of his death was a dark cold day.

Far from his illness
The wolves ran on through the evergreen forests,
The pleasant river was untempted by the fashionable quays;

10   By mourning tongues
The death of the poet was kept from his poems.

But for him it was his last afternoon as himself,
An afternoon of nurses and rumours;
The provinces of his body revolted,
The squares of his mind were empty,
Silence invaded the suburbs,
The current of his feeling failed; he became his admirers.

Now he is scattered among a hundred cities
And wholly given over to unfamiliar affections,
20   To find his happiness in another kind of wood
And be punished under a foreign code of conscience.
The words of a dead man
Are modified in the guts of the living.

But in the importance and noise of to-morrow
When the brokers are roaring like beasts on the floor of the Bourse,
And the poor have the sufferings to which they are fairly
    accustomed,
And each in the cell of himself is almost convinced of his freedom,
A few thousand will think of this day
As one thinks of a day when one did something slightly unusual.
30   What instruments we have agree
The day of his death was a dark cold day.

II

You were silly like us; your gift survived it all:
The parish of rich women, physical decay,
Yourself. Mad Ireland hurt you into poetry.
Now Ireland has her madness and her weather still,
For poetry makes nothing happen: it survives
In the valley of its making where executives
Would never want to tamper, flows on south
From ranches of isolation and the busy griefs,
40   Raw towns that we believe and die in; it survives,
A way of happening, a mouth.

III

Earth, receive an honoured guest:
William Yeats is laid to rest.

Let the Irish vessel lie
Emptied of its poetry.

In the nightmare of the dark
All the dogs of Europe bark,
And the living nations wait,
Each sequestered in its hate;

50   Intellectual disgrace
Stares from every human face,
And the seas of pity lie
Locked and frozen in each eye.

Follow, poet, follow right
To the bottom of the night,
With your unconstraining voice
Still persuade us to rejoice;

With the farming of a verse
Make a vineyard of the curse,
60   Sing of human unsuccess
In a rapture of distress;

In the deserts of the heart
Let the healing fountain start,
In the prison of his days
Teach the free man how to praise.

The Unknown Citizen

To JS/07/M/378
This Marble Monument
Is Erected by the State

He was found by the Bureau of Statistics to be
One against whom there was no official complaint,
And all the reports on his conduct agree
That, in the modern sense of an old-fashioned word, he was a saint,
For in everything he did he served the Greater Community.
Except for the War till the day he retired
He worked in a factory and never got fired,
But satisfied his employers, Fudge Motors Inc.
Yet he wasn't a scab or odd in his views,
10   For his Union reports that he paid his dues,

(Our report on his Union shows it was sound)
And our Social Psychology workers found
That he was popular with his mates and liked a drink.
The Press are convinced that he bought a paper every day
And that his reactions to advertisements were normal in every way.
Policies taken out in his name prove that he was fully insured,
And his Health-card shows he was once in hospital but left it cured.
Both Producers Research and High-Grade Living declare
He was fully sensible to the advantages of the Instalment Plan
20   And had everything necessary to the Modern Man,
A phonograph, a radio, a car and a frigidaire.
Our researchers into Public Opinion are content
That he held the proper opinions for the time of year;
When there was peace, he was for peace; when there was war, he went.
He was married and added five children to the population,
Which our Eugenist says was the right number for a parent of his generation,
And our teachers report that he never interfered with their education.
Was he free? Was he happy? The question is absurd:
Had anything been wrong, we should certainly have heard.

At the Grave of Henry James

The snow, less intransigeant than their marble,
Has left the defence of whiteness to these tombs,
    And all the pools at my feet
Accommodate blue now, echo clouds as occur
To the sky, and whatever bird or mourner the passing
    Moment remarks they repeat.

While rocks, named after singular spaces
Within which images wandered once that caused
    All to tremble and offend,
10   Stand here in an innocent stillness, each marking the spot
Where one more series of errors lost its uniqueness
    And novelty came to an end.

To whose real advantage were such transactions,
When worlds of reflection were exchanged for trees?
    What living occasion can
Be just to the absent? Noon but reflects on itself,
And the small taciturn stone, that is the only witness
    To a great and talkative man,

Has no more judgement than my ignorant shadow
20 Of odious comparisons or distant clocks
      Which challenge and interfere
With the heart's instantaneous reading of time, time that is
A warm enigma no longer to you for whom I
      Surrender my private cheer,

As I stand awake on our solar fabric,
That primary machine, the earth, which gendarmes, banks
      And aspirin pre-suppose,
On which the clumsy and sad may all sit down, and any who will
Say their a-ha to the beautiful, the common locus
30   Of the Master and the rose.

Shall I not especially bless you as, vexed with
My little inferior questions, I stand
      Above the bed where you rest,
Who opened such passionate arms to your *Bon* when It ran
Towards you with its overwhelming reasons pleading
      All beautifully in Its breast?

With what an innocence your hand submitted
To those formal rules that help a child to play,
      While your heart, fastidious as
40 A delicate nun, remained true to the rare noblesse
Of your lucid gift, and, for its love, ignored the
      Resentful muttering Mass,

Whose ruminant hatred of all that cannot
Be simplified or stolen is yet at large:
      No death can assuage its lust
To vilify the landscape of Distinction and see
The heart of the Personal brought to a systolic standstill,
      The Tall to diminished dust.

Preserve me, Master, from its vague incitement;
50 Yours be the disciplinary image that holds
      Me back from agreeable wrong
And the clutch of eddying Muddle, lest Proportion shed
The alpine chill of her shrugging editorial shoulder
      On my loose impromptu song.

All will be judged. Master of nuance and scruple,
Pray for me and for all writers, living or dead:

Because there are many whose works
Are in better taste than their lives, because there is no end
To the vanity of our calling, make intercession
60   For the treason of all clerks.

THEODORE ROETHKE
1908–1963
The Premonition

Walking this field I remember
Days of another summer.
Oh that was long ago! I kept
Close to the heels of my father,
Matching his stride with half-steps
Until we came to a river.
He dipped his hand in the shallow:
Water ran over and under
Hair on a narrow wrist bone;
10   His image kept following after,—
Flashed with the sun in the ripple.
But when he stood up, that face
Was lost in a maze of water.

Dolor

I have known the inexorable sadness of pencils,
Neat in their boxes, dolor of pad and paper-weight,
All the misery of manilla folders and mucilage,
Desolation in immaculate public places,
Lonely reception room, lavatory, switchboard,
The unalterable pathos of basin and pitcher,
Ritual of multigraph, paper-clip, comma,
Endless duplication of lives and objects.
And I have seen dust from the walls of institutions,
10   Finer than flour, alive, more dangerous than silica,
Sift, almost invisible, through long afternoons of tedium,
Dropping a fine film on nails and delicate eyebrows,
Glazing the pale hair, the duplicate grey standard faces.

Elegy for Jane

My Student, Thrown by a Horse

I remember the neckcurls, limp and damp as tendrils;
And her quick look, a sidelong pickerel smile;
And how, once startled into talk, the light syllables leaped for her,
And she balanced in the delight of her thought,
A wren, happy, tail into the wind,
Her song trembling the twigs and small branches.
The shade sang with her;
The leaves, their whispers turned to kissing;
And the mold sang in the bleached valleys under the rose.

10   Oh, when she was sad, she cast herself down into such a pure depth,
Even a father could not find her:
Scraping her cheek against straw;
Stirring the clearest water.

My sparrow, you are not here,
Waiting like a fern, making a spiny shadow.
The sides of wet stones cannot console me,
Nor the moss, wound with the last light.

If only I could nudge you from this sleep,
My maimed darling, my skittery pigeon.
20   Over this damp grave I speak the words of my love:
I, with no rights in this matter,
Neither father nor lover.

The Waking[1]

I wake to sleep, and take my waking slow.
I feel my fate in what I cannot fear.
I learn by going where I have to go.

We think by feeling. What is there to know?
I hear my being dance from ear to ear.
I wake to sleep, and take my waking slow.

1. This poem is a villanelle, a strict form with only two rhyming sounds,
   in which the last two lines of the poem are also the last lines of alternate stanzas.
   Roethke loosens the form just a bit.

Of those so close beside me, which are you?
God bless the Ground! I shall walk softly there,
And learn by going where I have to go.

10   Light takes the Tree; but who can tell us how?
The lowly worm climbs up a winding stair;
I wake to sleep, and take my waking slow.

Great Nature has another thing to do
To you and me; so take the lively air,
And, lovely, learn by going where to go.

This shaking keeps me steady. I should know.
What falls away is always. And is near.
I wake to sleep, and take my waking slow.
I learn by going where I have to go.

I Knew a Woman

I knew a woman, lovely in her bones,
When small birds sighed, she would sigh back at them;
Ah, when she moved, she moved more ways than one:
The shapes a bright container can contain!
Of her choice virtues only gods should speak,
Or English poets who grew up on Greek
(I'd have them sing in chorus, cheek to cheek).

How well her wishes went! She stroked my chin,
She taught me Turn, and Counter-turn, and Stand;
10   She taught me Touch, that undulant white skin;
I nibbled meekly from her proffered hand;
She was the sickle; I, poor I, the rake,
Coming behind her for her pretty sake
(But what prodigious mowing we did make).

Love likes a gander, and adores a goose:
Her full lips pursed, the errant note to seize;
She played it quick, she played it light and loose;
My eyes, they dazzled at her flowing knees;
Her several parts could keep a pure repose,
20   Or one hip quiver with a mobile nose
(She moved in circles, and those circles moved).

Let seed be grass, and grass turn into hay:
I'm martyr to a motion not my own;
What's freedom for? To know eternity.
I swear she cast a shadow white as stone.
But who would count eternity in days?
These old bones live to learn her wanton ways:
(I measure time by how a body sways).

The Manifestation

Many arrivals make us live: the tree becoming
Green, a bird tipping the topmost bough,
A seed pushing itself beyond itself,
The mole making its way through darkest ground,
The worm, intrepid scholar of the soil—
Do these analogies perplex? A sky with clouds,
The motion of the moon, and waves at play,
A sea-wind pausing in a summer tree.

What does what it should do needs nothing more.
10   The body moves, though slowly, toward desire.
We come to something without knowing why.

DYLAN THOMAS
1914–1953
The Force That through the Green Fuse Drives the Flower

The force that through the green fuse drives the flower
Drives my green age; that blasts the roots of trees
Is my destroyer.
And I am dumb to tell the crooked rose
My youth is bent by the same wintry fever.

The force that drives the water through the rocks
Drives my red blood; that dries the mouthing streams
Turns mine to wax.
And I am dumb to mouth unto my veins
10   How at the mountain spring the same mouth sucks.

The hand that whirls the water in the pool
Stirs the quicksand; that ropes the blowing wind

Hauls my shroud sail.
And I am dumb to tell the hanging man
How of my clay is made the hangman's lime.

The lips of time leech to the fountain head;
Love drips and gathers, but the fallen blood
Shall calm her sores.
And I am dumb to tell a weather's wind
20   How time has ticked a heaven round the stars.

And I am dumb to tell the lover's tomb
How at my sheet goes the same crooked worm.

This Bread I Break

This bread I break was once the oat,
This wine upon a foreign tree
Plunged in its fruit;
Man in the day or wind at night
Laid the crops low, broke the grape's joy.

Once in this wine the summer blood
Knocked in the flesh that decked the vine,
Once in this bread
The oat was merry in the wind;
10   Man broke the sun, pulled the wind down.

This flesh you break, this blood you let
Make desolation in the vein,
Were oat and grape
Born of the sensual root and sap;
My wine you drink, my bread you snap.

A Refusal to Mourn the Death, By Fire, of a Child in London

Never until the mankind making
Bird beast and flower
Fathering and all humbling darkness
Tells with silence the last light breaking
And the still hour
Is come of the sea tumbling in harness

And I must enter again the round
Zion of the water bead
And the synagogue of the ear of corn
10   Shall I let pray the shadow of a sound
Or sow my salt seed
In the least valley of sackcloth to mourn

The majesty and burning of the child's death.
I shall not murder
The mankind of her going with a grave truth
Nor blaspheme down the stations of the breath
With any further
Elegy of innocence and youth.

Deep with the first dead lies London's daughter,
20   Robed in the long friends,
The grains beyond age, the dark veins of her mother,
Secret by the unmourning water
Of the riding Thames.
After the first death, there is no other.

Do Not Go Gentle into That Good Night[1]

Do not go gentle into that good night,
Old age should burn and rave at close of day;
Rage, rage against the dying of the light.

Though wise men at their end know dark is right,
Because their words had forked no lightning they
Do not go gentle into that good night.

Good men, the last wave by, crying how bright
Their frail deeds might have danced in a green bay,
Rage, rage against the dying of the light.

10   Wild men who caught and sang the sun in flight,
And learn, too late, they grieved it on its way,
Do not go gentle into that good night.

Grave men, near death, who see with blinding sight
Blind eyes could blaze like meteors and be gay,
Rage, rage against the dying of the light.

1. Like Roethke's "The Waking," this is a villanelle. See above, p. 692.

And you, my father, there on the sad height,
Curse, bless, me now with your fierce tears, I pray.
Do not go gentle into that good night.
Rage, rage against the dying of the light.

Fern Hill

Now as I was young and easy under the apple boughs
About the lilting house and happy as the grass was green,
      The night above the dingle starry,
            Time let me hail and climb
      Golden in the heydays of his eyes,
And honoured among wagons I was prince of the apple towns
And once below a time I lordly had the trees and leaves
            Trail with daisies and barley
      Down the rivers of the windfall light.

10   And as I was green and carefree, famous among the barns
About the happy yard and singing as the farm was home,
      In the sun that is young once only,
            Time let me play and be
      Golden in the mercy of his means,
And green and golden I was huntsman and herdsman, the calves
Sang to my horn, the foxes on the hills barked clear and cold,
            And the sabbath rang slowly
      In the pebbles of the holy streams.

All the sun long it was running, it was lovely, the hay
20   Fields high as the house, the tunes from the chimneys, it was air
            And playing, lovely and watery
                  And fire green as grass.
            And nightly under the simple stars
As I rode to sleep the owls were bearing the farm away,
All the moon long I heard, blessed among stables, the night-jars
            Flying with the ricks, and the horses
                  Flashing into the dark.

And then to awake, and the farm, like a wanderer white
With the dew, come back, the cock on his shoulder: it was all
30   Shining, it was Adam and maiden,
            The sky gathered again
      And the sun grew round that very day.
So it must have been after the birth of the simple light

In the first, spinning place, the spellbound horses walking warm
    Out of the whinnying green stable
        On to the fields of praise.

And honoured among foxes and pheasants by the gay house
Under the new made clouds and happy as the heart was long,
    In the sun born over and over,
40   I ran my heedless ways,
    My wishes raced through the house high hay
And nothing I cared, at my sky blue trades, that time allows
In all his tuneful turning so few and such morning songs
    Before the children green and golden
        Follow him out of grace,

Nothing I cared, in the lamb white days, that time would take me
Up to the swallow thronged loft by the shadow of my hand,
    In the moon that is always rising,
        Nor that riding to sleep
50   I should hear him fly with the high fields
And wake to the farm forever fled from the childless land.
Oh as I was young and easy in the mercy of his means,
    Time held me green and dying
    Though I sang in my chains like the sea.

W. S. MERWIN
1927–
Separation

Your absence has gone through me
Like thread through a needle.
Everything I do is stitched with its color.

Departure's Girl-Friend

Loneliness leapt in the mirrors, but all week
I kept them covered like cages. Then I thought
Of a better thing.

And though it was late night in the city
There I was on my way
To my boat, feeling good to be going, hugging
This big wreath with the words like real
Silver: *Bon Voyage.*

             The night
Was mine but everyone's, like a birthday.
10 Its fur touched my face in passing. I was going
Down to my boat, my boat,
To see it off, and glad at the thought.
Some leaves of the wreath were holding my hands
And the rest waved good-bye as I walked, as though
They were still alive.

And all went well till I came to the wharf, and no one.

I say no one, but I mean
There was this young man, maybe
Out of the merchant marine,
20 In some uniform, and I knew who he was; just the same
When he said to me where do you think you're going,
I was happy to tell him.

But he said to me, it isn't your boat,
You don't have one. I said, it's mine, I can prove it:
Look at this wreath I'm carrying to it,
Bon Voyage. He said, this is the stone wharf, lady,
You don't own anything here.
                                    And as I
Was turning away, the injustice of it
Lit up the buildings, and there I was
30 In the other and hated city
Where I was born, where nothing is moored, where
The lights crawl over the stone like flies, spelling now,
Now, and the same fat chances roll
Their many eyes; and I step once more
Through a hoop of tears and walk on, holding this
Buoy of flowers in front of my beauty,
Wishing myself the good voyage.

When You Go Away

When you go away the wind clicks around to the north
The painters work all day but at sundown the paint falls
Showing the black walls
The clock goes back to striking the same hour
That has no place in the years

And at night wrapped in the bed of ashes

In one breath I wake
It is the time when the beards of the dead get their growth
I remember that I am falling
10   That I am the reason
And that my words are the garment of what I shall never be
Like the tucked sleeve of a one-armed boy

For a Coming Extinction

Gray whale
Now that we are sending you to The End
That great god
Tell him
That we who follow you invented forgiveness
And forgive nothing

I write as though you could understand
And I could say it
One must always pretend something
10   Among the dying
When you have left the seas nodding on their stalks
Empty of you
Tell him that we were made
On another day

The bewilderment will diminish like an echo
Winding along your inner mountains
Unheard by us
And find its way out
Leaving behind it the future
20   Dead
And ours

When you will not see again
The whale calves trying the light
Consider what you will find in the black garden
And its court
The sea cows the Great Auks the gorillas
The irreplaceable hosts ranged countless
And fore-ordaining as stars
Our sacrifices

30   Join your word to theirs
Tell him
That it is we who are important

Envoy from D'Aubigné[1]

Go book

go
now I will let you
I open the grave
live
I will die for us both

go but come again if you can
and feed me in prison

if they ask you why
you do not boast of me
10   tell them as they
have forgotten
truth habitually
gives birth in private

Go without ornament
without showy garment
if there is in you any
joy
may the good find it

for the others be
20   a glass broken in their mouths

Child
how will you
survive with nothing but your virtue
to draw around you
when they shout Die die
who have been frightened before
the many

I think of all I wrote in my time
dew
30   and I am standing in dry air

1. The *envoi* or *envoy* was once a customary way for a poet
   to "send" his book into the world. Merwin here offers a
   version attributed to a French Renaissance poet.

Here are what flowers there are
and what hope
from my years

and the fire I carried with me

Book
burn what will not abide your light

When I consider the old ambitions
to be on many lips
meaning little there
40   it would be enough for me to know
who is writing this
and sleep knowing it

far from glory and its gibbets

and dream of those who drank at the icy fountain
and told the truth

Tale

After many winters the moss
finds the sawdust crushed bark chips
and says old friend
old friend

Elegy

Who would I show it to

PHILIP LEVINE
1928–
For Fran

She packs the flower beds with leaves,
Rags, dampened papers, ties with twine
The lemon tree, but winter carves
Its features on the uprooted stem.

I see the true vein in her neck
And where the smaller ones have broken
Blueing the skin, and where the dark
Cold lines of weariness have eaten

Out through the winding of the bone.
10   On the hard ground where Adam strayed,
Where nothing but his wants remain,
What do we do to those we need,

To those whose need of us endures
Even the knowledge of what we are?
I turn to her whose future bears
The promise of the appalling air,

My living wife, Frances Levine,
Mother of Theodore, John, and Mark,
Out of whatever we have been
20   We will make something for the dark.

Losing You

Another summer gone.
the hills burned to burdock
and thistle, I hold you
a moment in the cup
of my voice,
you flutter
in the frail cave of the finch,
you lean to speak
in my ear
10   and the first rains blow
you away.

Dusk is a burning
of the sun.
West of the Chowchilla
The Lost Continent of Butterflies
streams across the freeway.
Radiators crusted,
windshields smeared with gold
and you come on
20   rising into the moons
of headlights.

My brother is always a small bear,
cleaning his paws,
I am a leopard
running through snow,
you are the face of an egg
collapsing sideways.
Now the last olive falls
gripping its seed
30   a black stone among stones
and you are lost.

In a white dress
my little girl goes to the window.
She is unborn,
she is the thin flame
of a candle,
she is her mother
singing a song.
Her words frost
40   the mirror of the night,
a huge wind waits
at the back of her breath.

Hold Me

The table is cleared of my place
and cannot remember. The bed sags
where I turned to death, the earth fills
my first footsteps, the sun drowns my sight.

A woman turns from the basket
of dried white laundry and sees the room
flooding with the rays of my eyes,
the burning of my hair and tongue.

I enter your bedroom, you look up
10   in the dark from tying your shoes
and see nothing, your boney shoulders
stiffen and hold, your fingers stop.

Was I dust that I should fall?
Was I silence that the cat heard?
Was I anger the jay swallowed?
The black elm choking on leaves?

In May, like this May, long ago
my tiny Russian Grandpa—the bottle king—
cupped a stained hand under my chin
20   and ran his comb through my golden hair.

Sweat, black shag, horse turds on the wind,
the last wooden cart rattling down
the alleys, the clop of his great gray mare,
green glass flashing in December sun . . .

I am the eye filled with salt,
his child climbing the rain, we are
all the moon, the one planet, the hand
of five stars flung on the night river.

No One Remembers

A soft wind
off the stones of the dead.
I pass by, stop the car,
and walk among none
of my own, to say
something useless
for them, something
that will calm me under
the same old beaten sky,
10   something to let me
go on with this day
that began so badly
alone in a motel 10 miles
from where I was born.

I say *Goodbye* finally
because nothing else is here,
because it is Goodbye,
Uncle Joe, big cigar, fist
on the ear, nodding *sure*
20   *bitch* and coming at me.
You can't touch me now,
and she's a thousand miles
from here, hell, she may be
dancing long past dawn
across the river
from Philly. It's morning

there too, even in Philly,
it's morning on Lake St. Clair
where we never went fishing,
30   along the Ohio River, the Detroit,
morning breaking on
the New York Central Express
crashing through the tunnel
and the last gasp of steam
before the entrance into hell
or Baltimore, but it's not
morning where you are, Joe,
unless you come with me.

I'm going to see her today.
40   She'll cry like always
when you raised your voice
or your fist, she'll
be robed near the window
of the ward when I come in.
No, she won't be dancing.
It's my hand she'll take
in hers and spread on her lap,
it's me she'll feel
slowly finger by finger
50   like so many threads back
to where the blood died
and our lives met
and went wrong, back
to all she said she'd be,
woman, promise, sigh,
dark hair in the mirror
of a car window all night
on the way back from Georgia.

You think because I
60   was a boy, I didn't hear,
you think because you had
a pocketful of loose change,
your feet on the desk,
your own phone, a yellow car
on credit, I didn't see
you open your hands
like a prayer and die
into them the way a child

dies into a razor, black hair,
70   into a tire iron, a chain.
You think I didn't smell
the sweat that rose
from your bed, didn't
know you on the stairs
in the dark, grunting
into a frightened girl.
Because you could push me
aside like a kitchen chair
and hit where you wanted,
80   you think I was a wren,
a mourning dove
surrendering the nest.

The earth is asleep, Joe,
it's rock, steel, ice,
the earth doesn't care
or forgive. No one remembers
your eyes before they tired,
the way you fought weeping.
No one remembers how much
90   it cost to drive all night
to Chicago, how much
to sleep all night in a car,
to have it all except
the money. No one remembers
your hand, opened, warm
and sweating on the back
of my neck when you first
picked me up and said
my name, *Philip*, and held
100   the winter sun up
for me to see outside
the French windows of
the old house on Pingree,
no one remembers.

Ricky

I go into the back yard
and arrange some twigs
and a few flowers. I go alone
and speak to you as I never could

when you lived, when you
smiled back at me shyly.
Now I can talk to you as I talked
to a star when I was a boy,
expecting no answer, as I talked
10   to my father who had become
the wind, particles of rain
and fire, these few twigs
and flowers that have no name.

*

Last night they said a rosary
and my boys went, awkward
in slacks and sport shirts,
and later sitting under the hidden
stars they were attacked and beaten.
You are dead, and a nameless rage
20   is loose. It is 105,
the young and the old burn
in the fields, and though they cry
enough the sun hangs on
bloodying the dust above the aisles
of cotton and grape.

*

This morning they will say a mass
and then the mile-long line of cars.
Teddy and John, their faces swollen,
and four others will let you
30   slowly down into the fresh earth
where you go on. Scared now,
they will understand some of it.
Not the mass or the rosary
or the funeral, but the rage.
Not you falling through the dark
moving underwater like a flower
no one could find until
it was too late and you had gone out,
your breath passing through dark water
40   never to return to the young man,
pigeon-breasted, who rode
his brother's Harley up the driveway.

*

Wet grass sticks to my feet, bright
marigold and daisy burst in the new day.
The bees move at the clumps
of clover, the carrots—
almost as tall as I—
have flowered, pale lacework.
Hard dark buds
50   of next year's oranges, new green
of slick leaves, yellow grass
tall and blowing by the fence. The grapes
are slow, climbing the arbor,
but some day there will be shade
here where the morning sun whitens
everything and punishes my eyes.

*

Your people worked so hard
for some small piece of earth,
for a home, adding a room
60   a boy might want. Butchie said
you could have the Harley
if only you would come back,
anything that was his.

*

A dog barks down the block
and it is another day. I hear
the soft call of the dove,
screech of mockingbird and jay.
A small dog picks up the tune,
and then *tow-weet tow-weet*
70   of hidden birds, and two finches
darting over the low trees—
there is no end.

*

What can I say to this mound
of twigs and dry flowers, what
can I say now that I would speak

to you? Ask the wind, ask
the absence or the rose burned
at the edges and still blood red.
And the answer is you
80   falling through black water
into the stillness that fathers
the moon, the bees ramming into
the soft cups, the eucalyptus
swaying like grass under water.
My John told me your cousin
punched holes in the wall
the night you died and was afraid
to be alone. Your brother
walks staring at the earth.
90   I am afraid of water.

                    *

And the earth goes on
in blinding sunlight.
I hold your image
a moment, the long
Indian face
the brown almond eyes
your dark skin full
and glowing as you grew
into the hard body
100   of a young man.

                    *

And now it is bird screech
and a tree rat suddenly
parting the tall grass
by the fence, lumbering
off, and in the distance
the crashing of waves
against some shore
maybe only in memory.

                    *

We lived by the sea.
110   Remember, my boys wrote

postcards and missed you
and your brother. I slept
and wakened to the sea,
I remember in my dreams
water pounded the windows
and walls, it seeped
through everything,
and like your spirit,
Ricky, like your breath,
120   nothing could contain it.

ADRIENNE RICH
1929–
The Afterwake

Nursing your nerves
to rest, I've roused my own; well,
now for a few bad hours!
Sleep sees you behind closed doors.
Alone, I slump in his front parlor.
You're safe inside. Good. But I'm
like a midwife who at dawn
has all in order: bloodstains
washed up, teapot on the stove,
10   and starts her five miles home
walking, the birthyell still
exploding in her head.

Yes, I'm with her now: here's
the streaked, livid road
edged with shut houses
breathing night out and in.
Legs tight with fatigue,
we move under morning's coal-blue star,
colossal as this load
20   of unexpired purpose, which drains
slowly, till scissors of cockcrow snip the air.

Novella

Two people in a room, speaking harshly.
One gets up, goes out to walk.
(That is the man.)
The other goes into the next room
and washes the dishes, cracking one.
(That is the woman.)
It gets dark outside.
The children quarrel in the attic.
She has no blood left in her heart.
10   The man comes back to a dark house.
The only light is in the attic.
He has forgotten his key.
He rings at his own door
and hears sobbing on the stairs.
The lights go on in the house.
The door closes behind him.
Outside, separate as minds,
the stars too come alight.

Night-Pieces: For a Child

1. *The Crib*

You sleeping I bend to cover.
Your eyelids work. I see
your dream, cloudy as a negative,
swimming underneath.
You blurt a cry. Your eyes
spring open, still filmed in dream.
Wider, they fix me—
—death's head, sphinx, medusa?
You scream.
10   Tears lick my cheeks, my knees
droop at your fear.
Mother I no more am,
but woman, and nightmare.

2. *Her Waking*

Tonight I jerk astart in a dark
hourless as Hiroshima,
almost hearing you breathe
in a cot three doors away.

You still breathe, yes—
and my dream with its gift of knives,
its murderous hider and seeker,
ebbs away, recoils

10   back into the egg of dreams,
the vanishing point of mind.
All gone.

But you and I—
swaddled in a dumb dark
old as sickheartedness,
modern as pure annihilation—

we drift in ignorance.
If I could hear you now
mutter some gentle animal sound!
If milk flowed from my breast again. . . .

5:30 A.M.

Birds and periodic blood.
Old recapitulations.
The fox, panting, fire-eyed,
gone to earth in my chest.
How beautiful we are,
she and I, with our auburn
pelts, our trails of blood,
our miracle escapes,
our whiplash panic flogging us on
10   to new miracles!
They've supplied us with pills
for bleeding, pills for panic.
Wash them down the sink.
This is truth, then:
dull needle groping in the spinal fluid,
weak acid in the bottom of the cup,
foreboding, foreboding.
No one tells the truth about truth,
that it's what the fox
20   sees from her scuffled burrow:
dull-jawed, onrushing
killer, being that
inanely single-minded
will have our skins at last.

Moving in Winter

Their life, collapsed like unplayed cards,
is carried piecemeal through the snow:
Headboard and footboard now, the bed
where she has lain desiring him
where overhead his sleep will build
its canopy to smother her once more;
their table, by four elbows worn
evenings after evening while the wax runs down;
mirrors grey with reflecting them,
10 bureaus coffining from the cold
things that can shuffle in a drawer,
carpets rolled up around those echoes
which, shaken out, take wing and breed
new altercations, the old silences.

Rape

There is a cop who is both prowler and father:
he comes from your block, grew up with your brothers,
had certain ideals.
You hardly know him in his boots and silver badge,
on horseback, one hand touching his gun.

You hardly know him but you have to get to know him:
he has access to machinery that could kill you.
He and his stallion clop like warlords among the trash,
his ideals stand in the air, a frozen cloud
10 from between his unsmiling lips.

And so, when the time comes, you have to turn to him,
the maniac's sperm still greasing your thighs,
your mind whirling like crazy. You have to confess
to him, you are guilty of the crime
of having been forced.

And you see his blue eyes, the blue eyes of all the family
whom you used to know, grow narrow and glisten,
his hand types out the details
and he wants them all
20 but the hysteria in your voice pleases him best.

You hardly know him but now he thinks he knows you:
he has taken down your worst moment
on a machine and filed it in a file.
He knows, or thinks he knows, how much you imagined;
he knows, or thinks he knows, what you secretly wanted.

He has access to machinery that could get you put away;
and if, in the sickening light of the precinct,
and if, in the sickening light of the precinct,
your details sound like a portrait of your confessor,
30   will you swallow, will you deny them, will you lie your way home?

Amnesia

I almost trust myself to know
when we're getting to that scene—
call it the snow-scene in *Citizen Kane:*

the mother handing over her son
the earliest American dream
shot in a black-and-white

where every flake of snow
is incandescent
with its own burden, adding-

10   up, always adding-up to the
cold blur of the past
But first there is the picture of the past

simple and pitiless as the deed
truly was
the putting-away of a childish thing

Becoming a man means leaving
someone, or something—
still, why

must the snow-scene blot itself out
20   the flakes come down so fast
so heavy, so unrevealing

over the something that gets left behind?

GARY SNYDER

1930–

Mid-August at Sourdough
Mountain Lookout

Down valley a smoke haze
Three days heat, after five days rain
Pitch glows on the fir-cones
Across rocks and meadows
Swarms of new flies.

I cannot remember things I once read
A few friends, but they are in cities.
Drinking cold snow-water from a tin cup
Looking down for miles
10   Through high still air.

Riprap[1]

Lay down these words
Before your mind like rocks.
    placed solid, by hands
In choice of place, set
Before the body of the mind
    in space and time:
Solidity of bark, leaf, or wall
    riprap of things:
Cobble of milky way,
10   straying planets,
These poems, people,
    lost ponies with
Dragging saddles—
    and rocky sure-foot trails.
The worlds like an endless
    four-dimensional
Game of *Go.*
    ants and pebbles
In the thin loam, each rock a word
20   a creek-washed stone
Granite: ingrained
    with torment of fire and weight

---

1. In trail-building some places are reinforced with a "riprap"
of stones to retard erosion.

Crystal and sediment linked hot
  all change, in thoughts,
As well as things.

An Autumn Morning in Shokoku-ji

Last night watching the Pleiades,
Breath smoking in the moonlight,
Bitter memory like vomit
Choked my throat.
I unrolled a sleeping bag
On mats on the porch
Under the thick autumn stars.
In dream you appeared
(Three times in nine years)
10 Wild, cold, and accusing.
I woke shamed and angry:
The pointless wars of the heart.
Almost dawn. Venus and Jupiter.
The first time I have
Ever seen them close.

Looking at Pictures
to Be Put Away

Who was this girl
In her white night gown
Clutching a pair of jeans

On a foggy redwood deck.
She looks up at me tender,
Calm, surprised,

What will we remember
Bodies thick with food and lovers
After twenty years.

It Was When

We harked up the path in the dark
    to the bamboo house
        green strokes down my back
        arms over your doubled hips
  under cow-breath thatch
    bent   cool
           breasts brush my chest
—and Naga walked in with a candle,
   "I'm sleepy"

10   Or jungle ridge by a snag—
    banyan canyon—a Temminck's Robin
      whirled down the waterfall gorge
  in zazen, a poncho spread out on the stones.
     below us the overturning
       silvery
     brush-bamboo slopes—
rainsqualls came up on us naked
     brown nipples in needles of ocean-
       cloud
20   rain.

  Or the night in the farmhouse
    with Franco on one side, or Pon
    Miko's head against me, I swung you
     around and came into you
  careless and joyous,
     late
      when Antares had set

  Or out on the boulders
    south beach at noon
30   rockt by surf
  burnd under by stone
  burnd over by sun
     saltwater caked
skin swing
    hips on my eyes
      burn between;

That we caught: sprout
      took grip in your womb and it held.
      new power in your breath called its place.
40   blood of the moon   stoppt;
      you pickt your steps well.

Waves
   and the
      prevalent easterly
        breeze.
    whispering into you,
      through us,
          the grace.

SYLVIA PLATH
1932–1963
Sheep in Fog

The hills step off into whiteness.
People or stars
Regard me sadly, I disappoint them.

The train leaves a line of breath.
O slow
Horse the colour of rust,

Hooves, dolorous bells—
All morning the
Morning has been blackening,

10   A flower left out.
My bones hold a stillness, the far
Fields melt my heart.

They threaten
To let me through to a heaven
Starless and fatherless, a dark water.

Daddy

You do not do, you do not do
Any more, black shoe
In which I have lived like a foot
For thirty years, poor and white,
Barely daring to breathe or Achoo.

Daddy, I have had to kill you.
You died before I had time—
Marble-heavy, a bag full of God,
Ghastly statue with one grey toe
10   Big as a Frisco seal

And a head in the freakish Atlantic
Where it pours bean green over blue
In the waters off beautiful Nauset.
I used to pray to recover you.
Ach, du.

In the German tongue, in the Polish town
Scraped flat by the roller
Of wars, wars, wars.
But the name of the town is common.
20   My Polack friend

Says there are a dozen or two.
So I never could tell where you
Put your foot, your root,
I never could talk to you.
The tongue stuck in my jaw.

It stuck in a barb wire snare.
Ich, ich, ich, ich,
I could hardly speak.
I thought every German was you.
30   And the language obscene

An engine, an engine
Chuffing me off like a Jew.
A Jew to Dachau, Auschwitz, Belsen.
I began to talk like a Jew.
I think I may well be a Jew.

The snows of the Tyrol, the clear beer of Vienna
Are not very pure or true.
With my gypsy ancestress and my weird luck
And my Taroc pack and my Taroc pack
40   I may be a bit of a Jew.

I have always been scared of *you*,
With your Luftwaffe, your gobbledygoo.
And your neat mustache
And your Aryan eye, bright blue.
Panzer-man, panzer-man, O You—

Not God but a swastika
So black no sky could squeak through.
Every woman adores a Fascist,
The boot in the face, the brute
50   Brute heart of a brute like you.

You stand at the blackboard, daddy,
In the picture I have of you,
A cleft in your chin instead of your foot
But no less a devil for that, no not
Any less the black man who

Bit my pretty red heart in two.
I was ten when they buried you.
At twenty I tried to die
And get back, back, back to you.
60   I thought even the bones would do.

But they pulled me out of the sack,
And they stuck me together with glue.
And then I knew what to do.
I made a model of you,
A man in black with a Meinkampf look

And a love of the rack and the screw.
And I said I do, I do.
So daddy, I'm finally through.
The black telephone's off at the root,
70   The voices just can't worm through.

If I've killed one man, I've killed two—
The vampire who said he was you
And drank my blood for a year,
Seven years, if you want to know.
Daddy, you can lie back now.

There's a stake in your fat black heart
And the villagers never liked you.
They are dancing and stamping on you.
They always *knew* it was you.
80   Daddy, daddy, you bastard, I'm through.

Kindness

Kindness glides about my house.
Dame Kindness, she is so nice!
The blue and red jewels of her rings smoke
In the windows, the mirrors
Are filling with smiles.

What is so real as the cry of a child?
A rabbit's cry may be wilder
But it has no soul.
Sugar can cure everything, so Kindness says.
10   Sugar is a necessary fluid,

Its crystals a little poultice.
O kindness, kindness
Sweetly picking up pieces!
My Japanese silks, desperate butterflies,
May be pinned any minute, anaesthetized.

And here you come, with a cup of tea
Wreathed in steam.
The blood jet is poetry,
There is no stopping it.
20   You hand me two children, two roses.

Edge

The woman is perfected.
Her dead

Body wears the smile of accomplishment,
The illusion of a Greek necessity

Flows in the scrolls of her toga,
Her bare

Feet seem to be saying:
We have come so far, it is over.

Each dead child coiled, a white serpent,
One at each little

Pitcher of milk, now empty.
She has folded

Them back into her body as petals
Of a rose close when the garden

Stiffens and odours bleed
From the sweet, deep throats of the night flower.

The moon has nothing to be sad about,
Staring from her hood of bone.

She is used to this sort of thing.
Her blacks crackle and drag.

Words

Axes
After whose stroke the wood rings,
And the echoes!
Echoes travelling
Off from the centre like horses.

The sap
Wells like tears, like the
Water striving
To re-establish its mirror
10   Over the rock

That drops and turns,
A white skull,
Eaten by weedy greens.
Years later I
Encounter them on the road—

Words dry and riderless,
The indefatigable hoof-taps.
While
From the bottom of the pool, fixed stars
20   Govern a life.

MICHAEL HARPER
1938–
Blue Ruth: America

I am telling you this:
the tubes in your nose,
in the esophagus,
in the stomach;
the small balloon
attached to its end
is your bleeding gullet;
yellow in the canned
sunshine of gauze,
10   stitching, bedsores,
each tactoe cut
sewn back
is America:
I am telling you this:
history is your own heart beat.

This Is My Son's Song:

"Ungie, Hi Ungie"

A two-year-old boy
is a blossom in the intensive
care aisle, small as
a ball-bearing,
round, open and smooth;
for a month, in his first
premature hours, his shaved
head made him a mohawk Indian
child, tubes the herbs
10   for his nest, a collapsed lung
the bulbous wing of a hawk.
Slivered into each sole
is an intravenous solution
to balance his losses
or what they take out
for the lab; the blue spot
on his spine is a birth
mark of needle readings;
the hardened thighs immune
20   from 70 shots of various
drugs of uneven depth; the chest
is thick with congestion: bad
air and mucus—good air and pure
oxygen; jerky pouch buffalo lungs—
It does not surprise me
when he waits patiently for his
grandmother, over her five-hour
painless operation; he has
waited in his isolette
30   before: the glow in his eyes
is for himself, will and love:
an exclamation of your name:
"*Ungie, hi Ungie*"; you are saved.

History as Apple Tree

Cocumscussoc is my village,
the western arm of Narragansett
Bay; Canonicus chief sachem;
black men escape into his tribe.

How does patent not breed heresy?
Williams[1] came to my chief
for his tract of land,
hunted by mad Puritans,
founded Providence Plantation;
10 Seekonk where he lost
first harvest, building, plant,
then the bay from these natives:
he set up trade.
With Winthrop he bought
an island, *Prudence;*
two others, *Hope* and *Patience*
he named, though small.
His trading post at the cove;
Smith's at another close by.
20 We walk the Pequot trail
as artery or spring.

Wampanoags, Cowesets,
Nipmucks, Niantics
came by canoe for the games;
matted bats, a goal line,
a deerskin filled with moss:
lacrosse. They danced;
we are told they gambled their souls.
In your apple orchard
30 legend conjures Williams' name;
he was an apple tree.
Buried on his own lot
off Benefit Street
a giant apple tree grew;
two hundred years later,
when the grave was opened,
dust and root grew
in his human skeleton:
bones became apple tree.

40 As black man I steal away
in the night to the apple tree,
place my arm in the rich grave,

1. Roger Williams (1603–1683), a Baptist, left
Massachusetts in search of religious freedom
and founded what is now Rhode Island.

black sachem on a family plot,
take up a chunk of apple root,
let it become my skeleton,
become my own myth:
my arm the historical branch,
my name the bruised fruit,
black human photograph: apple tree.

Roland

—a tune of watchfulness—

They told me to sit on the highest stool,
eating ice cream to my grandfather's
beckoning, his hands batons of light,
knuckles chiseled in saving
his people without money.

Who waits for the watch that a white man
brought to our stoop some weeks after
his stitches healed, his eye put back
from the sidewalk glimmering with vision,
10   his wrecked car cleaned from the corner
where he stacked his flesh
put back by a black man from Canada?

'moments of your life
added years to mine'
the watch says to my son
named for the man who wove
the eye back in its socket,
who drew me from my mother
in the upstairs infirmary bedroom,
20   who pointed to my mole
marked for his father.

To the white man
interfaced on the streetcorner:
a toast from the highest stool
from whenever my son sits wheeling
in his own chair ticking;
and to Roland, to Roland,

this word from his seat
of ancestral force
30   on his feeding frequency
of the high mode.

mahalia: MAHALIA

> a voice like hers comes along once a millennium—
> MLK, JR.

High-pitched waves of glory
bring you down in Chicago;
though satan should be bound
and it is spring
the death of him
inspired, dreamed
in glory to Memphis,
your choired practice
this spirit bowl-flesh
10   roughed echoing full faces
torn in shakes of saving—
her transcendent voice.

Words, sungstrewn, always the last word:
high-pitched resonant
whole sister fortified in Jesus
here in these deathmarch horsedrawn
blessings: most hearty bedrocked
sister with bad heart weakening
our ecstatic pain:

20   and who is listening?
head-dressed high-pitched whole sister
in the choir-chariot down
who is listening to your name.

4
DRAMA

Contexts of Drama

DRAMA, LITERATURE, AND REPRESENTATIONAL ART

Drama begins in make-believe, in the play acting of children, in the ritual of primitive religion. And it never forsakes its primitive beginnings, for imitative action is its essence. When an actor appears on stage, he makes believe he is someone other than himself, much as a child does, much as primitive people still do. Thus, like play-acting and ritual, drama creates its experience by doing things that can be heard and seen. "Drama," in fact, comes from a Greek word meaning "thing done." And the things it does, as with play-acting and ritual, create a world apart—a world modeled on ours yet leading its own charmed existence.

Drama, of course, is neither primitive ritual nor child's play, but it does share with them the essential quality of *enactment*. This quality should remind us that drama is not solely a form of literature. It is at once literary art *and* representational art. As literary art, a play is a fiction made out of words. It has a plot, characters, and dialogue. But it is a special kind of fiction—a fiction *acted out* rather than narrated. In a novel or short story, we learn about characters and events through the words of a narrator who stands between us and them, but in a play nothing stands between us and the total make-up of its world. Characters appear and events happen without any intermediate comment or explanation. Drama, then, offers us a *direct* presentation of its imaginative reality. In this sense it is representational art.

As students of drama, we are faced with something of a paradox. Because it is literature, a play can be read. But because it is representational art, a play is meant to be witnessed. We can see this problem in other terms. The text of a play is something like the score of a symphony—a finished work, yet only a potentiality until it is performed. Most plays, after all, are written to be performed. Those eccentric few that are not—that are written only to be read—we usually refer to as *closet dramas*. Very little can take place in a closet, but anything is possible in the theater. For most of us, however, the experience of drama is usually confined to plays in print rather than in performance. This means that we have to be unusually resourceful in our study of drama. Careful reading is not enough. We have to be creative readers as well. We have to imagine drama on the stage: not only must we attend to the meanings and implications of words—we also have to envision the words in performance. By doing so, we can begin to experience the understanding *and* pleasure that spectators gain when they attend a play. Their place, of course, is the theater, where our study properly begins.

DRAMA AND THEATRICAL PERFORMANCE

The magic of theater, its ability to conjure up even such incredible characters as the Ghost in *Hamlet,* or the Witches in *Macbeth,* or Death in *Everyman,* depends on the power of *spectacle*. And by spectacle we mean all the sights and sounds of performance—the slightest twitch or the boldest thrust of a sword, the faintest whisper or the loudest cry. Spectacle, in short, is the means by which the fictional world of a play is brought to life in the theater. When we witness a play, our thoughts and feelings are provoked as much by the spectacle as by the words themselves. Thus in reading a play, we should continually seek to create its spectacle in the imaginative theater of our minds. To do so, we must take a special approach to the text of a play.

It is not enough to read the text as simply a sequence of statements made by characters talking to one another or to themselves. We must also read the text as a *script* for performance, as if we were directors and actors involved in staging the play. Once we interpret it as a script, we can then see that the text contains innumerable cues from which we can construct a spectacle in our mind's eye. If we are attentive to those cues, they will tell us about the various elements that make up the total spectacle: *setting, costuming, props, blocking* (the arrangement of characters on the stage), *movement, gestures, intonation,* and *pacing* (the tempo and coordination of performance). By keeping those elements continuously in mind, we can imagine what the play looks and sounds like on stage. Then we will truly be entering into the world of the play, and by doing so we will not only understand, but also experience, its meaning.

Some dramatists, such as Ibsen, Shaw, and Williams, provide extensive and explicit directions for performance in parenthetical remarks preceding the dialogue and interspersed with it. But no matter how extensive their remarks may be, they are never complete guides to production. They still require us to infer elements of the spectacle from the dialogue itself. Other dramatists such as Sophocles, Shakespeare, and Molière provide little, if any, explicit guidance about staging. When we read their plays, we must gather our cues almost entirely from the dialogue. Thus we have chosen a passage from Shakespeare both to illustrate how the text of a play can embody a script for performance, and to demonstrate the analytic method appropriate for discovering its implicit cues. In the next paragraph we will provide a brief explanation of the context for the passage. With that background in hand, you should then examine the dialogue carefully to see what details you can infer on your own about the arrangement, gestures, and physical interaction of the characters.

The following passage from Act I, Scene 2, of *Othello* depicts a confrontation between Othello, leader of the Venetian military forces, and Brabantio, a Venetian senator. The confrontation is occasioned by the fact that Othello has secretly courted and married Brabantio's daughter Desdemona—a fact revealed to Brabantio in the previous scene by Roderigo, a jealous suitor of Desdemona, and Iago, the duplicitous subordinate of Othello. As the passage begins, Othello and his officers Cassio and Iago are on their way to meet with the Duke of Venice, who has sent messengers to summon Othello to a military planning session.

IAGO   Come, captain, will you go?
OTHELLO   Have with you.
CASSIO   Here comes another troop to seek for you.

Enter Brabantio, Roderigo, and others with lights and weapons.

IAGO   It is Brabantio. General, be advised.
      He comes to bad intent.
OTHELLO   Holla! stand there!
RODERIGO   Signior, it is the Moor.
BRABANTIO   Down with him, thief!

They draw on both sides.

IAGO   You, Roderigo! Come, sir, I am for you.
OTHELLO   Keep up your bright swords, for the dew will rust them.
      Good signior, you shall more command with years
      Than with your weapons.
BRABANTIO   O thou foul thief, where hast thou stowed my daughter?
      Damned as thou art, thou hast enchanted her!
      For I'll refer me to all things of sense,
      If she in chains of magic were not bound,
      Whether a maid so tender, fair, and happy,
      So opposite to marriage that she shunned
      The wealthy curlèd darlings of our nation,
      Would ever have, t'incur a general mock,
      Run from her guardage to the sooty bosom
      Of such a thing as thou—to fear, not to delight.
      Judge me the world if 'tis not gross in sense
      That thou hast practiced on her with foul charms,

> Abused her delicate youth with drugs or minerals
> That weaken motion. I'll have't disputed on;
> 'Tis probable, and palpable to thinking.
> I therefore apprehend and do attach thee
> For an abuser of the world, a practicer
> Of arts inhibited and out of warrant.
> Lay hold upon him. If he do resist,
> Subdue him at his peril.
> OTHELLO   Hold your hands,
> Both you of my inclining and the rest.
> Were it my cue to fight, I should have known it
> Without a prompter.

This passage depicts a confrontation that twice threatens to erupt into a pitched sword battle between Brabantio's followers and those of Othello. Thus it is a highly dramatic moment in the play, and our purpose should be to envision the performance as fully and as precisely as possible. From the initial remarks of Iago and Othello, it appears that they must be moving to exit from one side of the stage, while Cassio, who is standing nearby, has not yet turned to depart and thus sees a group of people with torches entering from the opposite side of the stage. Cassio does not identify them—presumably because they are still some distance away and the light of their torches obscures their faces. But Cassio's announcement of "another troop" must cause Iago and Othello to reverse their direction, by which time Brabantio and his followers have moved close enough to be recognized by Iago.

Iago, of course, is directly responsible for Brabantio's appearance on the scene, having previously aroused his anger with the revelation of Othello's elopement. But since Othello and his followers are unaware of Iago's double-dealing, they can only take his warning about Brabantio's "bad intent" as the straightforward advice of a loyal officer. Thus, when Iago utters his warning, we should imagine Cassio and the other attendants of Othello moving forward and unsheathing their swords as though to make ready for a battle with Brabantio and his troop. Once we do so, we can recognize that Othello's command—"stand there!"—which might seem to be addressed to Brabantio and his followers, is in fact addressed to his own men. Even though Othello is a military man, he does not wish to settle this personal matter by force of arms, as is clear from his subsequent remarks to Brabantio. We might, then, even imagine Othello raising his arm at this point to accentuate that command of restraint to his troops.

Brabantio, however, responding to Roderigo's recognition of Othello—"Signior, it is the Moor"—incites his own followers to attack Othello and his men. Thus, at the moment that Brabantio makes his command to attack—"Down with him, thief!"—we should picture the two groups of men not only drawing their swords but also moving toward one another. Iago's challenge to Roderigo—"You, Roderigo! Come, sir, I am for you"—should cause us to see him as leading the charge of Othello's men. He is, of course, simply feigning an attack to sustain the impression of being Othello's loyal officer.

At this point Othello gives his second command of the scene—"Keep up your bright swords." When he does so, we should not only hear the authority of his voice but also envision the authority of his movement. We should imagine Othello, without any sword at all, stepping between the two groups of men, raising his arms to quell the movement on both sides, and then turning to address Brabantio face to face with a courtly but gentle reproof—"Good signior, you shall more command with years/Than with your weapons." At the same time that Othello is turning to address Brabantio, we should also visualize the two groups of men responding to his command by stepping back and away from one another, as well as relaxing their sword arms, so that Othello and Brabantio become the exclusive focus in the foreground of the scene.

Othello's attempt to calm the two sides does not by any means subdue Brabantio's anger. Brabantio instead delivers a lengthy attack on Othello's character, uttering a series of insults and accusations so extreme that we might well expect them to arouse Othello to defend his honor with his sword. But Othello, we notice, is silent throughout the harangue—which is a powerful dramatic statement in itself. That restraint should also lead us to see Othello as standing in a dignified posture, arms by his sides, while Brabantio accentuates his insults with physical gestures and movements, first pointing his finger accusingly at him, then raising his arm in self-righteous judgment, and probably even moving back and forth in front of him as he gives voice to his accusations. Then, at the conclusion of his harangue, we should imagine Brabantio as once again turning to his troop of men to issue his second command—"Lay hold upon him. If he do resist,/Subdue him at his peril."

Once again we should imagine the two groups of men raising their swords and moving to attack one another. And once again, when Othello gives his third command—"Hold your hands,/Both you of my inclining and the rest"—we should see him moving between the two groups to prevent a battle from taking place. That visual image of the action is important for us to keep in mind, because it is a definitive spectacle. It embodies above all the exceptional authority and restraint of Othello: twice in this brief passage he is faced with a potentially explosive situation, and twice he subdues the situation and himself with extraordinary grace.

Our discussion has thus far treated the passage as a script to guide us in imagining the physical interaction of the characters. We have examined each bit of the dialogue with an eye to the cues it contains about the gestures, movements, and spatial relations of the characters at every moment in the scene. Our approach has emphasized the theatrical, rather than the literary, implications of the passage. Detailed as it is, however, our analysis has not yet envisioned the action *on* stage *in* a theater. And we must do that too, if we wish to experience and understand the total spectacle of the scene. At this point, then, it might be tempting to imagine the action on a modern stage, equipped with machinery for sets and special lighting effects. We might imagine the characters arranged in front of a set depicting, for example, houses and public buildings, for we know from earlier cues in the text that the scene takes place on a street in Venice. We might, in turn, imagine the stage as completely darkened, except for the torches carried by the attendants of Othello and Brabantio, for we know also from earlier cues in the text, as well as from the torches themselves, that the scene takes place at about midnight. And we might, finally, imagine ourselves sitting in a darkened theater and witnessing the scene, which is framed like a picture by the arch of the stage.

Then we would have a vividly dramatic image and experience of the potential conflict between Brabantio's men and the supporters of Othello. Then, for example, the space initially dividing the two groups of men would be dramatically set off by the darkness engulfing it. Then their aggressive movements toward each other would be dramatically accentuated by the fiery movement of their torches. Then their weapons, reflecting the light of their torches, would truly appear to be "bright swords," as Othello calls them, particularly by contrast with the surrounding darkness. And then, each time Othello stepped between them, their response to his command would be visible in the subduing of that fiery brightness. All in all, the spectacle would be as dazzling as the authority of Othello himself.

But that spectacle is not what Shakespeare's seventeenth-century audiences would have seen when they witnessed the play. The Globe Theater, where Shakespeare's plays were originally produced, was an open-air structure without sets or lights of any kind. Thus the spectators of Shakespeare's time could not have witnessed the "realistic" illusion of a midnight street scene such as we have imagined in the previous paragraph. They would have seen the action take place in broad daylight on a bare stage without a backdrop. Thus they would have depended wholly upon the language, the actors, and their torches to evoke a sense of that dark Venetian street suddenly lighted up by those two fiery groups of men. Even so, they would have had a more intimate involvement with the characters and the action, for the Globe stage, rather than being set behind an arch, extended out into the audience itself. Their experience of the scene would thus have been quite different from that provided by our modern stage version. In light of that difference, we might well ask which version is valid. Both, in fact, are valid, but for different reasons. The modern version is valid, primarily because it is true to the theatrical conditions of our own time. Most modern theaters, after all, are not designed like the Globe, and if we attend a performance of *Othello* we should not expect it to duplicate the scene as produced in Shakespeare's time. But when we are reading the play we *can* imagine how it would have been produced in the Globe and thus be true to the theatrical conditions for which Shakespeare created it.

Once we have imagined any play in the context of the theater for which it was written, we can also bring that understanding to any production we may happen to witness. We can compare our imagined production with the production on stage, and by doing so we can recognize how the director and actors have adapted the original context of the play to their own theatrical circumstances. If, for example, we were to attend a production of *Othello*, we might see that scene with Brabantio, Othello, and their followers performed on a bare stage, without sets or props of any kind. Having imagined the scene in its original theatrical context, we would then not be surprised or puzzled by that bare stage, but would recognize that the director was attempting to incorporate an important element of seventeenth-century theater in a contemporary production. By being historically informed play-readers, we can also become critically enlightened play-goers. With this in mind, we shall preface each of the plays in the "Classical to Neoclassical Drama" section with a description of the theater for which it was written. Those descriptions will provide a context for imagining the plays in their original theatrical setting. For this reason we recommend that before reading any play in that section, you read the theatrical description preceding it.

DRAMA AND OTHER LITERARY FORMS

In the preceding section we considered drama primarily as a theatrical event—a representational art to be performed and witnessed. In doing so, we were concerned with the uniquely dramatic experience created by a play in performance. But any performance, moving as it may be, is an *interpretation*—of how the lines should be enacted and delivered. Thus every production of a play stresses some words and minimizes others, includes some meanings and excludes others. No single production can possibly convey all the implications in the language of a play. This should remind us that drama is also a form of literature—an art made out of words—and should be understood in relation not only to the theater but also to the other literary forms: story, poem, and essay.

In relating drama to the other literary forms, we might first look again at the diagram in the general introduction to this book. That diagram, you will recall, locates and defines each form according to the unique way it uses words and communicates them to the reader. Drama in its pure form uses words to create action through the dialogue of characters talking to one another rather than to the reader: its essential quality is *interaction*. But the diagram, as we noted earlier, also represents the proximity of the forms to each other. Like a story, drama is concerned with plot and character. Like a poem, it is overheard rather than being addressed to a reader. Like an essay, it is capable of being used to explore issues and propose ideas. Using these relationships as points of departure, we can now examine some of the ways in which drama takes on the characteristics and devices of the other forms.

Drama and Narration

A play is at its most dramatic, of course, when it uses the give-and-take of dialogue to create interaction. But the interaction always takes place within a specific context—a background in time and place without which it cannot be properly understood. To bring about this understanding, drama turns to the narrative techniques of the story. This is not to say that we should expect to find storytellers addressing us directly in plays. Occasionally they do turn up (like the Stage Manager in *Our Town*), but more often the characters become storytellers in their dialogue with one another. The most obvious form of this storytelling occurs at the beginning of plays, and is appropriately called *exposition* because it sets forth and explains in a manner typical of narrative.

Exposition is important not only because it establishes the mood of a play but also because it conveys information about the world of that play. Through expository dialogue the dramatist may reveal information about the public state of affairs, as in the opening of *Oedipus Rex;* or exposition may disclose information about past actions and private relations of the characters, as in the opening of *Othello.* Often the information comes in bits and pieces of dialogue, as in life itself, so that we must put it together on our own. But once we have done so, we have a background for understanding the action that takes place during the play.

Related to exposition is another narrative device, called *retrospection.* Often, during the process of action, characters look back and survey significant events that took place well before the time of the play; and when this happens, drama is again using an element of narration. Sometimes retrospection may lead to major revelations about the characters and the motivations for their behavior, as in the lengthy conversation between Brick and Big Daddy toward the end of Act II of *Cat on a Hot Tin Roof.* Sometimes retrospection may be the principal activity of the play, as in *Oedipus Rex* and *The Stronger.* In both these plays the chief characters become preoccupied with piecing together elements from their past, and in each case the climax occurs when their retrospection leads them to discoveries about their past which totally reverse their view of themselves and their world.

Thus far we have looked at narrative elements referring to pre-play action, but there are also occasions when narration is used to convey the action of the play itself—when narration replaces interaction. Occasions such as these are produced when offstage action is reported rather than represented—for even when characters are offstage they are still doing things that we must know about in order to have a total view of the action. When offstage action is reported, a play becomes most nearly like a story. Words then are being used to develop a view of character and situation rather than to create action through dialogue. This process can be seen most clearly in *Oedipus Rex*, when the Second Messenger tells the Choragus about the death of Iokastê and the self-blinding of Oedipus. The interaction on stage ceases entirely for the length of almost fifty lines, and what we get instead has all the features of a miniature story.

The Messenger first establishes his narrative authority, then moves into his tale, supplying detailed information, offering explanations for facts he cannot provide, reporting dialogue, and concluding with a general reflection on the fate of Oedipus and Iokastê, whose experience he sees as epitomizing the "misery of mankind." In trying to explain why Sophocles has these events reported rather than showing them on stage, we might simply conclude that they are too gruesome to be displayed. But it is also true that through the Messenger's report Sophocles is able to provide a comment on the meaning of the events.

The Messenger's commentary brings us to the last important element of narration in drama—*choric commentary*. When the narrator of a story wishes to comment on characters and events, he can do so at will. But the dramatist, of course, cannot suddenly appear in the play—or on stage—to provide a point of view on the action. The dramatist's alternative is the *chorus*, or *choric characters*—personages, that is, who are relatively detached from the action and can thus stand off from it, somewhat like a narrator, to reflect on the significance of events. In Greek drama the chorus performed this function.

The existence of a chorus, however, is no guarantee that its opinions are always to be trusted. Sometimes it can be as wrongheaded as any of the more involved characters. Sometimes it is completely reliable, as in its concluding remarks in *Oedipus Rex* about the frailty of the human condition. Choric commentary, then, provides a point of view, but not necessarily an authoritative one, or one to be associated necessarily with the dramatist. In each case it has to be judged in the context of the entire play. But whether it is valid, or partially reliable, or completely invalid, the chorus does provoke us to reflect on the meaning of events by providing commentary for us to assess.

After the classical Greek period the formal chorus disappeared almost entirely from drama. Remnants of the chorus can, of course, be found in later plays—even in contemporary drama. But for us as readers the important matter is to recognize that choric characters persist in drama despite the absence of a formally designated chorus. Minor characters such as messengers, servants, clowns, or others not directly involved in the action, can carry out the functions of a chorus, as does the Doctor at the end of *Everyman*. Characters involved in the action can also function as choric commentators, particularly if they are, like Eliante in *The Misanthrope* or

Bluntschli in *Arms and the Man*, endowed with a highly reasonable disposition. Ultimately, any character is capable of becoming a commentator of a sort, simply by standing off from the action and viewing it as a spectator rather than as a participant. And their reflections should be taken no less seriously than those of a chorus. After all, like Nora in the last scene of *A Doll's House*, or Othello in his last speech of the play, characters can be the most discerning judges of their world.

Drama and Meditation

When we recall that interaction through dialogue is the basis of drama, we can readily see that a play is committed by its very nature to showing us the public side of its characters. Realizing this, we can see as well the artistic problem a dramatist faces when trying to reveal the private side of such characters. The narrator of a story can solve this problem simply by telling us the innermost thoughts of the characters. But a dramatist must turn to the conventions of the poem, using words addressed by a speaker talking or thinking to himself.

When reading a purely lyric poem, we automatically assume that the situation is private rather than public and that we can overhear the words even though they might never be spoken aloud. In reading or witnessing a play, we must make a similar imaginative effort. To assist our efforts, dramatists have traditionally organized their plays so as to make sure that a character thinking to himself is seen in private. That special situation is implied by our term *soliloquy*, which means (literally) to speak alone. But it is also true that we have private thoughts even in the presence of others, and this psychological reality has been recognized by modern dramatists whose characters may often be seen thinking to themselves in the most public situations. Whatever the circumstances, private or public, the soliloquy makes unusual demands on both actors and audience.

As readers we should be aware that the soliloquy can perform a variety of functions, and, since it is so unusual an element in drama, it achieves its purposes with great effectiveness. Customarily, the soliloquy is a means of giving expression to a complex state of mind and feeling, and in most cases the speaker is seen struggling with problems of the utmost consequence. This accounts for the intensity we often find in the soliloquy. We are all familiar, for example, with Hamlet's predicaments—to be or not to be, to kill or not to kill the king—and these are typical of the weighty issues that usually burden the speaker of a soliloquy. In soliloquy, then, the interaction among characters is replaced by the interaction of a mind with itself.

When a play shifts from dramatic interaction to meditation, its process of events is temporarily suspended, and the soliloquizing character necessarily becomes a spectator of his world. In this way the soliloquy, like choric commentary, offers the dramatist a means of providing a point of view on the action of the play. In reading a soliloquy, then, we should examine it not only as the private revelation of a character but also as a significant form of commentary on other characters and events. Even the soliloquies of a villain such as Iago can offer us valuable points of view, especially when the villain happens, like Iago, to be a discerning judge of his world.

In considering the soliloquy, we have been examining only an element of meditation in drama. It is also possible for plays to become primarily or even exclusively meditative—though at first this probably sounds like a contradiction of dramatic form. If drama depends on the interaction of dialogue, how is it possible for internalized thought and feeling to be the principal subject of a play? Actually, this can happen in a number of ways. One way—a very traditional way—is to create a cast of characters who represent not persons but abstractions—who embody aspects, or qualities, or thoughts, or feelings of a single mind. In *Everyman*, for example, the title character is shown in conversation with other characters named Beauty, Strength, Discretion, and Five Wits. Interaction among characters of that sort is clearly meant to represent the interaction of a mind with itself, and so it constitutes the dramatization of a meditative experience achieved through what we might call an allegory of the mind.

We can also recognize plays dramatizing the life of the mind through methods other than allegory. Many modern plays, such as *Death of a Salesman*, or *A Streetcar Named Desire*, or *A Slight Ache*, or *Equus*, entail sustained action that is meant to expose the mental life of the principal characters. In such plays we encounter not only soliloquies and other kinds of monologue but also imaginary sequences depicting dreams and fantasies. Plays such as these reflect the influence of modern psychological theories about the behavior of the mind. Writing in 1932, for example, Eugene O'Neill defined the "modern dramatist's problem" as discovering how to "express those profound hidden conflicts of the mind which the probings of psychology continue to disclose to us." Almost fifty years earlier, in 1888, the Swedish dramatist Strindberg anticipated the same idea: "I have noticed that what interests people most nowadays is the psychological action." Looking at their statements side by side, we can see that they share the same concern. O'Neill speaks of "hidden conflicts of the mind," and Strindberg of "psychological action." We might also call it *meditative drama*.

Whatever form a meditative drama may take, we as readers must be alert to the "hidden conflicts" it aims to dramatize. To recognize such conflicts we must be attentive not only to the external action but also to what we might call the internal action. We should examine both plot and dialogue for what they can tell us about the mental life of the characters. And rather than looking for a clearly defined sequence of events, we should expect to find a kind of movement as irregular and hazy as the workings of the mind itself.

Drama and Persuasion

A play could be exclusively a piece of persuasion only if it con-sisted of a single character—the dramatist!—addressing ideas directly to the audience. In such an event, of course, it would be difficult to distinguish the play from a lecture. This extreme case should remind us that drama is rarely, if ever, simply an exposition or assertion of ideas. Ideas can, of course, be found throughout the dialogue of almost any play, but, as we have seen in the preceding sections, it is best to assume that those ideas are sentiments of the characters rather than the opinions of the dramatist. A character is a character. A dramatist is a dramatist. And dramatists are never present to speak for themselves, except in prefaces, prologues, epilogues, stage directions—and other statements outside the framework of the play.

Although dramatists cannot speak for themselves, their plays can. The essential quality of drama—interaction—may be made to serve the purposes of an essay. Dialogue, plot, and character may be used to expound ideas and sway the opinions of an audience. The desire to persuade usually implies the existence of conflicting ideas, and plays with a persuasive intention customarily seek to demonstrate the superiority of one idea, or set of attitudes, over another. Thus characters may become spokesmen for ideas, dialogue a form of debating ideas, and action a form of testing ideas. Plays of this kind inevitably force audiences and readers to examine the merits of each position and align themselves with one side or the other. In reading such plays, we must be attentive not only to the motives and personalities of characters but also to the ideas they espouse. Similarly, we must be interested not only in the fate of the characters but also in the success or failure of their ideas. Ultimately, then, these plays do not allow us the pleasure of simply witnessing the interaction of characters. Like essays, they seek to challenge our ideas and change our minds.

Because they focus on conflicting ideas, plays with a persuasive intention can easily be distinguished from other forms of drama. Like *Arms and the Man* or *The Misanthrope*, they usually set up opposing values in their opening scenes. In the first scene of *The Misanthrope*, for example, Philinte espouses social conformity, Alceste opposes him by defending personal integrity; and their disagreement produces a debate that runs on for more than 150 lines. As spokesman for ideas, they behave like contes-tants in a formal argument rather than characters in a dramatic situation. And their dialogue sounds like disputation rather than conversation. By the end of the scene, then, the play has clearly invited us to take a stand, to choose between "outward courtesies" and "inward hearts." The choice, of course, is not an easy one, and the play is designed to keep us from making a simple choice.

Modes of Drama

DRAMA, THE WORLD, AND IMITATION

Drama, as we said at the start, creates a world modeled on our own: its essence is imitative action. But drama is not imitative in the ordinary sense of the word. It does not offer us a literal copy of reality, for the truth of drama does not depend upon reproducing the world exactly as it is. Drama is true to life by being false to our conventional notions of reality.

The sexual sit-down strike in *Lysistrata* is outlandish. The abstract characters of *Everyman* are fantastic. The dialogue in *A Slight Ache* is frequently absurd. Yet each of these plays creates a world that we recognize as being in some sense like our own. Our problem then is to define the special sense in which drama is imitative. We can begin by recognizing that its mode of imitation must be selective rather than all-inclusive, intensive rather than extensive. It has to be, since time is short and space is limited in the theater. Faced with limitations in stage size and performance time, the dramatist obviously cannot hope to reproduce the world exactly as it is. By selecting and intensifying things, however, the dramatist can emphasize the dominant patterns and essential qualities of human experience. Thus, our understanding of any play requires that we define the principle of emphasis that determines the make-up of its world and the experience of its characters.

In defining the emphasis of any play, we can ask ourselves whether the dramatist has focused on the beautiful or the ugly, on the orderly or the chaotic, on what is best or on what is worst in the world. A play that emphasizes the beautiful and the orderly tends toward an idealized vision of the world—which is the mode we call *romance*. A play focusing on the ugly and chaotic tends toward a debased view of the world, and this we call *satire*. Both these emphases depend for their effect upon extreme views of human nature and existence.

743

In contrast to the extreme conditions of romance and satire, another pair of dramatic processes takes place in a world neither so beautiful as that of romance nor so ugly as that of satire—in a world more nearly like our own. Rather than focusing on essential qualities in the world, these processes—*comedy* and *tragedy*—emphasize the dominant patterns of experience that characters undergo in the world. In comedy the principal characters ordinarily begin in a state of opposition either to one another or to their world—often both. By the end of the play, their opposition is replaced by harmony. Thus the characters are integrated with one another and with their world. In tragedy, however, the hero and his world begin in a condition of harmony that subsequently disintegrates, leaving him by the end of the play completely isolated or destroyed.

With these four possibilities in mind, we might draw a simple diagram such as this:

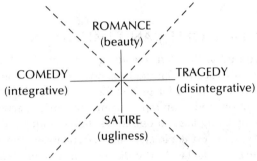

The vertical pair emphasize the essential qualities in the world; the horizontal pair emphasize the dominant patterns of human experience; the point of intersection—the absence of emphasis—refers to the world as it is. In this way we can immediately visualize each of the emphases, its distinguishing characteristics, and its relation to each of the others. Once we have recognized these possibilities, we might be tempted simply to categorize plays in terms of the characteristics we have identified with each emphasis. Yet it should be kept in mind that each emphasis is at best an abstraction—a definition formulated in order to generalize about a great number of plays, not an explanation of any one play in particular. Thus, when we turn to individual plays we should not necessarily expect that they can be accurately described and understood simply by labeling them comedy or tragedy, satire or romance.

As a way of anticipating some of the complexities, we can see in the diagram that each emphasis borders on two others. Comedy, for example, tends toward romance, on the one hand, and satire, on the other. The same is true of tragedy, and the others. Even the antithetical possibilities, as we will see, can interact. But this should hardly surprise us: if the world can incorporate both the beautiful and the ugly, so can a play. Ultimately, then, these categories will serve us best if we use them tactfully as guides to understanding rather than as a rigid system of classification. But before they can serve us as guides, we must familiarize ourselves with their characteristics in greater detail.

TRAGEDY AND COMEDY

Tragedies usually end in death and mourning, comedies in marriage and dancing. That difference accounts for the two familiar masks of drama, one expressing sorrow, the other joy, one provoking tears, the other laughter. That difference also accounts for the commonly held notion that tragedy is serious, and comedy frivolous. But when we consider that both modes are probably descended from primitive fertility rites—tragedy from ritual sacrifice, comedy from ritual feasting—we can recognize that they dramatize equally important dimensions of human experience. Tragedy embodies the inevitability of individual death, comedy the irrepressibility of social rebirth. So, like autumn and spring, tragedy and comedy are equally significant phases in a natural cycle of dramatic possibilities. Indeed, like the seasons of the year and the nature of human experience, they are inextricably bound up with one another.

Every comedy contains a potential tragedy—the faint possibility that harmony may not be achieved, that the lovers may not come together to form a new society. And every tragedy contains a potential comedy—the faint possibility that disaster may be averted, that the hero or heroine may survive. This in turn should remind us that we must be concerned not only with the distinctive endings of tragedy and of comedy, but also with the means by which each brings about its end. Catastrophe in and of itself does not constitute tragedy, nor does marriage alone make for comedy. The unique experience of each mode is produced by the design of its plot and the nature of the characters who take part in it. We can grasp this principle most clearly by looking first at the elements of tragedy, then at the elements of comedy.

Tragedy was first defined by the Greek philosopher Aristotle (384–322 B.C.), who inferred its essential elements from witnessing the plays of his own time. His observations, which he set down in the *Poetics,* cannot be expected to explain all the tragedies that have ever been written; no single theory could possibly do so. But Aristotle's theory has influenced more dramatists—and critics—than any other propounded since his time, and thus it remains the best guide we have to the nature of tragedy.

Aristotle considered *plot* to be the most important element of tragedy, because he believed that "all human happiness or misery takes the form of action," that "it is in our actions—what we do—that we are happy or the reverse." Thus, in discussing tragedy, he emphasized the design of the plot and established several important qualities that contribute to its effect. First, he stressed the *unity* of a tragic plot. By unity he meant that the plot represents a single action, or story, with a definite beginning, middle, and end, and further that all its incidents are "so closely connected that the transposal or withdrawal of any one of them will disjoin or dislocate the whole." By close connection he also meant that the incidents are causally related to one another, so that their sequence is probable and necessary. Ultimately, then, we can see that, in emphasizing the unity of a tragic plot, Aristotle was calling attention to the quality of the inevitable that we associate with tragedy. Thus in reading a tragedy we should attempt to define the chain of cause and effect linking each incident in the plot. In this way we will understand the process that makes its catastrophe inevitable, and thus gain insight into the meaning of the catastrophe.

In examining the plot of a tragedy such as *Oedipus Rex*, we may be tempted to regard its catastrophe as not only inevitable but also inescapable. Aristotle, however, did not see the inevitable change in the fortunes of the tragic hero as being the result of chance, or coincidence, or fate, or even of some profound flaw in the character of the hero. Rather, he saw the change of fortune as being caused by "some error of judgment," a "great error," on the part of the hero. In defining this element of tragedy, Aristotle clearly regarded the hero or heroine, and not some condition beyond human control, as responsible for initiating the chain of events leading to the change of fortune. Even a profound flaw in character, after all, is beyond human control. Accordingly, Aristotle described the tragic hero as an "intermediate kind of personage" in moral character, neither "preeminently virtuous and just," nor afflicted "by vice and depravity"—as someone morally "like ourselves," in whom we can engage our emotional concern. Thus, when we read tragedies such as *Oedipus Rex* or *Othello*, we should not regard their protagonists as victims of absurd circumstances, but rather should seek to identify the sense in which they are agents of their undoing.

While we seek to understand the nature of their error, we should not forget that most tragic heroes are genuinely admirable characters—persons, as Aristotle tells us, who deservedly enjoy "great reputation and prosperity." And their reputation is a function not simply of their social rank but also of their commitment to noble purposes. Oedipus is not merely a king but also a man committed to discovering the truth and ridding his city of the plague. Othello is not only a military leader but also a man committed to moral purity in all his actions as well as in all his personal relations. Romeo and Juliet are not simply the children of aristocratic families but also persons committed to a love that transcends the pettiness of family squabbles and political factions. Our response to them should thus combine judgment with sympathy and admiration.

Once we make the effort to discover their error, we shall find that we undergo an experience parallel to that of the protagonists themselves. We shall find that we are compelled by the process of events—by the turn of the plot—to recognize how they have undone themselves. The protagonist's act of recognition is defined by Aristotle as the *discovery*, because it entails "a change from ignorance to knowledge." And the discovery, as Aristotle recognized, is caused inevitably by a *reversal,* an incident or sequence of incidents that go contrary to the protagonist's expectations. Reversal and discovery are crucial elements of the tragic experience, because they crystalize its meaning for the protagonist—and for us. When events go contrary to their expectations, when the irony of their situation becomes evident, they—and we—have no choice but to recognize exactly how the noblest intentions can bring about the direst consequences. Thus, in its discovery, as in its entire plot, tragedy affirms both the dignity and the frailty of man.

Discovery scenes take place in comedy as well, but, rather than accounting for an inevitable disaster, comic discoveries reveal information that enables characters to avoid a probable catastrophe. Lost wills may be found, or mistaken identities corrected, or some other fortuitous circumstance may be revealed. Somehow comedy always manages to bring about a happy turn of events for its heroes and heroines—and thus those heroes and heroines are rarely the sole or primary agents of their success. Usually, in fact, they get a large helping hand from chance, or coincidence, or some other lucky state of affairs. Comedy thrives on improbability. And in doing so it defies the mortal imperatives of tragedy.

In this sense comedy embodies the spirit of spring with its eternal promise of rebirth and renewal, and it embodies, too, the festive air and festive activities we associate with spring. The term *comedy*, in fact, is derived from a Greek word, *komoidia*, meaning revel-song, and revelry always finds its way into comedy, whether in the form of feasts and dancing, tricks and joking, sex and loving—or all of them combined, as in *Lysistrata*. So the perils that develop in the world of comedy rarely seem very perilous to us. Although the characters themselves may feel temporarily threatened, the festive air makes us sense that ultimately no permanent damage will be done, and thus we share the perspective of Puck in *A Midsummer Night's Dream*, when he says:

> Jack shall have Jill,
> Naught shall go ill,
> The man shall have his mare again, and all shall be well.

Though comedy avoids the experience of death, it does not evade the significance of life. Comic plots, in fact, usually arise out of conflicts that embody opposing values and beliefs. Thus the conflicts among characters inevitably pit one set of attitudes against another, one kind of social vision against another. In reading comedies, therefore, we should attempt to identify the attitudes that bring characters into conflict. In *Lysistrata*, for example, the wives are committed to peace, their husbands to political honor. In *A Midsummer Night's Dream* the young lovers, Hermia and Lysander, are committed to their vows of true love, but Hermia's father is committed to his parental authority. In *Arms and the Man* one set of characters is committed to realistic facts about war and love, the other to romantic illusions. Once we have identified those conflicting values, we will discover that they can help us to understand the meaning of a comic plot.

Comedy usually begins with a state of affairs dominated by one kind of social idea, and thus the resolution of a comic plot—achieved through its scenes of discovery—embodies the triumph of a new social order. Whoever wins out in comedy is invariably on the right side, no matter how improbable the victory may seem. Thus it is that the characters who oppose the new order of things—the blocking figures—are usually subjected to comic ridicule throughout the play. Comedy, after all, expresses an irreverent attitude toward old and inflexible ideas, toward any idea that stifles natural and reasonable impulses in the human spirit. But comedy, as we said earlier, also embodies the generous and abundant spirit of spring. Its heroes and heroines—the proponents of the new society—always seek to include their opponents in the final comic festivities. Comedy seeks not to destroy the old, but rather to reclaim it. And therein is to be seen the ultimate expression of its exuberant faith in life.

SATIRE AND ROMANCE

Satire and romance, rather than dramatizing the dominant patterns of human experience, embody the essential qualities and potentialities of human nature. Romance bears witness to what humanity can be at its best, satire to what it can be at its worst. Romance offers us an idealized vision of human potentiality, satire a spectacle of inferior human conduct. Thus, when we encounter plays in these modes, we should not expect to find the morally "intermediate kind" of character of whom Aristotle speaks in his discussion of tragedy. Rather we should expect to encounter characters who tend toward moral, social, or psychological extremes of behavior. For the same reason, we should not expect finely detailed personalities with complex motivations. Rather, we should expect characters who represent types of human nature dominated by clear-cut attitudes and impulses.

Satire and romance are intended ultimately to produce clear-cut images of good or evil, virtue or vice, wisdom or folly; and those images may be embodied most vividly in characters who are boldly outlined rather than finely detailed. Such qualities may also be highlighted through *contrast*. Thus, the plots of satire and romance often bring together characters from both extremes, using their interaction to create emphatic contrasts. We can best understand these elements by looking first at satire, then at romance.

Satiric drama always expresses a critical attitude toward a particular aspect of human conduct and affairs. The satire may focus on morality, society, politics, or some other dimension of human nature and culture. Our first purpose in reading a satiric play should thus be to identify the focus of its criticism, as we can do by examining the characters themselves to see what particular types of behavior predominate among them. In Ben Jonson's *Volpone*, for example, all the leading characters in the first act—Volpone, Mosca, Corvino, Corbaccio, and Voltore—are obsessed by material greed. The principal character, Volpone, is motivated additionally by lust and pride. In short, the world of *Volpone* impresses us as being morally corrupt. In *The Misanthrope*, most of the characters are motivated by social ambitiousness. Célimène is a malicious gossip and an incurable coquette, Arsinoe a jealous and hypocritical prude, Oronte a vain poet and officious lover, Acaste and Clitandre a matched pair of pretentious fops. Even Alceste, the "misanthrope," the self-proclaimed enemy of social pretensions, is badly flawed by his extraordinary egotism. The world of these characters thus strikes us as a false and shallow society.

Once we have identified the dominant vices of the characters, we should explore the consequences of their behavior, and we can do so by examining the incidents of the plot. In *Volpone*, for example, the greed of the characters is shown to threaten the ethical and legal foundations of their society. In *The Misanthrope* the social pretensions of the characters are shown to make them incapable of loving one another or feeling genuine affection for one another. Thus in each case the plot is designed to dramatize not only the vice but also its moral or social implications. Satiric plots incorporate discovery scenes as well, and the discoveries of satire inevitably bring about the public exposure of the principal characters. Volpone, for example, is exposed in court and legally punished. Célimène is exposed in her own house and subjected to social ridicule.

As those discovery scenes indicate, satiric drama does not necessarily offer us a completely pessimistic spectacle of human affairs. Indeed, we will usually find that a satire incorporates at least a few virtuous characters. Celia and Bonario in *Volpone* are completely generous and trusting individuals—so much so that they are almost helpless to prevent themselves from being victimized by the others. And in *The Misanthrope*, Philinte and particularly Eliante are sensible enough to transcend the shallowness of their society. These characters, by representing the virtuous potentiality of human nature, not only highlight the ugliness surrounding them in the satiric world but also remind us in the end that humanity is not—and need not be—depraved. In other words, satire offers us an intensified but not completely negative view of human imperfection.

Romance, by analogy, offers us an intensified but not completely idealized vision of human excellence. The heroes of romance, for example, are typically shown in conflict with characters representing aspects of human imperfection or depravity. Prospero in *The Tempest* is threatened by his malign brother Antonio, who embodies the sin of pride; Everyman is tempted by Fellowship and Goods, who embody the evils of worldliness. Although these heroes triumph over the malign forces in their world, the struggle is perilous, and their success inevitably requires the assistance of miraculous events or supernatural powers. Prospero depends on his magic wand and on Ariel, the spirit who performs extraordinary deeds for him. And Everyman can redeem his soul only through the miraculous power of the sacraments. In this respect the heroes of dramatic romance resemble their counterparts in a well-known narrative form of romance, the medieval tale of chivalric love and adventure, which portrays virtuous knights doing battle with evil monsters and triumphing over them through the power of a magic sword or some other kind of talisman. Their miraculous power, of course, is derived from, and symbolic of, their commitment to the forces of goodness and truth in their world. And that condition should remind us that romance typically assumes the existence of a divinely ordered world, in which the hero succeeds because he recognizes that order and is obedient to it.

In reading or witnessing a romance play, such as *The Tempest* or *Everyman,* we must make a similar commitment ourselves. We must be willing to believe in the possibility of a supernatural power. That act of belief, however, is nothing more than an extension of our willingness to accept the imaginative premises of any story or play. Once we do so, we can see that romance drama develops plausibly within its special premises, that the miraculous achievements of its heroes are genuinely deserved. Prospero in the end is able to redeem his kingdom because he recognizes the persistence of evil in his world and the necessity to be eternally vigilant against it. And Everyman at last is able to redeem his soul because he recognizes the futility of clinging to bodily life, as well as the necessity to accept its inevitable demise. Thus the discovery scenes of romance, which reveal the hero's miraculous achievement, are prepared for by the hero's heightened state of moral or spiritual awareness. And that awareness always includes a recognition of human frailty. In this sense, as in its plot and characters, the idealized vision of romance never completely ignores the actual conditions of the world.

TRAGICOMEDY, NATURALISM, AND ABSURDIST DRAMA

Tragedy, comedy, satire, and romance—each of those primary modes embodies its own unique pattern of dramatic experience. As we have seen, each incorporates distinctly different kinds of plots and characters, distinctly different kinds of conflicts and discovery scenes, and each achieves a distinctly different view of human existence. Thus, when we read or witness a tragedy or comedy, a satire or romance, we undergo an experience that is more or less clear-cut. We feel sorrow or joy, scorn or admiration. We know, in short, exactly how we feel, exactly what we think.

But some plays—many modern plays, especially—do not arouse such clear-cut responses. As we read or witness them, our feelings and judgments may well be confused, or ambiguous, or mixed in one way or another. We may well feel torn between sorrow and joy, scorn and admiration. Indeed, we may not know exactly how we feel, or exactly what we think. When we find ourselves experiencing such mixed feelings, we will probably also discover that the play itself has been designed to leave us in an unresolved state of mind—that it does not embody a clear-cut pattern of catastrophe or rebirth (as in tragedy or comedy) or present clear-cut images of good or evil (as in romance or satire). Many plays, rather than being dominated by a single mode, actually combine differing or opposing modes of dramatic experience. In describing such works we use the term *tragicomedy*—not as a value judgment but as a means of defining the ambiguous experience that we witness in the play and feel within ourselves. Tragicomedy, then, leaves us with a complex reaction, similar to the uncertainty we often feel in response to life itself.

Uncertainty—about the nature of human existence—is a fundamental source of the tragicomic quality we find in many modern and contemporary plays. In some, that quality is produced by a *naturalistic* view of human nature and experience—a view of men and women as influenced by psychological, social, and economic forces so complex that their character and behavior cannot be easily judged or explained. That view of human nature led Strindberg, for example, to create characters whom he describes as being "somewhat 'characterless' "—characters, that is, who are influenced by "a whole series of motives," rather than by any single, or simple, purpose. Like other naturalistic dramatists, Strindberg is unwilling to offer us simple explanations to account for human behavior:

> A suicide is committed. Business troubles, says the man of affairs. Unrequited love, say the women. Sickness, says the invalid. Despair, says the down-and-out. But it is possible that the motive lay in all or none of these directions, or that the dead man concealed his actual motive by revealing quite another, likely to reflect more to his glory.

Just as we cannot definitely account for their actions, so too the characters in naturalistic drama cannot themselves perceive, much less control, all the forces influencing their behavior. Typically, then, the protagonists of naturalistic drama, such as Mrs. X in *The Stronger,* or Nora in *A Doll's House,* or Brick in *Cat on a Hot Tin Roof,* are placed in dramatic situations portraying them as being in some sense victims of their environment. They may wilfully deceive themselves about the nature of their circumstances, as does Mrs. X, or they may attempt to alter their circumstances, as does Nora, or they may acquiesce in them, as does Brick; but whatever action they take, it does not lead to a clear-cut resolution of the kind we associate with tragedy and comedy. Nor does their situation allow us to make the clear-cut moral judgment that we do of characters in satire and romance. "Vice has a reverse side very much like virtue," as Strindberg reminds us. Thus, naturalistic drama leaves us with a problematic view of human experience, and the most we can hope for is to understand, to the degree that we humanly can, the psychological, social, and economic circumstances that are contributing to the problematic situations of its characters.

In some contemporary plays the problematic situation is produced by conditions that transcend even naturalistic explanations. In these plays we sense the presence of some profound situation that afflicts the characters but is in the end indefinable. In Beckett's *Endgame*, for example, we find the principal characters existing in a world where all the elements of nature seem to be on the verge of extinction; yet the cause of that condition remains a mystery. In *A Slight Ache* we are faced with a character, the Matchseller, who never utters a single word, who barely makes a single movement, whose identity is never explained, yet whose presence brings about a profound change in the lives of the other two characters. These mysterious, even ridiculous, circumstances lead us to wonder whether there is *any* ultimate source of meaning *at all* in the world of those plays, or for that matter whether there is *any* rational source of explanation *at all* for the experience of the characters. For this reason, such plays are known as *absurdist* drama.

Their absurdity is usually evident not only in plot but in dialogue as well. Often, for example, the conversation of characters in absurdist drama does not make perfect sense, either because they are talking at cross purposes, or because their language has no clear point of reference to anything in their world. Yet even as we read the dialogue we will find it to be at once laughably out of joint and terrifyingly uncommunicative. In much the same way we may be puzzled by the resolution of these plays—wondering whether the characters' situation at the end is in any significant respect different from what it was at the beginning, wondering whether the play is tragic or comic, wondering even whether there is any single word, or concept, such as *tragicomedy*, that can adequately express the possibility that human existence may be meaningless. Ultimately, then, absurdist drama like the other modes does embody a view of human existence; but rather than perceiving existence as dominated by one pattern or another, one quality or another, that view implies that existence may have no pattern or meaning at all.

Elements of Drama

CONTEXTS, MODES, AND THE ELEMENTS OF DRAMA

Characters, dialogue, plot—these are the indispensable elements of drama. Together they make possible the imitative world of every play, for characters are like people, dialogue and plot like the things they say and do. But likeness does not mean identicalness. As we indicated in our discussion of dramatic modes, the truth of drama does not depend upon reproducing the world exactly as it is. For this reason, we should not expect to find characters who talk and act in just the same way that people do, nor should we expect to find plots that develop in just the same way that ordinary events do. The characters who populate romance and satire, for example, are modeled less on specific people than on human potentialities. Similarly, the plots elaborated in comedy and tragedy are based less on real occurrences than on basic patterns of human experience. The elements of drama, then, are highly specialized versions of the elements that make up the world as it is. The particular version we encounter in any single play will be determined by a variety of circumstances—by the mode of the play, the purpose of the play, the literary form of the play, and the design of the theater for which it was written. Thus we should always keep these circumstances in mind when we study the elements of drama.

DIALOGUE

The give-and-take of dialogue is a specialized form of conversation. Designed as it is to serve the needs created by the various contexts and modes of drama, it can hardly be expected to sound like our customary patterns of speech. In ordinary conversation, for example, we adjust our style to meet the needs of the people with whom we are talking, and we reinforce our words with a wide range of facial expressions, bodily gestures, and vocal inflections, many of which we perform unconsciously. If we recognize that we are not being understood, we may stammer momentarily while trying to rephrase our feelings and ideas. Then, before we can get the words out, someone may have interrupted us and completely changed the topic of conversation. Whatever the case, we find ourselves continually adjusting to circumstances that are as random as our thoughts and the thoughts of those with whom we are talking. If we were to transcribe and then listen to the tape of an ordinary conversation, even one that we considered coherent and orderly, we would probably find it far more erratic and incoherent than we had imagined.

Drama cannot afford to reproduce conversation as faithfully as a tape recorder. To begin with, the limitations of performance time require that characters express their ideas and feelings much more economically than we do in the leisurely course of ordinary conversation. The conditions of theatrical performance demand also that dialogue be formulated so that it can be not only heard by characters talking to one another but also overheard and understood by the audience in the theater. Thus the continuity of dialogue must be very clearly marked out at every point. On the basis of what is overheard, the audience—or the reader—must be able to develop a full understanding of the characters and the plot.

Dialogue, then, is an extraordinarily significant form of conversation, for it is the means by which every play conveys the total make-up of its imaginative world. And this is not all. Dialogue must fulfill the needs of not only the audience but also the director, the set designer, and the actors. This means that the dialogue must serve as a script for all the elements of production and performance—for the entire theatrical realization of a play.

Because it has to serve so many purposes all at once, dialogue is necessarily a more artificial form of discourse than ordinary conversation. Thus, in reading any segment of dialogue, we should always keep in mind its special purposes. It is a script for theatrical production, and that means that we should see what it can tell us about the total spectacle: the setting, the arrangement of characters on the stage, their physical movements, gestures, facial expressions, and inflections. It is also a text for conveying the imaginative world of the play, which means that we should see what it can tell us about the character speaking, the character listening, and the other characters not present; about the public and private relations among the characters, the past as well as present circumstances of the characters, and the quality of the world they inhabit; about the events that have taken place prior to the play, the events that have taken place offstage during the play, the events that have caused the interaction of the characters during the dialogue itself, and the events that are likely to follow from their interaction. If we read the dialogue with all these concerns in mind, we will find in the end that it takes us out of ourselves and leads us into the imaginative experience of the play.

PLOT

Plot is a specialized form of experience. We can see just how specialized it is if we consider for a moment what happens during the ordinary course of our daily experience. Between waking and sleeping, we probably converse with a number of people and perform a variety of actions. But most of these events have very little to do with one another, and they usually serve no purpose other than our pleasure, our work, or our bodily necessities. In general, the events that take place in our daily existence do not embody a significant pattern or process. If they have any pattern at all, it is merely the product of habit and routine.

In drama, however, every event is part of a carefully designed pattern and process. And this is what we call plot. Plot, then, is not at all like the routine, and often random, course of our daily existence. Rather it is a wholly interconnected system of events, deliberately selected and arranged for the purpose of fulfilling a complex set of imaginative and theatrical purposes. Plot is thus an extremely artificial element, and it has to be so. Within the limits of a few hours the interest of spectators—and readers—has to be deeply engaged and continuously sustained. That requires a system of events that quickly develops complications and suspense, and leads in turn to a climax and resolution. Interest must also be aroused by events that make up a process capable of being represented on stage. And the totality of events must create a coherent imitation of the world.

In order to understand how plot fulfills these multiple purposes, we should first recognize that it comprises *everything* that takes place in the imaginative world of a play. In other words, plot is not confined to what takes place on stage: it includes off-stage as well as on-stage action, reported as well as represented action. In *The Misanthrope,* for example, we witness a process that includes among other events a lawsuit brought against Alceste, tried in court, and judged in favor of his enemy. Yet we never actually see his enemy, nor do we hear the case being tried. We only hear *about* it—before and after it takes place—from the dialogue of Alceste and Philinte. Obviously the lawsuit does take place within the imaginative world of the play. It is part of the plot. But it is not part of what we call the *scenario*—the action occurring on stage. Thus, if we wish to identify the plot of a play, we have to distinguish it from the scenario. The scenario embodies the plot and presents it to us, but it is not itself the plot.

We can understand this distinction in another way if we realize that in a plot all the events are necessarily arranged *chronologically.* whereas in a scenario events are arranged *dramatically*—that is, in an order that will create the greatest impact on the audience. In some cases that may result in non-chronological order. We may well reach the end of a scenario before we learn about events that took place years before. For this reason, in studying the plot of a play, we must consider not only the events of which it consists but also the order in which those events are presented by the scenario.

The ordering of events can best be grasped if we think of the scenario as being constructed of a series of *dramatic units:* each time a character enters or leaves the stage a new dramatic unit begins. The appearance or departure of a character or group of characters is thus like a form of punctuation that we should take special note of whenever we are reading or witnessing a play. As one grouping of characters gives way to another, the dramatic situation necessarily changes—sometimes slightly, sometimes very perceptibly—to carry the play forward in the evolution of its process and the fulfillment of its plot. Thus we should examine each unit individually, to discover not only what on-stage action takes place within it but also what off-stage action is revealed within it. Then we should determine how the off-stage action that is reported affects the on-stage action, as well as how it shapes our own understanding of the characters and the plot.

In the opening dramatic unit of *Oedipus Rex,* for example, we witness a conversation between Oedipus and a Priest, in which the Priest pleads with Oedipus to rid Thebes of the plague, while Oedipus assures the Priest that he is eager to cure the city of its sickness. During that conversation we also learn from the Priest that, in years past, Oedipus had through his wisdom and knowledge liberated the city from the domination of the Sphinx, and we learn from Oedipus that he has recently sent his brother-in-law, Creon, to seek advice from the oracle at Delphi. These two reports of off-stage action establish the heroic stature of Oedipus, revealing him to be an exceptionally effective and responsible leader. The dramatic unit leads the Priest and Oedipus—and us as spectators—to expect that he will be equally successful in this crisis. In examining the unit we thus see that it not only identifies the motivating problem of the plot but also establishes Oedipus as the hero of the play; and that, moreover, it creates a set of positive expectations about his ability to overcome the problem. (He does, of course, overcome the problem but not without undoing himself in the process.) The unit, then, is crucial in creating a complicated mixture of true and false expectations within both the characters—and us.

In addition to examining dramatic units individually, we should also examine them in relation to one another—in context. Context is important because it is one of the dramatist's major techniques for influencing our perception and understanding of characters and plot. Dramatists usually select and arrange events so as to produce significant parallels or contrasts between them. Thus, if we look at the units in context, we will be able to perceive those relationships and their implications. Finally, of course, we must move beyond pairs and series of units to an overview of all the units together. By doing that we will be able to recognize the dominant process of the play. We will, that is, be able to perceive how it sets up the complications and works toward the discoveries and resolutions of tragedy, comedy, satire, romance, or tragicomedy. By examining the over-all design of the plot, we can thus recognize the dominant view of experience embodied in the play.

On the basis of our discussion, it should be obvious that plot is an extremely complicated element, one that can be understood only through a detailed analysis of dramatic units. Here, then, are some reminders and suggestions to follow in analyzing the plot of any play. Identify *all* the events that take place within the plot and the chronological order in which they occur. In order to do this, examine the scenario closely, paying attention to instances of implied and reported action. Once the details and make-up of the plot have been established, then examine how the plot is presented by the scenario. In order to do this, examine each dramatic unit in detail, beginning with the first and proceeding consecutively through the play. Remember that a single dramatic unit can serve a variety of purposes. Remember, too, that every unit exists within a context of units: within the context of units that immediately precede and follow it, and within the context of all the units of the play.

CHARACTER

Although characters in a play are like real people in some respects, they are by no means identical to people in real life. Real people, after all, exist in the world as it is, whereas characters exist in an imaginative world shaped by the theatrical contexts and imitative purposes of drama. In the classical Greek theater, for example, a character was defined visually by the fixed expression of his or her facial mask. Clearly, it would have been impossible for spectators to regard such characters as identical to complex human personalities. And if we look at Oedipus, we can see that he is conceived in terms of a few dominant traits that could be projected through the bold acting required by the enormous size of the ancient Greek theater.

Even when production conditions allow for greater psychological detail, as in the relatively intimate theaters of seventeenth-century France, there are usually other circumstances that work against the formation of completely lifelike characters. In *The Misanthrope*, for example, detailed characterization is less important than the essayistic form and satiric purpose of the play. Thus Alceste and Philinte have personality traits consistent with the ideas they espouse, and the other characters are exaggerated versions of objectionable human tendencies that show up in high society. They are character types consistent with Moliere's satiric purpose.

Because of its sustained interest in psychological behavior, modern drama tends to put a great deal of emphasis on character. Yet even plays—such as *A Doll's House* and *Cat on a Hot Tin Roof*—that are concerned specifically with the workings of the human mind, do not embody characters who can be taken as identical to real people. It would be misleading to think of Nora or Brick, for example, or any other principal characters in these plays, as fully developed personalities. Although they do represent complex studies in human psychology, they are conceived to dramatize specific ideas about the impact of the family and society upon the individual. In other words, they exhibit patterns of behavior that are *typical* rather than *actual*.

Although dramatic characters are not real people, they are endowed with human capacities. They talk and act and interact with one another. They experience pleasure and endure pain. They feel, and they act on their feelings. They believe, and they act according to their beliefs. It would thus be inhuman of us not to respond to their humanity. But we can only respond appropriately if we know what we are responding to: we have to consider all of the ways in which characters are revealed and defined by dialogue and plot.

The most immediate way to understand a character is to examine in detail everything the character says, in order to identify the important attitudes, beliefs, and feelings of that character. Examine not only the content but also the style of such utterances. Look, for example, at the kinds of words, and images, and sentence structures that mark the character's dialogue, for often these elements of style provide insight into subtle aspects of character. A further source of information is what others in the play say about the character. Since characters, like real people, are repeatedly talking about one another—to their faces and behind their backs—what they have to say often will provide valuable insights into the character. The things a character does may reveal as much as what the character says and what others have to say.

In examining their actions, pay careful attention to context, for characters are likely to behave differently in different situations. The problem in such a case is to determine whether the character has actually changed, for what appears to be a change in character may simply be the result of our knowing the character more fully. Another important key to understanding is to compare and contrast a character with others in the play. A study of this kind often sharpens and intensifies the perceptions we have gained from examining the character in isolation.

Character analysis can be a source of pleasure and understanding in its own right, but it should ultimately lead us more deeply into the play as a whole. For that reason, when we analyze characters, we should always keep in mind the theatrical contexts and imaginative purposes that shape their being. In this way we shall be truly able to appreciate the dramatic imitation of a world created by the wedding of literary and of representational art.

A Collection of Plays

1. *Classical to Neoclassical Drama*

TRAGEDY IN THE CLASSICAL GREEK THEATER

The theater of Dionysus at Athens, where *Oedipus Rex* was first produced (c. 425 B.C.), could accommodate an audience of almost fifteen thousand. So vast a structure could not, of course, be roofed over, but had to be open-air. This fact alone will take us a long way toward understanding the nature of a Greek dramatic performance. To begin with, we can see that the experience must have been very public and communal—nothing at all like the coziness of our fully enclosed modern theaters, where no more than five hundred—or a thousand at most—gather in darkened rows of cushioned seats. The size of the theater also required the drama to be conceived on a monumental scale and performed in a correspondingly emphatic style of acting. When Oedipus accused Teiresias of treason, his impetuous judgment had to be heard and seen by thousands of spectators. Facial expression obviously would not serve the purpose, nor would a conversational tone of voice. Instead, the actors wore large, stylized masks and costumes—an inheritance from primitive ritual—representing character *types;* and as their fortunes and emotions changed, they changed their masks to suit the situation. Further, those masks were probably equipped with a mouthpiece to aid in projecting the dialogue. In short, we should not imagine a style of performance corresponding in any way to that of our present-day ideas about dramatic realism. Exaggerated gestures, bold movements, declamatory utterances—everything was larger than life and highly formalized, if only to ensure a clear theatrical impression.

Size alone was not responsible for the highly formal style of Greek drama.

The design of the theater, and the religious origin of its design, also had a great deal to do with the ceremonial quality of the production. The Greek theater evolved from places of ritual celebration consisting of a circular area for dancers and singers, surrounded by a hillside to accommodate worshipers. A modified version of that arrangement is what we have in the classical Greek theater illustrated here. The theater consisted of three parts. Its focal element was the *orchestra* (literally, the dancing place), a circular space sixty-four feet in diameter. The *orchestra* was surrounded by the *theatron* (literally, the seeing place), a semicircular terraced hillside equipped with benches. Facing the *theatron* was the *skene* (literally, the hut), a one-story building with three openings entering on to the *orchestra*, wings projecting toward the *orchestra*, and a slightly raised stage-like platform extending between the wings. The classic simplicity of that design is unparalleled in the history of the theater.

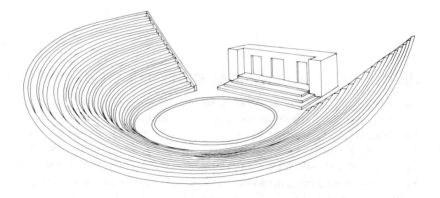

The *skene* was used for storing properties, changing costumes, providing entrances and exits, and serving as a scenic background. Stylized scenes were painted on the areas between the doors to suggest the outlines of a location, and the *skene* itself was understood to represent any structure central to the action (such as the palace in *Oedipus Rex*). Beyond these few hints, the Greek theater provided very little in the way of scenery or props to assist the spectator's imagination. At most, a chariot might be driven in to the *orchestra* to represent the arrival of a hero, or an actor lowered by machine from the roof of the *skene* to depict the intervention of a god, or a tableau wheeled out of the *skene* to suggest off-stage action.

The most important part of the theater was the *orchestra*, for it served as the primary acting area. Within that area the performance of a tragedy such as *Oedipus Rex* adhered to a highly formalized structure. The actors made their initial entrance to the *orchestra* from the *skene* and then performed a brief expository episode, the *prologos*. Then the chorus (of fifteen members) made its entrance—the *parados*—by marching in a stately rhythm through the passageways between the *theatron* and the *skene*. When all the members of the tragic chorus had entered the orchestra, they arranged themselves in rectangular formation and began their choral song and dance to the accompaniment of a flute. The chorus remained in the *orchestra* throughout the play, performing not only during its odes but also during the episodes, sometimes exchanging dialogue with the characters through its leader (the *choragos*), sometimes, no doubt, making gestures and movements in sympathetic response to the action. In this way the chorus provided a sustained point of reference, a source of mediation between the audience and the actors, who moved back and forth between the *orchestra* and the *skene* as their parts dictated.

In imagining the effect produced by the simultaneous presence of actors and chorus, we should remember that the chorus retained the skills inherited from the ritual celebrations of an earlier time, so that its members, like the actors, were accomplished dancers and singers. When we read *Oedipus Rex*, therefore, we should visualize the chorus as moving through a slow and graceful dance appropriate to tragedy. And we should try to hear how it sounded as it chanted its parts accompanied by a flute player. Musically and visually, the total performance must have been as complex as a modern opera—though by no means similar in emphasis, for in opera everything is subordinated to the music, whereas in Greek tragedy everything is subordinated to the action. Taken all in all—the choric singing and dancing, the simplified setting, the bold acting—dramatic productions in ancient Greece must have matched the grand dimensions of the theater and of the tragedies written for it by Sophocles.

SOPHOCLES
496–406 B.C.
Oedipus Rex

PERSONS REPRESENTED

OEDIPUS	MESSENGER
A PRIEST	SHEPHERD OF LAÏOS
KREON	SECOND MESSENGER
TEIRESIAS	CHORUS OF THEBAN ELDERS
IOKASTE	

The Scene. Before the palace of Oedipus, King of Thebes. A central door and two lateral doors open onto a platform which runs the length of the façade. On the platform, right and left, are altars; and three steps lead down into the "or-chêstra," or chorus-ground. At the beginning of the action these steps are crowded by suppliants who have brought branches and chaplets of olive leaves and who sit in various attitudes of despair.

Oedipus enters.

PROLOGUE

OEDIPUS   My children, generations of the living
   In the line of Kadmos, nursed at his ancient hearth:
   Why have you strewn yourselves before these altars
   In supplication, with your boughs and garlands?
   The breath of incense rises from the city
   With a sound of prayer and lamentation.
                                    Children,
   I would not have you speak through messengers,
   And therefore I have come myself to hear you—
   I, Oedipus, who bear the famous name.

To a Priest

10   You, there, since you are eldest in the company,
   Speak for them all, tell me what preys upon you,
   Whether you come in dread, or crave some blessing:
   Tell me, and never doubt that I will help you

An English version by Dudley Fitts and Robert Fitzgerald

In every way I can; I should be heartless
Were I not moved to find you suppliant here.
PRIEST   Great Oedipus, O powerful King of Thebes!
You see how all the ages of our people
Cling to your altar steps: here are boys
Who can barely stand alone, and here are priests
By weight of age, as I am a priest of God,
And young men chosen from those yet unmarried;
As for the others, all that multitude,
They wait with olive chaplets in the squares,
At the two shrines of Pallas, and where Apollo
Speaks in the glowing embers.
                                    Your own eyes
Must tell you: Thebes is tossed on a murdering sea
And can not lift her head from the death surge.
A rust consumes the buds and fruits of the earth;
The herds are sick; children die unborn,
And labor is vain. The god of plague and pyre
Raids like detestable lightning through the city,
And all the house of Kadmos is laid waste,
All emptied, and all darkened: Death alone
Battens upon the misery of Thebes.

You are not one of the immortal gods, we know;
Yet we have come to you to make our prayer
As to the man surest in mortal ways
And wisest in the ways of God. You saved us
From the Sphinx, that flinty singer, and the tribute
We paid to her so long; yet you were never
Better informed than we, nor could we teach you:
A god's touch, it seems, enabled you to help us.

Therefore, O mighty power, we turn to you:
Find us our safety, find us a remedy,
Whether by counsel of the gods or of men.
A king of wisdom tested in the past
Can act in a time of troubles, and act well.
Noblest of men, restore
Life to your city! Think how all men call you
Liberator for your boldness long ago;
Ah, when your years of kingship are remembered,
Let them not say *We rose, but later fell*—
Keep the State from going down in the storm!
Once, years ago, with happy augury,

You brought us fortune; be the same again!
No man questions your power to rule the land:
But rule over men, not over a dead city!
Ships are only hulls, high walls are nothing,
When no life moves in the empty passageways.

60   OEDIPUS   Poor children! You may be sure I know
All that you longed for in your coming here.
I know that you are deathly sick; and yet,
Sick as you are, not one is as sick as I.
Each of you suffers in himself alone
His anguish, not another's; but my spirit
Groans for the city, for myself, for you.

I was not sleeping, you are not waking me.
No, I have been in tears for a long while
And in my restless thought walked many ways.
70   In all my search I found one remedy,
And I have adopted it: I have sent Kreon,
Son of Menoikeus, brother of the Queen,
To Delphi, Apollo's place of revelation,
To learn there, if he can,
What act or pledge of mine may save the city.
I have counted the days, and now, this very day,
I am troubled, for he has overstayed his time.
What is he doing? He has been gone too long.
Yet whenever he comes back, I should do ill
80   Not to take any action the god orders.
PRIEST   It is a timely promise. At this instant
They tell me Kreon is here.
OEDIPUS   O Lord Apollo!
May his news be fair as his face is radiant!
PRIEST   Good news, I gather: he is crowned with bay,
The chaplet is thick with berries.
OEDIPUS   We shall soon know;
He is near enough to hear us now.

Enter Kreon.

                              O Prince:
Brother: son of Menoikeus:
What answer do you bring us from the God?
KREON   A strong one. I can tell you, great afflictions
90   Will turn out well, if they are taken well.

OEDIPUS   What was the oracle? These vague words
    Leave me still hanging between hope and fear.
KREON   Is it your pleasure to hear me with all these
    Gathered around us? I am prepared to speak,
    But should we not go in?
OEDIPUS   Speak to them all.
    It is for them I suffer, more than for myself.
KREON   Then I will tell you what I heard at Delphi.

    In plain words
    The god commands us to expel from the land of Thebes
100   An old defilement we are sheltering.
    It is a deathly thing, beyond cure;
    We must not let it feed upon us longer.
OEDIPUS   What defilement? How shall we rid ourselves of it?
KREON   By exile or death, blood for blood. It was
    Murder that brought the plague-wind on the city.
OEDIPUS   Murder of whom? Surely the god has named him?
KREON   My lord: Laïos once ruled this land,
    Before you came to govern us.
OEDIPUS   I know;
    I learned of him from others; I never saw him.
110 KREON   He was murdered; and Apollo commands us now
    To take revenge upon whoever killed him.
OEDIPUS   Upon whom? Where are they? Where shall we find a clue
    To solve that crime, after so many years?
KREON   Here in this land, he said. Search reveals
    Things that escape an inattentive man.
OEDIPUS   Tell me: Was Laïos murdered in his house,
    Or in the fields, or in some foreign country?
KREON   He said he planned to make a pilgrimage.
    He did not come home again.
OEDIPUS   And was there no one,
120   No witness, no companion, to tell what happened?
KREON   They were all killed but one, and he got away
    So frightened that he could remember one thing only.
OEDIPUS   What was that one thing? One may be the key
    To everything, if we resolve to use it.
KREON   He said that a band of highwaymen attacked them,
    Outnumbered them, and overwhelmed the King.
OEDIPUS   Strange, that a highwayman should be so daring—
    Unless some faction here bribed him to do it.
KREON   We thought of that. But after Laïos' death
130   New troubles arose and we had no avenger.

OEDIPUS   What troubles could prevent your hunting down the killers?
KREON   The riddling Sphinx's song
　　　Made us deaf to all mysteries but her own.
OEDIPUS   Then once more I must bring what is dark to light.
　　　It is most fitting that Apollo shows,
　　　As you do, this compunction for the dead.
　　　You shall see how I stand by you, as I should,
　　　Avenging this country and the god as well,
　　　And not as though it were for some distant friend,
140　　　But for my own sake, to be rid of evil.
　　　Whoever killed King Laïos might—who knows?—
　　　Lay violent hands even on me—and soon.
　　　I act for the murdered king in my own interest.

　　　Come, then, my children: leave the altar steps,
　　　Lift up your olive boughs!
　　　　　　　　　　　One of you go
　　　And summon the people of Kadmos to gather here.
　　　I will do all that I can; you may tell them that.

　　　　　　　　　　　　　　　　　　　　　　Exit a Page.

　　　So, with the help of God.
　　　We shall be saved—or else indeed we are lost.
150   PRIEST   Let us rise, children. It was for this we came,
　　　And now the King has promised it.
　　　Phoibos has sent us an oracle; may he descend
　　　Himself to save us and drive out the plague.

Exeunt Oedipus and Kreon into the palace by the central door. The Priest and the Suppliants disperse right and left. After a short pause the Chorus enters the orchêstra.

PÁRODOS

CHORUS   What is God singing in his profound　　　　　　STROPHE I
　　　Delphi of gold and shadow?
　　　What oracle for Thebes, the sunwhipped city?

　　　Fear unjoints me, the roots of my heart tremble.

　　　Now I remember, O Healer, your power and wonder:
　　　Will you send doom like a sudden cloud, or weave it
　　　Like nightfall of the past?

Speak, speak to us, issue of holy sound;
Dearest to our Expectancy: be tender!

10   Let me pray to Athenê, the immortal daughter of Zeus,   ANTISTROPHE I
And to Artemis her sister
Who keeps her famous throne in the market ring,

And to Apollo, archer from distant heaven—

O gods, descend! Like three streams leap against
The fires of our grief, the fires of darkness;
Be swift to bring us rest!

As in the old time from the brilliant house
Of air you stepped to save us, come again!

Now our afflictions have no end   STROPHE 2
20   Now all our stricken host lies down
And no man fights off death with his mind;

The noble plowland bears no grain,
And groaning mothers can not bear—

See, how our lives like birds take wing,
Like sparks that fly when a fire soars,
To the shore of the god of evening.

The plague burns on, it is pitiless,   ANTISTROPHE 2
Though pallid children laden with death
Lie unwept in the stony ways,

30   And old gray women by every path
Flock to the strand about the altars

There to strike their breasts and cry
Worship of Phoibos in wailing prayers:
Be kind, God's golden child!

There are no swords in this attack by fire,   STROPHE 3
No shields, but we are ringed with cries.

Send the besieger plunging from our homes
Into the vast sea-room of the Atlantic
40   Or into the waves that foam eastward of Thrace—

For the day ravages what the night spares—

Destroy our enemy, lord of the thunder!
Let him be riven by lightning from heaven!

Phoibos Apollo, stretch the sun's bowstring,   ANTISTROPHE 3
That golden cord, until it sing for us,
Flashing arrows in heaven!
                              Artemis, Huntress,
Race with flaring lights upon our mountains!

O scarlet god, O golden-banded brow,
O Theban Bacchos in a storm of Maenads,

Enter Oedipus, center.

      Whirl upon Death, that all the Undying hate!
50   Come with blinding torches, come in joy!

SCENE I

OEDIPUS Is this your prayer? It may be answered. Come,
      Listen to me, act as the crisis demands,
      And you shall have relief from all these evils.

      Until now I was a stranger to this tale,
      As I had been a stranger to the crime.
      Could I track down the murderer without a clue?
      But now, friends,
      As one who became a citizen after the murder,
      I make this proclamation to all Thebans:

10   If any man knows by whose hand Laïos, son of Labdakos,
      Met his death, I direct that man to tell me everything,
      No matter what he fears for having so long withheld it.
      Let it stand as promised that no further trouble
      Will come to him, but he may leave the land in safety.

      Moreover: If anyone knows the murderer to be foreign,
      Let him not keep silent: he shall have his reward from me.
      However, if he does conceal it; if any man

Fearing for his friend or for himself disobeys this edict,
Hear what I propose to do:

20   I solemnly forbid the people of this country,
Where power and throne are mine, ever to receive that man
Or speak to him, no matter who he is, or let him
Join in sacrifice, lustration, or in prayer.
I decree that he be driven from every house,
Being, as he is, corruption itself to us: the Delphic
Voice of Apollo has pronounced this revelation.
Thus I associate myself with the oracle
And take the side of the murdered king.

As for the criminal, I pray to God—
30   Whether it be a lurking thief, or one of a number—
I pray that that man's life be consumed in evil and wretchedness.
And as for me, this curse applies no less
If it should turn out that the culprit is my guest here,
Sharing my hearth.
                        You have heard the penalty.

I lay it on you now to attend to this
For my sake, for Apollo's, for the sick
Sterile city that heaven has abandoned.
Suppose the oracle had given you no command:
Should this defilement go uncleansed for ever?
40   You should have found the murderer: your king,
A noble king, had been destroyed!
                        Now I,
Having the power that he held before me,
Having his bed, begetting children there
Upon his wife, as he would have, had he lived—
Their son would have been my children's brother,
If Laïos had had luck in fatherhood!
(And now his bad fortune has struck him down)—
I say I take the son's part, just as though
I were his son, to press the fight for him
50   And see it won! I'll find the hand that brought
Death to Labdakos' and Polydoros' child,
Heir of Kadmos' and Agenor's line.
And as for those who fail me,
May the gods deny them the fruit of the earth,
Fruit of the womb, and may they rot utterly!
Let them be wretched as we are wretched, and worse!

For you, for loyal Thebans, and for all
Who find my actions right, I pray the favor
Of justice, and of all the immortal gods.

60 CHORAGOS Since I am under oath, my lord, I swear
I did not do the murder, I can not name
The murderer. Phoibos ordained the search;
Why did he not say who the culprit was?

OEDIPUS An honest question. But no man in the world
Can make the gods do more than the gods will.

CHORAGOS There is an alternative, I think—

OEDIPUS   Tell me.
Any or all, you must not fail to tell me.

CHORAGOS A lord clairvoyant to the lord Apollo,
As we all know, is the skilled Teiresias.

70   One might learn much about this from him, Oedipus.

OEDIPUS I am not wasting time:
Kreon spoke of this, and I have sent for him—
Twice, in fact; it is strange that he is not here.

CHORAGOS The other matter—that old report—seems useless.

OEDIPUS What was that? I am interested in all reports.

CHORAGOS The King was said to have been killed by highwaymen.

OEDIPUS I know. But we have no witnesses to that.

CHORAGOS If the killer can feel a particle of dread,
Your curse will bring him out of hiding!

OEDIPUS   No.

80   The man who dared that act will fear no curse.

Enter the blind seer Teiresias, led by a Page.

CHORAGOS But there is one man who may detect the criminal.
This is Teiresias, this is the holy prophet
In whom, alone of all men, truth was born.

OEDIPUS Teiresias: seer: student of mysteries,
Of all that's taught and all that no man tells,
Secrets of Heaven and secrets of the earth:
Blind though you are, you know the city lies
Sick with plague; and from this plague, my lord,
We find that you alone can guard or save us.

90   Possibly you did not hear the messengers?
Apollo, when we sent to him,
Sent us back word that this great pestilence
Would lift, but only if we established clearly
The identity of those who murdered Laïos.

They must be killed or exiled.
                              Can you use
Birdflight or any art of divination
To purify yourself, and Thebes, and me
From this contagion? We are in your hands.
There is no fairer duty
100   Than that of helping others in distress.
TEIRESIAS How dreadful knowledge of the truth can be
When there's no help in truth! I knew this well
But did not act on it: else I should not have come.
OEDIPUS What is troubling you? Why are your eyes so cold?
TEIRESIAS Let me go home. Bear your own fate, and I'll
Bear mine. It is better so: trust what I say.
OEDIPUS What you say is ungracious and unhelpful
To your native country. Do not refuse to speak.
TEIRESIAS When it comes to speech, your own is neither temperate
110   Nor opportune. I wish to be more prudent.
OEDIPUS In God's name, we all beg you—
TEIRESIAS   You are all ignorant.
No; I will never tell you what I know.
Now it is my misery; then, it would be yours.
OEDIPUS What! You do know something, and will not tell us?
You would betray us all and wreck the State?
TEIRESIAS I do not intend to torture myself, or you.
Why persist in asking? You will not persuade me.
OEDIPUS What a wicked old man you are! You'd try a stone's
Patience! Out with it! Have you no feeling at all?
120 TEIRESIAS You call me unfeeling. If you could only see
The nature of your own feelings . . .
OEDIPUS   Why,
Who would not feel as I do? Who could endure
Your arrogance toward the city?
TEIRESIAS   What does it matter?
Whether I speak or not, it is bound to come.
OEDIPUS Then, if 'it' is bound to come, you are bound to tell me.
TEIRESIAS No, I will not go on. Rage as you please.
OEDIPUS Rage? Why not!
                          And I'll tell you what I think:
You planned it, you had it done, you all but
Killed him with your own hands: if you had eyes,
130   I'd say the crime was yours, and yours alone.
TEIRESIAS So? I charge you, then,
Abide by the proclamation you have made:
From this day forth

Never speak again to these men or to me;
You yourself are the pollution of this country.

OEDIPUS   You dare say that! Can you possibly think you have
Some way of going free, after such insolence?

TEIRESIAS   I have gone free. It is the truth sustains me.

OEDIPUS   Who taught you shamelessness? It was not your craft.

140   TEIRESIAS   You did. You made me speak. I did not want to.

OEDIPUS   Speak what? Let me hear it again more clearly.

TEIRESIAS   Was it not clear before? Are you tempting me?

OEDIPUS   I did not understand it. Say it again.

TEIRESIAS   I say that you are the murderer whom you seek.

OEDIPUS   Now twice you have spat out infamy. You'll pay for it!

TEIRESIAS   Would you care for more? Do you wish to be really angry?

OEDIPUS   Say what you will. Whatever you say is worthless.

TEIRESIAS   I say you live in hideous shame with those
Most dear to you. You can not see the evil.

150   OEDIPUS   Can you go on babbling like this for ever?

TEIRESIAS   I can, if there is power in truth.

OEDIPUS   There is:
But not for you, not for you,
You sightless, witless, senseless, mad old man!

TEIRESIAS   You are the madman. There is no one here
Who will not curse you soon, as you curse me.

OEDIPUS   You child of total night! I would not touch you;
Neither would any man who sees the sun.

TEIRESIAS   True: it is not from you my fate will come.
That lies within Apollo's competence,
As it is his concern.

160   OEDIPUS   Tell me, who made
These fine discoveries? Kreon? or someone else?

TEIRESIAS   Kreon is no threat. You weave your own doom.

OEDIPUS   Wealth, power, craft of statesmanship!
Kingly position, everywhere admired!
What savage envy is stored up against these,
If Kreon, whom I trusted, Kreon my friend,
For this great office which the city once
Put in my hands unsought—if for this power
Kreon desires in secret to destroy me!

170   He has bought this decrepit fortune-teller, this
Collector of dirty pennies, this prophet fraud—
Why, he is no more clairvoyant than I am!
                                    Tell us:
Has your mystic mummery ever approached the truth?

When that hellcat the Sphinx was performing here,
What help were you to these people?
Her magic was not for the first man who came along:
It demanded a real exorcist. Your birds—
What good were they? or the gods, for the matter of that?
But I came by,
180   Oedipus, the simple man, who knows nothing—
I thought it out for myself, no birds helped me!
And this is the man you think you can destroy.
That you may be close to Kreon when he's king!
Well, you and your friend Kreon, it seems to me,
Will suffer most. If you were not an old man,
You would have paid already for your plot.

CHORAGOS   We can not see that his words or yours
Have been spoken except in anger, Oedipus,
And of anger we have no need. How to accomplish
190   The god's will best: that is what most concerns us.

TEIRESIAS   You are a king. But where argument's concerned
I am your man, as much a king as you.
I am not your servant, but Apollo's
I have no need of Kreon's name.

Listen to me. You mock my blindness, do you?
But I say that you, with both your eyes, are blind:
You can not see the wretchedness of your life,
Nor in whose house you live, no, nor with whom.
Who are your father and mother? Can you tell me?
200   You do not even know the blind wrongs
That you have done them, on earth and in the world below.
But the double lash of you parents' curse will whip you
Out of this land some day, with only night
Upon your precious eyes.
Your cries then—where will they not be heard?
What fastness of Kithairon will not echo them?
And that bridal-descant of yours—you'll know it then,
The song they sang when you came here to Thebes
And found your misguided berthing.
210   All this, and more, that you can not guess at now,
Will bring you to yourself among your children.

Be angry, then. Curse Kreon. Curse my words.
I tell you, no man that walks upon the earth
Shall be rooted out more horribly than you.

OEDIPUS   Am I to bear this from him?—Damnation
    Take you! Out of this place! Out of my sight!
TEIRESIAS   I would not have come at all if you had not asked me.
OEDIPUS   Could I have told that you'd talk nonsense, that
    You'd come here to make a fool of yourself, and of me?
220   TEIRESIAS   A fool? Your parents thought me sane enough.
OEDIPUS   My parents again!—Wait: who were my parents?
TEIRESIAS   This day will give you a father, and break your heart.
OEDIPUS   Your infantile riddles! Your damned abracadabra!
TEIRESIAS   You were a great man once at solving riddles.
OEDIPUS   Mock me with that if you like; you will find it true.
TEIRESIAS   It was true enough. It brought about your ruin.
OEDIPUS   But if it saved this town?
TEIRESIAS   *To the Page*   Boy, give me your hand.
OEDIPUS   Yes, boy; lead him away.
                    —While you are here
    We can do nothing. Go; leave us in peace.
230   TEIRESIAS   I will go when I have said what I have to say.
    How can you hurt me? And I tell you again:
    The man you have been looking for all this time,
    The damned man, the murderer of Laïos,
    That man is in Thebes. To your mind he is foreign-born,
    But it will soon be shown that he is a Theban,
    A revelation that will fail to please.
                    A blind man,
    Who has his eyes now; a penniless man, who is rich now;
    And he will go tapping the strange earth with his staff.
    To the children with whom he lives now he will be
240   Brother and father—the very same; to her
    Who bore him, son and husband—the very same
    Who came to his father's bed, wet with his father's blood.

    Enough. Go think that over.
    If later you find error in what I have said,
    You may say that I have no skill in prophecy.

Exit Teiresias, led by his Page. Oedipus goes into the palace.

ODE I

CHORUS   The Delphic stone of prophecies   STROPHE 1
    Remembers ancient regicide
    And a still bloody hand.

That killer's hour of flight has come.
He must be stronger than riderless
Coursers of untiring wind,
For the son of Zeus armed with his father's thunder
Leaps in lightning after him;
And the Furies hold his track, the sad Furies.

10   Holy Parnassos' peak of snow   ANTISTROPHE 1
Flashes and blinds that secret man,
That all shall hunt him down:
Though he may roam the forest shade
Like a bull gone wild from pasture
To rage through glooms of stone.
Doom comes down on him; flight will not avail him;
For the world's heart calls him desolate,
And the immortal voices follow, for ever follow.

But now a wilder thing is heard   STROPHE 2
20   From the old man skilled at hearing Fate in the wing-beat of a bird.
Bewildered as a blown bird, my soul hovers and can not find
Foothold in this debate, or any reason or rest of mind.
But no man ever brought—none can bring
Proof of strife between Thebes' royal house,
Labdakos' line, and the son of Polybos;
And never until now has any man brought word
Of Laïos' dark death staining Oedipus the King.

Divine Zeus and Apollo hold   ANTISTROPHE 2
Perfect intelligence alone of all tales ever told;
30   And well though this diviner works, he works in his own night;
No man can judge that rough unknown or trust in second sight,
For wisdom changes hands among the wise.
Shall I believe my great lord criminal
At a raging word that a blind old man let fall?
I saw him, when the carrion woman faced him of old,
Prove his heroic mind. These evil words are lies.

SCENE II

KREON   Men of Thebes:
    I am told that heavy accusations
    Have been brought against me by King Oedipus.

I am not the kind of man to bear this tamely.

If in these present difficulties
He holds me accountable for any harm to him
Through anything I have said or done—why, then,
I do not value life in this dishonor.

It is not as though this rumor touched upon
10   Some private indiscretion. The matter is grave.
The fact is that I am being called disloyal
To the State, to my fellow citizens, to my friends.
CHORAGOS   He may have spoken in anger, not from his mind.
KREON   But did you not hear him say I was the one
Who seduced the old prophet into lying?
CHORAGOS   The thing was said; I do not know how seriously.
KREON   But you were watching him! Were his eyes steady?
Did he look like a man in his right mind?
CHORAGOS   I do not know.
I can not judge the behavior of great men.
But here is the King himself.

Enter Oedipus.

20   OEDIPUS   So you dared come back.
Why? How brazen of you to come to my house,
You murderer!
                        Do you think I do not know
That you plotted to kill me, plotted to steal my throne?
Tell me, in God's name: am I coward, a fool,
That you should dream you could accomplish this?
A fool who could not see your slippery game?
A coward, not to fight back when I saw it?
You are the fool, Kreon, are you not? hoping
Without support or friends to get a throne?
30   Thrones may be won or bought: you could do neither.
KREON   Now listen to me. You have talked; let me talk, too.
You can not judge unless you know the facts.
OEDIPUS   You speak well: there is one fact; but I find it hard
To learn from the deadliest enemy I have.
KREON   That above all I must dispute with you.
OEDIPUS   That above all I will not hear you deny.
KREON   If you think there is anything good in being stubborn
Against all reason, then I say you are wrong.

OEDIPUS If you think a man can sin against his own kind
40   And not be punished for it, I say you are mad.
KREON I agree. But tell me: what have I done to you?
OEDIPUS You advised me to send for that wizard, did you not?
KREON I did. I should do it again.
OEDIPUS   Very well. Now tell me:
        How long has it been since Laïos—
KREON   What of Laïos?
OEDIPUS Since he vanished in that onset by the road?
KREON   It was long ago, a long time.
OEDIPUS   And this prophet,
        Was he practicing here then?
KREON   He was; and with honor, as now.
OEDIPUS Did he speak of me at that time?
KREON   He never did;
        At least, not when I was present.
OEDIPUS   But . . . the enquiry?
        I suppose you held one?
50 KREON   We did, but we learned nothing.
OEDIPUS Why did the prophet not speak against me then?
KREON I do not know; and I am the kind of man
        Who holds his tongue when he has no facts to go on.
OEDIPUS There's one fact that you know, and you could tell it.
KREON What fact is that? If I know it, you shall have it.
OEDIPUS If he were not involved with you, he could not say
        That it was I who murdered Laïos.
KREON If he says that, you are the one that knows it!—
        But now it is my turn to question you.
60 OEDIPUS Put your questions. I am no murderer.
KREON First, then: You married my sister?
OEDIPUS   I married your sister.
KREON And you rule the kingdom equally with her?
OEDIPUS Everything that she wants she has from me.
KREON And I am the third, equal to both of you?
OEDIPUS That is why I call you a bad friend.
KREON No. Reason it out, as I have done.
        Think of this first: Would any sane man prefer
        Power, with all a king's anxieties,
        To that same power and the grace of sleep?
70   Certainly not I.
        I have never longed for the king's power—only his rights.
        Would any wise man differ from me in this?
        As matters stand, I have my way in everything
        With your consent, and no responsibilities.

If I were king, I should be a slave to policy.
How could I desire a sceptre more
Than what is now mine—untroubled influence?
No, I have not gone mad; I need no honors,
Except those with the perquisites I have now.
I am welcome everywhere; every man salutes me,
And those who want your favor seek my ear,
Since I know how to manage what they ask.
Should I exchange this ease for that anxiety?
Besides, no sober mind is treasonable.
I hate anarchy
And never would deal with any man who likes it.

Test what I have said. Go to the priestess
At Delphi, ask if I quoted her correctly.
And as for this other thing: if I am found
Guilty of treason with Teiresias,
Then sentence me to death. You have my word
It is a sentence I should cast my vote for—
But not without evidence!
                    You do wrong
When you take good men for bad, bad men for good.
A true friend thrown aside—why, life itself
Is not more precious!
                    In time you will know this well:
For time, and time alone, will show the just man,
Though scoundrels are discovered in a day.
CHORAGOS   This is well said, and a prudent man would ponder it.
    Judgments too quickly formed are dangerous.
OEDIPUS   But is he not quick in his duplicity?
    And shall I not be quick to parry him?
    Would you have me stand still, holding my peace, and let
    This man win everything, through my inaction?
KREON   And you want—what is it, then? To banish me?
OEDIPUS   No, not exile. It is your death I want,
    So that all the world may see what treason means.
KREON   You will persist, then? You will not believe me?
OEDIPUS   How can I believe you?
KREON   Then you are a fool.
OEDIPUS   To save myself?
KREON   In justice, think of me.
OEDIPUS   You are evil incarnate.
KREON   But suppose that you are wrong?
OEDIPUS   Still I must rule.

KREON   But not if you rule badly.
OEDIPUS   O city, city!
KREON   It is my city, too!
CHORAGOS   Now, my lords, be still. I see the Queen,
    Iokastê, coming from her palace chambers;
    And it is time she came, for the sake of you both.
    This dreadful quarrel can be resolved through her.

Enter Iokastê.

IOKASTÊ   Poor foolish men, what wicked din is this?
    With Thebes sick to death, is it not shameful
120   That you should rake some private quarrel up?

To Oedipus

    Come into the house
              —And you, Kreon, go now:
    Let us have no more of this tumult over nothing.
KREON   Nothing? No, sister: what your husband plans for me
    Is one of two great evils: exile or death.
OEDIPUS   He is right.
           Why, woman I have caught him squarely
    Plotting against my life.
KREON   No! Let me die
    Accurst if ever I have wished you harm!
IOKASTÊ   Ah, believe it, Oedipus!
    In the name of the gods, respect this oath of his
130   For my sake, for the sake of these people here!

CHORAGOS   STROPHE 1
    Open your mind to her, my lord. Be ruled by her, I beg you!
OEDIPUS   What would you have me do?
CHORAGOS   Respect Kreon's word. He has never spoken like a fool,
    And now he has sworn an oath.
OEDIPUS   You know what you ask?
CHORAGOS   I do.
OEDIPUS   Speak on, then.

CHORAGOS   A friend so sworn should not be baited so,
    In blind malice, and without final proof.
OEDIPUS   You are aware, I hope, that what you say
    Means death for me, or exile at the least.

CHORAGOS

140   No, I swear by Helios, first in Heaven!   STROPHE 2
            May I die friendless and accurst,
        The worst of deaths, if ever I meant that!
                It is the withering fields
                    That hurt my sick heart:
                Must we bear all these ills,
                    And now your bad blood as well?

OEDIPUS   Then let him go. And let me die, if I must,
        Or be driven by him in shame from the land of Thebes.
        It is your unhappiness, and not his talk,
        That touches me.
150   As for him—
        Wherever he goes, hatred will follow him.
KREON   Ugly in yielding, as you were ugly in rage!
        Natures like yours chiefly torment themselves.
OEDIPUS   Can you not go? Can you not leave me?
KREON   I can.
        You do not know me; but the city knows me,
        And in its eyes I am just, if not in yours.

                                            Exit Kreon.

CHORAGOS   ANTISTROPHE 1
        Lady Iokastê, did you not ask the King to go to his chambers?
IOKASTÊ   First tell me what has happened.
CHORAGOS   There was suspicion without evidence; yet it rankled
160   As even false charges will.
IOKASTÊ   On both sides?
CHORAGOS   On both.
IOKASTÊ   But what was said?

CHORAGOS   Oh let it rest, let it be done with!
        Have we not suffered enough?
OEDIPUS   You see to what your decency has brought you:
        You have made difficulties where my heart saw none.

CHORAGOS
        Oedipus, it is not once only I have told you—   ANTISTROPHE 2
            You must know I should count myself unwise
        To the point of madness, should I now forsake you—
                You, under whose hand,

170   In the storm of another time,
              Our dear land sailed out free.
              But now stand fast at the helm!

IOKASTÊ   In God's name, Oedipus, inform your wife as well:
          Why are you so set in this hard anger?
OEDIPUS   I will tell you, for none of these men deserves
          My confidence as you do. It is Kreon's work,
          His treachery, his plotting against me.
IOKASTÊ   Go on, if you can make this clear to me.
OEDIPUS   He charges me with the murder of Laïos.
180 IOKASTÊ   Has he some knowledge? Or does he speak from hearsay?
OEDIPUS   He would not commit himself to such a charge,
          But he has brought in that damnable soothsayer
          To tell his story.
IOKASTÊ   Set your mind at rest.
          If it is a question of soothsayers, I tell you
          That you will find no man whose craft gives knowledge
          Of the unknowable.

                         Here is my proof:
          An oracle was reported to Laïos once
          (I will not say from Phoibos himself, but from
          His appointed ministers, at any rate)
190   That his doom would be death at the hands of his own son—
          His son, born of his flesh and of mine!

          Now, you remember the story: Laïos was killed
          By marauding strangers where three highways meet;
          But his child had not been three days in this world
          Before the King had pierced the baby's ankles
          And left him to die on a lonely mountainside.

          Thus, Apollo never caused that child
          To kill his father, and it was not Laïos' fate
          To die at the hands of his son, as he had feared.
200   This is what prophets and prophecies are worth!
          Have no dread of them.
                         It is God himself
          Who can show us what he wills, in his own way.
OEDIPUS   How strange a shadowy memory crossed my mind,
          Just now while you were speaking; it chilled my heart.
IOKASTÊ   What do you mean? What memory do you speak of?
OEDIPUS   If I understand you, Laïos was killed
          At a place where three roads meet.

IOKASTÊ   So it was said:
We have no later story.

OEDIPUS   Where did it happen?

IOKASTÊ   Phokis, it is called: at a place where the Theban Way
210   Divides into the roads toward Delphi and Daulia.

OEDIPUS   When?

IOKASTÊ   We had the news not long before you came
And proved the right to your succession here.

OEDIPUS   Ah, what net has God been weaving for me?

IOKASTÊ   Oedipus! Why does this trouble you?

OEDIPUS   Do not ask me yet.
First, tell me how Laïos looked, and tell me
How old he was.

OEDIPUS   He was tall, his hair just touched
With white; his form was not unlike your own.

OEDIPUS   I think that I myself may be accurst
By my own ignorant edict.

IOKASTÊ   You speak strangely.
220   It makes me tremble to look at you, my King.

OEDIPUS   I am not sure that the blind man can not see.
But I should know better if you were to tell me—

IOKASTÊ   Anything—though I dread to hear you ask it.

OEDIPUS   Was the King lightly escorted, or did he ride
With a large company, as a ruler should?

IOKASTÊ   There were five men with him in all: one was a herald;
And a single chariot, which he was driving.

OEDIPUS   Alas, that makes it plain enough!
                              But who—
Who told you how it happened?

IOKASTÊ   A household servant,
The only one to escape.

230   OEDIPUS   And is he still
A servant of ours?

IOKASTÊ   No; for when he came back at last
And found you enthroned in the place of the dead king,
He came to me, touched my hand with his, and begged
That I would send him away to the frontier district
Where only the shepherds go—
As far away from the city as I could send him.
I granted his prayer; for although the man was a slave,
He had earned more than this favor at my hands.

OEDPIUS   Can he be called back quickly?

IOKASTÊ   Easily.
But why?

240   OEDIPUS I have taken too much upon myself
         Without enquiry; therefore I wish to consult him.
    IOKASTÊ Then he shall come.
                      But am I not one also
         To whom you might confide these fears of yours?
    OEDIPUS That is your right; it will not be denied you,
         Now least of all; for I have reached a pitch
         Of wild foreboding. Is there anyone
         To whom I should sooner speak?

         Polybos of Corinth is my father.
         My mother is a Dorian: Meropê.
250   I grew up chief among the men of Corinth
         Until a strange thing happened—
         Not worth my passion, it may be, but strange.

         At a feast, a drunken man maundering in his cups
         Cries out that I am not my father's son!
         I contained myself that night, though I felt anger
         And a sinking heart. The next day I visited
         My father and mother, and questioned them. They stormed,
         Calling it all the slanderous rant of a fool;
         And this relieved me. Yet the suspicion
260   Remained always aching in my mind;
         I knew there was talk; I could not rest;
         And finally, saying nothing to my parents,
         I went to the shrine at Delphi.

         The god dismissed my question without reply;
         He spoke of other things.
                    Some were clear,
         Full of wretchedness, dreadful, unbearable:
         As that I should lie with my own mother, breed
         Children from whom all men would turn their eyes;
         And that I should be my father's murderer.

270   I heard all this, and fled. And from that day
         Corinth to me was only in the stars
         Descending in that quarter of the sky,
         As I wandered farther and farther on my way
         To a land where I should never see the evil
         Sung by the oracle. And I came to this country
         Where, so you say, King Laïos was killed.

I will tell you all that happened there, my lady.

There were three highways
Coming together at a place I passed;
And there a herald came towards me, and a chariot
Drawn by horses, with a man such as you describe
Seated in it. The groom leading the horses
Forced me off the road at his lord's command;
But as this charioteer lurched over towards me
I struck him in my rage. The old man saw me
And brought his double goad down upon my head
As I came abreast.
                                He was paid back, and more!
Swinging my club in this right hand I knocked him
Out of his car, and he rolled on the ground.
                                              I killed him.

I killed them all.
Now if that stranger and Laïos were—kin,
Where is a man more miserable than I?
More hated by the gods? Citizen and alien alike
Must never shelter me or speak to me—
I must be shunned by all.
                                And I myself
Pronounced this malediction upon myself!

Think of it: I have touched you with these hands,
These hands that killed your husband. What defilement!

Am I all evil, then? It must be so,
Since I must flee from Thebes, yet never again
See my own countrymen, my own country,
For fear of joining my mother in marriage
And killing Polybos, my father.
                                Ah,
If I was created so, born to this fate,
Who could deny the savagery of God?

O holy majesty of heavenly powers!
May I never see that day! Never!
Rather let me vanish from the race of men
Than know the abomination destined me!

CHORAGOS We too, my lord, have felt dismay at this.
But there is hope: you have yet to hear the shepherd.

OEDIPUS   Indeed, I fear no other hope is left me.

IOKASTÊ   What do you hope from him when he comes?

OEDIPUS   This much:
> If his account of the murder tallies with yours,
> Then I am cleared.

IOKASTÊ   What was it that I said
> Of such importance?

OEDIPUS   Why, "marauders," you said,
> Killed the King, according to this man's story.
> If he maintains that still, if there were several,
> Clearly the guilt is not mine: I was alone.

320
> But if he says one man, singlehanded, did it,
> Then the evidence all points to me.

IOKASTÊ   You may be sure that he said there were several;
> And can he call back that story now? He cán not.
> The whole city heard it as plainly as I.
> But suppose he alters some detail of it:
> He can not ever show that Laïos' death
> Fulfilled the oracle: for Apollo said
> My child was doomed to kill him; and my child—
> Poor baby!—it was my child that died first.

330
> No. From now on, where oracles are concerned,
> I would not waste a second thought on any.

OEDIPUS   You may be right.
>   But come: let someone go
> For the shepherd at once. This matter must be settled.

IOKASTÊ   I will send for him.
> I would not wish to cross you in anything,
> And surely not in this.—Let us go in.

Exeunt into the palace.

ODE II

CHORUS   Let me be reverent in the ways of right,   STROPHE 1
> Lowly the paths I journey on;
> Let all my words and actions keep
> The laws of the pure universe
> From highest Heaven handed down.
> For Heaven is their bright nurse,
> Those generations of the realms of light;
> Ah, never of mortal kind were they begot,

Nor are they slaves of memory, lost in sleep:
Their Father is greater than Time, and ages not.

The tyrant is a child of Pride   ANTISTROPHE 1
Who drinks from his great sickening cup
Recklessness and vanity,
Until from his high crest headlong
He plummets to the dust of hope.
That strong man is not strong.
But let no fair ambition be denied;
May God protect the wrestler for the State
In government, in comely policy,
Who will fear God, and on His ordinance wait.

Haughtiness and the high hand of disdain   STROPHE 2
Tempt and outrage God's holy law;
And any mortal who dares hold
No immortal Power in awe
Will be caught up in a net of pain:
The price for which his levity is sold.
Let each man take due earnings, then,
And keep his hands from holy things,
And from blasphemy stand apart—
Else the crackling blast of heaven
Blows on his head, and on his desperate heart.
Though fools will honor impious men,
In their cities no tragic poet sings.

Shall we lose faith in Delphi's obscurities,   ANTISTROPHE 2
We who have heard the world's core
Discredited, and the sacred wood
Of Zeus at Elis praised no more?
The deeds and the strange prophecies
Must make a pattern yet to be understood.
Zeus, if indeed you are lord of all,
Throned in light over night and day,
Mirror this in your endless mind:
Our masters call the oracle
Words on the wind, and the Delphic vision blind!
Their hearts no longer know Apollo,
And reverence for the gods has died away.

SCENE III

Enter Iokastê.

IOKASTÊ   Princes of Thebes, it has occurred to me
　　　　To visit the altars of the gods, bearing
　　　　These branches as a suppliant, and this incense.
　　　　Our King is not himself: his noble soul
　　　　Is overwrought with fantasies of dread,
　　　　Else he would consider
　　　　The new prophecies in the light of the old.
　　　　He will listen to any voice that speaks disaster,
　　　　And my advice goes for nothing.

She approaches the altar, right.

　　　　　　　　　　　　　　To you, then, Apollo,
10　　　Lycéan lord, since you are nearest, I turn in prayer.

　　　　Receive these offerings, and grant us deliverance
　　　　From defilement. Our hearts are heavy with fear
　　　　When we see our leader distracted, as helpless sailors
　　　　Are terrified by the confusion of their helmsman.

Enter Messenger.

MESSENGER   Friends, no doubt you can direct me:
　　　　Where shall I find the house of Oedipus,
　　　　Or, better still, where is the King himself?
CHORAGOS   It is this very place, stranger; he is inside.
　　　　This is his wife and mother of his children.
20　MESSENGER   I wish her happiness in a happy house,
　　　　Blest in all the fulfillment of her marriage.
IOKASTÊ   I wish as much for you: your courtesy
　　　　Deserves a like good fortune. But now, tell me:
　　　　Why have you come? What have you to say to us?
MESSENGER   Good news, my lady, for your house and your husband.
IOKASTÊ   What news? Who sent you here?
MESSENGER   　　　　　　　　　　　　I am from Corinth.
　　　　The news I bring ought to mean joy for you,
　　　　Though it may be you will find some grief in it.
IOKASTÊ   What is it? How can it touch us in both ways?

30 MESSENGER   The word is that the people of the Isthmus
            Intend to call Oedipus to be their king.
    IOKASTÊ   But old King Polybos—is he not reigning still?
    MESSENGER   No. Death holds him in his sepulchre.
    IOKASTÊ   What are you saying? Polybos is dead?
    MESSENGER   If I am not telling the truth, may I die myself.
    IOKASTÊ   *To a Maidservant*
            Go in, go quickly; tell this to your master.

            O riddlers of God's will, where are you now!
            This was the man whom Oedipus, long ago,
            Feared so, fled so, in dread of destroying him—
40   But it was another fate by which he died.

Enter Oedipus, center.

    OEDIPUS   Dearest Iokastê, why have you sent for me?
    IOKASTÊ   Listen to what this man says, and then tell me
            What has become of the solemn prophecies.
    OEDIPUS   Who is this man? What is his news for me?
    IOKASTÊ   He has come from Corinth to announce your father's death!
    OEDIPUS   Is it true, stranger? Tell me in your own words.
    MESSENGER   I can not say it more clearly: the King is dead.
    OEDIPUS   Was it by treason? Or by an attack of illness?
    MESSENGER   A little thing brings old men to their rest.
    OEDIPUS   It was sickness, then?
50 MESSENGER   Yes, and his many years.
    OEDIPUS   Ah!
            Why should a man respect the Pythian hearth, or
            Give heed to the birds that jangle above his head?
            They prophesied that I should kill Polybos,
            Kill my own father; but he is dead and buried,
            And I am here—I never touched him, never,
            Unless he died of grief for my departure,
            And thus, in a sense, through me. No. Polybos
            Has packed the oracles off with him underground.
            They are empty words.
    IOKASTÊ   Had I not told you so?
60 OEDIPUS   You had; it was my faint heart that betrayed me.
    IOKASTÊ   From now on never think of those things again.
    OEDIPUS   And yet—must I not fear my mother's bed?
    IOKASTÊ   Why should anyone in this world be afraid,
            Since Fate rules us and nothing can be foreseen?
            A man should live only for the present day.

Have no more fear of sleeping with your mother:
How many men, in dreams, have lain with their mothers!
No reasonable man is troubled by such things.

OEDIPUS   That is true; only—

70   If only my mother were not still alive!
But she is alive. I can not help my dread.

IOKASTÊ   Yet this news of your father's death is wonderful.

OEDIPUS   Wonderful. But I fear the living woman.

MESSENGER   Tell me, who is this woman that you fear?

OEDIPUS   It is Meropê, man; the wife of King Polybos.

MESSENGER   Meropê? Why should you be afraid of her?

OEDIPUS   An oracle of the gods, a dreadful saying.

MESSENGER   Can you tell me about it or are you sworn to silence?

OEDIPUS   I can tell you, and I will.

80   Apollo said through his prophet that I was the man
Who should marry his own mother, shed his father's blood
With his own hands. And so, for all these years
I have kept clear of Corinth, and no harm has come—
Though it would have been sweet to see my parents again.

MESSENGER   And is this the fear that drove you out of Corinth?

OEDIPUS   Would you have me kill my father?

MESSENGER   As for that
You must be reassured by the news I gave you.

OEDIPUS   If you could reassure me, I would reward you.

MESSENGER   I had that in mind, I will confess: I thought

90   I could count on you when you returned to Corinth.

OEDIPUS   No: I will never go near my parents again.

MESSENGER   Ah, son, you still do not know what you are doing—

OEDIPUS   What do you mean? In the name of God tell me!

MESSENGER   —If these are your reasons for not going home.

OEDIPUS   I tell you, I fear the oracle may come true.

MESSENGER   And guilt may come upon you through your parents?

OEDIPUS   That is the dread that is always in my heart.

MESSENGER   Can you not see that all your fears are groundless?

OEDIPUS   Groundless? Am I not my parents' son?

MESSENGER   Polybos was not your father.

100 OEDIPUS   Not my father?

MESSENGER   No more your father than the man speaking to you.

OEDIPUS   But you are nothing to me!

MESSENGER   Neither was he.

OEDIPUS   Then why did he call me son?

MESSENGER   I will tell you:
Long ago he had you from my hands, as a gift.

OEDIPUS   Then how could he love me so, if I was not his?

MESSENGER   He had no children, and his heart turned to you.

OEDIPUS   What of you? Did you buy me? Did you find me by chance?

MESSENGER   I came upon you in the woody vales of Kithairon.

OEDIPUS   And what were you doing there?

MESSENGER   Tending my flocks.

OEDIPUS   A wandering shepherd?

110   MESSENGER   But your savior, son, that day.

OEDIPUS   From what did you save me?

MESSENGER   Your ankles should tell you that.

OEDIPUS   Ah, stranger, why do you speak of that childhood pain?

MESSENGER   I pulled the skewer that pinned your feet together.

OEDIPUS   I have had the mark as long as I can remember.

MESSENGER   That was why you were given the name you bear.

OEDIPUS   God! Was it my father or my mother who did it?
     Tell me!

MESSENGER   I do not know. The man who gave you to me
     Can tell you better than I.

OEDIPUS   It was not you that found me, but another?

120   MESSENGER   It was another shepherd gave you to me.

OEDIPUS   Who was he? Can you tell me who he was?

MESSENGER   I think he was said to be one of Laïos' people.

OEDIPUS   You mean the Laïos who was king here years ago?

MESSENGER   Yes; King Laïos; and the man was one of his herdsmen.

OEDIPUS   Is he still alive? Can I see him?

MESSENGER   These men here
     Know best about such things.

OEDIPUS   Does anyone here
     Know this shepherd that he is talking about?
     Have you seen him in the fields, or in the town?
     If you have, tell me. It is time things were made plain.

130   CHORAGOS   I think the man he means is that same shepherd
     You have already asked to see. Iokastê perhaps
     Could tell you something.

OEDIPUS   Do you know anything
     About him, Lady? Is he the man we have summoned?
     Is that the man this shepherd means?

IOKASTÊ   Why think of him?
     Forget this herdsman. Forget it all.
     This talk is a waste of time.

OEDIPUS   How can you say that,
     When the clues to my true birth are in my hands?

IOKASTÊ   For God's love, let us have no more questioning!
     Is your life nothing to you?

140   My own is pain enough for me to bear.

OEDIPUS You need not worry. Suppose my mother a slave,
    And born of slaves: no baseness can touch you.
IOKASTÊ Listen to me, I beg you: do not do this thing!
OEDIPUS I will not listen; the truth must be made known.
IOKASTÊ Everything that I say is for your own good!
OEDIPUS   My own good
    Snaps my patience, then; I want none of it.
IOKASTÊ You are fatally wrong! May you never learn who you are!
OEDIPUS Go, one of you, and bring the shepherd here.
    Let us leave this woman to brag of her royal name.
150 IOKASTÊ Ah, miserable!
    That is the only word I have for you now.
    That is the only word I can ever have.

                                   Exit into the palace.

CHORAGOS Why has she left us, Oedipus? Why has she gone
    In such a passion of sorrow? I fear this silence:
    Something dreadful may come of it.
OEDIPUS   Let it come!
    However base my birth, I must know about it.
    The Queen, like a woman, is perhaps ashamed
    To think of my low origin. But I
    Am a child of Luck; I can not be dishonored.
160 Luck is my mother; the passing months, my brothers,
    Have seen me rich and poor.
                         If this is so,
    How could I wish that I were someone else?
    How could I not be glad to know my birth?

ODE III

CHORUS If ever the coming time were known   STROPHE
    To my heart's pondering,
    Kithairon, now by Heaven I see the torches
    At the festival of the next full moon,
    And see the dance, and hear the choir sing
    A grace to your gentle shade:
    Mountain where Oedipus was found,
    O mountain guard of a noble race!
    May the god who heals us lend his aid,
10 And let that glory come to pass
    For our king's cradling-ground.

Of the nymphs that flower beyond the years,   ANTISTROPHE
Who bore you, royal child,
To Pan of the hills or the timberline Apollo,
Cold in delight where the upland clears,
Or Hermês for whom Kyllenê's heights are piled?
Or flushed as evening cloud,
Great Dionysos, roamer of mountains,
He—was it he who found you there,
20   And caught you up in his own proud
Arms from the sweet god-ravisher
Who laughed by the Muses' fountains?

SCENE IV

OEDIPUS   Sirs: though I do not know the man,
I think I see him coming, this shepherd we want:
He is old, like our friend here, and the men
Bringing him seem to be servants of my house.
But you can tell, if you have ever seen him.

Enter Shepherd escorted by servants.

CHORAGOS   I know him, he was Laïos' man. You can trust him.
OEDIPUS   Tell me first, you from Corinth: is this the shepherd
We were discussing?
MESSENGER   This is the very man.
OEDIPUS   *To Shepherd*
Come here. No, look at me. You must answer
10   Everything I ask.—You belonged to Laïos?
SHEPHERD   Yes: born his slave, brought up in his house.
OEDIPUS   Tell me: what kind of work did you do for him?
SHEPHERD   I was a shepherd of his, most of my life.
OEDIPUS   Where mainly did you go for pasturage?
SHEPHERD   Sometimes Kithairon, sometimes the hills near-by.
OEDIPUS   Do you remember ever seeing this man out there?
SHEPHERD   What would he be doing there? This man?
OEDIPUS   This man standing here. Have you ever seen him before?
SHEPHERD   No. At least, not to my recollection.
20   MESSENGER   And that is not strange, my lord. But I'll refresh
His memory: he must remember when we two
Spent three whole seasons together, March to September,
On Kithairon or thereabouts. He had two flocks;
I had one. Each autumn I'd drive mine home

And he would go back with his to Laïos' sheepfold.—
Is this not true, just as I have described it?

SHEPHERD   True, yes; but it was all so long ago.

MESSENGER   Well, then: do you remember, back in those days,
That you gave me a baby boy to bring up as my own?

30   SHEPHERD   What if I did? What are you trying to say?

MESSENGER   King Oedipus was once that little child.

SHEPHERD   Damn you, hold your tongue!

OEDIPUS   No more of that!
It is your tongue needs watching, not this man's.

SHEPHERD   My King, my Master, what is it I have done wrong?

OEDIPUS   You have not answered his question about the boy.

SHEPHERD   He does not know . . . He is only making trouble . . .

OEDIPUS   Come, speak plainly, or it will go hard with you.

SHEPHERD   In God's name, do not torture an old man!

OEDIPUS   Come here, one of you; bind his arms behind him.

40   SHEPHERD   Unhappy king! What more do you wish to learn?

OEDIPUS   Did you give this man the child he speaks of?

SHEPHERD   I did.
And I would to God I had died that very day.

OEDIPUS   You will die now unless you speak the truth.

SHEPHERD   Yet if I speak the truth, I am worse than dead.

OEDIPUS   *To Attendant*
He intends to draw it out, apparently—

SHEPHERD   No! I have told you already that I gave him the boy.

OEDIPUS   Where did you get him? From your house? From somewhere else?

SHEPHERD   Not from mine, no. A man gave him to me.

OEDIPUS   Is that man here? Whose house did he belong to?

50   SHEPHERD   For God's love, my King, do not ask me any more!

OEDIPUS   You are a dead man if I have to ask you again.

SHEPHERD   Then . . . Then the child was from the palace of Laïos.

OEDIPUS   A slave child? or a child of his own line?

SHEPHERD   Ah, I am on the brink of dreadful speech!

OEDIPUS   And I of dreadful hearing. Yet I must hear.

SHEPHERD   If you must be told, then . . .
                              They said it was Laïos' child:
But it is your wife who can tell you about that.

OEDIPUS   My wife!—Did she give it to you?

SHEPHERD   My Lord, she did.

OEDIPUS   Do you know why?

SHEPHERD   I was told to get rid of it.

OEDIPUS   Oh heartless mother!

60   SHEPHERD   But in dread of prophecies . . .

OEDIPUS   Tell me.

SHEPHERD   It was said that the boy would kill his own father.
OEDIPUS   Then why did you give him over to this old man?
SHEPHERD   I pitied the baby, my King,
    And I thought that this man would take him far away
    To his own country.
                        He saved him—but for what a fate!
    For if you are what this man says you are,
    No man living is more wretched than Oedipus.
OEDIPUS   Ah God!
    It was true!
                All the prophecies!
                            —Now,
70   O Light, may I look on you for the last time!
    I, Oedipus,
    Oedipus, damned in his birth, in his marriage damned,
    Damned in the blood he shed with his own hand!

He rushes into the palace.

ODE IV

CHORUS   Alas for the seed of men.   STROPHE 1

    What measure shall I give these generations
    That breathe on the void and are void
    And exist and do not exist?

    Who bears more weight of joy
    Than mass of sunlight shifting in images,
    Or who shall make his thought stay on
    That down time drifts away?

    Your splendor is all fallen.

10   O naked brow of wrath and tears,
    O change of Oedipus!
    I who saw your days call no man blest—
    Your great days like ghósts góne.

    That mind was a strong bow.   ANTISTROPHE 1

    Deep, how deep you drew it then, hard archer,
    At a dim fearful range,

And brought dear glory down!

You overcame the stranger—
The virgin with her hooking lion claws—
And though death sang, stood like a tower
To make pale Thebes take heart.

Fortress against our sorrow!

True king, giver of laws,
Majestic Oedipus!
No prince in Thebes had ever such renown,
No prince won such grace of power.

And now of all men ever known   STROPHE 2
Most pitiful is this man's story:
His fortunes are most changed, his state
Fallen to a low slave's
Ground under bitter fate.

O Oedipus, most royal one!
The great door that expelled you to the light
Gave at night—ah, gave night to your glory:
As to the father, to the fathering son.

All understood too late.

How could that queen whom Laïos won,
The garden that he harrowed at his height,
Be silent when that act was done?

But all eyes fail before time's eye,   ANTISTROPHE 2
All actions come to justice there.
Though never willed, though far down the deep past,
Your bed, your dread sirings,
Are brought to book at last.

Child by Laïos doomed to die,
Then doomed to lose that fortunate little death,
Would God you never took breath in this air
That with my wailing lips I take to cry:

For I weep the world's outcast.

50   I was blind, and now I can tell why:
        Asleep, for you had given ease of breath
        To Thebes, while the false years went by.

ÉXODOS

Enter, from the palace, Second Messenger.

SECOND MESSENGER   Elders of Thebes, most honored in this land,
        What horrors are yours to see and hear, what weight
        Of sorrow to be endured, if, true to your birth,
        You venerate the line of Labdakos!
        I think neither Istros nor Phasis, those great rivers,
        Could purify this place of all the evil
        It shelters now, or soon must bring to light—
        Evil not done unconsciously, but willed.

        The greatest griefs are those we cause ourselves
10   CHORAGOS   Surely, friend, we have grief enough already;
        What new sorrow do you mean?
SECOND MESSENGER   The Queen is dead.
CHORAGOS   O miserable Queen! But at whose hand?
SECOND MESSENGER   Her own.
        The full horror of what happened you can not know,
        For you did not see it; but I, who did, will tell you
        As clearly as I can how she met her death.

        When she had left us,
        In passionate silence, passing through the court,
        She ran to her apartment in the house,
        Her hair clutched by the fingers of both hands.
20   She closed the doors behind her; then, by that bed
        Where long ago the fatal son was conceived—
        That son who should bring about his father's death—
        We heard her call upon Laïos, dead so many years,
        And heard her wail for the double fruit of her marriage,
        A husband by her husband, children by her child.

        Exactly how she died I do not know:
        For Oedipus burst in moaning and would not let us
        Keep vigil to the end: it was by him
        As he stormed about the room that our eyes were caught.
30   From one to another of us he went, begging a sword,
        Hunting the wife who was not his wife, the mother

Whose womb had carried his own children and himself.
I do not know: it was none of us aided him,
But surely one of the gods was in control!
For with a dreadful cry
He hurled his weight, as though wrenched out of himself,
At the twin doors: the bolts gave, and he rushed in.
And there we saw her hanging, her body swaying
From the cruel cord she had noosed about her neck.
40   A great sob broke from him, heartbreaking to hear,
As he loosed the rope and lowered her to the ground.

I would blot out from my mind what happened next!
For the King ripped from her gown the golden brooches
That were her ornament, and raised them, and plunged them down
Straight into his own eyeballs, crying, "No more,
No more shall you look on the misery about me,
The horrors of my own doing! Too long you have known
The faces of those whom I should never have seen,
Too long been blind to those for whom I was searching!
50   From this hour, go in darkness!" And as he spoke,
He struck at his eyes—not once, but many times;
And the blood spattered his beard,
Bursting from his ruined sockets like red hail.

So from the unhappiness of two this evil has sprung,
A curse on the man and woman alike. The old
Happiness of the house of Labdakos
Was happiness enough: where is it today?
It is all wailing and ruin, disgrace, death—all
The misery of mankind that has a name—
60   And it is wholly and for ever theirs.
CHORAGOS   Is he in agony still? Is there no rest for him?
SECOND MESSENGER   He is calling for someone to open the doors wide
So that all the children of Kadmos may look upon
His father's murderer, his mother's—no,
I can not say it!
                    And then he will leave Thebes,
Self-exiled, in order that the curse
Which he himself pronounced may depart from the house.
He is weak, and there is none to lead him,
So terrible is his suffering.
                    But you will see:
70   Look, the doors are opening; in a moment
You will see a thing that would crush a heart of stone.

The central door is opened; Oedipus, blinded, is led in.

CHORAGOS   Dreadful indeed for men to see.
      Never have my own eyes
      Looked on a sight so full of fear.

      Oedipus!
      What madness came upon you, what daemon
      Leaped on your life with heavier
      Punishment than a mortal man can bear?
      No: I can not even
80   Look at you, poor ruined one.
      And I would speak, question, ponder,
      If I were able. No.
      You make me shudder.
OEDIPUS   God. God.
      Is there a sorrow greater?
      Where shall I find harbor in this world?
      My voice is hurled far on a dark wind.
      What has God done to me?
CHORAGOS   Too terrible to think of, or to see.

90   OEDIPUS   O cloud of night,   STROPHE 1
      Never to be turned away: night coming on,
      I can not tell how: night like a shroud!

      My fair winds brought me here.
                              O God. Again
      The pain of the spikes where I had sight,
      The flooding pain
      Of memory, never to be gouged out.

CHORAGOS   This is not strange.
      You suffer it all twice over, remorse in pain,
      Pain in remorse.

100   OEDIPUS   Ah dear friend   ANTISTROPHE 1
      Are you faithful even yet, you alone?
      Are you still standing near me, will you stay here,
      Patient, to care for the blind?
                              The blind man!
      Yet even blind I know who it is attends me,
      By the voice's tone—
      Though my new darkness hide the comforter.

CHORAGOS   Oh fearful act!
   What god was it drove you to rake black
   Night across your eyes?

110   OEDIPUS   Apollo. Apollo. Dear   STROPHE 2
   Children, the god was Apollo.
   He brought my sick, sick fate upon me.
   But the blinding hand was my own!
   How could I bear to see
   When all my sight was horror everywhere?

CHORAGOS   Everywhere; that is true.

OEDIPUS   And now what is left?
   Images? Love? A greeting even,
   Sweet to the senses? Is there anything?
120   Ah, no, friends: lead me away.
   Lead me away from Thebes.
                              Lead the great wreck
   And hell of Oedipus, whom the gods hate.

CHORAGOS   Your misery, you are not blind to that.
   Would God you had never found it out!

OEDIPUS   Death take the man who unbound   ANTISTROPHE 2
   My feet on that hillside
   And delivered me from death to life! What life?
   If only I had died,
   This weight of monstrous doom
130   Could not have dragged me and my darlings down.

CHORAGOS   I would have wished the same.

OEDIPUS   Oh never to have come here
   With my father's blood upon me! Never
   To have been the man they call his mother's husband!
   Oh accurst! Oh child of evil,
   To have entered that wretched bed—
                              the selfsame one!
   More primal than sin itself, this fell to me.

CHORAGOS   I do not know what words to offer you.
   You were better dead than alive and blind.

140   OEDIPUS   Do not counsel me any more. This punishment

That I have laid upon myself is just.
If I had eyes,
I do not know how I could bear the sight
Of my father, when I came to the house of Death,
Or my mother; for I have sinned against them both
So vilely that I could not make my peace
By strangling my own life.
                              Or do you think my children,
Born as they were born, would be sweet to my eyes?
Ah never, never! Nor this town with its high walls,
Nor the holy images of the gods.
150   For I,
Thrice miserable!—Oedipus, noblest of all the line
Of Kadmos, have condemned myself to enjoy
These things no more, by my own malediction
Expelling that man whom the gods declared
To be a defilement in the house of Laïos.
After exposing the rankness of my own guilt,
How could I look men frankly in the eyes?
No, I swear it,
If I could have stifled my hearing at its source,
160 I would have done it and made all this body
A tight cell of misery, blank to light and sound:
So I should have been safe in my dark mind
Beyond external evil.
                              Ah Kithairon!
Why did you shelter me? When I was cast upon you,
Why did I not die? Then I should never
Have shown the world my execrable birth.

Ah Polybos! Corinth, city that I believed
The ancient seat of my ancestors: how fair
I seemed, your child! And all the while this evil
Was cancerous within me!
170   For I am sick
In my own being, sick in my origin.

O three roads, dark ravine, woodland and way
Where three roads met: you, drinking my father's blood,
My own blood, spilled by my own hand: can you remember
The unspeakable things I did there, and the things
I went on from there to do?
                              O marriage, marriage!
The act that engendered me, and again the act

Performed by the son in the same bed—

                                 Ah, the net

Of incest, mingling fathers, brothers, sons,

180   With brides, wives, mothers: the last evil

That can be known by men: no tongue can say

How evil!

              No. For the love of God, conceal me

Somewhere far from Thebes; or kill me; or hurl me

Into the sea, away from men's eyes for ever.

Come, lead me. You need not fear to touch me.

Of all men, I alone can bear this guilt.

Enter Kreon.

CHORAGOS   Kreon is here now. As to what you ask,

He may decide the course to take. He only

Is left to protect the city in your place.

190   OEDIPUS   Alas, how can I speak to him? What right have I

To beg his courtesy whom I have deeply wronged?

KREON   I have not come to mock you, Oedipus,

Or to reproach you, either.

To Attendants   —You standing there:

If you have lost all respect for man's dignity,

At least respect the flame of Lord Helios:

Do not allow this pollution to show itself

Openly here, an affront to the earth

And Heaven's rain and the light of day. No, take him

Into the house as quickly as you can.

200   For it is proper

That only the close kindred see his grief.

OEDIPUS   I pray you in God's name, since your courtesy

Ignores my dark expectation, visiting

With mercy this man of all men most execrable:

Give me what I ask—for your good, not for mine.

KREON   And what is it that you turn to me begging for?

OEDIPUS   Drive me out of this country as quickly as may be

To a place where no human voice can ever greet me.

KREON   I should have done that before now—only,

210   God's will had not been wholly revealed to me.

OEDIPUS   But his command is plain: the parricide

Must be destroyed. I am that evil man.

KREON   That is the sense of it, yes; but as things are,

We had best discover clearly what is to be done.

OEDIPUS   You would learn more about a man like me?

KREON   You are ready now to listen to the god.

OEDIPUS   I will listen. But it is to you
That I must turn for help. I beg you, hear me.

The woman in there—
220   Give her whatever funeral you think proper:
She is your sister.
                    —But let me go, Kreon!
Let me purge my father's Thebes of the pollution
Of my living here, and go out to the wild hills,
To Kithairon, that has won such fame with me,
The tomb my mother and father appointed for me,
And let me die there, as they willed I should.
And yet I know
Death will not ever come to me through sickness
Or in any natural way: I have been preserved
230   For some unthinkable fate. But let that be.

As for my sons, you need not care for them.
They are men, they will find some way to live.
But my poor daughters, who have shared my table,
Who never before have been parted from their father—
Take care of them, Kreon; do this for me.
And will you let me touch them with my hands
A last time, and let us weep together?
Be kind, my lord,
Great prince, be kind!
                    Could I but touch them,
240   They would be mine again, as when I had my eyes.

Enter Antigone and Ismene, attended.

Ah, God!
Is it my dearest children I hear weeping?
Has Kreon pitied me and sent my daughters?
KREON   Yes, Oedipus: I knew that they were dear to you
In the old days, and know you must love them still.
OEDIPUS   May God bless you for this—and be friendlier
Guardian to you than he has been to me!

Children, where are you?
Come quickly to my hands: they are your brother's—
250   Hands that have brought your father's once clear eyes
To this way of seeing—
                    Ah dearest ones,

I had neither sight nor knowledge then, your father
By the woman who was the source of his own life!
And I weep for you—having no strength to see you—,
I weep for you when I think of the bitterness
That men will visit upon you all your lives.
What homes, what festivals can you attend
Without being forced to depart again in tears?
And when you come to marriageable age,
260   Where is the man, my daughters, who would dare
Risk the bane that lies on all my children?
Is there any evil wanting? Your father killed
His father; sowed the womb of her who bore him;
Engendered you at the fount of his own existence!

That is what they will say of you.

                              Then, whom
Can you ever marry? There are no bridegrooms for you,
And your lives must wither away in sterile dreaming.

O Kreon, son of Menoikeus!
You are the only father my daughters have,
270   Since we, their parents, are both of us gone for ever.
They are your own blood: you will not let them
Fall into beggary and loneliness;
You will keep them from the miseries that are mine!
Take pity on them; see, they are only children,
Friendless except for you. Promise me this,
Great Prince, and give me your hand in token of it.

Kreon clasps his right hand.

Children:
I could say much, if you could understand me,
But as it is, I have only this prayer for you:
280   Live where you can, be as happy as you can—
Happier, please God, than God has made your father.
KREON   Enough. You have wept enough. Now go within.
OEDIPUS   I must; but it is hard.
KREON   Time eases all things.
OEDIPUS   You know my mind, then?
KREON   Say what you desire.
OEDIPUS   Send me from Thebes!
KREON   God grant that I may!

OEDIPUS   But since God hates me . . .
KREON   No, he will grant your wish.
OEDIPUS   You promise?
KREON   I can not speak beyond my knowledge.
OEDIPUS   Then lead me in.
KREON   Come now, and leave your children.
OEDIPUS   No! Do not take them from me!
KREON   Think no longer
290   That you are in command here, but rather think
           How, when you were, you served your own destruction.

*Exeunt into the house all but the Chorus; the Choragos chants directly to the
audience.*

CHORAGOS   Men of Thebes: look upon Oedipus.

        This is the king who solved the famous riddle
        And towered up, most powerful of men.
        No mortal eyes but looked on him with envy,
        Yet in the end ruin swept over him.

        Let every man in mankind's frailty
        Consider his last day; and let none
        Presume on his good fortune until he find
300   Life, at his death, a memory without pain.

COMEDY IN THE CLASSICAL GREEK THEATER

Lysistrata was first staged in 411 B.C. at the theater of Dionysus in Athens, where *Oedipus Rex* had been produced some fifteen years earlier. (A description of that theater can be found in our introduction to *Oedipus Rex*.) The method of staging, however, was quite different for the two plays—as different as tragedy and comedy. If we recall that classical Greek comedy developed from primitive fertility rites and masquerades, in which people wore fantastic costumes and went throughout the streets singing, dancing, carousing, and even jesting with bystanders, we can begin to sense the bizarre quality of the spectacle created in the original performance of *Lysistrata*. We can get an even more particular sense of its outlandishness when we realize that the male characters would have been costumed in extremely short tunics and flesh-colored tights padded to suggest comic deformity, and that between their legs they would have been sporting large leather phalluses so as to ridicule their sexual frustration. Their masks, too, would have been ridiculously ugly and contorted so as to suggest the lewd grimace of a coarse peasant type.

In their physical movements as in their costumes, they would have aimed to accentuate the bawdy element of the comedy. They would not have limited themselves simply to reciting their lines, but would also have performed ribald dance movements, kicking their buttocks, slapping their thighs, and possibly even pummeling one another. And the same would have been true of the choral dancing and singing.

The chorus, in fact, had a major role in the performance of *Lysistrata*, as in all Greek comedies. Its function can best be appreciated when seen within the typical structure of Greek comedy. Comedy always began with a short scene, a *prologos*, in which the comic protagonist proposed a fantastic solution to a pressing social or political issue. Lysistrata, for example, opens the play by gathering her cohorts together and proposing that they go on a sex strike against their husbands as a means of ending the war that was then literally consuming Athenian life.

Immediately after the *prologos*, the chorus entered in two groups, one group siding with the protagonist, the other with the antagonists; and a contest, or *agon*, developed between the two groups as they debated the fantastic proposal. Thus, immediately after Lysistrata and her cohorts depart, the chorus of old men appears carrying logs and torches, then the chorus of old women carrying pitchers of water; and soon the old women are dousing the old men with water. Indeed, the *agon* typically developed into a knock-down drag-out struggle, one that involved not only bawdy words and slapstick action but also a series of ridiculously complicated patter songs, the last of which was sung rapidly without drawing a single breath. The *agon* also included a debate between the protagonist and a single antagonist. Thus Lysistrata is shown humiliating the Athenian magistrate in word and in deed.

The climax of the *agon* took place only after the protagonist and supporting chorus had literally beaten down all opposition to their proposal. Then all the actors departed and the chorus supporting the protagonist stepped forward and addressed the spectators directly, exhorting them to side with the idea of the play. In this section, known as the *parabasis*, the dramatist actually had his say, as does Aristophanes when the Chorus of Women implore the citizens of Athens to "hear useful words for the state." After the *parabasis* the actors returned, and in a series of short scenes the fantastic proposal was put into action and shown to be successful. Thus *Lysistrata* concludes with the raucous festivities that might have taken place had Athens and Sparta actually made peace in 411 B.C.

Though *Lysistrata* was occasioned by the immediate circumstances of the war between Athens and Sparta, it makes a statement about war that has been true for all times. It makes that statement through the fantastic idea dreamed up by Lysistrata—to force the Athenian men to make peace by refusing to make love to them so long as they continue the war. Nearly twenty-five centuries ago, Aristophanes was pleading with his audience to make love not war. And he showed his audience that truth by staging a war of the sexes—and celebrating the peace that might follow such a war.

ARISTOPHANES

c. 448–*c.* 380 B.C.

Lysistrata

CHARACTERS

LYSISTRATA ⎫
CALONICE ⎬ Athenian women
MYRRHINE ⎭
LAMPITO, a Spartan woman
LEADER of Chorus of Old Men
CHORUS of Old Men
LEADER of Chorus of Old Women
CHORUS of Old Women
ATHENIAN MAGISTRATE

THREE ATHENIAN WOMEN
CINESIAS, an Athenian, husband
   of Myrrhine
SPARTAN HERALD
SPARTAN AMBASSADORS
ATHENIAN AMBASSADORS
TWO ATHENIAN CITIZENS
CHORUS of Athenians
CHORUS of Spartans

Scene. In Athens, beneath the Acropolis. In the center of the stage is the propylaea, or gate-way to the Acropolis; to one side is a small grotto, sacred to Pan. The orchestra represents a slope leading up to the gate-way.

It is early in the morning. Lysistrata is pacing impatiently up and down.

LYSISTRATA   If they'd been summoned to worship the God of Wine, or Pan, or to visit the Queen of Love, why, you couldn't have pushed your way through the streets for all the timbrels. But now there's not a single woman here—except my neighbour; here she comes.

Enter Calonice.

   Good day to you, Calonice.
CALONICE   And to you, Lysistrata. [*Noticing Lysistrata's impatient air*] But what ails you? Don't scowl, my dear; it's not becoming to you to knit your brows like that.
LYSISTRATA [*sadly*]   Ah, Calonice, my heart aches; I'm so annoyed at us women. For among men we have a reputation for sly trickery—
CALONICE   And rightly too, on my word!
LYSISTRATA   —but when they were told to meet here to consider a matter of no small importance, they lie abed and don't come.
CALONICE   Oh, they'll come all right, my dear. It's not easy for a woman to

Translated by Charles T. Murphy

get out, you know. One is working on her husband, another is getting up the maid, another has to put the baby to bed, or wash and feed it.

LYSISTRATA   But after all, there are other matters more important than all that.

CALONICE   My dear Lysistrata, just what is this matter you've summoned us women to consider? What's up? Something big?

LYSISTRATA   Very big.

CALONICE [*interested*]   Is it stout, too?

LYSISTRATA [*smiling*]   Yes indeed—both big and stout.

CALONICE   What? And the women still haven't come?

LYSISTRATA   It's not what you suppose; they'd have come soon enough for *that*. But I've worked up something, and for many a sleepless night I've turned it this way and that.

CALONICE [*in mock disappointment*]   Oh, I guess it's pretty fine and slender, if you've turned it this way and that.

LYSISTRATA   So fine that the safety of the whole of Greece lies in us women.

CALONICE   In us women? It depends on a very slender reed then.

LYSISTRATA   Our country's fortunes are in our hands; and whether the Spartans shall perish—

CALONICE   Good! Let them perish, by al! means.

LYSISTRATA   —and the Boeotians shall be completely annihilated.

CALONICE   Not completely! Please spare the eels.

LYSISTRATA   As for Athens, I won't use any such unpleasant words. But you understand what I mean. But if the women will meet here—the Spartans, the Boeotians, and we Athenians—then all together we will save Greece.

CALONICE   But what could women do that's clever or distinguished? We just sit around all dolled up in silk robes, looking pretty in our sheer gowns and evening slippers.

LYSISTRATA   These are just the things I hope will save us: these silk robes, perfumes, evening slippers, rouge, and our chiffon blouses.

CALONICE   Hᴜ v so?

LYSISTRATA   So never a man alive will lift a spear against the foe—

CALONICE   I'll get a silk gown at once.

LYSISTRATA   —or take up his shield—

CALONICE   I'll put on my sheerest gown!

LYSISTRATA   —or sword.

CALONICE   I'll buy a pair of evening slippers.

LYSISTRATA   Well then, shouldn't the women have come?

CALONICE   Come? Why, they should have *flown* here.

LYSISTRATA   Well, my dear, just watch: they'll act in true Athenian fashion—everything too late! And now there's not a woman here from the shore or from Salamis.

CALONICE   They're coming, I'm sure; at daybreak they were laying—to their oars to cross the straits.

LYSISTRATA   And those I expected would be the first to come—the women of Acharnae—they haven't arrived.

CALONICE   Yet the wife of Theagenes means to come: she consulted Hecate about it. [*Seeing a group of women approaching*] But look! Here come a few. And there are some more over here. Hurrah! Where do they come from?

LYSISTRATA   From Anagyra.

CALONICE   Yes indeed! We've raised up quite a stink from Anagyra anyway.

Enter Myrrhine in haste, followed by several other women.

MYRRHINE   [*breathlessly*]   Have we come in time, Lysistrata? What do you say? Why so quiet?

LYSISTRATA   I can't say much for you, Myrrhine, coming at this hour on such important business.

MYRRHINE   Why, I had trouble finding my girdle in the dark. But if it's so important, we're here now; tell us.

LYSISTRATA   No. Let's wait a little for the women from Boeotia and the Peloponnesus.

MYRRHINE   That's a much better suggestion. Look! Here comes Lampito now.

Enter Lampito with two other women.

LYSISTRATA   Greetings, my dear Spartan friend. How pretty you look, my dear. What a smooth complexion and well-developed figure! You could throttle an ox.

LAMPITO   Faith, yes, I think I could. I take exercises and kick my heels against my bum. [*She demonstrates with a few steps of the Spartan "bottom-kicking" dance.*]

LYSISTRATA   And what splendid breasts you have.

LAMPITO   La! You handle me like a prize steer.

LYSISTRATA   And who is this young lady with you?

LAMPITO   Faith, she's an Ambassadress from Boeotia.

LYSISTRATA   Oh yes, a Boeotian, and blooming like a garden too.

CALONICE   [*lifting up her skirt*]   My word! How neatly her garden's weeded!

LYSISTRATA   And who is the other girl?

LAMPITO   Oh, she's a Corinthian swell.

MYRRHINE   [*after a rapid examination*]   Yes indeed. She swells very nicely [*pointing*] here and here.

LAMPITO   Who has gathered together this company of women?

LYSISTRATA   I have.

LAMPITO   Speak up, then. What do you want?

MYRRHINE   Yes, my dear, tell us what this important matter is.

LYSISTRATA   Very well, I'll tell you. But before I speak, let me ask you a little question.

MYRRHINE   Anything you like.

LYSISTRATA   [earnestly]   Tell me: don't you yearn for the fathers of your children, who are away at the wars? I know you all have husbands abroad.

CALONICE   Why, yes; mercy me! my husband's been away for five months in Thrace keeping guard on—Eucrates.

MYRRHINE   And mine for seven whole months in Pylus.

LAMPITO   And mine, as soon as ever he returns from the fray, readjusts his shield and flies out of the house again.

LYSISTRATA   And as for lovers, there's not even a ghost of one left. Since the Milesians revolted from us, I've not even seen an eight-inch dingus to be a leather consolation for us widows. Are you willing, if I can find a way, to help me end the war?

MYRRHINE   Goodness, yes! I'd do it, even if I had to pawn my dress and—get drunk on the spot!

CALONICE   And I, even if I had to let myself be split in two like a flounder.

LAMPITO   I'd climb up Mt. Taygetus if I could catch a glimpse of peace.

LYSISTRATA   I'll tell you, then, in plain and simple words. My friends, if we are going to force our men to make peace, we must do without—

MYRRHINE   Without what? Tell us.

LYSISTRATA   Will you do it?

MYRRHINE   We'll do it, if it kills us.

LYSISTRATA   Well then, we must do without sex altogether. [General consternation.] Why do you turn away? Where go you? Why turn so pale? Why those tears? Will you do it or not? What means this hesitation?

MYRRHINE   I won't do it! Let the war go on.

CALONICE   Nor I! Let the war go on.

LYSISTRATA   So, my little flounder? Didn't you say just now you'd split yourself in half?

CALONICE   Anything else you like. I'm willing, even if I have to walk through fire. Anything rather than sex. There's nothing like it, my dear.

LYSISTRATA   [to Myrrhine]   What about you?

MYRRHINE   [sullenly]   I'm willing to walk through fire, too.

LYSISTRATA   Oh vile and cursed breed! No wonder they make tragedies about us: we're naught but "love-affairs and bassinets." But you, my dear Spartan friend, if you alone are with me, our enterprise might yet succeed. Will you vote with me?

LAMPITO   'Tis cruel hard, by my faith, for a woman to sleep alone without her nooky; but for all that, we certainly do need peace.

LYSISTRATA   O my dearest friend! You're the only real woman here.

CALONICE [*wavering*]   Well, if we do refrain from—[*shuddering*] what you say (God forbid!), would that bring peace?

LYSISTRATA   My goodness, yes! If we sit at home all rouged and powdered, dressed in our sheerest gowns, and neatly depilated, our men will get excited and want to take us; but if you don't come to them and keep away, they'll soon make a truce.

LAMPITO   Aye; Menelaus caught sight of Helen's naked breast and dropped his sword, they say.

CALONICE   What if the men give us up?

LYSISTRATA   "Flay a skinned dog," as Pherecrates says.

CALONICE   Rubbish! These make-shifts are no good. But suppose they grab us and drag us into the bedroom?

LYSISTRATA   Hold on to the door.

CALONICE   And if they beat us?

LYSISTRATA   Give in with a bad grace. There's no pleasure in it for them when they have to use violence. And you must torment them in every possible way. They'll give up soon enough; a man gets no joy if he doesn't get along with his wife.

MYRRHINE   If this is your opinion, we agree.

LAMPITO   As for our own men, we can persuade them to make a just and fair peace; but what about the Athenian rabble? Who will persuade them not to start any more monkey-shines?

LYSISTRATA   Don't worry. We guarantee to convince them.

LAMPITO   Not while their ships are rigged so well and they have that mighty treasure in the temple of Athene.

LYSISTRATA   We've taken good care for that too: we shall seize the Acropolis today. The older women have orders to do this, and while we are making our arrangements, they are to pretend to make a sacrifice and occupy the Acropolis.

LAMPITO   All will be well then. That's a very fine idea.

LYSISTRATA   Let's ratify this, Lampito, with the most solemn oath.

LAMPITO   Tell us what oath we shall swear.

LYSISTRATA   Well said. Where's our Policewoman? [*to a Scythian slave*] What are you gaping at? Set a shield upside-down here in front of me, and give me the sacred meats.

CALONICE   Lysistrata, what sort of an oath are we to take?

LYSISTRATA   What oath? I'm going to slaughter a sheep over the shield, as they do in Aeschylus.

CALONICE   Don't, Lysistrata! No oaths about peace over a shield.

LYSISTRATA   What shall the oath be, then?

CALONICE   How about getting a white horse somewhere and cutting out its entrails for the sacrifice?

LYSISTRATA   White horse indeed!

CALONICE   Well then, how shall we swear?

MYRRHINE   I'll tell you: let's place a large black bowl upside-down and then slaughter—a flask of Thasian wine. And then let's swear—not to pour in a single drop of water.

LAMPITO   Lord! How I like that oath!

LYSISTRATA   Someone bring out a bowl and a flask.

A slave brings the utensils for the sacrifice.

CALONICE   Look, my friends! What a big jar! Here's a cup that 'twould give me joy to handle. [*She picks up the bowl.*]

LYSISTRATA   Set it down and put your hands on our victim. [*As Calonice places her hands on the flask*] O Lady of Persuasion and dear Loving Cup, graciously vouchsafe to receive this sacrifice from us women. [*She pours the wine into the bowl.*]

CALONICE   The blood has a good colour and spurts out nicely.

LAMPITO   Faith, it has a pleasant smell, too.

MYRRHINE   Oh, let me be the first to swear, ladies!

CALONICE   No, by our Lady! Not unless you're allotted the first turn.

LYSISTRATA   Place all your hands on the cup, and one of you repeat on behalf of all what I say. Then all will swear and ratify the oath. *I will suffer no man, be he husband or lover,*

CALONICE   *I will suffer no man, be he husband or lover,*

LYSISTRATA   *To approach me all hot and horny.* [*As Calonice hesitates*] Say it!

CALONICE   [*slowly and painfully*]   *To approach me all hot and horny.* O Lysistrata, I feel so weak in the knees!

LYSISTRATA   *I will remain at home unmated,*

CALONICE   *I will remain at home unmated,*

LYSISTRATA   *Wearing my sheerest gown and carefully adorned,*

CALONICE   *Wearing my sheerest gown and carefully adorned,*

LYSISTRATA   *That my husband may burn with desire for me,*

CALONICE   *That my husband may burn with desire for me,*

LYSISTRATA   *And if he takes me by force against my will,*

CALONICE   *And if he takes me by force against my will,*

LYSISTRATA   *I shall do it badly and keep from moving.*

CALONICE   *I shall do it badly and keep from moving.*

LYSISTRATA   *I will not stretch my slippers toward the ceiling,*

CALONICE   *I will not stretch my slippers toward the ceiling,*

LYSISTRATA   *Nor will I take the posture of the lioness on the knife-handle.*

CALONICE   *Nor will I take the posture of the lioness on the knife-handle.*

LYSISTRATA   *If I keep this oath, may I be permitted to drink from this cup,*

CALONICE   *If I keep this oath, may I be permitted to drink from this cup,*

LYSISTRATA   *But if I break it, may the cup be filled with water.*

CALONICE   *But if I break it, may the cup be filled with water.*

LYSISTRATA   Do you all swear to this?

ALL   I do, so help me!

LYSISTRATA   Come then, I'll just consummate this offering.

She takes a long drink from the cup.

CALONICE [*snatching the cup away*] Shares, my dear! Let's drink to our continued friendship.

A shout is heard from off-stage.

LAMPITO   What's that shouting?

LYSISTRATA   That's what I was telling you: the women have just seized the
Acropolis. Now, Lampito, go home and arrange matters in Sparta; and
leave these two ladies here as hostages. We'll enter the Acropolis to join
our friends and help them lock the gates.

CALONICE   Don't you suppose the men will come to attack us?

LYSISTRATA   Don't worry about them. Neither threats nor fire will suffice to
open the gates, except on the terms we've stated.

CALONICE   I should say not! Else we'd belie our reputation as unmanageable
pests.

*Lampito leaves the stage. The other women retire and enter the Acropolis through
the Propylaea.*
Enter the Chorus of Old Men, carrying fire-pots and a load of heavy sticks.

LEADER OF MEN   Onward, Draces, step by step, though your shoulder's
aching.
Cursèd logs of olive-wood, what a load you're making!

FIRST SEMI-CHORUS OF OLD MEN [*singing*]
Aye, many surprises await a man who lives to a ripe old age;
For who could suppose, Strymodorus my lad, that the women we've
nourished (alas!),
Who sat at home to vex our days,
Would seize the holy image here,
And occupy this sacred shrine,
With bolts and bars, with fell design,
To lock the Propylaea?

LEADER OF MEN   Come with speed, Philourgus, come! to the temple hast'n-
ing.
There we'll heap these logs about in a circle round them,
And whoever has conspired, raising this rebellion,
Shall be roasted, scorched, and burnt, all without exception,
Doomed by one unanimous vote—but first the wife of Lycon.

SECOND SEMI-CHORUS [*singing*]
>   No, no! by Demeter, while I'm alive, no woman shall mock at me.
>   Not even the Spartan Cleomenes, our citadel first to seize,
>   Got off unscathed; for all his pride
>   And haughty Spartan arrogance,
>   He left his arms and sneaked away,
>   Stripped to his shirt, unkempt, unshav'd,
>   With six years' filth still on him.

LEADER OF MEN   I besieged that hero bold, sleeping at my station,
>   Marshalled at these holy gates sixteen deep against him.
>   Shall I not these cursèd pests punish for their daring,
>   Burning these Euripides-and-God-detested women?
>   Aye! or else may Marathon overturn my trophy.

FIRST SEMI-CHORUS [*singing*]   There remains of my road
>   Just this brow of the hill;
>   There I speed on my way.
>   Drag the logs up the hill, though we've got no ass to help.
>   (God! my shoulder's bruised and sore!)
>   Onward still must we go.
>   Blow the fire! Don't let it go out
>   Now we're near the end of our road.

ALL [*blowing on the fire-pots*]   Whew! Whew! Drat the smoke!

SECOND SEMI-CHORUS [*singing*]   Lord, what smoke rushing forth
>   From the pot, like a dog
>   Running mad, bites my eyes!
>   This must be Lemnos-fire. What a sharp and stinging smoke!
>   Rushing onward to the shrine
>   Aid the gods. Once for all
>   Show your mettle, Laches my boy!
>   To the rescue hastening all!

ALL [*blowing on the fire-pots*]   Whew! Whew! Drat the smoke!

The chorus has now reached the edge of the Orchestra nearest the stage, in front of the propylaea. They begin laying their logs and fire-pots on the ground.

LEADER OF MEN   Thank heaven, this fire is still alive. Now let's first put down these logs here and place our torches in the pots to catch; then let's make a rush for the gates with a battering-ram. If the women don't unbar the gate at our summons, we'll have to smoke them out.

>   Let me put down my load. Ouch! That hurts! [*To the audience*] Would any of the generals in Samos like to lend a hand with this log? [*Throwing down a log*] Well, *that* won't break my back any more, at any rate. [*Turning to his fire-pot*] Your job, my little pot, is to keep those coals alive and furnish me shortly with a red-hot torch.

O mistress Victory, be my ally and grant me to rout these audacious women in the Acropolis.

While the men are busy with their logs and fires, the Chorus of Old Women enters, carrying pitchers of water.

LEADER OF WOMEN   What's this I see? Smoke and flames? Is that a fire ablazing?
Let's rush upon them. Hurry up! They'll find us women ready.
FIRST SEMI-CHORUS OF OLD WOMEN *[singing]*
    With wingèd foot onward I fly,
    Ere the flames consume Neodice;
    Lest Critylla be overwhelmed
  By a lawless, accurst herd of old men.
  I shudder with fear. Am I too late to aid them?
  At break of the day filled we our jars with water
Fresh from the spring, pushing our way straight through the crowds.
    Oh, what a din!
    Mid crockery crashing, jostled by slave-girls,
    Sped we to save them, aiding our neighbours,
    Bearing this water to put out the flames.
SECOND SEMI-CHORUS OF OLD WOMEN *[singing]*
    Such news I've heard; doddering fools
    Come with logs, like furnace-attendants,
    Loaded down with three hundred pounds,
  Breathing many a vain, blustering threat,
  That all these abhorred sluts will be burnt to charcoal.
  O goddess, I pray never may they be kindled;
Grant them to save Greece and our men, madness and war help them to
    end.
    With this as our purpose, golden-plumed Maiden,
    Guardian of Athens, seized we thy precinct.
    Be my ally, Warrior-maiden,
    'Gainst these old men, bearing water with me.

The women have now reached their position in the Orchestra, and their Leader advances toward the Leader of the Men.

LEADER OF WOMEN   Hold on there! What's this, you utter scoundrels? No decent, God-fearing citizens would act like this.
LEADER OF MEN   Oho! Here's something unexpected: a swarm of women have come out to attack us.
LEADER OF WOMEN   What, do we frighten you? Surely you don't think we're

too many for you. And yet there are ten thousand times more of us whom you haven't even seen.

LEADER OF MEN   What say, Phaedria? Shall we let these women wag their tongues? Shan't we take our sticks and break them over their backs?

LEADER OF WOMEN   Let's set our pitchers on the ground; then if anyone lays a hand on us, they won't get in our way.

LEADER OF MEN   By God! If someone gave them two or three smacks on the jaw, like Bupalus, they wouldn't talk so much!

LEADER OF WOMEN   Go on, hit me, somebody! Here's my jaw! But no other bitch will bite a piece out of you before me.

LEADER OF MEN   Silence! or I'll knock out your—senility!

LEADER OF WOMEN   Just lay one finger on Stratyllis, I dare you!

LEADER OF MEN   Suppose I dust you off with this fist? What will you do?

LEADER OF WOMEN   I'll tear the living guts out of you with my teeth.

LEADER OF MEN   No poet is more clever than Euripides: "There is no beast so shameless as a woman."

LEADER OF WOMEN   Let's pick up our jars of water, Rhodippe.

LEADER OF MEN   Why have you come here with water, you detestable slut?

LEADER OF WOMEN   And why have you come with fire, you funeral vault? To cremate yourself?

LEADER OF MEN   To light a fire and singe your friends.

LEADER OF WOMEN   And I've brought water to put out your fire.

LEADER OF MEN   What? You'll put out my fire?

LEADER OF WOMEN   Just try and see!

LEADER OF MEN   I wonder: shall I scorch you with this torch of mine?

LEADER OF WOMEN   If you've got any soap, I'll give you a bath.

LEADER OF MEN   Give *me* a bath, you stinking hag?

LEADER OF WOMEN   Yes—a bridal bath!

LEADER OF MEN   Just listen to her! What crust!

LEADER OF WOMEN   Well, I'm a free citizen.

LEADER OF MEN   I'll put an end to your brawling.

The men pick up their torches.

LEADER OF WOMEN   You'll never do jury-duty again.

The women pick up their pitchers.

LEADER OF MEN   Singe her hair for her!
LEADER OF WOMEN   Do your duty, water!

The women empty their pitchers on the men.

LEADER OF MEN   Ow! Ow! For heaven's sake!

LEADER OF WOMEN   Is it too hot?

LEADER OF MEN   What do you mean "hot"? Stop! What are you doing?

LEADER OF WOMEN   I'm watering you, so you'll be fresh and green.

LEADER OF MEN   But I'm all withered up with shaking.

LEADER OF WOMEN   Well, you've got a fire; why don't you dry yourself?

Enter an Athenian Magistrate, accompanied by four Scythian policemen.

MAGISTRATE   Have these wanton women flared up again with their timbrels
and their continual worship of Sabazius? Is this another Adonis-dirge
upon the roof-tops—which we heard not long ago in the Assembly?
That confounded Demostratus was urging us to sail to Sicily, and the
whirling women shouted, "Woe for Adonis!" And then Demostratus
said we'd best enroll the infantry from Zacynthus, and a tipsy woman
on the roof shrieked, "Beat your breasts for Adonis!" And that vile and
filthy lunatic forced his measure through. Such license do our women
take.

LEADER OF MEN   What if you heard of the insolence of these women here?
Besides their other violent acts, they threw water all over us, and we
have to shake out our clothes just as if we'd leaked in them.

MAGISTRATE   And rightly, too, by God! For we ourselves lead the women
astray and teach them to play the wanton; from these roots such notions
blossom forth. A man goes into the jeweler's shop and says, "About
that necklace you made for my wife, goldsmith: last night, while she
was dancing, the fastening-bolt slipped out of the hole. I have to sail
over to Salamis today; if you're free, do come around tonight and fit in a
new bolt for her." Another goes to the shoe-maker, a strapping young
fellow with manly parts, and says, "See here, cobbler, the sandal-strap
chafes my wife's little—toe; it's so tender. Come around during the
siesta and stretch it a little, so she'll be more comfortable." Now we see
the results of such treatment: here I'm a special Councillor and need
money to procure oars for the galleys; and I'm locked out of the Treasury
by these women.

But this is no time to stand around. Bring up crow-bars there! I'll put
an end to their insolence. [*To one of the policemen*] What are you gaping
at, you wretch? What are you staring at? Got an eye out for a tavern, eh?
Set your crow-bars here to the gates and force them open. [*Retiring to a
safe distance*] I'll help from over here.

*The gates are thrown open and Lysistrata comes out followed by several other
women.*

LYSISTRATA   Don't force the gates; I'm coming out of my own accord. We don't need crow-bars here; what we need is good sound common-sense.

MAGISTRATE Is that so, you strumpet? Where's my policeman? Officer, arrest her and tie her arms behind her back.

LYSISTRATA By Artemis, if he lays a finger on me, he'll pay for it, even if he is a public servant.

The policeman retires in terror.

MAGISTRATE You there, are you afraid? Seize her round the waist—and you, too. Tie her up, both of you!

FIRST WOMAN *(as the second policeman approaches Lysistrata)* By Pandrosus, if you but touch her with your hand, I'll kick the stuffings out of you.

The second policeman retires in terror.

MAGISTRATE Just listen to that: "kick the stuffings out." Where's another policeman? Tie *her* up first, for her chatter.

SECOND WOMAN By the Goddess of the Light, if you lay the tip of your finger on her, you'll soon need a doctor.

The third policeman retires in terror.

MAGISTRATE What's this? Where's my policemen? Seize *her* too. I'll soon stop your sallies.

THIRD WOMAN By the Goddess of Tauros, if you go near her, I'll tear out your hair until it shrieks with pain.

The fourth policeman retires in terror.

MAGISTRATE Oh, damn it all! I've run out of policemen. But women must never defeat us. Officers, let's charge them all together. Close up your ranks!

The policemen rally for a mass attack.

LYSISTRATA By heaven, you'll soon find out that we have four companies of warrior-women, all fully equipped within!

MAGISTRATE [*advancing*] Twist their arms off, men!

LYSISTRATA [*shouting*] To the rescue, my valiant women!
O sellers-of-barley-green-stuffs-and-eggs,
O sellers-of-garlic, ye keepers-of-taverns, and vendors-of-bread,
Grapple! Smite! Smash!
Won't you heap filth on them? Give them a tongue-lashing!

The women beat off the policemen.

Halt! Withdraw! No looting on the field.

MAGISTRATE   Damn it! My police-force has put up a very poor show.

LYSISTRATA   What did you expect? Did you think you were attacking slaves?
Didn't you know that women are filled with passion?

MAGISTRATE   Aye, passion enough—for a good strong drink!

LEADER OF MEN   O chief and leader of this land, why spend your words in
vain?
Don't argue with these shameless beasts. You know not how we've
fared:
A soapless bath they've given us; our clothes are soundly soaked.

LEADER OF WOMEN   Poor fool! You never should attack or strike a peaceful
girl.
But if you do, your eyes must swell. For I am quite content
To sit unmoved, like modest maids, in peace and cause no pain;
But let a man stir up my hive, he'll find me like a wasp.

CHORUS OF MEN [*singing*]
O God, whatever shall we do with creatures like Womankind?
This can't be endured by any man alive. Question them!
Let us try to find out what this means.
To what end have they seized on this shrine,
This steep and rugged, high and holy,
Undefiled Acropolis?

LEADER OF MEN   Come, put your questions; don't give in, and probe her
every statement.
For base and shameful it would be to leave this plot untested.

MAGISTRATE   Well then, first of all I wish to ask her this: for what purpose
have you barred us from the Acropolis?

LYSISTRATA   To keep the treasure safe, so you won't make war on account of
it.

MAGISTRATE   What? Do we make war on account of the treasure?

LYSISTRATA   Yes, and you cause all our other troubles for it, too. Peisander
and those greedy office-seekers keep things stirred up so they can find
occasions to steal. Now let them do what they like: they'll never again
make off with any of this money.

MAGISTRATE   What will you do?

LYSISTRATA   What a question! We'll administer it ourselves.

MAGISTRATE   *You* will administer the treasure?

LYSISTRATA   What's so strange in that? Don't we administer the household
money for you?

MAGISTRATE   That's different.

LYSISTRATA   How is it different?

MAGISTRATE   We've got to make war with this money.

LYSISTRATA   But that's the very first thing: you mustn't make war.

MAGISTRATE   How else can we be saved?

LYSISTRATA   We'll save you.

MAGISTRATE   *You?*

LYSISTRATA   Yes, we!

MAGISTRATE   God forbid!

LYSISTRATA   We'll save you, whether you want it or not.

MAGISTRATE   Oh! This is terrible!

LYSISTRATA   You don't like it, but we're going to do it none the less.

MAGISTRATE   Good God! it's illegal!

LYSISTRATA   We *will* save you, my little man!

MAGISTRATE   Suppose I don't want you to?

LYSISTRATA   That's all the more reason.

MAGISTRATE   What business have you with war and peace?

LYSISTRATA   I'll explain.

MAGISTRATE   [*shaking his fist*]   Speak up, or you'll smart for it.

LYSISTRATA   Just listen, and try to keep your hands still.

MAGISTRATE   I can't. I'm so mad I can't stop them.

FIRST WOMAN   Then you'll be the one to smart for it.

MAGISTRATE   Croak to yourself, old hag! [*To Lysistrata*] Now then, speak up.

LYSISTRATA   Very well. Formerly we endured the war for a good long time with our usual restraint, no matter what you men did. You wouln't let us say "boo," although nothing you did suited us. But we watched you well, and though we stayed at home we'd often hear of some terribly stupid measure you'd proposed. Then, though grieving at heart, we'd smile sweetly and say, "What was passed in the Assembly today about writing on the treaty-stone?" "What's that to you?" my husband would say. "Hold your tongue!" And I held my tongue.

FIRST WOMAN   But I wouldn't have—not I!

MAGISTRATE   You'd have been soundly smacked, if you hadn't kept still.

LYSISTRATA   So I kept still at home. Then we'd hear of some plan still worse than the first; we'd say, "Husband, how could you pass such a stupid proposal!" He'd scowl at me and say, "If you don't mind your spinning, your head will be sore for weeks. *War shall be the concern of men.*"

MAGISTRATE   And he was right, upon my word!

LYSISTRATA   Why right, you confounded fool, when your proposals were so stupid and we weren't allowed to make any suggestions?

"There's not a *man* left in the country," says one. "No, not one," says another. Therefore all we women have decided in council to make a common effort to save Greece. How long should we have waited? Now, if you're willing to listen to our excellent proposals and keep silence for us in your turn, we still may save you.

MAGISTRATE   We men keep silence for you? That's terrible; I won't endure it!

LYSISTRATA   Silence!

MAGISTRATE   Silence for *you*, you wench, when you're wearing a snood? I'd rather die!

LYSISTRATA   Well, if that's all that bothers you—here! take my snood and tie it round your head. [*During the following words the women dress up the Magistrate in women's garments.*] And *now* keep quiet! Here, take this spinning-basket, too, and card your wool with robes tucked up, munching on beans. *War shall be the concern of Women!*

LEADER OF WOMEN   Arise and leave your pitchers, girls; no time is this to falter.

We too must aid our loyal friends; our turn has come for action.

CHORUS OF WOMEN [*singing*]

I'll never tire of aiding them with song and dance; never may
Faintness keep my legs from moving to and fro endlessly.
    For I yearn to do all for my friends;
    They have charm, they have wit, they have grace,
        With courage, brains, and best of virtues—
            Patriotic sapience.

LEADER OF WOMEN   Come, child of manliest ancient dames, offspring of stinging nettles,

Advance with rage unsoftened; for fair breezes speed you onward.

LYSISTRATA   If only sweet Eros and the Cyprian Queen of Love shed charm over our breasts and limbs and inspire our men with amorous longing and priapic spasms, I think we may soon be called Peacemakers among the Greeks.

MAGISTRATE   What will you do?

LYSISTRATA   First of all, we'll stop those fellows who run madly about the Marketplace in arms.

FIRST WOMAN   Indeed we shall, by the Queen of Paphos.

LYSISTRATA   For now they roam about the market, amid the pots and greenstuffs, armed to the teeth like Corybantes.

MAGISTRATE   That's what manly fellows ought to do!

LYSISTRATA   But it's so silly: a chap with a Gorgon-emblazoned shield buying pickled herring.

FIRST WOMAN   Why, just the other day I saw one of those long-haired dandies who command our cavalry ride up on horseback and pour into his bronze helmet the egg-broth he'd bought from an old dame. And there was a Thracian slinger too, shaking his lance like Tereus; he'd scared the life out of the poor fig-peddler and was gulping down all her ripest fruit.

MAGISTRATE   How can you stop all the confusion in the various states and bring them together?

LYSISTRATA   Very easily.

MAGISTRATE   Tell me how.

LYSISTRATA   Just like a ball of wool, when it's confused and snarled: we take it thus, and draw out a thread here and a thread there with our spindles; thus we'll unsnarl this war, if no one prevents us, and draw together the various states with embassies here and embassies there.

MAGISTRATE   Do you suppose you can stop this dreadful business with balls of wool and spindles, you nit-wits?

LYSISTRATA   Why, if *you* had any wits, you'd manage all affairs of state like our wool-working.

MAGISTRATE   How so?

LYSISTRATA   First you ought to treat the city as we do when we wash the dirt out of a fleece: stretch it out and pluck and thrash out of the city all those prickly scoundrels; aye, and card out those who conspire and stick together to gain office, pulling off their heads. Then card the wool, all of it, into one fair basket of goodwill, mingling in the aliens residing here, any loyal foreigners, and anyone who's in debt to the Treasury; and consider that all our colonies lie scattered round about like remnants; from all of these collect the wool and gather it together here, wind up a great ball, and then weave a good stout cloak for the democracy.

MAGISTRATE   Dreadful! Talking about thrashing and winding balls of wool, when you haven't the slightest share in the war!

LYSISTRATA   Why, you dirty scoundrel, we bear more than twice as much as you. First, we bear children and send off our sons as soldiers.

MAGISTRATE   Hush! Let bygones be bygones!

LYSISTRATA   Then, when we ought to be happy and enjoy our youth, we sleep alone because of your expeditions abroad. But never mind us married women: I grieve most for the maids who grow old at home unwed.

MAGISTRATE   Don't men grow old, too?

LYSISTRATA   For heaven's sake! That's not the same thing. When a man comes home, no matter how grey he is, he soon finds a girl to marry. But woman's bloom is short and fleeting; if she doesn't grasp her chance, no man is willing to marry her and she sits at home a prey to every fortune-teller.

MAGISTRATE [*coarsely*]   But if a man can still get it up—

LYSISTRATA   See here, you: what's the matter? Aren't you dead yet? There's plenty of room for you. Buy yourself a shroud and I'll bake you a honey-cake. [*Handing him a copper coin for his passage across the Styx*] Here's your fare! Now get yourself a wreath.

During the following dialogue the women dress up the Magistrate as a corpse.

FIRST WOMAN   Here, take these fillets.

SECOND WOMAN   Here, take this wreath.

LYSISTRATA   What do you want? What's lacking? Get moving; off to the ferry! Charon is calling you; don't keep him from sailing.

MAGISTRATE   Am I to endure these insults? By God! I'm going straight to the
magistrates to show them how I've been treated.

LYSISTRATA   Are you grumbling that you haven't been properly laid out?
Well, the day after tomorrow we'll send around all the usual offerings
early in the morning.

*The Magistrate goes out still wearing his funeral decorations. Lysistrata and the
women retire into the Acropolis.*

LEADER OF MEN   Wake, ye sons of freedom, wake! 'Tis no time for sleeping.
Up and at them, like a man! Let us strip for action.

The Chorus of Men remove their outer cloaks.

CHORUS OF MEN [*singing*]
Surely there is something here greater than meets the eye;
For without a doubt I smell Hippias' tyrrany.
Dreadful fear assails me lest certain bands of Spartan men,
Meeting here with Cleisthenes, have inspired through treachery
All these god-detested women secretly to seize
Athens' treasure in the temple, and to stop that pay
    Whence I live at my ease.
LEADER OF MEN   Now isn't it terrible for them to advise the state and chatter
about shields, being mere women?
And they think to reconcile us with the Spartans—men who hold
nothing sacred any more than hungry wolves. Surely this is a web of
deceit, my friends, to conceal an attempt at tyranny. But they'll never
lord it over me; I'll be on my guard and from now on,
    "The blade I bear   A myrtle spray shall wear."
I'll occupy the market under arms and stand next to Aristogeiton.
Thus I'll stand beside him [*He strikes the pose of the famous statue of the
tyrannicides, with one arm raised.*] And here's my chance to take this
accurst old hag and—[*striking the Leader of Women*] smack her on the
jaw!
LEADER OF WOMEN   You'll go home in such a state your Ma won't recognize
you!
Ladies all, upon the ground let us place these garments.

The Chorus of Women remove their outer garments.

CHORUS OF WOMEN [*singing*]
Citizens of Athens, hear useful words for the state.
Rightly; for it nurtured me in my youth royally.
As a child of seven years carried I the sacred box;

Then I was a Miller-maid, grinding at Athene's shrine;
Next I wore the saffron robe and played Brauronia's Bear;
And I walked as a Basket-bearer, wearing chains of figs,
    As a sweet maiden fair.

LEADER OF WOMEN   Therefore, am I not bound to give good advice to the city?

Don't take it ill that I was born a woman, if I contribute something better than our present troubles. I pay my share; for I contribute MEN. But you miserable old fools contribute nothing, and after squandering our ancestral treasure, the fruit of the Persian Wars, you make no contribution in return. And now, all on account of you, we're facing ruin.

What, muttering, are you? If you annoy me, I'll take this hard, rough slipper and—[striking the Leader of Men] smack you on the jaw!

CHORUS OF MEN [singing]

This is outright insolence! Things go from bad to worse.
If you're men with any guts, prepare to meet the foe.
Let us strip our tunics off! We need the smell of male
Vigour. And we cannot fight all swaddled up in clothes.

They strip off their tunics.

Come then, my comrades, on to the battle, ye once to Leipsydrion came;
    Then ye were MEN. Now call back your youthful vigour.
With light, wingèd footstep advance,
    Shaking old age from your frame.

LEADER OF MEN   If any of us give these wenches the slightest hold, they'll stop at nothing; such is their cunning.

They will even build ships and sail against us, like Artemisia. Or if they turn to mounting, I count our Knights as done for: a woman's such a tricky jockey when she gets astraddle, with a good firm seat for trotting. Just look at those Amazons that Micon painted, fighting on horseback against men!

But we must throw them all in the pillory—[seizing and choking the Leader of Women] grabbing hold of yonder neck!

CHORUS OF WOMEN [singing]

'Ware my anger! Like a boar 'twill rush upon you men.
Soon you'll bawl aloud for help, you'll be so soundly trimmed!
Come, my friends, let's strip with speed, and lay aside these robes;
Catch the scent of women's rage. Attack with tooth and nail!

They strip off their tunics.

Now then, come near me, you miserable man! You'll never eat garlic or
   black beans again.
And if you utter a single hard word, in rage I will "nurse" you as once
   The beetle requited her foe.
LEADER OF WOMEN   For you don't worry me; no, not so long as my Lampito
   lives and our Theban friend, the noble Ismenia.
   You can't do anything, not even if you pass a dozen—decrees! You
   miserable fool, all our neighbours hate you. Why, just the other day
   when I was holding a festival for Hecate, I invited as playmate from our
   neighbours the Boeotians a charming, wellbred Copaic—eel. But they
   refused to send me one on account of your decrees.
   And you'll never stop passing decrees until I grab your foot and—
   [tripping up the Leader of Men] toss you down and break your neck!

Here an interval of five days is supposed to elapse. Lysistrata comes out from the
Acropolis.

LEADER OF WOMEN [dramatically]   Empress of this great emprise and under-
   taking,
Why come you forth, I pray, with frowning brow?
LYSISTRATA   Ah, these cursèd women! Their deeds and female notions make
   me pace up and down in utter despair.
LEADER OF WOMEN   Ah, what sayest thou?
LYSISTRATA   The truth, alas! the truth.
LEADER OF WOMEN   What dreadful tale hast thou to tell thy friends?
LYSISTRATA   'Tis shame to speak, and not to speak is hard.
LEADER OF WOMEN   Hide not from me whatever woes we suffer.
LYSISTRATA   Well then, to put it briefly, we want—laying!
LEADER OF WOMEN   O Zeus, Zeus!
LYSISTRATA   Why call on Zeus? That's the way things are. I can no longer
   keep them away from the men, and they're all deserting. I caught one
   wriggling through a hole near the grotto of Pan, another sliding down
   a rope, another deserting her post; and yesterday I found one getting on
   a sparrow's back to fly off to Orsilochus, and had to pull her back by the
   hair. They're digging up all sorts of excuses to get home. Look, here
   comes one of them now.

A woman comes hastily out of the Acropolis.

Here you! Where are you off to in such a hurry?
FIRST WOMAN   I want to go home. My very best wool is being devoured by
   moths.
LYSISTRATA   Moths? Nonsense! Go back inside.

FIRST WOMAN   I'll come right back; I swear it. I just want to lay it out on the bed.

LYSISTRATA   Well, you won't lay it out, and you won't go home, either.

FIRST WOMAN   Shall I let my wool be ruined?

LYSISTRATA   If necessary, yes.

Another woman comes out.

SECOND WOMAN   Oh dear! Oh dear! My precious flax! I left it at home all unpeeled.

LYSISTRATA   Here's another one, going home for her "flax." Come back here!

SECOND WOMAN   But I just want to work it up a little and then I'll be right back.

LYSISTRATA   No indeed! If you start this, all the other women will want to do the same.

A third woman comes out.

THIRD WOMAN   O Eilithyia, goddess of travail, stop my labour till I come to a lawful spot!

LYSISTRATA   What's this nonsense?

THIRD WOMAN   I'm going to have a baby—right now!

LYSISTRATA   But you weren't even pregnant yesterday.

THIRD WOMAN   Well, I am today. O Lysistrata, do send me home to see a midwife, right away.

LYSISTRATA   What are you talking about? [*Putting her hand on her stomach*] What's this hard lump here?

THIRD WOMAN   A little boy.

LYSISTRATA   My goodness, what have you got there? It seems hollow; I'll just find out. [*Pulling aside her robe*] Why, you silly goose, you've got Athene's sacred helmet there. And you said you were having a baby!

THIRD WOMAN   Well, I *am* having one, I swear!

LYSISTRATA   Then what's this helmet for?

THIRD WOMAN   If the baby starts coming while I'm still in the Acropolis, I'll creep into this like a pigeon and give birth to it there.

LYSISTRATA   Stuff and nonsense! It's plain enough what you're up to. You just wait here for the christening of this—helmet.

THIRD WOMAN   But I can't sleep in the Acropolis since I saw the sacred snake.

FIRST WOMAN   And I'm dying for lack of sleep: the hooting of the owls keep me awake.

LYSISTRATA   Enough of these shams, you wretched creatures. You want your husbands, I suppose. Well, don't you think they want us? I'm sure

they're spending miserable nights. Hold out, my friends, and endure
for just a little while. There's an oracle that we shall conquer, if we don't
split up. [*Producing a roll of paper*] Here it is.

FIRST WOMAN   Tell us what it says.

LYSISTRATA   Listen.
"When in the length of time the Swallows shall gather together,
Fleeing the Hoopoe's amorous flight and the Cockatoo shunning,
Then shall your woes be ended and Zeus who thunders in heaven
Set what's below on top—"

FIRST WOMAN   What? Are we going to be on top?

LYSISTRATA   "But if the Swallows rebel and flutter away from the temple,
Never a bird in the world shall seem more wanton and worthless."

FIRST WOMAN   That's clear enough, upon my word!

LYSISTRATA   By all that's holy, let's not give up the struggle now. Let's go
back inside. It would be a shame, my dear friends, to disobey the
oracle.

The women all retire to the Acropolis again.

CHORUS OF MEN [*singing*]
I have a tale to tell,
Which I know full well.
It was told me
In the nursery.

Once there was a likely lad,
Melanion they name him;
The thought of marriage made him mad,
For which I cannot blame him.

So off he went to mountains fair;
(No women to upbraid him!)
A mighty hunter of the hare,
He had a dog to aid him.

He never came back home to see
Detested women's faces.
He showed a shrewd mentality.
With him I'd fain change places!

ONE OF THE MEN [*to one of the women*]   Come here, old dame; give me a kiss.

WOMAN   You'll ne'er eat garlic, if you dare!

MAN   I want to kick you—just like this!

WOMAN   Oh, there's a leg with bushy hair!

MAN   Myronides and Phormio
    Were hairy—and they thrashed the foe.

CHORUS OF WOMEN [*singing*]
    I have another tale,
    With which to assail
      Your contention
      'Bout Melanion.

    Once upon a time a man
      Named Timon left our city,
    To live in some deserted land.
      (We thought him rather witty.)

    He dwelt alone amidst the thorn;
      In solitude he brooded.
    From some grim Fury he was born:
      Such hatred he exuded.

    He cursed you men, as scoundrels through
      And through, till life he ended.
    He couldn't stand the sight of you!
      But women he befriended.

WOMAN [*to one of the men*]   I'll smash your face in, if you like.
MAN   Oh no, please don't! You frighten me.
WOMAN   I'll lift my foot—and thus I'll strike.
MAN   Aha! Look there! What's that I see?
WOMAN   Whate'er you see, you cannot say
    That I'm not neatly trimmed today.

Lysistrata appears on the wall of the Acropolis.

LYSISTRATA   Hello! Hello! Girls, come here quick!

Several women appear beside her.

WOMAN   What is it? Why are you calling?
LYSISTRATA   I see a man coming: he's in a dreadful state. He's mad with
    passion. O Queen of Cyprus, Cythera, and Paphos, just keep on this
    way!
WOMAN   Where is the fellow?
LYSISTRATA   There, beside the shrine of Demeter.

WOMAN Oh yes, so he is. Who is he?

LYSISTRATA Let's see. Do any of you know him?

MYRRHINE Yes indeed. That's my husband, Cinesias.

LYSISTRATA It's up to you, now: roast him, rack him, fool him, love him— and leave him! Do everything, except what our oath forbids.

MYRRHINE Don't worry; I'll do it.

LYSISTRATA I'll stay here to tease him and warm him up a bit. Off with you.

The other women retire from the wall. Enter Cinesias followed by a slave carrying a baby. Cinesias is obviously in great pain and distress.

CINESIAS [*groaning*] Oh-h! Oh-h-h! This is killing me! O God, what tortures I'm suffering!

LYSISTRATA [*from the wall*] Who's that within our lines?

CINESIAS Me.

LYSISTRATA A *man?*

CINESIAS [*pointing*] A *man*, indeed!

LYSISTRATA Well, go away!

CINESIAS Who are you to send me away?

LYSISTRATA The captain of the guard.

CINESIAS Oh, for heaven's sake, call out Myrrhine for me.

LYSISTRATA Call Myrrhine? Nonsense! Who are you?

CINESIAS Her husband, Cinesias of Paionidai.

LYSISTRATA [*appearing much impressed*] Oh, greetings, friend. Your name is not without honour here among us. Your wife is always talking about you, and whenever she takes an egg or an apple, she says, "Here's to my dear Cinesias!"

CINESIAS [*quivering with excitement*] Oh, ye gods in heaven!

LYSISTRATA Indeed she does! And whenever our conversations turn to men, your wife immediately says, "All others are mere rubbish compared with Cinesias."

CINESIAS [*groaning*] Oh! Do call her for me.

LYSISTRATA Why should I? What will you give me?

CINESIAS Whatever you want. All I have is yours—and you see what I've got.

LYSISTRATA Well then, I'll go down and call her. [*She descends.*]

CINESIAS And hurry up! I've had no joy of life ever since she left home. When I go in the house, I feel awful: everything seems so empty and I can't enjoy my dinner. I'm in such a state all the time!

MYRRHINE [*from behind the wall*] I *do* love him so. But he won't let me love him. No, no! Don't ask me to see him!

CINESIAS O my darling, O Myrrhine honey, why do you do this to me?

Myrrhine appears on the wall.

Come down here!

MYRRHINE   No, I won't come down.

CINESIAS   Won't you come, Myrrhine, when I call you?

MYRRHINE   No; you don't want me.

CINESIAS   *Don't want you?* I'm in agony!

MYRRHINE   I'm going now.

CINESIAS   Please don't. At least, listen to your baby. [*To the baby*] Here you,
    call your mamma! [*Pinching the baby*]

BABY   Ma-ma! Ma-ma! Ma-ma!

CINESIAS [*to Myrrhine*]   What's the matter with you? Have you no pity for
    your child, who hasn't been washed or fed for five whole days?

MYRRHINE   Oh, poor child; your father pays no attention to you.

CINESIAS   Come down then, you heartless wretch, for the baby's sake.

MYRRHINE   Oh, what it is to be a mother! I've got to come down, I suppose.

She leaves the wall and shortly reappears at the gate.

CINESIAS [*to himself*]   She seems much younger, and she has such a sweet
    look about her. Oh, the way she teases me! And her pretty, provoking
    ways make me burn with longing.

MYRRHINE [*coming out of the gate and taking the baby*]   O my sweet little angel.
    Naughty papa! Here, let Mummy kiss you, Mamma's little sweetheart!

She fondles the baby lovingly.

CINESIAS [*in despair*]   You heartless creature, why do you do this? Why fol-
    low these other women and make both of us suffer so?

He tries to embrace her.

MYRRHINE   Don't touch me!

CINESIAS   You're letting all our things at home go to wrack and ruin.

MYRRHINE   I don't care.

CINESIAS   You don't care that your wool is being plucked to pieces by the
    chickens?

MYRRHINE   Not in the least.

CINESIAS   And you haven't celebrated the rites of Aphrodite for ever so long.
    Won't you come home?

MYRRHINE   Not on your life, unless you men make a truce and stop the war.

CINESIAS   Well, then, if that pleases you, we'll do it.

MYRRHINE   Well then, if that pleases *you*, I'll come home—afterwards! Right now I'm on oath not to.

CINESIAS   Then just lie down here with me for a moment.

MYRRHINE   No—[*in a teasing voice*] and yet I won't say I don't love you.

CINESIAS   You love me? Oh, do lie down here, Myrrhine dear!

MYRRHINE   What, you silly fool! in front of the baby?

CINESIAS [*hastily thrusting the baby at the slave*]   Of course not. Here—home! Take him, Manes! [*The slave goes off with the baby.*] See, the baby's out of the way. Now won't you lie down?

MYRRHINE   But where, my dear?

CINESIAS   Where? The grotto of Pan's a lovely spot.

MYRRHINE   How could I purify myself before returning to the shrine?

CINESIAS   Easily: just wash here in the Clepsydra.

MYRRHINE   And then, shall I go back on my oath?

CINESIAS   On my head be it! Don't worry about the oath.

MYRRHINE   All right, then. Just let me bring out a bed.

CINESIAS   No, don't. The ground's all right.

MYRRHINE   Heavens, no! Bad as you are, I won't let you lie on the bare ground.

She goes into the Acropolis.

CINESIAS   Why, she really loves me; it's plain to see.

MYRRHINE [*returning with a bed*]   There! Now hurry up and lie down. I'll just slip off this dress. But—let's see: oh yes, I must fetch a mattress.

CINESIAS   Nonsense! No mattress for me.

MYRRHINE   Yes indeed! It's not nice on the bare springs.

CINESIAS   Give me a kiss.

MYRRHINE [*giving him a hasty kiss*]   There!

She goes.

CINESIAS [*in mingled distress and delight*]   Oh-h! Hurry back!

MYRRHINE [*returning with a mattress*]   Here's the mattress; lie down on it. I'm taking my things off now—but—let's see: you have no pillow.

CINESIAS   I don't *want* a pillow.

MYRRHINE   But I do.

She goes.

CINESIAS   Cheated again, just like Heracles and his dinner!

MYRRHINE [*returning with a pillow*]   Here, lift your head. [*To herself, wondering how else to tease him*] Is that all?

CINESIAS   Surely that's all! Do come here, precious!

MYRRHINE   I'm taking off my girdle. But remember: don't go back on your promise about the truce.

CINESIAS   I hope to die, if I do.

MYRRHINE   You don't have a blanket.

CINESIAS   [shouting in exasperation]   I don't want one! I WANT TO—

MYRRHINE   Sh-h! There, there, I'll be back in a minute.

She goes.

CINESIAS   She'll be the death of me with these bed-clothes.

MYRRHINE   [returning with a blanket]   Here, get up.

CINESIAS   I've got *this* up!

MYRRHINE   Would you like some perfume?

CINESIAS   Good heavens, no! I won't have it!

MYRRHINE   Yes, you shall, whether you want it or not.

She goes.

CINESIAS   O lord! Confound all perfumes anyway!

MYRRHINE   [returning with a flask]   Stretch out your hand and put some on.

CINESIAS   [suspiciously]   By God, I don't much like this perfume. It smacks of shilly-shallying, and has no scent of the marriage-bed.

MYRRHINE   Oh dear! This is Rhodian perfume I've brought.

CINESIAS   It's quite all right, dear. Never mind.

MYRRHINE   Don't be silly!

She goes out with the flask.

CINESIAS   Damn the man who first concocted perfumes!

MYRRHINE   [returning with another flask]   Here, try this flask.

CINESIAS   I've got another one all ready for you. Come, you wretch, lie down and stop bringing me things.

MYRRHINE   All right; I'm taking off my shoes. But, my dear, see that you vote for peace.

CINESIAS   [absently]   I'll consider it.

Myrrhine runs away to the Acropolis.

I'm ruined! The wench has skinned me and run away! [chanting, in tragic style] Alas! Alas! Deceived, deserted by this fairest of women, whom shall I—lay? Ah, my poor little child, how shall I nurture thee? Where's Cynalopex? I needs must hire a nurse!

LEADER OF MEN   [chanting]   Ah, wretched man, in dreadful wise beguiled, bewrayed, thy soul is sore distressed. I pity thee, alas! alas! What soul, what loins, what liver could stand this strain? How firm and unyielding he stands, with naught to aid him of a morning.

CINESIAS   O lord! O Zeus! What tortures I endure!

LEADER OF MEN   This is the way she's treated you, that vile and cursèd wanton.

LEADER OF WOMEN   Nay, not vile and cursèd, but sweet and dear.

LEADER OF MEN   Sweet, you say? Nay, hateful, hateful!

CINESIAS   Hateful indeed! O Zeus, Zeus!

Seize her and snatch her away,
Like a handful of dust, in a mighty,
Fiery tempest! Whirl her aloft, then let her drop
Down to the earth, with a crash, as she falls—
On the point of this waiting
    Thingummybob!

He goes out.
Enter a Spartan Herald, in an obvious state of excitement, which he is doing his best to conceal.

HERALD   Where can I find the Senate or the Prytanes? I've got an important message.

The Athenian Magistrate enters.

MAGISTRATE   Say there, are you a man or Priapus?

HERALD [*in annoyance*]   I'm a herald, you lout! I've come from Sparta about the truce.

MAGISTRATE   Is that a spear you've got under your cloak?

HERALD   No, of course not!

MAGISTRATE   Why do you twist and turn so? Why hold your cloak in front of you? Did you rupture yourself on the trip?

HERALD   By gum, the fellow's an old fool.

MAGISTRATE [*pointing*]   Why, you dirty rascal, you're all excited.

HERALD   Not at all. Stop this tom-foolery.

MAGISTRATE   Well, what's that I see?

HERALD   A Spartan message-staff.

MAGISTRATE   Oh, certainly! That's just the kind of message-staff I've got. But tell me the honest truth: how are things going in Sparta?

HERALD   All the land of Sparta is up in arms—and our allies are up, too. We need Pellene.

MAGISTRATE   What brought this trouble on you? A sudden Panic?

HERALD   No, Lampito started it and then all the other women in Sparta with one accord chased their husbands out of their beds.

MAGISTRATE   How do you feel?

HERALD   Terrible. We walk around the city bent over like men lighting matches in a wind. For our women won't let us touch them until we all agree and make peace throughout Greece.

MAGISTRATE   This is a general conspiracy of the women; I see it now. Well, hurry back and tell the Spartans to send ambassadors here with full powers to arrange a truce. And I'll go tell the Council to choose ambassadors from here; I've got something here that will soon persuade them!

HERALD   I'll fly there; for you've made an excellent suggestion.

The Herald and the Magistrate depart on opposite sides of the stage.

LEADER OF MEN   No beast or fire is harder than womankind to tame,
Nor is the spotted leopard so devoid of shame.

LEADER OF WOMEN   Knowing this, you dare provoke us to attack?
I'd be your steady friend, if you'd but take us back.

LEADER OF MEN   I'll never cease my hatred keen of womankind.

LEADER OF WOMEN   Just as you will. But now just let me help you find
That cloak you threw aside. You look so silly there
Without your clothes. Here, put it on and don't go bare.

LEADER OF MEN   That's very kind, and shows you're not entirely bad.
But I threw off my things when I was good and mad.

LEADER OF WOMEN   At last you seem a man, and won't be mocked, my lad.
If you'd been nice to me, I'd take this little gnat
That's in your eye and pluck it out for you, like that.

LEADER OF MEN   So that's what's bothered me and bit my eye so long!
Please dig it out for me. I own that I've been wrong.

LEADER OF WOMEN   I'll do so, though you've been a most ill-natured brat.
Ye gods! See here! A huge and monstrous little gnat!

LEADER OF MEN   Oh, how that helps! For it was digging wells in me.
And now it's out, my tears can roll down hard and free.

LEADER OF WOMEN   Here, let me wipe them off, although you're such a knave,
And kiss me.

LEADER OF MEN   No!

LEADER OF WOMEN   Whate'er you say, a kiss I'll have.

She kisses him.

LEADER OF MEN   Oh, confound these women! They've a coaxing way about them.
He was wise and never spoke a truer word, who said,
"We can't live with women, but we cannot live without them."
Now I'll make a truce with you. We'll fight no more; instead,

I will not injure you if you do me no wrong.
And now let's join our ranks and then begin a song.
COMBINED CHORUS [*singing*]

Athenians, we're not prepared,
To say a single ugly word
About our fellow-citizens.
Quite the contrary: we desire but to say and to do
Naught but good. Quite enough are the ills now on hand.

Men and women, be advised:
If anyone requires
Money—minae two or three—
We've got what he desires.

My purse is yours, on easy terms:
When Peace shall reappear,
Whate'er you've borrowed will be due.
So speak up without fear.

You needn't pay me back, you see,
If you can get a cent from me!

We're about to entertain
Some foreign gentlemen;
We've soup and tender, fresh-killed pork.
Come round to dine at ten.

Come early; wash and dress with care,
And bring the children, too.
Then step right in, no "by your leave."
We'll be expecting you.

Walk in as if you owned the place.
You'll find the door—shut in your face!

*Enter a group of Spartan Ambassadors; they are in the same desperate condition as
the Herald in the previous scene.*

LEADER OF CHORUS   Here comes the envoys from Sparta, sprouting long
beards and looking for the world as if they were carrying pig-pens in
front of them.
Greetings, gentlemen of Sparta. Tell me, in what state have you come?

SPARTAN   Why waste words? You can plainly see what state we've come in!

LEADER OF CHORUS   Wow! You're in a pretty high-strung condition, and it seems to be getting worse.

SPARTAN   It's indescribable. Won't someone please arrange a peace for us—in any way you like.

LEADER OF CHORUS   Here come our own, native ambassadors, crouching like wrestlers and holding their clothes in front of them; this seems an athletic kind of malady.

Enter several Athenian Ambassadors.

ATHENIAN   Can anyone tell us where Lysistrata is? You see our condition.

LEADER OF CHORUS   Here's another case of the same complaint. Tell me, are the attacks worse in the morning?

ATHENIAN   No, we're always afflicted this way. If someone doesn't soon arrange this truce, you'd better not let me get my hands on— Cleisthenes!

LEADER OF CHORUS   If you're smart, you'll arrange your cloaks so none of these fellows who smashed the Hermae can see you.

ATHENIAN   Right you are; a very good suggestion.

SPARTAN   Aye, by all means. Here, let's hitch up our clothes.

ATHENIAN   Greetings, Spartan. We've suffered dreadful things.

SPARTAN   My dear fellow, we'd have suffered still worse if one of those fellows had seen us in this condition.

ATHENIAN   Well, gentlemen, we must get down to business. What's your errand here?

SPARTAN   We're ambassadors about peace.

ATHENIAN   Excellent; so are we. Only Lysistrata can arrange things for us; shall we summon her?

SPARTAN   Aye, and Lysistratus too, if you like.

LEADER OF CHORUS   No need to summon her, it seems. She's coming out of her own accord.

Enter Lysistrata accompanied by a statue of a nude female figure, which represents Reconciliation.

> Hail, noblest of women; now must thou be
> A judge shrewd and subtle, mild and severe,
> Be sweet yet majestic: all manners employ.
> The leaders of Hellas, caught by thy love-charms,
> Have come to thy judgment, their charges submitting.

LYSISTRATA   This is no difficult task, if one catch them still in amorous passion, before they've resorted to each other. But I'll soon find out. Where's Reconciliation? Go, first bring the Spartans here, and don't seize them rudely and violently, as our tactless husbands used to do, but as befits a woman, like an old, familiar friend; if they won't give you their hands, take them however you can. Then go fetch these Athenians here, taking hold of whatever they offer you. Now then, men of Sparta, stand here beside me, and you Athenians on the other side, and listen to my words.

I am a woman, it is true, but I have a mind; I'm not badly off in native wit, and by listening to my father and my elders, I've had a decent schooling.

Now I intend to give you a scolding which you both deserve. With one common font you worship at the same altars, just like brothers, at Olympia, at Thermopylae, at Delphi—how many more might I name, if time permitted;—and the Barbarians stand by waiting with their armies; yet you are destroying the men and towns of Greece.

ATHENIAN   Oh, this tension is killing me!

LYSISTRATA   And now, men of Sparta,—to turn to you—don't you remember how the Spartan Pericleidas came here once as a suppliant, and sitting at our altar, all pale with fear in his crimson cloak, begged us for an army? For all Messene had attacked you and the god sent an earthquake too? Then Cimon went forth with four thousand hoplites and saved all Lacedaemon. Such was the aid you received from Athens, and now you lay waste the country which once treated you so well.

ATHENIAN   [hotly]   They're in the wrong, Lysistrata, upon my word, they are!

SPARTAN   [absently, looking at the statue of Reconciliation]   We're in the wrong. What hips! How lovely they are!

LYSISTRATA   Don't think I'm going to let you Athenians off. Don't you remember how the Spartans came in arms when you were wearing the rough, sheepskin cloak of slaves and slew the host of Thessalians, the comrades and allies of Hippias? Fighting with you on that day, alone of all the Greeks, they set you free and instead of a sheepskin gave your folk a handsome robe to wear.

SPARTAN   [looking at Lysistrata]   I've never seen a more distinguished woman.

ATHENIAN   [looking at Reconciliation]   I've never seen a more voluptuous body!

LYSISTRATA   Why then, with these many noble deeds to think of, do you fight each other? Why don't you stop this villany? Why not make peace? Tell me, what prevents it?

SPARTAN   [waving vaguely at Reconciliation]   We're willing, if you're willing to give up your position on yonder flank.

LYSISTRATA   What position, my good man?

SPARTAN   Pylus; we've been panting for it for ever so long.

ATHENIAN   No, by God! You shan't have it!

LYSISTRATA Let them have it, my friend.

ATHENIAN Then what shall we have to rouse things up?

LYSISTRATA Ask for another place in exchange.

ATHENIAN Well, let's see: first of all [pointing to various parts of Reconciliation's anatomy] give us Echinus here, this Maliac Inlet in back there, and
these two Megarian legs.

SPARTAN No, by heavens! You can't have everything, you crazy fool!

LYSISTRATA Let it go. Don't fight over a pair of legs.

ATHENIAN [taking off his cloak] I think I'll strip and do a little planting now.

SPARTAN [following suit] And I'll just do a little fertilizing, by gosh!

LYSISTRATA Wait until the truce is concluded. Now if you've decided on
this course, hold a conference and discuss the matter with your allies.

ATHENIAN Allies? Don't be ridiculous! They're in the same state we are.
Won't all our allies want the same thing we do—to jump in bed with
their women?

SPARTAN Ours will, I know.

ATHENIAN Especially the Carystians, by God!

LYSISTRATA Very well. Now purify yourselves, that your wives may feast
and entertain you in the Acropolis; we've provisions by the basketfull.
Exchange your oaths and pledges there, and then each of you may take
his wife and go home.

ATHENIAN Let's go at once.

SPARTAN Come on, where you will.

ATHENIAN For God's sake, let's hurry!

They all go into the Acropolis.

CHORUS [singing]
    Whate'er I have of coverlets
      And robes of varied hue
    And golden trinkets,—without stint
      I offer them to you.

    Take what you will and bear it home,
      Your children to delight,
    Or if your girl's a Basket-maid;
      Just choose whate'er's in sight.

    There's naught within so well secured
      You cannot break the seal
    And bear it off; just help yourselves;
      No hesitation feel.

But you'll see nothing, though you try,
Unless you've sharper eyes than I!

If anyone needs bread to feed
  A growing family,
I've lots of wheat and full-grown loaves;
  So just apply to me.

Let every poor man who desires
  Come round and bring a sack
To fetch the grain; my slave is there
  To load it on his back.

But don't come near my door, I say:
Beware the dog, and stay away!

An Athenian enters carrying a torch; he knocks at the gate.

ATHENIAN   Open the door! [*To the Chorus, which is clustered around the gate*]
  Make way, won't you! What are you hanging around for? Want me to
  singe you with this torch? [*To himself*] No; it's a stale trick, I won't do it!
  [*To the audience*] Still if I've got to do it to please *you*, I suppose I'll have
  to take the trouble.

A Second Athenian comes out of the gate.

SECOND ATHENIAN   And I'll help you.
FIRST ATHENIAN [*waving his torch at the Chorus*]   Get out! Go bawl your
  heads off! Move on there, so the Spartans can leave in peace when the
  banquet's over.

They brandish their torches until the Chorus leaves the Orchestra.

SECOND ATHENIAN   I've never seen such a pleasant banquet: the Spartans are
  charming fellows, indeed they are! And we Athenians are very witty in
  our cups.
FIRST ATHENIAN   Naturally: for when we're sober we're never at our best. If
  the Athenians would listen to me, we'd always get a little tipsy on our
  embassies. As things are now, we go to Sparta when we're sober and
  look around to stir up trouble. And then we don't hear what they say—
  and as for what they *don't* say, we have all sorts of suspicions. And then
  we bring back varying reports about the mission. But this time every-

thing is pleasant; even if a man should sing the Telamon-song when he ought to sing "Cleitagorus," we'd praise him and swear it was excellent.

The two Choruses return, as a Chorus of Athenians and a Chorus of Spartans.

Here they come back again. Go to the devil, you scoundrels!
SECOND ATHENIAN   Get out, I say! They're coming out from the feast.

Enter the Spartan and Athenian envoys, followed by Lysistrata and all the women.

SPARTAN [*to one of his fellow-envoys*]   My good fellow, take up your pipes; I want to do a fancy two-step and sing a jolly song for the Athenians.
ATHENIAN   Yes, do take your pipes, by all means. I'd love to see you dance.
SPARTAN [*singing and dancing with the Chorus of Spartans*]
        These youths inspire
    To song and dance, O Memory;
    Stir up my Muse, to tell how we
    And Athens' men, in our galleys clashing
    At Artemisium, 'gainst foemen dashing
        In godlike ire,
    Conquered the Persian and set Greece free.

        Leonidas
    Led on his valiant warriors
    Whetting their teeth like angry boars.
    Abundant foam on their lips was flow'ring,
    A stream of sweat from their limbs was show'ring.
        The Persian was
    Numberless as the sand on the shores.

    O Huntress who slayest the beasts in the glade,
    O Virgin divine, hither come to our truce,
    Unite us in bonds which all time will not loose.
    Grant us to find in this treaty, we pray,
    An unfailing source of true friendship today,
    And all of our days, helping us to refrain
    From weaseling tricks which bring war in their train.
        Then hither, come hither! O huntress maid.

LYSISTRATA   Come then, since all is fairly done, men of Sparta, lead away your wives, and you, Athenians, take yours. Let every man stand beside his wife, and every wife beside her man, and then, to celebrate our fortune, let's dance. And in the future, let's take care to avoid these misunderstandings.

CHORUS OF ATHENIANS [*singing and dancing*]
> Lead on the dances, your graces revealing.
> Call Artemis hither, call Artemis' twin,
> Leader of dances, Apollo the Healing,
> Kindly God—hither! let's summon him in!
>
>   Nysian Bacchus call,
> Who with his Maenads, his eyes flashing fire,
>   Dances, and last of all
> Zeus of the thunderbolt flaming, the Sire,
>   And Hera in majesty,
>   Queen of prosperity.
>   Come, ye Powers who dwell above
> Unforgetting, our witnesses be
> Of Peace with bonds of harmonius love—
> The Peace which Cypris has wrought for me.
>   Alleluia! Io Paean!
>   Leap in joy—hurrah! hurrah!
>   'Tis victory—hurrah! hurrah!
>   Euoi! Euoi! Euai! Euai!

LYSISTRATA [*to the Spartans*]   Come now, sing a new song to cap ours.

CHORUS OF SPARTANS [*singing and dancing*]
> Leaving Taygetus fair and renown'd
> Muse of Laconia, hither come:
> Amyclae's god in hymns resound,
> Athene of the Brazen Home,
> And Castor and Pollux, Tyndareus' sons,
> Who sport where Eurotas murmuring runs.
>
>   On with the dance! Heia! Ho!
>   All leaping along,
>   Mantles a-swinging as we go!
>   Of Sparta our song.
> There the holy chorus ever gladdens,
> There the beat of stamping feet,
> As our winsome fillies, lovely maidens,
> Dance, beside Eurotas, banks a-skipping,—
>   Nimbly go to and fro
> Hast'ning, leaping feet in measures tripping,

Like the Bacchae's revels, hair a-streaming.
Leda's child, divine and mild,
Leads the holy dance, her fair face beaming.
　On with the dance! as your hand
　　Presses the hair
　Streaming away unconfined.
　　Leap in the air
　Light as the deer; footsteps resound
　Aiding our dance, beating the ground.
Praise Athene, Maid divine, unrivalled in her might,
Dweller in the Brazen Home, unconquered in the fight.

All go out singing and dancing.

MORALITY DRAMA ON THE MEDIEVAL STAGE

Permanent theaters did not exist in England during the medieval period. When the morality play *Everyman* was first produced sometime near the end of the fifteenth century, it was probably performed on a makeshift platform set up in a village square or in the great dining hall of a castle. On the platform a couple of small set-like structures known as *mansions* (literally, dwelling places) would have been set up to stand for the two specific locations where action takes place—namely, heaven, from which God speaks at the opening of the play, and the house of salvation, to which Everyman goes in the middle of the play for confession and penance. As the action moved from one mansion to the other, the stage was understood to be an extension of one location and then of the other.

Sometimes, of course, the location of the action was neither specified nor implied, as when Everyman encounters Death, or Fellowship, or Kindred and Cousin. In such instances the stage would have been understood to represent a street or some other open area. And at the end of the play, when Everyman is about to die, he would have moved to the front of the stage, so that after his last speech he could step down from the stage to indicate that he had entered his grave. Thus the medieval method of staging *Everyman* was fundamentally symbolic in its use of space and processional in its movement from one mansion or location to another.

Costuming was also symbolic rather than realistic, and yet at the same time highly vivid. God, for example, might be dressed in the imperial vestments of a Pope, and Goods might be got up in a costume decorated with jewels or gold and silver coins. The audience, then, would have been treated to a spectacle that was at once visually appealing and spiritually significant.

The medieval method of staging brought actors and spectators closer to one another than ever before or since. They were not separated either by distance or by the architecture of a theater. Spectators witnessed the play from only a few feet away, and on occasion—as when Everyman enters his grave—an actor literally moved into the area of the audience. Although that movement into the audience may strike us today as being a violation of theatrical conventions, it would have affected medieval spectators quite differently: it would have shown them the imminence of their own death and the futility of clinging to their worldly possessions. That vision of *Everyman* would have been especially meaningful to medieval spectators, for they had also endured the bubonic plague, the so-called Black Death, which had ravaged England and the Continent during the fourteenth century.

Although we have not witnessed the Black Death, we all know the inescapable facts of death—the physical decay, the loss of consciousness, the end of being in the world—and *Everyman* does show us how those facts might affect a representative human being like ourselves. Everyman's initial denial of death, his desire to postpone it, his attempt to bargain with it, his final acceptance of it, and his ultimate recognition that it can be transcended only by the knowledge of having lived a decent life—the spectacle of these events makes the play as relevant for us as it must have been for its medieval audience.

Everyman

c. 1485

CHARACTERS

MESSENGER	GOOD DEEDS
GOD	KNOWLEDGE
DEATH	CONFESSION
EVERYMAN	BEAUTY
FELLOWSHIP	STRENGTH
KINDRED	DISCRETION
COUSIN	FIVE WITS
GOODS	ANGEL
DOCTOR	

Here beginneth a treatise how the High Father of Heaven sendeth Death to summon every creature to come and give account of their lives in this world, and is in manner of a moral play.

Enter Messenger

MESSENGER I pray you all give your audience
    And hear this matter with reverence,
    By figure a moral play:
    The Summoning of Everyman called it is,
    That of our lives and ending shows
    How transitory we be all day.
    This matter is wondrous precious,
    But the intent of it is more gracious
    And sweet to bear away.
10   The story saith: Man, in the beginning
    Look well, and take good heed to the ending,
    Be you never so gay!
    Ye think sin in the beginning full sweet,
    Which in the end causeth the soul to weep,
    When the body lieth in clay.
    Here shall you see how Fellowship and Jollity,
    Both Strength, Pleasure and Beauty
    Will fade from thee as flower in May;

Edited by Kate Franks

For ye shall hear how our Heaven's King
20   Calleth Everyman to a general reckoning.
Give audience, and hear what he doth say.

Exit Messenger

God speaks.

GOD   I perceive, here in my majesty,
How that all creatures be to me unkind,
Living without dread in worldly prosperity.
Of ghostly sight[1] the people be so blind,
Drowned in sin, they know me not for their God.
In worldly riches is all their mind;
They fear not my righteousness, the sharp rod.
My law that I showed when I for them died
30   They forget clean, and shedding of my blood red.
I hanged between two thieves, it cannot be denied;
To get them life I suffered to be dead;
I healed their feet, with thorns hurt was my head.
I could do no more than I did, truly;
And now I see the people do clean forsake me.
They use the seven deadly sins damnable,
As pride, covetise, wrath, and lechery
Now in the world be made commendable;
And thus they leave of angels the heavenly company.
40   Every man liveth so after his own pleasure,
And yet of their life they be nothing sure.
I see the more that I them forbear
The worse they be from year to year.
All that liveth appaireth[2] fast;
Therefore I will, in all the haste,
Have a reckoning of every man's person;
For, if I leave the people thus alone
In their life and wicked tempests,
Verily they will become much worse than beasts;
50   For now one would by envy another up eat;
Charity they do all clean forget.
I hoped well that every man
In my glory should make his mansion,
And thereto I had them all elect;
But now I see, like traitors deject,

1. Spiritual sight; knowledge of God
2. Worsens

They thank me not for the pleasure that I to them meant,
Nor yet for their being that I them have lent.
I proffered the people great multitude of mercy,
And few there be that asketh it heartily.
60   They be so cumbered with worldly riches
That needs on them I must do justice,
On every man living without fear.
Where art thou, Death, thou mighty messenger?

Enter Death

DEATH   Almighty God, I am here at your will,
Your commandment to fulfill.
GOD   Go thou to Everyman
And show him, in my name,
A pilgrimage he must on him take,
Which he in no wise may escape;
70   And that he bring with him a sure reckoning
Without delay or any tarrying.
DEATH   Lord, I will in the world go run over all
And cruelly search out both great and small.
Every man will I beset that liveth beastly
Out of God's laws, and dreadeth not folly.
He that loveth riches I will strike with my dart,
His sight to blind, and from Heaven to depart—
Except that alms be his good friend—
In hell for to dwell, world without end.

Enter Everyman.

80   Lo, yonder I see Everyman walking.
Full little he thinketh on my coming;
His mind is on fleshly lusts and his treasure,
And great pain it shall cause him to endure
Before the Lord, Heaven's King.
Everyman, stand still! Whither art thou going
Thus gaily? Hast thou thy Maker forgot?
EVERYMAN   Why askest thou?
Wouldest thou know?
DEATH   Yea, sir. I will you show:
90   In great haste I am sent to thee
From God out of his majesty.
EVERYMAN   What, sent to me?

DEATH Yea, certainly.
    Though thou have forgot him here,
    He thinketh on thee in the heavenly sphere,
    As, ere we depart, thou shalt know.

EVERYMAN What desireth God of me?

DEATH That I shall show to thee:
    A reckoning he will needs have

100   Without any longer respite.

EVERYMAN To give a reckoning longer leisure I crave;
    This blind[3] matter troubleth my wit.

DEATH On thee thou must take a long journey;
    Therefore thy book of account with thee thou bring,
    For turn again thou cannot, by no way.
    And look thou be sure of thy reckoning,
    For before God thou shalt answer and show
    Thy many bad deeds, and good but a few;
    How thou hast spent thy life, and in what wise,

110   Before the Chief Lord of Paradise.
    Have ado that thou were in that way,
    For know thou well, thou shalt make no attorney.[4]

EVERYMAN Full unready I am, such reckoning to give.
    I know thee not. What messenger art thou?

DEATH I am Death that no man dreadeth,[5]
    For every man I rest and no man spareth;
    For it is God's commandment
    That all to me should be obedient.

EVERYMAN O Death, thou comest when I had thee least in mind!

120   In thy power it lieth me to save;
    Yet of my goods will I give thee, if thou will be kind—
    Yea, a thousand pound shalt thou have!—
    And defer this matter till another day.

DEATH Everyman, it may not be, by no way.
    I set not by gold, silver, nor riches,
    Nor by pope, emperor, king, duke, nor princes;
    For, if I would receive gifts great,
    All the world I might get;
    But my custom is clean contrary:

130   I give thee no respite. Come hence, and not tarry!

EVERYMAN Alas, shall I have no longer respite?
    I may say Death giveth no warning!

3. Unknown, obscure
4. You won't be able to plead your case
5. Who fears no man

To think on thee, it maketh my heart sick,
For all unready is my book of reckoning.
But twelve years if I might have abiding,
My accounting book I would make so clear
That my reckoning I should not need to fear.
Wherefore, Death, I pray thee, for God's mercy,
Spare me till I be provided of remedy.

140   DEATH   Thee availeth not to cry, weep and pray;
But haste thee lightly[6] that thou were gone that journey,
And prove thy friends if thou can.
For know thou well the tide abideth no man,
And in the world each living creature
For Adam's sin must die of nature.

EVERYMAN   Death, if I should this pilgrimage take
And my reckoning surely make,
Show me, for sainted charity,
Should I not come again shortly?

150   DEATH   No, Everyman. If thou be once there
Thou mayst never more come here,
Trust me verily.

EVERYMAN   O gracious God in the high seat celestial,
Have mercy on me in this most need!
Shall I have no company from this vale terrestial
Of mine acquaintance, that way me to lead?

DEATH   Yea, if any be so hardy
That would go with thee and bear thee company.
Hie thee that thou were gone to God's magnificence,

160   Thy reckoning to give before his presence.
What, thinkest thou thy life is given thee
And thy worldly goods also?

EVERYMAN   I had thought so, verily.

DEATH   Nay, nay, it was but lent thee;
For as soon as thou art gone,
Another a while shall have it and then go therefrom,
Even as thou hast done.
Everyman, thou art mad! Thou hast thy wits five
And here on earth will not amend thy life;

170   For suddenly I do come.

EVERYMAN   O wretchéd caitiff, whither shall I flee,
That I might escape this endless sorrow?
Now, gentle Death, spare me till tomorrow,

6. Quickly

That I may amend me
With good advisement.
DEATH   Nay, thereto I will not consent,
Nor no man will I respite;
But to the heart suddenly I shall smite
Without any advisement.
180   And now out of thy sight I will me hie.
See thou make thee ready shortly;
For thou mayst say this is the day
That no man living may escape away.

Exit Death.

EVERYMAN   Alas, I may well weep with sighs deep!
Now have I no manner of company
To help me in my journey and me to keep;
And also my writing is full unready.
How shall I do now for to excuse me?
I would to God I had never been begot!
190   To my soul a full great profit it had been;
For now I fear pains huge and great.
The time passeth. Lord, help, that all wrought!
For though I mourn it availeth naught.
The day passeth and is almost ago;
I know not well what for to do.
To whom were I best my complaint to make?
What if I to Fellowship thereof spake
And showed him of this sudden chance?
For in him is all mine affiance;[7]
200   We have in the world so many a day
Been good friends in sport and play.

Enter Fellowship.

I see him yonder, certainly.
I trust that he will bear me company;
Therefore to him will I speak to ease my sorrow.
Well met, good Fellowship, and good morrow!
FELLOWSHIP   Everyman, good morrow, by this day!
Sir, why lookest thou so piteously?
If anything be amiss, I pray thee me say,
That I may help to remedy.
210   EVERYMAN   Yea, good Fellowship, yea,
I am in great jeopardy.

7. Faith or trust

FELLOWSHIP   My true friend, show to me your mind.
　　　I will not forsake thee to my life's end
　　　In the way of good company.
EVERYMAN That was well spoken and lovingly.
FELLOWSHIP   Sir, I must needs know your heaviness;
　　　I have pity to see you in any distress.
　　　If any have you wronged, ye shall revenged be,
　　　Though I on the ground be slain for thee,
220　　　Though that I know before that I should die.
EVERYMAN Verily, Fellowship, gramercy.
FELLOWSHIP   Tush! By thy thanks I set not a straw.
　　　Show me your grief, and say no more.
EVERYMAN If I my heart should to you break,
　　　And then you to turn your mind from me
　　　And would not me comfort when ye hear me speak,
　　　Then should I ten times sorrier be.
FELLOWSHIP   Sir, I say as I will do in deed.
EVERYMAN Then be you a good friend in need.
230　　　I have found you true herebefore.
FELLOWSHIP   And so ye shall evermore;
　　　For, in faith, if thou go to hell,
　　　I will not forsake thee by the way.
EVERYMAN Ye speak like a good friend; I believe you well.
　　　I shall deserve it, if I may.
FELLOWSHIP   I speak of no deserving, by this day!
　　　For he that will say and nothing do
　　　Is not worthy with good company to go;
　　　Therefore show me the grief of your mind,
240　　　As to your friend most loving and kind.
EVERYMAN I shall show you how it is:
　　　Commanded I am to go a journey,
　　　A long way hard and dangerous,
　　　And give a straight account without delay
　　　Before the high judge, Adonai.[8]
　　　Wherefore, I pray you, bear me company,
　　　As ye have promised, in this journey.
FELLOWSHIP   That is matter indeed! Promise is duty;
　　　But if I should take such a voyage on me,
250　　　I know it well, it should be to my pain;
　　　Also it maketh me afeared, certain.
　　　But let us take counsel here as well as we can,
　　　For your words would fear a strong man.

8. Hebrew name for God

EVERYMAN   Why, ye said if I had need
 Ye would me never forsake, quick nor dead,
 Though it were to hell, truly.
FELLOWSHIP   So I said, certainly,
 But such pleasures be set aside, the sooth to say;
 And also, if we took such a journey
260 When should we again come?
EVERYMAN   Nay, never again till the day of doom.
FELLOWSHIP   In faith, then will not I come there!
 Who hath you these tidings brought?
EVERYMAN   Indeed, Death was with me here.
FELLOWSHIP   Now, by God that all hath bought,
 If Death were the messenger,
 For no man that is living today
 I will not go that loath journey—
 Not for the father that begat me!
270 EVERYMAN   Ye promised otherwise, pardie.
FELLOWSHIP   I know well I said so, truly;
 And yet, if thou wilt eat and drink and make good cheer,
 Or haunt to women the lusty company[9]
 I would not forsake you while the day is clear,
 Trust me verily.
EVERYMAN   Yea, thereto ye would be ready!
 To go to mirth, solace and play
 Your mind will sooner apply
 Than to bear me company in my long journey.
280 FELLOWSHIP   Now, in good faith, I will not that way;
 But if thou will murder or any man kill,
 In that I will help thee with a good will.
EVERYMAN   O, that is a simple advice indeed.
 Gentle fellow, help me in my necessity!
 We have loved long, and now I need;
 And now, gentle Fellowship, remember me.
FELLOWSHIP   Whether ye have loved me or no,
 By Saint John, I will not with thee go!
EVERYMAN   Yet, I pray thee, take the labor and do so much for me
290 To bring me forward, for sainted charity,
 And comfort me till I come without the town.
FELLOWSHIP   Nay, if thou would give me a new gown,
 I will not a foot with thee go;
 But if thou had tarried, I would not have left thee so.

---

9. Seek women's company for pleasure; go a-whoring

And as now, God speed thee in thy journey,
For from thee I will depart as fast as I may.
EVERYMAN   Wither away, Fellowship? Will thou forsake me?
FELLOWSHIP   Yea, by my faith! To God I betake[10] thee.
EVERYMAN   Farewell, good Fellowship! For thee my heart is sore.
300   Adieu forever! I shall see thee no more.
FELLOWSHIP   In faith, Everyman, farewell now at the ending!
For you I will remember that parting is mourning.

Exit Fellowship.

EVERYMAN   Alack, shall we thus depart indeed—
Ah, Lady, help!—without any more comfort?
Lo, Fellowship forsaketh me in my most need.
For help in this world whither shall I resort?
Fellowship herebefore with me would merry make,
And now little sorrow for me doth he take.
It is said, "In prosperity men friends may find,
310   Which in adversity be full unkind."
Now whither for succor shall I flee,
Since that Fellowship hath forsaken me?
To my kinsmen I will, truly,
Praying them to help me in my necessity.
I believe that they will do so,
For kind will creep where it may not go.[11]

Enter Kindred and Cousin.

I will go say, for yonder I see them.
Where be ye now, my friends and kinsmen?
KINDRED   Here be we now at your commandment.
320   Cousin, I pray you show us your intent
In any wise and not spare.
COUSIN   Yea, Everyman, and to us declare
If ye be disposed to go anywhither;
For know you well, we will live and die together.
KINDRED   In wealth and woe we will with you hold,
For over his kin a man may be bold.
EVERYMAN   Gramercy, my friends and kinsmen kind.
Now shall I show you the grief of my mind:
I was commanded by a messenger,
330   That is a high king's chief officer;

10. Entrust
11. One's kin will crawl where they may not walk;
i.e., will do what they can.

He bade me go a pilgrimage, to my pain,
And I know well I shall never come again.
Also I must give a reckoning strait,
For I have a great enemy that hath me in wait,
Which intendeth me for to hinder.

KINDRED   What account is that which ye must render?
That would I know.

EVERYMAN   Of all my works I must show
How I have lived and my days spent;
340   Also of ill deeds that I have used
In my time, since life was me lent;
And of all virtues that I have refused.
Therefore, I pray you, go thither with me
To help to make mine account, for saint charity.

COUSIN   What, to go thither? Is that the matter?
Nay, Everyman, I had liefer fast bread and water
All this five years and more.

EVERYMAN   Alas, that ever I was born!
For now shall I never be merry
350   If that you forsake me.

KINDRED   Ah, sir, but ye be a merry man!
Take good heart to you, and make no moan.
But one thing I warn you, by Saint Anne—
As for me, ye shall go alone.

EVERYMAN   My Cousin, will you not with me go?

COUSIN   No, by our Lady! I have the cramp in my toe.
Trust not to me; for, so God me speed,
I will deceive you in your most need.

KINDRED   It availeth not us to entice.
360   Ye shall have my maid with all my heart;
She loveth to go to feasts, there to be nice,
And to dance and abroad to start.
I will give her leave to help you in that journey,
If that you and she may agree.

EVERYMAN   Now show me the very effect of your mind:
Will you go with me, or abide behind?

KINDRED   Abide behind? Yea, that will I, if I may!
Therefore farewell till another day.

Exit Kindred.

EVERYMAN   How should I be merry or glad?
370   For fair promises men to me make,
But when I have most need they me forsake.
I am deceived; that maketh me sad.

COUSIN   Cousin Everyman, farewell now,

For verily I will not go with you.
Also of mine own an unready reckoning
I have to account; therefore I make tarrying.
Now God keep thee, for now I go.

Exit Cousin.

EVERYMAN   Ah, Jesus, is all come hereto?
    Lo, fair words maketh fools fain;
380   They promise and nothing will do, certain.
    My kinsmen promised me faithfully
    For to abide with me steadfastly,
    And now fast away do they flee,
    Even so Fellowship promised me.
    What friend were best me of to provide?
    I lose my time here longer to abide.
    Yet in my mind a thing there is:
    All my life I have loved riches;
    If that my Goods now help me might,
390   He would make my heart full light.
    I will speak to him in this distress.
    Where art thou, my Goods and riches?

Goods revealed in a corner.

GOODS   Who calleth me? Everyman? What, hast thou haste?
    I lie here in corners, trussed and piled so high,
    And in chests I am locked so fast,
    Also sacked in bags. Thou mayst see with thine eye
    I cannot stir; in packs, low I lie.
    What would ye have? Lightly me say.
EVERYMAN   Come hither, Goods, in all the haste thou may,
400   For of counsel I must desire thee.
GOODS   Sir, if ye in the world have sorrow or adversity,
    That can I help you to remedy shortly.
EVERYMAN   It is another disease that grieveth me;
    In this world it is not, I tell thee so.
    I am sent for, another way to go,
    To give a strait account general
    Before the highest Jupiter of all;
    And all my life I have had joy and pleasure in thee.
    Therefore, I pray thee, go with me;
410   For, peradventure, thou mayst before God Almighty
    My reckoning help to clean and purify;
    For it is said ever among
    That "money maketh all right that is wrong."

GOODS   Nay, Everyman, I sing another song.
    I follow no man in such voyages;
    For if I went with thee,
    Thou shouldst fare much the worse for me.
    For because on me thou did set thy mind,
    Thy reckoning I have made blotted and blind,
420   That thine account thou cannot make truly—
    And that hast thou for the love of me!
EVERYMAN   That would grieve me full sore,
    When I should come to that fearful answer.
    Up, let us go thither together.
GOODS   Nay, not so! I am too brittle, I may not endure.
    I will follow no man one foot, be ye sure.
EVERYMAN   Alas, I have thee loved, and had great pleasure
    All my life-days in goods and treasure.
GOODS   That is to thy damnation, without lying,
430   For my love is contrary to the love everlasting.
    But if thou had me loved moderately during,
    As to the poor given part of me,
    Then shouldst thou not in this dolor be,
    Nor in this great sorrow and care.
EVERYMAN   Lo, now was I deceived ere I was aware,
    And all I may lay to my spending of time.
GOODS   What, thinkest thou that I am thine?
EVERYMAN   I had thought so.
GOODS   Nay, Everyman, I say no.
440   As for a while I was lent thee;
    A season thou hast had me in prosperity.
    My condition is a man's soul to kill;
    If I save one, a thousand I do spill.
    Thinkest thou that I will follow thee?
    Nay, from this world not, verily.
EVERYMAN   I had thought otherwise.
GOODS   Therefore to thy soul Goods is a thief;
    For when thou art dead, this is my guise—
    Another to deceive in this same wise
450   As I have done thee, and all to his soul's reprief.[12]
EVERYMAN   O false Goods, cursed thou be,
    Thou traitor to God, that hast deceived me
    And caught me in thy snare!
GOODS   Marry, thou brought thyself in care,

12. Harm

Whereof I am glad.
I must needs laugh; I cannot be sad.
EVERYMAN   Ah, Goods, thou hast had long my hearty love;
I gave thee that which should be the Lord's above.
But wilt thou not go with me indeed?
460   I pray thee truth to say.
GOODS   No, so God me speed!
Therefore farewell, and have good day.

Exit Goods.

EVERYMAN   O, to whom shall I make my moan
For to go with me in that heavy journey?
First Fellowship said he would with me go;
His words were very pleasant and gay,
But afterward he left me alone.
Then spake I to my kinsmen, all in despair,
And also they gave me words fair;
470   They lacked no fair speaking,
But all forsook me in the ending.
Then went I to my Goods that I loved best,
In hope to have comfort; but there had I least,
For my Goods sharply did me tell
That he bringeth many into Hell.
Then of myself I was ashamed,
And so I am worthy to be blamed;
Thus may I well myself hate.
Of whom shall I now counsel take?
480   I think that I shall never speed
Till that I go to my Good Deeds.
But, alas, she is so weak
That she can neither go nor speak;
Yet will I venture on her now.
My Good Deeds, where be you?

Good Deeds revealed on the ground.

GOOD DEEDS   Here I lie, cold in the ground.
Thy sins hath me so sore bound
That I cannot stir.
EVERYMAN   O Good Deeds, I stand in fear!
490   I must you pray of counsel,
For help now should come right well.
GOOD DEEDS   Everyman, I have understanding

That ye be summoned account to make
Before Messiah, of Jerusalem King;
If you do by me, that journey with you will I take.
EVERYMAN   Therefore I come to you my moan to make.
I pray you that ye will go with me.
GOOD DEEDS   I would full fain, but I cannot stand, verily.
EVERYMAN   Why, is there anything on you fallen?
500   GOOD DEEDS   Yea, sir, I may thank you of all.
If ye had perfectly cheered me,
Your book of account full ready would be.
Look, the books of your works and deeds eke,[13]
As how they lie under the feet
To your soul's heaviness.
EVERYMAN   Our Lord Jesus help me!
For one letter here I cannot see.
GOOD DEEDS   There is a blind reckoning in time of distress.
EVERYMAN   Good Deeds, I pray you help me in this need,
510   Or else I am forever damned indeed;
Therefore help me to make reckoning
Before the Redeemer of all things,
That King is, and was, and ever shall.
GOOD DEEDS   Everyman, I am sorry of your fall,
And fain would I help you if I were able.
EVERYMAN   Good Deeds, your counsel I pray you give me.
GOOD DEEDS   That shall I do verily.
Though that on my feet I may not go,
I have a sister that shall with you also,
520   Called Knowledge, which shall with you abide
To help you to make that dreadful reckoning.

Enter Knowledge.

KNOWLEDGE   Everyman, I will go with thee and be thy guide,
In thy most need to go by thy side.
EVERYMAN   In good condition I am now in everything
And am wholly content with this good thing;
Thanked be God my Creator.
GOOD DEEDS   And when she hath brought you there,
Where thou shalt heal thee of thy smart,
Then go you with your reckoning and your Good Deeds together
530   For to make you joyful at heart
Before the Blesséd Trinity.

13. Also

EVERYMAN   My Good Deeds, gramercy!
    I am well content, certainly,
    With your words sweet.

Everyman and Knowledge leave Good Deeds.

KNOWLEDGE   Now go we together lovingly
    To Confession, that cleansing river.
EVERYMAN   For joy I weep; I would we were there!
    But, I pray you, give me cognition
    Where dwelleth that holy man, Confession.
540   KNOWLEDGE   In the house of salvation;
    We shall find him in that place
    That shall us comfort, by God's grace.

Knowledge leads Everyman to Confession.

    Lo, this is Confession. Kneel down and ask mercy,
    For he is in good esteem with God Almighty.
EVERYMAN   O glorious fountain, that all uncleaness doth clarify,
    Wash from me the spots of vice unclean,
    That on me no sin may be seen.
    I come with Knowledge for my redemption,
    Redempt with hearty and full contrition;
550   For I am commanded a pilgrimage to take
    And great accounts before God to make.
    Now I pray you, Shrift, mother of salvation,
    Help my Good Deeds for my piteous exclamation.
CONFESSION   I know your sorrow well, Everyman.
    Because with Knowledge ye come to me,
    I will you comfort as well as I can,
    And a precious jewel I will give thee,
    Called penance, voider of adversity;
    Therewith shall your body chastised be,
560   With abstinence and perseverance in God's serviture.
    Here shall you receive that scourge of me
    Which is penance strong that ye must endure,
    To remember thy Saviour was scourged for thee
    With sharp scourges and suffered it patiently;
    So must thou, ere thou escape that painful pilgrimage.

Confession gives scourge to Knowledge.

    Knowledge, keep him in this voyage,

And by that time Good Deeds will be with thee.
But in any wise be sure of mercy,
For your time draweth fast; if ye will saved be,
570   Ask God mercy, and he will grant truly.
When with the scourge of penance man doth him bind,
The oil of forgiveness then shall he find.

Everyman and Knowledge leave Confession.

EVERYMAN   Thanked be God for his gracious work!
For now I will my penance begin.
This hath rejoiced and lighted my heart,
Though the knots be painful and hard within.
KNOWLEDGE   Everyman, look your penance that ye fulfill,
What pain that ever it to you be;
And Knowledge shall give you counsel at will
580   How your account ye shall make clearly.
EVERYMAN   O eternal God, O heavenly figure,
O way of righteousness, O goodly vision,
Which descended down in a virgin pure
Because he would every man redeem,
Which Adam forfeited by his disobedience;
O blessèd Godhead, elect and high divine,
Forgive me my grievous offence!
Here I cry thee mercy in this presence.
O ghostly[14] treasure, O ransomer and redeemer,
590   Of all the world hope and conductor,
Mirror of joy, foundation of mercy,
Which illumineth Heaven and earth thereby,
Hear my clamorous complaint though it late be;
Receive my prayers unworthy in this heavy life!
Though I be a sinner most abominable,
Yet let my name be written in Moses' table.
O Mary, pray to the Maker of all things,
Me for to help at my ending;
And save me from the power of my enemy,
600   For Death assaileth me strongly.
And, Lady, that I may by means of thy prayer
Of your Son's glory to be partner,
By the means of his passion, I it crave;
I beseech you, help my soul to save.

14. Spiritual, as in Holy Ghost

Knowledge, give me the scourge of penance;
My flesh therewith shall give acquittance.
I will now begin if God give me grace.

Knowledge gives scourge to Everyman.

KNOWLEDGE   Everyman, God give you time and space!
Thus I bequeath you in the hands of our Saviour;
610   Now may you make your reckoning sure.
EVERYMAN   In the name of the Holy Trinity,
My body sore punishéd shall be:
Take this, body, for the sins of the flesh!
Also thou delightest to go gay and fresh,
And in the way of damnation thou did me bring;
Therefore suffer now strokes of punishing.
Now of penance I will wade the water clear
To save me from Purgatory, that sharp fire.

Good Deeds rises from the ground.

GOOD DEEDS   I thank God, now I can walk and go
620   And am delivered of my sickness and woe.
Therefore with Everyman I will go and not spare;
His good works I will help him to declare.
KNOWLEDGE   Now, Everyman, be merry and glad!
Your Good Deeds cometh now; ye may not be sad.
Now is your Good Deeds whole and sound,
Going upright upon the ground.
EVERYMAN   My heart is light and shall be evermore;
Now will I smite faster than I did before.
GOOD DEEDS   Everyman, pilgrim, my special friend,
630   Blessed be thou without end!
For thee is prepared the eternal glory.
Ye have me made whole and sound,
Therefore I will bide by thee in every stound.[15]
EVERYMAN   Welcome, my Good Deeds! Now I hear thy voice
I weep for very sweetness of love.
KNOWLEDGE   Be no more sad, but ever rejoice;
God seeth thy living in his throne above.

Knowledge gives Everyman the garment of contrition.

15. Instance, occasion

Put on this garment to thy behove,[16]
Which is wet with your tears,
640   Or else before God you may it miss
When you to your journey's end come shall.
EVERYMAN   Gentle knowledge, what do ye it call?
KNOWLEDGE   It is the garment of sorrow;
From pain it will you borrow.
Contrition it is
That getteth forgiveness;
It pleaseth God passing well.
GOOD DEEDS   Everyman, will you wear it for your heal?[17]

Everyman puts on the garment of contrition.

EVERYMAN   Now blesséd be Jesu, Mary's Son,
650   For now have I on true contrition;
And let us go now without tarrying.
Good Deeds, have we clear our reckoning?
GOOD DEEDS   Yea, indeed, I have it here.
EVERYMAN   Then I trust we need not fear.
Now, friends, let us not part in twain.
KNOWLEDGE   Nay, Everyman, that will we not, certain.
GOOD DEEDS   Yet must thou lead with thee
Three persons of great might.
EVERYMAN   Who should they be?
660   GOOD DEEDS   Discretion and Strength they hight,[18]
And thy Beauty may not abide behind.
KNOWLEDGE   Also ye must call to mind
Your Five Wits as for your counsellors.
GOOD DEEDS   You must have them ready at all hours.
EVERYMAN   How shall I get them hither?
KNOWLEDGE   You must call them all together,
And they will hear you incontinent.[19]
EVERYMAN   My friends, come hither and be present:
Discretion, Strength, my Five Wits, and Beauty.

Enter Discretion, Strength, Five Wits, and Beauty.

670   BEAUTY   Here at your will we be all ready.
What would ye that we should do?

16. Benefit
17. Salvation
18. Are called
19. At once

GOOD DEEDS   That ye would with Everyman go
    And help him in his pilgrimage.
    Advise you, will ye with him or not in that voyage?
STRENGTH   We will bring him all thither
    To his help and comfort, ye may believe me.
DISCRETION   So will we go with him all together.
EVERYMAN   Almighty God, loved may thou be!
    I give thee laud that I have hither brought
680   Strength, Discretion, Beauty and Five Wits. Lack I naught;
    And my Good Deeds, with Knowledge clear,
    All be in company at my will here.
    I desire no more to my business.
STRENGTH   And I, Strength, will by you stand in distress,
    Though thou would in battle fight on the ground.
FIVE WITS   And though it were through the world round,
    We will not depart for sweet nor sour.
BEAUTY   No more will I unto death's hour,
    Whatsoever thereof befall.
690 DISCRETION   Everyman, advise you first of all;
    Go with a good advisement and deliberation.
    We all give you virtuous monition
    That all shall be well.
EVERYMAN   My friends, hearken what I will tell:
    I pray God reward you in his heavenly sphere.
    Now hearken, all that be here,
    For I will make my testament
    Here before you all present:
    In alms, half my goods I will give with my hands twain
700   In the way of charity with good intent,
    And the other half still shall remain
    In queth,[20] to be returned where it ought to be.
    This I do in despite of the fiend of hell,
    To go quite out of his peril
    Ever after and this day.
KNOWLEDGE   Everyman, hearken what I say:
    Go to Priesthood, I you advise,
    And receive of him in any wise
    The holy sacrament and ointment together;
710   Then shortly see ye turn again hither.
    We will all abide you here.
FIVE WITS   Yea, Everyman, hie you that ye ready were.

---

20. As a bequest; though the remainder of the line indicates that it is
    actually a restitution of illegally acquired property.

There is no emperor, king, duke, nor baron
That of God hath commission
As hath the least priest in the world being;
For of the blesséd sacraments pure and benign,
He beareth the keys, and thereof hath the cure
For man's redemption—it is ever sure—
Which God for our soul's medicine
720   Gave us out of his heart with great pine.[21]
Here in this transitory life, for thee and me,
The blessed sacraments seven there be:
Baptism, confirmation with priesthood good,
And the sacrament of God's precious flesh and blood,
Marriage, the holy extreme unction, and penance.
These seven be good to have in remembrance,
Gracious sacraments of high divinity.

EVERYMAN   Fain would I receive that holy body,
And meekly to my ghostly[22] father I will go.

730 FIVE WITS   Everyman, that is the best that ye can do.
God will you to salvation bring,
For priesthood exceedeth all other things:
To us holy scripture they do teach
And converteth man from sin, Heaven to reach;
God hath to them more power given
Than to any angel that is in Heaven.
With five words he may consecrate,
God's body in flesh and blood to make,
And handleth his Maker between his hands.
740   The priest bindeth and unbindeth all bands,
Both in earth and in Heaven.
Thou ministers all the sacraments seven;
Though we kissed thy feet, thou were worthy.
Thou art surgeon that cureth sin deadly;
No remedy we find under God
But all only priesthood.
Everyman, God gave priests that dignity
And setteth them in his stead among us to be;
Thus be they above angels in degree.

Exit Everyman.

750 KNOWLEDGE   If priests be good, it is so, surely.
But when Jesu hanged on the cross with great smart,
There he gave, out of his blesséd heart,

21. Anguish, torment
22. Spiritual

The seven sacraments in great torment;
He sold them not to us, that Lord omnipotent;
Therefore Saint Peter the apostle doth say
That Jesu's curse hath all they
Which God their Saviour do buy or sell,
Or they for any money do take or tell.[23]

760   Sinful priests giveth the sinners example bad;
Their children sitteth by other men's fires, I have heard;
And some haunteth women's company
With unclean life, as lusts of lechery;
These be with sin made blind.

FIVE WITS   I trust to God no such may we find;
Therefore let us priesthood honor
And follow their doctrine for our souls' succour.
We be their sheep, and they shepherds be
By whom we all be kept in surety.
Peace! For yonder I see Everyman come,

770   Which hath made true satisfaction.

GOOD DEEDS   Methinks it is he indeed.

Re-enter Everyman.

EVERYMAN   Now Jesu be your alder speed![24]
I have received the sacrament for my redemption
And then mine extreme unction.
Blesséd be all they that counselled me to take it!
And now, friends, let us go without longer respite.
I thank God that ye have tarried so long.
Now set each of you on this rood your hand
And shortly follow me.

780   I go before where I would be. God be our guide!

They go toward the grave.

STRENGTH   Everyman, we will not from you go
Till ye have done this voyage long.

DISCRETION   I, Discretion, will bide by you also.

KNOWLEDGE   And though this pilgrimage be never so strong,
I will never part you from.

STRENGTH   Everyman, I will be as sure by thee
As ever I did by Judas Maccabee.[25]

23. Count out, as in bank teller
24. Help to all of you
25. A Jewish leader of the second century B.C., known for his courage (1 Macc. 3)

They arrive at the grave.

EVERYMAN   Alas, I am so faint I may not stand;
   My limbs under me do fold.
790   Friends, let us not turn again to this land,
   Not for all the world's gold;
   For into this cave must I creep
   And turn to earth, and thereto sleep.
BEAUTY   What, into this grave? Alas!
EVERYMAN   Yea, there shall ye consume, more and less.[26]
BEAUTY   And what, should I smother here?
EVERYMAN   Yea, by my faith, and never more appear.
   In this world live no more we shall,
   But in Heaven before the highest Lord of all.
800   BEAUTY   I cross out all this. Adieu, by Saint John!
   I take my tap in my lap and am gone.[27]
EVERYMAN   What, Beauty, whither will ye?
BEAUTY   Peace! I am deaf. I look not behind me,
   Not if thou wouldest give me all the gold in thy chest.

                                           Exit Beauty.

EVERYMAN   Alas, whereto may I trust?
   Beauty goeth fast away from me.
   She promised with me to live and die.
STRENGTH   Everyman, I will thee also forsake and deny;
   Thy game liketh me not at all.
810   EVERYMAN   Why, then, ye will forsake me all?
   Sweet Strength, tarry a little space.
STRENGTH   Nay, sir, by the rood of grace!
   I will hie me from thee fast,
   Though thou weep till thy heart to-brast.[28]
EVERYMAN   Ye would ever bide by me, ye said.
STRENGTH   Yea, I have you far enough conveyed.
   Ye be old enough, I understand,
   Your pilgrimage to take in hand.
   I repent me that I hither came.
820   EVERYMAN   Strength, you to displease I am to blame;
   Yet promise is debt, this ye well wot.[29]
STRENGTH   In faith, I care not.

26. The grave devours all, both the great and the small.
27. A tap is an unspun tuft of wool or flax. Hence, like a peasant housewife, Beauty
    is saying, "I'm pocketing my spinning materials and am off."
28. Bursts in two
29. Know

Thou art but a fool to complain;
You spend your speech and waste your brain.
Go thrust thee into the ground!

Exit Strength.

EVERYMAN   I had thought surer I should you have found.
He that trusteth in his Strength,
She him deceiveth at the length.
Both Strength and Beauty forsaketh me;
830   Yet they promised me fair and lovingly.
DISCRETION   Everyman, I will after Strength be gone.
As for me, I will leave you alone.
EVERYMAN   Why, Discretion, will ye forsake me?
DISCRETION   Yea, in faith, I will go from thee;
For when Strength goeth before,
I follow after evermore.
EVERYMAN   Yet, I pray thee, for the love of the Trinity,
Look in my grave once piteously.
DISCRETION   Nay, so nigh will I not come.
840   Farewell, everyone!

Exit Discretion.

EVERYMAN   O, all things faileth, save God alone—
Beauty, Strength and Discretion;
For when Death bloweth his blast,
They all run from me full fast.
FIVE WITS   Everyman, my leave now of thee I take.
I will follow the others, for here I thee forsake.
EVERYMAN   Alas, then may I wail and weep,
For I took you for my best friend.
FIVE WITS   I will no longer thee keep.
850   Now farewell, and there an end.

Exit Five Wits.

EVERYMAN   O Jesu, help! All hath forsaken me.
GOOD DEEDS   Nay, Everyman, I will bide with thee.
I will not forsake thee in deed;
Thou shalt find me a good friend in need.
EVERYMAN   Gramercy, Good Deeds! Now may I true friends see.
They have forsaken me, every one;
I loved them better than my Good Deeds alone.
Knowledge, will ye forsake me also?
KNOWLEDGE   Yea, Everyman, when ye to Death shall go;
860   But not yet, for no manner of danger.
EVERYMAN   Gramercy, Knowledge, with all my heart.
KNOWLEDGE   Nay, yet I will not from hence depart
Till I see where ye shall be come.

EVERYMAN   Methinks, alas, that I must be gone
          To make my reckoning and my debts pay,
          For I see my time is nigh spent away.
          Take example, all ye that this do hear or see,
          How they that I loved best do forsake me,
          Except my Good Deeds that bideth truly.
870 GOOD DEEDS   All earthly things is but vanity:
          Beauty, Strength and Discretion do man forsake,
          Foolish friends and kinsmen that fair spake—
          All fleeth save Good Deeds, and that am I.
     EVERYMAN   Have mercy on me, God most mighty,
          And stand by me, thou mother and maid, Holy Mary!
     GOOD DEEDS   Fear not, I will speak for thee.
     EVERYMAN   Here I cry God mercy.
     GOOD DEEDS   Shorten our end, and diminish our pain;
          Let us go and never come again.

Good Deeds leads Everyman into grave.

880 EVERYMAN   Into thy hands, Lord, my soul I commend;
          Receive it, Lord, that it be not lost.
          As thou me boughtest, so me defend
          And save me from the fiend's boast,
          That I may appear with that bléssed host
          That shall be saved at the day of doom.
          In manus tuas, of mights most
          Forever, *commendo spiritum meum.*[30]
                              Exeunt Everyman and Good Deeds.
     KNOWLEDGE   Now hath he suffered that we all shall endure;
          The Good Deeds shall make all sure.
890   Now hath he made ending;
          Methinks that I hear angels sing
          And make great joy and melody
          Where Everyman's soul received shall be.

Enter Angel.

THE ANGEL   Come, excellent elect spouse, to Jesu!
          Here above thou shalt go
          Because of thy singular virtue.
          Now thy soul is taken thy body from,
          Thy reckoning is crystal clear.

---

30. *In manus tuas . . . commendo spiritum meum:* Into thy hands I commend my spirit.

Now shalt thou into the heavenly sphere,
900   Unto the which all ye shall come
That liveth well before the day of doom.

Exeunt Angel and Knowledge.

Enter Doctor.

DOCTOR   This moral men may have in mind.
Ye hearers, take it of worth, old and young,
And forsake Pride, for he deceiveth you in the end;
And remember Beauty, Five Wits, Strength, and Discretion,
They all at the last do Everyman forsake,
Save his Good Deeds there doth he take.
But beware, for if they be small,
Before God he hath no help at all:
No excuse may be there for Everyman.
910   Alas, how shall he do then?
For after death amends may no man make,
For then mercy and pity doth him forsake.
If his reckoning be not clear when he doth come,
God will say, "*Ite, maledicti, in ignem eternum.*"[31]
And he that hath his account whole and sound,
High in Heaven he shall be crowned;
Unto which place God bring us all thither,
That we may live body and soul together.
Thereto help the Trinity!
920   Amen, say ye, for saint charity.

Exit Doctor.

Thus endeth this moral play of Everyman.

31. Go, sinners, into eternal fire.

TRAGEDY IN THE RENAISSANCE ENGLISH THEATER

The first recorded production of Shakespeare's tragedy *Othello* took place in 1604 in the Globe theater, a public playhouse capable of accommodating between two and three thousand spectators. Despite its large seating capacity, the Globe, like other theaters in Renaissance England, created an intimate experience of drama, as we can tell by considering its physical dimensions and design. The Globe was a circular or polygonally shaped building, approximately eighty-four feet in diameter and thirty-three feet high. Its height was sufficient to accommodate three levels of galleries for spectators. The area enclosed by the galleries was approximately fifty-five feet in diameter. Into this space extended an acting platform approximately

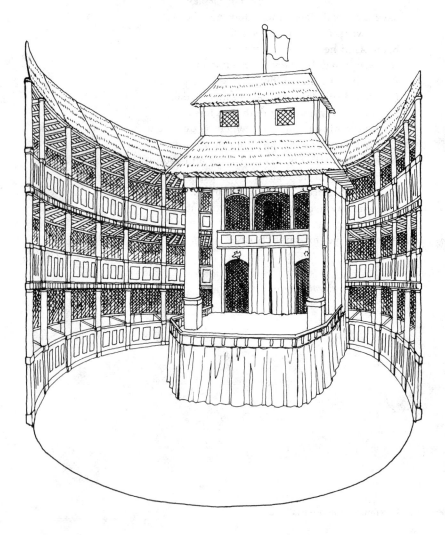

forty-three feet wide and about twenty-seven feet deep, leaving a sizable area of ground surrounding the stage for standing spectators.

We can readily see that this arrangement must have created an intimate relationship between actors and members of the audience. Since the actors were surrounded on three sides by spectators in the yard and the galleries, they were in fact much closer to one another than in our smaller modern theaters where actors and spectators are physically set off from one another by the framed and curtained stage. The Renaissance audience could see the actors up close—which meant that the actors had to pay meticulous attention to all their gestures and facial expressions. Most significantly, that physical intimacy necessarily must have aroused in the spectators a very immediate and personal engagement in the action of the play. In another respect, however, drama in the Renaissance English theater was a very public and communal affair, for the yard area was open to the sky, and plays were thus performed in full daylight. As they sat in the galleries or stood in the yard, the spectators could easily see one another, as well as the actors.

The stage itself consisted of two acting levels. The main area was the platform jutting into the yard; at the rear of the platform on each side were doors for entrances and exits. Between the doors was a curtained inner stage for use in "discoveries" and special dramatic situations, such as the bedchamber scene in the final act of *Othello*. Above this inner stage was the second acting level, a gallery, which could be used for balcony scenes, such as when Brabantio is awakened by Roderigo and Iago and appears at the window of his house in Act I of *Othello*. The gallery was used also for musicians, or even for spectators when it was not required for the performance. Directly above the gallery was a roof covering the rear half of the acting platform. As we can see from these arrangements, Shakespeare's stage was a remarkably flexible one, allowing action to be set in a number of different areas, and allowing, too, for rapid entrances and exits of the sort that take place during Cassio's drunken quarrel with Roderigo and Montano in Act II of *Othello*.

Flexibility in staging resulted also from the fact that scenery was not used in the Globe Theater. The stage was understood to stand for whatever setting was implied by the action and from whatever props were placed on stage. Thus when the Duke and Senators appeared in Act I, Scene 3, of *Othello*, the table and chairs provided for them on stage would have been enough to indicate that the scene was taking place at court. Their costuming, however, was sumptuous, and by that means the actors were able to create a vivid spectacle, particularly by contrast with their spare surroundings. In that scene at the Duke's court, for example, the actors would have been richly arrayed in Renaissance styles of dress appropriate to a Duke and his Senators.

Even though the English theater of the Renaissance did not create a realistic or by any means complete scenic illusion of the sort we are accustomed to on the modern stage, it set forth a vividly human and symbolic spectacle—a spectacle, in fact, that would have been regarded by the audience as embodying universal significance. For when the actors appeared on stage, they were also understood to be standing between the heavens implied by that roof above them and hell implied by the space beneath the stage. Thus, when the audience witnessed the action of *Othello*, they would have regarded it not only as representing the catastrophe of a particular man who is undone by an officer he trusts more than his wife, but also as presenting a spectacle of universal significance about the conflict of good and evil.

WILLIAM SHAKESPEARE

1560–1616

The Tragedy of Othello

The Moor of Venice

CHARACTERS

DUKE OF VENICE
BRABANTIO, a senator, father to Desdemona
SENATORS OF VENICE
GRATIANO, brother to Brabantio, a noble Venetian
LODOVICO, kinsman to Brabantio, a noble Venetian
OTHELLO, the Moor, in the military service of Venice
CASSIO, an honorable lieutenant to Othello
IAGO, Othello's ensign, a villain
RODERIGO, a gulled gentleman
MONTANO, governor of Cyprus
CLOWN, servant to Othello
DESDEMONA, daughter to Brabantio and wife to Othello
EMILIA, wife to Iago
BIANCA, a courtesan
GENTLEMEN, SAILORS, OFFICERS, MESSENGERS, HERALD, MUSICIANS, ATTENDANTS

Scene: Venice and Cyprus

ACT I

SCENE 1

Enter Roderigo and Iago.

RODERIGO Tush, never tell me! I take it much unkindly
    That thou, Iago, who hast had my purse
    As if the strings were thine, shouldst know of this.[1]
IAGO 'Sblood, but you will not hear me!
    If ever I did dream of such a matter,
    Abhor me.
RODERIGO Thou told'st me thou didst hold him[2] in thy hate.
IAGO Despise me if I do not. Three great ones of the city,
    In personal suit to make me his lieutenant,

---

1. Desdemona's elopement with Othello   2. Othello

10   Off-capped to him; and, by the faith of man,
I know my price; I am worth no worse a place.
But he, as loving his own pride and purposes,
Evades them with a bombast circumstance.
Horribly stuffed with epithets of war;
And, in conclusion,
Nonsuits[3] my mediators; for, "Certes," says he,
"I have already chose my officer."
And what was he?
Forsooth, a great arithmetician,[4]
20   One Michael Cassio, a Florentine
(A fellow almost damned in a fair wife)[5]
That never set a squadron in the field,
Nor the division of a battle knows
More than a spinster;[6] unless the bookish theoric,
Wherein the togèd consuls[7] can propose
As masterly as he. Mere prattle without practice
Is all his soldiership. But he, sir, had th' election;
And I (of whom his eyes had seen the proof
At Rhodes, at Cyprus, and on other grounds
30   Christian and heathen) must be belee'd and calmed[8]
By debitor and creditor; this counter-caster,[9]
He, in good time, must his lieutenant be,
And I—God bless the mark!—his Moorship's ancient.[10]
RODERIGO   By heaven, I rather would have been his hangman.
IAGO   Why, there's no remedy; 'tis the curse of service.
Preferment[11] goes by letter and affection,[12]
And not by old gradation,[13] where each second
Stood heir to th' first. Now, sir, be judge yourself,
Whether I in any just term am affined[14]
To love the Moor.
40   RODERIGO   I would not follow him then.
IAGO   O, sir, content you;
I follow him to serve my turn upon him.

---

3. Rejects
4. Person skilled in military calculations, but not in actual warfare
5. *almost . . . wife:* unexplainable phrase. Cassio is not married, nor is he about to be married. In the Italian novella that was the source for Shakespeare's play, Cassio is married, and perhaps Shakespeare intended to follow the novella when he began writing the play.
6. Spinner of thread; i.e., housewife
7. Senators dressed in togas; i.e., clothed for the council chamber, not the battlefield
8. Have the wind taken out of my sails and left becalmed
9. Accountant
10. Ensign, standard-bearer
11. Advancement
12. Personal favoritism
13. Seniority
14. Bound

We cannot all be masters, nor all masters
Cannot be truly followed. You shall mark
Many a duteous and knee-crooking knave
That, doting on his own obsequious bondage,
Wears out his time, much like his master's ass,
For naught but provender; and when he's old, cashiered.[15]
Whip me such honest knaves! Others there are
50   Who, trimmed in forms and visages of duty,
Keep yet their hearts attending on themselves;
And, throwing but shows of service on their lords,
Do well thrive by them, and when they have lined their coats,
Do themselves homage. These fellows have some soul;
And such a one do I profess myself. For, sir,
It is as sure as you are Roderigo,
Were I the Moor, I would not be Iago.
In following him, I follow but myself;
Heaven is my judge, not I for love and duty,
60   But seeming so, for my own peculiar[16] end;
For when my outward action doth demonstrate
The native act and figure of my heart
In compliment extern,[17] 'tis not long after
But I will wear my heart upon my sleeve
For daws to peck at; I am not what I am.
RODERIGO   What a full fortune does the thick-lips owe[18]
If he can carry't thus!
IAGO   Call up her father,
Rouse him. Make after him, poison his delight,
Proclaim him in the streets. Incense her kinsmen,
70   And though he in a fertile climate dwell,
Plague him with flies; though that his joy be joy,
Yet throw such changes of vexation on't
As it may lose some color.
RODERIGO   Here is her father's house. I'll call aloud.
IAGO   Do, with like timorous[19] accent and dire yell
As when, by night and negligence, the fire
Is spied in populous cities.
RODERIGO   What, ho, Brabantio! Signior Brabantio, ho!
IAGO   Awake! What, ho, Brabantio! Thieves! thieves! thieves!
80   Look to your house, your daughter, and your bags!
Thieves! thieves!

15. Dismissed
16. Personal
17. External show

18. Own
19. Terrifying

Brabantio at a window.

BRABANTIO [*above*]   What is the reason of this terrible summons?
 What is the matter there?
RODERIGO   Signior, is all your family within?
IAGO   Are your doors locked?
BRABANTIO   Why, wherefore ask you this?
IAGO   Zounds, sir, y'are robbed! For shame, put on your gown!
 Your heart is burst; you have lost half your soul.
 Even now, now, very now, an old black ram
 Is tupping your white ewe. Arise, arise!
90   Awake the snorting[20] citizens with the bell,
 Or else the devil will make a grandsire of you.
 Arise, I say!
BRABANTIO   What, have you lost your wits?
RODERIGO   Most reverend signior, do you know my voice?
BRABANTIO   Not I. What are you?
RODERIGO   My name is Roderigo.
BRABANTIO   The worser welcome!
 I have charged thee not to haunt about my doors.
 In honest plainness thou hast heard me say
 My daughter is not for thee; and now, in madness,
 Being full of supper and distemp'ring[21] draughts,
100   Upon malicious bravery[22] dost thou come
 To start[23] my quiet.
RODERIGO   Sir, sir, sir—
BRABANTIO   But thou must needs be sure
 My spirit and my place have in them power
 To make this bitter to thee.
RODERIGO   Patience, good sir.
BRABANTIO   What tell'st thou me of robbing? This is Venice;
 My house is not a grange.[24]
RODERIGO   Most grave Brabantio,
 In simple and pure soul I come to you.
IAGO   Zounds, sir, you are one of those that will not serve God if the
 devil bid you. Because we come to do you service, and you think we are
110   ruffians, you'll have your daughter covered with a Barbary horse; you'll
 have your nephews[25] neigh to you; you'll have coursers for cousins,[26]
 and gennets for germans.[27]
BRABANTIO   What profane wretch art thou?

20. Snoring
21. Intoxicating
22. Bravado
23. Upset

24. Isolated farmhouse
25. Grandsons
26. Horses for kinsmen
27. Spanish horses for close relatives

IAGO   I am one, sir, that comes to tell you your daughter and the Moor
    are now making the beast with two backs.

BRABANTIO   Thou art a villain.

IAGO   You are—a senator.

120   BRABANTIO   This thou shalt answer. I know thee, Roderigo.

RODERIGO   Sir, I will answer anything. But I beseech you,
    If't be your pleasure and most wise consent,
    As partly I find it is, that your fair daughter,
    At this odd-even[28] and dull watch o' th' night,
    Transported, with no worse nor better guard
    But with a knave of common hire, a gondolier,
    To the gross clasps of a lascivious Moor—
    If this be known to you, and your allowance,
    We then have done you bold and saucy[29] wrongs;
130   But if you know not this, my manners tell me
    We have your wrong rebuke. Do not believe
    That, from the sense of[30] all civility,
    I thus would play and trifle with your reverence.
    Your daughter, if you have not given her leave,
    I say again, hath made a gross revolt,
    Tying her duty, beauty, wit, and fortunes
    In an extravagant and wheeling[31] stranger
    Of here and everywhere. Straight satisfy yourself.
    If she be in her chamber, or your house,
140   Let loose on me the justice of the state
    For thus deluding you.

BRABANTIO   Strike on the tinder, ho!
    Give me a taper! Call up all my people!
    This accident[32] is not unlike my dream.
    Belief of it oppresses me already.
    Light, I say! Light!   *Exit above.*

IAGO   Farewell, for I must leave you.
    It seems not meet, nor wholesome to my place,
    To be produced—as, if I stay, I shall—
    Against the Moor. For I do know the state,
    However this may gall him with some check,[33]
150   Cannot with safety cast[34] him; for he's embarked
    With such loud reason to the Cyprus wars,
    Which even now stand in act,[35] that for their souls

28. Around midnight, when the end of one
    day is indistinguishable from the be-
    ginning of the next
29. Insolent
30. Contrary to
31. Wandering and roving
32. Occurrence
33. Reprimand
34. Dismiss
35. Are underway

Another of his fathom[36] they have none
To lead their business; in which regard,
Though I do hate him as I do hell-pains,
Yet, for necessity of present life,
I must show out a flag and sign of love,
Which is indeed but sign. That you shall surely find him,
Lead to the Sagittary[37] the raisèd search;
160   And there will I be with him. So farewell.   *Exit.*

Enter, below, Brabantio, and Servants with torches.

BRABANTIO   It is too true an evil. Gone she is;
And what's to come of my despisèd time
Is naught but bitterness. Now, Roderigo,
Where didst thou see her?—O unhappy girl!—
With the Moor, say'st thou?—Who would be a father?—
How didst thou know 'twas she?—O, she deceives me
Past thought!—What said she to you?—Get more tapers!
Raise all my kindred!—Are they married, think you?
RODERIGO   Truly I think they are.
170   BRABANTIO   O heaven! How got she out? O treason of the blood!
Fathers, from hence trust not your daughters' minds
By what you see them act. Is there not charms
By which the property[38] of youth and maidhood
May be abused? Have you not read, Roderigo,
Of some such thing?
RODERIGO   Yes, sir, I have indeed.
BRABANTIO   Call up my brother.—O, would you had had her!—
Some one way, some another.—Do you know
Where we may apprehend her and the Moor?
RODERIGO   I think I can discover him, if you please
180   To get good guard and go along with me.
BRABANTIO   Pray you lead on. At every house I'll call;
I may command at most.—Get weapons, ho!
And raise some special officers of night.—
On, good Roderigo; I'll deserve[39] your pains.   *Exeunt.*

SCENE 2

Enter Othello, Iago, and Attendants with torches.

IAGO   Though in the trade of war I have slain men,

36. Ability   38. Nature
37. An inn   39. Reward

Yet do I hold it very stuff o' th' conscience
To do no contrived murther. I lack iniquity
Sometimes to do me service. Nine or ten times
I had thought t' have yerked[40] him here under the ribs.

OTHELLO 'Tis better as it is.

IAGO   Nay, but he prated,
And spoke such scurvy and provoking terms
Against your honor
That with the little godliness I have
I did full hard forbear him.[41] But I pray you, sir,
Are you fast married? Be assured of this,
That the magnifico[42] is much beloved,
And hath in his effect a voice potential
As double as the duke's.[43] He will divorce you,
Or put upon you what restraint and grievance
The law, with all his might to enforce it on,
Will give him cable.[44]

OTHELLO   Let him do his spite.
My services which I have done the signiory[45]
Shall out-tongue his complaints. 'Tis yet to know[46]—
Which, when I know that boasting is an honor,
I shall promulgate—I fetch my life and being
From men of royal siege;[47] and my demerits[48]
May speak unbonneted[49] to as proud a fortune
As this that I have reached. For know, Iago,
But that I love the gentle Desdemona,
I would not my unhoused[50] free condition
Put into circumscription and confine
For the sea's worth.

Enter Cassio, Officers, with torches.

                          But look, what lights come yond?

IAGO   Those are the raisèd father and his friends.
You were best go in.

OTHELLO   Not I; I must be found.

---

40. Stabbed
41. *did . . . him:* had great difficulty restraining myself from attacking him
42. Venetian nobleman (Brabantio)
43. *voice . . . duke's:* influence so strong it is like having two votes, as does the Duke of Venice
44. Scope

45. Venetian government
46. Still not known
47. Rank
48. Merits
49. Without taking my hat off; i.e., on equal terms
50. Unconfined

My parts,[51] my title, and my perfect soul[52]
Shall manifest me rightly. Is it they?
IAGO   By Janus, I think no.
OTHELLO   The servants of the duke, and my lieutenant.
The goodness of the night upon you, friends!
What is the news?
CASSIO   The duke does greet you, general;
And he requires your haste-post-haste appearance
Even on the instant.
OTHELLO   What's the matter, think you?
CASSIO   Something from Cyprus, as I may divine.
40   It is a business of some heat. The galleys
Have sent a dozen sequent[53] messengers
This very night at one another's heels,
And many of the consuls, raised and met,
Are at the duke's already. You have been hotly called for;
When, being not at your lodging to be found,
The Senate hath sent about three several quests
To search you out.
OTHELLO   'Tis well I am found by you.
I will but spend a word here in the house,
And go with you.   *Exit.*
CASSIO   Ancient, what makes he here?
50   IAGO   Faith, he to-night hath boarded a land carack.[54]
If it prove lawful prize, he's made for ever.
CASSIO   I do not understand.
IAGO   He's married.
CASSIO   To who?

Enter Othello.

IAGO   Marry, to—Come, captain, will you go?
OTHELLO   Have with you.
CASSIO   Here comes another troop to seek for you.

Enter Brabantio, Roderigo, and others with lights and weapons.

IAGO   It is Brabantio. General, be advised.
He comes to bad intent.

51. Personal qualities   53. Consecutive
52. Clear conscience   54. Trading ship

OTHELLO   Holla! stand there!

RODERIGO   Signior, it is the Moor.

BRABANTIO   Down with him, thief!

They draw on both sides.

IAGO   You, Roderigo! Come, sir, I am for you.

OTHELLO   Keep up your bright swords, for the dew will rust them.

60   Good signior, you shall more command with years

            Than with your weapons.

BRABANTIO   O thou foul thief, where has thou stowed my daughter?

            Damned as thou art, thou hast enchanted her!

            For I'll refer me to all things of sense,[55]

            If she in chains of magic were not bound,

            Whether a maid so tender, fair, and happy,

            So opposite to marriage that she shunned

            The wealthy curlèd darlings of our nation,

            Would ever have, t' incur a general mock,

70   Run from her guardage to the sooty bosom

            Of such a thing as thou—to fear, not to delight.

            Judge me the world if 'tis not gross in sense[56]

            That thou hast practiced on her with foul charms,

            Abused her delicate youth with drugs or minerals

            That weaken motion.[57] I'll have't disputed on;[58]

            'Tis probable, and palpable to thinking.

            I therefore apprehend and do attach[59] thee

            For an abuser of the world, a practicer

            Of arts inhibited and out of warrant.[60]

80   Lay hold upon him. If he do resist,

            Subdue him at his peril.

OTHELLO   Hold your hands,

            Both you of my inclining and the rest.

            Were it my cue to fight, I should have known it

            Without a prompter. Where will you that I go

            To answer this your charge?

BRABANTIO   To prison, till fit time

            Of law and course of direct session

            Call thee to answer.

OTHELLO   What if I do obey?

---

55. *refer . . . sense:* appeal to common sense   59. Arrest
56. Obvious   60. *inhibited . . . warrant:* prohibited and
57. Senses and mental powers   illegal
58. Tried in court

How may the duke be therewith satisfied,
Whose messengers are here about my side
90   Upon some present business of the state
To bring me to him?

OFFICER   'Tis true, most worthy signior.
The duke's in council, and your noble self
I am sure is sent for.

BRABANTIO   How? The duke in council?
In this time of the night? Bring him away.
Mine's not an idle[61] cause. The duke himself,
Or any of my brothers of the state,
Cannot but feel this wrong as 'twere their own;
For if such actions may have passage free,
Bondslaves and pagans shall our statesmen be.   *Exeunt.*

SCENE 3

Enter Duke and Senators, set at a table, with lights and Attendants.

DUKE   There is no composition[62] in these news
That gives them credit.

1. SENATOR   Indeed they are disproportioned.
My letters say a hundred and seven galleys.

DUKE   And mine a hundred forty.

2. SENATOR   And mine two hundred.
But though they jump[63] not on a just account—
As in these cases where the aim[64] reports
'Tis oft with difference—yet do they all confirm
A Turkish fleet, and bearing up to Cyprus.

DUKE   Nay, it is possible enough to judgment.
10   I do not so secure me in the error[65]
But the main article I do approve[66]
In fearful sense.

SAILOR [*within*]   What, ho! what, ho! what, ho!

OFFICER   A messenger from the galleys.

Enter Sailor.

DUKE   Now, what's the business?

61. Trivial
62. Consistency
63. Agree

64. Conjecture
65. *secure . . . error:* rely on inconsistencies
66. Accept

SAILOR   The Turkish preparation makes for Rhodes.
　　So was I bid report here to the state
　　By Signior Angelo.
DUKE   How say you by this change?
1. SENATOR   This cannot be
　　By no assay[67] of reason. 'Tis a pageant
　　To keep us in false gaze.[68] When we consider
20　　Th' importancy of Cyprus to the Turk,
　　And let ourselves again but understand
　　That, as it more concerns the Turk than Rhodes,
　　So may he with more facile question bear it,[69]
　　For that it stands not in such warlike brace,[70]
　　But altogether lacks th' abilities
　　That Rhodes is dressed in—if we make thought of this,
　　We must not think the Turk is so unskillful
　　To leave that latest which concerns him first,
　　Neglecting an attempt of ease and gain
30　　To wake and wage[71] a danger profitless.
DUKE   Nay, in all confidence he's not for Rhodes.
OFFICER   Here is more news.

Enter a Messenger.

MESSENGER   The Ottomites, reverend and gracious,
　　Steering with due course toward the isle of Rhodes,
　　Have there injointed them with an after fleet.
1. SENATOR   Ay, so I thought. How many, as you guess?
MESSENGER   Of thirty sail; and now they do restem
　　Their backward course, bearing with frank appearance
　　Their purposes toward Cyprus. Signior Montano,
40　　Your trusty and most valiant servitor,
　　With his free duty[72] recommends[73] you thus,
　　And prays you to believe him.
DUKE   'Tis certain then for Cyprus.
　　Marcus Luccicos, is not he in town?
1. SENATOR   He's now in Florence.
DUKE   Write from us to him; post, post-haste dispatch.

Enter Barbantio, Othello, Cassio, Iago, Roderigo, and Officers.

---

67. Test	71. Risk
68. Looking the wrong way	72. Freely given expression of loyalty
69. More easily capture	73. Informs
70. Preparedness	

1. SENATOR Here comes Brabantio and the valiant Moor.

DUKE Valiant Othello, we must straight employ you
Against the general enemy Ottoman.

50   [To Brabantio] I did not see you. Welcome, gentle signior.
We lacked your counsel and your help to-night.

BRABANTIO So did I yours. Good your grace, pardon me.
Neither my place, nor aught I heard of business,
Hath raised me from my bed; nor doth the general care
Take hold on me; for my particular grief
Is of so floodgate[74] and o'erbearing nature
That it engluts and swallows other sorrows,
And it is still itself.

DUKE   Why, what's the matter?

BRABANTIO My daughter! O, my daughter!

ALL   Dead?

BRABANTIO   Ay, to me.

60   She is abused, stol'n from me, and corrupted
By spells and medicines bought of mountebanks;
For nature so prepost'rously to err,
Being not deficient, blind, or lame of sense,
Sans[75] witchcraft could not.

DUKE Whoe'er he be that in this foul proceeding
Hath thus beguiled your daughter of herself,
And you of her, the bloody book of law
You shall yourself read in the bitter letter
After your own sense; yea, though our proper[76] son
Stood in your action.[77]

70   BRABANTIO   Humbly I thank your grace.
Here is the man—this Moor, whom now, it seems,
Your special mandate for the state affairs
Hath hither brought.

ALL   We are very sorry for't.

DUKE [to Othello] What, in your own part, can you say to this?

BRABANTIO Nothing, but this is so.

OTHELLO Most potent, grave, and reverend signiors,
My very noble, and approved good masters,
That I have ta'en away this old man's daughter,
It is most true; true I have married her.

80   The very head and front[78] of my offending
Hath this extent, no more. Rude am I in my speech,

74. Overflowing
75. Without
76. My own
77. Were accused by you
78. The utmost

And little blessed with the soft phrase of peace;
For since these arms of mine had seven years' pith[79]
Till now some nine moons wasted, they have used
Their dearest action in the tented field;
And little of this great world can I speak
More than pertains to feats of broil and battle;
And therefore little shall I grace my cause
In speaking for myself. Yet, by your gracious patience,
90   I will a round[80] unvarnished tale deliver
Of my whole course of love—what drugs, what charms,
What conjuration, and what mighty magic
(For such proceeding am I charged withal)
I won his daughter.
BRABANTIO   A maiden never bold;
Of spirit so still and quiet that her motion
Blushed at herself;[81] and she—in spite of nature,
Of years, of country, credit, everything—
To fall in love with what she feared to look on!
It is a judgment maimed and most imperfect
100   That will confess perfection so could err
Against all rules of nature, and must be driven
To find out practices of cunning hell
Why this should be. I therefore vouch again
That with some mixtures pow'rful o'er the blood,
Or with some dram, conjured to this effect,
He wrought upon her.
DUKE   To vouch this is no proof,
Without more certain and more overt test
Than these thin habits[82] and poor likelihoods
Of modern seeming[83] do prefer against him.
110 1. SENATOR   But, Othello, speak.
Did you by indirect and forcèd courses
Subdue and poison this young maid's affections?
Or came it by request, and such fair question
As soul to soul affordeth?
OTHELLO   I do beseech you,
Send for the lady to the Sagittary
And let her speak of me before her father.
If you do find me foul in her report,
The trust, the office, I do hold of you

79. Strength
80. Plain
81. *her motion . . . herself:* her own emotions made her blush

82. Slight appearing
83. Commonplace suppositions

Not only take away, but let your sentence
Even fall upon my life.

120 DUKE   Fetch Desdemona hither.

OTHELLO   Ancient, conduct them; you best know the place.

Exit Iago, with two or three Attendants.

And till she come, as truly as to heaven
I do confess the vices of my blood,
So justly to your grave ears I'll present
How I did thrive in this fair lady's love,
And she in mine.

DUKE   Say it, Othello.

OTHELLO   Her father loved me, oft invited me;
Still questioned me the story of my life

130 From year to year—the battles, sieges, fortunes
That I have passed.
I ran it through, even from my boyish days
To th' very moment that he bade me tell it.
Wherein I spake of most disastrous chances,
Of moving accidents by flood and field;
Of hairbreadth scapes i' th' imminent deadly breach;
Of being taken by the insolent foe
And sold to slavery; of my redemption thence
And portance[84] in my travel's history;

140 Wherein of anters[85] vast and deserts idle,[86]
Rough quarries, rocks, and hills whose heads touch heaven,
It was my hint to speak—such was the process;
And of the Cannibals that each other eat,
The Anthropophagi,[87] and men whose heads
Do grow beneath their shoulders. This to hear
Would Desdemona seriously incline;
But still the house affairs would draw her thence;
Which ever as she could with haste dispatch,

150 She'ld come again, and with a greedy ear
Devour up my discourse. Which I observing,
Took once a pliant[88] hour, and found good means
To draw from her a prayer of earnest heart
That I would all my pilgrimage dilate,[89]
Whereof by parcels[90] she had something heard,
But not intentively.[91] I did consent,
And often did beguile her of her tears

84. Behavior
85. Caves
86. Barren
87. Man-eaters

88. Convenient
89. Relate
90. In bits and pieces
91. With full attention

When I did speak of some distressful stroke
That my youth suffered. My story being done,
She gave me for my pains a world of sighs.
160   She swore, i' faith, 'twas strange, 'twas passing strange;
'Twas pitiful, 'twas wondrous pitiful.
She wished she had not heard it; yet she wished
That heaven had made her such a man. She thanked me;
And bade me, if I had a friend that loved her,
I should but teach him how to tell my story,
And that would woo her. Upon this hint[92] I spake.
She loved me for the dangers I had passed,
And I loved her that she did pity them.
This only is the witchcraft I have used.
170   Here comes the lady. Let her witness it.

Enter Desdemona, Iago, Attendants.

DUKE   I think this tale would win my daughter too.
Good Brabantio,
Take up this mangled matter at the best.
Men do their broken weapons rather use
Than their bare hands.
BRABANTIO   I pray you hear her speak.
If she confess that she was half the wooer,
Destruction on my head if my bad blame
Light on the man! Come hither, gentle mistress.
Do you perceive in all this noble company
Where most you owe obedience?
180   DESDEMONA   My noble father,
I do perceive here a divided duty.
To you I am bound for life and education;
My life and education[93] both do learn me
How to respect you: you are the lord of duty;
I am hitherto your daughter. But here's my husband;
And so much duty as my mother showed
To you, preferring you before her father,
So much I challenge[94] that I may profess
Due to the Moor my lord.
BRABANTIO   God b' wi' ye! I have done.
190   Please if your grace, on to the state affairs.
I had rather to adopt a child than get[95] it.

92. Opportunity   94. Claim
93. Upbringing   95. Beget

Come hither, Moor.
I here do give thee that with all my heart
Which, but thou hast already, with all my heart
I would keep from thee. For your sake,[96] jewel,
I am glad at soul I have no other child;
For thy escape would teach me tyranny,
To hang clogs on them. I have done, my lord.

DUKE   Let me speak like yourself[97] and lay a sentence[98]
Which, as a grise[99] or step, may help these lovers
Into your favor.
When remedies are past, the griefs are ended
By seeing the worst, which late on hopes depended.
To mourn a mischief that is past and gone
Is the next way to draw new mischief on.
What cannot be preserved when fortune takes,
Patience her injury a mock'ry makes.
The robbed that smiles steals something from the thief;
He robs himself that spends a bootless[100] grief.

BRABANTIO   So let the Turk of Cyprus us beguile:
We lose it not so long as we can smile.
He bears the sentence well that nothing bears
But the free comfort which from thence he hears;
But he bears both the sentence and the sorrow
That to pay grief must of poor patience borrow.
These sentences, to sugar, or to gall,
Being strong on both sides, are equivocal.
But words are words. I never yet did hear
That the bruised heart was piecèd[101] through the ear.
Beseech you, now to the affairs of state.

DUKE   The Turk with a most mighty preparation makes for Cyprus. Othello, the fortitude of the place is best known to you; and though we have there a substitute of most allowed[102] sufficiency, yet opinion, a sovereign mistress of effects,[103] throws a more safer voice on you. You must therefore be content to slubber[104] the gloss of your new fortunes with this more stubborn and boisterous expedition.

OTHELLO   The tyrant custom, most grave senators,
Hath made the flinty and steel couch of war
My thrice-driven[105] bed of down. I do agnize[106]

96. Because of what you have done
97. As you should
98. Maxim
99. Degree
100. Unavailing
101. Relieved
102. Acknowledged
103. Of what should be done
104. Sully
105. Thrice-winnowed; i.e., softest
106. Recognize

A natural and prompt alacrity
I find in hardness;[107] and do undertake
These present wars against the Ottomites.
Most humbly, therefore, bending to your state,
I crave fit disposition[108] for my wife,
Due reference of place, and exhibition,[109]
With such accommodation and besort[110]
As levels with her breeding.

240 DUKE   If you please,
Be't at her father's.

BRABANTIO   I'll not have it so.

OTHELLO   Nor I.

DESDEMONA   Nor I. I would not there reside,
To put my father in impatient thoughts
By being in his eye. Most gracious duke,
To my unfolding lend your prosperous[111] ear,
And let me find a charter in your voice,
To assist my simpleness.

DUKE   What would you, Desdemona?

DESDEMONA   That I did love the Moor to live with him,
250   My downright violence, and storm of fortunes,
May trumpet to the world. My heart's subdued
Even to the very quality of my lord.
I saw Othello's visage in his mind,
And to his honors and his valiant parts
Did I my soul and fortunes consecrate.
So that, dear lords, if I be left behind,
A moth of peace, and he go to the war,
The rites for which I love him are bereft me,
And I a heavy interim shall support
260   By his dear absence. Let me go with him.

OTHELLO   Let her have your voices.
Vouch with me, heaven, I therefore beg it not
To please the palate of my appetite,
Nor to comply with heat[112]—the young affects[113]
In me defunct—and proper[114] satisfaction;
But to be free and bounteous to her mind;
And heaven defend[115] your good souls that you think

---

107. *alacrity . . . hardness:* readiness to en-
    dure hardship
108. Suitable provision
109. *reference . . . exhibition:* assignment of
    residence and allowance of money
110. Suitable company

111. Favorable
112. Sexual desire
113. Excesses of youthful passion
114. Personal
115. Forbid

I will your serious and great business scant
For[116] she is with me. No, when light-winged toys
270   Of feathered Cupid seel[117] with wanton dullness
My speculative and officed instruments,[118]
That[119] my disports corrupt and taint my business,
Let housewives make a skillet of my helm,
And all indign[120] and base adversities
Make head against my estimation![121]

DUKE   Be it as you shall privately determine,
Either for her stay or going. Th' affair cries haste,
And speed must answer it. You must hence to-night.

DESDEMONA   To-night, my lord?

DUKE   This night.

OTHELLO   With all my heart.

280   DUKE   At nine i' th' morning here we'll meet again.
Othello, leave some officer behind,
And he shall our commission bring to you,
With such things else of quality and respect
As doth import[122] you.

OTHELLO   So please your grace, my ancient;
A man he is of honesty and trust.
To his conveyance I assign my wife,
With what else needful your good grace shall think
To be sent after me.

DUKE   Let it be so.
Good night to every one. [To Brabantio] And, noble signoir,
290   If virtue no delighted[123] beauty lack,
Your son-in-law is far more fair than black.

1. SENATOR   Adieu, brave Moor. Use Desdemona well.

BRABANTIO   Look to her, Moor, if thou hast eyes to see:
She has deceived her father, and may thee.

OTHELLO   My life upon her faith!

                              Exeunt Duke, Senators, Officers, &c.
                    Honest Iago,
My Desdemona must I leave to thee.
I prithee let thy wife attend on her,
And bring them after in the best advantage.[124]
Come, Desdemona. I have but an hour

---

116. Because
117. Blind
118. *My . . . instruments:* perceptual and
        mental powers
119. So that
120. Shameful

121. Reputation
122. Concern
123. Delightful
124. *in . . . advantage:* at the most opportune
        time

Of love, of worldly matters and direction,
300   To spend with thee. We must obey the time.

Exit Moor and Desdemona.

RODERIGO   Iago,—

IAGO   What say'st thou, noble heart?

RODERIGO   What will I do, think'st thou?

IAGO   Why, go to bed and sleep.

RODERIGO   I will incontinently[125] drown myself.

IAGO   If thou dost, I shall never love thee after. Why, thou silly gentleman?

RODERIGO   It is silliness to live when to live is torment; and then have we a
      prescription to die when death is our physician.

IAGO   O villainous! I have looked upon the world for four times seven years;
310   and since I could distinguish betwixt a benefit and an injury, I never
      found man that knew how to love himself. Ere I would say I would
      drown myself for the love of a guinea hen, I would change my humanity
      with a baboon.

RODERIGO   What should I do? I confess it is my shame to be so fond, but it is
      not in my virtue to amend it.

IAGO   Virtue? a fig! 'Tis in ourselves that we are thus or thus. Our bodies are
      our gardens, to the which our wills are gardeners; so that if we will plant
      nettles or sow lettuce, set hyssop and weed up thyme, supply it with one
      gender[126] of herbs or distract it with many—either to have it sterile with
320   idleness or manured with industry—why, the power and corrigible[127]
      authority of this lies in our wills. If the balance of our lives had not one
      scale of reason to poise another of sensuality, the blood and baseness of
      our natures would conduct us to most preposterous conclusions. But we
      have reason to cool our raging motions, our carnal stings, our unbitted[128]
      lusts; whereof I take this that you call love to be a sect or scion.[129]

RODERIGO   It cannot be.

IAGO   It is merely a lust of the blood and a permission of the will. Come, be a
      man! Drown thyself? Drown cats and blind puppies! I have professed
      me thy friend, and I confess me knit to thy deserving with cables of
330   perdurable[130] toughness. I could never better stead[131] thee than now. Put
      money in thy purse. Follow these wars; defeat thy favor[132] with an
      usurped beard. I say, put money in thy purse. It cannot be that Des-
      demona should long continue her love to the Moor—put money in thy
      purse—nor he his to her. It was a violent commencement, and thou shalt
      see an answerable sequestration[133]—put but money in thy purse. These
      Moors are changeable in their wills—fill thy purse with money. The food

125. Immediately
126. Species
127. Corrective
128. Uncontrolled
129. Cutting or offshoot

130. Everlasting
131. Help
132. Disguise yourself
133. Equally abrupt ending

that to him now is as luscious as locusts[134] shall be to him shortly as bitter as coloquintida.[135] She must change for youth: when she is sated with his body, she will find the error of her choice. She must have change, she must. Therefore put money in thy purse. If thou wilt needs damn thyself, do it a more delicate way than drowning. Make[136] all the money thou canst. If sanctimony[137] and a frail vow betwixt an erring[138] barbarian and a supersubtle[139] Venetian be not too hard for my wits and all the tribe of hell, thou shalt enjoy her. Therefore make money. A pox of drowning! 'Tis clean out of the way. Seek thou rather to be hanged in compassing thy joy than to be drowned and go without her.

RODERIGO   Wilt thou be fast[140] to my hopes, if I depend on the issue?

IAGO   Thou art sure of me. Go, make money. I have told thee often, and I retell thee again and again, I hate the Moor. My cause is hearted;[141] thine hath no less reason. Let us be conjunctive in our revenge against him. If thou canst cuckold him, thou dost thyself a pleasure, me a sport. There are many events in the womb of time, which will be delivered. Traverse,[142] go, provide thy money! We have more of this to-morrow. Adieu.

RODERIGO   Where shall we meet i' th' morning?

IAGO   At my lodging.

RODERIGO   I'll be with thee betimes.

IAGO   Go to, farewell.—Do you hear, Roderigo?

RODERIGO   What say you?

IAGO   No more of drowning, do you hear?

RODERIGO   I am changed.

IAGO   Go to, farewell. Put money enough in your purse.

RODERIGO   I'll sell my land.   *Exit.*

IAGO   Thus do I ever make my fool my purse;
  For I mine own gained knowledge should profane
  If I would time expend with such a snipe[143]
  But for my sport and profit. I hate the Moor;
  And it is thought abroad that 'twixt my sheets
  H'as done my office. I know not if't be true;
  Yet I, for mere suspicion in that kind,
  Will do as if for surety.[144] He holds me well;[145]
  The better shall my purpose work on him.
  Cassio's a proper[146] man. Let me see now:

---

134. Sweet Mediterranean fruit
135. Bitter apple, used as a purgative
136. Raise, or get together
137. Religious ceremony
138. Vagabond
139. Highly refined
140. True

141. Rooted in my heart; i.e., deeply felt
142. March forward
143. Woodcock; silly bird; i.e., fool
144. As if it were a proven fact
145. In high regard
146. Handsome

To get his place, and to plume up my will[147]
In double knavery—How, how?—Let's see:—
After some time, to abuse Othello's ear
That he is too familiar with his wife.
He hath a person and a smooth dispose[148]
To be suspected—framed to make women false.
The Moor is of a free and open nature
That thinks men honest that but seem to be so;
And will as tenderly be led by th' nose
As asses are.
I have't! It is engendered! Hell and night
Must bring this monstrous birth to the world's light.

Exit.

147. Dress up my intentions   148. Manner

ACT II

SCENE 1

Enter Montano and two Gentlemen.

MONTANO   What from the cape can you discern at sea?
1. GENTLEMAN   Nothing at all: it is a high-wrought flood.
    I cannot 'twixt the heaven and the main
    Descry a sail.
MONTANO   Methinks the wind hath spoke aloud at land;
    A fuller blast ne'er shook our battlements.
    If it hath ruffianed so upon the sea,
    What ribs of oak, when mountains melt on them,
    Can hold the mortise?[1] What shall we hear of this?
2. GENTLEMAN   A segregation[2] of the Turkish fleet.
    For do but stand upon the foaming shore,
    The chidden billow seems to pelt the clouds;
    The wind-shaked surge, with high and monstrous mane,
    Seems to cast water on the burning Bear
    And quench the guards[3] of th' ever-fixèd pole.
    I never did like molestation[4] view
    On the enchafèd flood.

1. Hold the joints together   3. Stars near the North Star
2. Scattering   4. Disturbance

MONTANO   If that the Turkish fleet
    Be not ensheltered and embayed, they are drowned;
    It is impossible they bear it out.

Enter a third Gentleman.

20 3. GENTLEMAN   News, lads! Our wars are done.
    The desperate tempest hath so banged the Turks
    That their designment halts.[5] A noble ship of Venice
    Hath seen a grievous wrack and sufferance[6]
    On most part of their fleet.
    MONTANO   How? Is this true?
    3. GENTLEMAN   The ship is here put in,
    A Veronesa;[7] Michael Cassio,
    Lieutenant to the warlike Moor Othello,
    Is come on shore; the Moor himself at sea,
    And is in full commission here for Cyprus.
30 MONTANO   I am glad on't. 'Tis a worthy governor.
    3. GENTLEMAN   But this same Cassio, though he speak of comfort
    Touching the Turkish loss, yet he looks sadly
    And prays the Moor be safe, for they were parted
    With foul and violent tempest.
    MONTANO   Pray heaven he be;
    For I have served him, and the man commands
    Like a full soldier. Let's to the seaside, ho!
    As well to see the vessel that's come in
    As to throw out our eyes for brave Othello,
    Even till we make the main[8] and th' aerial blue
    An indistinct regard.[9]
40 3. GENTLEMAN   Come, let's do so;
    For every minute is expectancy
    Of more arrivance.

Enter Cassio.

CASSIO   Thanks, you the valiant of this warlike isle,
    That so approve the Moor! O, let the heavens
    Give him defense against the elements,
    For I have lost him on a dangerous sea!
    MONTANO   Is he well shipped?

5. Plan is crippled
6. Damage
7. Ship furnished by Verona

8. Sea
9. Indistinguishable

CASSIO   His bark is stoutly timbered, and his pilot
   Of very expert and approved allowance;[10]
50   Therefore my hopes, not surfeited to death,
   Stand in bold cure.[11]   [*Within*] A sail, a sail, a sail!

Enter a Messenger.

CASSIO   What noise?
MESSENGER   The town is empty; on the brow o' th' sea
   Stand ranks of people, and they cry 'A sail!'
CASSIO   My hopes do shape him for the governor.   [*A shot.*]
2. GENTLEMAN   They do discharge their shot of courtesy:
   Our friends at least.
CASSIO   I pray you, sir, go forth
   And give us truth who 'tis that is arrived.
2. GENTLEMAN   I shall.   *Exit.*
60 MONTANO   But, good lieutenant, is your general wived?
CASSIO   Most fortunately. He hath achieved a maid
   That paragons[12] description and wild fame;
   One that excels the quirks of blazoning pens,[13]
   And in th' essential vesture of creation
   Does tire the ingener.[14]

Enter Second Gentleman.

                How now? Who has put in?
2. GENTLEMAN   'Tis one Iago, ancient to the general.
CASSIO   H'as had most favorable and happy speed:
   Tempests themselves, high seas, and howling winds,
   The guttered[15] rocks and congregated sands,
70   Traitors ensteeped[16] to clog the guiltless keel,
   As having sense of beauty, do omit
   Their mortal[17] natures, letting go safely by
   The divine Desdemona.
MONTANO   What is she?
CASSIO   She that I spake of, our great captain's captain,

---

10. Skill
11. *not surfeited . . . cure:* not having been overindulged stand a good chance of being fulfilled
12. Surpasses
13. *quirks . . . pens:* ingenious descriptions of writers who seek to list all her beauties
14. *in . . . ingener:* her essential nature as it was created by God overwhelms the imagination of anyone who seeks to praise it
15. Jagged
16. Submerged
17. Deadly

Left in the conduct of the bold Iago,
Whose footing[18] here anticipates our thoughts
A se'nnight's[19] speed. Great Jove, Othello guard,
And swell his sail with thine own pow'rful breath,
That he may bless this bay with his tall ship,
80   Make love's quick pants in Desdemona's arms,
Give renewed fire to our extinct spirits,
And bring all Cyprus comfort!

Enter Desdemona, Iago, Roderigo, and Emilia with Attendants.

                              O, behold!
The riches of the ship is come on shore!
Ye men of Cyprus, let her have your knees.
Hail to thee, lady! and the grace of heaven,
Before, behind thee, and on every hand,
Enwheel thee round!
DESDEMONA   I thank you, valiant Cassio.
What tidings can you tell me of my lord?
CASSIO   He is not yet arrived; nor know I aught
90   But that he's well and will be shortly here.
DESDEMONA   O but I fear! How lost you company?
CASSIO   The great contention of the sea and skies
Parted our fellowship.   [*Within*] A sail, a sail! [*A shot.*]
              But hark. A sail!
2. GENTLEMAN   They give their greeting to the citadel;
This likewise is a friend.
CASSIO   See for the news.
                                        Exit Gentleman.
Good ancient, you are welcome. [*To Emilia*] Welcome, mistress.—
Let it not gall your patience, good Iago,
That I extend[20] my manners. 'Tis my breeding
100   That gives me this bold show of courtesy. [*Kisses Emilia.*]
IAGO   Sir, would she give you so much of her lips
As of her tongue she oft bestows on me,
You would have enough.
DESDEMONA   Alas, she has no speech!
IAGO   In faith, too much.
I find it still when I have list[21] to sleep.
Marry, before your ladyship, I grant,

18. Landing
19. Week's
                                   20. Show
                                   21. Desire

She puts her tongue a little in her heart
And chides with thinking.

EMILIA   You have little cause to say so.

110 IAGO   Come on, come on! You are pictures out of doors,
Bells in your parlors, wildcats in your kitchens,
Saints in your injuries, devils being offended,
Players[22] in your housewifery, and housewives[23] in your beds.

DESDEMONA   O, fie upon thee, slanderer!

IAGO   Nay, it is true, or else I am a Turk:
You rise to play, and go to bed to work.

EMILIA   You shall not write my praise.

IAGO   No, let me not.

DESDEMONA   What wouldst thou write of me, if thou shouldst praise me?

IAGO   O gentle lady, do not put me to't,

120 For I am nothing if not critical.

DESDEMONA   Come on, assay.[24]—There's one gone to the harbor?

IAGO   Ay, madam.

DESDEMONA   I am not merry; but I do beguile
The thing I am by seeming otherwise.—
Come, how wouldst thou praise me?

IAGO   I am about it; but indeed my invention
Comes from my pate as birdlime[25] does from frieze[26]—
It plucks out brains and all. But my Muse labors,
And thus she is delivered:

130 If she be fair[27] and wise, fairness and wit—
The one's for use, the other useth it.

DESDEMONA   Well praised! How if she be black[28] and witty?

IAGO   If she be black, and thereto have a wit,
She'll find a white that shall her blackness fit.

DESDEMONA   Worse and worse!

EMILIA   How if fair and foolish?

IAGO   She never yet was foolish that was fair,
For even her folly[29] helped her to an heir.

DESDEMONA   These are old fond[30] paradoxes to make fools laugh i' th'

140 alehouse. What miserable praise hast thou for her that's foul[31] and
foolish?

IAGO   There's none so foul, and foolish thereunto,
But does foul pranks which fair and wise ones do.

DESDEMONA   O heavy ignorance! Thou praisest the worst best. But what

22. Actors
23. Hussies
24. Try
25. Sticky paste used to catch birds
26. Coarse cloth

27. Blonde
28. Brunette
29. Wantonness
30. Foolish
31. Ugly

praise couldst thou bestow on a deserving woman indeed—one that in the authority of her merit did justly put on the vouch[32] of very malice itself?

IAGO   She that was ever fair, and never proud;
150   Had tongue at will, and yet was never loud;
        Never lacked gold, and yet went never gay;[33]
        Fled from her wish, and yet said 'Now I may';
        She that, being angered, her revenge being nigh,
        Bade her wrong stay,[34] and her displeasure fly;
        She that in wisdom never was so frail
        To change the cod's head for the salmon's tail;[35]
        She that could think, and ne'er disclose her mind;
        See suitors following, and not look behind:
        She was a wight[36] (if ever such wight were)—
160 DESDEMONA   To do what?

IAGO   To suckle fools[37] and chronicle small beer.[38]

DESDEMONA   O most lame and impotent conclusion! Do not learn of him, Emilia, though he be thy husband. How say you, Cassio? Is he not a most profane and liberal[39] counsellor?

CASSIO   He speaks home,[40] madam. You may relish him more in the[41] soldier than in the scholar.

IAGO [aside]   He takes her by the palm. Ay, well said, whisper! With as little
170   a web as this will I ensnare as great a fly as Cassio. Ay, smile upon her, do! I will gyve[42] thee in thine own courtship.[43]—You say true; 'tis so, indeed!—If such tricks as these strip you out of your lieutenantry, it had been better you had not kissed your three fingers so oft—which now again you are most apt to play the sir[44] in. Very good! well kissed! an excellent curtsy! 'Tis so, indeed. Yet again your fingers to your lips? Would they were clyster pipes[45] for your sake! [Trumpet within.] The
180   Moor! I know his trumpet.

CASSIO   'Tis truly so.

DESDEMONA   Let's meet him and receive him.

CASSIO   Lo, where he comes.

Enter Othello and Attendants.

32. *put . . . vouch:* compel the praise
33. Extravagantly dressed
34. Sense of injury cease
35. *To . . . tail:* to exchange something common but valuable for something rare but useless
36. Person
37. Babies
38. Keep petty household accounts in order

39. Free-speaking; i.e., lewd
40. Bluntly
41. In the character of
42. Trap
43. Courtly manners
44. Courtly gentleman
45. Syringes for an enema

OTHELLO   O my fair warrior!

DESDEMONA   My dear Othello!

OTHELLO   It gives me wonder great as my content
To see you here before me. O my soul's joy!
If after every tempest come such calms,
May the winds blow till they have wakened death!
And let the laboring bark climb hills of seas
190 Olympus-high, and duck again as low
As hell's from heaven! If it were now to die,
'Twere now to be most happy; for I fear
My soul hath her content so absolute
That not another comfort like to this
Succeeds in unknown fate.

DESDEMONA   The heavens forbid
But that our loves and comforts should increase
Even as our days do grow.

OTHELLO   Amen to that, sweet powers!
I cannot speak enough of this content;
It stops me here; it is too much of joy.
200 And this, and this, the greatest discords be   *They kiss.*
That e'er our hearts shall make!

IAGO   [*Aside*] O, you are well tuned now!
But I'll set down⁴⁶ the pegs that make this music,
As honest as I am.

OTHELLO   Come, let us to the castle.
News, friends! Our wars are done; the Turks are drowned.
How does my old acquaintance of this isle?—
Honey, you shall be well desired⁴⁷ in Cyprus;
I have found great love amongst them. O my sweet,
I prattle out of fashion, and I dote
In mine own comforts. I prithee, good Iago,
210 Go to the bay and disembark my coffers.
Bring thou the master to the citadel;
He is a good one, and his worthiness
Does challenge much respect.—Come, Desdemona,
Once more well met at Cyprus.
                         Exit Othello with all but Iago and Roderigo.

IAGO [*to an Attendant, who goes out*].   Do thou meet me presently at the harbor. [*To Roderigo*] Come hither. If thou be'st valiant (as they say base
men being in love have then a nobility in their natures more than is
native to them), list me. The lieutenant to-night watches on the court of

46. Loosen   47. Warmly welcomed

guard.[48] First, I must tell thee this: Desdemona is directly in love with
220   him.

RODERIGO   With him? Why, 'tis not possible.

IAGO   Lay thy finger thus,[49] and let thy soul be instructed. Mark me with
what violence she first loved the Moor, but for bragging and telling her
fantastical lies; and will she love him still for prating? Let not thy discreet heart think it. Her eye must be fed; and what delight shall she have
to look on the devil? When the blood is made dull with the act of sport,
there should be, again to inflame it and to give satiety a fresh appetite,
loveliness in favor, sympathy in years, manners, and beauties; all which
the Moor is defective in. Now for want of these required conveniences,[50]
230   her delicate tenderness will find itself abused, begin to heave the
gorge,[51] disrelish and abhor the Moor. Very nature will instruct her in it
and compel her to some second choice. Now, sir, this granted—as it is a
most pregnant and unforced position—who stands so eminent in the
degree of this fortune as Cassio does? A knave very voluble; no further
conscionable than in putting on the mere form of civil and humane[52]
seeming for the better compassing of his salt[53] and most hidden loose
affection? Why, none! why, none! A slipper[54] and subtle knave; a
finder-out of occasions; that has an eye can stamp and counterfeit advantages, though true advantage never present itself; a devilish knave! Be-
240   sides, the knave is handsome, young, and hath all those requisites in
him that folly and green[55] minds look after. A pestilent complete knave!
and the woman hath found him already.

RODERIGO   I cannot believe that in her; she's full of most blessed condition.

IAGO   Blessed fig's-end! The wine she drinks is made of grapes. If she had
been blessed, she would never have loved the Moor. Blessed pudding!
Didst thou not see her paddle with the palm of his hand? Didst not mark
that?

RODERIGO   Yes, that I did; but that was but courtesy.

IAGO   Lechery, by this hand! an index and obscure prologue to the history
250   of lust and foul thoughts. They met so near with their lips that their
breaths embraced together. Villainous thoughts, Roderigo! When these
mutualities so marshal the way, hard at hand comes the master and
main exercise, th' incorporate[56] conclusion. Pish! But, sir, be you ruled
by me: I have brought you from Venice. Watch you to-night; for the
command, I'll lay't upon you. Cassio knows you not. I'll not be far from
you: do you find some occasion to anger Cassio, either by speaking too

48. *watches . . . guard:* Has charge of the watch
49. On your lips
50. Compatibilities
51. Be nauseated
52. Courteous
53. Lecherous
54. Slippery
55. Wanton and youthful
56. Sexual

loud, or tainting⁵⁷ his discipline, or from what other course you please
which the time shall more favorably minister.

RODERIGO Well.

260 IAGO Sir, he is rash and very sudden in choler,⁵⁸ and haply with his trun-
cheon may strike at you. Provoke him that he may; for even out of that
will I cause these of Cyprus to mutiny; whose qualification⁵⁹ shall come
into no true taste again but by the displanting of Cassio. So shall you
have a shorter journey to your desires by the means I shall then have to
prefer⁶⁰ them; and the impediment most profitably removed without the
which there were no expectation of our prosperity.

RODERIGO I will do this if you can bring it to any opportunity.

IAGO I warrant thee. Meet me by and by at the citadel; I must fetch his
necessaries ashore. Farewell.

270 RODERIGO Adieu.   *Exit.*

IAGO That Cassio loves her, I do well believe it;
That she loves him, 'tis apt and of great credit.⁶¹
The Moor, howbeit that I endure him not,
Is of a constant, loving, noble nature,
And I dare think he'll prove to Desdemona
A most dear husband. Now I do love her too;
Not out of absolute lust, though peradventure
I stand accountant for as great a sin,
But partly led to diet my revenge,
280 For that I do suspect the lusty Moor
Hath leaped into my seat; the thought whereof
Doth, like a poisonous mineral, gnaw my inwards;
And nothing can or shall content my soul
Till I am evened with him, wife for wife;
Or failing so, yet that I put the Moor
At least into a jealousy so strong
That judgment cannot cure. Which thing to do,
If this poor trash of Venice, whom I trash⁶²
For his quick hunting, stand the putting on,⁶³
290 I'll have our Michael Cassio on the hip,⁶⁴
Abuse him to the Moor in the rank garb⁶⁵
(For I fear Cassio with my nightcap too),

57. Discrediting
58. Quick to anger
59. Satisfaction
60. Advance
61. *apt . . . credit:* probable and believable
62. Hang weights on, as was done to hounds to restrain them from hunting too fast
63. *stand the putting on:* performs properly in response to my command
64. In a vulnerable position (a term from wrestling)
65. Coarse manner

Make the Moor thank me, love me, and reward me
For making him egregiously an ass
And practicing upon[66] his peace and quiet
Even to madness. 'Tis here, but yet confused:
Knavery's plain face is never seen till used.   *Exit.*

SCENE 2

Enter Othello's Herald, with a proclamation.

HERALD   It is Othello's pleasure, our noble and valiant general, that, upon
certain tidings now arrived, importing the mere perdition[67] of the Turkish fleet, every man put himself into triumph; some to dance, some to
make bonfires, each man to what sport and revels his addiction leads
him. For, besides these beneficial news, it is the celebration of his nuptial. So much was his pleasure should be proclaimed. All offices[68] are
open, and there is full liberty of feasting from this present hour of five
till the bell have told eleven. Heaven bless the isle of Cyprus and our
noble general Othello!   *Exit.*

SCENE 3

Enter Othello, Desdemona, Cassio, and Attendants.

OTHELLO   Good Michael, look you to the guard to-night.
Let's teach ourselves that honorable stop,
Not to outsport discretion.
CASSIO   Iago hath direction what to do;
But not withstanding, with my personal eye
Will I look to't.
OTHELLO   Iago is most honest.
Michael, good night. To-morrow with your earliest
Let me have speech with you. [*To Desdemona*] Come, my dear love.
The purchase made, the fruits are to ensue;
10   That profit's yet to come 'tween me and you.—
Good night.
                              Exit Othello with Desdemona and Attendants.

Enter Iago.

CASSIO   Welcome, Iago. We must to the watch.

66. Plotting against   68. Kitchens and storerooms
67. Complete destruction

IAGO   Not this hour, lieutenant; 'tis not yet ten o' th' clock. Our general cast[69] us thus early for the love of his Desdemona; who let us not therefore blame. He hath not yet made wanton the night with her, and she is sport for Jove.

CASSIO   She's a most exquisite lady.

20   IAGO   And, I'll warrant her, full of game.

CASSIO   Indeed, she's a most fresh and delicate creature.

IAGO   What an eye she has! Methinks it sounds a parley to provocation.

CASSIO   An inviting eye; and yet methinks right modest.

IAGO   And when she speaks, is it not an alarum[70] to love?

CASSIO   She is indeed perfection.

30   IAGO   Well, happiness to their sheets! Come, lieutenant, I have a stoup[71] of wine, and here without are a brace of Cyprus gallants that would fain have a measure to the health of black Othello.

CASSIO   Not to-night, good Iago. I have very poor and unhappy brains for drinking; I could well wish courtesy would invent some other custom of entertainment.

IAGO   O, they are our friends. But one cup! I'll drink for you.

40   CASSIO   I have drunk but one cup to-night, and that was craftily qualified[72] too; and behold what innovation[73] it makes here. I am unfortunate in the infirmity and dare not task my weakness with any more.

IAGO   What, man! 'Tis a night of revels: the gallants desire it.

CASSIO   Where are they?

IAGO   Here at the door; I pray you call them in.

CASSIO   I'll do't, but it dislikes me.[74]   *Exit.*

50   IAGO   If I can fasten but one cup upon him
With that which he hath drunk to-night already,
He'll be as full of quarrel and offense
As my young mistress' dog. Now my sick fool Roderigo,
Whom love hath turned almost the wrong side out,
To Desdemona hath to-night caroused
Potations pottle-deep;[75] and he's to watch.
Three lads of Cyprus—noble swelling spirits,
That hold their honors in a wary distance,[76]
The very elements of this warlike isle—
60   Have I to-night flustered with flowing cups,
And they watch too. Now, 'mongst this flock of drunkards
Am I to put our Cassio in some action
That may offend the isle.

69. Dismissed
70. Trumpet signal
71. Two-quart tankard
72. Carefully diluted
73. Disturbing change

74. I don't want to
75. To the bottom of the tankard
76. *hold . . . distance:* are very touchy about their honor

Enter Cassio, Montano, and Gentlemen; Servants following with wine.

But here they come.
If consequence do but approve my dream,[77]
My boat sails freely, both with wind and stream.
CASSIO 'Fore God, they have given me a rouse[78] already.
MONTANO Good faith, a little one; not past a pint, as I am a soldier.
70 IAGO Some wine, ho!

[*Sings*] And let me the canakin clink, clink;
      And let me the canakin clink.
          A soldier's a man;
          A life's but a span,
      Why then, let a soldier drink.

Some wine, boys!
CASSIO 'Fore God, an excellent song!
IAGO I learned it in England, where indeed they are most potent in potting.
80   Your Dane, your German, and your swag-bellied Hollander—Drink,
      ho!—are nothing to your English.
CASSIO Is your Englishman so expert in his drinking?
IAGO Why, he drinks you with facility your Dane dead drunk; he sweats
      not to overthrow your Almain;[79] he gives your Hollander a vomit ere the
      next pottle can be filled.
CASSIO To the health of our general!
90 MONTANO I am for it, lieutenant, and I'll do you justice.
IAGO O sweet England!

[*Sings*] King Stephen was a worthy peer;
          His breeches cost him but a crown;
      He held 'em sixpence all to dear,
          With that he called the tailor lown.[80]
      He was a wight of high renown,
          And thou art but of low degree.
      'Tis pride that pulls the country down;
          Then take thine auld cloak about thee.

100   Some wine, ho!
CASSIO 'Fore God, this is a more exquisite song than the other.
IAGO Will you hear't again?

77. *If . . . dream:* if events work out as I   79. German
    hope   80. Rascal
78. Drink

CASSIO   No, for I hold him to be unworthy of his place that does those things. Well, God's above all; and there be souls must be saved, and there be souls must not be saved.

IAGO   It's true, good lieutenant.

110   CASSIO   For mine own part—no offense to the general, nor any man of quality—I hope to be saved.

IAGO   And so do I too, lieutenant.

CASSIO   Ay, but, by your leave, not before me. The lieutenant is to be saved before the ancient. Let's have no more of this; let's to our affairs.—God forgive us our sins!—Gentlemen, let's look to our business. Do not think, gentlemen, I am drunk. This is my ancient; this is my right hand, 120   and this is my left. I am not drunk now. I can stand well enough, and speak well enough.

ALL   Excellent well!

CASSIO   Why, very well then. You must not think then that I am drunk.

                                                                                        Exit.

MONTANO   To th' platform, masters. Come, let's set the watch.

IAGO   You see this fellow that is gone before.
　　　He is a soldier fit to stand by Caesar
　　　And give direction; and do but see his vice.
　　　'Tis to his virtue a just equinox,[81]
130　　　The one as long as th' other. 'Tis pity of him.
　　　I fear the trust Othello puts him in,
　　　On some odd time of his infirmity,
　　　Will shake this island.

MONTANO   But is he often thus?

IAGO   'Tis evermore the prologue to his sleep:
　　　He'll watch the horologe a double set[82]
　　　If drink rock not his cradle.

MONTANO   It were well
　　　The general were put in mind of it.
　　　Perhaps he sees it not, or his good nature
　　　Prizes the virtue that appears in Cassio
140　　　And looks not on his evils. Is not this true?

Enter Roderigo.

IAGO   [*aside to him*]   How now, Roderigo?
　　　I pray you after the lieutenant, go!   *Exit Roderigo.*

MONTANO   And 'tis great pity that the noble Moor
　　　Should hazard such a place as his own second

81. Exact equivalent
82. *watch . . . set:* stay awake two times
　　　around the clock

With one of an ingraft[83] infirmity.
It were an honest action to say
So to the Moor.

IAGO   Not I, for this fair island!
I do love Cassio well and would do much
To cure him of this evil.   [*Within*] Help! help!
                    But hark! What noise?

Enter Cassio, driving in Roderigo.

CASSIO Zounds, you rogue! you rascal!
150 MONTANO What's the matter, lieutenant?
CASSIO   A knave teach me my duty?
I'll beat the knave into a twiggen[84] bottle.
RODERIGO Beat me?
CASSIO   Dost thou prate, rogue?   *Strikes him.*
MONTANO   Nay, good lieutenant!
                    Stays him.

Pray, sir, hold your hand.
CASSIO   Let me go, sir.
Or I'll knock you o'er the mazzard.[85]
MONTANO   Come, come, you're drunk!
CASSIO Drunk?   *They fight.*
IAGO [*aside to Roderigo*] Away, I say! Go out and cry a mutiny!
                    Exit Roderigo.

Nay, good lieutenant. God's will, gentlemen!
Help, ho!—lieutenant—sir—Montano—sir—
Help, masters!—Here's a goodly watch indeed!

A bell rung.

160 Who's that which rings the bell? Diablo, ho!
The town will rise. God's will, lieutenant, hold!
You will be shamed for ever.

Enter Othello and Gentlemen with weapons.

OTHELLO   What is the matter here?
MONTANO Zounds, I bleed still. I am hurt to the death.
He dies!
OTHELLO Hold for your lives!

83. Ingrained   85. Head
84. Wicker covered

IAGO   Hold, hold! Lieutenant—sir—Montano—gentlemen!
    Have you forgot all sense of place and duty?
    Hold! The general speaks to you. Hold, hold, for shame!
OTHELLO   Why, how now, ho? From whence ariseth this?
170   Are we turned Turks, and to ourselves do that
    Which heaven hath forbid the Ottomites?
    For Christian shame put by this barbarous brawl!
    He that stirs next to carve for[86] his own rage
    Holds his soul light; he dies upon his motion.
    Silence that dreadful bell! It frights the isle
    From her propriety.[87] What's the matter, masters?
    Honest Iago, that looks dead with grieving,
    Speak. Who began this? On thy love, I charge thee.
IAGO   I do not know. Friends all but now, even now,
180   In quarter, and in terms like bride and groom
    Devesting them for bed; and then, but now—
    As if some planet had unwitted men—
    Swords out, and tilting one at other's breast
    In opposition bloody. I cannot speak
    Any beginning to this peevish odds.[88]
    And would in action glorious I had lost
    Those legs that brought me to a part of it!
OTHELLO   How comes it, Michael, you are thus forgot?
CASSIO   I pray you pardon me; I cannot speak.
190 OTHELLO   Worthy Montano, you were wont be civil;
    The gravity and stillness of your youth
    The world hath noted, and your name is great
    In mouths of wisest censure.[89] What's the matter
    That you unlace your reputation thus
    And spend your rich opinion[90] for the name
    Of a night-brawler? Give me answer to't.
MONTANO   Worthy Othello, I am hurt to danger.
    Your officer, Iago, can inform you,
    While I spare speech, which something now offends[91] me,
200   Of all that I do know; nor know I aught
    By me that's said or done amiss this night,
    Unless self-charity be sometimes a vice,
    And to defend ourselves it be a sin
    When violence assails us.
OTHELLO   Now, by heaven,

---

86. Indulge
87. Natural condition
88. Childish quarrel

89. Judgment
90. High reputation
91. Pains

My blood begins my safer guides to rule,
And passion, having my best judgment collied,[92]
Assays to lead the way. If I once stir
Or do but lift this arm, the best of you
Shall sink in my rebuke. Give me to know
210   How this foul rout began, who set it on;
And he that is approved in[93] this offense,
Though he had twinned with me, both at a birth,
Shall lose me. What! in a town of war,
Yet wild, the people's hearts brimful of fear,
To manage[94] private and domestic quarrel?
In night, and on the court and guard of safety?
'Tis monstrous. Iago, who began't?

MONTANO   If partially affined, or leagued in office,[95]
Thou dost deliver more or less than truth,
Thou art no soldier.

220   IAGO   Touch me not so near.
I had rather have this tongue cut from my mouth
Than it should do offense to Michael Cassio;
Yet I persuade myself, to speak the truth
Shall nothing wrong him. Thus it is, general.
Montano and myself being in speech,
There comes a fellow crying out for help,
And Cassio following him with determined sword
To execute[96] upon him. Sir, this gentleman
Steps in to Cassio and entreats his pause.
230   Myself the crying fellow did pursue,
Lest by his clamor—as it so fell out—
The town might fall in fright. He, swift of foot,
Outran my purpose; and I returned the rather
For that I heard the clink and fall of swords,
And Cassio high in oath; which till to-night
I ne'er might say before. When I came back—
For this was brief—I found them close together
At blow and thrust, even as again they were
When you yourself did part them.
240   More of this matter cannot I report;
But men are men; the best sometimes forget.
Though Cassio did some little wrong to him,

---

92. Darkened
93. Proved guilty of
94. Carry on

95. *partially . . . office:* biased because of
     personal or official ties
96. Work his will

As men in rage strike those that wish them best,
Yet surely Cassio I believe received
From him that fled some strange indignity,
Which patience could not pass.[97]

OTHELLO   I know, Iago,
Thy honesty and love doth mince this matter,
Making it light to Cassio. Cassio, I love thee;
But never more be officer of mine.

Enter Desdemona, attended.

250   Look if my gentle love be not raised up!
I'll make thee an example.

DESDEMONA   What's the matter?

OTHELLO   All's well now, sweeting; come away to bed.
[*To Montano*] Sir, for your hurts, myself will be your surgeon.
Lead him off.   *Montano is led off.*
Iago, look with care about the town
And silence those whom this vile brawl distracted.
Come, Desdemona: 'tis the soldiers' life
To have their balmy slumbers waked with strife.
                          Exit with all but Iago and Cassio.

IAGO   What, are you hurt, lieutenant?

260   CASSIO   Ay, past all surgery.

IAGO   Marry, God forbid!

CASSIO   Reputation, reputation, reputation! O, I have lost my reputation! I
have lost the immortal part of myself, and what remains is bestial. My
reputation, Iago, my reputation!

IAGO   As I am an honest man, I thought you had received some bodily
wound. There is more sense in that than in reputation. Reputation is an
270   idle and most false imposition; oft got without merit and lost without
deserving. You have lost no reputation at all unless you repute yourself
such a loser. What, man! there are ways to recover the general again. You
are but now cast in his mood[98]—a punishment more in policy than in
malice, even so as one would beat his offenseless dog to affright an
imperious lion. Sue to him again, and he's yours.

CASSIO   I will rather sue to be despised than to deceive so good a commander with so slight, so drunken, and so indiscreet an officer. Drunk!
280   and speak parrot![99] and squabble! swagger! swear! and discourse

97. Ignore   99. Talk nonsense
98. *cast . . . mood:* dismissed because of his
   anger

fustian[100] with one's own shadow! O thou invisible spirit of wine, if thou hast no name to be known by, let us call thee devil!

IAGO What was he that you followed with your sword? What had he done to you?

CASSIO I know not.

IAGO Is't possible?

290 CASSIO I remember a mass of things, but nothing distinctly; a quarrel, but nothing wherefore. O God, that men should put an enemy in their mouths to steal away their brains! that we should with joy, pleasance, revel, and applause transform ourselves into beasts!

IAGO Why, but you are now well enough. How came you thus recovered?

CASSIO It hath pleased the devil drunkenness to give place to the devil wrath. One unperfectness shows me another, to make me frankly

300 despise myself.

IAGO Come, you are too severe a moraler. As the time, the place, and the condition of this country stands, I could heartily wish this had not so befall'n; but since it is as it is, mend it for your own good.

CASSIO I will ask him for my place again: he shall tell me I am a drunkard! Had I as many mouths as Hydra,[101] such an answer would stop them all. To be now a sensible man, by and by a fool, and presently a beast! O strange! Every inordinate cup is unblest, and the ingredient is a devil.

310 IAGO Come, come, good wine is a good familiar creature if it be well used. Exclaim no more against it. And, good lieutenant, I think you think I love you.

CASSIO I have well approved[102] it, sir. I drunk!

IAGO You or any man living may be drunk at some time, man. I'll tell you what you shall do. Our general's wife is now the general. I may say so in this respect, for that he hath devoted and given up himself to the con-

320 templation, mark, and denotement of her parts and graces. Confess yourself freely to her; importune her help to put you in your place again. She is of so free,[103] so kind, so apt, so blessed a disposition she holds it a vice in her goodness not to do more than she is requested. This broken joint between you and her husband entreat her to splinter;[104] and my fortunes against any lay[105] worth naming, this crack of your love shall

330 grow stronger than 'twas before.

CASSIO You advise me well.

IAGO I protest, in the sincerity of love and honest kindness.

CASSIO I think it freely; and betimes in the morning will I beseech the

---

100. Bombastic gibberish
101. Many-headed monster of classical mythology
102. Proved
103. Generous
104. Bind up with splints
105. Wager

virtuous Desdemona to undertake for me. I am desperate of my fortunes
if they check me here.

340   IAGO   You are in the right. Good night, lieutenant; I must to the watch.

CASSIO   Good night, honest Iago.   *Exit Cassio.*

IAGO   And what's he then that says I play the villain,
When this advice is free I give and honest,
Probal[106] to thinking, and indeed the course
To win the Moor again? For 'tis most easy
Th' inclining Desdemona to subdue[107]
In any honest suit; she's framed as fruitful[108]
As the free elements. And then for her
To win the Moor—were't to renounce his baptism,
350   All seals and symbols of redeemèd sin—
His soul is so enfettered to her love
That she may make, unmake, do what she list,[109]
Even as her appetite shall play the god
With his weak function. How am I then a villain
To counsel Cassio to this parallel course,
Directly to his good? Divinity[110] of hell!
When devils will the blackest sins put on,
They do suggest at first with heavenly shows,
As I do now. For whiles this honest fool
360   Plies Desdemona to repair his fortunes,
And she for him pleads strongly to the Moor,
I'll pour this pestilence into his ear,
That she repeals[111] him for her body's lust;
And by how much she strives to do him good,
She shall undo her credit with the Moor.
So will I turn her virtue into pitch,
And out of her own goodness make the net
That shall enmesh them all.

Enter Roderigo.

How, now, Roderigo?

RODERIGO   I do follow here in the chase, not like a hound that hunts, but one
370   that fills up the cry.[112] My money is almost spent; I have been to-night
exceedingly well cudgelled; and I think the issue will be—I shall have so

---

106. Probable
107. Persuade
108. Generous
109. Pleases

110. Theology
111. Pleads for his reinstatement
112. Pack

much experience for my pains; and so, with no money at all, and a little
more wit, return again to Venice.

IAGO   How poor are they that have not patience!
What wound did ever heal but by degrees?
Thou know'st we work by wit, and not by witchcraft;
And wit depends on dilatory time.

380   Does't not go well? Cassio hath beaten thee,
And thou by that small hurt hast cashiered[113] Cassio.
Though other things grow fair against the sun,
Yet fruits that blossom first will first be ripe.
Content thyself awhile. By the mass, 'tis morning!
Pleasure and action make the hours seem short.
Retire thee; go where thou art billeted.
Away, I say! Thou shalt know more hereafter.
Nay, get thee gone!   *Exit Roderigo.*
                    Two things are to be done:
My wife must move for Cassio to her mistress;

390   I'll set her on;
Myself the while to draw the Moor apart
And bring him jump[114] when he may Cassio find
Soliciting his wife. Ay, that's the way!
Dull not device by coldness and delay.   *Exit.*

113. Brought about Cassio's discharge   114. At the exact moment

ACT III

SCENE 1

Enter Cassio, with Musicians.

CASSIO   Masters, play here, I will content[1] your pains:
Something that's brief; and bid 'Good morrow, general.'
                                                            They play.

Enter the Clown.

CLOWN   Why, masters, ha' your instruments been at Naples, that they speak
i' th' nose[2] thus?

1. Reward you for
2. *Naples . . . nose:* Naples was reputed to be a center of venereal disease, and ve- nereal diseases were thought to damage the structure of the nose, resulting in a peculiar nasal sound.

MUSICIAN   How, sir, how?

CLOWN   Are these, I pray, called wind instruments?

MUSICIAN   Ay, marry, are they, sir.

CLOWN   O, thereby hangs a tail.

MUSICIAN   Whereby hangs a tale, sir?

CLOWN   Marry, sir, by many a wind instrument that I know. But, masters, here's money for you; and the general so likes your music that he desires you, for love's sake, to make no more noise with it.

10   MUSICIAN   Well, sir, we will not.

CLOWN   If you have any music that may not be heard, to't again: but, as they say, to hear music the general does not greatly care.

MUSICIAN   We have none such, sir.

CLOWN   Then put up your pipes in your bag, for I'll away. Go, vanish into air, away!   *Exit Musician with his fellows.*

CASSIO   Dost thou hear, my honest friend?

CLOWN   No, I hear not your honest friend. I hear you.

CASSIO   Prithee keep up thy quillets.[3] There's a poor piece of gold for thee. If the gentlewoman that attends the general's wife be stirring, tell her

20   there's one Cassio entreats her a little favor of speech. Wilt thou do this?

CLOWN   She is stirring, sir. If she will stir hither, I shall seem to notify unto her.

CASSIO   Do, good my friend.   *Exit Clown.*

Enter Iago.

                              In happy time, Iago.

IAGO   You have not been abed then!

CASSIO   Why, no; the day had broke
Before we parted. I have made bold, Iago,
To send in to your wife: my suit to her
Is that she will to virtuous Desdemona
Procure me some access.

IAGO   I'll send her to you presently;
And I'll devise a mean to draw the Moor

30   Out of the way, that your converse and business
May be more free.

CASSIO   I humbly thank you for't.   *Exit Iago.*
                              I never knew
A Florentine more kind and honest.

Enter Emilia.

3. Puns

EMILIA   Good morrow, good lieutenant. I am sorry
    For your displeasure; but all will sure be well.
    The general and his wife are talking of it,
    And she speaks for you stoutly. The Moor replies
    That he you hurt is of great fame in Cyprus
    And great affinity,[4] and that in wholesome wisdom
40   He might not but refuse you; but he protests he loves you,
    And needs no other suitor but his likings
    To take the safest occasion by the front[5]
    To bring you in again.
CASSIO   Yet I beseech you,
    If you think fit, or that it may be done,
    Give me advantage of some brief discourse
    With Desdemona alone.
EMILIA   Pray you come in.
    I will bestow you where you shall have time
    To speak your bosom[6] freely.
CASSIO   I am much bound to you.   *Exeunt.*

SCENE 2

Enter Othello, Iago, and Gentlemen.

OTHELLO   These letters give, Iago, to the pilot
    And by him do my duties[7] to the Senate.
    That done, I will be walking on the works;[8]
    Repair there to me.
IAGO   Well, my good lord, I'll do't.
OTHELLO   This fortification, gentlemen, shall we see't?
GENTLEMEN   We'll wait upon your lordship.   *Exeunt.*

SCENE 3

Enter Desdemona, Cassio, and Emilia.

DESDEMONA   Be thou assured, good Cassio, I will do
    All my abilities in thy behalf.
EMILIA   Good madam, do. I warrant it grieves my husband
    As if the cause were his.
DESDEMONA   O, that's an honest fellow. Do not doubt, Cassio,

4. Family connections
5. Forelock
6. Most private thoughts

7. Pay my respects
8. Fortifications

But I will have my lord and you again
As friendly as you were.

CASSIO   Bounteous madam,
Whatever shall become of Michael Cassio,
He's never anything but your true servant.

10 DESDEMONA   I know't; I thank you. You do love my lord;
You have known him long; and be you well assured
He shall in strangeness⁹ stand no farther off
Than in a politic distance.

CASSIO   Ay, but, lady,
That policy may either last so long,
Or feed upon such nice¹⁰ and waterish diet,
Or breed itself so out of circumstance,
That, I being absent, and my place supplied,
My general will forget my love and service.

DESDEMONA   Do not doubt¹¹ that; before Emilia here
20   I give thee warrant of thy place. Assure thee,
If I do vow a friendship, I'll perform it
To the last article. My lord shall never rest;
I'll watch him tame¹² and talk him out of patience;
His bed shall seem a school, his board a shrift;¹³
I'll intermingle everything he does
With Cassio's suit. Therefore be merry, Cassio,
For thy solicitor shall rather die
Than give thy cause away.

Enter Othello and Iago at a distance.

EMILIA   Madam, here comes my lord.
30 CASSIO   Madam, I'll take my leave.
DESDEMONA   Why, stay, and hear me speak.
CASSIO   Madam, not now: I am very ill at ease,
Unfit for mine own purposes.
DESDEMONA   Well, do your discretion.   *Exit Cassio.*
IAGO   Ha! I like not that.
OTHELLO   What dost thou say?
IAGO   Nothing, my lord; or if—I know not what.
OTHELLO   Was not that Cassio parted from my wife?
IAGO   Cassio, my lord? No, sure, I cannot think it,

---

9. Aloofness
10. Trivial
11. Fear

12. Keep him awake (hawks were tamed by
    being kept awake)
13. Confessional

That he would steal away so guilty-like,
Seeing you coming.

40 OTHELLO   I do believe 'twas he.

DESDEMONA How now, my lord?
I have been talking with a suitor here,
A man that languishes in your displeasure.

OTHELLO Who is't you mean?

DESDEMONA Why, your lieutenant, Cassio. Good my lord,
If I have any grace or power to move you,
His present reconciliation[14] take;
For if he be not one that truly loves you,
That errs in ignorance, and not in cunning,
50 I have no judgment in an honest face.
I prithee call him back.

OTHELLO   Went he hence now?

DESDEMONA Yes, faith; so humbled
That he hath left part of his grief with me
To suffer with him. Good love, call him back.

OTHELLO Not now, sweet Desdemon; some other time.

DESDEMONA But shall't be shortly?

OTHELLO   The sooner, sweet, for you.

DESDEMONA Shall't be to-night at supper?

OTHELLO   No, not to-night.

DESDEMONA To-morrow dinner then?

OTHELLO   I shall not dine at home;
I meet the captains at the citadel.

60 DESDEMONA Why then, to-morrow night, or Tuesday morn,
On Tuesday noon or night, or Wednesday morn.
I prithee name the time, but let it not
Exceed three days. I' faith, he's penitent;
And yet his trespass, in our common reason
(Save that, they say, the wars must make examples
Out of their best), is not almost[15] a fault
T' incur a private check.[16] When shall he come?
Tell me, Othello. I wonder in my soul
What you could ask me that I should deny
70 Or stand so mamm'ring on.[17] What? Michael Cassio,
That came a-wooing with you, and so many a time,
When I have spoke of you dispraisingly,
Hath ta'en your part—to have so much to do
To bring him in? By'r Lady, I could do much—

14. Accept his repentance
15. Hardly

16. Even a private reprimand
17. *stand . . . on:* be so hesitant to do

OTHELLO   Prithee no more. Let him come when he will!
　　I will deny thee nothing.
DESDEMONA   Why, this is not a boon;
　　'Tis as I should entreat you wear your gloves,
　　Or feed on nourishing dishes, or keep you warm,
　　Or sue to you to do a peculiar profit
80　　To your own person. Nay, when I have a suit
　　Wherein I mean to touch your love indeed,
　　It shall be full of poise and difficult weight,
　　And fearful to be granted.
OTHELLO   I will deny thee nothing!
　　Whereon I do beseech thee grant me this,
　　To leave me but a little to myself.
DESDEMONA   Shall I deny you? No. Farewell, my lord.
OTHELLO   Farewell, my Desdemon: I'll come to thee straight.
DESDEMONA   Emilia, come.—Be as your fancies teach you;
　　Whate'er you be, I am obedient.   *Exit with Emilia.*
90 OTHELLO   Excellent wretch! Perdition catch my soul
　　But I do love thee! and when I love thee not,
　　Chaos is come again.
IAGO   My noble lord—
OTHELLO   What dost thou say, Iago?
IAGO   Did Michael Cassio, when you wooed my lady,
　　Know of your love?
OTHELLO   He did, from first to last. Why dost thou ask?
IAGO   But for a satisfaction of my thought;
　　No further harm.
OTHELLO   Why of thy thought, Iago?
IAGO   I did not think he had been acquainted with her.
100 OTHELLO   O, yes, and went between us very oft.
IAGO   Indeed?
OTHELLO   Indeed? Ay, indeed! Discern'st thou aught in that?
　　Is he not honest?
IAGO   Honest, my lord?
OTHELLO   Honest. Ay, honest.
IAGO   My lord, for aught I know.
OTHELLO   What dost thou think?
IAGO   Think, my lord?
OTHELLO   Think, my lord?
　　By heaven, he echoes me,
　　As if there were some monster in his thought
　　Too hideous to be shown. Thou dost mean something:
　　I heard thee say but now, thou lik'st not that,
110　　When Cassio left my wife. What didst not like?

And when I told thee he was of my counsel
In my whole course of wooing, thou cried'st 'Indeed?'
And didst contract and purse thy brow together,
As if thou then hadst shut up in thy brain
Some horrible conceit.[18] If thou dost love me,
Show me thy thought.

IAGO   My lord, you know I love you.

OTHELLO   I think thou dost;
And, for[19] I know thou'rt full of love and honesty
And weigh'st thy words before thou giv'st them breath,
120   Therefore these stops of thine fright me the more;
For such things in a false disloyal knave
Are tricks of custom; but in a man that's just
They are close dilations,[20] working from the heart
That passion cannot rule.

IAGO   For Michael Cassio,
I dare be sworn I think that he is honest.

OTHELLO   I think so too.

IAGO   Men should be what they seem;
Or those that be not, would they might seem none!

OTHELLO   Certain, men should be what they seem.

IAGO   Why then, I think Cassio's an honest man.

130   OTHELLO   Nay, yet there's more in this.
I prithee speak to me as to thy thinkings,
As thou dost ruminate, and give thy worst of thoughts
The worst of words.

IAGO   Good my lord, pardon me:
Though I am bound to every act of duty,
I am not bound to that all slaves are free to.
Utter my thoughts? Why, say they are vile and false,
As where's that palace whereinto foul things
Sometimes intrude not? Who has a breast so pure
But some uncleanly apprehensions
140   Keep leets[21] and law days, and in session sit
With meditations lawful?

OTHELLO   Thou dost conspire against thy friend, Iago,
If thou but think'st him wronged, and mak'st his ear
A stranger to thy thoughts.

IAGO   I do beseech you—
Though I perchance am vicious in my guess
(As I confess it is my nature's plague

---

18. Idea
19. Because

20. Secret feelings
21. Sessions of local courts

To spy into abuses, and oft my jealousy[22]
Shapes faults that are not), that your wisdom yet
From one that so imperfectly conjects[23]
150   Would take no notice, nor build yourself a trouble
Out of his scattering and unsure observance.
It were not for your quiet nor your good,
Nor for my manhood, honesty, or wisdom,
To let you know my thoughts.

OTHELLO   What dost thou mean?

IAGO   Good name in man and woman, dear my lord,
Is the immediate jewel of their souls.
Who steals my purse steals trash; 'tis something, nothing;
'Twas mine, 'tis his, and has been slave to thousands;
But he that filches from me my good name
160   Robs me of that which not enriches him
And makes me poor indeed.

OTHELLO   By heaven, I'll know thy thoughts!

IAGO   You cannot, if my heart were in your hand;
Nor shall not whilst 'tis in my custody.

OTHELLO   Ha!

IAGO   O, beware, my lord, of jealousy!
It is the green-eyed monster, which doth mock[24]
The meat it feeds on. That cuckold lives in bliss
Who, certain of his fate, loves not his wronger;
But O, what damnèd minutes tells he o'er
170   Who dotes, yet doubts—suspects, yet strongly loves!

OTHELLO   O misery!

IAGO   Poor and content is rich, and rich enough;
But riches fineless[25] is as poor as winter
To him that ever fears he shall be poor.
Good God, the souls of all my tribe defend
From jealousy!

OTHELLO   Why, why is this?
Think'st thou I'ld make a life of jealousy,
To follow still the changes of the moon
With fresh suspicions? No! To be once in doubt
180   Is once to be resolved. Exchange me for a goat
When I shall turn the business of my soul
To such exsufflicate and blown[26] surmises,
Matching thy inference. 'Tis not to make me jealous

22. Suspicion
23. Conjectures
24. Play with; i.e., torture

25. Boundless
26. Inflated and flyblown

To say my wife is fair, feeds well, loves company,
Is free of speech, sings, plays, and dances well;
Where virtue is, these are more virtuous.
Nor from mine own weak merits will I draw
The smallest fear or doubt of her revolt,
For she had eyes, and chose me. No, Iago;
190   I'll see before I doubt; when I doubt, prove;
And on the proof there is no more but this—
Away at once with love or jealousy!

IAGO I am glad of this; for now I shall have reason
To show the love and duty that I bear you
With franker spirit. Therefore, as I am bound,
Receive it from me. I speak not yet of proof.
Look to your wife; observe her well with Cassio;
Wear your eye thus, not jealous nor secure:
I would not have your free and noble nature,
200   Out of self-bounty,[27] be abused. Look to't.
I know our country disposition well:
In Venice they do let God see the pranks
They dare not show their husbands; their best conscience
Is not to leave't undone, but keep't unknown.

OTHELLO Dost thou say so?

IAGO She did deceive her father, marrying you;
And when she seemed to shake and fear your looks,
She loved them most.

OTHELLO   And so she did.

IAGO   Why, go to then!
She that, so young, could give out such a seeming
210   To seel[28] her father's eyes up close as oak[29]—
He thought 'twas witchcraft—but I am much to blame.
I humbly do beseech you of your pardon
For too much loving you.

OTHELLO   I am bound to thee for ever.

IAGO I see this hath a little dashed your spirits.

OTHELLO Not a jot, not a jot.

IAGO   I' faith, I fear it has.
I hope you will consider what is spoke
Comes from my love. But I do see y' are moved.
I am to pray you not to strain my speech
To grosser issues[30] nor to larger reach
220   Than to suspicion.

27. Natural goodness
28. Close; i.e., deceive
29. Close grained wood
30. Consequences

OTHELLO I will not.

IAGO   Should you do so, my lord,
My speech should fall into such vile success[31]
As my thoughts aim not at. Cassio's my worthy friend—
My lord, I see y' are moved.

OTHELLO   No, not much moved:
I do not think but Desdemona's honest.[32]

IAGO Long live she so! and long live you to think so!

OTHELLO And yet, how nature erring from itself—

IAGO Ay, there's the point! as (to be bold with you)
Not to affect[33] many proposèd matches
230   Of her own clime, complexion, and degree,
Whereto we see in all things nature tends—
Foh! one may smell in such a will[34] most rank,
Foul disproportion, thoughts unnatural—
But pardon me—I do not in position[35]
Distinctly speak of her; though I may fear
Her will, recoiling[36] to her better judgment,
May fall to match[37] you with her country forms,[38]
And happily[39] repent.

OTHELLO   Farewell, farewell!
If more thou dost perceive, let me know more.
240   Set on thy wife to observe. Leave me, Iago.

IAGO My lord, I take my leave.   *Going.*

OTHELLO Why did I marry? This honest creature doubtless
Sees and knows more, much more, than he unfolds.

IAGO [*returns*] My lord, I would I might entreat your honor
To scan this thing no further: leave it to time.
Although 'tis fit that Cassio have his place,
For sure he fills it up with great ability,
Yet, if you please to hold him off awhile,
You shall by that perceive him and his means.
250   Note if your lady strain his entertainment[40]
With any strong or vehement importunity;
Much will be seen in that. In the mean time
Let me be thought too busy in my fears
(As worthy cause I have to fear I am)
And hold her free.[41] I do beseech your honor.

31. Evil outcome
32. Chaste
33. Desire
34. Desire
35. In these assertions
36. Reverting
37. Happen to compare
38. Appearance of her countrymen
39. Perchance
40. Urge his reinstatement
41. Consider her guiltless

OTHELLO   Fear not my government.[42]

IAGO   I once more take my leave.   *Exit.*

OTHELLO   This fellow's of exceeding honesty,
And knows all qualities, with a learnèd spirit
260   Of human dealings. If I do prove her haggard,[43]
Though that her jesses[44] were my dear heartstrings,
I'd whistle her off and let her down the wind[45]
To prey at fortune. Haply, for I am black
And have not those soft parts of conversation[46]
That chamberers[47] have, or for I am declined
Into the vale of years—yet that's not much—
She's gone. I am abused, and my relief
Must be to loathe her. O curse of marriage,
That we can call these delicate creatures ours,
270   And not their appetites! I had rather be a toad
And live upon the vapor of a dungeon
Than keep a corner in the thing I love
For others' uses. Yet 'tis the plague of great ones;
Prerogatived[48] are they less than the base.
'Tis destiny unshunnable, like death.
Even then this forkèd plague[49] is fated to us
When we do quicken.[50] Look where she comes.

Enter Desdemona and Emilia.

If she be false, O, then heaven mocks itself!
I'll not believe't.

DESDEMONA   How now, my dear Othello?
280   Your dinner, and the generous[51] islanders
By you invited, do attend your presence.

OTHELLO   I am to blame.

DESDEMONA   Why do you speak so faintly?
Are you not well?

OTHELLO   I have a pain upon my forehead, here.

DESDEMONA   Faith, that's with watching;[52] 'twill away again.
Let me but bind it hard, within this hour
It will be well.

OTHELLO   Your napkin is too little

---

42. Self-control
43. Wild hawk
44. Straps connected to the legs of a hawk
    for keeping it under control
45. *whistle . . . wind:* turn her loose and let
    her fly wherever her will might take her
    (presumably to her self destruction)

46. *soft . . . conversation:* polished manners
47. Courtiers
48. Privileged
49. Horns of a cuckold
50. Are born
51. Noble
52. From lack of sleep

He pushes the handkerchief from him, and it falls unnoticed.

        Let it alone. Come, I'll go in with you.
DESDEMONA   I am very sorry that you are not well.   *Exit with Othello.*
290   EMILIA   I am glad I have found this napkin;
        This was her first remembrance from the Moor.
        My wayward husband hath a hundred times
        Wooed me to steal it; but she so loves the token
        (For he conjured her she should ever keep it)
        That she reserves it evermore about her
        To kiss and talk to. I'll have the work ta'en out[53]
        And give't Iago.
        What he will do with it heaven knows, not I;
        I nothing but[54] to please his fantasy.[55]

Enter Iago.

300   IAGO   How now? What do you here alone?
      EMILIA   Do not you chide; I have a thing for you.
      IAGO   A thing for me? It is a common thing—
      EMILIA   Ha?
      IAGO   To have a foolish wife.
      EMILIA   O, is that all? What will you give me now
        For that same handkerchief?
      IAGO   What handkerchief?
      EMILIA   What handkerchief!
        Why, that the Moor first gave to Desdemona;
        That which so often you did bid me steal.
310   IAGO   Hast stol'n it from her?
      EMILIA   No, faith; she let it drop by negligence,
        And to th' advantage, I, being here, took't up.
        Look, here it is.
      IAGO   A good wench! Give it me.
      EMILIA   What will you do with't, that you have been so earnest
        To have me filch it?
      IAGO   Why, what's that to you?   *Snatches it.*
      EMILIA   If it be not for some purpose of import,
        Give't me again. Poor lady, she'll run mad
        When she shall lack it.
      IAGO   Be not acknown on't;[56] I have use for it.

53. Pattern copied
54. My only desire is
55. Whim

56. *Be . . . it:* pretend that you know nothing about it

320   Go, leave me.   *Exit Emilia.*
        I will in Cassio's lodging lose this napkin
        And let him find it. Trifles light as air
        Are to the jealous confirmations strong
        As proofs of holy writ. This may do something.
        The Moor already changes with my poison:
        Dangerous conceits are in their natures poisons,
        Which at the first are scarce found to distaste,
        But with a little act upon the blood
        Burn like the mines of sulphur.

Enter Othello.

                                        I did say so.
330   Look where he comes! Not poppy nor mandragora,[57]
        Nor all the drowsy syrups of the world,
        Shall ever med'cine thee to that sweet sleep
        Which thou owedst yesterday.
OTHELLO   Ha! ha! false to me?
IAGO   Why, how now, general? No more of that!
OTHELLO   Avaunt! be gone! Thou hast set me on the rack.
        I swear 'tis better to be much abused
        Than but to know't a little.
IAGO   How now, my lord?
OTHELLO   What sense had I of her stol'n hours of lust?
        I saw't not, thought it not, it harmed not me;
340   I slept the next night well, fed well, was free[58] and merry;
        I found not Cassio's kisses on her lips.
        He that is robbed, not wanting what is stol'n,
        Let him not know't, and he's not robbed at all.
IAGO   I am sorry to hear this.
OTHELLO   I had been happy if the general camp,
        Pioneers[59] and all, had tasted her sweet body,
        So I had nothing known. O, now for ever
        Farewell the tranquil mind! farewell content!
        Farewell the plumèd troop, and the big wars
350   That make ambition virtue! O, farewell!
        Farewell the neighing steed and the shrill trump,
        The spirit-stirring drum, th' ear-piercing fife,
        The royal banner, and all quality,
        Pride, pomp, and circumstance[60] of glorious war!

57. A narcotic   59. Lowest rank of soldier
58. Carefree   60. Pageantry

And O you mortal engines[61] whose rude throats
Th' immortal Jove's dread clamors counterfeit,[62]
Farewell! Othello's occupation's gone!

IAGO Is't possible, my lord?

OTHELLO   Villain, be sure thou prove my love a whore!
360   Be sure of it; give me the ocular proof;
Or, by the worth of man's eternal soul,
Thou hadst been better have been born a dog
Than answer my waked wrath!

IAGO   Is't come to this?

OTHELLO   Make me to see't; or at the least so prove it
That the probation[63] bear no hinge nor loop
To hang a doubt on—or woe upon thy life!

IAGO My noble lord—

OTHELLO   If thou dost slander her and torture me,
Never pray more; abandon all remorse;
370   On horror's head horrors accumulate;
Do deeds to make heaven weep, all earth amazed;
For nothing canst thou to damnation add
Greater than that.

IAGO   O grace! O heaven forgive me!
Are you a man? Have you a soul or sense?—
God b' wi' you! take mine office. O wretched fool,
That liv'st to make thine honesty a vice!
O monstrous world! Take note, take note, O world,
To be direct and honest is not safe.
I thank you for this profit;[64] and from hence
380   I'll love no friend, sith love breed such offense.

OTHELLO   Nay, stay. Thou shouldst be honest.

IAGO I should be wise; for honesty's a fool
And loses that it works for.

OTHELLO   By the world,
I think my wife be honest, and think she is not;
I think that thou art just, and think thou art not.
I'll have some proof. Her name, that was as fresh
As Dian's visage, is now begrimed and black
As mine own face. If there be cords, or knives,
Poison, or fire, or suffocating streams,
390   I'll not endure it. Would I were satisfied!

IAGO I see, sir, you are eaten up with passion:

61. Deadly artillery   63. Proof
62. Imitate   64. Lesson

I do repent me that I put it to you.
You would be satisfied?

OTHELLO   Would? Nay, I will.

IAGO   And may; but how? how satisfied, my lord?
Would you, the supervisor, grossly gape on?
Behold her topped?

OTHELLO   Death and damnation! O!

IAGO   It were a tedious difficulty, I think,
To bring them to that prospect. Damn them then,
If ever mortal eyes do see them bolster[65]

400   More[66] than their own! What then? How then?
What shall I say? Where's satisfaction?
It is impossible you should see this,
Were they as prime[67] as goats, as hot as monkeys,
As salt[68] as wolves in pride,[69] and fools as gross
As ignorance made drunk. But yet, I say,
If imputation and strong circumstances
Which lead directly to the door of truth
Will give you satisfaction, you may have't.

OTHELLO   Give me a living reason she's disloyal.

410   IAGO   I do not like the office.
But sith I am entered in this cause so far,
Pricked to't by foolish honesty and love,
I will go on. I lay with Cassio lately,
And being troubled with a raging tooth,
I could not sleep.
There are a kind of men so loose of soul
That in their sleeps will mutter their affairs.
One of this kind is Cassio.
In sleep I heard him say, 'Sweet Desdemona,

420   Let us be wary, let us hide our loves!'
And then, sir, would he gripe[70] and wring my hand,
Cry 'O sweet creature!' and then kiss me hard,
As if he plucked up kisses by the roots
That grew upon my lips; then laid his leg
Over my thigh, and sighed, and kissed, and then
Cried 'Cursèd fate that gave thee to the Moor!'

OTHELLO   O monstrous! monstrous!

IAGO   Nay, this was but his dream.

65. Lie together   68. Lecherous
66. Other   69. Heat
67. Lustful   70. Grip

OTHELLO   But this denoted a foregone conclusion:
'Tis a shrewd doubt,[71] though it be but a dream.
430   IAGO   And this may help to thicken other proofs
That do demonstrate thinly.
OTHELLO   I'll tear her all to pieces!
IAGO   Nay, but be wise. Yet we see nothing done;
She may be honest yet. Tell me but this—
Have you not sometimes seen a handkerchief
Spotted with strawberries in your wife's hand?
OTHELLO   I gave her such a one; 'twas my first gift.
IAGO   I know not that; but such a handkerchief—
I am sure it was your wife's—did I to-day
See Cassio wipe his beard with.
OTHELLO   If't be that—
440   IAGO   If it be that, or any that was hers,
It speaks against her with the other proofs.
OTHELLO   O, that the slave had forty thousand lives!
One is too poor, too weak for my revenge.
Now do I see 'tis true. Look here, Iago:
All my fond love thus do I blow to heaven.
'Tis gone.
Arise, black vengeance, from the hollow hell!
Yield up, O love, thy crown and hearted throne
To tyrannous hate! Swell, bosom, with thy fraught,[72]
For 'tis of aspics'[73] tongues!
450   IAGO   Yet be content.
OTHELLO   O, blood, blood, blood!
IAGO   Patience, I say. Your mind perhaps may change.
OTHELLO   Never, Iago. Like to the Pontic sea,[74]
Whose icy current and compulsive course
Ne'er feels retiring ebb, but keeps due on
To the Propontic and the Hellespont,
Even so my bloody thoughts, with violent pace,
Shall ne'er look back, ne'er ebb to humble love,
Till that a capable[75] and wide revenge
460   Swallow them up. [*He kneels.*] Now, by yond marble heaven,
In the due reverence of a sacred vow
I here engage my words.
IAGO   Do not rise yet.   *Iago kneels.*

71. Strong reason for suspicion   74. Black Sea
72. Burden   75. Comprehensive
73. Asps' (deadly poisonous snakes)

Witness, you ever-burning lights above,
You elements that clip[76] us round about,
Witness that here Iago doth give up
The execution[77] of his wit, hands, heart
To wronged Othello's service! Let him command,
And to obey shall be in me remorse,[78]
What bloody business ever.   *They rise.*

OTHELLO   I greet thy love,
470   Not with vain thanks but with acceptance bounteous,
And will upon the instant put thee to't.
Within these three days let me hear thee say
That Cassio's not alive.

IAGO   My friend is dead; 'tis done at your request.
But let her live.

OTHELLO   Damn her, lewd minx! O, damn her!
Come, go with me apart. I will withdraw
To furnish me with some swift means of death
For the fair devil. Now art thou my lieutenant.

IAGO   I am your own for ever.   *Exeunt.*

SCENE 4

Enter Desdemona, Emilia, and Clown.

DESDEMONA   Do you know, sirrah, where Lieutenant Cassio lies?[79]

CLOWN   I dare not say he lies anywhere.

DESDEMONA   Why, man?

CLOWN   He's a soldier, and for me to say a soldier lies is stabbing.

DESDEMONA   Go to. Where lodges he?

CLOWN   To tell you where he lodges is to tell you where I lie.

10   DESDEMONA   Can anything be made of this?

CLOWN   I know not where he lodges; and for me to devise a lodging, and say
he lies here or he lies there, were to lie in mine own throat.[80]

DESDEMONA   Can you enquire him out, and be edified by report?

CLOWN   I will catechize the world for him; that is, make questions, and by
them answer.

DESDEMONA   Seek him, bid him come hither. Tell him I have moved my lord
20   on his behalf and hope all will be well.

CLOWN   To do this is within the compass of man's wit, and therefore I'll
attempt the doing of it.   *Exit.*

76. Encompass   79. Lodges
77. Action   80. Tell an obvious lie
78. Expression of pity (for Othello)

DESDEMONA   Where should I lose that handkerchief, Emilia?
EMILIA   I know not, madam.
DESDEMONA   Believe me, I had rather have lost my purse
　　Full of crusadoes;[81] and but my noble Moor
　　Is true of mind, and made of no such baseness
　　As jealous creatures are, it were enough
　　To put him to ill thinking.
EMILIA   Is he not jealous?
30 DESDEMONA   Who? he? I think the sun where he was born
　　Drew all such humors[82] from him.

Enter Othello.

EMILIA   Look where he comes.
DESDEMONA   I will not leave him now till Cassio
　　Be called to him.—How is't with you, my lord?
OTHELLO   Well, my good lady. [*Aside*] O, hardness to dissemble!—
　　How do you, Desdemona?
DESDEMONA   Well, my good lord.
OTHELLO   Give me your hand. This hand is moist, my lady.
DESDEMONA   It yet hath felt no age nor known no sorrow.
OTHELLO   This argues fruitfulness and liberal heart.
　　Hot, hot, and moist. This hand of yours requires
40 　　A sequester[83] from liberty, fasting and prayer,
　　Much castigation, exercise devout;
　　For here's a young and sweating devil here
　　That commonly rebels. 'Tis a good hand,
　　A frank one.
DESDEMONA   You may, indeed, say so;
　　For 'twas that hand that gave away my heart.
OTHELLO   A liberal hand! The hearts of old gave hands;
　　But our new heraldry is hands, not hearts.
DESDEMONA   I cannot speak of this. Come now, your promise!
OTHELLO   What promise, chuck?
50 DESDEMONA   I have sent to bid Cassio come speak with you.
OTHELLO   I have a salt and sorry rheum[84] offends me.
　　Lend me thy handkerchief
DESDEMONA   Here, my lord.
OTHELLO   That which I gave you.
DESDEMONA   I have it not about me.
OTHELLO   Not?

---

81. Portuguese gold coins   83. Removal
82. Temperamental inclinations   84. Head cold

DESDEMONA   No, faith, my lord.

OTHELLO   That is a fault.

That handkerchief
Did an Egyptian[85] to my mother give.
She was a charmer,[86] and could almost read
The thoughts of people. She told her, while she kept it,
'Twould make her amiable[87] and subdue my father
Entirely to her love; but if she lost it
Or made a gift of it, my father's eye
Should hold her loathly, and his spirits should hunt
After new fancies. She, dying, gave it me,
And bid me, when my fate would have me wive,
To give it her. I did so; and take heed on't;
Make it a darling like your precious eye.
To lose't or give't away were such perdition
As nothing else could match.

DESDEMONA   Is't possible?

OTHELLO   'Tis true. There's magic in the web of it.
A sibyl[88] that had numbered in the world
The sun to course two hundred compasses,
In her prophetic fury sewed the work;
The worms were hallowed that did breed the silk;
And it was dyed in mummy[89] which the skillful
Conserved[90] of maidens' hearts.

DESDEMONA   I' faith? Is't true?

OTHELLO   Most veritable. Therefore look to't well.

DESDEMONA   Then would to God that I had never seen't!

OTHELLO   Ha! Wherefore?

DESDEMONA   Why do you speak so startingly and rash?

OTHELLO   Is't lost? Is't gone? Speak, is it out o' th' way?

DESDEMONA   Heaven bless us!

OTHELLO   Say you?

DESDEMONA   It is not lost. But what an if it were?

OTHELLO   How?

DESDEMONA   I say it is not lost.

OTHELLO   Fetch't, let me see't!

DESDEMONA   Why, so I can, sir; but I will not now.
This is a trick to put me from my suit:
Pray you let Cassio be received again.

OTHELLO   Fetch me the handkerchief! My mind misgives.

85. Gypsy
86. Magician
87. Desirable

88. Prophetess
89. Fluid derived from embalmed bodies
90. Preserved

90 DESDEMONA   Come, come!
    You'll never meet a more sufficient man.
  OTHELLO   The handkerchief!
  DESDEMONA   I pray talk me of Cassio.
  OTHELLO   The handkerchief!
  DESDEMONA   A man that all his time
    Hath founded his good fortunes on your love,
    Shared dangers with you—
  OTHELLO   The handkerchief!
  DESDEMONA   I'faith, you are to blame.
  OTHELLO   Zounds!   *Exit.*
  EMILIA   Is not this man jealous?
100 DESDEMONA   I ne'er saw this before.
    Sure there's some wonder in this handkerchief;
    I am most unhappy in the loss of it.
  EMILIA   'Tis not a year or two shows us a man.
    They are all but stomachs, and we all but food;
    They eat us hungerly, and when they are full,
    They belch us.

Enter Iago and Cassio.

              Look you—Cassio and my husband!
  IAGO   There is no other way; 'tis she must do't.
    And lo the happiness![91] Go and importune her.
  DESDEMONA   How now, good Cassio? What's the news with you?
110 CASSIO   Madam, my former suit. I do beseech you
    That by your virtuous means I may again
    Exist, and be a member of his love
    Whom I with all the office of my heart
    Entirely honor. I would not be delayed.
    If my offense be of such mortal kind
    That neither service past, nor present sorrows,
    Nor purposed merit in futurity,
    Can ransom me into his love again,
    But to know so must be my benefit.
120   So shall I clothe me in a forced content,
    And shut myself up in some other course,
    To fortune's alms.
  DESDEMONA   Alas, thrice-gentle Cassio!
    My advocation[92] is not now in tune.
    My lord is not my lord; nor should I know him,

91. Good luck   92. Advocacy

Were he in favor[93] as in humor altered.
So help me every spirit sanctified
As I have spoken for you all my best
And stood within the blank[94] of his displeasure
For my free speech! You must awhile be patient.
130   What I can do I will; and more I will
Than for myself I dare. Let that suffice you.
IAGO   Is my lord angry?
EMILIA   He went hence but now,
And certainly in strange unquietness.
IAGO   Can he be angry? I have seen the cannon
When it hath blown his ranks into the air
And, like the devil, from his very arm
Puffed his own brother—and can he be angry?
Something of moment then. I will go meet him.
There's matter in't indeed if he be angry.
DESDEMONA   I prithee do so.   *Exit Iago.*
140   Something sure of state,
Either from Venice or some unhatched practice[95]
Made demonstrable here in Cyprus to him,
Hath puddled[96] his clear spirit; and in such cases
Men's natures wrangle with inferior things,
Though great ones are their object. 'Tis even so;
For let our finger ache, and it endues[97]
Our other, healthful members even to that sense
Of pain. Nay, we must think men are not gods,
Nor of them look for such observancy[98]
150   As fits the bridal. Beshrew me much, Emilia,
I was, unhandsome warrior as I am,
Arraigning his unkindness with my soul;
But now I find I had suborned the witness,
And he's indicted falsely.
EMILIA   Pray heaven it be state matters, as you think,
And no conception nor no jealous toy[99]
Concerning you.
DESDEMONA   Alas the day! I never gave him cause.
EMILIA   But jealous souls will not be answered so;
160   They are not ever jealous for the cause,
But jealous for they are jealous. 'Tis a monster
Begot upon itself, born on itself.

93. Appearance   97. Brings
94. Center of a target   98. Devoted attention
95. Plot in the making   99. Fancy
96. Muddied

DESDEMONA   Heaven keep that monster from Othello's mind!
EMILIA   Lady, amen.
DESDEMONA   I will go seek him. Cassio, walk here about:
If I do find him fit, I'll move your suit
And seek to effect it to my uttermost.
CASSIO   I humbly thank your ladyship.   *Exeunt Desdemona and Emilia.*

Enter Bianca.

BIANCA   Save you, friend Cassio!
CASSIO   What make you from home?
170   How is it with you, my most fair Bianca?
I' faith, sweet love, I was coming to your house.
BIANCA   And I was going to your lodging, Cassio.
What, keep a week away? seven days and nights?
Eightscore eight hours? and lovers' absent hours,
More tedious than the dial[100] eightscore times?
O weary reck'ning!
CASSIO   Pardon me, Bianca:
I have this while with leaden thoughts been pressed;
But I shall in a more continuate[101] time
Strike off this score of absence. Sweet Bianca,

Gives her Desdemona's handkerchief.

Take me this work out.
180   BIANCA   O Cassio, whence came this?
This is some token from a newer friend.
To the felt absence now I feel a cause.
Is't come to this? Well, well.
CASSIO   Go to, woman!
Throw your vile guesses in the devil's teeth,
From whence you have them. You are jealous now
That this is from some mistress, some remembrance.
No, by my faith, Bianca.
BIANCA   Why, whose is it?
CASSIO   I know not, sweet; I found it in my chamber.
I like the work well; ere it be demanded,
190   As like enough it will, I'd have it copied.
Take it and do't, and leave me for this time.
BIANCA   Leave you? Wherefore?
CASSIO   I do attend here on the general

100. Clock   101. Uninterrupted

And think it no addition, nor my wish,
To have him see me womaned.

BIANCA   Why, I pray you?

CASSIO   Not that I love you not.

BIANCA   But that you do not love me!
I pray you bring me on the way a little,
And say if I shall see you soon at night.

CASSIO   'Tis but a little way that I can bring you,
For I attend here; but I'll see you soon.

200 BIANCA   'Tis very good. I must be circumstanced.¹⁰²   *Exeunt.*

102. Governed by circumstances

ACT IV

SCENE 1

Enter Othello and Iago.

IAGO   Will you think so?

OTHELLO   Think so, Iago?

IAGO   What,
To kiss in private?

OTHELLO   An unauthorized kiss.

IAGO   Or to be naked with her friend in bed
An hour or more, not meaning any harm?

OTHELLO   Naked in bed, Iago, and not mean harm?
It is hypocrisy against the devil.
They that mean virtuously, and yet do so,
The devil their virtue tempts, and they tempt heaven.

IAGO   So they do nothing, 'tis a venial slip.

10   But if I give my wife a handkerchief—

OTHELLO   What then?

IAGO   Why, then 'tis hers, my lord; and being hers,
She may, I think, bestow't on any man.

OTHELLO   She is protectress of her honor too;
May she give that?

IAGO   Her honor is an essence that's not seen;
They have it very oft¹ that have it not.
But for the handkerchief—

OTHELLO   By heaven, I would most gladly have forgot it!

1. *They . . . oft:* they often have the appearance of it

20   Thou said'st—O, it comes o'er my memory
       As doth the raven o'er the infected house,
       Boding to all!—he had my handkerchief.
IAGO   Ay, what of that?
OTHELLO   That's not so good now.
IAGO   What
       If I had said I had seen him do you wrong?
       Or heard him say—as knaves be such abroad
       Who having, by their own importunate suit,
       Or voluntary dotage of some mistress,
       Convincèd or supplied[2] them, cannot choose
       But they must blab—
OTHELLO   Hath he said anything?
30 IAGO   He hath, my lord; but be you well assured,
       No more than he'll unswear.
OTHELLO   What hath he said?
IAGO   Faith, that he did—I know not what he did.
OTHELLO   What? what?
IAGO   Lie—
OTHELLO   With her?
IAGO   With her, on her; what you will.
OTHELLO   Lie with her? lie on her?—We say lie on her when they belie
       her.—Lie with her! Zounds, that's fulsome.—Handkerchief—
40   confessions—handkerchief!—To confess, and be hanged for his labor—
       first to be hanged, and then to confess! I tremble at it. Nature would not
       invest herself in such shadowing[3] passion without some instruction.[4] It
       is not words that shakes me thus.—Pish! Noses, ears, and lips? Is't
       possible?—Confess?—Handkerchief?—O devil!   *Falls in a trance.*
IAGO   Work on,
       My med'cine, work! Thus credulous fools are caught,
       And many worthy and chaste dames even thus,
       All guiltless, meet reproach.—What, ho! my lord!
       My lord, I say! Othello!

Enter Cassio.

                   How now, Cassio?
50 CASSIO   What's the matter?
IAGO   My lord is fall'n into an epilepsy.
       This is his second fit; he had one yesterday.
CASSIO   Rub him about the temples.

2. Overcome or gratified   4. Prompting, or cause
3. Overwhelming

IAGO   No, forbear.
   The lethargy must have his quiet course.
   If not, he foams at mouth, and by and by
   Breaks out to savage madness. Look, he stirs.
   Do you withdraw yourself a little while.
   He will recover straight. When he is gone,
   I would on great occasion speak with you.   *Exit Cassio.*
60   How is it, general? Have you not hurt your head?
OTHELLO   Dost thou mock me?
IAGO   I mock you? No, by heaven.
   Would you would bear your fortune like a man!
OTHELLO   A hornèd man's[5] a monster and a beast.
IAGO   There's many a beast then in a populous city,
   And many a civil monster.
OTHELLO   Did he confess it?
IAGO   Good, sir, be a man.
   Think every bearded fellow that's but yoked[6]
   May draw with you. There's millions now alive
   That nightly lie in those unproper[7] beds
70   Which they dare swear peculiar:[8] your case is better.
   O, 'tis the spite of hell, the fiend's arch-mock,
   To lip a wanton in a secure[9] couch,
   And to suppose her chaste! No, let me know;
   And knowing what I am, I know what she shall be.
OTHELLO   O, thou are wise! 'Tis certain.
IAGO   Stand you awhile apart;
   Confine yourself but in a patient list.[10]
   Whilst you were here, o'erwhelmèd with your grief—
   A passion most unsuiting such a man—
   Cassio came hither. I shifted him away
80   And laid good 'scuse upon your ecstasy;[11]
   Bade him anon return, and here speak with me;
   The which he promised. Do but encave[12] yourself
   And mark the fleers,[13] the gibes, and notable scorns
   That dwell in every region of his face;
   For I will make him tell the tale anew—
   Where, how, how oft, how long ago, and when

5. Cuckold
6. Married
7. Not exclusively their own
8. Exclusively their own
9. Free from suspicion

10. Within the bounds of patience
11. Trance
12. Conceal
13. Sneers

He hath, and is again to cope[14] your wife.
I say, but mark his gesture. Marry, patience!
Or I shall say you are all in all in spleen,[15]
And nothing of a man.

90   OTHELLO   Dost thou hear, Iago?
I will be found most cunning in my patience;
But—dost thou hear?—most bloody.

IAGO   That's not amiss;
But yet keep time in all. Will you withdraw?   *Othello retires.*
Now will I question Cassio of Bianca,
A huswife[16] that by selling her desires
Buys herself bread and clothes. It is a creature
That dotes on Cassio, as 'tis the strumpet's plague
To beguile many and be beguiled by one.
He, when he hears of her, cannot refrain
100 From the excess of laughter. Here he comes.
As he shall smile, Othello shall go mad;
And his unbookish[17] jealousy must conster[18]
Poor Cassio's smiles, gestures, and light behavior
Quite in the wrong. How do you now, lieutenant?

CASSIO   The worser that you give me the addition[19]
Whose want even kills me.

IAGO   Ply Desdemona well, and you are sure on't.
Now, if this suit lay in Bianca's power,
How quickly should you speed!

CASSIO   Alas, poor caitiff![20]

110 OTHELLO   Look how he laughs already!

IAGO   I never knew a woman love man so.

CASSIO   Alas, poor rogue! I think, i' faith, she loves me.

OTHELLO   Now he denies it faintly, and laughs it out.

IAGO   Do you hear, Cassio?

OTHELLO   Now he importunes him
To tell it o'er. Go to! Well said, well said!

IAGO   She gives it out that you shall marry her.
Do you intend it?

120 CASSIO   Ha, ha, ha!

OTHELLO   Do you triumph, Roman? Do you triumph?

14. Meet   18. Construe
15. Completely overcome by emotion 19. Title (of lieutenant)
16. Hussy   20. Wretch
17. Uninstructed

CASSIO   I marry her? What, a customer?[21] Prithee bear some charity to my wit; do not think it so unwholesome. Ha, ha, ha!

OTHELLO   So, so, so, so! They laugh that win!

IAGO   Faith, the cry goes that you shall marry her.

CASSIO   Prithee say true.

IAGO   I am a very villain else.

130 OTHELLO   Have you scored[22] me? Well.

CASSIO   This is the monkey's own giving out. She is persuaded I will marry her out of her own love and flattery, not out of my promise.

OTHELLO   Iago beckons me; now he begins the story.

CASSIO   She was here even now; she haunts me in every place. I was t' other day talking on the sea bank with certain Venetians, and thither comes

140 the bauble,[23] and, by this hand, she falls me thus about my neck—

OTHELLO   Crying 'O dear Cassio!' as it were. His gesture imports it.

CASSIO   So hangs, and lolls, and weeps upon me; so hales and pulls me! Ha, ha, ha!

OTHELLO   Now he tells how she plucked him to my chamber. O, I see that nose of yours, but not that dog I shall throw't to.

CASSIO   Well, I must leave her company.

Enter Bianca.

IAGO   Before me! Look where she comes.

150 CASSIO   'Tis such another fitchew![24] marry, a perfumed one. What do you mean by this haunting of me?

BIANCA   Let the devil and his dam haunt you! What did you mean by that same handkerchief you gave me even now? I was a fine fool to take it. I must take out the whole work? A likely piece of work that you should find it in your chamber and know not who left it there! This is some minx's token, and I must take out the work? There! Give it your hobby-

160 horse.[25] Wheresoever you had it, I'll take out no work on't.

CASSIO   How now, my sweet Bianca? How now? how now?

OTHELLO   By heaven, that should be my handkerchief!

BIANCA   An you'll come to supper to-night, you may; an you will not, come when you are next prepared for.   *Exit.*

IAGO   After her, after her!

170 CASSIO   Faith, I must; she'll rail i' th' street else.

IAGO   Will you sup there?

CASSIO   Yes, I intend so.

IAGO   Well, I may chance to see you; for I would very fain speak with you.

21. Prostitute
22. Beaten
23. Plaything

24. Polecat; slang term for a whore
25. Harlot

CASSIO   Prithee come. Will you?

IAGO   Go to! say no more.   *Exit Cassio.*

180   OTHELLO *[comes forward]*   How shall I murder him, Iago?

IAGO   Did you perceive how he laughed at his vice?

OTHELLO   O Iago!

IAGO   And did you see the handkerchief?

OTHELLO   Was that mine?

IAGO   Yours, by this hand! And to see how he prizes the foolish woman
your wife! She gave it him, and he hath giv'n it his whore.

OTHELLO   I would have him nine years a-killing!—A fine woman! a fair
woman! a sweet woman!

190   IAGO   Nay, you must forget that.

OTHELLO   Ay, let her rot, and perish, and be damned to-night; for she shall
not live. No, my heart is turned to stone; I strike it, and it hurts my
hand. O, the world hath not a sweeter creature! She might lie by an
emperor's side and command him tasks.

IAGO   Nay, that's not your way.

OTHELLO   Hang her! I do but say what she is. So delicate with her needle! an
admirable musician! O, she will sing the savageness out of a bear! Of so
200   high and plenteous wit and invention—

IAGO   She's the worse for all this.

OTHELLO   O, a thousand thousand times! And then, of so gentle²⁶ a condition!

IAGO   Ay, too gentle.²⁷

OTHELLO   Nay, that's certain. But yet the pity of it, Iago! O Iago, the pity of
it, Iago!

210   IAGO   If you are so fond over her iniquity, give her patent²⁸ to offend; for if it
touch not you, it comes near nobody.

OTHELLO   I will chop her into messes! Cuckold me!

IAGO   O, 'tis foul in her.

OTHELLO   With mine officer!

IAGO   That's fouler.

OTHELLO   Get me some poison, Iago, this night. I'll not expostulate with her,
lest her body and beauty unprovide²⁹ my mind again. This night, Iago!

IAGO   Do it not with poison. Strangle her in her bed, even the bed she hath
contaminated.

OTHELLO   Good, good! The justice of it pleases. Very good!

220   IAGO   And for Cassio, let me be his undertaker: you shall hear more by
midnight.

OTHELLO   Excellent good!   *A trumpet.*

What trumpet is that same?

26. Nobly born and bred   28. License
27. Generous   29. Unsettle

IAGO   Something from Venice, sure.

Enter Lodovico, Desdemona, and Attendants.

                              'Tis Lodovico,
     Come from the duke; and see, your wife is with him.
LODOVICO   God save you, worthy general!
OTHELLO   With all my heart, sir.
230 LODOVICO   The duke and senators of Venice greet you.   *Gives him a letter.*
OTHELLO   I kiss the instrument of their pleasures.

Opens the letter and reads.

DESDEMONA   And what's the news, good cousin Lodovico?
IAGO   I am very glad to see you, signior.
     Welcome to Cyprus.
LODOVICO   I thank you. How does Lieutenant Cassio?
IAGO   Lives, sir.
DESDEMONA   Cousin, there's fall'n between him and my lord
     An unkind breach; but you shall make all well.
OTHELLO   Are you sure of that?
DESDEMONA   My lord?
240 OTHELLO [*reads*]   'This fail you not to do, as you will—'
LODOVICO   He did not call; he's busy in the paper.
     Is there division 'twixt thy lord and Cassio?
DESDEMONA   A most unhappy one. I would do much
     T' atone[30] them, for the love I bear to Cassio.
OTHELLO   Fire and brimstone!
DESDEMONA   My lord?
OTHELLO   Are you wise?
DESDEMONA   What, is he angry?
LODOVICO   May be the letter moved him;
     For, as I think, they do command him home,
     Deputing Cassio in his government.
DESDEMONA   By my troth, I am glad on't.
OTHELLO   Indeed?
DESDEMONA   My lord?
OTHELLO   I am glad to see you mad.
250 DESDEMONA   Why, sweet Othello—
OTHELLO   Devil!   *Strikes her.*
DESDEMONA   I have not deserved this.
LODOVICO   My lord, this would not be believed in Venice,

30. To reconcile

Though I should swear I saw't. 'Tis very much.
Make her amends; she weeps.
OTHELLO   O devil, devil!
If that the earth could teem with[31] woman's tears,
Each drop she falls would prove a crocodile.
Out of my sight!
DESDEMONA   I will not stay to offend you.   *Going.*
LODOVICO   Truly, an obedient lady.
260   I do beseech your lordship call her back.
OTHELLO   Mistress!
DESDEMONA   My lord?
OTHELLO   What would you with her, sir?
LODOVICO   Who? I, my lord?
OTHELLO   Ay! You did wish that I would make her turn.
        Sir, she can turn, and turn, and yet go on
        And turn again; and she can weep, sir, weep;
        And she's obedient; as you say, obedient,
        Very obedient.—Proceed you in your tears.—
        Concerning this, sir—O well-painted passion!—
        I am commanded home.—Get you away;
270   I'll send for you anon.—Sir, I obey the mandate
        And will return to Venice.—Hence, avaunt!   *Exit Desdemona.*
        Cassio shall have my place. And, sir, to-night
        I do entreat that we may sup together.
        You are welcome, sir, to Cyprus.—Goats and monkeys!   *Exit.*
LODOVICO   Is this the noble Moor whom our full Senate
        Call all in all sufficient? Is this the nature
        Whom passion could not shake? whose solid virtue
        The shot of accident nor dart of chance
        Could neither graze nor pierce?
IAGO   He is much changed.
280   LODOVICO   Are his wits safe? Is he not light of brain?
IAGO   He's that he is; I may not breathe my censure.
        What he might be (if, what he might, he is not)
        I would to heaven he were!
LODOVICO   What, strike his wife?
IAGO   Faith, that was not so well; yet would I knew
        That stroke would prove the worst!
LODOVICO   Is it his use?[32]
        Or did the letter work upon his blood
        And new-create this fault?
IAGO   Alas, alas!

31. Be made pregnant by   32. Habit

It is not honesty in me to speak
What I have seen and known. You shall observe him,
290   And his own courses will denote him so
That I may save my speech. Do but go after
And mark how he continues.

LODOVICO   I am sorry that I am deceived in him.   *Exeunt.*

SCENE 2

Enter Othello and Emilia.

OTHELLO   You have seen nothing then?

EMILIA   Nor ever heard, nor ever did suspect.

OTHELLO   Yes, you have seen Cassio and she together.

EMILIA   But then I saw no harm, and then I heard
Each syllable that breath made up between them.

OTHELLO   What, did they never whisper?

EMILIA   Never, my lord.

OTHELLO   Nor send you out o' th' way?

EMILIA   Never.

OTHELLO   To fetch her fan, her gloves, her mask, nor nothing?

10   EMILIA   Never, my lord.

OTHELLO   That's strange.

EMILIA   I durst, my lord, to wager she is honest,
Lay down my soul at stake. If you think other,
Remove your thought; it doth abuse your bosom.
If any wretch have put this in your head,
Let heaven requite it with the serpent's curse!
For if she be not honest, chaste, and true,
There's no man happy; the purest of their wives
Is foul as slander.

OTHELLO   Bid her come hither. Go.   *Exit Emilia.*

20   She says enough; yet she's a simple bawd
That cannot say as much. This is a subtle whore,
A closet lock and key of villainous secrets;
And yet she'll kneel and pray; I have seen her do't.

Enter Desdemona and Emilia.

DESDEMONA   My lord, what is your will?

OTHELLO   Pray, chuck, come hither.

DESDEMONA   What is your pleasure?

OTHELLO   Let me see your eyes.
Look in my face.

DESDEMONA   What horrible fancy's this?

OTHELLO [to Emilia] Some of your function,[33] mistress.
    Leave procreants alone and shut the door;
    Cough or cry hem if anybody come.
30   Your mystery,[34] your mystery! Nay, dispatch!   *Exit Emilia.*

DESDEMONA Upon my knees, what doth your speech import?
    I understand a fury in your words,
    But not the words.

OTHELLO Why, what art thou?

DESDEMONA   Your wife, my lord; your true
    And loyal wife.

OTHELLO   Come, swear it, damn thyself;
    Lest, being like one of heaven, the devils themselves
    Should fear to seize thee. Therefore be double-damned—
    Swear thou art honest.

DESDEMONA   Heaven doth truly know it.

OTHELLO Heaven truly knows that thou art false as hell.

40 DESDEMONA To whom, my lord? With whom? How am I false?

OTHELLO Ah, Desdemon! away! away! away!

DESDEMONA Alas the heavy day! Why do you weep?
    Am I the motive[35] of these tears, my lord?
    If haply you my father do suspect
    An instrument of this your calling back,
    Lay not your blame on me. If you have lost him,
    Why, I have lost him too.

OTHELLO   Had it pleased heaven
    To try me with affliction, had they rained
    All kinds of sores and shames on my bare head,
50   Steeped me in poverty to the very lips,
    Given to captivity me and my utmost hopes,
    I should have found in some place of my soul
    A drop of patience. But, alas, to make me
    A fixèd figure for the time of scorn[36]
    To point his slow unmoving finger at!
    Yet could I bear that too; well, very well.
    But there where I have garnered up my heart,
    Where either I must live or bear no life,
    The fountain from the which my current runs
60   Or else dries up—to be discarded thence,
    Or keep it as a cistern for foul toads

---

33. Go about your business; i.e., perform   35. Cause
    your function as the madam of a brothel   36. Scornful world
  34. Trade

To knot and gender in—turn thy complexion there,[37]
Patience, thou young and rose-lipped cherubin!
Ay, there look grim as hell!

DESDEMONA   I hope my noble lord esteems me honest.

OTHELLO   O, ay; as summer flies are in the shambles,[38]
That quicken even with blowing.[39] O thou weed,
Who art so lovely fair, and smell'st so sweet,
That the sense aches at thee, would thou hadst ne'er been born!

70 DESDEMONA   Alas, what ignorant sin have I committed?

OTHELLO   Was this fair paper, this most goodly book,
Made to write 'whore' upon? What committed?
Committed? O thou public commoner![40]
I should make very forges of my cheeks
That would to cinders burn up modesty,
Did I but speak thy deeds. What committed?
Heaven stops the nose at it, and the moon winks;[41]
The bawdy wind, that kisses all it meets,
Is hushed within the hollow mine of earth
80 And will not hear it. What committed?
Impudent strumpet!

DESDEMONA   By heaven, you do me wrong!

OTHELLO   Are not you a strumpet?

DESDEMONA   No, as I am a Christian!
If to preserve this vessel for my lord
From any other foul unlawful touch
Be not to be a strumpet, I am none.

OTHELLO   What, not a whore?

DESDEMONA   No, as I shall be saved!

OTHELLO   Is't possible?

DESDEMONA   O, heaven forgive us!

OTHELLO   I cry you mercy[42] then.
I took you for that cunning whore of Venice
90 That married with Othello.—[Calling] You, mistress,
That have the office opposite to Saint Peter
And keep the gate of hell!

Enter Emilia.

You, you, ay, you!

37. *turn . . . there:* change your color at that point
38. Slaughterhouses
39. *quicken . . . blowing:* come to life as soon as their eggs are deposited
40. Whore
41. Closes her eyes
42. Beg your pardon

We have done our course; there's money for your pains:
I pray you turn the key, and keep our counsel.   *Exit.*
EMILIA   Alas, what does this gentleman conceive?
How do you, madam? How do you, my good lady?
DESDEMONA   Faith, half asleep.
EMILIA   Good madam, what's the matter with my lord?
DESDEMONA   With who?
100 EMILIA   Why, with my lord, madam.
DESDEMONA   Who is thy lord?
EMILIA   He that is yours, sweet lady.
DESDEMONA   I have none. Do not talk to me, Emilia.
I cannot weep; nor answer have I none
But what should go by water.[43] Prithee to-night
Lay on my bed my wedding sheets, remember;
And call thy husband hither.
EMILIA   Here's a change indeed!   *Exit.*
DESDEMONA   'Tis meet I should be used so, very meet.
How have I been behaved, that he might stick
The small'st opinion[44] on my least misuse?[45]

Enter Iago and Emilia.

110 IAGO   What is your pleasure, madam? How is't with you?
DESDEMONA   I cannot tell. Those that do teach young babes
Do it with gentle means and easy tasks:
He might have chid me so; for, in good faith,
I am a child to chiding.
IAGO   What is the matter, lady?
EMILIA   Alas, Iago, my lord hath so bewhored her,
Thrown such despite and heavy terms upon her
As true hearts cannot bear.
DESDEMONA   Am I that name, Iago?
IAGO   What name, fair lady?
DESDEMONA   Such as she says my lord did say I was.
120 EMILIA   He called her whore. A beggar in his drink
Could not have laid such terms upon his callet.[46]
IAGO   Why did he so?
DESDEMONA   I do not know; I am sure I am none such.
IAGO   Do not weep, do not weep. Alas the day!
EMILIA   Hath she forsook so many noble matches,

43. Tears   45. Slightest misconduct
44. Suspicion   46. Whore

Her father and her country, all her friends,
To be called whore? Would it not make one weep?

DESDEMONA   It is my wretched fortune.

IAGO   Beshrew him for't!
How comes this trick[47] upon him?

DESDEMONA   Nay, heaven doth know.

130   EMILIA   I will be hanged if some eternal villain,
Some busy and insinuating rogue,
Some cogging,[48] cozening slave, to get some office,
Have not devised this slander. I'll be hanged else.

IAGO   Fie, there is no such man! It is impossible.

DESDEMONA   If any such there be, heaven pardon him!

EMILIA   A halter pardon him! and hell gnaw his bones!
Why should he call her whore? Who keeps her company?
What place? what time? what form? what likelihood?
The Moor's abused by some most villainous knave,

140   Some base notorious knave, some scurvy fellow.
O heaven, that such companions thou'dst unfold,[49]
And put in every honest hand a whip
To lash the rascals naked through the world
Even from the east to th' west!

IAGO   Speak within door.[50]

EMILIA   O, fie upon them! Some such squire he was
That turned your wit the seamy side without
And made you to suspect me with the Moor.

IAGO   You are a fool. Go to.

DESDEMONA   O good Iago,
What shall I do to win my lord again?

150   Good friend, go to him; for, by this light of heaven,
I know not how I lost him. Here I kneel:
If e'er my will did trespass 'gainst his love
Either in discourse of thought or actual deed,
Or that mine eyes, mine ears, or any sense
Delighted them in any other form,
Or that I do not yet, and ever did,
And ever will (though he do shake me off
To beggarly divorcement) love him dearly,
Comfort forswear[51] me! Unkindness may do much;

160   And his unkindness may defeat my life,

47. Strange behavior   50. Quietly
48. Cheating   51. Happiness forsake
49. Expose

But never taint my love. I cannot say "whore."
It doth abhor me now I speak the word;
To do the act that might th' addition earn
Not the world's mass of vanity could make me.
IAGO   I pray you be content. 'Tis but his humor.
The business of the state does him offense,
And he does chide with you.
DESDEMONA   If 'twere no other—
IAGO   'Tis but so, I warrant.

Trumpets within.

Hark how these instruments summon you to supper.
170   The messengers of Venice stay the meal[52]
Go in, and weep not. All things shall be well.
                              Exeunt Desdemona and Emilia.

Enter Roderigo.

How now, Roderigo?
RODERIGO   I do not find that thou deal'st justly with me.
IAGO   What in the contrary?
RODERIGO   Every day thou daff'st me[53] with some device, Iago, and rather,
as it seems to me now, keep'st from me all conveniency[54] than suppliest
me with the least advantage of hope. I will indeed no longer endure it;
nor am I yet persuaded to put up in peace what already I have foolishly
suffered.
180   IAGO   Will you hear me, Roderigo?
RODERIGO   Faith, I have heard too much; for your words and performance
are no kin together.
IAGO   You charge me most unjustly.
RODERIGO   With naught but truth. I have wasted myself out of means. The
jewels you have had from me to deliver to Desdemona would half have
corrupted a votarist.[55] You have told me she hath received them, and
returned me expectations and comforts of sudden respect and acquaintance; but I find none.
IAGO   Well, go to; very well.

---

52. Wait to eat
53. Put me off

54. Opportunities (to meet with Desde-
    mona)
55. Nun

190 RODERIGO Very well! go to! I cannot go to, man; nor 'tis not very well. By this hand, I say 'tis very scurvy, and begin to find myself fopped[56] in it.

IAGO Very well.

RODERIGO I tell you 'tis not very well. I will make myself known to Desdemona. If she will return me my jewels, I will give over my suit and repent my unlawful solicitation; if not, assure yourself I will seek satisfaction of you.

IAGO You have said now.

RODERIGO Ay, and said nothing but what I protest intendment of doing.

IAGO Why, now I see there's mettle in thee; and even from this instant do
200   build on thee a better opinion than ever before. Give me thy hand, Roderigo. Thou hast taken against me a most just exception; but yet I protest I have dealt most directly in thy affair.

RODERIGO It hath not appeared.

IAGO I grant indeed it hath not appeared, and your suspicion is not without wit and judgment. But, Roderigo, if thou hast that in thee indeed which I have greater reason to believe now than ever, I mean purpose, courage, and valor, this night show it. If thou the next night following enjoy not Desdemona, take me from this world with treachery and devise engines for[57] my life.

210 RODERIGO Well, what is it? Is it within reason and compass?

IAGO Sir, there is especial commission come from Venice to depute Cassio in Othello's place.

RODERIGO Is that true? Why, then Othello and Desdemona return again to Venice.

IAGO O, no; he goes into Mauritania and takes away with him the fair Desdemona, unless his abode be lingered here by some accident; wherein none can be so determinate[58] as the removing of Cassio.

RODERIGO How do you mean removing of him?

IAGO Why, by making him uncapable of Othello's place—knocking out his
220   brains.

RODERIGO And that you would have me to do?

IAGO Ay, if you dare do yourself a profit and a right. He sups to-night with a harlotry, and thither will I go to him. He knows not yet of his honorable fortune. If you will watch his going thence, which I will fashion to fall out between twelve and one, you may take him at your pleasure. I will be near to second your attempt, and he shall fall between us. Come, stand not amazed at it, but go along with me. I will show you such a necessity in his death that you shall think yourself bound to put it on him. It is now high suppertime, and the night grows to waste. About it!

56. Fooled
57. Plots against

58. Effective

230 RODERIGO I will hear further reason for this.
IAGO And you shall be satisfied.   *Exeunt.*

SCENE 3

Enter Othello, Lodovico, Desdemona, Emilia, and Attendants.

LODOVICO I do beseech you, sir, trouble yourself no further.
OTHELLO O, pardon me; 'twill do me good to walk.
LODOVICO Madam, good night. I humbly thank your ladyship.
DESDEMONA Your honor is most welcome.
OTHELLO   Will you walk, sir?
     O, Desdemona—
DESDEMONA My lord?
OTHELLO Get you to bed on th' instant; I will be returned forthwith. Dis-
     miss your attendant there. Look't be done.
10 DESDEMONA I will, my lord.
                              Exit Othello, with Lodovico and Attendants.
EMILIA How goes it now? He looks gentler than he did.
DESDEMONA He says he will return incontinent.[59]
     He hath commanded me to go to bed,
     And bade me to dismiss you.
EMILIA   Dismiss me?
DESDEMONA It was his bidding; therefore, good Emilia,
     Give me my nightly wearing, and adieu.
     We must not now displease him.
EMILIA I would you had never seen him!
DESDEMONA So would not I. My love doth so approve him
20   That even his stubbornness,[60] his checks,[61] his frowns—
     Prithee unpin me—have grace and favor in them.
EMILIA I have laid those sheets you bade me on the bed.
DESDEMONA All's one. Good faith, how foolish are our minds!
     If I do die before thee, prithee shroud me
     In one of those same sheets.
EMILIA   Come, come! You talk.
DESDEMONA My mother had a maid called Barbary.
     She was in love; and he she loved proved mad[62]
     And did forsake her. She had a song of 'Willow';
     An old thing 'twas; but it expressed her fortune,
30   And she died singing it. That song to-night

59. Immediately   61. Rebukes
60. Roughness   62. Untrue

Will not go from my mind; I have much to do
But to go hang my head all at one side
And sing it like poor Barbary. Prithee dispatch.
EMILIA   Shall I go fetch your nightgown?
DESDEMONA   No, unpin me here.
This Lodovico is a proper man.
EMILIA   A very handsome man.
DESDEMONA   He speaks well.
EMILIA   I know a lady in Venice would have walked barefoot to Palestine for
40   a touch of his nether lip.
DESDEMONA [sings].

    The poor soul sat sighing by a sycamore tree,
        Sing all a green willow;
    Her hand on her bosom, her head on her knee,
        Sing willow, willow, willow.
    The fresh streams ran by her and murmured her moans;
        Sing willow, willow, willow;
    Her salt tears fell from her, and soft'ned the stones—

    Lay by these.

        Sing willow, willow, willow—

50   Prithee hie thee; he'll come anon.

    Sing all a green willow must be my garland.
    Let nobody blame him; his scorn I approve—

    Nay, that's not next. Hark! who is't that knocks?
EMILIA   It is the wind.
DESDEMONA [sings].

    I called my love false love; but what said he then?
        Sing willow, willow, willow:
    If I court moe women, you'll couch with moe men.

    So, get thee gone; good night. Mine eyes do itch.
    Doth that bode weeping?
EMILIA   'Tis neither here nor there.
60   DESDEMONA   I have heard it said so. O, these men, these men!
    Dost thou in conscience think—tell me, Emilia—
    That there be women do abuse their husbands
    In such gross kind?

EMILIA   There be some such, no question.

DESDEMONA   Wouldst thou do such a deed for all the world?

EMILIA   Why, would not you?

DESDEMONA   No, by this heavenly light!

EMILIA   Nor I neither by this heavenly light.
        I might do't as well i' th' dark.

DESDEMONA   Wouldst thou do such a deed for all the world?

EMILIA   The world's a huge thing; it is a great price for a small vice.

70 DESDEMONA   Good troth, I think thou wouldst not.

EMILIA   By my troth, I think I should; and undo't when I had done it. Marry,
        I would not do such a thing for a joint-ring,[63] nor for measures of lawn,[64]
        nor for gowns, petticoats, nor caps, nor any petty exhibition;[65] but, for
        all the whole world—'Ud's pity! who would not make her husband a
        cuckold to make him a monarch? I should venture purgatory for't.

DESDEMONA   Beshrew me if I would do such a wrong
        For the whole world.

80 EMILIA   Why, the wrong is but a wrong i' th' world; and having the world
        for your labor, 'tis a wrong in your own world, and you might quickly
        make it right.

DESDEMONA   I do not think there is any such woman.

EMILIA   Yes, a dozen; and as many to th' vantage[66] as would store[67] the
        world they played for.
        But I do think it is their husbands' faults
        If wives do fall. Say that they slack their duties
        And pour our treasures into foreign laps;
90   Or else break out in peevish jealousies,
        Throwing restraint upon us; or say they strike us,
        Or scant our former having[68] in despite[69]—
        Why, we have galls;[70] and though we have some grace,
        Yet have we some revenge. Let husbands know
        Their wives have sense like them. They see, and smell,
        And have their palates both for sweet and sour,
        As husbands have. What is it that they do
        When they change us for others? Is it sport?
        I think it is. And doth affection breed it?
100   I think it doth. Is't frailty that thus errs?
        It is so too. And have not we affections,
        Desires for sport, and frailty, as men have?

63. Cheap ring   67. Populate
64. Fine linen   68. Allowance
65. Gift   69. Spite
66. In addition   70. Capacity to feel resentment

Then let them use us well; else let them know,
The ills we do, their ills instruct us so.
DESDEMONA   Good night, good night. God me such usage[71] send,
Not to pick bad from bad, but by bad mend!   *Exeunt.*

71. Habits

ACT V

SCENE 1

Enter Iago and Roderigo.

IAGO   Here, stand behind this bulk;[1] straight will he come.
Wear thy good rapier bare, and put it home.
Quick, quick! Fear nothing; I'll be at thy elbow.
It makes us, or it mars us—think on that,
And fix most firm thy resolution.
RODERIGO   Be near at hand; I may miscarry in't.
IAGO   Here, at thy hand. Be bold, and take thy stand.   *Stands aside.*
RODERIGO   I have no great devotion to the deed,
And yet he hath given me satisfying reasons.
10   'Tis but a man gone. Forth my sword! He dies!
IAGO   I have rubbed this young quat[2] almost to the sense,[3]
And he grows angry. Now whether he kill Cassio,
Or Cassio him, or each do kill the other,
Every way makes my gain. Live Roderigo,
He calls me to a restitution large
Of gold and jewels that I bobbed[4] from him
As gifts to Desdemona.
It must not be. If Cassio do remain,
He hath a daily beauty in his life
20   That makes me ugly; and besides, the Moor
May unfold me to him; there stand I in much peril.
No, he must die. Be't so! I hear him coming.

Enter Cassio.

RODERIGO   I know his gait. 'Tis he. Villain, thou diest!
                                        Makes a pass at Cassio.

1. Projecting store front   3. Raw
2. Pimple   4. Swindled

CASSIO   That thrust had been mine enemy indeed
    But that my coat is better than thou know'st.
    I will make proof of thine.   *Draws, and wounds Roderigo.*
RODERIGO   O, I am slain!

Iago darts from concealment behind Cassio, wounds him in the leg, and exit.

CASSIO   I am maimed for ever. Help, ho! Murder! murder!   *Falls.*

Enter Othello.

OTHELLO   The voice of Cassio. Iago keeps his word.
RODERIGO   O, villain that I am!
OTHELLO   It is even so.
30   CASSIO   O, help, ho! light! a surgeon!
OTHELLO   'Tis he. O brave Iago, honest and just,
    That hast such noble sense of thy friend's wrong!
    Thou teachest me. Minion,[5] your dear lies dead,
    And your unblest fate hies.[6] Strumpet, I come.
    Forth of my heart those charms, thine eyes, are blotted.
    Thy bed, lust-stained, shall with lust's blood be spotted.   *Exit.*

Enter Lodovico and Gratiano.

CASSIO   What, ho? No watch? No passage?[7] Murder! murder!
GRATIANO   'Tis some mischance. The cry is very direful.
CASSIO   O, help!
40   LODOVICO   Hark!
RODERIGO   O wretched villain!
LODOVICO   Two or three groan. It is a heavy[8] night.
    These may be counterfeits. Let's think't unsafe
    To come in to the cry without more help.
RODERIGO   Nobody come? Then shall I bleed to death.
LODOVICO   Hark!

Enter Iago, with a light.

GRATIANO   Here's one comes in his shirt, with light and weapons.
IAGO   Who's there? Whose noise is this that cries on murder?
LODOVICO   We do not know.
IAGO   Did not you hear a cry?

5. Mistress   7. Passersby
6. Hurries on   8. Dark

CASSIO Here, here! For heaven's sake, help me!

50 IAGO   What's the matter?

GRATIANO This is Othello's ancient, as I take it.

LODOVICO The same indeed, a very valiant fellow.

IAGO What are you here that cry so grievously?

CASSIO Iago? O, I am spoiled, undone by villains!
    Give me some help.

IAGO O me, lieutenant! What villains have done this?

CASSIO I think that one of them is hereabout
    And I cannot make away.

IAGO   O treacherous villains!
    [*To Lodovico and Gratiano*] What are you there? Come in, and give some help.

60 RODERIGO O, help me here!

CASSIO That's one of them.

IAGO   O murd'rous slave! O villain!   *Stabs Roderigo.*

RODERIGO O damned Iago! O inhuman dog!

IAGO Kill men i' th' dark?—Where be these bloody thieves?—
    How silent is this town!—Ho! murder! murder!—
    What may you be? Are you of good or evil?

LODOVICO As you shall prove us, praise us.

IAGO Signior Lodovico?

LODOVICO He, sir.

IAGO I cry you mercy. Here's Cassio hurt by villains.

70 GRATIANO Cassio?

IAGO How is it, brother?

CASSIO My leg is cut in two.

IAGO   Marry, heaven forbid!
    Light, gentlemen. I'll bind it with my shirt.

Enter Bianca.

BIANCA What is the matter, ho? Who is't that cried?

IAGO Who is't that cried?

BIANCA O my dear Cassio! my sweet Cassio!
    O Cassio, Cassio, Cassio!

IAGO O notable strumpet!—Cassio, may you suspect
    Who they should be that thus have mangled you?

80 CASSIO No.

GRATIANO I am sorry to find you thus. I have been to seek you.

IAGO Lend me a garter. So. O for a chair
    To bear him easily hence!

BIANCA Alas, he faints! O Cassio, Cassio, Cassio!

IAGO Gentlemen all, I do suspect this trash
    To be a party in this injury.—

Patience awhile, good Cassio.—Come, come!
Lend me a light. Know we this face or no?
Alas, my friend and my dear countryman
90   Roderigo? No.—Yes, sure.—O heaven, Roderigo!
GRATIANO   What, of Venice?
IAGO   Even he, sir. Did you know him?
GRATIANO   Know him? Ay.
IAGO   Signior Gratiano? I cry you gentle pardon.
     These bloody accidents must excuse my manners
     That so neglected you.
GRATIANO   I am glad to see you.
IAGO   How do you, Cassio?—O, a chair, a chair!
GRATIANO   Roderigo?
IAGO   He, he, 'tis he! [A chair brought in.] O, that's well said;⁹ the chair.
     Some good man bear him carefully from hence.
100   I'll fetch the general's surgeon. [To Bianca] For you, mistress,
     Save you your labor.—He that lies slain here, Cassio,
     Was my dear friend. What malice was between you?
CASSIO   None in the world; nor do I know the man.
IAGO [To Bianca]   What, look you pale?—O, bear him out o' th' air.

Cassio and Roderigo are borne off.

Stay you, good gentlemen.—Look you pale, mistress?—
Do you perceive the gastness¹⁰ of her eye?—
Nay, if you stare, we shall hear more anon.
Behold her well; I pray you look upon her.
Do you see, gentlemen? Nay, guiltiness will speak,
110   Though tongues were out of use.

Enter Emilia.

EMILIA   'Las, what's the matter? What's the matter, husband?
IAGO   Cassio hath here been set on in the dark
     By Roderigo, and fellows that are scaped.
     He's almost slain, and Roderigo dead.
EMILIA   Alas, good gentleman! alas, good Cassio!
IAGO   This is the fruit of whoring. Prithee, Emilia,
     Go know of Cassio where he supped to-night.
     [To Bianca] What, do you shake at that?
BIANCA   He supped at my house; but I therefore shake not.
120   IAGO   O, did he so? I charge you go with me.

9. Well done   10. Terror

EMILIA   Fie, fie upon thee, strumpet!

BIANCA   I am no strumpet, but of life as honest
    As you that thus abuse me.

EMILIA   As I? Foh! fie upon thee!

IAGO   Kind gentlemen, let's go see poor Cassio dressed.
    [*To Bianca*] Come, mistress, you must tell's another tale.
    Emilia, run you to the citadel
    And tell my lord and lady what hath happed.   *Exit Emilia.*
    Will you go on afore?   *Exeunt all but Iago.*
                    This is the night
    That either makes me or fordoes[11] me quite.   *Exit.*

SCENE 2

Desdemona asleep in her bed. Enter Othello with a light.

OTHELLO   It is the cause,[12] it is the cause, my soul.
    Let me not name it to you, you chaste stars!
    It is the cause. Yet I'll not shed her blood,
    Nor scar that whiter skin of hers than snow,
    And smooth as monumental alabaster.
    Yet she must die, else she'll betray more men.
    Put out the light, and then put out the light.
    If I quench thee, thou flaming minister,
    I can again thy former light restore,
10   Should I repent me; but once put out thy light,
    Thou cunning'st pattern of excelling nature,
    I know not where is that Promethean heat[13]
    That can thy light relume.[14] When I have plucked the rose,
    I cannot give it vital growth again;
    It needs must wither. I'll smell thee on the tree.   *He kisses her.*
    O balmy breath, that dost almost persuade
    Justice to break her sword! One more, one more!
    Be thus when thou art dead, and I will kill thee,
    And love thee after. One more, and this the last!
20   So sweet was ne'er so fatal. I must weep,
    But they are cruel tears. This sorrow's heavenly;
    It strikes where it doth love. She wakes.

DESDEMONA   Who's there? Othello?

OTHELLO   Ay, Desdemona.

DESDEMONA   Will you come to bed, my lord?

11. Destroys   13. Divine fire
12. Cause of justice   14. Rekindle

OTHELLO   Have you prayed to-night, Desdemona?

DESDEMONA   Ay, my lord.

OTHELLO   If you bethink yourself of any crime
    Unreconciled as yet to heaven and grace,
    Solicit for it straight.

DESDEMONA   Alack, my lord, what may you mean by that?

30 OTHELLO   Well, do it, and be brief; I will walk by.
    I would not kill thy unprepared spirit.
    No, heaven forfend![15] I would not kill thy soul.

DESDEMONA   Talk you of killing?

OTHELLO   Ay, I do.

DESDEMONA   Then heaven
    Have mercy on me!

OTHELLO   Amen, with all my heart!

DESDEMONA   If you say so, I hope you will not kill me.

OTHELLO   Hum!

DESDEMONA   And yet I fear you; for you are fatal then
    When your eyes roll so. Why I should fear I know not,
    Since guiltiness I know not; but yet I feel I fear.

OTHELLO   Think on thy sins.

40 DESDEMONA   They are loves I bear to you.

OTHELLO   Ay, and for that thou diest.

DESDEMONA   That death's unnatural that kills for loving.
    Alas, why gnaw you so your nether lip?
    Some bloody passion shakes your very frame.
    These are portents; but yet I hope, I hope,
    They do not point on me.

OTHELLO   Peace and be still!

DESDEMONA   I will so. What's the matter?

OTHELLO   That handkerchief which I so loved and gave thee
    Thou gav'st to Cassio.

DESDEMONA   No, by my life and soul!
    Send for the man and ask him.

50 OTHELLO   Sweet soul, take heed,
    Take heed of perjury; thou art on thy deathbed.

DESDEMONA   Ay, but not yet to die.

OTHELLO   Yes, presently.
    Therefore confess thee freely of thy sin;
    For to deny each article with oath
    Cannot remove nor choke the strong conception[16]
    That I do groan withal. Thou art to die.

DESDEMONA   Then Lord have mercy on me!

---

15. Forbid   16. Belief (of her being guilty)

OTHELLO   I say amen.

DESDEMONA   And have you mercy too! I never did
    Offend[17] you in my life; never loved Cassio
60   But with such general warranty of heaven
    As I might love. I never gave him token.

OTHELLO   By heaven, I saw my handkerchief in's hand!
    O perjured woman! thou dost stone[18] my heart,
    And mak'st me call what I intend to do
    A murder, which I thought a sacrifice.
    I saw the handkerchief.

DESDEMONA   He found it then.
    I never gave it him. Send for him hither.
    Let him confess a truth.

OTHELLO   He hath confessed.

DESDEMONA   What, my lord?

OTHELLO   That he hath used thee.

70   DESDEMONA   How? unlawfully?

OTHELLO   Ay.

DESDEMONA   He will not say so.

OTHELLO   No, his mouth is stopped.
    Honest Iago hath ta'en order for't.[19]

DESDEMONA   O, my fear interprets. What, is he dead?

OTHELLO   Had all his hairs been lives, my great revenge
    Had stomach for them all.

DESDEMONA   Alas, he is betrayed, and I undone!

OTHELLO   Out, strumpet! Weep'st thou for him to my face?

DESDEMONA   O, banish me, my lord, but kill me not!

OTHELLO   Down, strumpet!

80   DESDEMONA   Kill me to-morrow; let me live to-night!

OTHELLO   Nay, an you strive[20]—

DESDEMONA   But half an hour!

OTHELLO   Being done, there is no pause.

DESDEMONA   But while I say one prayer!

OTHELLO   It is too late.

Smothers her.

DESDEMONA   O Lord, Lord, Lord!

Emilia at the door.

---

17. Wrong
18. Turn to stone

19. Take measures to bring it about
20. Struggle

EMILIA [calls within].   My lord, my lord! What, ho, my lord, my lord!

OTHELLO   What noise is this? Not dead? Not yet quite dead?

> I that am cruel am yet merciful;
>
> I would not have thee linger in thy pain.
>
> So, so.

EMILIA [within].   What, ho! my lord, my lord!

OTHELLO   Who's there?

90   EMILIA [within].   O, good my lord, I would speak a word with you!

OTHELLO   Yes, 'tis Emilia.—By and by.—She's dead.—

> 'Tis like she comes to speak of Cassio's death.
>
> The noise was here. Ha! no more moving?
>
> Still as the grave.—Shall she come in? Were't good?—
>
> I think she stirs again. No.—What's best to do?
>
> If she come in, she'll sure speak to my wife.
>
> My wife! my wife! what wife? I have no wife.
>
> O, insupportable! O heavy hour!
>
> Methinks it should be now a huge eclipse
>
100 > Of sun and moon, and that th' affrighted globe
>
> Should yawn²¹ at alteration.

EMILIA   [within] I do beseech you

> That I may speak with you, O good my lord!

OTHELLO   I had forgot thee. O, come in, Emilia.

> Soft, by and by.—Let me the curtains draw.—

Closes the bed-curtains.
Opens the door.

> Where art thou?

Enter Emilia.

> What's the matter with thee now?

EMILIA   O my good lord, yonder's foul murder done!

OTHELLO   What? Now?

EMILIA   But now, my lord.

OTHELLO   It is the very error²² of the moon.

> She comes more nearer earth than she was wont
>
110 > And makes men mad.

EMILIA   Cassio, my lord, hath killed a young Venetian

> Called Roderigo.

OTHELLO   Roderigo killed?

> And Cassio killed?

EMILIA   No, Cassio is not killed.

OTHELLO   Not Cassio killed? Then murder's out of tune,

> And sweet revenge grows harsh.

DESDEMONA   O, falsely, falsely murdered!

---

21. Open, as in an earthquake   22. Straying from its natural course

EMILIA   O Lord! what cry is that?

OTHELLO   That? What?

EMILIA   Out and alas! that was my lady's voice.

120   Help! help, ho! help! O lady, speak again!
            Sweet Desdemona! O sweet mistress, speak!

DESDEMONA   A guiltless death I die.

EMILIA   O, who hath done this deed?

DESDEMONA   Nobody—I myself. Farewell.
            Commend me to my kind lord. O, farewell!   *She dies.*

OTHELLO   Why, how should she be murd'red?

EMILIA   Alas, who knows?

OTHELLO   You heard her say herself, it was not I.

EMILIA   She said so. I must needs report the truth.

OTHELLO   She's like a liar gone to burning hell!
            'Twas I that killed her.

130   EMILIA   O, the more angel she,
            And you the blacker devil!

OTHELLO   She turned to folly, and she was a whore.

EMILIA   Thou dost belie her, and thou art a devil.

OTHELLO   She was false as water.

EMILIA   Thou art rash as fire to say
            That she was false. O, she was heavenly true!

OTHELLO   Cassio did top her. Ask thy husband else.
            O, I were damned beneath all depth in hell
            But that I did proceed upon just grounds
            To this extremity. Thy husband knew it all.

140   EMILIA   My husband?

OTHELLO   Thy husband.

EMILIA   That she was false to wedlock?

OTHELLO   Ay, with Cassio. Nay, had she been true,
            If heaven would make me such another world
            Of one entire and perfect chrysolite,
            I'ld not have sold her for it.

EMILIA   My husband?

OTHELLO   Ay, 'twas he that told me first.
            An honest man he is, and hates the slime
            That sticks on filthy deeds.

EMILIA   My husband?

150   OTHELLO   What needs this iterance?[23] Woman, I say thy husband.

EMILIA   O mistress, villainy hath made mocks with love!
            My husband say that she was false?

OTHELLO   He, woman.

23. Repetition

I say, thy husband. Dost understand the word?
My friend, thy husband; honest, honest, Iago.

EMILIA If he say so, may his pernicious soul
Rot half a grain a day! he lies to th' heart.
She was too fond of her most filthy bargain.

OTHELLO Ha!

EMILIA Do thy worst.

160   This deed of thine is no more worthy heaven
Than thou wast worthy her.

OTHELLO   Peace, you were best.

EMILIA Thou hast not half the power to do me harm
As I have to be hurt.[24] O gull! O dolt!
As ignorant as dirt! thou hast done a deed—
I care not for thy sword; I'll make thee known,
Though I lost twenty lives. Help! help! O, help!
The Moor hath killed my mistress! Murder! murder!

Enter Montano, Gratiano, Iago, and Others.

MONTANO What is the matter? How now, general?

EMILIA O, are you come, Iago? You have done well,
170   That men must lay their murders on your neck.

GRATIANO What is the matter?

EMILIA Disprove this villain, if thou be'st a man.
He says thou told'st him that his wife was false.
I know thou didst not; thou'rt not such a villain.
Speak, for my heart is full.

IAGO I told him what I thought, and told no more
Than what he found himself was apt and true.

EMILIA But did you ever tell him she was false?

IAGO I did.

180   EMILIA You told a lie, an odious damnèd lie!
Upon my soul, a lie! a wicked lie!
She false with Cassio? Did you say with Cassio?

IAGO With Cassio, mistress. Go to, charm[25] your tongue.

EMILIA I will not charm my tongue; I am bound to speak:
My mistress here lies murdered in her bed—

ALL O heavens forfend!

EMILIA And your reports have set the murder on.

OTHELLO Nay, stare not, masters. It is true indeed.

GRATIANO 'Tis a strange truth.

MONTANO O monstrous act!

---

24. To endure pain   25. Cast a spell on; i.e., silence

190 EMILIA   Villainy, villainy, villainy!
    I think upon't—I think I smell't!—O villainy!
    I thought so then.—I'll kill myself for grief.—
    O villainy, villainy!
IAGO   What, are you mad? I charge you get you home.
EMILIA   Good gentlemen, let me have leave to speak.
    'Tis proper I obey him, but not now.
    Perchance, Iago, I will ne'er go home.
OTHELLO   O! O! O!   *Falls on the bed.*
EMILIA   Nay, lay thee down and roar!
    For thou hast killed the sweetest innocent
    That e'er did lift up eye.
200 OTHELLO   O, she was foul!   *Rises.*
    I scarce did know you, uncle. There lies your niece,
    Whose breath, indeed, these hands have newly stopped.
    I know this act shows horrible and grim.
GRATIANO   Poor Desdemon! I am glad thy father's dead.
    Thy match was mortal to him, and pure grief
    Shore[26] his old thread in twain. Did he live now,
    This sight would make him do a desperate turn;[27]
    Yea, curse his better angel from his side,
    And fall to reprobation.[28]
210 OTHELLO   'Tis pitiful; but yet Iago knows
    That she with Cassio hath the act of shame
    A thousand times committed. Cassio confessed it;
    And she did gratify his amorous works
    With the recognizance and pledge of love
    Which I first gave her. I saw it in his hand.
    It was a handkerchief, an antique token
    My father gave my mother.
EMILIA   O God! O heavenly God!
IAGO   Zounds, hold your peace!
EMILIA   'Twill out, 'twill out! I peace?
220 No, I will speak as liberal[29] as the north.[30]
    Let heaven and men and devils, let them all,
    All, all, cry shame against me, yet I'll speak.
IAGO   Be wise, and get you home.
EMILIA   I will not.

Iago draws and threatens Emilia.

26. Cut   29. Unrestrainedly
27. Deed   30. Blowing of the north wind
28. Be rejected by God

GRATIANO   Fie!
  Your sword upon a woman?
EMILIA   O thou dull Moor, that handkerchief thou speak'st of
  I found by fortune, and did give my husband;
  For often with a solemn earnestness—
  More than indeed belonged to such a trifle—
  He begged of me to steal't.
IAGO   Villainous whore!
230 EMILIA   She give it Cassio? No, alas, I found it,
  And I did give't my husband.
IAGO   Filth, thou liest!
EMILIA   By heaven, I do not, I do not, gentlemen.
  O murd'rous coxcomb! what should such a fool
  Do with so good a wife?
OTHELLO   Are there no stones[31] in heaven
  But what serves for the thunder? Precious villain!

The Moor runs at Iago, but is disarmed by Montano. Iago kills his wife.

GRATIANO   The woman falls. Sure he hath killed his wife.
EMILIA   Ay, ay. O, lay me by my mistress' side.   *Exit Iago.*
GRATIANO   He's gone, but his wife's killed.
MONTANO   'Tis a notorious villain. Take you this weapon,
240   Which I have here recovered from the Moor.
  Come, guard the door without. Let him not pass,
  But kill him rather. I'll after that same villain,
  For 'tis a damnèd slave.

Exit Montano, with all but Othello and Emilia.

OTHELLO   I am not valiant neither;
  But every puny whipster[32] gets my sword.
  But why should honor outlive honesty?
  Let it go all.
EMILIA   What did thy song bode, lady?
  Hark, canst thou hear me? I will play the swan,
  And die in music [*sings*] 'Willow, willow, willow.'
  Moor, she was chaste. She loved thee, cruel Moor:
250   So come my soul to bliss as I speak true.
  So speaking as I think, I die, I die.   *She dies.*
OTHELLO   I have another weapon in this chamber;

31. Thunderbolts   32. Top-whipping boy

It is a sword of Spain, the Isebrook's[33] temper.
O, here it is.—Uncle, I must come forth.
GRATIANO [*within*] If thou attempt it, it will cost thee dear.
Thou hast no weapon, and perforce must suffer.
OTHELLO Look in upon me then and speak with me,
Or, naked[34] as I am, I will assault thee.

Enter Gratiano.

GRATIANO   What is the matter?
OTHELLO   Behold, I have a weapon;
260   A better never did itself sustain
Upon a soldier's thigh. I have seen the day
That with this little arm and this good sword
I have made my way through more impediments
Than twenty times your stop.[35] But O vain boast!
Who can control his fate? 'Tis not so now.
Be not afraid, though you do see me weaponed.
Here is my journey's end, here is my butt,[36]
And very seamark[37] of my utmost sail.
Do you go back dismayed? 'Tis a lost[38] fear.
270   Man but a rush[39] against Othello's breast,
And he retires. Where should Othello go?
Now, how dost thou look now? O ill-starred wench!
Pale as thy smock! When we shall meet at compt,[40]
This look of thine will hurl my soul from heaven,
And fiends will snatch at it. Cold, cold, my girl?
Even like thy chastity.
O cursèd, cursèd slave! Whip me, ye devils,
From the possession of this heavenly sight!
Blow me about in winds! roast me in sulphur!
280   Wash me in steep-down gulfs of liquid fire!
O Desdemona, Desdemona! dead!
O! O! O!

Enter Lodovico, Montano, Iago as prisoner, and Officers; Cassio in a chair.

LODOVICO   Where is this rash and most unfortunate man?
OTHELLO   That's he that was Othello. Here I am.

33. Innsbruck, where the finest steel blades   37. Beacon
    of the time were forged   38. Wasted
34. Unarmed   39. Wield a mere reed
35. Power to stop   40. Final accounting; i.e., Day of Judgment
36. Limit

LODOVICO   Where is that viper? Bring the villain forth.

OTHELLO   I look down towards his feet[41]—but that's a fable.
  If that thou be'st a devil, I cannot kill thee.   *Wounds Iago.*

LODOVICO   Wrench his sword from him.   *Othello is disarmed.*

IAGO   I bleed, sir, but not killed.

OTHELLO   I am not sorry neither. I'ld have thee live;
290   For in my sense, 'tis happiness to die.

LODOVICO   O thou Othello that wert once so good,
  Fall'n in the practice[42] of a damnèd slave,
  What shall be said to thee?

OTHELLO   Why, anything:
  An honorable murderer, if you will;
  For naught did I in hate, but all in honor.

LODOVICO   This wretch hath part confessed his villainy.
  Did you and he consent in Cassio's death?

OTHELLO   Ay.

CASSIO   Dear general, I never gave you cause.

300   OTHELLO   I do believe it, and I ask your pardon.
  Will you, I pray, demand that demi-devil
  Why he hath thus ensnared my soul and body?

IAGO   Demand me nothing. What you know, you know.
  From this time forth I never will speak word.

LODOVICO   What, not to pray?

GRATIANO   Torments will ope your lips.

OTHELLO   Well, thou dost best.

LODOVICO   Sir, you shall understand what hath befall'n,
  Which, as I think, you know not. Here is a letter
  Found in the pocket of the slain Roderigo;
310   And here another. The one of them imports
  The death of Cassio to be undertook
  By Roderigo.

OTHELLO   O villain!

CASSIO   Most heathenish and most gross!

LODOVICO   Now here's another discontented paper
  Found in his pocket too; and this, it seems,
  Roderigo meant t' have sent this damnèd villain;
  But that, belike, Iago in the nick[43]
  Came in and satisfied him.

OTHELLO   O thou pernicious caitiff!—
  How came you, Cassio, by that handkerchief
  That was my wife's?

---

41. *I . . . feet:* to see if they are cloven, as the
  Devil's feet were believed to be

42. Plot

43. Nick of time

320 CASSIO   I found it in my chamber;
        And he himself confessed but even now
        That there he dropped it for a special purpose
        Which wrought to his desire.
    OTHELLO   O fool! fool! fool!
    CASSIO   There is besides in Roderigo's letter,
        How he upbraids Iago that he made him
        Brave[44] me upon the watch; whereon it came
        That I was cast;[45] and even but now he spake,
        After long seeming dead—Iago hurt him,
        Iago set him on.
330 LODOVICO   You must forsake this room and go with us.
        Your power and your command is taken off,
        And Cassio rules in Cyprus. For this slave,
        If there be any cunning cruelty
        That can torment him much and hold him long,
        It shall be his. You shall close prisoner rest
        Till that the nature of your fault be known
        To the Venetian state. Come, bring away.
    OTHELLO   Soft you! a word or two before you go.
        I have done the state some service, and they know't.
340   No more of that. I pray you, in your letters,
        When you shall these unlucky deeds relate,
        Speak of me as I am. Nothing extenuate,
        Nor set down aught in malice. Then must you speak
        Of one that loved not wisely, but too well;
        Of one not easily jealous, but, being wrought,
        Perplexed[46] in the extreme; of one whose hand,
        Like the base Indian, threw a pearl away
        Richer than all his tribe; of one whose subdued eyes,
        Albeit unusèd to the melting mood,
350   Drop tears as fast as the Arabian trees
        Their med'cinable gum. Set you down this.
        And say besides that in Aleppo once,
        Where a malignant and a turbaned Turk
        Beat a Venetian and traduced the state,
        I took by th' throat the circumcisèd dog
        And smote him—thus.   *He stabs himself.*
    LODOVICO   O bloody period![47]
    GRATIANO   All that's spoke is marred.

---

44. Defy   46. Distraught
45. Dismissed   47. Ending

OTHELLO   I kissed thee ere I killed thee. No way but this,
   Killing myself, to die upon a kiss.   *He falls upon the bed and dies.*
360 CASSIO   This did I fear, but thought he had no weapon;
   For he was great of heart.
LODOVICO   [*to Iago*] O Spartan dog,[48]
   More fell[49] than anguish, hunger, or the sea!
   Look on the tragic loading of this bed.
   This is thy work. The object[50] poisons sight;
   Let it be hid. Gratiano, keep the house,
   And seize upon[51] the fortunes of the Moor,
   For they succeed on you. To you, lord governor,
   Remains the censure[52] of this hellish villain,
   The time, the place, the torture. O, enforce it!
370 Myself will straight abroad, and to the state
   This heavy act with heavy heart relate.   *Exeunt.*

48. Type of bloodhound, noted for its silence   50. Spectacle
    and relentlessness   51. Take possession
49. Cruel   52. Legal sentencing

SATIRE IN THE NEOCLASSICAL FRENCH THEATER

Molière's *The Misanthrope* was first performed in 1666 at the theater of the Palais-Royal, a fully enclosed structure within an elegant palace that had been erected by Cardinal de Richelieu, King Louis XIII's chief minister. The play, in short, had its premiere within a building that embodied the very same aristocratic and sophisticated culture that Molière was satirizing in his work. Indeed, the audience was made up largely of members of the aristocracy and nobility, and they could hardly have failed to interpret the play as a reflection on themselves. The theater itself was elegantly decked out, with neoclassical columns on each side of the stage, decorative trim around the galleries and the moldings of the upper walls, and chandeliers suspended from the ceiling of the auditorium and from the center of the stage. Thus the actors on stage and the audience watching them were illuminated by candlelight.

Despite the shared light of candles, the actors and audience were actually

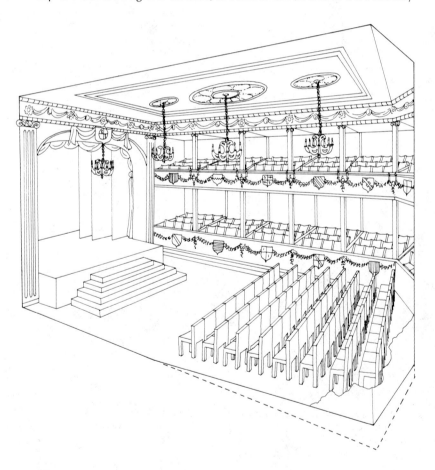

separated from one another by the physical design of the theater. The Palais-Royal theater was a long rectangle in shape, with a rather deep stage at one end. Spectators viewed the action either from the main floor or from two levels of galleries located on each side of the hall. The theater accommodated six hundred persons in all—an intimate audience whose members could see and be seen by one another under the glowing candlelight of the chandeliers.

As we can see from the design of the theater, however, the audience was distinctly separated from the actors by the proscenium arch, which framed the action like a picture. And the barrier created by the arch was reinforced by the use of a curtain to divide the separate acts of the play. The audience was thus placed in the position of looking into something like a box, one side of which had been stripped away when the curtain was pulled apart. In this respect the neoclassical audience could be said to have witnessed dramatic performances from a perspective similar to that of our modern theaters—except that spectators seated in the galleries probably had a very restricted angle from which to view the stage. And neoclassical French settings were not designed to create the kind of highly realistic illusion we associate with modern theatrical productions. The action of *The Misanthrope*, for example, was played in front of a flat piece of background scenery depicting something like the wall of a salon in Célimène's house, but it was not elaborated to create the impression of a three-dimensional space. It was, rather, a standard setting that would have been used repeatedly in comedies and satires having to do with sophisticated social experience.

Acting styles of the period were also highly formalized. If we try to imagine the style used in *The Misanthrope* we will do best to refer to *commedia dell'arte*, a popular form of drama which emerged during the Italian Renaissance (sixteenth century), and which exerted a strong influence on French actors, particularly on Molière. *Commedia* was an improvisational theater built upon an array of type characters, such as the clever servant, the braggart soldier, the ingenious maid, the foolish husband, the angry father, and so on. Associated with each type was a stylized, exaggerated mode of gesture and movement, which would have been especially appropriate to such characters as Arsinoe (the hypocritical prude), or Célimène (the flirtatious coquette), or Oronte (the vain fop). Thus the method of acting, like the theater itself, provided a stylized form of production ideally suited to the social satire dramatized in *The Misanthrope*.

MOLIÈRE
1622–1673
The Misanthrope

CHARACTERS

ALCESTE, in love with Célimène
PHILINTE, Alceste's friend
ORONTE, in love with Célimène
CÉLIMÈNE, Alceste's beloved
ÉLIANTE, Célimène's cousin
ARSINOÉ, a friend of Célimène's

ACASTE ⎫
CLITANDRE ⎬ marquesses
BASQUE, Célimène's servant
A GUARD of the Marshalsea
DUBOIS, Alceste's valet

The scene throughout is in Célimène's house at Paris.

ACT I

SCENE 1

PHILINTE, ALCESTE

PHILINTE   Now, what's got into you?
ALCESTE, *seated.*   Kindly leave me alone.
PHILINTE   Come, come, what is it? This lugubrious tone . . .
ALCESTE   Leave me, I said; you spoil my solitude.
PHILINTE   Oh, listen to me, now, and don't be rude.
ALCESTE   I choose to be rude, Sir, and to be hard of hearing.
PHILINTE   These ugly moods of yours are not endearing;
    Friends though we are, I really must insist . . .
ALCESTE, *abruptly rising.*   "Friends? Friends, you say? Well, cross me off your
        list.
    I've been your friend till now, as you well know;
10   But after what I saw a moment ago
    I tell you flatly that our ways must part.
    I wish no place in a dishonest heart.
PHILINTE   Why, what have I done, Alceste? Is this quite just?
ALCESTE   My God, you ought to die of self-disgust.
    I call your conduct inexcusable, Sir,
    And every man of honor will concur.
    I see you almost hug a man to death,
    Exclaim for joy until you're out of breath,

Translated by Richard Wilbur

And supplement these loving demonstrations
20   With endless offers, vows, and protestations;
Then when I ask you "Who was that?" I find
That you can barely bring his name to mind!
Once the man's back is turned, you cease to love him,
And speak with absolute indifference of him!
By God, I say it's base and scandalous
To falsify the heart's affections thus;
If I caught myself behaving in such a way,
I'd hang myself for shame, without delay.

PHILINTE It hardly seems a hanging matter to me;
30   I hope that you will take it graciously
If I extend myself a slight reprieve,
And live a little longer, by your leave.

ALCESTE How dare you joke about a crime so grave?

PHILINTE What crime? How else are people to behave?

ALCESTE I'd have them be sincere, and never part
With any word that isn't from the heart.

PHILINTE When someone greets us with a show of pleasure,
It's but polite to give him equal measure,
Return his love the best that we know how,
40   And trade him offer for offer, vow for vow.

ALCESTE No, no, this formula you'd have me follow,
However fashionable, is false and hollow,
And I despise the frenzied operations
Of all these barterers of protestations,
These lavishers of meaningless embraces,
These utterers of obliging commonplaces,
Who court and flatter everyone on earth
And praise the fool no less than the man of worth.
Should you rejoice that someone fondles you,
50   Offers his love and service, swears to be true,
And fills your ears with praises of your name,
When to the first damned fop he'll say the same?
No, no: no self-respecting heart would dream
Of prizing so promiscuous an esteem;
However high the praise, there's nothing worse
Than sharing honors with the universe.
Esteem is founded on comparison:
To honor all men is to honor none.
Since you embrace this indiscriminate vice,
60   Your friendship comes at far too cheap a price;
I spurn the easy tribute of a heart
Which will not set the worthy man apart:

I choose, Sir, to be chosen; and in fine,
The friend of mankind is no friend of mine.

PHILINTE   But in polite society, custom decrees
That we show certain outward courtesies. . . .

ALCESTE   Ah, no! we should condemn with all our force
Such false and artificial intercourse.
Let men behave like men; let them display
70   Their inmost hearts in everything they say;
Let the heart speak, and let our sentiments
Not mask themselves in silly compliments.

PHILINTE   In certain cases it would be uncouth
And most absurd to speak the naked truth;
With all respect for your exalted notions,
It's often best to veil one's true emotions.
Wouldn't the social fabric come undone
If we were wholly frank with everyone?
Suppose you met with someone you couldn't bear;
80   Would you inform him of it then and there?

ALCESTE   Yes.

PHILINTE   Then you'd tell old Emilie it's pathetic
The way she daubs her features with cosmetic
And plays the gay coquette at sixty-four?

ALCESTE   I would.

PHILINTE   And you'd call Dorilas a bore,
And tell him every ear at court is lame
From hearing him brag about his noble name?

ALCESTE   Precisely.

PHILINTE   Ah, you're joking.

ALCESTE   *Au contraire:*
In this regard there's none I'd choose to spare.
All are corrupt; there's nothing to be seen
90   In court or town but aggravates my spleen.
I fall into deep gloom and melancholy
When I survey the scene of human folly,
Finding on every hand base flattery,
Injustice, fraud, self-interest, treachery. . . .
Ah, it's too much; mankind has grown so base,
I mean to break with the whole human race.

PHILINTE   This philosophic rage is a bit extreme;
You've no idea how comical you seem;
Indeed, we're like those brothers in the play
100   Called *School for Husbands,* one of whom was prey . . .

ALCESTE   Enough, now! None of your stupid similes.

PHILINTE   Then let's have no more tirades, if you please.

The world won't change, whatever you say or do;
And since plain speaking means so much to you,
I'll tell you plainly that by being frank
You've earned the reputation of a crank,
And that you're thought ridiculous when you rage
And rant against the manners of the age.

ALCESTE   So much the better; just what I wish to hear.
110   No news could be more grateful to my ear.
All men are so detestable in my eyes,
I should be sorry if they thought me wise.

PHILINTE   Your hatred's very sweeping, is it not?

ALCESTE   Quite right: I hate the whole degraded lot.

PHILINTE   Must all poor human creatures be embraced,
Without distinction, by your vast distaste?
Even in these bad times, there are surely a few . . .

ALCESTE   No, I include all men in one dim view:
Some men I hate for being rogues; the others
120   I hate because they treat the rogues like brothers,
And, lacking a virtuous scorn for what is vile,
Receive the villain with a complaisant smile.
Notice how tolerant people choose to be
Toward that bold rascal who's at law with me.
His social polish can't conceal his nature;
One sees at once that he's a treacherous creature;
No one could possibly be taken in
By those soft speeches and that sugary grin.
The whole world knows the shady means by which
130   The low-brow's grown so powerful and rich,
And risen to a rank so bright and high
That virtue can but blush, and merit sigh.
Whenever his name comes up in conversation,
None will defend his wretched reputation;
Call him knave, liar, scoundrel, and all the rest,
Each head will nod, and no one will protest.
And yet his smirk is seen in every house,
He's greeted everywhere with smiles and bows,
And when there's any honor that can be got
140   By pulling strings, he'll get it, like as not.
My God! It chills my heart to see the ways
Men come to terms with evil nowadays;
Sometimes, I swear, I'm moved to flee and find
Some desert land unfouled by humankind.

PHILINTE   Come, let's forget the follies of the times
And pardon mankind for its petty crimes;

Let's have an end of rantings and of railings,
And show some leniency toward human failings.
This world requires a pliant rectitude;
150   Too stern a virtue makes one stiff and rude;
Good sense views all extremes with detestation,
And bids us to be noble in moderation.
The rigid virtues of the ancient days
Are not for us; they jar with all our ways
And ask of us too lofty a perfection.
Wise men accept their times without objection,
And there's no greater folly, if you ask me,
Than trying to reform society.
Like you, I see each day a hundred and one
160   Unhandsome deeds that might be better done,
But still, for all the faults that meet my view,
I'm never known to storm and rave like you.
I take men as they are, or let them be,
And teach my soul to bear their frailty;
And whether in court or town, whatever the scene,
My phlegm's as philosophic as your spleen.
ALCESTE   This phlegm which you so eloquently commend,
Does nothing ever rile it up, my friend?
Suppose some man you trust should treacherously
170   Conspire to rob you of your property,
And do his best to wreck your reputation?
Wouldn't you feel a certain indignation?
PHILINTE   Why, no. These faults of which you so complain
Are part of human nature, I maintain,
And it's no more a matter for disgust
That men are knavish, selfish and unjust,
Than that the vulture dines upon the dead,
And wolves are furious, and apes ill-bred.
ALCESTE   Shall I see myself betrayed, robbed, torn to bits,
180   And not . . . Oh, let's be still and rest our wits.
Enough of reasoning, now. I've had my fill.
PHILINTE   Indeed, you would do well, Sir, to be still.
Rage less at your opponent, and give some thought
To how you'll win this lawsuit that he's brought.
ALCESTE   I assure you I'll do nothing of the sort.
PHILINTE   Then who will plead your case before the court?
ALCESTE   Reason and right and justice will plead for me.
PHILINTE   Oh, Lord. What judges do you plan to see?
ALCESTE   Why, none. The justice of my cause is clear.
190   PHILINTE   Of course, man; but there's politics to fear. . . .

ALCESTE   No, I refuse to lift a hand. That's flat.
  I'm either right, or wrong.
PHILINTE   Don't count on that.
ALCESTE   No, I'll do nothing.
PHILINTE   Your enemy's influence
  Is great, you know . . .
ALCESTE   That makes no difference.
PHILINTE   It will; you'll see.
ALCESTE   Must honor bow to guile?
  If so, I shall be proud to lose the trial.
PHILINTE   Oh, really . . .
ALCESTE   I'll discover by this case
  Whether or not men are sufficiently base
  And impudent and villainous and perverse
200   To do me wrong before the universe.
PHILINTE   What a man!
ALCESTE   Oh, I could wish, whatever the cost,
  Just for the beauty of it, that my trial were lost.
PHILINTE   If people heard you talking so, Alceste,
  They'd split their sides. Your name would be a jest.
ALCESTE   So much the worse for jesters.
PHILINTE   May I enquire
  Whether this rectitude you so admire,
  And these hard virtues you're enamored of
  Are qualities of the lady whom you love?
  It much surprises me that you, who seem
210   To view mankind with furious disesteem,
  Have yet found something to enchant your eyes
  Amidst a species which you so despise.
  And what is more amazing, I'm afraid,
  Is the most curious choice your heart has made.
  The honest Éliante is fond of you,
  Arsinoé, the prude, admires you too;
  And yet your spirit's been perversely led
  To choose the flighty Célimène instead,
  Whose brittle malice and coquettish ways
220   So typify the manners of our days.
  How is it that the traits you most abhor
  Are bearable in this lady you adore?
  Are you so blind with love that you can't find them?
  Or do you contrive, in her case, not to mind them?
ALCESTE   My love for that young widow's not the kind
  That can't perceive defects; no, I'm not blind.
  I see her faults, despite my ardent love,

And all I see I fervently reprove.
And yet I'm weak; for all her falsity,
230   That woman knows the art of pleasing me,
And though I never cease complaining of her,
I swear I cannot manage not to love her.
Her charm outweighs her faults; I can but aim
To cleanse her spirit in my love's pure flame.
PHILINTE   That's no small task; I wish you all success.
You think then that she loves you?
ALCESTE   Heavens, yes!
I wouldn't love her did she not love me.
PHILINTE   Well, if her taste for you is plain to see,
Why do these rivals cause you such despair?
240   ALCESTE   True love, Sir, is possessive, and cannot bear
To share with all the world. I'm here today
To tell her she must send that mob away.
PHILINTE   If I were you, and had your choice to make,
Éliante, her cousin, would be the one I'd take;
That honest heart, which cares for you alone,
Would harmonize far better with your own.
ALCESTE   True, true: each day my reason tells me so;
But reason doesn't rule in love, you know.
PHILINTE   I fear some bitter sorrow is in store;
250   This love . . .

SCENE 2

ORONTE, ALCESTE, PHILINTE

ORONTE, *to Alceste.*   The servants told me at the door
That Éliante and Célimène were out,
But when I heard, dear Sir, that you were about,
I came to say, without exaggeration,
That I hold you in the vastest admiration,
And that it's always been my dearest desire
To be the friend of one I so admire.
I hope to see my love of merit requited,
And you and I in friendship's bond united.
10   I'm sure you won't refuse—if I may be frank—
A friend of my devotedness—and rank.

During this speech of Oronte's, Alceste is abstracted, and seems unaware that he is being spoken to. He only breaks off his reverie when Oronte says:

It was for you, if you please, that my words were intended.

ALCESTE　For me, Sir?

ORONTE　　　　　　Yes, for you. You're not offended?

ALCESTE　By no means. But this much surprises me. . . .
　　The honor comes most unexpectedly. . . .

ORONTE　My high regard should not astonish you;
　　The whole world feels the same. It is your due.

ALCESTE　Sir . . .

ORONTE　　　　　Why, in all the State there isn't one
　　Can match your merits; they shine, Sir, like the sun.

ALCESTE　Sir . . .

20　ORONTE　　　　　You are higher in my estimation
　　Than all that's most illustrious in the nation.

ALCESTE　Sir . . .

ORONTE　　　　　If I lie, may heaven strike me dead!
　　To show you that I mean what I have said,
　　Permit me, Sir, to embrace you most sincerely,
　　And swear that I will prize our friendship dearly.
　　Give me your hand. And now, Sir, if you choose,
　　We'll make our vows.

ALCESTE　　　　　　Sir . . .

ORONTE　　　　　　　What! You refuse?

ALCESTE　Sir, it's a very great honor you extend:
　　But friendship is a sacred thing, my friend;

30　　It would be profanation to bestow
　　The name of friend on one you hardly know.
　　All parts are better played when well-rehearsed;
　　Let's put off friendship, and get acquainted first.
　　We may discover it would be unwise
　　To try to make our natures harmonize.

ORONTE　By heaven! You're sagacious to the core;
　　This speech has made me admire you even more.
　　Let time, then, bring us closer day by day;
　　Meanwhile, I shall be yours in every way.

40　　If, for example, there should be anything
　　You wish at court, I'll mention it to the King.
　　I have his ear, of course; it's quite well known
　　That I am much in favor with the throne.
　　In short, I am your servant. And now, dear friend,
　　Since you have such fine judgment, I intend
　　To please you, if I can, with a small sonnet
　　I wrote not long ago. Please comment on it,
　　And tell me whether I ought to publish it.

ALCESTE   You must excuse me, Sir; I'm hardly fit
    To judge such matters.
ORONTE   Why not?
50   ALCESTE   I am, I fear,
    Inclined to be unfashionably sincere.
ORONTE   Just what I ask; I'd take no satisfaction
    In anything but your sincere reaction.
    I beg you not to dream of being kind.
ALCESTE   Since you desire it, Sir, I'll speak my mind.
ORONTE   *Sonnet.* It's a sonnet. . . . *Hope* . . . The poem's addressed
    To a lady who wakened hopes within my breast.
    Hope . . . this is not the pompous sort of thing,
    Just modest little verses, with a tender ring.
ALCESTE   Well, we shall see.
60   ORONTE   *Hope* . . . I'm anxious to hear
    Whether the style seems properly smooth and clear,
    And whether the choice of words is good or bad.
ALCESTE   We'll see, we'll see.
ORONTE   Perhaps I ought to add
    That it took me only a quarter-hour to write it.
ALCESTE   The time's irrelevant, Sir: kindly recite it.
ORONTE, *reading.*

    Hope comforts us awhile, 'tis true,
    Lulling our cares with careless laughter,
    And yet such joy is full of rue,
    My Phyllis, if nothing follows after.

70   PHILINTE   I'm charmed by this already; the style's delightful.
ALCESTE, *sotto voce, to Philinte.*   How can you say that? Why, the thing is
    frightful.

ORONTE   Your fair face smiled on me awhile,
    But was it kindness so to enchant me?
    'Twould have been fairer not to smile,
    If hope was all you meant to grant me.

PHILINTE   What a clever thought! How handsomely you phrase it!
ALCESTE, *sotto voce, to Philinte.*   You know the thing is trash. How dare you
    praise it?

ORONTE   If it's to be my passion's fate
    Thus everlastingly to wait,

982   A COLLECTION OF PLAYS

> Then death will come to set me free:
> For death is fairer than the fair;
> Phyllis, to hope is to despair
> When one must hope eternally.

PHILINTE   The close is exquisite—full of feeling and grace.

ALCESTE, *sotto voce, aside.*   Oh, blast the close; you'd better close your face
Before you send your lying soul to hell.

PHILINTE   I can't remember a poem I've liked so well.

ALCESTE, *sotto voce, aside.*   Good Lord!

ORONTE, *to Philinte.*   I fear you're flattering me a bit.

PHILINTE   Oh, no!

ALCESTE, *sotto voce, aside.*
              What else d'you call it, you hypocrite?

90 ORONTE, *to Alceste.*   But you, Sir, keep your promise now: don't shrink
From telling me sincerely what you think.

ALCESTE   Sir, these are delicate matters; we all desire
To be told that we've the true poetic fire.
But once, to one whose name I shall not mention,
I said, regarding some verse of his invention,
That gentlemen should rigorously control
That itch to write which often afflicts the soul;
That one should curb the heady inclination
To publicize one's little avocation;

100 And that in showing off one's works of art
One often plays a very clownish part.

ORONTE   Are you suggesting in a devious way
That I ought not . . .

ALCESTE   Oh, that I do not say.
Further, I told him that no fault is worse
Than that of writing frigid, lifeless verse,
And that the merest whisper of such a shame
Suffices to destroy a man's good name.

ORONTE   D'you mean to say my sonnet's dull and trite?

ALCESTE   I don't say that. But I went on to cite

110 Numerous cases of once-respected men
Who came to grief by taking up the pen.

ORONTE   And am I like them? Do I write so poorly?

ALCESTE   I don't say that. But I told this person, "Surely
You're under no necessity to compose;
Why you should wish to publish, heaven knows.
There's no excuse for printing tedious rot
Unless one writes for bread, as you do not.
Resist temptation, then, I beg of you;

Conceal your pastimes from the public view;
120   And don't give up, on any provocation,
Your present high and courtly reputation,
To purchase at a greedy printer's shop
The name of silly author and scribbling fop."
These were the points I tried to make him see.
ORONTE   I sense that they are also aimed at me;
But now—about my sonnet—I'd like to be told . . .
ALCESTE   Frankly, that sonnet should be pigeonholed.
You've chosen the worst models to imitate.
The style's unnatural. Let me illustrate:

130   For example, *Your fair face smiled on me awhile,*
Followed by, *'Twould have been fairer not to smile!*
Or this: *such joy is full of rue;*
Or this: *For death is fairer than the fair;*
Or, *Phyllis, to hope is to despair*
   When one must hope eternally!

This artificial style, that's all the fashion,
Has neither taste, nor honesty, nor passion;
It's nothing but a sort of wordy play,
And nature never spoke in such a way.
140   What, in this shallow age, is not debased?
Our fathers, though less refined, had better taste;
I'd barter all that men admire today
For one old love song I shall try to say:

   If the King had given me for my own
   Paris, his citadel,
   And I for that must leave alone
   Her whom I love so well,
   I'd say then to the Crown,
   Take back your glittering town;
150   My darling is more fair, I swear,
   My darling is more fair.

The rhyme's not rich, the style is rough and old,
But don't you see that it's the purest gold
Beside the tinsel nonsense now preferred,
And that there's passion in its every word?

   If the King had given me for my own
   Paris, his citadel,

And I for that must leave alone
    Her whom I love so well,
160   I'd say then to the Crown,
    Take back your glittering town;
My darling is more fair, I swear,
    My darling is more fair.

There speaks a loving heart. [*To Philinte*] You're laughing, eh?
Laugh on, my precious wit. Whatever you say,
I hold that song's worth all the bibelots
That people hail today with ah's and oh's.

ORONTE   And I maintain my sonnet's very good.

ALCESTE   It's not at all surprising that you should.
170   You have your reasons; permit me to have mine
For thinking that you cannot write a line.

ORONTE   Others have praised my sonnet to the skies.

ALCESTE   I lack their art of telling pleasant lies.

ORONTE   You seem to think you've got no end of wit.

ALCESTE   To praise your verse, I'd need still more of it.

ORONTE   I'm not in need of your approval, Sir.

ALCESTE   That's good; you couldn't have it if you were.

ORONTE   Come now, I'll lend you the subject of my sonnet;
I'd like to see you try to improve upon it.
180 ALCESTE   I might, by chance, write something just as shoddy;
But then I wouldn't show it to everybody.

ORONTE   You're most opinionated and conceited.

ALCESTE   Go find your flatterers, and be better treated.

ORONTE   Look here, my little fellow, pray watch your tone.

ALCESTE   My great big fellow, you'd better watch your own.

PHILINTE, *stepping between them.*   Oh, please, please, gentlemen! This will
never do.

ORONTE   The fault is mine, and I leave the field to you.
I am your servant, Sir, in every way.

ALCESTE   And I, Sir, am your most abject valet.

SCENE 3

PHILINTE, ALCESTE

PHILINTE   Well, as you see, sincerity in excess
Can get you into a very pretty mess;
Oronte was hungry for appreciation. . . .

ALCESTE   Don't speak to me.

PHILINTE   What?

ALCESTE   No more conversation.
PHILINTE Really, now . . .
ALCESTE   Leave me alone.
PHILINTE   If I . . .
ALCESTE   Out of my sight!
PHILINTE But what . . .
ALCESTE   I won't listen.
PHILINTE   But . . .
ALCESTE   Silence!
PHILINTE   Now, is it polite . . .
ALCESTE By heaven, I've had enough. Don't follow me.
PHILINTE Ah, you're just joking. I'll keep you company.

ACT II

SCENE 1

ALCESTE, CÉLIMÈNE

ALCESTE Shall I speak plainly, Madam? I confess
    Your conduct gives me infinite distress,
    And my resentment's grown too hot to smother.
    Soon, I foresee, we'll break with one another.
    If I said otherwise, I should deceive you;
    Sooner or later, I shall be forced to leave you,
    And if I swore that we shall never part,
    I should misread the omens of my heart.
CÉLIMÈNE You kindly saw me home, it would appear,
10   So as to pour invectives in my ear.
ALCESTE I've no desire to quarrel. But I deplore
    Your inability to shut the door
    On all these suitors who beset you so.
    There's what annoys me, if you care to know.
CÉLIMÈNE Is it my fault that all these men pursue me?
    Am I to blame if they're attracted to me?
    And when they gently beg an audience,
    Ought I to take a stick and drive them hence?
ALCESTE Madam, there's no necessity for a stick;
20   A less responsive heart would do the trick.
    Of your attractiveness I don't complain;
    But those your charms attract, you then detain
    By a most melting and receptive manner,
    And so enlist their hearts beneath your banner.

It's the agreeable hopes which you excite
That keep these lovers round you day and night;
Were they less liberally smiled upon,
That sighing troop would very soon be gone.
But tell me, Madam, why it is that lately
30   This man Clitandre interests you so greatly?
Because of what high merits do you deem
Him worthy of the honor of your esteem?
Is it that your admiring glances linger
On the splendidly long nail of his little finger?
Or do you share the general deep respect
For the blond wig he chooses to affect?
Are you in love with his embroidered hose?
Do you adore his ribbons and his bows?
Or is it that this paragon bewitches
40   Your tasteful eye with his vast German breeches?
Perhaps his giggle, or his falsetto voice,
Makes him the latest gallant of your choice?
CÉLIMÈNE   You're much mistaken to resent him so.
Why I put up with him you surely know:
My lawsuit's very shortly to be tried,
And I must have his influence on my side.
ALCESTE   Then lose your lawsuit, Madam, or let it drop;
Don't torture me by humoring such a fop.
CÉLIMÈNE   You're jealous of the whole world, Sir.
ALCESTE   That's true,
50   Since the whole world is well-received by you.
CÉLIMÈNE   That my good nature is so unconfined
Should serve to pacify your jealous mind;
Were I to smile on one, and scorn the rest,
Then you might have some cause to be distressed.
ALCESTE   Well, if I mustn't be jealous, tell me, then,
Just how I'm better treated than other men.
CÉLIMÈNE   You know you have my love. Will that not do?
ALCESTE   What proof have I that what you say is true?
CÉLIMÈNE   I would expect, Sir, that my having said it
60   Might give the statement a sufficient credit.
ALCESTE   But how can I be sure that you don't tell
The selfsame thing to other men as well?
CÉLIMÈNE   What a gallant speech! How flattering to me!
What a sweet creature you make me out to be!
Well then, to save you from the pangs of doubt,
All that I've said I hereby cancel out;
Now, none but yourself shall make a monkey of you:
Are you content?

ALCESTE   Why, why am I doomed to love you?
    I swear that I shall bless the blissful hour
70   When this poor heart's no longer in your power!
    I make no secret of it: I've done my best
    To exorcise this passion from my breast;
    But thus far all in vain; it will not go;
    It's for my sins that I must love you so.
CÉLIMÈNE   Your love for me is matchless, Sir; that's clear.
ALCESTE   Indeed, in all the world it has no peer;
    Words can't describe the nature of my passion,
    And no man ever loved in such a fashion.
CÉLIMÈNE   Yes, it's a brand-new fashion, I agree:
80   You show your love by castigating me,
    And all your speeches are enraged and rude.
    I've never been so furiously wooed.
ALCESTE   Yet you could calm that fury, if you chose.
    Come, shall we bring our quarrels to a close?
    Let's speak with open hearts, then, and begin . . .

SCENE 2

CÉLIMÈNE, ALCESTE, BASQUE

CÉLIMÈNE   What is it?
BASQUE   Acaste is here.
CÉLIMÈNE   Well, send him in.

SCENE 3

CÉLIMÈNE, ALCESTE

ALCESTE   What! Shall we never be alone at all?
    You're always ready to receive a call,
    And you can't bear, for ten ticks of the clock,
    Not to keep open house for all who knock.
CÉLIMÈNE   I couldn't refuse him: he'd be most put out.
ALCESTE   Surely that's not worth worrying about.
CÉLIMÈNE   Acaste would never forgive me if he guessed
    That I consider him a dreadful pest.
ALCESTE   If he's a pest, why bother with him then?
10 CÉLIMÈNE   Heavens! One can't antagonize such men;
    Why, they're the chartered gossips of the court,

And have a say in things of every sort.
One must receive them, and be full of charm;
They're no great help, but they can do you harm,
And though your influence be ever so great,
They're hardly the best people to alienate.

ALCESTE   I see, dear lady, that you could make a case
For putting up with the whole human race;
These friendships that you calculate so nicely . . .

SCENE 4

ALCESTE, CÉLIMÈNE, BASQUE

BASQUE   Madam, Clitandre is here as well.
ALCESTE   Precisely.
CÉLIMÈNE   Where are you going?
ALCESTE   Elsewhere.
CÉLIMÈNE   Stay.
ALCESTE   No, no.
CÉLMINÈNE   Stay, Sir.
ALCESTE   I can't.
CÉLIMÈNE   I wish it.
ALCESTE   No, I must go.
I beg you, Madam, not to press the matter;
You know I have no taste for idle chatter.
CÉLIMÈNE   Stay: I command you.
ALCESTE   No, I cannot stay.
CÉLIMÈNE   Very well; you have my leave to go away.

SCENE 5

ÉLIANTE, PHILINTE, ACASTE, CLITANDRE, ALCESTE, CÉLIMÈNE, BASQUE

ÉLIANTE, *to Célimène*.   The Marquesses have kindly come to call.
Were they announced?
CÉLIMÈNE   Yes. Basque, bring chairs for all.

Basque provides the chairs, and exits.

To Alceste.   You haven't gone?
ALCESTE   No; and I shan't depart
Till you decide who's foremost in your heart.
CÉLIMÈNE   Oh, hush.
ALCESTE   It's time to choose; take them, or me.

CÉLIMÈNE   You're mad.

ALCESTE   I'm not, as you shall shortly see.

CÉLIMÈNE   Oh?

ALCESTE   You'll decide.

CÉLIMÈNE   You're joking now, dear friend.

ALCESTE   No, no; you'll choose; my patience is at an end.

CLITANDRE   Madam, I come from court, where poor Cléonte
10   Behaved like a perfect fool, as is his wont.
        Has he no friend to counsel him, I wonder,
        And teach him less unerringly to blunder?

CÉLIMÈNE   It's true, the man's a most accomplished dunce;
        His gauche behavior charms the eye at once;
        And every time one sees him, on my word,
        His manner's grown a trifle more absurd.

ACASTE   Speaking of dunces, I've just now conversed
        With old Damon, who's one of the very worst;
        I stood a lifetime in the broiling sun
20   Before his dreary monologue was done.

CÉLIMÈNE   Oh, he's a wondrous talker, and has the power
        To tell you nothing hour after hour:
        If, by mistake, he ever came to the point,
        The shock would put his jawbone out of joint.

ÉLIANTE, to Philinte.   The conversation takes its usual turn,
        And all our dear friends' ears will shortly burn.

CLITANDRE   Timante's a character, Madam.

CÉLIMÈNE   Isn't he, though?
        A man of mystery from top to toe,
        Who moves about in a romantic mist
30   On secret missions which do not exist.
        His talk is full of eyebrows and grimaces;
        How tired one gets of his momentous faces;
        He's always whispering something confidential
        Which turns out to be quite inconsequential;
        Nothing's too slight for him to mystify;
        He even whispers when he says "good-by."

ACASTE   Tell us about Géralde.

CÉLIMÈNE   That tiresome ass.
        He mixes only with the titled class,
40   And fawns on dukes and princes, and is bored
        With anyone who's not at least a lord.
        The man's obsessed with rank, and his discourses
        Are all of hounds and carriages and horses;
        He uses Christian names with all the great,
        And the word Milord, with him, is out of date.

CLITANDRE   He's very taken with Bélise, I hear.
CÉLIMÈNE   She is the dreariest company, poor dear.
    Whenever she comes to call, I grope about
    To find some topic which will draw her out,
50   But, owing to her dry and faint replies,
    The conversation wilts, and droops, and dies.
    In vain one hopes to animate her face
    By mentioning the ultimate commonplace;
    But sun or shower, even hail or frost
    Are matters she can instantly exhaust.
    Meanwhile her visit, painful though it is,
    Drags on and on through mute eternities,
    And though you ask the time, and yawn, and yawn,
    She sits there like a stone and won't be gone.
ACASTE   Now for Adraste.
60 CÉLIMÈNE   Oh, that conceited elf
    Has a gigantic passion for himself;
    He rails against the court, and cannot bear it
    That none will recognize his hidden merit;
    All honors given to others give offense
    To his imaginary excellence.
CLITANDRE   What about young Cléon? His house, they say,
    Is full of the best society, night and day.
CÉLIMÈNE   His cook has made him popular, not he:
    It's Cléon's table that people come to see.
70 ÉLIANTE   He gives a splendid dinner, you must admit.
CÉLIMÈNE   But must he serve himself along with it?
    For my taste, he's a most insipid dish
    Whose presence sours the wine and spoils the fish.
PHILINTE   Damis, his uncle, is admired no end.
    What's your opinion, Madam?
CÉLIMÈNE   Why, he's my friend.
PHILINTE   He seems a decent fellow, and rather clever.
CÉLIMÈNE   He works too hard at cleverness, however.
    I hate to see him sweat and struggle so
    To fill his conversation with bons mots.
80   Since he's decided to become a wit
    His taste's so pure that nothing pleases it;
    He scolds at all the latest books and plays,
    Thinking that wit must never stoop to praise,
    That finding fault's a sign of intellect,
    That all appreciation is abject,
    And that by damning everything in sight
    One shows oneself in a distinguished light.

He's scornful even of our conversations:
Their trivial nature sorely tries his patience;
90   He folds his arms, and stands above the battle,
And listens sadly to our childish prattle.

ACASTE   Wonderful, Madam! You've hit him off precisely.

CLITANDRE   No one can sketch a character so nicely.

ALCESTE   How bravely, Sirs, you cut and thrust at all
These absent fools, till one by one they fall:
But let one come in sight, and you'll at once
Embrace the man you lately called a dunce,
Telling him in a tone sincere and fervent
How proud you are to be his humble servant.

100   CLITANDRE   Why pick on us? *Madame's* been speaking, Sir,
And you should quarrel, if you must, with her.

ALCESTE   No, no, by God, the fault is yours, because
You lead her on with laughter and applause,
And make her think that she's the more delightful
The more her talk is scandalous and spiteful.
Oh, she would stoop to malice far, far less
If no such claque approved her cleverness.
It's flatterers like you whose foolish praise
Nourishes all the vices of these days.

110   PHILINTE   But why protest when someone ridicules
Those you'd condemn, yourself, as knaves or fools?

CÉLIMÈNE   Why, Sir? Because he loves to make a fuss.
You don't expect him to agree with us,
When there's an opportunity to express
His heaven-sent spirit of contrariness?
What other people think, he can't abide;
Whatever they say, he's on the other side;
He lives in deadly terror of agreeing;
'Twould make him seem an ordinary being.
120   Indeed, he's so in love with contradiction,
He'll turn against his most profound conviction
And with a furious eloquence deplore it,
If only someone else is speaking for it.

ALCESTE   Go on, dear lady, mock me as you please;
You have your audience in ecstasies.

PHILINTE   But what she says is true: you have a way
Of bridling at whatever people say;
Whether they praise or blame, your angry spirit
Is equally unsatisfied to hear it.

130   ALCESTE   Men, Sir, are always wrong, and that's the reason
That righteous anger's never out of season;

All that I hear in all their conversation
Is flattering praise or reckless condemnation.
CÉLIMÈNE   But . . .
ALCESTE   No, no, Madam, I am forced to state
That you have pleasures which I deprecate,
And that these others, here, are much to blame
For nourishing the faults which are your shame.
CLITANDRE   I shan't defend myself, Sir; but I vow
I'd thought this lady faultless until now.
140 ACASTE   I see her charms and graces, which are many;
But as for faults, I've never noticed any.
ALCESTE   I see them, Sir; and rather than ignore them,
I strenuously criticize her for them.
The more one loves, the more one should object
To every blemish, every least defect.
Were I this lady, I would soon get rid
Of lovers who approved of all I did,
And by their slack indulgence and applause
Endorsed my follies and excused my flaws.
150 CÉLIMÈNE   If all hearts beat according to your measure,
The dawn of love would be the end of pleasure;
And love would find its perfect consummation
In ecstasies of rage and reprobation.
ÉLIANTE   Love, as a rule, affects men otherwise,
And lovers rarely love to criticize.
They see their lady as a charming blur,
And find all things commendable in her.
If she has any blemish, fault, or shame,
They will redeem it by a pleasing name.
160 The pale-faced lady's lily-white, perforce;
The swarthy one's a sweet brunette, of course;
The spindly lady has a slender grace;
The fat one has a most majestic pace;
The plain one, with her dress in disarray,
They classify as *beauté négligée*;
The hulking one's a goddess in their eyes,
The dwarf, a concentrate of Paradise;
The haughty lady has a noble mind;
The mean one's witty, and the dull one's kind;
170 The chatterbox has liveliness and verve,
The mute one has a virtuous reserve.
So lovers manage, in their passion's cause,
To love their ladies even for their flaws.
ALCESTE   But I still say . . .

CÉLIMÈNE   I think it would be nice
   To stroll around the gallery once or twice.
   What! You're not going, Sirs?
CLITANDRE AND ACASTE   No, Madam, no.
ALCESTE   You seem to be in terror lest they go.
   Do what you will, Sirs; leave, or linger on,
   But I shan't go till after you are gone.
180 ACASTE   I'm free to linger, unless I should perceive
   Madame is tired, and wishes me to leave.
CLITANDRE   And as for me, I needn't go today
   Until the hour of the King's *coucher.*
CÉLIMÈNE, *to Alceste.*   You're joking, surely?
ALCESTE   Not in the least; we'll see
   Whether you'd rather part with them, or me.

SCENE 6

ALCESTE, CÉLIMÈNE, ÉLIANTE, ACASTE, PHILINTE, CLITANDRE, BASQUE

BASQUE, *to Alceste.*   Sir, there's a fellow here who bids me state
   That he must see you, and that it can't wait.
ALCESTE   Tell him that I have no such pressing affairs.
BASQUE   It's a long tailcoat that this fellow wears,
   With gold all over.
CÉLIMÈNE, *to Alceste.*   You'd best go down and see.
   Or—have him enter.

SCENE 7

ALCESTE, CÉLIMÈNE, ÉLIANTE, ACASTE, PHILINTE, CLITANDRE, GUARD

ALCESTE, *confronting the Guard.*   Well, what do you want with me?
   Come in, Sir.
GUARD   I've a word, Sir, for your ear.
ALCESTE   Speak it aloud, Sir; I shall strive to hear.
GUARD   The Marshals have instructed me to say
   You must report to them without delay.
ALCESTE   Who? Me, Sir?
GUARD   Yes, Sir; you.
ALCESTE   But what do they want?
PHILINTE, *to Alceste.*   To scotch your silly quarrel with Oronte.
CÉLIMÈNE, *to Philinte.*   What quarrel?
PHILINTE   Oronte and he have fallen out

Over some verse he spoke his mind about;
10   The Marshals wish to arbitrate the matter.
ALCESTE   Never shall I equivocate or flatter!
PHILINTE   You'd best obey their summons; come, let's go.
ALCESTE   How can they mend our quarrel, I'd like to know?
    Am I to make a cowardly retraction,
    And praise those jingles to his satisfaction?
    I'll not recant; I've judged that sonnet rightly.
    It's bad.
PHILINTE   But you might say so more politely. . . .
ALCESTE   I'll not back down; his verses make me sick.
PHILINTE   If only you could be more politic!
    But come, let's go.
20   ALCESTE   I'll go, but I won't unsay
    A single word.
PHILINTE   Well, let's be on our way.
ALCESTE   Till I am ordered by my lord the King
    To praise that poem, I shall say the thing
    Is scandalous, by God, and that the poet
    Ought to be hanged for having the nerve to show it.

To Clitandre and Acaste, who are laughing.

    By heaven, Sirs, I really didn't know
    That I was being humorous.
CÉLIMÈNE   Go, Sir, go;
    Settle your business.
ALCESTE   I shall, and when I'm through,
    I shall return to settle things with you.

ACT III

SCENE 1

CLITANDRE, ACASTE

CLITANDRE   Dear Marquess, how contented you appear;
    All things delight you, nothing mars your cheer.
    Can you, in perfect honesty, declare
    That you've a right to be so debonair?
ACASTE   By Jove, when I survey myself, I find
    No cause whatever for distress of mind.
    I'm young and rich; I can in modesty

Lay claim to an exalted pedigree;
And owing to my name and my condition
10   I shall not want for honors and position.
Then as to courage, that most precious trait,
I seem to have it, as was proved of late
Upon the field of honor, where my bearing,
They say, was very cool and rather daring.
I've wit, of course; and taste in such perfection
That I can judge without the least reflection,
And at the theater, which is my delight,
Can make or break a play on opening night,
And lead the crowd in hisses or bravos,
20   And generally be known as one who knows.
I'm clever, handsome, gracefully polite;
My waist is small, my teeth are strong and white;
As for my dress, the world's astonished eyes
Assure me that I bear away the prize.
I find myself in favor everywhere,
Honored by men, and worshiped by the fair;
And since these things are so, it seems to me
I'm justified in my complacency.
CLITANDRE   Well, if so many ladies hold you dear,
30   Why do you press a hopeless courtship here?
ACASTE   Hopeless, you say? I'm not the sort of fool
That likes his ladies difficult and cool.
Men who are awkward, shy, and peasantish
May pine for heartless beauties, if they wish,
Grovel before them, bear their cruelties,
Woo them with tears and sighs and bended knees,
And hope by dogged faithfulness to gain
What their poor merits never could obtain.
For men like me, however, it makes no sense
40   To love on trust, and foot the whole expense.
Whatever any lady's merits be,
I think, thank God, that I'm as choice as she;
That if my heart is kind enough to burn
For her, she owes me something in return;
And that in any proper love affair
The partners must invest an equal share.
CLITANDRE   You think, then, that our hostess favors you?
ACASTE   I've reason to believe that that is true.
CLITANDRE   How did you come to such a mad conclusion?
50   You're blind, dear fellow. This is sheer delusion.
ACASTE   All right, then: I'm deluded and I'm blind.
CLITANDRE   Whatever put the notion in your mind?

ACASTE Delusion.

CLITANDRE   What persuades you that you're right?

ACASTE I'm blind.

CLITANDRE   But have you any proofs to cite?

ACASTE I tell you I'm deluded.

CLITANDRE   Have you, then,
  Received some secret pledge from Célimène?

ACASTE Oh, no: she scorns me.

CLITANDRE   Tell me the truth, I beg.

ACASTE She just can't bear me.

CLITANDRE   Ah, don't pull my leg.
  Tell me what hope she's given you, I pray.

60 ACASTE I'm hopeless, and it's you who win the day.
  She hates me thoroughly, and I'm so vexed
  I mean to hang myself on Tuesday next.

CLITANDRE Dear Marquess, let us have an armistice
  And make a treaty. What do you say to this?
  If ever one of us can plainly prove
  That Célimène encourages his love,
  The other must abandon hope, and yield,
  And leave him in possession of the field.

ACASTE Now, there's a bargain that appeals to me;
70 With all my heart, dear Marquess, I agree.
  But hush.

SCENE 2

CÉLIMÈNE, ACASTE, CLITANDRE

CÉLIMÈNE Still here?

CLITANDRE   'Twas love that stayed our feet.

CÉLIMÈNE I think I heard a carriage in the street.
  Whose is it? D'you know?

SCENE 3

CÉLIMÈNE, ACASTE, CLITANDRE, BASQUE

BASQUE   Arsinoé is here,
  Madame.

CÉLIMÈNE Arsinoé, you say? Oh, dear.

BASQUE Éliante is entertaining her below.

CÉLIMÈNE What brings the creature here, I'd like to know?

ACASTE   They say she's dreadfully prudish, but in fact
　　I think her piety . . .
CÉLIMÈNE   It's all an act.
　　At heart she's worldly, and her poor success
　　In snaring men explains her prudishness.
　　It breaks her heart to see the beaux and gallants
　　Engrossed by other women's charms and talents,
10　　And so she's always in a jealous rage
　　Against the faulty standards of the age.
　　She lets the world believe that she's a prude
　　To justify her loveless solitude,
　　And strives to put a brand of moral shame
　　On all the graces that she cannot claim.
　　But still she'd love a lover; and Alceste
　　Appears to be the one she'd love the best.
　　His visits here are poison to her pride;
　　She seems to think I've lured him from her side;
20　　And everywhere, at court or in the town,
　　The spiteful, envious woman runs me down.
　　In short, she's just as stupid as can be,
　　Vicious and arrogant in the last degree,
　　And . . .

SCENE 4

ARSINOÉ, CÉLIMÈNE, CLITANDRE, ACASTE

CÉLIMÈNE   Ah! What happy chance has brought you here?
　　I've thought about you ever so much, my dear.
ARSINOÉ   I've come to tell you something you should know.
CÉLIMÈNE   How good of you to think of doing so!

　　　　　　　　　　　　Clitandre and Acaste go out, laughing.

SCENE 5

ARSINOÉ, CÉLIMÈNE

ARSINOÉ   It's just as well those gentlemen didn't tarry.
CÉLIMÈNE   Shall we sit down?
ARSINOÉ   That won't be necessary.
　　Madam, the flame of friendship ought to burn
　　Brightest in matters of the most concern,
　　And as there's nothing which concerns us more

Than honor, I have hastened to your door
To bring you, as your friend, some information
About the status of your reputation.
I visited, last night, some virtuous folk,
10   And, quite by chance, it was of you they spoke;
There was, I fear, no tendency to praise
Your light behavior and your dashing ways.
The quantity of gentlemen you see
And your by now notorious coquetry
Were both so vehemently criticized
By everyone, that I was much surprised.
Of course, I needn't tell you where I stood;
I came to your defense as best I could,
Assured them you were harmless, and declared
20   Your soul was absolutely unimpaired.
But there are some things, you must realize,
One can't excuse, however hard one tries,
And I was forced at last into conceding
That your behavior, Madam, is misleading,
That it makes a bad impression, giving rise
To ugly gossip and obscene surmise,
And that if you were more *overtly* good,
You wouldn't be so much misunderstood.
Not that I think you've been unchaste—no! no!
30   The saints preserve me from a thought so low!
But mere good conscience never did suffice:
One must avoid the outward show of vice.
Madam, you're too intelligent, I'm sure,
To think my motives anything but pure
In offering you this counsel—which I do
Out of a zealous interest in you.
CÉLIMÈNE   Madam, I haven't taken you amìss;
I'm very much obliged to you for this;
And I'll at once discharge the obligation
40   By telling you about *your* reputation.
You've been so friendly as to let me know
What certain people say of me, and so
I mean to follow your benign example
By offering you a somewhat similar sample.
The other day, I went to an affair
And found some most distinguished people there
Discussing piety, both false and true.
The conversation soon came round to you.
Alas! Your prudery and bustling zeal

50   Appeared to have a very slight appeal.
Your affectation of a grave demeanor,
Your endless talk of virtue and of honor,
The aptitude of your suspicious mind
For finding sin where there is none to find,
Your towering self-esteem, that pitying face
With which you contemplate the human race,
Your sermonizings and your sharp aspersions
On people's pure and innocent diversions—
All these were mentioned, Madam, and, in fact,
60   Were roundly and concertedly attacked.
"What good," they said, "are all these outward shows,
When everything belies her pious pose?
She prays incessantly; but then, they say,
She beats her maids and cheats them of their pay;
She shows her zeal in every holy place,
But still she's vain enough to paint her face;
She holds that naked statues are immoral,
But with a naked *man* she'd have no quarrel."
Of course, I said to everybody there
70   That they were being viciously unfair;
But still they were disposed to criticize you,
And all agreed that someone should advise you
To leave the morals of the world alone,
And worry rather more about your own.
They felt that one's self-knowledge should be great
Before one thinks of setting others straight;
That one should learn the art of living well
Before one threatens other men with hell,
And that the Church is best equipped, no doubt,
80   To guide our souls and root our vices out.
Madam, you're too intelligent, I'm sure,
To think my motives anything but pure
In offering you this counsel—which I do
Out of a zealous interest in you.
ARSINOÉ   I dared not hope for gratitude, but I
Did not expect so acid a reply;
I judge, since you've been so extremely tart,
That my good counsel pierced you to the heart.
CÉLIMÈNE   Far from it, Madam. Indeed, it seems to me
90   We ought to trade advice more frequently.
One's vision of oneself is so defective
That it would be an excellent corrective.
If you are willing, Madam, let's arrange

Shortly to have another frank exchange
In which we'll tell each other, *entre nous,*
What you've heard tell of me, and I of you.
ARSINOÉ   Oh, people never censure you, my dear;
It's me they criticize. Or so I hear.
CÉLIMÈNE   Madam, I think we either blame or praise
100   According to our taste and length of days.
There is a time of life for coquetry,
And there's a season, too, for prudery.
When all one's charms are gone, it is, I'm sure,
Good strategy to be devout and pure:
It makes one seem a little less forsaken.
Some day, perhaps, I'll take the road you've taken:
Time brings all things. But I have time aplenty,
And see no cause to be a prude at twenty.
ARSINOÉ   You give your age in such a gloating tone
110   That one would think I was an ancient crone;
We're not so far apart, in sober truth,
That you can mock me with a boast of youth!
Madam, you baffle me. I wish I knew
What moves you to provoke me as you do.
CÉLIMÈNE   For my part, Madam, I should like to know
Why you abuse me everywhere you go.
Is it my fault, dear lady, that your hand
Is not, alas, in very great demand?
If men admire me, if they pay me court
120   And daily make me offers of the sort
You'd dearly love to have them make to you,
How can I help it? What would you have me do?
If what you want is lovers, please feel free
To take as many as you can from me.
ARSINOÉ   Oh, come. D'you think the world is losing sleep
Over that flock of lovers which you keep,
Or that we find it difficult to guess
What price you pay for their devotedness?
Surely you don't expect us to suppose
130   Mere merit could attract so many beaux?
It's not your virtue that they're dazzled by;
Nor is it virtuous love for which they sigh.
You're fooling no one, Madam; the world's not blind;
There's many a lady heaven has designed
To call men's noblest, tenderest feelings out,
Who has no lovers dogging her about;
From which it's plain that lovers nowadays

Must be acquired in bold and shameless ways,
And only pay one court for such reward
140   As modesty and virtue can't afford.
Then don't be quite so puffed up, if you please,
About your tawdry little victories;
Try, if you can, to be a shade less vain,
And treat the world with somewhat less disdain.
If one were envious of your amours,
One soon could have a following like yours;
Lovers are no great trouble to collect
If one prefers them to one's self-respect.

CÉLIMÈNE   Collect them then, my dear; I'd love to see
150   You demonstrate that charming theory;
Who knows, you might . . .

ARSINOÉ   Now, Madam, that will do;
It's time to end this trying interview.
My coach is late in coming to your door,
Or I'd have taken leave of you before.

CÉLIMÈNE   Oh, please don't feel that you must rush away;
I'd be delighted, Madam, if you'd stay.
However, lest my conversation bore you,
Let me provide some better company for you;
This gentleman, who comes most apropos,
160   Will please you more than I could do, I know.

SCENE 6

ALCESTE, CÉLIMÈNE, ARSINOÉ

CÉLIMÈNE   Alceste, I have a little note to write
Which simply must go out before tonight;
Please entertain *Madame*; I'm sure that she
Will overlook my incivility.

SCENE 7

ALCESTE, ARSINOÉ

ARSINOÉ   Well, Sir, our hostess graciously contrives
For us to chat until my coach arrives;
And I shall be forever in her debt
For granting me this little tête-à-tête.
We women very rightly give our hearts

To men of noble character and parts,
And your especial merits, dear Alceste,
Have roused the deepest sympathy in my breast.
Oh, how I wish they had sufficient sense
10   At court, to recognize your excellence!
They wrong you greatly, Sir. How it must hurt you
Never to be rewarded for your virtue!

ALCESTE   Why, Madam, what cause have I to feel aggrieved?
What great and brilliant thing have I achieved?
What service have I rendered to the King
That I should look to him for anything?

ARSINOÉ   Not everyone who's honored by the State
Has done great services. A man must wait
Till time and fortune offer him the chance.
20   Your merit, Sir, is obvious at a glance,
And . . .

ALCESTE   Ah, forget my merit; I'm not neglected.
The court, I think, can hardly be expected
To mine men's souls for merit, and unearth
Our hidden virtues and our secret worth.

ARSINOÉ   *Some* virtues, though, are far too bright to hide;
Yours are acknowledged, Sir, on every side.
Indeed, I've heard you warmly praised of late
By persons of considerable weight.

ALCESTE   This fawning age has praise for everyone,
30   And all distinctions, Madam, are undone.
All things have equal honor nowadays,
And no one should be gratified by praise.
To be admired, one only need exist,
And every lackey's on the honors list.

ARSINOÉ   I only wish, Sir, that you had your eye
On some position at court, however high;
You'd only have to hint at such a notion
For me to set the proper wheels in motion;
I've certain friendships I'd be glad to use
40   To get you any office you might choose.

ALCESTE   Madam, I fear that any such ambition
Is wholly foreign to my disposition.
The soul God gave me isn't of the sort
That prospers in the weather of a court.
It's all too obvious that I don't possess
The virtues necessary for success.
My one great talent is for speaking plain;
I've never learned to flatter or to feign;

And anyone so stupidly sincere
50   Had best not seek a courtier's career.
Outside the court, I know, one must dispense
With honors, privilege, and influence;
But still one gains the right, foregoing these,
Not to be tortured by the wish to please.
One needn't live in dread of snubs and slights,
Nor praise the verse that every idiot writes,
Nor humor silly Marquesses, nor bestow
Politic sighs on Madam So-and-So.

ARSINOÉ   Forget the court, then; let the matter rest.
60   But I've another cause to be distressed
About your present situation, Sir.
It's to your love affair that I refer.
She whom you love, and who pretends to love you,
Is, I regret to say, unworthy of you.

ALCESTE   Why, Madam! Can you seriously intend
To make so grave a charge against your friend?

ARSINOÉ   Alas, I must. I've stood aside too long
And let that lady do you grievous wrong;
But now my debt to conscience shall be paid:
70   I tell you that your love has been betrayed.

ALCESTE   I thank you, Madam; you're extrmely kind.
Such words are soothing to a lover's mind.

ARSINOÉ   Yes, though she *is* my friend, I say again
You're very much too good for Célimène.
She's wantonly misled you from the start.

ALCESTE   You may be right; who knows another's heart?
But ask yourself if it's the part of charity
To shake my soul with doubts of her sincerity.

ARSINOÉ   Well, if you'd rather be a dupe than doubt her,
80   That's your affair. I'll say no more about her.

ALCESTE   Madam, you know that doubt and vague suspicion
Are painful to a man in my position;
It's most unkind to worry me this way
Unless you've some real proof of what you say.

ARSINOÉ   Sir, say no more: all doubt shall be removed,
And all that I've been saying shall be proved.
You've only to escort me home, and there
We'll look into the heart of this affair.
I've ocular evidence which will persuade you
90   Beyond a doubt, that Célimène's betrayed you.
Then, if you're saddened by that revelation,
Perhaps I can provide some consolation.

ACT IV

SCENE 1

ÉLIANTE, PHILINTE

PHILINTE   Madam, he acted like a stubborn child;
　　　I thought they never would be reconciled;
　　　In vain we reasoned, threatened, and appealed;
　　　He stood his ground and simply would not yield.
　　　The Marshals, I feel sure, have never heard
　　　An argument so splendidly absurd.
　　　"No, gentlemen," said he, "I'll not retract.
　　　His verse is bad: extremely bad, in fact.
　　　Surely it does the man no harm to know it.
10　　Does it disgrace him, not to be a poet?
　　　A gentleman may be respected still,
　　　Whether he writes a sonnet well or ill.
　　　That I dislike his verse should not offend him;
　　　In all that touches honor, I commend him;
　　　He's noble, brave, and virtuous—but I fear
　　　He can't in truth be called a sonneteer.
　　　I'll gladly praise his wardrobe; I'll endorse
　　　His dancing, or the way he sits a horse;
　　　But, gentlemen, I cannot praise his rhyme.
20　　In fact, it ought to be a capital crime
　　　For anyone so sadly unendowed
　　　To write a sonnet, and read the thing aloud."
　　　At length he fell into a gentler mood
　　　And, striking a concessive attitude,
　　　He paid Oronte the following courtesies:
　　　"Sir, I regret that I'm so hard to please,
　　　And I'm profoundly sorry that your lyric
　　　Failed to provoke me to a panegyric."
　　　After these curious words, the two embraced,
30　　And then the hearing was adjourned—in haste.
ÉLIANTE   His conduct has been very singular lately;
　　　Still, I confess that I respect him greatly.
　　　The honesty in which he takes such pride
　　　Has—to my mind—its noble, heroic side.
　　　In this false age, such candor seems outrageous;
　　　But I could wish that it were more contagious.
PHILINTE   What most intrigues me in our friend Alceste
　　　Is the grand passion that rages in his breast.

The sullen humors he's compounded of
40   Should not, I think, dispose his heart to love;
But since they do, it puzzles me still more
That he should choose your cousin to adore.
ÉLIANTE   It does, indeed, belie the theory
That love is born of gentle sympathy,
And that the tender passion must be based
On sweet accords of temper and of taste.
PHILINTE   Does she return his love, do you suppose?
ÉLIANTE   Ah that's a difficult question, Sir. Who knows?
How can we judge the truth of her devotion?
50   Her heart's a stranger to its own emotion.
Sometimes it thinks it loves, when no love's there;
At other times it loves quite unaware.
PHILINTE   I rather think Alceste is in for more
Distress and sorrow than he's bargained for;
Were he of my mind, Madam, his affection
Would turn in quite a different direction,
And we would see him more responsive to
The kind regard which he receives from you.
ÉLIANTE   Sir, I believe in frankness, and I'm inclined,
60   In matters of the heart, to speak my mind.
I don't oppose his love for her; indeed,
I hope with all my heart that he'll succeed,
And were it in my power, I'd rejoice
In giving him the lady of his choice.
But if, as happens frequently enough
In love affairs, he meets with a rebuff—
If Célimène should grant some rival's suit—
I'd gladly play the role of substitute;
Nor would his tender speeches please me less
70   Because they'd once been made without success.
PHILINTE   Well, Madam, as for me, I don't oppose
Your hopes in this affair; and heaven knows
That in my conversations with the man
I plead your cause as often as I can.
But if those two should marry, and so remove
All chance that he will offer you his love,
Then I'll declare my own, and hope to see
Your gracious favor pass from him to me.
In short, should you be cheated of Alceste,
80   I'd be most happy to be second best.
ÉLIANTE   Philinte, you're teasing.
PHILINTE   Ah, Madam, never fear;

No words of mine were ever so sincere,
And I shall live in fretful expectation
Till I can make a fuller declaration.

SCENE 2

ALCESTE, ÉLIANTE, PHILINTE

ALCESTE   Avenge me, Madam! I must have satisfaction,
    Or this great wrong will drive me to distraction!
ÉLIANTE   Why, what's the matter? What's upset you so?
ALCESTE   Madam, I've had a mortal, mortal blow.
    If Chaos repossessed the universe,
    I swear I'd not be shaken any worse.
    I'm ruined. . . . I can say no more. . . . My soul . . .
ÉLIANTE   Do try, Sir, to regain your self-control.
ALCESTE   Just heaven! Why were so much beauty and grace
10   Bestowed on one so vicious and so base?
ÉLIANTE   Once more, Sir, tell us . . .
ALCESTE   My world has gone to wrack;
    I'm—I'm betrayed; she's stabbed me in the back:
    Yes, Célimène (who would have thought it of her?)
    Is false to me, and has another lover.
ÉLIANTE   Are you quite certain? Can you prove these things?
PHILINTE   Lovers are prey to wild imaginings
    And jealous fancies. No doubt there's some mistake. . . .
ALCESTE   Mind your own business, Sir, for heaven's sake.
    To Éliante.
    Madam, I have the proof that you demand
20   Here in my pocket, penned by her own hand.
    Yes, all the shameful evidence one could want
    Lies in this letter written to Oronte—
    Oronte! whom I felt sure she couldn't love,
    And hardly bothered to be jealous of.
PHILINTE   Still, in a letter, appearances may deceive;
    This may not be so bad as you believe.
ALCESTE   Once more I beg you, Sir, to let me be;
    Tend to your own affairs; leave mine to me.
ÉLIANTE   Compose yourself; this anguish that you feel . . .
30   ALCESTE   Is something, Madam, you alone can heal.
    My outraged heart, beside itself with grief,
    Appeals to you for comfort and relief.
    Avenge me on your cousin, whose unjust

And faithless nature has deceived my trust;
Avenge a crime your pure soul must detest.

ÉLIANTE But how, Sir?

ALCESTE   Madam, this heart within my breast
Is yours; pray take it; redeem my heart from her,
And so avenge me on my torturer.
Let her be punished by the fond emotion,
40   The ardent love, the bottomless devotion,
The faithful worship which this heart of mine
Will offer up to yours as to a shrine.

ÉLIANTE You have my sympathy, Sir, in all you suffer;
Nor do I scorn the noble heart you offer;
But I suspect you'll soon be mollified,
And this desire for vengeance will subside.
When some belovèd hand has done us wrong
We thirst for retribution—but not for long;
However dark the deed that she's committed,
50   A lovely culprit's very soon acquitted.
Nothing's so stormy as an injured lover,
And yet no storm so quickly passes over.

ALCESTE No, Madam, no—this is no lovers' spat;
I'll not forgive her; it's gone too far for that;
My mind's made up; I'll kill myself before
I waste my hopes upon her any more.
Ah, here she is. My wrath intensifies.
I shall confront her with her tricks and lies,
And crush her utterly, and bring you then
60   A heart no longer slave to Célimène.

SCENE 3

CÉLIMÉNE, ALCESTE

ALCESTE, *aside*. Sweet heaven, help me to control my passion.

CÉLIMÉNE, *aside*. Oh, Lord.
       To Alceste.
                     Why stand there staring in that fashion?
And what d'you mean by those dramatic sighs,
And that malignant glitter in your eyes?

ALCESTE I mean that sins which cause the blood to freeze
Look innocent beside your treacheries;
That nothing Hell's or Heaven's wrath could do
Ever produced so bad a thing as you.

CÉLIMÈNE   Your compliments were always sweet and pretty.

10   ALCESTE   Madam, it's not the moment to be witty.
No, blush and hang your head; you've ample reason,
Since I've the fullest evidence of your treason.
Ah, this is what my sad heart prophesied;
Now all my anxious fears are verified;
My dark suspicion and my gloomy doubt
Divined the truth, and now the truth is out.
For all your trickery, I was not deceived;
It was my bitter stars that I believed.
But don't imagine that you'll go scot-free;
20   You shan't misuse me with impunity.
I know that love's irrational and blind;
I know the heart's not subject to the mind,
And can't be reasoned into beating faster;
I know each soul is free to choose its master;
Therefore had you but spoken from the heart,
Rejecting my attentions from the start,
I'd have no grievance, or at any rate
I could complain of nothing but my fate.
Ah, but so falsely to encourage me—
30   That was a treason and a treachery
For which you cannot suffer too severely,
And you shall pay for that behavior dearly.
Yes, now I have no pity, not a shred;
My temper's out of hand; I've lost my head;
Shocked by the knowledge of your double-dealings,
My reason can't restrain my savage feelings;
A righteous wrath deprives me of my senses,
And I won't answer for the consequences.

CÉLIMÈNE   What does this outburst mean? Will you please explain?
40   Have you, by any chance, gone quite insane?

ALCESTE   Yes, yes, I went insane the day I fell
A victim to your black and fatal spell,
Thinking to meet with some sincerity
Among the treacherous charms that beckoned me.

CÉLIMÈNE   Pooh. Of what treachery can you complain?

ALCESTE   How sly you are, how cleverly you feign!
But you'll not victimize me any more.
Look: here's a document you've seen before.
This evidence, which I acquired today,
50   Leaves you, I think, without a thing to say.

CÉLIMÈNE   Is this what sent you into such a fit?

ALCESTE   You should be blushing at the sight of it.

CÉLIMÈNE   Ought I to blush? I truly don't see why.

ALCESTE   Ah, now you're being bold as well as sly;
    Since there's no signature, perhaps you'll claim . . .

CÉLIMÈNE   I wrote it, whether or not it bears my name.

ALCESTE   And you can view with equanimity
    This proof of your disloyalty to me!

CÉLIMÈNE   Oh, don't be so outrageous and extreme.

60 ALCESTE   You take this matter lightly, it would seem.
    Was it no wrong to me, no shame to you,
    That you should send Oronte this billet-doux?

CÉLIMÈNE   Oronte! Who said it was for him?

ALCESTE   Why, those
    Who brought me this example of your prose.
    But what's the difference? If you wrote the letter
    To someone else, it pleases me no better.
    My grievance and your guilt remain the same.

CÉLIMÈNE   But need you rage, and need I blush for shame,
    If this was written to a *woman* friend?

70 ALCESTE   Ah! Most ingenious. I'm impressed no end;
    And after that incredible evasion
    Your guilt is clear. I need no more persuasion.
    How dare you try so clumsy a deception?
    D'you think I'm wholly wanting in perception?
    Come, come, let's see how brazenly you'll try
    To bolster up so palpable a lie:
    Kindly construe this ardent closing section
    As nothing more than sisterly affection!
    Here, let me read it. Tell me, if you dare to,
    That this is for a woman . . .

80 CÉLIMÈNE   I don't care to.
    What right have you to badger and berate me,
    And so highhandedly interrogate me?

ALCESTE   Now, don't be angry; all I ask of you
    Is that you justify a phrase or two . . .

CÉLIMÈNE   No, I shall not. I utterly refuse,
    And you may take those phrases as you choose.

ALCESTE   Just show me how this letter could be meant
    For a woman's eyes, and I shall be content.

CÉLIMÈNE   No, no, it's for Oronte; you're perfectly right.

90   I welcome his attentions with delight,
    I prize his character and his intellect,
    And everything is just as you suspect.
    Come, do your worst now; give your rage free rein;
    But kindly cease to bicker and complain.

ALCESTE, *aside.*   Good God! Could anything be more inhuman?
Was ever a heart so mangled by a woman?
When I complain of how she has betrayed me,
She bridles, and commences to upbraid me!
She tries my tortured patience to the limit;
100 She won't deny her guilt; she glories in it!
And yet my heart's too faint and cowardly
To break these chains of passion, and be free,
To scorn her as it should, and rise above
This unrewarded, mad, and bitter love.

To Célimène.

Ah, traitress, in how confident a fashion
You take advantage of my helpless passion,
And use my weakness for your faithless charms
To make me once again throw down my arms!
But do at least deny this black transgression;
110 Take back that mocking and perverse confession;
Defend this letter and your innocence,
And I, poor fool, will aid in your defense.
Pretend, pretend, that you are just and true,
And I shall make myself believe in you.
CÉLIMÈNE   Oh, stop it. Don't be such a jealous dunce,
Or I shall leave off loving you at once.
Just why should I *pretend?* What could impel me
To stoop so low as that? And kindly tell me
Why, if I loved another, I shouldn't merely
120 Inform you of it, simply and sincerely!
I've told you where you stand, and that admission
Should altogether clear me of suspicion;
After so generous a guarantee,
What right have you to harbor doubts of me?
Since women are (from natural reticence)
Reluctant to declare their sentiments,
And since the honor of our sex requires
That we conceal our amorous desires,
Ought any man for whom such laws are broken
130 To question what the oracle has spoken?
Should he not rather feel an obligation
To trust that most obliging declaration?
Enough, now. Your suspicions quite disgust me;
Why should I love a man who doesn't trust me?
I cannot understand why I continue,

Fool that I am, to take an interest in you.
I ought to choose a man less prone to doubt,
And give you something to be vexed about.

ALCESTE   Ah, what a poor enchanted fool I am;
140   These gentle words, no doubt, were all a sham;
But destiny requires me to entrust
My happiness to you, and so I must.
I'll love you to the bitter end, and see
How false and treacherous you dare to be.

CÉLIMÈNE   No, you don't really love me as you ought.

ALCESTE   I love you more than can be said or thought;
Indeed, I wish you were in such distress
That I might show my deep devotedness.
Yes, I could wish that you were wretchedly poor,
150   Unloved, uncherished, utterly obscure;
That fate had set you down upon the earth
Without possessions, rank, or gentle birth;
Then, by the offer of my heart, I might
Repair the great injustice of your plight;
I'd raise you from the dust, and proudly prove
The purity and vastness of my love.

CÉLIMÈNE   This is a strange benevolence indeed!
God grant that I may never be in need. . . .
Ah, here's Monsieur Dubois, in quaint disguise.

SCENE 4

CÉLIMÈNE, ALCESTE, DUBOIS

ALCESTE   Well, why this costume? Why those frightened eyes?
What ails you?

DUBOIS   Well, Sir, things are most mysterious.

ALCESTE   What do you mean?

DUBOIS   I fear they're very serious.

ALCESTE   What?

DUBOIS   Shall I speak more loudly?

ALCESTE   Yes; speak out.

DUBOIS   Isn't there someone here, Sir?

ALCESTE   Speak, you lout!
Stop wasting time

DUBOIS   Sir, we must slip away.

ALCESTE   How's that?

DUBOIS   We must decamp without delay.

ALCESTE   Explain yourself.

DUBOIS   I tell you we must fly.

ALCESTE   What for?

DUBOIS   We mustn't pause to say good-by.

10   ALCESTE   Now what d'you mean by all of this, you clown?

DUBOIS   I mean, Sir, that we've got to leave this town.

ALCESTE   I'll tear you limb from limb and joint from joint
      If you don't come more quickly to the point.

DUBOIS   Well, Sir, today a man in a black suit,
      Who wore a black and ugly scowl to boot,
      Left us a document scrawled in such a hand
      As even Satan couldn't understand.
      It bears upon your lawsuit, I don't doubt;
      But all hell's devils couldn't make it out.

20   ALCESTE   Well, well, go on. What then? I fail to see
      How this event obliges us to flee.

DUBOIS   Well, Sir: an hour later, hardly more,
      A gentleman who's often called before
      Came looking for you in an anxious way.
      Not finding you, he asked me to convey
      (Knowing I could be trusted with the same)
      The following message. . . . Now, what *was* his name?

ALCESTE   Forget his name, you idiot. What did he say?

DUBOIS   Well, it was one of your friends, Sir, anyway.

30   He warned you to begone, and he suggested
      That if you stay, you may well be arrested.

ALCESTE   What? Nothing more specific? Think, man, think!

DUBOIS   No, Sir. He had me bring him pen and ink,
      And dashed you off a letter which, I'm sure,
      Will render things distinctly less obscure.

ALCESTE   Well—let me have it!

CÉLIMÈNE   What *is* this all about?

ALCESTE   God knows; but I have hopes of finding out.
      How long am I to wait, you blitherer?

DUBOIS, *after a protracted search for the letter.*   I must have left it on your table,
      Sir.

ALCESTE   I ought to . . .

40   CÉLIMÈNE   No, no, keep your self-control;
      Go find out what's behind his rigmarole.

ALCESTE   It seems that fate, no matter what I do,
      Has sworn that I may not converse with you;
      But, Madam, pray permit your faithful lover
      To try once more before the day is over.

ACT V

SCENE 1

ALCESTE, PHILINTE

ALCESTE   No, it's too much. My mind's made up, I tell you.
PHILINTE   Why should this blow, however hard, compel you . . .
ALCESTE   No, no, don't waste your breath in argument;
 Nothing you say will alter my intent;
 This age is vile, and I've made up my mind
 To have no further commerce with mankind.
 Did not truth, honor, decency, and the laws
 Oppose my enemy and approve my cause?
 My claims were justified in all men's sight;
10 I put my trust in equity and right;
 Yet, to my horror and the world's disgrace,
 Justice is mocked, and I have lost my case!
 A scoundrel whose dishonesty is notorious
 Emerges from another lie victorious!
 Honor and right condone his brazen fraud,
 While rectitude and decency applaud!
 Before his smirking face, the truth stands charmed,
 And virtue conquered, and the law disarmed!
 His crime is sanctioned by a court decree!
20 And not content with what he's done to me,
 The dog now seeks to ruin me by stating
 That I composed a book now circulating,
 A book so wholly criminal and vicious
 That even to speak its title is seditious!
 Meanwhile Oronte, my rival, lends his credit
 To the same libelous tale, and helps to spread it!
 Oronte! a man of honor and of rank,
 With whom I've been entirely fair and frank;
 Who sought me out and forced me, willy-nilly,
30 To judge some verse I found extremely silly;
 And who, because I properly refused
 To flatter him, or see the truth abused,
 Abets my enemy in a rotten slander!
 There's the reward of honesty and candor!
 The man will hate me to the end of time
 For failing to commend his wretched rhyme!
 And not this man alone, but all humanity

Do what they do from interest and vanity;
They prate of honor, truth, and righteousness,
40   But lie, betray, and swindle nonetheless.
Come then: man's villainy is too much to bear;
Let's leave this jungle and this jackal's lair.
Yes! treacherous and savage race of men,
You shall not look upon my face again.

PHILINTE   Oh, don't rush into exile prematurely;
Things aren't as dreadful as you make them, surely.
It's rather obvious, since you're still at large,
That people don't believe your enemy's charge.
Indeed, his tale's so patently untrue
50   That it may do more harm to him than you.

ALCESTE   Nothing could do that scoundrel any harm:
His frank corruption is his greatest charm,
And, far from hurting him, a further shame
Would only serve to magnify his name.

PHILINTE   In any case, his bald prevarication
Has done no injury to your reputation,
And you may feel secure in that regard.
As for your lawsuit, it should not be hard
To have the case reopened, and contest
This judgment . . .

60   ALCESTE   No, no, let the verdict rest.
Whatever cruel penalty it may bring,
I wouldn't have it changed for anything.
It shows the times' injustice with such clarity
That I shall pass it down to our posterity
As a great proof and signal demonstration
Of the black wickedness of this generation.
It may cost twenty thousand francs; but I
Shall pay their twenty thousand, and gain thereby
The right to storm and rage at human evil,
70   And send the race of mankind to the devil.

PHILINTE   Listen to me. . . .

ALCESTE   Why? What can you possibly say?
Don't argue, Sir; your labor's thrown away.
Do you propose to offer lame excuses
For men's behavior and the times' abuses?

PHILINTE   No, all you say I'll readily concede:
This is a low, conniving age indeed;
Nothing but trickery prospers nowadays,
And people ought to mend their shabby ways.
Yes, man's a beastly creature; but must we then

80   Abandon the society of men?
    Here in the world, each human frailty
    Provides occasion for philosophy,
    And that is virtue's noblest exercise;
    If honesty shone forth from all men's eyes,
    If every heart were frank and kind and just,
    What could our virtues do but gather dust
    (Since their employment is to help us bear
    The villainies of men without despair)?
    A heart well-armed with virtue can endure. . . .
90 ALCESTE   Sir, you're a matchless reasoner, to be sure;
    Your words are fine and full of cogency;
    But don't waste time and eloquence on me.
    My reason bids me go, for my own good.
    My tongue won't lie and flatter as it should;
    God knows what frankness it might next commit,
    And what I'd suffer on account of it.
    Pray let me wait for Célimène's return
    In peace and quiet. I shall shortly learn,
    By her response to what I have in view,
100   Whether her love for me is feigned or true.
    PHILINTE   Till then, let's visit Éliante upstairs.
    ALCESTE   No, I am too weighed down with somber cares.
    Go to her, do; and leave me with my gloom
    Here in the darkened corner of this room.
    PHILINTE   Why, that's no sort of company, my friend;
    I'll see if Éliante will not descend.

SCENE 2

CÉLIMÈNE, ORONTE, ALCESTE

    ORONTE   Yes, Madam, if you wish me to remain
    Your true and ardent lover, you must deign
    To give me some more positive assurance.
    All this suspense is quite beyond endurance.
    If your heart shares the sweet desires of mine,
    Show me as much by some convincing sign;
    And here's the sign I urgently suggest:
    That you no longer tolerate Alceste,
    But sacrifice him to my love, and sever
10   All your relations with the man forever.
    CÉLIMÈNE   Why do you suddenly dislike him so?
    You praised him to the skies not long ago.

ORONTE   Madam, that's not the point. I'm here to find
    Which way your tender feelings are inclined.
    Choose, if you please, between Alceste and me,
    And I shall stay or go accordingly.
ALCESTE, *emerging from the corner.*   Yes, Madam, choose; this gentleman's demand
    Is wholly just, and I support his stand.
    I too am true and ardent; I too am here
20   To ask you that you make your feelings clear.
    No more delays, now; no equivocation;
    The time has come to make your declaration.
ORONTE   Sir, I've no wish in any way to be
    An obstacle to your felicity.
ALCESTE   Sir, I've no wish to share her heart with you;
    That may sound jealous, but at least it's true.
ORONTE   If, weighing us, she leans in your direction . . .
ALCESTE   If she regards you with the least affection . . .
ORONTE   I swear I'll yield her to you there and then.
30 ALCESTE   I swear I'll never see her face again.
ORONTE   No, Madam, tell us what we've come to hear.
ALCESTE   Madam, speak openly and have no fear.
ORONTE   Just say which one is to remain your lover.
ALCESTE   Just name one name, and it will all be over.
ORONTE   What! Is it possible that you're undecided?
ALCESTE   What! Can your feelings possibly be divided?
CÉLIMÈNE   Enough: this inquisition's gone too far:
    How utterly unreasonable you are!
    Not that I couldn't make the choice with ease;
40   My heart has no conflicting sympathies;
    I know full well which one of you I favor,
    And you'd not see me hesitate or waver.
    But how can you expect me to reveal
    So cruelly and bluntly what I feel?
    I think it altogether too unpleasant
    To choose between two men when both are present;
    One's heart has means more subtle and more kind
    Of letting its affections be divined,
    Nor need one be uncharitably plain
50   To let a lover know he loves in vain.
ORONTE   No, no, speak plainly; I for one can stand it.
    I beg you to be frank.
ALCESTE   And I demand it.
    The simple truth is what I wish to know,
    And there's no need for softening the blow.

You've made an art of pleasing everyone,
But now your days of coquetry are done:
You have no choice now, Madam, but to choose,
For I'll know what to think if you refuse;
I'll take your silence for a clear admission
60   That I'm entitled to my worst suspicion.
ORONTE   I thank you for this ultimatum, Sir,
    And I may say I heartily concur.
CÉLIMÈNE   Really, this foolishness is very wearing:
    Must you be so unjust and overbearing?
    Haven't I told you why I must demur?
    Ah, here's Éliante; I'll put the case to her.

SCENE 3

ÉLIANTE, PHILINTE, CÉLIMÈNE, ORONTE, ALCESTE

CÉLIMÈNE   Cousin, I'm being persecuted here
    By these two persons, who, it would appear,
    Will not be satisfied till I confess
    Which one I love the more, and which the less,
    And tell the latter to his face that he
    Is henceforth banished from my company.
    Tell me, has ever such a thing been done?
ÉLIANTE   You'd best not turn to me; I'm not the one
    To back you in a matter of this kind:
10   I'm all for those who frankly speak their mind.
ORONTE   Madam, you'll search in vain for a defender.
ALCESTE   You're beaten, Madam, and may as well surrender.
ORONTE   Speak, speak, you must; and end this awful strain.
ALCESTE   Or don't, and your position will be plain.
ORONTE   A single word will close this painful scene.
ALCESTE   But if you're silent, I'll know what you mean.

SCENE 4

ARSINOÉ, CÉLIMÈNE, ÉLIANTE, ALCESTE, PHILINTE, ACASTE, CLITANDRE, ORONTE

ACASTE, *to Célimène.*   Madam, with all due deference, we two
    Have come to pick a little bone with you.
CLITANDRE, *to Oronte and Alceste.*   I'm glad you're present, Sirs; as you'll
        soon learn,
    Our business here is also your concern.
ARSINOÉ, *to Célimène.*   Madam, I visit you so soon again

Only because of these two gentlemen,
Who came to me indignant and aggrieved
About a crime too base to be believed.
Knowing your virtue, having such confidence in it,
10   I couldn't think you guilty for a minute,
In spite of all their telling evidence;
And, rising above our little difference,
I've hastened here in friendship's name to see
You clear yourself of this great calumny.
ACASTE   Yes, Madam, let us see with what composure
You'll manage to respond to this disclosure.
You lately sent Clitandre this tender note.
CLITANDRE   And this one, for Acaste, you also wrote.
ACASTE, *to Oronte and Alceste.*   You'll recognize this writing, Sirs, I think;
20   The lady is so free with pen and ink
That you must know it all too well, I fear.
But listen: this is something you should hear.

"How absurd you are to condemn my lightheartedness in society,
and to accuse me of being happiest in the company of others.
Nothing could be more unjust; and if you do not come to me
instantly and beg pardon for saying such a thing, I shall never
forgive you as long as I live. Our big bumbling friend the Viscount
30   . . ."

What a shame that he's not here.

"Our big bumbling friend the Viscount, whose name stands first
in your complaint, is hardly a man to my taste; and ever since the
day I watched him spend three-quarters of an hour spitting into a
well, so as to make circles in the water, I have been unable to think
highly of him. As for the little Marquess . . ."

40   In all modesty, gentlemen, that is I.

"As for the little Marquess, who sat squeezing my hand for such a
long while yesterday, I find him in all respects the most trifling
creature alive; and the only things of value about him are his cape
and his sword. As for the man with the green ribbons . . ."

To Alceste.   It's your turn now, Sir.

"As for the man with the green ribbons, he amuses me now and
50   then with his bluntness and his bearish ill-humor; but there are

many times indeed when I think him the greatest bore in the world.
And as for the sonneteer . . ."

To Oronte.   Here's your helping.

"And as for the sonneteer, who has taken it into his head to be
witty, and insists on being an author in the teeth of opinion, I
simply cannot be bothered to listen to him, and his prose wearies
me quite as much as his poetry. Be assured that I am not always so
60   well-entertained as you suppose; that I long for your company,
more than I dare to say, at all these entertainments to which people
drag me; and that the presence of those one loves is the true and
perfect seasoning to all one's pleasures."

CLITANDRE   And now for me.

"Clitandre, whom you mention, and who so pesters me with his
saccharine speeches, is the last man on earth for whom I could feel
any affection. He is quite mad to suppose that I love him, and so are
70   you, to doubt that you are loved. Do come to your senses; exchange
your suppositions for his; and visit me as often as possible, to help
me bear the annoyance of his unwelcome attentions."

It's a sweet character that these letters show,
And what to call it, Madam, you well know.
Enough. We're off to make the world acquainted
With this sublime self-portrait that you've painted.
ACASTE   Madam, I'll make you no farewell oration;
No, you're not worthy of my indignation.
Far choicer hearts than yours, as you'll discover,
80   Would like this little Marquess for a lover.

SCENE 5

CÉLIMÈNE, ÉLIANTE, ARSINOÉ, ALCESTE, ORONTE, PHILINTE

ORONTE   So! After all those loving letters you wrote,
You turn on me like this, and cut my throat!
And your dissembling, faithless heart, I find,
Has pledged itself by turns to all mankind!
How blind I've been! But now I clearly see;
I thank you, Madam, for enlightening me.
My heart is mine once more, and I'm content;
The loss of it shall be your punishment.

To Alceste.

Sir, she is yours; I'll seek no more to stand
10   Between your wishes and this lady's hand.

SCENE 6

CÉLIMÈNE, ÉLIANTE, ARSINOÉ, ALCESTE, PHILINTE

ARSINOÉ, *to Célimène.*   Madam, I'm forced to speak. I'm far too stirred
To keep my counsel, after what I've heard.
I'm shocked and staggered by your want of morals.
It's not my way to mix in others' quarrels;
But really, when this fine and noble spirit,
This man of honor and surpassing merit,
Laid down the offering of his heart before you,
How *could* you . . .
ALCESTE   Madam, permit me, I implore you,
To represent myself in this debate.
10   Don't bother, please, to be my advocate.
My heart, in any case, could not afford
To give your services their due reward;
And if I chose, for consolation's sake,
Some other lady, 'twould not be you I'd take.
ARSINOÉ   What makes you think you could, Sir? And how dare you
Imply that I've been trying to ensnare you?
If you can for a moment entertain
Such flattering fancies, you're extremely vain.
I'm not so interested as you suppose
20   In Célimène's discarded gigolos.
Get rid of that absurd illusion, do.
Women like me are not for such as you.
Stay with this creature, to whom you're so attached;
I've never seen two people better matched.

SCENE 7

CÉLIMÈNE, ÉLIANTE, ALCESTE, PHILINTE

ALCESTE, *to Célimène.*   Well, I've been still throughout this exposé,
Till everyone but me has said his say.
Come, have I shown sufficient self-restraint?
And may I now . . .
CÉLIMÈNE   Yes, make your just complaint.

Reproach me freely, call me what you will;
You've every right to say I've used you ill.
I've wronged you, I confess it; and in my shame
I'll make no effort to escape the blame.
The anger of those others I could despise;
My guilt toward you I sadly recognize.
Your wrath is wholly justified, I fear;
I know how culpable I must appear,
I know all things bespeak my treachery,
And that, in short, you've grounds for hating me.
Do so; I give you leave.

ALCESTE   Ah, traitress—how,
How should I cease to love you, even now?
Though mind and will were passionately bent
On hating you, my heart would not consent.

To Éliante and Philinte.

Be witness to my madness, both of you;
See what infatuation drives one to;
But wait; my folly's only just begun,
And I shall prove to you before I'm done
How strange the human heart is, and how far
From rational we sorry creatures are.

To Célimène.

Woman, I'm willing to forget your shame,
And clothe your treacheries in a sweeter name;
I'll call them youthful errors, instead of crimes,
And lay the blame on these corrupting times.
My one condition is that you agree
To share my chosen fate, and fly with me
To that wild, trackless, solitary place
In which I shall forget the human race.
Only by such a course can you atone
For those atrocious letters; by that alone
Can you remove my present horror of you,
And make it possible for me to love you.

CÉLIMÈNE   What! I renounce the world at my young age,
And die of boredom in some hermitage?

ALCESTE   Ah, if you really loved me as you ought,
You wouldn't give the world a moment's thought;
Must you have me, and all the world beside?

CÉLIMÈNE   Alas, at twenty one is terrified
    Of solitude. I fear I lack the force
    And depth of soul to take so stern a course.
    But if my hand in marriage will content you,
    Why, there's a plan which I might well consent to,
    And . . .
ALCESTE   No, I detest you now. I could excuse
    Everything else, but since you thus refuse
    To love me wholly, as a wife should do,
50   And see the world in me, as I in you,
    Go! I reject your hand, and disenthrall
    My heart from your enchantments, once for all.

SCENE 8

ÉLIANTE, ALCESTE, PHILINTE

ALCESTE, *to Éliante*.   Madam, your virtuous beauty has no peer;
    Of all this world, you only are sincere;
    I've long esteemed you highly, as you know;
    Permit me ever to esteem you so,
    And if I do not now request your hand,
    Forgive me, Madam, and try to understand.
    I feel unworthy of it; I sense that fate
    Does not intend me for the married state,
    That I should do you wrong by offering you
    My shattered heart's unhappy residue,
    And that in short . . .
10 ÉLIANTE   Your argument's well taken:
    Nor need you fear that I shall feel forsaken.
    Were I to offer him this hand of mine,
    Your friend Philinte, I think, would not decline.
PHILINTE   Ah, Madam, that's my heart's most cherished goal,
    For which I'd gladly give my life and soul.
ALCESTE, *to Éliante and Philinte*.   May you be true to all you now profess,
    And so deserve unending happiness.
    Meanwhile, betrayed and wronged in everything,
    I'll flee this bitter world where vice is king,
20   And seek some spot unpeopled and apart
    Where I'll be free to have an honest heart.
PHILINTE   Come, Madam, let's do everything we can
    To change the mind of this unhappy man.

2. Modern to Contemporary Drama

SETTING AND SYMBOLISM IN MODERN AND CONTEMPORARY DRAMA

Each play in this collection of modern and contemporary drama invites us to imagine not only a particular location but also a highly detailed setting within that locale. In the stage directions preceding the first act of *A Doll's House*, for example, Ibsen is not content simply to tell us that the play takes place in the living room of Torvald Helmer's home. He gives us, rather, an elaborate description of that room and all of its furnishings:

> A comfortably and tastefully, but not expensively furnished room. Backstage right a door leads out to the hall; backstage left, another door to Helmer's study. Between these two doors stands a piano. In the middle of the left-hand wall is a door, with a window downstage of it. Near the window, a round table with armchairs and a small sofa. In the right-hand wall, slightly upstage, is a door; downstage of this, against the same wall, a stove lined with porcelain tiles, with a couple of armchairs and a rocking chair in front of it. Between the stove and the side door is a small table. Engravings on the wall. A what-not with china and other bric-à-brac; a small bookcase with leather-bound books. A carpet on the floor; a fire in the stove.

That description is so complete that it asks us even to visualize a fire burning in the stove. And why not, since the action takes place shortly before Christmas? It seems to be a perfectly logical detail for Ibsen to note. But it seems logical to us because as twentieth-century playgoers we have become accustomed to the vividly realistic stage illusions of our present-day theaters.

To Ibsen's audience (which witnessed the first production of *A Doll's*

1023

House in 1879) that elaborately realistic set, depicting an upper-middle class interior of the nineteenth century, was almost as revolutionary as his frankly realistic approach to the marital problems of that upper-middle class family. Until the 1850s, in fact, theatrical settings of the nineteenth century consisted largely of painted flats depicting the exotic landscapes of Romantic melodrama. And before the nineteenth century, as we have seen in our introductory notes on classical-through-neoclassical theaters, there were virtually no attempts whatsoever to create a completely detailed visual illusion on stage. Shakespeare's plays were originally staged without sets at all and only a few props. And most of Molière's comedies were originally performed in front of a stock set—a flat painted to represent the wall of a drawing room with four doors cut in for entrances and exits. Thus, in a brief stage direction preceding the first act of *A Misanthrope*, Molière tells us simply that "the scene throughout is in Célimène's house at Paris."

Molière, of course, was writing two centuries before Ibsen, at a time—as we might assume—when the machinery of the theater provided him with limited opportunities for elaborately designed sets. But that is not the case at all. The theaters of Molière's time were equipped with highly sophisticated machinery capable of producing visual extravaganzas for the entertainment of the King and his court. Those visual spectacles, however, were limited to the staging of operas and ballets. Apparently, then, Molière and his contemporaries did not lack the technical means for creating detailed theatrical illusions within their plays. They simply did not choose to create them. But Ibsen and many dramatists since his time have deliberately aimed to create elaborate settings for their plays, and thus we should be aware of their purposes in doing so. We should not be content simply to attribute those sets to technical advances in the design of theaters.

In Ibsen's case that detailed setting is related directly to the naturalistic impulse of his play. Thus, in *A Doll's House* he not only portrays the psychological relationship between Helmer and Nora, but he also displays the environment in which that relationship is rooted. He is, in fact, at such pains to create a total sense of their environment that he turns the stage into a completely furnished living room with a wall at both sides as well as at the back. That box set is also crucial to an experiencing of the play. Were we to witness a production of the play, we would feel as though we were peering in on the characters, as though the space defined by the proscenium arch did not exist for them, as though they were in a room surrounded by four walls, as though they were conducting their personal lives in private.

But beyond having us experience this naturalistic illusion, Ibsen intends us also to see that elaborate set as symbolizing the impact of the Helmers' environment upon their marriage—indeed as symbolizing the very nature of that marriage. That set with all its expensive possessions embodies the profound pressures placed on Helmer and Nora by the material and social conditions of their world. Thus, when we read the play we should keep continually in our mind's eye the rich clutter of that room with its bric-à-brac and its overstuffed chairs that in the end are as stifling—and as deceiving—as the marriage of Nora and Helmer. We should be aware, for example, of how deeply attached Nora is to those possessions in the beginning of the play—like a child, she does not wish to give up the illusions of her doll's house—and thus of how much it takes for her to free herself of their very solid hold on her life: on her physical life *and* on her mental life.

Once we recognize setting as a potentially symbolic element of modern and contemporary drama, we shall find that our reading of plays is enriched when we pay close attention to all the descriptive details concerning the make-up of the set. Dramatists provide those elaborate descriptions not only for the guidance of set designers but also for the enlightenment of readers like us who may not have the opportunity to witness a production of their plays. And as we move from one play to the next, we shall find that the settings enlighten us in quite different ways. Just as dramatists write in different styles, so they use their settings for different symbolic effects. At the beginning of *Arms and the Man,* for example, Shaw gives us an extensive description of Raina's bedroom—a more extensive description than Ibsen's at the beginning of *A Doll's House*—yet Shaw's is clearly not a naturalistic display of his heroine's environment so much as it is a wryly satiric revelation of her foolish, romantic illusions and of her confused cultural pretensions. Although Shaw does not state those implications so bluntly as we have here, he does make them evident through the irony and sarcasm with which he records the details in just these few sentences near the opening of his stage directions:

> Through an open window with a little balcony a peak of the Balkans, wonderfully white and beautiful in the starlit snow, seems quite close at hand, though it is actually miles away. The interior of the room is not like anything to be seen in the west of Europe. It is half rich Bulgarian, half cheap Viennese.

Tennessee Williams also describes a bedroom at the beginning of *Cat on a Hot Tin Roof,* and his description is even longer than Shaw's; yet it is neither satiric like Shaw's nor completely naturalistic like Ibsen's. At one point it appears to be a naturalistically detailed set, for Williams offers a meticulous description of the furniture it includes, in particular "a *huge* console combination of radio-phonograph (Hi-Fi with three speakers) TV set *and* liquor cabinet." He even provides an interpretation of its symbolic significance:

> This piece of furniture . . . is a very complete and compact little shrine to virtually all the comforts and illusions behind which we hide from such things as the characters in the play are faced with.

Immediately after that interpretation, however, he complicates our understanding of the set by disclaiming its naturalistic connection with reality:

> The set should be far less realistic than I have so far implied. I think the wall below the ceiling should dissolve into air; the set should be roofed by the sky; stars and moon suggested by traces of milky pallor, as if they were observed through a telescope lens out of focus.

Suddenly, then, his realistic set design seems to melt into thin air, to become surrealistic, as though to imply that it is not a wholly reliable symbol of his characters' environment. Later still, he tells us that

> The designer should take as many pains to give the actors room to move about freely (to show their restlessness, their passion for breaking out) as if it were a set for a ballet.

Williams's set clearly has numerous implications—far more in fact than we have suggested by our few quotations from his description. Most settings in modern and contemporary drama are indeed just as richly significant as the actions that take place within them, but that should not surprise us, for we have come to know from our own lives that the environments in which we exist not only influence us but are in turn influenced by us. So it is with the settings and characters of the plays we have included in this collection. They are inextricably bound up with one another, and thus they can be understood only in relation to one another.

HENRIK IBSEN
1828–1906
A Doll's House

CHARACTERS

TORVALD HELMER, a lawyer

NORA, his wife

DR. RANK

MRS. LINDE

NILS KROGSTAD, also a lawyer

The HELMERS' three small children

ANNE-MARIE, their nurse

HELEN, the maid

A PORTER

The action takes place in the Helmers' apartment.

ACT I

A comfortably and tastefully, but not expensively furnished room. Backstage right a door leads out to the hall; backstage left, another door to Helmer's study. Between these two doors stands a piano. In the middle of the left-hand wall is a door, with a window downstage of it. Near the window, a round table with armchairs and a small sofa. In the right-hand wall, slightly upstage, is a door; downstage of this, against the same wall, a stove lined with porcelain tiles, with a couple of armchairs and a rocking-chair in front of it. Between the stove and the side door is a small table. Engravings on the wall. A what-not with china and other bric-a-brac; a small bookcase with leather-bound books. A carpet on the floor; a fire in the stove. A winter day.

    A bell rings in the hall outside. After a moment, we hear the front door being opened. Nora enters the room, humming contentedly to herself. She is wearing outdoor clothes and carrying a lot of parcels, which she puts down on the table right. She leaves the door to the hall open; through it, we can see a Porter carrying a Christmas tree and a basket. He gives these to the Maid, who has opened the door for them.

NORA Hide that Christmas tree away, Helen. The children mustn't see it before I've decorated it this evening. [*To the Porter, taking out her purse.*] How much—?

PORTER A shilling.

NORA Here's half a crown. No, keep it.

Translated by Michael Meyer

The Porter touches his cap and goes. Nora closes the door. She continues to laugh happily to herself as she removes her coat, etc. She takes from her pocket a bag containing macaroons and eats a couple. Then she tiptoes across and listens at her husband's door.

NORA   Yes, he's here. [*Starts humming again as she goes over to the table, right.*]

HELMER [*from his room*]   Is that my skylark twittering out there?

NORA [*opening some of the parcels*]   It is!

HELMER   Is that my squirrel rustling?

NORA   Yes!

HELMER   When did my squirrel come home?

NORA   Just now. [*Pops the bag of macaroons in her pocket and wipes her mouth.*] Come out here, Torvald, and see what I've bought.

HELMER   You mustn't disturb me! [*Short pause; then he opens the door and looks in, his pen in his hand.*] Bought, did you say? All that? Has my little squanderbird been overspending again?

NORA   Oh, Torvald, surely we can let ourselves go a little this year! It's the first Christmas we don't have to scrape.

HELMER   Well, you know, we can't afford to be extravagant.

NORA   Oh yes, Torvald, we can be a little extravagant now. Can't we? Just a tiny bit? You've got a big salary now, and you're going to make lots and lots of money.

HELMER   Next year, yes. But my new salary doesn't start till April.

NORA   Pooh; we can borrow till then.

HELMER   Nora! [*Goes over to her and takes her playfully by the ear.*] What a little spendthrift you are! Suppose I were to borrow fifty pounds today, and you spent it all over Christmas, and then on New Year's Eve a tile fell off a roof on to my head—

NORA [*puts her hand over his mouth*]   Oh, Torvald! Don't say such dreadful things!

HELMER   Yes, but suppose something like that did happen? What then?

NORA   If anything as frightful as that happened, it wouldn't make much difference whether I was in debt or not.

HELMER   But what about the people I'd borrowed from?

NORA   Them? Who cares about them? They're strangers.

HELMER   Oh, Nora, Nora, how like a woman! No, but seriously, Nora, you know how I feel about this. No debts! Never borrow! A home that is founded on debts can never be a place of freedom and beauty. We two have stuck it out bravely up to now; and we shall continue to do so for the short time we still have to.

NORA [*goes over towards the stove*]   Very well, Torvald. As you say.

HELMER [*follows her*]   Now, now! My little songbird mustn't droop her

wings. What's this? Is little squirrel sulking? [*Takes out his purse*] Nora;
guess what I've got here!

NORA [*turns quickly*]   Money!

HELMER   Look. [*Hands her some banknotes*] I know how these small expenses
crop up at Christmas.

NORA [*counts them*]   One—two—three—four. Oh, thank you, Torvald, thank
you! I should be able to manage with this.

HELMER   You'll have to.

NORA   Yes, yes, of course I will. But come over here, I want to show you
everything I've bought. And so cheaply! Look, here are new clothes for
Ivar—and a sword. And a horse and a trumpet for Bob. And a doll and a
cradle for Emmy—they're nothing much, but she'll pull them apart in a
few days. And some bits of material and handkerchiefs for the maids. Old
Anne-Marie ought to have had something better, really.

HELMER   And what's in that parcel?

NORA [*cries*]   No, Torvald, you mustn't see that before this evening!

HELMER   Very well. But now, tell me, you little spendthrift, what do you
want for Christmas?

NORA   Me? Oh, pooh, I don't want anything.

HELMER   Oh, yes, you do. Now tell me, what, within reason, would you
most like?

NORA   No, I really don't know. Oh, yes—Torvald—!

HELMER   Well?

NORA [*plays with his coat-buttons; not looking at him*]   If you really want to
give me something, you could—you could—

HELMER   Come on, out with it.

NORA [*quickly*]   You could give me money, Torvald. Only as much as you
feel you can afford; then later I'll buy something with it.

HELMER   But, Nora—

NORA   Oh yes, Torvald dear, please! Please! Then I'll wrap up the notes in
pretty gold paper and hang them on the Christmas tree. Wouldn't that
be fun?

HELMER   What's the name of that little bird that can never keep any money?

NORA   Yes, yes, squanderbird; I know. But let's do as I say, Torvald; then I'll
have time to think about what I need most. Isn't that the best way? Mm?

HELMER [*smiles*]   To be sure it would be, if you could keep what I give you
and really buy yourself something with it. But you'll spend it on all sorts
of useless things for the house, and then I'll have to put my hand in my
pocket again.

NORA   Oh, but Torvald—

HELMER   You can't deny it, Nora dear. [*Puts his arm round her waist.*] The
squanderbird's a pretty little creature, but she gets through an awful lot
of money. It's incredible what an expensive pet she is for a man to keep.

NORA For shame! How can you say such a thing? I save every penny I can.

HELMER [*laughs*] That's quite true. Every penny you can. But you can't.

NORA [*hums and smiles, quietly gleeful*] Hm. If you only knew how many expenses we larks and squirrels have, Torvald.

HELMER You're a funny little creature. Just like your father used to be. Always on the look-out for some way to get money, but as soon as you have any it just runs through your fingers, and you never know where it's gone. Well, I suppose I must take you as you are. It's in your blood. Yes, yes, yes, these things are hereditary, Nora.

NORA Oh, I wish I'd inherited more of Papa's qualities.

HELMER And I wouldn't wish my darling little songbird to be any different from what she is. By the way, that reminds me. You look awfully—how shall I put it?—awfully guilty today.

NORA Do I—

HELMER Yes, you do. Look me in the eyes.

NORA [*looks at him*] Well?

HELMER [*wags his finger*] Has my little sweet-tooth been indulging herself in town today, by any chance?

NORA No, how can you think of such a thing?

HELMER Not a tiny little digression into a pastry shop?

NORA No, Torvald, I promise—

HELMER Not just a wee jam tart?

NORA Certainly not.

HELMER Not a little nibble at a macaroon?

NORA No, Torvald—I promise you, honestly—

HELMER There, there. I was only joking.

NORA [*goes over to the table, right*] You know I could never act against your wishes.

HELMER Of course not. And you've given me your word—[*Goes over to her.*] Well, my beloved Nora, you keep your little Christmas secrets to yourself. They'll be revealed this evening, I've no doubt, once the Christmas tree has been lit.

NORA Have you remembered to invite Dr. Rank?

HELMER No. But there's no need; he knows he'll be dining with us. Anyway, I'll ask him when he comes this morning. I've ordered some good wine. Oh, Nora, you can't imagine how I'm looking forward to this evening.

NORA So am I. And, Torvald, how the children will love it!

HELMER Yes, it's a wonderful thing to know that one's position is assured and that one has an ample income. Don't you agree? It's good to know that, isn't it?

NORA Yes, it's almost like a miracle.

HELMER Do you remember last Christmas? For three whole weeks you shut yourself away every evening to make flowers for the Christmas tree, and all those other things you were going to surprise us with. Ugh, it was the most boring time I've ever had in my life.

NORA I didn't find it boring.

HELMER [smiles] But it all came to nothing in the end, didn't it?

NORA Oh, are you going to bring that up again? How could I help the cat getting in and tearing everything to bits?

HELMER No, my poor little Nora, of course you couldn't. You simply wanted to make us happy, and that's all that matters. But it's good that those hard times are past.

NORA Yes, it's wonderful.

HELMER I don't have to sit by myself and be bored. And you don't have to tire your pretty eyes and your delicate little hands—

NORA [claps her hands] No, Torvald, that's true, isn't it—I don't have to any longer? Oh, it's really all just like a miracle. [Takes his arm] Now, I'm going to tell you what I thought we might do, Torvald. As soon as Christmas is over— [A bell rings in the hall.] Oh, there's the doorbell. [Tidies up one or two things in the room.] Someone's coming. What a bore.

HELMER I'm not at home to any visitors. Remember!

MAID [in the doorway] A lady's called, madam. A stranger.

NORA Well, ask her to come in.

MAID And the doctor's here too, sir.

HELMER Has he gone to my room?

MAID Yes, sir.

Helmer goes into his room. The Maid shows in Mrs. Linde, who is dressed in travelling clothes, and closes the door.

MRS. LINDE [shyly and a little hesitantly] Good evening, Nora.

NORA [uncertainly] Good evening—

MRS. LINDE I don't suppose you recognize me.

NORA No, I'm afraid I— Yes, wait a minute—surely— [Exclaims.] Why, Christine! Is it really you?

MRS. LINDE Yes, it's me.

NORA Christine! And I didn't recognize you! But how could I—? [More quietly] How you've changed, Christine!

MRS. LINDE Yes, I know. It's been nine years—nearly ten—

NORA Is it so long? Yes, it must be. Oh, these last eight years have been such a happy time for me!. So you've come to town? All that way in winter! How brave of you!

MRS. LINDE I arrived by the steamer this morning.

NORA Yes, of course—to enjoy yourself over Christmas. Oh, how splendid! We'll have to celebrate! But take off your coat. You're not cold, are you? [Helps her off with it.] There! Now let's sit down here by the stove and be comfortable. No, you take the armchair. I'll sit here in the rocking-chair.

[Clasps Mrs. Linde's hands.] Yes, now you look like your old self. It was just at first that—you've got a little paler, though, Christine. And perhaps a bit thinner.

MRS. LINDE   And older, Nora. Much, much older.

NORA   Yes, perhaps a little older. Just a tiny bit. Not much. [Checks herself suddenly and says earnestly.] Oh, but how thoughtless of me to sit here and chatter away like this! Dear, sweet Christine, can you forgive me?

MRS. LINDE   What do you mean, Nora?

NORA [quietly]   Poor Christine, you've become a widow.

MRS. LINDE   Yes. Three years ago.

NORA   I know, I know—I read it in the papers. Oh, Christine, I meant to write to you so often, honestly. But I always put it off, and something else always cropped up.

MRS. LINDE   I understand, Nora dear.

NORA   No, Christine, it was beastly of me. Oh, my poor darling, what you've gone through! And he didn't leave you anything?

MRS. LINDE   No.

NORA   No children, either?

MRS. LINDE   No.

NORA   Nothing at all, then?

MRS. LINDE   Not even a feeling of loss or sorrow.

NORA [looks incredulously at her]   But, Christine, how is that possible?

MRS. LINDE [smiles sadly and strokes Nora's hair]   Oh, these things happen, Nora.

NORA   All alone. How dreadful that must be for you. I've three lovely children. I'm afraid you can't see them now, because they're out with nanny. But you must tell me everything—

MRS. LINDE   No, no, no. I want to hear about you.

NORA   No, you start. I'm not going to be selfish today, I'm just going to think about you. Oh, but there's one thing I must tell you. Have you heard of the wonderful luck we've just had?

MRS. LINDE   No. What?

NORA   Would you believe it—my husband's just been made manager of the bank!

MRS. LINDE   Your husband? Oh, how lucky—!

NORA   Yes, isn't it? Being a lawyer is so uncertain, you know, especially if one isn't prepared to touch any case that isn't—well—quite nice. And of course Torvald's been very firm about that—and I'm absolutely with him. Oh, you can imagine how happy we are! He's joining the bank in the New Year, and he'll be getting a big salary, and lots of percentages too. From now on we'll be able to live quite differently—we'll be able to do whatever we want. Oh, Christine, it's such a relief! I feel so happy! Well, I mean, it's lovely to have heaps of money and not to have to worry about anything. Don't you think?

MRS. LINDE   It must be lovely to have enough to cover one's needs, anyway.
NORA   Not just our needs! We're going to have heaps and heaps of money!
MRS. LINDE [smiles]   Nora, Nora, haven't you grown up yet? When we were at school you were a terrible little spendthrift.
NORA [laughs quietly]   Yes, Torvald still says that. [Wags her finger.] But "Nora, Nora" isn't as silly as you think. Oh, we've been in no position for me to waste money. We've both had to work.
MRS. LINDE   You too?
NORA   Yes, little things—fancy work, crocheting, embroidery and so forth. [Casually.] And other things too. I suppose you know Torvald left the Ministry when we got married? There were no prospects of promotion in his department, and of course he needed more money. But the first year he overworked himself quite dreadfully. He had to take on all sorts of extra jobs, and worked day and night. But it was too much for him, and he became frightfully ill. The doctors said he'd have to go to a warmer climate.
MRS. LINDE   Yes, you spent a whole year in Italy, didn't you?
NORA   Yes. It wasn't easy for me to get away, you know. I'd just had Ivar. But of course we had to do it. Oh, it was a marvelous trip! And it saved Torvald's life. But it cost an awful lot of money, Christine.
MRS. LINDE   I can imagine.
NORA   Two hundred and fifty pounds. That's a lot of money, you know.
MRS. LINDE   How lucky you had it.
NORA   Well, actually, we got it from my father.
MRS. LINDE   Oh, I see. Didn't he die just about that time?
NORA   Yes, Christine, just about then. Wasn't it dreadful, I couldn't go and look after him. I was expecting little Ivar any day. And then I had my poor Torvald to care for—we really didn't think he'd live. Dear, kind Papa! I never saw him again, Christine. Oh, it's the saddest thing that's happened to me since I got married.
MRS. LINDE   I know you were very fond of him. But you went to Italy—?
NORA   Yes. Well, we had the money, you see, and the doctors said we mustn't delay. So we went the month after Papa died.
MRS. LINDE   And your husband came back completely cured?
NORA   Fit as a fiddle!
MRS. LINDE   But—the doctor?
NORA   How do you mean?
MRS. LINDE   I thought the maid said that the gentleman who arrived with me was the doctor.
NORA   Oh yes, that's Doctor Rank, but he doesn't come because anyone's ill. He's our best friend, and he looks us up at least once every day. No, Torvald hasn't had a moment's illness since we went away. And the children are fit and healthy and so am I. [Jumps up and claps her hands.] Oh God, oh God, Christine, isn't it a wonderful thing to be alive and

happy! Oh, but how beastly of me! I'm only talking about myself. [*Sits on a footstool and rests her arms on Mrs. Linde's knee.*] Oh, please don't be angry with me! Tell me, is it really true you didn't love your husband? Why did you marry him, then?

MRS. LINDE   Well, my mother was still alive; and she was helpless and bedridden. And I had my two little brothers to take care of. I didn't feel I could say no.

NORA   Yes, well, perhaps you're right. He was rich then, was he?

MRS. LINDE   Quite comfortably off, I believe. But his business was unsound, you see, Nora. When he died it went bankrupt, and there was nothing left.

NORA   What did you do?

MRS. LINDE   Well, I had to try to make ends meet somehow, so I started a little shop, and a little school, and anything else I could turn my hand to. These last three years have been just one endless slog for me, without a moment's rest. But now it's over, Nora. My poor dear mother doesn't need me any more; she's passed away. And the boys don't need me either; they've got jobs now and can look after themselves.

NORA   How relieved you must feel—

MRS. LINDE   No, Nora. Just unspeakably empty. No one to live for any more. [*Gets up restlessly.*] That's why I couldn't bear to stay out there any longer, cut off from the world. I thought it'd be easier to find some work here that will exercise and occupy my mind. If only I could get a regular job—office work of some kind—

NORA   Oh but, Christine, that's dreadfully exhausting; and you look practically finished already. It'd be much better for you if you could go away somewhere.

MRS. LINDE   [*goes over to the window*]   I have no Papa to pay for my holidays, Nora.

NORA   [*gets up*]   Oh, please don't be angry with me.

MRS. LINDE   My dear Nora, it's I who should ask you not to be angry. That's the worst thing about this kind of situation—it makes one so bitter. One has no one to work for; and yet one has to be continually sponging for jobs. One has to live; and so one becomes completely egocentric. When you told me about this luck you've just had with Torvald's new job—can you imagine?—I was happy not so much on your account, as on my own.

NORA   How do you mean? Oh, I understand. You mean Torvald might be able to do something for you?

MRS. LINDE   Yes, I was thinking that.

NORA   He will too, Christine. Just you leave it to me. I'll lead up to it so delicately, so delicately; I'll get him in the right mood. Oh, Christine, I do so want to help you.

MRS. LINDE   It's sweet of you to bother so much about me, Nora. Especially since you know so little of the worries and hardships of life.

NORA   I! You say *I* know little of—?

MRS. LINDE   [*smiles*]   Well, good heavens—those bits of fancy work of yours—well, really—! You're a child, Nora.

NORA   [*tosses her head and walks across the room*]   You shouldn't say that so patronizingly.

MRS. LINDE   Oh?

NORA   You're like the rest. You all think I'm incapable of getting down to anything serious—

MRS. LINDE   My dear—

NORA   You think I've never had any worries like the rest of you.

MRS. LINDE   Nora dear, you've just told me about all your difficulties—

NORA   Pooh—that! [*Quietly.*] I haven't told you about the big thing.

MRS. LINDE   What big thing? What do you mean?

NORA   You patronize me, Christine; but you shouldn't. You're proud that you've worked so long and so hard for your mother.

MRS. LINDE   I don't patronize anyone, Nora. But you're right—I am both proud and happy that I was able to make my mother's last months on earth comparatively easy.

NORA   And you're also proud at what you've done for your brothers.

MRS. LINDE   I think I have a right to be.

NORA   I think so too. But let me tell you something, Christine. I too have done something to be proud and happy about.

MRS. LINDE   I don't doubt it. But—how do you mean?

NORA   Speak quietly! Suppose Torvald should hear! He mustn't, at any price—no one must know, Christine—no one but you.

MRS. LINDE   But what is this?

NORA   Come over here. [*Pulls her down on to the sofa beside her.*] Yes, Christine—I too have done something to be happy and proud about. It was I who saved Torvald's life.

MRS. LINDE   Saved his—? How did you save it?

NORA   I told you about our trip to Italy. Torvald couldn't have lived if he hadn't managed to get down there—

MRS. LINDE   Yes, well—your father provided the money—

NORA   [*smiles*]   So Torvald and everyone else thinks. But—

MRS. LINDE   Yes?

NORA   Papa didn't give us a penny. It was I who found the money.

MRS. LINDE   You? All of it?

NORA   Two hundred and fifty pounds. What do you say to that?

MRS. LINDE   But Nora, how could you? Did you win a lottery or something?

NORA   [*scornfully*]   Lottery? [*Sniffs.*] What would there be to be proud of in that?

MRS. LINDE   But where did you get it from, then?

NORA [hums and smiles secretively]   Hm; tra-la-la-la!

MRS. LINDE   You couldn't have borrowed it.

NORA   Oh? Why not?

MRS. LINDE   Well, a wife can't borrow money without her husband's consent.

NORA [tosses her head]   Ah, but when a wife has a little business sense, and knows how to be clever—

MRS. LINDE   But Nora, I simply don't understand—

NORA   You don't have to. No one has said I borrowed the money. I could have got it in some other way. [Throws herself back on the sofa.] I could have got it from an admirer. When a girl's as pretty as I am—

MRS. LINDE   Nora, you're crazy!

NORA   You're dying of curiosity now, aren't you, Christine?

MRS. LINDE   Nora dear, you haven't done anything foolish?

NORA [sits up again]   Is it foolish to save one's husband's life?

MRS. LINDE   I think it's foolish if without his knowledge you—

NORA   But the whole point was that he mustn't know! Great heavens, don't you see? He hadn't to know how dangerously ill he was. I was the one they told that his life was in danger and that only going to a warm climate could save him. Do you suppose I didn't try to think of other ways of getting him down there? I told him how wonderful it would be for me to go abroad like other young wives: I cried and prayed; I asked him to remember my condition, and said he ought to be nice and tender to me; and then I suggested he might quite easily borrow the money. But then he got almost angry with me, Christine. He said I was frivolous, and that it was his duty as a husband not to pander to my moods and caprices—I think that's what he called them. Well, well, I thought, you've got to be saved somehow. And then I thought of a way—

MRS. LINDE   But didn't your husband find out from your father that the money hadn't come from him?

NORA   No, never. Papa died just then. I'd thought of letting him into the plot and asking him not to tell. But since he was so ill—! And as things turned out, it didn't become necessary.

MRS. LINDE   And you've never told your husband about this?

NORA   For heaven's sake, no! What an idea! He's frightfully strict about such matters. And besides—he's so proud of being a man—it'd be so painful and humiliating for him to know that he owed anything to me. It'd completely wreck our relationship. This life we have built together would no longer exist.

MRS. LINDE   Will you never tell him?

NORA [thoughtfully, half-smiling]   Yes—some time, perhaps. Years from now, when I'm no longer pretty. You mustn't laugh! I mean of course, when Torvald no longer loves me as he does now; when it no longer amuses him to see me dance and dress up and play the fool for him. Then it might be useful to have something up my sleeve. [*Breaks off.*] Stupid, stupid, stupid! That time will never come. Well, what do you think of my big secret, Christine? I'm not completely useless, am I? Mind you, all this has caused me a frightful lot of worry. It hasn't been easy for me to meet my obligations punctually. In case you don't know, in the world of business there are things called quarterly instalments and interest, and they're a terrible problem to cope with. So I've had to scrape a little here and save a little there as best I can. I haven't been able to save much on the housekeeping money, because Torvald likes to live well; and I couldn't let the children go short of clothes—I couldn't take anything out of what he gives me for them. The poor little angels!

MRS. LINDE   So you've had to stint yourself, my poor Nora?

NORA   Of course. Well, after all, it was my problem. Whenever Torvald gave me money to buy myself new clothes, I never used more than half of it; and I always bought what was cheapest and plainest. Thank heaven anything suits me, so that Torvald's never noticed. But it made me a bit sad sometimes, because it's lovely to wear pretty clothes. Don't you think?

MRS. LINDE   Indeed it is.

NORA   And then I've found one or two other sources of income. Last winter I managed to get a lot of copying to do. So I shut myself away and wrote every evening, late into the night. Oh, I often got so tired, so tired. But it was great fun, though, sitting there working and earning money. It was almost like being a man.

MRS. LINDE   But how much have you managed to pay off like this?

NORA   Well, I can't say exactly. It's awfully difficult to keep an exact check on these kind of transactions. I only know I've paid everything I've managed to scrape together. Sometimes I really didn't know where to turn. [*Smiles*] Then I'd sit here and imagine some rich old gentleman had fallen in love with me—

MRS. LINDE   What! What gentleman?

NORA   Silly! And that now he'd died and when they opened his will it said in big letters: "Everything I possess is to be paid forthwith to my beloved Mrs. Nora Helmer in cash."

MRS. LINDE   But, Nora dear, who was this gentleman?

NORA   Great heavens, don't you understand? There wasn't any old gentleman; he was just something I used to dream up as I sat here evening after evening wondering how on earth I could raise the money. But what does it matter? The old bore can stay imaginary as far as I'm concerned, because now I don't have to worry any longer! [*Jumps up.*] Oh, Christine, isn't it wonderful? I don't have to worry any more! No more troubles! I can play all day with the children, I can fill the house with pretty things, just the way Torvald likes. And, Christine, it'll soon be spring, and the air'll be fresh and the skies blue,—and then perhaps we'll be able to take a little trip somewhere. I shall be able to see the sun again. Oh, yes, yes, it's a wonderful thing to be alive and happy!

The bell rings in the hall.

MRS. LINDE [*gets up*]   You've a visitor. Perhaps I'd better go.

NORA   No, stay. It won't be for me. It's someone for Torvald—

MAID [*in the doorway*]   Excuse me, madam, a gentleman's called who says he wants to speak to the master. But I didn't know—seeing as the doctor's with him—

NORA   Who is this gentleman?

KROGSTAD [*in the doorway*]   It's me, Mrs. Helmer.

Mrs. Linde starts, composes herself and turns away to the window.

NORA [*takes a step towards him and whispers tensely*]   You? What is it? What do you want to talk to my husband about?

KROGSTAD   Business—you might call it. I hold a minor post in the bank, and I hear your husband is to become our new chief—

NORA   Oh—then it isn't—?

KROGSTAD   Pure business, Mrs. Helmer. Nothing more.

NORA   Well, you'll find him in his study.

Nods indifferently as she closes the hall door behind him. Then she walks across the room and sees to the stove.

MRS. LINDE   Nora, who was that man?

NORA   A lawyer called Krogstad.

MRS. LINDE   It was him, then.

NORA   Do you know that man?

MRS. LINDE   I used to know him—some years ago. He was a solicitor's clerk in our town, for a while.

NORA   Yes, of course, so he was.

MRS. LINDE   How he's changed!

NORA   He was very unhappily married, I believe.

MRS. LINDE   Is he a widower now?

NORA   Yes, with a lot of children. Ah, now it's alight.

She closes the door of the stove and moves the rocking-chair a little to one side.

MRS. LINDE   He does—various things now, I hear?

NORA   Does he? It's quite possible—I really don't know. But don't let's talk about business. It's so boring.

Dr. Rank enters from Helmer's study.

RANK [*still in the doorway*]   No, no, my dear chap, don't see me out. I'll go and have a word with your wife. [*Closes the door and notices Mrs. Linde.*] Oh, I beg your pardon. I seem to be *de trop* here too.

NORA   Not in the least. [*Introduces them.*] Dr. Rank. Mrs. Linde.

RANK   Ah! A name I have often heard in this house. I believe I passed you on the stairs as I came up.

MRS. LINDE   Yes. Stairs tire me; I have to take them slowly.

RANK   Oh, have you hurt yourself?

MRS. LINDE   No, I'm just a little run down.

RANK   Ah, is that all? Then I take it you've come to town to cure yourself by a round of parties?

MRS. LINDE   I have come here to find work.

RANK   Is that an approved remedy for being run down?

MRS. LINDE   One has to live, Doctor.

RANK   Yes, people do seem to regard it as a necessity.

NORA   Oh, really, Dr. Rank. I bet you want to stay alive.

RANK   You bet I do. However miserable I sometimes feel, I still want to go on being tortured for as long as possible. It's the same with all my patients; and with people who are morally sick, too. There's a moral cripple in with Helmer at this very moment—

MRS. LINDE [*softly*]   Oh!

NORA   Whom do you mean?

RANK   Oh, a lawyer fellow called Krogstad—you wouldn't know him. He's crippled all right; morally twisted. But even he started off by announcing, as though it were a matter of enormous importance, that he had to live.

NORA   Oh? What did he want to talk to Torvald about?

RANK   I haven't the faintest idea. All I heard was something about the bank.

NORA   I didn't know that Krog—that this man Krogstad had any connection with the bank.

RANK   Yes, he's got some kind of job down there. [*To Mrs. Linde.*] I wonder if in your part of the world you too have a species of human being that spends its time fussing around trying to smell out moral corruption? And when they find a case they give him some nice, comfortable position so that they can keep a good watch on him. The healthy ones just have to lump it.

MRS. LINDE   But surely it's the sick who need care most?

RANK [*shrugs his shoulders*]   Well, there we have it. It's that attitude that's turning human society into a hospital.

Nora, lost in her own thoughts, laughs half to herself and claps her hands.

RANK   Why are you laughing? Do you really know what society is?

NORA   What do I care about society? I think it's a bore. I was laughing at something else—something frightfully funny. Tell me, Dr. Rank—will everyone who works at the bank come under Torvald now?

RANK   Do you find that particularly funny?

NORA   [smiles and hums]   Never mind! Never you mind! [Walks around the room] Yes, I find it very amusing to think that we—I mean, Torvald—has obtained so much influence over so many people. [Takes the paper bag from her pocket.] Dr. Rank, would you like a small macaroon?

RANK   Macaroons! I say! I thought they were forbidden here.

NORA   Yes, well, these are some Christine gave me.

MRS. LINDE   What? I—?

NORA   All right, all right, don't get frightened. You weren't to know Torvald had forbidden them. He's afraid they'll ruin my teeth. But, dash it—for once—! Don't you agree, Dr. Rank? Here! [Pops a macaroon into his mouth.] You too, Christine. And I'll have one too. Just a little one. Two at the most. [Begins to walk round again.] Yes, now I feel really, really happy. Now there's just one thing in the world I'd really love to do.

RANK   Oh? And what is that?

NORA   Just something I'd love to say to Torvald.

RANK   Well, why don't you say it?

NORA   No, I daren't. It's too dreadful.

MRS. LINDE   Dreadful?

RANK   Well, then, you'd better not. But you can say it to us. What is it you'd so love to say to Torvald?

NORA   I've the most extraordinary longing to say: "Bloody hell!"

RANK   Are you mad?

MRS. LINDE   My dear Nora—!

RANK   Say it. Here he is.

NORA   [hiding the bag of macaroons.]   Ssh! Ssh!

Helmer, with his overcoat on his arm and his hat in his hand, enters from his study.

NORA   [goes to meet him]   Well, Torvald dear, did you get rid of him?

HELMER   Yes, he's just gone.

NORA   May I introduce you—? This is Christine. She's just arrived in town.

HELMER   Christine—? Forgive me, but I don't think—

NORA   Mrs. Linde, Torvald dear. Christine Linde.

HELMER   Ah. A childhood friend of my wife's, I presume?

MRS. LINDE   Yes, we knew each other in earlier days.

NORA   And imagine, now she's traveled all this way to talk to you.

HELMER   Oh?

MRS. LINDE   Well, I didn't really—

NORA   You see, Christine's frightfully good at office work, and she's mad to come under some really clever man who can teach her even more than she knows already—

HELMER   Very sensible, madam.

NORA   So when she heard you'd become head of the bank—it was in her local paper—she came here as quickly as she could and—Torvald, you will, won't you? Do a little something to help Christine? For my sake?

HELMER   Well, that shouldn't be impossible. You are a widow, I take it, Mrs. Linde?

MRS. LINDE   Yes.

HELMER   And you have experience of office work?

MRS. LINDE   Yes, quite a bit.

HELMER   Well then, it's quite likely I may be able to find some job for you—

NORA [claps her hands]   You see, you see!

HELMER   You've come at a lucky moment, Mrs. Linde.

MRS. LINDE   Oh, how can I ever thank you—?

HELMER   There's absolutely no need. [Puts on his overcoat.] But now I'm afraid I must ask you to excuse me—

RANK   Wait. I'll come with you.

He gets his fur coat from the hall and warms it at the stove.

NORA   Don't be long, Torvald dear.

HELMER   I'll only be an hour.

NORA   Are you going too, Christine?

MRS. LINDE [puts on her outdoor clothes]   Yes, I must start to look round for a room.

HELMER   Then perhaps we can walk part of the way together.

NORA [helps her]   It's such a nuisance we're so cramped here—I'm afraid we can't offer to—

MRS. LINDE   Oh, I wouldn't dream of it. Goodbye, Nora dear, and thanks for everything.

NORA   Au revoir. You'll be coming back this evening, of course. And you too, Dr. Rank. What? If you're well enough? Of course you'll be well enough. Wrap up warmly, though.

They go out, talking, into the hall. Children's voices are heard from the stairs.

NORA   Here they are! Here they are!

She runs out and opens the door. Anne-Marie, the nurse, enters with the children.

NORA   Come in, come in! [Stoops down and kisses them.] Oh, my sweet darlings—! Look at them, Christine! Aren't they beautiful?

RANK   Don't stand here chattering in this draught!
HELMER   Come, Mrs. Linde. This is for mothers only.

Dr. Rank, Helmer, and Mrs. Linde go down the stairs. The Nurse brings the children into the room. Nora follows, and closes the door to the hall.

NORA   How well you look! What red cheeks you've got! Like apples and roses! [*The children answer her inaudibly as she talks to them.*] Have you had fun? That's splendid. You gave Emmy and Bob a ride on the sledge? What, both together? I say! What a clever boy you are, Ivar! Oh, let me hold her for a moment, Anne-Marie! My sweet little baby doll! [*Takes the smallest child from the Nurse and dances with her.*] Yes, yes, Mummy will dance with Bob too. What? Have you been throwing snowballs? Oh, I wish I'd been there! No, don't—I'll undress them myself, Anne-Marie. No, please let me; it's such fun. Go inside and warm yourself; you look frozen. There's some hot coffee on the stove. [*The Nurse goes into the room on the left. Nora takes off the children's outdoor clothes and throws them anywhere while they all chatter simultaneously.*] What? A big dog ran after you? But he didn't bite you? No, dogs don't bite lovely little baby dolls. Leave those parcels alone, Ivar. What's in them? Ah, wouldn't you like to know! No, no; it's nothing nice. Come on, let's play a game. What shall we play? Hide and seek. Yes, let's play hide and seek. Bob shall hide first. You want me to? All right, let me hide first.

Nora and the children play around the room, and in the adjacent room to the left, laughing and shouting. At length Nora hides under the table. The children rush in, look, but cannot find her. Then they hear her half-stifled laughter, run to the table, lift up the cloth and see her. Great excitement. She crawls out as though to frighten them. Further excitement. Meanwhile, there has been a knock on the door leading from the hall, but no one has noticed it. Now the door is half-opened and Krogstad enters. He waits for a moment; the game continues.

KROGSTAD   Excuse me, Mrs. Helmer—
NORA   [*turns with a stifled cry and half jumps up*]   Oh! What do you want?
KROGSTAD   I beg your pardon; the front door was ajar. Someone must have forgotten to close it.
NORA   [*gets up*]   My husband is not at home, Mr. Krogstad.
KROGSTAD   I know.
NORA   Well, what do you want here, then?
KROGSTAD   A word with you.
NORA   With—? [*To the children, quietly.*] Go inside to Anne-Marie. What? No, the strange gentleman won't do anything to hurt Mummy. When he's gone we'll start playing again.

She takes the children into the room on the left and closes the door behind them.

NORA [*uneasy, tense*]   You want to speak to me?

KROGSTAD   Yes.

NORA   Today? But it's not the first of the month yet.

KROGSTAD   No, it is Christmas Eve. Whether or not you have a merry Christmas depends on you.

NORA   What do you want? I can't give you anything today—

KROGSTAD   We won't talk about that for the present. There's something else. You have a moment to spare?

NORA   Oh, yes. Yes, I suppose so; though—

KROGSTAD   Good. I was sitting in the café down below and I saw your husband cross the street—

NORA   Yes.

KROGSTAD   With a lady.

NORA   Well?

KROGSTAD   Might I be so bold as to ask: was not that lady a Mrs. Linde?

NORA   Yes.

KROGSTAD   Recently arrived in town?

NORA   Yes, today.

KROGSTAD   She is a good friend of yours, is she not?

NORA   Yes, she is. But I don't see—

KROGSTAD   I used to know her too once.

NORA   I know.

KROGSTAD   Oh? You've discovered that. Yes, I thought you would. Well then, may I ask you a straight question: is Mrs. Linde to be employed at the bank?

NORA   How dare you presume to cross-examine me, Mr. Krogstad? You, one of my husband's employees? But since you ask, you shall have an answer. Yes, Mrs. Linde is to be employed by the bank. And I arranged it, Mr. Krogstad. Now you know.

KROGSTAD   I guessed right, then.

NORA [*walks up and down the room*]   Oh, one has a little influence, you know. Just because one's a woman it doesn't necessarily mean that— When one is in a humble position, Mr. Krogstad, one should think twice before offending someone who—hm—

KROGSTAD   —who has influence?

NORA   Precisely.

KROGSTAD [*changes his tone*]   Mrs. Helmer, will you have the kindness to use your influence on my behalf?

NORA   What? What do you mean?

KROGSTAD   Will you be so good as to see that I keep my humble position at the bank?

NORA   What do you mean? Who is thinking of removing you from your position?

KROGSTAD   Oh, you don't need to play the innocent with me. I realize it can't be very pleasant for your friend to risk bumping into me; and now I also realize whom I have to thank for being hounded out like this.

NORA   But I assure you—

KROGSTAD   Look, let's not beat about the bush. There's still time, and I'd advise you to use your influence to stop it.

NORA   But, Mr. Krogstad, I have no influence!

KROGSTAD   Oh? I thought you just said—

NORA   But I didn't mean it like that! I? How on earth could you imagine that I would have any influence over my husband?

KROGSTAD   Oh, I've known your husband since we were students together. I imagine he has his weaknesses like other married men.

NORA   If you speak impertinently of my husband, I shall show you the door.

KROGSTAD   You're a bold woman, Mrs. Helmer.

NORA   I'm not afraid of you any longer. Once the New Year is in, I'll soon be rid of you.

KROGSTAD [*more controlled*]   Now listen to me, Mrs. Helmer. If I'm forced to, I shall fight for my little job at the bank as I would fight for my life.

NORA   So it sounds.

KROGSTAD   It isn't just the money; that's the last thing I care about. There's something else—well, you might as well know. It's like this, you see. You know of course, as everyone else does, that some years ago I committed an indiscretion.

NORA   I think I did hear something—

KROGSTAD   It never came into court; but from that day, every opening was barred to me. So I turned my hand to the kind of business you know about. I had to do something; and I don't think I was one of the worst. But now I want to give up all that. My sons are growing up; for their sake, I must try to regain what respectability I can. This job in the bank was the first step on the ladder. And now your husband wants to kick me off that ladder back into the dirt.

NORA   But my dear Mr. Krogstad, it simply isn't in my power to help you.

KROGSTAD   You say that because you don't want to help me. But I have the means to make you.

NORA   You don't mean you'd tell my husband that I owe you money?

KROGSTAD   And if I did?

NORA   That'd be a filthy trick! [*Almost in tears.*] This secret that is my pride and my joy—that he should hear about it in such a filthy, beastly way—hear about it from you! It'd involve me in the most dreadful unpleasantness—

KROGSTAD   Only—unpleasantness?

NORA [*vehemently*]   All right, do it! You'll be the one who'll suffer. It'll show my husband the kind of man you are, and then you'll never keep your job.

KROGSTAD   I asked you whether it was merely domestic unpleasantness you were afraid of.

NORA   If my husband hears about it, he will of course immediately pay you whatever is owing. And then we shall have nothing more to do with you.

KROGSTAD   [takes a step closer]   Listen, Mrs. Helmer. Either you've a bad memory or else you know very little about financial transactions. I had better enlighten you.

NORA   What do you mean?

KROGSTAD   When your husband was ill, you came to me to borrow two hundred and fifty pounds.

NORA   I didn't know anyone else.

KROGSTAD   I promised to find that sum for you—

NORA   And you did find it.

KROGSTAD   I promised to find that sum for you on certain conditions. You were so worried about your husband's illness and so keen to get the money to take him abroad that I don't think you bothered much about the details. So it won't be out of place if I refresh your memory. Well—I promised to get you the money in exchange for an I.O.U., which I drew up.

NORA   Yes, and which I signed.

KROGSTAD   Exactly. But then I added a few lines naming your father as security for the debt. This paragraph was to be signed by your father.

NORA   Was to be? He did sign it.

KROGSTAD   I left the date blank for your father to fill in when he signed this paper. You remember, Mrs. Helmer?

NORA   Yes, I think so—

KROGSTAD   Then I gave you back this I.O.U. for you to post to your father. Is that not correct?

NORA   Yes.

KROGSTAD   And of course you posted it at once; for within five or six days you brought it along to me with your father's signature on it. Whereupon I handed you the money.

NORA   Yes, well. Haven't I repaid the instalments as agreed?

KROGSTAD   Mm—yes, more or less. But to return to what we were speaking about—that was a difficult time for you just then, wasn't it, Mrs. Helmer?

NORA   Yes, it was.

KROGSTAD   Your father was very ill, if I am not mistaken.

NORA   He was dying.

KROGSTAD   He did in fact die shortly afterwards?

NORA   Yes.

KROGSTAD   Tell me, Mrs. Helmer, do you by any chance remember the date of your father's death? The day of the month, I mean.

NORA   Papa died on the twenty-ninth of September.

KROGSTAD   Quite correct; I took the trouble to confirm it. And that leaves me with a curious little problem— [*Takes out a paper*] —which I simply cannot solve.

NORA   Problem? I don't see—

KROGSTAD   The problem, Mrs. Helmer, is that your father signed this paper three days after his death.

NORA   What? I don't understand—

KROGSTAD   Your father died on the twenty-ninth of September. But look at this. Here your father has dated his signature the second of October. Isn't that a curious little problem, Mrs. Helmer? [*Nora is silent.*] Can you suggest any explanation? [*She remains silent.*] And there's another curious thing. The words "second of October" and the year are written in a hand which is not your father's, but which I seem to know. Well, there's a simple explanation to that. Your father could have forgotten to write in the date when he signed, and someone else could have added it before the news came of his death. There's nothing criminal about that. It's the signature itself I'm wondering about. It *is* genuine, I suppose, Mrs. Helmer? It was your father who wrote his name here?

NORA   [*after a short silence, throws back her head and looks defiantly at him*]   No, it was not. It was I who wrote Papa's name there.

KROGSTAD   Look, Mrs. Helmer, do you realize this is a dangerous admission?

NORA   Why? You'll get your money.

KROGSTAD   May I ask you a question? Why didn't you send this paper to your father?

NORA   I couldn't. Papa was very ill. If I'd asked him to sign this, I'd have had to tell him what the money was for. But I couldn't have told him in his condition that my husband's life was in danger. I couldn't have done that!

KROGSTAD   Then you would have been wiser to have given up your idea of a holiday.

NORA   But I couldn't! It was to save my husband's life. I couldn't put it off.

KROGSTAD   But didn't it occur to you that you were being dishonest towards me?

NORA   I couldn't bother about that. I didn't care about you. I hated you because of all the beastly difficulties you'd put in my way when you knew how dangerously ill my husband was.

KROGSTAD   Mrs. Helmer, you evidently don't appreciate exactly what you have done. But I can assure you that it is no bigger nor worse a crime than the one I once committed, and thereby ruined my whole social position.

NORA You? Do you expect me to believe that you would have taken a risk like that to save your wife's life?

KROGSTAD The law does not concern itself with motives.

NORA Then the law must be very stupid.

KROGSTAD Stupid or not, if I show this paper to the police, you will be judged according to it.

NORA I don't believe that. Hasn't a daughter the right to shield her father from worry and anxiety when he's old and dying? Hasn't a wife the right to save her husband's life? I don't know much about the law, but there must be something somewhere that says that such things are allowed. You ought to know about that, you're meant to be a lawyer, aren't you? You can't be a very good lawyer, Mr. Krogstad.

KROGSTAD Possibly not. But business, the kind of business we two have been transacting—I think you'll admit I understand something about that? Good. Do as you please. But I tell you this. If I get thrown into the gutter for a second time, I shall take you with me.

He bows and goes out through the hall.

NORA [*stands for a moment in thought, then tosses her head*] What nonsense! He's trying to frighten me! I'm not that stupid. [*Busies herself gathering together the children's clothes; then she suddenly stops.*] But—? No, it's impossible. I did it for love, didn't I?

THE CHILDREN [*in the doorway, left*] Mummy, the strange gentleman's gone out into the street.

NORA Yes, yes, I know. But don't talk to anyone about the strange gentleman. You hear? Not even to Daddy.

CHILDREN No, Mummy. Will you play with us again now?

NORA No, no. Not now.

CHILDREN Oh but, Mummy, you promised!

NORA I know, but I can't just now. Go back to the nursery. I've got a lot to do. Go away, my darlings, go away. [*She pushes them gently into the other room, and closes the door behind them. She sits on the sofa, takes up her embroidery, stitches for a few moments, but soon stops.*] No! [*Throws the embroidery aside, gets up, goes to the door leading to the hall and calls.*] Helen! Bring in the Christmas tree! [*She goes to the table on the left and opens the drawer in it; then pauses again.*] No, but it's utterly impossible!

MAID [*enters with the tree*] Where shall I put it, madam?

NORA There, in the middle of the room.

MAID Will you be wanting anything else?

NORA No, thank you. I have everything I need.

The Maid puts down the tree and goes out.

NORA [*busy decorating the tree*]   Now—candles here—and flowers here. That loathsome man! Nonsense, nonsense, there's nothing to be frightened about. The Christmas tree must be beautiful. I'll do everything that you like, Torvald. I'll sing for you, dance for you—

Helmer, with a bundle of papers under his arm, enters.

NORA   Oh—are you back already?

HELMER   Yes. Has anyone been here?

NORA   Here? No.

HELMER   That's strange. I saw Krogstad come out of the front door.

NORA   Did you? Oh yes, that's quite right—Krogstad was here for a few minutes.

HELMER   Nora, I can tell from your face, he's been here and asked you to put in a good word for him.

NORA   Yes.

HELMER   And you were to pretend you were doing it of your own accord? You weren't going to tell me he'd been here? He asked you to do that too, didn't he?

NORA   Yes, Torvald. But—

HELMER   Nora, Nora! And you were ready to enter into such a conspiracy? Talking to a man like that, and making him promises—and then, on top of it all, to tell me an untruth!

NORA   An untruth?

HELMER   Didn't you say no one had been here? [*Wags his finger.*] My little songbird must never do that again. A songbird must have a clean beak to sing with; otherwise she'll start twittering out of tune. [*Puts his arm round her waist.*] Isn't that the way we want things? Yes, of course it is. [*Lets go of her.*] So let's hear no more about that. [*Sits down in front of the stove.*] Ah, how cosy and peaceful it is here. [*Glances for a few moments at his papers.*]

NORA [*busy with the tree; after a short silence*]   Torvald.

HELMER   Yes.

NORA   I'm terribly looking forward to that fancy dress ball at the Stenborgs on Boxing Day.

HELMER   And I'm terribly curious to see what you're going to surprise me with.

NORA   Oh, it's so maddening.

HELMER   What is?

NORA   I can't think of anything to wear. It all seems so stupid and meaningless.

HELMER   So my little Nora's come to that conclusion, has she?

NORA [*behind his chair, resting her arms on its back*]   Are you very busy, Torvald?

HELMER   Oh—

NORA   What are those papers?

HELMER   Just something to do with the bank.

NORA   Already?

HELMER   I persuaded the trustees to give me authority to make certain immediate changes in the staff and organization. I want to have everything straight by the New Year.

NORA   Then that's why this poor man Krogstad—

HELMER   Hm.

NORA   [still leaning over his chair, slowly strokes the back of his head]   If you hadn't been so busy, I was going to ask you an enormous favour, Torvald.

HELMER   Well, tell me. What was it to be?

NORA   You know I trust your taste more than anyone's. I'm so anxious to look really beautiful at the fancy dress ball. Torvald, couldn't you help me to decide what I shall go as, and what kind of costume I ought to wear?

HELMER   Aha! So little Miss Independent's in trouble and needs a man to rescue her, does she?

NORA   Yes, Torvald. I can't get anywhere without your help.

HELMER   Well, well, I'll give the matter thought. We'll find something.

NORA   Oh, how kind of you! [Goes back to the tree. Pause.] How pretty these red flowers look! But, tell me, is it so dreadful, this thing that Krogstad's done?

HELMER   He forged someone else's name. Have you any idea what that means?

NORA   Mightn't he have been forced to do it by some emergency?

HELMER   He probably just didn't think—that's what usually happens. I'm not so heartless as to condemn a man for an isolated action.

NORA   No, Torvald, of course not!

HELMER   Men often succeed in re-establishing themselves if they admit their crime and take their punishment.

NORA   Punishment?

HELMER   But Krogstad didn't do that. He chose to try and trick his way out of it; and that's what has morally destroyed him.

NORA   You think that would—?

HELMER   Just think how a man with that load on his conscience must always be lying and cheating and dissembling; how he must wear a mask even in the presence of those who are dearest to him, even his own wife and children! Yes, the children. That's the worst danger, Nora.

NORA   Why?

HELMER   Because an atmosphere of lies contaminates and poisons every corner of the home. Every breath that the children draw in such a house contains the germs of evil.

NORA [*comes closer behind him*]   Do you really believe that?

HELMER   Oh, my dear, I've come across it so often in my work at the bar. Nearly all young criminals are the children of mothers who are constitutional liars.

NORA   Why do you say mothers?

HELMER   It's usually the mother; though of course the father can have the same influence. Every lawyer knows that only too well. And yet this fellow Krogstad has been sitting at home all these years poisoning his children with his lies and pretences. That's why I say that, morally speaking, he is dead. [*Stretches out his hands towards her.*] So my pretty little Nora must promise me not to plead his case. Your hand on it. Come, come, what's this? Give me your hand. There. That's settled, now. I assure you it'd be quite impossible for me to work in the same building as him. I literally feel physically ill in the presence of a man like that.

NORA [*draws her hand from his and goes over to the other side of the Christmas tree*]   How hot it is in here! And I've so much to do.

HELMER [*gets up and gathers his papers*]   Yes, and I must try to get some of this read before dinner. I'll think about your costume too. And I may even have something up my sleeve to hang in gold paper on the Christmas tree. [*Lays his hand on her head.*] My precious little songbird!

He goes into his study and closes the door.

NORA [*softly, after a pause*]   It's nonsense. It must be. It's impossible. It *must* be impossible!

NURSE [*in the doorway, left*]   The children are asking if they can come in to Mummy.

NORA   No, no, no; don't let them in! You stay with them, Anne-Marie.

NURSE   Very good, madam. [*Closes the door.*]

NORA [*pale with fear*]   Corrupt my little children—! Poison my home! [*Short pause. She throws back her head.*] It isn't true! It *couldn't* be true!

ACT II

The same room. In the corner by the piano the Christmas tree stands, stripped and disheveled, its candles burned to their sockets. Nora's outdoor clothes lie on the sofa. She is alone in the room, walking restlessly to and fro. At length she stops by the sofa and picks up her coat.

NORA [*drops the coat again*]   There's someone coming! [*Goes to the door and listens*] No, it's no one. Of course—no one'll come today, it's Christmas

Day. Nor tomorrow. But perhaps—! [*Opens the door and looks out.*] No. Nothing in the letter-box. Quite empty. [*Walks across the room.*] Silly, silly. Of course he won't do anything. It couldn't happen. It isn't possible. Why, I've three small children.

The Nurse, carrying a large cardboard box, enters from the room on the left.

NURSE   I found those fancy dress clothes at last, madam.

NORA   Thank you. Put them on the table.

NURSE [*does so*]   They're all rumpled up.

NORA   Oh, I wish I could tear them into a million pieces!

NURSE   Why, madam! They'll be all right. Just a little patience.

NORA   Yes, of course. I'll go and get Mrs. Linde to help me.

NURSE   What, out again? In this dreadful weather? You'll catch a chill, madam.

NORA   Well, that wouldn't be the worst. How are the children?

NURSE   Playing with their Christmas presents, poor little dears. But—

NORA   Are they still asking to see me?

NURSE   They're so used to having their Mummy with them.

NORA   Yes, but, Anne-Marie, from now on I shan't be able to spend so much time with them.

NURSE   Well, children get used to anything in time.

NORA   Do you think so? Do you think they'd forget their mother if she went away from them—for ever?

NURSE   Mercy's sake, madam! For ever!

NORA   Tell me, Anne-Marie—I've so often wondered. How could you bear to give your child away—to strangers?

NURSE   But I had to when I came to nurse my little Miss Nora.

NORA   Do you mean you wanted to?

NURSE   When I had the chance of such a good job? A poor girl what's got into trouble can't afford to pick and choose. That good-for-nothing didn't lift a finger.

NORA   But your daughter must have completely forgotten you.

NURSE   Oh no, indeed she hasn't. She's written to me twice, once when she got confirmed and then again when she got married.

NORA [*hugs her*]   Dear old Anne-Marie, you were a good mother to me.

NURSE   Poor little Miss Nora, you never had any mother but me.

NORA   And if my little ones had no one else, I know you would—no, silly, silly, silly! [*Opens the cardboard box.*] Go back to them, Anne-Marie. Now I must—Tomorrow you'll see how pretty I shall look.

NURSE   Why, there'll be no one at the ball as beautiful as my Miss Nora.

She goes into the room, left.

NORA [*begins to unpack the clothes from the box, but soon throws them down again*]   Oh, if only I dared go out! If I could be sure no one would come and nothing would happen while I was away! Stupid, stupid! No one will come. I just mustn't think about it. Brush this muff. Pretty gloves, pretty gloves! Don't think about it, don't think about it! One, two, three, four, five, six— [*Cries*] Ah—they're coming—!

She begins to run towards the door, but stops uncertainly. Mrs. Linde enters from the hall, where she has been taking off her outdoor clothes.

NORA   Oh, it's you, Christine. There's no one else out there, is there? Oh, I'm so glad you've come.

MRS. LINDE   I hear you were at my room asking for me.

NORA   Yes, I just happened to be passing. I want to ask you to help me with something. Let's sit down here on the sofa. Look at this. There's going to be a fancy dress ball tomorrow night upstairs at Consul Stenborg's, and Torvald wants me to go as a Neapolitan fisher-girl and dance the tarantella. I learned it on Capri.

MRS. LINDE   I say, are you going to give a performance?

NORA   Yes, Torvald says I should. Look, here's the dress. Torvald had it made for me in Italy; but now it's all so torn, I don't know—

MRS. LINDE   Oh, we'll soon put that right; the stitching's just come away. Needle and thread? Ah, here we are.

NORA   You're being awfully sweet.

MRS. LINDE [*sews*]   So you're going to dress up tomorrow, Nora? I must pop over for a moment to see how you look. Oh, but I've completely forgotten to thank you for that nice evening yesterday.

NORA [*gets up and walks across the room*]   Oh, I didn't think it was as nice as usual. You ought to have come to town a little earlier, Christine. . . . Yes, Torvald understands how to make a home look attractive.

MRS. LINDE   I'm sure you do, too. You're not your father's daughter for nothing. But, tell me. Is Dr. Rank always in such low spirits as he was yesterday?

NORA   No, last night it was very noticeable. But he's got a terrible disease; he's got spinal tuberculosis, poor man. His father was a frightful creature who kept mistresses and so on. As a result Dr. Rank has been sickly ever since he was a child—you understand—

MRS. LINDE [*puts down her sewing*]   But, my dear Nora, how on earth did you get to know about such things?

NORA [*walks about the room*]   Oh, don't be silly, Christine—when one has three children, one comes into contact with women who—well, who know about medical matters, and they tell one a thing or two.

MRS. LINDE [*sews again; a short silence*]   Does Dr. Rank visit you every day?

NORA Yes, every day. He's Torvald's oldest friend, and a good friend to me too. Dr. Rank's almost one of the family.

MRS. LINDE But, tell me—is he quite sincere? I mean, doesn't he rather say the sort of thing he thinks people want to hear?

NORA No, quite the contrary. What gave you that idea?

MRS. LINDE When you introduced me to him yesterday, he said he'd often heard my name mentioned here. But later I noticed your husband had no idea who I was. So how could Dr. Rank—?

NORA Yes, that's quite right, Christine. You see, Torvald's so hopelessly in love with me that he wants to have me all to himself—those were his very words. When we were first married, he got quite jealous if I as much as mentioned any of my old friends back home. So naturally, I stopped talking about them. But I often chat with Dr. Rank about that kind of thing. He enjoys it, you see.

MRS. LINDE Now listen, Nora. In many ways you're still a child; I'm a bit older than you and have a little more experience of the world. There's something I want to say to you. You ought to give up this business with Dr. Rank.

NORA What business?

MRS. LINDE Well, everything. Last night you were speaking about this rich admirer of yours who was going to give you money—

NORA Yes, and who doesn't exist—unfortunately. But what's that got to do with—?

MRS. LINDE Is Dr. Rank rich?

NORA Yes.

MRS. LINDE And he has no dependants?

NORA No, no one. But—

MRS. LINDE And he comes here to see you every day?

NORA Yes, I've told you.

MRS. LINDE But how dare a man of his education be so forward?

NORA What on earth are you talking about?

MRS. LINDE Oh, stop pretending, Nora. Do you think I haven't guessed who it was who lent you that two hundred pounds?

NORA Are you out of your mind? How could you imagine such a thing? A friend, someone who comes here every day! Why, that'd be an impossible situation!

MRS. LINDE Then it really wasn't him?

NORA No, of course not. I've never for a moment dreamed of—anyway, he hadn't any money to lend then. He didn't come into that till later.

MRS. LINDE Well, I think that was a lucky thing for you, Nora dear.

NORA No, I could never have dreamed of asking Dr. Rank— Though I'm sure that if I ever did ask him—

MRS. LINDE But of course you won't.

NORA   Of course not. I can't imagine that it should ever become necessary. But I'm perfectly sure that if I did speak to Dr. Rank—

MRS. LINDE   Behind your husband's back?

NORA   I've got to get out of this other business; and *that's* been going on behind his back. I've *got* to get out of it.

MRS. LINDE   Yes, well, that's what I told you yesterday. But—

NORA   [*walking up and down*]   It's much easier for a man to arrange these things than a woman—

MRS. LINDE   One's own husband, yes.

NORA   Oh, bosh. [*Stops walking.*] When you've completely repaid a debt, you get your I.O.U. back, don't you?

MRS. LINDE   Yes, of course.

NORA   And you can tear it into a thousand pieces and burn the filthy, beastly thing!

MRS. LINDE   [*looks hard at her, puts down her sewing and gets up slowly*]   Nora, you're hiding something from me.

NORA   Can you see that?

MRS. LINDE   Something has happened since yesterday morning. Nora, what is it?

NORA   [*goes towards her*]   Christine! [*Listens.*] Ssh! There's Torvald. Would you mind going into the nursery for a few minutes? Torvald can't bear to see sewing around. Anne-Marie'll help you.

MRS. LINDE   [*gathers some of her things together*]   Very well. But I shan't leave this house until we've talked this matter out.

She goes into the nursery, left. As she does so, Helmer enters from the hall.

NORA   [*runs to meet him*]   Oh, Torvald dear, I've been so longing for you to come back!

HELMER   Was that the dressmaker?

NORA   No, it was Christine. She's helping me mend my costume. I'm going to look rather splendid in that.

HELMER   Yes, that was quite a bright idea of mine, wasn't it?

NORA   Wonderful! But wasn't it nice of me to give in to you?

HELMER   [*takes her chin in his hand*]   Nice—to give in to your husband? All right, little silly, I know you didn't mean it like that. But I won't disturb you. I expect you'll be wanting to try it on.

NORA   Are you going to work now?

HELMER   Yes. [*Shows her a bundle of papers.*] Look at these. I've been down to the bank— [*Turns to go into his study.*]

NORA   Torvald.

HELMER   [*stops*]   Yes.

NORA   If little squirrel asked you really prettily to grant her a wish—

HELMER   Well?

NORA Would you grant it to her?

HELMER First I should naturally have to know what it was.

NORA Squirrel would do lots of pretty tricks for you if you granted her wish.

HELMER Out with it, then.

NORA Your little skylark would sing in every room—

HELMER My little skylark does that already.

NORA I'd turn myself into a little fairy and dance for you in the moonlight, Torvald.

HELMER Nora, it isn't that business you were talking about this morning?

NORA [comes closer] Yes, Torvald—oh, please! I beg of you!

HELMER Have you really the nerve to bring that up again?

NORA Yes, Torvald, yes, you must do as I ask! You must let Krogstad keep his place at the bank!

HELMER My dear Nora, his is the job I'm giving to Mrs. Linde.

NORA Yes, that's terribly sweet of you. But you can get rid of one of the other clerks instead of Krogstad.

HELMER Really, you're being incredibly obstinate. Just because you thoughtlessly promised to put in a word for him, you expect me to—

NORA No, it isn't that, Helmer. It's for your own sake. That man writes for the most beastly newspapers—you said so yourself. He could do you tremendous harm. I'm so dreadfully frightened of him—

HELMER Oh, I understand. Memories of the past. That's what's frightening you.

NORA What do you mean?

HELMER You're thinking of your father, aren't you?

NORA Yes, yes. Of course. Just think what those dreadful men wrote in the papers about Papa! The most frightful slanders. I really believe it would have lost him his job if the Ministry hadn't sent you down to investigate, and you hadn't been so kind and helpful to him.

HELMER But my dear little Nora, there's a considerable difference between your father and me. Your father was not a man of unassailable reputation. But I am; and I hope to remain so all my life.

NORA But no one knows what spiteful people may not dig up. We could be so peaceful and happy now, Torvald—we could be free from every worry—you and I and the children. Oh, please, Torvald, please—!

HELMER The very fact of your pleading his cause makes it impossible for me to keep him. Everyone at the bank already knows that I intend to dismiss Krogstad. If the rumor got about that the new manager had allowed his wife to persuade him to change his mind—

NORA Well, what then?

HELMER Oh, nothing, nothing. As long as my little Miss Obstinate gets her way—! Do you expect me to make a laughing-stock of myself before my entire staff—give people the idea that I am open to outside influence? Believe me, I'd soon feel the consequences! Besides—there's something else that makes it impossible for Krogstad to remain in the bank while I am its manager.

NORA   What is that?

HELMER   I might conceivably have allowed myself to ignore his moral obloquies—

NORA   Yes, Torvald, surely?

HELMER   And I hear he's quite efficient at his job. But we—well, we were schoolfriends. It was one of those friendships that one enters into over-hastily and so often comes to regret later in life. I might as well confess the truth. We—well, we're on Christian name terms. And the tactless idiot makes no attempt to conceal it when other people are present. On the contrary, he thinks it gives him the right to be familiar with me. He shows off the whole time, with "Torvald this," and "Torvald that." I can tell you, I find it damned annoying. If he stayed, he'd make my position intolerable.

NORA   Torvald, you can't mean this seriously.

HELMER   Oh? And why not?

NORA   But it's so petty.

HELMER   What did you say? Petty? You think I am petty?

NORA   No, Torvald dear, of course you're not. That's just why—

HELMER   Don't quibble! You call my motives petty. Then I must be petty too. Petty! I see. Well, I've had enough of this. [Goes to the door and calls into the hall.] Helen!

NORA   What are you going to do?

HELMER   [searching among his papers]   I'm going to settle this matter once and for all. [The Maid enters.] Take this letter downstairs at once. Find a messenger and see that he delivers it. Immediately! The address is on the envelope. Here's the money.

MAID   Very good, sir. [Goes out with the letter.]

HELMER   [putting his papers in order]   There now, little Miss Obstinate.

NORA   [tensely]   Torvald—what was in that letter?

HELMER   Krogstad's dismissal.

NORA   Call her back, Torvald! There's still time. Oh, Torvald, call her back! Do it for my sake—for your own sake—for the children! Do you hear me, Torvald? Please do it! You don't realize what this may do to us all!

HELMER   Too late.

NORA   Yes. Too late.

HELMER   My dear Nora, I forgive you this anxiety. Though it is a bit of an insult to me. Oh, but it is! Isn't it an insult to imply that I should be frightened by the vindictiveness of a depraved hack journalist? But I forgive you, because it so charmingly testifies to the love you bear me. [Takes her in his arms.] Which is as it should be, my own dearest Nora. Let what will happen, happen. When the real crisis comes, you will not find me lacking in strength or courage. I am man enough to bear the burden for us both.

NORA [*fearfully*]   What do you mean?

HELMER   The whole burden, I say—

NORA [*calmly*]   I shall never let you do that.

HELMER   Very well. We shall share it, Nora—as man and wife. And that is as it should be. [*Caresses her.*] Are you happy now? There, there, there; don't look at me with those frightened little eyes. You're simply imagining things. You go ahead now and do your tarantella, and get some practice on that tambourine. I'll sit in my study and close the door. Then I won't hear anything, and you can make all the noise you want. [*Turns in the doorway.*] When Dr. Rank comes, tell him where to find me. [*He nods to her, goes into his room with his papers and closes the door.*]

NORA [*desperate with anxiety, stands as though transfixed, and whispers*]   He said he'd do it. He will do it. He will do it, and nothing'll stop him. No, never that. I'd rather anything. There must be some escape—! Some way out—! [*The bell rings in the hall.*] Dr. Rank—! Anything but that! Anything, I don't care—!

She passes her hand across her face, composes herself, walks across and opens the door to the hall. Dr. Rank is standing there, hanging up his fur coat. During the following scene it begins to grow dark.

NORA   Good evening, Dr. Rank. I recognized your ring. But you mustn't go in to Torvald yet. I think he's busy.

RANK   And—you?

NORA [*as he enters the room and she closes the door behind him*]   Oh, you know very well I've always time to talk to you.

RANK   Thank you. I shall avail myself of that privilege as long as I can.

NORA   What do you mean by that? As long as you *can?*

RANK   Yes. Does that frighten you?

NORA   Well, it's rather a curious expression. Is something going to happen?

RANK   Something I've been expecting to happen for a long time. But I didn't think it would happen quite so soon.

NORA [*seizes his arm*]   What is it? Dr. Rank, you must tell me!

RANK [*sits down by the stove*]   I'm on the way out. And there's nothing to be done about it.

NORA [*sighs with relief*]   Oh, it's you—?

RANK   Who else? No, it's no good lying to oneself. I am the most wretched of all my patients, Mrs. Helmer. These last few days I've been going through the books of this poor body of mine, and I find I am bankrupt. Within a month I may be rotting up there in the churchyard.

NORA   Ugh, what a nasty way to talk!

RANK   The facts aren't exactly nice. But the worst is that there's so much else that's nasty to come first. I've only one more test to make. When that's done I'll have a pretty accurate idea of when the final disintegration is likely to begin. I want to ask you a favor. Helmer's a sensitive chap, and I know how he hates anything ugly. I don't want him to visit me when I'm in hospital—

NORA   Oh but, Dr. Rank—

RANK   I don't want him there. On any pretext. I shan't have him allowed in. As soon as I know the worst, I'll send you my visiting card with a black cross on it, and then you'll know that the final filthy process has begun.

NORA   Really, you're being quite impossible this evening. And I did hope you'd be in a good mood.

RANK   With death on my hands? And all this to atone for someone else's sin? Is there justice in that? And in every single family, in one way or another, the same merciless law of retribution is at work—

NORA   [holds her hands to her ears]   Nonsense! Cheer up! Laugh!

RANK   Yes, you're right. Laughter's all the damned thing's fit for. My poor innocent spine must pay for the fun my father had as a gay young lieutenant.

NORA   [at the table, left]   You mean he was too fond of asparagus and foie gras?

RANK   Yes; and truffles too.

NORA   Yes, of course, truffles, yes. And oysters too, I suppose?

RANK   Yes, oysters, oysters. Of course.

NORA   And all that port and champagne to wash them down. It's too sad that all those lovely things should affect one's spine.

RANK   Especially a poor spine that never got any pleasure out of them.

NORA   Oh yes, that's the saddest thing of all.

RANK   [looks searchingly at her]   Hm—

NORA   [after a moment]   Why did you smile?

RANK   No, it was you who laughed.

NORA   No, it was you who smiled, Dr. Rank!

RANK   [gets up]   You're a worse little rogue than I thought.

NORA   Oh, I'm full of stupid tricks today.

RANK   So it seems.

NORA   [puts both her hands on his shoulders]   Dear, dear Dr. Rank, you mustn't die and leave Torvald and me.

RANK   Oh, you'll soon get over it. Once one is gone, one is soon forgotten.

NORA   [looks at him anxiously]   Do you believe that?

RANK   One finds replacements, and then—

NORA   Who will find a replacement?

RANK   You and Helmer both will, when I am gone. You seem to have made a start already, haven't you? What was this Mrs. Linde doing here yesterday evening?

NORA Aha! But surely you can't be jealous of poor Christine?

RANK Indeed I am. She will be my successor in this house. When I have moved on, this lady will—

NORA Ssh—don't speak so loud! She's in there!

RANK Today again? You see!

NORA She's only come to mend my dress. Good heavens, how unreasonable you are! [Sits on the sofa.] Be nice now, Dr. Rank. Tomorrow you'll see how beautifully I shall dance; and you must imagine that I'm doing it just for you. And for Torvald, of course; obviously. [Takes some things out of the box.] Dr. Rank, sit down here and I'll show you something.

RANK [sits] What's this?

NORA Look here! Look!

RANK Silk stockings!

NORA Flesh-coloured. Aren't they beautiful? It's very dark in here now, of course, but tomorrow—! No, no, no; only the soles. Oh well, I suppose you can look a bit higher if you want to.

RANK Hm—

NORA Why are you looking so critical? Don't you think they'll fit me?

RANK I can't really give you a qualified opinion on that.

NORA [looks at him for a moment] Shame on you! [Flicks him on the ear with the stockings.] Take that. [Puts them back in the box.]

RANK What other wonders are to be revealed to me?

NORA I shan't show you anything else. You're being naughty.

She hums a little and looks among the things in the box.

RANK [after a short silence] When I sit here like this being so intimate with you, I can't think—I cannot imagine what would have become of me if I had never entered this house.

NORA [smiles] Yes, I think you enjoy being with us, don't you?

RANK [more quietly, looking into the middle distance] And now to have to leave it all—

NORA Nonsense. You're not leaving us.

RANK [as before] And not to be able to leave even the most wretched token of gratitude behind; hardly even a passing sense of loss; only an empty place, to be filled by the next comer.

NORA Suppose I were to ask you to—? No—

RANK To do what?

NORA To give me proof of your friendship—

RANK Yes, yes?

NORA No, I mean—to do me a very great service—

RANK Would you really for once grant me that happiness?

NORA But you've no idea what it is.

RANK Very well, tell me, then.

NORA No, but, Dr. Rank, I can't. It's far too much—I want your help and advice, and I want you to do something for me.

RANK The more the better. I've no idea what it can be. But tell me. You do trust me, don't you?

NORA Oh, yes, more than anyone. You're my best and truest friend. Otherwise I couldn't tell you. Well then, Dr. Rank—there's something you must help me to prevent. You know how much Torvald loves me—he'd never hesitate for an instant to lay down his life for me—

RANK [leans over towards her] Nora—do you think he is the only one—?

NORA [with a slight start] What do you mean?

RANK Who would gladly lay down his life for you?

NORA [sadly] Oh, I see.

RANK I swore to myself I would let you know that before I go. I shall never have a better opportunity. . . . Well, Nora, now you know that. And now you also know that you can trust me as you can trust nobody else.

NORA [rises; calmly and quietly] Let me pass, please.

RANK [makes room for her but remains seated] Nora—

NORA [in the doorway to the hall] Helen, bring the lamp. [Goes over to the stove.] Oh, dear Dr. Rank, this was really horrid of you.

RANK [gets up] That I have loved you as deeply as anyone else has? Was that horrid of me?

NORA No—but that you should go and tell me. That was quite unnecessary—

RANK What do you mean? Did you know, then—?

The Maid enters with the lamp, puts it on the table and goes out.

RANK Nora—Mrs. Helmer—I am asking you, did you know this?

NORA Oh, what do I know, what did I know, what didn't I know—I really can't say. How could you be so stupid, Dr. Rank? Everything was so nice.

RANK Well, at any rate now you know that I am ready to serve you, body and soul. So—please continue.

NORA [looks at him] After this?

RANK Please tell me what it is.

NORA I can't possibly tell you now.

RANK Yes, yes! You mustn't punish me like this. Let me be allowed to do what I can for you.

NORA You can't do anything for me now. Anyway, I don't need any help. It was only my imagination—you'll see. Yes, really. Honestly. [Sits in the rocking chair, looks at him and smiles.] Well, upon my word you are a fine gentleman, Dr. Rank. Aren't you ashamed of yourself, now that the lamp's been lit?

RANK Frankly, no. But perhaps I ought to say—adieu?

NORA   Of course not. You will naturally continue to visit us as before. You know quite well how Torvald depends on your company.

RANK   Yes, but you?

NORA   Oh, I always think it's enormous fun having you here.

RANK   That was what misled me. You're a riddle to me, you know. I'd often felt you'd just as soon be with me as with Helmer.

NORA   Well, you see, there are some people whom one loves, and others whom it's almost more fun to be with.

RANK   Oh yes, there's some truth in that.

NORA   When I was at home, of course I loved Papa best. But I always used to think it was terribly amusing to go down and talk to the servants; because they never told me what I ought to do; and they were such fun to listen to.

RANK   I see. So I've taken their place?

NORA   [jumps up and runs over to him]   Oh, dear sweet Dr. Rank, I didn't mean that at all. But I'm sure you understand—I feel the same about Torvald as I did about Papa.

MAID   [enters from the hall]   Excuse me, madam. [Whispers to her and hands her a visiting card.]

NORA   [glances at the card]   Oh! [Puts it quickly in her pocket.]

RANK   Anything wrong?

NORA   No, no, nothing at all. It's just something that—it's my new dress.

RANK   What? But your costume is lying over there.

NORA   Oh—that, yes—but there's another—I ordered it specially—Torvald mustn't know—

RANK   Ah, so that's your big secret?

NORA   Yes, yes. Go in and talk to him—he's in his study—keep him talking for a bit—

RANK   Don't worry. He won't get away from me. [Goes into Helmer's study.]

NORA   [to the Maid]   Is he waiting in the kitchen?

MAID   Yes, madam, he came up the back way—

NORA   But didn't you tell him I had a visitor?

MAID   Yes, but he wouldn't go.

NORA   Wouldn't go?

MAID   No, madam, not until he'd spoken with you.

NORA   Very well, show him in; but quietly. Helen, you mustn't tell anyone about this. It's a surprise for my husband.

MAID   Very good, madam. I understand. [Goes.]

NORA   It's happening. It's happening after all. No, no, no, it can't happen, it mustn't happen.

She walks across and bolts the door of Helmer's study. The Maid opens the door from the hall to admit Krogstad, and closes it behind him. He is wearing an overcoat, heavy boots and a fur cap.

NORA [goes towards him.] Speak quietly. My husband's at home.

KROGSTAD Let him hear.

NORA What do you want from me?

KROGSTAD Information.

NORA Hurry up, then. What is it?

KROGSTAD I suppose you know I've been given the sack.

NORA I couldn't stop it, Mr. Krogstad. I did my best for you, but it didn't help.

KROGSTAD Does your husband love you so little? He knows what I can do to you, and yet he dares to—

NORA Surely you don't imagine I told him?

KROGSTAD No, I didn't really think you had. It wouldn't have been like my old friend Torvald Helmer to show that much courage—

NORA Mr. Krogstad, I'll trouble you to speak respectfully of my husband.

KROGSTAD Don't worry, I'll show him all the respect he deserves. But since you're so anxious to keep this matter hushed up, I presume you're better informed than you were yesterday of the gravity of what you've done?

NORA I've learned more than you could ever teach me.

KROGSTAD Yes, a bad lawyer like me—

NORA What do you want from me?

KROGSTAD I just wanted to see how things were with you, Mrs. Helmer. I've been thinking about you all day. Even duns and hack journalists have hearts, you know.

NORA Show some heart, then. Think of my little children.

KROGSTAD Have you and your husband thought of mine? Well, let's forget that. I just wanted to tell you, you don't need to take this business too seriously. I'm not going to take any action, for the present.

NORA Oh, no—you won't, will you? I knew it.

KROGSTAD It can all be settled quite amicably. There's no need for it to become public. We'll keep it among the three of us.

NORA My husband must never know about this.

KROGSTAD How can you stop him? Can you pay the balance of what you owe me?

NORA Not immediately.

KROGSTAD Have you any means of raising the money during the next few days?

NORA None that I would care to use.

KROGSTAD Well, it wouldn't have helped anyway. However much money you offered me now I wouldn't give you back that paper.

NORA What are you going to do with it?

KROGSTAD Just keep it. No one else need ever hear about it. So in case you were thinking of doing anything desperate—

NORA I am.

KROGSTAD Such as running away—

NORA   I am.

KROGSTAD   Or anything more desperate—

NORA   How did you know?

KROGSTAD   —just give up the idea.

NORA   How did you know?

KROGSTAD   Most of us think of that at first. I did. But I hadn't the courage—

NORA   [dully]   Neither have I.

KROGSTAD   [relieved]   It's true, isn't it? You haven't the courage either?

NORA   No. I haven't. I haven't.

KROGSTAD   It'd be a stupid thing to do anyway. Once the first little domestic explosion is over. . . . I've got a letter in my pocket here addressed to your husband—

NORA   Telling him everything?

KROGSTAD   As delicately as possibly.

NORA   [quickly]   He must never see that letter. Tear it up. I'll find the money somehow—

KROGSTAD   I'm sorry, Mrs. Helmer, I thought I'd explained—

NORA   Oh, I don't mean the money I owe you. Let me know how much you want from my husband, and I'll find it for you.

KROGSTAD   I'm not asking your husband for money.

NORA   What do you want, then?

KROGSTAD   I'll tell you. I want to get on my feet again, Mrs. Helmer. I want to get to the top. And your husband's going to help me. For eighteen months now my record's been clean. I've been in hard straits all that time; I was content to fight my way back inch by inch. Now I've been chucked back into the mud, and I'm not going to be satisfied with just getting back my job. I'm going to get to the top, I tell you. I'm going to get back into the bank, and it's going to be higher up. Your husband's going to create a new job for me—

NORA   He'll never do that!

KROGSTAD   Oh, yes he will. I know him. He won't dare to risk a scandal. And once I'm in there with him, you'll see! Within a year I'll be his right-hand man. It'll be Nils Krogstad who'll be running that bank, not Torvald Helmer!

NORA   That will never happen.

KROGSTAD   Are you thinking of—?

NORA   Now I have the courage.

KROGSTAD   Oh, you can't frighten me. A pampered little pretty like you—

NORA   You'll see! You'll see!

KROGSTAD   Under the ice? Down in the cold, black water? And then, in the spring to float up again, ugly, unrecognizable, hairless—?

NORA   You can't frighten me.

KROGSTAD   And you can't frighten me. People don't do such things, Mrs. Helmer. And anyway, what'd be the use? I've got him in my pocket.

NORA   But afterwards? When I'm no longer—?

KROGSTAD   Have you forgotten that then your reputation will be in my hands? [*She looks at him speechlessly.*] Well, I've warned you. Don't do anything silly. When Helmer's read my letter, he'll get in touch with me. And remember, it's your husband who's forced me to act like this. And for that I'll never forgive him. Goodbye, Mrs. Helmer. [*He goes out through the hall.*]

NORA   [*runs to the hall door, opens it a few inches and listens*]   He's going. He's not going to give him the letter. Oh, no, no, it couldn't possibly happen. [*Opens the door a little wider.*] What's he doing? Standing outside the front door. He's not going downstairs. Is he changing his mind? Yes, he—!

A letter falls into the letter-box. Krogstad's footsteps die away down the stairs.

NORA   [*with a stifled cry, runs across the room towards the table by the sofa. A pause*]   In the letter-box. [*Steals timidly over towards the hall door.*] There it is! Oh, Torvald, Torvald! Now we're lost!

MRS. LINDE   [*enters from the nursery with Nora's costume*]   Well, I've done the best I can. Shall we see how it looks—?

NORA   [*whispers hoarsely*]   Christine, come here.

MRS. LINDE   [*throws the dress on the sofa*]   What's wrong with you? You look as though you'd seen a ghost!

NORA   Come here. Do you see that letter? There—look—through the glass of the letter-box.

MRS. LINDE   Yes, yes, I see it.

NORA   That letter's from Krogstad—

MRS. LINDE   Nora! It was Krogstad who lent you the money!

NORA   Yes. And now Torvald's going to discover everything.

MRS. LINDE   Oh, believe me, Nora, it'll be best for you both.

NORA   You don't know what's happened. I've committed a forgery—

MRS. LINDE   But, for heaven's sake—!

NORA   Christine, all I want is for you to be my witness.

MRS. LINDE   What do you mean? Witness what?

NORA   If I should go out of my mind—and it might easily happen—

MRS. LINDE   Nora!

NORA   Or if anything else should happen to me—so that I wasn't here any longer—

MRS. LINDE   Nora, Nora, you don't know what you're saying!

NORA   If anyone should try to take the blame, and say it was all his fault—you understand—?

MRS. LINDE   Yes, yes—but how can you think—?

NORA   Then you must testify that it isn't true, Christine. I'm not mad—I know exactly what I'm saying—and I'm telling you, no one else knows anything about this. I did it entirely on my own. Remember that.

MRS. LINDE   All right. But I simply don't understand—

NORA   Oh, how could you understand? A miracle—is—about to happen.

MRS. LINDE   Miracle?

NORA   Yes. A miracle. But it's so frightening, Christine. It *mustn't* happen, not for anything in the world.

MRS. LINDE   I'll go over and talk to Krogstad.

NORA   Don't go near him. He'll only do something to hurt you.

MRS. LINDE   Once upon a time he'd have done anything for my sake.

NORA   He?

MRS. LINDE   Where does he live?

NORA   Oh, how should I know—? Oh yes, wait a moment—! [*Feels in her pocket.*] Here's his card. But the letter, the letter—!

HELMER [*from his study, knocks on the door*]   Nora!

NORA [*cries in alarm*]   What is it?

HELMER   Now, now, don't get alarmed. We're not coming in; you've closed the door. Are you trying on your costume?

NORA   Yes, yes—I'm trying on my costume. I'm going to look so pretty for you, Torvald.

MRS. LINDE [*who has been reading the card*]   Why, he lives just round the corner.

NORA   Yes; but it's no use. There's nothing to be done now. The letter's lying there in the box.

MRS. LINDE   And your husband has the key?

NORA   Yes, he always keeps it.

MRS. LINDE   Krogstad must ask him to send the letter back unread. He must find some excuse—

NORA   But Torvald always opens the box at just about this time—

MRS. LINDE   You must stop him. Go in and keep him talking. I'll be back as quickly as I can.

She hurries out through the hall.

NORA [*goes over to Helmer's door, opens it and peeps in*]   Torvald!

HELMER [*offstage*]   Well, may a man enter his own drawing room again? Come on, Rank, now we'll see what— [*In the doorway.*] But what's this?

NORA   What, Torvald dear?

HELMER   Rank's been preparing me for some great transformation scene.

RANK [*in the doorway*]   So I understood. But I seem to have been mistaken.

NORA   Yes, no one's to be allowed to see me before tomorrow night.

HELMER   But, my dear Nora, you look quite worn out. Have you been practising too hard?

NORA   No, I haven't practised at all yet.

HELMER   Well, you must.

NORA   Yes, Torvald, I must, I know. But I can't get anywhere without your help. I've completely forgotten everything.

HELMER   Oh, we'll soon put that to rights.

NORA   Yes, help me, Torvald. Promise me you will? Oh, I'm so nervous. All those people—! You must forget everything except me this evening. You mustn't think of business—I won't even let you touch a pen. Promise me, Torvald?

HELMER   I promise. This evening I shall think of nothing but you—my poor, helpless little darling. Oh, there's just one thing I must see to— [*Goes towards the hall door.*]

NORA   What do you want out there?

HELMER   I'm only going to see if any letters have come.

NORA   No, Torvald, no!

HELMER   Why, what's the matter?

NORA   Torvald, I beg you. There's nothing there.

HELMER   Well, I'll just make sure.

He moves towards the door. Nora runs to the piano and plays the first bars of the tarantella.

HELMER [*at the door, turns*]   Aha!

NORA   I can't dance tomorrow if I don't practise with you now.

HELMER [*goes over to her*]   Are you really so frightened, Nora dear?

NORA   Yes, terribly frightened. Let me start practising now, at once—we've still time before dinner. Oh, do sit down and play for me, Torvald dear. Correct me, lead me, the way you always do.

HELMER   Very well, my dear, if you wish it.

He sits down at the piano. Nora seizes the tambourine and a long multi-coloured shawl from the cardboard box, wraps the latter hastily around her, then takes a quick leap into the center of the room.

NORA   Play for me! I want to dance!

Helmer plays and Nora dances. Dr. Rank stands behind Helmer at the piano and watches her.

HELMER [*as he plays*]   Slower, slower!

NORA   I can't!

HELMER   Not so violently, Nora.

NORA   I must!

HELMER [*stops playing*]   No, no, this won't do at all.

NORA [*laughs and swings her tambourine*]   Isn't that what I told you?

RANK   Let me play for her.

HELMER [*gets up*]   Yes, would you? Then it'll be easier for me to show her.

Rank sits down at the piano and plays. Nora dances more and more wildly. Helmer has stationed himself by the stove and tries repeatedly to correct her, but she seems not to hear him. Her hair works loose and falls over her shoulders; she ignores it and continues to dance. Mrs. Linde enters.

MRS. LINDE [*stands in the doorwary as though tongue-tied*]   Ah—!

NORA [*as she dances*]   Christine, we're having such fun!

HELMER   But, Nora darling, you're dancing as if your life depended on it.

NORA   It does.

HELMER   Rank, stop it! This is sheer lunacy. Stop it, I say!

Rank ceases playing. Nora suddenly stops dancing.

HELMER [*goes over to her*]   I'd never have believed it. You've forgotten everything I taught you.

NORA [*throws away the tambourine*]   You see!

HELMER   I'll have to show you every step.

NORA   You see how much I need you! You must show me every step of the way. Right to the end of the dance. Promise me you will, Torvald?

HELMER   Never fear. I will.

NORA   You mustn't think about anything but me—today or tomorrow. Don't open any letters—don't even open the letter-box—

HELMER   Aha, you're still worried about that fellow—

NORA   Oh, yes, yes, him too.

HELMER   Nora, I can tell from the way you're behaving, there's a letter from him already lying there.

NORA   I don't know. I think so. But you mustn't read it now. I don't want anything ugly to come between us till it's all over.

RANK [*quietly, to Helmer*]   Better give her her way.

HELMER [*puts his arm round her*]   My child shall have her way. But tomorrow night, when your dance is over—

NORA   Then you will be free.

MAID [*appears in the doorway, right*]   Dinner is served, madam.

NORA   Put out some champagne, Helen.

MAID   Very good, madam. [*Goes.*]

HELMER   I say! What's this, a banquet?

NORA   We'll drink champagne until dawn! [*Calls.*] And, Helen! Put out some macaroons! Lots of macaroons—for once!

HELMER [*takes her hands in his*]   Now, now, now. Don't get so excited. Where's my little songbird, the one I know?

NORA All right. Go and sit down—and you too, Dr. Rank. I'll be with you in a minute. Christine, you must help me put my hair up.

RANK [quietly, as they go] There's nothing wrong, is there? I mean, she isn't—er—expecting—?

HELMER Good heavens no, my dear chap. She just gets scared like a child sometimes—I told you before—

They go out right.

NORA Well?

MRS. LINDE He's left town.

NORA I saw it from your face.

MRS. LINDE He'll be back tomorrow evening. I left a note for him.

NORA You needn't have bothered. You can't stop anything now. Anyway, it's wonderful really, in a way—sitting here and waiting for the miracle to happen.

MRS. LINDE Waiting for what?

NORA Oh, you wouldn't understand. Go in and join them. I'll be with you in a moment.

Mrs. Linde goes into the dining-room.

NORA [stands for a moment as though collecting herself. Then she looks at her watch] Five o'clock. Seven hours till midnight. Then another twenty-four hours till midnight tomorrow. And then the tarantella will be finished. Twenty-four and seven? Thirty-one hours to live.

HELMER [appears in the doorway, right] What's happened to my little songbird?

NORA [runs to him with her arms wide] Your songbird is here!

ACT III

The same room. The table which was formerly by the sofa has been moved into the centre of the room; the chairs surround it as before. The door to the hall stands open. Dance music can be heard from the floor above. Mrs. Linde is seated at the table, absent-mindedly glancing through a book. She is trying to read, but seems unable to keep her mind on it. More than once she turns and listens anxiously towards the front door.

MRS. LINDE [looks at her watch] Not here yet. There's not much time left. Please God he hasn't—! [Listens again.] Ah, here he is. [Goes out into the hall and cautiously opens the front door. Footsteps can be heard softly ascending the stairs. She whispers.] Come in. There's no one here.

KROGSTAD [*in the doorway*]   I found a note from you at my lodgings. What does this mean?

MRS. LINDE   I must speak with you.

KROGSTAD   Oh? And must our conversation take place in this house?

MRS. LINDE   We couldn't meet at my place; my room has no separate entrance. Come in. We're quite alone. The maid's asleep, and the Helmers are at the dance upstairs.

KROGSTAD [*comes into the room*]   Well, well! So the Helmers are dancing this evening? Are they indeed?

MRS. LINDE   Yes, why not?

KROGSTAD   True enough. Why not?

MRS. LINDE   Well, Krogstad. You and I must have a talk together.

KROGSTAD   Have we two anything further to discuss?

MRS. LINDE   We have a great deal to discuss.

KROGSTAD   I wasn't aware of it.

MRS. LINDE   That's because you've never really understood me.

KROGSTAD   Was there anything to understand? It's the old story, isn't it—a woman chucking a man because something better turns up?

MRS. LINDE   Do you really think I'm so utterly heartless? You think it was easy for me to give you up?

KROGSTAD   Wasn't it?

MRS. LINDE   Oh, Nils, did you really believe that?

KROGSTAD   Then why did you write to me the way you did?

MRS. LINDE   I had to. Since I had to break with you, I thought it my duty to destroy all the feelings you had for me.

KROGSTAD [*clenches his fists*]   So that was it. And you did this for money!

MRS. LINDE   You mustn't forget I had a helpless mother to take care of, and two little brothers. We couldn't wait for you, Nils. It would have been so long before you'd had enough to support us.

KROGSTAD   Maybe. But you had no right to cast me off for someone else.

MRS. LINDE   Perhaps not. I've often asked myself that.

KROGSTAD [*more quietly*]   When I lost you, it was just as though all solid ground had been swept from under my feet. Look at me. Now I am a shipwrecked man, clinging to a spar.

MRS. LINDE   Help may be near at hand.

KROGSTAD   It was near. But then you came, and stood between it and me.

MRS. LINDE   I didn't know, Nils. No one told me till today that this job I'd found was yours.

KROGSTAD   I believe you, since you say so. But now you know, won't you give it up?

MRS. LINDE   No—because it wouldn't help you even if I did.

KROGSTAD   Wouldn't it? I'd do it all the same.

MRS. LINDE   I've learned to look at things practically. Life and poverty have taught me that.

KROGSTAD And life has taught me to distrust fine words.

MRS. LINDE Then it's taught you a useful lesson. But surely you still believe in actions?

KROGSTAD What do you mean?

MRS. LINDE You said you were like a shipwrecked man clinging to a spar.

KROGSTAD I have good reason to say it.

MRS. LINDE I'm in the same postion as you. No one to care about, no one to care for.

KROGSTAD You made your own choice.

MRS. LINDE I had no choice—then.

KROGSTAD Well?

MRS. LINDE Nils, suppose we two shipwrecked souls could join hands?

KROGSTAD What are you saying?

MRS. LINDE Castaways have a better chance of survival together than on their own.

KROGSTAD Christine!

MRS. LINDE Why do you suppose I came to this town?

KROGSTAD You mean—you came because of me?

MRS. LINDE I must work if I'm to find life worth living. I've always worked, for as long as I can remember; it's been the greatest joy of my life—my only joy. But now I'm alone in the world, and I feel so dreadfully lost and empty. There's no joy in working just for oneself. Oh, Nils, give me something—someone—to work for.

KROGSTAD I don't believe all that. You're just being hysterical and romantic. You want to find an excuse for self-sacrifice.

MRS. LINDE Have you ever known me to be hysterical?

KROGSTAD You mean you really—? Is it possible? Tell me—you know all about my past?

MRS. LINDE Yes.

KROGSTAD And you know what people think of me here?

MRS. LINDE You said just now that with me you might have become a different person.

KROGSTAD I know I could have.

MRS. LINDE Couldn't it still happen?

KROGSTAD Christine—do you really mean this? Yes—you do—I see it in your face. Have you really the courage—?

MRS. LINDE I need someone to be a mother to; and your children need a mother. And you and I need each other. I believe in you, Nils. I am afraid of nothing—with you.

KROGSTAD [clasps her hands] Thank you, Christine—thank you! Now I shall make the world believe in me as you do! Oh—but I'd forgotten—

MRS. LINDE [listens] Ssh! The tarantella! Go quickly, go!

KROGSTAD Why? What is it?

MRS. LINDE   You hear that dance? As soon as it's finished, they'll be coming down.

KROGSTAD   All right, I'll go. It's no good, Christine. I'd forgotten—you don't know what I've just done to the Helmers.

MRS. LINDE   Yes, Nils. I know.

KROGSTAD   And yet you'd still have the courage to—?

MRS. LINDE   I know what despair can drive a man like you to.

KROGSTAD   Oh, if only I could undo this!

MRS. LINDE   You can. Your letter is still lying in the box.

KROGSTAD   Are you sure?

MRS. LINDE   Quite sure. But—

KROGSTAD [looks searchingly at her]   Is that why you're doing this? You want to save your friend at any price? Tell me the truth. Is that the reason?

MRS. LINDE   Nils, a woman who has sold herself once for the sake of others doesn't make the same mistake again.

KROGSTAD   I shall demand my letter back.

MRS. LINDE   No, no.

KROGSTAD   Of course I shall. I shall stay here till Helmer comes down. I'll tell him he must give me back my letter—I'll say it was only to do with my dismissal, and that I don't want him to read it—

MRS. LINDE   No, Nils, you mustn't ask for that letter back.

KROGSTAD   But—tell me—wasn't that the real reason you asked me to come here?

MRS. LINDE   Yes—at first, when I was frightened. But a day has passed since then, and in that time I've seen incredible things happen in this house. Helmer must know the truth. This unhappy secret of Nora's must be revealed. They must come to a full understanding; there must be an end of all these shiftings and evasions.

KROGSTAD   Very well. If you're prepared to risk it. But one thing I can do—and at once—

MRS. LINDE [listens]   Hurry! Go, go! The dance is over. We aren't safe here another moment.

KROGSTAD   I'll wait for you downstairs.

MRS. LINDE   Yes, do. You can see me home.

KROGSTAD   I've never been so happy in my life before!

He goes out through the front door. The door leading from the room into the hall remains open.

MRS. LINDE [tidies the room a little and gets her hat and coat]   What a change! Oh, what a change! Someone to work for—to live for! A home to bring joy into! I won't let this chance of happiness slip through my fingers. Oh, why don't they come? [*Listens.*] Ah, here they are. I must get my coat on.

She takes her hat and coat. Helmer's and Nora's voices become audible outside. A key is turned in the lock and Helmer leads Nora almost forcibly into the hall. She is dressed in an Italian costume with a large black shawl. He is in evening dress, with a black cloak.

NORA [*still in the doorway, resisting him*]   No, no, no—not in here! I want to go back upstairs. I don't want to leave so early.

HELMER   But my dearest Nora—

NORA   Oh, please, Torvald, please! Just another hour!

HELMER   Not another minute, Nora, my sweet. You know what we agreed. Come along, now. Into the drawing-room. You'll catch cold if you stay out here.

He leads her, despite her efforts to resist him, gently into the room.

MRS. LINDE   Good evening.

NORA   Christine!

HELMER   Oh, hullo, Mrs. Linde. You still here?

MRS. LINDE   Please forgive me. I did so want to see Nora in her costume.

NORA   Have you been sitting here waiting for me?

MRS. LINDE   Yes. I got here too late, I'm afraid. You'd already gone up. And I felt I really couldn't go back home without seeing you.

HELMER [*takes off Nora's shawl*]   Well, take a good look at her. She's worth looking at, don't you think? Isn't she beautiful, Mrs. Linde?

MRS. LINDE   Oh, yes, indeed—

HELMER   Isn't she unbelievably beautiful? Everyone at the party said so. But dreadfully stubborn she is, bless her pretty little heart. What's to be done about that? Would you believe it, I practically had to use force to get her away!

NORA   Oh, Torvald, you're going to regret not letting me stay—just half an hour longer.

HELMER   Hear that, Mrs. Linde? She dances her tarantella—makes a roaring success—and very well deserved—though possibly a trifle too realistic—more so than was aesthetically necessary, strictly speaking. But never mind that. Main thing is—she had a success—roaring success. Was I going to let her stay on after that and spoil the impression? No, thank you. I took my beautiful little Capri signorina—my capricious little Capricienne, what?—under my arm—a swift round of the ballroom, a curtsey to the company, and, as they say in novels, the beautiful apparition disappeared! An exit should always be dramatic, Mrs. Linde. But unfortunately that's just what I can't get Nora to realize. I say, it's hot in here. [*Throws his cloak on a chair and opens the door to his study.*] What's this? It's dark in here. Ah, yes, of course—excuse me. [*Goes in and lights a couple of candles.*]

NORA [*whispers swiftly, breathlessly*] Well?

MRS. LINDE [*quietly*] I've spoken to him.

NORA Yes?

MRS. LINDE Nora—you must tell your husband everything.

NORA [*dully*] I knew it.

MRS. LINDE You've nothing to fear from Krogstad. But you must tell him.

NORA I shan't tell him anything.

MRS. LINDE Then the letter will.

NORA Thank you, Christine. Now I know what I must do. Ssh!

HELMER [*returns*] Well, Mrs. Linde, finished admiring her?

MRS. LINDE Yes. Now I must say good night.

HELMER Oh, already? Does this knitting belong to you?

MRS. LINDE [*takes it*] Thank you, yes. I nearly forgot it.

HELMER You knit, then?

MRS. LINDE Why, yes.

HELMER Know what? You ought to take up embroidery.

MRS. LINDE Oh? Why?

HELMER It's much prettier. Watch me, now. You hold the embroidery in your left hand, like this, and then you take the needle in your right hand and go in and out in a slow, easy movement—like this. I am right, aren't I?

MRS. LINDE Yes, I'm sure—

HELMER But knitting, now—that's an ugly business—can't help it. Look— arms all huddled up—great clumsy needles going up and down—makes you look like a damned Chinaman. I say, that really was a magnificent champagne they served us.

MRS. LINDE Well, good night, Nora. And stop being stubborn. Remember!

HELMER Quite right, Mrs. Linde!

MRS. LINDE Good night, Mr. Helmer.

HELMER [*accompanies her to the door*] Good night, good night! I hope you'll manage to get home all right? I'd gladly—but you haven't far to go, have you? Good night, good night. [*She goes. He closes the door behind her and returns.*] Well, we've got rid of her at last. Dreadful bore that woman is!

NORA Aren't you very tired, Torvald?

HELMER No, not in the least.

NORA Aren't you sleepy?

HELMER Not a bit. On the contrary, I feel extraordinarily exhilarated. But what about you? Yes, you look very sleepy and tired.

NORA Yes, I am very tired. Soon I shall sleep.

HELMER You see, you see! How right I was not to let you stay longer!

NORA   Oh, you're always right, whatever you do.

HELMER [*kisses her on the forehead*]   Now my little songbird's talking just like a real big human being. I say, did you notice how cheerful Rank was this evening?

NORA   Oh? Was he? I didn't have a chance to speak with him.

HELMER   I hardly did. But I haven't seen him in such a jolly mood for ages. [*Looks at her for a moment, then comes closer.*] I say, it's nice to get back to one's home again, and be all alone with you. Upon my word, you're a distractingly beautiful young woman.

NORA   Don't look at me like that, Torvald!

HELMER   What, not look at my most treasured possession? At all this wonderful beauty that's mine, mine alone, all mine.

NORA [*goes round to the other side of the table*]   You mustn't talk to me like that tonight.

HELMER [*follows her*]   You've still the tarantella in your blood, I see. And that makes you even more desirable. Listen! Now the other guests are beginning to go. [*More quietly.*] Nora—soon the whole house will be absolutely quiet.

NORA   Yes, I hope so.

HELMER   Yes, my beloved Nora, of course you do! Do you know—when I'm out with you among other people like we were tonight, do you know why I say so little to you, why I keep so aloof from you, and just throw you an occasional glance? Do you know why I do that? It's because I pretend to myself that you're my secret mistress, my clandestine little sweetheart, and that nobody knows there's anything at all between us.

NORA   Oh, yes, yes, yes—I know you never think of anything but me.

HELMER   And then when we're about to go, and I wrap the shawl round your lovely young shoulders, over this wonderful curve of your neck— then I pretend to myself that you are my young bride, that we've just come from the wedding, that I'm taking you to my house for the first time—that, for the first time, I am alone with you—quite alone with you, as you stand there young and trembling and beautiful. All evening I've had no eyes for anyone but you. When I saw you dance the tarantella, like a huntress, a temptress, my blood grew hot, I couldn't stand it any longer! That was why I seized you and dragged you down here with me—

NORA   Leave me, Torvald! Get away from me! I don't want all this.

HELMER   What? Now, Nora, you're joking with me. Don't want, don't want—? Aren't I your husband—?

There is a knock on the front door.

NORA [*starts*]   What was that?

HELMER [*goes towards the hall*]   Who is it?

RANK [*outside*] It's me. May I come in for a moment?

HELMER [*quietly, annoyed*] Oh, what does he want now? [*Calls.*] Wait a moment. [*Walks over and opens the door.*] Well! Nice of you not to go by without looking in.

RANK I thought I heard your voice, so I felt I had to say goodbye. [*His eyes travel swiftly around the room.*] Ah, yes—these dear rooms, how well I know them. What a happy, peaceful home you two have.

HELMER You seemed to be having a pretty happy time yourself upstairs.

RANK Indeed I did. Why not? Why shouldn't one make the most of this world? As much as one can, and for as long as one can. The wine was excellent—

HELMER Especially the champagne.

RANK You noticed that too? It's almost incredible how much I managed to get down.

NORA Torvald drank a lot of champagne too, this evening.

RANK Oh?

NORA Yes. It always makes him merry afterwards.

RANK Well, why shouldn't a man have a merry evening after a well-spent day?

HELMER Well-spent? Oh, I don't know that I can claim that.

RANK [*slaps him across the back*] I can, though, my dear fellow!

NORA Yes, of course, Dr. Rank—you've been carrying out a scientific experiment today, haven't you?

RANK Exactly.

HELMER Scientific experiment! Those are big words for my little Nora to use!

NORA And may I congratulate you on the finding?

RANK You may indeed.

NORA It was good, then?

RANK The best possible finding—both for the doctor and the patient. Certainty.

NORA [*quickly*] Certainty?

RANK Absolute certainty. So aren't I entitled to have a merry evening after that?

NORA Yes, Dr. Rank. You were quite right to.

HELMER I agree. Provided you don't have to regret it tomorrow.

RANK Well, you never get anything in this life without paying for it.

NORA Dr. Rank—you like masquerades, don't you?

RANK Yes, if the disguises are sufficiently amusing.

NORA Tell me. What shall we two wear at the next masquerade?

HELMER You little gadabout! Are you thinking about the next one already?

RANK We two? Yes, I'll tell you. You must go as the Spirit of Happiness—

HELMER You try to think of a costume that'll convey that.

RANK Your wife need only appear as her normal, everyday self—

HELMER   Quite right! Well said! But what are you going to be? Have you decided that?

RANK   Yes, my dear friend. I have decided that.

HELMER   Well?

RANK   At the next masquerade, I shall be invisible.

HELMER   Well, that's a funny idea.

RANK   There's a big, black hat—haven't you heard of the invisible hat? Once it's over your head, no one can see you any more.

HELMER [represses a smile]   Ah yes, of course.

RANK   But I'm forgetting what I came for. Helmer, give me a cigar. One of your black Havanas.

HELMER   With the greatest pleasure. [Offers him the box.]

RANK [takes one and cuts off the tip]   Thank you.

NORA [strikes a match]   Let me give you a light.

RANK   Thank you. [She holds out the match for him. He lights his cigar.] And now—goodbye.

HELMER   Goodbye, my dear chap, goodbye.

NORA   Sleep well, Dr. Rank.

RANK   Thank you for that kind wish.

NORA   Wish me the same.

RANK   You? Very well—since you ask. Sleep well. And thank you for the light. [He nods to them both and goes.]

HELMER [quietly]   He's been drinking too much.

NORA [abstractedly]   Perhaps.

Helmer takes his bunch of keys from his pocket and goes out into the hall.

NORA   Torvald, what do you want out there?

HELMER   I must empty the letter-box. It's absolutely full. There'll be no room for the newspapers in the morning.

NORA   Are you going to work tonight?

HELMER   You know very well I'm not. Hullo, what's this? Someone's been at the lock.

NORA   At the lock—?

HELMER   Yes, I'm sure of it. Who on earth—? Surely not one of the maids? Here's a broken hairpin. Nora, it's yours—

NORA [quickly]   Then it must have been the children.

HELMER   Well, you'll have to break them of that habit. Hm, hm. Ah, that's done it. [Takes out the contents of the box and calls into the kitchen.] Helen! Helen! Put out the light on the staircase. [Comes back into the drawing room with the letters in his hand and closes the door to the hall.] Look at this! You see how they've piled up? [Glances through them.] What on earth's this?

NORA [at the window]   The letter! Oh, no, Torvald, no!

HELMER   Two visiting cards—from Rank.

NORA   From Dr. Rank?

HELMER [*looks at them*]   Peter Rank, M.D. They were on top. He must have dropped them in as he left.

NORA   Has he written anything on them?

HELMER   There's a black cross above his name. Look. Rather gruesome, isn't it? It looks just as though he was announcing his death.

NORA   He is.

HELMER   What? Do you know something? Has he told you anything?

NORA   Yes. When these cards come, it means he's said good-bye to us. He wants to shut himself up in his house and die.

HELMER   Ah, poor fellow. I knew I wouldn't be seeing him for much longer. But so soon—! And now he's going to slink away and hide like a wounded beast.

NORA   When the time comes, it's best to go silently. Don't you think so, Torvald?

HELMER [*walks up and down*]   He was so much a part of our life. I can't realize that he's gone. His suffering and loneliness seemed to provide a kind of dark background to the happy sunlight of our marriage. Well, perhaps it's best this way. For him, anyway. [*Stops walking.*] And perhaps for us too, Nora. Now we have only each other. [*Embraces her.*] Oh, my beloved wife—I feel as though I could never hold you close enough. Do you know, Nora, often I wish some terrible danger might threaten you, so that I could offer my life and my blood, everything, for your sake.

NORA [*tears herself loose and says in a clear, firm voice*]   Read your letters now, Torvald.

HELMER   No, no. Not tonight. Tonight I want to be with you, my darling wife—

NORA   When your friend is about to die—?

HELMER   You're right. This news has upset us both. An ugliness has come between us; thoughts of death and dissolution. We must try to forget them. Until then—you go to your room; I shall go to mine.

NORA [*throws her arms round his neck*]   Good night, Torvald! Good night!

HELMER [*kisses her on the forehead*]   Good night, my darling little songbird. Sleep well, Nora. I'll go and read my letters.

He goes into the study with the letters in his hand, and closes the door.

NORA [*wild-eyed, fumbles around, seizes Helmer's cloak, throws it round herself and whispers quickly, hoarsely*]   Never see him again. Never. Never. Never. [*Throws the shawl over her head.*] Never see the children again. Them too. Never. Never. Oh—the icy black water! Oh—that bottomless—that—! Oh, if only it were all over! Now he's got it—he's reading it. Oh, no, no! Goodbye, Torvald! Goodbye, my darlings!

She turns to run into the hall. As she does so, Helmer throws open his door and stands there with an open letter in his hand.

HELMER   Nora!

NORA *[shrieks]*   Ah—!

HELMER   What is this? Do you know what is in this letter?

NORA   Yes, I know. Let me go! Let me go!

HELMER *[holds her back]*   Go? Where?

NORA *[tries to tear herself loose]*   You mustn't try to save me, Torvald!

HELMER *[staggers back]*   Is it true? Is it true, what he writes? Oh, my God! No, no—it's impossible, it can't be true!

NORA   It *is* true. I've loved you more than anything else in the world.

HELMER   Oh, don't try to make silly excuses.

NORA *[takes a step towards him]*   Torvald—

HELMER   Wretched woman! What have you done?

NORA   Let me go! You're not going to suffer for my sake. I won't let you!

HELMER   Stop being theatrical. *[Locks the front door.]* You're going to stay here and explain yourself. Do you understand what you've done? Answer me! Do you understand?

NORA *[looks unflinchingly at him and, her expression growing colder, says]*   Yes. Now I am beginning to understand.

HELMER *[walking round the room]*   Oh, what a dreadful awakening! For eight whole years—she who was my joy and my pride—a hypocrite, a liar—worse, worse—a criminal! Oh, the hideousness of it! Shame on you, shame!

Nora is silent and stares unblinkingly at him.

HELMER *[stops in front of her]*   I ought to have guessed that something of this sort would happen. I should have foreseen it. All your father's recklessness and instability—be quiet!—I repeat, all your father's recklessness and instability he has handed on to you. No religion, no morals, no sense of duty! Oh, how I have been punished for closing my eyes to his faults! I did it for your sake. And now you reward me like this.

NORA   Yes. Like this.

HELMER   Now you have destroyed all my happiness. You have ruined my whole future. Oh, it's too dreadful to contemplate! I am in the power of a man who is completely without scruples. He can do what he likes with me, demand what he pleases, order me to do anything—I dare not disobey him. I am condemned to humiliation and ruin simply for the weakness of a woman.

NORA   When I am gone from this world, you will be free.

HELMER   Oh, don't be melodramatic. Your father was always ready with that kind of remark. How would it help me if you were "gone from this world," as you put it? It wouldn't assist me in the slightest. He can still make all the facts public; and if he does, I may quite easily be suspected of having been an accomplice in your crime. People may think that I was behind it—that it was I who encouraged you! And for all this I have to thank you, you whom I have carried on my hands through all the years of our marriage! Now do you realize what you've done to me?

NORA [*coldly calm*] Yes.

HELMER It's so unbelievable I can hardly credit it. But we must try to find some way out. Take off that shawl. Take it off, I say! I must try to buy him off somehow. This thing must be hushed up at any price. As regards our relationship—we must appear to be living together just as before. Only *appear*, of course. You will therefore continue to reside here. That is understood. But the children shall be taken out of your hands. I dare no longer entrust them to you. Oh, to have to say this to the woman I once loved so dearly—and whom I still—! Well, all that must be finished. Henceforth there can be no question of happiness; we must merely strive to save what shreds and tatters— [*The front door bell rings. Helmer starts.*] What can that be? At this hour? Surely not—? He wouldn't—? Hide yourself, Nora. Say you're ill.

Nora does not move. Helmer goes to the door of the room and opens it. The Maid is standing half-dressed in the hall.

MAID A letter for madam.

HELMER Give it me. [*Seizes the letter and shuts the door.*] Yes, it's from him. You're not having it. I'll read this myself.

NORA Read it.

HELMER [*by the lamp*] I hardly dare to. This may mean the end for us both. No. I must know. [*Tears open the letter hastily; reads a few lines; looks at a piece of paper which is enclosed with it; utters a cry of joy.*] Nora! [*She looks at him questioningly.*] Nora! No—I must read it once more. Yes, yes, it's true! I am saved! Nora, I am saved!

NORA What about me?

HELMER You too, of course. We're both saved, you and I. Look! He's returning your I.O.U. He writes that he is sorry for what has happened—a happy accident has changed his life—oh, what does it matter what he writes? We are saved, Nora! No one can harm you now. Oh, Nora, Nora—no, first let me destroy this filthy thing. Let me see—! [*Glances at the I.O.U.*] No, I don't want to look at it. I shall merely regard the whole business as a dream. [*He tears the I.O.U. and both letters into pieces, throws them into the stove and watches them burn.*] There. Now they're destroyed. He wrote that ever since Christmas Eve you've been—oh, these must have been three dreadful days for you, Nora.

NORA Yes. It's been a hard fight.

HELMER It must have been terrible—seeing no way out except—no, we'll forget the whole sordid business. We'll just be happy and go on telling ourselves over and over again: "It's over! It's over!" Listen to me, Nora. You don't seem to realize. It's over! Why are you looking so pale? Ah, my poor little Nora, I understand. You can't believe that I have forgiven you. But I have, Nora. I swear it to you. I have forgiven you everything. I know that what you did you did for your love of me.

NORA That is true.

HELMER You have loved me as a wife should love her husband. It was simply that in your inexperience you chose the wrong means. But do you think I love you any the less because you don't know how to act on your own initiative? No, no. Just lean on me. I shall counsel you. I shall guide you. I would not be a true man if your feminine helplessness did not make you doubly attractive in my eyes. You mustn't mind the hard words I said to you in those first dreadful moments when my whole world seemed to be tumbling about my ears. I have forgiven you, Nora. I swear it to you; I have forgiven you.

NORA Thank you for your forgiveness.

She goes out through the door, right.

HELMER No, don't go— [*Looks in.*] What are you doing there?

NORA [*offstage*] Taking off my fancy dress.

HELMER [*by the open door*] Yes, do that. Try to calm yourself and get your balance again, my frightened little songbird. Don't be afraid. I have broad wings to shield you. [*Begins to walk around near the door.*] How lovely and peaceful this little home of ours is, Nora. You are safe here; I shall watch over you like a hunted dove which I have snatched unharmed from the claws of the falcon. Your wildly beating little heart shall find peace with me. It will happen, Nora; it will take time, but it will happen, believe me. Tomorrow all this will seem quite different. Soon everything will be as it was before. I shall no longer need to remind you that I have forgiven you; your own heart will tell you that it is true. Do you really think I could ever bring myself to disown you, or even to reproach you? Ah, Nora, you don't understand what goes on in a husband's heart. There is something indescribably wonderful and satisfying for a husband in knowing that he has forgiven his wife— forgiven her unreservedly, from the bottom of his heart. It means that she has become his property in a double sense; he has, as it were, brought her into the world anew; she is now not only his wife but also his child. From now on that is what you shall be to me, my poor, helpless, bewildered little creature. Never be frightened of anything again, Nora. Just open your heart to me. I shall be both your will and your conscience. What's this? Not in bed? Have you changed?

NORA [*in her everyday dress*]   Yes, Torvald. I've changed.

HELMER   But why now—so late—?

NORA   I shall not sleep tonight.

HELMER   But, my dear Nora—

NORA [*looks at her watch*]   It isn't that late. Sit down here, Torvald. You and I have a lot to talk about.

She sits down on one side of the table.

HELMER   Nora, what does this mean? You look quite drawn—

NORA   Sit down. It's going to take a long time. I've a lot to say to you.

HELMER [*sits down on the other side of the table*]   You alarm me, Nora. I don't understand you.

NORA   No, that's just it. You don't understand me. And I've never understood you—until this evening. No, don't interrupt me. Just listen to what I have to say. You and I have got to face facts, Torvald.

HELMER   What do you mean by that?

NORA [*after a short silence*]   Doesn't anything strike you about the way we're sitting here?

HELMER   What?

NORA   We've been married for eight years. Does it occur to you that this is the first time that we two, you and I, man and wife, have ever had a serious talk together?

HELMER   Serious? What do you mean, serious?

NORA   In eight whole years—no, longer—ever since we first met—we have never exchanged a serious word on a serious subject.

HELMER   Did you expect me to drag you into all my worries—worries you couldn't possibly have helped me with?

NORA   I'm not talking about worries. I'm simply saying that we have never sat down seriously to try to get to the bottom of anything.

HELMER   But, my dear Nora, what on earth has that got to do with you?

NORA   That's just the point. You have never understood me. A great wrong has been done to me, Torvald. First by Papa, and then by you.

HELMER   What? But we two have loved you more than anyone in the world!

NORA [*shakes her head*]   You have never loved me. You just thought it was fun to be in love with me.

HELMER   Nora, what kind of a way is this to talk?

NORA   It's the truth, Torvald. When I lived with Papa, he used to tell me what he thought about everything, so that I never had any opinions but his. And if I did have any of my own, I kept them quiet, because he wouldn't have liked them. He called me his little doll, and he played with me just the way I played with my dolls. Then I came here to live in your house—

HELMER   What kind of a way is that to describe our marriage?

NORA [*undisturbed*]   I mean, then I passed from Papa's hands into yours. You arranged everything the way you wanted it, so that I simply took over your taste in everything—or pretended I did—I don't really know—I think it was a little of both—first one and then the other. Now I look back on it, it's as if I've been living here like a pauper, from hand to mouth. I performed tricks for you, and you gave me food and drink. But that was how you wanted it. You and Papa have done me a great wrong. It's your fault that I have done nothing with my life.

HELMER   Nora, how can you be so unreasonable and ungrateful? Haven't you been happy here?

NORA   No; never. I used to think I was; but I haven't ever been happy.

HELMER   Not—not happy?

NORA   No. I've just had fun. You've always been very kind to me. But our home has never been anything but a playroom. I've been your doll-wife, just as I used to be Papa's doll-child. And the children have been my dolls. I used to think it was fun when you came in and played with me, just as they think it's fun when I go in and play games with them. That's all our marriage has been, Torvald.

HELMER   There may be a little truth in what you say, though you exaggerate and romanticize. But from now on it'll be different. Playtime is over. Now the time has come for education.

NORA   Whose education? Mine or the children's?

HELMER   Both yours and the children's, my dearest Nora.

NORA   Oh, Torvald, you're not the man to educate me into being the right wife for you.

HELMER   How can you say that?

NORA   And what about me? Am I fit to educate the children?

HELMER   Nora!

NORA   Didn't you say yourself a few minutes ago that you dare not leave them in my charge?

HELMER   In a moment of excitement. Surely you don't think I meant it seriously?

NORA   Yes. You were perfectly right. I'm not fitted to educate them. There's something else I must do first. I must educate myself. And you can't help me with that. It's something I must do by myself. That's why I'm leaving you.

HELMER [*jumps up*]   What did you say?

NORA   I must stand on my own feet if I am to find out the truth about myself and about life. So I can't go on living here with you any longer.

HELMER   Nora, Nora!

NORA   I'm leaving you now, at once. Christine will put me up for tonight—

HELMER   You're out of your mind! You can't do this! I forbid you!

NORA   It's no use your trying to forbid me any more. I shall take with me nothing but what is mine. I don't want anything from you, now or ever.

HELMER   What kind of madness is this?

NORA   Tomorrow I shall go home—I mean, to where I was born. It'll be easiest for me to find some kind of a job there.

HELMER   But you're blind! You've no experience of the world—

NORA   I must try to get some, Torvald.

HELMER   But to leave your home, your husband, your children! Have you thought what people will say?

NORA   I can't help that. I only know that I must do this.

HELMER   But this is monstrous! Can you neglect your most sacred duties?

NORA   What do you call my most sacred duties?

HELMER   Do I have to tell you? Your duties towards your husband, and your children.

NORA   I have another duty which is equally sacred.

HELMER   You have not. What on earth could that be?

NORA   My duty towards myself.

HELMER   First and foremost you are a wife and a mother.

NORA   I don't believe that any longer. I believe that I am first and foremost a human being, like you—or anyway, that I must try to become one. I know most people think as you do, Torvald, and I know there's something of the sort to be found in books. But I'm no longer prepared to accept what people say and what's written in books. I must think things out for myself, and try to find my own answer.

HELMER   Do you need to ask where your duty lies in your own home? Haven't you an infallible guide in such matters—your religion?

NORA   Oh, Torvald, I don't really know what religion means.

HELMER   What are you saying?

NORA   I only know what Pastor Hansen told me when I went to confirmation. He explained that religion meant this and that. When I get away from all this and can think things out on my own, that's one of the questions I want to look into. I want to find out whether what Pastor Hansen said was right—or anyway, whether it is right for me.

HELMER   But it's unheard of for so young a woman to behave like this! If religion cannot guide you, let me at least appeal to your conscience. I presume you have some moral feelings left? Or—perhaps you haven't? Well, answer me.

NORA   Oh, Torvald, that isn't an easy question to answer. I simply don't know. I don't know where I am in these matters. I only know that these things mean something quite different to me from what they do to you. I've learned now that certain laws are different from what I'd imagined them to be; but I can't accept that such laws can be right. Has a woman really not the right to spare her dying father pain, or save her husband's life? I can't believe that.

HELMER   You're talking like a child. You don't understand how society works.

NORA   No, I don't. But now I intend to learn. I must try to satisfy myself which is right, society or I.

HELMER   Nora, you're ill; you're feverish. I almost believe you're out of your mind.

NORA   I've never felt so sane and sure in my life.

HELMER   You feel sure that it is right to leave your husband and your children?

NORA   Yes. I do.

HELMER   Then there is only one possible explanation.

NORA   What?

HELMER   That you don't love me any longer.

NORA   No, that's exactly it.

HELMER   Nora! How can you say this to me?

NORA   Oh, Torvald, it hurts me terribly to have to say it, because you've always been so kind to me. But I can't help it. I don't love you any longer.

HELMER   [controlling his emotions with difficulty]   And you feel quite sure about this too?

NORA   Yes, absolutely sure. That's why I can't go on living here any longer.

HELMER   Can you also explain why I have lost your love?

NORA   Yes, I can. It happened this evening, when the miracle failed to happen. It was then that I realized you weren't the man I'd thought you to be.

HELMER   Explain more clearly. I don't understand you.

NORA   I've waited so patiently, for eight whole years—well, good heavens, I'm not such a fool as to suppose that miracles occur every day. Then this dreadful thing happened to me, and then I knew: "Now the miracle will take place!" When Krogstad's letter was lying out there, it never occurred to me for a moment that you would let that man trample over you. I knew that you would say to him: "Publish the facts to the world." And when he had done this—

HELMER   Yes, what then? When I'd exposed my wife's name to shame and scandal—

NORA   Then I was certain that you would step forward and take all the blame on yourself, and say: "I am the one who is guilty!"

HELMER   Nora!

NORA   You're thinking I wouldn't have accepted such a sacrifice from you? No, of course I wouldn't! But what would my word have counted for against yours? That was the miracle I was hoping for, and dreading. And it was to prevent it happening that I wanted to end my life.

HELMER   Nora, I would gladly work for you night and day, and endure sorrow and hardship for your sake. But no man can be expected to sacrifice his honor, even for the person he loves.

NORA   Millions of women have done it.

HELMER   Oh, you think and talk like a stupid child.

NORA   That may be. But you neither think nor talk like the man I could share my life with. Once you'd got over your fright—and you weren't frightened of what might threaten me, but only of what threatened you—once the danger was past, then as far as you were concerned it was exactly as though nothing had happened. I was your little songbird just as before—your doll whom henceforth you would take particular care to protect from the world because she was so weak and fragile. [*Gets up.*] Torvald, in that moment I realized that for eight years I had been living here with a complete stranger, and had borne him three children—! Oh, I can't bear to think of it! I could tear myself to pieces!

HELMER [*sadly*]   I see it, I see it. A gulf has indeed opened between us. Oh, but Nora—couldn't it be bridged?

NORA   As I am now, I am no wife for you.

HELMER   I have the strength to change.

NORA   Perhaps—if your doll is taken from you.

HELMER   But to be parted—to be parted from you! No, no, Nora, I can't conceive of it happening!

NORA [*goes into the room, right*]   All the more necessary that it should happen.

She comes back with her outdoor things and a small traveling-bag, which she puts down on a chair by the table.

HELMER   Nora, Nora, not now! Wait till tomorrow!

NORA [*puts on her coat*]   I can't spend the night in a strange man's house.

HELMER   But can't we live here as brother and sister, then—?

NORA [*fastens her hat*]   You know quite well it wouldn't last. [*Puts on her shawl.*] Goodbye, Torvald. I don't want to see the children. I know they're in better hands than mine. As I am now, I can be nothing to them.

HELMER   But some time, Nora—some time—?

NORA   How can I tell? I've no idea what will happen to me.

HELMER   But you are my wife, both as you are and as you will be.

NORA   Listen, Torvald. When a wife leaves her husband's house, as I'm doing now, I'm told that according to the law he is freed of any obligations towards her. In any case, I release you from any such obligations. You mustn't feel bound to me in any way, however small, just as I shall not feel bound to you. We must both be quite free. Here is your ring back. Give me mine.

HELMER   That too?

NORA   That too.

HELMER   Here it is.

NORA   Good. Well, now it's over. I'll leave the keys here. The servants know about everything to do with the house—much better than I do. Tomorrow, when I have left town, Christine will come to pack the things I brought here from home. I'll have them sent on after me.

HELMER   This is the end then! Nora, will you never think of me any more?

NORA   Yes, of course. I shall often think of you and the children and this house.

HELMER   May I write to you, Nora?

NORA   No. Never. You mustn't do that.

HELMER   But at least you must let me send you—

NORA   Nothing. Nothing.

HELMER   But if you should need help—?

NORA   I tell you, no. I don't accept things from strangers.

HELMER   Nora—can I never be anything but a stranger to you?

NORA   [picks up her bag]   Oh, Torvald! Then the miracle of miracles would have to happen.

HELMER   The miracle of miracles?

NORA   You and I would both have to change so much that—oh, Torvald, I don't believe in miracles any longer.

HELMER   But I want to believe in them. Tell me. We should have to change so much that—?

NORA   That life together between us two could become a marriage. Goodbye.

She goes out through the hall.

HELMER   [sinks down on a chair by the door and buries his face in his hands] Nora! Nora! [Looks round and gets up.] Empty! She's gone! [A hope strikes him.] The miracle of miracles—?

The street door is slammed shut downstairs.

AUGUST STRINDBERG
1849–1912
The Stronger

CHARACTERS

MRS. X., actress, married
MISS Y., actress, unmarried
A WAITRESS

Scene: A corner of a ladies' café (in Stockholm in the eighteen eighties). Two small wrought-iron tables, a red plush settee and a few chairs.

Miss Y. is sitting with a half-empty bottle of beer on the table before her, reading an illustrated weekly which from time to time she exchanges for another.

Mrs. X. enters, wearing a winter hat and coat and carrying a decorative Japanese basket.

MRS. X Why, Millie, my dear, how are you? Sitting here all alone on Christmas Eve like some poor bachelor.

Miss Y. looks up from her magazine, nods, and continues to read.

MRS. X You know it makes me feel really sad to see you. Alone. Alone in a café and on Christmas Eve of all times. It makes me feel as sad as when once in Paris I saw a wedding party at a restaurant. The bride was reading a comic paper and the bridegroom playing billiards with the witnesses. Ah me, I said to myself, with such a beginning how will it go, and how will it end? He was playing billiards on his wedding day! And she, you were going to say, was reading a comic paper on hers. But that's not quite the same.

A waitress brings a cup of chocolate to Mrs. X. and goes out.

MRS. X Do you know, Amelia, I really believe now you would have done better to stick to him. Don't forget I was the first who told you to forgive him. Do you remember? Then you would be married now and have a home. Think how happy you were that Christmas when you stayed with your fiancé's people in the country. How warmly you spoke of domestic happiness! You really quite longed to be out of the theatre. Yes, Amelia

Translated by Elizabeth Sprigge

dear, home is best—next best to the stage, and as for children—but you couldn't know anything about that.

Miss Y.'s expression is disdainful. Mrs. X. sips a few spoonfuls of chocolate, then opens her basket and displays some Christmas presents.

MRS. X   Now you must see what I have bought for my little chicks. [*Takes out a doll.*] Look at this. That's for Lisa. Do you see how she can roll her eyes and turn her head. Isn't she lovely? And here's a toy pistol for Maja.[1] [*She loads the pistol and shoots it at Miss Y., who appears frightened.*]

MRS. X   Were you scared? Did you think I was going to shoot you? Really, I didn't think you'd believe that of me. Now if *you* were to shoot *me* it wouldn't be so surprising, for after all I did get in your way, and I know you never forget it—although I was entirely innocent. You still think I intrigued to get you out of the Grand Theatre, but I didn't. I didn't, however much you think I did. Well, it's no good talking, you will believe it was me . . . [*Takes out a pair of embroidered slippers.*] And these are for my old man, with tulips on them that I embroidered myself. As a matter of fact I hate tulips, but he has to have tulips on everything.

Miss Y. looks up, irony and curiosity in her face.

MRS. X [*putting one hand in each slipper*]   Look what small feet Bob has, hasn't he? And you ought to see the charming way he walks—you've never seen him in slippers, have you?

Miss Y. laughs.

MRS. X   Look, I'll show you. [*She makes the slippers walk across the table, and Miss Y. laughs again.*]

MRS. X.   But when he gets angry, look, he stamps his foot like this. "Those damn girls who can never learn how to make coffee! Blast! That silly idiot hasn't trimmed the lamp properly!" Then there's a draught under the door and his feet get cold. "Hell, it's freezing, and the damn fools can't even keep the stove going!" [*She rubs the sole of one slipper against the instep of the other. Miss Y. roars with laughter.*]

MRS. X.   And then he comes home and has to hunt for his slippers, which Mary has pushed under the bureau . . . Well, perhaps it's not right to make fun of one's husband like this. He's sweet anyhow, and a good, dear husband. You ought to have had a husband like him, Amelia. What are you laughing at? What is it? Eh? And, you see, I know he is faithful to me. Yes, I know it. He told me himself—what *are* you giggling

1. Pronounced Maya

at?—that while I was on tour in Norway that horrible Frederica came and tried to sebuce him. Can you imagine anything more abominable? [*Pause.*] I'd have scratched her eyes out if she had come around while I was at home. [*Pause.*] I'm glad Bob told me about it himself, so I didn't just hear it from gossip. [*Pause.*] And, as a matter of fact, Frederica wasn't the only one. I can't think why, but all the women in the Company seem to be crazy about my husband. They must think his position gives him some say in who is engaged at the Theatre. Perhaps you have run after him yourself? I don't trust you very far, but I know he has never been attracted by you, and you always seemed to have some sort of grudge against him, or so I felt.

Pause. They look at one another guardedly.

MRS. X.   Do come and spend Christmas Eve with us tonight, Amelia—just to show that you're not offended with us, or anyhow not with me. I don't know why, but it seems specially unpleasant not to be friends with you. Perhaps it's because I did get in your way that time . . . [*slowly*] or—I don't know—really, I don't know at all why it is.

Pause. Miss Y. gazes curiously at Mrs. X.

MRS. X.   [*thoughtfully*]   It was so strange when we were getting to know one another. Do you know, when we first met, I was frightened of you, so frightened I didn't dare let you out of my sight. I arranged all my goings and comings to be near you. I dared not be your enemy, so I became your friend. But when you came to our home, I always had an uneasy feeling, because I saw my husband didn't like you, and that irritated me—like when a dress doesn't fit. I did all I could to make him be nice to you, but it was no good—until you went and got engaged. Then you became such tremendous friends that at first it looked as if you only dared show your real feelings then—when you were safe. And then, let me see, how was it after that? I wasn't jealous—that's queer. And I remember at the christening, when you were the godmother, I told him to kiss you. He did, and you were so upset . . . As a matter of fact I didn't notice that then . . . I didn't think about it afterwards either . . . I've never thought about it—until *now!* [*Rises abruptly.*] Why don't you say something? You haven't said a word all this time. You've just let me go on talking. You have sat there with your eyes drawing all these thoughts out of me—they were there in me like silk in a cocoon— thoughts . . . Mistaken thoughts? Let me think. Why did you break off your engagement? Why did you never come to our house after that? Why don't you want to come to us tonight?

Miss Y. makes a motion, as if about to speak.

MRS. X.   No. You don't need to say anything, for now I see it all. That was why—and why—and why. Yes. Yes, that's why it was. Yes, yes, all the pieces fit together now. That's it. I won't sit at the same table as you. [*Moves her things to the other table.*] That's why I have to embroider tulips, which I loathe, on his slippers—because you liked tulips. [*Throws the slippers on the floor.*] That's why we have to spend the summer on the lake—because you couldn't bear the seaside. That's why my son had to be called Eskil—because it was your father's name. That's why I had to wear your colours, read your books, eat the dishes you liked, drink your drinks—your chocolate, for instance. That's why—oh my God, it's terrible to think of, terrible! Everything, everything came to me from you—even your passions. Your soul bored into mine like a worm into an apple, and ate and ate and burrowed and burrowed, till nothing was left but the skin and a little black mould. I wanted to fly from you, but I couldn't. You were there like a snake, your black eyes fascinating me. When I spread my wings, they only dragged me down. I lay in the water with my feet tied together, and the harder I worked my arms, the deeper I sank—down, down, till I reached the bottom, where you lay in waiting like a giant crab to catch me in your claws—and now here I am. Oh how I hate you! I hate you, I hate you! And you just go on sitting there, silent, calm, indifferent, not caring whether the moon is new or full, if it's Christmas or New Year, if other people are happy or unhappy. You don't know how to hate or to love. You just sit there without moving—like a cat at a mouse-hole. You can't drag your prey out, you can't chase it, but you can out-stay it. Here you sit in your corner—you know they call it the rat-trap after you—reading the papers to see if anyone's ruined or wretched or been thrown out of the Company. Here you sit sizing up your victims and weighing your chances—like a pilot his shipwrecks for the salvage. [*Pause.*]Poor Amelia! Do you know, I couldn't be more sorry for you. I know you are miserable, miserable like some wounded creature, and vicious because you are wounded. I can't be angry with you. I should like to be, but after all you are the small one—and as for your affair with Bob, that doesn't worry me in the least. Why should it matter to me? And if you, or somebody else, taught me to drink chocolate, what's the difference? [*Drinks a spoonful. Smugly.*] Chocolate is very wholesome anyhow. And if I learnt from you how to dress, *tant mieux!*—that only gave me a stronger hold over my husband, and you have lost what I gained. Yes, to judge from various signs, I think you have now lost him. Of course, you meant me to walk out, as you once did, and which you're now regretting. But I won't do that, you may be sure. One shouldn't be narrow-minded, you know. And why should nobody else want what I have? [*Pause.*] Perhaps, my dear, taking everything into consideration, at this moment it is I who am the stronger. You never got anything from me, you just gave away—from yourself. And now, like the thief in the night, when you woke up I had what you had lost. Why was it then that everything you touched became worthless and sterile? You couldn't keep a man's love—for all your tulips and your passions—but I could. You couldn't learn the art of living from your books—but I learnt it. You bore no little Eskil, although that was your father's name. [*Pause.*] And why is it you are silent—everywhere, always silent? Yes, I used to think this was strength, but perhaps it was because you hadn't anything to say, because you couldn't think of anything. [*Rises and picks up the slippers.*] Now I am going home, taking the tulips with me—*your* tulips. You couldn't learn from others, you couldn't bend, and so you broke like a dry stick. I did not. Thank you, Amelia, for all your good lessons. Thank you for teaching my husband how to love. Now I am going home—to love him.

Exit.

GEORGE BERNARD SHAW
1856–1950
Arms and the Man

CHARACTERS

MAJOR PAUL PETKOFF
CATHERINE PETKOFF, his wife
RAINA, their daughter
SERGIUS SARANOFF, Major in the Bulgarian army, and Raina's fiancé
CAPTAIN BLUNTSCHLI, a Swiss, officer in the Serbian army
LOUKA, Servant girl
NICOLA, Man-servant
A RUSSIAN OFFICER
A SERBIAN OFFICER

*Action takes place at the Petkoff's home in a small town in Bulgaria from
November 1885 to March 1886.*

ACT I

*Night: A lady's bedchamber in Bulgaria, in a small town near the Dragoman Pass,
late in November in the year 1885. Through an open window with a little balcony
a peak of the Balkans, wonderfully white and beautiful in the starlit snow, seems
quite close at hand, though it is really miles away. The interior of the room is not
like anything to be seen in the west of Europe. It is half rich Bulgarian, half cheap
Viennese. Above the head of the bed, which stands against a little wall cutting off
the left hand corner of the room, is a painted wooden shrine, blue and gold, with
an ivory image of Christ, and a light hanging before it in a pierced metal ball
suspended by three chains. The principal seat, placed towards the other side of the
room and opposite the window, is a Turkish ottoman. The counterpane and
hangings of the bed, the window curtains, the little carpet, and all the ornamental
textile fabrics in the room are oriental and gorgeous; the paper on the walls is
occidental and paltry. The washstand, against the wall on the side nearest the
ottoman and window, consists of an enamelled iron basin with a pail beneath it in
a painted metal frame, and a single towel on the rail at the side. The dressing table,
between the bed and the window, is a common pine table, covered with a cloth of
many colours, with an expensive toilet mirror on it. The door is on the side nearest
the bed; and there is a chest of drawers between. This chest of drawers is also
covered by a variegated native cloth; and on it there is a pile of paper backed
novels, a box of chocolate creams, and a miniature easel with a large photograph
of an extremely handsome officer, whose lofty bearing and magnetic glance can be*

felt even from the portrait. The room is lighted by a candle on the chest of drawers, and another on the dressing table with a box of matches beside it.

The window is hinged doorwise and stands wide open. Outside, a pair of wooden shutters, opening outwards, also stand open. On the balcony a young lady, intensely conscious of the romantic beauty of the night, and of the fact that her own youth and beauty are part of it, is gazing at the snowy Balkans. She is in her nightgown, well covered by a long mantle of furs, worth, on a moderate estimate, about three times the furniture of the room.

Her reverie is interrupted by her mother, Catherine Petkoff, a woman over forty, imperiously energetic, with magnificent black hair and eyes, who might be a very splendid specimen of the wife of a mountain farmer, but is determined to be a Viennese lady, and to that end wears a fashionable tea gown on all occasions.

CATHERINE   [*entering hastily, full of good news*]   Raina! [*She pronounces it Rah-eena, with the stress on the ee.*] Raina! [*She goes to the bed, expecting to find Raina there.*] Why, where—? [*Raina looks into the room.*] Heavens, child! are you out in the night air instead of in your bed? You'll catch your death. Louka told me you were asleep.

RAINA   [*dreamily*]   I sent her away. I wanted to be alone. The stars are so beautiful! What is the matter?

CATHERINE   Such news! There has been a battle.

RAINA   [*her eyes dilating*]   Ah! [*She comes eagerly to Catherine.*]

CATHERINE   A great battle at Slivnitza! A victory! And it was won by Sergius.

RAINA   [*with a cry of delight*]   Ah! [*They embrace rapturously.*] Oh, mother! [*Then, with sudden anxiety*] is father safe?

CATHERINE   Of course! he sends me the news. Sergius is the hero of the hour, the idol of the regiment.

RAINA   Tell me, tell me. How was it? [*Ecstatically*] Oh, mother! mother! mother! [*She pulls her mother down on the ottoman; and they kiss one another frantically.*]

CATHERINE   [*with surging enthusiasm*]   You can't guess how splendid it is. A cavalry charge! think of that! He defied our Russian commanders—acted without orders—led a charge on his own responsibility—headed it himself—was the first man to sweep through their guns. Can't you see it, Raina: our gallant splendid Bulgarians with their swords and eyes flashing, thundering down like an avalanche and scattering the wretched Serbs and their dandified Austrian officers like chaff. And you! you kept Sergius waiting a year before you would be betrothed to him. Oh, if you have a drop of Bulgarian blood in your veins, you will worship him when he comes back.

RAINA   What will he care for my poor little worship after the acclamations of a whole army of heroes? But no matter: I am so happy! so proud! [*She *rises and walks about excitedly.*] It proves that all our ideas were real after all.

CATHERINE [*indignantly*] Our ideas real! What do you mean?

RAINA   Our ideas of what Sergius would do. Our patriotism. Our heroic ideals. I sometimes used to doubt whether they were anything but dreams. Oh, what faithless little creatures girls are! When I buckled on Sergius's sword he looked so noble: it was treason to think of disillusion or humiliation or failure. And yet—and yet—[*She sits down again suddenly.*] Promise me you'll never tell him.

CATHERINE   Don't ask me for promises until I know what I'm promising.

RAINA   Well, it came into my head just as he was holding me in his arms and looking into my eyes, that perhaps we only had our heroic ideas because we are so fond of reading Byron and Pushkin, and because we were so delighted with the opera that season at Bucharest. Real life is so seldom like that! indeed never, as far as I knew it then. [*Remorsefully*] Only think, mother: I doubted him: I wondered whether all his heroic qualities and his soldiership might not prove mere imagination when he went into a real battle. I had an uneasy fear that he might cut a poor figure there beside all those clever officers from the Tsar's court.

CATHERINE   A poor figure! Shame on you! The Serbs have Austrian officers who are just as clever as the Russians; but we have beaten them in every battle for all that.

RAINA [*laughing and snuggling against her mother*] Yes: I was only a prosaic little coward. Oh, to think that it was all true! that Sergius is just as splendid and noble as he looks! that the world is really a glorious world for women who can see its glory and men who can act its romance! What happiness! what unspeakable fulfilment!

They are interrupted by the entry of Louka, a handsome proud girl in a pretty Bulgarian peasant's dress with double apron, so defiant that her servility to Raina is almost insolent. She is afraid of Catherine, but even with her goes as far as she dares.

LOUKA   If you please, madam, all the windows are to be closed and the shutters made fast. They say there may be shooting in the streets. [*Raina and Catherine rise together, alarmed.*] The Serbs are being chased right back through the pass; and they say they may run into the town. Our cavalry will be after them; and our people will be ready for them, you may be sure, now they're running away. [*She goes out on the balcony, and pulls the outside shutters to; then steps back into the room.*]

CATHERINE [*businesslike, housekeeping instincts aroused*]   I must see that everything is made safe downstairs.

RAINA　I wish our people were not so cruel. What glory is there in killing wretched fugitives?

CATHERINE　Cruel! Do you suppose they would hesitate to kill you—or worse?

RAINA　[to Louka] Leave the shutters so that I can just close them if I hear any noise.

CATHERINE　[authoritatively, turning on her way to the door] Oh no, dear: you must keep them fastened. You would be sure to drop off to sleep and leave them open. Make them fast, Louka.

LOUKA　Yes, madam. [She fastens them.]

RAINA　Don't be anxious about me. The moment I hear a shot, I shall blow out the candles and roll myself up in bed with my ears well covered.

CATHERINE　Quite the wisest thing you can do, my love. Good night.

RAINA　Goodnight. [Her emotion comes back for a moment.] Wish me joy. [They kiss.] This is the happiest night of my life—if only there are no fugitives.

CATHERINE　Go to bed, dear; and don't think of them. [She goes out.]

LOUKA　[secretly to Raina] If you would like the shutters open, just give them a push like this [she pushes them: they open; she pulls them to again]. One of them ought to be bolted at the bottom; but the bolt's gone.

RAINA　[with dignity, reproving her] Thanks, Louka; but we must do what we are told. [Louka makes a grimace.] Goodnight.

LOUKA　[carelessly] Goodnight. [She goes out, swaggering.]

Raina, left alone, takes off her fur cloak and throws it on the ottoman. Then she goes to the chest of drawers, and adores the portrait there with feelings that are beyond all expression. She does not kiss it or press it to her breast, or shew it any mark of bodily affection; but she takes it in her hands and elevates it, like a priestess.

RAINA　[looking up at the picture] Oh, I shall never be unworthy of you any more, my soul's hero: never, never, never. [She replaces it reverently. Then she selects a novel from the little pile of books. She turns over the leaves dreamily; finds her page; turns the book inside out at it; and, with a happy sigh, gets into bed and prepares to read herself to sleep. But before abandoning herself to fiction, she raises her eyes once more, thinking of the blessed reality, and murmurs] My hero! my hero!

A distant shot breaks the quiet of the night. She starts, listening; and two more shots, much nearer, follow, startling her so that she scrambles out of bed, and hastily blows out the candle on the chest of drawers. Then, putting her fingers in her ears, she runs to the dressing table, blows out the light there, and hurries back

to bed in the dark, nothing being visible but the glimmer of the light in the pierced
ball before the image, and the starlight seen through the slits at the top of the
shutters. The firing breaks out again: there is a startling fusillade quite close at
hand. Whilst it is still echoing, the shutters disappear, pulled open from without;
and for an instant the rectangle of snowy starlight flashes out with the figure of a
man silhouetted in black upon it. The shutters close immediately; and the room is
dark again. But the silence is now broken by the sound of panting. Then there is a
scratch; and the flame of a match is seen in the middle of the room.

RAINA   [*crouching on the bed*]   Who's there? [*The match is out instantly.*]
Who's there? Who is that?

A MAN'S VOICE   [*in the darkness, subduedly, but threateningly*]   Sh—sh! Don't
call out; or you'll be shot. Be good; and no harm will happen to you. [*She
is heard leaving her bed, and making for the door.*] Take care: it's no use
trying to run away.

RAINA   But who—

THE VOICE   [*warning*]   Remember: if you raise your voice my revolver will go
off. [*Commandingly*] Strike a light and let me see you. Do you hear?
[*Another moment of silence and darkness as she retreats to the chest of
drawers. Then she lights a candle; and the mystery is at an end. He is a man of
about 35, in a deplorable plight, bespattered with mud and blood and snow,
his belt and the strap of his revolver case keeping together the torn ruins of
the blue tunic of a Serbian artillery officer. All that the candlelight and his
unwashed unkempt condition make it possible to discern is that he is of
middling stature and undistinguished appearance, with strong neck and
shoulders, roundish obstinate looking head covered with short crisp bronze
curls, clear quick eyes and good brows and mouth, hopelessly prosaic nose
like that of a strong minded baby, trim soldierlike carriage and energetic
manner, and with all his wits about him in spite of his desperate predicament:
even with a sense of the humor of it, without, however, the least intention of
trifling with it or throwing away a chance. Reckoning up what he can guess
about Raina: her age, her social position, her character, and the extent to
which she is frightened, he continues, more politely but still most determined-
ly*] Excuse my disturbing you; but you recognize my uniform? Serb! If
I'm caught I shall be killed. [*Menacingly*] Do you understand that?

RAINA   Yes.

THE MAN   Well, I don't intend to get killed if I can help it. [*Still more
formidably*] Do you understand that? [*He locks the door quickly but
quietly.*]

RAINA   [*disdainfully*]   I suppose not. [*She draws herself up superbly, and looks
him straight in the face, adding, with cutting emphasis*] Some soldiers, I
know, are afraid to die.

THE MAN   [*with grim goodhumor*]   All of them, dear lady, all of them, believe
me. It is our duty to live as long as we can. Now, if you raise an alarm—

RAINA   [*cutting him short*] You will shoot me. How do you know that *I* am afraid to die?

THE MAN   [*cunningly*] Ah; but suppose I don't shoot you, what will happen then? A lot of your cavalry will burst into this pretty room of yours and slaughter me here like a pig; for I'll fight like a demon: they shan't get me into the street to amuse themselves with: I know what they are. Are you prepared to receive that sort of company in your present undress? [*Raina, suddenly conscious of her nightgown, instinctively shrinks and gathers it more closely about her neck. He watches her and adds pitilessly*] Hardly presentable, eh? [*She turns to the ottoman. He raises his pistol instantly, and cries*] Stop! [*She stops.*] Where are you going?

RAINA   [*with dignified patience*] Only to get my cloak.

THE MAN   [*passing swiftly to the ottoman and snatching the cloak*] A good idea! I'll keep the cloak; and you'll take care that nobody comes in and sees you without it. This is a better weapon than the revolver: eh? [*He throws the pistol down on the ottoman.*]

RAINA   [*revolted*] It is not the weapon of a gentleman!

THE MAN   It's good enough for a man with only you to stand between him and death. [*As they look at one another for a moment, Raina hardly able to believe that even a Serbian officer can be so cynically and selfishly unchivalrous, they are startled by a sharp fusillade in the street. The chill of imminent death hushes the man's voice as he adds*] Do you hear? If you are going to bring those blackguards in on me you shall receive them as you are. [*Clamor and disturbance. The pursuers in the street batter at the house door, shouting*] Open the door! Open the door! Wake up, will you! [*A man servant's voice calls to them angrily from within*] This is Major Petkoff's house: you can't come in here. [*But a renewal of the clamor, and a torrent of blows on the door, end with his letting a chain down with a clank, followed by a rush of heavy footsteps and a din of triumphant yells, dominated at last by the voice of Catherine, indignantly addressing an officer with*] What does this mean, sir? Do you know where you are? [*The noise subsides suddenly.*]

LOUKA   [*outside, knocking at the bedroom door*] My lady! my lady! get up quick and open the door. If you don't they will break it down.

The fugitive throws up his head with the gesture of a man who sees that it is all over with him, and drops the manner he has been assuming to intimidate Raina.

THE MAN   [*sincerely and kindly*] No use, dear: I'm done for. [*Flinging the cloak to her*] Quick! wrap yourself up: they're coming.

RAINA   Oh, thank you. [*She wraps herself up with intense relief.*]

THE MAN   [*between his teeth*] Don't mention it.

RAINA   [*anxiously*] What will you do?

THE MAN   [*grimly*] The first man in will find out. Keep out of the way; and don't look. It won't last long; but it will not be nice. [*He draws his sabre and faces the door, waiting.*]

RAINA   [*impulsively*]   I'll help you. I'll save you.

THE MAN   You can't.

RAINA   I can. I'll hide you. [*She drags him towards the window.*] Here! behind the curtains.

THE MAN   [*yielding to her*]   There's just half a chance, if you keep your head.

RAINA   [*drawing the curtain before him*]   S-sh! [*She makes for the ottoman.*]

THE MAN   [*putting out his head*]   Remember—

RAINA   [*running back to him*]   Yes?

THE MAN   —nine soldiers out of ten are born fools.

RAINA   Oh! [*She draws the curtain angrily before him.*]

THE MAN   [*looking out at the other side*]   If they find me, I promise you a fight: a devil of a fight.

She stamps at him. He disappears hastily. She takes off her cloak, and throws it across the foot of the bed. Then, with a sleepy, disturbed air, she opens the door. Louka enters excitedly.

LOUKA   One of those beasts of Serbs has been seen climbing up the waterpipe to your balcony. Our men want to search for him; and they are so wild and drunk and furious. [*She makes for the other side of the room to get as far from the door as possible.*] My lady says you are to dress at once and to— [*She sees the revolver lying on the ottoman, and stops, petrified.*]

RAINA   [*as if annoyed at being disturbed*]   They shall not search here. Why have they been let in?

CATHERINE   [*coming in hastily*]   Raina, darling, are you safe? Have you seen anyone or heard anything?

RAINA   I heard the shooting. Surely the soldiers will not dare come in here?

CATHERINE   I have found a Russian officer, thank Heaven: he knows Sergius. [*Speaking through the door to someone outside*] Sir: will you come in now. My daughter will receive you.

A young Russian officer, in Bulgarian uniform, enters, sword in hand.

OFFICER   [*with soft feline politeness and stiff military carriage*]   Good evening, gracious lady. I am sorry to intrude; but there is a Serb hiding on the balcony. Will you and the gracious lady your mother please to withdraw whilst we search?

RAINA   [*petulantly*]   Nonsense, sir: you can see that there is no one on the balcony. [*She throws the shutters wide open and stands with her back to the curtain where the man is hidden, pointing to the moonlit balcony. A couple of shots are fired right under the window; and a bullet shatters the glass opposite*

Raina, who winks and gasps, but stands her ground; whilst Catherine screams, and the officer, with a cry of Take care! *rushes to the balcony.]*

THE OFFICER [*on the balcony, shouting savagely down to the street*] Cease firing there, you fools: do you hear? Cease firing, damn you! [*He glares down for a moment; then turns to Raina, trying to resume his polite manner.*] Could anyone have got in without your knowledge? Were you asleep?

RAINA No: I have not been to bed.

THE OFFICER [*impatiently, coming back into the room*] Your neighbors have their heads so full of runaway Serbs that they see them everywhere. [*Politely*] Gracious lady: a thousand pardons. Goodnight. [*Military bow, which Raina returns coldly. Another to Catherine, who follows him out.*]

Raina closes the shutters. She turns and sees Louka, who has been watching the scene curiously.

RAINA Don't leave my mother, Louka, until the soldiers go away.

Louka glances at Raina, at the ottoman, at the curtain; then purses her lips secretively, laughs insolently, and goes out. Raina, highly offended by this demonstration, follows her to the door, and shuts it behind her with a slam, locking it violently. The man immediately steps out from behind the curtain, sheathing his sabre. Then, dismissing the danger from his mind in a businesslike way, he comes affably to Raina.

THE MAN A narrow shave; but a miss is as good as a mile. Dear young lady: your servant to the death. I wish for your sake I had joined the Bulgarian army instead of the other one. I am not a native Serb.

RAINA [*haughtily*] No: you are one of the Austrians who set the Serbs on to rob us of our national liberty, and who officer their army for them. We hate them!

THE MAN Austrian! not I. Don't hate me, dear young lady. I am a Swiss, fighting merely as a professional soldier. I joined the Serbs because they came first on the road from Switzerland. Be generous: you've beaten us hollow.

RAINA Have I not been generous?

THE MAN Noble! Heroic! But I'm not saved yet. This particular rush will soon pass through; but the pursuit will go on all night by fits and starts. I must take my chance to get off in a quiet interval. [*Pleasantly*] You don't mind my waiting just a minute or two, do you?

RAINA [*putting on her most genteel society manner*] Oh, not at all. Won't you sit down?

THE MAN Thanks. [*He sits on the foot of the bed.*]

Raina walks with studied elegance to the ottoman and sits down. Unfortunately she sits on the pistol, and jumps up with a shriek. The man, all nerves, shies like a frightened horse to the other side of the room.

THE MAN   [*irritably*] Don't frighten me like that. What is it?

RAINA   Your revolver! It was staring that officer in the face all the time. What an escape!

THE MAN   [*vexed at being unnecessarily terrified*] Oh, is that all?

RAINA   [*staring at him rather superciliously as she conceives a poorer and poorer opinion of him, and feels proportionately more and more at her ease*] I am sorry I frightened you. [*She takes up the pistol and hands it to him.*] Pray take it to protect yourself against me.

THE MAN   [*grinning wearily at the sarcasm as he takes the pistol*] No use, dear young lady: there's nothing in it. It's not loaded. [*He makes a grimace at it, and drops it disparingly into his revolver case.*]

RAINA   Load it by all means.

THE MAN   I've no ammunition. What use are cartridges in battle? I always carry chocolate instead; and I finished the last cake of that hours ago.

RAINA   [*outraged in her most cherished ideals of manhood*] Chocolate! Do you stuff your pockets with sweets—like a schoolboy—even in the field?

THE MAN   [*grinning*] Yes: isn't it contemptible? [*Hungrily*] I wish I had some now.

RAINA   Allow me. [*She sails away scornfully to the chest of drawers, and returns with the box of confectionery in her hand.*] I am sorry I have eaten them all except these. [*She offers him the box.*]

THE MAN   [*ravenously*] You're an angel! [*He gobbles the contents.*] Creams! Delicious! [*He looks anxiously to see whether there are any more. There are none: he can only scrape the box with his fingers and suck them. When that nourishment is exhausted he accepts the inevitable with pathetic goodhumor, and says, with grateful emotion*] Bless you, dear lady! You can always tell an old soldier by the inside of his holsters and cartridge boxes. The young ones carry pistols and cartridges: the old ones, grub. Thank you. [*He hands back the box. She snatches it contemptuously from him and throws it away. He shies again, as if she had meant to strike him.*] Ugh! Don't do things so suddenly, gracious lady. It's mean to revenge yourself because I frightened you just now.

RAINA   [*loftily*] Frighten me! Do you know, sir, that though I am only a woman, I think I am at heart as brave as you.

THE MAN   I should think so. You haven't been under fire for three days as I have. I can stand two days without shewing it much; but no man can stand three days: I'm as nervous as a mouse. [*He sits down on the ottoman, and takes his head in his hands.*] Would you like to see me cry?

RAINA   [*alarmed*] No.

THE MAN   If you would, all you have to do is to scold me just as if I were a
little boy and you my nurse. If I were in camp now, they'd play all sorts
of tricks on me.

RAINA   [a little moved] I'm sorry. I won't scold you. [Touched by the sympathy
in her tone, he raises his head and looks gratefully at her: she immediately
draws back and says stiffly] You must excuse me: our soldiers are not like
that. [She moves away from the ottoman.]

THE MAN   Oh yes they are. There are only two sorts of soldiers: old ones and
young ones. I've served fourteen years: half of your fellows never smelt
powder before. Why, how is it that you've just beaten us? Sheer
ignorance of the art of war, nothing else. [Indignantly] I never saw
anything so unprofessional.

RAINA   [ironically] Oh! was it unprofessional to beat you!

THE MAN   Well, come! is it professional to throw a regiment of cavalry on a
battery of machine guns, with the dead certainty that if the guns go off
not a horse or man will ever get within fifty yards of the fire? I couldn't
believe my eyes when I saw it.

RAINA   [eagerly turning to him, as all her enthusiasm and her dreams of glory
rush back on her] Did you see the great cavalry charge? Oh, tell me about
it. Describe it to me.

THE MAN   You never saw a cavalry charge, did you?

RAINA   How could I?

THE MAN   Ah, perhaps not. No: of course not! Well, it's a funny sight. It's
like slinging a handful of peas against a window pane: first one comes;
then two or three close behind him; and then all the rest in a lump.

RAINA   [her eyes dilating as she raises her clasped hands ecstatically] Yes, first
One! the bravest of the brave!

THE MAN   [prosaically] Hm! you should see the poor devil pulling at his
horse.

RAINA   Why should he pull at his horse?

THE MAN   [impatient of so stupid a question] It's running away with him, of
course: do you suppose the fellow wants to get there before the others
and be killed? Then they all come. You can tell the young ones by their
wildness and their slashing. The old ones come bunched up under the
number one guard: they know that they're mere projectiles, and that it's
no use trying to fight. The wounds are mostly broken knees, from the
horses cannoning together.

RAINA   Ugh! But I don't believe the first man is a coward. I know he is a
hero!

THE MAN   [goodhumoredly] That's what you'd have said if you'd seen the
first man in the charge today.

RAINA   [breathless, forgiving him everything] Ah, I knew it! Tell me. Tell me
about him.

THE MAN   He did it like an operatic tenor. A regular handsome fellow, with flashing eyes and lovely moustache, shouting his war-cry and charging like Don Quixote at the windmills. We did laugh.

RAINA   You dared to laugh!

THE MAN   Yes; but when the sergeant ran up as white as a sheet, and told us they'd sent us the wrong ammunition, and that we couldn't fire a round for the next ten minutes, we laughed at the other side of our mouths. I never felt so sick in my life; though I've been in one or two very tight places. And I hadn't even a revolver cartridge: only chocolate. We'd no bayonets: nothing. Of course, they just cut us to bits. And there was Don Quixote flourishing like a drum major, thinking he'd done the cleverest thing ever known, whereas he ought to be courtmartialled for it. Of all the fools ever let loose on a field of battle, that man must be the very maddest. He and his regiment simply committed suicide; only the pistol missed fire: that's all.

RAINA   [deeply wounded, but steadfastly loyal to her ideals] Indeed! Would you know him again if you saw him?

THE MAN   Shall I ever forget him!

She again goes to the chest of drawers. He watches her with a vague hope that she may have something more for him to eat. She takes the portrait from its stand and brings it to him.

RAINA   That is a photograph of the gentleman—the patriot and hero—to whom I am betrothed.

THE MAN   [recognizing it with a shock] I'm really very sorry. [Looking at her] Was it fair to lead me on? [He looks at the portrait again.] Yes: that's Don Quixote: not a doubt of it. [He stifles a laugh.]

RAINA   [quickly] Why do you laugh?

THE MAN   [apologetic, but still greatly tickled] I didn't laugh, I assure you. At least I didn't mean to. But when I think of him charging the windmills and imagining he was doing the finest thing— [He chokes with suppressed laughter.]

RAINA   [sternly] Give me back the portrait, sir.

THE MAN   [with sincere remorse] Of course. Certainly. I'm really very sorry. [He hands her the picture. She deliberately kisses it and looks him straight in the face before returning to the chest of drawers to replace it. He follows her, apologizing.] Perhaps I'm quite wrong, you know: no doubt I am. Most likely he had got wind of the cartridge business somehow, and knew it was a safe job.

RAINA   That is to say, he was a pretender and a coward! You did not dare say that before.

THE MAN   [with a comic gesture of despair] It's no use, dear lady: I can't make you see it from the professional point of view. [As he turns away to get back to the ottoman, a couple of distant shots threaten renewed trouble.]

RAINA [*sternly, as she sees him listening to the shots*] So much the better for you!

THE MAN [*turning*] How?

RAINA You are my enemy; and you are at my mercy. What would I do if I were a professional soldier?

THE MAN Ah, true, dear young lady: you're always right. I know how good you've been to me: to my last hour I shall remember those three chocolate creams. It was unsoldierly; but it was angelic.

RAINA [*coldly*] Thank you. And now I will do a soldierly thing. You cannot stay here after what you have just said about my future husband; but I will go out on the balcony and see whether it is safe for you to climb down into the street. [*She turns to the window.*]

THE MAN [*changing countenance*] Down that waterpipe! Stop! Wait! I can't! I daren't! The very thought of it makes me giddy. I came up it fast enough with death behind me. But to face it now in cold blood—! [*He sinks on the ottoman.*] It's no use: I give up: I'm beaten. Give the alarm. [*He drops his head on his hands in the deepest dejection.*]

RAINA [*disarmed by pity*] Come: don't be disheartened. [*She stoops over him almost maternally: he shakes his head.*] Oh, you are a very poor soldier: a chocolate cream soldier! Come, cheer up! it takes less courage to climb down than to face capture: remember that.

THE MAN [*dreamily, lulled by her voice*] No: capture only means death; and death is sleep: oh, sleep, sleep, sleep, undisturbed sleep! Climbing down the pipe means doing something—exerting myself—thinking! Death ten times over first.

RAINA [*softly and wonderingly, catching the rhythm of his weariness*] Are you as sleepy as that?

THE MAN I've not had two hours undisturbed sleep since I joined. I haven't closed my eyes for forty-eight hours.

RAINA [*at her wit's end*] But what am I to do with you?

THE MAN [*staggering up, roused by her desperation*] Of course. I must do something. [*He shakes himself; pulls himself together; and speaks with rallied vigor and courage.*] You see, sleep or no sleep, hunger or no hunger, tired or not tired, you can always do a thing when you know it must be done. Well, that pipe must be got down: [*he hits himself on the chest*] do you hear that, you chocolate cream soldier? [*He turns to the window.*]

RAINA [*anxiously*] But if you fall?

THE MAN I shall sleep as if the stones were a feather bed. Goodbye. [*He makes boldly for the window; and his hand is on the shutter when there is a terrible burst of firing in the street beneath.*]

RAINA [*rushing to him*] Stop! [*She seizes him recklessly, and pulls him quite round.*] They'll kill you.

THE MAN [*coolly, but attentively*] Never mind: this sort of thing is all in my day's work. I'm bound to take my chance. [*Decisively*] Now do what I tell you. Put out the candle; so that they shan't see the light when I open the shutters. And keep away from the window, whatever you do. If they see me they're sure to have a shot at me.

RAINA [*clinging to him*] They're sure to see you: it's bright moonlight. I'll save you. Oh, how can you be so indifferent! You want me to save you, don't you?

THE MAN I really don't want to be troublesome. [*She shakes him in her impatience.*] I am not indifferent, dear young lady, I assure you. But how is it to be done?

RAINA Come away from the window. [*She takes him firmly back to the middle of the room. The moment she releases him he turns mechanically towards the window again. She seizes him and turns him back, exclaiming*] Please! [*He becomes motionless, like a hypnotized rabbit, his fatigue gaining fast on him. She releases him, and addresses him patronizingly.*] Now listen. You must trust to our hospitality. You do not yet know in whose house you are. I am a Petkoff.

THE MAN A pet what?

RAINA [*rather indignantly*] I mean that I belong to the family of the Petkoffs, the richest and best known in our country.

THE MAN Oh yes, of course. I beg your pardon. The Petkoffs, to be sure. How stupid of me!

RAINA You know you never heard of them until this moment. How can you stoop to pretend!

THE MAN Forgive me: I'm too tired to think; and the change of subject was too much for me. Don't scold me.

RAINA I forgot. It might make you cry. [*He nods, quite seriously. She pouts and then resumes her patronizing tone.*] I must tell you that my father holds the highest command of any Bulgarian in our army. He is [*proudly*] a Major.

THE MAN [*pretending to be deeply impressed*] A Major! Bless me! Think of that!

RAINA You shewed great ignorance in thinking that it was necessary to climb up to the balcony because ours is the only private house that has two rows of windows. There is a flight of stairs inside to get up and down by.

THE MAN Stairs! How grand! You live in great luxury indeed, dear young lady.

RAINA Do you know what a library is?

THE MAN A library? A roomful of books?

RAINA Yes. We have one, the only one in Bulgaria.

THE MAN Actually a real library! I should like to see that.

RAINA [*affectedly*] I tell you these things to shew you that you are not in the house of ignorant country folk who would kill you the moment they saw your Serbian uniform, but among civilized people. We go to Bucharest every year for the opera season; and I have spent a whole month in Vienna.

THE MAN   I saw that, dear young lady. I saw at once that you knew the world.

RAINA   Have you ever seen the opera of Ernani?

THE MAN   Is that the one with the devil in it in red velvet, and a soldiers' chorus?

RAINA   [contemptuously]   No!

THE MAN   [stifling a heavy sigh of weariness]   Then I don't know it.

RAINA   I thought you might have remembered the great scene where Ernani, flying from his foes just as you are tonight, takes refuge in the castle of his bitterest enemy, an old Castilian noble. The noble refuses to give him up. His guest is sacred to him.

THE MAN   [quickly, waking up a little]   Have your people got that notion?

RAINA   [with dignity]   My mother and I can understand that notion, as you call it. And if instead of threatening me with your pistol as you did you had simply thrown yourself as a fugitive on our hospitality, you would have been as safe as in your father's house.

THE MAN   Quite sure?

RAINA   [turning her back on him in disgust]   Oh, it is useless to try to make you understand.

THE MAN   Don't be angry: you see how awkward it would be for me if there was any mistake. My father is a very hospitable man: he keeps six hotels; but I couldn't trust him as far as that. What about your father?

RAINA   He is away at Slivnitza fighting for his country. I answer for your safety. There is my hand in pledge of it. Will that reassure you? [She offers him her hand.]

THE MAN   [looking dubiously at his own hand]   Better not touch my hand, dear young lady. I must have a wash first.

RAINA   [touched]   That is very nice of you. I see that you are a gentleman.

THE MAN   [puzzled]   Eh?

RAINA   You must not think I am surprised. Bulgarians of really good standing—people in our position—wash their hands nearly every day. So you see I can appreciate your delicacy. You may take my hand. [She offers it again.]

THE MAN   [kissing it with his hands behind his back]   Thanks, gracious young lady: I feel safe at last. And now would you mind breaking the news to your mother? I had better not stay here secretly longer than is necessary.

RAINA   If you will be so good as to keep perfectly still whilst I am away.

THE MAN   Certainly. [He sits down on the ottoman.]

Raina goes to the bed and wraps herself in the fur cloak. His eyes close. She goes to the door. Turning for a last look at him, she sees that he is dropping off to sleep.

RAINA [*at the door*] You are not going asleep, are you? [*He murmurs inarticulately: she runs to him and shakes him.*] Do you hear? Wake up: you are falling asleep.

THE MAN Eh? Falling aslee—? Oh no: not the least in the world: I was only thinking. It's all right: I'm wide awake.

RAINA [*severely*] Will you please stand up while I am away. [*He rises reluctantly.*] All the time, mind.

THE MAN [*standing unsteadily*] Certainly. Certainly: you may depend on me.

Raina looks doubtfully at him. He smiles weakly. She goes reluctantly, turning again at the door, and almost catching him in the act of yawning. She goes out.

THE MAN [*drowsily*] Sleep, sleep, sleep, sleep, slee—[*The words trail off into a murmur. He wakes again with a shock on the point of falling.*] Where am I? That's what I want to know: where am I? Must keep awake. Nothing keeps me awake except danger: remember that: [*intently*] danger, danger, danger, dan—[*trailing off again: another shock*] Where's danger? Mus' find it. [*He starts off vaguely round the room in search of it.*] What am I looking for? Sleep—danger—don't know. [*He stumbles against the bed.*] Ah yes: now I know. All right now. I'm to go to bed, but not to sleep. Be sure not to sleep, because of danger. Not to lie down either, only sit down. [*He sits on the bed. A blissful expression comes into his face.*] Ah! [*With a happy sigh he sinks back at full length; lifts his boots into the bed with a final effort; and falls fast asleep instantly.*]

Catherine comes in, followed by Raina.

RAINA [*looking at the ottoman*] He's gone! I left him here.

CATHERINE Here! Then he must have climbed down from the—

RAINA [*seeing him*] Oh! [*She points.*]

CATHERINE [*scandalized*] Well! [*She strides to the bed, Raina following until she is opposite her on the other side.*] He's fast asleep. The brute!

RAINA [*anxiously*] Sh!

CATHERINE [*shaking him*] Sir! [*Shaking him again, harder*] Sir!! [*Vehemently, shaking very hard*] Sir!!!

RAINA [*catching her arm*] Don't, mamma; the poor darling is worn out. Let him sleep.

CATHERINE [*letting him go, and turning amazed to Raina*] The poor darling! Raina!!! [*She looks sternly at her daughter.*]

The man sleeps profoundly.

ACT II

The sixth of March, 1886. In the garden of Major Petkoff's house. It is a fine spring morning: the garden looks fresh and pretty. Beyond the paling the tops of a couple of minarets can be seen, shewing that there is a valley there, with the little town in it. A few miles further the Balkan mountains rise and shut in the landscape. Looking towards them from within the garden, the side of the house is seen on the left, with a garden door reached by a little flight of steps. On the right the stable yard, with its gateway, encroaches on the garden. There are fruit bushes along the paling and house, covered with washing spread out to dry. A path runs by the house, and rises by two steps at the corner, where it turns out of sight. In the middle, a small table, with two bent-wood chairs at it, is laid for breakfast with Turkish coffee pot, cups, rolls, etc.; but the cups have been used and the bread broken. There is a wooden garden seat against the wall on the right.

Louka, smoking a cigaret, is standing between the table and the house, turning her back with angry disdain on a man servant who is lecturing her. He is a middle-aged man of cool temperament and low but clear and keen intelligence, with the complacency of the servant who values himself on his rank in servitude, and the imperturbability of the accurate calculator who has no illusions. He wears a white Bulgarian costume: jacket with embroidered border, sash, wide knicker-bockers, and decorated gaiters. His head is shaved up to the crown, giving him a high Japanese forehead. His name is Nicola.

NICOLA   Be warned in time, Louka: mend your manners. I know the mistress. She is so grand that she never dreams that any servant could dare be disrespectful to her; but if she once suspects that you are defying her, out you go.

LOUKA   I do defy her. I will defy her. What do I care for her?

NICOLA   If you quarrel with the family, I never can marry you. It's the same as if you quarrelled with me!

LOUKA   You take her part against me, do you?

NICOLA   [*sedately*]   I shall always be dependent on the good will of the family. When I leave their service and start a shop in Sofia, their custom will be half my capital: their bad word would ruin me.

LOUKA   You have no spirit. I should like to catch them saying a word against me!

NICOLA   [*pityingly*]   I should have expected more sense from you, Louka. But you're young: you're young!

LOUKA   Yes; and you like me the better for it, don't you? But I know some family secrets they wouldn't care to have told, young as I am. Let them quarrel with me if they dare!

NICOLA   [*with compassionate superiority*]   Do you know what they would do if they heard you talk like that?

LOUKA   What could they do?

NICOLA   Discharge you for untruthfulness. Who would believe any stories you told after that? Who would give you another situation? Who in this house would dare be seen speaking to you ever again? How long would your father be left on his little farm? [*She impatiently throws away the end of her cigaret, and stamps on it.*] Child: you don't know the power such high people have over the like of you and me when we try to rise out of our poverty against them. [*He goes close to her and lowers his voice.*] Look at me, ten years in their service. Do you think I know no secrets? I know things about the mistress that she wouldn't have the master know for a thousand levas. I know things about him that she wouldn't let him hear the last of for six months if I blabbed them to her. I know things about Raina that would break off her match with Sergius if—

LOUKA   [*turning on him quickly*]   How do you know? I never told you!

NICOLA   [*opening his eyes cunningly*]   So that's your little secret, is it? I thought it might be something like that. Well, you take my advice and be respectful; and make the mistress feel that no matter what you know or don't know, she can depend on you to hold your tongue and serve the family faithfully. That's what they like; and that's how you'll make most out of them.

LOUKA   [*with searching scorn*]   You have the soul of a servant, Nicola.

NICOLA   [*complacently*]   Yes: that's the secret of success in service.

A loud knocking with a whip handle on a wooden door is heard from the stable yard.

MALE VOICE OUTSIDE   Hollo! Hollo there! Nicola!

LOUKA   Master! back from the war!

NICOLA   [*quickly*]   My word for it, Louka, the war's over. Off with you and get some fresh coffee. [*He runs out into the stable yard.*]

LOUKA   [*as she collects the coffee pot and cups on the tray, and carries it into the house*]   You'll never put the soul of a servant into me.

Major Petkoff comes from the stable yard, followed by Nicola. He is a cheerful, excitable, insignificant, unpolished man of about 50, naturally unambitious except as to his income and his importance in local society, but just now greatly pleased with the military rank which the war has thrust on him as a man of consequence in his town. The fever of plucky patriotism which the Serbian attack roused in all the Bulgarians has pulled him through the war; but he is obviously glad to be home again.

PETKOFF   [*pointing to the table with his whip*]   Breakfast out here, eh?

NICOLA   Yes, sir. The mistress and Miss Raina have just gone in.

PETKOFF   [*sitting down and taking a roll*]   Go in and say I've come; and get me some fresh coffee.

NICOLA   It's coming, sir. [*He goes to the house door. Louka, with fresh coffee, a clean cup, and a brandy bottle on her tray, meets him.*] Have you told the mistress?

LOUKA   Yes: she's coming.

Nicola goes into the house. Louka brings the coffee to the table.

PETKOFF   Well: the Serbs haven't run away with you, have they?

LOUKA   No, sir.

PETKOFF   That's right. Have you brought me some cognac?

LOUKA   [*putting the bottle on the table*] Here, sir.

PETKOFF   That's right. [*He pours some into his coffee.*]

Catherine, who, having at this early hour made only a very perfunctory toilet, wears a Bulgarian apron over a once brilliant but now half worn-out dressing gown, and a colored handkerchief tied over her thick black hair, comes from the house with Turkish slippers on her bare feet, looking astonishingly handsome and stately under all the circumstances. Louka goes into the house.

CATHERINE   My dear Paul: what a surprise for us! [*She stoops over the back of his chair to kiss him.*] Have they brought you fresh coffee?

PETKOFF   Yes: Louka's been looking after me. The war's over. The treaty was signed three days ago at Bucharest; and the decree for our army to demobilize was issued yesterday.

CATHERINE   [*springing erect, with flashing eyes*] Paul: have you let the Austrians force you to make peace?

PETKOFF   [*submissively*] My dear: they didn't consult me. What could *I* do? [*She sits down and turns away from him.*] But of course we saw to it that the treaty was an honorable one. It declares peace—

CATHERINE   [*outraged*] Peace!

PETKOFF   [*appeasing her*] —but not friendly relations: remember that. They wanted to put that in; but I insisted on its being struck out. What more could I do?

CATHERINE   You could have annexed Serbia and made Prince Alexander Emperor of the Balkans. That's what I would have done.

PETKOFF   I don't doubt it in the least, my dear. But I should have had to subdue the whole Austrian Empire first; and that would have kept me too long away from you. I missed you greatly.

CATHERINE   [*relenting*] Ah! [*She stretches her hand affectionately across the table to squeeze his.*]

PETKOFF   And how have you been, my dear?

CATHERINE   Oh, my usual sore throats: that's all.

PETKOFF   [*with conviction*] That comes from washing your neck every day. I've often told you so.

CATHERINE   Nonsense, Paul!

PETKOFF   [over his coffee and cigaret]   I don't believe in going too far with these modern customs. All this washing can't be good for the health: it's not natural. There was an Englishman at Philippopolis who used to wet himself all over with cold water every morning when he got up. Disgusting! It all comes from the English: their climate makes them so dirty that they have to be perpetually washing themselves. Look at my father! he never had a bath in his life; and he lived to be ninety-eight, the healthiest man in Bulgaria. I don't mind a good wash once a week to keep up my position; but once a day is carrying the thing to a ridiculous extreme.

CATHERINE   You are a barbarian at heart still, Paul. I hope you behaved yourself before all those Russian officers.

PETKOFF   I did my best. I took care to let them know that we have a library.

CATHERINE   Ah; but you didn't tell them that we have an electric bell in it? I have had one put up.

PETKOFF   What's an electric bell?

CATHERINE   You touch a button; something tinkles in the kitchen; and then Nicola comes up.

PETKOFF   Why not shout for him?

CATHERINE   Civilized people never shout for their servants. I've learnt that while you were away.

PETKOFF   Well, I'll tell you something I've learnt too. Civilized people don't hang out their washing to dry where visitors can see it; so you'd better have all that [indicating the clothes on the bushes] put somewhere else.

CATHERINE   Oh, that's absurd, Paul: I don't believe really refined people notice such things.

SERGIUS   [knocking at the stable gates]   Gate, Nicola!

PETKOFF   There's Sergius. [Shouting] Hollo, Nicola!

CATHERINE   Oh, don't shout, Paul: it really isn't nice.

PETKOFF   Bosh! [He shouts louder than before.] Nicola!

NICOLA   [appearing at the house door]   Yes, sir.

PETKOFF   Are you deaf? Don't you hear Major Saranoff knocking? Bring him round this way. [He pronounces the name with the stress on the second syllable: Sarahnoff.]

NICOLA   Yes, Major. [He goes into the stable yard.]

PETKOFF   You must talk to him, my dear, until Raina takes him off our hands. He bores my life out about our not promoting him. Over my head, if you please.

CATHERINE   He certainly ought to be promoted when he marries Raina. Besides, the country should insist on having at least one native general.

PETKOFF   Yes; so that he could throw away whole brigades instead of regiments. It's no use, my dear: he hasn't the slightest chance of promotion until we're quite sure that the peace will be a lasting one.

NICOLA [at the gate, announcing] Major Sergius Saranoff! [He goes into the house and returns presently with a third chair, which he places at the table. He then withdraws.]

Major Sergius Saranoff, the original of the portrait in Raina's room, is a tall romantically handsome man, with the physical hardihood, the high spirit, and the susceptible imagination of an untamed mountaineer chieftain. But his remarkable personal distinction is of a characteristically civilized type. The ridges of his eyebrows, curving with an interrogative twist round the projections at the outer corners; his jealously observant eye; his nose, thin, keen, and apprehensive in spite of the pugnacious high bridge and large nostril; his assertive chin would not be out of place in a Parisian salon, shewing that the clever imaginative barbarian has an acute critical faculty which has been thrown into intense activity by the arrival of western civilization in the Balkans. The result is precisely what the advent of nineteenth century thought first produced in England: to wit, Byronism. By his brooding on the perpetual failure, not only of others, but of himself, to live up to his ideals; by his consequent cynical scorn for humanity; by his jejune credulity as to the absolute validity of his concepts and the unworthiness of the world in disregarding them; by his wincings and mockeries under the sting of the petty disillusions which every hour spent among men brings to his sensitive observation, he has acquired the half tragic, half ironic air, the mysterious moodiness, the suggestion of a strange and terrible history that has left nothing but undying remorse, by which Childe Harold fascinated the grandmothers of his English contemporaries. It is clear that here or nowhere is Raina's ideal hero. Catherine is hardly less enthusiastic about him than her daughter, and much less reserved in shewing her enthusiasm. As he enters from the stable gate, she rises effusively to greet him. Petkoff is distinctly less disposed to make a fuss about him.

PETKOFF Here already, Sergius! Glad to see you.

CATHERINE My dear Sergius! [*She holds out both her hands.*]

SERGIUS [*kissing them with scrupulous gallantry*] My dear mother, if I may call you so.

PETKOFF [*drily*] Mother-in-law, Sergius: mother-in-law! Sit down; and have some coffee.

SERGIUS Thank you: none for me. [*He gets away from the table with a certain distaste for Petkoff's enjoyment of it, and posts himself with conscious dignity against the rail of the steps leading to the house.*]

CATHERINE You look superb. The campaign has improved you, Sergius. Everybody here is mad about you. We were all wild with enthusiasm about that magnificent cavalry charge.

SERGIUS [*with grave irony*] Madam: it was the cradle and the grave of my military reputation.

CATHERINE How so?

SERGIUS I won the battle the wrong way when our worthy Russian generals were losing it the right way. In short, I upset their plans, and wounded their self-esteem. Two Cossack colonels had their regiments routed on the most correct principles of scientific warfare. Two major-generals got killed strictly according to military etiquette. The two colonels are now major-generals; and I am still a simple major.

CATHERINE   You shall not remain so, Sergius. The women are on your side; and they will see that justice is done you.

SERGIUS   It is too late. I have only waited for the peace to send in my resignation.

PETKOFF   [dropping his cup in his amazement]   Your resignation!

CATHERINE   Oh, you must withdraw it!

SERGIUS   [with resolute measured emphasis, folding his arms]   I never withdraw.

PETKOFF   [vexed]   Now who could have supposed you were going to do such a thing?

SERGIUS   [with fire]   Everyone that knew me. But enough of myself and my affairs. How is Raina; and where is Raina?

RAINA   [suddenly coming round the corner of the house and standing at the top of the steps in the path]   Raina is here.

She makes a charming picture as they turn to look at her. She wears an underdress of pale green silk, draped with an overdress of thin ecru canvas embroidered with gold. She is crowned with a dainty eastern cap of gold tinsel. Sergius goes impulsively to meet her. Posing regally, she presents her hand: he drops chivalrously on one knee and kisses it.

PETKOFF   [aside to Catherine, beaming with parental pride]   Pretty, isn't it? She always appears at the right moment.

CATHERINE   [impatiently]   Yes; she listens for it. It is an abominable habit.

Sergius leads Raina forward with splendid gallantry. When they arrive at the table, she turns to him with a bend of the head: he bows; and thus they separate, he coming to his place and she going behind her father's chair.

RAINA   [stooping and kissing her father]   Dear father! Welcome home!

PETKOFF   [patting her cheek]   My little pet girl. [He kisses her. She goes to the chair left by Nicola for Sergius, and sits down.]

CATHERINE   And so you're no longer a soldier, Sergius.

SERGIUS   I am no longer a soldier. Soldiering, my dear madam, is the coward's art of attacking mercilessly when you are strong, and keeping out of harm's way when you are weak. That is the whole secret of successful fighting. Get your enemy at a disadvantage; and never, on any account, fight him on equal terms.

PETKOFF   They wouldn't let us make a fair stand-up fight of it. However, I suppose soldiering has to be a trade like any other trade.

SERGIUS   Precisely. But I have no ambition to shine as a tradesman; so I have taken the advice of that bagman of a captain that settled the exchange of prisoners with us at Pirot, and given it up.

PETKOFF   What! that Swiss fellow? Sergius: I've often thought of that exchange since. He over-reached us about those horses.

SERGIUS   Of course he over-reached us. His father was a hotel and livery stable keeper; and he owed his first step to his knowledge of horse-dealing. [*With mock enthusiasm*] Ah, he was a soldier: every inch a soldier! If only I had bought the horses for my regiment instead of foolishly leading it into danger, I should have been a field-marshal now!

CATHERINE   A Swiss? What was he doing in the Serbian army?

PETKOFF   A volunteer, of course: keen on picking up his profession. [*Chuckling*] We shouldn't have been able to begin fighting if these foreigners hadn't shewn us how to do it: we knew nothing about it; and neither did the Serbs. Egad, there'd have been no war without them!

RAINA   Are there many Swiss officers in the Serbian Army?

PETKOFF   No. All Austrians, just as our officers were all Russians. This was the only Swiss I came across. I'll never trust a Swiss again. He humbugged us into giving him fifty ablebodied men for two hundred worn out chargers. They weren't even eatable!

SERGIUS   We were two children in the hands of that consummate soldier, Major: simply two innocent little children.

RAINA   What was he like?

CATHERINE   Oh, Raina, what a silly question!

SERGIUS   He was like a commercial traveller in uniform. Bourgeois to his boots!

PETKOFF   [*grinning*] Sergius: tell Catherine that queer story his friend told us about how he escaped after Slivnitza. You remember. About his being hid by two women.

SERGIUS   [*with bitter irony*] Oh yes: quite a romance! He was serving in the very battery I so unprofessionally charged. Being a thorough soldier, he ran away like the rest of them, with our cavalry at his heels. To escape their sabres he climbed a waterpipe and made his way into the bedroom of a young Bulgarian lady. The young lady was enchanted by his persuasive commercial traveller's manners. She very modestly entertained him for an hour or so, and then called in her mother lest her conduct should appear unmaidenly. The old lady was equally fascinated; and the fugitive was sent on his way in the morning, disguised in an old coat belonging to the master of the house, who was away at the war.

RAINA   [*rising with marked stateliness*] Your life in the camp has made you coarse, Sergius. I did not think you would have repeated such a story before me. [*She turns away coldly.*]

CATHERINE [*also rising*] She is right, Sergius. If such women exist, we should be spared the knowledge of them.

PETKOFF Pooh! nonsense! what does it matter?

SERGIUS [*ashamed*] No, Petkoff: I was wrong. [*To Raina, with earnest humility*] I beg your pardon. I have behaved abominably. Forgive me, Raina. [*She bows reservedly.*] And you too, madam. [*Catherine bows graciously and sits down. He proceeds solemnly, again addressing Raina*] The glimpses I have had of the seamy side of life during the last few months have made me cynical; but I should not have brought my cynicism here: least of all into your presence, Raina. I— [*Here, turning to the others, he is evidently going to begin a long speech when the Major interrupts him.*]

PETKOFF Stuff and nonsense, Sergius! That's quite enough fuss about nothing: a soldier's daughter should be able to stand up without flinching to a little strong conversation. [*He rises.*] Come: it's time for us to get to business. We have to make up our minds how those three regiments are to get back to Philippopolis: there's no forage for them on the Sofia route. [*He goes towards the house.*] Come along. [*Sergius is about to follow him when Catherine rises and intervenes.*]

CATHERINE Oh, Paul, can't you spare Sergius for a few moments? Raina has hardly seen him yet. Perhaps I can help you to settle about the regiments.

SERGIUS [*protesting*] My dear madam, impossible: you—

CATHERINE [*stopping him playfully*] You stay here, my dear Sergius: there's no hurry. I have a word or two to say to Paul. [*Sergius instantly bows and steps back.*] Now, dear [*taking Petkoff's arm*]: come and see the electric bell.

PETKOFF Oh, very well, very well.

They go into the house together affectionately. Sergius, left alone with Raina, looks anxiously at her, fearing that she is still offended. She smiles, and stretches out her arms to him.

SERGIUS [*hastening to her*] Am I forgiven?

RAINA [*placing her hands on his shoulders as she looks up at him with admiration and worship*] My hero! My king!

SERGIUS My queen! [*He kisses her on the forehead.*]

RAINA How I have envied you, Sergius! You have been out in the world, on the field of battle, able to prove yourself there worthy of any woman in the world; whilst I have had to sit at home inactive—dreaming—useless—doing nothing that could give me the right to call myself worthy of any man.

SERGIUS   Dearest: all my deeds have been yours. You inspired me. I have gone through the war like a knight in a tournament with his lady looking down at him!

RAINA   And you have never been absent from my thoughts for a moment. [*Very solemnly*] Sergius: I think we two have found the higher love. When I think of you, I feel that I could never do a base deed, or think an ignoble thought.

SERGIUS   My lady and my saint! [*He clasps her reverently.*]

RAINA   [*returning his embrace*] My lord and my—

SERGIUS   Sh—sh! Let me be the worshipper, dear. You little know how unworthy even the best man is of a girl's pure passion!

RAINA   I trust you. I love you. You will never disappoint me, Sergius. [*Louka is heard singing within the house. They quickly release each other.*] I can't pretend to talk indifferently before her: my heart is too full. [*Louka comes from the house with her tray. She goes to the table, and begins to clear it, with her back turned to them.*] I will get my hat; and then we can go out until lunch time. Wouldn't you like that?

SERGIUS   Be quick. If you are away five minutes, it will seem five hours. [*Raina runs to the top of the steps, and turns there to exchange looks with him and wave him a kiss with both hands. He looks after her with emotion for a moment; then turns slowly away, his face radiant with the loftiest exaltation. The movement shifts his field of vision, into the corner of which there now comes the tail of Louka's double apron. His attention is arrested at once. He takes a stealthy look at her, and begins to twirl his moustache mischievously, with his left hand akimbo on his hip. Finally, striking the ground with his heels in something of a cavalry swagger, he strolls over to the other side of the table, opposite her, and says*] Louka: do you know what the higher love is?

LOUKA   [*astonished*] No, sir.

SERGIUS   Very fatiguing thing to keep up for any length of time, Louka. One feels the need of some relief after it.

LOUKA   [*innocently*] Perhaps you would like some coffee, sir? [*She stretches her hand across the table for the coffee pot.*]

SERGIUS   [*taking her hand*] Thank you, Louka.

LOUKA   [*pretending to pull*] Oh, sir, you know I didn't mean that. I'm surprised at you!

SERGIUS   [*coming clear of the table and drawing her with him*] I am surprised at myself, Louka. What would Sergius, the hero of Slivnitza, say if he saw me now? What would Sergius, the apostle of the higher love, say if he saw me now? What would the half dozen Sergiuses who keep popping in and out of this handsome figure of mine say if they caught us here? [*Letting go her hand and slipping his arm dexterously round her waist*] Do you consider my figure handsome, Louka?

LOUKA   Let me go, sir. I shall be disgraced. [*She struggles: he holds her inexorably.*] Oh, will you let go?

SERGIUS   [*looking straight into her eyes*]   No.

LOUKA   Then stand back where we can't be seen. Have you no common sense?

SERGIUS   Ah! that's reasonable. [*He takes her into the stable yard gateway, where they are hidden from the house.*]

LOUKA   [*plaintively*]   I may have been seen from the windows: Miss Raina is sure to be spying about after you.

SERGIUS   [*stung: letting her go*]   Take care, Louka. I may be worthless enough to betray the higher love; but do not you insult it.

LOUKA   [*demurely*]   Not for the world, sir, I'm sure. May I go on with my work, please, now?

SERGIUS   [*again putting his arm round her*]   You are a provoking little witch, Louka. If you were in love with me, would you spy out of windows on me?

LOUKA   Well, you see, sir, since you say you are half a dozen different gentlemen all at once, I should have a great deal to look after.

SERGIUS   [*charmed*]   Witty as well as pretty. [*He tries to kiss her.*]

LOUKA   [*avoiding him*]   No: I don't want your kisses. Gentlefolk are all alike: you making love to me behind Miss Raina's back; and she doing the same behind yours.

SERGIUS   [*recoiling a step*]   Louka!

LOUKA   It shews how little you really care.

SERGIUS   [*dropping his familiarity, and speaking with freezing politeness*]   If our conversation is to continue, Louka, you will please remember that a gentleman does not discuss the conduct of the lady he is engaged to with her maid.

LOUKA   It's hard to know what a gentleman considers right. I thought from your trying to kiss me that you had given up being so particular.

SERGIUS   [*turning from her and striking his forehead as he comes back into the garden from the gateway*]   Devil! devil!

LOUKA   Ha! ha! I expect one of the six of you is very like me, sir; though I am only Miss Raina's maid. [*She goes back to her work at the table, taking no further notice of him.*]

SERGIUS   [*speaking to himself*]   Which of the six is the real man? that's the question that torments me. One of them is a hero, another a buffoon, another a humbug, another perhaps a bit of a blackguard. [*He pauses, and looks furtively at Louka as he adds, with deep bitterness*]   And one, at least, is a coward: jealous, like all cowards. [*He goes to the table.*]   Louka.

LOUKA   Yes?

SERGIUS   Who is my rival?

LOUKA   You shall never get that out of me, for love or money.

SERGIUS   Why?

LOUKA   Never mind why. Besides, you would tell that I told you; and I should lose my place.

SERGIUS [holding out his right hand in affirmation] No! on the honor of a—[He checks himself; and his hand drops, nerveless, as he concludes sardonically] —of a man capable of behaving as I have been behaving for the last five minutes. Who is he?

LOUKA I don't know. I never saw him. I only heard his voice through the door of her room.

SERGIUS Damnation! How dare you?

LOUKA [retreating] Oh, I mean no harm: you've no right to take up my words like that. The mistress knows all about it. And I tell you that if that gentleman ever comes here again, Miss Raina will marry him, whether he likes it or not. I know the difference between the sort of manner you and she put on before one another and the real manner.

Sergius shivers as if she had stabbed him. Then, setting his face like iron, he strides grimly to her, and grips her above the elbows with both hands.

SERGIUS Now listen you to me.

LOUKA [wincing] Not so tight: you're hurting me.

SERGIUS That doesn't matter. You have stained my honor by making me a party to your eavesdropping. And you have betrayed your mistress.

LOUKA [writhing] Please—

SERGIUS That shews that you are an abominable little clod of common clay, with the soul of a servant. [He lets her go as if she were an unclean thing, and turns away, dusting his hands of her, to the bench by the wall, where he sits down with averted head, meditating gloomily.]

LOUKA [whimpering angrily with her hands up her sleeves, feeling her bruised arms] You know how to hurt with your tongue as well as with your hands. But I don't care, now I've found out that whatever clay I'm made of, you're made of the same. As for her, she's a liar; and her fine airs are a cheat; and I'm worth six of her. [She shakes the pain off hardily; tosses her head; and sets to work to put the things on the tray.]

He looks doubtfully at her. She finishes packing the tray, and laps the cloth over the edges, so as to carry all out together. As she stoops to lift it, he rises.

SERGIUS Louka! [She stops and looks defiantly at him.] A gentleman has no right to hurt a woman under any circumstances. [With profound humility, uncovering his head] I beg your pardon.

LOUKA That sort of apology may satisfy a lady. Of what use is it to a servant?

SERGIUS [rudely crossed in his chivalry, throws it off with a bitter laugh, and says slightingly] Oh! you wish to be paid for the hurt! [He puts on his shako, and takes some money from his pocket.]

LOUKA   [*her eyes filling with tears in spite of herself*] No: I want my hurt made
well.
SERGIUS   [*sobered by her tone*] How?

*She rolls up her left sleeve; clasps her arm with the thumb and fingers of her right
hand; and looks down at the bruise. Then she raises her head and looks straight at
him. Finally, with a superb gesture, she presents her arm to be kissed. Amazed, he
looks at her; at the arm; at her again; hesitates; and then; with shuddering
intensity, exclaims* Never! *and gets away as far as possible from her.*

*Her arm drops. Without a word, and with unaffected dignity, she takes her tray,
and is approaching the house when Raina returns, wearing a hat and jacket in the
height of the Vienna fashion of the previous year, 1885. Louka makes way proudly
for her, and then goes into the house.*

RAINA   I'm ready. What's the matter? [*Gaily*] Have you been flirting with
Louka?
SERGIUS   [*hastily*] No, no. How can you think such a thing?
RAINA   [*ashamed of herself*] Forgive me, dear: it was only a jest. I am so
happy today.

*He goes quickly to her, and kisses her hand remorsefully. Catherine comes out and
calls to them from the top of the steps.*

CATHERINE   [*coming down to them*] I am sorry to disturb you, children; but
Paul is distracted over those three regiments. He doesn't know how to
send them to Philippopolis; and he objects to every suggestion of mine.
You must go and help him, Sergius. He is in the library.
RAINA   [*disappointed*] But we are just going out for a walk.
SERGIUS   I shall not be long. Wait for me just five minutes. [*He runs up the
steps to the door.*]
RAINA   [*following him to the foot of the steps and looking up at him with timid
coquetry*] I shall go round and wait in full view of the library windows.
Be sure you draw father's attention to me. If you are a moment longer
than five minutes, I shall go in and fetch you, regiments or no regiments.
SERGIUS   [*laughing*] Very well. [*He goes in.*]

*Raina watches him until he is out of her sight. Then, with a perceptible relaxation
of manner, she begins to pace up and down the garden in a brown study.*

CATHERINE   Imagine their meeting that Swiss and hearing the whole story!
The very first thing your father asked for was the old coat we sent him off
in. A nice mess you have got us into!

RAINA [*gazing thoughtfully at the gravel as she walks*] The little beast!

CATHERINE Little beast! What little beast?

RAINA To go and tell! Oh, if I had him here, I'd cram him with chocolate creams til he couldn't ever speak again!

CATHERINE Don't talk such stuff. Tell me the truth, Raina. How long was he in your room before you came to me?

RAINA [*whisking round and recommencing her march in the opposite direction*] Oh, I forget.

CATHERINE You cannot forget! Did he really climb up after the soldiers were gone; or was he there when that officer searched the room?

RAINA No. Yes: I think he must have been there then.

CATHERINE You think! Oh, Raina! Raina! Will anything ever make you straightforward? If Sergius finds out, it will be all over between you.

RAINA [*with cool impertinence*] Oh, I know Sergius is your pet. I sometimes wish you could marry him instead of me. You would just suit him. You would pet him, and spoil him, and mother him to perfection.

CATHERINE [*opening her eyes very widely indeed*] Well, upon my word!

RAINA [*capriciously: half to herself*] I always feel a longing to do or say something dreadful to him—to shock his propriety—to scandalize the five senses out of him. [*To Catherine, perversely*] I don't care whether he finds out about the chocolate cream soldier or not. I half hope he may. [*She again turns and strolls flippantly away up the path to the corner of the house.*]

CATHERINE And what should I be able to say to your father, pray?

RAINA [*over her shoulder, from the top of the two steps*] Oh, poor father! As if he could help himself! [*She turns the corner and passes out of sight.*]

CATHERINE [*looking after her, her fingers itching*] Oh, if you were only ten years younger! [*Louka comes from the house with a salver, which she carries hanging down by her side.*] Well?

LOUKA There's a gentleman just called, madam. A Serbian officer.

CATHERINE [*flaming*] A Serb! And how dare he—[*checking herself bitterly*] Oh, I forgot. We are at peace now. I suppose we shall have them calling every day to pay their compliments. Well: if he is an officer why don't you tell your master? He is in the library with Major Saranoff. Why do you come to me?

LOUKA But he asks for you, madam. And I don't think he knows who you are: he said the lady of the house. He gave me this little ticket for you. [*She takes a card out of her bosom; puts it on the salver; and offers it to Catherine.*]

CATHERINE [*reading*] "Captain Bluntschli"? That's a German name.

LOUKA Swiss, madam, I think.

CATHERINE [*with a bound that makes Louka jump back*] Swiss! What is he like?

LOUKA [*timidly*] He has a big carpet bag, madam.

CATHERINE   Oh Heavens! he's come to return the coat. Send him away: say
we're not at home: ask him to leave his address and I'll write to him. Oh
stop: that will never do. Wait! [*She throws herself into a chair to think it
out. Louka waits.*] The master and Major Saranoff are busy in the library,
aren't they?

LOUKA   Yes, madam.

CATHERINE   [*decisively*] Bring the gentleman out here at once. [*Peremptorily*]
And be very polite to him. Don't delay. Here [*impatiently snatching the
salver from her*]: leave that here; and go straight back to him.

LOUKA   Yes, madam [*going*].

CATHERINE   Louka!

LOUKA   [*stopping*] Yes, madam.

CATHERINE   Is the library door shut?

LOUKA   I think so, madam.

CATHERINE   If not, shut it as you pass through.

LOUKA   Yes, madam [*going*].

CATHERINE   Stop [*Louka stops.*] He will have to go that way [*indicating the
gate of the stable yard*]. Tell Nicola to bring his bag here after him. Don't
forget.

LOUKA   [*surprised*] His bag?

CATHERINE   Yes: here: as soon as possible. [*Vehemently*] Be quick! [*Louka
runs into the house. Catherine snatches her apron off and throws it behind a
bush. She then takes up the salver and uses it as a mirror, with the result that
the handkerchief tied round her head follows the apron. A touch to her hair
and a shake to her dressing gown make her presentable.*] Oh, how? how?
how can a man be such a fool! Such a moment to select! [*Louka appears at
the door of the house, announcing* Captain Bluntschli. *She stands aside at
the top of the steps to let him pass before she goes in again. He is the man of
the midnight adventure in Raina's room, clean, well brushed, smartly
uniformed, and out of trouble, but still unmistakably the same man. The
moment Louka's back is turned, Catherine swoops on him with impetuous,
urgent, coaxing appeal.*] Captain Bluntschli: I am very glad to see you; but
you must leave this house at once. [*He raises his eyebrows.*] My husband
has just returned with my future son-in-law; and they know nothing. If
they did, the consequences would be terrible. You are a foreigner: you
do not feel our national animosities as we do. We still hate the Serbs: the
effect of the peace on my husband has been to make him feel like a lion
baulked of his prey. If he discovers our secret, he will never forgive me;
and my daughter's life will hardly be safe. Will you, like the chivalrous
gentleman and soldier you are, leave at once before he finds you here?

BLUNTSCHLI   [*disappointed, but philosophical*] At once, gracious lady. I only
came to thank you and return the coat you lent me. If you will allow me
to take it out of my bag and leave it with your servant as I pass out, I
need detain you no further. [*He turns to go into the house.*]

CATHERINE [*catching him by the sleeve*] Oh, you must not think of going back that way. [*Coaxing him across to the stable gates*] This is the shortest way out. Many thanks. So glad to have been of service to you. Good-bye.

BLUNTSCHLI But my bag?

CATHERINE It shall be sent on. You will leave me your address.

BLUNTSCHLI True. Allow me. [*He takes out his cardcase, and stops to write his address, keeping Catherine in an agony of impatience. As he hands her the card, Petkoff, hatless, rushes from the house in a fluster of hospitality, followed by Sergius.*]

PETKOFF [*as he hurries down the steps*] My dear Captain Bluntschli—

CATHERINE Oh Heavens! [*She sinks on the seat against the wall.*]

PETKOFF [*too preoccupied to notice her as he shakes Bluntschli's hand heartily*] Those stupid people of mine thought I was out here, instead of in the—haw!—library. [*He cannot mention the library without betraying how proud he is of it.*] I saw you through the window. I was wondering why you didn't come in. Saranoff is with me: you remember him, don't you?

SERGIUS [*saluting humorously, and then offering his hand with great charm of manner*] Welcome, our friend the enemy!

PETKOFF No longer the enemy, happily. [*Rather anxiously*] I hope you've called as a friend, and not about horses or prisoners.

CATHERINE Oh, quite as a friend, Paul. I was just asking Captain Bluntschli to stay to lunch; but he declares he must go at once.

SERGIUS [*sardonically*] Impossible, Bluntschli. We want you here badly. We have to send on three cavalry regiments to Philippopolis; and we don't in the least know how to do it.

BLUNTSCHLI [*suddenly attentive and businesslike*] Philippopolis? The forage is the trouble, I suppose.

PETKOFF [*eagerly*] Yes: that's it. [*To Sergius*] He sees the whole thing at once.

BLUNTSCHLI I think I can shew you how to manage that.

SERGIUS Invaluable man! Come along! [*Towering over Bluntschli, he puts his hand on his shoulder and takes him to the steps, Petkoff following.*]

Raina comes from the house as Bluntschli puts his foot on the first step.

RAINA Oh! The chocolate cream soldier!

Bluntschli stands rigid. Sergius, amazed, looks at Raina, then at Petkoff, who looks back at him and then at his wife.

CATHERINE [*with commanding presence of mind*] My dear Raina, don't you see that we have a guest here? Captain Bluntschli: one of our new Serbian friends.

Raina bows: Bluntschli bows.

RAINA   How silly of me! [*She comes down into the center of the group, between Bluntschli and Petkoff.*] I made a beautiful ornament this morning for the ice pudding; and that stupid Nicola has just put down a pile of plates on it and spoilt it. [*To Bluntschli, winningly*] I hope you didn't think that you were the chocolate cream soldier, Captain Bluntschli.

BLUNTSCHLI   [*laughing*] I assure you I did. [*Stealing a whimsical glance at her*] Your explanation was a relief.

PETKOFF   [*Suspiciously, to Raina*]   And since when, pray, have you taken to cooking?

CATHERINE   Oh, whilst you were away. It is her latest fancy.

PETKOFF   [*testily*]   And has Nicola taken to drinking? He used to be careful enough. First he shews Captain Bluntschli out here when he knew quite well I was in the library; and then he goes downstairs and breaks Raina's chocolate soldier. He must—[*Nicola appears at the top of the steps with the bag. He descends; places it respectfully before Bluntschli; and waits for further orders. General amazement. Nicola, unconscious of the effect he is producing, looks perfectly satisfied with himself. When Petkoff recovers his power of speech, he breaks out at him with*] Are you mad, Nicola?

NICOLA   [*taken aback*]   Sir?

PETKOFF   What have you brought that for?

NICOLA   My lady's orders, major. Louka told me that—

CATHERINE   [*interrupting him*]   My orders! Why should I order you to bring Captain Bluntschli's luggage out here? What are you thinking of, Nicola?

NICOLA   [*after a moment's bewilderment, picking up the bag as he addresses Bluntschli with the very perfection of servile discretion*]   I beg your pardon, captain, I am sure. [*To Catherine*] My fault, madame: I hope you'll overlook it. [*He bows, and is going to the steps with the bag, when Petkoff addresses him angrily.*]

PETKOFF   You'd better go and slam that bag, too, down on Miss Raina's ice pudding! [*This is too much for Nicola. The bag drops from his hand almost on his master's toes, eliciting a roar of*] Begone, you butter-fingered donkey.

NICOLA   [*snatching up the bag, and escaping into the house*]   Yes, Major.

CATHERINE   Oh, never mind. Paul: don't be angry.

PETKOFF   [*blustering*]   Scoundrel! He's got out of hand while I was away. I'll teach him. Infernal blackguard! The sack next Saturday! I'll clear out the whole establishment—[*He is stifled by the caresses of his wife and daughter, who hang round his neck, petting him.*]

CATHERINE }
            } [*together*] { Now, now, now, it mustn't be angry. He meant no harm. Be good to please me, dear. Sh-sh-sh-sh!
RAINA   }   { Wow, wow, wow: not on your first day at home. I'll make another ice pudding. Tch-ch-ch!

PETKOFF [*yielding*] Oh well, never mind. Come, Bluntschli: let's have no
more nonsense about going away. You know very well you're not going
back to Switzerland yet. Until you do go back you'll stay with us.

RAINA   Oh, do, Captain Bluntschli.

PETKOFF [*to Catherine*] Now, Catherine: it's of you he's afraid. Press him:
and he'll stay.

CATHERINE   Of course I shall be only too delighted if [*appealingly*] Captain
Bluntschli really wishes to stay. He knows my wishes.

BLUNTSCHLI [*in his driest military manner*] I am at madam's orders.

SERGIUS [*cordially*] That settles it!

PETKOFF [*heartily*] Of course!

RAINA   You see you must stay.

BLUNTSCHLI [*smiling*] Well, if I must, I must.

Gesture of despair from Catherine.

ACT III

*In the library after lunch. It is not much of a library. Its literary equipment consists
of a single fixed shelf stocked with old paper covered novels, broken backed, coffee
stained, torn and thumbed; and a couple of little hanging shelves with a few gift
books on them: the rest of the wall space being occupied by trophies of war and the
chase. But it is a most comfortable sitting room. A row of three large windows
shews a mountain panorama, just now seen in one of its friendliest aspects in the
mellowing afternoon light. In the corner next the right hand window a square
earthenware stove, a perfect tower of glistening pottery, rises nearly to the ceiling
and guarantees plenty of warmth. The ottoman is like that in Raina's room, and
similarly placed; and the window seats are luxurious with decorated cushions.
There is one object, however, hopelessly out of keeping with its surroundings. This
is a small kitchen table, much the worse for wear, fitted as a writing table with an
old canister full of pens, an eggcup filled with ink, and a deplorable scrap of
heavily used pink blotting paper.*

*At the side of this table, which stands to the left of anyone facing the window,
Bluntschli is hard at work with a couple of maps before him, writing orders. At the
head of it sits Sergius, who is supposed to be also at work, but is actually gnawing
the feather of a pen, and contemplating Bluntschli's quick, sure, businesslike
progress with a mixture of envious irritation at his own incapacity and awestruck
wonder at an ability which seems to him almost miraculous, though its prosaic
character forbids him to esteem it. The Major is comfortably established on the
ottoman, with a newspaper in his hand and the tube of his hookah within easy
reach. Catherine sits at the stove, with her back to them, embroidering. Raina,
reclining on the divan, is gazing in a daydream out at the Balkan landscape, with a
neglected novel in her lap.*

SHAW: ARMS AND THE MAN ACT III

The door is on the same side as the stove, farther from the window. The button of the electric bell is at the opposite side, behind Bluntschli.

PETKOFF [*looking up from his paper to watch how they are getting on at the table*] Are you sure I can't help in any way, Bluntschli?

BLUNTSCHLI [*without interrupting his writing or looking up*] Quite sure, thank you. Saranoff and I will manage it.

SERGIUS [*grimly*] Yes: we'll manage it. He finds out what to do; draws up the orders; and I sign em. Division of labor! [*Bluntschli passes him a paper.*] Another one? Thank you. [*He plants the paper squarely before him; sets his chair carefully parallel to it; and signs with his cheek on his elbow and his protruded tongue following the movements of his pen.*] This hand is more accustomed to the sword than to the pen.

PETKOFF It's very good of you, Bluntschli: it is indeed, to let yourself be put upon in this way. Now are you quite sure I can do nothing?

CATHERINE [*in a low warning tone*] You can stop interrupting, Paul.

PETKOFF [*starting and looking round at her*] Eh? Oh! Quite right. [*He takes his newspaper up again, but presently lets it drop.*] Ah, you haven't been campaigning, Catherine: you don't know how pleasant it is for us to sit here, after a good lunch, with nothing to do but enjoy ourselves. There's only one thing I want to make me thoroughly comfortable.

CATHERINE What is that?

PETKOFF My old coat. I'm not at home in this one: I feel as if I were on parade.

CATHERINE My dear Paul, how absurd you are about that old coat! It must be hanging in the blue closet where you left it.

PETKOFF My dear Catherine, I tell you I've looked there. Am I to believe my own eyes or not? [*Catherine rises and crosses the room to press the button of the electric bell.*] What are you shewing off that bell for? [*She looks at him majestically, and silently resumes her chair and her needlework.*] My dear: if you think the obstinacy of your sex can make a coat out of two old dressing gowns of Raina's, your waterproof, and my mackintosh, you're mistaken. That's exactly what the blue closet contains at present.

Nicola presents himself.

CATHERINE Nicola: go to the blue closet and bring your master's old coat here: the braided one he wears in the house.

NICOLA Yes, madame. [*He goes out.*]

PETKOFF Catherine.

CATHERINE Yes, Paul.

PETKOFF I bet you any piece of jewellery you like to order from Sofia against a week's housekeeping money that the coat isn't there.

CATHERINE Done, Paul!

PETKOFF [*excited by the prospect of a gamble*] Come: here's an opportunity for some sport. Who'll bet on it? Bluntschli: I'll give you six to one.

BLUNTSCHLI [*imperturbably*] It would be robbing you, Major. Madame is sure to be right. [*Without looking up, he passes another batch of papers to Sergius.*]

SERGIUS [*also excited*] Bravo, Switzerland! Major: I bet my best charger against an Arab mare for Raina that Nicola finds the coat in the blue closet.

PETKOFF [*eagerly*] Your best char—

CATHERINE [*hastily interrupting him*] Don't be foolish, Paul. An Arabian mare will cost you 50,000 levas.

RAINA [*suddenly coming out of her picturesque revery*] Really, mother, if you are going to take the jewellery, I don't see why you should grudge me my Arab.

Nicola comes back with the coat, and brings it to Petkoff, who can hardly believe his eyes.

CATHERINE Where was it, Nicola?

NICOLA Hanging in the blue closet, madame.

PETKOFF Well, I am d—

CATHERINE [*stopping him*] Paul!

PETKOFF I could have sworn it wasn't there. Age is beginning to tell on me. I'm getting hallucinations. [*To Nicola*] Here: help me to change. Excuse me, Bluntschli. [*He begins changing coats, Nicola acting as valet.*] Remember: I didn't take that bet of yours, Sergius. You'd better give Raina that Arab steed yourself, since you've roused her expectations. Eh, Raina? [*He looks round at her; but she is again rapt in the landscape. With a little gush of parental affection and pride, he points her out to them, and says*] She's dreaming, as usual.

SERGIUS Assuredly she shall not be the loser.

PETKOFF So much the better for her. *I* shan't come off so cheaply, I expect. [*The change is now complete. Nicola goes out with the discarded coat.*] Ah, now I feel at home at last. [*He sits down and takes his newspaper with a grunt of relief.*]

BLUNTSCHLI [*to Sergius, handing a paper*] That's the last order.

PETKOFF [*jumping up*] What! Finished?

BLUNTSCHLI Finished.

PETKOFF [*with childlike envy*] Haven't you anything for me to sign?

BLUNTSCHLI Not necessary. His signature will do.

PETKOFF [*inflating his chest and thumping it*] Ah well, I think we've done a thundering good day's work. Can I do anything more?

BLUNTSCHLI You had better both see the fellows that are to take these. [*Sergius rises.*] Pack them off at once; and shew them that I've marked on the orders the time they should hand them in by. Tell them that if they stop to drink or tell stories—if they're five minutes late, they'll have the skin taken off their backs.

SERGIUS [stiffening indignantly] I'll say so. [He strides to the door.] And if one of them is man enough to spit in my face for insulting him, I'll buy his discharge and give him a pension. [He goes out.]

BLUNTSCHLI [confidentially] Just see that he talks to them properly, Major, will you?

PETKOFF [officiously] Quite right, Bluntschli, quite right. I'll see to it. [He goes to the door importantly, but hesitates on the threshold.] By the bye, Catherine, you may as well come too. They'll be far more frightened of you than of me.

CATHERINE [putting down her embroidery] I daresay I had better. You would only splutter at them. [She goes out, Petkoff holding the door for her and following her.]

BLUNTSCHLI What an army! They make cannons out of cherry trees; and the officers send for their wives to keep discipline! [He begins to fold and docket the papers.]

Raina, who has risen from the divan, marches slowly down the room with her hands clasped behind her, and looks mischievously at him.

RAINA You look ever so much nicer than when we last met. [He looks up, surprised.] What have you done to yourself?

BLUNTSCHLI Washed; brushed; good night's sleep and breakfast. That's all.

RAINA Did you get back safely that morning?

BLUNTSCHLI Quite, thanks.

RAINA Were they angry with you for running away from Sergius's charge?

BLUNTSCHLI [grinning] No: they were glad; because they'd all just run away themselves.

RAINA [going to the table, and leaning over it towards him] It must have made a lovely story for them: all that about me and my room.

BLUNTSCHLI Capital story. But I only told it to one of them: a particular friend.

RAINA On whose discretion you could absolutely rely?

BLUNTSCHLI Absolutely.

RAINA Hm! He told it all to my father and Sergius the day you exchanged the prisoners. [She turns away and strolls carelessly across to the other side of the room.]

BLUNTSCHLI [deeply concerned, and half incredulous] No! You don't mean that, do you?

RAINA [turning, with sudden earnestness] I do indeed. But they don't know that it was in this house you took refuge. If Sergius knew, he would challenge you and kill you in a duel.

BLUNTSCHLI   Bless me! then don't tell him.

RAINA   Please be serious, Captain Bluntschli. Can you not realize what it is to me to deceive him? I want to be quite perfect with Sergius: no meanness, no smallness, no deceit. My relation to him is the one really beautiful and noble part of my life. I hope you can understand that.

BLUNTSCHLI   [*sceptically*] You mean that you wouldn't like him to find out that the story about the ice pudding was a—a—a—You know.

RAINA   [*wincing*] Ah, don't talk of it in that flippant way. I lied: I know it. But I did it to save your life. He would have killed you. That was the second time I ever uttered a falsehood. [*Bluntschli rises quickly and looks doubtfully and somewhat severely at her.*] Do you remember the first time?

BLUNTSCHLI   I! No. Was I present?

RAINA   Yes; and I told the officer who was searching for you that you were not present.

BLUNTSCHLI   True. I should have remembered it.

RAINA   [*greatly encouraged*] Ah, it is natural that you should forget it first. It cost you nothing: it cost me a lie! A lie!

She sits down on the ottoman, looking straight before her with her hands clasped around her knee. Bluntschli, quite touched, goes to the ottoman with a particularly reassuring and considerate air, and sits down beside her.

BLUNTSCHLI   My dear young lady, don't let this worry you. Remember: I'm a soldier. Now what are the two things that happen to a soldier so often that he comes to think nothing of them? One is hearing people tell lies [*Raina recoils.*]: the other is getting his life saved in all sorts of ways by all sorts of people.

RAINA   [*rising in indignant protest*] And so he becomes a creature incapable of faith and of gratitude.

BLUNTSCHLI   [*making a wry face*] Do you like gratitude? I don't. If pity is akin to love, gratitude is akin to the other thing.

RAINA   Gratitude! [*Turning on him*] If you are incapable of gratitude you are incapable of any noble sentiment. Even animals are grateful. Oh, I see now exactly what you think of me! You were not surprised to hear me lie. To you it was something I probably did every day! every hour! That is how men think of women. [*She paces the room tragically.*]

BLUNTSCHLI   [*dubiously*] There's reason in everything. You said you'd told only two lies in your whole life. Dear young lady: isn't that rather a short allowance? I'm quite a straightforward man myself; but it wouldn't last me a whole morning.

RAINA   [*staring haughtily at him*] Do you know, sir, that you are insulting me?

BLUNTSCHLI   I can't help it. When you strike that noble attitude and speak in that thrilling voice, I admire you; but I find it impossible to believe a single word you say.

RAINA   [superbly] Captain Bluntschli!

BLUNTSCHLI   [unmoved] Yes?

RAINA   [standing over him, as if she could not believe her senses] Do you mean what you said just now? Do you know what you said just now?

BLUNTSCHLI   I do.

RAINA   [gasping] I! I!!! [She points to herself incredulously, meaning "I, Raina Petkoff tell lies!" He meets her gaze unflinchingly. She suddenly sits down beside him, and adds, with a complete change of manner from the heroic to a babyish familiarity] How did you find me out?

BLUNTSCHLI   [promptly] Instinct, dear young lady. Instinct, and experience of the world.

RAINA   [wonderingly] Do you know, you are the first man I ever met who did not take me seriously?

BLUNTSCHLI   You mean, don't you, that I am the first man that has ever taken you quite seriously?

RAINA   Yes: I suppose I do mean that. [Cosily, quite at her ease with him] How strange it is to be talked to in such a way! You know, I've always gone on like that.

BLUNTSCHLI   You mean the—?

RAINA   I mean the noble attitude and the thrilling voice. [They laugh together.] I did it when I was a tiny child to my nurse. She believed in it. I do it before my parents. They believe in it. I do it before Sergius. He believes in it.

BLUNTSCHLI   Yes: he's a little in that line himself, isn't he?

RAINA   [startled] Oh! Do you think so?

BLUNTSCHLI   You know him better than I do.

RAINA   I wonder—I wonder is he? If I thought that—! [Discouraged] Ah, well; what does it matter? I suppose, now you've found me out, you despise me.

BLUNTSCHLI   [warmly, rising] No, my dear young lady, no, no, no a thousand times. It's part of your youth: part of your charm. I'm like all the rest of them: the nurse, your parents, Sergius: I'm your infatuated admirer.

RAINA   [pleased] Really?

BLUNTSCHLI   [slapping his breast smartly with his hand, German fashion] Hand aufs Herz! Really and truly.

RAINA   [very happy] But what did you think of me for giving you my portrait?

BLUNTSCHLI   [astonished] Your portrait! You never gave me your portrait.

RAINA   [quickly] Do you mean to say you never got it?

BLUNTSCHLI   No. [He sits down beside her, with renewed interest, and says, with some complacency] When did you send it to me?

RAINA [*indignantly*] I did not send it to you. [*She turns her head away, and adds, reluctantly*] It was in the pocket of that coat.

BLUNTSCHLI [*pursing his lips and rounding his eyes*] Oh-o-oh! I never found it. It must be there still.

RAINA [*springing up*] There still! for my father to find the first time he puts his hand in his pocket! Oh, how could you be so stupid?

BLUNTSCHLI [*rising also*] It doesn't matter: I suppose it's only a photograph: how can he tell who it was intended for? Tell him he put it there himself.

RAINA [*bitterly*] Yes: that is so clever! isn't it? [*Distractedly*] Oh! what shall I do?

BLUNTSCHLI Ah, I see. You wrote something on it. That was rash.

RAINA [*vexed almost to tears*] Oh, to have done such a thing for you, who care no more—except to laugh at me—oh! Are you sure nobody has touched it?

BLUNTSCHLI Well, I can't be quite sure. You see, I couldn't carry it about with me all the time: one can't take much luggage on active service.

RAINA What did you do with it?

BLUNTSCHLI When I got through to Pirot I had to put it in safe keeping somehow. I thought of the railway cloak room; but that's the surest place to get looted in modern warfare. So I pawned it.

RAINA Pawned it!!!

BLUNTSCHLI I know it doesn't sound nice: but it was much the safest plan. I redeemed it the day before yesterday. Heaven only knows whether the pawnbroker cleared out the pockets or not.

RAINA [*furious: throwing the words right into his face*] You have a low shopkeeping mind. You think of things that would never come into a gentleman's head.

BLUNTSCHLI [*phlegmatically*] That's the Swiss national character, dear lady. [*He returns to the table.*]

RAINA Oh, I wish I had never met you. [*She flounces away, and sits at the window fuming.*]

Louka comes in with a heap of letters and telegrams on her salver, and crosses, with her bold free gait, to the table. Her left sleeve is looped up to the shoulder with a brooch, shewing her naked arm, with a broad gilt bracelet covering the bruise.

LOUKA [*to Bluntschli*] For you. [*She empties the salver with a fling on to the table.*] The messenger is waiting. [*She is determined not to be civil to an enemy, even if she must bring him his letters.*]

BLUNTSCHLI [*to Raina*] Will you excuse me: the last postal delivery that reached me was three weeks ago. These are the subsequent accumulations. Four telegrams: a week old. [*He opens one.*] Oho! Bad news!

RAINA [*rising and advancing a little remorsefully*] Bad news?

BLUNTSCHLI My father's dead. [*He looks at the telegram with his lips pursed, musing on the unexpected change in his arrangements. Louka crosses herself hastily.*]

RAINA Oh, how very sad!

BLUNTSCHLI Yes: I shall have to start for home in an hour. He has left a lot of big hotels behind him to be looked after. [*He takes up a fat letter in a long blue envelope.*] Here's a whacking letter from the family solicitor. [*He puts out the enclosures and glances over them.*] Great Heavens! Seventy! Two hundred! [*In a crescendo of dismay*] Four hundred! Four thousand!! Nine thousand six hundred!!! What on earth am I to do with them all?

RAINA [*timidly*] Nine thousand hotels?

BLUNTSCHLI Hotels! nonsense. If you only knew! Oh, it's too ridiculous! Excuse me: I must give my fellow orders about starting. [*He leaves the room hastily, with the documents in his hand.*]

LOUKA [*knowing instinctively that she can annoy Raina by disparaging Bluntschli*] He has not much heart, that Swiss. He has not a word of grief for his poor father.

RAINA [*bitterly*] Grief! A man who has been doing nothing but killing people for years! What does he care? What does any soldier care? [*She goes to the door, restraining her tears with difficulty.*]

LOUKA Major Saranoff has been fighting too; and he has plenty of heart left. [*Raina, at the door, draws herself up haughtily and goes out.*] Aha! I thought you wouldn't get much feeling out of your soldier. [*She is following Raina when Nicola enters with an armful of logs for the stove.*]

NICOLA [*grinning amorously at her*] I've been trying all the afternoon to get a minute alone with you, my girl. [*His countenance changes as he notices her arm.*] Why, what fashion is that of wearing your sleeve, child?

LOUKA [*proudly*] My own fashion.

NICOLA Indeed! If the mistress catches you, she'll talk to you. [*He puts the logs down, and seats himself comfortably on the ottoman.*]

LOUKA Is that any reason why you should take it on yourself to talk to me?

NICOLA Come! don't be so contrary with me. I've some good news for you. [*She sits down beside him. He takes out some paper money. Louka, with an eager gleam in her eyes, tries to snatch it; but he shifts it quickly to his left hand, out of her reach.*] See! a twenty leva bill! Sergius gave me that, out of pure swagger. A fool and his money are soon parted. There's ten levas more. The Swiss gave me that for backing up the mistress' and Raina's lies about him. He's no fool, he isn't. You should have heard old Catherine downstairs as polite as you please to me, telling me not to mind the Major being a little impatient; for they knew what a good servant I was—after making a fool and a liar of me before them all! The twenty will go to our savings; and you shall have the ten to spend if you'll only talk to me so as to remind me I'm a human being. I get tired of being a servant occasionally.

LOUKA Yes: sell your manhood for 30 levas, and buy me for 10! [*Rising scornfully*] Keep your money. You were born to be a servant. I was not. When you set up your shop you will only be everybody's servant instead of somebody's servant. [*She goes moodily to the table and seats herself regally in Sergius's chair.*]

NICOLA [*picking up his logs, and going to the stove*] Ah, wait til you see. We shall have our evenings to ourselves; and I shall be master in my own house, I promise you. [*He throws the logs down and kneels at the stove.*]

LOUKA You shall never be master in mine.

NICOLA [*turning, still on his knees, and squatting down rather forlornly on his calves, daunted by her implacable disdain*] You have a great ambition in you, Louka. Remember: if any luck comes to you, it was I that made a woman of you.

LOUKA You!

NICOLA [*scrambling up and going to her*] Yes, me. Who was it made you give up wearing a couple of pounds of false black hair on your head and reddening your lips and cheeks like any other Bulgarian girl! I did. Who taught you to trim your nails, and keep your hands clean, and be dainty about yourself, like a fine Russian lady! Me: do you hear that? me! [*She tosses her head defiantly; and he turns away, adding more cooly*] I've often thought that if Raina were out of the way, and you just a little less of a fool and Sergius just a little more of one, you might come to be one of my grandest customers, instead of only being my wife and costing me money.

LOUKA I believe you would rather be my servant than my husband. You would make more out of me. Oh, I know that soul of yours.

NICOLA [*going closer to her for greater emphasis*] Never you mind my soul; but just listen to my advice. If you want to be a lady, your present behaviour to me won't do at all, unless when we're alone. It's too sharp and impudent; and impudence is a sort of familiarity: it shews affection for me. And don't you try being high and mighty with me, either. You're like all country girls: you think it's genteel to treat a servant the way I treat a stableboy. That's only your ignorance; and don't you forget it. And don't be so ready to defy everybody. Act as if you expected to have your own way, not as if you expected to be ordered about. The way to get on as a lady is the same as the way to get on as a servant: you've got to know your place: that's the secret of it. And you may depend on me to know my place if you get promoted. Think over it, my girl. I'll stand by you: one servant should always stand by another.

LOUKA [*rising impatiently*] Oh, I must behave in my own way. You take all the courage out of me with your cold-blooded wisdom. Go and put those logs in the fire: that's the sort of thing you understand.

Before Nicola can retort, Sergius comes in. He checks himself a moment on seeing Louka; then goes to the stove.

SERGIUS [*to Nicola*] I am not in the way of your work, I hope.

NICOLA [*in a smooth, elderly manner*] Oh no, sir: thank you kindly. I was only speaking to this foolish girl about her habit of running up here to the library whenever she gets a chance, to look at the books. That's the worst of her education, sir: it gives her habits above her station. [*To Louka*] Make that table tidy, Louka, for the Major. [*He goes out sedately.*]

Louka, without looking at Sergius, pretends to arrange the papers on the table. He crosses slowly to her, and studies the arrangement of her sleeve reflectively.

SERGIUS Let me see: is there a mark there? [*He turns up the bracelet and sees the bruise made by his grasp. She stands motionless, not looking at him: fascinated, but on her guard.*] Ffff! Does it hurt?

LOUKA Yes.

SERGIUS Shall I cure it?

LOUKA [*instantly withdrawing herself proudly, but still not looking at him*] No. You cannot cure it now.

SERGIUS [*masterfully*] Quite sure? [*He makes a movement as if to take her in his arms.*]

LOUKA Don't trifle with me, please. An officer should not trifle with a servant.

SERGIUS [*indicating the bruise with a merciless stroke of his forefinger*] That was no trifle, Louka.

LOUKA [*flinching; then looking at him for the first time*] Are you sorry?

SERGIUS [*with measured emphasis, folding his arms*] I am never sorry.

LOUKA [*wistfully*] I wish I could believe a man could be as unlike a woman as that. I wonder are you really a brave man?

SERGIUS [*unaffectedly, relaxing his attitude*] Yes: I am a brave man. My heart jumped like a woman's at the first shot; but in the charge I found that I was brave. Yes: that at least is real about me.

LOUKA Did you find in the charge that the men whose fathers are poor like mine were any less brave than the men who are rich like you?

SERGIUS [*with bitter levity*] Not a bit. They all slashed and cursed and yelled like heroes. Psha! the courage to rage and kill is cheap. I have an English bull terrier who has as much of that sort of courage as the whole Bulgarian nation, and the whole Russian nation at its back. But he lets my groom thrash him, all the same. That's your soldier all over! No, Louka: your poor men can cut throats; but they are afraid of their officers; they put up with insults and blows; they stand by and see one another punished like children: aye, and help to do it when they are ordered. And the officers!!! Well [*with a short harsh laugh*] I am an officer.

Oh, [*fervently*] give me the man who will defy to the death any power on earth or in heaven that sets itself up against his own will and conscience: he alone is the brave man.

LOUKA   How easy it is to talk! Men never seem to me to grow up: they all have schoolboy's ideas. You don't know what true courage is.

SERGIUS   [*ironically*] Indeed! I am willing to be instructed. [*He sits on the ottoman, sprawling magnificently.*]

LOUKA   Look at me! How much am I allowed to have my own will? I have to get your room ready for you: to sweep and dust, to fetch and carry. How could that degrade me if it did not degrade you to have it done for you? But [*with subdued passion*] if I were Empress of Russia, above everyone in the world, then!! Ah then, though according to you I could shew no courage at all, you should see, you should see.

SERGIUS   What would you do, most noble Empress?

LOUKA   I would marry the man I loved, which no other queen in Europe has the courage to do. If I loved you, though you would be as far beneath me as I am beneath you, I would dare to be the equal of my inferior. Would you dare as much if you loved me? No: if you felt the beginnings of love for me you would not let it grow. You would not dare: you would marry a rich man's daughter because you would be afraid of what other people would say of you.

SERGIUS   [*bounding up*] You lie: it is not so, by all the stars! If I loved you, and I were the Czar himself, I would set you on the throne by my side. You know that I love another woman, a woman as high above you as heaven is above earth. And you are jealous of her.

LOUKA   I have no reason to be. She will never marry you now. The man I told you of has come back. She will marry the Swiss.

SERGIUS   [*recoiling*] The Swiss!

LOUKA   A man worth ten of you. Then you can come to me; and I will refuse you. You are not good enough for me. [*She turns to the door.*]

SERGIUS   [*springing after her and catching her fiercely in his arms*] I will kill the Swiss; and afterwards I will do as I please with you.

LOUKA   [*in his arms, passive and steadfast*] The Swiss will kill you, perhaps. He has beaten you in love. He may beat you in war.

SERGIUS   [*tormentedly*] Do you think I believe that she—she! whose worst thoughts are higher than your best ones, is capable of trifling with another man behind my back?

LOUKA   Do you think she would believe the Swiss if he told her now that I am in your arms?

SERGIUS   [*releasing her in despair*] Damnation! Oh, damnation! Mockery! mockery everywhere! everything I think is mocked by everything I do. [*He strikes himself frantically on the breast.*] Coward! liar! fool! Shall I kill myself like a man, or live and pretend to laugh at myself? [*She again turns to go.*] Louka! [*She stops near the door.*] Remember: you belong to me.

LOUKA [*turning*] What does that mean? An insult?

SERGIUS [*commandingly*] It means that you love me, and that I have had you here in my arms, and will perhaps have you there again. Whether that is an insult I neither know nor care: take it as you please. But [*vehemently*] I will not be a coward and a trifler. If I choose to love you, I dare marry you, in spite of all Bulgaria. If these hands ever touch you again, they shall touch my affianced bride.

LOUKA We shall see whether you dare keep your word. And take care. I will not wait long.

SERGIUS [*again folding his arms and standing motionless in the middle of the room*] Yes: we shall see. And you shall wait my pleasure.

Bluntschli, much preoccupied, with his papers still in his hand, enters, leaving the door open for Louka to go out. He goes across to the table, glancing at her as he passes. Sergius, without altering his resolute attitude, watches him steadily. Louka goes out, leaving the door open.

BLUNTSCHLI [*absently, sitting at the table as before, and putting down his papers*] That's a remarkable looking young woman.

SERGIUS [*gravely, without moving*] Captain Bluntschli.

BLUNTSCHLI Eh?

SERGIUS You have deceived me. You are my rival. I brook no rivals. At six o'clock I shall be in the drilling-ground on the Klissoura road, alone, on horseback, with my sabre. Do you understand?

BLUNTSCHLI [*staring, but sitting quite at his ease*] Oh, thank you: that's a cavalry man's proposal. I'm in the artillery; and I have the choice of weapons. If I go, I shall take a machine gun. And there shall be no mistake about the cartridges this time.

SERGIUS [*flushing, but with deadly coldness*] Take care, sir. It is not our custom in Bulgaria to allow invitations of that kind to be trifled with.

BLUNTSCHLI [*warmly*] Pooh! don't talk to me about Bulgaria. You don't know what fighting is. But have it your own way. Bring your sabre along. I'll meet you.

SERGIUS [*fiercely delighted to find his opponent a man of spirit*] Well said, Switzer. Shall I lend you my best horse?

BLUNTSCHLI No: damn your horse! thank you all the same, my dear fellow. [*Raina comes in, and hears the next sentence.*] I shall fight you on foot. Horseback's too dangerous; I don't want to kill you if I can help it.

RAINA [*hurrying forward anxiously*] I have heard what Captain Bluntschli said, Sergius. You are going to fight. Why? [*Sergius turns away in silence, and goes to the stove, where he stands watching her as she continues, to Bluntschli*] What about?

BLUNTSCHLI I don't know: he hasn't told me. Better not interfere, dear young lady. No harm will be done: I've often acted as sword instructor.

He won't be able to touch me; and I'll not hurt him. It will save explanations. In the morning I shall be off home; and you'll never see me or hear of me again. You and he will then make it up and live happily ever after.

RAINA   [*turning away deeply hurt, almost with a sob in her voice*] I never said I wanted to see you again.

SERGIUS   [*striding forward*] Ha! That is a confession.

RAINA   [*haughtily*] What do you mean?

SERGIUS   You love that man!

RAINA   [*scandalized*] Sergius!

SERGIUS   You allow him to make love to you behind my back, just as you treat me as your affianced husband behind his. Bluntschli: you knew our relations; and you deceived me. It is for that that I call you to account, not for having received favors I never enjoyed.

BLUNTSCHLI   [*jumping up indignantly*] Stuff! Rubbish! I have received no favors. Why, the young lady doesn't even know whether I'm married or not.

RAINA   [*forgetting herself*] Oh! [*Collapsing on the ottoman*] Are you?

SERGIUS   You see the young lady's concern, Captain Bluntschli. Denial is useless. You have enjoyed the privilege of being received in her own room, late at night—

BLUNTSCHLI   [*interrupting him pepperily*] Yes, you blockhead! she received me with a pistol at her head. Your cavalry were at my heels. I'd have blown out her brains if she'd uttered a cry.

SERGIUS   [*taken aback*] Bluntschli! Raina: is this true?

RAINA   [*rising in wrathful majesty*] Oh, how dare you, how dare you?

BLUNTSCHLI   Apologize, man: apologize. [*He resumes his seat at the table.*]

SERGIUS   [*with the old measured emphasis, folding his arms*] I never apologize!

RAINA   [*passionately*] This is the doing of that friend of yours, Captain Bluntschli. It is he who is spreading this horrible story about me. [*She walks about excitedly.*]

BLUNTSCHLI   No: he's dead. Burnt alive.

RAINA   [*stopping, shocked*] Burnt alive!

BLUNTSCHLI   Shot in the hip in a woodyard. Couldn't drag himself out. Your fellows' shells set the timber on fire and burnt him, with half a dozen other poor devils in the same predicament.

RAINA   How horrible!

SERGIUS   And how ridiculous! Oh, war! war! the dream of patriots and heroes! A fraud, Bluntschli. A hollow sham, like love.

RAINA   [*outraged*] Like love! You say that before me!

BLUNTSCHLI   Come, Saranoff: that matter is explained.

SERGIUS   A hollow sham, I say. Would you have come back here if nothing had passed between you except at the muzzle of your pistol? Raina is mistaken about your friend who was burnt. He was not my informant.

RAINA   Who then? [*Suddenly guessing the truth*] Ah, Louka! my maid! my servant! You were with her this morning all that time after—after—Oh, what sort of god is this I have been worshipping! [*He meets her gaze with sardonic enjoyment of her disenchantment. Angered all the more, she goes closer to him, and says, in a lower, intenser tone*] Do you know that I looked out of the window as I went upstairs, to have another sight of my hero; and I saw something I did not understand then. I know now that you were making love to her.

SERGIUS   [*with grim humor*] You saw that?

RAINA   Only too well. [*She turns away, and throws herself on the divan under the centre window, quite overcome.*]

SERGIUS   [*cynically*] Raina: our romance is shattered. Life's a farce.

BLUNTSCHLI   [*to Raina, whimsically*] You see: he's found himself out now.

SERGIUS   [*going to him*] Bluntschli: I have allowed you to call me a blockhead. You may now call me a coward as well. I refuse to fight you. Do you know why?

BLUNTSCHLI   No; but it doesn't matter. I didn't ask the reason when you cried on; and I don't ask the reason now that you cry off. I'm a professional soldier! I fight when I have to, and am very glad to get out of it when I haven't to. You're only an amateur: you think fighting's an amusement.

SERGIUS   [*sitting down at the table, nose to nose with him*] You shall hear the reason all the same, my professional. The reason is that it takes two men—real men—men of heart, blood and honor—to make a genuine combat. I could no more fight with you than I could make love to an ugly woman. You've no magnetism: you're not a man: you're a machine.

BLUNTSCHLI   [*apologetically*] Quite true, quite true. I always was that sort of chap. I'm very sorry.

SERGIUS   Psha!

BLUNTSCHLI   But now that you've found that life isn't a farce, but something quite sensible and serious, what further obstacle is there to your happiness?

RAINA   [*rising*] You are very solicitous about my happiness and his. Do you forget his new love—Louka? It is not you that he must fight now, but his rival, Nicola.

SERGIUS   Rival!!! [*bounding half across the room*].

RAINA   Don't you know that they're engaged?

SERGIUS   Nicola! Are fresh abysses opening? Nicola!

RAINA   [*sarcastically*] A shocking sacrifice, isn't it? Such beauty! such intellect! such modesty! wasted on a middle-aged servant man. Really, Sergius, you cannot stand by and allow such a thing. It would be unworthy of your chivalry.

SERGIUS   [*losing all self-control*] Viper! Viper! [*He rushes to and fro, raging.*]

BLUNTSCHLI   Look here, Saranoff: you're getting the worst of this.

RAINA [*getting angrier*] Do you realize what he has done, Captain Bluntschli? He has set this girl as a spy on us; and her reward is that he makes love to her.

SERGIUS False! Monstrous!

RAINA Monstrous! [*Confronting him*] Do you deny that she told you about Captain Bluntschli being in my room?

SERGIUS No; but—

RAINA [*interrupting*] Do you deny that you were making love to her when she told you?

SERGIUS No; but I tell you—

RAINA [*cutting him short contemptuously*] It is unnecessary to tell us anything more. That is quite enough for us. [*She turns away from him and sweeps majestically back to the window.*]

BLUNTSCHLI [*quietly, as Sergius, in an agony of mortification, sinks on the ottoman, clutching his averted head between his fists*] I told you you were getting the worst of it, Saranoff.

SERGIUS Tiger cat!

RAINA [*running excitedly to Bluntschli*] You hear this man calling me names, Captain Bluntschli?

BLUNTSCHLI What else can he do, dear lady? He must defend himself somehow. Come [*very persuasively*]: don't quarrel. What good does it do?

Raina, with a gasp, sits down on the ottoman, and after a vain effort to look vexedly at Bluntschli, falls a victim to her sense of humor, and actually leans back babyishly against the writhing shoulder of Sergius.

SERGIUS Engaged to Nicola! Ha! ha! Ah well, Bluntschli, you are right to take this huge imposture of a world coolly.

RAINA [*quaintly to Bluntschli, with an intuitive guess at his state of mind*] I daresay you think us a couple of grown-up babies, don't you?

SERGIUS [*grinning savagely*] He does: he does. Swiss civilization nursetending Bulgarian barbarism, eh?

BLUNTSCHLI [*blushing*] Not at all, I assure you. I'm only very glad to get you two quieted. There! there! let's be pleasant and talk it over in a friendly way. Where is this other young lady?

RAINA Listening at the door, probably.

SERGIUS [*shivering as if a bullet had struck him, and speaking with quiet but deep indignation*] I will prove that that, at least, is a calumny. [*He goes with dignity to the door and opens it. A yell of fury bursts from him as he looks out. He darts into the passage, and returns dragging in Louka, whom he flings violently against the table, exclaiming*] Judge her, Bluntschli. You, the cool impartial man: judge the eavesdropper.

Louka stands her ground, proud and silent.

BLUNTSCHLI   [*shaking his head*]   I mustn't judge her. I once listened myself
    outside a tent when there was a mutiny brewing. It's all a question of the
    degree of provocation. My life was at stake.
LOUKA   My love was at stake. I am not ashamed.
RAINA   [*contemptuously*]   Your love! Your curiosity, you mean.
LOUKA   [*facing her and returning her contempt with interest*]   My love, stronger
    than anything you can feel, even for your chocolate cream soldier.
SERGIUS   [*with quick suspicion, to Louka*]   What does that mean?
LOUKA   [*fiercely*]   I mean—
SERGIUS   [*interrupting her slightingly*]   Oh, I remember: the ice pudding. A
    paltry taunt, girl!

Major Petkoff enters, in his shirtsleeves.

PETKOFF   Excuse my shirtsleeves, gentlemen. Raina: somebody has been
    wearing that coat of mine: I'll swear it. Somebody with a differently
    shaped back. It's all burst open at the sleeve. Your mother is mending it.
    I wish she'd make haste: I shall catch cold. [*He looks more attentively at
    them.*] Is anything the matter?
RAINA   No. [*She sits down at the stove, with a tranquil air.*]
SERGIUS   Oh no. [*He sits down at the end of the table, as at first.*]
BLUNTSCHLI   [*who is already seated*]   Nothing. Nothing.
PETKOFF   [*sitting down on the ottoman in his old place*]   That's all right. [*He
    notices Louka.*] Anything the matter, Louka?
LOUKA   No, sir.
PETKOFF   [*genially*]   That's all right. [*He sneezes.*] Go and ask your mistress
    for my coat, like a good girl, will you?

*Nicola enters with the coat. Louka makes a pretence of having business in the
room by taking the little table with the hookah away to the wall near the windows.*

RAINA   [*rising quickly as she sees the coat on Nicola's arm*]   Here it is papa.
    Give it to me Nicola; and do you put some more wood on the fire. [*She
    takes the coat, and brings it to the Major, who stands up to put it on. Nicola
    attends to the fire.*]
PETKOFF   [*to Raina, teasing her affectionately*]   Aha! Going to be very good to
    poor old papa just for one day after his return from the wars, eh?
RAINA   [*with solemn reproach*]   Ah, how can you say that to me, father?

PETKOFF   Well, well, only a joke, little one. Come: give me a kiss. [*She kisses him.*] Now give me the coat.

RAINA   No: I am going to put it on for you. Turn your back. [*He turns his back and feels behind him with his arms for the sleeves. She dexterously takes the photograph from the pocket and throws it on the table before Bluntschli, who covers it with a sheet of paper under the very nose of Sergius, who looks on amazed, with his suspicions roused in the highest degree. She then helps Petkoff on with his coat.*] There, dear! Now are you comfortable?

PETKOFF   Quite, little love. Thanks. [*He sits down; and Raina returns to her seat near the stove.*] Oh, by the bye, I've found something funny. What's the meaning of this? [*He puts his hand into the picked pocket.*] Eh? Hallo! [*He tries the other pocket.*] Well, I could have sworn—! [*Much puzzled, he tries the breast pocket.*] I wonder— [*trying the original pocket*]. Where can it—? [*He rises, exclaiming*] Your mother's taken it!

RAINA   [*very red*] Taken what?

PETKOFF   Your photograph, with the inscription: "Raina, to her Chocolate Cream Soldier: a Souvenir." Now you know there's something more in this than meets the eye; and I'm going to find it out. [*Shouting*] Nicola!

NICOLA   [*coming to him*] Sir!

PETKOFF   Did you spoil any pastry of Miss Raina's this morning?

NICOLA   You heard Miss Raina say that I did, sir.

PETKOFF   I know that, you idiot. Was it true?

NICOLA   I am sure Miss Raina is incapable of saying anything that is not true, sir.

PETKOFF   Are you? Then I'm not. [*Turning to the others*] Come: do you think I don't see it all? [*He goes to Sergius, and slaps him on the shoulder.*] Sergius: you're the chocolate cream soldier, aren't you?

SERGIUS   [*starting up*] I! A chocolate cream soldier! Certainly not.

PETKOFF   Not! [*He looks at them. They are all very serious and very conscious.*] Do you mean to tell me that Raina sends things like that to other men?

SERGIUS   [*enigmatically*] The world is not such an innocent place as we used to think, Petkoff.

BLUNTSCHLI   [*rising*] It's all right, Major. I'm the chocolate cream soldier. [*Petkoff and Sergius are equally astonished.*] The gracious young lady saved my life by giving me chocolate creams when I was starving: shall I ever forget their flavour! My late friend Stolz told you the story of Pirot. I was the fugitive.

PETKOFF   You! [*He gasps.*] Sergius: do you remember how those two women went on this morning when we mentioned it? [*Sergius smiles cynically. Petkoff confronts Raina severely.*] You're a nice young woman, aren't you?

RAINA   [*bitterly*] Major Saranoff has changed his mind. And when I wrote that on the photograph, I did not know that Captain Bluntschli was married.

BLUNTSCHLI   [*startled into vehement protest*] I'm not married.

RAINA [with deep reproach] You said you were.

BLUNTSCHLI I did not. I positively did not. I never was married in my life.

PETKOFF [exasperated] Raina: will you kindly inform me, if I am not asking too much, which of these gentlemen you are engaged to?

RAINA To neither of them. This young lady [introducing Louka, who faces them all proudly] is the object of Major Saranoff's affections at present.

PETKOFF Louka! Are you mad, Sergius? Why, this girl's engaged to Nicola.

NICOLA I beg your pardon, sir. There is a mistake. Louka is not engaged to me.

PETKOFF Not engaged to you, you scoundrel! Why, you had twenty-five levas from me on the day of your betrothal; and she had that gilt bracelet from Miss Raina.

NICOLA [with cool unction] We gave it out so, sir. But it was only to give Louka protection. She had a soul above her station; and I have been no more than her confidential servant. I intend, as you know, sir, to set up a shop later on in Sofia; and I look forward to her custom and recommendation should she marry into the nobility. [He goes out with impressive discretion, leaving them all staring after him.]

PETKOFF [breaking the silence] Well, I am—hm!

SERGIUS This is either the finest heroism or the most crawling baseness. Which is it, Bluntschli?

BLUNTSCHLI Never mind whether it's heroism or baseness. Nicola's the ablest man I've met in Bulgaria. I'll make him manager of a hotel if he can speak French and German.

LOUKA [suddenly breaking out at Sergius] I have been insulted by everyone here. You set them the example. You owe me an apology.

Sergius, like a repeating clock of which the spring has been touched, immediately begins to fold his arms.

BLUNTSCHLI [before he can speak] It's no use. He never apologizes.

LOUKA Not to you, his equal and his enemy. To me, his poor servant, he will not refuse to apologize.

SERGIUS [approvingly] You are right. [He bends his knee in his grandest manner.] Forgive me.

LOUKA I forgive you. [She timidly gives him her hand, which he kisses.] That touch makes me your affianced wife.

SERGIUS [springing up] Ah! I forgot that.

LOUKA [coldly] You can withdraw if you like.

SERGIUS Withdraw! Never! You belong to me. [He puts his arm about her.]

Catherine comes in and finds Louka in Sergius' arms, with all the rest gazing at them in bewildered astonishment.

CATHERINE   What does this mean?

Sergius releases Louka.

PETKOFF   Well, my dear, it appears that Sergius is going to marry Louka instead of Raina. [*She is about to break out indignantly at him: he stops her by exclaiming testily*] Don't blame me: I've nothing to do with it. [*He retreats to the stove.*]

CATHERINE   Marry Louka! Sergius: you are bound by your word to us!

SERGIUS   [*folding his arms*] Nothing binds me.

BLUNTSCHLI   [*much pleased by this piece of common sense*] Saranoff: your hand. My congratulations. These heroics of yours have their practical side after all. [*To Louka*] Gracious young lady: the best wishes of a good Republican! [*He kisses her hand, to Raina's great disgust, and returns to his seat.*]

CATHERINE   Louka: you have been telling stories.

LOUKA   I have done Raina no harm.

CATHERINE   [*haughtily*] Raina!

Raina, equally indignant, almost snorts at the liberty.

LOUKA   I have a right to call her Raina: she calls me Louka. I told Major Saranoff she would never marry him if the Swiss gentleman came back.

BLUNTSCHLI   [*rising, much surprised*] Hallo!

LOUKA   [*turning to Raina*] I thought you were fonder of him than of Sergius. You know best whether I was right.

BLUNTSCHLI   What nonsense! I assure you, my dear Major, my dear Madame, the gracious young lady simply saved my life, nothing else. She never cared two straws for me. Why, bless my heart and soul, look at the young lady and look at me. She, rich, young, beautiful, with her imagination full of fairy princes and noble natures and cavalry charges and goodness knows what! And I, a commonplace Swiss soldier who hardly knows what a decent life is after fifteen years of barracks and battles: a vagabond, a man who has spoiled all his chances in life through an incurably romantic disposition, a man—

SERGIUS   [*starting as if a needle had pricked him and interrupting Bluntschli in incredulous amazement*] Excuse me, Bluntschli: what did you say had spoiled your chances in life?

BLUNTSCHLI   [*promptly*] An incurably romantic disposition. I ran away from home twice when I was a boy. I went into the army instead of into my father's business. I climbed the balcony of this house when a man of sense would have dived into the nearest cellar. I came sneaking back here to have another look at the young lady when any other man of my age would have sent the coat back—

PETKOFF   My coat!

BLUNTSCHLI   —yes: that's the coat I mean—would have sent it back and gone quietly home. Do you suppose I am the sort of fellow a young girl falls in love with? Why, look at our ages! I'm thirty-four: I don't suppose the young lady is much over seventeen. [*This estimate produces a marked sensation, all the rest turning and staring at one another. He proceeds innocently.*] All that adventure which was life or death to me, was only a schoolgirl's game to her—chocolate creams and hide and seek. Here's the proof! [*He takes the photograph from the table.*] Now, I ask you, would a woman who took the affair seriously have sent me this and written on it "Raina, to her Chocolate Cream Soldier: a Souvenir"? [*He exhibits the photograph triumphantly, as if it settled the matter beyond all possibility of refutation.*]

PETKOFF   That's what I was looking for. How the deuce did it get there? [*He comes from the stove to look at it, and sits down on the ottoman.*]

BLUNTSCHLI   [*to Raina, complacently*] I have put everything right, I hope, gracious young lady.

RAINA   [*going to the table to face him*] I quite agree with your account of yourself. You are a romantic idiot. [*Bluntschli is unspeakably taken aback.*] Next time, I hope you will know the difference between a school girl of seventeen and a woman of twenty-three.

BLUNTSCHLI   [*stupefied*] Twenty-three!

Raina snaps the photograph contemptuously from his hand; tears it up; throws the pieces in his face; and sweeps back to her former place.

SERGIUS   [*with grim enjoyment of his rival's discomfiture*] Bluntschli: my one last belief is gone. Your sagacity is a fraud, like everything else. You have less sense than even I!

BLUNTSCHLI   [*overwhelmed*] Twenty-three! Twenty-three!! [*He considers.*] Hm! [*Swiftly making up his mind and coming to his host*] In that case, Major Petkoff, I beg to propose formally to become a suitor for your daughter's hand, in place of Major Saranoff retired.

RAINA   You dare!

BLUNTSCHLI   If you were twenty-three when you said those things to me this afternoon, I shall take them seriously.

CATHERINE   [*loftily polite*] I doubt, sir, whether you quite realize either my daughter's position or that of Major Sergius Saranoff, whose place you propose to take. The Petkoffs and the Saranoffs are known as the richest and most important families in the country. Our position is almost historical: we can go back for twenty years.

PETKOFF   Oh, never mind that, Catherine. [*To Bluntschli*] We should be most happy, Bluntschli, if it were only a question of your position; but hang it, you know, Raina is accustomed to a very comfortable establishment. Sergius keeps twenty horses.

BLUNTSCHLI   But who wants twenty horses? We're not going to keep a circus.

CATHERINE   [*severely*] My daughter, sir, is accustomed to a first-rate stable.

RAINA   Hush, mother: you're making me ridiculous.

BLUNTSCHLI   Oh well, if it comes to a question of an establishment, here goes! [*He darts impetuously to the table; seizes the papers in the blue envelope; and turns to Sergius.*] How many horses did you say?

SERGIUS   Twenty, noble Switzer.

BLUNTSCHLI   I have two hundred horses. [*They are amazed*] How many carriages?

SERGIUS   Three.

BLUNTSCHLI   I have seventy. Twenty-four of them will hold twelve inside, besides two on the box, without counting the driver and conductor. How many tablecloths have you?

SERGIUS   How the deuce do I know?

BLUNTSCHLI   Have you four thousand?

SERGIUS   No.

BLUNTSCHLI   I have. I have nine thousand six hundred pairs of sheets and blankets, with two thousand four hundred eider-down quilts. I have ten thousand knives and forks, and the same quantity of dessert spoons. I have three hundred servants. I have six palatial establishments, besides two livery stables, a tea garden, and a private house. I have four medals for distinguished services; I have the rank of an officer and the standing of a gentleman; and I have three native languages. Shew me any man in Bulgaria that can offer as much!

PETKOFF   [*with childish awe*] Are you Emperor of Switzerland?

BLUNTSCHLI   My rank is the highest known in Switzerland: I am a free citizen.

CATHERINE   Then, Captain Bluntschli, since you are my daughter's choice—

RAINA   [*mutinously*] He's not.

CATHERINE   [*ignoring her*] —I shall not stand in the way of her happiness. [*Petkoff is about to speak.*] That is Major Petkoff's feeling also.

PETKOFF   Oh, I shall be only too glad. Two hundred horses! Whew!

SERGIUS   What says the lady?

RAINA   [*pretending to sulk*] The lady says that he can keep his tablecloths and his omnibuses. I am not here to be sold to the highest bidder. [*She turns her back on him.*]

BLUNTSCHLI   I won't take that answer. I appealed to you as a fugitive, a beggar, and a starving man. You accepted me. You gave me your hand to kiss, your bed to sleep in, and your roof to shelter me.

RAINA   I did not give them to the Emperor of Switzerland.

BLUNTSCHLI   That's just what I say. [*He catches her by the shoulders and turns her face-to-face with him.*] Now tell us whom you did give them to.

RAINA   [*succumbing with a shy smile*]   To my chocolate cream soldier.

BLUNTSCHLI   [*with a boyish laugh of delight*]   That'll do. Thank you. [*He looks at his watch and suddenly becomes businesslike.*] Time's up, Major. You've managed those regiments so well that you're sure to be asked to get rid of some of the infantry of the Timok division. Send them home by way of Lom Palanka. Saranoff: don't get married until I come back: I shall be here punctually at five in the evening on Tuesday fortnight. Gracious ladies [*his heels click*] good evening. [*He makes them a military bow, and goes.*]

SERGIUS   What a man! Is he a man!

TENNESSEE WILLIAMS
1914–
Cat on a Hot Tin Roof

CHARACTERS

MARGARET

BRICK

MAE, sometimes called Sister Woman

BIG MAMA

DIXIE, a little girl

BIG DADDY

REVEREND TOOKER

GOOPER, sometimes called Brother Man

DOCTOR BAUGH, pronounced "Baw"

LACEY, a Negro servant

SOOKEY, another

CHILDREN

NOTES FOR THE DESIGNER

The set is the bed-sitting-room of a plantation home in the Mississippi Delta. It is along an upstairs gallery which probably runs around the entire house; it has two pairs of very wide doors opening onto the gallery, showing white balustrades against a fair summer sky that fades into dusk and night during the course of the play, which occupies precisely the time of its performance, excepting, of course, the fifteen minutes of intermission.

Perhaps the style of the room is not what you would expect in the home of the Delta's biggest cotton-planter. It is Victorian with a touch of the Far East. It hasn't changed much since it was occupied by the original owners of the place, Jack Straw and Peter Ochello, a pair of old bachelors who shared this room all their lives together. In other words, the room must evoke some ghosts; it is gently and poetically haunted by a relationship that must have involved a tenderness which was uncommon. This may be irrelevant or unnecessary, but I once saw a reproduction of a faded photograph of the verandah of Robert Louis Stevenson's home on that Samoan Island where he spent his last years, and there was a quality of tender light on weathered wood, such as porch furniture made of bamboo and wicker, exposed to tropical suns and tropical rains, which came to mind when I thought about the set for this play, bringing also to mind the grace and comfort of light, the reassurance it gives, on a late and fair afternoon in summer, the way that no matter what, even dread of death, is gently touched and soothed by it. For the set is the background for a play that deals with human extremities of emotion, and it needs that softness behind it.

The bathroom door, showing only pale-blue tile and silver towel racks, is in one side wall; the hall door in the opposite wall. Two articles of furniture need mention: a big double bed which staging should make a functional part of the set as often as suitable, the surface of which should be slightly raked to make figures on it seen more easily; and against the wall space between the two huge double doors upstage: a monumental monstrosity peculiar to our times, a *huge* console combination of radio-phonograph (hi-fi with three speakers) TV set *and* liquor cabinet, bearing and containing many glasses and bottles, all in one piece, which is a compostition of muted silver tones, and the opalescent tones of reflecting glass, a chromatic link, this thing, between the sepia (tawny gold) tones of the interior and the cool (white and blue) tones of the gallery and sky. This piece of furniture (?!), this monument, is a very complete and compact little shrine to virtually all the comforts and illusions behind which we hide from such things as the characters in the play are faced with. . . .

The set should be far less realistic than I have so far implied in this description of it. I think the walls below the ceiling should dissolve mysteriously into air; the set should be roofed by the sky; stars and moon suggested by traces of milky pallor, as if they were observed through a telescope lens out of focus.

Anything else I can think of? Oh, yes, fanlights (transoms shaped like an open glass fan) above all the doors in the set, with panes of blue and amber, and above all, the designer should take as many pains to give the actors room to move about freely (to show their restlessness, their passion for breaking out) as if it were a set for a ballet.

An evening in summer. The action is continuous, with two intermissions.

ACT I

At the rise of the curtain someone is taking a shower in the bathroom, the door of which is half open. A pretty young woman, with anxious lines in her face, enters the bedroom and crosses to the bathroom door.

MARGARET [*shouting above roar of water*]   One of those no-neck monsters hit me with a hot buttered biscuit so I have t' change!

Margaret's voice is both rapid and drawling. In her long speeches she has the vocal tricks of a priest delivering a liturgical chant, the lines are almost sung, always continuing a little beyond her breath so she has to gasp for another. Sometimes she intersperses the lines with a little wordless singing, such as "da-da-daaaa!"

Water turns off and Brick calls out to her, but is still unseen. A tone of politely feigned interest, masking indifference, or worse, is characteristic of his speech with Margaret.

BRICK Wha'd you say, Maggie? Water was on s' loud I couldn't hearya. . . .

MARGARET Well, I!—just remarked that!—one of th' no-neck monsters messed up m' lovely lace dress so I got t'—cha-a-ange. . . . [*She opens and kicks shut drawers of the dresser.*]

BRICK Why d'ya call Gooper's kiddies no-neck monsters?

MARGARET Because they've got no necks! Isn't that a good enough reason?

BRICK Don't they have any necks?

MARGARET None visible. Their fat little heads are set on their fat little bodies without a bit of connection.

BRICK That's too bad.

MARGARET Yes, it's too bad because you can't wring their necks if they've got no necks to wring! Isn't that right, honey? [*She steps out of her dress, stands in a slip of ivory satin and lace.*] Yep, they're no-neck monsters, all no-neck people are monsters . . .

Children shriek downstairs.

Hear them? Hear them screaming? I don't know where their voice boxes are located since they don't have necks. I tell you I got so nervous at that table tonight I thought I would throw back my head and utter a scream you could hear across the Arkansas border an' parts of Louisiana an' Tennessee. I said to your charming sister-in-law, Mae, honey, couldn't you feed those precious little things at a separate table with an oilcloth cover? They make such a mess an' the lace cloth looks *so* pretty! She made enormous eyes at me and said, "Ohhh, noooooo! On Big Daddy's birthday? Why, he would never forgive me!" Well, I want you to know, Big Daddy hadn't been at the table two minutes with those five no-neck monsters slobbering and drooling over their food before he threw down his fork an' shouted, "Fo' God's sake, Gooper, why don't you put them pigs at a trough in th' kitchen?"—Well, I swear, I simply could have di-ieed!

Think of it, Brick, they've got five of them and number six is coming. They've brought the whole bunch down here like animals to display at a county fair. Why, they have those children doin' tricks all the time!

"Junior, show Big Daddy how you do this, show Big Daddy how you do that, say your little piece fo' Big Daddy, Sister. Show your dimples, Sugar. Brother, show Big Daddy how you stand on your head!"—It goes on all the time, along with constant little remarks and innuendos about the fact that you and I have not produced any children, are totally childless and therefore totally useless!—Of course it's comical but it's also disgusting since it's so obvious what they're up to!

BRICK [*without interest*]   What are they up to, Maggie?

MARGARET   Why, you know what they're up to!

BRICK [*appearing*]   No, I don't know what they're up to.

He stands there in the bathroom doorway drying his hair with a towel and hanging onto the towel rack because one ankle is broken, plastered and bound. He is still slim and firm as a boy. His liquor hasn't started tearing him down outside. He has the additional charm of that cool air of detachment that people have who have given up the struggle. But now and then, when disturbed, something flashes behind it, like lightning in a fair sky, which shows that at some deeper level he is far from peaceful. Perhaps in a stronger light he would show some signs of deliquescence, but the fading, still warm, light from the gallery treats him gently.

MARGARET   I'll tell you what they're up to, boy of mine!—They're up to cutting you out of your father's estate, and—

She freezes momentarily before her next remark. Her voice drops as if it were somehow a personally embarrassing admission.

—Now we know that Big Daddy's dyin' of—*cancer*. . . .

There are voices on the lawn below: long-drawn calls across distance. Margaret raises her lovely bare arms and powders her armpits with a light sigh.

She adjusts the angle of a magnifying mirror to straighten an eyelash, then rises fretfully saying:

There's so much light in the room it—

BRICK [*softly but sharply*]   Do we?

MARGARET   Do we what?

BRICK   Know Big Daddy's dyin' of cancer?

MARGARET   Got the report today.

BRICK   Oh . . .

MARGARET [*letting down bamboo blinds which cast long, gold-fretted shadows over the room*]   Yep, got th' report just now . . . . it didn't surprise me, Baby. . . .

Her voice has range, and music; sometimes it drops low as a boy's and you have a sudden image of her playing boy's games as a child.

I recognized the symptoms soon's we got here last spring and I'm willin' to bet you that Brother Man and his wife were pretty sure of it, too. That more than likely explains why their usual summer migration to the coolness of the Great Smokies was passed up this summer in favor of—hustlin' down here ev'ry whipstitch with their whole screamin' tribe! And why so many allusions have been made to Rainbow Hill lately. You know what Rainbow Hill is? Place that's famous for treatin' alcoholics an' dope fiends in the movies!

BRICK   I'm not in the movies.

MARGARET   No, and you don't take dope. Otherwise you're a perfect candidate for Rainbow Hill, Baby, and that's where they aim to ship you—over my dead body! Yep, over my dead body they'll ship you there, but nothing would please them better. Then Brother Man could get a-hold of the purse strings and dole out remittances to us, maybe get power of attorney and sign checks for us and cut off our credit wherever, whenever he wanted! Son-of-a-bitch!—How'd you like that, Baby?— Well, you've been doin' just about ev'rything in your power to bring it about, you've just been doin' ev'rything you can think of to aid and abet them in this scheme of theirs! Quittin' work, devoting yourself to the occupation of drinkin'!—Breakin' your ankle last night on the high school athletic field: doin' what? Jumpin' hurdles? At two or three in the morning? Just fantastic! Got in the paper. *Clarksdale Register* carried a nice little item about it, human interest story about a well-known former athlete stagin' a one-man track meet on the Glorious Hill High School athletic field last night, but was slightly out of condition and didn't clear the first hurdle! Brother Man Gooper claims he exercised his influence t' keep it from goin' out over AP or UP or every goddam "P."

But, Brick? You still have one big advantage!

During the above swift flood of words, Brick has reclined with contrapuntal leisure on the snowy surface of the bed and has rolled over carefully on his side or belly.

BRICK [*wryly*]   Did you *say* something, Maggie?

MARGARET   Big Daddy dotes on you, honey. And he can't stand Brother Man and Brother Man's wife, that monster of fertility, Mae. Know how I know? By little expressions that flicker over his face when that woman is holding fo'th on one of her choice topics such as—how she refused twilight sleep!—when the twins were delivered! Because she feels motherhood's an experience that a woman ought to experience fully!—

in order to fully appreciate the wonder and beauty of it! HAH!—and how she made Brother Man come in an' stand beside her in the delivery room so he would not miss out on the "wonder and beauty" of it either!—producin' those no-neck monsters. . . .

A speech of this kind would be antipathetic from almost anybody but Margaret; she makes it oddly funny, because her eyes constantly twinkle and her voice shakes with laughter which is basically indulgent.

—Big Daddy shares my attitude toward those two! As for me, well—I give him a laugh now and then and he tolerates me. In fact!—I sometimes suspect that Big Daddy harbors a little unconscious "lech" fo' me. . . .

BRICK   What makes you think that Big Daddy has a lech for you, Maggie?
MARGARET   Way he always drops his eyes down my body when I'm talkin' to him, drops his eyes to my boobs an' licks his old chops! Ha ha!
BRICK   That kind of talk is disgusting.
MARGARET   Did anyone ever tell you that you're an ass-aching Puritan, Brick?

I think it's mighty fine that that ole fellow, on the doorstep of death, still takes in my shape with what I think is deserved appreciation!

And you wanta know something else? Big Daddy didn't know how many little Maes and Goopers had been produced! "How many kids have you got?" he asked at the table, just like Brother Man and his wife were new acquaintances to him! Big Mama said he was jokin', but that ole boy wasn't jokin', Lord, no!

And when they infawmed him that they had five already and were turning out number six!—the news seemed to come as a sort of unpleasant surprise . . .

Children yell below.

Scream, monsters!

Turns to Brick with a sudden, gay, charming smile which fades as she notices that he is not looking at her but into fading gold space with a troubled expression.

It is constant rejection that makes her humor "bitchy."

Yes, you should of been at that supper-table, Baby.

Whenever she calls him "baby" the word is a soft caress.

Y'know, Big Daddy, bless his ole sweet soul, he's the dearest ole thing in the world, but he does hunch over his food as if he preferred not to notice anything else. Well, Mae an' Gooper were side by side at the table, direckly across from Big Daddy, watchin' his face like hawks while they jawed an' jabbered about the cuteness an' brillance of th' no-neck monsters!

She giggles with a hand fluttering at her throat and her breast and her long throat arched.

She comes downstage and recreates the scene with voice and gesture.

And the no-neck monsters were ranged around the table, some in high chairs and some on th' *Books of Knowledge,* all in fancy little paper caps in honor of Big Daddy's birthday, and all through dinner, well, I want you to know that Brother Man an' his partner never once, for one moment, stopped exchanging pokes an' pinches an' kicks an' signs an' signals!—Why, they were like a couple of cardsharps fleecing a sucker.—Even Big Mama, bless her ole sweet soul, she isn't th' quickest an' brightest thing in the world, she finally noticed, at last, an' said to Gooper, "Gooper, what are you an' Mae makin' all these signs at each other about?"—I swear t' goodness, I nearly choked on my chicken!

Margaret, back at the dressing table, still doesn't see Brick. He is watching her with a look that is not quite definable—Amused? shocked? contemptuous?—part of those and part of something else.

Y'know—your brother Gooper still cherishes the illusion he took a giant step up the social ladder when he married Miss Mae Flynn of the Memphis Flynns.

But I have a piece of Spanish news for Gooper. The Flynns never had a thing in this world but money and they lost that, they were nothing at all but fairly successful climbers. Of course, Mae Flynn came out in Memphis eight years before I made my debut in Nashville, but I had friends at Ward-Belmont who came from Memphis and they used to come to see me and I used to go to see them for Christmas and spring vacations, and so I know who rates an' who doesn't rate in Memphis society. Why, y'know ole Papa Flynn, he barely escaped doing time in the Federal pen for shady manipulations on th' stock market when his chain stores crashed, and as for Mae having been a cotton carnival queen, as they remind us so often, lest we forget, well, that's one honor that I don't envy her for!—Sit on a brass throne on a tacky float an' ride down Main Street, smilin', bowin', and blowin' kisses to all the trash on the street—

She picks out a pair of jeweled sandals and rushes to the dressing table.

Why, year before last, when Susan McPheeters was singled out fo' that honor, y' know what happened to her? Y'know what happened to poor little Susie McPheeters?

BRICK [*absently*]   No. What happened to little Susie McPheeters?

MARGARET   Somebody spit tobacco juice in her face.

BRICK [*dreamily*]   Somebody spit tobacco juice in her face?

MARGARET   That's right, some old drunk leaned out of a window in the Hotel Gayoso and yelled, "Hey, Queen, hey, hey, there, Queenie!" Poor Susie looked up and flashed him a radiant smile and he shot out a squirt of tobacco juice right in poor Susie's face.

BRICK   Well, what d'you know about that.

MARGARET [*gaily*]   What do I know about it? I was there, I saw it!

BRICK [*absently*]   Must have been kind of funny.

MARGARET   Susie didn't think so. Had hysterics. Screamed like a banshee. They had to stop th' parade an' remove her from her throne an' go on with—

She catches sight of him in the mirror, gasps slightly, wheels about to face him. Count ten.

—Why are you looking at me like that?

BRICK [*whistling softly, now*]   Like what, Maggie?

MARGARET [*intensely, fearfully*]   The way y' were lookin' at me just now, befo' I caught your eye in the mirror and you started t' whistle! I don't know how t' describe it but it froze my blood!—I've caught you lookin' at me like that so often lately. What are you thinkin' of when you look at me like that?

BRICK   I wasn't conscious of lookin' at you, Maggie.

MARGARET   Well, I was conscious of it! What were you thinkin'?

BRICK   I don't remember thinking of anything, Maggie.

MARGARET   Don't you think I know that—? Don't you—?—Think I know that—?

BRICK [*cooly*]   Know *what*, Maggie?

MARGARET [*struggling for expression*]   That I've gone through this— hideous!—transformation, become—hard! Frantic! [*Then she adds, almost tenderly:*]   —cruel!!

That's what you've been observing in me lately. How could y' help but observe it? That's all right. I'm not—thin-skinned any more, can't afford t' be thin-skinned any more. [*She is now recovering her power.*] —But Brick? Brick?

BRICK   Did you say something?

MARGARET   I was *goin'* t' say something: that I get—lonely. Very!

BRICK   Ev'rybody gets that . . .

MARGARET   Living with someone you love can be lonelier—than living entirely *alone*!—if the one that y' love doesn't love you. . . .

There is a pause. Brick hobbles downstage and asks, without looking at her:

BRICK   Would you like to live alone, Maggie?

Another pause: then—after she has caught a quick, hurt breath:

MARGARET   No!—God!—I wouldn't!

Another gasping breath. She forcibly controls what must have been an impulse to cry out. We see her deliberately, very forcibly, going all the way back to the world in which you can talk about ordinary matters.

Did you have a nice shower?

BRICK   Uh-huh.

MARGARET   Was the water cool?

BRICK   No.

MARGARET   But it made y' feel fresh, huh?

BRICK   Fresher. . . .

MARGARET   I know something would make y' feel *much* fresher!

BRICK   What?

MARGARET   An alcohol rub. Or cologne, a rub with cologne!

BRICK   That's good after a workout but I haven't been workin' out, Maggie.

MARGARET   You've kept in good shape, though.

BRICK   [*indifferently*]   You think so, Maggie?

MARGARET   I always thought drinkin' men lost their looks, but I was plainly mistaken.

BRICK   [*wryly*]   Why, thanks, Maggie.

MARGARET   You're the only drinkin' man I know that it never seems t' put fat on.

BRICK   I'm gettin' softer, Maggie.

MARGARET   Well, sooner or later it's bound to soften you up. It was just beginning to soften up Skipper when—   [*She stops short.*]   I'm sorry. I never could keep my fingers off a sore—I wish you *would* lose your looks.

If you did it would make the martyrdom of Saint Maggie a little more bearable. But no such goddam luck. I actually believe you've gotten better looking since you've gone on the bottle. Yeah, a person who didn't know you would think you'd never had a tense nerve in your body or a strained muscle.

There are sounds of croquet on the lawn below: the click of mallets, light voices, near and distant.

Of course, you always had that detached quality as if you were playing a game without much concern over whether you won or lost, and now that you've lost the game, not lost but just quit playing, you have that rare sort of charm that usually only happens in very old or hopelessly sick people, the charm of the defeated.—You look so cool, so cool, so enviably cool.

REVEREND TOOKER [*off stage right*]   Now looka here, boy, lemme show you how to get outa that!

MARGARET   They're playing croquet. The moon has appeared and it's white, just beginning to turn a little bit yellow. . . .

You were a wonderful lover. . . .

Such a wonderful person to go to bed with, and I think mostly because you were really indifferent to it. Isn't that right? Never had any anxiety about it, did it naturally, easily, slowly, with absolute confidence and perfect calm, more like opening a door for a lady or seating her at a table than giving expression to any longing for her. Your indifference made you wonderful at lovemaking—*strange?*—but true. . . .

REVEREND TOOKER   Oh! That's a beauty.

DOCTOR BAUGH   Yeah. I got you boxed.

MARGARET   You know, if I thought you would never, never, *never* make love to me again—I would go downstairs to the kitchen and pick out the longest and sharpest knife I could find and stick it straight into my heart, I swear that I would!

REVEREND TOOKER   Watch out, you're gonna miss it.

DOCTOR BAUGH   You just don't know me, boy!

MARGARET   But one thing I don't have is the charm of the defeated, my hat is still in the ring, and I am determined to win!

There is the sound of croquet mallets hitting croquet balls.

REVEREND TOOKER   Mmm—You're too slippery for me.

MARGARET   —What is the victory of a cat on a hot tin roof?—I wish I knew. . . .

Just staying on it, I guess, as long as she can. . . .
DOCTOR BAUGH   Jus' like an eel, boy, jus' like an eel!

More croquet sounds.

MARGARET   Later tonight I'm going to tell you I love you an' maybe by that
time you'll be drunk enough to believe me. Yes, they're playing croquet. . . .

Big Daddy is dying of cancer. . . .

What were you thinking of when I caught you looking at me like that?
Were you thinking of Skipper?

Brick takes up his crutch, rises.

Oh, excuse me, forgive me, but laws of silence don't work! No, laws of
silence don't work. . . .

Brick crosses to the bar, takes a quick drink, and rubs his head with a towel.

Laws of silence don't work. . . .

When something is festering in your memory or your imagination, laws
of silence don't work, it's just like shutting a door and locking it on a
house on fire in hope of forgetting that the house is burning. But not
facing a fire doesn't put it out. Silence about a thing just magnifies it. It
grows and festers in silence, becomes malignant. . . .

He drops his crutch.

BRICK   Give me my crutch.

*He has stopped rubbing his hair dry but still stands hanging onto the towel rack in
a white towel-cloth robe.*

MARGARET   Lean on me.
BRICK   No, just give me my crutch.
MARGARET   Lean on my shoulder.
BRICK   *I don't want to lean on your shoulder, I want my crutch!*

This is spoken like sudden lightning.

Are you going to give me my crutch or do I have to get down on my knees on the floor and—

MARGARET *Here, here, take it, take it!* [*She has thrust the crutch at him.*]

BRICK [*hobbling out*] Thanks . . .

MARGARET We mustn't scream at each other, the walls in this house have ears. . . .

He hobbles directly to liquor cabinet to get a new drink.

—but that's the first time I've heard you raise your voice in a long time, Brick. A crack in the wall?—Of composure?

—I think that's a good sign. . . .

A sign of nerves in a player on the defensive!

Brick turns and smiles at her coolly over his fresh drink.

BRICK It just hasn't happened yet, Maggie.

MARGARET What?

BRICK The click I get in my head when I've had enough of this stuff to make me peaceful. . . .

Will you do me a favor?

MARGARET Maybe I will. What favor?

BRICK Just, just keep your voice down!

MARGARET [*in a hoarse whisper*] I'll do you that favor, I'll speak in a whisper, if not shut up completely, if *you* will do *me* a favor and make that drink your last one till after the party.

BRICK What party?

MARGARET Big Daddy's birthday party.

BRICK Is this Big Daddy's birthday?

MARGARET You know this is Big Daddy's birthday!

BRICK No, I don't, I forgot it.

MARGARET Well, I remembered it for you. . . .

They are both speaking as breathlessly as a pair of kids after a fight, drawing deep exhausted breaths and looking at each other with faraway eyes, shaking and panting together as if they had broken apart from a violent struggle.

BRICK Good for you, Maggie.

MARGARET You just have to scribble a few lines on this card.

BRICK You scribble something, Maggie.

MARGARET It's got to be your handwriting; it's your present, I've given him my present; it's got to be your handwriting!

The tension between them is building again, the voices becoming shrill once more.

BRICK I didn't get him a present.
MARGARET I got one for you.
BRICK All right. You write the card, then.
MARGARET And have him know you didn't remember his birthday?
BRICK I didn't remember his birthday.
MARGARET You don't have to prove you didn't!
BRICK I don't want to fool him about it.
MARGARET Just write "Love, Brick!" for God's—
BRICK No.
MARGARET You've *got* to!
BRICK I don't have to do anything I don't want to do. You keep forgetting the conditions on which I agreed to stay on living with you.
MARGARET [*out before she knows it*] I'm not living with you. We occupy the same cage.
BRICK You've got to remember the conditions agreed on.
SONNY [*off stage*] Mommy, give it to me. I had it first.
MAE Hush.
MARGARET They're impossible conditions!
BRICK Then why don't you—?
SONNY I want it, I want it!
MAE Get away!
MARGARET HUSH! Who is out there? Is somebody at the door?

There are footsteps in hall.

MAE [*outside*] May I enter a moment?
MARGARET OH, *you!* Sure. Come in, Mae.

Mae enters bearing aloft the bow of a young lady's archery set.

MAE Brick, is this thing yours?
MARGARET Why, Sister Woman—that's my Diana Trophy. Won it at the intercollegiate archery contest on the Ole Miss campus.
MAE It's a mighty dangerous thing to leave exposed round a house full of nawmal rid-blooded children attracted t'weapons.
MARGARET "Nawmal rid-blooded children attracted t'weapons" ought t'be taught to keep their hands off things that don't belong to them.

MAE Maggie, honey, if you had children of your own you'd know how funny that is. Will you please lock this up and put the key out of reach?

MARGARET Sister Woman, nobody is plotting the destruction of your kiddies. —Brick and I still have our special archers' license. We're goin' deer-huntin' on Moon Lake as soon as the season starts. I love to run with dogs through chilly woods, run, run leap over obstructions— [*She goes into the closet carrying the bow.*]

MAE How's the injured ankle, Brick?

BRICK Doesn't hurt. Just itches.

MAE Oh, my! Brick—Brick, you should've been downstairs after supper! Kiddies put on a show. Polly played the piano, Buster an' Sonny drums, an' then they turned out the lights an' Dixie an' Trixie puhfawmed a toe dance in fairy costume with *spahkluhs!* Big Daddy just beamed! He just beamed!

MARGARET [*from the closet with a sharp laugh*] Oh, I bet. It breaks my heart that we missed it! [*She reenters.*] But Mae? Why did y'give dawgs' names to all your kiddies?

MAE *Dogs'* names?

MARGARET [*sweetly*] Dixie, Trixie, Buster, Sonny, Polly!—Sounds like four dogs and a parrot . . .

MAE Maggie?

Margaret turns with a smile.

Why are you so catty?

MARGARET Cause I'm a cat! But why can't *you* take a joke, Sister Woman?

MAE Nothin' pleases me more than a joke that's funny. You know the real names of our kiddies. Buster's real name is Robert. Sonny's real name is Saunders. Trixie's real name is Marlene and Dixie's—

Gooper downstairs calls for her. "Hey, Mae! Sister Woman, intermission is over!"—She rushes to door, saying:

Intermission is over! See ya later!

MARGARET I wonder what Dixie's real name is?

BRICK Maggie, being catty doesn't help things any . . .

MARGARET I know! *WHY!*—Am I so catty?—Cause I'm consumed with envy an' eaten up with longing?—Brick, I'm going to lay out your beautiful Shantung silk suit from Rome and one of your monogrammed silk shirts. I'll put your cuff links in it, those lovely star sapphires I get you to wear so rarely. . . .

BRICK I can't get trousers on over this plaster cast.

MARGARET Yes, you can, I'll help you.

BRICK   I'm not going to get dressed, Maggie.

MARGARET   Will you just put on a pair of white silk pajamas?

BRICK   Yes, I'll do that, Maggie.

MARGARET   *Thank* you, thank you so *much!*

BRICK   Don't mention it.

MARGARET   *Oh, Brick!* How long does it have t' go on? This punishment? Haven't I done time enough, haven't I served my term, can't I apply for a—pardon?

BRICK   Maggie, you're spoiling my liquor. Lately your voice always sounds like you'd been running upstairs to warn somebody that the house was on fire!

MARGARET   Well, no wonder, no wonder. Y'know what I feel like, Brick?

I feel all the time like a cat on a hot tin roof!

BRICK   Then jump off the roof, jump off it, cats can jump off roofs and land on their four feet uninjured!

MARGARET   Oh, yes!

BRICK   Do it!—fo' God's sake, do it . . .

MARGARET   Do what?

BRICK   Take a lover!

MARGARET   I can't see a man but you! Even with my eyes closed, I just see you! Why don't you get ugly, Brick, why don't you please get fat or ugly or something so I could stand it? [*She rushes to hall door, opens it, listens.*] The concert is still going on! Bravo, no-necks, bravo! [*She slams and locks door fiercely.*]

BRICK   What did you lock the door for?

MARGARET   To give us a little privacy for a while.

BRICK   You know better, Maggie.

MARGARET   No, I don't know better. . . .

She rushes to gallery doors, draws the rose-silk drapes across them.

BRICK   Don't make a fool of yourself.

MARGARET   I don't mind makin' a fool of myself over you!

BRICK   I mind, Maggie. I feel embarrassed for you.

MARGARET   Feel embarrassed! But don't continue my torture. I can't live on and on under these circumstances.

BRICK   You agreed to—

MARGARET   I know but—

BRICK   —Accept that condition!

MARGARET   *I CAN'T! I CAN'T! CAN'T!*   [*She seizes his shoulder.*]

BRICK   Let go!

He breaks away from her and seizes the small boudoir chair and raises it like a lion-tamer facing a big circus cat.

Count five. She stares at him with her fist pressed to her mouth, then bursts into shrill, almost hysterical laughter. He remains grave for a moment, then grins and puts the chair down.

Big Mama calls through closed door.

BIG MAMA   Son? Son? Son?

BRICK   What is it, Big Mama?

BIG MAMA [*outside*]   Oh, son! We got the most wonderful news about Big Daddy. I just had t' run up an' tell you right this—   [*She rattles the knob.*]   —What's this door doin', locked, faw? You all think there's robbers in the house?

MARGARET   Big Mama, Brick is dressin', he's not dressed yet.

BIG MAMA   That's all right, it won't be the first time I've seen Brick not dressed. Come on, open this door!

Margaret, with a grimace, goes to unlock and open the hall door, as Brick hobbles rapidly to the bathroom and kicks the door shut. Big Mama has disappeared from the hall.

MARGARET   Big Mama?

Big Mama appears through the opposite gallery doors behind Margaret, huffing and puffing like an old bulldog. She is a short, stout woman; her sixty years and 170 pounds have left her somewhat breathless most of the time; she's always tensed like a boxer, or rather, a Japanese wrestler. Her "family" was maybe a little superior to Big Daddy's, but not much. She wears a black or silver lace dress and at least half a million in flashy gems. She is very sincere.

BIG MAMA [*loudly, startling Margaret*]   Here—I come through Gooper's and Mae's gall'ry door. Where's Brick? *Brick*—Hurry on out of there, son, I just have a second and want to give you the news about Big Daddy.—I hate locked doors in a house. . . .

MARGARET [*with affected lightness*]   I've noticed you do, Big Mama, but people have got to have *some* moments of privacy, don't they?

BIG MAMA   No, ma'am, not in *my* house. [*without pause*] Whacha took off you' dress faw? I thought that little lace dress was so sweet on yuh, honey.

MARGARET   I thought it looked sweet on me, too, but one of m' cute little table-partners used it for a napkin so—!

BIG MAMA [*picking up stockings on floor*]   What?

MARGARET   You know, Big Mama, Mae and Gooper's so touchy about those children—thanks, Big Mama . . .

Big Mama has thrust the picked-up stockings in Margaret's hand with a grunt.

—that you just don't dare to suggest there's any room for improvement in their—

BIG MAMA   Brick, hurry out!—Shoot, Maggie, you just don't like children.

MARGARET   I do SO like children! Adore them!—well brought up!

BIG MAMA [*gentle—loving*]   Well, why don't you have some and bring them up well, then, instead of all the time pickin' on Gooper's an' Mae's?

GOOPER [*shouting up the stairs*]   Hey, hey, Big Mama, Betsy an' Hugh got to go, waitin' t' tell yuh g'by!

BIG MAMA   Tell 'em to hold their hawses, I'll be right down in a jiffy!

GOOPER   Yes ma'am!

She turns to the bathroom door and calls out.

BIG MAMA   Son? Can you hear me in there?

There is a muffled answer.

We just got the full report from the laboratory at the Ochsner Clinic, completely negative, son, ev'rything negative, right on down the line! Nothin' a-tall's wrong with him but some little functional thing called a spastic colon. Can you hear me, son?

MARGARET   He can hear you, Big Mama.

BIG MAMA   Then why don't he say something? God Almighty, a piece of news like that should make him shout. It made *me* shout, I can tell you. I shouted and sobbed and fell right down on my knees!—Look! [*She pulls up her skirt.*]   See the bruises where I hit my kneecaps? Took both doctors to haul me back on my feet!

She laughs—she always laughs like hell at herself.

Big Daddy was furious with me! But ain't that wonderful news?

Facing bathroom again, she continues:

After all the anxiety we been through to git a report like that on Big Daddy's birthday? Big Daddy tried to hide how much of a load that news took off his mind, but didn't fool *me*. He was mighty close to crying about it *himself*!

Goodbyes are shouted downstairs, and she rushes to door.

GOOPER   Big Mama!
BIG MAMA   *Hold those people down there, don't let them go!*—Now, git dressed, we're all comin' up to this room fo' Big Daddy's birthday party because of your ankle.—How's his ankle, Maggie?
MARGARET   Well, he broke it, Big Mama.
BIG MAMA   I know he broke it.

A phone is ringing in hall. A Negro voice answers: "Mistuh Polly's res'dence."

I mean does it hurt him much still.
MARGARET   I'm afraid I can't give you that information, Big Mama. You'll have to ask Brick if it hurts much still or not.
SOOKEY [*in the hall*]   It's Memphis, Mizz Polly, it's Miss Sally in Memphis.
BIG MAMA   Awright, Sookey.

Big Mama rushes into the hall and is heard shouting on the phone:

Hello, Miss Sally. How are you, Miss Sally?—Yes, well, I was just gonna call you about it. *Shoot!*
MARGARET   Brick, don't!

Big Mama raises her voice to a bellow.

BIG MAMA   *Miss Sally? Don't ever call me from the Gayoso Lobby, too much talk goes on in that hotel lobby, no wonder you can't hear me!* Now listen, Miss Sally. They's nothin' serious wrong with Big Daddy. We got the report just now, they's nothin' wrong but a thing called a—spastic! SPASTIC!—colon . . . [*She appears at the hall door and calls to Margaret.*] —Maggie, come out here and talk to that fool on the phone. I'm shouted breathless!
MARGARET [*goes out and is heard sweetly at phone*]   Miss Sally? This is Brick's wife, Maggie. So nice to hear your voice. Can you hear *mine?* Well, *good!*—Big Mama just wanted you to know that they've got the report from the Ochsner Clinic and what Big Daddy has is a spastic colon. Yes. Spastic colon, Miss Sally. That's right, spastic colon. *G'bye, Miss Sally, hope I'll see you real soon!*

Hangs up a little before Miss Sally was probably ready to terminate the talk. She returns through the hall door.

She heard me perfectly. I've discovered with deaf people the thing to do is not shout at them but just enunciate clearly. My rich old Aunt Cornelia was deaf as the dead but I could make her hear me just by sayin' each word slowly, distinctly, close to her ear. I read her the *Commercial Appeal* ev'ry night, read her the classified ads in it, even, she never missed a word of it. But was she a mean ole thing! Know what I got when she died? Her unexpired subscriptions to five magazines and the Book-of-the-Month Club and a LIBRARY full of ev'ry dull book ever written! All else went to her hellcat of a sister . . . meaner than she was, even!

Big Mama has been straightening things up in the room during this speech.

BIG MAMA [*closing closet door on discarded clothes*]   Miss Sally sure is a case! Big Daddy says she's always got her hand out fo' something. He's not mistaken. That poor ole thing always has her hand out fo' somethin'. I don't think Big Daddy gives her as much as he should.
GOOPER   Big Mama! Come on now! Betsy and Hugh can't wait no longer!
BIG MAMA [*shouting*]   I'm comin'!

She starts out. At the hall door, turns and jerks a forefinger, first toward the bathroom door, then toward the liquor cabinet, meaning: "Has Brick been drinking?" Margaret pretends not to understand, cocks her head and raises her brows as if the pantomimic performance was completely mystifying to her.

Big Mama rushes back to Margaret.

Shoot! Stop playin' so dumb!—I mean has he been drinkin' that stuff much yet?
MARGARET [*with a little laugh*]   Oh! I think he had a highball after supper.
BIG MAMA   Don't laugh about it!—Some single men stop drinkin' when they git married and others start! Brick never touched liquor before he—!
MARGARET [*crying out*]   THAT'S NOT FAIR!
BIG MAMA   Fair or not fair I want to ask you a question, one question: D'you make Brick happy in bed?
MARGARET   Why don't you ask if he makes *me* happy in bed?
BIG MAMA   Because I know that—
MARGARET   *It works both ways!*
BIG MAMA   Something's not right! You're childless and my son drinks!
GOOPER   Come on, Big Mama!

Gooper has called her downstairs and she has rushed to the door on the line above. She turns at the door and points at the bed.

—When a marriage goes on the rocks, the rocks are *there*, right *there!*
MARGARET   *That's—*

Big Mama has swept out of the room and slammed the door.

        —not—*fair . . .*

Margaret is alone, completely alone, and she feels it. She draws in, hunches her shoulders, raises her arms with fists clenched, shuts her eyes tight as a child about to be stabbed with a vaccination needle. When she opens her eyes again, what she sees is the long oval mirror and she rushes straight to it, stares into it with a grimace and says: "Who are you?"—Then she crouches a little and answers herself in a different voice which is high, thin, mocking: "I am Maggie the Cat!"—Straightens quickly as bathroom door opens a little and Brick calls out to her.

BRICK   Has Big Mama gone?
MARGARET   She's gone.

He opens the bathroom door and hobbles out, with his liquor glass now empty, straight to the liquor cabinet. He is whistling softly. Margaret's head pivots on her long, slender throat to watch him.

She raises a hand uncertainly to the base of her throat, as if it was difficult for her to swallow, before she speaks:

    You know, our sex life didn't just peter out in the usual way, it was cut off short, long before the natural time for it to, and it's going to revive again, just as sudden as that. I'm confident of it. That's what I'm keeping myself attractive for. For the time when you'll see me again like other men see me. Yes, like other men see me. They still see me, Brick, and they like what they see. Uh-huh. Some of them would give their—

    Look, Brick!

She stands before the long oval mirror, touches her breast and then her hips with her two hands.

    How high my body stays on me!—Nothing has fallen on me—not a fraction. . . .

Her voice is soft and trembling: a pleading child's. At this moment as he turns to glance at her—a look which is like a player passing a ball to another player, third down and goal to go—she has to capture the audience in a grip so tight that she can hold it till the first intermission without any lapse of attention.

    Other men still want me. My face looks strained, sometimes, but I've kept my figure as well as you've kept yours, and men admire it. I still turn heads on the street. Why, last week in Memphis everywhere that I went men's eyes burned holes in my clothes, at the country club and in restaurants and department stores, there wasn't a man I met or walked by that didn't just eat me up with his eyes and turn around when I passed him and look back at me. Why, at Alice's party for her New York cousins, the best-lookin' man in the crowd—followed me upstairs and tried to force his way in the powder room with me, followed me to the door and tried to force his way in!

BRICK   Why didn't you let him, Maggie?

MARGARET   Because I'm not that common, for one thing. Not that I wasn't almost tempted to. You like to know who it was? It was Sonny Boy Maxwell, that's who!

BRICK   Oh, yeah, Sonny Boy Maxwell, he was a good end-runner but had a little injury to his back and had to quit.

MARGARET   He has no injury now and has no wife and still has a lech for me!

BRICK   I see no reason to lock him out of a powder room in that case.

MARGARET   And have someone catch me at it? I'm not that stupid. Oh, I might sometime cheat on you with someone, since you're so insultingly eager to have me do it!—But if I do, you can be damned sure it will be in a place and a time where no one but me and the man could possibly know. Because I'm not going to give you any excuse to divorce me for being unfaithful or anything else. . . .

BRICK   Maggie, I wouldn't divorce you for being unfaithful or anything else. Don't you know that? Hell. I'd be relieved to know that you'd found yourself a lover.

MARGARET   Well, I'm taking no chances. No, I'd rather stay on this hot tin roof.

BRICK   A hot tin roof's 'n uncomfo'table place t' stay on. . . .   [He starts to whistle softly.]

MARGARET   [through his whistle]   Yeah, but I can stay on it just as long as I have to.

BRICK   You could leave me, Maggie.

He resumes whistle. She wheels about to glare at him.

MARGARET   Don't want to and will not! Besides if I did, you don't have a cent to pay for it but what you get from Big Daddy and he's dying of cancer!

For the first time a realization of Big Daddy's doom seems to penetrate to Brick's consciousness, visibly, and he looks at Margaret.

BRICK   Big Mama just said he wasn't, that the report was okay.

MARGARET   That's what she thinks because she got the same story that they gave Big Daddy. And was just as taken in by it as he was, poor ole things. . . .

But tonight they're going to tell her the truth about it. When Big Daddy goes to bed, they're going to tell her that he is dying of cancer. [*She slams the dresser drawer.*]—It's malignant and it's terminal.

BRICK   Does Big Daddy know it?

MARGARET   Hell, do they *ever* know it? Nobody says, "You're dying." You have to fool them. They have to fool *themselves.*

BRICK   Why?

MARGARET   *Why?* Because human beings dream of life everlasting, that's the reason! But most of them want it on earth and not in heaven.

He gives a short, hard laugh at her touch of humor.

Well. . . . [*She touches up her mascara.*] That's how it is, anyhow. . . . [*She looks about.*] Where did I put down my cigarette? Don't want to burn up the home-place, at least not with Mae and Gooper and their five monsters in it!

She has found it and sucks at it greedily. Blows out smoke and continues:

So this is Big Daddy's last birthday. And Mae and Gooper, they know it, oh, *they* know it, all right. They got the first information from the Ochsner Clinic. That's why they rushed down here with their no-neck monsters. Because. Do you know something? Big Daddy's made no will? Big Daddy's never made out any will in his life, and so this campaign's afoot to impress him, forcibly as possible, with the fact that you drink and I've borne no children!

He continues to stare at her a moment, then mutters something sharp but not audible and hobbles rather rapidly out onto the long gallery in the fading, much faded, gold light.

MARGARET [*continuing her liturgical chant*]   Y'know, I'm *fond* of Big Daddy, I am genuinely fond of that old man, I really *am*, you know. . . .

BRICK [*faintly, vaguely*]   Yes, I know you are. . . .

MARGARET   I've always sort of admired him in spite of his coarseness, his four-letter words and so forth. Because Big Daddy *is* what he *is*, and he makes no bones about it. He hasn't turned gentleman farmer, he's still a Mississippi redneck, as much of a redneck as he must have been when he was just overseer here on the old Jack Straw and Peter Ochello place. But he got hold of it an' built it into th' biggest an' finest plantation in the Delta.—I've always *liked* Big Daddy. . . .

She crosses to the proscenium.

Well, this is Big Daddy's last birthday. I'm sorry about it. But I'm facing the facts. It takes money to take care of a drinker and that's the office that I've been elected to lately.

BRICK   You don't have to take care of me.

MARGARET   Yes, I do. Two people in the same boat have got to take care of each other. At least you want money to buy more Echo Spring when this supply is exhausted, or will you be satisfied with a ten-cent beer?

Mae an' Gooper are plannin' to freeze us out of Big Daddy's estate because you drink and I'm childless. But we can defeat that plan. We're *going* to defeat that plan!

Brick, y'know, I've been so God damn disgustingly poor all my life!—That's the *truth*, Brick!

BRICK   I'm not sayin' it isn't.

MARGARET   Always had to suck up to people I couldn't stand because they had money and I was poor as Job's turkey. You don't know what that's like. Well, I'll tell you, it's like you would feel a thousand miles away from Echo Spring!—And had to get back to it on that broken ankle . . . without a crutch!

That's how it feels to be as poor as Job's turkey and have to suck up to relatives that you hated because they had money and all you had was a bunch of hand-me-down clothes and a few old moldly three-per-cent government bonds. My daddy loved his liquor, he fell in love with his liquor the way you've fallen in love with Echo Spring!—And my poor Mama, having to maintain some semblance of social position, to keep appearances up, on an income of one hundred and fifty dollars a month on those old government bonds!

When I came out, the year that I made my debut, I had just two evening dresses! One Mother made me from a pattern in *Vogue,* the other a hand-me-down from a snotty rich cousin I hated!

—The dress that I married you in was my grandmother's weddin' gown. . . .

So that's why I'm like a cat on a hot tin roof!

Brick is still on the gallery. Someone below calls up to him in a warm Negro voice, "Hiya, Mistuh Brick, how yuh feelin'?" Brick raises his liquor glass as if that answered the question.

MARGARET   You can be young without money, but you can't be old without
it. You've got to be old *with* money because to be old without it is just
too awful, you've got to be one or the other, either *young* or *with money*,
you can't be old and *without* it.—That's the *truth*, Brick. . . .

Brick whistles softly, vaguely.

Well, now I'm dressed, I'm all dressed, there's nothing else for me to
do. [*Forlornly, almost fearfully.*]   I'm dressed, all dressed, nothing else
for me to do. . . .

She moves about restlessly, aimlessly, and speaks, as if to herself.

What am I—? Oh!—my bracelets. . . .

*She starts working a collection of bracelets over her hands onto her wrists, about
six on each, as she talks.*

I've thought a whole lot about it and now I know when I made my
mistake. Yes, I made my mistake when I told you the truth about that
thing with Skipper. Never should have confessed it, a fatal error, tellin'
you about that thing with Skipper.

BRICK   Maggie, shut up about Skipper. I mean it, Maggie; you got to shut up
about Skipper.

MARGARET   You ought to understand that Skipper and I—

BRICK   You don't think I'm serious, Maggie? You're fooled by the fact that I
am saying this quiet? Look, Maggie. What you're doing is a dangerous
thing to do. You're—you're—you're—foolin' with something that—
nobody ought to fool with.

MARGARET   This time I'm going to finish what I have to say to you. Skipper
and I made love, if love you could call it, because it made both of us feel
a little bit closer to you. You see, you son of a bitch, you asked too much
of people, of me, of him, of all the unlucky poor damned sons of bitches
that happen to love you, and there was a whole pack of them, yes, there
was a pack of them besides me and Skipper, you asked too goddam
much of people that loved you, you—superior creature!—you godlike
being!—And so we made love to each other to dream it was you, both of
us! Yes, yes, yes! Truth, truth! What's so awful about it? I like it, I think
the truth is—yeah! I shouldn't have told you. . . .

BRICK [*holding his head unnaturally still and uptilted a bit*]   It was Skipper that
told me about it. Not you, Maggie.

MARGARET   I told you!

BRICK   After he told me!

MARGARET   What does it matter who—?

DIXIE   I got your mallet, I got your mallet.

TRIXIE   Give it to me, give it to me. IT's mine.

Brick turns suddenly out upon the gallery and calls:

BRICK   Little girl! Hey, little girl!

LITTLE GIRL [*at a distance*]   What, Uncle Brick?

BRICK   Tell the folks to come up!—Bring everybody upstairs!

TRIXIE   It's mine, it's mine.

MARGARET   I can't stop myself! I'd go on telling you this in front of them all, if I had to!

BRICK   Little girl! Go on, go on, will you? Do what I told you, call them!

DIXIE   Okay.

MARGARET   Because it's got to be told and you, you!—you never let me!

She sobs, then controls herself, and continues almost calmly.

It was one of those beautiful, ideal things they tell about in the Greek legends, it couldn't be anything else, you being you, and that's what made it so sad, that's what made it so awful, because it was love that never could be carried through to anything satisfying or even talked about plainly.

BRICK   Maggie, you gotta stop this.

MARGARET   Brick, I tell you, you got to believe me, Brick, I *do* understand all about it! I—I think it was—*noble!* Can't you tell I'm sincere when I say I respect it? My only point, the only point that I'm making, is life has got to be allowed to continue even after the *dream* of life is —all—over. . . .

Brick is without his crutch. Leaning on furniture, he crosses to pick it up as she continues as if possessed by a will outside herself:

Why I remember when we double-dated at college, Gladys Fitzgerald and I and you and Skipper, it was more like a date between you and Skipper. Gladys and I were just sort of tagging along as if it was necessary to chaperone you!—to make a good public impression—

BRICK [*turns to face her, half lifting his crutch*]   Maggie, you want me to hit you with this crutch? Don't you know I could kill you with this crutch?

MARGARET   Good, Lord, man, d' you think I'd care if you did?

BRICK   One man has one great good true thing in his life. One great good thing which is true!—I had friendship with Skipper.—You are naming it dirty!

MARGARET   I'm not naming it dirty! I am naming it clean.

BRICK   Not love with you, Maggie, but friendship with Skipper was that one great true thing, and you are naming it dirty!

MARGARET   Then you haven't been listenin', not understood what I'm saying! I'm naming it so damn clean that it killed poor Skipper!—You two had something that had to be kept on ice, yes, incorruptible, yes!—and death was the only icebox where you could keep it. . . .

BRICK   I married you, Maggie. Why would I marry you, Maggie, if I was—?

MARGARET   Brick, let me finish!—I know, believe me I know, that it was only Skipper that harbored even any *unconscious* desire for anything not perfectly pure between you two!—Now let me skip a little. You married me early that summer we graduated out of Ole Miss, and we were happy, weren't we, we were blissful, yes, hit heaven together ev'ry time that we loved! But that fall you an' Skipper turned down wonderful offers of jobs in order to keep on bein' football heroes—pro-football heroes. You organized the Dixie Stars that fall, so you could keep on bein' teammates forever! But somethin' was not right with it!—*Me included!*—between you. Skipper began hittin' the bottle . . . you got a spinal injury—couldn't play the Thanksgivin' game in Chicago, watched it on TV from a traction bed in Toledo. I joined Skipper. The Dixie Stars lost because poor Skipper was drunk. We drank together that night all night in the bar of the Blackstone and when cold day was comin' up over the Lake an' we were comin' out drunk to take a dizzy look at it, I said, "SKIPPER! STOP LOVIN' MY HUSBAND OR TELL HIM HE'S GOT TO LET YOU ADMIT IT TO HIM!"—one way or another!

HE SLAPPED ME HARD ON THE MOUTH!—then turned and ran without stopping once, I am sure, all the way back into his room at the Blackstone. . . .

—When I came to his room that night, with a little scratch like a shy little mouse at his door, he made that pitiful, ineffectual little attempt to prove that what I had said wasn't true. . . .

Brick strikes at her with crutch, a blow that shatters the gemlike lamp on the table.

—In this way, I destroyed him, by telling him truth that he and his world which he was born and raised in, yours and his world, had told him could not be told?

—From then on Skipper was nothing at all but a receptacle for liquor and drugs. . . .

—Who shot cock robin? I with my—   [*She throws back her head with tight shut eyes.*]   —merciful arrow!

Brick strikes at her; misses.

Missed me!—Sorry,—I'm not tryin' to whitewash my behavior, Christ, no! Brick, I'm not good. I don't know why people have to pretend to be good, nobody's good. The rich or the well-to-do can afford to respect moral patterns, conventional moral patterns, but I could never afford to, yeah, but—I'm honest! Give me credit for just that, will you *please?*— Born poor, raised poor, expect to die poor unless I manage to get us something out of what Big Daddy leaves when he dies of cancer! But Brick?!—*Skipper is dead! I'm alive!* Maggie the cat is—

Brick hops awkwardly forward and strikes at her again with his crutch.

—*alive! I am alive, alive! I am . . .*

He hurls the crutch at her, across the bed she took refuge behind, and pitches forward on the floor as she completes her speech.

—*alive!*

A little girl, Dixie, bursts into the room, wearing an Indian war bonnet and firing a cap pistol at Margaret and shouting: "Bang, bang, bang!"

Laughter downstairs floats through the open hall door. Margaret had crouched gasping to bed at child's entrance. She now rises and says with cool fury:

Little girl, your mother or someone should teach you—[*gasping*]—to knock at a door before you come into a room. Otherwise people might think that you—lack—good breeding. . . .

DIXIE   Yanh, yanh, yanh, what is Uncle Brick doin' on th' floor?

BRICK   I tried to kill your Aunt Maggie, but I failed—and I fell. Little girl, give me my crutch so I can get up off th' floor.

MARGARET   Yes, give your uncle his crutch, he's a cripple, honey, he broke his ankle last night jumping hurdles on the high school athletic field!

DIXIE   What were you jumping hurdles for, Uncle Brick?

BRICK   Because I used to jump them, and people like to do what they used to do, even after they've stopped being able to do it. . . .

MARGARET   That's right, that's your answer, now go away, little girl.

Dixie fires cap pistol at Margaret three times.

Stop, you stop that, monster! You little no-neck monster! [*She seizes the cap pistol and hurls it through gallery doors.*]

DIXIE [*with a precocious instinct for the cruelest thing*]   You're *jealous!*—You're just jealous because you can't have babies!

She sticks out her tongue at Margaret as she sashays past her with her stomach stuck out, to the gallery. Margaret slams the gallery doors and leans panting against them. There is a pause. Brick has replaced his spilt drink and sits, faraway, on the great four-poster bed.

MARGARET   You see?—they gloat over us being childless, even in front of their five little no-neck monsters!

Pause. Voices approach on the stairs.

Brick?—I've been to a doctor in Memphis, a—a gynecologist. . . .

I've been completely examined, and there is no reason why we can't have a child whenever we want one. And this is my time by the calendar to conceive. Are you listening to me? Are you? Are you LISTENING TO ME!

BRICK   Yes. I hear you, Maggie. [*His attention returns to her inflamed face.*]   —But how in hell on earth do you imagine—that you're going to have a child by a man that can't stand you?

MARGARET   That's a problem that I will have to work out.   [*She wheels about to face the hall door.*]

MAE [*off stage left*]   Come on, Big Daddy. We're all goin' up to Brick's room.

From off stage left, voices: Reverend Tooker, Doctor Baugh, Mae.

MARGARET   *Here they come!*

The lights dim.

Curtain

ACT II

There is no lapse of time. Margaret and Brick are in the same positions they held at the end of Act I.

MARGARET [*at door*]   *Here they come!*

Big Daddy appears first, a tall man with a fierce, anxious look, moving carefully not to betray his weakness even, or especially, to himself.

GOOPER   I read in the *Register* that you're getting a new memorial window.

Some of the people are approaching through the hall, others along the gallery: voices from both directions. Gooper and Reverend Tooker become visible outside gallery doors, and their voices come in clearly.

They pause outside as Gooper lights a cigar.

REVEREND TOOKER [*vivaciously*] Oh, but St. Paul's in Grenada has three memorial windows, and the latest one is a Tiffany stained-glass window that cost twenty-five hundred dollars, a picture of Christ the Good Shepherd with a Lamb in His arms.

MARGARET Big Daddy.

BIG DADDY Well, Brick.

BRICK Hello Big Daddy.—Congratulations!

BIG DADDY —Crap. . . .

GOOPER Who give that window, Preach?

REVEREND TOOKER Clyde Fletcher's widow. Also presented St. Paul's with a baptismal font.

GOOPER Y'know what somebody ought t' give your church is a *coolin'* system, Preach.

MAE [*almost religiously*] —Let's see now, they've had their *tyyy*-phoid shots, and their tetanus shots, their diptheria shots and their hepatitis shots and their polio shots, they got *those* shots every month from May through September, and—Gooper? Hey! Gooper!—What all have the kiddies been shot faw?

REVEREND TOOKER Yes, siree, Bob! And y'know what Gus Hamma's family gave in his memory to the church at Two Rivers? A complete new stone parish-house with a basketball court in the basement and a—

BIG DADDY [*uttering a loud barking laugh which is far from truly mirthful*] Hey, Preach! What's all this talk about memorials, Preach? Y' think somebody's about t' kick off around here? 'S that it?

Startled by this interjection, Reverend Tooker decides to laugh at the question almost as loud as he can.

How he would answer the question we'll never know, as he's spared that embarrassment by the voice of Gooper's wife, Mae, rising high and clear as she appears with "Doc" Baugh, the family doctor, through the hall door.

MARGARET [*overlapping a bit*] Turn on the hi-fi, Brick! Let's have some music t' start off th' party with!

BRICK You turn it on, Maggie.

The talk becomes so general that the room sounds like a great aviary of chattering birds. Only Brick remains unengaged, leaning upon the liquor cabinet with his faraway smile, an ice cube in a paper napkin with which he now and then rubs his forehead. He doesn't respond to Margaret's command. She bounds forward and stoops over the instrument panel of the console.

GOOPER   We gave 'em that thing for a third anniversary present, got three speakers in it.

The room is suddenly blasted by the climax of a Wagnerian opera or a Beethoven symphony.

BIG DADDY   *Turn that dam thing off!*

Almost instant silence, almost instantly broken by the shouting charge of Big Mama, entering through hall door like a charging rhino.

BIG MAMA   *Wha's my Brick, wha's mah precious baby!!*
BIG DADDY   *Sorry! Turn it back on!*

Everyone laughs very loud. Big Daddy is famous for his jokes at Big Mama's expense, and nobody laughs louder at these jokes than Big Mama herself, though sometimes they're pretty cruel and Big Mama has to pick up or fuss with something to cover the hurt that the loud laugh doesn't quite cover.

On this occasion, a happy occasion because the dread in her heart has also been lifted by the false report on Big Daddy's condition, she giggles, grotesquely, coyly, in Big Daddy's direction and bears down upon Brick, all very quick and alive.

BIG MAMA   Here he is, here's my precious baby! What's that you've got in your hand? You put that liquor down, son, your hand was made fo' holdin' somethin' better than that!
GOOPER   Look at Brick put it down!

Brick has obeyed Big Mama by draining the glass and handing it to her. Again everyone laughs, some high, some low.

BIG MAMA   Oh, you bad boy, you, you're my bad little boy. Give Big Mama a kiss, you bad boy, you!—Look at him shy away, will you? Brick never liked bein' kissed or made a fuss over, I guess because he's always had too much of it!

Son, you turn that thing off!

Brick has switched on the TV set.

I can't stand TV, radio was bad enough but TV has gone it one better, I mean—[*plops wheezing in chair*]—one worse, ha ha! Now what'm I sittin' down here faw? I want t' sit next to my sweetheart on the sofa, hold hands with him and love him up a little!

Big Mama has on a black and white figured chiffon. The large irregular patterns, like the markings of some massive animal, the luster of her great diamonds and many pearls, the brilliants set in the silver frames of her glasses, her riotous voice, booming laugh, have dominated the room since she entered. Big Daddy has been regarding her with a steady grimace of chronic annoyance.

BIG MAMA [*still louder*]   Preacher, Preacher, hey, Preach! Give me you' hand an' help me up from this chair!
REVEREND TOOKER   None of your tricks, Big Mama!
BIG MAMA   What tricks? You give me you' hand so I can get up an'—

Reverend Tooker extends her his hand. She grabs it and pulls him into her lap with a shrill laugh that spans an octave in two notes.

Ever seen a preacher in a fat lady's lap? Hey, hey, folks! Ever seen a preacher in a fat lady's lap?

Big Mama is notorious throughout the Delta for this sort of inelegant horseplay. Margaret looks on with indulgent humor, sipping Dubonnet "on the rocks" and watching Brick, but Mae and Gooper exchange signs of humorless anxiety over these antics, the sort of behavior which Mae thinks may account for their failure to quite get in with the smartest young married set in Memphis, despite all. One of the Negroes, Lacy or Sookey, peeks in, cackling. They are waiting for a sign to bring in the cake and champagne. But Big Daddy's not amused. He doesn't understand why, in spite of the infinite mental relief he's received from the doctor's report, he still has these same old fox teeth in his guts. "This spastic condition is something else," he says to himself, but aloud he roars at Big Mama:

BIG DADDY   *BIG MAMA, WILL YOU QUIT HORSIN'?*—You're too old an' too fat fo' that sort of crazy kid stuff an' besides a woman with your blood pressure—she had two hundred last spring!—is riskin' a stroke when you mess around like that. . . .

Mae blows on a pitch pipe.

BIG MAMA   *Here comes Big Daddy's birthday!*

Negroes in white jackets enter with an enormous birthday cake ablaze with candles and carrying buckets of champagne with satin ribbons about the bottle necks.

Mae and Gooper strike up song, and everybody, including the Negroes and Children, joins in. Only Brick remains aloof.

EVERYONE
     Happy birthday to you.
     Happy birthday to you.
     Happy birthday, Big Daddy—

Some sing: "Dear, Big Daddy!"

     Happy birthday to you.

Some sing: "How old are you?"

Mae has come down center and is organizing her children like a chorus. She gives them a barely audible: "One, two, three!" and they are off in the new tune.

CHILDREN
     Skinamarinka—dinka—dink
     Skinamarinka—do
     We love you.
     Skinamarinka—dinka—dink
     Skinamarinka—do.

All together, they turn to Big Daddy.

     Big Daddy, you!

They turn back front, like a musical comedy chorus.

     We love you in the morning;
     We love you in the night.
     We love you when we're with you,
     And we love you out of sight.
     Skinamarinka—dinka—dink
     Skinamarinka—do.

Mae turns to Big Mama.

     Big Mama, too!

Big Mama bursts into tears. The Negroes leave.

BIG DADDY   Now Ida, what the hell is the matter with you?

MAE   She's just so happy.

BIG MAMA   I'm just so happy, Big Daddy, I have to cry or something.

Sudden and loud in the hush:

> Brick, do you know the wonderful news that Doc Baugh got from the
> clinic about Big Daddy? Big Daddy's one hundred per cent!

MARGARET   Isn't that wonderful?

BIG MAMA   He's just one hundred per cent. Passed the examination with
flying colors. Now that we know there's nothing wrong with Big Daddy
but a spastic colon, I can tell you something. I was worried sick, half out
of my mind, for fear that Big Daddy might have a thing like—

Margaret cuts through this speech, jumping up and exclaiming shrilly:

MARGARET   Brick, honey, aren't you going to give Big Daddy his birthday
present?

Passing by him, she snatches his liquor glass from him.

She picks up a fancily wrapped package.

> Here it is, Big Daddy, this is from Brick!

BIG MAMA   This is the biggest birthday Big Daddy's ever had, a hundred
presents and bushels of telegrams from—

MAE [*at same time*]   What is it, Brick?

GOOPER   I bet 500 to 50 that Brick don't *know* what it is.

BIG MAMA   The fun of presents is not knowing what they are till you open
the package. Open your present, Big Daddy.

BIG DADDY   Open it you'self. I want to ask Brick somethin'! Come here,
Brick.

MARGARET   Big Daddy's callin' you, Brick.   [*She is opening the package.*]

BRICK   Tell Big Daddy I'm crippled.

BIG DADDY   I see you're crippled. I want to know how you got crippled.

MARGARET [*making diversionary tactics*]   *Oh, look, oh, look, why, it's a
cashmere robe!* [*She holds the robe up for all to see.*]

MAE   You sound surprised, Maggie.

MARGARET   I never saw one before.

MAE   That's funny.—*Hah!*

MARGARET [*turning on her fiercely, with a brilliant smile*]   Why is it funny? All
my family ever had was family—and luxuries such as cashmere robes
still surprise me!

BIG DADDY [*ominously*]   Quiet!

MAE [*heedless in her fury*]   I don't see how you could be so surprised when you bought it yourself at Loewenstein's in Memphis last Saturday. You know how I know?

BIG DADDY   I said, Quiet!

MAE   —I know because the salesgirl that sold it to you waited on me and said, Oh, Mrs. Pollitt, your sister-in-law just bought a cashmere robe for your husband's father!

MARGARET   Sister Woman! Your talents are wasted as a housewife and mother, you really ought to be with the FBI or—

BIG DADDY   QUIET!

Reverend Tooker's reflexes are slower than the others'. He finishes a sentence after the bellow.

REVEREND TOOKER [*to Doc Baugh*]   —the Stork and the Reaper are running neck and neck!

He starts to laugh gaily when he notices the silence and Big Daddy's glare. His laugh dies falsely.

BIG DADDY   Preacher, I hope I'm not butting in on more talk about memorial stained-glass windows, am I, Preacher?

Reverend Tooker laughs feebly, then coughs dryly in the embarrassed silence.

Preacher?

BIG MAMA   Now, Big Daddy, don't you pick on Preacher!

BIG DADDY [*raising his voice*]   You ever hear that expression all hawk and no spit? You bring that expression to mind with that little dry cough of yours, all hawk an' no spit. . . .

The pause is broken only by a short startled laugh from Margaret, the only one there who is conscious of and amused by the grotesque.

MAE [*raising her arms and jangling her bracelets*]   I wonder if the mosquitoes are active tonight?

BIG DADDY   What's that, Little Mama? Did you make some remark?

MAE   Yes, I said I wondered if the mosquitoes would eat us alive if we went out on the gallery for a while.

BIG DADDY   Well, if they do, I'll have your bones pulverized for fertilizer!

BIG MAMA [*quickly*]   Last week we had an airplane spraying the place and I think it done some good, at least I haven't had a—

BIG DADDY [*cutting her speech*]   Brick, they tell me, if what they tell me is true, that you done some jumping last night on the high school athletic field?

BIG MAMA   Brick, Big Daddy is talking to you, son.

BRICK [*smiling vaguely over his drink*]   What was that, Big Daddy?

BIG DADDY   They said you done some jumping on the high school track field last night.

BRICK   That's what they told me, too.

BIG DADDY   Was it jumping or humping that you were doing out there? What were you doing out there at three A.M., layin' a woman on that cinder track?

BIG MAMA   Big Daddy, you are off the sick-list, now, and I'm not going to excuse you for talkin' so—

BIG DADDY   Quiet!

BIG MAMA   —*nasty* in front of Preacher and—

BIG DADDY   QUIET!—I ast you, Brick, if you was cuttin' you'self a piece o' poon-tang last night on that cinder track? I thought maybe you were chasin' poon-tang on that track an' tripped over something in the heat of the chase—'sthat it?

Gooper laughs, loud and false, others nervously following suit. Big Mama stamps her foot, and purses her lips, crossing to Mae and whispering something to her as Brick meets his father's hard, intent, grinning stare with a slow, vague smile that he offers all situations from behind the screen of his liquor.

BRICK   No, sir, I don't think so. . . .

MAE [*at the same time, sweetly*]   Reverend Tooker, let's you and I take a stroll on the widow's walk.

She and the preacher go out on the gallery as Big Daddy says:

BIG DADDY   Then what the hell were you doing out there at three o'clock in the morning?

BRICK   Jumping the hurdles, Big Daddy, runnin' and jumpin' the hurdles, but those high hurdles have gotten too high for me, now.

BIG DADDY   Cause you was drunk?

BRICK [*his vague smile fading a little*]   Sober I wouldn't have tried to jump the low ones. . . .

BIG MAMA [*quickly*]   Big Daddy, blow out the candles on your birthday cake!

MARGARET [*at the same time*]   I want to propose a toast to Big Daddy Pollitt on his sixty-fifth birthday, the biggest cotton planter in—

BIG DADDY [*bellowing with fury and disgust*]   I told you to stop it, now stop it, quit this—!

BIG MAMA [*coming in front of Big Daddy with the cake*]   Big Daddy, I will not
   allow you to talk that way, not even on your birthday, I—
BIG DADDY   I'll talk like I want to on my birthday, Ida, or any other goddam
   day of the year and anybody here that don't like it knows what they can
   do!
BIG MAMA   You don't mean that!
BIG DADDY   What makes you think I don't mean it?

*Meanwhile various discreet signals have been exchanged and Gooper has also gone
out on the gallery.*

BIG MAMA   I just know you don't mean it.
BIG DADDY   You don't know a goddam thing and you never did!
BIG MAMA   Big Daddy, you don't mean that.
BIG DADDY   Oh, yes, I do, oh, yes, I do, I mean it! I put up with a whole lot of
   crap around here because I thought I was dying. And you thought I was
   dying and you started taking over, well, you can stop taking over now,
   Ida, because I'm not gonna die, you can just stop now this business of
   taking over because you're not taking over because I'm not dying, I went
   through the laboratory and the goddam exploratory operation and
   there's nothing wrong with me but a spastic colon. And I'm not dying of
   cancer which you thought I was dying of. Ain't that so? Didn't you think
   that I was dying of cancer, Ida?

*Almost everybody is out on the gallery but the two old people glaring at each other
across the blazing cake.*

Big Mama's chest heaves and she presses a fat fist to her mouth.

Big Daddy continues, hoarsely:

   Ain't that so, Ida? Didn't you have an idea I was dying of cancer and now
   you could take control of this place and everything on it? I got that
   impression, I seemed to get that impression. Your loud voice everywhere,
   your fat old body butting in here and there!
BIG MAMA   Hush! The Preacher!
BIG DADDY   Fuck the goddam preacher!

Big Mama gasps loudly and sits down on the sofa which is almost too small for her.

   Did you hear what I said? I said fuck the goddam preacher!

*Somebody closes the gallery doors from outside just as there is a burst of fireworks
and excited cries from the children.*

BIG MAMA   I never seen you act like this before and I can't think what's got in you!

BIG DADDY   I went through all that laboratory and operation and all just so I would know if you or me was boss here! Well, now it turns out that I am and you ain't—and that's my birthday present—and my cake and champagne!—because for three years now you been gradually taking over. Bossing. Talking. Sashaying your fat old body around the place I made! I made this place! I was overseer on it! I was the overseer on the old Straw and Ochello plantation. I quit school at ten! I quit school at ten years old and went to work like a nigger in the fields. And I rose to be overseer of the Straw and Ochello plantation. And old Straw died and I was Ochello's partner and the place got bigger and bigger and bigger and bigger and bigger! I did all that myself with no goddam help from you, and now you think you're just about to take over. Well, I am just about to tell you that you are not just about to take over, you are not just about to take over a God damn thing. Is that clear to you, Ida? Is that very plain to you, now? Is that understood completely? I been through the laboratory from A to Z. I've had the goddam exploratory operation, and nothing is wrong with me but a spastic colon—made spastic, I guess, by *disgust!* By all the goddam lies and liars that I have had to put up with, and all the goddam hypocrisy that I lived with all these forty years that we been livin' together!

Hey! Ida!! Blow out the candles on the birthday cake! Purse up your lips and draw a deep breath and blow out the goddam candles on the cake!

BIG MAMA   Oh, Big Daddy, oh, oh, oh, Big Daddy!

BIG DADDY   What's the matter with you?

BIG MAMA   *In all these years you never believed that I loved you??*

BIG DADDY   Huh?

BIG MAMA   *And I did, I did so much, I did love you!*—I even loved your hate and your hardness, Big Daddy!   [*She sobs and rushes awkwardly out onto the gallery.*]

BIG DADDY   [*to himself*]   *Wouldn't it be funny if that was true. . . .*

A pause is followed by a burst of light in the sky from the fireworks.

BRICK! HEY, BRICK!

He stands over his blazing birthday cake.

After some moments, Brick hobbles in on his crutch, holding his glass.

Margaret follows him with a bright, anxious smile.

I didn't call you, Maggie. I called Brick.
MARGARET   I'm just delivering him to you.

She kisses Brick on the mouth which he immediately wipes with the back of his hand. She flies girlishly back out. Brick and his father are alone.

BIG DADDY   Why did you do that?
BRICK   Do what, Big Daddy?
BIG DADDY   Wipe her kiss off your mouth like she'd spit on you.
BRICK   I don't know. I wasn't conscious of it.
BIG DADDY   That woman of yours has a better shape on her than Gooper's but somehow or other they got the same look about them.
BRICK   What sort of look is that, Big Daddy?
BIG DADDY   I don't know how to describe it but it's the same look.
BRICK   They don't look peaceful, do they?
BIG DADDY   No, they sure in hell don't.
BRICK   They look nervous as cats?
BIG DADDY   That's right, they look nervous as cats.
BRICK   Nervous as a couple of cats on a hot tin roof?
BIG DADDY   That's right, boy, they look like a couple of cats on a hot tin roof. It's funny that you and Gooper being so different would pick out the same type of woman.
BRICK   Both of us married into society, Big Daddy.
BIG DADDY   Crap . . . I wonder what gives them both that look?
BRICK   Well. They're sittin' in the middle of a big piece of land, Big Daddy, twenty-eight thousand acres is a pretty big piece of land and so they're squaring off on it, each determined to knock off a bigger piece of it than the other whenever you let it go.
BIG DADDY   I got a surprise for those women. I'm not gonna let it go for a long time yet if that's what they're waiting for.
BRICK   That's right, Big Daddy. You just sit tight and let them scratch each other's eyes out. . . .
BIG DADDY   You bet your life I'm going to sit tight on it and let those sons of bitches scratch their eyes out, ha ha ha. . . .

But Gooper's wife's a good breeder, you got to admit she's fertile. Hell, at supper tonight she had them all at the table and they had to put a couple of extra leafs in the table to make room for them, she's got five head of them, now, and another one's comin'.
BRICK   Yep, number six is comin'. . . .
BIG DADDY   Six hell, she'll probably drop a litter next time. Brick, you know, I swear to God, I don't know the way it happens?

BRICK   The way what happens, Big Daddy?

BIG DADDY   You git you a piece of land, by hook or crook, an' things start growin' on it, things accumulate on it, and the first thing you know it's completely out of hand, completely out of hand!

BRICK   Well, they say nature hates a vacuum, Big Daddy.

BIG DADDY   That's what they say, but sometimes I think that a vacuum is a hell of a lot better than some of the stuff that nature replaces it with.

Is someone out there by that door?

GOOPER   Hey Mae.

BRICK   Yep.

BIG DADDY   Who? [*He has lowered his voice.*]

BRICK   Someone int'rested in what we say to each other.

BIG DADDY   Gooper?——*GOOPER!*

After a discreet pause, Mae appears in the gallery door.

MAE   Did you call Gooper, Big Daddy?

BIG DADDY   Aw, it was you.

MAE   Do you want Gooper, Big Daddy?

BIG DADDY   No, and I don't want you. I want some privacy here, while I'm having a confidential talk with my son Brick. Now it's too hot in here to close them doors, but if I have to close those fuckin' doors in order to have a private talk with my son Brick, just let me know and I'll close 'em. Because I hate eavesdroppers, I don't like any kind of sneakin' an' spyin'.

MAE   Why, Big Daddy—

BIG DADDY   You stood on the wrong side of the moon, it threw your shadow!

MAE   I was just—

BIG DADDY   You was just nothing but *spyin'* an' you *know* it!

MAE   [*begins to sniff and sob*]   Oh, Big Daddy, you're so unkind for some reason to those that really love you!

BIG DADDY   Shut up, shut up, shut up! I'm going to move you and Gooper out of that room next to this! It's none of your goddam business what goes on in here at night between Brick an' Maggie. You listen at night like a couple of rutten peekhole spies and go and give a report on what you hear to Big Mama an' she comes to me and says they say such and such and so and so about what they heard goin' on between Brick an' Maggie, and Jesus, it makes me sick. I'm goin' to move you an' Gooper out of that room, I can't stand sneakin' an' spyin', it makes me puke. . . .

Mae throws back her head and rolls her eyes heavenward and extends her arms as if invoking God's pity for this unjust martyrdom; then she presses a handkerchief to her nose and flies from the room with a loud swish of skirts.

BRICK [*now at the liquor cabinet*]   They listen, do they?

BIG DADDY   Yeah. They listen and give reports to Big Mama on what goes on in here between you and Maggie. They say that— [*He stops as if embarrassed.*]   —You won't sleep with her, that you sleep on the sofa. Is that true or not true? If you don't like Maggie, get rid of Maggie!—What are you doin' there now?

BRICK   Fresh'nin' up my drink.

BIG DADDY   Son, you know you got a real liquor problem?

BRICK   Yes, sir, yes, I know.

BIG DADDY   Is that why you quit sports-announcing, because of this liquor problem?

BRICK   Yes, sir, yes, sir, I guess so.

He smiles vaguely and amiably at his father across his replenished drink.

BIG DADDY   Son, don't guess about it, it's too important.

BRICK [*vaguely*]   Yes, sir.

BIG DADDY   And listen to me, don't look at the damn chandelier. . . .

Pause. Big Daddy's voice is husky.

—Somethin' else we picked up at th' big fire sale in Europe.

Another pause.

Life is important. There's nothing else to hold onto. A man that drinks is throwing his life away. Don't do it, hold onto your life. There's nothing else to hold onto. . . .

Sit down over here so we don't have to raise our voices, the walls have ears in this place.

BRICK [*hobbling over to sit on the sofa beside him*]   All right, Big Daddy.

BIG DADDY   Quit!—how'd that come about? Some disappointment?

BRICK   I don't know. Do you?

BIG DADDY   I'm askin' you, God damn it! How in hell would I know if you don't?

BRICK   I just got out there and found that I had a mouth full of cotton. I was always two or three beats behind what was goin' on on the field and so I—

BIG DADDY   Quit!

BRICK [*amiably*]   Yes, quit.

BIG DADDY   Son?

BRICK   Huh?

BIG DADDY [*inhales loudly and deeply from his cigar; then bends suddenly a little forward, exhaling loudly and raising a hand to his forehead]*   —Whew!—ha ha!—I took in too much smoke, it made me a little lightheaded. . . .

The mantel clock chimes.

Why is it so damn hard for people to talk?
BRICK   Yeah. . . .

The clock goes on sweetly chiming till it has completed the stroke of ten.

—Nice peaceful-soundin' clock, I like to hear it all night. . . .

He slides low and comfortable on the sofa; Big Daddy sits up straight and rigid with some unspoken anxiety. All his gestures are tense and jerky as he talks. He wheezes and pants and sniffs through his nervous speech, glancing quickly, shyly, from time to time, at his son.

BIG DADDY   We got that clock the summer we wint to Europe, me an' Big Mama on that damn Cook's Tour, never had such an awful time in my life, I'm tellin' you, son, those gooks over there, they gouge your eyeballs out in their grand hotels. And Big Mama bought more stuff than you could haul in a couple of boxcars, that's no crap. Everywhere she wint on this whirlwind tour, she bought, bought, bought. Why, half that stuff she bought is still crated up in the cellar, under water last spring!   [*He laughs.*]

That Europe is nothin' on earth but a great big auction, that's all it is, that bunch of old worn-out places, it's just a big firesale, the whole fuckin' thing, an' Big Mama wint wild in it, why, you couldn't hold that woman with a mule's harness! Bought, bought, bought!—lucky I'm a rich man, yes siree, Bob, an' half that stuff is mildewin' in th' basement. It's lucky I'm a rich man, it sure is lucky, well, I'm a rich man, Brick, yep, I'm a mighty rich man.   [*His eyes light up for a moment.*]

Y'know how much I'm worth? Guess, Brick! Guess how much I'm worth!

Brick smiles vaguely over his drink.

Close on ten million in cash an' blue-chip stocks, outside, mind you, of twenty-eight thousand acres of the richest land this side of the valley Nile!

But a man can't buy his life with it, he can't buy back his life with it when his life has been spent, that's one thing not offered in the Europe fire-sale or in the American markets or any markets on earth, a man can't buy his life with it, he can't buy back his life when his life is finished.

That's a sobering thought, a very sobering thought, and that's a thought that I was turning over in my head, over and over and over— until today. . . .

I'm wiser and sadder, Brick, for this experience which I just gone through. They's one thing else that I remember in Europe.

BRICK   What is that, Big Daddy?

BIG DADDY   The hills around Barcelona in the country of Spain and the children running over those bare hills in their bare skins beggin' like starvin' dogs with howls and screeches, and how fat the priests are on the streets of Barcelona, so many of them and so fat and so pleasant, ha ha!—Y'know I could feed that country? I got money enough to feed that goddam country, but the human animal is a selfish beast and I don't reckon the money I passed out there to those howling children in the hills around Barcelona would more than upholster the chairs in this room, I mean pay to put a new cover on this chair!

Hell, I threw them money like you'd scatter feed corn for chickens, I threw money at them just to get rid of them long enough to climb back into th' car and—drive away. . . .

And then in Morocco, them Arabs, why, I remember one day in Marrakech, that old walled Arab city, I set on a broken-down wall to have a cigar, it was fearful hot there and this Arab woman stood in the road and looked at me till I was embarrassed, she stood stock still in the dusty hot road and looked at me till I was embarrassed. But listen to this. She had a naked child with her, a little naked girl with her, barely able to toddle, and after a while she set this child on the ground and give her a push and whispered something to her.

This child come toward me, barely able t' walk, come toddling up to me and—

Jesus, it makes you sick to' remember a thing like this!
It stuck out its hand and tried to unbotton my trousers!

That child was not yet five! Can you believe me? Or do you think that I am making this up? I wint back to the hotel and said to Big Mama, Git packed! We're clearing out of this country. . . .

BRICK   Big Daddy, you're on a talkin' jag tonight.

BIG DADDY [*ignoring this remark*]   Yes, sir, that's how it is, the human animal is a beast that dies but the fact that he's dying don't give him pity for others, no, sir, it—

—Did you say something?

BRICK   Yes.

BIG DADDY   What?

BRICK   Hand me over that crutch so I can get up.

BIG DADDY   Where you goin'?

BRICK   I'm takin' a little short trip to Echo Spring.

BIG DADDY   To where?

BRICK   Liquor cabinet. . . .

BIG DADDY   Yes, sir, boy— [*he hands Brick the crutch.*]   —the human animal is a beast that dies and if he's got money he buys and buys and buys and I think the reason he buys everything he can buy is that in the back of his mind he has the crazy hope that one of his purchases will be life everlasting!—Which it never can be. . . . The human animal is a beast that—

BRICK [*at the liquor cabinet*]   Big Daddy, you sure are shootin' th' breeze here tonight.

There is a pause and voices are heard outside.

BIG DADDY   I been quiet here lately, spoke not a word, just sat and stared into space. I had something heavy weighing on my mind but tonight that load was took off me. That's why I'm talking.—The sky looks diff'rent to me. . . .

BRICK   You know what I like to hear most?

BIG DADDY   What?

BRICK   Solid quiet. Perfect unbroken quiet.

BIG DADDY   Why?

BRICK   Because it's more peaceful.

BIG DADDY   Man, you'll hear a lot of that in the grave. [*He chuckles agreeably.*]

BRICK   Are you through talkin' to me?

BIG DADDY   Why are you so anxious to shut me up?

BRICK   Well, sir, ever so often you say to me, Brick, I want to have a talk with you, but when we talk, it never materializes. Nothing is said. You sit in a chair and gas about this and that and I look like I listen. I try to look like I listen, but I don't listen, not much. Communication is—awful hard between people an'—somehow between you and me, it just don't— happen.

BIG DADDY   Have you ever been scared? I mean have you ever felt downright terror of something? [*He gets up.*]   Just one moment.   [*He looks off as if he were going to tell an important secret.*]

BIG DADDY   Brick?

BRICK   What?

BIG DADDY   Son, I thought I had it!

BRICK   Had what? Had what, Big Daddy?

BIG DADDY   Cancer!

BRICK   Oh . . .

BIG DADDY   I thought the old man made out of bones had laid his cold and heavy hand on my shoulder!

BRICK   Well, Big Daddy, you kept a tight mouth about it.

BIG DADDY   A pig squeals. A man keeps a tight mouth about it, in spite of a man not having a pig's advantage.

BRICK   What advantage is that?

BIG DADDY   Ignorance—of mortality—is a comfort. A man don't have that comfort, he's the only living thing that conceives of death, that knows what it is. The others go without knowing which is the way that anything living should go, go without knowing, without any knowledge of it, and yet a pig squeals, but a man sometimes, he can keep a tight mouth about it. Sometimes he—

There is a deep, smoldering ferocity in the old man.

—can keep a tight mouth about it. I wonder if—

BRICK   What, Big Daddy?

BIG DADDY   A whiskey highball would injure this spastic condition?

BRICK   No, sir, it might do it good.

BIG DADDY   [*grins suddenly, wolfishly*]   Jesus, I can't tell you! The sky is open! Christ, it's open again! It's open, boy, it's open!

Brick looks down at his drink.

BRICK   You feel better, Big Daddy?

BIG DADDY   Better? Hell! I can breathe!—All of my life I been like a doubled up fist. . . .   [*He pours a drink.*]   —Poundin', smashin', drivin'!—now I'm going to loosen these doubled-up hands and touch things *easy* with them. . . .

He spreads his hands as if caressing the air.

You know what I'm contemplating?

BRICK   [*vaguely*]   No, sir. What are you contemplating?

BIG DADDY   Ha ha!—*Pleasure!*—pleasure with *women!*

Brick's smile fades a little but lingers.

—Yes, boy. I'll tell you something that you might not guess. I still have desire for women and this is my sixty-fifth birthday.

BRICK   I think that's mighty remarkable, Big Daddy.

BIG DADDY   Remarkable?

BRICK   *Admirable*, Big Daddy.

BIG DADDY   You're damn right it is, remarkable and admirable both. I realize now that I never had me enough. I let many chances slip by because of scruples about it, scruples, convention—crap. . . . All that stuff is bull, bull, bull!—It took the shadow of death to make me see it. Now that shadow's lifted, I'm going to cut loose and have, what is it they call it, have me a—ball!

BRICK   A ball, huh?

BIG DADDY   That's right, a ball, a ball! Hell!—I slept with Big Mama till, let's see, five years ago, till I was sixty and she was fifty-eight, and never even liked her, never did!

The phone has been ringing down the hall. Big Mama enters, exclaiming:

BIG MAMA   Don't you men hear that phone ring? I heard it way out on the gall'ry.

BIG DADDY   There's five rooms off this front gall'ry that you could go through. Why do you go through this one?

Big Mama makes a playful face as she bustles out the hall door.

Hunh!—Why, when Big Mama goes out of a room, I can't remember what that woman looks like—

BIG MAMA   Hello.

BIG DADDY   —But when Big Mama comes back into the room, boy, then I see what she looks like, and I wish I didn't.

Bends over laughing at this joke till it hurts his guts and he straightens with a grimace. The laugh subsides to a chuckle as he puts the liquor glass a little distrustfully down the table.

BIG MAMA   Hello, Miss Sally.

Brick has risen and hobbled to the gallery doors.

BIG DADDY   Hey! Where you goin'?

BRICK   Out for a breather.

BIG DADDY Not yet you ain't. Stay here till this talk is finished, young fellow.

BRICK I thought it was finished, Big Daddy.

BIG DADDY It ain't even begun.

BRICK My mistake. Excuse me. I just wanted to feel that river breeze.

BIG DADDY Set back down in that chair.

Big Mama's voice rises, carrying down the hall.

BIG MAMA Miss Sally, you're a case! You're a caution, Miss Sally.

BIG DADDY Jesus, she's talking to my old maid sister again.

BIG MAMA Why didn't you give me a chance to explain it to you?

BIG DADDY Brick, this stuff burns me.

BIG MAMA Well, goodbye, now, Miss Sally. You come down real soon. Big Daddy's dying to see you.

BIG DADDY Crap!

BIG MAMA Yaiss, goodbye, Miss Sally. . . .

She hangs up and bellows with mirth. Big Daddy groans and covers his ears as she approaches.

Bursting in:

Big Daddy, that was Miss Sally callin' from Memphis again! You know what she done, Big Daddy? She called her doctor in Memphis to git him to tell her what that spastic thing is! Ha-*HAAAA!*—And called back to tell me how relieved she was that—Hey! Let me in!

Big Daddy has been holding the door half closed against her.

BIG DADDY Naw I ain't. I told you not to come and go through this room. You just back out and go through those five other rooms.

BIG MAMA Big Daddy? Big Daddy? Oh, Big Daddy!—You didn't mean those things you said to me, did you?

He shuts door firmly against her but she still calls.

Sweetheart? Sweetheart? Big Daddy? You didn't mean those awful things you said to me?—I know you didn't. I know you didn't mean those things in your heart. . . .

The childlike voice fades with a sob and her heavy footsteps retreat down the hall. Brick has risen once more on his crutches and starts for the gallery again.

BIG DADDY All I ask of that woman is that she leave me alone. But she can't

admit to herself that she makes me sick. That comes of having slept with
her too many years. Should of quit much sooner but that old woman she
never got enough of it—and I was good in bed . . . I never should of
wasted so much of it on her. . . . They say you got just so many and each
one is numbered. Well, I got a few left in me, a few, and I'm going to
pick me a good one to spend 'em on! I'm going to pick me a choice one, I
don't care how much she costs, I'll smother her in—minks! Ha ha! I'll
strip her naked and smother her in minks and choke her with diamonds!
Ha ha! I'll strip her naked and choke her with diamonds and smother her
with minks and hump her from hell to breakfast. *Ha aha ha ha ha!*

MAE [*gaily at door*]   Who's that laughin' in there?
GOOPER   Is Big Daddy laughin' in there?
BIG DADDY   Crap!—them two—*drips.* . . .

He goes over and touches Brick's shoulder.

Yes, son. Brick, boy.—I'm—*happy!* I'm happy, son, I'm happy!

*He chokes a little and bites his under lip, pressing his head quickly, shyly against
his son's head and then, coughing with embarrassment, goes uncertainly back to
the table where he set down the glass. He drinks and makes a grimace as it burns
his guts. Brick sighs and rises with effort.*

What makes you so restless? Have you got ants in your britches?
BRICK   Yes, sir . . .
BIG DADDY   Why?
BRICK   —Something—hasn't—happened. . . .
BIG DADDY   Yeah? What is that!
BRICK [*sadly*]   —the click. . . .
BIG DADDY   Did you say click?
BRICK   Yes, click.
BIG DADDY   What click?
BRICK   A click that I get in my head that makes me peaceful.
BIG DADDY   I sure in hell don't know what you're talking about, but it
disturbs me.
BRICK   It's just a mechanical thing.
BIG DADDY   What is a mechanical thing?
BRICK   This click that I get in my head that makes me peaceful. I got to drink
till I get it. It's just a mechanical thing, something like a—like a—like a—
BIG DADDY   Like a—
BRICK   Switch clicking off in my head, turning the hot light off and the cool
night on and— [*He looks up, smiling sadly.*] —all of a sudden there's
—peace!
BIG DADDY [*whistles long and soft with astonishment; he goes back to Brick and*

clasps his son's two shoulders]   Jesus! I didn't know it had gotten that bad
with you. Why, boy, you're—*alcoholic!*

BRICK   That's the truth, Big Daddy. I'm alcoholic.

BIG DADDY   This shows how I—let things go!

BRICK   I have to hear that little click in my head that makes me peaceful.
Usually I hear it sooner than this, sometimes as early as—noon, but—

—Today it's—dilatory. . . .

—I just haven't got the right level of alcohol in my bloodstream yet!

This last statement is made with energy as he freshens his drink.

BIG DADDY   Uh—huh. Expecting death made me blind. I didn't have no idea
that a son of mine was turning into a drunkard under my nose.

BRICK   [*gently*]   Well, now you do, Big Daddy, the news has penetrated.

BIG DADDY   UH-huh, yes, now I do, the news has—penetrated. . . .

BRICK   And so if you'll excuse me—

BIG DADDY   No, I won't excuse you.

BRICK   —I'd better sit by myself till I hear that click in my head, it's just a
mechanical thing but it don't happen except when I'm alone or talking to
no one. . . .

BIG DADDY   You got a long, long time to sit still, boy, and talk to no one, but
now you're talkin' to me. At least I'm talking to you. And you set there
and listen until I tell you the conversation is over!

BRICK   But this talk is like all the others we've ever had together in our lives!
It's nowhere, nowhere!—it's—it's *painful*, Big Daddy. . . .

BIG DADDY   All right, then let it be painful, but don't you move from that
chair!—I'm going to remove that crutch. . . .   [*He seizes the crutch and
tosses it across room.*]

BRICK   I can hop on one foot, and if I fall, I can crawl!

BIG DADDY   If you ain't careful you're gonna crawl off this plantation and
then, by Jesus, you'll have to hustle your drinks along Skid Row!

BRICK   That'll come, Big Daddy.

BIG DADDY   Naw, it won't. You're my son and I'm going to straighten you
out; now that *I'm* straightened out, I'm going to straighten out you!

BRICK   Yeah?

BIG DADDY   Today the report come in from Ochsner Clinic. Y'know what
they told me? [*His face glows with triumph.*]   The only thing that they
could detect with all the instruments of science in that great hospital is a
little spastic condition of the colon! And nerves torn to pieces by all that
worry about it.

A little girl bursts into room with a sparkler clutched in each fist, hops and shrieks like a monkey gone mad and rushes back out again as Big Daddy strikes at her.

Silence. The two men stare at each other. A woman laughs gaily outside.

I want you to know I breathed a sigh of relief almost as powerful as the Vicksburg tornado!

There is laughter outside, running footsteps, the soft, plushy sound and light of exploding rockets.

Brick stares at him soberly for a long moment; then makes a sort of startled sound in his nostrils and springs up on one foot and hops across the room to grab his crutch, swinging on the furniture for support. He gets the crutch and flees as if in horror for the gallery. His father seizes him by the sleeve of his white silk pajamas.

Stay here, you son of a bitch!—till I say go!
BRICK   I can't.
BIG DADDY   You sure in hell will, God damn it.
BRICK   No, I can't. We talk, you talk, in—circles! We get no where, no where! It's always the same, you say you want to talk to me and don't have a fuckin' thing to say to me!
BIG DADDY   Nothin' to say when I'm tellin' you I'm going to live when I thought I was dying?!
BRICK   Oh—*that!*—Is that what you have to say to me?
BIG DADDY   Why, you son of a bitch! Ain't that, ain't that—*important?!*
BRICK   Well, you said that, that's said, and now I—
BIG DADDY   Now you set back down.
BRICK   You're all balled up, you—
BIG DADDY   I ain't balled up!
BRICK   You are, you're all balled up!
BIG DADDY   Don't tell me what I am, you drunken whelp! I'm going to tear this coat sleeve off if you don't set down!
BRICK   Big Daddy—
BIG DADDY   Do what I tell you! I'm the boss here, now! I want you to know I'm back in the driver's seat now!

Big Mama rushes in, clutching her great heaving bosom.

BIG MAMA   Big Daddy!
BIG DADDY   What in hell do you want in here, Big Mama?
BIG MAMA   Oh, Big Daddy! Why are you shouting like that? I just cain't stainnnnnnnd—it. . . .

A COLLECTION OF PLAYS

BIG DADDY [*raising the back of his hand above his head*]   GIT!—outa here.

She rushes back out, sobbing.

BRICK [*softly, sadly*]   Christ. . . .
BIG DADDY [*fiercely*]   Yeah! Christ!—is right . . .

Brick breaks loose and hobbles toward the gallery.

Big Daddy jerks his crutch from under Brick so he steps with the injured ankle. He utters a hissing cry of anguish, clutches a chair and pulls it over on top of him on the floor.

Son of a—tub of—hog fat. . . .
BRICK   Big Daddy! Give me my crutch.

Big Daddy throws the crutch out of reach.

Give me that crutch, Big Daddy.
BIG DADDY   Why do you drink?
BRICK   Don't know, give me my crutch!
BIG DADDY   You better think why you drink or give up drinking!
BRICK   Will you please give me my crutch so I can get up off this floor?
BIG DADDY   First you answer my question. Why do you drink? Why are you throwing your life away, boy, like somethin' disgusting you picked up on the street?
BRICK [*getting onto his knees*]   Big Daddy, I'm in pain, I stepped on that foot.
BIG DADDY   Good! I'm glad you're not too numb with the liquor in you to feel some pain!
BRICK   You—spilled my—drink . . .
BIG DADDY   I'll make a bargain with you. You tell me why you drink and I'll hand you one. I'll pour the liquor myself and hand it to you.
BRICK   Why do I drink?
BIG DADDY   Yea! Why?
BRICK   Give me a drink and I'll tell you.
BIG DADDY   Tell me first!
BRICK   I'll tell you in one word.
BIG DADDY   What word?
BRICK   DISGUST!

The clock chimes softly, sweetly. Big Daddy gives it a short, outraged glance.

Now how about that drink?

BIG DADDY   What are you disgusted with? You got to tell me that, first. Otherwise being disgusted don't make no sense!

BRICK   Give me my crutch.

BIG DADDY   You heard me, you got to tell me what I asked you first.

BRICK   I told you, I said to kill my disgust!

BIG DADDY   DISGUST WITH WHAT!

BRICK   You strike a hard bargain.

BIG DADDY   What are you disgusted with?—an' I'll pass you the liquor.

BRICK   I can hop on one foot, and if I fall, I can crawl.

BIG DADDY   You want liquor that bad?

BRICK   [dragging himself up, clinging to bedstead]   Yeah, I want it that bad.

BIG DADDY   If I give you a drink, will you tell me what it is you're disgusted with, Brick?

BRICK   Yes, sir, I will try to.

The old man pours him a drink and solemnly passes it to him.

There is silence as Brick drinks.

Have you ever heard the word "mendacity"?

BIG DADDY   Sure. Mendacity is one of them five dollar words that cheap politicians throw back and forth at each other.

BRICK   You know what it means?

BIG DADDY   Don't it mean lying and liars?

BRICK   Yes, sir, lying and liars.

BIG DADDY   Has someone been lying to you?

CHILDREN   [chanting in chorus offstage]
   We want Big Dad-dee!
   We want Big Dad-dee!

Gooper appears in the gallery door.

GOOPER   Big Daddy, the kiddies are shouting for you out there.

BIG DADDY   [fiercely]   Keep out, Gooper!

GOOPER   'Scuse me!

Big Daddy slams the doors after Gooper.

BIG DADDY   Who's been lying to you, has Margaret been lying to you, has your wife been lying to you about something, Brick?

BRICK   Not her. That wouldn't matter.

BIG DADDY   Then who's been lying to you, and what about?

BRICK   No one single person and no one lie. . . .

BIG DADDY   Then what, what then, for Christ's sake?

BRICK   —The whole, the whole—thing. . . .

BIG DADDY   Why are you rubbing your head? You got a headache?

BRICK   No, I'm tryin' to—

BIG DADDY   —Concentrate, but you can't because your brain's all soaked with liquor, is that the trouble? Wet brain!   [*He snatches the glass from Brick's hand.*]   What do you know about this mendacity thing? Hell! I could write a book on it! Don't you know that? I could write a book on it and still not cover the subject? Well, I could, I could write a goddam book on it and still not cover the subject anywhere near enough!!—Think of all the lies I got to put up with!—Pretenses! Ain't that mendacity? Having to pretend stuff you don't think or feel or have any idea of? Having for instance to act like I care for Big Mama!—I haven't been able to stand the sight, sound, or smell of that woman for forty years now!—even when I *laid* her!—regular as a piston. . . .

Pretend to love that son of a bitch of a Gooper and his wife Mae and those five same screechers out there like parrots in a jungle? Jesus! Can't stand to look at 'em!

Church!—it bores the bejesus out of me but I go!—I go an' sit there and listen to the fool preacher!

Clubs!—Elks! Masons! Rotary!—*crap!*

A spasm of pain makes him clutch his belly. He sinks into a chair and his voice is softer and hoarser.

You I *do* like for some reason, did always have some kind of real feeling for—affection—respect—yes, always. . . .

You and being a success as a planter is all I ever had any devotion to in my whole life!—and that's the truth. . . .

I don't know why, but it is!

I've lived with mendacity!—Why can't *you* live with it? Hell, you *got* to live with it, there's nothing *else* to *live* with except mendacity, is there?

BRICK   Yes, sir. Yes, sir there is something else that you can live with!

BIG DADDY   What?

BRICK   [*lifting his glass*]   This!—Liquor. . . .

BIG DADDY   That's not living, that's dodging away from life.

BRICK   I want to dodge away from it.

BIG DADDY   Then why don't you kill yourself, man?

BRICK   I like to drink. . . .

BIG DADDY   Oh, God, I can't talk to you. . . .

BRICK   I'm sorry, Big Daddy.

BIG DADDY   Not as sorry as I am. I'll tell you something. A little while back
   when I thought my number was up—

This speech should have torrential pace and fury.

—before I found out it was just this—spastic—colon. I thought about
   you. Should I or should I not, if the jig was up, give you this place when
   I go—since I hate Gooper an' Mae an' know that they hate me, and since
   all five same monkeys are little Maes an' Goopers.—And I thought,
   No!—Then I thought, Yes!—I couldn't make up my mind. I hate Gooper
   and his five same monkeys and that bitch Mae! Why should I turn over
   twenty-eight thousand acres of the richest land this side of the valley
   Nile to not my kind?—But why in hell, on the other hand, Brick—should
   I subsidize a goddam fool on the bottle?—Liked or not liked, well,
   maybe even—*loved!*—Why should I do that?—Subsidize worthless behavior? Rot? Corruption?

BRICK [*smiling*]   I understand.

BIG DADDY   Well, if you do, you're smarter than I am, God damn it, because
   I don't understand. And this I will tell you frankly. I didn't make up my
   mind at all on that question and still to this day I ain't made out no
   will!—Well, now I don't *have* to. The pressure is gone. I can just wait and
   see if you pull yourself together or if you don't

BRICK   That's right, Big Daddy.

BIG DADDY   You sound like you thought I was kidding.

BRICK [*rising*]   No, sir, I know you're not kidding.

BIG DADDY   But you don't care—?

BRICK [*hobbling toward the gallery door*]   No, sir, I don't care. . . .

*He stands in the gallery doorway as the night sky turns pink and green and gold
with successive flashes of light.*

BIG DADDY   *WAIT!*—Brick. . . .

*His voice drops. Suddenly there is something shy, almost tender, in his restraining
gesture.*

Don't let's—leave it like this, like them other talks we've had, we've
   always—talked around things, we've—just talked around things for
   some fuckin' reason, I don't know what, it's always like something was
   left not spoken, something avoided because neither of us was honest
   enough with the—other. . . .

BRICK   I never lied to you, Big Daddy.

BIG DADDY   Did I ever to *you?*

BRICK   No, sir. . . .

BIG DADDY   Then there is at least two people that never lied to each other.

BRICK   But we've never *talked* to each other.

BIG DADDY   We can *now.*

BRICK   Big Daddy, there don't seem to be anything much to say.

BIG DADDY   You say that you drink to kill your disgust with lying.

BRICK   You said to give you a reason.

BIG DADDY   Is liquor the only thing that'll kill this disgust?

BRICK   Now. Yes.

BIG DADDY   But not once, huh?

BRICK   Not when I was still young an' believing. A drinking man's someone
    who wants to forget he isn't still young an' believing.

BIG DADDY   Believing what?

BRICK   Believing. . . .

BIG DADDY   Believing *what?*

BRICK   [*stubbornly evasive*]   Believing. . . .

BIG DADDY   I don't know what the hell you mean by believing and I don't
    think you know what you mean by believing, but if you still got sports
    in your blood, go back to sports announcing and—

BRICK   Sit in a glass box watching games I can't play? Describing what I
    can't do while players do it? Sweating out their disgust and confusion in
    contests I'm not fit for? Drinkin' a coke, half bourbon, so I can stand it?
    That's no goddam good any more, no help—time just outran me, Big
    Daddy—got there first . . .

BIG DADDY   I think you're passing the buck.

BRICK   You know many drinkin' men?

BIG DADDY   [*with a slight, charming smile*]   I have known a fair number of that
    species.

BRICK   Could any of them tell you why he drank?

BIG DADDY   Yep, you're passin' the buck to things like time and disgust with
    "mendacity" and—crap!—if you got to use that kind of language about a
    thing, it's ninety-proof bull, and I'm not buying any.

BRICK   I had to give you a reason to get a drink!

BIG DADDY   You started drinkin' when your friend Skipper died.

*Silence for five beats. Then Brick makes a startled movement, reaching for his
crutch.*

BRICK   What are you suggesting?

BIG DADDY   I'm suggesting nothing.

The shuffle and clop of Brick's rapid hobble away from his father's steady, grave attention.

—But Gooper an' Mae suggested that there was something not right exactly in your—
BRICK [*stopping short downstage as if backed to a wall*]   "Not right"?
BIG DADDY   Not, well, exactly *normal* in your friendship with—
BRICK   They suggested that, too? I thought that was Maggie's suggestion.

Brick's detachment is at last broken through. His heart is accelerated; his forehead sweat-beaded; his breath becomes more rapid and his voice hoarse. The thing they're discussing, timidly and painfully on the side of Big Daddy, fiercely, violently on Brick's side, is the inadmissible thing that Skipper died to disavow between them. The fact that if it existed it had to be disavowed to "keep face" in the world they lived in, may be at the heart of the "mendacity" that Brick drinks to kill his disgust with. It may be the root of his collapse. Or maybe it is only a single manifestation of it, not even the most important. The bird that I hope to catch in the net of this play is not the solution of one man's psychological problem. I'm trying to catch the true quality of experience in a group of people, that cloudy, flickering, evanescent—fiercely charged!—interplay of live human beings in the thundercloud of a common crisis. Some mystery should be left in the revelation of character in a play, just as a great deal of mystery is always left in the revelation of character in life, even in one's own character to himself. This does not absolve the playwright of his duty to observe and probe as clearly and deeply as he legitimately can: but it should steer him away from "pat" conclusions, facile definitions which make a play just a play, not a snare for the truth of human experience.

The following scene should be played with great concentration, with most of the power leashed but palpable in what is left unspoken.

Who else's suggestion is it, is it *yours*? How many others thought that Skipper and I were—
BIG DADDY [*gently*]   Now, hold on, hold on a minute, son.—I knocked around in my time.
BRICK   What's that got to do with—
BIG DADDY   I said "Hold on!"—I bummed, I bummed this country till I was—
BRICK   Whose suggestion, who else's suggestion is it?
BIG DADDY   Slept in hobo jungles and railroad Y's and flophouses in all cities before I—
BRICK   Oh, *you* think so, too, you call me your son and a queer. Oh! Maybe that's why you put Maggie and me in this room that was Jack Straw's

and Peter Ochello's, in which that pair of old sisters slept in a double bed where both of 'em died!

BIG DADDY *Now just don't go throwing rocks at—*

Suddenly Reverend Tooker appears in the gallery doors, his head slightly, playfully, fatuously cocked, with a practised clergyman's smile, sincere as a bird call blown on a hunter's whistle, the living embodiment of the pious, conventional lie.

Big Daddy gasps a little at this perfectly timed, but incongruous, apparition.

—What're you lookin' for, Preacher?

REVEREND TOOKER   The gentleman's lavatory, ha ha!—heh, heh . . .

BIG DADDY [*with strained courtesy*]   —Go back out and walk down to the other end of the gallery, Reverend Tooker, and use the bathroom connected with my bedroom, and if you can't find it, ask them where it is!

REVEREND TOOKER   Ah, thanks.   [*He goes out with a deprecatory chuckle.*]

BIG DADDY   It's hard to talk in this place . . .

BRICK   Son of a—!

BIG DADDY [*leaving a lot unspoken*]   —I seen all things and understood a lot of them, till 1910. Christ, the year that—I had worn my shoes through, hocked my—I hopped off a yellow dog freight car half a mile down the road, slept in a wagon of cotton outside the gin—Jack Straw an' Peter Ochello took me in. Hired me to manage this place which grew into this one.—When Jack Straw died—why, old Peter Ochello quit eatin' like a dog does when its master's dead, and died, too!

BRICK   Christ!

BIG DADDY   I'm just saying I understand such—

BRICK [*violently*]   Skipper is dead. I have not quit eating!

BIG DADDY   No, but you started drinking.

Brick wheels on his crutch and hurls his glass across the room shouting.

BRICK   YOU THINK SO, TOO?

Footsteps run on the gallery. There are women's calls.

Big Daddy goes toward the door.

Brick is transformed, as if a quiet mountain blew suddenly up in volcanic flame.

BRICK   You think so, too? You think so, too? You think me an' Skipper did, did, did!—*sodomy!*—together?

BIG DADDY   Hold—!

BRICK   That what you—

BIG DADDY   —ON—a minute!

BRICK   You think we did dirty things between us, Skipper an'—

BIG DADDY   Why are you shouting like that? Why are you—

BRICK   —Me, is that what you think of Skipper, is that—

BIG DADDY   —so excited? I don't think nothing. I don't know nothing. I'm simply telling you what—

BRICK   You think that Skipper and me were a pair of dirty old men?

BIG DADDY   Now that's—

BRICK   Straw? Ochello? A couple of—

BIG DADDY   Now just—

BRICK   —fucking sissies? Queers? Is that what you—

BIG DADDY   Shhh.

BRICK   —think?

He loses his balance and pitches to his knees without noticing the pain. He grabs the bed and drags himself up.

BIG DADDY   Jesus!—Whew. . . . Grab my hand!

BRICK   Naw, I don't want your hand. . . .

BIG DADDY   Well, I want yours. Git up!

He draws him up, keeps an arm about him with concern and affection.

You broken out in a sweat! You're panting like you'd run a race with—

BRICK *[freeing himself from his father's hold]* Big Daddy, you shock me, Big Daddy, you, you—*shock* me! Talkin' so— *[He turns away from his father.]* —casually!—about a—thing like that . . .

—Don't you know how people *feel* about things like that? How, how *disgusted* they are by things like that? Why, at Ole Miss when it was discovered a pledge to our fraternity, Skipper's and mine, did a, *attempted* to do a, unnatural thing with—

We not only dropped him like a hot rock!—We told him to git off the campus, and he did, he got!—All the way to— *[He halts, breathless.]*

BIG DADDY   —Where?

BRICK   —North Africa, last I heard!

BIG DADDY   Well, I have come back from further away than that, I have just now returned from the other side of the moon, death's country, son, and I'm not easy to shock by anything here. *[He comes downstage and faces out.]* Always. anyhow, lived with too much space around me to be infected by ideas of other people. One thing you can grow on a big place more important than cotton!—is *tolerance!*—I grown it. [*He returns toward Brick.*]

BRICK   Why can't exceptional friendship, *real, real, deep, deep friendship!* between two men be respected as something clean and decent without being thought of as—

BIG DADDY   It can, it is, for God's sake.

BRICK   —Fairies. . . .

In his utterance of this word, we gauge the wide and profound reach of the conventional mores he got from the world that crowned him with early laurel.

BIG DADDY   I told Mae an' Gooper—

BRICK   Frig Mae and Gooper, frig all dirty lies and liars!—Skipper and me had a clean, true thing between us!—had a clean friendship, practically all our lives, till Maggie got the idea you're talking about. Normal? No!—It was too rare to be normal, any true thing between two people is too rare to be normal. Oh, once in a while he put his hand on my shoulder or I'd put mine on his, oh, maybe even, when we were touring the country in pro-football an' shared hotel-rooms we'd reach across the space between the two beds and shake hands to say goodnight, yeah, one or two times we—

BIG DADDY   Brick, nobody thinks that that's not normal!

BRICK   Well, they're mistaken, it was! It was a pure an' true thing an' that's not normal.

MAE [*off stage*]   Big Daddy, they're startin' the fireworks.

They both stare straight at each other for a long moment. The tension breaks and both turn away as if tired.

BIG DADDY   Yeah, it's—hard t'—talk. . . .

BRICK   All right, then, let's—let it go. . . .

BIG DADDY   Why did Skipper crack up? Why have you?

Brick looks back at his father again. He has already decided, without knowing that he has made this decision, that he is going to tell his father that he is dying of cancer. Only this could even the score between them: one inadmissible thing in return for another.

BRICK [*ominously*]   All right. You're asking for it, Big Daddy. We're finally going to have that real true talk you wanted. It's too late to stop it, now, we got to carry it through and cover every subject.

He hobbles back to the liquor cabinet.

Uh-huh.

He opens the ice bucket and picks up the silver tongs with slow admiration of their frosty brightness.

Maggie declares that Skipper and I went into pro-football after we left "Ole Miss" because we were scared to grow up . . .

He moves downstage with the shuffle and clop of a cripple on a crutch. As Margaret did when her speech became "recitative," he looks out into the house, commanding its attention by his direct, concentrated gaze—a broken, "tragically elegant" figure telling simply as much as he knows of "the Truth":

—Wanted to—keep on tossing—those long, long!—high, high!—passes that—couldn't be intercepted except by time, the aerial attack that made us famous! And so we did, we did, we kept it up for one season, that aerial attack, we held it high!—Yeah, but—

—that summer, Maggie, she laid the law down to me, said, Now or never, and so I married Maggie. . . .

BIG DADDY   How was Maggie in bed?

BRICK [*wryly*]   Great! the greatest!

Big Daddy nods as if he thought so.

She went on the road that fall with the Dixie Stars. Oh, she made a great show of being the world's best sport. She wore a—wore a—tall bearskin cap! A shako, they call it, a dyed moleskin coat, a moleskin coat dyed red!—Cut up crazy! Rented hotel ballrooms for victory celebrations, wouldn't cancel them when it—turned out—defeat. . . .

MAGGIE THE CAT! Ha ha!

Big Daddy nods.

—But Skipper, he had some fever which came back on him which doctors couldn't explain and I got that injury—turned out to be just a shadow on the X-ray plate—and a touch of bursitis. . . .

I lay in a hospital bed, watched our games on TV, saw Maggie on the bench next to Skipper when he was hauled out of a game for stumbles, fumbles!—Burned me up the way she hung on his arm!—Y'know, I think that Maggie had always felt sort of left out because she and me never got any closer together than two people just get in bed, which is not much closer than two cats on a—fence humping. . . .

So! She took this time to work on poor dumb Skipper. He was a less than average student at Ole Miss, you know that, don't you?!—Poured in his mind the dirty, false idea that what we were, him and me, was a frustrated case of that ole pair of sisters that lived in this room, Jack Straw and Peter Ochello!—He, poor Skipper, went to bed with Maggie to prove it wasn't true, and when it didn't work out, he thought it *was* true!—Skipper broke in two like a rotten stick—nobody ever turned so fast to a lush—or died of it so quick. . . .

—Now are you satisfied?

Big Daddy has listened to this story, dividing the grain from the chaff. Now he looks at his son.

BIG DADDY   Are *you* satisfied?
BRICK   With what?
BIG DADDY   That half-ass story!
BRICK   What's half-ass about it?
BIG DADDY   Something's left out of that story. What did you leave out?

The phone has started ringing in the hall.

GOOPER [*off stage*]   Hello.

As if it reminded him of something, Brick glances suddenly toward the sound and says:

BRICK   Yes!—I left out a long-distance call which I had from Skipper—
GOOPER   Speaking, go ahead.
BRICK   —In which he made a drunken confession to me and on which I hung up!
GOOPER   No.
BRICK   —Last time we spoke to each other in our lives . . .
GOOPER   No, sir.
BIG DADDY   You musta said something to him before you hung up.
BRICK   What could I say to him?
BIG DADDY   Anything. Something.
BRICK   Nothing.
BIG DADDY   Just hung up?
BRICK   Just hung up.
BIG DADDY   Uh-huh. Anyhow now!—we have tracked down the lie with which you're disgusted and which you are drinking to kill your disgust with, Brick. You been passing the buck. This disgust with mendacity is disgust with yourself.

You!—dug the grave of your friend and kicked him in it!—before you'd face truth with him!

BRICK   *His* truth, not *mine!*

BIG DADDY   His truth, okay! But you wouldn't face it with him!

BRICK   Who *can* face truth? Can *you?*

BIG DADDY   Now don't start passin' the rotten buck again, boy!

BRICK   *How about these birthday congratulations, these many, many happy returns of the day, when ev'rybody knows there won't be any except you!*

Gooper, who has answered the hall phone, lets out a high, shrill laugh; the voice becomes audible saying: "No, no, you got it all wrong! Upside down! Are you crazy?"

Brick suddenly catches his breath as he realizes that he has made a shocking disclosure. He hobbles a few paces, then freezes, and without looking at his father's shocked face, says:

Let's, let's—go out, now, and—watch the fireworks. Come on, Big Daddy.

Big Daddy moves suddenly forward and grabs hold of the boy's crutch like it was a weapon for which they were fighting for possession.

BIG DADDY   Oh, no, no! No one's going out! What did you start to say?

BRICK   I don't remember.

BIG DADDY   "Many happy returns when they know there won't be any"?

BRICK   Aw, hell, Big Daddy, forget it. Come on out on the gallery and look at the fireworks they're shooting off for your birthday. . . .

BIG DADDY   First you finish that remark you were makin' before you cut off. "Many happy returns when they know there won't be any"?—Ain't that what you just said?

BRICK   Look, now. I can get around without that crutch if I have to but it would be a lot easier on the furniture an' glassware if I didn' have to go swinging along like Tarzan of th'—

BIG DADDY   FINISH! WHAT YOU WAS SAYIN'!

An eerie green glow shows in sky behind him.

BRICK [*sucking the ice in his glass, speech becoming thick*]   Leave th' place to Gooper and Mae an' their five little same little monkeys. All I want is—

BIG DADDY   "LEAVE TH' PLACE," did you say?

BRICK [*vaguely*]   All twenty-eight thousand acres of the richest land this side of the valley Nile.

BIG DADDY   Who said I was "leaving the place" to Gooper or anybody? This is my sixty-fifth birthday! I got fifteen years or twenty years left in me! I'll outlive *you!* I'll bury you an' have to pay for your coffin!

BRICK   Sure. Many happy returns. Now let's go watch the fireworks, come on, let's—

BIG DADDY   Lying, have they been lying? About the report from th'—clinic? Did they, did they—find something——*Cancer.* Maybe?

BRICK   Mendacity is a system that we live in. Liquor is one way out an' death's the other. . . .

He takes the crutch from Big Daddy's loose grip and swings out on the gallery leaving the doors open.

A song, "Pick a Bale of Cotton," is heard.

MAE [*appearing in door*]   *Oh, Big Daddy, the field hands are singin' fo' you!*

BRICK   I'm sorry, Big Daddy. My head don't work any more and it's hard for me to understand how anybody could care if he lived or died or was dying or cared about anything but whether or not there was liquor left in the bottle and so I said what I said without thinking. In some ways I'm no better than the others, in some ways worse because I'm less alive. Maybe it's being alive that makes them lie, and being almost *not* alive makes me sort of accidentally truthful—I don't know but—anyway— we've been friends . . .

—And being friends is telling each other the truth. . . .

There is a pause.

You told *me!* I told *you!*

BIG DADDY [*slowly and passionately*]   CHRIST—DAMN—

GOOPER [*off stage*]   Let her go!

Fireworks off stage right.

BIG DADDY   —ALL—LYING SONS OF—LYING BITCHES!

He straightens at last and crosses to the inside door. At the door he turns and looks back as if he had some desperate question he couldn't put into words. Then he nods reflectively and says in a hoarse voice:

Yes, all liars, all liars, all lying dying liars!

This is said slowly, slowly, with a fierce revulsion. He goes on out.

    —Lying! Dying! Liars!

Brick remains motionless as the lights dim out and the curtain falls.

Curtain

ACT III

There is no lapse of time. Big Daddy is seen leaving as at the end of ACT II.

BIG DADDY   ALL LYIN'—DYIN'!—LIARS! LIARS!—LIARS!

Margaret enters.

MARGARET   Brick, what in the name of God was goin' on in this room?

Dixie and Trixie enter through the doors and circle around Margaret shouting. Mae enters from the lower gallery window.

MAE   Dixie, Trixie, you quit that!

Gooper enters through the doors.

    Gooper, will y' please get these kiddies to bed right now!
GOOPER   Mae, you seen Big Mama?
MAE   Not yet.

Gooper and kids exit through the doors. Reverend Tooker enters through the windows.

REVEREND TOOKER   Those kiddies are so full of vitality. I think I'll have to be starting back to town.
MAE   Not yet, Preacher. You know we regard you as a member of this family, one of our closest an' dearest, so you just got t' be with us when Doc Baugh gives Big Mama th' actual truth about th' report from the clinic.
MARGARET   Where do you think you're going?
BRICK   Out for some air.
MARGARET   Why'd Big Daddy shout "Liars"?
MAE   Has Big Daddy gone to bed, Brick?

GOOPER [*entering*]   Now where is that old lady?

REVEREND TOOKER   I'll look for her.   [*He exits to the gallery.*]

MAE   Cain'tcha find her, Gooper?

GOOPER   She's avoidin' this talk.

MAE   I think she senses somethin'.

MARGARET [*going out on the gallery to Brick*]   Brick, they're goin' to tell Big Mama the truth about Big Daddy and she's goin' to need you.

DOCTOR BAUGH   This is going to be painful.

MAE   Painful things caint always be avoided.

REVEREND TOOKER   I see Big Mama.

GOOPER   Hey, Big Mama, come here.

MAE   Hush, Gooper, don't holler.

BIG MAMA [*entering*]   Too much smell of burnt fireworks makes me feel a little bit sick at my stomach.—Where is Big Daddy?

MAE   That's what I want to know, where has Big Daddy gone?

BIG MAMA   He must have turned in, I reckon he went to baid . . .

GOOPER   Well, then, now we can talk.

BIG MAMA   What *is* this talk, *what* talk?

Margaret appears on the gallery, talking to Doctor Baugh.

MARGARET [*musically*]   My family freed their slaves ten years before abolition. My great-great-grandfather gave his slaves their freedom five years before the War between the States started!

MAE   Oh, for God's sake! Maggie's climbed back up in her family tree!

MARGARET [*sweetly*]   What, Mae?

The pace must be very quick: great Southern animation.

BIG MAMA [*addressing them all*]   I think Big Daddy was just worn out. He loves his family, he loves to have them around him, but it's a strain on his nerves. He wasn't himself tonight, Big Daddy wasn't himself, I could tell he was all worked up.

REVEREND TOOKER   I think he's remarkable.

BIG MAMA   Yaisss! Just remarkable. Did you all notice the food he ate at that table? Did you all notice the supper he put away? Why he ate like a hawss!

GOOPER   I hope he doesn't regret it.

BIG MAMA   What? Why that man—ate a huge piece of cawn bread with molasses on it! Helped himself twice to hoppin' John.

MARGARET   Big Daddy loves hoppin' John.—We had a real country dinner.

BIG MAMA [*overlapping Margaret*]   Yaiss, he simply adores it! an' candied yams? Son? That man put away enough food at that table to stuff a *field* hand!

GOOPER [*with grim relish*]   I hope he don't have to pay for it later on . . .

BIG MAMA [*fiercely*]   What's *that*, Gooper?

MAE   Gooper says he hopes Big Daddy doesn't suffer tonight.

BIG MAMA   Oh, shoot, Gooper says, Gooper says! Why should Big Daddy suffer for satisfying a normal appetite? There's nothin' wrong with that man but nerves, he's sound as a dollar! And now he knows he is an' that's why he ate such a supper. He had a big load off his mind, knowin' he wasn't doomed t'—what he thought he was doomed to . . .

MARGARET [*sadly and sweetly*]   Bless his old sweet soul . . .

BIG MAMA [*vaguely*]   Yais, bless his heart, where's Brick?

MAE   Outside.

GOOPER   —Drinkin' . . .

BIG MAMA   I know he's drinkin'. Cain't I see he's drinkin' without you continually tellin' me that boy's drinkin'?

MARGARET   Good for you, Big Mama! [*She applauds.*]

BIG MAMA   Other people *drink* and *have* drunk an' will *drink*, as long as they make that stuff an' put it in bottles.

MARGARET   That's the truth. I never trusted a man that didn't drink.

BIG MAMA   *Brick? Brick!*

MARGARET   He's still on the gall'ry. I'll go bring him in so we can talk.

BIG MAMA [*Worriedly*]   I don't know what this mysterious family conference is about.

Awkward silence. Big Mama looks from face to face, then belches slightly and mutters, "Excuse me . . ." She opens an ornamental fan suspended about her throat. A black lace fan to go with her black lace gown, and fans her wilting corsage, sniffing nervously and looking from face to face in the uncomfortable silence as Margaret calls "Brick?" and Brick sings to the moon on the gallery.

MARGARET   Brick, they're gonna tell Big Mama the truth an' she's gonna need you.

BIG MAMA   I don't know what's wrong here, you all have such long faces! Open that door on the hall and let some air circulate through here, will you please, Gooper?

MAE   I think we'd better leave that door closed, Big Mama, till after the talk.

MARGARET   Brick!

BIG MAMA   Reveren' Tooker, will *you* please open that door?

REVEREND TOOKER   I sure will, Big Mama.

MAE   I just didn't think we ought t' take any chance of Big Daddy hearin' a word of this discussion.

BIG MAMA   *I swan!* Nothing's going to be said in Big Daddy's house that he caint hear if he want to!

GOOPER   Well, Big Mama, it's—

Mae gives him a quick, hard poke to shut him up. He glares at her fiercely as she circles before him like a burlesque ballerina, raising her skinny bare arms over her head, jangling her bracelets, exclaiming:

MAE   *A breeze! A breeze!*

REVEREND TOOKER   I think this house is the coolest house in the Delta.—Did you all know that Halsey Banks's widow put air-conditioning units in the church and rectory at Friar's Point in memory of Halsey?

General conversation has resumed; everybody is chatting so that the stage sounds like a bird cage.

GOOPER   Too bad nobody cools your church off for you. I bet you sweat in that pulpit these hot Sundays, Reverend Tooker.

REVEREND TOOKER   Yes, my vestments are drenched. Last Sunday the gold in my chasuble faded into the purple.

GOOPER   Reveren', you musta been preachin' hell's fire last Sunday.

MAE   *[at the same time to Doctor Baugh]*   You reckon those vitamin B12 injections are what they're cracked up t' be, Doc Baugh?

DOCTOR BAUGH   Well, if you want to be stuck with something I guess they're as good to be stuck with as anything else.

BIG MAMA   *[at the gallery door]*   *Maggie, Maggie, aren't you comin' with Brick?*

MAE   *[suddenly and loudly, creating a silence]*   *I have a strange feeling, I have a peculiar feeling!*

BIG MAMA   *[turning from the gallery]*   What feeling?

MAE   That Brick said somethin' he shouldn't of said t' Big Daddy.

BIG MAMA   Now what on earth could Brick of said t' Big Daddy that he shouldn't say?

GOOPER   Big Mama, there's somethin'—

MAE   NOW, WAIT!

She rushes up to Big Mama and gives her a quick hug and kiss. Big Mama pushes her impatiently off.

DOCTOR BAUGH   In my day they had what they call the Keeley cure for heavy drinkers.

BIG MAMA   Shoot!

DOCTOR BAUGH   But now I understand they just take some kind of tablets.

GOOPER   They call them "Annie Bust" tablets.

BIG MAMA   *Brick* don't need to take *nothin'*.

Brick and Margaret appear in gallery doors, Big Mama unaware of his presence behind her.

That boy is just broken up over Skipper's death. You know how poor Skipper died. They gave him a big, big dose of that sodium amytal stuff at his home and then they called the ambulance and give him another big, big dose of it at the hospital and that and all of the alcohol in his system fo' months an' months just proved too much for his heart . . . I'm scared of needles! I'm more scared of a needle than the knife . . . I think more people have been needled out of this world than— [*She stops short and wheels about.*]
Oh—here's Brick! My precious baby—

She turns upon Brick with short, fat arms extended, at the same time uttering a loud, short sob, which is both comic and touching. Brick smiles and bows slightly, making a burlesque gesture of gallantry for Margaret to pass before him into the room. Then he hobbles on his crutch directly to the liquor cabinet and there is absolute silence, with everybody looking at Brick as everybody has always looked at Brick when he spoke or moved or appeared. One by one he drops ice cubes in his glass, then suddenly, but not quickly, looks back over his shoulder with a wry, charming smile, and says:

BRICK   I'm sorry! Anyone else?
BIG MAMA [*sadly*]   No, son. I *wish* you wouldn't!
BRICK   I wish I didn't have to, Big Mama, but I'm still waiting for that click in my head which makes it all smooth out!
BIG MAMA   Ow, Brick, you—BREAK MY HEART!
MARGARET [*at same time*]   Brick, go sit with Big Mama!
BIG MAMA   I just cain't staiiiiii-nnnnnnnd-it . . . [*She sobs.*]
MAE   Now that we're all assembled—
GOOPER   We kin talk . . .
BIG MAMA   Breaks my heart . . .
MARGARET   Sit with Big Mama, Brick, and hold her hand.

Big Mama sniffs very loudly three times, almost like three drumbeats in the pocket of silence.

BRICK   You do that, Maggie. I'm a restless cripple. I got to stay on my crutch.

Brick hobbles to the gallery door; leans there as if waiting.

Mae sits beside Big Mama, while Gooper moves in front and sits on the end of the couch, facing her. Reverend Tooker moves nervously into the space between them; on the other side, Doctor Baugh stands looking at nothing in particular and lights a cigar. Margaret turns away.

BIG MAMA Why're you all *surroundin'* me—like this? Why're you all starin' at me like this an' makin' signs at each other?

Reverend Tooker steps back startled.

MAE Calm yourself, Big Mama.

BIG MAMA Calm you'self, *you'self*, Sister Woman. How could I calm myself with everyone starin' at me as if big drops of blood had broken out on m'face? What's this all about, annh! What?

Gooper coughs and takes a center position.

GOOPER Now, Doc Baugh.

MAE Doc Baugh?

GOOPER Big Mama wants to know the complete truth about the report we got from the Ochsner Clinic.

MAE [*eagerly*] —on Big Daddy's condition!

GOOPER Yais, on Big Daddy's condition, we got to face it.

DOCTOR BAUGH Well . . .

BIG MAMA [*terrified, rising*] Is there? Something? Something that I? Don't—know?

In these few words, this startled, very soft, question, Big Mama reviews the history of her forty-five years with Big Daddy, her great almost embarrassingly true-hearted and simple-minded devotion to Big Daddy, who must have had something Brick has, who made himself loved so much by the "simple expedient" of not loving enough to disturb his charming detachment, also once coupled, like Brick, with virile beauty.

Big Mama has a dignity at this moment; she almost stops being fat.

DOCTOR BAUGH [*after a pause, uncomfortably*] Yes?—Well—

BIG MAMA I!!!—want to—*knowwwwww* . . .

Immediately she thrusts her fist to her mouth as if to deny that statement. Then for some curious reason, she snatches the withered corsage from her breast and hurls it on the floor and steps on it with her short, fat feet.

Somebody must be lyin'!—I want to know!

MAE Sit down, Big Mama, sit down on this sofa.

MARGARET Brick, go sit with Big Mama.

BIG MAMA *What is it, what is it?*

DOCTOR BAUGH   I never have seen a more thorough examination than Big
    Daddy Pollitt was given in all my experience with the Ochsner Clinic.
GOOPER   It's one of the best in the country.
MAE   It's THE best in the country—bar *none*!

*For some reason she gives Gooper a violent poke as she goes past him. He slaps at
her hand without removing his eyes from his mother's face.*

DOCTOR BAUGH   Of course they were ninety-nine and nine-tenths per cent
    sure before they even started.
BIG MAMA   Sure of what, sure of what, sure of—*what?—what?*

*She catches her breath in a startled sob. Mae kisses her quickly. She thrusts Mae
fiercely away from her, staring at the Doctor.*

MAE   Mommy, be a brave girl!
BRICK [*in the doorway, softly*]   "By the light, by the light, Of the sil-ve-ry
    mo-oo-n . . ."
GOOPER   Shut up!—Brick.
BRICK   Sorry . . . [*He wanders out on the gallery.*]
DOCTOR BAUGH   But now, you see, Big Mama, they cut a piece off this
    growth, a specimen of the tissue and—
BIG MAMA   Growth? You told Big Daddy—
DOCTOR BAUGH   Now wait.
BIG MAMA [*fiercely*]   You told me and Big Daddy there wasn't a thing wrong
    with him but—
MAE   Big Mama, they always—
GOOPER   Let Doc Baugh talk, will yuh?
BIG MAMA   —little spastic condition of—[*Her breath gives out in a sob.*]
DOCTOR BAUGH   Yes, that's what we told Big Daddy. But we had this bit of
    tissue run through the laboratory and I'm sorry to say the test was
    positive on it. It's—well—malignant . . .

Pause.

BIG MAMA   —Cancer?! Cancer?!

Doctor Baugh nods gravely. Big Mama gives a long gasping cry.

MAE AND GOOPER   Now, now, now, Big Mama, you had to know . . .
BIG MAMA   WHY DIDN'T THEY CUT IT OUT OF HIM? HANH? HANH?
DOCTOR BAUGH   Involved too much, Big Mama, too many organs affected.
MAE   Big Mama, the liver's affected and so's the kidneys, both! It's gone way
    past what they call a—

GOOPER   A surgical risk.

MAE   —Uh-huh . . .

Big Mama draws a breath like a dying gasp.

REVEREND TOOKER   Tch, tch, tch, tch, tch!

DOCTOR BAUGH   Yes it's gone past the knife.

MAE   *That's why he's turned yellow, Mommy!*

BIG MAMA   *Git away from me, git away from me, Mae!* [*She rises abruptly.*]   I want Brick! Where's Brick? Where is my only son?

MAE   Mama! Did she say "*only* son"?

GOOPER   What does that make *me*?

MAE   A sober responsible man with five precious children!—*Six!*

BIG MAMA   I want Brick to tell me! Brick! Brick!

MARGARET [*rising from her reflections in a corner*]   Brick was so upset he went back out.

BIG MAMA   *Brick!*

MARGARET   Mama, let *me* tell you!

BIG MAMA   No, no, leave me alone, you're not my blood!

GOOPER   *Mama, I'm your son!* Listen to *me!*

MAE   Gooper's your son, he's your first-born!

BIG MAMA   Gooper never liked Daddy.

MAE [*as if terribly shocked*]   *That's not TRUE!*

There is a pause. The minister coughs and rises.

REVEREND TOOKER [*to Mae*]   I think I'd better slip away at this point.   [*Discreetly*]   Good night, good night, everybody, and God bless you all . . . on this place . . .

He slips out.

Mae coughs and points at Big Mama.

DOCTOR BAUGH   Well, Big Mama . . .   [*He sighs.*]

BIG MAMA   It's all a mistake, I know it's just a bad dream.

DOCTOR BAUGH   We're gonna keep Big Daddy as comfortable as we can.

BIG MAMA   Yes, it's just a bad dream, that's all it is, it's just an awful dream.

GOOPER   In my opinion Big Daddy is having some pain but won't admit that he has it.

BIG MAMA   Just a dream, a bad dream.

DOCTOR BAUGH   That's what lots of them do, they think if they don't admit they're having the pain they can sort of escape the fact of it.

GOOPER [*with relish*]   Yes, they get sly about it, they get real sly about it.

MAE   Gooper and I think—

GOOPER   Shut up, Mae! Big Mama, I think—Big Daddy ought to be started on morphine.

BIG MAMA   Nobody's going to give Big Daddy morphine.

DOCTOR BAUGH   Now, Big Mama, when that pain strikes it's going to strike mighty hard and Big Daddy's going to need the needle to bear it.

BIG MAMA   I tell you, nobody's going to give him morphine.

MAE   Big Mama, you don't want to see Big Daddy suffer, you know you—

Gooper, standing beside her, gives her a savage poke.

DOCTOR BAUGH [*placing a package on the table*]   I'm leaving this stuff here, so if there's a sudden attack you all won't have to send out for it.

MAE   I know how to give a hypo.

BIG MAMA   Nobody's gonna give Big Daddy morphine.

GOOPER   Mae took a course in nursing during the war.

MARGARET   Somehow I don't think Big Daddy would want Mae to give him a hypo.

MAE   You think he'd want *you* to do it?

DOCTOR BAUGH   Well . . .

Doctor Baugh rises.

GOOPER   Doctor Baugh is goin'.

DOCTOR BAUGH   Yes, I got to be goin'. Well, keep your chin up, Big Mama.

GOOPER [*with jocularity*]   She's gonna keep *both* chins up, aren't you, Big Mama?

Big Mama sobs.

Now stop that, Big Mama.

GOOPER [*at the door with Doctor Baugh*]   Well, Doc, we sure do appreciate all you done. I'm telling you, we're surely obligated to you for—

Doctor Baugh has gone out without a glance at him.

—I guess that doctor has got a lot on his mind but it wouldn't hurt him to act a little more human . . .

Big Mama sobs.

Now be a brave girl, Mommy.

BIG MAMA   It's not true, I know that it's just not true!

GOOPER   Mama, those tests are infallible!

BIG MAMA   Why are you so determined to see your father daid?

MAE Big Mama!

MARGARET [*gently*] I know what Big Mama means.

MAE [*fiercely*] Oh, do you?

MARGARET [*quietly and very sadly*] Yes, I think I do.

MAE For a newcomer in the family you sure do show a lot of understanding.

MARGARET Understanding is needed on this place.

MAE I guess you must have needed a lot of it in your family, Maggie, with your father's liquor problem and now you've got Brick with his!

MARGARET Brick does not have a liquor problem at all. Brick is devoted to Big Daddy. This thing is a terrible strain on him.

BIG MAMA Brick is Big Daddy's boy, but he drinks too much and it worries me and Big Daddy, and, Margaret, you've got to cooperate with us, you've got to co-operate with Big Daddy and me in getting Brick straightened out. Because it will break Big Daddy's heart if Brick don't pull himself together and take hold of things.

MAE Take hold of *what* things, Big Mama?

BIG MAMA The place.

There is a quick violent look between Mae and Gooper.

GOOPER Big Mama, you've had a shock.

MAE Yais, we've all had a shock, but . . .

GOOPER Let's be realistic—

MAE —Big Daddy would never, would *never*, be foolish enough to—

GOOPER —put this place in irresponsible hands!

BIG MAMA Big Daddy ain't going to leave the place in anybody's hands; Big Daddy is *not* going to die. I want you to get that in your heads, all of you!

MAE Mommy, Mommy, Big Mama, we're just as hopeful an' optimistic as you are about Big Daddy's prospects, we have faith in *prayer*—but nevertheless there are certain matters that have to be discussed an' dealt with, because otherwise—

GOOPER Eventualities have to be considered and now's the time . . . Mae, will you please get my brief case out of our room?

MAE Yes, honey. [*She rises and goes out through the hall door.*]

GOOPER [*standing over Big Mama*] Now, Big Mom. What you said just now was not at all true and you know it. I've always loved Big Daddy in my own quiet way. I never made a show of it, and I know that Big Daddy has always been fond of me in a quiet way, too, and he never made a show of it neither.

Mae returns with Gooper's brief case.

MAE Here's your brief case, Gooper, honey.

GOOPER [*handing the brief case back to her*]   Thank you . . . Of cou'se, my relationship with Big Daddy is different from Brick's.

MAE   You're eight years older'n Brick an' always had t' carry a bigger load of th' responsibilities than Brick ever had t' carry. He never carried a thing in his life but a football or a highball.

GOOPER   Mae, will y' let me talk, please?

MAE   Yes, honey.

GOOPER   Now, a twenty-eight-thousand-acre plantation's a mighty big thing t' run.

MAE   Almost singlehanded.

Margaret has gone out onto the gallery and can be heard calling softly to Brick.

BIG MAMA   You never had to run this place! What are you talking about? As if Big Daddy was dead and in his grave, you had to run it? Why, you just helped him out with a few business details and had your law practice at the same time in Memphis!

MAE   Oh, Mommy, Mommy, Big Mommy! Let's be fair!

MARGARET   Brick!

MAE   Why, Gooper has given himself body and soul to keeping this place up for the past five years since Big Daddy's health started failing.

MARGARET   Brick!

MAE   Gooper won't say it, Gooper never thought of it as a duty, he just did it. And what did Brick do? Brick kept living in his past glory at college! Still a football player at twenty-seven!

MARGARET   [*returning alone*]   Who are you talking about now? Brick? A football player? He isn't a football player and you know it. Brick is a sports announcer on T.V. and one of the best-known ones in the country!

MAE   I'm talking about what he was.

MARGARET   Well, I wish you would just stop talking about my husband.

GOOPER   I've got a right to discuss my brother with other members of MY OWN family, which don't include *you.* Why don't you go out there and drink with Brick?

MARGARET   I've never seen such malice toward a brother.

GOOPER   How about his for me? Why, he can't stand to be in the same room with me!

MARGARET   This is a deliberate campaign of vilification for the most disgusting and sordid reason on earth, and I know what it is! It's *avarice, greed, greed!*

BIG MAMA   *Oh, I'll scream! I will scream in a moment unless this stops!*

Gooper has stalked up to Margaret with clenched fists at his sides as if he would strike her. Mae distorts her face again into a hideous grimace behind Margaret's back.

BIG MAMA [*sobs*]   Margaret. Child. Come here. Sit next to Big Mama.
MARGARET   Precious Mommy. I'm sorry, I'm, sorry, I—!

She bends her long graceful neck to press her forehead to Big Mama's bulging shoulder under its black chiffon.

MAE   How beautiful, how touching, this display of devotion! Do you know why she's childless? She's childless because that big beautiful athlete husband of hers won't go to bed with her!
GOOPER   You jest won't let me do this in a nice way, will yah? Aw right—I don't give a goddam if Big Daddy likes me or don't like me or did or never did or will or will never! I'm just appealing to a sense of common decency and fair play. I'll tell you the truth. I've resented Big Daddy's partiality to Brick ever since Brick was born, and the way I've been treated like I was just barely good enough to spit on and sometimes not even good enough for that. Big Daddy is dying of cancer, and it's spread all through him and it's attacked all his vital organs including the kidneys and right now he is sinking into uremia, and you all know what uremia is, it's poisoning of the whole system due to the failure of the body to eliminate its poisons.
MARGARET   [*to herself, downstage, hissingly*]   Poisons, poisons! Venomous thoughts and words! In hearts and minds!—That's poisons!
GOOPER   [*overlapping her*]   I am asking for a square deal, and, by God, I expect to get one. But if I don't get one, if there's any peculiar shenanigans going on around here behind my back, well, I'm not a corporation lawyer for nothing, I know how to protect my own interests.

Brick enters from the gallery with a tranquil, blurred smile, carrying an empty glass with him.

BRICK   Storm coming up.
GOOPER   Oh! A late arrival!
MAE   Behold the conquering hero comes!
GOOPER   The fabulous Brick Pollitt! Remember him?—Who could forget him!
MAE   He looks like he's been injured in a game!
GOOPER   Yep, I'm afraid you'll have to warm the bench at the Sugar Bowl this year, Brick!

Mae laughs shrilly.

Or was it the Rose Bowl that he made that famous run in?—

Thunder.

MAE   The punch bowl, honey. It was in the punch bowl, the cut-glass punch bowl!

GOOPER   Oh, that's right, I'm getting the bowls mixed up!

MARGARET   Why don't you stop venting your malice and envy on a sick boy?

BIG MAMA   *Now you two hush, I mean it, hush, all of you, hush!*

DAISY, SOOKEY   Storm! Storm comin'! Storm! Storm!

LACEY   Brightie, close them shutters.

GOOPER   Lacey, put the top up on my Cadillac, will yuh?

LACEY   Yes, suh, Mistah Pollitt!

GOOPER   [*at the same time*].   Big Mama, you know it's necessary for me t' go back to Memphis in th' mornin' t' represent the Parker estate in a lawsuit.

Mae sits on the bed and arranges papers she has taken from the brief case.

BIG MAMA   Is it, Gooper?

MAE   Yaiss.

GOOPER   That's why I'm forced to—to bring up a problem that—

MAE   Somethin' that's too important t' be put off!

GOOPER   If Brick was sober, he ought to be in on this.

MARGARET   Brick is present; we're present.

GOOPER   Well, good. I will now give you this outline my partner, Tom Bullitt, an' me have drawn up—a sort of dummy—trusteeship.

MARGARET   Oh, that's it! You'll be in charge an' dole out remittances, will you?

GOOPER   This we did as soon as we got the report on Big Daddy from th' Ochsner Laboratories. We did this thing, I mean we drew up this dummy outline with the advice and assistance of the Chairman of the Boa'd of Directors of th' Southern Plantahs Bank and Trust Company in Memphis, C. C. Bellowes, a man who handles estates for all th' prominent fam'lies in West Tennessee and th' Delta.

BIG MAMA   Gooper?

GOOPER   [*crouching in front of Big Mama*]   Now this is not—not final, or anything like it. This is just a preliminary outline. But it does provide a basis—a design—a—possible, feasible—*plan!*

MARGARET   Yes, I'll bet it's a plan.

Thunder.

MAE   It's a plan to protect the biggest estate in the Delta from irresponsibility an'—

BIG MAMA   Now you listen to me, all of you, you listen here! They's not goin' to be any more catty talk in my house! And Gooper, you put that away before I grab it out of your hand and tear it right up! I don't know what the hell's in it, and I don't want to know what the hell's in it. I'm talkin' in Big Daddy's language now; I'm his *wife* not his *widow*, I'm still his *wife!* And I'm talkin' to you in his language an'—

GOOPER   Big Mama, what I have here is—

MAE [*at the same time*]   Gooper explained that it's just a plan . . .

BIG MAMA   I don't care what you got there. Just put it back where it came from, an' don't let me see it again, not even the outside of the envelope of it! Is that understood? Basis! Plan! Preliminary! Design! I say—what is it Big Daddy always says when he's disgusted?

BRICK [*from the bar*]   Big Daddy says "crap" when he's disgusted.

BIG MAMA [*rising*]   That's right—CRAP! I say CRAP too, like Big Daddy!

Thunder.

MAE   Coarse language doesn't seem called for in this—

GOOPER   Somethin' in me is *deeply outraged* by hearin' you talk like this.

BIG MAMA   *Nobody's goin' to take nothin'!*—till Big Daddy lets go of it—maybe, just possibly, not—not even then! No, not even then!

Thunder.

MAE   Sookey, hurry up an' git that po'ch furniture covahed; want th' paint to come off?

GOOPER   Lacey, put mah car away!

LACEY   Caint, Mistah Pollitt, you got the keys!

GOOPER   Naw, you got 'em, man. Where th' keys to th' car, honey?

MAE   You got 'em in your pocket!

BRICK   "You can always hear me singin' this song, Show me the way to go home."

Thunder distantly.

BIG MAMA   Brick! Come here, Brick, I need you. Tonight Brick looks like he used to look when he was a little boy, just like he did when he played wild games and used to come home when I hollered myself hoarse for him, all sweaty and pink cheeked and sleepy, with his—red curls shining . . .

Brick draws aside as he does from all physical contact and continues the song in a whisper, opening the ice bucket and dropping in the ice cubes one by one as if he were mixing some important chemical formula.

Distant thunder.

Time goes by so fast. Nothin' can outrun it. Death commences too early—almost before you're half acquainted with life—you meet the other . . . Oh, you know we just got to love each other an' stay together, all of us, just as close as we can, especially now that such a *black* thing has come and moved into this place without invitation.

Awkwardly embracing Brick, she presses her head to his shoulder.

A dog howls off stage.

Oh, Brick, son of Big Daddy, Big Daddy does so love you. Y'know what would be his fondest dream come true? If before he passed on, if Big Daddy has to pass on . . .

A dog howls.

. . . you give him a child of yours, a grandson as much like his son as his son is like Big Daddy . . .

MARGARET   I know that's Big Daddy's dream.

BIG MAMA   That's his dream.

MAE   Such a pity that Maggie and Brick can't oblige.

BIG DADDY [*off down stage right on the gallery*]   Looks like the wind was takin' liberties with this place.

SERVANT [*off stage*]   Yes, sir, Mr. Pollitt.

MARGARET [*crossing to the right door*]   Big Daddy's on the gall'ry.

Big Mama has turned toward the hall door at the sound of Big Daddy's voice on the gallery.

BIG MAMA   I can't stay here. He'll see somethin' in my eyes.

Big Daddy enters the room from up stage right.

BIG DADDY   Can I come in?

He puts his cigar in an ash tray.

MARGARET   Did the storm wake you up, Big Daddy?

BIG DADDY   Which stawm are you talkin' about—th' one outside or th' hullballoo in here?

Gooper squeezes past Big Daddy.

GOOPER   'Scuse me.

Mae tries to squeeze past Big Daddy to join Gooper, but Big Daddy puts his arm firmly around her.

BIG DADDY   I heard some mighty loud talk. Sounded like somethin' important was bein' discussed. What was the powwow about?

MAE [*flustered*]   Why—nothin', Big Daddy . . .

BIG DADDY [*crossing to extreme left center, taking Mae with him*]   What is that pregnant-lookin' envelope you're puttin' back in your brief case, Gooper?

GOOPER [*at the foot of the bed, caught, as he stuffs papers into envelope*]   That? Nothin', suh—nothin' much of anythin' at all . . .

BIG DADDY   Nothin'? It looks like a whole lot of nothin'!

He turns up stage to the group.

You all know th' story about th' young married couple—

GOOPER   Yes, sir!

BIG DADDY   Hello, Brick—

BRICK   Hello, Big Daddy.

The group is arranged in a semicircle above Big Daddy, Margaret at the extreme right, then Mae and Gooper, then Big Mama, with Brick at the left.

BIG DADDY   Young married couple took Junior out to th' zoo one Sunday, inspected all of God's creatures in their cages, with satisfaction.

GOOPER   Satisfaction.

BIG DADDY [*crossing to up stage center, facing front*]   This afternoon was a warm afternoon in spring an' that ole elephant had somethin' else on his mind which was bigger'n peanuts. You know this story, Brick?

Gooper nods.

BRICK   No, sir, I don't know it.

BIG DADDY   Y'see, in th' cage adjoinin' they was a young female elephant in heat!

BIG MAMA [*at Big Daddy's shoulder*]   Oh, Big Daddy!

BIG DADDY   What's the matter, preacher's gone, ain't he? All right. That female elephant in the next cage was permeatin' the atmosphere about her with a powerful and excitin' odor of female fertility! Huh! Ain't that a nice way to put it, Brick?

BRICK   Yes, sir, nothin' wrong with it.

BIG DADDY   Brick says th's nothin' wrong with it!

BIG MAMA   Oh, Big Daddy!

BIG DADDY [*crossing to down stage center*]   So this ole bull elephant still had a couple of fornications left in him. He reared back his trunk an' got a whiff of that elephant lady next door!—began to paw at the dirt in his cage an' butt his head against the separatin' partition and, first thing y'know, there was a conspicuous change in his *profile*—very *conspicuous!* Ain't I tellin' this story in decent language, Brick?

BRICK   Yes, sir, too fuckin' decent!

BIG DADDY   So, the little boy pointed at it and said, "What's that?" His mama said, "Oh, that's—nothin'!"—His papa said, "She's spoiled!"

Big Daddy crosses to Brick at left.

You didn't laugh at that story, Brick.

Big Mama crosses to down stage right crying. Margaret goes to her. Mae and Gooper hold up stage right center.

BRICK   No, sir, I didn't laugh at that story.

BIG DADDY   What is the smell in this room? Don't you notice it, Brick? Don't you notice a powerful and obnoxious odor of mendacity in this room?

BRICK   Yes, sir, I think I do, sir.

GOOPER   Mae, Mae . . .

BIG DADDY   There is nothing more powerful. Is there, Brick?

BRICK   No, sir. No, sir, there isn't, an' nothin' more obnoxious.

BIG DADDY   Brick agrees with me. The odor of mendacity is a powerful and obnoxious odor an' the stawm hasn't blown it away from this room yet. You notice it, Gooper?

GOOPER   What, sir?

BIG DADDY   How about you, Sister Woman? You notice the unpleasant odor of mendacity in this room?

MAE   Why, Big Daddy, I don't even know what that is.

BIG DADDY   You can smell it. Hell it smells like death!

Big Mama sobs. Big Daddy looks toward her.

What's wrong with that fat woman over there, loaded with diamonds? Hey, what's-you-name, what's the matter with you?

MARGARET   [*crossing toward Big Daddy*]   She had a slight dizzy spell, Big Daddy.

BIG DADDY   You better watch that, Big Mama. A stroke is a bad way to go.

MARGARET   [*crossing to Big Daddy at center*]   Oh, Brick, Big Daddy has on your birthday present to him, Brick, he has on your cashmere robe, the softest material I have ever felt.

BIG DADDY   Yeah, this is my soft birthday, Maggie . . . Not my gold or my silver birthday, but my soft birthday, everything's got to be soft for Big Daddy on this soft birthday.

Maggie kneels before Big Daddy at center.

MARGARET   Big Daddy's got on his Chinese slippers that I gave him, Brick. Big Daddy, I haven't given you my big present yet, but now I will, now's the time for me to present it to you! I have an announcement to make!

MAE   What? What kind of announcement?

GOOPER   A sports announcement, Maggie?

MARGARET   Announcement of life beginning! A child is coming, sired by Brick, and out of Maggie the Cat! I have Brick's child in my body, an' that's my birthday present to Big Daddy on this birthday!

Big Daddy looks at Brick who crosses behind Big Daddy to down stage portal, left.

BIG DADDY   Get up, girl, get up off your knees, girl.

Big Daddy helps Margaret to rise. He crosses above her, to her right, bites off the end of a fresh cigar, taken from his bathrobe pocket, as he studies Margaret.

Uh-huh, this girl has life in her body, that's no lie!

BIG MAMA   BIG DADDY'S DREAM COME TRUE!

BRICK   JESUS!

BIG DADDY [*crossing right below wicker stand*]   Gooper, I want my lawyer in the mornin'.

BRICK   Where are you goin', Big Daddy?

BIG DADDY   Son, I'm goin' up on the roof, to the belvedere on th' roof to look over my kingdom before I give up my kingdom—twenty-eight thousand acres of th' richest land this side of the valley Nile!

He exits through right doors, and down right on the gallery.

BIG MAMA [*following*]   Sweetheart, sweetheart, sweetheart—can I come with you?

She exits down stage right.

Margaret is down stage center in the mirror area. Mae has joined Gooper and she gives him a fierce poke, making a low hissing sound and a grimace of fury.

GOOPER [*pushing her aside*]   Brick, could you possibly spare me one small shot of that liquor?

BRICK Why, help yourself, Gooper boy.

GOOPER I will.

MAE [*shrilly*] Of course we know that this is—a lie.

GOOPER *Be still, Mae.*

MAE I won't be still! I know she's made this up!

GOOPER Goddam it, I said shut up!

MARGARET Gracious! I didn't know that my little announcement was going to provoke such a storm!

MAE *That* woman isn't *pregnant!*

GOOPER Who said she was?

MAE *She* did.

GOOPER The doctor didn't. Doc Baugh didn't.

MARGARET I haven't gone to Doc Baugh.

GOOPER Then who'd you go to, Maggie?

MARGARET One of the best gynecologists in the South.

GOOPER Uh huh, uh huh!—I see . . . [*He takes out a pencil and notebook.*] —May we have his name, please?

MARGARET No, you may not, Mister Prosecuting Attorney!

MAE He doesn't have any name, he doesn't exist!

MARGARET Oh, he exists all right, and so does my child, Brick's baby!

MAE You can't conceive a child by a man that won't sleep with you unless you think you're—

Brick has turned on the phonograph. A scat song cuts Mae's speech.

GOOPER *Turn that off!*

MAE We know it's a lie because we hear you in here; he won't sleep with you, we hear you! So don't imagine you're going to put a trick over on us, to fool a dying man with a—

A long drawn cry of agony and rage fills the house. Margaret turns the phonograph down to a whisper. The cry is repeated.

MAE Did you hear that, Gooper, did you hear that?

GOOPER Sounds like the pain has struck.

MAE Go see, Gooper!

GOOPER Come along and leave these lovebirds together in their nest!

He goes out first. Mae follows but turns at the door, contorting her face and hissing at Margaret.

MAE *Liar!*

She slams the door.

Margaret exhales with relief and moves a little unsteadily to catch hold of Brick's arm.

MARGARET   Thank you for—keeping still . . .
BRICK   O.K., Maggie.
MARGARET   It was gallant of you to save my face!

He now pours down three shots in quick succession and stands waiting, silent. All at once he turns with a smile and says:

BRICK   *There!*
MARGARET   What?
BRICK   The *click* . . .

His gratitude seems almost infinite as he hobbles out on the gallery with a drink. We hear his crutch as he swings out of sight. Then, at some distance, he begins singing to himself a peaceful song. Margaret holds the big pillow forlornly as if it were her only companion, for a few moments, then throws it on the bed. She rushes to the liquor cabinet, gathers all the bottles in her arms, turns about undecidedly, then runs out of the room with them, leaving the door ajar on the dim yellow hall. Brick is heard hobbling back along the gallery, singing his peaceful song. He comes back in, sees the pillow on the bed, laughs lightly, sadly, picks it up. He has it under his arm as Margaret returns to the room. Margaret softly shuts the door and leans against it, smiling softly at Brick.

MARGARET   Brick, I used to think that you were stronger than me and I didn't want to be overpowered by you. But now, since you've taken to liquor—you know what?—I guess it's bad, but now I'm stronger than you and I can love you more truly! Don't move that pillow. I'll move it right back if you do!—Brick?

She turns out all the lamps but a single rose-silk-shaded one by the bed.

I really have been to a doctor and I know what to do and—Brick?—this is my time by the calendar to conceive?
BRICK   Yes, I understand, Maggie. But how are you going to conceive a child by a man in love with his liquor?
MARGARET   By locking his liquor up and making him satisfy my desire before I unlock it!
BRICK   Is that what you've done, Maggie?
MARGARET   Look and see. That cabinet's mighty empty compared to before!
BRICK   Well, I'll be a son of a—

He reaches for his crutch but she beats him to it and rushes out on the gallery, hurls the crutch over the rail and comes back in, panting.

MARGARET   And so tonight we're going to make the lie true, and when that's done, I'll bring the liquor back here and we'll get drunk together, here, tonight, in this place that death has come into . . . —What do you say?
BRICK   I don't say anything. I guess there's nothing to say.
MARGARET   Oh, you weak people, you weak, beautiful people!—who give up with such grace. What you want is someone to—

She turns out the rose-silk lamp.

—take hold of you.—Gently, gently with love hand your life back to you, like somethin' gold you let go of. I *do* love you, Brick, I *do!*
BRICK   [*smiling with charming sadness*]   Wouldn't it be funny if that was true?

The End

HAROLD PINTER

1930–

A Slight Ache

CHARACTERS

FLORA

EDWARD

THE MATCHSELLER

A country house, with two chairs and a table laid for breakfast at the center of the stage. These will later be removed and the action will be focused on the scullery on the right and the study on the left, both indicated with a minimum of scenery and props. A large well kept garden is suggested at the back of the stage with flower beds, trimmed hedges, etc. The garden gate, which cannot be seen by the audience, is off right.

Flora and Edward are discovered sitting at the breakfast table. Edward is reading the paper.

FLORA   Have you noticed the honeysuckle this morning?

EDWARD   The what?

FLORA   The honeysuckle.

EDWARD   Honeysuckle? Where?

FLORA   By the back gate, Edward.

EDWARD   Is that honeysuckle? I thought it was . . . convolvulus, or something.

FLORA   But you know it's honeysuckle.

EDWARD   I tell you I thought it was convolvulus.

Pause.

FLORA   It's in wonderful flower.

EDWARD   I must look.

FLORA   The whole garden's in flower this morning. The clematis. The convolvulus. Everything. I was out at seven. I stood by the pool.

EDWARD   Did you say—that the convolvulus was in flower?

FLORA   Yes.

EDWARD   But good God, you just denied there was any.

FLORA   I was talking about the honeysuckle.

EDWARD   About the what?

FLORA   [*calmly*]   Edward—you know that shrub outside the toolshed . . .

1231

EDWARD   Yes, yes.
FLORA   That's convolvulus.
EDWARD   That?
FLORA   Yes.
EDWARD   Oh. [Pause.]   I thought it was japonica.
FLORA   Oh, good Lord no.
EDWARD   Pass the teapot, please.

Pause. She pours tea for him.

I don't see why I should be expected to distinguish between these plants. It's not my job.
FLORA   You know perfectly well what grows in your garden.
EDWARD   Quite the contrary. It is clear that I don't.

Pause.

FLORA [rising]   I was up at seven. I stood by the pool. The peace. And everything in flower. The sun was up. You should work in the garden this morning. We could put up the canopy.
EDWARD   The canopy? What for?
FLORA   To shade you from the sun.
EDWARD   Is there a breeze?
FLORA   A light one.
EDWARD   It's very treacherous weather, you know.

Pause.

FLORA   Do you know what today is?
EDWARD   Saturday.
FLORA   It's the longest day of the year.
EDWARD   Really?
FLORA   It's the height of summer today.
EDWARD   Cover the marmalade.
FLORA   What?
EDWARD   Cover the pot. There's a wasp. [He puts the paper down on the table.] Don't move. Keep still. What are you doing?
FLORA   Covering the pot?
EDWARD   Don't move. Leave it. Keep still. [Pause.] Give me the "Telegraph."
FLORA   Don't hit it. It'll bite.
EDWARD   Bite? What do you mean, bite? Keep still.

Pause.

It's landing.

FLORA   It's going in the pot.
EDWARD   Give me the lid.
FLORA   It's in.
EDWARD   Give me the lid.
FLORA   I'll do it.
EDWARD   Give it to me! Now . . . Slowly . . .
FLORA   What are you doing?
EDWARD   Be quiet. Slowly . . . carefully . . . on . . . the . . . pot! Ha-ha-ha.
    Very good.

He sits on a chair to the right of the table.

FLORA   Now he's in the marmalade.
EDWARD   Precisely.

Pause. She sits on a chair to the left of the table and reads the "Telegraph."

FLORA   Can you hear him?
EDWARD   Hear him?
FLORA   Buzzing.
EDWARD   Nonsense. How can you hear him? It's an earthenware lid.
FLORA   He's becoming frantic.
EDWARD   Rubbish. Take it away from the table.
FLORA   What shall I do with it?
EDWARD   Put it in the sink and drown it.
FLORA   It'll fly out and bite me.
EDWARD   It will not bite you! Wasps don't bite. Anyway, it won't fly out. It's
    stuck. It'll drown where it is, in the marmalade.
FLORA   What a horrible death.
EDWARD   On the contrary.

Pause.

FLORA   Have you got something in your eyes?
EDWARD   No. Why do you ask?
FLORA   You keep clenching them, blinking them.
EDWARD   I have a slight ache in them.
FLORA   Oh, dear.
EDWARD   Yes, a slight ache. As if I hadn't slept.
FLORA   Did you sleep, Edward?
EDWARD   Of course I slept. Uninterrupted. As always.
FLORA   And yet you feel tired.
EDWARD   I didn't say I felt tired. I merely said I had a slight ache in my eyes.

FLORA   Why is that, then?

EDWARD   I really don't know.

Pause.

FLORA   Oh goodness!

EDWARD   What is it?

FLORA   I can see it. It's trying to come out.

EDWARD   How can it?

FLORA   Through the hole. It's trying to crawl out, through the spoon-hole.

EDWARD   Mmmnn, yes. Can't do it, of course. [*Silent pause.*] Well, let's kill it, for goodness' sake.

FLORA   Yes, let's. But how?

EDWARD   Bring it out on the spoon and squash it on a plate.

FLORA   It'll fly away. It'll bite.

EDWARD   If you don't stop saying that word I shall leave this table.

FLORA   But wasps do bite.

EDWARD   They don't bite. They sting. It's snakes . . . that bite.

FLORA   What about horseflies? [*Pause.*]

EDWARD   [*to himself*]   Horseflies suck. [*Pause.*]

FLORA   [*tentatively*]   If we . . . if we wait long enough, I suppose it'll choke to death. It'll suffocate in the marmalade.

EDWARD   [*briskly*]   You do know I've got work to do this morning, don't you? I can't spend the whole day worrying about a wasp.

FLORA   Well, kill it.

EDWARD   You want to kill it?

FLORA   Yes.

EDWARD   Very well. Pass me the hot water jug.

FLORA   What are you going to do?

EDWARD   Scald it. Give it to me.

She hands him the jug. Pause.

Now . . .

FLORA   [*whispering*]   Do you want me to lift the lid?

EDWARD   No, no, no. I'll pour down the spoon hole. Right . . . down the spoon-hole.

FLORA   Listen!

EDWARD   What?

FLORA   It's buzzing.

EDWARD   Vicious creatures. [*Pause.*] Curious, but I don't remember seeing any wasps at all, all summer, until now. I'm sure I don't know why. I mean, there must have been wasps.

FLORA   Please.

EDWARD   This couldn't be the first wasp, could it?

FLORA   Please.

EDWARD   The first wasp of summer? No. It's not possible.

FLORA   Edward.

EDWARD   Mmmmnnn?

FLORA   Kill it.

EDWARD   Ah, yes. Tilt the pot. Tilt. Aah . . . down here . . . right down . . . blinding him . . . that's . . . it.

FLORA   Is it?

EDWARD   Lift the lid. All right, I will. There he is! Dead. What a monster. [He squashes it on a plate.]

FLORA   What an awful experience.

EDWARD   What a beautiful day it is. Beautiful. I think I shall work in the garden this morning. Where's that canopy?

FLORA   It's in the shed.

EDWARD   Yes, we must get it out. My goodness, just look at that sky. Not a cloud. Did you say it was the longest day of the year today?

FLORA   Yes.

EDWARD   Ah, it's a good day. I feel it in my bones. In my muscles. I think I'll stretch my legs in a minute. Down to the pool. My God, look at that flowering shrub over there. Clematis. What a wonderful . . . [He stops suddenly.]

FLORA   What? [Pause.] Edward, what is it? [Pause.] Edward . . .

EDWARD   [thickly]   He's there.

FLORA   Who?

EDWARD   [low, murmuring]   Blast and damn it, he's there, he's there at the back gate.

FLORA   Let me see.

She moves over to him to look. Pause.

    [Lightly] Oh, it's the matchseller.

EDWARD   He's back again.

FLORA   But he's always there.

EDWARD   Why? What is he doing there?

FLORA   But he's never disturbed you, has he? The man's been standing there for weeks. You've never mentioned it.

EDWARD   What is he doing there?

FLORA   He's selling matches, of course.

EDWARD   It's ridiculous. What's the time?

FLORA   Half past nine.

EDWARD   What in God's name is he doing with a tray full of matches at half past nine in the morning?

FLORA   He arrives at seven o'clock.

EDWARD   Seven o'clock?

FLORA   He's always there at seven.

EDWARD   Yes, but you've never . . . actually seen him arrive?

FLORA   No, I . . .

EDWARD   Well, how do you know he's . . . not been standing there all night?

Pause.

FLORA   Do you find him interesting, Edward?

EDWARD [*casually*]   Interesting? No. No, I . . . don't find him interesting.

FLORA   He's a very nice old man, really.

EDWARD   You've spoken to him?

FLORA   No. No, I haven't spoken to him. I've nodded.

EDWARD [*pacing up and down*]   For two months he's been standing on that
    spot, do you realize that? Two months. I haven't been able to step
    outside the back gate.

FLORA   Why on earth not?

EDWARD [*to himself*]   It used to give me great pleasure, such pleasure, to
    stroll along through the long grass, out through the back gate, pass into
    the lane. That pleasure is now denied me. It's my own house, isn't it? It's
    my own gate.

FLORA   I really can't understand this, Edward.

EDWARD   Damn. And do you know I've never seen him sell one box? Not a
    box. It's hardly surprising. He's on the wrong road. It's not a road at all.
    What is it? It's a lane, leading to the monastery. Off everybody's route.
    Even the monks take a short cut to the village, when they want to go . . .
    to the village. No one goes up it. Why doesn't he stand on the main road
    if he wants to sell matches, by the *front* gate? The whole thing's
    preposterous.

FLORA [*going over to him*]   I don't know why you're getting so excited about
    it. He's a quiet, harmless old man, going about his business. He's quite
    harmless.

EDWARD   I didn't say he wasn't harmless. Of course he's harmless. How
    could he be other than harmless?

Fade out and silence.

Flora's voice, far in the house, drawing nearer.

FLORA [*off*]   Edward, where are you? Edward? Where are you, Edward?

She appears.

Edward?

Edward, what are you doing in the scullery?

EDWARD [*looking through the scullery window*]   Doing?

FLORA   I've been looking everywhere for you. I put up the canopy ages ago. I came back and you were nowhere to be seen. Have you been out?

EDWARD   No.

FLORA   Where have you been?

EDWARD   Here.

FLORA   I looked in your study. I even went into the attic.

EDWARD [*tonelessly*]   What would I be doing in the attic?

FLORA   I couldn't imagine what had happened to you. Do you know it's twelve o'clock?

EDWARD   Is it?

FLORA   I even went to the bottom of the garden, to see if you were in the toolshed.

EDWARD [*tonelessly*]   What would I be doing in the toolshed?

FLORA   You must have seen me in the garden. You can see through this window.

EDWARD   Only part of the garden.

FLORA   Yes.

EDWARD   Only a corner of the garden. A very small corner.

FLORA   What are you doing in here?

EDWARD   Nothing. I was digging out some notes, that's all.

FLORA   Notes?

EDWARD   For my essay.

FLORA   Which essay?

EDWARD   My essay on space and time.

FLORA   But . . . I've never . . . I don't know that one.

EDWARD   You don't know it?

FLORA   I thought you were writing one about the Belgian Congo.

EDWARD   I've been engaged on the dimensionality and continuity of space . . . and time . . . for years.

FLORA   And the Belgian Congo?

EDWARD [*shortly*]   Never mind about the Belgian Congo.

Pause.

FLORA   But you don't keep notes in the scullery.

EDWARD   You'd be surprised. You'd be highly surprised.

FLORA   Good Lord, what's that? Is that a bullock let loose? No. It's the matchseller! My goodness, you can see him . . . through the hedge. He looks bigger. Have you been watching him? He looks . . . like a bullock. [*Pause.*] Edward? [*Pause. Moving over to him*] Are you coming outside?

I've put up the canopy. You'll miss the best of the day. You can have an hour before lunch.

EDWARD   I've no work to do this morning.

FLORA   What about your essay? You don't intend to stay in the scullery all day, do you?

EDWARD   Get out. Leave me alone.

A slight pause.

FLORA   Really Edward. You've never spoken to me like that in all your life.

EDWARD   Yes, I have.

FLORA   Oh, Weddie. Beddie-Weddie . . .

EDWARD   Do not call me that!

FLORA   Your eyes are bloodshot.

EDWARD   Damn it.

FLORA   It's too dark in here to peer . . .

EDWARD   Damn.

FLORA   It's so bright outside.

EDWARD   Damn.

FLORA   And it's dark in here.

Pause.

EDWARD   Christ blast it!

FLORA   You're frightened of him.

EDWARD   I'm not.

FLORA   You're frightened of a poor old man. Why?

EDWARD   I am not!

FLORA   He's a poor, harmless old man.

EDWARD   Aaah my eyes.

FLORA   Let me bathe them.

EDWARD   Keep away. [*Pause. Slowly.*] I want to speak to that man. I want to have a word with him. [*Pause.*] It's quite absurd, of course. I really can't tolerate something so . . . absurd, right on my doorstep. I shall not tolerate it. He's sold nothing all morning. No one passed. Yes. A monk passed. A non-smoker. In a loose garment. It's quite obvious he was a non-smoker but still, the man made no effort. He made no effort to clinch a sale, to rid himself of one of his cursed boxes. His one chance, all morning, and he made no effort.

Pause.

I haven't wasted my time. I've hit, in fact, upon the truth. He's not a matchseller at all. The bastard isn't a matchseller at all. Curious I never realized that before. He's an impostor. I watched him very closely. He made no move towards the monk. As for the monk, the monk made no move towards him. The monk was moving along the lane. He didn't pause, or halt, or in any way alter his step. As for the matchseller—how ridiculous to go on calling him by that title. What a farce. No, there is something very false about that man. I intend to get to the bottom of it. I'll soon get rid of him. He can go and ply his trade somewhere else. Instead of standing like a bullock . . . a bullock, outside my back gate.

FLORA   But if he isn't a matchseller, what is his trade?

EDWARD   We'll soon find out.

FLORA   You're going out to speak to him?

EDWARD   Certainly not! Go out to *him*? Certainly . . . not. I'll invite him in here. Into my study. Then we'll . . . get to the bottom of it.

FLORA   Why don't you call the police and have him removed?

He laughs. Pause.

Why don't you call the police, Edward? You could say he was a public nuisance. Although I . . . I can't say I find him a nuisance.

EDWARD   Call him in.

FLORA   Me?

EDWARD   Go out and call him in.

FLORA   Are you serious? [*Pause.*] Edward, I could call the police. Or even the vicar.

EDWARD   Go and get him.

She goes out. Silence.

Edward waits.

FLORA [*in the garden*]   Good morning. [*Pause.*] We haven't met. I live in this house here. My husband and I. [*Pause.*] I wonder if you could . . . would you care for a cup of tea? [*Pause.*] Or a glass of lemon? It must be so dry, standing here. [*Pause.*] Would you like to come inside for a little while? It's much cooler. There's something we'd very much like to . . . tell you, that will benefit you. Could you spare a few moments? We won't keep you long. [*Pause.*] Might I buy your tray of matches, do you think? We've run out, completely, and we always keep a very large stock. It happens that way, doesn't it? Well, we can discuss it inside. Do come. This way. Ah now, do come. Our house is full of curios, you know. My husband's been rather a collector. We have goose for lunch. Do you care for goose?

She moves to the gate.

Come and have lunch with us. This way. That's . . . right. May I take your arm? There's a good deal of *nettle* inside the gate. [*The Matchseller appears.*] Here. This way. Mind now. Isn't it beautiful weather? It's the longest day of the year today. [*Pause.*] That's honeysuckle. And that's convolvulus. There's clematis. And do you see that plant by the conservatory? That's japonica.

Silence. She enters the study.

FLORA   He's here.

EDWARD   I know.

FLORA   He's in the hall.

EDWARD   I know he's here. I can smell him.

FLORA   Smell him?

EDWARD   I smelt him when he came under my window. Can't you smell the house now?

FLORA   What are you going to do with him, Edward? You won't be rough with him in any way? He's very old. I'm not sure if he can hear, or even see. And he's wearing the oldest—

EDWARD   I don't want to know what he's wearing.

FLORA   But you'll see for yourself in a minute, if you speak to him.

EDWARD   I shall.

Slight pause.

FLORA   He's an old man. You won't . . . be rough with him?

EDWARD   If he's so old, why doesn't he seek shelter . . . from the storm?

FLORA   But there's no storm. It's summer, the longest day . . .

EDWARD   There was a storm, last week. A summer storm. He stood without moving, while it raged about him.

FLORA   When was this?

EDWARD   He remained quite still, while it thundered all about him.

Pause.

FLORA   Edward . . . are you sure it's wise to bother about all this?

EDWARD   Tell him to come in.

FLORA   I . . .

EDWARD   Now.

She goes and collects the Matchseller.

FLORA   Hullo. Would you like to go in? I won't be long. Up these stairs here. [*Pause.*] You can have some sherry before lunch. [*Pause.*] Shall I take your tray? No. Very well, take it with you. Just . . . up those stairs. The door at the . . . [*She watches him move.*] the door . . . [*Pause.*] the door at the top. I'll join you . . . later. [*She goes out.*]

The Matchseller stands on the threshold of the study.

EDWARD [*cheerfully*] Here I am. Where are you? [*Pause.*] Don't stand out there, old chap. Come into my study. [*He rises.*] Come in.

The Matchseller enters.

That's right. Mind how you go. That's . . . it. Now, make yourself comfortable. Thought you might like some refreshment, on a day like this. Sit down, old man. What will you have? Sherry? Or what about a double scotch? Eh?

Pause.

I entertain the villagers annually, as a matter of fact. I'm not the squire, but they look upon me with some regard. Don't believe we've got a squire here any more, actually. Don't know what became of him. Nice old man he was. Great chess-player, as I remember. Three daughters. The pride of the county. Flaming red hair. Alice was the eldest. Sit yourself down, old chap. Eunice I think was number two. The youngest one was the best of the bunch. Sally. No, no, wait a minute, no, it wasn't Sally, it was . . . Fanny. Fanny. A flower. You must be a stranger here. Unless you lived here once, went on a long voyage and have lately returned. Do you know the district?

Pause.

Now, now, you mustn't . . . stand about like that. Take a seat. Which one would you prefer? We have a great variety, as you see. Can't stand uniformity. Like different seats, different backs. Often when I'm working, you know, I draw up one chair, scribble a few lines, put it by, draw up another, sit back, ponder, put it by . . . [*absently*] . . . sit back . . . put it by . . .

Pause.

I write theological and philosophical essays . . .

Pause.

Now and again I jot down a few observations on certain tropical phenomena—not from the same standpoint, of course. [*Silent pause.*] Yes. Africa, now. Africa's always been my happy hunting ground. Fascinating country. Do you know it? I get the impression that you've . . . been around a bit. Do you by any chance know the Membunza Mountains? Great range south of Katambaloo. French Equatorial Africa, if my memory serves me right. Most extraordinary diversity of flora and fauna. Especially fauna. I understand in the Gobi Desert you can come across some very strange sights. Never been there myself. Studied the maps though. Fascinating things, maps.

Pause.

Do you live in the village? I don't often go down, of course. Or are you passing through? On your way to another part of the country? Well, I can tell you, in my opinion you won't find many prettier parts than here. We win the first prize regularly, you know, the best kept village in the area. Sit down. [*Pause.*] I say, can you hear me? [*Pause.*] I said, I say, can you hear me? [*Pause.*] You possess most extraordinary repose, for a man of your age, don't you? Well, perhaps that's not quite the right word . . . repose. Do you find it chilly in here? I'm sure it's chillier in here than out. I haven't been out yet, today, though I shall probably spend the whole afternoon working, in the garden, under my canopy, at my table, by the pool.

Pause.

Oh, I understand you met my *wife*? Charming woman, don't you think? Plenty of grit there, too. Stood by me through thick and thin, that woman. In season and out of season. Fine figure of a woman she was, too, in her youth. Wonderful carriage, flaming red hair. [*He stops abruptly.*]

Pause.

Yes, I . . . I was in much the same position myself then as you are now, you understand. Struggling to make my way in the world. I was in commerce too. [*With a chuckle*] Oh, yes, I know what it's like—the weather, the rain, beaten from pillar to post, up hill and down dale . . . the rewards were few . . . winters in hovels . . . up till all hours working at your thesis . . . yes, I've done it all. Let me advise you. Get a good woman to stick by you. Never mind what the world says. Keep at it. Keep your shoulder to the wheel. It'll pay dividends.

Pause.

[*With a laugh*] You must excuse my chatting away like this. We have few
visitors this time of the year. All our friends summer abroad. I'm a home
bird myself. Wouldn't mind taking a trip to Asia Minor, mind you, or to
certain lower regions of the Congo, but Europe? Out of the question.
Much too noisy. I'm sure you agree. Now look, what will you have to
drink? A glass of ale? Curaçao Fockink Orange? Ginger beer? Tia Maria?
A Wachenheimer Fuchsmantel Reisling Beeren Auslese? Gin and it?
Chateauneuf-du-Pape? A little Asti Spumante? Or what do you say to a
straightforward Piesporter Goldtropfschen Feine Auslese (Reichsgraf
von Kesselstaff)? Any preference?

Pause.

You look a trifle warm. Why don't you take off your balaclava? I'd find
that a little itchy myself. But then I've always been one for freedom of
movement. Even in the depth of winter I wear next to nothing.

Pause.

I say, can I ask you a personal question? I don't want to seem inquisitive
but aren't you rather on the wrong road for matchselling? Not terribly
busy, is it? Of course you may not care for petrol fumes or the noise of
traffic. I can quite understand that.

Pause.

Do forgive me peering but is that a glass eye you're wearing?

Pause.

Do take off your balaclava, there's a good chap, put your tray down and
take your ease, as they say in this part of the world. [*He moves towards
him.*] I must say you keep quite a good stock, don't you? Tell me,
between ourselves, are those boxes full, or are there just a few half-
empty ones among them? Oh yes, I used to be in commerce. Well now,
before the good lady sounds the gong for petit déjeuner will you join me
in an apéritif? I recommend a glass of cider. Now . . . just a minute . . . I
know I've got some—Look out! Mind your tray!

The tray falls, and the matchboxes.

Good God, what . . .? [*Pause.*] You've dropped your tray.

Pause. He picks the matchboxes up.

> [*Grunts.*] Eh, these boxes are all wet. You've no right to sell wet matches, you know. Uuuuugggh. This feels suspiciously like fungus. You won't get very far in this trade if you don't take care of your goods. [*Grunts, rising.*] Well, here you are. [*Pause.*] Here's your tray.

He puts the tray into the Matchseller's hands, and sits. Pause.

> Now listen, let me be quite frank with you, shall I? I really cannot understand why you don't sit down. There are four chairs at your disposal. Not to mention the hassock. I can't possibly talk to you unless you're settled. Then and only then can I speak to you. Do you follow me? You're not being terribly helpful. [*Slight pause.*] You're sweating. The sweat's pouring out of you. Take off that balaclava.

Pause.

> Go into the corner then. Into the corner. Go on. Get into the shade of the corner. Back. Backward. [*Pause.*] Get back! [*Pause.*] Ah, you understand me. Forgive me for saying so, but I had decided that you had the comprehension of a bullock. I was mistaken. You understand me perfectly well. That's right. A little more. A little to the right. Aaah. Now you're there. In shade, in shadow. Good-o. Now I can get down to brass tacks. Can't I?

Pause.

> No doubt you're wondering why I invited you into this house? You may think I was alarmed by the look of you. You would be quite mistaken. I was not alarmed by the look of you. I did not find you at all alarming. No, no. Nothing outside this room has ever alarmed me. You disgusted me, quite forcibly, if you want to know the truth.

Pause.

> Why did you disgust me to that extent? That seems to be a pertinent question. You're no more disgusting than Fanny, the squire's daughter, after all. In appearance you differ but not in essence. There's the same . . . [*Pause.*] The same . . . [*Pause. In a low voice.*] I want to ask you a question. Why do you stand outside my back gate, from dawn till dusk, why do you pretend to sell matches, why . . .? What is it, damn you. You're shivering. You're sagging. Come here, come here . . . mind your tray! [*Edward rises and moves behind a chair.*] Come, quick quick. There. Sit here. Sit . . . sit in this.

The Matchseller stumbles and sits. Pause.

Aaaah! You're sat. At last. What a relief. You must be tired. [*Slight pause.*] Chair comfortable? I bought it in a sale. I bought all the furniture in this house in a sale. The same sale. When I was a young man. You too, perhaps. You too, perhaps. [*Pause.*] At the same time, perhaps! [*Pause. Muttering*] I must get some air. I must get a breath of air.

He goes to the door.

Flora!

FLORA   Yes?

EDWARD [*with great weariness*]   Take me into the garden.

Silence. They move from the study door to a chair under a canopy.

FLORA   Come under the canopy.

EDWARD   Ah. [*He sits. Pause.*] The peace. The peace out here.

FLORA   Look at our trees.

EDWARD   Yes.

FLORA   Our own trees. Can you hear the birds?

EDWARD   No, I can't hear them.

FLORA   But they're singing, high up, and flapping.

EDWARD   Good. Let them flap.

FLORA   Shall I bring your lunch out here? You can have it in peace, and a quiet drink, under your canopy. [*Pause.*] How are you getting on with your old man?

EDWARD   What do you mean?

FLORA   What's happening? How are you getting on with him?

EDWARD   Very well. We get on remarkably well. He's a little . . . reticent. Somewhat withdrawn. It's understandable. I should be the same, perhaps, in his place. Though, of course, I could not possibly find myself in his place.

FLORA   Have you found out anything about him?

EDWARD   A little. A little. He's had various trades, that's certain. His place of residence is unsure. He's . . . he's not a drinking man. As yet, I haven't discovered the reason for his arrival here. I shall in due course . . . by nightfall.

FLORA   Is it necessary?

EDWARD   Necessary?

FLORA [*quickly sitting on the right arm of the chair*]   I could show him out now, it wouldn't matter. You've seen him, he's harmless, unfortunate . . . old, that's all. Edward—listen—he's not here through any . . . design, or anything, I know it. I mean, he might just as well stand outside our back gate as anywhere else. He'll move on. I can . . . make him. I promise you. There's no point in upsetting yourself like this. He's an old man, weak in the head . . . that's all.

Pause.

EDWARD   You're deluded.

FLORA   Edward—

EDWARD   [*rising*]   You're deluded. And stop calling me Edward.

FLORA   You're not still frightened of him?

EDWARD   Frightened of him? Of *him*? Have you *seen* him? [*Pause.*] He's like jelly. A great bullockfat of jelly. He can't see straight. I think as a matter of fact he wears a glass eye. He's almost stone deaf . . . almost . . . not quite. He's very nearly dead on his feet. Why should he frighten me? No, you're a woman, you know nothing. [*Slight pause.*] But he possesses other faculties. Cunning. The man's an imposter and he knows I know it.

FLORA   I'll tell you what. Look. Let me speak to him. I'll speak to him.

EDWARD   [*quietly*]   And I know he knows I know it.

FLORA   I'll find out all about him, Edward. I promise you I will.

EDWARD   And he knows I know.

FLORA   Edward! Listen to me! I can find out all about him, I promise you. I shall go and have a word with him now. I shall . . . get to the bottom of it.

EDWARD   You? It's laughable.

FLORA   You'll see—he won't bargain for me. I'll surprise him. He'll . . . he'll admit everything.

EDWARD   [*softly*]   He'll admit everything, will he?

FLORA   You wait and see, you just—

EDWARD   [*hissing*]   What are you plotting?

FLORA   I know exactly what I shall—

EDWARD   What are you plotting?

He seizes her arms.

FLORA   Edward, you're hurting me!

Pause.

[*With dignity*] I shall wave from the window when I'm ready. Then you can come up. I shall get to the truth of it, I assure you. You're much too heavy-handed, in every way. You should trust your wife more, Edward.

You should trust her judgment, and have a greater insight into her capabilities. A woman . . . a woman will often succeed, you know, where a man must invariably fail.

Silence. She goes into the study.

Do you mind if I come in?

The door closes.

Are you comfortable? [*Pause.*] Oh, the sun's shining directly on you. Wouldn't you rather sit in the shade?

She sits down.

It's the longest day of the year today, did you know that? Actually the year has flown. I can remember Christmas and that dreadful frost. And the floods! I hope you weren't here in the floods. We were out of danger up here, of course, but in the valleys whole families I remember drifted away on the current. The country was a lake. Everything stopped. We lived on our own preserves, drank elderberry wine, studied other cultures.

Pause.

Do you know, I've got a feeling I've seen you before, somewhere. Long before the flood. You were much younger. Yes, I'm really sure of it. Between ourselves, were you ever a poacher? I had an encounter with a poacher once. It was a ghastly rape, the brute. High up on a hillside cattle track. Early spring. I was out riding on my pony. And there on the verge a man lay—ostensibly injured, lying on his front, I remember, possibly the victim of a murderous assault, how was I to know? I dismounted, I went to him, he rose, I fell, my pony took off, down to the valley. I saw the sky through the trees, blue. Up to my ears in mud. It was a desperate battle. [*Pause.*] I lost. [*Pause.*] Of course, life was perilous in those days. It was my first canter unchaperoned.

Pause.

Years later, when I was a Justice of the Peace for the county, I had him in front of the bench. He was there for poaching. That's how I know he was a poacher. The evidence though was sparse, inadmissible, I acquitted him, letting him off with a caution. He'd grown a red beard, I remember. Yes. A bit of a stinker.

Pause.

I say, you are perspiring, aren't you? Shall I mop your brow? With my chiffon? Is it the heat? Or the closeness? Or confined space? Or . . . ? [*She goes over to him.*] Actually, the day is cooling. It'll soon be dusk. Perhaps it is dusk. May I? You don't mind? [*Pause. She mops his brow.*] Ah, there, that's better. And your cheeks. It is a woman's job, isn't it? And I'm the only woman on hand. There.

Pause. She leans on the arm of chair.

[*Intimately*] Tell me, have you a woman? Do you like women? Do you ever . . . think about women? [*Pause.*] Have you ever . . . stopped a woman? [*Pause.*] I'm sure you must have been quite attractive once. [*She sits.*] Not any more, of course. You've got a vile smell. Vile. Quite repellent, in fact.

Pause.

Sex, I suppose, means nothing to you. Does it ever occur to you that sex is a very vital experience for other people? Really, I think you'd amuse me if you weren't so hideous. You're probably quite amusing in your own way. [*Seductively*] Tell me all about love. Speak to me of love.

Pause.

God knows what you're saying at this very moment. It's quite disgusting. Do you know when I was a girl I loved . . . I loved . . . I simply adored . . . what *have* you got on, for goodness sake? A jersey? It's clogged. Have you been rolling in mud? [*Slight pause.*] You haven't been rolling in mud, have you? [*She rises and goes over to him.*] And what have you got under your jersey? Let's see. [*Slight pause.*] I'm not tickling you, am I? No. Good . . . Lord, is this a vest? That's quite original. Quite original. [*She sits on the arm of his chair.*] Hmmnn, you're a solid old boy, I must say. Not at all like a jelly. All you need is a bath. A lovely lathery bath. And a good scrub. A lovely lathery scrub. [*Pause.*] Don't you? It will be a pleasure. [*She throws her arms round him.*] I'm going to keep you. I'm going to keep you, you dreadful chap, and call you Barnabas. Isn't it dark, Barnabas? Your eyes, your eyes, your great big eyes.

Pause.

My husband would never have guessed your name. Never. [*She kneels at his feet. Whispering*] It's me you were waiting for, wasn't it? You've been standing waiting for me. You've seen me in the woods, picking daisies, in my apron, my pretty daisy apron, and you came and stood, poor creature, at my gate, till death us do part. Poor Barnabas. I'm going to put you to bed. I'm going to put you to bed and watch over you. But first you must have a good whacking great bath. And I'll buy you pretty little things that will suit you. And little toys to play with. On your deathbed. Why shouldn't you die happy?

A shout from the hall.

EDWARD   Well?

Footsteps upstage.

    Well?
FLORA   Don't come in.
EDWARD   Well?
FLORA   He's dying.
EDWARD   Dying? He's not dying.
FLORA   I tell you, he's very ill.
EDWARD   He's not dying! Nowhere near. He'll see you cremated.
FLORA   The man is desperately ill!
EDWARD   Ill? You lying slut. Get back to your trough!
FLORA   Edward . . .
EDWARD   [*violently*]   To your trough!

She goes out. Pause.

    [*Coolly*] Good evening to you. Why are you sitting in the gloom? Oh, you've begun to disrobe. Too warm? Let's open these windows, then, what?

He opens the windows.

    Pull the blinds.

He pulls the blinds.

    And close . . . the curtains . . . again.

He closes the curtains.

    Ah. Air will enter through the side chinks. Of the blinds. And filter through the curtains. I hope. Don't want to suffocate, do we? [*Pause.*]

More comfortable? Yes. You look different in darkness. Take off all your togs, if you like. Make yourself at home. Strip to your buff. Do as you would in your own house.

Pause.

Did you say something? [*Pause.*] Did you say something? [*Pause.*] Anything? Well then, tell me about your boyhood. Mmnn? [*Pause.*] What did you do with it? Run? Swim? Kick the ball? You kicked the ball? What position? Left back? Goalie? First reserve?

Pause.

I used to play myself. Country house matches, mostly. Kept wicket and batted number seven. [*Pause.*] Kept wicket and batted number seven. Man called—Cavendish, I think had something of your style. Bowled left arm over the wicket, always kept his cap on, quite a dab hand at solo whist, preferred a good round of prop and cop to anything else. [*Pause.*] On wet days when the field was swamped.

Pause.

Perhaps you don't play cricket. [*Pause.*] Perhaps you never met Cavendish and never played cricket. You look less and less like a cricketer the more I see of you. Where did you live in those days? God damn it, I'm entitled to know something about you! You're in my blasted house, on my territory, drinking my wine, eating my duck! Now you've had your fill you sit like a hump, a mouldering heap. In my room. My den. I can rem . . . [*He stops abruptly.*]

Pause.

You find that funny? Are you grinning?

Pause.

[*In disgust*] Good Christ, is that a grin on your face? [*Further disgust*] It's lopsided. It's all—down on one side. You're grinning. It amuses you, does it? When I tell you how well I remember this room, how well I remember this den. [*Muttering*] Ha. Yesterday now, it was clear, clearly defined, so clearly. [*Pause.*] The garden, too, was sharp, lucid, in the rain, in the sun. [*Pause.*] My den, too, was sharp, arranged for my purpose . . . quite satisfactory. [*Pause.*] The house too, was polished, all the banisters were polished, and the stair rods, and the curtain rods. [Pause.] My desk was polished, and my cabinet.

Pause.

I was polished. [Nostalgic] I could stand on the hill and look through my telescope at the sea. And follow the path of the three-masted schooner, feeling fit, well aware of my sinews, their suppleness, my arms lifted holding the telescope, steady, easily, no trembling, my aim was perfect, I could pour hot water down the spoon-hole, yes, easily, no difficulty, my grasp firm, my command established, my life was accounted for, I was ready for my excursions to the cliff, down the path to the back gate, through the long grass, no need to watch for the nettles, my progress was fluent, after my long struggling against all kinds of usurpers, disreputables, lists, literally lists of people anxious to do me down, and my reputation down, my command was established, all summer I would breakfast, survey my landscape, take my telescope, examine the overhanging of my hedges, pursue the narrow lane past the monastery, climb the hill, adjust the lens [he mimes a telescope], watch the progress of the three-masted schooner, my progress was as sure, as fluent . . .

Pause. He drops his arms.

Yes, yes, you're quite right, it is funny. [Pause.] Laugh your bloody head off! Go on. Don't mind me. No need to be polite. [Pause.] That's right. [Pause.] You're quite right, it is funny. I'll laugh with you!

He laughs.

Ha-ha-ha! Yes! You're laughing with me, I'm laughing with you, we're laughing together!

He laughs and stops.

[Brightly] Why did I invite you into this room? That's your next question, isn't it? Bound to be. [Pause.] Well, why not, you might say? My oldest acquaintance. My nearest and dearest. My kith and kin. But surely correspondence would have been as satisfactory . . . more satisfactory? We could have exchanged postcards, couldn't we? What? Views, couldn't we? Of sea and land, city and village, town and country, autumn and winter . . . clocktowers . . . museums . . . citadels . . . bridges . . . rivers . . . [Pause.] Seeing you stand, at the back gate, such close proximity, was not at all the same thing.

Pause.

What are you doing? You're taking off your balaclava . . . you've decided not to. No, very well then, all things considered, did I then invite you into this room with express intention of asking you to take off your balaclava, in order to determine your resemblance to—some other person? The answer is no, certainly not, I did not, for when I first saw you you wore no balaclava. No headcovering of any kind, in fact. You looked quite different without a head—I mean without a hat—I mean without a headcovering, of any kind. In fact every time I have seen you you have looked quite different to the time before. [*Pause.*] Even now you look different. Very different.

Pause.

Admitted that sometimes I viewed you through dark glasses, yes, and sometimes through light glasses, and on other occasions bare eyed, and on other occasions through the bars of the scullery window, or from the roof, the roof, yes in driving snow, or from the bottom of the drive in thick fog, or from the roof again in blinding sun, so blinding, so hot, that I had to skip and jump and bounce in order to remain in one place. Ah, that's good for a guffaw, is it? That's good for a belly laugh? Go on, then. Let it out. Let yourself go, for God's . . . [*He catches his breath.*] You're crying . . .

Pause.

[*Moved.*] You haven't been laughing. You're crying. [*Pause.*] You're weeping. You're shaking with grief. For me. I can't believe it. For my plight. I've been wrong.

Pause.

[*Briskly.*] Come, come, stop it. Be a man. Blow your nose for goodness sake. Pull yourself together.

He sneezes.

Ah.

He rises. Sneeze.

Ah. Fever. Excuse me.

He blows his nose.

I've caught a cold. A germ. In my eyes. It was this morning. In my eyes. My eyes.

Pause. He falls to the floor.

Not that I had any difficulty in seeing you, no, no, it was not so much my sight, my sight is excellent—in winter I run about with nothing on but a pair of polo shorts—no, it was not so much any deficiency in my sight as the airs between me and my object—don't weep—the change of air, the currents obtaining in the space between me and my object, the shades they make, the shapes they take, the quivering, the eternal quivering— please stop crying—nothing to do with heat-haze. Sometimes, of course, I would take shelter, shelter to compose myself. Yes, I would seek a tree, a cranny of bushes, erect my canopy and so make shelter. And rest. [*Low murmur.*] And then I no longer heard the wind or saw the sun. Nothing entered, nothing left my nook. I lay on my side in my polo shorts, my fingers lightly in contact with the blades of grass, the earthflowers, the petals of the earthflowers flaking, lying on my palm, the underside of all the great foliage dark, above me, but it is only afterwards I say the foliage was dark, the petals flaking, then I said nothing, I remarked nothing, things happened upon me, then in my times of shelter, the shades, the petals, carried themselves, carried their bodies upon me, and nothing entered my nook, nothing left it.

Pause.

But then, the time came. I saw the wind. I saw the wind, swirling, and the dust at my back gate, lifting, and the long grass, scything together . . . [*Slowly, in horror*] You *are* laughing. You're laughing. Your face. Your body. [*Overwhelming nausea and horror.*] Rocking . . . gasping . . . rocking . . . shaking . . . rocking . . . heaving . . . rocking . . . You're laughing at me! Aaaaahhhh!

The Matchseller rises. Silence.

You look younger. You look extraordinarily . . . youthful.

Pause.

You want to examine the garden? It must be very bright, in the moonlight. [*Becoming weaker*] I would like to join you . . . explain . . .

show you . . . the garden . . . explain . . . The plants . . . where I run
. . . my track . . . in training . . . I was number one sprinter at Howells
. . . when a stripling . . . no more than a stripling . . . licked . . . men
twice my strength . . . when a stripling . . . like yourself.

Pause.

[*Flatly*] The pool must be glistening. In the moonlight. And the lawn. I
remember it well. The cliff. The sea. The three-masted schooner.

Pause.

[*With great, final effort—a whisper*] Who are you?
FLORA [*off*]   Barnabas?

Pause. She enters.

Ah, Barnabas. Everything is ready.

Pause.

I want to show you my garden, your garden. You must see my japonica,
my convolvulus . . . my honeysuckle, my clematis.

Pause.

The summer is coming. I've put up your canopy for you. You can lunch
in the garden, by the pool. I've polished the whole house for you.
[*Pause.*] Take my hand.

Pause. The Matchseller goes over to her.

Yes. Oh, wait a moment.

Pause.

Edward. Here is your tray.

*She crosses to Edward with the tray of matches, and puts it in his hands. Then she
and the Matchseller start to go out as the curtain falls slowly.*

ED BULLINS
1935—
In the Wine Time

CHARACTERS

CLIFF DAWSON	BEATRICE
LOU DAWSON, Cliff's wife	TINY
RAY, Lou's nephew	SILLY WILLY CLARK
MISS MINNY GARRISON	RED
BUNNY GILLETTE	BAMA
MRS. KRUMP	DORIS
EDDIE KRUMP	A POLICEMAN

THE PROLOGUE

She passed the corner every evening during my last wine time, wearing a light summer dress with big pockets, in small ballerina slippers, swinging her head back and to the side all special-like, hearing a private melody singing in her head. I waited for her each dusk, and for this she granted me a smile, but on some days her selfish tune would drift out to me in a hum; we shared the smile and sad tune and met for a moment each day but one of that long-ago summer.

The times I would be late she lingered, in the sweating twilight, at the corner in the barbershop doorway, ignoring the leers and coughs from within, until she saw me hurrying along the tenement fronts. On these days her yellows and pinks and whites would flash out from the smoked walls, beckoning me to hurry hurry to see the lights in her eyes before they fleeted away above the single smile, which would turn about and then down the street, hidden by the little pretty head. Then, afterwards, I would stand before the shop refusing to believe the slander from within.

"Ray . . . why do you act so stupid?" Lou asked each day I arose to await the rendezvous.

"I don't know . . . just do, that's all," I always explained.

"Well, if you know you're bein' a fool, why do you go on moonin' out there in the streets for *that?* . . ."

"She's a friend of mine, Lou . . . she's a friend."

August dragged in the wake of July in steaming sequence of sun and then hell and finally sweltering night. The nights found me awake with Cliff and Lou and our bottles of port, all waiting for the sun to rise again and then to sleep in dozes during the miserable hours. And then for me to wake hustling my liquor money and then to wait on the corner for my friend to pass.

"What'd the hell you say to her, Ray?" Cliff asked.

"Nothin'."

"Nothing?"

"Nawh . . . nothin'."

"Do you ever try?"

"Nawh," I said.

"Why? She's probably just waiting for you to . . ."

"Nawh, she's not. We don't need to say anything to each other. We know all we want to find out."

And we would go on like that until we were so loaded our voices would crack and break as fragile as eggs and the subject would escape us, flapping off over the roofs like a fat pigeon.

Summer and Cliff and Lou and me together—all poured from the same brew, all hating each other and loving, and consuming and never forgiving—but not letting go of the circle until the earth swung again into winter, bringing me closer to manhood and the freedom to do all the things that I had done for the past three summers.

We were the group, the gang. Cliff and Lou entangled within their union, soon to have Baby Man, and Henrietta, and Stinky, and Debra, and may be who knows who by now. Summer and me wrapped in our embrace like lovers, accepting each as an inferior, continually finding faults and my weaknesses, pretending to forgive though never forgetting, always at each other's vitals . . . My coterie and my friend . . .

She with the swinging head and flat-footed stance and the single smile and private song for me. She was missing for a day in the last week of summer.

I waited on the corner until the night boiled up from the pavements and the wine time approached too uncomfortably.

Cliff didn't laugh when learning of my loss; Lou stole a half a glass more than I should have received. The night stewed us as we blocked the stoop fighting for air and more than our shares of the port, while the bandit patrol cruised by as sinister as gods.

She was there waiting next day, not smiling nor humming but waving me near. I approached and saw my very own smile.

"I love you, little boy," she said.

I nodded, trying to comprehend.

"You're my little boy, aren't you?" She took my hand. "I have to go away but I wanted to tell you this before I left." She looked into my eyes and over my shaggy uncut hair. "I must be years older than you, but you look so much older than I. In two more years you won't be able to stop with only wine," she said. "Do you have to do it?"

"I don't know . . . just do, that's all," I explained.

"I'm sorry, my dear," she said. "I must go now."

"Why?"

"I just must."

"Can I go with you?"

She let go of my hand and smiled for the last time.

"No, not now, but you can come find me when you're ready."

"But where?" I asked.

"Out in the world, little boy, out in the world. Remember, when you're ready, all you have to do is leave this place and come to me, I'll be waiting. All you'll need to do is search!"

Her eyes lighted for the last time before hiding behind the pretty head, swinging then away from me, carrying our sorrowful, secret tune.

I stood listening to the barbershop taunts follow her into the darkness, watching her until the wicked city night captured her; then I turned back to meet autumn and Cliff and Lou in our last wine time, meeting the years which had to hurry hurry so I could begin the search that I have not completed.

ACT I

The people in this play are black except for the Krumps and the Policeman.

Scene: Derby Street. A small side street of a large northern American industrial city, in the early 1950s.

At left, the houses stand together on one side of the street in unbroken relief, except for a tunnel-like alley which opens between the Krumps' and the Garrisons' houses, forming a low, two-storied canyon, the smoke-stained chimneys the pinnacles of the ridges. Four-letter words, arrow-pierced hearts and slangy street-talk, scrawled in haste, smear a wooden fence, painted green, across the narrow street. Tattered posters of political candidates wearing scribbled, smudged mustaches, circuses of seasons passed and fading, golden and orange snuff containers decorate the enclosure. Each building's front is dull red, not brick colored, but a gray- and violet-tinged red, the shade the paint becomes after successive seasons of assault by the city's smoke- and grit-laden atmosphere. Precise white lines, the older ones yellowing, outline each brick of the walls, and every house has a squat stoop of five white stone steps.

A raised level, upstage right, between the fence and the houses, represents "The Avenue."

From within the Dawsons' house black music of the period—called rhythm 'n blues by disc jockeys at that time—is heard not too loudly, and continues throughout the play, interrupted only seldom by amusing, jive-talking commercials for used cars, televisions, appliances, hair straighteners and skin lighteners. Some of the recording stars of this season are King Pleasure, Johnnie Otis, Fats Domino, Little Esther, Ray Charles and "The Queen," Miss Dinah Washington. When Miss Minny Garrison raises her window gospel music can be heard.

At Rise: It is a sultry evening in late August. All the steps are occupied by members of the various Derby Street households.

At the end of the street, downstage, is a corner lighted by a streetlamp, the gas-burning variety found still then in some sections of Philadelphia, Baltimore, New York and Boston.

All lights are down but the corner streetlamp, though dim shadows of people on the stoops can be seen carrying on their evening activities: talking, gossiping, playing checkers and cards, drinking sodas, wine and beer.

Mr. Krump enters and stands at the streetlamp. He is very drunk.

Lights on the Krumps' doorstoop, the nearer to the corner.

The Krumps' front door opens and Mrs. Krump leans out.

THE RADIO   And here we are folks . . . on a black juicy, jammin' 'n' groovin' hot August night . . . yeah . . . one of them nights fo' bein' wit' tha one ya loves . . .

MRS. KRUMP [*strident, over the radio*]   *Krumpy! What cha doin' on da corner? Hey, Krumpy! Hey, Krumpy! . . . Krumpy . . . Get the hell on over here!*

Light on third doorstoop.

CLIFF   Heee . . . heee . . . look a' ole man Krump work out.

Bunny Gillette and Doris enter Derby Street at the corner and see Mr. Krump.

LOU   Hush up, Cliff.

CLIFF   Sheeet.

BUNNY GILLETTE   Look'a there, Doris!

LOU   Be quiet, Cliff. Will ya, huh?

DORIS   Awww, shit, girl. That's nothin' . . . it just that god-damn Mr. Krump again . . . drunk out of his fucken' mind.

THE RADIO   It's eighty-two degrees . . . maaan, that's hot-oh-rooney . . . yeah, burnin' up this evenin' . . . red hot! . . . Ouch! . . . But we're cool on the Hep Harrison red-hot, up-tight, out-a-sight weather lookout indicator. That's eighty-two degrees . . . that's eight two out there . . . And here's a cool number that will hit you right where you're at . . . for your listenin' pleasure . . .

Mrs. Krump has stepped to the center of Derby Street and calls up to her second-floor window as the music begins.

MRS. KRUMP [*raspy, urban voice*]   *Hey, Edward . . . Hey, Edward . . . ! Hey, Edward . . . come on down here and get your fa'tha! Hey, Edward . . .*

DORIS   Hey, lissen ta that cow yell.

BUNNY   Ain't it a shame, girl?

Bunny starts off.

CLIFF [*disgust*]   God dammit . . . Lou. You always tellin' me to be quiet . . . I
   don't even make half the noise that some of our *good* neighbors do.
DORIS [*to Bunny*]   Where ya goin', broad?
LOU [*sitting beside Cliff*]   Awww . . . she should leave Mr. Krump alone. All
   he's doin' is peein' aside the pole . . . and then he's goin' in and go ta
   bed.
BUNNY   Up on "The Avenue."
DORIS   Where?

*Eddie Krump sticks his head from his upstairs window. He has dirty blond hair and
a sharp, red nose. He is about eleven.*

EDDIE   Ohhh, Christ, Ma . . . what'cha want?
BUNNY   "The Avenue," Doris.
MRS. KRUMP [*furious*]   Don't you Christ me, Edward . . . Come down here
   right away, young man!
CLIFF [*to Lou*]   I bet he ain't gonna do it.
DORIS   Ain't you gonna see Ray? That's what you come down this way for.
LOU   He might, Cliff. Besides . . . you the one that's always sayin' every-
   body here on Derby Street only does what they want to do most of the
   time, anyway.
BUNNY   He's up there on the step . . . he could see me if he wanted . . .
   C'mon, girl . . . let's split.   [*They exit.*]
CLIFF   'Specially mindin' other people's business.

Ray sits between Cliff and Lou, one step below them.

LOU   Wasn't that Bunny, Ray?
RAY   Think I should go and help Mr. Krump out, Cliff?
CLIFF   Nawh. [*Pause.*]
LOU   Why, Cliff?
CLIFF   You stay yo' ass here where ya belong, Ray.
LOU   Don't you talk like that, Cliff.
MRS. KRUMP [*to Eddie in window*]   Eddie . . . are you comin' down here?
EDDIE   Nawh.
CLIFF [*incredulous*]   Did you hear that?
LOU   Remember . . . we mind our own business.

*From the upstairs window of the Garrisons' house, Miss Minny Garrison pushes
her head; she has a bandanna tied about her head, and she is a huge black woman.*

MRS. KRUMP [*starting for her door*]   I'm going to come up there and beat the
   hell out of you, Edward.

Eddie ducks his head in the window as his mother enters the door below.

Sounds of Mrs. Krump's screams, the shouts of Eddie Krump and of running feet.

Silence.

Rhythm 'n blues and gospel music mingle softly.

Red and Bama enter at the corner. They see Mr. Krump and nod to each other, then slowly, stiff-leggedly, stalk about the streetlamp, tightening the circle about Mr. Krump on each full swing around.

MISS MINNY   Ray . . . wha don't you help Mr. Krump git home?

Ray stands and looks up at her.

RAY   Yas'sum.
CLIFF [*to Ray*]   Wha' . . . you gonna go down there and help? . . . [*Ray hesitates.*]
LOU   Awww, Cliff . . . there ain't no harm in it.
CLIFF   No harm?
LOU   Ray always does it.
CLIFF   Well, it's about time he stopped.
MISS MINNY   Go on, Ray. Go on and git Mr. Krump.
RAY   Yas'sum. [*He trots to the corner.*]
CLIFF [*mimics Ray in high falsetto*]   Yas'sum.
LOU [*angry*]   Stop that, Cliff!
CLIFF   Sheeet!
RED   Hey . . . Ray . . . is this lump ah shit a friend of yours? . . .
RAY   Nawh.
LOU   Why don't you stop that stuff, Cliff? Ain't nothin' bein' hurt because Ray's helpin' out Mr. Krump.
BAMA   Maybe they're related.
RED [*chuckling*]   Hey, man, cool it. I know Ray don't play that. Do you, Ray?
RAY [*trying to support Mr. Krump*]   Nawh, Red. Nawh.
RED [*to Bama*]   See, Bama, Ray don't play the dozens. You better be careful.
BAMA   Shit.

Ray and Bama exchange stares. Bama is several years older than Ray.

RED   You seen Bunny and Doris, Ray?
RAY   Yeah . . . they headed for "The Avenue."
CLIFF   Nothin' bein' hurt? Just look at that. Look at that, Lou!

Ray has slung Mr. Krump across his shoulder. He is husky and carries his load well.

[*Standing, shouting.*] Hey, Ray! Make sure his pants fly is zipped up or you'll be a
    victim of a horrible calamity!

LOU   You think you so smart, Cliff.

BAMA [*to Ray*]   Tote dat bar', boy . . . lift dat bale.

RED [*booting Ray in the seat of the pants*]   Git along, little doggie.

*Cliff is pleased with himself but starts as Red kicks Ray and stands, but Lou tugs at
his trouser leg and he sits back down, chuckling over his wit, though scowling at
Red and Bama, who turn laughing and exit.*

*Ray carries his load to the Krumps' door. Cliff lights a cigarette and takes a drink.
Lou tries to ignore him.*

Mrs. Krump, wearing a perpetual worried expression, at her door.

MRS. KRUMP   Why, thank you, Ray. Just bring him in here and put him on
    the couch. Thank you, Ray. That Edward is just . . .

*They go in, Mrs. Krump at the rear, peering at Mr. Krump's head that dangles
down Ray's back.*

CLIFF   That goddamn Miss Minny's always startin' some shit!

LOU   Shusss . . . Cliff. She'll hear you.

CLIFF [*bitter*]   I don't care if the big sow does. Always pretendin' her ears are
    filled with nothin' but holy holy *gospel* music . . . when they're nothin'
    but brimmin' with Derby Street dirt. [*Mutters.*] Ole bitch!

LOU [*uneasy*]   Cliff!

CLIFF [*looks up at Miss Minny*]   Always startin' some trouble.

Miss Minny closes her window. Her light goes off.

LOU   See, she did hear you!

CLIFF   I don't give a damn . . . who she thinks she is anyway?

LOU   Cliff, you just tryin' to start some trouble with Mr. Garrison. You
    wouldn't say those things if Homer were home.

CLIFF [*challenging*]   Wouldn't I?

LOU   No, you wouldn't!

CLIFF   I would do anything I do now if ole four-eyed Homer was sittin' right
    over there on that step pickin' his big nose.

LOU   He don't pick his nose no more.

CLIFF   How do you know? Is that what Miss Minny told you?

LOU   No, Miss Minny didn't tell me a thing. His sister, Marigold, showed me a picture of him in his sergeant's uniform . . . and I know nobody in the United States Army who makes sergeant still picks their nose.

CLIFF   Sheeet! [*Silence.*]

LOU   Cliff?

CLIFF [*angry*]   Look what you've done to that boy, Lou. Look what you and his mother . . .

LOU [*angry*]   Now don't you start in talkin' 'bout my dead sister!

CLIFF [*angrier*]   Shut up! [*Pause and stare.*] Don't you see what all of you are tryin' to do . . . Miss Minny . . .

LOU   Who's tryin' to do what, Cliff?

CLIFF [*continues*]   Miss Minny . . . you . . . all the so-called high-falutin' pussy on this block . . .

LOU [*indignant*]   Now you watch your mouth . . .

CLIFF   Pussy! Cunt! Bitches! Always startin' some trouble.

LOU [*apologetic*]   That was no trouble, Cliff.

CLIFF   It was so . . . Who the hell Miss Minny thinks she is anyway tellin' Ray to go down there an' get ole man Krump? And gettin' kicked by that punk Red . . . Ray's nearly a man . . . he shouldn't . . .

LOU [*cutting*]   She didn't mean nothin' by it.

CLIFF   Just like she didn't mean nothin' the time she passed around that petition to have us run off'a Derby Street when we first moved here.

LOU   She didn't know us then . . . we was strangers. Why don't you forget it?

CLIFF [*raising voice*]   What's so strange about us, huh? What was so strange about us back then when we moved in? What was so strange? Was we strange because I was goin' ta school on the G.I. Bill and not totin' a lunch pail like all these other asses? . . .

LOU   Shusss . . . Cliff.

CLIFF   I will not shusss . . . that's what they are, aren't they? Asses! Mules! Donkeys!

LOU   I'm goin' in if you keep that up, Cliff.

THE RADIO   . . . and Fat Abe . . . your local honest used car dealer is now offering a custom bargain fo' one of you real swingers out there . . .

Cliff reaches up and pulls the door shut with a slam, muffling the radio.

CLIFF   You ain't goin' nowhere just because you don't want to hear the truth. [*Silence. Lou sulks.*] Well, they are asses . . . [*Ridicule.*] Derby Street Donkeys!

LOU [*apologetic*]   Well, I was workin', Cliff. And . . .

CLIFF [*cutting*]   And they made a hell of a noise about that, too. Always whisperin' how you work so hard all day in a laundry for no count me who goes around carryin' books. And gets home in the middle of the afternoon and jest lays around like a playboy . . .

LOU   They did see you with them girls all the time, Cliff.

CLIFF   I ain't been with no bitches.

LOU   Cliff . . .

CLIFF   They're lies! That's all . . . every one a lie . . . and don't you let me hear you tell me them lies again. [Silence.]

LOU   Never?

CLIFF   Never!

LOU   What should I say when I find lipstick on your shirt . . . shades I don't use? [Silence.] What should I say when I see you flirtin' with the young girls on the street and with my friends? [Silence.]

CLIFF   [tired]   Light me a cigarette, will ya? [She does.]

LOU   This street ain't so bad now.

CLIFF   Was we so strange because your nephew Ray stays with us . . . and don't have to work [Bitter.] like an ass or mule or fool . . . like a Derby Street Donkey!

LOU   Cliff!

CLIFF   Why was we so strange?

LOU   Nawh, we wasn't . . .

CLIFF   Who wasn't?

LOU   We wasn't!

CLIFF   Yes, we was!

LOU   Nawh . . . we seemed strange because we always drinkin' this . . . [Raising her glass.]

CLIFF   Everybody else drinks somethin' around here . . . ole man Garrison puts at least a pint of white lightnin' away a night . . . pure'dee cooked corn whiskey!

LOU   But their ignorant oil don't make them yell and holler half the night like this wine makes us.

CLIFF   [yells]   Who yells!

LOU   [amused]   . . . and we sing and laugh and you cuss like a sailor.

CLIFF   Who sings and laughs? . . .

LOU   We do!

CLIFF   You a liar!

LOU   Nawh, I'm not, Cliff.

He grabs her arm and twists it behind her back.

CLIFF   Say you a liar.

LOU   Nawh, Cliff . . . don't do that.

CLIFF   [twists it more]   Who's a liar?

LOU   I am, Cliff.

CLIFF [a slight jerk]   Who?
LOU   I am, Cliff. I am!

He releases her.

CLIFF   That's right . . . sing out when I want you to. Ha ha ha . . . [*He tries to caress her.*]
LOU [*rubs arm and shoves him*]   Leave me alone.
CLIFF [*kisses her*]   I'm glad you finally confessed . . . It'll do your soul some good.
LOU [*sulking*]   You shouldn't do that, Cliff.
CLIFF   Do what?
LOU   You know what.
CLIFF   Give you spiritual comfort? . . . Apply some soul ointment?
LOU [*disgusted*]   Awwww . . .
CLIFF   I don't know if you never tell me, hon.
LOU   You know all right.
CLIFF   That I cuss like a sailor?
LOU [*remembering*]   That's right . . . and . . .
CLIFF [*cutting*]   Well, you didn't say that.
LOU   I didn't? [*Pause.*] I did too, Cliff.
CLIFF   What?
LOU   Say that we yell and holler and sing and laugh and cuss like sailors half the night.
CLIFF [*toasts her*]   Ohhh, Lou. To Lou Lou, my Hottentot queen.
LOU   I'm not!
CLIFF   My queen?
LOU   Hottentot! . . . My features are more northern . . . more Ethiopian.
CLIFF [*ridicule*]   Haaaah! [*Pause.*] Haaaaah! More northern . . . more Ethiopian! That beak nose of yours comes from that shanty Irishman who screwed your grandmammy down on the plantation.
LOU   Watch your mouth, Cliff.
CLIFF   Watch my mouth?
LOU   Yeah, watch your mouth. Some things I just won't allow you to say.
CLIFF [*mocking*]   "Some things I just won't allow you to say." [*Offended.*] Watch my mouth? Well, take a look at yours. Yours comes from that Ubangi great granddaddy on your father's side . . . your "northern" nose, well, we've gone through its . . .
LOU [*warning*]   Stop it, Cliff!
CLIFF   . . . but your build is pure Hottentot, darling . . . and that's why I shall forever love you . . . however the Derby Street Donkeys bray about me being with other girls . . . younger, prettier girls, mind you . . . But Lou, baby, you are married to an "A" number one ass man . . . and *yours* is one of the Hottentot greats of northern America.

LOU [*indignant*]   Fuck you!

CLIFF [*fake dialect*]   Wahl, hon-nee chile . . . I just wanted ta tell yawhal dat
yo' husband is one ob dem connoisseurs of dem fleshy Hottentot parts
which'n yous is so wonderfully invested wit'.

LOU   Fuck you, Cliff! . . . Ohhh, just listen to that. You make me say bad
things, man. You think you so smart and know all them big words since
you been goin' to school. You still ain't nothin' but a lowdown bastard at
heart as far as I'm concerned.

Silence. Cliff takes a drink. Lou is wary but defiant.

CLIFF [*smiles*]   We do cuss too much, don't we?

LOU [*smiles*]   And we drink too much.

He pulls her over and fondles her; she kisses him but pushes him away.

CLIFF   Like sailors?

LOU   Yes!

CLIFF [*amused*]   I thought we cussed like sailors.

LOU   We do.

CLIFF [*raises voice*]   Make up yo' mind, broad. Now what is it . . . do we cuss
and drink like sailors or cuss like sailors and drink like . . . like . . . like
. . . what?

LOU   Like niggers.

*At the last word lights go up on other stoops, revealing the occupants looking at
Cliff and Lou.*

*Then lights dim and come up on "The Avenue." The figures of Red, Bama, Doris
and Bunny Gillette are seen.*

BUNNY GILLETTE   Go on now, Red . . . stop messin' with me.

RED   Awww . . . woman . . . stop all your bullshit. You know you like me to
feel your little ass . . . c'mere.

DORIS   Stop fucken with that girl, Red.

RED   What's wrong, Doris? You jealous or somethin'?

DORIS   Man . . . if you melted and turned to water and ran down the gutter I
wouldn't even step over you.

RED   Why . . . scared I'd look up your dress and see your tonsils?

BUNNY GILLETTE [*giggling*]   Ohhh . . . girl, ain't he bad.

BAMA   C'mere, Doris. I wanna talk to you.

DORIS   You ain't never wanted to talk to me before, Bama.

Red has his arm about Bunny Gillette's waist. Bama takes Doris's hand.

RED C'mon, Bunny . . . I'll buy you a fish sandwich. [*To Bama.*] Hey, Bam ah lam . . . do you think these broads deserve a fish sandwich?

BAMA Nawh, man, they don't deserve shit.

DORIS Hey, Bunny, we really hooked us some sports . . . you better make it back to Ray, girl.

Lights down on "The Avenue."

Lights up on Derby Street. Cliff and Lou laugh as Ray comes out of the Krumps'. The radio is muffled in the background.

MRS. KRUMP [*off*] You sure you don't want another slice of cake and a glass of milk, Raymond?

RAY Nawh, thank you, Mrs. Krump.

Eddie Krump sticks his head out of his window.

EDDIE Thanks ah lot, Ray.

RAY That's okay; why don't you come on down for a while?

EDDIE Nawh . . . I can't . . . I gotta headache.

CLIFF [*to Ray*] Little white Eddie don't want to come down after you carry his pissy pukey drunk daddy in for him, huh?

LOU Cliff!

RAY [*embarrassed*] Nawh.

LOU Cliff . . . no wonder they sent around that petition. Just look how you act.

CLIFF [*angry*] Yeah, just look how I act . . . fuck how I act!

LOU You got the dirtiest mouth, Cliff.

CLIFF [*angrier*] Fuck how I act . . . fuck it!

Cliff stands and glares about at his neighbors. They turn their heads and resume their activities.

LOU Just like a sailor.

CLIFF [*satisfied*] Yup . . . just like I always said . . . folks on Derby Street sure know how to mind their own business.

LOU Just like the no-'count sailor I met and married.

CLIFF Well, I am a mathafukken shit-ass sailor. The same you met and married, Lou.

LOU Not any more.

CLIFF Still! I still am. Once a sailor . . . always a sailor.

LOU Not any more. Besides . . . you stayed most of your time in the guardhouse.

CLIFF [*to Ray*] Listen to that . . . listen to that, Ray. Guardhouse.

LOU   That was the reason I married you. Felt sorry for you and knew your
commanding officer would go light on you if he knew you had been
married when you deserted and not put you in the guardhouse for so
long.

CLIFF   Yeah?

LOU   Yeah!

CLIFF   Don't think you did me any favors, baby.

LOU   Well, who else did? I went to your ship and testified . . . I kept you
from gettin' a bad discharge. In fact, I'm the one who made a man out of
you even though your mother and the whole entire United States Navy
failed.

CLIFF [mutters]   Bitch!

LOU   Do you hear that? Failed . . . to make a man or a sailor of ya.

CLIFF [ridicule]   Ray. This broad, pardon the expression, this woman named
Lou . . . Lou Ellen Margarita Crawford Dawson . . . who calls herself
your aunt, by the way . . .

LOU   I am his aunt!

CLIFF   This bitch don't know what a sailor is.

LOU   I don't? . . . I don't? Then I guess you know even though you spent
most of your navy time in the guardhouse.

RAY   Brig, Lou . . .

CLIFF   Thank you, son. Thank you.

LOU   What? . . .

RAY   Brig, Lou . . . not guardhouse.

CLIFF   That's right . . . that's fucken "A" right . . .

LOU [mutters and takes a drink]   Dirtiest mouth I ever heard.

CLIFF   That's a lie . . . your sister has the dirtiest mouth in north, south,
west and all of this town. [To Ray.] That's your play-aunt Doris I'm
talkin' about, Ray, not your dear dead mother . . . may she rest in peace
. . .

LOU   You two-faced bastard. Listen to you soundin' like one of them white
missionaries . . . "May she rest in peace . . ." Dirty-mouthed liar!

CLIFF   Liar? About what? My not being in the guardhouse?

RAY   Brig.

LOU   You know that's not what I mean.

CLIFF   Pour yourself a drink, Ray. Put some hair on your . . . ding-a-ling.
[Begins humming.]

LOU   I pity the day you talked me into allowing Ray to take a drink.

CLIFF   Whatta ya mean? He was a lush when he came here. His mother and
him both almost drank themselves to death.

LOU   Cliff!

CLIFF [defensive]   Ain't that right, Ray?

RAY   Sort'a. I did kinda drink along with Mamma for a while until they put
her away.

CLIFF Sort'a? Stop jivin' . . . for a youngblood you can really hide some port.

RAY [flattered] Yeah . . . I do my share.

LOU Now, Ray, I want you to . . .

CLIFF [loud] Quiet! You heard him . . . he does his share. Here's a toast to you, youngblood. [Lifts his glass.] To Ray who does his share. [They drink, except for Lou.]

RAY Thanks, Cliff.

CLIFF Don't mention it, Ray. Just don't mention it at all. It's your world, son. It's really your world. [To Lou.] Well, isn't it? [Silence.] You don't feel like toasting Ray? [Silence.] Ray . . . you know, Lou is a lot like your mother used to be. Quiet, except that your mother usually had a glass up to her mouth instead of her mouth clamped tight.

LOU You shouldn't of said that, Cliff. You're goin'a pay for that.

CLIFF Pay? Ray, it's your world . . . does your ole Uncle Cliff have to pay?

RAY Well, I don't . . .

LOU [cutting] Stop it, Cliff. Ray, I'm sorry. Cliff gets too much to drink in him . . .

CLIFF [loud, cutting] Nice night we havin' out here on our white well-scrubbed steps . . .

Both together.

LOU . . . and he runs off at the mouth somethin' terrible. I know you wasn't much past twelve when I came an' got you and kept them from puttin' you in a home. And you had already started in drinkin' 'n smokin' and foolin' around with girls . . . and I knew you drank too much for a growin' boy, much less a man. But I couldn't see you in a home—it would have messed you up . . . or sent down South to Cousin Frank's. I don't mean you so young you don't know what you want to do, Ray. I'm only six years older than you . . . but Cliff still shouldn't be givin' you so much wine and teachin' you

CLIFF . . . with all of God's white stars shinin' above your black heads. Ain't that right, Lord? You old shyster. You pour white heat on these niggers, these Derby Street Donkeys, in the daytime and roast and fry them while they shovel shit for nex' to nothin', and steam them at night like big black lobsters . . . ha ha . . . the Krumps are little red lobsters of Yourn . . . and they just drink, an' screw in the dark, and listen to jive talk an' jive music an' jive *holy* music . . . but they still think they have to face You in the mornin'. That's right, face You, You jive-ass sucker! They don't know they got to face Your jive-hot, bad habits. It ain't good for none of us, not even me. I hardly know where I'm at some of the times when I start in drinkin' after I come from work . . . but it sho' do relaxes me. And your mother is gonna call me to account for it when we meet up in heaven . . . I really know that. The devil's in Cliff, I know that, to do what he's doin' to us . . . and I ain't helpin' things much. Listen to what I say, Ray, and not to the devil. Listen to me, Ray.

blazin' face . . . simple niggers . . . but they do 'cause they believe in You and Your lies. Stupid donkeys! They only got to look my god in the face once and forget about You, You jive-time sucker . . . [Remembering an old joke.] . . . ha ha . . . she's black as night and as cool and slick as a king snake . . . [Singing.] . . . Yes, Lord, yes, Lord, yes, Lord, yes, Lord . . .

LOU   *Stop it, Cliff! You're drunk 'n' crazy 'n' drivin' me out of my head!*

Silence. Cliff stares at her.

RAY [*to both*]   It's all right. It's all right.

LOU   Ray, when I get to heaven your mother's gonna have a lot to say to me.

CLIFF [*laughs*]   Heaven?

LOU   Yeah, heaven. And you better get some of the fear of the Lord in you, Cliff.

CLIFF [*disgust*]   Every night. Every goddamn night when you start feelin' your juice.

LOU   'Cause I know better, that's why.

CLIFF   Is that why when I get you in bed every night you holler: [*Whining falsetto.*] "Yes, Lord. Yes, Lord. Ohhh . . . Jesus . . . one more time." [*Ray giggles.*]

LOU   You're bad, Cliff. You're bad. Bad!

CLIFF   Sho' I'm bad, hon-nee chile. [*Singing.*] I'm forty hands across mah chest . . . don't fear nothin' . . . not God nor death . . . I got a tombstone mind an' a graveyard disposition . . . I'm a bad mathafukker an' I don't mind . . . dyin'.

LOU [*cutting*]   You're just a dirty-mouthed . . .

CLIFF [*cutting*]   Yeah, I know . . . and I'll have you know that just because I spent one third of my navy time in various brigs, not just one, understand, baby girl, but at least an even dozen between here and Istanbul, that I was still one of the saltiest salt water sailors in the fleet . . . on dry land, in the fleet or in some fucken marine brig!

LOU   You wasn't shit, Cliff . . . You know that, don't you?

CLIFF   Sticks 'n' stones, Lou . . . sticks 'n' stones.

LOU   Pour me a drink, Ray . . . and give your no-'count step-uncle one too.

Ray pours drinks for the three of them.

CLIFF   Step-uncle? Now how in Jesus' name did I get demoted from uncle to step?

LOU   You just did . . . suddenly you just stepped down.

RAY   Do you think I can get into the navy, Cliff?

CLIFF   [*grabs Lou's arm*]   Sometimes, Lou . . .

RAY   Huh, Cliff?

CLIFF   [*recovering*]   Navy? . . . Why sure . . . sure, Ray. When you come of age I'll sign the papers myself.

LOU   Steps can't, Cliff. But I can.

CLIFF   I can, Lou . . . I should know. [*Proudly.*] I joined on my sixteenth birthday.

LOU   Steps can't.

CLIFF   [*pinches her shoulder*]   Bitch!

LOU   [*feigning*]   Owww, Cliff. Owww.

RAY   If I'm of age then you won't have to sign, will ya?

CLIFF   No, I won't. Not if you're of age, Ray.

LOU   He can't sign anyway.

CLIFF   I can too, Ray. You just watch me when the time comes.

RAY   I'll be sixteen next week, Cliff.

CLIFF   You will?

RAY   Yeah.

CLIFF   Already?

RAY   Yeah.

CLIFF   [*to Lou*]   He will?

LOU   If that's what he says.

CLIFF   Damn . . . so soon.

LOU   Sixteen ain't old enough. You have to be seventeen before they'll even let me sign for you, Ray.

CLIFF   I went when I was sixteen . . . my sixteenth birthday.

LOU   [*peeved*]   That's because you were down in Virginia in the woods . . . fool! They don't even have birth certificates down there . . . you could of went when you were thirteen if your mother had'a sworn you was old enough.

CLIFF   I was too old enough!

LOU   No, you wasn't. And Ray ain't either. He's got to wait until he's seventeen. And then I might sign for him.

RAY   I got to wait? But Uncle Cliff said I could go.

CLIFF   Yeah, you can go, Ray. I'll sign the papers myself. You're goin' to the navy and see how real men live.

LOU [*angry*]   He's not goin' . . . he's not old enough . . . and you ain't signin' no papers for him, Cliff. His mother wouldn't . . .

CLIFF   I'll sign anything I want fo' him. I'm his guardian . . .

LOU [*ridicule*]   Guardian? How? With what? You ain't never had a job in your life over six months. What you raise him with . . . the few lousy bucks you don't drink up from your government check? You somebody's guardian . . . I . . .

Cliff slaps her violently.

CLIFF [*low, menacing*]   You talk too much, Lou.

LOU [*defiant*]   It's my responsibility, Cliff. Mine. Mine. My responsibility. I'm not going to sign or let you sign. His mother . . .

CLIFF   Damn that! Damn it! I don't care what his dead mother wants. Who the hell cares what the dead want? It's what Ray wants that counts. He's got to get out of here . . . don't you, Ray? . . . Off'a Derby Street and away from here so he can grow up to be his own man.

LOU [*crying*]   Like you?

CLIFF   No, not like me . . . not tied down to a half-grown, scared, childish bitch!

LOU   You don't have to be.

CLIFF   But I love you.

Lights down, up on "The Avenue." Red slaps Bunny Gillette.

DORIS   *Red . . . you mathafukker . . . Stop that!*

BUNNY GILLETTE [*crying*]   Go on now, Red. Leave me alone . . .

RED   Bitch! Who you think you tellin' to kiss your ass? You want me to kiss your nasty ass?

BAMA [*reaching for him*]   Hey, lighten up, Red.

DORIS   Leave her alone!

RED [*being held by Bama*]   You want me to kiss your . . .

BUNNY GILLETTE   Nawh, Red. Nawh.

DORIS [*a short knife in her hand*]   You better not touch her again . . . you better not. You goin'a be sorry for this.

Lights down on "The Avenue" and up on Derby Street.

RAY   I'm sorry, Lou.

LOU   It's all right, Ray. We've fought before . . . I'm just sorry you have to see us act like this.

CLIFF   Awww, honey . . . I'll forget it if you do.

LOU   You beat on me and I'm supposed to forget it? In my condition.

CLIFF   You got nearly six months before the baby. He can't get hurt by just a little . . .

LOU   You know the doctor told you not to be hittin' on me no mo'. You did it on purpose 'cause you don't want it.

CLIFF   I'm sorry, Lou.

LOU   It's a wonder you didn't hit me in the stomach.

CLIFF   Well, it's a wonder I didn't.

LOU   See there. You don't want it.

CLIFF   Nawh, I don't want a baby I can't take care of . . . do you?

LOU   You can get a job.

CLIFF   At a dollar an hour? Dollar-an-hour Dawson, that's me. Nawh, I don't want any kids until I can afford them. That's why I'm goin' ta school.

LOU   You studying business so you can take care of me an' your kids? What kind of job can you get in business? You got money to open you a business?

CLIFF   Lou, we've gone over this before. I'll manage.

LOU   Like you have gettin' a job?

CLIFF   Well, you want me to get a job in the laundry? Like all your cousins?

LOU   And me!

CLIFF   Startin' at a buck an hour. Hell no, I won't work!

LOU   [scared]   But what are we goin'a do when your checks run out, Cliff?

CLIFF   Me? I'll do the best I can. Maybe ship out again.

LOU   No, Cliff!

CLIFF   If I can't turn up anything . . . well, you and the kid can get on relief. [Silence.]

LOU   Where's your pride? A big strong man like . . .

CLIFF   A dollar an hour don't buy that much pride, Lou. There's a big rich world out there . . . I'm goin'a get me part of it or not at all.

Both together.

LOU   You ain't no man. My daddy he worked twenty years with his hands . . . his poor hands are hard and rough with corns and callouses. He was a man . . . he worked and brought us up to take pride in ourselves and to fear God. What did I marry? I thought you was a man, Cliff. I thought because you was loud and was always

CLIFF   I'm goin' ta get me part of that world or stare your God in the eye and scream *why*. I am not a beast . . . an animal to be used for the plows of the world. But if I am then I'll act like one, I'll be one and turn this fucken world of dreams and lies and fairy tales into a jungle or a desert. And I don't give much of a happy fuck fightin' and drinkin' and was so big and strong that you was a man . . . but you ain't nothin' but a lowdown and less than nothin'!

which. There's a world out there, woman. Just beyond that lamppost . . . just across "The Avenue" and it'll be nice and Ray's.

LOU [*screams*] *You're nothin'!*

CLIFF   In the navy Ray can travel and see things and learn and meet lots of different . . .

LOU   *No!!!*

CLIFF   . . . girls and make somethin' . . .

LOU   *Is that what it did for you?*

CLIFF   Yeah, that's what it did for me!

LOU   Well, I don't want him to be like you.

CLIFF   How would you want him to be like . . . one of the Derby Street Donkeys? Or one of the ditty boppers or an avenue hype . . . or . . . a drug addict . . . or what?

LOU   [*standing*]   He ain't turned out so bad so far. [*Determined.*] He's not goin', Cliff. [*Pause.*] Ray, just get it out of your mind. I'm not signin' no navy papers . . . you're too young.

She enters the house as the lights fade to blackness.

                                                        Curtain

ACT II

Mythic blues plays. Lights up on "The Avenue." The couples are in embrace.

BUNNY GILLETTE [*to Red*]   I like you a lot . . . really I do . . . but what will Ray say?

RED   Fuck that little punk!

DORIS [*to Red*]   What you say 'bout my nephew?

BAMA   He wasn't talkin' to you, Doris.

BUNNY GILLETTE   You ain't gonna fight me anymo' . . . are ya, Red?

DORIS   I'd cut that nigger's nut off if he had'a hit me like that, Bunny!

BAMA   You wouldn'a do nothin', Doris . . . you just . . .

DORIS   Yeah, I would . . . and that goes double for any jive nigger who lays a finger on me or mine!

RED [*places his hands on Bunny's rear*]   Why don't all you mathafukkers shut up! Can't you see I'm concentratin'?

Lights down, up on Derby Street.

Cliff and Ray sit upon their stoop. The remainder of the street is in shadow.

Silence.

From the last stoop up the street Beatrice detaches herself from the shadows and walks toward the corner.

She is a buxom, brown girl and carries herself proudly. She speaks as she passes each shadowy group of forms upon the stoops.

THE RADIO   It's seventy-eight degrees . . . that's seven . . . eight . . .
BEATRICE [*passing*]   Hello, Mr. Cooper. Miz Cooper.
SHADOWS   Hello, Beatrice. How you doin' tonight?
BEATRICE [*passing*]   Hello, Miss Francis.
SHADOWS   Why hello, Bea. How ya doin', girl?
BEATRICE [*passing*]   Hello, Mr. Roy.
SHADOWS   Howdy, Beatrice. How's your folks?
BEATRICE   Just fine. [*She passes on.*]

Miss Minny puts her head out her window. Beatrice passes Cliff and Ray without speaking, her pug nose up, her head sighting on something upon the Derby Street fence, on the far side of the street.

Beatrice comes abreast the Garrison's house and looks up.

Hello, Miss Minny.
MISS MINNY   Hello, Beatrice . . . how y'all?
BEATRICE [*stops*]   Just fine, Miss Minny. How's Marigold and Ruth?
MISS MINNY   Awww . . . they're fine, Beatrice. They off visitin' mah sister this week.
BEATRICE   That's nice, Miss Minny. Tell them I asked about them, will ya?
MISS MINNY   All right, dear. Did you know that Homer asked about you in his last letter?
BEATRICE   No, I didn't. Is he still in Korea?
MISS MINNY   Yeah, he's still over there. They done made him a sergeant.
BEATRICE   Yes, I know. Marigold told me. He's doing okay, isn't he?
MISS MINNY   Oh, yes, he's just doin' fine and everything. Says he likes it over there.
BEATRICE   Tell him I asked about him, will you?
MISS MINNY   All right, Beatrice.

Beatrice continues, and reaching the corner, she exits. Miss Minny withdraws and shuts her window.

THE RADIO . . . And now the genius of the great . . . [*Music plays, softly.*]
CLIFF   Sheeet.
RAY   What'cha say, Cliff? [*Silence.*]

Both together.

CLIFF   I said that . . .   RAY   I wonder if . . .

Silence.

Both together.

  [*annoyed*]   Go on!   [*embarrassed*]   Excuse me.

Lengthy silence. Both take drinks and drag upon their cigarettes.

CLIFF [*hurriedly*]   How old's that broad?
RAY   How old? . . .
CLIFF   Yeah.
RAY   Oh, Bea? . . . About my age, I guess.
CLIFF   She's certainly a snotty little stuckup heifer, ain't she?
RAY   Yeah, I guess so. [*Silence.*]

Both together.

CLIFF [*almost leering*]   I wonder   RAY [*explaining*]   She's always . . .
    what . . .

Both halt. Cliff stubs out his cigarette.

CLIFF [*yells over his shoulder*]   Hey, Lou!

No answer.

    [*To Ray.*] Guess she's out back in the kitchen or the john.
RAY   Yeah.
CLIFF   Ray?
RAY   Huh?
CLIFF   Did you ever get any ah that?
RAY   Beatrice?
CLIFF   Yeah.
RAY   Nawh.
CLIFF   What she doin', savin' it for Homer?

RAY   Homer? [*Laughing.*] She can't stand Homer. Calls him "Ole Country."

CLIFF   What'cha waitin' on, boy?

RAY   Nothin'.

CLIFF   When I was yo' age I'd ah had every little pussy on Derby Street all to myself.

RAY   You'd have them all sewed up, huh?

CLIFF   [*not perceiving Ray's humor*]   Yeah, sho' would.

RAY   Ahhhuh.

CLIFF   How 'bout Marigold and Ruth?

RAY   What about them?

CLIFF   You ain't gettin' none of that either?

RAY   Nawh.

CLIFF   Why not, boy? What's the matter with you?

RAY   Nothin'.

CLIFF   Nothing?

RAY   Nawh, nothin'.

CLIFF   With all this good stuff runnin' 'round here you lettin' the chance of a lifetime slip by . . .

RAY   Yeah, I guess I am.

CLIFF   . . . always over there on Thirteenth Street messin' round with li'l Bunny when you should be takin' care of business back home.

RAY   I don't like any of the girls 'round here.

CLIFF   What's wrong with them? A girl's a girl . . . well, most of them are anyway.

RAY   [*embarrassed*]   Well, I like Bunny. Me and her's in love.

CLIFF   In love? In love? [*Cracking the door and over the music.*] Hey, Lou Ellen . . . *Your nephew's in love!*

No answer.

[*Muttering.*] Must'a fell in. [*Looking at Ray.*] Boy . . . you got a lot to learn.

RAY   I can't help it, Cliff. And she loves me too.

CLIFF   Ohhh, yeah . . . you really got a lot to learn.

RAY   Cliff . . . I . . .

CLIFF   Just because she comes down here with you on the nights that me and Lou are out don't make you be in love. You didn't think I knew, huh? Well, who the hell you think been turnin' those pillows on the couch over an' wipin' them off? Not your Aunt Lou . . . nawh nawh, she'd damn near die if she knew you were doin' what comes naturally.

RAY   I'm sorry, Cliff.

CLIFF   Forget it. Oh yeah, now that reminds me. Clean up your own mess from now on. You're big enough.

RAY   Okay.

CLIFF   Bunny's the first girl you've had?

RAY   Nawh.

CLIFF   How many?

RAY   'Bout half a dozen. [*Silence.*]

CLIFF   Well . . . you ain't exactly backward . . . but still when I was your age . . . but let's forget about that.

RAY   Okay.

CLIFF   Now what about Marigold and Ruth, don't they like you?

RAY   All the girls on the street like me, I guess . . . 'cept'n Beatrice n' she used to let me kiss her . . .

CLIFF   She did, huh? Well, what happened?

RAY   I don't know.

CLIFF   Well, why don't you get one of the girls next door? Screw one of Homer's sisters. [*Chuckling.*] Get some of his stuff while he's away.

RAY   Yeah . . . yeah, Marigold likes me a lot. Homer even wants me to get Marigold so I might have to marry her and he'd have a brother-in-law he'd like, but she don't want it, not like that, and I don't see the sense of goin' with a girl if I can't do it to her.

CLIFF   You showin' some sense there, Ray. An' forget about that marriage stuff too.

RAY   Yeah, and Ruth wants to get married too bad. I'm scared as hell of her. [*Silence.*]

CLIFF   Yeah, you better stick with fast little Bunny. Gettin' you in the service is gonna be hard enough . . . If your aunt knew that anyone was thinkin' about you and marriage . . . we'd really have a case on our hands. She'd probably lock you up in the cellar.

RAY   [*contemplating*]   And Beatrice thinks she's better than anybody else.

CLIFF   Yeah. I guess you do know what you're doin' stickin' with Bunny. But you'll be gone in a month anyway.

RAY   In a week.

CLIFF   Yeah, that's right . . . in a week . . . And things will be different then for you. [*Pause.*] Hey, do you know what, Ray?

RAY   [*slowly*]   I met a girl the other day.

CLIFF   Do you know what, Ray?

RAY   I met a girl the other day, Cliff.

CLIFF   You did?

RAY   [*more sure*]   Yeah, I met her the other day . . . she's almost a woman.

CLIFF   She is?

RAY   A pretty girl.

CLIFF   You met her where, Ray?

Lights down, and up on "The Avenue."

The Girl appears and stands under soft light. She has huge eyes and her skin is a soft black.

The couples are fixed in tableau but Red and Bama pull away from Bunny Gillette and Doris and dance about the Girl in a seduction dance, until the two girls break their position and dance against the attraction of the girl in a symbolic castration of the boys.

Lights down to fantasy hues on "The Avenue" and up on Cliff and Ray.

RAY   I met her over on "The Avenue."

CLIFF   Yeah, and she was pretty?

RAY   Yeah.

CLIFF   That's good. But you better not get stuck on her.

RAY   Why? Why, Cliff?

CLIFF   'Cause you goin' away in a month. You goin' to the navy, remember?

RAY   But she can wait for me.

CLIFF   Well . . . most women are funny. They don't wait around too long. They get anxious . . . you know, nervous that they won't get something that they think belongs to them. Never could understand what that somethin' was, but most of them are on the lookout for it, whinin' for it all the time, demandin' it. And I guess some of them even get it.

RAY   She'll wait.

CLIFF   Don't be too sure, son. Most of them don't.

RAY   Lou waited for you, didn't she? [*Silence.*] Didn't she? [*Silence.*]

CLIFF   Yeah . . . but that was a little different.

RAY   How?

CLIFF   It was just different . . . that's all.

RAY   But how would it be different for you and Lou and not for me and my girl?

CLIFF   Well, for one, I don't know your girl so I can't say positively just how she'd act . . . And, two, and you better not breathe a word of this to your aunt . . . you hear? [*Pause.*] Well, Lou Ellen is different because . . . well, because she's got character.

RAY   My girl . . .

CLIFF   [*cutting*]   And your aunt's got principle and conviction and you have to be awfully special for that.

RAY   But, Cliff . . .

CLIFF   [*continuing*]   . . . Now don't tell her, your aunt, I said these things, but she's special in that way.

RAY   I won't tell her.

CLIFF   For someone to have all them qualities in these times is close to bein' insane. She's either got to be hopelessly ignorant or have the faith of an angel . . . and she's neither.

RAY   Nawh, I don't guess she is.

CLIFF   I don't deserve her, I know.

RAY   You two pretty happy together, aren't you?

CLIFF   Ray?

RAY   Yeah.

CLIFF   Don't think about her too much.

RAY   Lou?

CLIFF   Nawh . . . you know. Your girl.

RAY   Oh.

CLIFF   Yeah.

RAY [distant]   Yeah, I guess so.

CLIFF   Why do you say it like that?

RAY   Awww, I was just thinkin'. Lou says I can't go . . . and . . . and this girl . . . she . . . well, I see her every day now and . . .

CLIFF   Have you . . .

RAY [upset, cutting]   Nawh! We don't . . . we don't need to do anything. We just look at each other and smile . . . that's all.

CLIFF   Smile?

RAY   Yeah.

CLIFF   What else?

RAY   That's all. I just wait on the corner for her every afternoon and she comes dancing along with her little funny walk and sometimes she hums or sings to me a while . . . then smiles some more and goes away . . .

Lights down on "The Avenue" and the dancers.

CLIFF   Boy, you better git yourself another drink.

RAY   I won't see her no more if I go to the navy, Cliff.

CLIFF   There's other things to see. Get her out of your head, Ray. There's a lot more fish in the ocean . . . ha ha . . . and a lot more girls where she came from. Girls all sizes and shapes . . .

RAY [protesting]   You don't know where she came from!

CLIFF   Why don't I? I just need to take one look at any girl and I know all about her. And with yours . . . well, your just tellin' me about her makes me know. I know all about her, Ray. And let me give you some advice . . . now you trust me, don't you? [Pause.] Good. I want you to stay away from her. There's all kinds of girls on this stinkin' planet . . . speakin' all kinds of tongues you never would think of, comin' in all kinds of shades and colors and everything. When you become a swabby, the world will open up to you.

Say, maybe you'll go to France . . . to Nice or Marseilles . . . the Riviera. Lie out in the hot sun . . . you won't need a suntan but you can lie out there anyway so those tourists and Frenchmen can see you and envy you. And you'll see all those sexy French broads in their handkerchief bathin' suits. Yeah, I can see you now, Ray, out there in your bright red trunks with sunglasses on peekin' at those girls. Or maybe you'll go to Italy and git you some of that dago stuff. Ha ha ha . . . best damn poon tang in the world, boy.

He ruffles Ray's woolly head and takes a good-sized drink.

Ha ha ha . . . put hair on your tonsils. [*Pause. Laughing.*] Yeah, there's nothin' like walkin' down a street in your navy blues. You know . . . you know . . . you should get tailor-made, skin tights, Ray, with buttons up both sides, and have your wallet slung around back of your pants . . . I can see you now. Your wallet will be fat as a Bible. And . . . and the pretty little broads will be callin' out to you. "Hey, Yankee! Hey, sailor! Hey, Joe! Fucky fucky . . . two American dollah!" Ha ha ha ha . . . yeah!

Yeah, that's livin', Ray. That's livin'.

RAY [*enthused*]   Is it, Cliff? Is it?

CLIFF   In some ports you can get a quart of the best imported whisky for two bucks and in some ports you can get the best brandy for only a buck or so.

And the nights . . . ahhh . . . the nights at sea, boy. Ain't nothin' like it. To be on watch on a summer night in the South Atlantic or the Mediterranean when the moon is full enough to give a year of your life for, Ray. The moon comes from away off and is all silvery, slidin' across the rollin' ocean like a path of cold, wet white fire, straight into your eye. Nothin' like it. Nothin' like it to be at sea . . . unless it's to be in port with a good broad and some mellow booze.

RAY   Do you think I can get in, Cliff?

CLIFF   Sure you can. Sure. Don't worry none about what your Aunt Lou says . . . I've got her number. I'll fix it up.

RAY   I sure hope you can.

CLIFF   Sure I can. As long as I tell your aunt I'm fixin' to ship out she'll sell you, herself, and probably her soul to keep me with her.

RAY [*frowning*]   You goin'a ship out, Cliff?

CLIFF   Nawh . . . nawh . . . I had my crack at the world . . . and I've made it worse, if anything . . . you youngbloods own the future . . . remember that . . . I had my chance. All I can do now is sit back and raise fat babies. It's your world now, boy.

Tiny rounds the corner.

Well, here comes Tiny. [*Knocks on door behind him with his elbow.*] Lou. Lou. Here comes little Tiny.

It has gotten darker and the shadowy figures have disappeared from the other stoops, into the doors of the houses, one after another.

LOU [*off*]   What'cha want, Cliff? I just washed my hair.
CLIFF   It's Tiny . . . she's comin' down the street.

Tiny is a small, attractive girl in her late teens. As she comes abreast of the alley a large man in wide-brimmed hat jumps out at her and shouts.

CLARK   *Boo!*
TINY   *Aaaaaiieeeeee!!!*

After the scream there is recognition between the two and Clark laughs, nearly hysterically, and begins trotting first in a circle about Tiny, who looks furious enough to cry, then across the street to the fence where he leans and laughs, pounding the boards with his fists.

Windows go up.

MRS. KRUMP   Is anything wrong?
MISS MINNY   What's all dat noise out dere?
LOU (*at door, her hair disheveled*)   Clark, you shouldn't go 'round scarin' people like that!

The Policeman passes the corner and stops and looks over the scene.

TINY [*regains breath*]   You ole stupid mathafukker!
MRS. KRUMP   Is anyone hurt?
CLIFF [*stands, his arm around Tiny's shoulder*]   Nawh, Krumpy . . . the goddamn natives are restless, that's all.
MRS. KRUMP   Ohhhh . . . I'm sorry . . . I just wanted to help. [*Her window closes.*]
MISS MINNY   You and your friends shouldn't all the time be usin' that kinda language, Cliff . . . gives the street a bad name. We got enough bad streets and boys around here without you makin' it worse.
CLIFF   If you kept your head in where it belongs you wouldn't hear so much, Miss Minny. Now would you?
MISS MINNY   I'm gonna talk to somebody 'bout you, Cliff. Somethin' should be done about you. [*Her window closes.*]
THE POLICEMAN   Is everything okay, Cliff?
CLIFF   Yeah, Officer Murphy. Everything's great.
THE POLICEMAN   Well keep it that way. I want it quiet around here, Cliff. [*The Policeman turns the corner.*]

RAY   His name's not Murphy, Cliff.

CLIFF   To me it is . . . If he doesn't know to call my right name I don't know his.

RAY   He said Cliff.

CLIFF   Yeah, he said Cliff like he was sayin' boy. He didn't say Mr. Dawson.

LOU [ridicule]   Mr. Dawson . . . and his mob.

TINY   I'm sorry, Cliff. I didn't mean to make all that noise . . . but that stupid ole Clarkie over there . . .

CLIFF   That's okay, Tiny. It's not your fault. Old nose for news up there has been after us as long as I can remember. [To Clark.] Hey, Silly Willy . . . come the hell on over here and stop tryin' to tear down those people's fence . . . besides, it wasn't that funny anyway.

RAY   You sho' can holler, Tiny.

TINY   I was afraid, man. Some big old stupid thing like that jumps out at you. Damn, man . . . I'm just a little thing . . . he makes two of me.

LOU   From the way you holler, sister, I know they'll have to want you really bad to get you.

TINY   Fucken "A," baby. If they want mah little ass they gonna have to bring ass.

CLIFF   With Clark's big bad feet he couldn't catch a cold.

TINY   I should'a known better than to be walkin' along beside some alley, anyway. If I hadn't seen you folks up here on the steps I would'a been out in the middle of the street with runnin' 'n' hollerin' room all around.

RAY   You still didn't do so bad.

Clark comes over, snuffling and wheezing. He has a large moon face and is in his early thirties.

CLARK [giggles]   I'm sorry, Tiny . . . ha ha ha . . . but I couldn't help myself when I saw you over on Ninth Street turn the corner.

TINY [peeved]   You been following me that long, man?

CLARK [nearly convulsed]   Heee heee . . . yeah, I ran through the alley and waited . . . and . . . heee heee . . . and when . . . heee heee . . . I heard your walk I jumped out.

LOU [angry]   Somebody's goin'a shoot you, you old dumb nut.

RAY   Wow, Tiny, you almost scared me. You sure can holler.

TINY   Yeah, man, I really can when somethin's after me.

LOU   C'mon, girl. C'mon in while I fix my hair.

Lou's hair is long and bushy, just having been washed. It covers her head like a gigantic crown.

TINY [steps across Ray]   Okay, girl. Hey, Ray, don't cha look up my dress.

RAY [jest]   Why not, Tiny?

TINY   You must think you're gettin' big, boy.

RAY [*drawl*]   I is.

LOU   Not that big, boy.

CLIFF   Why do you keep pesterin' the boy, Lou? If he didn't try and look I'd be wonderin' what's wrong with him.

LOU   Is that what you do, look?

CLIFF   What do you think? [*Silence.*]

Clark begins snuffling.

LOU   The only thing that's wrong with Ray is you, Cliff. I know some of those nasty things you been tellin' him. [*Silence. Lou and Cliff stare at each other.*]

TINY   I saw Doris and Bunny, Lou. [*Pause.*] They said they'd be over. Said they had some business to take care of. [*Pause.*]

CLARK   Doris comin' over?

TINY [*to Clark*]   Yeah . . . yeah, stupid ass. She said she'd be down. And Ray, Bunny said you'd better keep yo' ass home too. She wants to ask you some questions about that girl you been seein' out on "The Avenue."

RAY   What did she say?

CLIFF [*grinning*]   So it's finally got back home.

LOU [*hostile*]   Yeah, it's gotten back. You don't like it?

TINY   She said you'd better keep yo' black ass home, Ray. That's what she said.

CLIFF [*weary*]   Awww . . . Lou . . . please.

LOU   Followin' after you the way he does it's a wonder he ain't always in some trouble.

CLIFF [*caressing her leg*]   But, baby . . . [*She pulls her leg back.*]

RAY [*angry*]   What she mean I better keep mah black ass home? I'll go where I want . . . with who I want. She better watch it . . . or I won't be lettin' her come down here.

CLARK   Hey, listen to Tiger.

LOU   I ain't gonna let you start anything with little Bunny, you hear, Ray? Don't be hittin' on that little girl.

RAY   Awww . . . sheeet.

LOU   What'd you say?

CLIFF   What'd it sound like he said?

LOU   Now you keep out of this, Cliff.

CLARK   You women folks are sho somethin' else.

TINY   You shut your mouth and mind your business, Clark.

LOU   Now listen here, Ray. Don't you talk to me like that, frownin' up your face an' rollin' yo' eyes. You gittin' too mannish 'round here. You hear? [*Ray doesn't answer, but gives a deep sigh.*] Don't you bother that girl.

CLIFF   Ray?

RAY   Yeah?

CLIFF   If Bunny fucks with you . . . you knock her on her ass, ya hear?

RAY   Yeah, that's what I'm aimin' ta do, Cliff. Right on her ass.

Lou and Tiny go in.

CLARK   Hey, how 'bout pourin' me some of that wine you hidin' down there?

RAY   We ain't hidin' no wine.

CLIFF   Pour your own troubles, garbage gut.

CLARK   Why, hell, you ain't got nothin' here 'cept enough for maybe Ray here.

CLIFF   Ray, here? What do you mean "Ray here?" Why this youngblood nephew of mine will drink you underneath the table and into the middle of nex' week, ole Silly Willy Clark.

CLARK   Sheeet.

CLIFF   Can't you, Ray?

RAY   [*proudly*]   Sure as hell can.

CLARK   Well, we'll see . . . come on, let's go on up to the store and get us a big man.

RAY   A big man?

CLARK   That's right . . . a whole gallon.

Cliff stands and beckons Ray.

CLIFF   Never stand in the way of a man who wants to part with some coins . . . and buy ya a drink at the same time, I say.

CLARK   Yeah, c'mon . . . [*As an afterthought.*] . . . I'm buyin'.

CLIFF   [*humming*]   Hummmm hummm hummm . . . don't mind if I do get a little refreshing night air . . . c'mon, Ray, let's take a stroll.

CLARK   Well, which liquor store we goin' to? The one up on "The Avenue" or the one down by the bridge?

CLIFF   Let's go up on "The Avenue." [*Pause.*] That's okay with you, Ray?

RAY   Yeah, fine with me.

CLARK   Boy, we gonna get pissy pukey fallin' down drunk tonight.

CLIFF   If you see your girl up on "The Avenue" you'll point her out to me, Ray, wont'cha?

RAY   Yeah, Cliff. Yeah.

They exit. The street is clear. Music plays, then a commercial begins.

And lights down.

Curtain

ACT III

Time: *Forty-five minutes later.*
Scene: *Derby Street, Lou, Tiny, Doris, Bunny Gillette, Red, and Bama sit upon the Dawson's stoop.*

A gallon jug of red wine is on the pavement beside the steps, and everyone except Red and Lou has a paper cup in hand.

Doris is a small girl, not as small as Tiny, and has a full figure. Red looks like a hungry wolf and Bama seems to be mostly elbows and knees.

LOU   I don't see how you folks drink that nasty ole muscatel wine.
DORIS [*demonstrating*]   There's nothin' to it, baby sis.
RED   That's about the only goddamn thing we got in common, Lou. I don't drink that fucken hawg wash neither.
LOU [*primly*]   If you must sit on my steps this late at night, Red, I wish you'd respect me and the other girls here by not bein' so foul mouthed.
RED [*indignant*]   Shit, woman, talk to your ole man, Cliff . . . I'm usin' Mr. Dawson's rule book.
LOU   Don't blame Cliff!
BAMA [*to Red*]   Forget it, huh?
RED   You sometimes forget who your husband is, don't you, woman?
TINY   Yeah . . . knock it off, you guys.
RED [*to Tiny*]   Fuck you, bitch!
LOU [*to Red*]   I got a good memory, little red nigger.
RED   So use it . . . and don't bug me.
BUNNY GILLETTE   If you fools gonna keep this up all night I'm goin'a go home!
BAMA   Bye!
LOU   But I got to live with Cliff, Red . . . not you . . . hear?
DORIS [*in high voice, nearly drunk*]   Do y'all want a hot dog? Do y'all want a hot dog?
TINY   Why don't we all stop arguing? I knew this would happen if you bought more wine, Bama.
BUNNY   You been drinkin' much as anybody.
BAMA   Ahhh, don't blame me. If I didn't get it somebody else would.
BUNNY   They up on "The Avenue" gettin' some more now.
LOU   Cliff and Ray's probably out lookin' for some ole funky bitches.
TINY   That's the way those punk-ass men are, girl.
BUNNY   Sho' is!
LOU   Who you callin' punk-ass?
TINY   Not anybody . . . well, I don't mean punk . . . it's just that all men are messed up.

BAMA   What chou talkin' 'bout, broad?

RED   Hey, Bama, you better straighten your ole lady out before I have to do it.

DORIS   Do y'all want a hot dog?

BUNNY   Yeah, who's this girl Ray's been seein', Lou?

LOU   Don't ask me, chile. Don't even let him know I said anything.

RED   Tell Ray I want to meet her, Bunny.

Bunny threatens to pour her wine on him.

TINY   When will Cliff be back?

DORIS   I said do y'all want a hot dog?

LOU   You waitin' for Cliff now, Tiny?

TINY   Yeah . . . Doris, I want one . . . but give them time to cook, will . . .

LOU   I asked you a question, Tiny.

TINY   Nawh . . . nawh . . . can't you see I'm with Bama. Ain't I, Bama?

RED [*mutters*]   Goddamn . . . what a collection of cop-outs.

BAMA   Hey, get me a hot dog too.

DORIS   The mathafukkers should be done by now.

TINY [*nervous laugh*]   Woman, stop usin' all that bad language. You know Lou don't like it.

DORIS   Shit on you and Lou both, it's my mouth.

LOU   Now I ain't gonna warn none of you no longer . . . Next one says one bad word has got to go home.

BAMA   Will you listen to this now?

RED   Hey, Doris, get me one of those fucken hot dogs, will ya?

LOU   That did it, Red . . . Go home!

RED   Okay.

TINY   Doris, you can't say two words without cussin'. Don't you know any better?

RED [*stands*]   But before I go, Lou, tell me what did I say that was so bad?

LOU   I don't have to repeat it.

DORIS   I wouldn't be talkin' 'bout people so fucken much if I was you, Tiny. Remember I know somethin' . . . now don't I?

LOU   That goes for you too, Doris.

TINY [*frightened*]   Whatta ya mean, Doris?

BUNNY   Uuuhhh uhhh . . . y'all sure do act funny when you start in drinkin' this mess.

BAMA   Yeah . . . whatta ya mean, Doris?

DORIS   I ain't talkin' ta you, Bama.

BAMA   I'm talkin' ta you. [*To Tiny.*] What she got on you, Mamma?

TINY   Whatta ya mean?

DORIS [*drunk*]   Whatta ya think I mean?

BAMA   That's what I'm tryin' to find out . . . what ya mean.

RED   Shall we go . . . children?

TINY   That's what I'm askin' ya . . . whatta ya mean?

LOU   Now look. You broads can take that business back where you got it.

BAMA [amused]   That's tellin' them, Lou.

TINY   Don't you be callin' me a broad!

BUNNY [to Red]   Red . . . don't you think . . .

RED   Shut up, woman!

LOU [amazed]   Wha' . . . I didn't . . .

BAMA [joking]   Yeah, you did. I hear you.

DORIS [jest]   Don't be talkin' to mah baby sister like that.

TINY [scared and belligerent]   What you gonna do 'bout it, bitch! You gonna tell her 'bout Cliff and me?

BAMA   Hey, cool it, baby.

LOU   What did you say?

BUNNY   Now Lou . . . don't get mad . . .

LOU [disgust]   Okay, let's forget about it. You guys don't have to go home . . . I want you to wait on Cliff.

RED [sitting]   Wasn't plannin' on goin', anyway.

LOU   Now looka here, Red.

RED [angry]   Goddammit! Make up your mind!

DORIS [to Tiny]   You tryin' to be bad, ain't you, you li'l sawed-off heifer?

TINY [rising]   Little heifer!

Cliff, Ray, and Silly Willy Clark turn the corner. They have a gallon jug of wine, half-emptied, which they pass between themselves and take large draughts.

They visibly feel their drinks and stop under the streetlamp and drink and talk.

CLIFF   Ray . . . just learn this one thing in life . . . When the time comes . . . be a man . . . however you've lived up till then . . . throw it out of your mind . . . Just do what you have to do as a man.

RAY [not sober]   Sure, Cliff . . . sure.

CLARK [still drunker]   That sho is right, Dawson . . . that's right . . . but why can't we be men all the time, Dawson?

CLIFF [annoyed]   You don't know what I'm talkin' 'bout, silly ass, do you . . . do you now?

BUNNY   Here comes Cliff, Ray, and Silly Willy Clark.

DORIS [moving toward Tiny]   I'm tired of your little ass jumpin' bad around here, Tiny.

TINY [scared but standing her ground]   You are?

BAMA [between them]   Hey, knock off the bullshit . . . ya hear?

RED   Nawh, Bama . . . let them get it on and see who's the best.

TINY [crying]   Bama, why you always takin' somebody's side against me?

LOU   Shut up, all of you!

BAMA I'm not takin' nobody's side against you, baby.

DORIS You ain't takin' my side, Bama? And what you callin' her baby fo'?

TINY [to Bama] Y'are!

BAMA I ain't. We all just out to have a good time . . . that's all . . . a good time, huh? [He pulls Doris down beside him and puts his arm about her.]

TINY [scratching at his face] You bastard . . . I thought you was comin' down here to see me.

Doris pulls her small knife.

LOU Doris, stop!

DORIS What the fuck's wrong with you, bitch!

Cliff comes up and sees Doris's knife but doesn't appear to notice; she puts it away.

I'm goin' in an' get a hot dog. [Same high voice.] Y'all want a hot dog?

No answer. She enters the house.

Bama, Tiny, and Lou glare at each other. Red and Bunny sit together.

RED Well, if it ain't Mr. Dawson and nephew . . . the Derby Street killjoys. And hello, Mr. Silly Willy Clark . . . you simple mathafukker.

CLARK Hey, everybody. . . [Passing them the bottle.] . . . knock yourselves out.

BAMA We got ours.

Lou silently stands, looks at Cliff and the drunken Ray and enters the house.

RED [hugs Bunny, looks at Ray] Hey, what'cha mathafukkers doin'? Why don't you all have a sit down?

CLARK Don't mind if I do, Red . . . Hey, Cliff, is it okay if I sit down on your steps?

CLIFF Be my guest . . . you know me, don't you?

BUNNY [pulls away from Red] C'mon now, Red . . . stop all that stuff, man.

RED You like it. [He feels her breasts as the two people pull apart.]

LOU [looking out the door] I don't want to hear any more of that nasty shit from your mouth tonight, Red. And watch how you act!

RED Watch how I act?

CLIFF Yeah, that's what she said . . . watch how you act.

LOU Yeah, you keep your hands to yourself. I saw that.

RED Hey, what's wrong with you goddamn people tonight? Is there a full moon or somethin'?

BAMA Hey, Red, let's split.

RED   Mr. and Mrs. Dawson . . . and nephew . . . I'm sorry. Forgive me. Will you please accept my humble-ass apology, huh? Will you Dawsons do that? [*Red places his hand upon Lou's leg; she pulls away.*] Now what have I done?

BUNNY   What's wrong with you, Ray?

DORIS   [*sticks head out of door*]   Do y'all want a hot dog?

TINY   Ray's gone off somewhere behind that wine . . . look at him slobber spit . . . probably with his . . .

BUNNY   With his what?

TINY   Nothin', hon . . . I was just kiddin' . . . [*Shakes Ray.*] . . . Wasn't I, Ray?

RAY   Yeah . . . yeah.

BAMA   [*mimics Doris*]   "Do yawhl wants a hot dawg?"

TINY   Don't be so mean, Bama.

DORIS   Y'all can kiss mah ass.

LOU   [*caricature*]   Don't be so mean, Bama.

BAMA   [*furious*]   *Who you tellin' to kiss your ass, woman? I thought you saw what Bunny got tonight up on "The Avenue" for* . . .

Miss Minny's window goes up.

TINY   Don't be so noisy, baby.

RED   I thought you was gonna get me one ah those mathafukkin' hot dogs, woman.

MISS MINNY   Cliff . . . Cliff . . . I see you out there . . . I'm callin' the police right now about all this disturbance! [*Her window goes down.*]

DORIS   You better watch your little self, Tiny.

LOU   I told you about your mouth, Red.

TINY   Watch myself?

RED   My mouth . . . awww . . . Lou. You can't be serious.

CLIFF   Well, children, it's time that Daddy got to bed . . . I suggest that everyone goes home to bed or just home. Good night, all.

LOU   Ain't you gonna stay out here and wait for the cops, Cliff?

CLIFF   Good night, my love. Don't be too long . . . I think your hair's sexy.

Lou has her hair in curlers. He goes in, followed by Doris.

DORIS   [*off*]   Do y'all wants a hot dog, Cliff?

RED   If I hadn't seen Cliff beat so many bad niggers' asses I would think he's a chicken-hearted punk.

LOU   There's more than one way to be a coward.

BAMA   You better not let him hear you say that, lady.

CLARK   It's been a hard night, heh, Bunny?

BUNNY   Honey, these wine times is somethin' else.

RAY [*mumbling*]   Sho is, baby. Sho is.

DORIS [*back again, peering bleary-eyed at each one*]   Do y'all want a hot dog?
  Do y'all want a hot dog? If y'all don't, speak up . . . dese here hot dogs
  gonna be all gone 'cause I'm eatin' them fast as I can.

RED   Shove 'em up your ass . . . you silly bitch.

LOU   Okay, you all have to go now!

*Red rises and is followed by the rest, except Ray, who snores on the step. Lou goes
back into the house and her fussing with Cliff about Ray's condition, his friends,
and Tiny can be more sensed than heard.*

BUNNY   Ray . . . Ray?

RAY   Yeah?

BUNNY   I gotta tell you somethin' . . . Ray? . . . Ray? . . . I got somethin' to
  tell ya.

BAMA   Leave him alone, Bunny.

TINY   Yeah, let him sleep. He'll find out.

RAY   Yeah . . . what is it?

BUNNY   I'm Red's girl now.

Silly Willy Clark gets up and enters the house.

  Did you hear me, Ray? Did you hear me?

Red faces the building, and urinates in one of the wine bottles.

RAY [*groggy*]   Yeah . . . I heard you, Bunny. You're Red's girl now.

BAMA [*giggling*]   I guess Ray's really got himself a new girl, Bunny.

Red hands Ray the wine bottle he has just finished with.

RED   Let's toast to that, Ray.

Blindly, Ray lifts the jug to his lips, as Bama and Tiny gasp.

BUNNY   No! . . . No, Raayyy!!!

*She knocks the jug out of his grasp, smashing it upon the pavement. Ray wakes
instantly, perceives her action, and lashes out at her face. He lands a solid punch
that knocks her sprawling in the street.*

*Red rushes Ray and hits him with a haymaker aside the head. Ray grabs him for
support and the two fall to the pavement, grappling.*

Tiny screams. And Miss Minny's window goes up.

There are shouts and noise of running feet. The fighters roll about the pavement and Bama reaches down and pulls Ray off Red and holds him as the older boy smashes him in the face.

Silly Willy Clark rushes from the house and grabs Bama from behind. Upon his release from Bama, Ray butts Red in the midriff and staggers him to the entrance of the alley. Red pulls a bone-handled switch-blade; Ray grabs his arm and they fight their way into the alley.

Doris comes out of the house holding her small knife.

DORIS [*to Bunny*]   Where's Ray . . . Where's Ray!

Bunny, dazed, points to the alley. Doris enters the alley as Cliff runs out of the door in only pants in time to see her disappear in the tunnel.

The street is lit; the Krumps' upper windows are open.

EDDIE   Kill'em. . .Kill'em!
MRS. KRUMP   Keep back, Edward . . . there may be stray bullets!

Silly Willy Clark has choked Bama into surrender.

RED [*from the alley, muffled*]   All right . . . all right . . .

As Cliff runs into the alley there is a sharp sigh, then noise of more struggle and a groan.

Lou, Tiny, Bunny, and Derby Street residents crowd around the alley entrance.

MISS MINNY   Oh, Lord . . . what's happened . . . what's happened?
MRS. KRUMP   Close the window, Edward . . . Close the window! [*The Krumps' window closes.*]

The Policeman turns the corner at a run.

RESIDENT [*to another resident*]   Did you see what happen, Mr. Roy?
MR. ROY   Nawh, Miz Cooper . . . but I knew somethin' had to happen with all this goin' on down here.

Ray emerges from the alley, blood on his shirt. Doris follows him, her dress splotched with blood.

THE POLICEMAN [*running up with hand on pistol*]   What's happened here?

Cliff steps out of the alley, holding Red's knife.

CLIFF [*hands knife to Policeman and points in alley*]   I killed him.
LOU [*incredulous*]   You killed him . . .

Cliff nods.

RESIDENT   Did you hear that?
MISS MINNY   What happened? What happened, Miss Francis?
RESIDENT   Cliff Dawson's done killed a boy.
MISS MINNY   Ohhh . . . my Lord.
TINY [*disbelief*]   You killed him?
THE POLICEMAN [*leads Cliff to stoop*]   Okay, everybody . . . get back and don't
    nobody leave. By the looks of most of you . . . we'll want to talk to you.
    Get back . . . Will somebody call an ambulance and wagon?
MISS MINNY   I already did.

*Bama has revived; he looks sick and sits beside the alley entrance. Bunny, Clark,
and Doris support Ray, who looks to be in shock.*

LOU   Cliff . . . Cliff . . . don't do it . . . don't leave me! Tell the truth.

Cliff caresses her.

CLIFF   It won't be for long . . . I was protectin' my family . . . our family.

Lou cries, joining Tiny, Bunny and one of the neighbors.

Doris appears resigned to the situation.

RAY   She's gone . . . she's gone . . .

A siren is heard.

DORIS   Who's gone, Ray? Who?
RAY   She is . . . my girl . . . my girl on "The Avenue."
DORIS   She'll be back.
RAY   No, she's not. She won't be back.
THE POLICEMAN   I have to warn you, Mr. Dawson, that anything you say can
    be used against you.
CLIFF [*genuine*]   Yes, sir.

Beatrice turns the corner.

RAY   Never . . . she'll never be back.
CLIFF   Lou . . . Lou, I want one thing from you . . .

Lou looks at him, then at Ray.

LOU   He's all I got left, Cliff . . . He's all the family I got left.

He looks at her until she places her head upon his chest and sobs uncontrollably.

BEATRICE [*walking up, to Miss Minny in her window*]   What's the trouble,
    Miss Minny?
MISS MINNY   Ohhh, somethin' terrible, girl . . . I can't tell you now.
CLIFF [*handcuffed to the Policeman*]   It's your world, Ray . . . It's yours, boy
    . . . Go on out there and claim it.

Sirens nearer. Lights down and music rises.

MISS MINNY   Come down tomorrow for tea, Beatrice, dear, and I'll tell you all
    about it.
BEATRICE   All right, Miss Minny. The Lord bless you tonight.
MISS MINNY   He will, dear . . . 'cause he works in mysterious ways.
BEATRICE [*starting off*]   Amen!

Lights down to blackness and a commercial begins.

Curtain

5
FILM

THE ELEMENTS OF FILM

An Introduction

Since film is a fairly recent phenomenon, it has borrowed a great deal from other forms of expression. Perhaps even more markedly than in discussions of prose or poetry, when people write or talk about films they often use criteria and terminology originally developed with respect to painting or drama or the novel. There is nothing inherently wrong in this: such a tendency may even point to film as a medium combining in complex ways a great many characteristics which other forms can exhibit only in particular ways (oil painting represents through images, novels through words) but which film manages to do simultaneously (film can combine images and words).

At the same time, in order to write about films with some fluency, certain specific mechanisms peculiar to film need to be examined and scrutinized. Most people think they know what a "shot" is; they know that they know what a word is. It is important to distinguish between one word and another which may closely resemble it in meaning or sound; indeed, it is important to stress precisely this sort of difference when reading, or else meaning fails. The important thing when watching a film is both to understand what a shot may potentially be, while discriminating between one shot and another. This would perhaps seem too much for any reasonable person to undertake. Furthermore, analogy between shot and word breaks down when we realize that any language has a more or less finite number of words, while the number of possible shots is literally infinite. There will never be an Oxford Dictionary of Shots. Still, it is important to begin to discriminate, perhaps for the simple purpose of getting our movies straight in our heads if not to satisfy loftier theoretical purposes.

The images in most films represent objects and people as we might recognize them in everyday life. This power to record faithfully is almost an automatic legacy of the camera and the technology of reproduction which goes into the "finished product" we see in the theater. Anyone can aim a camera at the traffic moving in the street, send the film to a developer, put the developed film in a projector, sit down in a darkened room and watch the traffic moving in the street. But is that what we're really watching? If we say that in fact we are watching "the traffic moving in the street" (in that darkened room) the addition of quotation marks might stand as a way of indicating that everything we see in films has gone through an extremely complicated fictional process having, as its chief aim and end result, the effect of reproducing the objects and people photographed in such a way that all the intervening fictional processes are invisible.

In order to write a poem you need pen and paper; in order to do theater you need actors and a space, and sometimes a script. But to achieve the most "natural" effects on film you need (besides a "something" to be photographed) a camera, film, editing equipment, laboratories, a projector, a screen. All these apparatuses and procedures are part of the machinery we might call the material "fiction" of film-making. These are the things that put the quotation marks around the images. None of them except the screen, though, is ever visible to the spectator. And a bare screen looks incomplete, like a blank page in a book. We wait (with some impatience) for it to be covered up, made invisible, by the images projected onto it.

So when we see on a movie screen traffic moving in the street, we know that it is "traffic moving in the street," but we accept it as though it were traffic moving in the street (without any intervening quotation marks). In short, it is difficult for us to acknowledge that we have to "read" movie images in the same way we "read" images in a poem or story. Everyone understands that the rocking horse in D. H. Lawrence's "The Rocking-Horse Winner" is meant to refer to a children's toy and to something more abstract, some instinctual frenzy to which the horse connects its young rider. In reading Lawrence's story it is sometimes necessary to remind oneself of the literal level of the fiction, that the rocking horse is indeed meant always to be a literal rocking horse: it is easy to forget this, and to see the rocking horse merely as a kind of free-floating metaphor. In a filmed version of the story it would be necessary to be reminded constantly that the photographed object (a rocking horse) was in fact this extraordinary and visionary vehicle (the "rocking horse," with quotation marks). Because in a film the rocking horse would have a physical immediacy that the words "rocking horse" on a printed page can only evoke. Words refer; images reproduce.

Of course, there are many images in films that do not purport to reproduce. If we think of King Kong, we are constantly aware that this is an ape which is like no other ape. Part of his unique status lies in the fact that he must be constructed; we know this as we watch the film, and if we marvel at all, we marvel at how ape-like the ape is. It's the same with *Jaws*. We are convinced by the "special effects" of the film that a mechanically constructed movie property can be made to seem so "shark-like." At the same time we know that this is a shark like no other shark; and partly we know this because we know that it has been elaborately constructed.

These films rely heavily on things out of the ordinary. But most films rely heavily on their ability to convince us that they simulate the real world to the point of versimilitude. The makers of *All the President's Men*, for example, constructed an exact replica of the city room of the *Washington Post*, used authentic locations, used special camera lenses to get the proper reportorial "feel" to the film. Details of the script were checked constantly for accuracy with the two *Post* reporters (Bob Woodward and Carl Bernstein) who had broken the Watergate cover-up story. And yet the film places Robert Redford and Dustin Hoffman in the midst of this realistic detail, and asks us to believe that they "are" Woodward and Bernstein. These immediately recognizable faces have two effects: they elicit sympathy and identification, and they force us to acknowledge that something other than the event itself is taking place before our eyes. At least, we are forced to admit that some sort of reconstruction of a real event is being placed before us; and if we're willing to go that far, we may begin to look further. Like the presence of ketchup in a good restaurant, it's an indication that things may not be what they purport to be.

The idea of versimilitude in film has always posed problems. Where should the lines be drawn? In many gangster films of the 1930s and in *films noirs* of the 1940s the most extraordinary and effective lighting was used as a means of heightening psychological states or simply in order to make interesting formal patterns in the demarcation of physical space. Directors like Josef von Sternberg, Fritz Lang, Frank Borzage, Max Ophuls, and Billy Wilder utilized cigarette smoke and bold shadows to enhance cafés, city streets, and automobile interiors. But never in this wide array of lighting effects was the shadow of a microphone or a camera ever permitted to be seen. On the sets of costume dramas special employees in charge of what was termed "continuity" were employed to sit at the edges of the set and prevent a Roman centurion or a pirate from appearing in a scene wearing a Rolex watch or a pair of eyeglasses. And though great care was taken to record the pitch of an actor's voice with absolute fidelity, all thoughts of strictly accurate recording went out the window when two actors moved toward an amorous close-up and suddenly the air was filled with the sound of a thousand throbbing violins. Of course whole careers were ruined in the transition from silent to sound pictures, when it was felt that an actor or actress could not deliver suitably for "talkies."

It has to be noted, then, that narrative film has always bent the rules a little: photographic verisimilitude occurs within a highly prescribed series of conventions. Some of these are linked specifically to the manufacture of the image and to its reproduction; some have to do essentially with the construction of the film as a product, in both the aesthetic and commercial senses; and others may be seen as concerns growing out of the fundamental task of storytelling, problems of action and movement that overlap with some of the central situations of prose fiction. In the essay which follows we shall deal briefly with these problems of representation under two headings: camera and image, editing and narrative.

CAMERA AND IMAGE
The Non-presence of the Camera

Most films assume an invisible point of division between that which is photographed and that which is perceiving (the spectator, a character or, occasionally, some implied observer). The camera marks the line of this division. Everything in front of the camera can potentially be shown; and when the camera moves to face what was in the previous shot "behind" the camera, we do not see the director, the extras, and all the people on the set. Instead, we are once again presented with an area free from all traces of the image's production. We might imagine a circle bisected horizontally, with the camera at the bisecting point and the film crew standing behind; when the space originally occupied by the film crew is filmed, or even when the camera is pointed in that direction, everything must be reversed: the camera will point in the opposite direction, the crew will occupy space where previously the camera had pointed, and the actors or objects to be photographed will be pointed in the opposite direction.

Feature films are not shot precisely following the order of shots in the final print, so that varying the look of the film does not always involve total disruption for every new shot. But the so-called 180° rule, in which the camera is limited to what it can take in from one edge of a hypothetical semicircle, still generally obtains. Recently directors have returned self-consciously to the use of a single shot that rotates the camera horizontally on its base in a complete circle (a 360° pan) so that we feel we are being shown "everything." People accustomed to watching traditional movies and television feel a slight quiver when the camera moves past the 180° mark; but nothing is "revealed" in this procedure. We wait for a revelation, when the point of the shot often is precisely to preserve the mystery of the camera and its sacred, invisible place.

The Shape of the Image

Images are framed, kept within particular boundaries. In the first place, the screen serves as a receptacle; any empty screen, we might say, demands to be filled by an image. As spectators, we will be disconcerted if the picture spills over the edge of the screen onto a wall or some curtains; similarly, we will be upset if the tops of heads get cut off. The fact of the frame enables us to place the image in a central position. We do not care so much whether the sound comes from speakers at the side, rear or front of an auditorium, but the image must usually be centralized.

Aside from the physical fact of the frame, the shape of the image, its proportions, have received attention from those who produce them. The relative size of the horizontal to the vertical edge of the frame (called the "aspect ratio" of the image) has undergone recent modification. Almost every film through the early 1950s was shot in a controlled format of 1.33:1. Now we are largely accustomed to a "standard" ratio of 1.85:1, and road-show extravaganzas like *Cinerama* can be shot in ratios up to 2.55:1. Put simply, in these last cases the image is about 2½ times as wide as it is high. Despite these technological changes, however, the impulse of the director and cameraman who shoot the film—and the tendency of the spectator as well—will be to look toward the center of the image. Very few directors lavish a great deal of attention on the edges of a widescreen frame (Stanley Kubrick, in such films as *Barry Lyndon,* might be the exception to prove the rule). The tendency to look at the center of the image has been re-enforced over hundreds of years by the tradition of perspective that originated in paintings and drawings of the fifteenth century. This culturally inherited way of seeing is congruent with the convergent focal planes of the eye which, unless trained in other ways, seeks out a vanishing point lying directly ahead and to the center. When driving or playing basketball we must develop special visual cues and movements to counteract this centralizing tendency.

Most images, then, no matter what their aspect ratio, move toward the center, if we consider the screen merely as a single-planed horizontal field. But of course the culturally inherited laws of perspective lead us to infer planar depth from almost any image. A painting by Jackson Pollock or Andy Warhol arrests us partly because it tries to combat, or at least to suspend, what might be termed the gravitational pull exerted at the vanishing point of a perspectival painting. Films that utilize perspective, and thus ally themselves with the inherited codes of post-Renaissance Western painting, are doubly centered. Their images are composed along the horizontal plane so as to place the most significant action in the center of the physical frame (the frame, we recall, is itself a centering procedure); and the composition also moves in depth along any number of sightlines toward a limitless horizon found at the very rear and center of the image.

We might imagine a stock situation in a Western. Two "bad guys" are in the process of hanging a "good guy" from a tree in the left foreground. If space exists at the center of the frame, our eyes will ineluctably be drawn there in order to look for the oncoming rescuers. In part, of course, we do this because the genre of the Western has led us to expect this; but we are led there visually, as well, since we expect the center of the image to be filled. Of course, infinite variations can be played on this theme: we can hear a shot or a bugle first, or we can be moved to the position of the rescuers. But in traditional films, some way will be found to satisfy expectations while avoiding clichés, of obeying cinematic laws while cloaking them in surprising ways.

The image can at least be modified, then, by the arrangement of the people and objects within it. *Composition*, as this art traditionally has been called, evokes the distribution of parts within the fixed frame. The shape of the image is not changed through composition, but its texture will be. An image can be made to seem very rigid: marching troops in Leni Rienfenstahl's *Triumph of the Will* or a dancing chorus line in a musical are extreme examples of fixity within the frame. Some directors enjoy imparting a quality of sculptural immobility to their images, as if the characters and objects were frozen in time and suspended in space: again, Kubrick's portraiture in *Barry Lyndon* comes to mind, as do the tableaux of von Sternberg, the massive structures of Orson Welles, and the solemn architecture of many German expressionist films. Other directors would seem rather to permit objects and people to move fluidly through the space held by the camera: people in Howard Hawks movies tend to be in motion through the frame; so too does Jean Renoir use the frame as an insufficient container, suggesting action offscreen taking place simultaneously with the action which the camera has "happened" to observe. With the exception of Kubrick, these directors tend to conceive of the frame as if it were an opening onto the scene of the action; events move past the camera, rather than the camera moving to take in an object and thus creating an "event" through movement. Perhaps John Ford best displays a combination of still, painterly compositions with the fluid harmonies of an open frame. In his Western films especially he utilizes open spaces in order to achieve breadth of composition, and places his people together in a contrasting manner to provide a kind of posed, epic portraiture.

The Image and Its Physical Representation

We should note, first of all, that the conventional image is focused with sharp outlines. If loss of focus becomes part of a film's aesthetic design, that loss will usually be done for atmospheric effect (the fog in the harbor of *Anna Christie*, the blurring of consciousness when a hero is knocked out or drugged). Rarely will focus be lost in the center of an image, and rarely will it be lost on a leading actor or actress. Rather, as the leading players walk through a shot, the focus will be kept quite clearly on them, with the remainder of the frame left to take care of itself.

So-called "deep focus" is used throughout *Citizen Kane*. We may note that the use of special lenses enables the director and cinematographer to maintain consistently sharp focus on objects, whether they be in the foreground or background of the frame. This use of lenses pushes the convention of focus to an extreme and artificially stylized degree. We all know that by focusing with intensity on an object six inches away from our eyes our field of vision is foreshortened, so that background objects are only more or less in focus. But movie focus stands for a psychologically determined way of seeing things, rather than for a scrupulously accurate record of physiological perception.

Obviously, light must come through the lens aperture to leave a photo-chemical impression on the film stock. The greater the amount of light, the darker the negative becomes; and in printing, when the negative is in effect reversed, the area of densest light once again appears as it had to the eye. But not quite—the photochemical process, depending on the type of film used, can be made to differ subtly from the physical registration of light as it strikes the retina. Moreover, anyone who has used a darkroom knows that the process of developing has much to do with the look of an image, that tones and values can be controlled and even drastically changed.

In much of what we have been describing we can see an effort to stan-dardize, to make the production of movies a uniform procedure. In this, the film industry in the 1920s doesn't differ much from Ford Motors or General Electric. A number of interesting and aberrant private systems, often put together entirely by brilliant individuals, had to be geared for mass produc-tion and delivery to an audience that was willing to pay regularly for a pleasing and familiar product. Therefore, the screen was set at a standard ratio, the film moving through the camera and subsequently through the projectors was regulated at a constant speed (twenty-four frames of film stock or print per second), and the focus and exposure of the stock was regulated, too. One early studio directed all its cinematographers to shoot everything at f1.6, ignoring such variables as weather and the sun. They wanted a standardized image, something that wouldn't be too experi-mental. Heretofore many cameramen operated with great freedom and guarded their secrets jealously. D. W. Griffith's favorite cameraman, Billy Bitzer, who shot The Birth of a Nation and Intolerance, used to develop footage as he shot, and would never let anyone know how he achieved certain effects.

As the large studios and their massive production schedules got into high gear, however, all footage was developed by technicians in laboratories who required a regularized product to achieve uniform results. This is not to say that all movies began to look alike; but variations had to be achieved under more controlled conditions. The early films (and many of the fea-tures) of the great silent comedians have a special look because their stunts (hanging from buildings like human flies, rescuing maidens from waterfalls) had to be performed in the open spaces of Beverly Hills. They were shot with available light: one of the reasons the film business moved from New York and New Jersey to California was the clear, smogless uniformity of the sun. For companies utilizing natural light, the climate was ideal. As film-making moved into the constructed environments of the newly built studios, the range of effects was considerably narrowed. We shouldn't generalize (as have some historians and critics) that movies were dead after the so-called "Golden Age of Comedy" (Chaplin, Keaton, Lloyd, Sennett). Film simply became a more fully controlled product, the range of its meanings shifted. If anything, within their increasingly fixed format, movies became more sophisticated: while it doesn't take much cinematic schooling to enjoy an incredible gymnastic feat by Keaton, a miming face of Chaplin's, or Lloyd's constant risking of life and limb, it does require a practiced eye to spot variations in lighting, camera movement, subtle editing, and other grammatical devices which would be perfected over the years as the studios attempted to find a homogeneous model.

Some studios tried to duplicate the even lighting of the California sunshine, in effect using a consistently lighted image that avoided shadows and highlights. Others attempted to mold lighting so that the play of light source and shadow would yield visual meaning. Often a key light would pick out a star so that he or she might be presented in as flattering a position as possible. It's interesting to contrast Greta Garbo with Marlene Dietrich in this respect. Garbo worked for a studio (M-G-M) that aimed at the production of images with a consistently high gloss: lighting was kept even except for moments of particular dramatic atmosphere, or when the theme demanded a certain romantic drabness (again the fog in Garbo's *Anna Christie* would be an example of a film lit in a manner unusual for M-G-M). On the other hand, Dietrich's work in the early 1930s was done at Paramount under the direction of Josef von Sternberg, who also served as lighting cameraman. He was a remarkable stylist whose lighting effects were extremely complex and varied, and he literally constructed Dietrich's face through lighting. A complicated series of spotlights threw her face into perfect and frozen relief: often Sternberg used her face as the whitest element of the image, so that it would stand metaphorically as the "key light" for the other elements of the composition. Thus she was called on less to act than to emanate, she had fewer emotions than Garbo, but rather elicited emotion from others.

It should be emphasized that in both cases—Garbo and Dietrich—lighting is utilized as a means of shaping the image in artificial ways. The image itself—any image—tends, through framing and composition, to the artificial.

The Distance between Camera and Object

One of the basic procedures for introducing rhythmic texture and visual meaning into a film lies in the simple variation of distance between the camera and the thing it records. In very early films (those of Lumière in

France, Porter in America) the camera seems always to be about 10 or 15 feet from the object, though longer distances were quite permissible. The famous (and possibly apocryphal) response of the directors of the Biograph Company to D. W. Griffith's early use of facial close-ups ("What's happened to her body? Fire the cameraman.") may stand as an indication that most moviegoers had not assimilated close-ups into their notions of cinematic grammar. Just thirty-five years later Orson Welles and Gregg Toland would employ such shots as an entire screen filled with two lips and, though people may have been startled, the shot could without too much difficulty be seen as an "extreme close-up."

No one has quite been able to define the point separating a "close-up" from a shot slightly further away. There is no magical dividing line between a close shot and a medium shot. But since in movies there is no such thing as a neutral event, the position taken by the camera will go a long way toward shaping not only our attitude toward the events but the very shape of the events themselves. If we imagine a murder or robbery filmed with the camera constantly kept in a fixed position, more than a hundred feet from the activity, we might feel frustrated and wish to go in for a closer look. But if we were kept at a distance congruent with the participants in the activity, we might feel the need to "step back" and place things in perspective. On the theory that a mixture of focal lengths provides a blending of perspectives which satisfies the viewer's need to identify and participate vicariously on the one hand, and to detach himself from a situation that might jeopardize him on the other hand, classical film construction usually varies distance with some care. As viewers, we learn how to "read" this movement, so that we almost anticipate the moment when we see the murderer's face in close-up, or the hands of the frightened bank teller raised above his head.

Variations on these movements can produce startling effects. Usually, for example, a director will begin with an "establishing shot," taken from a position so as to include as much of the potential field as possible. If a murder is to take place in a room, we may get a shot which shows the physical layout and the protagonists; if the victim and aggressor are physically separated at the outset of the action, we probably will get a separate shot of the advancing murderer. But what if in place of the establishing shot the director or editor placed a close-up of the murder weapon? It might be a utilitarian or innocuous household object like a bread knife or a lamp, resting securely in its everyday location. By placing it at the beginning of an action, though, the film-maker calls it to our attention to such a degree that it plays in our minds throughout the length of the scene. The murder will then seem to confirm a suspicion, will gain through incremental repetition what it might lose in explicit shock. The choice of a camera's location defines the action; it is one element of the shot, and presents us with the field of vision.

The Movement of the Camera

When we speak of "moving pictures" we mean primarily that, as opposed to photographic images, film images can record movement. This term also acknowledges that the movement of the recording agency (the camera) can itself be registered simultaneously in the image. We take this quite for granted, but the double movement—of camera and of object photographed—accounts for much of film's complexity.

We should distinguish initially between camera movement on a fixed base, and movement of the sort involving acutal transportation of the camera from one point to another. Strictly speaking, the former is not movement but a series of gestures the camera can make along fixed axes of rotation—but they often appear as movement to the spectator, and the shape of the image changes just as much as though the camera were in fact to be transported. For example, the camera can tilt vertically on its base so that the image will be registered from varying angles ranging from directly overhead through high-angled, eye-level, to low-angled shots, in which objects tower above us (in the post-election confrontation between Charles Foster Kane and Jedediah Leland, Welles and Toland placed the camera below the level of the floor on which the actors stood). Camera style has been a traditional criterion for the interpretation of the image. It is a cliché to note that low camera angles produce objects that dominate the audience physically and psychologically. Yet perhaps the most politically potent image in the history of cinema is taken from an extremely high angle, as the small but distinguishable figure of Hitler walks in isolated review amongst the ordered and anonymous thousands of his followers in *Triumph of the Will*. We can at any rate say that an extremely angled shot (whether overhead or very low) indicates that an attitude toward the thing photographed is being encouraged. To revert to the terminology of our opening distinction, we are being shown the quotation marks around the image. Most conventional narrative avoids extremes, employing eye-level shots or slight deflections from it for purposes of narrative construction or exposition (e.g., the inevitable low-angle shot in a Western from the floor of a canyon to show the Indians riding along the rim above).

In addition, the camera can, while remaining fixed on its base, swivel from side to side horizontally. Often this movement is undetectable; when the camera is in close-up on a face, a slight lateral movement emphasizes the direction of a glance. Anything greater would be distracting. This movement is characterized, when used well, by great economy in the delineation of physical space and the revelation of an object's presence within that space. In Ford's *Stagecoach* the camera looks down at the stagecoach moving far below along the valley floor; the camera, maintaining its fixed position, moves laterally to the right (the verb which characterizes this lateral movement is "pans") to reveal a band of hostile Indians. The "revelation" itself isn't very surprising (axiom: where there's a stagecoach in a Western, there must be Indians) but the movement of the camera has established our position as spectators in relation to the two objects in a way which anticipates our closer proximity during the ensuing chase.

If we extend the basic movements of the camera on its base (vertical tilt and horizontal pan) beyond the fixed base, some special apparatus is needed. A "crane" shot places the camera and its operator in a flexible bucket that arcs out over the area to be photographed. The camera can then describe fluid movement away from or toward an object, while varying the angle of the movement. If the camera is to follow the movement of actors along a horizontal plane, tracks are laid down for the camera to move along the frontal plane of the image, or along an axis that moves the camera toward an object or away from it. When these shots are done in a studio, tracks similar to railroad tracks are laid down, and the camera is placed on a flat-bed dolly (hence the interchangeability of the terms "tracking shot" or "dollying" to describe the recorded trace of these movements). Occasionally these shots can be extraordinarily complex: they might register the point-of-view of a single character and, through movement, intensify that identification; they might, as in many of the films of Max Ophuls, inscribe a space between camera and protagonist that holds the latter's actions up to scrutiny. A famous moment in Ophuls's *Letter from an Unknown Woman* (1948) contains three basic elements: composition of characters within the frame, camera movement, and the imagined voice of the central character—she is dead, and her lover is reconstructing the events of her life from a letter. The moment to be delineated is a meeting of old lovers at the opera, after many years. The woman and her husband climb the stairs and, just as they reach the top step, overhear that the lover has returned to Vienna. Ophuls films this in one lengthy shot, picking the couple up in the foyer, losing sight of them in the crowd, climbing with them as they climb the stairs (the camera then both tracks and cranes), until, just as they reach a group of people who make the remark about her former lover, the camera is close enough to her face to pick up the subtle change of expression. It is a moment that simultaneously examines character and the mechanisms which unfold it, the emotions and the machinery which holds emotion up to scrutiny.

Tracking shots that combine movement of the vertical axis require extremely complicated arrangements of the entire cinematic mechanism. Many films which use lateral movement of the camera may prefer for convenience's sake to avoid laying down tracks and mounting the camera on a flatbed dolly. They might wish to film a chase through the window of an automobile or from the back of a pick-up truck. New lightweight equipment that can be mounted on portable bases permits movement far beyond the limits of the sound stage. At the end of François Truffaut's *400 Blows* the central character simply runs away from the detention center in which he is being held. The camera "runs" along-side him, never varying its position, keeping him in frame as he runs easily toward the sea. On the roadway and on the beach itself Truffaut accomplishes this movement by mounting the camera on the back of a truck and by making sure that the truck's tires are under-inflated to absorb excess vibration.

A variety of things have combined to diminish the number of films which utilize elaborate tracking shots. Development of lighter equipment has meant that many shots which follow a character or an object can be shot with a camera actually held by the camera operator. Chase scenes photographed with a hand-held camera have a nervous, edgy quality that is quite the opposite of the lyricism imparted, through movement, in the examples cited from Truffaut and Ophuls. The demise of the studios, with their vast sound stages and hosts of technicians, meant inevitably that films began to be shot in less elaborate ways. Some elements of film have come to be identified with a particular way of making "studio" films. The tracking shot may be one of these, and many young directors wanted their films to look like something else, something more immediate and less elaborately constructed. Finally, the advent of special wide-angle and telephoto lenses in effect provide a substitute for movement by seeming to manipulate the visual field in ways that might have been accounted for previously by movement of the apparatus.

Wide-angle lenses take in a broader visual field, and provide an image with relative depth. Telephoto lenses flatten the image and substitute a contraction of the visual field for movement of the apparatus.

EDITING AND NARRATIVE

Everything we have talked about to this point relates to the recording mechanisms of the cinema. When people remember a moment from a film they will often refer to these moments as "shots," as in "I remember the shot in which . . ." But in shooting a film, units of measurement can quite simply be made by a single distinction: that time when the camera motor is running, and that time when it is not. All the events recorded during the first period—taken from different angles, shot with movement or in stasis, shot with different lenses, composed in different ways with differing lighting—will be regarded as footage to be sifted through and arranged during the period of editing.

Of course, no one shows up to make a feature film without some general idea of how things ought to go. There is usually a script, for example. But few scripts contain directions about the placement of the cameras or the actors, and most directors rightly disregard such directions if they find them.

In discussing editing as an element of film, then, we must first distinguish among certain key terms that have fairly precise meanings but are often used in rather slippery ways. Part of the reason for the confusion stems from an attempt on the part of film-makers to give us the visual event in a way that makes it seem unmediated, what we earlier termed the impossible ideal of the film without quotation marks. The Greek painter Apelles was said to have painted fruit so real that birds would peck at them, seeking to feast; this ideal expresses a yearning for continuity between creator, object, and beholder. The mechanisms of cinema have operated all along on what we might call the "Apelles principle": to synchronize the divisions that are mandatory in the construction of a film. When we attend carefully to the distinctions that follow, we are working against the stream of the cinematic machinery, but we are working to make things more accessible and open to analysis.

The Take

Of all the elements in the pattern of a film's continuity, this is the least likely to show up in the final edited version. Each time the camera motor is turned on, a take begins; when the motor stops, the take is over. If the event to be filmed is a man walking across a room, picking up a newspaper and sitting down, this event may be recorded as many times as desired, in as many ways as possible. Each one of these recordings will be called a take. Film operates on the premise of a surplus, from which the "real film" will be "cut." An over-cautious director might wish to record a simple event like the one described above as many as a dozen times; usually, though, such considerations as budget and temperament dictate a smaller number of takes.

Some directors may be characterized as exponents of the "long take." A "long take" seems long because it stands out from the normal patterns of editing dictated by most of the classical narrative models in the history of cinema. In *Citizen Kane,* shots 6 and 7 of the snow sequence (see below) are long takes; the time taken to unfold them on the screen duplicates exactly the time taken to record them on the set of the movie. Nothing has interrupted the temporal and spatial unity of the recorded event.

A take thus points to the harmony and synchronization between the registration of an event by the camera and its reception by the audience. A long take sustains the impossible premise that a film has been "untouched by human hands," that it comes straight from the camera to you.

The Shot

A shot differs from a take in that it designates an edited unit of the finished film. Some takes never become shots; all shots are takes. If we imagine ourselves as directors, faced once again with the task of the man crossing the room, we might film it in a single continuous action that would show up in the final product as one shot. In fact, it would be quite remarkble if we permitted him to move two or three feet, then called a halt while the camera was turned off, moved to a new position, and was started up once again. If we did this, the breaks designated by the interruptions would force us to articulate this movement, assuming we wanted to keep it in the finished film, as more than one shot. If we decided to opt for sanity and shoot the event as single and continuous, we would still have the opportunity of doing other takes, in which the angle or position of the camera might vary, the lighting might be changed, and so forth.

We tend to think of the shot as something connected with the shooting of the film. This may on occasion be true: when Welles and Toland made the decision to shoot the snow sequence in *Kane* utilizing the long take, they had to meticulously plan the position of the actors and the camera during every moment of the shot. The extent of preparation (and we must include here the actors' preparation) may be realized if we imagine what shot 6 might be like if it were broken. We might imagine Welles and Toland interspersing the conversation in the cabin with shots of young Charles Foster Kane playing with his sled in the snow. In many ways this hypothetical construction would draw closer attention between the young boy and the adults who are in the process of sealing his future. Even if Welles had filmed all the cabin conversation in a single take, had he then begun to intersperse it with other material, it would lose its status as a single unit and would become a series of shots. Thus, what was filmed in a single take would be represented in the text of the film as a series of shots. For we designate a shot as something which, in the final version of the film, begins and ends with specifically marked cinematic punctuation (a cut, or an optical device of some sort). When analyzing a film, we need not even concern ourselves about whether every shot in a specific piece of action (let's say, the car/elevated train chase in *The French Connection*) was filmed on the same day and under the same conditions. We understand that its importance lies not in the unmediated unity of the shot but in the synchronized unity of a series of shots.

The term "shot," then, designates a portion of the edited version of a film; it refers not to the "shooting" process, but to the process of structuring which we term "editing." The problem with the term "shot" is that it can refer to such a wide variety of potential elements of meaning. Shots can be as brief as the twenty-four frames which elapse in a single second, or they can be as lengthy as the capacity of the camera's magazine. A shot can include movement, or can be still; it can be taken at any distance from the object. All these differences are normally denoted by the single word "shot."

The Fact of Synchronization

Image and sound are recorded separately—that is, by different mechanisms. During the first years of the sound film it was necessary to register directly every sound made on the set during the recording of an event. Increasingly, though, dubbing and re-recording have made possible a diversification of sources on the soundtrack; but the fact remains that little experimentation has to this date taken place. The overlapping dialogue of *Citizen Kane* (where one actor speaks while another is speaking, or trying to speak) remains an adventurous and startling example of sound experimentation. A film like Francis Ford Coppola's *The Conversation* (1974) has the virtue of showing us (visually and aurally) how sound can be manipulated, though in the end the recording source (a "bug" planted in the protagonist's apartment) remains undiscovered: sound preserves its mysterious origins.

Few attempts have been made at deliberate discontinuity and disharmony between image track and soundtrack. Many viewers will fail to distinguish between the two, or will fail to see even that the two are, in fact, two separate things at all. If words don't match a character's lip movements, if a character speaks with a different voice, if sounds from another shot are heard, our tendency is to think that something has gone drastically wrong with the film. Many people—including film "purists"—cannot stand dubbed films (in which a French film, for example, will be re-recorded in English) because it disturbs the illusionist quality of the film. The playing of word *against* image, in some dialectical fashion, would be presumably even more treasonable.

In fact, image and sound are usually married in such a way that they appear to have been harmoniously together from the beginning of the event. This is accomplished at two stages—at the filming and in the printing of the finally edited version. The recording apparatus is kept in time with the camera through a cable or by employing generators which use crystal clocks to ensure perfectly synchronous timing. When the sound record is printed on special magnetic tape so that it can be edited, sprocket holes maintain a precise link between image and sound in any take; thus, sound may be edited completely apart from the image so long as the means of defining the rate of the unwinding of tape and celluloid can be strictly regulated—and the means for that regulation is the sprocket holes, which also enables the film to be projected for viewing at just the proper speed to ensure synchronization.

Synchronization stands as the regulation of the cinematic apparatus. Things that had been taken apart for the purpose of editing are put back in such a way as to disguise the fact that they had ever been separated. If we marvel at the dancer who sings beautifully and without difficulty during a strenuous dance number, or at the encouragement shouted back and forth by a platoon under heavy artillery bombardment, we are applauding in large measure a technology that has encouraged the covering up of artifice.

The Cut

A cut is the most fundamental procedure of editing: the joining of two hitherto separate pieces of film in order to present them as related. Although cutting might in the literal sense suggest the interruption of a single shot at various points in order that it be broken down into smaller units or interspersed with other shots, the term "cutting" as it is often applied to the editing process refers as much to the *construction* of two (or more) shots end to end.

Again, the cut is an important quotation mark, signifying a definite break in the construction of the film as a whole. Classic narrative cutting, though, has usually been done in such a way as to make these breaks as invisible as possible. The cut is made at a point where the end of one shot and the beginning of the next will match. Obviously, if the cut moves the audience great distances in time and space, a break of some sort is unavoidable. In such a case the cut is usually overlooked in the general shift of the plot. But when Welles makes a cut in the middle of a formulaic season's greeting—"Merry Christmas/And a Happy New Year"—with the first shot preceding the second in time by close to twenty years, we can assume that the idea of "matched cuts" is being played with deliberately. Usually cutting continuity in the classical film follows more restrictive guidelines. For example, a cut that unites two shots of a couple talking—one over character A's shoulder on character B, the second reversing this—will rarely be seen by the viewer as the inclusion of 360° of space. The cut moves us back and forth over the 180° line (see section "Non-presence of the Camera"), but we probably register the cut less as a movement than as an almost negligible joining of two opposed points of view.

Within the 180 degrees that are deemed the camera's field of vision, certain axes provide general guidelines for cutting continuity. We might imagine the typical family dinner scene in an American film, with Dad at the head of the table and Mom at the foot, nearest the kitchen, and all the brood lined up picturesquely at either side. Shots of either Dad or Mom in close-up would place the camera, in effect, in the point of view of the one directly opposite, though this may not "register" on the screen. Shots of the children might be taken directly in front (from across the table, as it were) or at an angle that will include Mom or Dad; and the kids themselves can be shot in such a way as to include Mom or Dad in the foreground. A full "establishing" shot, which might occur at the beginning or end of the meal, would be taken from a slight distance away from the table in order to include as many members as possible (probably some plants in the dining room and a maid might be shown as well).

A diagram showing permissible axes of shooting in such a scene might look like this:

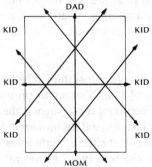

Even with a strict adherence to the 180°, 90°, and 45° angles there is a wide range of possibilities for camera placement. What is of importance here is that too small an angle of variance not be present as a cut that separates. A close-up of Dad should not be interrupted by a cut, if the next shot will show Dad from only a slightly different angle (say a 5° variance to the left or right). The viewer will "read" this, interestingly, as a lapse in time; and it will appear that continuity has been lost, that synchronous quality that the sound narrative film has always been at pains to preserve.

Cuts that do not work to preserve continuity are often labeled "jump" cuts. These may vary from small "flaws" in the continuity (such as a cut of less than 30° variance, which does not significantly alter composition) to the massive exclusions of expository material occasionally found in modernist films. Whereas Capra or Hitchcock would film a dinner scene so as to explore through conventional cutting the relationship between characters, using the standard model as the basis for their particular signification (as they do in *Mr. Smith Goes to Washington* or *Shadow of a Doubt*), a modern director might take great liberties by cutting out what he considers "waste" footage, jumbling the temporal progress of the meal, and other devices.

Optical Effects

Other than through the introduction of a cut, pieces of film can be joined by modifying the image as it is printed in the laboratory. A *dissolve* superimposes one image on another (shots 9 and 10 of the "snow sequence" in *Citizen Kane*); the time taken to effect the transition may be brief, or it may be slowed down so much that one image remains fully visible while another is superimposed upon it (a *lap* [short for "overlapping"] *dissolve*). The image can *fade* away so that the frame contains momentarily a blankness that may be either light or dark; similarly, an image may be made (quickly or slowly) to emerge from this blankness (a *fade in*, as opposed to a *fade out*). An image may be retained on the screen while the resolution of the focus is made slightly less definite (a *freeze*); this often occurs at the end of a series of shots or at the end of a film as a whole. Such special effects as the *iris* (*in* or *out*), in which the rectangular frame either begins or ends as a point of circular light, and the *wipe* (of which there are literally a thousand varieties), whereby a line appears to move across the screen, changing the image, are less common. They are sometimes used by current directors as a means of evoking old-fashioned movies.

Usually the insertion of an optical device moves the film markedly in time or space: the dissolve at shots 6/7 of our sample passage indicate the elapsing of perhaps an hour. Sometimes a dissolve will be accompanied by a pictorial emblem (whirling leaves, or wind blowing the pages of a calendar) to indicate movement into the past. Because these past events belong to the film text itself, rather than to any one character exclusively, we call them *flashback* rather than the more simple "memory." They can, of couse, be the memory of a single character, but he will be shown to "remember" in a visual style congruent with the rest of the film.

The Sequence

The purpose of editing since its inception has been the construction of a series of images into a coherent whole. Though in the largest sense this whole ought to be the film itself, a film's patterning effects often make themselves available through smaller units that have often been called sequences. If we think of a narrative event in a film, we may remember individual shots but we are more likely to recall the cumulative effect of a limited number of shots sequentially arranged. Thus, the sequence as a concept brings us to the problems of narrative which go beyond the specific language of cinema and connect with problems of prose narrative discussed elsewhere in this book.

A sequence may be a single lengthy shot, but is more likely to be a compilation of several shots: by establishing continuity and unity within this relatively limited area, a film-maker will attempt to endow the enterprise as a whole with some organic development. Those film-makers interested in promoting discontinuity (and there are more and more of them) will attempt to subvert cinematic articulation at this point, at the level of the narrative sequence.

When film-makers first began constructing lengthy films through the patterned articulation of a series of shots, it was inevitable that they would build each pattern into some sort of climax or intense conclusion. Early in the history of editing, then, such devices as movement back and forth between parallel activities (taking place in different locales) would "build" the action into a pattern that could be resolved when the two actions came together at a significant moment.

Constructing this rhythmic parallelism had the virtue of giving shape and control to elements of the narrative which were first introduced as disparate entities. Two characters and their fates might be traced separately until that inevitable moment when they stood face to face. Within smaller narrative units (a chase, a rescue) immense distances could be covered quickly, and (as it seemed) simultaneity could be suggested simply by cutting from one object or person to another, provided that a cut was made with reasonable speed back to the original object (A plus B must be followed again by A). This simple structuring device, known as cross cutting, was also given the more elevated name "montage." Whatever the origin of the term, in stand-ard narrative film it often refers to a series of shots which would seem to stand in some significant relation to the resolution of the narrative pattern, a series of events (shots) welded together so as to form a thematic and formal whole. Occasionally, when this highly visible style of editing grew out of favor, montage "set-pieces" would be inserted into a film for color and variety (the twice repeated opening night at the opera in *Citizen Kane* takes on this coloration, as do more visibly the encounters between Kane and Emily Norton at breakfast).

An important theorist of editing like Eisenstein developed a method of placing shots together in order to make them discontinuous even as they suggested affinities: the relation between shots was never an easy one, and was always subject to the dialectical pressure of attraction and re-definition. But even among his own countrymen Eisenstein was a minority, though influential. Other theoreticians of editing were concerned more with establishing unified patterns. Their impulse was to use the sequence not only as a means of furthering the narrative and enhancing it (through such devices as tone and speed) but also as a means of endowing the film with points of resolution. This simple-minded linkage, of course, can be elaborated in extremely complicated ways, but they all move us toward a sense of closure. We want our Rosebud in a traditional film, and we are finally shown it in most cases.

Some Examples of Cinematic Narration

Cinematic narration is not only a question of the arrangement of visual events to tell a story. It involves also the way in which these events are presented to us. In discussing the short story or the novel, we are accustomed to distinguishing between the order of events and the voice or viewpoint through which they are presented. In considering film, we may make similar distinctions. But in speaking of film, "voice" and "point of view" are no longer metaphors but have become facts. In the language of written fiction, description is hard and commentary is easy. In film, the events are before us. We see and hear them. The film-maker's problem is to give them human significance without overstating their significance for the viewer. This a problem not in the narrative arrangement of events but in the manner in which the narrative is conducted. The following four examples are intended to illustrate—but not exhaust—the range of narrational procedures that film-makers have employed.

NARRATION BY EXTERNAL NARRATOR

A disembodied narrative voice tends to rob the eye of its joys in discovering and, too often, underlines points already well set forth. The authoritative spokesman who was once a staple ingredient of newsreels and documentaries (a voice deftly parodied in the "News on the March" newsreel of *Citizen Kane*) would define the problem, establish setting and introduce the central characters, then would be replaced by the straightforward, dramatically conceived progression of events.

The most fruitful way of employing a narration by someone totally outside the plot relinquishes omniscience in favor of distance and detachment. Welles's *The Magnificent Ambersons,* for example, begins with a voice that helps the audience to establish its attitude toward the past and those who lived there. Describing mores and fashions, the slow tempo of life ("In those days they had time for everything"), and quick tongues of the Mid-western small-town chorus, the narrator tempers irony with a gentle, self-conscious affection. He prevents, above all, our impulse to think of the past as merely quaint and nothing more—though its quirkiness is never denied, in fact it is relished by the film—so that when the opening narrated segment dies away with "it was the last of the great, long-remembered dances that 'everybody talked about . . . ,' " we have been prepared to be swept up by the glittering energy of the ballroom sequence immediately following with-out losing sight of its transience and superficiality.

NARRATION BY INTERNAL NARRATOR

A more common technique, this has affinities with novels that utilize first-person narration. Here camera and narration usually work in counterpoint; that is, the camera records the world while the voice of a central character interprets and explains on the soundtrack. If the camera were to become a true first-person narrator, it would record the world as though the lens were the eyes of the protagonist; and while the narration would become a re-enforcing verbal record, the mannered constrictions of Robert Montgomery's notorious experiment, *Lady in the Lake* (1945), in which the camera sees only what is related by an invisible narrator, make this a highly stylized and unwieldy method.

The shared internal narrative may be conveniently traced to its most famous source in *Citizen Kane.* The reporter's search for the meaning of "Rosebud" offers the superficial reason for seeking out a group of Kane's associates. Welles mixes their narration with other dramatized sources of information, while establishing narrative reportage as nothing more than an interesting pretext for investing a shadowy figure with the substance of reason. As the various narratives proceed, the viewer finds himself drawn less to the search for "meaning" and more to the suggestiveness of Welles's style—besides the fact that the film offers glimpses of Kane's life from perspectives beyond the consciousness of individual narrators (for exam-ple, the famous traveling shot, which gives the stagehands' reaction to Susan Alexander's singing, or the shot from behind the poisonous glass after her attempted suicide). We feel Welles's imagination giving idiosyn-cratic visual shape to related occurrences.

Recently certain films have featured lengthy narratives told directly into the camera by a central character. Bergman (*Hour of the Wolf, Persona*) and Godard (*Weekend, Le Gai Savoir*) are particularly fond of this device, which perhaps should be seen as a narrative subset, or narrative within narrative.

Certainly they are meant to display themselves as "narrative," while an ostensibly narrated film like Truffaut's *Such a Gorgeous Kid Like Me* (in which a rollicking female criminal dictates her life's story to a timid investigating sociologist) or Arthur Penn's *Little Big Man* (the tape-recorded memoirs of a 112-year-old survivor of Little Big Horn) seems to exist, during the body of the story itself, as straightforward telling, without the intervention and filtering of a narrative consciousness.

CAMERA AS NARRATOR

At those moments when the camera establishes a relation between two formerly discrete areas through movement, or repeats with deliberate care a movement made in another part of the film, or pulls back to obscure an act, we are made aware of its efficiency as a narrative principle. Of course, this ties the camera referentially to what lies before it waiting to be photographed, and also forces the viewer to become conscious of what might have been hitherto an invisible and unthought-of mechanism. By taking the consciousness of means and meaning as a good thing, however, and by acknowledging that we have before our eyes a constantly modified series of visionary projections, we may extend our definition of narrative to incorporate purely visual process. Thus we may wish to conclude that a film like *Jules and Jim* has at least two simultaneous narrative procedures—one conducted by voice-over and one by camera movement.

MODERNIST NARRATIVE

We are moving now through a period in which film narrative has become very problematic. The look and shape of movies changed during the decade beginning in 1960, either through the internalizing of incidents that had earlier found expression through the pressures of men and objects meeting the external world squarely and acting within its dimensions, or through the depiction of consciousness itself as baffled and without points of reference (the most extreme representative would be Alain Resnais's *Last Year at Marienbad*).

No longer supported by inherited images and traditional structures, some film-makers have experimented with new, composite narratives. Most radically, Jean-Luc Godard fashioned a series of films in which he played with inherited American generic models (musicals in *A Woman Is a Woman*, "philosophical" thriller / melodramas in *Breathless* and *The Little Soldier*), didactic pieces modeled on the plays of Brecht (*My Life to Live*, *La Chinoise*), futuristic versions of old German silents like *Metropolis* or *Dr. Mabuse* (*Alphaville*), social commentary (*Two or Three Things I Know About Her*, *Weekend*), and filmed conversation (*Le Gai Savoir*) before arriving at a position of finally distrusting any narrative whatsoever. Each film utilizes whatever it can to get itself told—monologues, straight characterization, action sequences, songs, silences. *Pierrot le Fou*, arguably Godard's masterpiece and certainly the film most heavily laden with emotion, utilizes the following: songs sung by Anna Karina to a usually sulking Jean-Paul Belmondo, in the tradition of the duet in a Hollywood musical; printed titles; radio announcements; passages read aloud from Céline; stream of consciousness voice-over; monologues in which a character addresses the audience directly; guerrilla theater; fairy tales and parables; a printed and narrated diary; poems; a film (also by Godard) within the main film; various and lengthy anecdotes told by characters seen only once during the course of the film.

These narrative postures have irritated and confused viewers, but they promote within the film an extraordinary freedom—as if something eventful and moving may happen at any moment in any way—which replaces conventional narration with narrative process. Unlike some Godard films, *Pierrot le Fou*'s absorption with itself as a narrative hypothesis never precludes intense emotion. Many of the best European films of the 1960s, in fact, deal precisely and emotionally with narrative crisis—*Blow-up*, *8½*, *Pierrot le Fou*, *The Spider's Stratagem*. A central character tries to find a story, tries to tell it, to make it coherent, and to find an audience that will become both a part of what he tells and the group to which he tells it.

A return to easy residence within the boundaries of "American" narrative would be literally unthinkable now; film-makers today are too smart to be instinctive, and what they know is movies. A split between "popular" and "intellectual" films always existed, but critics and film-makers have only recently begun to admit what some of them used to say in odd moments: popular films had all the best of the narrative clarity, emotional depth, and intellectual verve. Above all now, one cannot extract them from themselves. They cannot exist as myth (the last refuge of scoundrels), or as a purely formal idea, or as intellectual history. Finding new ways to deploy knowledge, engaging fictions in ways both self-conscious and coherent, conveying simultaneously intellectual and physical vitality—the best films of the 1960s may have begun the difficult job of recasting the cinema's narrative conventions.

CLOSE ANALYSIS: A SCENE FROM *CITIZEN KANE*

In theory it ought to be possible to take any brief excerpt from a narrative film which follows most of the conventions we have been discussing (and 90 percent of the films we see are such films) and subject it to careful and revealing analysis. At the very least, we might begin to *describe* a film more accurately if we were able to note where one shot ends and another begins, what the relation between sound track and image track might be at the moment when a cut occurs, whether the camera is moving or not, what sort of lighting is being employed.

Trying to do this over a lengthy period of time—let's say, an attempt to describe in this way a feature-length film as a whole—brings us up against almost insuperable limitations: lack of access to the print (an economic and technological problem), non-reproducibility for other readers (how do you *quote* a sequence from a film, as opposed to a line from a poem?) and lack of a set of terms upon which most people can agree. Despite these hindrances, it would seem that our responses to film have to go beyond generalized responses.

What follows is an attempt to open a minute portion of Orson Welles's *Citizen Kane*. Though more has been written about this film than any other in the history of American film, little has been analyzed at the level of movement from one shot to the next. Most people call it a "great film" or a "daring undertaking" without having the text fixed in their minds in any way. *Kane* is partly the very object responsible for this: it is so dazzling, so lightning-like in its movement, that it effectively prevents our "getting at it" in detail. But the details turn out to be worth getting at; they broaden our sense of how the film functions, permit us to analyze its artifices and to reflect on its construction. It may be, too, that the more we know about any film, the more we are capable of understanding the reasons for our pleasure when we watch it.

Orson Welles was invited to Hollywood by R-K-O Radio Pictures in 1939 to help a studio whose financial condition was lethargic. Welles had achieved a measure of success with his theatrical productions and much notoriety for his 1938 radio adaptation of H. G. Wells's *War of the Worlds*. It was hoped that this "boy wonder" (Welles was 23 when put under contract) would put R-K-O on a better artistic and fiscal footing. Welles was initially unable to decide on a project for his first film until 1940, when he settled on a script called "American," by Herman J. Mankiewicz. It was this property that eventually emerged as *Citizen Kane*, released after much delay in July 1941.

Citizen Kane is the "failed" attempt to decipher the mystery of a man's life. This deciphering and decoding is ostensibly an assignment to a newspaperman. He must "get the story" of the final word of a dying public man, as overheard by his nurse. To do so, he interviews four people (an ex-wife, an old friend, a former business associate, and a butler) and reads the private diary of a fifth person. Each of these interviews and the "reading" take the form of narratives, told from slightly differing perspectives. Each person analyzes motive and event, offers moral evaluation and psychological analysis. Clearly, the reporter's hope and ours is that the composite narratives will add up to something like the truth which, for the purposes of the film, we understand to be the meaning of "Rosebud," the last word in the mouth of the dying man.

The attempts at reading and deciphering fail. Kane takes the secret of Rosebud with him to his death. Of course, it is important to distinguish that, even though the characters in the film never understand, the audience is apparently granted the answer. Yet by the time we realize what the "answer" might be, we understand that it's insufficient, that it doesn't in fact explain anything. It is expressive, perhaps, of something that can never be recaptured; or, it may be an utterance symbolically evocative of Kane's lost innocence. Even these interpretations seem trite, though. Rosebud as an answer may be something of a joke.

We might imagine someone in the audience who calls out early in the film, "Rosebud's the sled!" Since most people remember the Peanuts cartoon in which Snoopy hugs his sled while intoning "Rosebud" over it, or simply remember or have been told the "answer to the riddle," we can assume that the film is being watched for other reasons. We watch *Citizen Kane* again and again for the intricacy of its construction, the energy of its visual and aural expression, and for its ability to meditate on the very nature of film without apparently relinquishing its staccato drive toward the completion of the task, the "solving of the riddle." It combines the abstract thoughtfulness of experimental and avant-garde films with a vulgar raciness common to the genre of "newspaper films" of the 1930s, with lots of action, deadlines, and fast talk.

It's important, of course, that Welles makes sure that the audience does not leave the theater saying "What was that 'Rosebud,' anyway?" He makes sure that we are told, and that we understand that despite the accumulation of details about Kane lodging in our consciousness over the course of the film's unfolding, we know little more about the center of the man than we did at the beginning. The question may then be redirected: "I wonder what made Kane tick?" "Which one of the stories did you believe?" or "I wonder if stories ever tell us the whole truth?"

Citizen Kane is very deceptive, then, and perhaps intentionally so. We think we are seeing a film about a man, but we get instead a film which records the process of a personality's construction by the words of other people. We think that we are getting a story with a question and an answer, or several answers; instead, we get a film that holds up to scrutiny the entire process of question and answer. And the result is that we are constantly having our attention drawn to process rather than to end result, to how the thing is done rather than to some specific point of arrival. The film always grounds its revelations in specific cinematic technique, and these techniques are not disguised or easy to overlook: they jump right off the screen and grab the audience by the neck. The construction of Kane the man through narration never takes precedence over the construction of *Citizen Kane* by Orson Welles and Gregg Toland (the cinematographer who is given special credit for the visual style of the film). The many aspects of Kane—sentimentalist, humorist, tyrant, muckraker—are echoed by the very form of the film, which deploys its effects variously to elicit tears, laughter, revulsion, enthusiasm.

Still, a distinction ought to be made between *Citizen Kane* as the story of a man and *Citizen Kane* as an important moment in the history of the cinema. If we don't watch *Citizen Kane* to find out what Rosebud is, and if the film doesn't finally tell us who Charles Foster Kane "really" was, why do we watch it? Perhaps we might say that the content of the film—whether narrative or psychological—stays with us less fully than do the particular quality of the images, the cinematic devices, the entire panoply of tricks which Welles pulls out of his magician's repertoire. The manipulations of time, the pitting of one narration against another, the animation of still pictures and the freezing of animate people and objects so that they come to resemble the statues collected by Kane—all these devices which might seem at first viewing distracting or superficial or even excessively flashy, are in fact the things which make *Citizen Kane* fresh after thirty-five years. They indicate a playful desire to transform space and time, to juggle the sequence of events, to shock the audience out of its complacency. At the same time, they never fully violate certain basic cinematic laws. *Kane* was a commercial film, after all, made for an American studio, and it could not alienate its audience or confuse them. Part of the caution and conservatism projects itself as biography (in the Hollywood tradition of films about Pasteur, Edison, and others) and part as mystery (what was the secret of the man?). It becomes apparent that these questions are both secondary and, in the long run, less interesting than some others: about the ways in which the narrative structures itself, about the integration and dis-integration of image and sound, about the arrangement of the film's parts into something that never quite becomes a whole.

These are not merely technical questions, though they will involve for descriptive purposes some basic knowledge of film technique. But again, it would be simplistic to assume that the answers to the various problems posed by *Citizen Kane* can be explained by mere close attention to the level of cinematic expression. Just as an examination of a poem's meter will indicate certain moments of intensity and the shaping or disrupting of patterns of articulation, so attention paid to the technical procedures of a film will indicate, in themselves, particularized moments of meaning. It is important to read these carefully. At the same time, these elements of expression never count for anything in themselves. Shots in *Citizen Kane* may be long (say, twenty seconds) or short, but we call them all "shots." In order to make some connection between content and expression, we must try to integrate the uniquely cinematic area of film technique with areas of imaginative expression common to other artistic forms (duration, narrative, theatricality). By fusing these, by playing them off against each other, we can watch the film shaping itself.

One of the chief problems confronting a student trying to "read" a film is the sheer weight of information. *Kane*, for example, is 119 minutes in length, and throws a barrage of facts and opinions at the viewer with such speed that it is literally impossible to take them all in at a single viewing. It's difficult enough to remember everything said about Kane by the five chief sources of information; but we must attend also to the film constructed by Welles and Toland, and this means noting with care such points as the movement or immobility of the camera, the length of shots, the composition of objects within the frame, the focal length of the lens in any shot, the lighting, the presence or absence of music. Moreover, this information does not come at us serially, but in clusters. We may be trying to evaluate what Susan Alexander Kane has to say about "Charlie," while we are at the same time trying to take account of someone else's version of the event being described, the intonations of her delivery, the music (ironic? sentimental? neutral?), the composition (close shot? medium two-shot?), and a wide variety of other items.

Everything in a film, it turns out, is *motivated*. At least, until it's disproven, we ought to proceed on the basis that everything counts. Reading a lyric poem or a play by Shakespeare forces us to attend to every word, painstaking as this may be, for fear of "missing" something that helps the work add up to a satisfying totality. It's more difficult to do this with a narrative of some length, whether novel or film. Who would maintain that attention ought to be paid to every noun and adjective in *War and Peace*? Yet even in an extreme example of this sort, a reader—ideally, at least—has the leisure and the opportunity to stop and think about things and to interrupt the automatic flow of information in order to reflect on what he or she has been reading. This is almost impossible when it comes to describing a film. The result of this is a heavy reliance on generalization when people come to write about film. Sometimes the generalizations are interesting, sometimes not. But they leave a great deal out of the analysis (or evaluation) that is taken for granted in the study of poetry.

One way to combat this problem is to undertake as precise an examination as possible of a particular sequence in a film. A sequence might reasonably be described as a series of shots that seem to fit together, whether by virtue of their all having to do with the same thing (a car chase, let's say), or their being placed within a special time frame (a flashback, for example), or told from within a single perspective, or shown from the same point of view. The virtue of analyzing a single sequence or a select number of sequences, rather than attempting to generalize about an entire film, should be obvious. By narrowing the area to be discussed, we cut down on the sheer number of items to be taken into account, curb the impulse to make weighty generalizations based on impressions, and are able to take account of the precise elements of cinematic expression. At the same time, we ought to hold the rest of the film as much in our minds as possible, so that the information gleaned from the sequence under discussion can be folded back into the film as a whole. This will help us avoid confusing analysis with paraphrase, since a mere recapitulation of "what happens" on the screen, without an effort at integration, will hardly satisfy us. We will in that case inevitably feel that we've left a great deal unaccounted for. Of course, it's inevitable that to some extent we will always feel that something has been "left out."

No critical analysis fully accounts for the text it analyzes; it usually provides something different but in harmony—like the left- and right-hand passages in a two-part invention for piano. But if we try to bring the weight of the film as a whole (both its form and its content) to bear on every shot in every sequence we will have done a great deal. And we should remember, too, that the feeling of "something left out" specifically pertains to *Citizen Kane*. Like the jigsaw puzzles Susan Alexander Kane works at, a piece seems always to be missing. There's a missing element (perhaps more than one) in Charles Foster Kane which no one's narrative manages to capture and which even the audience, with its knowledge of "Rosebud," can't quite ascertain. And Welles and Toland have managed to present an extremely complex and satisfying film which leaves things out and which, partly on account of these very omissions, drives one again and again to think about the structure and themes of the film.

We might choose as an exemplary sequence the famous "snow" passage. But before analyzing this passage, we should go back to one or two scenes which precede it. After the film's opening credits, the camera had seemed to move past the "No Trespassing" sign into the heart of Kane's estate, Xanadu. In fact, after the first few shots, the camera scarcely moves; Welles "moves" us toward Kane's deathbed by a series of linked dissolves. A dissolve (one image blurring into another, which takes the former's place as the "text" of the film) marks a break either of time or of space. A dissolve moves the film without the camera's having to move. In the opening sequence, dissolves move us from the outskirts of Xanadu, through the lighted bedroom window to the very lips of the dying man: in huge close-up they utter the fatal and illusory clue, "Rosebud!" But just before the shot of the lips, we are shown a shot of falling snow. At first, this is disorientating, since we had thought we were inside a room. In fact, this snow turns out to be an "impossible" shot of a snow-covered house with snowmen surrounding it; when the camera pulls back slightly, the snow "landscape" is revealed to be a glass ball held in the dying man's hand. This trick of perspective—a momentarily confusing landscape being clarified by the movement of the camera to reveal a difference of scale—is the first of the film's visual reversals.

It should be noted that the camera has placed the audience in a position of privilege. No one could (or ought to legally) glide past the "No Trespassing" sign and through the bedroom window just in time to see the glass "snow globe" slip from the dying man's hand. The nurse, who evidently enters with the sound of the breaking glass, arrives in time to hear the word

"Rosebud!" but she does not have the close, gruesome perspective we are afforded. Moreover, since most of the remainder of the film will be given over to events filtered through the consciousness of narrators who are themselves characters in the action, the opening stands—along with the final moments after the departure of the reporters from Xanadu—as a sequence belonging to no particular internal narrator. Yet the sequence is clearly directive (pointing us toward conclusions) and manipulative (extreme close-ups and trick perspectives), every bit as partial to its view of the truth as will be Bernstein, Jed Leland, Susan Alexander, Raymond the butler, or the notebooks of Walter Thatcher.

The film's second sequence presents the public record, the "News on the March" newsreel. An extraordinary compilation of visual styles and techniques, ranging from shots which look like home movies and candid camera to formal portraiture, it nevertheless prompts an investigation precisely because it seems to omit the "secret" of the man. Thus the quest for "Rosebud"—the missing element—is undertaken as a newspaper reporter's search for a story.

Of the five narratives within the film, the Thatcher diary records the earliest portion of Kane's life revealed to us. The diary is located in the Thatcher Memorial Library, a mausoleum-like structure guarded by a formidable security agent and an even more formidable female librarian. The newspaper man, Thompson, gains access and seats himself at a long table in a barren, high-ceilinged room. The light streams in diagonally and unnaturally; opening the vault where the meager diary is stored seems like opening a crypt or the deepest depository in Thatcher's financial empire. Although the sequence may properly be said to start the moment Thompson enters the library, our analysis begins with the fourth shot of the sequence, as the camera moves over Thompson's shoulder toward the book open in front of him (shot 1).

The "snow" sequence proper begins with four brief shots moving us backward in time and placing us at the Colorado boarding house owned by Kane's mother. As Thompson opens the diary to the correct page, we dissolve to the title (shot 2) and then move quickly along the first sentence, the camera emulating the reading eye (shot 3). Here the dissolves are used to move us back from 1941 to 1871, and shots 4 and 5 present us with a snow-bound landscape which picks up the motif introduced by the glass "snow-scene." The movement backward in time is facilitated both by the spidery, aged handwriting of Thatcher (a passage presumably written some time during the 1930s) and the playful shouts of young Charles Kane (1871, aged about 6). In the course of a single dissolve, then, we move from Philadelphia (location of the Thatcher Memorial Library) to the wilds of Colorado, and approximately seventy years into the past.

Shots 6 and 7 are two of the lengthiest shots in the film. They are examples of the "long take," and we need to comment further on this. Welles came to

Hollywood without any real ideas about the technology of film-making or about the precise project he was to undertake. He did bring with him great energy, intelligence, and notoriety; he also brought an accomplished group of actors who had worked with him on radio and the stage as the Mercury Players. The technical problems were eased when Gregg Toland wrote a letter to Welles, announcing his availability and his eagerness to work with Welles.

Toland had worked in the 1930s, in films directed by William Wyler, John Ford, and others, at achieving a cinematographic style that would produce a strong illusion of depth in field. Objects at the "front" of the image, no matter how large, would be in focus equally with smaller objects at the "rear" of the image. Before the mid-1930s, the shallow focus of the largely immobile 35mm cameras had to be compensated for through lighting and blocking; and of course the audience mostly wanted to see the stars; so, if their faces were clearly in focus, it was felt that the background could take care of itself—if it was "interesting" décor, fine; but it was usually just additional "atmosphere." Because of technological developments—film stock had been developed for color cinematography which was more sensitive to light, advancements had been made in set construction, the cameras had become somewhat more flexible—Toland and others began to develop a technique which permitted a greater area of the shot to be consistently in focus. Actors could now move around more freely, the frame could be loosened up to permit a wider range of activities.

All this appealed to Welles. Part of the re-definition of film style that goes on in *Citizen Kane* must have come simply from his notion that he didn't have to follow slavishly all the "rules" (for example, cutting to a close-up on the face of the star at a crucial dramatic moment) set forth more or less prescriptively in other narrative films. Perhaps he didn't want to break all the rules, but he was certainly going to bend them. And here was a knowledgeable cinematographer inviting him to collaborate on this iconoclastic activity.

The "long take," then, is simply an adventurous kind of shot. We are impressed with shots 6 and 7 because they last so long, because so much is accomplished within them. After all the brief establishing shots, they settle the narrative down into an older time, a slower way of life. These particular shots are dominated by two things: 1. the placement and movement of the actors within the frame; 2. the performance of Agnes Moorhead as the mother. Throughout the entire length of *Citizen Kane* the mother appears in only three consecutive shots, the ones we have numbered 6, 7, and 8 (though we do glimpse an old daguerreotype of her with her son in the "News on the March" newsreel). Yet despite the brevity of her appearance, her presence persists remarkably in our memories of the film. We might say that she is part of what is lost to Kane, part of what he tries to recapture. Welles succeeds in permeating the film with her, and uses both a lens with great depth of focus and a placement of the camera in extreme close-up to accomplish his end: both devices give great presence (in the sense of "stage presence") to the actors in front of the camera.

In these two shots, Mrs. Kane decides her son's fate: she hands him over to the Eastern banker who will act as guardian and ensures that the bank will handle his education and financial affairs. Kane is thus moved away from his mother and toward the world of acquisitions. He acquires wealth and loses his mother; the world of finance acquires him, and something difficult to define is lost. In her poem "Amnesia" Adrienne Rich speaks of this scene as "The mother handing over her son / The earliest American dream (see p. ??? above)." As the mother moves away from the window where she has shown concern for her son's health ("Pull your muffler around your neck, Charles") she follows the camera back to a rear room in the boarding house. Almost in the middle of the frame we can see young Charles playing in the snow while the adults decide his future. We can even hear him shouting things like "Union forever," a fitting slogan for the years immediately following the Civil War, but ironic in its reference to the impending severance from his family.

Mrs. Kane sits erectly at the extreme right edge of the frame, flanked by a young-ish Walter Thatcher. To the other side of the frame, and to the left of the window which shows young Charles, stands the father. Weakly, he argues that the boy ought to stay. His placement in the frame shows him in opposition to the other two adults, and the informal dress and manner show his lack of power and resolution. Between these two groups of adults lie 1. the object of their discussion, in focus to the rear; 2. the papers that will transfer authority from family to institution, in focus on a table at the very front of the frame. Unknown to young Kane, he is in a direct visual line with the documents that will determine his future. When Thatcher indicates that the parents will receive $50,000 per year, the father stops his weak protest, moves to the window and closes it. The sound of Charles's play is stilled, his future decided.

The cut that now moves us from shot 6 to 7 is a mark which indicates a reversal of point of view. At the same time, it is not as though one narrator of a story were to stop in the middle and another narrator were to take over. Usually in a film the change in point of view from one shot to another in fact ensures that narrative continuity is preserved. It is as though the film-maker were sensing that we might be growing tired of looking at everything from the same position, and were asking for a change. Welles effectively preserves continuity within change by effecting a shift on the visual track even as the soundtrack continues. Thatcher is talking toward the end of shot 6, saying that the bank will administer "in trust for your son, Charles Foster Kane, until he reaches his twenty-fifth birthday, at which time . . .". His voice drones on mechanically, reading from the agreement which has just been signed; he is not interested—just another business deal—and Mrs.

Kane, the other chief mover, is not interested. She has turned her attention to her son, and Welles indicates this by cutting *before Thatcher finishes his sentence.* Our attention is directed away from Thatcher, toward what the mother sees. At the same time, we are not shown what she sees; we are shown her looking, so that her look becomes the most important element of shot 7. Thatcher concludes, now in shot 7: ". . . he is to come into complete possession." Mrs. Kane calls to her son: "Charles!" Her voice is sharp, and her face is unforgettable in its mixture of severity, determination, and abstraction. She sees her son and she does not see him; and we know this latter to be the case precisely because we do not see him, either. He is as absent to her (already taken from her) as he is to us. We might break down the elements of this shot as it begins as follows:

> 1. A banker speaks of Kane's coming into "complete possession" at the age of 25; we know that he will never possess what he really wants, and that what he thinks he wants will be dictated (as a legal document) by the decisions made by others.
> 2. A mother looks at her son in a way that fixes her face in his consciousness and ours. She could as easily be looking at some idea of him that she holds away in her imagination, just as others will later have their own "ideas" about what his life meant.
> 3. The mother is placed forward in the frame, isolating her from each of the two men (husband-father and banker-guardian). In the previous shot she had allied herself with the guardian against the father. Now she is seen in isolation, and Thatcher's importance is discounted, in comparison with the strange and remote bond between mother and son.

Thus Welles manages to change the relationship between the characters, and shift the object of our attention, by means of a single cut.

At the end of shot 7 the four principals are standing in the snow in front of the boarding house. Charles has had his fate announced to him, and asks in a puzzled voice, "Where'm I going?" His father reels off his itinerary as a series of train stops: "You're going to see Chicago and New York, and Washington maybe. Ain't he, Mr. Thatcher?" When we see the film a second time we recall that New York will be the scene of his greatest triumphs with the *Inquirer* and of his greatest folly (the campaign for Governor and the scandal of Susan Alexander); Chicago is the place where Susan makes her debut as a singer, and where Kane's friendship with Jed Leland comes to an end; and Washington represents the political power to which Kane aspires, into which he marries, but which finally eludes him ("Washington maybe"). At any rate, Charles only senses that he is being severed from what he knows; so he lunges at Thatcher with his sled. The father threatens discipline, and the mother clutches her son. Once again, Welles breaks a line of dialogue in the middle by a cut in order to guarantee both our sense that something is being shifted and our sense that some unity of expression is being preserved. And once again the film plays the

1328 ELEMENTS OF FILM

visual track against the image track, but in such a way that we don't lose sight of essential continuity. When the father threatens Charles with "a good thrashing," the mother challenges him. He repeats his aim, and she says, more to herself than anyone, "That's why he's going to be brought up where you can't get at him." Between the words "why" and "he's," Welles cuts to a close-up of mother and son (shot 8). The snow is falling softly, Bernard Herrmann's intelligent music is plaintive and fragile. The camera pans left to right, picking up the young boy's face staring with a mixture of hostility and curiosity at Thatcher.

At this point Welles uses two dissolves that are among the most expressive in the film. As Charles's face fades, we hear the whistle of a train signifying his departure from home. Filling the screen is an image of the sled, lying isolated in the snow (shot 9). It is our second "snow scene," reminiscent, of course, of the ball dropped by the dying man in the first sequence. Another brief dissolve takes place. The snow has piled higher on the now fully abandoned sled (shot 10). This object, invested later with so much senti-ment and ultimately false significance, becomes a sign of time passing, of departure, of loss and absence. The people have left. The object will persist only in memory. No wonder Adrienne Rich entitles her poem "Amnesia," that state in which we cannot remember, and know that we cannot re-member, "the picture of the past":

> Why
> Must the snow blot itself out
> The flakes come down so fast
> So heavy, so unrevealing
> Over the something that gets left behind?

Like *Citizen Kane*, many other great films try to reach back to "the something that gets left behind." In *Kane* we could call it Kane's childhood, or the sled—we could call it anything. All films try to present us with objects that will make up for that lost something, whether it be an object or a state of mind. Film projects itself as a recovery (shot follows shot, event follows event), but it's never enough, we can't quite reach what we're after. Perhaps Adrienne Rich is right in saying that film—this sequence from *Kane* taken as a departure point—is finally "unrevealing." Something is always hidden, though what gets shown is filled with wit and insight. And at a certain point, when we become familiar with a text or the elements of a medium, we can "almost trust" ourselves "to know / When we're getting to that scene." We can begin to examine it and place it, both in our memories and, briefly, in the forefront of our minds.

In fact, this sequence of Thatcher's diary presents us (and young Charles) with something resembling a recovery. The next shot (shot 11) puts us in a room at Christmas, the time of gifts and acquisitions. Paper is torn off a package, the camera moves back to show young Charles staring sourly at a shiny new sled. The camera pans up the legs of Thatcher, the obvious giver of the gift, wishing a detached "Merry Christmas." Charles mechanically returns the salutation. The disparity between the sled lost and the sled recovered suggests to us other disparities: between memory and fact, mother and guardian, love and expediency. The recovery is at the same time a gain in economic status (this sled is more expensive, and Charles already looks like a wealthy spoiled brat) and a loss of use (where is the snow? at what can he throw a snowball?). The sled is a false recovery, the first of the thousands of objects Kane will accumulate in his attempts at restoration.

We are presented next with yet another of Welles's extraordinary compressions and ellipses. After young Charles's reiterated "Merry Christmas," we cut to a much older Thatcher standing near an office window, dictating the close of a letter. Once again, we begin the shot in mid-sentence: ". . . and a Happy New Year." But we learn that Kane is approaching the time of his inheritance, and that we have jumped almost twenty years with a single cut.

These few shots mark only part of a sequence, and that sequence plays only a partial role in the articulation of the whole film. Yet we can find within these shots the basic materials for analysis: the distance of the camera from the objects it photographs; use of music and dialogue; presence and absence of characters; means of cutting to achieve leaps in space and time; use of an optical device like a dissolve in order to produce movement—again either of space or time—without movement of the camera; use of different points of view. In addition, we can bring to bear on almost any small sequence the larger thematic patterns of the film: memory and loss, the importance of objects—to give just two obvious examples. Though this sequence has a rather evocative quality, any number of sequences might be similarly analyzed.

Close examination of this sort makes a film seem manageable. And while it's right and proper to generalize about literary or cinematic experience, close analysis of the text will provide the most solid basis for such generalizations.

Shot 1. Camera moves over Thompson's shoulder as he examines the notebook in Thatcher Memorial Library.

Shot 2. The title of one chapter in the Thatcher notebook. The whiteness of page (and screen) initiates the sound of "Christmas-y" music on the soundtrack as a prelude to introduction of the figure of young Charles Foster Kane.

Shot 3. Camera has moved along the first sentence of the notebook chapter, which reads "I first encountered Mr. Kane in 1871." At the close of this "reading" of the sentence we "encounter" the figure of Kane, as the whiteness of the falling snow presents Welles with an opportunity for an invisible "dissolve" (the overlapping of one shot by another). In this case the dissolve simultaneously records the two shots with equal clarity, since "1871" (a remnant of *Shot 3*) and the figure of Kane (*Shot 4*) are disposed in different halves of the frame.

Shots 4 and 5. The snowbound landscape—the child and "home," which, fittingly enough, is revealed as a rest stop for transients. The snowball finds its target as nothing else in the film ever will.

Shot 6 (beginning). The start of this lengthy shot appears almost as a response to Charles's snowball. The mother leans out a window frame precisely congruent with the film frame. As the camera pulls back, another (obviously outlandish) figure balances the composition, and we know that we are in for something more complex than a domestic scene.

Shot 6 (middle). The weight of the foregrounded figures denotes their authority as Mrs. Kane signs her son's future over to the bank. Even Thatcher's hat seems more imposing than the forlorn father on the left. In a direct line with the papers, Charles plays obliviously; Welles jokes about his presence by having him fall in the snow as the shot proceeds, so that he seems to appear and disappear in the window frame.

Shot 6 (conclusion). Camera has followed Mrs. Kane from the table after the signing. She returns to the window, her vantage point and position of relation with her son. She has in effect stopped listening to Thatcher.

Shot 7 (beginning). Mrs. Kane gazes outside the boarding house window, beyond her son. She is just about to call his name, but she is unseen by him; she is seen by the men, but has no interest in either of them. The blank intensity of her vision signifies a moment of separation.

Shot 7 (middle and conclusion). Camera moves back to permit the adults access to the boy. Charles rebuffs Thatcher by fending him off with his sled, eventually knocking him down. The father attempts to intervene with disciplinary measures, but the mother enfolds the boy protectively.

Shot 8. The mother affirms her right to make decisions, and the camera agrees. The slight movement downward and to the right affirms the connection between mother and son, and reveals where Kane gets his will and determination.

Shots 9 and 10. The dissolve between shots is again almost invisible; we measure the passage of time by the increased quantity of snow. All people have disappeared, and the inanimate object lacks the anthropomorphic pathos with which Kane will later invest it. The sound of a train whistle tells us that the itinerary has begun.

Shot 11. Charles receives his new Christmas sled from Thatcher—the first "substitute object" in the film.

Glossary and Index
of Critical Terms

ESSAY

ANALOGY A type of comparison that emphasizes particular resemblances between otherwise dissimilar things and is used as the principal kind of support in the literary form of the argumentative essay. See pp. 9, 13–14.

ARGUMENTATIVE ESSAY A form of the essay that is addressed directly to the reader and straightforwardly attempts to make a case for something by using various kinds of supporting material, such as factual information, expert testimony, personal appeal, and analogy. See pp. 5–6, 9–10, 48.

COMMENTARY Interpretative part(s) of a narrative essay, in which the essayist implicitly or explicitly explains the point of a story contained in the essay. See pp. 15–16, 22–23, 48.

DIALOGUE A form of the dramatic essay in which conversation between imaginary characters is used as a means of testing ideas, expounding ideas, or demonstrating the superiority of one set of ideas over another. See pp. 5, 32–33, 36–37, 49.

DRAMATIC ESSAY A form of the essay that uses the basic elements of drama (either dialogue, plot, and character; or dramatic monologue) as a persuasive means of presenting ideas. See pp. 5, 32–33, 36–37, 38–39, 49.

ESSAY A prose statement that uses words to present ideas persuasively. See pp. 1–6.

ESSAYIST Author of an essay (as distinguished from the FICTIONAL SELF of an essayist). See pp. 6–8.

FICTIONAL SELF   Role or character an essayist plays in any particular essay. See pp. 6–8, 38–39; see also IMPERSONATION.

IMPERSONATION Specialized form of role playing in which an essayist deliberately assumes a disagreeable, despicable, or stupid character whose opinions are not to be identified with those of the essayist but instead are to be seen as embodying the wrongheaded view of a situation. See pp. 38–39, 49; see also IRONY and MONOLOGUE.

IRONY   The deliberately extreme disparity existing between an essayist and an essayist's fictional self in the monologue form of a dramatic essay. See pp. 38–39; see also IMPERSONATION and MONOLOGUE.

MEDITATIVE ESSAY   A form of the essay that presents ideas and images in an associative order so as to reveal an author's process of thinking and feeling about something. See pp. 5–6, 24–25, 30–33, 48–49.

MONOLOGUE   A form of the dramatic essay in which an essayist uses impersonation as a persuasive means of showing the superiority of one set of ideas over another. See pp. 5, 38–39, 49; see also IMPERSONATION and IRONY.

NARRATIVE ESSAY   A form of the essay that uses the basic elements of narration (a story and a storyteller) as a means of making a commentary upon some aspect of experience. See pp. 5–6, 15–16, 19–24, 48; see also COMMENTARY.

PERSUASION   The act of using language as a means of moving a reader to accept a particular view of something. See pp. 5–6.

FICTION

ALLEGORY   A story in which the events and characters are symbolic of another order of meaning, in a frame of reference outside that of the fictional world, the way killing a dragon may symbolize defeating the devil. See pp. 111–12.

CHARACTER   A name or title and a set of qualities that make a fictional person. See pp. 109–10, 136, 142, 146.

COMEDY   The story of a person's rise to a higher station in life through education or improvement of personality. See pp. 106–7.

DESIGN   The shape of a story when it is considered as a completed object rather than an ongoing process. See pp. 117–19.

DIALOGUE   The parts of a story in which the words of characters are directly reported. See p. 113.

FABLE   A story that makes a moral point through the actions of characters, often using animals to represent human behavior. See pages 123–24.

FABULATION   Fiction that violates normal probabilities to make some point about the nature of existence. See p. 177.

FACT   A thing that has been done, or a true statement. See pp. 101–2.

FANTASY   A story of events that violate our sense of natural possibilities in this world; the more extreme the violation, the more fantastic the story. See pp. 103–5.

FICTION   Something made up, usually a made-up story. See pp. 101–2.

HISTORY   The events of the past, or a re-telling of those events in the form of a story; the most factual kind of fiction. See pp. 103–5, 137.

IRONY   The result of some difference in point of view or values between a character in fiction and the narrator or reader. See pp. 113–14.

JUXTAPOSITION   The way episodes or elements of a plot are located next to one another to contribute to the design of a story. See pp. 117–19.

METAFICTION   A special kind of fabulation that calls into question the nature of fiction itself. See p. 177.

METAPHOR   The way rich and complex thoughts can be conveyed by the linking of different images and ideas. See pp. 113–17, 160, 169.

MYTH   A story that expresses a deep human concern, often involving the actions of gods or other superhuman figures. See pp. 120–21.

NARRATION   The parts of a story that summarize events and conversations. See p. 113.

NARRATOR   The person who tells a story. See p. 113.

PARABLE   A story that takes the form of a simple allegory, using humble characters and situations as a way of suggesting more important moral or religious concerns. See pp. 123–24.

PATHOS   The emotion generated by the story of a character's fall or persecution through no fault of his own. See p. 106–7.

PICARESQUE   A kind of story that blends comedy and satire to narrate the adventures of a rogue passing though a low or debased version of contemporary reality. See p. 107.

PLOT   The order of events in a story as an ongoing process. See p. 108–9.

POINT OF VIEW   The voice and vision through which the events of a story reach the reader. See pp. 113–17.

REALISM   A mode of fiction that is not specifically factual but presents a world recognizably bound by the same laws as the world of the author. See pp. 105, 158.

REPETITION   The way certain features or elements of a story may be presented more than once to make a thematic point. See pp. 117–19.

ROMANCE   A story that is neither wildly fantastic nor bound by the conventions of realism, but offers a heightened version of reality. See pp. 105, 158.

SATIRE   A story that offers a world that is debased in relation to the world of the author. See pp. 106–7.

STORY   A complete sequence of events, as told about a single character or group of characters. See p. 102.

STREAM OF CONSCIOUSNESS   A fictional technique in which the thoughts of a character are entirely opened to the reader, usually being presented as a flow of ideas and feelings, apparently without logical organization. See p. 109.

SYMBOL   A particular object or event in a story which acquires thematic value through its function or the way it is presented. See pp. 119, 169.

TALE   A story that is told for its own sake, because it has a satisfying shape. See pp. 128–29.

THEME   The ideas, values, or feelings that are developed or questioned by a work of fiction. See pp. 110–12.

TONE   The way in which attitudes are conveyed through language without being presented directly as statements, as in sarcasm. See pp. 113–15.

TRAGEDY   The story of a character's fall from a high position through some flaw of personality. See pp. 106–7.

POETRY

ACCENT   The rhythmical alternation of light and heavy (soft and loud) sounds in verse. See pp. 549–56; see also STRESS.

ALLITERATION   The use of the same sound at the beginning of two or more words in the same line (or two adjacent lines) of verse. See pp. 558–59.

ANIMATION   The endowment of inanimate objects with some of the qualities of living creatures. See p. 541.

BALLAD   A poem that tells a story, usually meant to be sung. See p. 528.

BLANK VERSE   Unrhymed iambic pentameter lines. See p. 556; see also FOOT and LINE.

CAESURA   The point or points within a line of verse where a pause is noticeable. See pp. 556–57.

CONCEIT   An elaborately developed and sometimes farfetched metaphor. See pp. 538–39.

DESCRIPTION   The use of visual images and appeals to other senses in poetry. See pp. 531–33.

DRAMA   The quality of poetry that is like theatrical drama, requiring the reader to grasp the nature of speaker, listener, and situation. See pp. 525–29; see also DRAMA Glossary.

DRAMATIC MONOLOGUE   A poem in which a single speaker addresses remarks to one or more listeners at some significant moment in the speaker's life. See pp. 526–27.

END-STOPPED   A line of verse that ends where one would normally pause in speech or punctuate in writing. See p. 548.

ENJAMBMENT   The use of run-on lines in verse. See p. 548.

FEMININE RHYME   When rhyme words end in an unaccented syllable, two rhyming sounds are required, as in *yellow* and *fellow*. See pp. 553, 559.

FOOT A unit of meter or rhythm, of which five kinds are normally recognized: the iamb (da-dum), the anapest (da-da-dum), the trochee (dum-da), the dactyl (dum-da-da), and the spondee (dum-dum). See pp. 550–56.

FREE VERSE Unrhymed lines in which no particular meter is maintained. See p. 548.

HEROIC COUPLET A rhymed, iambic pentameter pair of lines, usually both end-stopped, with a period or other full stop at the end of the second line. See pp. 557–58; see also FOOT and LINE.

IMAGERY The use of sensory details (images) in poetry: sounds, scents, tastes, textures, and especially sights. See p. 537.

IRONY A deliberate gap or disparity between the language in which a thing is discussed and language usually considered appropriate for that particular subject. See pp. 542–45.

LINE The line of verse as normally printed on a page. Lines may be divided into feet and labeled according to the number of feet per line. In English the most common lines are pentameter (five feet) and tetrameter (four feet). See p. 548; see also FOOT.

MEDITATION The movement from images to ideas in poetry. See pp. 532–33.

METAPHOR The discovery of likeness or similarity in different things—a major resource of poetical expression. See pp. 534–38.

METRICS The part of poetry that has to do with sound rather than sense. See pp. 547–59.

NARRATION The quality of poetry that is like fiction, requiring the reader to follow shifts in time and space, and to observe significant details, so as to understand a poem as a kind of story. See pp. 528–30.

NARRATOR One who tells a story. See pp. 528–29.

PERSONIFICATION The endowment of non-human things or creatures with distinctly human qualities. See pp. 541–42.

PUN A word used in a context that obliges it to carry two conflicting meanings. See pp. 540–41.

RHYME A sound pattern in which both vowel and consonant sounds at the end of words match (as in *rhyme* and *chime*), especially when these words come at the ends of nearby lines. See pp. 558–59.

RUN-ON A line of verse that ends where one would not normally pause in speech or punctuate in writing. See p. 548.

SCANSION To "scan" a poem is to determine its metrical structure and rhyme scheme. See pp. 549–59.

SIMILE A kind of metaphor in which the likeness of two things is made explicit by such words as *like, as, so.* See pp. 534–35.

SITUATION In a narrative or dramatic poem, the circumstances of the characters or speaker. See pp. 525–27.

SONNET A verse form featuring intricate rhyming, usually employing fourteen iambic pentameter lines. See pp. 565–67.

STANZA A regularly repeated metrical pattern of the same number of lines in groups throughout a poem, sometimes including repeated patterns of rhyme as well. See pp. 553–54.

STRESS   The ways in which verse sounds are accented, of which three types may be recognized in poetry: *grammatical stress,* the normal pronunciation of a word or phrase; *rhetorical stress,* change in pronunciation to emphasize some part of the meaning of an utterance; *poetical stress,* the regular rhythm established in metrical verse. See pp. 549–50.

SYMBOL   An extension of metaphor in which one thing is implicitly discussed by means of the explicit discussion of something else. See pp. 539–40.

TACT   A reader's ability to observe the conventions operating in any particular poem and to pay attention to the idiom of every poet. See pp. 524–25.

DRAMA

ABSURDIST DRAMA   A mode of drama which does not provide any rational source of explanation for the behavior and fate of its characters and thus expresses the possibility that human existence may be meaningless. See pp. 750–52.

BLOCKING   Arrangement of characters on stage during any particular moment in the production of a play. See pp. 732–35.

CHARACTER   A dramatic being, known by name, word, and deed. See pp. 757–58.

CHORIC CHARACTER   A character who takes part in the action of a play but is not directly involved in the outcome of the action, and thus can provide a source of commentary upon it. See pp. 739–46.

CHORIC COMMENTARY   Commentary upon characters and events provided either by a chorus or by choric characters. See p. 739.

CHORUS   A group of characters who comment upon the action of a play but do not take part in it. See pp. 739, 760–61.

CLOSET DRAMA   Drama written only to be read, rather than to be produced in a theater. See pp. 731–32.

COMEDY   Dramatization of a hero's and heroine's change in fortune (from frustration to satisfaction) brought about not only by the effort of the hero and heroine themselves but also by some element of chance, coincidence, or luck. See pp. 744–48, 806–7.

COSTUME   A piece of physical apparel worn by actors to create a visual illusion appropriate to the characters they are pretending to be. See pp. 732, 759, 806, 845, 873.

CUE   A word, phrase, or statement in the text of a play which provides explicit or implicit information relevant to theatrical production of the play. See pp. 732–35.

DIALOGUE   Specialized form of conversation peculiar to drama, in that it is designed to convey everything about the imaginative world of a play, as well as to provide all of the cues necessary for production of a play. See pp. 732–35, 738–39, 753–54.

DISCOVERY   A change from ignorance to knowledge on the part of a dramatic hero and/or heroine which brings about a significant change in the fortune of the hero and/or heroine. See pp. 747, 749, 750; see also REVERSAL.

DRAMA   Imitative action created through the words of imaginary beings talking to one another rather than to a reader or spectator. See pp. 731–32, 737–38, 743–45, 753.

DRAMATIC UNIT   A segment of the scenario that is determined by the entrance or exit of a character or group of characters. See pp. 756–57; see also SCENARIO.

EXPOSITION   Dialogue at the beginning of a play that includes background information about characters and events in the imaginative world of a play. See pp. 738, 756.

GESTURE   A physical movement made by actors appropriate to the attitudes and intentions of the characters they are pretending to be. See pp. 732, 734–35, 759, 806, 873, 971.

INTERACTION   Verbal and physical deeds performed by dramatic characters in relation to one another. See pp. 734–35, 737–40.

INTONATION   Particular manner (including pronunciation, rhythm, and volume) in which actors deliver the lines of the characters they are pretending to be. See pp. 732, 759.

MEDITATIVE DRAMA   A form of drama that is primarily concerned with representing the internalized thoughts and feelings of its characters. See pp. 740–41.

NARRATION   An element in drama that is like the act of storytelling, in that it tells about characters and events, or comments upon characters and events, rather than showing them directly. See pp. 737–40; see also CHORIC CHARACTER, CHORIC COMMENTARY, CHORUS, EXPOSITION, REPORTED ACTION, and RETROSPECTION.

NATURALISTIC DRAMA   A mode of drama which embodies a view of men and women as being influenced by psychological, social, and economic forces beyond their control and comprehension. See pp. 750–52, 1023–25.

PACING   Tempo of activity on stage during any particular moment in the production of a play. See pp. 732, 734–35.

PERSUASIVE DRAMA   A form of drama that uses dialogue, plot, and character primarily as a means of testing ideas, expounding ideas, or demonstrating the superiority of one set of ideas over another. See p. 742.

PLOT   Specialized form of experience peculiar to drama, in that it consists of a wholly interconnected system of events, deliberately selected and arranged to fulfill both the imaginative and theatrical purposes of a play. See pp. 745–48, 753, 755–57; see also SCENARIO.

PROP   Any physical item (other than costume and set) which is used by actors on stage during the production of a play. See pp. 732, 760, 873, 1024.

REPORTED ACTION   Action taking place during the time of the play which is reported by one or more of the characters rather than being directly presented. See pp. 738–39, 755–57.

REPRESENTED ACTION   Action taking place during the time of the play which is directly presented rather than reported by one or more of the characters. See pp. 731–33, 738–39, 755–57.

RETROSPECTION   Post-expository dialogue in which characters survey, explore, and seek to understand action which took place well before the time of the play. See p. 738.

REVERSAL   An incident or sequence of incidents that go contrary to the expectations of a hero and/or heroine. See p. 747.

ROMANCE   A mode of drama that uses characters and events to present an intensified but not completely idealized view of human excellence. See pp. 743, 748–50.

SATIRE   A mode of drama that uses characters and events to present an intensified but not completely negative view of human imperfection. See pp. 743, 748–50, 970–71.

SCENARIO   Action that is directly presented (i.e., on stage), and thus embodies everything that takes place in the imaginative world of a play (i.e., the plot). See pp. 755–57.

SCRIPT   Text of a play interpreted as a set of cues for theatrical production. See pp. 732–35.

SET   Physical construction placed on stage to represent an interior or exterior location in the imaginative world of a play. See pp. 732, 736–37, 760, 845, 873–74, 971, 1023–26.

SOLILOQUY   Lines spoken by a character that are meant to represent the unspoken thoughts and feelings of the character. See pp. 740–41.

SPECTACLE   Sights and sounds of performance by means of which the imaginative world of a play is brought to life in the theater. See pp. 732–37, 759–61, 806–7, 845, 873–74, 971, 1023–26. See also BLOCKING, COSTUME, GESTURE, INTONATION, PACING, PROP, SET.

TRAGEDY   Dramatization of a hero's or heroine's change in fortune (from prosperity to catastrophe) brought about by some great error in judgment on the part of the hero or heroine. See pp. 744–47, 760–61.

TRAGICOMEDY   A mode of drama that does not embody a clear-cut pattern of catastrophe or rebirth (as in tragedy or comedy), or present clear-cut images of good or evil (as in romance or satire), and thus presents an ambiguous and problematic view of human experience. See pp. 750–52; see also ABSURDIST DRAMA; NATURALISTIC DRAMA.

FILM

ASPECT RATIO   The relative size of the screen's height (constant) and width (varying). Most feature films were shot in Academy ratio (1.33:1) prior to the early 1950s. Standard ratios now are 1.66:1 (European) and 1.85:1 (American), but may range up to 2.55:1 in formats like Super Panavision. See p. 1301.

BOOM   A support for camera, microphone, and operators, which can swing out over the actors to provide horizontal and vertical movement coupled with height. Sometimes referred to as a CRANE. See p. 1307.

CAMERA ANGLE   The vertical position of the camera on its fixed base as it points toward the object being photographed. The vast majority of shots in any narrative film will avoid extremity of angle along the vertical axis. See p. 1306.

CLOSE-UP   A position taken by the camera along the horizontal axis, placing it in immediate proximity with the object photographed. In standard narrative film, an actor's CLOSE-UP would take in only the head; a CLOSE-UP of an object would simply exclude everything but the object. See p. 1305.

CONTINUITY   The assurance that a film will unfold smoothly, without disquieting transitions from one shot to the next, or inexplicable detail. Thus, "continuity cutting" emphasizes narrative logic, unobtrusively controls the unfolding of space and time, assures the audience's ability to identify with a character. See pp. 1308–9.

CROSS CUTTING   The movement in editing from one locale to another or from one story line to another, with the implication usually that the two events are taking place within a generally simultaneous period of time. See p. 1314.

CUT   The break in the film which often marks where one shot ends and the next begins; the editing process works to smooth over this potential disruption. See pp. 1311–14; see also CONTINUITY.

DEEP FOCUS   Photography that uses lenses permitting all objects within the FRAME to remain in focus. See p. 1325.

DISSOLVE, LAP DISSOLVE   One image gradually FADES, lingering on the screen while another is replacing it; at the mid-point of the process the two images overlap. See pp. 1313, 1323.

DOLLY   A flatbed on a set of wheels, upon which the camera can be mounted for movement along specially laid tracks. Hence moving DOLLY SHOTS or TRACKING SHOTS, which tend to follow actors within reasonably limited spaces. See p. 1307.

EDITING   The joining of pieces of film through a literal match, as in a CUT, to a merging in the laboratory with optical devices like FADES or DISSOLVES. In a larger sense, the construction of the film as a whole after shooting has taken place. See pp. 1308–15.

ESTABLISHING SHOT   Usually a shot taken at a longer distance from the object, placed at the beginning of a SEQUENCE in order to give the viewer some fixed point against which he can then calculate deviations. See p. 1305.

FADE   A laboratory process which either moves the image from normal registration to darkness or brightness (FADE OUT), or reverses the process so that the final step will be a fully articulated image (FADE IN). FADES may vary in duration, depending on the expressive intent. See p. 1313.

FAST STOCK   Film that is highly sensitive to light, and does not need much light in order to receive acceptable exposure. See pp. 1303–4.

FLASHBACK   An editing technique that suggests movement in time, whether through an optical device (a DISSOLVE, for example) or through a MONTAGE of images associated with temporal passage (a calendar's pages, swirling leaves). See pp. 1313–14.

FOCAL LENGTH   The length of the lens, from the outside surface of the lens itself to its plane of focus. See pp. 1305–8.

FOCUS   An image which looks acceptably resolved; that is, one speaks of FOCUS when an image has definition, and sharp outlines, and acceptable clarity. See pp. 1302–3.

FOOTAGE   All film stock exposed during shooting. See p. 1308.

FRAME   1. Any single unit, from one sprocket hole to the next, on the film itself. Twenty-four of these FRAMES pass through camera and projector in one second of shooting or viewing. 2. The outer limits of the image when projected; literally, the borders surrounding the image. See pp. 1300–1302.

IRIS   An optical device that either reduces a full-size image to a small portion of the frame (IRIS OUT) or expands that portion to "fill" the frame (IRIS IN). These actions usually occur at the end or the beginning of a sequence respectively. See p. 1313.

JUMP CUT   A cut that violates standard CONTINUITY cutting, so as to present overtly a break in the temporal or spatial progression of the film. See p. 1313.

LONG TAKE   A shot that continues past the point of normal expectations of continuity, so as to draw attention to its length. See pp. 1309, 1324–25.

MATCH CUT   A CUT that perfectly integrates the succeeding shot with the preceding one, so that the division between the two becomes almost invisible. The opposite of a JUMP CUT. See p. 1312.

MONTAGE   Most generally, a term loosely used to indicate a highly patterned SEQUENCE of SHOTS. More strictly, a term developed by Soviet theorists to demonstrate that a series of hitherto disconnected shots could, through proximity, be constructed so as to produce meaning. See pp. 1314–15.

PAN   A movement of the camera from side to side along an imaginary fixed horizontal axis. See pp. 1300, 1306–7.

SCREEN   A general term for any surface upon which a film image is projected. See p. 1301.

SEQUENCE   A unit of narrative measurement, consisting of any number of shots usually having some thematic connection or formal likeness. See pp. 1314–15, 1322.

SET   The location of the shooting process; traditionally, a sound stage, but now generally used to imply the space needed to make a film. See pp. 1306–7.

SHOT   A single piece of celluloid uninterrupted by cuts or optical devices, in the final print of a film. See pp. 1309–10.

SOUNDTRACK   1. A tape or magnetic recording which encodes sound, whether recorded at the time of shooting or added at a later stage of the editing process. 2. A strip of recorded impulses affixed to the image track on the final print, often appearing as wavy lines next to the image. See pp. 1310–11.

SPROCKETS   Holes punched in the side of film stock and magnetic sound tracks to regulate the forward movement of the recording process. See p. 1311.

SYNCHRONIZATION   The adjustment of the recording, editing, and projecting mechanisms of the cinema into mutually re-enforcing congruency. LOSS OF SYNCHRONIZATION generally shows as a breakdown or non-alignment of sound and image. See pp. 1310–11.

TAKE   An exposure of the camera; what appears in the finished film as a SHOT will usually have been selected from a number of takes. See p. 1309.

TRACKING SHOT   See DOLLY.

TWO-SHOT   A shot with two people, usually taken from the waist to the head, and usually with the actors facing each other at a slight angle. See page 1310.

WIDE-ANGLE LENS   A lens that increases the illusion of depth and distorts the normal patterns of perspective. See p. 1308.

WIPE   An optical device in which one image appears to push another off the screen by means of a bar or line. See p. 1313.

Index

Names of authors and film directors appear in SMALL CAPITALS, titles of readings and films in *italics*, and first lines of poems in roman type. If title and first line coincide, the title alone is entered; if title begins the first line, it appears in *italics*, the rest of the line in [roman bracketed]. Titles supplied for untitled works appear in [*italic bracketed*].